W9-ANB-748

2nd edition

ENCYCLOPEDIA OF PHILOSOPHY

SHAFTESBURY – ZUBIRI

volume 9

2nd edition

ENCYCLOPEDIA OF PHILOSOPHY

DONALD M. BORCHERT

Editor in Chief

MACMILLAN REFERENCE USA

An imprint of Thomson Gale, a part of The Thomson Corporation

Detroit • New York • San Francisco • San Diego • New Haven, Conn. • Waterville, Maine • London • Munich

Encyclopedia of Philosophy, Second Edition

Donald M. Borchert, Editor in Chief

For more information, contact
Macmillan Reference USA
An imprint of Thomson Gale
27500 Drake Rd.
Farmington Hills, MI 48331-3535
Or you can visit our internet site at
http://www.gale.com

LIBRARY OF CONGRESS CATALOGING-IN-PUBLICATION DATA

Encyclopedia of philosophy / Donald M. Borchert, editor in chief.—2nd ed.
p. cm.
Includes bibliographical references and index.
ISBN 0-02-865780-2 (set hardcover : alk. paper)—
ISBN 0-02-865781-0 (vol 1)—ISBN 0-02-865782-9 (vol 2)—
ISBN 0-02-865783-7 (vol 3)—ISBN 0-02-865784-5 (vol 4)—
ISBN 0-02-865785-3 (vol 5)—ISBN 0-02-865786-1 (vol 6)—
ISBN 0-02-865787-X (vol 7)—ISBN 0-02-865788-8 (vol 8)—
ISBN 0-02-865789-6 (vol 9)—ISBN 0-02-865790-X (vol 10)
1. Philosophy–Encyclopedias. I. Borchert, Donald M., 1934-

B51.E53 2005
103–dc22

2005018573

This title is also available as an e-book.
ISBN 0-02-866072-2
Contact your Thomson Gale representative for ordering information.

Printed in the United States of America
10 9 8 7 6 5 4 3 2 1

contents

ENCYCLOPEDIA OF

PHILOSOPHY

2nd edition

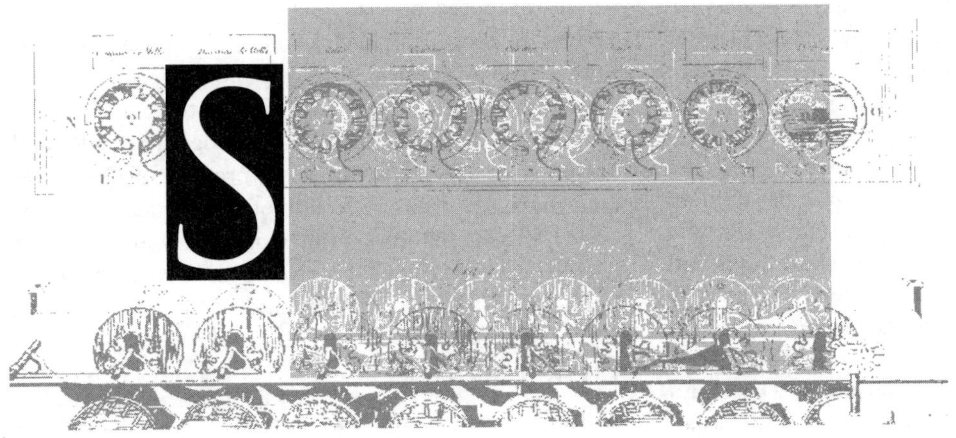

SHAFTESBURY, THIRD EARL OF (ANTHONY ASHLEY COOPER)

(1671–1713)

Anthony Ashley Cooper (the Third Earl of Shaftesbury) was born in London in the home of his grandfather, the first earl, a prominent Whig politician, who put his secretary and friend, John Locke, in charge of his grandson's education. Fluent at eleven in both Greek and Latin, Shaftesbury was an avid student of ancient philosophy, particularly Plato and the Stoics. In 1686, accompanied by a tutor, he embarked on a three-year tour of the Continent, learning French and acquiring a sophisticated taste for the arts. He was elected to Parliament in 1695 and served for three years, although asthma prevented him from standing for reelection. In 1698 he moved to Holland, where he met Pierre Bayle, an advocate for religious tolerance and one of the first to argue that it is possible for an atheist to be virtuous. After becoming the Third Earl of Shaftesbury in 1699, he attended meetings of the House of Lords until 1702, but once again ill health prevented him from continuing to serve and being more active in Whig causes. He married Jane Ewer in 1709; they had one son. His bad health forced him to move in 1711 to Italy, where he died in 1713.

BACKGROUND

Shaftesbury's first published work was an edited collection of the sermons of the Cambridge Platonist Benjamin Whichcote (1609–1683). In his preface Shaftesbury attacked Thomas Hobbes's conception of morality as a matter of law springing from the will of a sovereign, backed up by sanctions imposed on us to restrain our natural, selfish tendencies. His letters make clear, however, that he thought John Locke was an even greater threat to morality since he made Hobbes's views more respectable. Rejecting Locke's view that moral laws spring from the will of God and that morality requires sanctions, Shaftesbury complained that Locke not only "threw all order and virtue out of the world" but also made moral ideas "unnatural," without any "foundation in the mind" (1900, p. 403). In the Cambridge Platonists, however, he found doctrines that were both congenial to his own outlook and an antidote to those of Hobbes and Locke. Proposing a conception of morality that centered on love, the Cambridge Platonists emphasized the natural goodness and sociability of human beings and our ability to act virtuously without sanctions.

Shaftesbury's chief work is *Characteristicks of Men, Manners, Opinions, Times*, an anthology of his essays. It was first published in 1711 in three volumes; ten more editions were printed by 1790. *Characteristicks* includes "An Inquiry concerning Virtue or Merit," which John Toland originally published in 1699, although there is dispute about whether Shaftesbury authorized that version. He revised the "Inquiry" for inclusion in *Characteristicks*. The other four essays were written between 1705 and 1710 and cover a variety of topics in different genres. He discusses issues in morality, politics, religion, aesthetics, culture, and what he calls "politeness"—the conventions of good manners and refined conversation. The essays take different forms: the traditional treatise, as well as an epistle, a dialogue, and a soliloquy. He includes his own commentaries or "miscellaneous reflections" on each essay, which were written especially for the collection.

CONCEPTION OF PHILOSOPHY

Shaftesbury's unorthodox writing style goes hand in hand with his conception of philosophy as practical. He laments that philosophy "is no longer active in the world" (1711/1999, p. 232). On his view, philosophy should help people fashion themselves into moral and unified beings. Conceiving of moral self-transformation in Socratic terms as the pursuit of self-knowledge, he suggests that the best way to know yourself is by means of an inner dialogue. Dialogues and soliloquies, rather than lectures and sermons, are therefore the appropriate vehicles for inspiration and edification. His intended audience was cultivated readers rather than philosophers and other academics, so he thought his writing needed to be accessible—easy, smooth, and polite.

Shaftesbury's practical conception of the philosophical enterprise led him to reject metaphysical and epistemological studies on the grounds that they make people "neither better, nor happier, nor wiser" (1900, p. 269). He was largely indifferent to the successes in the natural sciences that were made during this period and opposed mechanistic conceptions of nature. In contrast to many eighteenth-century philosophers, he was uninterested in putting morality on a scientific footing. He preferred ancient philosophy to that of his contemporaries.

Shaftesbury is best read as a transitional figure, a bridge between the philosophical thinking of the ancients and the moderns, as well as between the seventeenth and the eighteenth centuries. Although he rejected the seventeenth-century natural law view of morality, he retained its Stoic conception of the universe as teleologically structured. The natural world is an integrated and harmonious whole composed of many subsystems, all of which are ordered to good ends. Each subsystem or species, including the human species, is designed to play specific functional roles in still larger systems, which together form the universal nature, the system of all things. The order and harmony in universal nature is a product of God's creative intelligence. As a reflection of God's intelligence, the universe itself embodies rational principles. Shaftesbury's teleological picture of the universe underwrites many of his views on religion, morality, and aesthetics.

ETHICAL THEORY

As Henry Sidgwick remarks in his *Outlines of the History of Ethics [for English Readers]* (1886), Shaftesbury's *Characteristicks* "marks a turning point" in the history of ethics, since he is the first to take "psychological experience as the basis of ethics" (p. 190). He makes morality dependent on the mind in two ways. First, first-order sentiments—the passions and affections that motivate people to act—and actions expressive of these sentiments—have moral value. Second, what gives these motives their value are reflective, second-order sentiments—sentiments we have about our own or other people's sentiments. Shaftesbury's inward turn was the inspiration for sentimentalist moral theories, especially Francis Hutcheson's and David Hume's, as well as Bishop [Joseph] Butler's electric theory.

Shaftesbury's best-known work today is his most traditional piece of writing, "An Inquiry concerning Virtue or Merit." The question that frames the "Inquiry" is whether virtue is able to support itself without the aid of religion. In the course of answering that question he explains both the nature of virtue and our obligation to it. Distinguishing between natural goodness and moral goodness, he defines natural goodness in a functional or teleological way. To say that something is naturally good is to say that it contributes to the good of the system of which it is a part. Where a subsystem is part of a larger system, judgments of natural goodness are relative to that larger system. He even says that something is "really" good or bad only if it benefits or hinders universal nature. However, when we judge the natural goodness or badness of a sensible creature, our judgments concern the structure or economy of its affections. Sensible creatures are good if their affections are adapted to contribute to the good of their species. Their goodness is a matter of being in a healthy state, one that enables them to realize their natural ends. Not surprisingly, Shaftesbury often equates the good with the natural and evil with the unnatural.

While sensible creatures are capable of natural goodness, Shaftesbury claims that only rational creatures are capable of moral goodness—virtue—because only they have the capacity to make their affections objects of reflection. When affections are "brought into the mind by reflection … there arises another kind of affection towards those very affections themselves and … now become the subject of a new liking or disliking" (1711/1999, p. 172). As rational creatures, human beings have second-order, reflective sentiments, sentiments about sentiments. Shaftesbury calls this reflexive capacity a "moral sense." He conceives of it in aesthetic terms—a sense of what is beautiful or harmonious, foul or dissonant in our sentiments. The harmony and proportion of the affections, like the natural beauty in the universe, is evidence of a creative designing mind: God. In feeling moral approval we are able to share in the divine intelligence that created the beauty in the universe. On Shaftesbury's view the moral sense is an active, intelligent, and creative power, not the passive faculty that Hutcheson took it to be.

Shaftesbury argues that what the reflective sense approves of, and so makes morally good, is our natural goodness. We are naturally good when our "natural" or social affections and our self-directed affections are balanced in such a way as to promote our own good and the good of our species. While he thinks that our concern for others may be too strong and our self-concern may be too weak, more typically people are vicious when their social affections are too weak or their self-directed affections too strong. Moral evil arises not only from an imbalance between the social and self-interested affections but also from such "unnatural" affections as malice, sadism, and "delight in disorder."

After explaining the nature of virtue Shaftesbury turns to the question of our obligation to virtue, which he takes to mean "what reason there is to embrace" a virtuous life (1711/1999, p. 192). He then proceeds to show that virtue and self-interest coincide. He begins by arguing that mental pleasures are superior to physical pleasures. He thinks that there are two kinds of mental pleasures: those that consist in the operation of first-order affections and those that result from second-order affections such as those of the moral sense. The first-order affections that are social are a superior source of pleasure since they are pleasant in themselves, never go stale, and enable us to share sympathetically in the pleasures of others. More important, virtuous people experience the pleasures of their own approval as well as the approval of others, while vicious people suffer the torments and pangs of their own disapproval and those of others. He concludes that what obligates us to the practice of virtue is that being virtuous makes us happy. Being a virtuous person is not only good but also good for you.

Returning to the topic of the relation between morality and religion, Shaftesbury argues that it is possible for an atheist to be virtuous and that superstitious or false religious beliefs do more harm than having none at all. He characterizes theism as the belief that the universe is designed by a benevolent God and ordered "for the best," whereas atheists deny that there is a natural order and believe that the universe is a product of chance. Theism is the "perfection and height of virtue," since the theist is attuned to the order and harmony of the universe (1711/1999, p. 192). As moral agents, this is an order and harmony to which we ought to aspire.

VIEWS ON POLITICS, AGENCY, AND AESTHETICS

In other essays Shaftesbury, like his grandfather, champions religious tolerance and liberty of thought. Tolerance and free discussion are the basis of moral and cultural improvement. The way to disarm religious fanatics or those who are superstitious is with "ridicule," lighthearted, good-mannered humor, and tolerance, rather than with punishment and persecution. Although highly critical of the enthusiasm that results from fanaticism or superstition, Shaftesbury argues for true or reasonable enthusiasm—a state of mind that raises people beyond their ordinary capacities and enables them to feel the divine presence. Shaftesbury's conception of reasonable enthusiasm informs his views on nature, religion, morality, and aesthetics.

Some commentators, notably Stephen Darwall, find Shaftesbury's thoughts on the self, its unity and self-government, to be suggestive even though his ideas on these topics are not developed in a systematical way. Shaftesbury thinks that soliloquy is necessary both for self-government and for an agent's unity and integrity. He describes soliloquy, a kind of self-analysis, as a process whereby we are able to divide ourselves into "two parties," an idea that foreshadows Adam Smith's conception of conscience. One part is the better self, the sage, demon, or genius—an ideal of character to which each person is committed. In dividing ourselves into two, we erect the better part as the "counsellor and governor" (1711/1999, p. 77). Soliloquy enables us to step back and critically assess our desires—scrutinizing their causes and their place in the scheme of our aims and concerns. Likewise, soliloquy aims to make us unified agents, true to our ideals of character.

Shaftesbury has been described as the first great English aesthetician. Not only does he think of moral goodness as a species of the beautiful but he also thinks that moral and aesthetic taste amount to the same thing. Thus, he says that "the science of the virtuosi and that of virtue itself become, in a manner, one and the same." The real virtuoso understands and appreciates the inner harmony and order that constitute the goodness in works of art and in people's characters. The source of Beauty and what we ultimately find beautiful is the creative, intelligent mind. Thus, he says that "the beautifying, not the beautiful is the really beautiful" (1711/1999, p. 322). When we admire order and proportion in natural objects, we are really admiring the creator, God. Shaftesbury developed a concept of disinterested pleasure to explain the kind of pleasure we experience in a true apprehension of beauty.

Shaftesbury's *Characteristicks* was influential both in England and on the Continent during the eighteenth century. It is thought that virtually every educated man in the eighteenth century was acquainted with it. While the sentimentalists, Hutcheson and Hume, kept Shaftesbury's idea that moral goodness springs from second-order affections, they detached their accounts of natural goodness from his teleological picture of the universe. Thus, Hutcheson identifies natural goodness with pleasure. There has been renewed attention to Shaftesbury's work since the 1980s, not only by traditional philosophers interested in his moral and aesthetic views but also by those interested in literary theory and gender studies.

See also Aesthetics, History of; Bayle, Pierre; Cambridge Platonists; Locke, John.

Bibliography

WORKS BY SHAFTESBURY

Select Sermons of Dr. Whichcot. London: Awnsham and John Churchill, 1698.

Characteristics of Men, Manners, Opinions, Times (1711), edited by Lawrence E. Klein. New York: Cambridge University Press, 1999.

The Life, Unpublished Letters, and Philosophical Regimen of Anthony, Earl of Shaftesbury, edited by Benjamin Rand. London: Swan Sonnenschein, 1900.

Second Characters. Cambridge, U.K.: Cambridge University Press, 1914.

WORKS ABOUT SHAFTESBURY

Darwall, Stephen. "Shaftesbury: Authority and Authorship." In *The British Moralists and the Internal "Ought": 1640–1740*. New York: Cambridge University Press, 1995.

Gill, Michael B. "Shaftesbury's Two Accounts of the Reason to Be Virtuous." *Journal of the History of Philosophy* 38 (4) (2000): 529–548.

Grean, Stanley. "Self-Interest and Public Interest in Shaftesbury's Philosophy." *Journal of the History of Philosophy* 2 (1964): 37–46.

Grean, Stanley. *Shaftesbury's Philosophy of Religion and Ethics: A Study in Enthusiasm*. Athens: Ohio University Press, 1967.

Schneewind, J. B. *The Invention of Autonomy: A History of Modern Moral Philosophy*. New York: Cambridge University Press, 1998.

Sidgwick, Henry. *Outlines of the History of Ethics*. Indianapolis: Hackett Publishing Company, 1988.

Taylor, Charles. "Moral Sentiments." In *Sources of the Self: The Making of the Modern Identity*. Cambridge, MA: Harvard University Press, 1989.

Trianosky, Gregory W. "On the Obligation to Be Virtuous: Shaftesbury and the Question, Why Be Moral?" *Journal of the History of Philosophy* 16 (3) (1978): 289–300.

Voitle, Robert. *The Third Earl of Shaftesbury, 1671–1713*. Baton Rouge: Louisiana University Press, 1984.

Charlotte R. Brown (2005)

SHAME

Shame is the painful emotion occasioned by the realization that one has fallen far below one's ideal self—the person that one wants to be. Although shame no doubt originally involves a concern with being observed by others (its link with embarrassment), such observation need no longer be a part of shame once ideals of the self have been internalized.

SHAME AND GUILT

Shame is perhaps best understood initially by contrasting it with guilt. Both are painful emotions, but the relationship of shame to morality is more complicated than is the case with guilt. Guilt is necessarily a moral emotion, since it is essentially a painful negative self-assessment with a moral basis—namely, the belief that one has done something morally wrong. One may, of course, be mistaken about the actual moral status of what one has done—one may, for example, have mistaken moral beliefs—but this is a moral mistake. Even those feelings of guilt that we classify as irrational or neurotic are typically labeled as such because we believe that the person experiencing the guilt has made a moral mistake—for example, our belief that the conduct is in fact not wrong; or our belief that the person is assuming responsibility when not really responsible; or our belief that, even if the conduct is wrong, the guilt that one feels is radically disproportionate to the nature of the wrong. So we might classify great guilt over, say, masturbation as irrational or neurotic. We surely would not, however, label as irrational or neurotic the Nazi death camp commandant who comes to feel great guilt over his evil acts.

Although shame may also have a moral dimension, this is not necessarily the case. Shame is best understood as the painful negative self-assessment that arises when it is brought to consciousness that one's actual self is radically at odds with the ideal that one has of oneself—what Freud called one's ego-ideal. Although shame typically involves an ideal self that is at least in part constructed from social norms, these norms are frequently not moral in nature; and thus it is quite common that one may feel great shame over aspects of oneself that are morally innocent and over which one may have little control. Examples are shame over one's appearance, weight, social awkwardness, or poverty. Although such shames can sometimes prompt people to do things that are good for them (e.g., diet), they can also be so destructive of self as to be properly labeled toxic. This does not make them moral, however. Not everything that is important—even very important—is moral in nature.

MORAL SHAME

Shame becomes a moral emotion when one's ideal self, one's ego ideal, is moral in nature. If one seeks to preserve an image of oneself as a decent person with largeness and generosity of spirit, for example, then one will feel great moral shame when it is brought to consciousness that one has revealed a nature that is in fact petty, grasping, and indifferent to the hurt that one may cause others in pursuit of one's own narrow interest.

The gnawing pain of bad conscience—the *agenbite of inwit*, some medieval writers called it—may be seen as guilt over the wrong that one has done, coupled with shame over something about oneself that the wrong has revealed: the kind of person that one is, and how far this person differs from the moral person one thinks one ought to be. "Shame creeps through guilt and feels like retribution," as the novelist William Trevor puts it.

Given these important differences between guilt and moral shame—the former directed primarily toward wronging others, the latter directed to flaws of the self—one can see why the agent's healing and restorative responses to the two feelings tend to be quite different as well. Guilt typically engages such responses as apology, atonement, restitution, and even the acceptance of punishment. Moral shame imposes an even more difficult burden, however: the construction of a different and better self.

Because of its potential for moral transformation, moral shame deserves more respect than it often receives. Critics of shame tend to focus on non-moral shame, and they are quite right to stress the potentially toxic nature of some instances of non-moral shame. Some instances can even be toxic, and quite literally so, to the body. Witness the large numbers of young women who get sick and even die of eating disorders (anorexia and bulimia) because they are ashamed of their body image.

SHAME AND PUNISHMENT

Respect even for moral shame should not lead to uncritical enthusiasm, however. We should be suspicious, for example, of the trendy movement in late twentieth-century American criminal law toward shaming punishments—for example, making prisoners wear signs saying "I molest children" or dressing them in black-and-white striped uniforms and putting them on public chain gang work details. However they may be described, such practices are often merely exercises in cruel and vindictive public humiliation—something more likely to harden the heart rather than transform it in morally admirable ways. (Shaming punishments have been given their most powerful defense by Dan Kahan [1996] and their most powerful critique by Toni Massaro [1991].) As John Braithwaite (1989) has pointed out, some impressive results have been achieved with shaming punishments in small homogeneous societies that provide for rituals of reintegration. The homogeneity guarantees that one is being shamed before a group in which one values membership and whose good opinion one values, and the rituals of reintegration provide a hopeful light at the end of the tunnel. It would be a fantasy to think that modern American criminal law satisfies either condition, however.

See also Guilt; Moral Sentiments; Punishment.

Bibliography

Braithwaite, John. *Crime, Shame and Reintegration.* Cambridge, U.K.: Cambridge University Press, 1989.

Freud, Sigmund. *The Ego and the Id.* Translated by Joan Riviere. Revised and edited by James Strachey. New York: W. W. Norton, 1960.

Kahan, Dan. "What Do Alternative Sanctions Mean?" *University of Chicago Law Review* 63 (1996): 591–653.

Massaro, Toni. "The Meanings of Shame: Implications for Legal Reform." *Psychology, Public Policy and Law* 3 (1997): 645–704.

Massaro, Toni. "Shame, Culture, and American Criminal Law." *Michigan Law Review* 89 (1991): 1880–1944.

Morris, Herbert, ed. *Guilt and Shame*. Belmont, CA: Wadsworth, 1971.

Murphy, Jeffrie G. "Shame Creeps through Guilt and Feels Like Retribution." *Law and Philosophy* 18 (1999): 327–344.

Taylor, Gabriele. *Pride, Shame and Guilt: Emotions of Self Assessment*. Oxford: Clarendon Press, 1988.

Trevor, William. *Death in Summer*. New York: Viking Press, 1998.

Williams, Bernard. *Shame and Necessity*. Berkeley: University of California Press, 1993.

Jeffrie G. Murphy (2005)

SHAO YONG

(1011–1077)

Shao Yong was a Chinese philosopher, historian, and poet born in 1011 (January 21, 1012, by European dating). He was the scion of a humble but educated family that had resided in northern China, near the modern-day national capital of Beijing, for several generations. However, the border conflicts that pitted the Chinese Song dynasty (960–1279) against various hostile and encroaching non-Chinese peoples forced the Shaos into a series of moves southward toward the safer center of the empire. Thus, in 1049, Shao relocated to nearby Luoyang, the secondary imperial capital and nascent cultural hub, where he lived until his death in 1077.

Shao was influenced early by teachers—among them his father Shao Gu (986–1064) and the scholar and minor official Li Zhicai (1001–1045). But his philosophical development was surely determined much less by any one person than it was by the singular divinatory text that constitutes one of the five works included in the vaunted corpus of ancient Chinese classics—the *Book of Change* or *Yijing*. Shao was unquestionably invested in the *Book of Change*. Nonetheless, he evinced an uncommon independence of mind in how he responded to it. In contrast to others who were similarly inspired by the classic, Shao diverged from his prominent contemporaries by never writing a separate commentary specifically on the *Book of Change*. Instead, one can rightly regard the magnum opus of Shao's own scholarly output—the *Book of Supreme World-ordering Principles* (*Huangji jingshi shu*)—as entirely an expansion on the seminal premises contained in the *Book of Change* and in related writings, including the remaining four classics. Moreover, as was customary among the Chinese educated elite, Shao composed poetry. His poems were collected as *Striking the Earth at Yi River* (*Yichuan jirang ji*); this work is also one in which his cardinal philosophical ideas are exhibited. Thus, the survival of Shao's only two verifiable writings permits us to divide his thought into its early- and late-emerging components.

EARLY THOUGHT

Shao is usually accorded a position in the movement called the "Learning of the Way" (*daoxue*, a term that Europeans equate with neo-Confucianism). But he is far more noteworthy for his unique departures from the solutions arrived at by this movement. The early *daoxue* movement was chiefly preoccupied with achieving consensus on a metaphysical "first principle" that would support a cosmogony and yet also account for the assumed ethical endowment of humankind. The concept settled upon was *li* (pattern or principle), which thinkers construed as the fundamental reality underlying both physical and human nature.

Shao, however, was alone in his advocacy of the concept of number (*shu*). For him, number—and not principle—became elemental, the foundation on which the universe rested and thus the key to uncovering its secrets. Shao's faith in the regulative power of number led him to proffer that the natural processes operative in the world were number-dependent—hence, his theme of "world ordering" (*jingshi*). His conviction that number was the basis of reality also led him to advance a kind of predictive knowledge that he promoted as "before Heaven" (*xiantian*) learning. This learning, he contended, is a priori in the sense that it has always existed, even prior to the formation of the universe.

LATER THOUGHT

The final component to emerge in Shao's philosophy was a concept of methodologically reflexive observation, the chief characteristics of which were its claims to ubiquity of application and the attainment of pure objectivity and gnosis. Shao called this concept the "observation of things" (*guanwu*). Its prescribed procedure of "reverse observation" (*fanguan*) purportedly empowered the observer to know or understand any and all animate or inanimate things objectively and yet also be able to apprehend them from their own distinctly individuated and particularized standpoints. Thus, through its putative capacity to observe each and every object fully in terms of the observed object itself, the "observation of things" promised its practitioners knowledge that was truly objective, universalistic, and omniscient in its perspective.

See also Cheng Hao; Cheng Yi; Confucius; Zhang Zai; Zhou Dunyi.

Bibliography

Arrault, Alain. *Shao Yong (1012–1077), Poète et Cosmologue.* Paris: Collège de France, Institut des Hautes Études Chinoises, 2002.

Birdwhistell, Anne D. *Transition to Neo-Confucianism: Shao Yung on Knowledge and Symbols of Reality.* Stanford, CA: Stanford University Press, 1989.

Wyatt, Don J. "Historicism, Contextualization, and the Western Reception of Master Shao." *Intellectual News: Review of the International Society for Intellectual History* 4 (5) (1999): 26–36.

Wyatt, Don J. *The Recluse of Loyang: Shao Yung and the Moral Evolution of Early Sung Thought.* Honolulu: University of Hawaii Press, 1996.

Smith, Jr., Kidder; Peter K. Bol, Joseph A. Adler, and Don J. Wyatt. *Sung Dynasty Uses of the I Ching.* Princeton, NJ: Princeton University Press, 1990.

Don J. Wyatt (2005)

SHARIATI, ALI

(1933–1977)

Ali Shariati did not live to see the Islamic Revolution in Iran of 1979, but he was definitely one of its intellectual authors. Like many Iranians in the twentieth century he combined an education in the traditional religious sciences in Iran with more modern ideas from a European context—in his case Paris. His connections with the anticolonialist movement in Paris led him to argue that Islam is a basically revolutionary and liberating doctrine; Shariati did not abandon religion as many of his fellow radical Iranians did, nor did he accept the reverence for the imam or spiritual leader so prevalent in Shiʿi Islam. This set him firmly aside from Khomeini and the ideology of the Islamic Revolution itself.

He was a great borrower of ideas that he then applied in his own way. Thus while he rejected the dialectical materialism of Marxism, he did use the notion of history having a direction and a pattern—albeit one based on divine will and class struggle by individuals progressively perfecting their consciousness. Islam is a religion based on liberation, and Shariati reads the Qurʾan as a book representing a community struggling permanently to achieve social justice, a fraternal society, and freedom. Shariati was not impressed with the power of imported ideologies to generate political solidarity among the people against oppressive regimes. Like his distinguished Iranian predecessor, Jalal Al-e Ahmad, he recognized the importance of politicizing Islam as an ideology of emancipation and liberation of the Iranian people. Unlike another influence on him, Frantz Fanon, Shariati approved of religion, provided it is reinterpreted appropriately.

His version of Shiʿism placed emphasis on Imam ʿAli as a revolutionary leader as well as a religious thinker. This view of Shiʿism is different from that of the religious orthodoxy, especially as it places authority in the opinion of the individual, a vindication of *ijtihad* or independent judgment rather distant from normal understandings of the notion in Islam. Here he was undoubtedly influenced by Jean-Paul Sartre and the existentialist emphasis on the importance of authentic decisions being made by free agents. Shariati argued that Islam could be vindicated as a faith if it is seen as involving autonomous choices by individuals and a genuine progressive direction in both social and personal policies.

Bibliography

WORKS BY SHARIATI

On the Sociology of Islam: Lectures. Translated by Hamid Algar. Berkeley, CA: Mizan Press, 1979.

From Where Shall We Begin? Houston: Book Distribution Press, 1980.

Marxism and Other Western Fallacies: An Islamic Critique. Translated by R. Campbell. Berkeley, CA: Mizan Press, 1980.

Oliver Leaman (2005)

SHELLEY, PERCY BYSSHE

(1792–1822)

Percy Bysshe Shelley is usually thought of as a romantic and lyric poet rather than as a philosophical one. He was, however, the author of a number of polemical prose pamphlets on politics and religion; and both his prose and his poetry reflect a coherent background of social and metaphysical theory.

In general, Shelley's beliefs are those of the radical English intelligentsia of the period immediately before and after the French Revolution, and in particular of William Godwin, who became his father-in-law. It has often been said that Shelley was really antipathetic to Godwin's atheism and determinism and that he gradually threw off Godwin's influence in favor of a more congenial Platonic transcendentalism. This view, however, seems to rest on a misunderstanding of both Godwin and Shelley.

ATTACK ON CHRISTIANITY

In *The Necessity of Atheism,* for which he was expelled from Oxford in 1811, Shelley argued, on Humean lines, that no argument for the existence of God is convincing. He developed this position in *A Refutation of Deism* (1814), a dialogue that purports to defend Christianity against deism, but which actually presents a strong case against both and in favor of atheism. In both these works, and in some of his essays (many of which were not published in his lifetime), Shelley was concerned with what he later called "that superstition which has disguised itself under the name of the system of Jesus." In the longer *Essay on Christianity,* published posthumously, he explained what he thought that system really was: an allegorical expression of the virtues of sympathy and tolerance, and of an anarchistic belief in the equality of men and in the wickedness of punishment and all other forms of coercion. Christ, Shelley claimed, had "the imagination of some sublimest and most holy poet"; he was also a reformer who, like most reformers, practiced a little mild deception by pandering to "the prejudices of his auditors." The doctrine of a personal God, in particular, is not to be taken as "philosophically true," but as "a metaphor easily understood."

THE NATURAL AND THE MORAL ORDER

Shelley explained this coupling of poetry and religion, and the view that both are essentially allegory, in *A Defence of Poetry* (1821). It is the function of both poetry and religion to provide men with a coherent view of the world that will help them to understand both themselves and their fellow men, and to provide it in a form that will kindle the imagination as well as the intellect—that is, through metaphor. There is a natural order in the universe, which science and philosophy reveal; there is also a moral order, which men themselves must impose. The metaphor of a personal God is meant to impress this twofold order on men's minds. Since this metaphor had, unfortunately, been perverted by a superstitious interpretation, Shelley himself preferred such symbols as the World Soul or the Spirit of Intellectual Beauty.

ANARCHISM

The details of the moral order itself are made clear in Shelley's political pamphlets. Shelley began to write these when, as a youth of nineteen, he set out to settle the Irish question by instructing the Irish in the fundamental principles of Godwinian anarchism. Godwin's main thesis was that social institutions, and particularly the coercive ones imposed by governments, fasten blinkers on men's minds which prevent them from seeing their fellows as they really are. The ultimate solution is a community small enough for each member to know the other members as individuals. Such intimate personal knowledge will bring understanding and sympathy, so that men will be prepared to cooperate for the common good, without the coercion of law. As Shelley put it, "no government will be wanted but that of your neighbor's opinion." Men will indeed value their neighbors' opinions, but they will not take their neighbors' opinions on trust. To do so would be useless, because even a true opinion is of little value unless one understands the grounds for holding it. It is only when men see things as they are, in all their intricate interconnections, that they will feel the right emotions and thus lead happy and virtuous lives.

POLITICAL PAMPHLETEERING

In accordance with these general principles, Shelley urged the Irish not to seek emancipation by means of violence, but to agitate for freedom of assembly, freedom of the press, and parliamentary representation as the first steps toward the ideal society. It was also in accordance with these principles that Shelley wrote his *Letter to Lord Ellenborough* (1812), in which he protested vehemently against the sentence passed on the publisher of Thomas Paine's *Age of Reason.* Both this pamphlet and the *Address on the Death of Princess Charlotte* (1817), in which he suggested that Englishmen would do better to mourn for their lost liberties than for even the most beautiful and blameless of princesses, were eloquent attacks on judicial persecution and on the suppression of free speech. In another pamphlet, *On the Punishment of Death* (left unpublished), he opposed capital punishment. In the long essay *A Philosophical View of Reform,* another of the unpublished manuscripts found among Shelley's journals, he recapitulated the common radical objections to priests, kings, and the aristocracy, and gave his support to such measures as a more democratic suffrage and a capital levy on unearned wealth.

UNITY OF THE WORLD

Shelley's writings on politics and religion provide meanings for many of the symbols and metaphors to be found in his poetry. His frequent references to life and the world around us as "a painted veil," an illusion through which we must penetrate to the reality behind (this reality being the "one" that remains when "the many change and pass"), is probably to be interpreted as a Godwinian allegory. Godwin had said that men see life as if through a veil—the veil of their own prejudices, which are imposed by social institutions. The constant theme of Godwin's novels was that men must transcend these prejudices in order to understand and love their fellow men. Shelley's idealization of love, which has been taken as a departure from Godwin, is actually his attempt to present this Godwinian theme in a form that will kindle the imagination. It is, moreover, quite in accord with Godwin's views to say that once the veil is removed, the world will be seen as a unity—both in the sense in which science may be said to be a unity (the truth about one field of study cohering with and illuminating the truth about another), and in the sense that a true understanding of our fellow men will give rise to virtuous behavior. This seems to be what Shelley had in mind when he spoke of "the indestructible order" that it is the business of poetry to reveal. There is no need to suppose that he thought of this order as being imposed upon the world by a moral being.

THE UNIVERSAL MIND

It is true that Shelley was also influenced by Plato, Benedict de Spinoza, George Berkeley, and (in spite of his derogatory remarks about Immanuel Kant in *Peter Bell the Third*) by the newer type of idealism that was beginning to be made fashionable by Samuel Taylor Coleridge. In *On Life* he suggested that there are no distinct individual minds, but one universal mind in which all minds participate. As early as 1812 he had identified this "mass of infinite intelligence" with Deity. In this, Shelley was certainly departing from the doctrine of materialists like Baron d'Holbach; but Godwin, although he was not an idealist, was hardly a materialist either. Godwin would certainly have said that when men see things as they are, they hold the same opinions and, in a sense, think the same thoughts. Each man, seeing things from his own point of view, grasps only part of the truth. He will come nearer to grasping the whole of the truth as he comes to understand and sympathize with the minds of other men. In a sense, the truth as a whole is the property not of any one mind but of the sum of all minds. Probably Shelley himself meant little more than this.

PROMETHEUS UNBOUND

Shelley's beliefs find expression in his poetry in a way that is seen fairly clearly in *Prometheus Unbound* (1820), which can be interpreted as a Godwinian allegory. Prometheus, chained to his rock, is suffering humankind, and as the discoverer of fire, he is also knowledge and the civilizing arts. These discoveries, in themselves, are not enough to liberate man from the oppressive rule of Jupiter, which is built "on faith and fear." Prometheus is freed when, instead of cursing his oppressor, he begins to pity and so to understand him. This reflects the favorite Godwinian theme that the oppressor, no less than the oppressed, is the victim of social institutions. A better order is possible only when men come to understand this fact and substitute mutual sympathy for recrimination and punishment. It is also necessary to understand the secrets of Demogorgon, who personifies the natural forces that control the universe, and to cooperate with the Hours, who, with their chariots, personify Godwin's conviction of the inevitability of gradualism.

See also Anarchism; Atheism; Berkeley, George; Coleridge, Samuel Taylor; Deism; Godwin, William; Holbach, Paul-Henri Thiry, Baron d'; Kant, Immanuel; Paine, Thomas; Plato; Spinoza, Benedict (Baruch) de; Wollstonecraft, Mary.

Bibliography

WORKS BY SHELLEY

The definitive edition of Shelley's writings is *The Complete Works of Shelley,* edited by R. Ingpen and W. E. Peck, 10 vols. (London and New York, 1926–1930). A useful collection is *Shelley's Prose, or The Trumpet of a Prophecy,* edited by D. L. Clark (Albuquerque: University of New Mexico Press, 1954).

WORKS ON SHELLEY

A detailed biography is N. I. White, *Shelley,* 2 vols. (New York: Knopf, 1940). Works dealing especially with his thought are C. Baker, *Shelley's Major Poetry* (Princeton, NJ: Princeton University Press, 1948); H. N. Brailsford, *Shelley, Godwin, and Their Circle* (New York: Holt, 1913); P. Butter, *Shelley's Idols of the Cave* (Edinburgh: Edinburgh University Press, 1954); A. M. D. Hughes, *The Nascent Mind of Shelley* (Oxford: Clarendon Press, 1947); D. King-Hele, *Shelley: His Thought and Work* (London: Macmillan, 1960); A. Sen, *Studies in Shelley* (Calcutta: University of Calcutta, 1936); and M. T. Wilson, *Shelley's Later Poetry* (New York: Columbia University Press, 1959).

D. H. Monro (1967)

SHEPHERD, MARY

(1777–1847)

Mary Shepherd was born in Scotland at her family's estate on December 31, 1777, the second daughter of Neil Primrose, Earl of Rosebery; she died in London on January 7, 1847. Relatively few details of her life and education are available. She married an English barrister, Henry Shepherd, in 1808. She published at least two works in philosophy, *An Essay upon the Relation of Cause and Effect*

(1824), and *Essays on the Perception of an External Universe and other Subjects Connected with the Doctrine of Causation* (1827). A third work, originally published anonymously in 1819, *Enquiry respecting the Relation of Cause and Effect*, has been credited to her, but it differs so significantly from her other work, both in style and content, as to make this attribution dubious. She was as well a participant in an exchange of views with a contemporary, John Fearn, which appeared in various venues.

Shepherd's work reflects the continued interest in the first quarter of the nineteenth century in developing alternative arguments to those of Hume, conceived largely skeptically. Her first work establishes the line of argument that was to direct her work. In it, she seeks to refute Hume's position on causality by arguing that Hume is mistaken in holding that we lack an intuitive understanding that events have causes. Shepherd reads Hume as holding that we cannot be intuitively certain that everything that begins to exist has a cause, and subjects to criticism the contained concept of a causeless beginning-to-be of some existence. Her argument is that this beginning is itself an action and hence must be a state of something that, by hypothesis, does not as yet exist until it has begun to be. Hence, she claims, the basic assumption of Hume's account is contradictory. Shepherd offers a realist account of cause as the productive principle of effects, themselves not subsequent to causes, but rather coexistent with the productive object. She uses her realist understanding of causation to criticize not only Hume, but also her own contemporaries, Thomas Brown and William Lawrence.

Shepherd's second work, *Essays on the Perception of an External World*, was originally intended as an appendix to her first work and consists primarily, although not exclusively, of an application of her ideas about causation to the question of the existence of an external world. By far the largest part is directed to providing an alternative answer to Hume's question about the sources of our idea of a continuous external existence. Appended are a series of essays about Berkeley, Reid, Stewart, Hume, and what Shepherd terms in the title of her work "various modern atheists." Shepherd argues, against Hume, that the possibility of causal reasoning, as demonstrated in her first book, makes such reasoning available to substantiate the existence of a continuously existing independent world. She feels it necessary, however, to give a different solution from that of Reid. This is because she thinks Reid failed to appreciate the importance of Berkeley's claim that an idea can only be like another idea. Shepherd takes this to mean that Reid is wrong to suppose that we can give content to our ideas of a mind-independent world. Thanks to the possibility of causal reasoning, however, we are able to assert the existence of causes responsible for our ideas. In particular, because our ideas change, there must be causes for these changes, independent of our ever-present mind. The variety we experience must be due to causes other than ourselves, whose nature, while unknown, must be, she thinks proportional to their effects.

Shepherd develops and clarifies these ideas further in her exchange of views with John Fearn, a retired naval officer and philosophical aficionado. This exchange is unusual as well as interesting, presenting one of the first occasions where a woman's ideas are attacked in print, and illustrating some of the different venues available to ordinary practitioners for publishing philosophy in the early nineteenth century. The first two parts of the exchange appear in 1828 in a volume loosely related to the clergyman, Samuel Parr, called *Parriana*, apparently supplied by Fearn to its compiler, Ernest Barker, and included by him, despite the lack of relevance to Parr. These consist of a four-page paper, critical of Fearn by Shepherd, apparently sent to him privately, and a longer defense of his views against Shepherd by Fearn. Shepherd was sufficiently concerned by this unauthorized use of her work that she published a rebuttal, "Lady Mary Shepherd's Metaphysics" in a well-known literary journal, *Fraser's Magazine*, in July 1832.

The exchange focuses on a disagreement over the idea of extension. It is Fearn's view that the content of the idea of extension is determined by our perception of it. There can be no extended external material cause of such an idea. The only possible cause consists of the energies of an extended mind, analogous to our own. Shepherd maintains that Fearn has not adequately distinguished the idea of extension from its unknown cause. On the one hand, Shepherd holds that extension can only apply to objects considered as causes, for it is as causes that they take up space and move. Ideas, on the other hand, neither move nor take up space, or we would be left with the ridiculous position that the idea of a fat man is itself fat. Shepherd, in defense of this claim, gives a fresh defense of her causal realism. While it is true that the mind perceives internal changes to its own states, it nevertheless reasons to the existence of external unperceived causes of these changes.

See also Berkeley, George; Brown, Thomas; Causation: Metaphysical Issues; Epistemology; Hume, David; Metaphysics; Reid, Thomas; Stewart, Dugald; Women in the History of Philosophy.

Bibliography

WORKS BY SHEPHERD

An Essay upon the Relation of Cause and Effect, controverting the Doctrine of Mr. Hume, concerning the Nature of the Relation; with Observations upon the Opinions of Dr. Brown and Mr. Lawrence, Connected with the Same Subject. London: printed for T. Hookham, Old Bond Street, 1824.

Essays on the Perception of an External Universe, and Other Subjects connected with the Doctrine of Causation. London: John Hatchard and Son, 1827.

"Observations of Lady Mary Shepherd on the 'First Lines of the Human Mind.'" In *Parriana: Or Notices of the Rev. Samuel Parr, L.L.D.*. Collected from various sources and in part written by E. H. Barker, esq., 624–627. 1828.

"Lady Mary Shepherd's Metaphysics." *Fraser's Magazine for Town and Country* 5 (30) (1832): 697–708.

Modern edition of all of the above: *The Philosophical Works of Lady Mary Shepherd.* Vols. 1–2, edited by Jennifer McRobert. Bristol, U.K.: Thoemmes Press, 2000.

WORKS ABOUT SHEPHERD

Atherton, Margaret. "Lady Mary Shepherd's Case against George Berkeley." *British Journal for the History of Philosophy* 4 (2) (1996): 347–366.

Atherton, Margaret. "Mary Shepherd." In *Dictionary of NineteenthCentury British Philosophers.* Bristol, U.K.: Thoemmes Press, 2002.

McRobert, Jennifer. Introduction to *The Philosophical Works of Lady Mary Shepherd.* Vols. 1–2. Bristol, U.K.: Thoemmes Press, 2000.

Margaret Atherton (2005)

SHESTOV, LEV ISAAKOVICH

(1866–1938)

Lev Isaakovich Shestov, the Russian philosopher and religious thinker, was born in Kiev. His real name was Lev Isaakovich Schwarzmann. Shestov studied law at Moscow University but never practiced it. He lived in St. Petersburg from the late 1890s until he migrated to Berlin in 1922; he later settled in Paris. He gave occasional lectures in Berlin, Paris, and Amsterdam and made two lecture tours in Palestine, but he held no regular academic position.

Shestov called William Shakespeare his "first teacher of philosophy"; in his later years he interpreted Hamlet's enigmatic "the time is out of joint" as a profound existential truth. Shestov apparently turned to philosophy relatively late, perhaps in 1895, when he reportedly underwent a spiritual crisis. He himself never referred to such a crisis; in general, his works are less confessional and autobiographical than those of most existential thinkers. However, they are neither impersonal nor unimpassioned; intensity and engagement (in a religious and moral rather than a political sense) are hallmarks of his thought.

Shestov was perhaps most strongly influenced by Blaise Pascal, Fëdor Dostoevsky, and Friedrich Nietzsche. He discovered Søren Kierkegaard quite late and found his position highly congenial, but he had worked out his own existentialist position independently of Kierkegaard. Shestov's philosophical works are written in an aphoristic, ironic, questioning style reminiscent of Pascal's *Pensées* and Nietzsche's *Beyond Good and Evil.* Shestov believed, with Kierkegaard, that subjective truth borders on paradox. "People seem shocked," he once wrote, "when I enunciate two contradictory propositions simultaneously.… But the difference between them and me is that I speak frankly of my contradictions while they prefer to dissimulate theirs, even to themselves.… They seem to think of contradictions as the *pudenda* of the human spirit" (quoted in de Schloezer, "Un penseur russe …," pp. 89–90).

Shestov was not a systematic thinker. He attacked the views of others, sometimes massively; but he was content to suggest or sketch his own position. His writings focus positively on the question of religion and morality or religiously based morality; negatively on the critique of theoretical and practical rationalism. Among the rationalists whom he attacked by name are Parmenides, Plato, Aristotle, Plotinus, Benedict de Spinoza, Immanuel Kant, G. W. F. Hegel, and Edmund Husserl.

The basic either/or of Shestov's thought is suggested by the title of his major work in philosophy of religion: *Afiny i Ierusalim* (Athens and Jerusalem). Athens is the home of reason, of a philosophical rationalism that insists on a neat and knowable cosmos ruled by eternal and unalterable laws. Jerusalem is the home of faith, of an existential irrationalism that stresses contingency, arbitrariness, mystery, and pure possibility. For God "all things are possible," even what René Descartes had called a logical absurdity, that is, causing what has in fact happened not to have happened.

Sometimes Shestov's attack on reason took the form of questioning reason's theoretical competence. Thus, he complained that theorists of biological and cosmic evolution, with their loose talk about "millions and billions of years" and about "eternal nature," were perpetrating a "monstrous absurdity."

More frequently Shestov made the rather different claim that rational knowledge neglects what is essential—

the individual, contingent, incomprehensible, and mysterious. "However much we may have attained in science," he wrote, "we must remember that *science cannot give us truth*.... For truth lies in the singular, uncontrollable, incomprehensible, ... and 'fortuitous'" (*In Job's Balances,* p. 193). "We live," Shestov declared, "surrounded by an infinite multitude of mysteries" (*Afiny i Ierusalim,* p. 25).

Most frequently Shestov attacked the moral consequences of theoretical reason, its erosion and subversion of human values. Reason exhibits necessity and imposes nonfreedom. Faith assumes contingency and makes freedom possible. Rationalists recognize an eternal structure of being, a system of necessary laws that antedates any possible cosmic lawgiver. The necessity of such laws requires obedience. What is nonnecessary, whether contingent or arbitrary, admits of free decision and creativity. Shestov repudiated all obedience to necessity in the sense of acceptance of necessary evil, injustice, and inhumanity. There are scales, he declared, upon which human suffering weighs heavier than all the necessities of theoretical reason; such are "Job's balances."

In particular, Shestov rejected the Greek view, which he traced back to Anaximander, that coming to be (*genesis*) is a kind of affront to the gods, a cosmic hubris, justly rewarded by the punishment of passing away (*phthora*). He called this the "dreadful law which inseparably links death to birth." "In man's very existence," Shestov added, "thought has discovered something improper, a defect, a sickness, or sin, and ... has demanded that this be overcome at its root [by] a renunciation of existence" (*Kirgegard ekzistentsial'naia filosofiia,* p. 8).

In such passages Shestov may appear to have confused natural (descriptive) laws with moral (prescriptive) ones. However, his point could be made in terms of such a distinction; descriptive laws, insofar as the regularities which they describe are universal and necessary and not merely local or statistical, demand unconditional acceptance and thus in a sense function prescriptively.

In any case, Shestov wished to assert that rationalists, in absolutizing theoretical truth, inevitably relativize human life. In yielding to "self-evidence," they accept the "horrors of human existence" as something necessary and legitimate. Shestov, in contrast, was quite prepared to relativize theoretical truth if that was the price to be paid for absolutizing moral and religious values and thus "redeeming" the existing individual.

The Nietzschean strain in Shestov's thought appears most clearly in his denial of the validity of universal norms. Such norms function to limit and repress creativity. "The fundamental property of life," he wrote, "is daring; all life is creative daring and thus an eternal mystery, irreducible to anything finished or intelligible" (*In Job's Balances,* p. 158). Under the tyranny of ethical rationalism (a part of the general tyranny of reason, which develops naturally out of the initial autonomy of reason), we come to fear chaos because it is a loss of order. But "chaos is not a limited possibility; it is an unlimited opportunity" (ibid., p. 226).

For Shestov the decisive either/or—reason and necessity or faith and freedom—is not a choice, as rationalists would claim, between sanity and insanity. It is a choice between two kinds of madness (the distinction is reminiscent of Kierkegaard's distinction between "objective" and "subjective" madness). The first kind of madness is that of theoretical reason, which takes as ultimate, eternal, and universally obligatory those objective truths which rationalize and legitimize the "horrors of human existence." The second kind of madness is the Kierkegaardian leap of faith which ventures to take up the struggle against rationalized and legitimized horror at the point where such struggle is "self-evidently" doomed to defeat. Between these two kinds of madness, Shestov's own choice is clear and final.

See also Anaximander; Aristotle; Descartes, René; Dostoevsky, Fyodor Mikhailovich; Existentialism; Hegel, Georg Wilhelm Friedrich; Husserl, Edmund; Kant, Immanuel; Kierkegaard, Søren Aabye; Nietzsche, Friedrich; Parmenides of Elea; Pascal, Blaise; Plato; Plotinus; Rationalism; Russian Philosophy; Spinoza, Benedict (Baruch) de.

Bibliography

WORKS BY SHESTOV

Dostoevskii i Nietsshe: Filosofiia tragedii. St. Petersburg, 1903. Translated by R. von Walter as *Dostojewski und Nietzsche: Philosophie der Tragödie.* Cologne, 1924. Also translated into French as *Dostoevski et Nietzsche (La Philosophie de la tragédie).* Paris, 1926.

Apofeoz bespochvennosti: Opyt adogmaticheskogo myshleniia (The apotheosis of groundlessness: an essay in undogmatic thought). St. Petersburg, 1905. Translated by S. S. Koteliansky as *All Things Are Possible.* New York: R.M. McBride, 1920. With a foreword by D. H. Lawrence.

Na Vesakh Iova. Paris: Sovremennyia zapiski, 1929. Translated by A. Coventry and C. A. Macartney as *In Job's Balances.* London: J.M. Dent, 1932.

Kirkegard i ekzistentsial'naia filosofiia (Glas vopiiushchego v pustyne). Paris: Dom knigi i Sovremennyia zapiski, 1939. Translated by T. Rageot and Boris de Schloezer from the manuscript as *Kierkegaard et la philosophie existentielle (Vox Clamantis in Deserto).* Paris: J. Vrin, 1936; reprinted 1948.

English translation by Elinor Hewitt as *Kierkegaard and the Existential Philosophy.* Athens: Ohio University Press, 1966.

Afiny i Ierusalim. Paris: YMCA Press, 1951. Translated from the manuscript by Boris de Schloezer as *Athènes et Jerusalem: Essai de philosophie religieuse.* Paris: J. Vrin, 1938.

WORKS ON SHESTOV

Schloezer, Boris de. "Un penseur russe: Léon Chestov." *Mercure de France* 159 (1922): 82–115.

Zenkovsky, V. V. *Istoriia russkoi filosofii.* 2 vols. Paris: YMCA Press, 1948–1950. Translated by G. L. Kline as *A History of Russian Philosophy.* 2 vols., 780–791. New York: Columbia University Press, 1953.

George L. Kline (1967)

SHESTOV, LEV ISAAKOVICH [ADDENDUM]

Shestov has become the object of academic philosophical attention only since 1968. After the 1917 Russian Revolution Shestov became a significant voice in European philosophical existentialism, in his later life engaging with Blaise Pascal and Søren Kierkegaard, actively influencing the thought of Albert Camus, and corresponding with Martin Buber. Some of these philosophical relationships have received concentrated, though not exhaustive, critical attention (Maia Neto 1995). In addition, Shestov corresponded with and wrote an article on Edmund Husserl, which is the focus of one critical article.

Because of the Soviet ban on research and publication relating to Shestov, scholars inevitably found it difficult to define and establish Shestov as a philosopher. To begin with there was very little criticism outside the Paris émigré community. The two-volume biography on Shestov written by his daughter, Natalie Baranova-Shestova (1983), drew attention to the man and his work. Since the end of the Soviet Union Shestov has won renewed consideration among Russian philosophers.

Existentialist aspects of Shestov's thought have generally garnered the most critical attention and have generated other critical approaches. Some existentialist commentaries focus on the experience of suffering, isolation, and tragedy while others concentrate on the aspect of the absurd. Shestov has received attention as a religious thinker particularly in two contexts. First, scholars have viewed him in the context of the "Russian religious renaissance," a group of Russian religious philosophers of the early twentieth century who brought a personalist, anti-dogmatic and antirational approach to the question of religious experience and faith. Second, scholars have seen him as a major modern Jewish thinker. In the late twentieth century, philosophical research focused on two contrasting aspects of Shestov's thought, the paradoxical but invigorating interaction between skepticism and religious faith. His philosophy has been viewed together with that of Pascal and Kierkegaard, as part of the tradition of skeptical thought, Pyrrhonism, that goes beyond pure skepticism to employ reasoned doubt in a positive role within categories of faith.

Bibliography

WORKS BY LEV SHESTOV

Sobranie sochinenii. 6 vols. St. Petersburg: Izd. Shipovnik, 1911.

Athens and Jerusalem. Translated with an introduction by Bernard Martin. Athens: Ohio University Press, 1966. Originally published as *Afiny I Ierusalim.* Parizh: YMCA Press, 1951.

A Shestov Anthology, edited with an introduction by Bernard Martin. Athens: Ohio University Press, 1971.

WORKS ABOUT LEV SHESTOV

Baranova-Shestova, Natalie. *Zhizn' L'va Shestova: po perepiske i vospominaniiam sovremennikov* (The life of Lev Shestov from his correspondence and reminiscences of contemporaries). 2 vols. Paris: Presse Libre, 1983.

Clowes, Edith. "Philosophy as Tragedy." In *Fiction's Overcoat: Russian Literary Culture and the Question of Philosophy.* Ithaca: Cornell University Press, 2004, 130–154.

Kline, George L. *Religious and Anti-Religious Thought in Russia.* Chicago: University of Chicago Press, 1968.

Maia Neto, Jose R. *The Christianization of Pyrrhonism: Skepticism and Faith in Pascal, Kierkegaard, and Shestov.* Dordrecht: Kluwer Academic, 1995.

Martin, Bernard, ed. *Great Twentieth Century Jewish Philosophers: Shestov, Rosenzweig, Buber, with Selections from Their Writings.* New York: Macmillan, 1970.

Zakydalsky, Taras D. "Lev Shestov and the Revival of Religious Thought in Russia." In *Russian Thought after Communism: The Recovery of a Philosophical Heritage*, edited by James P. Scanlan, 153–164. Armonk, NY: M. E. Sharpe, 1994.

Edith Clowes (2005)

SHINRAN

(1173–1262)

Shinran, born Hino Arinori, is the foremost proponent of Japanese Pure Land Buddhism and is widely regarded as the founder of Jôdo-Shinshû, more commonly known outside of Japan as Shin Buddhism. Pure Land Buddhism has the largest following in East Asia (China, Korea, and Japan), and the Shin sect is the largest sect of Japanese Buddhism. As a development of Mahayana Buddhism, the core of Shinran's thought is based on the twofold truth:

Conventional truth	Highest truth
Form	Emptiness
Distinctions	No distinctions
Words	Beyond words
suffering	liberation
samsara	nirvana
defiled world	Pure Land
blind passion	boundless compassion
self-power	other-power
foolish being	Amida Buddha
Namu	Amida Butsu

TWOFOLD TRUTH

These truths are twofold because they are like the two sides of the same coin. There is an aspect of truth defined conceptually by the discursive intellect, and there is a truth beyond words, beyond the grasp of the discursive intellect. In this view, all conceptual reality is nothing more than agreed on convention, hence the term *conventional truth*. When the mind is emptied of all preconceptions, the truth can be grasped for the first time with one's whole being. This is the highest truth, emptied of the concepts that act like an intervening smoke screen between subject and object. When the conceptual smoke screen is removed, the separation between subject and object also disappears. Paradoxically, this merging of subject and object does not mean the obliteration of perception. Rather, perception becomes more fluid, dynamic, and vivid. For example, when one is viewing a flower and is caught up in trying to determine its genus, species, and variety, one fails to see the vivid dynamism of the beautiful flower unfolding before one. However, when one lets go of one's obsession with grasping the flower taxonomically or conceptually, suddenly one feels that the flower is closer, more intimate, vivid, and fluid in its evanescence.

WORDS AND BEYOND WORDS

In Buddhism the problem does not lie with the categories or words themselves, such as *flower*, *peony*, and so on. Rather, it is the mind that becomes obsessed or attached to fixed conceptions of reality that causes one to become lost or separated from the dynamic flow of reality. Suffering, defiled perception, and blinded passion all result from this fixation. Conversely, words, properly used, can convey reality beyond words. They are like the words of a love poem. Although the individual words of a love poem cannot capture love itself, a beautiful love poem can nevertheless convey the sensibility of love. The words are no mere signs; they are vessels of a higher truth.

THE NAME OF AMIDA BUDDHA

In Shinran's Shin thought, the twofold truth is expressed through the Name of Amida Buddha, the Buddha of Infinite Light and Immeasurable Life. The practitioner of Shin invokes or chants the name Namu Amida Butsu. It originates in India and comes from the Sanskrit, Namas Amitâbha Buddha, meaning, "I entrust myself to the awakening of infinite light." When the practitioner, caught in the net of fixed ideas, is illuminated by the dynamic flow of reality, he or she is released from his or her blind passions and awakens to the light of emptiness, or the boundless oneness of reality.

The highest truth of reality is formless, without shape, definition, color, or scent. However, the experience of release from the ego-bonds of fixation and blind passion is one of illumination or light. This is neither merely symbolic nor merely material or physical. Similar to the experience of being relieved of a heavy mental burden, one's conscious awareness and field of vision become clearer, lighter, and more responsive.

According to Shinran the consciousness of an ego self-enclosed in its own solipsistic world works under the delusion of self-power (Japanese: *jiriki*), as though it sustains itself completely unrelated to the world around it. When the bonds of this delusion are exposed and illuminated by the dynamic unfolding of emptiness/oneness, the self awakens to the working of other-power (Japanese: *tariki*), so-called because it is other than (the delusory) ego.

However, one does not and cannot abandon the foolish delusions of the ego; as long as one lives in this limited body and mind, one will continue to suffer the ego's foolishness. Furthermore, it is this very foolishness, when one recognizes it, that connects the practitioner to his or her deepest humanity and that of others. For it is in the suffering of blind passion and foolishness that one finds the deepest bonds of humanity, and ultimately, with all sentient beings. In the illumination of Amida Buddha, the blind passion of the foolish being becomes the gateway to wisdom and compassion. Thus, Namu represents the foolish being who, in his very foolishness, is illuminated by Amida Butsu, infinite light and boundless compassion. The saying of the name Namu Amida Butsu embodies the realization of the oneness of foolish being and boundless compassion. Without the Namu, Amida Buddha is merely a cold abstraction; only when the practitioner engages the vivid flow of reality by allowing his or her blindness to be illuminated does the reality of Amida Buddha come to life. For this reason, the real name of Amida Buddha is said to be Namu Amida Butsu.

SHINRAN'S SOCIAL VISION

Shinran's philosophical thought translated itself into an egalitarian social vision. According to him, no human being, even religious masters, were completely enlightened. Indeed, those who had engaged in intensive religious practice were considered particularly susceptible to the hubris of religious attainment. Shinran abandoned the monastic life, married openly, had four children, and lived among the farmers in outlying districts. Nevertheless, he and his wife, Esshinni, continued to wear religious robes and ministered to peasants and farmers until Shinran was about sixty. He describes himself as "neither monk nor layman" (Hirota, 289 [translation adapted]) and states, "I do not have even a single disciple"(Hirota, 664 [translation adapted]) since the power of compassion comes from Amida as the deepest reality of the self, and not from the finite human being Shinran.

He spent his final thirty years living in his brother's house, writing voluminously on his understanding of the wondrous working of Amida's boundless compassion, mythologically expressed as the working of Amida's Primal Vow. This is a way of expressing the relentless flow of reality that sooner or later breaks down and dissolves the brittle facade of self-power ego.

See also Buddhism; Buddhist Epistemology; Japanese Philosophy; Social and Political Philosophy; Truth.

Bibliography

Dobbins, James C. *Jōdo Shinshū: Shin Buddhism in Medieval Japan*. Honolulu: University of Hawaii Press, 2002.

Hirota. Dennis, trans. *The Collected Works of Shinran.*, 2 vols. Kyoto, Japan: Jōdo Shinsū Hongwanji-Ha, 1997.

Keel, Hee-Sung. *Understanding Shinran: A Dialogical Approach.* Fremont, CA: Asian Humanities Press, 1995.

Unno, Taitetsu. *River of Fire, River of Water: An Introduction to the Pure Land Tradition of Shin Buddhism.* New York: Doubleday, 1998.

Mark T. Unno (2005)

SHĪRĀZĪ, SADR AL-DĪN

See *Mullā Ṣadrā*

SHOAH

See *Holocaust*

SHOEMAKER, SYDNEY

(1931–)

Sydney Shoemaker is the Susan Linn Sage Professor of Philosophy Emeritus at Cornell University. Before joining the Philosophy Department at Cornell in 1961, he taught at Ohio State University and he held the Santayana Fellowship at Harvard University. He also delivered the John Locke Lectures at Oxford University (1972) on "Mind and Behavior" and the Royce Lectures at Brown University (1993) on "Self-Knowledge" and "Inner Sense." He has pioneered work in a variety of areas in metaphysics and the philosophy of mind, particularly on the nature of mind, the nature of the self and of self-knowledge, and the nature of properties. Some of the most important of his contributions in these areas are charted in this entry.

Shoemaker's work on the topic of the self and self-knowledge is informed by a rejection of the Cartesian notion of an immaterial self and the accompanying view that self-knowledge involves a kind of "inner observation" of the contents of one's mind that is perception-like in certain characteristic ways. The nature of the self and self-knowledge forms the subject matter of his seminal *Self-Knowledge and Self-Identity* (1963). In this work Shoemaker conducts a sustained attack on the Cartesian view that the unity of the self, or personal identity, is due to or involves an immaterial unity. Shoemaker argues, against this, that personal identity involves both physical factors concerning persons' bodies and psychological factors concerning their memories and that although the primary criterion for such identity is bodily identity, a memory criterion is also applicable. His arguments make use of a distinctive methodological strategy that has come to be known as "the method of cases" (Johnston 1987), involving the use of thought experiments to determine answers to questions about personal identity (a method that John Locke [1985] used in his discussion of personal identity).

Shoemaker's examples and the style of argumentation in this work have been highly influential in discussions of personal identity. His views in this area are further developed in later work, such as his "Persons and Their Pasts" (1970), *Personal Identity* (1984; with Richard Swinburne), *The First-Person Perspective and Other Essays* (1996), and the Royce Lectures, where he revisits another important theme found in *Self-Knowledge and Self-Identity*: the Cartesian, "inner sense" view of self-knowledge. In these lectures he argues that if self-knowledge were perception-like, and the object of such knowledge were the self, it would be possible to err in one's attempt to identify oneself, just as it is possible to err in one's attempt to identify the objects of ordinary perception. However, he claims, it is not possible to misidentify oneself in this way. He also argues that the "inner sense" model of self-knowledge, being a perceptual one, requires commitment to two conditions that are essential to a "broad" perceptual model, a causal condition and an independence condition, but that knowledge of one's own mental states does not meet these conditions. His own view is that self-knowledge is not based on evidence of any kind, whether this be from "outer" behavioral facts or from "inner" ones, as the perceptual model encourages one to suppose.

Shoemaker's arguments involve an appeal to a particular view of the nature of mind known as functionalism, a view that he has developed and defended extensively in several works, notably in "Functionalism and Qualia" (1975), "Some Varieties of Functionalism" (1981a), "Absent Qualia Are Impossible" (1981b), and "The Inverted Spectrum" (1981c). Functionalism in the philosophy of mind is, broadly construed, the doctrine that mental-state types or kinds can be exhaustively characterized and uniquely individuated by their functional properties—by the relations that they are apt to bear to certain characteristic kinds of physical stimuli, other mental states, and behavioral responses. Shoemaker (1981b, 1981c) defends this doctrine against two major objections, known as the inverted qualia and absent qualia objections. The inverted qualia objection supposes that two states—say, perceptual experiences—might vary in their visual qualia (one being reddish, perhaps, while the other is greenish) yet remain invariant with respect to their functional roles. Shoemaker agrees but argues that this possibility is compatible with the truth of functionalism. The absent qualia objection goes further and supposes that two states could be functionally identical yet differ to the extent that one has qualitative content while the other lacks it altogether. Shoemaker concedes that if this were a genuine possibility, it would show that functionalism is false, but it is not a genuine possibility.

A third area in which Shoemaker has done pioneering work, connected with his functionalist view of the nature of mind, concerns the nature of properties. In the case of mental states Shoemaker argues that their nature is causal-functional. In the case of properties Shoemaker is an advocate of what is known as the causal theory of properties (Armstrong 2000), a view championed in his influential "Causality and Properties" (1980). According to it, properties have causal powers essentially, rather than accidentally, in that it is in the nature of properties to bestow causal capacities on their instances or exemplifications. So, for example, it is in the nature of the property, pain, to confer on its instances, individual pains, the capacity to cause their subjects to believe that they are in pain, to wince, and so on. The view contrasts with a "categoricalist" one (Armstrong 2000), which takes properties to be contingently, rather than essentially, related to the capacities they bestow on their instances.

Although some have construed Shoemaker as holding the view that properties just are dispositions (rather than the weaker view that properties are essentially dispositional), which is a controversial and difficult view to defend, this is a mistake. Shoemaker argues that, strictly speaking, the dispositional/nondispositional distinction only applies to linguistic items, specifically, to predicates such as *soluble*, *fragile*, *round*, and so on. Some predicates (e.g., *soluble* or *fragile*) are dispositional whereas others (e.g., *round* or *red* are not. But all properties bestow causal capacities on their instances, for it is in their nature to do so. So, for example, the property round bestows on its instances in, say, marbles, the capacity to roll into round holes, but not triangular ones. Shoemaker argues that the identity conditions of properties can be given in terms of such capacities, that is, that properties are identical if and only if they bestow on their instances the same causal capacities or powers and that it follows that the relations that hold between properties are necessary rather than contingent, so that, if laws involve relations between properties, such laws are necessary rather than contingent.

See also Cartesianism; Philosophy of Mind; Qualia.

Bibliography

Shoemaker, Sydney, and Richard Swinburne. *Personal Identity*. Oxford, U.K.: Blackwell, 1984.

WORKS BY SHOEMAKER

Self-Knowledge and Self-Identity. Ithaca, NY: Cornell University Press, 1963.

"Persons and Their Pasts." *American Philosophical Quarterly* 7 (4) (1970): 269–285.

"Functionalism and Qualia." *Philosophical Studies* 27 (5) (1975): 291–315.

"Causality and Properties." In *Time and Cause: Essays Presented to Richard Taylor*, edited by Peter van Inwagen, 109–135. Dordrecht, Netherlands: Reidel, 1980.

"Some Varieties of Functionalism." *Philosophical Topics* 12 (1981a): 83–118.

"Absent Qualia Are Impossible." *Philosophical Review* 90 (1981b): 581–599.

"The Inverted Spectrum." *Journal of Philosophy* 74 (1981c): 357–381.

Identity, Cause, and Mind: Philosophical Essays. New York: Cambridge University Press, 1984.

"Self-Knowledge and Inner Sense." *Philosophy and Phenomenological Research* 54 (1994): 249–314.

The First-Person Perspective and Other Essays. New York: Cambridge University Press, 1996.

WORKS ABOUT SHOEMAKER

Armstrong, David. "The Causal Theory of Properties: Properties According to Shoemaker, Ellis, and Others." *Metaphysica* 1 (2000): 5–20.

Johnston, Mark. "Human Beings." *Journal of Philosophy* 84 (1987): 59–83.

Locke, John. *An Essay concerning Human Understanding*, edited by Peter H. Nidditch. Oxford, U.K.: Clarendon Press, 1985.

Cynthia Macdonald (2005)

SHPET, GUSTAV GUSTAVOVICH

(1879–1937)

In his most important phenomenological work, *Iavlenie i smysl* (Appearance and sense, 1914), Gustav Shpet took up Edmund Husserl's idea of pure phenomenology and developed it in the direction of a "phenomenology of hermeneutical reason." In this theoretical framework he formulated, between 1914 and 1918, hermeneutic and semiotic problems, which in the 1920s he elaborated more specifically within the fields of philosophy of language and theory of art. In doing so, he was combining Husserl's conceptions with ideas from other philosophical movements, particularly Wilhelm Dilthey's hermeneutics and Wilhelm von Humboldt's philosophy of language.

Shpet's reception and transformation of phenomenology must be seen in the context of Russian intellectual and cultural life during the first two decades of the twentieth century. The Platonic "Moscow Metaphysical School" (which included Vladimir Solov'ëv and Sergei Trubetskoi) provided the intellectual atmosphere in which Shpet's turn to Husserl's phenomonology took place. His ideas on theories of language and signs are close to those of contemporary Russian formalism. His phenomenological and structural theories influcenced Prague structuralism through the "Moscow Linguistic Circle," and his work is seen as a precursor to Soviet semiotics.

SHPET'S LIFE

Gustav Shpet was born in 1879 in Kiev. He studied there at Vladimir University from 1901 to 1905, completing his studies with a monograph entitled *Problema prichinnosti u Iuma i Kanta* (The problem of causality in Hume and Kant). In 1907 he moved to Moscow, and taught at Moscow University from 1910. During a stay in Göttingen (1912–1913), where he studied with Husserl, he turned to Husserl's transcendental phenomenology. His first phenomenological publication, *Iavlenie i smysl* (Appearance and meaning, 1914) marked the beginning of a productive reception of Husserl's phenomenology in Russia. In 1916 he defended his master's thesis *Istoriia kak problema logiki* (History as a problem of logic, Part I). In 1918 he finished *Germenevtika i eë problemy* (Hermeneutics and its problems), in which he discussed the problems of hermeneutics as they have been developed throughout history from antiquity (especially in Origen and Augustine) to modern times, thereby at the same time elaborating the basic outline of his "hermeneutical philosophy"—a philosophy that is caught in the field of tension exerted, on the one side, by Husserl's "Phenomenology of Reason" and, on the other, by Dilthey's "Philosophy of Life."

After the Revolution of 1917, Shpet was active in various fields of cultural and intellectual life. He received a professorship of philosophy at Moscow University. In 1920 he joined the "Moscow Linguistic Circle" (MLK), a center of Russian formalism, and in 1921 he was appointed director of the Institute for Scientific Philosophy, a new research institute at Moscow University. Expelled from the university in 1923 for political reasons, he concentrated his activities on the State Academy of the Arts (GAKhN), where he served as vice president until 1929, and where he temporarily chaired the Department of Philosophy. His most important contributions to the theory of art and language are his *Ėsteticheskie fragmenty* (Aesthetic fragments), published in 1922 and 1923 in Petrograd, and *Vnutrenniaia forma slova* (The internal form of the word) (1927).

Ėsteticheskie fragmenty includes a phenomenology of "living discourse" and an analysis of those rules that determine the constitution of meaning in poetic discourse. These phenomenological and structural analyses of language, which aim to construct a poetics, were further developed through a critical assessment of Wilhelm von Humboldt's philosophy of language in Shpet's last substantial work, *The Internal Form of the Word* (1927). Following a "cleansing" of the GAKhN in 1929, Shpet was forced to retire from his academic post, and he subsequently worked as a translator, editor, and critic. It was during this period that he translated Dickens, Byron, and Shakespeare into Russian. In March 1935 he was arrested by the NKVD (People's Commissariat of Internal Affairs) and was charged with having led an anti-Soviet group during his time at the GAKhN in the 1920s. After a lengthy detention, he was exiled for five years to Eniseisk, and later to Tomsk. There, in 1937, he finished his Russian translation of Hegel's *Phenomenology of Spirit.* In October of that year he was arrested and shot by the NKVD.

SHPET'S DEVELOPMENT TOWARD PHENOMENOLOGY

Representative of Shpet's notion of philosophy before his turn to phenomenology, as well as expectations he held for a reform of philosophy and psychology, is his article *Odin put' psikhologii i kuda on vedët* (One way of psychology and where it leads), published in 1912. The article criticizes experimental and explanatory psychology for having replaced "living and concrete facts" with "empty schemata and abstractions." Only a descriptive psychology that focuses on the pure data of consciousness would be able to fathom psychic life in its concreteness and totality. He saw the basis for this new direction in psychological theory in Wilhelm Dilthey's *Ideas of a Descriptive and Analytical Psychology* (1894). Shpet argued for a philosophy that would take into account the totality of psychic life: a "realistic metaphysics," whose task it would be to grasp "the real in its true essence and its totality." Shpet thought that such a philosophy, which draws on the evident facts of "inner experience," had been realized in important movements of nineteenth- and early twentieth-century Russian philosophy. Philosophers of the "Moscow Metaphysical School" (especially Vladimir Solov'ëv and Sergei Trubetskoi) are cited as exponents of this trend in Russian thought.

Another, no less important, influence on Shpet's reception of Husserl was his interest in the logic of the historical sciences. During his stay in Göttingen (1912–1913) he discovered in Husserl's phenomenology the theory for which he had been searching, and his hermeneutical interest motivated him to try to develop Husserl's "Phenomenology of Reason," as outlined in *Ideas Pertaining to a Pure Phenomenology*, volume 1 (1913), into a theory of hermeneutic reason that focuses on the problem of understanding signs. Although the ideas Shpet encountered in Göttingen primarily concerned transcendental phenomenology—the seminar on "Nature and Spirit," which Shpet attended with other influential phenomenologists like Roman Ingarden and Hans Lipps, certainly met his hermeneutical interests—the ontological trend in the intellectual atmosphere among Husserl's fellow students in Göttingen also should be taken into account.

SHPET'S VERSION OF PHENOMENOLOGY

Shpet's encounter with Husserl's phenomenology, in light of Shpet's expectation of a reform of philosophy and psychology, leads to a singular notion of phenomenology, which is documented in *Iavlenie i smysl* (Appearence and sense, 1914). On the one hand, Shpet tries to reconstruct Husserl's noetic-noematic studies within the framework of an ontological inquiry, based on the Neoplatonism of the Moscow Metaphysical School; on the other hand, he demonstrates the incompleteness of Husserl's analyses of intentional objects, as presented in *Ideas*, volume 1, and completes these analyses with his own. The "noematic sense" intended in acts of consciousness, as presented by Husserl, presupposes for Shpet a class of intentional experiences hardly dealt with in *Ideas*: acts of consciousness through understanding, which play a role in the constitution of all classes of concrete objects. The structure of these "hermeneutic acts" is illustrated by a range of phenomena that are of only minor importance in *Ideas*: the mode of appearance of items of practical use, the specific character of historical sources, and the understanding of linguistic utterances. Thus Husserl's "Phenomenology of Reason" provides a basis for historical cognition in scientific logic, leading eventually to a grounding of the humanities throughan analysis of their conceptual framework and methodology.

Shpet's ensuing works on hermeneutics, philosophy of language, and theory of art, published or written between 1916 and 1927, can be seen as a further development of his hermeneutical phenomenology, the primary idea of which is the correlation of signs (as a combination of expression and meaning) and sign-interpreting consciousness. Shpet also characterizes his project as a semiotic "Philosophy of Culture" in which language, art, myths, and manners are to be described as systems of signs. He develops the basic model of a sign out of Husserl's concept of linguistic expression, which acts as a prototype for all other forms of signs. The idea of a "purely logical grammar," which formulates laws for the grammatical meanings of natural languages, should be applied analogously to all other cultural systems.

HERMENEUTICS, PHILOSOPHY OF LANGUAGE, AND POETICS

The concrete form of Shpet's phenomenology of hermeneutical reason in his philosophy of language and his poetics was also much influenced by Dilthey's "Philosophy of Life." In Shpet's hermeneutical philosophy, as outlined in *Germenevtika i ee problemy* (Hermeneutics and its problems) (1918), he worked with Schleiermacher's, Boeckh's and Dilthey's theories of understanding. Above all, he tried to deepen and refine Dilthey's late grounding of the humanities—then the culmination in the development of hermeneutics—with insights in the domain of semiotic theories, which he found not only in Husserl's first *Logical Investigation on Expression and Meaning*, but also in other semantic works of the Brentano School (particularly Anton Marty and Alexius Meinong). A combination of Husserl's semantics with Dilthey's hermeneutics would be an enrichment for both sides, as Shpet wrote at the end of the manuscript. The theory of understanding could find a new answer to the question of the mutual relation of the different methods of interpretation, whereas semantics would experience in this combination a "philosophically lively and concrete embodiment."

This actualization of Husserl's philosophical semantics, with a hermeneutical intention, has left its traces in Shpet's *Ėsteticheskie fragmenty* (1922–1923), with which he entered contemporary discussions on literary theory, as initiated by Russian formalism. He was particularly concerned with the definition of the specific character of poetical discourse as opposed to others, be they scientific, rhetorical, or everyday discourses. If one puts this question phenomenologically, one has to ask under what conditions a linguistic utterance appears as artistic or poetic to a listener or reader. Since a poetic utterance is experienced only as a contrast to everyday use of language, one must first analyze the reception of everyday language. Shpet follows this procedure in the second part of *Ėsteticheskie fragmenty*. The difference between understanding the message and understanding its author plays a pivotal role in Shpet's description of the various forms and aspects of linguistic consciousness.

In contrast to such a phenomenological analysis of lingusitic consciousness, Shpet presents a structural analysis of linguistic expression as "ontology of the word," which he, in turn, subsumed under a general theory of semiotics. In this confrontation between a phenomenological inquiry, which is confined to the side of experience, and an ontology, which focuses on the object, the ever-increasing influence of Husserl's early concept of phenomenology on Shpet becomes visible. In Shpet's "ontology of the word" a particular concept of structure is of central importance. "The structure is a concrete construction whose individual parts can vary in their extent and even in their quantity, but not a single part of the whole *in potentia* can be removed without destroying this whole." (1922–1923, II, 11). By "structure of the word" Shpet did not mean the morphological, syntactic, or stylistic construction—in short, not the arrangement of linguistic units "in the plane," but "the organic, depth-wise, as it were, arrangement of the word—from the sensually conceivable wording to the eidetic object." The structure of the word, therefore, consists of the relations between phonemes and meaning, as well as of those between the word's meaning and "object," where the latter is ideal and ontologically distinct from concrete individual things.

When Shpet spoke of the structure of the *word*, he took it in the wide sense of the Russian expression for "word" *slovo*, which can mean sentences or combinations of sentences in discourse, as well as literary texts and even natural language in its entirety. Shpet used it with all these different meanings, yet was mainly concerned with the "communicating word": meaningful discourse able to convey something to another person. Thus Shpet took up Plato's definition of predicative statements, as "the shortest and most simple *logos*" (Sophistēs 262c). Shpet described its structure as follows: in a simple predication the subject denotes a concrete, individual object; the predicate indicates a property belonging to this object. In denoting, speakers refer to a thing; in predication, they say something about it. What can be said about this thing, and conversely, which predications are possible, is determined by the species to which the thing belongs. Therefore the act of intending a species, which Shpet called also the "eidetic object," is indispensable for the construction of a meaningful sentence.

With these definitions Shpet outlined the "word's structure," which is common to everyday and scientific communication, as well as to rhetorical and poetic discourse. In order to explain how this general structure manifests itself in the artistic usage of words, sentences, and discourse, Shpet developed a theory of linguistic functions that stems from a critical assessment of Husserl's and Marty's philosophy of language. He started from three different functions of language, each fulfilled by a particular type of discourse. These three communicative functions are the factual—the expressive, and the poetic, the latter working through the creative formation of language. Depending on which of these three functions is dominant, discourse is either scientific (concerned with factual communication), rhetorical (concerned with influencing other people's emotions), or poetic (primarily concerned with the arrangement of linguistic expressions as such).

The predominance of one of the three functions implies in each case a different mutual relation between the above-mentioned parts of the word structure. Whereas, for example, in everyday language the arrangement on the level of expression aims primarily at structuring the expressed meaning, and thereby at the communication of facts, in poetic discourse all levels gain a relative importance of their own. The rhythmic forms and syntactic peculiarities of this discourse should attract attention as such. At the same time, the meaning expressed in poetic discourse is more dependent on the external forms of language: whereas the meaning of a factual—above all scientific—communication is not affected by each change of wording and syntactic arrangement.

FROM HUSSERL TO HUMBOLDT

By giving pure logic, which deals with the condition of the possibility of science, a phenomenological foundation, Husserl excluded important aspects of living discourse from his language analysis. Shpet's project was more extensive than Husserl's in that he analyzed scientific communication merely as one possible form alongside the poetic, rhetorical, and everyday discourses. This widening of the horizon entails a turning away from (not only a modification of) Husserl's concept of language. Shpet questioned, for example, one of the central presuppositions of *Logical Investigations*—that scientific discourse can be marked off from living discourse. These two ways of speaking are only tendencies, as Shpet emphasized; they are not fully realized in any empirical speech sample. "Figurativeness is not only a trait of 'poetry'… it is a general property of language, which belongs to scientific discourse as well." (1922–1923, III, 32).

The thesis of the irreducibility of figurative-ambivalent discourse has to do with Shpet's emphasis on the fact that thought is inseparably bound to language. With this concept of language as the "formative organ of thought," as outlined by Shpet in his interpretation of Humboldt in 1927, he turned away most clearly from Husserl's *Logical Investigations*, according to which "the fact of being expressed is arbitrary for the meaning."

See also Existentialism; Phenomenology.

Bibliography

WORKS BY SHPET

Ėsteticheskie fragmenty I–III (Aesthetic fragments). Petrograd: Kolos, 1922–1923. Reprinted in *Sochineniia* (Works), 343–472. Moscow: Pravda, 1989. Shpet's contribution to the theory of art and language.

"Germenevtika i eë problemy" (Hermeneutics and its problems, 1918). In *Gustav Shpet: Mysli Slovo: Izbrannye Trudy* (Thought and word: selected works), edited by Tatiana Shchedrina. Moscow: Rosspen, 2005. Translated into German as *Die Hermeneutik und ihre Probleme*, edited by R. Daube-Schackat and A. Haardt. Freiburg, Munich: Alber, 1993. Critical presentation of the problems of hermeneutics as they have developed throughout history.

Iavlenie i smysl: Fenomenologiia kak osnovnaia nauka i eëe problemy (1914). 2nd ed. Tomsk: Vodolei, 1996. Translated as *Appearance and Sense: Phenomenology as the Fundamental Science and Its Problems* by T. Nemeth. Dordrecht, Boston, London: Kluwer Academic Publishers, 1991. Shpet oulines his "phenomenology of hermeneutical reason."

Istoriia kak problema logiki (History as a problem of logic). Moscow, 1916. Shpet's master's thesis.

"Odin put' psikhologii i kuda on vedët" (One way of psychology and where it leads). In *Filosofskii sbornik L. M. Lopatinu*, 245–264. Moscow, 1912. Representative of Shpet's notion of philosophy before his turn to phenomenology.

Problema prichinnosti u Iuma i Kanta (The problem of causality in Hume and Kant). Kiev: Universitet Sv. Vladimira, 1907. Shpet's first work, a monograph.

Vnutrenniaia forma slova (The internal form of the word). Moscow: GAKhN, 1927. 2nd ed. Ivanovo: Ivanovskii gosudarstvennyi universitet, 1999. A critical assessment of Humboldt's philosophy of language.

WORKS ABOUT SHPET

Haardt, A. *Husserl in Rußland: Phänomenologie der Sprache und Kunst bei Gustav Špet und Alekseij Losev* (Husserl in Russia: Phenomenology of language and art in Gustav Shpet and Aleksei Losev). Munich: Fink, 1993.

Shchedrina, T. G. *"Ja pishu kak ėkho drugogo…": Ocherki intellektual'noi biografii Gustava Shpeta* ("I'm writing like an echo of other people…": Studies on the Intellectual Biography of Gustav Shpet). Moscow: Progress-Tradiciia, 2004.

Alexander Haardt (2005)

SIBLEY, FRANK
(1923–1996)

Frank Sibley was trained as a philosopher in postwar Oxford. His principal teacher was Gilbert Ryle, who, understandably, had a profound influence on Sibley's way of doing philosophical analysis—an influence that is as apparent in his last papers as in his first ones.

Sibley must be credited with inaugurating the renaissance in aesthetics and philosophy of art in the English-speaking world after World War II, a renaissance that is still in full cry. He did it in 1959, in an article that, in the years since, has never ceased being discussed and cited in the literature, and, at the time of its appearance, produced a veritable deluge of essays, and even books in response or defense, that completely reinvigorated the discipline.

"Aesthetic Concepts" (1959a), as Sibley titled his inaugural article, dealt, in a surprisingly few pages, with three of the most basic and difficult issues in the discipline: taste, criticism, and the distinction between the aesthetic and nonaesthetic. He began, with a sensitive ear for "ordinary language" that was to characterize to the end all of his work in aesthetics, by distinguishing between the kinds of things one says about works of art such as "that a novel has a great number of characters and deals with life in a manufacturing town" or "that a painting uses pale colors, predominantly blues and greens," and such remarks, in contrast, as "that a poem is tightly knit" or "that a picture lacks balance or has a certain serenity and repose." About these different kinds of remarks, Sibley claims, "It would be natural enough to say that the making of judgments such as these [latter ones] requires the exercise of taste, perceptiveness, or sensitivity of aesthetic discrimination or appreciation; one would not say this of my first group" (pp. 63–64).

Sibley calls the terms that he thinks require a perceptiveness, sensitivity, or taste beyond that of "normal eyes, ears, and intelligence," aesthetic concepts or terms. And it is the central, most controversial of his claims that aesthetic concepts or terms are, as he puts it, not condition-governed, which is to say, "There are no sufficient conditions, no non-aesthetic features such that the presence of some set or number of them will beyond question logically justify or warrant the application of an aesthetic term" (1959a, p. 67).

Sibley was, throughout his professional life, reticent to publish because of a deeply ingrained perfectionism. Even though his philosophical reputation stems mainly from the groundbreaking "Aesthetic Concepts," it is not the only one of his publications to have influenced the field. Particularly worthy of mention are "Aesthetics and the Looks of Things" (1959b) and "Aesthetic and Nonaesthetic" (1965), in both of which Sibley further explores the whole question of aesthetic reason-giving. As well, Sibley's work in aesthetics and philosophy of art is now likely to have a renewed influence on the field through the posthumous publication of essays he was in the process of preparing for the press at the time of his death. The range of subjects broached in these essays demonstrates that, to the last, Sibley was at the cutting edge of research and is likely to remain a potent philosophical force for many years to come.

See also Aesthetic Qualities.

Bibliography

WORKS BY SIBLEY

"Aesthetic Concepts." *Philosophical Review* 68 (1959a).

"Aesthetics and the Looks of Things." *Journal of Philosophy* 66 (1959b).

"Aesthetic and Nonaesthetic." *Philosophical Review* 74 (2) (1965): 135–159.

Perception: A Philosophical Symposium. London: Methuen, 1971.

Approach to Aesthetics: Collected Papers on Philosophical Aesthetics, edited by John Benson, Betty Redfern, and Jeremy Roxbee Cox. Oxford, U.K.: Clarendon Press, 2001.

WORKS ABOUT SIBLEY

Brady, Emily, and Jerrold Levinson, eds. *Aesthetic Concepts: Essays after Sibley*. Oxford, U.K.: Clarendon Press, 2001.

Cohen, Ted. "Aesthetic/Non-aesthetic and the Concept of Taste: A Critique of Sibley's Position." *Theoria* 39 (1973): 113–151.

Kivy, Peter. *Speaking of Art*. The Hague: Nijhoff, 1973.

Peter Kivy (2005)

SIDGWICK, HENRY

(1838–1900)

Henry Sidgwick, the English philosopher and educator, was born in Yorkshire and attended Rugby and Trinity College, Cambridge. After a brilliant undergraduate career, he was appointed a fellow at Trinity in 1859. He had already begun to have religious doubts, and in the years following 1860 he studied Hebrew and Arabic intensively, hoping to resolve these doubts through historical research. At the same time Sidgwick was teaching philosophy, and he had for many years been a leading member of the small group that met for philosophical discussions with John Grote. Gradually he came to think that if answers to his religious questions were to be found at all, they would be found through philosophy—but he never fully quieted his doubts. In 1869 he resigned his fellowship because he felt he could no longer honestly subscribe to the Thirty-nine Articles, as fellows were required to do. His college promptly appointed him to a lectureship, and when religious tests were dropped, he was reappointed fellow. In 1876 he married Eleanor Balfour, sister of Arthur Balfour. He succeeded T. R. Birks as Knightbridge professor of moral philosophy in 1883, and continued actively teaching in the moral sciences course until his death.

WORK AND ACTIVITIES

Philosophy was only one of Sidgwick's many interests—he also wrote on education, literature, political theory, and history of political institutions. He was active in the cause of women's education at Cambridge and had a large part in the founding of Newnham College for women, to which he devoted considerable time and money. Another main interest was psychical research—he performed some experiments with F. W. H. Myers as early as 1873, and in 1882 he helped found the Society for Psychical Research. He served twice as the society's president, and investigated and reported on many alleged psychical phenomena, very few of which, however, he believed to be both genuine and significant.

Sidgwick's most important work is *The Methods of Ethics* (1874). His other philosophical writings, although interesting for the light they throw on his moral philosophy, are too slight, too occasional, or too little original to be of independent significance; but the *Methods* has been held by C. D. Broad and other writers to be the greatest single work on ethics in English—and possibly in any language. Sidgwick's work in economics and political science is generally thought not to be of comparable importance.

PHILOSOPHICAL METHOD

The Methods of Ethics exemplifies Sidgwick's views on the nature of philosophy. The philosopher's aim is not to discover new truths; rather, it is to give systematic organization to knowledge that we already possess. Theoretical philosophy attempts to unify the knowledge obtained through the sciences, so that all of it may be seen as a whole and all the methods used in science may be seen as parts of one method. Practical philosophy has a similar task to perform with our common moral knowledge of what ought to be and what ought to be done, and with the methods we use in obtaining this knowledge.

In carrying out the task of practical philosophy, Sidgwick offered a resolution of a perennial controversy that had been particularly sharp in the middle years of the nineteenth century—that between utilitarians, such as J. S. Mill, and intuitionists, such as William Whewell. However, he found himself unable to reach a solution to another central controversy, that between those who held that morality is independent of religious belief and those who held that without religion no coherent morality is possible.

A brief summary of the course of the argument of *The Methods of Ethics* will make these points plain. Sidgwick took a method of ethics to be a reasoned procedure for reaching specific decisions about what one ought to do. The methods used by common sense, he argued, may be reduced to three. One method takes excellence or perfection as an ultimate goal, and claims that we have intuitive knowledge of a variety of independently valid moral principles and maxims. We reach specific conclusions by subsuming particular cases under the relevant principles. According to the other two methods, we are to infer the rightness or wrongness of acts from the amount of happiness they would cause. According to one method, we calculate the consequences to the agent alone. According to the other, we consider the consequences for everyone affected by the act. Moral rules and principles, for these two methods, are only useful indications of the effects that certain kinds of actions may generally be expected to have. After discussing some basic ethical concepts, Sidgwick examined each method separately and then considered their mutual relations. He concluded that the first method, intuitionism, and the third, utilitarianism, supplement one another, and that their conclusions form a systematic whole. Thus, it is reasonable to act as those conclusions dictate. The remaining method, egoism, can also be systematically developed, and it is reasonable to act according to its conclusions. Either of the two views thus reached dictates obligations that are binding quite independently of any religious sanctions.

However, empirical evidence alone does not show that the conclusions of the egoistic method will always agree with those of the intuitional-utilitarian method. Using methods that are perfectly reasonable, we are sometimes led to serious contradictions. Unless we can find some evidence for the existence of a moral power that will repay self-sacrifice and punish transgression, we will be unable to bring all our practical beliefs and methods into any coherent system. The mere fact that the existence of a power that rewards and punishes behavior is needed to make our practical beliefs coherent does not justify the assertion that there is such a power. Sidgwick personally held that the theistic view is natural for man, but he despaired of finding any evidence to support it and refused to use it in his philosophy. The consequence of the existence of these practical contradictions is (as Sidgwick put it in the melancholy concluding words of the first edition of the *Methods*) that "the prolonged effort of the human intellect to frame a perfect ideal of rational conduct is seen to have been foredoomed to inevitable failure."

BASIS OF CLASSIFICATION

Sidgwick's classification of the methods implicit in commonsense morality rests on two considerations. First, the methods reflect two sides of human nature. Those taking happiness as the final end reflect the sentient side of man, the capacity for enjoying and suffering, while the method taking excellence as the final end reflects the fact that man is also an active being, with a need to do as well as a need to feel. Second, the classification indicates an epistemological distinction that Sidgwick constantly took as basic, the distinction between propositions that we are entitled to assert only because we have correctly inferred them from others that we know, and propositions that we are entitled to assert because we know them without any inference, directly or "intuitively." The intuitional method claims that we have noninferential knowledge of moral principles, while the other methods emphasize the ways in which moral rules and maxims are arrived at by inference.

NONINFERENTIAL TRUTH

If there is inferential knowledge, Sidgwick believed, there must be noninferential knowledge; and since he also held that there are no infallible sources of noninferential knowledge, the problem arises of how to test claims to possess noninferential truth or claims to have found self-evident propositions. Sidgwick proposed four tests that apparently self-evident propositions must pass before we can be justified in accepting them: (1) the terms in which they are stated must be clear and precise; (2) their self-evidence must be very carefully ascertained; (3) they must be mutually consistent; and (4) there must be general agreement of experts on their truth. Sidgwick argued at great length that commonsense moral principles, which according to traditional intuitionism are self-evident, fail to pass these tests. Hence, if they are true principles, as we all take them to be, they must be inferential and dependent, not self-evident and independent.

SELF-EVIDENT MORAL PRINCIPLES

What do commonsense moral principles depend on? There are four principles that do pass Sidgwick's tests and that he accepted as self-evident. (1) Whatever action anyone judges right for himself, he implicitly judges to be right for anyone else in similar circumstances. (2) One ought to have as much regard for future good or evil as for present, allowing for differences in certainty. (3) The good enjoyed by any individual is as important as the good enjoyed by any other. (4) A rational being is bound to aim generally at good.

PRINCIPLE OF BENEVOLENCE

From the principles that the good of each person is equally important and that a rational being must aim generally at good, Sidgwick deduced an abstract principle of benevolence. Commonsense morality, he argued, appeals to this principle to settle cases in which its usual rules give no answers, and allows its rules to be overridden by the principle if they conflict with it. These facts indicate that common sense considers its rules to depend for their validity on this principle. However, the abstract principle of benevolence is also at the center of utilitarianism, and commonsense morality—the stronghold of traditional intuitionists—is thus seen to be fundamentally utilitarian. The utilitarian, in turn, can have no objection to any of the self-evident principles, and the two methods can thus be completely synthesized. Even the egoist can accept three of the self-evident truths; his rejection of the fourth is an indication of the basic contradiction in the realm of practical reason.

CRITICISMS OF UTILITARIANISM

Sidgwick is usually considered a utilitarian, and he frequently referred to himself as one. However, his views differ considerably from those of the earlier utilitarians.

EMPIRICISM. Sidgwick rejected the empiricist epistemology that J. S. Mill developed and that seemed to underlie Jeremy Bentham's thought. Empiricism, as Sidgwick understood it, holds that the basic premises from which all knowledge is built are cognitions of particular facts and that these cognitions alone are infallible. Sidgwick argued that these cognitions are not infallible and that empiricism cannot give a satisfactory account of the principles of inference that guide the construction of knowledge from the basic data. Metaphysically, he rejected not only materialism but also the reductive sensationalism to which he believed the empiricist epistemology led. Following Thomas Reid, he held to what he called a commonsense dualism of mind and matter, although he found the connections between the two most obscure.

DEFINITION OF ETHICAL TERMS. Sidgwick also rejected what he took to be the traditional utilitarian attempt to define ethical concepts such as "good" and "ought" in terms of nonethical concepts such as "pleasant" or "conducive to most pleasure" and in this way to justify the construction of a purely factual, scientific morality. No reduction of "ought" to "is," of ideal to actual, had yet been successful, he held, although he hesitated to say that no reduction could possibly succeed. However, he did affirm that it is impossible to make an ethical first principle true by definition. To define "good" as "pleasure" is self-defeating if you wish to hold, as a first principle that the good is pleasure, since what you hold as a principle would then be a tautology, and a tautology cannot be an ethical first principle. Recognition of these points, Sidgwick believed, would force the utilitarian to admit the need of a basic intuition in his philosophy.

MOTIVATION. Sidgwick rejected the motivational theories of Bentham and the Mills. He did not think that we always necessarily act to obtain what we take to be our own pleasure or our own good.

THE RELEVANCE OF PSYCHOLOGY. Sidgwick strongly objected to the tendency, which he attributed to Mill, to substitute psychological (or perhaps, with Auguste Comte, sociological) investigation into the origins of ideas and beliefs for properly philosophical investigation of their applicability or truth. Quite aside from his doubts as to the adequacy of the associationist psychology that the earlier utilitarians accepted, Sidgwick held that psychological discoveries about the antecedents and concomitants of ideas and beliefs are, in general, irrelevant to questions of their truth and validity—and psychology can tell us only about antecedents and concomitants. It cannot supersede the deliverances of direct introspective awareness on the question of what our ideas now are.

DETERMINISM. Sidgwick agreed with the earlier utilitarians that there seems to be overwhelming evidence in support of a deterministic view of human action. However, he held that this evidence must be balanced against the fact that in the moment of choosing between alternative actions we inevitably think ourselves free to choose either alternative. He argued that the issue is, therefore, not yet settled, but he held that it is not important for ethical theory that it should be.

INDEPENDENCE OF POLITICS. Sidgwick held that utilitarianism does not necessarily lead to reforming radicalism in politics. He pointed out the strong utilitarian element to such conservative thinkers as David Hume and Edmund Burke, and he argued at great length that a utilitarian would be extremely cautious in recommending important changes.

AGREEMENTS WITH UTILITARIANISM

Sidgwick's position was, of course, utilitarian in its major ethical aspects. He held that the only ultimate or intrinsic good is desirable or pleasant states of consciousness; that acts are objectively right only if they produce more good than any other alternative open to the agent; and that moral rules, such as those of truth-telling or promise-keeping, are subordinate to the principle of utility and are dependent on it for whatever validity they possess. He also held that the value of character and motive is derived from, and to be judged in terms of, the consequences of the actions to which they tend to lead. Sidgwick's disagreements with the traditional forms of utilitarianism are part of his attempt to show that the utilitarian view of morality is independent of metaphysical doctrines, psychological theories, and political platforms and therefore is capable of being what he argued it is—the position toward which commonsense morality in every age and in every society has tended.

See also Balfour, Arthur James; Bentham, Jeremy; Broad, Charlie Dunbar; Burke, Edmund; Common Sense; Consequentialism; Egoism and Altruism; Empiricism; Ethics, History of; Grote, John; Hume, David; Mill, James; Mill, John Stuart; Moral Principles: Their Justification; Pleasure; Reid, Thomas; Utilitarianism; Whewell, William.

Bibliography

WORKS BY SIDGWICK

The Methods of Ethics. London, 1874. Extensively revised for the editions of 1877, 1884, and 1890. The sixth edition (1901) was the last revised by Sidgwick; it contains an autobiographical sketch of great interest.

Principles of Political Economy. London: Macmillan, 1883, 1887, 1901.

Outlines of the History of Ethics. London, 1886. Many subsequent editions.

Elements of Politics. London: Macmillan, 1891 and 1897.

Practical Ethics. London: S. Sonnenschein, 1898.

Philosophy, Its Scope and Relations. London: Macmillan, 1902.

Lectures on the Ethics of Green, Spencer, and Martineau. London, 1902.

Development of European Polity. London, 1903.

Miscellaneous Essays and Addresses. London and New York: Macmillan, 1904.

Lectures on the Philosophy of Kant, edited by James Ward. London: Macmillan, 1905.

WORKS ON SIDGWICK

Bradley, F. H. "Mr. Sidgwick's Hedonism." In his *Collected Essays.* Oxford, 1935. Vol. I. Polemic against Sidgwick.

Broad, C. D. *Ethics and the History of Philosophy.* London: Routledge, 1952. This and the two following works are useful and lengthy discussions of Sidgwick.

Broad, C. D. *Five Types of Ethical Theory.* London: Kegan Paul, 1930.

Broad, C. D. *Religion, Philosophy, and Psychical Research.* London: Routledge, 1953.

Havard, W. C. *Henry Sidgwick and Later Utilitarian Political Philosophy.* Gainesville: University of Florida Press, 1959.

Hayward, F. H. *The Ethical Philosophy of Sidgwick.* London, 1901. Not very useful.

Sidgwick, A., and E. M. Sidgwick. *Henry Sidgwick; A Memoir.* London, 1906. The standard biography, written by his brother and his widow. It contains letters, unpublished papers, and a complete bibliography of his writings.

J. B. Schneewind (1967)

SIDGWICK, HENRY [ADDENDUM]

Henry Sidgwick is renowned for giving classical utilitarianism its most sophisticated dress and greatly advancing substantive ethical theory. Celebrated for his clarity and cool impartiality, he developed an approach to ethical theory that profoundly shaped influential philosophers from G. E. Moore and Bertrand Russell down to R. M. Hare, John Rawls, Marcus Singer, Derek Parfit, and Peter Singer. It was Sidgwick, rather than Moore, who set the course for twentieth-century debates over the ethics and metaethics of the utilitarian view that maximizing happiness is the ultimate normative demand—that is, over such matters as the conflict between egoistic and utilitarian reasons, the distinction between total and average utility, the role of commonsense in utilitarian reasoning, the meaning of *good*, and the moral standing of other beings that are not human. Yet Sidgwick himself had more comprehensive intellectual, religious, and cultural concerns than most of his later analytical admirers. He was haunted by the specter of skepticism in religion and morality, and if he turned utilitarianism into a respectable academic philosophy, he also reluctantly brought it into the crisis of the Enlightment.

Educated in classics and mathematics at Trinity College, Cambridge, Sidgwick spent his entire adult life at Cambridge, becoming Knightbridge Professor in 1883. Molded by the influential discussion society known as the Cambridge Apostles, he developed serious interests in theology, biblical criticism, poetry, education, ethics, political economy, jurisprudence, political theory, sociology, epistemology, metaphysics, and parapsychology (he was a founder and president of the Society for Psychical Research). He vastly influenced the Cambridge moral sciences curriculum and was a guiding force in the cause of women's higher education and the founding of Newnham College. In 1876 he married Eleanor Mildred Balfour, a force in her own right in psychical research and educational reform. Moreover, he was deeply involved with the work of his close friend John Addington Symonds, a pioneer of cultural history and gay studies.

Sidgwick's masterpiece, *The Methods of Ethics* (1874), was a sustained effort at independent, secular moral theory resulting from his decade of "storm and stress" over the defense and reform of Christianity. It also reveals that, however indebted Sidgwick was to his chief mentor, J. S. Mill, his hedonism was more consistently Benthamite, whereas his overall position was more eclectic, reconciling utilitarianism with arguments from Plato, Aristotle, Descartes, Immanuel Kant, Joseph Butler, Samuel Clarke, William Whewell, John Grote, F. D. Maurice, and T. H. Green. It rejects the empiricism and reductionism of earlier utilitarianism, and adheres to a sophisticated fallibilist intuitionism involving various tests for reducing the risk of error with respect to basic non-inferentially known propositions:

1) clarity and precision.

2) ability to withstand careful reflection.

3) mutual consistency.

4) consensus of experts.

The Methods of Ethics is largely a systematic critical comparison of the methods of ethical egoism, common sense or intuitional morality, and utilitarianism—for Sidgwick, the ongoing procedures for determining, on principle, what one ought to do (though he would later devote as much attention to idealism and evolutionism). He takes the notion of *ought* or *right* as fundamental and irreducible and, for the most part, gives an internalist account of moral approbation. But he also holds that it is a plausible and significant (not tautological) proposition that ultimate good is pleasure or desirable consciousness; egoism and utilitarianism hence reduce to egoistic and universalistic hedonism. He then shows that earlier utilitarians exaggerated the conflict with common sense, confused the utilitarian and egoist positions, and failed to give their view rational foundations. His exhaustive examination of commonsense morality, after the manner of Aristotle, reveals time and again that such principles as veracity, fidelity, justice, and benevolence are either too vague and indeterminate, or too conflicting and variably interpreted to form a system of rational intuitions.

Indeed, common sense is even unconsciously utilitarian because it is apt to resort to that view to complete its own system—for example, to settle conflicts between the duty to speak the truth and the duty to keep one's promises.

Thus, commonsense morality ends in utilitarianism, though utilitarianism grounded on philosophical intuitionism, and utilitarianism can in turn rationalize much of commonsense morality as the (indirect) means to the greatest happiness. But no such reconciliation of utilitarianism and egoism is forthcoming, each being, on reflection, equally defensible. Kantian universalizability, the essence of justice, comports with either egoism or utilitarianism and cannot decide between them, though it is another self-evident principle. Sidgwick dismally concludes that there is a dualism of practical reason rendering it incoherent. Without help from epistemology or theology, he has no rational way to settle conflicts between individual self-interest and universal good. Arguably, his demand that these be reconciled in a manner doing justice to the force of both means that his view is better described as dualist, rather than simply utilitarian.

Still, Sidgwick's other intellectual and reformist interests often radiated from his fears about the implications of the dualism of practical reason. His research in parapsychology was largely devoted to seeking evidence of personal survival of death, since such evidence, he believed, might bolster a theism affording the needed reconciliation. And although *The Principles of Political Economy* (1883) and *The Elements of Politics* (1891) tend rather to assume a utilitarian standpoint, they also bespeak his concern that human emotions be shaped in a more deeply altruistic direction, encouraging sympathetic, benevolent sentiments and reigning in narrow or materialistic egoistic ones.

Both his reformism and his philosophical and scientific pursuits were brought to bear on the potential for such societal evolution and the perhaps limited place of reason and religion within it. Never as sanguine as Comte, Mill, or Spencer, his concern for reform was tempered by fear that skepticism and crude egoism would lead to social deterioration. If Sidgwick was as good at defending an agent-relative egoism as an agent-neutral utilitarianism, this was scarcely the result he sought, unless some high-minded reconciliation could be effected as well.

But Sidgwick's views on civilization and its direction suggest both continuities and discontinuities with earlier utilitarianism. It would be hard to deny that troubling racist undercurrents can be found in his work, or that his educational and political writings and activities, in particular, reflected the pervasive late Victorian culture of imperialism. Sidgwick was a friend and colleague of such imperialist luminaries as Sir John Seeley, and went so far as to edit Seeley's posthumous *Introduction to Political Science*. Arthur Balfour, the future prime minister, was his student, brother-in-law, and colleague in psychical research, and also influenced his politics. Ironically, given the priority of politics in Benthamism, the political and economic dimensions of Sidgwick's utilitarianism have been comparatively neglected. This is doubly ironic because Sidgwick was, in fact, an influential economic and political theorist who shaped the views of Alfred Marshall, F. Y. Edgeworth, and other seminal figures in modern economics.

Only by reading *The Methods of Ethics* in the context of Sidgwick's other work and activities is there some hope of determining whether he was a true "government house" utilitarian, holding that the publicity of moral principles be subject to felicific calculations congenial to paternalistic governments, or a defender of the plain person's capacity for moral self-direction, as his focus on common sense and method might suggest. Still, it is clear that Sidgwick articulated a truly comprehensive practical philosophy, and a sophisticated metaethics and epistemology, one deeply informed by Kantianism and idealism as well as utilitarianism. He was not a naïve encyclopedist lacking any grasp of social theory or the historicity of his own philosophy. But whether he began, in his last decades, to doubt the philosophical quest for certainty enough to approximate the pragmatist via media is a very difficult question that has put Sidgwick back in the middle of debates over the imperialistic origins of contemporary political Liberalism.

See also Aristotle; Balfour, Arthur James; Bentham, Jeremy; Butler, Joseph; Clarke, Samuel; Comte, Auguste; Darwinism; Descartes, René; Enlightenment; Ethical Egoism; Green, Thomas Hill; Grote, John; Hare, Richard M.; Hedonism; Idealism; Justice; Kant, Immanuel; Liberalism; Mill, John Stuart; Moore, George Edward; Parfit, Derek; Plato; Rawls, John; Singer, Peter; Skepticism, History of; Utilitarianism; Whewell, William.

Bibliography

PRIMARY WORKS

The Ethics of Conformity and Subscription. London: Williams & Norgate, 1870.

The Methods of Ethics. London: Macmillan, 1874.

The Principles of Political Economy. London: Macmillan, 1883.

Outlines of the History of Ethics for English Readers. London: Macmillan, 1886.
The Elements of Politics. London: Macmillan, 1891.
Practical Ethics: A Collection of Addresses and Essays. London: Swan Sonnenschein, 1898.
Philosophy, Its Scope and Relations. London: Macmillan, 1902.
Lectures on the Ethics of T. H. Green, H. Spencer, and J. Martineau. London: Macmillan, 1902.
The Development of European Polity. London: Macmillan, 1903.
Miscellaneous Essays and Addresses. London: Macmillan, 1904.
Lectures on the Philosophy of Kant and Other Philosophical Lectures and Essays. London: Macmillan, 1905.
Sidgwick, Henry, A Memoir. London: Macmillan, 1906.
The Complete Works and Select Correspondence of Henry Sidgwick, edited by Bart Schultz. Charlottesville, VA: InteLex, 1996.
Essays on Ethics and Method by Henry Sidgwick, edited by Marcus G. Singer. Oxford: Oxford University Press, 2000.

SECONDARY WORKS

Crisp, Roger, and Bart Schultz, eds. "Sidgwick 2000." *Utilitas* 12 (3) (2000): 251–401.
Harrison, Ross, ed. *Henry Sidgwick*. Oxford: Oxford University Press, 2001.
Hurka, Thomas. "Moore in the Middle." *Ethics* 113 (2003): 599–628.
Parfit, Derek. *Reasons and Persons*. Oxford: Oxford University Press, 1984.
Schneewind, J. B. *Sidgwick's Ethics and Victorian Moral Philosophy*. Oxford: Oxford University Press, 1977.
Schultz, Bart, ed. *Essays on Henry Sidgwick*. New York: Cambridge University Press, 1992.
Schultz, Bart. *Henry Sidgwick, Eye of the Universe: An Intellectual Biography*. New York: Cambridge University Press, 2004.
Shaver, Robert. *Rational Egoism*. New York: Cambridge University Press, 1999.
Williams, Bernard. "The Point of View of the Universe: Sidgwick and The Ambitions of Ethics." *Cambridge Review*, 7 (1982):183–91.

R. Barton Schultz (1996, 2005)

SIGER OF BRABANT

(c. 1240–c. 1281/1284)

Of Siger's life, we know very few facts for certain. His exact place of birth remains unknown, as well as the locale and circumstances of his death. (Did he die peacefully in Liege, Belgium, or was he assassinated in Italy at the Roman curia?) Even the chronology of his works is uncertain. Although they are thought to have been written between 1265 and 1277, the precise dates remain conjectural.

Concerning his university career, facts are again unclear. Although it is certain that he never left the faculty of arts for one of the higher faculties (theology, medicine, law), his role in the debates that shook the University of Paris and led to the statutes of 1272 remains the subject of discussion (Putallaz and Imbach 1997 versus Bianchi 1999). At the beginning of his career, he was one of Thomas Aquinas's most outspoken adversaries, but the question as to what degree he would have abandoned Averroism to adopt Thomist views remains open. Certain passages seem to support the view that he would have abandoned Averroism, while others are incompatible with this hypothesis (Van Steenberghen and Maurer defend the developmental interpretation, whereas Mandonnet and Bukowski defend the idea that Siger never changed his mind and was the strictest Averroist of his time, a philosopher who could without any guilt subscribe to heretical propositions).

All of these often radical oppositions about the interpretation of Siger's doctrines—whether metaphysical, psychological, ethical, or logical—illustrate the difficulty involved in understanding the complex thought of a Master of Arts who taught in a time as intellectually rich as it was eventful. Siger was influenced by the famous Dominican theologian Albert the Great, was directly attacked by another famous Dominican theologian, Thomas Aquinas, in his *De unitate intellectus*, was singled out by the condemnations of 1277 (although many of their propositions cannot be related to any of his works), was taken as a model for John of Jandun, later became one of the most important Averroists in the fourteenth century, and was placed by Dante in paradise beside Thomas Aquinas. Faced with this abundance of information, one must consider Siger's texts in themselves by situating them in their context, of course, but also by distinguishing what Siger said from what others say he said. It is well known that the opponents of a thesis tend to present it in a less than advantageous light to make it seem absurd and, in the Middle Ages, heretical. It is also important to take into account how Siger expresses his ideas. For example, Imbach (1996) showed clearly that Siger habitually took certain passages from Thomas Aquinas and twisted them from their original meaning to defend a thesis opposed to that of his illustrious opponent. Such a rhetorical procedure should not be surprising in the context of the condemnations. If we follow these methodological principles, we can draw a clearer and more nuanced portrait of Siger.

PRINCIPLE PHILOSOPHICAL THESES

Siger sought to be a career philosopher. At the end of the thirteenth century, this involved being autonomous from theology and being independent from established philosophical authorities. This stance influenced Siger's philosophical thought.

Siger's claim that philosophy is independent of theology does not in any way involve a rejection of faith. Rather, it seeks to confine theology to the domain of revelation, where it is the supreme guarantor of truth, and only to where it applies there (Siger 1981/1983, VI, comm. 1). For example, we know through revelation that the world was created. However, revelation does not tell us whether the world was created in time or out of eternity. To decide this question, we would have to investigate the divine will, which is impossible. So we have a choice: either to believe the first thesis on the authority of Augustine, although it rests on no rational argument, or to believe, contrary to Aristotle, for whom the world was not created, the second thesis, a conclusion arrived at by means of natural reason (1972a, *QTDA*, q. 2; 1972a, *DEM*; 1981/1983, III). Between Aristotle, who opposes faith, and the theologians, who pretend to demonstrate their thesis in a philosophical manner that is false, Siger proposes an intermediary path that conforms to the demands of both faith and philosophy: creation out of eternity.

Siger sought to be independent of philosophical authorities, including Aristotle, as we have just seen, as well as Averroes. Indeed, he held that the philosopher must demonstrate for himself the proofs of his predecessors and oppose or correct them if they prove to be erroneous (1981/1983, IV, q. 34). Thus, even in his first work dedicated to noetic (philosophy-of-mind) questions (1972a, *QTDA*, written before 1270), where he is deeply influenced by Averroes, Siger never supported the monopsychist position that Thomas Aquinas attributed to Averroes, a position according to which all of humanity shares a single intellect. This position would imply that there is no individual thinking, as well as no individual immortality, no corporeal fires of hell, and no resurrection of the body.

The best evidence that Siger rejected monopsychism is Aquinas's introduction to his criticism of Siger's doctrine in the *De unitate intellectus* (On the unity of the intellect; written in 1270): "Some, seeing that on Averroes's position it cannot be sustained that this man understands, take another path and say that intellect is united to body as its mover" (III, sec. 66). This view of Siger's position also explains how, in his last work (1972b, presumably written in 1277), Siger could sincerely declare Averroes's noetic doctrine "absurd and heretical" without abandoning his previous doctrine (1972b, q. 27). Here too Siger takes a middle path. The intellect is not united to the body like a sailor to his boat (the error of Plato), nor is it united to the body like a mould to wax (the error of Alexander of Aphrodisias). Rather, the intellect functions intrinsically within the body. Siger held that the intellect is not a unique form completely separate from the body (the position of Averroes according to Aquinas, a position similar to Plato's, and a position against faith and individual morality). He also held that the intellect is not a multiple form completely immanent to the body (the position of Aquinas and Albert according to Siger, a position similar to Alexander's, and a position against philosophy). Rather, intellect, according to Siger, is a mixed form, separate from the body in substance, but joined with it in function (1972a, *QTDA*, q. 7; 1972a, *DAI*, III and VII; 1972b, q. 26).

With regard to morality, about which he wrote very little, as well as psychology, Siger resolutely defended the thesis that the intellect holds sway over the will (1974, *Quaestiones morales*; Ryan 1983), a position that many theologians of the time considered to be equivalent to determinism. In metaphysics, Siger held that there is no real distinction between existence and essence (1981/1983, I, qq. 7–8). He also held that universals, as such, are not substances; they exist only in the soul and are acquired by abstraction from the particular natures of things (1981/1983, III, qq. 15 and 28; 1972a, *DEM*).

See also Agent Intellect; Averroes; Averroism; Eternity; John of Jandun; Thomas Aquinas, St.

Bibliography

Although most significant texts have been critically edited, there are only very few monographs dedicated to Siger's thought. Most studies still more or less depend on Van Steenberghen's evolutionist interpretation and, not surprisingly, concentrate on one of the following subjects: the eternity of the world, the rational soul, and the relation between reason and faith. The most complete bibliography to date is available from http://www.mapageweb.umontreal.ca/pironetf.

WORKS BY SIGER

Quaestiones in tertium de anima. De anima intellectiva. De aeternitate mundi edited by Bernardo C. Baz án. Louvain, Belgium: Publications universitaires, 1972a. (Referred to as *QTDA, DAI, DEM* respectively.)

Les "quaestiones super librum 'De causis' " de Siger de Brabant edited by Antonio Marlasca. Louvain, Belgium: Publications universitaires, 1972b.

Écrits de logique, de morale et de physique edited by Bernardo C. Baz án. Louvain, Belgium: Publications universitaires, 1974. This volume contains *Sophisma omnis homo de necessitate est animal*; *Quaestio utrum haec sit vera: Homo est animal, nullo homine existente*; *Quaestiones logicales*;

Impossibilia; *Quaestiones morales*; *Quaestiones naturales*; *Compendium super "De generatione et corruptione"*; and *Quaestiones in physicam*.

Quaestiones in metaphysicam, edited by William Dunphy. Louvain-la-Neuve, Belgium: Éditions de l'Institut sup Érieur de philosophie, 1981.

Quaestiones in metaphysicam, edited by Armand Maurer. Louvain-la-Neuve, Belgium: Éditions de l'Institut sup Érieur de philosophie, 1983.

WORKS ON SIGER

Bianchi, Luca. *Censure et libert É intellectuelle à l'Universit É de Paris, XIIIe–XIVe siècles*, 165–201. Paris: Belles Lettres, 1999.

Bukowski, T. P. "Siger of Brabant vs. Thomas Aquinas on Theology." *New Scholasticism* 61 (1987): 25–32.

Dodd, Tony. *The Life and Thought of Siger of Brabant, Thirteenth-Century Parisian Philosopher: An Examination of His Views on the Relationship of Philosophy and Theology.* Lewiston, NY: Mellen Press, 1998.

Imbach, Ruedi. "Notice sur le commentaire du *Liber de causis* de Siger de Brabant et ses rapports avec Thomas d'Aquin." *Freiburger Zeitschrift für Philosophie und Theologie* 43 (1996): 304–323.

Mandonnet, Pierre. *Siger de Brabant et l'Averroïsme Latin au XIIIe siècle.* 2 vols. Louvain, Belgium: Institut sup Érieur de philosophie, 1908–1911.

Maurer, A. "Siger of Brabant and Theology." *Mediaeval Studies* 50 (1988): 257–278.

Putallaz, François-Xavier, and Imbach, Ruedi. *Profession, philosophe: Siger de Brabant.* Paris: Cerf, 1997.

Ryan, C. "Man's Free Will in the Works of Siger of Brabant." *Mediaeval Studies* 45 (1983): 155–199.

Van Steenberghen, Fernand. *Maître Siger de Brabant.* Louvain, Belgium: Publications universitaires, 1977.

Fabienne Pironet (2005)

SIGNIFICANCE TESTS

See *Statistics, Foundations of*

SIGWART, CHRISTOPH

(1830–1904)

Christoph Sigwart, the German philosopher and logician, was born and died in Tübingen. He studied philosophy, theology, and mathematics there and taught in Halle from 1852 to 1855, before joining the theological seminar in Tübingen in 1855. He accepted a professorship at Blaubeuren in 1859 and returned to Tübingen as professor of philosophy, a position he held from 1865 to 1903. His doctoral dissertation was on Giovanni Pico della Mirandola. He also wrote on Friedrich Schleiermacher, Benedict de Spinoza, Huldrych Zwingli, and Giordano Bruno, as well as on ethics. His most important work was the two-volume *Logik,* a comprehensive treatise on the theory of knowledge.

The aim of logic, Sigwart maintained, is normative rather than descriptive. Logic is a regulative science whose aim should be to present a useful methodology for the extension of our knowledge. It is "the ethics rather than the physics of thought" and concerns itself not with an account of psychological processes but with finding the rules in accordance with which thought may achieve objective validity. Like ethics, logic is concerned with the question "What ought I to do?" The adequacy of thought lies not in its correspondence with an antecedently objective reality but in its satisfaction of human purposes. The overriding purpose of reasoning is to reach ideas that are necessary and universal for us, for human beings. Objective validity is essentially a matter of intersubjective agreement. The possibility of discovering the rules for necessary and universally valid thinking, however, depends also on an immediate awareness of self-evidence, a property that is possessed by necessary judgments. The experience of self-evidence is a postulate beyond which we cannot inquire. Logic strives to disclose the conditions under which this feeling occurs.

In Sigwart's philosophy there is a voluntarist element combined with respect for natural science, both of which evidently impressed William James. (James quoted from Sigwart in his essay "The Dilemma of Determinism.") Sigwart held that an activity of free and conscious willing is presupposed not only by ethics and metaphysics but by logic as well. Free will is presupposed by any distinction between correct and incorrect reasoning, since thinking must be a voluntary activity and not necessitated. The will is supreme in the realm of theory as well as in that of practice. The ultimate presupposition of all experience, and therefore of all thinking too, is not merely Immanuel Kant's "I think," which can accompany all ideas, but also "I will," which governs all acts of thought.

Sigwart's classification of the forms of judgments and categories presents judging as the basic cognitive function. Judgments are divided into simple narrative judgments, expressive of an immediate recognition ("This is Socrates"), and complex judgments, presupposing twofold and higher syntheses ("This cloud is red"). The discussion of existential judgments agrees with Kant in denying that existence, or "to be," adds anything to the content of an idea.

Sigwart was also interested in the work of men outside his own country; for example, the *Logik* contains a lengthy discussion of J. S. Mill on induction. Sigwart's ethical and metaphysical views were somewhat conventional: He held that progress in the development of the social order is an inevitable fact of history, and he argued that the attempt to make all our knowledge coherent inevitably leads to the idea of God.

See also Bruno, Giordano; Determinism and Freedom; Epistemology; Epistemology, History of; James, William; Kant, Immanuel; Mill, John Stuart; Pico della Mirandola, Count Giovanni; Schleiermacher, Friedrich Daniel Ernst; Spinoza, Benedict (Baruch) de.

Bibliography

WORKS BY SIGWART

Spinozas neuentdeckter Traktat von Gott, dem Menschen und dessen Glückseligkeit. Gotha: R. Besser, 1866.

Logik. 2 vols. Tübingen, 1873 and 1878. 5th ed., Tübingen, 1924, contains Heinrich Maier's biography of Sigwart and a bibliography. Translated by Helen Dendy as *Logic.* 2 vols. London, 1890.

Vorfragen der Ethik. Freiburg, 1886.

WORKS ON SIGWART

Häring, T. L. *Christoph Sigwart.* Tübingen, 1930.

Levinson, R. B. "Sigwart's Logic and William James." *Journal of the History of Ideas* 8 (1947): 475–483.

Arnulf Zweig (1967)

SIMMEL, GEORG
(1858–1918)

Georg Simmel, the German philosopher and sociologist, was born in Berlin and resided there except for the last four years of his life. He was educated there, and in 1881 he received his doctorate from the University of Berlin. Three years later he began to teach at that university as a *Privatdozent* and from 1900 he was associate professor without faculty status. Although successful as a lecturer and a writer, he was never promoted to a full professorship at Berlin, nor was he able to secure such a position at any other leading German university. Only in 1914, when his career was almost ended, was he offered a chair in philosophy at the provincial University of Strasbourg. However, World War I disrupted university life there, so that Strasbourg benefited little from Simmel's teaching. Just before the end of the war, Simmel died of cancer.

Simmel's failure as an academic was connected with the nature of his interests, his style of lecturing and writing, and his philosophic position. He had many influential friends—he knew and corresponded with Max Weber, Heinrich Rickert, Edmund Husserl, Adolf von Harnack, and Rainer Maria Rilke—and his applications for openings were always well supported by the testimony of his crowded lecture halls and the success of his many writings, both technical and popular. However, from the straitlaced viewpoint of the German academic hierarchy Simmel was suspect. He seemed to be interested in everything: He wrote books or essays on Rembrandt and Johann Wolfgang von Goethe, on Michelangelo, Auguste Rodin, and Stefan George; on Florence, Rome, Venice, and the Alps; on the philosophy of money, adventure, love, landscapes, and the actor; on ruins, handles, coquetry, and shame; as well as on the more standard philosophic subjects of ethics, philosophy of history, Immanuel Kant, Arthur Schopenhauer, and Friedrich Nietzsche, and, at the end of his life, metaphysics.

Throughout his career Simmel made contributions of lasting importance to sociology, a subject that had not yet achieved academic respectability. His style, too, was not that expected of a professor of philosophy. It was insightful rather than expository; digressive rather than systematic; witty rather than solemn. Because Simmel's position on any particular point was frequently not easy to see, he was often considered to be a critic whose primary impulse was analytic, if not destructive. By some he was thought to have no philosophic position at all.

Other, more sympathetic, readers of his work called him a *Kulturphilosoph*, primarily on the basis of his preoccupation with the objects of culture. Yet because toward the end of his career Simmel began to sketch a philosophic position having a conception of human life at its center, he is also referred to as a *Lebensphilosoph.* Both of these activities, however, are but two sides of the same lifelong dual concern: to illuminate the objects of culture by showing their relation to human experience and to shed light upon the nature of human life by seeing it in relation to its products.

Simmel conceived of human life as being a process and as being, necessarily, productive. By calling life a process (which he expressed by partially defining life as "more-life"), Simmel sought to convey the view that life has the characteristics of what the Greeks called "becoming": It is continuous and continuously changing; strictly speaking, it can only be lived (experienced), not known. However, this same life produces objects that are not in constant flux, that have form and hence are intelligible. (In virtue of this productiveness of human life, Simmel completed his definition by saying that life is "more-than-life.") These products constitute the realm of culture and include not only works of science, history, and art, but social and political institutions and religious theories and practices as well. These objects stand in a twofold relationship to human life: Their genesis lies in human experience and, once in existence, they are independently subject to being experienced in various ways. Simmel's philosophy dealt in detail with both of these relationships.

To account for the existence of the objects of culture, Simmel made use, in his own particular way, of the categories of form and content. He posited a realm of contents (rather like George Santayana's realm of essences) as the material that enters into all experience. Contents, however, are not experienced as they are in themselves; they are shaped by the experiencing psyche. Experience (Simmel here followed Kant) is formative; to see how form arises thus requires an understanding of the natural history of experience.

Simmel conceived of a stage in human life in which all needs are instantly satisfied, in which there is no gap between desire and fulfillment. Such a stage of life would be prior to experience and hence prior to any differentiation of subject and object. In that stage there would be neither self nor sugar but only sweetness. However, the world is clearly not so organized that life could actually be lived in this way, and in the gap between need and fulfillment both experience and form are born. In becoming conscious, we distinguish between ourselves as subject and that which we experience as objects.

Experience, however, is not all of a piece: We experience in different modes. It is one thing to know an object, another to appreciate it as beautiful, and still another to revere it as an object of worship. In Simmel's view, the contents experienced in each of the three cases may be the same, although they are not the same in experience. The objects of the three experiences differ in that the contents are given shape—are objectified—by means of three different ways of experiencing. The same contents differ in form.

For the most part, people act to fulfill their needs. Their experience gives shape to contents only to the extent to which the immediate requirements of a situation demand it. In the scholastic language Simmel sometimes adopted, both the terminus a quo (the origin) and the terminus ad quem (the goal) of the objects produced by ordinary experience—of whatever mode—remain within the biography of the individual producing them. As a result of this subservience to the needs of individuals, form in ordinary experience is not pure, and the objects that are formed in this way are not yet properly the objects of culture. As long as life sets the goals of action (characteristic of the phase of life Simmel called teleological or pragmatic), knowledge is tentative and limited—not yet science; art is homespun and primitive—not yet fully aesthetic; religion is simple and sporadic—not yet embodied in a theology and in institutions. The form is proto-form and the objects are proto-culture.

However, the bonds of the teleology of life can be broken. The terminus ad quem of people's actions need not reside within their lives: They can act for the sake of a form, a type of action Simmel called free action. Instead of knowing for the sake of acting, some people act in order to know; instead of seeing for the sake of living, some people—artists—live in order to see. In acting for the sake of a form, experience in the relevant form is refined; the structure inchoate in ordinary experience is made explicit and worked out. Form proper is born and the objects of culture are produced.

There are many kinds of form; there is and can be no definitive list. Knowledge, art, religion, value, and philosophy are among the important forms (or "world forms," as Simmel called them) by means of which men have shaped the realm of contents. Reality, too, is only one such form and enjoys no privileged status; the objects of reality constitute the world of practice—those objects which we perceive and manipulate in our daily lives. There are other forms and other worlds, however; one of the tasks of the philosopher is to distinguish and analyze them.

Human life is not self-sufficient; it needs things outside itself to exist and to continue to exist. The objects life forms first come into being to meet its needs; but, because they are objects, they continue to exist independently of life and to make their demands upon the race that has produced them. Humans work out the forms implicit in the various modes of ordinary experience; they become artists, historians, philosophers, and scientists. But once works of art, history, philosophy, or science exist, they make a second demand upon humans: they are the objects by whose assimilation individuals become cultivated. Here Simmel saw a source of inevitable conflict. People differ from each other, and the way in which each person can fulfill himself is peculiar to him. Thus, to fulfill himself each person must utilize a different selection of already existing objects of culture. However, not every road, not just any selection, leads to the assimilation of these objects. To properly understand the objects an individual requires in order to become cultivated, he may need to learn to apprehend a vast number of other objects not so required. In order to serve life, his life, an individual may have to make his own needs subservient to those of forms. This is the tragedy of culture.

In his philosophic position Simmel attempted to do justice to the antitheses that have occupied philosophers since the pre-Socratics. Life as a process is the pole of flux and becoming; it can be lived, but not known. Form is stable and has structure; it is the pole of being and is intelligible. Life is one; experience in all modes is the experience of the same subject. Forms and worlds are many; they are severed from the life that produced them and take on existence independent of it. Neither Being nor Becoming, neither the One nor the Many, holds exclusive sway. The tension between the poles of these antitheses is a permanent feature of the world.

This position underlies the greatest part of Simmel's work. His writings in *Kulturphilosophie* are explorations into the nature of different forms and of different works, whether of philosophy or of art. They are investigations into the relationships between the lives and works of men like Rembrandt and Goethe. In sum, his essays in the philosophy of culture are a series of applications of his philosophy of life.

See also Experience; Philosophy of History.

Bibliography

IMPORTANT WORKS BY SIMMEL

Die Probleme der Geschichtsphilosophie. Eine erkenntnistheoretische Studie. Leipzig: Duncker and Humblot, 1892; 2nd ed. (completely revised), 1905.

Einleitung in die Moralwissenschaft. Eine Kritik der ethischen Grundbegriffe. 2 vols. Berlin: Hertz, 1892–1893.

Philosophie des Geldes. Leipzig: Duncker and Humblot, 1900.

Kant. Sechzehn Vorlesungen gehalten an der Berliner Universität. Leipzig: Duncker and Humblot, 1903.

Die Religion. Frankfurt am Main: Rütten and Loening, 1906. Translated by Curt Rosenthal as *Sociology of Religion.* New York: Philosophical Library, 1959.

Soziologie. Untersuchungen über die Formen der Vergesellschaftung. Leipzig: Duncker and Humblot, 1908. Partly translated, with other essays, by Kurt H. Wolff in *The Sociology of Georg Simmel.* Glencoe, IL: Free Press, 1950.

The Problems of the Philosophy of History: An Epistemological Essay. New York: Free Press, 1977.

The Philosophy of Money. London; Boston: Routledge & Kegan Paul, 1978.

With Otthein Rammstedt. *Gesamtausgabe.* Frankfurt am Main: Suhrkamp, 1989.

COLLECTIONS OF ESSAYS BY SIMMEL

Philosophische Kultur. Gesammelte Essays. Leipzig: Kröner, 1911.

Zur Philosophie der Kunst. Philosophische und kunstphilosophische Aufsätze, edited by Gertrud Simmel. Potsdam: Kiepenheuer, 1922.

Fragmente und Aufsätze aus dem Nachlass und Veröffentlichungen der letzten Jahre, edited by Gertrud Kantorowicz. Munich: Drei Masken, 1923.

Brücke und Tür. Essays des Philosophen zur Geschichte, Religion, Kunst und Gesellschaft, edited by Michael Landmann and Margarete Susman. Stuttgart: Koehler, 1957.

The Conflict in Modern Culture, and Other Essays. New York: Teachers College Press, 1968.

On Individuality and Social Forms: Selected Writings. Chicago:, University of Chicago Press, 1971.

Simmel on Culture: Selected Writings, edited by David Frisby and Mike Featherstone. London; Thousand Oaks, CA: Sage Publications, 1997.

WORKS ON SIMMEL'S PHILOSOPHY

Aron, Raymond. *Essai sur la théorie de l'histoire dans l'Allemagne.* Paris: J. Vrin, 1938. Includes a discussion of Simmel's philosophy of history.

Frisby, David. *Fragments of Modernity: Theories of Modernity in the Work of Simmel, Kracauer, and Benjamin.* Cambridge, MA: MIT Press, 1986.

Frisby, David. *Georg Simmel.* Rev. ed. London; New York: Routledge, 2002.

Frisby, David. *Georg Simmel: Critical Assessments.* London; New York: Routledge, 1994.

Frisby, David. *Simmel and Since: Essays on Georg Simmel's Social Theory.* London; New York: Routledge, 1992.

Frisby, David. *Sociological Impressionism: A Reassessment of Georg Simmel's Social Theory.* 2nd ed. London; New York: Routledge, 1992.

Gassen, Kurt. "Georg-Simmel-Bibliographie." In *Buch des Dankes an Georg Simmel*, edited by Kurt Gassen and Michael Landmann. Berlin: Duncker and Humblot, 1958. Excellent bibliography.

Jankélévitch, Vladimir. "Georg Simmel, philosophe de la vie." *Revue de métaphysique et de morale* 32 (1925): 213–257, 373–386.

Lawrence, Peter A. *Georg Simmel: Sociologist and European.* New York: Barnes & Noble Books, 1976.

Mandelbaum, Maurice. *The Problem of Historical Knowledge: An Answer to Relativism.* New York: Liveright, 1938. Includes a discussion of Simmel's philosophy of history.

Weingartner, Rudolph H. *Experience and Culture: The Philosophy of Georg Simmel.* Middletown, CT: Wesleyan University Press, 1962.

Weinstein, Deena, and Michael A. Weinstein. *Postmodern(ized) Simmel.* London; New York: Routledge, 1993.

Wolff, Kurt H., ed. *Georg Simmel, 1858–1918. A Collection of Essays with Translations and a Bibliography.* Columbus: Ohio State University Press, 1959.

Rudolph H. Weingartner (1967)

Bibliography updated by Michael J. Farmer (2005)

SIMON, RICHARD

(1638–1712)

The French biblical scholar Richard Simon was born in Dieppe, France, and studied with the Oratorians and the

Jesuits and at the Sorbonne, specializing in Hebrew and Near Eastern studies. Before being ordained a priest in 1670, he taught philosophy at an Oratorian college. He soon became one of the foremost experts in Hebrew, Judaism, and Eastern Church history. Influenced by Benedict (Baruch) de Spinoza's critique of the Bible and by the theory of his friend and fellow Oratorian, Isaac La Peyrère, that there were men before Adam, Simon began developing his views about the Bible and church doctrine. His first published work, a defense of the Jews of Metz (1670), attacked Christian anti-Semitism. It was followed by a study of the Eastern Church, another of Jewish ceremonies and customs, and an attack on the monks of Fécamp. His most important and revolutionary work, *Histoire critique du vieux testament*, was printed in 1678. Jacques Bénigne Bossuet caused it to be banned immediately, and almost all copies were destroyed. A few reached England, and the work was published in French with an English translation by Henry Dickinson in 1682. The scandal forced Simon to leave the Oratory and become a simple priest. Thereafter, he argued with various Protestant and Catholic thinkers and wrote many works on the history of religion and on the Bible, which culminated in his translation of the New Testament (1702). Bossuet caused this work to be banned also.

Simon's revolutionary contention was that no original text of the Bible exists, that the texts one possesses have developed and have been altered through the ages, and that it is therefore necessary to apply the method of critical evaluation to biblical materials to establish the most accurate human form of the revelation. This method involves philology, textual study, historical researches, and comparative studies. Protestants saw that Simon's claim that there is no perfect copy of scripture fundamentally challenged their position that truth is found only by examining the Bible. Catholics feared that he was undermining all bases of Judeo-Christianity by raising problems about all its documents and traditions. Simon contended that he was merely trying to clarify religious knowledge by showing its foundations and development and the need for a tradition to interpret and understand it. Whether intentional or not, Simon's method launched the whole enterprise of biblical higher criticism, which was often directed toward undermining confidence in the uniqueness and ultimate truth of the Judeo-Christian revelation.

See also Bossuet, Jacques Bénigne; Philosophy of Religion, History of; Revelation.

Bibliography

WORKS BY SIMON

Histoire critique du vieux testament. Paris: N.p., 1678.*Lettres choisies de M. Simon.* 4 vols. 2nd ed. Frankfurt am Main, Germany: Minerva G.N.B.H, 1967.

WORKS ABOUT SIMON

Bredvold, Louis I. *The Intellectual Milieu of John Dryden: Studies in Some Aspects of Seventeenth-Century Thought.* Ann Arbor: University of Michigan Press, 1956.

Hazard, Paul. *La Crise de la conscience européene (1680–1715).* 2 vols. Paris: Boivin, 1935.

Mirri, F. Saverio. *Richard Simon e il metodo storico-critico di B. Spinoza: Storia di un libro e di una polemica sullo sfondo delle lotte politico-religiose della Francia di Luigi XIV.* Florence, Italy: F. Le Monnier, 1972.

Ranson, Patric. *Richard Simon, ou, Du caractère illégitime de l'augustinisme en théologie.* Lausanne, Switzerland: L'Age d'homme, 1990.

Steinmann, Jean. *Richard Simon et les origines de l'exégèse biblique.* Paris: Desclee de Brouwer, 1960.

Richard H. Popkin (1967, 2005)

SIMON MAGUS

Simon Magus, the earliest Gnostic leader known to us, was a native of the Samaritan village of Gitta. He is first mentioned in Acts (8:4–25), where he appears as a wonder-worker who had gained a considerable following in Samaria and who sought to augment his stock in trade by purchasing the power of conferring the Holy Spirit from the apostles. The identity of the Simon of the book of Acts and the founder of the Gnostic sect has been questioned, but Irenaeus, among others, has no doubt of it. According to Hippolytus, Simon died in Rome when he failed, in an abortive attempt at a miracle, to rise from the pit in which he had been buried alive. In the pseudo-Clementine literature Simon serves as the target for veiled Jewish-Christian attacks on Paul and Marcion. According to Origen, in his time the Simonians numbered only thirty, but Eusebius, years later, still knew of their existence.

The Simonian theory is of special interest not only as one of the earliest Gnostic systems but also as providing an illustration of the ways in which such systems developed and were modified. Assessment of the evidence is complicated by the meagerness of our sources and by various problems of evaluation and interpretation, but in general we may distinguish three main stages. Simon himself appears to have been a "magician" of the common Hellenistic type, who claimed to be a divine incarnation. His teaching would be not so much Gnostic in the second-century sense (that is, the Gnosticism of the heretical Christian systems) but rather a form of syncretistic gnosis into which he sought to incorporate Christian elements. The accounts of Justin and Irenaeus introduce his companion, the ex-prostitute Helen, whom he declared to be the first conception (*Ennoia*) of his mind, emanating from him like Athena from the head of Zeus. A notable feature here is the blending of biblical elements with elements from Homer and Greek mythology.

Descending to the lower regions, Ennoia generated the angels and powers by whom this world was made but was then detained by them and compelled to suffer a round of incarnations (thus she is, inter alia, Helen of Troy) until Simon himself came to redeem her. The problem here is to know how much can be credited to Simon himself and how much to reflection among his followers.

A third and more philosophical stage is represented by the "Great Affirmation" preserved by Hippolytus, which probably has nothing to do with the original Simon but may be the work of later disciples attributed, as was often the case, to the master himself. Here the primal ground of being is fire, from which emanate three pairs of "roots," or Powers, which are the origin of all existence: Mind and Thought, Voice and Name, Reason and Desire (text in W. Völker, *Quellen zur Geschichte des christlichen Gnosis,* Tübingen, 1932, pp. 3ff.). In this scheme, elements from Greek philosophy (Heraclitus, Plato, Aristotle) are blended with biblical and Homeric elements into a thoroughly Gnostic system. It is of interest to note that Simonianism provides one of the sources of the later Faust legend.

See also Aristotle; Gnosticism; Heraclitus of Ephesus; Homer; Marcion; Origen; Plato.

Bibliography

GENERAL WORKS

Grant, R. M. *Gnosticism and Early Christianity,* 70ff. New York: Columbia University Press, 1959.

Jonas, Hans. *The Gnostic Religion,* 103ff. Boston: Beacon Press, 1958.

Leisegang, H. *Die Gnosis,* 60ff. Stuttgart, 1955.

Wilson, R. McL. *The Gnostic Problem,* 99ff. London: A.R. Mowbray, 1958.

SPECIALIZED WORKS

Casey, R. P. "Simon Magus." In *The Beginnings of Christianity,* edited by F. J. F. Jackson and Kirsopp Lake. Vol. V, 151ff. London, 1933.

Cerfaux, L. *Receuil Cerfaux.* 2 vols. Vol. I, 191ff. Gembloux, 1954.

Haenchen, E. "Gab es eine vorchristliche Gnosis?" *Zeitschrift für Theologie und Kirche* 49 (1952): 316ff.

Haenchen, E. *Die Apostelgeschichte,* 250ff. Göttingen, 1959.

Hall, G. N. L. "Simon Magus." In *Encyclopaedia of Religion and Ethics,* edited by James Hastings. Vol. XI, 514ff. Deals fairly extensively with the "Great Affirmation."

Headlam, A. C. "Simon Magus." In *Dictionary of the Bible,* edited by James Hastings. Vol. IV, 520ff. On p. 527 Headlam lists four points in the later Faust legend that point back to the legend of Simon Magus.

Lietzmann, H. "Simon Magus." In *Realencyclopädie der classischen Altertumswissenschaft,* edited by August Pauly and Georg Wissowa. 2nd series. Vol. III, Cols. 180ff.

R. McL. Wilson (1967)

SIMPLICIUS

(fl. c. 530)

Simplicius of Cilicia (in Asia Minor) tells us that he studied Platonic philosophy in Alexandria under Ammonius the son of Hermias (fl. c. 550). Afterward, he attended the lectures of Damascius, probably in Athens at the original and still flourishing school founded by Plato himself, the Academy. (An earlier scholarly opinion that there were doctrinal differences between the teachings on Plato in Alexandria and Athens is no longer held.)

All these figures were active neoplatonists, and Hermias and Damascius did in fact publish commentaries on various dialogues of Plato. But Ammonius and Simplicius (and to a lesser extent Damascius as well) devoted most of their writings to the explication of Aristotle's works. Simplicius, in addition to a commentary on Epictetus's Handbook (*Enchiridion*), wrote extensive commentaries on five of those works of Aristotle that most challenge philosophers: *Metaphysics* (no longer extant, although fragments are known), *Physics*, *Categories*, *De Anima*, and *De Caelo*, with the four extant commentaries totaling over 2,800 sizable pages in the series *Commentaria in Aristotelem Graeca*. (References in some modern books to a commentary by Simplicius on *Sophistici Elenchi* are mistaken.) In addition to the time obviously needed to complete these commentaries, a brief examination of Simplicus's learned exegeses shows that he also was in need of an extensive philosophical library, one that included not only Plato and Aristotle, their predecessors (the pre-Socratics) but also everything (it seems) ever written by an Academician or Peripatetic, as well as some Stoic texts.

Where could this library have been? An obvious answer is Athens, but one of the few hard facts concerning these philosophers is that, owing to increasing Christian hostility to pagan philosophizing, the emperor

Justinian in 529 forbade teaching by non-Christians, which gave Simplicius time to write his commentary of Epictetus, who as a philosopher struggling under tyranny could serve as a model for Simplicius and his colleagues. Agathias (c. 536–c. 582), the Christian historian (and epigrammatist), states that "Damascius of Syria, Simplicius of Cilicia, Eulamius of Phrygia, Prisican of Lydia, Hermias and Diogenes of Phoenicia, and Isidore of Gaza … concluded that, since Christianity was not to their liking [a euphemism], Persia was a better place for them." Unfortunately, the stories about King Chosroes I (reigned 531–579) that made him sound like a Platonic philosopher-king were greatly exaggerated. In time, even Greece, with all its dangers, seemed preferable; "and so all returned home," trusting in a treaty between Justinian I (483–565) and Chosroes that, among other things, stipulated that the philosophers could return to their homes and live there as long as they wished "on their own," this last vague phrase probably meaning that the treaty guaranteed them the freedom to congregate as philosophers and conduct themselves (mostly) as before (Agathias *Historiae* 2.30.3–31.4 Keydell).

Thus, although some scholars still believe that Simplicius chose to stay somewhere safe in the Persian Empire, probably in Haran, the explicit evidence of Agathias, who refers to these Academics as his (younger) contemporaries, strongly suggests that Simplicius returned to Athens. There, still denied the right to teach, he dedicated himself to scholarship.

For the most part, Simplicius's writings are straightforward analyses, lemma by lemma, of Aristotelian passages, a form of commentary designed for readers rather than for the students to whom he no longer could lecture. Here Simplicius not only dispassionately and at great length explains the meaning of selected passages he also attempts to harmonize or minimize the differences between Plato and Aristotle. Indeed, Simplicius often turns Aristotle into a neoplatonist, as when, for example, he argues that Aristotle's causes were six in number. The lemmas both explicate the meaning and summarize other scholars' views of the passage in question. In both aspects Simplicius is of immeasurable importance for the history of earlier Greek philosophy, for he, far more than any other commentator on Plato or Aristotle, took the trouble to go back both to the texts Aristotle quotes or alludes to as well as to the texts that comment on Aristotle.

Simplicius is thus the most important source for verbatim quotations of the pre-Socratics, Academics, Peripatetics, Stoics, and others. Time after time, where others comment on Aristotle's allusion to (say) Parmenides merely by elaborating on Aristotle's words, inferring from them what Parmenides meant, Simplicius, explicitly referring to the rarity of Parmenides' book, says that he will quote from it *in extenso*. By far the vast majority of the fragments of Parmenides, Empedocles, Zeno, Melissus, Anaxagoras, and Diogenes of Apollonia is known thanks to Simplicius alone. Earlier attempts to argue that he found these passages in Theophrastus's lost doxographical treatise on earlier thought falter when one looks at the extant *Metaphysics* and *De Sensibus* of Theophrastus, whose verbatim quotations of pre-Socratics are infrequent and not of great length, unlike many in Simplicius. In short, present-day knowledge of the actual words of the pre-Socratics would be halved or worse without him. It would doubtless be increased were a copy of his *In Metaphysica* found.

Similarly, Simplicius is now the only source for many of the earlier but now lost Aristotelian commentaries. Much of what is known of Theophrastus's *Physics* comes from Simplicius's commentary, and his quotations from John Philoponus's lost *Against Aristotle, on the Eternity of the World* are so extensive that they have been excerpted and published separately.

Although Simplicius is strictly neutral toward the pre-Socratics, he is capable of criticizing Aristotelian commentators of several centuries earlier, such as Alexander of Aphrodisias, whom he accuses, sometimes ironically, of not having considered all available sources, a virtue he explicitly declares necessary for the serious commentator in the beginning of *In Cat*, along with an ability to make dispassionate judgments. He is naturally more deferential to his teachers Ammonius and Damascius. He reserves his most critical if not contemptuous statements for Philoponus, who was also a student of Ammonius, but whose Christian interpretations, such as that the cosmos had a fixed beginning, he finds most abhorrent.

Since all of Simplicius's works are in the form of commentaries on two philosophers not of his own school, it is not easy to isolate beliefs and preoccupations that would distinguish him from other neoplatonists. Apart from his almost religious adoration of the Platonic Demiurge (reminiscent of Cleanthes' *Hymn to Zeus*), Simplicius writes very much in the tradition of Alexandrian and Athenian commentators on Aristotle who in place of sustained argument are more likely merely to state their interpretation of his text. Simplicius, then, a scholar like few before him, read every relevant text that would illuminate Aristotle, who he argued should be seen as a complement to Plato's noble philosophy.

See also Greek Academy; Neoplatonism; Peripatetics; Platonism and the Platonic Tradition; Stocism.

Bibliography

Cameron, Alan. "The Last Days of the Academy at Athens." *Proceedings of the Cambridge Philological Society* 195 (15) (1969): 7–29.

Hadot, Ilsetraut. *Le problème du néoplatonisme alexandrin: Hiéroclès et Simplicius.* Paris: Études Augustiniennes, 1978.

Hadot, Ilsetraut, ed. *Simplicius: Sa vie, son oeuvre, sa survie: Actes du colloque international de Paris.* Berlin: De Gruyter, 1987.

Hadot, Ilsetraut. "The Life and Work of Simplicius in Greek and Arabic Sources." In *Aristotle Transformed: The Ancient Commentators and Their Influence*, edited by Richard Sorabji, 275–304. London: Duckworth, 1990.

Hoffmann, Philippe. "Simplicius' Polemics." In *Philoponus and the Rejection of Aristotelian Science*, edited by Richard Sorabji, 57–83. Ithaca, NY: Cornell University Press, 1987.

Praechter, K. "Simplikios (10)." *Pauly-Wissowa, Real-Encyclopädie der classischen Altertumswissenschaft* 3A (1) (1927): 204–213.

Sorabji, Richard, ed. *Ancient Commentators on Aristotle.* London: Duckworth. In this series of translations the following works of Simplicius have appeared thus far, with others forthcoming: *In De Caelo* 1.1–1.4 (translated by R. J. Hankinson, 2002), 1.5–1.9 (translated by R. J. Hankinson), 1.10–1.12 (translated by R. J. Hankinson, 2003); *In Physica* 2 (translated by Barrie Fleet, 1997), 3 (translated by J. O. Urmson, notes by Peter Lautner, 2002), 4.1–4.5, 10–14 (translated by J. O. Urmson, 1992), 5 (translated by J. O. Urmson, notes by Peter Lautner, 1997), 4.6–4.9 (on the void; translated by J. O. Urmson, notes by Peter Lautner, 1994), 4, pp. 601.1–645.19 and 773.8–800.25 (corollaries on place and time, respectively; translated by J. O. Urmson, notes by L. Siorvanes, 1992), 6 (translated by David Konstan, 1989), 7 (translated by Charles Hagen, 1994), 8.6–8.10 (translated by translated by R. McKirahan, 2001), 8.10, pp. 1326.38–1336.34 (against Philoponus on the eternity of the world; translated by C. Wildberg, 1991); *In De Anima* 1.1–2.4 (translated by J. O. Urmson, notes by Peter Lautner, 1995), 2.5–2.12 (translated by Carlos Steel and J. O. Urmson, notes by Peter Lautner, 1997), 3.1–3.5 (translated by H. J. Blumenthal, 2000); *In Categorias* 1–4 (translated by M. Chase, 2003), 5–6 (translated by F. de Haas and Barry Fleet, 2002), 7–8 (translated by Barry Fleet, 2002), 9–15 (translated by R. Gaskin, 2000); *Handbook on Epictetus* 1–26 (translated by C. Brittain and T. Brennan, 2002), 27–53 (translated by C. Brittain and T. Brennan, 2002).

Thiel, Rainer. *Simplikios und das Ende der neuplatonische Schule in Athen.* Mainz, Germany: Abhandlungen der Geistes- und Sozialwissenschaftliche Klasse. Akademie der Wissenschaften und der Literatur, 1999. Nr. 8.

David Sider (2005)

SIMULATION THEORY

A prominent part of everyday thought is thought about mental states. We ascribe states like desire, belief, intention, hope, thirst, fear, and disgust both to ourselves and to others. We also use these ascribed mental states to predict how others will behave. Ability to use the language of mental states is normally acquired early in childhood, without special training. This naïve use of mental state concepts is variously called *folk psychology*, *theory of mind*, *mentalizing*, or *mindreading* and is studied in both philosophy and the cognitive sciences, including developmental psychology, social psychology, and cognitive neuroscience. One approach to mindreading holds that mental-state attributors use a naïve psychological "theory" to infer mental states in others from their behavior, the environment, or their other mental states, and to predict their behavior from their mental states. This is called the *theory theory* (TT). A different approach holds that people commonly execute mindreading by trying to simulate, replicate or reproduce in their own minds the same state, or sequence of states, as the target. This is the *simulation theory* (ST).

Another possible label for simulation is *empathy*. In one sense of the term, *empathy* refers to the basic maneuver of feeling one's way into the state of another, by "identifying" with the other, or imaginatively putting oneself in the other's shoes. One does not simply try to depict or represent another's state, but actually to experience or share it. Of course, mental life may feature empathic acts or events that are not deployed for mindreading. But the term *simulation theory* primarily refers to an account of mindreading that accords to empathy, or simulation, a core role in how we understand, or mindread, the states of others.

HISTORICAL ANTECEDENTS OF THE DEBATE

A historical precursor of the ST/TT debate was the debate between positivists and hermeneutic theorists about the proper methodology for the human sciences. Whereas positivists argued for a single, uniform methodology for the human and natural sciences, early-twentieth-century philosophers like Wilhelm Dilthey and R. G. Collingwood advocated an autonomous method for the social sciences, called *Verstehen*, in which the scientist or historian projects herself into the subjective perspective or viewpoint of the actors being studied. Contemporary ST, however, makes no pronouncements about the proper methodology of social science; it only concerns the prescientific practice of understanding others. The kernel of this idea has additional historical antecedents. Adam Smith, Immanuel Kant, Arthur Schopenhauer, Friedrich Nietzsche, and W. V. Quine all wrote of the mind's empathic or projective propensities. Kant wrote:

> [I]f I wish to represent to myself a thinking being, I must put myself in his place, and thus substitute, as it were, my own subject for the object I am seeking to consider… (Kant 1787/1961, p. 336)

Nietzsche anticipated modern psychology in the following passage:

> To understand another person, that is to *imitate his feelings in ourselves*, we … produce the feeling in ourselves after the *effects* it exerts and displays on the other person by imitating with our own body the expression of his eyes, his voice, his bearing.… Then a similar feeling arises in us in consequence of an ancient association between movement and sensation. (Nietzsche 1881/1977, pp. 156–157.…)

Quine (1960) briefly endorsed an empathy account of indirect discourse and propositional attitude ascription. He described attitude ascriptions as an "essentially dramatic idiom" rather than a scientific procedure, and this encouraged him to see the attitudes as disreputable posits that deserve to be eliminated from our ontology.

THE BEGINNING OF THE DEBATE

It was in the 1980s that three philosophers—Robert Gordon, Jane Heal, and Alvin Goldman—first offered sustained defenses of ST as an account of the method of mindreading. They were reacting partly to functionalist ideas in philosophy of mind and partly to emerging research in psychology. According to analytic functionalism, our understanding of mental states is based on commonsense causal principles that link states of the external world with mental states and mental states with one another. For example, if a person is looking attentively at a round object in ordinary light, he is caused to have a visual experience as of something round. If he is very thirsty and believes there is something potable in a nearby refrigerator, he will decide to walk toward that refrigerator. By using causal platitudes of this sort, attributors can infer mental states from the conditions of an agent's environment or from his previous mental states. One might start with beliefs about a target's initial mental states plus beliefs in certain causal psychological principles, feed this information into one's theoretical reasoning system, and let the system infer the "final" states that the target went into or will go into. This TT approach assumes that attribution relies on information about causal principles, so TT is said to be a "knowledge rich" approach.

Simulationists typically doubt that ordinary adults and children have as much information, or the kinds of information, that TT posits, even at a tacit or unconscious level. ST offers a different possibility, in which attributors are "knowledge-poor" but engage a special mental skill: the construction of pretend states. To predict an upcoming decision of yours, I can pretend to have your goals and beliefs, feed these pretend goals and beliefs into my own decision-making system, let the system make a pretend decision, and finally predict that you will make this decision. This procedure differs in three respects from the theorizing procedure. First, it involves no reliance on any belief by the attributor in a folk-psychological causal principle. Second, it involves the creation and deployment of pretend, or make-believe, states. Third, it utilizes a mental system, here a decision-making system, for a non-standard purpose, for the purpose of mindreading rather than action. It takes the decision-making system "off-line."

Daniel Dennett (1987) challenged ST by claiming that simulation collapses into a form of theorizing. If I make believe I am a suspension bridge and wonder what I will do when the wind blows, what comes to mind depends on the sophistication of my knowledge of the physics of suspension bridges. Why shouldn't make-believe mindreading equally depend on theoretical knowledge? Goldman (1989) parried this challenge by distinguishing two kinds of simulation: theory-driven and process-driven simulation. A successful simulation need not be theory driven. If both the initial states of the simulating system and the process driving the simulation are the same as, or relevantly similar to, those of the target system, the simulating system's output should resemble the target's output, enabling the prediction to be accurate.

Heal (1994) also worried about a threat of ST collapsing into TT. If ST holds that one mechanism is used to simulate another mechanism of the same kind, she claimed, then the first mechanism embodies tacit knowledge of theoretical principles of how that type of mechanism operates. Since defenders of TT usually say that folk-psychological theory is known only tacitly, this cognitive science brand of simulation would collapse into a form of TT. This led Heal to reject such empirical claims about sub-personal processes. Instead, she proposed

(1998) that ST is in some sense an a priori truth. When we think about another's thoughts, we "co-cognize" with our target; that is, we use contentful states whose contents match those of the target. Heal has claimed that such co-cognition is simulation, and is an a priori truth about how we mindread.

Martin Davies and Tony Stone (2001) criticize Heal's proposed criterion of tacit knowledge possession. Yet another way to rebut the threat of collapse is to question the assumption that the integrity or robustness of simulation can be sustained only if it is not underpinned by theorizing. The assumption is that simulation is a sham if it is implemented by theorizing; ST implies that no theorizing is used. Against this, Goldman (2006) argues that theorizing at an implementation level need not conflict with higher-level simulation, and the latter is what ST insists upon.

TRANSFERENCE

According to the standard account, simulational mindreading proceeds by running a simulation that produces an output state (e.g., a decision) and "transferring" that output state to the target. "Transference" consists of two steps: classifying the output state as falling under a certain concept and inferring that the target's state also falls under that concept. Gordon (1995) worries about these putative steps. Classifying one's output state under a mental concept ostensibly requires introspection, a process of which Gordon is leery. Inferring a similarity between one's own state and a target's state sounds like an analogical argument concerning other minds, which Ludwig Wittgenstein and others have criticized. Also, if the analogy rests on theorizing, this undercuts the autonomy of simulation. Given these worrisome features of the standard account, Gordon proposes a construal of simulation without introspection or inference "from me to you."

Gordon replaces transference with "transformation." When I simulate a target, I "recenter" my egocentric map on the target. In my imagination, the target becomes the referent of the first-person pronoun "I" and his time of action, or decision, becomes the referent of "now." The transformation Gordon discusses is modeled on the transformation of an actor into a character he is playing. Once a personal transformation is accomplished, there is no need to "transfer" my state to him or to infer that his state is similar to mine. But there are many puzzling features of Gordon's proposal. He describes the content of what is imagined, but not what literally takes place. Mindreaders are not literally transformed into their targets (in the way princes are transformed into frogs) and do not literally lose their identity. We still need an account of a mindreader's psychological activities. Unless he identifies the type of his output state and imputes it to the target, how does the activity qualify as mindreading, that is, as believing of the target that she is in state M? Merely being oneself in state M, in imagination, does not constitute the mindreading of another person. One must impute a state to the target, and the state selected for imputation is the output state of the simulation, which must be detected and classified. First-person mental-state detection thereby becomes an important item on the ST agenda, an item on which simulationists differ, some, such as Harris (1992) and Goldman (2006), favoring introspection and others, such as Gordon (1995), resisting it.

Different theorists favor stronger or weaker versions of ST, in which "information" plays no role versus a moderate role. Gordon favors a very pure version of ST, whereas Goldman favors more of a hybrid approach, in which some acts of mindreading may proceed wholly by theorizing, and some acts may have elements of both simulation and theorizing. For example, a decision predictor might use a step of simulation to determine what he himself would do, but then correct that preliminary prediction by adding background information about differences between the target and himself. Some theory theorists have also moved toward a hybrid approach by acknowledging that certain types of mindreading tasks are most naturally executed by a simulation-like procedure (Nichols and Stich 2003).

What exactly does ST mean by the pivotal notion of a "pretend state"? Mental pretense may not be essential for simulational mindreading, for example, for the reading of people's emotional states as discussed at the end of this article. But most formulations of ST appeal to mental pretense. Mental pretense is often linked to imagining, but imagining comes in different varieties. One can imagine that something is the case, for example, that Mars is twice as large as it actually is, without putting oneself in another person's shoes. Goldman (2006) proposes a distinction between two types of imagining: suppositional-imagining and enactive-imagining.

Suppositional imagining is what one does when one supposes, assumes, or hypothesizes something to be the case. It is a purely intellectual posture, though its precise connection to other intellectual attitudes, like belief, is a delicate matter. Enactive imagining is not purely intellectual or doxastic. It is an attempt to produce in oneself a mental state normally produced by other means, where the mental states might be perceptual, emotional, or purely attitudinal. You can enactively imagine seeing something—you can visualize it—or you can enactively imagine wanting or dreading something. For purposes of ST, the relevant notion of imagination is enactive imagination. To pretend to be in mental state M is to enactively imagine being in M. If the pretense is undertaken for mindreading, one would imagine being in M and "mark" the imaginative state as belonging to the target of the mindreading exercise.

Can a state produced by enactive imagining really resemble its counterpart state, the state it is meant to enact? And what are the respects of resemblance? Gregory Currie (1995) advanced the thesis that visual imagery is the simulation of vision, and Currie and Ian Ravenscroft extended this proposal to motor imagery. They present evidence from cognitive science and cognitive neuroscience to support these ideas, highlighting evidence of behavioral and neural similarity (Currie and Ravenscroft 2002). Successful simulational mindreading would seem to depend on significant similarity between imagination-produced states and their counterparts. However, perfect similarity, including phenomenological similarity, is not required (Goldman 2006).

PSYCHOLOGICAL EVIDENCE

Gordon's first paper on ST (1986) appealed to research in developmental psychology to support it. Psychologists Heinz Wimmer and Josef Perner (1983) studied children who watched a puppet show in which a character is outside playing while his chocolate gets moved from the place he put it to another place in the kitchen. Older children, like adults, attribute to the character a false belief about the chocolate's location; three-year-olds, by contrast, do not ascribe a false belief. Another experiment showed that older autistic children resemble three-year-olds in making mistakes on this false-belief task (Baron-Cohen, Leslie, and Frith 1985). This was interesting because autistic children are known for a striking deficit in their capacity for pretend play. Gordon suggested that the capacity for pretense must be critical for adequate mindreading, just as ST proposes. Most developmental psychologists offered a different account of the phenomena, postulating a theorizing deficit as the source of the poor performances by both three-year-olds and autistic children. It was argued that three-year-olds simply do not possess the full adult concept of belief as a state that can be false, and this conceptual "deficit" is responsible for their poor false-belief task performance.

ENDOWMENT EFFECT

The conceptual-deficit account, however, appears to have been premature. First, when experimental tasks were simplified, three-year-olds and even younger children sometimes passed false-belief tests. Second, researchers found plausible alternative explanations of poor performance by three-year-olds, explanations in terms of memory or executive control deficiencies rather than conceptual deficiencies. Thus, the idea of conceptual change—assumed to be theoretical change—was undercut. This had been a principal form of evidence for TT and, implicitly, against ST. It has proved difficult to design more direct tests between TT and ST.

Shaun Nichols, Stephen Stich, and Alan Leslie (1995) cite empirical tests that allegedly disconfirm ST. One of these types of empirical tests involves the "endowment effect." The endowment effect is the finding that when people are given an item, for example, a coffee mug, they come to value it more highly than people who do not possess one. Owners hold out for significantly more money to sell it back than do nonowners who are offered a choice between receiving a mug and receiving a sum of money. When asked to predict what they would do, before being in such a situation, subjects underpredict the price that they themselves subsequently set. Nichols, Stich, and Leslie argue that TT readily explains this underprediction; people simply have a false theory about their own valuations. But ST, they argue, cannot explain it. If simulation is used to predict a choice, there are only two ways it could go wrong. The predictor's decision-making system might operate differently from that of the target, or the wrong inputs might be fed into the decision-making system. The first explanation does not work here, because it is the very same system. The second explanation also seems implausible because the situation is so transparent. This last point, however, runs contrary to the evidence. Research by George Loewenstein and other investigators reveals countless cases in which self- and other-predictions go wrong because people are unable to project themselves accurately into the shoes of others, or into their own future shoes. The actual current situation constrains their imaginative construction of future or hypothetical states, which can obviously derail a simulation routine (Van Boven, Dunning, and Loewenstein 2000). So ST has clear resources for explaining underpredictions in endowment effect cases.

EMOTION RECOGNITION

One of the best empirical cases for simulation is found in a domain little studied in the first two decades of empirical research on mindreading. This is the domain of detecting emotions by facial expressions. Goldman and Sripada (2005; also Goldman, 2006) survey findings pertaining to three types of emotions: fear, disgust, and anger. For each of these emotions, brain-damaged patients who are deficient in experiencing a given emotion are also selectively impaired in recognizing the same emotion in others' faces. Their mindreading deficit is specific to the emotion they are impaired in experiencing. ST provides a natural explanation of these "paired deficits": normal recognition proceeds by using the same neural substrate that subserves a tokening of that emotion, but if the substrate is damaged, mindreading should be impaired. TT, by contrast, has no explanation that is not ad hoc. TT is particularly unpromising because the impaired subjects retain conceptual ("theoretical") understanding of the relevant emotions.

By what simulational process could normal face-based emotion recognition take place? One possibility involves facial mimicry followed by feedback that leads to (subthreshold) experience of the observed emotion. In other words, normal people undergo traces of the same emotion as the person they observe. This resembles Nietzsche's idea, now supported by research showing that even unconscious perception of faces produces covert, automatic imitation of facial musculature in the observer, and these mimicked expressions can produce the same emotions in the self.

Another possible explanation of emotion recognition is unmediated mirroring, or resonance, in which the observer undergoes the same emotion experience as the observed person without activation of facial musculature. Such "mirror matching" phenomena have been identified for a variety of mental phenomena, in which the same experience that occurs in one person is also produced in someone who merely observes the first. Such mirror matching occurs for events ranging from action with the hands (Rizzolatti et al., 2001), to somatosensory experiences (Keysers et al., 2004), to pain (Singer et al., 2004). For example, if one observes somebody else acting, the same area of the premotor cortex is activated that controls that kind of action; if one observes somebody being touched on the leg, the same area of somatosensory cortex is activated that is activated in the normal experience of being touched on the leg; the same sort of matching applies to pain. This leads Vittorio Gallese (2003) to speak of a "shared manifold" of intersubjectivity, a possible basis for empathy and social cognition more generally. It is unclear whether mirror matching always yields recognition, or attribution, of the experience in question, so perhaps mindreading is not always implicated. But the basic occurrence of mental simulation, or mental mimicry, is strikingly instantiated.

See also Cognitive Science; Folk Psychology; Psychology.

Bibliography

Baron-Cohen, Simon, Alan Leslie, and Uta Frith. "Does the Autistic Child Have a 'Theory of Mind'?" *Cognition* 21(1985): 37–46.

Carruthers, Peter, and Peter K. Smith, eds. *Theories of Theories of Mind*. New York: Cambridge University Press, 1996.

Currie, Gregory. "Visual Imagery as the Simulation of Vision." *Mind and Language* 10(1995): 25–44.

Currie, Gregory, and Ian Ravenscroft. *Recreative Minds: Imagination in Philosophy and Psychology*. Oxford: Oxford University Press, 2002.

Davies, Martin, and Tony Stone. "Mental Simulation, Tacit Theory, and the Threat of Collapse." *Philosophical Topics* 29 (2001): 127–173.

Davies, Martin, and Tony Stone, eds. *Folk Psychology*. Oxford: Blackwell, 1995.

Davies, Martin, and Tony Stone, eds. *Mental Simulation: Evaluations and Applications*. Oxford: Blackwell, 1995.

Dennett, Daniel. "Making Sense of Ourselves." In his *The Intentional Stance*. Cambridge, MA: MIT Press, 1987.

Gallese, Vittorio. "The Manifold Nature of Interpersonal Relations: The Quest for a Common Mechanism." *Philosophical Transactions of the Royal Society of London B* 358 (2003): 517–528.

Goldman, Alvin. "Interpretation Psychologized." *Mind and Language* 4 (1989): 161–185.

Goldman, Alvin. *Simulating Minds: The Philosophy, Psychology and Neuroscience of Mindreading*. New York: Oxford University Press, 2006.

Goldman, Alvin, and Chandra Sripada. "Simulationist Models of Face-based Emotion Recognition." *Cognition* 94 (2005): 193–213.

Gopnik, Alison. "How We Know Our Minds: The Illusion of First-Person Knowledge of Intentionality." *Behavioral and Brain Sciences* 16 (1993): 1–14.

Gopnik, Alison, and Andrew N. Meltzoff. *Words, Thoughts, and Theories*. Cambridge, MA: MIT Press, 1997.

Gordon, Robert. "Folk Psychology as Simulation." *Mind and Language* 1 (1986): 158–171.

Gordon, Robert. "Simulation without Introspection or Inference from Me to You." In *Mental Simulation*, edited by Martin Davies and Tony Stone. Oxford: Blackwell, 1995.

Harris, Paul. "From Simulation to Folk Psychology: The Case for Development." *Mind and Language* 7 (1992): 120–144.

Heal, Jane. "Simulation vs. Theory Theory: What Is at Issue?" In *Objectivity, Simulation and the Unity of Consciousness: Current Issues in the Philosophy of Mind*, edited by Christopher Peacocke. Oxford: Oxford University Press, 1994.

Heal, Jane. "Co-cognition and Off-line Simulation: Two Ways of Understanding the Simulation Approach." *Mind and Language* 13 (1998): 477–498.

Kant, Immanuel. *Critique of Pure Reason*. Translated by Norman Kemp Smith. London: Macmillan, 1961.

Keysers, C., B. Wicker, V. Gazzola, J.-L. Anton, L. Fogassi, and V. Gallese. "A Touching Sight: SII/PV Activation During the Observation and Experience of Touch." *Neuron*. 42 (2004): 335–346.

Nietzsche, Friedrich. "Daybreak" (1881). In *A Nietzsche Reader*. Translated by R. J. Hollingdale. Harmondsworth: Penguin, 1977.

Nichols, Shaun, and Stephen P. Stich. *Mindreading: An Integrated Account of Pretence, Self-Awareness, and Understanding Other Minds*. Oxford: Oxford University Press, 2003.

Nichols, Shaun, Stephen Stich, and Alan Leslie. "Choice Effects and the Ineffectiveness of Simulation: Response to Kuhberger et al." *Mind and Language* 10 (1995): 437–445.

Perner, Josef. *Understanding the Representational Mind*. Cambridge, MA: MIT Press, 1991.

Quine, Willard Van Orman. *Word and Object*. Cambridge, MA: Technology Press, 1960.

Rizzolatti, G., L. Fogassi, and V. Gallese. "Neurophysiological Mechanisms Underlying the Understanding and Imitation of Action." *Nature Reviews Neuroscience* 2 (2001): 661–670.

Singer, T., B. Seymour, J. O'doherty, H. Kaube, R. J. Dolan, And C. D. Frith. "Empathy for Pain Involves the Affective but not Sensory Components of Pain." *Science*, 303 (2004): 1157–1162.

Van Boven, L., D. Dunning, and G. Loewenstein. "Egocentric Empathy Gaps between Owners and Buyers: Misperceptions of the Endowment Effect." *Journal of Personality and Social Psychology* 79 (2000): 66–76.

Wimmer, Heinz, and Josef Perner. "Beliefs about Beliefs: Representation and Constraining Function of Wrong Beliefs in Young Children's Understanding of Deception." *Cognition* 13 (1983): 103–128.

Alvin I. Goldman (2005)

SINGER, PETER

(1946–)

Peter Singer is one of the most influential philosophers of the twentieth century. While other philosophers have been more important in the development of the discipline, none has changed more lives. *Newsweek* magazine observed that the modern animal rights movement may be dated from the publication of *Animal Liberation*. This book has sold more than 500,000 copies in sixteen languages thus far. Altogether Singer is responsible in whole or part for producing thirty-six books, and a vast number of articles and reviews in journals ranging from *The Philosophical Review* to the *New York Times*.

Peter Singer was born in Melbourne, Australia, on July 6th, 1946. His parents were Viennese Jews who escaped in 1938, shortly after the *Anschluss* incorporated Austria into the German Reich. He went on to Melbourne University, where as an undergraduate he studied law, history, and philosophy. In 1969 he received an MA in philosophy, writing a thesis on *Why Should I Be Moral?* A scholarship allowed Singer to complete his graduate studies in Oxford, where he received his bachelor's in philosophy in 1971 and served as Radcliffe lecturer from 1971 to 1973.

In 1972 Singer published *Famine, Affluence, and Morality* in the first volume of a new journal, *Philosophy and Public Affairs*. This article, which has been reprinted more than two dozen times, is important for several reasons. In terms of style it was an unconventional philosophical essay in that it was written in simple, direct prose, with few references to philosophical texts. Rather than beginning from Immanuel Kant, Aristotle, or a hypothetical moral question, it addressed events that were occurring as Singer was writing. The article began with these words: "As I write this, in November, 1971, people are dying in East Bengal from lack of food, shelter, and medical care." Singer went on to present his readers with a stark moral challenge. On the basis of some apparently simple, plausible premises, he argued that affluent people ought to transfer their resources to those who are worse off until they reach the point at which further transfers would hurt them more than they would benefit others. Singer was asking his readers to give up their opera tickets, their wine cellars, and private schools for their children—the accoutrements of the sophisticated, upper-middle-class life favored by many academics. Furthermore, Singer was completely unapologetic about making such demands: "The whole way we look at moral issues … needs to be altered, and with it, the way of life that has come to be taken for granted in our society."

In autumn 1973, Singer moved to the United States in order to teach at New York University. He was in America only sixteen months, but his visit had a large impact. He wrote most of *Animal Liberation* during his stay and, while working on the book, Singer presented draft chapters to philosophy departments around the country. Also during his time in New York, Singer wrote "Philosophers Are Back on the Job" for the *New York Times Magazine* (1974). This essay brought the practical ethics movement to the attention of a wide, non-professional audience.

In 1975 Singer returned to Melbourne where he remained until 1999, except to take up various visiting appointments in universities around the world. Since 1999 he has been the Ira W. DeCamp Professor of Bioethics at Princeton University.

Virtually all of Singer's work exemplifies the following three important characteristics. First, it is revisionary. The point of practical ethics is not simply to understand the world, but to change it. A second characteristic of Singer's work is that facts matter. Philosophy may begin where facts run out, as Singer wrote in "Philosophers Are Back on the Job" (p. 20), but it is hard to see what philosophy would be for Singer if it didn't start with a vivid appreciation of the way things are. Finally, Singer's work presupposes that individual action can make a difference. As his work has unfolded, Singer has increasingly addressed social policy dimensions of the problems that he considers, but he usually writes as one person in conversation with another. His goal is to change our attitudes and behavior because that is how one changes the world.

Although he has written widely, Singer is most closely associated with his defense of animals and his attack on the traditional ethic of the sanctity of human life. According to Singer, other things being equal, it is better to experiment on a profoundly brain-damaged human infant than on a normal chimpanzee. The normative theory that underwrites these judgments is utilitarianism. The good to be maximized, in the case of self-conscious creatures (persons), is satisfied preferences; in the case of non-persons, it is pleasure and the absence of suffering. In metaethics, Singer follows the universal prescriptivism of his teacher, R. M. Hare.

Singer's recent writing has ranged from practical ethics to work that is more personal. His most recent book, *The President of Good and Evil* (2004), takes President George W. Bush's moralism at face value, and subjects it to rigorous philosophical examination. His 2002 book, *One World*, is an ethical assessment of the environmental, economic, and legal dimensions of globalization. *Pushing Time Away* (2003) is the most personal of his books. It is a moving biography of Singer's maternal grandfather, David Oppenheim, a Viennese intellectual and teacher, who was murdered in the Holocaust. In recovering the life, thought, and sensibility of Oppenheim, Singer discovers strong affinities with his own thought and intellectual formation, perhaps because of a common source in the *Haskalah* (Jewish Enlightenment). Only in his late-50s as of 2005, Singer is likely to continue to produce important work in all areas of moral philosophy.

See also Animal Rights and Welfare; Moral Sentiments.

Bibliography

PRIMARY WORKS

Practical Ethics. 2nd ed. New York: Cambridge University Press, 1993.

Rethinking Life and Death: The Collapse of Our Traditional Ethics. New York: St. Martins Press, 1995.

Animal Liberation: A New Ethics for Our Treatment of Animals. 2nd ed. Ecco: New York, 2001.

SECONDARY WORKS

Jamieson, Dale, ed. *Singer and his Critics*. Oxford: Blackwelll, 1999.

Peter Singer. http://www.petersingerlinks.com/

Dale Jamieson (2005)

SKEPTICISM

See *Skepticism, Contemporary; Skepticism, History of*

SKEPTICISM, CONTEMPORARY

Skepticism regarding a subject matter is the view that knowledge about the subject matter is not possible. Many subject matters have come under skeptical attack. It has been argued, for example, that it is not possible to obtain knowledge about the external world, about as-yet-unobserved states of affairs, and about minds other than one's own. This entry will focus upon skepticism about knowledge of the external world.

THE CARTESIAN SKEPTICAL ARGUMENT

The following skeptical argument is suggested by Descartes's first Meditation. Consider the skeptical hypothesis SK: There are no physical objects; all that exists is my mind and that of an evil genius, who causes me to have sense experience just like that which I actually have (sense experience representing a world of physical objects). This hypothesis, says the skeptic, is logically possible and incompatible with propositions implying the existence of the external world, such as that I have hands. The skeptic then claims that (1) if I know that I have hands, then I know that not-SK. To justify premise (1), the skeptic points out that the proposition that I have hands entails not-SK, and he asserts this closure principle: If S knows that ϕ and S knows that ϕ entails ψ, then S knows that ψ. The skeptical argument's other premise is that (2) I do not know that not-SK. To justify this premise, the skeptic points out that, if SK were true, then I would have sense experience exactly similar to that which I actually have. Because my sensory evidence does not discriminate between the hypothesis that SK and the hypothesis that not-SK, this evidence does not justify me in believing not-SK rather than SK. Lacking justification for my belief that not-SK, I do not know that not-SK. From (1) and (2) it follows that I do not know that I have hands. A similar argument may be given for each external-world proposition that I claim to know.

Those who think that minds are physical in nature may well balk at the skeptic's claim that the evil-genius hypothesis is logically possible. Accordingly, the skeptic will replace that hypothesis with this updated version of SK: I am a brain in a vat connected to a computer that is the ultimate cause of my (thoroughly unveridical) sense experience.

To see how the foregoing pattern of skeptical reasoning may be extended to other subject matters, let the target knowledge claim be that there are minds other than my own, and let the skeptical hypothesis be that the complex patterns of bodily behavior that I observe are not accompanied by any states of consciousness. The analogue to premise (2) will in this case be supported by the claim that, if the skeptical hypothesis were true, then I would have behavioral evidence exactly similar to that which I actually have.

DENYING THE LOGICAL POSSIBILITY OF SK

Let us consider two radical responses to the Cartesian skeptical argument. The evil-genius and vat hypotheses both depend on the assumption that the external world is mind-independent in such a way that it is logically possible for sense experience to represent there to be a physical world of a certain character even though there is no physical world, or at least no physical world of that character. An idealist denies this assumption of independence. The idealist maintains that facts about physical objects hold simply in virtue of the holding of the right facts about sense experience, then denies that skeptical hypotheses such as SK are logically possible: any world in which the facts of sense experience are as they actually are is a world in which there is an external reality of roughly the sort people take there to be. Thus premise (2) is false: I know that not-SK in virtue of knowing the necessary falsity of SK.

The second radical response to the skeptical argument rests on a verificationist constraint on the meaningfulness of sentences. Like the idealist, the verificationist holds that the sentence "I am a victim of thoroughgoing sensory deception" fails to express a logically possible hypothesis. Given that the sentence fails to express a proposition for which sense experience could in principle provide confirming or disconfirming evidence, the verificationist counts the sentence as meaningless. Because the sentence expresses no proposition at all, it does not express a proposition that is possibly true.

The antirealist puts forward a similar view, maintaining that one's understanding of a sentence's meaning consists in a recognitional capacity manifestable in one's use of the sentence. Suppose that the conditions under which a sentence X is true transcend people's powers of recognition. Then one's understanding of X's meaning could not be identified with one's grasping of X's recognition-transcendent truth conditions (because such a grasping could not, in turn, be identified with a manifestable recognitional capacity). This conception may be applied to sentences that allegedly express skeptical hypotheses. If people cannot detect the obtaining of their truth conditions, then what is understood when skeptical sentences' meanings are understood must be something other than their truth conditions. Grasping such sentences' meanings must instead consist in grasping the detectable conditions under which they are warrantedly assertible. Thus, it would turn out that an allegedly problematic skeptical hypothesis fails to make any coherent claims about putative conditions in the world that outstrip the human capacity for knowledge.

ATTACKING PREMISE (1)

Premise (1) has come under attack by those who think that the skeptic has succeeded in stating a hypothesis that is genuinely logically possible and not known to be false. On this strategy the closure principle is denied. This opens up the possibility that I know that I have hands even though I do not know that not-SK. For example, one may deny closure by maintaining that knowing that ϕ requires knowing only that the *relevant* alternative hypotheses to ϕ do not obtain. Skeptical hypotheses, it is then said, are not relevant alternatives to the propositions involved in ordinary knowledge claims.

Another way of denying closure is to hold that S knows that P if and only if (i) S correctly believes that P, and (ii) S would not mistakenly believe that P if P were false. To satisfy the tracking condition (ii), S must not mistakenly believe that P in the possible worlds in which P is false that are *most similar* to the actual world, according to the standard semantics for counterfactuals. (Robert Nozick adds the further tracking requirement that S believes that P in the possible worlds in which P is true that are most similar to the actual world.) Now suppose that some hypothetical normal believer S satisfies these conditions with respect to the proposition that he has hands (S correctly believes that he has hands and would not mistakenly believe that he has hands in the no-hands possible worlds most similar to his world, worlds in which, say, he has lost his hands in a terrible accident). Then S knows that he has hands. But in all the possible worlds in which not-SK is false (SK worlds), S mistakenly believes that not-SK (he mistakenly believes that he is not in a vat). So S does not know that not-SK, even though this proposition is entailed by the proposition that S has hands. This is a counterexample to the closure principle.

ATTACKING PREMISE (2)

Let us turn to antiskeptical strategies that do not challenge premise (1) and that accept that SK is indeed logically possible. On these strategies, premise (2) is attacked. For example, Kant tried to show via a transcendental argument that, in allowing knowledge of certain key features of one's own mind, the Cartesian is already committed to the possibility of knowledge of the external world. Kant argued (in "Refutation of Idealism" in *Critique of Pure Reason*) that, in order to have knowledge of one's own temporally-ordered inner states, one must also have knowledge of spatial objects outside one's mind, whose temporal ordering is related to that of one's inner states. A prima facie difficulty for the Kantian strategy is that arguing for a connection between knowledge of one's mind and knowledge of the external world seems to require the assumption of verificationism or idealism, which would render superfluous the rest of the transcendental argument.

The inference to the best explanation strategy relies on the idea that, even if two incompatible explanatory hypotheses are equally supported by the available evidence, I am still justified in rejecting one hypothesis if the other offers a better explanation of the evidence. It might be maintained that the ordinary hypothesis that the world is roughly as I take it to be offers a better explanation of my sensory evidence than does SK, in virtue of its greater simplicity. Thus, I can justifiably reject SK. The proponent of this strategy needs to specify the respect in which SK is more complex than the ordinary hypothesis and to make it plausible that hypotheses that are complex in the specified way are less likely to be true than simpler ones.

Another way to attack premise (2) is to adopt a reliabilist theory of knowledge, according to which knowing that ϕ is a matter of having a reliably produced true belief that ϕ. If reliabilism is correct, then in arguing that I do not know that not-SK, the skeptic would have the difficult burden of showing that there is in fact some flaw in the belief-producing mechanism that yields my belief that not-SK (thereby precluding that belief's amounting to knowledge).

Let us return to the skeptic's *defense* of his premise (2). To validate the premise, the skeptic needs to appeal to an epistemic principle that is (apparently) distinct from the closure principle. This is the underdetermination principle:

> (UP) If S's evidence for Φ does not favor Φ over a competing incompatible hypothesis Ψ, then S is not justified in believing Φ.

The skeptic maintains that one's perceptual evidence would be the same regardless of whether SK holds or not-SK holds. By (UP), then, one's perceptual evidence fails to justify one in believing that not-SK. Hence, one does not know that not-SK.

According to one response to this line of thought, experiences justify perceptual beliefs (such as that a cat is near) without providing evidence or reasons for these beliefs because evidence and reasons always come in the form of *beliefs* which inferentially justify other beliefs. Thus the skeptic cannot appeal to (UP) in the foregoing way. Some philosophers maintain that perceptual Perceptual experiences, some philosophers maintain, justify perceptual beliefs in virtue of having *propositional content*, although they are not themselves propositions. A visual perception, say, has the representational content expressible by the sentence "A cat is near," and accordingly justifies an associated perceptual belief's having that same content.

One problem for this view is that it is plausible to suppose that nonhuman animals have perceptual experiences with representational contents that are similar to those of humans (given the physiological similarities between the relevant perceptual systems). But the animals' perceptual representations do not possess *propositional* content. One may reply that experiences nevertheless justify perceptual beliefs by virtue of having *nonpropositional* representational content, such as that possessed by maps and pictures. This view is, in one way, less attractive than the propositional view, however, because it is easier to see how a belief-like state with propositional content can justify a perceptual belief than to see how a state with a nonpropositional content can perform the same justifying feat.

Further, both views about perceptual justification have the following difficulty. (UP) can be reformulated as:

> (UP*) If S's putative justifier for Φ does not favor Φ over a competing incompatible hypothesis Ψ, then S is not justified in believing Φ.

Now the skeptic may hold that one's nonevidential, perceptual putative justifier would be present regardless of whether SK holds or not-SK holds. Thus, one is not justified in believing not-SK, as the skeptic originally claimed.

Against this, it has been held that the perceptual states that one has when not-SK holds differ in their intrinsic nature from those that one has when SK holds. On this view, the veridical perceptual states possessed by a normal perceiver are *object-involving*, in that objects such as cats are constituents of their perceptual contents. This view might be put forward as a direct realist answer to skepticism, according to which our awareness of external objects is not mediated by awareness of our own experiences. But such direct realism has little antiskeptical force: the skeptic may maintain that even if veridical experience, should it occur, involves direct awareness of cats, it is nevertheless possible that all of one's experiences are unveridical, none possessing an object-involving perceptual content. When the object-involving view is put forward a little differently, however, there is a greater payoff. A disjunctive view challenges the skeptic's use of (UP*). Unlike a veridical perceptual experience of a cat, a nonveridical perceptual state of a brain in a vat is obviously *not* object-involving. The two states, then, are not tokens of a single perceptual state type; there is no common factor between the states. Because it is not true that the same putative perceptual justifier would be present regardless of whether SK holds or not-SK holds, (UP*) cannot be used to show that one lacks justification for believing not-SK. Thus, on the disjunctivist approach, premise (2) of the skeptical argument is not adequately supported.

One may use considerations from the philosophy of language and the philosophy of mind to argue that SK is in fact false. According to semantic externalism, the Cartesian commits an error in attempting to construct thought experiments involving massive deception. The Cartesian naively assumes that, starting with a subject S of thought and experience who is ensconced in a normal external environment, we may hold fixed the contents of S's thoughts and the meanings of his sentences while varying (in thought) S's external environment in such a way that S's thoughts about his environment come out to be predominantly false. According to the semantic externalist, the Cartesian fails to realize that the contents of one's thoughts and the meanings of one's sentences depend in certain ways on one's external environment.

For example, Donald Davidson argues that, when we interpret a speaker's sentences as expressing various beliefs that he holds, we are constrained to attribute beliefs to him that are by and large true of the environment with which he interacts (Davidson 1986). This is because there is no rational basis for preferring one interpretation that finds him to be massively mistaken in his beliefs over another such interpretation. It is constitutive of beliefs and of sentential meanings that they are what are correctly attributed in correct interpretation, on Davidson's view. Thus, it follows from the nature of belief and meaning that, contrary to what SK states, one can never be so massively mistaken.

To see another manifestation of this anti-Cartesian line of thought, consider Hilary Putnam's Twin Earth, a planet like Earth except for the circumstances that the clear, thirst-quenching liquid that the Twin Earthians call "water" is composed of XYZ molecules rather than H_2O molecules. The Twin Earthians' term "water" does not refer to water, but rather to the liquid on Twin Earth with which they interact. Hence, my Twin Earth counterpart's word "water" does not have the same meaning as my word, and when the Twin Earthian says "Water is wet," it is not to thereby express the thought that I think when I think that water is wet. Similarly, the semantic externalist maintains that, when my envatted twin in a treeless world uses the word "tree" in thought, it is not to refer to trees. Instead, the brain in a vat refers to those entities in the external environment that play a causal role with respect to his uses of "tree" analogous to that played by trees with respect to normal uses of "tree" in a tree-filled world. These entities may be states of the computer that systematically cause the brain in a vat to have "tree-like" sense experience. When the brain in the vat thinks the sentence "A tree has fallen," he does not thereby mistakenly express the thought that a tree has fallen. Instead, he expresses a thought about computer states, which may well be true of his environment. In general, then, the brain in a vat is not massively mistaken about the world, contrary to what the Cartesian maintains.

We may use these considerations, together with the assumption that I have knowledge of the contents of my own thoughts, against premise (2) in the following way: I am now thinking that a tree has fallen; if SK is true, then I am not now thinking that a tree has fallen; thus, SK is false. This argument, however, is powerless against versions of the skeptical hypothesis on which the brain in a vat is indirectly causally linked to ordinary objects. If, for example, there are programmers of the computer who refer to trees, then it becomes plausible to suppose that the brain does so as well. Further, there is a prima facie problem as to whether I may claim knowledge of the contents of my own thoughts, given semantic externalism. Such knowledge seems to require independent knowledge of the content-determining causal environment in which I am located, knowledge the antiskeptical argument was meant to provide.

AMBIVALENCE ABOUT THE SKEPTICAL ARGUMENT

Contextualism is a response to skepticism that is based upon a novel view of the semantics of knowledge-attributing sentences of the form "S knows that P." According to the contextualist, such sentences are like sentences of the form "X is flat." The truth value of the latter sort of sentence depends upon both (1) the shape of the pertinent object, and (2) contextually determined standards regarding contour. Relative to one conversational context (in which bicycle racing is under discussion, for instance), "The road is flat" can come out true; relative to another context (where inclined planes are under discussion), the sentence (concerning the same road) can come out false. Similarly, the truth value of an utterance of, say, "John knows that the bank is open this Saturday" depends upon both (1) John's epistemic situation (e.g., his evidential beliefs, his perceptual experience, whether the bank is indeed open), and (2) contextually determined epistemic standards (set by the interests, intentions, and expectations of the knowledge-attributing conversationalists).

Suppose that John's basis for claiming that the bank is open this Saturday is that he visited it on a Saturday a month ago. Suppose that my business partner and I wish to deposit a check this Saturday or some time the following week. Then my partner's utterance of "John knows that the bank is open this Saturday" may well be true, given John's epistemic situation and given the low stakes in our conversational context. Holding John's epistemic situation fixed, imagine a different case in which our business will go bankrupt if the check is not deposited on Saturday. In this case, my partner's utterance of "John knows that the bank is open this Saturday" may well be false, given the higher stakes in this context, in which evidence superior to John's may well be required for knowledge about the bank.

The contextualist claims that his view both (a) explains why the skeptical argument may seem compelling, and (b) implies that there is much ordinarily-attributed knowledge in the world. When skepticism and skeptical possibilities are under discussion, the conversational context is such that abnormally high epistemic standards are in place. Accordingly, an utterance of the argument's premise (2)—"I do not know that not-SK"—comes out true. According to the contextualist, utterances of the argument's closure-based premise (1) are true in all conversational contexts. Thus, relative to a skeptical context, an utterance of the argument's conclusion is true. However, in an ordinary, nonskeptical conversational context, the epistemic standards are lowered, and utterances of premise (2) are false. Thus, knowledge-attributions in ordinary conversational contexts are not threatened by the skeptical argument.

One problem for contextualism is that it is hard to coherently state the view. For example, I cannot now correctly say that Michael Jordan knows that he has hands, since I am currently involved in a skeptical (written) conversational context. What I must instead say is that neither I, nor anybody else, knows that he has hands. I cannot even justifiably say that some ordinary-context utterances of "Michael Jordan knows that he has hands" are true, relative to the low epistemic standards in effect in such contexts. This is because I, in my present context, do not know whether anyone has hands.

Another problem for contextualism is that it seems to imply that speakers are mistaken about the very meanings of their knowledge-attributing sentences. That is, suppose that I think that the skeptical argument is compelling and yet at the same time find its conclusion to be repugnant: it just can't be true that I do not know that I have hands. This means that I am failing to realize that the sentence stating the argument's conclusion is perfectly true as uttered in my current philosophical context. This betrays a misunderstanding of what my sentence means when used in the philosophical context.

See also Epistemology; Reliabilism; Verifiability Principle.

Bibliography

Ayer, Alfred Jules. *Language, Truth, and Logic*. New York: Dover, 1952. Verificationism.

Berkeley, George. *Three Dialogues between Hylas and Philonous*. Indianapolis: Bobbs-Merrill, 1954.

Brewer, Bill. *Perception and Reason*. Oxford: Oxford University Press, 1999. Perceptual beliefs.

Brueckner, Anthony. "Semantic Answers to Skepticism." *Pacific Philosophical Quarterly* 72 (1992): 200–201. Semantic externalism.

Brueckner, Anthony. "The Structure of the Skeptical Argument." *Philosophy and Phenomenological Research* 54 (1994): 827–835. *Underdetermination Principle.*

Cohen, Stewart. "How to be a Fallibilist." *Philosophical Perspectives* 2 (1988): 91–123. Contextualism.

Davidson, Donald. "A Coherence Theory of Truth and Knowledge." In *Truth and Interpretation*, edited by Ernest LePore. Oxford: Oxford University Press, 1986. Semantic externalism.

Descartes, René. *Meditations on First Philosophy*. In *The Philosophical Works of Descartes*. Vol. 1, translated by Haldane and Ross. New York: Dover, 1955. The Cartesian skeptical argument.

Dretske, Fred. "Epistemic Operators." *Journal of Philosophy* 67 (1970): 1007–1023. Denying the closure principle.

Dummett, Michael. "What Is a Theory of Meaning? (II)." In *Truth and Meaning*, edited by G. Evans and J. McDowell. Oxford: Oxford University Press, 1976. Antirealism.

Goldman, Alvin. "What Is Justified Belief?" In *Justification and Knowledge*, edited by G. Pappas. Dordrecht, Holland: Kluwer, 1979. Reliabilism.

Huemer, Michael. *Skepticism and the Veil of Perception*. Lanham, MD: Rowman and Littlefield, 2001. Perceptual beliefs; direct realism.

Kant, Immanuel. *Critique of Pure Reason*. Translated by N. K. Smith. New York: St. Martin's Press, 1965. Transcendental arguments.

McDowell, John. "Singular Thought and the Extent of Inner Space." In *Subject, Thought and Context*, edited by P. Pettit and J. McDowell. Oxford: Oxford University Press, 1986. Disjunctive view.

Nozick, Robert. *Philosophical Explanations*. Chap. 3. Cambridge, MA: Belknap Press of Harvard University Press, 1981). Denying the closure principle; tracking condition.

Putnam, Hilary. "Meaning and Reference." *Journal of Philosophy* 70 (1973): 699–711. Semantic externalism.

Putnam, Hilary. *Reason, Truth, and History*. Chap. 1. Cambridge, MA: 1981. Semantic externalism.

Schiffer, Stephen. "Contextualist Solutions to Skepticism." *Proceedings of the Aristotelian Society* 96 (1996): 317–333. Contextualism.

Stroud, Barry. "Transcendental Arguments." *Journal of Philosophy* 65 (1968): 241–256. Transcendental arguments.

Vogel, Jonathan. "Cartesian Skepticism and Inference to the Best Explanation." *Journal of Philosophy* 87 (1990): 658–666.

Anthony Brueckner (1996, 2005)

SKEPTICISM, HISTORY OF

Skepticism (also spelled "Scepticism") is the philosophical attitude of doubting knowledge claims set forth in various areas. Skeptics have challenged the adequacy or reliability of these claims by asking what they are based upon or what they actually establish. They have raised the question whether such claims about the world are either indubitable or necessarily true, and they have challenged the alleged grounds of accepted assumptions. Practically everyone is skeptical about some knowledge claims; but the skeptics have raised doubts about any knowledge beyond the contents of directly felt experience. The original Greek meaning of *skeptikos* was "an inquirer," someone who was unsatisfied and still looking for truth.

From ancient times onward skeptics have developed arguments to undermine the contentions of dogmatic philosophers, scientists, and theologians. The skeptical arguments and their employment against various forms of dogmatism have played an important role in shaping both the problems and the solutions offered in the course of western philosophy. As ancient philosophy and science developed, doubts arose about basic accepted views of the world. In ancient times skeptics challenged the claims of Platonism, Aristotelianism, and Stoicism, and in the Renaissance those of Scholasticism and Calvinism. After René Descartes, skeptics attacked Cartesianism and other theories justifying the "new science." Later, a skeptical offensive was leveled against Kantianism and then against Hegelianism. Each skeptical challenge led to new attempts to resolve the difficulties. Skepticism, especially since the Enlightenment, has come to mean disbelief—primarily religious disbelief—and the skeptic has often been likened to the village atheist.

VARIOUS SENSES AND APPLICATIONS

Skepticism developed with regard to various disciplines in which men claimed to have knowledge. It was questioned, for example, whether one could gain any certain knowledge in metaphysics (the study of the nature and significance of being as such) or in the sciences. In ancient times a chief form was medical skepticism, which questioned whether one could know with certainty either the causes or cures of diseases. In the area of ethics, doubts were raised about accepting various mores and customs and about claiming any objective basis for making value distinctions. Skepticisms about religion have questioned the doctrines of different traditions. Certain philosophies, like those of David Hume and Immanuel Kant, have seemed to show that no knowledge can be gained beyond the world of experience and that one cannot discover the causes of phenomena. Any attempt to do so, as Kant argued, leads to antinomies, contradictory knowledge claims. A dominant form of skepticism, the subject of this article, concerns knowledge in general, questioning whether anything actually can be known with complete or adequate certainty. This type is called epistemological skepticism.

Kinds of epistemological skepticism can be distinguished in terms of the areas in which doubts are raised; that is, whether they be directed toward reason, toward the senses, or toward knowledge of things-in-themselves. They can also be distinguished in terms of the motivation of the skeptic—whether he or she is challenging views for ideological reasons or for pragmatic or practical ones to attain certain psychological goals. Among the chief ideological motives have been religious or antireligious concerns. Some skeptics have challenged knowledge claims so that religious ones could be substituted—on faith. Others have challenged religious knowledge claims in order to overthrow some orthodoxy. Kinds of skepticism also can be distinguished in terms of how restricted or how thoroughgoing they are—whether they apply only to certain areas and to certain kinds of knowledge claims or whether they are more general and universal.

ANCIENT SKEPTICISM

Historically, skeptical philosophical attitudes began to appear in pre-Socratic thought. In the fifth century BCE, the Eleatic philosophers, known for reducing reality to a static One, questioned the reality of the sensory world, of change and plurality, and denied that reality could be described in the categories of ordinary experience. On the other hand, the Ephesian philosopher of change Heraclites and his pupil Cratylus thought that the world was in such a state of flux that no permanent, unchangeable truth about it could be found; and Xenophanes, a wandering poet and philosopher, doubted whether man could distinguish true from false knowledge.

A more developed skepticism appeared in some of Socrates' views and in several of the Sophists. Socrates, in the early Platonic dialogues, was always questioning the knowledge claims of others; and in the *Apology*, he said that all that he really knew was that he knew nothing. Socrates' enemy, the Sophist Protagoras, contended that man is the measure of all things. This thesis was taken as a kind of skeptical relativism: no views are ultimately true, but each is merely one man's opinion. Another Sophist, Gorgias, advanced the skeptical-nihilist thesis that nothing exists; and if something did exist, it could not be known; and if it could be known, it could not be communicated.

ACADEMIC SKEPTICISM. Academic skepticism, so-called because it was formulated in the Platonic Academy in the third century BCE, developed from the Socratic observation, "All I know is that I know nothing." Its theoretical formulation is attributed to Arcesilas (c. 315–241 BCE) and Carneades (c. 213–129 BCE), who worked out a series of arguments, directed primarily against the knowledge claims of the Stoic philosophers, to show that nothing could be known. As these arguments have come down to us, especially in the writings of Cicero, Diogenes Laertius, and Saint Augustine, the aim of the Academic skeptical philosophers was to show, by a group of arguments and dialectical puzzles, that the dogmatic philosopher (that is, the philosopher who asserted that he knew *some* truth about the real nature of things), could not know with absolute certainty the propositions he said he knew. The Academics formulated a series of difficulties to show that the information we gain by means of our senses may be unreliable, that we cannot be certain that our reasoning is reliable, and that we possess no guaranteed criterion or standard for determining which of our judgments is true or false.

The basic problem at issue is that any proposition purporting to assert some knowledge about the world contains some claims that go beyond the merely empirical reports about what appears to us to be the case. If we possessed any knowledge, this would mean for the skeptics, that we knew a proposition, asserting some non-empirical, or trans-empirical claim, which we were certain could not possibly be false. If the proposition might be false, then it would not deserve the name of knowledge, but only that of opinion, i.e., that it might be the case. Since the evidence for any such proposition would be based, according to the skeptics, on either sense information or reasoning, and both of these sources are unreliable to some degree, and no guaranteed or ultimate criterion of true knowledge exists, or is known, there is always some doubt that any non-empirical or trans-empirical proposition is absolutely true and hence constitutes real knowledge. As a result, the Academic skeptics said that nothing is certain. The best information we can gain is only probable and is to be judged according to probabilities. Hence, Carneades developed a type of verification theory and a type of probabilism that is somewhat similar to the theory of scientific '"knowledge" of present-day pragmatists and positivists.

The skepticism of Arcesilas and Carneades dominated the philosophy of the Platonic Academy until the first century before Christ. In the period of Cicero's studies, the Academy changed from skepticism to the eclecticism of Philo of Larissa and Antiochus of Ascalon. The arguments of the Academics survived mainly through Cicero's presentation of them in his *Academica* and *De*

Natura Deorum, and through their refutation in St. Augustine's *Contra Academicos*, as well as in the summary given by Diogenes Laertius. The locus of skeptical activity, however, moved from the Academy to the school of the Pyrrhonian skeptics, which was probably associated with the Methodic school of medicine in Alexandria.

THE PYRRHONIAN SCHOOL. The putative father of Greek skepticism is Pyrrho of Elis (c. 360–c. 272 BCE) and his student Timon (c. 315–225 BCE). He avoided committing himself to any views about what was actually going on and acted only according to appearances. In this way he sought happiness or at least mental peace. The stories about Pyrrho that are reported indicate that he was not a theoretician, but rather a living example of the complete doubter, the man who would not commit himself to any judgment that went beyond what seemed to be the case. His interests seem to have been primarily ethical and moral, and in this area he tried to avoid unhappiness that might be due to the acceptance of value theories and to judging according to them. If such value theories were to any degree doubtful, accepting them and using them could only lead to mental anguish.

Pyrrhonism, as a theoretical formulation of skepticism, is attributed to Aenesidemus (c. 100–40 BCE). The Pyrrhonists considered that both the Dogmatists and the Academics asserted too much, one group saying, "Something can be known," the other that "Nothing can be known." Instead, the Pyrrhonians proposed to suspend judgment on all questions on which there seemed to be conflicting evidence, including the question whether or not something could be known.

Building on the type of arguments developed by Arcesilas and Carneades, Aenesidemus and his successors put together a series of "Tropes" or ways of proceeding to bring about suspense of judgment on various questions. In the sole surviving texts from the Pyrrhonian movement, those of Sextus Empiricus, these are presented in groups of ten, eight, five, and two tropes, each set offering reasons why one should suspend judgment about knowledge claims that go beyond appearances. The Pyrrhonian skeptics tried to avoid committing themselves on any and all questions, even as to whether their arguments were sound. Skepticism for them was an ability, or mental attitude, for opposing evidence both pro and con on any question about what was nonevident, so that one would suspend judgment on the question. This state of mind then led to a state of *ataraxia*, quietude, or unperturbedness, in which the skeptic was no longer concerned or worried about matters beyond appearances. Skepticism was a cure for the disease called Dogmatism or rashness. But, unlike Academic skepticism, which came to a negative dogmatic conclusion from its doubts, Pyrrhonian skepticism made no such assertion, merely saying that skepticism is a purge that eliminates everything including itself. The Pyrrhonist, then, lives undogmatically, following his natural inclinations, the appearances of which he is aware, and the laws and customs of his society, without ever committing himself to any judgment about them.

The Pyrrhonian movement flourished up to about 200 CE, the approximate date of Sextus Empiricus, and flourished mainly in the medical community around Alexandria as an antidote to the dogmatic theories, positive and negative, of other medical groups. The position has come down to us principally in the writings of Sextus Empiricus in his *Hypotyposes (Outlines of Pyrrhonism)* and the larger *Adversus mathematicos*, in which all sorts of disciplines from logic and mathematics to astrology and grammar are subjected to skeptical devastation. In his *Outlines of Pyrrhonism* and *Adversus mathematicos*, Sextus presented the tropes developed by previous Pyrrhonists. The ten tropes attributed to Aenesidemus showed the difficulties to be encountered in ascertaining the truth or reliability of judgments based on sense information, owing to the variability and differences of human and animal perceptions.

Other arguments raised difficulties in determining whether there are any reliable criteria or standards—logical, rational, or otherwise—for judging whether anything is true or false. To settle any disagreement, a criterion seems to be required. Any purported criterion, however, would appear to be based on another criterion, thus requiring an infinite regress of criteria, or else it would be based upon itself, which would be circular. Sextus offered arguments to challenge any claims of dogmatic philosophers to know more than what is evident; and in so doing he presented in one form or another practically all of the skeptical arguments that have ever appeared in subsequent philosophy.

Sextus said that his arguments were aimed at leading people to a state of *ataraxia* (unperturbability). People who thought that they could know reality were constantly disturbed and frustrated. If they could be led to suspend judgment, however, they would find peace of mind. In this state of suspension they would neither affirm nor deny the possibility of knowledge but would remain peaceful, still waiting to see what might develop. The Pyrrhonist did not become inactive in this state of suspense but lived undogmatically according to appearances, customs, and natural inclinations.

MEDIEVAL SKEPTICISM

Pyrrhonism ended as a philosophical movement in the late Roman Empire, as religious concerns became paramount. In the Christian Middle Ages the main surviving form of skepticism was the Academic, described in St. Augustine's *Contra academicos*. Augustine, before his conversion, had found Cicero's views attractive and had overcome them only through revelation. With faith, he could seek understanding. Augustine's account of skepticism and his answer to it provided the basis for medieval discussions.

In Islamic Spain, where there was more contact with ancient learning, a form of antirational skepticism developed among Muslim and Jewish theologians. Al-Ghazālī, an Arab theologian of the eleventh and early twelfth centuries, and his Jewish contemporary Judah ha-Levi (c. 1075/c. 1085–c. 1141), who was a poet and physician as well as a philosopher, offered skeptical challenges (much like those later employed by the occasionalist Nicolas Malebranche and by David Hume) against the contemporary Aristotelians in order to lead people to accept religious truths in mystical faith. This view that truth in religion is ultimately based on faith rather than on reasoning or evidence—what is known as fideism—also appears in the late Middle Ages in the German cardinal and philosopher Nicolaus of Cusa's advocacy of learned ignorance as the way to religious knowledge.

Another line of thinking that includes skeptical elements was that of the followers of William of Ockham (1285–1347) in the fourteenth century, who were exploring the consequences of accepting divine omnipotence and a divine source for all knowledge. They examined puzzles about whether God could deceive mankind, regardless of the evidence, and could make all human reasoning open to question.

MODERN SKEPTICISM

Modern Skepticism emerged in part from some of the Ockhamite views but mainly from the rediscovery of the skeptical classics. Very little of the Pyrrhonnian tradition had been known in the Middle Ages, but in the fifteenth century the texts of Sextus Empiricus in Greek were brought from the Byzantine Empire into Italy. Sextus' *Outlines of Pyrrhonism* was published in Latin in 1562, his *Adversus matematicos* in 1569, and the Greek texts of both in 1621. Interest in Cicero was revived and his *Academica* and *De natura deorum* were also published in the sixteenth century.

The voyages of exploration; the humanistic rediscovery of the learning of ancient Greece, Rome, and Palestine; and the new science—all combined to undermine confidence in man's accepted picture of the world. The religious controversy between the Protestants and Catholics raised fundamental epistemological issues about the bases and criteria of religious knowledge.

RENAISSANCE AND REFORMATION. Toward the end of the fifteenth century, there was a revival of interest in ancient skepticism among Florentine humanists. Politian was lecturing on philosophy using notes from Sextus with which he had recently become acquainted from manuscripts brought from Byzantium. Humanists, including Gianfrancesco Pico della Mirandola, were acquiring and studying Sextus' texts. Some of these manuscripts were deposited in the convent of San Marco where the Dominican friar and prophet Girolamo Savonarola was heading up an exciting intellectual forum in which ancient philosophies were being analyzed. Savonarola, who did not read Greek, asked two of his monks to prepare a Latin translation of Sextus from one of these manuscripts. This apparently was to be used as a weapon against philosophy independent of religion. Before Savonarola's project could be completed the convent was destroyed and he was executed.

Gianfrancesco Pico, one of Savonarola's disciples and the nephew of the great Pico della Mirandola, published the first work using skepticism as a way of challenging all of philosophy. Gianfrancesco Pico's *Examen Vanitatis* (1520) is the first work to present Sextus in Latin for the European audience. In 1562 Henri Estienne (Stephanus) published a Latin translation of the *Pyrrhoniarum Hypotyposes* in Paris, and in 1569 Gentian Hervet published a Latin translation of *Adversus Mathematicos* in Antwerp. The Greek texts were first printed at Cologne, Paris, and Geneva in 1621. Some texts of Sextus appeared in English in 1592 in a work attributed to Sir Walter Raleigh titled "The Skepticke." A full translation of Book One of Sextus appeared in 1659 in Thomas Stanley's *History of Philosophy*; instead of explaining skepticism he just presented the whole book to the readers. A French translation was started by Pierre Gassendi's disciple Samuel Sorbière but was never finished or published. The first complete French translation, by Claude Huart, did not appear until 1725.

RELIGIOUS CONTROVERSY: ERASMUS AND LUTHER. The skeptical issue became more central when raised in the debate between Erasmus and Martin Luther. Using Academic skeptical materials, Erasmus insisted that the issues in dispute could not be resolved and that one should therefore suspend judgment and remain with the church. In 1524, Erasmus finally published a work, *De Libero Arbitrio*, attacking Martin Luther's views on free will. Erasmus' general anti-intellectualism and dislike of rational theological discussions led him to suggest a kind of skeptical basis for remaining within the Catholic Church. This contempt for intellectual endeavor was coupled with his advocacy of a simple, non-theological Christian piety. Theological controversies were not Erasmus' meat, and he states that he would prefer to follow the attitude of the skeptics and suspend judgment, especially where the inviolable authority of Scripture and the decrees of the Church permit. He says he is perfectly willing to submit to the decrees, whether or not he understands them or the reasons for them.

Scripture is not as clear as Luther would have us believe, and there are some places that are just too shadowy for human beings to penetrate. Theologians have argued and argued the question without end. Luther claims he has found the right answer and has understood Scripture correctly. But how can we tell that he really has? Other interpretations can be given that seem much better than Luther's. In view of the difficulty in establishing *the* true meaning of Scripture concerning the problem of free will, why not accept the traditional solution offered by the Church? Why start such a fuss over something one cannot know with any certainty? For Erasmus, what is important is a simple, basic, Christian piety, a Christian spirit. The rest, the superstructure of the essential belief, is too complex for a man to judge. Hence it is easier to rest in a skeptical attitude, and accept the age-old wisdom of the Church on these matters, than to try to understand and judge for oneself.

This attempt, early in the Reformation, at a skeptical "justification" of the Catholic rule of faith brought forth a furious answer from Luther, the *De Servo Arbitrio* of 1525. Erasmus' book, Luther declared, was shameful and shocking, the more so since it was written so well and with so much eloquence. *De Libero Arbitrio* begins with the announcement that the problem of the freedom of the will is one of the most involved of labyrinths. The central error of Erasmus' book, according to Luther, was that Erasmus did not realize that a Christian cannot be a skeptic. Christianity involves the affirmation of certain truths because one's conscience is completely convinced of their veracity. The content of religious knowledge, according to Luther, is far too important to be taken on trust. One must be absolutely certain of its truth. Hence, Christianity is the complete denial of skepticism. To find the truths, one only has to consult Scripture.

Of course there are parts that are hard to understand, and there are things about God that we do not, and perhaps shall not, know. But this does not mean that we cannot find the truth in Scripture. The central religious truth can be found in clear and evident terms, and these clarify the more obscure ones. However, if many things remain obscure to some people, it is not the fault of Scripture, but of the blindness of those who have no desire to know the revealed truths. Luther's view, and later that of Calvin, proposed a new criterion—that of inner experience—while the Catholics of the Counter-Reformation employed Pyrrhonian and Academic arguments to undermine the criterion. Following after Erasmus, H. C. Agrippa von Nettesheim, a stormy occult philosopher and physician, employed the skeptical arguments against Scholasticism, Renaissance Naturalism, and many other views to win people to the "true religion."

HERVET. Gentian Hervet, secretary to the Cardinal of Lorraine, and participant at part of the Council of Trent, linked his work on Sextus with what Gianfrancesco Pico had earlier done. During the 1560s, Hervet, a humanist, fought intellectually against the encroachments of Calvinism, challenging various Protestants to debate with him, and publishing many pamphlets against their views. He saw Sextus' work as ideal for demolishing this new form of heretical dogmatism, that of the Reformer. If nothing can be known, then, he insisted, Calvinism cannot be known. The only certainty we can have is God's Revelation. Skepticism, by controverting all human theories, will cure people from dogmatism, give them humility, and prepare them to accept the doctrine of Christ. Hervet's employment of Pyrrhonism against Calvinism was soon to be shaped into a skeptical machine of war for use by the Counter-Reformation. This view of Pyrrhonism, by one of the leaders of French Catholicism, was to set the direction of one of its major influences on the next three-quarters of a century.

MONTAIGNE AND SANCHES. The new concern with skepticism was given a general philosophical formulation by Michel de Montaigne and his cousin Francisco Sanches. Michel de Montaigne was the most significant figure in the sixteenth century revival of ancient skepticism. Not only was he the best writer and thinker of those who were interested in the ideas of the Academics and Pyrrhonians, but he was also the one who felt most fully the impact of the Pyrrhonian arguments of complete doubt—and its relevance to the religious debates of the time. Montaigne was simultaneously a creature of the Renaissance and the Reformation. He was a thorough-going humanist, with a vast interest in, and concern with, the ideas and values of Greece and Rome, and their application to the lives of men in the rapidly changing world of sixteenth-century France. Montaigne was sent to the Collège de Guyenne in 1539 when he was six years old and was there for the next seven years. The college reflected the religious tensions of the time. Two of its leaders were André de Gouvea, a Portuguese New Christian, and George Buchanan, the Scottish Latin poet.

Montaigne's 1576 essay "Apologie of Raimond Sebond" unfolds in his inimitable rambling style as a series of waves of skepticism, with occasional pauses to consider and digest various levels of doubt, but with the overriding theme an advocacy of a new form of fideism—Catholic Pyrrhonism. The essay begins with a probably inaccurate account of how Montaigne came to read and translate the audacious work of the fifteenth century Spanish theologian, Raimond Sebond. Starting from a quibble about the validity of the arguments of Sebond, Montaigne moved to a general skeptical critique of the possibility of human beings understanding anything. In a rather back-handed manner, Montaigne excuses Sebond's theological rationalism by saying that although he, Montaigne, is not versed in theology, it is his view that religion is based solely on faith given to us by the Grace of God; true religion can only be based on faith, and any human foundation for religion is too weak to support divine knowledge. If human beings had the real light of faith, then human means, like the arguments of Sebond, might be of use. Montaigne explored the human epistemological situation and showed that man's knowledge claims in all areas were extremely dubious and so made pure faith the cornerstone of religion. Montaigne recommended living according to nature and custom and accepting whatever God reveals.

Sanches, in *Quod nihil scitur*, also written in 1576, advocated recognizing that nothing can be known and then trying to gain what limited information one can through empirical scientific means. In his book, Sanches develops his skepticism by means of an intellectual critique of Aristotelianism, rather than by an appeal to the history of human stupidity and the variety and contrariety of previous theories. Sanches begins by asserting that he does not even know if he knows nothing. Then he proceeds, step by step, to analyze the Aristotelian conception of knowledge to show why this is the case.

Every science begins with definition and definitions are nothing but names arbitrarily imposed upon things in a capricious manner, having no relation to the things named. The names keep changing, so that when we think we are saying something about the nature of things by means of combining words and definitions, we are just fooling ourselves. And if the names assigned to an object such as man, like "rational animal," all mean the same thing, then they are superfluous and do not help to explain what the object is. On the other hand, if the names mean something different from the object, then they are not the names of the object. By means of such an analysis, Sanches worked out a thorough-going nominalism.

Sanches' first conclusion was the usual fideistic one of the time—that truth can be gained only by faith. His second conclusion was to play an important role in later though: just because nothing can be known in an ultimate sense, we should not abandon all attempts at knowledge but should try to gain what knowledge we can, namely, limited, imperfect knowledge of some of those things with which we become acquainted through observation, experience and judgment. The realization that *nihil scitur* ("nothing is known") thus can yield some constructive results. This early formulation of "constructive" or "mitigated" skepticism was to be developed into an important explication of the new science by Marin Mersenne, Pierre Gassendi, and the leaders of the Royal Society.

THE SEVENTEENTH CENTURY

Montaigne's skepticism was extremely influential in the early seventeenth century. His followers, Pierre Charron in *De la Sagesse* (1601) and Jean-Pierre Camus in *Essay sceptique* (1603), became most popular in the early seventeenth century, especially among the avant-garde intellectuals in Paris. The so-called libertines, including Gabriel Naudé, Mazarin's secretary; Guy Patin, rector of the Sorbonne medical school; and François La Mothe Le Vayer, teacher of the dauphin, espoused Montaigne's attitude and were often accused of being skeptical even of fundamental religious tenets. Others, like François Veron, used the arguments of Sextus and Montaigne to challenge the Calvinist claim of gaining true knowledge from reading Scripture. French Counter-Reformers, by raising skeptical epistemological problems about whether one could determine what book is the Bible, what it actually says, what it means, and so on, forced Calvinists to seek an indisputable basis for knowledge as a prelude to defending their theological views.

GASSENDI AND MERSENNE. In the 1620s efforts to refute or mitigate this new skepticism appeared. Some authors simply stated that Aristotle would have resolved the difficulties by applying his theory of sense perception and knowledge to the problems raised. Others, like François Garasse, decried the irreligious tendencies they discerned in all this doubting. Still others, like Francis Bacon, tried to overcome the skeptical difficulties by appealing to new methods and new instruments that might correct errors and yield firm and unquestionable results. Herbert of Cherbury, in *De Veritate* (1624), offered an elaborate scheme for overcoming skepticism which combined Aristotelian and Stoic elements, and ultimately appealed to common notions, or truths known by all men, as the criteria by which reliable and indubitable judgment would be possible.

Perhaps the most forceful presentation of skepticism in the early seventeenth century is Pierre Gassendi's earliest work, *Exercitationes Paradoxicae Adversus Aristoteleos* (1624). A Christian Epicurean, Gassendi, himself originally a skeptic, challenged almost every aspect of Aristotle's view, as well as many other theories. He applied a battery of ancient and Renaissance skeptical arguments, concluding, "No science is possible, least of all in Aristotle's sense." In this work, Gassendi indicated in embryo what became his and Marin Mersenne's constructive solution to the skeptical crisis, the development of an empirical study of the world of appearances rather than an attempt to discover the real nature of things.

Mersenne, one of the most influential figures in the intellectual revolution of the times, while retaining epistemological doubts about knowledge of reality, yet recognized that science provided useful and important information about the world. Mersenne granted that the problems raised by Sextus could not be answered and that, in a fundamental sense, knowledge of the real nature of things cannot be attained. However, he insisted, information about appearances and deductions from hypotheses can provide an adequate guide for living in this world and can be checked by verifying predictions about futures experiences. Gassendi, in his later works, developed this constructive skepticism as a *via media* between complete doubt and dogmatism, and offered his atomic theory as the best hypothetical model for interpreting experience. Mersenne and Gassendi combined skepticism about metaphysical knowledge of reality with a way of gaining useful information about experience through a pragmatic scientific method. The constructive skepticisms of Gassendi and Mersenne, and later of members of the Royal Society of England like Bishop John Wilkins and Joseph Glanvill, thus developed the attitude of Sanches into a hypothetical, empirical interpretation of the new science.

DESCARTES. René Descartes offered a fundamental refutation of the new skepticism, contending that, by applying the skeptical method of doubting all beliefs that could possibly be false (due to suffering illusions or being misled by some power), one would discover a truth that is genuinely indubitable, namely, "I think, therefore I am" (*cogito ergo sum*), and that from this truth one could discover the criterion of true knowledge, namely, that whatever is clearly and distinctly conceived is true. Using this criterion, one could then establish: God's existence, that he is not a deceiver, that he guarantees our clear and distinct ideas, and that an external world exists that can be known through mathematical physics. Descartes, starting from skepticism, claimed to have found a new basis for certitude and for knowledge of reality.

REPLIES TO DESCARTES. Throughout the seventeenth century skeptical critics—Mersenne, Gassendi, the reviver of Academic philosophy Simon Foucher, and Pierre-Daniel Huet, one of the most learned men of the age—sought to show that Descartes had not succeeded and that, if he sincerely followed his skeptical method, his new system could only lead to complete skepticism. They challenged whether the *cogito* proved anything, or whether it was indubitable; whether Descartes' method could be successfully applied, or whether it was certain; and whether any of the knowledge claims of Cartesianism were *really* true. Nicolas Malebranche, the developer of occasionalism, revised the Cartesian system to meet the skeptical attacks only to find his efforts challenged by the new skeptical criticisms of Foucher and by the contention of the Jansenist philosopher Antoine Arnauld that Malebranchism led to a most dangerous Pyrrhonism.

Huet's *Censura Philosophae Cartesiana* (1689) and his unpublished defense of it raised doubts about each element of the proposition, "I think, therefore perhaps I may be." Gassendi, Huet, and others questioned whether Descartes' criterion could determine what was true or false. Could we really tell what was clear and distinct, or could we only tell that something appeared clear and distinct to us? Mersenne pointed out that even with the criterion we could not be sure that what was clear and distinct to us, and hence true, was really true for God. Hence, in an ultimate sense, even the most certain Cartesian knowledge might be false. Gassendi, in what Descartes called the "objections of objections," pointed out that for all anyone could ascertain, the whole Cartesian system of truths might be only a subjective vision in somebody's mind and not a true picture of reality. Huet argued that since all the fundamental Cartesian data consisted of ideas, and ideas are not real physical things, the Cartesian world of ideas, even if clear and distinct, cannot represent something quite different from itself.

FOLLOWERS OF DESCARTES. As Cartesianism was attacked from many sides, adherents modified it in various ways. The radical revision of Nicolas Malebranche, designed partially to avoid skeptical difficulties involved in connecting the world of ideas with reality, was immediately attacked by the skeptic Simon Foucher. The orthodox Cartesian Antoine Arnaud claimed that Malebranchism could only lead to a most dangerous Pyrrhonism. Foucher, who wished to revive Academic skepticism, applied various skeptical gambits to Malebranche's theory, one of which was to be important in subsequent philosophy. He argued that the skeptical difficulties which Descartes and Malebranche used to deny that sense qualities (the so-called secondary qualities—color, sound heat, taste, smell) were features of real objects, applied as well to the mathematically describable primary qualities like extension and motion, which the Cartesians considered the fundamental properties of things. These mathematical qualities, as perceived, are as variable and as subjective as the others. If the skeptical arguments are sufficient to cause doubt about the ontological status of secondary qualities, Foucher contended, they are also sufficient to lead us to doubt that primary ones are genuine features of reality.

ENGLISH SKEPTICISM. Various English philosophers, culminating in John Locke, tried to blunt the force of skepticism by appealing to common sense and to the "reasonable" man's inability to doubt everything. They admitted that there might not be sufficient evidence to support the knowledge claims extending beyond immediate experience. But this did not actually require that everything be doubted; by using standards of common sense, an adequate basis for many beliefs could be found.

This theory of limited certitude was articulated especially by two figures, John Wilkins and Joseph Glanvill. The theory is a development from the earlier solution to the skeptical problems advanced by Sebastian Castillio and William Chillingworth. Wilkins set forth the theory of limited certainty as both an answer to dogmatism and to excessive skepticism. Wilkins completely rejected the dogmatists' outlook, and then offered a way of defusing the potentially disastrous results of complete skepticism. In order to find a moderate skeptical stance from which religion and science could flourish, Wilkins felt it was necessary to analyze what kind of certainty human beings could actually attain. The highest level of certainty, absolute infallible certainty, which could not possibly be false, is beyond human attainment. Only God has such certainty. The highest human level Wilkins called conditional infallible certainty. This requires that "our faculties be true, and that we do not neglect the exerting of them."

Glanvill saw the reliability of our faculties as central for avoiding any ultimate and overwhelming skepticism. Glanvill, like Wilkins, saw that the kind of certainty we would need to be absolutely sure of our faculties is unattainable—"for it may not be absolutely impossible, but that our Faculties may be so construed, as always to deceive us in the things we judg most certain and assured." We may not be able to attain infallible certitude, but we can attain indubitable certitude—that our faculties are true. This is indubitable in two senses—one, that we find we have to believe them, and, two, that we have no reason or cause for doubting them. In terms of this distinction, Wilkins, Glanvill, and their colleagues built up a theory of empirical science and jurisprudence for studying nature and deciding human problems within the limits of "reasonable doubt." Their limited skepticism appears in the Anglo-American theory of legal evidence and in the theory of science of the early Royal Society. They believed that by applying their probabilistic empirical method to religious questions they could justify a tolerant, latitudinarian form of Christianity.

OTHER RESOLUTIONS OF SKEPTICISM. Other answers were offered to the skeptics and to their challenge of some of the basic tenets of the new philosophy. Thomas Hobbes had admitted the force of the problem of finding *the* criterion for judging what was genuinely true, and he insisted that the solution was ultimately political—the sovereign would have to decide. Blaise Pascal in his scientific works gave one of the finest expositions of the hypothetical probabilistic nature of science and mathematics. Pascal, who presented the case for skepticism most forcefully in his *Pensées*, still denied that there can be a complete skepticism; for nature prevents it. Lacking rational answers to complete skepticism, man's only recourse lies in turning to God for help in overcoming doubts. Spinoza, on the other hand, with his completely rational vision of the world, could not regard skepticism as a serious problem. If one had clear and adequate ideas, there would be no need or excuse for doubting. Doubt was only an indication of lack of clarity, not of basic philosophical difficulties.

The philosopher who took the skeptics most seriously was Gottfried Wilhelm von Leibniz, and he was regarded as a closer friend intellectually by the skeptics of his age than any of the other metaphysicians of the period. Leibniz, although certainly not a philosophical skeptic, agrees with some of the major contentions of the skeptics, and is willing to admit, unlike other metaphysicians of the seventeenth century, that there are general, and perhaps unanswerable, objections that can be raised against any philosophical theory. The skeptics and Leibniz could agree on the major failings of Cartesianism, although they were hardly in agreement as to what to do about them. Leibniz and the skeptics were all humanists and found great value in the tradition of man's effort to understand his universe; hence they rejected the Cartesian attitude towards the past. In his discussions, especially with Simon Foucher and Pierre Bayle, Leibniz agreed that there are first principles of philosophical reasoning that have not been satisfactorily demonstrated.

Leibniz was willing to regard metaphysics as a hypothetical enterprise, that is, as an attempt to present theories which agree with the known facts, which avoid certain difficulties in previous theories, and which give a satisfactory or adequate explanation of the world that is experienced. In the debate with Pierre Bayle over the article "Rorarius," in Bayle's *Dictionnaire historique et critique*, Leibniz does not argue for his theory as the true picture of reality, but rather as the most consistent hypothesis to explain the known scientific facts and the general conclusions of the "new philosophers" about the relation of the mind and the body, and to avoid the "unfortunate" complications or conclusions of the views of Descartes, Malebranche, or Spinoza. Leibniz was unwilling to see these limitations on our knowledge as a reason for skeptical despair or to see these points as constituting a radical skepticism that cast whatever knowledge we had in any serious doubt. For Leibniz, whatever merits the skeptical arguments had, they did not have to lead to negative or destructive conclusions. At best, skepticism should be a spur to constructive theorizing, and not a reason for doubting or despairing of the possibility of knowledge.

BAYLE AND THE ENLIGHTENMENT. The culmination of seventeenth-century skepticism appears in the writings of Pierre Bayle, especially in his monumental *Dictionnaire historique et critique* (1697–1702). Bayle, a superb dialectician, challenged philosophical, scientific, and theological theories, both ancient and modern, showing that they all led to perplexities, paradoxes, and contradictions. He argued that the theories of Descartes, Spinoza, Leibniz, and Malebranche, when skeptically analyzed, cast in doubt all information about the world, even whether a world exists. Bayle skillfully employed skeptical arguments about such things as sense information, human judgments, logical explanations, and the criteria of knowledge in order to undermine confidence in human intellectual activity in all areas. Bayle suggested that man should abandon rational activity and turn blindly to faith and revelation; he can therefore only follow his conscience without any criterion for determining true faith. Bayle showed that the interpretations of religious knowledge were so implausible that even the most heretical views, like Manichaeism—known for its cosmic dualism of good and evil—and Atheism made more sense. As a result Bayle's work became "the arsenal of the Enlightenment," and he was regarded as a major enemy of religion.

Bayle, in his later works, indicated that he held some positive views even though he presented no answers to his skepticism. There is still much scholarly debate as to what his actual position was, but he influenced many people in the eighteenth century. His skeptical arguments were soon applied to traditional religion by Voltaire and others. But in place of Bayle's doubts or his appeal to faith, they offered a new way of understanding man's world—that of Newtonian science—and professed an inordinate optimism about what man could comprehend and accomplish through scientific examination and induction. Though Bayle remained the heroic figure who had launched the Age of Reason by criticizing all the superstitions of past philosophy and theology, the leaders of the Enlightenment, both in France and Britain, felt that his skepticism was *passé* and only represented the summit of human understanding before "God said, Let Newton be, and all was light."

THE EIGHTEENTH CENTURY

Most eighteenth-century thinkers gave up the quest for metaphysical knowledge after imbibing Bayle's arguments. George Berkeley, an Empiricist and Idealist, fought skeptical doubts by identifying appearance and reality and offering a spiritualistic metaphysics. He was immediately seen as just another skeptic, since he was denying the world beyond experience.

HUME. Bayle's chief eighteenth-century successor was David Hume. Combining empirical and skeptical arguments, Hume, in the *Treatise of Human Nature and the Enquiry Concerning Human Understanding*, charged that neither inductive nor deductive evidence could establish the truth of any matter of fact. Knowledge could only consist of intuitively obvious matters or demonstrable relations of ideas but not of anything beyond experience; the mind can discover no necessary connections within experience nor any root causes of experience. Beliefs about the world are based not upon reason or evidence, nor even upon appeal to the uniformity of nature, but only on habit and custom. Basic beliefs cannot be justified by reasoning. Belief that there is an external world, a self, a God is common; but there is no adequate evidence for it. Although it is natural to hold these convictions, they are inconsistent and epistemologically dubious. "Philosophy would render us entirely Pyrrhonian, were not Nature too strong for it." The beliefs that a man is forced to hold enable him to describe the world scientifically, but when he tries to justify them he is led to complete skepticism. Before he goes mad with doubts, however, Nature brings him back to common sense, to unjustifiable beliefs. Hume's fideism was a natural rather than a religious one; it is only animal faith that provides relief from complete doubt. The religious context of skepticism from Montaigne to Bayle had been removed, and man was left with only his natural beliefs, which might be meaningless or valueless.

THE *PHILOSOPHES*. The French Enlightenment philosophers, the *philosophes*, built on the skeptical reading of Locke and Bayle, and on their interpretation of Berkeley as a radical skeptic. While they produced vast accumulations of new forms of knowledge, they also placed this alongside a skepticism about whether one could ever establish that this knowledge was about an external reality. Perhaps the most skeptical of them was the great French mathematician Marquis de Condorcet who held that mathematics, physics, and moral philosophies were all just probable. He also raised the possibility that our present mental faculties by which we judged our knowledge might change over time and, hence, that what we found true today might not be so tomorrow.

REID AND THE COMMON-SENSE SCHOOL. The central themes in Hume's skeptical analysis—the basis of induction and causality, knowledge of the external world and the self, proofs of the existence of God—became the key issues of later philosophy. Hume's contemporary Thomas Reid hoped to rebut Hume's skepticism by exposing it as the logical conclusion of the basic assumptions of modern philosophy from Descartes onward. Such disastrous assumptions should be abandoned for commonsensical principles that have to be believed. When the conclusions of philosophy run counter to common sense, there must be something wrong with philosophy. Since nobody could believe and act by complete skepticism, the fact that this skepticism was the consistent issue of the Cartesian and Lockean way of ideas only showed the need to start anew. Reid offered his commonsense realism as a way of avoiding Hume's skepticism by employing as basic principles the beliefs we are psychologically unable to doubt.

Hume was unimpressed by Reid's argument. As Hume and Kant saw, Reid had not answered Hume's skepticism but had only sidestepped the issue by appealing to commonsensical living. This provided, however, neither a theoretical basis for beliefs nor a refutation of the arguments that questioned them. The Scottish common-sense school of Oswald, Beattie, Stewart, Brown, and others kept reiterating its claim to have refuted Hume's skepticism by appealing to natural belief, while at the same time conceding that Hume's fundamental arguments could not be answered. Thomas Brown, an early-nineteenth-century disciple of Reid, admitted that Reid and Hume differed more in words than in opinions, saying, "'Yes,' Reid bawled out, 'we must believe in an outward world': but added in a whisper, 'we can give no reason for our belief.' Hume cries out, 'we can give no reason for such a notion': and whispers, 'I own that we cannot get rid of it.'"

THE GERMAN ENLIGHTENMENT AND KANT. The Scottish school was perhaps the first to make Hume's version of modern skepticism the central view to be combated if philosophy was to make coherent sense of man's universe. The more fundamental attempt, for subsequent philosophy, to deal with Hume's skepticism was developed in Germany in the second half of the eighteenth century and culminated in Kant's critical philosophy. Such leaders of the Prussian Academy as Jean Henry Samuel Formey, Johann Bernhard Mérian, and Johann Georg Sulzer had long been arguing against Pyrrhonism. They were among the first to read, translate (into French and German), and criticize Hume's writings. They saw in the skeptical tradition up to Bayle and Huet, and in Hume's version of it, a major challenge to all man's intellectual achievements. Although their answers to skepticism were hardly equal to the threat they saw in it, these writers helped revive interest in and concern with skepticism in an age that thought it had solved, or was about to solve, all problems. Others in Germany contributed to an awareness of the force of skepticism: Johann Christoff Eschenbach by his edition of the arguments of Sextus, Berkeley, and Arthur Collier (Berkeley's contemporary) against knowledge of an external corporeal world; Ernst Platner by his skeptical aphorisms and his German edition of Hume's *Dialogues on Natural Religion* (1781); hosts of German professors by dissertations against skepticism; and the translators of the Scottish critics of Hume.

Kant saw that Hume had posed a most fundamental challenge to all human knowledge claims. To answer him, it had to be shown not that knowledge is possible but *how* it is possible. Kant combined a skepticism toward metaphysical knowledge with the contention that certain universal and necessary conditions are involved in having experience and describing it. In terms of these it is possible to have genuine knowledge about the forms of all possible experience, space and time, and about the categories in which all experience is described. Any effort to apply this beyond all possible experience, however, leads into contradictions and skepticism. It is not possible to know about things-in-themselves nor about the causes of experience.

SKEPTICAL REJOINDERS TO KANT. Though Kant thought that he had resolved the skeptical problems, some of his contemporaries saw his philosophy as commencing a new skeptical era. G. E. Schulze (or Schulze-Aenesidemus) a notable critic of Kantianism, insisted that, on Kant's theory, no one could know any objective truths about anything; he could only know the subjective necessity of his views. So Schulze, by insisting on the inability of the Kantian analysis to move from subjective data about what people have to believe to any objective claims about reality, contended that Kant had not advanced beyond Hume's skepticism, and that this failure of the Kantian revolution actually constituted a vindication of Hume's views.

Salomon Maimon contended that, though there are such things as a priori concepts, their application to experience is always problematical, and whether they apply can only be found through experience. Hence, the possibility of knowledge can never be established with certainty. Assured truth on the basis of concepts is possible only of human creations, like mathematical ideas, and it is questionable whether these have any objective truth. Thus Maimon developed a mitigated Kantianism (to some extent like that of the Neo-Kantian movement a century later) in which the reality of a priori forms of thought is granted but in which the relation of these forms to matters of fact is always in question. Knowledge (that is, propositions that are universal and necessary, rather than ones that are just psychologically indubitable) is possible in mathematics but not in sciences dealing with the world. Unlike the logical positivists, who were to claim that mathematics was true because it consisted only of vacuous logical tautologies, Maimon contended that mathematics was true because it was about creations of our mind. Its objective relevance was always problematical.

Maimon's partial skepticism exposed some of the fundamental limitations of Kant's critical philosophy as a solution to the skeptical crisis. Developing the thesis that human creativity is the basis of truth, Johann Georg Hamann posited a new way of transcending skepticism. Hamann accepted Hume's and Kant's arguments as evidence that knowledge of reality cannot be gained by rational means but only by faith. Hamann exploited the skeptical thought of these philosophies to press for a complete antirational fideism. He used Hume's analyses of miracles and of the evidence for religious knowledge to try to convince Kant of the futility of the search for truth by rational means. During the height of nineteenth-century positivism, materialism, and idealism, Hamann's type of fideism was revitalized by Kierkegaard and in France by Catholic opponents of the French Revolution and liberalism—like Joseph de Maistre and H.-F.-R. Lamennais, who used it as a critique of French liberal, empirical, and Enlightenment views and as a new defense of orthodoxy and political conservatism. Kierkegaard brilliantly combined themes from Sextus, Hume, and Hamann to attack the rationalism of the Hegelians, to develop a thoroughgoing skepticism about rational achievements, and to show the need for faith in opposition to reason. Fideism has become a major element in twentieth-century neo-orthodox and existentialist theology, which tries to show that the traditional skeptical problems still prevent us from finding an ultimate basis for our beliefs except by faith.

IDEALISM. In the mainstream of philosophy after Kant, although skepticism continues to play a vital role, few philosophers have been willing to call themselves skeptics. The German metaphysicians, from Fichte and Hegel onward, sought to escape from the skeptical impasse produced by Hume and Kant and to reach knowledge of reality through the creative process and the recognition of historical development. They attempted to portray skepticism as a stage in the awareness and understanding of the process of events. For Fichte, skepticism made one recognize the need for commitment to a fundamental outlook about the world. The commitment to see the world in terms of creative thought processes led to a revelation of the structure of the universe as an aspect of the Absolute Ego.

For Hegel skepticism was the nadir of philosophy, actually its antithesis. According to Hegel, human knowledge is a historically developing process. At each stage of the process both our knowledge and the world itself are limited and contain contradictions, which are overcome at the next stage. Only the final, Absolute stage, when no further contradictions can be developed, permits genuine knowledge that is not partly true and partly false. Then, presumably, skepticism is no longer possible. The English Hegelian F. H. Bradley, in his *Appearance and Reality* (1893), used the traditional skeptical arguments to show that the world was unintelligible in terms of empirical or materialistic categories, and hence that one had to go beyond the world appearance to find true knowledge.

RECENT AND CONTEMPORARY PHILOSOPHY

Irrational skepticism was developed into Existentialism by Søren Kierkegaard in the nineteenth century. Using traditional skeptical themes to attack Hegelianism and liberal Christianity, Kierkegaard stressed the need for faith. Only by an unjustified and unjustifiable "leap into faith" could certainty be found—which would then be entirely subjective rather than objective. Modern neo-orthodox and Existentialist theologians have argued that skepticism highlights man's inability to find any ultimate truth except through faith and commitment. Nonreligious forms of this view have been developed by Existentialist writers like Albert Camus, combining the epistemological skepticism of Kierkegaard and Leon Shestov with the skepticism regarding religion and objective values of Friedrich Nietzsche.

In his *Myth of Sisyphus*, Camus portrays man as trying to measure the nature and meaning of an essentially absurd universe by means of questionable rational and scientific criteria. Camus regards the skeptical arguments used by Kierkegaard and Shestov as showing decisively the contradictory nature of human rational attempts to understand the world, but he rejects their fideistic solution: overcoming the skeptical crisis by "a leap into faith." Instead, he accepts Nietzsche's picture of the ultimate meaninglessness of the world because "God is dead." The rational and scientific examination of the world shows it to be unintelligible and absurd but it is necessary to struggle with it. It is thus through action and commitment that one finds whatever personal meaning one can, though it has no objective significance. The mythological Sisyphus, eternally pushing a huge rock uphill, only to have to fall to the bottom again, typifies the human situation. He does not expect to find truth, nor does he expect to end his struggle. He finds no ultimate point or value in his situation, but he perseveres with a "silent joy," realizing that his struggle has meaning only for him, in terms of his human condition. The struggle is neither sterile nor futile for him, though it is meaningless in terms of understanding or possible achievement.

George Santayana, an American critical Realist, in *Scepticism and Animal Faith*, presented a naturalistic skepticism. Any interpretation of immediate or intuited experience is open to question. To make life meaningful, however, men make interpretations by "animal faith," according to biological and social factors. The resulting beliefs, though unjustified and perhaps illusory, enable them to persevere and find the richness of life. When the full force of complete skepticism is realized, Santayana claimed, one can appreciate what is in fact absolutely indubitable, the immediately experienced or intuited qualities that Santayana called "essences." The interpretation of these essences leads to various questionable metaphysical systems. A thoroughgoing skepticism makes one realize the unjustifiable assumptions involved in interpreting the realm of essences, and also that we do interpret them and thereby construct meaningful pictures of the world. Santayana called the process of interpretation "animal faith," which is consistent with complete skepticism and involves following natural and social tendencies and inclinations.

Types of skepticism also appear in logical positivism and various forms of linguistic philosophy. The attack on speculative metaphysics developed by the physicist and early Positivist Ernst Mach, Bertrand Russell, and Rudolf Carnap, a leader in the Vienna Circle, where logical positivism was nourished, incorporated a skepticism about the possibility of gaining knowledge beyond experience or logical tautologies. Russell and the important philosopher of science Karl Popper have further stressed the unjustifiability of the principle of induction, and Popper has criticized theories of knowledge based upon empirical verification. A founder of linguistic analysis, Fritz Mauthner, has set forth a skepticism in which any language is merely relative to its users and thus subjective. Every attempt to tell what is true just leads one back to linguistic formulations, not to objective states of affairs. The result is a complete skepticism about reality—a reality that cannot even be expressed except in terms of what he called godless mystical contemplation. Mauthner's linguistic skepticism bears some affinities to the views expressed in Ludwig Wittgenstein's *Tractatus Logico-Philosophicus*.

A different way of dealing with skepticism was set forth by the English philosopher, G. E. Moore at Cambridge. He contended that no matter what skeptical arguments may be they do not eliminate people's certitude about what they immediately perceive. There is a kind of "certain knowledge" that each of us has and can build on even though we know that it can be questioned in some theoretical way. Wittgenstein explored this kind of resolution in his essay *On Certainty* and sought to get beyond what Moore had done. Many contemporary philosophers are still writing and arguing about what constitutes knowledge and whether, in some way, we can find any basis for certainty.

POSTMODERNISM

A new, radical form of skepticism has developed in the last half century: postmodernism. This view challenges whether there can be any rational framework for discussing intellectual problems or whether the frameworks that people use are related to their life situations. Developing out of literary criticism and psychological investigations, the postmodernists have been undermining confidence in the investigation of the world in which we live by showing that the investigations are part of what needs to be scrutinized. Using ideas from Martin Heidegger, Michel Foucault, Jacques Derrida, Jean-François Lyotard, and Richard Rorty, they see philosophy and science as human activities to be judged in terms of their role in human life, rather than by some standard that can be said to be true or false. Rather than attempting to find a holistic truth or set of truths that are knowable and eternal, Postmodernists stress reflexivity, fragmentation, discontinuity, and ambiguity. Critics see this as a most dangerous development in that there will be no objective standpoint for evaluating theories. But that, of course, is part of the postmodernist outlook. Psychologists and sociologists have been adding to this view by stressing how intellectual outlooks vary according to sexual orientation, racial background, gender, and other fundamental features of human outlooks. Skepticism results from seeing that there is no objective standpoint from which to sort out the better or worse of these points of view.

CRITICISM AND EVALUATION. In Western thought, skepticism has raised basic epistemological issues. In view of the varieties of human experience, it has questioned whether it is possible to tell which are veridical. The variations that occur in different perceptions of what is presumed to be one object raise the question of which is the correct view. The occurrence of illusory experiences raises the question of whether it is really possible to distinguish illusions and dreams from reality. The criteria employed can be questioned and require justification. On what basis does one tell whether one has the right criteria? By other criteria? Then, are these correct? On what standards? The attempt to justify criteria seems either to lead to an infinite regress or to just stop arbitrarily. If an attempt is made to justify knowledge claims by starting with first principles, what are these based upon? Can it be established that these principles cannot possibly be false? If so, is the proof itself such that it cannot be questioned? If it is claimed that the principles are self-evident, can one be sure of this, sure that one is not deceived? And can one be sure that one can recognize and apply the principles correctly? Through such questioning, skeptics have indicated the basic problems that an investigator would have to resolve before he could be certain of possessing knowledge; that is, information that could not possibly be false.

Critics have contended that skepticism is both a logically and a humanly untenable view. Any attempt to formulate the position will be self-refuting since it will assert at least some knowledge claims about what is supposed to be dubious. Montaigne suggested that the skeptics needed a nonassertive language, reflecting the claim of Sextus that the skeptic does not make assertions but only chronicles his feelings. The strength of skepticism lies not in whether it can be stated consistently but upon the effects of its arguments on dogmatic philosophers. As Hume said, skepticism may be self-refuting, but in the process of refuting itself it undermines dogmatism. Skepticism, Sextus said, is like a purge that eliminates itself as well as everything else.

Critics have claimed that anyone who tried to be a complete skeptic, denying or suspending all judgments about ordinary beliefs, would soon be driven insane. Even Hume thought that the complete skeptic would have to starve to death and would walk into walls or out of windows. Hume, therefore, separated the doubting activity from natural practical activities in the world. Skeptical philosophizing went on in theory, while believing occurred in practice. Sextus and the contemporary Norwegian skeptic Arne Naess have said, on the other hand, that skepticism is a form of mental health. Instead of going mad, the skeptic—without commitment to fixed positions—can function better than the dogmatist.

Some thinkers like A. J. Ayer and J. L Austin have contended that skepticism is unnecessary. If knowledge is defined in terms of satisfying meaningful criteria, then knowledge is open to all. The skeptics have raised false problems, because it is, as a matter of fact, possible to tell that some experiences are illusory since we have criteria for distinguishing them from actual events. We do resolve doubts and reach a state of knowledge through various verification procedures, after which doubt is meaningless. Naess, in his book *Scepticism*, has sought to show, however, that, on the standards offered by Ayer and Austin, one can still ask if knowledge claims may not turn out to be false and hence that skepticism has still to be overcome.

Skepticism throughout history has played a dynamic role in forcing dogmatic philosophers to find better or stronger bases for their views and to find answers to the skeptical attacks. It has forced a continued reexamination of previous knowledge claims and has stimulated creative thinkers to work out new theories to meet the skeptical problems. The history of philosophy can be seen, in part, as a struggle with skepticism. The attacks of the skeptics also have served as a check on rash speculation; the various forms of modern skepticism have gradually eroded the metaphysical and theological bases of European thought. Most contemporary thinkers have been sufficiently affected by skepticism to abandon the search for certain and indubitable foundations of human knowledge. Instead, they have sought ways of living with the unresolved skeptical problems through various forms of naturalistic, scientific, or religious faiths.

See also Aenesidemus; Agrippa von Nettesheim, Henricus Cornelius; al-Ghazālī, Muhammad; Ancient Skepticism; Antiochus of Ascalon; Aristotelianism; Aristotle; Arnauld, Antoine; Augustine, St.; Augustinianism; Austin, John Langshaw; Averroism; Ayer, Alfred Jules; Bacon, Francis; Bayle, Pierre; Beattie, James; Berkeley, George; Bradley, Francis Herbert; Brown, Thomas; Calvin, John; Camus, Albert; Carnap, Rudolf; Carneades; Cartesianism; Charron, Pierre; Cicero, Marcus Tullius; Collier, Arthur; Condorcet, Marquis de; Cratylus; Derrida, Jacques; Descartes, René; Diogenes Laertius; Enlightenment; Erasmus, Desiderius; Fichte, Johann Gottlieb; Fideism; Foucault, Michel; Foucher, Simon; Gassendi, Pierre; Glanvill, Joseph; Gorgias of Leontini; Greek Academy; Halevi, Yehuda; Hamann, Johann Georg; Hegel, Georg Wilhelm Friedrich; Hegelianism; Heidegger, Martin; Herbert of Cherbury; Huet, Pierre-Daniel; Hume, David; Kant, Immanuel; Kierkegaard, Søren Aabye; Lamennais, Hugues Félicité Robert de; La Mothe Le Vayer, François de; Leibniz, Gottfried Wilhelm; Locke, John; Logical Positivism; Luther, Martin; Lyotard, Jean Francois; Mach, Ernst; Maimon, Salomon; Maistre, Comte Joseph de; Malebranche, Nicolas; Mani and Manichaeism; Medieval Philosophy; Mersenne, Marin; Montaigne, Michel Eyquem de; Moore, George Edward; Moral Skepticism; Neo-Kantianism; Nicholas of Cusa; Nietzsche, Friedrich; Ockhamism; Pascal, Blaise; Philo of Larissa; Pico della Mirandola, Count Giovanni; Pico della Mirandola, Gianfrancesco; Platonism and the Platonic Tradition; Popper, Karl Raimund; Protagoras of Abdera; Pyrrho; Reformation; Reid, Thomas; Renaissance; Rorty, Richard; Russell, Bertrand Arthur William; Sanches, Francisco; Santayana, George; Schulze, Gottlob Ernst; Sextus Empiricus; Shestov, Lev Isaakovich; Skepticism, Contemporary; Socrates; Spinoza, Benedict (Baruch) de; Stewart, Dugald; Stoicism; Sulzer, Johann Georg; Timon of Phlius; William of Ockham; Wittgenstein, Ludwig Josef Johann; Xenophanes of Colophon.

Bibliography

The basic statements and arguments of various forms of skepticism are given in:

Academic skepticism: Cicero, *Academica* and *De natura deorum*, both with trans. by H. Rackham, Loeb Classical Library (1956).

Pyrrhonian skepticism: *Sextus Empiricus, Outlines of Scepticism*, ed. by J. Annas, J. Barnes, K. Ameriks, D. M. Clarke (2000); *The Skeptic Way: Sextus Empiricus's Outlines of Pyrrhonism*, translated, introduction, and commentary by Benson Mates (1996); *Adversus Mathematicos*, with trans. by R. G. Bury, Loeb Classical Library: vol. 1–2, *Against the Logicians* and *Outlines of Pyrrhonism* (1933–1936); vol. 3, *Against the Physicists, Against the Ethicists* (1936); vol. 4, *Against the Professors* (1959–1960); and *Scepticism, Man, and God: Selections from the Major Writings of Sextus Empiricus*, ed. by P. Hallie, translated by S. G. Etheridge (1964); L. Floridi, *Sextus Empiricus: The Transmission and Recovery of Pyrrhonism* (2002).

Renaissance skepticism: Michel de Montaigne, "L'apologie de Raimond Sebond," in *Les essais de Michel de Montaigne*, edited by Pierre Villey, new ed. (1922); Fréderic Brahami, *Le scepticisme de Montaigne* (1997); Donald Frame, *Montaigne: A Biography* (1984); Elaine Limbrick and Douglas F. Thomson, *That Nothing Is Known: Francisco Sanches* (1988).

Skepticism and Fideism: Blaise Pascal, *Pensées*, edited by L. Brunschvicg (1951).

Skepticism in relation to modern philosophy: Pierre Bayle, *Dictionnaire historique et critique*, esp. the articles "Pyrrho" and "Zeno of Elea," both of which appear in Bayle's *Historical and Critical Dictionary: Selections*, translated and edited by Richard H. Popkin (1965); David Hume, *Dialogues concerning Natural Religion*, edited by Richard H. Popkin (1980); *Enquiries concerning the Human Understanding and concerning the Principles of Morals*, 2nd ed., edited by L. A. Selby-Bigge (1957), and *A Treatise of Human Nature*, edited by David Fate Norton and Mary J. Norton (2000); Sylvia Giocanti, *Penser l'irrésolution: Montaigne, Pascal, La Mothe le Vayer, Trois itinéraires sceptiques* (2001); John C. Laursen, *The Politics of Scepticism in the Ancients, Montaigne, Hume and Kant* (1992); Gianni Paganini, *The Return of Scepticism: From Hobbes and Descartes to Bayle* (2003); Antony Mckenna and Alain Mothu, *La philosophie clandestine a l'âge classique*; José Maia Neto, *The Christianization of Pyrrhonism: Scepticism and Faith in Pascal, Kierkegaard, and Shestov* (1995); Gianluca Mori, *Bayle philosophe* (1999); Martin Mulsow, *Moderne aus dem Untergrund: radikale frühaufklärung in Deutschland 1680–1720* (2002); René Pintard, *Les libertinage érudits dans le première moitié du XVII siècle* (1943); Don Cameron Allen, *Doubt's Boundless Sea: Skepticism and Faith in the Renaissance* (1964); Richard H. Popkin, *The History of Scepticism from Savonarola to Bayle*, rev. ed. (2003) and *The High Road to Pyrrhonism* (1980); Popkin, Silvia Berti, and Françoise Charles-Daubert, *Heterodoxy, Spinozism, and Free Thought in Early-Eighteenth-Century Europe: Studies on the Traite Des Trois Imposteurs* (1996); Popkin and Arjo Vanderjagt, *Skepticism and Irreligion in the Seventeenth and Eighteenth Centuries* (1993); Popkin and José Maia Neto, *Skepticism in Renaissance and Post-Renaissance Thought: New Interpretations* (2004); Popkin, Ezequiel Olaso, and Giorgio Tonelli, *Skepticism in the Enlightenment* (1997).

The standard studies of ancient skepticism are: Victor Brochard, *Les Sceptiques grecs* (1887); Norman Maccoll, *The Greek Sceptics from Pyrrho to Sextus* (1869); Mary Mills Patrick, *The Greek Sceptics* (1929); Leon Robin, *Pyrrhon et le scepticisme grec* (1944); and Eduard Zeller, *The Stoics, Epicureans and Sceptics*, trans. by O. J. Reichel (1880); Charlotte L. Stough, *Greek Skepticism* (1969); Raoul Richter, *Der Skeptizismus in der Philosophie* (1904–1908); Cornelia De Vogel, *Greek Philosophy*.

For general studies of skepticism, see: Richard H. Popkin, "Skepticism," *Encyclopedia of Philosophy*, vol. 7, pp. 449–461 (1967); Arne Naess, *Scepticism* (1968); and Benson Mates, *Skeptical Essays* (1981).

Richard Popkin (1967, 2005)

SKINNER, B. F.

(1904–1990)

The name of B. F. (Burrhus Frederic) Skinner has become virtually synonymous with behaviorism. By introducing the concept of "operant conditioning" (in the late 1930s), Skinner fundamentally transformed behaviorist approaches to experimental psychology. Operant conditioning is based on the fact that the behavior of organisms (including people) typically has environmental consequences and is explained in important part by reference to them. Its fundamental principle is that the probability of occurrence of a specified kind of behavior is a function of the environmental consequences of previous occurrences of behavior of the same type, most notably, that the probability increases if the previous occurrences have been followed by "reinforcement." Skinner, surpassing older behaviorist "stimulus-response" approaches, inaugurated an experimental research program aiming to discover the laws of operant conditioning and, thus, generalizations concerning the three-term relation: discriminative stimulus-behavior-reinforcement.

The earliest laws of operant conditioning include generalizations about the relationship of the probability of a behavior's occurrence to its "schedule of reinforcement"—for example, to the conditions (discriminative stimulus) of its occurrence, the temporal duration between behavior and reinforcement, the proportion of behaviors that are followed by reinforcement, and whether these durations and proportions are fixed or variable. Later developments include generalizations about behavior that occurs under multiple schedules of reinforcement. The research program of operant conditioning constitutes Skinner's definitive and most lasting contribution. It also informs an applied program (of "behavioral technology"), based on the notion that behavior can be controlled by appropriate arrangement of the contingencies of reinforcement. The journals, *Journal of the Experimental Analysis of Behavior* (1958–) and *Journal of Applied Behavior Analysis* (1968–) are principally devoted, respectively, to publishing results of these and related programs.

Skinner considered his research program to underlie "radical behaviorism," a viewpoint that is distinct from the better-known (among philosophers) "logical behaviorism" and "methodological behaviorism." Unlike logical behaviorism, radical behaviorism does not hold that "mentalistic" terms—terms that may be taken to designate mental states or events (e.g., sensations, thoughts, memories, beliefs)—can be analyzed in terms of relations between behavior and the environment, or as referring to dispositions to behave in certain ways under specified environmental conditions. Unlike methodological behaviorism, it does not hold that any knowledge we may have about mental states and events is gained by means of inference (e.g., hypothetico-deductive) from knowledge of observed behavior, or that mental phenomena may be investigated by way of the behavioral phenomena causally linked with them. Radical behaviorism is not a philosophical thesis about meaning or about the epistemological primacy of behavior. It is a program aiming to "interpret" voluntary behavior (intentional action) in the light of the principle (in the most general terms) that voluntary behavior is under the control of environmental variables and the history of their relations with a person's behavior; or (more specifically) that it is explicable in terms of the history of contingencies of reinforcement to which a person has been exposed and the general laws (identified in the experimental program) of operant conditioning governing these contingencies. The philosophical journal *Behaviorism* (1972–1989) provided a forum for extensive discussion of radical behaviorism.

For Skinner, the philosophical impact of the program of radical behaviorism becomes apparent in the light of two proposals: (a) that adopting the program has the backing of scientific authority, and (b) that it is from science—rather than, say, from deploying ordinary intentional idiom—that we gain the best understanding of human phenomena. Regarding (a), he wrote a series of methodological articles (reprinted in Skinner 1969, 1972) arguing that the methodological and theoretical resources of the experimental program of operant (combined with respondent) conditioning at least match, and usually surpass, those of programs guided by methodological behaviorism. Thus, he concluded that theories that deploy mentalistic terms are unnecessary, and that a more complete account of behavior can be obtained within the framework of radical behaviorism. Regarding (b), in order to deal with the fact that language is integral to human behavior and that, in ordinary speech and communication acts, mentalistic terms are indispensable, he offered in *Verbal Behavior* (1957) a series of "interpretations" (speculative hypotheses) attempting to make it plausible that utterances containing these terms may be treated simply as instances of "verbal behavior," whose occurrences and other causal roles, can be explained (predicted and controlled) in terms of the principles of operant conditioning.

Radical behaviorism, applied to linguistic phenomena, had some influence on philosophical developments—for example, on the form of behaviorism adopted in W. V. Quine's *Word and Object* (1960), and on Quine's endorsement of "naturalistic epistemology." For the most part, however, philosophers are aware of *Verbal Behavior* mainly by way of Noam Chomsky's (1959) scathing review. Chomsky's most important criticism was that radical behaviorist "interpretations" are unable to encompass a number of fundamental aspects of linguistic phenomena: (e.g., the "creative" use of language, the rapidity and ease of the acquisition of language by children, and certain specific features of grammar, such as embedding of clauses). Furthermore, the linguistic phenomena cited by Chomsky became focal points of rival programs of experimental and theoretical psychology (psycholinguistics, cognitive psychology), which were designed to possess the theoretical resources needed to encompass them and to bypass Skinner's methodological objections. Chomsky, thus, rejected claim (a), that Skinner's program has the backing of scientific authority. Not so well known are behaviorist responses to Chomsky's arguments and further elaborations (and modifications) of Skinner's program (in, e.g., Place 1981), so much so that many philosophers consider Chomsky's review to have sounded the death knell of behaviorism.

Other critics questioned claim (b), that it is from experimentally based science that we get the best understanding of human phenomena. Barry Schwartz and Hugh Lacey (1982, 1987) argued against Skinner: (1) that his methodological criticism of the use of mentalistic terms in psychological theories does not apply at all to the use of intentional idiom in ordinary language; (2) that in fact human action cannot be reduced to behavior that is explicable in terms of laws (behaviorist or otherwise); and (3) that, using arguments that are formulated irreducibly in intentional idiom, the limits of applicability of radical behaviorist principles can be identified (Schwartz and Lacey 1982; Lacey and Schwartz 1987). These limits are ignored in *Verbal Behavior*, and also in Skinner's most controversial book *Beyond Freedom and Dignity* (1971). In the latter Skinner argued that fundamental notions of liberal democracy (freedom, dignity, autonomy) that are integral to standard defenses of civil rights are ill-founded and in conflict with the best scientifically grounded view of human nature. Such arguments suggested to his critics that the primary motivation for engaging in the program of radical behaviorism comes from commitment to the social value of the control of human behavior.

Although radical behaviorism ceased to have many high-profile adherents after the 1980s, and programs of cognitive psychology have become much more prominent than Skinner's experimental program in major universities, the residue of Skinner's contribution is deeply entrenched. The experimental program of operant conditioning continues at a high level of (increasingly mathematical) sophistication, exploring, for example, choices made under the influence of multiple contingencies of reinforcement in accord with the "matching law"; and Skinner's central theoretical term "reinforcement" has become a staple in practices that range from education to clinical psychology. In addition, newer behaviorist programs that are in continuity with Skinner's have emerged—for example, Howard Rachlin's (1994) "teleological behaviorism" and John Staddon's (1993) "theoretical behaviorism."

See also Behaviorism; Chomsky, Noam; Philosophy of Education, Epistemological Issues in; Psychology; Quine, Willard Van Orman.

Bibliography

Chomsky, Noam. "Review of B. F. Skinner's *Verbal Behavior*." *Language* 35 (1959): 26–58.

Lacey, Hugh, and Barry Schwartz. "The Explanatory Power of Radical Behaviorism." In *B. F. Skinner: Consensus and Controversy*, edited by S. Modgil and C. Modgil. New York: Falmer Press, 1987.

Place, U. T. "Skinner's *Verbal Behavior*." *Behaviorism* 9 (1981): 1–24, 131–152.

Quine, W. V. *Word and Object*. Cambridge, MA: MIT Press, 1960.

Rachlin, Howard. *Behavior and Mind: The Roots of Modern Psychology*. New York: Oxford University Press, 1994.

Schwartz, Barry, and Hugh Lacey. *Behaviorism, Science, and Human Nature*. New York: Norton, 1982.

Staddon, J. E. R. *Behaviorism: Mind, Mechanism and Society*. London: Duckworth, 1993.

WORKS BY SKINNER

Verbal Behavior. New York: Appleton-Century-Crofts, 1957.

Contingencies of Reinforcement: A Theoretical Analysis. New York: Appleton-Century-Crofts, 1969.

Beyond Freedom and Dignity. New York: Knopf, 1971.

Cumulative Record: A Selection of Papers. 3rd. ed. New York: Appleton-Century-Crofts, 1972.

Hugh Lacey (2005)

SKOLEM-LÖWENHEIM THEOREM

See *Logic, History of: Modern Logic: From Frege to Gödel*

SKOVORODA, HRYHORII SAVYCH (GRIGORII SAVVICH)

(1722–1794)

Grigorii (Hryhorii) Savvich Skovoroda, the Ukrainian poet, fabulist, philosopher, and religious thinker, was educated at the Kiev Theological Academy. As a young man he traveled in eastern and western Europe and paid brief visits to St. Petersburg and Moscow, but eighteenth-century European culture left few traces on his thought. He taught, mainly literature, at Pereiaslavl' (Pereiaslavl'-Khmel'nitskii) about 1755 and at the Khar'kov (Khar'kiv) Collegium from about 1759 to 1765, but he fell out with his ecclesiastical superiors and was dismissed. He spent his last thirty years as a mendicant scholar and "teacher of the people."

Skovoroda's disciple, M. I. Kovalinski, has left an engaging account of Skovoroda's manner of life:

> He dressed decently but simply; … he did not eat meat or fish, not from superstitious belief but because of his own inner constitution; … he allowed himself no more than four [hours a day] for sleep; … he was always gay, good-natured, easy-going, quick, restrained, abstemious, and content with all things, benign, humble before all men, willing to speak so long as he was not required to …; he visited the sick, consoled the grieving, shared his last crust with the needy, chose and loved his friends for the qualities of their hearts, was pious without superstition, learned without ostentation, complaisant without flattery. ("The Life of Gregory Skovoroda," translated by G. L. Kline, in *Russian Philosophy*, Vol. I, p. 20)

Skovoroda aspired to be a "Socrates in Russia" both as a moralist, a gadfly provoking thoughtless and selfish men to scrutinize their lives, and as an intellectual forerunner, clearing the path for the more profound and systematic philosophizing of a future "Russian Plato." In many ways he was not only the last, but also the first, of the medievals in Russia. His metaphysics and philosophical anthropology are explicitly Christian and Neoplatonic, and his philosophical idiom is studded with Greek and Church Slavonic terms and constructions. He knew both German and Latin (he left over a hundred Latin letters and poems) and had some knowledge of Greek and Hebrew, but he wrote all of his philosophical works in Russian. As it happened, few of his own philosophic coinages were accepted by later Russian thinkers.

All of Skovoroda's philosophical and theological writings are in dialogue form. They are Socratic in method and in theme, genuinely dramatic and dialogic, written with wit, imagination, and moral intensity. They offer an acute critique of both ontological materialism and sense-datum empiricism, and they outline a dualistic cosmology with a pantheistic (or "panentheistic") and mystical coloring. One of Skovoroda's favorite metaphors for the relation of appearance to reality is that of a tree's many passive, shifting shadows to the firm, single, living tree itself.

In deliberate opposition to the Baconian summons to "know nature in order to master it," Skovoroda urged individuals to "know themselves in order to master themselves" and to put aside desires for comfort, security, fame, and knowledge. His position is thus Stoic as well as Socratic. Seneca, no less than Socrates, would have savored the epitaph which Skovoroda wrote for himself: "The world set a trap for me, but it did not catch me."

See also Appearance and Reality; Neoplatonism; Pantheism; Plato; Russian Philosophy; Socrates; Stoicism.

Bibliography

WORKS BY SKOVORODA

Hryhori Skovoroda: Tvori v Dvokh Tomakh (Grigorii Skovoroda: works in two volumes), edited by O. I. Biletski, D. K. Ostryanin, and P. M. Popov. Kiev, 1961. Text in Russian and Latin; introduction, commentary, notes, and translation of Latin text in Ukrainian.

"A Conversation among Five Travellers concerning Life's True Happiness" (abridged translation by George L. Kline of "Razgovor pyati putnikov o istinnom shchastii v zhizni," *Tvori v Dvokh Tomakh,* Vol. I, 207–247). In *Russian Philosophy,* edited by James M. Edie, James P. Scanlan, Mary-Barbara Zeldin, and George L. Kline. 3 vols. Vol. I, 26–57. Chicago: Quadrangle, 1965.

WORKS ON SKOVORODA

Chyzhevsky, D. *Filosofiia H. S. Skovorody* (The philosophy of G. S. Skovoroda). Warsaw, 1934. In Ukrainian.

Ern, V. *Grigorii Savvich Skovoroda: Zhizn' i uchenie* (Grigorii Savvich Skovoroda: his life and teaching). Moscow, 1912.

Zenkovsky, V. V. *Istoriia russkoi filosofii,* 2 vols. Paris: YMCA Press, 1948–1950. Translated by George L. Kline as *A History of Russian Philosophy,* 2 vols., 53–69. New York: Columbia University Press, 1953.

George L. Kline (1967)

SKOVORODA, HRYHORII SAVYCH (GRIGORII SAVVICH) [ADDENDUM]

Hryhorii Savych Skovoroda's outdated language and literary style make it difficult to grasp his philosophical thought. He expresses his ideas mostly through images, symbols, proverbs, and stories instead of philosophical concepts and propositions, and he does not organize them logically into a system. Because of this he has been subject to many conflicting interpretations: He has been called both an eclectic and a strict rationalist, a mystic and a materialist, a theologian and a moral teacher. While some of his doctrines are obscure (the heart in man, personal immortality, the nature of matter), his ideas do fall into a logically coherent system that is intended to serve a practical purpose.

The aim of philosophy, according to Skovoroda, is to show people the way to happiness. This is why his moral teachings are articulated more fully than the other parts of his philosophy. His metaphysical, epistemological, and anthropological teachings are developed only to the extent that is necessary for grounding his moral principles. For Skovoroda happiness is not merely the absence of pain or a state of inner peace, but joy and gaiety, which are not free of tension. To attain happiness two things are necessary: to be content with everything and to fulfill one's true self. The first rests on a belief in a providential order that supplies each creature with whatever is necessary for its happiness. The Epicurean doctrine that what is necessary is easy and what is difficult is unnecessary liberates us from fear and anxiety. The other condition for happiness is the pursuit of one's God-given, innate, congenial task (*srodnyi trud*) in life. To work at one's natural task brings joy, while to work at an unnatural task brings misery regardless of the accompanying external rewards such as wealth and fame. Every congenial task corresponds to a necessary social role (e.g., ruler, teacher, soldier, farmer, and so on); hence, by fulfilling their natural potential people also ensure the harmonious and efficient functioning of society.

This moral teaching rests on a dualistic metaphysics. Skovoroda divides reality into three isomorphic worlds: the macrocosm or the all-encompassing universe, the human microcosm or man, and the symbolical microcosm or Bible. All three worlds have an inner and outer, spiritual and material, intelligible and sensible nature: in the macrocosm the two natures are called God and the physical universe; in man soul and body; and in the Bible the true and the apparent meaning. The inner principle in each world is the more important one: It sustains and rules the outer one and is eternal and immutable. Self-knowledge is the foundation of all knowledge: By delving into oneself one discovers the essential truths not only about one's own nature and one's congenial task, but also about the other two worlds. Skovoroda considered the Bible, his favorite book, to be a treasury of universal wisdom and a source of false beliefs for those who take its statements at their face value. His dialogues are largely discussions of its symbolic meaning.

Skovoroda's poetry, composed in a language close to the Ukrainian vernacular, became popular among the common people, while his dialogues circulated in manuscript within the narrow circle of his friends. The first collection of his works to appear in print (1861) contained only half of his dialogues. Fuller collections came out in 1894, 1912, and 1961 and the first complete collection did not appear until 1973. Skovoroda's ideas began to attract the attention of philosophers only at the end of the nineteenth century. Although Skovoroda's influence in Russian and Ukrainian philosophy has been negligible, his colorful and independent personality has served as an inspiration to Ukrainian writers during the cultural revival of the 1920s and 1960s.

See also Happiness; Macrocosm and Microcosm; Russian Philosophy; Self-Knowledge.

Bibliography

WORKS BY SKOVORODA

Hryhorii Skovoroda: Povne zibrannia tvoriv u dvokh tomakh (Hryhorii Skovoroda: The complete collection of his work in two volumes). Edited by V. Shynkaruk et al. Kyiv, Ukraine: Naukova dumka, 1973. Text in the literary Russian of his time and Latin. Introduction, commentary, notes, and translation of Latin texts in Ukrainian.

Fables and Aphorisms. Translated by Dan B. Chopyk. New York: Peter Lang, 1990.

WORKS ABOUT SKOVORODA

Special Issue on Hryhorii Skovoroda. *Journal of Ukrainian Studies* 22 (1–2) (1997).

Dva stolittia Skovorodiiany / Two Centuries of Skovorodiana: Bibliographical Guide. Project director, Leonid Ushkalov. Kharkiv, Ukraine: Acta, 2002.

Hryhorij Savyč Skovoroda: An Anthology of Critical Articles, edited by Richard M. Marshall and Thomas E. Bird. Edmonton: Canadian Institute of Ukrainian Studies Press. 1994.

Taras Zakydalsky (2005)

SMART, JOHN JAMIESON CARSWELL

(1920–)

John Jamieson Carswell Smart was born into an academic Scottish family on September 16, 1920. His father, W. M. Smart, was an astronomer in Cambridge until 1937 when the family moved to Glasgow. J. J. C. Smart entered the University of Glasgow in 1938.

War service interrupted Smart's education from 1940 to 1945, after which he rapidly completed his degrees at Glasgow, then proceeded to the University of Oxford, where he read for the newly established BPhil degree and came under the influence of Gilbert Ryle. After a short period at Corpus Christi College, he accepted, at the age of twenty-nine, the Hughes Professorship of Philosophy at the University of Adelaide.

Smart spent twenty-two years at the University of Adelaide, moving to La Trobe University in Melbourne in 1972. In 1976 he was appointed to a Chair in the Research School of Social Sciences of the Australian National University, which he held until his retirement in 1985. Since then he has continued to be active in philosophy at the Australian National University and in Melbourne.

Soon after his arrival in Australia Smart's thought moved away from its linguistic, Oxford orientation and began to take on its characteristic science-based form. Showing the influence of both eighteenth-century Scot David Hume and twentieth-century American W. V. Quine, Smart's mature philosophy has been consistently empiricist, taking human experience as the wellspring and touchstone of knowledge, giving primacy to statements of actual fact and treating modal claims regarding necessity or mere possibility as human artifacts, and embracing nominalism concerning universals. In the philosophy of science, he has upheld regularity views of causation and natural law. Unlike many empiricists, however—who regard imperceptible entities as human constructs—Smart has always been staunchly realist in his account of some theoretical entities, claiming that electrons, for example, are straightforwardly real components of the world.

Smart's ethics has been similarly consistent: He has defended a rather pure act-utilitarian consequentialism throughout. His major contributions to philosophy have involved three themes: in cosmology, four-dimensional physical realism; in the philosophy of mind, materialism; and in ethics, utilitarianism.

For forty years, culminating with *Our Place in the Universe* (1989), Smart has argued that the four-dimensional conception of space-time introduced by Minkowski for the interpretation of the theory of special relativity is superior to all others. This conception implies the equal reality of past, present, and future and rejects as unreal the flow of time that seems to underpin the human experience of time passing.

Smart's second major theme is materialism, the claim that there are no spiritual realities, and that in particular human minds are not spiritual. The mind—the organ with which one thinks—proves to be the brain. All the various states of mind are states, processes, or functions of the brain and its associated nervous system. This *central state materialism* emerged in its contemporary form from two landmark papers: Smart's colleague U. T. Place published his "Is Consciousness a Brain Process?" in the *British Journal of Psychology* in 1956; Smart's "Sensations and Brain Processes," which appeared in *The Philosophical Review* in 1959 (reprinted in *Essays, Metaphysical and Moral* [1987]), gave the view wide notoriety. The importance of Smart's paper consisted in his exposing the inadequacy of the reasons then prevalent for holding that the mental and the physical belong to essentially incompatible categories. Smart expanded and defended materialism in subsequent discussions both of the general issue and of its implications for the secondary qualities, particularly color.

From *An Outline of a System of Utilitarian Ethics* (1961) onward, Smart has presented a utilitarian theory of moral judgment and action: What matters is not people's intentions, or character, nor any fixed set of moral rules, but the actual consequences of behavior. The consequences to be considered concern the happiness of all sentient beings, as judged from a natural, secular point of view. To adhere to a social or traditional rule of conduct, even in those cases where doing so would result in increased misery, Smart deprecates as "rule worship." He recognizes the notorious difficulties that questions of justice generate for any rigorously utilitarian theory; in *Ethics, Persuasion and Truth* (1984) discussing the enormity of accepting the idyllic happiness of many at the cost of the continuing torture of one lost soul. There is no definitive resolution in his ethical thought of this conflict between the claims of happiness and of justice.

Philosophy and Scientific Realism (1963) marked the first appearance of a line of thinking that continues through *Our Place in the Universe* (1989) and subsequent pieces: what is now known as the Argument to the Best Explanation. The issue is realism over theoretical entities such as electrons and quarks, which must forever be beyond any direct observational validation. Smart's position is that the complex, interlocking set of experimental results that have been obtained and validated about electrons, for instance, would constitute an incredible set of interlocking coincidences for which there could be no intelligible accounting, unless electron theory were (close to being) literally referentially correct.

In *Ethics, Persuasion, and Truth* (1984) Smart argues for a sophisticated subjectivist theory in metaethics. As an empiricist, Smart rejects the idea that moral judgments state some special kind of "moral fact," and develops a preference semantics and pragmatics for them. *Our Place in the Universe* (1989) presents a coherent naturalistic vision of the physical world and life on earth, suffused with a kind of natural piety or philosophic awe.

Since 1990, Smart has continued to write on all the major themes of his philosophy. In 1996 he joined with J. J. Haldane in a debate on the issue of atheism. In all his work, Smart argues for firmly held views with the calm, well-informed courtesy and candor that have made him one of the best loved, as well as most respected, of contemporary philosophers.

See also Colors; Consequentialism; Empiricism; Inference to the Best Explanation; Philosophy of Mind; Utilitarianism.

Bibliography

BOOKS BY SMART

An Outline of a System of Utilitarian Ethics. Melbourne: Melbourne University Press on behalf of the University of Adelaide, 1961.

Philosophy and Scientific Realism. London: Routledge & Kegan Paul, 1963.

Between Science and Philosophy: An Introduction to the Philosophy of Science. New York: Random House, 1968.

Utilitarianism: For and Against, with Bernard Williams. Cambridge, U.K.: Cambridge University Press, 1973.

Ethics and Science. Hobart, Australia: University of Tasmania, 1981.

Ethics, Persuasion, and Truth. London: Routledge & Kegan Paul, 1984.

Essays, Metaphysical and Moral: Selected Philosophical Papers. Oxford: B. Blackwell, 1987.

Our Place in the Universe: A Metaphysical Discussion. Oxford: Blackwell, 1989.

Atheism and Theism. With J. J. Haldane. Oxford: Blackwell, 1996.

BOOKS EDITED BY SMART

Problems of Space and Time: Readings. New York: Macmillan, 1964.

BOOKS ABOUT SMART

Petit, Philip, Richard Sylvan, and Jean Norman, eds. *Metaphysics and Morality: Essays in Honour of J. J. C. Smart.* Oxford: B. Blackwell, 1987.

Keith Campbell (1996, 2005)

SMITH, ADAM

(1723–1790)

Adam Smith, one of the most influential political economists of Western society, first became known as a moral philosopher. Smith was born in Kirkcaldy, Scotland. His father died shortly before he was born, and his mother's loss doubtless explains the lifelong attachment that flourished between her and her son. Smith entered the University of Glasgow in 1737, where he attended Francis Hutcheson's lectures. In 1740 he entered Balliol College, Oxford, as a Snell exhibitioner. He remained at Oxford for seven years and then returned to Kirkcaldy. In 1748 he moved to Edinburgh, where he became the friend of David Hume and Lord Kames (Henry Home). In 1751 he was elected professor of logic at the University of Glasgow, and in the next year he exchanged logic for the professorship in moral philosophy, an appointment that he held for the next ten years.

The *Theory of Moral Sentiments,* drawn from his course of lectures, was published in 1759. The work received wide acclaim and so impressed the stepfather of the young duke of Buccleuch that he invited Smith to become the duke's tutor, with the promise of a pension for life. Smith resigned his professorship at Glasgow and accompanied the duke on a visit to the Continent that lasted from 1764 to 1766. His tutoring duties ended, he returned again to Kirkcaldy, where he spent the next ten years in retirement at work on *The Wealth of Nations,* which was published in 1776 and for which he became famous. In 1778 he was appointed a commissioner of customs for Scotland. He died in 1790 and was buried in the Canongate churchyard, Edinburgh.

The greater part of the *Theory of Moral Sentiments* is an account of moral psychology. Only after he has settled the psychological questions does Smith turn, in the last seventh of the work, to moral philosophy. The mainstay of Smith's moral psychology is sympathy. Sympathy is our fellow feeling with the passions or affections of another person. Smith characterizes the mechanism of sympathy in this way: "Whatever is the passion which arises from any object in the person principally concerned, *an analogous emotion* springs up at the thought of his situation, in the breast of every attentive spectator." The important phrase here is "at the thought of his situation." Sympathetic feelings may seem to arise from our seeing the expression of a certain emotion in another person, but Smith argues that if the appearance of grief or joy, for example, arouses similar feelings in us, it is because these feelings suggest to us the general idea of some good or evil that has befallen the person in whom we observe them. What is more, there are some passions whose expression excites disgust rather than sympathy until we are acquainted with their cause. The furious behavior of an angry man, for example, is more likely to exasperate us against him than against his enemies. Thus, Smith concludes that sympathy does not arise so much from the view of the passion as from the view of the situation that excites it, and he reinforces this claim by noting that we sometimes feel for another a passion that he himself seems to be altogether incapable of, as when we feel embarrassed at someone's behaving rudely although he has no sense of the impropriety of his behavior.

Sympathy is the basis for our judgments of both the propriety and the merit of other people's feelings and the actions that follow from them. When the original passions of the principal person are in perfect accord with the sympathetic emotions of the spectator, the passions of the principal appear to the spectator as just and proper. Smith even goes as far as to say that to approve of the passions of another as suitable to their objects is the same as to observe that we entirely sympathize with them. Indeed, even though our own emotions may make it impossible for us to have on occasion a certain sympathetic emotion, we may "by general rules" recognize the appropriateness of some person's having a given emotion because, for example, we could sympathize with the other person's joy but for our own grief.

Although our sense of the propriety of some piece of conduct arises from our sympathy with the affections and motives of the agent, our sense of merit (that is, our sense of a certain action's making the agent worthy of a reward) stems from our sympathy with the gratitude of the person affected by the action. When we see someone aided by another, our sympathy with his joy at the receipt of the aid animates our fellow feeling with his gratitude toward his benefactor.

Having shown how sympathy gives rise to the senses of propriety and of merit in our judgment of the passions and conduct of others, Smith turns to showing how these sentimental mechanisms may be employed in our judgment of ourselves. We must take care to avoid a self-interested partiality in our judgments. According to Smith, impartiality can be achieved only if we look at our own behavior as though it were someone else's. Thus, we may judge ourselves from the same point of view that we judge others, and our approval or disapproval of our own conduct will depend on whether we can sympathize with the sentiments from which our actions flow. Conscience, "the judge within us," enables us to make a proper comparison between our own interests and the interests of others. With its aid we may approach the ideal of the man of perfect virtue, who is possessed of both a command of his own feelings and a sensibility for the feelings of others.

We may guard against self-deceit by keeping before us the general rules for what is appropriate in human conduct. These rules have their basis in the sentiments that certain kinds of behavior evoke, and our own respect for the rules should follow from the correspondence between them and our own feelings as we observe the conduct of others. Smith stresses that the rules are generalizations from particular instances in which conduct has excited the sense of propriety and merit in humankind. A just regard for these general rules is a sense of duty. By acting from a sense of duty, one can make up for any lack of the appropriate sentiment on a given occasion. Of all the general rules, those that define justice have the greatest exactness.

Throughout his discussion of our moral psychology, Smith assumes the general acceptance of beneficence and justice as social virtues. He glides quickly over the problem of their description, and he introduces sympathy into his moral psychology as a kind of absolute without considering whether someone might sympathize with "wrong" affections.

In his moral philosophy Smith treats of two questions: Wherein does virtue consist? What power or faculty of the mind recommends virtue to us?

The different accounts of virtue may be reduced to three principles. First, virtue is the proper government and direction of all our affections (propriety). Second, virtue is the judicious pursuit of our own private interest (prudence). Third, virtue lies in the exercise of only those affections that aim at the happiness of others (benevolence). These principles make it evident either that virtue may be ascribed to all our affections when properly governed (as the principle of propriety implies) or that virtue is limited to one of two classes of our affections, either the prudent ones or the benevolent ones.

After surveying the various systems of morals, Smith offers the following conclusions. The systems based on propriety give no precise measure of it. Smith remedies this defect by pointing out that the standard of what is appropriate in sentiments and motives can be found nowhere but in the sympathetic feelings of the impartial spectator. The most that can be claimed for the definition of virtue as propriety is that there is no virtue without propriety, and where there is propriety, some approbation is due. But those who make propriety the sole criterion of virtue can be refuted by the single consideration that they cannot account for the superior esteem granted to benevolent actions. However, neither prudence nor benevolence can be allowed to be the sole criterion of virtue, for whichever we choose, we make it impossible to explain our approbation of the other. Smith's implied conclusion is that there can be no single criterion of virtue and that each of the three principles that he notes must be allowed its just scope.

When Smith turns to the question of what power or faculty of the mind recommends virtue to us, he remarks that this question is of purely speculative interest and has no practical importance whatsoever. Several candidates had been proposed by Smith's predecessors as the source of virtue, notably self-love, reason, or some sentiment. Smith rejects self-love as the ultimate basis of behavior, and hence as the basis of virtue, on the ground that its proponents have neglected sympathy as a cause of action. For Smith, sympathy is not a selfish principle. Smith also rejects reason as a source of the distinction between virtue and vice because reason cannot render any action either agreeable or disagreeable to the mind for its own sake. The first perceptions of right and wrong must be derived from an immediate sense of the agreeableness or disagreeableness of actions. Thus, Smith is left with the conclusion that there must be some sentiment that recommends virtue to us.

Smith considers the proposal that there is a special sense of virtue, the moral sense, as proposed by his former teacher Hutcheson. But Smith regards the moral sense as objectionable on two counts. First, no one seemed to be aware that he had a moral sense before the moral philosophers began to talk about it; and if the moral sense is a genuine sense, this state of affairs seems very odd indeed. Second, Smith finds that sympathy, a recognized human phenomenon, is the source of a range of feelings that provide a foundation for virtue. Therefore, since a sentimental basis for virtue is already provided by nature, there is no need to invent one in the form of a moral sense.

An Inquiry into the Nature and Causes of the Wealth of Nations is partly a description of the actual conditions of manufacture and trade in Smith's own time, partly a history of European economics, and partly recommendations to governments. Smith opposes the mercantilist beliefs that money is wealth and that the best economic policy for a country is the retention within its borders of as much gold and silver as possible. He argues, rather, that wealth is consumable goods and that the wealthiest country is one that either produces itself or can command from others the greatest quantity of consumable goods.

The development of a full-blown economic system requires some people in a society to possess a supply of either raw materials or manufactured goods greater than is required to fulfill their own immediate needs. The surplus stocks provide the opportunity for trade among people with various needs. Where the demand for a certain kind of thing is great enough to assure a producer that his other wants may be supplied in exchange for producing this certain good, he will specialize in its production. This kind of division of labor will continue, according to Smith, until some laborers are producing a very small part of a manufactured product because the master finds that a division of labor enables his workers to produce a greater quantity of goods in a shorter time.

Smith believes that the general welfare will be best served by permitting each person to pursue his own interest. Sympathy, which figured largely in Smith's account of moral psychology, is not mentioned in his economics. Self-interest is the motive required to explain economic action. Smith argues, "Every individual is continually exerting himself to find out the most advantageous employment for whatever capital he can command." Since the most advantageous employment of capital is to be found in producing and selling the goods that satisfy the greatest needs of a people, the capitalist is bound to work to satisfy those needs. Intending only his own gain, he contributes nonetheless to the general welfare. Thus, the capitalist is "led by an invisible hand to promote an end which was no part of his intention."

Smith was instrumental in bringing his contemporaries to see the modern European economic system for the first time, and we are the heirs of their vision. Of course, Smith is guilty of oversimplifications and omissions, but his work is nonetheless a model of both observation and systematization in the social sciences.

See also Ethics, History of; Ethics and Economics; Home, Henry; Hume, David; Hutcheson, Francis; Moral Sense; Philosophy of Economics; Virtue Ethics.

Bibliography

The edition of *The Wealth of Nations* prepared by Edwin Cannan (London: Methuen, 1904) is recommended. See also William R. Scott, ed., *Adam Smith as Student and Professor, with Unpublished Documents* (Glasgow: Jackson, 1937), a biographical account, and Eli Ginzberg, *The House of Adam Smith* (New York: Columbia University Press, 1934), which is the classic analysis of Smith's economics based on consideration of his predecessors and contemporaries. For Smith's moral philosophy, see James Bonar, *Moral Sense* (London: Allen and Unwin, 1930), Chs. X and XI.

Elmer Sprague (1967)

SMITH, ADAM [ADDENDUM]

Adam Smith's claim on the history of aesthetics lies in his essay, "Of the Nature of that Imitation which takes place in what are called the Imitative Arts," arguably the most logically acute and penetrating discussion of what one would call pictorial representation that eighteenth-century Britain produced. It was first published, posthumously, in 1795, in Smith's *Essays on Philosophical Subjects*.

The main thesis of Smith's account is that "the disparity between the imitating and the imitated object is the foundation of the beauty of imitation. It is because the one object does not naturally resemble the other, that we are so much pleased by it, when by art it is made to do so" (1795, p. 144).

Smith's most elaborately worked-out example concerns the contrast between painting and sculpture, much discussed in the eighteenth century. The idea is that statues represent three-dimensional objects in a three-dimensional medium, whereas paintings represent three-dimensional objects in two dimensions. Hence a higher level of resemblance would be required of a statue to its represented object than would be required of a painting to its, to achieve the same level of representational beauty. "The disparity between the object imitating, and the object imitated," Smith wrote, "is much greater in the one art than in the other; and the pleasure arising from the imitation seems to be greater in proportion as this disparity is greater" (1795, p. 137). Smith pays considerable attention in his essay, as well, to music and dance, concluding that "the imitative powers of Dancing are much superior to those of instrumental Music, and are at least equal, perhaps superior, to those of any other art" (Smith, p. 175).

See also Aesthetics, History of; Art, Expression in; Art, Representation in.

Bibliography

Smith, Adam. *Essays on Philosophical Subjects*. London, 1795.

Peter Kivy (2005)

SMITH, JOHN
(c. 1616–1652)

John Smith, the moral and religious philosopher of the Cambridge Platonist school, was born at Achurch, near Oundle, in Northamptonshire. Very little is known with certainty about his origins. It would seem that his father was a locally respected small farmer, that both of his parents were elderly when he was born, that he lost his mother in his early childhood and his father soon after. His short life was a continual struggle against poverty and ill health. In 1636 he was somehow enabled to enter Emmanuel College, where he came under the influence of Benjamin Whichcote. Although he was about the same age as his fellow Platonist Ralph Cudworth, Cudworth was already a fellow of Emmanuel before Smith took his

BA in 1640; Smith was very likely his pupil and certainly came under his influence. The influence may have been in some measure reciprocal.

Smith took his MA degree in 1644; the same year he was elected a fellow of Queen's College, Cambridge, having been declared by the London Assembly of Divines a suitable person to replace one of the fellows who had been ejected by the Puritan Parliament. He taught Greek, Hebrew, and mathematics. Like his master Whichcote he had gifts of character and personal warmth, which won for him not only the respect but also the affection of pupils and friends. The funeral sermon preached by Simon Patrick on his death on August 7, 1652, is, even allowing for the extravagance of phrase common to such occasions, an impressive tribute to his intellectual and personal gifts. He published nothing, but after his death a series of *Discourses* that he had delivered as dean of his college in the chapel of Queen's was collected, edited, and published by John Worthington. Another volume was promised but never appeared.

Matthew Arnold described Smith's *Discourses* as "the most admirable work left to us by the Cambridge School." This is the judgment of a man whose interests lay in religion and culture rather than in philosophy. As a philosopher Smith will not stand comparison with Cudworth or Henry More. Basically, he was an eloquent apologist for the liberal theology of the Cambridge school. The flow of that eloquence, however, is interrupted, in the Cambridge Platonist manner, by quotations in a variety of tongues from Plato, especially the *Phaedo* and the *Republic*, and the Neoplatonists, the Hebrew Scriptures, the Talmud, and, the sole contemporary, René Descartes. Smith's reasoning is by no means close. "It is but a thin, airy knowledge," he writes in the first *Discourse*, "that is got by mere speculation, which is ushered in by syllogisms and demonstrations." God's nature, he thinks, is to be understood by "spiritual sensation" rather than by verbal description; Smith's object is to arouse such a "spiritual sensation" in human souls, and philosophy is only ancillary to that task.

THOUGHT

The first six of the *Discourses* Smith composed as a continuous essay. They were to be the first segment of a book that he did not live to complete. As editor, Worthington broke up the essay into chapters and added, from Smith's papers, four sermons to act as a substitute for the unwritten segments of the essay. Smith's general thesis is the Platonic one that goodness and knowledge are intimately united; only the purified soul can achieve true knowledge. Every soul, he thought, has within it innate concepts of religion and morality. Ordinarily obscured by sensuality, they nevertheless act as a guide to the direction in which purification is to be sought. Such principles Smith thinks of as innate ideas. Knowledge, in his view, is derived by reflection of the character of our souls; it does not arise out of sensory experience. One can see why he admired the Neoplatonists and welcomed the teachings of Descartes. He did not live long enough to share in the revulsion against Descartes's teachings as mechanistic, which More and Cudworth were to exhibit; indeed, in his *Discourses* he draws on Descartes's physiology.

According to Smith, the three great enemies of religion are superstition, legalism, and atheism. Superstition consists of treating God as a capricious power who has to be cajoled by flattery, bribery, or magical spells. Legalism conceives of religion as laying down doctrines that have simply to be accepted as rules for governing our conduct. It can take a variety of forms, "Scripture-Christianity" is quite as legalistic as Jewish formalism if it consists of picking out of the Scriptures a set of doctrines on the acceptance of which salvation is supposed to depend. Smith attacks this sort of Christianity with particular vigor, especially in his Sermon "Pharisaical Righteousness" (*Discourses* VIII).

As for atheism, Smith, unlike Cudworth and More, did not have Thomas Hobbes to contend with. He knew of atheism only as it appears in the writings of the Epicureans; much of his (very brief) argument against atheism is directed against the Epicurean version of atomism. He regards the belief in God as a "natural belief" that scarcely needs to be defended. He is much more preoccupied with the belief in immortality, perhaps because Richard Overton in a notorious pamphlet, *Man's Mortality* (1643), published in London although as if from Amsterdam, had denied that humans are by nature immortal, arguing that the soul and the body are so compounded that they die and are resurrected together. Smith defends what Overton had rejected—the traditional distinction between soul and body—calling upon Descartes for support.

If people are led to doubt the immortality of their souls, Smith argues, this is only because they are conscious that their souls do not deserve to be immortalized. Once they improve the quality of their lives, they will come to be conscious of their souls as exhibiting a kind of goodness that is obviously destined to be eternal. Similarly, if questions arise about God's nature, these can be settled, as Plotinus had suggested, only by reflection on the workings of our own souls in their most godlike moments. God is the perfect soul, the perfectly loving soul, the perfectly rational soul; that this is God's nature we see by reflection upon our own perfections and imperfections.

It is easy to see why men as different as John Wesley and Matthew Arnold expressed admiration for Smith and sought to introduce his writings to a wider audience. Smith's appeal to inwardness, to the capture of the soul by God, recommends him to the evangelical; his rejection of merely creedal religions, the moral emphasis of his teaching, recommends him to the liberal theologian.

See also Cambridge Platonists.

Bibliography

The *Select Discourses* were first published and edited by John Worthington in 1660 (London). The best edition is that edited by Henry Griffin Williams for the Cambridge University Press in 1859. Various extracts have been published, for example, by John Wesley in Vol. XI of his Christian Library (London, 1819–1827). A selection with the title *The Natural Truth of Christianity*, edited by W. M. Metcalfe (Paisley, U.K., 1882), includes an introductory commendation by Matthew Arnold.

For works on Smith, see bibliography to the "Cambridge Platonists" entry; Rufus Matthew Jones, *Spiritual Reformers in the Sixteenth and Seventeenth Centuries* (London: Macmillan, 1914), Ch. 16; the Address to the Reader prefixed to John Worthington's edition of the *Discourses* (reprinted in the 1859 edition); John K. Ryan, "John Smith, Platonist and Mystic," in *New Scholasticism* 20 (1) (1946): 1–25; J. E. Saveson, "Descartes' Influence on John Smith, Cambridge Platonist," in *Journal of the History of Ideas* 20 (2) (1959): 258–263; C. A. Patrides, *The Cambridge Platonists* (Cambridge, U.K.: Cambridge University Press, 1980); and Brenton J. Stearns, "Mediate Immediacy: A Search for Some Models," in *International Journal for Philosophy of Religion* 3 (1972): 195–211.

John Passmore (1967)
Bibliography updated by Tamra Frei (2005)

SMUTS, JAN CHRISTIAAN
(1870–1950)

Jan Christiaan Smuts, the South African statesman, soldier, and scholar, introduced the concept of "holism" into philosophy. Smuts was born on a farm near Riebeek West, Cape Colony (now Western Cape Province). He was graduated from Victoria College, Stellenbosch, in 1891 and from Cambridge in 1894, where he studied law. At both places his record was brilliant, but he had the reputation of being a bookish recluse who made few friends. Returning home in 1895, he was admitted to the bar, entered political life, and during the Boer War commanded a force against the British with the rank of general. However, when World War I broke out in 1914 he became a staunch defender of the Allied cause. In 1918 he published a pamphlet titled *The League of Nations: A Practical Suggestion,* which helped to form President Woodrow Wilson's ideas. From 1919 to 1924, and again from 1939 to 1948, he was prime minister of South Africa. In the intervening period he completed his only philosophical work, *Holism and Evolution* (New York, 1926). Smuts was a dominant figure in the politics of his country for over half a century and an influential figure on the world scene. His enemies considered him arrogant and ruthless, more interested in ideas than in people. Yet the theme of his politics, as of his philosophy, was the integration of parts into wholes.

This theme is central to *Holism and Evolution,* where it is used to integrate the results of the sciences, especially the biological sciences, and where it becomes the basis of "a new *Weltanschauung* within the general framework of Science." The background was supplied by the theory of evolution, so interpreted as to preclude mechanistic or materialistic formulations of it. Such formulations, Smuts held, are incompatible with the fact that evolution is creative, having successively brought into existence items that are genuinely novel and that were not even potentially existent before they appeared on the scene. These items he called "wholes." Their appearance was explained by postulating a primordial whole-making, or "holistic," factor in the universe. This factor he also called a "creative tendency or principle" operative throughout the history of nature.

Smuts apparently wished to distinguish wholes in the strict sense from mere aggregates, mechanical systems, and chemical compounds. In a true whole the parts lose forever their prior identity. In aggregates, mechanical systems, and chemical compounds, however, the identity of the parts or elements is not lost but is always recoverable. There are certain entities, such as biochemical systems, which appear to have an intermediate status. For they display "a mixture of mechanism and holism." These systems form "the vast ladder of life." At the bottom of the ladder, mechanistic features predominate; at the top, holistic features predominate. True wholes, free of any admixture of mechanism, are exemplified in minds or psychic structures, which first appear among higher organisms, and in human personality, "the supreme embodiment of Holism."

Smuts sometimes spoke of atoms and molecules as wholes, presumably using the term in other than the strict sense he had defined. The broader use allowed him to affirm that the factor of holism is "responsible for the total course of evolution, inorganic as well as organic. All the great main types of existence are due to it." Long before organisms or minds arose, the holistic factor was producing elementary wholes of a purely physical kind. Later, through a series of "creative leaps," it became more fully embodied in biological structures, minds, and persons. Indeed, "it is in the sphere of spiritual values that Holism finds its clearest embodiment," for in this sphere love, beauty, goodness, and truth have their source.

Smuts nowhere attributed to the holistic factor any teleological orientation. Nor did he apply to it any personal or spiritual categories. It was represented as an ultimate principle, metaphysical rather than religious, at work and still working in the cosmos.

There is a considerable resemblance between Smuts's philosophical views and those of Henri Bergson and C. Lloyd Morgan. All three philosophers stressed the creativity of evolution, its engendering of novelties whose presence invalidates mechanistic materialism. All were critical of Darwinism and opposed it with arguments and assertions couched in highly general terms. Smuts differed from the other two philosophers in refusing to state explicitly that the holistic factor is spiritual or akin to mind. But at bottom it remains as inscrutable as Bergson's *élan vital* or Morgan's directing Activity.

See also African Philosophy; Bergson, Henri; Darwinism; Holism and Individualism in History and Social Science; Morgan, C. Lloyd.

Bibliography

McDougall, William. "The Confusion of the Concept." *Journal of Philosophical Studies* 3 (1928): 440–442.

Morgan, C. Lloyd. Review of *Holism and Evolution. Journal of Philosophical Studies* (1927): 85–89.

T. A. Goudge (1967)

SOCIAL AND POLITICAL PHILOSOPHY

It is generally agreed that the central task of social and political philosophy is to provide a justification for coercive institutions. Coercive institutions range in size from the family to the nation-state and world organizations, like the United Nations, with their narrower and broader agendas for action. Yet essentially, they are institutions that at least sometimes employ force or the threat of force to control the behavior of their members to achieve either minimal or wide-ranging goals. To justify such coercive institutions, we need to show that the authorities within these institutions have a right to be obeyed and that their members have a corresponding duty to obey them. In other words, we need to show that these institutions have legitimate authority over their members.

In philosophical debate at the beginning of the twenty-first century, a number of competing justifications for coercive institutions have been defended: (1) a libertarian justification, which appeals to an ideal of liberty; (2) a socialist justification, which appeals to an ideal of equality; (3) a welfare liberal justification, which appeals to an ideal of contractual fairness; (4) a communitarian justification, which appeals to an ideal of the common good; and (5) a feminist justification, which appeals to an ideal of a gender-free society. Each of these justifications needs to be examined in order to determine which, if any, are morally defensible.

LIBERTARIANISM

Libertarians frequently cite the work of F. A. Hayek, particularly his *Constitution of Liberty* (1960), as an intellectual source of their view. Hayek argues that the libertarian ideal of liberty requires "equality before the law" and "reward according to market value" but not " substantial equality" or "reward according to merit." Hayek further argues that the inequalities due to upbringing, inheritance, and education that are permitted by an ideal of liberty actually tend to benefit society as a whole.

In basic accord with Hayek, contemporary libertarians, like John Hospers (1971), Robert Nozick (1974), Tibor Machan (2004), and Jan Narveson (1998), define liberty negatively as "the state of being unconstrained by other persons from doing what one wants" rather than positively as "the state of being assisted by other persons in doing what one wants." Libertarians go on to characterize their social and political ideal as requiring that each person should have the greatest amount of liberty commensurate with the same liberty for all. From this ideal, libertarians claim that a number of more specific requirements, in particular a right to life, a right to freedom of speech, press, and assembly, and a right to property, can be derived.

The libertarian's right to life is not a right to receive from others the goods and resources necessary for preserving one's life; it is simply a right not to be killed. So understood, the right to life is not a right to receive welfare. In fact, there are no welfare rights according to the libertarian view. Correspondingly, the libertarian's understanding of the right to property is not a right to receive from others the goods and resources necessary for one's welfare, but rather a right to acquire goods and resources either by initial acquisition or by voluntary agreement. By defending rights such as these, libertarians support only a limited role for coercive institutions. That role is simply to prevent and punish initial acts of coercion—the only wrongful actions for libertarians. Thus, libertarians are opposed to all forms of censorship and paternalism, unless they can be supported by their ideal of liberty.

Libertarians do not deny that it is a good thing for people to have sufficient goods and resources to meet their basic nutritional needs, but libertarians do deny that coercive institutions should be used to provide for such needs. Some good things, such as the provision of welfare to the needy, are requirements of charity rather than justice, libertarians claim. Accordingly, failure to make such provisions is neither blameworthy nor punishable.

SOCIALISM

In contrast with libertarians, socialists take equality to be the ultimate social and political ideal. In the *Communist Manifesto* (1848), Karl Marx and Friedrich Engels maintain that the abolition of bourgeois property and bourgeois family structure is a necessary first requirement for building a society that accords with the political ideal of equality. In *Critique of the Gotha Program*, Marx provides a much more positive account of what is required to build a society based upon the political ideal of equality. In such a society, Marx claims that the distribution of social goods must conform, at least initially, to the principle "from each according to his ability, to each according to his contribution." But when the highest stage of communist society has been reached, Marx adds, distribution will conform to the principle "from each according to his ability, to each according to his need." Contemporary socialists like Kai Nielson and Carol Gould continue to endorse these tenets of Marxism.

At first hearing, these tenets of Marxism might sound ridiculous to someone brought up in a capitalist society. The obvious objection is, how can you get persons to contribute according to their ability if income is distributed on the basis of their needs and not on the basis of their contributions? The answer, according to socialists, is to make the work that must be done in a society as much as possible enjoyable in itself. As a result, people will want to do the work they are capable of doing because they find it intrinsically rewarding. For a start, socialists might try to get people to accept presently existing, intrinsically rewarding jobs at lower salaries—top executives, for example, to work for $300,000, rather than $900,000 or more, a year. Yet ultimately, socialists hope to make all jobs as intrinsically rewarding as possible, so that after people are no longer working primarily for external rewards, while making their best contributions to society, distribution can proceed on the basis of need.

Socialists propose to implement their egalitarian ideal by giving workers democratic control over the workplace. They believe that if workers have more to say about how they do their work, they will find their work intrinsically more rewarding. As a consequence, they will be more motivated to work, because their work itself will be meeting their needs. Socialists believe that extending democracy to the workplace will necessarily lead to socialization of the means of production and the end of private property. By making jobs intrinsically as rewarding as possible, in part through democratic control of the workplace and an equitable assignment of unrewarding tasks, socialists believe people will contribute according to their ability even when distribution proceeds according to need. Liberation theology has also provided an interpretation of Christianity that is sympathetic to this socialist ideal.

Nor are contemporary socialists disillusioned by the collapse of the Soviet Union and the transformation of the countries in Eastern Europe. Judging the acceptability of the socialist ideal of equality by what took place in these countries would be as unfair as judging the acceptability of the libertarian ideal of liberty by what takes place in countries like Guatemala or Singapore, where there is a free market but very little political liberty. By analogy, it would be like judging the merits of college football by the way Vanderbilt's or Columbia s team play rather than by the way Florida's or USC's team play. Actually, a fairer comparison would be to judge the socialist ideal of equality by what takes place in countries like Sweden and to judge the libertarian ideal of liberty by what takes place in the United States. Even these comparisons, however, are not wholly appropriate because none of these countries fully conforms to those ideals.

WELFARE LIBERALISM

Finding merit in both the libertarian's ideal of liberty and the socialist's ideal of equality, welfare liberals attempt to combine both liberty and equality into one political ideal that can be characterized by contractual fairness. A classical example of this contractual approach is found in the political works of Immanuel Kant. Kant claims that a civil state ought to be founded on an original contract satisfying the requirements of freedom, equality, and independence. According to Kant, it suffices that the laws of a civil state are such that people would agree to them under conditions in which the requirements of freedom, equality, and independence obtain.

The Kantian ideal of a hypothetical contract as the moral foundation for coercive institutions has been further developed by John Rawls in *A Theory of Justice* (1971). Rawls, like Kant, argues that principles of justice are those principles that free and rational persons who are concerned to advance their own interests would accept in an initial position of equality. Yet Rawls goes beyond Kant by interpreting the conditions of his "original position" to explicitly require a "veil of ignorance." This veil of ignorance, Rawls claims, has the effect of depriving persons in the original position of the knowledge they would need to advance their own interests in ways that are morally arbitrary.

According to Rawls, the principles of justice that would be derived in the original position are the following: (1) a principle of equal political liberty; (2) a principle of equal opportunity; (3) a principle requiring that the distribution of economic goods work to the greatest advantage of the least advantaged. Rawls holds that these principles would be chosen in the original position because persons so situated would find it reasonable to follow the conservative dictates of the "maximin" strategy and maximize the minimum), thereby securing for themselves the highest minimum payoff. In his *Political Liberalism* (1993), Rawls explains how these principles could be supported by an overlapping consensus, and thus would be compatible with a pluralistic society whose members endorse diverse comprehensive conceptions of the good, and in his *The Law of Peoples* (1999), Rawls attempts to extend his theory of justice to the international realm.

COMMUNITARIANISM

Another prominent social and political ideal defended by contemporary philosophers is the communitarian ideal of the common good. As one might expect, many contemporary defenders of a communitarian social and political ideal regard their conception as rooted in Aristotelian moral theory. Alasdair MacIntyre in *After Virtue* (1981) sees his social and political theory as rooted in Aristotelian moral theory, but it is an Aristotelian moral theory that has been refurbished in certain respects. Specifically, MacIntyre claims that Aristotelian moral theory must, first of all, reject any reliance on a metaphysical biology. Instead of appealing to a metaphysical biology, MacIntyre proposes to ground Aristotelian moral theory on a conception of a practice. A practice, for MacIntyre, is "any coherent and complex form of socially established cooperative human activity through which goods internal to that form of activity are realized in the course of trying to achieve those standards of excellence which are appropriate to and partially definitive of that form of activity, with the result that human powers to achieve excellence, and human conceptions of the ends and goods involved are systematically extended" (1981, p.175). As examples of practices, MacIntyre cites arts, sciences, games, and the making and sustaining of family life.

MacIntyre then partially defines the virtues in terms of practices. A virtue, such as courage, justice or honesty, is "an acquired human quality the possession and exercise of which tends to enable us to achieve those goods which are internal to practices and the lack of which prevents us from achieving any such goods" (1981, p.178). However, MacIntyre admits that the virtues which sustain practices can conflict (e.g., courage can conflict with justice) and that practices so defined are not themselves above moral criticism.

Accordingly, to further ground his account, MacIntyre introduces the conception of a telos, or good of a whole human life conceived as a unity. It is by means of this conception that MacIntyre proposes to morally evaluate practices and resolve conflicts between virtues. For MacIntyre, the telos of a whole human life is a life spent in seeking that telos; it is a quest for the good human life and it proceeds with only partial knowledge of what is sought. Nevertheless, this quest is never undertaken in isolation but always within some shared tradition. Moreover, such a tradition provides additional resources for evaluating practices and for resolving conflicts while remaining open to moral criticism itself.

MacIntyre's characterization of the human telos in terms of a quest undertaken within a tradition marks a second respect in which he wants to depart from Aristotle's view. This historical dimension to the human telos that MacIntyre contends is essential for a rationally acceptable communitarian account is absent from Aristotle' s view. A third respect in which MacIntyre's account departs from that of Aristotle concerns the possibility of tragic moral conflicts. As MacIntyre points out, Aristotle only recognized moral conflicts that are the outcome of wrongful or mistaken action. Yet MacIntyre, following Sophocles, wants to recognize the possibility of additional conflicts between rival moral goods that are rooted in the very nature of things.

Initially, rather than draw out the particular requirements of his own social and political theory, MacIntyre defended his theory by attacking rival theories, and, by and large, he focused his attacks on liberal social and political theories; in this respect he shares common ground with contemporary deconstructionists. Thus, MacIntyre argues in his "Privatization of the Good" that virtually all forms of liberalism attempt to separate rules defining right action from conceptions of the human good. MacIntyre contends that these forms of liberalism not only fail but have to fail because the rules defining right action cannot be adequately grounded apart from a conception of the good. For this reason, MacIntyre claims, only some refurbished Aristotelian theory that grounds rules supporting right action in a complete conception of the good can ever hope to be adequate.

In his most recent book, *Rational Dependent Animals* (1999), however, MacIntyre's defense of the communitarian ideal of the common good has now moved in a socialist or Marxist direction. In this book, Macintyre argues that for independent practical reasoners, Marx's principle for a socialist society—to each according to his or her contribution—is appropriate, but between those capable of giving and those most dependent, it is Marx's principle for a communist society—from each according to his or her ability, to each according to his or her need—that is appropriate.

FEMINISM

Defenders of a feminist social and political ideal present a distinctive challenging critique to defenders of other social and political ideals. In *The Subjection of Women* (1869), John Stuart Mill, one of the earliest male defenders of women's liberation, argues that the subjection of women was never justified but was imposed upon women because they were physically weaker than men; later this subjection was confirmed by law. Mill argues that society must remove the legal restrictions that deny women the same opportunities enjoyed by men. However, Mill does not consider whether, because of past discrimination against women, it may be necessary to do more than simply remove legal restrictions: he does not consider whether positive assistance may also be required.

Usually it is not enough simply to remove unequal restrictions to make a competition fair among those who have been participating. Positive assistance to those who have been disadvantaged in the past may also be required, as would be the case in a race in which some were unfairly impeded by having to carry ten-pound weights for part of the race. To render the outcome of such a race fair, we might want to transfer the ten-pound weights to the other runners in the race, and thereby advantage the previously disadvantaged runners for an equal period of time. Similarly, positive assistance, such as affirmative action or preferential treatment programs, may be necessary if women who have been disadvantaged in the past by sexism are now going to be able to compete fairly with men. According to feminists, the argument for using affirmative action or preferential treatment to overcome sexism in society is perfectly analogous to the argument for using affirmative action or preferential treatment to overcome racism in society.

In *Justice, Gender and the Family* (1989), Susan Okin argues for the feminist ideal of a gender-free society. A gender-free society is a society in which basic rights and duties are not assigned on the basis of a person's biological sex. Being male or female is not the grounds for determining what basic rights and duties a person has in a gender-free society. Since a conception of justice is usually thought to provide the ultimate grounds for the assignment of rights and duties, we can refer to this ideal of a gender-free society as "feminist justice."

Okin goes on to consider whether John Rawls's welfare liberal conception of justice can support the ideal of a gender-free society Noting Rawls's initial failure to apply his "original position" concept to family structures, Okin is skeptical about the possibility of using a welfare liberal ideal to support feminist justice. She contends that in a gender-structured society like our own, male philosophers cannot achieve the sympathetic imagination required to see things from the standpoint of women. In a gender-structured society, Okin claims, male philosophers cannot do the "original position-type thinking required by the welfare liberal ideal because they lack the ability to put themselves in the position of women. According to Okin, the "original position" can only really be achieved in a gender-free society.

Yet at the same time that Okin despairs of doing "original position-type thinking in a gender-structured society, like our own, she herself purportedly does a considerable amount of just that type of thinking. For example, she claims that Rawls's principles of justice "would seem to require a radical rethinking not only of the division of labor within families but also of all the nonfamily institutions that assume it." She also claims that "the abolition of gender seems essential for the fulfillment of Rawls's criterion of political justice" (1989, p. 104).

PRACTICAL REQUIREMENTS

Unfortunately, unless we can show that either libertarianism, socialism, welfare liberalism, communitarianism, or feminism, or some combination of these ideals is most morally defensible, it will be difficult to know which practical requirements one should endorse. However, assuming we have obligations to distant peoples and future generations, it may be possible to show that the libertarian's own ideal of liberty leads to a right to welfare that is acceptable to welfare liberals, and that when this right is extended to distant peoples and future generations, it requires something like the equality that socialists endorse. This would effect a practical reconciliation of sorts among seemingly opposing social and political ideals.

There is also the question of whether we have obligations to animals and other nonhuman living beings. Until recently, there was very little discussion of whether humans have such obligations. It was widely assumed, without much argument, that we have obligations only to humans. However, this lack of argument has recently been challenged by defenders of animal rights on grounds of speciesism. Speciesism, they claim, is the prejudicial favoring of the interests of members of one' s own species over the interests of other species. Obviously, determining whether this charge of speciesism can be sustained is vital to providing a justification of coercive institutions, particularly the coercive institutions of animal experimentation and factory farming, and thus it is vital to fulfilling the central task of social and political philosophy as well.

See also Aristotle; Civil Disobedience; Communitarianism; Cosmopolitanism; Democracy; Engels, Friedrich; Feminist Social and Political Philosophy; Kant, Immanuel; Liberation Theology; Libertarianism; Liberty; MacIntyre, Alasdair; Marx, Karl; Mill, John Stuart; Multiculturalism; Nationalism; Nozick, Robert; Pluralism; Postcolonialism; Rawls, John; Republicanism; Socialism; Speciesism.

Bibliography

Gould, Carol. *Globalizing Democracy and Human Rights*. Cambridge, U.K.: Cambridge University Press, 2004.

Hayek, Friedrich A. *The Constitution of Liberty*. Chicago: University of Chicago Press, 1960.

Hospers, John. *Libertarianism*. Los Angeles: Nash, 1971.

Machan, Tibor. *Passion for Liberty*. Lanham: Rowman & Littlefield, 2004.

MacIntyre, Alasdair. *After Virtue*. Notre Dame, IN: University of Notre Dame Press, 1981.

MacIntyre, Alasdair. *Dependent Rational Animals*. Chicago: Open Court, 1999.

MacIntyre, Alasdair. "The Privatization of the Good." *Review of Politics* 52 (1990): 1–20.

MacIntyre, Alasdair. *Three Rival Versions of Moral Enquiry*. Notre Dame, IN: University of Notre Dame Press, 1990.

Marx, Karl, and Friedrich Engels. *The Communist Manifesto*. Originally published as *Manifest der Kommunistischen Partie* (1848). Translated by Paul Sweeney. New York: Monthly Review Press, 1998.

Mill, John Stuart. *The Subjection of Women* (1869). Orchard Park, NY: Broadview Press, 2000.

Narveson, Jan. *The Libertarian Idea*. Philadelphia: Temple University Press, 1988.

Nielson, Kai. *Liberty and Equality*. Totowa, NJ: Rowman and Littlefield, 1985.

Nozick, Robert. *Anarchy, State, and Utopia*. New York: Basic Books, 1974.

Okin, Susan. *Justice, Gender, and the Family*. New York: Basic Books, 1989.

Rawls, John. *The Law of Peoples*. Cambridge, MA: Harvard University Press, 1999.

Rawls, John. *Political Liberalism*. New York: Columbia University Press, 1993.

Rawls, John. *A Theory of Justice*. Cambridge, MA: Harvard University Press, 1971.

Sterba, James P. *Justice for Here and Now*. New York: Cambridge University Press, 1998.

James P. Sterba (1996, 2005)

SOCIAL CONSTRUCTIONISM

Social constructionism (sometimes "constructivism") is a version of constructivism. The idea that human beings in some measure construct the reality they perceive can be found in many philosophical traditions. The pre-Socratic philosopher Xenophones, for instance, argued that humans construct gods in their own image (Fragment 16), a possibility that is also criticized in the Jewish, Christian, and Islamic religious traditions (among others). But the idea that human beings epistemologically construct the reality they perceive is first given extended philosophical articulation in the work of Immanuel Kant (1724–1804). In the nineteenth century a constructivism of sorts emerged as political theory in the work of Karl Marx (1818–1883) and others. Then, in the twentieth century, constructivism took new forms in psychology, in sociology, and in science, technology, and society (STS) studies.

CONSTRUCTIVISM IN PSYCHOLOGY

A root form of social constructionism is found in psychological constructivism. Illuminating research by the British psychologist Frederick Bartlett (1886–1969) revealed how humans use prior knowledge to make sense of new phenomena. In his landmark study *Remembering* (1932), Bartlett presented an unfamiliar indigenous American folk tale to students at Cambridge University. Later each subject was asked to recall the story in as much detail as possible. Bartlett was able to show how each retelling was a unique *reconstruction* of the story rather than a *reproduction* of the original. Subjects tended to replace unfamiliar elements of the story with objects drawn from their own experience. Bartlett concluded that in coming to understand the story, his students tended to make use of pre-existing mental structures or *schemata*, which proved essential both for originally comprehending the story and for subsequent recall.

The notion of schemata is central as well to Jean Piaget's (1896–1980) theory of intelligence. The Swiss psychologist undertook pioneering work on childhood intellectual development. From years of careful observations of and conversations with children and watching them function in problem-solving activities, Piaget argued that cognitive development is an adaptive process of schema correction by means of assimilation and accommodation. We assimilate new information by fitting it within existing cognitive structures. Where preexisting schema cannot incorporate a new experience, we adjust our mental structures to accommodate them. For Piaget, learning is not a passive activity of replication and data storage but an active process of invention and creation. Piaget's resultant genetic epistemology describes how increasingly complex intellectual processes are built on top of more primitive structures in regularly occurring stages.

Lev Semyonovitch Vygotsky (1896–1934), a Piaget contemporary, also studied the cognitive development of children in Soviet Russia during the Stalin years and noted how children engaged in a problem-solving activity invariably speak about what they are doing. This led to his theory of speech as a means for making sense of the activity. Although children's use of tools during their preverbal period is comparable to that of apes, as soon as speech and signs are incorporated into any action, the action becomes transformed and organized along entirely new lines.

Language is thus central to complex reasoning and higher order thinking. Intelligence is the readiness to use culturally transmitted knowledge and practice as prostheses of the mind, and learning is inherently social; learned social speech becomes inner speech through development. Vygotsky came to believe that speech precedes thought and that human thought is a social phenomenon that develops from society to the individual. The idea that cognition emerges out of social activity is central to Vygotsky's work. This is also a view that has become at once widely adopted—being applied especially in educational theory—and controversial, especially various forms of cognitive psychology.

SOCIAL CONSCTRUCTIONISM IN SOCIAL THEORY

The American social philosopher George Herbert Mead (1863–1931) took constructivism into sociology with a theory of self consciousness as originating from social interaction. In his posthumously published *Mind, Self, and Society* (1934), Mead argued that personal identity is constructed through social relationships. In the context of play, for instance, children take on the roles of others, eventually learning to view themselves from the standpoint of a "generalized other." Children's games thus function as instruments for personal and social development, especially when children adopt attitudes of those who in some sense control them or on whom they depend. For Mead the self is a dialectical conversation between the "me" and the "I"—"me" being the social self and "I" the creative self that responds to the "me" in multiple contexts to form, over time, the ontogenic, historical image of one's self.

The theorists Peter Berger and Thomas Luckmann cite Mead as a major source for their seminal sociological text *The Social Construction of Reality* (1966). In this treatise, Berger and Luckmann extend Mead's ontogenetic observations on the self to include all phenomena that we encounter in a social world. They describe the dialectic relationship between the subjective reality of the individual and the objective reality of society that emerges in a universe of discourse that is continuously under construction. Through interaction and conversation with others, knowledge is internalized, then externalized, becoming at once a subjective perception and an objective reality. From such a process of socialization we construct our daily lives.

Much social constructionism implies some degree of subjectivism. From an analysis of intentionality and how it plays out in a social context, however, the philosopher John Searle (1995) has argued that socially constructed reality exhibits its own distinctive type of objectivity. Searle's realism distinguishes between "brute facts" that exist independently of what any humans think and "social facts" that depend on human thinking while being independent of what any one human thinks. Human beings construct a social reality through common intentions that assign functions to physical objects, as when a certain type of paper comes to be treated as money.

SOCIAL CONSTRUCTIONISM IN SCIENCE AND TECHNOLOGY

Epistemological constructivism has taken special forms in the development of cybernetics, evolutionary epistemology, and the philosophy of mathematics. But insofar as cybernetics moved from analyses of interactions between organisms and their physical environments to consideration of communication in a social environment, social cybernetics offered as well a science and a technology of social interactive constructions. Yet the cybernetic approach has been only marginally influential on social constructionism in general.

One of the most contested areas of social constructionism is not in science and technology but in studies about science and technology. Ludwik Fleck (1979) first proposed, in a controversial interpretation of the medical conceptualization of disease, that even some supposedly brute facts of science were socially constructed. This idea was picked up and developed by Thomas Kuhn (1962), which subsequently led to the development of a research program in the sociology of scientific knowledge (SSK). The sociology of scientific institutions, as initiated by Robert K. Merton (1910–2003) in the 1930s, came under increasing criticism in the 1970s for its idealization of science and its failures to treat the production of scientific truth and falsity in a symmetrical manner. Drawing on the ideas from the later Ludwig Wittgenstein about the influence of language games and forms of life on human understanding, David Bloor (1983) and others proposed that social factors influenced not only the production of falsehood (a weak SSK program) but also any consensus about truth (the strong SSK program).

The SSK program in conceptual and analytic criticism was quickly complemented by empirical studies of laboratory practices and how such practices themselves contribute to the production of scientific knowledge. Employing ethnographic approaches, Bruno Latour and Steve Woolgar (1979) and Karin Knorr Cetina (1981) argued that knowledge production is seldom the rational, linear process of hypothesis testing leading to article publication found in the standard image of science. Behind the scenes science is a mangle of practical skills, instrumental jiggering, personal relationships, interpretative debates, and consensus building that deploys a variety of rhetorical strategies to frame both problems and experimental results.

The full extent to which scientific knowledge is a social construction or laboratory production—and what this might imply for science, scientists, as science as a social institution—has been subject to extensive debate in the so-called "science wars" between scientists and their social scientific critics. Among the most philosophically astute assessments of this research program and ensuing debate has been Ian Hacking's *Social Construction of What?* (1995).

The program for a parallel analysis of the social construction of technology (SCOT) has been almost as controversial as social constructivism applied to science, but for different reasons. As Louis Bucciarelli (1994) has shown with his ethnographic examination of the engineering design process, social and personal factors of all sorts readily influence engineering products, processes, and systems. The question is whether this means that those such as Jacques Ellul (1954) or Hans Jonas (1984) who have raised ethical and political questions about the dominance of modern technology in human affairs are simply mistaken in their worries. For proponents of SCOT or one of its related programs such as actor-network theory, critics have too often criticized technology as a kind of "black box" that they failed to examine in sufficient detail. But critics such as Langdon Winner (1994) have responded that "opening the black box" can also be an exercise in avoidance of more fundamental questions.

Relations between social constructivism in psychology, sociology, and STS deserve further examination. Moreover, arguments concerning the social construction of science and technology exhibit unexplored affinities with the pragmatic epistemologies of the "fixation of belief" (C. S. Peirce), the merger of science and technology in the general category of tools (John Dewey), and criticisms of strict empiricism (Willard van Orman Quine). Indeed, social constructivism presents a broad philosophical interpretation of personal and public life, from the epistemological to the ethical, in ways that will likely continue to exercise considerable influence in twenty-first century thought.

See also Constructivism and Conventionalism; Critical Theory; Dewey, John; Feuerbach, Ludwig Andreas; Kant, Immanuel; Kuhn, Thomas; Marx, Karl; Mead, George Herbert; Peirce, Charles Sanders; Personal Identity; Piaget, Jean; Psychology; Quine, Willard Van Orman; Searle, John; Social and Political Philosophy;

Wittgenstein, Ludwig Josef Johann; Xenophanes of Colophon.

Bibliography

Bartlett, Frederick. *Remembering: A Study in Experimental and Social Psychology*. Cambridge, U.K.: Cambridge University Press, 1932.

Berger, Peter, and Thomas Luckmann. *The Social Construction of Reality*. New York: Doubleday, 1966.

Bloor, David. *Ludwig Wittgenstein: A Social Theory of Knowledge*. New York: Columbia University Press, 1983.

Bucciarelli, Louis L. *Designing Engineers*. Cambridge, MA: MIT Press, 1994.

Ellul, Jacques. *La technique, ou l'enjeu du siècle*. Paris: A. Colin, 1954. English translation: *The Technological Society*. Translated by J. Wilkerson. New York: Knopf, 1964.

Fleck, Ludwik. *Genesis and Development of a Scientific Fact*, edited T. J. Trenn and R. K. Merton, 1935. Translated by F. Bradley. Chicago: University of Chicago Press, 1979.

Hacking, Ian. *The Social Construction of What?* Cambridge, MA: Harvard University Press, 1999.

Jonas, Hans. *Das Prinzip Verantwortung: Versuch einer Ethik für die technologische Zivilisation*. Frankfurt: Insel Verlag, 1979. English translation: *The Imperative of Responsibility: In Search of an Ethics for the Technological Age*. Translated by H. Jonas and D. Herr. Chicago: University of Chicago Press, 1984.

Knorr Cetina, Karin. *The Manufacture of Knowledge: An Essay on the Constructivist and Contextual Nature of Science*. Oxford: Pergamon Press, 1981.

Kuhn, Thomas. *The Structure of Scientific Revolutions*. Chicago: University of Chicago Press, 1962.

Latour, Bruno, and Steve Woolgar. *Laboratory Life: The Construction of Scientific Facts*. Beverly Hills, CA: Sage, 1979.

Mead, George Herbert. *Mind, Self, and Society*, edited by C. W. Morris. Chicago: University of Chicago Press, 1934.

Piaget, Jean. *Genetic Epistomology*. Translated by E. Duckworth. New York: Columbia University Press, 1970.

Piaget, Jean. *The Construction of Reality in the Child*. London: Routledge and Kegan Paul, 1955.

Searle, John. *The Construction of Social Reality*. New York: Free Press, 1995.

Vygotsky, Lev S. *Mind in Society: The Development of Higher Psychological Processes*, edited by M. Cole. Cambridge, MA: Harvard University Press, 1978.

Winner, Langdon. "Upon Opening the Black Box and Finding It Empty: Social Constructivism and the Philosophy of Technology." *Science, Technology, and Human Values*, 18, 362–378.

Carl Mitcham (2005)
Martin Ryder (2005)

SOCIAL CONTRACT

"Social contract" is the name given to a group of related and overlapping concepts and traditions in political theory. Like other such aggregations in philosophy and intellectual history, it has at its center an extremely simple conceptual model, in this case that the collectivity is an agreement between the individuals who make it up. This model suggests that it is proper to ask whether the agreement was or is voluntary in character and whether, therefore, the individual can decide to withdraw either because he no longer agrees or because the conditions that are or were understood in the agreement are not being maintained. It suggests furthermore that the individual should be thought of as logically prior to the state or to society, and that it is meaningful to speculate on situations in which individuals existed but no collectivity was in being. From a historical point of view, it is therefore relevant to discuss periods during which no collectivity existed, when what is traditionally called a "state of nature" prevailed, and to contrast these periods with times when by agreement the collectivity had come into existence, that is, with what is traditionally called a "state of society."

The concept of a prepolitical state of nature that can be brought to an end by agreement can thus be applied to geographical areas of human society as well as to periods of time. Individuals in such areas must be considered, as Thomas Hobbes himself said, "to have no government at all and to live at this day in that brutish manner." Although this may seem to be the least persuasive of the elements belonging to the social contract, its parallel in relationships between politically constituted societies or states, that is to say, in the international state of nature, is perhaps the most useful and persistent. It seems still to command allegiance in the study of international relations. The actual process of agreeing ("contracting," "compacting," "covenanting") to end the state of nature and establish a state of society has been the subject of extensive analysis and elaboration by political and social theorists. Distinctions have been drawn, more precisely perhaps by academic commentators in modern times than by contractarian writers themselves, between a social contract and a governmental contract.

The social contract proper (*pactum societatis, pacte d'association, Gesellschaftsvertrag*) is thought of as bringing individuals together in society, and the governmental contract (*pactum subjectionis, pacte du gouvernement, Herrschaftsvertrag*) as establishing a formal government. As might be expected, the nature and form of the contract or contracts has been thought of in a variety of ways. In some systems the contract is a once-and-for-all, irrevocable act understood to have been performed in the remote past (Richard Hooker), but in others it appears as a continuing understanding that is perpetually being renewed and is regarded rather as a trust than as a contract (John Locke). The parties to the various contracts differ also: Sometimes agreements are made between individuals only, sometimes between individuals and governments or sovereigns, sometimes between a body of individuals acting as a fictitious person (*persona ficta*) and either the sovereign or a member of the body. In such ways as these a whole set and succession of interrelated contractual agreements have occasionally been presumed, as in the case of the seventeenth-century German political theorist Samuel Pufendorf and his followers in the eighteenth century.

The theory of a social contract belongs with the individualist attitude to state and society; indeed the simple conceptual model of agreement for the collectivity in all its possible shapes seems to inform the entire individualistic outlook. Contractual political theory is, therefore, universally associated with the rights of the individual person, with consent as the basis of government, and with democratic, republican, or constitutional institutions. It has also been regarded as a part of early capitalist individualism, and in Victorian England a great watershed was held to exist between a condition in which status ruled relationships and one in which contract ruled them. Notwithstanding this assumption, the social contract is perfectly reconcilable with the most absolute of despotic rule and with the complete negation of constitutionalism or the rule of law. Hobbes is the classic case here, for his two alternative accounts of how society and government came simultaneously into being are designed to tie every citizen to unquestioning obedience to a supreme, irresistible, indivisible sovereign whose dictates are the law. Benedict de Spinoza makes a rather similar use of contractual principles, but the political theory of Jean-Jacques Rousseau, although expounded in contractual form, has collectivist tendencies, since it endows political society with the capacity to make people moral. Rousseau's major political work, *Du Contrat social,* must be looked upon as the point of departure of the quite separate and traditionally quite irreconcilable outlook whose model is the theory of the general will.

EXPLANATORY VALUE

If the collectivity is understood as embodying agreement, it does not necessarily follow that any such agreement between parties ever actually took place in historical time. Nor does it follow that there may be people in the world still living in a prepolitical, precontractual situation or that those now within constituted society could ever revert to the nonpolitical condition. A contractarian political theory, therefore, can be entirely hypothetical, analyzing state and society as if agreement must always be presumed. Such an argument can provide a penetrating critique of existing arrangements and of their rationale: It can be used in a reformist direction, to suggest what ought to be the aims and ends of statesmen. No reversion to a literal state of nature need be implied by criticism of this kind, only that this or that action or abuse requires a remedy in accordance with the suggested criterion of an assumed agreement.

In this hypothetical form the contract theory is still of importance to political philosophy. It has recently been used by John Rawls in his articles "Justice as Fairness" and "Distributive Justice" to develop an account of justice alternative to the utilitarian (previously assumed to have outmoded contractarianism). Contemporary appreciations of the great contractarian writers (for example, by Howard Warrender, C. B. Macpherson, and A. G. Wernham), especially of Hobbes but also of Locke, Spinoza, and David Hume, and even of Rousseau, have tended to insist that the classic theories are hypothetical, which makes it possible to free the theories to a surprising extent from the lumber that had attached to them—the unacceptable histories of the human race, the fanciful anthropology and sociology. Moreover, the assumptions of natural law can thus be put aside.

NATURAL LAW

The reinterpretation of social contract theory is an important example of the way in which past political theory can enter into present theoretical analysis independently of chains of influence and continuous traditions. Still, the reinterpretation may lead to a serious distortion of the truth about the actual contents of contractarian treatises on politics. All the many members of the school of natural law, including those named above, did in fact assume that their contractual claims were literal as well as hypothetical. They all made dogmatic statements about the history of humanity and the condition of savages. Moreover all of them, though here writers like Hobbes and Hume are in special categories, subscribed to the general system of natural law in one form or another.

The concept of natural law provided the fixed and enduring framework within which the contract ending the state of nature could be concluded, and subsequent breaches or revisions of the contract could be related to the original act. Therefore, natural law had to be assumed if the contract was to be taken at all literally. The duty to keep promises, on which any contract rests, could hardly come into being with the contract itself, and this duty must persist should the contract be broken, if only to make a new one possible. When the Commons of England in January 1689 accused their former king, James II, of "breaking the original contract betwixt King and people," they did so in the secure belief that this was an offense that was and always would be punishable under natural law. It is understandable, then, that the history of the idea of a social contract has been largely the same as that of natural law itself.

HISTORY

The origins of social contract theory and of natural law can be sought in the Roman Stoicism of Cicero and in the system of Roman law. The development of social contract into a standard feature of the Western Christian attitude can be seen in the Middle Ages, and its apotheosis can be observed in the period between the Reformation and the eighteenth century. It is usual in fact to insist that the rise of the contractarian attitude to predominance in European political thought came about because of the Reformation. Certainly the justification of the right of a Protestant minority in a Catholic country, and of that of a Catholic minority in a Protestant country, to its own form of religious worship came about because of the gradual acceptance of contractarian notions by Reformation and post-Reformation political and legal thinkers and even by some politicians and sovereigns. The slow and hesitant growth of religious toleration would undoubtedly have been even more retarded if natural law and the social contract had not been at hand to provide a definition of the individual citizen, his individual rights, and the nature of his relationship to political authority. Accordingly, we find that the French religious wars of the 1560s, 1570s, and 1580s, together with the revolt of the Dutch against the throne of Spain, which began in 1568, brought about the elaboration of contractarian ideas. In both these cases embattled Calvinists were asserting their political as well as their religious rights against Catholic authorities, but in England at the same time it was the Catholics who needed contractarian justification for their rights, even finally their rights to resist government.

The *Monarchomachi* ("bearers of the sword against monarchs"), as the French writers were called, developed the contract between people and sovereign in various directions, and in the famous *Vindiciae Contra Tyrannos* (1579) it justified a recognizably revolutionary doctrine. In Holland the contract was codified further and became in the works of Johannes Althusius and Hugo Grotius an informing principle of political life as well as of the relations between sovereign and people. (Grotius's great work, however, the *De Jure Belli ac Pacis* of 1625, acquired and retains its fame because of its application of natural law and contractarian principles to international law.)

All these ideas and all these experiences—particularly the experience of religious separatism developing into civil war—can be seen at work in Hobbes, the most impressive of all contractarian theorists. In Hobbes's *Leviathan* (1651), the state of nature was a state of war, a propertyless anarchy brought to an end only by the contract of absolute submission. Hobbes made such devastating use of the destructive potentialities of the social contract in criticism of the conventional thinking about natural law that all succeeding systems can be looked upon to some extent as commentaries upon him. This is truest of Spinoza (*Tractatus Theologico-Politicus*, 1670; *Tractatus Politicus*, 1677) and until recently was thought to be true of Hobbes's eminent and enormously influential successor in England, Locke.

Locke's *Two Treatises of Government* (written 1679–1683, published 1689) are now known to have been written as an attack on Robert Filmer, not on Hobbes, and Locke's relatively peaceful and sociable state of nature, brought to an end by a very limited contract, has only a somewhat distant relationship with Hobbes's "war of all against all." It is interesting that Filmer should have been the most effective critic of the concept of a state of nature and of the possibility and relevance of contract and that his traditional, patriarchal authoritarianism was to a large extent immune from contractarian notions.

It was not traditionalism, however, which broke down contractarian assumptions within a generation of the death of Locke in 1704, but rather the rapid defeat of the natural law outlook by utilitarian criticism in England and by general will notions in France and elsewhere. Contract lost its persuasiveness as the rationalist outlook on the nature of law gave way to the historical outlook early in the nineteenth century. The development of observational anthropology and empirical sociology in more recent times makes it entirely unlikely that contract in anything but a strictly hypothetical form will ever be adopted again by political theorists.

This conventional account of the history of contract could be corrected and extended by reference to the simple model of the collectivity as agreement with which this entry began. This is so obvious an image that it can be found in some form in any political system, even in the refusal of Socrates to escape from his prison and avoid the poison on the ground that he owed obedience to his native city because of the benefits he had received as a citizen. It seems likely that every political theory must be contractual, at least to some degree, in this very wide sense.

Nevertheless, since contract proceeds by abstracting the individual from society, and then by reassembling individuals again as society although they are by definition asocial abstractions, the general contractual social and political scheme seems incurably faulty, quite apart from the empirical objections to it on the part of contemporary social scientists.

See also Althusius, Johannes; Cicero, Marcus Tullius; Filmer, Robert; General Will, The; Grotius, Hugo; Hobbes, Thomas; Hooker, Richard; Hume, David; Locke, John; Natural Law; Philosophy of Law, History of; Pufendorf, Samuel von; Rawls, John; Reformation; Rousseau, Jean-Jacques; Socrates; Spinoza, Benedict (Baruch) de; State; Stoicism.

Bibliography

The standard account in English is J. W. Gough, *The Social Contract* (1st ed., Oxford: Clarendon Press, 1936; rev. ed., 1957). Ernest Barker analyzes classical notions of contract very succinctly in a compilation he edited for the World's Classics series titled *Social Contract: Essays by Locke, Hume, and Rousseau* (New York: Oxford University Press, 1948); he has also translated the relevant part of Otto Gierke's monumental general treatise, *Das Deutsche Genossenschaftsrecht* (1913), as *Natural Law and the Theory of Society,* 2 vols. (Cambridge, U.K.: Cambridge University Press, 1934). In addition, see A. G. Wernham, ed., *Spinoza, Political Works* (Oxford: Clarendon Press, 1958); Peter Laslett, ed., *John Locke, Two Treatises of Government* (Cambridge, U.K.: Cambridge University Press, 1960); Howard Warrender, *Political Philosophy of Hobbes* (Oxford: Clarendon Press, 1957); and C. B. Macpherson, *Political Theory of Possessive Individualism: Hobbes to Locke* (Oxford: Clarendon Press, 1962).

More recent theoretical analyses of contract are Margaret Macdonald, "The Language of Political Theory," in *Logic and Language,* edited by Antony Flew, first series (Oxford, 1956), and the essays in the collection *Philosophy, Politics and Society,* edited by Peter Laslett and W. S. Runciman (Oxford: Blackwell, 1957–), especially those by John Rawls.

Peter Laslett (1967)

SOCIAL CONTRACT [ADDENDUM]

Contemporary social contract theory is practically identified with the work of John Rawls (1921–2002). In his best known book, *A Theory of Justice*, Rawls attempts to generalize and carry to a higher level of abstraction the social contract theory of Locke, Rousseau, and Kant. In Rawls's version of social contract theory, people are to select the principles of justice they are to live by in imagined ignorance of whether natural or social contingencies have worked in their favor. His theory requires that we should choose as though we were standing behind an imaginary "veil of ignorance" with respect to most particular facts about ourselves, anything that would bias our choice or stand in the way of unanimous agreement. Rawls calls this choice situation "the original position" because it is the position we should start from when determining what principles of justice we should live by. Rawls explicitly argues that the principles of justice that would be selected are significantly different from the classical or average principle of utility.

Almost immediately, there was a utilitarian challenge to Rawls's theory led by R.M. Hare (2003) and Richard Brandt (1972), which maintained that the theory had the same practical consequences as utilitarianism. Soon after, there was a libertarian challenge led by Robert Nozick (1974), which claimed that Rawls's theory conflicted with an ideal of liberty, and later a communitarian challenge led by Michael Sandel (1982) and Michael Walzer (1983) contended that the theory ignored the situatedness of human beings, along with an Aristotelian challenge led by Alistair MacIntyre (1981) which objected to Rawls's theory for denying the priority of the good.

There was also a feminist challenged led by Susan Okin (1989), who, among others, maintained that Rawls's theory was biased against women, and a multicultural challenge led by a diverse array of Western and non-Western philosophers who maintained that the theory was biased against non-Western cultures. Since Rawls was reluctant to respond directly to his critics, these challenges created opportunities for others to step in and respond to them or to suggest ways in which Rawls's work needed to be modified to address these criticisms.

There was also the important question of the practical implications of Rawls's work for how we should live our lives individually and collectively. Rawls had always claimed to be developing primarily an ideal moral theory. *A Theory of Justice* only touched briefly on nonideal theory to provide an account of civil disobedience. But the farther removed one's society is from ideally just institutions, the greater is the need to spell out the practical requirements of justice for one's time, lest one stand accused of legitimating existing unjust institutions and practices. By deciding to focus his work on ideal moral theory, Rawls created opportunities for others either to work out the practical implications of views developed in opposition or as a corrective to Rawls's view for the nonideal world in which we live.

Rawls's second book, *Political Liberalism*, was written to correct a fundamental problem that Rawls perceived in *A Theory of Justice*. Rawls believed that his earlier book assumed a relatively complete Kantian conception of the good. In *Political Liberalism*, Rawls tries to ground his same theory of justice on a more minimal foundation—an overlapping consensus of reasonable comprehensive conceptions of the good. According to Rawls, citizens are to conduct their fundamental discussions within a framework of a conception of justice that everyone, irrespective of one's particular comprehensive conceptions of the good, could be reasonably expected to endorse. An important implication of Rawls's view is that religious considerations are generally excluded from public debate over fundamental issues in society. This feature of Rawls's view has engendered considerable debate, not only among philosophers, but also among theologians, political scientists, and lawyers, but it has not had any discernible effect on public policy, at least in the United States, where religious considerations continue to have an impact on public policy beyond anything that could be justified by a reasonable overlapping consensus.

Rawls's third major book, *The Law of Peoples*, attempts to extend his theory of justice to the international realm. Rejecting any straightforward application of his principles of justice to the international realm, Rawls favors more minimal obligations to other peoples. According to Rawls, there is virtually "no society anywhere in the world … with resources so scarce that it could not, were it reasonably organized and governed, become well-ordered." Rawls also allows for exceptions to international principles of justice, specifically a requirement of noncombatant immunity, in order to attain "some substantial good." At the same time he disallows any comparable exceptions to intersocietal principles of justice. Here again, Rawls's views have given rise to a wide-ranging discussion over possible exceptions to principles of justice, which has become even more important given the connection that exists between terrorisim and international justice.

Bibliography

Brandt, Richard. "Utilitarianism and the Rules of War." *Philosophy and Public Affairs*, 1 (1972) 145–165.

Hare, R. M. "Justice and Equality." In *Justice: Alternative Political Perspectives*, edited by James P. Sterba. 4th ed. Belmont: Wadsworth, 2003.

MacIntyre, Alasdair. *After Virtue*. Notre Dame: University of Notre Dame Press, 1981.

Nozick, Robert *Anarchy, State and Utopia*. New York: Basic Books, 1974.

Okin, Susan Moller. *Justice, Gender, and the Family*. New York: Basic Books, 1989.

Rawls, John. *Justice as Fairness: A Restatement*. Cambridge, MA: Harvard University Press, 2001.

Rawls, John. *The Law of Peoples*. Cambridge. MA: Harvard University Press, 1999.

Rawls, John. *Political Liberalism*. New York: Columbia University Press, 1993.

Rawls, John. *A Theory of Justice*. Cambridge, MA: Harvard University Press, 1971.

Sandel, Michael. *Liberalism and the Limits of Justice*. New York: Cambridge University Press, 1982.

Sterba, James P. *How to Make People Just*. Lanham: Rowman & Littlefield, 1988.

Walzer, Michael. *Spheres of Justice*. New York: Basic Books, 1983.

James P. Sterba (2005)

SOCIAL EPISTEMOLOGY

Since the early 1980s, social epistemology has become an important field in Anglo-American philosophy. It encompasses a wide variety of approaches, all of which regard the investigation of social aspects of inquiry to be relevant to discussions of justification and knowledge. The approaches range from the conservative acknowledgment that individual thinkers are aided by others in their pursuits of truth to the radical view that both the goals of inquiry and the manner in which those goals are attained are profoundly social.

Individualistic rather than social epistemologies have dominated philosophical discourse since at least the time of Descartes. The writings of Mill, Peirce, Marx, Dewey, and Wittgenstein, which began to develop social epistemologies, are among a few exceptions to individualistic approaches. They had little effect on epistemological work at the time they were published. Even the move to naturalism, taken by many epistemologists after W. V. Quine's polemics in its favor, persisted—quite unnecessarily—in individualistic assumptions about the nature of knowledge and justification. Quine argued in "Epistemology Naturalized" that epistemologists should attend to actual, rather than ideal, conditions of production of knowledge but he concluded that "epistemology … falls into place as a chapter of psychology," ignoring the sociology of knowledge altogether.

Movements outside of epistemology motivated and cleared the way for social epistemology. First and most important, the proliferation of interdisciplinary research on social aspects of scientific change following the publication of Kuhn's *The Structure of Scientific Revolutions* pressured naturalistic epistemologists to take sociology of knowledge seriously. In particular, the skeptical and relativistic conclusions of sociologists and anthropologists of science—among them Barry Barnes, David Bloor, Steven Shapin, Simon Schaffer, Bruno Latour, Steve Woolgar, Harry Collins, Karin Knorr-Cetina, and Andrew Pickering—moved naturalistic epistemologists of science—including Ronald Giere, Larry Laudan, Philip Kitcher, and Paul Thagard—to take social accounts of scientific change seriously yet to draw their own epistemic conclusions. Second, influential work during the late 1970s in the philosophy of language and philosophy of mind—core fields of philosophy—by Hilary Putnam, Tyler Burge, and others eschewed individualism and began producing social accounts. A more general openness to social approaches in philosophy followed.

RANGE OF SOCIAL EPISTEMOLOGIES

Social epistemologies vary along several dimensions. First, they may emphasize either the *procedures* or the *goals* of inquiry. Whether the emphasis is on procedures or goals, the range here is as large as the range in epistemology as a whole: from consensus practices to critical engagement to truth to pragmatic success to socially constituted goals. Second, attempts to follow the procedures or attain the goals are evaluated for different units of inquiry. Some social epistemologists evaluate the attempts of individual human beings, assessing the influence of social processes on individual reasoning and decision making. Others evaluate the aggregate efforts of groups of people who may work together or separately.

Social epistemologies also tend to investigate particular domains and/or to work at particular levels of generality. Many (for example, Giere, David Hull, Kitcher, Helen Longino, Miriam Solomon, and Thagard) are social epistemologists of science rather than of ordinary knowledge or some other area of specialized knowledge. Feminist epistemologists (for example, Donna Haraway, Lynn Hankinson Nelson, and Naomi Scheman) look at the gender-relatedness of methodologies or assumptions in several fields, not only those explicitly dealing with sex or sex roles. Alvin Goldman (1992, 1999, 2002) works in the widest range of domains—from science to law to education to politics—and moves from the most general considerations of epistemics (in which he argues that truth is the ultimate epistemic goal) to the most concrete practical considerations (in which, for example, he argues that the common-law system is veritistically inferior to the Continental civil law system). Many social epistemologists work primarily at the general (abstract) level in their studies of areas such as testimony (Coady 1992), trust (Hardwig 1991), and knowledge (Kusch 2002).

Two journals are devoted to publishing material in social epistemology, *Social Epistemology* (1986–) and *Episteme* (2004–); many other journals publish special issues and individual articles in the area.

PROCEDURES OR GOALS OF INQUIRY

Longino's normative approach is to evaluate the procedures of a knowledge community. Her "critical contextual empiricism" (2002) evaluates four features of the knowledge community: the "tempered" equality of intellectual authority (equality moderated by deference for expertise), presence of forums for criticism, some shared norms (including empirical success in a scientific community), and responsiveness to criticism. Normative judgments will be of epistemic communities rather than of individuals and will be positive for communities following the appropriate procedures, irrespective of outcome.

Goldman, Kitcher, and Hilary Kornblith all take truth (or significant truth) to be the central goal of all kinds of inquiry. They assess various social processes and practices for their conduciveness to truth attainment. For example, Goldman (1992) shows that in some situations, such as some legal contexts, groups reach the truth more reliably when some true information is deliberately withheld from them—for example, misleading prejudicial information. So Goldman concludes that social epistemologists need to think about communication control, for paternalistic epistemic reasons. Goldman (1992, 1999) and Kitcher (1993) explore the consequences of intellectual rivalry and credit seeking in science. They both conclude that rivalry and credit seeking can lead scientists to distribute their cognitive effort well over the available research approaches, coming to a veritistic conclusion more quickly than they otherwise would. Kornblith (in Schmitt 1994) argues that the widespread practice of deference to experts may be reliable in one social setting and unreliable in another, depending on the institutions through which a society confers the title of "expert."

Some hold that, although truth is the ultimate epistemic goal, it is mediated by coherence of belief. They examine social processes for their conduciveness to coherence. For example, Keith Lehrer (1990) argues that individual reasoning yields more coherent belief if it makes use of all the information residing in a community; Thagard (1993) argues that delays in the transmission of information across a community can be conducive to a good distribution of cognitive labor and thereby eventually to maximal explanatory coherence and truth.

Although most social epistemologists who employ normative goals regard truth as the most important epistemic goal, there is a range of other, less traditional, positions. Giere (1988), for example, claims that the goal of scientific inquiry is theories that model the world rather than directly correspond to it and that social practices such as credit seeking should be assessed for their conduciveness to producing good models. Solomon (2001) argues that scientific theories aim for empirical success. Steve Fuller (2002) writes of a range of epistemic goals espoused by scientific communities and argues that those goals should themselves be debated by scientists.

The most radical position on epistemic goals is one that claims that our social epistemic practices *construct* truths rather than discover them and, furthermore, negotiate the goals of inquiry rather than set them in some nonarbitrary manner. Work in the "strong program" in sociology of science during the 1970s and 1980s—notably by Barnes and Bloor, Latour and Woolgar, Shapin and Schaffer, Latour and Woolgar, and Collins and Trevor Pinch—was frequently guided by such social constructivism. (Recent work in the sociology of science is usually more philosophically sophisticated: See, for example, Shapin [1994].) Most contemporary social epistemologists in the Anglo-American philosophical tradition are motivated by their disagreement with the social constructivist tradition, and they argue for the less radical positions just described.

THE DISTRIBUTION OF COGNITIVE LABOR

The distribution of cognitive labor is a common theme in social epistemology and is a link between social epistemology and evolutionary epistemology. It is wasteful to duplicate the efforts of others, beyond the minimum required to check robustness of results. It is most efficient to have different individuals or research groups pursue different avenues of inquiry, especially when, as is usually the case, there is more than one promising direction to follow. Hull (1988), following the founder of evolutionary epistemology, Donald Campbell, was one of the first to apply this idea in the social epistemology of science, where he argued that new theories are like new organisms—produced by random variation on past theories—where only the fittest survive. And there is no way of knowing in advance which theory will be the fittest.

Others have also given accounts of how cognitive labor is distributed, although they have not emphasized the evolutionary analogy. Kitcher (1993) and Goldman (1992, 1999) have argued that the desire for credit leads to an effective division of cognitive labor; Thagard (1993) has argued that the same result is achieved by delays in dissemination of information; Giere (1988) thinks that interests and variation in cognitive resources distribute research effort; Solomon (2001) has argued that cognitive biases such as salience, availability, and representativeness can result in effective distribution of belief and thereby of research effort. (Not all these stories are, of course, true; some combination of them may be.) For all of the aforementioned thinkers, it is the *distribution* of cognitive labor across a community that is epistemically valuable rather than the decisions of any particular individual.

Cognitive labor can be divided not only for discovery and development of new ideas but also for storage of facts, theories, and techniques that are widely accepted. Just as books contain information that no individual could retain, information is also stored in communities in ways that are accessible to most or all members of that community but could not be duplicated within each head. One important way in which this is brought about is when people with expertise on different subjects—or with different experiences or techniques—increase the knowledge within a community. Knowledge and expertise is thus socially distributed. Edwin Hutchins's account of navigation (1995), in which skills and knowledge are distributed across the officers and enlisted men on board a naval vessel, is an example of this process.

A final way in which cognitive labor can be distributed is for the process of coming to consensus. In traditional philosophies of science, consensus is presented as the outcome of the identical decision of each member of a scientific community: A good consensus is the result of each scientist choosing the best theory through the same process, and a bad consensus is the result of each scientist choosing the wrong theory through the same inappropriate process. Of course, this is just the simplest model of group consensus formation, and it presumes the same starting point, the same endpoint, and the same processes of change. The only time that the members of the group may differ is during the period of dissent, when, as Hull (1998, p. 521) would say, a thousand theories may bloom. Giere, Hull, Kitcher, and others would also say that, when coming to consensus, each scientist picks the same theory for the same overriding good reasons. Other accounts of consensus formation in which cognitive labor is distributed include that of Hussein Sarkar (1983), who finds that different scientists may select the same theory for different good reasons, and Solomon (2001), who finds that, although individual scientists may make biased and idiosyncratic decisions, there is a social perspective from which to evaluate the overall normativity of the decisions.

THE UNITS OF INQUIRY

Who knows? And who is justified in his or her knowledge? Nelson (1990) argues provocatively that only societies can really know. Some social epistemologists consider the outcomes of social epistemic processes for individuals and some for communities. The most conservative social epistemologies look only at the effects of social processes on individual reasoning and knowledge. For example, Kornblith (in Schmitt 1994) looks at those circumstances under which one scientist can judge that it is reasonable to rely on the expertise of another scientist. Coady's work on the role of testimony (1992) argues that individuals are typically justified in relying on the word of others. The claim is that individual human beings reason better when placed in favorable epistemic social situations. Epistemic terms such as "knows" and "is justified" are applied to individual human beings.

More radically, social groups can be understood as having emergent epistemic qualities that are due to something other than the epistemic properties of their members. Gilbert (1989) argues that group knowledge need have no coincidences with the knowledge ascribed to individual members of the group. Longino (1990, 2002) presents four conditions for objective knowledge that are satisfied by (some) knowledge societies rather than by individuals: tempered equality of intellectual authority, forums for criticism, responsiveness to criticism, and some shared values of inquiry. Nelson (1990) argues that communities set the standards of evidence and are the primary knowers. Kusch's "communitarian epistemology" (2002) argues for a similar conclusion through a performative analysis of testimony. Goldman (1999) shows that some kinds of social organization (for example, that of the American justice system) lead to poorer results than other kinds (for example, the Continental justice system). Schmitt (1994) argues that group justificatory processes can achieve, through interactions, more than the sum of individual justifications. Solomon (2001) shows that differently organized scientific communities make better and worse scientific decisions.

CONCLUSION

It is not surprising to find that the wide variety of social epistemologiesis connected to work in other disciplines. Economics, artificial intelligence (especially distributed computation), race and gender studies, sociology of science, anthropology, and European philosophical traditions (for example, Foucault and Habermas) are frequently cited, either for the data or for the methodologies that they supply.

When epistemologies are deeply social, recommendations for inquiry will often be applicable to communities or institutions rather than to individuals. Social epistemologists, especially those who are both naturalistic and applied, have begun to spell out these recommendations. The traditional focus on individual epistemic responsibility is being transformed by the addition of new, socially informed directions of inquiry.

See also Descartes, René; Dewey, John; Epistemology, History of; Foucault, Michel; Goldman, Alvin; Habermas, Jürgen; Kuhn, Thomas; Marx, Karl; Mill, John Stuart; Peirce, Charles Sanders; Putnam, Hilary; Quine, Willard Van Orman; Subjectivist Epistemology; Wittgenstein, Ludwig Josef Johann.

Bibliography

Coady, C. A. J. *Testimony: A Philosophical Study*. Oxford: Oxford University Press, 1992

Fuller, Steve. *Social Epistemology*. 2nd ed. Bloomington: Indiana University Press, 2002.

Giere, Ronald. *Explaining Science: A Cognitive Approach*. Chicago: University of Chicago Press, 1988.

Gilbert, Margaret. *On Social Facts*. London: Routledge, 1989.

Goldman, Alvin I. *Knowledge in a Social World*. New York: Oxford University Press, 1999.

Goldman, Alvin I. *Liaisons: Philosophy Meets the Cognitive and Social Sciences*. Cambridge, MA: MIT Press, 1992.

Goldman, Alvin I. *Pathways to Knowledge*. New York: Oxford University Press, 2002.

Haraway, Donna. *Simians, Cyborgs, and Women: The Reinvention of Nature*. New York: Routledge, 1991.

Hardwig, John. "The Role of Trust in Knowledge." *Journal of Philosophy* 88 (1991): 693–704.

Hull, David. *Science as a Process: An Evolutionary Account of the Social and Conceptual Development of Science*. Chicago: University of Chicago Press, 1988.

Hutchins, Edwin. *Cognition in the Wild*. Cambridge, MA: MIT Press, 1995.

Kitcher, P. *The Advancement of Science*. New York: Oxford University Press, 1993.

Kusch, Martin. *Knowledge by Agreement: The Programme of Communitarian Epistemology*. Oxford: Oxford University Press, 2002.

Lehrer, Keith, *Theory of Knowledge*. Boulder, CO: Westview Press, 1990.

Longino, Helen E. *The Fate of Knowledge*. Princeton, NJ: Princeton University Press, 2002.

Longino, Helen E. *Science as Social Knowledge: Values and Objectivity in Scientific Inquiry*. Princeton, NJ: Princeton University Press, 1990.

Nelson, Lynn Hankinson. *Who Knows: From Quine to a Feminist Empiricism*. Philadelphia, PA: Temple University Press, 1990.

Sarkar, Hussein. *A Theory of Method*. Berkeley and Los Angeles: University of California Press, 1983.

Scheman, Naomi. *Engenderings: Constructions of Knowledge, Authority, and Privilege*. New York: Routledge, 1993.

Schmitt, Fred, ed. *Socializing Epistemology*. Lanham, MD: Rowman and Littlefield, 1994.

Shapin, Steven. *A Social History of Truth: Civility and Science in Seventeenth-Century England*. Chicago and London: The University of Chicago Press, 1994.

Solomon, Miriam. *Social Empiricism*. Cambridge, MA: MIT Press, 2001.

Thagard, Paul. "Collaborative Knowledge." *Nous* 31 (1997): 242–261.

Thagard, Paul. "Societies of Minds: Science as Distributed Computing." *Studies in the History and Philosophy of Science* (1993): 49–67.

Miriam Solomon (1996, 2005)

SOCIALISM

This entry is concerned with "socialism" from the time at which, so far as anyone knows, the word was first used in print to describe a view of what human society should be like. This was in 1827, in the English *Co-operative Magazine,* a periodical aimed at expounding and furthering the views of Robert Owen of New Lanark, generally regarded as the father and founder of the cooperative movement. (Owenite cooperation, incidentally, was an institution different from, and far more idealistic than, the distributive stores which in the Victorian age took over the name.) Some historians have traced the ancestry of socialism much further back: For example, to primitive communist societies, to the Jesuits of Paraguay, to the ideal communities described by Thomas More and others, to the Diggers of Cromwell's army, and even to Plato's *Republic.* Although there are elements of socialism to be found in all these, particularly in More's *Utopia,* the scope of this article is limited to socialism in modern times and to the sense in which the word is normally used, omitting both distant possible origins and, of course, bastard movements such as the National Socialism (Nazism) of twentieth-century Germany and Austria which, save for the bare fact that they enforced central control of social policy, had nothing of socialism in them.

ORIGIN OF SOCIALISM

The seedbed of socialism, as of so much else in modern thought, was the French Revolution and the revolutionary French thinkers who preceded it—Voltaire, Jean-Jacques Rousseau, and the Encyclopedists. Rousseau was no socialist, but from his cornucopia of seminal though sometimes unclear and inconsistent thought socialists drew the ideas of people born free but everywhere in chains, of a "general will" making for perfection in society, of the importance of education, and a host of others. From the Encyclopedists they learned to question all institutions in the light of reason and justice, and even from "Gracchus" Babeuf to demand equality for the downtrodden and to seek it by means of dedicated conspirators. Owen himself was no revolutionary; insofar as his ideas can be traced to anyone but himself, they probably came from early reading of the William Godwin who wrote *Political Justice*; Owen envisaged a society consisting of small, self-governing, cooperating communities, established by the free and rational consent of all, of whatever class or station. Originally, the word *socialism* appears to have laid particular emphasis on communal cooperation in contrast to the more-or-less liberalism that was coming to be the creed of the industrial revolution—hence Owen's rather contemptuous dismissal of Jeremy Bentham and the utilitarians. The idea of socialism came rapidly to fit the aspirations of the working classes and their radical champions not only in its country of origin but far beyond it.

SOCIALIST TENETS

Since its beginnings in the early 1800s, a period that has seen vast changes not merely in the industrial and political organization of society but also in people's minds, their modes of thought, and their interpretation both of themselves and of what they have seen around them, "socialism" has naturally borne many meanings, and dozens of views have been held and expressed about the form of society that socialists hope to see and about the means by which it should be attained and secured. Long before Karl Marx and Friedrich Engels introduced the great schism between what they called utopian and scientific socialism, there were wide differences of opinion; and the differences are no less wide today. George Bernard Shaw, for example, in *The Intelligent Woman's Guide to Socialism and Capitalism,* laid down absolute equality of money incomes as a sine qua non—a dictum accepted by few of his fellow socialists, and not by Shaw himself in any practical sense. There are many other definitions that could be quoted. Nevertheless, the word is certainly not meaningless. It describes a living thing that grows and changes as it lives; and it is possible to discern certain beliefs that are fundamental to all who can be called socialists, as well as to note the divergences in what may be called secondary beliefs and to relate these, in part at least, to the conditions of the time.

CRITIQUE OF EXISTING SOCIETY. The first of the fundamental beliefs of socialists is that the existing system of society and its institutions should be condemned as unjust, as morally unsound. The institutions that are thus condemned vary from time to time and from place to place according to circumstances, the greatest stress being laid sometimes on landlordism, sometimes on factory industry, on the churches, the law, or the political government, or a combination of these (as William Cobbett, in an earlier century, denounced "The Thing"), depending on what seems to be the most potent engine or engines of oppression. This condemnation may be associated with the values of revealed religion, as in the case of the various forms of Christian socialism, or may positively repudiate those values, as Marx did; in either case the emphasis is on injustice. Pierre-Joseph Proudhon's dictum, "Property is theft," expresses this condemnation most concisely.

Many socialist movements, such as the Saint-Simonians in the 1830s and the Fabians half a century later, attacked the existing system for its economic and social inefficiency as well; but this criticism was less fundamental. Socialists such as François Marie Charles Fourier in France and William Morris in England laid much more stress on freedom, happiness, and beauty than on material wealth. Even the economists among them, however, long asserted that granted decent (that is, socialist) distribution of the product of industry and agriculture, there would easily be "enough to go round" and to provide everyone with a standard of living recognized to be reasonable. By the mid-twentieth century the enormous multiplication of potential demand, coupled with realization of the existence of hundreds of millions living far below European standards of life, had referred that type of prophecy to the far-distant future.

A NEW AND BETTER SOCIETY. The second fundamental of socialism is the belief that there can be created a different form of society with different institutions, based on moral values, which will tend to improve humankind instead of, as now, to corrupt it. Since it is living men who are to create the new institutions—men who must, therefore, recognize and follow the appeal of moral value—this belief is in effect an assertion of the perfectibility, or at least near-perfectibility, of man. It was most dogmatically stated by Owen, in books such as *A New View of Society*; and the history of socialism shows that it can survive innumerable disappointments. It is not the same as a belief in "progress," which has been held by many who were not socialists; it is more like *Magna est veritas et praevalebit* ("The truth is great and will prevail")—truth being here equated with justice.

Does justice, in social institutions, imply equality? Does it also imply democracy? For socialists, the answer to both these questions has generally been positive but the answer has not been absolute. Equality of rights—yes; equality before the law—yes, again. We have already observed, however, that complete equality of income was not a universal socialist tenet; and from the very earliest days there were sharp differences among socialists on the relationship between work and income. On the dictum "From each according to his ability" they more or less agreed. But some added "to each according to his needs"; others countered with "to each according to his effort—or his product." This debate, in which sides were taken, on the whole, in accordance with the temperament and/or environment of the individual and in which many intermediate positions were adopted, remained unresolved throughout the history of socialism—not surprisingly, since the problem of controlling the level of incomes has defeated all except completely static societies. On the question of democracy, again, the great majority of socialists have been democrats in the ordinarily accepted sense of the word. But some rejected any formal democratic process in favor of a communal consensus resembling the Quaker "sense of the meeting" (or Rousseau's general will). Owen, in practice, was an autocratic egalitarian; and post-Marxist socialism has evolved a procedure known as democratic centralism, which bears little relation to what any pre-Marxist would recognize as democracy.

Deep differences arose early on the kind of institution which would be best suited for a world devoted to justice. There was one main difference at first: Some put their faith in small communities of neighbors, as far as possible self-sufficient, cooperating freely with other similar communities in such functions as exchange of goods, and relying to the minimum on any regional or central authority for such necessities as defense and the supply of credit; others looked rather to a development of science, technology, and large-scale industrial production and banking to increase rapidly the supply of material goods and thereby the prosperity of a socialist economy through centralized planning techniques. Of these two schools—whose views have necessarily been greatly simplified for the compass of this article—the first, or "utopian," is best known from the writings of Owen, Fourier, and Proudhon, and the second, or "scientific," from those of the Comte de Saint-Simon and his followers. The first clearly derived from rural society: Owen's villages of cooperation and Fourier's phalansteries were based upon small-scale agriculture, with such industrial and craft production as could conveniently be carried on in villages or small communities. This was the kind of society envisaged, much later, in William Morris's *News from Nowhere*; and much later still, there were curious echoes of it in V. I. Lenin's dreams of cheap electricity transforming the life of the Russian peasantry and even in the Chinese "great leap forward," with a piece of factory in every backyard.

The weakness of this school is that its fear of size, of external authority, and of the apparatus of the state and of central government, whatever concessions it may in theory make to "natural necessities," such as the conduct of a national railway system, are liable to lead in practice as well as in theory to anarchism and the repudiation of any government at all—which in the modern world means chaos. The second school, that of large-scale production and planning, was, from the beginning, in harmony with the way the world was tending. Its dangers are today only too obvious, and the recurrent malaise of large-scale industry in times of prosperity, the demands for "shares in control," and the like, show the vacuum created by the nonfulfillment of the utopian ideals of a just society.

REVOLUTION. Whatever form of institution the several schools of socialism envisaged for the future, all agreed that what was required was a fundamental transformation of society amounting to revolution, a program of action to effect such a transformation, and a revolutionary will so to transform it existing in the members of present-day society. This is the third fundamental socialist assumption; how it is to be put into effect has been the subject of much division of opinion. As socialism was generally believed to have a strong rational basis, it was natural that all schools of socialists should set great store by education, persuasion, and propaganda; Owen, indeed, carried the trust in rationality so far that he could not believe that anyone, whatever his condition or his preconceived opinions, could fail to be converted by "Mr. Owen's powers of persuasion," if only Mr. Owen could employ them sufficiently often and at sufficient length. Others, less confident, sought to achieve their end by preaching to and working upon groups already conditioned by the circumstances of their working lives to accept the whole or a part of the socialist gospel—the most obvious of these being, of course, the trade unions and other organizations of the working class. In this spirit Marx looked upon the British trade unions that supported the International Working Men's Association (the "First International") as "a lever for the proletarian revolution." Strikes, threats of strikes, and other forms of what much later came to be known as "direct action," supplemented persuasion by inducing the ruling classes to make concessions which could not otherwise have been wrung from them.

The practicability, either of persuasion or of group action, depended very largely on the political conditions of time and place. And although there was a running argument between gradualists, who believed that revolutionary change could be brought about peacefully and piecemeal, and revolutionaries, who thought head-on collision between the holders of power and their victims was inevitable in the long run if not immediately, the difference was not as absolute as was often supposed. In Britain, after the defeat of Chartism had registered the end of insurrectionism in any form, after the press had been freed and the franchise widened, the organizations of the working class leaned to peaceful evolution far more than to violence—the "inevitability of gradualism" was an accepted belief long before Sidney Webb put it into words in the 1920s. In tsarist Russia, at the other extreme, a generally authoritarian government, operating a police state, appeared to bar the door to anything but physical revolution. There were many possible in-between positions; and the role of the convinced individual socialist varied similarly, from that of open persuader, adviser, and organizer, like Keir Hardie at the end of the nineteenth century, to that of secret conspirator, like Auguste Blanqui in France after 1848 and organizers of communist cells in the twentieth century.

INTERNATIONALISM. One other characteristic should briefly be mentioned. Socialism was initially a world philosophy, not concerning itself with race or nation, not advocating the brotherhood of man so much as assuming it. The opening of the *Communist Manifesto,* "Workers of the world, unite," crystallized this into words; the nationalism of Poles, Irish, Italians, Hungarians, was only an aspect of the struggle against corrupt institutions. Later, of course, nationalism grew so strong that it clashed, sometimes violently, with other fundamentals of socialism; nevertheless, the idea remained potent for generations, and it may still be suggested that socialist movements that have become exclusively nationalist have ceased to be socialist at all.

MARXIAN SOCIALISM

The *Communist Manifesto* marks a great divide between pre-Marxian and post-Marxian socialism. Marx and Engels dismissed all their predecessors as utopians and formulated a system of socialism that they claimed was "scientific." There is no room here to expound Marxist philosophy or Marxist economics; but it must be pointed out that neither "utopian" nor "scientific" is an accurate description. Marxist socialism accepted the fundamentals as set out above; it differed from most of its forerunners in that it did not, save in a few very vague allusions, seek to describe the new, uncorrupt institutions that would appear after the revolution; it assumed—and what could be more utopian?—that after the proletariat had conquered, it would make all anew and "the government of man be replaced by the administration of things."

"Scientific," in Marxist language, meant not so much acceptance of technology and large-scale production—although this was included—as the proving, by logical argument and study of history, of two quite simple propositions: First, that under the existing capitalist system, the proletariat, the laboring class, is systematically and continuously robbed of its just share of the fruits of production; second, that "changes in the modes of production and exchange," and not any other factor, such as "man's insight into eternal truth and justice," are leading inevitably to a reversal of the system that will remove the bourgeois capitalist class from the seats of power and replace it by the organs of the proletariat. This is the base on which the whole enormous superstructure of Marxism is founded; it is not science, but messianic prophecy. It is easy to understand, however, the compelling effect that this fundamentally simple appeal had to the downtrodden at various times and in various places. At the same time, Marx's powerful and penetrating analysis, which discredited a great deal of current economic and historical theory, profoundly attracted many of the best brains among those who were dissatisfied with the human results of the existing system, and the teaching of the Marxists that morality in action was relative to the needs of the time, even if slightly inconsistent with their denunciation, on grounds of injustice, of slavery and wage slavery, gave their followers both the inspiration of those who were fighting a continuing battle and the sanction to use any and every method that could advance their cause. Marx did not invent the conception of classes, but Marxists fought the class war.

The work of Marx and Engels has had as great and lasting an effect on the thinking of non-Marxists, particularly after the Russian Revolution, as has that of Sigmund Freud on non-Freudians. This entry cannot deal with the developments in socialist thought, Marxist or non-Marxist, in the post-Marxian era. These are of enormous importance for the study of history and present-day politics; but they are concerned principally with method and strategy. The fundamental tenets of socialism as a view of society have remained substantially unaltered, although the process of translating them has been far more lengthy and complicated than the nineteenth century ever foresaw.

See also Anarchism; Bentham, Jeremy; Communism; Encyclopédie; Engels, Friedrich; Fourier, François Marie Charles; Freud, Sigmund; Godwin, William; Justice; Lenin, Vladimir Il'ich; Marx, Karl; Marxist Philosophy; More, Thomas; Plato; Proudhon, Pierre-Joseph; Rousseau, Jean-Jacques; Saint-Simon, Claude-Henri de Rouvroy, Comte de; Utilitarianism; Voltaire, François-Marie Arouet de.

Bibliography

By far the most complete work on socialism is G. D. H. Cole, *History of Socialist Thought.* 7 vols. (London, 1953–1960), last volume published posthumously. Each volume except the last has a full bibliography for every chapter.

Earlier books are Max Beer, *History of British Socialism* (London: G. Bell, 1929); Édouard Dolléans, *Histoire du mouvement ouvrier,* 2 vols. (Paris: A. Colin, 1936–1939); Sir Alexander Gray, *The Socialist Tradition: Moses to Lenin* (London: Longmans, Green, 1946); Élie Halévy, *Histoire du socialisme européen* (Paris: Gallimard, 1948); Thomas Kirkup, *History of Socialism,* rev. ed. by E. R. Pease (London: A. and C. Black, 1913); H. W. Laidler, *Social Economic Movements* (New York: Thomas Y. Crowell, 1944), first issued as *History of Socialist Thought* (New York: Thomas Y. Crowell, 1927); and Paul Louis, *Histoire du socialisme en France,* rev. ed. (Paris, 1950).

For documents, see Raymond Postgate, *Revolution from 1789 to 1906,* reissued, with a new introduction (Gloucester, MA: P. Smith, 1969).

Margaret Cole (1967)

SOCIALISM [ADDENDUM]

Socialism has seen enormous changes since the above entry was written. Its cachet has gone up and down and, after an all-time low during the early 1990s, is now perhaps going to go up again. The socialist ideal fell on hard times when "actually existing socialism" collapsed in the Soviet Union and its satellite states in 1989 and somewhat later in Yugoslavia. The headlong rush of China towards free-market development has further deepened the crisis of contemporary socialism. Only Cuba, North Korea, and perhaps Vietnam and Laos remain as "actually existing socialisms."

There have been similar upheavals in socialist theory. Most Western socialists, including most Marxists, while not being cold warriors, did not regard these "actually existing socialisms" as genuinely socialist but as statist noncapitalist societies that were authoritarian, nondemocratic and excessively bureaucratic regimes parading as paradigms of socialist societies. Instead of the dictatorship *of* the proletariat (what was supposed to be the mass but democratic governing of the working class by the working class in the interim before "the withering away of the state" and the attaining of a classless society), there were what anarchist socialists (most notably Mikhail Bakunin) called the dictatorship *over* the proletariat, namely the rule over the proletariat by a small elite calling themselves communists.

Among most Western socialist theoreticians something like the following view became prevalent: The Soviet Union was not even a flawed socialism but an authoritarian statist postcapitalist society that had betrayed many of the most fundamental beliefs of socialism. Others, including Noam Chomsky, denied that it even had a somewhat progressive "postcapitalist" character at all, but actually the Soviet Union became a form of state capitalism; this latter claim is disputable as it is not for contemporary China. But state capitalist or postcapitalist, it became an authoritarian cumbersomely bureaucratic regime that betrayed many of the ideals of socialism. Both sorts of socialist intellectuals sought to reinvigorate socialist though and to help create a way to reinvigorate socialist practice. For them, in a standard sense of the word *democratic*, the term "democratic socialism" was a pleonasm.

In light of these historical realities, what it is to be a socialist has become more ambiguous than it was at the high tide of Marxism. Andrew Levine has well used "socialism" to designate those political tendencies and movements that, since the beginning of the nineteenth century, sought to deepen what the most radical of the French revolutionists began. Like the liberals, their tamer confreres on the Left, socialists always have been steadfast in their dedication to "liberty, equality, and fraternity." But, like their revolutionary forebears—and unlike liberals—they have usually favored radical, structural transformations, at least in principle. This broad characterization allows us to regard the more radical social democrats (for example, Jürgen Habermas), some anarchists (for example, Noam Chomsky), and Orthodox Marxists (for example, Bertell Ollman) as all socialists. Whether there is a spectrum here or some fundamental cleavage is a much debated matter.

The more Orthodox Marxists would take it to be axiomatic that a socialist of any sort is someone who favors public or social ownership, and at least indirect control, of at least the principal means of production. In such a society there would be no one because of this public and shared ownership who *simply* has to sell his or her labor. Public ownership in different forms of socialism can mean different things. For some it has meant state ownership and for others various schemes of worker ownership and control. For some social democrats socialism has meant a mixed-economy containing small-scale private ownership of the means of production but with larger-scale ownership being firmly public. Others would move so far from traditional conceptions of socialism as to not identify socialism necessarily with a distinctive form of ownership at all but with radical democracy and a thoroughly egalitarian-solidaristic conception of justice.

Some orthodox socialists would not regard a mixed economy at all; nor would they regard as socialist normative conceptions of socialism that identify it with radical democracy and egalitarian-solidaristic justice. They would classify the latter as social democratic and not genuinely socialist at all. A socialist society, on this view, must be a society without capitalism (or at least on the way to abolishing it). It would be a society in which everyone is either a worker, a potential worker (children), a former worker or person incapable of work (such as the retired or disabled), or someone soon destined to become a worker in a social order in transition to a classless society. Many Marxists believe that such a development would have to be global to be sustained.

Others would respond that contemporary society has too many strata doing various kinds of work to make "worker" a very useful category or class analysis the trenchant critical took that Marxists took it to be. Others insist on the centrality of a class analysis while arguing that in contemporary society classes have become more ramified than in Marx's time (Wright 1989).

Although the foregoing characterizations of socialism are matters of definition, they are not simply that. Each vision of a socialist future bears different implications for social policy and for the society and the world as a whole. At the far end of the social democratic spectrum capitalism would remain in place, but with much of its power curbed (or so the plan goes); on the more robustly socialist end of the spectrum, capitalism would have to be replaced with socialism either by the ballot box or by some form of revolution. And where socialism is identified with the ownership and control of the means of production, it matters considerably whether public ownership takes the form of state ownership or direct workers' ownership and control or some combination of both.

Socialism, taken in the more robust sense, is commonly thought to be tyrannical or authoritarian. But that claim has little merit. Contemporary socialists in the West have, like liberals, a commitment to liberty and democratic procedures, as did Marx and Engels, although the latter two seemed to have an unrealistically simplistic view of the implementation of radical democracy and paid little attention to procedures or to constitutional matters of protecting human rights. They thought that, as the dust of the socialist revolution settled, society would evolve in an ever more democratic direction. But contemporary socialists do not think that. Moreover, Marx and Engels thought that the socialist revolution would start in advanced capitalist societies, but when it arose in Russia instead, Rosa Luxemburg argued perceptively that if it did not quickly spread to the wealthy capitalist West, it would be doomed. But socialism did not spread westward from the Soviet Union; it originated in a backward authoritarian state with little in the way of a democratic tradition and without much in the way of developed productive forces.

Marxist socialists of whatever stripe are historical materialists and anticipated that socialism would piggyback on developed capitalism. No socialist society can succeed, they claim, without highly developed forces of production and a democratic tradition. Where those are absent, a socialist revolution will sour or collapse. But where these conditions obtain, Marxists claim, there is no fear of a socialist society succumbing to authoritarianism.

Another issue for contemporary socialist thought is whether socialism can work efficiently in the absence of markets. Only market societies have had a successful track record of providing consumer goods and services swiftly to a large portion of the population. The response by many contemporary socialists has been to propose market socialism. Alec Nove, John Roemer, and David Schweikart have proposed carefully worked out diverse models about how this hybrid could work. Market socialists (as in reality contemporary capitalists do) work with both market and plan. They disdain the Soviet command model, which regards markets (except in very limited domains) as dysfunctional, and are cautious about central planning.

Market socialism has been resisted by some Orthodox Marxists (for example, Mandel and Ollman). They believe that any market socialism will reproduce the inequalities and instabilities of large-scale capitalism. But Roemer responds that if markets are used solely to guide allocation, there is no reason why market socialism will lead to a society addicted to consumerism. Indeed some socialists believe that it might even surpass concentrated capitalist enterprises in meeting people's needs. The problem for others is rather a worry about what appears at least to be its *political* impossibility. A major worry is whether such an alternative could ever gain a serious hearing in societies dominated by capitalist states and by large capitalist media conglomerates.

See also Bakunin, Mikhail Aleksandrovich; Chomsky, Noam; Civil Disobedience; Cosmopolitanism; Engels, Friedrich; Marx, Karl; Marxist Philosophy; Postcolonialism; Republicanism.

Bibliography

Bernstein, Eduard. *Evolutionary Socialism.* New York: Schocken Books, 1961.

Cohen, G. A. *Karl Marx's Theory of History: A Defense.* Oxford, U.K.: Clarendon Press. 1978.

Cunningham, Frank. *Theories of Democracy.* London, U.K.: Routledge, 2002.

Dolgoff, Sam, ed. and trans. *Bakunin on Anarchy.* London: George Allen and Unwin, 1971.

Gay, Peter. *The Dilemma of Democratic Socialism.* New York: Octagon Books, 1983

Habermas, Jürgen. "What Does Socialism Mean Today? The Revolutions of Recuperation and the Need for New Thinking." In *After the Fall: the Failure of Communism and Future of Socialism*, edited by Robin Blackburn, 23–46. London: Verso. 1991.

Howard, Dick, ed. *Selected Political Writings: Rosa Luxemburg.* New York: Monthly Review Press, 1971.

Kolakowski, Leszek. *Main Currents of Marxism.* 3 Vols. Translated by P. S. Falla. Oxford: Clarendon Press. 1978.

Levine, Andrew. *Arguing for Socialism: Theoretical Considerations.* Boston: Routledge and Kegan Paul, 1984.

Mandel, Ernest. "The Myth of Market Socialism" *New Left Review* 169 (1988): 108–120.

Nove, Alec. *The Economics of Feasible Socialism.* London: George Allen & Unwin, 1983.

Ollman, Bertell, ed. *Market Socialism: The Debate Among Socialists.* London: Routledge, 1998.

Pierson, Christopher. *Socialism after Communism.* University Park: The Pennsylvania State University Press, 1995.

Roemer, John. *A Future for Socialism*. Cambridge, MA: Harvard University Press. 1984.

Schweikart, David. *Against Capitalism*. Cambridge, U.K.: Cambridge University Press, 1993.

Trotsky, Leon. *The History of the Russian Revolution*. New York: Anchor Foundation, 1980.

Tucker, Robert C., ed. *The Lenin Anthology*. New York: W. W. Norton, 1975.

Wright, Erik Olin. *The Debate on Classes*. London: Verso, 1989.

Kai Nielsen (2005)

SOCIAL SCIENCE EXPLANATIONS OF RELIGION

See *Religion, Psychological Explanations of*

SOCIAL SCIENCES, PHILOSOPHY OF

See *Philosophy of Social Sciences*

SOCIETY

A group of perennial problems in social philosophy arises from the concept "society" itself and from its relation to the "individual." What is the ontological status of a society? When one speaks of it as having members, is that to recognize it as a whole with parts, or is the relation of some different kind? Or is this a case of what Alfred North Whitehead called the fallacy of misplaced concreteness?

SOCIAL ACTION AND SOCIAL RELATIONS

"Society" is used both abstractly and to refer to entities that can be particularized, identified, and distinguished from each other as social systems or organizations. The phrase "man in society" is an instance of the more abstract use, for it refers neither to some particular form of association nor to a particular collectivity in which individuals find themselves. It refers, rather, to the social dimension of human action—to a certain generalized type of human relationship. Purely spatial or physical relations between human beings, like contiguity, are not social; for social relations give to human actions a dimension possessed neither by the mere behavior of things nor, indeed, of animals.

Max Weber defined a social action as one which, "by virtue of the subjective meaning attached to it by the acting individual (or individuals), … takes account of the behavior of others and is thereby oriented in its course" (*Theory of Social and Economic Organization*, p. 88). That is to say, the agent understands his own action as having a particular point, which in turn depends on an understanding of what another individual or other individuals have done in the past (as, for instance, in an act of vengeance), are doing now, or are expected to do in the future (as, for instance, in a proposal of marriage). So, said Weber, the efforts of two cyclists to avoid hitting one another would have a social character, whereas the collision between them would not.

An action would not be social merely because it was the effect on an individual of the existence of a crowd as such. For instance, laughing less inhibitedly in a crowd than one would when alone would not be an action oriented to the fact of the existence of the crowd "on the level of meaning"; while the crowd may be one of the causes of the action, the point or meaning of the action does not presuppose some conception of, say, the crowd's purposes or the reasons for its presence. Nor would merely imitative behavior be social; one could learn to whistle by imitating a man, a bird, or a whistling kettle. Learning and performance need neither an understanding of what is imitated as an action nor an orientation toward expected future action of the model. Nevertheless, says Weber, if the action is imitated because it is "fashionable, or traditional, or exemplary, or lends social distinction … it is meaningfully oriented either to the behavior of the source of imitation or of third persons or of both" (pp. 112–114). Weber then goes on to define "social relationship." This would exist wherever, among a number of actors, there existed a probability that their actions would be social actions.

Weber's concept of the "meaning" of an action is rather obscure. It may be a meaning "imputed to the parties in a given concrete case," or it may be what the action means "on the average, or in a theoretically formulated pure type—it is never a normatively 'correct' or metaphysically 'true' meaning" (p. 118). This concept is connected with Weber's much criticized conception of empathic understanding (*Verstehen*). But this connection is not strictly necessary, for the meaning we give to the actions of others depends not so much on an attempted reconstruction of what is in their minds as on a knowledge of the norms and standards regulating their behavior in a given context. Thus I know what a man is about when he presents a bank teller with a signed paper of a certain size, shape, and color, not because I can reconstruct his state of mind in imagination but because I can recognize the procedures for cashing checks.

Weber insists that it is the probability itself of a course of social action that constitutes the social relation, not any particular basis for the probability. Yet we can rely on situational responses (like the bank teller's, for instance) very largely because we expect them to conform to norms and procedures, by which such responses are deemed appropriate or otherwise. Assuming, as many sociologists would, that even war is a social relation, the acts of opposing commanders are mutually oriented by an understanding of the aims and practices of warfare and by the supposition that the other's actions will be appropriate, not only in terms of means and ends but also in consideration of whatever rules of war may be current. Thus we can move from the concept of social relations as frameworks for interaction to Talcott Parsons's conception of a social system constituted by differentiated statuses and roles.

SOCIETIES AS ORGANIZATIONS

The concept of "*a* society" implies a system of more or less settled statuses, to each of which correspond particular patterns of actions appropriate to a range of situations. By virtue of qualifying conditions a man enjoys a status; in virtue of that status he has a role to play. These concepts, however, are meaningful only in the context of rules or norms of conduct—a man's role is not simply what he habitually does (for this may be no more socially significant than a tic), nor even what he is expected to do, if an expectation is only what one might predict about his future conduct from a knowledge of his past. His role is what is expected of him, in the sense of what is required of him by some standard. The role of secretary to an association, for instance, requires that he read the minutes of the last meeting, because the rules of procedure assign this action to whosoever enjoys this status. Less formally, a father's role may be to provide the family with an income, and failure to do so will be regarded not merely as falsifying predictions but also as disappointing reasonable or legitimate expectations—reasonable, because grounded on an understanding of the norms constituting the structure of the family. Indeed, though what we knew of some particular father might give us good grounds for predicting that he would neglect his role, that would not mean that its requirements did not apply to him. Of course, when we speak of "the family" or "the modern state," we commonly have in mind ideal types or paradigms. There may be significant deviations from these in practice. Any particular family may have its own standards, deviant from the social norm, according to which the role of father does not include providing the family income.

Looked at in these terms, a society is an aggregate of interacting individuals whose relations are governed by role-conferring rules and practices which give their actions their characteristic significance. Thus, to demand money with menaces is one thing if done by a common blackmailer or footpad, another if done by a tax collector.

Nevertheless, the act of John Smith, tax collector, is still the act of John Smith, who acts also in different roles in other situations—as father, member of Rotary, and so forth. So one may take two views of a society. On the one hand, one may see it, as a biographer might, as an aggregate of life histories of its individual members, each, in the course of his life, acting in a variety of roles that explain (but only partially) what he does. Or one may adopt the sociological standpoint. A society is then a pattern of roles, and what President Brown does is less important than that it instantiates the role of president.

INDIVIDUALIST AND HOLISTIC ACCOUNTS

Are there any statements about societies, or what Émile Durkheim termed "social facts," that are not ultimately reducible to statements about individuals? According to an extreme individualist or nominalist, such as Thomas Hobbes, social wholes have no substantial reality; propositions attributing properties or actions to a collectivity can be reduced, without residue, to a series of propositions about the relations and actions of individuals: "A multitude of men are made one person, when they are by one man, or one person, represented.… and *unity,* can not otherwise be understood in multitude" (*Leviathan,* edited by Michael Oakeshott, Ch. 16, p. 107). Karl Popper's methodological individualism is as uncompromising. So-called social wholes, he declares, are theoretical constructs; "social phenomena, including collectives, should be analysed in terms of individuals and their actions and relations" (*Conjectures and Refutations,* p. 341).

There is no agreement, however, on whether such analysis is possible. Some philosophers, while admitting that every action is the action of an individual, nevertheless deny that "statements which contain societal terms" can be reduced "to a conjunction of statements which only include terms referring to the thoughts and actions of specific individuals" (Maurice Mandelbaum, "Societal Facts," p. 482). While the "societal fact" of cashing a check can be expressed in terms of what individuals do, nevertheless the description will always contain such societal terms as *bank* and *money,* which cannot themselves be translated without remainder into wholly individual terms. Furthermore, such societal facts, it is said, interact with individual behavior; a banking system can have an effect on a concrete individual. For it is clearly true that for every individual, the institutions and mores of his society present themselves as independent and external facts, just as much as his physical environment does. And if that is true for every individual, it is true for the totality of individuals composing the society. That is not to say that a totality is a thing independent of individuals or that it has a group mind; it is only to say that for any participant or for any observer of an individual's actions, it makes sense to talk of him confronting and confronted by independent social facts (Ernest Gellner elaborates this point). Moreover, the principle that social action can ultimately be explained by referring to the dispositions of individuals to behave in certain ways in given circumstances overlooks the possibility that these dispositions may themselves depend on social facts.

The view that social facts are not reducible to individual facts is commonly called holism. In its more extreme forms it relies heavily on biological organic analogies. An organism, it is said, is prior to its constituent parts in the sense that any understanding of their nature and function presupposes an understanding of the whole organism. The whole organism is more than the mere sum of its parts, since no account in terms of the parts considered separately could add up to some of the things that could be said about the whole. (The same might be said, however, of some of the properties of a triangle that arise from the three sides considered in relation to one another.) Just as the liver is a more significant object considered as an organ of a working body than as a detached piece of tissue, so the acts of individuals are significant or intelligible only when considered as the acts of role-bearers or as manifesting characteristics of their social or cultural environment. So drinking wine has a different range of social meaning in England from the one it has in France. The thought-experiment of the social contract theorists, who put man into an asocial state of nature the better to understand his real purposes in society, was radically misconceived, precisely because it abstracted man from the very context in which alone he would be a man but still attributed human properties to him.

According to the Hegelians (Bernard Bosanquet, for example), so far are we from being able to reduce social facts to individual facts that it is the individual himself who must be explained as an expression of the concrete social universal—an idea manifesting itself organically in its differentiated parts, as the idea of an oak tree is differentially but organically manifest in its leaves, bark, trunk, and so forth, all in a sense different from one another yet all linked by the idea of the oak and collectively differentiated thereby from the corresponding parts of an elm. "Man" is an abstraction—we are men as we are Germans, Englishmen, Frenchmen; that is, we instantiate the spirit of our own society.

Holistic organicism of this kind has laid great stress on history. Social wholes, it is said (by Friedrich Karl von Savigny, for instance), are not like mechanical wholes. Mechanical wholes can be understood by reducing them to their smallest constituent parts that conform in their behavior to general laws from which the varying behavior of the aggregates can be deduced. A social whole, on the contrary, is sui generis, to be understood not by analysis but by studying it *as* a developing whole. Consequently, there can be no general theory of social action, and history is the only legitimate mode of sociological inquiry.

According to Popper, these arguments are totally misconceived. There is simply no way of studying wholes as wholes; any attempt at understanding implies abstracting from a particular configuration of properties and circumstances those that seem significant for the particular study and relating them to general laws and hypotheses that are valid for all cases, irrespective of time, in which the stated initial conditions are satisfied. A law of development could be a statement about the general tendencies of certain types of society, given certain initial conditions; but it is a misunderstanding of the nature of both scientific and historical inquiry to propose a study of a society as a whole, partly because a social whole is a theoretical construct and partly because to attribute to it its own peculiar law of growth, in some sense true regardless of, or despite, any initial conditions whatsoever, is to make any explanatory statement about its behavior impossible.

COMMUNITY AND ASSOCIATION

The individualist account of social action is most persuasive when the form of social organization under consideration is a joint-stock corporation or a trade association. There is little temptation to attribute group personalities to such bodies, except in a strictly legal sense, and therefore little resistance to treating them as nothing but procedural forms. Their members and officials are clearly identified individuals with limited common interests. These interests explain their interaction, without suggesting that the association is anything more than a means for promoting them. Moreover, such interests remain intelligible even abstracted from the context of the society.

Ferdinand Tönnies distinguished this type of organization, which he called a *Gesellschaft* (association), from its polar opposite, the *Gemeinschaft* (community). Paradigms of the latter type are the family, the village, the tribe, and the nation. These are much less formally organized than a joint-stock company. They have no clearly defined, limited aim; qualifications for membership may be poorly defined, depending very largely on subjective criteria. Yet individuals do not deliberately join such bodies—more usually they are born into them or acquire membership by residence. At the same time, membership in such a community may mean much more to the individual. So far from his using the organization as a means for the pursuit of personal interest, privately conceived, what he conceives to be his interest may depend very much on the influence of the collectivity upon him. He may feel bound to it by ties and responsibilities not of his own choosing which nevertheless demand his respect. Moreover, such communities appear to have a lifespan greater than that of any generation of individual members, which cannot be explained, as might that of a corporation, by the continuities of constitutional procedures. It is, rather, that from generation to generation there passes an attachment to a common set of symbols and a common history, a participation in what Durkheim termed "collective representations" in a collective consciousness—a common culture, in short—which enables members to identify one another where other criteria are uncertain, which gives the society its cohesion, and which provides the standards by which its members' actions are regulated and assessed.

A FUNCTIONALLY INCLUSIVE COLLECTIVITY

"Boundary maintenance," to use Talcott Parsons's term, is a necessity for every society. To possess an identity, a society must furnish criteria whereby its members can identify one another, since their actions and attitudes toward one another will be different from those toward outsiders. But Parsons also conceives of boundary maintenance by social subsystems within a broader system. Thus he defines "a society" as a collectivity "which is the primary bearer of a distinctive institutionalized culture and which cannot be said to be a differentiated subsystem of a higher-order collectivity oriented to most of the functional exigencies of a social system" (*Theories of Society,* Vol. I, p. 44). Such a collectivity is organized by political, economic, familial, and similar subsystems. Parsons distinguishes polity and society, but he asserts that "the boundaries of a society tend to coincide with the territorial jurisdiction of the highest-order units of political organization" (p. 46). For, in Parsons's view, a society's existence depends so crucially on commitment to common values and on the maintenance of order between its individual and collective components that the political boundary tends to settle automatically the limits of the society.

The relation between state and society presented no problems for the Greeks. Political, religious, cultural, and athletic activities were largely undifferentiated and occurred within the single organizational structure of the polis. The first serious problems in this respect emerged with the Christian dichotomies between God and Caesar, church and state, the *Civitas Dei* and the *Civitas Terrena.* The medieval view was that, ideally, there was one universal community of humankind with two modes of organization, or "subsystems," church and empire. Reality never corresponded very closely to this ideal. It became irretrievably divorced from it with the rise of the nation-state and the Reformation. Since then, when people have talked of the society to which they belong, they have thought primarily (like Parsons) of the social order contained within the boundaries of a state and sustained by its organized power.

Nevertheless, liberal thinkers have striven hard to maintain the conceptual distinction between state, or polity, and society. One reason has been to resist the claim that the state could be the only focus of loyalty, competent by virtue of an overriding authority to lay down the terms on which other associations might function. On the other hand, there has emerged a new totalitarianism which identifies state and society. Every form of economic, religious, artistic, or scientific activity thereby acquires a political dimension, promoting or impeding the public good as embodied in state policy. G. W. F. Hegel provided a metaphysical justification for this kind of doctrine when he distinguished between, on one hand, civil society—a level of social organization including the market economy and the forces of civil order—and, on the other, the transcendent state—"the realized ethical idea or ethical spirit," "the true meaning and ground" of lower forms of social organization like the family and civil society (*Philosophy of Right,* Secs. 257, 256). By contrast, not only do liberals insist on the subordination of the state to society; they have also tended, according to Sheldon S. Wolin, to depreciate the political and to attach increasingly to other social subsystems, like the business corporation or the voluntary association, concepts like statesmanship, authority, and legitimacy, which have been considered hitherto characteristic of the state. Meanwhile, Wolin argues, the concept of an organization directed to the most general interests of the community tends to get lost, to be replaced by a model of conflicting pressure groups operating within a very nebulously defined arena. If Parsons is right, our notion of a society as the most inclusive framework of social interaction depends on the political not only for its boundary maintenance but also for its very identity. There may be a danger that in pressing the antitotalitarian, pluralistic account so far that it dissolves the state, it will lose thereby its capacity to define the society.

See also Bosanquet, Bernard; Durkheim, Émile; Hegel, Georg Wilhelm Friedrich; Hobbes, Thomas; Holism and Individualism in History and Social Science; Popper, Karl Raimund; Savigny, Friedrich Karl von; Social Contract; Sovereignty; Weber, Max; Whitehead, Alfred North.

Bibliography

Bendix, Reinhard. *Max Weber—An Intellectual Portrait.* New York: Doubleday, 1960.

Black, Max, ed. *The Social Theories of Talcott Parsons.* Englewood Cliffs, NJ: Prentice Hall, 1961.

Bosanquet, Bernard. *The Philosophical Theory of the State.* 4th ed. London: Macmillan, 1923.

Durkheim, Émile. *Les règles de la méthode sociologique.* Paris: Alcan, 1895. Translated by S. A. Solovay and J. H. Mueller as *Rules of Sociological Method,* edited by G. E. G. Catlin. Chicago: University of Chicago Press, 1938.

Durkheim, Émile. *De la division du travail social.* 5th ed. Paris: Alcan, 1926. Edited and translated by George Simpson as *The Division of Labor in Society.* Glencoe, IL: Free Press, 1947.

Gellner, Ernest. "Holism versus Individualism in History and Sociology." In *Theories of History,* edited by Patrick Gardiner, 489–503. Glencoe, IL: Free Press, 1959.

Hegel, G. W. F. *Grundlinien der Philosophie des Rechts.* Berlin, 1821. Translated with notes by T. M. Knox as *Hegel's Philosophy of Right.* Oxford: Clarendon Press, 1942.

Hobbes, Thomas. *Leviathan.* London, 1651. Edited with introduction by Michael Oakeshott. Oxford, 1946.

MacIver, R. M., and C. H. Page. *Society: An Introductory Analysis.* New York: Rinehart, 1949.

Mandelbaum, Maurice. "Societal Facts." In *Theories of History,* op. cit., 476–488.

Parsons, Talcott. *The Structure of Social Action.* Glencoe, IL: Free Press, 1949. Includes extended discussions of the views of Alfred Marshall, Vilfredo Pareto, Émile Durkheim, and Max Weber.

Parsons, Talcott. *The Social System.* Glencoe, IL: Free Press, 1951. Parsons's intricate style and elaborate terminology will deter any but the most determined.

Parsons, Talcott, Edward Shils, K. D. Naegele, and J. R. Pitts, eds. *Theories of Society.* 2 vols. New York: Free Press, 1961.

Popper, Karl R. *The Poverty of Historicism.* London: Routledge, 1957.

Popper, Karl R. *The Open Society and Its Enemies.* 2 vols., 4th rev. ed. London, 1962.

Popper, Karl R. "Prediction and Prophecy in the Social Sciences." In his *Conjectures and Refutations.* London: Routledge, 1963. Ch. 16. Also in *Theories of History,* op. cit., 276–285.

Simmel, Georg. *The Sociology of Georg Simmel.* Translated and edited by K. H. Wolff. Glencoe, IL: Free Press, 1950. An anthology of Simmel's principal works on sociological theory.

Stark, Werner. *The Fundamental Forms of Social Thought.* London: Routledge and K. Paul, 1962. A study of the traditional organicist-mechanistic dichotomy and an attempt to overcome it.

Tönnies, Ferdinand. *Gemeinschaft und Gesellschaft.* Leipzig, 1887. Translated by C. P. Loomis as *Fundamental Concepts of Sociology.* New York: American Book, 1940. Reissued as *Community and Association.* London: Routledge and K. Paul, 1955.

Watkins, J. W. N. "Historical Explanation in the Social Sciences." In *Theories of History,* op. cit., 503–514.

Weber, Max. *Grundriss der Sozialökonomik—III Abt: Wirtschaft und Gesellschaft.* Tübingen: Mohr, 1925. Part I edited and translated by Talcott Parsons and A. M. Henderson (with introduction by Parsons) as *Theory of Social and Economic Organization.* New York: Oxford University Press, 1947.

Wolin, Sheldon S. *Politics and Vision.* Boston: Little, Brown, 1960.

Stanley I. Benn (1967)

SOCIETY [ADDENDUM]

Toward the end of the twentieth century, while earlier discussions of holism *versus* individualism did not die out, the interplay among three different but related notions of society—civil society, the corporation, and cosmopolitan society or the society of nations—an interplay adumbrated in the last two paragraphs above, began increasingly to dominate philosophical inquiry. The development that, more than any other, propelled the notion of civil society back into greater prominence late in that century was an ever more publicly articulated dissatisfaction with the totalitarian nature of the political regimes and their corresponding societies in Eastern Europe. It was widely contended that the suppressed elements of "civil society" in those countries needed to be regenerated and kept independent of the state. Hence the eventual, generally peaceful dissolution of the governments in question was seen as a triumph of the ideals of civil society.

As in the past, so in the late twentieth and early twenty-first centuries, understandings of the meaning of "civil society" (as well as of "society") have varied widely. Some philosophers, such as Jürgen Habermas, have wished to exclude from the scope of civil society important aspects of the economic institutions that were so central to Hegel's use of the term and to focus on its informal, less easily quantifiable "life-world" elements. For others, the increasing power, in a world characterized by ever-accelerating "globalization," of transnational corporations—"*sociétés anonymes à responsabilité limitée*" in French or "*Gesellschaften mit beschränkter Haftung*" in German—with their essentially capitalist economic purposes and typically nondemocratic structures poses a threat to the viability of political, cultural, and other components of individual (national) civil societies; therefore, according to this line of thinking, corporations need to be treated as focal points in the philosophical analysis of the concepts of both "society" and "civil society." In addition, some have identified, and found great significance in, an emerging *global* civil society, exemplified especially by large transnational nongovernmental organizations (NGOs) that are not essentially profit-oriented, as well as by more informal institutions and practices with similar global concerns.

GLOBAL SOCIETY?

The idea of a global civil society implies that of a global, or cosmopolitan, society as such, contrary to the previously mentioned Parsonian insistence on "boundary maintenance." Resistance to the idea of a global society stems from both methodological and ethicopolitical considerations. John Rawls, for instance, explicitly took the self-contained "closed society"—that is, the nation-state or something similar—as the appropriate abstract entity within which to develop his original theory of justice, which advocates unequal distribution of goods only to the extent to which such distribution will benefit the least advantaged member of that society. This intentional limitation of scope was a methodological preference of his, as it had been of so many of his predecessors in social theory; but it also helped enable him, when he later undertook to analyze international issues in his *The Law of Peoples* (1999), to reject the application of his principles of justice to the world as a whole and to refrain from endorsing cosmopolitanism as a desirable or viable ethicopolitical ideal. (Rawls did, however, introduce the somewhat novel term "Society of Peoples" to refer to those existing "peoples," by no means all, who observe the principles and ideals specified in his book.) Others have used Rawls's theoretical framework in order to develop a more cosmopolitan viewpoint than his own, one that regards "global society" as the name of an emerging contemporary reality, its parts linked by the Internet and other technological innovations, its fate bound up with newly identified shared risks, such as global warming, that some of these innovations have exacerbated, and its extreme imbalances of wealth and poverty perpetuating injustice and instability.

In sharpest reaction to globalizing tendencies and their corresponding theories have been ideologies of resurgent nationalism and religious fundamentalism. The former have, by definition, insisted on the preeminence of individual societies characterized, most frequently, by a perceived common ethnic identity. But considerations of history and genetics alike indicate to how great a measure such perceptions are the products of a particular, time-limited collective imagination, rather than reflections of some underlying truths of social ontology. As for the religious fundamentalist notion that "societies" can be differentiated according to common religious beliefs, a notion shared by some Western writers who subscribe to the vague notion (with constantly shifting boundary definitions), of a global "clash of civilizations," the existence of numerous "warring sects" within the major world religions, combined with basic questions of hermeneutics (that is, how are the sacred scriptures to be interpreted?), casts strong doubt on this way of viewing and intellectually segmenting the world.

It was a British Prime Minister, Margaret Thatcher, rather than a professional philosopher, who is famously reported to have asserted, "There is no such thing as society." This seems a rather extreme claim concerning a supposed reality with references to which so many conversations in ordinary language are replete. It is rather the case, it would seem, that "society" is an exceptionally complex and multivocal term, the complexity and multivocity of which analyses by sociologists, such as Habermas's formalist, structuralist opponent in the broad Parsonian tradition, Niklas Luhmann, and by life-world- and *praxis*-oriented philosophers such as Habermas himself, the phenomenologist Alfred Schutz, and Jean-Paul Sartre in his late-life contribution to social theory, *Critique of Dialectical Reason* (1976), have served to underscore and articulate.

See also Civil Disobedience; Cosmopolitanism; Multiculturalism; Postcolonialism; Republicanism.

Bibliography

Beck, Ulrich. *World Risk Society*. London: Polity, 1999.

Castoriadis, Cornelius. *The Imaginary Institution of Society*. Translated by K. Blamey. Cambridge, MA: MIT Press, 1987.

Cohen, Jean, and Andrew Arato. *Civil Society and Political Theory*. Cambridge, MA: MIT Press, 1992.

Habermas, Jürgen. *Between Facts and Norms: Contributions to a Discourse Theory of Law and Democracy*. Translated by W. Rehg. Cambridge, MA: MIT Press, 1996.

Jarvie, Ian Charles. *Concepts and Society*. London: Routledge, 1972.

Keane, John. *Global Civil Society?* Cambridge, U.K.: Cambridge University Press, 2003.

Luhmann, Niklas. *The Differentiation of Society*. Translated by S. Holmes and C. Larmore. New York: Columbia University Press, 1982.

Rawls, John. *The Law of Peoples*. Cambridge, MA: Harvard University Press, 1999.

Sartre, Jean-Paul. *Critique of Dialectical Reason*. Vol. 1, *Theory of Practical Ensembles*, translated by A. Sheridan-Smith. London: New Left Books, 1976.

Schutz, Alfred. *The Phenomenology of the Social World*. Translated by G. Walsh and F. Lehnert. Evanston, IL: Northwestern University Press, 1967.

McBride, William L. (2005)

SOCINIANISM

"Socinianism," an evangelical rationalist movement, was one of the forerunners of modern Unitarianism. Three phases can be distinguished: (1) the thought of Laelius Socinus (1525–1562) and his nephew Faustus Socinus (1539–1604); (2) the thought and institutions of the Minor (Reformed) Church of Poland, especially as embodied in the Racovian Catechism (1605), which represented a fusion of Faustus's theology with that of the local anti-Trinitarian and partly Anabaptist Minor Church; and (3) the rationalist theology of the Socinianized Minor Church. This last phase was especially important after the Socinianized Minor Church was crushed in Poland in 1658 and the spirit of Socinianism became influential in the Netherlands among the Remonstrants; in the British Isles, in the seventeenth century, among certain Anglican divines and nonconformist intellectuals; and, in the eighteenth century, among the Arminian divines of New England, who were forerunners of the Unitarian congregationalists.

Socinian evangelical rationalism originated from an amalgam of the rationalist humanism of Juan de Valdés, Florentine Platonism, and Paduan Aristotelianism; in Poland it was augmented by certain Calvinist and Anabaptist ingredients. In all three phases Socinianism was characterized by (1) a rationalist interpretation of Scripture (which was nevertheless accepted as true and authoritative), with a predilection for the pre-Mosaic and the New Covenantal parts of the Bible; (2) an acceptance of Jesus as the definitive word or revelation of God but nevertheless solely a man, not divine but chosen by God to rule as king, priest, and prophet over the world and the church; (3) belief in the principle of pacific separation of church and state; (4) acceptance of the doctrine of the death of the soul with the body with, however, selective resurrection and immortality for all those who persevered "through the power of the Spirit" in observing all of Jesus' earthly commandments.

LAELIUS AND FAUSTUS SOCINUS

Laelius Socinus, born in Siena, was a well-to-do student with a wide and critical interest in theology. He established contact and became friendly with several reformers, notably Philipp Melanchthon, John Calvin, and Johann Bullinger, and also with the Rhaetian heretic Camillo Renato. Himself suspected of heresy, Laelius was obliged to prepare a Confession of Faith (in which, however, he reserved the right to further inquiry), one of the few extant documents from his hand. At his death he left his library, and perhaps some unpublished papers, to his nephew.

Faustus Socinus, born in Siena, was a student of logic and law, a member of the local academy, and an indifferent poet. He first clearly manifested his rejection of traditional Christian doctrines in a letter of 1563, in which he argued against the postulate of natural immortality. In 1570 he wrote his first major work, *De Auctoritate Sacrae Scripturae*, and in 1578 he issued his basic treatise on Christology and soteriology, *De Jesu Christu Servatore*. Because of the latter work he was invited to Transylvania to defend the legitimacy of prayer addressed to the ascended Christ against the faction in the Unitarian Reformed Church led by Francis Dávid. On the journey he was persuaded to make Poland his permanent home. There he became a major defender of the Minor Church, although he declined on principle to become a communicant member of it, refusing to submit to believers' baptism by immersion. Socinus was cocommissioned with local pastors to revise the Latin *Catechesis* (1574) of Racov, the communitarian settlement and spiritual center of the Minor Church, northeast of Kraków. The radical revision was published in Polish in 1605, a year after Socinus's death, as the *Racovian Catechism*, the first Latin edition of which (1609) was dedicated to James I of England.

THE SOCINIANIZED MINOR CHURCH

The Socinianized Minor Church, centered in Racov, had an academy that at one time attracted a thousand students and a publishing house that turned out tracts and books in a score of languages; it became in fact more a school than a church. Among the faculty of the academy and the pastorate of the synod, which met annually in Racov, the most prominent were Socinus's own grandson, Andreas Wiszowaty (d. 1678), who wrote *Religio Rationalis*; Stanislas Lubieniecki (d. 1675), who wrote *Historia Reformationis Polonicae*; Samuel Przypkowski (d. 1670), who wrote *Vita Fausti Socini*; and quite a few converts from German Protestantism who resettled in Poland and were rebaptized: Christoph Ostorodt (d. 1611); Johann Völkel, who wrote *De Vera Religione* (1630); Johann Crell (d. 1631), who wrote *De Uno Deo Patre* and a defense of Socinus against Hugo Grotius, *De Satisfactione*; and Christoph Sand (d. 1680), who compiled the *Bibliotheca Antitrinitariorum*.

SPREAD OF SOCINIANISM

Well before the crushing of the Minor Church in 1658, Socinians were established in the Netherlands. At Amsterdam the basic works of the movement, the eight-volume *Bibliotheca Fratrum Polonorum*, edited by Wiszowaty, were printed in 1688. In England, Socinian rationality, latitudinarianism, Unitarianism, and mortalism (psychopannychism) variously appealed to Arminian prelates, Oxford rationalists (such as William Chillingworth), Cambridge Platonists (such as Benjamin Whichcote), philosophers and scientists (such as Isaac Newton and John Locke), and to the first avowed native Socinians, Paul Best, John Biddle ("the father of English Unitarianism"), and Stephen Nye, whose *History of Unitarianism commonly called Socinianism* set off the Trinitarian controversy in the Established church in 1687.

See also Arminius and Arminianism; Calvin, John; Cambridge Platonists; Grotius, Hugo; Locke, John; Melanchthon, Philipp; Newton, Isaac; Rationalism; Whichcote, Benjamin.

Bibliography

Bianchi, Daniela. "Some Sources for a History of English Socinianism: A Bibliography of 17th Century English Socinian Writings." *Topoi* 4 (1985): 91–120.

Chmaj, Ludwik. *Faust Socyn*. Warsaw: Ksiazka i Wiedza, 1963.

Edwards, John. *Some Thoughts concerning the Several Causes and Occasions of Atheism: Socinianism Unmask'd*. New York: Garland, 1984.

Kühler, W. J. *Socinianisme in Nederland*. Leiden, 1912.

McLachlan, H. John. *Socinianism in Seventeenth-Century England*. London: Oxford University Press, 1951.

Stewart, M. A. *English Philosophy in the Age of Locke*. New York: Oxford University Press, 2000.

Wilbur, Earl M. *A History of Unitarianism: Socinianism and Its Antecedents*. Cambridge, MA: Harvard University Press, 1945.

Yolton, John W., ed. *Philosophy, Religion and Science in the Seventeenth and Eighteenth Centuries*. New York: University of Rochester Press, 1990.

George Hunston Williams (1967)
Bibliography updated by Tamra Frei (2005)

SOCINUS, LAELIUS AND FAUSTUS

See *Socinianism*

SOCIOLOGY, FUNCTIONALISM IN

See *Functionalism in Sociology*

SOCIOLOGY OF KNOWLEDGE

The "sociology of knowledge" is concerned with determining whether human participation in social life has any influence on human knowledge, thought, and culture and, if it does, what sort of influence it is.

DEVELOPMENT

Although the term *sociology of knowledge* was coined in the twentieth century, the origins of the discipline date back to classical antiquity. Plato, for instance, asserted that the lower classes are unfit to pursue the higher kinds of knowledge, because their mechanical crafts not only deform their bodies but also confuse their souls. Plato also held the more refined doctrine of the correspondence of the knower (or more precisely, the faculties and activities of the knower's mind, which are in part determined by society) and the known. This latter theory became part of the Platonic tradition and ultimately stimulated some modern pioneers in the sociology of knowledge, notably Max Scheler. Both theories anticipated an essential claim of the sociology of knowledge—that social circumstances, by shaping the subject of knowing, also determine the objects that come to be known.

In the Middle Ages, patterns of life were fixed and defined, and patterns of thought tended to be equally so; ideas appeared as absolute, and the factors that conditioned them remained hidden. As soon, however, as rifts developed in the social fabric, awareness of these factors reemerged. Niccolò Machiavelli's remark in the *Discourses* that the thought of the palace was one thing, the thought of the market place quite another, revealed this new awareness.

In the following centuries, the stream of ideas that was to lead to the modern sociology of knowledge was divided between rationalism and empiricism. The rationalists regarded mathematical propositions as the archetype of truth. As mathematical propositions do not change in content from age to age and from country to country, the rationalists could not concede that different societies might have different systems of knowledge, all equally valid. But if truth was one, error could be multiform, and its roots could be sought in social life—for instance, in the machinations of privileged classes in whose interest it was to keep the people in ignorance. Francis Bacon's doctrine of "idols," or sources of delusion, set forth in his *Novum Organum*, illustrates this tendency. The rationalists thus became the first "unmaskers" of "ideologies."

According to the empiricists, the contents of the mind depend on the basic life experiences, and as these are manifestly dissimilar in dissimilarly circumstanced societies, they almost had to assume that reality would offer a different face in each society. Thus, Giambattista Vico asserted that every phase of history has its own style of thought which provides it with a specific and appropriate cultural mentality. The treatment of the biblical account of creation by the two schools shows their contrast. Voltaire called it a piece of stultifying priestcraft that no rational person anywhere would accept: How could the light exist before the sun? Johann Gottfried Herder answered that for a desert nation like the ancient Hebrews the dawn breaks before the solar disk appears above the horizon. For them, therefore, the light *was* before the sun.

Though the problems of the genesis of error and the genesis of truth should be kept apart, the overly sharp distinction between them and the partisan handling of them before the end of the eighteenth century prevented any tangible progress. And even though Immanuel Kant achieved a synthesis of rationalism and empiricism, the sociology of knowledge failed to gain from his advances. Kant's whole approach prevented such a gain: The problem of knowledge arose for Kant from the meeting of the individual mind with the physical world. The social element was missing at either pole. The sociology of knowledge explains Kant's narrowness itself as socially determined. The decay of feudal society and the emergence of a class of independent producers (peasants and artisans) had created the desire to "liberate" man from the "artificial restrictions" of social life. A presocial, asocial, or antisocial type of man was thought possible and even superior to social man. The primacy of being was ascribed to the individual, and society was considered to be no more than a collection of individuals linked by contract. In these circumstances, no one could see the influence of social forces on the human mind.

The nineteenth century brought a strong reaction against this radical individualism. As the forces of social control reasserted themselves, man was once again conceived of as essentially a social creature. The result of this new trend was Karl Marx's mislabeled "materialistic interpretation of history." Marx wrote in his *Introduction to the Critique of Political Economy*: "It is not men's consciousness which determines their existence, but on the contrary their social existence which determines their consciousness." For Marx, the real "substructure" upon which the intellectual "superstructure" rests is a special set of human relationships. Though his definition of these relationships is too narrow, and though he has been variously interpreted, Marx's formulation provided the starting point in the development of the modern sociology of knowledge.

SOCIAL ORIGIN OF IDEAS

While there is general agreement among scholars in the field that social relationships provide the key to the understanding of the genesis of ideas, there are also far-reaching disagreements among several distinct schools, within which there are again individual differences. An attempt will be made here only to characterize the three most important basic attitudes.

MATERIALIST SCHOOL. A materialist group of writers emphasizes that human beings are creatures of nature before they are creatures of society and tends to see human beings as dominated by certain genetic drives, with decisive consequences for their emergent mentalities. Friedrich Nietzsche, for instance, ascribed to man an elementary will to power; if this will is frustrated by a barrier, self-consolatory ideas are apt to appear. Christianity is one such idea; it is essentially a philosophy of "sour grapes," a "slave morality." It assures the defeated that they are really superior to those who have defeated them.

Vilfredo Pareto's *Trattato di sociologia generale* is the most elaborate statement of this position. According to Pareto, people act first and think of reasons for their action only afterward. These reasons he calls "derivations" because they are derived from, or secondary to, the "residues," or quasi instincts, which in fact determine human modes of conduct and, through them, human modes of thought as well. This school continued the line initiated by the rationalists. Theirs is a doctrine of ideologies that devalues thought while it accounts for its formation.

IDEALIST SCHOOL. A second group of writers asserts that every society has to come to some decision about the Absolute and that this decision will act as a basic premise that determines the content of the culture. Juan Donoso Cortés tried to explain the classical Greek worldview as the product of heathen preconceptions about the Absolute, and the medieval worldview as the product of Christian-Catholic preconceptions. An ambitious presentation of this theory is Pitirim Sorokin's *Social and Cultural Dynamics*. He distinguishes three basic metaphysics that, prevailing in given societies, color all their thinking. If a realm beyond space and time is posited as the Absolute, as in ancient India, an "ideational" mentality will spring up; if the realm inside space and time is posited as the Absolute, as in the modern West, a "sensate" mentality will come into being; and if, finally, reality is ascribed both to the here and now and to the beyond, as in the high Middle Ages, an "idealistic" mentality will be the result. Sorokin's doctrine is itself idealistic in character and finds its ultimate inspiration in a religious attitude.

SOCIOLOGISTS OF KNOWLEDGE. The third group of writers occupies the middle ground. These writers do not go beyond the human sphere but divide it into a primary and conditioning half and a secondary and conditioned one. There is, however, great diversity of opinion over exactly which social facts should be regarded as conditioning thought. Marx, for instance, held that relations of production, which themselves reflect still more basic property relations, were primary, but many other factors, such as power relations, have been singled out by other thinkers. Still others regard the social constitution as a whole as the substructure of knowledge, thought, and culture. A typical representative of this numerous group is W. G. Sumner. In his classic *Folkways*, he suggested that wherever individuals try to live together, they develop mutual adjustments that harden into a set of customs, supported and secured by social sanctions, which permanently coordinate and control their conduct. These habits of action have as their concomitants habits of the mind, a generalized ethos that permeates the mental life of the society concerned. This theory can be sharpened by formulating it in axiological terms. A society is a society because, and insofar as, it is attuned to certain selected and hierarchically ordered values. These values determine what lines of endeavor will be pursued both in practice and in theory.

This third group represents the sociology of knowledge in the narrower and proper sense of the word. The theory just summed up has received some empirical confirmation through the discovery that societies do gain mental consistency to the degree that they achieve better human coordination and integration.

RELATION OF A SOCIETY TO IDEAS EXPRESSED IN IT

The problem next in importance to the identification of the substructure of knowledge is the explanation of its relation to the superstructure. Here again there are three schools that may, but do not always, correspond to those already discussed. One tendency is toward causalism. The positivists Gustav Ratzenhofer and Hippolyte Taine, for example, expected of the future a science of culture no less deterministic than the sciences of matter. But though the term *determination* is frequently and generally used in all the literature of this school, it hardly ever means strict determination. While this first school concedes, in principle, no independence to the mind and its contents, a second, Platonic tendency ascribes complete independence to the mind. To Scheler, Florian Znaniecki, and others, thinking means participating in eternal preexistent ideas. If these ideas are to become active in the world, they must ally themselves to a social movement seeking appropriate ideas. Max Weber has called this doctrine the doctrine of elective affinity. The third theory argues in terms of interdependence and appears regularly in connection with functionalism. If society is to function as a unity, its modes of acting and thinking must be in, or on the way to, agreement. Neither substructure nor superstructure is given ontological priority, but there is a tendency to see thought in action as prior to thought as theory.

EXTENT OF INFLUENCE. Another problem concerns the extent of the influence of social factors on ideas. Here opinions range from the view that these factors influence only a few political slogans to the view that their influence is all-pervading. An important systematic dividing line separates the authors who assert that the categories of thought themselves are socially determined from those who deny that they are.

EPISTEMOLOGICAL SIGNIFICANCE

The main philosophical importance of the sociology of knowledge consists in its claim to supplement, if not to replace, traditional epistemology. If society partially or totally determines knowing and thinking, how does this affect their validity? All sociologists of knowledge are inclined to stress that initially the human mind is never aware of more than a sector of reality and that the selection of a sector to be investigated is dependent on the axiological system that a given society has made its own. From this point they diverge once again into three schools, and once more there is no simple correlation with the tendencies previously identified.

EFFECT OF SOCIAL FACTORS ON THOUGHT. Some writers, such as Pareto, hold that, in the last analysis, only the senses are reliable sources of knowledge. They tend to split the mental universe into a scientific and a nonscientific department and accord the ideas belonging to the latter at best conventional status, but no truth-value in the narrower sense of the term. The axiological system of society, insofar as it is not taken up with scientific and technological pursuits, appears as an opaque and distorting medium that interposes itself between the intellect and reality. The effect of society on the mind is thus something negative, to be regretted and, if possible, overcome.

Whereas this group denigrates the social element in human beings, and hence in human knowledge, another, including Émile Durkheim and Karl Mannheim, sees it as supreme. The latter group conceives the individual as the most likely source of error and society as the most reliable source of truth, if for no other reason than because personal blunders are neutralized in a common attitude. They regard society as the test of the validity of a belief: It is valid if those who hold it manage to operate smoothly within their social system. But if the true is what works and if different societies work differently (as manifestly they do), then truth is once again merely convention. At any rate, there can be no general truths.

The third group, including Weber and Scheler, considers that the social influence on mental activity consists essentially in giving directions. What knowledge will be sought in a society depends on the axiological system that reigns in that society. In its most radical form, this doctrine sees our very awareness of facts as socially determined: Only those aspects of reality that are marked by their possession of some value, social in origin, will be noticed and enter into the canon of knowledge. There appears, however, no cogent reason why a person should not see a thing thus selected for study on an axiological basis as what it really is. It can therefore be said that every society has its own truth, without giving the word a relativistic tinge. Any human being who integrates himself, factually or intellectually, with a certain society and accepts its constitutive values will have to agree that, from the chosen angle, the world does, and must, look as it is described by the searchers and thinkers of that society. Hence sociality is neither a truth-destroying nor a truth-guaranteeing, but merely a truth-limiting factor. The resulting limitations can, in principle, be overcome by combining the valid "aspectual" insights of all societies into a comprehensive whole.

KNOWLEDGE OF NATURE AND KNOWLEDGE OF CULTURE

An important distinction sometimes made is that between knowledge of nature and knowledge of culture. The facts of nature do not change from age to age and from country to country; the facts of culture do. Knowledge of the former, therefore, need not be marked by relativity. The Paretian theory, by making physical knowledge the model of all knowledge, does less than justice to the study of cultures; the theory of Mannheim and Durkheim, by making cultural knowledge the model of all knowledge, is apt to fall into the opposite mistake (though its best protagonists have managed to avoid this). The theory of Weber and Scheler escapes both weaknesses. In every society's axiological system, some interest in nature, especially in methods of dominating nature, will be present, and insights gained in the pursuit of this domination will be comparable, transferable, and absolute in the sense of binding on all human beings. Other values will vary from society to society; insights gained in pursuit of them will be correspondingly incomparable, nontransferable, and relative (even though they can all be fitted together as alternative actualized possibilities inherent in one creature, man).

Because people must take the facts of nature as they find them, while the facts of culture are their own work, the social determination of knowledge will be different in the two instances. In scientific research, only the origin of an insight will be determined by the social factor (say, a pressing social need); in cultural studies, however, both the origin and the content will be socially determined. In the case of science, tendencies arising from the social sphere induce a person to open his eyes and see; in the case of cultural studies, they induce him to open his eyes and decide what he shall see. These considerations go far toward overcoming the conflict between the unduly negative and the unduly positive epistemological versions of the sociology of knowledge and show the superiority of the third approach.

SOCIOLOGY OF KNOWLEDGE AS A SCIENCE

In conclusion, it should be emphasized that the sociology of knowledge is not only a substantive philosophical discipline but also an analytical tool that can be used by the descriptive sciences concerned with the observable products of the mind. Because it can throw light on the genesis, and often on the content, of concrete thought structures, the sociology of knowledge may enable the historian or the anthropologist to achieve a deeper understanding of the facts before him. Considered from this angle, the sociology of knowledge appears, above all, as a hermeneutic method and need not become involved in the difficult ontological problems that the social "determination" of knowledge, thought, and culture is otherwise bound to raise.

See also Functionalism in Sociology.

Bibliography

DEVELOPMENT

Barth, Hans. *Wahrheit und Ideologie*. Zürich: Manesse, 1945. Important, particularly with regard to Nietzsche.

Grünwald, Ernst. *Das Problem der Soziologie des Wissens*. Vienna: Braumüller, 1934. First comprehensive critical survey.

Lukács, Georg. *Geschichte und Klassenbewusstsein*. Berlin: Malik, 1923. Most distinguished Marxist study of the twentieth century.

Stark, Werner. "The Conservative Tradition in the Sociology of Knowledge." *Kyklos* 13 (1960): 90–101.

Stark, Werner. "Die idealistische Geschichtsauffassung und die Wissenssoziologie." *Archiv für Rechts- und Sozialphilosophie* 46 (1961): 355–374. This paper and the preceding one attempt to balance the picture of the doctrine's development.

Stark, Werner. *Montesquieu: Pioneer of the Sociology of Knowledge*. London: Routledge and Paul, 1960.

MAIN TRENDS

Adler, Franz. "A Quantitative Study in Sociology of Knowledge." *American Sociological Review* 19 (1954): 42–48. From the viewpoint of logical positivism.

Alpert, Harry. *Emile Durkheim and His Sociology*. New York: Columbia University Press, 1939.

Eisermann, Gottfried. "Vilfredo Pareto als Wissenssoziologe." *Kyklos* 15 (1962): 427–464.

Lieber, Hans-Joachim. *Wissen und Gesellschaft*. Tübingen: Niemeyer, 1952. Good all around, mainly on Scheler and Mannheim.

Mannheim, Karl. *Essays on the Sociology of Knowledge*, edited by Paul Kecskemeti. London: Routledge, 1952.

Mannheim, Karl. *Ideologie und Utopie*. Bonn: Cohen, 1929. Translated by Louis Wirth and Edward Shils as *Ideology and Utopia*. London: Routledge, 1936. Basic; from the historicist point of view, with comprehensive bibliography.

Maquet, Jacques J. *Sociologie de la connaisance*. Louvain, 1949. Translated by John F. Locke as *The Sociology of Knowledge*. Boston: Beacon Press, 1951. On Mannheim and Sorokin.

Rüschmeyer, Dietrich. *Probleme der Wissenssoziologie*. Cologne, 1958. Strong bias toward naive empiricism.

Scheler, Max, ed. *Versuche zu einer Soziologie des Wissens*. Munich: Duncker and Humblot, 1924. Decisive pioneering effort.

Scheler, Max. *Die Wissensformen und die Gesellschaft*. Leipzig: Neue Geist, 1926. Basic; from the phenomenological point of view.

Znaniecki, Florian. *The Social Role of the Man of Knowledge*. New York: Columbia University Press, 1940.

PHILOSOPHICAL ASPECTS

Child, Arthur. "The Existential Determination of Thought." *Ethics* 52 (1941–1942): 153–185.

Child, Arthur. "The Problem of Imputation in the Sociology of Knowledge." *Ethics* 51 (1940–1941): 200–219.

Child, Arthur. "The Problems of Imputation Resolved." *Ethics* 54 (1943–1944): 96–109.

Child, Arthur. "The Theoretical Possibility of the Sociology of Knowledge." *Ethics* 51 (1940–1941): 392–418.

Geiger, Theodor. *Ideologie und Wahrheit*. Stuttgart: Homboldt-Verlag, 1953. Rationalistic approach.

Horowitz, Irving L. *Philosophy, Science, and the Sociology of Knowledge*. Springfield, IL: Thomas, 1961. Methodological problems.

Schelting, Alexander von. *Max Webers Wissenschaftslehre*. Tübingen, 1933. Basic.

Stark, Werner. "The Sociology of Knowledge and the Problem of Ethics." In *Transactions of the Fourth World Congress of Sociology*, Vol. IV. London, 1959.

GENERAL SURVEYS

De Gré, Gerard L. *Society and Ideology*. New York, 1943.

Merton, Robert K. "The Sociology of Knowledge." In *Twentieth Century Sociology*, edited by Georges Gurvitch and Wilbert E. Moore. New York: Philosophical Library, 1946.

Stark, Werner. *The Sociology of Knowledge*. London: Routledge and Paul, 1958. Attempt at a total evaluation.

OTHER RECOMMENDED TITLES

Alston, William P. "Belief-Forming Practices and the Social." In *Socializing Epistemology*, edited by Frederick Schmitt. Lanham, MD: Rowman & Littlefield, 1994.

Bloor, D. *Knowledge and Social Imagery*. Chicago: University of Chicago Press, 1991.

Brown, J. R. *Scientific Rationality: The Sociological Turn*. Dordrecht: Reidel, 1984.

Fuller, Steve. "Recent Work on Social Epistemology." *American Philosophical Quarterly* 33 (1996): 149–166.

Hollis, M., and S. Lukes. *Rationality and Relativism*. Oxford: Blackwell, 1982.

Katz, Jonathan. "Rational Common Ground in the Sociology of Knowledge." *Philosophy of the Social Sciences* 19 (1989): 257–271.

Kurzman, Charles. "Epistemology and the Sociology of Knowledge." *Philosophy of the Social Sciences* 24 (1994): 267–290.

Latour, B. *Science in Action*. Cambridge, MA: Harvard University Press, 1987.

Longino, H. *Science as Social Knowledge*. Princeton, NJ: Princeton University Press, 1990.

McMullin, Ernan, ed. *The Social Dimensions of Knowledge*. South Bend, IN: Notre Dame University Press, 1992.

Okasha, S. "The Underdetermination of Theory by Data and the 'Strong Programme' in the Sociology of Knowledge." *International Studies in the Philosophy of Science* 14 (2000): 283–297.

Rouse, J. *Knowledge and Power: Toward a Political Philosophy of Science*. Ithaca, NY: Cornell University Press, 1987.

Schmitt, F. F., ed. *Socializing Epistemology*. Lanham, MD: Rowman & Littlefield, 1994.

Susser, Bernard. "The Sociology of Knowledge and Its Enemies." *Inquiry* 32 (1989): 245–260.

Werner Stark (1967)
Bibliography updated by Benjamin Fiedor (2005)

SOCRATES

(c. 470–399 BCE)

Socrates is the first Western philosopher to have left to posterity any sense of his individual personality, and he is a central figure in the subsequent development of philosophy. Both of these aspects are due primarily to Plato. It is via his portrayal by Plato's literary genius that Socrates is a living figure for subsequent generations, and thereby an exemplar of the ideals of philosophy, above all dedication to truth and intellectual integrity. It was under the influence of Socrates that Plato applied systematic techniques of argument pioneered by Socrates and his contemporaries, the Sophists, to the fundamental questions of human nature and conduct that primarily interested Socrates, thereby placing ethics and psychology at the center of the philosophical agenda. But while Plato brings Socrates to center stage he also hides him; because Socrates wrote nothing himself we depend on others for our knowledge of him, and it is above all Plato's representation of Socrates that constitutes the figure of perennial philosophical significance. But that representation was itself the expression of Plato's understanding of an actual historical individual and the events of his life. It is necessary, therefore, to begin with a brief account of the little that is known of that individual and those events.

LIFE

Socrates was born in Athens around 470 BCE and lived in the city all his life, apart from military service abroad. Little is known of the circumstances of his life. His father, Sophroniscus, is said by some ancient sources to have been a stonemason, and in Plato's *Theaetetus* (149a) Socrates says that his mother, Phainarete, was a midwife. That may indeed be true, though the fact that the name literally means "revealing excellence" suggests the possibility that Plato has invented the story in allusion to Socrates' role as midwife to the ideas of others (*Theaetetus* 149–151). Because Socrates served in the infantry, who had to provide their own arms and equipment, his circumstances, at least initially, must have been reasonably prosperous, but Plato and other writers emphasize his poverty in later life, which they attribute to his spending all his time in philosophical discussion. The same sources stress that, unlike the Sophists, he never took payment for his philosophical activity, and he may have depended largely on support from wealthier friends. During his lifetime Athens became the principal center of intellectual and cultural life in Greece, attracting from all over the Greek world intellectuals who developed and popularized the tradition of natural philosophy begun by the Ionian philosophers of the previous century, together with exciting new argumentative techniques and radical questioning of traditional beliefs about theology, morals, and society.

Socrates was actively interested in most of these areas. Plato and others attest to his interest at one stage in questions of cosmology and physiology, though the sources agree that his interests subsequently shifted to fundamental questions of conduct. Socrates never engaged in formal philosophical instruction, or set up any school; his philosophical activity consisted in informal conversation, partly with a circle of mainly younger associates whom he attracted by the force of his intellect and personality, but also with others, including Sophists and prominent citizens. Some of his associates, including Plato and some of his relations, were opposed to the

Athenian democratic system, and it may be that Socrates shared that attitude to some extent.

Socrates married relatively late in life; at the time of his death at about the age of seventy his eldest son was an adolescent, and he had two more small sons, the younger probably a baby. His wife (who must have been at least thirty years younger than he) was Xanthippe. Her bad temper (attested by Xenophon and others, but not by Plato) became legendary; stories of her abuse of Socrates, and his equanimity in putting up with it, were a stock comic theme from antiquity to modern times. Thus Chaucer's Wife of Bath describes in the Prologue to her tale (727–732) how Socrates sat quietly while Xanthippe "caste pisse upon his heed," merely remarking mildly, "Before the thunder stops it comes on to rain." (The story goes back to Diogenes Laertius's life of Socrates, *Lives of the Philosophers* 2.36.) One element in this comic tradition is the story that Socrates had another wife, or possibly a concubine, while married to Xanthippe; stories of how the two women switched from quarrelling with one another to concerted assaults on Socrates afforded rich material. Ancient sources attribute the origin of this tale to Aristotle, but the supposed original source is lost, and the historical basis extremely dubious.

Nothing is known of specific events in Socrates' life till after the outbreak of the Peloponnesian War with Sparta in 432. He served with distinction in various campaigns, most notably the Battle of Delium in 424, where it was said (Plato, *Laches* 181b) that if everyone had behaved like Socrates the battle would not have been lost. By the 420s he had become sufficientiy well known to be caricatured in several comic dramas. In the single example to survive complete, the *Clouds* of Aristophanes, first produced in 423, he appears as a representative of subversive contemporary tendencies, the head of a disreputable academy whose curriculum combines training in argumentative trickery with atheistic natural philosophy. Later, in his *Apology* (Defense of Socrates), Plato represents this portrayal as the origin of prejudice against Socrates that culminated in his condemnation on charges of impiety and corruption of the young (19a–19d); there is no reason to discount that evidence.

The only occasion on which Socrates is known to have intervened in public life took place in 406. After a naval engagement the Athenian commanders had failed to pick up survivors, and the popular assembly voted to try them collectively, instead of individually as required by law. At that period most civic offices were assigned by lot, and Socrates happened to be a member of the executive committee whose function was to prepare business for the assembly. In that capacity he was the only one to oppose the illegal proposal. A few years later when, after final defeat in the war, the democracy was temporarily overthrown by a junta known as the Thirty Tyrants, he showed the same adherence to legality and morality by refusing, at the risk of his own life, to obey an order from the tyrants to take part in the arrest of an innocent man. It is likely that he remained neutral during the civil war in which the tyranny was overthrown, because he had friends in both camps; in particular, two of the most prominent among the tyrants, Critias and Charmides, both relatives of Plato, were among his close associates.

It is probable that this was at least a contributory factor in the accusation brought against him under the restored democracy. The explicit charges were failure to recognize (or perhaps "to believe in") the gods of the state religion and the introduction of new divinities, coupled with corruption of the young. The case was tried early in 399, and the prosecution demanded the death penalty. There is no evidence of the detail of the prosecution's case. On the religious aspect the prosecutors may have sought to represent Socrates as the leader of an illegal private cult, and may have used his claim, amply attested by Plato, to be guided by a private divine sign or voice in support of that charge. It is highly likely that the charge of corruption centered on his associations with notorious enemies of the state, particularly the tyrants mentioned above, as well as Alcibiades, an intimate of Socrates who had instigated a disastrous invasion of Sicily in 415 and had later defected to Sparta. Knowledge of the trial is based on two versions of Socrates' defense, by Plato and Xenophon, each of whom, while preserving a core of fact, presents the defense in the light of his own agenda; Xenophon relies wholly on Socrates' adherence to conventional piety and morality, whereas Plato gives a radically unconventional picture of Socrates' philosophical activity as the fulfillment of a divine mission to perfect the souls of his fellow citizens by subjecting their basic beliefs and values to philosophical criticism.

Socrates was condemned to death. Plato's *Phaedo* gives a moving picture of his last hours, spent among his followers in discussion of the immortality of the soul and the task of philosophy to free it from the trammels of the body, followed by his tranquil death from self-administration of hemlock. While there is dispute about the relative degrees of realism and idealization in the description of the effects of the poison, there is little doubt that the primary aim of the whole work is less historical accuracy than depiction of the ideal philosophical death.

SOCRATIC LITERATURE

Besides Plato and Xenophon no fewer than nine associates of Socrates are reported by various ancient sources as having written imaginative accounts of Socrates' conversations, creating a body of literature collectively known as "Socratic conversations" (or "discourses") (*Sokratikoi logoi*). For the most part only the titles of these works survive, indicating that Socrates' relations with certain individuals, especially Alcibiades, who figures prominently in some Platonic dialogues—notably *Alcibiades* and *Symposium*—were a theme common to Plato and the other Socratic writers. Apart from Plato and Xenophon, the only Socratic writer of whose works any significant fragments survive is Aeschines of Sphettus; the fragments of his *Alcibiades* show Socrates using his characteristic critical method (see below) to convince Alcibiades of the vanity of his political ambitions. They thus provide evidence that the program of defending Socrates against the slanders occasioned by his associations with political undesirables was not confined to Plato and Xenophon, but they provide no evidence for Socrates' thought to complement those sources.

For information specifically about the thought of Socrates scholars are in fact almost wholly dependent on Plato, because the other principal source, Xenophon, focuses on the practical and moral import of Socrates' conversations, with comparatively little theoretical content, in keeping with his overall purpose (see above) of portraying Socrates as a good man and sound citizen. There is a systematic difficulty in determining which of the views attributed to Socrates in Plato's dialogues were actually held by the historical person, and scholarly opinion has embraced all possible positions. In the nineteenth century the dominant consensus (primarily on the part of German scholars) divided the Platonic writings into three broad groups, distinguished both chronologically and doctrinally. The first "early" group, including *Laches*, *Charmides*, *Protagoras*, and those dialogues dealing directly with the trial of Socrates (*Euthyphro*, *Apology*, and *Crito*), was generally held to give a veridical account of the personality, views, and philosophical activity of the historical Socrates.

Thereafter Plato's philosophy developed in directions independent of Socrates, and the importance of the dramatic figure of Socrates in the dialogues correspondingly declined, until its virtual disappearance in works such as the *Sophist* and the *Statesman* (which were taken to be late), and its total disappearance from the *Laws* (unfinished on Plato's death and generally regarded as his last work). This "developmental" model was supported by the stylometric studies of the later nineteenth century, in which a number of scholars, working largely independently of one another, converged on the identification of six dialogues—*Sophist*, *Statesman*, *Timaeus*, *Critias*, *Philebus*, and *Laws*—as a group distinct in various features of style and vocabulary from the rest of the Platonic corpus; these dialogues were fixed as late by the presence of the *Laws*. *Parmenides*, *Phaedrus*, *Republic*, and *Theaetetus*, which are by the same criteria closer in style to the late group than the rest of the dialogues, were identified as "middle" dialogues, and the remainder as "early."

While this developmental model, with its assumption that the early dialogues accurately represent the historical Socrates, is still highly significant in the twenty-first century, notably in the influential work of Gregory Vlastos and others, it has undergone challenge from two opposite extremes, on the one side the thesis maintained by John Burnet and A. E. Taylor in the early twentieth century that all the doctrines attributed by Plato to Socrates in the dialogues were actually maintained by the historical Socrates, and on the other side the views of those who, stressing that all information about Socrates derives from sources with their own literary and philosophical agenda, urge that the historical Socrates is inaccessible and should therefore disappear from the history of philosophy.

The Burnet/Taylor thesis has few if any adherents in the twenty-first century; not only does it present an implausible picture of a Plato who devoted the great part of his literary career to recounting the views of someone else, but it rests on an assumption about the nature of Plato's attitude to Socrates, namely that it would have been disrespectful to Socrates for Plato to do other than represent his views with historical accuracy, which seems totally foreign to the character of the dialogues themselves. It is clear from the dialogues that Plato's attitude to Socrates was that the latter's life and activity represented the paradigm of philosophy, and it is totally in keeping with that attitude that Plato should ascribe to Socrates what he (Plato) regards as the philosophical truth, whether or not Socrates himself had maintained it. What we may call the skeptical view of Socrates, however, is widely accepted today, and while its extreme versions are exaggerated and oversimplified, it is based on an important insight into the nature of our sources.

The insight is simply that all knowledge of Socrates is based on sources in which historical veridicality is at best one among the author's concerns, and generally not the principal concern. Oversimplification consists in the characterization of these sources as fiction, as opposed to factual biography, and exaggeration in the conclusion that the historical Socrates is inaccessible. The dichotomy between biography and fiction seems inapplicable to the Socratic literature, including Plato's Socratic dialogues (and indeed this author doubts its appropriateness to most ancient biographical writing); Socratic conversation is a form of biography, but biography whose factual constraints are looser than is standardly the case in the modern world.

That is not to say that there are no factual constraints; Plato's dialogues do present an actual historical individual, some of the events in whose life are known, and they are no doubt faithful to the spirit and nature of the philosophical conversation that was that individual's principal activity. But when it comes to specific doctrines, while there are some doctrines found maintained by Plato's Socrates that it is virtually certain the historical Socrates did not maintain, there are none that is certain that he did. In the first class the paradigm case is the theory of separate Forms, (i.e., intelligible universal natures existing separately from their sensible instances) which we find maintained by Socrates in several dialogues, but which Aristotle (whose evidence this author regards as independent of the dialogues on this point) explicitly says Socrates did not hold (*Metaphysics* 1078b27–1078b32).

However, theses characteristically regarded as "Socratic"—for example, that Virtue is Knowledge (see below)—are not ascribed to Socrates by sources that are clearly independent of their appearance in the Platonic dialogues. They may in fact have been maintained by Socrates, or they may have been suggested to Plato, in the form in which they appear in the dialogues, by things that Socrates said. We cannot be sure, and in any case it is not of the first importance, because the philosophical significance of these doctrines consists in the role that they play, and the arguments by which they are supported, in the dialogues in which they appear. The brief account of Socrates' thought that follows is to be understood as based on that assumption. It identifies some central themes in the portrayal of Socrates in those dialogues, generally considered comparatively early compositions, in which the personality and argumentative style of Socrates are more prominent than in dialogues devoted to the more systematic exposition of Plato's own thought (see above). The attribution of any specific doctrine to the historical Socrates must be correspondingly tentative.

THOUGHT

DISAVOWAL OF WISDOM. In these dialogues Socrates is presented for the most part not as a systematic or authoritative teacher, but as a questioner and enquirer. His enquiries are all focused on questions of conduct, broadly understood, and frequently consist of attempts to reach an agreed definition of some fundamental value, such as courage, or goodness in general. Typically Socrates is depicted as engaged with one or more people in conversation on some specific, often practical topic, which leads on to the more general issues just mentioned. Socrates elicits the views of his interlocutors on these issues and subjects them to critical examination, conducted with a minimum of philosophical technicality, and utilizing other assumptions, usually of a commonsense kind, which the parties to the discussion agree on. Usually this procedure reveals inconsistency among the set of beliefs (including the general thesis or proposed definition) that the person examined holds, which is taken as requiring the abandonment of the thesis or definition. Frequently the dialogue ends with the acknowledgement by Socrates and the others that, having failed to settle the general issue raised, they are unable to proceed further; they thus end up in a state of *aporia*—that is, a state with no way out. This procedure of enquiry, rather than instruction, and its frequent aporetic outcome are in keeping with Socrates' denial (*Apology* 21b) that he possesses any wisdom (i.e., expertise). It is the mark of an expert to be able to define the concepts in the area of his expertise and to expound that area systematically, neither of which Socrates can do.

In later antiquity Socrates was regularly reported as having said that he knew nothing, or, paradoxically, that he knew nothing except that he knew nothing. Either formulation goes beyond anything found in Plato. Though Socrates frequently says in the dialogues that he does not know the answer to this or that particular question, he never says that he knows nothing, and occasionally makes emphatic claims to knowledge, most notably in the *Apology*, where he twice claims to know that abandoning his divine mission to philosophize would be bad and disgraceful (29b, 37b).

What he does disavow is having any wisdom. He seems to apply the notion of wisdom firstly to divine wisdom, a complete and perspicuous understanding of everything, that belongs to the gods alone, and is consequently unavailable to humans, and then to human expertise of the sort possessed by craftsmen such a builders and shoemakers, a systematic mastery of a technique that enables its possessor to apply it successfully and to expound and pass it on to others. The Sophists claimed to possess, and to teach to others, a practical expertise applying not to any specialized area of human activity but to human life as such, mastery of which guaranteed overall success in personal and political life; this was "the political craft" (*Apology* 19d–20c, *Protagoras* 319a). Socrates rejects that claim, not on the ground that such expertise is not available to humans; but because the Sophists' activity fails to meet the ordinary criteria for human expertise, particularly that of being systematically learned and taught (*Protagoras*319d–320b, *Meno* 89c–94e). He denies that he possesses this expertise himself (*Apology* 20c), but does not say that it is impossible that he, or any human being, should possess it.

This disavowal of expertise is not incompatible with the claim to know particular things. The nonexpert can know some particular things, but not in the way the expert knows them; specifically the nonexpert is not able, as the expert is, to relate his or her particular items of knowledge to a comprehensive system that provides explanations of their truth by relating them to other items of knowledge and to the system as a whole. But that raises the problem of the source of Socrates' nonexpert knowledge of moral truths. Usually, nonexperts know some particular things because they have been told by an expert, or because they have picked them up from some intermediate source whose authority is ultimately derived from that of the expert. But Socrates does not recognize any moral experts, among human beings at any rate. So what is the source of his nonexpert knowledge? The dialogues provide no clear or uniform answer to this question. Sometimes he suggests that the application of his critical method is sufficient, not merely to reveal inconsistency in his interlocutor's beliefs, but to prove that some are false, and hence that their negations are true. Thus at the end of the argument with Callicles in the *Gorgias* he claims (508e–509a) that the conclusion that it is always better to suffer wrong than to do it has been established by "arguments of iron and adamant" (i.e., of irresistible force), while conjoining that claim with a disavowal of knowledge: "I do not know how these things are, but no-one I have ever met, as in the present case, has been able to deny them without making himself ridiculous."

This presents a contrast between expert knowledge, which Socrates disclaims, and a favorable epistemic position produced by repeated application of Socrates' critical method of argument. There are some propositions that repeated experiment shows no one capable of denying without self-contradiction. While it is always theoretically possible that someone might come up with a way of escape from this position, realistically the arguments establishing those propositions are so firmly entrenched as to be irresistible. While it is an attractive suggestion that Socrates considers the moral truths that he nonexpertly knows to be of this kind, it receives no clear confirmation from the dialogues. There is, for instance, no indication in the *Crito* that Socrates' unshakable commitment to the fundamental principle that one must never act unjustly (49a) is based on critical examination of his and Crito's moral beliefs. It has to be acknowledged that while Socrates indicates that critical examination is sometimes capable of establishing truth beyond at least the practical possibility of rebuttal, and sometimes suggests that he knows some moral truths on the strength of good arguments for them, he gives no general account of the grounds of his nonexpert moral knowledge.

RELIGION. One might perhaps speculate that the source of Socrates' nonexpert moral knowledge is supposed to be divine revelation, but though Socrates' attitudes to the divine are an important element in his portrayal by both Plato and Xenophon, neither in fact suggests that Socrates believed that his moral beliefs were divinely inspired. What he did believe, according to both writers, is that throughout his life he was guided by a private sign or voice that he accepted, apparently without question, as being of divine origin, but the content of that guidance appears to have been, not moral principles, but day-to-day practical affairs, and it had the peculiar feature that its guidance was always negative, warning Socrates against some course of action that he might otherwise have undertaken (Plato, *Apology* 31c–31d). Thus Xenophon reports him (*Apology* 4) as explaining his failure to prepare his defense because the divine sign had told him not to, while in Plato's *Apology* (40a–40b) he says that he is confident that his conduct at his trial has been correct because the divine sign has not opposed it.

Such a claim to continuous private divine guidance (as opposed to occasional private revelations, e.g., in dreams) was certainly unusual, and, as suggested above, it is likely that it at least contributed to the charge of religious unorthodoxy that was one of the grounds of his condemnation. The actual stance of the historical Socrates toward conventional religion is not altogether easy to reconstruct from the sources. Xenophon, as pointed out above, stresses his conventional piety, as measured by public observance and private conversation; for example, his demonstration to an irreligious acquaintance of the providential ordering of the world, down to such details as the design of the eyelashes to shield the eyes from the wind (*Memorabilia* 1.4). On that account it is difficult to see how the charge of impiety could have been brought at all.

Plato's presentation is more complex. He does indeed represent Socrates as concerned on occasion with prophetic dreams (*Crito* 44a–44b; *Phaedo* 60e–61b) and with ritual, most famously in his report of Socrates' last words: "Crito, we owe a cock to Asclepius; pay it and don't forget" (*Phaedo* 118a). But it is notable that all of these instances arise in the context of Socrates' imminent death. When Plato represents Socrates as praying on various occasions throughout his life he almost always makes him pray for nothing but wisdom and virtue, while in his most extensive discussion of piety, in *Euthyphro*, he suggests that Socrates thinks that what the gods require from humans is nothing other than moral virtue. That fits well with his *Apology*, where Socrates' rebuttal of the charge of impiety has nothing at all to say about ritual, consisting wholly in the claim that Socrates' life has been the fulfillment of a divine mission to promote the welfare, identified with the moral virtue, of his fellow citizens.

Plato's view of Socratic religion seems then to be that the essence of service to the gods is moral virtue, and that ritual fills its proper role, as in Socrates' life and death, as a complement to the fulfillment of that primary task. If that reflects Socrates' own view, then it is possible that it was seen by conservatively minded contemporaries as presenting a radical challenge to traditional ideas of the relations between gods and humans, which were founded on the belief that divine favor and protection for individuals and the community were secured by performance of the appropriate prayers and rituals, and thereby as justifying his condemnation for neglecting the state religion in favor of a new religion of his own.

DEFINITIONS. In the procedure of enquiry sketched in (i) above, the search for general definitions is central. This arises naturally from Socrates' search for expertise; the expert knows about his or her subject, and according to Socrates the primary knowledge concerning any subject is precisely knowledge of what that subject is. The general pattern of argument in the dialogues is that some specific question about a subject—for example, how is one to acquire goodness—is problematic in the absence of an agreed conception of what that subject is. Hence before the problematic question can be pursued, the definition of the subject must first be sought. The problematic question may be of various kinds; it may be, as in the example above (from the *Meno*) how goodness as such is to be acquired, or how a specific virtue is to be acquired (courage in the *Laches*), or whether a virtue is advantageous to its possessor (justice in the *Republic*). The *Euthyphro* exemplifies another pattern; it is disputed whether a particular action, Euthyphro's prosecution of his father for homicide, is an instance of piety or holiness, and Socrates maintains that the question will be settled when, and only when, the definition of piety is arrived at. This pattern has given rise to the accusation that Socrates is guilty of the "Socratic fallacy" of maintaining that in general it is impossible to tell whether anything is an instance of a property unless one already possesses a general definition of that property.

That general position would be methodologically disastrous for Socrates, because his approved strategy for reaching a definition is to consider what instances of the kind or property in question have in common, and it is impossible to do that if a person has to know the definition before he or she can even identify the instances from which the definition is to be derived. In fact the argument of the *Euthyphro* does not involve that fallacy; even if it is granted that there are some disputed cases where the question "Is this an instance of F?" cannot be settled without answering the prior question "What is F?" it does not follow that there are no undisputed cases where instances of F can be recognized without a definition. In the *Hippias Major*, however, Socrates does argue (286c–286e) that people cannot tell whether anything is fine or beautiful (*kalon*) unless they know—that is, can give a definition of—what fineness or beauty is; so though the Socratic fallacy is not a pervasive defect of Socrates' argumentative method, there does seem to be one instance of it in the dialogues.

The question "What is F?" can itself be understood in various ways; it may be a request for an elucidation of the linguistic meaning of the term "F," or a request for a substantive account of what the property of F-ness consists in, including, where appropriate, the decomposition of a complex property into its components (e.g., goodness consists of justice, self-control, etc.) and explanatory accounts of properties (e.g., self-control consists of the control of the bodily appetites by reason). The practical nature of the questions that often give rise to the search for definitions suggests that the latter kind of definition is what is sought. Someone who wants to know how virtue is to be acquired will not be helped by a specification of the meaning of "virtue" as "a property contributing to overall success in life"; what they are looking for is precisely an account of what it is that constitutes or guarantees success in life. That is confirmed by the fact that *Laches*, *Meno*, and *Protagoras*, all of which start from the practical question of how either a specific virtue or goodness in general is to be acquired, converge on the suggestion that courage (in *Laches*) and goodness (in *Meno* and *Protagoras*) are identical with knowledge, which is itself part of a substantive theory of the nature of goodness (see next section). It must, however, be acknowledged that Plato shows no awareness of the theoretical distinction between a purely conceptual definition and the kind of substantive account that is favored by the structure of the dialogues just mentioned. Even in the *Meno*, the dialogue in which definition is treated in the greatest detail, he gives model definitions of either kind without any explicit differentiation. Substantive accounts are favored over conceptual definitions by his practice, not in the light of any theoretical discrimination between the two.

ETHICS. The picture of Socrates as a nonexpert enquirer outlined above needs to be qualified to this extent, that in some dialogues, specifically *Protagoras*, *Gorgias*, and *Meno*, he is represented as arguing positively, though not conclusively, in favor of certain propositions that amount to at least the outline of a theory of human nature and of human good. The basic theses of this theory are:

(1) Every agent has a single overall aim, the achievement of a completely satisfactory life for him or herself.

(2) Knowledge of what constitutes such a life is both necessary and sufficient for the achievement of it.

(3) Such a life consists in the practice of the virtues of justice, self-control, courage, and holiness, which are identical with one another in that they are the application to different kinds of situation of the fundamental virtue of knowledge (of what the good for humans is and how it is to be achieved).

Thesis 2 is the famous thesis that "Virtue is knowledge," from which together with thesis 1 follows the still more famous thesis that "No-one does wrong willingly" (the latter two often referred to as "The Socratic Paradoxes"). The idea expressed in the second paradox is that, because everyone necessarily has the single aim of achieving the best life for him or herself, any action that does not in fact promote that aim must be explained by the agent's mistaken belief that it does promote it. Socrates is thus the first of a succession of philosophers throughout the ages to deny the possibility of acting against one's better judgment (often ascribed to weakness of will); that position remains as controversial in the twenty-first century as it was in antiquity. The identification of the conventional moral and social virtues as applications of the fundamental knowledge of what the human good is (with the implication that the virtues are identical with one another, conventionally labeled "The Unity of the Virtues"), though central to the prototheory, is never adequately argued for. It is supported at *Crito* (47e) by an analogy between virtue of soul and health of body; justice and injustice are respectively the health and sickness of the soul. So, just as it is not worth living with a diseased and corrupted body, it is not worth living with a diseased and corrupted soul. But that is not an argument. Even granted that health is an intrinsically desirable and disease an intrinsically undesirable state, the crucial claims that justice is the health of the soul and injustice its disease require defense, not mere assertion.

Plato supplies some arguments in the *Gorgias*, but they are weak. Socrates first agues that successful tyrants, who manifest the extreme of injustice, do not get what they really want—that is, the best life for themselves—because their injustice is bad for them. The crucial argument for that conclusion (473a–475c) starts from the premise, conceded by Socrates' opponent Polus, that acting unjustly, while good (i.e., advantageous) for the agent, is disgraceful. It is next agreed that whatever is disgraceful is so either because it is unpleasant or because it is harmful. Because acting unjustly is clearly not unpleasant, it must therefore be harmful. Hence the life of injustice is harmful to the unjust agent. This argument fails because it ignores the relativity of the concepts of unpleasantness and harmfulness. To be acceptable the first premise must be read as "Whatever is disgraceful to anyone is so either because it is unpleasant to someone or because it is harmful to someone." From that premise it clearly does not follow that because injustice is not unpleasant to the unjust person it must be harmful to that person. It could be harmful to someone else, and its being so could be the ground of its being disgraceful to the unjust person (as indeed people ordinarily think).

Later in the dialogue (503e–504d) Socrates argues against Callicles that because the goodness of anything, such as a boat or a house, depends on the proper proportion and order of its components, the goodness of body and soul alike depend on the proper proportion and order of their components, respectively health in the case of the body and justice and self-control in the case of the soul. The analogy of health and virtue, simply asserted in the *Crito*, is here supported by the general principle that goodness depends on the organization of components, but that principle is insufficient to ground the analogy, because the proper organization of components is determined by the function, point, or aim of the thing that those components make up. So in order to know which organization of psychic components is the appropriate one for humans we need a prior conception of what our aims in life should be. One conception of these aims may indeed identify the optimum organization as that defined by the conventional moral virtues, but another may identify as optimum a different organization, say one that affords the maximum scope to certain kinds of self-expression, as exemplified by a figure such as the Nietzschean Superman. Socrates provides no argument to exclude that possibility.

In addition to the failure to establish that virtue is always in the agent's interest, the prototheory is more deeply flawed, in that it proves to be incoherent. This emerges when we consider Proposition 2, "Virtue Is Knowledge," and ask what virtue is knowledge of. The answer suggested by *Meno* and *Protagoras* is that virtue is knowledge of the best life for the agent; given the standing motivation to achieve that life, knowledge of what it consists in will be necessary if one is to pursue it reliably, and sufficient to guarantee success in that pursuit. But that requires that the best life for the agent is something distinct from the knowledge which guarantees that one will achieve that life. "Virtue is knowledge of the best life for the agent" will be parallel to "Medicine is knowledge of health," and the value of that knowledge will be purely instrumental and derivative from the intrinsic value of the success in life which it guarantees. But Socrates, as we have seen, treats virtue as analogous, not to medicine, but to health itself, and hence as intrinsically, not merely instrumentally valuable. Virtue is not, then, a means to some independently specifiable condition of life which we can identify as the best life, well-being, or happiness (in Greek, *eudaimonia*); rather it is a constituent of such a life, and one of the most difficult questions about Socratic ethics is whether Socrates recognizes any other constituents. That is to say, for Socrates a life is worth living either solely or at least primarily in virtue of the fact that it is a life of virtue.

The incoherence of the prototheory thus consists in the fact that Socrates maintains both that virtue is knowledge of what the agent's good is and that it is that good itself, whereas these two theses are inconsistent with one another. It could indeed be the case both that virtue is knowledge of what the agent's good is and that the agent's good is knowledge, but in that case the knowledge which is the agent's good has to be a distinct item or body of knowledge from the knowledge of what the agent's good is. So if Socrates is to maintain that virtue is knowledge, he must either specify that knowledge as knowledge of something other than what the agent's good is, or he must abandon the thesis that virtue is the agent's good. There are indications in the dialogues that Plato was conscious of this difficulty. In the *Euthydemus* he represents Socrates as grappling inconclusively with the problem, and in the *Republic* he offers a solution in a conception of human good as consisting in a state of the personality in which the nonrational impulses are directed by the intellect, informed indeed by knowledge, but by knowledge not of human good, but of goodness itself, a universal principle of rationality. This conception retains from the prototheory the thesis that human good is virtue, but abandons the claim that knowledge is virtue, because virtue is not identical with knowledge but directed by it, the knowledge in question being knowledge of the universal good.

Protagoras may plausibly be seen as exploring another solution to this puzzle, because in that dialogue Socrates sets out an account of goodness whose central theses are (i) virtue is knowledge of human good, and (ii) human good is a life in which pleasure predominates over distress. Whether Socrates is represented as adopting this solution in his own person, or merely as proposing it as a theory that ordinary people and Sophists such as Protagoras ought to accept (a question on which there has been much dispute), it represents a way out of the impasse that blocks the prototheory, though not a way that Plato was himself to adopt. Having experimented with this solution, which retains the identity of virtue with knowledge while abandoning the identity of virtue with human good, he settled instead for the *Republic*'s solution, which maintains the latter identity while abandoning the former.

The prototheory is not strictly inconsistent with Socrates' disavowal of wisdom or expertise, because it is presented in outline only, not established by conclusive argument as expertise requires. But the presentation of Socrates as even a prototheorist has at least a different emphasis from the depiction of him simply as a questioner and generator of *aporiai*. This author believes that it is impossible to tell how much of this theory is Plato's own and how much was actually held by Socrates; that it was at least suggested to Plato by certain ideas that had emerged in Socrates' conversations seems highly likely, but we are not justified in asserting more than that.

LATER INFLUENCE

The prototheory just sketched was an important element in the development of Plato's own ethical theory, and via Plato on those of Aristotle and the post-Aristotelian philosophical schools. With the exception of the Epicureans, each of the main schools adopted Socrates as, in effect, a patron saint, stressing aspects of his thought and personality congenial to its particular philosophical standpoint; the skeptics, especially those in the Platonic

Academy, which was converted to skepticism by Arcesilaus just over a century after its foundation and remained skeptical for two centuries, stressed Socrates' disavowal of wisdom and the undogmatic character of his questioning technique. The Cynics, whose doctrines and way of life derived from Antisthenes, one of Socrates' associates, claimed to emulate the austerity of his lifestyle and to accept his doctrine that virtue is sufficient for happiness. Via the Cynics, Socrates became a major influence on Stoicism, which combined the Cynic doctrine that happiness consists in living according to nature with the doctrine that for rational beings the life according to nature is the life in accordance with rationality. Accepting the essentials of the prototheory outlined above they drew the conclusion that moral virtue is the only good, everything else being indifferent—that is, neither good nor bad. A particularly significant figure in the Stoics' canonization of Socrates is Epictetus, who adopted Socrates at the exemplar of the philosophical life and reproduced in his protreptic discourses features of Socratic method such as elenctic and inductive arguments.

The influence of Socrates was not confined to the ancient philosophical schools. The second-century Christian apologist Justin claimed him as a forerunner of Christianity, a characterization that was revived by Renaissance Neoplatonists such as Marsilio Ficino. In Medieval Islam he was revered, though not well understood, as a sage and a defender of (and martyr for) monotheism against idolatry. In the Enlightenment era he was appropriated by rationalists such as Voltaire as an exemplar of natural virtue and a martyr in the struggle of rationality against superstition. In the nineteenth century Hegel, Kierkegaard, and Nietzsche identified him as a central figure in developments in the history of philosophy to which their own respective theories responded, and in the last quarter of the twentieth century he was a major influence on the later thought of Foucault.

The perennial fascination of Socrates owes less, however, to any specific doctrines than to Plato's portrayal of him as the exemplar of a philosophical life—that is, a life dedicated to following the argument wherever it might lead, even when it in fact led to hardship, poverty, judicial condemnation, and consequent death. Plato's depiction of how Socrates lived for philosophy would in any case have made him immortal; his presentation of how he died for it has given him a unique status in its history.

See also Plato; Sophists; Xenophon.

Bibliography

ANCIENT SOURCES

Aristophanes. *Clouds*, edited by K. J. Dover. Oxford: Clarendon Press, 1968. Translated by B. B. Rogers. London and Cambridge, MA: Loeb, 1924.

Diogenes Laertius. *Lives of Eminent Philosophers: Diogenes Laertius*. Loeb Classical Library. Translated by R. D. Hicks. Cambridge, MA: Harvard University Press, 1925. All volumes in the Loeb Classical Library contain the text in the original language with facing English translation.

Ferguson, John. *Socrates: A Source Book*. London: Macmillan for the Open University Press, 1970. This book contains a comprehensive collection of passages of ancient works (in English translation) referring to Socrates.

Plato. *Platonis Opera*, edited by John Burnet. 5 vols. Oxford: Clarendon Press, 1902–1906. Often called the Oxford Classical Text. New edition of Vol. 1, edited by E. A. Duke et al. (New York: Oxford University Press, 1995). New edition of *Republic*, edited by S. Slings (New York: Oxford University Press, 2003).

All the dialogues are available in numerous English translations.

Xenophon. *Apology*. Loeb Classical Library, edited by O. J. Todd. Cambridge, MA: Harvard University Press, 1961.

Xenophon. *Memorabilia*. Loeb Classical Library, edited by E. C. Marchant. London: Heinemann, 1923. Greek with facing English translation.

Xenophon. *Symposium*. Loeb Classical Library, edited by O. J. Todd. Cambridge, MA: Harvard University Press, 1961.

Xenophon, Conversations of Socrates, Translated by Hugh Tredennick and Robin Waterfield. Harmondsworth: Penguin Classics, 1990.

Minor Socratic writers. *Socratis et Socraticorum Reliquiae*. Edited by Gabriele Giannantoni. 4 vols. Naples: Bibliopolis, 1990. English translation of the principal fragments of Aeschines in *Plato and His Contemporaries*, by G. C. Field, chap. 11. London: Methuen, 1930.

MODERN WORKS

Comprehensive Survey

Guthrie, W. K. C. *A History of Greek Philosophy*. Vol. 3, pt. 2. Cambridge, U.K.: Cambridge University Press, 1969. Published separately in 1971 under title *Socrates*.

Socratic Literature and the Problem of the Historical Socrates

Burnet, John. *Greek Philosophy: Thales to Plato*. London: Macmillan, 1914.

Burnet, John. "The Socratic Doctrine of the Soul." *Proceedings of the British Academy* 7 (1915–1916): 235–260.

Döring, Klaus. "Sokrates, die Sokratiker und die von ihnen begründeten Traditionen." In *Grundriss der Geschichte der Philosophie. Die Philosophie der Antike 2/1: Sophistik, Sokrates, Sokratik, Mathematik, Medizin*, edited by Helmut Flashar, 139–364. Basel, Switzerland: Schwabe, 1998.

Kahn, Charles H. *Plato and the Socratic Dialogue: The Philosophical Use of a Literary Form*. Cambridge, U.K.: Cambridge University Press, 1996.

Patzer, Andreas, ed. *Der historische Sokrates*. Darmstadt, Germany: Wissenschaftliche Buchgesellschaft, 1987.

Rutherford, R. B. *The Art of Plato: Ten Essays in Platonic Interpretation*. London: Duckworth, 1995.

Taylor, A. E. "Plato's Biography of Socrates." *Proceedings of the British Academy* 8 (1917–1918): 93–132.

Taylor, A. E. *Socrates*. London: Peter Davies, 1932.

Taylor, A. E. *Varia Socratica*. Oxford: James Parker, 1911.

Taylor, C. C. W. *Socrates*. Oxford: Oxford University Press, 1998.

Vander Waerdt, Paul A. *The Socratic Movement*. Ithaca, NY: Cornell University Press, 1994.

Critical and Analytical Studies, Primarily on Plato's Presentation of Socrates

Benson, Hugh H. *Socratic Wisdom: The Model of Knowledge in Plato's Early Dialogues*. New York: Oxford University Press, 2000.

Brickhouse, Thomas C., and Nicholas D. Smith. *The Philosophy of Socrates*. Boulder, CO: Westview Press, 2000.

Brickhouse, Thomas C., and Nicholas D. Smith. *Plato's Socrates*. New York: Oxford University Press, 1994.

Irwin, Terence. *Plato's Ethics*. New York: Oxford University Press, 1995.

McPherran, Mark L. *The Religion of Socrates*. University Park: Pennsylvania State University Press, 1996.

Santas, Gerasimos Xenophon. *Socrates: Philosophy in Plato's Early Dialogues*. London: Routledge, 1979.

Vlastos, Gregory. *Socrates, Ironist and Moral Philosopher*. Cambridge, U.K.: Cambridge University Press, 1991.

Vlastos, Gregory. *Socratic Studies*, edited by Myles Burnyeat. Cambridge, U.K.: Cambridge University Press, 1994.

Works on the Trial of Socrates

Brickhouse, Thomas C., and Nicholas D. Smith. *Socrates on Trial*. Princeton, NJ: Princeton University Press, 1989; and Oxford: Clarendon Press, 1989. This work contains a useful guide to modern literature on Socrates.

Brickhouse, Thomas C., and Nicholas D. Smith, eds. *The Trial and Execution of Socrates: Sources and Controversies*. New York: Oxford University Press, 2002.

Hansen, Mogens Herman. *The Trial of Sokrates: From the Athenian Point of View*. Copenhagen: The Royal Danish Academy of Sciences and Letters, 1995.

Stone, I. F. *The Trial of Socrates*. London: Jonathan Cape, 1988.

Collections of Articles

Benson, Hugh H., ed. *Essays on the Philosophy of Socrates* New York: Oxford University Press, 1992.

Gower, Barry S., and Michael C. Stokes, eds. *Socratic Questions: New Essays on the Philosophy of Socrates and Its Significance*. London: Routledge, 1992.

Prior, William J., ed. *Socrates: Critical Assessments*. 4 Vols. London: Routledge, 1996.

Smith, Nicholas D., and Paul B. Woodruff, eds. *Reason and Religion in Socratic Philosophy*. New York: Oxford University Press, 2000.

Vlastos, Gregory, ed. *The Philosophy of Socrates: A Collection of Critical Essays*. Garden City, NY: Doubleday, 1971.

Later Influence

Fitzpatrick, P.J., "The Legacy of Socrates." In Gower and Stokes, *Socratic Questions*.

Long, A. A. "Socrates in Hellenistic Philosophy." *Classical Quarterly* 38 (1988): 150–171.

Montuori, Mario. *Socrates: Physiology of a Myth*. Translated by J. M. P. Langdale and M. Langdale. Amsterdam: J. C. Gieben, 1981. Original Italian edition, Florence: G. C. Sanzoni, 1974.

Nehamas, Alexander. *The Art of Living: Socratic Reflections from Plato to Foucault*. Berkeley: University of California Press, 1998.

C. C. W. Taylor (2005)

SOLGER, KARL WILHELM FERDINAND

(1780–1819)

Karl Wilhelm Ferdinand Solger, the German romantic philosopher, was born in Schwedt. He studied jurisprudence, philology, and philosophy at the University of Halle and at Jena, where he heard Friedrich von Schelling lecture. After some time in the Prussian civil service, he lectured on philosophy at the University of Frankfurt an der Oder (1809), where he met Ludwig Tieck, the writer. From 1811 until his death he was a professor at the University of Berlin.

Like many romantics, Solger was preoccupied with the polarity of the finite and the infinite. Man is finite but filled with a desire for the infinite. The world in which he finds himself is fragmented. Grasping splinters of reality, common understanding operates in terms of polarities—concrete and universal, appearance and concept, body and soul, individual and nature. Only in the infinite Idea are polarities reconciled. Common understanding is tied to the finite. Man must escape from its rule if he is to recognize the infinite Idea. God made a sacrifice of himself to create the finite, and man must sacrifice himself and the phenomenal to return to the infinite. In this annihilation the Godhead reveals itself. The reconciliation of the finite and the infinite is the goal of the philosopher when he tries to capture truth in his systems; it is the duty of the moral man who confronts it as a task; it is achieved by the artist who, in creating the beautiful, reveals the Idea in the phenomenal.

The philosophy of art was at the center of Solger's philosophical program. Enthusiasm and irony are the two mainsprings of artistic creation. Enthusiasm, like Plato's Eros, ties man to the reality in which he has his ground. The enthusiast is possessed by the Idea. Irony recognizes the negativity of phenomenal reality and negates it. Thus it pushes away the veil that normally hides the Idea from us.

For Solger, as for Plato, philosophy is fundamentally conversation. It is a joint struggle for something that is dimly apprehended and yet escapes adequate articulation. Truth is never a possession; it only reveals itself in the process of striving for it. Thus, the most adequate vehicle for the expression of philosophical thought is the dialogue.

See also Plato; Romanticism; Schelling, Friedrich Wilhelm Joseph von.

Bibliography

WORKS BY SOLGER

Erwin, Vier Gespräche über das Schöne und die Kunst. 2 vols. Berlin: In der Realschulbuchhandlung, 1815.

Philosophische Gespräche. Berlin, 1817.

Nachgelassene Schriften und Briefwechsel, edited by L. Tieck and F. von Raumer. Leipzig, 1826.

Vorlesungen über Aesthetik, edited by K. W. L. Heyse. Leipzig, 1829.

The Complete Correspondence (between Solger and Ludwig Tieck). Edited by P. Matenko. New York: Westermann, 1932.

WORKS ON SOLGER

Allemann, Beda. *Ironie und Dichtung.* Pfullingen, Germany: Neske, 1956.

Boucher, Maurice. *K. W. F. Solger, ésthetique et philosophie de la présence.* Paris: Stock, 1934.

Hartmann, Hans. *Kunst und Religion bei Wackenroder, Tieck und Solger.* Erlangen, 1916. A dissertation.

Hegel, G. W. F. *Sämmtliche Werke.* Vol. XII, pp. 100–106, 221; Vol. XX, pp. 132–202. Stuttgart, 1927–1930.

Heller, J. E. *Solgers Philosophie der ironischen Dialektik.* Berlin, 1928.

Kierkegaard, Søren. "Om Begrebet Ironi." *Samlede Vaerker,* 15 vols. Vol. XIII, pp. 376–387. Copenhagen, 1901–1906.

Müller, Gustav. "Solger's Aesthetics—A Key to Hegel." *Corona, Studies in Celebration of the 80th Birthday of Samuel Singer.* Durham, NC, 1941.

Schönebeck, Erich. *Tieck und Solger.* Berlin: H. Blanke's Spezial-druckerei für Dissertationen, 1910. A dissertation.

Walzel, Oskar. "'Allgemeines' und 'Besonderes.'" *Deutsche Vierteljahrsschrift* 17 (1939): 152–182.

Wildbolz, Rudolf. *Der philosophische Dialog als literarisches Kunstwerk.* Bern and Stuttgart, 1952.

Karsten Harries (1967)

SOLIPSISM

There are a number of importantly different views associated with the term *solipsism.* Its Latin roots—*solus,* meaning "alone," and *ipse,* meaning "self"—suggest the rough idea that a solipsistic doctrine is going to put some sort of emphasis on the self standing alone, but there are radically different ways in which a philosopher might develop that emphasis. In particular, we must distinguish an extreme metaphysical thesis, a view about the nature of mental states (sometimes misleadingly referred to as methodological solipsism), an epistemological/methodological thesis, and an ethical thesis.

METAPHYSICAL SOLIPSISM

The simplest and most radical of doctrines associated with solipsism is the puzzling doctrine that only the self exists. Stated in these terms, the doctrine is scarcely intelligible. The obvious question concerns whose self precisely it is that is supposed to be the only existing thing. It is easiest to state the doctrine from the first-person perspective. If I embrace solipsism, I am endorsing the view that I am the only existing thing. If you embrace solipsism, then you are endorsing the view that you are the only existing thing. If we both endorse solipsism, therefore, then we are both wrong. In asserting solipsism, the solipsist is usually not trying to deny the existence of *properties* exemplified by the self. So the self that exists may believe, fear, hope, plan, and so on. We can also distinguish the solipsist who intends only to deny the existence of other minds from the solipsist who denies the existence of all other objects, for example, physical objects. It would be odd, however, to hold the former without the latter for, as we shall see, the epistemological position that drives one to a skepticism about other selves often involves a skepticism with respect to the external world.

There is almost a comical aspect to the most extreme form of solipsism. It is certainly odd to hear any philosopher defending (to whom?) the view. One could certainly never take comfort in the fact that one succeeded in convincing anyone of the truth of the view. But in this respect solipsism is probably no worse off than any other extreme form of skepticism—say skepticism with respect to the past, the future, or the external world. In fact, solipsism is probably a view that one starts to take seriously precisely in the context of more general epistemological concerns. So, for example, while Descartes was no solipsist, he came perilously close to painting himself into a solipsistic corner.

In the *Meditations,* Descartes famously sought secure foundations for knowledge. To find those foundations he employed what is sometimes called the method of doubt. He tried to strip from his belief system all those beliefs that admit of the possibility of error. So, for example, he thought that no belief about the physical world belongs in the foundations of knowledge because our evidence for believing what we do about that world never gets any better than vivid sense experience. But the kind of sense experience upon which we must rely is always compatible with our dreaming, or our being the victims of massive demon-induced hallucination. Since our knowledge of the existence of other people seems to rest critically on our knowledge of other bodies, skepticism with respect to the physical world might seem to entail a skepticism with respect to the existence of other selves. After rejecting a number of candidates for foundational truth, Descartes finally hit upon his own existence as one truth that he could not rationally doubt. No matter how hard he tried to convince himself that he did not exist, such efforts merely reinforced for him the fact that he did exist. One can only doubt one's own existence if one exists to do the doubting. "Cogito, ergo sum," Descartes concluded—I think, therefore I am.

While the exact nature of the evidence or justification to which Descartes appeals in claiming foundational knowledge of his own existence is a matter of some controversy, his attempt to begin a reconstruction of the rest of what he knows from this foundation is one that could have easily led him to a solipsistic conclusion. Descartes thought that he could find a way of legitimately inferring the rest of what he believes from knowledge of his own thoughts and experiences, but it is an understatement to suggest that his efforts did not meet with universal acceptance. Indeed, many contemporary philosophers are convinced that if we restrict ourselves to premises describing our own existence and the conscious states exemplified there, there is no path to knowledge of, or even justified belief in, the rest of what we commonsensically think we know.

The kind of radical foundationalism that Descartes embraced might naturally lead, then, to the conclusion that we can only know of our own existence and the perceptions and thoughts that reside there. And if one restricts one's metaphysical positions to what is licensed by knowledge, then one might be left affirming only one's own existence. Again, that claim is usually expanded, even by the solipsist, to include the conscious mental states exemplified by that self. When we discuss epistemological solipsism, we will say more about the epistemological assumptions that might lead one to take seriously the position of metaphysical solipsism. But let us first examine some influential criticisms leveled at the view.

CRITICISMS. One charge often leveled against metaphysical solipsism is the charge of self-refutation. There are a number of different ways in which a view might be self-refuting. The strongest form of self-refutation is logical—a self-refuting view entails that it is itself false. So, for example, the proposition that all claims are false is self-refuting in this sense. The claim entails its own falsehood. On the face of it, it is difficult to see how the solipsist's claim can be self-refuting in this way. Nevertheless, critics have claimed that for the solipsist's claim to be *meaningful* it must be false. Inspired by Wittgenstein, for example, some philosophers claim that language and meaning are essentially social; there can be no such thing as a private language or a private linguist.

Unfortunately, it is by no means easy to figure out just what the basis for this claim is. One crude characterization of the argument emphasizes the importance of rules in determining meaning. One uses a term meaningfully only if one uses it in accord with a rule that determines when the term is used correctly or incorrectly. If one is the sole arbiter of when a term is used correctly, the argument goes, one will be unable to make a mistake. But if one cannot make a mistake using the term, then it makes no sense to suppose that one is using the term correctly; correct use makes sense only against the possibility of incorrect use. It is only when there is a community of language users that one can understand the distinction between correct and incorrect use of language; incorrect use can be identified with divergence from standard or common use.

So to illustrate with an example, suppose that I see a creature I have never seen before and resolve to call it and anything relevantly like it a "gretl." One might initially suppose that I have successfully introduced a word into my own private language. Tomorrow, I see another creature—somewhat like the first, but also in many ways dissimilar. Is it a "gretl" or not? It seems that if I am the only one deciding whether it is enough like the first creature to count as a "gretl," then I cannot get it wrong—whatever I decide goes. Again, the Wittgensteinian will claim that where there is no possibility of error, there is no possibility of truth.

There are no uncontroversial interpretations of the private language argument, and a full evaluation of it would take us far afield. All versions of the argument, however, rest on highly controversial assumptions. It is not clear, for example, that judgment involves comparison to a paradigm. In any event, one must surely worry that the version stated above would rule out even the possibility of a *solitary* linguist—a sole language user. But it is hard to see how it could be impossible for there to exist one and only one person who was capable of both thought and language. We can imagine, for example, an infant who is the sole human survivor of a worldwide natural disaster and who, adopted by apes, somehow manages to mature into an adult. In such a world, if that human being could formulate the thought that there are no other people, he or she would have formulated a true thought. And do we really want to argue that in the situation described it would be metaphysically impossible for the person to formulate either the thought or a language that could express the thought? If we reflect on the scenario just described, we might become suspicious of any argument that purports to show that the solipsist's doctrine that there exists only one self is in some sense unintelligible or necessarily false.

There is a more recent philosophical claim about the nature of thought that, like the earlier arguments inspired by Wittgenstein, might seek to cast doubt on the intelligibility of metaphysical solipsism. It is sometimes called semantic, psychological, or content externalism. The basic idea behind the view is encapsulated in Putnam's famous slogan that meanings are not "in the head," and its proponents sometimes seem to claim that one can only have thoughts about certain kinds of things if those kinds of things exist. If the view were true, one might be able to infer from the fact that one can form thoughts about physical objects (even the thought that there are no physical objects) that physical objects exist. Similarly, one might be able to infer from the fact that one can form thoughts about other people (even the thought that there are no other people) that other people exist. The view underlying this criticism of metaphysical solipsism is held in opposition to another thesis associated with solipsism, a thesis sometimes called "methodological solipsism."

METHODOLOGICAL SOLIPSISM

The term *methodological solipsism* was introduced by Hilary Putnam and made more familiar by Jerry Fodor. It is precisely the view rejected by the content externalist. The methodological solipsist (or internalist in the philosophy of mind) is convinced that psychological states (beliefs, desires, fears, pains, etc.) are entirely constituted by internal features of the person in those states. Two people cannot be in identical internal states while one of them has a certain desire, say, and the other does not. The externalist argues, somewhat paradoxically perhaps, that at least some of the conditions that constitute or determine your psychological states are factors that lie outside you—factors that include, for example, the causal origin of your internal states. So Putnam famously argued that two people could be in precisely the same internal states while one is thinking about water (the stuff with molecular structure H_2O) and the other is thinking about "twater" (something with an entirely different molecular structure). The difference in the content of their thoughts would be a function of the environments in which the respective internal states arise. In a much-discussed attempt to extend these considerations to issues involving skepticism, Putnam (1981) appeared to argue that if one were a brain in a vat whose experiences were produced by the machinations of some mad neurophysiologist, one could not even entertain that hypothesis. His idea is that without some sort of sensory interaction with the physical world, one could not even form a thought that was about a physical object like a brain or a vat.

If such an argument were successful it would not be hard to extend it as an attack on the intelligibility of the more extreme forms of metaphysical solipsism. When the solipsists make clear their views about what does not exist, their ability to form the thought, for example the thought that there is no external world, presupposes that there is one. Without interaction with external reality, no thought could be about such reality and one thus could not even coherently deny its existence. Since skepticism about the existence of others typically runs through skepticism about the external world, one will have undercut an argument for solipsism.

CRITICISMS. Content externalism is no less controversial than the various presuppositions Wittgenstein and others brought to their philosophical views about meaning. But even if we grant some of the basic tenets of the externalist's conception of the conditions necessary for thought, *careful* statements of the view will not take one very far toward interesting metaphysical conclusions about what there is. For one thing, the careful content externalist is going to radically restrict the view to a subclass of thoughts. No one thinks, for example, that in order for one to have thoughts about mermaids, one must have interacted in some way (or be connected with someone else who has interacted in some way) with actual mermaids. The most natural move, borrowed from the earlier empiricists who thought that all ideas are "copies" of prior impressions, is to make a distinction between complex ideas and simple ideas. The earlier empiricist conceded that the idea of a mermaid is not a copy of some prior impression or experience of a mermaid, but went on to claim that the idea is complex (the idea of woman's torso combined with a fish's tail), and the ideas out of which the complex idea is composed *are* copies of prior impressions. Of course, the idea of a torso itself might be complex, composed of still simpler ideas. The natural thought for both the earlier empiricist and the content externalist is to restrict their thesis to the simple ideas that are the "building blocks" of other ideas.

The difficulty is that it is not clear what the best candidates are for the simple ideas out of which others are built. Suppose, for example, that I have the idea of a sensation. I might also be able to form the idea of causation. I can put those two ideas together to form the idea of that which causes the sensation. Arguably, in this way I can form the complex idea of an external object. But I have formed the idea in such a way that it might not correspond to anything—the sensation in question might have no cause. There seems to be nothing in the externalist's view that blocks the possibility of forming thoughts of this sort, thoughts that might well not correspond to anything. Consequently, it is not at all clear that the metaphysical solipsist would face any problems of self-refutation in framing various radical views about what does not exist.

EPISTEMOLOGICAL SOLIPSISM

The first two theses discussed above are metaphysical claims—claims about what exists. As we have just seen, one use of the expression "methodological solipsism" involves a claim about the nature of mental states. There was, however, an earlier use of the term "methodological solipsism" (by Hans Driesch, Rudolph Carnap, and others) expressing an epistemological thesis. Indeed, that earlier use of the expression is a much more natural way to describe what these philosophers had in mind—a *method* for arriving at truth. To avoid confusion, it is best to describe the view that I have in mind as epistemological solipsism.

The fundamental idea behind epistemological solipsism is the claim that in reaching conclusions about what exists, each of us is restricted to a foundation of knowledge about our own mental states. The foundationalist in epistemology is convinced that there must be some truths that are known or justifiably believed without their needing to be inferred from other different truths that are known or justifiably believed. This foundational knowledge is needed to block a vicious epistemological regress. To justifiably believe *P* by inferring it from *E1*, one would need, the argument goes, justification for believing *E1*. Some would argue that one would also need justification for believing that *E1* confirms *P*. But if the only way to justifiably believe something is to infer it from something else, then to justifiably believe *E1*, one would need to infer it from something else *E2*, which one would need to infer from something else *E3*, and so on, ad infinitum. Finite minds cannot complete infinitely long chains of reasoning. It is not even clear that infinite minds can complete infinitely long chains of reasoning. So if we are to justifiably believe anything at all, some of our beliefs must be non-inferentially justified—justified without inference.

The radical empiricist/epistemological solipsist is convinced that the only contingent truths that one can know without inference are truths about one's own existence and the thoughts and experiences contained there. Arguments for restricting the foundations of knowledge in this way depend, typically, on specific presuppositions about the nature of foundational knowledge. As we saw earlier, Descartes sought foundations in beliefs that are infallible. If one's justification for believing something is compatible with the belief's being false, then the belief is not a candidate for non-inferential knowledge. The radical empiricist was convinced that beliefs about the external world, the past, other minds, and the future, all fail this test for foundational knowledge. By contrast, one's beliefs that one exists, that one is in pain (when one is), that one has thoughts, all were supposed to pass the test.

A closely related version of foundationalism seeks to identify foundational knowledge with belief accompanied by direct acquaintance with facts that are the truthmakers for the belief. On this view, when one is in pain, for example, one's non-inferential justification consists in the fact that the pain itself is directly present to consciousness. Again, the claim is that objects in the physical world, other minds, facts about the past, and facts about the future, are never directly presented to consciousness in this way. Their existence must be inferred from what is known directly about present conscious states.

The epistemological solipsist's position was probably almost taken for granted by most prominent philosophers in the history of philosophy. The task of the philosopher is essentially egocentric. If one is to avoid begging questions, one has no choice but to begin one's search for truth with the various ways that things appear. This epistemological position does not entail metaphysical solipsism, but as we saw, there is the danger that one will be unable to reason oneself out from behind this "veil" of subjective appearance.

CRITICISMS. The version of foundationalism endorsed by the epistemological solipsist has come under sustained attack in the last several decades. In discussing metaphysical solipsism, we have already had occasion to examine Wittgenstein's worries about the possibility of a private language. To the extent that judgment involves categorizing things, categorizing things involves appeal to the correctness of following certain rules, and knowledge of what rules sanction involves facts about communities of rule followers, one will have difficulty finding the kind of foundations sought by the epistemological solipsist. But as we saw, this criticism of private language and thought is by no means uncontroversial.

In the previous section, we also discussed a view about the nature of mental states that might also cast doubt on the radical version of foundationalism endorsed by many empiricists. If external reality is literally partially constitutive of mental states like belief, then it might seem to follow that our knowledge of mental states could be no more secure than the knowledge of that external reality upon which their content depends. That this follows from psychological externalism, however, is a matter of great dispute, and among those who take it to be an implication of externalism in the philosophy of mind, there are many who take this consequence of the view to be a *reductio* of the view. In any event, as we also noted, psychological externalism is no more uncontroversial than the presuppositions of Wittgenstein's argument against the possibility of knowing truths about a "private" experience.

There are other efforts to cast doubt on the claim that empirical knowledge begins (and perhaps even ends) with knowledge of one's inner mental states. In a famous attack on the radical empiricist's doctrine of what is "given," Wilfred Sellars (1963) claimed that it is an illusion to suppose that we can form thoughts about appearances that are independent of thoughts about objective reality. So suppose, for example, that the epistemological solipsist claims to know that something looks red to him, or that it appears as if something is red. That epistemological solipsist claims that knowledge that there actually is a physical object that is red is more tenuous, less secure, than knowledge of the subjective appearance presented by such an object. But Sellars wants to know precisely what it means to say that it looks as if something is red. Sometimes we use "seems"/ "appears" language to indicate tentative belief—R. M. Chisholm (1957) called this the epistemic use of "appears." But in its epistemic sense, the judgment that it appears as if *X* is red is just the tentative judgment that *X* is red—it is not a truth about an appearance to which one might appeal as evidence for the claim that there exists before one a red object.

There is another use of "appears," however—the comparative use. But it will not be of any use to the philosopher intent on restricting a knowledge claim to subjective experience. In the comparative sense, to judge that it appears to me as if *X* is red is just to judge that I am having the kind of experience that is usually caused by red things under normal conditions. It takes but a moment's reflection to realize that this thought about how things appear is not a thought confined to subjective reality at all. To know that it looks as if something is red, I would have to know something about objective reality—I would have to know how red things look under normal conditions—something that presupposes that I have had epistemic access to how things have been, not just how things appear.

If the only way that we could conceptualize experience was comparatively in the above sense, then it would be folly to suggest that our knowledge of reality begins with knowledge of subjective appearance. But, of course, it is not difficult to see how the epistemological solipsist should respond to the above criticism. The very characterization of the comparative use of "appears" seems to make reference to a "way" that red things look and the radical empiricist/epistemological solipsist thinks that we have no difficulty conceptualizing that way in terms of its intrinsic character. However the word "appears" is normally used, the epistemological solipsist can borrow that term to describe what Chisholm called the noncomparative intrinsic character of the experience (1957).

There are countless other attacks on the radical foundationalist's idea that all empirical knowledge rests on a foundation of knowledge about the character of subjective experience. Some, for example, argue that we must reject such a view because it will ultimately lead to a radical skepticism—perhaps even the metaphysical solipsism discussed earlier. The charge is that the foundations countenanced by such a view coupled with available epistemic principles simply will not allow us to get back the knowledge that we commonsensically take ourselves to have. To determine whether epistemological solipsism does lead to skepticism would take us too far afield, but one might wonder whether a commitment to the falsity of skepticism should rule philosophical thought.

Still others complain that the epistemological solipsist radically overintellectualizes the nature of our thought about external reality. Not only do we not *always* infer objective reality from subjective experience, we rarely pay attention to how things appear. As anyone who has tried to paint soon realizes, it takes a certain amount of learning and sophistication to see the world as it appears instead of as we take it to be objectively. But it is not clear what relevance this observation has for the epistemological solipsist's central thesis. To be sure, if the solipsist makes a claim about what we actually do know, the above observations might cast doubt on that claim by casting doubt on the question of whether we typically form the required thoughts. But the careful epistemological solipsist might make a claim only about the possibility of knowledge. That epistemological solipsist might argue that whatever we think we know or justifiably believe, the only truths that *can* be known, at least directly and without inference, are truths about the character of subjective experience.

Just as there is an internalism/externalism controversy concerning the nature of mental states, so also there is an internalism/externalism controversy in epistemology. Many epistemological externalists argue that whether or not a belief is justified depends critically on the causal history of the belief—the way in which the belief was produced. Alvin Goldman (1979) advances one version of such a view—reliabilism. The reliabilist is a kind of foundationalist but argues that foundationally justified beliefs are just beliefs produced by reliable belief-producing processes that take as their input something other than beliefs. A belief-producing process of this sort is reliable when it does or would produce mostly true beliefs. Reflection on the reliabilist's criterion for non-inferential justification reveals that there can be no *a priori* restrictions on which beliefs might turn out to be non-inferentially justified. Against the traditional foundationalists, the reliabilist will argue that non-inferential justification has nothing to do with infallibility. A belief can be non-inferentially justified if it is just barely more likely to be true than false. Beliefs about the past, the physical world, and other minds all might be non-inferentially justified according to the reliabilist. Whether they are or not depends on empirical facts about the way in which such beliefs are caused.

It is certainly true that arguments for epistemological solipsism are challenged by contemporary versions of epistemological externalism. It is hardly the case, however, that philosophers agree on the success of externalist analyses of epistemic concepts. The epistemological solipsists have an array of weapons ready to deploy against the externalist. But underlying their criticism is often the common theme that the externalist's analysis of epistemic concepts has stripped them of their philosophical interest. The epistemological solipsist is likely to be convinced that satisfying the externalist's epistemic concepts does nothing to provide assurance of the sort the philosopher seeks. I may have a reliably produced belief. I may be evolutionarily programmed to believe reliably various truths about the world around me. But unless I have some reason to believe that the way in which my beliefs are formed is reliable, the mere fact of reliability does nothing to give me the kind of assurance I was looking for when I was interested in having justified beliefs.

EGOISM

Another quite different sort of doctrine that might be associated with the idea of the self standing alone is the ethical theory or theory of rational behavior known as egoism. A crude version of the theory is that rational people have only one goal or end in acting—their own happiness or well-being. Egoists can certainly take into account the well-being of others but only insofar as they have some reason to believe that the well-being of others impacts their own well-being.

Like other versions of solipsism, egoism has been accused by some of internal incoherence. As a theory, one argument goes, egoism must enjoin everyone to achieve his or her own well-being. But we can easily imagine a case in which my doing *X* maximizes my well-being, while *R*'s preventing me from doing *X* will maximize *R*'s well-being. I cannot coherently recommend, exhort, or want *R* to prevent me from doing what I want to do.

The above criticism presupposes that a principle of morality or rationality must be universalizable in certain respects. More specifically, it presupposes that if someone accepts the principle that everyone ought to seek only his or her own well-being, that commits that person to recommending such behavior to others, or acquiescing in such behavior on the part of others, or wanting others to behave in such ways. Such presuppositions are not uncontroversial even in the domain of morality, but are arguably downright implausible if the "ought" judgment in question is intended to assert only the rationality of egoistic behavior. There seems nothing at all inconsistent in my believing that it would be rational for all people to act egoistically while encouraging them not to so act and doing what I can to prevent them from acting that way. I know all too well what people ought to do to beat me in a game of tennis, but I never advise them concerning how to do it; I never want them to do it, and I do whatever I can to thwart them from behaving as they ought to.

As an ethical theory, the plausibility of egoism might in the end depend on metaphysical issues concerning the nature of ethical properties. G. E. Moore (1912) famously argued that if my happiness is objectively good, it is so in virtue of the property of being happy that I exemplify. But if objective goodness "supervenes" in this sense on the property of being happy, then it supervenes on that property no matter whose happiness we are talking about. An ethical egoist cannot recognize the goodness of his or her own happiness without recognizing the value inherent in another person's being happy. But most egoists are not objectivists about value. On one view, diametrically opposed to ethical objectivism, something has intrinsic value for a person *S* only insofar as *S* subjectively values that thing for its own sake. And it is just a brute fact about most human beings, the egoist claims, that people care more about their own happiness than they do about the happiness of others.

That alleged empirical truth, however, is not uncontroversial. It might not be all that difficult for most parents, for example, to conclude that they value intrinsically the happiness of their children—perhaps even more than they value their own happiness. If they do, and if subjective valuing confers intrinsic value on that which is valued, then the egoist's view that rational people concern themselves only with their own well-being is implausible. It is worth noting, however, that the view according to which a thing's intrinsic value for a person is determined by that person's valuing it is itself a kind of solipsistic view. It is not egoism, because we might find ourselves valuing intrinsically the well-being of others, but it is still a view that makes the individual person the creator of the goals or ends that partially define for that person how life ought to be lived.

See also Augustine, St.; Ayer, Alfred Jules; Bradley, Francis Herbert; Bridgman, Percy William; Broad, Charlie Dunbar; Carnap, Rudolf; Descartes, René; Driesch, Hans Adolf Eduard; Egoism and Altruism; Epistemology; Fichte, Johann Gottlieb; Hamilton, William; Hume, David; Kant, Immanuel; Lewis, Clarence Irving; Locke, John; Mach, Ernst; Malcolm, Norman; Mill, John Stuart; Moore, George Edward; Other Minds; Pastore, Valentino Annibale; Private Language Problem; Royce, Josiah; Russell, Bertrand Arthur William; Santayana, George; Schiller, Ferdinand Canning Scott; Schuppe, Ernst Julius Wilhelm; Stace, Walter Terence; Stebbing, Lizzie Susan; Wittgenstein, Ludwig Josef Johann.

Bibliography

Ayer, A. J. *Privacy*. London, 1959; also in *Proceedings of the British Academy* 45 (1959): 43–65.

Ayer, A. J. *Problem of Knowledge*. London: Macmillan, 1956.

Bradley, F. H. *Appearance and Reality*. London: Swan Sonnenschien, 1893.

Carnap, Rudolf. *Der Logische aufbau der Welt*. Berlin: Weltkreis, 1928.

Carnap, Rudolf. "Die physikalische Sprache als Universalsprache der Wissenschaft." *Erkenntnis 2* (1932). Translated by Max Black as *The Unity of Science*. London: K. Paul, Trench, and Trubner, 1934.

Chisholm, R. M. *Perceiving*. Ithaca, NY: Cornell University Press, 1957.

Dretske, Fred. *Naturalizing the Mind*. Cambridge, MA: MIT Press, 1995.

Feigl, H. "Physicalism, Unity of Science and the Foundations of Psychology." In *The Philosophy of Rudolf Carnap*, edited by Paul A. Schilpp, 227–267. La Salle, IL: Open Court, 1963–1964.

Fodor, Jerry A. "Methodological Solipsism Considered as a Research Strategy in Cognitive Psychology." *The Behavioral and Brain Sciences* 3 (1) (1980): 63–72.

Fumerton, Richard. *Metaepistemology and Skepticism*. Lanham, MD: Rowman & Littlefield, 1995.

Fumerton, Richard. *Reason and Morality: A Defense of the Egocentric Perspective*. Ithaca, NY: Cornell University Press, 1990.

Gallie, W. B. "Solipsistic and Social Theories of Meaning." *PAS* 38 (1937–1938): 61–84.

Gauthier, David, ed. *Morality and Rational Self-Interest*. Englewood Cliffs, NJ: Prentice-Hall, 1970.

Goldman, Alvin. "What Is Justified Belief?" In *Justification and Knowledge*, edited by George Pappas, 1–23. Dordrecht: Reidel, 1979.

Kalin, Jesse. "In Defense of Egoism." In *Morality and Rational Self-Interest*, edited by David Gauthier, 64–87. Englewood Cliffs, NJ: Prentice-Hall, 1970.

Kripke, Saul A. *Naming and Necessity*. Cambridge, MA: Harvard University Press, 1980.

Lewis, C. I. *An Analysis of Knowledge and Evaluation*. La Salle, IL: Open Court, 1946. See Book II, especially chap. 7, sec. 11; chap. 9, sec. 8; chap. 11, sec. 5.

Ludlow, Peter, and Norah Martin, eds. *Externalism and Self-Knowledge*. Stanford, CA: CSLI Publications, 1998.

Malcolm, Norman. "Knowledge of Other Minds." *Journal of Philosophy* 55 (1958): 969–978.

Medlin, Brian. "Ultimate Principles and Ethical Egoism." *Australian Journal of Philosophy* 35 (1957): 111–118.

Moore, G. E. *Ethics*. London: Oxford University Press, 1912.

Moore, G. E. *Philosophical Papers*. London: Allen & Unwin, 1959. Especially "Defense of Common Sense" (1925) and "Proof of an External World" (1939).

Putnam, Hilary. "The Meaning of 'Meaning.'" In *Minnesota Studies in the Philosophy of Science*. Vol. 7, edited by K. Gunderson, 131–193. Minneapolis: University of Minnesota Press, 1975.

Putnam, Hilary. *Reason, Truth, and History*. Cambridge, U.K.: Cambridge University Press, 1981.

Rhees, Rush. "Can There Be a Private Language?" *PAS*, supp. vol. 28 (1954): 63–94. Symposium with Ayer.

Russell, Bertrand. *Human Knowledge*. New York: Simon & Schuster, 1948. See Part III, chap. 2.

Russell, Bertrand. *Our Knowledge of the External World*. Chicago: Open Court, 1914. Lectures III and IV.

Schlick, Moritz. "Meaning and Verification." *Philosophical Review* 45 (1936): 339–369. Reprinted in *Readings in Philosophical Analysis*, edited by H. Feigl and W. Sellars. New York: Appleton, 1949. See especially Sec. 5.

Sellars, Wilfred. *Science, Perception, and Reality*. London: Routledge and Kegan Paul, 1963.

Strawson, P. F. *Individuals*. Garden City, NY: Doubleday, 1963. See Part I, chap. 3.

Wisdom, John. *Other Minds*. Oxford: Blackwell, 1953.

Wittgenstein, Ludwig. *Tractatus Logico-philosophicus*. London: Routledge and Kegan Paul, 1922. See passages 5.6–5.641. Translated by D. F. Pears and B. F. McGuinness. London: Routledge and Kegan Paul, 1961. A survey of useful comments on the relevant passage in this work will be found in Max Black, *A Companion to Wittgenstein's Tractatus* (Cambridge, U.K.: Cambridge University Press, 1964), 307–311.

Wright, Crispin, Barry C. Smith, and Cynthia Macdonald, eds. *Knowing Our Own Minds*. Oxford: Clarendon Press, 1998.

Richard A. Fumerton (2005)

SOLOV'ËV (SOLOVYOV), VLADIMIR SERGEEVICH

(1853–1900)

Vladimir Sergeevich Solov'ëv was a Russian philosopher, poet, polemical essayist, and literary critic. His father, S. M. Solov'ëv, was an eminent historian and professor at Moscow University.

After graduating in 1873 from the historico-philological department of Moscow University, Solov'ëv studied for a year at the Moscow Theological Academy. In 1874 he defended his master's dissertation, *Krizis zapadnoi filosofii. Protiv pozitivistov* (The crisis of western philosophy: Against positivists) and was elected a docent of philosophy at Moscow University. During 1875–1876 he conducted research at the British Library, where he concentrated on mystical and Gnostic literature, including Jakob Boehme, Paracelsus, Emanuel Swedenborg, and the kabbalah.

Having a poetic and impressionable nature, Solov'ëv apparently possessed mediumistic gifts. Several times he had visions of Sophia, or the Eternal Feminine; he tells about one such vision, which he had in Egypt in 1875, in his poem "Three Meetings." After his return to Russia, he resumed lecturing at Moscow University; but in 1877, because of conflicts among the professors, he left the university and went to Petersburg to serve on the Scholarly Committee of the Ministry of National Education, meanwhile giving lectures at Petersburg University and at the Higher Courses for Women.

In 1877 he published the essay "Filosofskie nachala tsel'nlgo znaniia" (Philosophical principles of integral knowledge); during 1877–1880 he wrote the study *Kritika otvlechennykh nachal* (Critique of abstract principles); and in 1878 he began reading the cycle of *Chteniia o bogochelovechestve* (Lectures on godmanhood).

On March 28, 1881, after the assassination of Tsar Alexander II, Solov'ëv, in a public lecture on the incompatibility of capital punishment with Christian morality, called on the new tsar to refrain from executing the assassins. His lecture provoked a fierce reaction; the relations between the philosopher and the authorities were ruined, and he left public and academic service, becoming a professional writer.

In the 1880s his attention was focused on sociopolitical and religious questions. His most important works of this period were *Dukhovnye osnovy zhizni* (Spiritual foundations of life; 1882–1884), *Velikii spor i khristianskaia politika* (The great dispute and Christian politics; 1883), *Istoriia i budushchnost' teokratii* (The history and the future of theocracy; Zagreb, 1886), *Tri rechi v pamiat' Dostoevskogo* (Three speeches in memory of Dostoevsky; 1881–1883), *La Russie et l'Eglise Universelle* (Paris, 1889; Russian translation, 1911), and the cycle of essays *Natsional'nyi vopros v Rossii* (The national question in Russia; 1883–1891).

In the 1890s Solov'ëv returned to philosophical: work proper. He wrote the essay "Smysl liubvi" (The meaning of love; 1892–1894) and the treatise on ethics *Opravdanie dobra* (The justification of the good; 1894–1895); he proposed a new interpretation of the theory of knowledge in essays unified under the title *Pervoe nachalo teoreticheskoi filosofii* (The first principle of theoretical philosophy; 1897–1899); and his last significant work, *Tri razgovora* (Three conversations; 1899–1900), was devoted to the problem of evil. Excessive work and unsettled life ruined Solov'ëv's health, which had always been poor. He died near Moscow as a guest on the estate of his friends, the Princes Trubetskoi.

In his spiritual development, Solov'ëv experienced many influences that determined the orientation and character of his thought. In early youth he assimilated socialist ideas: the quest for social truth and faith in progress, which were characteristic for Russian thought and in fact for the nineteenth century in general. From the Slavophiles Solov'ëv assimilated the idea of "integral knowledge," which offered an answer to the question of the meaning of human existence, as well as to that of the goal of the cosmic and historical process. According to Solov'ëv the subject of this process is humanity as a single organism, a concept borrowed from Auguste Comte. This approach is based on Solov'ëv's belief in the reality of the universal, a belief formed under the influence of

Benedict (Baruch) de Spinoza and of German idealism, especially Georg Wilhelm Friedrich Hegel.

Solov'ëv was also greatly influenced by thinkers who attributed a metaphysical significance to the concept of the will: Immanuel Kant, Arthur Schopenhauer, Eduard von Hartmann, and especially Friedrich Wilhelm Joseph von Schelling. If Solov'ëv owes his dialectical method primarily to Hegel, his theology, metaphysics, and aesthetics bear the stamp of the influence of voluntaristic metaphysics. Solov'ëv converges with Schelling in his romantic aesthetic approach to problems of religion and in his erotic mysticism that culminates in the cult of the Eternal Feminine, the world soul. A significant role in the formation of Solov'ëv's views belonged to the Christian Platonism of P. D. Iurkevich, especially the latter's doctrine of the heart as the center of spiritual life. Solov'ëv creatively transformed these multifarious influences in his doctrine by developing a systematic philosophy, which, however, was not free of a number of difficulties and contradictions. In his works one finds a sober assessment and constructive critique of many philosophical conceptions that had previously contributed to forming his worldview.

BEING AND EXISTENCE

Solov'ëv constructs his philosophical system according to a schema of history as the development of the world spirit, that is, as a theo-cosmo-historical process. He rejects the secularism that permeates modern European philosophy and, following the early Slavophiles, seeks to attain integral knowledge that presupposes the unity of theory and practical activity. His goal is "to introduce the eternal content of Christianity into a new rational unconditional form proper to this content" (1908–1923, p. 2:89).

In other words, his goal is to justify this content by means of "theosophy," an investigation of the nature of God. Like the Slavophiles, Solov'ëv critiques abstract thought (particularly Hegel's idealism) from the vantage point of spiritualistic realism, which requires that thought, the thinking subject, and the thought content be separated into distinct elements—elements that coincide for Hegel in the absolute idea. According to Solov'ëv, that which genuinely exists is not a concept or an empirical given but a real spiritual entity, the subject of will, existent (*sushchee*). The bearers of power and volition, spirits and souls alone possess reality; following Kant and Schopenhauer, Solov'ëv considers the empirical world to be only a phenomenon and describes it as being, in contradistinction to existent. The first and supreme "existent," God, is defined by Solov'ëv in the spirit of neoplatonism and the kabbalah as a positive nothingness, which is the direct opposite of Hegel's negative nothingness—pure being obtained by abstraction from all positive definitions. Having defined existence as that which appears, and being as a phenomenon, Solov'ëv thus interprets the connection between God and the world as the connection between essence and phenomenon, establishing a relation of necessity between the transcendent foundation of the world and the world itself, which can be known by means of reason—with the aid of so-called organic logic.

However, there is a certain contradiction between Solov'ëv's mystical realism and his rationalistic method: If that which is, is a transcendent spiritual entity, one can have knowledge of it only on the basis of revelation. It is inaccessible to rational knowledge. However, Solov'ëv is convinced that the rationally unfathomable existent can be an object of mystical contemplation, of intellectual intuition understood in a special manner and identified by Solov'ëv with the state of inspiration. Following Schelling and the Romantics, Solov'ëv takes intellectual intuition to be akin to the productive capacity of the imagination and, accordingly, he takes philosophy to be akin to artistic creation, interpreting here the creative act by analogy with the passively mediumistic trance state. Solov'ëv considers the ecstatic inspired state to be the origin of philosophical knowledge:

> The action upon us of ideal entities, producing in us the intellectual or contemplative knowledge (and creation) of their ideal forms or ideas, is what is called inspiration. This action takes us out of our ordinary natural center and raises us to a higher sphere, thereby producing ecstasy. Thus … the directly defining principle of true philosophical knowledge is inspiration. (1911–1914, p. 1:294)

By identifying the direct action of transcendent entities on people with the intellectual contemplation of ideas, Solov'ëv removes the boundary between rational thought and mystical vision; and the removal of the distinction between mystically interpreted intellectual intuition and the productive capacity of the imagination leads to the confusion of artistic imagination with religious revelation and to a magical and occultist interpretation of art, characteristic not only of Solov'ëv but also of the symbolists whom he influenced. It is precisely in this manner that Solov'ëv understands the synthesis of philosophy, religion, and art. According to Solov'ëv the divine "That Which Is" is revealed directly, with the aid of sensation or emotion; and therefore no proofs of the existence of God are required: His reality cannot be logically derived from pure reason but is given only by an act of faith. Nevertheless, the content of the divine "Existent" is revealed with the aid of reason.

ALL-UNITY

Solov'ëv describes the Absolute as the "eternal all-one" (1911–1914, p. 3:234), or as the "One and all." This means that all that which exists is contained in the Absolute: The all-unity is unity in multiplicity. According to Solov'ëv the one is independent of the all (the term *absolute* means "detached," "liberated"), and consequently it is defined negatively in relation to the other. But since it cannot have anything outside itself, it is defined positively in relation to the other. Thus, two poles or centers are eternally present in it: (1) independence of all forms, of all manifestation; and (2) the power that produces being, that is, the multiplicity of forms. The first pole is the One; the second is the potency of being, or the first matter, which, as in Boehme, is included in the Absolute as "its other," as the first substrate, or the "ground" of God.

Solov'ëv clarifies the concept of the first matter in terms of Schellingian-Schopenhaurean definitions—as power, attracting, striving, and originating in Boehme's doctrine of the "dark nature" in God, the doctrine of the unconscious depths of Divinity as the principle of evil. The inseparability of the two poles of That Which Exists signifies that the Absolute cannot appear except as actualized in matter, and matter cannot appear except as idea, as the actualized image of the One. In his *Critique of Abstract Principles* Solov'ëv describes the second pole of the all-unity, that is, the first matter (which is idea, or nature), as the becoming all-one, in contrast to the first pole, which is the existent all-one (1911–1914, p. 2:299). This means that the Absolute cannot exist except as actualized in its other. The pantheistic basis of this conception is obvious: This view of the relation between God and the world differs from the Christian idea of creation. The becoming all-one is the world soul, which, being the foundation of the entire cosmic process, only "in man first receives its proper inner activity, finds itself, is conscious of itself" (pp. 2:302–303).

SOPHIOLOGY

In his *Lectures on Godmanhood* Solov'ëv attempts to translate the self-sundering of the Absolute into the language of Christian theology, giving his own interpretation of the dogma of the Trinity. He distinguishes God as the absolute existent from His content (essence or idea), which appears in the person of the Son, or the Logos. The incarnation of this content is realized in the world soul, Sophia, the third person of the divine Trinity—the Holy Spirit. Distinguishing in God the active unity of the creative Word (Logos) and the actualized unity, His organic body, Solov'ëv views the latter as "the produced unity to which we have given the mystical name Sophia" (1911–1914, p. 3:111); it "is the principle of humanity, the ideal or normal man" (p. 3:111). Perfect humanity is not an empirical individual or man as a generic concept, but an eternal idea, a special kind of universal individuality, "the universal form of the union of material nature with Divinity … God-man-hood and Divine matter" (1911–1914, p. 8:231). The empirical world, where people appear as individuals, is "the somber and excruciating dream of a separate egotistical existence" (1911–1914, p. 3:120), an illusory and inauthentic world.

For Solov'ëv, as well as for Schopenhauer, the cause of this world is "the sin of individuation," producing the external, material existence of separateness and enmity. But if individuality is the source of evil and suffering, then in no wise can it be immortal: Salvation lies in the liberation from individual existence, not in its eternal continuation. Solov'ëv's philosophy of the last period is impersonalistic; it is not by chance that, on this question, there arose a polemic between him and Lev Mikhailovich Lopatin, who was convinced of the substantiality of the human self and of the immortality of the individual soul.

Solov'ëv sees the source of world evil in the meonic foundation of the divine all-unity. The world soul, Sophia, falls away from God, seeking to ground herself outside of Him, and "falls out of the all-one center of Divine being into the multiple periphery of creation, losing her freedom and her power over this creation" (1911–1914, p. 3:131). Meanwhile, the Divine Universe falls apart into a multiplicity of separate elements. The central personage of the theocosmic process—the eternally feminine principle in God, the body of Christ, the ideal humanity—acquires demonic characteristics. The image of the Eternal Feminine becomes dual. To eliminate this duality, Solov'ëv, in *Russia and the Universal Church*, introduces the distinction between Sophia on the one hand and the world soul on the other hand. The latter now appears as the antipode of Sophia, the Wisdom of God, who is a "radiant and heavenly entity." The essence of the cosmic process is the battle between the Divine Word and the infernal principle for power over the world soul, a battle that must end with the reunification of the fallen world soul with God and the restoration of the divine all-unity. The historical process leads with internal necessity to the triumph of good, to the victory of unity and love over disintegration and enmity. Solov'ëv's theodicy converges not only with Hegel's teleological determinism but also with the evolutionism of the natural sciences.

PHILOSOPHY OF HISTORY

Solov'ëv's philosophy of history is an attempt to understand cosmic history as a series of free acts on the way to the restoration of the unity of God and humanity. At the first stage, that of natural revelation, humanity knows God as a natural entity: Such are the pagan beliefs of the ancient world and the materialistic doctrines of the modern period. At the second stage, God is revealed as the transcendent, extranatural principle; such are the Asian ascetic-pessimistic religions, especially Buddhism, which seek to overcome the active, personal principle. Finally, in the religion of the Old Testament, humanity received a positive revelation, whose full meaning was disclosed in Christianity. In Christ was manifested the synthesis of the religiously contemplative principle of Russia and the personal and human principle, which developed in the bosom of European culture.

However, the schism between the Eastern and Western Churches marked the epoch of a new disintegration, which now affected the Christian world because of the imperfection of "historical Christianity." Triumphant in Russia was the supraindividual divine principle that left no room for human freedom; whereas Europe was marked by excessive individualism and by freedom in its negative sense, which led to capitalism atheistic egotism. Russia had a messianic calling to unify the two separated sides and to realize the final act of the cosmic historical drama in which humanity will be reunited with God. In the 1880s Solov'ëv's philosophy of history takes the form of a utopian doctrine about a universal theocracy in which the secular power of the Russian tsar is joined with the spiritual power of the pope in Rome. The first step toward this theocracy was supposed to take place as the reunification of the Eastern and Western Churches.

ETHICS

Solov'ëv touched on the problems of ethics in many works, but he has one work that is specially devoted to moral philosophy: *The Justification of the Good.* In this work he critiques two extreme points of view: moral subjectivism, which asserts that only the person can be the bearer of good; and objectivism, which recognizes only social institutions as guarantors of moral conduct. According to Solov'ëv these two elements must complement each other. Here, he underscores the importance of the objective forms of moral life, taking as his point of departure the belief in the reality of the universal, that is, of Godmanhood as one organism. If in his early works Solov'ëv emphasized the dependence of ethics on religious metaphysics, he now insists on the autonomy of ethics, because as "in creating a moral philosophy, reason does nothing more than develop, on the basis of experience, the idea of the good that is originally inherent in it" (1911–1914, p. 7:29). Nevertheless, even if it is autonomous the philosophy of morality cannot be fully separated from metaphysics and religion, because only the doctrine of the cosmic divine-human process and of the final victory of the divine all-unity grounds morality—the reality of superhuman good.

Solov'ëv gives a deep analysis of moral emotions: shame, pity, piety, or veneration. Man is ashamed of that which constitutes his lower nature; characteristic in this respect is sexual shame. Human experience pity, that is, they empathize with the suffering of all living beings; as the source of altruism, pity is the basis of social relationships. Shame represents individual chastity, whereas pity represents social chastity. Finally, the sense of piety, that is, veneration of the supreme principle, is the moral foundation of religion. Examining the problem of the relation between morality and law, Solov'ëv sees their distinction in the fact that, in contrast to legal obligations, moral ones are unlimited, as well as in the coercive character of juridical laws. Law is the lower bound or minimum of morality, which is realized by means of compulsion. However, contrary to the common opinion, there is no contradiction between moral and juridical laws.

Although Solov'ëv does not have a work specially devoted to aesthetics, the theme of beauty permeates all of his works. For Solov'ëv, philosophical intuition converges, in the spirit of romanticism, with artistic creativity; and he sees in the latter a kinship with mystical experience and considers art to be a real power, illuminating and regenerating the world (see 1911–1914, p. 3:189). The supreme goal of art is theurgy, that is, the transformation of everyday reality into ideal, transfigured corporeality. Solov'ëv's aesthetics is connected with his sophiology and with his doctrine of Eros, to which his treatise *The Meaning of Love* is devoted. His aesthetic ideas were also expressed in his essays in the field of literary criticism devoted to the poetry of Aleksandr Pushkin, Fedor Tiutchev, Mikhail Lermontov, and Afanasy Fet.

Not long before his death, Solov'ëv became disenchanted with theocratic utopia and, in general, with the idea of progress. In his final work, *Three Conversations*, the central plane is occupied by the eschatological theme: The coming of the Kingdom of God is now conceived as the end of history. Solov'ëv had a powerful influence on philosophical thought in Russia. The religious philosophy of the end of the nineteenth century and of the beginning of the twentieth century developed under his influence; this is true, in particular, of Sergei Trubetskoi and Evgenii Trubetskoi, Nikolai Losskii, S. L. Frank, Sergei Bulgakov, Pavel Florenskii, Nikolai Berdiaev, and so on. Just as significant was Solov'ëv's influence on Russian literature, especially on the symbolists Aleksandr Blok, Andrei Belyi, Viacheslav Ivanov, and so on. It is precisely from Solov'ëv that the Russian silver age got its mystical and Gnostic tendency, which was characteristic for the atmosphere of the spiritual life of the pre-Revolutionary period in Russia.

See also Absolute, The; Berdyaev, Nikolai Aleksandrovich; Boehme, Jakob; Bulgakov, Sergei Nikolaevich; Comte, Auguste; Florenskii, Pavel Aleksandrovich; Frank, Semën Liudvigovich; Gnosticism; Hartmann, Eduard von; Hegel, Georg Wilhelm Friedrich; Kabbalah; Kant, Immanuel; Losskii, Nikolai Onufrievich; Mysticism, Nature and Assessment of; Paracelsus; Russian Philosophy; Schelling, Friedrich Wilhelm Joseph von; Schopenhauer, Arthur; Spinoza, Benedict (Baruch) de; Swedenborg, Emanuel; Trubetskoi, Evgenii Nikolaevich; Trubetskoi, Sergei Nikolaevich.

Bibliography

WORKS BY SOLOV'ËV

Pis'ma (Letters). Vols. 1–4. St. Petersburg: 1908–1923.

Sobranie sochinenii (Collected works). Vols. 1–10. St. Petersburg: 1911–1914.

Stikhotvoreniia i shutochnye piesy (Poems and comic plays). Leningrad: 1974.

Sochineniia (Works), 2 vols. Moscow: 1988.

Literaturnaia kritika (Literary criticism). Moscow: 1990.

WORKS BY SOLOV'ËV IN ENGLISH TRANSLATION

The Justification of the Good: An Essay in Moral Philosophy. Translated by Natalie A. Duddington. London: Constable, 1918. This was originally published under the title *Opravdanie dobra: Nravstvennaya filosofiia* in 1897.

God, Man, and the Church: The Spiritual Foundations of Life. Translated by Donald Attwater. Milwaukee, WI: Bruce Publishing, 1938; London: James Clarke, 1938, 1973. This was originally published in French under the title *Dukhovnye osnovy zhizni* in 1884.

Russia and the Universal Church. Translated by Herbert Rees. London: G. Bles, 1948. This was originally published in French under the title *La Russie et l'Eglise universelle* in 1888.

A Solovyov Anthology. Compiled by S. L. Frank. Translated by Natalie Duddington. London: SCM Press, 1950.

"Foundations of Theoretical Philosophy," Part 1. In *Russian Philosophy*, 3 vols. Translated by Vlada Tolley and James P. Scanlan; edited by James M. Edie, James P. Scanlan, and Mary-Barbara Zeldin, with the collaboration of George L. Kline, 99–134. Chicago: Quadrangle Books, 1965. This was originally published under the title "Osnovy teoreticheskoi filosofii" in 1897–1899.

The Meaning of Love. Translated by Thomas R. Beyer Jr. West Stockbridge, MA: Lindisfarne Press, 1985. This was originally published under the title *Smysl liubvi* in 1892–1894.

Three Conversations concerning War, Progress, and the End of History, Including a Short Story of the Antichrist. Hudson, NY: Lindisfarne Press, 1990. This was originally published under the title *Tri razgovora o voine, progresse, i kontse istorii, i kratkaia povest' ob Antikhriste* in 1900.

Lectures on Divine Humanity. Translated by Peter Zouboff; edited by Boris Jakim. Hudson, NY: Lindisfarne Press, 1995. This was originally published under the title *Chteniia o Bogochelovechestve* in 1877–1881.

The Crisis of Western Philosophy: Against the Positivists. Translated by Boris Jakim. Hudson, NY: Lindisfarne Press, 1996a. This was originally published under the title *Krizis zapadnoi filosofii: Protiv pozitivistov* in 1874.

Poems of Sophia. Translated by Boris Jakim and Laury Magnus. New Haven, CT: Variable Press, 1996b. Includes "Three Meetings."

WORKS ON SOLOV'ËV

Asmus, V. F. "V. S. Solov'ev: Opyt filosofskoi biografii" (V. S. Solov'ëv: An attempt at a philosophical biography). *Voprosy filosofii* 6 (1988).

Balthasar, Hans Urs von. *Studies in Theological Lay Styles, Vol. 3: The Glory of the Lord: A Theological Aesthetics.* Translated by Andrew Louth et al.; edited by John Riches, 279–352. Edinburgh: T. and T. Clark, 1986. This essay was originally published in German under the title *Herrlichkeit: Eine theologische Aesthetik* in 1962.

Gaidenko, P. P. "Chelovek i chelovechestvo v uchenii V.S. Solov'eva" (Man and humanity in Solov'ëv's doctrine). *Voprosy filosofii* 6 (1994).

Gaidenko, P. P. *Vladimir Solov'ev i filosofiia Serebrianogo veka* (Vladimir Solovyov and the philosophy of the silver age). Moscow: 2001.

George, M. *Mystische und religiöse Erfahrung im Denken Vladimir Solov'evs.* Göttingen: 1988.

Losev, A. F. *Vladimir Solov'ev.* Moscow: 1983.

Losey, A. F. *Vladimir Solov'ev i ego vremia* (Vladimir Solov'ëv and his time). Moscow: 1990.

Lossky, N. O. *History of Russian Philosophy.* New York: International Universities Press, 1951.

Madey, J. *W. S. Solowjew und seine Lehre von der Weltseele.* Düsseldorf, Germany: 1961.

Mochul'sky, K. V. *Vladimir Solov'ev. Zhizn' i uchenie* (Vladimir Solov'ëv: Life and teaching). 2nd ed. Paris: YMCA Press, 1951.

Radlov, E. L. *Vl. Solovyov. Zhizn' i uchenie* (Vl. Solov'ëv: Life and teaching). St. Petersburg: 1913.

Solov'ev, S. M. *Vladimir Solovyov. Zhizn' i tvorvcheskaia evoliustii* (Vladimir Solov'ëv: Life and creative evolution). Moscow: Respublika, 1997.

Strémooukhoff, D. *Vladimir Soloviev and His Messianic Work.* Translated by Elizabeth Meyendorff; edited by Phillip Guilbeau and Heather Elise MacGregor. Belmont, MA: Nordland, 1980. This was originally published in French under the title *Vladimir Soloviev et son oeuvre messianique* in 1935 and 1975.

Sutton, Jonathan. *The Religious Philosophy of Vladimir Solovyov: Towards a Reassessment.* New York: St. Martin's, 1988.

Trubetskoi, E. N. *Mirosozertsanie Vl. S. Solovyova* (The world view of V. S. Solov'ëv). 2 vols. Moscow: 1913.

Utkina, N. F. "Tema vseedinstva v filosofii Vl. Solovyova" (The theme of all-unity in Solov'ëv's philosophy). *Voprosy filosofii* 6 (1989).

Velichko, V. L. *Vladimir Solovyov. Zhizn' i tvoreniia* (Vladimir Solov'ëv: Life and works). St. Petersburg: 1903.

Wenzler, L. *Die Freiheit und das Böse nach Vl. Solov'ev.* Freiburg-Munich: 1978.

Zen'kovskii, V. V. *A History of Russian Philosophy.* 2 vols. Translated by George L. Kline. New York: Columbia University Press, 1953. This was originally published under the title *Istoriia russkoi filosofii* in 1948–1950.

Piama Gaidenko (2005)
Translated by Boris Jakim

SOMBART, WERNER

(1863–1941)

Werner Sombart, the German economic and social theorist, was born in Ermsleben near the Harz Mountains. He was professor of economics at the University of Breslau from 1890 to 1906 and at Berlin University from 1906 to 1931. Sombart made a strong impact on German economic thought and policies; he played a leading role in the Verein für Sozialpolitik and the Deutsche Soziologische Gesellschaft, and he was joint editor with Max Weber and Edgar Jaffe of the journal *Archiv für Sozialwissenschaft und Sozialpolitik.*

Sombart's interests covered economic and social history and theory, sociology, and the methodology of the social sciences, although his contributions to methodology were more polemical than constructive. Together with Wilhelm Dilthey, Heinrich Rickert, Karl Jaspers, and Max and Alfred Weber, he helped to establish modern German historical and cultural sociology. Sombart was a highly prolific writer, and few of his writings are free from marks of careless workmanship, though nearly all sparkle with suggestive ideas.

STUDY OF CAPITALISM

Sombart concentrated on the study of the development and the structural makeup of European industrial society and in particular on the development of capitalism and the transition from capitalism to socialism. In his early work he was influenced by Karl Marx, but in his mature period he sought to go beyond Marx's theoretical and historical edifice and fundamentally to undermine the Marxist weltanschauung.

Sombart's magnum opus was *Der moderne Kapitalismus,* whose first and second versions (1902 and 1916–1927) both demonstrated methodological and substantive advances. In contrast to Max Weber's comparative-institutional approach, Sombart conceived of the European capitalist system as a "historical individual," that is, the collective expression of the values of the expansive "Faustian" spirit of enterprise and the acquisitive bourgeois spirit. He traced the development of capitalism through early, high (mature), and late periods, each representing different cultural attitudes and styles. The basic qualities of each period were seen as determined by its system of economic values (*Wirtschaftsgesinnung*)—which he understood as being in continuous interpenetration with the other areas of cultural and social activity; by the forms of its legal and social organization; and by its technology and methods. In a dialectical process of transition, one period generates another as its antithesis. His emphasis on the concrete historical elements caused Sombart to neglect the theoretical and analytical structure of economics, which he regarded as supplementary to his own kind of investigation. Thus, economists tend to regard Sombart's work as history, but historians do not.

Sombart supported his study of capitalism by a large number of sociological monographs on such subjects as the city, precious metals, the location of industry, Jews, fashion, advertising, the bourgeois, the proletariat, war and capitalism, and luxury and capitalism. Following the Russian and German revolutions at the end of World War I, Sombart sharply dissociated himself from Marxian socialism, which, like capitalism, he regarded as "uninhibited Mammonism," the victory of evil forces (utilitarianism and hatred) over idealism and love. He advocated "German socialism" or "anticapitalism," based on the rejection of materialism, "technomania," and belief in progress. His specific prescriptions became increasingly totalitarian.

SOCIAL PHILOSOPHY

In social and cultural philosophy Sombart stressed the idea of an "economic system" (*Wirtschaftssystem*) whose forms and organization are the creation of the mind and reflect the clusters of cultural values (*Wirtschaftsgesinnungen*) mentioned above. The concept of *Wirtschaftssystem* is related to that of structure and to Max Weber's "ideal types." Originally Sombart conceived of this concept in terms of the early psychology of Dilthey and, like Weber, took account of the subjective intentions of historical agents. Later, however, he turned to an almost phenomenological interpretation of the "objective" meaning of cultural systems. Like Weber, Sombart regarded the "ideal type" both as a conceptual tool for evaluating historical processes and as a reflection of the essential structure of historicocultural reality. Sombart, however, emphasized the "realist" function and interpreted history as an expression of the national spirit rather than a multicausal sequence. In the first edition of *Der moderne Kapitalismus* this attitude led him to a naturalistic confusion of theory and history, which was assailed by Weber. Though Sombart was an economist by profession, he regarded economic laws as determined by the exigencies of the spirit of the age, and like Auguste Comte and the German historical school, he rejected the claim of economics to be an independent discipline. In his *Die drei Nationaloekonomien,* which he regarded as the theoretical key to his work, he distinguished between ethical (*richtende*), analytical (*ordnende*), and interpretive (*verstehende*) economics. He rejected the first because science should be ethically neutral, the second because it fastened on applied science only and opened the door to the mechanical methods of the natural sciences, which cannot lead to the required understanding of meanings, of cultural institutions, and of motivations (*Sinn-, Sach-,* and *Seelverstehen*). His insistence on the exclusion of value judgments, on the one hand, and on an intuition of essences, on the other hand, led Sombart into unresolved intellectual difficulties and caused him finally to stress the superiority of biased observation over the limited vistas of scientific thought. Sombart came to regard the dispute over methods as a contest between German (heroic-spiritual) and Western (utilitarian-mercenary) thought. He reproached Western philosophy for the "deconsecration of the mind," a destructive tendency to resolve the spiritual realm of ideas into their psychological and sociological elements.

Accordingly, Sombart saw sociology as more than a limited specialized discipline; to him, it was a universal discipline whose aim is to explain the whole of human relationships and cultural categories. He viewed society as a creation of the mind, and accordingly, his "noo-sociology" embraced religion, art, the law, and the state, as well as economics. In his final work, *Vom Menschen,* Sombart assigned the same universal function to philosophical (*geistwissenschaftliche*) anthropology, which was to be developed into a "basic science" coordinating all knowledge concerning human groups and peoples, both their structures and their origins. This work, a bitter indictment of civilization, was, however, merely programmatic.

Sombart exerted considerable influence upon a generation of German economists and sociologists, but his chief significance lies in his suggestive contributions to the morphology and genesis of capitalism and to the history of economic and social ideas.

See also Comte, Auguste; Dilthey, Wilhelm; Jaspers, Karl; Marx, Karl; Marxist Philosophy; Philosophical Anthropology; Philosophy of Economics; Rickert, Heinrich; Weber, Alfred; Weber, Max.

Bibliography

WORKS BY SOMBART

Sozialismus und soziale Bewegung im 19. Jahrhundert. Jena, Germany: Fischer, 1896; 10th ed. titled *Der proletarische Sozialismus,* 2 vols. Jena, 1924. Translated by M. Epstein as *Socialism and the Social Movement in the 19th Century.* London: Putnam, 1898.

Der moderne Kapitalismus, 2 vols., Munich, 1902; 7th ed., 6 vols., Munich: Duncker and Humblot, 1928. Condensed translation by F. L. Nussbaum as *A History of the Economic Institutions of Modern Europe.* New York: Crofts, 1933.

Das Proletariat. Frankfurt: Rütten and Loening, 1906.

Die Juden und das Wirtschaftsleben. Munich, 1911. Translated by M. Epstein as *The Jews and Modern Capitalism.* London: Unwin, 1913; paperback, with introduction by B. Hoselitz, New York, 1962.

Der Bourgeois. Munich: Duncker and Humblot, 1913. Translated by M. Epstein as *The Quintessence of Capitalism.* London: Unwin, 1915.

Studien zur Entwicklungsgeschichte des modernen Kapitalismus, 2 vols. Munich: Duncker and Humblot, 1913. Translated by W. R. Dittmar as *Luxury and Capitalism.* New York, 1938.

Die drei Nationaloekonomien. Munich: Duncker and Humblot, 1930.

Die Zukunft des Kapitalismus. Berlin: Buchholz and Weisswange, 1932. Translated as *The Future of Capitalism.* Berlin and London, 1932.

Deutscher Sozialismus. Berlin: Buchholz and Weisswange, 1934. Translated by Karl F. Geiser as *A New Social Philosophy.* Princeton, NJ: Princeton University Press, 1937.

Vom Menschen. Berlin: Buchholz and Weisswange, 1938.

Noo-Soziologie. Edited by Nicolaus Sombart. Berlin, 1956.

Why Is There No Socialism in the United States?, Translated by Patricia M. Hocking and C. T. Husbands; edited by C. T. Husbands. White Plains, NY: International Arts and Sciences Press, 1976.

WORKS ON SOMBART

Brocke, Bernhard vom. "Werner Sombart (1863–1941): Capitalism, Socialism, His Life, Works and Influence since Fifty Years," translated by Lode Vereeck. *Jahrbuch für Wirtschaftsgeschichte* (1) (1992): 113–182.

Mitzman, Arthur. "Werner Sombart (1863–1941)." In his *Sociology and Estrangement: Three Sociologists of Imperial Germany.* New York: Knopf, 1973.

Nussbaum, Frederick Louis. *A History of the Economic Institutions of Modern Europe; An Introduction to* Der moderne Kapitalismus *of Werner Sombart.* New York: A.M. Kelley, 1968.

Plotnik, Mortin J. *Werner Sombart and His Type of Economics.* New York: Eco Press, 1937. Has good bibliography.

Weippert, Georg. *Werner Sombarts Gestaltidee des Wirtschaftssystems.* Göttingen, 1953.

H. O. Pappé (1967)
Bibliography updated by Philip Reed (2005)

SOPHIA

See Appendix, Vol. 10

SOPHISTS

In English, the term *sophist* is most often used pejoratively, for one who argues with devious abuses of logic. The Greek *Sophistês* took on a similar sense in the fifth century BCE., but its original meaning is simply *expert* or *wise person.* In the study of Greek philosophy, the sophists denote a group of teachers and intellectuals of the fifth and fourth century BCE (the term is also used for later practitioners of their profession; this soon comes to be interchangeable with rhetoric or public speaking, as in the so-called Second Sophistic movement of the second century CE).

The sophists are perennially ambiguous and controversial figures, and it has long been debated whether they should be deemed philosophers. Two central points seem clear: First, the sophists did not constitute a philosophical school with a shared set of metaphysical and ethical positions; second, a number of them did develop serious, innovative, and influential ideas and arguments on a wide range of topics, and so demand inclusion in the history of ancient philosophy.

The sophists are best seen as an intellectual movement, comparable to the philosophies of the eighteenth century or the progressive thinkers of Victorian England (some of whom, such as George Grote, were champions of the ancient sophists). As always with such movements, it is debatable who should be counted as a member, and membership is in any case more a matter of shared interests and tendencies than common doctrines. The leading figures of the sophistic movement so understood include Protagoras, Gorgias, Hippias, Antiphon, and Prodicus. Gorgias was primarily a rhetorician (i.e., an expert in and teacher of public speaking), but the two professions must have overlapped widely, and his surviving texts are among the most important for reconstructing sophistic ideas. Socrates was often counted among the sophists by his contemporaries, and is used to represent the whole movement in Aristophanes' *Clouds*; in a number of dialogues Plato aims to show that he differs from them radically.

Sophistic ideas have also come from some important anonymous texts, such as the *Dissoi Logoi* and the *Anonymus Iamblichi* (a long discussion of virtue, apparently of sophistic origin, inserted by the Neoplatonist Iamblichus in his *Protrepticus*), or of contested authorship (notably the fragment on religion from the satyr play *Sisyphus*, attributed to both Critias and Euripides).

They can also be found in contemporary historical and medical texts (e.g., Thucydides' *Melian Dialogues*, the Hippocratic *On the Art*), as well as comedy and tragedy (especially Euripides). So there is no firm dividing line between sophistic thought and the broader fifth-century Greek culture around them, which was marked by a vigorous questioning of tradition and empirical, naturalistic researches into many subjects (*historiê*).

Sociologically, the sophists were professional teachers, the first in Greece to offer a higher education in the liberal arts. Sophists (who came from all over the Greek world) traveled from city to city presenting themselves to prospective students through public displays; this could involve giving a set speech (*epideixis*), performing feats of memory, undertaking to answer any question the audience might pose, or offering question-and-answer refutations of others. This practice of refutation, usually given the pejorative name *eristic*, is formally identical to the Socratic *elenchus*; to differentiate the two, Plato emphasizes that Socrates argues in pursuit of the truth and moral improvement, whereas sophists argue for victory and for money. Some sophists gave displays at the Olympic games, and the sophistic practices themselves were intensely agonistic.

Plato's *Protagoras* gives a vivid depiction of a gathering of sophists engaged in argument, banter, and competitive intellectual showing-off. Such sessions served as advertisements to the wealthy young men who made up the audience, encouraging them to sign on for further teaching. This would be an expensive proposition: The sophists (and above all Protagoras) seem to have charged far more than any other contemporary professionals, and became enormously rich from their teaching. Sophists also served on embassies for their native cities, drafted laws, and wrote books; they were famous and influential—and bitterly controversial—public intellectuals as well as teachers.

Most sophists are said to have claimed to teach virtue (*arête*), but their curricula and teaching methods varied. In the *Protagoras*, Protagoras chides Hippias for forcing students to study subjects like mathematics and astronomy; he himself claims to teach them good judgment (*euboulia*), enabling them both to manage their private affairs and to succeed in politics, and accepts that this amounts to the teaching of virtue. He also claims that the greatest part of education is the ability to analyze and criticize poetry. So the sophistic teaching of virtue was not a matter of moralistic indoctrination; rather, the sophists taught their students to reflect on traditional values, to analyze and criticize the literary texts that discussed them, and to apply this learning in a political career.

In practice, their teaching seems to have centered on rhetoric or public speaking (hence the blurriness of the line between rhetorician and sophist), which was the key skill for a political career. The connection between teaching rhetoric and teaching virtue is easier to understand if we bear in mind the traditional, Homeric sense of *arête* as excellence—that is, the skills and personal qualities that make a gentleman successful in his career and a valuable asset to his community. By teaching the arts of political success, the sophists *were* teaching virtue in a quite traditional sense. In doing so they prompted debate about just what virtue or excellence really consists in, and in particular about the status of qualities such as justice, *dikaiosunê*, which seem to benefit the community at the expense of their possessor.

The evidence for sophistic ideas is uneven and very defective. There are several brief, but substantial, works by Gorgias (*On Not Being*; *Defense of Helen*), and a few pages worth of Antiphon's *On Truth*; but for Protagoras, the leading figure of the movement, only a handful of brief fragments (that is, trustworthy-looking quotations in later authors) survive. Moreover, many of our texts are ambiguous or difficult to interpret. For instance, both the *Dissoi Logoi* and Antiphon's discussion of justice seem to argue for contradictory conclusions; perhaps they are exercises in *antilogikê*, opposing arguments, a sophistic genre associated with Protagoras. Gorgias's *On Not Being* and the *Defense of Helen* both seem to be exercises in defending the indefensible; whether they also have serious philosophical agendas is still debated.

A further difficulty is posed by the all-important evidence of Plato, who fixed forever the stereotype of the Sophist. Plato vividly depicts sophists in a number of dialogues (*Protagoras, Gorgias, Republic* [Thrasymachus], *Hippias Major* and *Minor*, and *Euthydemus*), and the *Sophist* is devoted to defining their nature. But Plato's evidence is not consistent: For instance, the *Protagoras* and the *Euthydemus* give very different pictures of sophistic argument, and the *Protagoras* and *Theaetetus* seem to give conflicting accounts of Protagoras's ethical views. Moreover, Plato's presentation of the sophists is sometimes warped by hostile prejudice (though, as Grote [1865] and T.H. Irwin [1995] have noted, he is not as uniformly hostile as scholars sometimes assume), and by his anxiety to distinguish them as sharply as possible from Socrates.

Unsurprisingly, given the focus of their teaching, sophistic thought seems to have centered on ethical and political topics. However, sophistic interests varied greatly; in some cases they were very broad, and several sophists are associated with ideas in mathematics or natural science. So the traditional scholarly contrast between the sophists and the pre-socratics, with their researches into natural science, is probably misguided or at least overstated. The sophists also were founders of what are now called the social sciences; they offered theories of the origins of human institutions such as law and religion, and took a particular scientific interest in language and the norms applicable to it. Here in the social realm, the closest thing to a unifying pattern in sophistic thought is found—their concern to distinguish *phusis* and *nomos* (i.e., the natural and the merely conventional or, as one might now say, socially constructed).

Surviving sophistic texts analyze a wide range of human institutions and values—above all, justice—in these terms, with the assumption that nature represents a deeper or more binding norm than convention. Combined with the sophists' recognition of the differing norms of various cultures (see the *Dissoi Logoi*) and their skepticism about traditional religion, this privileging of the natural could be seen as undermining the authority of moral tradition. However, hostility toward the sophists probably had less to do with their particular theories than with their teaching to all comers the ability to speak persuasively, and with it the power to manipulate both political assemblies and legal proceedings.

It is now generally recognized that it is wrong to describe the sophists collectively as moral skeptics, immoralists, or relativists (Bett 1989, 2002). Protagoras is presented as a relativist in Plato's *Theaetetus*, but not in his earlier and probably more historically accurate *Protagoras*. The *Dissoi Logoi* presents a wealth of evidence for the cultural relativity of values, but argues against relativistic conclusions as well as for them. Sophistic uses of *nomos* and *phusis* were often in the service of conflicting ethical and political theories, and attempts to pin the sophists down to any common moral theory are doomed by the sheer diversity of sophistic thought. If anything, the sophists (as one would expect given the competitive character of their profession) tended to take up positions in opposition to each other—even if the battle lines are often now blurred by the incompleteness of evidence available.

On matters of natural science, metaphysics, and epistemology, it is still more difficult to identify shared sophistic positions. Antiphon's *On Truth* seems to have offered a complete cosmogony on natural science: Aristotle, in *Physics*, reports him as claiming that the true essence of a wooden bed is wood because if planted it would reproduce a tree rather than another bed. Presumably the force of the scientific part of the work was to spell out this kind of distinction between the underlying natures of things (the realm of *phusis*) and merely superficial human arrangements and projections, (*nomos*).

Gorgias's *On Not Being* seems intended to support a skeptical conclusion, at least as a critique of metaphysicians like Parmenides. His main criticism was: If beings do have a real nature independent of humans, it can neither be known or communicated. Plato's *Theaetetus* attributes a sophisticated relativism or subjectivism in epistemology (and ethics) to Protagoras: its slogan, "Man is the measure of all things," must go back to Protagoras's work *Truth*, but how much of the detailed theory presented by Plato that is genuinely Protagorean is uncertain. Even setting aside other sophistic views (where evidence is even scantier), the most these positions could be said to share is a critical orientation—a tendency to diagnose beliefs and perceptions (both everyday and scientific, or philosophical) as irreducibly subjective.

In keeping with their activities as teachers and writers, and their interest in the analysis of human conventions, the sophists were noted for their researches into language. Prodicus was celebrated for drawing fine distinctions in the meanings of words. It is thought that Protagoras analyzed the parts of speech, and claimed that the words for *wrath* and *helmet*, feminine in Greek, were properly masculine. The sophists are often associated with claims that falsehood and contradiction are impossible, but the evidence for this is unclear and confusing, and these claims are hard to square with the eristic practice of inducing contradictions in others. One might suspect that distinctive views about the nature of truth were entailed by Protagoras's *Measure Thesis*, and lay behind his practice of argument on both sides of a question (*antilogikê*); but attempts to reconstruct sophistic ideas on these questions are highly speculative.

See also Antiphon; Gorgias of Leontini; Nomos and Phusis; Protagoras of Abdera; Socrates.

Bibliography

Barney, R. "The Sophistic Movement." In *The Blackwell Companion to Ancient Philosophy*, edited by Mary Louise Gill and Pierre Pellegrin. Oxford: Blackwell, 2005.

Bett, R. "Is There a Sophistic Ethics?" *Ancient Philosophy* 22 (2002): 235–262.

Bett, R. "The Sophists and Relativism." *Phronesis* 34 (1989): 139–169.

Broadie, Sarah. "The Sophists and Socrates." In *The Cambridge Companion to Greek and Roman Philosophy*, edited by D.N. Sedley. Cambridge, U.K.: Cambridge University Press, 2003.

Diels, H. *Die fragmente der Vorsokratiker*, 6th ed. revised by W. Kranz. Berlin: Weidmann, 1951–1952.

Dillon, J., and T. Gergel. *The Greek Sophists*. Penguin, 2003.

Gagarin, M., and P. Woodruff. *Early Greek Political Thought from Homer to the Sophists*. Cambridge, U.K.: Cambridge University Press, 1995.

Grote, George. *A History of Greece*, 4th ed. London: John Murray, 1872.

Grote, George. *Plato and the Other Companions of Socrates*. London: John Murray, 1865.

Guthrie, W.K.C. *A History of Greek Philosophy*. Vol. 3. Cambridge, U.K.: Cambridge University Press, 1969.

Irwin, T.H. "Plato's Objections to the Sophists." In *The Greek World*, edited by C.A. Powell. London: Routledge, 1995.

Kerferd, G.B. *The Sophistic Movement*. Cambridge, U.K.: Cambridge University Press, 1981.

Morrison, J. S. "The Truth of Antiphon." *Phronesis* 8 (1963): 35–49.

Nehamas, A. "Eristic, Antilogic, Sophistic, Dialectic: Plato's Demarcation of Philosophy from Sophistry." *History of Philosophy Quarterly* 7 (1990): 3–16.

Pendrick, G. *Antiphon The Sophist: The Fragments*. Cambridge, U.K.: Cambridge University Press, 2002.

Robinson, T.M., ed. *Contrasting Arguments: an Edition of the Dissoi Logoi*. New York: Arno Press, 1979.

Sidgwick, Henry. "The Sophists." *Journal of Philology* (1872): 288–307.

Sidgwick, Henry. "The Sophists." *Journal of Philology* (1873): 66–80.

Striker, G. "Methods of Sophistry." In *Essays on Hellenistic Epistemology and Ethics*. Cambridge, U.K.: Cambridge University Press, 1996.

Waterfield, R. *The First Philosophers: The Presocratics and Sophists*. Oxford: Oxford Paperbacks, 2000.

Rachel Barney (2005)

SÔPHROSYNÊ

See Appendix, Vol. 10

SOREL, GEORGES
(1847–1922)

Georges Sorel, the French pragmatist philosopher and social theorist, was born in Cherbourg and was trained at the École Polytechnique. He served as an engineer with the French roads and bridges department for twenty-five years in Corsica, the Alps, Algeria, and Perpignan before retiring at the age of forty-five to devote himself to scholarship. In the following thirty years he produced a series of highly curious books on the philosophy of science, the history of ideas, social theory, and Marxism, of which one, *Réflexions sur la violence* (1908; *Reflections on Violence*), immediately became world famous. Before and after his retirement Sorel's life was quite uneventful, for despite his hatred of the bourgeois, his conduct was a model of provincial respectability. Nevertheless, he never married his lifelong companion, Marie David, to whom he dedicated his work after her death in 1897. Sorel's Roman ideas on the importance of chastity, marriage, and the family were no match for his family's objections to Marie's proletarian origins.

ECONOMICS AND POLITICAL VIEWS

Sorel's first books, on the Bible and the trial of Socrates, were written while he was still in charge of irrigation around Perpignan. They are works of erudition, marked by a streak of passionate eccentricity. Soon after retiring to the suburbs of Paris, Sorel discovered the work of Karl Marx and edited (1895–1897) a magazine, *Le devenir social,* that introduced theoretical Marxism to France. At the same time Sorel collaborated with Benedetto Croce and Antonio Labriola in propagating Marx's ideas in Italy. (Italy was always Sorel's second intellectual home, although he never visited it or even left French territory, and much of his work has been published only in Italian.) Sorel soon became dissatisfied with Marxism's scientific pretensions and joined with Croce, Eduard Bernstein, Tomáš Masaryk, and Saverio Merlino in precipitating the revisionist crisis. The other revisionists drew reformist conclusions from their critique of Marxism and abandoned revolutionary activity, but Sorel did the opposite. He transferred his interest from orthodox socialism to the most revolutionary wing of the French labor movement, the anarchosyndicalists. He argued that this was consistent because the syndicalists did not use Marxism as science but as myth. It was to account for this mythical character of extremist social doctrines that Sorel elaborated one of his most influential theories.

By the eve of World War I, Sorel had lost faith in syndicalism, and for a time he associated with such extreme right-wing groups as the monarchists and ultranationalists, as well as with groups of Catholic revivalists. Silent during the war, Sorel emerged after the Bolshevik Revolution to devote his last energies to the defense of the cause of V. I. Lenin, as he understood it. He supposed that it meant transfer of power away from central authority to the workers' and peasants' soviets and thus that it was in the federalist spirit of Pierre-Joseph Proudhon rather than in the spirit of Marx.

Years earlier, Sorel had predicted an important political career for Benito Mussolini, who, in turn, called *Reflections on Violence* his bedside book. Yet despite tenacious legend, Sorel had no influence over either fascism or communism. He himself disclaimed any part in Mussolini's nationalist doctrines, and Lenin denied drawing ideas from "that confusionist." Apologists of later revolutionary movements, notably African and Asian nationalism, have echoed Sorel's doctrines, and students of all such movements still find useful his conceptions of myth and violence. Croce said that Sorel and Marx were the only original thinkers socialism ever had.

PHILOSOPHY OF SCIENCE

Sorel accepted Jean-Joseph-Marie-Auguste Jaurès's scornful description of him as "the metaphysician of socialism," for he thought of himself as primarily a philosopher, though not of socialism alone. Socialism engaged no more of his attention than the philosophy of science or the history of Christianity. Sorel's philosophy of science was technological rationalism: Scientific laws were accounts of the working of experimental machinery into which a part of nature, after being purified to make it homogeneous with the manmade mechanism, had been incorporated. There was no cause to suppose that such machines were models of nature's hidden mechanisms, and in fact there was no sign that determinism of any sort operated in nature left to herself. Determinism existed only where men created it, in machines that did violence to nature by shutting out chance interference. Thus, science is concerned with "artificial nature," the manmade phenomena of experiment and industry. It has nothing to say about "natural nature," where hazard, waste, and entropy are uncontrolled, where our knowledge is limited to statistical probability and our intervention to rule of thumb. Sorel accepted the pessimistic conclusions often drawn at that time from the second law of thermodynamics, to the effect that there was absolute chance in nature and that the universe was "running down" to heat-death.

It was against that malevolent nature of chance and waste that humanity struggled in a hopeless effort of "dis-entropy," seeking to establish regions of determinism (experimental science) and of economy of forces (productive industry). Being a professional engineer, Sorel could work out these ideas in great technical detail. He even applied them to mathematics, saying that geometry was about architecture, not nature.

SOCIAL THEORY

Sorel's social theory derived from his philosophy of science. There are "entropic" trends in society comparable to those in nature. Culture is constantly threatened by a relapse into barbarism and disorder that would make history sheer meaningless succession. Against perpetual decadence men struggle heroically to establish limited zones of law, order, and cultural significance. To succeed in this for a time, they must do violence to their own natures by imposing on themselves a hard discipline and accepting moral isolation amid their mediocre fellows. This means living in conformity to "the ethic of the producers" and seeing the good life to be a cooperative creative enterprise carried on in a self-reliant spirit. Against this ethic stands "the ethic of the consumers," which takes the good to be things to be obtained rather than a way of acting. In the consumers' view typical goods are welfare, prosperity, distributive justice, and the classless society, things to be aimed at for the future and enjoyed if secured. Sorel replied that enterprises undertaken in that spirit were based on envy and inevitably fell under the control of adventurers (usually intellectuals) who duped the masses. He cited as instances slave revolts, peasant wars, Jacobinism, anti-Semitism, and contemporary welfare-state socialism.

In contrast, producers' movements concentrated on building the independent institutions that embodied their morality of productivity and solidarity. Such movements might be concerned with religious, artistic, scientific, or industrial activities, and Sorel took capitalism and syndicalist socialism as successive and equally admirable types of an industrial producers' movement. The workers were in revolt against capitalism not because of exploitation or inequality of riches (such matters concerned consumers only) but because the bourgeoisie had become unenterprising, cowardly, hypocritical—in a word, decadent. Until some more youthful, vigorous movement wrested social preeminence from the bourgeoisie (and Sorel did not think that socialism was the only contender), Western history would be a meaningless sequence of parliamentary deals and predatory wars. All movements "ran down" in the end, as their nerve failed, even (or especially) without challenge from a new movement. This succession of periods of heroic creativity and decadent barbarism did not constitute a true historical cycle, but Sorel adopted the accounts of the heroic and decadent phases of society given by Giambattista Vico in his cyclical theory. Sorel and Croce stimulated the revival of interest in Vico, and Sorel regarded his own social theory as a Viconian revision of Marxism.

VIOLENCE

Sorel is remembered less for his general philosophical system than for two notions lifted from it, violence and myth. Sorel found the syndicalists using violence during industrial strikes, and he set out to answer the common charge that a movement that resorted to violence was ipso facto evil and retrograde. He pointed out that Christianity and French republicanism, for example, had welcomed violent confrontations in order to mark clearly their rejection of the social milieu and their refusal to compromise. In such cases violence was a sign of moral health that frightened away lukewarm supporters and gave notice of earnest determination to adopt a new way of life. Physical violence—head breaking and bloodshed—was only one extreme of a range of vehement attitudes of which the other extreme was "a violence of principles," such as parading the least acceptable part of one's doctrines (in the Christian religion, miracles) to discourage one's "reasonable" friends. Sorel's theory of violence was intended to cover that whole range of attitudes, and the only special stress on physical violence was the statement that without being at all typical of social relationships, physical violence is a logical extreme from which no rising movement will shrink in certain unfavorable circumstances. Such circumstances would be confrontation with the armed force of a state that preached pacifism and social unity while it sought to smother a rebellious minority. The classic case was primitive Christianity, which could have secured tolerance within Roman polytheism but enthusiastically courted violent persecution to mark its unbridgeable differences with paganism. Parliamentary democracy was an even greater threat to independent social movements than polytheism had been to Christianity, because it claimed to have devised, in parliament, a perfect market where all social demands could be reconciled by elected representatives, thus ensuring social harmony. A movement that refused to come to that market because it wanted things other than parliamentary seats and budget subsidies would have to be unequivocal, vehement, and even violent to escape from the nets of democratic prejudice. Most shocking of all, violence might be exercised not only against supposed enemies but against the men of good will, the peacemakers sent to befriend the minority and corrupt it into conformity.

Sorel's theory of violence caused scandalized misunderstanding among respectable people and some morbid enthusiasm among protofascists. Yet Sorel had not defended indiscriminate violence. He had said that since violence is ubiquitous in society, in the form of war and the enforcement of law and order, one could not selectively deplore violence on the part of an opposition without first looking to see who that opposition was. One should ask if it were associated, as so often in the past, with a progressive and heroic morality obliged to be ruthless to force recognition of its independence and to signify its rejection of mediocrity. Sorel noted that such movements built up sanguinary legends about how much violence they had known. Just as strikers exaggerated police brutalities committed on "our martyred dead," so the early Christians had endured far too little persecution to justify the tradition that the church was nourished by the blood of martyrs. Such violent tales were only symbolically true; a few clashes that proved a willingness to go to extremes had revealed the Christian community to itself and its enemies.

Last, Sorel argued (in 1908, when the seeds of world war, Bolshevism, and fascism were germinating) that Edwardian democrats were deluding themselves in thinking that civilized men had progressed beyond the stage at which they would use violence to promote or oppose causes. Violence would never be outgrown (and if it were, that would not be progress) because it was not, absolutely and in itself, brutish. It could be lucid, noble, and applied to the defense of high purposes; it could mark the birth of a new civilizing agency. Of course, it could also be bestial and oppressive, in which case Sorel called it force.

MYTH

Sorel found that myth was being used by the syndicalists, and he recalled similar uses from history. In no sense did he urge political activists to adopt extremist beliefs they knew to be false. That ambiguity, of which Sorel was accused, was really in the sociological facts themselves, he said. One found movements uttering views about the future without trying to establish their prophecies as scientifically plausible, without even caring to argue whether the forecasts were sound. They cared for those visions of the future passionately, but they cared for them only as inspiring pictures of what the world would be like if the new morality won all men's hearts. Such visions were myths, a present morality stated in the future tense. The case in point was the general strike. Syndicalists said socialism would come if all workers went on strike at once, whereupon the capitalist state would be paralyzed. Parliamentary socialists replied, reasonably enough, that for the workers to strike all at once and successfully defy the state, they would have to be ardent socialists to a man and the regime ripe for overthrow. But in that event socialism would already have arrived, and the general strike would not be needed. It was not a means to anything because it presupposed that all the problems were solved. Precisely this, answered Sorel, is the social function of the general strike. It is the dramatic picture of a morality triumphant. It is not a plan or scientific forecast, and therefore rational criticism of it is pointless. Besides, intellect has nothing better to put in its place, because the future is radically unpredictable and there is no science of the unknowable. A myth, being the expression of the aspirations of an enthusiastic mass of men and women, could well foreshadow something like itself, at least something equally sublime, whereas scientific blueprints for the future foreshadowed nothing but disappointment, the rule of intellectual planners, and the spread of the consumer outlook among those who waited for the planned good time to start. Granted that prevision is impossible, there are only two sorts of attitude toward the future—myths and utopias. Myths command respect as the product of intense social wills that could achieve something in history; utopias deserve scorn as the divagations of solitary intellectuals.

Sorel's tolerant view of myths and his anxiety to protect their improbabilities from rational examination were dependent on his conviction (drawn from Henri Bergson's philosophy) that the future is undetermined and thus totally unknowable. Few philosophers accept that position, and they would thus feel entitled to be more critical of myths than Sorel allowed. Yet he provided social theory with a valuable new concept—the galvanizing mass faith about which even its own believers are ambivalent, half admitting it to be improbable and yet clinging to it as the dramatic epitome of the cause they live for.

See also Bergson, Henri; Continental Philosophy; Croce, Benedetto; Labriola, Antonio; Lenin, Vladimir Il'ich; Marx, Karl; Marxist Philosophy; Masaryk, Tomáš Garrigue; Myth; Nationalism; Philosophy of Science, History of; Philosophy of Science, Problems of; Political

Philosophy, History of; Proudhon, Pierre-Joseph; Socrates; Vico, Giambattista; Violence.

Bibliography

WORKS BY SOREL

Contribution à l'étude profane de la Bible. Paris: Ghio, 1889.

Le procès de Socrate. Paris: Alcan, 1889.

La ruine du monde antique. Paris: Jacques, 1901.

Essai sur l'église et l'état. Paris: Jacques, 1902.

Saggi di critica del marxismo. Palermo: Sandron, 1902.

Introduction à l'économie moderne. Paris, 1903.

Le système historique de Renan, 4 vols. Paris: Jacques, 1905–1906.

Insegnamenti sociali della economia contemporanea. Palermo: Sandron, 1907.

Réflexions sur la violence. Paris: Librarie de "Pages Libres," 1908. Translated by T. E. Hulme and J. Roth as *Reflections on Violence.* New York: Huebsch, 1914.

Les illusions du progrès. Paris: Rivière, 1908. Translated by John and Charlotte Stanley as *The Illusions of Progress.* Berkeley: University of California Press, 1969.

La décomposition du marxisme. Paris: Rivière, 1908.

La révolution dreyfusienne. Paris: Rivière, 1909.

Matériaux d'une théorie du prolétariat. Paris: Rivière, 1919.

Les préoccupations métaphysiques des physiciens modernes. Paris, 1921.

De l'utilité du pragmatisme. Paris: Rivière, 1921.

D'Aristote à Marx. Edited by Édouard Berth. Paris: Rivière, 1935.

Propos de Georges Sorel. Edited by Jean Variot. Paris: Gallimard, 1935. Sorel's conversations.

From Georges Sorel: Essays in Socialism and Philosophy. Edited by John L. Stanley. New York: Oxford University Press, 1976.

From Georges Sorel, Vol. 2: *Hermeneutics and the Science.* Edited by John L. Stanley; translated by John and Charlotte Stanley. New Brunswick, NJ: Transaction, 1990.

WORKS ON SOREL

V. Delesalle, *Bibliographic sorélienne* (Leiden, 1939), lists hundreds of articles and reviews by Sorel scattered through dozens of journals, including material of philosophical interest, and records the extensive literature on Sorel up to 1939; J. H. Meisel, *The Genesis of Georges Sorel* (Ann Arbor, MI: Wahr, 1951), adds later items. Of the many hundreds of studies, the most instructive are Richard Humphrey, *Georges Sorel, Prophet without Honor* (Cambridge, MA: Harvard University Press, 1951); Victor Sartre, *Georges Sorel* (Paris, 1937); Michael Freund, *Der revolutionäre Konservativismus* (Frankfurt, 1932); Giuseppe Santonastaso, *Georges Sorel* (Bari, Italy, 1932); Pierre Andreu, *Notre maître, M. Sorel* (Paris: Grasset, 1953); Jean Deroo, *Le renversement du matérialisme historique* (Paris: Rivière, 1942); Max Ascoli, *Georges Sorel* (Paris, 1921); Georges Guy-Grand, *La philosophie syndicaliste* (Paris: Grasset, 1911); Gaétan Piron, *Georges Sorel* (Paris: Rivière, 1927); Georges Goriely, *Le pluralisme dramatique de Georges Sorel* (Paris: Riviere, 1962); Fernand Rossignol, *La pensée de Georges Sorel* (Paris, 1948); various authors, special issue of *Fédération* (November 1947).

ADDITIONAL SOURCES

Berlin, Isaiah. "Georges Sorel." In *Against the Current: Essays in the History of Ideas,* edited by Henry Hardy. New York: Viking Press, 1980.

Jennings, Jeremy R. *Georges Sorel; The Character and Development of His Thought.* London: Macmillan, 1985.

Kolakowski, Leszek. "Georges Sorel: A Jansenist Marxism." In *Main Currents of Marxism,* Vol. 2, translated by P. S. Falla. Oxford: Clarendon Press, 1978.

Stanley, John L. *The Sociology of Virtue: The Political and Social Theories of Georges Sorel.* Los Angeles: University of California Press, 1981.

Vernon, Richard. *Commitment and Change: Georges Sorel and the Idea of Revolution.* Toronto: University of Toronto Press, 1978.

Vincent, Steven K. "Interpreting Georges Sorel: Defender of Virtue or Apostle of Violence?" *History of European Ideas* 12 (2) (1990): 239–257.

Neil McInnes (1967)

Bibliography updated by Philip Reed (2005)

SOSA, ERNEST

(1940–)

Ernest Sosa is Romeo Elton Professor of Natural Theology and Professor of Philosophy at Brown University and regular Distinguished Visiting Professor at Rutgers University. He received his Ph.D. from the University of Pittsburgh and has taught at Brown since 1964. Since 1983, he has been the editor of *Philosophy and Phenomenological Research* and since 1999, with Jaegwon Kim, the co-editor of *Nous.* Sosa has published essays on issues in a wide variety of philosophical areas such as metaphysics, logic, philosophy of mind, theory of action, and philosophy of language, but he has been most influential in epistemology, where he is known for advocating a virtue-based approach to the analysis of knowledge and justification with an emphasis on the importance of a reflective perspective.

What is distinctive of virtue epistemology is the order of explanation: A belief's epistemic status is to be understood in terms of the epistemic properties of the subject, which in turn are to be captured by employing the concept of an intellectual virtue. How is this concept to be understood? In pure virtue epistemology, construed in analogy to pure virtue ethics, the concept of an intellectual virtue is basic (Foley 1994). Sosa, however, conceives of an intellectual virtue as a stable disposition to form true beliefs in a certain field of propositions, F, under suitable circumstances, C. Thus his brand of virtue epistemology, which he has labeled virtue perspectivism, is not an example of the pure kind but may be viewed as a form of reliabilism.

The two main elements of Sosa's virtue perspectivism are the concepts of an intellectual virtue and an epistemic perspective. As already indicated, Sosa conceives of intellectual virtues in terms of reliability. Reliably functioning faculties, such as vision, hearing, introspection, and memory are examples of intellectual virtues. Sosa calls beliefs that are grounded in the exercise of such virtues apt. Apt beliefs, if true, qualify as knowledge, or, more precisely, as animal knowledge, to be distinguished from reflective knowledge. With the distinction between these two kinds of knowledge, the second main element of virtue perspectivism comes to the fore: the concept of an epistemic perspective.

Let S refer to the subject whose beliefs we wish to evaluate. Suppose S's visual belief that p is true and, due to the reliability of S's vision, apt. Hence by employing her faculty of vision, S acquires animal knowledge that p. For S's belief to rise to the level of reflective knowledge, a further condition must be met: S must form a meta-belief to the effect that her belief and its being true have their origin in a reliable faculty. In general terms, if from S's epistemic perspective, a faculty is coherently viewed as reliable within field F and circumstances C, then by employing this faculty S can acquire reflective knowledge within field F and circumstances C.

Animal knowledge, then, results from external aptness: the exercise of faculties that are in fact reliable. Reflective knowledge also requires aptness, but, in addition, the adoption of an internally coherent perspective with respect to the reliability of one's faculties. Sosa's virtue perspectivism, then, combines both an externalist and an internalist element.

In the large body of work in which Sosa articulates and defends his approach to the philosophical explanation of knowledge and justification, he has addressed various problems that arise for virtue perspectivism. First, there is the problem of what a reliabilist should say about what are referred to as *evil demon victims*: subjects whose beliefs seem justified although, due to the massive deception to which the victims are subjected, their beliefs are grounded in unreliable faculties. Sosa responds that, whereas the demon victims' beliefs are *actual world* justified (as the victims' faculties would be reliable in the actual world, they are *same world* unjustified because the faculties the victims employ are unreliable in their own world (1994a). In more recent terminology, Sosa classifies the victims' beliefs as adroit though not apt (Sosa 2003).

Second, Sosa's reliability-grounded virtue perspectivism is challenged by what Sosa calls the *problem of meta-incoherence*, which arises from cases in which a subject's beliefs are produced by a faculty whose de facto reliability is not (or at least not yet) recognized by the subject. Since such subjects do not meet the perspectival condition of having formed reliability-attributing meta-beliefs about the relevant belief sources, Sosa judges that the beliefs in question are unjustified, or not reflectively justified (Sosa 1991).

Third, there is the generality problem, which for Sosa amounts to the challenge of finding the right level of specificity in describing field and circumstances. Here, Sosa's solution is to require that the relevant descriptions be useful within the subject's epistemic community and to the subject herself (Sosa 1991). Three further, important problems to which Sosa has articulated detailed solutions are the following: First, how can we distinguish between accidental and non-accidental reliability? Second, what justifies reliability-attributing perspectival meta-beliefs (Sosa 1994a)? Third, why is the process by which reliability-attributing meta-beliefs are formed (using, for example, perception to attest to the reliability of our perceptual faculties) not viciously circular (1994b and 1997)?

Recently, Sosa has also contributed important work on the following question: If a belief is to be an instance of knowledge, what modal link must there exist between the belief and its truth? According to some, knowledge requires sensitivity: S would not believe that p if p were false. Viewing this condition as too demanding, Sosa objects to it on the basis of the following case: Having dropped a trash bag in the garbage shoot, you believe the bag will momentarily reach its destination in the basement. This belief, Sosa suggests, amounts to knowledge even though it is not sensitive: if p (the bag will land momentarily) were false (because, say, the bag snagged in the shoot), you would still believe p. As an alternative, Sosa proposes safety: If S were to believe p, p would be true (or: Not easily would S believe incorrectly in believing that p). Though your belief that the bag will land momentarily is not sensitive, it is indeed safe, for possible worlds in which S believes that the bag will shortly arrive downstairs, but believes this mistakenly, are indeed remote (Sosa 1999).

The distinction between safety and sensitivity assumes particular significance for Sosa, for he appeals to it for the purpose of rejecting the contextualist solution to the puzzle of skepticism. Contextualists have argued that, when confronted with a skeptical argument, we face a paradox because, although we find the premises plausible, we wish to reject the conclusion. According to the contextualist response, the puzzle is to be solved by appeal to the context-sensitivity of the word *know*. Sosa suggests an alternative solution: Skeptical arguments may (misleadingly) seem cogent because we fail to recognize that knowledge requires not sensitivity, but merely safety (Sosa 1999 and 2003).

See also Contextualism; Kim, Jaegwon; Moral Epistemology; Reliabilism; Skepticism, Contemporary; Virtue Epistemology.

Bibliography

PRIMARY WORKS

Knowledge in Perspective: Selected Essays in Epistemology. Cambridge,U.K.: Cambridge University Press, 1991.

"Philosophical Skepticism and Epistemic Circularity." *Aristotelian Society Supplementary Volume*, 68 (1994a): 263–290.

"Virtue Perspectivism: A Response to Foley and Fumerton."*Philosophical Issues*, 5 (1994b): 29–50.

"Perspectives in Virtue Epistemology: A Response to Dancy and BonJour." *Philosophical Studies* 78 (1995): 221–235.

"Reflective Knowledge in the Best Circles." *The Journal of Philosophy* 96 (1997): 271–293.

"How to Defeat Opposition to Moore." *Philosophical Perspectives* (1999) 141–153.

"Relevant Alternatives, Contextualism Included" *Philosophical Studies* 119 (2003): 35–65.

SECONDARY WORKS

BonJour, Laurence. *Epistemic Justification: Internalism vs. Externalism, Foundations vs. Virtue.* Malden, MA: Blackwell, 2003

BonJour, Laurence. "Sosa on Knowledge, Justification, and 'Aptness.'" *Philosophical Studies* 78 (1995): 207–220.

Dancy, Jonathan. "Supervenience, Virtues, and Consequences." *Philosophical Studies* 78 (1995): 198–205.

Foley, Richard. "The Epistemology of Sosa." *Philosophical Issues* 5 (1994): 1–14.

Fumerton, Richard. "Sosa's Epistemology." *Philosophical Issues* 5 (1994): 14–27.

Greco, John. *Ernest Sosa and His Critics.* Malden, MA: Blackwell, 2004.

Matthias Steup (2005)

SOTO, DOMINIC DE

(1494–1560)

Dominic de Soto, the Dominican scholastic theologian, was born at Segovia, Spain, and died at Salamanca. He studied at Alcalá de Henares and became a professor of philosophy there after advanced studies at the University of Paris. Entering the Dominican order in 1524, Soto taught theology from 1525 onward at the University of Salamanca. He was very active in the deliberations of the Council of Trent. Soto's writings include two commentaries on Aristotle (*In Dialecticam Aristotelis,* Salamanca, 1543; *In Libros Physicorum,* Salamanca, 1545). Theological works containing some philosophical thought are *Summulae* (4 vols., Burgos, 1529); *De Natura et Gratia* (Venice, 1547); and the treatise *De Justitia et Jure* (Justice and the law; Salamanca, 1556).

One of the founders of the school of Spanish Thomism, Soto had his own opinions on many philosophical questions. Like John Duns Scotus, he denied the usual Thomistic distinction between essence and existence. In theory of knowledge, he also showed the influence of Scotism, teaching that the primary object of human understanding is indeterminate being in general. His psychology followed that of Thomas Aquinas, with strong emphasis on the intellectual functions: the intellect is a nobler power than the will. Soto is an important figure in the philosophy of law and politics. He violently criticized the theory of the state of pure human nature, as popularized by Cardinal Cajetan and Francisco Suárez. Unlike his teacher, Francisco de Vitoria, Soto taught that law stems from the understanding rather than from the will of the legislator; he clearly differentiated natural law, which depends on the real natures and relations of things, from positive law, which results from a decision of the legislator (*De Justitia* I, 1, 1). In political philosophy he represents a growing tendency toward democratic thinking in Renaissance scholasticism: Both civil and ecclesiastical power derive ultimately from God, but the civil power proceeds through the medium of society; the people concretize the authority received from God in the persons whom they designate as rulers. Soto is also regarded as one of the founders of the general theory of international law.

See also Aristotle; Cajetan, Cardinal; Philosophy of Law, History of; Philosophy of Law, Problems of; Renaissance; Scotism; Suárez, Francisco; Thomas Aquinas, St.; Thomism; Vitoria, Francisco de.

Bibliography

De Justitia et Jure has been translated into Spanish by Jaime T. Ripoll as *Tratado de la justicia y del derecho.* 2 vols. (Madrid, 1926).

For literature on Soto, see A. J. Carlyle, *History of Mediaeval Political Theory* (Edinburgh, 1950), Vol. VI, pp. 254–258; T. Davitt, *The Nature of Law* (St. Louis: Herder, 1951), pp. 161–177; and Beltrán de Heredia, "El maestro Domingo

(Francisco) de Soto," in *La ciencia tomista* 43 (1931): 357–373.

Vernon J. Bourke (1967)

SOUL

See *Immortality; Psychē; Psychology*

SOUND

"Sound" according to Aristotle's *De Anima* (418a12) and George Berkeley's *First Dialogue*, is the special, or proper, object of hearing. G. J. Warnock, in his *Berkeley*, interprets this as meaning that sound is the "tautological accusative" of hearing: Sounds can only be heard and must be heard if anything is heard.

Hearing receives attention in philosophy mainly for its differences from seeing. Two respects in which listening and hearing differ from looking and seeing are (1) that there is nothing analogous, in seeing, to hearing the sound of something, and (2) that, in telling where something is, there is nothing analogous, in listening, to our having to look in the right direction.

Warnock's explanation of the first of these differences is that we establish the presence and existence of an object by sight and touch, and then proceed to distinguish the object thus established from its smell and taste and the noises it makes. He mentions, as reasons for not ascribing such primacy to hearing, that inanimate objects often do not make any noises, that animate ones make them only intermittently, and that it is often difficult to tell where a sound is coming from. There would be a further reason if, as P. F. Strawson maintains (in *Individuals*, p. 65), a universe in which experience was exclusively auditory would have no place at all for spatial concepts. This reason would be decisive if in a nonspatial world there could be no concept of an object (*Individuals*, Ch. 2). Strawson asserts that we can discover some spatial features of things by listening (for instance, sounds seem to come from the left or right), but denies that such expressions as "to the left of" have any intrinsically auditory significance. In accordance with this, G. N. A. Vesey labels knowing where a sound comes from by listening "borrowed-meaning" knowledge. Berkeley makes use of the fact that we talk of hearing sounds caused by things, together with the principle that "the senses perceive nothing which they do not perceive immediately: for they make no inferences," to gain acceptance of the view that we cannot properly be said to hear the causes of sounds.

We can see directly (otherwise than by reflection) only what is on the same side of our heads as our eyes. Knowing in what position we have had to put our heads—in what direction we have had to look—to see an object, we know in what direction the object is. Hearing is not limited in this fashion, and so we identify the position of a merely seen object and a merely heard object very differently. Furthermore, if Strawson and Vesey are right about spatial expressions not having an intrinsically auditory significance, we cannot hear that one object is to the left of another as we can see that one object is to the left of another. It might be concluded that knowledge that the source of a sound is to one's left, gained by listening, must be mediated knowledge—that is, must have involved the making of an inference. To be valid, this conclusion would require the further premise that acquiring a perceptual capacity is invariably a matter of learning to interpret one thing as a sign of another. An alternative hypothesis would be that the only interpretation involved is at the physiological level; that is, that differences in the stimuli to the two ears which, in a person whose experience was exclusively auditory, would have no counterpart in experience, would, in a person who knew what it was to see and feel things as being on his left or right, subserve his hearing things as being on his left or right.

B. O'Shaughnessy ("The Location of Sound") asserts that hearing where a sound comes from is noninferential and immediate. He contends that the seeming mysteriousness of the fact that listening can tell us where a sound is coming from is the result of our thinking of what is heard as a complex of two elements, "the sound itself" and "its coming from the left" (defining "the sound itself" as what is auditory—evidence of a "metaphysical theory of the sensory substratum"), and then having to think of its coming from the left either as "part and parcel of the sound" or as something we experience "other than and additional to the sound itself" but somehow related to it. That the sound is coming from the left, O'Shaughnessy holds, is neither part of the sound, nor something else we experience; nor is it something "we simply know." The mistake lies in our thinking of what is heard as a complex, and O'Shaughnessy sees this as a result of our having "the idea that a thought or meaning is a complexity."

Sound is a Lockean secondary quality. Hylas, in Berkeley's *First Dialogue*, accordingly distinguishes between sound as it is perceived by us ("a particular kind of sensation") and sound as it is in itself ("merely a vibrative or undulatory motion in the air"). Consideration of this philosophical position would not seem to raise issues peculiar to sound.

Bibliography

Grice, H. P. "Some Remarks about the Senses." In *Analytic Philosophy.* 1st series. Oxford: Blackwell, 1962.

Jonas, Hans. "The Nobility of Sight: A Study in the Phenomenology of the Senses." *Philosophy and Phenomenological Research* 14 (4) (June 1954): 507–519.

Malpas, R. M. P. "The Location of Sound." In *Analytic Philosophy*, edited by R. J. Butler, 131–144, 2nd series. Oxford, 1965.

O'Shaughnessy, B. "An Impossible Auditory Experience." *PAS* 57 (1956–1957): 53–82.

O'Shaughnessy, B. "The Location of Sound." *Mind* 66 (264) (October 1957): 471–490.

Pasnau, Robert. "What Is Sound?" *Philosophical Quarterly* 49 (1999): 309–324.

Strawson, P. F. *Individuals.* London: Methuen, 1959. Ch. 2.

Swartz, R., ed. *Perceiving, Sensing, and Knowing.* Berkeley: University of California Press, 1965.

Urmson, J. O. "The Objects of the Five Senses." *Proceedings of the British Academy* 54 (1968): 117–131.

Vesey, G. N. A. "Knowledge without Observation." *Philosophical Review* 72 (2) (April 1963): 198–212.

Warnock, G. J. *Berkeley*, 33–36. Harmondsworth, U.K., 1953.

G. N. A. Vesey (1967)
Bibliography updated by Benjamin Fiedor (2005)

SOUTH AMERICAN PHILOSOPHY

See *Latin American Philosophy*

SOVEREIGNTY

Analysis of "sovereignty" brings one into contact with nearly all the major problems in political philosophy. At least seven related concepts may be distinguished:

(1) A person or an institution may be said to be sovereign if he or it exercises authority (as a matter of right) over every other person or institution in the legal system, there being no authority competent to override him or it. For some writers, though not for all, this concept also implies unlimited legal competence; for, it is said, an authority competent to determine the limits of its own competence must be omnicompetent. (2) Difficulties arising from the first concept have led some writers to ascribe sovereignty to a constitution or basic norm from which all other rules of a system derive validity. (3) Sovereignty is sometimes ascribed to a person, or a body or a class of persons, said to exercise supreme power in a state, as distinct from authority, in the sense that their wills can usually be expected to prevail against any likely opposition.

The state itself is often said to be sovereign. This may mean any of at least four distinct (though possibly related) things: (4) that the state as an organized association will in fact prevail in conflict with any person or any other association in its territory; (5) that the rights of all such associations and persons derive from the legal order that is supported by the state or that (according to Hans Kelsen) *is* the state; (6) that the state is a moral order with claims to obedience and loyalty which have precedence over all others; (7) that the state is autonomous vis-à-vis other states; according to some theories, the state has only such obligations, whether in law or in morals, as it chooses to recognize.

CLASSICAL AND MEDIEVAL THEORIES

Aristotle regarded legislative authority as supreme in a state and classified states according to whether it was located in a monarch, in an oligarchical assembly, or in an assembly of the whole people. But to speak of a "supreme legislative authority" is a little misleading here; for the Greeks, legislation was the local application of a divinely ordained order, rather than the authoritative creation of new laws. The Roman concept of imperium was nearer sovereignty: The princeps (ruler) personally embodied the supreme authority of the Roman people. He was *legibus solutus* (not bound by the laws), at least in the sense that no one could question his enactments. Still, there were strong elements of natural law in Roman jurisprudence; the emperor was supreme because his function was to command what was *right* and for the public good.

There was rather less room for sovereignty in medieval political thought. According to Thomas Aquinas, for instance, the king was not only subject to divine and natural law but for most purposes to the custom of his realm as well. Medieval statutes commonly purported to restore laws that had been abused, rather than to innovate. In Thomas's view the Roman maxim *Quod principi placuit legis habet vigorem* (What pleases the prince has the force of law) was valid only if the prince's command was reasonable. According to Henry de Bracton, "the king ought to have no equal in his realm … [but] he ought to be subject to God and the law, since law makes the king … there is no king where will rules and not the law" (*De Legibus et Consuetudinibus Angliae,* edited by G. Woodbine, New Haven, CT, 1915–1942, Vol. II, pp. 32–33). Similarly, the *plenitudo potestatis* ascribed to the pope usually meant that supreme ecclesiastical authority was undivided, or that he held a reserve jurisdiction in secular matters—not that he was *legibus solutus.*

Alongside the doctrine of royal supremacy was another that derived royal authority from the people corporately. According to Marsilius of Padua, supreme authority rested in the *legislator,* which was either the whole organized community or an assembly (not necessarily elected) that spoke for it. Marsilius's stress on legislation as the will of a supreme authority brought him closer than his predecessors to Jean Bodin and Thomas Hobbes.

BODIN: PARADOX OF LAWFUL SOVEREIGNTY EGOISM

Bodin's *Six livres de la république* (1576) is generally considered the first statement of the modern theory that within every state there must be a determinate sovereign authority. Writing during the French religious wars, he insisted that an ordered commonwealth must have a sovereign competent to overrule customary and subordinate authorities. Sovereignty is "a supreme power over citizens and subjects unrestrained by law"; it is "the right to impose laws generally on all subjects regardless of their consent." Law is "nothing else than the command of the sovereign in the exercise of his sovereign power." Accordingly the sovereign could be subject to no one else, for he makes the law, amends it, and abrogates it for everyone. Nevertheless, he is subject to the laws of God and of nature. For instance, he may not seize his subjects' property without reasonable cause and must keep his promises to them. Moreover, he must respect the fundamental laws of the constitution, like the succession law, for sovereignty, as a *legal* authority, stems from these.

In defining sovereignty as a supreme power unrestrained by law, while yet admitting these limitations, Bodin is not as inconsistent as he is commonly said to be. Within the legal system, sovereignty may be unlimited; yet the sovereign may be bound in morals and religion to respect the laws of God and nature. Bodin's suggestion that sovereignty can be limited by constitutional laws raises more serious difficulties; for if "law is nothing else than the command of the sovereign, in the exercise of his sovereign power," how can any law be beyond his power to amend? The qualification, "in the exercise of sovereign power," may be important. Constitutional laws seem to be what H. L. A. Hart calls "rules of recognition" (see his *Concept of Law*), that is, they are rules that lay down the criteria of validity for rules of substance; they constitute the sovereign office, designate who shall occupy it, and identify his acts as those of a sovereign authority. For the sovereign to interfere with them, Bodin said, would be for him to undermine his own authority. If the acts of the sovereign are those done "in the exercise of sovereign power," that is, in accordance with the rules of recognition, it would be logically impossible to act in a valid sovereign way inconsistently with these rules. Nevertheless, the sovereign could still amend them so long as he used the unamended procedures to do so. Yet Bodin regarded the rules constituting the sovereign office as unamendable in principle; should the prince infringe them, "his successor can always annul any act prejudicial to the traditional form of the monarchy since on this is founded and sustained his very claim to sovereign majesty" (all quotations from *Six Books,* Bk. I, Ch. 8).

Bodin's reasoning, though confused, bears closely on certain twentieth-century constitutional controversies in the United Kingdom and Commonwealth countries, which have hinged on the contention that a sovereign legislature, though admittedly competent to prescribe its own powers and procedures, must yet do so only by the procedures currently laid down. Such procedures, it is argued, are among the criteria for identifying the legislature and for determining what constitutes one of its acts. Bodin's analysis of sovereignty also suggests how an omnicompetent authority like the British Parliament can yet limit its omnicompetence, as it purported to do in the Statute of Westminster of 1931. In that statute it renounced supreme authority over the dominions by making their advice and consent part of the procedure for any future legislative acts affecting them.

HOBBES: SOVEREIGNTY AND SUPREME POWER

Where Bodin was concerned mainly with supreme legal authority, Hobbes was more concerned to show a necessary relation between order, political power, sovereign authority, and political obligation. Hobbes argued that since no man can safely rely on his own strength or wits alone, men's obligations under the law of nature to forbear from harming one another must be subject to mutual guarantees; otherwise, for anyone to forbear in the competitive struggle would be to endanger his life. There is no reliable guarantee unless all parties agree not to exercise their "natural right to all things," but to submit unconditionally to a sovereign authorized to act on behalf of each of them, with the power to make them keep their agreements. Mutual forbearance would then be a duty. Sovereignty, therefore, is necessary for a social order among equals. Sovereignty cannot be made effectively subject to conditions without depriving it of its point; for on whom could be conferred the authority to judge whether such conditions had been violated? If on the individual subjects, no one individual could rely on the submission of any other. If on the sovereign, the conditions themselves would be merely formal. And there could be no independent arbiter, for any independent arbiter who could impose his ruling would himself be sovereign. Sovereignty is likewise indivisible, for if anyone had the power to mediate effectively in conflicts of authority, he would be sovereign. The united strength of all is therefore the sovereign's to use as he thinks fit. His duties under God and natural law are strictly God's business. The subject, having freely surrendered the right to interpret the law of nature for himself, must accept the sovereign's pronouncements on what is right and wrong. He could, however, be under no obligation to take his own life or to submit willingly if the sovereign should seek to kill him. Both commitments would be unnatural, being contrary to the supreme end, which is to avoid sudden death; and having no sanction in reserve, the sovereign would have no way of enforcing either obligation.

The sovereign remains one only so long as "the power lasteth, by which he is able to protect" his subjects. The purpose of submission is protection; protection requires overwhelming power; so overwhelming power is the actual condition for supreme authority. Conversely, supreme authority, brooking no rivals, commanding the power of everyone, wields supreme power. Further, natural law enjoins us to keep our covenants, above all the covenant establishing the civil order. In its concrete political expression, natural law is identical with the command of the sovereign and therefore with the civil law. So the sovereign authority is also the supreme moral authority.

JOHN AUSTIN AND THE IMPERATIVE THEORY OF LAW

The imperative theory of law expounded by Hobbes was developed by Jeremy Bentham to disarm opponents of legal reform who treated natural law and morality as built-in justifications of the unreformed common law. For if, as Bentham argued, law were simply whatever the sovereign commanded, or, in the case of the common law, what he chose not to rescind, then it might be reformed by command in accordance with rational principles of utility. In the hands of Bentham's disciple John Austin the theory of sovereignty became a tool for juristic analysis. "Law properly so-called" was distinguished from rules of other kinds as a "rule laid down for the guidance of an intelligent being by an intelligent being having power over him." Within any legal system there must be one supreme power, "a *determinate* human superior, *not* in a habit of obedience to a like superior (receiving) *habitual* obedience from the *bulk* of the society" (*Province*). His will was the ultimate validating principle of law; otherwise the quest for validity would lead to an infinite regress. Austin avoided it by resting sovereignty on the sociological fact of obedience.

The English Parliament, which is subject to legal limitation or restraint by no other authority is, prima facie, the paradigm of a sovereign legislature. Yet if its will is law, that is because law makes it so. Moreover, it is the law that defines the conditions for determining what that will is. For an institution has a will only by analogy; it is constituted by the decisions of individuals playing roles defined by rules. A change in the rules might change the will, though the individual decisions remained the same. Austin himself falters, admitting that to identify the members of the sovereign Parliament would require a knowledge of the British constitution. Habitual obedience, in short, may be rendered not to determinate individuals but to an institution, which is a legal creation. In the United States supreme legislative authority rests in the constitutional amending organ—composed of the two houses of Congress, each acting by a two-thirds majority, plus three-quarters of the states, acting through their legislatures or by conventions. So complex, discontinuous, and impersonal an authority cannot enjoy habitual obedience; its authority, like its very being, presupposes the law. To say that the law is what it commands, simply because it is formally competent to annul any rule, is to use "command" in a very strained sense.

In any case, there could be a constitution without an amending organ that nevertheless could allocate areas of competence to a number of organs. All authorities would then be limited. If one could still speak of sovereignty, it would be divided among them, with no "determinate human superior"; each would be supreme in its own sphere. The notion that sovereignty must be indivisible and omnicompetent is a corollary, then, of the false theory that every law is an enforceable command. Federal states retain their character not because their component institutions obey a sovereign authority able to enforce its will but because there is a general disposition to conform to accepted rules and in cases of dispute to accept the arbitration of the courts. The latter, however, being formally incompetent to legislate, cannot themselves be the requisite Austinian common superior.

The imperative theory was in part an attempt to determine the conditions that a legal system must satisfy if rules valid within the system are to be identifiable and conflicts of rules resolved. An alternative answer, however, is that every system must have what Hans Kelsen called a *Grundnorm* (a basic law), which is "the supreme reason of validity of the whole legal order" and which gives it its systematic unity. In these schematic analyses of legal systems, the basic law (usually a constitution) and the Austinian sovereign have very similar functions. Some writers indeed have transferred the concept of sovereignty from rulers to constitutions, thus abandoning the imperative theory. This either leaves a purely structural analysis of a legal order or it substitutes for Austin's "habitual obedience" respect for the constitution as the sociological starting point.

SOVEREIGNTY AND POLITICAL POWER

As Austinian analyses of sovereignty became metalegal and remote from political facts, attempts were made to split, not indeed the sovereign, but the concept of sovereignty into two types: legal and political (or practical). The first would be attributable to the supreme legislature; the second to the class or body in the society that "could make [its] will prevail whether with or against the law" (James Bryce) or "the will of which is ultimately obeyed by the citizens" (A. V. Dicey). In a democracy this would normally be the people, or the electorate.

The notion of sovereignty as supreme power in the latter sense, however, suggests certain problems. First, one must generally take account not only of what one can do by oneself but also of other people's possible resistance or cooperation. No one can ever do just what he wants; even the supreme army commander must keep the troops loyal. Every social choice is between only those alternatives that the powers of other men leave open. Political decisions reflect not only actual pressures but also those that might be anticipated were things decided differently. Again, a group may exercise very great power in that policy sphere in which it has an interest as a group; but in others its members' interests may be diverse and conflicting, and there may be quite different configurations of interests and pressures. This does not mean that there could never be a particular group strong enough to get its way regardless of counterpressures, and with group interests spanning most of the important areas of policy. Even so, many political scientists see decisions emerging not from the domination of any one particular will or group interest but rather from an interplay of interests and pressures. In their view, the concept of supreme power simply suggests the wrong model. At best the concept would mean that in the search for explanations one need not look outside the internal politics of the supreme group; other groups could safely be ignored.

SOVEREIGNTY AS MORAL SUPREMACY: ROUSSEAU

The transposition of the concept of sovereignty from the context of seventeenth-century and eighteenth-century despotisms to the modern, popularly based state accounts for many of the perplexing features of the concept. The sovereign was then a king by divine right who at his strongest was subject to very few restraints and no legal limitations and to whom, it was said, his subjects owed unconditional obedience as a moral and religious duty.

Jean-Jacques Rousseau shifted sovereignty from the king to the people, which was now to exercise supreme power, somewhat paradoxically, over itself. For Rousseau, the citizens of a state had put themselves freely but unconditionally "under the supreme direction of the general will." And he radically altered the emphasis of the old doctrine that the people is the source of supreme authority by suggesting that the general will would be authentic and binding only if every citizen participated equally in expressing it. Moreover, since its object was the common good, there could be no higher claim on the citizen; he realized his own highest ends in total submission to it. As a legislating participant and a beneficiary of the moral order sustained by the general will, he attained freedom, not in the unrestricted slavery of impulse and appetite, but in obedience to a moral law that he prescribed to himself. It is true that Rousseau did not identify the will of all with the general will. The latter would be expressed only if the citizens addressed themselves to the question Wherein does the common good lie?, not to the question What would suit me personally? Democracy, too, can be corrupt, and the state in decay.

From Rousseau on, to ascribe sovereignty to the people was not (or not only) to state a political fact or a legal theory but to make a moral claim. Moreover, Rousseau reshaped the whole conceptual order of politics when he wrote that "the public person" created by the act of political association "is called by its members *State* when passive, *Sovereign* when active, and *Power* when compared with others like itself. Those who are associated in it take collectively the name of *people,* and severally are called *citizens,* as sharing in the sovereign power, and *subjects,* as being under the laws of the state" (*Social Contract,* Bk. I, Ch. 7). It was the citizen, not the king, who might say, henceforth, *L'état, c'est moi.* Consequently, the object of the state, if not corrupted by tyrants or by selfish sectional interests, was a good in which all its members might participate on terms of justice and equality. Its sovereignty amounted to a claim to override, in the name of the public interest, all lesser associations and interests.

THE STATE OF HEGELIAN IDEALISM

Rousseau was hostile to sectional associations as rivals to the general will; G. W. F. Hegel accepted them as partial expressions of, or vehicles for, the more inclusive Idea that was the state. The state's sovereignty lay in its moral preeminence over all other forms of human association. As the highest stage in the moral evolution of man, the state embodied concretely, as a living institution, man's autonomous, rational will. Man progressed dialectically through the conflict of states, the most vigorous and forward-looking state taking the leadership of humanity from the aging and debilitated and setting its own mark on a new age. The state was sovereign, therefore, in its relations with other states because it owed them nothing; its highest moral commitment was to its own survival as the agent of history, which alone could judge its works.

CRITICS. The Hegelian view of sovereignty was challenged early in the twentieth century by political and legal theorists and historians, such as Otto von Gierke, Hugo Krabbe, Léon Duguit, F. W. Maitland, J. N. Figgis, and H. J. Laski. They substituted a pluralistic for the monistic model of the state. They held that state and society must be distinguished; that society is made up of many associations, each serving its own range of human needs and interests. They denied that the state's moral purpose, whether ideal or actual, gives it a special claim on the allegiance of its members, overriding the churches' claim on those of them who are believers, or the unions' on those of them who are workers. In a given situation, a church might mean even more to believers than the state. Moreover, the suggestion that the corporate legal status and existence of associations depends on state recognition was vigorously repudiated. Associations came into existence to fulfill needs the state could not satisfy.

According to Duguit, the existence and corporate rights of associations and, indeed, law itself were social facts that the state simply registered; it did not create them. According to Figgis and Laski, the state's claim to regulate the constitutions, aims, and internal relations of other associations was an invasion of their corporate moral autonomy. Each was strictly sovereign in its own sphere. The pluralists conceded that the state must continue, but as an umpire, maintaining the minimal conditions of order, determining conflicts of jurisdiction, and protecting members of one association from the encroachments of another. Hobbes would certainly have interpreted this as an admission of the need for a single sovereign authority; for as arbiter, the state must have the power to judge what is an encroachment and therefore the powers of review and disallowance. Enjoying an overriding authority, the state could not be merely one among others. Despite Duguit, the law must ultimately be determined by state officials. For Kelsen, who identified state and law, corporations are necessarily subsystems within the state system, since their rules have legal effect only by the state's extending recognition to them. But, of course, the same could conceivably be said, in reverse, of other associations. For instance, the state could just as well be seen from a religious standpoint as encapsulated within the greater religious and moral order sustained by the church.

SOVEREIGNTY IN INTERNATIONAL RELATIONS

Is state sovereignty consistent with international law? In Hobbes's view, states confront one another in the posture of gladiators—lacking a common superior, they could not be subject to any law. Austin regarded international law as a kind of positive morality; without a sovereign, it could not be "law properly so-called." Attempts have been made to get around this difficulty by what Georg Jellinek termed *auto-limitation*: International law is binding because sovereign states have imposed it on themselves. The relation between international law and a municipal legal order can be expressed, in Kelsen's terms, as follows: Seen from the standpoint of a municipal legal order, international law is validated in a self-subsistent municipal legal system by the *Grundnorm* of that system, in other words, by being received into the system. Kelsen repudiated this conclusion, however, because he wanted to maintain that there is one all-inclusive world of law and that international law itself provides the principles validating the laws of so-called sovereign states as subsystems. But one could as well describe the one world of law from the standpoint of any legal system one chose, on the condition that it recognized other legal systems. For each system could encapsulate the rest, including international law.

Article 2 of the United Nations Charter claims that the organization is based on the sovereign equality of all members. This must surely mean that states are sovereign if, unlike colonies or trust territories, they are not liable to have any binding obligations laid upon them by other states without their consent. If international law is really a legal system, however, it cannot mean that a state has obligations only if, and for as long as, it chooses. For then there is no law. The notions of unlimited competence or overriding authority associated with "sovereignty" in a state's internal relations are out of place here. A sovereign state in international law must therefore be a particular kind of legal personality, like corporations in municipal law, with characteristic powers, rights, immunities, and obligations, including those implied in the principle of equality—namely, freedom from interference in its domestic jurisdiction, and, in the absence of an international legislature, immunity from new obligations except by consent. Nevertheless, states are considered bound by the established law and custom of nations, and the obligations of new states date from their inception and do not wait upon any consent or deliberate act of acceptance.

Finally, the alleged equality of sovereign states is not, of course, equality in power. Sovereignty in law is consistent with a large measure of actual control over a state from outside, though a minimum of independence might be a qualifying condition for sovereign status. Even the most powerful state, however, cannot ignore altogether the need to placate its friends and to avoid provoking its foes to the point of inconvenient obstruction. Freedom to act is relative in international as in internal affairs.

See also Aristotle; Austin, John; Bentham, Jeremy; Bodin, Jean; Democracy; Hart, Herbert Lionel Adolphus; Hegel, Georg Wilhelm Friedrich; Hobbes, Thomas; Kelsen, Hans; Marsilius of Padua; Natural Law; Political Philosophy, History of; Social and Political Philosophy; Rousseau, Jean-Jacques; Society; State; Thomas Aquinas, St.

Bibliography

Dias, R. W. M. *A Bibliography of Jurisprudence.* London: Butterworth, 1964. A valuable annotated bibliography. For sovereignty, see Chs. 4 and 14.

HISTORY OF THE CONCEPT

Bennett, W. H. *American Theories of Federalism.* University: University of Alabama Press, 1964. Largely concerned with the concept of sovereignty in history of U.S. constitutional theories.

Cohen, H. E. *Recent Theories of Sovereignty.* Chicago: University of Chicago Press, 1937. Contains an extensive bibliography.

Galizia, Mario, *Teoria della sovranità dal medioevo alla rivoluzione francese.* Milan, 1951.

McIlwain, Charles H. *The Growth of Political Thought in the West.* New York: Macmillan, 1932.

Merriam, Charles E. *History of the Theory of Sovereignty since Rousseau.* New York: Columbia University Press, 1900.

Riesenberg, P. N. *The Inalienability of Sovereignty in Medieval Political Thought.* New York: Columbia University Press, 1956.

STUDIES DISTINGUISHING TYPES OF SOVEREIGNTY

Benn, S. I. "The Uses of 'Sovereignty.'" *Political Studies* 3 (1955): 109–122.

Bryce, James. *Studies in History and Jurisprudence.* Oxford: Oxford University Press, 1901. Vol. II.

Dicey, A. V. *Law of the Constitution,* edited by E. C. S. Wade, 10th ed. London: Macmillan, 1959.

Rees, W. J. "The Theory of Sovereignty Restated." In *Philosophy, Politics and Society,* edited by P. Laslett, first series. Oxford: Blackwell, 1956.

THE CONCEPT IN IMPERATIVE THEORIES OF LAW

Austin, John. *Lectures on Jurisprudence,* edited by R. Campbell, 5th ed. London: J. Murray, 1885.

Austin, John. *The Province of Jurisprudence Determined,* edited with an introduction by H. L. A. Hart. London: Weidenfeld and Nicolson, 1954. First published in 1832.

Bodin, Jean. *Six Livres de la république.* Lyon, 1576. Translated and abridged by M. J. Tooley as *Six Books of the Commonwealth.* Oxford: Blackwell, 1955.

Burns, J. H. "Sovereignty and Constitutional Law in Bodin." *Political Studies* 7 (1959): 174–177.

Hart, H. L. A. *Concept of Law.* Oxford: Clarendon Press, 1961.

Hobbes, Thomas. *Leviathan,* edited with an introduction by M. Oakeshott. Oxford: Blackwell, 1946. First published in 1651.

Kelsen, Hans. *General Theory of Law and State.* Cambridge, MA: Harvard University Press, 1945.

Kelsen, Hans. *Das Problem der Souveränität und die Theorie des Völkerrechts.* Tübingen, 1920.

Marshall, G. *Parliamentary Sovereignty and the Commonwealth.* Oxford: Clarendon Press, 1957.

Spinoza, Benedict. "Tractatus Politicus." In his *Opera Posthuma.* Amsterdam, 1677. This work and the one above may be found in translation in *Spinoza: The Political Works,* edited by A. G. Wernham. London: Clarendon Press, 1958.

Spinoza, Benedict. *Tractatus Theologico-Politicus.* Amsterdam, 1670.

Warrender, Howard. *Political Philosophy of Hobbes.* Oxford: Clarendon Press, 1957.

SOVEREIGNTY AS MORAL SUPREMACY

Bosanquet, Bernard. *Philosophical Theory of the State.* 4th ed. London, 1923. First published in 1899.

Green, T. H. *Lectures on the Principles of Political Obligation.* London: Longmans, 1941. First published in 1882.

Hegel, G. W. F. *Grundlinien der Philosophie des Rechts.* Berlin, 1821. Translated with notes by T. M. Knox as *Hegel's Philosophy of Right.* Oxford: Clarendon Press, 1942.

Rousseau, J.-J. *Le contrat social.* Amsterdam, 1762. Available in French in *Political Writings of Jean-Jacques Rousseau,* edited by C. E. Vaughn. Oxford, 1962. Translated and edited by F. Watkins in *Rousseau: Political Writings.* Edinburgh, 1953.

PLURALIST CRITICS OF SOVEREIGN-STATE THEORY

Duguit, Léon. *Les transformations du droit public.* Paris, 1913. Translated by H. J. Laski and F. Laski as *Law in the Modern State.* New York: B.W. Huebsch, 1919.

Figgis, J. N. *Churches in the Modern State.* London: Longmans, Green, 1913.

Gierke, Otto von. *Das deutsche Genossenschaftsrecht.* 4 vols. Berlin, 1868–1913. Part of Vol. III translated with an introduction by F. W. Maitland as *Political Theories of the Middle Ages.* Cambridge, U.K., 1900. Part of Vol. IV translated with an introduction by Ernest Barker as *Natural Law and the Theory of Society, 1500 to 1800.* Cambridge, U.K.: Cambridge University Press, 1934.

Krabbe, Hugo. *Lehre des Rechtssouveränität.* Groningen, Netherlands, 1906.

Krabbe, Hugo. *Die Moderne Staats-Idee.* The Hague, 1915. Edited and translated by G. H. Sabine and W. J. Shepard as *The Modern Idea of the State.* New York, 1922.

Laski, Harold J. *The Foundations of Sovereignty and Other Essays.* New York: Harcourt Brace, 1921.

Laski, Harold J. *Grammar of Politics,* 5th ed. London, 1948.

Laski, Harold J. *Studies in the Problem of Sovereignty.* New Haven, CT: Yale University Press, 1917.

Stanley I. Benn (1967)

SOVEREIGNTY [ADDENDUM]

Sovereignty is one of the central organizing concepts of modern Western political thought. To say that it is a concept central to the organization of political thought is not to say that it is one of the concepts on which political theorists have lavished the greatest amount of explicit attention. But it is to say that certain claims about sovereignty are crucial to the way philosophers in the modern period have modeled or pictured the political world about which they are theorizing. That way of picturing the political world gained currency following the Peace of Westphalia, which was brokered to end the wars of religion that wracked Europe after the Protestant Reformation. It can therefore be called the post-Westphalian model.

The Peace of Westphalia gave impetus and sanction to the emergence of national states in Europe. The post-Westphalian model is a model of the world of states as philosophers such as Thomas Hobbes and Jean Bodin thought that world should be. The most important claims made by proponents of the post-Westphalian model are that the world is (a) divided into states that (b) should be ruled by agents who exercise sovereignty within the boundaries of the states they govern, and (c) are themselves sovereign with respect to one another. Recall that according to (1) and (3) in Stanley Benn's entry above, to say that an agent exercises sovereignty is to say that that agent exercises political authority or power, and that there is no agent who is authorized to override the decisions of the agent to whom sovereignty is ascribed, or who can generally be expected to prevail against that agent. According to the post-Westphalian model, then, the political world (a) consists of states (b) each of which is ruled by an agent exercising supreme power or authority within that state's borders, and (c) those states are not themselves subject to an agent who exercises such authority or power over international relations.

The central elements of the post-Westphalian model raise a number of interesting and important philosophical questions. That the European political world seemed increasingly to conform to the post-Westphalian model in the modern period guaranteed that the questions raised by (a), (b), and (c) would have a high place on the agenda of Western political theory. It is because these questions are raised by the claims about sovereignty that lie at the heart of the post-Westphalian model that sovereignty has become a central organizing concept of political philosophy—a concept the analysis of which, as Benn said, brings one into contact with nearly all the major problems of the discipline.

While political philosophers continue to debate the details of the post-Westphalian model, it is widely agreed that the sovereignty, which the model ascribes to rulers and states, confers on the sovereign a presumption of control over a state's people, territory, and boundaries. To question the presumption of such control—by, for example, asserting that other states may interfere in a state's internal affairs at will—is to question the sovereignty of the ruler or the state in question. Contemporary developments in politics and philosophy have led to criticism of the post-Westphalian model. Critics proceed by questioning whether states are the only corporate agents of interest in the political world and whether rulers and states can or should enjoy the presumption of control—hence the sovereignty—the model is generally taken to imply.

Why question whether states can exercise the control presupposed by the post-Westphalian model? The increasing importance of non-state actors in international affairs, and the various processes that constitute what is often called globalization, make it increasingly difficult for governments to control their own affairs or their political agenda. The rise of international terrorism in the early twenty-first century clearly makes it difficult for states to pursue their security interests or to identify rival states that threaten them. The ability of individuals and private organizations to move goods, services, information, and capital across national borders makes it increasingly difficult for contemporary nations to manage their own economies. The liability of some states to the environmental consequences of actions undertaken by other states and the corporations they house implies that there are important parts of a state—the quality of its air and water—that some governments cannot be presumed control.

Even when states are able significantly to control their economies or their environmental quality, they may think it wise to cede a certain amount of control over their economies, their environments, or the pursuit of their national security interests to multinational unions such as NATO and the European Union. Such surrender of control is a surrender of some of the powers of sovereignty. Thus are the increasing importance of non-state actors, globalization, and the emergence of economic, political, and military unions all thought to erode the sovereignty the post-Westphalian model ascribes to states.

Why question whether states should enjoy the sovereignty the post-Westphalian model ascribes to them? The sovereignty of a state is usually taken to imply that it has a very strong presumption of control over the natural resources that lie within its borders. According to this view, a state can extract, consume, or conserve those resources as it sees fit. But it is surely open to question whether states are morally entitled to deplete a resource the rest of the world needs, to control a river on which citizens of another state downstream depend, or to exacerbate global inequalities of wealth by profiting excessively from a resource it happens to possess. Furthermore, it is open to question whether states are morally entitled to control access to its resources and opportunities by forbidding or restricting the movement of people across its borders. So-called "failed states" may lack the capacity to address humanitarian crises that affect their citizens. They can also harbor terrorist and criminal organizations that threaten international order. The incapacities of failed states, and the dangers they pose, are sometimes thought to license foreign intervention even if such intervention entails a violation of state sovereignty.

Perhaps the most profound challenge to the post-Westphalian model is posed by growing international recognition of human rights. These rights are rights that people enjoy simply in virtue of their humanity. While the list and the philosophical foundations of human rights remains disputed, it is increasingly accepted that there are such rights, that they limit what governments may do to their people and that the gross and widespread violation of such rights by a government may give non-governmental organizations, other states, and international bodies the right to intervene. The easier it is to defeat the presumption of non-intervention in such cases, the greater the challenge a global regime of human rights poses to the post-Westphalian model and to the forms of sovereignty that model implies. With the rejection of the post-Westphalian model as descriptively or normatively inadequate, its displacement by another model of the political world, or the loosening of its hold on the imagination of political theorists, sovereignty would cease to be the central organizing concept it long has been.

See also Civil Disobedience; Cosmopolitanism; Multiculturalism; Postcolonialism; Republicanism

Bibliography

Biersteker, Thomas, and Cynthia Weber, eds. *State Sovereignty as Social Construct.* Cambridge, MA: Cambridge University Press, 1996.

Camilleri, Joseph, and Jim Falk. *The End of Sovereignty?.* Hants, U.K.: Edward Elgar, 1992.

Goldstein, Judith, and Michael Doyle, eds. *Ideas and Foreign Policy.* Ithaca, NY: Cornell University Press, 1993.

Nickel, James. "Is Today's International Human Rights System a Global Governance Regime?" *The Journal of Ethics* 6 (2002): 353–371.

Tanguy, Joelle. "Redefining Sovereignty and Intervention." *Ethics and International Affairs* 17 (2003): 141–48.

Paul Weithman (2005)

SPACE

When men began to think about the nature of "space," they thought of it as an all-pervading ether or as some sort of container. Since a thing can move from one part of space to another, it seemed that there was something, a place or a part of space, to be distinguished from the material objects that occupy space. For this reason places might be thought of as different parts of a very subtle jellylike medium within which material bodies are located.

HISTORY OF THE CONCEPT OF SPACE

Some of the Pythagoreans seem to have identified empty space with air. For more special metaphysical reasons Parmenides and Melissus also denied that there could be truly empty space. They thought that empty space would be nothing at all, and it seemed to them a contradiction to assert that a nothing could exist. On the other hand, there seems to be something wrong with treating space as though it were a material, which, however subtle, would still itself have to be *in* space. Democritus and the atomists clearly distinguished between the atoms and the void that separated them. However, the temptation to think of space as a material entity persisted, and Lucretius, who held that space was infinite, nevertheless wrote of space as though it were a container. Yet he seems to have been clear on the fact that space is unlike a receptacle in that it is a pure void. Since material bodies, in his view, consist of atoms, there must be chinks of empty space even between the atoms in what appear to be continuous bodies.

Plato's views on space have to be gotten mainly from the obscure metaphors of the *Timaeus*; he, too, appears to have thought of space as a receptacle and of the matter in this receptacle as itself mere empty space, limited by geometrical surfaces. If so, he anticipated the view of René Descartes, where the problem arises of how empty space can be distinguished from nonempty space. Even if, like Lucretius and other atomists, we make a distinction between the atoms and the void, what is this void or empty space? Is it a thing or not a thing?

ARISTOTLE. Aristotle tried to dodge the difficulty by treating the concept of space in terms of place, which he defined as the adjacent boundary of the containing body. For two things to interchange places *exactly,* they would have to be identical in volume and shape. Consider two exactly similar apples that are interchanged in this way. The *places* are not interchanged; rather, the first apple is now at the very same place at which the second apple was and vice versa. We seem, therefore, to be back at the notion of space as a substratum or ether, but it is probable that Aristotle was trying to avoid this and that he meant to define place by reference to the cosmos as a whole. Aristotle thought of the cosmos as a system of concentric spheres, and the outermost sphere of the cosmos would, on his view, define all other places in relation to itself. In the Aristotelian cosmology each of the various "elements" tends toward its own place. Thus, heavy bodies tend toward the center of Earth, and fire goes away from it. This is not, however, for any other reason than that the center of Earth happens to be the center of the universe; the places toward which the elements tend are independent of what particular bodies occupy what places. In more recent times we view these as two different and seemingly irreconcilable ways of thought—the notions of space as a stuff and of space as a system of relations between bodies.

DESCARTES AND LEIBNIZ. Descartes held that the essence of matter is extension, and so, on his view, space and stuff are identical, for if the essence of matter is to be extended, then any volume of space must be a portion of matter, and there can be no such thing as a vacuum. This raises the question of how we can distinguish one material object (in the ordinary sense of these words) from another. How, on Descartes's view, can we elucidate such a statement as that one bit of matter has moved relative to another one? In what sense, if matter just *is* extension, can one part of space be more densely occupied by matter than another? Descartes considered these objections but lacked the mathematical concepts necessary to answer them satisfactorily. We shall see that a reply to these objections can be made by denying that space is the same everywhere, and this can be done by introducing the Riemannian concept of a space of variable curvature.

As against Descartes, Gottfried Wilhelm Leibniz held a relational theory of space, whereby space is in no sense a stuff or substance but is merely a system of relations in which indivisible substances, or "monads," stand to one another. Few philosophers have followed Leibniz in his theory of monads, but in a slightly different form the relational theory of space has continued to rival the Cartesian, or "absolute," theory. The issue between the two theories has by no means been decisively settled, at least if we consider not space but space-time. It is still doubtful whether the general theory of relativity can be stated in such a way that it does not require absolute space-time.

KANT. In his *Prolegomena,* Immanuel Kant produced a curious argument in favor of an absolute theory of space. Suppose that the universe consisted of only one human hand. Would it be a left hand or a right hand? According to Kant it must be one or the other, yet if the relational theory is correct it cannot be either. The relations between the parts of a left hand are exactly the same as those between corresponding parts of a right hand, so if there were nothing else to introduce an asymmetry, there could be no distinction between the case of a universe consisting only of a left hand and that of a universe consisting only of a right hand. Kant, however, begged the question; in order to define "left" and "right" we need the notions of clockwise and counterclockwise rotations or of the bodily asymmetry which is expressed by saying that one's heart is on the left side of one's body. If there were only one hand in the world, there would be no way of applying such a concept as left or clockwise. The relationist could therefore quite consistently reply to Kant that if there were only one thing in the universe, a human hand, it could not *meaningfully* be described as either a right one or a left one. (The discovery in physics that parity is not conserved suggests that the universe is not symmetrical with respect to mirror reflection, so there is probably, in tact, something significant in nature analogous to the difference between a left and a right hand.)

Later, in his *Critique of Pure Reason,* Kant argued against both a naive absolute theory of space and a relational view. He held that space is something merely subjective (or "phenomenal") wherein in thought we arrange nonspatial "things-in-themselves." He was led to this view partly by the thought that certain antinomies or contradictions are unavoidable as long as we think of space and time as objectively real. However, since the work of such mathematicians as Karl Theodor Wilhelm Weierstrass, Augustin-Louis Cauchy, Julius Wilhelm Richard Dedekind, and Georg Cantor, we possess concepts of the infinite which should enable us to deal with Kant's antinomies and, indeed, also to resolve the much earlier, yet more subtle, paradoxes of Zeno of Elea.

NEWTON'S CONCEPTION OF SPACE

Isaac Newton held absolute theories of space and time—metaphysical views that are strictly irrelevant to his dynamical theory. What is important in Newtonian dynamics is not the notion of absolute space but that of an inertial system. Consider a system of particles acting on one another with certain forces, such as those of gravitational or electrostatic attraction, together with a system of coordinate axes. This is called an inertial system if the various accelerations of the particles can be resolved in such a way that they all occur in pairs whose members are equal and lie in opposite directions in the same straight line. Finding an inertial system thus comes down to finding the right set of coordinate axes. This notion of an inertial system, not the metaphysical notion of absolute space, is what is essential in Newtonian dynamics, and as Ernst Mach and others were able to show, we can analyze the notion of an inertial system from the point of view of a relational theory of space. Psychologically, no doubt, it was convenient for Newton to think of inertial axes as though they were embedded in some sort of ethereal jelly—absolute space. Nevertheless, much of the charm of this vanishes when we reflect that, as Newton well knew, any system of axes that is moving with uniform velocity relative to some inertial system is also an inertial system. There is reason to suppose, however, that in postulating absolute space Newton may have been partly influenced by theological considerations that go back to Henry More and, through More, to cabalistic doctrines.

We can remove the metaphysical trappings with which Newton clothed his idea of an inertial system if we consider how in mechanics we determine such a system. But even before we consider how we can define an inertial system of axes, it is interesting to consider how it is possible for us to define any system of axes and spatial positions at all. As Émile Borel has remarked, how hard it would be for a fish, however intelligent, which never perceived the shore or the bottom of the sea to develop a system of geometrical concepts. The fish might perceive other fish in the shoal, for example, but the mutual spatial relations of these would be continually shifting in a haphazard manner. It is obviously of great assistance to us to live on the surface of an earth that, if not quite rigid, is rigid to a first order of approximation. Geometry arose after a system of land surveying had been developed by the Egyptians, who every year needed to survey the land boundaries obliterated by the flooding of the Nile. That such systems of surveying were possible depended on certain physical facts, such as the properties of matter (the nonextensibility of chains, for example) and the rectilinear propagation of light. They also depended on certain geodetic facts, such as that the tides, which affect even the solid crust of Earth, were negligible. The snags that arise when we go beyond a certain order of approximation were unknown to the Egyptians, who were therefore able to get started in a fairly simple way.

It might be tempting to say that it was fortunate that the Egyptians were unaware of these snags, but of course in their rudimentary state of knowledge they could not have ascertained these awkward facts anyway. When, however, we consider geodetic measurements over a wide area of the globe we need to be more sophisticated. For example, the exact shape of Earth, which is not quite spherical, needs to be taken into account. Moreover, in determining the relative positions of points that are far apart from one another it is useful to make observations of the heavenly bodies as seen simultaneously from the different points. This involves us at once in chronometry. There is thus a continual feedback from physics and astronomy. Increasingly accurate geodetic measurements result in more accurate astronomy and physics, and more accurate astronomy and physics result in a more accurate geodesy.

Such a geodetic system of references is, however, by no means an inertial one. An inertial system is one in which there are no accelerations of the heavenly bodies except those which can be accounted for by the mutual gravitational attractions of these bodies. It follows, therefore, that the directions of the fixed stars must not be rotating with respect to these axes. In principle we should be able to determine a set of inertial axes from dynamical considerations, even if we lived in a dense cloud, as on Venus, and were unaware of the existence of the fixed stars. This may have influenced Newton to think of space as absolute. However, Newton was not on Venus, and he could see the fixed stars. It is therefore a little surprising that he did not take the less metaphysical course of supposing an inertial system to be determined by the general distribution of matter in the universe. This was the line taken in the nineteenth century by Mach and is referred to (after Albert Einstein) as Mach's principle. It is still a controversial issue in cosmology and general relativity.

Mach's principle clearly invites, though it does not compel, a relational theory of space, such as Mach held. The origin of the axes of an inertial system in Newtonian mechanics was naturally taken to be the center of gravity of the solar system, which is nearly, but not quite, at the center of the sun. In fact, it is continually changing its position with reference to the center of the sun. Now that the rotation of the galaxy has been discovered, we have to consider the sun as moving around a distant center. We shall here neglect the possibility that our galaxy is accelerating relative to other galaxies. In any case, once we pass to cosmological considerations on this scale we need to abandon Newtonian theory in favor of the general theory of relativity.

The philosophical significance of the foregoing discussion is as follows: When we look to see how inertial axes are in fact determined we find no need to suppose any absolute space. Because such a space would be unobservable, it could never be of assistance in defining a set of inertial axes. On the other hand, the complexities in the determination of inertial axes are such that it is perhaps psychologically comforting to think of inertial axes, or rather some one preferred set of such axes, as embedded in an absolute space. But Newton could equally have taken up the position, later adopted by Mach, that inertial systems are determined not by absolute space but by the large-scale distribution of matter in the universe.

SPACE AND TIME IN THE SPECIAL THEORY OF RELATIVITY

We have already noticed the dependence of space measurements on time measurements which sometimes obtains in geodesy. This situation is accentuated in astronomy because of the finite velocity of light. In order to determine the position of a heavenly body we have to make allowance for the fact that we see it in the position it was in some time ago. For example, an observation of a star that is ten light-years away is the observation of it in its position years ago. Indeed, it was the discrepancy between the predicted and observed times at which eclipses of the satellites of Jupiter should occur that led Olaus Rømer to assign a finite, and approximately correct, value to the velocity of light. The correction of position and time on account of the finite velocity of light presupposes in any particular case our knowing what this velocity is, relative to Earth. This would seem to depend not only on the velocity of light relative to absolute space (or to some preferred set of inertial axes) but also on Earth's velocity relative to absolute space (or to the preferred set of inertial axes). The experiment of Albert Abraham Michelson and Edward Williams Morley showed, however, that the velocity of light relative to an observer is independent of the velocity of the observer. This led to the special theory of relativity, which brings space and time into intimate relation with one another. For present purposes it is necessary to recall only that according to the special theory of relativity events that are simultaneous with reference to one inertial set of axes are not simultaneous with reference to another inertial frame. The total set of point-instants can be arranged in a four-dimensional space-time. Observers in different inertial frames will partition this four-dimensional space-time into a "space" and a "time," but they will do so in different ways.

Before proceeding further it is necessary to clear up a certain ambiguity in the word *space.* So far in this entry space has been thought of as a continuant. In this sense of the word *space* it is possible for things to continue to occupy space and to move from one point of space to another and for regions of space to begin or cease to be occupied or to stay occupied or unoccupied. Here space is something that endures through time. On the other hand, there is a different, timeless use of the word *space.* In solid geometry a three-dimensional space is thought of as timeless. Thus, if a geometer said that a sphere had changed into a cube, he would no longer be thinking within the conceptual scheme of solid geometry. In geometry all verbs must be tenseless. In this tenseless way let us conceive of a four-dimensional space-time, three of whose dimensions correspond roughly to the space of our ordinary thought whereas the other corresponds to what we ordinarily call time. What we commonly think of as the state of space at an instant of time is a three-dimensional cross section of this four-dimensional space-time.

Taking one second to be equivalent to 186,300 miles, which is the distance light travels in that time, any physical object, such as a man or a star, would be rather like a four-dimensional worm—its length in a timelike direction would be very much greater than its spacelike cross section. Thinking in terms of space-time, then, two stars that are in uniform velocity with respect to each other and also with respect to our frame of reference will appear as two straight worms, each at a small angle to the other. An observer on either star will regard himself as at rest, so he will take his own world line—the line in space-time along which his star lies—as the time axis. He will take his space axes as (in a certain sense) perpendicular to the time axis. It follows that observers on stars that move relative to one another will slice space-time into spacelike cross sections at different angles. This makes the relativity of simultaneity look very plausible and no longer paradoxical. As Hermann Minkowski observed, the relativity of simultaneity could almost have been predicted from considerations of mathematical elegance even before the experimental observations that led to the special theory of relativity. Indeed, Minkowski showed that the Lorentz transformations of the theory of relativity can be understood as simply a rotation of axes in space-time. (In trying to picture such a rotation of axes it is important to remember that Minkowski space-time is not Euclidean but semi-Euclidean.) In Minkowski's words, "Henceforth space by itself, and time by itself, are doomed to fade away into mere shadows, and only a kind of union of the two will preserve an independent reality." We must not forget that space-time is a space in the mathematical sense of the word *space,* not in the sense in which space is a continuant. Thus, certain objectionable locutions are often used in popular expositions. For example, we sometimes hear it said that a light signal is propagated from one part of space-time to another. The correct way to put the matter is to say that the light signal *lies* (tenselessly) along a line between these two parts of space-time. Space-time is not a continuant and is not susceptible of change or of staying the same.

EUCLIDEAN AND NON-EUCLIDEAN SPACE

Geometry, as we observed earlier, developed out of experiences of surveying, such as those of the ancient Egyptians. The assumptions underlying the surveying operations were codified by Greek mathematicians, whose interests were mainly theoretical. This codification was developed by Euclid in the form of an axiomatic system. Euclid's presentation of geometry shows a high degree of sophistication, though it falls considerably short of modern standards of rigor. Euclid's geometry was a metrical one. There are, of course, geometries that are more abstract than metrical geometry. The most abstract of all is topology, which deals with those properties of a space that remain unchanged when the space is distorted, as by stretching. Thus, from the point of view of topology a sphere, an ellipsoid, and a parallepiped are identical with one another and are different from a torus. Metrical geometry uses a bigger battery of concepts—not only such notions as those of betweenness and of being longer than (which itself goes beyond topology) but also those of being, say, twice or three and a half times as long as.

Euclid regarded one of his axioms as more doubtful than the others. This is the axiom that is equivalent to the so-called axiom of parallels. It will be more convenient to discuss the axiom of parallels than Euclid's own axiom. The axiom of parallels states that if *C* is a point not on an infinite straight line *AB,* then there is one and only one straight line through *C* and in the plane of *AB* that does not intersect *AB.* Geometers made many efforts to deduce the axiom of parallels from the other, more evident ones. In the seventeenth and eighteenth centuries Gerolamo Saccheri and J. H. Lambert each tried to prove the axiom by means of a reductio ad absurdum proof. By assuming the falsity of the axiom of parallels they hoped to derive a contradiction. They did not succeed; in fact, Saccheri and Lambert proved a number of perfectly valid theorems of non-Euclidean geometry, though they were not bold enough to assert that this was what they were doing.

János Bolyai and N. I. Lobachevski replaced the axiom of parallels with the postulate that *more than one* parallel can be drawn. The type of geometry that results is called hyperbolic. Another way to deny the axiom of parallels is to say that *no* parallel can be drawn. This yields elliptic geometry. (Some adjustments have to be made in the other axioms. For instance, straight lines become finite, and two points do not necessarily determine a straight line.) It is easy to prove (by giving a non-Euclidean geometry an interpretation within Euclidean geometry) that both hyperbolic and elliptic geometries are consistent if Euclidean geometry is. (And all can easily be shown to be consistent if the theory of the real-number continuum is.) A priori, therefore, there is nothing objectionable about non-Euclidean geometries. Unfortunately, many philosophers followed Kant in supposing that they had an intuition that space was Euclidean, and mathematicians had to free themselves from this conservative climate of opinion.

The question then arose whether our actual space is Euclidean or non-Euclidean. In order to give sense to this question we must give a physical interpretation to our geometric notions, such as that of a straight line. One way of defining a straight line is as follows: Suppose that rigid bodies *A, B, C* have surfaces S_A, S_B, S_C, such that when *A* is applied to *B*, then S_A and S_B fit; when *B* is applied to *C*, then S_B and S_C fit; and when *C* is applied to *A*, then S_C and S_A fit. Suppose also that S_A, S_B, S_C can all be slid and twisted over one another—that is, that they are not like cogged gears, for example. Then S_A, S_B, S_C are all by definition plane surfaces. The intersection of two planes is a straight line. (In the above we have used the notion of a rigid body, but this can easily be defined without circularity.) With the above definition of a straight line and the like we can make measurements to tell whether the angles of a triangle add up to two right angles. If they make more than two right angles, space is elliptic; if less than two right angles, space is hyperbolic; and if exactly two right angles, space is Euclidean. However, such experiments could not determine the question to any high degree of accuracy. All that this method shows is that, as every schoolchild knows, physical space is *approximately* Euclidean.

To make measurements that could settle the question to any high degree of accuracy we should have to make them on an astronomical scale. On this scale, however, it is not physically possible to define straight lines by means of the application of rigid bodies to one another. An obvious suggestion is that we should define a straight line as the path of a light ray in empty space. One test of the geometry of space might then come from observations of stellar parallax. On the assumption that space is Euclidean, the directions of a not very distant star observed from two diametrically opposite points on Earth's journey round the sun will be at a small but observable angle. If space is hyperbolic, this angle, which is called the parallax, will be somewhat greater. If space is elliptic, the parallax will be less or even negative. If we knew the distance of the star, we could compare the observed parallax with the theoretical parallax, on various assumptions about the geometry. But we cannot know the distances of the stars except from parallax measurements. However, if space were markedly non-Euclidean, we might get some hint of this because the distribution of stars in space, calculated from parallax observations on Euclidean assumptions, would be an improbable one. Indeed, at the beginning of the twentieth century Karl Schwarzschild made a statistical analysis of parallaxes of stars and was able to assign an upper limit to the extent to which physical space deviates from the Euclidean.

A good indication that space, on the scale of the solar system at least, is very nearly Euclidean is the fact that geometrical calculations based on Euclidean assumptions are used to make those predictions of the positions of the planets that have so strongly confirmed Newtonian mechanics. This consideration points an important moral, which is that it is impossible to test geometry apart from physics; we must regard geometry as a part of physics. In 1903, Jules Henri Poincaré remarked that Euclidean geometry would never be given up no matter what the observational evidence was; he thought that the greater simplicity of Euclidean, as against non-Euclidean, geometry would ensure our always adopting some physical hypothesis, such as that light does not always travel in straight lines, to account for our observations. We shall not consider whether—and if so, in what sense—non-Euclidean geometry is necessarily less simple than Euclidean geometry. Let us concede this point to Poincaré. What he failed to notice was that the greater simplicity of the geometry might be bought at the expense of the greater complexity of the physics. The total theory, geometry plus physics, might be made more simple even though the geometrical part of it was more complicated. It is ironical that not many years after Poincaré made his remark about the relations between geometry and physics he was proved wrong by the adoption of Einstein's general theory of relativity, in which overall theoretical simplicity is achieved by means of a rather complicated space-time geometry.

In three-dimensional Euclidean space let us have three mutually perpendicular axes, Ox_1, Ox_2, Ox_3. Let *P* be the point with coordinates (x_1, x_2, x_3), and let *Q* be a nearby point with coordinates $(x_1 + dx_1, x_2 + dx_2, x_3 + dx_3)$. Then if *ds* is the distance *PQ*, the Pythagorean theorem

$$ds^2 = dx_1^{\,2} + dx_2^{\,2} + dx_3^{\,2}$$

holds. In a "curved," or non-Euclidean, region of space this Pythagorean equation has to be replaced by a more general one. But before considering this let us move to four dimensions, so that we have an additional axis, Ox_4. This four-dimensional space would be Euclidean if

$$ds^2 = dx_1^{\,2} + dx_2^{\,2} + dx_3^{\,2} + dx_4^{\,2}.$$

In the general case

$$\begin{aligned} ds^2 = {} & g_{11}dx_1^{\,2} + g_{22}dx_2^{\,2} + g_{33}dx_3^{\,2} + g_{44}dx_4^{\,2} \\ & + 2g_{12}dx_1dx_2 + 2g_{13}dx_1dx_3 + 2g_{14}dx_1dx_4 \\ & + 2g_{23}dx_2dx_3 + 2g_{24}dx_2dx_4 + 2g_{34}dx_3dx_4. \end{aligned}$$

The *g*'s are not necessarily constants but may be functions of x_1, x_2, x_3, x_4. That it is impossible to choose a coordinate system such that for a certain region g_{12}, g_{13}, g_{14}, g_{23},

g_{24}, g_{34} are all zero is what is meant by saying that the region of space in question is curved. That a region of space is curved can therefore in principle always be ascertained by making physical measurements in that region—for instance, by testing whether the Pythagorean theorem holds. There is, therefore, nothing obscure or metaphysical about the concept of curvature of space. The space-time of special relativity, it is worth mentioning, is semi-Euclidean and of zero curvature. In it we have

$$g_{11} = g_{22} = g_{33} = -1, \; g_{44} = +1,$$

and g_{12}, g_{13}, g_{14}, g_{23}, g_{24}, g_{34} are all zero.

According to the general theory of relativity, space-time is curved in the neighborhood of matter. (More precisely, it has a curvature over and above the very small curvature that, for cosmological reasons, is postulated for empty space.) A light wave or any free body, such as a space satellite, is assumed in the general theory to lie along a geodesic in space-time. A geodesic is either the longest or the shortest distance between two points. In Euclidean plane geometry it is the shortest, whereas in the geometry of space-time it happens to be the longest. Owing to the appreciable curvature of space-time near any heavy body, a light ray that passes near the sun should appear to us to be slightly bent—that is, there should be an apparent displacement of the direction of a star whose light passes very near the sun. During an eclipse of the sun it is possible to observe stars very near to the sun's disk, since the glare of the sun is blacked out by the moon. In the solar eclipse of 1919, Sir Arthur Stanley Eddington and his colleagues carried out such an observation that gave results in good quantitative accord with the predictions of relativity. In a similar way, also, the general theory of relativity accounted for the anomalous motion of the perihelion of Mercury, the one planetary phenomenon that had defied Newtonian dynamics. In other cases the predictions of Newtonian theory and of general relativity are identical, and general relativity is, on the whole, important only in cosmology (unlike the special theory, which has countless verifications and is an indispensable tool of theoretical physics).

IS SPACE ABSOLUTE OR RELATIVE?

The theory of relativity certainly forces us to reject an absolute theory of space, if by this is meant one in which space is taken as quite separate from time. Observers in relative motion to one another will take their space and time axes at different angles to one another; they will, so to speak, slice space-time at different angles. The *special* theory of relativity, at least, is quite consistent with either an absolute or a relational philosophical account of space-time, for the fact that space-time can be sliced at different angles does not imply that it is not something on its own account.

It might be thought that the *general* theory of relativity forces us to a relational theory of space-time, on the grounds that according to it the curvature of any portion of space-time is produced by the matter in it. But if anything the reverse would seem to be the case. If we accept a relational theory of space-time, we have to suppose that the inertia of any given portion of matter is determined wholly by the total matter in the universe. Consider a rotating body. If we suppose it to be fixed and everything else rotating, then we must say that some distant bodies are moving with transitional velocities greater than that of light, contrary to the assumptions of relativity. Hence, it is hard to avoid the conclusion that the inertia of a body is partly determined by the local metrical field, not by the total mass in the universe. But if we think of the local metrical field as efficacious in this way, we are back to an absolute theory of space-time. Furthermore, most forms of general relativity predict that there would be a curvature (and hence a structure) of space-time even if there were a total absence of matter. Indeed, relativistic cosmology often gives a picture of matter as consisting simply of regions of special curvature of space-time. (Whether this curvature is the cause of the existence of matter or whether the occurrence of matter produces the curvature of space-time is unclear in the general theory itself.) The variations of curvature of space-time enable us to rebut the objection to Descartes's theory that it cannot differentiate between more and less densely occupied regions of space.

Nevertheless, there are difficulties about accepting such a neo-Cartesianism. We must remember that quantum mechanics is essentially a particle physics, and it is not easy to see how to harmonize it with the field theory of general relativity. One day we may know whether a particle theory will have absorbed a geometrical field theory or vice versa. Until this issue is decided we cannot decide the question whether space (or space-time) is absolute or relational—in other words, whether particles are to be thought of as singularities (perhaps like the ends of J. A. Wheeler's "wormholes" in a multiply connected space) or whether space-time is to be understood as a system of relations between particles. This issue can be put neatly if we accept W. V. Quine's criterion of ontological commitment. Should our scientific theory quantify over point-instants of space-time, or should we, on the other hand, quantify over material particles, classes of them, classes of classes of them, and so on? The latter involves a commitment to particle physics, but if a unified field theory is successful, our ontology may consist simply of point-instants, classes of them, classes of classes of them, and so on, and physical objects will be definable in terms of all of these. So far neither Descartes nor Leibniz has won an enduring victory.

See also Aristotle; Atomism; Cantor, Georg; Cartesianism; Descartes, René; Eddington, Arthur Stanley; Einstein, Albert; Geometry; Kant, Immanuel; Lambert, Johann Heinrich; Leibniz, Gottfried Wilhelm; Leucippus and Democritus; Logical Paradoxes; Lucretius; Mach, Ernst; Melissus of Samos; More, Henry; Newton, Isaac; Parmenides of Elea; Philosophy of Physics; Plato; Poincaré, Jules Henri; Pythagoras and Pythagoreanism; Quantum Mechanics; Quine, Willard Van Orman; Relativity Theory; Time; Zeno of Elea.

Bibliography

An excellent, mainly historical, account of the philosophy of space is given in Max Jammer, *Concepts of Space* (Cambridge, MA: Harvard University Press, 1954; rev. ed., New York, 1960). Ch. 1, "The Concept of Space in Antiquity," is particularly valuable as a guide to the very scattered and obscure references to space in Greek philosophy. Also useful is John Burnet, *Early Greek Philosophy,* 3rd ed. (London: A. and C. Black, 1920). For Descartes, see his *Principles of Philosophy,* Part II, Secs. 4–21. For Leibniz, see especially his correspondence with Clarke, third paper, Secs. 3–6, and fifth paper, Secs. 32–124. The Leibniz-Clarke correspondence has been edited, with introduction and notes, by H. G. Alexander (Manchester, U.K., 1956). See also Bertrand Russell's *The Philosophy of Leibniz* (London, 1900). Newton's metaphysical views on space are to be found in the Scholium to the definitions of the *Principia* (*Mathematical Principles of Natural Philosophy,* translated by Florian Cajori, Berkeley: University of California Press, 1934). For Kant's example of the left hand and the right hand, see his *Prolegomena to Any Future Metaphysics,* translated by P. G. Lucas (Manchester, U.K., 1953), Sec. 13. Kant's most characteristic doctrines about space are to be found in his *Critique of Pure Reason,* in Secs. 2–7 of the "Transcendental Aesthetic" and in the "First Antinomy." In N. Kemp Smith's translation (London, 1929) these passages will be found on pp. 67–82 and 396–402. A criticism of Kant, Zeno, and other philosophers is to be found in Bertrand Russell's *Our Knowledge of the External World,* Lecture VI, "The Problem of Infinity Considered Historically" (London: Allen and Unwin, 1914). See also Adolf Grünbaum, "A Consistent Conception of the Extended Linear Continuum as an Aggregate of Unextended Elements," in *Philosophy of Science* 19 (1952): 288–306. For Mach's criticism of Newton, see especially Secs. 2–6 of his *Science of Mechanics,* translated by J. T. McCormack, 6th ed. (La Salle, IL: Open Court, 1960).

On a fairly elementary level, and although somewhat out of date in places, Émile Borel, *Space and Time* (New York: Dover, 1960)—a translation, by Angelo S. Rappoport and John Dougall, of the French edition published in 1922—can be recommended. So can the more difficult *Philosophy of Space and Time,* by Hans Reichenbach (New York, 1958), and *Philosophical Problems of Space and Time,* by Adolf Grünbaum (New York: Knopf, 1963). See also Grünbaum's paper "Geometry, Chronometry and Empiricism," in *Minnesota Studies in the Philosophy of Science,* edited by Herbert Feigl and Grover Maxwell, Vol. III (Minneapolis: University of Minnesota Press, 1962). A criticism of Grünbaum's views is given by Hilary Putnam in his paper "An Examination of Grünbaum's Philosophy of Geometry," in *Philosophy of Science, the Delaware Seminar,* edited by Bernard Baumrin, Vol. II (1962–1963; published New York: Interscience, 1963). Chs. 8 and 9 of Ernest Nagel's *Structure of Science* (New York: Harcourt Brace, 1961) are very useful. An interesting dialogue by A. S. Eddington, "What Is Geometry?," is a prologue to his *Space, Time and Gravitation* (Cambridge, U.K.: Cambridge University Press, 1920). On relativity, see Hermann Minkowski, "Space and Time," in *The Principle of Relativity,* by Albert Einstein, et al. (London: Methuen, 1923); Hans Reichenbach, "The Philosophical Significance of Relativity," and H. P. Robertson, "Geometry as a Branch of Physics," both in *Albert Einstein: Philosopher-Scientist,* edited by P. A. Schilpp, 2nd ed. (New York: Tudor, 1951); and Adolf Grünbaum, "The Philosophical Retention of Absolute Space in Einstein's General Theory of Relativity," in *Philosophical Review* 66 (1957): 525–534 (a revised version appears in *Problems of Space and Time,* edited by J. J. C. Smart, New York: Macmillan, 1963). See also J. A. Wheeler, "Curved Empty Space-Time as the Building Material of the Physical World: An Assessment," in *Logic, Methodology, and Philosophy of Science* edited by Ernest Nagel, Patrick Suppes, and Alfred Tarski (Stanford, CA: Stanford University Press, 1962), pp. 361–374.

For a discussion of the asymmetry between clockwise and counterclockwise rotations in relation to the nonconservation of parity, which has some relevance to Kant's problem of the left and right hands, see the brilliant popular exposition by O. R. Frisch, "Parity Is Not Conserved, a New Twist to Physics?," in *Universities Quarterly* 11 (1957): 235–244, and the article by Philip Morrison, "Overthrow of Parity," in *Scientific American* 196 (April 1957). For Poincaré's views, see *Science and Hypothesis* (New York: Dover, 1952), especially pp. 72–73. In connection with the sharpening of the issue between absolute and relational theories of space and time into an issue of ontology, see W. V. Quine, *Word and Object* (Cambridge, MA: Technology Press of the Massachusetts Institute of Technology, 1960), especially Sec. 52, "Geometrical Objects." A book of readings on space and time is *Problems of Space and Time,* edited by J. J. C. Smart (New York: Macmillan, 1964).

I should like to thank Professor B. C. Rennie, who read an earlier draft of this entry and made helpful comments.

J. J. C. Smart (1967)

SPACE IN PHYSICAL THEORIES

Space here means the space of the science of mechanics, which encompasses planetary and celestial (i.e., "outer") space, but is presupposed by the motion—spatial change—of any bodies whatsoever, from the tiniest particles through human-sized bodies to the whole universe. The investigation of space has been perhaps the most fruitful interaction between physics and philosophy. Physics endows space with specific properties playing a crucial role in determining the motions of bodies, but, despite being omnipresent, space (prerelativistically) is frustratingly inert—not having even the indirect causal effects of subatomic particles, say. Thus physics ascribes substantive properties to space on the basis of indirect evidence, allowing metaphysical bias to influence understanding, and calling (in part) for philosophical clarification.

One of the main strands of this clarification involves the "absolute-relative" debate. In fact a number of (interconnected) debates go under this title, of which two are focused on in the historical development of mechanics: Of all the motions a body has (relative to different frames of reference), which if any are privileged or "absolute"? Are such absolute motions determined by the motions of bodies relative to one another, or by motions with respect to space itself: is space a real, substantial entity in addition to bodies? (A third important strand: Are all spatial properties extrinsic—that is, "relative"—or intrinsic?)

SPACE IN ARISTOTELIAN PHYSICS

In the European tradition, Eudoxus's (408–355 BCE) account of the motions of the heavens—which was later significantly extended by Ptolemy (c. 85–165 CE)—is probably the first "physical theory" (in anything like a modern sense) in which space plays a significant role. According to this theory the Earth is at rest at the center of the universe, surrounded by a series of concentric spheres, interconnected along their axes. The moon, sun, planets, and totality of fixed stars are each located on their own sphere, with the stars farthest out. The daily apparent motions of the heavens are explained by a daily rotation of the stellar sphere, which carries all the other spheres with it; the "wanderings" of the other bodies through the fixed stars are explained by the additional, slower rotations of the other spheres about their axes. Aristotle (384–322 BCE) provided the philosophical interpretation of this system: a finite, spherical universe with an absolute center (which Aristotle suggests is determined by its position relative to the circumference). Thus bodies do have an absolute motion, namely relative to the center, which is essential for Aristotle's mechanics: heavy bodies move naturally toward the center, light bodies away, and the heavenly element, ether, around circularly. (Note that Aristotle denied the existence of space separate from body: no vacuum and no pure extension.)

Although astronomers often took this model instrumentally, Aristotle's account was the context of debate over the nature of space until the eighteenth century, even after Nicolaus Copernicus (1473–1543) proposed that the earth moved around the sun. Questions seen as important during this period that had bearing on later developments include the possibility of the vacuum and whether God could move the entire universe.

SPACE IN CARTESIAN PHYSICS

In the Early Modern period, René Descartes (1596–1650) is a logical place to start despite numerous important predecessors, especially Galileo Galilei (1564–1642), because of his influence on both physics and its philosophy. Notable contributions include the development of mechanical explanation, conservation laws, and, with Pierre Gassendi (1592–1655), the correct "law of inertia": Bodies experiencing no net forces move at constant speeds along straight paths. According to Descartes, because matter and space have the same essence—"extension"—they are one and the same (Plato's *Timaeus* describes a similar view). This identification poses a problem: As a body moves, so does the matter that composes it and hence the space it occupies, but if it does not change with respect to space then it does not move! In his *Principles of Philosophy* (1644), Descartes's first solution is to relativize to reference bodies (selected arbitrarily): In thought people identify a relatively moving piece of matter=space as the same body, while they identify as the same spatial region those different pieces of matter=space that bear some fixed relations to the reference bodies. However, in addition to this "ordinary" concept of motion, Descartes defines motion "properly speaking" as displacement of a body from the bodies in contact with it (in accord with Aristotle's *Physics*, Book IV Chapter 4). Why there are dual accounts is a subject of dispute.

According to one interpretation, Descartes took relative motion to be fundamental, but sought to avoid the heretical denial of the earth's rest; because he wrote only a decade after Galileo was condemned (1633), such concern was real. Descartes claimed that the universe was a plenum in constant agitation, and explained the motions of the planets (including the earth) by postulating a giant vortex of fine matter carrying them around the sun, like leaves in a whirlpool. Hence the earth is in relative motion around the sun and roughly at rest with its surroundings, and so both Copernicus and Aristotle were correct—in the "ordinary" and "proper" senses, respectively. The second interpretation claims that Descartes took proper motion more seriously, as the correct, "true" sense of motion in physics; in particular, his laws of collision are blatantly contradictory if taken to concern relative motion, but not if they concern proper motion, because it is "absolute" in the sense of being privileged over all other relative motions. (As Christiaan Huygens [1629–1695] realized, Descartes should have changed the laws to make them consistently describe relative motions, not relied on his absolute notion.)

SPACE IN NEWTONIAN PHYSICS

Although Descartes's views were influential, Isaac Newton's (1643–1727) physics and philosophy (arguably his epistemology as well as his metaphysics) were infinitely more successful. In his *Principia* (1687) and in an unpublished essay, *De Gravitatione* (undated), he attacks Descartes's views concerning space and motion and lays out his own. Newton claims that space is three-dimensional and Euclidean, persists through time, and is neither a substance such as mind or matter (because it has no causal powers—the law of inertia holds because space does not act on bodies) nor a property of substances (because in a vacuum there is space but no substance): Space is outside of the categories of traditional metaphysics. He takes it to be a pseudosubstance, causally inert, but metaphysically necessary for the existence of anything, including God, because everything exists somewhere. Commentators often stretch metaphysical categories, and count Newton's "absolute space" as a nonmaterial, nonmental substance, regions of which may be occupied by other substances: they rather inaccurately ascribe "substantivalism" to Newton.

Newton famously argues against the Cartesian view of space using the example of a bucket of water, though it is only one of a series of arguments he gives. If bucket and water, initially at rest, are set spinning about their axis, initially the water will remain at rest, and hence be in motion relative to its contiguous surroundings (the side of the bucket); the water will be rotating properly speaking. Later, friction with the sides of the bucket will have set the water rotating at the same rate as the bucket, and so it will be at "proper" rest, according to Descartes. In the first instance, because it is not yet rotating, the surface of the water will be flat, whereas in the second it will be concave (just like tea stirred in a cup). By Descartes's and Newton's (and most of their contemporaries') explicit principles, it follows that only in the second case is the water "truly," physically rotating. And so in the experiment the water has physical motion if and only if it has no motion properly speaking. Cartesian "ordinary" motion fares no better: The water spins at a unique height in the bucket, indicating a unique rate of rotation, while it moves at different rates relative to different reference bodies. Newton concludes that because true motion is neither kind of Cartesian motion, it must be the only other option on the table: motion relative to absolute space (which he calls "absolute motion," though it was seen above that proper motion too is "absolute" in the sense of being privileged).

LEIBNIZ'S RELATIONIST RESPONSE

Gottfried Leibniz's (1646–1716) position is complex: He argued persuasively against substantivalism, but was motivated by idiosyncratic metaphysics; and he gave a sophisticated account of "relationism"—space is not a substance, and all spatial properties and motions are determined by relations—but it conflicted with his theory of collisions (the so-called "Newtonian" or "classical" theory of elastic collisions). At the end of his life Leibniz arguably held: (1) that every body possesses a unique quantity of "living force" or "*vis viva*", measured by *mass* × *speed*^{2} (basically kinetic energy), and hence a unique speed; (2) that living force and pure Cartesian extension are "form" and "substance" in an updated Aristotelian metaphysics; (3) that force entails the laws of mechanics (living force and momentum are conserved in elastic collisions); (4) to avoid being an occult power, the actual force must have no detectable effects, so the laws must satisfy the "equivalence of hypotheses" and hold in all frames (Leibniz was mistaken to think this was true of his laws); and (5) that space is not only merely relative, so bodies and their relations exhaust all spatial facts, but also ideal (not a "well-founded phenomenon" in his terms), arguing in part that because no two things can literally stand in the same relation to a third, only a mental identification allows two things to stand in the same relative place one after the other. Thus Leibniz opposes both Descartes and Newton: Against Descartes he rejects the claims that space is matter (space is ideal, whereas matter is well-founded) and that "proper" motion is privileged (Descartes also held that *vis viva* was *mass* × *speed*); against Newton he rejects the view that space is absolute.

In his *Correspondence* (1715–1716) with Samuel Clarke (1675–1729), Leibniz gives relativity arguments against Newton. He argues that because two systems differing only in their absolute positions or velocities cannot be told apart, they must not differ at all: that absolute locations and velocities, and absolute space itself, are unreal. While this argument impressed later empiricists, Leibniz himself argued from the theological "principle of sufficient reason." Leibniz claims that his relationism avoids Newton's arguments, but this is highly doubtful: He only hints at (in his *Specimen of Dynamics*, 1695) a relational account of rotating bodies (such as the bucket), and fails to see that Newton's arguments disprove the relativity of his own mechanics.

MODERN ARGUMENTS

In his *Science of Mechanics* (1893) Ernst Mach (1836–1916) criticized Newton for making a non sequitur: Rotation relative to the bucket fails to explain the curvature of the water, but it does not follow that the water must be rotating relative to absolute space—could not the curvature show motion relative to some other body? Mach's reading fails to understand how Newton refuted Descartes, and ignores his attack on relative ("ordinary") motion, but asks a reasonable question as a non-Cartesian relationist. Mach proposed that sufficiently massive bodies act to cause distant bodies to move in constant, linear relative motion unless acted on by forces: in particular, that the fixed stars determine which motions are inertial, not absolute space. (Newton considered this idea, but dismissed it because it involved action at a distance—a questionable argument given his theory of gravity.) Mach's arguments were influential on contemporary physicists who were developing the idea of an "inertial frame": a frame in which Newton's laws hold, and in particular in which bodies experiencing no net forces move inertially. In practice, physicists have since taken inertial frames to be sufficient, and viewed absolute space (if at all) as an early formulation of that idea, though whether this approach amounts to relationism is debatable.

Mach was also a hero of empiricist philosophers, however; beginning in the 1960s, a reappraisal of Newton led to a defense of absolute space (simultaneous with a general philosophical turn from strict empiricism toward realism). In the late twentieth and early twenty-first centuries, Newton is often taken to argue abductively that his theory gives the best explanation of the bucket; better than Descartes's, and by extension, because he offered no real theory, better than Mach's. It is (arguably) no non sequitur to infer that motion is absolute because Newtonian mechanics in absolute space explains better than any relational theory. Note that although Newton might have endorsed this argument as a response to Mach, it is weaker than Newton's demonstration of the inconsistency of Descartes.

A major innovation has been to transfer the arguments into the context of (nonrelativistic) spacetime. One can then distinguish (a) "Newtonian spacetime" with a preferred standard of rest—geometrically speaking, a "rigging" that picks out stationary trajectories—from (b) "Galilean spacetime" with only a preferred standard of constant motion—no rigging but an "affine connection" that picks out nonaccelerated, inertial trajectories. In (a) both velocity and acceleration are well defined and hence "absolute," but in (b) only acceleration is, avoiding (part of) Leibniz's relativity argument. Thus, plausibly, Newtonian mechanics—which distinguishes different states of absolute acceleration but not velocity—in Galilean spacetime offers the best mechanical explanations.

Modern substantivalists infer first from the need for well-defined accelerations in Newtonian mechanics, to spacetimes with "absolute structures" such as a connection, and then further to the substantiality of those spacetimes, particularly of Galilean spacetime. Several relationists have responded by arguing that acceleration can be understood without substantial spacetime: that Newtonian mechanics has a relational interpretation. Other relationists have attempted to construct a theory that does explain this as well as Newton: Most attempts rely on the fact that if it is postulated that the total angular momentum of a system (such as the whole universe) is zero, then Newtonian mechanics determines a well-defined evolution for the relative state of the system.

RELATIVITY

How does the absolute-relative debate change in relativity theory? Consider the special theory of relativity (henceforth "STR"). First distinguish "relativity" from relationism. Broadly speaking, a theory is relativistic if it admits no unmeasureable quantities. Then Newtonian mechanics in absolute space or Newtonian spacetime is not relativistic, because it admits absolute velocity, whereas Newtonian mechanics in Galilean spacetime and electromagnetism in Minkowski spacetime are relativistic. The relativity of STR is thus of a specific kind: So that no body can be said to be at rest, all must agree on the speed of light. Thus the difference between the relativity of STR and Newtonian mechanics lies in whether one takes account of electromagnetic phenomena, a difference that has no immediate bearing on whether space is absolute or relative. Indeed, Minkowski spacetime has an affine connection, so acceleration is as absolute as in Galilean spacetime, thus the same question of whether a connection provides evidence for the substantiality of spacetime arises.

In the general theory of relativity ("GTR") spacetime is not a fixed background but is acted on by matter and has more robust causal powers. For example, rapidly rotating bodies (e.g., a black hole) can produce gravitational waves with the power to stretch and squeeze bodies as they pass through them. The causal powers of spacetime are a serious problem for relational interpretations of GTR: If a gravitational wave knocks a person down it would be odd to say that person's body merely moved relative to the ground "as if" a wave were present. Thus only a strictly relational theory in agreement with the evidence for GTR will suffice for the relationist. However, the causal nature of the spacetime of GTR makes it metaphysically different from Newton's, and so hardly vindicates prerelativistic substantivalism either.

GTR is sometimes mistakenly claimed to be relational. First, the action of matter on space means that the affine connection, and hence inertial motion, is dependent on the distribution of matter in distant regions (in the causal past), as Mach claimed. However, the distribution does not determine inertial motion, because the connection also depends on the geometry of spacetime in the causal past: for instance, even if there is no matter at all, the connection in a region is not fixed. Thus Mach's relationism is not vindicated by GTR. Second, the theory is "generally covariant": Its equations take the same form in every frame. Thus, unlike Newtonian mechanics, one cannot define absolute acceleration as acceleration in some privileged class of frames, and any relative frame will do for formulating the theory. But these points do not settle the absolute-relative debate: GTR has an affine connection, and every body still has an absolute acceleration. Further, Newtonian mechanics can be formulated generally covariantly too, so arguably general covariance shows nothing.

It is true, however, that, unlike Newtonian mechanics and STR, the dynamic nature of spacetime in GTR makes general covariance necessary: Intuitively, how can spacetime have privileged frames if spacetime is not independently given? More or less equivalently, GTR is "diffeomorphism invariant": If all the dynamical quantities in a model (the distribution of matter and the geometry of spacetime) are continuously rearranged over the points of spacetime then the result is still a model. (Spacetime theories with static geometries are also "diffeomorphism invariant" in the weaker sense that the diffeomorphism of a model is also a model if the dynamical quantities and the nondynamical geometry are permuted.) Diffeomorphism invariance drives the "hole argument" against substantivalism, because it entails a kind of indeterminism if the spacetime of GTR has a substantival interpretation. That antisubstantivalists and some substantivalists avoid such indeterminism by claiming that distinct diffeomorphic models represent the same physical world, which is to say that the physical content of the models is captured by the relation between matter and the geometry of space, because this is what the models have in common. If so, GTR is a theory of the relations between dynamical quantities, which is what the prerelativistic relationists sought, though in terms of different dynamic quantities, namely relative distances. Thus it can be argued that GTR is as sympathetic to prerelativistic relationism as to prerelativistic substantivalism (note that physicists tend to emphasize the relational nature of GTR far more than philosophers).

QUANTUM GRAVITY

What of the absolute-relative debate in a sought-after quantum theory of gravity, such as string theory? First, the interpretation of diffeomorphism invariance is important for certain approaches to quantizing general relativity, which some argue gives physical import to the philosophical debate concerning the hole argument. Second, space is likely to be an "effective" notion, which does not appear as a fundamental element of the theory, but only phenomenologically in particular circumstances. If so, then neither relationism nor substantivalism will be correct interpretations of quantum gravity, and the debate may seem doomed. However, quantum gravity could shed new light on the matter in the following sense. One could ask what quantities count as observables in the effective context: If the theory can be given completely in terms of observables relating bodies then effective space could be said to be relational, whereas if the theory contains observables concerning points of space, then it seems that effective space is substantial.

See also Hole Argument, The; Philosophy of Physics; Relativity Theory; Time in Physics.

Bibliography

Barbour, Julian B. *Absolute or Relative Motion?* Vol. 1: *The Discovery of Dynamics.* Oxford: Oxford University Press, 1989. Republished as *The Discovery of Dynamics.* Oxford: Oxford University Press, 2003.

Dainton, Barry. *Time and Space.* Montreal: McGill-Queen's University Press, 2001.

Earman, John. *World Enough and Spacetime: Absolute versus Relational Theories of Space and Time*. Cambridge, MA: MIT Press, 1989.

Friedman, Michael. *Foundations of Space-Time Theories*. Princeton, NJ: Princeton University Press, 1983.

Garber, Daniel. "Leibniz: Physics and Philosophy." In *The Cambridge Companion to Leibniz*, edited by Nicholas Jolley. Cambridge, U.K.: Cambridge University Press, 1995.

Huggett, Nicholas. *Space from Zeno to Einstein: Classic Readings with a Contemporary Commentary*. Cambridge, MA: MIT Press, 1999. This book contains relevant extracts from most of the historical works mentioned here.

Rovelli, Carlo. "Quantum Spacetime: What Do We Know?" In *Physics Meets Philosophy at the Planck Scale: Contemporary Theories in Quantum Gravity*, edited by Craig Callender and Nicholas Huggett. Cambridge, U.K.: Cambridge University Press, 2001.

Rynasiewicz, Robert. "By Their Properties, Causes, and Effects: Newton's Scholium on Time, Space, Place, and Motion–I. The Text" and "By Their Properties, Causes and Effects: Newton's Scholium on Time, Space, Place, and Motion–II. The Context." *Studies in History and Philosophy of Science* 26 (1995): 133–153 and 295–321.

Sklar, Lawrence. *Space, Time and Spacetime*. Berkeley: University of California Press, 1977.

Sorabji, Richard. *Matter, Space and Motion: Theories in Antiquity and Their Sequel*. Ithaca, NY: Cornell University Press, 1988.

Stein, Howard. "Newtonian Spacetime." *Texas Quarterly* 10 (1967): 174–200.

Nick Huggett (2005)

SPANN, OTHMAR

(1878–1950)

Othmar Spann, the Austrian philosopher and sociologist, was born in Vienna and educated at the universities of Vienna, Zürich, and Tübingen. He was a professor at Brünn from 1909 to 1919, when he was appointed to a chair of economics and sociology at Vienna.

Spann contrasted his "neoromantic universalism"—called neoromantic by Spann to indicate his debt to Adam Müller—with "individualism," that is, with the doctrine that society derives its character from the independently existing qualities of the individual men composing it. He classified as individualist such allegedly erroneous doctrines as the economic liberalism of Adam Smith and David Ricardo, utilitarianism, the various "social contract" theories, "natural law" theories of social life, egalitarianism, anarchism, Machiavellianism, and Marxism. As this heterogeneous grouping suggests, Spann was less interested in discussing the individual merits and faults of these doctrines than in placing them with respect to his total intellectual system. Such an aim was entirely consistent with his universalistic tenet that wholes are logically prior to and more real than their parts. Particular intellectual doctrines, on this view, can be understood only in relation to the total worldview to which they belong.

Spann's main application of universalism was in his theory of society, widely acclaimed by fascists. What is spiritual (*das Geistige*) in an individual is never due to himself alone but is always "an echo of what another spirit excites in him." The development and persistence of spirituality must be understood in the context of personal relations falling under the heading of what Spann called *Gezweiung*. Individuals so related form a genuine whole, the reality of which is presupposed by, rather than a result of, the spiritual characteristics of the related individuals. Examples of *Gezweiung* are the relations between artist and public, mother and child, teacher and pupil. Spann was not merely making the formal logical point that if, for instance, one calls a man "a teacher," one implies that he has a pupil, and vice versa. He was saying something about the quality of the teacher's and the pupil's experiences; the teacher "learns by teaching," and the pupil incorporates some of the teacher's spiritual qualities into his own soul.

Spann held that it is the prior existence of such institutions as art, the family, and education that makes possible relations of *Gezweiung*. These institutions have both a higher degree of reality and a higher value than do individuals. One does not understand what education is unless one understands that there can be more and less satisfactory instances of the teacher-pupil relationship and that there could be no actual instance beyond conceivable improvement. Therefore, a knowledge of the ideal must precede understanding of particular cases, and the study of social institutions must be normative.

An institution is itself only a partial whole (*Teilganz*) belonging to a higher reality, society. Society, too, has a normative aspect; it involves a hierarchy of values in terms of which the *Teilgänze* are mutually related. There must be a corresponding hierarchy among the social sciences; particular social institutions and aspects can be studied only in the context of a general theory of society.

Spann's emphasis on hierarchy was reinforced by his insistence that all *Gezweiung* involves a relation between a leader and one who is led. It belongs to the nature of society that there should be "obedience of those low in the spiritual scale toward those more highly developed." In Spann's theory distributive justice, based on the idea of inequality of function, replaces liberty as the fundamental social value.

Spann's stress on inequality is reflected in his political program. His doctrine of estates (*Stände*) was intended to combine decentralization with a strengthening of authority in order to check socially deleterious individualist tendencies. Each industry would be directed by the "mentally most highly developed individuals" from labor unions and employers' unions, which would send representatives to a central representative *Ständehaus*. Property would be owned communally by the various estates, and each industry's legal problems would be handled by its own special courts.

See also Equality, Moral and Social; Holism and Individualism in History and Social Science; Smith, Adam.

Bibliography

WORKS BY SPANN

Die Haupttheorien der Volkswirtschaftslehre auf lehrgeschichtlicher Grundlage. 1910. Translated from the 19th German edition by Eden Paul and Cedar Paul as *Types of Economic Theory.* London, 1930. This translation also appeared under the title *History of Economics.* New York: Norton, 1930.

Kurzgefasstes System der Gesellschaftslehre. Berlin, 1914.

Fundament der Volkswirtschaftslehre. Jena, Germany, 1918.

Der wahre Staat. Leipzig, 1921.

Gesellschaftsphilosophie. Jena, Germany, 1932.

Kämpfende Wissenschaft. Jena, Germany: Fischer, 1934. Collected papers.

Erkenne Dich selbst! Eine Geistesphilosophie als Lehre vom Menschen und seiner Weltstellung. Jena, Germany, 1935.

Naturphilosophie. Jena, Germany, 1937.

Kategorienlehre, 2nd ed. Jena, Germany, 1939.

WORKS ON SPANN

Gerber, Carl. *Der Universalismus bei Othmar Spann in Hinblick auf seine Religionsphilosophie.* Berlin, 1934.

Haag, John. "Othmar Spann and the Quest for a 'True State.'" *Austrian History Yearbook* 12–13 (2) (1976–1977): 227–250.

König, Albert. *Emil Brunners Staatsauffassung und der Universalismus Othmar Spanns.* Bleicherode, 1938.

Räber, Hans. *Othmar Spanns Philosophie des Universalismus. Darstellung und Kritik.* Jena, Germany: Fischer, 1937.

Riha, Thomas J. F. "Spann's Universalism: The Foundation of the Neoromantic Theory of Corporative State." *Australian Journal of Politics and History* 31 (2) (1985): 255–268.

Vikor, Desider. *Economic Romanticism in the Twentieth Century: Spann's Attempt to Revolutionize Economic Theory.* New Delhi: New Book Society of India, 1964.

Wagner, H. G. *Essai sur l'universalisme économique. Othmar Spann.* Paris, 1931.

Wrangel, Georg. *Das universalistische System von Othmar Spann.* Jena, Germany, 1929.

Peter Winch (1967)
Bibliography updated by Philip Reed (2005)

SPAVENTA, BERTRANDO

(1817–1883)

Bertrando Spaventa, the Italian Hegelian philosopher, was born at Bomba in Abruzzo, educated in the seminary at Chieti, and taught for a time in the seminary at Monte Cassino before moving to Naples in 1840. There he became one of a small circle of liberal students associated with Ottavio Colecchi (1773–1847), who taught privately in opposition to the "official" philosophy of Pasquale Galluppi. Colecchi was himself a devotee of Immanuel Kant, but he read all the German idealists carefully and in the original. Spaventa, like the other young men in Colecchi's circle, was convinced that the real meaning of Kant's work was to be found in the later idealists, especially in G. W. F. Hegel, and the Hegelian interpretation of the *Critique of Pure Reason* always remained the nodal point of his own speculations.

Spaventa's younger brother, Silvio, was imprisoned at Naples for his part in the revolution of 1848, and Bertrando was forced to take refuge at Turin for ten years. This was the period during which most of his ideas took shape. By 1850 he had renounced the priestly office to which he had, with great reluctance, been ordained some years earlier in the hope that by preferment he could relieve the poverty of his family. In Turin he turned his hand to political journalism, writing philosophical and historical polemics against the church and particularly against the Jesuits. He was already an enthusiastic student of Giordano Bruno and Tommaso Campanella.

THE "CIRCULATION OF ITALIAN PHILOSOPHY"

The first fruits of Spaventa's labors were his "Studi sopra la filosofia di Hegel" (in *Rivista italiana,* n.s., [November 1850]: 1–30, and [December 1850]: 31–78) and his "I principî della filosofia pratica di Giordano Bruno" (in *Saggi di filosofica civile,* Genoa, 1851). His studies of Hegel were specifically concerned with the *Phenomenology,* but they contained the germ of Spaventa's most original and fruitful conception, which he termed "circulation of Italian philosophy." This germ was the claim, first voiced by Silvio Spaventa about 1844, that the real tradition of Italian philosophy had been cut off and driven into exile by the Counter-Reformation, so that "Not our own philosophers of the last two centuries, but Spinoza, Kant, Fichte, Schelling, and Hegel, have been the real disciples of Bruno, Vanini, Campanella, Vico and other great thinkers." In this view of the history of philosophy Spaventa's patriotism was neatly reconciled with his political and intellectual liberalism. He could use it both against the defenders of the status quo and against the patriotic chauvinism of Antonio Rosmini-Serbati and Vincenzo Gioberti, who believed that their native tradition enshrined a truth that had become corrupted in the rest of Europe. Spaventa himself held at this time that, on the contrary, nothing of value had survived in contemporary Italian philosophy.

He began to shift from this position toward his doctrine of a completed circle when he studied Rosmini's work in connection with an article on Kant that he wrote in 1855. He decided then that everything good in Rosmini's theory of knowledge had been stolen from Kant. This unjust judgment at least involved the admission that there were valuable elements in Rosmini's thought. When Spaventa began, in 1857, to work on a critical survey of Galluppi and Gioberti in connection with a projected study of Hegel's *Phenomenology,* his attitude changed dramatically, and he ended by writing in 1858 one massive volume of a planned two-volume work, *La filosofia di Gioberti* (Naples, 1863). The view that he now took was that all the fruits of European speculation from René Descartes to Kant were to be found in the work of Galluppi and Rosmini when it was rightly understood, and that Gioberti was even moving at the end of his life toward a critical reconstruction of his system that would have made it clearly the culmination of post-Kantian speculation.

Thus, in its fully developed form, the thesis that Spaventa proclaimed to the new nation when he returned as professor at Bologna in 1860, and at Naples from 1861 onward, was that the metaphysics of modern idealism was born in Bruno, that Campanella's theory of knowledge foreshadowed all the problems of rationalism and empiricism which were finally resolved by Kant, and that the achievement of the Germans had been anticipated by Giambattista Vico and had at last returned to be integrated with its sources in Galluppi, Rosmini, and Gioberti. As history, this thesis becomes more dubious with every succeeding clause. It must be taken rather as an account of the historical genesis of Spaventa's own idealism and as a model of how an idealist of the Hegelian type must strive, in studying the history of philosophy, to integrate different aspects of the truth as they appear. From this standpoint we can see how the emphasis on concrete experience that Spaventa found in Bruno and Campanella led him to feel that the rather abstract formalism of Kant's transcendental unity of apperception must be integrated with Rosmini's theory of the self as rooted in a "fundamental feeling"; once this was done, the Rosminian-Giobertian doctrine of knowledge as the intellectual intuition of Being could be jettisoned. Spaventa's most fundamental philosophical insight is to be found in his critical analysis of the difficulties that arise from an intuitive theory of knowledge.

LATER STUDIES

The "circulation of Italian philosophy" and the critical reconstruction of Gioberti is, properly speaking, a sort of Italian version of the coming to consciousness of the Absolute in Hegel's *Phenomenology*; Spaventa is remarkable among the Hegelians of his generation in that he regarded the *Phenomenology* as being of equal importance with the *Logic* in Hegel's system and as the key to a right interpretation of the system. He always rejected the religious interpretation of Hegel given by the "Right" and defended at Naples by his better-known colleague Augusto Vera. To admit that the Idea was really superior to and independent of the laborious progress of the Spirit in history would have entailed falling back into just the sort of Platonic intuitionism that Spaventa had so trenchantly criticized. The Being from which Hegel's *Logic* begins must therefore be taken as the thinking being of the Absolute Spirit itself that emerges at the end of the *Phenomenology.* Thus a completely human or immanent interpretation of the *Logic* as an actual process of thinking, rather than as an ideal pattern of thought, can be given.

Just how the *Philosophy of Nature* fits into Hegel's system thereby becomes even more obscure; Spaventa did not concern himself with this problem as such, but his ready acceptance of the Darwinian theory forced it on him in another way when the positivists began to produce evolutionary explanations of the Kantian a priori. Pointing to the vicious circle involved in a causal explanation of our belief in causes, Spaventa began in his last years to work out a phenomenalist account of experience that would do justice to the positivist claims while remaining firmly founded on Kant's first *Critique.* He died, however, before his work was finished. *Esperienza e metafisica* was published at Turin in 1888.

Spaventa was never widely understood or appreciated in his own lifetime. His most sympathetic follower was Donato Jaja (1839–1914), who inspired Giovanni Gentile to collect and republish Spaventa's scattered essays, along with some unpublished manuscripts. As a result of Gentile's work, Spaventa's true stature and importance have been recognized; and in Gentile's own "actual idealism" the three distinct strands of Spaventa's thought—the Italian tradition, the Hegelian dialectic, and critical phenomenalism—are woven into a single synthesis.

See also Bruno, Giordano; Campanella, Tommaso; Darwinism; Descartes, René; Fichte, Johann Gottlieb; Gentile, Giovanni; Gioberti, Vincenzo; Hegel, Georg Wilhelm Friedrich; Hegelianism; Kant, Immanuel; Phenomenalism; Rosmini-Serbati, Antonio; Schelling, Friedrich Wilhelm Joseph von; Spinoza, Benedict (Baruch) de; Vanini, Giulio Cesare; Vico, Giambattista.

Bibliography

ADDITIONAL WORKS BY SPAVENTA

Saggi di critica filosofica. Naples, 1867.

Scritti filosofici. Edited by Giovanni Gentile. Naples: Morano, 1900. Contains biography and full bibliography to 1900.

Principi di etica. Naples, 1904. A study of Hegel's ethics.

La filosofia italiana nelle sue relazione colla filosofia europea. Bari: Laterza, 1908.

Logica e metafisica. Bari: Laterza, 1911.

WORKS ON SPAVENTA

Cubeddu, I. *Bertrando Spaventa.* Florence: Sansoni, 1964. The most comprehensive monograph on Spaventa.

Grilli, M. "The Nationality of Philosophy and Bertrando Spaventa." *Journal of the History of Ideas* 2 (1941): 339–371.

H. S. Harris (1967)

SPECIAL SCIENCES

The special sciences are generally taken to include all the sciences above physics, including biochemistry, genetics and the various biological sciences, the brain sciences, cognitive science, psychology, and economics, amongst many others. Because of their growing success over the last century, the special sciences, and their results, play an increasingly central role in philosophy. This is true of issues in the philosophy of mind and psychology, such as the mind-body problem or the nature of emotion, but also in central debates in ethics concerning a person's moral psychology and its implications, in metaphysics, for instance in discussions of personal identity and the possibility of freewill, and in epistemology, through the manifold issues affected by the nature of human cognitive capabilities. Consequently, debates over the nature, and status, of special sciences are understandably vigorous, though unfortunately they are also especially challenging because of the wide range of issues they incorporate, the often technical formulations of positions, and the implicit nature of many of their commitments. Given these difficulties, one must, first, illuminate the key questions about special sciences and then, second, provide a road map to the major positions and ongoing areas of dispute.

There have arguably been two primary, and hard-fought, foundational issues about the nature of special sciences, though for historical reasons only one of these questions has received widespread explicit discussion. First, there is the issue of the dispensability of the various special sciences themselves. That is, whether humans will be able to completely replace the special sciences, their theories, explanations, laws, and, ultimately, predicates (i.e., words or terms), with the predicates, laws, explanations, and theories of physics. Because there is clearly no practical opportunity of actually dispensing with the special sciences in the foreseeable future, the contested question is whether *in principle* special sciences, at some future point, could be dispensed with in favor of a more fully developed physics. Can humans, in principle, dispense with the special sciences, their predicates, such as *neuron* or *diabetic*, and the explanations couched in terms of them? (In discussing this issue, the in principle dispensability of special science predicates will be referred to for simplicity). On one side, the inter-theoretic reductionist argues that in order to fully explain and understand the natural world one ultimately only needs physics and its predicates, whereas, on the other side, the inter-theoretic anti-reductionist argues that humans cannot do without the special sciences and their proprietary vocabulary.

In contrast, rather than focusing upon words or explanations, the second foundational topic asks which entities, for example properties and individuals such as neurons and being diabetic, should be accepted as the truth makers of the best scientific explanations and theories. In this debate, in one corner is the ontological reductionist who argues that, when properly understood, the sole truth makers for scientific theories and explanations are the entities of physics—thus, really, only individuals like quarks and their properties of spin, charm, and charge should be taken to exist. In the other corner is the ontological non-reductivist who argues that, in addition to the entities of physics, it must also be accepted that the world contains the properties and individuals apparently posited by the special sciences—for example, individuals such as neurons and properties such as being diabetic.

Given the thoroughly ontological nature of this second question, it must be carefully noted that some philosophers accept the existence of only one genuine issue—the first. For example, many scientific anti-realists, such as the positivists and their intellectual descendents, take broad ontological questions to be, in some sense, illegitimate and argue that one must rest simply with the first kind of question about theories, explanations, and predicates. However, since the mid-1970s, scientific realism has reemerged and argues that the best scientific theories allow humans to know about entities in the world. As a consequence, many scientific realist philosophers now accept the legitimacy of both questions about what scientific predicates are in principle indispensable and the consequent issue of which worldly entities should be taken to be the truth makers of the true, and in principle indispensable, scientific theories and explanations using such predicates.

Bearing these two issues in mind, modern discussions of special sciences can be examined and arguably start, in the 1950s, with the positivists' account of special sciences, which grows from Ernest Nagel's (1961) model of inter-theoretic reduction. In its most plausible version, Nagel provided machinery that putatively allowed the laws of special sciences to be explained by using identity statements relating special science predicates and predicates of lower level sciences, in combination with the law statements of lower level sciences, to derive the law statements of special sciences. For this entry's purposes, what is important is that it was claimed that, in principle, one could consequently derive, and explain, all the laws of the special sciences from the laws of physics. Thus it was concluded that special sciences and their predicates are in principle dispensable. As a result, the Nagelian picture of special sciences takes them to be analogous to the line chefs who are needed in restaurants to speedily prep difficult and complex subject matter, but where ultimately the master chef, in physics and its predicates, would, in principle, suffice to get the job done (i.e., to explain and understand all phenomena).

As befits positivism's suspicion of ontology, the Nagelian picture is focused upon the relations of predicates, law statements, theories, and other semantic entities. However, obvious ontological conclusions flow from the Nagelian account, though, for the ideological reasons noted earlier, these implications were rarely made explicit. When one establishes identity statements, then one shows that there is only one entity referred to by two predicates, rather than two entities as was previously supposed. Through such identity statements one thus plausibly reduces one's ontology. Furthermore, if as a result of such identity statements one only needs physics and its predicates in order to account, in principle, for everything about the natural world, then, at least intuitively, parsimony considerations suggest that the entities of physics are the only entities that actually exist. In this manner, the Nagelian view of special sciences provides the background to recent debates with a trenchant defense of inter-theoretic reductionism, and the in principle dispensability of special sciences and their predicates, implicitly combined with a thorough ontological reductionism that merely accepts the existence of the entities of physics, such as quarks and their properties.

During the 1960s, 1970s, and 1980s, philosophers of science more closely examined the actual nature of particular special sciences, primarily psychology and biology, to show that, contrary to the Nagelian claims, such disciplines and their predicates are in principle indispensable. Though a range of evidence was used to defend this conclusion, Jerry Fodor's (1974) so-called Multiple Realization Argument was the most prominent of these defenses. The latter argument's crucial premise is the observation that the predicates of the special sciences refer to properties that are composed, or multiply realized, by heterogeneous combinations of the properties studied by physics. For example, the economic predicate "has monetary value" refers to the properties composed by the physically heterogeneous combinations of properties found in paper, metal, plastic, and even shells. Such multiple realization means that there is a failure in getting the identity claims necessary to drive the Nagelian program—having monetary value, and other special science properties, simply are not identical to any particular combination of physical properties.

As well as undermining the Nagelian's key argument for the dispensability of special sciences and their predicates, multiple realization was also used to provide positive arguments for the in principle indispensability of such predicates by Fodor, William Wimsatt (1976), Philip Kitcher (1984), and others. Though differing in their details, these positive arguments putatively show that—given the physical heterogeneity of the combinations of physical properties that realize special science properties—the predicates of physics will fail to articulate the commonalities between the multiply realized properties, like having monetary value, studied by the special sciences. For the predicates of physics simply frame the physical differences amongst the heterogeneous realizers of special science properties. Consequently, it is argued in various ways that the proprietary predicates of the special sciences are also necessary, in principle, to fully account for the multiply realized properties these disciplines study.

Though many philosophers of science have worked to articulate this position, for simplicity the latter account of special sciences will be referred to as the Fodorian view; and, as well as its claims about predicates, this position again lends itself to further ontological conclusions. In fact, the realization of special sciences properties by the properties of physics is explicitly combined by Fodor, and others, with the idea of the implementation of special science mechanisms by mechanisms of physics (and implicitly with the constitution of individuals of the special sciences by the individuals of physics).

As a result, the Fodorian view is apparently a version of ontological non-reductivism, for it assumes that the world is a compositional hierarchy containing many levels of distinct properties, individuals, and mechanisms bearing complex compositional relations to other levels of entities until one bottoms out (so far as we now know) with the entities studied by physics. The Fodorian picture thus takes a diametrically opposed view of the special sciences than the Nagelian account, arguing that, rather than leaving too many cooks preparing the broth, the special sciences and their proprietary predicates are, in principle, necessary in order to fully understand and explain the variegated levels of multiply realized properties, multiply constituted individuals, and multiply implemented mechanisms that the special sciences take as their objects of inquiry.

As the dominant position, the Fodorian view has received sustained critical attention and two tendencies are worth noting here. First, there is a significant, and continuing body of work that follows various strands of the Nagelian view, either by seeking to provide technical machinery that establishes the in principle dispensability of special science predicates, or by looking at a wider range of scientific cases to drive such machinery, or both (Hooker 1981, Bickle 1998). However, Jaegwon Kim has recently pioneered a second approach that diverges radically from the Nagelian framework's semantic focus. As a response to the Fodorian view, Kim (1998) instead champions what might be dubbed the "metaphysics of science"—the careful examination of ontological issues as they arise in sciences. The resulting strategy proceeds, first, by more carefully examining the nature of an ontological claim about the special sciences central to the Fodorian picture, and then, second, by seeking to show that when the metaphysics of this notion is properly understood it fails to support the conclusions claimed by the Fodorians.

Perhaps the most important of these critical arguments focuses on the realization relation itself. Crudely put, certain property instances, the realizers, realize another property instance only if the causal powers contributed by the realizers non-causally suffice for the powers individuative of the realized property, but not vice versa. Kim (1998) has consequently argued that, given this core feature of the realization relation, considerations of ontological parsimony make it prima facie plausible that it should only be accepted that there are realizer property instances. This grounds a new form of ontological reductionism, what Kim terms the functionalization model, which uses the Fodorian view's own commitment to realization relations in the special sciences to reduce the ontology of the sciences simply to the ultimate realizers—the properties of physics. Other important examples of such arguments driven by work in the metaphysics of science are found in Kim (1992) and Lawrence Shapiro (2000), which each use more precise metaphysical examinations of multiple realization to attack the scientific legitimacy of multiply realized properties, as well as explanations using predicates referring to them and any science that seeks to study them—again turning the Fodorian account of special sciences against itself.

Naturally, there have been responses to such critical arguments focused on the metaphysics of science (see, for instance, Fodor [1997] and Gillett [2003]) and, as yet, it is far from clear where this renewed ontological focus will finally lead. However, ongoing debates over special sciences have arguably changed in a fundamental way, not least by the range of new questions faced. Can the ontological non-reductivism, the levels position, which many assume is the backbone of the Fodorian view, be sustained or does it collapse upon itself as Kim's functionalizing reductionism seeks to show? And is there space for a third, previously unappreciated, type of view about special sciences that combines ontological reductionism, driven by the metaphysical argument underpinning Kim's functionalizing reduction, and a commitment to the in principle indispensability of special sciences, founded upon the Fodorian's reasoning that complex aggregates can only be fully understood using special science predicates? As well as these concerns about global views of special sciences, one also now confronts a prior set of more specific issues about the foundations of the special sciences. For example, what is the nature of composition generally in the special sciences, as well as particular compositional relations such as the realization relations between properties in the sciences?

The answers to the more particular questions in the metaphysics of science are important because, as has been seen, they underpin many of the ongoing disputes between proponents of competing global accounts of the special science themselves. Moreover, all of these questions about the foundations of the special sciences will only become more pressing. For as humans increasingly look to the sciences to understand their own nature, then what is said about special sciences, like genetics, neurophysiology, and psychology, will also have more and more obvious implications for what they must consequently conclude about themselves.

See also Emergence; Philosophy of Biology; Reduction.

Bibliography

Bickle, J. *Psychoneural Reduction: The New Wave*. Cambridge, MA: MIT Press, 1998.

Fodor, J. "Special Sciences: Or, the Disunity of Science as a Working Hypothesis." *Synthese* 28 (1974): 97–115.

Fodor, J. "Special Sciences: Still Autonomous after all these Years." *Philosophical Perspectives* 11 (1997): 149–163.

Gillett, C. "The Metaphysics of Realization, Multiple Realizability and The Special Sciences." *Journal of Philosophy* 22 (2003): 591–603.

Hooker, C.A. "Towards A General Theory of Reduction. Part I: Historical and Scientific Settings. Part II: Identity. Part III: Cross Categorial Reduction." *Dialogue* 20 (1981): 38–59, 201–36, 496–529.

Kim, J. *Mind in a Physical World*. Cambridge, MA: MIT Press, 1998.

Kim, J. "Multiple Realization and the Metaphysics of Reduction." *Philosophy and Phenomenological Research* 52 (1992):1–26.

Kitcher, P. "1953 and All That: A Tale of Two Sciences." *Philosophical Review* 93 (1984): 335–73.

Nagel, E. *The Structure of Science*. New York: Harcourt Brace, 1961.

Shapiro, L. "Multiple Realizations." *Journal of Philosophy* 19 (2000): 635–654.

Wimsatt, W. "Reductionism, Levels of Organization, and the Mind-Body Problem." In *Consciousness and The Brain*, edited by G. Globus, I. Savodnik, and G. Maxwell. New York: Plenum, 1976.

Carl Gillett (2005)

SPECIESISM

"Speciesism" is the name of a form of bias or discrimination that is much discussed in the contemporary debates over the moral status of animals. It amounts to discriminating on the basis of species; that is, it takes the fact that, say, baboons and humans belong to different species as a reason in itself to draw moral differences between them and on several counts.

First, speciesism sometimes manifests itself in consideration of who or what may be members of the moral community, of who or what is morally considerable (see Clark, Frey, Regan, Singer). For example, it is sometimes said that creatures who have experiences or are sentient count morally; to go on to affirm that (some) animals have experiences and are sentient but to deny that they count morally solely because they are not of the right species is a form of speciesism. If it really is the fact that creatures have experiences and are sentient that matters, then animals count; what has to be shown is why the fact that it is a baboon and not a human who has these characteristics matters morally.

Second, speciesism sometimes manifests itself in claims about pain and suffering. For instance, we usually take pain and suffering to be evils, to be things that blight a life and lower its quality, and animals can feel pain and suffer. Thus, suppose one pours scalding water on a child and on a cat: It seems odd to say that it would be wrong to scald the child but not wrong to scald the cat, since both feel pain and suffer, both have the quality of their lives diminished, and both instinctively reveal pain-avoidance behavior. To claim that scalding the child is wrong, but that scalding the cat is not wrong solely on the basis of the species to which each belongs is not in itself to give a reason why or how species-membership is morally relevant, let alone morally decisive (see Rachels 1990, Sapontzis 1987).

Third, speciesism sometimes manifests itself in claims about the value of life. Most of us think human life is more valuable than animal life; yet to think this solely on the basis of species exposes one to an obvious problem. If it is true that normal adult human life is more valuable than animal life, it by no means follows that all human life is more valuable than animal life, since it is by no means the case that all human lives are even remotely approximate in their quality. Thus, some human lives have a quality so low that those who are currently living those lives seek to end them; this, of course, is what the contemporary concern with euthanasia and physician-assisted suicide is all about. Indeed, some humans live in permanently vegetative states, where, as best we can judge, all talk of the quality of life seems beside the point. Are even these human lives more valuable than the lives of perfectly healthy baboons? To say that they are solely because they are human lives, lives lived by members of the species *Homo sapiens,* even though it is true that healthy baboons can do all manner of things, can have all manner of experiences, is in effect to say that species-membership makes the crucial difference in value. It is not apparent exactly how it does this (see Frey). Of course, certain religions and cultural traditions may hold that humans have greater value than do animals, no matter what the quality or kind of lives lived: But these very same religions have put forward moral views that many today do not endorse, and these very same cultural traditions have held that, for example, whites are superior to blacks.

See also Animal Mind; Animal Rights and Welfare; Euthanasia; Racism; Singer, Peter.

Bibliography

Clark, S. R. L. *The Moral Status of Animals.* Oxford: Clarendon Press, 1977.

Clark, S. R. L. *The Nature of the Beast.* Oxford: Oxford University Press, 1982.

Frey, R. G. *Interests and Rights: The Case against Animals.* Oxford: Clarendon Press, 1980.

Frey, R. G. "Moral Standing, the Value of Lives, and Speciesism." *Between the Species* 4 (1988): 191–201.

Frey, R. G. *Rights, Killing, and Suffering: Moral Vegetarianism and Applied Ethics.* Oxford: Blackwell, 1983.

Rachels, J. *Created from Animals: The Moral Implications of Darwinism.* New York: Oxford University Press, 1990.

Regan, T. *The Case for Animal Rights.* Berkeley: University of California Press, 1983.

Regan, T., and P. Singer, eds. *Animal Rights and Human Obligations,* 2nd ed. Englewood Cliffs, NJ: Prentice Hall, 1989.

Sapontzis, S. F. *Morals, Reason, and Animals.* Philadelphia: Temple University Press, 1987.

Singer, P. *Animal Liberation,* 2nd ed. New York: New York Review of Books, 1990.

Singer, P. *Practical Ethics,* 2nd ed. Cambridge, U.K.: Cambridge University Press, 1993.

R. G. Frey (1996)

SPECIOUS PRESENT

See *Time, Consciousness of*

SPENGLER, OSWALD

(1880–1936)

The German writer Oswald Spengler was born at Blankenburg, Germany. Spengler is known almost entirely for his contribution to philosophy of history. After studying at the universities of Munich, Berlin, and Halle—chiefly natural science and mathematics, although he also read widely in history, literature, and philosophy—Spengler obtained a doctorate in 1904, with a thesis on Heraclitus, and embarked upon a career as a high school teacher. In 1911 he abandoned teaching to take up the penurious life of a private scholar in Munich, where the first volume of his only considerable work, *Der Untergang des Abendlandes* (*The Decline of the West*), gradually took shape. This volume was published in 1918 at the moment of his country's defeat in World War I. Its pessimistic conclusions so exactly suited the prevailing mood that its author rocketed to instant but short-lived fame.

An ardent nationalist, Spengler has sometimes been accused, especially because of his reactionary and quite undistinguished political writings after 1923, of having helped to prepare the way intellectually for fascism. He actually opposed Adolf Hitler's rise, but chiefly on the ground (as he put it) that what Germany needed was a hero, not a heroic tenor. He died in Munich in 1936, bitterly resentful of the drastic decline his reputation had suffered. It is doubtful that Spengler would have been greatly mollified by the revival of interest in his work that followed World War II, for this was due as much to the general stimulus given to speculation about history by Arnold Toynbee's popular *A Study of History* as to any belated recognition of the independent merits of Spengler's views.

HISTORY AS COMPARATIVE MORPHOLOGY

The Decline of the West, although fascinating in stretches, is an unsystematic, repetitive, obscurely written book. Its style is oracular rather than analytical; it offers more "insights" than arguments. Yet its major claims are reasonably clear. From the outset it calls for a "Copernican revolution" in our way of viewing human history that will at once undermine both the traditional ancient–medieval–modern framework generally employed by empirical historians (a framework that Spengler finds provincial) and the prevailing linear interpretation of most Western philosophers of history, whether progressive or regressive (which he finds naive). According to Spengler, history, steadily and objectively regarded, will be seen to be without center or ultimate point of reference. It is the story of an indefinite number of cultural configurations, of which western Europe is only one, that "grow with the same superb aimlessness as the flowers of the field." The careers of such cultures, he contends, constitute the only meaning to be found in the course of history as a whole; they are pockets of unconnected significance in a wilderness of human life, most of which is "historyless." All that philosophical study of history can attempt is a "comparative morphology of cultures"—an inquiry into the typical form of their life, their rhythms, and possibly their laws—aimed at giving categories and an interpretative framework to empirical historiography. In outline at least, this is the aim of Spengler's two massive volumes.

But what exactly are the cultures that provide subject matter for the morphological approach to history? In view of the common complaint that Spengler "biologizes" history, it should be noted that he represents cultures as spiritual phenomena, although rooted in a definite "natural landscape." A culture is the spiritual orientation of a group of people who have achieved some unitary conception of their world that informs all their activities—their art, religion, and philosophy, their politics and economics, even their warfare—and which is expressible in a distinctive concept of the space in which they are to live and act. This concept of space functions as the culture's "prime symbol" and is the key to the understanding of its history.

Thus, classical man, to whom Spengler applies Friedrich Nietzsche's term *Apollinian,* is said to have conceived of himself as living in a local, finite space, a visible, tangible here-and-now, of which the life-sized nude statue and the small columned temple are eminent expressions. The concept shows itself equally in such things as the circumscribed political life of the city-state and the practice of burning rather than burying the dead, as if the idea of eternity could not be squarely faced. By contrast, modern Western man conceives of himself as living in a space of boundless extent, his whole culture expressing a Faustian urge to reach out and fill it with his activity. Thus, the spires of Gothic cathedrals soar skyward, Western painting develops distant perspectives, music produces the expansive form of the fugue. Also typically Faustian are long-distance sailing and long-range weapons, the conquest of space by telephone, and the insatiable ambitions of Western statesmen (for whom, like Cecil Rhodes, "expansion is everything").

Other cultures each have their characteristic space concept. The ancient Egyptians saw their world in one dimension, and their architecture, which assumed the basic form of a corridor enclosed in masonry, expressed the notion of "moving down a narrow and inexorably prescribed life-path." The Russians, whom Spengler classifies as non-Western, have a "flat plane" culture, which, when free to do so, expresses itself in low-lying buildings and an ethics of undiscriminating brotherhood. The Arabian culture of the Middle East, which Spengler calls Magian, views the world mysteriously, as a cavern in which "light … battles against the darkness." Its architecture is consequently interior-oriented; its religion, magical and dualistic. Altogether, Spengler claims to identify nine (possibly ten) such cultures, which have emerged at various times from "the proto-spirituality of ever-childish humanity." But he does not rule out the possibility of others being discovered.

Spengler's concept of human cultures has some affinity with G. W. F. Hegel's concept of the state. Both envisage an organic unity of human attitudes and activities that express a definite form of the human spirit. Spengler never wrote the promised metaphysical work that might have made clearer the general status of "spirit" in his philosophy of history. But his concept of it certainly differs from Hegel's, for he denies that the spirituality of successive historical units taken together reveals the developing nature of spirit itself. The units have no rational connection with one another, Spengler maintains, denying categorically that one culture can ever really understand, learn from, or (strictly speaking) be influenced by another. The divergence of his approach from Hegel's is even greater in his account of the typical career of a culture. Whereas Hegel attempted to represent not only the succession of historical units, but also the succession of stages within each unit, as a rationally (that is, dialectically) ordered sequence, Spengler finds, instead, a pattern analogous to the life cycle of a plant or animal. Like biological organisms, cultures grow old. The qualitative changes that accompany the "aging" will be as apparent, to a historian possessing "physiognomic tact," as is a culture's original orientation.

CULTURAL CYCLE

Spengler often speaks of the aging of cultures in terms of the succession of the four seasons. They have their spring in an early heroic period when life is rural, agricultural, and feudal. In the Apollinian culture this was the Homeric period; in the Faustian it was the high Middle Ages. This is a time of seminal myths, of inspiring epic and saga, and of powerful mystical religion. With summer comes the rise of towns not yet alienated from the countryside, an aristocracy of manners growing up beside an older, lustier leadership, and great individual artists succeeding their anonymous predecessors. In the Apollinian culture this was the period of the early city-states; in the Faustian it was the time of the Renaissance, of William Shakespeare and Michelangelo, and of the Galilean triumphs of the uncorrupted intellect.

Autumn witnesses the full ripening of the culture's spiritual resources and the first hints of possible exhaustion; it is a time of growing cities, spreading commerce, and centralizing monarchies, with religion being challenged by philosophy and tradition undermined by "enlightenment." In the classical world this was the age of the Sophists, of Socrates and Plato; in the West it was the eighteenth century, which reached the apogee of creative maturity in the music of Mozart, the poetry of Johann Wolfgang von Goethe, and the philosophy of Immanuel Kant. Transition to winter is characterized by the appearance of the megalopolis, the world city, with its rootless proletariat, plutocracy, esoteric art, and growing skepticism and materialism. It is an age, furthermore, of imperialism, of increasing political tyranny, and of almost constant warfare, as political adventurers skirmish for world empire. In general, culture loses its soul and hardens into mere "civilization," the highest works of which are feats of administration and the application of science to industry.

Faustian culture is, according to Spengler, currently well into its autumn period, at a point roughly equivalent to 200 BCE in the Apollinian culture. An early sign of our advanced cultural age is the career of Napoleon Bonaparte, who is morphologically contemporary with Alexander the Great; our Julius Caesar is yet to come. The moral is plain.

> We are civilized, not Gothic or Rococo, people; we have to reckon with the hard cold facts of *late* life, to which the parallel is to be found not in Pericles' Athens but in Caesar's Rome. Of great painting or great music there can no longer be, for Western people, any question.... Only *extensive* possibilities are open to them.

Young Faustians who wish to play a significant role in the gathering winter should, in other words, either join the army or enroll in a technological institute. Spengler hopes that enough of his countrymen will heed his advice to ensure that the Faustian equivalent of the Roman Empire will be German.

CULTURAL CYCLE AND DETERMINISM. Clearly, Spengler regards comparative morphology as a basis for predicting the future of a culture, given the stage it has reached. Spengler, in fact, represents his study as the first serious attempt to "predetermine history," and he offers comparative charts in support of his claim that the life cycle of a culture takes about one thousand years to work itself through.

It is nevertheless misleading to call Spengler's account of history deterministic without qualification. Unlike Toynbee's, for example, it offers no explanation of the origin of cultures; the sudden rise of a new "world experience" is left a cosmic mystery. Nor do Spengler's cultures disappear on schedule after reaching the stage of civilization; civilizations may last indefinitely, as the examples of India and China show. Even while alive, the working out of a culture's "destiny" leaves open many alternative possibilities; the themes, Spengler says, are given, but not the modulations, which "depend on the character and capacities of individual players." Thus, Germany was bound to be united in the nineteenth century; how it would be united depended on what Frederick William IV would do in 1848 and Otto von Bismarck in 1870. Spengler's historical "laws" are thus not envisaged as determining, but only as limiting, the actions of individuals. This is part of the rationale of his political activism.

The notion, furthermore, of a developing culture's being a *self*-determining system is qualified by Spengler's recognition of two ways in which its normal development may be frustrated. Thus, he claims that the Mexican culture had perished through external assault, "like a sunflower whose head is struck off by one passing." Spengler also concedes that a culture can sustain spiritual damage from too close proximity to a stronger one, resulting in what he calls pseudomorphosis. What originally led him to elaborate this idea was the confused development of the Magian culture, which came to life on the ground of the Apollinian before the older culture had passed away. In such cases, Spengler observes, the younger culture "cannot get its breath, and fails not only to achieve pure and specific expression-forms, but even to develop fully its own self-consciousness." The Russian culture—which, according to Spengler, was "prematurely born"—has similarly been deformed by intrusions of the Faustian culture, first in the "reforms" of Peter the Great and again in the Bolshevik Revolution. Since weaker cultures take on only certain outer forms of dominant ones, however, Spengler would deny that the doctrine of pseudomorphosis contradicts his claim that one culture never really influences another.

DIFFICULTIES IN SPENGLER'S THEORY

Like all large synoptic systems, Spengler's theory of history has been criticized for rearing its speculative superstructure on too shaky an empirical foundation. Even Toynbee has not escaped this charge, and in breadth of historical knowledge (if not always in perceptiveness) Spengler is vastly the inferior of the two. His knowledge of his cultures is much more uneven; all he really knows well is the Apollinian and Faustian. More important, what he does say at the detailed level all too often gives the appearance of special pleading. In some cases his morphological judgments are just a bit too ingenious to be convincing, as when he declares that Rembrandt's brown is the color of Ludwig van Beethoven's string quartets. In other cases dubious value judgments seem to be traceable chiefly to the requirements of the overarching thesis, as when the Roman Empire, being a winter phenomenon, is represented as culturally sterile, in spite of Vergil, Horace, and Ovid. In still other cases critics have suspected Spengler, if not of falsifying, then at least of suppressing, known historical facts, as when he claims that classical man, by contrast with Magian man, was polytheistic, ignoring the almost uniform monotheism of the great Greek philosophers. Highhanded treatment of the details is made easier by the fact that what passes for empirical verification in Spengler's work is really only casual exemplification of his general ideas; he makes no attempt to test systematically, and possibly to falsify, a precisely articulated hypothesis about cultural development. And when the details become intransigent, much can be explained away as pseudomorphosis. Thus, high-rise buildings in Russia are called Western-inspired, and Hadrian's Pantheon (the "first mosque") is labeled an irruption of the Magian.

Even if Spengler's actual procedure were scientifically more acceptable, there would remain the basic weakness of any attempt to generalize about the whole of history from a mere eight to ten instances of cultural development, two of which are conceded in any case to be abnormal. Spengler's defenders, of course, have often denied the relevance of this sort of criticism. What he attempted, they claim, was not social science, not even philosophy of history in the sense of arguing to general conclusions from philosophical premises in the manner of Kant and Hegel. It was, rather, a vision of events, whose truth is the truth of poetry. From this standpoint Spengler's charts and tables are an unfortunate lapse that should not be taken too seriously; part of the value of his work lies in its imaginative imprecision. Certainly, Spengler himself declared that whereas nature should be studied scientifically, history should be studied poetically. As a defense against the empirical objection, however, this will not do. For poetry is not predictive. Spengler's theory is distinctive in insisting that the significant features of history are those that are focused by the historian's aesthetic judgment. But classification and simple induction of the sort characteristic of the underdeveloped sciences is as essential to his final conclusions as is aesthetic insight.

The weakness of Spengler's inductions might not have been so serious had he not been an uncompromising holist as well. He offers no explanation of the changes his cultures undergo; he makes no attempt to isolate the factors that might throw light on their "mechanism" and that might have afforded reasons for expecting such developments to continue. In fact, part of the function of the puzzling contrast he draws between the "causality" of nature and the "destiny" of history is to persuade us not to look for this sort of thing. Spengler seems to think of causality rather narrowly as a matter of physical interaction. His own model for historical development is the biological destiny of a seed, its tendency to grow into a plant of a definite kind, barring accidents and in spite of deformations—it being assumed that this is not explicable mechanistically. It is ironical that although Spengler himself, in elaborating this concept of explanation, claimed to be resisting inappropriate scientific approaches to history, it is precisely because of this approach that some critics have charged him with scientism. Idealist philosophers of history, for example, have regarded Spengler as a cryptopositivist because, in searching out the life cycle of cultures without trying to understand in detail and from the inside why the human participants acted as they did, he treats what he originally defined spiritualistically as if it were part of nature. The causation of action by human reason, these critics would say, is central to all explanations of historical change. By ignoring this, Spengler's theory falls into incompatible parts.

Many critics have held that an even more obvious contradiction vitiates much of what Spengler had to say about specifically historical understanding. According to him, the reason cultures never really influence one another is that they are never able to grasp one another's prime symbol—a doctrine of cultural isolation that Spengler extended even to such apparently recalcitrant subjects as mathematics (to Apollinians and Faustians, he says, number means entirely different things). But the notion that we can never understand what is culturally alien to us surely raises barriers to the sort of understanding claimed by Spengler himself; comparative morphology presupposes a correct grasp of what is being compared. Spengler tries to meet this difficulty with the ad hoc claim that a few intuitive geniuses may rise above the barrier of cultural relativism. Yet the fact that he offered his book to the general public surely betrays confidence in a rather wider distribution of transcultural insight than is strictly compatible with the impossibility of cultures' learning from one another. Nor is it helpful to suggest that cultures may learn without being influenced, for the reason for denying influence was the impossibility of understanding. The difficulty is compounded by Spengler's sometimes also denying that we can understand what is culturally "out of phase" with us, even though it belongs to the past of our own culture. Thus, we are told that although Tacitus knew of the revolution of Tiberius Gracchus two and a half centuries earlier, he no longer found it meaningful. Together, Spengler's two limitations on the understanding lead to the conclusion that we can understand only ourselves. This is scarcely a promising position from which to develop a theory of historical inquiry.

See also Goethe, Johann Wolfgang von; Hegel, Georg Wilhelm Friedrich; Heraclitus of Ephesus; Kant, Immanuel; Nietzsche, Friedrich; Philosophy of History; Plato; Socrates; Sophists; Toynbee, Arnold Joseph.

Bibliography

The first volume of Spengler's *Der Untergang des Abendlandes,* subtitled *Gestalt und Wirklichkeit* (Munich: Beck, 1918), was revised in the definitive Munich edition of 1923. The second volume, *Welthistorische Perspektiven,* had been published there the previous year. A good English translation by C. F. Atkinson is available under the title *The Decline of the West* (London: Allen and Unwin, 1932), and there is an abridged edition of this prepared by Helmut Werner and Arthur Helps (New York: Knopf, 1962).

For an introductory discussion of the background and influence of Spengler's work, as well as a select bibliography, see H. S. Hughes, *Oswald Spengler: A Critical Estimate* (New York: Scribners, 1952). For further references see Patrick Gardiner, ed., *Theories of History* (Glencoe, IL: Free Press, 1959), p. 524. For criticism from the standpoint of both idealist philosophy of history and empirical historiography, see R. G. Collingwood, "Oswald Spengler and the Theory of Historical Cycles," in *Antiquity* 1 (1927): 311–325, 435–446.

W. H. Dray (1967)

SPINOZA, BENEDICT (BARUCH) DE

(1632–1677)

Dutch Jewish philosopher Benedict de Spinoza was best known for his *Ethics* (1677), which laid out in geometric form arguments for the existence of an impersonal God, the identity of mind and body, determinism, and a way of overcoming the dominance of the passions and achieving freedom and blessedness. His *Theological-Political Treatise* (1670) was a landmark in the history of biblical criticism. He was also, in that work, the first major philosopher in the Western tradition to argue for democracy and for freedom of thought and expression.

IN THE PORT OF AMSTERDAM (1632–1656)

Spinoza was born into the Portuguese Jewish community in Amsterdam in the same year Galileo published his *Dialogue Concerning the Two Chief World Systems.* His father, Michael, was an immigrant who had fled Portugal, with other members of his family, to escape the persecution of the Inquisition. At that time the Dutch Republic was one of the few places in Europe where Jews could worship freely. In Amsterdam Michael became a fairly prosperous merchant in the import-export business and a prominent member of the Portuguese synagogue.

But Baruch, as Benedict was first called, encountered his own problems with religious intolerance. In 1656, when he was twenty-three, the synagogue expelled him for what the sentence of excommunication described as "abominable heresies" and "monstrous deeds." Although Spinoza had received an orthodox religious education in his congregation's school, he rebelled early on against central tenets of Judaism and began to take an interest in the new philosophy of Descartes, Hobbes, and Galileo. After his excommunication he was known by the Latin version of his name, Benedict (which means "blessed" in Latin, as Baruch does in Hebrew).

Excommunication was a common form of discipline in the Amsterdam synagogue, often imposed for minor offenses and for short periods, with a provision that the sentence could be lifted if the offender performed some penance. Spinoza's excommunication was unconditional and quite harsh. The elders cursed him with exceptional severity; no one in the Jewish community (including members of his own family) could associate with him. For a long time historians did not know exactly what heresies he was accused of. But in the mid-twentieth century, research in the archives of the Inquisition disclosed a report from a Spanish priest who had spent several months in Amsterdam. His report revealed that the main doctrinal charges against Spinoza were: (1) that he held that God exists "only philosophically"; (2) that he maintained that the soul dies with the body; and (3) that he denied that the law of Moses was a true law. The "monstrous deeds" probably included his unrepentant resistance to authority when threatened with excommunication.

BECOMING A PHILOSOPHER (1656–1661)

Michael de Spinoza died two years before the excommunication. At that time Baruch took over the family business in partnership with his younger brother, Gabriel. But the punishment prescribed for his heresy made it impossible for Benedict to continue running his father's firm (which was, in any case, in financial trouble as a result of the first Anglo-Dutch war). There is little definite information about Spinoza's life during the years immediately after his excommunication. Probably he remained in Amsterdam for most of this period, and began working as a lens grinder, a craft in which he earned a reputation for excellence. Perhaps he lodged at first with Francis van den Enden, a former Jesuit at whose school he had been learning Latin. Van den Enden may also have helped to shape his inclinations toward the new philosophy, religious heterodoxy, and democratic politics. Perhaps Spinoza earned room and board by assisting Van den Enden in teaching Latin. Very probably he played parts in the comedies of Terence, which Van den Enden had his students perform in 1657 and 1658. Possibly he assisted the Quakers in their attempts to convert the Jews by translating some of their literature into Hebrew.

Sometime between 1656 and 1661 it appears that Spinoza did some formal study of philosophy at the University of Leiden. The Dutch Republic was the first place where Cartesianism took hold, having been introduced in 1640 by Regius, a professor of medicine at the University of Utrecht. Cartesianism was highly controversial. Voetius, a professor of theology at Utrecht, challenged Regius's doctrine that the union of soul and body is one of two separate substances, defending the scholastic-Aristotelian doctrine that the soul is the substantial form of the body. In 1642 the university forbade the teaching of Cartesianism. Later in the 1640s there were similar controversies at the University of Leiden. In 1646 Heereboord, a professor of logic at that university, defended the Cartesian method of doubt as a way of achieving certainty. Revius, a professor of theology at Leiden, replied that the method of doubt would lead to atheism and accused Descartes of Pelagianism. In 1647 their controversy led the university to ban the discussion of Descartes' philosophy, pro or con. Nevertheless, in the late 1650s Leiden was a place where one could study Cartesian philosophy.

By the end of the 1650s, Spinoza had established a circle of friends, the most notable of whom were Jan Rieuwertsz, a bookseller and publisher of Dutch translations of Descartes' works, who was later to become Spinoza's publisher; Jan Glazemaker, translator into Dutch of Descartes'works, who was later to translate most of Spinoza's works into Dutch; Peter Balling, the Amsterdam agent of various Spanish merchants, who was to translate Spinoza's first published work, an exposition of Descartes, into Dutch; the brothers Jan and Adriaan Koerbagh, the latter of whom died in prison for publishing Spinozistic views; and Lodewijk Meyer, a prominent member of Amsterdam literary circles, who wrote, in 1666, a work entitled *Philosophy, Interpreter of Holy Scripture*.

Meyer's work anticipates some of the themes of Spinoza's *Theological-Political Treatise* (TPT), though it differs from Spinoza in the solution it proposes. Meyer complains that theologians try to settle their controversies by appeals to scripture but that their interpretations of scripture are so insecurely based that the controversies never end. Meyer thinks Descartes' work holds the key to ending these debates. He proposes to doubt everything alleged to be the teaching of scripture if it is not based on a solid foundation. Accepting the Cartesian doctrine that God is not a deceiver, and assuming that the books of the Old and New Testaments are the word of God, Meyer concludes that if a proposed interpretation of scripture conflicts with what philosophy shows to be the truth, we can reject that interpretation as false. This is a modernized version of the Maimonidean approach to scripture that Spinoza rejected in the TPT.

Spinoza's friends in Amsterdam shared an interest in Cartesian philosophy and in a religion which involves minimal theological doctrine, emphasizing the love of God and neighbor. Many were affiliated with the Collegiants, a liberal protestant group which had broken away from the Reformed Church after the Synod of Dort in 1618, and which had neither a clergy nor a creed. Many of Spinoza's friends also had a connection with the University of Leiden.

Evidently Spinoza began writing his earliest philosophical works during this period: almost certainly the never-finished *Treatise on the Emendation of the Intellect*; probably his *Short Treatise on God, Man, and his Well-Being*, a systematic presentation of his philosophy, foreshadowing his *Ethics*, but never put into final form; and an early version of the *Theological-Political Treatise*, which may have developed out of a defense of his religious opinions he wrote in Spanish, addressed to the synagogue. The *Treatise on the Intellect* was first published in his *Opera posthuma*; the *Short Treatise* was not discovered until the nineteenth century, in two manuscripts which apparently stem from a Dutch translation of a lost Latin original. The defense to the synagogue has never been found, though it seems possible to infer some of its likely content from the version of the *Theological-Political Treatise* published in 1670.

THE TREATISE ON THE EMENDATION OF THE INTELLECT

The order of composition of Spinoza's earliest works has been debated, but there now seems to be a consensus that the *Treatise on the Emendation of the Intellect* (TEI) is the earliest of his surviving works. It is a good place to start the exposition of Spinoza's philosophy, since it explains his motivation for becoming a philosopher. Spinoza begins the TEI by writing that experience had taught him that all the things men commonly pursue—wealth, honor and sensual pleasure—are empty and futile. The pursuit of these supposed goods does not lead to true peace of mind. Sensual pleasure is transitory and, when past, is followed by great sadness. The desires for honor and wealth are never satisfied; when we achieve some measure of them, our success leads only to a never-ending quest for more of the same. When we are unsuccessful, we experience great sadness. The pursuit of honor has the special disadvantage that it puts us at the mercy of others' opinion.

The pursuit of wealth is subject to the uncertainties of fortune, as Spinoza might have learned from his experience as a merchant during the first Anglo-Dutch war. So Spinoza says he finally resolved to seek a good which would give him a joy unalloyed with sadness and which he thought could be found in love for something eternal and infinite. Achieving that highest good, he concluded, would involve perfecting his own nature by acquiring knowledge of the union the mind has with the whole of nature. This decision evidently came only after the excommunication, though it probably culminated a period of reflection which began several years earlier.

Spinoza's primary purpose in this work is to develop a theory of knowledge which will enable him—"with others if possible"—to attain the knowledge which is the highest good. He conceives that project as requiring a healing and purification of the intellect. To this end he offers a classification of the different ways we can 'perceive' things so that he can choose the best. He enumerates four ways by which he has been lead to affirm something without doubt: (1) because someone has told him so; (2) because he has come to believe it by random experience; (3) because he has inferred the essence of a thing from something else (but not adequately); and (4) because he has come to perceive the thing through its essence alone or through knowledge of its proximate cause.

Of the numerous examples Spinoza gives of things he has come to believe in these ways, one must suffice here. Suppose we are given three numbers, *a*, *b*, and *c*, and wish to find a fourth number, *d*, which is to *c* as *b* is to *a*. (1) Some will be able to find *d* because they have been taught a rule which tells them to multiply *b* and *c*, and divide the product by *a*. (2) Others will construct that rule for themselves by generalizing from simple cases where the answer is obvious. (3) Still others will have learned the rule by working through its demonstration in Euclid's *Elements*. And finally, (4), some will simply see, intuitively, the answer to the problem, without going through any inferential process. Surprisingly, given his fondness for demonstration in the *Ethics*, Spinoza rejects *all* of the first three paths to knowledge, and he claims that only the fourth way of affirming things will lead us to the perfection we seek. But, he says ruefully, the things he has so far been able to understand by this kind of knowledge are very few.

The middle portion of the TEI is a search for a method of acquiring knowledge in this fourth way. The reasoning here is obscure and seems to present difficulties which may explain why Spinoza never finished this work. For example, he claims that truth needs no sign and that having a true idea is sufficient to remove all doubt. But the method is supposed to teach us what a true idea is and how to distinguish it from other perceptions. That quest seems to assume that we do need a sign to recognize a true idea.

The concluding sections of the work, however, contain suggestive hints about Spinoza's metaphysical views during this period. A proper application of the method, it seems, will require us to order our ideas in a way which reflects the order of things in nature, reflects, that is, the causal structure of nature. This in turn requires that we begin by understanding what he calls "the source and origin of Nature," which he identifies with "the first elements of the whole of nature." He then makes a distinction between 'uncreated' things that "require nothing but their own being for their explanation" and 'created' things, which depend on a cause (other than their own nature) for their existence. The first elements of the whole of nature would evidently be uncreated things which exist in themselves, independently of anything else. Spinoza explains that if something exists in itself, it is its own cause. Everything else in nature presumably would depend in some way on the first elements. But how do 'created' things depend on 'uncreated' things? And how can something be its own cause?

Toward the end of the TEI Spinoza makes another distinction, which may help to answer these questions. He distinguishes between what he calls the series of fixed and eternal things and the series of singular, changeable things. The singular changeable things are apparently the particular, finite things we encounter in our daily experience. The fixed and eternal things are said to be present everywhere, to be the causes of all things, and to have laws "inscribed in them," according to which the singular, changeable things come to be and are ordered. There are, it appears, two causal orders, one of which relates singular, changeable things to other singular, changeable things, the other of which relates them to fixed and eternal things. The true progress of the intellect requires understanding how singular, changeable things are related to the series of fixed and eternal things. To trace their connection with the series of other singular, changeable things would be impossible, because of the infinity of that series. But it would also not give us insight into the essences of the singular changeable things.

What does this mean? In particular, what are these fixed and eternal things? One plausible conjecture is this: central to Descartes' philosophy is the claim that philosophy is like a tree whose roots are metaphysics, whose trunk is physics, and whose branches are all the other sciences. What underlies this metaphor is Descartes' idea—present both in his cosmological treatise, *The World*, and in his *Principles of Philosophy*—that the fundamental laws of physics—such as the principle of inertia and the principle of conservation of motion—can be deduced from the attributes of God (in particular, from his immutability). From these fundamental laws of physics, which apply to all bodies, we can deduce other, more specific laws which apply to particular kinds of bodies (such as magnets) and which are the subjects of the special sciences (such as medicine and mechanics). In principle it should be possible to deduce all the laws governing the operations of physical objects from the fundamental laws of physics. And everything which happens in the physical world (except insofar as it involves the intervention of mental acts, which are outside the causal network) is governed by scientific laws.

Suppose Spinoza accepted the broad outlines of this Cartesian vision of a unified science. He would not have accepted the idea that minds can operate as uncaused causes, interfering with what would otherwise be the course of physical nature. And he would not have accepted the idea that the will of a personal God is the ultimate cause of the fundamental laws of physics. But he does seem to have accepted the idea that there are fundamental laws of physics, from which all the other laws of physical nature can in principle be deduced, and that all the operations of physical objects can be understood in terms of these laws. On this hypothesis, the first elements of the whole of nature, which are among the fixed and eternal things, would be those general features of extended nature which the fundamental laws of physics describe. The other fixed and eternal things, which are connected in a finite series running between the first elements and the singular changeable things, would be the general features of nature which the derivative laws of physics describe. And the singular, changeable things would be the particular physical objects whose operations are explained by these laws. The order of ideal science reflects the causal structure of nature.

This account may give the impression that Spinoza thought of science as a wholly a priori enterprise which proceeds by the intuition of first principles and deduction of theorems from those first principles. But the final sections of the TEI make it clear that Spinoza recognized that achieving knowledge of singular, changeable things would require some appeal to experience. The laws of nature describe general, unchanging facts, which hold at all times and places. They are not sufficient by themselves to explain why events in the physical world happen at the particular times and places they do. To understand that, Spinoza thinks, we must appeal to "other aids," to experiments which will enable us to determine by what laws of eternal things the particular event occurred. But before we can conduct fruitful experiments, we must first come to understand the nature of our senses so that we will know how to use them. Since that would appear to require knowledge of singular things, there seems to be a problem of circularity here, which may be one reason why Spinoza never succeeded in finishing this treatise.

One puzzle about the TEI, not resolved by the above interpretation, is what the relation is between the "first elements of the whole of nature" and Spinoza's later metaphysical categories. In the TEI Spinoza never uses the terms "substance," "attribute," and "mode," which are fundamental to the metaphysics of the *Ethics*. If the first elements are the uncreated things Spinoza mentions in the TEI's theory of definition, then we might be inclined to identify them with the one substance, God. The uncreated things exist in themselves, or are their own cause, and the concept of existing in itself is one Spinoza later used to define substance. Moreover, the first elements are supposed to be "the source and origin of Nature." Although Spinoza does not refer to them as God, it is natural to think that "the source and origin of Nature" must be God in any philosophy which acknowledges the existence of God. The problem is that there is, evidently, a plurality of first elements, and only one substance, only one God. The next work we consider may provide a solution to this puzzle.

THE SHORT TREATISE ON GOD, MAN, AND HIS WELL-BEING

It is clear that Spinoza intended the *Treatise on the Emendation of the Intellect* as a prelude to a systematic exposition of his philosophy; from the correspondence it seems almost certain that some version of *The Short Treatise on God, Man, and His Well-being* (ST) was the systematic exposition the TEI was intended to introduce. Spinoza probably began writing it while he was still living in Amsterdam, but he must have finished it after he moved to Rijnsburg in the summer of 1661, when he apparently sent a copy of the Latin manuscript back to his friends in Amsterdam. This manuscript would then have been translated into Dutch for the members of his circle who could not read Latin. It is that Dutch manuscript, or manuscripts descended from it, which provides the basis for our knowledge of the ST.

Spinoza was still uncertain about publishing the ST as late as April 1662, when he had already made a start on expounding his philosophy in the geometric style of his *Ethics*. He had initially written the ST at the request of his friends, but only for private circulation, not publication. It appears that he sent them the manuscript some time after he moved to Rijnsburg. He hesitated to publish this work because he knew it was theologically unorthodox and he was reluctant to invite the attacks he knew would come from the conservative Calvinist clergy.

The surviving manuscripts present many textual difficulties. Frequently we do not know whether what we are reading is originally from Spinoza's hand, an addition by an early reader, a mistranslation of the Latin original, or a copyist's error. It appears that even in those portions of the manuscripts we can confidently ascribe to Spinoza, the views he holds, or the ways he expresses or argues for those views, reflect an early, formative stage of his thought. There also seem to be different strata in the manuscripts themselves, reflecting different stages in his thought. Often the argument is quite obscure.

In spite of these difficulties, the ST can be very instructive. Many of the central theses of the *Ethics* are already present in this work; it is interesting to see the form they take here. Like Descartes, Spinoza holds that God exists necessarily. He accepts versions of the ontological and causal arguments Descartes had used to prove this in the *Meditations*. The work does not yet have the distinctively Spinozistic arguments used in the *Ethics*. He defines God as a being consisting of infinite attributes, each perfect in its kind. This is not a definition Descartes had explicitly given, though it is one he might have accepted. From the correspondence we know Spinoza thought it followed from the definition Descartes did give, that God is by definition a supremely perfect being.

Unlike Descartes, and anticipating the *Ethics* (though often with different arguments), Spinoza contends that no substance can be finite; that there are no two substances of the same kind; that one substance cannot produce another; that God is an immanent cause; that both thought *and* extension are attributes of God; that man is not a substance, but a mode of substançe; that the human soul (or mind) is a mode of thought, the idea of its body, which is, a mode of extension. Spinoza also argues in this work for theses which appear in the *Ethics* without argument, such as the identification of God with Nature. Early in the ST he contends that, because no attributes can exist in the divine intellect which do not exist in Nature, Nature must be a being which consists of infinite attributes, each perfect in its kind. So Nature satisfies the definition of God.

The identification of God with Nature and the claim that God is an extended substance are only two of several claims Spinoza makes in this work which he might have expected to arouse theological opposition. Also provocative are his contentions that because God is supremely perfect, he could not omit doing what he does; and that the properties of God commonly included in lists of his attributes—omnipotence, omniscience, eternity, simplicity, and so on—are not, strictly speaking, divine *attributes*, which tell us what God is in himself, but only modes, which can be attributed to him in virtue of some or all of his attributes. Omniscience, for example, presupposes thought; so it must be a mode, not an attribute; but it applies to God only in virtue of the attribute of thought, not in virtue of the attribute of extension. Eternity, on the other hand, would apply to God in virtue of all of his attributes. But it is not an attribute, because it does not tell us *what* God is. It only tells us something about the manner of God's existence, that he exists timelessly and immutably. Spinoza also argues that, because God is omnipotent, he does not give laws to men which they are capable of breaking (who could disobey the will of an omnipotent being?); that he does not love or hate his creatures; and that he does not make himself known to man through words, miracles, or any other finite things.

The God of the ST, like the God of the *Ethics*, is a philosopher's God, an eternal first cause of all things, quite remote from the God who revealed himself to the Jews through his prophets, chose them as his people, performed miracles on their behalf, rewarded them when they obeyed his laws, and punished them when they disobeyed. Presumably something like this is what Spinoza meant when he said to the elders of the synagogue that God exists "only philosophically" and that the law of Moses is not a true law, that it does not, as Judaism supposes, represent a divine command which people may either obey or disobey at their peril.

If there is no divine law which is binding on us, how, then, should we conduct ourselves? Here Spinoza develops at considerable length a theme he only hinted at it in the TEI: that we must set aside worldly goods to seek a good which can give us joy unmixed with sadness, transferring our love for finite, transitory things to something eternal and infinite, perfecting our nature by acquiring knowledge of "the union the mind has with the whole of nature." Progressing towards this perfection requires us to rid ourselves of irrational passions, which depend on the lowest form of cognition, opinion.

Like the *Ethics*, the ST (normally) counts three forms of cognition, not the four counted in the TEI. The first, opinion, combines the first two forms of perception enumerated in the TEI: beliefs we form on the basis of what others have told us and beliefs based on what the TEI called "random experience." As an example of an irrational passion based on opinion, Spinoza offers the hatred which Jews, Christians, and Muslims often have for one another, based on unreliable reports about the others' religions and customs, and/or hasty generalizations from an inadequate acquaintance with members of the other religion. 'Opinion' in the ST corresponds to what Spinoza calls 'imagination' in the *Ethics*.

We can make progress towards overcoming these irrational passions if we pass from opinion to what the ST sometimes calls 'belief' and sometimes calls 'true belief.' However designated, this stage of cognition involves more than what the phrases suggest: in Spinoza's usage 'true belief' implies not only that the belief is true but that the believer has a firm rational basis for it. True belief, the second of three modes of cognition in the ST, is equivalent to the third of the four modes of cognition in the TEI (and to what Spinoza calls 'reason' in the *Ethics*). So it would involve rational demonstration from certain premises.

How does true belief enable us to overcome our irrational passions? Partly, it seems, by eliminating beliefs formed through unreliable ways of perceiving things, but partly also by enabling us to recognize that man is a part of nature (where this implies that man must follow the laws of nature, that his actions are as necessary as those of any other thing in nature) and partly by teaching us that good and evil are not something inherent in the things we judge to be good and evil, but that they are related to human nature. The good is what helps us to attain what our intellect conceives to be perfection for a human being; evil is what hinders our attaining it (or does not assist it).

But as in the TEI, Spinoza does not think this form of cognition can take us all the way to our goal. That requires the highest form, which this work usually calls 'clear knowledge,' or 'science,' which we achieve when we are not merely convinced by reasons but are aware of and enjoy the thing itself. If we achieve this kind of knowledge of God, we will come to love Him and be united with Him, as we now love and are united with the body. In our union with Him, we will be released from the body and achieve an eternal and immutable constancy.

This affirmation that we can achieve immortality looks like a startling departure from one of the views for which Spinoza was condemned by the synagogue—that the soul dies with the body. In other respects the ST seems to remain committed to the early heresies and to enable us to understand Spinoza's reasons for holding them. In this instance, it looks as though Spinoza has reverted to what his community regarded as orthodox belief. But as we will see when we come to the *Ethics*, it does not appear that the 'immortality' Spinoza allows is a personal immortality.

In the preceding section we noted a puzzle about Spinoza's early metaphysics: How are the "first elements of the whole of nature," which the TEI said were the "source and origin of nature," related to the categories of Spinoza's later metaphysics? If the first elements are "uncreated things," then Spinoza's theory of definition in the TEI implies that they exist in themselves, which would mean that they are substances. But the first elements are evidently many; and there is supposed to be only one substance.

In the ST the answer appears to be that the first elements of nature are the attributes, which Spinoza defines as existing through themselves and known through themselves, in contrast with the modes, which exist through and are understood through the attributes of which they are modes. So the attributes taken individually satisfy the definition of substance that Spinoza will give in the *Ethics*. The reason there is nevertheless only one substance is that the many attributes are attributes of one being, God or Nature.

The ST also tells us what the other "fixed and eternal" things of the TEI might be. Here for the first time Spinoza makes his distinction between *natura naturans*, defined as a being we conceive clearly and distinctly through itself (all the attributes, or God), and *natura naturata*, the modes which depend on and are understood through God. He divides *natura naturata* into universal and particular modes, identifying only one universal mode in each attribute: motion in extension and intellect in thought. These he describes as infinite, eternal, and immutable, proceeding immediately from God, and in turn the cause of the particular modes, which are 'corruptible': they are changeable, have a beginning, and will have an end. The idea underlying the identification of motion as a "universal" mode of extension is that, in accordance with the mechanistic program of the new philosophy, the particular properties of individual extended objects are a function of the different degrees of motion of their component parts.

RIJNSBURG YEARS (1661–1663)

By mid-summer of 1661 Spinoza had moved to Rijnsburg, a quiet village near Leiden, which had been the center of the Collegiant sect. The extant correspondence begins during this period, so we are much better informed about these years in Spinoza's life. Much of the correspondence is with his Amsterdam friends, but his correspondents also include Henry Oldenburg, who became the first secretary of the nascent Royal Society, and Robert Boyle, the British chemist and advocate of the mechanical philosophy. By the fall Spinoza had begun to put his philosophy into geometric form. An early experiment with a geometric presentation appears as an appendix to the ST; another version can be reconstructed from the correspondence with Oldenburg, whom Spinoza had sent a draft which improved on the draft in the appendix of the ST.

In the following year, Spinoza undertook to teach Cartesian philosophy to a student named Casearius. He prepared for Casearius a geometric presentation of Part II of Descartes' *Principles of Philosophy*, which deals with the foundations of Cartesian physics, along with some thoughts on topics in metaphysics. When his friends learned of this work, they urged him to add to it a geometric presentation of Part I of Descartes' *Principles*; Lodewijk Meyer offered to write a preface for the work and help him polish it for publication. Spinoza agreed, hoping that by establishing himself as an expert in Cartesian philosophy, he would ease the way toward the publication of his own ideas.

PARTS I AND II OF DESCARTES' *PRINCIPLES OF PHILOSOPHY* DEMONSTRATED GEOMETRICALLY (1663)

Although the preface Meyer wrote for this work proclaimed that Spinoza's work was no more than an exposition of Descartes' *Principles*—and that this was true even for the appendix, which Spinoza called *Metaphysical Thoughts*—in fact his work is more than that. For one thing, Spinoza also draws on other Cartesian works in constructing his account of Descartes' philosophy. Sometimes his reconstruction implies a criticism of the way Descartes himself argued for his positions. Sometimes he is openly critical of Descartes' assumptions. And sometimes (particularly in the appendix) he uses this venue to develop his own ideas, independently of Descartes. An interesting example involves the question of miracles. He offers a reason for doubting them along the lines he subsequently published in the TPT. But in this work he does not endorse the argument; he merely leaves it as a problem for the theologians.

Perhaps his most important differences with Descartes in this mainly expository work are those he asked Meyer to call attention to in his preface: that he does not think the will is distinct from the intellect, or endowed with the freedom Descartes attributed to it; and that he does not think the human mind is a substance, any more than the human body is a substance. Just as the human body is "extension determined in a certain way, according to the laws of extended nature, by motion and rest, so also the human mind, or soul, is … thought determined in a certain way, according to the laws of thinking nature, by ideas" (Gebhardt I, 132). He also disassociates himself from the Cartesian claim that some things—such as the nature of the infinite—surpass human understanding. He claims that these and many other things can be conceived clearly and distinctly, provided the intellect is guided in the search for truth along a different path from the one Descartes followed. He does not say precisely how that path would have to differ, but he does say that the foundations of the sciences Descartes laid are not sufficient to solve all the problems arise in metaphysics. We need to find different foundations for the sciences.

VOORBURG (1663–C.1670)

In April 1663, shortly before the publication of his exposition of Descartes, Spinoza moved from Rijnsburg to Voorburg, a village outside the Hague. During his first two years in Voorburg, Spinoza must have worked intensively on his *Ethics*, for by the summer of 1665 he had a draft far enough advanced that he was thinking about finding someone to translate it into Dutch. Having grown up in a community whose main languages were Spanish, Portuguese, and Hebrew, Spinoza did not feel entirely comfortable writing philosophy in Dutch. In 1665 he seems to have conceived the *Ethics* as being divided into three parts, the last of which would probably have corresponded roughly to the last three parts of the final version.

During this period he also entered into a correspondence with a Dutch merchant and would-be philosopher, Willem van Blijenbergh, who had read his exposition of Descartes and had many questions for the author. Van Blijenbergh wondered about the existence of evil, and about how, if evil existed, this fact could be reconciled with the creation of the world by God—and indeed, its continuous creation, from one moment to the next. He wanted to know what it meant to say that evil is only a negation in relation to God, and how he could distinguish which portions of *Descartes' Principles* merely articulated Descartes' views and which ones expressed Spinoza's views. He wondered what Spinoza's view of the relation between mind and body implied about the immortality of the soul.

Van Blijenbergh was a committed Christian who believed that scripture was the ultimate authority on any philosophical question it addressed. His approach to scripture was the opposite of Meyer's: If his reason persuaded him of something contrary to what scripture taught, he would mistrust his reason rather than scripture. This was not a promising basis for a dialogue with Spinoza. Spinoza found the exchange of letters an unproductive use of his time and broke it off as soon as he could. But the correspondence with Van Blijenbergh seems to have persuaded him that he must diminish the authority of scripture before he could get a fair hearing for his own philosophy. By the fall of that year he had set the *Ethics* aside to return to work on his *Theological-Political Treatise*, which he intended to "expose the prejudices of the theologians," clear himself of the charge of atheism, and argue for freedom of thought and expression, which he saw as threatened by the authority of the preachers.

Another stimulus for this shift in his writing may have been an incident involving his landlord, Daniel Tydeman, a painter and member of the Reformed Church. The minister of the local church had died, and Tydeman was on the committee appointed to select his successor. Tydeman seems to have been a theological liberal, perhaps with Collegiant inclinations. The committee nominated a man they found sympathetic theologically but encountered opposition from conservatives in the congregation, who sought to discredit the committee's candidate by claiming, among other things, that Tydeman had living in his house a former Jew, now turned atheist, who "mocked all religions" and was "a disgraceful element in the republic." The committee's candidate was rejected.

These were difficult years for the Dutch Republic. The plague had returned to Europe in 1663 and had been so virulent that Spinoza felt it necessary to leave Voorburg to spend several months of the winter of 1664 at the country house of relatives of a friend. Competition between the Dutch and the English for control of maritime trade led to war between the two countries from 1664 to 1667, the second such war in a little over a decade. No sooner had that war ended than there were threats of a new war with France, whose king, Louis XIV, had expansionist ambitions. And there was tension between the leaders of the Republic and the princes of the house of Orange.

This tension went back to the early days of the Republic. In the mid-sixteenth century the area now occupied by the independent nations of the Netherlands, Belgium, and Luxemburg was a unit within the Holy Roman Empire, ruled by the King of Spain. Toward the end of the century, the seven northern provinces (the modern Netherlands) succeeded in breaking away from Spanish rule, largely under the leadership of William I, Prince of Orange and Stadholder of the provinces of Holland, Utrecht, and Zeeland, though his son, Maurice of Nassau, also played a key role. The Stadholders were originally governors of the provinces, representing the Spanish crown and charged with the administration of justice. During the revolt against Spain, the Stadholders of the house of Orange sided with the rebels and provided the military leadership the provinces needed. Sometimes they worked in collaboration with the States-General, an assembly representing all the provinces. Sometimes they competed with the leadership of the States-General for power. Later princes of Orange developed monarchic ambitions.

In the late 1640s the Prince of Orange was William II, who unsuccessfully opposed the Treaty of Westphalia (1648), which ended the eighty-year war for Dutch independence from Spain (as well as the Thirty Years War, which had embroiled most of Europe since before Spinoza was born). The States-General, dominated by the province of Holland and Dutch mercantile interests, favored the treaty. When William died unexpectedly in 1650, the position of the Orange party was weakened. His son, William III, was not born until just after his father's death. For many years the minority of the young prince provided the leaders of the States-General with an excuse to leave the office of Stadholder vacant. The functions the Stadholder had performed fell to the States-General, under the leadership of Jan de Witt, who generally had great success in defending his country against many challenges. But as William III neared adulthood, the tensions between the De Witt party and the Orange party increased, particularly when the affairs of the Republic were not going well, as was the case at the end of the 1660s.

Spinoza was sympathetic to the De Witt regime, strongly preferring it to the Orangist alternative. But some historians have exaggerated his closeness to De Witt, trusting too much to contemporary accounts. De Witt's political enemies, bent on discrediting him, sometimes claimed a close association between him and Spinoza—suggesting, for example, that De Witt had assisted in the editing and publishing of the TPT. And Spinoza's friends sometimes told similar stories—for example, that De Witt had often visited Spinoza to discuss affairs of state—apparently with the intention of magnifying Spinoza's reputation by associating him with a political leader whom many regarded as a hero. Though De Witt and Spinoza would have agreed in opposing the monarchic ambitions of the Prince of Orange, Spinoza was a democrat, whereas De Witt favored an oligarchic republic. They would have agreed in opposing the desire of the more conservative members of the clergy, in alliance with the princes of Orange, to enforce a strict Calvinist orthodoxy. But Spinoza favored a very expansive freedom of thought, whereas De Witt recognized the necessity, if only as a matter of practical politics, of making accommodations to the Reformed Church.

In the *Theological-Political Treatise* (TPT) Spinoza speaks in glowing terms about the freedom of the Dutch Republic:

> Since we happen to have that rare good fortune, that we live in a Republic in which everyone is granted complete freedom of judgment, and is permitted to worship God according to his understanding, and in which nothing is thought to be dearer or sweeter than freedom, I believed I would be doing something neither unwelcome, nor useless, if I showed not only that this freedom can be granted without harm to piety and the peace of the Republic, but also that it cannot be abolished unless piety and the Peace of the Republic are abolished.
>
> (GEBHART III, 7)

But Spinoza knew all too well that the Republic was not as free as he claimed.

In 1668 his friend Adriaan Koerbagh had published *A Flower Garden of All Kinds of Loveliness*, ostensibly a treatise explaining the meanings of foreign words which had become part of Dutch but in fact a critique of all the organized religions known in the Dutch Republic. In this acerbically written book, Koerbagh anticipated a number of the claims Spinoza made two years later in the TPT: He denied that the books of the Bible were written by the men to whom they were traditionally ascribed; he proposed that Ezra, the postexilic priest and scribe who wrote the book of Ezra, was responsible for the existing form of the Hebrew Bible, having compiled and attempted to reconcile the inconsistent manuscripts which had come down to him; and he argued that a proper interpretation of the Bible would require a thorough knowledge of the languages it was written in and the historical contexts its authors wrote in. Like Spinoza, he did not deny that there was something solid and consistent with reason in scripture; but that solid element in scripture was not its theology.

Koerbagh was arrested—along with his brother, Jan, who was suspected of complicity in the work—and, with the encouragement of the Reformed clergy, tried for blasphemy by the civil authorities in Amsterdam. Jan was released after a few weeks, but Adriaan was found guilty after a lengthy inquest, during which he was questioned about his association with Spinoza and Van den Enden. Sentenced to a fine of 4,000 guilders and ten years in prison, to be followed by ten years' exile, he died a little more than a year after his imprisonment from the harsh conditions in the prison.

The influence of the Reformed clergy on Dutch politics perhaps explains why Spinoza and the other members of his circle showed the interest they did in the work of Hobbes. Probably Spinoza had known some of Hobbes' work for years, since Hobbes' first published work of political philosophy, *De cive* (On the Citizen), had been available in a language he could read since 1642. It is likely that this would have been one of the works Van den Enden called to his attention when he was encouraging his interest in the new philosophy. But before 1667, Spinoza's inability to read English would have prevented him from gaining first-hand knowledge of *Leviathan*, which developed Hobbes' religious views more fully than *De cive* had. Two events in the late 1660s changed that: in 1667 Abraham van Berckel, a friend of Spinoza's (and of the Koerbagh brothers), translated *Leviathan* into Dutch; and in 1668 an edition of Hobbes' complete Latin works (including a Latin translation of *Leviathan*) was published in the Netherlands. Although it may seem paradoxical to Anglophone readers of Hobbes, who think of him primarily as a defender of absolute monarchy, Hobbes' theory was attractive to republicans in the United Provinces because of his advocacy of state control over religion. In Holland in the 1660s conservative Christianity was a problem for them, much as it had been for the royalists in England in the 1640s.

THE THEOLOGICAL-POLITICAL TREATISE (1670)

It is no accident that Spinoza treats religion and politics in one work. The preface to the TPT illustrates one way in which these subjects are linked. Spinoza begins with reflections on the psychological origin of superstition, which he attributes to the uncertainty of our lives and the role fortune plays in them. Much of what happens to us depends on circumstances over which we have no control. We do not know whether things will go well or badly for us, and we fear what may happen if they go badly. So we would like to believe in some story which offers us the hope of gaining control over our lives. In this mood we may believe that the future can be predicted from the entrails of birds or affected by prayer and the performance of rituals. That belief puts us at the mercy of unscrupulous priests and the politicians who use them. "The greatest secret of monarchic rule," Spinoza writes in the preface, "is to keep men deceived, and to cloak in the specious name of religion the fear by which they must be checked, so that they will fight for slavery as they would for salvation, and will think it not shameful, but a most honorable achievement, to give their life and blood that one man may have a ground for boasting."

If the politicians use the priests to provide divine authority for their rule, the priests also use the politicians, trading their support for the enactment of laws condemning opinions contrary to those they endorse. These condemnations enhance their authority, giving official sanction to the idea that the priests have a special expertise in matters of religion. Spinoza speaks with respect of Christianity, which he sees as a religion whose true spirit calls for love, peace, restraint, and honesty toward all. But he deplores the fact that the Christians of his day are no more prone to display these virtues than the members of any other religion, a fact he attributes to the wealth, honor, and power accorded to its clergy. These incentives attract the worst kind of men to the ministry, men who for their personal ends are willing to exploit the credulity of the people for personal gain, to teach them contempt for reason, and to stir up hatred of those who disagree with them.

Spinoza proposes to remedy this evil by challenging the assumptions with which the priests approach scripture. They assume as a principle of interpretation that scripture is, in every passage, true and divine. Since scripture often appears to be inconsistent, they invent forced, reconciling interpretations whose only value is their apparent smoothing over of contradictions. And because scripture often appears to be contrary to reason in other ways, they are prone to invent metaphorical readings of scripture to make it conform to their beliefs. This procedure reverses the proper order of things. We should seek first to determine the meaning of scripture and only after that should we make a judgment about its truth and divinity.

But how should we determine the meaning of scripture? Spinoza's fundamental rule is that we should attribute to scripture as its teaching nothing we have not clearly understood from its history. By a "history of scripture" Spinoza understands, first, an account of the vocabulary and grammar of the language in which its books were written and which its authors spoke. This will tell us what meanings its words can have in ordinary usage and what ways of combining those words are legitimate. Second, a history of scripture must organize what scripture says topically, so that we can easily find all the passages bearing on the same subject; it must also note any passages which seem ambiguous or obscure or inconsistent with one another. Next, it must describe the circumstances under which the book was written, who its author was, what his character was, when he wrote and for what reason, for what audience, and in what language. And, finally, it must tell us how the book was first received, into whose hands it fell, how many different readings there are of various passages, and how it came to be accepted as sacred. What Spinoza is proposing here is that we apply to the interpretation of scripture the scholarly criteria Renaissance humanists had applied to the classics of pagan antiquity (with the exception that for the pagan works the question of their acceptance as sacred does not arise).

The result of applying these rules does not inspire confidence in the historical accuracy of scripture: the historical books were not written by the authors to whom tradition ascribed them—Moses, Joshua, Samuel, and so on—but were compiled by a much later editor, whose knowledge of the events these books described was based on manuscripts which had come into his possession but are now lost. Spinoza conjectures that this editor was

Ezra. Moreover, not only was Ezra's knowledge of the early history of the Jews second-hand knowledge of long-ago events, but he also reworked the texts to smooth out inconsistencies and make them tell the story he wanted to tell: that when the people of Israel obeyed God's laws, they prospered, whereas evil befell them when they disobeyed.

Not all of Spinoza's conclusions about the Bible were radically new. In the twelfth century Abraham ibn Ezra had hinted in his commentary on the Torah that the first five books of the Bible, in the form in which we have them, were written much later than the events they described. In the 1650s Isaac de la Peyrère and Thomas Hobbes had drawn similar conclusions more openly. But Spinoza was more systematic, thorough, and blunt than any of these predecessors. Unlike La Peyrère and Hobbes, he had the advantage of knowing the texts well in the original Hebrew, of knowing the medieval Jewish interpretive tradition, and of having a well-developed theory of interpretation, a theory which set a new standard for Biblical scholarship. Unlike Ibn Ezra, he did not pull his punches:

> Those who consider the Bible, as it is, as a letter God has sent men from heaven, will doubtless cry out that I have committed a sin against the Holy Ghost, because I have maintained that the word of God is faulty, mutilated, corrupted and inconsistent, which we have only fragments of it, and finally, which the original text of the covenant God made with the Jews has been lost.
>
> (GEBHARDT III, 138)

It's hardly surprising that when Hobbes read the TPT, he commented that he had not dared to write so boldly.

Spinoza did not object only that our knowledge of biblical history was based on unreliable texts, he also criticized biblical theology as embodying the opinions of men whose conception of God was based on the imagination rather than the intellect. The prophets, he argued, were outstanding for their personalities, their moral qualities, and their knack for expressing themselves in powerful language. But they were not philosophers. They thought of God as the maker of all things, existing at all times, who surpassed all other beings in power; but they did not understand that God was omniscient and omnipresent, or that He directed all human actions by his decree. They imagined that He had a body, which was visible (though you would die if you looked upon it), and that He had emotions, like compassion, kindness, and jealousy. Moreover, they were not strict monotheists. They believed that there were other Gods who were subordinate to the God of Israel and that He had entrusted the care of other nations to these lesser Gods. So their conceptions of God were very inadequate. And they often accommodated their theology to the even more primitive capacities of their audience.

In his rejection of Biblical theology, Spinoza even goes so far as to suggest that it is anthropomorphism to think of God as having a mind. What, then, can God be? Spinoza never answers that question directly, but he does say that God's guidance is "the fixed and immutable order of nature." When we say that all things are ordered according to the decree and guidance of God, this is the same as saying that all things happen according to the laws of nature. It is a natural consequence of this view that there can be no miracles, no divine interventions in the order of nature. If there were an event contrary to the laws of nature, that would be an event contrary to divine decree. If God is omnipotent, this is impossible.

God's omnipotence also makes it irrational to conceive of God as a lawgiver of the kind portrayed in the Bible. The biblical God is conceived as being like a king who issues commands which his subjects have the power to obey or disobey. They will prosper if they obey and suffer if they disobey. But the laws which are truly divine are principles of natural necessity—like the laws according to which motion is transferred from one body to another in a collision. No one has any choice but to "obey" these laws; it is not a contingent matter whether someone acts in accordance with them. (Nevertheless, even after stating this conclusion quite clearly early in the TPT, Spinoza regularly adopts some of this anthropomorphic language himself, later in his work, when he argues that the primary purpose of scripture is to encourage obedience to God, not to inculcate correct beliefs about God.)

Although Spinoza questions much of the history and theology of the Hebrew Bible—and delicately avoids any extended discussion of the Christian New Testament—he denies that he has spoken unworthily of scripture. Scripture is divine and sacred when it moves men toward devotion toward God, as it can do and often does. But it is not inherently sacred. If men neglect it, or interpret it superstitiously, as they can and often do, it is no more sacred than any other writing. There is a core ethical teaching in scripture which is so pervasive that it cannot have been corrupted by any misinterpretation: that we should love God above all else, and love our neighbors as ourselves; that we should practice justice, aid the poor, kill no one, covet no one's possessions, and so on. These prescriptions deserve our utmost respect. If we seek to follow them wholeheartedly, we will be treating scripture as sacred, whether we think of those prescriptions as the commands of a heavenly king or regard them (in the manner of Hobbes) as theorems about what is conducive to our self-preservation and to living in the best way possible.

Spinoza does not endorse only the ethical teachings of scripture. He also thinks there are core theological teachings which are central to scripture and which are in some sense true: for example, that God exists; that he provides for all; that he is omnipotent; that things go well for those who observe their religious duties but badly for the unprincipled; that our salvation depends only on God's grace; and so on. In his way, he does endorse these teachings. But his approval of them is hedged. There is a popular way of understanding them which assumes that the God of whom they speak is a changeable personal agent who acts from freedom of the will, who prescribes laws as a prince does, and who has desires which humans will frustrate if they disobey his commands. And there is a philosophical way of understanding them, according to which God is the fixed and immutable order of nature who acts from the necessity of his own nature and whose "laws" are eternal truths, the violation of which is followed only by natural punishments, not supernatural ones. Presumably the philosophical way of understanding these doctrines is the right way to understand them from the standpoint of truth. But the popular way of understanding them is not to be despised *if* it produces conduct in accordance with the ethical teachings of scripture. If it does, it is to be respected, honored, and encouraged.

Insofar as Spinoza endorses a minimalist theology, which avoids most controversial doctrines, concentrating on those which elicit broad agreement and which emphasizes the importance of works as the path to salvation, the TPT is in the tradition of Erasmian liberalism. This outlook provides him with a religious argument for tolerating diversity of opinion in the realm of religion. Philosophy and theology are separate areas, neither of which should be the handmaiden of the other. Theology is concerned with revelation, which in turn is concerned with obedience, not with speculative truth. In judging whether or not a person's faith is pious, we must look only to his works. If they are good, his faith is as it should be.

In the political portions of the TPT, Spinoza supplements this religious argument for freedom of thought and expression with a political argument. He seeks to show, from fundamental political principles, that allowing this freedom is compatible, not only with religion, but also with the well-being of the state. Indeed, he will go further and argue that the well-being of the state *requires* freedom of thought and expression.

The foundations of his political thought look very Hobbesian; the liberal conclusions he draws from them seem rather un-Hobbesian. Like Hobbes, Spinoza believes that the condition of man in the state of nature—that is, in any state where there is no effective government—is wretched and insecure. Human beings are very egoistic. Everyone seeks what considerations he would develop to be to his own advantage, with little concern for the well-being of others or the long-term consequences of his actions or the moral repercussions for civil society. Moreover, humans generally have an impoverished understanding of what is in their interest, valuing such goods as wealth, honor, and sensual pleasure more than they should, and knowledge and the control of their passions less than they should. If they did not have laws to restrain them, laws which alter their calculations of self-interest, they would not practice justice and loving-kindness; their lives would be full of conflict, hatred, anger, deception, and misery. In the state of nature there is, by definition, no human law to restrain them. And Spinoza takes himself to have shown that God cannot be conceived as a lawgiver. It follows that in the state of nature, though each person is permitted to do whatever he has the power to do, he has no joy from this freedom.

But, like Hobbes, Spinoza also assumes that people are smart enough to see that their condition in the state of nature is wretched and to see what they must do to escape it: create a civil society by agreeing with other people to transfer their power to defend themselves to society, creating a collective entity which will have sufficient power to make and enforce laws for the common protection and advantage. Not only will this arrangement provide them with security, but it will also make possible cooperative enterprises which improve the lives of everyone in the state, enabling them to seek the highest good: the knowledge of things through their first causes, that is, the knowledge of God, which leads to the love of God. (Positing this—or anything else—as our highest good is very un-Hobbesian.)

In some respects, Spinoza goes further than Hobbes in his conception of what the creation of the state involves. He thinks that when individuals agree to form a civil society, they must surrender to it whatever rights they possessed in the state of nature. If they wanted to reserve certain rights to themselves, they would have to establish some means of protecting those rights; establishing these means would divide and consequently destroy the sovereignty of the state. (Although Hobbes favored absolute sovereignty, he argued that some rights, like the right to defend oneself against attack, were inalienable.) Just as Spinoza thinks that the right of individuals in the state of nature is limited only by their power, so the right of the state is limited only by its power. Since it is not, and cannot be, bound by any laws, what it can do, it may do.

Is the formation of the state, then, really as rational an act as Spinoza presents it as being? The state, which can call upon the collective might of all (or at least, most) of its members, seems potentially much more dangerous to each of its members than any individual in the state of nature. As Locke wrote in response to the similar views of Hobbes, "this is to think that men are so foolish that they take care to avoid what mischiefs may be done them by polecats, or foxes, but are content, nay think it safety, to be devoured by lions." But Spinoza thinks people can rationally run this risk because he thinks that even in a monarchy or aristocracy the state will normally avoid commanding things contrary to the interests of the people. If it did, it would risk losing its power and hence its right to command.

Moreover, in the TPT Spinoza is mainly thinking of the state which emerges from this process as a democratic one, that is, one in which decisions of the state are to be made by a general assembly of all the people. He acknowledges that in certain circumstances other forms of political organization may be desirable. In his posthumously published *Political Treatise* (PT) he recommended ways of structuring monarchies and aristocracies which provide the citizens with protection from their rulers. But in the TPT he focuses most of his attention on democracy, which he regards as the most natural form of government.

In the state of nature all men were equal; they retain that equality in civil society when the state is a democracy because no one in a democracy is subject to his equals. In the state of nature, all people are free because they are subject to no laws; they retain their freedom in civil society insofar as they are subject only to laws in whose formation they have participated—laws, moreover, guided by the principle that the well-being of the people is the supreme law, not the well-being of the ruler. A man can be free even when he is acting according to a command, if the command is rationally aimed at his advantage. Indeed, he is truly free only when he is acting wholeheartedly according to the guidance of reason. (Unlike Hobbes, Spinoza favors a positive conception of liberty, not a negative one which regards it merely as the absence of impediments to the agent's preferred actions.) Rule by one man, or by a few men, might be justifiable if that man (or those men) had some ability which went beyond ordinary human nature. But Spinoza seems to think that this is not normally the case. And, like Machiavelli, Spinoza thinks that the people are less prone to unwise actions than are autocratic rulers.

To those of us who are accustomed to a system in which the actions of government are constrained by a written constitution which provides protection for individual liberties, it may seem that a political theory that calls for men to give up all their rights to the state is an unpromising basis for a defense of freedom of thought and expression—even if the state is a democratic one. Spinoza may have thought, as Rousseau did, that if the legislators are making laws which bind themselves as much as they do others, that fact will provide a sufficient incentive for them not to impose undue burdens. But this thought seems to ignore the possibility that a majority will make decisions that it believes to be for the common good, even if the minority regards them as tyrannical.

In the TPT Spinoza's primary remedy for this problem is not an institutional one. He relies on the facts that in his theory the right of the state is limited by its power and that its power is inevitably limited by the recalcitrance of human nature. Some of the things a state might wish to command are things its citizens cannot change at will, such as their beliefs and their emotions. The threat of punishment for believing or loving as a person does cannot cause that person to believe or love otherwise. But if the state lacks the power to control its citizens' beliefs and actions, then it also lacks the right to control these things.

The fact that the state lacks the right to control what it lacks the power to control, in itself, is no protection. But Spinoza emphasizes that it is impossible for people to surrender their right (or transfer their power) to the state in such a way that they are not feared by the people to whom they have surrendered their right. Any government is in greater danger from its own citizens than it is from any external enemy, for its control over its citizens and its ability to respond to enemies both depend ultimately on the voluntary obedience of a substantial number of its own citizens. Hobbes put the point well in *Behemoth*, his history of the English Civil War: "The power of the mighty hath no foundation but in the opinion and belief of the people.… If men know not their duty, what is there that can force them to obey the laws? An army, you will say? But what shall force the army?" Spinoza would almost certainly not have known *Behemoth*—which was finished in 1668 but first published in a pirated edition in

1679, and then only in English—but he might have come to appreciate the basic point by reading and reflection on Hobbesian works he did know, or by reflection on the works of classical historians like Tacitus and Quintus Curtius, whose writings may also have helped Hobbes see this point.

If all governments are vulnerable to destruction from within, those which seek to rule by violence are the most vulnerable. And no rulers are more violent than those which make it a crime to hold controversial opinions, since they criminalize behavior the citizen cannot change at will. When the government seeks to do what it cannot do, not only does it exceed its right, it also creates resentment among those citizens who feel they are being treated unjustly. It cannot do this without harm to its own power to maintain itself. The most the government can accomplish is to suppress the expression of opinion, not the opinions themselves. But to the extent that it succeeds in suppressing expression, it creates a culture in which people think one thing and say another. It destroys the honesty necessary to the well-being of the state, encouraging deception, flattery and treachery, all of which are destructive of the social order.

What is particularly pernicious about this result is that it makes enemies of just those citizens whose education, integrity of character, and virtue would make them most useful to the state. Spinoza is sometimes portrayed as the epitome of cool rationality, but on this subject he is passionate:

> What greater evil can be imagined for the State than that honorable men should be exiled as unprincipled because they hold different opinions and do not know how to pretend to be what they are not? What, I ask, can be more fatal than that men should be considered enemies and condemned to death, not because of any wickedness or crime, but because they have a mind worthy of a free man? Or that the gallows, the scourge of the evil, should become the noblest stage for displaying the utmost endurance and a model of virtue, to the conspicuous shame of the authorities?
>
> (GEBHARDT III, 245)

Spinoza may be thinking here of cases like that of Judah the Faithful, whom he refers to in his correspondence. Judah was a Spanish *converso* (that is, a Jew forcibly converted to Christianity) who reverted to Judaism. Burned at the stake by the Inquisition when Spinoza was twelve, his case was well-known in the Amsterdam Jewish community. As the flames roared up around him, he sang a hymn which begins "I offer up my soul to you, Oh Lord." He died still singing this hymn. Spinoza cites this case in response to a Christian correspondent who tried to persuade him of the truth of Christianity by citing the many martyrs who had died for their faith. Spinoza's reply was that Judaism claimed, with justice, to count many more martyrs to its faith.

THE HAGUE (C. 1670–1677)

Sometime during the winter of 1669–1670, Spinoza moved to the Hague, first renting a room from a widow and, after about a year, relocating to the home of the painter Hendrik van der Spyck, where he was to live for the rest of his life. In early 1670 the TPT was published in Amsterdam by Jan Rieuwertsz, but with a title page claiming publication in Hamburg, by a fictitious publisher named Heinrich Künraht. Reaction was immediate and vehement. In June the ecclesiastic court of the Reformed Church in Amsterdam condemned the work as "blasphemous and dangerous." Similar denunciations followed from church groups in The Hague, Leiden, and Utrecht. Nor was it only conservative Calvinists who were shocked by his work. Theological liberals, including those sympathetic to the new philosophy, such as Frans Burman and Philip van Limborch, also opposed it. Burman called it an "utterly pestilential book" which must be attacked and destroyed. Between 1670 and 1672 the church authorities repeatedly called for the suppression of the TPT, along with Meyer's *Philosophy, the Interpreter of Holy Scripture* and Hobbes' *Leviathan.*

Nevertheless, there was no formal prohibition of the TPT until 1674, and it did in fact circulate widely among the learned audience to whom it was addressed. This does not mean that the civil authorities tolerated it. De Witt's position seems to have been that the city governments had ample authority, under anti-Socinian legislation passed in 1653, to confiscate copies of Spinoza's book. There was no need to increase the notoriety of this book, and its sales, by calling special attention to it. In many parts of the Republic the civil authorities did make efforts to suppress it, as they did in the other countries to which it spread. That these efforts did not prevent the work from being widely read was due to the ingenuity and dedication of Spinoza's publisher. However, when Spinoza learned that Rieuwertsz had commissioned a Dutch translation of the TPT which would have made it available to a wider audience, he asked that it be withheld, as it was until sixteen years after his death.

1672 has been called a "year of disaster" in the history of the Dutch Republic. In March, England resumed its naval war with the Republic, attacking a Dutch convoy. In April France declared war. In May the French army began its invasion, followed quickly by two German armies, under the Prince-Bishop of Münster and the Elector of Cologne. The overwhelming forces of the invaders quickly conquered most of the Dutch provinces. Only by opening the dykes to flood a large swath of land, from the Zuider Zee in the north to the river Waal in the south, was the government able to prevent the invaders from occupying the province of Holland.

These were extreme and unpopular measures. The people were deeply divided between those who wanted to surrender and those who wanted to resist. In June, Jan de Witt, wounded in an assassination attempt, resigned his position as Grand Pensionary, leader of the States of Holland. William III had been appointed captain-general of the army in February; in July he became Stadholder of the provinces of Zeeland and Holland, and the dominant political power in the Republic. In August De Witt's brother, Cornelis, who had been imprisoned on a charge of plotting against the Stadholder's life, was acquitted. When an angry mob gathered outside the prison where he was being held, Jan went to the prison to escort his brother to safety. The mob murdered both brothers, dismembering their bodies, roasting them and eating them. When Spinoza learned of this, he tried to rush into the street, carrying a sign reading *ultimi barbarorum*, "the worst of barbarians." Fortunately, his landlord prevented him from carrying out this act of protest.

In 1673 Spinoza had an opportunity to leave the Netherlands when the University of Heidelberg offered him a professorship. It appears that the Elector Palatine, who was responsible for the offer, knew Spinoza as the author of a highly regarded exposition of Descartes but not as the author of the TPT. He charged a professor at the university, Louis Fabritius, with the task of making the offer. Fabritius knew that Spinoza was the author of the TPT. He couched his offer in terms which he probably knew Spinoza would refuse, assuring him that he would have "complete freedom to philosophize" but noting that the Elector assumed Spinoza would not "misuse use that freedom to disturb the publicly established religion." In declining, Spinoza gave two reasons: first, he feared that teaching would interfere with his research, and second, he did not know what limits he would have to impose on himself to avoid appearing to disturb the established religion.

By 1675 Spinoza was satisfied enough with his revisions of the *Ethics* that he visited Amsterdam to give the manuscript to Rieuwertsz for publication. But the theologians learned of his plans and complained to the civil authorities. So Spinoza gave up on this attempt to publish his masterwork, leaving it to appear in his *Opera posthuma*.

In his last years Spinoza began two additional works which he did not live to finish: his *Compendium of Hebrew Grammar* and his *Political Treatise*. Both these works are in some sense byproducts of the TPT. The biblical criticism of the TPT had emphasized that to understand scripture it was essential to understand the language in which it was originally written. But Spinoza believed no existing grammar explained it adequately. The *Hebrew Grammar* was intended to fill that gap. And although the TPT had provided foundations for political philosophy, it had not dealt with practical questions about the merits of the different forms of government and the best ways of organizing them. The *Political Treatise* aimed to remedy that lack.

In February 1677 Spinoza died of a debilitating lung disease, probably aggravated by inhaling the glass dust produced by grinding lenses. By December his posthumous works were published in nearly simultaneous Latin and Dutch editions, the *Opera posthuma* and the *Nagelate schriften*. Because the Dutch translations must have been done from manuscripts rather than from the printed text of the Latin edition, the Dutch translations provide a check on the proofreading of the editors of the *Opera posthuma*, a fact which has aided recent critical editions of Spinoza's works. The Latin edition included the *Ethics*, the correspondence (originally seventy-five letters to and from Spinoza), and three unfinished works, the *Treatise on the Intellect*, the *Political Treatise*, and the *Hebrew Grammar*. Neither edition included the *Short Treatise*, manuscripts of which were not discovered until the nineteenth century. Subsequent scholarship has also added twelve letters to the correspondence. We'll conclude with an account of the works which first appeared posthumously, beginning with the *Political Treatise*.

THE POLITICAL TREATISE (1677)

Though Spinoza expressed a strong preference for democracy in the TPT, he also recognized that it might not be the most suitable form of government for all situations. Like Machiavelli, whose work he studied closely, he thought it was not an easy matter to impose a new form of government on people who had become accustomed to a different form. So part of what he seeks to do in the *Political Treatise* (PT) is to work out principles for organizing the alternatives he regards as inherently less desirable. He offers detailed proposals for the best way to organize a monarchy or an aristocracy so that it can be stable and serve the interests of its citizens as well as possible.

The sensible design of any form of government must take into account the known features of human nature. For example, because no one has so powerful a mind that he always sees the good and never yields to his passions, and because "kings are not Gods, but men, who are often captivated by the Sirens' song," even in a monarchy it is unwise to put all decision-making power in the hands of one man. If it is necessary to have a monarchy, the king should be guided in his decisions by a large, broadly based council of advisors. Indeed, Spinoza proposes that the king be required to choose from among the proposals recommended by his council. He does not explain how this requirement is to be enforced.

Similarly, he thinks an aristocracy will work best if the power to make and repeal laws, and to appoint ministers of state, is granted to a large council drawn from the patrician class. He regards the size of that council as critical to its proper functioning, on the theory that the larger the deliberative body, the more apt it is to have in it some men outstanding for their wisdom, and the less apt it is to favor irrational policies. But he would provide a smaller council of syndics, also drawn from the patrician class, to insure that the legislative council follows the prescribed procedures and that the ministers faithfully execute the laws.

Spinoza intended to add a discussion of democracy to this work but lived to complete only a few paragraphs on that topic. What he does say about democracy has embarrassed many of his modern admirers because he excludes women from the political process on the ground that they are naturally unequal to men (and because men are apt to overrate the intelligence of beautiful women). We can only speculate about what else he might have said, but it seems likely that he would have acknowledged that even democracy—understood as a form of government in which all adult males who are neither servants nor criminals nor men of ill repute are entitled to vote in the legislative assembly and to hold political offices—has inherent problems that require some form of constitutional protections.

THE COMPENDIUM OF HEBREW GRAMMAR (1677)

As indicated above, Spinoza undertook this work because he believed that a thorough understanding of biblical Hebrew was essential for interpreting scripture, that no existing Hebrew grammar provided an adequate understanding of the language, and that he could succeed where his predecessors had failed. The first of these reasons would generally be acknowledged as valid. The second may have been true in Spinoza's day but is probably not true now. To what extent Spinoza's grammar has contributed to our improved understanding of the Hebrew language and the Bible is a matter for historians of Hebrew linguistics and biblical scholarship to judge. The primary question here is whether this work contributes anything to our understanding of Spinoza's philosophy. Regrettably the answer to that question seems to be "no."

ETHICS (1677)

The most important work included in the *Opera posthuma* is the *Ethics*, a systematic account of Spinoza's philosophy written in a style modeled on Euclidean geometry, beginning with a set of axioms and definitions, and attempting to show, by formal demonstrations, what conclusions these assumptions lead to. From time to time Spinoza interrupts the construction of proofs to elaborate on particularly important topics, in prefaces, scholia, and appendices. These tend to contain his most accessible and memorable passages. But the bulk of the work is written in a format which increases its difficulty for many readers, however much they may admire the commitment to rigor. The formal definitions Spinoza gives of his key terms sometimes raise more questions than they answer. The axioms are not always intuitively obvious. And the demonstrations are not always perspicuous. The forbidding style of the work may explain why, for the first hundred years after Spinoza's death, the TPT was the most influential of his main works. It was only toward the end of the eighteenth century that the *Ethics* began to find an appreciative audience.

Some of the difficulty of the work may be alleviated by recognizing that Spinoza does not expect his readers to find all the axioms obvious or all the demonstrations compelling. He arrived at his final set of axioms only by trying out different axiomatizations on his correspondents and modifying them in response to criticism, supplying arguments for assumptions the correspondents questioned. Often he provides more than one demonstration of a proposition, recognizing that his readers may not be convinced by the first demonstration. And at one point, having come to a conclusion he expects his readers to find particularly surprising, he implores them to refrain from judgment until they have followed the argument carefully to its conclusion. The implication seems to be that the system is to be judged partly by its ability to explain, comprehensively and consistently, a wide range of data.

The work is divided into five parts. The first attempts to demonstrate the existence of God and determine his properties; the second explores the nature of the mind, with particular attention to the human mind; the third gives an account of man's emotional nature, systematizing what Spinoza takes to be the laws of human psychology; the fourth seeks to explain why we are so often the victims of self-destructive passions and propounds an ideal of human nature we can and should strive to attain; the fifth part tries to show how we can control our passions and achieve blessedness.

In the Appendix to Part I, Spinoza provides a useful summary of its main conclusions: that God, defined as a substance consisting of infinite attributes, exists necessarily; that God is the only substance, everything else being a mode of God; that God is the free cause of all things; that everything else is so dependent on God that it cannot be or be conceived without him; and that God has predetermined all things, not from freedom of the will, but from the necessity of his nature.

To this we might add that Spinoza also claims to show in Part I that infinitely many modes follow from the necessity of the divine nature. Some of these modes follow from God's *absolute* nature—that is, follow from God's nature unconditionally—and hence are themselves infinite and eternal. Other things—particular, finite things—express God's attributes in a determinate way, and do not follow from God's absolute nature, but from one of God's attributes insofar as it is modified by another modification which is also finite. So each finite mode has as part of its causal history an infinite series of other prior, particular, finite things.

Spinoza is often referred to as a pantheist, a term usually taken to mean that God is identical with nature, understood as the totality of things. But Spinoza identifies God with nature only in the sense that he identifies God with His attributes, those eternal elements in nature which exist in themselves and are conceived through themselves. When Spinoza identifies God with Nature, it is with what he calls *Natura naturans* (active or productive nature). The modes which follow from and express God's attributes he calls *Natura naturata* (passive or produced nature) (*Ethics* I, Prop. 29, Schol.). They are not God. Their defining properties are logically opposed to God's: they exist in another, through which they are conceived. Nor are they a part of God, since it is incompatible with God's nature to have parts (*Ethics* I, Prop. 29, Schol.).

Because everything which exists is either an attribute, whose existence is absolutely necessary, or a mode, and because all modes either follow from God unconditionally or else are necessary in relation to other modes of God, Spinoza concludes that there is nothing contingent in nature. All things are determined by the necessity of the divine nature to exist and act as they do. God could not have produced them in any other way than He did.

This is what Spinoza says. What does it mean? From the seventeenth century to the twenty-first many interpreters have understood the doctrine that there is only one substance, of which everything else is a mode—Spinoza's monism, in effect—as implying that there is only one ultimate subject of predication and that everything else is in some way a predicate of that one subject. This is a prima facie plausible way to understand his monism, given the close historical connection between the idea of substance and the idea of an ultimate subject of predication. But it is not obviously an attractive way of understanding Spinoza's monism on reflection. In what sense might a particular thing, like a human being, for example, be predicated of God?

When Pierre Bayle advanced this line of interpretation in the seventeenth century, he took it to imply that the properties of finite things must really be properties of God. And he understandably thought Spinoza's monism, so interpreted, was absurd. God would be constantly changing his properties as the properties of finite things changed (though Spinoza insists that God is immutable). He would have unseemly human properties, insofar as people behaved improperly or criminally (though Spinoza is resolutely opposed to anthropomorphism). And he would have contradictory properties at the same time, as one finite thing had one property and another had its opposite.

In the late twentieth century Jonathan Bennett (1985) advanced a variation on Bayle's interpretation which avoids some but not all of these unhappy consequences. He suggested that when we say of a finite thing that it has a certain property, what we are really saying is that the universe, conceived under one of God's attributes, has some property at a certain location. That property is not necessarily the one we ascribe to the finite thing. For example, when we attribute a property to a physical object, we are saying that the universe, conceived under the attribute of extension—that is, space itself—has some property at that particular point. If I say that the peach I am about to peel is ripe, I am saying that space has, in that region, some quality I conceptualize as ripeness; I am not attributing ripeness either to that region of space or to space as a whole.

This interpretation avoids the problem of ascribing contradictory properties to God by understanding apparently contradictory predications as applying to the universe *at different locations*: Space is qualified here by whatever property I conceptualize as ripeness; it is qualified there by whatever property I conceptualize as unripeness. (How this works for modes of attributes other than extension is unclear.) It avoids the problem of ascribing human properties to God by remaining agnostic about the properties of space which underlie the properties we ascribe to humans and other finite things. (We do not know what properties of the universe underlie the fact that I love someone whom you do not love, but they are evidently not human properties.) But it does not avoid the problem that, on this view, God is constantly changing. Whenever some finite thing changes, God is changing at that location.

The main alternative interpretation (Curley 1969, 1988) emphasizes the equally strong traditional connection between the idea of substance and the idea of independent existence. When the TEI first introduced the contrast between things which exist in themselves and things which exist in something else, Spinoza glossed that contrast as one between things which are their own cause and things which are caused by something other than themselves. He did not explain it in terms of predication. The things which exist in themselves—the first elements of the whole of nature—were supposed to be fixed and eternal and to have laws "inscribed in them." If we identify the first elements of the whole of nature with the attributes, then we can infer that Spinoza conceived attributes like thought and extension as eternal entities involving laws of nature so fundamental that they do not admit of explanation in terms of anything more basic. On this reading Spinoza dreamed of a final scientific theory whose most basic principles would be, and could be seen to be, absolutely necessary. That is why the attributes exist in themselves and are conceived through themselves.

According to this interpretation, some things follow from the fundamental laws without the aid of any other propositions. These are the eternal, immutable things which follow from God's *absolute* nature, the infinite modes of the *Ethics* (or universal modes in the ST). They are those general features of reality corresponding to the derived laws of nature, like motion and rest, which involve laws pertaining to anything possessing motion or rest. They follow from the attributes because the lower level laws can be deduced from and hence explained by the most fundamental laws. (Spinoza provides us with a sketch of such a deduction in Part II of the *Ethics.*) Although these modes themselves are infinite (in the sense that the laws they involve apply throughout nature) and eternal (in the sense that the laws are immutable), the series of causes which produces them is finite. Explanation of one law by another deduces the less general law (say, a law governing the transfer of motion in a particular kind of impact) from more general laws (say, the law that motion is conserved in all causal interactions). The series of general causes must come to an end because there is a logical limit to the generality of laws. Once you have formulated a law so general that it applies to everything which possesses a certain attribute, no more general law is possible. It is thus in the nature of the attributes that they cannot be explained through anything else.

Other things—the finite modes of the *Ethics*, the singular changeable things of the TEI—do not follow from the *absolute* nature of God's attributes but do follow from God's attributes as modified by the infinite modes *and* other finite modes. This is a reflection of the fact that particular events cannot be explained by laws alone but require information about other particular events for their explanation. Their necessity is not absolute but relative to the existence of the other events essential to their explanation.

Something of this sort must be true if Spinoza's system is to allow for the reality of change. Spinoza insists that things follow from God's nature with the same necessity with which the properties of a triangle follow from its nature. This is why he is often criticized for assimilating the causal relation to that of entailment. If *everything* followed logically from the *absolute* nature of God, which is eternal and immutable, nothing could fail to share in that eternity and immutability. Because the infinite modes *do* follow from God's absolute nature, they share the eternity and infinitude of their cause. But not everything follows from God's absolute nature. Specifically, the particular finite things do not follow unconditionally from the infinite and eternal things. So its members are not infinite and eternal. This is why change is possible.

This dependence of the finite on other finite things also explains why the world must have no beginning. It contains particular things whose behavior can only be explained if we add information about antecedent conditions to the general facts we appeal to in our explanation. Those particular things constitute a series which cannot have an end, because each member of the series must have an explanation and can only be explained by the existence of some particular thing(s) prior to it (plus the laws of nature).

This reading of Spinoza's metaphysics has the advantage of identifying something in nature—the first elements of nature, or the attributes—which can plausibly be thought to be eternal, immutable, ultimate principles of explanation for everything else in the universe. Because Spinoza's system requires something eternal and infinite as an object of the love which is supposed to provide us with pure joy, this seems an important consideration. This reading also has the advantage of identifying something in nature which can plausibly be thought to follow logically from the first elements alone and to function as an intermediate between the ultimate principles of explanation and the finite things whose behavior is to be explained. The idea that there is a series of infinite and eternal things intermediate between God and finite things is one of the most distinctive features of Spinoza's metaphysics in contrast to Cartesianism.

This reading also has what may be thought to be a disadvantage: it implies that not everything in nature is absolutely necessary. The finite modes are portrayed here as not following unconditionally from the fixed and eternal things but as requiring other finite modes for their explanation and as being necessary only in relation to those other finite modes and the infinite modes. But this feature of the interpretation may not really be a disadvantage; Spinoza's discussion of necessity suggests that he thought things are necessary in two very different ways (*Ethics* I, Prop. 33, Schol. 1). Some are necessary in virtue of their own nature; others are necessary in virtue of their cause. Particular finite things, such as this or that human being, do not involve any inherent necessity (*Ethics* II, Ax. 1). They are necessary just insofar as the order of nature (the series of prior finite causes) makes them necessary.

The theory of mind-body identity in Part II of the *Ethics* is best approached by viewing it as a subversion of Cartesian dualism. Descartes sought to make belief in personal immortality rational by showing that the mind and the body are really distinct from one another. His strategy was to set up a thought experiment in which we clearly and distinctly conceive the possibility of the mind's existing without the body. We can, he claimed, find reasonable grounds for doubting the existence of the whole physical world by reflecting on the powers of God. An omnipotent being could, if he chose, create in us representations of physical objects without creating any physical objects. But we cannot find reasonable grounds for doubting our own existence as thinking things. Any hypothesis we entertain to cast doubt on our existence, such as deception by God, will entail that we think, and hence, that we exist. So we are compelled to affirm our existence as thinking things but not compelled to affirm the existence of our body (or any other extended object).

If we can clearly and distinctly conceive of the mind as existing without the body, then it is logically possible for it to exist without the body. If it is logically possible for it exist without the body, then it *could* exist without the body. (If it is logically possible for two things to exist separately, then an omnipotent being could cause them to exist separately. And Descartes thinks he has shown that there is an omnipotent being. So the possibility of their existing separately is not merely a logical one. There is a being which has the power to bring this about, if he wishes.) But if two things are such that one can exist without the other, they are really distinct. This entails that the mind is not necessarily destroyed when the body is destroyed, and that establishes the *possibility* of immortality. Whether that possibility is realized depends on the inscrutable will of God. So Descartes makes no serious attempt to prove actual immortality.

Descartes did, however, modify the strictness of this dualism when he added that the mind is not present in the body "as a sailor is present in his ship," that it is, instead, closely united to it, so that mind and body together constitute one thing and are "substantially united." What seems to have motivated this doctrine of substantial union—which is not obviously consistent with the dualism—was Descartes' recognition that there is a particularly intimate connection between the human mind and the human body. When something happens in my body, normally I am not aware of it in the external way in which I am aware of things which happen in bodies not mine. I feel my body's need for food as hunger, its need for drink as thirst, damage done to it as pain, and so on. These interested, action-motivating bodily sensations are what make this particular body peculiarly mine.

Spinoza, too, seems to have been deeply impressed by the intimacy of the relationship Descartes described, and particularly by the facts that the mind's capacities are a function of those of the body and that changes in the mind strictly parallel those in the body. For example, my mind's capacity for higher-level thought seems to be a function of my brain's complexity; its ability to think clearly and its mood are both closely correlated with my body's blood alcohol level. A Cartesian might dismiss some of these phenomena as mere coincidences. Others he might regard as examples of the body acting on the mind. But Spinoza thinks that because mind and body belong to such fundamentally disparate conceptual categories, we cannot posit a causal relationship between them. And he would not dismiss any such regularity in nature as a coincidence. What we should say instead is that the mind and the body are one and the same thing conceived under different attributes.

Spinoza has a metaphysical argument for supposing that this identity of modes of thought with modes of extension exists not only in human beings but also runs throughout the whole of nature. Suppose that God is an infinite, perfect substance who possesses the attributes of thought and of extension. As an infinite and perfect thinking thing, he must have in his intellect an idea of every existing mode of extension. If he did not, there would be gaps in his knowledge. Equally, as an infinite and perfect thinking thing, he cannot have in his intellect an idea of a mode of extension as existing if no such mode exists. If he did, he would be in error. So in God there must be a one-to-one correspondence between the modes of extension which exist and their representations in God. Moreover, since this correspondence is necessary, it is not possible for the modes of thought to exist without their corresponding modes of extension. The converse is also impossible. This entails that the modes of thought and the modes of extension are not, in Cartesian terms, really distinct from one another. They are conceptually distinct, insofar as they are conceived under different attributes. This is why there can be no causal relation between them. But they are not capable of existing apart from one another.

This argument leads to some surprising conclusions from which Spinoza does not shrink. For example, it entails that every extended thing in nature corresponds to a mode of thought which is, in some sense, its "mind." This doctrine is known as panpsychism. Spinoza clearly does think that all finite physical things other than humans have something *like* the minds humans have. Insofar as he affirms a continuity between humans and other animals, his panpsychism seems quite reasonable, much more reasonable than the Cartesian view that nonhuman animals are merely machines without any sensations. Moreover, other philosophers before Spinoza—like Montaigne—had argued that animals were capable of displaying intelligence and emotions. What is puzzling about Spinoza's panpsychism is its apparent implication that even the simplest material objects have something like a mind. We can diminish the shock of this claim to some degree by recollecting that Spinoza would probably not think that the minds of the simplest material objects are *very much like* human minds. If our capacity for higher-order thinking depends on our having a very complex brain, then presumably a carbon atom does not have the capacity to solve quadratic equations. But it is still unclear what the ascription of mentality to very simple physical objects comes to.

One unsurprising consequence of this view of the relation between mind and body is that Spinoza denies that the mind is capable of acting freely in the way Descartes tended to understand freedom. Descartes was quite ambiguous about the kind of freedom he wanted to claim for us. In the Fourth Meditation he seemed, initially, to interpret freedom of the will indeterministically, as a power to either do something or not do it, independently of any external causes. Then he reflected that there were two cases where he might not, in fact, be able to act otherwise, though he did not want to deny that he was free in those cases: one is the case where he sees something so clearly that he cannot help but assent to it; the other is the case where God, in an act of grace, disposes his inmost thoughts in a certain way. So he revised his initial definition, adding a clause which would make freedom compatible with certain kinds of determinism: we can be free if our intellect presents something so clearly to the will that it cannot judge otherwise; and we can be free even if God is determining our actions, so long as we are not aware of that determination, so long as we seem to ourselves to be the initiators of our actions. But this was another area where he was unable to maintain consistency. In the *Principles of Philosophy* he reverted to an indeterminist conception of freedom and pronounced the problem of reconciling human freedom with God's preordination of all things insoluble.

Spinoza rejects any indeterminist conception of freedom. This was evident already in Part I of the *Ethics*, where he held that all finite things are determined to exist and act the way they do by an infinite series of prior finite things. But his acceptance of mind-body identity provides an additional reason for denying indeterminism in humans. Descartes would have allowed that determinism reigned in the physical world except insofar as minds were capable of intervening in it to cause events which would have gone differently but for that intervention. If the mind and the body are one and the same thing, conceived in different ways, then the mind will not be able to intervene in the physical world as an uncaused cause. The decisions of the mind are just the appetites of the body, conceived under a different attribute. When they are conceived under the attribute of extension, they are conceived as part of a causal network which determines their character. Since the order and connection of ideas mirrors the order and connection of extended things, modes of thought must also be part of a causal network that determines their character, a network whose members are conceptually distinct from, but really identical with, the corresponding modes of extension. Spinoza concedes that it often seems to us that our acts of will have no antecedent causes; but he thinks all this shows is the inadequacy of our self-knowledge.

Consistently with this deterministic picture of things, Spinoza turns in Part III of the *Ethics* to an attempt to provide a systematic human psychology, explaining the laws according to which the human mind operates. He writes in the Preface to Part III,

> Nothing happens in nature which can be attributed to any defect in it, for nature [read *Natura naturans*] is always the same, and its virtue and power of acting are everywhere one and the same, i.e., the laws and rules of nature, according to which all things happen, and change from one form to another, are always and everywhere the same.
>
> (GEBHARDT II, 138)

So, if we are to understand anything, we must understand it in terms of the universal laws of nature. When we understand human actions and emotions in this way, we will no longer be disposed to curse them or find them ridiculous. We will see them as an inevitable result of the circumstances under which they occurred.

Like Hobbes, Spinoza makes the striving to persevere in existence the fundamental law of human behavior. He sees an analogy between that striving and the principle of inertia which was fundamental in the new physics and treats it as constituting the essence of each individual. His conviction that there is this analogy leads him to a revised understanding of what constitutes human activity: We should think of ourselves as active just to the extent that our actions can be adequately understood in terms of our striving to persevere in being. But he also thinks of the striving as encompassing more than just continuation in existence. In addition, it seeks to increase our perfection, or power of action. When we succeed in doing that, we experience the increase as joy; when our power of acting is diminished, we experience the decrease as sadness. In a way, Spinoza is a hedonist. We seek to maximize our joy and minimize our sadness. But the underlying changes in perfection, or power of action, are really at the core of these strivings.

Spinoza's psychology is generally egoistic in the sense that he thinks what we basically seek, insofar as we are active or self-determined (that is, insofar as what we do is determined by our own nature) is something we imagine to be good for ourselves (that is, to involve or lead to our joy). But his egoism does not exclude our taking an interest in the interests of others. If we conceive an external object—a person, or an institution, say—as a cause of joy in us, we will love that object and seek our own good by seeking its good. Similarly, if something in itself neutral is associated in our experience with something either positive or negative, we will come to have positive or negative feelings toward the inherently neutral thing. And to the extent that a thing is like us in some degree, we will tend to share its feelings: to feel sadness when it is sad, and joy when it is joyful. This is the psychological basis for pity and benevolence. We can minimize our own sadness and maximize our own joy by seeking to minimize the sadness of others like us and maximizing their joy.

These are fairly simple and benign cases. But the same psychological laws which explain pity and benevolence also explain, less happily, racial and religious hatred. We are less apt to feel sympathy for those we think of as unlike us. And we are apt to generalize to a whole group the negative emotions we have experienced toward some members of that group. What interests Spinoza most in human psychology is the complexity of our emotions and the psychological conflicts we regularly experience. If something affects us with both joy and sadness, we will feel conflicting emotions of love and hatred; a similar process will unfold if we imagine that something which usually affects us with sadness is like another thing that usually affects us with joy. The uncertainty of our knowledge of human affairs makes us prey to both hope and fear, which are inseparable from each other. But we are subject to wishful thinking, which inclines us to believe the things which give us hope. That is the root cause of superstition. And acting on irrational beliefs is a recipe for disappointment and despondency. Hatred, envy, and jealousy are as natural to us as love, benevolence, and friendship. These conflicting emotions are constantly fluctuating as external circumstances change, with the result that "we toss about, like waves on the sea, driven by contrary winds." For the most part we are not the masters of our fate.

Because Spinoza is a determinist who takes his doctrine to imply that we should bear calmly both good fortune and bad and condemn no one for his behavior, and because he frequently embraces subjectivist-sounding theories of ethical language—as when he writes that good and evil are nothing positive in things, considered in themselves, but just modes of thinking—it has often been thought that he has no ethical theory—or at least that he cannot consistently have one. But Spinoza called his masterwork *Ethics*, and Part IV of that work is full of what look like ethical judgments. He tells us that the knowledge of God is the mind's greatest good, that joy in itself is good and sadness evil, that pleasure can be excessive and evil, that pain can be good, that love can be excessive, that hatred can never be good, and so on. How can these judgments be true if good and evil are only "modes of thinking"?

The answer seems to be that Spinoza makes a distinction between the ordinary, nonphilosophical use of ethical terms, which is highly subjective and undisciplined, and the philosophical use of the same language. If we reflect on the use of terms like *good* and *evil* in connection with members of a natural kind, like man, we will recognize that they signify varying degrees of approximation to an ideal of perfection or completeness. Unaided by philosophy, we are apt to have varying conceptions of that ideal. But there is a way of conceiving the ideal human being which will necessarily attract us as soon as we form a clear idea of it. Spinoza uses the term "free man" as a label for that ideal and the term "good" as a label for those things we know will help to achieve our goal.

The free person is defined as one who is led by reason alone and characterized by his disregard of death and concentration on life; by his willingness to accept risks, when that is called for, and his wisdom in determining when it is not called for; by his determination to avoid the favors of the ignorant, when accepting them might compromise his integrity; by his gratitude to other free men for their acts of genuine love and friendship; by his honesty; and by his obedience to the laws of the state, not from fear of punishment but from his commitment to the common good.

The psychology of Part III holds that all men, to the extent that they determine their own actions and are not the slaves of fortune, pursue what they take to be their own good. The ethical theory of Part IV holds out the ideal of the free man as an enlightened egoist. Freedom is not mere self-determination but informed self-determination. The free man recognizes that, left to himself, he would lead a miserable life, that achieving his optimal state requires the cooperation of other men, that nothing is more useful to him than his fellow men, and that they are the more useful the more they share his dedication to the pursuit of knowledge, a noncompetitive good which is only increased, not diminished, by being shared. He is not an ascetic. He knows that his body requires the moderate use of pleasant food and drink, and that beautiful natural objects and works of art, music, theater, and other such things are goods anyone can enjoy without detriment to others. He understands that the greater the joy with which we are affected, the greater the perfection to which we gravitate, and the more we participate in the divine nature. Spinoza is apprehensive about human sexuality, knowing how easily sexual desire can become obsessive and self-destructive.

The central problem of ethics for Spinoza is not that of knowing what is good but that of pursuing it single-mindedly. "I see and approve the better," he writes, quoting Ovid, "but I follow the worse." Parts III and IV are concerned with explaining why we are often unable to pursue the good we clearly see. Part V tries to help us overcome the unhealthy dominance of the passions which underlies this weakness of the will. Descartes, whose moral philosophy was heavily influenced by the Renaissance revival of stoicism, thought that the mind could exercise an absolute control over the passions. Spinoza is not so optimistic. But he does think that we can increase our power over them and make them less harmful to us.

One promising remedy for our harmful passions is to correct the false beliefs they often involve. Most of the emotions Spinoza analyzes in Part III incorporate some cognitive element. He defines hatred, for example, as sadness accompanied by the idea of something external to us as the cause of our sadness. Indignation is hatred toward someone whom we imagine as having done evil to someone (or something) else. If we come to understand that the person we hate or toward whom we feel indignation is at most a partial cause of those negative consequences, that his actions are no more than the most recent link in a chain of causes which extends into the infinite past, this will diminish our negative emotions toward that individual, redirecting them toward the prior causes and diffusing them over those causes. This process may not immediately diminish our overall level of negative emotions. But if it diminishes the negative feelings we have toward the proximate cause of our sadness, it may make it easier for us to behave well toward that person and break the vicious circle of harm and retaliation which is the cause of so much human misery.

Part V of the *Ethics* concludes with a puzzling series of propositions dealing with the eternity of the mind. Astonishingly, given his earlier doctrine that the mind and body are one and the same thing, conceived under different attributes, Spinoza now maintains that the human mind is not entirely destroyed with the body but that something of it remains which is eternal. The eternal portion of the mind is apparently the part which understands things "under a species of eternity," that is, that sees them as necessary by understanding them under the second or third of the three kinds of cognition which the *Ethics* assumes, reason or intuitive science. Because Spinoza assumes that it is possible to increase our understanding of things by the second and third kinds of cognition—understanding more things in those ways at one time than we do at another—this implies that we can increase the portion of our mind which is eternal, even though eternity is supposed to entail that whatever is eternal has no relation to time. We can make sense of much of Spinoza's philosophy, but so far this part of the *Ethics* has resisted the best efforts of sympathetic interpreters. It is clear that it is not a doctrine of personal immortality, for Spinoza regards memory of the individual's past as essential to personal identity, and he is quite emphatic that the portion of the mind which is eternal has no memory of any past. Perhaps the best thing we can say is that Spinoza thought that there was some truth, badly articulated, in the traditional doctrine of personal immortality and thought (wrongly) that his philosophy could give a coherent explanation of that truth.

In another way, however, Spinoza may achieve some reconciliation with traditional religion in these final portions of the *Ethics*. Because he identifies God with nature (*natura naturans*), he can claim that the more we understand Nature, the more we understand God. When we understand nature by the third kind of cognition, intuitive science, we not only have the highest form of cognition we can have, but we also experience the greatest possible satisfaction. We then experience joy accompanied by the idea of God as the cause of our joy. This means that we love God. Together the knowledge of God and the love which is inseparable from that knowledge constitute our highest good, not because God is a king who will reward us with a happiness extrinsic to our love for him but because the knowledge and love of God inherently involve the highest happiness we can know.

This attempt at an accommodation with traditional religion may not succeed. It is true that Spinoza's "God" has many of the properties of God, as the concept of God came to be developed by philosophically minded theologians in Judaism and Christianity: He is a perfect being, infinite, eternal, the first cause of all things, himself neither needing nor being susceptible of any explanation. Because, in Spinoza's view, knowledge of God can be the cause of the greatest joy we can experience, he can be the object of a love which surpasses any love we can have for finite things. But because, according to Spinoza, God is supremely perfect, he is as incapable of joy (passage to a greater perfection) as he is of sadness (passage to a lesser perfection). So he is also incapable of love or hate, which are species of joy and sadness. We cannot rationally expect Spinoza's God to return our love. Nor can we expect him to watch over us like a loving father. Spinoza's God, being perfect, has no goals, no states he desires to reach (or maintain). To ascribe desire to Spinoza's God would be to conceive him as imperfect, a contradiction in terms. A fortiori, he is not seeking our welfare and cannot provide a refuge from the uncertainty of fortune. He cannot be affected by prayer or ritual. He does not issue laws accompanied by promises of reward for obedience and threats of punishment for disobedience. His laws are ones we cannot break.

Because Spinoza's God differs in so many respects from the God of traditional religion, even in its most philosophical forms, it is understandable that many religious-minded critics have regarded his philosophy as a form of atheism. But from Spinoza's point of view these criticisms only show a misunderstanding of the nature of God. The founders of the traditional religions, he thinks, were in a position like that of the first students of geometry, when geometry was still an empirical science. Relying on what Spinoza would call imagination, the early geometers had only very crude ideas of the objects they were studying. They could not have given a properly scientific definition of a triangle or a circle from which they could demonstrate precise theorems about the nature of these objects. So they made mistakes about them, thinking, for example, that the ratio of the circumference of a circle, to its diameter is 3:1.

But though they may not have had the same definitions of these objects as later geometers, they were still attempting to develop a theory of the same objects. They were just handicapped by the inadequate ideas they had about those things. Similarly handicapped by their reliance on imagination—on the dreams of prophets and reports of revelation passed down through tradition—the philosophers and theologians of the organized religions got some things right and many things wrong. They saw the truth, not clearly, but as if through a cloud. Spinoza's claim not to be an atheist depends on whether he was, as he believed, the Euclid of theology. Spinoza's admirers have inclined to the view that he was.

On the two hundredth anniversary of his death a collection was taken to erect a statue to Spinoza in the Hague. When the statue was unveiled in 1882, Ernest Renan concluded his address with words which sum up the feelings of those admirers: "Woe to him who in passing should hurl an insult at this gentle and pensive head… This man, from his granite pedestal, will point out to all men the way of blessedness which he found; and ages hence, the cultivated traveler, passing by this spot, will say in his heart, 'The truest vision ever had of God came, perhaps, here.'"

See also Bayle, Pierre; Bennett, Jonathan; Boyle, Robert; Cartesianism; Democracy; Descartes, René; Determinism and Freedom; Essence and Existence; Ethics, History of; Galileo Galilei; Hobbes, Thomas; Human Nature; Jewish Philosophy; La Peyrère, Isaac; Laws, Scientific; Machiavelli, Niccolò; Mind-Body Problem; Panpsychism; Philosophy of Mind; Regius, Henricus (Henry de Roy); Rousseau, Jean-Jacques; Spinozism.

Bibliography

WORKS BY SPINOZA

The Collected Works of Spinoza. Vol. 1. Edited and Translated by Edwin Curley. Princeton, NJ: Princeton University Press, 1985. The second and final volume is in progress.

Spinoza Opera. 4 vols. Edited by Carl Gebhardt. Heidelberg: Carl Winters Universitäts-buchhandlung, 1925.This is the current standard original-language edition, which will eventually be superseded by Moreau's edition.

Spinoza Oeuvres. Edited by Pierre-François Moreau. Paris: Presses Universitaires de France. As of June 2005 only one volume had appeared (in 1999), containing the *Theological-Political Treatise*, with a critical edition of the text by Fokke Akkerman and a translation by Moreau and Jacqueline Lagrée. A comprehensive edition is planned, with critically edited versions of the original language texts and French translations on the facing pages.

Spinoza, Complete Works. Edited by Michael L. Morgan and translated by Samuel Shirley. Indianapolis: Hackett, 2002. This is the only complete English-language edition.

WORKS ABOUT SPINOZA

Allison, Henry. *Benedict de Spinoza: An Introduction*. New Haven, CT: Yale University Press, 1987.

Bennett, Jonathan. *A Study of Spinoza's Ethics*. Indianapolis, IN: Hackett, 1984.

Curley, Edwin. *Behind the Geometrical Method*. Princeton, NJ: Princeton University Press, 1988.

Curley, Edwin. "*Homo Audax*: Leibniz, Oldenburg and the *Theological-Political Treatise*." *Studia Leibnitiana*, supp. 1991.

Curley, Edwin. "Maimonides, Spinoza and the Book of Job." In *Jewish Themes in Spinoza's Philosophy*, edited by Heidi Ravven and Lenn Goodman. Albany: SUNY Press, 2002.

Curley, Edwin. "Notes on a Neglected Masterpiece, I: Spinoza and the Science of Hermeneutics." In *Spinoza: The Enduring Questions*, edited by Graeme Hunter. Toronto: University of Toronto Press, 1994.

Curley, Edwin. "Notes on a Neglected Masterpiece, II: The *Theological-Political Treatise* as a Prolegomenon to the *Ethics*." In *Central Themes in Early Modern Philosophy*, edited by J. A. Cover and Mark Kulstad, Indianapolis, IN: Hackett, 1990.

Curley, Edwin. *Spinoza's Metaphysics*. Cambridge, MA: Harvard University Press, 1969.

Curley, Edwin. "The State of Nature and its Law in Hobbes and Spinoza." *Philosophical Topics* 19 (1991): 97–117.

Curley, Edwin, and Pierre-François Moreau. *Spinoza: Issues and Directions*. Leiden: Brill, 1990.

Curley, Edwin, and Greg Walski. "Spinoza's Necessitarianism Reconsidered." In *New Essays on the Rationalists*, edited by Rocco Gennaro and Charles Huenemann. Oxford: Oxford University Press, 1999.

Damasio, Antonio. *Looking for Spinoza: Joy, Sorrow and the Feeling Brain*. Orlando, FL: Harcourt, 2003.

Della Rocca, Michael. *Representation and the Mind-Body Problem in Spinoza*. Oxford: Oxford University Press, 1996.

Donagan, Alan. *Spinoza*. Chicago: University of Chicago Press, 1988.

Garrett, Don, ed. *The Cambridge Companion to Spinoza*. Cambridge, U.K.: Cambridge University Press, 1996.

Garrett, Don. "*Ethics* IP5: Shared Attributes and the Basis of Spinoza's Monism." In *Central Themes in Early Modern Philosophy*, edited by J. A. Cover and Mark Kulstad, Indianapolis: Hackett, 1990.

Garrett, Don, "Teleological Explanation in Spinoza and Early Modern Rationalism." In *New Essays on the Rationalists*, edited by Rocco Gennaro and Charles Huenemann. Oxford: Oxford University Press, 1999.

Grene, Marjorie, ed. *Spinoza, a Collection of Critical Essays*. Garden City, NY: Anchor, 1973.

Israel, Jonathan. *The Radical Enlightenment, Philosophy and the Making of Modernity, 1650–1750*. Oxford: Oxford University Press, 2001.

Koistinen, Olli, and John Biro, eds. *Spinoza: Metaphysical Themes*. Oxford: Oxford University Press, 2002.

Lloyd, Genevieve. *Part of Nature, Self-knowledge in Spinoza's Ethics*. Ithaca, NY: Cornell University Press, 1994.

Mandelbaum, Maurice, and Eugene Freeman, eds. *Spinoza: Essays in Interpretation*. LaSalle, IL: Open Court, 1975.

Nadler, Steven. *Spinoza, A Life*. Cambridge, U.K.: Cambridge University Press, 1999.

Nadler, Steven. *Spinoza's Heresy*. Oxford: Oxford University Press, 2001.

Smith, Steven, *Spinoza, Liberalism and the Question of Jewish Identity*. New Haven, CT: Yale University Press, 1997.

Wolfson, Harry Austryn. *The Philosophy of Spinoza*. 2 vols. Cambridge, MA: Harvard University Press, 1934.

Yovel, Yirmiyahu, ed. *Desire and Affect: Spinoza as Psychologist*. New York: Little Room Press, 1999.

Yovel, Yirmiyahu, ed. *God and Nature*. Leiden: E. J. Brill, 1991.

Yovel, Yirmiyahu. *Spinoza and Other Heretics*. Vol. 1: *The Marrano of Reason*. Vol. 2: *The Adventures of Immanenece*. Princeton, NJ: Princeton University Press, 1989.

Yovel, Yirmiyahu, and Gideon Segal, eds. *Spinoza*. Aldershot, U.K.: Ashgate, 2002.

Yovel, Yirmiyahu, and Gideon Segal, eds. *Spinoza on Knowledge and the Human Mind*. Leiden: E. J. Brill, 1994.

Yovel, Yirmiyahu, and Gideon Segal, eds. *Spinoza on Reason and the Free Man*. New York: Little Room Press, 2004.

Edwin Curley (2005)

SPINOZISM

The term *Spinozism* has almost invariably been used, by both defenders and detractors, to refer to doctrines held or allegedly held by Benedict de Spinoza. Unlike "Platonism," for example, it has not generally been used to refer to a developing doctrine arising out of Spinoza's philosophy. In the seventeenth and eighteenth centuries the term was frequently used to disparage various types of atheistic doctrines that were held to be attributable to Spinoza. For almost a century after his death, his work was neglected by philosophers, execrated by orthodox theologians of diverse denominations, and slighted even by freethinkers. It is not always possible, however, to distinguish between those genuinely opposed to Spinoza's alleged atheism and those who really espoused atheism while pretending to disparage it.

BAYLE AND THE "PHILOSOPHES"

Spinoza's early reputation rested almost entirely on the long article in Pierre Bayle's *Dictionnaire philosophique* (1697), for some time the only readily accessible account of Spinoza's system. Bayle, like many others, admired Spinoza's life but abhorred his doctrine. In Spinoza he saw an application of his own thesis that atheism may coexist with the highest moral excellence. All agree, he wrote, that Spinoza was a "sociable, affable, friendly, and thoroughly good man. This may be strange, but no stranger than to see a man lead an evil life even though he is fully persuaded of the truth of the Gospel." But Bayle described Spinoza's philosophy as "the most absurd and monstrous hypothesis that can be envisaged, contrary to the most evident notions of our mind." Bayle's antagonism to Spinoza's philosophy arose primarily from his dissatisfaction with monism as a solution to the problem of evil. That such an extreme evil as war could exist among men who are but modes of one and the same infinite, eternal, and self-sufficient substance seemed particularly outrageous to him.

Voltaire, like Bayle, expressed esteem for Spinoza's life but had misgivings about his philosophy, although he did accord a measure of praise to the *Tractatus Theologico-Politicus.* Voltaire's understanding of Spinoza's *Ethics,* however, may be questionable, for he quoted from the inaccurate, popularized version by the Count de Boulainvilliers, published under the title *Réfutation de Spinoza* (Brussels, 1731). According to Voltaire, Spinoza's system was built on complete ignorance of physics and was the most monstrous abuse of metaphysics. In regarding the universe as a single substance Spinoza was, as he put it in his *Le philosophe ignorant* (Geneva, 1766), "the dupe of his geometrical spirit."

Denis Diderot, in the *Encyclopédie,* also closely followed Bayle's article in his criticism of Spinoza's philosophy, yet his own views unmistakably reveal Spinozist elements in denying the existence of a being outside, or separate from, the material universe. "There is," he wrote in *Entretiens entre d'Alembert et Diderot,* "no more than one substance in the universe, in man or in animal." Diderot's monism was not quite the same as Spinoza's metaphysical monism, for it was more pragmatic in nature. His "one substance" was merely material substance, not substance in Spinoza's sense of "that which is in itself, and conceived through itself … (and) of which a conception can be formed independently of any other conception (*Ethics,* Part I, Definition 3). The universe, for Diderot, was monistic in its material unity. Nonetheless, Spinoza's metaphysical monism could be considered as the logical basis for Diderot's materialist monism.

GERMANY

While Voltaire's and the Encyclopedists' interpretation of Spinoza was gaining currency in France, attempts were being made in Germany to reappraise his philosophy. This reexamination was an integral part of the German Enlightenment that, while sharing with its French and English counterparts the affirmation of the individual's right to question established truths, also sought to link this affirmation with religious faith rather than with skeptical disbelief. In the course of this quest Spinoza's image underwent a distinct change. From David Hume's ironically labeled "universally infamous" atheist, Spinoza became Novalis's *gottbetrunkener Mensch.* A number of leading German thinkers came increasingly to see in Spinoza's pantheism a profoundly religious conception and interpretation of the cosmos.

To some extent, the reversal in Spinoza's fortunes was also a corollary of the developments in science. Few of Spinoza's contemporaries who accepted the new scientific theories realized their theological implications. The intellectual reorientation in eighteenth-century Germany, on the other hand, was accompanied by a corresponding change in theological thinking. In the light of these changes Spinoza's philosophy appeared much less inimical to the essential truths of religion.

PANTHEISMUSSTREIT. Probably the strongest factor contributing toward the revival of interest in Spinoza's thought was the controversy that raged over Gotthold Lessing's alleged Spinozism. This dispute, sparked by the disagreement between Moses Mendelssohn and F. H. Jacobi, came to involve almost every notable figure in the German literary world. Jacobi, in his account of a conversation with Lessing, claimed that the latter had been a Spinozist. According to this account Lessing said that the orthodox conceptions of deity were no longer satisfactory for him and that, if he were to call himself after any master, he knew of no other than Spinoza. Although Jacobi conceded that Spinoza's philosophy was logically unanswerable, he found it unacceptable on religious grounds; in religion, he felt, he had to take refuge in an act of faith, a "salto mortale" as he called it. Lessing sardonically replied that he was unable to trust his old limbs and heavy head for such a leap.

It should not, however, be inferred that Lessing's philosophical outlook was in every detail or even in essentials merely a reflection of Spinozist ideas. Lessing was far too independent a thinker to be subject to any single pervasive influence. He was also far less metaphysically oriented than Spinoza, and his faith in man's perfectibility was tempered by a shrewder realization of man's limitations than that of his world-shunning precursor. Nor must it be assumed that Lessing's exchanges with Jacobi can be taken at their face value. Lessing was fully aware of Jacobi's misconceptions in his approach to Spinoza and hardly took him seriously. He may have been speaking with tongue in cheek, and it would therefore be unwise to attach too great an importance to the views he espoused.

Lessing did succeed in eliciting Jacobi's admission that Spinoza's philosophy was the most rigorous and consistent intellectual enterprise ever attempted and in inducing him to study it more deeply. Although Jacobi's further studies did little to alter his conviction that Spinoza was an atheist and that final truths were to be found in the philosophy of the heart rather than in that of the understanding, they nonetheless helped to focus attention on Spinoza to an unprecedented degree. Two men in particular, Johann Gottfried Herder and Johann Wolfgang von Goethe, who were both on intimate terms with Jacobi, were the most directly affected. Herder openly called himself a Spinozist, although his ontology and cosmology had much more in common with the Earl of Shaftesbury's and Gottfried Wilhelm Leibniz's than with Spinoza's. Yet he insisted that by substituting his concept of *Kraft* for Spinoza's substance he was not fundamentally departing from Spinozist premises. Herder clearly did not realize how very different were his metaphysical presuppositions in postulating an ever-changing *Kraft* in place of Spinoza's unchanging substance and hence how profoundly at variance was his brand of monism with that of his great precursor, despite superficial similarities. Goethe, too, in his autobiography and in his correspondence with Jacobi, acknowledged a far greater debt to Spinoza than he really owed. In Book XIV of his *Dichtung und Wahrheit* he paid his eloquent tribute to Spinoza's influence:

> After I had looked around the whole world in vain for a means of developing my strange nature, I finally hit upon the *Ethics* of this man.... Here I found the serenity to calm my passions; a wide and free view over the material and moral world seemed to open before me. Above all, I was fascinated by the boundless disinterestedness that emanated from him. That wonderful sentence "he who truly loves God must not desire God to love him in return" with all the propositions on which it rests, with all the consequences that spring from it, filled my whole subsequent thought.

Yet Goethe's pantheism had far greater affinity with Herder's—and thus with Shaftesbury's and Leibniz'—than with Spinoza's. Like Herder's confessed Spinozism, Goethe's was much more the result of a poetical imagination and of an emotional craving than of logical analysis and philosophical understanding. Indeed, although G. W. F. Hegel regarded Spinoza's philosophy as philosophy par excellence and although Johann Gottlieb Fichte and Friedrich von Schelling took it as their starting points, the general nature of the Spinozist revival in Germany was literary rather than philosophical.

ENGLAND

Much the same was true of the Spinozist renaissance in England and to a lesser extent in France during the nineteenth century. Admittedly, deism in England had already displayed marked Spinozist characteristics, even if one cannot agree with Leslie Stephen that the "whole essence of the deist position may be found in Spinoza's *Tractatus.*" Few deists were consciously aware of the Spinozist heritage, and it was not until German thought had begun to make itself felt in the English literary world that Spinozism acquired significance as a subject of intellectual discourse.

Samuel Taylor Coleridge was undoubtedly the chief link in this transmission. To judge from Henry Crabb Robinson's account, Coleridge, when receiving from him Spinoza's *Ethics,* kissed Spinoza's face on the title page, said the book was his gospel, but—almost in the same breath—proclaimed his philosophy false and hence incapable of affecting in the slightest his faith "in all the doctrines of Christianity, even of the Trinity." The ambivalence in Coleridge's attitude toward Spinoza, whom he praised as the "Hercules' pillar of human reason" and simultaneously assailed for his moral and religious views, followed a pattern characteristic of many Spinozists before him, most notably Jacobi. Like Jacobi, Coleridge paid tribute to the rigor of Spinoza's logic and commended his works as "medicinal" reading, while deploring their inadequacy as a philosophical basis of religious belief. Spinoza's *unica substantia,* Coleridge maintained, was not an object at all but a mere notion, a subject, of the mind. Spinoza committed the "most grievous error" of seeing God "in his *Might* alone … and not likewise in his moral, intellectual, existential and personal Godhead." In the *Biographia Literaria* Coleridge related that he had talked much to William Wordsworth about Spinoza, which would help to account for the undeniably Spinozist elements in Wordsworth's poetry. But like Coleridge and other English writers of this period, Wordsworth added nothing new to the conception of Spinozism.

NINETEENTH-CENTURY FRANCE

The reception of Spinoza in nineteenth-century France also witnessed no startling reinterpretations except that, as in Germany, the charge of atheism appeared to many to be quite unfounded. Like Lessing, Herder, and Goethe, Victor Cousin and his followers decisively dismissed the accusations to which Spinoza's *Ethics* had been subjected by orthodox Christians. Nonetheless, Théodore Jouffroy and Émile Saisset, both disciples of Cousin, had serious misgivings about Spinoza's pantheism, for it seemed to absorb the individual in too determinate a manner in the cosmic forces of the whole and thus to threaten the very possibility of human freedom. Paul Janet echoed these misgivings and declared that "the genius of Spinoza was therefore not well adapted to the French mind." But Jouffroy's detailed attention in his lectures at the Sorbonne to Spinoza's thought, and Saisset's publication of a French translation of Spinoza's works, helped to create an intellectual climate in which Spinoza's philosophy could no longer be ignored or lightly dismissed. Thenceforth very many French writers of note, from Edgar Quinet, Alphonse-Marie-Louis de Prat de Lamartine, and Jules Michelet to Georges Sand, Ernest Renan, and the Saint-Simonians felt impelled to grapple with Spinozist ideas.

RUSSIA

The spread and proliferation of interest in Spinozism could not help making its imprint on Russia, a country whose thinkers had for some time been increasingly fascinated by Western philosophical thought. Even more remarkable is the extent to which Russia maintained its preoccupation with Spinoza despite—or perhaps because of—the Bolshevik Revolution. No other pre-Marxian philosopher, with the possible exception of Hegel, has received as much attention in the Soviet Union. From 1917 to 1938, 55,200 copies of Spinoza's works were published in the Soviet Union, compared to 8,000 in the period from 1897 to 1916. Prerevolutionary literature on Spinoza had for the most part been critical and negative, but what non-Marxists considered Spinoza's chief philosophical defects later appeared to many Soviet writers as his strong points. Spinoza's political doctrines particularly appealed to the Marxists. Georgi Plekhanov came to see in Spinozism, when freed from its theological wrappings, a historical forebear of dialectical materialism, and he spoke of Marxism as a "variety of Spinozism." Following Marx and Engels, many Soviet writers credited Spinoza with having correctly solved the fundamental ontological problem concerning the relation of consciousness to being, and of thought to things. Indeed, admiration for Spinoza prompted some to call him "Marx without a beard." Spinoza's rejection of an act of creation, his denial of a continuing intervention in the governance of the world by a supernatural being, his acceptance of nature as something ultimate, self-caused, and "given," without limits of time or space, were all features not lost upon dialectical materialists. No less congenial was the determinism and naturalism of Spinoza's ethical and social philosophy that, while insisting on the possibility of arriving at objective and absolute truth, had analyzed the moral concepts of good and evil in terms of human desire and judgment. Finally, and most important, the allegedly passive role of thought in Spinoza's system, which several prerevolutionary writers had critically commented upon, was regarded in the Soviet Union as the most convincing proof of Spinoza's profound understanding of the historical process. Even if it is conceded that the Marxists revealed as many differences of emphasis in their positive appraisal of Spinoza's thought as did the non-Marxists in their negative approaches, the essentials of Spinoza's doctrines substantially engaged Russian philosophical thinking since the nineteenth century.

Spinozism, then, embodies no single consistent school of thought. Many who professed to admire and accept Spinoza's philosophical premises were as apt to misunderstand and misinterpret them as those who despised them. Yet despite the diversity of meaning that the term underwent in different intellectual contexts and periods, its catalytic significance cannot be gainsaid.

See also Bayle, Pierre; Coleridge; Samuel Taylor; Lessing, Gotthold Ephraim; Pantheismusstreit; Spinoza, Benedict (Baruch) de.

Bibliography

Bayle, Pierre. *Dictionnaire historique et critique.* 2nd ed. Rotterdam, 1702.

Coleridge, Samuel Taylor. *Biographia Literaria.* London, 1817.

Colie, R. L. "Spinoza and the Early English Deists." *Journal of the History of Ideas* 20 (1959): 23–46.

Diderot, Denis. *Oeuvres complètes,* edited by J. Assezat and M. Tourneux. Vol. II. Paris, 1875–1877.

Dilthey, Wilhelm. "Aus der Zeit der Spinoza-Studien Goethes." *Archiv für Geschichte der Philosophie* 7 (1894): 317–341.

Goethe, Johann Wolfgang von. *Aus meinem Leben: Dichtung und Wahrheit.* 4 vols. Tübingen and Stuttgart, 1811–1833.

Herder, Johann Gottfried von. *Gott, einige Gespräche.* Gotha, 1787. Translated with an introduction by F. H. Burkhardt as *God, Some Conversations.* New York: Veritas Press, 1940.

Jacobi, Friedrich Heinrich. *Ueber die Lehre des Spinoza.* Breslau, 1785.

Jakobi, Max, ed. *Briefwechsel zwischen Goethe und F. H. Jakobi.* Leipzig, 1846.

Janet, Paul. "Spinoza et le Spinozisme." *Revue des deux mondes* 70 (1867): 470–498.

Janet, Paul. "Le Spinozisme en France." *Revue philosophique* 13 (1882): 109–132.

Kline, G. L. *Spinoza in Soviet Philosophy.* London: Routledge and Paul, 1952.

Lévy-Bruhl, Lucien. "Jacobi et le Spinozisme." *Revue philosophique* 27 (1894): 46–72.

Metzger, Lore, ed. "Coleridge's Vindication of Spinoza: An Unpublished Note." *Journal of the History of Ideas* 21 (1960): 279–293.

Morley, Edith J., ed. *Henry Crabb Robinson on Books and Their Writers.* 2 vols. London: Dent, 1938. These volumes contain the references to contemporary English books and their writers in Crabb Robinson's diary, travel journals, and reminiscences.

Rehorn, Karl. *G. E. Lessings Stellung zur Philosophie des Spinoza.* Frankfurt, 1877.

Stephen, Leslie. *History of English Thought in the Eighteenth Century.* London, 1876. Ch. 1, Par. 33.

Suphan, Bernhard. *Goethe und Spinoza, 1783–86.* Berlin, 1882.

Voltaire. *Le philosophe ignorant.* Geneva, 1766. Cited from Voltaire, *Mélanges.* Paris, 1961.

Frederick M. Barnard (1967)

SPIR, AFRIKAN ALEXANDROVICH

(1837–1890)

Afrikan Alexandrovich Spir, the Russian metaphysician was born in Elizavetgrad (present-day Kirovohrad) in the Ukraine, the son of a Russian doctor and a mother of Greek descent. Spir became interested in philosophy when, at the age of sixteen, he read Immanuel Kant's *Critique of Pure Reason,* a work that was to have a profound influence on him. He received no formal education in philosophy, however, and consequently never gained entry into philosophical circles, either in his native country or in Germany, where he settled in 1867. Spir attended a naval cadet school. He received both the Order of St. George and the Order of St. Andrew for his services as a naval officer. Before leaving Russia, he freed all his serfs and gave them land and lodging. He also gave away most of his money and lived on the income from the remainder. In 1869 Spir wrote that only two human activities have real worth—socially useful work and intimate discourse among people who think alike, yet in his lifetime Spir was denied both of these; indeed, few philosophers have been so isolated or ignored.

During the fifteen years Spir lived in Germany he published many articles and several books, including his major philosophical work, *Denken und Wirklichkeit* (Thought and reality; Leipzig, 1873), but notices and reviews were few. Bad health cut him off even further from the world. Hoping for a more receptive audience among French-speaking readers, Spir moved to Switzerland in 1882, but his work remained unknown and his views not understood. He died in Geneva, a Swiss citizen, just as his writing was beginning to attract attention.

Spir's later writings are on the whole restatements and clarifications of the metaphysical views presented in *Denken und Wirklichkeit,* which he felt might have been neglected because of its difficulty. In *Denken und Wirklichkeit* Spir argued that the task of philosophy is to seek absolutely true knowledge. In order to carry out this task, two immediately certain facts must be recognized: consciousness and the supreme law of thought, the principle of identity. This principle is the expression of a norm, of the a priori concept of the unconditioned, that is, of an object that is its own essence and is self-identical. To deny this concept is to deny that it can be conceived and, hence, that it can be denied. The principle of identity is seen to be the one synthetic a priori principle.

To the subjective necessity of this norm is added an objective proof: All our experience disagrees with it and, therefore, it cannot be a mere generalization from experience. Finally, the principle of identity adds something to experience: All phenomena are organized as if they were self-identical; therefore the principle of identity is the condition of all the regularity of experience.

The unconditioned is, then, the norm, true essence, or God. The unconditioned, however, is not the source or ground of the conditioned: The norm cannot be the source of the abnormal, which contains elements of falsity foreign to the absolute. The relation of the absolute to the phenomenal can best be described analogously, as the relation of an object to its false idea. Having no relation to true being, the phenomenal world simply cannot be explained, its principle can only be thought of as its very abnormality, as its nonself-identity, as becoming. Hence the phenomenal world has no beginning and no end. At the same time, since it is conditioned by becoming, it strives for and evolves to what it is not, the normal. In man, empirical nature has evolved to consciousness, to the awareness of its abnormality. In this awareness man recognizes a norm. Thus he rises above empirical nature and sees the law of his true being as the law not of nature but of the norm, as the laws of morality and logic. Thus morality rises above natural science and, since the moral law is the norm, morality becomes religion.

See also Kant, Immanuel; Metaphysics, History of; Russian Philosophy.

Bibliography

WORKS BY SPIR

Recht und Unrecht. Leipzig: J.G. Findel, 1879. Translated into English by A. F. Falconer as *Right and Wrong.* Edinburgh: University Court of the University of St. Andrews, Oliver and Boyd, 1954.

Gesammelte Werke von A. Spir. 2 vols., 4th ed. Leipzig, 1908–1909.

WORKS ON SPIR

Jodl, Friedrich. "African Spir." *Zeitschrift für Philosophie* 98 (1891).

Lapshin, I. I. "A. Spir, sa vie, sa doctrine." *Bulletin de l'Association russe pour les recherches scientifiques à Prague* 7 (42) (1938).

Lessing, Theodor. *African Spirs Erkenntnislehre.* Erlangen, Germany, 1899. Dissertation.

Zacharoff, Andreas. *Spirs theoretische Philosophie.* Jena, Germany, 1910. Dissertation.

Mary-Barbara Zeldin (1967)

SPIRITO, UGO
(1896–1979)

Ugo Spirito, the Italian idealist philosopher, was born in Arezzo. He began his academic career as assistant to Giovanni Gentile at Rome and first established his reputation as an acute interpreter and trenchant defender of "actual idealism." He was also one of the founders of "corporative" economic studies in fascist Italy and always maintained an active interest in economics and in political and social science.

Spirito held that Gentile's "pure act" was not merely a philosophical concept but was also necessarily a concept of philosophy itself as an activity. This belief led Spirito in 1929 to proclaim the identity of philosophy and science, because all actual knowledge must be the solution of a determinate historical problem and neither philosophy nor science as they occur in actual experience can claim an absolute status independent of the history of their genesis and of the progress of further research. According to Spirito, the actual unity of philosophy and science is what is realized in the process of scientific research; his claim that the "pure act" is the conscious achievement of this unity led to the conception of life as research, set forth in his best-known book *La vita come ricerca.* In this work the absolute philosophical knowledge of traditional metaphysics was presented as the ideal limit toward which scientific research must forever tend but which it can never attain.

In later works, Spirito was led to an ever more strictly negative or critical conception of the task of philosophy because of the difficulty of defining this ideal goal and the paradox involved in discussing it without knowledge of it (which could only come from the secure possession of an eternal standpoint). The philosopher must confine himself to the task of identifying and exposing all claims to absolute knowledge and all forms of antihistorical dogmatism or superhistorical metaphysics wherever they occur. Such claims will otherwise impede the free advance of positive research, which includes all types of inquiry leading to the acquisition of knowledge, whether theoretical or practical. In aesthetics, for example, the philosopher must concentrate on removing prejudices created by definitions and philosophies of art; he must leave to artists, critics, and competent students the construction of the positive science of aesthetics.

This negative conception of the philosopher's task necessarily presupposes a positive philosophy of scientific research itself as a cooperative and progressive solution of problems that organized social groups of researchers define for themselves. Theoretical problems are solved when science replaces personal opinion. Similarly, practical disagreements will be properly resolved only when scientific planning replaces the selfish initiatives of private individuals. The ideal of social competence must replace the ideal of personal culture in ethics and education, for only through commitment to membership in the community of positive research can an objective criterion of moral and practical values be found without recourse to any metaphysical or religious absolutes. Thus, Spirito inverted the conception of the relation between philosophy and science and between technical competence and general culture, which he found in Benedetto Croce and Gentile. He became one of the leaders of a new Hegelian left in Italy.

Bibliography

WORKS BY SPIRITO

Scienza e filosofia. Florence, 1933.

La vita come ricerca. Florence, 1937.

La vita come arte. Florence, 1941.

Opere complete, 12 vols. (as of 1965). Florence, 1950–.

La vita come amore. Florence: Sansoni, 1953.

Critica della democrazia. Florence: Sansoni, 1963.

Storia antologica dei problemi filosofici. Firenze: Sansoni, 1965–.

Il comunismo. Firenze: Sansoni, 1965.

Dal mito alla scienza. Firenze: Sansoni, 1966.

Machiavelli e Guicciardini. Firenze: Sansoni, 1968.

Giovanni Gentile. Firenze: G.C. Sansoni, 1969.

La vita come amore; Il tramonto della civilt‡ cristiana. Firenze: G.C. Sansoni, 1970.

L'idealismo italiano e i suoi critici. 2nd ed. Roma: Bulzoni, 1974.

La fine del comunismo. Roma: G. Volpe, 1978.

Tamassia, Franco. *L'opera di Ugo Spirito: Bibliografia*. Roma: Fondazione U. Spirito,1986.

Il Pensiero di Ugo Spirito. Roma: Istituto della Enciclopedia italiana, 1988–1990.

Memoirs of the Twentieth Century. Amsterdam; Atlanta, GA: Rodopi, 2000.

H. S. Harris (1967)
Bibliography updated by Michael J. Farmer (2005)

SPRANGER, (FRANZ ERNST) EDUARD
(1882–1963)

Eduard Spranger, the German philosopher and educator, was born in Grosslichterfelde, Berlin. He studied both mathematics and science at a *Realschule* and the humanities at a classical Gymnasium. At the University of Berlin he studied under Wilhelm Dilthey and Friedrich Paulsen and earned his right to lecture with *Wilhelm von Humboldt und die Humanitätsidee* (Berlin, 1909), a classic in the history of German humanism. He was called to the University of Leipzig as professor of philosophy in 1911 and to Berlin as professor of philosophy and pedagogy in 1920. He spent the most creative years of his career and exercised his greatest influence on the *Geisteswissenschaften* and on all levels of German education while at Berlin. In 1933 he submitted his resignation in protest against interference with university freedom by the new National Socialist government but was persuaded by many followers to retain his influential university position. In 1937/1938 he lectured in Japan. He was arrested and imprisoned in 1944 but was released upon the intercession of the Japanese ambassador. Appointed rector of the University of Berlin by the Allied military government in 1945, he found it impossible to accept interference by the East Berlin authorities and in 1946 accepted a professorship in philosophy at Tübingen, where he lectured until his retirement.

Spranger sought to further two projects begun by his teacher, Dilthey. One was an "understanding" (*verstehende*) psychology that would approach human life not with scientific abstractions but perceptively and with an appreciation of cultural values; the other was an attempt to provide a normative interpretation of the *Geisteswissenschaften*. The interdependence of these two problems led Spranger to a Hegelian position (toward which Dilthey himself had begun to turn before his death), and he became a leading figure of the German neo-Hegelian revival of the 1920s.

In his chief work, *Die Lebensformen* (Halle, 1914; translated by J. W. Pigors as *Types of Men*, Halle, 1928), Spranger undertook a typological analysis of personality through the use of the method of *Verstehen*. He held this method to be empirical in that it results in "an at least minimally categorialized after-experience." It is essentially an aesthetic perception of cultural forms in individual life and is motivated by a Platonic *eros*—a love for the personal values involved; this, Spranger insisted, does not interfere with its objectivity. Six forms of value—all of which are objectively rooted in the historical and cultural order, and each of which may dominate a person's life and evoke a reordering of the others in subordination to itself—determine six types of personality in modern culture—the theoretical, economic, aesthetic, social, political, and religious—which center, respectively, in the values of truth, utility, beauty, love; power, and, in religion, in the devotion to a vital totality of value. The moral is not a distinct type of value but enters into all valuations. Spranger schematized these types into an ideal order without denying individual freedom in value selection.

Spranger's *Psychologie des Jugendalters* (Leipzig, 1924; 8th ed., 1926) applied his method and conclusions to the problems of youth. Four important attainments mark the sound growth of the adolescent: the discovery of self, the development of a life plan, the ordering of the self into the different spheres of human relations, and the awakening of the sexual life and *eros.* The six personality types developed in the *Lebensformen* can serve as a schema for comprehending the individual person in exploring these critical developments.

Spranger's analysis of the *Geisteswissenschaften* found application in his discussions of the ethical bases of modern culture and education. It combined criticism of the historical philosophies of society and culture with the development of a modified Hegelian theory of objective spirit. Subjective and objective spirit are in close interaction within every historically relative situation. To them Spranger added a third dimension of spirit, the normative. This, the relativized absolute spirit of G. W. F. Hegel, comprised the factors that serve a regulative role in history through art, religion, and philosophy. Responsibility for the actualization of the normative, however, lies in the individual; no cultural content becomes meaningful except "insofar as it is again and again created out of the attitude and the conscience of the individual soul."

After World War II Spranger turned to religious themes, particularly in *Die Magie der Seele* (Tübingen, 1947). This "magic of the soul," which is essential to the life of a culture, is constituted by the religious consciousness and serves not to meet immediate external goals but to augment the powers of the person himself. Faith is a "withdrawal into inwardness."

Spranger's work in the philosophy of education kept the classical humanistic ideal alive and exercised a liberating effect on all levels and dimensions of education. It found notable expression in classic studies of great figures in education—Wilhelm von Humboldt, Jean-Jacques Rousseau, Friedrich Froebel, Johann Heinrich Pestalozzi, and Johann Wolfgang von Goethe. Spranger was also involved in most of the ethical and cultural problems of German life, addressing himself to such challenges as labor education, vocational education, personal and vocational guidance, and juvenile delinquency. The eloquence of Spranger's lectures and writings, his personal warmth, felt by a wide circle of friends of all ages, and his combination of keen perception with deep moral concern made him one of the most admired and influential of German thinkers. His deep sense of the German tragedy, and his long preoccupation with its moral and historical causes and the moral cost of redemption, won for him, before he died, the most distinguished honors that his country could bestow.

See also Dilthey, Wilhelm; Froebel, Friedrich; Geisteswissenschaften; Goethe, Johann Wolfgang von; Hegel, Georg Wilhelm Friedrich; Hegelianism; Humanism; Humboldt, Wilhelm von; Paulsen, Friedrich; Pestalozzi, Johann Heinrich; Rousseau, Jean-Jacques.

Bibliography

Among Spranger's other works are *Wilhelm von Humboldt und die Reform des Bildungswesen* (Berlin, 1910); *Goethes Weltanschauung. Reden und Aufsätze* (Leipzig and Wiesbaden, 1942); *Gibt es ein Kulturpathologie?* (Tübingen, 1947); and *Aus Friedrich Froebels Gedankenwelt* (Heidelberg, 1951).

For a complete bibliography of Spranger's works, see Theodore Neu, *Bibliographie Eduard Spranger* (Tübingen: Niemeyer, 1958).

For discussions of Spranger's thought and influence, see *Erziehung zur Menschlichkeit–Festschrift für Eduard Spranger zum 75. Geburtstag,* edited by H. W. Bähr (Tübingen: Niemeyer, 1957); and *Eduard Spranger, Bildnis eines geistigen Menschen unserer Zeit,* edited by Hans Wenke (Heidelberg: Quelle and Meyer, 1957).

L. E. Loemker (1967)

STACE, WALTER TERENCE

(1886–1967)

Walter Terence Stace, the Anglo American empiricist philosopher, was born in London. He was graduated from Trinity College, Dublin, in 1908 and from 1910 to 1932 served in the civil service in Ceylon. During this period he published *A Critical History of Greek Philosophy* (London, 1920) and *The Philosophy of Hegel* (London, 1924). In 1932 he retired from the civil service to teach philosophy at Princeton University, where he remained until his academic retirement in 1955. He was president of the American Philosophical Association in 1949.

Stace's *The Theory of Knowledge and Existence* (Oxford, 1932) is the definitive statement of his general position on philosophical method. His argument rests on the claim that on strict empirical grounds the solipsist position is logically unassailable. Whereas philosophers such as George Santayana, starting with the same claim, appealed to a doctrine of "animal faith" and emphasized the irrational element in belief in an external world, Stace carefully and in detail offered an analysis of the steps whereby we construct our conception of an external physical world out of the available data. He often spoke of his doctrine as a theory of *fictions*, but in print he preferred the word *constructions*. The point is that the construction of the fiction of an external world is neither irrational nor animal. It is a step-by-step inference that, although it fails to provide a logical answer to solipsism's claims, does satisfy human demands for reasons for belief. Ultimately our reasons for belief rest, according to Stace, upon two general claims that can be empirically supported—the claims that human minds are similar and that they labor together in common. These two empirical facts, and not logical proofs, support our commonsense beliefs. This thesis lies at the heart of most of Stace's later work.

Stace in this earlier period was an advocate of the sense-datum theory. In spite of continued association of his name with G. W. F. Hegel, he was chiefly indebted to David Hume, G. E. Moore, and Bertrand Russell. His main object of attack was Russell's *Our Knowledge of the External World*, which, according to Stace, constantly violates the principle of empiricism. In 1934 he published one of his best-known articles, "The Refutation of Realism" (*Mind* 43 [1934]: 145–155), in response to Moore's influential "The Refutation of Idealism." Moore's argument was based upon a distinction between sense data and our awareness of them. Stace replied that one can grant the distinction and still deny any force to the claim that sense data exist when not being perceived. He generalized the claim that there can be no good reason for believing any version of the proposition that entities exist unperceived. They may so exist, but it is absurd to claim that this can be empirically proved. It follows that where "such proof is impossible, the belief ought not to be entertained."

This argument seems, on the face of it, to contradict the thesis of *The Theory of Knowledge and Existence*. Stace always subsequently maintained, however, that his article had been misunderstood because it was not recognized as irony. He also insisted that Moore's article had been intended as humorous. The irony of his own consisted in showing that the simplest natural belief cannot be supported by strict logical proofs.

Stace's next major work was *The Concept of Morals* (New York, 1937). In one sense the main argument of the book might be, and has been, characterized as a version of subjectivism because it associates a general theory of the meaning of moral judgments with a general theory of man's wants and approvals. Perhaps the most permanently valuable aspect of the argument, however, is the attempt to disassociate the view he is defending from the label "subjectivist." Stace held that the proper contrast between subjectivism and objectivism is between views which make reasoned adjudication of ethical disputes impossible, and views which provide rational grounds for holding that one moral claim can be correct and its rivals mistaken. According to Stace, what makes his view objectivist in this significant sense is the connection between it and a general theory of man's nature, including his desires, wants, and approvals. The result is a modified version of utilitarianism based upon the same two principles emphasized in the theory of knowledge, the similarity of men's minds and the fact that they labor together in common.

In two articles ("Positivism," *Mind* 53 [1944]: 215–237; and "Some Misinterpretations of Empiricism," *Mind* 67 [1958]: 465–484) Stace distinguished empiricism from recent positivistic tendencies. The intention of both is to attack the attempt on the part of more recent logical empiricists, who, Stace claimed, associate empiricism with the demand for strict logical proofs.

In September 1948 Stace published in the *Atlantic Monthly* (pp. 53–58) an article titled "Man against Darkness." The thesis of the article, which Stace considered neither very original nor very shocking, was that the worldview endorsed by the physical sciences since the time of Galileo Galilei is incompatible with Christianity's traditional worldview. The violent reaction to this article stunned him. There followed *The Gate of Silence* (Boston, 1952), a book-length poem; *Philosophy and the Modern Mind* (New York, 1952), a careful historical study of the thesis that had been popularly stated in "Man against Darkness"; and *Time and Eternity* (Princeton, NJ, 1952), an essay in the philosophy of religion which many consider his most profound work.

No doubt partially because of the years he had lived in Ceylon, Stace was attracted to Hinayana Buddhism, and both *The Gate of Silence* and *Time and Eternity* reveal the extent of that influence on his later metaphysical thought. The theme of paradox runs throughout these works: "Men have always found that, in their search for the Ultimate, contradiction and paradox lie all around them.… Either God is a Mystery or He is nothing at all" (*Time and Eternity*, p. 8).

Thus, Stace now held that belief must transcend the confines of strict logic, and the rigorous empiricist ended by courting mysticism. Fully aware of this fact, Stace set himself to what he conceived to be his final philosophical task—the reconciliation of empiricism and mysticism. The result was *Mysticism and Philosophy* (New York, 1960). He claimed (1) that the mystical experience is a fact, is unique, and is the same in all cultures; (2) that the interpretations of the mystical experience vary widely from culture to culture; and (3) that a genuine empiricism cannot ignore the mystical experience simply because it is logically paradoxical.

Throughout the somewhat otherworldly philosophical reflection of his later life, Stace retained an interest in practical problems. His *The Destiny of Western Man* (New York, 1942) was an expression of horror against the irrational totalitarianism that swept Europe in the 1930s. In February 1947 he published an article in the *Atlantic Monthly*, vigorously attacking the legal basis of Zionist arguments. In early 1960s he was concerned with the universal condemnation of colonialism, insisting that high generalizations be checked against the evidence. In a letter to the *New York Times* (February 4, 1964), he wrote that colonialism "civilized half the world at the cost of the loss of some *amour propre*, of some snobbishness, of some arrogance, of some hard feeling, but—in the case of the Romans and British, at any rate—of very little real cruelty, injustice or tyranny."

See also Buddhism; Empiricism; Mysticism, Nature and Assessment of; Solipsism.

Bibliography

ADDITIONAL WORKS BY STACE

"The Metaphysics of Meaning." *Mind* 44 (1935): 417–438.

A Critical History of Greek Philosophy. London, Macmillan; New York, St. Martin's Press, 1965.

Man against Darkness, and Other Essays. Pittsburgh: University of Pittsburgh Press, 1967.

The Nature of the World: An Essay in Phenomenalist Metaphysics. New York, Greenwood Press, 1969.

Time and Eternity: An Essay in the Philosophy of Religion. New York, Greenwood Press, 1969.

The Destiny of Western Man. Westport, CT, Greenwood Press, 1970.

The Theory of Knowledge and Existence. Westport, CT, Greenwood Press, 1970.

Mysticism and Philosophy. New York: Macmillan, 1972.

The Concept of Morals. Gloucester, Mass., P. Smith, 1975.

Religion and the Modern Mind. Westport, CT: Greenwood Press, 1980.

Works on Stace are A. J. Ayer, "The Principle of Verifiability," in *Mind* 45 (1936): 199–203, a reply to Stace's "The Metaphysics of Meaning"; C. J. Ducasse, a review of *Mysticism and Philosophy*, in *Journal of Philosophy* 59 (1962): 323–335; H. H. Price, "Mr. Stace on the Construction of the External World," in *Mind* 42 (1933): 273–298; and Ralph E. Stedman and H. B. Acton, "Mr. Stace's Refutation of Realism," in *Mind* 43 (1934): 349–353. On *The Theory of Knowledge and Existence*, see the critical notice by F. C. S. Schiller in *Mind* 42 (1933): 94–100, and the review by L. Susan Stebbing in *Philosophy* 8 (1933): 354–357.

James Ward Smith (1967)
Bibliography updated by Michael J. Farmer (2005)

STAËL-HOLSTEIN, ANNE LOUISE GERMAINE NECKER, BARONNE DE
(1766–1817)

Anne Louise Germaine Necker Baronne de Staël-Holstein, the French novelist and essayist, was born in Paris, the daughter of Suzanne Curchot and Jacques Necker, finance minister to Louis XVI. In 1786 she married Eric Magnus, baron of Stäel-Holstein, the Swedish ambassador to France, from whom she separated in 1797. In the year of her marriage she published her first novel, *Sophie,* and four years later a tragedy, *Jeanne Grey.*

Her interest in philosophy began with a study of Jean-Jacques Rousseau, whose fervent admirer she remained throughout her life. She incurred the hostility of Napoleon Bonaparte both by her frank criticism and by her liberalism, and her advocacy of a constitutional monarchy led to her being exiled in 1802. She made her first trip to Germany at this time, a trip that was the occasion of her book *De l'Allemagne.* This work was sent to the printer in 1810, but it was condemned by the censor and did not appear until 1813. After years of traveling, Mme. de Staël returned to Paris, where she remained until her death.

The philosophical ideas of Mme. de Staël are to be found mainly in two books, *De la littérature considérée dans ses rapports avec les institutions sociales* (1800) and *De l'Allemagne.* In the former she attempted to show the influence of religion, morals, and laws on literature and that of literature upon religion, morals, and laws. This book presupposed the perfectibility of man, as Mme. de Staël admitted, but human progress was not automatic; to come into being it required the constant and deliberate aid of education (*les lumières*), which could be provided only through literature. A second premise was that of national characters, the Greek being given to art, emulation, and amusement; the Roman, to dignity, gravity of speech, and rational deliberation. Later she contrasted the Northerner and the Southerner, in *De l'Allemagne* exemplified respectively by the German and the Frenchman.

Nevertheless, there is nowhere in Mme. de Staël's writings the notion of national souls or collective spirits (*Geister*). People to her were individuals, and whatever community of interests and talents they showed was to be attributed to the influence of other individuals.

Mme. de Staël never questioned the absolute value of personal liberty. This belief she attributed to Protestantism, her family religion. To her, Protestantism rested on the principle of personal interpretation, and the source of one's convictions was to be looked for in the heart, just as it was in the teachings of Rousseau's Savoyard vicar. She held that individual differences in temperament were irreconcilable, and believed that only statistics could help a statesman solve his people's ethical problems. It may have been this firmly rooted idea that made her fear the natural scientist as the tool of despots. The scientist, who rejects everything that cannot be reduced to mathematics, is always willing to pursue his own ends, regardless of the vital interests of his fellow men.

The chief contribution of *De l'Allemagne* to philosophy was that it acquainted Mme. de Staël's countrymen with the works of Immanuel Kant, Johann Gottlieb Fichte, Friedrich von Schelling, and Friedrich Schlegel. She presented their ideas simply and sketchily but on the whole correctly. In this way she helped break the hold that the sensationalism of the school of Étienne Bonnot de Condillac had had upon the French. Mme. de Staël wrote no book that can be considered as technical philosophy, but she represents the mind that has absorbed a philosophy as a technique of thinking and as a corrective to authoritarianism.

Bibliography

WORKS BY MME. DE STAËL

Lettres sur les ouvrages et le charactère de J.-J. Rousseau. Paris, 1788.

De l'influence des passions sur le bonheur. 2 vols. Lausanne, 1796. A defense of reason as a critical agent.

De la littérature considérée dans ses rapports avec les institutions sociales. Paris, 1800.

De l'Allemagne. 3 vols. London, 1813.

Oeuvres complètes, 17 vols. Paris, 1820–1821.

WORKS ON MME. DE STAËL

Blennerhasset, Charlotte. *Frau von Staël, ihre Freunde und ihre Bedeutung in Politik und Literatur.* 3 vols. Berlin: Gebrüder Paetel, 1887–1889. Translated by J. E. Gordon Cumming as *Mme. de Staël, Her Friends and Her Influence on Politics and Literature.* London: Chapman and Hall, 1889.

Gautier, Paul. *Mme. de Staël et Napoléon.* Paris: Plon-Nourrit, 1903.

Herold, J. Christopher. *Mme. de Staël, Mistress to an Age.* Indianapolis, 1958. A popular but well-documented biography.

Ollion, E. *Les idées philosophiques morales et pedagogiques de Mme. de Staël.* Mâcon, 1910. Thesis.

George Boas (1967)

STAHL, GEORG ERNST

(1660–1734)

Georg Ernst Stahl was a leading German medical scientist and chemist of his day. Stahl was appointed professor of medicine at the University of Halle in 1694, and from 1716 until his death he served as personal physician to Frederick William I of Prussia. His numerous medical writings had a strongly doctrinal tendency, which made them the source of lively, often bitter, controversy. His famous phlogiston theory, an erroneous explanation of the nature of combustion and calcination, was nonetheless, before Antoine Lavoisier's discoveries, instrumental in placing chemistry on a scientific basis. The same may be said of his studies concerning the properties and composition of acids, alkalis, and salts.

Led by his medical, rather than chemical, interests to philosophy, Stahl elaborated (particularly in his *Theoria Medica Vera*, 1707) a rigorous position of animism, affirming that the animal organism was formed, governed, and preserved by an immaterial principle, or soul. If Stahlian thought was indebted to the *archei* of J. B. van Helmont's occultist biology, and more broadly to both neo-Aristotelian and Neoplatonic versions of animism in the late Renaissance, his notion of soul, reflecting the impact of post-Cartesian dualism, was typical of his own period. He conceived of it as essentially a rational and spiritual substance distinct from matter, but simultaneously he assigned to it the ability to control the organism by an "unconscious" mode of activity. Thus, the soul not only thinks and wills but, having constructed its body, also excites, regulates, and sustains all involuntary and vital processes. It does so by the intermediary of movement, which Stahl regarded as an immaterial entity, for matter itself is held to be essentially passive and inert. The soul, by a specific energy, is supposed to communicate the "spiritual act" of movement to the organism in pursuance of its own aims.

This rather obscure view of things (which Gottfried Wilhelm Leibniz, among others, criticized) was not improved by Stahl's manner of expression, a mixture of dogmatic haughtiness and repetitious turgidity. If he failed, moreover, to consider properly the various contradictions and difficulties peculiar to his position, this was due largely to his lack of interest in metaphysics as such. His animism was intended less as a philosophical contribution than as a theoretical standpoint from which to perceive and evaluate the phenomena of disease and health in accordance with an expectative approach to therapeutics. Even more significantly, it represented a protest against the dominant iatromechanist and iatrochemical schools, which at the time tended to see animate beings too naively and rigidly in terms of facile mechanical analogies and unexplained chemical reactions. But although Stahl's animism had the merit of emphasizing the presence of an irreducible "life force" having no equivalent in the machine, the omnipresent role allowed to this life force at the expense of a purely organic dynamism proved untenable.

The influence of Stahlianism was checked during the first half of the eighteenth century by the success of the mechanistic and empirical doctrines of Hermann Boerhaave and Friedrich Hoffmann. Subsequently, Stahl's medical philosophy was reinterpreted at the important Faculty of Montpellier, with the general result that its spiritualist aspect was abandoned as unscientific while its insistence on a metamechanical "vital principle" in the organism was adopted as profoundly valid. Stahl thereby came to be recognized as the founder of the vitalistic school of modern biology.

See also Cartesianism; Lavoisier, Antoine; Leibniz, Gottfried Wilhelm; Macrocosm and Microcosm; Panpsychism; Philosophy of Biology; Renaissance; Vitalism.

Bibliography

WORKS BY STAHL

Oeuvres médico-philosophiques et pratiques. 5 vols. Paris, 1859–1863.

WORKS ON STAHL

Duchesneau, Francois. "Stahl, Leibniz, and the Territories of Soul and Body." In *Psyche and Soma: Physicians and Metaphysicians on the Mind-Body Problem from Antiquity to Enlightenment*, edited by John Wright. Oxford: Clarendon Oxford Press, 2000.

Gottlieb, B. J. *Bedeutung und Auswirkungen Stahls auf den Vitalismus*. Halle, 1943.

Lemoine, Albert. *Le vitalisme et l'animisme de Stahl*. Paris: Baillière, 1864.

Metzger, Hélène. *Newton, Stahl, Boerhaave et la doctrine chimique*. Paris: Alcan, 1930.

Aram Vartanian (1967)
Bibliography updated by Tamra Frei (2005)

STAMMLER, RUDOLF
(1856–1938)

Rudolf Stammler was a German neo-Kantian legal philosopher. His first major work, *Die Lehre vom richtigen Recht*, outlined his philosophy of law, which was elaborated in subsequent works. Stammler sought to apply Immanuel Kant's distinction between pure and practical reason to the law. The embodiment of pure reason in legal theory is the concept of law, which Stammler defined as "combining sovereign and inviolable volition." The counterpart of practical reason is the idea of law, that is, the realm of purposes realized by volition. But whereas for Kant practical reason was not, like pure reason, a matter of intellectual perception, but of morality, Stammler sought to formulate a theoretically valid idea of justice. He based it on the community of purposes and the fact that man is a reasonable being, an end in himself. From this he derived two "principles of respect" and two "maxims of participation." The former are that no one's volition must be subject to the arbitrary desire of another and that any legal demand must be of such a nature that the addressee could be his own neighbor. The latter are that no member of a legal community must be arbitrarily excluded from the community and that a legal power may be exclusive only insofar as the excluded person can still be his own neighbor.

For Stammler these were not merely formal principles; they could be used to solve actual legal problems. He attempted, for example, to apply them to the legality of cartels and to the solution of disputes between upper and lower riparian owners over the use of water. His solutions were generally those of a moderate liberal.

Max Weber has shown in "Rudolf Stammlers Überwindung des materialistischen Geschichtsauffassung" (*Gesammelte Aufsätze zur Wissenschaftslehre*, Tübingen, 1922, pp. 291–359) that Stammler's alleged formal categories are in fact categories of progressive generalizations, the more general being relatively more formal than the less general. Stammler's main error was his attempt to make the idea of justice a matter of theoretical knowledge; it was therefore inevitable that he should confuse principles generally acceptable to a moderate liberal with universally valid principles of justice. His idea of justice is therefore a cross between a formal proposition and a definite social ideal, kept abstract and rather vague by the desire to remain formal. Stammler's chief merit remains his reintroduction of legal philosophy as a vital aspect of the study of law.

See also Continental Philosophy; Justice; Kant, Immanuel; Neo-Kantianism; Philosophy of Law, History of; Weber, Max.

Bibliography

WORKS BY STAMMLER

Wirtschaft und Recht. Halle, 1896. Law and economics are related as form and matter.

Die Lehre vom richtigen Recht. Halle, 1902. Translated by I. Husik as *The Theory of Justice.* New York: Macmillan, 1925.

Theorie der Rechtswissenschaft. Halle: Buchhandlung des Waisenhauses, 1911.

Lehrbuch der Rechtsphilosophie. Berlin and Leipzig: de Gruyter, 1922.

WORKS ABOUT STAMMLER

Ginsberg, Morris. "Stammler's Philosophy of Law." In *Reason and Unreason in Society: Essays in Sociology and Social Philosophy.* Cambridge, MA: Harvard University Press, 1948.

Stone, Julius. *Human Law and Human Justice.* London: Stevens, 1965.

Wolfgang Friedmann (1967)
Bibliography updated by Philip Reed (2005)

STATE

Before the sixteenth century the word *state* was used to refer to the *estates* of the realm or to kingly office or dignity, but not to an independent political community. Niccolò Machiavelli was largely responsible for establishing this modern usage. The change, however, was not in words only but also in ways of thinking about political organization and political relations. In feudal society a man figured in a network of quasi-contractual relations in which his political rights and duties were closely linked to land tenure and fealty. He was his lord's man and his king's man. The powers of kingship were only with difficulty distinguished from property rights. From the twelfth century on, the conceptions of Roman law began once more to influence political thought. Public authority was more sharply distinguished from private rights; the peculiar position of the king among his barons, which feudal writers recognized but found difficult to conceptualize, came to be expressed in Roman terms—the *princeps* was said to speak on behalf of the whole people and to exercise *imperium,* as distinct from a feudal privilege, because his care was for the whole *respublica.*

However, so long as barons could still simultaneously hold fiefs from different kings in different lands, the notion could not develop of the territorially defined state, making an exclusive claim to the allegiance of all who resided within its borders. The idea that men could be not only subjects of their king but also citizens of their state became possible with the consolidation of national monarchies in England, France, and Spain. Its development was assisted in the thirteenth century by the quickening of interest in Aristotle's ideas about the city-state and, in the early sixteenth century, by the Renaissance interest in the ancient Roman republic. Classical elements, then, were grafted onto the late medieval stock to produce the Renaissance state.

With the declining influence of such customary forms of regulation as feudal and manorial ties, the guild, and the family, the state became an indispensable category for any kind of speculative thought about society. Moreover, as the grip of custom slackened, men came to think that law might be made by an authoritative will rather than discovered by the understanding or known by tradition. The political order, as the authority structure through which law was created and which therefore conferred legal status and rights on all other forms of association, gained a corresponding preeminence. Out of the split in the universal church and the consequent alliance for mutual survival between protestant princes and religious reformers, there emerged the idea of a national church closely related to the state, further stressing that the state was a community or polity and not simply an aggregation of men who happened to owe allegiance to a common overlord. The consolidation of national states created a new state of nature—a world peopled by sovereign states recognizing no overriding authority and only tenuously subject, if at all, to a common law. Francisco Suárez, Francisco de Vitoria, Hugo Grotius, and Samuel von Pufendorf, the pioneers of international law, explored the relations between states in such a world; what was implied for the internal structure of a state was worked out by Jean Bodin and Thomas Hobbes.

IDENTITY OF THE STATE

Since the seventeenth century, political philosophers have been largely preoccupied with the relations of the state and the individual, with the citizen's rights, if any, against the state, with the right of the state to punish, to promote morality, or to regulate the affairs of other associations such as families, trade unions, and churches. These matters have been all the more troublesome because there is disagreement about the proper analysis of propositions about the state. For instance, what does it mean to say that a state has acted in a certain way, made a decision, adopted a policy, assumed responsibility, and so on? These are not statements about every one of its citizens, nor are they simply statements about the acts of certain individuals who govern the state; for not all the actions of the person who for the time being is president are acts of the United States, nor is an act of the state always attributable to one person in particular. Hobbes was certainly mistaken when he argued that what made an aggregate of many men into one corporate person was that one man acted for the rest: "The *unity* of the representer, not the *unity* of the represented … maketh the person *one*" (*Leviathan* I, 16).

Again, what kind of sustained identity has the state, that one can speak of its enduring through many generations of natural lives? It is tempting to meet such a question with an organic analogy: Although the cells die and are replaced, the organism survives; although an action of an organism requires nothing more than the coordinated operations of its organs, it is not identical with the actions of any one or of all of them (unless their functions as elements in an organism are presupposed in the descriptions of their actions). The organism, it is often said, is a form of life transcending its parts; purposes are attributed to it that are not the purposes of any one of its parts or of all of them taken severally. Many writers, notably the Hegelians, have described the state in this way, exalting the interests of the state at the expense of the interests of its members considered as individuals.

A quite different account of the state has been given by writers who have employed atomic or contractual models, with explanatory analogies drawn from joint-stock corporations, clubs, or perhaps from mechanical contrivances. Thus, Hobbes talks of the state as an *artificial* man, contrived by an agreement of self-determining individuals. It can have no purposes not ultimately reducible to the purposes of individuals; its acts are those of a sovereign authorized to act on their behalf. The contractual analogy in Hobbes and John Locke is a device for explaining how and under what conditions the acts of one or a few ruling individuals could be attributed to a body composed of a multitude of free and autonomous persons, all with their own separate interests, yet each committed by his own consent to a public interest in which he has a personal stake.

The problem of meaning, however, must be distinguished from the moral problem of obligation. The notion of corporate action does not necessarily entail consent or authorization on the part of individual members, although it could be argued that without consent the individual could have no moral commitment or responsibility. Acts of the state are acts of persons in an official capacity, acting according to procedures and within the competence prescribed by the rules of its constitution. A president's actions are those of the United States only when they form part of a particular procedural routine; they then indicate appropriate responses by other officials. When the president acts in nonofficial roles—as father or as member of his golf club—his actions are incidents in what a Wittgensteinian would call different "games" and therefore have appropriately different implications. The enduring identity of a state can be correspondingly analyzed in terms of the endurance of its procedural order. The Constitution of the United States has had an unbroken history since its adoption in 1788; the changes it has suffered have all been valid according to the criteria it prescribes for itself.

This sort of analysis explains the personality and life of a state without resorting to organic analogies or to metaphysical notions of an order of being where a whole is greater than the sum of its parts. However, it does not deal with all the problems. Despite several revolutions since 1789, there is a sense in which the French state has a continuous history, unlike the Austro-Hungarian state that was destroyed after World War I and replaced by a number of successor states. If the population of an area continues to be governed undivided, as an independent political unit, there seem to be grounds for saying that it remains the same state, despite changes in regime. In the case of France, although formal continuity of legitimization broke down between, for instance, the Second Empire and the Third Republic, there is a continuity of tradition and, despite deep cleavages, a sense that however bitterly rival groups contend, they are nevertheless committed by their awareness of history and common culture to remaining in political association. A struggle to control or reconstruct the machinery of government is not necessarily, then, an attempt to break up the political association, as it was in the Austro-Hungarian Empire.

THE STATE AS AN ASSOCIATION

To call the state an association is to put it on the same footing as clubs, churches, and trade unions. There are features of the state, however, which, although no one of them is peculiar to the state alone, together make it a rather special case. For instance, because people do not usually become or remain members of a state by choice, and because a state exercises exclusive authority over everyone in a given territory, the concept of membership is hazier than in the case of voluntary associations. The state insists that not only its citizens but also everyone else in its territorial jurisdiction shall conform to its rules. Indeed, the notion of a citizen suggests a certain minimum degree of active participation. This may be restricted, as it was in Athens, to a relatively small number of the resident native population. In that case, would the association include only the citizens? Are the rest outsiders on whom the state imposes its will, much as a trade union might insist that nonunionists shall not work for lower wages than its members? Or are citizens and noncitizens merely two classes of members, one with rights of participation, such as the right to vote, the others with private rights only?

Unlike trade unions, literary societies, joint-stock corporations, and guilds, the state's range of interests is very wide and, in principle, unlimited. This, too, is connected with its nonvoluntary character. Even allowing for migration and naturalization, people do not easily join or leave a state, and when they do, it is usually only with its permission. And whether they join it or not, they are subject to it if they reside in its territory. Consequently, the state does not need to define the terms and aims of their membership. Neither is there any higher authority which can rule, as the state's judicial authorities may do in relation to other associations, that a proposed act falls outside its terms of association and therefore infringes its members' rights. This indeterminancy of scope is a characteristic that the state shares with the family and even with some churches. Such associations have no defined set of aims: The behavior norms they sustain may govern a very wide, if fluctuating, segment of the social life of their members. And since the mid-1800s the effective sphere of the state has encroached increasingly on the spheres of other associations.

THE STATE AND CONFLICTS OF INTEREST

The state's territorial inclusiveness and the uncertain limits to its concern have led many political philosophers to assign to it a unique role among the forms of human association. Plato's *Republic* sketched an ideal state in which men's conflicting interests and energies were harnessed and reconciled by philosopher-rulers who would integrate them into a single-minded unity, the principles of which could be discovered by a philosophical insight. Aristotle claimed that, at its best, the Greek *polis* was the most perfect association because, while including lesser associations like the family and the village, it was large enough to provide within itself everything necessary for the good life. For Aristotle, citizenship was a matter not of passively enjoying rights but of participating energetically in the many-sided life of the *polis.* The Greek writers had in mind a small state, a face-to-face community capable of satisfying emotional needs that the impersonal mass state of the twenty-first century cannot. Nevertheless, the same completeness that Aristotle found in the *polis* has often been attributed to the modern state.

Jean-Jacques Rousseau, though tempted to identify the modern state with the *polis,* hesitated to do so unconditionally. He believed that the state was sufficient for the expression of all human excellencies. The vocation of the citizen was the highest to which a man could aspire. Participating in the expression of the general will for the common good of the whole association, the citizen rose above private interest and became a moral person, "substituting justice for instinct in his conduct.... man, who so far had considered only himself, finds that he is forced ... to consult his reason before listening to his inclination" (*Social Contract* I, 8). Membership of the state was for Rousseau, as for Plato and Aristotle, a moral education; bad laws corrupted nature, good laws provided conditions for moral development and nobility of soul. Not only was nothing needed beyond the state but also, Rousseau suspected, lesser associations, by setting up partial or sectional interests as objects of loyalty, frustrated the public interest and corrupted the state. Nevertheless, the ideal state of Rousseau's *Social Contract* remained a city-state, small enough for everyone to know everyone else. The attempt by others to extend the conception to the nation-state led to confusion in theory and, in practice, to Jacobin totalitarianism.

G. W. F. Hegel transformed Rousseau's doctrine by substituting for personal, face-to-face relations a metaphysical dependence of parts on the whole. The state was the concrete universal, the individual a mere partial expression of it. Sectional associations had a function in organizing human interests. They operated, however, on a lower plane of reality than the state, a plane that Hegel termed "civil society." This was not a different order from the state but the same social organization viewed from the standpoint of the subjective ends that individuals set themselves. It was the plane of the free market economy motivated by the pursuit of profit and sectional advantage, where competitive conflicts are checked, ordered, and adjusted by the police. Nevertheless, unknowingly and despite themselves, individuals promoted ideal ends. Interests that from the subjective point of view of civil society were sectional and egoistic appeared objectively in the state as moments or partial expressions or functions of the greater whole. The state would then rightly regulate although not supplant such interests. For Plato and Rousseau the conflict of interests was a pathological symptom in a state; for Hegel it was an unreality masking a fundamental unity that the state would safeguard if necessary. For all three there was a transcendent public interest in which the apparent interests of individuals are dissolved and fused.

There is, however, another view that takes the conflict of interests as a fundamental fact of nature; it can be controlled but never finally superseded. Machiavelli, Hobbes, and Jeremy Bentham were in this tradition. The state existed to regulate competition, since without it individual objectives would be mutually frustrating. The harmony it achieved, however, was artificial; the state remedied a desperate situation by altering the conditions under which men sought their own interests, deflecting them from antisocial ends by fear of punishment. Karl Marx and Friedrich Engels, agreeing that the state suppressed conflict, saw it as a strictly coercive instrument maintained by the dominant economic class to safeguard its privileges. But they believed that with the advent of a classless society, scarcity would give way to abundance, and conflict to harmony. The state would then wither away, to be replaced by a new administrative order without organized violence. The state, then, was a response to a pathological although historically necessary condition. Ultimately, however, the evolution of society would bring about the changes that would make Rousseau's vision possible. For Augustine the earthly state was the palliative for sin; for Marx it was the palliative for class conflict. But for both there was a condition of ultimate redemption, where the coercive state would have no place.

For John Locke civil society (equivalent in Locke's terms to the state) existed to safeguard the natural rights of individuals, which they could not successfully preserve in the state of nature. Nevertheless, because Locke considered people rational by nature and therefore ideally capable of living in peace according to the law of nature, the condition of conflict was pathological, not natural. However, the norm was not participation in a transcendent good but a condition in which everyone enjoyed their own area of legitimate privacy, troubled by neither private nor public intrusions. For Locke, as for Hobbes, the state's ends were reducible to those of individuals. Bentham put this quite unequivocally: "This public interest … is only an abstract term; it represents only the mass of the interests of individuals" (*Principles of the Civil Code, Works,* Vol. I, p. 321). The state had and could have no moral function except to arrange that as many people as possible should obtain as much as possible of whatever it was that they wanted. For some purposes all that was needed was for the state to uphold property and the sanctity of contract; economic motives in a free market would do the rest. But Benthamite utilitarianism was committed to active state policies wherever, as in public health, laissez-faire would not work. The Benthamite state was readily convertible to a Fabian policy of social engineering. But the objective would still be, in Roscoe Pound's phrase, "such an adjustment of relations and ordering of conduct as will make the goods of existence … go round as far as possible with the least friction and waste" (*Social Control through Law,* New Haven, CT, 1942, p. 65).

The view that politics is a matter of who gets what is substantially that of the group theorists in political science, such as A. E. Bentley and, more recently, Harold Lasswell, David Truman, and Robert Dahl. In their accounts, the state is dissolved into a "political process" which can be analyzed without residue in terms of the competitive pressures of interests. Whereas Locke and Rousseau would have agreed that the public interest was the proper end of state action (although possibly disagreeing in their accounts of it), many modern political scientists, Glendon Schubert, for instance, have rejected the concept of public interest as being so vague as to be useless or as being a device of politicians for advocating policies actually pursued for quite other reasons. Policy decisions, they argue, are the resultants of competing interests—there is no single interest that everyone would acknowledge, nor one that would be to everyone's advantage. Thus, there can be no public interest that the state ought to pursue.

An analysis like Schubert's depends, on the one hand, on the identification of interest and desire and, on the other hand, on interpreting "public" to mean "enjoyed by everyone." This was clearly not Rousseau's meaning. A citizen's interest was in being a person of a certain kind with characteristic excellences, attainable only in a healthy state. One might misguidedly desire what was not in his interest; so might all the citizens, for the will of all was not necessarily the same as the general will. But as long as their vision was clear, conflict was impossible because the public interest was whatever would be to *anyone's* advantage, insofar as he was capable of human excellence.

Political scientists mistrust such a theory, partly because it tends to describe the actual state as if it were the ideal and partly because it is evaluative, whereas they want theories to be descriptive and explanatory. What is in a man's interest, they say, is simply what he strives to get, irrespective of why he does so or with what wisdom. However, treating the state as simply an arena for sectional pressures has the drawback of disregarding or misconstruing the widespread opinion that to act in the public interest is to be impartial between competing groups—that the state (or its rulers) is therefore in a special position as arbiter between group interests. This frequently gives state decisions a moral authority that a mere political barometer, responding to the greatest pressures, could never enjoy, and it provides politicians and public servants, potentially at least, with a range of motives that are quite unlike interests as usually understood.

Sheldon S. Wolin, in *Politics and Vision,* advanced the somewhat paradoxical thesis that despite the vast extension of governmental activity, there has been a steady depreciation of politics and the political order since the seventeenth century. This has been matched, he asserts, by a corresponding heightening of regard for nonpolitical institutions and associations—for society as distinct from the state. This "groupism" is regrettable, in Wolin's view, because the specialized roles adopted by the individual are no substitute for citizenship. Citizenship, as the individual's most general role, calls on him to choose regardless of special interests. As a member of a society bounded for most purposes by the state's frontiers, he is confronted with this demand only as a member of the state. As a trade unionist, for instance, he shares sectional loyalties with coworkers and is led to strive for advantages at the expense of other groups. To be conscious of oneself as a citizen, however, is to enjoy an integrative experience, which "demands that the separate roles be surveyed from a more general point of view." The political art, in Wolin's opinion, is that "which strives for an integrative form of direction, one that is broader than that supplied by any group or organization." Wolin comes close indeed to the view of Rousseau and Hegel that there is a concrete morality in the state. As a citizen one is asked to judge what would be to the advantage of *anyone,* their special circumstances aside. In this manner one approaches a moral judgment, an impartial assessment of claims in matters of general concern.

A further disadvantage of a fragmented vision of the political process is its tendency to miss the influence of the state, both as an idea and as a tradition, on the life of the society. As a trade union or a church is not simply an arena for its own sectional interests, so each state embodies a set of values and objects of loyalty which may greatly influence what its members consider their interests to be. Its manners and traditions leave their mark on them. Associations that participate in its political processes reflect its style, its modes of organization, and its procedures. Moreover, the state lays down terms on which its members deal with one another and with foreigners, establishing an area within its borders in which trade, communications, and movement are free, and regulating traffic that crosses them. Because of its regulative power, the texture of social relations is far closer within its boundaries than across them. It thus supplies not only a legal but also a general conceptual framework for much of our social thought and action. Thus, where we speak of Australian primary producers' associations, Australian football teams, and the Australian Political Studies Association, we speak not of the Australian state but of Australia.

This seems to support the Hegelian view of the state as a national community within which certain particular functions are promoted by sectional associations operating within it. But then one must distinguish the state in this sense from its governmental authority structure, which would be but one of its organs alongside trade unions, graziers' associations, and the like. For voluntary and sectional associations are not, like departments of state, of the navy, or of the post office, subordinate parts of the governmental structure, nor are their actions the acts of the state. This distinction would be quite consistent with a generalized although conditional duty on the part of sectional associations to submit to governmental authority. However, it would not be a duty owed by subordinate agencies to a superior but rather one owed by members of a society in which an authority is recognized as arbiter and coordinator of interests and as initiator of policies of general concern. This would also be consistent with the moral right of associations to defy the government should these functions be abused. The fact that the government is the executive agent of the politically organized state does not mean that its own views of the public interest or of a just settlement of conflicting claims must always and necessarily prevail.

The word *nation* is often used to refer to the state-community; so, in slightly different contexts, is the word *country.* Both words, however, have other meanings and overtones, *nation* being used of cultural groups which can transcend state frontiers or which may be minorities within a state, *country* referring more particularly to the state's territory or to the state as an international personality.

LIMITS OF STATE ACTION

Liberal political philosophers have tried to define necessary limits beyond which the activities of the state must not extend. Some, like Locke, account for the existence of the state in terms of some specific function, such as the safeguarding of natural rights. They then infer, by analogy with the statement of aims in the articles of association of a club or joint-stock company, that the state would be exceeding its competence if it did more than that. Others have tried to define an area of private action that the state ought not invade. According to J. S. Mill, for instance, the state is never justified in restraining the action of a normal adult solely on the grounds that it is in his interests that it should. Some, like T. H. Green and Ernest Barker and, in a more sophisticated form, F. A. Hayek, have claimed that the state as a coercive organization has intrinsic limitations. Although it can hinder hindrances to the good life, it cannot force people to live that life; any form of activity, such as religion, art, or science, whose value lies in spontaneity or freedom of belief must therefore fall outside its scope. Barker argued that because the state's essential mode of action was through general rules, it was not apt for any field that, like industry, required ad hoc discretionary decisions. Such an argument depends, however, on a very doubtful kind of essentialism. The state has no one modus operandi. For the varied range of activities that states have undertaken since the mid-1800s, they have devised an equally varied range of techniques. They encourage the arts as well as censoring them. Nearly all modern states have very extensive responsibilities in education, industrial management, health insurance, and medical services, all of which have at one time been private undertakings and none of which involves coercion except in very remote or indirect ways. It does not follow from the state's monopoly of legitimate coercion that it can do nothing for which coercion is inappropriate. Nor need we suppose that, if there are indeed forms of social activity that the state has at present no satisfactory means of regulating, encouraging, or promoting, it may not yet invent them. Therefore, one cannot say in advance whether a given task would be more properly left to individual initiative or organized by governmental agencies. That depends on what can be done with the techniques available.

See also Aristotle; Augustine, St.; Bentham, Jeremy; Bodin, Jean; Engels, Friedrich; General Will, The; Green, Thomas Hill; Grotius, Hugo; Hegel, Georg Wilhelm Friedrich; Hobbes, Thomas; Locke, John; Machiavelli, Niccolò; Marx, Karl; Mill, John Stuart; Nationalism; Plato; Political Philosophy, History of; Pufendorf, Samuel von; Punishment; Renaissance; Rousseau, Jean-Jacques; Social Contract; Society; Sovereignty; Suárez, Francisco; Vitoria, Francisco de.

Bibliography

Virtually all the works listed in the bibliography to the Sovereignty entry are also relevant to this topic. The works listed here are therefore additional references.

HISTORICAL TREATMENTS

Cassirer, Ernst. *The Myth of the State.* New Haven, CT: Yale University Press, 1946.

Jouvenel, Bertrand de. *Du pouvoir. Histoire naturelle de sa croissance.* Geneva, 1945. Translated by J. F. Huntington as *On Power: Its Nature and the History of Its Growth.* New York: Viking, 1949.

Nisbet, Robert. *The Quest for Community.* New York: Oxford University Press, 1953. Republished as *Community and Power.* New York: Oxford University Press, 1967.

Plamenatz, John. *Man and Society.* 2 vols. London: Longman, 1963.

Wolin, Sheldon S. *Politics and Vision.* Boston: Little, Brown, 1960.

ANALYTICAL WORKS

Benn, S. I., and R. S. Peters. *Social Principles and the Democratic State.* London: Allen and Unwin, 1959. Republished as *Principles of Political Thought.* New York: Collier, 1964.

Jouvenel, Bertrand de. *De la souveraineté.* Paris: M. T. Génin, 1955. Translated by J. F. Huntington as *Sovereignty: An Inquiry into the Political Good.* Chicago: University of Chicago Press, 1957.

Jouvenel, Bertrand de. *The Pure Theory of Politics.* New Haven, CT: Yale University Press, 1963.

Mabbott, J. D. *The State and the Citizen.* London: Hutchinson's University Library, 1948.

THE APPROACH OF MODERN POLITICAL SCIENTISTS

Bentley, A. F. *The Process of Government.* Chicago: University of Chicago Press, 1908.

Dahl, Robert A. *Modern Political Analysis.* Englewood Cliffs, NJ: Prentice-Hall, 1963.

Friedrich, Carl J. *Man and His Government.* New York: McGraw-Hill, 1963. Includes extensive bibliography.

Friedrich, Carl J., ed. *The Public Interest.* New York: Atherton Press, 1962. This is Vol. V of American Society of Political and Legal Philosophy, ed., *Nomos.*

Lasswell, Harold D., and Abraham Kaplan. *Power and Society: A Framework for Political Inquiry.* New Haven, CT: Yale University Press, 1950.

Schubert, Glendon. *The Public Interest.* Glencoe, IL: Free Press, 1960.

WORKS IN THE CLASSICAL LIBERAL TRADITION

Barker, Ernest. *Principles of Social and Political Theory.* Oxford, 1951.

Bentham, Jeremy. *A Fragment on Government* (London, 1776). Edited by W. Harrison. Oxford: Blackwell, 1948. This volume also contains *Introduction to the Principles of Morals and Legislation.*

Bentham, Jeremy. *Traités de législation, civile et pénale,* edited by E. Dumont. Paris, 1802. Translated by R. Hildreth as *The Theory of Legislation.* Boston: Weeks, Jordan, 1840; London: Trubner, 1864.

Bentham, Jeremy. *Works,* edited by John Bowring, 11 vols. London, 1843.

Hayek, F. A. *The Constitution of Liberty.* London: Routledge and K. Paul, 1960.

Locke, John. *Two Treatises of Government* (1690), edited by Peter Laslett. Cambridge, U.K.: Cambridge University Press, 1960.

Mill, J. S. *On Liberty* (1859) and *Considerations on Representative Government* (1861). Edited by R. B. McCallum. Oxford, 1946; London, 1947.

Popper, Karl. *The Open Society and Its Enemies.* 2 vols., 4th rev. ed. London: Routledge and K. Paul, 1962.

MARXIST VIEWS

Bottomore, T. B., and M. Rubel, eds. and trs. *Karl Marx: Selected Writings in Sociology and Social Philosophy.* 2nd ed. London: Penguin, 1961. Includes selected bibliography of Marx's writings.

Engels, Friedrich. *Der Ursprung der Familie, des Privateigenthums und des Staats.* Zürich, 1884. Translated by Lewis H. Morgan as *Origin of the Family, Private Property and the State.* 4th ed. London, 1946.

Lenin, V. I. *Gosudarstvo i Revoliutsiia.* Petrograd, 1918. Translated as *State and Revolution* in *Selected Works,* edited by J. Fineberg. Vol. VII. London, 1946.

Marx, Karl, and Friedrich Engels. *Die deutsche Ideologie* (1845–1846). In *Marx–Engels Gesamtausgabe.* Berlin, 1932. Part I, Vol. V. Parts I and III were edited by R. Pascal and translated by William Lough and Charles P. Magill as *The German Ideology.* London: Lawrence and Wishart, 1938.

Marx, Karl, and Friedrich Engels. *Manifest der kommunistischen Partei.* London, 1848. Edited with introduction by Harold J. Laski as *Communist Manifesto: Socialist Landmark.* London: Allen and Unwin, 1948.

CATHOLIC THEORIES OF NATURAL LAW

Entrèves, A. P. d'. *La dottrina dello stato; elementi di analisi e di interpretazione.* Turin: Giappichelli, 1962.

Maritain, Jacques. *Man and the State.* Chicago: University of Chicago Press, 1951.

FASCIST VIEWS

Gentile, Giovanni. *Genesi e struttura della società.* Florence: Sansoni, 1946. Translated and edited by H. S. Harris as *Genesis and Structure of Society.* Urbana: University of Illinois Press, 1960. The views of the official philosopher of Italian fascism from the standpoint of "actual idealism."

Stanley I. Benn (1967)

STATE [ADDENDUM]

In the past three centuries, states have replaced empires and tribes as the dominant form of political organization. But one clear lesson of the twentieth century is that the vast powers of states can be put to disastrous as well as beneficent ends.

Philosophical reflection about states often begins with Thomas Hobbes and the rational justification of social order as mutually advantageous. Many more contemporary philosophers have ignored the state, however, focusing instead on justice and the rights and liberties that states should respect. Indeed, the most important work in political philosophy in the twentieth century (Rawls 1972) does not discuss the state—it lacks even one entry for "the state" in its index.

In recent years there has, however, been a renewed interest in the state that has developed along several lines. Some have used modern game theory to pursue Hobbes's question of the possibility of a rational justification of the state. Others have studied the nature of the state itself and its relationship with other forms of social control, while some have questioned both the authority and the legitimacy of states. Another topic is the impact on states of global economic, social, and legal transformations.

Questions about the nature of states can be addressed either by considering the similarities and differences among states, nations and governments or by comparing states with other ways of maintaining social order. Nations and peoples are distinct from states, as evidenced by the fact that we often speak of "stateless" peoples such as Kurds and Palestinians. Nations and peoples are marked by common cultures and histories that provide the basis of a shared identity. Governments are also distinct from states: the head of the government in the United Kingdom (the prime minister) is not the head of state (the monarch is), just as the U.S. president is the head of state but not of the government as a whole. What, then, are states?

Unlike both ancient empires and the overlapping allegiances of feudal Europe, states claim sovereignty, and of a specific sort. Empires lacked clear territorial boundaries and often shared sovereignty with local rulers. In feudal Europe political power was fragmented among different and often overlapping jurisdictions that encompassed kings, lords, local rulers, bishops, and popes who demanded allegiance or taxes or both. Sovereign states differ from these forms of political control because they have a centralized and hierarchical organization ruling over a defined territory with established boundaries. A state also claims to be the ultimate source of legal authority and demands loyalty from all permanent inhabitants within its territory.

Although many assume that states' claims to authority and legitimacy could be vindicated—that states could be made just—anarchists have questioned both claims. Robert Paul Wolff (1976) attacked the state's authority by attacking authority in general. He argued that because people are responsible for their own decisions based on reasons that they understand to be relevant, the claimed authority of states is illegitimate. One cannot both accept responsibility for one's own actions and submit to the authority of the state, said Wolff. This claim has spurred Joseph Raz (1979) and others to look more closely at authority. Raz agrees that authority involves a type of surrender or acquiescence of judgment, though he denies that this is always contrary to reason. He explains by distinguishing first-order reasons (where we weigh competing reasons and act accordingly) from second-order reasons that "preempt" first-order reasons. The eclipsing of first-order reasons by the authority's judgment suggests that Wolf is right in casting doubt on the state's claim that it is always an authority, although it also implies that it is sometimes not a violation of autonomy to decide to act for second-order reasons.

Robert Nozick (1974) raised questions not only about the state's authority but also about the widely presumed legitimacy of the state's use of coercive power. The only legitimate exercise of coercive power, he argued, would be vastly different from powers states commonly claim. A legitimate state's power is limited, for example, by people's rights to refuse to join the state or to join only on terms that are voluntarily. While Nozick defends the state's use of coercion to protect rights to property and life, he questions whether the many other, familiar coercive measures are legitimate—measures ranging from paternalistic efforts to protect people against themselves to laws preventing self-regarding but immoral acts to taxes aimed at redistributing wealth and providing social services. In painting an attractive and purportedly workable picture of an anarchist society, both Wolff and Nozick have encouraged a fresh look at states' claims to authority and legitimacy as well as at alternative methods of maintaining social order.

Economic, legal, and social forces are also affecting states. States traditionally claim both internal sovereign control over populations and immunity from external power, yet both ideas have come under increasing pressure from many different angles. As the world has become smaller and more integrated and corporations do business in different states, it is often important for states to harmonize laws governing commerce and immigration. Adding to these pressures for more cooperation has come a need to meet growing international problems such as environmental degradation and terrorism—neither of which can be effectively addressed without the cooperation of other states. This greater interdependence of states, and their mutual vulnerability, has even sparked renewed interest in possible preemptive actions against states as a form of self-defense.

Alongside these challenges to the external sovereignty of states has come greater emphasis on human rights, further weakening states' claims of internal sovereignty over their own populations. International tribunals, nongovernment aid organizations, and sometimes unilateral military action in the name of helping citizens or protecting them from their own states have all challenged the supremacy of state power. Yet despite all these forces working to limit states' sovereignty, terrorism has also brought home the importance of avoiding "failed states" in which terrorists can train and plan. So although states are losing authority and sovereignty because of globalization, mutual interdependence, and growing legal limits on their power, the prospect of failed states breeding terrorists abroad and anarchy at home has strengthened the case of defenders of the state power.

See also Anarchism; Authority; First-Order Logic; Hobbes, Thomas; Justice; Liberty; Nozick, Robert; Political Philosophy, History of; Rights; Sovereignty; Terrorism.

Bibliography

Fukuyama, Francis. *State-Building: Governance and World Order in the 21st Century*. Ithaca: Cornell University Press, 2004.

Green, Leslie. *The Authority of the State*. Oxford: Clarendon Press, 1990.

Morris, Christopher. *An Essay on the Modern State*. Cambridge, U.K.: Cambridge University Press, 1998.

Nozick, Robert. *Anarchy, State, and Utopia*. New York: Basic Books, 1974.

Rawls, John. *A Theory of Justice*. Cambridge, MA: Harvard University Press, 1972.

Raz, Joseph. *The Authority of Law*. Oxford: Oxford University Press, 1979.

Wolff, Robert Paul. *In Defense of Anarchism*. 2nd ed. New York: Harper and Row, 1976.

John Arthur (2005)

STATEMENTS

See *Propositions*

STATISTICAL MECHANICS, PHILOSOPHY OF

See *Philosophy of Statistical Mechanics*

STATISTICS, FOUNDATIONS OF

Thorny conceptual issues arise at every turn in the ongoing debate between the three major schools of statistical theory: the Bayesian (B), likelihood (L), and frequentist (F). (F) rather uneasily combines the Neyman-Pearson-Wald conception of statistics as "the science of decision making under uncertainty" with Ronald A. Fisher's theories of estimation and significance testing, viewed by him as inferential. However, in keeping with his frequentist conception of probability, Fisher viewed the inferential theory of Thomas Bayes and Pierre Simon de Laplace as applicable only where the needed prior probability inputs are grounded in observed relative frequencies. Maximum likelihood estimates and significance tests were intended as substitutes for Bayesian inference in all other cases. (F), (B) and (L) all provide a framework for comparatively appraising statistical hypotheses, but Fisher questioned whether one can fruitfully assimilate the weighing of evidence to decision making.

Given the response probabilities for a diagnostic test shown in Table 1:

TABLE 1

	Positive	Negative
Infected (h)	0.95	0.05
Uninfected (k)	0.02	0.98

one may, following Richard M. Royall (1997, p. 2), usefully distinguish three questions of evidence, belief, and decision when a subject (S) tests positive:

Q1. Is this result evidence that S has the disease?

Q2. What degree of belief that S has the disease is warranted?

Q3. Should S be treated for the disease?

(L) addresses only Q1 and does so by what Ian Hacking (1965) dubs the law of likelihood (LL):

> evidence e supports hypothesis h over k if and only if $(Pe|h) > P(e|k)$; moreover, *the likelihood ratio* (LR), $P(e|h) : P(e|k)$, measures the strength of the support e accords h over k.

The LL follows from Bayes's fundamental rule for revising a probability assignment given new data. Indeed, Laplace arrived (independently) at this rule by appeal to the intuition that the updated odds in favor of h against k in light of e should be the product of the initial odds by the LR (Hald 1998, p. 158):

(1)
$$P(h \mid e) : P(k \mid e) = \frac{P(e \mid h)}{P(e \mid k)} \times \frac{P(h)}{P(k)}$$

If the rival (mutually exclusive) hypotheses h and k are treated as exhaustive, so that their probabilities sum to one, then (1) yields the usual form of Bayes's rule:

(2)
$$P(h \mid e) = \frac{P(e \mid h)P(h)}{P(e)}$$

with $P(e)$ usually given in the general case by the partitioning formula:

(3) $$P(e) = P(e|h_1)P(h_1) + \ldots + P(e|h_n)P(h_n)$$

with the (mutually exclusive) considered hypotheses h_1, $\ldots$, h_n treated as exhaustive.

One also sees how (B) answers Q2 by multiplying the initial odds, based on what is known about the incidence of the disease, by the LR of 95/2 provided by a positive reaction. If the incidence of the disease is even as low as 1 per 1,000, the posttest (or "posterior") probability of infection may still lie well below 50 percent. Notice, too, that knowledge of the infection rate may rest on the same sort of empirical frequency data that underwrites the conditional probabilities of Table 1. When this is true, (L) and (F) have no qualms about applying (2) to answer Q2. They do not question the validity of (2), only whether the initial probabilities needed to apply it can be freed of the taint of subjectivism.

THE LIKELIHOOD PRINCIPLE

Statistical hypotheses typically assign values to one or more parameters of an assumed probability model of the experiment, for example, to the mean of a normal distribution or the probability of success in a sequence of Bernoulli trials. If θ is such a parameter and X the experimental random variable then

$$P(x|\theta)$$

is called the sampling distribution when considered as a function of the observation x and the likelihood function qua function of θ.

The case of randomly sampling an urn with replacement, with p the population proportion of white balls, affords a simple illustration. Then the probability of x white and n-x black in a sample of n is given by the binomial (sampling) distribution:

$$P(x \mid n, p) = \binom{n}{x} p^x (1-p)^{n-x}$$

For comparing two hypotheses about p by the LR, the binomial coefficients cancel and so one may ignore them and define the likelihood function for this experiment by:

$$L(p) = p^x(1-p)^{n-x}$$

The value of p, which maximizes $L(p)$, is called the maximum likelihood (ML) estimate of p and is easily found, by calculus, to be x/n, the observed sample proportion (of white balls) or successes.

Consider, next, a second experiment in which one samples until the first success is observed. This happens on trial n with probability, $p(1-p)^{n-1}$, since $n-1$ failures must precede the first success. More generally, if one samples until the *rth* success is observed, this happens on trial n with probability:

$$P(r \mid n, p) = \binom{n-1}{r-1} p^r (1-p)^{n-r}$$

which reduces to $p(1-p)^{n-1}$ when $r = 1$. This sampling distribution is called the negative binomial (or waiting time) distribution; it gives rise to the same likelihood function as the first experiment.

Now suppose Jay elects to observe $n = 30$ trials and finds $x = 12$ successes, while May elects to sample until she finds $r = 12$ successes but that happens to occur on the thirtieth trial. In a literal sense, both experimenters have observed the same thing: twelve successes in thirty Bernoulli trials. One would think they would then draw the same conclusions. (F) violates this prescription, called the likelihood principle (LP). In so doing (F) allows the experimenter's intentions when to stop sampling to influence the evidential import of what is observed. It also makes the import of the outcome observed dependent on the entire sample space, hence, on outcomes that might have been but were not observed (see de Groot 1986, p. 417). By the same token, the unbiased estimators favored by (F), those centered on the true value of the parameter, violate the LP (p. 417), since this concept depends on all possible values of the estimator. Thus, the unbiased estimates of p are, respectively, k/n and $(k-1)/(n-1)$ for the two previous experiments. The LP virtually defines the difference between (B) and (L), on the one hand, and (F), on the other.

In effect, (B) and (L) charge (F) with inconsistency, with basing different assessments of the evidence (or different decisions to accept or reject hypotheses) on equivalent outcomes, for two outcomes are accounted equivalent by the LP if they define the same likelihood function. This charge of inconsistency can be carried to a higher metalevel since (F) accepts Bayes's rule (2), and with it the LP, when the prior probabilities are known from past frequency data. Hence (F) finds itself in the odd position of accepting or rejecting the LP according as the prior probabilities are "known" or "unknown." Charges of inconsistency are the weapon of choice in the ongoing battles between the three schools, beginning with the charge that Bayes's postulate for assigning a uniform distribution to a parameter about which nothing is known leads to inconsistent assignments. In the sequel, one will explore how consistency may be used instead to forge agreement.

FISHERIAN SIGNIFICANCE TESTS

Fisher (1935, chapter 2, the *locus classicus*) presented significance tests as analogues of the logicians' *modus tollens*: if A then B, not-B/∴not-A. When the probability, $P(e|h_0)$, falls below α, one counts e as evidence against h_0, the smaller α, the stronger the evidence. As Fisher describes it, the logic is "that of a simple disjunction: Either an exceedingly rare chance has occurred, or the theory is not true." Using (2), the probabilistic analogue of *modus tollens* is:

$$P(A \mid \bar{B}) = P(A)\left[\frac{P(\bar{B} \mid A)}{P(\bar{B})}\right]$$

which shows that for not-B to seriously infirm A requires, not merely that $P(\bar{B}|A)$ be small, but small relative to $P(\bar{B})$, so that some alternative to A must accord not-B a higher probability.

Much of Fisher's practice conforms to this precept. In his famous example of the tea-tasting lady (1935), the lady claims that she can tell whether tea or milk was infused first in a mixture of the two. To test her claim she is asked to classify eight cups of which four are tea-first and the other four milk-first, but, of course, she does not know which four. The relevant statistic is the number R of correct classifications and its sampling distribution on the null hypothesis that she lacks such ability is:

$$P(R = r \mid h_0) = \frac{\binom{4}{r}\binom{4}{4-r}}{\binom{8}{4}}$$

Notice, the probability that $R = r$ on the alternative hypothesis of skill cannot be computed so that likelihood ratios do not exist. All that one has to work with is an intuitive rank ordering of the outcomes with larger values of R more indicative of skill. What $P(R \geq r^*|h_0)$ measures may be verbalized as "the probability of obtaining, by chance, agreement with the hypothesis of skill as good as that observed" (Fisher 1935, p.13). Although Fisher rejected the implication that by "disproving" the null hypothesis one "demonstrates" the alternative (p. 16), he also says that "we should admit that the lady had made good her claim" (p. 14) if she classified all eight cups correctly. He argues that one can (effectively) disprove the null hypothesis because it is "exact," while the alternative of skill is vague. However, this does not preclude one from adopting the natural view of most researchers that a significant result is evidence in favor of the alternative hypothesis. The null hypothesis is then cast in the subtly different role of a fixed point of comparison that permits computation of the relevant chance probability (Rosenkrantz 1977, chapter 9).

This is, in fact, the logic of most nonparametric tests, the Wilcoxon rank sum test for comparing two treatments being paradigmatic (see Hodges and Lehmann 1970, §§12.3–12.4, especially p. 333). Table 2 compares the survival times (in years) following a heart attack of $t = 6$ patients receiving a new treatment and $s = 4$ controls receiving the standard treatment, with their ranks in parentheses.

TABLE 2

Treated	7.3 (4)	17.2 (1)	6.1 (6)	11.4 (3)	15.8 (2)	5.2 (7)
Controls	1.4 (9)	0.6 (10)	5.0 (8)	6.7 (5)		

The sum, W_t of the ranks of the t-treated patients is a suitable test statistic, and under the null hypothesis that the new treatment is no better than the old, all $\binom{10}{6} = 210$ assignments of ranks 1 through 10 to the six treated patients are equiprobable. Hence, the paucity of possible rank sums as small as the observed value, $W_t = 1 + 2 + 3 + 4 + 6 + 7 = 23$, measures the strength of the evidence, the smaller this proportion the stronger the evidence of improved efficacy. Since only three other possible rank sums are as small as the observed value of W_t, the relevant proportion is 4/210 = .019, or about 2 percent.

This same form of argument also enjoys widespread currency in the sciences, as when an anthropologist maintains that certain cultural commonalities are too numerous and striking to be ascribed to parallel development and point instead to contact between two civilizations, or when an evolutionist argues that the structural similarities between two organs that do not even perform the same function in two species are homologous and not merely analogous, hence indicative of common ancestry. Indeed, the rationale behind the principle of parsimony—that a phylogeny is more plausible if it requires fewer evolutionary changes—is this same piling up of otherwise improbable coincidences. And how improbable that various methods of reconstructing a phylogeny—for example, the ordering of fish, amphibians, reptiles, and mammals—based on the fossil record, homologies, serology, or DNA and protein sequencing should all agree if the phyla in question were separately created?

Fisher's foremost contribution to the design of experiments, randomization, also fits this logic (Fisher 1935, pp. 17–21, 41–44, 62–66). If, for example, the treated subjects of Table 2 were all younger than the controls, they might be expected to live longer in any case. However if, after controlling for such plainly relevant differences, the patients were assigned at random to the two groups, the chances are just one in $\binom{s+t}{t}$ that all treated subjects will share some hidden trait conducive to longevity that is lacking in the controls, thus removing any suspicion of selection bias. In addition, randomization underwrites the probability model of the experiment from which the sampling distribution of the chosen test statistic, W_T, is deduced (for a more leisurely discussion of randomization, see Hodges and Lehmann 1970, §12.1).

Since significance tests apply, on this reading, only when the likelihood function does not exist, they can be viewed as complements rather than alternatives to the methods of (B) or (L). Seen in this positive light, significance tests have a deeper Bayesian rationale. For the paucity of possible outcomes a model with zero or more adjustable parameters accommodates measures the support in its favor when the observed outcome belongs to this set (Rosenkrantz 1977, chapter 5). Echoing I. J. Good (who echoed Fisher), to garner support requires not just accuracy but improbable accuracy.

Moreover, the present formulation resolves many of the controversies that have swirled about significance testing (see Morrison and Henkel 1970), above all, the question whether a significant outcome with a small sample constitutes stronger evidence against null than one with a large sample (see Royall 1997, pp. 70–71). If, in fact, the chance probability of agreement with the causal hypothesis of interest is the same in both cases, the evidence in favor of that causal hypothesis is also equally strong.

All these advantages notwithstanding, significant test results are still most widely viewed as evidence against the null hypothesis and, indeed, without reference to alternative hypotheses (see Fisher 1935, pp. 15–16; 1956, pp. 40–42; and for a critique of this viewpoint, Royall 1997, chapter 3). Thus, one classifies the observed outcome as evidence for or against h_0 not by comparing its probability on h_0 to its probability on alternative hypotheses but by comparing its probability on h_0 with that of other possible outcomes.

NEYMAN-PEARSON THEORY

In the late 1920s Jerzy Neyman and Egon S. Pearson (henceforth, NP) set forth a new approach to the testing of statistical hypotheses. Although initially presented as a refinement of Fisherian significance testing, NP actually addressed the different problem of testing one hypothesis against one or more alternatives in situations where the likelihoods do exist. In such cases, Fisher's practice, in accord with (L), was to compare the relevant hypotheses by their likelihoods. NP proposed, instead, to lay down in advance a rule of rejection, that is, a critical region R of the space of outcomes such that the tested hypothesis is rejected just in case the outcome actually observed falls in R.

In the simplest case of testing one point hypothesis, $h_0 : \theta = \theta_0$ against another, $h_1 : \theta = \theta_1$, called simple dichotomy, one can err not only by rejecting h_0 when it is true but also by accepting h_0 when the alternative hypothesis, h_1, is true. Plainly, one cannot reduce both these error probabilities,

$$\alpha = P(X \in R|h_0)$$

and

$$\beta = P(X \notin R|h_1)$$

without increasing the sample size. NP's recommended procedure was to so label the hypotheses that rejecting h_0 is the more serious error, fix α at a tolerable level, α_0, called the size or significance level of the test, and then among all tests of this size, $\alpha \leq \alpha_0$, choose the one that minimizes β, or, equivalently, maximizes the power $1 - \beta$. The test is thus chosen as the solution of a well-defined optimization problem, a feature modeled on Fisher's approach to estimation. The fundamental lemma of NP theory then affirms the existence of a unique solution, that is, the existence of a most powerful test of a given size. Finally, test statistics could then be compared in terms of their power. The overall effect was to unify point estimation, interval estimation (confidence intervals), and testing under the broader rubric of "decision making under uncertainty," a viewpoint made explicit in the later work of Abraham Wald. In this scheme of things, estimates, confidence intervals, and tests are to be judged solely in terms of such performance characteristics as their mean squared error or their error probabilities. That is, arguably, the feature of the approach that continues to exercise the most powerful influence on the orthodox (i.e., frequentist) school (see Hodges and Lehmann 1970, chapters 11–13; de Groot 1986, chapter 7).

These developments occurred in such rapid succession that they have yet to be fully digested. NP had uppermost in mind massed tests like screening a population for a disease, testing a new drug, or industrial sampling inspection where the same practical decision, such as classifying a patient as infected or uninfected, must be faced repeatedly. For such situations, a reliable rule that controls for the probability of error seemed preferable to an explicitly (Bayesian) decision theoretic treatment that would require prior probabilities that the statistician could not base on any objective rule, as well as on loss or utility functions that would vary even more from one policy maker to another. To be sure, one might know the distribution of the proportion of defectives from past experience with a manufacturing process and be able to supply objective cost functions, but such cases would be uncommon.

But even in cases where an assembly line approach seems appropriate, NP's recommended procedure is open to question. If the more serious type 1 error is deemed, say, a hundred times more serious than the less serious type 2 error, should one not prefer a test whose probability of committing the more serious error is correspondingly less than its probability of committing the less serious error? In short, why not minimize the weighted sum, $100\alpha + \beta$? After all, the result of fixing α at some tolerable level, then minimizing β, might be to drive β much lower than α, which is wasteful, or else to drive β so high as to render the test powerless. This point is not merely academic, for a random sample of some seventy-one clinical trials revealed that overemphasis on controlling type 1 error probability led to a 10 percent risk of missing a 50 percent therapeutic improvement (Good 1983, p. 144).

To minimize the total risk, $a\alpha + b\beta$, one finds, writing $f_i(x) = P(X = x_i|h_i)$, $i = 1, 2$, that

$$a\alpha + b\beta = aP(X \in R \mid h_0) + bP(X \notin R \mid h_1)$$
$$= aP(X \in R \mid h_0) + b[1 - P(X \in R \mid h_1)]$$
$$= b + \sum_{x \in R} [af_0(x) - bf_1(x)]$$

Hence, the total risk is minimized by making $af_0(x) - bf_1(x) < 0$ for all $x \in R$. Then h_0 is rejected when

$$f_1(x){:}f_0(x) > a{:}b$$

which says: Reject h_0 (in favor of h_1) when the LR in favor of h_1 exceeds the relative seriousness, $a{:}b$, of the two kinds of error. More advanced readers will recognize this as a Bayesian decision rule for the special case of constant regret functions, appropriate in situations where "a miss is as good as a mile," and equal prior probabilities. In the general case, one may interpret $a{:}b$: as the product of the prior odds by the ratio of the regrets. The fundamental lemma then drops out as an easy corollary (de Groot 1986, p. 444), where the most powerful test of size α has critical region, $R = \{x{:}f_1(x){:}f_0(x) > k\}$, with k the least number for which $P(X \in R|h_0) \leq \alpha$. The main virtue of this approach, however, is that it allows one to adjust the sample size so as to achieve a tolerable level of overall risk. Roughly speaking, one goes on sampling until the marginal cost of one more item exceeds the marginal risk reduction.

NP's decision theoretic formulation notwithstanding, users of statistical tests have continued to interpret them as evidence and to view NP tests as a refinement of Fisher's significance tests. One reason for this is that NP continued to use the language of hypothesis testing, of accepting or rejecting hypotheses. A more important reason is that in many, if not most, scientific inquiries, practical decisions are nowhere in view. Even where questions of public policy impinge, as in the smoking-cancer or charter school controversies, it is deemed necessary to first weigh the evidence before deciding what policy or legislation to adopt. The tendency of NP is to subsume the individual test under a rule of specifiable reliability. Rejection of h_0 at a 5 percent level does not mean that the probability is 0.05 that a type 1 error was committed in this case, much less that h_0 has probability 0.05 given the outcome. The error probability refers to the procedure, not the result. However, this raises new concerns.

Consider a test of normal means of common (unknown) variance, σ^2, $h_0{:}\mu = \mu_0$ *versus* $h_1{:}\mu = \mu_1$. The optimal 5 percent test rejects h_0 when $\bar{x} \geq \mu_0 + 1.64\sigma/\sqrt{n}$, where n is the sample size and $\bar{x} = (x_1 + \ldots + x_n)/n$ is the sample mean. For as Carl Friedrich Gauss first showed, $\bar{x} \sim N(\mu, \sigma^2/n)$, that is, the sample mean for independent and identically distributed normal variates, $X_i \sim N(\mu, \sigma^2/n)$, is normally distributed about their common mean, μ, with variance, σ^2/n, or precision, n/σ^2, n times that of a single measurement. For example, if $\mu_0 = 0$, $\mu_1 = \sigma^2 = 1$, and $n = 30$ so that $\sigma^2/n = 0.18$, then h_0 is rejected when $\bar{x} \geq .30$. However, $\bar{x} = .30$ is $.70/.18 = 3.89$ standard deviation units below the mean of $\mu = 1$ posited by h_1, and thus much closer to $\mu_0 = 0$. It is strange that such an observation should be interpreted as strong evidence against h_0. Indeed, the LR given a random sample of n measurements is:

$$\frac{(2\pi\sigma^2)^{n/2}\prod \exp(-\frac{1}{2\sigma^2}(x_i - \mu_0)^2)}{(2\pi\sigma^2)^{n/2}\prod \exp(-\frac{1}{2\sigma^2}(x_i - \mu_1)^2)} = \exp\{-\frac{1}{2\sigma^2}\sum[(x_i - \mu_0)^2 - (x_i - \mu_1)^2]\}$$

which, using $\sum x_i = n\bar{x}$, simplifies further to:

(4)
$$f_0 / f_1 = \exp\left\{\frac{n(\mu_1 - \mu_0)}{\sigma^2}\left(\bar{x} - \frac{\mu_0 + \mu_1}{2}\right)\right\}$$

And with the values chosen, this specializes at the boundary point, $\bar{x} = 1.645\sigma/\sqrt{n}$, to

$$f_0/f_0 = \exp(1.645\sqrt{n} - 0.5n)$$

which tends to zero as $n \to \infty$. Even at a modest $n = 30$ one finds:

$$f_0/f_1 = \exp(1.645(\sqrt{30}) - 15) = 0.0025 = 1/400$$

or an LR in favor of the rejected h_0 of roughly 400:1.

Thus, one has a recognizable subset of the critical region, namely outcomes at or near the boundary, which more and more strongly favor the rejected hypothesis. The 5 percent significance level is achieved by a surreptitious averaging, for the critical region is built up by incorporating outcomes that give LR's greater than a critical value, starting with the largest LR and continuing until the size of the test is .05. Those first included give evidence against h_0 stronger than the significance level indicates, but the last few included often favor h_0. Better disguised examples of this phenomenon drawn from actual frequentist practice are given in chapter 9 of Jaynes (1983, especially pp. 182f), a critical comparison of orthodox and Bayesian methods that focuses on actual performance. For other criticisms of NP along these lines, see Fisher (1959, chapter 4), and John Kalbfleisch and D.A. Sprott, both of which repay careful study.

It is clear as well that NP violates the LP. In the example of binomial versus negative binomial given earlier,

Jay's most powerful 5 percent test of $h_0{:}p = \frac{1}{4}$ against $h_1{:}p = \frac{3}{4}$ rejects h_0 when $X \geq 12$ successes occur in the $n = 30$ trials, while May's best 5 percent test rejects h_0 when $n_0 \leq 29$, that is, when the twelfth success occurs on or before the twenty-ninth trial. Hence, they reach opposite conclusions when Jay records twelve successes and May obtains the twelfth success on the thirtieth trial. Notice, too, the outcomes 12 and 13 of Jay's experiment both favor h_0, even though the error probabilities of Jay's test are eminently satisfactory, with $\alpha \leq .05$ and $\beta = .0001$.

In keeping with the LP, it seems perfectly permissible to stop sampling as soon as the accumulated data are deemed sufficiently strong evidence for or against the tested hypothesis. This is, after all, the idea behind Wald's extension of NP theory to sequential tests (see Hodges and Lehmann 1970, §6.10). Could it really make a difference whether one had planned beforehand to stop when the sample proportion of defectives exceeds B or falls below A or decided this on the spur of the moment? To continue sampling till the bitter end in keeping with a preset sample size may place experimental subjects in needless jeopardy or even cause their death (for a chilling real-life example, see Royall 1997, §4.6). Thus, the ongoing debate over optional stopping raises serious ethical, as well as methodological, concerns.

(B) and (L) also permit enlarging a promising study to solidify the evidence, but because this can only increase the type 1 error probabilities, NP disallows it. This further points to the need to separate the presampling design of an experiment from the postsampling analysis of the resulting data.

But what about the fraud who resolves to go on sampling until some targeted null hypothesis is rejected? The reply to this objection to optional stopping is that while such deception is, indeed, possible using standard NP tests, for the power of such a test, as illustrated earlier, approaches one as the sample size increases, the chances of such deception using a likelihood criterion are remote. Using the familiar mathematics of gambler's ruin (de Groot 1986, §2.4), one can show, for example, that the probability of achieving an LR of 32 in favor of a cure rate of 75 percent for a new drug against the 25 percent rate of the drug currently in use, which requires an excess of $s - t \geq 4$ cures over noncures, is given by:

$$\frac{(q/p)^m - 1}{(q/p)^{m+4} - 1} = \frac{3^m - 1}{3^{m+4} - 1}$$

with $q = 1 - p$, which increases rapidly to its limit of 1/81 as $m \to \infty$.

In espousing an evidential interpretation of NP, Egon S. Pearson speaks of "a class of results which makes us more and more inclined . . . to reject the hypothesis tested in favor of alternatives which differ from it by increasing amounts" (1966, p. 173). Deborah G. Mayo, who defends an evidential version of NP, remarks that "one plausible measure of this inclination is the likelihood" (1996, p. 389), but Pearson rejects this on the grounds that "if we accept the criterion suggested by the method of likelihood it is still necessary to determine its sampling distribution in order to control the error involved in rejecting a true hypothesis" (quoted by Mayo 1996, p. 393). What Pearson, Mayo, and others fail to appreciate, however, is the possibility of retaining the law of likelihood while still assessing and controlling beforehand the probability of obtaining misleading results.

If a LR, $L = f_1/f_0$ greater than L^* is accounted strong evidence in favor of h_1 against h_0, then one may compute $P(f_1/f_0 \geq L^*|h_0)$ as readily as one computes $\alpha = P(X \in R|h_0)$, and in place of $\beta = P(X \notin R|\, h_1)$ one may compute $P(f_1/f_0 < L^*|h_1)$, which is the probability of misleading evidence against h_1. (It should be emphasized that it is the evidence itself that is misleading, not one's interpretation of it.)

An important general result, noted independently by C. A. B. Smith and Alan Birnbaum, affirms that the probability of obtaining an LR of at least k in favor of h_0 when h_1 holds is at most $1/k$:

(5) $$P(f_1/f_0 \geq k|h_0) \leq k^{-1}$$

For if S is the subset of outcomes for which the LR is at least k, then

$$P(L \geq k \mid h_0) = \sum_{x \in S} P(x \mid h_0) \leq k^{-1} \sum_{x \in S} P(x \mid h_1) \leq k^{-1}$$

Naturally, this universal bound can be considerably sharpened in special cases, as in the example of a would-be fraud. A specially important case is that of testing hypotheses about a normal mean of known variance with LR given by (4). If the distance $\Delta = |\mu_1 - \mu_0|$ is measured in units of the standard deviation of $\bar{x}$, $\Delta = c\sigma/\sqrt{n}$, one finds:

$$f_1 / f_0 \geq k \Leftrightarrow n\frac{\Delta}{\sigma^2}\left(\bar{x} - \frac{\mu_0 + \mu_1}{2}\right) \geq \ln k$$

$$\Leftrightarrow \bar{x} \geq \frac{\sigma^2}{n\Delta} \ln k + \frac{\mu_0 + \mu_1}{2}$$

$$\Leftrightarrow \frac{\bar{x} - \mu_0}{\sigma / \sqrt{n}} \geq \frac{\ln k}{c} + \frac{c}{2}$$

whence

$$P(f_1 / f_0 \geq k \mid h_0) = 1 - \Phi\left(\frac{\ln k}{c} + \frac{c}{2}\right) = \Phi\left(-\frac{c}{2} - \frac{\ln k}{c}\right)$$

with $\Phi(x)$ the (cumulative) normal distribution. Hence, the probability of misleading evidence in this case is a maximum when $c/2 + ln\ k/c$ is a minimum. By calculus this happens when $c = \sqrt{2lnk}$, in which case $c = c/2 + lnk/c$. Thus,

(6) $\quad \max P(f_1/f_0 \geq k|h_0) = \Phi(-\sqrt{2lnk})$

For example, for $k = 8$, $\Phi(-\sqrt{2ln8}) = .021$, while for $k = 32$, $\Phi(-\sqrt{2ln32}) = .0043$, which improve considerably on the universal bounds of 1/8 and 1/32. In fact, the ratio, $\Phi(-\sqrt{2lnk})/k^{-1}$ is easily seen to be decreasing, so that the relative improvement over the universal bound is greater for larger k. Royall (1997) greatly extends the reach of (6) by invoking the fact that the log-likelihood is asymptotically normal about its maximum (the ML estimate of the parameter) with precision given by the Fisher information, with an analogous result for the multiparameter case (Lindley 1965, §7.1; Hald 1998, p. 694).

The upshot is that one can retain the law of likelihood and the likelihood principle and still control for the probability of misleading evidence, the feature that lent NP so much of its initial appeal. This "Royall road" opens the way to further reconciliation of (F) with (B) and (L) and to the removal of many perplexing features of NP significance tests (Royall 1997, chapter 5). In retrospect, one sees that the significance level was made to play a dual role in NP theory as both an index of the evidence against null (Fisher's interpretation) and the relative frequency of erroneous rejections of the tested hypothesis. Fisher vigorously rejected the latter interpretation of significance levels and offered a pertinent counterexample (1956, pp. 93–96). He even says, "[T]he infrequency with which, in particular circumstances, decisive evidence is obtained, should not be confused with the force, or cogency, of such evidence" (p. 96).

NP's ban on optional stopping as well as on what Pearson brands "the dangerous practice of basing the choice of test . . . on inspection of the observations" (1966, p. 127) is rooted in a conception of testing as subsumption under a reliable rule. One's particular experiment is viewed as one trial of a repeatable sequence of identical experiments in which the considered hypotheses and a division of the outcomes into those supporting and those not supporting the tested hypothesis are specified in advance (compare Fisher 1956, pp. 81–82, who rejects this formulation in no uncertain terms). Thus, it is considered cheating to publish the error probabilities computed for a *post facto* test as if that test had been predesignated. See Mayo (1996, chapter 9) for numerous statements and illustrations of this stance, especially when she maintains, "Using the computed significance level in post-designated cases . . . conflicts with the intended interpretation and use of significance levels (as error probabilities)" (p. 317). Most textbooks are curiously silent on this issue (see Hodges and Lehmann 1970, chapters 11, 13; de Groot 1986, chapter 8), but Mayo's strictures seem to be widely shared by users of statistical tests. The question is whether a statistician, even an orthodox statistician, can function within the confines of such a strict predesignationism.

From Fisher on, modern statisticians have emphasized the importance of checking the assumptions of one's model, and, of course, these are not the object of one's test. Moreover, the most sensitive test of such common assumptions as independence, normality, or equality of variances, is often suggested by the deviations observed in one's data, thus violating Pearson's proscription. But, ironically, the most telling counterexamples come from the bible of NP theory, Erich Lehmann's classic, *Testing Statistical Hypotheses* (1959, p. 7). In testing a hypothesis about a normal mean of unknown variance, one cannot tell how large a sample is needed for a sharp result until one has estimated the variance. Or, again, if X is uniformly distributed in a unit interval of unknown location, one can stop sampling if the first two observations are (very nearly) a unit distance apart, but if the first n observations all lie within a tiny distance of each other, no more has been learned than the first two observations convey and one must go on sampling. In these workaday examples of Lehmann's, optional stopping is not optional; it is the only option.

Obviously, the issue just raised has strong links to the philosophy of science that holds that "evidence predicted by a hypothesis counts more in its support than evidence that accords with a hypothesis constructed after the fact" (Mayo 1996, p. 251). It would be digressive to enter into this issue here, so one must refer to Mayo (chapter 8) for further discussion and references, and to Stephen G. Brush (1994).

GOODNESS-OF-FIT TESTS

Karl Pearson's goodness-of-fit test (de Groot 1986, §§9.1–4; Hodges and Lehmann 1970, §11.3) rejects a multinomial model h_0 of categorical data when the deviation between observed (n_i) and predicted category counts (np_i) is improbably large conditional on h_0. The measure of deviation employed by Pearson is the chi-squared measure:

(7)
$$X^2 = \sum_{i=1}^{k} \frac{(n_i - np_i)^2}{np_i} = n\sum_{i=1}^{k} \frac{(f_i - p_i)^2}{p_i}$$

with $f_i = n_i/n$. Pearson showed that if h_0 is true, X^2 has, asymptotically, a chi-squared distribution with $v = k - 1$ degrees of freedom. The mean and variance are v and $2v$ and a rule of thumb is that roughly 90 to 95 percent of the probability mass of the chi-squared distribution lies to the left of the mean plus two standard deviations. These and other mathematically convenient features are, essentially, the only thing that recommends this particular measure of deviation (see the two texts just cited and Jaynes 2003, p. 299).

On the surface, Pearson's chi-squared test appears to test the goodness-of-fit of a model without reference to alternatives. (B) offers a less well known test whose rationale is best brought out by considering Jaynes's example of a thick coin (2003, p. 300) that may land on its edge with a probability of .002 and is otherwise balanced (h_0). In $n = 29$ tosses, $D = (n_1, n_2, n_3) = (14, 14, 1)$ is observed, that is, the coin lands on its edge once and lands heads and tails equally often, in an almost "best possible" agreement with h_0. However, $X^2 = 15.33$, which is more than seven standard deviations beyond the mean of 2. Defenders of the test will be quick to point out that the chi-square approximation to the distribution of X^2 breaks down when one or more of the expected counts is less than 5, but that is not the problem here. For one can use brute force to compute $P(X^2 \geq 15.33|h_0)$ exactly, since the only outcomes that give a smaller value of X^2 are $(l, 29 - l, 0)$ and $(29 - l, l, 0)$ with $4 \leq l \leq 14$. The sum of their probabilities on h_0 is 0.9435, whence $P(X^2 \geq 15.33|h_0) = 0.0565$. Hence, Pearson's test just fails by a whisker to reject h_0 at the 5 percent significance level conventionally associated with strong evidence against h_0. The source of the trouble is that X^2 wrongly orders the possible outcomes; some accounted less deviant than (14, 14, 1) are actually less probable on h_0. Ideally, outcomes less probable on h_0 should be accounted more deviant.

Given data $D = (n_1, \ldots, n_k)$, one might ask a somewhat different question than the one Pearson asked, namely: How much support is apt to be gained in passing to some alternative hypothesis? For as Fisher and others emphasize, before rejecting a model as ill fitting one should attempt to find a plausible alternative that fits the data better. Plausibility aside, there is always one alternative hypothesis—call it the tailored hypothesis—that fits D better than h_0 by positing the observed relative frequencies, $f_i = n_i/n$, as its category probabilities. In effect, one wants to test the given model against the ideally best-fitting alternative, and this prompts one to look at the LR in favor of $F = (f_1, \ldots, f_2)$ against the probability distribution $P = (p_1, \ldots, p_2)$ of h_0, namely, $\prod_{i=1}^{k} \frac{f_i^{n_i}}{p_i^{n_i}}$, or, better, at its logarithm, $\sum_{i=1}^{k} n_i \ln(f_i / p_i)$, which is additive in independent samples. This proves to be n times

(8)
$$H(F,P) = \sum_{i=1}^{k} f_i \ln(f_i / p_i)$$

which may be viewed as a measure of the nearness of F to P. Though (8) was used by Alan Turing and his chief statistical assistant, I. J. Good during World War II, Solomon Kullback, another wartime code breaker, was the first to publish a systematic treatment of its properties and applications to statistics, dubbing it discrimination information (see the entry on information theory). Since F is tailored to achieve perfect fit, $H(F, P)$ sets an upper limit to how much one can improve the fit to the data by scrapping h_0 in favor of a simple or composite alternative hypothesis (Jaynes 2003, pp. 293–297).

Happily, $\psi = 2nH(F, P)$ is also asymptotically distributed as χ^2_{k-1}, the chi-square variate with $k - 1$ *d.f.* (degrees of freedom). This hints that Pearson's X^2 approximates ψ (Jaynes 1983, pp. 262–263). For example, Mendel's predicted phenotypic ratios of *AB:Ab:aB:ab* = *9:3:3:1* for a hybrid cross, *AaBb* × *AaBb*, gave rise to counts of 315, 101, 108, and 32 among $n = 556$ offspring. This gives $X^2 = .4700$ and $\psi = .4754$. But when the expected category counts include a small value or the deviations are large, the approximation degrades, and with it the performance of Pearson's test. Thus, in Jaynes's (2003) thick coin example, X^2 rates the outcomes $(l, 29 - l, 0)$ and $(29 - l, l, 0)$ for $4 \leq l \leq 8$ as less deviant than (14, 14, 1) even though they are also less probable on h_0; by contrast, ψ errs only in failing to count (9, 20, 0) and (20, 9, 0) as less deviant than (14, 14, 1). Hence, the exact probability that ψ is less than its value of 3.84 at (14, 14, 1) is twice the sum of the probabilities (on h_0) of the outcomes $(l, 29 - l, 0)$ for $10 \leq l \leq 14$, or 0.7640, whence $P(\psi \geq 3.84|h_0) = .2360$. Clearly, the ψ-test gives no reason to believe support can be much increased by passing to an alternative hypothesis, but it will be instructive to carry the analysis a step further.

The only plausible alternative that presents itself is the composite hypothesis, $H{:}p_1 = p_2 = \frac{1}{2}(1 - \theta), p_3 = \theta$ $(0 < \theta < 1)$, which includes h_0 as the special case $\theta = .002$. Since one d.f. is lost for each parameter estimated from the data in using Pearson's test (de Groot 1986, §9.2), this is one way of trading off the improved accuracy that results when a parameter is added against the loss of simplicity. It is insensitive, however, to whatever constraints may govern the parameters. A Bayesian treatment tests h_0 against the composite alternative $H - h_0$ (i.e., H exclusive of the value $\theta = .002$) and goes by averaging the likelihoods of the special cases of $H - h_0$ against a uniform prior of θ over its allowed range—unless more specific knowledge of θ is available. (The affect is to exact a maximum penalty for the given complication of h_0.) On canceling the multinomial coefficient and using the beta integral (*v.s.*), the ratio of the likelihoods reduces to:

$$P(D \mid h_0) : P(D \mid H - h_0) = .499^{28}(.002) : \int_0^1 [\tfrac{1}{2}(1-\theta)]^{28}\theta d\theta$$

$$= 30 \cdot 29 \cdot 2^{28}(.499^{28})(.002) = 1.645$$

Thus, the data $D = (14, 14, 1)$ favors h_0 over the composite alternative, and this remains true, albeit less strongly, if one integrates, say, from 0 to 0.1. By contrast, the chi-square test favors $H - h_0$ over h_0 by mere dint of the fact that the composite hypothesis includes the tailored hypothesis as a special case, namely, $\theta = 1/29$, for then the value of X^2 is zero. Thus, any complication of an original model that happens to include the tailored hypothesis will be preferred to the original model.

Notice, the parameter distribution must reflect only what is known before sampling. Unfortunately, more cannot be said about the different ways (F) and (L) handle the problem of trading off the improved accuracy gained in complicating a model, retaining the original model as a special case, against the loss of simplicity as compared to the Bayesian method just illustrated of averaging the likelihoods. For more on this, see Roger D. Rosenkrantz (1977, chapters 5, 7, and 11) and Arnold Zellner, Hugo A. Keuzenkamp, and Michael McAleer (2001) for other approaches.

PROBABILITY AS LOGIC

Bayesians view probability as the primary (or primitive) concept and induction or inference as derived (see Finetti 1938/1980, p. 194). They emphasize that their methods, properly applied, have never been rejected on the basis of their actual performance (Jaynes 1983, chapter 9; 2003, p. 143). As a corollary, they maintain that the canons of scientific method and inductive reasoning have a Bayesian rationale, while this is vigorously contested by frequentists (e.g., Mayo 1996, chapters 3 and 11). In particular, Bayesians evolved a mathematical analysis of inductive reasoning with its source in the original memoir of Thomas Bayes that includes purported solutions of the notorious problem of induction by Laplace (see Hald 1998, chapter 15) and de Finetti (1937/1981), as well as the equally notorious paradoxes of confirmation (see Good 1983, chapter 11; Rosenkrantz 1977, chapter 2).

Plainly, one's view of statistics is highly colored by one's interpretation of probability. The approaches of Fisher, Neyman, and Pearson, as well as that of most (L) proponents, like Royall, are grounded in a frequency interpretation that equates probabilities with asymptotically stable relative frequencies. The criticisms of the frequency theory, nicely summed up by L. J. Savage (1954, pp. 61–62), are, first, that it is limited (and limiting) in refusing to treat as meaningful the probabilities of singular or historical events, or (in most cases) scientific theories or hypotheses, like the hypothesis that smoking causes lung cancer, and, second, that it is circular. The model of random independent (Bernoulli) trials considered earlier is often held to justify the definition of probability as a limiting relative frequency, but all that theorem does is assign a high probability to the proposition that the observed relative frequency will lie within any preassigned error of the true probability of success in a sufficiently long sequence of such trials.

Savage's criticism along these lines is more subtle. Bayes saw that a distinctly inverse or inductive inference is needed to infer probabilities from observed frequency behavior. Thus, even Bayesians, like Good or Rudolf Carnap, who admit physical probabilities, insist that epistemic probabilities are needed to measure or infer the values of physical probabilities. A more sophisticated view is that physical probabilities arise from the absence of microscopic control over the outcome of one's experiment (see the final section).

Modern Bayesians have sought deeper foundations for probability qua degree of belief and the rules governing it in the bedrock of consistency. It is not merely "common sense reduced to a calculus" (Laplace) but a "logic of consistency" (F. P. Ramsey). Needed, in particular, is a warrant for (2), for it is in Bayesian eyes the basic (not to say the "bayesic") mode of learning from experience. Epistemologists of the naturalist school seriously question this, as when Ronald N. Giere contends that "there are many different logically possible ways of 'conditionalizing' on the evidence, and no *a priori* way of singling out one way as uniquely rational" (1985, p. 336). Rather than multiply one's initial odds by the LR, why not by some positive power of the LR? At any rate, this marks a major parting of the ways in contemporary epistemology.

One Bayesian response has been to argue that alternatives to the usual rules of probability open one to sure loss in a betting context, to a so-called Dutch book. However, this justification imports strategic or game theoretic considerations of doubtful relevance, which is why Bruno de Finetti (1972), an early sponsor of the argument, turns, instead, to the concept of a proper scoring rule, a means of evaluating the accuracy of a probabilistic forecast that offers forecasters no incentive to announce degrees of prediction different from their actual degrees of belief. (It is rumored that some weather forecasters overstate the probability of a storm, for example, to guard against blame for leaving the citizenry unwarned and unprepared.) This move to scoring rules opens the way to a means-end justification of (2) as the rule that leaves one, on average, closest to the truth after sampling.

By far the most direct way of sustaining Ramsey's declaration that "the laws of probability are laws of consistency" is that developed by the physicist Richard T. Cox (1946). Besides a minimal requirement of agreement with common sense, his main appeal is to a requirement of consistency (CON), that two ways of doing a calculation permitted by the rules must yield the same result. In particular, one must assign a given proposition the same probability in two equivalent versions of a problem.

In a nutshell, Cox's argument for the product rule, $P(AB|C) = P(A|BC)P(B|C)$, from which (2) is immediate, exploits the associativity of conjunction.

First phase: Letting $AB|C$ denote the plausibility of the conjunction AB supposing that C, show that $AB|C$ depends on (and only on) $A|BC$ and $B|C$, so that

(i) $$AB|C = F(A|BC, B|C)$$

Moreover, by the requirement of agreement with qualitative common sense, the function $F(x, y)$ must be continuous and monotonically increasing in both arguments, x and y.

Second phase: Using first one side then the other of the equivalence of $(AB)D$ and $A(BD)$:

$$ABD|C = F(AB|DC, D|C) = F(F(A|BDC, B|DC), D|C)$$

$$ABD|C = F(A|BDC, BD|C) = F(F(A|BDC, F(B|DC, D|C))$$

leading by (CON) to the associativity functional equation first studied by Niels Henrik Abel in 1826:

(ii) $$F(F(x, y), z) = F(x, F(y, z))$$

Cox solved (ii) by assuming that, in addition, $F(x, y)$ is differentiable. An elementary approach sketched by C. Ray Smith and Gary J. Erickson (1990) based on functional iteration, due to J. Aczel, dispenses with this assumption and leads to the solution: $w(F(x, y)) = w(x)w(y)$, with w continuous and monotonic, hence to

(iii) $$w(AB|C) = w(A|BC)w(B|C)$$

Third phase: Specializing (iii) to the cases where A is certain or impossible given C, one deduces that $w(A|A) = 1$ and $w(A|\bar{A}) = 0$ or ∞. But these two choices lead to equivalent theories, so one may as well assume that $w(A|\bar{A}) = 0$ in line with the usual convention.

Cox (1946) gives a similar derivation of the negation rule. $P(A) + P(\bar{A}) = 1$, and in conjunction with the product rule just derived, this yields the sum rule as follows:

$$\begin{aligned}
P(A \vee B \mid C) &= 1 - P(\bar{A}\bar{B} \mid C) \\
&= 1 - P(\bar{A} \mid \bar{B}C)P(\bar{B} \mid C) \\
&= 1 - [1 - P(A \mid \bar{B}C)]P(\bar{B} \mid C) \\
&= P(B \mid C) + P(A \mid \bar{B}C)P(\bar{B} \mid C) \\
&= P(B \mid C) + P(A\bar{B} \mid C) \\
&= P(B \mid C) + P(A \mid C)[1 - P(B \mid AC)] \\
&= P(A \mid C) + P(B \mid C) - P(AB \mid C)
\end{aligned}$$

Notice, Cox's derivation is restricted to finite algebras of sets, though not to finite sample spaces.

Non-Bayesian methods (or surrogates) of inference, which *ipso facto* violate one or more of Cox's desiderata, tend to break down in extreme cases. For example, unbiased estimates can yield values of the estimated parameter that are deductively excluded and frequentist confidence intervals can include impossible values of the parameter. A weaker but more general result to account for this affirms that one maximizes one's expected score after sampling (under any proper scoring rule) with (2) in preference to any other inductive rule (Rosenkrantz 1992, p. 535). This optimality theorem, which seems to have many discoverers, affords a purely cognitive justification of (2) as the optimally efficient means to one's cognitive end of making inferences that leave one as close to the truth as possible. This rationale has been extended by inductive logicians to the justification of more specialized predictive rules that are seen as optimal for universes or populations of specifiable orderliness (see Festa 1993).

An interesting implication of the optimality theorem is that it pays to sample, or that informed forecasts are better than those that lack or waste given information. To see this, compare (2) to the impervious rule that fixes updated probabilities at their initial values. Moreover, since the utility scoring rule, $S(R, h_i) = U(a_R, h_i)$, is proper, where a_R maximizes expected utility against the probability distribution, $R = (r_1, \ldots, r_n)$, over states of nature, one can expect higher utility after sampling as well, a result first given by Good (1983, chapter 17). Thus, both cognitive and utilitarian ends are encompassed.

The optimality theorem presents Bayesian conditioning as the solution of a well-defined optimization problem, thus connecting it to related results on optimal searching and sorting and continuing the tradition of Fisher, Neyman, Pearson, and Wald of viewing rules of estimation, statistical tests, and decision functions (strategies) as solutions of well-posed optimization problems.

THE CONTROVERSIAL STATUS OF PRIOR PROBABILITIES

Objections to (B) center on the alleged impossibility of objectively representing complete ignorance by a uniform probability distribution (Fisher 1956, chapter 2; Mayo 1996, pp. 72ff; Royall 1997, chapter 8). For if one is ignorant of V (volume), then, equally, one is ignorant of $D = 1/V$ (density), but a uniform distribution of V entails a nonuniform distribution of D and vice versa, since equal intervals of V correspond to unequal intervals of D, so it appears one is landed in a contradiction (for some of the tangled history of this charge of noninvariance, see Hald 1998, §15.6; Zabell 1988).

Bayesian subjectivists also deny that any precise meaning can be attached to ignorance (Savage 1954, pp. 64–66), but often avail themselves of uniform priors when the prior information is diffuse (e.g., Lindley 1965, p. 18). This affords a reasonably good approximation to any prior that is relatively flat in the region of high likelihood and not too large outside that region, provided there is such a region (or, in other words, that the evidence is not equally diffuse). For a precise statement, proof, and discussion of this so-called principle of stable estimation, see Ward Edwards, Harold Lindman and Leonard J. Savage (1965, pp. 527–534), as well as Dennis V. Lindley (1965, §5.2) for the important special case of sampling a normal population.

Bayesians have also used Harold Jeffreys's log-uniform prior with density

(9) $$p(\theta|I_0) \propto \theta^{-1}$$

for a positive variate or parameter, $\theta > 0$, where I_0 represents a diffuse state of prior knowledge. (9) is equivalent to assigning $\ln\theta$ a uniform distribution, whence the name *log-uniform*. If θ is known to lie within finite bounds, $a \leq \theta \leq b$, the density (9) becomes

(9a) $$p(\theta)d\theta = \frac{1}{\theta \ln R_\theta}$$

where $R_0 = b/a$, hence, the probability that θ lies in a subinterval, $[c, d]$ of $[a, b]$ is given by:

(9b) $$P(c \leq \theta \leq d \mid I_0) = \frac{\ln d - \ln c}{\ln b - \ln a}$$

It follows that θ is log-uniformly distributed in $[a, b]$ if and only if, for any integer k, θ^k is log-uniformly distributed in $[a^k, b^k]$, since

$$\begin{aligned} P(c \leq \theta^k \leq d \mid I_0) &= P(c^{1/k} \leq \theta \leq d^{1/k} \mid I_0) \\ &= \frac{\ln d^{1/k} - \ln c^{1/k}}{\ln b - \ln a} \\ &= \frac{\ln d - \ln c}{k[\ln b - \ln a]} \\ &= \frac{\ln d - \ln c}{\ln b^k - \ln a^k} \end{aligned}$$

This at once resolves the objection from the (alleged) arbitrariness of parameterization mentioned at the outset. For V (volume) is a positive quantity, hence, the appropriate prior is, not uniform, but log-uniform, and it satisfies the required invariance: all (positive or negative) powers of V, including V^{-1}, have the same (log-uniform) distribution.

Its invariance would be enough to recommend (9), but Jeffreys provided further justifications (for his interesting derivation of 1932, see Jaynes 2003, p. 498). He did not, however, derive (9) from a basic principle clearly capable of broad generalization (Kendall and Stuart 1967, p. 152). Nevertheless, his insistence that parameters with the same formal properties be assigned the same prior distribution hinted at a *Tieferlegung*. And while the leaders of the Bayesian revival of the 1950s, Savage, Good, and Lindley, did not find in Jeffreys's assorted derivations of (9) a principle definite enough to qualify as a postulate of rationality, they did clearly believe that given states of partial knowledge are better represented by some priors than by others they denigrated as pig-headed (Lindley 1965, p. 18) or highly opinionated (e.g., Zabell 1988, p. 157). Such out-of-court priors might be highly concentrated in the face of meager information or import a dependence between two parameters (de Groot 1986, p. 405). There matters stood when Jaynes published his fundamental paper, "Prior Probabilities" in 1968 (chapter 7 of Jaynes 1983).

Bayesian subjectivists are as committed to consistency as Bayesian objectivists, and to assign different probabilities to equivalent propositions or to the same proposition in two equivalent formulations of a problem is to commit the most obvious inconsistency. Savage (1954, p. 57), for one, viewed it as unreasonable to not remove an inconsistency, once detected.

Consider a horse race about which one knows only the numbers—better, the labels—of the entries. Since the labels convey no information (or so one is assuming), any relabeling of the horses leads to an equivalent problem, and the only distribution invariant under all permutations of the labels is, of course, the uniform distribution. Thus reinvented as an equivalence principle, Laplace's hoary principle of indifference is given a new lease on life: The vague notion of indifference between events or possibilities gives way to the relatively precise notion of indifference between problems (Jaynes 1983, p. 144). Two versions of a problem that differ only in details left unspecified in the statement of the problem are *ipso facto* equivalent (p. 144). In this restricted form Laplace's principle can be applied to the data or sampling distributions to which (F) and (L) are confined as well as to the prior distributions on which (B) relies. Indeed, from this point of view, "exactly the same principles are needed to assign either sampling distributions or prior probabilities, and one man's sampling probability is another man's prior probability" (Jaynes 2003, p. 89).

Invariance also plays a leading role in frequentist accounts of estimation and testing (Lehmann 1959, chapter 6). In testing a bivariate distribution of shots at a target for central symmetry, Lehmann notes, the test itself should exhibit such symmetry, for if not, "acceptance or rejection will depend on the choice of [one's coordinate] system, which under the assumptions made is quite arbitrary and has no bearing on the problem" (p. 213).

To see how the principle can be used to arrive at a sampling distribution, consider, again, Frank Wilcoxon's statistic, W_t, for the sum of the ranks of the t treated subjects, with W_c the corresponding statistic for the c controls, where $t + c = N$. Clearly, it is a matter of arbitrary convention whether subjects who show a greater response are assigned a higher or lower number as rank. In Table 2, the inverse ranks of the $t = 8$ treated subjects are, respectively, 10, 13, 8, 11, 12, and 7, where each rank and its inverse sum to $N + 1 = 14$. This inversion of the ranks leaves the problem unchanged. On the null hypothesis, h_0, that the treatment is without affect, both W_t and the corresponding statistic, $W_t^{'}$, for the sum of the inverse ranks, are sums of t numbers picked at random from the numbers 1 through N. Hence, W_t and $W_t^{'}$ have the same distribution, which we write as:

$$W_t \simeq W_t^{'}$$

This is the invariance step where the Jaynesian principle of indifference is applied. Furthermore, since $W_t + W_t^{'} = t(N+1)$, it follows that

$$E(W_t) = E(W_t^{'}) = t\frac{N+1}{2}$$

whence

$$W_t - t\frac{N+1}{2} = -\left[W_t^{'} - t\frac{N+1}{2}\right] \simeq -\left[W_t - t\frac{N+1}{2}\right]$$

which implies that W_t is symmetrically distributed about its mean. Next, recenter the distribution by subtracting the minimum rank sum of $1 + 2 + \ldots + t = t(t + 1)/2$ from W_t, that is, define:

$$U_t = W_t - t\frac{t+1}{2}$$

and, similarly,

$$U_c = W_c - c\frac{c+1}{2}$$

for the controls. Then both U_t and U_c range from 0 to tc, have mean ½tc, and inherit the symmetry of W_t and $W_t^{'}$ about their mean, which suggests, but does not prove, that $U_t \simeq U_c$. This follows from

$$W_c - c\frac{N+1}{2} \simeq W_t - t\frac{N+1}{2}$$

using

$$W_c - c\frac{N+1}{2} = -\left[W_t - t\frac{N+1}{2}\right]$$

and the symmetry of W_t, while at the same time,

$$W_t - t\frac{N+1}{2} = U_t - \frac{tc}{2}$$

and

$$W_c - c\frac{N+1}{2} = U_c - \frac{tc}{2}$$

so that $U_t - ½tc \simeq U_c - ½tc$, or $U_t \simeq U_c$. Finally, from the common distribution of U_t and U_c, which is easily tabulated for small values of t and c using an obvious recurrence, and for large values using a normal approximation (Hodges and Lehmann 1970, chapter 12, especially p. 349), the distributions of W_t and W_c, with either convention governing the ranks, can be obtained.

Consider, next, Jaynes's (1983, p.126) derivation of the distribution of the rate parameter, λ, of the Poisson distribution (POIS):

$$p(n \mid \lambda, t) = e^{-\lambda t}\frac{(\lambda t)^n}{n!}$$

which gives the probability that n events (e.g., accidents, cell divisions, or arrivals of customers) occur in an interval of time of length t. Nothing being said about the time scale, two versions of the problem that differ in their units of time are equivalent. Then the times t and t' in the two versions are related by

(i) $$t = qt'$$

so that corresponding pairs $(\lambda, t)$and (λ', t') satisfy $\lambda t = \lambda' t'$, or

(ii) $$\lambda' = q\lambda$$

Indeed, (ii) is what defines λ as a scale parameter. Then $d\lambda' = qd\lambda$, that is, corresponding intervals of time also differ by the scale conversion factor. Hence, if $f(\lambda)d\lambda$ and $g(\lambda')d\lambda'$ are the probabilities of lying in corresponding small intervals, $d\lambda$ and $d\lambda'$, then (step 1):

(iii) $$f(\lambda)d\lambda = g(\lambda')d\lambda'$$

since one is observing the same process in the two time frames, or, using (ii),

(iv) $$f(\lambda) = qg(q\lambda)$$

Now (step 2) invoke the consistency requirement to affirm that $f = g$, leading to the functional equation

$$f(\lambda) = qf(q\lambda)$$

whose (unique) solution (step 3) is readily seen to be $f(\lambda) \propto 1/\lambda$, the log-uniform distribution of Jeffreys. Thus, if all one knows about a parameter is that it is a scale parameter, then consistency demands that one assigns it a scale-invariant distribution. Following Jaynes (2003, §17.3) , it is instructive to compare the estimates of λ and powers thereof to which the log-uniform distribution leads with the unbiased estimates favored by frequentist theory.

Using the gamma integral,

$$\int_0^\infty \lambda^{k-1}e^{-\lambda}d\lambda = \Gamma(k) = (k-1)!$$

for integers $k = 1, 2, 3, \ldots$, one sees that the rate parameter, λ, is also the mean and variance of POIS. Hence, the mean of any (integer) power of λ after observing n incidents in a chosen unit interval of time (used now in place of an interval of length t) is given by:

$$E(\lambda^k) = \frac{(n+k)!}{n!}$$

In particular, the posterior mean of λ is $n + 1$, that of λ^{-1} is n^{-1}, and that of λ^2 is $(n + 2)(n + 1)$, so that the variance of the posterior distribution is equal to $n + 1$, the same as that of λ, itself a kind of invariance. (F) favors using unbiased statistics (estimators) to estimate a parameter and then among them, choosing the one of minimum variance. That is, on the analogy to target shooting, one uses statistics centered on the bull's eye and most tightly concentrated there (Hodges and Lehmann 1970, chapter 8; de Groot 1986, §7.7). However, as Jaynes shows (2003, §17.3) this "nice property" is not so nice. For while the unbiased estimator of λ is n, which is reasonable and close to its (B) counterpart, the only unbiased estimator $f(n)$ of λ^2 when n is the number of incidents recorded in the unit of time, is

$$f(n) = n(n-1)$$

and $f(n) = 0$ otherwise. Thus, when $n = 1$ incident is observed, the unbiased estimate of λ^2 is zero, which entails that $\lambda = 0$. That is, one is led to an estimate of λ^2 that is deductively excluded by the observation. (It only gets better—or worse!—when one looks at higher powers of λ.) Moreover, no unbiased estimator of λ^{-1} exists. In essence, unbiased estimators are seen to be strongly dependent on which power of the unknown parameter one chooses to estimate, Bayes estimators (equating these with the mean of the posterior distribution) only weakly so.

It is also well known that, for any distribution, the sample variance, $n^{-1}\sum_{i=1}^{n}(x_i - \bar{x})^2$, is a biased estimator of the population variance, σ^2, while $(n-1)^{-1}\sum_{i=1}^{n}(x_i - \bar{x})^2$ is unbiased. If, however, one's goal is to minimize the mean-squared error, $E_\theta[(\hat{\theta}-\theta)^2]$, of one's estimate $\hat{\theta}$ of θ (de Groot 1986, p. 412), the avowed goal of (F), then it can be shown that the biased estimator, $(n+1)^{-1}\sum_{i=1}^{n}(x_i - \bar{x})^2$, of a normal population variance has, for every value of σ^2, a smaller MSE than either of the two cases of the class $c\sum_{i=1}^{n}(x_i - \bar{x})^2$ given earlier (de Groot 1986, pp. 414–415). Hence, the unbiased sample variance is dominated by a biased one; it is, in this precise sense of decision theory, inadmissible. Thus, the two leading (F) criteria of unbiasedness and admissibility are seen to conflict. This insight of Charles Stein's shows, too, that an unbiased estimator is by no means certain to have lower MSE than a biased one, for the MSE is a sum of two terms, the bias and the variance, and in the case at hand, the biased sample variance more than makes up in its smaller variance what it gives up in bias (for more on this, including the waste of information that often accompanies unbiased estimation, see Jaynes 2003, pp. 511ff).

If the density of a variate, *X*, can be written:

(10)
$$f(x \mid \mu, \sigma) = g\left(\frac{x-\mu}{\sigma}\right)$$

then μ is called a location parameter and σ a scale parameter of the distribution. For changes in μ translate the density curve along the x-axis without changing its shape, while changes in σ alter the shape (or spread) without changing the location. The exemplars are, of course, the mean and standard deviation of a normal distribution. Pretty clearly, Jaynes's derivation of the log-uniform distribution of a Poisson rate applies to any scale parameter (1983, pp. 125–127). That is the justification Jeffreys lacked, though anticipating it in his requirement that formally identical parameters should have the same distribution. The essential point is that not every transformation of a parameter leads to an equivalent problem. Even a subjectivist with no prior information about the population proportion *p* of some trait would balk at having his or her beliefs represented by a uniform prior of some high power of *p*.

Notice, the range of $\ln\sigma$ for $0 < \sigma < \infty$ is the whole real line, as is that of a uniform prior of a variate that can assume any real value. Such functions are, of course, nonintegrable (nonnormalizable) and are termed *improper*. They cause no trouble—lead to a normalizable posterior density—when the likelihood function tails off sufficiently fast, as it will when the sample information is nonnegligible. In sampling a normal population of known precision, $h = \sigma^{-2}$, a normal prior, $N(\mu_0, h_0)$, of the unknown mean, μ, combines with the normal likelihood based on a random sample of size n to yield a normal posterior density, $N(\mu_1, h_1)$ with precision given by $h_1 = h_0 + nh$, the sum of the prior and the sample precision, and mean:

(11)
$$\mu_1 = \frac{h_0\mu_0 + nh\bar{x}}{h_0 + nh}$$

a precision-weighted average of the prior mean and the sample mean (Lindley 1965, §5.1; Edwards, Lindman, and Savage 1965, pp. 535–538). Small prior precision, h_0, represents a poverty of prior information about the mean, and letting it approach zero yields a uniform prior as a limiting case. Then the posterior mean, μ_1, becomes the sample mean. This is a way of realizing Fisher's ideal of "allowing the data to speak for themselves" and can be applied in the spirit of the "jury principle" when the experimenter is privy to prior information not widely shared by the relevant research community. Priors that achieve this neutrality are termed *uninformative* or *reference priors* (see Loredo 1990, p. 119).

This example of closure—a normal prior combining with the (normal) likelihood to yield a normal postsampling distribution—is prototypic and one speaks of the relevant distribution as conjugate to the given likelihood function or data distribution. Other examples (de Groot 1986, pp. 321–327) include the beta:

$$f_\beta(p \mid a, b)dp = B(a, b)^{-1}p^{a-1}(1-p)^{b-1}$$

with $B(a,b) = \int_0^1 p^{a-1}(1-p)^{b-1}\,dp = \frac{\Gamma(a)\Gamma(b)}{\Gamma(a+b)}$ and $\Gamma(n) = (n-1)!$ when n is an integer, which combines with a binomial likelihood, $L(p) = p^r(1-p)^s$, to yield a beta posterior density, $f_\beta(p \mid a+r, b+s)$; or, again, the gamma distribution with density

$$f_\gamma(\lambda \mid a, b)d\lambda = \frac{b^a}{\Gamma(a)}\lambda^{a-1}e^{-b\lambda}$$

which combines with a Poisson likelihood to yield a gamma posterior density (de Groot 1986, p. 323). In general, any (one-parameter) data distribution of the form:

(12)
$$f(x \mid \theta) = F(x)G(\theta)\exp[u(x)\phi(\theta)]$$

will combine with a prior of the form, $p(\theta \mid I)d\theta \propto G(\theta)^a \exp(b\phi(\theta))$, to yield a density of the same so-called Koopman-Darmois form (Lindley 1965, p. 55). These are precisely the data distributions that admit a fixed set of sufficient statistics, namely, estimators of the unknown parameter(s) that yield the same posterior distribution as the raw data (Lindley 1965, §5.5; de Groot 1986, §6.7; or, for more advanced readers, Jaynes 2003, chapter 8).

The parameters of a conjugate prior represent a quantity of information. For example, for the beta prior, $a + b$ may be the size of a pilot sample or a virtual sample. By letting these parameters approach zero, one obtains an uninformed prior in the limit that represents, so to speak, the empty state of prior knowledge. The log-uniform prior (9) of a normal variance can be obtained in this way from the conjugate chi-squared prior (Lindley 1965, §5.3, p. 32), thus complementing its derivation as the distribution of a scale parameter about which nothing else is assumed.

In all the cases considered, the improper prior arises as a well-defined limit of proper priors. When this finite sets policy, which Jaynes traces to Gauss, is violated, paradoxes result, that is, in Jaynesian parlance, "errors so pervasive as to become institutionalized" (2003, p. 485). Such paradoxes can be manufactured at will in accordance with the following prescription:

(1) Start with a mathematically well-defined problem involving a finite set, a discrete or a normalizable distribution, where the correct solution is not in doubt;

(2) Pass to a limit without specifying how the limit is approached;

(3) Ask a question whose answer depends on how that limit is approached.

Jaynes adds that "as long as we look only at the limit, and not the limiting process, the source of the error is concealed from view" (p. 485).

Jaynes launches his deep-probing analysis of these paradoxes with the following exemplar, a proof that an infinite series, $S = \sum a_n$, converges to any real number x one cares to name. Denoting the partial sums, $s_n = a_1 + a_2 + \ldots + a_n$ with $s_0 = 0$, one has for $n \geq 1$:

$$a_n = (s_n - x) - (s_{n-1} - x)$$

and so the series becomes

$$S = (s_1 - x) + (s_2 - x) + (s_3 - x) + \ldots$$

$$-(s_0 - s) - (s_1 - x) - (s_2 - x) - \ldots$$

Since the terms $s_1 - x, s_2 - x, \ldots$ all cancel out, one arrives at $S = -(s_0 - x) = x$.

Apart from assuming convergence, the fallacy here lies in treating the series as if it were a finite sum. The nonconglomerability paradox, which purports to show that the average, $P(A|I)$, of a bounded infinite set of conditional probabilities, $P(A|C_jI)$, can lie outside those bounds, also turns on the misguided attempt to assign these probabilities directly on an infinite matrix rather than approaching them as well-defined limits of the same probabilities on finite submatrices (Jaynes 2003, §15.3). Jaynes goes on to consider countable additivity, the Borel-Kolmogorov paradox, which involves conditioning on a set of measure zero, and the marginalization paradoxes aimed at discrediting improper priors. These paradoxes have little to do with prior probabilities *per se* and everything to do with ambiguities in the foundations of continuous probability theory.

Leaving these subtle fallacies to one side, one can apply Jaynes's policy of starting with finite sets and then passing to well-defined limits to another old chestnut, the water-and-wine paradox in which one is told only that the ratio of water (H) to wine (W) in a mixture lies between 1 and 2. Then the inverse ratio of wine to water lies between ½ and 1, and, in the usual way, a uniform distribution of one ratio induces a nonuniform distribution of the other. One can eliminate ambiguity, however, by quantizing the problem. There are, after all, just a finite number N of molecules of liquid, of which N_H are water molecules and N_W are wine molecules. Then the inequality, $1 \leq N_H{:}N_W \leq 2$, is equivalent to $N_W \leq N_H \leq 2N_W$, and so the admissible pairs $(N_H, N_W)$are:

$$\{(N_H, N - N_H){:}\tfrac{1}{2}N \leq N_H \leq \tfrac{2}{3}N\}$$

Moreover, this remains true when one starts with the other (equivalent) version of the problem in which the given is the inequality, $\tfrac{1}{2} \leq N_W{:}N_H \leq 1$, governing the inverse ratio. One then assigns equal probabilities to these $(\tfrac{2}{3} - \tfrac{1}{2})N = \tfrac{1}{6}N$ allowed pairs. Then to find, for example, the probability that $\tfrac{1}{2} \leq N_W{:}N_H \leq \tfrac{3}{4}$, one takes the ratio of the allowed pairs meeting this condition, which is equivalent to

$$\tfrac{4}{7}N \leq N_H \leq \tfrac{2}{3}N$$

to the total number, $N/6$, of allowed pairs to find, not 1/2, but

$$\left(\frac{2}{3} - \frac{4}{7}\right) / \frac{1}{6} = \frac{2/21}{1/6} = \frac{4}{7}$$

which is surprisingly close to:

$$\frac{\ln\frac{3}{4}-\ln\frac{1}{2}}{\ln 1-\ln\frac{1}{2}}=\frac{\ln 3-\ln 2}{\ln 2}=.58496$$

Or, again, the probability that $N_W{:}N_H$ lies between 5/8 and 11/13 is found to be 23/52 = .442, which is close to (ln11/13 – ln5/8)/ln2 = .437. Thus, by assigning equal probabilities in a discrete version of the problem—the only invariant assignment—one appears to be led once more to the log-uniform prior.

Another familiar puzzle of geometric probability is Joseph Bertrand's chord paradox, which asks for the probability that a chord of a circle of radius R drawn at random exceeds the side $s = \sqrt{3}R$ of the inscribed equilateral triangle. Depending on how one defines "drawn at random," different answers result, and Bertrand himself seems to have attached no deeper significance to the example than that "la question est mal posee."

Like the water-and-wine example, this puzzle is more redolent of the faculty lounge than the laboratory, so following Jaynes (1983, chapter 8; 2003, §12.4.4), one can connect it to the real world by giving it a physical embodiment in which broom straws are dropped onto a circular target from a great enough height to preclude skill. Nothing being said about the exact size or location of the target circle, the implied translation and scale invariance uniquely determine a density:

(13) $$f(r,\theta)=\frac{1}{2\pi rR}$$

for the center (r, θ) of the chord in polar coordinates. And since

$$\int_{r_1}^{r_2} f(r,\theta)dr=(2\pi R)^{-1}\ln(r_2/r_1)$$

it follows that annuli whose inner and outer radii, r_1 and r_2, stand in the same ratio should experience the same frequency of hits by the center of a chord. With $L = 2\sqrt{R^2-r^2}$ the length of a chord whose center is at (r, θ), the relative length, $x = L/2R$, of a chord has the induced density:

(13a) $$p(x)dx=\frac{x}{\sqrt{1-x^2}}$$

Finally, since $L = \sqrt{3}R$ is the side-length of the inscribed equilateral triangle, the probability sought is:

$$\int_{\sqrt{3}/2}^{1} p(x)dx=\tfrac{1}{2}\int_0^{1/4} u^{-1/2}du=\frac{1}{2}$$

with $u = 1 - x^2$.

All these predictions of Jaynes's solution can be put to the test (for one such test and its outcome, see Jaynes 1983, p. 143). In particular, (13) tells one to which hypothesis space a uniform distribution should be assigned to get an empirically correct result, namely, to the linear distance between the centers of the chord and circle. There is no claim, however, to be able to derive empirically correct distributions *a priori*, much less to conjure them out of ignorance. All that has been shown is that any distribution other than (13) must violate one or more of the posited invariances. If, for example, the target circle is slightly displaced in the grid of straight lines defined by a rain of straws, then the proportion of hits predicted by that other distribution will be different for the two circles. However if, Jaynes argues (p. 142), the straws are tossed in a manner that precludes even the skill needed to make them fall across the circle, then, surely, the thrower will lack the microscopic control needed to produce a different distribution on two circles that differ just slightly in size or location.

The broom straw experiment, which readers are urged to repeat for themselves, is highly typical of those to which one is tempted to ascribe physical probabilities or objective chances, for example, the chance of 1/2 that the chord fixed by a straw that falls across the circle exceeds the side of the inscribed triangle. However, as Zabell (1988, pp. 156–157) asks, if there is a "propensity" or "dispositional property" present, of what is it a property? Surely not of the straws, nor, he argues, of the manner in which they are tossed. A skilled practitioner of these arts can make a coin or a die show a predominance of heads or sixes (see Jaynes 2003, chapter 10). Nor is it at all helpful to speak of identical trials of the experiment, for if truly identical, they will yield the same result every time. Zabell concludes that "the suggested chance setup is in fact nothing other than a sequence of objectively differing trials which we are subjectively unable to distinguish between." However, one may well be able to distinguish between different throws of a dart in terms of how tightly one gripped it, for example, without being able to produce different distributions on slightly differing targets. It is the absence of such skill that seems to matter, and that feature of the chance setup is objective. On this basis, Jaynes is led to characterize the resulting invariant distribution as "by far the most likely to be observed experimentally in the sense that it requires by far the least skill" (1983, p. 133).

For a different example, consider the law of first digits. Naive application of the principle of indifference at the level of events leads to an assignment of equal probabilities to the hypotheses, h_d, $d = 1, 2, \ldots, 9$, that d is the first significant digit of an entry, X, in a table of numerical data. Nothing being said about the scale units employed, the implied scale invariance implies a log-uniform distribution of X with normalization constant, $1/\ln 10$, since $a = 10^k \leq X < 10^{k+1} = b$ forces $1 = \int_a^b \frac{dx}{x} = \ln(b/a) = \ln 10$ (which is independent of k). Hence, d is the first significant digit with probability:

(14)
$$p_d = \int_{da}^{(d+1)a} \frac{dx}{x \ln 10} = \frac{1}{\ln 10} \ln(1 + d^{-1}) = \log_{10}(1 + d^{-1})$$

so that $p_1 = log_{10}\ 2 = .301, \ldots, p_9 = 1 - log_{10}\ 9 = .046$. Known earlier to Simon Newcomb, (14) was rediscovered in 1938, though not explained, by Frank Benford, who tested it against twenty tables ranging from the surface areas of rivers and lakes to the specific heats of thousands of compounds. Surprisingly, Benford found that (14) even applies to populations of towns or to street addresses, which are certainly not ratio scaled. The explanation lies in the recent discovery of T. P. Hill (1995) that "base invariance implies Benford's law." That is, (14) is invariant under any change of the base $b > 1$ of the number system. Moreover, since scale invariance implies base invariance—but not conversely—the scale-invariant tables for which (14) holds are a proper subset of the base-invariant ones. Indeed, Hill derives a more general form of (14) that applies to initial blocks of $k \geq 1$ digits of real numbers expressed in any base, namely:

(14a)
$$P\left(\bigcap_{i=1}^{k} \{D_b^{(i)} = d_i\}\right) = \log_b\left[1 + \left(\sum_{i=1}^{k} b^{k-i} d_i\right)^{-1}\right]$$

where $D_b^{(i)}(x)$ is the ith significant digit of x in base b. For example, for base ten, and $k = 2$, the probability that the first two digits are 3 and 7 is $\log_{10}[1 + (37)^{-1}] = .01158$, while, as one may verify, the probability that the second digit is d is given by:

(14b)
$$\sum_{k=1}^{9} p_{kd} = \sum_{k=1}^{9} \log_{10}[1 + (10k + d)^{-1}]$$

Hill's derivation of (14) is a beautiful and instructive exercise in measure theoretic probability, but the main point to register here is that (14) is not the chance distribution of any readily conceivable physical process or random experiment. One can be just as certain, though, that any list or table of numbers that violates (14) must yield different frequencies of first (second, . . .) digits when the scale or number system is changed. More generally, the output of a deterministic process, like that which generates the digits of π or random numbers, for that matter, can be as random as one likes under the most stringent criterion or definition of randomness. These categories, so commonly contrasted, are not mutually exclusive. However, it is far from clear how to characterize an intrinsically random physical process in a way that is free of circularity and amenable to experimental confirmation (Jaynes 2003, §10.5). Jaynes views such random processes as mythic products of what he labels the "Mind Projection Fallacy."

BAYES EQUIVALENCE

Part of the motivation of the frequency theory was to develop objective means of assessing the evidence from an experiment, leaving readers of the report free to supply their own priors or utility functions. However, this ideal of separating evidence from opinion is unrealizable because, first, the support of a composite hypothesis or model with adjustable parameters depends on the weights assigned its various simple components, and, second, because of the presence of so-called nuisance parameters.

For an example of the former (Royall 1997, pp. 18–19), one can compare the hypothesis (H) that the proportion p of red balls in an urn is either ¼ or ¾ with the simple hypothesis (k) that $p = ½$, given that a ball drawn at random is red. The bearing of this outcome is wholly dependent on the relative weights assigned the two simple components of H, namely, $p = ¼$ and $p = ¾$. Or, again, how does drawing an ace of clubs bear on the hypothesis that the deck is a trick deck (fifty-two copies of the same card) versus the hypothesis that it is a normal deck? If one's intuition is that a single card can tell one nothing, then one is implicitly assigning equal probabilities to all fifty-two components of the trick deck hypothesis, but if, for example, one has information that most trick decks are composed of aces or picture cards, then drawing that ace of clubs will favor (for one) the trick deck hypothesis by a factor ranging from 1 to 52.

In practice, (F) resorts to comparing two models by the ratios of their maximum likelihoods, as in the orthodox t-test for comparing two normal means (de Groot 1986, §8.6). This is often a good approximation to the Bayes factor, the ratio of average likelihoods, when the two models are of roughly equal simplicity (Rosenkrantz 1977, p. 99), but this practice is otherwise highly biased (in the colloquial sense) in favor of the more complicated hypothesis, as in the trick deck example.

An equally formidable bar to the separation of sample information and prior information is the presence of parameters other than the one of interest. In testing the equality of two normal means, the difference, $\bar{x} - \bar{y}$, of the sample means *means* different things depending on one's beliefs about the variances of the two populations. An even simpler example is random sampling of an urn of size N without replacement. If interest centers on the number R of red balls in the urn and N is also unknown, then an outcome, $D = (n, r)$, of r red in a sample of n, will mean different things depending on one's prior beliefs about the relationship, if any, between R and N. If, for example, extensive previous experience renders it almost certain that the incidence of a certain birth defect lies well below one in a thousand, then a sample of modest size in which such a defect occurs, for example, $(n, r) = (500, 1)$, tells one not merely that $N \geq 500$, the sample size, but (almost surely) that $N \geq 1{,}000$. Even so simple a problem as this appears to lie entirely beyond the scope of (F) or (L), but as Jaynes amply demonstrates, this shopworn topic of introductory probability-statistics courses takes on a rich new life when the inverse problem of basing inferences about N and R on observed samples is considered and different kinds of prior information are incorporated in the resulting data analysis (2003, chapters 3 and 6).

In general, (B) handles nuisance parameters by marginalization, that is, by finding the joint posterior density, say, $p(\theta_1, \theta_2|DI)$ for the case of two parameters, and then integrating with respect to θ_2:

$$p(\theta_1 \mid DI) = \int p(\theta_1, \theta_2 \mid DI)\, d\theta_2$$

the discrete analogue being $P(A|DI) = \sum P(AB_i|DI)$ for mutually exclusive and exhaustive B_i's. Thus, intuition expects that a more focused belief state will result when there is prior knowledge of θ_2 than when its value is completely unknown before sampling.

Consider the case of sampling a normal population when nothing is known about $\theta_1 = \mu$ *and* $\theta_2 = \sigma^2$, so that their joint prior is the Jeffreys prior:

$$p(\theta_1, \theta_2|I) = p(\theta_1|I)p(\theta_2|I) = \theta_2^{-1}$$

while the (normal) likelihood is

$$L(\theta_1, \theta_2) = (2\pi\theta_2)^{-\frac{n}{2}} \exp\left[-\frac{1}{2\theta_2}\sum (x_i - \theta_1)^2\right]$$

$$\propto \theta_2^{-\frac{n}{2}} \exp[-\{\nu s^2 + n(\bar{x} - \theta_1)^2\}/2\theta_2]$$

using the obvious identity, $\sum (x_i - \theta_1)^2 = \sum (x_i - \bar{x} + \bar{x} - \theta_1)^2 = \sum (x_i - \bar{x})^2 + n(\bar{x} - \theta_1)^2$, with $s^2 = \sum_{i=1}^{n} (x_i - \bar{x})^2 / \nu$ and $\nu = n - 1$. Multiplying this by the prior yields the joint postsampling density

$$p(\theta_1, \theta_2 \mid DI) \propto \theta_2^{-\left(\frac{n-2}{2}\right)} \exp[-\{\nu s^2 + n(\bar{x} - \theta_1)^2\}/2\theta_2]$$

up to a normalization constant. Then using

(*) $$\int_0^\infty e^{-A/\theta}\theta^{-u}\, d\theta = \frac{\Gamma(u-1)}{A^{u-1}}$$

obtained from $\Gamma(u) = \int_0^\infty x^{u-1}e^{-x}\,dx$ by the substitution, $x = A/\theta$, the marginal posterior density of θ_1 is:

$$p(\theta_1 \mid DI) \propto \int_0^\infty \theta_2^{-\left(\frac{n+2}{2}\right)} \exp[-\{\nu s^2 + n(\bar{x} - \theta_1)^2\}/2\theta_2]\, d\theta_2$$

$$\propto \{\nu s^2 + n(\bar{x} - \theta_1)^2\}^{-\nu/2}$$

using (*) with $A = \nu s^2 + n(\bar{x} - \theta_1)^2$ and $u = (n + 2)/2$, whence

$$p(\theta_1|DI) \propto (1 + t^2/\nu)^{\frac{1}{2}(\nu+1)}$$

with $t = n^{\frac{1}{2}}(x - \theta_1)/s$. To find the normalization constant, one integrates on the right using the substitution, $t = \nu^{1/2}\left[\frac{x}{1-x}\right]^{1/2}$, with $dt = \frac{1}{2}\nu^{\frac{1}{2}}x^{-\frac{1}{2}}(1 - x)^{-\frac{3}{2}}dx$ and $1 + \frac{t^2}{\nu} = \frac{1}{1-x}$ to obtain:

$$2\int_0^\infty (1 + t^2/\nu)^{-\frac{1}{2}(\nu+1)}\, dt = \nu^{1/2}\int_0^1 x^{-\frac{1}{2}}(1-x)^{\frac{\nu}{2}-1}\, dx$$

$$= \nu^{\frac{1}{2}}\Gamma(\tfrac{1}{2})\Gamma(\tfrac{\nu}{2})/\Gamma(\tfrac{\nu+1}{2})$$

using the beta integral,

$$\int_0^1 x^{a-1}(1-x)^{b-1}\, dx = \Gamma(a)\Gamma(b)/\Gamma(a+b).$$

Hence, the posterior density of the mean, using $\Gamma(\frac{1}{2}) = \sqrt{\pi}$, is given by:

(15) $$p(\theta_1 \mid DI) = \frac{\Gamma(\frac{\nu+1}{2})}{\sqrt{\pi\nu}\,\Gamma(\frac{\nu}{2})} \frac{1}{\left(1 + \frac{t^2}{\nu}\right)^{\frac{1}{2}(\nu+1)}}$$

which is the density of the t-distribution with $v = n - 1$ degrees of freedom.

Thus, one has arrived in a few lines of routine calculation at the posterior (marginal) density of the mean when the variance is (completely) unknown. Were the variance known, the uniform prior of the mean leads, as was seen earlier, to a normal posterior distribution about the sample mean, x, with variance σ^2/n, or in symbols:

$$n^{\frac{1}{2}}(\theta_1 - \bar{x})\sigma \sim N(0, 1)$$

while the result, $n^{\frac{1}{2}}(\theta 1 - \bar{x})/s$, of replacing the population s.d., s, by the sample s.d., s when the former is unknown, has the t-distribution with $v = n - 1$ d.f. The density (15) is, like the normal density, bell-shaped and symmetric, but has larger tails (i.e., does not approach its asymptote, the x-axis, as rapidly as the normal curve) and is thus less concentrated. For example, for $v = 10$ degrees of freedom (d.f.), the 95 percent central region of the t-distribution is (–2.228, 2.228) while that of the normal is $(-1.96, 1.96) \approx (-2, 2)$. Thus, Bayesian updating confirms one's intuition that the postsampling belief function should be less concentrated when the variance is (completely) unknown than when it is known. Moreover, the t-distribution approaches normality rather rapidly as $v \to \infty$, and so the difference in the two states of prior knowledge is quickly swamped by a large sample. Already at $v = 20$, the 95 percent central region of (15) is (–1.98, 1.98), which is almost indistinguishable from the normal.

Because of a mathematical quirk, (F) interval estimates (confidence intervals) for a normal mean with variance unknown are numerically indistinguishable from (B) interval estimates (credence intervals) obtained from the posterior density, although their interpretation is radically different. For a normal distribution, the sample mean, $\bar{x}$, and sample variance, $s_n^2 = n^{-1}\sum_{i=1}^{n}(x_i - \bar{x})^2$, are independent (for a proof, see de Groot 1986, §7.3). As the normal distribution is the only one for which this independence of sample mean and sample variance obtains, it may justly be called a quirk. One shows, next, that if $Y \sim N(0, 1)$ and $Z \sim \chi_n^2$, then

$$X = \frac{Y}{\left(\frac{Z}{n}\right)^{1/2}}$$

has the t-distribution (15) with n degrees of freedom (§7.4). Now $Y = n^{\frac{1}{2}}(\bar{x} - \mu)/\sigma \sim N(0, 1)$ is standard normal, and it can be shown (de Groot 1986, pp. 391–392) that $Z = s_n^2 / \sigma^2 \sim \chi_{(n-1)}^2$, hence

$$U = \frac{Y}{\left(\frac{Z}{n-1}\right)^{1/2}}$$

has the t-distribution with $n - 1$ d.f. The crucial point is that σ^2 cancels out when one divides Y by $Z^{\frac{1}{2}}$ and so the distribution of U does not depend on the unknown variance. The nuisance is literally eliminated. Finally, (F) estimates of μ can be obtained from the distribution of U since $-c \leq U \leq c$ just in case $\bar{x} - c\sigma'/\sqrt{n} \leq \mu \leq \bar{x} + c\sigma'/\sqrt{n}$, writing $\sigma' = \left(\frac{s_n^2}{n-1}\right)^{1/2}$. Notice, however, the different interpretation. One thinks of $(\bar{x} - c\sigma', \bar{x} + c\sigma')$ as a random interval that contains μ with the specified probability, or long-run relative frequency in an imagined sequence of repetitions of the experiment.

The first thing that strikes one is how much more complicated this derivation of the sampling distribution of the relevant statistic is than the (B) derivation of the postsampling distribution (15) of μ. Even the modern streamlined derivation given in de Groot's (1986) text occupies nearly ten pages. William Seeley Gossett guessed the distribution by an inspired piece of mathematical detective work (for some of the relevant history, see Hald 1998, §27.5). The first rigorous proof was given in 1912 by a bright Cambridge undergraduate named R. A. Fisher. Gossett began his 1908 paper by noting that earlier statisticians had simply assumed "a normal distribution about the mean of the sample with standard deviation equal to $s/\sqrt{n}$" but that for smaller and smaller samples "the value of the s.d. found from the sample . . . becomes itself subject to an increasing error, until judgments reached in this way may become altogether misleading" (Hald 1998, p. 665). Fisher never tired of extolling "Student" (Gossett's pen name) for his great discovery, as well he might, for it is safe to say that without it, the (F) approach to statistics would never have gotten off the ground. For (F) would not then have been able to address the inferential problems associated with sampling a normal population for the vital case of small samples of unknown precision.

In essence, the pre-Gossett practice of replacing σ in $n^{\frac{1}{2}}(\bar{x} - \mu)/\sigma$ by its ML estimate, s_n, would be about the only option open to (F) or (L) if this nuisance parameter could not be eliminated. However, that is to treat the unknown parameter as if it were known to be equal to its estimated value—precisely what Gossett's predecessors had done. Complete ignorance of σ should result in a fuzzier belief state than when it is known (compare Royall 1997, p. 158). The only remedy (L) offers (p. 158) when nuisance parameters really are a nuisance (and cannot be eliminated) is to use the maximum of the likelihood function taken over all possible values of the relevant nuisance parameter(s). However, this is to equate a model with its best-fitting special case, which is to favor the more complicated of two models being compared. Moreover, in the real world outside of textbooks, normal samples do not come earmarked "variance known" or "variance unknown."

To borrow "Example 1" from Jaynes (1983, p. 157), the mean life of nine units supplied by manufacturer A is 42 hours with s.d. 7.48, while that of four units supplied by B is 50 hours with s.d. 6.48. (F) proceeds in such cases to test the null hypothesis that the two s.d.'s are equal using the F-test originated by Fisher (de Groot 1986, §8.8). When the null hypothesis is accepted, (F) then treats the two s.d.'s as equal and proceeds to a two sample t-test of the equality of the means (de Groot 1986, §8.9), which is predicated on the equality of the two (unknown) variances. In the present example, the hypothesis of equal s.d.'s is accepted at the 5 percent significance level, but then the two-sample t-test (unaccountably) accepts the hypothesis that the two means are equal at a 10 percent level. Jaynes calculates odds of 11.5 to 1 that B's components have a greater mean life, and without assuming equality of the variances. Then he asks, "Which statistician would you hire?"

The (F) solution extends to the case where independent samples are drawn from two normal populations of unknown variance, provided the variances are known to be equal or to stand in a given ratio. However, when the variances are known (or assumed) to be unequal, (F) fragments into a number of competing solutions with no general agreement as to which is best (Lindley 1965, pp. 94–95; Kendall and Stuart 1967, pp. 139ff). W.-U. Behrens proposed a solution in 1929 that Fisher rederived a few years later using his highly controversial fiducial argument (see the entry on R. A. Fisher). As Harold Jeffreys points out (1939, p. 115), the Behrens solution follows in a few lines from (2) using the Jeffreys prior for the unknown parameters (also see Lindley 1965, §6.3).

However, what of the intermediate cases where the variances are not known to be equal (the two-sample problem) and not known to be unequal (the Behrens-Fisher problem). In his definitive treatment, G. Larry Bretthorst (1993) takes up three problems: (1) determine if the two samples are from the same normal population, (2) if not, find how they differ, and (3) estimate the magnitude of the difference. Thus, if they differ, is it the mean or the variance (or both)?

Consider, once more, Jaynes's example. Bretthorst finds a probability of 0.58 that the s.d.'s, σ_1 and σ_2, are the same, given the sample s.d.'s of 7.48 and 6.48, the inconclusive verdict intuition expects. (F) is limited to an unnuanced approach where one or the other of these alternatives must be assumed. The posterior distribution Bretthorst computes is a weighted average of those premised on equal and unequal population variances and thus lies between them (Bretthorst 1993, p. 190, and figure 1). By marginalization, it yields a 72 percent probability that the parent means are different. The analysis is based on independent uniform and log-uniform priors for the means and variances truncated, respectively, at 34 = 46 – 12 and 58 = 46 + 12, and at $\sigma_L = 3$ and $\sigma_H = 10$. This is not just for the sake of greater realism but to ensure that the posterior density is normalizable (p. 191). Doubling the range of the means lowers the probability that the parent populations differ from 0.83 to 0.765, a change of roughly eight percent, while doubling the range of the s.d.'s makes about a 2 percent difference. Hence, the inference appears to be reasonably robust. Finally, the Bayesian solution smoothly extends the partial solutions (F) offers when the variances are unknown; the (F) solutions appear as the limiting cases of the (B) solution when the probability that the variances are equal is either zero or one. This makes it hard for an (F) theorist to reject the Bayesian solution.

The (F) solutions also correspond to (B) solutions based on an uninformative prior. This Bayes equivalence of (F) interval estimates or tests is more widespread than one might suppose (Jaynes 1983, pp. 168–171, 175), but is by no means universal. Generalizing from the case of known variances, it would seem to hold when sufficient estimators of the parameter(s) of interest exist, no nuisance parameters are present, and prior knowledge is vague or insubstantial.

Confidence intervals for a binomial success rate, θ, are harder to construct than the CI's for a normal mean because here the population variance, $n\theta(1 - \theta)$, depends on the parameter being estimated. The solution is to find for each value of θ, values $p_L(\theta)$ and $p_H(\theta)$, such that

$$P(p \geq p_L|\theta) = ½(1 - \alpha)$$

and

$$P(p \leq p_H|\theta) = ½(1 - \alpha)$$

as nearly as possible, where p is the proportion of successes in n trials. In other words, one finds a direct> 100(1

– α)% confidence interval for p for each value of the unknown success rate θ. Then the corresponding CI for θ comprises all those values whose direct CI contains the observed proportion p. For an example (n = 20) and a chart, see Kendall and Stuart (1967, pp. 103–105), whose obscure exposition makes this rather convoluted method seem even more mysterious. Plainly, finding such CI's is an undertaking, involving round off errors and approximations. By contrast, the Bayesian posterior density, given in the original memoir of Bayes, based on the uniform prior of θ, for r successes in n trials is

$$p(\theta \mid n,r) = \frac{(n+1)!}{r!(n-r)!}\theta^r(1-\theta)^{n-r}$$

with mean $(r + 1)/(n + 2)$ and variance, $f(1 - f)/(n + 3)$, where $f = r/n$. Hence, the Bayesian credence intervals assume the simple form,

$$f \pm k\sqrt{\frac{f(1-f)}{n+3}}$$

where k is 1.645, 1.96, and 2.57 for the 90, 95, and 99 percent intervals (using the normal approximation to the beta distribution). Jaynes finds (1983, p. 171) these Bayesian intervals are numerically indistinguishable from the CI's of the same confidence coefficient, leading him to wryly observe that the Bayesian solution Fisher denigrated as "founded on an error" delivers exactly the same interval estimates as the (F) solution at a fraction of the computational and mathematical effort. The reason for the equivalence is that, despite its great difference in motivation and interpretation, the (F) method of confidence intervals is based in this case on a sufficient statistic, the observed relative frequency f of success.

As Jaynes notes, the official doctrine of (F) is that CI's need not be based on sufficient statistics (Kendall and Stuart 1967, p. 153), and, indeed, the advertised confidence coefficient is valid regardless. Bayesian credence intervals, being based on the likelihood function, automatically take into account all the relevant information contained in the data, whether or not sufficient statistics exist. Thus, (F) methods not based on a sufficient statistic must perforce be wasting information, and the result one expects, given the optimality theorem, is a degradation of performance. The point is that the data may contain additional information that leads one to recognize that the advertised confidence coefficient is invalid (Loredo 1990, p. 117). The next several examples illustrate this and related points in rather striking fashion.

For a simple example (de Groot 1986, p. 400), let independent observations X_1 and X_2 be taken from a uniform distribution on the interval, $(\theta - ½, \theta + ½)$, with θ unknown. Then if $Y_1 = min(X_1, X_2)$ and $Y_2 = max(X_1, X_2)$, we have:

$$P(Y_1 \leq \theta \leq Y_2) = P(X_1 \leq \theta)P(X_2 \geq \theta) + P(X_2 \leq \theta)P(X_1 \geq \theta)$$

$$= ½ \cdot ½ + ½ \cdot ½ = ½$$

Thus, if $Y_1 = y_1$ and $Y_2 = y_2$ is observed, (y_1, y_2) is a 50 percent CI for θ. However, what if $y_2 - y_1 \approx 1$? Then (y_1, y_2) is virtually certain to contain θ; indeed, one easily checks that it is certain to contain θ when $y_2 - y_1 \geq 1/2$. Thus, one has a recognizable subset of the outcome space on which the 50 percent confidence coefficient is misleadingly conservative.

For an example of the opposite kind, where confidence is misplaced, one can turn to "Example 5" of Jaynes (1983, p. 172f). A chemical inhibitor that protects against failures wears off after an unknown time θ and decay is exponential (with mean one) beyond that point, so that a failure occurs at a time x with probability

$$f(x|\theta) = \exp(\theta - x)h(x, \theta)$$

where $h(x, \theta) = 1$ if $\theta < x$ and is otherwise zero. Since this data distribution for n failure times factors as

$$f_n(x_1, \ldots, x_n|\theta) = \exp[-\textstyle\sum x_i][e^{n\theta}h(y_1, \theta)$$

the factorization criterion (de Groot 1986, p. 358) shows that $Y_1 = \min(X_1, \ldots, X_n)$ is a sufficient statistic. (Intuitively, the least time to a failure contains all the information in the n recorded failure times relevant to the grace period of θ.) With a uniform distribution of θ (which enters here as a positive location parameter), the posterior density of θ is proportional to $exp[n(\theta - y_1)]$ and yields for three observations, $(X_1, X_2, X_3) = (12, 14, 16)$, a 90 percent credence interval of $11.23 > \theta > 12.0$, in good accord with qualitative intuition. However, (F) doctrine directs one to an unbiased estimator, and the point of the example is to show what can happen when a CI is not based on a sufficient statistic. Since

$$E(X) = \int_\theta^\infty xe^{\theta - x}dx = \theta + 1$$

an unbiased estimator of θ is given by $\theta^* = n^{-1}\sum_{i=1}^{n}(X_i - 1)$. Notice, however, that this can be negative for permitted (positive) failure times, even though θ is necessarily nonnegative. The shortest 90 percent CI based on this statistic's sampling distribution (found by computer, using an approximation) is $\theta^*-0.8529 < \theta < \theta^* + 0.8264$, or, since $\theta^* = 13$ for the three observations,

$$12.1471 < \theta < 13.8264$$

This consists entirely of values deductively excluded by the data! By contrast, the CI based on the sufficient statistic, the least of the failure times, is indistinguishable from its (B) counterpart.

Thus, Fisher was right to insist that his fiducial intervals be based on sufficient statistics. But, unfortunately, sufficient statistics do not always exist. A famous example is provided by the Cauchy distribution (the special case, $v = 1$, of Gossett's t-distribution), with density:

$$f(x \mid \theta) = \frac{1}{\pi} \frac{1}{1+(x-\theta)^2}$$

with θ a location parameter to be estimated. The Cauchy distribution has the peculiarity that the mean of any finite number of observations has the same (Cauchy) distribution as a single observation. Given, say, two observations, X_1 and X_2, the sampling distributions of either one or their mean, $\theta^* = \frac{1}{2}(X_1 + X_2)$, are all the same, and so, if one's choice of estimator is to be guided solely by the sampling distributions of the candidates, as (F) doctrine dictates, then any of these statistics is as good as another for the purpose of estimating θ. However, would anyone be willing to use just the first observation and throw away the second? Or doubt that their mean is a better estimator of θ than either observation taken alone? In fact, the mean is the optimal Bayes estimator for any loss function that is a monotonically increasing function of the absolute error, $|\hat{\theta} - \theta|$, in the sense that it minimizes one's expected loss after sampling. (Lacking a prior for θ, (F) lacks any such clear-cut criterion of optimality.) Now, besides their mean, the two observations provide further information in the form of their range or half-range, $Y = \frac{1}{2}(X_1 - X_2)$. Jaynes then calculates the conditional distribution of θ^* given Y, from which he calculates the probability that the 90 percent CI contains The true value of θ given the value of the half-range Y (1983, p. 279). The calculations show that for samples of small range, the .90 confidence coefficient is conservative: The CI for $y \leq 4$ will cover the true θ more than 95 percent of the time. However, for samples of wide range, $y \geq 10$, which comprise about 6.5 percent of the total, the CI covers θ less than 12 percent of the time.

By abandoning the principle of being guided only by the sampling distribution, (F) can also avail itself of the conditional distribution and base different estimates of θ on different values of Y, choosing for each observed y the shortest CI that, within that y-subclass, covers the true θ 90 percent of the time. For samples of narrow range, this delivers much shorter intervals than the standard 90 percent CI, while for samples of wide range, it covers the true θ more often with a join of two separate intervals. The resulting rule is uniformly reliable in never under or overstating its probability of covering the true θ, but by now one will have guessed that the uniformly reliable rule is the Bayesian rule!

A recurring theme of Jaynes's writings is that the (F) devotees of error probabilities and performance characteristics have never bothered to investigate the performance of the Bayesian solutions they denigrate as "founded on an error" or to compare their performance with their own preferred solutions. (B) methods based on uninformed priors capture Fisher's desideratum of "allowing the data to speak for themselves" as evidenced by their agreement with (F) methods based on sufficient statistics. It is then rather an onerous thesis to maintain that they fail to do this in cases where (F) lacks a solution or where, as it has just been seen, the (F) solution not so based leads to palpably absurd results or misleading statements of confidence. One can also sometimes criticize a frequentist solution as equivalent to a Bayesian solution based on an absurdly opinionated prior (see Jaynes 1983, p. 103).

Jaynes explains why (F) methods inevitably waste information as follows, "Orthodoxy requires us to choose a single estimator, $b(D) \equiv b(X_1, \ldots, X_n)$, *before we have seen the data*, and then use only $b(D)$ for the estimation" (2003, p. 510). The observed value of this statistic then places one on a manifold (or subspace) of n-dimensional space of dimension $n - 1$. If position on this manifold is irrelevant for θ, then $b(D)$ is a sufficient statistic, but if not, then D contains additional information relevant to θ that is not conveyed by specifying $b(D)$. (B) is then able to choose the optimal estimator for the present data set. The sampling distribution of $b(D)$ is simply not relevant, since one is free to choose different estimators or different CI's for different data sets.

INFORMED PRIORS AND ENTROPY

Of the many approaches to constructing uninformed priors, group invariance has been stressed because of its intimate ties to consistency. The same rationale underwrites a powerful extension of (2) to a more general rule of minimal belief change that goes by minimizing the cross-entropy deviation from an initial (pre) distribution among all those satisfying empirically given distributional constraints (see the entry on information theory). Recall, the cross entropy or discrimination information of a distribution $P = (p_1, \ldots, p_n)$ with respect to $Q = (q_1, \ldots, q_n)$ is defined by

$$H(P,Q) = \sum_{i=1}^{n} p_i \ln\left(\frac{p_i}{q_i}\right)$$

And when $Q = (n^{-1}, \ldots, n^{-1})$ is a uniform distribution, the rule (*MINXENT*) of minimizing cross entropy specializes to the rule (*MAXENT*) of maximizing the (Shannon) entropy,

$$H(P) = -\sum_{i=1}^{n} p_i \ln p_i$$

which is a measure of the uncertainty embodied in P. Entropy figures centrally in Claude Shannon's mathematical theory of communication (information theory), and looks to be a fundamental concept of probability theory as well. Thus, sufficient statistics, informally defined as "preserving all the information in the data relevant to inferences about θ," do actually preserve information in the sense of entropy (Jaynes 2003, §14.2). Also see Jaynes (§17.4) for further links between sufficiency, entropy, Fisher information, and the Cramer-Rao inequality.

When the psi-test discussed earlier leads one to expect a significant improvement in support by moving to an alternative (and possibly more complicated) model, MINXENT can lead one to it, as in the example of a biased die discussed in information theory entry. Thus, MINXENT literally enables one to carve a model out of empirically given measurements or mean values. Jaynes's original (1957) application to equilibrium thermodynamics (Jaynes 1983, chapters 1–6) with later extensions to nonequilibrium thermodynamics (chapter 10, §D) remains the exemplar, but a veritable floodtide of additional applications to all areas of scientific research have since followed, as recorded in the proceedings of workshops on Bayesian and maximum entropy methods held annually since 1981. The inferential problems this opens to attack lie even further beyond the range of (F) or (L).

Moreover, many classical models like the exponential or Gaussian arise most naturally as maxent distributions. Thus, the exponential, with density, $f(x|\theta) = \theta exp(-\theta x)$, is the maxent distribution of a positive continuous X of know mean; the normal (or Gaussian) that of a distribution whose first two moments are known. Jaynes (2003, p. 208) makes a serious case that this best accounts for the ubiquity of the Gaussian as a distribution of errors or noise, so that it is neither "an experimental fact" nor a "mathematical theorem," but simply the most honest representation of what is typically known about one's errors, namely, their "scale" and that positive and negative ones tend to cancel each other.

MAXENT functions primarily, though, as a means of arriving at informed priors. The superiority of a Bayes solution will be more manifest, in general, when substantial prior knowledge is formally incorporated in the analysis. Research might disclose, for example, that horse 1 finished ahead of horse 2 in two-thirds of the races both entered. If that is all that is known, then one's prior for tonight's race must satisfy $p_1 = 2p_2$. (How should this information affect the odds on the other horses?) In the inventory example of Jaynes (2003, §14.7), successive pieces of information, bearing on the decision which of three available colors to paint the day's run of 200 widgets so as to ensure twenty-four-hour delivery, are assimilated, starting with the current stocks of each color, the average number of each color sold per day, the average size of an individual order for each color, and so on. This is not just an amusing and instructive example of entropy maximization, but, evidently, one with serious practical applications.

At the other extreme of uninformativeness, the Bayesian econometrician Arnold Zellner has used entropy to define a maximal data informative prior (MDIP) as one that maximizes

$$\int I(\theta)p(\theta)d\theta - \int p(\theta)\ln p(\theta)d\theta$$

the difference between the average information in the data density and the (variable) prior density, where

$$I(\theta) = \int f(x\,|\,\theta)\ln f(x\,|\,\theta)d\theta$$

measures the information conveyed by the data density, $f(x|\theta)$. Such a prior also maximizes the expected log-ratio of the likelihood function to the prior density (for a number of examples and yet another derivation of the Jeffreys log-uniform prior, see Zellner and Min 1993).

To Lindley's oft-repeated question, "Why should one's knowledge or ignorance of a quantity depend on the experiment being used to determine it?" Jaynes answers that the prior should be based on all the available prior information and "the role a parameter plays in a sampling distribution is always a part of that information" (1983, p. 352). However, it should not depend on the size of the sample contemplated (pp. 379–382).

Apart from the satisfaction of seeing that variously motivated lines of attack all lead to the same priors in the best understood cases, like location or scale parameters or regression coefficients (for which see Jaynes 1983, pp. 195–196), different methods can be expected to generalize in different ways when harder problems are addressed. Obviously, there is room for much creative thought here in what might be described as the new epistemology, the endeavor to accurately represent whatever is known in probabilistic terms—what Jaynes calls "that great neglected half of probability theory." Such research can be expected to further the development of artificial intelligence and the formation of consensus priors in decision theoretic or policymaking contexts.

SUMMARY: A BAYESIAN REVOLUTION?

Is the much heralded Bayesian revolution a *fait accompli*? In his account of scientific revolutions, Thomas Kuhn may have erred in some of the details but certainly convinced his readers that there is a pattern here, something to construct a theory of. That applies, in particular, to revolutionary theory change, the overthrow of an old paradigm in favor of the new. Brush (1994, p. 137) touches on several of the reasons that usually enter in speaking of the acceptance of wave mechanics. Based on what has been surveyed in this entry, Bayesians would lodge the following parallel claims:

- (B) offers simpler solutions to the salient problems of the old (F) paradigm
- (B) offers a unified approach to all inferential problems—indeed, to all three problems of evidence, belief, and decision mentioned at the outset
- (B) is able to pose and solve problems of obvious importance that lie beyond the range of (F) or (L), among them problems involving nuisance parameters and those amenable to MINXENT.

(B) also lays claim to greater resolving power in the detection of periodicities in time series or in separating periodicities from trends (Jaynes 2003, p. 125 and chapter 17).

(B) views (2) as embodying the entire logic of science. It has demonstrated that (2), as well as its extension to MINXENT, is anchored in the bedrock of consistency and that the price of inconsistency is inefficiency, the waste of information present in the data. Finally, (B) claims to be able to ascertain the limits of validity of the methods of (F) by viewing them as approximations to Bayesian methods. That, too, is highly characteristic of the claims a new paradigm lodges against the old. In any case, many time-honored procedures of (F), like significance tests or chi-square tests, retain an honorable place in the Bayesian corpus as approximate Bayes procedures, and where the elements needed for a Bayesian solution are lacking, one may use Bayesian logic to find a useful surrogate.

Critics will allege that Bayesians have not solved the "problem of the hypothesis space," namely, to which hypotheses should one assign probabilities? Jaynesians admit they have not solved this problem, but neither has anyone else. Jaynes's point, rather, is that the only way to discover that we have not gone to a deep enough hypothesis space is to draw inferences from the one we have. We learn most when our predictions fail, but to be certain that failed predictions reflect inadequacies of our hypothesis space rather than poor reasoning, "those inferences [must be] our *best* inferences, which make full use of all the information we have" (Jaynes 2003, p. 326).

See also Experimentation and Instrumentation; Probability and Chance.

Bibliography

Bretthorst, G. Larry. "On the Difference in Means." In *Physics and Probability: Essays in Honor of Edwin T. Jaynes*, edited by W. T. Grandy Jr. and P. W. Milonni. New York: Cambridge University Press, 1993.

Brush, Stephen G. "Dynamics of Theory Change: The Role of Predictions." *PSA 1994*. Vol. 2, edited by David Hull, Micky Forbes, and Richard Burian. East Lansing, MI: Philosophy of Science Association, 1994.

Cox, Richard T. "Probability, Frequency, and Reasonable Expectation." *American Journal of Physics* 14 (1946): 1–13.

De Finetti, Bruno. "La Prevision: ses lois logiques, ses sources subjectives." *Annales de l'Institut Henri Poincare* 7 (1937), 1–68. Translated as "Prevision: Its Logical Laws, Its Subjective Sources." In *Studies in Subjective Probability*. 2nd ed., edited by Henry Kyburg and Howard Smokler. New York: Wiley, 1981.

De Finetti, Bruno. "Sur la condition d'equivalence partielle." *Actualites scientifiques et industrielles*, No. 739 (Colloque Geneve d'Octobre 1937 sur la Théorie des Probabilites, 6tieme partie.) Paris: Hermann, 1938. Translated as "On the Condition of Partial Exchangeability." In *Studies in Inductive Logic and Probability*, edited by Richard C. Jeffrey. Berkeley: University of California Press, 1980.

De Finetti, Bruno. *Probability, Induction, and Statistics*. New York: Wiley, 1972.

De Groot, Morris. *Probability and Statistics*. 2nd ed. Reading, MA: Addison-Wesley, 1986.

Edwards, Ward, Harold Lindman, and Leonard J. Savage. "Bayesian Statistical Inference for Psychological Research." In *Readings in Mathematical Psychology*. Vol. 2, edited by. R. Duncan Luce, R. Bush, and Eugene Galanter. New York: Wiley, 1965.

Festa, Roberto. *Optimum Inductive Methods*. Dordrecht, Netherlands: Kluwer Academic, 1993.

Fisher, Ronald A. *The Design of Experiments*. Edinburgh, Scotland: Oliver and Boyd, 1935.

Fisher, Ronald A. *Statistical Methods and Scientific Inference*. 2nd ed. Edinburgh, Scotland: Oliver and Boyd, 1959. All of Fisher's three main books on statistics have been reprinted by Oxford University Press (2003) under the title *Statistical Methods, Experimental Design and Statistical Inference*.

Giere, Ronald N. "Philosophy of Science Naturalized." *Philosophy of Science* 52 (1985): 331–356.

Good, I. J. *Good Thinking*. Minneapolis: University of Minnesota Press, 1983.

Hacking, Ian. *Logic of Statistical Inference*. New York: Cambridge University Press, 1965.

Hald, Anders. *A History of Mathematical Statistics from 1750 to 1930*. New York: Wiley, 1998.

Hill, T. P. "Base Invariance Implies Benford's Law." *Proceedings of the American Mathematical Society* 123 (1995): 887–895.

Hodges, J. L., and Erich Lehmann. *Basic Concepts of Probability and Statistics*. 2nd ed. San Francisco: Holden-Day, 1970.

Jaynes, E. T. *Papers on Probability, Statistics, and Statistical Physics*, edited by R. D. Rosenkrantz. Dordrecht, Netherlands: D. Reidel, 1983.

Jaynes, E. T. *Probability Theory: The Logic of Science*, edited by G. Larry Bretthorst. New York: Cambridge University Press, 2003.

Jeffreys, Harold. *Theory of Probability*. Oxford, U.K.: Clarendon Press, 1939.

Kalbfleish, John G., and D. A. Sprott. "On Tests of Significance." *In Foundations of Probability Theory, Statistical Inference, and Statistical Theories of Science*. Vol. 2, edited by William L. Harper and Clifford A. Hooker. Dordrecht, Netherlands: D. Reidel, 1976.

Kendall, Maurice G., and Alan Stuart. *Advanced Theory of Statistics*. 2nd ed. New York: Hafner, 1967.

Lehmann, Erich. *Testing Statistical Hypotheses*. New York: Wiley, 1959.

Lindley, Dennis V. *Introduction to Probability and Statistics. Vol. 2, Inference*. Cambridge, U.K.: Cambridge University Press, 1965.

Loredo, T. J. "From Laplace to Supernova SN 1987A: Bayesian Inference in Astrophysics." In *Maximum Entropy and Bayesian Methods*, edited by Paul Fougere. Dordrecht, Netherlands: Kluwer Academic, 1990.

Mayo, Deborah G. *Error and the Growth of Experimental Knowledge*. Chicago: University of Chicago Press, 1996.

Morrison, D., and R. Henkel, eds. *The Significance Test Controversy*. Chicago: Aldine Press, 1970.

Pearson, Egon S. *The Selected Papers of E. S. Pearson*. Berkeley: University of California Press, 1966.

Rosenkrantz, R. D. *Inference, Method, and Decision*. Dordrecht, Netherlands: D. Reidel, 1977.

Rosenkrantz, R. D. "The Justification of Induction." *Philosophy of Science* 59 (1992): 527–539.

Royall, Richard M. *Statistical Evidence: A Likelihood Paradigm*. London: Chapman and Hall, 1997.

Savage, L. J. *The Foundations of Statistics*. New York: Wiley, 1954.

Smith, C. Ray, and Gary J. Erickson. "Probability Theory and the Associativity Equation." In *Maximum Entropy and Bayesian Methods*, edited by Paul Fougere. Dordrecht, Netherlands: Kluwer Academic, 1990.

Zabell, S. L. "Symmetry and Its Discontents." In *Causation, Chance, and Credence*, edited by Brian Skyrms and W. L. Harper, 155–190. Dordrecht, Netherlands: Kluwer Academic, 1988.

Zellner, Arnold, and Chung-ki Min. "Bayesian Analysis, Model Selection, and Prediction." In *Physics and Probability: Essays in Honor of Edwin T. Jaynes*, edited by W. T. Grandy Jr. and P. W. Milonni. New York: Cambridge University Press, 1993.

Zellner, Arnold, Hugo A. Keuzenkamp, and Michael McAleer, eds. *Simplicity, Inference, and Modeling: Keeping It Sophisticatedly Simple*. New York: Cambridge University Press, 2001.

Roger D. Rosenkrantz

STEBBING, LIZZIE SUSAN

(1885–1943)

Lizzie Susan Stebbing, the English logician and philosopher, was born in London. A very delicate child, she received a discontinuous education until she went to Girton College, Cambridge, in 1906. While at Cambridge she happened to read F. H. Bradley's *Appearance and Reality*, which led to her interest in philosophy. She became a pupil of the logician W. E. Johnson. From 1913 to 1915 she lectured in philosophy at King's College, London; and she became a lecturer at Bedford College, London, in 1915 and a professor in 1933.

In London Stebbing's philosophical development was stimulated by the meetings of the Aristotelian Society, which were often attended by Bertrand Russell, A. N. Whitehead, and G. E. Moore; and she always acknowledged the philosophical influence of Moore as particularly strong. In 1931 she published *A Modern Introduction to Logic* and in 1937 *Philosophy and the Physicists*, which were by a considerable degree the most substantial of her books. She wrote numerous papers, the best of which are to be found in *Mind* and the *Proceedings of the Aristotelian Society*.

In philosophy Stebbing's main interests lay in the metaphysical questions posed by logic and in the foundations of science. Much of her work in these topics is contained in *A Modern Introduction to Logic*. The book's merit does not lie in any originality in formal logic, or even in its method of presenting formal structures, but rather in its clear exposition of the logical theories of the early twentieth century, together with a stimulating, lucid, perceptive account of the metaphysical problems the new logical techniques either dispersed or clarified, and of the metaphysics that lay behind these logical theories. It was the first book on modern logic that introduced together and comprehensively both the formalism and its related philosophical problems. It is probably still the best introduction for a reader prepared to give serious thought to such problems.

In the professional journals Stebbing published papers on a range of topics closely related to those of *A Modern Introduction to Logic,* but her interests were not confined to such purely academic, though deeply absorbing, matters. She wrote several books on what one might call logic in practice. (Her book *Thinking to Some Purpose* is a good example both in its title and in its content.) She was strongly convinced of the importance of rationality and clarity in the conduct of human affairs and of the immense importance of knowledge. She attempted, therefore to expose the artifices by which hard facts are obscured in soft language, either so that the unscrupulous may deceive us or so that we may hide from ourselves what we do not wish to see. Her books in this field are especially valuable for their actual examples of irrationality and emotional persuasion in high places and on vital matters.

This commitment to rational clarity was combined with her more purely professional interests and skills in *Philosophy and the Physicists.* In the course of writing books with the ostensible aim of popularizing contemporary science, Sir James Jeans and Sir Arthur Eddington had argued that modern physics shows the world to be quite other than the sort of place it seems to be, not merely physically but also metaphysically. Both argued for idealist views of physics and, consequently, for a comfortable if imperfectly clear form of theism. In much of her book Stebbing exposed the fallacies, needless obscurities and mystifications with which the pages of Jeans and Eddington abound. *Philosophy and the Physicists* is an excellent piece of rational cool criticism, but a significant characteristic of the book is its implicit faith that we need not seek protection behind intellectual smoke screens and, indeed, that this sort of evasion prevents any really dignified adjustment to the human situation based on knowledge and reason. Stebbing deeply believed that such an adjustment is possible.

See also Bradley, Francis Herbert; Eddington, Arthur Stanley; Jeans, James Hopwood; Logic, History of: Modern Logic; Moore, George Edward; Russell, Bertrand Arthur William; Whitehead, Alfred North; Women in the History of Philosophy.

Bibliography

Books by Susan Stebbing are *A Modern Introduction to Logic* (London: Methuen, 1931; 2nd ed., revised, London, 1933); *Philosophy and the Physicists* (London: Methuen, 1937); *Thinking to Some Purpose* (Harmondsworth, U.K.: Penguin, 1939); and *Ideals and Illusions* (London: Watts, 1941).

The Aristotelian Society collected the material for *Philosophical Studies: Essays in Memory of L. Susan Stebbing* (London: Allen and Unwin, 1948), a volume of essays that contains an appreciation by John Wisdom and a full bibliography of Stebbing's writings.

G. C. Nerlich (1967)

STEFANINI, LUIGI

(1891–1956)

Luigi Stefanini, the Italian personalist philosopher, taught at Messina and Padua. He was a founder of the Gallarate movement and the founder and first editor of the *Rivista di estetica.* Much of Stefanini's own philosophy is to be found in his work on the history of philosophy. He tried to demonstrate by careful historical analysis that authentic religious and metaphysical needs are adequately met by certain historical positions, especially those of St. Augustine and St. Bonaventure. His guiding principle, "paradigmatism," is of Platonic and Neoplatonic origin and may be stated thus: that which is created in the image of another (as is man) has as its constitutive imperative, or life vocation, the expression in itself of its transcendental model.

Stefanini professed in turn Christian idealism, spiritualism, and personalism. His Christian idealism was based on a critique of Giovanni Gentile's claim that the self generates the self and the world and hence is the paradigm of the world. Stefanini held that the self apprehends itself not as self-generating but as created and therefore has its paradigm in an other. Art is an immediate expression of that other and provides an approach to the Christian experience, in which the image of God in the human subject is remodeled on the higher paradigm of Christ.

Stefanini's spiritualism began in a critique of historicism, phenomenology, and existentialism. All of these, he claimed, divide the transcendental from the existential. He sought to heal this split by the analysis of the self. The self is not existence as given (*Dasein*) but existence that utters itself. The self is spirit, or word, and this word does not utter, but alludes to, the Absolute; in this way it reveals its dependence. The purest form of this allusion to the Absolute is the Word of God, Christ. The vocation of the Christian is to utter that Word in himself.

Stefanini called his most mature thought "personalism." The self is central to every form of participation and is the only ultimate point of reference. But the self cannot sustain itself; it rests upon the other, and the transcendent is therefore the principle of the self's being. The self realizes itself as a person by its relation to the transcendent. It seeks to realize the transcendent in itself according to the limits and form of its own being.

See also Absolute, The; Augustine, St.; Bonaventure, St.; Existentialism; Gentile, Giovanni; Historicism; Idealism; Personalism; Phenomenology; Self.

Bibliography

WORKS BY STEFANINI

Idealismo cristiano. Padua: Zannoni, 1931.

Platone. 2 vols. Padua: Milani, 1932–1935.

Spiritualismo cristiano. Brescia, 1942.

La metafisica della persona. Brescia: Morcelliana, 1949.

La metafisica dell'arte. Brescia: Morcelliana, 1949.

WORKS ON STEFANINI

Bortolaso, Giovanni. "Uno spiritualista cristiano: Luigi Stefanini." *Civiltà cattolica* (1956) (1): 295–304.

Carlini, Armando. "Incontri e scontri con Stefanini e con Sciacca." *Giornale critico della filosofia italiana,* series III, 4 (1950): 841–893.

Chaix-Ruy, Jules. "Les philosophes italiens d'aujourd'hui." *Revue thomiste* 55 (1947): 407ff.

De Ruggiero, Guido. "Stefanini." *La critica* (1934): 383ff.

Luigi Stefanini. Filosofi d'oggi series. Turin. Contains a complete bibliography.

A. Robert Caponigri (1967)

STEFFENS, HENRICH
(1773–1845)

Henrich Steffens, the philosopher, scientist, and novelist and short-story writer was of Danish and German descent. He was born in Stavanger, Norway, the son of a physician in the service of the Dano-Norwegian monarchy. From 1790 to 1794 Steffens studied natural science, especially mineralogy and geology, in Copenhagen. He next studied natural history in Kiel, where he became interested in philosophy. In 1798 he moved to Jena, drawn not least by the natural philosophy of Friedrich von Schelling, whose *Erster Entwurf eines Systems der Naturphilosophie* had appeared in 1797. In Jena, Steffens met Schelling, Johann Wolfgang von Goethe, and August Schlegel; and in Berlin in 1799 he met Friedrich von Schlegel and Friedrich Schleiermacher.

In 1802 Steffens returned to Copenhagen to lecture on natural philosophy. Through his large audience he influenced the development of the romantic movement in Denmark, but he failed to obtain the university position he had hoped for, and in 1804 he accepted a chair in natural philosophy and mineralogy at the University of Halle. In 1811 he was appointed professor of physics in Breslau, where he remained, except for a brief period of service as a volunteer in the war against Napoleon Bonaparte in 1813–1814, until 1832. In that year Steffens became professor at Berlin, where he lectured on natural philosophy, anthropology, and geology until his death.

Steffens's philosophy was markedly influenced by Benedict de Spinoza and by Spinozistic pantheism, as well as by Schelling. Schelling's *Von der Weltseele, eine Hypothese der höheren Physik zur Erklärung des allgemeinen Organismus* (On the world-soul, a hypothesis of higher physics in explanation of the general organism) appeared in 1798, and in Steffens's *Beiträge zur innern Naturgeschichte der Erde* (Contributions to the inner natural history of the earth; 1801) the influence of Schelling is readily discernible. The title of Schelling's work gives an indication of the substance and trend of Steffens's philosophical thinking; it is a blend of natural science and speculative philosophy imbued with the general spirit of the romantic movement, somewhat less speculative than that of Schelling.

Steffens viewed the history of nature as a development or evolution from inorganic stages to organic and animate forms, governed by a divine purpose. His pantheism found characteristic expression in the view that nature itself is creative, the acme of the natural creative process being the free individual human personality, or spirit. According to Steffens's *Anthropologie* (1822) man is a living unity of spirit and nature—a microcosm, in the sense that the history of humankind mirrors the development of nature itself. He found in myths and mythological traditions a true, though symbolically expressed, understanding and knowledge of nature; however, he believed that a proper scientific study of nature was a necessary prerequisite for a correct interpretation of the meaning of myths.

See also Goethe, Johann Wolfgang von; Pantheism; Philosophy of Physics; Schelling, Friedrich Wilhelm Joseph von; Schlegel, Friedrich von; Schleiermacher, Friedrich Daniel Ernst; Spinoza, Benedict (Baruch) de.

Bibliography

WORKS BY STEFFENS

Beiträge zur innern Naturgeschichte der Erde. Freiburg, 1801.

Grundzüge der philosophischen Naturwissenschaft. Berlin: Realschulbuchhandlung, 1806.

Anthropologie. Breslau: J. Max, 1822.

Was ich erlebte, 10 vols. Breslau, 1840–1844. Steffens's autobiography; an important source for the study of the romantic movement in Germany.

WORKS ON STEFFENS

Petersen, Richard. *Henrich Steffens.* Copenhagen, 1881.

Waschnitus, Victor. *Henrich Steffens.* Neumünster, Germany, 1939.

Knut Erik Tranöy (1967)

STEIN, EDITH

(1891–1942)

Edith Stein was born into a German Jewish family on October 12, 1891, on Yom Kippur, in the Silesian capital Breslau, Germany (after 1945, Wroclaw, Poland). She was the youngest of eleven children, four of whom died in early childhood. Her father, Siegfried Stein (1844–1893), had a small trade with coals and wood and died too early for his youngest child to have any memory of him. Her mother, Auguste Stein, née Courant (1849–1936), was a matriarchal, warm-hearted woman who tried to educate her children in the traditional Jewish faith and in the celebration of the rituals. Nonetheless, the industrious and highly intelligent girl became an agnostic from her puberty onward and already in school became a champion of women's liberation.

After a brilliant performance on school examinations, she studied psychology with William Stern, philosophy with Richard Hönigswald, along with German literature and history, at the Universität Breslau from 1911 to 1913. One can obtain a good sense of her feelings from that period, up to her doctorate in 1916 from the Albert-Ludwigs-Universität Freiburg, from her fragmentary autobiography *Life in a Jewish Family*, written in 1933 but first published in 1965. In 1913 Stein went to Göttingen to study under the famous founder of phenomenology, Edmund Husserl (1859–1938), and with his assistant Adolf Reinach (1883–1917), whose death in World War I affected her very deeply. In 1915 she worked as a Red-Cross nurse in an international soldiers' recovery hospital in Weißkirchen, Mähren (now located in the Czech Republic). After completing her state examinations, she followed Husserl to Universität Freiburg in 1916, where she completed her dissertation *On the Problem of Empathy* summa cum laude. From 1917 to 1918 she served as Husserl's private assistant, transcribing, ordering, and completing his manuscripts, preparing for publication his *Ideas Pertaining to a Pure Phenomenology and to a Phenomenological Philosophy*, books 2 and 3, along with his *On the Phenomenology of the Consciousness of Internal Time*, later published in 1927 by Martin Heidegger.

Between 1918 and 1932 Stein attempted four times to qualify for a habilitation (the highest qualification in the German university), at the universities in Göttingen, Freiburg, Breslau, and Kiel, but she failed partly because she was female and partly because she was a Jew. During a deepening personal as well as academic crisis as her relationships with the phenomenologists Roman Ingarden and Hans Lipps weakened, she started studying classical Christian literature, especially St. Teresa of Ávila, as well as Martin Luther, Søren Kierkegaard, and St. Augustine. Her Catholic baptism on January 1, 1922, separated her in a painful way from her family, especially from her mother, who received a second, almost unsustainable blow in October 1933, when Stein entered the Carmelite order in Cologne. From 1923 until 1931, she worked as a teacher of German and history at a girls' college, Mädchen-Lyzeum, in Speyer on the Rhine, and from 1932 until March 1933 she taught as a docent at the Deutsches Institut für wissenschaftliche Pädagogik (German Institute for Scientific Pedagogy) in Münster. From 1928 through 1933, her spiritual mentor was Raphael Walzer OSB, arch abbot of the Benedictine monastery at Beuron. During the same period she became well known in Catholic circles in Germany, Austria (Salzburg, Vienna), and Switzerland (Zurich) through her lectures on Christian anthropology and Christian feminism.

After the removal of non-Aryans from official positions in the spring of 1933, Stein left the institute to fulfill her wish for a Carmelite existence. In April 1933 she wrote a famous letter to Pope Pius XI asking him to protest against the humiliation of Jews and predicting a coming prosecution of the Catholic Church too. From 1933 through 1938 she stayed in the Carmelite cloisters in Cologne, using the name Sister Teresia Benedicta a cruce of the Cross OCD. In 1939 she moved to the Carmelite cloisters at Echt, Netherlands. After the protest of Dutch Catholic bishops against prosecution of Jews, she and her sister Rosa were arrested by the Gestapo on August 2, 1942, brought first to the Dutch camps of Amersfort and Westerbork, and taken from there by train to Auschwitz. The day of her arrival on August 9, 1942, is most probably the day she was killed. In 1987 she was beatified, in

1998 sanctified, and in 1999 named copatroness of Europe by Pope John Paul II.

PHILOSOPHICAL WORKS

In the first, strictly phenomenological period of her writing while she was one of Husserl's leading students (1916–1922), Stein employed Husserl's phenomenological method in fundamental analyses in anthropology, focusing on psychology, psychophysical interactions, intersubjectivity, and personhood. Her dissertation investigated empathy (a field neglected by Husserl) as the basis for intersubjectivity and the experience of the other's and one's own body, referring to the tradition of Theodor Lipps, Max Scheler, and Alexander Pfänder, and then developing independent conclusions. In 1919, in *Einführung in die Philosophie*,Stein critiqued Husserl's idealistic position on the ego, contrasting his view of the monadic ego with arguments for a real external world. Her habilitation *Philosophy of Psychology and the Humanities* (1922/2000) differentiated the psyche and the soul with reference to causality and motivation. Causality determines the bound psyche with the help of conditions and psychic laws, while motivation inspires the free, creative will of the personal soul. Respectively they constitute the sensual, receptive subject and the rational, active subject. She takes an analogous approach in her treatment of the community and its transindividual reality in *Individuum und Gemeinschaft* (Individuality and community; 1922). The essential difference between psychic bindings and rationally deciding leads to the difference between psychology and the humanities (*Geisteswissenschaften*). The voluminous study *Eine Untersuchung über den Staat* (A study of the state; 1925) illuminates the ontological basis of sociology by differentiating between community and society and showing the roots of society in community and the roots of community in the individual.

In her second period after her baptism (1922–1937), Stein, in analyzing important parts of the Christian tradition but still doing so in a phenomenological way, was drawn to classical ontology and metaphysics. Inspired by the Jesuit Erich Przywara, in the 1920s Stein translated John Henry Newman's *Letters from the Anglican Period* and *Idea of a University*, and Thomas Aquinas's *Quaestiones disputatae de veritate* (Disputations on truth; 1931–1934) and *De ente et essentia* (On being and essence; unpublished yet). Her studies in Christian feminism and female education, including essays on Elisabeth of Thüringen and Teresa of Avila, revealed a remarkable phenomenology of womanhood, especially in reference to the interrelation of body, soul, self-concept, and being divinely gifted. While teaching in Münster from 1932 to 1933, she wrote a philosophical anthropology and a fragmentary theological anthropology in *Der Aufbau der menschlichen Person* (The structure of human person) and *Was ist der Mensch?* (What is a human being?). The difference, but also the possible connection, between phenomenological method and scholastic ontology is shown in *Was ist Philosophie? Ein Gespräch zwischen Edmund Husserl und Thomas von Aquino* (1929) a Platonic dialogue between Husserl and Aquinas, with Aquinas as the leading speaker. In *Potenz und Akt* (Potentiality and act; 1931) and *Endliches und ewiges Sein* (Finite and eternal being; 1936/37), Stein tried to reconcile phenomenology and scholastic philosophy in a contemporary fashion. Referring to Aristotle, Aquinas, Augustine, pseudo-Dionysius, Heidegger, Jean Hering, and Hedwig Conrad-Martius (her godmother, famous for a philosophy of nature and of space and time), Stein tried to analyze different conceptions of being and to reconcile phenomenology and classical and medieval ontology into a philosophy for all time. Though she started with Aquinas, who maintained an Aristotelian ontology, she ultimately ended up closer to Augustine's personalism and his trinitarian view of creation. The aim of her philosophy was a theory of the person, not of ontological being.

In her third period (1940–1942), Stein composed two important studies on Christian spirituality and mystics. To prepare for a modern analysis of the great Spanish Carmelite reformer John of the Cross (1542–1591), she translated the complete works of pseudo-Dionysius (the Areopagite), the father of occidental mysticism, and dedicated to him the essay "Wege der Gotteserkenntnis" (Ways to recognize God; 1940/41). She reconstructed and commented on the three classical Areopagitic ways of pursuing theology: the positive, the negative, and the mystical. As an immediate fruit of rethinking the basics of mysticism, Stein provided an immanent interpretation of the theory and poetry of mystical ascent by John of the Cross, in her last, almost completed work *The Science of the Cross* (1950/2002). In his three-dark-nights theory of spiritual development, one must pass through the night of sentiment, the night of mind, and the night of faith before ascending to God. She also held that one must annihilate the self before reaching the glory of God—a theory that sheds light on Stein's own inner spiritual development. Her reflections retain language and methods close to phenomenological research.

LEGACY

Until 1930 the writings and translations of Stein were published for the most part during her lifetime. All of her other works, letters, and uncompleted projects began to be published from 1950 to 1998 in *Edith Steins Werke* in 18 volumes by Herder in Freiburg. A new critical edition of all her writings, based on the complete material in the Carmelite Archive in Cologne and including translations and scattered pieces, is being projected from 2000 to 2010 as *Edith Stein Gesamtausgabe* (Complete works of Edith Stein) in 25 volumes, also by Herder. The interest in her life initially led to many hagiographic studies. Meanwhile, since the 1990s her philosophical work on Husserl and Heidegger has met with strong interest and received an increasingly positive appraisal. Stein's importance and influence in the history of phenomenology has yet to be fully explored.

See also Phenomenology; Thomism.

Bibliography

WORKS BY STEIN

The Collected Works of Edith Stein. Washington, DC: ICS Publications, 1986–2002. Vol. 1: *Life in a Jewish Family, 1891–1916: An Autobiography*, translated by Josephine Koeppel (1986). Vol. 2: *Essays on Woman*, translated by Freda Mary Oben (1996). Vol. 3: *On the Problem of Empathy*, translated by Waltraud Stein, 3rd, rev. ed. (1989). Vol. 4: *The Hidden Life*, translated by Waltraud Stein (1992). Vol. 5: *Self Portrait in Letters, 1916–1942*, translated by Josephine Koeppel (1993). Vol. 6: *The Science of the Cross* (1950), translated by Josephine Koeppel (2002). Vol. 7: *Philosophy of Psychology and the Humanities*, translated by Mary Catharine Baseheart and Marianne Sawicki (2000). Vol. 8: *Knowledge and Faith*, translated by Walter Redmond (2000). Vol. 9: *Finite and Eternal Being: An Attempt at an Ascent to the Meaning of Being*, translated by Kurt F. Reinhardt (2002).

Edith Steins Werke, edited by Lucy Gelber and Michael Linssen. Freiburg, Germany: Herder, 1950–.

Einführung in die Philosophie, edited by Claudia Mariéle Wulf. Freiburg, Germany: Herder, 2004.

Gesamtausgabe. Freiburg, Germany: Herder, 2000–.

Individuum und Gemeinschaft. Halle, Germany: M. Niemeyer, 1922.

Eine Untersuchung über den Staat. Halle, Germany: M. Niemeyer, 1925.

WORKS ON STEIN

Baseheart, Mary Catharine. *Person in the World: Introduction to the Philosophy of Edith Stein*. Dordrecht: Kluwer, 1997.

Beckmann, Beate. *Phänomenologie des religiösen Erlebnisses: Religionsphilosophische Überlegungen im Anschluß an Adolf Reinach und Edith Stein*. Würzburg, Germany: Königshausen und Neumann, 2003.

Beckmann, Beate, and Hanna-Barbara Gerl-Falkovitz, eds. *Edith Stein: Themen, Bezüge, Dokumente*. Würzburg, Germany: Königshausen und Neumann, 2003.

Fetz, Reto Luzius, Matthias Rath, and Peter Schulz, eds. *Studien zur Philosophie von Edith Stein*. Freiburg, Germany: Alber, 1993.

Gerl-Falkovitz, Hanna-Barbara. *Unerbittliches Licht: Edith Stein; Philosophie, Mystik, Leben*. 3rd ed. Mainz, Germany: Grünewald, 1999.

Herbstrith, Waltraud, ed. *Never Forget: Christian and Jewish Perspectives on Edith Stein*. Translated by Susanne Batzdorff. Washington, DC: ICS Publications, 1998.

Neyer, Amata. *Edith Stein: Her Life in Photos and Documents*. Translated by Waltraud Stein. Washington: ICS Publications, 1999.

Sawicki, Marianne. *Body, Text, and Science: The Literacy of Investigative Practices and the Phenomenology of Edith Stein*. Dordrecht, Netherlands: Kluwer, 1997.

Hanna-Barbara Gerl-Falkovitz (2005)

STEINER, RUDOLF
(1861–1925)

Rudolf Steiner, the German philosopher and occultist, was born in Kraljevic, Hungary, of Catholic parents. His early education was obtained at technical secondary schools and the Polytechnic Institute of Vienna. Steiner's anthroposophical teaching, presented as "spiritual science," is an extraordinary synthesis of "organic" ideas in nineteenth-century German thought with theosophical material and fresh occult intuitions. In 1902 Steiner became a lecturer and general secretary of the Theosophical Society's German branch, but his earlier thought had been basically formed between 1890 and 1897, years devoted to the study and editing of Johann Wolfgang von Goethe's scientific writings at the Goethe-Archiv in Weimar. In this time, and during a period (1897–1900) as editor of the *Magazin: Monatschrift für Litteratur*, he developed his own views of evolution, natural organization, and science through confrontation with the ideas of Charles Darwin, Ernst Heinrich Haeckel, Friedrich Nietzsche, and contemporary German philosophies.

Steiner presented his synthesis as a modern scientific and monistic world conception, despite the range of esoteric content it eventually included. His early work, *Philosophie der Freiheit* (1896), contained no occult material, but it left room for inclusion of such material by the theories of knowledge and of spiritual freedom which it expounded: Mechanistic science gives only abstract knowledge of some uniform relations in nature. The model for fuller knowledge of individual beings is the organic idea of a self-evolving and self-directing organism, which Goethe saw in the "primal plant." The method for generalizing such knowledge is one of intuitive thinking. Steiner espoused a "monism of thought": A valid world image is ever building as individual spirits live in (*miterleben*) the organic world process.

Heralding Nietzsche's independence of thought, Steiner followed him in rejecting both natural teleology and objective moral laws. Yet he maintained that Nietzsche was always protestingly and tragically dashing his free spirit against an alien culture and a limited science of nature. Nietzsche's doctrine of "eternal recurrence," however, was a factor that led Steiner to give sympathetic attention to Indian thought. Nature is, after all, but one manifestation of spiritual reality, which reveals itself more directly in thought and in art. Among Indian ideas which Steiner adopted while a theosophist is the fourfold construction of man on Earth as having the physical, the ether, the astral bodies, and the "I," with their respective powers of development and transformation.

After 1907 conflict with Annie Besant's pro-Hindu policies led Steiner to withdraw from the Theosophical Society, but he continued on an independent line of esoteric thinking, to which in 1913 he gave the name "anthroposophy." Natural evolution, he then taught, has thus far been a progression of bodily organizations into which "pure spirit" descends through successive reincarnations with the aim of producing individual self-consciousness. Reaching its apogee in the Renaissance, this development showed its dangerous limitations in nineteenth-century individualism. The societal remedy, Steiner declared in 1919, was not the collectivism of a totalitarian state but a "three-fold social organism," in which the juridical, spiritual, and economic spheres of life are independently organized as three autonomous interacting systems. Equality is a concept applying particularly to the juridical sphere of rights (which includes just compensation for work), liberty to the spiritual domain, and fraternity or voluntary cooperation to the economic organization of production.

Steiner's own interest lay primarily in the liberty of the spiritual sphere, which included great reaches of "cosmic memory." In future stages of evolution, spirit, without loss of self-consciousness, must ascend again through knowledge of its cosmic relations to its universality and transcendence over matter. Special organs ("the lotuses") must be cultivated to apprehend the higher worlds of spirit and the traces left by their events in the cosmic ether. These include the anti-Lucifer impulsions given by Buddha, Zarathustra, Plato, and Christ and the regenerative solar influence of the blood shed in the mystery of Golgotha.

After World War I Steiner was able to establish a cultural center, the Goetheanum, in Switzerland at Dornach, near Basel. His movement spread from Germany to England, the United States, and other countries. Anthroposophy was practiced at various levels of initiation; those not ready for the higher insights could participate in the preliminary disciplines. These included eurythmic dance, mystery plays, organic agriculture and therapy, and distinctive educational measures in a number of notable elementary schools, beginning with the Waldorf School in Stuttgart. While the higher aim of Steiner's pedagogy was to develop special powers of spiritual insight, the cultivation of moral balance, a harmony of virtuous dispositions intermediate between excesses and defects, was considered a prerequisite.

Bibliography

The writings of Rudolf Steiner are extensive. His autobiography, *Mein Lebensgang* (Dornach: Philosophisch-Anthroposophischer, 1925), was translated by Olin D. Wannamaker as *The Course of My Life* (New York, 1928).

Of basic interest to students of general philosophy are *Philosophie der Freiheit* (Berlin, 1896), translated as *Philosophy of Spiritual Activity* (2nd ed., rev. and enl., London, 1916); *Goethes Weltanschauung* (Stuttgart, 1897); and *Friedrich Nietzsche: Ein Kämpfer gegen seine Zeit* (1895; expanded 2nd ed., Dornach: Philosophisch-Anthroposophischer, 1926).

For further developments of his thought in various directions, see *Knowledge of the Higher Worlds and Its Attainment* (London and New York: Putnam, 1932); *The New Art of Education* (London: Anthroposophical, 1928); *The Problems of Our Time* (London and New York, 1919); and *The Writings and Lectures of Rudolf Steiner,* compiled by P. M. Allen (New York: Whittier, 1956).

A collected edition of Steiner's major writings was begun in observation of the centennial of his birth. Vol. I in English has appeared as *Cosmic Memory: Prehistory of Earth and Man,* (West Nyack, NY: Rudolf Steiner Publications, 1961); it is a translation by Karl E. Zimmer of *Aus der Akasha-Chronik.* Four additional volumes have been published. For additional information, the reader may consult the *Bibliographie der Werke Rudolf Steiners,* prepared by Guenther Wachsmuth (Dornach, 1942).

A secondary work of interest is J. W. Hauer, *Werden und Wesen der Anthroposophie* (Stuttgart, 1922).

Horace L. Friess (1967)

STEPHEN, LESLIE

(1832–1904)

Leslie Stephen, an English man of letters, was the son of James and Jane Venn Stephen, both of whom came from families in the innermost group of the reforming Evangelicals who formed the so-called Clapham Sect. He attended Eton, briefly and unhappily, and then went to Trinity Hall, Cambridge, where he was made a fellow in 1854. Fellows had then to be ordained in the Church of England, and Stephen took holy orders and eventually became a priest, although he was not deeply religious. At the same time, religious doubt and disaffection began to trouble him. In 1862, as a result of these doubts, he resigned his fellowship, and in 1864 he left Cambridge for good. By 1865 he had completely lost all religious belief. He settled in London and began writing for various journals. Thereafter he wrote continually, copiously, and on a very wide range of topics.

In 1867 he married William Makepeace Thackeray's daughter Harriet Marian. She died in 1875, leaving him with one child. Three years later he married Julia Jackson Duckworth, a widow. They had four children, one of whom became the writer Virginia Woolf. Julia Stephen died in 1895.

Stephen was for many years editor of the *Cornhill Magazine.* In 1882 he accepted an invitation to edit the newly projected *Dictionary of National Biography.* The success of the project was largely due to his lengthy period of arduous service in this position (he wrote 387 of the biographies himself). Stephen was knighted in 1901.

Stephen was not a considerable innovator, in philosophy, in historical method, or in literary criticism. He had, however, very great gifts of rapid narration and clear and lively exposition. His work on the history of thought is based on massive reading and wide acquaintance with the social, political, and religious aspects of the periods of which he wrote. If it is neither original in its criticism nor profound in its understanding of positions, it is still useful and has not been entirely superseded because of its grasp of the broader contexts of thought and the skill with which it brings out the continuities from one period to another and from earlier formulations of problems to later ones.

It was Stephen who made Thomas Huxley's coinage *agnostic* an English word, and the problems and beliefs springing from his agnosticism underlay both his major historical works and his philosophical writings. He rejected theism of the sort he had originally been taught because he rejected the doctrine of original sin and because the problem of evil seemed to him insoluble. To evade this problem by confessing the transcendence and incomprehensibility of God was, he thought, to change from a believer into a skeptic, and in that case the part of honesty was simply to avow oneself an agnostic. But true Victorian that he was, he felt that morality, by this view, becomes gravely problematical. If there is no deity to sanction moral principles, why will—why should—men obey them?

To answer these questions was part of Stephen's aim in his investigations of eighteenth-century thought. He dealt more systematically with them, and with others, in his least successful and most tedious book, *The Science of Ethics.* The agnostic, he held, must place morality on a scientific basis, and this means that there must be nothing in his ethics that is outside the competence of scientific inquiry. Brought up on John Stuart Mill and profoundly influenced by Charles Darwin, Stephen attempted to cut through what he impatiently dismissed as academic debates about morality by showing that moral beliefs were the result neither of excessively rational utilitarian calculation nor of mysterious intuition but of the demands of the social organism in its struggle for survival. Since the healthy survival of the social organism must increasingly coincide with conditions that bring the greatest happiness to the greatest number of those individuals who are the "cells" in the "social tissue," utilitarianism is not entirely false. But its atomistic analysis of society is erroneous, and its criterion of rightness is neither adequate nor entirely accurate. The healthy survival of society, and of oneself as part of it, can alone serve as sanction for morality, and the rules for that health, which are mirrored in our instincts and our deepest habits and appear in consciousness as intuitively known moral rules, can be put on a scientific basis only when we come to possess, as we do not yet, a scientific sociology.

Bibliography

WORKS BY STEPHEN

Stephen's works are far too numerous to be listed completely here. *Essays on Freethinking and Plainspeaking* (London: Longmans, Green, 1873) and *An Agnostic's Apology and Other Essays* (London: Smith, Elder, 1893) contain most of his better-known popular essays. *The Science of Ethics* (London: Smith, Elder, 1882) is his only purely philosophical work. His important historical studies are *History of English Thought in the Eighteenth Century* (2 vols., New York: Putnam, 1876; 3rd ed., 1902); *The English Utilitarians* (3 vols., London: Duckworth, 1900); and *Hobbes* (London: Macmillan, 1904). To these the lectures in *English*

Thought and Society in the Eighteenth Century (London, 1904) provide a valuable supplement.

WORKS ON STEPHEN

The standard biography is F. W. Maitland's charming *Life and Letters of Leslie Stephen* (London: Duckworth, 1906), which contains an adequate bibliography of Stephen's work. Noel Annan, in *Leslie Stephen* (London: MacGibbon and Kee, 1951), studies Stephen as a representative Victorian thinker and as a link between the Clapham Sect and the Bloomsbury Group.

J. B. Schneewind (1967)

STERN, LOUIS WILLIAM

(1871–1938)

Louis William Stern, the German philosopher and psychologist, was born in Berlin and received his PhD under Hermann Ebbinghaus in Berlin in 1892. From 1897 to 1915 he taught philosophy and psychology at the University of Breslau, and in 1915 he moved to Hamburg, where, in 1919, he helped to found the University of Hamburg. He was forced into exile in 1933 by the Nazi government and became professor of psychology and philosophy at Duke University. He died in Durham, North Carolina.

As a psychologist Stern revolted against the elementarism (the belief in the adequacy of analysis of consciousness into its elementary parts) current in Germany before the general acceptance of Gestalt psychology. In his early studies of the perception of change and motion, he employed phenomenological methods and anticipated some later developments in Gestalt psychology. He soon gave up psychophysical experimentation, however, and pioneered in various fields of applied psychology, such as psychology of childhood, forensic psychology, intelligence testing (he introduced the concept of the intelligence quotient), and vocational psychology. Stern's work in psychology was always timely and often ahead of his times; he therefore earned a reputation as a psychologist that he never enjoyed as a philosopher, for most of his philosophizing was either opposed to, or out of touch with, contemporary movements. Some resemblance to *Lebens-philosophie* can be discerned, but he had little contact with Wilhelm Dilthey and his circle. Stern's philosophy must be understood in conjunction with his own psychological work, as providing the presuppositions for his lifelong scientific focus on the individual person—not on elements in his behavior and not on abstract universal laws relating them, but on the unique man. Even against Gestalt psychology, which likewise rejected elementarism, Stern's motto was: "No *Gestalt* without a *Gestalter.*" The *Gestalter* was the person.

Stern called his philosophy critical personalism to distinguish it from other personalistic theories, such as animism, vitalism, and Cartesianism, which were based upon the familiar dualism of mind and body. For him the person was an integral totality (*unitas multiplex*) whose defining property was purposive activity. What is not a person is a thing. A thing is not a whole but merely an aggregate; not autonomous but determined from without; not concretely individual but fragmentary or abstract. The person-thing distinction does not correspond to the mind-body distinction; rather, Stern held, the person is "psychophysically neutral," and both mind and body are thinglike abstractions from the original concreteness of a person sufficiently complex to be called an organism. Only some persons are conscious; indeed, only some of them are living. The person-thing distinction is repeated hierarchically, and the world is a system of persons included in and inclusive of others. A thing is a person seen from the standpoint of the supervenient person; that is, a person which includes other persons as parts.

With this conception, which suggests Aristotle, Gottfried Wilhelm Leibniz, and Gustav Fechner, Stern formulated his theory of teleomechanics as a way of avoiding an ontological dichotomy between teleology and mechanism. Mechanical uniformities, patterns of thing-behaviors, are derivative from teleological activities of supervenient personal beings in which the things are components. By this theory Stern attempted to derive the formal concepts and principles of the thing-world as we know it, such as magnitude, uniformity, class, causality, space, and time. By making these concepts and principles derivative, not fundamental, Stern's theory gave metaphysical priority to teleological and irreducibly individualistic notions.

Since the concrete substances of the world are teleological both as goal-setting and as goal-realizing, Stern identified the concept of intrinsic value with that of genuine, or personal, being. There are values corresponding to every level of person, indeed to every individual in the hierarchy of persons. But whereas in the theory of teleomechanism persons become things in the context of supervenient persons and thereby have at most extrinsic value, Stern later explored interpersonal relations in which the autonomy of each person is preserved and heightened through those relations which constitute a higher person. To the teleomechanical (cosmological) relation between persons Stern now added the introceptive (axiological) relation, by which ends and intrinsic values of other persons as such are used by each person as factors in his own selfhood and autonomous self-determination and growth. In the formation of more inclusive and autonomous persons, the value of the whole suffuses the included persons with a radiative value (*Strahlwert*) instead of depersonalizing them as merely instrumentally valuable.

Stern's studies of love, religion, art, history, and ethics are deep and perceptive applications of his account of introception and radiative values. The theory of radiative value is especially fruitful in his accounts of symbolism and expression in many fields, and in his theory of introception he attempted to rationalize the value-oriented assessment of total personality characteristic of his psychology of individual differences.

Stern's personalism differs from that of personal idealism in that it is neither theistic nor idealistic, nor so radically pluralistic. It has closer resemblances to Jan Christiaan Smuts's holism and to some phases of Max Scheler's theory of value.

Bibliography

Works by Stern are *Person und Sache*, 3 vols. (Leipzig: Barth, 1906–1924); *Personalistik als Wissenschaft* (Leipzig: Barth, 1932); and *Allgemeine Psychologie auf personalistischer Grundlage* (The Hague: Nijhoff, 1936), translated by H. D. Spoerl as *General Psychology from the Personalistic Standpoint* (New York: Macmillan, 1938). An autobiographical essay may be found in Carl Murchison, *History of Psychology in Autobiography* (Worcester, MA, 1930), Vol. I, pp. 335–388.

Lewis White Beck (1967)

STEVENSON, CHARLES L.

(1908–1979)

Charles L. Stevenson authored the first thorough emotivist, or noncognitivist, account of ethical language. Traditionally the study of ethics had involved a quest for the truth about what is good and right, but Stevenson abandoned that search and set out to investigate the practical use of ethical language to shape attitudes. In a series of articles, and in his 1944 book *Ethics and Language*, he proposed answers to classical philosophical questions about meaning and justification that set the agenda for the next several generations of moral philosophers.

Stevenson earned degrees at Yale and Cambridge before receiving his doctorate from Harvard in 1935. He then taught at Harvard and Yale, where his original and challenging ideas about ethics were not popular. In 1946 he joined the philosophy department at the University of Michigan, where he remained till his retirement.

By the time *Ethics and Language* appeared, a form of emotivism had been sketched by A. J. Ayer, who claimed that ethical utterances are disguised commands and exclamations. Other students of ethics and language had introduced behavioral accounts of meaning, drawing attention to the actual use of moral language and questioning the place of reason in ethics. Stevenson's contribution was to integrate these ideas into a coherent theory and to emphasize the complexity and importance of the expressive function and the dynamic power of ethical language.

Disagreements in ethics, according to Stevenson, involve "an opposition of purposes, aspirations, wants, preferences, desires, and so on" (Stevenson 1944, p. 3). He called such disagreements "disagreements in attitude" and contrasted them with "disagreements in belief." Ethical disagreements can be resolved by rational argument when they can be traced to disagreements in belief, but when disagreements in attitude remain after agreement about the facts has been reached, rational means will be of no use. When rational means fail, Stevenson noted, and even when they do not, we resort to a variety of non-rational methods. Non-rational persuasion exploits language that carries what Stevenson called "emotive meaning." Emotive meaning "is the power that a word acquires, on account of its history in emotional situations, to evoke or directly express attitudes, as distinct from describing or designating them" (Stevenson, 1944, p. 33). Stevenson explored the many ways in which words with positive or negative emotive meaning can be used by speakers aiming to persuade others (or themselves) to alter (or preserve) some attitude.

Turning to the question of meaning, Stevenson argued that we can explain the meaning of an utterance such as *X is good* if we can find a relevant, similar expression that is free from ambiguity and confusion, and that allows us to do and say everything we can do and say with the original expression. By leaving out any mention of emotive meaning, a "subjectivist" definition such as *X is good = I approve of X* fails because it distorts the nature of ethical disagreement, which is fundamentally a clash of attitudes. Stevenson's suggestion, which he characterized as his "first pattern of analysis," was that any adequate analysis of *X is good* will satisfy the following pattern:

X is good = I approve of X, do so as well.

The first element (*I approve of X*) gives a subjectivist descriptive meaning and is but one example from a long list of candidates. The second (*Do so as well*) represents the emotive meaning and indicates that exposure to utterances like *X is good* tends to bring about approval for *X*.

According to a first-pattern analysis, one persuades by making a straightforward ethical judgment, counting on the emotive meaning of the key terms to influence the attitudes of the audience. A second method of persuasion is illustrated by a "second pattern of analysis." Many words carry strong emotive meaning, and just as we can influence attitudes by an explicit ethical judgment, so we can operate more subtly by exploiting what Stevenson called a "persuasive definition." When we give or use a persuasive definition, we attach a new descriptive meaning to a term like *courage* or *justice* while keeping the emotive meaning unchanged. The point of doing this is to change the direction of peoples' interests. As Stevenson says, "Words are prizes which each man seeks to bestow on the qualities of his own choice" (Stevenson 1944, p. 213) If we can redefine *courage* to cover our strategic retreat, then we too can be called courageous. "True courage," we might say, "is knowing when to run."

Stevenson observed that when our persuasion fits the first pattern, "attitudes are altered by ethical judgments," and when it fits the second pattern, attitudes "are altered not only by judgments but by definitions" (Stevenson 1944, p. 210). The two patterns turn out to be equivalent in the sense that "for every second pattern *definition* there is a first pattern *judgment*, the latter being the persuasive counterpart of the former" (Stevenson 1944, p. 229).

Stevenson's analysis of meaning had consequences for his view of another metaethical issue, the question of justification. When disagreement in attitude is not rooted in disagreement in belief, then the notion of a "reason" expands to include "any statement about any matter of fact which any speaker considers likely to alter attitudes" (Stevenson 1944, p. 114). This claim led some critics to accuse Stevenson of wanting to replace ethical reasoning with propaganda, but actually he claimed only that rational methods have limits and that persuasion is in play even when rational methods are used and even when we are trying to change or preserve our own attitudes. The choice of methods, he pointed out, is always a normative one, but he consistently identified his own study as a descriptive analytical one and refused to moralize about the ways of moralists.

In addition to his landmark works on metaethics, Stevenson wrote on aesthetics, music, and verse. He was a serious amateur musician, frequently performing chamber music with his friends and family.

See also Ayer, Alfred Jules; Emotive Theory of Ethics; Ethical Subjectivism; Metaethics; Noncognitivism.

Bibliography

WORKS BY STEVENSON

"The Emotive Meaning of Ethical Terms." *Mind*46 (1937): 14–31.

Ethics and Language. New Haven, CT: Yale University Press, 1944.

Facts and Values. New Haven, CT: Yale University Press, 1963.

"Persuasive Definitions." *Mind* 47 (1938): 331–350.

WORKS ON STEVENSON

Ayer, A. J. *Language, Truth and Logic*. London: Golancz, 1936.

Goldman, Alvin I. and Jaegwon Kim, eds. *Value and Morals: Essays in Honor of William Frankena, Charles Stevenson, and Richard Brandt*. Dordrecht; Boston: D. Reidel, 1978.

Urmson, J. O. *The Emotive Theory of Ethics*. London: Hutchinson, 1968.

Richard T. Garner (1996, 2005)

STEWART, DUGALD

(1753–1828)

Dugald Stewart was an Edinburgh professor of moral philosophy who expounded the common sense theory of Thomas Reid and the libertarian political economy of Adam Smith. He taught from 1785 until illness forced his retirement in 1809. An eloquent spokesman for Reid and Smith rather than an original thinker, he left no legacy of his own but conveyed theirs. He provided his classes with a feast of psychology, ethics, and intellectual history and was the first professor in Britain to offer a course in political economy, which he began in 1800. A defender of academic freedom (see Brown [2004, 657] and Veitch [1858, lxxv–lxxix on the Leslie affair]), he both consoled and disturbed his audience by sustaining its metaphysical prejudices against Humean skepticism while revising its economic and political ones. He was no utilitarian yet advocated private liberty and the open market as the route to general happiness. His renown as a teacher was sustained by his books, which were translated into German, French, and Italian. He was honored by learned societies in Russia, Italy, and America, as well as by the Royal Societies of Edinburgh and London. Poet Robert Burns summed Stewart up as four parts Socrates, four parts Nathaniel, and two parts Brutus. He meant that

Stewart combined philosophical wisdom, a prophetic sense of morality, and a republican inclination.

Stewart's birth in Edinburgh on November 22, 1753 was in every sense an academic one. Not only was his father, Matthew, a college professor, but he was actually born in the college itself since their house was one of the college buildings. His father's family came from the southwest of Scotland where his grandfather was a minister. His mother was the daughter of an Edinburgh lawyer from whom she inherited the small Ayrshire estate of Catrine where the family spent the summer and where he befriended Burns whose home was at nearby Mossgiel.

Stewart attended the High School of Edinburgh where he learned Latin and Greek and the literature of both civilizations. He formed a lifelong attachment to the classics, a taste he shared with his revered friend Smith. In old age both philosophers turned to the early authors for pleasure and consolation, Smith to Sophocles and Euripides, Stewart to the Latin poets. He would later find this school education helpful in following the lectures of Adam Ferguson, whose class in moral philosophy he attended at the College in Edinburgh, which later became Edinburgh University. Ferguson was steeped in Roman history and literature, which formed the background to his lectures on moral and political philosophy and on civil society and its progress.

At the college, Stewart was introduced by John Stevenson, professor of logic and metaphysics, to the philosophy of John Locke, which was dominant at the time but which Stewart was to reject largely under the influence of Reid but also under that of Ferguson, who inspired his love of moral philosophy and whose chair he was to occupy. Before replacing Ferguson and after completing his college studies, Stewart had unexpectedly to take his father's place as professor of mathematics because illness forced his premature retirement. His father had achieved a minor international reputation as a Euclidean geometer although he was a reactionary who disdained algebraic geometry. He probably schooled his son informally in his own subject. Although Stewart was a good mathematician, he preferred philosophy, in which subject Ferguson discovered his talent.

Ferguson's philosophy was eclectic but principally Stoic. The classical moralists on whom he modeled himself advanced their own individual conceptions of virtue, of which they were taken to be exemplars. Assuming that moral philosophy is a kind of practical wisdom, their aim was to advise their students morally and lead them towards virtue. Stewart followed Ferguson's lead in adopting this ideal and in regarding right and wrong as like *primary* qualities, such as hardness, and not like the *secondary* qualities of colour and taste. With Ferguson and Reid, he criticized the school of moral sense led by the Lockean Francis Hutcheson, professor of moral philosophy in Glasgow and Smith's teacher. Hutcheson, followed by David Hume, said that virtue and vice are perceived through moral sensations of pleasure and pain or displeasure. Reason, they thought, is indifferent to virtue, which is only discovered by the responsive heart. Their critics—Ferguson, Reid, and Stewart—proposed, on the contrary, that humans use rational intuition to see which actions are morally right or wrong. These qualities exist independently of feeling and sensation. If the two sides did not agree about how virtue is perceived and why it is pursued, they did agree that the fundamental virtues are those of benevolence and justice.

Though no populist, Stewart managed to be more supportive of the idea of liberal reform than Ferguson. He agreed with Ferguson on the need for political leadership by wise philosophers, though he was quite clear about the citizen's right to political representation and clear that personal liberty is sacred. If the citizen is to be led, then it is to be out of servitude toward liberty. He was therefore deeply interested in the French liberal movement, which was headed intellectually by Anne-Robert-Jacques Turgot, François Quesnay, and Marie-Jean-Antoine-Nicolas Caritat, Marquis de Condorcet. They saw the nation's economy as the means of raising the standard of living of all its citizens. The movement was taken over by extremist deputies in the Assembly and culminated in violence against the throne. This was not the intention of the economists, who were not arguing for populist control but for rule by platonic philosophers guiding the monarch.

Stewart visited Paris in 1788 and 1789 and met some of the reformist thinkers, who encouraged his belief in the peaceful benefits of economic reform under wise government. He subsequently explained his innocuous views on political reform in *Elements of the Philosophy of the Human Mind* (1792; 1818, Vol. 1, 234–276). But this had an un-looked-for consequence because it led Scotland's judiciary to suppose that he actually supported violent revolution. Included among those were two judges known personally to Stewart who wished him to tone down his political writings. He declined to alter the second edition (1802) of the offending text, explaining his reason in a footnote. Although he sympathized with French liberalism and, unusually for someone of his position, with the American assertion of political and economic independence, he rejected violence as an instrument of change.

Stewart went to Glasgow to hear Reid lecture in 1772 just before he took over as deputy for his father. As professor of moral philosophy, Reid was famous for his theory of common sense and his criticism of Hume's skepticism and the theory that ideas are copies of sensations. It was Reid's theory of belief, or laws of belief, as Stewart preferred to phrase it, that specially appealed, and he dedicated his first book, *Elements*, to Reid in 1792. Stewart felt that describing Reid's work as an inquiry into the principles of common sense suggested quite wrongly that it was not a philosophical theory about a philosophical matter: There is no room for theory if it is only common sense. According to Stewart—though Reid did much in showing that sensation cannot explain central beliefs in personal identity, the external world, the past and the future—Reid made no progress on René Descartes's position on proof of the existence of the external world: In other words, we can only trust to our beliefs, not prove them. To advance further, Stewart revives a suggestion he attributes to Father Ruggero Giussepe Boscovich the eighteenth-century Jesuit natural philosopher, that belief in external objects comes from the experience of their resistance. Stewart enlarges the suggestion with an idea from Turgot that, if experience suggests its cause, it is repetition of the experience that suggests the continuity of that cause (*Philosophical Essays*, chs. 1 and 2, 115–148). This account does not, he admits, completely prove that there are external objects but, rather, explains the belief as an expectation that what resists being touched or pushed will do so again because it continues to exist when it is not being felt.

As did the despised Lockeans, Stewart believed that the philosophy of mind is a science in which data are our sensations, our thoughts, and our volitions. It tries to analyze states of consciousness without either aspiring to understand the ultimate nature of mind or trying to explain all belief by sensation and feeling. We are not directly conscious of mind, nor are we of matter. Although we do not know what matter is, nor what mind is, we do know that there are two fundamentally different kinds of experience. One suggests matter, the other mind. To materialists who said that if we do not know what matter or mind are, they might be the same thing, he replied in a footnote in the first part of the introduction to *Elements*: if they were the same, "it would no more be proper to say of mind, that it is material, than to say of body, that it is spiritual" (p. 5). It did not occur to Stewart that, since it is improper to say of what is spiritual that it is material, if mind is matter, it would be improper to say that it is spiritual but not improper to say that it is material. It was inconceivable to him, though not to others such as David Hartley and Joseph Priestley, that mind might be located in the nervous system and the brain.

See also Condorcet, Marquis de; Descartes, René; Ethics; Ferguson, Adam; Hartley, David; Hume, David; Hutcheson, Francis; Locke, John; Philosophy of Mind; Priestley, Joseph; Reid, Thomas; Smith, Adam; Social and Political Philosophy; Socrates; Stoicism; Turgot, Anne Robert Jacques, Baron de L'Aulne.

Bibliography

WORKS

Collected Works of Dugald Stewart, edited by Sir William Hamilton. Edinburgh: Constable, 1858.

Philosophical Essays. 2nd ed. Edinburgh: Constable, 1816.

Elements of the Philosophy of the Human Mind. 1st ed., 1792. 6th ed. [London], 1818.

STUDIES

Brown, Michael P. "Stewart Dugald." In *Oxford Dictionary of National Biography*. Vol. 52., edited by H. C. G. Matthew and Brian Harrison. Oxford: Oxford University Press, 2004.

Veitch, John. "A Memoir of Dugald Stewart." In *The Collected Works of Dugald Stewart*. Vol. X., edited by Sir William Hamilton. Edinburgh: Constable, 1858

V. M. Hope (2005)

STILLINGFLEET, EDWARD

(1635–1699)

Edward Stillingfleet, an English Protestant theologian, was born in Cranborne, Dorset. He entered St. John's College, Cambridge, in 1649. On graduating in 1653 he was elected a college fellow, but after a year went into private employment. He was appointed rector of Sutton, Bedfordshire, in 1657. The Church of England was then under Presbyterian administration, but Stillingfleet received episcopal ordination in a clandestine ceremony and readily conformed after the restoration of the monarchy in 1660. A popular preacher in London legal circles, he became rector of St. Andrew's, Holborn, London, in 1665, and in 1678 rose to be dean of St. Paul's. On the accession of William III (1650–1702) in 1689 Stillingfleet was created bishop of Worcester. He was active in the politico-theological controversies of the time, most of which had a philosophical dimension. None of his writings was narrowly or exclusively philosophical.

His first work was *Irenicum* (1659). Though ostensibly an attempt to restore Protestant unity after several decades of sectarian divisions, it had a disguised episcopalian agenda. Stillingfleet resumed the debate with less disguise in the 1680s amid growing fears of a Catholic revival, publishing *The Mischief of Separation* (1680), *The Unreasonableness of Separation* (1681), and *Origines Britannicae* (1685). In *Irenicum* he allowed that episcopacy, presbytery, and independency could all point to precedents from the apostolic period; thus, all three could coexist compatibly. By 1685, however, he was arguing that the original English church had been an episcopal foundation, independent of Rome.

Stillingfleet's most consistent claim was that the primitive churches constituted a single society within each political state. Citing the authority of both natural and scriptural law, he portrayed the church of his own day as a subsociety operating within and compatibly with the laws of civil society, under which its members receive or lose privileges in proportion to their conformity. This was "latitudinarianism," a scheme that, by distinguishing essential from inessential matters, aimed to comprehend all believers in a national church and opposed the legal toleration of dissenting denominations. On matters not dictated by natural or revealed law—including the balance between episcopal and other forms—the overriding issue was one of civil peace, for which the civil administration was legislator. But many dissenters believed that there were theological issues here on which the civil power was incompetent to arbitrate. By the time of Stillingfleet's later writings against separation, there was a growing lobby in favor of the tolerationist alternative. John Locke prepared a critique of Stillingfleet in 1681 that survives in manuscript.

A second important early work, *Origines Sacrae* (1662), attempted to demonstrate the rational foundations of Judeo-Christian monotheism. Stillingfleet presented a detailed philosophy of history, exploring the nature of historical evidence and the grounds of assent to testimony. He claimed to establish the general superiority of written records over tradition and of the biblical record over ancient pagan history. On these principles he defended the authenticity of the biblical miracles, but not others, as confirming the authority of a revelation. Central to his argument was the concept of moral certainty. This was a genuine certainty attainable in matters beyond reasonable doubt by persons in possession of normal reason and of the evidence, where part of the function of reason is to judge the type of evidence appropriate to the context. By this means one can attain certainty in doctrinal matters that are above reason but not contrary to it. One's confidence is underwritten by the certainty one has of the existence of God.

This was a different kind of certainty based on clear and distinct ideas, yet compatible with the recognition that the object of certainty is largely incomprehensible. Part of the inspiration here was Cartesian, but Stillingfleet's enthusiasm for Cartesianism moderated in his last years after he absorbed Henry More's criticisms of René Descartes's cosmology and saw the direction taken by some post-Cartesian thinkers such as Benedict (Baruch) de Spinoza. In 1697 he was at work on a new *Origines Sacrae*, but only a fragment survives.

The epistemology developed in *Origines Sacrae* provided the basis for a relentless polemic against Catholic views of the rule of faith, from *A Rational Account of the Grounds of Protestant Religion* (1664) to *The Doctrine of the Trinity and Transubstantiation Compared* (1687), with many intervening titles. Stillingfleet appealed to weakly formulated principles of reason and common sense to reiterate his conviction that the doctrine of the trinity, being derived from a historically sound scripture, albeit above reason, was an assured certainty of faith; whereas that of transubstantiation, being contrary to reason and sense, was not. The Catholics argued for an exact parallelism and believed that the Protestants had no reliable arbiter in their disagreements about biblical interpretation.

By 1687 Stillingfleet had opened up the debate over the identification of substance and the distinction of persons. This was an opportunity for a growing Unitarian movement on the edge of Anglicanism to weigh in, seeking to demonstrate on clear and distinct principles that both the trinity and transubstantiation were equally indefensible and to promote a revisionist account of the atonement. Simultaneously with this, a rising tide of deism—religious belief based on natural reason alone without revelation—was beginning to pose awkward questions about the credibility of revelation.

Stillingfleet had already attacked Socinianism, a continental form of Unitarianism, in 1669 and deism in 1677, without obvious effect. Beset with opposition on so many fronts, he published *A Discourse in Vindication of the Doctrine of the Trinity* (1696). He incorporated an attack on John Toland's deistic *Christianity Not Mysterious* (1696), implicating Locke as the supposed inspiration for Toland's rejection of truths above reason. As a result, his final years were taken up with a highly public dispute with Locke, each side contributing three pieces. The dispute was over whether Locke's philosophy was capable of supporting what Stillingfleet considered the basic propositions of the creed. Confused by Locke's Cartesian language about clear and distinct ideas, he challenged Locke to show how such ideas could come by sensation or reflection. Locke, he complained, had a "new way" of ideas, one that left him apparently ambivalent over mind-body dualism, agnostic about substance and essence, and unable to demonstrate immortality or to explicate the distinction of persons on his philosophy: in short, unable to bring any certainty to matters of faith. Locke gave no quarter to Stillingfleet in his replies, insisting on the coherence of his philosophy and its compatibility with biblical doctrine but refusing to be drawn into theological debate. Where, however, Stillingfleet had identified ill-chosen uses of the phrase "clear and distinct ideas" in Locke's *Essay concerning Human Understanding,* Locke silently amended them in the fourth edition (1700).

See also Cartesianism; Deism; Descartes, René; Locke, John; More, Henry; Revelation; Socinianism; Spinoza, Benedict (Baruch) de; Toland, John.

Bibliography

WORKS BY STILLINGFLEET

The Works of That Eminent and Most Learned Prelate, Dr. Edw. Stillingfleet, Late Lord Bishop of Worcester: Together with His Life and Character. 6 vols. London: Henry and George Mortlock, 1710. A consolidated reissue of separately titled works and collections published in a uniform format between 1707 and 1710.

Three Criticisms of Locke. Hildesheim, Germany: Georg Olms, 1987.

The Philosophy of Edward Stillingfleet. 6 vols. Bristol, U.K.: Thoemmes Press, 2000.

WORKS ABOUT STILLINGFLEET

Carroll, Robert Todd. *The Common-Sense Philosophy of Religion of Bishop Edward Stillingfleet, 1635–1699.* The Hague, Netherlands: Nijhoff, 1975.

Griffin, Martin I. J., Jr. *Latitudinarianism in the Seventeenth-Century Church of England,* edited by Lila Freedman. Leiden, Netherlands: E. J. Brill, 1992.

Hutton, Sarah. "Science, Philosophy, and Atheism: Edward Stillingfleet's Defence of Religion." In *Scepticism and Irreligion in the Seventeenth and Eighteenth Centuries,* edited by Richard H. Popkin and Arjo Vanderjagt. Leiden, Netherlands: E. J. Brill, 1993.

Popkin, Richard H. "The Philosophy of Bishop Stillingfleet." *Journal of the History of Philosophy* 9 (1971): 303–319.

Reedy, Gerard. *The Bible and Reason: Anglicans and Scripture in Late Seventeenth-Century England.* Philadelphia: University of Pennsylvania Press, 1985.

Schwitzgebel, Gottfried. *Edward Stillingfleet als Kritiker der Ideenlehre John Lockes.* Frankfurt am Main, Germany: Peter Lang, 2000.

Stewart, M. A. "Stillingfleet and the Way of Ideas." In *English Philosophy in the Age of Locke,* edited by M. A. Stewart. Oxford, U.K.: Clarendon Press, 2000.

M. A. Stewart (2005)

STIRNER, MAX

(1806–1856)

Max Stirner was the nom de plume of the German individualist philosopher Johann Kaspar Schmidt. Born in Bayreuth, Bavaria, Schmidt had a poor childhood. His academic career was long and fragmented. From 1826 to 1828 he studied philosophy at the University of Berlin, where he fell under the influence of G. W. F. Hegel. After brief periods at the universities of Erlangen and Königsberg, he returned to Berlin in 1832 and with some difficulty gained a certificate to teach in Prussian Gymnasiums. Several years of poverty and unemployment followed, until Schmidt found a position as teacher in a Berlin academy for young ladies run by a Madame Gropius. After this he lived something of a double life: The respectable teacher of young ladies had for another self the aspiring philosophical writer who assumed the name of Stirner.

The immediate stimulus that provoked Stirner to write his one important book, *Der Einzige und sein Eigentum* (Leipzig, 1845; translated by Steven T. Byington as *The Ego and His Own,* New York, 1907), was his association with the group of young Hegelians known as Die Freien (the "free ones"), who met under the leadership of the brothers Bruno and Edgar Bauer. In this company Stirner met Karl Marx, Friedrich Engels, Arnold Ruge, Georg Herwegh, and many other revolutionary intellectuals. In the same circle he also met Marie Dahnhardt, whom he married in 1843 and who left him in 1847. Before the publication of his book Stirner produced only a few brief periodical pieces, including an essay on educational methods printed by Marx in *Rheinische Zeitung.*

THOUGHT

Der Einzige und sein Eigentum, a treatise in defense of philosophic egoism, carried to its extreme the young Hegelian reaction against Hegel's teachings. In part it was a bitter attack on contemporary philosophers, particularly those with social inclinations. Stirner's associates among Die Freien were rejected as strongly as Hegel and Ludwig Feuerbach.

Stirner's approach was characterized by a passionate anti-intellectualism that led him to stress the will and the instincts as opposed to the reason. He attacked systematic philosophies of every kind, denied all absolutes, and rejected abstract and generalized concepts of every kind. At the center of his vision he placed the human individual, of whom alone we can have certain knowledge; each individual, he contended, is unique, and this uniqueness is the very quality he must cultivate to give meaning to his life. Hence, he reached the conclusion that the ego is a law unto itself and that the individual owes no obligations outside himself. All creeds and philosophies based on the concept of a common humanity are, in Stirner's view, false and irrational; rights and duties do not exist; only the might of the ego justifies its actions.

There is much in common between Stirner's embattled ego and Friedrich Nietzsche's superman; indeed, Stirner was seen as a forerunner of Nietzsche during the 1890s.

Stirner has often been included with the anarchist philosophers, and he has much in common with them. However, he differs from writers like William Godwin, Pierre-Joseph Proudhon, and Pëtr Alekseevich Kropotkin in that the idea of a system of natural law, or immanent justice, which human law negates, is essential to their points of view. Stirner, however, rejected the idea of any such law, and in this respect he stands nearer to certain existentialists and the nihilists. Furthermore, while the anarchist seeks freedom as his ultimate goal, Stirner regarded such an aim as always being limited by external necessities; in its place he sought uniqueness or "ownness." "Every moment," he said, "the fetters of reality cut the sharpest welts in my flesh. But *my own* I remain."

Stirner agreed with the anarchists, however, in regarding the state as the great enemy of the individual who seeks to fulfill his "own will." The state and the self-conscious and willful ego cannot exist together; therefore the egoist must seek to destroy the state, but by rebellion rather than by revolution. This distinction is essential to Stirner's doctrine. Revolution, in overthrowing an established order, seeks to create another order; it implies a faith in institutions. Rebellion is the action of individuals seeking to rise above the condition they reject; it "demands that one rise, or exalt oneself." Revolution is a social or political act; rebellion is an individual act, and therefore appropriate to the egoist. If rebellion prospers, the state will collapse.

In rebellion the use of force is inevitable, and Stirner envisaged "the war of each against all," in which the egoist fights with all the means at his command. This viewpoint led Stirner to justify and even to exalt crime. Crime is the assertion of the ego, the rejection of the sacred. The aim of egoist rebellion is the free wielding of power by each individual.

In Stirner's view the end of this process is not conflict but a kind of dynamic balance of power between men aware of their own might, for the true egoist realizes that excessive possessions and power are merely limitations on his own uniqueness. His assertion is based on the absence of submissiveness in others; the withdrawal of each man into his uniqueness lessens rather than increases the chance of conflict, for "as unique you have nothing in common with the other any longer, and therefore nothing divisive or hostile either." Stirner argued that far from producing disunity among individuals, egoism allows the freest and most genuine of unions, the coming together without any set organization of the "Union of Egoists," which will replace not only the state with its political repression but also society with its less obvious claims.

LATER YEARS

Der Einzige und sein Eigentum is not just a most extreme expression of individualism, it is also the single manifestation of Stirner's own revolt against a frustrating life that finally submerged him. In his totally undistinguished later years he embarked on a series of unsuccessful commercial ventures and translated English and French economists. His remaining book, *Die Geschichte der Reaktion* (Berlin, 1852), lacked the fire of discontent that made his earlier work so provocative. Stirner's last years were shadowed by declining powers and haunted by creditors; he died poor and forgotten in 1856.

Bibliography

For further information on Stirner, see Victor Basche, *L'individualisme anarchiste: Max Stirner* (Paris: Alcan, 1904); James Gibbons Huneker, *Egoists* (New York, 1921); and John Henry Mackay, *Max Stirner, sein Leben und sein Werk* (Berlin: Schuster and Loeffler, 1898).

George Woodcock (1967)

STÖHR, ADOLF

(1855–1921)

Adolf Stöhr, the Austrian philosopher, psychologist, and linguist, was born at St. Pölten and studied law and philology, then botany, and finally philosophy, at the University of Vienna. In 1885 he was appointed *Privatdozent* in theoretical philosophy at the same university, rising to associate professor in 1901 and to full professor of the philosophy of the inductive sciences in 1911. He published some thirty works in logic, natural philosophy, psychology, and philosophy.

LANGUAGE AND THOUGHT

Stöhr developed his system of logic in the closest connection with the psychology of thought processes and linguistics. His work deals in great detail with the dependence of thought upon language (what he calls the glossomorphy of thought), and he warned against the dangerous consequences that flow from confusing forms of speech with forms of thought. Not only do we make use of language to fix our thoughts and to communicate our knowledge; we also think in our language, so that the structure of our thought reflects the logical forms of our language. When the course of thought becomes automatic, the result may be that self-critical thought is replaced by an "idle flow of speech" ("glossurgy"), which is frequently even self-contradictory.

Through such reflections Stöhr began the "critique of language" pursued later with such success by other important thinkers. With the aid of this critique, he sought above all to oppose the misuse of language in philosophy and to unmask the muddled philosophical thinking that gives rise to the reification of concepts, metaphors, and allegories. Because "our language compels us to designate consciousness as if it were constructed of a subject, of mental acts and of physical objects" (as in the sentence "I see an object"), the illusion arises that "thoughts have the form (*morphe*) of the language (*glossa*)." The final outcome is that fictions are taken for facts; metaphors, for that which is actually meant. Thus the fact of the psychological "I" is confused with the fiction of the mental "subject," and the fact of phenomenal matter as a complex of visual and tactile sensations is confused with the materialistic fiction of a metaphysical matter (*Wege des Glaubens*, pp. 20ff.).

METAPHYSICS

Stöhr distinguished three roots of metaphysical thinking: wonder at the facts (the "theorogonous" metaphysics of the "constructing imagination"); pain (the "pathogonous" metaphysics of the "suffering heart"); and glossomorphic confusion (the "glossogonous" metaphysics of the "rolling word"). Metaphysics can supply no universally valid knowledge because the transcendental is in principle unknowable; one can only "have faith" in the existence of something beyond experience. This metaphysical faith is the expression of a subjective reaction of the heart and is "lived." Knowledge cannot engender faith, and faith cannot substitute for knowledge; for the two are of an entirely different nature" ("Ist Metaphysik möglich?," p. 30). "Everyone proceeds along that path of faith which his whole constitution obliges him to take. There is neither an inductive nor a deductive proof for or against a faith" (*Wege des Glaubens*, p. 36).

Stöhr rejected both "pathogonous" and "glossogonous" metaphysics, and thus the whole of metaphysics in the traditional sense, with its claim to knowledge of the transcendental. Anyone who pretends to provide such knowledge is philosophizing both "pathogonously" and "glossogonously." Anyone who is unable to find the meaning of life in life itself, in the work and tasks of life, and therefore suffers in being alive, seeks that meaning beyond the world and life. Since he would like to convince others of the truth of his outlook on life and the world, which is directed to the beyond, he intentionally or unintentionally misuses language in order to offer rhetorical pseudo solutions to metaphysical pseudo problems as if they were genuine solutions to real problems.

Stöhr himself professed "theorogonous" metaphysics. He defined it as "the satisfaction of an artistic propensity by means of the elegant construction of a world view"—which, of course, must not contradict the facts. "Thus metaphysics, in contrast to the empirical sciences, does not grow through apposition, but continuous building, rebuilding and building anew" (*Lehrbuch der Logik*, p. 304). Stöhr constructed his own view of nature in this manner, not dogmatically but as an exercise, assigning more importance to the creation than to the validity of a system. (He often said in discussion: "I am only playing with these ideas. I do not say that this is the way things are. I do not say even that this is the way they probably are. All that I say is that this is the way they may be.")

NATURAL PHILOSOPHY

Stöhr attempted to explain the structure of matter and the peculiarities of organic happenings in conformity with his undogmatic approach. Since for him mechanism was the sole intelligible conception of nature, he sought to understand both the organic world and the inorganic world with the help of mechanistic conceptual models. Stöhr proved to be as original a thinker in the philosophy of nature as in logic and psychology. That many of his ingenious solutions to problems have become outmoded by the progress of the sciences does not alter the epistemological excellence of his clear and exact style of thought.

Bibliography

Stöhr's major works include *Umriss einer Theorie der Namen* (Leipzig and Vienna: Deuticke, 1889); *Alegbra der Grammatik* (Leipzig: Deuticke, 1898); *Philosophie der unbelebten Materie* (Leipzig, 1907); *Der Begriff des Lebens* (Heidelberg: Winter, 1909); *Lehrbuch der Logik* (Leipzig: Deuticke, 1910); "Ist Metaphysik möglich?" in *Jahrbuch der philosophischen Gesellschaft an der Universität zu Wien 1914 und 1915* (Leipzig, 1916), pp. 25–36; *Psychologie. Tatsachen, Probleme und Hypothesen* (Vienna and Leipzig, 1917; 2nd ed., Vienna and Leipzig: W. Braumüller, 1922); and *Wege des Glaubens* (Vienna and Leipzig, 1921).

Works on Stöhr include Franz Ferdinand Worlitzky, *Über die Philosophie Adolf Stöhrs,* a dissertation (Vienna, 1925), and Franz Austeda, "Der Oesterreicher Adolf Stöhr—einer der bedeutendsten Denker unseres Jahrhunderts," in *Neue Wege* (Vienna) (104) (1955): 3–5.

Franz Austeda (1967)
Translated by Albert E. Blumberg

STOICISM

Stoicism was a philosophical movement founded in Athens in the late fourth century BCE by Zeno of Citium. Although Stoicism was shaped by many philosophical influences (including the thought of Heraclitus), it was throughout its history an essential part of the mainstream Socratic tradition of ancient philosophy. Inspired as well by the Cynics (Zeno was taught by Crates, a student of Diogenes of Sinope), Stoicism developed alongside and in competition with Platonism and Aristotelianism over the next 500 years. For centuries it was the main rival to Epicurean thought as well. Virtually no works survive from the early period of the school's history. Yet its doctrines have been reconstructed with a fair level of reliability on the basis of later accounts, critical discussions by non-Stoics, and the surviving works of later Stoic writers.

HISTORY

When Zeno arrived in Athens, attracted from his home on Cyprus by Socratic philosophy, Plato's Academy was led by Polemo and was soon to make its historic shift away from what we now recognize as Platonism toward a form of skepticism under the leadership of Arcesilaus. Aristotle's legacy was still in the hands of Theophrastus, head of the Lyceum, though in the third century BCE the school would decline in philosophical power as it concentrated on more narrowly scientific problems. Nevertheless, the Aristotelian drive for broad-based philosophical synthesis had an impact on the shape of Stoicism. A significant group of philosophers, forming no particular school but many coming from nearby Megara, concentrated on dialectic as their principal activity. These included Stilpo, also interested in ethics and metaphysics, and Diodorus Cronus, whose sharply formulated arguments provided powerful challenges in physics and metaphysics and challenged the Stoics to develop dialectic as a central part of their system. The Cynics in turn championed nature (as opposed to narrow polis-based social norms) as the foundation of ethics. All of this contributed to Zeno's formation of a powerful philosophical system whose internal articulation into three parts (logic, physics, ethics) was inspired by the Academic Xenocrates.

Stoicism was named for Zeno's favorite meeting place, the Painted Stoa in the Athenian marketplace. The movement was concentrated in a formal philosophical school in Athens for more than 200 years until political changes resulting from Rome's rise to power led prominent philosophers to spread out around the Mediterranean world, especially to Rhodes, Alexandria, and Rome itself. The climax of this process came when the Roman general Sulla sacked Athens in 86 BCE during the Mithridatic Wars. By the end of the first century BCE, Stoic activity was widely dispersed and had become a central part of intellectual culture in the Greco-Roman world. In the early second century CE, the emperor Hadrian founded a chair of Stoic philosophy in Rome (as well as chairs for the other major schools). With the rise of Neoplatonism, Stoicism gradually faded in prominence, though its influence persisted until the end of antiquity. Its impact on medieval philosophy was sporadic, but in the Renaissance it became an important part of the philosophical legacy of the ancient world to modern philosophy.

PRINCIPAL STOICS AND THEIR WORKS

The founder of the school, Zeno, was a prolific author whose best-known work was his utopian *Republic*, influenced by his Cynic teachers and by Plato's *Republic*. He wrote extensively on ethics and politics (e.g., *On the Life according to Nature*; *On Law*; *On Human Nature*; *On Passions*; *On Greek Education*), on cosmology (*On the Universe*), on poetry (*Homeric Problems*; *On Listening to Poetry*), and on dialectic (*On Signs*; *Refutations,*; *Solutions*). Of his many students, some (Persaeus and Sphaerus) also involved themselves in politics. Cleanthes was a highly prolific writer in the areas of cosmology, physics, ethics, and dialectic. He was also known for his poetry, especially the *Hymn to Zeus* (which has survived entire) and for his interest in Heraclitus. Cleanthes' contemporary Aristo of Chios favored the Cynic side of the school's heritage and rejected physics and dialectic in favor of a teaching based solely on ethics. Though eclipsed by Cleanthes (who succeeded Zeno as head of the school) and Chrysippus (the third head of the school), Aristo's influence continued to be felt at least until the first century CE.

Chrysippus, the great systematizer of the Stoic tradition, put the school's doctrines on a solid footing after a long period of debate and criticism, especially by the Academic Arcesilaus. Respected as a second founder of the school, he and his students dominated its leadership for many decades. He argued that Zeno's philosophy (as he interpreted it) was essentially correct and thereby stabilized the essential doctrines of the school, which nevertheless continued to be open to internal debate. A highly prolific author (more than 700 books are attributed to him and a partial catalog survives in book 7 of Diogenes' *Lives*), Chrysippus revised and rounded out the areas of physics and ethics and put dialectic, especially the study of formal inference and the theory of language, on a new foundation. He wrote a work in defense of Zeno's *Republic*, evidently declining to abandon the school's Cynic roots, a large number of works on logic and dialectic (including *Logical Investigations*, of which a few fragments have survived among the Herculaneum papyri), and a nearly equal number on logic and physics. The best attested work is certainly his *On Passions*, from which Galen quotes many passages in the course of his criticism of Stoic views on psychology and ethics.

The next phase in the school's history came in the late second and early first centuries BCE, when Panaetius of Rhodes and subsequently Posidonius of Apamea adopted a more open stance toward Platonic and Aristotelian approaches than seems to have been characteristic of Chrysippus. There was, however, no dramatic departure from the earlier school. Prominent among later Stoics is Seneca the Younger, a Roman politician of the first century CE. Many of his works, including the *Moral Epistles to Lucilius*, were highly influential in the early modern period. Other works of Seneca's include *On Benefits* (which offers important arguments in ethics) and *Natural Questions* (on physics and meteorology). His works form the earliest corpus of Stoic writing that has survived to the modern era. Another Stoic was Epictetus, a prolific writer and teacher, mostly of ethics, in the late first century CE. He owed a great deal to Musonius Rufus, a Roman citizen from Etruria who wrote in Greek in the early first century CE. Epictetus's lectures were very influential in later antiquity and the early modern period; this is especially true of his *Handbook*, a compendium drawn from the *Discourses*, which in turn was compiled by his student Arrian from his lectures. The emperor Marcus Aurelius left a set of personal philosophical reflections, *To Himself*, more commonly titled *Meditations*. In no sense a professional philosopher, Marcus combines a profoundly Stoic point of view, deeply influenced by Epictetus, with a more generalized "philosophical" stance reflecting influences from many traditions.

CENTRAL IDEAS

The concept of nature played a central role in Stoicism. The key to human fulfillment or happiness (*eudaimonia*) is living according to nature, and Stoic philosophy was based on this conception of the goal of life. The study of the natural world, physics, was a major occupation of virtually all Stoics (Aristo of Chios being a notable early exception). Human nature for the Stoics is characterized by a rationality that, when fully developed, is divine in its perfection. A deep expression of our nature and of that of the cosmos is our capacity for logic. Nature was formally defined as "a craftsmanlike fire, proceeding methodically to creation (*genesis*)" (Diogenes 7.156). God, a fully rational and providential force causally responsible for the world and its orderliness, was equated with nature. Whereas the divine craftsman of Plato's *Timaeus* stood outside the physical cosmos, the rational creator god of Stoicism is completely immanent in the material world.

The Stoics, more than any other ancient school, emphasized the interdependence among the parts of philosophy. They used various similes to illustrate the point. Philosophy is like an animal—logic is the bones and sinews; ethics the flesh; physics the soul. Or it is like an egg—logic is the shell; ethics the white; physics the yolk. Or like agricultural land—logic is the wall around the field; ethics the fruit; physics the land or trees that bear the fruit. Ideas varied about the ordering and relative importance of the three parts and their subdivisions, but all agreed that philosophy, when properly taught, demanded an intimate blend of all three disciplines, regardless of the pedagogical order chosen (Diogenes 7.39–41).

The Stoics based all areas of their thought on a rigorous metaphysical principle that sharply distinguished the corporeal and the incorporeal. The key to this distinction is the argument that only bodies can interact causally, an argument that seems to have emerged from a critique of Plato's metaphysics. Hence god, the soul, nature, and the principles that organize raw matter into intelligible natural kinds are all forms of matter for the Stoics. Even cognitive states such as knowledge are treated as corporeal dispositions of the material mind, since they have causal impact; so too for virtue and other dispositions. Their theory of perception similarly posits corporeal entities, lending weight to their essentially empiricist epistemology. The Stoics recognized only four incorporeal entities: void, space, time, and "sayables" (*lekta*, roughly, the meanings of thought and speech). Each of these incorporeal entities is parasitic on bodies, a necessary feature of the world but in itself causally inefficacious.

In ethics the central concept was virtue, understood in a distinctively Stoic manner. Human life has a single goal (*telos*): to live according to nature. Following Aristotle, the Stoics called achieving this goal "happiness" (*eudaimonia*). Perfection of our intrinsically rational nature is the only way to do this. This perfection, which they called "virtue" (*aretē*), is the necessary and sufficient condition for achieving our goal. This robust conception of virtue is at the center of Stoic thought and became the defining feature of the school.

LOGIC

Stoic logic has two parts: dialectic and rhetoric. Dialectic is broader in scope than logic in the modern sense. Yet the Stoics made crucial advances even in logic understood in the narrower modern sense.

Traditionally, rhetoric had been the art of persuasion through speech. As such it was either condemned, as by Plato, or reformed, as by Aristotle. The Stoics restricted rhetoric by insisting that it, like other crafts, must be conducted under norms of truth and virtue. Hence rhetoric became the art of persuading an audience of the truth through orderly discourse and argument, differing from dialectic only in form; rhetoric is merely a more expansive way of achieving such conviction. As Zeno said, rhetoric is an open hand, while dialectic is a closed fist (Sextus 1935, 2.7 [= *Adv. Mathematicos* 2.7]). Stoic ideas about rhetoric understandably had limited influence.

In contrast, their dialectic had considerable influence, since it aimed to be a comprehensive study of human discourse and its relation to truth about the world. It covered the content of discourse as well as the utterances that express that content, both what is signified and what does the signifying. The relationship between linguistic signifiers and their meaning lies at the heart of Stoic dialectic. Accordingly, dialectic covered much of what we classify as epistemology and philosophy of language (including semantics), as well as the study of propositions and their relations. But since what is signified by speech are incorporeal sayables, dialectic also included aspects of metaphysics and philosophy of mind. The broad Stoic conception of dialectic also covered what we would consider linguistics and grammar, the parts of speech and various forms of speech acts; their theories had great influence on the development of grammar as a discipline.

In perception, on the Stoic theory, we receive through the senses representations of objects and events. A rational animal becomes aware of this representational content by way of a sayable (usually a proposition [*axiōma*], defined as what admits of being true or false), which is dependent on the physical change in the mind. We either assent to this proposition, reject it as being unrepresentative of its alleged correlate in the world, or suspend judgment about its truth. This is the heart of Stoic epistemology. Academic critics of the Stoic theory argued that no sensory representation could be satisfactorily reliable. In defending their theory (in part by positing self-verifying cataleptic representations) and in elaborating how perceptual experience formed the basis for concepts, memories, and the like, the Stoics expanded on the foundations for empirical epistemology that Aristotle had laid.

The most important aspect of Stoic logic is its study of the forms of argument, inference, and validity. Stoics undertook this to defend the truth of their substantive doctrines and to demonstrate the pervasiveness of rational structures in the world. Chrysippus went beyond that goal and plunged into had been the starting point, and the subject had been advanced by the development of challenging paradoxes and puzzles by Megarian and other dialecticians. Chrysippus made the logic of propositions and arguments into a discipline.

Stoic logic takes the proposition (*axiōma*, often symbolized by an ordinal number) as its basic unit of analysis and works with a small set of operators used to connect them: "if," "and," "not," and exclusive "or." Five basic inference forms were recognized; all valid arguments were supposed to be derivable from these indemonstrable arguments by purely logical means. Stoics attempted to prove this completeness claim with the aid of higher-order logical principles. The five indemonstrables are the following:

If the first, the second.
But the first.
Therefore, the second.

If the first, the second.
But not the second.
Therefore, not the first.

Not both the first and the second.
But the first.
Therefore, not the second.

Either the first or the second.
But the first.
Therefore, not the second.

Either the first or the second.
But not the second.
Therefore, the first.

PHYSICS

Stoic physics was, in its day, the most up-to-date and influential version of the nonatomistic physics pioneered by Empedocles and developed by Aristotle. Stoics posited a geocentric cosmos made up of earth, air, fire, and water arranged in four roughly concentric spheres. Although the cosmos has no void within it, it is surrounded by an indefinitely large void, which provides room for expansion when the cosmos reaches the end of its finite life span. The Stoics held that the cosmos was generated by the creative intelligence of Zeus and eventually ends by returning to the fire from which it was born. This process repeats itself forever—a doctrine that responds in part to Aristotle's arguments for the eternity of the cosmos. Since things expand when heated, the conflagration that occurs at the end of each cycle requires that there be empty space outside the physical world.

Zeus is a craftsman-god modeled on the creator god of Plato's *Timaeus* and initially identified with a kind of fire. Cosmogony begins when this fire transforms itself in a quasi-biological process that generates the four elements that are the stuff of the world. Fire has a dual role, both as the original divine source and as one of the four elements. Each element is analyzable into two principles, the active and the passive, but these principles are themselves corporeal. The active principle (like Aristotelian form) is immanent everywhere and is responsible for the structure and comprehensibility of things; hence it is often identified as god and reason, a creative form of fire that embodies a divine plan for every aspect of the physical world. This emphasis on unified and immanent divine power made the Stoics pioneers for later forms of pantheism.

Later Stoics (including Chrysippus) revised the role of fire and claimed that the immanent shaping power was better understood as *pneuma*, a unique blend of fire and air with an optimal combination of fluidity and tensile strength. *Pneuma* gives order and shape to things in varying degrees. In lifeless things like rocks it is a disposition (*hexis*), giving them coherence and shape. In plants it is their "nature" (*phusis*) and accounts for their ability to grow and change. In animals it accounts for the full range of dynamic attributes, including perception and desire; hence it is there called "soul" (*psuchē*). In humans and gods this divine shaping power is labeled "reason" (*logos*). These various forms of a single power unite all entities into a single order, the cosmos. Since both the active shaping power and the passive component of a thing are corporeal, the Stoics had to give an account of how two such bodies could be fused into a perfect mixture. Their sophisticated theory of "total blending" was frequently criticized, but the concept of *pneuma* itself had considerable influence in later centuries.

The Stoics analyzed each individual entity by means of a complex theory that today would fall under the heading of metaphysics. They posit four "genera" or kinds (less helpfully, "categories"), all of which apply to every object. First, each object can be treated as a "substrate"; this merely asserts that it is a material object, a being, without specifying its attributes. Second, each object is "qualified," endowed (by the active principle or by *pneuma*) with structure sufficient to make it a definite thing. Qualities are either common (making the object a kind of thing, such as a human) or peculiar (making it a unique individual, such as Socrates). The third genus specifies dispositions or conditions of an entity (Socrates may be courageous or have frost-bitten feet), while the fourth is termed "relative disposition" and picks out relations such as being the father of someone or being on the right of someone. Though we cannot be certain of all its details, this theory clearly provided the analytical framework for Stoic corporealist physics.

Since the cosmos is a whole united by reason (i.e., the *pneuma* that pervades it), it can be regarded as a single living entity. In this perspective, everything else is a part of the whole, even humans, whose reason is the same in nature as that of Zeus. Hence humans are uniquely situated in the world, subordinate to it as parts but able to understand in principle the unified plan determining all that happens.

From a theological perspective, this plan appears as a providential divine arrangement, but in Stoic physics, it is actually a mere consequence of Stoic causal determinism. There are no uncaused events, so all that happens is determined by antecedent events and states of affairs in the world. The world, then, is a network of causal relationships capable in principle of being explained. If this were not the case, there would be uncaused events, which Stoics thought unacceptable; even the principle of bivalence (the claim that every proposition is either true or false) would be threatened, and Chrysippus (contrary to Aristotle and Epicurus) held that this logical principle obtains even for future-tense propositions.

Human thoughts, actions, and decisions are a part of this causally deterministic system, but moral responsibility is not threatened (according to the Stoics), since the decisive causal factor is the character and disposition of the agent as he or she reacts to the world. Critics in the ancient world argued that causal determinism jeopardized moral accountability, but Chrysippus stoutly maintained a distinction between being caused (as human actions are) and being necessitated by factors wholly external to the agent. Stoic compatibilism still seems reasonable to many philosophers, but it remained contentious in the ancient world.

ETHICS

It is tempting to suppose that for the Stoics ethics is the most important branch of philosophy, subserved by logic and physics. But of all the similes used to described the relationship among the parts of philosophy, only two support this claim: Posidonius's assertion that ethics is like the soul of an animal (Sextus 1935, 1..19 [= *Adv. Mathematicos* 7.19]) and the claim that ethics is like fruit on the trees (Diogenes 7.39–41). Other Stoics make physics the culmination of philosophical activity. Three factors incline us to regard ethics as the core of Stoic thought: the pattern of ancient philosophical controversy, the accidental bias of the surviving sources, and the fact that Stoic physics is today more obviously obsolete than Stoic ethics. To yield to this tendency is to take sides in a debate within the ancient school, to support the Socratic mission of Aristo of Chios against, for example, Chrysippus, who regarded theology (part of physics) as the culmination of philosophy (Plutarch 1035a).

Philosophy is a craft for living (*technē tou biou*). As a craft, it is based on a body of knowledge, consists in a stable disposition of a rational agent, and has a determinate function (*ergon*) and goal (*telos*). Stoicism is firmly embedded in the eudaimonistic tradition of ancient ethics, where the goal is *eudaimonia*, conventionally translated as "happiness." For Stoics, the goal is to live in accordance with nature, and their claim is that this consists in living in accordance with virtue, since human virtue is the excellence of our nature. But our nature is fundamentally rational. Hence perfection of human reason is another summary expression of the goal. This remains a merely formal account until substantive Stoic views about human nature are considered. In contrast to Plato and Aristotle, Stoics denied that the mature human soul contains essentially irrational components. In Stoic thought, there is no lower part of the soul to be tamed and managed by reason; rather, our rational faculties have an affective component, and so emotion and desire are features of some of our cognitive processes. Further, the Stoics held that our rational nature is qualitatively the same as the divine reason embedded in nature, so that our goal requires living in accordance with both human nature and cosmic nature (Diogenes 7.88).

Like all living things, humans are shaped by a fundamental drive to preserve and enhance their nature, a drive visible even in infants but taking on its characteristic form when they mature. This basic drive involves a commitment to pursue the good, understood as what is truly beneficial. Stoics accept the Socratic argument that only virtue is consistently and genuinely beneficial, since an excellence cannot be misused. Other advantageous things (health, pleasure, social standing, etc.) admit of misuse, so their value is merely provisional. They are preferred but not good. There is a similar account of vice (the only truly bad thing) and disadvantageous things like disease and poverty, which are dispreferred but not genuinely bad. This basic duality in Stoic value theory is a central feature of Stoic ethics. Though it is rational to avoid dispreferred things and embrace preferred things in the course of a well-planned human life, only genuine goods demand unconditional commitment.

This is the basis for the notorious Stoic rejection of passions, which are understood as unreasonable and excessive reactions to preferred and dispreferred things. If sickness and poverty are not bad but merely dispreferred, we should not grieve over them (but, of course, we should do our best to avoid them). If wealth is not a strict good, we should not be elated at achieving it (though there is nothing wrong with enjoying it). If a favorable reputation in our community is not an unconditional good, then we need not fear losing it. If romantic attachments are worth having but are not the sine qua non of human flourishing, then we should pursue potential partners without obsession. And so forth. Life according to our purely rational nature will be free of passions, but not devoid of affect. For in a life of virtuous choices and actions, there will be many things to want, to shun, and to rejoice over. Such positive affective states were called *eupatheiai*.

Most Stoics accepted the doctrine of the unity of virtues, though there was serious debate about the nature of that unity. But all Stoics held that virtuous action was limited to the sage—a normative ideal of perfected virtue used as a benchmark for good action. The Stoics distinguished between appropriate actions (*kathēkonta*), which can be determined by the proper application of moral guidelines and maxims, and genuinely good actions (*katorthōmata*), which are appropriate actions performed from the perfected disposition of a sage. Nonsages may have little real chance to attain wisdom, but their constant striving to determine the appropriate thing and to do is guided by the ideal of the sage. Stoic recommendations for appropriate actions (such as participation in civic life, unless it is hopelessly corrupt) are routinely presented as descriptions of what the sage will do, yet Stoicism does not categorically prescribe any particular actions. Only the commands to follow (or accommodate oneself to) nature and to act virtuously are unconditional.

Stoic ethics is often portrayed as mired in paradox, but we can make better sense of the persistent philosophical appeal of Stoicism if we focus instead on Stoics' stringent and carefully formulated theories in all branches of philosophy and their insistence that these parts should fit together into a coordinated whole, that they should combine the best understanding of the natural world available in their day with a deep commitment to the exercise of human reason as the key to human fulfillment.

See also Arcesilaus; Aristotelianism; Chrysippus; Cleanthes; Cynics; Diodorus Cronus; Epictetus; Epicureanism and the Epicurean School; Greek Academy; Heraclitus of Ephesus; Marcus Aurelius Antoninus; Musonius Rufus; Panaetius of Rhodes; Posidonius; Seneca, Lucius Annaeus; Zeno of Citium.

Bibliography

WORKS BY STOICS

Diogenes Laertius. *Lives of Eminent Philosophers*. Translated by R. D. Hicks. Cambridge, MA: Harvard University Press, 1972.

Epictetus. *The Discourses of Epictetus*. London: J. M. Dent, 1995.

Epictetus. *Handbook of Epictetus*. Translated by Nicholas P. White. Indianapolis, IN: Hackett, 1983.

Marcus Aurelius. *Meditations*. Translated by A. S. L. Farquharson. New York: Knopf, 1992.

Plutarch. "On Stoic Self-Contradictions." In his *Moralia*. Vol. 13, Pt. 2: *Stoic Essays*, translated by Harold Cherniss. Cambridge, MA: Harvard University Press, 1976.

Seneca, Lucius Annaeus. *Seneca's Letters to Lucilius*. Translated by E. Phillips Barker. Oxford, U.K.: Clarendon Press, 1932.

Sextus Empiricus. *Against the Logicians*. Translated by R. G. Bury. Cambridge, MA: Harvard University Press, 1935.

Sextus Empiricus. *Against the Physicists. Against the Ethicists*. Translated by R. G. Bury. Cambridge, MA: Harvard University Press, 1936.

Sextus Empiricus. *Against the Professors*. Translated by R. G. Bury. Cambridge, MA: Harvard University Press, 1949.

Sextus Empiricus. *The Skeptic Way: Sextus Empiricus's "Outlines of Pyrrhonism."* Translated by Benson Mates. New York: Oxford University Press, 1996.

WORKS ON STOIC PHILOSOPHY

Algra, Keimpe, et al. *Cambridge History of Hellenistic Philosophy*. Cambridge, U.K.: Cambridge University Press, 1999.

Becker, Lawrence C. *A New Stoicism*. Princeton, NJ: Princeton University Press, 1998.

Bobzien, Susanne. *Determinism and Freedom in Stoic Philosophy*. Oxford, U.K.: Clarendon Press, 1998.

Frede, Michael. *Die stoische Logik*. Göttingen, Germany: Vandenhoeck und Ruprecht, 1974.

Hahm, David E. *The Origins of Stoic Cosmology*. Columbus: Ohio State University Press, 1977.

Inwood, Brad, ed. *The Cambridge Companion to the Stoics*. Cambridge, U.K.: Cambridge University Press, 2003.

Inwood, Brad. *Ethics and Human Action in Early Stoicism*. Oxford: Clarendon Press, 1985.

Long, A. A., ed. *Problems in Stoicism*. London: Athlone Press, 1971.

Long, A. A., and D. N. Sedley. *The Hellenistic Philosophers*. Chaps. 26–67. Cambridge, U.K.: Cambridge University Press, 1987.

Mates, Benson. *Stoic Logic*. Berkeley: University of California Press, 1953.

Rist, John M., ed. *The Stoics*. Berkeley: University of California Press, 1978.

Sandbach, F. H. *The Stoics*. London: Chatto and Windus, 1975.

Striker, Gisela. "Following Nature: A Study in Stoic Ethics." *Oxford Studies in Ancient Philosophy* 10 (1996): 1–73.

Brad Inwood (2005)

STOUT, GEORGE FREDERICK

(1860–1944)

George Frederick Stout was an English philosopher and psychologist. Records of Stout's early life are scant. He was born in South Shields, Durham. A clever boy at school, he went in 1879 to St. John's College, Cambridge, where he obtained first-class honors in the classical tripos with distinction in ancient philosophy and followed this with first-class honors in the moral sciences tripos with distinction in metaphysics. In 1884 he was elected a fellow of his college, and in 1891 he succeeded George Croom Robertson as editor of *Mind*. He was appointed Anderson lecturer in comparative psychology at Aberdeen in 1896; Wilde reader in mental philosophy at Oxford in 1899; and professor of logic and metaphysics at the University of St. Andrews in 1903. He remained at St. Andrews, where he was instrumental in establishing a laboratory of experimental psychology, until his retirement in 1936. In 1939 he went to Sydney, Australia, to live with his son Alan, who had been appointed to the chair of moral and political philosophy at the University of Sydney. He spent the remaining years of his life joining vigorously in the discussions of a lively circle of younger philosophers at that university.

Stout's position in the history of philosophy and psychology is at the end of the long line of philosophers who, by reflective analysis, introspection, and observation, established the conceptual framework of what became in his time the science of psychology. He was a pupil of James Ward but not a mere disciple. He assimilated the essentials of Ward's system into his own philosophy of mind, but in the assimilation he transformed and extended them so that he created an entirely original and distinctive philosophy. Although he was formidable in polemical discussion, his bent was to constructive thinking. He assimilated many systems, boasting in later years, "I have got them all in my system" (idealism, realism, rationalism, and empiricism). He acknowledged indebtedness to philosophers as diverse as Benedict de Spinoza and Thomas Hobbes and to the last was preoccupied with the ideas of his contemporaries Bertrand Russell, G. E. Moore, and Ludwig Wittgenstein, and he was far from being unsympathetic to the increasingly influential schools of psychology: behaviorism and the hormic and gestalt psychologies.

In Stout's work there is a progressive development of three main theses: the doctrine concerning thought and sentience; the concept of the embodied self; and a doctrine concerning "conative activity." These central theses entail in their elaboration the reinterpretation of many of the concepts important, historically and analytically, in the philosophy of mind. It is difficult to distinguish clearly, although the attempt is rewarding, between changes (or developments) in Stout's views and changes merely in his terminology. In his earlier writings, for example, he was content to describe the ultimate data of our knowledge of the external world as "sensations." Later he followed Ward in using the term *presentations,* and finally he accepted *sense data* and *sensa* to facilitate discussion with the exponents of the prevailing phenomenalism of the day. The readiness to change his terminology was most striking in his many attempts to convey his distinctive doctrine of thought reference.

THOUGHT AND SENTIENCE

Since the time of George Berkeley there has been a widely accepted doctrine that cognition begins with simple sensations which are mental states and "in the mind"; that these sensations and their corresponding images are associated in order to form complex ideas; that some of these sensations and images are projected so as to appear as phenomena of the external world; and that these sensations are the ultimate basis of our beliefs about and our knowledge of the external world. Against this Stout set up the proposition that sense experience involves "thought reference" to real objects. As René Descartes had held that "thought" (as he used the term) implies a thinker, so Stout held that "thought" (in the same sense) implies something real and objective which is thought about.

This thesis, prominent in his *Analytic Psychology,* was expressed in terms of the concept of "noetic synthesis." In his characteristic conciliatory way he conceded the abstract possibility of "anoetic sentience" (sense experience without thought reference), but in subsequent writings he was inclined to deny both the occurrence of anoetic sentience and (to coin a phrase for him) "non-sentient noesis" (imageless thought or any form of thought reference independent of sense experience). In the elaboration of this thesis he offered a paradoxical theory of error—one difficult to refute or prove—to the effect that there can be no complete error, no sheer illusion, no pure hallucination. All errors are misinterpretations of fact. This thesis was later expressed in terms of "original meaning," in saying that every sense experience is apprehended as "conditioned by something other than itself," or as an "inseparable phase of something other than itself." It was developed with subtlety and in detail in the genetic psychology of the *Manual of Psychology.*

Following Ward, Stout attempted to give a natural history of the development of human awareness of the world which also offered grounds for our knowledge of what the world is really like. The central thesis here is that we must accept as primary not only the particular sense data of experience but also the categories or ultimate principles of unity: space, time, thinghood, and causality. These are not so much a priori cognitions as dispositions to organize experience in certain ways. We do not, for instance, have a priori knowledge that every event has a cause, but we have a disposition to look for causes. So, *mutatis mutandis,* with the other categories.

THE EMBODIED SELF

Stout, like Ward, accepted a two-dimensional, tripartite division of mental functions into cognition, feeling, and conation; and he distinguished self, attitude, and object in each function. However, in the analysis of every concept in this scheme Stout modified every idea he took from Ward. He was more thoroughgoing in his adoption of Franz Brentano's principle that the essential component that distinguishes a mental function from a nonmental one is the attitude or way in which the subject is concerned with its objects. His most fundamental divergence from Ward was in his account of the knowing, feeling, and willing subject (self or ego). His differences from Ward are set out in detail in his important article "Ward as a Psychologist" (*Monist,* January 1926). Here he opposed to Ward's account of the pure ego his own view that the self as first known in sensible experience is that thing whose boundary from other things is the skin.

The *Manual of Psychology* contains a puzzling and confusing chapter, "Body and Mind," that combines a critique of the classical theories of interactionism, epiphenomenalism, and parallelism, all of which presupposed Cartesian dualism, with a defense of a version of parallelism that did not. This chapter puzzled students until, many years later, Stout was able to set out more clearly (especially in the Gifford Lectures) his basic philosophical thesis. This was a rejection of a dualistic ontology (that there are two sorts of substance, material things and minds) and a defense of a dualism of attributes—physical and mental—combined in a single entity, the embodied mind, which has both physical and mental attributes united somewhat as the primary and secondary characteristics are united in a material object as it is apprehended in naive perceptual situations. This view of the self entailed a corresponding reanalysis of the mental attitudes of cognition, feeling, and conation.

Stout discarded the dualism of substances but retained the dualism of qualities in his account of mental dispositions. These came to be described as "psychophysical dispositions" in accounts of the instincts, sentiments, attitudes, and other proposed ultimate sources of behavior. In this he anticipated and inspired the hormic psychology of William McDougall and, less directly, the theory of personality elaborated by Gordon Allport. McDougall was to describe the ultimate springs of human conduct in terms of certain innate primary psychophysical dispositions to perceive and attend to certain objects, to feel emotional excitement in the presence of such objects, and to experience an impulse to act in certain ways in regard to those objects. Allport later defined these sources of behavior as mental and neural "states of readiness" for such experiences and activities. In Stout these concepts are embodied in a more radical account of conative activity and conative dispositions.

CONATION

Although he accepted the classical tripartite division of mental functions, Stout accorded a certain priority to conation, so much so that he encouraged what has been described as the "conative theory of cognition," such as that developed by his contemporary Samuel Alexander. (The last paper published by Stout was "A Criticism of Alexander's Theory of Mind and Knowledge," *Australian Journal of Psychology and Philosophy,* September 1944.) The term *conative activity* covers all psychophysical processes which are directed to a goal (whether anticipated or not). It includes such cognitive processes as observation, recollection, and imagination, which are directed to the attainment of clearer and fuller perception of things present, the reconstruction of the past, and the comprehension of future possibilities. Conation is divided into practical and theoretical conation. Practical conative activity is directed to producing actual changes in the objects and situations with which the subject has to deal in the real world. Theoretical conation is directed to the fuller and clearer apprehension of such objects and situations. Stout's account of theoretical conation was in effect his account of attention. Attention is theoretical conation, although it incorporates practical conation through determining sensory-motor adjustments and the manipulation of instruments that facilitate clarity of perception.

Traditional accounts of association and reproductive and productive thinking were similarly revised and restated in conative terms. The law of association by contiguity was reformulated as the law of association by continuity of interest. One basic idea in all later theories of productive or creative thinking derives from Stout's account of "relative suggestion," an expression introduced by Thomas Brown that led to confusion between Stout's usage and Brown's.

In his treatment of all these concepts, Stout advanced beyond Ward and contributed significantly to the transition of psychology from a branch of philosophy to a science of human experience and behavior. These contributions were largely ignored, however, because of the powerful movements in psychology that were adverse to what had come to be described as "armchair psychology," that is, the purely formal analysis of psychological concepts. Stout's influence on philosophical thought outside his own circle of associates was also limited because of the reaction against "speculative" philosophy and the increasing restriction of philosophical discussion to analysis, more especially to the analysis of linguistic usage.

Stout's philosophy was, mistakenly, treated as being in the tradition of metaphysical speculation and the creation of systems in the grand manner. His final position is most fully set out in the two volumes of Gifford Lectures. These embody many clarifications of concepts in the philosophy of mind and some acute criticism of earlier expositions of materialism and of contemporary phenomenalism. They contain the only records of Stout's views on aesthetics and ethics and his more tentative speculations concerning God, teleology, and the nature of material things. There is probably no philosopher who in his own thinking so smoothly made the transition from the prevailing idealism of the late nineteenth century to the prevailing critical, nonspeculative philosophy of the mid-twentieth century. Something of the idealist tradition is preserved in his sophisticated defense of philosophical animism, but more important are his detailed contributions to the transition from the philosophy of mind of the nineteenth century to that of the twentieth.

Bibliography

WORKS BY STOUT

Analytic Psychology. 2 vols. London: Sonnenschein, 1896.

A Manual of Psychology. London: University Correspondence College Press, 1899; 4th ed., rev. by C. A. Mace, London, 1929; 5th (and last) ed., London: University Tutorial Press, 1938. The 5th edition contains an appendix on gestalt psychology by R. H. Thouless and a supplementary note by Stout.

Studies in Philosophy and Psychology. London: Macmillan, 1930.

Mind and Matter. London and New York: Cambridge University Press, 1931. Vol. I of the Gifford Lectures.

God and Nature. Edited by Alan Stout. London: Cambridge University Press, 1952. Vol. II of the Gifford Lectures with a memoir by J. A. Passmore and a full bibliography.

WORKS ON STOUT

Broad, C. D. "The Local Historical Background of Contemporary Cambridge Philosophy." In *British Philosophy in the Mid Century,* edited by C. A. Mace. London: Allen and Unwin, 1957; 2nd ed., 1966.

Hamlyn, D. W. "Bradley, Ward and Stout." In *Historical Roots of Contemporary Psychology,* edited by B. B. Wolman. New York: Harper and Row, 1968.

Mace, C. A. "George Frederick Stout." *Proceedings of the British Academy* 31.

Mace, C. A. "The Permanent Contributions to Psychology of George Frederick Stout." *British Journal of Educational Psychology* 24, Part 2 (June 1954).

Passmore, J. A. *A Hundred Years of Philosophy,* 192–202 and passim. London: Duckworth, 1957.

C. A. Mace (1967)

STRATO AND STRATONISM

Little is known for sure about the life and work of Strato of Lampsacus, third head of Aristotle's school. He lived in Alexandria as tutor to the young Ptolemy Philadelphus for some time before he took over the leadership of the Peripatos; during this time he likely came into contact with the doctors and scientists patronized by the Ptolemaic court. He was head of Aristotle's school in Athens from Theophrastus's death in 286 BCE until his death in 268 or 269 BCE. The school seems to have dwindled into obscurity after Strato's time: Explanations offered for this include a suspect story that the school lost its library after Theophrastus's death.

Strato was known in antiquity as "the natural philosopher," possibly because of his insistence on separating the study of the natural world from any dependence on the divine. He reportedly ascribed all natural events to forces of weight and motion. He rejected Aristotle's doctrine of the fifth element, and also the idea that air and fire have an independent tendency to move upward, claiming instead that they are squeezed out by the fall of heavy bodies. His physics seems to have been basically Aristotelian, because he stressed the role of hot and cold in effecting change; yet he seems to have made changes in the doctrine of the void, because he held that it is at least possible within the cosmos. One report claims that he held that matter has passageways to allow the passage of light and heat. Controversy surrounds the relationship between Strato's view of the void and that of later Hellenistic theories of pneumatic effects. His best-known contributions to natural philosophy include attempts to prove the downward acceleration of falling bodies.

Besides work on logic, metaphysics, and ethics, Strato wrote a number of works on medical topics. Perhaps following Hellenistic medical research, he seems to have offered a naturalistic account of the soul, ascribing its functions to a substance, *pneuma*, carried in passageways throughout the body. He located the center of the soul's activity between the eyebrows, rejecting Aristotle's view that the heart is the center. He regarded reasoning as a causal movement in the soul, and offered lists of objections to Plato's arguments for the immortality of the soul.

Strato may have had some impact amongst the scientific figures in Alexandria, but his greatest notoreity was acquired some two millenium later. Ralph Cudworth characterized Strato's approach—which he called "hylozoism," the idea that matter is inherently alive—as a particularly pernicious brand of atheism. Although there is little evidence that this is Strato's view, his name became identified in the Enlightenment with a kind of naturalistic atheism.

See also Aristotelianism; Aristotle.

Bibliography

Until the expected reedition of the fragments of Strato of Lampsacus by R. W. Sharples, Rutgers University Studies in the Classical Humanities, the standard edition is F. Wehrli, *Die Schule des Aristoteles*. Vol. 5: *Straton von Lampsakos*. 2nd ed. (Basel, Germany: Schwabe, 1969). Recent studies include David Furley, "Strato's Theory of Void," in his *Cosmic Problems: Essays on Greek and Roman Philosophy of Nature*, 149–160 (Cambridge, U.K.: Cambridge University Press, 1989), and H. B. Gottschalk, "Strato of Lampsacus: Some Texts," *Proceedings of the Leeds Philosophical and Literary Society* 9 (1965): 95–182.

Sylvia Berryman (2005)

STRAUSS, DAVID FRIEDRICH

(1808–1874)

David Friedrich Strauss, the German theologian, historian of religion, and moralist, was born at Ludwigsburg in Württemberg. He studied from 1821 to 1825 at Blaubeuren, where he fell under the influence of the Hegelian theologian F. C. Baur, and at the Tübingen Stift from 1825 to 1831. He next attended the University of Berlin, where he heard lectures by G. W. F. Hegel and Friedrich Schleiermacher. In 1832 he went to the University of Tübingen as lecturer, remaining there until 1835, the year of the publication of the first volume of his most important work, *Das Leben Jesu kritisch bearbeitet* (2 vols., Tübingen, 1835–1836; translated from the 4th German edition by George Eliot as *The Life of Jesus Critically Examined,* London, 1848). The universal storm of public indignation that this book occasioned resulted in his dismissal from the university and his permanent retirement from academic life. Master of a clear and forthright prose style, Strauss had no difficulty supporting himself as a journalist and popular exponent of the view that religion—Christianity in particular—is an expression of the human mind's capacity to generate myths and treat them as truths revealed by God to man.

When he began his study of the Gospels, Strauss was neither a liberal nor a materialist. His original interests had been those of a Hegelian idealist; he had meant to study the available records of Jesus' life in order to distinguish their historically valid content from the theological accretions that had become associated with them during the first two centuries of the Christian era. His investigations convinced him, however, that the principal importance of the Gospels was aesthetic and philosophical, not historical. On the one hand, the Gospels provided insight into the Messianic expectation of the Jewish people in the late Hellenistic period; on the other hand, they reflected a memory of the exceptional personality of a great man, Jesus. Thus envisaged, the Gospels were a synthesis of notions peculiar to the Jews regarding the nature of world history and of certain moral teachings associated with the name of a purely human, yet historically vague, personality, presented in an aesthetically pleasing form for members of a new religious community that was both Jewish and Greek in its composition. For Strauss, the Gospels were, in short, interesting primarily as evidence of the workings of consciousness in the sphere of religious experience: they showed how the mind could fabricate miracles and affirm them as true, contrary to the Hegelian dictum, then regarded as an established truth, that the real was rational and the rational was real.

Had Strauss halted at this point, his work might have been ignored as merely another vestige of the free thought of the Enlightenment. Instead, he went on to argue that even if the historicity of the account of Jesus's life in the Gospels were denied, it need not follow that the Gospels were a product of conscious invention or fraud. He held, rather, that they could be said to belong to a third order of mental activity, called by Hegel unconscious invention or myth and defined by him as an attempt to envision the Absolute in terms of images derived from sensible experiences. As unconscious invention, the Gospels were to be viewed as poetic renderings of man's desire to transcend the finitude of the historical moment, as evidence of the purely human desire to realize the immanent goal of Spirit in its journey toward the Hegelian Being-in-and-for-itself. Thus, although Strauss had denied that the Gospels were evidence of the direct intrusion of the divine into history or even of the true nature of Jesus' life, he had, in his own view, at least salvaged them as documents in the history of human expression. In doing so, of course, he had reduced them to the same status as the pagan myths, legends, and epics.

In a second work, *Die christliche Glaubenslehre* (2 vols., 1840–1841), Strauss tried to clarify the theoretical basis of his original historical inquiry. He argued that Christianity was a stage in the evolution of a true pantheism that had reached its culmination in Hegelian philosophy. What the poet and mystic took for God was nothing but the world—specifically, man in the world—conceived in aesthetic terms. Science studied the same phenomena that are governed by physical laws, and philosophy was, as Hegel had taught, mind reflecting on these prior activities of thought and imagination.

Das Leben Jesu became a cause célèbre in a Germany growing increasingly reactionary both politically and intellectually. The attack launched against Strauss from all quarters soon made him a symbol to German liberals; he was regarded as a martyr of science and freedom of thought. Accordingly, Strauss was drawn into political as well as theological polemics. In 1848 he published at Halle a defense of bourgeois liberalism, *Der politische und der theologische Liberalismus.* He later turned to the study of philosophical materialism (that of Friedrich Albert Lange and of Charles Darwin) and to the production of a series of historical works on leading advocates of freedom of thought in European history (for example, a long biography of Ulrich von Hutten, 1858, and a study of Voltaire, 1870). As he progressed, he repudiated the Hegelianism of his first book. In a preface to a later edition of *Das Leben Jesu,* he stated that he had undertaken it to show "to those to whom the conceptions … as to the supernatural character … of the life of Jesus had become intolerable … [that] the best means of effectual release will be found in historical inquiry." Abandoning the last residues of his earlier idealism, he argued that "everything that happens, or ever happened, happened naturally." He still recognized the aesthetic value of the Gospel account, but he now saw it as providing the image of the good life that had finally become possible on this earth because of the triumphs of science and industrial technology and the advance of political liberalism. It was this position that won for him the enmity of both Karl Marx and Friedrich Nietzsche. To Marx, he was the bourgeois *idéologue* par excellence, who tried to combine Christian sentimental ethics and the practices of capitalism in a single package. For Nietzsche, Strauss represented the German *Bildungsphilister* who made a show of intellectual radicalism but always left the conventional morality intact.

Strauss remained to the end of his life the spokesman of popular religious criticism, materialistic in his intention but Hegelian in method, a combination which allowed him to accommodate almost any position that appealed to him. After 1850 his political and social criticism became increasingly conservative—aristocratic, monarchical, and nationalistic. In part this transformation was due to the suspicion that popular democracy would be in general as unable to recognize genius as it had been unable to recognize, in particular, the value of Strauss's own works; but this transformation was also a result of his attempt to move from Hegelianism to positivism. In the second half of the eighteenth century, positivist social thought had become—as, for example, in Hippolyte Taine—a kind of crude determinism, hostile to any revolutionary impulse.

To the young Hegelians, who were already becoming aware of the methodological limitations of Hegel's late thought, *Das Leben Jesu* provided an impulse to the critical, empirical study of the historical milieus within which *Geist* supposedly manifested itself, and it thus prepared them to accept Leopold von Ranke's historicism. To German liberals, Strauss remained a symbol of the risks that had to be run by any German who presumed to espouse radical causes. The later Marxists regarded Strauss as merely a confused bourgeois who had blundered onto forbidden ground. For them, the way to a true revision of Hegelianism was provided by Ludwig Feuerbach. Feuerbach saw that the true importance of Strauss's *Das Leben Jesu* lay in a problem that remained implicit in the work and was hardly touched upon by Strauss himself: the psychological problem about the nature of the mythmaking mechanism that distinguishes man from the rest of nature. It was Feuerbach, then, rather than Strauss, who posed the question with which German philosophy had to come to terms in the 1840s—the question of the relation between human consciousness and its material matrix.

See also Darwin, Charles Robert; Enlightenment; Feuerbach, Ludwig Andreas; Hegel, Georg Wilhelm Friedrich; Hegelianism; Idealism; Lange, Friedrich Albert; Marx, Karl; Materialism; Miracles; Nietzsche, Friedrich; Positivism; Schleiermacher, Friedrich Daniel Ernst; Taine, Hippolyte-Adolphe; Voltaire, François-Marie Arouet de.

Bibliography

WORKS BY STRAUSS

Ulrich von Hutten. 2 vols. Leipzig, 1858. Translated by Mrs. G. Sturge as *Ulrich von Hutten, His Life and Times.* London, 1874.

Hermann Samuel Reimarus. Leipzig: Brockhaus, 1862.

Kleine Schriften biographischen, literarischen, und kunstgeschichtlichen Inhalts. Leipzig, 1862.

Der Christus des Glaubens und der Jesus der Geschichte. Berlin, 1865.

Kleine Schriften, Neue Folge. Berlin, 1866.

Voltaire: sechs Vortrage. Leipzig, 1870.

Gesammelte Schriften, edited by Eduard Zeller. 12 vols. Bonn: E. Strauss, 1876–1878.

Ausgewählte Briefe. Bonn, 1895.

WORKS ON STRAUSS

Barth, Karl. *Die protestantische Theologie im 19. Jahrhundert.* Zürich: Evangelischer, 1947. Translated by Brian Cozens as *Protestant Thought from Rousseau to Ritschl.* New York: Harper, 1959.

Feuter, Eduard. *Geschichte der neueren Historiographie.* 3rd ed. Munich and Berlin, 1936.

Nietzsche, Friedrich. *Unzeitgemüsse Betrachtungen, Erstes Stück.* Leipzig, 1873. Translated by A. M. Ludovici as *Thoughts out of Season.* New York, 1924.

Schweitzer, Albert. *Von Reimarus zu Wrede.* Tübingen: Mohr, 1906. Translated by W. Montgomery as *The Quest for the Historical Jesus.* London: Black, 1910.

Zeller, Eduard. *David Friedrich Strauss in seinem Leben und seinen Schriften.* 2 vols. Heidelberg, 1876–1878.

Hayden V. White (1967)

STRAWSON, PETER FREDERICK

(1919–)

Peter Frederick Strawson, the British philosopher, was educated at Christ's College, Finchley, and St. John's College, Oxford. He holds the BA and MA degrees and is a fellow of University College, Oxford.

LANGUAGE AND LOGIC

Strawson is a leading member of the circle of philosophers whose work is sometimes described as "ordinary language philosophy" or as "Oxford philosophy." Of his early work, the most influential and most controversial is the famous article "On Referring" (*Mind*, 1950), a criticism of the philosophical aspects of Bertrand Russell's theory of definite descriptions. According to Russell's theory any sentence of the form "The *f* is *g*"—for example, "The king of France is bald"—is properly analyzed as follows (in terms of our example): "There is a king of France. There is not more than one king of France. There is nothing which is king of France and which is not bald."

Strawson argues that this analysis confuses referring to an entity with asserting the existence of that entity. In referring to an entity, a speaker presupposes that the entity exists, but he does not assert that it exists, nor does what he asserts entail that it exists. Presupposition is to be distinguished from entailment. In asserting something of the form "The *f* is *g*," a speaker refers or purports to refer to an entity with the subject noun phrase, and to do so involves presupposing that there is such an entity, but this is quite different from asserting that there is such an entity.

According to Strawson this confusion between referring and asserting is based on an antecedent confusion between a sentence and the statement made in a particular use of that sentence. Russell erroneously supposes that every sentence must be either true, false, or meaningless. But, Strawson argues, sentences can be meaningful or meaningless and yet cannot strictly be characterized as true or false. Statements, which are made using sentences, but which are distinct from sentences, are, or can be, either true or false. The sentence "The king of France is bald" is indeed meaningful, but a statement made at the present time using that sentence does not succeed in being either true or false because, as there is presently no king of France, the purported reference to a king of France fails. According to Russell the sentence is meaningful and false. According to Strawson the sentence is meaningful, but the corresponding statement is neither true nor false because one of its presuppositions—namely, that there is a king of France—is false.

In another well-known article of this early period, "Truth" (*Analysis*, 1949), Strawson criticizes the semantic theory of truth and proposes an alternative analysis to the effect that "true" does not describe any semantic properties or, indeed, any other properties at all, because its use is not to describe; rather, we use the word *true* to express agreement, to endorse, concede, grant, or otherwise accede to what has been or might be said. Strawson explicitly draws an analogy between the use of the word *true* and J. L. Austin's notion of performatives. Like performatives, *true* does not describe anything; rather, if we examine its use in ordinary language, we see that it is used to perform altogether different sorts of acts.

This article gave rise to a controversy with Austin, a defender of the correspondence theory. The gist of Strawson's argument against the correspondence theory is that the attempt to explicate truth in terms of correspondence between statements on the one hand and facts, states of affairs, and situations on the other must necessarily fail because such notions as "fact" already have the "word–world relationship" built into them. Facts are not something which statements name or refer to; rather, "facts are what statements (when true) state."

In his first book, *Introduction to Logical Theory* (New York and London, 1952), Strawson continued his investigation of the logical features of ordinary language by studying the relations between ordinary language and formal logic. The book, he says, has two complementary aims: first, to compare and contrast the behavior of ordinary words with the behavior of logical symbols, and, second, to make clear the nature of formal logic itself. It is in the first of these two enterprises that he has shown the more originality and aroused the more controversy. The theme of this part of the book is that such logical systems as the propositional and predicate calculi do not completely represent the complex logical features of ordinary language and indeed represent them less accurately than has generally been supposed. He argues that the logical connectives, especially "$\vee$," "$\supset$," and "$\equiv$," are much less like "or," "if," and "if and only if" than is often claimed. In his discussion of predicate logic (Chs. 5 and 6), he continues the themes of "On Referring," arguing that certain orthodox criticisms which are made of traditional Aristotelian syllogistic fail because of a failure to appreciate the fact that statements made in the use of a sentence of the form "All *f*s are *g*" presuppose the existence of members of the subject class.

Thus, for example, the question whether it is true that all John's children are asleep does not even arise if John has no children. Once it is seen that statements of the form "All *f*s are *g*" have existential presuppositions, it is possible to give a consistent interpretation of the traditional Aristotelian system. The failure to understand this and the misconception regarding the relation of the predicate calculus to ordinary language are in large part due to the same mistakes that underlie the theory of descriptions: the failure to see the distinction between sentence and statement; the "bogus trichotomy" of true, false, or meaningless; and the failure to see the distinction between presupposition and entailment.

The final chapter of the book contains a discussion of probability and induction in which Strawson argues that attempts to justify induction are necessarily misconceived, since there are no higher standards to which one can appeal in assessing inductive standards. The question whether inductive standards are justified is as senseless as the question whether a legal system is legal. Just as a legal system provides the standards of legality, so do inductive criteria provide standards of justification. Underlying this point is the fact that inductive standards form part of our concept of rationality. It is, he says, a necessary truth that the only ways of forming rational opinions concerning what happened or will happen in given circumstances are inductive.

METAPHYSICS

In the middle 1950s Strawson's concerns shifted from investigations of ordinary language to an enterprise he named descriptive metaphysics. This enterprise differs from "revisionary metaphysics" in that it is content to describe the actual structure of our thought about the world rather than attempting to produce a better structure, and it differs from ordinary conceptual analysis in its much greater scope and generality, since it attempts to "lay bare the most general features of our conceptual structure."

These investigations resulted in the publication of a second book, *Individuals* (London, 1959). The book is divided into two parts. Part One, titled "Particulars," deals with the nature of and preconditions for the identification of particular objects in speech; Part Two, "Logical Subjects," concentrates on the relations between particulars and universals and on the corresponding and related distinctions between reference and predication and subjects and predicates. The first important thesis of the book is that from the point of view of particular identification, material objects are the basic particulars. What this means is that the general conditions of particular identification require a unified system of publicly observable and enduring spatiotemporal entities. The material universe forms such a system. Material objects can therefore be identified independently of the identification of particulars in other categories, but particulars in other categories cannot be identified without reference to material objects. This provides us, then, with a sense in which material objects are the basic particulars as far as particular identification is concerned.

A second thesis, one of the most provocative of the book, concerns the traditional mindogon;body problem. In Chapter 3, titled "Persons," Strawson attacks both the Cartesian notion that states of consciousness are ascribed to mental substances, which are quite distinct from but nonetheless intimately connected to bodies, and the modern "no-ownership" theory, according to which states of consciousness are not, strictly speaking, ascribed to anything at all. Both views, he argues, are ultimately incoherent. The solution to the dilemma posed by these views is that the concept of a person is a primitive concept. It is a concept such that both states of consciousness and physical properties are ascribable to one and the same thing—namely, a person. The concept of a mind is derivative from the primitive concept of a person, and the concept of a person is not to be construed as a composite concept made up of the concept of a mind and the concept of a body. The recognition of the primitiveness of the concept of a person enables us to see both why states of consciousness are ascribed to anything at all and why they are ascribed to the very same thing to which certain physical states are ascribed.

Most of Part Two of *Individuals* is devoted to an investigation of the problems of the relations of subjects and predicates. Strawson considers two traditional ways of making the distinction between subject and predicate: a grammatical criterion in terms of the different kinds of symbolism for subject and predicate expressions and a category criterion in terms of the distinction between particulars and universals. He investigates the "tensions and affinities" between these two criteria, and he concludes that the crucial distinction between the way a subject expression introduces a particular into a proposition and the way a predicate expression introduces a universal into a proposition is that the identification of a particular involves the presentation of some empirical fact which is sufficient to identify the particular (this harks back to the doctrine of what is presupposed by identifying references in "On Referring" and *Introduction to Logical Theory*), but the introduction of the universal term by the predicate term does not in general involve any empirical fact. The meaning of the predicate term suffices to identify the universal that the predicate introduces into the proposition. One might say that identifying reference to particulars involves the presentation of empirical facts; the predication of universals involves only the presentation of meanings. This enables us to give a deeper sense to Gottlob Frege's notion that objects are complete—in contrast to concepts, which are incomplete—and it enables us to account for the Aristotelian doctrine that only universals and not particulars are predicable.

In tone, method, and overall objectives, *Individuals* stands in sharp contrast to Strawson's earlier work. Piecemeal investigation of ordinary language occurs here only as an aid and adjunct to attacking large traditional metaphysical problems. One might say that *Individuals* employs essentially Kantian methods to arrive at Aristotelian conclusions. Yet much of the book is at least foreshadowed by Strawson's earlier work, particularly "On Referring" and certain portions of his first book. The notion of descriptive metaphysics itself has been as influential as the actual theses advanced in *Individuals*. More than any other single recent work, this book has resurrected metaphysics (albeit descriptive metaphysics) as a respectable philosophical enterprise.

See also Performative Theory of Truth.

Bibliography

ADDITIONAL WORKS BY STRAWSON

"Necessary Propositions and Entailment Statements." *Mind* (1948).

"Ethical Intuitionism." In *Readings in Ethical Theory*, edited by Wilfrid Sellars and John Hospers. New York: Appleton-Century-Crofts, 1952.

"Particular and General." *PAS* supp. 27 (1953–1954).

"Critical Notice of Wittgenstein." *Mind* (1954).

"Presupposing: A Reply to Mr. Sellars." *Philosophical Review* (1954).

"A Logician's Landscape." *Philosophy* (1955).

"Construction and Analysis." In *The Revolution in Philosophy*, by A. J. Ayer et al. London: Macmillan, 1956.

"In Defense of a Dogma." *Philosophical Review* (1956). Written with H. P. Grice.

"Singular Terms, Ontology and Identity." *Mind* (1956).

"Logical Subjects and Physical Objects." *Philosophy and Phenomenological Research* (1956–1957).

"*Logic and Knowledge* by Bertrand Russell." *Philosophical Quarterly* (1957).

"Metaphysics." In *The Nature of Metaphysics*, edited by D. F. Pears. London: Macmillan, 1957. Written with H. P. Grice and D. F. Pears.

"Professor Ayer's *The Problem of Knowledge*." *Philosophy* (1957).

"Proper Names." *PAS* supp. 31 (1957).

"Propositions, Concepts and Logical Truths." *Philosophical Quarterly* (1957).

"Singular Terms and Predication." *Journal of Philosophy* (1961).

"Social Morality and Individual Ideal." *Philosophy* (1961).

"Freedom and Resentment." *Proceedings of the British Academy* (1962). Annual philosophical lecture.

"Determinism." In *Freedom and the Will*, edited by D. F. Pears. New York: St. Martin's Press, 1963. A discussion with G. J. Warnock and J. F. Thomson.

"Identifying Reference and Truth Values." *Theoria* (1964).

"Truth: A Reconsideration of Austin's Views." *Philosophical Quarterly* (1965).

Meaning and Truth. Oxford: Clarendon, 1970.

Logico-Linguistic Papers. London: Methuen, 1971.

Freedom and Resentment. London: Methuen, 1974.

Subject and Predicate in Logic and Grammar. London: Methuen, 1974.

"Does Knowledge Have Foundations?" *Teorema* MONO1 (1974): 99–110.

"Universals." *Midwest Studies in Philosophy* 4 (1979): 3–10.

Skepticism and Naturalism: Some Varieties. New York: Columbia University Press, 1985.

"Ma Philosophie: Son Developpment, Son Theme Centrale et Nature Generale," *Revue de Theologie et de Philosophie* 120 (1988): 437–452.

"Two Conceptions of Philosophy." In *Perspectives on Quine*, edited by Robert Barrett and Roger Gibson. Cambridge, MA: Blackwell, 1990.

Analysis and Metaphysics: An Introduction to Philosophy. Oxford: Oxford University Press, 1992.

"Comments on Some Aspects of Peter Unger's 'Identity, Consciousness and Value,'" *Philosophy and Phenomenological Research* 52 (1) (March 1992): 145–148.

"The Incoherence of Empiricism." *Proceedings of the Aristotelian Society*, Supp. Vol. 66 (1992).

"Knowing from Words." In *Knowing from Words*, edited by B.K. Matilal and A. Chakrabarti. Dordrecht: Kluwer, 1992.

"Individuals." In *Philosophical Problems Today*, Vol. I, edited by G. Fløistad. Dordrecht: Kluwer, 1994.

"The Problem of Realism and the A Priori." In *Kant and Contemporary Epistemology*, edited by Paolo Parrini. Dordrecht: Kluwer, 1994.

"My Philosophy" and "Replies." In *The Philosophy of P. F. Stawson*, edited by Pranab Kumar Sen and Roop Rekha Verma, New Delhi: Indian Council of Philosophical Research, 1995.

Entity and Identity and Other Essays. Oxford: Clarendon, 1997.

"Intellectual Autobiography" and "Replies." *In The Philosophy of P. F. Strawson*, edited by Lewis Edwin Hahn, Library of Living Philosophers Vol. 26, Chicago and LaSalle, IL: Open Court, 1998.

"Entailment and its Paradoxes." In *Realism: Responses and Reactions (Essays in Honor of Pranab Kumar Sen)*. New Delhi: Indian Council of Philosophical Research, 2000.

"What Have We Learned from Philosophy in the Twentieth Century?" In *The Proceedings of the Twentieth World Congress of Philosophy, Vol. 8: Contemporary Philosophy*, edited by Daniel Dahlstrom. Charlottesville: Philosophy Documentation Center, 2000.

"A Bit of Intellectual Autobiography." In *Strawson and Kant*, edited by Hans-Johann Glock. Oxford: Clarendon, 2003.

Logico-Linguistic Papers. Rev. ed. Aldershot, Hampshire and Burlington, VT: Ashgate, 2004.

Subject and Predicate in Logic and Grammar. Rev. ed. Aldershot, Hampshire, and Burlington, VT: Ashgate, 2004.

Strawson, Peter Frederick, and Arindam Chakrabarti, eds. *Universals, Concepts and Qualities: New Essays on the Meaning of Predicates*. Aldershot, Hampshire, and Burlington, VT: Ashgate, 2005.

WORKS ON STRAWSON

Aune, Bruce. "Feelings, Moods and Introspection." *Mind* (1963).

Ayer, A. J. "The Concept of a Person." In *The Concept of a Person and Other Essays*. London: Macmillan, 1963.

Bradley, M. C. "Mr. Strawson and Skepticism." *Analysis* (1959).

Campbell, Scott. "Strawson, Parfit and Impersonality." *Canadian Journal of Philosophy* 30 (2) (June 2000): 207–224.

Caton, C. E. "Strawson on Referring." *Mind* (1959).

Coval, S. C. "Persons and Criteria in Strawson." *Philosophy and Phenomenological Research* (1964).

Geach, P. T. "Mr. Strawson on Symbolic and Traditional Logic." *Mind* (1963).

Hacker, Peter. "Strawson's Concept of a Person." *Proceedings of the Aristotelian Society* 102 (2002): 21–40.

Hahn, Lewis Edwin, ed. *The Philosophy of P. F. Strawson*. Library of Living Philosphers, Vol. 26. Chicago and La Salle, IL: Open Court, 1998.

Hutcheson, Peter. "Vindicating Strawson." *Philosophical Topics* 13 (spring 1985): 175–184.

Jarvis, Judith. "Notes on Strawson's *Logic*." *Mind* (1961).

Lewis, H. D. "Mind and Body." *PAS* (1962–1963).

Millican, Peter. "Statements and Modality: Strawson, Quine and Wolfram." *International Journal of Moral and Social Studies* 8 (3) (autumn 1993): 315–326.

Pears, D. F. Review of *Individuals. Philosophical Quarterly* (1961).

Quine, W. V. "Mr. Strawson on Logical Theory." *Mind* (1953).

Russell, Bertrand. "Mr. Strawson on Referring." *Mind* (1957).

Sellars, Wilfrid. "Presupposing." *Philosophical Review* (1954).

Sen, Pranab Kumar, and Roop Rekha Verma, eds. *The Philosophy of P. F. Strawson*, New Delhi: Indian Council of Philosophical Research, 1995.

Szubka, Tadeusz. "P. F. Strawson." In *British Philosophers, 1900–2000*, edited by Peter S. Fosi. Columbia, SC: Bruccoli Clark Layman/Gale, 2002.

Urmson, J. O. Review of *Individuals. Mind* (1961).

Van Straaten, Zak, ed. *Philosophical Subjects: Essays Presented to P. F. Strawson*. Oxford: Clarendon, 1980.

Williams, B. A. O. Review of *Individuals. Philosophy* (1961).

John R. Searle (1967)
Bibliography updated by Vicki Lynn Harper (2005)

STRING THEORY

Physicists believe there to be four fundamental forces. Three of these—the electromagnetic, the strong force, and the weak force—are amalgamated in the standard model of elementary particle physics, a family of quantum field theories that has enjoyed stupendous empirical success. Gravity, the fourth and feeblest fundamental force, is the subject of a stupendously successful *non-quantum* field theory, Einstein's general theory of relativity (GTR). Desiring to fit all of fundamental theoretical physics into a quantum mechanical framework, and suspecting that GTR would break down at tiny ("Planck scale," i.e., 10^{-33} cm) distances where quantum effects become significant, physicists have been searching for a quantum theory of gravity since the 1930s. In the last quarter of the twentieth century, string theory became the predominant approach to quantizing gravity, as well as to forging a unified picture of the four fundamental forces. A minority approach to quantizing gravity is the program of loop quantum gravity, which promises no grand unification. Both attempts to quantize gravity portend a science of nature radically different from the Newtonian one that frames much of classical philosophical discourse. They also present gratifying instances of working physicists actively concerned with recognizably philosophical questions about space, time, and theoretical virtue.

THE STANDARD MODEL

String theory would quantize gravity by treating the gravitational force as other forces are treated. In the standard model, pointlike elementary particles, quarks, and leptons constitute matter. Each particle is characterized by invariants, such as mass, spin, charge, and the like. The matter-constituting particles have half-integer multiples of spin, which makes them fermions. Beside fermions, the standard model posits gauge bosons, "messenger particles" or carriers of the interaction, for each force in its ambit. Bosons are distinguished from fermions by having whole-integer multiples of spin. As early as 1934, preliminary work on the sort of coupling with matter required by a quantum theory suggested that, if the gravitational force had a gauge boson, it must be a mass 0 spin 2 particle, dubbed the *graviton*. No such particle is predicted by the standard model.

According to string theory, the elementary particles of the standard model are not the ultimate constituents of nature. Filamentary objects—strings—are. Different vibrational modes of these strings correspond to the different masses (charges, spins) of elementary particles. The standard model is recovered, and fundamental physics unified, in a string theory incorporating vibrational modes corresponding to every species of particle in the standard particle zoo (and so incorporating the strong, weak, and electromagnetic forces), as well as to the graviton (and so incorporating gravity).

THE EARLY YEARS OF STRING THEORY

String theory evolved from attempts, undertaken within the standard model in the 1970s, to model the strong nuclear force in terms of a band between particles. As a theory of the strong nuclear force, these attempts suffered in comparison to quantum chromodynamics. They also predicted the existence of a particle that had never been detected: a mass 0 spin 2 particle. In 1974, John Schwartz and Joël Scherk proposed to promote this empirical embarrassment to a theoretical resource: The undetected particle, they suggested, was in fact the graviton! (Further evidence that string theory encompasses gravity comes in the form of a consistency constraint on the background spacetime in which string theoretic calculations are carried out, which consistency constraint resembles the equations of GTR.)

String theory evolved piecemeal in the 1970s and 1980s, roughly by adapting perturbative approximation techniques developed for the standard model's point particles to stringy entities. One benefit of the adaptation was the suppression of infinities that arise in perturbative calculations for point particles. In the standard model, these infinities call for the expedient of renormalization, the barelyprincipled subtraction of other infinities to yield finite outcomes. Perturbative string theories require no such expedient. Worries that they harbored inconsistencies all their own, called *anomalies*, were allayed by Schwartz's and Michael Green's 1984 argument that string theories were anomaly-free—a result that galvanized research in the field.

By the early 1990s there were five different consistent realizations of perturbative string theory. These realizations shared some noteworthy features. First, their equations were consistent only in ten space-time dimensions. To accord with the appearance that space is three-dimensional, the extra six dimensions are supposed to be Planck-scale and compactified ("rolled up"). (The usual analogy invokes the surface of a cylinder, which is a two-dimensional object: one dimension runs along the length of the cylinder; the other is "rolled up" around its circumference. Supposing the rolled-up dimension to be small enough, a cylinder looks like a one-dimensional object, a line.) Details of the geometries of these extra dimensions influence the physics string theory predicts. These details are adjustable; only with certain choices of the geometries can string theory mimic the standard model.

The initial string theories dealt only with bosons. So that they might incorporate fermions as well, *supersymmetry* was imposed. That is, the equations of string theory were required to be invariant under half-integer changes in spin. Thus the theory predicts for every particle in the standard zoo that it has a supersymmetric partner. For the (spin 1/2) electron, a spin 0 "selectron;" for the (spin-1) photon, a spin 1/2 "photino," and so on. Of these supersymmetric partners, none are observable using present technologies. But there is hope of detecting the lightest, the neutralino, with the Large Hadron Collider, slated to come on-line at CERN in 2007.

Parameters describing, for example, coupling strengths or the volume of the compactified extra dimensions appear in string theories. This means that each string theory can be thought of as a member of a family of related string theories, obtained from the first by varying the values of these parameters. A *duality* is said to obtain between theories so related. In the mid-1990s, Ed Witten and others uncovered evidence of dualities connecting pairs in the set of five consistent perturbative string theories. This embolded Witten to propose that the existing, approximate, string theories were all approximations to a single underlying exact theory he dubbed "M-theory." Although the equations of M-theory are unknown, it is believed that they hold in an eleven-dimensional spacetime, and have eleven-dimensional supergravity (ironically enough, a leading contender for the title "theory of everything" which string theory dislodged in the early 1980s) as their low-energy limit. In addition to strings, M-theory boasts higher-dimensional supersymmetric objects—membranes—some theorists have put to cosmological use, for example, by maintaining that the three spatial dimensions of this world are a three-brane moving through an eleven-dimensional universe harboring other worlds such as this one.

Most predictions of fledgling programs in quantum gravity are experimentally inaccessible, and liable to stay that way. But a nonempirical circumstance is widely believed to confirm string theory. In black hole thermodynamics (developed by Stephen Hawking, Jacob Bekenstein, and others), black holes are attributed properties, such as temperature and entropy, that obey thermodynamic laws. (For instance, entropy, identified as the surface area of a black hole's future event horizon, never decreases.) For certain black holes known as extremal black holes, string theoretic calculations exactly reproduce the Bekenstein entropy formula. Although there has never been an observation confirming (or disconfirming) black hole thermodynamics, the recovery of the black hole entropy formula is widely held to be evidence that string theory is on the right track.

More empirical tests have been proposed, none strong. For example, if the extra dimensions posited by string theory are large enough, new mechanisms for the production of microscopic black holes could be unleashed at energies attainable in the Large Hadron Collider. But string theory is not required to posit large extra-dimensions. So the failure of microscopic black holes to appear would not force the abandonment of string theory.

Despite its successes, there are causes for complaint about string theory. It is not an exact theory yet. Its predictions might seem unduly sensitive to the discretionary matter of the geometry of the extra dimensions. In addition to predicting the existence of the standard particles and the graviton, it predicts the existence of infinitely many particles, including supersymmetric particles, humans have not seen (yet). It requires seven extra spatial dimensions humans have not seen (yet). And as formulated *at present*, it takes place in a fixed space-time background.

STRING THEORY AND LOOP QUANTUM GRAVITY

The game of background-independent M-theory is afoot; some (e.g., Smolin 2001) hope that its pursuit will reveal connections between string theory and its main rival, loop quantum gravity. Background-independence is the rallying cry of the (much less populated) loop quantum gravity camp. Largely trained as general relativists, adherents of this approach take the fundamental moral of GTR to be that space-time is not a setting in which physics happens but is itself a dynamical object, malleable in response to the matter and energy filling it. Whereas string theory seeks a quantum theory of gravity on the model of early twenty-first century quantum theory of other forces—a model that adds a graviton to a particle zoo revealed by approximations carried out in a fixed spacetime background—loop quantum gravity seeks a quantum theory of gravity by quantizing gravity: that is, by casting GTR as a classical theory in Hamiltonian form, and following a canonical procedure for quantizing such theories. Insofar as GTR's variables determine the geometry of space-time, should the quantization procedure succeed, space-time itself would be the commodity quantized.

The quantization procedure is complicated by the fact that GTR is a constrained Hamiltonian system: its canonical momenta are not independent. Instead, they satisfy constraint equations that must be reflected in the final quantum theory. The origin of these constraint equations is the diffeomorphism invariance of GTR, that is, if one starts with a solution to the equations of GTR and smoothly reassigns the dynamical fields comprising that solution to the manifold on which they are defined, one winds up with a solution to the equations of GTR. Adherents of loop quantum gravity take diffeomorphism invariance to express the background independence of GTR.

Loop quantum gravity exploits a Hamiltonian formulation of GTR due to Abhay Ashtekar, a physicist at Syracuse University. Its quantization is set in a Hilbert space spanned by spin-network states: graphs whose edges are labeled by integer multiples of 1/2. Not set in some background space, these spin-network states are supposed to be the constituents from which space is built. Defined on their Hilbert space are area and volume (but not length) operators that have discrete spectra. A free parameter in the theory can be adjusted so that this quantization occurs at the Planck scale. On these grounds, its adherents claim loop quantum gravity to be a background-independent exact theory that quantizes space. Like string theory, loop quantum gravity finds quasi-confirmation in its accord with black hole thermodynamics: for all black holes, loop quantum gravity reproduces the Bekenstein entropy within a factor of 4.

Despite its successes, there are causes for complaint about loop quantum gravity. It does not incorporate the predictions of the standard model. So whereas it may be a quantum theory of gravity, it is not a theory of everything. More telling, loop quantum gravity as yet fails to reflect the full diffeomorphism invariance of GTR in a way that is both consistent and has GTR as its classical limit. The sticking point is the classical Hamiltonian constraint, related to diffeomorphisms that can be interpreted as time translations. Until this constraint is wrangled, loop quantum gravity lacks a dynamics: it consists of a space of possible instantaneous spacetime geometries, without an account of their time development. Given loop quantum gravity's ideology of background-independence, this is disappointing.

There is no established philosophy of quantum gravity. But there is much to provoke the philosopher. What, according to string theory or loop quantum gravity, is the nature of space(-time)? How many dimensions has it? (These questions are complicated by dualities between string theories revealed by varying the volumes of their compactified geometries, as well as by the holographic hypothesis, according to which physics in the interior of a region—an n-dimensional space—is dual to physics on that region's boundary—an (n-1)-dimensional space.) The search for quantum gravity was set off by no glaring empirical shortcoming in existing theories, and has reached theories for which no empirical evidence is readily forthcoming. In the absence of empirical adequacy, other theoretical virtues occupy center stage: the ideal of unification, the capacity to reproduce the results, or preserve the insights, of other theories (even unconfirmed ones); the susceptibility of puzzles posed in one theoretical framework to solution techniques available in another. The nature of these virtues, and how best to pursue them, are often live questions for quantum gravity researchers. Their work holds interest for the methodologist and the metaphysician alike.

See also Atomism; Philosophy of Physics; Quantum Mechanics; Relativity Theory.

Bibliography

Callendar, Craig, and Nicholas Huggett, eds. *Physics Meets Philosophy at the Planck Scale: Contemporary Theories in Quantum Gravity*. Cambridge, U.K.: Cambridge University Press: 2001.

Greene, Brian. *The Elegant Universe*. New York: Vintage, 2000.

Polchinski, Joseph. *String Theory*. Cambridge, U.K.: Cambridge University Press, 1999.

Rovelli, Carlo. "Quantum Spacetime: What Do We Know?" Cornell University on-line arXiv, 1999. Available from http://lanl.arxiv.org/PS_cache/gr-qc/pdf/9903/9903045.pdf.

Rovelli, Carlo. "Strings, Loops and Others: A Critical Survey of the Present Approaches to Quantum Gravity." Cornell University on-line arXiv, 1998. Available from http://lanl.arxiv.org/PS_cache/gr-qc/pdf/9803/9803024.pdf.

Smolin, Lee. *Three Roads to Quantum Gravity*. New York: Basic Books, 2001.

Stachel, John. "Early History of Quantum Gravity." In *Black Holes, Gravitational Radiation and the Universe*, edited by B. R. Iyer and B. Bhawal. Dordrecht, Netherlands: Kluwer, 1999.

Wald, Robert M. *Quantum Theory in Curved Spacetime and Black Hole Thermodynamics*. Chicago: University of Chicago Press, 1994.

Laura Ruetsche (2005)

STRUCTURALISM, MATHEMATICAL

Structuralism is a view about the subject matter of mathematics according to which what matters are structural relationships in abstraction from the intrinsic nature of the related objects. Mathematics is seen as the free exploration of structural possibilities, primarily through creative concept formation, postulation, and deduction. The items making up any particular system exemplifying the structure in question are of no importance; all that matters is that they satisfy certain general conditions—typically spelled out in axioms defining the structure or structures of interest—characteristic of the branch of mathematics in question. Thus, in the basic case of arithmetic, the famous "axioms" of Richard Dedekind (taken over by Giuseppe Peano, as he acknowledged) were conditions in a definition of a "simply infinite system," with an initial item, each item having a unique next one, no two with the same next one, and all items finitely many steps from the initial one. (The latter condition is guaranteed by the axiom of *mathematical induction*.) All such systems are structurally identical, and, in a sense to be made more precise, *the shared structure* is what mathematics investigates. (In other cases, multiple structures are allowed, as in abstract algebra with its many groups, rings, fields, and so forth.) This structuralist view of arithmetic thus contrasts with the absolutist view, associated with Gottlob Frege and Bertrand Russell, that natural numbers must in fact be certain definite objects, namely classes of equinumerous concepts or classes.

Historically, structuralism can be traced to nineteenth-century developments, including the rise of the axiomatic method and of non-Euclidean geometries leading to the recognition of multiple abstract spaces independent of *physical* space and of spatial intuition. David Hilbert, whose work in the foundations of geometry (1959 [1899]) was especially influential in this regard, remarked that "points, lines, and planes" could be read as "tables, chairs, and beer mugs" (suitably interrelated; Shapiro, p. 157). In instructive correspondence with Frege, Hilbert championed the structuralist view of axioms in pure mathematics as defining structures of interest rather than as assertions whose terms must already be understood. In the twentieth century, the development of modern algebra and set theory informed the influential views of the Bourbaki, who explicitly espoused a set-theoretic version of structuralism. Virtually any mathematical structure (or "space," e.g. metric, topological, and so forth) can be conceived or modeled as a set of objects with certain distinguished relations and/or operations on the set, and set theory has the resources for describing a wealth of interrelationships among structures, vital to advanced mathematics. The branch of logic known as *model theory* develops these ideas systematically.

Despite the success of set-theoretic structuralism in providing a unified framework for all major branches of mathematics, as an articulation of structuralism, it confronts certain problems. Notable among these is that it makes a major exception in its own case: despite the multiplicity of set theories (differing over axioms such as well-foundedness, choice, large cardinals, constructibility, and others), the axioms are standardly read as assertions of truths about "the real world of sets" rather than receiving a structuralist treatment. Questions then arise about this "fixed universe as background": How does one know about this real-world structure, how rich it is at its various levels, and how far its levels extend? The (putative) set-theoretic universe cannot be a set; yet as a totality of a different order, is it not indefinitely extendable, contrary to its purported universality? These and related questions have led some philosophers, logicians, and mathematicians to develop alternative ways of articulating structuralism.

ALTERNATIVE ARTICULATIONS TO STRUCTURALISM

The main alternatives to set-theoretic structuralism to be described here are, first, the view of structures as *patterns* or *sui generis universals*, developed by Michael Resnik and Stewart Shapiro, respectively; second, an eliminative, nominalistic *modal structuralism*, traceable in part to Russell and Hilary Putnam and developed by Geoffrey Hellman; and, finally, a version based on *category theory*, as a universal framework for mathematics independent of set theory, suggested by Saunders Mac Lane and others.

THE VIEW OF STRUCTURES AS PATTERNS OR UNIVERSALS. On the view of structures as patterns or universals, apparent reference to special objects in mathematics is taken at face value. Moreover, the reason that such objects are typically identified only by reference to operations and relations within a structure is that in fact they are *inherently incomplete*. They are to be thought of as *positions* or *places* in a pattern, on analogy with, say, the vertices of a triangle. For Resnik, identity and difference among positions make sense only in the context of a structure given by a theory. The number 2, say, is identified as the successor of 1, the predecessor of 3, and so on, but not intrinsically. Indeed, whether the natural number 2 = the real number 2 is indeterminate, except relative to a subsuming structure specified by a broader theory; and then it would still be indeterminate whether the numbers of the new theory were the same as or different from the respective old ones. This theory-relativity of reference and identity—besides leading to complications in the account of the common mathematical practice of embedding structures of a prior theory in those of a later one, as well as in the account of applications of mathematics—reflects Resnik's reluctance to think of patterns as an ontological foundation for mathematics. Talk of patterns may be only analogical, helping free one from the grip of traditional Platonism. Thus, a mathematical theory of structures is not given, in part because *its* objects could not then be identified with those of existing mathematical theories, defeating its purpose.

In contrast, Shapiro takes ontology seriously and develops an axiom system governing the existence of *ante rem* structures, abstract archetypes with places as objects, answering to that which particular realizations have in common. The background logic is second-order and the axioms resemble those of Zermelo-Fraenkel set theory but with an added *Coherence Postulate* guaranteeing an existing structure modeling any *coherent* second-order axiom system, where this new primitive is understood as analogous to the logical notion of *satisfiability*. Knowledge of key instances of this postulate arises naturally, it is argued, from their learning how to use mathematical language together with certain axioms characterizing the structure of interest (e.g. the principle of continuity of the real number system).

Although this view circumvents some of the objections raised against the set-theoretic version, it confronts a number of objections of its own. One (due to Jukka Keränen and John Burgess) points out that, whereas objects in a structure should be distinguishable entirely in terms of internal structural relationships, this is possible only in cases admitting no nontrivial automorphisms (1-1 structure preserving maps from the class of places to itself other than the identity map). The natural numbers and the reals are "rigid" in this sense, but many nonrigid structures arise in mathematics (e.g. the complex numbers, permuting *i* and –*i*, or homogeneous Euclidean spaces under isometries, and so forth). A further objection finds a circularity in the account of abstraction offered; the relevant structural relations can only be distinguished from others generated, say, from permutations of objects if those objects (the places) can be picked out independently, contrary to the idea of "structural objects." (This revives a well-known argument of Paul Benacerraf against numbers as objects generally.) Finally, although not committed to any maximal universe of sets, *ante rem* structuralism seems committed to a universe of all places in structures, contrary to the view that any such totality should be extendable.

MODAL-STRUCTURALISM. Turning to modal-structuralism, this view dispenses with special structural objects and indeed even with structures as objects, recognizing instead the possibility that enough objects—of whatever sort one likes—could be interrelated in the right ways as demanded by axioms or conditions appropriate to the mathematical investigation at hand. As suggested by Russell, the irrelevance of any intrinsic features of "mathematical objects" arises through *generalization*: statements "about numbers," for instance, are not about special objects but about whatever objects there might be, collectively standing in the right sort of ordering. By speaking of wholes and parts and utilizing a logic of plurals—reasoning about many things at once without having to talk of sets or classes of them—such generalizations, even over functions and relations, can be framed in nominalistic terms. The effect is to generalize over "structures there might be" without actually introducing structures as entities. Extendability is respected, as it makes no sense to collect "all structures, or items thereof, that there might be." Assuming the logical possibility of countably infinitely many objects, one can recover full classical analysis and, with coding devices, modern functional analysis and more. The main price paid for all of this is the adoption of a primitive notion of *possibility*, something set theory *explains* in terms of the existence of models. The gain is a circumvention of problems of reference to *abstracta* and a natural way of respecting indefinite extendability of mathematical domains.

CATEGORY-THEORETIC STRUCTURALISM. The final approach considered here is based on category theory. Having arisen in mathematics proper to help solve problems in algebraic topology and geometry, it can also serve as a general framework for mathematics. Its basic concepts are *mappings* (*morphisms* or *arrows*) between *objects*, and their *compositions*. The objects are typically what the other approaches call structures, described in relation to other such objects via morphisms ("arrows only"), not internally via set membership. Morphisms typically preserve relevant structure (algebraic, topological, differentiable, and so forth). *Toposes* are families of objects and morphisms with richness comparable to models of Zermelo set theory; they can serve as universes of discourse for mathematics. Generalizations of set-theoretic ideas are provided (such as Cartesian product, function classes, and logical operations, which generally obey intuitionistic laws, i.e. excluding the "law of excluded middle," *p* or not *p*, for arbitrary *p*). In contrast to set theory with its fixed universe, topos theory promotes a pluralistic conception of "many worlds," functionally interrelated (cf. Bell).

It is clear that there are some interesting similarities between category-theoretic structuralism and modal-structuralism, and indeed the latter can be adapted to accommodate the former. Whether category-theoretic structuralism can stand on its own, however, is an open question that turns on such issues as whether its basic concepts are really intelligible without set theory, just what its background logic presupposes, and whether a theory of category of categories can serve as an autonomous framework.

In sum, structuralism has become a major arena for exploring central questions of ontology and epistemology of mathematics.

See also Mathematics, Foundations of; Nominalism, Modern; Realism and Naturalism, Mathematical.

Bibliography

Awodey, S. "Structure in Mathematics and Logic: A Categorical Perspective." *Philosophia Mathematica* 3 (4) (1996): 209–237.

Bell, J. L. "From Absolute to Local Mathematics." *Synthese* 69 (1986): 409–426.

Benacerraf, Paul. "What Numbers Could Not Be." In *Philosophy of Mathematics*, 2nd edition, edited by P. Benacerraf and H. Putnam, 272–294. Cambridge, U.K.: Cambridge University Press, 1983.

Burgess, John P. Review of *Philosophy of Mathematics: Structure and Ontology*, by Stewart Shapiro. *Notre Dame J. Formal Logic* 40 (2) (1999): 283–291.

Dedekind, Richard. *Was sind und was sollen die Zahlen?* Brunswick, Germany: Friedrich Vieweg and Sons, 1888. Translated as *The Nature and Meaning of Numbers*. In *Essays on the Theory of Numbers*, edited by W. W. Beman, 31–115 (New York: Dover, 1963).

Frege, Gottlob. *Wissenschaftlicher Briefwechsel*. Edited by G. Gabriel, H. Hermes, F. Kambartel, and C. Thiel. Hamburg, Germany: Felix Meiner, 1976. Translated as *Philosophical and Mathematical Correspondence* (Oxford: Blackwell, 1980).

Hellman, Geoffrey. "Structuralism." In *The Oxford Handbook of Philosophy of Mathematics and Logic*. Edited by Stewart Shapiro, 536-562. Oxford: Oxford University Press, 2005.

Hilbert, David. *Grundlagen der Geometrie*. Leipzig: Teubner, 1899. Translated by E. Townsend as *Foundations of Geometry* (La Salle, IL: Open Court, 1959).

Keränen, Jukka. "The Identity Problem for Realist Structuralism." *Philosophia Mathematica* 3 (9) (2001): 308–330.

MacBride, Fraser. "Structuralism Reconsidered." In *The Oxford Handbook of Philosophy of Mathematics and Logic*. Edited by Stewart Shapiro, 563-589. Oxford: Oxford University Press, 2005.

Mac Lane, Saunders. *Mathematics: Form and Function*. New York: Springer, 1986.

Putnam, Hilary. "Mathematics without Foundations." In *Philosophy of Mathematics*. 2nd edition. Edited by P. Benacerraf and H. Putnam, 295–311. Cambridge, U.K.: Cambridge University Press, 1983.

Resnik, Michael D. *Mathematics as a Science of Patterns*. Oxford: Oxford University Press, 1997.

Russell, Bertrand. *Introduction to Mathematical Philosophy*. New York: Dover, 1993. First published 1919.

Shapiro, Stewart. *Philosophy of Mathematics: Structure and Ontology*. New York: Oxford University Press, 1997.

Geoffrey Hellman (2005)

STRUCTURALISM AND POSTSTRUCTURALISM

Structuralism emerged as a dominant intellectual paradigm in France in the late 1950s in part in response to the existentialist emphasis on subjectivity and individual autonomy—personified in the work and person of Jean-Paul Sartre—and in part as a reflection of the rising influence of research in the human sciences. In fact, structuralism has its origins in the work of the Swiss linguist Ferdinand de Saussure (1857–1913), whose 1906–1911 lectures at the University of Geneva, published on the basis of student notes in 1916 as the *Cours de linguistique générale*, provide structuralism's basic methodological insights and terminology. While Saussure's *Cours* makes frequent reference to a science that will study language as a system, it was the Russian-born linguist Roman Jakobson (1896–1982) who first used the term *structuralism* in 1929, and it was Jakobson who introduced the basic principles of Saussurean linguistics to both the anthropologist Claude Lévi-Strauss (1908–) and the psychoanalyst Jacques Lacan. Lévi-Strauss and Lacan, along with the philosopher Louis Althusser (1918–1990) and the literary theorist Roland Barthes, together are viewed as the dominant figures in French structuralism whose work in the 1950s and 1960s revolutionized how one thought about the human sciences, psychoanalysis, literature, and Marxism.

What unites these structuralist theorists is less a shared set of philosophical theses than a shared set of methodological assumptions and a willingness to work with the concepts of Saussurean linguistics. Drawing on the four binary oppositions central to Saussurean linguistics—signifier (*signifiant*) and signified (*signifié*), langue and parole, synchronic and diachronic, and infrastructure and superstructure—and privileging in their analyses the former term in each binary pair, the structuralists were able to develop theories that diminished the role of the individual subject or agent while highlighting the underlying relations that govern social and psychic practices.

Saussure defined the linguistic sign as the unity of a sound-image (signifier) and a concept (signified). The signifier is that aspect of a sign that can become perceptible, the psychological imprint of the word-sound or the impression it makes on one's senses, while the signified is a set of psychological associations, the mental picture or description associated with a signifier. In general, then, the signifier is the material (auditory or visual) component of a sign, while the signified is the mental concept associated with that sign. By langue, Saussure meant the set of interpersonal rules and norms that speakers of a language must obey if they are to communicate; langue is the theoretical system or structure of a language like English, French, or Italian. By contrast, parole is the actual manifestation of the system in speech and writing, the speech act, language as used. The distinction between langue and parole is the distinction between structure and event, between a collective product passively assimilated by the individual and the individual act.

By synchronic Saussure named the structural properties of a system at a particular historical moment, while the diachronic referred to the historical dimension of a language, the historical evolution of its elements through various stages. Finally, infrastructure refers to the set of underlying relations that explain the superstructure or surface structure that is open to observation and description. For Saussure, langue functions as the infrastructure to parole as superstructure, while, oversimplifying greatly, on Althusser's reading of Marx, the relations of means and modes of material production are the infrastructure, while ideology (family, religion, law, social organizations, etc.) is the resultant superstructure, or on Lacan's reconstruction of Sigmund Freud, the dynamic relations among the id, ego, and superego play themselves out at the infrastructural level, while the observable superstructural effects are displayed through behavior.

Their social scientific emphasis on structures also led the structuralists to downplay the role of consciousness, which figured so prominently in existentialism and phenomenology. This deflation of the importance of consciousness and subjectivity—the so-called "death of the subject"—can be seen in all the structuralists' work. Lévi-Strauss's structural analysis of myths, for example, suggests we interpret myths as parole or speech acts that are not the articulations of any particular conscious subject but are instead expressions and variations of a few basic structural relations that form a culture's langue, the set of interpersonal rules and norms that operate unconsciously and that actors in a culture must obey if they are to function. So, in *The Raw and the Crooked* (*Le cru et le cuit*) (1964), Lévi-Strauss analyzes 187 separate myths, showing them all to be variations, transformations, reversals, inversions, and so on of a deep structural opposition between the raw and the cooked, which is itself at the superstructural level of myth the expression of the underlying infrastructural opposition of nature and culture.

This methodological privileging of structure—the underlying rules or general laws—over event—the act of articulating the myth—leads structuralism to place emphasis on synchronic relations rather than on diachronic developments. The structuralists are thus concerned with studying particular systems or structures under somewhat artificial and ahistorical conditions in the hope of explaining their present functioning, as we see in Althusser's concentration on the various ideological state apparatuses at work at a given time in a society rather than the historical evolution of these various cultural formations, or in Barthes's emphasis on writing (*écriture*) as a function that exceeds the author's desire to express or communicate (which Barthes associates with style).

Poststructuralism is the name bestowed in the English-speaking philosophical and literary communities on the ideas of several French philosophers whose work arose as a distinctly philosophical response to the privileging of the human sciences that characterized structuralism. Under the name *poststructuralism* are brought together a number of theorists and theoretical positions that, in France, are often positioned far apart. The name is, however, preferable to either *deconstructionism* or *postmodernism*, which are frequently taken to be synonymous with *poststructuralism* as a rubric under which are grouped together the work of Jacques Derrida, Michel Foucault, Gilles Deleuze, and Jean-François Lyotard, as well as Luce Irigaray, Julia Kristeva, and Hélène Cixous. By contrast, in France only Derrida would be associated with deconstruction, and only Lyotard with postmodernism and, contrary to their English-speaking reception, each of these philosophers is considered to have a distinct project that results only rarely in any two of them being treated together by interpreters sympathetic to their work.

One can locate the emergence of poststructuralism in Paris in the late 1960s: Foucault published *Les mots et les choses: Une archéologie des sciences humaines* in 1966; Derrida published *De la grammatologie*, *L'écriture et la différence* and *La voix et le phénomène* in 1967; and Deleuze published *Différence et répétition* in 1968 and *Logique du sens* in 1969.

While not wanting to overlook the important differences between these thinkers, there are nevertheless certain themes and trends that do emerge in various ways in the work of many of the French philosophers and theorists who follow structuralism. In some cases these should be seen as correctives to the excesses of structuralism, in other cases as various ways in which thinkers coming into prominence in the late 1960s and early 1970s were to give expression to the Nietzschean-Freudian-Marxian spirit of the times, and in still other cases as a way of retrieving themes from some of the French traditions that had fallen out of favor during the scientistic orientation of the 1950s and early 1960s—the return of certain ethical, spiritual, and religious themes, along with some positions associated with phenomenology and existentialism. What cannot be denied, and should not be underestimated, is that the hegemony of structuralist social scientific thinking in the late 1950s and early 1960s was followed by the reemergence of the value of specifically philosophical thinking.

One way to understand their specifically philosophical orientation is to note that while the poststructuralists, like their structuralist predecessors, drew heavily on the ideas of Marx and Freud, unlike the structuralists, they drew at least as much from the third so-called master of suspicion—Friedrich Nietzsche. Nietzsche's critique of truth, his emphasis on interpretation and differential relations of power, and his attention to questions of style in philosophical discourse became central motifs within the work of the poststructuralists as they turned their attention away from the human sciences and toward a philosophical-critical analysis of writing and textuality (Derrida); relations of power, discourse, and the construction of the subject (Foucault); desire and language (Deleuze); questions of aesthetic and political judgment (Lyotard); and questions of sexual difference and gender construction (Irigaray, Kristeva, and Cixous).

And so, while the structuralist theorists had turned away from philosophy, theorists following structuralism readily identify themselves as philosophers. This is not surprising when one remembers that most of the poststructuralist philosophers "came of age" in an intellectual environment dominated by Sartre's existentialism and they all studied and were profoundly influenced by Maurice Merleau-Ponty's thinking on language and corporeality as well as Martin Heidegger's critique of the history of metaphysics. But unlike most philosophical thinkers in France who preceded the rise of structuralism, French philosophers after structuralism engage in philosophical reflection and analysis while taking account of the institutional and structural forces that inform philosophical thinking itself.

Although it is impossible to locate any set of themes that unite all the poststructuralist philosophers, it would not be inaccurate to note certain motifs that appear frequently in their works: an attention to questions of language, power, and desire that emphasizes the context in which meaning is produced and makes problematic all universal truth and meaning claims; a suspicion toward binary, oppositional thinking, often opting to affirm that which occupies a position of subordination within a differential network; a suspicion toward the figure of the humanistic human subject, challenging the assumptions of autonomy and transparent self-consciousness while situating the subject as a complex intersection of discursive, libidinal, and social forces and practices; and a resistance to claims of universality and unity, preferring instead to acknowledge difference and fragmentation. Situating these philosophical thinkers after structuralism, then, three themes in particular can be highlighted: the return to thinking historically, the return of thinking about the subject, and the emphasis on difference.

THE RETURN TO THINKING HISTORICALLY

There are many ways in which philosophical thinking in France after structuralism can be viewed as a corrective to the overemphasis on synchrony that one finds in structuralist writing. There is no single reason behind this, nor a single form in which French philosophy after structuralism seeks to think time, temporality, or history. But where the structuralists sought to understand the extratemporal functioning of systems (whether social, psychic, economic, or literary), thinkers like Foucault, Derrida, Deleuze, or Lyotard attend to the historical unfolding of the phenomena they choose to examine. In part, the attention to time, temporality, and history can be viewed as a consequence of the intellectual resources to which these thinkers appeal, resources that were not necessarily central to the work of their structuralist predecessors. Foucault, for example, draws on the study of the history of science and scientific change in the work of Georges Canguilhem (1904–1995) and Gaston Bachelard, while Deleuze returns to Henri Bergson's theories of time and *durée* (duration) as well as Nietzsche's eternal return. For Derrida, it is primarily Heidegger's focus on Being and the history of philosophy as a history of the forgetting of the ontological difference (the difference between Being and beings) that leads him to think in terms of the history of metaphysics as a history of logocentrism and ontotheology.

THE RETURN OF THINKING ABOUT THE SUBJECT

Where the rhetoric of the "death of the subject" was characteristic of the structuralists, this was never really the case with most of the philosophers labeled *post*structuralist. To be sure, thinkers like Derrida, Foucault, or Deleuze were never comfortable with the subject-centered thinking of the existentialists or phenomenologists. But they were equally uncomfortable with the straightforwardly antihumanist rhetoric of structuralist thinkers like Althusser or Lévi-Strauss. Thus, Derrida could reply to a question concerning the "death of the subject" that the subject is "absolutely indispensable" and that he does not destroy the subject but situates it in terms of "where it comes from and how it functions."

Even Foucault, who can arguably be associated with the rhetoric of the "death of the subject" in his works of the early 1960s, can at the same time be shown to have been thinking about the question of the construction of the modern subject throughout his oeuvre. That is to say, a distinction can and should be drawn between the "end of man" and the "death of the subject." It may be the case that Foucault's early work engages in thinking the end of man, as we can see, for example, in the closing pages of *The Order of Things* (*Les mots et les choses*). But it would be a mistake to equate the referent of "man" in these early contexts with what Foucault means by "subject." There is no question that the subject named "man" in philosophical discourse, from René Descartes's *cogito* to Immanuel Kant's autonomous rational moral agent, is a concept toward which Foucault has little sympathy. But even in a supposedly antihumanist work like the essay "What Is an Author?" (1969) Foucault's desire to deflate the subject as epistemically and discursively privileged is not conjoined with an attempt to eliminate the subject entirely. Instead, Foucault seeks to analyze the subject as a variable and complex function of discourse and power, which, he writes, means to ask not "How can a free subject penetrate the substance of things and give it meaning?" but "How, under what conditions and in what forms, can something like a subject appear in the order of discourse? What place can it occupy in each type of discourse, what functions can it assume, and by obeying what rules?"

What this means, and what has been largely misunderstood by many of Foucault's critics, is that his so-called antihumanism was not a rejection of the human *per se*; it was instead an assault on the philosophically modern idea that sought to remove man from the natural world and place him in a position of epistemic, metaphysical, and moral privilege that earlier thought had set aside for God. Foucault's work is less an antihumanism than an attempt to think humanism and the subject after the end of (modern) man. Far from being a thinker of the "death of the subject," Foucault simply refuses to accept the subject as given, as the foundation for ethical or rational thinking. The subject is, instead, something that has been historically created and Foucault's work, in its entirety, is engaged in analyzing the various ways that human beings are transformed into subjects, whether subjects of knowledge, of power, of sexuality, or of ethics.

For feminist thinkers writing after structuralism, the question of the subject was also central to their work as they sought to challenge both philosophical and psychoanalytic assumptions concerning the subject as sexed or gendered male or masculine. The feminists don't object to the subject simply being sexed or gendered; it is the subject's being sexed/gendered male that is the object of their criticisms. Although there are important differences between the theoretical positions of Cixous, Irigaray, or Kristeva, insofar as these "difference feminists" argue for sexual difference and the significant and important differences between male and female desire, they had to argue that there were important differences between male and female subjects. And to make this argument required that they refuse to follow the structuralist project of entirely eliminating the subject.

So, for example, while Irigaray acknowledges that insofar as the logic of subjectivity has relegated women to the position of object, one should not give up the possibility of occupying the position of the subject insofar as this is a position that women have heretofore never been able to occupy. In fact, she suggests that insofar as the circulation of women as objects of social-sexual exchange has been foundational to the Western patriarchal social order, one should not underestimate the possibilities for radical social transformation if women were to finally emerge as "speaking subjects."

The "speaking subject" is also a central focus of Kristeva's work, as she defines her project of analytical semiology or semanalysis, in part, as one of reinserting subjectivity into matters of language and meaning. Such a subject would not, of course, be a Cartesian or Husserlian subject, who could function as a pure source of meaning. Rather, following the discoveries of Freud, Lacan, and structural linguistics (Saussure and Émile Benveniste [1902–1976]), the "speaking subject" will always be a "split subject," split between conscious motivations and the unconscious, between structure and event, and between the subject of the utterance (*sujet d'énonciation*) and the subject of the statement (*sujet d'énoncé*). Elsewhere, in *Revolution and Poetic Language* (*La révolution du langage poétique: L'avant-garde à la fin du XIXe siècle, Lautréamont et Mallarmé*) (1974), this subject is developed as a subject-in-process/on-trial (*sujet-en-procès*), a dynamic subject at the intersection of the semiotic and the symbolic, making itself and being made, but a subject nonetheless.

THE EMPHASIS ON DIFFERENCE

One of the essential themes of Saussure's linguistics was that "in language there are only differences *without positive terms*" (Saussure 1959). By this, he meant that language functions as a system of interdependent units in which the value of each constituent unit results solely from the simultaneous presence of other units and the ways each unit differs from the others. This attention to difference led the structuralists to emphasize in their analyses relations rather than things and to focus on the differential relations between the objects they studied rather than the objects themselves. While the structuralists all took note of this theme, the emphasis on difference did not become truly dominant until after the hegemony of the structuralist paradigm began to wane. It has already been noted that sexual difference is a theme that almost all the feminist thinkers after structuralism have addressed. Indeed, Irigaray goes so far as to suggest that, if Heidegger is right in thinking that each epoch has but a single issue to think through, then "sexual difference is … the issue of our age" (Irigary 1993, p. 5). Similarly, Cixous sees the rigid conceptualization of sexual difference as what supports the identification of the male/masculine with the Same, while the female/feminine is rendered Other. For Cixous, the way out of this patriarchal system is not through the elimination of difference but through escaping the dominant logic of difference as hierarchal opposition to a new logic of difference in which "difference would be a bunch of new differences" (Cixous and Clément 1986).

Sexual difference is only one form in which the poststructuralist attention to difference has appeared. Insofar as Derrida's philosophical project began as an attempt to deconstruct the logocentric history of metaphysics as a metaphysics of presence that invariably privileges the temporal present, his coining of the neologism *différance* sought to situate at the foundation of deconstructive analysis an attention to difference by highlighting both meanings of the French verb *différer*: to defer in terms of delay over time and to differ in terms of spatial nonidentity. Insofar as *différance* names the movement of both temporal deferring and spatial differing, it stands as the transcendental condition for the possibility of differentiation, that is, *différance* is what makes differences possible.

This attention to difference—rather than a focus on identity or the Same—is particularly central to the projects of Lyotard and Deleuze. For Deleuze, whose work often takes a form of presentation much more in the mold of traditional philosophical analysis than the other philosophers writing after structuralism, difference has been a central and constant focus of his thinking. His *Nietzsche et la philosophie* (1962), which was the first of the major French interpretations of Nietzsche to appear, appeals to the concept of difference to show how Nietzsche departs from the Hegelian tradition (where Hegel's dialectic supersedes difference, Nietzsche's philosophy affirms it), to explicate Nietzsche's will to power (as the differential element between active and reactive forces), and to interpret Nietzsche's thought of the eternal recurrence (not as the eternal return of the same but as the repetition of difference). Deleuze develops these themes much further in *Différence et répétition* as he attempts to think the concept of difference in itself while challenging the metaphysical tradition for associating difference with opposition and the negative and privileging identity and the Same as primary.

For Lyotard, whose work is more closely tied to postmodernism than the other French philosophers, what characterizes the postmodern, as he puts it in the introduction to *The Postmodern Condition* (*La condition postmoderne: Rapport sur le savoir*) (1979), is an "incredulity toward metanarratives." Rather than naming a specific epoch, the postmodern names, instead, an antifoundationalist attitude that exceeds the legitimating orthodoxy of the moment. Postmodernity, then, does not follow modernity but resides constantly at the heart of the modern, challenging those totalizing and comprehensive master narratives (like the Enlightenment narrative of the emancipation of the rational subject or the Marxist narrative of the emancipation of the working class) that serve to legitimate its practices. In place of these grand meta- and master narratives, Lyotard suggests one looks instead to less ambitious "little narratives" that refrain from totalizing claims in favor of recognizing the specificity and singularity of events. To refuse to sanction the move to a metanarrative in the ethical, political, aesthetic, and metaphysical domains commits one to a philosophy of difference in that it accepts that oppositions will not be resolved in some higher unity and concludes that multiple and discordant voices are not only inevitable but desirable.

Beyond his postmodernist polemic, reflecting on difference operates at the core of what Lyotard considered his most important work, *Le Différend* (1983), in which he attempts to account for radical and incommensurable differences in the discourses of ethics and politics, that is, those incommensurable differences that will not admit any shared standard to which one could appeal in making judgments concerning what is different. The *différend* is thus defined as "a case of conflict, between (at least) two parties, that cannot be equitably resolved for lack of a rule of judgment applicable to both arguments" (Lyotard 1988). For Lyotard, once one has given up on master narratives, one must also give up on a master narrative of justice or the good to which all parties will agree. While such a master narrative is presupposed for a democratic politics based on consensus and agreement, the political question for Lyotard is ultimately the question of how to make decisions in the case of a *différend* in which, by definition, no consensus is possible. The choice, it would seem, is either violence or a new kind of political thinking that can accommodate *différends* in a shared social space where norms work to minimize evil rather than maximize good and where evil is itself defined in terms of the continued interdiction of different possibilities.

INFLUENCE

The impact of poststructuralism on philosophy, aesthetics, literary studies, and social theory has been extensive. While Continental philosophy was, during the 1970s, dominated by issues related to phenomenology, existentialism, and the works of Edmund Husserl, Heidegger, and Sartre, in the early 2000s the scope of Continental philosophy is increasingly focused on issues that originate in the works of post-1960 French thinkers. Derrida, and deconstruction, has been a major force in literary theory and criticism since the early 1970s. Since the early 1980s, Derrida has become a major influence in philosophical studies and he and Foucault have had the widest influence on English-language writers. Since 1980 other poststructuralist texts have appeared in translation and, as a consequence, we now see the impact on philosophers of Deleuze's important and innovative readings of major philosophical figures (David Hume, Benedict [Baruch] de Spinoza, Gottfried Wilhelm Leibniz, Kant, Nietzsche, and Bergson) as well as his analyses, alone and in collaboration with Félix Guattari, of psychoanalysis, cinema, art, literature, and contemporary culture; Lyotard's essays on politics, aesthetics, and art history, plus his important reflections on Kant's *Critique of Judgment* and questions of modernity and postmodernity; Irigaray's critical rereadings of Freud, the philosophical canon (Plato, Descartes, Heidegger, Nietzsche, Merleau-Ponty, and Emmanuel Levinas), and her reflections on language and sexual difference; Cixous's engendering writing and reflecting on its relations to the body, particularly the feminine body; and Kristeva's thinking on semiotics, abjection, and desire in language.

See also Art, Interpretation of; Deconstruction; Derrida, Jacques; Foucault, Michel; Literature, Philosophy of.

Bibliography

PRIMARY WORKS

Althusser, Louis. *Pour Marx*. Paris: F. Maspero, 1965. English-language translation: *For Marx*. Translated by Ben Brewster. London: Verso, 1990.

Cixous, Hélène, and Catherine Clément. *La jeune née*. Paris: Union générale d'Éditions, 1975. English-language translation: *The Newly Born Woman*. Translated by Betsy Wing. Minneapolis: University of Minnesota Press, 1986

Deleuze, Gilles. *Différence et répétition*. Paris: Presses universitaires de France, 1968. English-language translation: *Difference and Repetition*. Translated by Paul Patton. New York: Columbia University Press, 1994.

Deleuze, Gilles. *Logique du sens*. Paris: Éditions de Minuit, 1969. English-language translation: *The Logic of Sense*, edited by Constantin V. Boundas. Translated by Mark Lester with Charles Stivale. New York: Columbia University Press, 1990.

Deleuze, Gilles. *Nietzsche et la philosophie*. Paris: Presses universitaires de France, 1962. English-language translation: *Nietzsche and Philosophy*. Translated by Hugh Tomlinson. New York: Columbia University Press, 1983.

Deleuze, Gilles, and Félix Guattari. *Capitalisme et schizophrénie. 1. L'anti-Oedipe*. Paris: Éditions de Minuit, 1972. English-language translation: *Anti-Oedipus*. Translated by Robert Hurley, Mark Seem, and Helen R. Lane. New York: Viking Press, 1977.

Deleuze, Gilles, and Félix Guattari. *Capitalisme et schizophrénie. 2. Mille plateaux*. Paris: Éditions de Minuit, 1980. English-language translation: *A Thousand Plateaus: Capitalism and Schizophrenia*. Translated Brian Massumi. Minneapolis: University of Minnesota Press, 1987.

Deleuze, Gilles, and Félix Guattari. *Qu'est-ce que la philosophie?* Paris: Éditions de Minuit, 1991. English-language translation: *What Is Philosophy?* Translated by Hugh Tomlinson and Graham Burchell. New York: Columbia University Press, 1994.

Derrida, Jacques. *De la grammatologie*. Paris: Éditions de Minuit, 1967. English-language translation: *Of Grammatology*. Translated by Gayatri Chakravorty Spivak. Baltimore, MD: Johns Hopkins University Press, 1976.

Derrida, Jacques. *L'écriture et la différence*. Paris: Éditions du Seuil, 1967. English-language translation: *Writing and Difference*. Translated by Alan Bass. Chicago: University of Chicago Press, 1978.

Derrida, Jacques. *Marges de la philosophie*. Paris: Éditions de Minuit, 1972. English-language translation: *Margins of Philosophy*. Translated by Alan Bass. Chicago: University of Chicago Press, 1982.

Foucault, Michel. *The Essential Works of Michel Foucault, 1954–1988*. 3 vols., edited by Paul Rabinow. *Vol. 1: Ethics: Subjectivity and Truth*, edited by Paul Rabinow; translated by Robert Hurley (New York: New Press, 1997). *Vol. 2: Aesthetics, Method, and Epistemology*, edited by James D. Faubion; translated by Robert Hurley (New York: New Press, 1998). *Vol. 3: Power*, edited by James D. Faubion; translated by Robert Hurley (New York: New Press, 2000).

Foucault, Michel. *Histoire de la sexualité. 1. La volonté de savoir*. Paris: Éditions Gallimard, 1976. English-language translation: *The History of Sexuality. Vol. One: An Introduction*. Translated by Robert Hurley. New York: Vintage Books, 1980.

Foucault, Michel. *Les mots et les choses: Une archéologie des sciences humaines*. Paris: Éditions Gallimard, 1966. English-language translation: *The Order of Things: An Archeology of the Human Sciences*. New York: Vintage Books, 1970.

Foucault, Michel. *Surveiller et punir: Naissance de la prison*. Paris: Éditions Gallimard, 1975. English-language translation: *Discipline and Punish: The Birth of the Prison*. Translated by Alan Sheridan. New York: Vintage Books, 1977.

Irigaray, Luce. *Ce sexe qui n'en est pas un*. Paris: Éditions de Minuit, 1977. English-language translation: *This Sex Which Is Not One*. Translated by Catherine Porter with Carolyn Burke. Ithaca: Cornell University Press, 1985.

Irigaray, Luce. *An Ethis of Sexual Difference.* Translated by Carolyn Burke and Gillian C. Gill. Ithaca, NY: Cornell University Press, 1993.

Irigaray, Luce. *Speculum de l'autre femme.* Paris: Éditions de Minuit, 1974. English-language translation: *Speculum of the Other Woman.* Translated by Gillian C. Gill. Ithaca: Cornell University Press, 1985.

Kristeva, Julia. *Desire in Language: A Semiotic Approach to Literature and Art*, edited by Leon S. Roudiez. Translated by Thomas Gora, Alice Jardine, and Leon S. Roudiez. New York: Columbia University Press, 1980.

Kristeva, Julia. *Pouvoirs de l'horreur: Essai sur l'abjection.* Paris: Éditions du Seuil, 1980. English-language translation: *Powers of Horror: An Essay on Abjection.* Translated by Leon S. Roudiez. New York: Columbia University Press, 1982

Kristeva, Julia. *La révolution du langage poétique: L'avant-garde à la fin du XIXe siècle, Lautréamont et Mallarmé.* Paris: Éditions du Seuil, 1974. English-language translation: *Revolution in Poetic Language.* Translated by Margaret Waller. New York: Columbia University Press, 1984.

Lacan, Jacques. *Écrits.* Paris: Éditions du Seuil, 1966. English-language translation: *Ecrits: A Selection.* Translated by Alan Sheridan. New York: W. W. Norton, 1977.

Lévi-Strauss, Claude. *Anthropologie structurale.* Paris: Plon, 1958. English-language translation: *Structural Anthropology.* Translated by Claire Jacobson and Brooke Grundfest Schoepf. New York: Basic Books, 1963.

Lévi-Strauss, Claude. *Mythologiques. 1. Le Cru et le cuit.* Paris: Plon, 1964. English-language translation: *The Raw and the Cooked.* Translated by John and Doreen Weightman. New York: Harper and Row, 1969

Lévi-Strauss, Claude. *Les structures élémentaires de la parenté.* Paris: Presses universitaires de France, 1949. English-language translation: *The Elementary Structures of Kinship.* Edited by Rodney Needham. Translated by James Harle Bell and John Richard von Sturmer. Boston: Beacon Press, 1969.

Lyotard, Jean-François. *La condition postmoderne: Rapport sur le savoir.* Paris: Éditions de Minuit, 1979. English-language translation: *The Postmodern Condition. A Report on Knowledge.* Translated by Geoff Bennington and Brian Massumi. Minneapolis: University of Minnesota Press, 1984.

Lyotard, Jean-François. *Le différend.* Paris: Éditions de Minuit, 1983. English-language translation: *The Differend: Phrases in Dispute.* Translated by Georges Van Den Abbeele. Minneapolis: University of Minnesota Press, 1988.

Lyotard, Jean-François. *Discours, figure.* Paris, 1971.

Lyotard, Jean-François. *Economie libidinale.* Paris: Éditions de Minuit, 1974. English-language translation: *Libidinal Economy.* Translated by Iain Hamilton Grant. Bloomington: Indiana University Press, 1993.

Saussure, Ferdinand de. *Cours de linguistique générale.* Paris: Payot, 1915. English-language translation: *Course in General Linguistics*, edited by Charles Bally and Albert Sechehaye with the collaboration of Albert Riedlinger. Translated by Wade Baskin. New York: Philosophical Library, 1959.

SECONDARY LITERATURE

Bennington, Geoff. *Lyotard: Writing the Event.* Manchester, 1988.

Bogue, Ronald. *Deleuze and Guattari.* New York: Routledge, 1989.

Bogue, Ronald. *Deleuze on Cinema.* New York: Routledge, 2003.

Bogue, Ronald. *Deleuze on Literature.* New York: Routledge, 2003.

Bogue, Ronald. *Deleuze on Music, Painting and the Arts.* New York: Routledge, 2003.

Caws, Peter. *Structuralism: The Art of the Intelligible.* Atlantic Highlands, NJ: Humanities Press International, 1988.

Critchley, Simon, and William Schroeder, eds. *A Companion to Continental Philosophy.* Oxford: Blackwell, 1999.

Descombes, Vincent. *Le même et l'autre: Quarante-cinq ans de philosophie française (1933–1978).* Paris: Éditions du Minuit, 1979. English-language translation: *Modern French Philosophy.* Translated by L. Scott-Fox and J. M. Harding. Cambridge, U.K.: Cambridge University Press, 1980.

Dews, Peter. *Logics of Disintegration: Post-Structuralist Thought and the Claims of Critical Theory.* London: Verso, 1987.

Dosse, Francois. *History of Structuralism. Vol. 1. The Rising Sign, 1945–1966. Vol. 2. The Sign Sets, 1967–present.* Translated by Deborah Glassman. Minneapolis: University of Minnesota Press, 1997.

Frank, Manfred. *Was ist Neostrukturalismus?* Frankfurt: Suhrkamp, 1983. English-language translation: *What Is Neostructuralism?* Translated by Sabine Wilke and Richard. Minneapolis: University of Minnesota Press, 1989.

Gutting, Gary. *French Philosophy in the Twentieth Century.* Cambridge, U.K.: Cambridge University Press, 2001.

Hardt, Michael. *Gilles Deleuze: An Apprenticeship in Philosophy.* Minneapolis: University of Minnesota Press, 1993.

Hoy, David Couzens, ed. *Foucault: A Critical Reader.* Oxford: Blackwell, 1986.

Lawlor, Leonard. *Thinking through French Philosophy: The Being of the Question.* Bloomington: Indiana University Press, 2003.

Lechte, John. *Fifty Key Contemporary Thinkers: From Structuralism to Postmodernity.* New York: Routledge, 1994.

Macksey, Richard, and Eugenio Donato. *The Structuralist Controversy: The Languages of Criticism and the Sciences of Man.* Baltimore, MD: Johns Hopkins Press, 1972.

Massumi, Brian. *A User's Guide to Capitalism and Schizophrenia. Deviations from Deleuze and Guattari.* Cambridge, MA, 1992.

Patton, Paul, ed. *Deleuze: A Critical Reader.* Oxford: Blackwell, 1996.

Readings, Bill. *Introducing Lyotard: Art and Politics.* New York: Routledge, 1991.

Schrift, Alan D. *Twentieth Century French Philosophy: Key Themes and Thinkers.* Oxford: Blackwell, 2005.

Sturrock, John, ed. *Structuralism and Since: From Lévi-Strauss to Derrida.* Oxford: Oxford University Press, 1979.

Williams, James. *Lyotard: Towards a Postmodern Philosophy.* Cambridge: Polity Press, 1998.

Alan D. Schrift (1996, 2005)

STUMPF, KARL

(1848–1936)

Karl Stumpf, the German psychologist and philosopher, was born in Wiesentheid, Bavaria. He studied law at Würzburg, but under the influence of Franz Brentano his interests turned to philosophy and psychology. In 1868 he took a degree at Göttingen, under Rudolf Hermann Lotze, with a dissertation on the relation between Plato's God and the Idea of the Good. In 1869 he entered the Catholic seminary in Würzburg, where he studied St. Thomas Aquinas and the Scholastics. A year later, having lost his faith in orthodox Christianity and having abandoned the idea of becoming a priest, he left the seminary and became docent at Göttingen, where he taught for three years. His acquaintances included the philosopher and psychologist Gustav Fechner, who used Stumpf as a subject for his experiments in aesthetics.

Stumpf's passionate fondness for music motivated his pioneering research in the psychology of sound perception. In 1873 he became professor of philosophy at Würzburg and in 1879, at Prague. His associates included Ernst Mach and Anton Marty. In 1884 he moved to Halle, where Edmund Husserl (who later dedicated his *Logische Untersuchungen* to Stumpf) became his student. Stumpf moved to Munich in 1889, but his heretical religious views made him uncongenial to some of his orthodox colleagues and to the authorities. He therefore accepted a professorship in Berlin in 1894. There he founded the Phonogram Archive, devoted to collecting recordings of primitive music, and the Psychological Institute, and for a time he directed research in Immanuel Kant and Gottfried Wilhelm Leibniz at the Academy of Sciences. Besides Husserl, his most famous student was Wolfgang Köhler, the Gestalt psychologist. William James, who praised Stumpf's *Tonpsychologie* very highly, was a friend and correspondent.

Stumpf contributed greatly to the development of psychology from a branch of philosophy into an empirical science. His own experimental work was largely concerned with acoustical phenomena, but he also wrote on other topics in psychology, such as the theory of emotions. As a philosopher, Stumpf was an empiricist who preferred John Locke and George Berkeley to the tradition of German idealism. He praised Kant for emphasizing the concepts of necessity and duty but rejected the view that the categories are a priori (by which Stumpf meant innate) and not derived from perceptions. The category of substance, or "thing," he maintained, is a concept that can be traced back to such actual experiences as that of perceiving the close interpenetration of the parts of a whole. The constituent characteristics of a sensory feeling, such as quality and intensity, form a whole rather than a mere aggregate. Experience includes the perceiving of relations; it does not consist merely of individual sensations that need to be related by the understanding.

In the realm of mental functions, all simultaneous states of consciousness and intellectual and emotional activities are perceived as a unity. The concept of a substance, whether of a physical or a psychical substance, is not that of a bundle of qualities, as with David Hume, but is a unity of qualities and relations. As for the concept of cause, Stumpf believed that both Kant and Hume were wrong; we can sometimes actually perceive a causal nexus as opposed to a mere sequence, and this experience is the origin of the category of cause. For example, when our thought processes are governed by some interest or mood, we do not first experience the interest and only subsequently its effects; rather, we are aware of the interest and its effects all at once. Thus we directly experience causality in our own internal activity. Without this we would not be conscious of reality. We transfer this awareness of causality to natural phenomena, although this projection is superfluous for scientific purposes where only lawlike sequences of events are needed.

Stumpf accepted a dualism of mind and nature but regarded the task of philosophy as the investigation of what mind and nature have in common. Philosophy is the science that studies the most general laws of the psychical and of the real. To be real means to have effects. The reality of our own mental states is the first datum. We recognize the reality of external objects as they affect us, having first acquired the idea of causality internally.

From Brentano, Stumpf took the fundamental notion of self-evidence. We experience the self-evidence of such judgments as $2 \times 2 = 4$, and this self-evidence cannot be further reduced. It is the subjective aspect of truth. Truth itself is that property of contents of consciousness whereby they compel assent. Truth is a function of that which is thought, not a function of the thinker. Stumpf explicitly rejected the positivist and pragmatist theories of truth.

Knowledge is of two sorts, a priori and a posteriori. A priori knowledge consists of deductions from self-evident propositions and from bare concepts. It ought to be expressed in hypothetical propositions, since no determination of fact is here made. Mathematical knowledge is of this type. If there are more geometries than one, all are a priori; only their applicability to objective space is an empirical question. A priori knowledge may be secured from any concept. The mere concept of three tones implies a definite order according to which a tone of one pitch must be located between the other two. The concept of a tone series contains the possibility of its continuation ad infinitum. These are propositions that we know but that neither have nor require proof. They are analytic, not only known by means of our concepts but known because they are about our concepts. A posteriori knowledge, on the other hand, is of facts and laws. Both sensory contents and mental activities or functions are experienced directly. Stumpf introduced the term *Sachverhalte* (state of affairs) into philosophy, although he claimed only to have replaced Brentano's notion of "content of judgment" with the term.

Stumpf rejected the idea of vitalism or of any sort of life force, although he did not oppose empirical psychovitalism, the view that feelings, thoughts, and volitions can be stimuli for physical nerve processes. He argued that evolution did not dispose of the problem of teleology, since life itself, whose origin from nonliving atoms is so mathematically improbable, requires an explanatory hypothesis.

Bibliography

WORKS BY STUMPF

Über den psychologischen Ursprung der Raumvorstellung. Leipzig: Hinzel, 1873.

Tonpsychologie. 2 vols. Leipzig: Hirzel, 1883 and 1890.

Leib und Seele. Leipzig: Barth, 1903.

Erscheinungen und psychische Funktionen. Berlin, 1907.

Philosophische Reden und Vorträge. Leipzig: Barth, 1910. Contains various papers on evolution, the aesthetics of tragedy, and child psychology.

Die Anfänge der Musik. Leipzig: Barth, 1911.

Empfindung und Vorstellung. Berlin, 1918.

Franz Brentano. Munich: Beck, 1919.

Spinozastudien. Berlin, 1919.

Autobiography in *Die Philosophie der Gegenwart in Selbstdarstellung,* edited by Raymund Schmidt, Vol. V, 205–265. Leipzig, 1924. Gives the best summary of his philosophical views. An English translation is available in Charles Murchison, *Psychology in Autobiography,* Vol. I, 389–441. Worcester, MA, 1930.

William James. Berlin: Pan-verlag Rolf Heise, 1927.

Erkenntnislehre. 2 vols. Leipzig: Barton, 1939–1940.

WORKS ON STUMPF

Boring, E. G. *History of Experimental Psychology.* New York and London: Century, 1929. Gives fullest account of Stumpf's psychology and his classification of experiences in relation to that of Husserl and Brentano.

Spiegelberg, Herbert. *The Phenomenological Movement.* 2 vols. The Hague: Nijhoff, 1960. Vol. I.

Titchener, E. B. *Experimental Psychology.* New York and London: Macmillan, 1905. Vol. II, 161–163. Stumpf's psychophysics.

Titchener, E. B. "Prof. Stumpf's Affective Psychology." *American Journal of Psychology* 28 (1917): 263–277. Stumpf's theory of emotions.

Arnulf Zweig (1967)

STURZO, LUIGI

(1871–1959)

Luigi Sturzo, the Italian political figure and philosopher who elaborated a systematic historical anthropology, was born in Caltagirone, Sicily. He was ordained a priest in 1894 and received a doctorate in philosophy from the Gregorian University in Rome in 1898. He taught philosophy at the seminary in Caltagirone from 1898 to 1903. Sturzo served as mayor of Caltagirone from 1905 to 1920. He founded the Italian Popular Party in 1919 and served as its political secretary from 1919 to 1923. As early as 1926, in *Italy and Fascism,* Sturzo exposed the total economic concentration of power in the ruling radical right and the method of violence by which the power elite governed. His major works were written in exile in the period from 1924 to 1946 in Paris, London, and New York and were first published in translations. In recognition of his historic role in the birth of the Italian Republic, Sturzo was named a senator for life in 1952.

In philosophy Sturzo elaborated a "dialectic of the concrete" based primarily on the thought of St. Augustine, Gottfried Wilhelm Leibniz, Giambattista Vico, and Maurice Blondel. He opposed this dialectic to both absolute idealism, which he regarded as a necessitarian monism, and scholastic realism, which he considered a spectatorlike abstractionism. At the basis of his thought is historical man projected into "the fourth dimension, that of time." Man is at one and the same time individual and social, free and conditioned, structural and in process; he is a singular history in process rather than a nature fixed in essence. Man is never pure becoming, however, but a radical tendency toward reason in action.

Organically, man is constitutionally relational in his total organic connections. Socially, he is a manifold and simultaneous projection of collective purposes that are made concrete in social structures that embody his many needs in a dynamic interplay of primary and subsidiary associations.

When collective purposes become institutionalized and each social form presses for exclusive domination, conflicts are engendered. If one form gains such domination, forces of renewal and reform are unwittingly released. Thus, driven by precarious and incomplete achievements, man advances by conquering new dimensions of experience, both personal and collective.

The most radical novelty and the most powerful solvent of conflicting interests is the concrete ingression of the divine into the total human process. This "historicization of the divine" in its empirical reality is both singular and collective and constitutes the driving force of human progress.

Although he recognized the recurrence of regression, Sturzo professed an enlightened optimism, similar to that of Pierre Teilhard de Chardin, born out of his vision of one humankind moving toward ever greater socialization through the growth of international consciousness as revealed in the rationalization of force and the repudiation of war.

Bibliography

WORKS BY STURZO

Opera Omnia. Edited under the auspices of the Istituto Luigi Sturzo. Bologna, 1953–. Of a projected 30 vols., 12 have been published.

The following works were first published in Italian in *Opera Omnia,* First Series.

La comunità internazionale e il diritto di guerra (1928). Vol. II. 1954. Translated by Barbara B. Carter as *The International Community and the Right of War.* London: Allen and Unwin, 1929.

La società: Sociologica storicista (1935). Vol. III. 1960. Translated by Barbara B. Carter as *The Inner Laws of Society.* New York: P.J. Kenedy, 1944.

Chiesa e stato: Studio sociologico-storico (1937). Vols. V–VI. 1959. Translated by Barbara B. Carter as *Church and State.* New York, 1939.

La vera vita (1943). Vol. VII. 1960. Translated by Barbara B. Carter as *The True Life.* Washington, DC: Catholic University of America Press, 1943.

Del metodo sociologico. Bergamo, Italy, 1950.

WORKS ON STURZO

De Rosa, Gabriele. *Storia del partito popolare.* Bari: Laterza, 1958.

Di Lascia, Alfred. "Sturzo." *Cross Currents* 9 (1959): 400–410.

Pollock, Robert C., ed. "Luigi Sturzo: An Anthology." *Thought.* 28 (1953): 165–202. Pollock's commentary is invaluable.

Timasheff, Nicholas S. *The Sociology of Luigi Sturzo.* Baltimore: Helicon Press, 1962.

Walsh, John, and Joan Quick. "A Sturzo Bibliography." *Thought* 28 (1953): 202–208.

Alfred Di Lascia (1967)

SUÁREZ, FRANCISCO

(1548–1617)

Francisco Suárez, the Spanish scholastic philosopher and theologian, "Doctor Eximius," was born at Granada. His father was a wealthy lawyer and Francisco was the second of eight sons, six of whom entered the religious life. In 1564 he applied for admission to the Jesuit order. Perhaps because of ill health he showed little promise at first, and he failed to pass the examinations. Suárez appealed the verdict of his examiners, but his second examinations were not much better than the first. The provincial agreed, however, to admit Suárez at a lower rank. Shortly after his admission to the order, he began his study of philosophy. He showed little promise in the next few months and considered abandoning his studies for a lesser occupation in the order. However, he was persuaded by his superior to continue his studies, and within the next few years he became an outstanding student. Completing his course in philosophy with distinction, he transferred to the theology curriculum at the University of Salamanca and soon became an outstanding theologian.

In 1571 he was appointed professor of philosophy at the Jesuit college in Segovia and shortly thereafter was ordained to the priesthood. From 1576 to 1580 he served at the University of Valladolid and was then honored with an appointment to the chair of theology at the Jesuit college in Rome. Five years later he was transferred to a similar chair at the University of Alcalá. He had now achieved considerable reputation as a theologian and in 1593 was singled out by Philip II of Spain for appointment to the chair of theology at the University of Évora in Portugal. The years at Évora saw the publication of such major works as the *Disputationes Metaphysicae* (1597); the *De Legibus ac Deo Legislatore* (1612); the *Defensor Fidei* (1613), a refutation of the *Apologia* of King James I of England; and the *Varia Opuscula Theologica* (1599), which embodied Suárez's contributions to the congruist movement. In 1616 Suárez retired from active teaching; he died the following year.

At the time of his death, Suárez's reputation as a philosopher and theologian was extraordinary, and his metaphysics dominated thought at Catholic and many Protestant universities for the next two centuries. René Descartes is said to have carried a copy of the *Disputationes* with him during his travels. The *Ontologia* of Christian Wolff owed much to Suárez, and Gottfried Wilhelm Leibniz read him avidly. Arthur Schopenhauer declared that the *Disputationes* was an "authentic compendium of the whole scholastic wisdom." After Thomas Aquinas, to whom he owed much, Suárez is generally recognized as the greatest of the Scholastics. His philosophy will be considered under two headings, the metaphysics (including epistemology) and the philosophy of law.

METAPHYSICS

The metaphysics of Suárez is basically Aristotelian and Thomistic yet also highly original. It reveals remarkable erudition and a profound knowledge of his medieval predecessors. Some of the outstanding features of Suárez's metaphysics may be shown in a brief exposition of his views on the nature of metaphysics, the theory of distinctions, the principle of individuation, the problem of universals, the knowledge of singulars, the doctrine of analogy, the existence of God, and the problem of freedom.

NATURE OF METAPHYSICS. Suárez defined metaphysics as the science of being qua being. Taken as a noun, being signifies a real essence; taken as a participle, being refers to the act of existing. A real essence is noncontradictory, and by real Suárez means that which can or actually does exist in reality. Being may also be distinguished as real being and conceptual being. Real being may be immaterial, material, substantial, or accidental. The concept of being is analogical, derived from knowledge of the various kinds of real being; it is not univocal. The metaphysician is concerned primarily with immaterial being, and metaphysics is necessary for an understanding of sacred theology.

THEORY OF DISTINCTIONS. Like his predecessors Suárez held that in God essence and existence are one. Aquinas held that in finite beings essence and existence are really distinct. Suárez, however, maintained that the distinction is solely one of reason, a mental or logical distinction, for to assert a real distinction presupposes a knowledge of existence, and this would entail an essence of existence. To the Thomist objection that the denial of real existence destroys the contingency of created beings, Suárez replied that it is unnecessary to add a real distinction to establish the contingency, for it is in the nature of created being to be contingent. The emphasis upon essence in contrast to existence led Étienne Gilson to refer to Suárez's metaphysics as "essentialistic" in contrast to the "existentialistic" metaphysics of Aquinas.

PRINCIPLE OF INDIVIDUATION. The principle of individuation is neither the *materia signata* of Aquinas nor the *haecceitas* of John Duns Scotus, although Suárez agreed with Scotus that "individuality adds to the common nature [essence] something which is mentally distinct from that nature … and which together with the nature constitutes the individual metaphysically." In composite substances both form and matter individuate, for the essence of the individual is made up of both matter and form, with form the principal determinant. Individuals may be distinguished on the basis of their matter—for example, quantity—but their individuation is determined by form and matter, not by our mode of cognition.

PROBLEM OF UNIVERSALS. Universals have no existence either in reality or in individuals. There are only individuals; universals do have a foundation in reality, however, for the mind abstracts them from the likenesses of individuals. Suárez criticizes the Ockhamists for insisting that universals are only words or mental constructs, but it is difficult to dissociate his position from theirs, for he strongly insists that there are as many essences as individuals and that each individual being is an individual essence.

KNOWLEDGE OF SINGULARS. With Scotus, Suárez maintained that the intellect has a direct knowledge of singulars. "Our intellect knows the individual material object by a proper species of it … our intellects know individual material objects without reflection." Suárez maintained that the active intellect can have this kind of knowledge, for there is nothing contradictory about such knowledge and it is in conformity with experience. Furthermore, it is the function of the active intellect to make the passive intellect as similar as possible to the representation of the phantasms. Unlike Aquinas, Suárez maintained that the passive intellect can abstract the universal and that the active intellect can know the individual material object.

DOCTRINE OF ANALOGY. Suárez rejected the Scotist doctrine of the univocity of being. Like Aquinas he accepts the analogicity of being, but he insists that there is only an analogy of attribution—not of proportionality—which possesses an element of metaphor. "Every creature is being in virtue of a relation to God, inasmuch as it participates in or in some way imitates the being of God."

EXISTENCE OF GOD. A metaphysical rather than a physical proof is needed to establish the existence of God. The major defect in the Aristotelian argument from motion is the principle that "everything which is moved is moved by another." For this principle Suárez substituted the metaphysical principle that "everything which is produced is produced by another." From this principle he argued that there must be an unproduced or uncreated being, for an infinite regress either of a series or a circle of finite beings cannot be accounted for. And even if an infinite series were accepted, such a series would depend on a cause external to it. From the conclusion that there exists an uncreated being, Suárez proceeded to demonstrate that there is only one such being. Regarding the nature of such a being, its perfection, wisdom, infinitude, and so on, he followed Aquinas.

PROBLEM OF FREEDOM. Like Luis de Molina, Suárez was convinced that the Thomist doctrine that God physically predetermines the free act of the individual nullified man's freedom. Suárez maintained that through the *scientia media* God knows from all eternity what an individual will do if his grace is extended to him, and he consequently gives sufficient grace to effect the congruent action of the individual's will with his grace.

PHILOSOPHY OF LAW

Although Aquinas's influence on Suárez is apparent, Suárez was a highly original and influential thinker in the philosophy of law. He effected the transition from the medieval to the modern conception of natural law, and his influence is particularly noticeable in the work of Hugo Grotius.

NATURE OF LAW. Suárez maintained that Aquinas's definition of law as "an ordinance of reason directed to the common good" placed an inordinate emphasis on reason or intellect. Suárez did not deny that reason has a part in the law, but he did hold that obligation is the essence of law and that obligation is essentially an act of will. He defined law as "an act of a just and right will by which a superior wills to oblige his inferior to do this or that."

ETERNAL LAW. Like Aquinas, Suárez distinguished between eternal, divine, natural, and human law. However, the treatment of each is based on Suárez's contention that law is fundamentally an act of will. Eternal law is the divine providence that extends to all creatures and from which the other laws are derived. Defined as "a free decree of the will of God, who lays down the order to be observed," it is immutable and has always existed with God. It differs from the other laws, whose origins depend upon their promulgation; the eternal law receives its promulgation only through the other laws. Man's knowledge of such a law is limited and is reflected in his acceptance of the divine law, the discovery of the natural law, and his promulgation of the human law.

DIVINE LAW. Divine law is the direct revelation of God—the Mosaic law. The power and the will of God are the source of man's obligation to obey the divine law. In contrast, the power and the obligation of the human law are directly the will of the legislator, although indirectly the will of God.

NATURAL LAW. Natural law receives considerable attention from Suárez. This law is the participation of the moral nature of man in the eternal law. The natural law is based on the light of reason, but it is the work of the divine will and not the human will; its ultimate source is God, the supreme legislator. The natural law is not identified with man's nature; it transcends his will. The precepts of the natural law are the general and primary principles—to do good and avoid evil; the more definite and specific principles—that God must be worshiped; and certain moral precepts that may be deduced from the primary principles—that usury is unjust, adultery wrong, and so on. There is no dispensation from the natural law; its precepts are immutable. Thus, the introduction of private property did not reflect a change in the natural law, for although the natural law conferred all things upon men in common, it did not positively enjoin that only this form of ownership should endure.

HUMAN LAW. Human law must be based on either the divine law or the natural law and is best exemplified in political philosophy. Following Aristotle, Suárez held that man is a social animal. He rejected the view that political society is artificial, the result of a social contract or an enlightened egoism. The state is natural, and the legislative power is derived from the community and exists for the good of the community. The ultimate source of such power is God, who bestows it as a natural property upon the community. Such power is actualized only upon the formation of a political society. The form of government is essentially a matter of choice by the people. The modernity of Suárez is revealed in his rejection of the medieval ideal of the imperial power. He accepted the sovereignty of individual rulers and was skeptical of the feasibility of a world state. In discussing the rule of tyrants, he distinguished between a legitimate ruler who behaves tyrannically and a usurping tyrant. Revolt against the latter is self-defense; it is even legitimate to resort to tyrannicide provided that the injustice is extreme and the appeal to authority impossible. In the case of the legitimate ruler, the people have a right to rebel, for they bestowed the power upon the ruler. Tyrannicide is rejected here, and the rules of a just war must be followed. Suárez maintained that war is not intrinsically evil; just and defensive wars are permissible, and considerable attention is given to the conditions for waging a just war. Suárez also rejected the extremist views of papal power over temporal rulers, but he argued for the spiritual supremacy and jurisdiction of the papacy. This implied that the papacy has an indirect power to direct secular rulers for spiritual ends.

See also Aristotelianism; Duns Scotus, John; Essence and Existence; Gilson, Étienne Henry; Leibniz, Gottfried Wilhelm; Molina, Luis de; Natural Law; Ockhamism; Peace, War, and Philosophy; Philosophy of Law, History of; Schopenhauer, Arthur; Scientia Media and Molinism; Thomas Aquinas, St.; Thomism; Universals, A Historical Survey; Wolff, Christian.

Bibliography

MODERN EDITIONS

Works mentioned in text and others are to be found in the *Opera Omnia.* 28 vols. (Paris, 1856–1878). The *Disputationes Metaphysicae* have appeared in a Latin and Spanish edition (Madrid, 1960–1964). For the philosophy of law see especially the *Selections from Three Works of Francisco Suárez, S.J.* (*De Legibus, Defensor Fidei*, and *De Triplici Virtute Theologica*). 2 vols. (Classics of International Law, No. 20, Oxford: Clarendon Press, 1944). There is an introduction by J. B. Scott.

BIBLIOGRAPHICAL WORKS

McCormick, J. J. *A Suarezian Bibliography.* Chicago, 1937.

Mugica, P. *Bibliografica suareciana.* Granada, 1948.

Scorraille, R. de. *François Suarez de la compagnie de Jésus, d'après ses lettres, ses autres écrits inédits et un grand nombre de documents nouveaux.* 2 vols. Paris: Lethielleux, 1912–1913. The most authoritative bibliographical study.

METAPHYSICAL AND EPISTEMOLOGICAL STUDIES

Alejandro, J. M. *La gnoseologica del Doctor Eximio y la accusación nominalista.* Comillas, Spain, 1948.

Breuer, A. *Der Gottesbeweiss bei Thomas und Suarez.* Fribourg, Switzerland, 1930.

Conza, E. *Der Begriff der Metaphysik bei Franz Suarez.* Leipzig, Germany, 1928.

Descoqs, P. "Thomisme et Suarezisme." *Archives de philosophie* 4 (1926): 434–544.

Dumont, P. *Liberté humaine et concours divin d'après Suarez.* Paris, 1960.

Grabmann, M. "Die Disputationes Metaphysicae des Franz Suarez." In *Mittelalterliches Geistesleben.* 3 vols., Vol. I, 525–560. Munich: Hueber, 1926–1956.

Hellin, J. *La analogía del ser y el conocimiento de Dios en Suárez.* Madrid, 1947.

Mahieu, L. *François Suarez, sa philosophie et les rapports qu'elle a avec la théologie.* Paris, 1921.

Mullaney, T. *Suárez on Human Freedom.* Baltimore: Carroll Press, 1950.

PHILOSOPHY OF LAW STUDIES

Perena Vicente, L. *Teoría de la guerra en Francisco Suárez.* 2 vols. Madrid: Consejo Superior de Investigaciones Cientificas, Instituto Francisco de Vitoria, 1954.

Recaséns Siches, L. *La filosofía del derecho en Francisco Suárez.* Madrid, 1927.

Rommen, Heinrich. *Die Staatslehre des Franz Suarez.* Munich and Gladbach: Volksvereins-Verlag, 1926.

COLLECTED ESSAYS

Estudios eclesiásticos 22 (85–86) (1948).

Gemelli, A., ed. *Scritti vari.* Milan: Vita e pensiero, 1918.

Pensamiento, special issue, 4 (1948).

John A. Mourant (1967)

SUBCONSCIOUS

See *Unconscious*

SUBJECT AND PREDICATE

The contrast between "subject and predicate" is a significant one in at least four different realms of discourse: grammar, epistemology, logic, and metaphysics. A large number of philosophical problems have to do with how the distinction on one level is related to that on some other level; whether there really are four such distinct realms and, if so, how they bear on one another are matters of controversy.

GRAMMAR

In the realm of grammar, subject and predicate are sentence parts; they are, therefore, words or groups of words, and their definition and identification is a matter of syntax. In the simplest case, where the sentence consists of just two words, such as

(1) Bats fly,

(2) Fraser swims,

the subject is the noun and the predicate is the verb. Very few sentences are so simple, but an indicative sentence with just one noun and one verb remains a good paradigm for the grammatical categories of subject and predicate because we can see in it the form of the sentence stripped down to its essentials: If either of the two words were omitted, we would no longer have an indicative sentence. Furthermore, very many sentences of English, as well as of other familiar European languages, break neatly and obviously into two parts corresponding to the noun and the verb in the paradigm, and modern linguistic analysis of sentence syntax generally begins by viewing a sentence as a noun phrase plus a verb phrase:

$$S \rightarrow NP + VP$$

Although subject-predicate sentences are very common in English and in other languages, this form of sentence is not the only one, other forms being exemplified in English by normal idiomatic expressions for commands, requests, salutations, and so on. These other forms of sentence, however, have traditionally been assimilated to the subject-predicate form through the assumption of an "unexpressed subject" or some other missing element. It once seemed reasonable to try to save appearances in this way because subject and predicate seemed to be universal grammatical categories, found not only in the European languages but also, for example, in Sanskrit. Recent familiarity with a wider variety of languages has shown that these categories are by no means universal, and it is doubtful whether any grammatical categories or linguistic forms are universal. Some linguists have proposed that topic and comment are found universally, although subject and predicate are not. These categories, however, do not have to do just with the arrangement of words in sentences but rather with knowing what is being discussed and understanding what is said about it; hence topic and comment are not purely grammatical categories. The present situation in linguistics may therefore be summed up by saying that subject and predicate are useful grammatical concepts but do not represent universal grammatical categories.

In philosophy the grammatical distinction between subject and predicate has been prominent at least since Plato, who, in the *Sophist*, distinguished nouns and verbs as two classes of names. It is fair to say, however, that in that discussion, as well as in subsequent ones, philosophers have been interested in this grammatical distinction primarily because of the use they might make of it in treating problems of epistemology, logic, and metaphysics.

EPISTEMOLOGY

In epistemology the contrast between subject and predicate is a contrast between that part of a sentence which serves to identify or designate what is being discussed and that part which serves to describe or characterize the thing so identified. The categories of subject and predicate have more claim to universality at the level of epistemology (semantics) than at the level of grammar (syntax). It is here that the hypothesis about topic and comment, mentioned earlier, has its significance, for the fact that every language has some grammatical device or other for identifying a subject, or topic, and predicating something of it, or commenting on it, largely accounts for our remarkable ability to translate the content of any message from one language into another.

The epistemological sense of subject and predicate has much in common with the grammatical sense: Sentences (1) and (2) can be taken as paradigms for both senses, and the grammatical subject very frequently identifies the subject of discourse. Nevertheless, the two senses are not identical. They diverge, for example, in sentences with a dummy subject. In "It is raining" the expletive "it" is the grammatical subject of the sentence, but since it does not designate anything at all, it does not designate or identify what the sentence is about. Other instances are more relevant to philosophical issues and may be controversial. Consider

(3) What is not pink is not a flamingo.

(4) What is not just is not to be done.

There is no difficulty with (4), for it says something about unjust acts, and hence its grammatical and epistemological subjects coincide. But (3) seems to be about flamingos rather than about nonpink things, even though it has the same grammatical form as (4). Perhaps this is because we directly recognize and classify things as flamingos and as unjust acts, and even as pink, whereas in order to call something "not pink" one would normally first recognize it as gray or blue or some other color. If this is correct, the epistemological subject of (3) is mentioned in the grammatical predicate rather than in the grammatical subject.

Another instance of the divergence of the epistemological and grammatical senses is in relational sentences, such as

(5) Andrew was hit by Bernard.

(6) The cat is between the bird and the snake.

Sentences (5) and (6) may be taken to be about the two persons and the three animals, respectively, and what is said about their epistemological subjects is that a certain relation is true of them. Treating (5) and (6) as having multiple subjects in this manner is much more congenial than is a grammatical analysis to what Bertrand Russell, among others, said about the importance of relations.

It should be noted that what counts as the epistemological subject of a statement may be determined in part by the context in which it is made: If Bernard is the "topic" of conversation, (5) would naturally be construed as a "comment" about him, but other conversations in which (5) occurs will be focused differently. The importance of context in determining what counts as a subject differentiates the epistemological conception of subject from all the others.

Predicates as well as subjects have required special treatment in epistemology. Immanuel Kant distinguished real predicates from grammatical or logical predicates, a real predicate being one that says something about the subject—that is, one which attributes some property to the subject. Kant's contention that "exists" is not a real predicate but only a grammatical or logical one provides the basis for his refutation of the Ontological Argument. Statements of identity have also been held by Gottlob Frege, Russell, Ludwig Wittgenstein, and others not to be genuine predications—or at least not to be straightforward ones. Hence, in

(7) Tully is Cicero

the words "is Cicero" would not express an epistemological predicate, although they assuredly constitute the grammatical predicate. These are matters that are still not so clear as they might be.

Some very important topics in semantics and the philosophy of language are connected with the epistemological contrast between subject and predicate. In order to know what a person is talking about, I must know to what (or to whom) certain words in his utterances refer; the problem of how words can have such reference is an important one. In order to understand what is said about the subject under consideration, I must further know what is signified or entailed or meant by certain other words the person uses, whence arises another important problem, how words come to have sense or connotation. The distinction between two such modes of meaning, characteristic respectively of subjects and of predicates, has a long history and is still a live issue. Plato, in the *Theaetetus* and the *Sophist*, distinguished the mode of meaning of nouns from that of verbs. More recently J. S. Mill's distinction between connotation and denotation and Frege's distinction between sense and reference have taken up the same theme and made it central to the philosophy of language.

LOGIC

In formal logic there has been a distinction between subject and predicate ever since Aristotle's pioneering work in the field, but a dispute about the nature and scope of the distinction separates traditional from modern logicians. Aristotle would regard sentences (1) and (2) as both having subject-predicate form, but only (1) could serve as a paradigm for his formal logic. In traditional formal logic what is important about the subject term in the paradigm is, roughly, that it comes at the beginning of the sentence and indicates what (or who) is being discussed and that its quantity can be expressed by "some" or "all" preceding the noun. The pattern involved is

$$S \text{ is } P,$$

and since every proposition must have a topic about which something is asserted, this pattern is held to be manifested universally in categorical propositions. In modern logic, on the other hand, what is important about the subject term is that it is a proper name and stands for an individual, and so only sentence (2) can serve as a paradigm of the subject-predicate form. The pattern involved is

$$Fa$$

(where "F" stands for some attribute and "a" is a proper name); this pattern never applies to general propositions, since fully general propositions contain quantifiers, variables, and predicate terms but no proper names. According to this view general propositions pertain just to predicates and are not subject-predicate propositions at all. Russell's famous attack on "subject-predicate logic" was an attack on the view that every proposition must have a logical subject.

From a formal point of view the issue can be seen as a dispute about whether the principle of transposition (or contraposition) applies to subject-predicate propositions. In traditional logic it does, for the complement of a predicate can serve as a subject. This is not the case in modern logic, however, where only singular terms count as subjects and where transposition applies only to complex propositions compounded with the "if-then" sentence connective. There is a related divergence in the treatment of existence. Kant, a typical traditional logician in this respect, called existence a "logical" predicate, although not a "real" one; in effect, the grammatical analysis of assertions of existence into subject and predicate is carried over into logic. In modern logic, on the other hand, existence is generally represented through quantification, rather than through a predicate.

Epistemological and metaphysical considerations are involved in this dispute about how to represent subjects and predicates in formal logic. Roughly speaking, traditional logic seems to favor some sort of realistic view of universals, since terms representing universals can serve as both logical subjects and logical predicates. In the notation of modern logic, on the other hand, only singular expressions can serve as logical subjects, and this rule seems to give prominence to individuals rather than to universals. But a variety of epistemological and metaphysical views can consistently be advanced by both traditional and modern logicians, and the ascendancy of modern logic can be attributed to its greater flexibility, adaptability, and power as a calculus, rather than to epistemological and metaphysical views associated with it. It seems prudent, therefore, to keep matters of perspicuous symbolism and logical transformation separate from other considerations.

To illustrate the problems about the relation of logical structure to epistemological structure, one might consider

(8) All ravens are black.

The epistemological subject of (8) is ravens, and hence one would go about confirming the proposition by examining ravens and finding them black. If, using the rule of transposition, we derive from (8) the logically equivalent form

(9) All nonblack things are nonravens,

one is tempted to assume that the epistemological subject and predicate of (8) have been similarly transposed, so that nonblack things is the epistemological subject of (9). This assumption gives rise to the so-called paradox of confirmation, for it then appears as though we might confirm (8) and (9) by examining nonblack things and finding them not to be ravens, contrary to our normal procedure for confirming such simple generalizations. One solution is to hold that transposition does not apply to the epistemological structure of a proposition, that the epistemological structure of a proposition is therefore not always parallel to its logical structure, and that the epistemological subject of (9) is the same as that of (8)—that is, ravens. But the desire to have epistemological structure unambiguously represented in logical notation is a powerful consideration for some philosophers, and hence the matter is still controversial.

METAPHYSICS

The distinctions between subject and predicate in grammar, epistemology, and logic have given rise to a variety of metaphysical doctrines. These doctrines deserve separate consideration because although they are closely related to the distinctions already sketched and are suggested by them, none follows from them.

Plato noted that applying different predicates to a subject often entails a change in the subject, whereas applying a predicate to different subjects does not entail a change in the predicate. He took this changelessness to be a mark of reality (as well as epistemological priority), and hence his theory of Forms gives great ontological prominence to predicates (concepts, universals—i.e., that which a grammatical predicate stands for). This bold thesis opened a long and continuing dispute about the nature of universals, the problem being to determine what ontological commitments, if any, are entailed by our use of predicative expressions (in the epistemological sense).

Aristotle, in contrast to Plato, gave ontological standing to subjects as well as to predicates. Discussing substance in his *Categories*, he defined "first substances" as things satisfying two conditions: (*a*) being subjects but never predicates and (*b*) not being in or of something else (as a color or surface must be the color or surface of some other thing). He then defined "second substances" as things satisfying the second condition but not the first. First substances are individuals. Second substances are species or universals and hence incorporate an element of Plato's metaphysics (although not all universals are substances). An attractive feature of Aristotle's metaphysical treatment of subjects is that it fits his conception of subjects in epistemology and logic: What we talk about and investigate (especially in biology, Aristotle's scientific forte) are individuals and species, and his logic allows both individual names and universal terms, including species names, to occur as logical subjects. But, in spite of its merits, Aristotle's metaphysical conception of subjects is often regarded as unsatisfactory, largely because of qualms about putting individuals and species in one basket, about distinguishing predicates that stand for substances from those that do not, and about the usefulness of traditional logic.

Gottfried Wilhelm Leibniz's doctrine of monads builds on Aristotle's conception of individual substance. But Leibniz considered Aristotle's definition inadequate, and he defined a monad or individual substance as a subject that contains all its predicates—that is, as an individual from whose "notion" it is possible to deduce all that may ever be truly predicated of it. Few philosophers have thought there were any such substances. One difficulty may be that Leibniz attributed to his monads, which are epistemological subjects, the sort of identity that characteristically belongs to a predicate—namely, a definite set of entailments that define it.

Whereas Leibniz had only one kind of substance, G. W. F. Hegel allowed only one individual substance, the Absolute. The Absolute is the ultimate subject of every statement and resembles Leibniz's monads in that it contains all its predicates in the same sense as the monads are supposed to. Other philosophers have not been convinced of the existence of such a universal subject; Russell, who acknowledges Hegelian idealism to be a plausible account of the metaphysical implications of traditional logic, regards the doctrine as a reductio ad absurdum argument against a logic that analyzes every proposition as having a subject and a predicate.

Another interesting element of idealism is the concept of the concrete universal. Like the idea of a monad, this concept is an attempt to overcome the subject-predicate dualism by amalgamating features of both subjects and predicates in a single sort of entity. Whereas a monad is a subject with characteristics of a predicate (in that its identity is determined by what is logically contained in it, or entailed by it), a concrete universal is a predicate treated as a concrete individual thing.

One philosopher who accepted the subject-predicate dualism as a basis for his metaphysics was Frege. There are, he maintained, two radically different sorts of things, objects and concepts. Objects are complete, or "saturated," and stand on their own, so to speak; we have names for them and talk about them, but the name of an object can never be a grammatical or logical predicate. Concepts, or, more generally, what Frege called "functions," are incomplete, or "unsaturated"; they require an object to complete them and hence cannot stand alone, and a concept term is always a predicate, never a subject. Frege's dualistic view has been very influential with other philosophical logicians, including Russell, Wittgenstein, Rudolf Carnap, and P. T. Geach, but difficulties in Frege's formulation of it have impeded its general acceptance.

One difficulty is that even Frege wished to talk about concepts, and hence he had to suppose that each concept has a special object associated with it that serves only as an object to talk about when we mean to discuss the concept. A more serious difficulty is that the object-concept dualism does not fit with Frege's semantic distinction between sense and reference, which also arises from a consideration of subjects and predicates. One might expect that reference would be the mode of meaning characteristic of names of objects, and sense the mode of meaning characteristic of concept terms; however, both names and concept terms have both sense and reference. Frege had powerful reasons for what he said, but the final impression is that his two distinctions are distressingly unrelated; hence, the philosophers most influenced by him have differed from him. Russell, for example, vigorously rejected Frege's distinction between sense and reference (in his essay "On Denoting"), and Wittgenstein in his *Tractatus Logico-Philosophicus*, although indebted to Frege when he characterized his metaphysical objects, left no room for any other entities corresponding to Fregean functions.

Many analytic philosophers (which included Carnap, Ernest Nagel, and Max Black) hold that neither grammatical nor logical categories have metaphysical implications. P. F. Strawson, however, revived the issue among them by considering the implications and presuppositions of grammatical, logical, and epistemological subjects in his metaphysical essay *Individuals*. On balance, metaphysical skepticism must probably be considered as controversial as any of the metaphysical doctrines proposed.

See also Existence; Logic, History of; Meaning; Proper Names and Descriptions; Relations, Internal and External; Substance and Attribute; Universals, A Historical Survey.

Bibliography

For the linguistic aspects consult a standard work, such as Leonard Bloomfield, *Language* (New York: Holt, 1933), or R. A. Hall Jr., *Introductory Linguistics* (Philadelphia: Chilton, 1964). Russell's strictures against subject-predicate logic can be found in his discussions of Aristotle and Hegel in his *History of Western Philosophy* (New York: Simon and Schuster, 1945), and his *An Inquiry into Meaning and Truth* (New York: Norton, 1940) contains discussions of both logical and epistemological aspects of the question, as well as comments on Wittgenstein. Russell's paper "On Denoting" can be found in *Logic and Knowledge* (New York: Macmillan, 1956), together with other relevant papers. Frege's views are readily accessible in *Translations from the Philosophical Writings of Gottlob Frege*, edited by P. T. Geach and Max Black (Oxford: Blackwell, 1952). Wittgenstein's *Tractatus Logico-Philosophicus* has had a more profound influence with respect to semantics and logical form than any other twentieth-century work. Mill's discussion of connotation and denotation can be found in Book I of his *System of Logic*.

The chief items by Aristotle are *On Interpretation, Categories*, the opening paragraph of *Prior Analytics*, and Book Zeta of the *Metaphysics*; by Hegel, *The Phenomenology of the Mind*, especially the preface; by Leibniz, *Monadology*; by Carnap, P. A. Schilpp, ed., *The Philosophy of Rudolf Carnap* (La Salle,

IL: Open Court, 1963), the autobiographical essay and the replies; by Black, *Models and Metaphors* (Ithaca, NY: Cornell University Press, 1962); by Geach, *Reference and Generality* (Ithaca, NY: Cornell University Press, 1962).

G. E. M. Anscombe and P. T. Geach, *Three Philosophers* (Ithaca, NY: Cornell University Press, 1961), contains useful comments on the relevant views of Aristotle and Frege. One of the best more recent discussions of the influence of grammar on metaphysics is Morris Lazerowitz, "Substratum," in *Philosophical Analysis*, edited by Max Black (Ithaca, NY: Cornell University Press, 1950). For further references, see the articles cited in text and entries on the philosophers mentioned.

Newton Garver (1967)

SUBJECTIVISM IN ETHICS

See *Ethical Subjectivism*

SUBJECTIVIST EPISTEMOLOGY

A "subjectivist epistemology" is one that implies the standards of rational belief are those of the individual believer or those of the believer's community. Thus, subjectivism can come in either an individualistic form or a social form. A key negative test of subjectivism is whether an account implies that by being rational one is assured of having beliefs that are more reliable than they would be otherwise—that is, more reliable than they would be if one were not rational. Thus, reliabilist accounts of rational beliefs are paradigmatically objective. So are traditional foundationalist accounts. By contrast, if an account implies that the standards one must meet if one's beliefs are to be rational are those that one would regard as intellectually defensible were one to be ideally reflective (Foley 1987, 1993), then the account is subjective. Similarly, an account is subjective if it implies that one's beliefs are rational if they meet the standards of one's community (Rorty 1979) or the standards of the recognized experts in one's community (Stich 1985). Likewise, an account is subjective if it implies that one's beliefs are rational if they meet the standards of the human community at large, provided nothing else in the account implies that adhering to such standards will reliably produce true beliefs.

One of the considerations favoring a subjectivist epistemology is that it provides an attractive way of describing what is going on in skeptical scenarios—for example, one in which everything appears normal from my subjective point of view even though my brain has been removed from my body and placed in a vat, where it is being fed sensory experiences by a deceiving scientist. In such a scenario, almost everything I believe about my immediate surroundings would be false. Hence, I would have little knowledge about these surroundings, but what I believe about them might nonetheless be rational. Indeed, my beliefs would be as rational as my current beliefs about my surroundings. The most plausible explanation as to why this is so is that there is at least one important sense of rational belief according to which having rational beliefs is essentially a matter of meeting subjectively generated standards. Thus, by being envatted I may be deprived of the opportunity of having knowledge about my surroundings, but I am not necessarily also deprived of an opportunity of having rational beliefs.

See also Classical Foundationalism; Epistemology; Reliabilism; Social Epistemology.

Bibliography

Foley, R. *The Theory of Epistemic Rationality*. Cambridge, MA: Harvard University Press, 1987.

Foley, Richard. *Working without a Net*. New York: Oxford University Press, 1993.

Rorty, R. *Philosophy and the Mirror of Nature*. Princeton, NJ: Princeton University Press, 1979.

Stich, S. "Could Man Be an Irrational Animal?" *Synthese* 64 (1985): 115–135.

Richard Foley (1996)

SUBJECTIVITY

Subjectivity is, primarily, an aspect of consciousness. In a sense, conscious experience may be described as the way the world appears from a particular mental subject's point of view. The idea that there is a distinction between appearance and reality seems to presuppose the distinction between subjective and objective points of view.

THE TWO CONTROVERSIES

There are two principal controversies surrounding subjectivity: first, whether subjectivity, as it is manifested in consciousness, is an essential component of mentality; and second, whether subjectivity presents an obstacle to naturalistic theories of the mind.

THE FIRST CONTROVERSY. Most philosophers agree that intentionality—the ability to represent—is characteristic of mentality. However, there is strong disagreement over whether subjectivity is also necessary. Those philosophers who think it is (e.g., Searle 1992) argue that true—or what they call "original"—intentionality can only be attributed to a conscious subject. In this view, representational properties can only be ascribed to unconscious states and to unconscious machines—such as computers and robots—in a derivative sense. With respect to computers, the claim is that their internal states only have meaning to the extent that people (conscious subjects) interpret them to mean something. On their own, these states are merely meaningless formal symbols. When it comes to unconscious states—such as the unconscious beliefs and desires hypothesized in Freudian psychology—the claim is that only by virtue of their effects on one's conscious beliefs and intentions do they have content. The source of all genuine meaning resides in conscious, subjective mental activity.

The basic argument for this position is that for something to count as a representation—as meaning something—there must be a subject for whom its meaning is significant; a subject who is aware of and appreciates what it means. Otherwise, the argument goes, without a subject who understands, interprets, and makes use of the meaning, there is no basis for saying it means anything at all. In particular, given that most conditions stateable in objective terms for what a brain state or a computer state represents leave room for alternative interpretations, it is only by reference to the awareness of a conscious subject that a representation acquires determinate content.

Other philosophers reject this assimilation of intentionality and subjectivity, arguing that a theory of intentionality—one that applies equally to conscious and unconscious states—can be developed independently of a theory of subjectivity (e.g., Dretske 1981 and Fodor 1987). Some theorists see no need at all to appeal to the interpretive activity of a conscious subject to fix the content of a representational state. In this view, meaning ultimately comes down to information, a notion that may be treated in objective terms.

Others agree that some appeal to the purposes of the agent is necessary in order to ground an assignment of meaning to brain states. However, they claim that it is not necessary to invoke the subjective character of a subject's conscious states for this purpose. Rather, it suffices to show that by assigning the relevant interpretation to the subject's internal states one may provide appropriate psychological explanations of the subject's behavior and explain that subject's success in his or her interactions with the environment. What a subject's beliefs and desires are about is determined, in this view, by the nature of the subject's interactions with the environment and the role these states play in her or his internal psychological economy. These are facts clearly stateable from an objective point of view; no special appeal to the subjective experience of the agent is required.

Just how serious the first controversy is depends considerably on one's stand with respect to the second one. Suppose that one adopts the position that only creatures possessing subjective, conscious states are capable of any mentality at all. Still, if one also thinks that possession of subjective consciousness is a perfectly natural phenomenon—itself explicable in physical, or objective terms—the sting is largely removed from this position. There is now no reason to think properly programmed computers or robots couldn't possess the full range of mental states, so long as they satisfied the naturalistic conditions for conscious subjectivity.

THE SECOND CONTROVERSY. With respect to this second question—whether or not subjectivity presents a problem for a naturalistic framework—one may reason as follows. A complete inventory of the world should, if it is truly complete, capture everything there is and everything going on. It seems natural to suppose that such a complete description is in principle possible, and is in fact the ideal aim of natural science. But some argue that facts that are essentially accessible only from a particular subject's point of view cannot be included in this allegedly complete objective description (Nagel 1974, 1986). If they cannot, this would seem to undermine the idea that the natural world constitutes a coherent, lawful, and objective whole.

For example, take the fact of one's own existence. You could read through this hypothetical exhaustive description of the world, and it would include a description of a body at a particular spatio-temporal location, with particular physiological (or even nonphysical) processes going on inside it. However, what would be missing is that this is your body—this is you. No collection of facts stateable in objective terms seem to add up to this body being yours.

Or take the problem of personal identity. From a point of view outside the subject, what it is that makes one the same person across time—whether it be a matter of bodily or psychological continuity—seems to admit of borderline cases or matters of degree, or other sorts of indeterminacy. Thought experiments involving split brains, machines that take "memories" from one brain and implant them in another, and the like, reveal just how difficult it is to pin down personal identity as a determinate matter of objective fact. Yet, from the point of view of the subject, what it is to be oneself seems to be a clear-cut, all-or-nothing matter. Either one continues to exist or one doesn't. It is hard to reconcile the objective and subjective perspectives on this question.

One particularly difficult manifestation of the problem of subjectivity is how to account for the fact that there is "something it is like" to be certain objects (say a human being), or occupy certain states (say, visual experiences), but not others (say, a rock, and its states). This is also known as the problem of "qualia." From an objective point of view, there would seem to be nothing special about the neurological activity responsible for conscious experience that would explain what it's like for the subject. Two influential thought experiments starkly illustrate the problem.

Nagel (1974) presents the problem this way. Bats navigate in the dark by emitting high-pitched sounds and detecting their echos—a sensory system known as "echolocation." From an objective, third-person point of view, there is nothing especially difficult about understanding how this system works. While there are of course difficult technical questions, the idea that the bat extracts information concerning the location and movement of its target from the returning sound waves bouncing off of it is fairly clear. The problem emerges when one considers what echolocation is like for the bat, from its point of view. People know that there is something particular it is like to see a sunset, smell a rose, or feel a pain. There is every reason to believe that there is also something particular it is like to sense by echolocation. Yet, when the question is posed this way, it doesn't seem as if any of the details learned about the information-processing capabilities of the bat are helpful in answering this simple question: What is it like for the bat? It seems as if only by adopting the bat's point of view, by humans' experiencing echolocation, could one obtain a clue concerning what it is like.

Jackson (1982) asks people to consider the following situation. Imagine Mary, a neuroscientist who learns everything there is to know about the physiology and information processing involved in color vision. However, she learns this while restricted to a completely black and white environment, so that she herself never experiences color sensations. In a sense, she would be in the same position vis-à-vis everyone else that everyone else is vis-à-vis bats. At some point Mary is released from her purely black and white environment and allowed to see color. Suppose she now sees a red rose for the first time. It seems undeniable that her reaction would be one of wonder and novelty. "So that's what red looks like!" she might say. But now, if the subjective experience were adequately captured by the objective, third-person descriptions presented in her science texts, why should she experience novelty and wonder? That she would have this experience seems to demonstrate that what is apprehended from the first-person, subjective point of view is distinct from what is describable in objective, third-person terms.

Many philosophers argue that subjectivity does not present a special puzzle. For some (e.g., Searle 1992), it is just a fact that the world contains both objective facts and irreducibly subjective facts; their relation requires no explanation and produces no mystery. For most, though, the demystification of the subjective is accomplished by some sort of reductionist strategy (e.g., Lycan 1987 and 1990, and Rosenthal 1986), one that shows how to incorporate so-called subjective facts into an all-embracing, naturalistic and objective scientific framework. One influential model of subjectivity is the internal monitoring, or higher-order thought model. In this view, which fits well with a functionalist approach to the mind-body problem in general, subjectivity is principally a matter of some mental states representing other mental states. That is, to be aware of, or to apprehend from the first-person point of view, that one is having a certain experience, is merely to occupy a mental state that represents one as having that experience. If this is what subjectivity amounts to, then any model of the mind that builds in the requisite architectural features will explain subjectivity. A model of this sort of internal scanning already exists with computers.

Advocates for the view that subjectivity presents no special mystery sometimes point to the perspectival character of indexical expressions such as "I" and "here" for support. The idea is that it is generally acknowledged that the meaning of such expressions cannot be captured in nonindexical terms (Perry 1979), yet this doesn't give rise to any special philosophical problem or mystery. Because one cannot derive a statement containing an indexical expression from statements free of indexicals, one need not conclude that there are any special indexical facts that are indescribable in indexical-free terms. There are theories that take into account the special behavior of such terms consistent with a general theory that applies to nonindexical terms as well.

In the same way, goes the argument, subjective mental phenomena can be incorporated into a more general theory of the world that applies to nonsubjective phenomena as well. For instance, whereas it may be true that Mary, in the Jackson example described above, could not predict what it would be like to see red from her knowledge of the neurophysiology of color vision, this need not be taken to show that there are irreducibly subjective facts. It could be that human beings possess a distinct representational system that is employed only when information comes directly from the sensory systems (Rey 1993). It is no surprise that the same fact can be represented in distinct ways, and that being represented in distinct ways may obscure its identity from the subject.

ELIMINATING SUBJECTIVITY

Yet another approach to the problem of subjectivity is eliminativism (e.g., Churchland 1985, Dennett 1991). Proponents of this view will grant that none of the models proposed to account for subjectivity really explains it; but, they argue, that is due to the human intuitive conception of subjectivity—indeed of consciousness in general—being too confused, or incoherent, to be susceptible to scientific explanation. Subjectivity just isn't a real phenomenon, so there's nothing in the end to explain.

See also Knowledge Argument; Qualia; Self.

Bibliography

Churchland, P. "Reduction, Qualia, and the Direct Introspection of Brain States." *Journal of Philosophy* 82 (1985).

Dennett, D. C. *Consciousness Explained*. Boston: Little, Brown, 1991.

Dretske, F. *Knowledge and the Flow of Information*. Cambridge, MA: Bradford Books/The MIT Press, 1981.

Fodor, J.A. *Psychosemantics: The Problem of Meaning in the Philosophy of Mind*. Cambridge, MA: Bradford Books/The MIT Press, 1987.

Jackson, F. "Epiphenomenal Qualia." *Philosophical Quarterly* 32 (1982): 127–136.

Levin, J. "Could Love Be Like a Heatwave?: Physicalism and the Subjective Character of Experience." *Philosophical Studies* 49 (1986).

Lycan, W. G. *Consciousness*. Cambridge, MA: Bradford Books/The MIT Press, 1987.

Lycan, W. G. "What Is the 'Subjectivity' of the Mental?" *Philosophical Perspectives*. Vol. 4, edited by J. Tomberlin. Atascadero, CA: Ridgeview Publishing, 1990.

McGinn, C. *The Problem of Consciousness*. Oxford: Basil Blackwell, 1991.

McGinn, C. *The Subjective View*. New York: Oxford University Press, 1983.

Nagel, T. *The View from Nowhere*. New York: Oxford University Press, 1986.

Nagel, T. "What Is It Like to Be a Bat?" *The Philosophical Review* Vol. 82 (1974), pp. 435–450

Perry, J. "The Problem of the Essential Indexical." *Nous* 13 (1979).

Rey, G. "Sensational Sentences." In *Consciousness: Psychological and Philosophical Essays*, edited by M. Davies and G. Humphreys, 240–257. Oxford: Blackwell, 1993.

Rosenthal, D. "Two Concepts of Consciousness." *Philosophical Studies* 49 (1986): 329–359.

Searle, J. *The Rediscovery of the Mind*. Cambridge, MA: Bradford Books/The MIT Press, 1992.

van Gulick, R. "Physicalism and the Subjectivity of the Mental." *Philosophical Topics* 16 (1985).

Joseph Levine (1996, 2005)

SUBLIME, THE

This title already raises the conundrum that "the sublime" has regularly, although in different ways, posed. The substantivized form of the adjective suggests something one could point to where sublimity resides. The sublime might even be misconstrued (as it was by Edmund Burke) as a property of certain objects. But the sublime refers to no thing; it is instead an effect produced by the limits of our capacities for perception and representation. As such the sublime has played a vital role in the history of aesthetic theory as well as in postmodernist debates about representation and the limits of knowledge.

The sublime was first theorized by the pseudonymous Longinus in *On the Sublime*, written in the first century CE. Longinus conceives sublimity as a quality of elevated prose of great rhetorical power. Not until the seventeenth century does the sublime become associated with natural phenomena, and then with the incomprehensible excesses of natural force. In *A Philosophical Enquiry into the Origin of Our Ideas of the Sublime and the Beautiful* (1757), Burke provided an empiricist account of kinds of objects and situations that induce sublime perceptual experiences. Where beauty is found for Burke in things, the perception of which seems to harmonize with human sensory capacities, the sublime object of perception challenges our senses or exceeds our perceptual grasp. Burke equivocated on the implications of his empiricism, however, by conceiving sublimity as a property of these perceptually challenging objects or scenes, rather than understanding sublimity as a kind of secondary quality to be located in the relationship between perceiver and perceived.

Immanuel Kant provided in his *Critique of Judgment* (1790) the essential formulation of the sublime that has organized most subsequent discussion. Beauty, sublimity, and aesthetic qualities generally are for Kant no properties of objects; they are the felt effects of judgments that reflective perceivers make on the form and content of their experience. A judging subject finds something beautiful when its appearance or design, without or before applying conceptual rules to it, invigorates her cognitive capacities generally, and inspires an imaginative appreciation of the object. Judgments of beauty, then, reflect a harmony between feeling and cognition that is absent in the judgment of the sublime. People feel sublimity, to the contrary, in cases where their efforts to comprehend something are stymied by vastness, complexity, or by the natural might of that which threatens to overwhelm them.

These varieties of sublimity reflect Kant's germinal distinction between the mathematical and the dynamical sublime. The subject encounters mathematical sublimity when attempting to comprehend perceptually an object too vast (the starry heavens) or too grand (the great pyramids, from the correct distance) to take in all at once. The mathematical sublime exceeds one's conceptual grasp by inducing in the subject perceptual riches too extensive to subsume satisfactorily under available categories. It points up the limits of human capacity to perceive comprehensively and to represent to humans conceptually what is perceived. The frustration of this nevertheless gives rise to aesthetic pleasure for Kant, because the humbling of certain human cognitive capacities reminds people of the superiority of reason's capacity to think the infinite. For this reason, the sublime has regularly invited a theological interpretation throughout the European tradition.

The judging subject feels dynamical sublimity when threatened by the extraordinary forces of violent nature. This strain of Kant's theory of sublimity inspired the subsequent generation of Romantic poets, not to mention the later Nietzschean appreciation of Dionysian artistic impulses. Throughout the nineteenth century, the sublime is associated with excesses of natural force, tormented outpourings of emotion, and the transgression of norms of representation. Hence in the twentieth century the effects of sublime experiences were embraced by the sequence of artistic avant-garde movements that sought to induce ecstatic or liminal aesthetic responses designed to challenge conventional artistic or cultural norms. What a culture already possesses the conceptual apparatus to represent adequately cannot be sublime; the goal of the avant-garde was to allude to something that defies available means of representation.

Not surprisingly, then, the sublime was of great interest to postmodern theorists of the late twentieth century. Developments in multiple fields (the crisis of representation in anthropology, attacks on the representational theory of the mind in philosophy) encouraged postmodernists to embrace sublimity as the irrational and humiliating counterpoint to modernist categorizing zeal and its bureaucratic rationality. To embrace sublimity and to induce its manifestation in judging subjects is, as Jean-François Lyotard put it in *The Postmodern Condition* (1984), "To present the fact that the unpresentable exists" (p. 78). Rather than regard that humbled subject as the last word on the sublime, however, future theorists of this perennial notion may see the sublime, that which challenges human perceptual and conceptual reach, as a regular inducement to strive to extend that reach, rather than a reason to cease the attempt.

See also Aesthetics, History of; Beauty; Burke, Edmund; Kant, Immanuel.

Bibliography

Burke, Edmund. *A Philosophical Enquiry into the Origin of Our Ideas of the Sublime and the Beautiful*, edited by Alan Phillips. Oxford: Oxford University Press, 1990.

Kant, Immanuel. *Critique of Judgment*. Translated by Werner S. Pluhar. Indianapolis: Hackett, 1987.

Longinus. *On Great Writing (On the Sublime)*. Translated by G. M. A. Grube. Indianapolis: Hackett, 1991.

Lyotard, Jean-François. *The Postmodern Condition*. Translated by Geoff Bennington and Brian Massumi. Minneapolis: University of Minnesota Press, 1984.

Kirk E. Pillow (2005)

SUBSTANCE AND ATTRIBUTE

The concepts of "substance and attribute" are the focus of a group of philosophical problems that have their origins in Greek philosophy and in particular the philosophy of Aristotle. The concepts are, of course, familiar to prephilosophical common sense. Yet although we are acquainted with the distinction between things and their properties and are able to identify the same things among the changing appearances they manifest in time, these commonsense notions give rise to a group of philosophical problems when we come to scrutinize them. Thus we may wonder what it is that remains the same when, for example, we say that the car has new tires and lights and does not run as smoothly as it used to, but is still the same car; or when we say that although we could hardly recognize him, this man is the same one we went to school with thirty years ago.

It is interesting to note that the principal term for substance in the writings of Aristotle is *ousia,* a word that in earlier Greek writers means "property" in the legal sense of the word, that which is owned. (This sense is familiar in English in the old-fashioned expression "a man of substance.") The word *ousia* also occurs in philosophical writings before Aristotle as a synonym for the Greek word *physis,* a term that can mean either the origin of a thing, its natural constitution or structure, the stuff of which things are made, or a natural kind or species. The Latin word *substantia,* from which the English term is derived, is a literal translation of the Greek word *hypostasis* ("standing under"). This term acquired its philosophical connotations in later Greek and occurs principally in controversies among early Christian theologians about the real nature of Christ. A third philosophical term, *hypokeimenon* ("that which underlies something"), is used by both Plato and Aristotle to refer to that which presupposes something else.

There is, however, little of philosophical importance to be learned from the etymology of the terms in which problems are formulated and discussed. We shall first consider the questions to which the concepts of substance and attribute give rise in some of the philosophers for whom they have been important. We may then ask which of these questions remain as live philosophical issues at the present time and what answers can be given to these surviving questions.

ARISTOTLE

Aristotle's account of substance has been the most influential in the history of philosophy. His account is, however, obscure and probably inconsistent. The difficulties of elucidating and reconciling the various parts of his doctrine have been part of the cause of its influence—it has offered a continuing challenge to commentators and critics from Aristotle's time to the present. "Substance in the truest and primary and most definite sense of the word is that which is neither predicable of a subject nor present in a subject; for instance, the individual man or horse" (*Categories* 2A11). The explanation is obscure, but the examples cited leave no doubt of what Aristotle means here: Substance in the most basic sense of the word is the concrete individual thing. However, he goes on at once to mention a second sense of the word: "Those things are called substances within which, as species, the primary substances are included; also those which, as genera, include the species. For instance the individual man is included in the species 'man' and the genus to which the species belongs is 'animal'; these, therefore,—the species 'man' and the genus 'animal'—are termed secondary substances." These secondary substances are predicable of a subject. "For instance, 'man' is predicated of the individual man" (*Categories* 2A21–22), as when we say "Socrates is a man." Aristotle seems to have the idea here that essences or natures are substances, and the more qualities they comprise, the more substantial they really are; he explains, "Of secondary substances, the species is more truly substance than the genus, being more nearly related to primary substance" (*Categories* 2B7). For example, the species *Canis domesticus* shares more qualities in common with the individual dog Tray than does the genus *Canis.*

This notion of essences as substances is treated at length by Aristotle in the *Metaphysics* and seems to be his preferred sense of the term. The intimation that the more qualities something has, the more substantial it is, has the advantage of suggesting that being a substance is a matter of degree and not an all-or-nothing matter. This hint, which Aristotle does not develop, contains an important idea, as will be seen later. But the doctrine of secondary substances has little else to recommend it and involves a serious logical confusion between the relations of class membership and class inclusion, as well as the notorious difficulties of the doctrine of essences.

Aristotle's main purpose in the *Categories* is to contrast the independent way of existing proper to substances with the parasitic mode of being of qualities and relations. Substances can exist on their own; qualities and relations, only as the qualities of or relations between substances. The key to this distinction is given by the phrase "present in a subject." (The Greek word for "subject" here is *hypokeimenon,* literally "underlay.") Substances are never "present in a subject." This does not mean, as Aristotle explains, that a substance is never "present in" something else as a part of a whole. On the contrary, he cites heads and hands (*Categories* 8B15) as substances although they are parts of bodies. Rather, x is present in y when it is "incapable of existence apart from" y. This notion introduces a third sense of substance as that which is capable of independent existence. This sense is of considerable importance in later philosophy, but Aristotle does not develop it. He uses it chiefly to emphasize the distinction between substances on the one hand and their qualities and relations on the other. A quality—"red," "sweet," or "virtuous"—cannot exist apart from an x that has the quality. Relations such as "larger than" or "to the left of" cannot occur in the absence of the *x* and *y* that they relate.

It is true, of course, as Aristotle's critics have pointed out, that it is no more possible for a substance to exist without qualities than for qualities to exist without a substance. However, it is possible to point to prima facie examples of qualities existing without substances—the blue of the sky, for instance, or a red afterimage floating in my visual field. Surely the sky is not a substance, nor is my visual field. However, one cannot point to any instances of substances existing without qualities. Even if it makes sense to suppose that such a thing could occur, it is clearly incapable of being identified. Aristotle does not consider these problems. What he seems to have meant, although he does not express himself clearly, is that what is capable of independent existence is the concrete individual thing, a substance with its qualities and in its network of relations to other substances. But even here there is an obvious difficulty. Once we introduce the notion of relations involving other substances, we put a restriction on independent existence.

A fourth criterion of substance is that "while remaining numerically one and the same, it is capable of admitting contrary qualities" (*Categories* 4A10). This Aristotle calls "the most distinctive mark of substance." This notion is developed, more by later philosophers than by Aristotle himself, into the conception of a center of change and so of a substratum that underlies and supports its qualities. Finally, Aristotle emphasizes the notion of substance as a logical subject, "that which is not asserted of a subject, but of which everything else is asserted" (*Metaphysics* 1029A8), and he links this sense of the term with the concept of substratum. This logical criterion has been criticized as making the notion of substance dependent on the structure of Greek (and some other Indo-European languages), in which subject-predicate sentences are a standard mode of expression, and upon a restricted and now outmoded view of logic in which all statements canonically expressed are in a form in which a predicate is affirmed of a subject. It is not the case that sentences in all languages fall into a subject-predicate form or that this form of expression is adequate for a developed logic.

OTHER PHILOSOPHERS

The various notions of substance as (1) the concrete individual, (2) a core of essential properties, (3) what is capable of independent existence, (4) a center of change, (5) a substratum, and (6) a logical subject are never thoroughly worked out and reconciled in Aristotle. He appears to emphasize now one and now another mark of substance as of paramount importance. The quotations cited above have been chiefly from the *Categories*; the topic is taken up and discussed at length in the *Metaphysics*. The discussion is tentative and not finally conclusive, but Aristotle seems to favor alternative (2), substance as essence, as his preferred sense. But the whole treatment is important not for the answers that he gives but for the questions that he raises. Discussions of substance in later philosophers have tended, with few exceptions, to take over one or more of the six senses proposed by Aristotle as the clue to the problem.

ATOMISTS AND MEDIEVALS. Of the philosophical theories of antiquity, one other is of some consequence. Ancient atomism, founded by Leucippus and Democritus, developed by Epicurus, and expressed in its most attractive form in the *De Rerum Natura* of the Roman poet Lucretius, suggests that the truly real and substantial elements of nature are the atoms out of which everything is composed. It is these that are fundamental, unchangeable, and, in the last resort, capable of independent existence. The problem of substance and attribute was not much discussed by the ancient atomists, but their theories provide material for an answer to the question raised by Aristotle.

During the Middle Ages, discussion of this problem was very naturally centered upon the theological repercussions of rival theories. In particular, the doctrines of the Incarnation of Christ and of transubstantiation depended for their rational justification upon a plausible theory of substance. But these theological outworks produced no new basic insights that can be regarded as an improvement on the work of Aristotle. Indeed, they are just variations upon Aristotelian themes.

DESCARTES. The revival of philosophy in the seventeenth century in a form that was relatively independent of the religious framework of medieval philosophy produced several systems for which the notion of substance is fundamental. In the work of René Descartes the concepts of substance and attribute become associated naturally with those of the conscious self and its states, and the problem of substance becomes associated with the problem of personal identity. Descartes had been thoroughly trained in the form of Aristotelian scholasticism current in his day, and his notions of substance are in part derived from this and in part inconsistent with it. He gives a formal definition of substance as follows: "Everything in which there resides immediately, as in a subject, or by means of which there exists anything that we perceive, i.e. any property, quality, or attribute of which we have a real idea is called a *Substance*; neither do we have any other idea of substance itself, precisely taken, than that it is a thing in which this something that we perceive or which is present objectively in some of our ideas, exists formally or eminently. For by means of our natural light we know that a real attribute cannot be an attribute of nothing" (*Philosophical Works*, translated by Haldane and Ross, 2nd ed., Cambridge, U.K., 1931, Vol. II, p. 53). In other words, what we are directly aware of are attributes of things and not the things themselves. But it is a logically self-evident principle (known by "the natural light" of reason) that an attribute must be an attribute of something, and the something is a substance—known by this inference and not directly. So far Descartes does not depart from scholastic doctrine, but he goes on to affirm that substances have essential attributes. For example, thought is the essential attribute of mind, and extension is the essential attribute of matter. But he does not explain what a substance is apart from its essential property. What is the mind apart from thinking or matter apart from extension? Unless this question is answered, how can Descartes answer the later empiricist criticism that the concept of substance is meaningless because empty of content?

In another context (ibid., p. 101) he gives an alternative definition of substance. "Really the notion of *substance* is just this—that which can exist by itself, without the aid of any other substance." This second definition is a bad one, being circular in expression; but clearly Descartes has in mind both here and in the quotation above simply the Aristotelian criteria (3) and (5). On the basis of these definitions, Descartes postulates three types of substance: material bodies, minds, and God. But the first two, being in a certain sense dependent on God for their existence, clearly have a lower grade of substantiality. Descartes's conception of substance and attribute is made impossible to understand by the vagueness of the notion "attribute" by which he seeks to clarify the idea of substance. If "attribute" means "property or relation," it simply is not true that all attributes are attributes of substances. For example, a color may have properties that are not properties of the colored thing. It is true of the color *red* that it is produced by light of wavelength about 7000 angstrom units, but this is not true of red objects. In any case, it seems that Descartes has simply defined *substance* and *attribute* relative to each other so that his explanation is circular and thus uninformative: Attributes are what qualify substances and substances are what have attributes.

SPINOZA. Descartes's second account of substance as that which is capable of independent existence was taken up and developed by Benedict de Spinoza in his *Ethics*. Spinoza was a student of Descartes and may be regarded as one who developed some of Descartes's ideas to consistent but surprising conclusions. Reflecting on Descartes's second account of substance, Spinoza showed that if by *substance* we mean, according to his definition, "that which is in itself and is conceived through itself," it is easy to show that there can be only one such being, the whole universe. Thus Spinoza equated substance with God and nature, the three terms being synonymous for him. This "hideous hypothesis," in David Hume's ironical phrase, has won for Spinoza the inconsistent titles of atheist and pantheist. What he did, in fact, was to demonstrate the alarming consequences for religious orthodoxy of Descartes's second definition and to indicate obliquely that substantiality in this sense is a matter of degree. Nothing in the universe is completely independent of its environment, although some things are more independent than others. A human being has a certain degree of independence of his environment but can exist only within a certain range of temperature, pressure, and humidity, and with access to air, food, and water. Other things may be more or less independent of their surroundings, and the extent of their freedom in each case is an empirical question. Spinoza did not draw this conclusion, but it is implicit in his development of Descartes.

LEIBNIZ. Another rationalist philosopher, Gottfried Wilhelm Leibniz, makes the concept of substance fundamental to his philosophical system. He uses two of the Aristotelian criteria of substance, substance as a center of change and substance as a logical subject, but adds the concept of simplicity. The basic elements of Leibniz's metaphysical system were what he called monads. In his *Monadology* he defines *monad* as "nothing but a simple substance.... By 'simple' is meant 'without parts.'" That there are such simple substances follows, for Leibniz, from the admitted fact that there are compound things, which can be nothing but collections of simple things. Leibniz seems here to have been influenced by the arguments of the ancient materialists for the existence of atoms. His monads, however, were supposed to be immaterial substances, centers of change and thus subjects of predicates. Unfortunately, by describing his substances in this way, he deprives the term of meaning just as Descartes had done. He does indeed affirm that his monads are centers of activity, but this activity is manifested only in their tendency to move from one state to another. But if the essence of something is to be the x that undergoes changes and of which predicates can be affirmed, it can have no positive character of its own. In Bertrand Russell's words, "substance remains, apart from its predicates, wholly destitute of meaning" (*The Philosophy of Leibniz,* p. 50).

LOCKE, BERKELEY, HUME. Leibniz had criticized the British empiricist philosopher John Locke for professing to find substance an empty concept. The weakness of Locke's criticisms of the concept was that he concentrated his attack on the notion of a substratum of qualities. This is not the most important of the Aristotelian senses of the term. But if "substratum" can be shown to be an empty notion, it is easy to raise skeptical doubts about some of the associated senses, particularly those of substance as a center of change, as the concrete individual, and as a logical subject. Locke points out that we find in experience groups of qualities that occur together in time and place. We therefore presume these qualities to belong to one thing and come to use one word, "gold," "apple," or "water" (whatever it may be) to refer to the collection of properties "which indeed is a complication of many ideas together." Further, "not imagining how these simple ideas *can* subsist by themselves, we accustom ourselves to suppose some *substratum* wherein they do subsist, and from which they do result, which we therefore call *substance*" (*Essay concerning Human Understanding,* Book II, Ch. 23).

Substance, then, is not a positive concept but merely an "obscure and relative" notion of "the supposed but unknown support of those qualities we find existing, which we imagine cannot exist *sine re substante* without something to support them." Since Locke has already tried to show that all our meaningful concepts originate in experience, substance is an awkward counterexample to his theory of knowledge. Indeed, he would probably have rejected it altogether but for certain associated moral and theological doctrines that his cautious and conformist temperament made him forbear to reject outright. Moreover, he seems to have been unable to reject Descartes's principle that attributes must inhere in a substance, although he does not submit this supposed logical truth to any rigorous examination.

However, Locke's empiricist successors, George Berkeley and Hume, were fully aware of the importance of Locke's criticism and his reduction of the notion to "an uncertain supposition of we know not what." Berkeley's attack on the concept of material substance owes much to Locke, and Hume was content to write off the whole idea as an "unintelligible chimaera." Moreover, Hume extended the skepticism of Locke and Berkeley in respect of material substance to question, on analogous grounds, the existence of spiritual substances or selves. It is clear that a mind whose function is merely to be the bearer of states of consciousness is as vacuous a notion as Locke's material "we know not what."

KANT. Immanuel Kant's *Critique of Pure Reason* (1781) transformed the notion of substance, as it did so many other philosophical concepts. In Kant's view, "substance" does not refer to a feature of the objective world independent of human thinking. On the contrary, the unity and permanence of substances are features contributed by the human understanding to the world of phenomena. This represents a very radical revision of the concept of substance. Substance shrinks from being a fundamental feature of the objective world to an aspect under which men cannot help classifying their experience—and they cannot help themselves not because of the nature of external reality but because of the structure of their own cognitive apparatus.

MODERN CRITICISM

Since Kant's day the permanent and valuable features of philosophy have been those that have grown out of the immense development of the formal and natural sciences from the end of the eighteenth century to the present, a development that has shown the falsity of the scientific assumptions on which the Kantian revolution was built. For example, Kant believed that Newtonian physics, Euclidean geometry, and Aristotelian logic were finally and beyond all question true of the world, and some features of his system depend on these assumptions. This development has presented the problem of substance as a problem soluble, if at all, in the light of empirical evidence drawn from the relevant sciences. It has, moreover, made clear that there is no one problem of substance but a number of subproblems that can be treated independently.

These problems can still be stated in something like their original Aristotelian form, but we may find ourselves looking in different areas of knowledge for their answers. There is no one unitary science, such as metaphysics or ontology, that can be looked to for a solution. For example, the notion of substance as a logical subject of predicates (as when we say of a piece of gold, "*It* is heavy," "*It* is yellow," "*It* is malleable," "*It* melts at 1063° C," and so on) is now seen to be a problem of interest to formal logic and to linguistics. It is a technical question of logic whether all sentences about individual things can be (or must be) expressed in subject-predicate form. And it is a technical question of linguistics whether all languages use such a form to express these notions, or indeed have a subject-predicate syntax at all. (The answer in both cases seems to be "No.")

INDEPENDENT EXISTENTS. The question "What, if anything, is capable of independent existence?" can be seen, insofar as it relates to material things, to be a question to which physics, chemistry, and biology give us the answers. (If the question is asked about the existence of nonmaterial things such as numbers or propositions, we have first to make clear what is meant by "existence" in such contexts.) We see that *independent* is not a term with a clear meaning but, rather, is an elliptical expression. "X is capable of independent existence" means "X is capable of existing without regard to features $y_1, y_2, \cdots, y_n$ of its environment." Since these conditions are so numerous, it is easier to express the concept negatively: "X is not independent" means "X is incapable of existing apart from conditions $z_1, z_2, \cdots, z_n$" or "$z_1, \cdots, z_n$ are necessary conditions for the existence of X." On this interpretation, a substance in the sense of something that is capable of completely independent existence is something for whose existence there are no necessary conditions. The specific values of the variable z will vary with the value of X. For example, if X is a piece of ice or a lump of metal, one of the z's will be temperature; if X is a green plant, the z's will include light and oxygen; and so on. It may well be that nothing in the universe is independent of all conditions, but whether this is so is an empirical question.

ESSENCES. Aristotle's favorite, but least satisfactory, account of substance was that of substance as essence, an essence being a set of qualities that conjointly embody the nature of the thing they qualify, are grasped by intellectual intuition, and are expressed in the definition of the thing. But developments in the sciences (especially in biology) and in the philosophy of science over the past century have shown that this notion is illusory. Definitions, in the contemporary view, are either descriptions of current linguistic usage or recommendations for linguistic conventions. They cannot seek to explicate the essential nature of the definiendum because naturally occurring objects have no such invariable natures. Definitions in formal sciences like mathematics and logic do delineate the invariant properties of the definienda precisely because they are proposals for conventions.

SUBSTRATUM. There remains for consideration substance in the senses of (*a*) a center of change, (*b*) a substratum of qualities, and (*c*) the concrete individual thing. Senses (*a*) and (*b*) are closely akin and are both vulnerable to the empiricist line of criticism made famous by Locke. We may regard a particular thing as qualified by different properties at different times (for example, when an insect changes from egg to caterpillar to pupa to moth), or as qualified by a group of qualities at the same time (for example, when we say that a lump of sugar is white and sweet and soluble). Both of these ways of looking at substance lead to the unanswerable question "What is it that is the bearer of the qualities in each case?" But the answer to this cannot even be as satisfactory as Locke's "something we know not what," for by thus separating the subject (or hypothetical bearer of the qualities) from its predicates, we effectively prevent ourselves from saying anything about it. For to say anything about it is merely to assign to it one more predicate. This way of explaining substance makes it an empty concept.

Yet the obvious alternative to this blind alley seems no more promising. Suppose that when we say "Some apples are red" we do not mean what contemporary logic teaches us to mean: There is an x that has both the property of being an apple and the property of being red. Suppose that instead we mean: That set of particular properties which we call "apple" includes the further property of being red. Then the relation "being predicated of" turns out to be nothing more than the familiar relation of being a member of a group. This conclusion looks innocuous until we realize that this interpretation would make all subject-predicate affirmations either necessarily true or logically false. For the proposition "The set of properties $Q_1, Q_2, \cdots, Q_n$ contains the property Q_n" is a logically true statement. And if we amend it to make it informative thus: "The set of properties $Q_1, \cdots, Q_n$ contains the property Q_{n+1}" we do not have an informative proposition but, rather, a logically false one.

The way out of this dilemma is not to ask such misleadingly general questions as "What is the locus of change?" or "What is the bearer of properties?" We can ask for the detailed history of a particular thing, an insect, a plant, a man or what not, and the answer will be given to us by the relevant sciences—embryology, anatomy, physiology. We can ask for the detailed structure of a particular thing, a piece of gold, a moth, a man, or what not; again the relevant science—physics, chemistry, anatomy—will give us the answer if the answer is known. But we cannot ask for the history or structure of things in general, for there is no science of things in general.

CONCRETE INDIVIDUALS. A similar criticism awaits the last of the Aristotelian answers to the question about substance: A substance is a concrete individual thing. We cannot sensibly ask what makes things-in-general concrete individuals. The notion of a concrete individual thing is clear in its standard cases, like men, tables, mice, or stones. But it is unclear in its nonstandard applications. Is a cloud a concrete individual or is it just the particles that make it up that can be so called? Is a rainbow? Or a dream table? Can electrons be called individual things when it is impossible in principle to identify them and trace their continuous histories? Examples such as these show the futility of trying to find a general formula that will clarify the notion of a concrete individual thing. We can, of course, ask the psychologists what perceptual characteristics of things lead us to class them as individuals. That a set of jointly occurring properties stands out in our perceptual field, that it moves as one, that it persists through time—all these and other characteristics will lead us to regard a thing as a thing. But there is no decisive test which will enable us to decide, if we are doubtful, whether a certain *x* is really a concrete individual or not. In borderline cases this must be a matter for decision, not diagnosis.

Bibliography

BOOKS

Aristotle. *Metaphysics* and *Categories* (Oxford translations). Oxford, 1908 and 1928.

Blanshard, Brand. *The Nature of Thought.* London: Allen and Unwin, 1939. Ch. 3.

Broad, C. D. *An Examination of McTaggart's Philosophy.* Cambridge, U.K.: Cambridge University Press, 1933. Vol. I, Ch. 7.

Leibniz, G. W. *Monadology,* edited by Robert Latta. Oxford, 1898.

Locke, John. *An Essay concerning Human Understanding,* edited by J. Yolton. London, 1962. Book II, Ch. 23.

Russell, Bertrand. *The Analysis of Matter.* London: Kegan Paul 1927. Ch. 23.

Russell, Bertrand. *Human Knowledge.* London: Allen and Unwin, 1948.

Russell, Bertrand. *An Inquiry into Meaning and Truth.* London: Allen and Unwin, 1940.

Russell, Bertrand. *The Philosophy of Leibniz.* Cambridge, U.K., 1900.

Shoemaker, Sydney. *Self-Knowledge and Self-Identity.* Ithaca, NY: Cornell University Press, 1963.

Strawson, P. F. *Individuals.* London: Methuen, 1959.

ARTICLES

Anscombe, G. E. M. "Aristotle. " In *Three Philosophers.* Oxford, 1963.

Anscombe, G. E. M., and S. Körner. "Substance." *PAS* supp. 38 (1964).

Basson, A. H. "The Problem of Substance." *PAS* (1948–1949).

Bennett, Jonathan. "Substance, Reality, and Primary Qualities." *American Philosophical Quarterly* (1965).

Cousin, D. R. "Aristotle's Doctrine of Substance." *Mind* (1933).

Kneale, William. "The Notion of a Substance." *PAS* (1939–1940).

Lazerowitz, Morris. "Substratum." In *Philosophical Analysis,* edited by Max Black. Ithaca, NY: Cornell University Press, 1950.

Mei, Tsu-Lin. "Chinese Grammar and the Linguistic Movement in Philosophy." *Review of Metaphysics* 14 (1961). An original and penetrating critique of the notions of subject and predicate.

Sellars, Wilfrid. "Substance and Form in Aristotle." *Journal of Philosophy* (1957).

Stebbing, L. Susan. "On Substance." *PAS* (1929–1930).

D. J. O'Connor (1967)

SUBSTANCE DUALISM

See *Dualism in the Philosophy of Mind*

SUFI PHILOSOPHY

See *Sufism*

SUFISM

The origins of Sufism (*taṣawwuf* in Arabic), or Islamic mysticism, appear clearly in the spiritual practise of the Prophet Muhammad in seventh-century Arabia (Massignon 1954, Lings 1993). Sufism's key contemplative discipline, remembrance of God (*dhikr*), was practiced continually by the Prophet and is alluded to in fifteen verses of the Qur'ān. From this practise the Sufis developed an entire science of invocations and supplications (*adhkār*) designed to cultivate the heart, refine the soul, and elevate ordinary human consciousness into awareness of the ever-immanent divinity (Chittick 1987). There are nonetheless a number of formative influences on early Sufism that are extraneous to early Qur'ānic spirituality. Michael Sells (1996) has demonstrated that the heritage of pre-Islamic poetry provided numerous subthemes (for example, drunkenness, love-madness, perpetual wandering, the secret shared between lover and beloved) for later Sufi literature and poetry. Scholars such as D. Miguel Asin Palacios, Tor Andrae, Duncan Macdonald, Louis Massignon, Henry Corbin and Luce López-Baralt have revealed how some of the ascetic and mystical tendencies in early Sufism bear close resemblances to

Christian mysticism, a thesis adumbrated by Tor Andrea's *In the Garden of Myrtles: Studies in Early Islamic Mysticism* (1987).

QUR'ĀNIC ORIGINS AND FORMATIVE INFLUENCES FROM THE SEVENTH TO TENTH CENTURY

The word *Ṣūfī* as a technical term does not itself come into use before the end of the eighth century CE. The last of the following four possible etymologies of the word (there is no consensus) reflects the relation of the movement with Greek philosophy: from *Ahl-i Ṣuffa*, "the People of the Veranda," the Prophet's most intimate companions in seventh-century Medina; from *ṣafā*, meaning purity; from *ṣūf*, meaning wool; and from the Greek *sofos*, that is, *sagesse*, a cognate of *sophia* ("wisdom"). In the context of the last-cited etymology, Sufism appears to be related to Islamic "philosophy" or *falsafa* in Arabic, *faylasūf* (philosopher) being the Arabic transcription of the Greek *philosophos*. Although the terms *Sufi* and *Sufism* are historically applicable only to the type of mystic and mysticism developed within Islam, based upon pursuit of the Prophet's exemplary practice (*sunna*), it is undeniable that many of the theosophical elements in Sufism, especially as the mystical tradition changed and developed over the course of later centuries, are largely derived from Greek thought.

Mystical teachings are usually ascribed to a number of the Companions (*al-aṣḥāb*) of the Prophet and their "followers" (*al-tabā'iyun*) (Ernst 1999), the first and foremost being the fourth Sunni Caliph ʿAlī ibn Abī Ṭālib (d. 661) whose sermons, letters, poems, and maxims were compiled by Sharīf al-Raḍī (d. 1015) in the *Nahj al-balāghah*. ʿAlī features as the starting-point of all the esoteric initiatic chains of Sufism, whether Sunni or Shīʿite, and is recognized as the founder of two fundamental Sufi doctrines: renunciation of the world (*zuhd*) and spiritual poverty (*faqr*). His possession of gnostic insight and esoteric knowledge (*ʿilm-i ladunī*) is acknowledged by all Muslim theologians, Sufi mystics, and philosophers.

Ḥasan al-Baṣrī (d. 728), the principal founder of the early ascetic movement of Islam that later became known as Sufism, is listed as Imam ʿAlī's succeeding link in most Sufi initiatic chains among the "followers" of the Prophet's "Companions."

The next most significant figure in Sufi thought is the sixth Shīʿite Imam Abū Jaʿfar al-Ṣādiq (d. 765), the author of the earliest mystical Qur'ān commentary, described as "the soundest of all the Shaykhs, upon whom all of them rely. … He is the path-master of the people of love (*pīshvā-yi ahl-i ʿishq*) (ʿAttār 1993, p. 12). In fact, the love mysticism of Sufism may be traced back to both al-Ṣādiq and to his contemporary, Rābiʿa al-Adawiyya (d. 788–792), the most famous female Sufi in all history, of whom Ibn ʿArabī commented, "She is the one who analyzes and classes the categories of love to the point of being the most famous interpreter of love."

It was in the ninth century, when Greek philosophy was being introduced into Islam and when all the technical vocabulary of philosophy and theology in the Arabic language was being fashioned, that most of the basic technical terms, concepts, and categories of Sufism were also elaborated. It was probably in response to the Neoplatonic philosophers of the "School of Baghdad" (revolving around Caliph al-Ma'mūn, who supported the translation of Greek works into Arabic and Syriac) that the Sufis of the ninth century first began to use the term *mystical knowledge* (or *maʿrifat*) instead of *rational knowledge* (or *ʿilm*) to refer to the type of experiential, gnostic knowledge they possessed, in order to distinguish it from the mental, purely theoretical knowledge of their contemporaries, the Neoplatonists. (Danner 1987, p. 254).

It is not mere historical coincidence that both of these celebrated Schools of Baghdad—that of the philosophers and that of the Sufis—evolved at exactly the same time and place. From the early ninth century, Muslim Peripatetic philosophy and Sufi mysticism shared a common psychological vocabulary simultaneously fed by the two streams of Qur'ānic spirituality and Greek philosophical writings, which had been translated into Arabic. Although the intellectual contexts and applications of this vocabulary differed greatly, the lexicon of both was often identical; a huge stream of common terms flowed through both systems from the two sources. For instance, in psychology, both Sufi mystics and Peripateric philosophers shared a common terminology: for soul, *nafs*; for spirit, *rūḥ;* for heart, *qalb*, for phantasy, *wahm*; for imagination, *khiyāl;* for reason, *ʿaql*. While all these terms also figure prominently in the Qur'ān, they were corralled and culled as suitable translations (as Harry Wolfson [1935] established in a seminal article) by Muslim thinkers such as al-Farabi, Avicenna, and Ghazālī.

In the ninth century three mystics were of primary importance for the development of Sufi esoteric and mystical terminology. The first two are vaunted for their role in the development of psychospiritual terminology of Sufism, whereas the third is famous for his unusual but highly influential mystical theology. All three affected the formulation of Sufi philosophy, if *philosophia* is understood in its literal sense as love of divine wisdom.

The first figure was al-Ḥarīth al-Muḥāsibī (d. 857), who lived and taught in Baghdad. From the standpoint of formulation of mystical doctrine, psychological examination of the spiritual life, and authorship of definitive textbooks on both subjects, he was indubitably the most illustrious Sufi of the ninth century. As "the real master of primitive Islamic mysticism," as Margaret Smith put it, most later elaboration and exposition of Sufi technical terminology—such as self-examination (*muḥāsaba*), contemplation (*muraqaba*), fear (*khawf*), hope (*raja'*), patience (*ṣabr*), contentment (*riḍā'*)—can be traced back to terminology that first appeared in his works.

The second figure, Dhū'l-Nūn al-Miṣrī (d. 861), "the founder of theosophical Súfiism," as Nicholson (1906) rightly calls him, played a formative role in the evolution of Sufi doctrine. He had been the first to provide a systematic teaching about the mystical states and spiritual stations (*aḥwāl u maqāmāt*) of Sufism and was also the first to discourse on mystical knowledge, or *maʿrifat*, and to distinguish it from academic knowledge, or *ʿilm*. He was also founder of the practice and theory of the "art of audition to music" and the first to describe in poetic detail the types of "ecstatic rapture" (*samāʿ* and *wajd*), which ensued from this aesthetic tool of contemplative vision. He was the also the first mystic to use the imagery of the wine of love and cup of mystical of gnosis poured out for the lover (Smith 1991).

However, it was the third figure, Abū Yazīd (or Bāyazīd) Bisṭāmī (d. 848 or 875), who personified the Muslim mystic par excellence and who served as the real cornerstone of the free-spirited classical Sufism of later generations. He is the most frequently cited mystic in Sufi poetry. Bāyazīdian Sufism still represents the zenith of anticlerical thinking in Islam. His paradoxical utterances (he wrote nothing down), transmitted by word of mouth by disciples, soon became the subject of intricately argued prose commentaries and complicated Sufi metaphysical compositions in prose and verse. A century after his death, a separate Bāyazīdian school came into being; some two centuries later this school's contours became intellectually formalized in ʿAlī Hujwīrī's (d. 1071) *Kashf al-maḥjūb*, a Persian manual of Sufi teachings and doctrine, in which Bāyazīd's followers are classified as comprising a separate school of thought known as the Ṭayfūriyya and described as advocates of rapture (*ghalabat*) and intoxication (*sukr*) as opposed to Junayd's School of Sobriety (*saḥw*). Of particular importance in Sufi philosophy is Bāyazīd's doctrine of *fanā'*, or annihilation, of the selfhood or individual ego identity in God's Self-identity, enabling the mystic to contemplate God directly through God's own eye (Rūzbihān 1966, p. 115).

Aside from these three key Sufis, there were a number of other significant mystics in the history of ninth-century Sufism, most notably Ḥakīm al-Tirmidhī (d. 908), from the Transoxanian town of Tirmirdh, one of the most interesting and prolific authors to write on themes such as sanctity and prophethood. His works became the subject of commentaries by later Sufis such as Ibn ʿArabī.

The main center for the development of Sufi doctrine in the ninth and tenth centuries was Khurāsān, in northern Iran, and the city of Nishāpūr, which, following the fall of Baghdad to the Buwayhids in 945, became the center of Sunni Islam for the next two centuries. Nishāpūr was the center of the antiascetic Sufi school of the *Malāmatiyya* (lovers of blame), whose masters enjoined their students to practice psychological introspection into the blemishes of the "lower soul" (*nafs*), or ego, and to expose their personal faults in public. Its central teacher, Abū Ḥafṣ Ḥaddād (d. 874–879), advocated opening oneself to public blame, concealing all one's own praiseworthy virtues from public scrutiny while accusing oneself of spiritual shortcomings. Its two other main representatives in Nishāpūr, Hamdūn al-Qaṣṣār (d. 884) and Abū 'Uthmān al-Ḥīrī (d. 910), were famous for nonconformist mysticism: Qaṣṣār criticized as egotistical those who overtly perform *dhikr*, and al-Ḥīrī reproached as hypocritically impious those who engaged in acts of devotion with any degree of awareness of self.

Three important developments in Sufism—institutional, aesthetic and pedagogical—took place in Nishāpūr at the end of the ninth century. Regarding the institutional developments, Margaret Malamud (1977) and Jacqueline Chabbi (1994) have shown that, in the early ninth century, some of the earliest Sufi *khānaqāh*s (meeting houses) were established in Nishāpūr. Abū Saʿīd Abī'l-Khayr (967–1049) was the first person to formalize a program for institutional and communal living of disciples, codifying rules for novices in his Sufi *khānaqāh*. In mystical aesthetics, Abū Saʿīd is significant for having definitively integrated the practice of "audition to poetry with music" (*al-samāʿ*) into the Sufi devotional life. He pioneered the expression of mystical ideas in Persian verse, using the quatrain form (*rubāʿī*), in which he was the chief forerunner of Sanāʾī, ʿAṭṭār, and Rūmī (Graham 1999).

Fritz Meier (1999) has shown how a radical transformation in Sufism took place in Nishāpūr regarding the theory of pedagogy and practice of the master-disciple relationship from end of the late ninth century onwards. The spiritual master, who had formerly figured merely as an academic instructor of a group of students, now became the main fulcrum of the *via mystica*. He was transformed into a spiritual trainer of adepts, a saint in whom the student—now disciple—is obliged to confide with childlike trust his inmost thoughts and grant unquestioning obedience, considering him as the absolute authority and ultimate judge in all matters. By the eleventh century, this aristocratic Nishāpūrian model of the spirituality came to prevail throughout the Sufi tradition worldwide.

The leader and founder of the other important mystical school of Sufism, which was centred in Baghdad, was Abū'l-Qāsim Junayd (d. 910), who perfected Muḥāsibī's orthodox teachings and utilized his terminology. Junayd's translation of Bāyazīd's sayings from Persian into Arabic and commentary on them were preserved in Abū Naṣr Sarrāj al-Ṭusī's (d. 378/988) *Illumination of Sufism* (*Kitāb al-luma' fī'l-taṣawwuf*), "the oldest surviving general account of Sufism" (Arberry 1950). Junayd elaborated Bāyazīd's doctrine of *fanā'* in depth and detail, careful to guard against the negative consequences of the doctrine, which, superficially considered, might be interpreted by Sufism's enemies as either a kind of an ontological nihilism or else a subjective interiorised pantheism; he thus rejected both the doctrine of *ḥulūl* ("incarnationism," whereby God infuses himself in man as one substance into another) and *iṭṭiḥād* ("unitive absorption" of the individual's finite selfhood in God). Junayd's sober integration of the theosophical teachings of Sufism with Islamic legalism constitutes the basis for the orthodox understanding of Sufism down to the present day.

Because of the century and city (Baghdad) in which he flourished, Junayd was highly influenced by the school of Islamic Neoplatonism that had been established there. The theory of Al-Fārābī (d. 950), known as the "second teacher" (*al-muʿallim al-thānī*) after Aristotle, was that religions constitute elaborate symbol systems to be interpreted by an elite group of sages. This rationalist esotericism found a fit gnostic reprise in Junayd's use of mystical terminology that employed Sufi symbolic sayings couched in an enigmatic and hermetic writing style (*ishārāt*). A comparison of Junayd's basic concepts (as Ali Hassan Abdel-Kader [1976] has shown) with those of Plotinus—the stages of the mystical path, the doctrine of the preexistence and postexistence of the soul, the theory of contemplation (*mushāhada*), and the idea that mundane beauty stimulates the longing of the soul for its home Yonder—reveals Junayd's intellectual fraternity with the great pagan philosopher of late antiquity.

Junayd's school of sobriety stands in contrast to the boldly unconventional mystical theology of his most celebrated contemporary, the great martyr of Sufism Manṣūr al-Ḥallāj (d. 922), to whose life and thought Louis Massignon consecrated a huge four-volume monograph, *La Passion de Husayn Ibn Manṣūr Ḥallāj: martyr mystique de l'Islam* (1982). As Massignon (1986) pointed out, Ḥallāj figures as a precursor of Ghazālī in his endeavor to bring dogma into harmony with Greek philosophy on the basis of mystic experience. Ḥallāj was a disciple of Sahl ibn 'Abd Allāh Tustarī (d. 896), famed for his esoteric Qur'ānic exegesis. Tustarī identified "the search for knowledge" (*ṭalab al-'ilm*) as incumbent upon all Muslims with mystical feeling and spiritual consciousness (*'ilm al-ḥāl*). He defined this consciousness as the deep-felt realization that God is the witness (*shāhid*) of the devotee's thoughts, words, and deeds, which, with practice, can be transmuted into realized sapience or existential verification of knowledge (*taḥqīq al-ʿilm*).

At least two key philosophical doctrines in Sufism are traceable to Ḥallāj: first, the idea of Love (*ʿishq*) as "essential desire" (that is, human erotic aspiration as identical with the divine Essence), which Ḥallāj's follower Abū al-Ḥasan al-Daylamī (tenth century), was first to attribute to him in the *Kitāb ʿaṭf al-alif al-maʾlūf ʿalāʾl-lām al-maʿṭūf* (The book of the inclination of the familiar alif toward the inclined lam), the first book on mystical love in Islam which drew on Sufism, philosophy, and Arabic court culture (*adab*). Ḥallāj's controversial usage of the Arabic *ʿishq* (passionate love) for the human-divine relationship has startling similarities to the objections raised by Christian theologians against the use of the Platonic *eros* and the Latin *amor* as equivalents to the Pauline *agape*. Ibn Sīnā's (Avicenna, d. 1037) philosophical conception of love (*ʿishq*) as the universal principle of being, animate and inanimate; his view of God as the First Beloved (*Maʿshūq-i awwal*) who is simultaneously loved, lover, and love, is connected with Ḥallāj's theory (Anwar 2003, Ernst 1994). Second, Ḥallāj's conception of divine union as embodying realization of the essential oneness or unification of the human spirit with God (*ʿayn al-jamʿ*) was expressed notably in his shocking theopathic locution *Anā al-Ḥaqq* ("I am God"), for utterance of which he was martyred.

During the tenth century Persian mystics continued to compose manuals and systematic treatises on Sufism in Arabic: Abū Bakr Muḥammad al-Kalābādhī (1989) (d. 990, a native of Bukhara) wrote his pioneering *Introduc-*

tion to the Creed of the Sufis (*Kitāb al-taʿarruf li-madhhab ahl al-taṣawwuf*), an important introduction to—and integration of Islamic exotericism with—Sufism. In this work he prudently avoided any mention of Ḥallāj, still considered a heretic by the jurists. Another Sufi scholar, Abū Naṣr Sarrāj (d. 988) from Khurasan, wrote "the oldest surviving general account of Sufism" (Arberry 1950, p. 67). *Illumination of Sufism* (*Kitāb al-luma' fi'l-taṣawwuf*). One of Ḥallāj's masters, Abū Ṭālib al-Makkī (d. 996), composed the most celebrated Sufi textbook of the Baghdad School entitled *The Food of Hearts* (*Qūt al-qulūb*), which anticipated the reconciliation of mystical and legalistic Islam that would later appear in Ghazālī's works.

ABŪ ḤĀMID AL-GHAZĀLĪ'S ATTACK ON PHILOSOPHY AND THE RENAISSANCE OF SUFISM IN THE TWELFTH CENTURY

The birth of Islam's greatest mystical theologian, Abū Ḥāmid al-Ghazālī (in Ṭūs in Khurasan in 1058) occurred at the peak of the arch of the development of Islamic mystical tradition in eleventh-century Khurasan, at the precise cusp when one half of the tangent of the Persian-Arabic mystical tradition, buttressed by the rise of Arabic mystical literature (mostly composed by Persian Sufis), faced the other half of the arch's tangent, the first beginnings of Sufi literature in Persian. The two pillars of this arch were, respectively, the *malāmātī* Sufism of Abū Saʿīd Abī'l-Khayr and the Hellenistic philosophy of Abū ʿAlī Sīnā (Avicenna)—who, being affected and profoundly influenced the Sufism of his day, wrote a number of visionary works in Arabic (and the earliest philosophical work in Persian) that provided the speculative premises for the development of the love mysticism espoused by the later Persian Sufi poets.

So it is on the foundation of the Persian Sufi tradition that Ghazālī's theological achievement rests. Nearly all the major founders of Khurasani Sufism flourished during Ghazālī's era, having been born either in decades immediately before or after his birth. These included the likes of Abū 'Abd al-Raḥmān al-Sulamī (d. 1021), one of the main chroniclers of early Sufism, best known for his Arabic tract *The Generations of Sufis* (*Ṭabaqāt as-ṣūfiyya*), a compendium of the biographies of Sufis of five earlier generations that is a fundamental source for early Sufi history. 'Abd Allāh Anṣārī (d. 1089) of Heart, the leading stylist of Persian rhyming prose, translated and adapted Sulamī's tract into a Khurasanian dialect of New Persian. Almost as important as Sulamī's *Ṭabaqāt* is the best compendium of early Sufi doctrine, namely the *Treatise* (*Risāla*) on Sufism in Arabic by Abū'l-Qāsim al-Qushayrī (d. 1072) of Nishāpūr. All of these sources Ghazālī read and knew and often reproduced them verbatim in his works.

In his autobiography, *Al-Munqidh min al-ḍalāl*, Ghazālī records how he investigated the truth claims and methods advanced by four different schools of thought: scholastic theology (*Kalām*), Isma'ili pedagogy (*taʿlīm*), philosophy (*falsafa*), and Sufism (*taṣawwuf*); he concluded that the Sufi way is the highest and most perfect of them. The distinguishing dimension of Sufi teaching, he asserted, was that "it was not apprehended by study, but only by immediate experience (*dhawq*, literally "tasting"), by ecstasy, and by a moral change. (*Mā lā yumkin al-wuṣūl ilayih bā'l-taʿallum bul bā'l-dhawq wa'l-ḥāl wa tabaddal al-ṣafāt.*) I apprehended that the Sufis were men who had real experiences, not men of words (*arbāb al-aḥwāl, lā aṣḥāb al-aqwāl*)." The unstated implication of the Sufi experience was that it allowed the adept, without recourse to either theology or philosophy, to personally verify and partially access the experience of prophecy (Hodgson 1977). Ghazālī's approach to prophecy accorded with Avicenna's view of the faculty of intuition and imagination possessed by certain adept Sufis that enabled them to have access to illumination of the active intelligence (Griffel 2002). He believed that only the science of disclosure (*ʿilm al-mukāshafa*) allowed one to "gain knowledge of the meaning of prophecy and the prophet, and of the meaning of revelation" (*al-waḥy*) (Heer 1999, p. 247 and Ghazālī 1962, p. 47), which led to the privileging of esoteric visionary thinking in later Islamic epistemology.

Ghazālī consecrated two works to the Neo-Platonic philosophers, al-Fārābī and Avicenna in particular. The first of these works was his *Objectives of the Philosophers* (*Maqāṣid al-falāsifa*); written in Arabic, it closely followed Avicenna's Persian work *Dānish-nāma 'Alālī*, providing an overall account of the history of Muslim philosophy and a lucid exposition of the philosophical doctrines that he later means to criticize. The second work, *The Incoherence of the Philosophers* (*Tahāfut al-falāsifa*), was a decisive attack on the emanative metaphysics, causal theory, and the psychology of the philosophers (especially Avicenna); in this work he sets out to prove that the philosophers are unable to prove religious truths from a theoretical point of view.

Modern scholars disagree about Ghazālī's contribution to the development of later Islamic philosophy. Lenn Goodman (1992), Ahmed El-Ehwany (1995), and Fazlur Rahman (2000) view his emphasis on Sufism as fettering philosophic method and stifling the development of science in Islam, whereas M. Hodgson (1977), S. H. Nasr, and Henry Corbin (1996) perceive his contribution as having provided an excellent philosophical basis for the rise of later Islamic intellectual mysticism (*ḥikmat* and *ʿirfān*). Although it is true that Ghazālī's *Tahāfut* put later Islamic philosophy on the defensive, his reinterpretion of *falsafa* made philosophical ideas more accessible in the Islamic intellectual milieu than they had previously been and provided a necessary niche for philosophy to flourish in orthodox Islamic theological thought. Because Sufi theories of knowledge took center stage in his epistemological thinking, from the post-Ghazālī period in Islam down to early modern times, esoteric modes of expression invariably came to enjoy great popularity. Ghazālī believed the sapience of the heart (*dhawq*) to be superior to rational knowledge (*ʿilm*) and thought that gnosis (*maʿrifat*) could be obtained by means of the Sufi practices of remembrance of God and contemplation (*al-dhikr wa'l-fikr*), visionary unveiling (*kashf*) and abstaining from all but God Almighty. In this respect, his views are identical to those of Ibn ʿArabī a century later, whose writings on these subjects closely resemble Ghazālī's.

His most important composition was a monumental opus divided into forty books entitled *Iḥyāʾ ʿulūm al-dīn* (*The Revivification of the Sciences of Religion*), which, in its day, was unique in its cosmopolitan scope and integration of technical terminology, ideas, and writings derived from diverse sources. The *Iḥyāʾ*, a highly successful attempt to revive Islamic faith and piety on the basis of Sufism, had a profound impact on the later Islamic theological tradition. It began, in fact, what has been described as "the thirteenth-century revival of Sufism" (Danner 1988) and "the reorientation of the piety of Islam on the basis of Sufism." Because of men such as Ghazālī, Sufism became "acceptable to the '*ulama*' themselves," so that "gradually Sufism, from being one form of piety among others, and by no means the most accepted one either officially or popularly, came to dominate religious life not only within the Jama'i-Sunni fold, but to a lesser extent even among Shi'is" (Hodgson 1977, 2:203).

Mention here must be made of an equally important figure in the history of Sufism, namely Ghazālī's brother Aḥmad Ghazālī (d. 1126), who was the foremost metaphysician of love in the Sufi tradition (Lombard 2003). His impact on the later Persian Sufi tradition was even more profound than that of his brother the theologian. Aḥmad was the teacher of two important figures in particular: Abū'l-Najīb al-Suhrawardī (d. 1168) (Pourjavady 2001), who was in turn the master of his nephew Shihāb al-Dīn Abū Ḥafṣ ʿUmar Suhrawardī (d. 1234), the founder of the Suhrawardī order (famed as the "Mother of Sufi Orders"), who also authored the *'Awārif al-maʿārif*, a manual of Sufism so fundamental and all-encompassing that it was translated and adapted into Persian several times and taught throughout madrasas and *khānaqāh*s in the Indian subcontinent for centuries afterward. Aḥmad Ghazālī was also the master of the enigmatic mystical theologian and founder of Sufi speculative metaphysics: 'Ayn al-Quḍāt al-Hamadhānī (executed in 1132 by fanatical Muslim clerics for his uncompromising Sufi beliefs).

ILLUMINATIONISM AND THE RISE OF THE SUFI ORDERS

In terms of Islamic *philosophia*, the most important figure following Ghazālī was Shihāb al-Dīn Yaḥyā Suhrawardī (born in Suhraward, in northwest Persia, in 1154 and died in Aleppo in 1191), renowned as *Shaykh al-Ishrāq*, the "master of illuminationist theosophy" or the "sage of the theosophy of oriental lights." He was the most significant Platonic philosopher in the Eastern lands of medieval Islam. Described by Henry Corbin (1971, p. 340) as "an irregular Sufi of no formal affiliation," Suhrawardī traced his thought back to various sources: Islamicized Peripatetic philosophers (he followed Avicenna's metaphysics in many respects), the Hermetic tradition of Egypt (Hermes, Asclepius), the pre-Islamic Persians of Mazdean Iran (Kayomarth, Kaykhusraw and Zoroaster), and Greek thought (Socrates, Plato, Aristotle). His theosophy anticipated in Islam the universalistic philosophy of fifteenth-century Renaissance Platonists such as Gemistos Pletho and Marsilio Ficino. In the world of Islam, his writings were highly influential on the intellectual development of the Neoplatonist thinkers of seventeenth-century the School of Isfahan. Despite his Peripatetic roots, Suhrawardī featured Sufis in his works, considering them to be the true philosophers of Islam. In this context, he related a dream he had had of Aristotle in which the latter identified Bāyazīd Bisṭāmi, Sahl Tustarī, and Ḥallāj as the highest Muslim thinkers (Walbridge 2000).

Suhrawardī's epistemology was based on Sufi visionary experience, and in his major work, the *Philosophy of Oriental Illumination* (*Ḥikmat al-ishrāq*), he goes to considerable lengths of philosophical argument to prove the verity of mystical intuition (*kashf*). He calls this intuition "knowledge by presence" (*ʿilm-i ḥuḍūrī*), according to which the self can know things directly by virtue of the very presence of itself (Yazdi 1992). The doctrine of knowledge by presence is one of Suhrawardī's distinctive contributions to philosophy, and his *ishrāqī* theosophy generated a philosophical school that still dominates traditional schools of Iranian thought today. His influence "was greater than that of Averroes, for while the latter was largely forgotten in the Islamic world, Suhrawardī has continually attracted Islamic readers, followers, and opponents up to our own day" (Walbridge 2000, p. 5).

The twelfth century was also graced by the presence of the founders of two of the most influential Sufi orders in later medieval Islam: Abū Yaʿqūb al-Hamadhānī (d. 1140), founder of the Naqshbandī order, and 'Abd al-Qādir al-Jīlānī (d. 1166), founder of the Qādirī order. Two of the greatest poets of Persian literary history flourished in the same century. Ḥakīm ("the Sage") Sanā'ī of Ghazna (d. between 1131 and 1150) was a pioneer in the development of the gnostic ghazal and the first Persian Sufi poet to blend poetic imagery of the sacred and the profane into a refined philosophical lyricism. Sanā'ī's follower, Niẓāmī (d. 1202), wrote a series of unrivaled romantic epics and much mystical poetry. Another important figure is Rūzbihān Baqlī (d. 1210), whose writings constitute "a vast synthesis and rethinking of early Islamic religious thought from the perspective of pre-Mongol Sufism" (Ernst 1996, p. x), furnishing us with "a vital resource for understanding the experiential basis, not simply of Persian Sufi literature, but of Sufism and indeed mysticism in general" (Ernst 1996, p. 11). His monumental *Commentary on the Paradoxes of the Sufis* (*Sharḥ-i shaṭḥiyyāt*) is an indispensable source for the interpretation of the higher reaches of Sufi apophatic theology.

The most important Persian Sufi poet of the twelfth century was Farīd al-Dīn ʿAṭṭār (d. 1221), the prolific author of numerous epic Persian poetic works. His seminal masterpiece, *The Conference of the Birds* (*Manṭiq al-ṭayr*), has been translated into most European languages. ʿAṭṭār's major prose work was the monumental compendium, in Persian, of biographies of the famous Sufis, *Tadhkirat al-awliyā'* (*Memoirs of the Saints*).

ʿAṭṭār's contemporary was Najm al-Dīn Kubrā (d. 1221), another important figure in medieval Sufism. The founder of the Kubrawiyya, also known as the Central Asian school of Sufism, Kubrā was known for his theory of light apparitions that are beheld by the spiritual imagination in the imaginal realm (*ʿālam al-mithāl*). These theories were elaborated by later Sufis of this order, who included some of the most important names of the twelfth and thirteenth centuries. Their interpretation of these phenomena, especially when combined with their adherence to the theomonist doctrine and technical terminology of Ibn ʿArabī, constitute one of the most important chapters in the history of Islamic mysticism.

Perhaps the most famous Kubrawī mystic was Najm al-Dīn Rāzī (d. 1256), author of the *Devotees' Highroad* (*Mirṣād al-ʿibād*), an important manual of Sufi methodology in which he elaborated the peculiarly Kubrawī notion of a series of subtle centers of perception (*laṭā'if*) (Rāzī 1986, p. 299ff.). He also explained the varieties of visionary contemplation (*mushāhadāt-i anwār*) (Rāzī 1986) and continued an esoteric commentary on the Qur'ān that had been begun by Najm al-Dīn Kubrā and completed by another Kubrawī master, 'Alā' al-Dawla Simnānī (d. 1326), who elaborated his own theory of the scripture's seven esoteric levels of meaning, each of which, he said, corresponded to a subtle center of light (*laṭīfa*) (Waley 1991, Elias 1995) and expressed the inner reality (*ḥaqīqa*) of one of the prophets.

The Kubrawī school also featured a number of other notable Sufis who flourished in Iran and Central Asia: Saʿd al-Dīn Ḥammūya (d. 1253), author of the *Al-Miṣbāḥ fi'l-taṣawwuf*; Sayf al-Dīn Bākharẓī (d. 1260), author of the *Waqā'iʿ al-khalwa*; Abū'l-Mafākhir Yaḥyā Bakhrazī (d. 1335–1336), the author of an important Sufi manual, *Fuṣūṣ al-ādāb*; and 'Azīz-i Nasafī (d. between 1282 and1300), a Sufi philosopher from Uzbekistan who wrote a number of profoundly original works in Persian that still remain popular. In India, the Kubrawiyya played an important role down to fourteenth century. A disciple of Simnānī named Sayyid 'Alī Hamadānī (d. 1385) was the last great thinker of the order in Central Asia; he founded the Hamadānī line, and, according to legend, was responsible for the Islamization of Kashmir.

This order was also influential in China, where Sufism first established a foothold in the early fifteenth century. The writings of two Kubrawī masters, Rāzī and Nasafī, were among the first Islamic works that were translated into Chinese in the seventeenth century, thus forming the intellectual bedrock of the Chinese Islamic tradition. The development of Islam in China is inextricably connected with the translation of Sufi texts into Chinese. Prior to the twentieth century, only four Islamic books had been translated into Chinese, all of them Persian Sufi classics belonging to the Kubrawī and Ibn ʿArabī schools (Murata 1999). Sufism in China today remains dominated by the Naqshbandī and Qādirī orders (Gladney 1999).

RŪMĪ AND IBN ʿARABĪ

The thirteenth century was the golden age of Sufism, when the most celebrated Persian poet in Islamic history,

Jalāl al-Dīn Rūmī (d. 1273), appeared. He was the author of the most extensive collection of mystical poetry, with the widest pattern of meters yet seen in Persian poetry. His collection of mystical-erotic lyrics, the *Dīvān-i Shams-i Tabrīz* (compiled under the name of Shams-i Tabrīzī because the signature verse of nearly each poem bore the name "Shams," symbolic of the poet's absorption in his spiritual teacher of this name) totals some 35,000 verses. Each of these *ghazals* (Arabic for "love-lyric") is between five and sixty lines long and expresses the mystery of their relationship, as well as the paradoxes and subtleties of the mystical theology of Sufism. Each poem was the product of an ecstatic experience realized by the poet under the influence of the Sufi music-and-dance (*samā*ʿ) ceremony, which came to be the hallmark of his order, called the Mevlevi in Turkey and later known in the West as the Whirling Dervishes. In the eighteenth and nineteenth centuries, the Mevlevi Order's (from Rūmī's sobriquet *Mawlānā*, "our teacher") exotic flowing skirts and hypnotic revolving dance became the most popular European tourist attraction east of Athens, prompting Alexander Pope in his *Essay on Man* to observe that "Eastern priests in giddy circles run, / And turn their heads to imitate the Sun."

During the last decade and a half of his life, Rūmī began to compose the *Mathnawī-yi maʿnawī* (Rhyming spiritual couplets), dictated to his disciples under the sway of rapture. Eventually comprising more than 26,000 couplets of didactic poetry, this mystical epic became Rūmī's chief literary monument. "Judged by modern standards," wrote R. A. Nicholson in 1925 in his introduction to his critical edition and translation of the poem, "the *Mathnawī* is a very long poem: it contains almost as many verses as the *Iliad* and *Odyssey* together and about twice as many as the *Divina Commedia*."

Islam's greatest mystical thinker, known as the *Magister Magnus* or Shaykh al-Akbar, Muḥyī al-Dīn Ibn ʿArabī of Spain (d. 1240), generated a new era of writing in the field of Islamic gnosis with a string of Sufi commentators on his works and a whole school of theosophy still vital in Iran, India, Turkey, North Africa, Malaysia, and neighboring areas. Ibn ʿArabī was a very prolific author and, with the possible exception of Ghazālī, has been the most extensively studied thinker in the Islamic world (Morris 1986–1987). He composed some 850 works; 700 of these are extant, and at least 450 of them are genuine. His writings were responsible for formalizing and crystallizing the largely orally transmitted doctrines of the founders of the various Sufi Orders and thus fostered a common heritage for Sufism, which was then in the process of "creating new structures and attracting a wider flock of followers." (Chodkiewicz 1991, p. 51).

His major work, *The Meccan Revelations* (*al-Futūḥāt al-makkiyya*), covers 2,580 pages of small Arabic script (in its new critical edition the work is projected to cover thirty-seven volumes of about 500 pages each). His most famous work, however, is a short work entitled *Fuṣūṣ al-ḥikam*, made up of twenty-seven chapters, each of which is devoted to the divine wisdom revealed in a particular prophet and specific divine word. Each of these prophets represents a different mode of knowing. The title may be translated as "Bezels of Wisdom," implying that each prophet in his human setting is a kind of gemstone in which "each kind of wisdom is set, thus making of each prophet the signet or sign, by selection, of a particular aspect of God's wisdom" (Austin 1980, p. 16). The first chapter of the book concerns Adam and the last concerns Muḥammad, although the prophets discussed in between are not dealt with in chronological order. For nearly five hundred years it was the most frequently commented upon work in Sufi and theological circles in the Middle East, Central Asia, and India. In fact, the *Fuṣūṣ* was the chief intellectual preoccupation of the Sufis in India, where commentaries were written on the book by Sayyid ʿAlī Hamadānī in Kashmir, Shaykh ʿAlī Mahaymī in Gujerat, and Muhammad Gisūdarāz in the Deccan (Ahmad 1963).

Ibn ʿArabī's name is inextricably associated with the doctrine of the "Unity of Being," "Oneness of Existence," or "theomonism" (*waḥdat al-wujūd*), which should not be confused with pantheism. In this view, God is identical to created beings in His manifestation but completely separate and distinguished from them in their essences, so there is no substantial continuity between God and creation. All living beings participate with God through the theophany of His divine Names (the Living, the Speaking, the Hearing, the Omniscient, and so on), for we are all manifestations of one Light—the orifices of being through which His illumination is shone. Existence thus manifests itself by means of epiphany or theophany (*tajallī*), of which there are two types: intellectual theophany (*tajallī ʿilmī*), which is a manifestation of Being that is termed the "Most Holy Emanation" (*fayḍ al-aqdās*), and existential theophany (*tajallī wujūdī*), which is termed the "Sacred Emanation" (*fayḍ al-muqaddas*). The first type of theophany belongs to the Divine Essence, appertaining to the World of Unity (*ʿālam al-aḥadiyya*); the second type hails from the World of Unicity (*ʿālam al-waḥda*). Unlike the Peripatetic philosophers and most Sunni theologians, Ibn ʿArabī believed nothing to be external to the divinity or outside the Absolute. Existential multiplicity is not a kind of divine action outside of Being in its Essence and Attributes. He considered "Being as an unconditional absolute (*mawjūd-la-bi-sharṭ*) beyond all duality or multiplicity. According to him, the multiplicity which we observe at the sensible or spiritual levels does not affect the Unity of Being in its creative act. It simply represents its various degrees and many states. The existential theophanies, therefore, only constitute a facet of the Absolute-God who is One in His existence and many in His manifestations" (Yahia 1991, p. 36).

Knowledge of both existence and God can only be grasped imaginatively, that is, by intuitive disclosure (*kashf*) and contemplative insight (*shuhūd*), not through reason (*ʿaql*), because a likeness of God can be gained only by recourse to imagination, not reason. Ibn ʿArabī's doctrine of the metaphysical, transpersonal imagination (*khiyāl munfaṣil*), which possesses its own distinct independent ontological level (comparable to Jung's collective unconscious) lead him to espouse an epistemology that harmonizes reason and mystical insight (Chittick 1996, p. 666). God's self-manifestation (*ẓuhūr*) can thus be intuited through the theophany of His divine names, which are manifest to the visionary imagination of the mystic, who can thereby experience a supersensory reality (Izutsu 1994).

Ibn ʿArabī's writings, employing "all the tools of the theologians, philosophers, grammarians, and other specialists" (Chittick 1989, p. 289), generated "by far the most elaborate Islamic 'philosophy of religion' and religious life, a comprehensive metaphysics which offered an all-encompassing justification and explanation for the observed diversity of religions, philosophic, and spiritual 'paths' to God—whether within the multiple sects and schools of later Islamic culture, or in the wider, even multi-confessional context of the Ottoman, Safavid and Mogul empires." (Morris 1998, p. 23) As. T. Izutsu (1995, p. 552) has pointed out, "Even today the metaphysics of Ibn ʿArabī together with—or mingled with—that of Suhrawardī, the Master of Illumination (*Shaykh al-Ishrāq*), form the basis of the philosophical-gnostic world-view of Iranian Muslim intellectuals. In fact, one of his surnames, *Muḥyī al-Dīn*, meaning literally 'revivifier of religion,' manifests its living force when it is seen in terms of the role his thought has played in the historical formation of Iranian Islam."

Many of the greatest names in the annals of Persian Islam have counted themselves as disciples or at least interpreters of his doctrines. These include the likes of Awḥād al-Dīn Kirmānī (d. 1238), Ṣadr al-Dīn Qūnawī (d. 1274), Fakhr al-Dīn ʿIrāqī (d. 1289), Saʿīd al-Dīn al-Farghānī (d. 1299), 'Azīz al-Dīn Nasafī (d. circa 1300), Mu'ayyid al-Dīn Jandī (d. 1301), 'Abd al-Razzāq al-Kashānī (d. 1339), 'Alā al-Dawla Simnānī, Dāwūd Qayṣārī (d. 1350), Rukn al-Dīn (Bābā Ruknā) Masʿūd Shirāzī (d. 1367), Maḥmūd Shabistarī (d. after 1339), Muḥammad Shirin Maghribī (d. 1408), Khwāja Muḥammad Parsā (d. 1419), Ṣā'īn al-Dīn Turkah Iṣfahānī (d. 1427), Shāh Nimatu'llāh Walī (d. 1431), and Shāh Dāʿī Shirāzī (d. 1464).

SUFISM IN THE SCHOOL OF ISFAHAN

Prior to the advent of the modern age, the most significant development in Islamic thought occurred in the philosophical collegium of Isfahan in Safavid Iran (1501–1722), a unique amalgam of Sufism, Shīʿism, Platonist Ishrāqī theosophy, and Islamic rationalism that was heavily grounded in the theosophical theories of classical Sufism. Although all its members exhibited a profound respect for the ethical, intellectual, and spiritual ideals of classical Persian Sufism, few of them seem to have openly accepted the requirement of following the *ṭarīqa* discipline involving obedience to a living master (*pīr, murshid*). The writings of its members are permeated with Shīʿite piety, imamology, and theology, and were intellectually inspired by the Illuminationist (*Ishrāqī*) theosophy of Shaykh Yaḥyā Suhrawardī, which mixed Peripatetic rationalism with Islamic Platonism. Its main thinker, Mullā Ṣadrā (d. 1650), drew heavily on other renowned Sufi authors such as Abū Naṣr Sarrāj, 'Ayn al-Quḍāt Hamadhānī, Abū Ḥāmid al-Ghazālī, and Ibn ʿArabī (Pourjavady 1999). In fact, as S. H. Nasr has noted, if viewed correctly in historical context, the entire later school of Ṣadrā's Transcendental Theosophy, both in Iran and India, might be better classified as a sort of "speculative Sufism" (*taṣawwuf-i naẓārī*) (Nasr 1993, p. 124) rather than as simply a species of philosophical mysticism (*ḥikmat*).

Hodgson (1977, 3:52) has noted how the Platonists of Isfahan may be compared at points with their contemporaries, the Cambridge Platonists of England in their ecumenical interests. Mīr Findiriskī (d. 1640–1641) was one of the major philosophers of the School of Isfahan and was committed to the transmission and translation of the Hindu holy books and scriptures into Persian; he composed a commentary on the *Yoga-Vāshishtha* of Vālmiki. The Muslimization of Hindu mystical thought that resulted from the efforts of such philosophers and translators both in Iran and India can be compared to Marsilio Ficino's Christianization of the Greek Neoplatonic classics in his translations of Plato and Plotinus into Latin.

SUFISM IN EASTERN EUROPE, THE MIDDLE EAST, IRAN, AND INDIA FROM THE SEVENTEENTH CENTURY TO THE PRESENT

Since the late eighteenth century Muslim Sufi orders throughout the world have been in the throes of crisis and transformation because of the combined influences of modernism, Islamist reformism, nationalism, and European colonialism. A key to these upheavals has been the continuing impact of fundamentalist Islamism on Sufism throughout the Islamic world, a trend that began in the early twentieth century.

Throughout the Sunni world, *Salafī*s (puritans claiming to be followers of the "pious forbears" of the Prophet)—particularly in Egypt—have attacked Sufism as "inauthentic," a "Trojan horse for unwarranted innovations that owe their origins to non-Muslim civilizations such as Greece, Persia, and India" (Cornell 2004, p. 59). The same attacks have occurred in other Sunni-dominated countries of the Middle East. In Algeria and Syria, Sufis are beleaguered on the one hand by the all-encroaching influence of Western secularism, which endorses the Western modernist view of mysticism as an anachronistic superstition, and Wahhābī scriptural literalists on the other.

In Eastern Europe, Sufism has been a significant force since the early fifteenth century, especially in Bosnia, where a number of leading intellectuals, thinkers, and poets, mostly followers of the Mevlevīya and Naqshbandī Orders, penned influential mystical treatises and books and wrote glosses on classical tracts. After the collapse of the Ottoman Empire, Albania became an important center of Sufism, with the majority of its inhabitants belonging to one or another Sufi order (Clayer 2001).

Since the early sixteenth century Sufism has been firmly established in Turkey "as a fundamental element of Ottoman Islamic society, where in the urban context, the Mevlevīya played an important role in the education of Ottoman elites and in the cultivation of Sufi and Persian literatures" (Lapidus 1992, p. 29). In Ottoman society, Rūmī's Mevlevī order, to which most of the country's intellectual and artistic elite belonged, became the greatest preserver of musical creativity in a religious context. The Mevlevīya produced some of Turkey's finest musicians and calligraphers and the most sophisticated religious poet of early modern times, Ghālib Dede (1799), whose poem *Beauty and Love* is a supreme work of world literature (Holbrooke 1994, Winter 1994). Although, by the end of the nineteenth century, almost every city in the Ottoman Empire possessed its own Mevlevī center (Zarcone 2000), by the early twentieth century, because of the Kemalist laws against the Orders, many of the Sufi centers were closed down or destroyed (Raudvere 2002). The law of September 1925, which stated that "from this day forth, there are not *tarikat*s, or *dervishes*, and *murid*s belonging to them, within the boundaries of the Turkish Republic" (Algar 1994, p. 55) explicitly banned all dervish gatherings, practices, and teachings. The Naqshbandī Order was subject to particular governmental persecution and harassment. Since the 1950s there has been a relaxation of some of these restrictions because of the Turkish government's attempt to harness Sufism's spiritual potential to further its own secularist sociopolitical agenda. Because the agenda of the Kemalist secular state is to counter Islamist fundamentalism with Sufism's mystical and moral universalism (ignoring its institutional, contemplative, and practical aspects), there has been a consequent revival of Sufi activities such as Mevlevī dervish dancing, and renewed interest in the cultural heritage of Sufi architecture, poetry, literature and music.

In Egypt, hardline Islamist ideologues such as Muḥammad Rashīd Riḍā (d. 1935) and Ḥasan al-Banna (d. 1949), founder of the Muslim brotherhood, condemned Sufism wholesale as a repository of corrupting opinions and ideas in Islam. Another Egyptian fundamentalist thinker, Sayyid Quṭb (d. 1966), argued that Sufism represented a debilitating, antirational, antiprogressive force in the Islamic tradition (Abu-Rabi 1988). For more than a century, Sufism in Egypt has been controlled by an elaborate state apparatus. Since 1903 the leaders of the Orders have been governed and often appointed by a Supreme Council of the Sufi Orders. In the interests of religious and state conformism, most of the transcendentalist, illuminationist, ecstatic, and unitive aspects of the Sufi tradition are publicly denigrated and suppressed in favor of a sober, reformist mysticism focused on communal moral virtues and study of *ḥadīth* and the Qur'ān. The doctrines of rapture and intoxication maintained by the great founders of Sufi theosophy such as Ḥallāj and Bāyazīd are frowned upon by the Sufi Council (Hoffman 1995).

In Saudi Arabia, Sufism is banned today by the ḥadīth-driven scripturalism of the Wahhābī literalist theologians. The entire corpus of Sufi writings, philosophy, poetry, theosophy, and literature—whether these be the more orthodox works of Ghazālī or the visionary meditations of Ibn ʿArabī, which were once accepted as a mainstay of traditional Islamic theology by a broad spectrum of believers—have been anathematized by the Wahhābī hierarchy that controls the mosques, schools, and universities (Cornell 2004). Even the writings of great Sufi masters such as Aḥmad Ibn Idrīs (d. 1837) (the renowned Sufi saint of Moroccan origin who lived in Arabia and defended Ibn ʿArabī's Sufi doctrines in face of Wahhābī persecution) remain anathema to the Saudi fundamentalist state (Radtke 2000).

In Algeria during the nineteenth century, the Sufi orders played a leading role, among other Muslim groups, in fighting French imperialism, and stood in the vanguard of opposition to France's cultural and political colonialism (Benaissa 1997). During the twentieth century all the Sufi orders suffered persecution by the *Salafi* reformists, who accused them of backwardness and deviance from orthodoxy (Andezian 1994). In recent decades terrorist organizations, inspired by these same Algerian *Salafi*s, have continued their attack on Sufism, whereas the modernist secularist elements equate Sufism with decadence and backwardness, so that today "for many if not most educated Algerians, Sufism is virtually synonymous with 'maraboutism'—saint-worshipping idolatry, superstitious donning of amulets, snake-charming, etc." (Shah-Kazemi 1994, p. 171)

In Iran, most of the main nineteenth-century political reformers, such as Akhundzāda (d. 1878), Mīrzā Malkum Khān (d. 1908), and Mirzā Āqā Khān Kirmāni (d. 1896) attacked Sufism, castigating its alleged passivity and religious conformism (Lewisohn 1998–1999). Radical Iranian secular intellectuals of the early twentieth century, such as Aḥmad Kasravī (d. 1946) widened this critique to sweepingly condemned Sufism as "one of the deep-rooted and greatly misguided beliefs to have appeared in Islam" (Kasravī 1990, p. 79). In the Islamic Republic in the early twenty-first century, mystical philosophy (*ḥikmat*) is encouraged, and there has been a renaissance in the publication of works on classical *taṣawwuf*, with Sufis abounding in all major urban centers, but their activities and gatherings are often closely monitored by the fundamentalist state. Since 1978 the theocratic regime has tried to write Sufism out of the textbooks of Iranian history and to destroy the mausoleums of the masters and living institutions of the Orders which dot the country; nevertheless, both above and below ground the Sufi orders have managed to survive.

In Pakistan, there has been a renaissance in the publication of Sufi literature, much of it patronized by the state and nationalist interests, which underwrite editions and Urdu translations of prominent Sufi poets who composed verse in regional vernaculars. Works by the famous masters of the Chishtī, Suhrawardī, and Naqshbandī Orders from the thirteenth to the nineteenth centuries "are widely available for popular use through modern Urdu translations in India and Pakistan, and occasionally in other languages as well (Ernst 2000, p. 335). Pakistani modernists such as Muhammad Iqbal (d. 1938) have made use of classical figures such as Rūmī, Ḥallāj, and Junayd in their own writings to further their own personal philosophical agenda but have denounced khānaqāh-based Sufism and the master-disciple relationship; some have attacked as decadent the Sufi love mysticism of Persian poets such as Ḥāfiẓ. Recently, Sufism has sometimes been press-ganged to support nationalism—as in Z. A. Bhutto's claim that Sufi saints were forerunners of the modern Islamic state of Pakistan (Ernst 1997, pp. 79, 209).

From the tenth century onward, the Islamization of India "was achieved largely by the preaching of the dervishes, not by the word" (Schimmel 1975, p. 346). The two main Indian orders that dominated the cultural and religious life of the land were the Chishtiyya and Suhrawardīyya, which had been introduced into India with the foundation of the Sultanate of Dehli; within a short time thousands of their khānaqāhs and zāwiyahs had woven themselves into the complex religious culture of India, smoothing and softening relations between opposing religious identities. The rise of the Indian Bhakhti movements in the fourteenth and fifteenth centuries took place in the background and under the direct influence of *khānaqāh*-based Sufism of the Suhrawardī and Chishtī Orders (Nizami 1957).

The school of Ibn ʿArabī in India was sustained by Sufis of all the major Orders. The renewer of the Chishtī Order in northern India, 'Abd al-Quddūs Gangūhī (d. 1437), who had mastered the famous Hatha Yoga treatise Amrit Kund and who wrote Hindi poetry influenced by Nathpanthi Yogic and Bhakti traditions, strongly defended the philosophy of the 'Unity of Being' in his treatises and correspondence (Farooqi 2004, pp. 4–6). Some of the great Chishtī Sufis were ardent supporters of Ibn ʿArabī's theomonism. Shaykh Muḥibb-Allāh Ilāhābādī (d. 1648), a vicar of the grandson of 'Abd al-Quddūs Gangūhī, was known as the "Supreme Master" (Shaykh-i Kabīr) for works that defended and commented on Ibn ʿArabī's *Fuṣūṣ al-ḥikam*. (Farooqi 2004).

The rulers of the Mughal Empire, from Akbar the Great (d. 1604) down to Shāh Jahān (d. 1658), patronized Sufis of the Chishtī, Qādarī, and Naqshbandī Orders, and utilized Sufi ecumenical "unity of religions" theory to unite their Hindu and Muslim subjects. Many Sufis in India tried to bridge the differences between Hindu and

Muslim mysticism; hence one important service that the Sufi Orders and Sufis in South Asia performed was the promotion of sectarian harmony and interfaith tolerance (Islam 2002, p. 447). Mystics such as Niẓām al-Dīn Awliyā' and Dārā Shikūh were known for their tolerance of religious diversity and their appreciation of Hindu spirituality. Dārā Shikūh (d. 1659), the eldest son of the Mughal Emperor Shāh Jahān, wrote a comparative study of Sufi and Vedantic technical terms (*Conjunction of the two Oceans* [*Majma' al-baḥrayn*]) and a Persian translation of fifty-two Upanishads (*The Supreme Arcanum* [*Sirr-i akbar*]). This work was later translated into Latin by Anquetil-Duperron, inspiring Schopenhauer and a whole string of European and American philosophers after him throughout the nineteenth century. Sufis of the Chishtī and Qādirī Orders rendered the Bhagavadgītā into Persian three times during the Mughal period in the seventeenth century, with Ibn ʿArabī's theory of an underlying mystical unity of religions used by its translators to interpret Hinduism in the context of Islamic theomonism (Vassie 1999).

SUFISM IN THE CONTEMPORARY WEST

Up until the late eighteenth century, the cultural and intellectual influence of the Sufi tradition upon Western Europe had been marginal (Chodkiewicz 1994), although certain Sufi thinkers such as Ghazālī did have a formative influence upon certain Christian philosophers such as Raymond Llull (Urvoy 2004). In the nineteenth century, Persian Sufi theosophy and poetry entered the course of Western European thought through key representatives of the German Idealist and American Transcendentalist movements, particularly in the figures of Goethe in Germany and Emerson in North America, both of whom were profoundly influenced by translations of Persian Sufi mystical literature (Jahanpour 1999). During the twentieth century, the traditionalist school founded by the French metaphysician René Guénon (d. 1951)—who converted to Islam and spent the last twenty years of his life in Cairo as a Sufi shaykh of the North African Shadhili Order—have constituted the avant-garde of Sufi teaching in the West. Sufi Muslims among Guénon's followers included Frithjof Schuon, Titus Burckhardt, Martin Lings, and S. H. Nasr, whose writings endeavor to revive Muslim orthodox traditional Sufi teachings in the light of the *Sophia perennis*, aiming to address both Islamic orthodoxy and the ecumenical concerns of comparative religion. Other advocates of the *Sophia perennis* and followers of the traditionalist school who were deeply influenced by Sufism are Ananda Coomaraswamy and Aldous Huxley.

The renowned Greek-Armenian spiritual teacher G. I. Gurdjieff (d. 1949), who was steeped in Sufi theosophy, spread his teachings during the 1930s and 1940s throughout Europe and the United States through a wide circle of followers, such as P. D. Oupensky (d. 1947), P. L. Travers, René Daumal, and Maurice Nicoll. Many of Gurdjieff's followers articulated his esoteric teachings as being a kind of Sufism divorced from traditional Islam. During the same period, the so-called "Sufi Order of the West," founded by Ināyat Khān (d. 1927), an Indian musician of the Chishtī Order, preached Sufism in Europe and North America as a sort of woolly universal mysticism that could be detached from its Islamic roots. Idries Shah (d. 1996), a prolific author of more than twenty-five books on Sufism, did much to introduce Sufism to the educated middle classes in the West, particularly artists and intellectuals, teaching that Sufism lies at the heart of all religion, although his interpretation of Sufism was primarily a *malāmatī* rather than an orthodox Muslim one.

Over the past few decades, under the leadership of Dr. Javad Nurbakhsh, the Iranian Niʿmatu'llāhī order has become a major publisher of Sufi works in English, French, German, Russian, Spanish, and Italian. This order lays little emphasis on the Islamic dimension of Sufism, stressing its universalism and ethnic Persian origins. Since the 1980s, there has also been a renaissance of scholarship on classical Sufi texts in French, English, and German, and the publication of critical studies and editions of the works of the great Sufi saints in all the major European languages has blossomed. Rūmī has become the best-selling poet in the history of American poetry publishing.

There are today at least fifty different Sufi movements in North America, the literary output of which, as Marcia Hermansen (2000, p. 158) observes, "is by now so vast that it would require a volume rather than an essay to adequately discuss the history and doctrines of each of the groups in detail." Sufism and its Orders are today found throughout all the major countries of Europe; in Britain alone, there are at least twenty-five active orders whose followers' ethnic origins can be traced back to Pakistan, India, the Middle East, Iran, and West Africa (Geaves 2000).

See also al-Fārābī; al-Ghazālī, Aḥmad; al-Ghazālī, Muḥammad; Aristotle; Averroes; Avicenna; Corbin, Henry; Ficino, Marsilio; Galen; Ibn al-ʿArabī; Islamic Philosophy; Lull, Ramón; Mullā Ṣadrā; Mysticism, History of; Nasr, Seyyed Hossein; Neoplatonism; Plato;

Pletho, Giorgius Gemistus; Plotinus; Pope, Alexander; Socrates; Suhrawardī, Shihāb al-Dīn Yaḥyā; Zoroastrianism.

Bibliography

Abdel Kader, A. H. *The Life, Personality and Writings of al-Junayd*. London: Luzac & Co., 1976.

Abu-Rabi, Ibrahim M. "Al-Azhar Sufism in Modern Egypt: The Sufi Thought." *Islamic Quarterly* 32 (4) (1988): 207–235.

Ahmad, Aziz. "The Sufi and the Sultan in Pre-Mughal India." *Der Islam* 38 (1963): 142–153.

Algar, Hamid. "The Naqshbandi Order in Republican Turkey." *Islam World Report: Turkey: The Pendulum Swings Back* 1 (3) (1994): 51–67.

Andezian, Sossie. "Sufi Brotherhoods in Contemporary Algeria." *Islam World Report: Algeria: A Revolution Revisited* 1 (1) (1997): 114–127.

Andrea, Tor. *In the Garden of Myrtles: Studies in Early Islamic Mysticism*. Translated by B. Sharpe. Albany: State University of New York Press, 1987.

Anwar, Etin. "Ibn Sina's Philosophical Theology of Love: A Study of *Risalah fi al-ʿishq*." *Islamic Studies* 62 (2) (2003): 331–345.

Arberry, A. J. *Sufism: An Account of the Mystics of Islam*. London: Allen & Unwin, 1950.

ʿAṭṭār, Farīd al-Dīn. *Tadhkirat al-awliyā'*, edited by Muḥammad Istiʿlāmī. Tehran: Zawwār, 1993.

Benaissa, Omar. "Algerian Sufism in the Colonial Period." In *Islam World Report: Algeria: A Revolution Revisited*, edited by Reza Shah-Kazemi 1(1)(1997): 47–68.

Chabbi, Jacqueline. "Sufi Organizations and Structures of Authority in Medieval Nishāpūr." *International Journal of Middle Eastern Studies* 26 (3) (1994): 427–442.

Chittick, W. C. "Dhikr." In *Encyclopedia of Religion*, edited by M. Eliade, Vol. 4, 341–342. New York: Macmillan, 1987.

Chittick, W. C. "Ebn al-ʿArabī." *Encyclopædia Iranica* 7 (1996): 664–670.

Chittick, W. C. *The Sufi Path of Knowledge: Ibn al-ʿArabī's Metaphysics of Imagination*. Albany: State University of New York Press, 1989.

Chodkiewicz, Michel. "The Diffusion of Ibn ʿArabī's Doctrine." *The Journal of the Muhyiddin Ibn ʿArabī Society (JMIAS)* 9 (1991): 36–57.

Chodkiewicz, Michel. "La réception du soufisme par l'occident: conjectures et certitudes." In *The Introduction of Arabic Philosophy into Europe*, edited by C. Butterworth and Blake Kessel, 136–149. Leiden: Brill, 1994.

Clayer, Nathalie. "Taṣawwuf, Music and Social Change in the Balkans since the Beginning of the Twentieth Century with Special Consideration of Albania." In *Sufism, Music, and Society in Turkey and the Middle East*, edited by Anderes Hammarlund, Tord Olsson, and Elisabeth Ozdalga, 137–146. Istanbul: Swedish Research Institute, 2001.

Corbin, Henry. *History of Islamic Philosophy*.Translated by L. Sherrard and P. Sherrard. London: KPI and the Institute of Ismaili Studies, 1996.

Cornell, Vincent. "Practical Sufism: An Akbarian Foundation for a Liberal Theology of Difference." *JMIAS* 36 (2004): 59–84.

Danner, Victor. "The Early Development of Sufism." In *Islamic Spirituality*, Vol. 1: *Foundations*, edited by S. H. Nasr, 239–264. New York: Crossroad, 1987.

Danner, Victor. *The Islamic Tradition*. New York: Amity House, 1988.

El-Ehwany, Ahmed. "Ibn Rushd. E. The Way to Science." In *A History of Muslim Philosophy*, edited by M. M. Sharif, 540–564. Dehli: D.K. Publications, 1995.

Elias, Jamal. *The Throne Carrier of God: The Life and Thought of ʿAlā' ad-Dawla as-Simnānī*. Albany: State University of New York Press, 1995.

Ernst, Carl. *Rūzbihān Baqlī: Mysticism and the Rhetoric of Sainthood in Persian Sufism*. London: Curzon Press, 1996.

Ernst, Carl. "Rūzbihān Baqlī on Love as 'Essential Desire'." In *God Is Beautiful and He Loves Beauty: Festschrift in Honour of Annemarie Schimmel*, edited by A. Geise and J. C. Bürgel, 181–189. Berlin: Peter Lang, 1994.

Ernst, Carl. *The Shambhala Guide to Sufism*. Boston: Shambhala, 1997.

Ernst, Carl. "Taṣawwuf." Sec. 7 in "Muslim India." In *The Encyclopedia of Islam*. 2nd ed. Vol. 10, 334–337. Leiden: Brill, 2000.

Ernst, Carl, tr. *Teachings of Sufism*. Boston: Shambhala, 1999.

Farooqi, N. R. "The Resurgence of the Chishtīs: A Survey of the Expansion and Fulfillment of a Sufi Order in Mughal India." *Islamic Culture* 78 (1) (2004): 1–26.

Geaves, Ron. *The Sufis of Britain: An Exploration of Muslim Identity*. Cardiff: Cardiff Academic Press, 2000.

Ghazālī, Abū Ḥāmid. *The Book of Knowledge, Being a Translation with Notes of the Kitāb al-ʿIlm of al-Ghazzālī's Iḥyā' ʿUlūm al-Dīn*. Translated by N. A. Faris. Lahore: Sh. Muhammad Ashraf, 1962.

Gladney, Dru C. "Central Asia and China." In *The Oxford History of Islam*, edited by J. Esposito, 448–457. Oxford: Oxford University Press, 1999.

Goodman, Lenn. *Avicenna*. London: Routledge, 1992.

Graham, Terry. "Abū Saʿīd ibn Abī'l-Khayr and the School of Khurāsān." In *The Heritage of Sufism*, edited by L. Lewisohn, Vol. 1, 116–126. Oxford: Oneworld, 1999.

Griffel, Frank. "The Introduction of Avicennean Psychology into Muslim Theological Discourse." *Transcendent Philosophy* 4 (4) (2002): 359–370.

Hammarlund, Anders, Tord Olsson, and Elisabeth Ozdalga, eds. *Sufism, Music and Society in Turkey and the Middle East*. Istanbul: Swedish Research Institute, 2001.

Heer, Nicholas. "Abū Ḥāmid al-Ghazālī's Esoteric Exegesis of the Koran." In *The Heritage of Sufism*. Vol. 1: *Classical Persian Sufism: From Its Origins to Rumi*, edited by Leonard Lewisohn, 235–257. Oxford: Oneworld, 1999.

Hermansen, Marcia. "Hybrid Identity Formations in Muslim America: The Case of American Sufi Movements." *Muslim World* 90 (2000): 158–178.

Hodgson, Marshall G. S. *The Venture of Islam*. 3 vols. Chicago: University of Chicago Press, 1977.

Hoffman, Valerie. *Sufism, Mystics and Saints in Modern Egypt*. Columbia: University of South Carolina Press, 1995.

Holbrooke, Victoria. *The Unreadable Shore of Love*. Austin: University of Texas, 1994.

Ibn al-ʿArabī. *The Bezels of Wisdom*. Translated by R. J. W. Austin. New York: Paulist Press, 1980.

Islam, Riazul. *Sufism in South Asia: Impact on Fourteenth Century Muslim Society*. Karachi: Oxford University Press, 2002.

Izutsu, Toshiko. "An Analysis of *Wahdat al-Wujúd*: Towards a Metaphilosophy of Oriental Philosophies." In his *Creation and the Timeless Order of Things: Essays in Islamic Mystical Philosophy*, 66–97. Ashland, OR: White Cloud Press, 1994.

Izutsu, Toshiko. "The Basic Structure of Metaphysical Thinking in Islam." In his *Creation and the Timeless Order of Things: Essays in Islamic Mystical Philosophy*, 1–37. Ashland, OR: White Cloud Press, 1994.

Izutsu, Toshiko. "Ibn al-ʿArabī." In *Encyclopædia of Religion*, edited by M. Eliade. Vol. 6, 552–557. New York: Macmillan, 1995.

Jahanpour, Farhang. "Western Encounters with Persian Sufi Literature." In *The Heritage of Sufism*. Vol. 3: *Late Classical Persianate Sufism (1501–1750)*, edited by L. Lewisohn and David Morgan, 28–59. Oxford: Oneworld, 1999.

Kalābādhī. *Al-Taʿarruf li-madhhab ahl al-taṣawwuf.* Translated by A. J. Arberry as *The Doctrine of the Sufis*. Cambridge, U.K.: Cambridge University Press, 1989.

Kasravi, Ahmad. *On Islam and Shiʿism*. Translated by M. R. Ghanoonparvar. Costa Mesa, CA: Mazda, 1990.

Lapidus, Ira. "Sufism and Ottoman Islamic Society." In *The Dervish Lodge: Architecture, Art, and Sufism in Ottoman Turkey*, edited by Raymond Lifchez, 15–32. Berkeley: University of California Press, 1992.

Lewisohn, Leonard, ed. *The Heritage of Sufism*. Vol. 1: *Classical Persian Sufism from its Origins to Rumi 700–1300*; Vol. 2: *The Legacy of Mediæval Persian Sufism 1150–1500*; Vol. 3: *Late Classical Persianate Sufism 1501–1750*. Edited by L. Lewisohn and David Morgan. Oxford: Oneworld, 1999.

Lewisohn, Leonard. "An Introduction to the History of Modern Persian Sufism." A 2-part study in *The Bulletin of the School of Oriental & African Studies* 61, pt. 3 (October 1998): 437–464; 62, pt. 1 (February 1999): 36–59.

Lewisohn, Leonard. "Sufism and the School of Isfahan: *Taṣawwuf* and *ʿIrfān* in Late Safavid Iran (ʿAbd al-Razzāq Lahījī and Fayḍ-i Kashānī on the Relation of *Taṣawwuf*, *Ḥikmat* and *ʿIrfān*." In *The Heritage of Sufism*, Vol. III: *Late Classical Persianate Sufism: the Safavid and Mughal Period*, edited by L. Lewisohn and David Morgan, 63–134. Oxford: Oneworld, 1999.

Lifchez, Raymond, ed. *The Dervish Lodge: Architecture, Art, and Sufism in Ottoman Turkey*. Berkeley: University of California Press, 1992.

Lings, Martin. "The Koranic Origins of Sufism." *Sufi* 18 (1993): 5–9.

Lombard, Joseph. "Aḥmad al-Ghazālī and the Metaphysics of Love." PhD diss. Yale University, 2003.

Malamud, Margaret. "Remarques sur le développement historique des mouvements ascétiques et mystiques au Khurasan." *Studia Islamica* 46 (1977): 5–72.

Massignon, Louis. "Al-Ḥallādj." In *Encyclopedia of Islam*. 2nd ed. Vol. 3, 99–104. Leiden: Brill, 1986.

Massignon, Louis. *Essai sur les origines du lexique technique de la mystique musulmane*, nouvelle édition. Paris: J. Vrin, 1954. Translated by Benjamin Clark as *Essay on the Origins of the Technical Language of Islamic Mysticism*. Notre Dame, IN: University of Notre Dame Press, 1997.

Massignon, Louis. *La passion de Ḥusayn Ibn Mansūr Ḥallāj: martyr mystique de l'Islam*. Paris: Gallimard, 1975. Translated by H. Mason as *The Passion of Ḥallāj: Mystic and Martyr of Islam*. 4 vols. Princeton, NJ: Princeton University Press, 1982.

Meier, Fritz. "Khurāsān and the End of Classical Sufism." In *Essays on Islamic Piety and Mysticism*, translated by John O'Kane, 189–219. Leiden: Brill, 1999.

Morris, James. "...Except His Face: The Political and Aesthetic Dimensions of Ibn ʿArabī's Legacy." *Journal of the Muhyiddin Ibn ʿArabī Society* 23 (1998): 19–31.

Morris, James. "Ibn ʿArabī and His Interpreters." *Journal of the American Oriental Society* 106–107 (1986): I: 539–551; II: 732–756; (1987) II conclusion: 101–119.

Murata, Sachiko. "Sufi Texts in Chinese." In *The Heritage of Sufism*, edited by L. Lewisohn. Vol. 3, 376–388. Oxford: Oneworld, 1999.

Nasr, S. H. "ʿIrfān-i naẓārī u sayr u sulūk dar taṣawwuf." *Iran Nameh* 11 (1) (1993): 121–128.

Nasr, S. H., ed. *Islamic Spirituality*. Vol. I: *Foundations*; *Islamic Spirituality*. Vol. II: *Manifestations*. New York: Crossroad, 1987 and 1991.

Nasr, S. H. "The Place of the School of Isfahan in Islamic Philosophy and Sufism." In *The Heritage of Sufism*. Vol. 3: *Late Classical Persianate Sufism (1501–1750)*, edited by L. Lewisohn and David Morgan, 3–15. Oxford: Oneworld, 1999.

Nicholson, R. A. "A Historical Enquiry concerning the Origin and Development of Sufism, with a List of Definitions of the Terms *Ṣūfī* and *Taṣawwuf*, Arranged Chronologically." *Journal of the Royal Asiatic Society* Part I (1906): 303–353.

Nizami, K. H. "Some Aspects of Khanqah Life in Medieval India." *Studia Islamica* 8 (1957): 52–69.

Pourjavady, Nasrollah. "Ḥallāj va Bāyazīd Bisṭāmī az naẓār-i Mullā Ṣadrā." *Nashr-i Danish* 16 (3) (1999): 14–24.

Radtke, Bernd, John O'Kane, Knut S. Vikor, and R. S. O'Fahey. *The Exoteric Ahmad Ibn Idris: A Sufi's Critique of the Madhāhib and the Wahhābīs*. Leiden: Brill, 2000.

Rahman, Fazlur. *Revival and Reform: A Study of Islamic Fundamentalism*. Oxford: Oneworld, 2000.

Raudvere, Catharina. *The Book and the Roses: Sufi Women, Visibility and Zakir in Contemporary Istanbul*. Sweden: Bjärnums Tryckeri AB, 2002.

Rāzī, Najm al-Dīn. *Mirṣād al-ʿibād min al-mabdāʾ ilāʾl-maʿād*. 2nd ed., edited by Muḥammad Amīn Riyāḥi. Tehran: Intishārāt-i ʿIlmī u farhangī, 1986.

Rūzbihān Baqlī Shīrāzī. *Sharḥ-i shaṭḥiyyāt*, edited by H. Corbin. Bibliothéque Iranienne 12. Tehran: Departement d'iranologie de l'Institut Franco-iranien, 1966.

Abū Naṣr Sarrāj al-Ṭūsī. *Kitāb al-Lumaʿ*, edited by R. A. Nicholson. Translated into Persian by M. Maḥabbati. Tehran: Intishārāt-i Asāṭīr, 2003.

Schimmel, Annemarie. *Mystical Dimensions of Islam*. Chapel Hill: University of North Carolina Press, 1975.

Sells, Michael, ed. *Early Islamic Mysticism: Sufi, Qur'an, Mi'raj, Poetic and Theological Writings*. New York: Paulist Press, 1996.

Shah-Kazemi, Reza. "From Sufism to Terrorism: The Distortion of Islam in the Political Culture of Algeria." *Islam World Report: Algeria: A Revolution Revisited* #1 (1) (1997): 160–192.

Smith, Margaret. "Dhū'l-Nūn." *Encyclopedia of Islam*. 2nd ed. Vol. 2, 242. Leiden: Brill, 1991.

Trimingham. J. S. *The Sufi Orders in Islam*. Oxford: Oxford University Press, 1973.

Urvoy, Dominique. "Soufisme et Dialogue Islamo-Chrétien." *Islamochristiana* 30 (2004): 55–64.

Vassie, Roger. "'Abd al-Raḥmān Chishtī and the Bhagavadgita: 'Unity of Religion' Theory in Practice." In *The Heritage of Sufism*. Vol. 2: *The Legacy of Mediæval Persian Sufism (1150–1500)*, edited by L. Lewisohn, 367–377. Oxford: Oneworld, 1999.

Walbridge, John, *The Leaven of the Ancients: Suhrawardī and the Heritage of the Greeks*. Albany: State University of New York Press, 2000.

Waley, Muhammad Isa. "Najm al-Dīn Kubrā and the Central Asian School of Sufism the Kubrawiyyah." In *Islamic Spirituality*. Vol. 2: *Manifestations*, edited by S. H. Nasr, 80–104. New York: Crossroad, 1991.

Winter, T. J. "Spiritual Life in Ottoman Turkey." In *Islam World Report: Turkey: The Pendulum Swings Back*, edited by Reza Shah-Kazemi, 1 (1) (1994): 32–41.

Wolfson, Harry. "The Internal Senses in Latin, Arabic, and Hebrew Philosophic Texts." *Harvard Theological Review* 28 (2) (1935): 69–133.

Yahia, Osman. "Theophanies and Lights in the Thought of Ibn 'Arabī." *JMIAS* 10 (1991): 35–44.

Yazdi, Mahdi Ha'iri. *The Principles of Epistemology in Islamic Philosophy: Knowledge by Presence*. Albany: State University of New York Press, 1992.

Zarcone, Th. "Ṭarīḳa, 5. In the Turkish Lands, from Anatolia to Eastern Turkestan." *Encyclopedia of Islam*. 2nd ed. Vol. 10, 250–253. Leiden: Brill, 2000.

Leonard Lewisohn (2005)

SUHRAWARDĪ, SHIHĀB AL-DĪN YAḤYĀ

(c. 549 AH/1155 CE–587 AH/1191 CE)

Shihāb al-Dīn Yahyā Suhrawardī was born in Suhraward, ancient Media, in northwestern Iran. He died in Aleppo, in the full bloom of youth, a victim of the vindictiveness of the doctors of the Law and of the fanaticism of Ṣalāḥ al-Dīn (the "Saladin" of the Crusaders). It is important that this philosopher not be confused with two other Sufis with similar names (Shihāb al-Dīn 'Omar and Abu'l-Najīb Suhrawardī).

A guiding thought dominates Suhrawardī's work: to restore the philosophy and theosophy of the sages of ancient Persia. Three centuries before it was effected in the works of the great Byzantine philosopher Georgius Gemistus Pletho, the conjunction of the names of Plato and Zoroaster was realized in the works of this thinker of Islamic Persia. Broadly outlined, this work (where the influence of Hermeticism and late Neoplatonism was also joined) brought forth an interpretation of the theory of Platonic Ideas in terms of Zoroastrian angelology. If his design reconciled itself with difficulty to the spirit of legalistic Islam, of religion and the Law, it was not, on the other hand, contrary to a spiritual Islam, bringing into play all its resources and profoundly influencing it. This employment in effect imposed on philosophy an exigency that assured it thenceforth of a completely characteristic place in Islam. Suhrawardī did not separate philosophy and spirituality; a philosophy that does not terminate in or at least tend toward a mystical and spiritual experience is a vain undertaking. Seeking out a mystical and spiritual experience without a preliminary philosophical position puts one in great danger of losing one's way. The influence of this doctrine has been considerable, especially in Iran, and endures even to the present.

The key word in Suhrawardī's entire work is (in Arabic) *Ishrāq*. Literally, it means the illumination of the sun when it arises (*Aurora consurgens*). Transposed to the spiritual plane, it means a type of knowledge which is the very *Orient* of knowledge. Suhrawardī's principal work is titled *Ḥikmat al-Ishrāq*, "Oriental" philosophy or theosophy (the term *ḥikmat ilāhīya* being the exact equivalent of the Greek *theosophia*). It deals with a philosophy that is Oriental because it is illuminative and illuminative because it is Oriental. Between these two terms there is reciprocity rather than opposition (as C. Nallino believed). The disciples and perpetuators of Suhrawardī are known as the *Ishrāqīyūn* or *Mashriqīyūn*, the "Orientals." Suhrawardī himself is designated as preeminently the *shaikh al-Ishrāq*. Prior to Islam, these "Orientals" are to him essentially the sages of ancient Persia. Their "philosophy of enlightenment" originated with the concept of *Xwarnah* (Light-of-Glory in the Avesta and Mazdaistic cosmology; *Khorreh* in Persian). In its turn, this concept dominates the entire work of the *shaikh al-Ishrāq*. "Oriental" knowledge, which is its subject matter, is essentially a discovered "presential" knowledge (*'ilm hoḍūrī*), and intuitive perception, such as knowledge of oneself, in opposition to a type of representative knowledge (*'ilm ṣūrī*), through the intermediary of a Form or a *species*.

This is why an entire section of our shaikh's work (among approximately fifty titles, a trilogy, each of whose constituent elements is composed of a logic, a physics, and a metaphysics) is dedicated to freeing philosophy from all accumulated obstacles attributable to the abstractions of the Peripatetics and the scholastic scholars of Islam (the *Mutukallimūn*). This preliminary study was crowned with the work cited above, where, from the analysis of the concept of being as Light, the theory of the procession of beings of Light is disengaged (complex angelic hierarchies, deduced somehow from the esoteric interpretation of the laws of optics). To the structure of these hierarchies correspond those of the plans of the universe, which are "symbolic of each other." Suhrawardī, more particularly, seemed to have been the first to found, systematically, an ontology of the *mundus imaginalis* (*ʿālam al-mithāl*), a world of the Image and a world of the Souls (the *malakūt*), acting as an intermediary between the world of pure Intelligences (the *jabarūt*) and the sensible world. This is a world without which the visionary experiences of the prophets and mystics, as well as the suprasensible events that the philosophy of the Resurrection treats, would remain unexplained. From this another complete section of Suhrawardī's works, deliberately written in Persian, was introduced, especially to this world, as the first phase of spiritual initiation. It forms a cycle of symbolic tales in which Suhrawardī consciously followed Avicenna (Ibn Sīnā). He knew very well what he owed to Avicenna and why he was able to go further than he: Avicenna also had formulated the project of an "Oriental" philosophy, but he could not realize it, not having known its true source.

Thus did the work of the *shaikh al-Ishrāq* give rise in Islam to a current of philosophy and spirituality distinct from the three currents that are usually considered, that of *Kalām* (the rational scholastic scholars), that of the *falāsifa* (philosophers known as the Hellenists), and Sufism. It is currently said that the *Ishrāq* is to the philosophy of the *falāsifa* what Sufism is to the theology of the *kalam*. By doing this, Suhrawardī defended the cause of philosophy against the pious agnosticism of the literalist theologians, as well as against that of certain Sufi pietists. It was only because his work was ignored for so long a time in the West (where one was accustomed to assessing Islamic philosophy from the viewpoint of what was known of it by Latin Scholastics) that an exaggerated importance was attached to Averroes, whose work was considered as having attained the self-proclaimed pinnacle and terminal point of philosophy in Islam. Neither the Peripateticism of Averroes (with which the ontology of *Malakūt* was lost) nor the critique of the philosophy of Muḥammad al-Ghāzalī has had any influence on Oriental Islam, notably on Iranian philosophy. Even there, what develops is a "Suhrawardian Avicennism" to which is joined the influence of Ibn al-ʿArabī (of Andalusia, died 1240 CE, one of the greatest mystical theosophists of all time), which spread forth into the "prophetic philosophy" of Shīʿism. The influence of Suhrawardī's doctrines was later dominant in the School of Ispahan, in the sixteenth and seventeenth centuries, in the Iran of the Safavids (with the great names of Mīr Dāmād, Mullā Ṣadrā Shīrāzī, Moḥsen Fayż, Qāẓī Saʿid Qommī, and so forth), as it was also later preponderant in India in those circles influenced by the generous religious reform of Shāh Akbar. It still makes itself felt in Iran at the present time.

Bibliography

For an edition of the works of Suhrawardī, see *Opera Metaphysica et Mystica*, Vol. I, edited by Henry Corbin (Istanbul: Maarif Matbaasi, 1945), and *Oeuvres philosophiques et mystiques* (which is *Opera Metaphysica et Mystica*, Vol. II), edited by Henry Corbin (Teheran: Institut franco-iranien, 1952). The two volumes contain a long introduction in French.

See also Henry Corbin, *Histoire de la philosophie islamique*, Vol. I (Paris: Gallimard, 1964), pp. 284–304 and the detailed bibliography on pp. 360–361, and *Terre céleste et corps de résurrection: de l'Iran mazdeen a l'Iran shiʿite* (Paris: Buchet/Chastel, 1960), which contains translations of several of Suhrawardī's works.

Henry Corbin (1967)

SUHRAWARDĪ, SHIHĀB AL-DĪN YAḤYĀ [ADDENDUM]

(1155 or 1156–1191)

Shihāb al-Dīn Suhrawardī is one of the most well known, innovative, yet controversial Persian philosophers of the history of philosophy in Iran. He was executed in 1191 at the age of thirty-six by the express command of King Saladin, most probably for his illuminationist political doctrine. This doctrine is Platonist in principle, and is based on Fārābī's structure of the ideal republic, commonly known as the "Virtuous City," in which justice is achieved based on the enlightened rule of the inspired philosopher-sage. Later Shī'a scholastic political thought draws heavily on Suhrawardī's illuminationist political doctrine.

Suhrawardī authored nearly fifty works, many of them devoted to the systematic refinement and reconstruction of philosophical arguments of the prevailing Avicennan peripatetic system of his time. Suhrawardī's stipulated aim was to refine the Greek-inspired Avicennan texts, and as such he is one of the first philosophers to challenge the unquestioned superiority of Aristotle.

Suhrawardī's philosophical aim was not to refute rational philosophy, nor to reduce it to ill-defined mysticism; rather, his creative thinking represented a positive philosophical approach aimed primarily at constructing a consistent system to prove the rational validity of revealed knowledge, as well as the intuitive and the inspired, non-predicative cognitive modes.

Medieval historians and scholastic commentators recognize Suhrawardī's innovative thinking and named him the founder of a new system, the "philosophy of Illumination." Recent analytical studies of Suhrawardī's Arabic and Persian works that together define the new system have led to the revision of earlier Orientalist misrepresentations of Suhrawardī as a mystic or a theosopher. Suhrawardī was above all a rationalist thinker whose ambition in philosophy was to construct a consistent holistic system to remove presumed logical gaps in the Aristotelian scientific system known to him in Avicenna's peripatetic philosophical corpus. The aim of Suhrawardī's reconstructed system was to define a new scientific method named the "Science of Lights" (*al-ʿilm al-anwār*) that then is employed in the construction of a unified epistemological theory, named Knowledge by Presence (*al-ʿilm a-ḥuḍūrī*), capable of scientifically explaining an inclusive range of phenomena that cover the domains of sensation, intellection, intuition, inspiration, and revelation.

The Knowledge by Presence theory has been widely acclaimed in all major philosophical works in Arabic and Persian—from Suhrawardī's own time to the present—as the crowning achievement of the philosophy of illumination, and was later employed by the major Persian thinkers in their probing of theories of knowledge. For example, the much acclaimed seventeenth-century Persian scholastic philosopher, Mullā Ṣadrā, uses the illuminationist theory of Knowledge by Presence to, among other things, explain God's knowledge of things as well as man's knowledge of God. This knowledge by presence is of essence, and its construction exemplifies Suhrawardī's aim to refine and reconstruct peripatetic arguments, not to refute them. Suhrawardī attempted to prove that the Avicennan Essentialist Definition (*al-ḥadd al-tāmm*, similar to Aristotle's *horos* and *horismos*) does not provide knowledge of essence of primary principles; and that Aristotelian theory of intellectual knowledge—which in its Avicennan peripatetic formulation is seen as conjunction with the Active Intellect (acting as *dator formarum*), does not bestow principles of science to the knower.

In his analysis Suhrawardī first examined the logical law of identity and criticized knowledge by predication; he then took up the notion of union and conjunction in physics, finally constructing a unified theory as metaphysical law. The unified theory of Knowledge by Presence, then, is stated as an identity-preserving relation (literally an "illuminationist relation," *al-iḍāfa al-ishrāqiyya*) between the domains "knower" and "known," or the intellect and the intellected—or simply knowing and being. This type of knowledge is the technical refinement of Plato's "intellectual vision" plus Aristotle's logical notion of "quick wit" (*agkhinoia*); it posits priority to the self-conscious subject's immediate grasp of the real, manifest essence of objects. Suhrawardī's epistemological theory may be compared with Kant's notion of "immediate relation to objects," but is not to be reduced to Bertrand Russel's "knowledge by acquaintance," and in general anticipates Descartes's views on knowledge.

Suhrawardī's legacy defines the height of Arabic and Persian philosophy's twelfth-century rational response to the Ashʿarite and other Ghazzālī-inspired theological antirational dogma. This philosophical legacy continues to this day, where the philosophy of illumination is an accepted school of Islamic philosophy and is taught in Shiʿite scholastic circles in Iran. While the most major innovation of Suhrawardī's technical philosophical work may be seen in his unified epistemological theory, and while it is his illuminationist political doctrine that has had the widest impact on Persian intellectual and religious traditions, still illuminationist philosophy includes many technical innovations. To name a few: the definition of an independent modal operator in the construction of a superiterated modal proposition as the single form to which all types of propositions are reduced; the proof of the impossibility of the necessary and always true validity of the universal, affirmative proposition; reduction of the Figures of Syllogism, as well as other technical innovations.

Some of his ideas in ontology and cosmology should also be mentioned: In his system, God and the intellects are types of lights; creation is the propagation of abstract, countless, continuous lights as self-conscious entities, extended in durationless time from the source, becoming less intense with distance, and the source, the Light of Lights, is the most essentially luminous, thus the most visible and self-cognizant of all. The process of becoming indicates continuum being, and is defined by rapidly increasing sequences of light-essences within a time-space continuum, where measured time and Euclidean space apply to the corporeal realm, and time without measure and non-Euclidean space define a separate realm Suhrawardī names "Mundus Imaginalis," which is an "amazing" boundary "wonderland" realm joining the domain "intellect" with the domain "soul." This realm of being is named in many later works as the locus of experiential knowledge, and the idea also impacted textual traditions beyond the purely philosophical, notably wide-ranging Persian mystical poetry.

See also Illuminationism.

Bibliography

Two of Suhrawardī's philosophical texts are now available in bilingual editions. These texts are the best source for the study of his thinking:

The Book of Radiance: A Parallel English-Persian Text, edited and translated, with introduction, by Hossein Ziai. Costa Mesa, CA: Mazda Publishers, 1998.

The Philosophy of Illumination: A New Critical Edition of the Text of Ḥikmat al-ishrāq *with English Translation, Notes, Commentary, and Introduction by John Walbridge & Hossein Ziai*. Provo, UT: BYU Press, 1999.

A number of studies have been published, and the reader may consult them as further reading on Suhrawardī and his philosophy of illumination:

Walbridge, John. *The Science of Mystic Lights: Qu'b al-Dīn Shīrāzī and the Illuminationist Tradition in Islamic Philosophy*. Harvard Middle Eastern Monographs 26. Cambridge, MA: Harvard University Press, 1992.

Ziai, Hossein. "al-Suhrawardī, Shihāb al-Dīn." In *Encyclopedia of Islam*, 2nd ed. 781–784.

Ziai, Hossein. "The Illuminationist Tradition." In *The Routledge History of Islamic Philosophy*, edited by S. H. Nasr and Oliver Leaman, 465–496. London: Routledge, 1995.

Ziai, Hossein. *Shams al-Dīn Muḥammad Shahrazūrī's* Sharḥ Ḥikmat al-Ishrāq: *Commentary on the Philosophy of Illumination*. Critical edition, with English and Persian introductions, notes, and indexes. *Cultural Studies and Research Institute* 736 (1993): xxxix, 766.

Ziai, Hossein. "Shihāb al-Dīn Yaḥyā Suhrawardī." In *The Routledge History of Islamic Philosophy*, edited by S. H. Nasr and Oliver Leaman, 434–464. London: Routledge, 1995.

Ziai, Hossein. "Source and Nature of Authority: A Study of Suhrawardī's Illuminationist Political Doctrine." In *The Political Aspects of Islamic Philosophy*, edited by Charles Butterworth, 304–344. Cambridge, MA: Harvard University Press, 1992.

Hossein Ziai (2005)

SUICIDE

What role may a person play in the end of his or her own life? Is suicide wrong, always wrong, profoundly morally wrong? Or is it almost always wrong, but excusable in a few cases? Or is it sometimes morally permissible? Is it not intrinsically wrong at all though perhaps often imprudent? Is it sick? Is it a matter of mental illness? Is it a private or a social act? Is it something the family, community, or society could ever expect of a person? Or is it solely a personal matter, perhaps a matter of right, based in individual liberties, or even a fundamental human right?

What role a person may play in the end of his or her own life is the central ethical issue in suicide around which a set of related issues also form: What should the role of other persons be towards those intending suicide? What should the role of medical and psychiatric clinicians be toward a patient who intends suicide since it is they who are said to be charged with protecting human life? What intervention may the state make to interfere with a person's intention to end his or her own life? What responsibility do others—both immediate others such as family and friends or more distant or generalized others such as employers or institutions or society as a whole—bear when a person commits suicide?

This spectrum of views about the *ethics* of suicide—from the view that suicide is profoundly morally wrong to the view that it is a matter of basic human right, and from the view that it is primarily a private matter to the view that it is largely a social one—lies at the root of contemporary practical controversies over suicide. These practical controversies include at least three specific matters of high contemporary saliency:

- *Physician-assisted suicide in terminal illness*, the focus of intense debate in parts of the world with people who have long life expectancies and with high-tech medical systems, particularly the Netherlands, the United States, the United Kingdom, Canada, Switzerland, Belgium, Germany, and Australia;
- *Hunger strikes and suicides of social protest*, as in Turkey, Northern Ireland, and wartime Vietnam;
- *Suicide bombings* and related forms of self-destruction employed as military, guerilla, or terrorist tactics in ongoing political friction, including kamikaze attacks by wartime Japan; suicide missions by groups from Tamil separatists to al-Qaeda, and suicide bombings in the conflicts in Israel, Palestine, Iraq, and elsewhere.

Ethical issues have occupied the center of attention in the philosophical discussion of suicide, but conceptual and epistemological ones also play a role, as do a broad range of further issues raised within world historical, religious, and cultural traditions.

CONCEPTUAL AND LINGUISTIC ISSUES

The term *suicide* carries extremely negative connotations. However, there is little agreement on a formal definition. Some authors count all cases of voluntary, intentional self-killing as suicide; others include only cases in which the individual's primary intention is to end his or her life. Still others recognize that much of what is usually termed suicide neither is wholly voluntary nor involves a genuine intention to die, such as suicides associated with depression or other mental illness. Many writers exclude cases of self-inflicted death that, while voluntary and intentional, appear aimed to benefit others or to serve some purpose or principle—for instance, Socrates drinking the hemlock, Captain Lawrence Oates's (1890–1912) walking out into the Antarctic blizzard to allow his fellow explorers to continue without him, or the self-immolation of war protesters. These cases are usually not called suicide but *self-sacrifice* or *martyrdom*, terms with strongly positive connotations.

Attempts to differentiate these positive cases from negative ones often seem to reflect moral judgments, not genuine conceptual differences, and the linguistic framing of a practice plays a substantial role in social policies about suicide. For example, supporters of physician-assisted suicide often use the term *aid-in-dying* as well as earlier euphemisms such as *self-deliverance* to avoid the negative connotations of *suicide* while opponents insist on the more negative term *suicide*. Islamic militants attacking civilians are called *martyrs* by their supporters and those who recruit them but *suicide bombers* by their targets and by the Western press.

Differences among languages also play a role in the conceptualization of suicide. While for example English, French, Spanish, and many other languages have just a single, primary word for suicide, German has four: *Selbstmord* (self-murder), *Selbsttötung* (self-killing), *Suizid* (the Latinate term), and *Freitod* (free death). This latter German term has comparatively positive, even somewhat heroic, connotations, making it possible for German-speakers to think about the deliberate termination of their lives in a linguistic way not easily available to speakers of English or other languages that rely on a single, principal term with strongly negative connotations.

Linguistic issues also arise in attempts to refer to the performance of the act of suicide. The expression *to "commit" suicide* has been common, echoing the phrase *to commit a crime*; contemporary suicidologists typically use a variety of less-stigmatizing alternatives, including *suicided, completed suicide*, and *died by suicide*.

Some authors claim that it is not possible to reach a rigorous formal definition of suicide and prefer a *criterial* or operational approach to characterizing the term, noting its varied, shifting, and often inconsistent range of uses. Translation from one language to another may also prove difficult since there is sometimes little way to preserve comparatively positive connotations of some terms. Cases of death from self-caused accident, self-neglect, chronic self-destructive behavior, victim-precipitated homicide, high-risk adventure, refusal of life-saving medical treatment, and self-administered euthanasia—all of which share many features with suicide but are not usually termed such—cause still further conceptual difficulty.

Nevertheless, conceptual and linguistic issues concerning suicide are of considerable practical importance in policy formation, affecting, for instance, coroners' practices in identifying causes of death, insurance disclaimers, psychiatric protocols, religious prohibitions, codes of medical ethics, laws prohibiting or permitting assistance in suicide, social stigma and respect, and public response to international and political issues such as suicide bombing and protest suicide.

EPISTEMOLOGICAL ISSUES

Closely tied to conceptual issues, the central epistemological issues raised by suicide involve the kinds of knowledge available to those who contemplate killing themselves. The issue of what, if anything, can be known to occur after death has generally been regarded as a religious issue answerable only as a matter of faith; few philosophical writers have discussed it directly, despite its clear relation to theory of mind. Some writers have argued that since we cannot have antecedent knowledge of what death involves, we cannot knowingly and voluntarily choose our own deaths; suicide is therefore always irrational. Others, rejecting this argument, instead attempt to establish conditions for the rationality of suicide. Others consider whether death is always an evil for the person involved and whether death is appropriately conceptualized as the cessation of life. Still other writers examine psychological and situational constraints on decision making concerning suicide. For instance, the depressed, suicidal individual is described as seeing only a narrowed range of possible future outcomes in the current dilemma, the victim of a kind of *tunnel vision* constricted by depression. The possibility of preemptive suicide in the face of deteriorative mental conditions such as Alzheimer disease is characterized as a problem of having to use that very mind which may already be deteriorating to decide whether to bear deterioration or die to avoid it. Still others suggest that suicide would be the most straightforward expression of normative skepticism, expressing the view that life has no meaning and nothing is of value.

SUICIDE IN WORLD HISTORICAL TRADITIONS: THE WEST

Much of the extremely diverse discussion of suicide in the history of Western thought has been directed to ethical issues. Plato acknowledges Athenian burial restrictions—the suicide was to be buried apart from other citizens with the hand severed and buried separately—and in the *Phaedo,* he also reports the Pythagorean view that suicide is categorically wrong. But Plato also accepts suicide under various conditions, including shame, extreme distress, poverty, unavoidable misfortune, and *external compulsions* of the sort imposed on Socrates by the Athenian court: Socrates was condemned to drink the hemlock. In the *Republic* and the *Laws,* respectively, Plato obliquely insists that the person suffering from chronic, incapacitating illness or uncontrollable criminal impulses ought to allow his life to end or cause it to do so. Aristotle held more generally that suicide is wrong, claiming in the *Nichomachean Ethics* that it is *cowardly* and *treats the state unjustly.* The Greek and Roman Stoics, in contrast, recommended suicide as the responsible, appropriate act of the wise man, not to be undertaken in emotional distress but as an expression of principle, duty, or responsible control of the end of one's own life, as exemplified by Marcus Porcius Cato Uticencis (Cato the Younger) (95 BCE–46 BCE), Lucretia (sixth century BCE), and Lucius Annaeus Seneca.

Although Old Testament texts describe individual cases of suicide (Abimilech, Samson, Saul and his armor-bearer, Ahithophel, and Zimri), nowhere do they express general disapproval of suicide. However, the Greek-influenced Jewish soldier and historian Flavius Josephus (37 CE–100 CE) rejects it as an option for his defeated army, and clear prohibitions of suicide appear in Judaism by the time of the Talmud during the first several centuries CE, often appealing to the Biblical text Genesis 9:5: "For your lifeblood I will demand satisfaction." New Testament does not specifically condemn suicide, and mentions only one case: the self-hanging of Judas Iscariot after the betrayal of Jesus. There is evident disagreement among the early Church Fathers about the permissibility of suicide, especially in one specific circumstance: among others, Eusebius Pamphilus (c. 264–340), Ambrose (c. 340–397), and Jerome (c. 342–420) all considered whether a virgin may kill herself in order to avoid violation.

While Christian values clearly include patience, endurance, hope, and submission to the sovereignty of God, values that militate against suicide, they also stress willingness to sacrifice one's life, especially in martyrdom, and absence of the fear of death. Some early Christians (e.g., the Circumcellions, a subsect of the rigorist Donatists) apparently practiced suicide as an act of religious zeal. Suicide committed immediately after confession and absolution, they believed, permitted earlier entrance to heaven. Rejecting such reasoning, St. Augustine asserted that suicide violates the commandment *Thou shalt not kill* and is a greater sin than any that could be avoided by suicide. Whether he was simply clarifying earlier elements of Christian faith or articulating a new position remains a matter of contemporary dispute. In any case, it is clear that with this assertion, the Christian opposition to suicide became unanimous and absolute.

This view of suicide as morally and religiously wrong intensified during the Christian Middle Ages. St. Thomas Aquinas argued that suicide is contrary to the natural law of self-preservation, injures the community, and usurps God's judgment "over the passage from this life to a more blessed one" (*Summa theologiae* 2a 2ae q64 a5). By the High Middle Ages the suicide of Judas, often viewed earlier as appropriate atonement for the betrayal of Jesus, was seen as a sin worse than the betrayal itself. Enlightenment writers began to question these views. Thomas More incorporated euthanatic suicide in his *Utopia.* In *Biathanatos,* John Donne (c. 1572–1631) treated suicide as morally praiseworthy when done for the glory of God—as, he claimed, was the case for Christ; David Hume mocked the medieval arguments, justifying suicide on autonomist, consequentialist, and beneficent grounds.

Later thinkers such as Mme. de Staël (Anne Louise Germaine, née Necker, the baroness Staël-Holstein)—although she subsequently reversed her position—and Arthur Schopenhauer construed suicide as a matter of human right. Throughout this period, other thinkers insisted that suicide was morally, legally, and religiously wrong: among them, John Wesley (1703–1791) said that suicide attempters should be hanged, and Sir William Blackstone (1723–1780) described suicide as an offense against both God and the king. Immanuel Kant used the wrongness of suicide as a specimen of the moral conclusions the categorical imperative could demonstrate. In contrast, the Romantics tended to glorify suicide, and

Friedrich Nietzsche insisted that "suicide is man's right and privilege."

Although religious moralists have continued to assert that divine commandment categorically prohibits suicide, that suicide repudiates God's gift of life, that suicide ruptures covenantal relationships with other persons, and that suicide defeats the believer's obligation to endure suffering in the image of Christ, the volatile discussion of the moral issues in suicide among more secular thinkers ended fairly abruptly at the close of the nineteenth century. This was due in part to Émile Durkheim's insistence that suicide is a function of social organization, and also to the views of psychological and psychiatric theorists, developing from Jean Esquirol (1772–1840) to Sigmund Freud, that suicide is a product of mental illness. These new *scientific* views reinterpreted suicide as the product of involuntary conditions for which the individual could not be held morally responsible. The ethical issues, which presuppose choice, reemerged only in the later part of the twentieth century, stimulated primarily by discussions in bioethics of terminal illness and other dilemmas at the end of life.

SUICIDE AND MARTYRDOM IN MONOTHEIST RELIGIOUS TRADITIONS

The major monotheisms, Judaism, Christianity, and Islam, all repudiate suicide though in each, martyrdom is recognized and venerated. Judaism rejects suicide but venerates the suicides at Masada and accepts *Kiddush Hashem*, self-destruction to avoid spiritual defilement. At least since the time of Augustine, Christianity has clearly rejected suicide but accepts and venerates martyrdom to avoid apostasy and to testify to one's faith. Islam also categorically prohibits suicide but at the same time defends and expects martyrdom to defend the faith. Yet whether the distinction between suicide and martyrdom falls in the same place for Judaism, Christianity, and Islam is not clear. Judaism appears to accept self-killing to avoid defilement or apostasy; Christianity teaches submission to death where the faith is threatened but also celebrates the voluntary embrace of death in such circumstances; some Islamic fundamentalists support the political use of suicide bombing, viewing it as consistent with Islam and its teachings of *jihad*, or holy war to defend the faith, though others view this as a corruption of Islamic doctrine.

Thus, while all three traditions revere those who die for the faith as martyrs and all three traditions formally repudiate suicide, at least by that name, the practices they accept may be quite different: Christians would not accept the mass suicide at Masada; Jews do not use the suicide-bombing techniques of their Islamic neighbors in Palestine; and Muslims do not extol the passive submission to death of the Christian martyrs, appealing on Quranic grounds to a more active self-sacrificial defense of the faith.

OTHER RELIGIOUS AND CULTURAL VIEWS OF SUICIDE

Many other world religions hold the view that suicide is prima facie wrong but that there are certain exceptions. Still others encourage or require suicide in specific circumstances. Known as *institutionalized suicide*, such practices in the past have included the *sati* of a Hindu widow who was expected to immolate herself on her husband's funeral pyre; the *seppuku* or hara-kiri of traditional Japanese nobility out of loyalty to a leader or because of infractions of honor; and, in traditional cultures from South America to Africa to China, the apparently voluntary submission to sacrifice by a king's retainers at the time of his funeral in order to accompany him into the next world. Inuit, Native American, and some traditional Japanese cultures have practiced voluntary abandonment of the elderly, a practice closely related to suicide, in which the elderly are left to die, with their consent, on ice floes, on mountaintops, or beside trails.

In addition, some religious cultures have held comparatively positive views of suicide, at least in certain circumstances. The Vikings recognized violent death, including suicide, as guaranteeing entrance to Valhalla. Some Pacific Island cultures regarded suicide as favorably as death in battle and preferable to death by other means. The Jains, and perhaps other groups within traditional Hinduism, honored deliberate self-starvation as the ultimate asceticism and also recognized religiously motivated suicide by throwing oneself off a cliff. On Mangareva, members of a traditional Pacific Islands culture also practiced suicide by throwing themselves from a cliff, but in this culture not only was the practice largely restricted to women, but a special location on the cliff was reserved for noble women and a different location assigned to commoners. The Maya held that a special place in heaven was reserved for those who killed themselves by hanging (though other methods of suicide were considered disgraceful), and, though the claim is disputed, may have recognized a goddess of suicide, Ixtab. Many other pre-Columbian peoples in the Western hemisphere engaged in apparently voluntary or semi-voluntary ritual self-sacrifice, notably the Aztec practice of heart sacrifice, which was generally characterized at least at some historical periods by enhanced status and social approval. The view that suicide is intrinsically and without exception wrong is associated most strongly with post-Augustinian Christianity of the medieval period, surviving into the present; this absolutist view is not by and large characteristic of other cultures.

ETHICAL ISSUES IN CONTEMPORARY APPLICATION: PHYSICIAN-ASSISTED SUICIDE

The *right to die* movement emerging in the 1970s, 1980s, and 1990s, counting among its achievements the passage of *natural death*, *living will*, and *durable power of attorney* statues that gave patients greater control in decision making about their end-of-life medical care, also raised the question of what role the dying person might play in shaping his or her own death and what role the physician might play in directly assisting the patient's dying. These notions have often appealed to the concept of *death with dignity*, though the coherence of that notion is sometimes challenged. Public rhetoric quickly labeled the practice at issue *physician-assisted suicide* although less negatively freighted labels such as *physician-aid-in-dying* or *physician-negotiated death* have also been advanced as more appropriate.

Proponents of legalizing the practice have argued in its favor on two principal grounds: (1) autonomy, the right of a dying person to make his or her own choices about matters of deepest personal importance, including how to face dying, and (2) the right of a person to avoid pain and suffering that cannot be adequately controlled. Opponents offer two principal competing claims: (1) that fundamental moral principle prohibits killing, including self-killing, and (2) that allowing even sympathetic cases of physician assistance in suicide would lead down the *slippery slope*, as overworked doctors, burdened or resentful family members, and callous institutions eager to save money would manipulate or force vulnerable patients into choices of suicide that were not really their own. Pressures would be particularly severe for patients with disabilities, even those who were not terminally ill, and the result would be widespread abuse.

Compromise efforts, launched by bioethicists, physicians, legal theorists, and others on both sides, have focused primarily on the mercy argument from avoiding pain: It is claimed that improving pain control in terminal illness, including accelerated research, broader education of physicians, rejection of outdated concerns about addiction associated with opioid drugs, and recourse to terminal sedation or induced permanent unconsciousness if all else fails will serve to decrease requests for physician assistance in suicide. These compromise views also hold that assistance in suicide should remain, if available at all, a last resort in only the most recalcitrant cases.

However, although proponents of physician-assisted suicide welcome advances in pain control, many reject this sort of compromise arguing that it restricts the freedom of a person who is dying to face death in the way he or she wants. They point out that other apparent compromises, such as the use of terminal sedation, are both repugnant and can be abused, since full, informed consent may not actually be sought. Proponents also object on grounds of equity: It is deeply unfair, they insist, that patients dependent on life-support technology such as dialysis or a respirator can achieve a comparatively easy death at a time of their own choosing by having these supports discontinued—an action fully legal—but patients not dependent on life supports cannot die as they wish but must wait until the inevitable end when the disease finally kills them.

Many opponents of physician-assisted suicide reject attempts at compromise as well, sometimes arguing on religious grounds that suffering is an aspect of dying that ought to be accepted, sometimes holding that patients' wishes for self-determination ought not override the scruples of the medical profession, and sometimes objecting to any resort at all to assisted dying, even in very rare, difficult cases. And some who accept the claim that death is sometimes a benefit to which a person can be morally entitled still object that placing this choice in the hands of patient would make him or her worse off by obliging him or her to choose at all, even if the choice is against. There is little resolution, however, of the competing claims of autonomist and mercy claims on the one hand and wrongness-of-killing and social-consequences views on the other. Like the social arguments over abortion, disagreement continues both at the level of public ferment and at the deeper level of philosophical principle although the raising of the issue itself has meant far greater attention to issues about death and dying.

ETHICAL ISSUES IN CONTEMPORARY APPLICATION: SUICIDE IN OLD AGE

While comparatively rarely discussed in contemporary moral theory, the more difficult applied question concerns suicide in old age for reasons of old age alone though this is said to be an issue that will increasingly confront an aging society. In both historical argumentation and the very small amount of contemporary theorizing, the fundamental issues of suicide in old age concern two distinct sets of reasons for suicide, in practice often intertwined: (1) *Reasons of self-interest*: suicide in order to avoid the sufferings, physical limitations, loss of social roles, and stigma of old age; (2) *Other-regarding reasons*: suicide in order to avoid becoming a burden to others, including family members, caretakers, immediate social networks, or society as a whole.

Contemporary reflection, at least explicitly, countenances neither of these as adequate reasons for suicide in old age. With regard to self-interested reasons, modern gerontology maintains a resolutely upbeat and optimistic view of old age, insisting that it is possible to ameliorate many of the traditional burdens of old age—chronic illness, isolation, poverty, depression, and chronic pain—by providing better medical care, better family and caregiver education, and more comprehensive social programs. With respect to other-regarding reasons, including altruistic reasons, contemporary views consider it unconscionable—especially in the wealthy societies of the developed world—to regard elderly persons as burdens to families or to social units or to the society; nor is it thought ethically permissible to allow or encourage elderly persons to see themselves this way. While the notion that the elderly are to be venerated is associated primarily with the traditional cultures of the Asia, especially China, Western societies also insist, though sometimes ineffectually in a youth-oriented culture, on respect for the aged and on enhancing long lives. Simply put, the prevalent assumption in the Western cultures in the twenty-first century is that there can be no good *reasons* for suicide in old age even though suicide is frequent, especially in men in old age. Daniel Callahan (1930–), although opposing suicide in old age, points to contemporary medicine's relentless drive for indefinite extension of life, arguing that the elderly should forgo heroic life-prolonging care and refocus their attention instead on turning matters over to the next generation. Carlos Prado (1937–), exploring issues of declining competence, raises the issue of *preemptive* suicide in advanced age. Colorado Governor Richard Lamm's widely (mis)quoted remark that the elderly have a "duty to die," unleashed a small storm of academic and public discussion concerning suicide in terminal illness and in old age (Hardwig 1997).

Hints of real social friction can be seen over both self-interested and other-regarding and altruistic reasons for suicide in old age. Having fully legalized physician-assisted suicide and voluntary active euthanasia, the Netherlands is now considering whether to honor advance directives such as living wills in which a now-competent person requests physician-aided death after the onset of Alzheimer disease, a condition particularly frequent among the elderly. Double-exit suicides, often of married partners in advanced age even though only one is ill, startle public awareness. Disputes over generational equity in the face of rising health care costs question whether life prolongation means merely the extension of morbidity and whether health care ought to be preferentially allocated to the young rather than the old. The issue of whether a person may ethically and reasonably refuse medical treatment in order to spare health care costs to preserve an inheritance for his or her family is already beginning to be discussed; the same issue also raises the question of suicide. And issues about suicide in old age are posed by far-reaching changes in population structure, the *graying* of societies in Europe and the developed world: As birthrates fall and the proportion of retirees threatens to overwhelm the number of still-working younger people, could there be any obligation, as Euripides (c. 480–406 BCE) put it in *The Suppliants* nearly 2,500 years ago, go "hence, and die, and make way for the young"?

No party now encourages suicide for the elderly, and, indeed, no party even raises the issue; but the issue of suicide as a response to self-interested avoidance of the conditions of old age and to other-interested questions about social burdens of old age cannot be very far away. Drawing as they might on both Stoic and Christian roots in the West and on non-Western practices now coming to light, the ethical disputes over suicide in old age, independent of illness, are likely to intensify the currently vigorous debate over suicide in terminal illness: Can suicide in old age represent, as one author puts it, the last rational act of autonomous elders, or does it represent the final defeated event in a series of little tragedies of all kinds?

See also Aristotle; Augustine, St.; Consequentialism; Durkheim, Émile; Epistemology; Freud, Sigmund; Hume, David; Kant, Immanuel; More, Thomas; Nietzsche, Friedrich; Plato; Pythagoras and Pythagoreanism; Romanticism; Schopenhauer, Arthur; Staël-Holstein, Anne Louise Germanie Necker, Baronne de; Socrates; Stoicism;Thomas Aquinas, St.

Bibliography

Alvarez, Albert. *The Savage God: A Study of Suicide*. London: Weidenfeld and Nicolson, 1971.

Améry, Jean. *On Suicide: A Discourse on Voluntary Death* (1976). Translated by John D. Barlow. Bloomingon: Indiana University Press, 1999.

Thomas Aquinas. *Summa Theologiae*. 2a2ae, question 64, article 5, translated by Michael Rudick.

Aristotle. *Ethica Nicomachea* Book III, 1115a-1116a; Book V, 1138a, edited and translated by W.D. Ross. Oxford: Clarendon Press, 1925.

Baechler, Jean. *Suicides*. Translated by Barry Cooper. Oxford: Blackwell, 1979.

Barraclough, Brian M. "The Bible Suicides." *Acta Psychiatrica Scandinavia* 86 (1) (1992): 64–69.

Battin, Margaret Pabst. *Ending Life: Ethics and the Way We Die*. New York: Oxford University Press, 2005.

Battin, Margaret Pabst. *Ethical Issues in Suicide*. Englewood Cliffs, NJ: Prentice-Hall, 1982.

Battin, Margaret Pabst. *The Least Worst Death: Essays in Bioethics on the End of Life*. New York: Oxford University Press, 1994.

Battin, Margaret Pabst, and Ronald W. Maris, eds. "Suicide and Ethics." *Suicide and Life-Threatening Behavior*. Spec. issue 13 (4) (1983).

Battin, Margaret Pabst, and David J. Mayo, eds. *Suicide: The Philosophical Issues*. New York: St. Martin's Press, 1980.

Battin, Margaret P., Rosamond Rhodes, and Anita Silvers, eds. *Physician-Assisted Suicide: Expanding the Debate*. New York: Oxford University Press, 1998. Includes Oregon Death with Dignity Act.

Beauchamp, Tom L. *Intending Death: The Ethics of Assisted Suicide and Euthanasia*. Upper Saddle River, NJ: Prentice-Hall, 1996.

Brandt, Richard B. "The Morality and Rationality of Suicide." In *A Handbook for the Study of Suicide*, edited by Seymour Perlin. New York: Oxford University Press, 1975.

Brock, Dan W. *Life and Death: Philosophical Essays in Biomedical Ethics*. Cambridge, U.K.: Cambridge University Press, 1993.

Brock, Dan W. "Physician-Assisted Suicide as a Last-Resort Option at the End of Life." In *Physician-Assisted Dying. The Case for Palliative Care and Patient Choice*, edited by Timothy E. Quill and Margaret Pabst Battin, 130–149. Baltimore: Johns Hopkins University Press, 2004.

Brody, Baruch A., ed. *Suicide and Euthanasia: Historical and Contemporary Themes*. Dordrecht, Netherlands: Kluwer, 1989.

Callahan, Daniel. *False Hopes: Why America's Quest for Perfect Health Is a Recipe for Failure*. New York: Simon and Schuster, 1998.

Cholbi, Michael. "Suicide." *Stanford Encyclopedia of Philosophy*. (Summer 2004 Edition), edited by Edward N. Zalta. Available at http://plato.stanford.edu/.

Cicero, Marcus Tullius. *On Old Age*. Trans. Frank O. Copley. Ann Arbor, The University of Michigan Press, 1967.

Daube, David. "The Linguistics of Suicide." *Philosophy and Public Affairs* 1 (4) (1972): 387–437.

DeLeo, Diego, ed. *Suicide and Euthanasia in Older Adults: A Transcultural Journey*. Göttingen: Hogrefe and Huber, 2001.

Donne, John. *Biathanatos* (1647), edited by Michael Rudick and Margaret Pabst Battin. New York: Garland, 1982.

Droge, Arthur J., and James D. Tabor. *A Noble Death. Suicide and Martyrdom among Christians and Jews in Antiquity*. San Francisco: HarperCollins, 1992.

Durkheim, Emile. *Suicide: A Study in Sociology*. Translated by John A. Spaulding and edited by George Simpson. New York: Free Press, 1951.

Emanuel, Ezekiel J. "What is the Great Benefit of Legalizing Euthanasia or Physician-Assisted Suicide?" *Ethics* 109 (3) (1999): 629–642.

Emanuel, Linda L., ed. *Regulating How We Die: The Ethical, Medical, and Legal Issues Surrounding Physician-Assisted Suicide*. Cambridge, MA: Harvard University Press, 1998.

Euripides. *The Suppliants*, line 1113. Translated by Arthur S. Way. In *Euripides*. London: William Heinemann; New York: Macmillan, 1912, vol. 3, p. 589.

Fedden, Henry Romilly. *Suicide: A Social and Historical Study*. London: Peter Davies, 1938.

Fischer, John Martin, ed. *The Metaphysics of Death*. Stanford, CA: Stanford University Press, 1993.

Fletcher, David B. "Holy Dying, Assisted Dying? An Anglican Perspective on Physician-Assisted Suicide." *Ethics and Medicine* 1 (2004): 35–43.

Foley, Kathleen, and Herbert Hendin. *The Case against Assisted Suicide: For the Right to End-of-Life Care*. Baltimore: Johns Hopkins University Press, 2002.

Francis, Leslie Pickering. "Assisted Suicide: Are the Elderly a Special Case?" In *Physician Assisted Suicide: Expanding the Debate*, edited by Margaret P. Battin, Rosamond Rhodes, and Anita Silvers, 75–90. New York: Routledge, 1998.

Gentzler, Jyl. "What Is a Death with Dignity?" *Journal of Medicine and Philosophy* 28 (4) (2003): 461–487.

Griffiths, John, Alex Bood, and Heleen Weyers. *Euthanasia and the Law in the Netherlands*. Amsterdam: Amsterdam University Press, 1998.

Hardwig, John. "Is There a Duty to Die?" *Hastings Center Report* 27 (2) (1997): 34–42.

Hill, Thoms E. "Self-Regarding Suicide: A Modified Kantian View." In *Autonomy and Self-Respect*, 85–103. Cambridge, U.K.: Cambridge University Press, 1991.

Humber, James M., and Robert F. Almeder, eds. *Is There a Duty to Die?* Totowa, NJ: Humana Press, 2000.

Hume, David. "Of Suicide." (1777). In *Essays: Moral, Political, and Literary*, 586–596. London: Oxford University Press, 1963.

Humphry, Derek. *Final Exit: The Practicalities of Self-Deliverance and Assisted Suicide for the Dying*. Eugene, OR: National Hemlock Society, 1991.

Humphry, Derek, with Ann Wickett. *Jean's Way*. London: Quartet Books, 1978.

Kamisar, Yale. "Some Non-religious Views Against Proposed 'Mercy-Killing' Legislation." *Minnesota Law Review* 42 (1958): 969–1041.

Kamm, F. M. "Physician-Assisted Suicide, the Doctrine of Double Effect, and the Ground of Value." *Ethics* 109 (3) (1999): 586–605.

Kant, Immanuel. *Lectures on Ethics*. Translated by Louis Infield. Indianapolis, IN: Hackett, 1980.

Kant, Immanuel. *Ethical Philosophy: The Complete Texts of the Grounding for the Metaphysics of Morals, and Metaphysical Principles of Virtue, Part II of the Metaphysics of Morals*. Translated by James W. Ellington. Indianapolis, IN: Hackett, 1983.

Kant, Immanuel. *The Critique of Practical Reason*. Translated by Lewis White Beck. New York: Macmillan, 1993.

Kass, Leon. "Death with Dignity and the Sanctity of Life." *Commentary* (March 1990): 33–43.

Korsgaard, Christine M. *The Sources of Normativity*. Cambridge, U.K.: Cambridge University Press, 1996.

Landsberg, Paul-Louis. *The Experience of Death; The Moral Problem of Suicide*. Translated by Cynthia Rowland. New York: Philosophical Library, 1953.

Maris, Ronald W., Alan L. Berman, and Morton M. Silverman. *Comprehensive Textbook of Suicidology*. New York: Guilford Press, 2000.

McIntosh, John L. Annual updated U.S. suicide statistics. Available from www.iusb.edu/~jmcintos/. Official data also available in hardcopy from *National Vital Statistics Reports*, National Center for Health Statistics, Hyattsville, Maryland.

Minois, George. *History of Suicide. Voluntary Death in Western Culture*. Translated by Lydia G. Cochrane. Baltimore: Johns Hopkins University Press, 1999.

More, Thomas. *Utopia*. Book II. Translated by Ralph Robinson, in *Three Early Modern Utopias*, edited by Susan Bruce. Oxford University Press, 1999, pp. 89-90

Murray, Alexander. *Suicide in the Middle Ages: The Violent against Themselves*. Vol. 1. Oxford: Oxford University Press, 1998.

Narveson, Jan. "Self-Ownership and the Ethics of Suicide." *Suicide and Life-Threatening Behavior* 13 (4) (1983): 240–253.

Nietzsche, Friedrich. *The Day of Dawn (Morgenrote)* Original edition, 1881. Stuttgart: Kroner Verlag, 1953, p. 210.

Oregon Health Department. Annual data on the Death with Dignity Act. Available from http://www.oregon.gov/.

Perlin, Seymour, ed. *A Handbook for the Study of Suicide*. Oxford: Oxford University Press, 1975.

Plato. *The Dialogues of Plato*. Phaedo 61B-69E, 116A–118A; Republic III 405A–410A; Laws IX 853A-854D, 862D-863A, 872D–873E. Translated by. Benjamin Jowett. New York: Random House, 1892, 1920, vol. I, pp. 444–453 and 499–501; 669–674; vol. II, pp. 599–600, 608, 617–618.

Prado, Carlos G. *The Last Choice: Preemptive Suicide in Advanced Age*. Westport, CT: Greenwood Press, 1990.

Putnam, Constance E. *Hospice or Hemlock? Searching for Heroic Compassion*. Westport, CT: Praeger, 2002.

Quill, Timothy E. *A Midwife Through the Dying Process: Stories of Healing and Hard Choices at the End of Life*. Baltimore: Johns Hopkins University Press, 1996.

Quill, Timothy E., and Margaret P. Battin, eds. *Physician-Assisted Dying. The Case for Palliative Care and Patient Choice*. Baltimore: Johns Hopkins University Press,2004.

Raymond, Diane. "'Fatal Practices': A Feminist Analysis of Physician-Assisted Suicide and Euthanasia." *Hypatia: A Journal of Feminist Philosophy* 14 (2) (1999): 1–25.

Regan, Donald H. "Suicide and the Failure of Modern Moral Theory." *Suicide and Life-Threatening Behavior* 13 (4) (1983): 276–292.

Sartorius, Rolf. "Coercive Suicide Prevention: A Libertarian Perspective." *Suicide and Life-Threatening Behavior* 13 (4) (1983): 293–303.

Seneca, Lucius Annaeus. *Ad Lucilium Epistulae Morales* (Moral letters to Lucilius). Vol. 2. Letters 70 ("On the Proper Time to Slip the Cable"), 77 ("On Taking One's Own Life"), 78 ("On the Healing Power of the Mind"). Translated by Richard M. Gummere, 57–73, 169–199. New York: G. P. Putnam's Sons, 1920.

Shneidman, Edwin S., ed. *Suicidology: Contemporary Developments*. New York: Grune and Stratton, 1976.

Shneidman, Edwin S., and Norman I. Farberow, eds. *Clues to Suicide*. New York: McGraw-Hill, 1957.

Seneca, Lucius Annaeus. "Letter on Suicide" and "On the Proper Time to Slip the Cable." In *Ad Lucilium Epistulae Morales*. Translated by Richard M. Gummere. London: Heinemann, 1920.

Sprott, Samuel E. *The English Debate on Suicide: From Donne to Hume*. La Salle, IL.: Open Court, 1961.

Steinbock, B. "The Case for Physician-Assisted Suicide: Not (Yet) Proven." *Journal of Medical Ethics* 331 (2005): 235–241.

Thomasma, David C., Thomasine Kimbrough-Kushner, Gerrit K. Kimsma, and Chris Ciesielski-Carlucci, eds. *Asking to Die: Inside the Dutch Debate About Euthanasia*. Dordrecht, Netherlands: Kluwer, 1998.

van der Maas, Paul J., Gerrit van der Wal, et al. "Euthanasia, Physician-Assisted Suicide and Other Medical Practices Involving the End of Life in the Netherlands, 1990–1995." *New England Journal of Medicine* 335 (22) (1996): 1699–1705.

Velleman, J. David. "Against the Right to Die." *Journal of Medicine and Philosophy* 17 (1992): 665–81.

Velleman, J. David. "A Right of Self-Termination? *Ethics* 109 (1999): 606–628.

Wellman, Carl. "A Legal Right to Physician-Assisted Suicide Defended." *Social Theory and Practice* 29 (1) (2003): 19–38.

Werth, James L. Jr. *Contemporary Perspectives on Rational Suicide*. Philadelphia: Taylor and Francis, 1999.

Windt, Peter, "The Concept of Suicide." In *Suicide: The Philosophical Issues*, edited by M. Pabst Battin and David J. Mayo, 39–47. New York: St. Martin's Press, 1980.

Margaret Pabst Battin (2005)

SULZER, JOHANN GEORG

(1720–1779)

Johann Georg Sulzer, the Swiss aesthetician, was born in Winterthur. After studying in Zürich under J. J. Bodmer, he became a tutor in a private home in Magdeburg in 1743. He then went to Berlin, where he became acquainted with Pierre-Louis Moreau de Maupertuis and Leonhard Euler. In 1747 he was appointed professor of mathematics at the Joachimsthaler Gymnasium and in 1763 he moved to the new Ritterakademie. Illness forced him to resign in 1773, but in 1775 he was appointed director of the philosophical section of the Berlin Academy, to which he had been elected in 1750.

Sulzer's *Allgemeine Theorie der Schönen Künste* (General theory of the fine arts) was originally planned as a revision of Jacques Lacombe's *Dictionnaire portatif des beaux-arts* (1752), but it developed into an original encyclopedia covering both general aesthetics and the theory and history of each of the arts and of literature. The edition of 1796–1798, completed with biographical supplements by Christian Friedrich von Blankenburg, is still the best *summa* of German Enlightenment aesthetics and theory of art, as well as being an original contribution to aesthetics.

Sulzer's style, his psychological interests, and his unsystematic method were typical of the "popular philosophers." Because of his lack of system, and because his ideas are spread through the various articles of his encyclopedia, it is difficult to reduce his views to an organic and systematic whole.

Sulzer's aesthetics was inspired by Gottfried Wilhelm Leibniz, A. G. Baumgarten, G. F. Meier, Moses Mendelssohn, Joseph Addison, Edwards Young, and others. But the psychological character of Sulzer's work is even stronger than that of Baumgarten, Meier, or Mendelssohn. He was the first to find the source of beauty in the perceiving subject only, abandoning every residue of French classicism still present in his German predecessors.

Following Leibniz, Sulzer held that the essence and perfection of the soul consists in its activity of representation. The soul is representing sensibly when it is representing a multiplicity of partial representations taken as a whole. If it is representing every part of a representation as a distinct unit, it is thinking. Sensible representation is more effective than thought, and leads more readily to action. Thus the "lower faculty" of representation of traditional German psychology became more important relative to intellect in Sulzer than in Baumgarten or Meier.

Aesthetics, for Sulzer as for Baumgarten and Meier, was the theory of sensible representation. It explained how to arouse the soul to greater activity. This activity would make sensible representations more lively, and because the activity of representation was intimately connected with the feeling of pleasure, more pleasurable and beautiful.

By studying the psychological constitution of the soul it would be possible to deduce the general rules of the different arts—the more special rules can neither be deduced nor taught. The most important rule concerns the harmony of unity and multiplicity in the beautiful object as it arises out of the representative action of the soul. The object must conform to a spontaneous (*ungezwungen*) order and it must be coherent (*zusammenhängend*).

Sulzer held that beauty is judged by a special feeling—taste—that he sometimes seems to have held to be a function of a faculty different from intellect and the faculty of moral feeling but closely connected with both, particularly with the latter through the moral value of beauty. Taste itself is a transition between thinking and feeling.

Beauty, according to Sulzer, is a product of genius which is the highest stage of the spontaneous representative state of the soul. Genius is a natural force within the soul, and it acts unconsciously in a rational way. It does not, contrary to Baumgarten and Meier, create a new world. Art is an imitation of nature not because it copies nature, but because the artist of genius imitates nature's creative process. He creates nothing outside of nature, but something new within the natural world. In general, art is the expression of a psychological state of man; it imitates human nature in that it expresses nature through the representation of an object.

Sulzer, influenced by Johann Joachim Winckelmann, held that some works of art represent an ideal—that is, they express sensibly a general concept not mixed with anything particular.

In the theory of the individual arts Sulzer's most important contributions were in the aesthetics of music. Music, according to Sulzer, was the expression of passion. Opera, which is a union of all the arts, is the highest form of drama. Besides influencing musical theoreticians, Sulzer's aesthetics influenced Immanuel Kant and Friedrich Schiller; and although Sulzer was attacked by Johann Wolfgang von Goethe in 1772, his work was the foundation of the aesthetics of the *Sturm und Drang.*

Bibliography

WORKS BY SULZER

Versuch einiger moralischer Betrachtungen über die Werke der Natur. Berlin, 1745.

Untersuchungen über die Schönheit der Natur. Berlin, 1750.

Allgemeine Theorie der Schönen Künste. 2 vols. Leipzig: Weidmannschen, 1771–1774; 4th enlarged edition with supplements by C. F. von Blankenburg, 4 vols., Leipzig, 1796–1798.

Vermischte philosophische Schriften. 2 vols. Leipzig, 1773–1781.

WORKS ON SULZER

Dahne, M. *J. G. Sulzer als Pädagoge.* Leipzig, 1902.

Gross, Karl Josef. *Sulzers Allgemeine Theorie der schönen Künste.* Berlin: E. Ebering, 1905.

Heym, L. M. *Darstellung und Kritik der ästhetischen Ansichten J. G. Sulzers.* Leipzig, 1894.

Leo, Johannes. *Zur Entstehungsgeschichte der "Allgemeinen Theorie der schönen Künste" J. G. Sulzers.* Heidelberg, 1906.

Palme, Anton. *J. G. Sulzers Psychologie und die Anfänge der Dreivermögenslehre.* Friedenau, Germany: L. Schultz, 1905.
Tumarkin, Anna. *Der Asthetiker J. G. Sulzers.* Frauenfeld and Leipzig: Huber, 1933.
Wolf, R. *J. G. Sulzer aus Winterthur.* Zürich, 1860.

Giorgio Tonelli (1967)

SUMNER, WILLIAM GRAHAM
(1840–1910)

The American social philosopher, economist, and cultural anthropologist William Graham Sumner was graduated from Yale in 1863 and continued his studies at Geneva, Göttingen, and Oxford, with the aim of entering the Episcopal ministry. He did so in 1867, having returned to America the preceding year. Increasingly, however, this calling conflicted with his wider interests, and when in 1872 he was offered the chair of political and social science at Yale University, he gladly accepted it. He soon gained a considerable reputation as a teacher, publicist, and local politician, but his chief claim to renown derived from his studies in social development, culminating in his masterpiece, *Folkways* (1907).

Two conflicting impulses—polemical and scientific—dominated Sumner's approach to the study of society. It was undoubtedly the polemical impulse that fed the scientific. Dissatisfaction with the reformist dogmatism of his age prompted his search for a scientific basis for his own no less dogmatic advocacy of laissez-faire. In place of "political engineering" based on a facile and sentimental philosophy, Sumner advocated "social evolutionism" free from moralizing preconceptions.

Sumner identified the basic social forces with certain group habits, or "folkways," which, he held, operate on a subconscious level and reflect the spontaneous and the primary needs and interests of a given society, such as hunger, sex, vanity, and fear. These needs and interests, rather than conceptually formed purposes, determine the course of social development. Once the folkways attain persistence and stability, they become reinforced by more conscious processes, such as religious sanctions. Through repeated transmission they assume the status of sociomoral traditions, or "mores." The mores, supported by group authority, then function as the chief agencies of "legitimation"; they determine what shall be deemed right or wrong, or socially acceptable or unacceptable. The mores form the matrix into which an individual is born, and they pervade and control his ways of thinking in all the exigencies of life. The individual becomes critically conscious of his mores only when he comes into contact with another society with different mores or, if he lives in a society at a higher level of civilization, through literature.

Attempts to change a particular set of mores meet with considerable resistance, for they present themselves "as final and unchangeable, because they present answers which are offered as 'the truth'" (*Folkways,* Ch. 2, Sec. 83). Hence, Sumner argued, it was not likely that they could be substantively affected by revolutions or other predetermined acts or changed "by any artifice or device, to a great extent, or suddenly, or in any essential element" (ibid., Sec. 91). Legislation by itself can do little to bring about a transformation of social and moral values. To be truly effective, legislation must grow out of a people's mores; only then is it in keeping with their basic "interests." Nonetheless, Sumner did not deny the significance of legislation, as some commentators have suggested. Indeed, he believed it had a highly educative role, even when it was ineffective in achieving its intended ends. For "it is only in so far as things have been transferred from the mores into laws and positive institutions that there is discussion about them or rationalizing upon them" (ibid., Sec. 80). These unintended consequences, far from being a threat to the established system of mores, constitute a vital component of that system, since it is through such a "rationalizing" process that the mores develop "their own philosophical and ethical generalizations, which are elevated into 'principles' of truth and right" (ibid., Sec. 83).

Although Sumner had little faith in the efficacy of social and economic change produced by state intervention, he was by no means a fatalist or a blind defender of the status quo. A relativist in the tradition of Baron de Montesquieu and Johann Gottfried Herder, a conservative in the tradition of Edmund Burke and Alexander Hamilton, an individualist in the tradition of Thomas Jefferson and Wilhelm von Humboldt, a historicist in the tradition of Friedrich Karl von Savigny and the romanticists, a Spencerian and Darwinist by confession, Sumner believed that man could mold his social life only by paying heed to the "organic" nature of social growth, that he could modify its operative values only "by slow and long continued effort" (ibid., Sec. 91).

Starting from premises not unlike those of Karl Marx, Sumner was, in a sense, a social determinist. However, he recognized the dynamic role of beliefs and the operative value of ideas and, like Marx, he denied their independence from or superiority to material interests.

Material interests constituted both the primary source and the ultimate sanction of social action. Although they drew opposite inferences from their shared premises, and although they were both mistaken in their several dogmatisms and prophecies, Sumner and Marx nevertheless laid bare in an equally fearless manner many features of social development that their generation ignored.

See also Burke, Edmund; Darwinism; Herder, Johann Gottfried; Humboldt, Wilhelm von; Jefferson, Thomas; Marx, Karl; Montesquieu, Baron de; Savigny, Friedrich Karl von; Sociology of Knowledge.

Bibliography

WORKS BY SUMNER

A History of American Currency. New York: Holt, 1874.

Andrew Jackson as a Public Man. Boston: Houghton Mifflin, 1882.

What Social Classes Owe to Each Other. New York: Harper, 1883.

Alexander Hamilton. New York: Dodd Mead, 1890.

The Financier and the Finances of the American Revolution, 2 vols. New York: Dodd Mead, 1891.

A History of Banking in the United States. New York, 1896.

Folkways. Boston: Ginn, 1907.

Earth-Hunger and Other Essays. Edited by A. G. Keller. New Haven, CT: Yale University Press, 1913.

The Forgotten Man, and Other Essays. Edited by A. G. Keller. New Haven, CT: Yale University Press, 1918.

On Liberty, Society, and Politics: The Essential Essays of William Graham Sumner. Edited by Robert C. Bannister. Indianapolis: Liberty Fund, 1992.

WORKS ON SUMNER

Ball, H. V., G. E. Simpson, and K. Ikeda. "Law and Social Change: Sumner Reconsidered." *American Journal of Sociology* 67 (5) (March 1962).

Barnes, H. E. *An Introduction to the History of Sociology.* Chicago: University of Chicago Press, 1948. Ch. 6, "William Graham Sumner; Spencerianism in American Dress."

Curtis, Bruce. *William Graham Sumner.* Boston: Twayne, 1981.

Ellwood, C. A. *A History of Social Philosophy.* New York: Prentice-Hall, 1938. Ch. 28, "William Graham Sumner and Laissez Faire."

Hofstadter, Richard. *Social Darwinism in American Thought.* Boston: Beacon Press, 1955. Ch. 3, "William Graham Sumner."

Keller, A. G. *Reminiscences (Mainly Personal) of William Graham Sumner.* New Haven, CT: Yale University Press, 1933.

Pickens, Donald K. "Scottish Common Sense Philosophy and 'Folkways.'" *Journal of Thought* 22 (1987): 39–44.

Starr, H. E. *William Graham Sumner.* New York: Holt, 1925.

Frederick M. Barnard (1967)
Bibliography updated by Philip Reed (2005)

SUPERVENIENCE

There is supervenience when and only when there cannot be a difference of some sort A (for example, mental) without a difference of some sort B (for example, physical). When there cannot be an A-difference without a B-difference, then but only then A-respects supervene on B-respects. Supervenience claims are thus modal claims. They are claims to the effect that *necessarily*, there is exact similarity in A-respects whenever there is exact similarity in B-respects. So if, for example, mental properties supervene on physical properties, then, necessarily, individuals that are physically indiscernible (exactly alike with respect to every physical property) are mentally indiscernible (exactly alike with respect to every mental property). Thus, A-properties supervene on B-properties just in case how something is with respect to A-properties is a function of how it is with respect to B-properties.

Supervenience has been invoked in nearly every area of analytical philosophy. In addition to its having been claimed that mental properties supervene on physical properties, it has also been claimed that normative properties—moral, aesthetic, epistemic, and so on—supervene on natural properties, that general truths supervene on particular truths, and that modal truths supervene on nonmodal truths. Supervenience, moreover, has been used to distinguish various kinds of internalism and externalism: epistemic, semantic, and mental. And it has been invoked to test claims of reducibility and claims of conceptual analysis, both of which entail supervenience claims. Much of the philosophical work on supervenience itself, as opposed to its philosophical applications, has focused on distinguishing various varieties of supervenience, and examining their pairwise logical relations. But, before turning to the main varieties of supervenience, we can make some central points working just with the idea that there cannot be an A-difference without a B-difference.

1. MODEL FORCE

The term *cannot* in a supervenience claim can express logical impossibility, nomological impossibility (impossibility by virtue of laws of nature), or some other kind of impossibility. If it is logically impossible for there to be an A-difference without a B-difference, then A-properties logically supervene on B-properties; if that is only nomologically impossible, then there is merely nomological supervenience. The property *being a bachelor* logically supervenes on the set of properties {*being unmarried, being a man*} because it is logically impossible for individuals to differ with respect to *being a bachelor* without differing with respect to some property in that set. According to the Wiedemann-Franz law, the electrical conductivity of metals covaries with their thermal conductivity; thus, in metals, electrical-conductivity properties nomologically supervene on thermal conductivity properties (and vice versa).

2. THE RELATA OF THE SUPERVENIENCE RELATION

A difference can be a difference in any respect in which there can be a difference: a difference with respect to what properties something has, in what truths hold, in what conditions obtain, in what events occur, in what laws of nature there are, and so on. The *relata* of the supervenience relation thus seem many and varied. Indeed in "There cannot be an A-difference without a B-difference," A and B may range over nearly all manner of entities. It is often claimed, however, that nonempty sets of properties are the *primary relata* of the supervenience relation: either A-respects and B-respects will be properties in some nonempty sets of properties A and B, or else A-respects will supervene on B-respects in virtue of A-properties supervening on B-properties (Kim 1984). This view requires an "abundant" (as opposed to a "sparse") conception of properties, according to which properties "may be as extrinsic, as gruesomely gerrymandered, as miscellaneously disjunctive, as you please. … [They] far outrun the predicates of any language we could possibly possess. … In fact, the properties are as abundant as the sets themselves, because for any set whatever, there is the property of belong to that set" (Lewis 1986, 59–60).

Indeed, on this conception, there are even necessarily uninstantiated properties such as *being an electron and not being an electron*, and so properties are not always ways things might be. In the literature on supervenience, an abundance of properties is often assumed, and such will be assumed in this essay. But whether there is supervenience does not turn on whether there are abundant properties, or, if nominalists are right, even on whether there are properties at all. A nominalist could maintain that what A-predicates are true of something supervenes on what B-predicates are true of it. Nor does it turn on whether there is some uniform category of being the members of which are the *primary relata* of the supervenience relation. It does not even turn on whether there is a relation of supervenience in anything other than a merely pleonastic sense: talk of A bearing the supervenience relation to B might be taken to be just a way of saying that there cannot be an A-difference without a B-difference. What matters is that there be true statements of the form, "There cannot be an A-difference without a B-difference." And such there are in abundance, including many of philosophical interest.

3. LOGICAL PROPERTIES OF THE SUPERVENIENCE RELATION

Supervenience is reflexive, transitive, and nonsymmetric. Trivially, it holds when A = B and so is reflexive. It is also transitive, because if there cannot be an A-difference without a B-difference, and cannot be a B-difference without a C-difference, then there cannot be an A-difference without a C-difference. However, it is neither symmetric nor asymmetric, and so is nonsymmetric. Every reflexive case of supervenience is trivially symmetric. But, for instance, *being a bachelor* asymmetrically supervenes on {*being unmarried, being a man*}. James is a man and Vanessa is not, and so they differ with respect to B-properties. But since James is married, they are exactly alike with respect to *being a bachelor*: neither of them has that property.

4. SUPERVENIENCE AND ENTAILMENT

A notion of property entailment can be defined as follows: property P entails property Q if and only if it is logically necessary that whatever has P has Q. Supervenience shares with entailment the properties of being reflexive, transitive, and nonsymmetric. Property supervenience, however, is neither necessary nor sufficient for property entailment. The property *being a brother* entails the property *being a sibling*. But *being a sibling* does not supervene on *being a brother*. Thus, suppose that Sarah has a sister and that Jack is an only child. Then Sarah is a sibling and Jack is not, though neither is a brother. Property entailment thus does not suffice for supervenience.

It is often claimed in the literature that *logical* supervenience suffices for entailment (see, for example, Chalmers 1996). But that is not in general true. If A = {P&Q} and B = {P, Q}, then the A-property logically supervenes on B-properties, but no B-property entails the A- property. Indeed, every property F will supervene with logical necessity on its complement, not-F: Two things cannot differ with respect to F without differing with respect to not-F (and vice versa). But of course *being F* does not entail *being not-F* (McLaughlin 1995).

There seem, moreover, to be philosophically interesting cases of logical supervenience without entailment. Particular truths do not entail general truths. But general truths (arguably) supervene on particular truths (Skyrms 1981, Lewis 1986a). Bertrand Russell correctly noted:

"you cannot ever arrive at a general fact by [deductive] inference from particular facts, however, numerous" (1918/1992, p. 235, quoted in Bricker 2005). He concluded from this that "you must admit general facts as distinct from and over and above particular facts" (1981/1992, p. 236). If, however, general facts logically supervene on particular facts, then there is a sense in which that is not so, for once all the particular facts of a world are fixed, the general facts are fixed as well. A compelling case has been made that general facts logically supervene on particular facts, despite not being entailed by them (Bricker 2005).

5. SUPERVENIENCE AND ONTOLOGICAL PRIORITY

Many of the most interesting cases of supervenience are ones in which the subvenient factors are *ontologically prior* to the supervenient factors. Supervenience itself, however, is not an ontological priority relation. Ontological priority is irreflexive and asymmetric: Nothing can be ontologically prior to itself or be ontologically prior to something that is ontologically prior to it. But supervenience is reflexive and not asymmetric. Supervenience claims do not, in general, entail "in virtue of" claims. Every property supervenes on its complement, but of course nothing has a property F in virtue of having its complement not-F because nothing has both F and not-F (at least at the same time). Further, properties that everything necessarily has, and ones that nothing could possibly have, supervene on any property whatsoever. The necessary property *being an electron or not an electron* trivially supervenes on the property *being an antique*; and the necessarily uninstantiated property *being an electron and not being an electron* does well. The reason is that no two things can differ with respect to either such noncontingent property; and so, trivially, for any property, no two things can differ with respect to them without differing with respect to it. But there is no ontological priority in such cases. (McLaughlin 1995)

6. SUPERDUPER VENIENCE

Supervenience is just the relation of functional dependence: A-properties supervene on B-properties just in case how something is with respect to A-properties is a function of how it is with respect to B-properties. Given that, when A-properties supervene on B-properties, we expect there to be some explanation of why that is so. In the case of logical supervenience, the explanation might be that A-properties are necessary properties or that they are properties nothing could have. Or the explanation might be that A-properties are identical with B properties. Or the explanation might be that A-properties are determinables of B-properties and B-properties are all the determinates of A-properties, as *being colored* is a determinable of all the shades of color (*being red*, and so on), and they are determinates of *being colored*. And in the case of merely nomological supervenience, the explanation will appeal to a law of nature. (This list of possible explanations is not intended to be exhaustive.) When a supervenience relation is explainable, there is "superdupervenience" (Horgan 1993). Appeals to in principle unexplainable supervenience—supervenience without the possibility of superdupervience—would arguably be mystery-mongering.

7. SUPERVIENCE, CONCEPTUAL ANALYSIS, AND REDUCTION

Although logical supervenience does not suffice for conceptual analysis, the latter requires the former: if A-factors can be conceptually analyzed in terms of B-factors, then A-factors logically supervene on B-factors. Supervenience is thus useful in testing claims that a certain a kind of conceptual analysis is possible. According to a simple causal theory of perceptual knowledge, a subject's perceptual knowledge that P can be analyzed as P's bearing an appropriate causal connection to the subject's perceptual belief that P. To test the claim, one need not await a specific proposal as to what kind of causal connection is appropriate. For such a conceptual analysis is possible only if two believers that P cannot differ with respect to perceptually knowing that P without differing with respect to how the fact that P is causally connected to their belief that P. This supervenience thesis is open to refutation by a single counterexample. The well-known "fake barn country" case (Goldman 1976) yields a putative counterexample to this thesis. Thus, the claim that a certain kind of conceptual analysis is possible can be refuted by appeal to a false implied supervenience thesis (or, FIST). Claims that certain kinds of reductions are possible can be similarly tested by their implied supervenience theses. (McLaughlin 1995)

8. INDIVIDUAL/GLOBAL SUPERVENIENCE

There is a distinction between *individual* supervenience and *global* supervenience. The former concerns differences in individuals; the latter concern differences in possible worlds. The claim that individuals cannot differ with respect to their moral properties without differing with respect to their natural properties (Hare 1952) is an individual supervenience thesis. The claim that possible worlds cannot differ with respect to what general truth hold in them without differing with respect to what particular truths hold in them is a global supervenience thesis.

9. STRONG/WEAK INDIVIDUAL SUPERVENIENCE

Two nonequivalent kinds of individual supervenience have been formulated as follows (see Kim 1987):

POSSIBLE-WORLDS WEAK INDIVIDUAL SUPERVENIENCE. A-properties weakly supervene on B-properties if and only if in any possible world *w*, B-indiscernible individuals in *w* are A-indiscernible in *w*.

POSSIBLE-WORLD STRONG INDIVIDUAL SUPERVENIENCE. A-properties strongly supervene on B-properties if and only if for any possible worlds *w* and *w**, and any individuals *x* and *y*, if *x* in *w* is B-indiscernible from *y* in *w**, then *x* in *w* is A-indiscernible from *y* in w*.

The possible worlds quantified over might be all logically possible worlds or only all nomologically possible worlds (and so on); thus, weak and strong supervenience relations can have different modal strengths. As the names suggest, strong supervenience is stronger than weak supervenience (*modulo* sameness of modality). When the range of worlds is the same, strong supervenience of A-properties on B-properties entails weak supervenience of A-properties on B-properties, but the latter does not in general entail the former. Notions of weak and strong individual supervenience have also been formulated as follows, using the modal operator *necessarily* rather than quantification over possible worlds (Kim 1984).

OPERATOR-WEAK INDIVIDUAL SUPERVENIENCE. A-properties weakly supervene on B-properties if and only if necessarily, for any A-property *F*, if something has *F*, then there is a B-property G such that it has G, and whatever has G has *F*.

OPERATOR-STRONG INDIVIDUAL SUPERVENIENCE. A-properties strongly supervene on B-properties if and only if necessarily, for any *A*-property *F*, if something has *F*, then there is a B-property G such that it has G, and necessarily whatever has G has *F*.

The strong version is formulated exactly like the weak version except that it contains one more necessity operator. The two modal operators in the strong case can be the same or different. When all of the modal operators are the same, strong supervenience entails weak supervenience, but the latter does not in general entail the former.

If necessity is understood as universal quantification over possible worlds, then operator-weak supervenience entails world-weak supervenience, and operator-strong supervenience entails world-strong supervenience. However, the converse entailments do not hold in general. The operator definitions go beyond the idea that B-indiscernible individuals must be A-indiscernible. Operator-strong supervenience with logical necessity guarantees that every A-property is entailed by a B-property. And both operator-weak supervenience and operator-strong supervenience entail that if something has an A-property, then it has some B-property. Neither world-weak supervenience nor world-strong supervenience has that entailment, and so world-strong supervenience fails even to entail operator-weak supervenience (McLaughlin 1995). The property *being a bachelor* fails to even operator-weakly supervene on {*being unmarried*, *being a man*}, even though the former world-strongly supervenes on the later. The weak and strong operator definitions are, however, equivalent to the corresponding world-definitions in the special case of nonempty sets of properties closed under the Boolean operations of complementation and conjunction and/or disjunction, and ones involving quantification (Kim 1987). (The qualifiers *world* and *operator* will now be dropped.)

10. SUPERVENIENCE AND INTERNALISM/EXTERNALISM DISTINCTIONS

Individual supervenience has proved useful for formulating various kinds of internalism/externalism distinctions. For example, according to internalists about mental content, what content a mental state has will strongly supervene on intrinsic properties of the subject of the mental state. Content externalists deny such supervenience, and indeed typically deny there is even weak supervenience: they typically hold that two subjects within a possible world can be intrinsic duplicates while being in mental states with different contents. (Twin-Earth cases [Putnam 1975] are invoked in would-be arguments by appeal to FISTs against internalist theories of content.) Similarly, an internalist about epistemic justification asserts that whether a belief is justified strongly supervenes on what mental states the subject is in. Epistemic externalists deny that, and indeed deny that whether a belief is epistemically justified even weakly supervenes on what mental states the subject is in. Moreover, supervenience has been employed to capture the traditional distinction between internal and external relations (Lewis 1986a): internal relations (such as *being taller than*) strongly supervene on the intrinsic natures of its *relata*, whereas external relations (such as *being three kilometers from*) fail to even weakly supervene on the intrinsic natures of its *relata*.

11. WEAK SUPERVENIENCE WITHOUT STRONG SUPERVENIENCE

There can be weak supervenience without strong supervenience. But when this is the case, we expect an explanation of why weak supervenience holds that does not entail that strong supervenience holds as well. In any possible world, if two individuals assert exactly the same propositions, then they are exactly alike in having asserted a true proposition: The one will have asserted a true proposition if and only if the other did. The explanation is that any proposition will have a unique truth value relative to a world. But since contingent propositions are true in some worlds but not in others, strong supervenience fails in the case in question. It has been claimed that, although moral properties weakly supervene on natural properties, they do not strongly supervene on them (Hare 1952). And it has been claimed that, although mental properties weakly supervene on physical properties, they do not strong supervene on them (Davidson 1985). Defense of these claims requires an explanation of why weak supervenience holds despite the failure of strong supervenience. Although attempts have been made to provide such an explanation in the moral case (Blackburn 1993), there has been no attempt in the mental case. Many philosophers doubt such an explanation is possible in the mental case.

12. GLOBAL SUPERVENIENCE

Global supervenience has been invoked in the formulation of various philosophical doctrines (see, for example, Horgan 1982, 1984; Haugeland 1982; Post 1987). David Lewis's (1986a, x) doctrine of Humean Supervenience, according to which everything supervenes on the pattern of perfectly natural qualitative properties across space-times points, is a global supervenience thesis. Although Donald Davidson (1970) proposed a weak individual supervenience thesis to characterize the dependency of mental properties on physical properties, several attempts have been made to characterize physicalism as a global supervenience thesis (Lewis 1983, Chalmers 1996, Jackson 1996).

For example, Frank Jackson has proposed the following formulation: Any possible world that is a minimal physical duplicate of our world is a duplicate *simpliciter* of it (1998, p. 12). A physical duplicate of our world is any world exactly like it in every physical respect—with respect to its worldwide pattern of distribution of physical properties and relations, its physical laws, and so on. A minimal physical duplicate is any physical duplicate that contains nothing other than what is metaphysically necessary to be a physical duplicate. It is controversial whether this thesis suffices for physicalism; unlike physicalism, it seems compatible with the existence of a necessarily existing God. But even if it does not suffice, if physicalism requires it, then it earns its keep. A substantive condition of adequacy on physicalism would be that it explain why the supervenience thesis is true. And physicalism itself would rendered testable, even in the absence of a fully adequate formulation. Given that we are phenomenally conscious, if, as some philosophers (Chalmers 1996) maintain, a "zombie world" is possible—a world that is a minimal physical duplicate of our world but entirely devoid of phenomenal consciousness—then physicalism is false. Of course, the success of this would-be refutation by appeal to a FIST turns on the controversial issue of whether a zombie world is indeed possible.

Global property supervenience has often been formulated as follows:

GLOBAL SUPERVENIENCE. A globally supervenes on B if and only if, for any possible worlds w_1 and w_2, if w_1 and w_2, have exactly the same worldwide pattern of distribution of B-properties, then w_1 and w_2 have exactly the same worldwide pattern of distribution of A-properties.

It is now usually acknowledged that the notion of a worldwide pattern of distribution of properties should be understood in terms of a kind of property-preserving isomorphism between worlds as follows (McLaughlin 1996, 1997; Stalnaker 1996):

> An isomorphism I between the inhabitants of any worlds w_1 and w_2 preserves F-properties if and only if, for any x in w_1, x has an F-property in w_1 just in case the image of x under I.(the individual to which I maps x) has P in w_2.

13. WEAK, INTERMEDIATE, AND STRONG GLOBAL SUPERVENIENCE

A variety of different kinds of global supervenience has been formulated:

A-properties weakly globally supervene on B-properties if and only if, for any worlds w_1 and w_2, if there is a B-preserving isomorphism between w_1 and w_2, then there is an A-preserving isomorphism between them (McLaughlin 1996, 1997; Stalnaker 1996; Sider 1999).

A-properties intermediately globally supervene on B-properties if and only if, for any worlds w_1 and w_2, if there is a B-preserving isomorphism between w_1 and w_2, then there is at least one isomorphism between them that is both A-and-B-preserving (Shagrir 2002, Bennett 2004).

A-properties strongly globally supervene on B-properties if and only if, for any worlds w_1 and w_2, every B-preserving isomorphism between w_1 and w_2 is an A-preserving isomorphism between them. (McLaughlin 1996, 1997; Stalnaker 1996; Sider 1999). Strong global supervenience entails intermediate global supervenience, which entails weak global supervenience. But the converse entailments all fail to hold in general.

There seem to be no cases of philosophical interest in which weak global supervenience holds, but both strong and intermediate global supervenience fail to hold. In some cases of interest, however, intermediate global supervenience holds, even though strong global supervenience may fail to hold. Many philosophers maintain that two numerically distinct objects can have the same spatiotemporal location and so be spatiotemporally coincident. A frequently cited would-be example is a clay statue and the lump of clay that makes it up. Even if they are spatiotemporally coincident throughout their existence—created at the same time and destroyed at the same time—they nevertheless have different modal properties: for example, the lump could survive being squashed, while the statue could not. But they have exactly the same categorical properties (mass, size, shape, and so on). If the statue is indeed not the lump, then the statue's modal properties will neither individually strongly nor individually weakly supervene on its categorical properties. (Multiple-domain individual supervenience will hold, however [see Kim 1988 and Zimmerman 1995].) And modal properties will fail to strongly globally supervene on categorical properties. But weak global supervenience (Sider 1999) and intermediate global supervenience (Bennett 2004) will both hold. An appeal to intermediate global supervenience would not by itself, however, solve "the grounding problem," the problem of how individuals with exactly the same categorical properties can differ in their modal properties (Bennett 2004). A solution to the grounding problem would have to explain why intermediate global supervenience holds and do so in a way that does not entail that coincident objects are identical.

14. SOME EQUIVALANCIES

The plethora of technical definitions of kinds of supervenience gives the appearance of more variety than there is. Strong individual supervenience entails strong global supervenience (Kim 1984), but strong global supervenience does not in general entail strong individual supervenience (Paull and Sider 1992). Nevertheless, strong individual supervenience and strong global supervenience are equivalent in cases in which the base set of properties B is closed under Boolean operations and ones involving quantification and identity (Stalnaker 1996). Strong individual supervenience is also equivalent to strong global supervenience in cases in which A and B are sets of intrinsic properties (Shagrir 2002, Bennett 2004). It has, moreover, been compellingly argued that in cases in which A and B are sets of intrinsic properties, weak and strong individual supervenience are equivalent as well. Weak individual supervenience, strong individual supervenience, and strong global supervenience are equivalent for sets of intrinsic properties.

See also Davidson, Donald; Knowledge and Modality; Lewis, David; Modality, Philosophy and Metaphysics of; Physicalism; Reduction; Russell, Bertrand Arthur William.

Bibliography

Bennett, K. "Global Supervenience and Dependence." *Philosophy and Phenomenological Research* 68 (2004): 510–529.

Blackburn, S. "Supervenience Revisited." Reprinted in Blackburn ed. *Essays in Quasi–Realism*. Oxford: Oxford University Press, 1993.

Bricker, P. "The Relation Between General and Particular: Entailment vs. Supervenience." In *Oxford Studies in Metaphysics*. Vol. 2, edited by D. Zimmerman. Oxford: Oxford University Press, 2005.

Chalmers, D. *The Conscious Mind*. New York: Oxford University Press, 1996.

Davidson, D. "Mental Events." In *Experience and Theory*, edited by L. Foster and J. W. Swanson. Amhurst: University of Massachusetts, (1970): 79–101.

Davidson, D. "Replies to Essays X–XIII." In *Essays on Davidson: Actions and Events*, edited by B. Vermazen and M.B. Hintikka. New York: Oxford University Press, 1985.

Goldman, A. "Discrimination and Perceptual Knowledge." *Journal of Philosophy* 18 (1976): 771–91.

Hare, R. M. *The Language of Morals*. Oxford: Clarendon Press, 1952.

Haugeland, J. "Weak Supervenience." *American Philosophical Quarterly* 19 (1982): 93–103.

Horgan, T. "Supervenience and Microphysics." *Pacific Philosophical Quarterly* 63 (1982): 29–43.

Horgan, T. "Cosmic Hermenutics." *Southern Journal of Philosophy 22: The Spindel Conference on Supervenience Supplement* 22 (1984): 19–38.

Horgan, T. "From Supervenience to Superdupervenience: Meeting the Demands of a Material World." *Mind* 102 (1993): 555–86.

Jackson, F. *From Ethics to Metaphysics.* Oxford: Oxford University Press, 1996.

Kim, J. "Concepts of Supervenience." *Philosophy and Phenomenological Research* 45 (1984): 153–76. Reprinted in *Supervenience and Mind*, edited by J. Kim, 33–52. Cambridge, U.K.: Cambridge University Press, 1993.

Kim, J. "Strong and 'Global' Supervenience Revisited." *Philosophy and Phenomenological Research* 48 (1987): 315–26. Reprinted in Kim ed.1993, 79–91.

Kim, J., ed. *Supervenience and Mind.* Cambridge, U.K.: Cambridge University Press, 1993.

Kim, J. "Supervenience for Multiple Domains." *Philosophical Topics* 16 (1988): 129–50. Reprinted in Kim ed. 1993, 79–91.

Kim, J. "Supervenience as a Philosophical Concepts." *Metaphilosophy* 21 (1990): 1–27. Reprinted in Kim 1993 ed., 109–130.

Lewis, D. "New Work for a Theory of Universals." *Australasian Journal of Philosophy* 61 (1983): 343–77.

Lewis, D. *On the Plurality of Worlds.* Oxford: Oxford University Press, 1986b.

Lewis, D., ed. *Philosophical Papers*, vol. II. Oxford: Oxford University Press, 1986a.

Marsh, R. C. *Logic and Knowledge.* London: Routledge, 1992.

McLaughlin, B. P. "Supervenience." In *Macmillian Encyclopedia of Philosophy, Supplementary Volume* 1996, edited by D. Borchert, 558–60.

McLaughlin, B. P. "Supervenience, Vagueness, and Determination." *Philosophical Perspectives* 11 (1997): 209–230.

McLaughlin, B. P. "Varieties of Supervenience." In *Supervenience: New Essays*, edited by E. Savellos and U. Yalcin. Cambridge, U.K.: Cambridge University Press, 1995.

Moyer, M. "The Strengths and Weakness of Weak and Strong Supervenience." Forthcoming.

Paull, R. C., and T. R. Sider. "In Defense of Global Supervenience." *Philosophy and Phenomenological Research* 52 (1992): 833–54.

Post, J. *The Faces of Existence.* Ithaca, NY: Cornell University Press, 1987.

Putnam, H. "The Meaning of 'Meaning.'" *Minnesota Studies in the Philosophy of Science* 7 (1975): 215–71.

Russell, B. *The Philosophy of Logical Atomism* (1918). Reprinted in Marsh ed. (1992): 177–281.

Shagrir, O. "Global Supervenience, Coincident Entities and Anti–individualism." *Philosophical Studies* 109 (2002): 171–196.

Sider, T. R. "Global Supervenience and Identity Across Times and Worlds." *Philosophy and Phenomenological Research* 59 (1999): 913–37.

Skyrms, B. "Tractarian Nominalism." *Philosophical Studies* 40 (1981): 199–206.

Stalnaker, R. "Varieties of Supervenience." *Philosophical Perspectives* 10 (1996): 221–41.

Zimmerman, D. "Theories of Masses and the Problems of Constitution." *Philosophical Review* 104 (1995): 53–110.

Brian P. McLaughlin (1996, 2005)

SUPPES, PATRICK

(1922–)

Patrick Suppes is an American philosopher and scientist. Born in Tulsa, Oklahoma, Suppes was educated at Tulsa Central High School and pursued undergraduate studies at the University of Oklahoma, the University of Tulsa, and the University of Chicago, with particular emphasis on physics and meteorology. He graduated from Chicago in 1943, then spent 1944 to 1946 in the United States Army Air Force. During graduate studies in philosophy at Columbia University in the years 1947 through 1950 Suppes studied with Ernest Nagel, combining courses in philosophy with further work in physics and mathematics. Somewhat surprisingly in the light of his later research in psychology, he did not study that subject at either the undergraduate or the graduate level.

Suppes received his Ph.D. in philosophy from Columbia University in 1950. His entire academic career has been spent at Stanford University, where he began as an assistant professor of philosophy in 1950. He subsequently held concurrent positions in the departments of psychology, statistics, and education, and from 1959 until his retirement directed the Institute for Mathematical Studies in the Social Sciences at Stanford, a research center he co-founded with the economist Kenneth Arrow. He has been a pioneer in computer-assisted education and in 1967, with the psychologist Richard Atkinson, founded a successful company, Computer Curriculum Corporation. He has received numerous honors during his career, culminating with the award of the National Medal of Science in 1990. Suppes retired from Stanford in 1992, but he has continued an active research program, including work on robotics and experimental work on the neural bases of language processing.

WORK

Suppes's work is unusual in its combination of significant scientific research with rigorous philosophical analysis, in its scope, and in its constructive orientation. It spans philosophy, psychology, probability and statistics, education, and computer science. The focus here is on his contributions to the philosophy of science, although his positions in that area are always deeply rooted in his scientific work. Throughout his career, Suppes has emphasized the pluralistic and complex nature of actual, rather than idealized, scientific methods. For example, as early as 1962 he argued that there was a hierarchy of models between data and theory, anticipating in certain ways the later philosophical literature emphasizing the importance of scientific models. Many of Suppes's principal philosophical contributions have been in the area of formal methods, both as a way of injecting precision into philosophical questions and as an effective set of tools for producing answers to those questions.

At the heart of his philosophical work lies the semantic account of theories, of which Suppes—building on joint work with J. C. C. McKinsey and employing Alfred Tarski's work on formal models—was the primary developer. The semantic account, which is the chief rival to the syntactic account of theories, also served as the foundation for the later structuralist approach to theories. In Suppes's version of the semantic account, a theory is identified with a class of set-theoretical structures—models in the sense of mathematical logic. Thus, rather than a theory being a set of sentences or propositions represented in first order logic—the identification made by the logical empiricists and their successors, particularly Quine—a theory in Suppes's sense abstracts from a particular linguistic representation and focuses instead on what makes that theory true, using the full apparatus of set theory. Thus, Newton's, Hamilton's, and Lagrange's versions of classical mechanics are simply different linguistic representations of the same underlying semantic theory. This powerful foundational apparatus allows for an easy representation of the kind of mathematics needed for scientific theories—in contrast to first order logic, which is an apparatus that is too weak to capture large parts of standard mathematics. The apparatus employed in the semantic approach is especially useful in such areas as measurement theory, a subject to which Suppes has made contributions of permanent value. The semantic approach also leads naturally to a focus on axiomatized theories because this allows the content of the theories to be fully captured in an explicit, and often recursive, set of constraints. This emphasis on formal methods follows naturally from Suppes's view that there are only practical, rather than theoretical, differences between representations of mathematical theories and representations of scientific theories.

A key concept in Suppes's work is that of a representation theorem. A representation theorem for a set of models M asserts that there exists a subset R of M such that for any model m in M there is a model r in R that is isomorphic to m. Such representation theorems play a central role in measurement theory when R is a class of numerical measurement structures and M is the class of empirical models upon which measurement procedures are to be placed. Philosophically, the emphasis on identity up to isomorphism (or, more generally, homomorphism) entails that the abstract structure of systems is captured, rather than any intrinsic features that are unique to the system.

Suppes's other important contributions include his monograph on probabilistic causality that, together with Reichenbach's earlier treatment, began this distinctive and widely discussed approach to causation; his pioneering work on the identification of aural and visual language recognition using electroencephalographic brain data; his work exploring variant probability spaces in quantum theory; an exploration of Bayesian inference; and the role of invariances in classical and relativistic physics. As the culmination of developing a number of stochastic models of learning, Suppes proved in 1969 that any finite automaton could be represented by a stimulus-response learning model, a result of importance to controversies about the nature of language learning. Together with the work on theory structure and measurement theory, these form an impressive and permanent set of contributions to the philosophy of science.

Suppes's publications are demanding but always lucid; they invariably repay careful study. Inevitably, they only partially convey his considerable influence as a teacher and professional colleague, an influence grounded in equal parts of rigor, style, humor, and clarity. A comprehensive and detailed presentation of his mature views is given in *Representation and Invariance of Scientific Structures* (2002).

See also Causation: Philosophy of Science; First–Order Logic; Mathematics, Foundations of; Semantics; Structuralism, Mathematical.

Bibliography

WORKS BY SUPPES

"Models of Data." In *Logic, Methodology and Philosophy of Science: Proceedings of the 1960 International Congress.* Edited by E. Nagel, P. Suppes, and A. Tarski, 252–261. Stanford, CA: Stanford University Press, 1962.

"Stimulus-Response Theory of Finite Automata." *Journal of Mathematical Psychology* 6 (1969): 327–355.

A Probabilistic Theory of Causality. Amsterdam: North-Holland, 1970.

Foundations of Measurement. vols. 1–3. With D. H. Krantz, R. D. Luce, and A. Tversky. New York: Academic Press, 1971, 1989, 1990.

Stanford Faculty Web Pages. A complete bibliography of Patrick Suppes's publications through 2000. Available from http://www.stanford.edu/~psuppes.

Representation and Invariance of Scientific Structures. Stanford: CSLI Publications, 2002.

WORKS ABOUT SUPPES

Bogdan, R., ed. *Patrick Suppes.* Dordrecht, Netherlands: D. Reidel, 1979. Contains a personal and intellectual autobiography up to 1978.

Humphreys, P., ed. *Patrick Suppes: Scientific Philosopher.* Vols. 1–3. Dordrecht, Netherlands: Kluwer, 1994. Contains articles on most aspects of Suppes's research and his replies to each article.

Paul Humphreys (2005)

SUSO, HEINRICH

(1295/1300–1366)

Heinrich Suso, the Rhineland mystic, was born at Constance and early entered the Dominican order. A mystical experience at the age of eighteen set him on the path of asceticism, but a later one, between 1335 and 1340, led him to abandon self-mortification and to embark on an active career as preacher and spiritual adviser. As a result of attacks on some of his teachings and on his personal character, he was transferred to Ulm in 1348.

During his period of studies in Cologne, Suso had come into contact with Johannes Tauler and also came under the influence of Meister Eckhart. Indeed, in *Das Büchlein der Wahrheit* (*The Little Book of Truth,* c. 1327) he was bold enough to defend Eckhart against the doctrinal charges leveled against him, setting Eckhart's disputed doctrines alongside other quite orthodox statements made by him and providing interpretations that did not entail pantheistic conclusions.

Although Suso made use of the Eckhartian-sounding distinction between the undifferentiated Godhead and God as manifested in the persons of the Trinity, he did not hold that there was an ontological distinction within the divine Being. Rather, he held that the distinction was an intellectual one, made from the human point of view and dependent on our mode of trying to understand God's nature. Although Suso also used extreme Neoplatonic language in speaking of God as Nothing, he made it clear that this was simply to say that, because of God's complete simplicity, we cannot ascribe predicates to him in the sense in which they are applied to creatures. Suso went on to try to explain the contrasting and paradoxical multiplicity of God's nature, as exhibited in the Trinity, by the usual concept of eternal procession. Like his doctrine that the distinction between the Godhead and God as the Trinity is not an ontological one, the notion of procession should be taken in a way that does not imply the priority of God considered as a simple Nothing over God considered as the Father, Son, and Holy Spirit. Thus, Suso drew a strong distinction between the procession occurring within the divine Being and the creation of the world. The latter is a free act of God, and creatures owe their being to him; thus God is ontologically prior to the world. On the other hand, the internal dynamics of the Trinity are a perfect and eternal feature of God's life.

The idea of God as Nothing reflected, as did similar doctrines held by other medieval mystics, not only a view about predication in theology but also about the mystical experience itself. Thus, Suso characteristically spoke of that state in which the contemplative is taken out of himself and is made calm in the ground of the eternal Nothing. The fact that the contemplative experience is free from images and discursive thought is a sufficient explanation of the negative language used. Suso generally avoided the suggestion that the soul is merged with the Godhead and described the union as one of wills in which, however, the soul retains its identity. Nevertheless, there were times when he, orthodox as he generally was and wished to be, spoke of a substantial identification with the Godhead. Some explanation of this apparent inconsistency is found in his assertion that in the mystical state the individual is no longer aware of his own identity. It is afterward, and through going beyond a merely phenomenological description of the experience, that the mystic is able to give what he considers to be the correct theological account of it.

Suso's chief works were the autobiographical *Das Buch von dem Diener* (*The Life of the Servant*); the *Horologium Sapientiae,* which also occurs in a somewhat different German version as *Das Büchlein der ewigen Weisheit* (*The Little Book of the Eternal Wisdom*); and *Das Büchlein der Wahrheit* (*The Little Book of Truth*). The second of these, which is a dialogue about and meditation on the sufferings of Christ, attained a wide circulation, almost rivaling that of Thomas à Kempis's *The Imitation of Christ.* Because of the degree of openness in the description of his inner life, Suso's writings constitute a valuable source for the study of Christian mysticism.

Bibliography

The German writings can be found in Karl Bihlmayer, *Heinrich Suso: deutsche Schriften* (Stuttgart, 1907). The *Horologium Sapientiae* was edited by J. Strange (Cologne, 1861). Useful translations are J. M. Clark, *Little Book of Eternal Wisdom and Little Book of Truth* (London: Faber and

Faber, 1953) and *The Life of the Servant* (London, 1952). For a general introduction, see J. M. Clark, *The Great German Mystics* (Oxford: Blackwell, 1949), Ch. 4.

Ninian Smart (1967)

SWEDENBORG, EMANUEL

(1688–1772)

Emanuel Swedenborg, the scientist, biblical scholar, and mystic, was a member of a famous Swedish family of clergymen and scholars; his father was a prominent bishop and a prolific writer. Swedenborg studied the classics and Cartesian philosophy at Uppsala and became interested in mathematics and natural science. In 1710 he went abroad, spending most of the next five years in England, where he learned the Newtonian theories and developed a modern scientific outlook. After his return to Sweden in 1715, Swedenborg was appointed an assessor in the College of Mines by Charles XII. He held this office until 1747, when he resigned in order to devote his time to the interpretation of the Scriptures.

PHILOSOPHY OF NATURE

Swedenborg's many writings are characterized by great scholarship and by a fervent search for a synthesis of ancient wisdom and modern experience, empirical science, rationalistic philosophy, and Christian revelation. After some minor treatises on geological and cosmological problems, he published his first important work in 1734, *Opera Philosophica et Mineralia* (3 vols., Dresden and Leipzig); the first part of this work, *Principia Rerum Naturalium*, contains his philosophy of nature. Here Swedenborg used the concept of the mathematical point, which he described as coming into existence by motion from the Infinite. This point forms a nexus, or connection, between the Infinite and the finite world, and by its motion it creates aggregates of elements that build up the Cartesian vortexes, which are interpreted as the fundamentals of nature. The original motion in the Infinite, however, is not a mechanical motion but a kind of Leibnizian conatus, a motive force in nature that corresponds to will in human minds. In the first point there is a corresponding tendency, which transmits itself to the subsequent aggregates in this great chain of being.

The outlines of Swedenborg's natural philosophy are derived from René Descartes, Gottfried Wilhelm Leibniz, and other rationalists, but in the *Principia* Swedenborg was also inspired by empirical philosophy, especially that of John Locke. A similar English influence can be observed in Swedenborg's cosmology, which is set forth in the *Principia* and in a short hexaemeron titled *De Cultu et Amore Dei* (London, 1745). In these works Swedenborg presents a nebular hypothesis according to which the planets are formed of solar matter. It has been maintained that the planet theory of Immanuel Kant and Pierre Simon de Laplace might have been derived from Swedenborg via the comte de Buffon, but most probably the similarities between Swedenborg and Buffon depend on their common source of inspiration, Thomas Burnet's *Telluris Theoria Sacra* (The sacred theory of the earth; 1681). This treatise was widely known (even Samuel Taylor Coleridge admired it), and there is no doubt that it guided Swedenborg in his cosmology. Swedenborg's cosmology was essentially mechanistic, but like the great speculative philosophers of the seventeenth century, he attempted very early to find a theory that could combine these scientific hypotheses with Christianity.

Together with this mechanistic outlook there are several elements in Swedenborg's philosophy of nature that anticipate the organic theories set forth in his anatomic and psychological works. These works include *Oeconomia Regni Animalis* (2 vols., London and Amsterdam, 1740–1741), *Regnum Animale* (3 vols., The Hague and London, 1744–1745), and many other posthumously published treatises on the animal kingdom. The main problem concerning Swedenborg here is the relationship between soul and body. Since he was not satisfied by any of the current philosophical hypotheses, he turned to the study of contemporary microanatomy and physiology. His own theory, which is sometimes called the *harmonia constabilita* (coestablished harmony), is similar to Leibniz's theory of preestablished harmony. The two models are not identical, however, since there is a component of successive growing in Swedenborg's notion that is missing in the preestablished harmony.

In his physiological research Swedenborg starts with the study of the blood, which in its relation to the organization of the human body corresponds in some important ways to the role of the mathematical point as a nexus between the spiritual and the physical worlds. Swedenborg distinguishes several degrees of purity in the blood, with the highest degree corresponding to the Cartesian spiritous fluid. This fluid functions both as a concrete communication line between soul and body and as an abstract principle, a formative force of the body (*vis formatrix*). Swedenborg combined this concept of life force with Aristotle's concept of form and developed a teleological system very much like Leibniz's monadology.

DOCTRINE OF SERIES AND DEGREES. Swedenborg's system may be called the doctrine of series and degrees. The degrees are distinct links in the universal chain and form connected series of several kinds. Three of these series—the mineral kingdom, the plant kingdom, and the animal kingdom—belong to the earth. In these great series there are also subordinate series, down to the lowest elements. Each series has its first substance, which is dependent on the first series of nature. The first series of nature is an organic development of the concept of the mathematical point. Here, Swedenborg comes very close to the Neoplatonic conception of a world soul, a creative intellect from which the material world is called forth by the process of emanation. It seems probable that Aristotle's notion of the hierarchy of organisms was a decisive influence in the structuring of this gigantic system, in which Swedenborg has tried to arrange all series and degrees in a fixed order that determines all their interrelations. Swedenborg refused to follow Leibniz and Christian Wolff in calling his first substances monads because he did not look upon them as absolutely simple. For him they are created not directly from the Infinite but via the first substance of nature, in the same way that, according to the *Principia*, all natural elements are produced indirectly via the mathematical point.

The first substance of the series, its *vis formatrix*, determines the development of the whole series. There exists nothing in nature that does not belong to such a series. In the *Oeconomia* the human series consists of four degrees, the soul (*anima*), the reason (*mens rationalis*), the vegetative soul (*animus*), and the corresponding sense organs of the body, but in the theosophic writings after 1745 the series is reduced to three degrees with the *animus* subordinated to the *mens rationalis*. Nor is there any first substance of nature in these later works. The chain of the series extends up to God, who himself becomes the highest series.

PSYCHOLOGY

The philosophy of the theosophic period thus presents a kind of Neoplatonic emanation system, although in his earlier works Swedenborg was more influenced by contemporary philosophy. In his psychology he also turned to Locke, and his epistemology coincides with Locke's tabula rasa theory. According to Swedenborg, there are no innate ideas in the *mens rationalis*. He also thought, however, that all a priori knowledge is in the *anima* but that after the Fall of humanity the soul (*anima*) was separated from the body; this synthetic source of knowledge—in some ways corresponding to Locke's notion of intuitive knowledge—was thereby closed for ordinary people. If we could return to Adam's integrity before the Fall, it would be opened up anew. This dream of regaining paradise haunted Swedenborg in the decade before 1745, and he attempted to devise several methods for discovering this lost knowledge.

DOCTRINE OF CORRESPONDENCE

One of the best-known elements in Swedenborg's philosophy is his doctrine of correspondence. This doctrine parallels the speculations about *harmonia constabilita*, but it also has other connections with contemporary thought. The meaning of the term *correspondence* is stated in a short manuscript written in 1741 and titled *Clavis Hieroglyphica* (A Hieroglyphic Key; London, 1784). This work is an attempt to illustrate how linguistic terms may be used with three different meanings—the natural, the spiritual, and the divine. Later, this doctrine becomes the fundamental exegetic principle of the theosophic works. Swedenborg's doctrine of correspondence is an attempt to describe and explain the relations between the spiritual world and our material universe by means of linguistic analogies, the construction of which may be illustrated by the following example from *Clavis Hieroglyphica*.

> (1) There is no motion without *conatus*, but there is *conatus* without motion. For if all *conatus* were to break out into open motion the world would perish, since there would be no equilibrium. (2) There is no action without will, but there is will without action. If all will were to break out into open action man would perish, since there would be no rational balance or moderating reason. (3) There is no divine operation without providence, but there is indeed a providence not operative or effective. If all providence were operative and effective, human society would not be able to subsist such as it now is, since there would be no true exercise of human liberty. (*Psychological Transactions by Emanuel Swedenborg*, pp. 162–163)

The notions conatus, will, and providence correspond; so do world, humankind, and human society. By such means, the principles of the philosophy of nature are given a wider field of application, so that they reveal heavenly and divine secrets. Fundamentally, this doctrine may be interpreted as a variation of the Platonic theory of the relations between the world of ideas and the world of senses, but it is important to stress that Swedenborg looked upon his system primarily as a synthesis of ancient wisdom and contemporary thought.

The *Clavis Hieroglyphica* is related to the interpretations of hieroglyphics that were made during the Renaissance. This is apparent in Swedenborg's use of excerpts from Wolff's *Psychologia Empirica* (1732) where the famous German rationalist discusses the Egyptian hieroglyphs and their mystic signification and gives examples from John Amos Comenius and others. More important, Wolff inspired speculation about the universal philosophical language, *mathesis universalium* (Swedenborg) or *characteristica universalis* (Leibniz). In a posthumously published manuscript (Stockholm, 1869), Swedenborg tried to formulate his psychophysical conclusions in algebraic formulas of sorts, and he declared his conviction that such an attempt might eventually succeed. But in the meantime he introduced in the *Clavis Hieroglyphica* what he called a key to natural and spiritual arcana by way of correspondences and representations. Thus, there is no doubt that the doctrine of correspondence must be regarded as Swedenborg's contribution to the solution of the problem of the philosophical language. It should be noted, however, that he seems to have been influenced by Nicolas Malebranche in respect to the correspondent relations between the mind and the cerebral base. Swedenborg also follows another fundamental thought of Malebranche, according to which the omnipotence of God functions in conformity with an eternal order (*l'ordre immuable*); this idea becomes prominent in Swedenborg's theosophic writings.

THEOSOPHIC WORKS

Swedenborg's scientific and theosophic works are closely related. The decisive difference is that Swedenborg after a profound spiritual experience in 1745 directed his reasoning exclusively toward the interpretation of Scripture according to the doctrine of correspondence. His first exegetic work is *Arcana Coelestia quae in Genesi et Exodo Sunt Detecta* (8 vols., London, 1749–1756), and it was followed by many others. In all his exegetic treatises Swedenborg also gives vivid descriptions of his experiences in the spiritual world. Apart from these descriptions we meet with the same main theories, although they have been developed into an emanationist theology. Like most of his contemporaries, Swedenborg had always been certain of the existence of spirits and angels, and in the exegetic works he went so far as to describe a comprehensive spiritual system. The spirits live in cities where they have an active social life with social functions (even marriage) corresponding to earthly conditions. The relegation of spirits to heaven or hell from the intervening spiritual world depends on the spirits themselves, since their utmost desire (*amor regnans*) leads them into suitable company.

Christ and the doctrine of atonement play a very insignificant role in Swedenborg's theology, and he dismissed the Trinity dogma. Christ is the *Divinum Humanum*, a manifestation in time of God himself. Swedenborg's theology is extremely intellectual and totally dependent on the interpretation of the divine word as the mediating link between the Creator and humankind. In the course of time decadent churches have destroyed the original meaning of this word, and Swedenborg saw his mission as the restoration of its primary sense. He identified his own exegetic activity with the return of Messiah and the foundation of the New Jerusalem. However, Swedenborg did not aspire to effect conversions but confined himself to explaining the spiritual meaning of the Scriptures. He felt he had been commanded to do this in his decisive vision of 1745.

CONCLUSION

This is not the place to discuss the difficult problem of Swedenborg's mental status. For many modern observers it is only too easy to look upon his theosophy as the result of a pathological development of a pronouncedly schizoid personality whose intense desire for synthesis could not be satisfied within the boundaries of science and normal experience. But this must remain speculation. What is certain is that hundreds of thousands of followers have seen in him a prophet and visionary explorer of divine secrets. He has had a wide influence in several fields of thought and art, especially in romantic and symbolist literature; for poets like Charles-Pierre Baudelaire and August Strindberg he was a teacher and predecessor. Swedenborg is, of course, not a philosopher in the modern meaning of the word, but he is an interesting representative of the mystical trend in eighteenth-century thought.

See also Aristotle; Buffon, Georges-Louis Leclerc, Comte de; Coleridge, Samuel Taylor; Comenius, John Amos; Kant, Immanuel; Laplace, Pierre Simon de; Leibniz, Gottfried Wilhelm; Locke, John; Mysticism, History of; Nature, Philosophical Ideas of; Neoplatonism; Wolff, Christian.

Bibliography

Swedenborg's manuscripts are deposited in the library of the Royal Academy of Science in Stockholm. The greater part of them have been published (as photolithographs of the original or in edited translations or both) by the New Church societies, especially the Swedenborg Scientific Association in the United States, which is a great aid to scholars. Swedenborg wrote in Latin, but almost all of his works are available in English translations; a detailed but unfortunately obsolete bibliography is J. Hyde, *A Bibliography of the Works of Emanuel Swedenborg Original and Translated* (London: Swedenborg Society, 1906).

The following English translations of his many philosophical and scientific works can be recommended: *The Principia; or, The First Principles of Natural Things, Being New Attempts Toward a Philosophical Explanation of the Elementary World*, translated by A. Clissold, 2 vols. (London, 1846); *The Infinite and the Final Cause of Creation, Also the Intercourse between the Soul and the Body*, translated by J. J. G. Wilkinson (London, 1908); *Psychologica, Being Notes and Observations on Christian Wolff's "Psychologia Empirica" by Emanuel Swedenborg*, translated and edited by A. Acton (Philadelphia, 1923); *The Economy of the Animal Kingdom, Considered Anatomically, Physically, and Philosophically by Emanuel Swedenborg*, translated by A. Clissold, 2 vols. (London, 1845–1846); *The Fibre*, Vol. III of *The Economy of the Animal Kingdom, Considered Anatomically, Physically, and Philosophically by Emanuel Swedenborg*, translated and edited by A. Acton (Philadelphia, 1918); *A Philosopher's Note Book. Excerpts from Philosophical Writers and from the Sacred Scriptures on a Variety of Philosophical Subjects; Together with Some Reflections, and Sundry Notes and Memoranda by Emanuel Swedenborg*, translated and edited by A. Acton (Philadelphia, 1931); *The Brain Considered Anatomically, Physiologically, and Philosophically by Emanuel Swedenborg*, translated and edited by R. L. Tafel, 2 vols. (London, 1882–1887); *Three Transactions on the Cerebrum. A Posthumous Work by Emanuel Swedenborg*, translated and edited by A. Acton, 2 vols. (Philadelphia, 1937–1940); *Psychological Transactions by Emanuel Swedenborg*, translated and edited by A. Acton, 2nd ed. (Philadelphia, 1955); *Rational Psychology. A Posthumous Work by Emanuel Swedenborg*, translated and edited by N. H. Rogers and A. Acton (Philadelphia, 1950); *The Animal Kingdom Considered Anatomically, Physically, and Philosophically by Emanuel Swedenborg*, translated by J. J. G. Wilkinson, 2 vols. (Boston, 1858); *The Animal Kingdom*, Parts 4 and 5, translated and edited by A. Acton (Bryn Athyn, PA, 1928); *The Five Senses*, translated and edited by E. S. Price (Philadelphia, 1914); and *The Worship and Love of God*, translated by F. Sewall and A. H. Stroh (Boston, 1925).

The vast literature about Swedenborg is of unequal quality. An excellent survey is given in M. Lamm, *Swedenborg* (Stockholm, 1915); it has been translated by Ilse Meyer-Lüne as *Swedenborg: Eine Studie über seine Entwicklung zum Mystiker und Geisterseher* (Leipzig, 1922), and into French by E. Söderlindh as *Swedenborg* (Paris, 1936). This is still the best work available. In Ernst Benz, *Emanuel Swedenborg: Naturforscher und Seher* (Munich, 1948), there is more stress on theology and church history, but in general the author follows Lamm. A popular biography is S. Toksvig, *Emanuel Swedenborg, Scientist and Mystic* (New Haven, CT: Yale University Press, 1948). A modern solid monograph, although inspired by New Church teachings, is C. O. Sigstedt, *The Swedenborg Epic* (New York: Bookman Associates, 1952). An analysis of *De Cultu et Amore Dei*, which also deals with many of the philosophical and scientific problems in the rest of Swedenborg's production up to 1745, is I. Jonsson, *Swedenborgs Skapelsedrama "De Cultu et Amore Dei"* (Stockholm, 1961), written in Swedish with a summary in English.

Swedenborg's correspondence has been published in translations and with very informative commentaries in A. Acton, *The Letters and Memorials of Emanuel Swedenborg* (Bryn Athyn, PA: Swedenborg Scientific Association, 1948).

The biographical sources are collected in R. L. Tafel, *Documents concerning the Life and Character of Emanuel Swedenborg*, 3 vols. (London, 1875–1890).

Among the many useful studies by A. H. Stroh may be mentioned "The Sources of Swedenborg's Early Philosophy of Nature," Vol. III of *Emanuel Swedenborg: Opera Quaedam aut Inedita aut Obsoleta de Rebus Naturalibus*, published by the Royal Swedish Academy of Science (Stockholm, 1911), and "Swedenborg's Contributions to Psychology," in *Transactions of the International Swedenborg Congress* (London, 1911).

See also Clarke Garrett, "Swedenborg and the Mystical Enlightenment in Eighteenth-Century England," *Journal of the History of Ideas* (45 [1984]: 67–82).

Inge Jonsson (1967)
Bibliography updated by Tamra Frei (2005)

SWIFT, JONATHAN
(1667–1745)

Jonathan Swift, the British clergyman, moralist, satirist, poet, and political journalist, was born in Dublin, a few months after his father's death. He was educated at Kilkenny Grammar School and received his MA *speciali gratiâ* from Trinity College, Dublin, in 1686 and MA from Hart Hall, Oxford, in 1692. Periodically, from 1689 to 1699, he acted as secretary to Sir William Temple at Moore Park, Surrey. Ordained deacon and priest in the established church of Ireland, he was left by Temple's death in 1699 to make a career for himself. As domestic chaplain to the earl of Berkeley, lord justice of Ireland, he returned to Dublin and was granted the DD degree in 1701 by Trinity College.

In 1704 there appeared anonymously (his customary mode of publishing) *A Tale of a Tub* and *The Battle of the Books*, brilliant satires upholding the ancients against the moderns; assaulting both Catholic and Puritan theologies while upholding the *via media* of the Anglican Church; and castigating the shallowness of contemporary scholarship and literature. Thereafter Swift associated with the Whiggish wits in the circle of Joseph Addison and Richard Steele, contributing to the *Tatler* and laughing the astrologer John Partridge out of business in the hilarious *Bickerstaff Papers* (1708–1709). Gradually, however, when the Whig ministry displayed no interest either in the welfare of the Irish church or in Swift's own ecclesiastical preferment, he veered toward the Tories. His literary friends now included Alexander Pope, John Gay, William Congreve, Matthew Prior, and John Arbuthnot, many of whom later joined with him in the famous Scriblerus Club dedicated to eternal warfare against the dunces.

In 1710 Swift assumed the editorship of the *Examiner*, thus becoming party spokesman for the new Tory ministry of Robert Harley and Lord Bolingbroke. He shortly resigned this post to work on *The Conduct of the Allies* (1711), a pamphlet designed so to sway public opinion as to bring about the end of the "Whiggish" War of the Spanish Succession, an event that occurred in 1713 with the Treaty of Utrecht. Swift was unable, however, to reconcile the ever increasing animosities between Harley (now Lord Oxford) and Bolingbroke, each of whom was surreptitiously treating with both Jacobite and Hanoverian claimants to the British crown. The death of Queen Anne in 1714 and the accession of George I (of Hanover) led to the downfall and disgrace of the Tory Party. Swift, having been installed the previous year as dean of St. Patrick's Cathedral in Dublin, retired to Ireland, a country whose people he despised. A fascinating record of events and personalities of the turbulent years of ecclesiastical and political intrigues, 1710–1713, is preserved in his letters to Esther Johnson, known as the *Journal to Stella*.

During the long years of "exile," Swift, paradoxically, became the national hero of Ireland, rising to her defense against the ruthless exploitation by the English. Two works are especially notable in this campaign. First, there was *The Drapier's Letters to the People of Ireland* (1724), which caused the king of England, the prime minister, and the Parliament to back down from the insult to the people of Ireland in the proposed coining of William Wood's copper halfpence. And second, there was *A Modest Proposal For preventing the Children Of Poor People From Being a Burthen to Their Parents or Country, And For making them Beneficial to the Publick* (1729), which employed shock technique to apprise the Irish people of the fact that slaughtering and dressing infants for the dinner tables of English absentee landlords was really little different from prevailing conditions, which allowed them to die of starvation. In the *Proposal* and other politico-economic publications Swift advocated what was later to be called the boycott. In 1726 the immortal social and political satire *Gulliver's Travels* was published in London. Minor works—economic, political, and satirical—continued to appear until about 1739. In 1742 Swift's health had deteriorated to the extent that, for his own protection, he was declared of unsound mind and memory and incapable of caring for himself or his estate. Today it is recognized that Swift was suffering from labyrinthine vertigo (Ménière's disease), a purely physical disease, and that in modern terminology he was not insane. He lingered on until 1745, when he died in his seventy-eighth year and was buried in St. Patrick's Cathedral, ironically leaving most of his estate for the founding of a hospital for the insane. His last words were "I am a fool." He had prepared for himself an epitaph in Latin that is translated "When savage indignation can no longer torture the heart, proceed, traveller, and, if you can, imitate the strenuous avenger of noble liberty." "Savage indignation" and the fight for "noble liberty" are truly the prime characteristics of Jonathan Swift.

RELIGION AND MORALITY

Never professing to be a philosopher, Swift was nevertheless a serious thinker on the problems of religion and morality; however, because of his pervasive use of irony, his writings in this area have not infrequently been misunderstood and maligned. Swift always maintained, and quite properly, that he was not attacking religion but the corruptions and excesses of religion and the abuses of reason. As dean, he performed all the functions of that office and was in every respect a sincere Christian. In his surviving sermons, only eleven of which are unquestionably authentic, he takes a commonsense (derived from the funded experience of humankind) approach to theology. The lingering Trinitarian controversy, which caused such bitterness and name-calling among the "orthodox" that Parliament prohibited further publication on the subject, Swift found thoroughly repugnant. In *A Letter to a Young Gentleman, lately enter'd into Holy Orders* (1720), Swift advised that the Christian mysteries should not be explicated by divines but should remain incomprehensible, for otherwise they would not be "mysteries." Though God-given, human reason is not infallible, because of the interests, passions, and vices of the individual. Although there is clearly a skeptical bent in Swift, he is not to be regarded as a skeptic. Mysteries (for instance, the Trinity) are to be accepted on faith (which is above reason) and asserted on the authority of the Scriptures. As Swift stated in a private letter, "The grand points of Christianity ought to be taken as infallible revelations." It was this orthodox insistence on revelation that made Swift the intractable enemy of the English deists, who maintained that knowledge is prior to assent or faith.

Swift's religious antirationalism, anti-intellectualism, and fideism are well illustrated in his writings against the deists: John Toland, Matthew Tindal, and Anthony Collins were his chief butts. Collins who, in his *Discourse of Free thinking* (1713), had twice taunted Swift by name, is subjected to Swiftian irony in *Mr. C——n's Discourse of Freethinking; put into plain English by way of Abstract, for the Use of the Poor* (1713). Grossly unjust to Collins though it is deliberately intended to be, Swift's work is a witty exploitation of antirationalistic and anti-intellectualistic arguments. The optimistic apriorism inherent in deism was repugnant to Swift, who as an essentially Christian pessimist was always less concerned with philosophical and theological niceties than with the practical problems of morality.

Swift's vital interest in morality is observable in *An Argument against Abolishing Christianity* (1711). This masterpiece of irony attacks the rationalistic deistical concept of a self-sufficient religion of nature that needs no special revelation by assuming the position that "real" Christianity is no longer capable of justification to a sophisticated age. However, "nominal" Christianity is justifiable on grounds of expediency: It may help to preserve pride, wealth, and power and, possibly, to prevent a drop in the stock market of as much as 1 percent. *A Project for the Advancement of Religion and the Reformation of Manners* (1709) urges Queen Anne to lead a moral crusade against existing vices in the nation. That Swift was not ironic but completely earnest in this project is certain because of the abhorrence of human vices and the necessity for reformation he expressed in many other writings.

Believing that man is not *animal rationale* but merely *rationis capax*, Swift discerns a negative philosophy of history in the human tendency to degenerate after a certain degree of order and virtue has been achieved. In this restrictive sense only is he to be called a Christian misanthrope or simply a misanthrope. Swift devoted his life to exposing cruelty, inhumanity, inordinate love of power, pride, corrupt politics, and political oppression and to inculcating integrity and virtue in its major aspects of magnanimity and heroism—yet with no illusion that human nature is capable of reaching virtue in an eminent degree. This satiric-moralistic aim, enhanced by Swift's comic vision, finds its most brilliant literary achievement in *Gulliver's Travels*, a work that always has, and always will, vex, shock, divert, and entertain the world.

See also Addison, Joseph; Bolingbroke, Henry St. John; Collins, Anthony; Gay, John; Pope, Alexander; Religion and Morality; Tindal, Matthew; Toland, John.

Bibliography

MODERN EDITIONS OF SWIFT

The Letters of Jonathan Swift to Charles Ford, edited by D. Nichol Smith. Oxford: Clarendon Press, 1935.

The Prose Works of Jonathan Swift. 14 vols., edited by Herbert Davis. Oxford: Blackwell, 1939–1968.

Journal to Stella, edited by Harold Williams. Oxford: Clarendon Press, 1948.

The Poems of Jonathan Swift. 3 vols., edited by Harold Williams. Oxford, 1958.

The Correspondence of Jonathan Swift. 5 vols., edited by Harold Williams. Oxford, 1963–1965.

MODERN WORKS ON SWIFT

Davis, Herbert. *The Satire of Jonathan Swift*. New York: Macmillan, 1947.

Donoghue, Denis. *Jonathan Swift: A Critical Anthology*. Harmondsworth: Penguin, 1971.

Downie, J. A. *Jonathan Swift, Political Writer*. Boston: Routledge & K. Paul, 1984.

Ehrenpreis, Irwin. *The Personality of Jonathan Swift*. London: Methuen, 1958.

Ehrenpreis, Irwin. *Swift: The Man, His Works, and the Age*. Vol. 1: *Mr. Swift and His Contemporaries*. London: Methuen, 1962.

Fauske, Christopher J. *Jonathan Swift and the Church of Ireland, 1710–1724*. Dublin: Irish Academic Press, 2002.

Ferguson, Oliver W. *Jonathan Swift and Ireland*. Urbana: University of Illinois Press, 1962.

Fox, Christopher, ed. *The Cambridge Companion to Jonathan Swift*. New York: Cambridge University Press, 2003.

Gilbert, Jack G. *Knaves, Fools, and Heroes: Jonathan Swift's Ethics*. Unpublished PhD diss., University of Texas, 1962.

Landa, Louis. *Swift and the Church of Ireland*. Oxford: Clarendon Press, 1954.

Landa, Louis. "Swift, the Mysteries, and Deism." In *Studies in English*, 239–256. University of Texas, 1944.

Looten, C. *La pensée religieuse de Swift*. Paris, 1935.

Quintana, Ricardo. *The Mind and Art of Jonathan Swift*. 2nd ed. London: Methuen, 1953.

Quintana, Ricardo. *Swift: An Introduction*. London and New York: Oxford University Press, 1955.

Quintana, Ricardo. *Two Augustans: John Locke, Jonathan Swift*. London: University of Wisconsin Press, 1978.

Rawson, Claude, ed. *Jonathan Swift: A Collection of Critical Essays*. Englewood Cliffs, NJ: Prentice Hall, 1995.

Wedel, T. O. "On the Philosophical Background of Gulliver's Travels." *Studies in Philology* 23 (1926): 434–450.

Williams, Kathleen. *Jonathan Swift and the Age of Compromise*. Lawrence: University of Kansas Press, 1958.

Ernest Campbell Mossner (1967)
Bibliography updated by Tamra Frei (2005)

SWINESHEAD, RICHARD
(mid-1300s)

Richard Swineshead (Swyneshed; on the Continent, more commonly Suiseth) is the name now commonly ascribed to the author of the *Book of Calculations* (*Liber Calculationum*) although in various manuscripts and printed editions he is also given the first names John, Raymund, Roger, and William, among others. Based on the work of James A. Weisheipl, a different person with the name Roger Swyneshed, who was a Benedictine monk at Glastonbury, is now credited with writing a work that is in some ways similar, titled *Descriptions of Motions* or *On Natural Motions* (*Descriptiones motuum* or *De motibus naturalibus*) dated to the mid-1330s and found in Erfurt manuscript Amplonian F 135, ff. 25va–47rb. This same Roger Swyneshed is credited with logical works *On Insolubles* and *On Obligations* (*De insolubilibus* and *De obligationibus*) connected to standard academic exercises within medieval universities. If the same person wrote all of these works, then his views must have matured and changed considerably between the writing of the various works. The following entry will be limited to a discussion of the author of the *Book of Calculations*. Those interested in the history of logic should turn first to the articles, listed below, by Paul Spade on Roger Swyneshed's works.

Documentary evidence indicates that Swineshead was a fellow of Merton College, Oxford, probably in 1340—certainly in 1344—and again in 1355. Manuscript copies of the *Book of Calculations* are often incomplete and arranged differently from the printed editions. The work shows clear influence of Thomas Bradwardine's *On the Proportions of Velocities in Motions* (1961 [1328]) and of William Heytesbury's *Rules for Solving Sophisms* (1494 [1335]). Influence of the *Book of Calculations* begins to show up in Paris before 1350. Through the early sixteenth century, the work was widely studied on the Continent, in Italy and Spain as well as France, leading to various propedeutic works explaining its methods to potential readers. G. W. Leibniz several times recommended that the book be reprinted, both as a gem of the early history of printing and because the author was among the first to introduce mathematics into natural philosophy or metaphysics. To that end Leibniz went so far as hire someone to copy the Venice, 1520, printed edition by hand in preparation for the reprinting. Although Leibniz's project never came to fruition, the hand copy still exists in the Niedersächsische Landesbibliothek in Hannover, Germany.

In the printed versions of the *Book of Calculations* there are sixteen treatises, which cover:

I. Intension and remission of forms.

II. (Measures of) difform qualities.

III. Intensity of elemental bodies having two unequally intense qualities.

IV. Intensity of mixed bodies.

V. Rarity and density.

VI. Augmentation.

VII. Reaction.

VIII. Powers of things.

IX. Difficulty of action.

X. Maxima and minima.

XI. Place of an element.

XII. Light sources.

XIII. Action of light sources.

XIV. Local motion.

XV. Motion in nonresisting media (in media with varying resistances).

XVI. Induction of the maximum degree.

What these treatises have in common is an effort to attach quantitative measures to physical entities. Swineshead first tries to establish scales of measure for static magnitudes, such as intensities of heat and cold. He then attempts to measure speeds of change in the three categories in which medieval Aristotelians believed motion to occur, namely place, quality, and quantity. Treatise XIV, on dynamics, assumes the truth of Bradwardine's rule stating that the velocities in motions depend on the ratios of forces to resistances, using a special sense of the variation of ratios connected with the notion of *compounding* ratios used in Euclid's *Elements* (Book VI, proposition 23). The *Book of Calculations* represents a stage in medieval intellectual development in which logic (including the theory of supposition) together with mathematics begin to move physics from the matrix of natural philosophy to the status of an exact science.

Most of the treatises of the *Book of Calculations* follow the standard scholastic format in which arguments are given for and against competing opinions before Swineshead settles on and argues for the theory he believes to be more correct. Like Heytesbury's *Rules for Solving Sophisms*, the *Book of Calculations* seems to have been composed to provide university undergraduates with the analytical tools they needed to participate in disputations. As such, it is a good text to use for learning about the concepts and tools of fourteenth-century natural philosophy, including mathematics. Although the book does not expound its natural philosophical, let alone its metaphysical, foundations in detail, Swineshead appears to have agreed with the other Oxford Calculators, who (with the exception of Walter Burley) adopted the Scotistic addition theory of qualitative change and favored the ontological parsimony usually associated with William of Ockham. For more detail on the logical tools assumed by Swineshead, one should look to the work of Heytesbury, and for the natural philosophical background, to John Dumbleton's *Summa logicae et philosophiae naturalis*, as described in the work of Edith Sylla (1991b). A final fourteenth-century Oxford scholar whose work is related to that of Swineshead is Richard Kilvington, on whom there is significant recent scholarly work.

See also Aristotle; Bradwardine, Thomas; Burley, Walter; Heytesbury, William; Kilvington, Richard; Leibniz, Gottfried Wilhelm; Philosophy of Science; William of Ockham.

Bibliography

WORKS BY RICHARD SWINESHEAD

Book of Calculations. Only Treatise XI has been published in full, in the article by Hoskin and Molland (listed below). Edith Sylla has published a detailed outline of the entire work in her dissertation (listed below), as well as a similar outline for the *Descriptiones motuum* ascribed to Roger Swyneshed.

ROGER SWYNESHED'S LOGICAL WORKS

Spade, Paul Vincent, ed. "Roger Swyneshed's *Insolubilia*: Edition and Comments." *Archives d'histoire doctrinale et littéraire du moyen âge* 46 (1979): 177–220.

Spade, Paul Vincent, ed. "Roger Swyneshed's *Obligationes*: Edition and Comments." *Archives d'histoire doctrinale et littéraire du moyen âge* 44 (1977): 243–85.

WORKS ON RICHARD SWINESHEAD

Clagett, Marshall. "Richard Swineshead and Late Medieval Physics." *Osiris* 9 (1950): 131–161.

Clagett, Marshall. *The Science of Mechanics in the Middle Ages.* Madison: University of Wisconsin Press, 1959.

Crosby, H. Lamar Jr., ed. *Thomas of Bradwardine. His* Tractatus de Proportionibus. *Its Significance for the Development of Mathematical Physics.* Madison: University of Wisconsin Press, 1961.

Heytesbury, William. *Regule solvendi sophismatum.* Venice, 1494; many manuscripts.

Hoskin, Michael, and A. George Molland. "Swineshead on Falling Bodies: An Example of Fourteenth-Century Physics." *British Journal for the History of Science* 3 (1966): 150–182.

Murdoch, John, and Edith Sylla. "Swineshead, Richard." In *Dictionary of Scientific Biography*, Vol. 13. New York: Charles Scribner's Sons, 1976, pp. 184–213.

Spade, Paul. "Insolubilia," and "Obligations: Developments in the fourteenth century." In *The Cambridge History of Later Medieval Philosophy*, edited by Norman Kretzmann, Anthony Kenny, and Jan Pinborg. Cambridge, U.K.: Cambridge University Press, 1982.

Sylla, Edith. "Mathematical Physics and Imagination in the Work of the Oxford Calculators: Roger Swineshead's *On Natural Motions*." In *Mathematics and Its Application to Science and Natural Philosophy in the Middle Ages*, edited by Edward Grant and John Murdoch. Cambridge, U.K.: Cambridge University Press, 1987, pp. 69–101

Sylla, Edith. "The Oxford Calculators." In *The Cambridge History of Later Medieval Philosophy*, edited by Norman Kretzmann, Anthony Kenny, and Jan Pinborg. Cambridge: Cambridge University Press, 1982.

Sylla, Edith. "The Oxford Calculators and Mathematical Physics: John Dumbleton's *Summa Logicae et Philosophiae Naturalis*, Parts II and III." In *Physics, Cosmology and Astronomy, 1300-1700: Tension and Accommodation*, edited by Sabetai Unguru. Boston Studies in the Philosophy of Science, Vol. 126, Dordrecht; Boston: Kluwer Academic Publishers, 1991b, pp. 129–161.

Sylla, Edith. *The Oxford Calculators and the Mathematics of Motion, 1320–1350. Physics and Measurement by Latitudes.* Harvard University Dissertations in History of Science. New York: Garland Press, 1991a.

Weisheipl, James. "Roger Swyneshed, O. S. B., Logician, Natural Philosopher, and Theologian." In *Oxford Studies Presented to Daniel Callus*. Oxford: Clarendon Press, 1964. pp. 231–52.

Edith D. Sylla (2005)

SYLLOGISM

See *Logic, Traditional; Logical Terms, Glossary of*

SYLVESTER OF FERRARA, FRANCIS

(c. 1474–1528)

Francis Sylvester of Ferrara, a leading Thomistic commentator, sometimes listed under Francis, sometimes under his family name Silvestri, and cited in the Latin literature as Ferrariensis, was born in Ferrara, Italy. He entered the Dominican order in 1488, and took his magistrate in theology at Bologna in 1507. He later taught philosophy and theology at Bologna and other cities in northern Italy. Sylvester's "Commentary on *Summa Contra Gentiles*" has been printed with the definitive edition of that work of St. Thomas Aquinas in the Leonine edition of *Opera Omnia S. Thomae* (Vols. XIII–XV, Rome, 1918–1926). Among his other philosophical writings are two commentaries on Aristotle: *Annotationes in Libros Posteriorum* (Venice, 1535), and *Quaestionum Libri de Anima* (Venice, 1535).

A critic of Scotist and Ockhamist thought, Sylvester of Ferrara held some highly personal views, modifying Thomism in directions different from those of his contemporary Cajetan. In psychology and epistemology, Sylvester taught a theory of intellectual abstraction by compresence in which the actual object of understanding is quite different from the intelligible determinant that is impressed on the possible intellect (*species impressa* is not the *intelligibile*). The agent intellect performs two distinct actions, one on the phantasm and the other on the possible intellect. He modified Thomas's view that the proper object of the understanding is the universalized nature of sensible things, by teaching that the possible intellect forms a proper concept of the singular. In metaphysics, he also modified Thomism, saying that pure essences—for example, the natures of angels—may be multiplied numerically in existence, although how this is done is unknown. Concerning the individuation of bodies, Sylvester held that this is accomplished by matter as marked by definite dimensions (*materia signata quantitate determinata*).

Perhaps Sylvester is best known for his explanation of metaphysical analogy as that general characteristic of beings whereby they all somewhat resemble each other and yet are different. Contrary to the theory of Cajetan that all analogy reduces to that of proportionality, Sylvester argued that in every instance of analogy there is a first analogate which determines the meaning of the other analogates (*analogia unius ad alterum*). In endeavoring to harmonize various texts of Thomas, Sylvester may have minimized the essential character of analogy, moving in the direction of attribution and metaphor.

Among twentieth-century followers of Sylvester's theory of analogy are such important Thomists as F. A. Blanche, J. M. Ramirez, and N. Balthasar.

Bibliography

For a concordance to the Latin text of the Commentary on *Summa Contra Gentiles,* use *Indices … in Commentariis … Caietani et … Ferrariensis,* in Vol. XVI of the Leonine edition of *Opera S. Thomae* (Rome, 1948). See also G. P. Klubertanz, *St. Thomas Aquinas on Analogy* (Chicago: Loyola University Press, 1960), pp. 10ff., and F. A. Blanche, "Surle Sens de quelques locutions concernant l'analogie," in *Revue des sciences philosophiques et théologiques* 10 (1921): 52–59 and 169–193.

Vernon J. Bourke (1967)

SYMBOLIC LOGIC

See *Logic, History of: Modern Logic*

SYMPATHY AND EMPATHY

The notions of empathy and sympathy have a muddled history, and they are often used interchangeably. Recently, efforts at clarifying the difference have focused on empathy first and proceeded to characterize sympathy by contrast. The contemporary philosophical conception of empathy has three aspects. If Sam empathizes with Maria's anger, then: 1) Sam has a representation of Maria as angry; 2) Sam comes to have his empathic experience because of his representation of Maria as angry; 3) Sam's experience involves experiencing a state that is similar to anger.

On most accounts, sympathy differs from empathy by being triggered solely by emotions that are linked with pain and involves—either as consequence or through sharing the other person's pain—feeling sorry for the other person or wanting to alleviate the other person's suffering. The phrases *feeling with* and *feeling for*, respectively, are often used to capture the difference between the two notions.

Concerning number one above, the main point of contention is whether it is a requirement that the representation of Maria as angry be true, or whether Sam can empathize with Maria even if Maria is not angry now. Concerning number two, the main issue is how to describe the process of coming to feel empathic because of someone else's emotion. Does it require imagining the other person's emotion/situation or is it the case that a purely causal story not involving imagination sufficient for empathy? Concerning number three, the question is how to characterize the kind of affective experience empathy is. Is it an emotion of the same type as that of the person empathized with? Or are there rather natural empathic counterpart emotions corresponding to the emotions of the person empathized with? Or does empathic experience involve having some nonemotional feelings associated with the emotion empathized?

Although all these questions are still debated, there are two points of agreement: Empathy is not an emotion, but a phenomenon concerning the way one comes to be in touch with other people's emotions; in contrast, sympathy is, on one common conception, an emotional experience and amounts to something close to compassion. This contemporary understanding of empathy and sympathy has had many historical precursors under various confusing names. Most of these have focused on number two (i.e. the special way in which empathic experience is caused). Benedict de Spinoza's theory of affect imitation and David Hume's principle of sympathy, both central to these authors' conceptions of moral agency, exemplify the view that a fundamental trait of humanity resides in its capacity to experience other people's affects simply through the process of imagining these people experiencing these affects. The Scottish philosopher and economist, Adam Smith, held a similar view although his focus was on imagining other people's situations rather than affects.

The concept of empathy became prominent at the turn of the nineteenth century in German psychology and philosophy. It played an important role in elucidating human creatures' emotional engagement with the arts and how they come to interpret and understand each other as psychological beings. It was in this context that the term *empathy* itself was coined to translate the German word *Einfühlung* (i.e., "to feel one's way into"). Edmund Husserl, his student Edith Stein, and later Max Scheler are three philosophers whose contributions have shaped our present understanding of empathy. In particular, they each offered a particular elucidation of number three, insisting, each in their own way, that empathic experience cannot be of the same sort as the feeling that is the object of the empathic experience. Empathizing with someone who is angry would thus not involve oneself being angry, although it might involve the feelings associated with anger.

Interest in empathy and sympathy—and the broader interest in psychological simulation—has recently been driven by the thought that these phenomena are keys to the understanding of the development of moral agents. The idea—associated with a Humean take on morality—is that empathy is the most important source of one's understanding of others as beings with joys and sufferings directly dependent on the way one treats them. Hence the thought that moral sentiments and moral agency stem from a capacity to empathize with others. Contemporary empirical research on empathy has reinforced this idea. So has the existence of people (psychopaths) lacking both empathy and moral concern. However, the existence of people suffering from the same deprivation (some high-functioning autistic people) but manifesting a clear concern with morality suggests that empathy might only be a significant aid to moral growth, but not a necessary component of it.

See also Altruism; Moral Psychology; Moral Sentiments.

Bibliography

Darwall, Stephen. "Empathy, Sympathy, Care." *Philosophical Studies* 89 (1998): 261–282.

Hume, David. *A Treatise of Human Nature.* 2nd ed. Oxford: Oxford University Press, 1978.

Kennett, Jeanette. "Autism, Empathy, and Moral Agency." *The Philosophical Quarterly* 52 (2002): 340–357.

Nilsson, Peter. *Empathy and Emotions: On The Notion of Empathy as Emotional Sharing.* Sweden: Umea University, 2003.

Scheler, Max. *The Nature of Sympathy.* Translated by Peter Heath. London: Routledge, 1948.

Smith, Adam. *The Theory of Moral Sentiments.* Indianapolis: Liberty Fund, 1984.

Snow, Nancy E. "Empathy." *American Philosophical Quarterly* 37 (2000): 65–78.

Sober, Eliot, and David S. Wilson. *Unto Others: The Evolution and Psychology of Unselfish Behavior.* Cambridge, MA: Harvard University Press, 1998.

Stein, Edith. *On the Problem of Empathy. The Collected Works of Edith Stein.* 3rd ed. Translated by W. Stein. Washington, DC: ICS Publications, 1989.

Julien A. Deonna (2005)

SYNONYMITY

"Synonymity" has been a major topic in philosophy since the publication of Rudolf Carnap's *Meaning and Necessity* in 1947, though it was discussed earlier in the writings of W. V. Quine and C. I. Lewis. After Quine and Morton White launched their attacks on the tenability of the analytic-synthetic distinction, around 1950, the two topics became closely linked.

SYNONYMITY AND THE ANALYTIC-SYNTHETIC DISTINCTION

Analytic statements, in Quine's account, fall into two classes. Those of the first class, exemplified by (1), are logically true.

(1) No unmarried man is married.

Quine has no objection to the notion of analytic truth as used here, for he has what he regards as an acceptable account of the notion of logical truth in terms of which the notion of analytic truth is partially explicated. "The relevant feature of this example is that it not merely is true as it stands, but remains true under any and all reinterpretations of 'man' and 'married.' If we suppose a prior inventory of *logical* particles, comprising 'no,' 'un-,' 'not,' 'if,' 'then,' 'and,' etc. then in general a logical truth is a statement which is true and remains true under all reinterpretations of its components other than the logical particles" (all quotations from Quine are from "Two Dogmas of Empiricism").

All logical truths are analytic. The problems that beset analyticity, however, concern those purported analytic truths which are not logical truths. These are typified by

(2) No bachelor is married.

This is not a logical truth, for it does not remain true under every reinterpretation of its nonlogical components, "bachelor" and "married." If (2) is nevertheless to be considered analytic, it is because we can turn it into the logical truth (1) by replacing synonyms with synonyms. Thus, since "bachelor" and "unmarried man" are synonyms, we may replace the former with the latter in (2) in order to arrive at (1), a truth of logic.

It might appear that a generalization of the above considerations would yield a satisfactory account of the notion of an analytic statement. The generalization would go as follows: a statement is analytic if and only if it either (1) is a logical truth or (2) is transformable into a logical truth by the substitution of synonyms for synonyms. This account is rejected by Quine and White on the ground that synonymity (or synonymy, as Quine prefers) is no clearer a notion than analyticity. In Quine's words, "We still lack a proper characterization of this second class of analytic statements, and therewith of analyticity generally, inasmuch as we have had in the above description to lean on a notion of 'synonymy' which is no less in need of clarification than analyticity itself."

INTERCHANGEABILITY CRITERION OF SYNONYMITY

A natural response to Quine is that we can give an acceptable account of synonymity in terms of interchangeability. The suggestion is that the synonymity of two linguistic forms consists simply in their interchangeability in all contexts without change of truth-value—interchangeability, in Gottfried Wilhelm Leibniz's phrase, *salva veritate.* Benson Mates has offered an argument to show that if two expressions are synonymous they are interchangeable everywhere *salva veritate.* Following Gottlob Frege, Mates assumes that the meaning of a declarative sentence is a function of the meanings of the words which compose the sentence. Furthermore, two declarative sentences having the same meaning will necessarily have the same truth-value. It follows from these two assumptions that the replacement of a word in a sentence by another word synonymous with it cannot change the meaning of that sentence and hence cannot change its truth-value. Thus, if two words are synonymous they are interchangeable everywhere *salva veritate.*

In spite of the reasonableness of the above argument, the proposed interchangeability criterion soon runs into difficulty. Consider the synonymous pair "bachelor" and "unmarried man." The following statement is true:

(3) "Bachelor" has fewer than ten letters.

But the result of replacing the word *bachelor* by its synonym *unmarried man* is the false statement

(4) "Unmarried man" has fewer than ten letters.

This case can presumably be set aside on the ground that quoted expressions should themselves be understood as words functioning as names for their quoted contents. The interchangeability test is then interpreted as not applying to words such as *bachelor* when they appear as fragments of other words, such as "*bachelor.*" This makes the account of synonymity rest on the notion of wordhood, but Quine does not object on this account.

Perhaps Quine does not take seriously enough the difficulties involved here. Consider the synonymous pair "brothers" and "male siblings." Replacement of the former by the latter in

(5) *The Brothers Karamazov* is Dostoevsky's greatest novel

turns a true statement into one which is not true,

(6) *The Male Siblings Karamazov* is Dostoevsky's greatest novel.

Quine cannot object to this replacement for the same reason he objects to substitution of synonyms for synonyms within the context of quotation marks, for he cannot reasonably claim that titles are all single words.

The most serious problem connected with the interchangeability criterion is that the requirement is, apparently, too strong. Problems about wordhood aside, it is doubtful that paradigmatic synonym pairs like "bachelor" and "unmarried man" can pass the test. Consider the statement

(7) Jones wants to know whether a bachelor is an unmarried man.

Suppose it true, as it may well be, of some man named "Jones." Replacement of synonym for synonym here yields a statement that is no doubt false,

(8) Jones wants to know whether a bachelor is a bachelor.

CARNAP'S "INTENSIONAL ISOMORPHISM"

Carnap intended the concepts of intensional isomorphism and intensional structure to be explications of the ordinary notion of synonymity. Intensional isomorphism is explained in terms of logical equivalence (L-equivalence) when the usual application of the latter notion is extended beyond full sentences to cover various sentence parts. For example, two names "*a*" and "*b*" are L-equivalent if and only if "$a = b$" is logically true (L-true). Two (one-place) predicate expressions "*P*" and "*Q*" are L-equivalent if and only if "$(x)(Px \equiv Qx)$" is L-true. (This means that it is L-true that whatever has the property *P* also has the property *Q*, and conversely.) An analogous definition extends the notion of L-equivalence to many-place predicates (expressions for relations). Expressions for which the relation of L-equivalence has been defined in this manner are called "designators." If two designators are L-equivalent they are said to have the same intension.

Intensional structure is explained thus: "If two sentences are built in the same way out of corresponding designators with the same intensions, then we shall say that they have the same intensional structure" (all quotations from Carnap are from *Meaning and Necessity*). For example, consider the expressions "2 + 5" and "II sum V." These occur in a language *S* in which "2," "5," "II," and "V" are designations for numbers and "+" and "sum" signs for arithmetical operations. We suppose that according to the semantical rules of *S*, "2" is L-equivalent to "II" (and thus the two have the same intension), "5" is L-equivalent to "V," and "+" is L-equivalent to "sum." With regard to this example Carnap says, "…we shall say that the two expressions are *intensionally isomorphic* or that they have *the same intensional structure,* because they are not only L-equivalent as a whole, both being L-equivalent to '7,' but consist of three parts in such a way that corresponding parts are L-equivalent to one another and hence have the same intension." In our example corresponding parts correspond spatially, but this is not a necessary condition. Thus, Carnap regards "5 > 3" as intensionally isomorphic to "Gr(V,III)" because the (two-place) predicates ">" and "Gr" are L-equivalent and so are "5" and "V" and "3" and "III." The (two-place) predicates "correspond," regardless of their positions in the sentences. The sentence "(2 + 5) > 3" is intensionally isomorphic to "Gr(Sum(II,V),III)" because "2 + 5" is intensionally isomorphic to "Sum(II,V)" and the predicate expressions are L-equivalent, as are "3" and "III." On the other hand "7 > 3" is not intensionally isomorphic to "Gr(Sum(II,V),III)" even though "Gr" is L-equivalent to ">," "3" to "III," and "Sum(II,V)" to "7." They are not intensionally isomorphic because "Sum(II,V)" is not intensionally isomorphic to "7," although these expressions have the same intension (are L-equivalent). Intensional isomorphism of two expressions requires the intensional isomorphism of all corresponding subdesignators.

OBJECTIONS. Consider Carnap's extension of the use of "≡" so as to hold between predicators. According to this extension, if A_i and A_j are two predicators of degree 1, the following abbreviation is allowable:

$$A_i \equiv A_j \qquad \text{for } (X)(A_iX \equiv A_jX).$$

Now let us assume as L-true a sentence of the following form:

(1) $$A_i \equiv A_j.$$

This sentence will be intensionally isomorphic to

(2) $$A_i \equiv A_i.$$

But (1) is not intensionally isomorphic to

(3) $$(X)(A_iX \equiv A_iX),$$

which is the definitional expansion of (2). Sentence (1) will not be intensionally isomorphic to (3), because (3) contains a designator, "(X)," which cannot be matched to a designator in (1). The point of this criticism is that an expression can be intensionally isomorphic to another expression without being isomorphic to a third expression which has the same meaning as the second according to a definition. For this reason intensional isomorphism seems not to be an adequate explication of synonymity.

In "A Reply to Leonard Linsky," Carnap says that the ordinary notion of synonymity is imprecise. He concludes that more than one explicans must be considered. He proposes a series of seven possible explicata, at least some of which would not be affected by the above criticism.

The most serious argument against Carnap's program is that of Benson Mates: Let "*D*" and "*D'*" be abbreviations for two intensionally isomorphic sentences. Then the following are also intensionally isomorphic:

(1) Whoever believes that *D* believes that *D*.

(2) Whoever believes that *D* believes that *D'*.

Now the following sentence is true:

(3) Nobody doubts that whoever believes that *D* believes that *D*.

But (4), which is intensionally isomorphic to (3), is very likely false:

(4) Nobody doubts that whoever believes that *D* believes that *D'*.

If anybody even doubts that whoever believes that *D* believes that *D'*, then (4) is false, and the consequence is that two intensionally isomorphic sentences will differ in truth-value. But since two synonymous sentences cannot differ in truth-value, it follows that intensional isomorphism is not adequate as an explication for synonymity.

According to Hilary Putnam, Carnap believes that his theory in its present form cannot refute Mates's criticism. However, other philosophers (notably Alonzo Church) disagree with Putnam and (apparently) Carnap over the soundness of Mates's argument.

GOODMAN'S THEORY

One of the most widely discussed contributions to the topic of synonymity is Nelson Goodman's "On Likeness of Meaning." His view is particularly attractive to nominalistic philosophers who would avoid "abstract" entities, such as thoughts, senses, and meanings, in their semantical theories. Goodman proposes to explicate the notion of synonymity solely in terms of words and their "extensions"—the objects to which they apply. His account is confined to predicate expressions.

Suppose we say that two predicate expressions have the same meaning if and only if they have the same extensions—are true of the same things. A fatal objection to this view is that there are clear cases where two words have the same extension but do not have the same meaning. *Centaur* and *unicorn*, for example, have the same (null) extension, yet they differ in meaning.

We thus see that any simple identification of sameness of meaning of two expressions with sameness of extension must fail. But Goodman argues that we can still give an extensional account of sameness of meaning; although two words may have the same extension, certain predicates composed by making identical additions to these two words may have different extensions. *Centaur* and *unicorn* have the same (null) extension, but there are centaur pictures that are not unicorn pictures. Thus, "centaur picture" and "unicorn picture" have different extensions. Goodman concludes that "difference of meaning among extensionally identical predicates can be explained as difference in the extensions of certain other predicates. Or, if we call the extension of a predicate by itself its *primary* extension, and the extension of any of its compounds a *secondary* extension, the thesis is formulated as follows: two terms have the same meaning if and only if they have the same primary and secondary extensions." Suppose that in accordance with our nominalistic inclinations we exclude thoughts, concepts, attributes, meanings from the extensions under consideration. This means that when considering the identity of meaning of, for example, *centaur* and *unicorn* we will ignore such secondary extensions as those of "thought of a unicorn" and "thought of a centaur" or "concept of a unicorn" and "concept of a centaur." "If the thesis is tenable, we have answered our question by stating, without reference to anything other than terms and the things to which they apply, the circumstances under which two terms have the same meaning" (all quotations from Goodman are from "On Likeness of Meaning").

Let us see how Goodman's solution works. The predicates "(is the) morning star" and "(is the) evening star" have the same (primary) extension but differ in meaning. This difference is explained by Goodman as being due to a difference in the secondary extensions of these predicates. There are morning-star pictures that are not evening-star pictures and vice versa.

Now consider any predicates "*P*" and "*Q*." Consider the actual ink marks which constitute any inscription of the phrase "a *P* that is not a *Q*." Such an inscription will itself be part of the (secondary) extension of the predicate "*P*," for it will be part of the extension of the expression "*P*-description." But no inscription of the phrase "a *P* that is not a *Q*" will be part of the extension of the expression "*Q*-description." It follows from this that "*P*" and "*Q*" have different (secondary) extensions and hence that they are not synonymous. Since "*P*" and "*Q*" are any predicate expressions, no two predicates are synonymous. For example, any inscription of the phrase "a centaur that is not a unicorn" will be part of the extension of the expression "centaur description," but it will not be part of the extension of the expression "unicorn description." Hence, "centaur" and "unicorn" have different secondary extensions (though they have the same primary extension), so they differ in meaning.

ORDINARY-LANGUAGE VIEW

The discussions of the interchangeability criterion of synonymity and of Goodman's extensional criterion lead to the same radical conclusion. No two expressions are synonymous. Many philosophers regard this result as a reductio ad absurdum of the proposed criteria. Goodman seems to regard the result as a reductio ad absurdum of what is "commonly supposed" about synonymity. It is not clear whether he thinks that these views are commonly supposed only by the philosophers who discuss such questions or that they are held by those who in ordinary language sometimes declare two words to be synonymous. What is "commonly supposed," according to Goodman, is that (1) some predicates are synonymous with others and (2) synonymous expressions can replace each other "in all nonextensional contexts without change of truth-value."

Goodman holds that the two requirements are incompatible, and we can see why. "A *P* that is not a *Q*" is a *P*-description, not a *Q*-description; "a *Q* that is not a *P*" is a *Q*-description, not a *P*-description. On the supposition that "*P*" and "*Q*" are synonymous the following two statements have the same truth-value, if the interchangeability criterion is correct.

(1) "A *P* that is not a *Q*" is a *P*-description.

(2) "A *P* that is not a *Q*" is a *Q*-description.

However, the first statement is true and the second false. Thus, the predicates "*P*" and "*Q*" are not interchangeable everywhere, even in extensional contexts. But since "*P*" and "*Q*" are any predicates, no predicates are interchangeable everywhere. It follows from this that either no predicates are synonymous or synonymous predicates are not interchangeable everywhere.

In the face of this dilemma Goodman takes the alternative of declaring that "the relation of exact synonymy between diverse predicates is null." This is to say that no two predicates (or expressions of any kind, presumably) are "exactly synonymous." To many it has seemed more reasonable to abandon the interchangeability criterion. If no two expressions are synonymous or mean exactly the same thing, it is hard to see how the expressions "synonymous expressions" and "mean exactly the same thing" could have any currency in our language. Is it really credible that whenever we say two expressions are synonymous we are wrong? Is it not much more likely that the philosophers who discuss these issues have supposed that our concepts are governed by criteria which in fact do not apply? Consider a dictionary of synonyms. Is it credible that it is wrong in every entry because no two terms are synonymous? Surely not.

The above, or something like it, represents the response of the ordinary-language philosophers to the radical conclusions discussed in the earlier parts of this article. Such philosophers observe that a pair of terms may be regarded as synonymous "for certain purposes." This requires that they be interchangeable not everywhere but only in contexts relevant to the given discussion. It is wrong, these philosophers argue, to treat language as though it were a calculus governed by exact rules. But it is one thing to complain that the philosophers have distorted our actual use of the concept of synonymity and quite another to supply a careful and complete account of what that use is. Such an account remains to be given.

Bibliography

Several of the papers cited below are reprinted in *Semantics and the Philosophy of Language,* edited by Leonard Linsky (Urbana: University of Illinois Press, 1952).

ANALYTIC-SYNTHETIC DISTINCTION

Quine, W. V. "Two Dogmas of Empiricism." In *From a Logical Point of View.* Cambridge, MA: Harvard University Press, 1953. Ch. 2.

White, Morton. "The Analytic and the Synthetic." In Linsky, *Semantics* (see above). Ch. 14.

White, Morton. *Toward Reunion in Philosophy.* Cambridge, MA: Harvard University Press, 1956.

INTERCHANGEABILITY

Frege, Gottlob. "On Sense and Reference." In *Translations from the Philosophical Writings of Gottlob Frege,* edited by Max Black and P. T. Geach. New York: Philosophical Library, 1952.

Mates, Benson. "Synonymity." In Linsky, *Semantics* (see above). Ch. 7.

Quine, W. V. "Notes on Existence and Necessity." In Linsky, *Semantics* (see above). Ch. 5.

INTENSIONAL ISOMORPHISM

Carnap, Rudolf. *Meaning and Necessity.* Chicago: University of Chicago Press, 1947.

Carnap, Rudolf. "A Reply to Leonard Linsky." *Philosophy of Science* 16 (4) (1949): 347–350.

Church, Alonzo. "Intensional Isomorphism and Identity of Belief." *Philosophical Studies* 5 (5) (1954): 65–73.

Church, Alonzo. "On Carnap's Analysis of Statements of Assertion of Belief." *Analysis* 10 (1950): 97–99.

Lewis, C. I. *An Analysis of Knowledge and Valuation.* La Salle, IL: Open Court, 1946.

Lewis, C. I. "The Modes of Meaning." In Linsky, *Semantics* (see above). Ch. 3.

Linsky, Leonard. "Some Notes on Carnap's Concept of Intensional Isomorphism and the Paradox of Analysis." *Philosophy of Science* 16 (4) (1949): 343–347.

Putnam, Hilary. "Synonymity and the Analysis of Belief Sentences." *Analysis* (April 1954): 114–122.

Sellars, Wilfrid. "Putnam on Synonymity and Belief." *Analysis* (1955): 117–120.

GOODMAN'S THEORY

Goodman, Nelson. "On Likeness of Meaning." In Linsky, *Semantics* (see above). Ch. 4.

Goodman, Nelson. "On Some Differences about Meaning." *Analysis* (March 1953): 90–96.

Rudner, Richard. "A Note on Likeness of Meaning." *Analysis* 10 (1950): 115–118.

Thomson, James. "Some Remarks on Synonymy." *Analysis* 12 (1952): 73–76.

ORDINARY-LANGUAGE VIEW

Rollins, C. D. "The Philosophical Denial of Sameness of Meaning." *Analysis* 11 (1950): 38–45.

Shwayder, David. "Some Remarks on 'Synonymity' and the Language of Semanticists." *Philosophical Studies* 5 (1) (1954): 1–5.

Leonard Linsky (1967)

SYNONYMITY [ADDENDUM]

Intuitively, two expressions are synonymous if and only if (iff) they have the same meaning. Despite the apparently straightforward nature of this definition, the notion of synonymy has been hard pressed in contemporary philosophy of language. Difficulties arise from two directions: general skepticism about intensional semantics and specific concerns involving substitution into intensional contexts.

QUINE AGAINST INTENSIONAL SEMANTICS

In "Two Dogmas of Empiricism" (1951), W. V. O. Quine leveled an influential attack on intensional semantic concepts, concepts that express meaning relations (e.g., "analytic," "synonymous," and "antonymous"). While Quine acknowledged that such concepts are as a group interdefinable, he argued that no members of the class can be made philosophically respectable on empiricist principles.

His argument can be stated as follows. To be acceptable, semantic concepts must be definable in terms that are either formal (i.e., purely logical or linguistic) or observational. Quine first argued that there is no noncircular, nonarbitrary formal definition of the relevant semantic concepts. Thus, any definition will have to be stated in observational terms. But the semantic concepts under consideration presuppose that sentences have meanings individually. Yet, except at the theoretical periphery, where one finds observation sentences, observation does not bear on sentences one by one (holism). Consequently, there is no way to assign observational meanings to sentences individually. It follows that no acceptable definition of intensional concepts is possible.

MATES'S PUZZLE

In "Two Dogmas," Quine noted the possibility of defining an analytic statement as one that may be turned into a logical truth by replacing synonyms with synonyms. Quine then considered the possibility of defining synonymy in terms of substituting *salve veritate* (i.e., substituting without changing the truth value) in all nonquotational contexts. The suggestion is a natural one, since substitution of synonymous expressions ought to preserve compositional meaning, which in turn ought to preserve truth. Moreover, Quine's reasons for rejecting this proposal were not particularly forceful.

Benson Mates (1952) soon formulated a powerful and independently puzzling argument against substitution *salve veritate* as an adequate basis on which to define synonymy. Take any two purportedly synonymous expressions, say "chew" and "masticate." Now consider the following truism:

> (1) Nobody doubts that whoever believes that *x* chews, believes that *x* chews.

According to the proposed definition of synonyms, (1) implies (2):

> (2) Nobody doubts that whoever believes that *x* chews, believes that *x* masticates.

But clearly (2) may be false even though (1) is true, as when someone is unsure whether or not "chew" and "masticate" are synonymous. Consequently, "chews" and "masticates" are not synonymous. Moreover, this same argument will work for *any* pair of purportedly synonymous expressions.

Mates's puzzle is philosophically interesting apart from the question of whether or not substitution *salve veritate* underwrites an adequate definition of synonymy. For, in a compositional semantics for a language, substitution *salve veritate* appears to be at least a necessary condition for any pair of words to be synonymous.

RESPONSES

Attempts to revive a definition of synonymy have relied on hidden quotation, have sought to define synonymy in terms of responses to stimuli, and have involved rejecting the requirement of a reductive definition.

METALINGUISTIC RESPONSES. A natural first response to Mates's puzzle is to treat sentences like (1) and (2) as in some way covertly involving direct quotation. Wilfrid Sellars (1955), for instance, thought that sentences (1) and (2) should be reinterpreted as (1*) and (2*):

> (1*) Nobody doubts that whoever believes "*x* chews," believes "*x* chews."
>
> (2*) Nobody doubts that whoever believes "*x* chews," believes "*x* masticates."

Church (1954) offers a slightly more complex variant of this approach.

Despite their initial appeal, such metalinguistic responses do not appear to do justice the issue. For instance, while (1*) and (2*) explicitly involve English expressions, the original sentences do not; there is not even the presumption that people who are counterexamples to (2) must speak English. On this point, Tyler Burge (1978) seems quite right to note that while linguistic considerations may well be involved in such claims as (1) and (2), this does not show that these considerations enter into the content of the attitude report.

NEO-QUINEANISM. A second approach to synonymy derives from the work of Quine himself. Despite his attack on intensional semantics, Quine (1960) was able to preserve a vestigial concept of synonymy. He called two sentences *stimulus synonymous* for a speaker at a particular time iff the speaker would accept or reject them both under the same range of observational conditions. (A similar but more tenuous definition can be given for words.) Yet for many sentences, our assent or dissent does not depend on observation. Quine's concept of stimulus synonymy is far less widely applicable than the intuitive notion.

Peter Pagin (2001) attempted to extend this general sort of definitional strategy. According to Quine's holism, sentences may be partially ordered by how closely tied they are to observation. Observation sentences are either accepted or rejected on the basis of current observation. Most of the remaining sentences of the language, however, are assigned truth values more or less likely to be revised in light of further observation. On this basis, Pagin defined two statements *A* and *B* to be equally revisable ($=_r$), for a speaker at a particular time, as follows: $A =_r B$ iff for any statement C, $A <_r C$ iff $B <_r C$. Equivalently, $A =_r B$ iff for any statement C, $C <_r A$ iff $C <_r B$. Here $<_r$ is the relation of being less revisable than (for a speaker at a time). Pagin then offers the following definition (in which $A(\alpha/\beta)$ is any statement that results from substituting α for β in A, not necessarily uniformly):

> Expressions α and β are synonymous iff for any statement A, $A =_r A(\alpha/\beta)$.

Pagin's definition runs into problems at the level of statement synonymy. Let *A* and *B* be two distinct sentences that happen to be equally prone to revision. Then, setting $\alpha = B$ and $\beta = A$, we have it that any two statements that are equirevisable are synonymous. But surely it is possible to have two nonsynonymous statements that are equally prone to revision in light of recalcitrant data. In addition, Pagin's definition appears to flounder on a variant of Mates's argument. For let α = "masticates" and β = "chews" and let A = sentence (1) above. Then (2) will arise by substitution of α for β in *A*. But (1) and (2) are plainly not equally revisable, and so fail to qualify as synonyms on the proposed definition. And this result will clearly generalize to any pair of distinct expressions. This result is not surprising, for if substitution of synonyms cannot preserve truth, it can hardly be expected to preserve revisability.

NEOINTENSIONALISM. A final approach to restoring a definition of synonyms involves rejecting Quine's demand for a reductive definition altogether. Over the years, Jerrold Katz has developed a distinctive non-Fregean version of this approach. Katz's neointensionalism (2004) consists of two major theses: (i) Expressions of the language have a sense structure specified in terms of their parts. (ii) The sense structure of an expression is specified independently of its referential properties. Thus, senses are not modes of presentation. Rather, they constitute an *autonomous* semantic level posited (on the basis of the judgments of competent speakers of the language) to account for the sense properties of expressions (e.g., being meaningful, being synonymous). On such a view, it is straightforward to define synonymy in terms of having the same meaning (sense), since there is no further requirement to analyze meanings in terms of nonintensional concepts.

But clearly it will not do to allow the two semantic levels (sense and reference) to come apart completely. We cannot have an expression that, for instance, is synonymous with the definite description "the first celestial body visible in the evening" but that refers to, say, Margaret Thatcher. Consequently, Katz proposed that while sense does not *determine* reference, it does *mediate* it; that is, having a sense is necessary (though maybe not sufficient) for reference. The picture that Katz paints is one where we develop an autonomous theory of sense on the evidence of competent speakers' use of the language and then use that theory to constrain our theory of reference.

Katz's semantic theory does not appear, however, to avoid many of the objections that led to the downfall of its Fregean predecessors. Consider, for example, the fact that ordinary competent speakers of a language are occasionally radically mistaken about the nature of the entities about which they are speaking. Jonathan Cohen (2000), for instance, notes that in the past the best evidence from competent native speakers of English would have supported the hypothesis that the kind term "whale" included as a component of its sense the semantic marker FISH. Intuitively, however, those speakers were still referring to the same natural kind (the whale) as we do. But this judgment is inconsistent with Katz's proposal.

See also Analytic and Synthetic Statements; Analyticity; Meaning.

Bibliography

Burge, Tyler. "Belief and Synonymy." *Journal of Philosophy* 75 (1978): 119–138.

Cohen, Jonathan. "Analyticity and Katz's New Intensionalism: or, If You Sever Sense from Reference, Analyticity Is Cheap but Useless." *Philosophy and Phenomenological Research* 61 (2000): 115–135.

Church, Alonzo. "Intensional Isomorphism and Identity of Belief." *Philosophical Studies* 5 (1954): 65–73.

Katz, Jerrold. *Sense, Reference, and Philosophy*. Oxford, U.K.: Oxford University Press, 2004.

Mates, Benson. "Synonymity." In *Semantics and the Philosophy of Language*, edited by Leonard Linsky. Urbana: University of Illinois Press, 1952.

Pagin, Peter. "A Quinean Definition of Synonymy." *Erkenntnis* 55 (2001): 7–32.

Quine, W. V. O. "Two Dogmas of Empiricism." *Philosophical Review* 60 (1951): 20–43.

Quine, W. V. O. *Word and Object*. Cambridge, MA: MIT Press, 1960.

Sellars, Wilfrid. "Putnam on Synonymity and Belief." *Analysis* 15 (1955): 117–120.

Marc A. Moffett (2005)

SYNTACTICAL AND SEMANTICAL CATEGORIES

The basis for any theory of syntactical categories is the linguistic fact that in all natural languages there are strings of (one or more) words which are mutually interchangeable in all well-formed contexts *salva beneformatione*—that is, with well-formedness (grammaticality, syntactical correctness) being preserved in the interchange—and that there are innumerable other strings which do not stand in this relation. Any theory of semantical categories rests on a similar fact, with *well-formed* replaced by *meaningful* or *semantically correct*, and *beneformatione* by *significatione*.

The relation between *well formed* and *meaningful* is, in general, complex, and neither term is simply reducible to the other. The English expression "Colorful green ideas sleep furiously" (to use an example given by Noam Chomsky) is, at least prima facie, syntactically well formed. Yet it is semantically meaningless, even though certain meanings can be assigned to it by special conventions or in special contexts. In contrast, many everyday utterances are syntactically ill formed (because of false starts, repetitions, and the like) but semantically perfectly meaningful, again at least prima facie.

Chomsky and his followers have recently stressed that for natural languages well-formedness and meaningfulness are mutually irreducible, but this view has not gone unchallenged. For constructed language systems, particularly those meant to serve as languages of science, it has generally been assumed that the notions of well-formedness and meaningfulness coincide.

Since the time of Aristotle it has been customary among philosophers to explain the linguistic facts about interchangeability by resort to ontological assumptions. Certain strings of words, it is said, are not well formed (or meaningful) because the entities denoted by the substrings (the meanings, denotata, etc., of these substrings) do not fit together. Edmund Husserl, one of the authors who dealt most explicitly with interchangeability, coined the term *meaning categories* (*Bedeutungskategorien*). He maintained that we determine whether or not two expressions belong to the same meaning category, or whether or not two meanings fit together, by "apodictic evidence." But his examples and terminology—for instance, the use of the expression "adjectival matter" (*adjektivische Materie*)—indicate that his apodictic evidence was nothing more than a sort of unsophisticated grammatical intuition, which he hypostatized as insights into the realm of meanings.

Husserl certainly deserves great credit for distinguishing between nonsense (*Unsinn*) and "countersense" (*Widersinn*), or, in modern terms, between strings that violate rules of formation and strings that are refutable by the rules of deduction. But he is also responsible for the initiation of a fateful tradition in the treatment of semantical (and syntactical) categories. This tradition assumes—sometimes without even noticing the problematic status of the assumption, more often with only the flimsiest justification—that if two strings are interchangeable in some one context *salva beneformatione*, they must be so in all contexts.

This entry will discuss the chief modern contributions to the theory of syntactical and semantical categories. It will first outline the achievements of the Polish logician Stanisław Leśniewski and his pupil Kazimierz Ajdukiewicz. It will then evaluate the contributions by Rudolf Carnap and, in particular, stress the added flexibility gained by his decision not to adhere to Leśniewski's "main principle." Finally, the synthesis by Yehoshua Bar-Hillel of the insights of Ajdukiewicz and Carnap into a theory of syntactical categories and the demonstration by Chomsky of the essential inadequacy of categorial grammars for a description of the syntactical structure of natural languages will be mentioned.

LEŚNIEWSKI

In 1921, Leśniewski made an attempt to simplify Bertrand Russell's ramified theory of types but was not satisfied with the outcome. A type theory, however simplified and otherwise improved, remained for him an "inadequate palliative." He therefore began, the following year, to develop a theory of semantical categories that had greater appeal to his intuitive insights into the syntactical and semantical structure of "proper" language. For this purpose he turned from Russell to Husserl, of whose teachings he had learned from his teacher and Husserl's pupil, Kazimierz Twardowski, and, in particular, to Husserl's conception of meaning categories. As a prototype of a proper language, to which his theory of semantical categories was to be applied, Leśniewski constructed the canonical language *L*. Husserl's tacit assumption that if two strings are interchangeable in some one context *salva beneformatione*, they must be so in all contexts was elevated to the rank of the "main principle of semantical categories." Today Leśniewski's term *semantical categories* must be regarded as a misnomer, since the categorization was based on purely syntactical considerations. At the time, however, Leśniewski, like many other authors, believed that well-formedness and meaningfulness are completely coextensive for any proper language.

According to Leśniewski, each string, whether a single word or a whole phrase, of a proper language, and hence of his canonical language *L*, belongs to at most one category out of an infinitely extensible complex hierarchy. Strings are understood as tokens rather than as types. Moreover, two equiform tokens may well belong to different categories. This homonymy, however, never leads to ambiguity, since in any well-formed formula the context always uniquely determines the category of the particular token. In fact, Leśniewski exploited this homonymy for systematic analogy, with an effect similar to that obtained by Russell's exploitation of the typical ambiguity of strings (qua types).

Leśniewski excluded from the hierarchy only strings outside a sentential context, terms inside quantifiers binding variables, and parentheses and other punctuation signs. Defined constants were automatically assigned to categories by means of "introductory theses," as Leśniewski called those object-language sentences which, in his view, served to introduce new terms into an existing language. He gave rigid directives for the formation of introductory theses, assignment to a category being valid only after these theses were specified. The constructive relativity thus introduced was intended to take the place of the order restrictions by which Russell had sought to avoid the semantical antinomies.

In his canonical language Leśniewski worked with two basic categories, "sentences" and "nominals," and a potential infinity of functor categories. He admitted only indicative sentences; interrogatives, imperatives, hortatives, and the like were excluded. He explicitly rejected any categorial distinction between proper names and common nouns or between empty, uniquely denoting, and multiply denoting nominal phrases, although he later drew these distinctions on another basis. In the notation subsequently devised by Ajdukiewicz the category, say, of the sentential negation sign (that is, of a functor which, from a sentence as argument, forms a complex expression itself belonging to the category of sentences) is denoted by its "index" "*s/s*." The denominator of this "fraction" indicates the category of the argument and the numerator that of the resulting string. The index of such binary connectives as the conjunction sign is "*s/ss*." With "*n*" as the category index of nominals, "*n/n*" is assigned to "attributive adjectives" (but also to "nominal negators" such as "non-____"), "*s/n*" to "predicative intransitive verbs," "*s/nn*" to "predicative transitive verbs," "*s/n//s/n*" to certain kinds of "verbal adverbs," etc.

AJDUKIEWICZ

With the help of this notation Ajdukiewicz was able to formulate, in 1935, an algorithm for the determination of the syntactical structure of any given string in certain languages and, in particular, of its "syntactical connexity"—that is, its well-formedness. These languages had to embody, among other conditions, the Polish notation, in which functors always precede their arguments (thereby freeing parentheses from their customary duty as scope signals and making them available for other duties) and had to be "monotectonic," in H. B. Curry's later terminology—that is, to allow just one structure for each well-formed formula. These conditions of course excluded the natural languages from coming under Ajdukiewicz's algorithm.

To illustrate: Let

$$Afagbc$$

be a string in a given language fulfilling the above conditions. Let "*n*" be the index of "*a*," "*b*," and "*c*," let "*s/n*" be the index of "*f*," let "*s/nn*" be the index of "*g*," and let "*s/ss*" be the index of "*A*." The index string corresponding to the given string is, then,

$$\begin{array}{cccccc} A & f & a & g & b & c \\ s/ss & s/n & n & s/nn & n & n. \end{array}$$

Let the only rule of operation be the following: replace $\alpha/\beta\beta$ (where α and β are any index or string of indexes) by α (always applying the rule as far "left" as possible). One then arrives in two steps at the "exponent" "*s*," thus verifying that the given string is a sentence with the "parsing" *(A(fa)(gbc))*. The whole derivation can be pictured as follows:

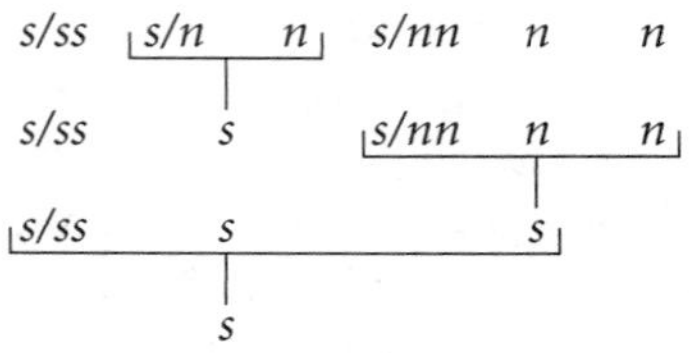

$$\begin{array}{cccccc} s/ss & \lfloor s/n & n \rfloor & s/nn & n & n \\ s/ss & & s & \lfloor s/nn & n & n \rfloor \\ \lfloor s/ss & & s & & s \rfloor & \\ & & s & & & \end{array}$$

In 1951, Bar-Hillel adapted Ajdukiewicz's notation to natural languages by taking into account the facts that in such languages arguments can stand on both sides of the functor, that each element, whether word, morpheme, or other appropriate atom in some linguistic scheme, can be assigned to more than one category, and that many well-formed expressions will turn out to be syntactically ambiguous or to have more than one structural description. These changes greatly increased the linguistic importance of the theory of syntactical categories and initiated the study of a new type of grammars, the so-called categorial grammars.

Ajdukiewicz never questioned the validity of Leśniewski's main principle. Neither did Alfred Tarski at first. It was taken for granted in the main body of Tarski's famous 1935 paper, "Der Wahrheitsbegriff in den formalisierten Sprachen." (The concept of truth in formalized languages; whose Polish original dates from 1931.) The appendix to this paper voiced some doubts as to its intuitive appeal, but these doubts probably derived more from a growing preference for set-theoretical logics over type-theoretical ones than from straight linguistic considerations.

CARNAP

Rudolf Carnap, in *Der logische Aufbau der Welt* (1928), had few misgivings about applying the simple theory of types to natural languages. Like Russell, he made a halfhearted attempt to provide a quasilinguistic justification for the type hierarchy, and his notion of "spheres" (*Sphären*) occupies a position approximately midway between Russell's types and Leśniewski's semantical categories. Carnap's explanation of certain philosophical pseudo problems as based on a "confusion of spheres" (*Sphärenvermengung*) antedates Gilbert Ryle's discussion of "category mistakes" in his *Concept of Mind* (London, 1949) by more than twenty years. Both explanations rest on an uncritical implicit adherence to the "main principle," even though Leśniewski's formulation was not known to Carnap at the time he wrote his book, probably because Leśniewski's publications prior to 1929 were all in Russian or Polish. At the same time, neither Leśniewski, Ajdukiewicz, nor Tarski quotes Carnap's book in their pertinent articles. Ryle, in his book, does not mention any of these publications.

Carnap was apparently the first logician to use the term *syntactical categories*, in 1932. At that time he believed that all logical problems could be treated adequately as syntactical problems, in the broad sense he gave the term.

He was also the first to free himself from the main principle. It eventually occurred to him that this principle embodied an arbitrary restriction on freedom of expression. Any attempt to impose this restriction on natural languages resulted in an intolerable and self-defeating proliferation of homonymies, similar to the outcome of the attempt by Russell and some of his followers to impose type-theoretical restrictions on natural languages, other than the tolerable "typical" ambiguities. In some cases it sounded rather natural to invoke equivocation (which is, of course, a "nontypical" ambiguity)—in the tradition of Aristotle, who used this notion to explain the deviancy of "The musical note and the knife are sharp." But in innumerable other cases there were no independent reasons for such invocation, and the induced artificialities exploded the whole structure. For instance, very strong reasons seem to be required if one were to assign the string "I am thinking of" to a different type or syntactical category each time the string following it belonged to a different type or category. For one may have after "I am thinking of" such varied strings as "you," "freedom," "the theory of syntactical categories," and "the world going to pieces."

In 1934, in *Logische Syntax der Sprache*, Carnap took implicit account of the possibility that two strings might be interchangeable in some contexts but not in all. He coined the term *related* for this relation and used *isogenous* for the relation of total interchangeability. Languages in which all strings are either pairwise isogenous or unrelated have, in this respect, a particularly simple structure. But there is no reason to assume that natural languages will exhibit this particularly simple structure. In fact, observing the main principle becomes a nuisance even for rich constructed language systems; as Carnap showed, the principle is not observed in some of the better-known calculi (perhaps contrary to the intention of their creators) with no real harm done.

BAR-HILLEL AND CHOMSKY

The relation "related" is clearly reflexive and symmetrical; hence, it is a similarity relation. The relation "isogenous" is, in addition, transitive; hence, it is an equivalence relation. Starting from these two relations, Bar-Hillel, in 1947, developed a theory of syntactical categories, illustrated by a series of model languages, all of which were, in a certain natural sense, sublanguages of English. In 1954, Chomsky developed a more powerful theory by taking into account, in addition, relations between the linguistic environments of the strings compared.

Recently, primarily owing to the insights of Chomsky and coming as a surprise to most workers in the field, it has become clear that interchangeability in context cannot by itself serve as the basic relation of an adequate grammar for natural languages. It may play this role for a number of constructed languages, and it certainly does so, for example, in the case of the standard propositional calculi. More exactly, it provides a satisfactory basis for what have become known as "phrase-structure languages," or what Curry calls "concatenative systems."

A phrase-structure language is a language (a set of sentences) determined by a phrase-structure grammar, the grammar being regarded as a device for generating or recursively enumerating a subset of the set of all strings over a given vocabulary. A phrase-structure grammar, rigorously defined, is an ordered quadruple $\langle V,T,P,S\rangle$, where V is a finite vocabulary, T (the terminal vocabulary) is a subset of V, P is a finite set of productions of the form $X \rightarrow x$ (where X is a string over $V-T$, the auxiliary vocabulary, and x is a string over V consisting of at least one word), and S (the initial string) is a distinguished element of $V-T$. Any terminal string (string over T) that can be obtained from S by a finite number of applications of the productions is a sentence. When the X's in all the productions consist of only one word the grammar is called a context-free, or simple, phrase-structure grammar.

Interchangeability in context seems also to be adequate for describing the surface structure of all English sentences but not for describing their "deep structure." It is powerful enough to enable us to analyze correctly the sentence "John loves Mary" (S) as a concatenate of a noun phrase (NP), consisting in this particularly simple illustration of a single noun (N), and a verb phrase (VP), consisting of a transitive verb (Vt) and another noun phrase itself consisting of a noun. Two customary representations of this analysis are the "labeled bracketing,"

$$({}_S({}_{NP}({}_N\text{John})({}_{VP}({}_{Vt}\text{loves})({}_{NP}({}_N\text{Mary}))))),$$

and the "inverted tree,"

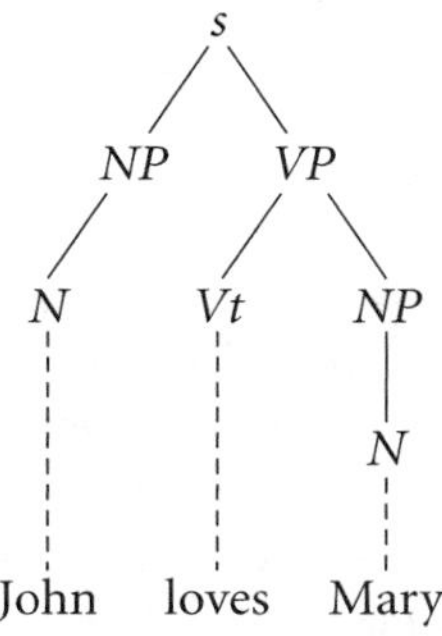

(both representations are simplified for present purposes). Interchangeability in context is likewise powerful enough to provide "Mary is loved by John" with the correct structure,

$$({}_S({}_{NP}({}_N\text{Mary})({}_{VP}({}_{\text{Pass}Vt}\text{is}({}_{Vt}\text{love})\text{-ed by})({}_{NP}({}_N\text{John}))))).$$

However, these analyses will not exhibit the syntactically (and semantically) decisive fact that "Mary is loved by John" stands in a very specific syntactical relation to "John loves Mary," namely that the former is the passive of the latter. No grammar can be regarded as adequate that does not, in one way or another, account for this fact. Transformational grammars, originated by Zellig Harris and considerably refined by Chomsky and his associates, appear to be in a better position to describe the deep structures of these sentences and of innumerable others.

Such grammars adequately account for the relation between the active and passive sentences and explain the fact that one intuitively feels "John" to be in some sense the subject of "Mary is loved by John," a feeling often expressed by saying that "John," though not the "grammatical" subject, is still the "logical" subject of the sentence. Transformational analysis shows that "John," though indeed not the subject in the surface structure of the given sentence, is the subject of another, underlying sentence of which the given sentence is a transform.

It has recently been proved that categorial grammars and context-free phrase-structure grammars are equivalent, at least in the weak sense of generating the same languages qua sets of sentences over a given vocabulary, though perhaps not always assigning the same structure(s) to each sentence. These sets can also be generated (or accepted) by certain kinds of automata, the so-called push-down store transducers. The connection that this and other results establish between algebraic linguistics and automata theory should be of considerable importance for any future philosophy of language.

DEVELOPMENTS IN THE 1960S

The early 1960s witnessed a revival of interest in the semantical categorization of expressions in natural languages, mostly under the impact of the fresh ideas of Chomsky and his associates. The whole field of theoretical semantics of natural languages is still very much in the dark, with innumerable methodological and substantive problems unsolved and sometimes hardly well enough formulated to allow for serious attempts at their solution. However, there is now a tendency to include indexes of semantical categories in the lexicon part of a complete description of such languages. These indexes, after application of appropriate rules, determine whether a given string is meaningful and, if it is, what its meaning is in some paraphrase of standardized form or, if it is not, how it deviates from perfect meaningfulness. In addition to semantical category indexes there are morphological, inflectional, and syntactical category indexes that determine whether the given string is morphologically and syntactically completely well formed, that present its syntactical structure in some standardized form, or that indicate the ways in which it deviates from full well-formedness.

Whether at least some semantical categories can, or perhaps must, be considered in some sense universal (language-independent) is a question that, like its syntactical counterpart, is now growing out of the speculative stage, with the first testable contributions beginning to appear. Investigations by Uriel Weinreich (1966) have cast serious doubts on the possibility of making a clear distinction between syntactical and semantical categories. Should these doubts be confirmed, the whole problem of the relation between these two types of categories will have to be reexamined.

See also Categories; Semantics, History of; Type Theory.

Bibliography

Ajdukiewicz, Kazimierz. "Die syntaktische Konnexität." *Studia Philosophica* 1 (1935): 1–27.

Bar-Hillel, Yehoshua. *Language and Information*. Reading, MA: Addison-Wesley, 1964.

Carnap, Rudolf. *Der logische Aufbau der Welt*. 2nd ed. Hamburg, 1961.

Carnap, Rudolf. *Logische Syntax der Sprache*. Vienna: Springer, 1934. Translated by Amethe Smeaton as *The Logical Syntax of Language*. New York: Harcourt Brace, 1937.

Chomsky, Noam. *Aspects of the Theory of Syntax*. Cambridge, MA: MIT Press, 1965.

Chomsky, Noam. "Formal Properties of Grammars." In *Handbook of Mathematical Psychology*, edited by R. Duncan Luce, R. R. Bush, and E. Galanter. Vol. II. New York: Wiley, 1963. Ch. 12.

Curry, H. B. *Foundations of Mathematical Logic*. New York: McGraw-Hill, 1963.

Husserl, Edmund. *Logische Untersuchungen*. 2nd ed., Vol. II. Halle: Niemeyer, 1913.

Luschei, E. C. *The Logical Systems of Leśniewski*. Amsterdam: North-Holland, 1962.

Suszko, Roman. "Syntactic Structure and Semantic Reference." *Studia Logica* 8 (1958): 213–244, and 9 (1960): 63–91.

Tarski, Alfred. *Logic, Semantics, Metamathematics*. Translated by J. H. Woodger. Oxford: Clarendon Press, 1956. Contains a translation of "Der Wahrheitsbegriff in den formalisierten Sprachen."

Weinreich, Uriel. "Explorations in Semantic Theory." In *Current Trends in Linguistics*, edited by Thomas A. Sebeok, Vol. III. The Hague: Mouton, 1966.

Yehoshua Bar-Hillel (1967)

SYNTACTICAL AND SEMANTICAL CATEGORIES [ADDENDUM]

Categorical distinctions in syntax and semantics are drawn on the basis of the distribution of linguistic expressions. According to the classical definitions, two expressions belong to the same syntactic category just in case they can be interchanged in every well-formed context *salva beneformatione* (without loss of well-formedness) and they belong to the same semantic category just in case they can be interchanged in every meaningful context *salva significatione* (without loss of meaningfulness) (Bar-Hillel 1953). The question is what counts as interchange in a context. Interpreting this phrase naïvely will result in inadequate definitions: Intuitively, one cannot conclude that "You are bald" and "I am bald" belong to different syntactic categories because "Most people who like you are bald" is well-formed, whereas "Most people who like I am bald" is not. Likewise, it cannot be concluded that *cat* and *dog* belong to different semantic categories from the fact that *location* is meaningful, whereas *lodogion* is not. Interchange of non-constituents is irrelevant for syntactic or semantic categorization.

One might try to modify the classical definition minimally, by saying that two expressions belong to the same syntactic category just in case they occupy the same range of syntactic positions within well-formed complex expressions, and they belong to the same semantic category just in case they occupy the same range of syntactic positions within meaningful complex expressions. But this still leads to excessively fine-grained categories. If one insists that *book* and *books* must belong to different syntactic categories because the first but not the second can occur with the indefinite article, or that *year* and *century* belong to distinct semantic categories because the morpheme *-ly* can attach meaningfully to the first but (arguably) not the second, they will miss a number of crucial generalizations.

The most useful categories will group together linguistic expressions that share much, but perhaps not all their distribution. Consider, for example, the syntactic category of prepositions. A distributional pattern used in identifying these is that prepositions can be intensified by *right* or *straight*, whereas other kinds of words cannot. "He went straight down the ladder" and "He lives right in the center of town," for instance, are well-formed, whereas "He went straight crazy" and "He is right the center of attention" are ungrammatical. This is an important test even though it yields both false negatives and false positives. "He went straight home" and "He came right with a friend." The exceptions can be neglected because *home* is idiosyncratic (for some reason "He went to home" is ungrammatical, but "He went to his home" is fine), and the facts about *with* allow for a different explanation (*with* cannot be intensified with *straight* or *right* because, given its meaning, it cannot be intensified at all).

One common way to achieve flexibility in talking about the distribution of linguistic expressions is to introduce *features*. Features are properties of words and morphemes that are marked in the lexicon (according to a common conception of lexical items, they are nothing more than structured bundles of features). Complex expressions inherit some of the features of their constituents. Some features are both semantically and syntactically significant (e.g. [PAST] which is a property of 'loved Hugo' but not 'loves Hugo'), some are syntactically but not semantically significant (e.g. [ACCUSATIVE] which is a property of the first person pronoun in 'They want me to come' but not in 'They want that I come'), and some are semantically but not syntactically significant (e.g. [ADULT], which is a property of 'horse' but not of 'foal').

Classical definitions can be modified by saying that two expressions belong to the same syntactic (semantic) category whenever they share a syntactically (semantically) significant set of features. This allows someone to say, for example, that nouns form a single syntactic category exhibiting important subcategorial distinctions (e.g., between proper nouns and common nouns, or between count nouns and mass nouns) and also cross-categorical similarities (e.g., prepositions and nouns do not allow the prefix "un-).

CATEGORIAL GRAMMARS

Even if certain differences of distribution are allowed within categories, about a dozen of them are still needed, and if significant subcategories are taken into account, the tally will go well above 100. To systematize these, one needs to involve them in describing the syntax and the semantics of the language (or languages) to which they belong. One of the simplest conceivable ways this could be done is through a *categorial grammar* (Ajdukiewicz 1967, Bar-Hillel 1953, Lambek 1958)

Categorial Grammars make the following four fundamental assumptions. First, words and morphemes are assigned, *pace ambiguity*, a single syntactic category in the lexicon. Second, there are a few basic syntactic categories, and the rest are derived through a few schemata. Categorial grammars vary widely in what they allow as basic categories, but for the sake of illustration, let us take the base consisting of the categories *S*, *N*, and *NP*—the category of sentences, nouns, and noun phrases. All categorial grammars include derived types that can be generated by the schema: If *A* and *B* are categories, so is *A/B*. Third, there are a few syntactic operations, including the one for right-concatenation: If *e* is of syntactic category *A/B* and *e'* is of syntactic category *B*, then there is an expression *ee'* of syntactic category *A*. Fourth, every expression within a given syntactic category has the same type of semantic value, and its semantic category is determined by its type.

Again, categorial grammars differ in the system of semantic types they assume, but a fairly typical idea is to assign the type t to S, the type $\langle e,t \rangle$ to N, the type $\langle\langle e,t \rangle,t \rangle$ to NP, and to lay down the schema that if the type of A is α and the type of B is β then the type of A/B is (β,α). If the semantics is extensional, semantic values of type e are entities, semantic values of type t are truth values, and semantic values of type (β,α) are functions from semantic values of type β to semantic values of type α (note that although the syntactic categories N and NP are basic, their semantic types are not). This divergence could be avoided if we had a basic syntactic category P of proper names with the associated semantic type e—N and NP could then perhaps be identified with the derived syntactic categories S/P and $S/(S/P)$, respectively (Ajdukiewicz 1967). Assigning the semantic type e to proper names would seem to be desirable anyway—it seems plausible that if semantics is extensional, the semantic value of *John* should be John himself, not the (characteristic function of the) set of (characteristic functions of) sets containing John. But if proper names and noun phrases are allowed to belong to different syntactic categories, it must be explained why their distribution is so very similar, which is why Montague (1973) decided against this option. One could get around this difficulty by introducing type-lifting rules (Hendriks 1987, Partee 1987).

In a minimal categorial grammar, the only syntactic rule is right-concatenation (interpretated as functional application). This is clearly inadequate because it cannot capture syntactic generalizations about word order. A natural idea to rectify this shortcoming is to introduce the schemata that if A and B are categories, then so is $A\backslash B$, and that if e is of syntactic category $A\backslash B$ and e' is of syntactic category A then there is an expression $e'e$ of syntactic category B (left-concatenation is also interpreted as functional application). But the resulting framework is still much too restrictive.

Until the very end of the 1960s it was widely assumed that categorial grammars are inadequate as syntactic theories of natural languages. There have been three basic strategies to challenge this attitude. The first is to add a transformational component to categorial grammars, whereas the second involves adding free permutations and propose syntactic filters to eliminate the ungrammatical (but interpretable) expressions. (For the former strategy see Lewis [1970]; for the latter see Cresswell [1973]). Both of these lines concede that categorial grammar is incomplete and perhaps nonexplanatory as a syntactic theory, but they argue that it still is the best structure to base compositional semantics on. The third strategy is more ambitious: It extends the set of permissible syntactic operations beyond concatenation and thereby seeks to achieve descriptive adequacy and explanatory power. This is the avenue most categorial grammarians have followed since the early 1970s.

The most important extension of permissible syntactic operations is the introduction of a different sort of concatenation—one that is not interpreted as functional application, but as functional composition. The simplest one of these is: If e is of syntactic category A/B and e' is of syntactic category B/C, then ee' is of syntactic category A/C; if the semantic value of e is the function f and the semantic type of e' is the function g, then the semantic value of ee' is a function h such that for every x: $h(x)=f(g(x))$.

A categorial grammar can have mixed composition rules as well, allowing the composition of a left-slash category with a right-slash category. These rules allow for the construction of sentences containing more than one quantifier to have different derivational histories, which in turn can account for scope ambiguities. They also open up the possibility to construct and interpret non-constituents (such as "Ron loves" in "Ron loves spinach"), which in turn allows categorial grammar to deal with difficult coordination phenomena, such as "Ron loves and Mia hates spinach" (Dowty 1987). All this is done without the introduction of a separate level of logical form with phonologically empty elements. Obviously, to prevent overgeneration, the application of composition rules must be tightly constrained (Steedman 1987).

Although very much a minority view among syntacticians, categorial grammar can explain a good deal about the structure of natural languages; for a survey, see Jacobson (1996). The attempt to do away with any structure other than what is visible on the surface is philosophically intriguing, especially considering that it is often supposed to lead to the complete elimination of variables (Szabolcsi 1989, Jacobson 1999). That the elimination of variables from certain logical languages was possible without limiting their expressive power is well-known from Quine (1966), but the claim that all sentences lack these devices may have much more significant consequences for philosophy. For one thing, those who believe in being ontologically committed to the values of the variables that are quantified over must find where these variables are. Quine's answer was that they are within the formulae of a formal first-order language that are associated with sentences through regimentation—a process where the outcome depends on one's particular interests. The result was the doctrine of ontological relativity (Quine 1969).

STRUCTURAL VALIDITY

Suppose categorial grammarians are empirically adequate and there is no need for a separate level of logical form to account for syntactic generalizations. There still might be the need for logical forms to distinguish between lexical and structural entailments. Consider, for example, the contrast between "Lou is a bachelor; therefore Lou is unmarried" and "Martin walked quickly; therefore Martin walked." Intuitively, the first is valid in part because of what *bachelor* means, whereas the validity of the second is independent of the lexicon. The established account of structural validity rests on logical form: An entailment is structurally valid if, and only if, it is valid in virtue of logical form (i.e., if, and only if, the logical forms of the premise(s) logically entail(s) the logical form of the conclusion). For example, if the (simplified) logical forms within the second entailment are:

$$\frac{\exists e \;(\text{walk}\,(\text{Martin}, e) \wedge \text{quick}\,(e))}{\exists e \;\text{walk}\,(\text{Martin}, e),}$$

As Davidson (1967) has argued, the entailment is indeed structurally valid on the established account. However, if there is no separate logical form, structural validity must be understood in a different manner.

The obvious thing to say is that semantic categories can provide a definition of structural validity without taking a detour through logical forms. One can say that an entailment is structurally valid just in case any uniform substitution of expressions of the same semantic category within it results in a valid entailment (Evans 1976). If, as categorial grammar assumes, syntactic categories are associated with a unique semantic type, which in turn determines semantic category, one may replace *semantic* with *syntactic* in the above definition. An interesting consequence of this definition is that logical consequence expressed in natural language (setting aside cases like "Hugo walks; therefore Hugo walks") will not be structural. But this is arguably as it should be: the inference "Hugo walks and talks; therefore Hugo walks" is valid in part because of what *and* means—replace it with *or* and the resulting entailment is no longer valid. Although logical entailments are said to be valid in virtue of their form, except for the special case of concluding something from itself, their validity also rests upon the lexical meaning of logical constants.

See also Semantics; Syntax.

Bibliography

Ajdukiewicz, K. "Die syntaktische konnextität." In *Polish Logic, 1920–1939*. Translated by S. McCall. Oxford: Clarendon, 1967.

Bar-Hillel, Y. "A Quasi-Arithmetical Notation for Syntactic Description." *Language*, 29 (1953): 47–58.

Cresswell, M. *Logics and Languages*. London: Methuen, 1973.

Davidson, D. "The Logical Form of Action Sentences." In *The Logic of Decision and Action*, edited by N. Rescher. Pittsburgh, PA: University of Pittsburgh Press, 1967.

Dowty, D. "Type Raising, Functional Composition, and Non-constituent Conjunction." In *Categorial Grammars and Natural Language Structures*, edited by R. Oherle. Dordrecht, Netherlands: Reidel, 1987.

Evans, G. "Semantic Structure and Logical Form." In *Truth and Meaning: Essays in Semantics*, edited by G. Evans and J. McDowell. Oxford: Oxford University Press, 1976.

Hendriks, H. "Type Change in Semantics: the Scope of Quantification and Coordination." In *Categories, Polymorphism, and Unification*, edited by E. Klein and J. van Benthem. Amsterdam: University of Amsterdam ITLI, 1987.

Jacobson, P. "The Syntax-Semantics Interface in Categorial Grammar." In *The Handbook of Contemporary Semantic Theory*, edited by S. Lappin. Oxford U.K.: Blackwell, 1996.

Jacobson, P. "Toward A Variable-Free Semantics." *Linguistics and Philosophy* 22 (1999): 117–185.

Lambek, J. "The Mathematics of Sentence Structure." *American Mathematical Monthly* 65 (1958): 154–169.

Lewis, D. "General Semantics." In *Philosophical Papers*. Vol. 1. Oxford: Oxford University Press, 1970.

Montague, R. "The Proper Treatment of Quantification in Ordinary English." In *Formal Philosophy: Selected Papers of Richard Montague*, edited by R.H. Thomason. New Haven, CT: Yale University Press, 1973.

Partee, B. "Noun Phrase Interpretation and Type-Shifting Principles." In *Studies in Discourse Representation Theory and the Theory of Generalized Quantifiers*, edited by J. Groenendijk. Dordrecht, Netherlands: Foris, 1987.

Quine, W. V. O. "Variables Explained Away." *In Selected Logic Papers*. New York: Random House, 1966.

Quine, W. V. O. "Ontological Relativity." In *Ontological Relativity*. New York: Columbia University Press, 1969.

Steedman, M. "Combinatory Grammars and Parasitic Gaps." *Natural Language and Linguistic Theory*, 5 (1987): 403–440.

Szabolcsi, A. "Bound Variables in Syntax: Are There Any?" In *Semantics and Contextual Expression*, edited by R. Bartsch. Dordrecht, Netherlands: Foris, 1989.

Zoltán Gendler Szabó (2005)

SYNTAX

"Syntax" is the theory of the construction of sentences out of words. In linguistics, syntax is distinguished from morphology, or the theory of the construction of words out of minimal units of significance, only some of which are words. According to this division, it is a matter of morphology that the word *solubility* decomposes into "dissolve" + "able" + "ity"; but it is a matter of syntax to analyze the construction of the sentence, "That substance is able to dissolve."

Although syntax is a traditional grammatical topic, it was only with the rise of formal methods growing out of the study of mathematical logic that the subject attained sufficient explicitness to be studied in depth, in works by Zelig Harris (1957) and Noam Chomsky (1957). Since then a flourishing field has been created; for it was rapidly discovered that the syntax of human languages was far more complex than at first appeared. In this respect, the development of syntax is comparable to other fields of cognitive science such as human vision, problem-solving capacities, and the organization of commonsense knowledge, all of which gave rise to difficult problems once the goal of fully explicit representation was put in place.

The dawn of syntax is marked by the realization that the structure of sentences is hierarchical; that is, that behind the linear order of words and morphemes that is visible in natural languages there is another organization in terms of larger or smaller constituents nested one within another. Description of sentences at this level is said to give their phrase structure. Moreover, phrases of a given kind can occur within others of the same kind: It is this recursive feature of language that enables sentences of arbitrary complexity to be constructed. The realization that phrase structure is recursive is very old. Assuming the categories of a complete noun phrase (NP) and sentence (S), Antoine Arnauld (1662) gives the examples (rendered here in English):

(1) ($_S$The divine law commands that [$_S$kings are to be honored])

(2) ($_S$[$_{NP}$Men [$_S$who are pious]] are charitable)

remarking that in (1) the embedded element "kings are to be honored" is a sentence occurring within a sentence, and that in (2) the relative clause has all the structure of a sentence, except that the relative pronoun "who" has replaced the subject.

In linguistic theory the recursive structure of syntax is expressed by principles of combination modeled after the clauses of an inductive definition. However, far more complex devices seem to be required for a compact description that helps to reveal the basis of the native speaker's ability. Chomsky's introduction of grammatical transformations opened the way to a variety of formalisms and developments (see Atkinson, Kilby, and Roca 1988 for a useful overview). Chomsky also initiated the conception of linguistic theory as a study of the acquisition of a system of linguistic knowledge, or competence. Any human language is acquirable under ordinary experiential conditions by any normal child. The space between empirical evidence and the resulting linguistic competence is sufficiently great that a kind of readiness for language, universal grammar in Chomsky's terminology, is presupposed. Contemporary theory seeks to probe the basis for this readiness in terms of innate rules and principles of grammar. For a more recent statement, see Chomsky and H. Lasnik (in Jacobs et al. 1993).

Within philosophy too the theory of syntax came to play an important role in the systematization of mathematics, and assumed central importance in Rudolf Carnap (1934). Carnap distinguished between grammatical syntax, of the sort that a linguist might give in a description of a language, and logical syntax, whose aim was not only to specify the class of sentences (or well-formed formulas of a calculus) but also to use formal methods in constructing a theory of logical consequence and logical truth. Carnap employed the distinction between grammatical form and logical form, which plays a crucial part in Ludwig Wittgenstein's views both in the *Tractatus* and in the *Philosophical Investigations,* and has become part of the lore of analytic philosophy. The scope of logical syntax in Carnap's terms took on much of the role of semantics in later philosophical discussion. Even with the later distinction between syntax and model-theoretic semantics, syntactic properties of formalized languages are still crucial for properties of systems of logic (soundness and completeness), and proof theory is established as a part of the syntax of mathematics.

In linguistic theory syntax and semantics have become increasingly intertwined disciplines, as it was realized that there are explanatory issues in relating linguistic forms to the specific meanings, or range of meanings, associated with them. S. Lappin (1995) contains a number of useful expositions on this theme; see also R. Larson and G. Segal (1995). The current research climate is in practice very different from conceptions associated with "ordinary language" philosophy: The contemporary view is not that ordinary speech lacks an exact logic, but rather that a diligent, collaborative effort is required to find out what the logic is. The concentration on logic implies that syntactic investigations have a metaphysical dimension. The patterns of inference of ordinary language call for formalization as part of a general account of the structure of individual human languages, or human language in general, and this formalization may in turn lead to proposals for reification, as in Donald Davidson's (1967) hypothesis that references to events are pervasive in ordinary action sentences.

On the side of linguistics proper, the problems of morphology have been treated in a progressively more syntactic manner as, for instance, our example *solubility* can be seen as built up by rules of a sort familiar from syntax. The result is the area now called morphosyntax, where the question whether morphology is a distinct level of linguistic organization is under active debate; see R. Hendrick (1995) for more recent discussion.

See also Arnauld, Antoine; Carnap, Rudolf; Chomsky, Noam; Davidson, Donald; Language; Logic, History of; Logical Form; Philosophy; Philosophy of Language; Proof Theory; Semantics; Wittgenstein, Ludwig Josef Johann.

Bibliography

Arnauld, A. *La logique, ou l'art de penser* (1662). Translated by J. Dickoff and P. James as *The Art of Thinking.* Indianapolis: Bobbs-Merrill, 1964.

Atkinson, M., D. Kilby, and I. Roca. *Foundations of General Linguistics.* 2nd ed. London: Unwin Hyman, 1988.

Carnap, R. *The Logical Syntax of Language.* London: K. Paul, Trench, Trubner, 1937.

Chomsky, N. *Syntactic Structures.* The Hague: Mouton, 1957.

Chomsky, N., and H. Lasnik. "The Theory of Principles and Parameters." In *Syntax: An International Handbook of Contemporary Research,* edited by J. Jacobs, A. von Stechow, W. Sternfeld, and T. Vennemann. Berlin and New York, 1993.

Davidson, D. "The Logical Form of Action Sentences." In *The Logic of Decision and Action,* edited by N. Rescher. Pittsburgh: University of Pittsburgh Press, 1967.

Harris, Z. "Co-Occurrence and Transformations in Linguistic Structure." *Language 33* 3 (1957).

Hendrick, R. "Morphosyntax." In *Government and Binding Theory and the Minimalist Program,* edited by G. Webelhuth. Oxford: Blackwell, 1995.

Lappin, S., ed. *The Handbook of Contemporary Semantic Theory.* Oxford: Blackwell, 1995.

Larson, R., and G. Segal. *Knowledge of Meaning.* Cambridge, MA: MIT Press, 1995.

James Higginbotham (1996)

SYNTAX AND SYNTACTICS

See *Semantics*

SYNTHETIC STATEMENTS

See *Analytic and Synthetic Statements*

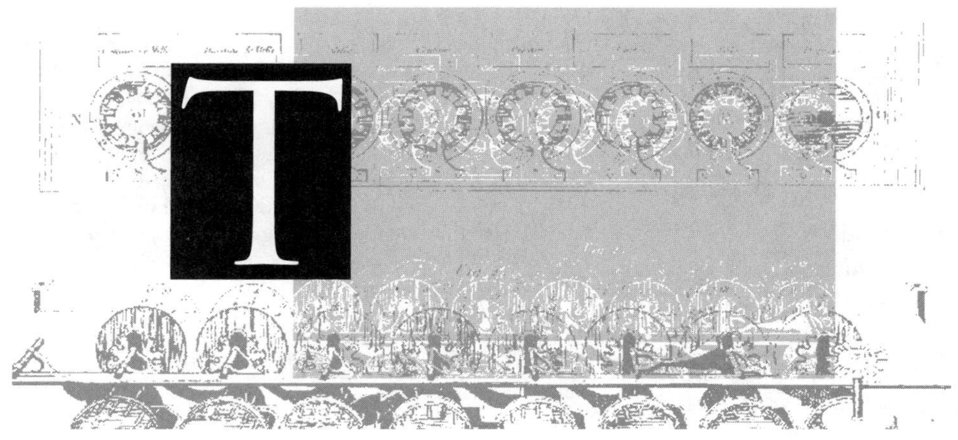

TAGORE, RABINDRANATH

(1861–1941)

Rabindranath Tagore was an Indian writer and philosopher. Romain Rolland, referring to the Orient and the Occident, said that Tagore contributed more than anyone else toward "the union of these two hemispheres of spirit." Sarvepalli Radhakrishnan called Tagore "the greatest figure of the Indian renaissance."

Tagore was born in Calcutta, studied in London, returned to India, and was married in 1883. He founded Visvabharati, a university at Santiniketan (near Bolpur), became India's most popular poet, won the Nobel Prize for literature in 1913, and was knighted in 1915. He visited and lectured in Canada, the United States, South America, England and several countries of Europe, the Soviet Union, Turkey, Iran, Ceylon, China, and Japan. He was in personal contact with Henri Bergson, Benedetto Croce, Albert Einstein, Bertrand Russell, and other leading intellectual figures of his period.

Tagore wrote about fifteen books of philosophical lectures and essays, about one hundred books of verse (mostly in Bengali, and partly translated by himself from his own Bengali version into English), about fifty plays (in some of which he acted the main role), and about forty works of fiction. His main writings of philosophical interest are *Sadhana: The Realisation of Life* (1913), *Personality* (1917), *Creative Unity* (1922), *The Religion of Man* (1931), all published in London and New York, and *Man* (1937), published in Madras. His best-known poems appear in *Gitanjali* (Song offerings), translated by the author from the original Bengali, with an introduction by W. B. Yeats (1913); *The Crescent Moon,* likewise translated by the author from the original Bengali (1913); and *Fruit-Gathering* (1916), all published in London and New York. He produced some drawings and paintings, beginning about his seventieth year, and planned and produced ballets.

Tagore's basic philosophical position is one that recognizes the useful insights of the main opposing views on a given question. For example, concerning the transcendence or immanence of God, Tagore accepted, on the one hand, the value of the doctrine of Brahman as "the absolute Truth, the impersonal It, in which there can be no distinction of this and that, the good and the evil, the beautiful and its opposite, having no other quality except its ineffable blissfulness in the eternal solitude of its consciousness"; but he also felt, on the other hand, that "whatever name may have been given to the divine Reality it has found its highest place in the history of our religion owing to its human character, giving meaning to the idea of sin and sanctity, and offering an eternal background to all the ideals of perfection which have their harmony with man's own nature" (*The Religion of Man*).

Similarly, he combined the best insights of humanists, who exalt man, and of otherworldly seekers of the World Force, who belittle man; of naturalists, who deny spirit, and of extreme partisans of spirit, who cut man off from nature; of individualists and universalists; of determinists and defenders of free will; of hedonists and ascetics; and of romanticists and realists.

In his social philosophy, as well as in his metaphysics, Tagore attempted to synthesize polar opposites. Neither wholly conservative nor wholly liberal, he favored gradual reform. This evolutionary note is reflected in his views on the economic order, public health, education, the social structure, national politics, and international affairs.

Tagore's emphasis on the mediating unity that embraces variety appears, for example, in *Sadhana,* where he wrote: "Facts are many, but the truth is one.... Man must clearly realise some central truth which will give him an outlook over the widest possible field. And that is the object which the Upanishad has in view when it says, Know thine own Soul. Or, in other words, realise the one great principle of unity that there is in every man."

In May 1930 Tagore delivered the Hibbert Lectures at Oxford. In the following year, the lectures were published in expanded form as a book, *The Religion of Man.* Tagore's mediationism appears in the book in such passages as the following: "The final freedom which India aspires after ... is beyond all limits of personality, divested of all moral or aesthetic distinctions; it is the pure consciousness of Being, the ultimate reality." The yogi has claimed that through intensive concentration and quietude we do reach "that infinity where knowledge ceases to be knowledge, subject and object become one—a state of existence that cannot be defined.... India attunes man to the grand harmony of the universal, leaving no room for untrained desires of a rampant individualism to pursue their destructive career unchecked, but leading them on to their ultimate modulation in the Supreme."

See also Bergson, Henri; Brahman; Croce, Benedetto; Einstein, Albert; Humanism; Indian Philosophy; Russell, Bertrand Arthur William.

Bibliography

The philosophical works by Tagore that are mentioned above, as well as others, have been published in various editions, in English and in translation into European languages.

Works on Tagore's philosophy include the following (arranged in chronological order): Sarvepalli Radhakrishnan, *The Philosophy of Rabindranath Tagore* (London: Macmillan, 1918; reissued Baroda: Good Companions, 1961); Sachin Sen, *The Political Thought of Tagore* (Calcutta: General Printers and Publishers, 1947); B. G. Ray, *The Philosophy of Rabindranath Tagore* (Bombay: Hind Kitabs, 1949); V. S. Naravane, *Rabindranath Tagore, A Philosophical Study* (Allahabad: Central Book Depot, n.d.); and Sasadhar Sinha, *Social Thinking of Rabindranath Tagore* (New York: Asia Publishing House, 1962).

Of the many biographies of Tagore, mention may be made of Krishna Kripalani, *Rabindranath Tagore: A Biography* (New York: Oxford University Press, 1962).

William Gerber (1967)

TAINE, HIPPOLYTE-ADOLPHE

(1828–1893)

Hippolyte-Adolphe Taine was a philosopher, psychologist, historian, and critic. Taine and Ernest Renan were the leading French positivistic thinkers of the second half of the nineteenth century. As a result of Taine's great independence of mind, his life was not always comfortable. Discriminatory treatment from the authorities of the Second Empire led to his withdrawal from teaching from 1852 to 1863, when he was appointed an examiner at Saint-Cyr. The next year he became a lecturer at the École des Beaux Arts; from his lectures there came his famous *Philosophie de l'art,* At the intervention of the Catholic clergy, a French Academy award for his *Histoire de la littérature anglaise* was denied him, and he was elected to the academy only in 1878, after the fall of the Second Empire. By that time he had antagonized both liberals and Bonapartists by his ruthless destruction of the revolutionary and Napoleonic legends. Nevertheless, his influence was great and diversified. His positivistic and physiological approach to psychology was adopted by Théodule Ribot, Pierre Janet, and others, and his opposition to centralization and to revolutionary experiments attracted Catholic traditionalists such as Paul Bourget and Maurice Barrès, who, however, ignored his severe condemnation of the old regime and his outspoken sympathies for Protestant and parliamentary England.

Although Taine's philosophical views were formed early in life under the joint influence of Benedict de Spinoza, G. W. F. Hegel, and classical science, they were first systematically expounded in his *De l'intelligence.* The theory of mind presented in this book is based on Taine's general monism and determinism. Thus in the preface to the fourth edition (Paris, 1883), he stated his opposition to faculty psychology on the grounds that words such as *capacity, self, reason,* and *memory* suggest by their simplicity the existence of indivisible mental entities and thus prevent us from grasping the enormous complexities of the underlying psychological mechanisms. The self is nothing but a series of mental events. In his attack on the substantialization of the self and the reification of abstractions, Taine drew on psychopathology and neural physiology. Psychopathology shows how mental disease can dissociate the components of a complex phenomenon that appears subjectively as simple; neural physiology reveals the enormous complexity of the neural mechanism that underlies mental phenomena. Taine held a double-aspect theory of the relation between introspective data and public physical events; the mental and the physical are two sides of the same process, "two translations of the same text" (*De l'intelligence,* Book 4, Ch. 2). Taine's use of physiological analysis, his strictures on introspection, and his mechanistic determinism place him among the naturalists.

Like most of his contemporaries, Taine regarded classical science as complete, and its picture of nature as definitive. Like Herbert Spencer, Wilhelm Ostwald, and others, he regarded the law of conservation of energy as ultimate, as "the immutable ground of being," and the equivalence of cause and effect as a consequence of this law.

Taine applied his rigorous determinism to all phenomena—physical, mental, and social. There is little in his writings dealing directly with physical phenomena, but there is no question that the determinism of classical physics was for him an ideal model to which other sciences should conform. Thus in the introduction to his *Histoire de la littérature anglaise,* he proposed that every social phenomenon should be explained as the result of race, environment, and time—that is, of the particular psychosocial state of a society. Taine had already applied this method in previous essays, and he applied it in his *Philosophie de l'art* and later in his major historical work, *Les origines de la France contemporaine,* inspired by his reflections on the French defeat in 1870. The thesis of this monumental and controversial work is that there was one persistent theme—excessive centralization—underlying all the violent upheavals of modern France. Introduced by the Bourbons, it was strengthened by the French Revolution, which destroyed the natural provinces and replaced them by departments which were mere administrative appendixes of the central government; in the hands of Napoleon Bonaparte the centralized administrative structure was an efficient tool of internal control and external conquest, but it became an unwieldy bureaucratic machine as soon as it was deprived of Napoleon's ruthless energy.

Taine's detailed study of social conditions under the old regime, of revolutionary excesses, and of mob psychology after 1789 strengthened the inclination to pessimism present in his previous writings. This inclination found its most eloquent expression in the following passage: "Man is a nervous machine, governed by a mood, disposed to hallucinations, transported by unbridled passions, essentially unreasonable" (*History of English Literature,* Vol. II, p. 173). In *De l'intelligence* Taine had said that every image tends to acquire a hallucinatory intensity unless checked by the inhibiting influence of other images. Thus mental equilibrium and social stability are mere "happy accidents." Civilization is a mere surface beneath which lurk irrational drives always ready to break through.

See also Determinism in History; Hegel, Georg Wilhelm Friedrich; Ostwald, Wilhelm; Renan, Joseph Ernest; Ribot, Théodule Armand; Sociology of Knowledge; Spinoza, Benedict (Baruch) de.

Bibliography

WORKS BY TAINE

Essais de critique et d'histoire. Paris: Hachette, 1858.

Histoire de la littérature anglaise, 4 vols. Paris: Hachette, 1863–1864. Translated by H. van Laun as *History of English Literature,* 2 vols. Edinburgh, 1873.

Nouveaux essais de critique et d'histoire. Paris, 1865.

Philosophie de l'art. Paris: Baillière, 1865; 2nd ed., enlarged, Paris, 1880. First edition translated by J. Durand as *The Philosophy of Art.* New York, 1865.

De l'intelligence, 2 vols. Paris: Hachette, 1870. Translated by T. D. Hayes as *Intelligence.* London, 1871.

Les origines de la France contemporaine, 5 vols. Paris, 1876–1893.

Derniers essais de critique et d'histoire. Paris, 1894.

WORKS ON TAINE

Barzelotti, Giacomo. *Ippolito Taine.* Rome, 1896.

Bourget, Paul. *Essais de psychologie contemporaine.* Vol. I. Paris, 1883.

Chevrillon, André. *Taine: Formation de sa pensée.* Paris: Plon, 1932.

Faguet, Émile. *Politiques et moralistes du XIXe* siècle. 3rd series. Paris, 1900.

Giraud, Victor. *Essai sur Taine: Son oeuvre et son influence.* Paris: Hachette, 1901.

Kahn, Sholem J. *Science and Aesthetic Judgment: A Study in Taine's Critical Method.* New York: Columbia University Press, 1953.

Lacombe, Paul. *La psychologie des individus et des sociétés chez Taine.* Paris: Alcan, 1906.

Lacombe, Paul. *Taine, historien et sociologue.* Paris: V. Giard and E. Brière, 1909.

Milič Čapek (1967)

TAOISM

See *Chinese Philosophy: Daoism; Laozi; Mysticism, History of*

TARSKI, ALFRED
(1902–1983)

Alfred Tarski, the Polish-American mathematician and logician, was born in Warsaw, received his doctorate in mathematics from the University of Warsaw in 1924, and two years later was named docent. In 1939 he emigrated to the United States. Appointed lecturer in mathematics at the University of California (Berkeley) in 1942, he remained at that institution for the rest of his life, serving as professor of mathematics from 1946 and becoming professor emeritus in 1968.

MATHEMATICS

Tarski worked in both pure mathematics, especially set theory and algebra, and mathematical logic, especially metamathematics. This entry will not discuss his mathematical contributions, although some of them (in particular his famous theorem, established jointly with Stefan Banach, on the decomposition of the sphere, as well as his theory of inaccessible cardinals) have a definite bearing on the epistemology of mathematics. (See S. Banach and A. Tarski, "Sur la décomposition des ensembles des points en parties respectivement congruentes," *Fundamenta Mathematicae* 6 [1924]: 244–277.)

It should be noted that in these papers Tarski has not criticized the assumptions of set theory. Like most mathematicians he has simply accepted them as true. This attitude and a systematic use of set-theoretic concepts have profoundly influenced his work in logic and metamathematics. Unlike the followers of David Hilbert and of L. E. J. Brouwer, Tarski has not refrained from the use of infinitistic set-theoretical concepts. He finds a definition or a theorem to be acceptable if it is expressed or proved on the basis of set theory. This attitude, of course, is completely different from that of Hilbert's formalism or Brouwer's intuitionism.

As a consequence of this methodological attitude, Tarski has gained much freedom in introducing new notions and thus has put himself in a much more advantageous position than the adherents of Hilbert or Brouwer. Consider the following very simple but typical example. In *Logic, Semantics, Metamathematics* (p. 38) Tarski defines the set of consequences of a given set of axioms as the smallest set containing the axioms and closed with respect to the rules of proof, and on this definition he bases the whole theory of the consequence relation in the propositional calculus. A follower of Hilbert or Brouwer would never accept such a definition because he would regard the clarification of the notion of set (involved in this definition) as the ultimate aim of his activity.

The free use of set theory has enabled Tarski to extend the field of application of metamathematics (see, for instance, his investigations of "infinitary languages," discussed below) and has formed a natural basis for the development of his semantic method. This method can indeed be formulated only in a language that has considerable deductive strength and is provided with means to express definitions of a very complicated structure. The general theory of sets satisfies both these requirements.

Obviously Tarski's methodological attitude is rejected by the adherents of finitism and by all logicians who seek in metamathematics a justification or explanation of set theory.

METAMATHEMATICS

Metamathematics is a branch of mathematical logic that studies formal theories and solves problems pertaining to such theories. Tarski contributed so much to this field that he deserves to be regarded, with Hilbert, as its cofounder.

AXIOMATIC THEORY OF FORMAL SYSTEMS. In his early papers Tarski presented an axiomatic theory of arbitrary formal systems. A "theory" for him is a set (whose elements are called formulas) and a function (called the consequence function) that correlates a set of formulas with each such set; this new set is called the set of consequences of the first set. The consequence function is not wholly arbitrary; it must satisfy certain axioms that will not be reproduced here. Several metamathematical notions, such as consistency, completeness, and independence, can be defined for theories in this abstract sense. All formal theories that were known in 1930 can be subsumed under this scheme. While this is no longer true today (see below), a relatively small rectification of Tarski's axioms would suffice to restore the universality of his scheme.

SYSTEMS BASED ON PROPOSITIONAL LOGIC. Besides discussing the most general scheme of formal theories, Tarski axiomatically described theories based on the classical propositional logic. Here the assumptions must, of course, be specialized. It is assumed, for example, that certain operations are defined on the set of formulas (the joining of two formulas by means of a connective). An example of an important property of consequence that Tarski took as an axiom is the deduction theorem. Its importance is that it provides the possibility of defining the consequence function in terms of one fixed set S_0 of sentences, specifically the set of consequences of the empty set. In concrete cases, S_0 consists of logical tautologies expressible in the given theory. In what follows, we shall speak of theories as being based on a logic L if S_0 is the set of tautologies of the logic L.

DESCRIPTION OF SYSTEMS. Tarski calls a set X of formulas a system if it is deductively closed, that is, if it is equal to its set of consequences. In "Grundzüge des Systemenkalküls" he formulated a general program aimed at describing all systems of a given theory. Tarski showed in this paper that in order to achieve this aim it is sufficient to describe all complete systems, and he illustrated his program in several simple but interesting cases of decidable theories. Many ideas developed in this paper were later incorporated by Tarski in the general theory of models.

SEMANTICS

In the early 1930s Tarski formulated the semantic method, which is his most important achievement in logic. The essence of the method consists in discussion of the relations between expressions and the objects they denote.

Tarski himself said that his semantics was a modest discipline. Yet the philosophical claims of semantics were ambitious from the start. Tarski's aim was "to construct—with reference to a given language—*a materially adequate and formally correct definition of the term 'true sentence,'*" a problem "which belongs to the classical questions of philosophy."

Almost from the beginning the methods of semantics exerted a profound influence on philosophers engaged in the construction and study of exact scientific languages. Semantics opened new possibilities in these studies, which formerly were limited to purely syntactic problems and thus were unable to express relations between languages and extralinguistic objects. Semantics offered a natural tool for the discussion of such relations. The price one had to pay was the use of a much stronger metalanguage than the one sufficient for syntax. At any rate, semantic methods became an accepted tool in the study of scientific languages: "Contemporary studies in the methodology of science are primarily concerned with the syntax and semantics of the language of science" (R. M. Martin, *Truth and Denotation*, Chicago, 1958, p. 16).

Tarski published little concerning the applicability of semantics to the study of empirical languages (see, however, his remarks in "The Semantic Conception of Truth and the Foundations of Semantics"). Rather, he limited himself to applications of his method to logic and mathematics. His most outstanding contributions in these areas will be described briefly.

INTERPRETATIONS OF PROPOSITIONAL CALCULI. The propositional calculus provides us with simple examples of semantic notions. Thus, the two-element Boolean algebra is an interpretation of the calculus; the propositional connectives are interpreted as functions whose arguments and values range over the algebra. We may accordingly conceive of the propositional calculus as a language that describes the two-element algebra. Instead of the two-element algebra we may take any other matrix for the propositional calculus. Thus, a formal calculus may have (and in general does have) many interpretations. Tarski early became acquainted with these notions through his collaboration with Jan Łukasiewicz, who in the 1920s initiated the metatheoretical investigation of propositional calculi. In a joint publication Tarski and Łukasiewicz gave a general set-theoretical definition of a matrix and showed its usefulness in various special problems.

MODELS. Models play the same role for theories based on (extensions of) the first-order functional calculus as that played by matrices for propositional calculi. If a theory T has as its primitive constants k predicates with $r_1, \cdot\cdot\cdot, r_k$ arguments, then a model for T is defined as an ordered k + 1-tuple $\langle A, R_1, \cdot\cdot\cdot, R_k \rangle$, where R_i is a relation with r_i arguments ranging over A ($i = 1, \cdot\cdot\cdot, k$). A model determines a partition of sentences into two sets, one consisting of sentences that are true in the model and the other of sentences that are false in the model. A formula that contains free variables is by itself neither true nor false in the model, but if arbitrary elements of A are correlated with the free variables of the formula, it becomes either true or false. In the first case we say that the elements of A correlated with the free variables satisfy the formula in the model. We have here an analogy with the situation in the propositional calculus: if a matrix is given and if its elements are correlated in an arbitrary way with the free variables of a formula, then the formula has a value that is an element of the matrix. This analogy between models and matrices was stressed in "The Concept of Truth in Formalized Languages," in *Logic, Semantics, Metamathematics,* pp. 152–278. (This is an English translation of an earlier paper.)

The notion of a model and some related semantic notions were known to mathematicians and logicians long before the work of Tarski. No one, however, was concerned to strive for such a degree of precision as Tarski maintained. The fruits of Tarski's approach are first, a precise set-theoretical description of the semantic notions, together with a meticulous discussion of the language in which these definitions are expressible; second, the discovery of general properties of these notions which sometimes are very startling; and third, the discovery of a broad field of applications.

The semantic notions, which before Tarski were used in solving relatively special problems concerning consistency and independence, now turned out to be powerful tools in dealing with many metamathematical investigations. For a philosopher the most important application of the semantic method is Tarski's theory of truth.

LOGICAL CONSEQUENCE. Logical consequence is defined as follows: a sentence F is a logical consequence of a set X of sentences if F is true in every model in which all sentences of X are true. For theories based on first-order logic this notion is coextensive with the syntactic notion of derivability (Gödel's completeness theorem). For theories based on the higher-order logics or on the various extensions of first-order logic, these notions are essentially different. Analyzing the intuitions underlying the notion of consequence, one arrives with Tarski at the conclusion that it is the semantic and not the syntactic notion that adequately describes the notion that is intuitively given. At the same time, many logics in which the consequence functions are defined semantically turn out to be free from defects resulting from the incompleteness phenomenon discovered by Kurt Gödel. This shows the essential gains brought by the acceptance of the semantically defined notion of logical consequence. What is lost is the finitary ("combinatorial") description of the consequence function.

DEFINABILITY. Like the notion of consequence, definability can be treated syntactically and semantically. Although investigations in both these directions were pursued in special cases before Tarski, it is only following Tarski's work that we can speak of a systematic theory of definability.

Syntactic theory of definability. Let T be a formal theory among whose constants there is a one-place predicate C. We say that C depends on other constants of T if there is a formula F free of C with exactly one free variable x such that the equivalence $C(x) \equiv F$ is provable in T. In special cases this notion was used long before Tarski; but Tarski was the first to formulate this notion precisely and in the general case, to discuss its properties, and to discover a far-reaching parallelism between the notions of consequence and definability. One of the most interesting results of his theory is a general formulation of a method (due in principle to A. Padoa) allowing one to establish the independence of a constant. Tarski also showed the universality of this method in cases in which the theory under consideration is based on second-order logic or its extensions; the case of theories based on first-order logic was decided much later by E. W. Beth.

Semantic notion of definability. Let M be a model as defined above. A subset S of A is called definable in M if there is a formula F with exactly one free variable such that an element a of A satisfies F in M if and only if a is an element of S. The formula F is called a definition of S in M.

The determination of the class of definable sets is an interesting problem that occupies a central place in investigations concerning the so-called hierarchies of sets. Without going into details, the aim of these investigations is to discuss sets obtainable from simple sets (which constitute the lowest level of the hierarchy) by means of fixed operations that lead to higher and higher levels. Hierarchies of this kind are discussed in mathematics (the Borel and the projective hierarchies) and in metamathematics (the arithmetical, the hyperarithmetical, and the analytic hierarchies). Tarski and Kazimierz Kuratowski in a joint paper described a method that in many cases allows one to infer directly, from the form of definition of a set, to which level of a given hierarchy this set belongs. Their method introduced essential simplifications into the theory of hierarchies.

The importance of these investigations for metamathematics will be clear if we reflect that, for example, Gödel's incompleteness theorem is an obvious corollary of the fact that the set of (numbers of) sentences derivable from the axioms of arithmetic does not belong to the lowest level of the arithmetical hierarchy. Tarski's work on definability is thus closely connected with problems of incompleteness. The most important result in this field is his theorem on truth, which says that under very general assumptions the set of (numbers of) sentences that are true in a model *M* is not definable in *M*. Gödel's incompleteness theorem for arithmetic and many related results are immediate corollaries of this theorem ("On Undecidable Statements in Enlarged Systems of Logic and the Concept of Truth," 1.939). Tarski's semantic theorem, however, requires for its formulation as well as for its proof a much stronger logical basis than the syntactic theorem of Gödel.

GENERAL THEORY OF MODELS. Notions closely related to models (as defined above) appeared in abstract mathematics independently of the logical investigations. Mathematicians were led to notions of this degree of generality by the development of abstract algebra. Tarski developed these algebraic investigations and tied them to metamathematics.

It is easy to explain the close connections between the general theory of models and the theory of systems. If we consider a theory whose consequence function is defined semantically, then every system is determined by the class of those models in which all sentences of the system are true. Conversely, every model determines a (complete) system consisting of sentences that are true in the model. However, different models may yield one and the same system.

Tarski and his students exploited these relationships especially for the case in which the theory under consideration is based on first-order logic. In this case it is irrelevant whether we accept the semantic or the syntactic notion of consequence, and we thus have the advantage of being able to use on the one hand the connection between systems and models and on the other the various properties of the consequence function that result from its syntactic definition. One of these properties is the so-called compactness of the consequence function, which states that if a set *X* of sentences is contradictory, then the same is true of a finite subset of *X*.

In his publications on the theory of models, which date as far back as 1949, Tarski sought to develop the theory in purely mathematical terms and avoided notions current in logic but less so in mathematics. Consequently his papers on the theory of models are more accessible to mathematicians than to logicians. The details of his highly technical works on the theory of models cannot be related here, and we must content ourselves with the brief indications given above.

GENERALIZATIONS OF FIRST-ORDER LOGIC. As was stated earlier, the general setting of model theory is meaningful for theories that are not necessarily based on first-order logic. Tarski suggested two important generalizations of first-order logic and showed that the model-theoretic approach to these logics leads to important discoveries.

The first of these logics is one with infinitely long formulas ("A Sentential Calculus with Infinitely Long Expressions"). Such formulas are, of course, abstract entities definable only in strong systems of set theory; nevertheless, Tarski showed that most of the questions formerly raised exclusively for theories based on ordinary logic are also meaningful for this abstractly described logic. The mathematically important work "Some Problems and Results Relating to the Foundations of Set Theory" resulted from a negative solution of the analogue of the compactness problem ("Some Model-Theoretical Results concerning Weak Second Order Logic," *Notices of the American Mathematical Society* 5, Abstract 550–6) for logics with infinitely long formulas.

Another important logic introduced by Tarski is weak second-order logic, that is, second-order logic in which the set variables are restricted to finite sets. For this logic as well, the semantic notion of consequence is definable only in a fairly strong system of set theory. Thus weak second-order logic, like the preceding one, is only an abstract construction. Tarski established various metamathematical properties of this logic (for instance, the analogue of the Skolem-Löwenheim theorem) and showed that they imply important mathematical consequences in algebra.

FURTHER CONTRIBUTIONS

DECISION PROBLEM AND UNDECIDABLE THEORIES. The decision problem for a theory *T* is the question whether there exists an algorithm allowing one to decide whether a sentence of *T* is or is not provable in *T*. Tarski discussed this problem for a large number of theories using the so-called method of the elimination of quantifiers, which originated with Thoralf Skolem ("The Concept of Truth in Formalized Languages," in *Logic, Language, Metamathematics,* p. 204). The most important result in this direction was a positive solution of the problem in the case in which T is the first-order theory of the field of real numbers (*A Decision Method for Elementary Algebra and Geometry*). This result found numerous applications in algebra and geometry.

A theory for which the decision problem does not admit a positive solution is called undecidable. It was related above how Tarski deduced the incompleteness (and hence the undecidability) of arithmetic from his general theorem. His further efforts were directed toward establishing the undecidability of various very weak but mathematically interesting theories. To this end he introduced the important notion of essential undecidability. A theory is said to be essentially undecidable if all consistent extensions of it are undecidable. Tarski showed in *Undecidable Theories* (1953) that a theory that has a joint consistent extension with an essentially undecidable theory based on a finite number of axioms is itself undecidable, although in general not essentially undecidable. This theorem provided a basis for numerous undecidability results obtained partly by Tarski and partly by his collaborators.

INTUITIONIST AND MODAL LOGICS. Of the numerous papers that Tarski devoted to the propositional calculus, only those on the intuitionistic and modal propositional calculi can be mentioned here. In "Sentential Calculus and Topology" (*Logic, Semantics, Metamathematics,* pp. 421–454) he established a startling connection between intuitionistic logic and topology: he constructed matrices for the intuitionistic propositional calculus, using as elements closed subsets of a topological space. In his further work on this calculus, done jointly with J. C. C. McKinsey, he no longer used topological notions but worked instead with certain algebraic structures. The class of all subsets of a topological space and the class of all closed subsets of such a space are examples of such structures, which Tarski and McKinsey called closure algebras and Brouwerian algebras, respectively. Using them, they established several properties of the intuitionistic and modal propositional logics.

CYLINDRIC ALGEBRAS. The above papers give a good illustration of Tarski's growing tendency to deal with metamathematical problems by means of algebraic tools. Another example is his work on cylindric algebras. These algebraic structures are related to the predicate calculus with identity in the way Boolean algebras are related to the usual propositional calculus. Logics with infinitely long expressions can also be investigated by means of suitable cylindric algebras.

CALCULUS OF BINARY RELATIONS. The calculus of binary relations was created by Ernst Schröder but soon fell into oblivion. Tarski gave axioms for this calculus, investigated its relations to the predicate calculus, and initiated extensive work on the models of his axioms. Of the several applications of the calculus found by Tarski, the axiomatization of set theory without variables, the existence of undecidable subsystems of the two-valued propositional calculus, and a general method of reduction of the number of primitive terms of a theory should be mentioned.

PHILOSOPHY

In the rich bibliography of Tarski's publications there are almost no philosophical papers. The exceptions are "The Establishment of Scientific Semantics" and "The Semantic Conception of Truth and the Foundations of Semantics," which deal with the philosophical significance of semantics. A partial exception is Tarski's paper on the notion of truth (in *Logic, Semantics, Metamathematics,* pp. 153–278), although the bulk of it is devoted to a systematic exposition of semantics.

Tarski, in oral discussions, often indicated his sympathies with nominalism. While he never accepted the "reism" of Tadeusz Kotarbiński, he was certainly attracted to it in the early phase of his work. However, the set-theoretical methods that form the basis of his logical and mathematical studies compelled him constantly to use the abstract and general notions that a nominalist seeks to avoid. In the absence of more extensive publications by Tarski on philosophical subjects, this conflict appears to have remained unresolved.

See also Boole, George; Brouwer, Luitzen Egbertus Jan; Correspondence Theory of Truth; First-Order Logic; Gödel's Theorem; Hilbert, David; Kotarbiński, Tadeusz; Logic, History of; Łukasiewicz, Jan; Mathematics, Foundations of; Model Theory; Second-Order Logic; Semantics; Set Theory.

Bibliography

Tarski's scientific writings consist of more than one hundred articles and books, plus many abstracts and reviews. Among these the most important for logic and philosophy are the following:

"Sur les truth-functions au sens de MM. Russell et Whitehead." *Fundamenta Mathematicae* 5 (1924): 59–74.

"Grundzüge des Systemenkalküls." *Fundamenta Mathematicae* 25 (1935): 503.

"Der Wahrheitsbegriff in den formalisierten Sprachen." *Studio Philosophica* 1 (1935–1936): 261–405.

"Über unerreichbare Kardinalzahlen." *Fundamenta Mathematicae* 30 (1938): 68–89.

"On Undecidable Statements in Enlarged Systems of Logic and the Concept of Truth." *Journal of Symbolic Logic* 4 (1939): 105–112.

"On the Calculus of Relations." *Journal of Symbolic Logic* 6 (1941): 73–89.

"The Semantic Conception of Truth and the Foundations of Semantics." *Journal of Philosophy and Phenomenological Research* 4 (1944): 341–375. Reprinted in *Readings in Philosophical Analysis,* edited by H. Feigl and W. Sellars, 52–84. New York: Appleton-Century-Crofts, 1949.

"On Closed Elements in Closure Algebras." *Annals of Mathematics* 45 (1944): 141–191, and 47 (1946): 122–162. Written with J. C. C. McKinsey, with remarks by Tarski, 163–165.

"Some Theorems about the Sentential Calculi of Lewis and Heyting." *Journal of Symbolic Logic* 13 (1948): 1–15. Written with J. C. C. McKinsey.

"Some Notions and Methods on the Borderline of Algebra and Metamathematics." In *Proceedings of the International Congress of Mathematicians,* 705–720. Cambridge, MA, 1950.

A Decision Method for Elementary Algebra and Geometry. Santa Monica, CA, 1948; 2nd ed., Berkeley: University of California Press, 1951.

Undecidable Theories. Amsterdam: North-Holland, 1953. Written with A. Mostowski and R. M. Robinson.

Logic, Semantics, Metamathematics. Oxford: Clarendon Press, 1956. Tarski's papers on logic from 1923 to 1938, collected and translated by J. H. Woodger.

"A Sentential Calculus with Infinitely Long Expressions." *Colloquium Mathematicum* 6 (1958): 165–170. Written with Dana Scott. Remarks by Tarski, 171–176.

"Cylindric Algebras." In *Proceedings of Symposia in Pure Mathematics: II Lattice Theory,* 83–113. Providence, RI: American Mathematical Society, 1961. Written with Leon Henkin.

"Some Problems and Results Relating to the Foundations of Set Theory." In *Proceedings of the 1960 Congress on Logic, Methodology, and Philosophy of Science,*125–135. Palo Alto, CA, 1962.

"From Accessible to Inaccessible Cardinals." *Fundamenta Mathematicae* 53 (1964): 225–308. Written with H. J. Keisler.

Andrzej Mostowski (1967)

TARSKI, ALFRED [ADDENDUM]

Alfred Tarski was born in 1901 (not 1902, as stated in the original entry). The name on his birth certificate was Alfred Teitelbaum (variant: Tajtelbaum); he changed it to Alfred Tarski in 1924. That same year his dissertation, written under the direction of Stanisław Lesńiewski, was published in two parts, the first under his birth name and the second under Alfred Tajtelbaum-Tarski; thereafter, all his articles and books were published under the name Alfred Tarski.

Tarski's immigration to the United States was somewhat accidental: He was attending a meeting of the Unity of Science at Harvard University in September 1939 when the Nazis invaded Poland and World War II began. Tarski was stranded and separated from his wife and two children, who were left behind in Warsaw (they were reunited after the war, but most of his family perished in the Holocaust). In 1942, after three years of casting about for a position, he received a one-year appointment as a lecturer at the University of California, Berkeley (UCB), from which he quickly rose to professor of mathematics in 1946. Working intensively with increasing success, he built a substantial graduate program in logic and, within a decade, Berkeley became a mecca for logicians worldwide. In 1957 Tarski was instrumental in creating the interdepartmental Program in Logic and Methodology of Science at UCB that mainly bridged the departments of mathematics and philosophy.

Tarski retired in 1968 but was recalled to teach for the next five years. He continued to do research and advise students until a year before his death in 1983. In the last decade of his life he received a number of honors, including honorary doctorates from the Universidad Católica de Chile, the Université d'Aix-Marseille II, and the University of Calgary; in addition, in 1981 he was awarded the Berkeley Citation, the highest honor that UCB can bestow. For a full biography see Anita Burdman Feferman and Solomon Feferman (2004).

From the 1960s to the end of his life, with the collaboration of colleagues and students, Tarski concentrated on the topics of axiomatic geometry and algebraic logic, while continuing to contribute to the areas of model theory, set theory, and universal algebra. His work on first-order systems of Euclidean geometry and the work that it led to in non-Euclidean geometry is described in a joint article with Steven R. Givant, "Tarski's System of Geometry" (1999). The research on relation algebra was capped by the joint monograph with Givant, *A Formalization of Set Theory without Variables* in 1987. In that it is shown how a wide variety of formal theories in the first-order predicate calculus, including set theory, can be axiomatized equivalently in purely quantifier-free relation-algebraic terms, even though those do not suffice in general to axiomatize first-order logic. The work on the algebraization of the full first-order logic with equality is exposited in the two substantial volumes of *Cylindric*

Algebras (1971–1985), written in collaboration with Leon Henkin and Donald Monk.

See also Model Theory.

Bibliography

WORKS BY TARSKI

Logic, Semantics, Metamathematics: Papers from 1923 to 1938. 2nd ed. Translated by J. H. Woodger, edited by John Corcoran. Indianapolis, IN: Hackett, 1983.

Collected Papers, Vols. 1–4, edited by Steven R. Givant and Ralph N. McKenzie. Basel: Birkhäuser, 1986.

WORKS BY TARSKI WITH OTHERS

Henkin, Leon, Donald Monk, and Alfred Tarski. *Cylindric Algebras.* 2 vols. Amsterdam: North-Holland, 1971–1985.

Tarski, Alfred, and Steven R. Givant. *A Formalization of Set Theory without Variables.* Providence, RI: American Mathematical Society, 1987.

Tarski, Alfred, and Steven R. Givant. "Tarski's System of Geometry." *Bulletin of Symbolic Logic* 5 (1999): 175–214.

WORKS ON TARSKI

Feferman, Anita Burdman, and Solomon Feferman. *Alfred Tarski: Life and Logic.* New York: Cambridge University Press, 2004.

Givant, Steven. "Bibliography of Alfred Tarski." *Journal of Symbolic Logic* 51 (4) (1986): 913–941.

Tarski's work is surveyed in a number of articles in the *Journal of Symbolic Logic* 51 (4) (1986) and 53 (1) (1988). There is a considerable secondary literature on Tarski's work, including the proceedings of the Tarski Centenary Conference held in Warsaw in 2001 that appeared in the *Annals of Pure and Applied Logic* 126 (1–3) (2004) and 127 (1–3) (2004).

Anita Burdman Feferman (2005)
Solomon Feferman (2005)

TAULER, JOHANNES

(c. 1300–1361)

The German mystic Johannes Tauler entered the Dominican order at Strasbourg about the age of fifteen and probably studied in the Dominican *studium generale* at Cologne, where he may have been taught by Meister Eckhart. He was certainly influenced by the latter and by the contemplative movement known as the *Gottesfreunde* (Friends of God). He was in Strasbourg at the time of Pope Innocent XXII's interdict on the city for taking the wrong side in the war between different sections of the Holy Roman Empire, but there is no good evidence for the story that during the Black Death he defied the interdict by administering sacraments to the dying. He remained a loyal and orthodox member of the church. Much legendary material surrounds his life, and various spurious works are attributed to him. It was on the basis of these sources that some earlier scholars mistakenly thought of Tauler as a precursor of the Reformation.

In his sermons, Tauler geared mystical teachings, which made use of Eckhartian and Neoplatonic concepts, to practical purposes. He was deeply committed to the view that mystical experiences are a nourishment to the soul in supporting the individual in a life of active love and that there are behavioral criteria for estimating their worth. He believed that in this active life we may possess God through a fusion of the divine and human wills. However, far from reducing contemplative religion to the exercise of good works, Tauler believed that the love of God and the love of men go together and that the former finds its consummation in the inner union of the soul with the Creator.

In principle, all men should be capable of this return of the soul to its Source (the notion of return was typical of the Neoplatonic tradition with which Tauler was acquainted). Two qualifications, however, must be made. First, the way of return, according to Tauler's account, involves great heroism and suffering. The creaturely side of man must be crucified. Self-mortification is a sign of burning love of God, and eventually the friend of God may acquire a real desire for, rather than an aversion to, suffering. In this emphasis on suffering, Tauler was strongly Christocentric in his preaching. But second, the fall of man has so tainted the human being that the divine light, which illuminates the contemplative and brings about the return to God, is something that man cannot achieve on his own. It is the gift of divine grace. Thus, the culmination of the mystic's quest is not a personal achievement of the mystic, but an enjoyment granted from beyond.

The importance of the need for grace gave Tauler's mysticism a firmly orthodox character. Nevertheless, he maintained that the operation of divine grace requires a right attitude on the part of men. Tauler speaks of God as a fisherman who lets down a baited hook into the ocean. Those fish who are not disposed toward the bait will not be hooked. This simile had its basis in Tauler's account of human psychology.

According to his psychology, three aspects of the soul can be distinguished. At the deepest level is the Ground of the soul—otherwise referred to as the Spark, the Apex (*Punkt*), and God in the soul—a concept deriving from Eckhart's teaching. However, Tauler is eager to assert that the Ground is God-given and is not an intrinsic, natural property of the individual. At another level, the soul possesses intellect, sense faculties, and will. Third, there is what Tauler refers to as the heart *(das Gemüt).* The attitude of the individual toward the divine Being is determined by whether his heart is turned toward the Ground or away from it. If the former, God will descend, draw the spirit up to himself, and unite it with him. Man's choice is therefore essentially a choice of disposition. Once this choice has been made, God through his grace will conform the human will to his own. Thus, the end of the contemplative life is a state in which the mystic is, so to speak, "taken over" by God, so that all his actions express God's purposes rather than his own.

See also Eckhart, Meister; Mysticism, History of; Neoplatonism; Reformation.

Bibliography

Tauler's works include *Twenty-five Sermons,* translated by Susanna Winkworth, 2nd ed. (London, 1906); *The Sermons and Conferences of John Tauler,* edited and translated by Walter Elliott (Washington, DC: Apostolic Mission House, 1910); *Die Predigten Taulers,* edited by F. Vetter (Berlin: Weidmann, 1910); and *Johannes Tauler—Predigten,* edited by G. Hofmann (Freiburg, 1961).

See also J. M. Clark, *The Great German Mystics* (Oxford: Blackwell, 1949).

Ninian Smart (1967)

TAUTOLOGY

See *Logical Terms, Glossary of*

TAYLOR, ALFRED EDWARD
(1869–1945)

Alfred Edward Taylor, the British philosopher, was born at Oundle, Northamptonshire, and educated at New College, Oxford. His teaching experience was unusually varied: He was a fellow of Merton College, Oxford, 1891–1898; lecturer at Owens College, Manchester, 1898–1903; professor of logic and metaphysics at McGill University, Montreal, 1903–1908; professor of moral philosophy at St. Andrews University, 1908–1924; and professor of moral philosophy at Edinburgh, 1924–1941. His interests were also varied; not only was he an authority on Greek philosophy but he also made extensive contributions to current thinking on ethics, metaphysics, and the philosophy of religion. Taylor's thought was within the tradition of British neo-Hegelianism, but as his philosophy developed, other influences came in also, though he remained firmly attached to a theistic and spiritualist interpretation of reality.

In the field of Greek philosophy, Taylor is noted chiefly for his work on Plato. He gives a full-scale exposition of Plato's thought in *Plato: The Man and His Work* (London, 1926) and a detailed study of Plato's cosmology in *A Commentary on Plato's Timaeus* (Oxford, 1928). Even in these works Taylor's own philosophical interests assert themselves, notably in his attempt to minimize alleged differences between the Platonic and biblical ways of understanding creation and in his contention that the Demiurge of Plato is a creator in the full sense of the word.

Taylor's philosophy found early expression in *The Problem of Conduct* (London, 1901) and in *Elements of Metaphysics* (London, 1903). At this stage he was influenced primarily by F. H. Bradley and English idealism. Later, Platonism, Thomism, and even Bergsonism became important additional influences on his mature thought as expressed in *The Faith of a Moralist* (London, 1930), a work based on his Gifford Lectures of 1926–1928.

Here Taylor claims that if we take moral experience seriously, we must recognize that it points beyond itself to, and is completed in, religion and that we are thus led to theism. Moral experience does deserve to be taken seriously, for facts and values are given together and never occur in separation in our concrete experience of the world. A naturalistic philosophy that allows reality to fact but denies it to value is guilty of a false abstraction. This argument about the concreteness of experience is a necessary prolegomenon to Taylor's position as a whole, for if the values of the moral life were divorced from the facts of the world, then no argument from moral experience to the nature of reality could succeed.

Taylor's attempt to move from the facts of moral experience to a religious metaphysic turns on two main considerations. The first concerns the nature of the good at which the moral life aims. Is it a temporal good or is it an eternal good? Taylor contends that even to be able to ask this question and to be aware of the temporal dimension of our existence is to have begun to transcend the form of temporality. Further reflection shows that no merely temporal goods can satisfy the demands of man's nature. Such goods are defective in various ways; for instance, they can be attained only successively and cannot be enjoyed simultaneously. One might answer, of course, that this merely shows that human aspirations are doomed to frustration, but Taylor rejects this and claims that the facts of moral striving point to an eternal good.

The second consideration concerns the question of how such an eternal good is to be attained. Can man of himself attain to an eternal good? Taylor answers in the negative, for he sees sin and guilt as inhibiting the moral life and preventing man from reaching his goal. But again he does not accept this frustration as final. Man's unavailing endeavors to reach toward the eternal good are met by what Taylor calls the initiative of the eternal. This is the divine grace that reaches down to man and enables his moral fulfillment. Thus, the moral life finds its completion in religion; if we deny this, we are bound to say that the moral life is self-stultifying. To take its demands seriously is to believe that it makes sense, and according to Taylor, it makes sense only in the light of a theistic worldview.

The individual destined for an eternal good and enabled by divine grace to move toward that good is also assured of immortality. Hence, from consideration of the implications of the moral life alone we arrive at a kind of minimal theology, so to speak, of God, grace, and immortality. But Taylor, who was himself a devout churchman of the Anglican communion, asks whether this minimal theology does not, like morality, point beyond itself for completion. The concreteness that characterizes Taylor's starting point is apparent again in his conclusions, as he argues that a bare philosophical theism needs to be embodied in an actual historical religion. Although the philosopher does not appeal to revelation, his analysis can, Taylor believed, bring us to the point at which we see the need for a concrete revelation to complete the bare schema of philosophical theology. Philosophy makes it reasonable to expect that there would be such a revelation, and Taylor thinks that Christian revelation especially fulfills this expectation. He continued to wrestle with the problems of religion, which provide the themes for two of his last books, *The Christian Hope of Immortality* (London, 1938) and *Does God Exist?* (London, 1943).

See also Bradley, Francis Herbert; Cosmology; Ethics, History of; Good, The; Idealism; Moral Arguments for the Existence of God; Plato; Platonism and the Platonic Tradition; Thomism.

Bibliography

Additional works by Taylor are *Varia Socratica* (Oxford: J. Parker, 1911); *The Laws of Plato* (London: Dent, 1934); *Philosophical Studies* (London: Macmillan, 1934); and *Aristotle* (London: T. Nelson, 1943).

W. D. Ross, "Alfred Edward Taylor, 1869–1945," in *Proceedings of the British Academy* 31 (1945): 407–424, contains a bibliography of Taylor's writings.

John Macquarrie (1967)

TEILHARD DE CHARDIN, PIERRE
(1881–1955)

Pierre Teilhard de Chardin, the paleoanthropologist and Roman Catholic priest who advocated a doctrine of cosmic evolution, was born in Sarcenat, France. At the age of eighteen he entered the Jesuit order, and he remained a faithful member of it for the rest of his life. By the time he was ordained, his interest in science and the reading of Henri Bergson resulted in his becoming a fervent evolutionist. Association with the Bergsonian scholar Édouard Le Roy also deeply influenced his thought. It became one of Teilhard's aims to show that evolutionism does not entail a rejection of Christianity. He likewise sought to convince the church that it can and should accept the implications of the revolution begun by Charles Darwin, but he met with uniform opposition from ecclesiastical superiors.

In 1926 he was expelled from the Catholic Institute in Paris, at which he had taught after returning from service in World War I. Until 1946 he was "exiled" in China, where he participated in paleontological researches that led to the discovery of Beijing man. He also completed the manuscript of his major work, *Le phénomène humain (The Phenomenon of Man)*; but despite repeated applications to Rome he was refused permission to publish it. After his death the appearance of the work, along with his other essays, gave rise to controversies both inside and outside the church.

The evolutionism that Teilhard advocated is all-embracing and characterizes much more than living things. Teilhard contended that long before living things appeared on Earth, the basic stuff of the cosmos was undergoing irreversible changes in the direction of greater complexity of organization. Hence, nonliving nature is profoundly historical. It is not a system of stable elements in a closed equilibrium. On the contrary, it conforms at all stages to a "law of complexification," comparable in importance to the law of gravity and illustrated by the vast array of organic forms that have appeared in evolutionary history. The most recent of these forms is man.

When viewed "from without" by the physical sciences, man is a material system in the midst of other material systems. But each individual man experiences himself "from within" as a conscious being. Consciousness is thus directly identifiable as "spiritual energy." Teilhard maintained that *all* constituents of the cosmos, from elementary particles to human beings, have "a conscious inner face that everywhere duplicates the material external face." Since this is so, the physical evolution of the cosmic stuff will at the same time be an evolution of consciousness. The more highly integrated a material system, the more developed its psychical interior will be. Thus, in the human brain an intense concentration, or "involution," of cells has led to the emergence of self-conscious thought, the most advanced stage reached by evolution thus far.

But greater developments are in store from the evolutionary convergence of disparate cultures and forms of consciousness. Man is now a single, interbreeding species expanding on the finite, spherical surface of the planet and still showing signs of biological immaturity. Furthermore, his capacity for self-conscious thought and the production of cultures has added a new "layer" to Earth's surface, which Teilhard calls the "noosphere," distinct from, yet superimposed on, the biosphere. The noosphere, or "thinking layer," forms the unique environment of man, marking him off from all other animals. The evolutionary convergence that it makes possible will be manifested externally in the unification of all human cultures into a single world culture. Paralleling this, a movement toward psychical concentration will occur, so that the noosphere will become involuted in a Hyperpersonal Consciousness "at a point which we might call *Omega*." Here evolution will reach the terminal phase of convergent integration.

Teilhard's concept of Point Omega is obscure, like other aspects of his evolutionism, because it is essentially the expression of a mystical vision. Omega is not identical with God but, rather, is God insofar as he determines the direction and goal of cosmic history. Hence, the evolutionary process is orthogenetic, although neither vitalistic nor wholly devoid of chance events. The integration of all personal consciousnesses at Omega will be achieved, Teilhard urged, through love, which forms *le milieu divin*, the spirit of Christ at work in nature.

Teilhard's doctrine tends to become pantheistic in certain of its formulations. On the whole, it is difficult to reconcile Teilhard's views either with orthodox Christian teaching or with a scientific theory of evolution. Yet the prose poetry of *The Phenomenon of Man* has stirred the imagination of theologians, philosophers, and scientists, even when it has not won their assent.

See also Bergson, Henri; Darwin, Charles Robert; Evolutionary Theory; Le Roy, Édouard; Pantheism.

Bibliography

WORKS BY TEILHARD DE CHARDIN

Oeuvres, 9 vols. Paris, 1955–. Ten volumes are projected.

Le phénomène humain. Paris: Seuil, 1955. Translated by Bernard Wall as *The Phenomenon of Man*. New York: Harper, 1959.

Lettres de voyage. Paris: Grasset, 1956. Translated by René Hague and others as *Letters from a Traveller*. London: Collins, 1962.

Le milieu divin. Paris: Seuil, 1957. Translated by Bernard Wall and others as *The Realm of the Divine*. New York: Harper, 1960.

L'avenir de l'homme. Paris: Seuil, 1959. Translated by Norman Denny as *The Future of Man*. New York: Harper, 1964.

Hymne de l'univers. Paris: Seuil, 1964. Translated by Simon Bartholemew as *Hymn of the Universe*. London: Collins, 1965.

WORKS ON TEILHARD DE CHARDIN

Cuénot, Claude. *Pierre Teilhard de Chardin, les grandes étapes de son évolution*. Paris: Plon, 1958. Translated by Vincent Colimore and edited by René Hague as *Teilhard de Chardin: A Biographical Study*. Baltimore: Helicon Press, 1965.

Francoeur, R. T., ed. *The World of Teilhard*. Baltimore: Helicon Press, 1961.

Raven, C. E. *Teilhard de Chardin: Scientist and Seer*. London: Collins, 1962.

Tresmontant, C. *Pierre Teilhard de Chardin, His Thought*. Baltimore: Helicon Press, 1959.

OTHER RECOMMENDED WORKS

Chauchard, Paul. *Man and Cosmos: Scientific Phenomenology in Teilhard de Chardin*. New York: Herder and Herder, 1965.

Delfgaauw, Bernard. *Evolution: The Theory of Teilhard de Chardin*. New York: Harper & Row, 1969.

Grau, Joseph A. *Morality and the Human Future in the Thought of Teilhard de Chardin: A Critical Study*. Rutherford: Fairleigh Dickinson University Press; Cranbury, NJ: distributed by Associated University Presses, 1976.

Lukas, Mary, and Ellen Lukas. *Teilhard*. Garden City, NY: Doubleday, 1977.

Rideau, Emile. *The Thought of Teilhard de Chardin*. New York: Harper & Row, 1967.

Speaight, Robert. *The Life of Teilhard de Chardin*. New York: Harper & Row, 1967.

Teilhard de Chardin, Pierre, and Henri de Lubac. *Letters from Paris, 1912–1914*. New York: Herder and Herder, 1967.

Teilhard de Chardin, Pierre, and Pierre Leroy. *Letters from My Friend, Teilhard de Chardin, 1948–1955: Including Letters Written during His Final Years in America*. New York: Paulist Press, 1980.

Teilhard de Chardin, Pierre. *Letters from Hastings, 1908–1912*. New York: Herder and Herder, 1968.

Teilhard de Chardin, Pierre. *Pierre Teilhard de Chardin: Writings*. Edited by Ursula King. Maryknoll, NY: Orbis Books, 1999.

Teilhard de Chardin, Pierre. *The Making of a Mind: Letters from a Soldier-priest, 1914–1919*. London, Collins, 1965.

Wildiers, N. M. *An Introduction to Teilhard de Chardin*. New York: Harper & Row, 1968.

T. A. Goudge (1967)
Bibliography updated by Michael Farmer (2005)

TELEOLOGICAL ARGUMENT FOR THE EXISTENCE OF GOD

The "Teleological Argument for the existence of God" is a member of the classic triad of arguments, which is completed by the Ontological Argument and the Cosmological Argument. Stated most succinctly, it runs:

> The world exhibits teleological order (design, adaptation).
>
> Therefore, it was produced by an intelligent designer.

To understand this argument, we must first understand what teleological order is.

TELEOLOGICAL ORDER

Generally speaking, to say that a group of elements is ordered in a certain way is to say that they are interrelated so as to form a definite pattern, but the notion of a definite pattern is vague. Any set of elements is interrelated in one way rather than another, and any complex of interrelations might be construed by someone as a definite pattern. Certain patterns are of special interest for one reason or another, and when one of these is exhibited, the complex would ordinarily be said to be ordered. Thus, when the elements form a pattern in whose perception we take intrinsic delight, we can speak of aesthetic order. When there are discernible regularities in the way, certain elements occur in spatiotemporal proximity, we can speak of causal order. The distinctive thing about teleological (Greek, *telos,* "end" or "goal") order is that it introduces the notion of processes and structures being fitted to bring about a certain result.

The usual illustrations of teleological order are from living organisms. It is a common observation that the anatomical structures and instinctive activities of animals are often nicely suited to the fulfillment of their needs. For example, the ears of pursuing, carnivorous animals, like the dog and the wolf, face forward so as to focus sounds from their quarry, while the ears of pursued, herbivorous animals, like the rabbit and the deer, face backward so as to focus sounds from their pursuers.

Examples of instinctive behavior are even more striking. The burying beetle deposits its eggs on the carcass of a small animal and then covers the whole "melange" with dirt to protect it until the young hatch out and find an ample supply of (hardly fresh) meat at hand.

If we are going to distinguish teleological order from causal order, we shall have to make explicit the tacit assumption that the result the structure or process in question is fitted to bring about is of value. Otherwise, *any* cause-effect relationship would be a case of teleological order. It is just as true to say that wind is fitted to produce the result of moving loose dirt into the air as it is to say that the mechanism of the eye is fitted to produce sight. The latter would be counted as an example of "design," whereas the former would not, because we regard sight as something worth having, whereas the movement of dirt through the air is not generally of any value. This has the important implication that insofar as it is impossible to give an objective criterion of value, it will not be an objective matter of fact that teleological order is or is not exhibited in a given state of affairs.

It is important to note that the term *design,* as used in this argument, does not by definition imply a designer. If it did, there could be no argument from design to the existence of God; we would have to know that the phenomena in question were the work of a designer before we could call them cases of design. We must define *design* in such a way as to leave open the question of its source. We have design in the required sense when things are so ordered that they tend to perform a valuable function. We might put this by saying that things are ordered as they would be if some conscious being had designed them, but in saying this we are not committing ourselves to the proposition that a mind has designed them. The equivalent terms *adaptation* and *teleological order* are not so liable to mislead in this way.

Arguments for the existence of God have been based on kinds of order other than the teleological. Exhortations to move from a consideration of the starry heavens to belief in God constitute an appeal to aesthetic order. It is sometimes claimed that we must postulate an intelligent creator to explain the regularity with which the solar system operates. Here it is causal order that is involved. Arguments like these are often not clearly distinguished from those based on teleological order, to which we shall confine our attention.

ARGUMENTS FROM PARTICULAR CASES OF DESIGN

The simplest form of the argument is that in which we begin with particular cases of design and argue that they can be adequately explained only by supposing that they were produced by an intelligent being. Thus William Paley, an eighteenth-century philosopher, in a classic formulation of the argument concentrated on the human eye as a case of design, stressing the ways in which various parts of the eye cooperate in a complex way to produce sight. He argued that we can explain this adaptation of means to end only if we postulate a supernatural designer. This is the heart of the teleological argument—the claim that adaptation can be explained only in terms of a designer. It always rests, more or less explicitly, on an analogy with human artifacts. Thus, Paley compared the eye to a watch and argued as follows: If one were to find a watch on a desert island, one would be justified in supposing that it was produced by an intelligent being. By the same token (the adjustment of means to ends) one is entitled, upon examination of the human eye, to conclude that it was produced by an intelligent being.

If it is asked why we should take artifacts as our model, the answer would seem to be this. Artifacts are certainly cases of design. In a watch, for example, the structure is well suited to the performance of a valuable function: showing the time. With artifacts, unlike natural examples of design, we have some insight into what is responsible for the adjustment of means to end. We can understand it because we can see how this adjustment springs from the creative activity of the maker, guided by his deliberate intention to make the object capable of performing this function. Hence, in natural cases of adaptation where the source of the adaptiveness is not obvious, we have no recourse but to employ the only way we know of rendering such phenomena intelligible—supposing them to stem from conscious planning. Since we do not observe any planner at work, we must postulate an invisible planner behind the scenes.

CRITICISMS. The comparison to artifacts was attacked by David Hume in his *Dialogues concerning Natural Religion,* in which he suggested that the production of artifacts by human planning is no more inherently intelligible than the production of organisms by biological generation. Why, asked Hume, should we take the former rather than the latter as the model for the creation of the world? Even if we admit that the world exhibits design, why are we not as justified in supposing that the world was generated from the sexual union of two parent worlds as in supposing that it was created by a mind in accordance with a plan? In answer to Hume it might be argued that creation gives a more satisfactory and a more complete explanation than generation because the generation consists of a reproduction of the same kind of thing and hence introduces another entity that raises exactly the same kind of question. If we are initially puzzled as to why a rabbit has organs that are so well adapted to the satisfaction of its needs, it does not help to be told that it is because the rabbit sprang from other rabbits with just the same adaptive features. If, on the other hand, we could see that the rabbit had been deliberately constructed in this way so that its needs would be satisfied, we would be making progress. To this Hume would reply that the mind of the designer also requires explanation. Why should the designer have a mind that is so well fitted for designing? Thus, this explanation also leaves problems dangling, but at least it is not just the same problem. If we were to reject every explanation that raised fresh problems, we would have to reject all of science.

DARWINIAN THEORY OF EVOLUTION. The development of the Darwinian theory of evolution opened up the possibility of a more serious alternative to the theistic explanation. According to this theory, the organic structures of today developed from much simpler organisms by purely natural processes. In this theory (as developed since Charles Darwin) two factors are considered to play the major role: mutations and overpopulation. (A mutation occurs when an offspring differs from its parents in such a way that it will pass this difference along to its offspring, and they will pass it along, and so on. It is a relatively permanent genetic change.)

The way these factors are thought to work can be illustrated by taking one of the cases of adaptation cited above. If we go back far enough in the ancestry of the dog, we will discover ancestors that did not have ears facing forward. Now let us suppose that a mutation occurred that consisted of an ear turned somewhat more forward than had been normal. Granting that organisms tend to reproduce in greater numbers than the environment can support, and hence that there is considerable competition for the available food supply, it follows that any feature of a given organism that gives it any advantage over its fellows in getting food or in avoiding becoming prey will make it more likely to survive and pass along its peculiarity to its offspring. Thus, within a number of generations we can expect the front-turned-ear proto-dogs to replace the others and be left in sole possession of the field. Since mutations do occur from time to time, and since some of them are favorable, we have a set of purely natural factors by whose operation the organic world can be continuously transformed in the direction of greater and greater adaptation.

The Darwinian theory aspires to do no more than explain how more complex organisms develop from less complex organisms. It has nothing to say about the origins of the simplest organisms. However, no matter how simple the organism, its structure must be fitted to the satisfaction of its needs, or it will not survive. Therefore, Darwinian theory is not a complete explanation of the existence of teleological order in the world; it merely tells us how some cases develop from other cases. Hence, it alone is not an alternative to the theistic explanation, but in principle there is no reason why it should not be supplemented by a biochemical theory of the origin of life from lifeless matter. No such theory has yet been completely established, but progress is being made. When and if this is done, there will be an explanation of design in living organisms for which there is empirical support, and it can no longer be claimed that theism represents the only real explanation of such facts.

WHAT FOLLOWS FROM THE ARGUMENT. The other major deficiency in Paley's form of the argument is that, even if valid, it does not go very far toward proving the existence of a theistic God. The most we are warranted in concluding is that each case of design in the natural world is due to the activity of an intelligent designer. Nothing is done to show that all cases of design are due to one and the same designer; the argument is quite compatible with polytheism or polydaemonism, in which we would have one supernatural designer for flies, another for fish, and so on. Even if there is one, and only one, designer, nothing is done to show that this being is predominantly good rather than evil; neither is anything done to show that he is infinitely powerful or wise, rather than limited in these qualities. Of course the theist might seek to supplement this argument by others, but by itself it will not bear the weight.

ARGUMENT FROM THE UNIVERSE AS A WHOLE

No argument that, like the Teleological Argument, is designed to show that facts in nature require a certain explanation, can establish the existence of a deity absolutely unlimited in power, knowledge, or any other respect. By such reasoning we can infer no more in the cause than is required to produce the effect. This deficiency is irremediable. However, there is a simple way of eliminating competing scientific claims—by starting from the universe as a whole rather than from individual instances of design within the universe. There are different ways of doing this. We might think of the whole universe as instrumental to some supreme goal, or we might think of the universe as a unified system of mutually adjusted and mutually supporting adaptive structures.

Taking the whole universe as instrumental to some supreme goal would give us the strongest argument, for here the analogy with consciously designed artifacts is strongest. An artifact like a house, ship, or watch is designed for the realization of goals outside its internal functioning; it is intended to be used for something. Therefore, if the analogy with artifacts is the main support for the notion that the universe was the result of conscious planning, that support would be firmest if grounds were presented for thinking that the universe as a whole was well fitted to be used for something. And if this something were of maximum value, we would then have a basis for attributing supreme goodness to the designer.

However, this alternative is rarely taken, largely because it is difficult to decide on a suitable candidate for, in Alfred, Lord Tennyson's words, the "far-off divine event, toward which the whole creation moves." The most common suggestions are the greater glory of God and the development of moral personality. But in regard to the first, no one can really understand just what it would mean for a God who is eternally perfect to receive greater glory, and in regard to the second, even if we can overcome doubts that moral development is worth the entire cosmic process, it would seem impossible ever to get adequate grounds for the proposition that everything that takes place throughout all space and time contributes to this development.

The second interpretation, that the universe is a unified system of mutually adjusted and mutually supporting adaptive structures—has been tried more often. So conceived, the argument will run as follows.

(1) The world is a unified system of adaptations.

(2) We can give an intelligible explanation of this fact only by supposing that the world was created by an intelligent being according to some plan.

(3) Therefore, it is reasonable to suppose that the world was created by an intelligent being.

The famous formulation of the argument in Hume's *Dialogues* makes explicit the analogy on which, as we have seen, step two depends. Hume's formulation, which is substantially equivalent to the above, runs as follows.

(1) The world is like a machine.

(2) Machines are made by human beings, in accordance with plans.

(3) Like effects have like causes.

(4) Therefore, the world probably owes its existence to something like a human being, who operates in accordance with a plan.

TYPES OF ADAPTATION. If one is to think of the whole universe as a system of connected adaptations, he will consider kinds of adaptation other than that exemplified by the fitness of organisms to the conditions of life; this kind alone will not bear the whole weight. F. R. Tennant, who has developed the weightiest recent presentation of the teleological argument in his *Philosophical Theology,* discusses six kinds of adaptation:

(1) The intelligibility of the world. The world and the human mind are so related that we can learn more and more without limit.

(2) The adaptation of living organisms to their environments. This is the kind on which we have been concentrating.

(3) The ways in which the inorganic world is conducive to the emergence and maintenance of life. Life is possible only because temperatures do not exceed certain limits, certain kinds of chemical processes go on, and so on.

(4) The aesthetic value of nature. Nature is not only suited to penetration by the intellect; it is also constituted so as to awaken valuable aesthetic responses in man.

(5) The ways in which the world ministers to the moral life of men. For example, through being forced to learn something about the uniformities in natural operations, men are forced to develop their intelligence, a prerequisite to moral development. And moral virtues are acquired in the course of having to cope with the hardships of one's natural environment.

(6) The overall progressiveness of the evolutionary process.

Tennant admits that no one of these forms of adaptiveness is a sufficient ground for the theistic hypothesis, but he maintains that when we consider the ways in which they dovetail, we will see theism to be the most reasonable interpretation. Thus, the adjustment of lower organisms to the environment takes on added significance when it is seen as a stage in an evolutionary process culminating in man, which in turn is seen to be more striking when we realize the ways in which nature makes possible the further development of the moral, intellectual, and aesthetic life of man.

When the argument takes this form, it is no longer subject to competition from scientific explanations of the same facts. If our basic datum is a certain configuration of the universe as a whole, science can, by the nature of the case, offer no explanation. Science tries to find regularities in the association of different parts, stages, or aspects within the physical universe. On questions as to why the universe as a whole exists, or exists in one form rather than another, it is silent. Ultimately this is because science is committed to the consideration of questions that can be investigated empirically. One can use observation to determine whether two conditions within the universe are regularly associated (increase of temperature and boiling), but there is no way to observe connections between the physical universe as a whole and something outside it. Therefore, there is no scientific alternative to the theistic answer to the question "Why is the universe a unified system of adaptations?"

ALTERNATIVE EXPLANATIONS OF ADAPTATION. What alternatives to the theistic explanation of adaptation are there? In the literature on the subject one often encounters the suggestion that we have this kind of universe by chance. If we dismiss the animistic notion of chance as a mysterious agent, the suggestion that we have this kind of universe by chance boils down to a refusal to take the question seriously. It may be said that the fact that the universe as a whole exhibits teleological order is not the sort of thing that requires explanation. It is difficult to see what justification could be given for this statement other than an appeal to the principle that sense observation is the only source of knowledge and/or meaning.

One cannot perceive by the senses any relation between the physical universe as a whole, or any feature thereof, and something outside it on which it depends. Hence, an extreme form of empiricism would brand the question posed by the Teleological Argument as fruitless or even meaningless. If, on the other hand, the question is taken seriously, any answer will be as metaphysical as the theistic answer, for it is really a question as to what characteristics are to be attributed to the cause (or causes) of the universe. Do the relevant facts about the world most strongly support the theistic position that the cause is a perfectly good personal being who created the universe in the carrying out of a good purpose? Or is there some other view that is equally, or more strongly, supported by the evidence? The Manichaeans held that the physical universe was the work of a malevolent deity and that man must separate himself from the body in order to escape this diabolical power and come into contact with the purely spiritual benevolent deity. It has also been held in many religions that the universe is the joint product of two or more deities who differ markedly in their characteristics. In Zoroastrianism it is held that the world is the battleground of a good deity and an evil deity, the actual state of affairs bearing traces of both. Indian religious philosophy typically regards the universe as resulting from a nonpurposive manifestation of, or emanation from, an absolute unity that is not personal in any strict sense.

EXTENT OF ADAPTIVENESS IN THE UNIVERSE. To evaluate the Teleological Argument in the light of competing explanations, we must ask whether the extent of adaptiveness in the universe is sufficient to warrant the theistic conclusion. As the problem is formulated in Hume's *Dialogues,* is there a close enough analogy between the universe and a machine? This requires judging the relative proportion of adaptive features to nonadaptive or maladaptive features. In addition to taking account of Tennant's enumeration of the ways in which the shape of things is instrumental to the realization of valuable ends, we must look at the other side of the picture and try to form an adequate impression of (1) the ways in which the shape of things is neutral, providing neither for good nor for evil, and (2) the ways in which the shape of things frustrates the search for value.

As for (1), as far as we can see, the distribution of matter and the variety of chemical elements in the world, to take two examples at random, could have been very different from what they are without reducing the chances of sentient beings leading satisfying lives.

As for (2), we begin to trespass onto the problem of evil, except that here we are interested in suffering and frustration not as possible disproofs of theism but as affecting the cogency of the Teleological Argument for the existence of God. There are many ways in which the organization of the world makes for disvalue rather than value in the lives of men and other sentient creatures. One need only mention the numerous sources of disease, the incidence of malformed offspring, the difficulty of attaining optimum conditions for the development of healthy personalities, and the importance of antisocial tendencies in human nature. It is quite possible, of course, that all the things that seem to be unfortunate features of the world as it exists are necessary elements in the best of all possible worlds. If we already believe that the world is the creation of a perfect deity, that carries with it the belief that these apparent evils are necessary even though we cannot see how they are. However, if we are trying to establish the existence of a perfect deity, we have to proceed on the basis of what we can see. And since, so far as we can see, the world would be better if the features listed above were altered, we cannot argue that the state of adaptiveness in the world requires explanation in terms of a perfectly good, omnipotent deity. But we have already seen, on other grounds, that the Teleological Argument cannot be used to establish the existence of a being unlimited in any respect.

The serious problem that remains is whether the total picture of adaptation and maladaptation, so far as we have it, gives sufficient support to the hypothesis that the world represents the at least partial implementation of a plan that is at least predominantly good. To resolve this problem we must weigh opposite factors and arrive at a final judgment of their relative importance. Unfortunately there are no real guidelines for this task. No one knows how much adaptation, relative to maladaptation, would warrant such a conclusion; and even if he did, he would not know what units to employ to perform the measurement. What is to count as one unit of adaptation? Do we count each individual separately, or is each species one unit? How can we compare the value of human knowledge with the disvalue of disease? It would seem that on this issue different positions will continue to be taken on the basis of factors outside the evidence itself.

See also Cosmological Argument for the Existence of God; Darwin, Charles Robert; Darwinism; Evil, The Problem of; God/Isvara in Indian Philosophy; Hume, David; Mani and Manichaeism; Ontological Argument for the Existence of God; Paley, William; Physicotheology; Popular Arguments for the Existence of God; Tennant, Frederick Robert; Theism, Arguments For and Against; Zoroastrianism.

Bibliography

In the Middle Ages there was general acceptance of an Aristotelian physics, according to which even purely physical processes were explained in terms of the natural tendency of a body toward an end. (Fire naturally tends to come to rest at the periphery of the universe.) Given this background, it was argued that the consideration of any natural processes led to the postulation of a designer. The argument in this form is found in Thomas Aquinas, *Summa Theologiae,* Part I, Question 2, Article 3. Contemporary Thomistic statements try to adjust this line of thought to modern physics. See G. H. Joyce, *The Principles of Natural Theology*

(New York: AMS Press, 1972); Réginald Garrigou-Lagrange, *God, His Existence and His Nature,* 2 vols. (St. Louis: Herder, 1934–1936); and D. J. B. Hawkins, *The Essentials of Theism* (New York: Sheed and Ward, 1949).

The influential presentation by the eighteenth-century thinker William Paley is to be found in his *Natural Theology: Or, Evidences of the Existence and Attributes of the Deity, Collected from the Appearances of Nature* (Indianapolis: Bobbs-Merrill, 1963). Important more recent formulations include F. R. Tennant, *Philosophical Theology,* 2 vols. (New York, 1928–1930), Vol. II, Ch. 4, and A. E. Taylor, *Does God Exist?* (New York: Macmillan, 1947).

Acute criticisms of the argument are to be found in David Hume, *Dialogues concerning Natural Religion*; Immanuel Kant, *Critique of Pure Reason,* Book II. Ch. 3; C. D. Broad, *Religion, Philosophy, and Psychical Research* (New York: Harcourt Brace, 1953); John Laird, *Theism and Cosmology* (New York, 1942); and J. J. C. Smart, "The Existence of God," in *New Essays in Philosophical Theology,* edited by Antony Flew and Alasdair MacIntyre (London: SCM Press, 1955).

William P. Alston (1967)

TELEOLOGICAL ARGUMENT FOR THE EXISTENCE OF GOD [ADDENDUM]

The argument from the causal order of the universe to the existence of an intelligent designer has experienced a revival in the work of Richard Swinburne and others (see also Collins 2002). Swinburne's cumulative case for God's existence is an argument to the best explanation, citing various pieces of data or evidence that are (a) relatively improbable on an assumption of naturalism but (b) relatively probable if theism is true (Swinburne 1979). One such datum is that the universe conforms to simple, mathematically formulable scientific laws—that is it exhibits *causal order.* (This differs from *spatial order*, an arrangement of parts that serves the purpose of a greater whole, as in an organism's suitability for its environment.) While theories of evolution partially undermine the argument from spatial order, they leave the following argument from causal order untouched:

(1) The universe conforms to formulas. ("The orderliness of nature is a matter of the vast uniformity in powers and liabilities of bodies throughout endless time and space, and also in the paucity of kinds of components of bodies" [Swinburne 1979, p. 140].)

(2) There are only two kinds of explanation for phenomena: scientific explanation and personal explanation (Swinburne 1979, pp. 140–141).

(3) No scientific explanation of (1) is possible. (The data in (1) concern the most basic or ultimate constituents of material bodies and the most fundamental physical laws; scientific explanation reaches no further.)

(4) Thus, either there is a personal explanation for (1) or it has no explanation (i.e., it occurs by chance).

(5) That there is a personal explanation for (1) is more probable than that it has no explanation.

(6) Hence, (1) confirms the hypothesis of a personal cause of the universe.

Naturalism offers no explanation for the causal order and fundamental intelligibility of the universe. Indeed, this type of order is surprising if the universe did not result from purpose or design. On the other hand, a personal being has reasons to produce causal order in the universe, due to aesthetic considerations—for example, order is more beautiful than chaos—and other value considerations (a universe with intelligent beings who can understand their world is preferable to a universe with no intelligent beings or with rational creatures whose attempts to "read the book of Nature" cannot succeed). Causal order combines with additional data that exhibit properties (a) and (b) above to support the further conclusion that *theism is more probable than naturalism*, even if the probability of theism is not greater than 0.5 or fifty percent.

Critics point to the difficulty of assigning a priori objective probabilities to large-scale metaphysical theories. Perhaps this can be blunted by appealing to epistemic probability—given what is known minus the assumption of intelligent design, it does not seem likely that the universe would exhibit such precise and ubiquitous causal order. Further scrutiny falls on the argument's conclusion, which posits only a personal cause, not a being with every perfection. Swinburne claims that considerations of simplicity lead to a positing of only one person—a person who has infinite knowledge and power, because any finite amount would require further explanation as to why the person has exactly this degree of knowledge or power.

Finally, the cumulative case argument draws upon further features of the universe that similarly confirm theism and disconfirm naturalism. Such features include the existence of a material universe, consciousness and moral awareness, and evidence of providence, miracles, and religious experiences. (Note that in chapters ten and eleven, Swinburne argues that evil and suffering do not disconfirm theism. The claim that they do, he writes, "stems from a failure to appreciate the deepest needs of men … and the strength of the logical constraints on the kinds of world which God can make" (1979, p. 224).

See also Naturalism; Philosophy of Religion, History of; Physicotheology; Popular Arguments for the Existence of God; Religious Experience, Argument for the Existence of God; Theism, Arguments For and Against.

Bibliography

Collins, Robin. "Design and the Many-Worlds Hypothesis" In *Philosophy of Religion: A Reader and Guide*, edited by William Lane Craig. New Brunswick, NJ: Rutgers University Press, 2002.

Smart, John Jamieson Carswell, and John J. Haldane. *Atheism and Theism*. Oxford: Blackwell, 1996. Smart offers a critique of Haldane's theistic arguments that would apply equally to many of Swinburne's and Collins's arguments.

Swinburne, Richard. *The Existence of God*. Oxford: Clarendon Press, 1979.

Laura Garcia (2005)

TELEOLOGICAL ETHICS

Theories about what is right and wrong are standardly divided into two kinds: those that are teleological and those that are not. Teleological theories are ones that first identify what is good in states of affairs and then characterize right acts entirely in terms of that good. The paradigm case of a teleological theory is therefore an impartial consequentialist theory, such as hedonistic utilitarianism; defended by John Stuart Mill (1969) and Henry Sidgwick (1907), it says the right act is always the one whose consequences contain the greatest total pleasure possible. But the category of teleological ethics is normally thought to be broader than that of consequentialism, so there can be teleological theories that are not consequentialist. This can be so, however, in several different ways.

Hedonistic utilitarianism has three principal features: First, it identifies good states of affairs independently of claims about the right, so even pleasure in a wrong act, such as a sadist's pleasure in torturing, is intrinsically good; and these goods are always consequences in the ordinary sense of acts that produce them, that is, separate states that follow after the acts. Second, in evaluating consequences, utilitarianism weighs all people's pleasures impartially, so for any person, a stranger's pleasure counts just as much as his child's or even his own. Finally, utilitarianism characterizes right acts in terms only of promoting the good and, more specifically, of maximizing it, so the right act is always the one that produces the most good possible.

Although teleological theories must identify the good independently of the right, they can recognize many goods other than pleasure. Some possible goods, such as knowledge and artistic creativity, are, like pleasure, states of individual persons. Others involve patterns of distribution across persons, such as that they enjoy equal pleasures or, on a different view, pleasures proportioned to their merit. Yet others, such as the existence of beauty or of complex ecosystems, are independent of persons. (Goods of all three types are affirmed in the *ideal consequentialisms* of G. E. Moore (1903) and Hastings Rashdall (1907). These initial goods are all, like pleasure, consequences in the ordinary sense of acts that produce them, but other possible goods are not. Imagine that a theory values difficult activities because they are difficult. Then engaging in a difficult activity, such as playing chess, will promote value not just by producing it as an external consequence but also by instantiating it, or by having difficulty as an intrinsic feature. The same holds if a theory values action from a virtuous motive, such as a benevolent desire for another's pleasure. Then a benevolent act will contribute to value in part through an intrinsic feature—its being benevolent. This is a first way in which a theory can be teleological but not consequentialist: If consequentialism can value only the external consequences of acts, as some definitions assume, then a theory fits the broader but not the narrower concept if it values some intrinsic properties of acts. It can still evaluate acts by the total state of the world that will obtain if they are performed, but some relevant features of that state are now internal to them.

A teleological theory can also abandon the second feature of utilitarianism—its impartiality about the good. Thus, a teleological theory can be egoistic, telling individual agents to promote only their own pleasure, knowledge, or other goods, or, conversely, can say that they should promote only others' good and not their own. It can also embrace what C. D. Broad (1971) called "self-referential altruism," which says that while people should give some weight to everyone's good, they should care more about that of those who are close to them, such as their family and friends. These theories can still identify the good independently of the right and say right acts maximize the good, but if it is essential to consequentialism to be impartial, as again some assume, they are teleological but not consequentialist.

These first two possibilities come together in a group of theories often categorized as teleological but not consequentialist—the eudaimonist theories of Aristotle and other ancient philosophers. They derive all moral requirements from a final end or good they call a person's *eudaimonia*, translated either as happiness or as flourishing. They are therefore formally egoistic since each person's final end is just that person's own eudaimonia. But they hold that a principal component of eudaimonia is moral virtue, which will express itself in virtuous acts such as helping others from benevolent motives. Eudaimonist theories can in principle yield the same substantive duties as utilitarianism, telling each person to maximize pleasure impartially. But their explanatory claims do not use the causal relation central to utilitarianism, saying, instead, that acts of helping others are required because they can instantiate moral virtue, which in turn instantiates part of eudaimonia.

Finally, a theory can abandon the third, maximizing feature of utilitarianism. This feature is extremely demanding since it implies that any time we do not do everything we can to benefit other people, which includes any time we relax or amuse ourselves, we act wrongly. One possibility, proposed by Michael Slote (1985), is to replace the maximizing principle with a *satisficing* one that says an act is right so long as its consequences are good enough, either in absolute terms or because they make some reasonable proportion of the greatest improvement the agent can make in the circumstances. Many writers see satisficing as consistent with consequentialism, but if it is essential to the latter to be maximizing, as some definitions imply, a satisficing principle again generates a nonconsequentialist teleology. A related possibility, proposed by Samuel Scheffler (1982), is to retain a maximizing principle but simultaneously grant agents an option to give somewhat more weight to their own good. Then, if they prefer a smaller benefit for themselves to a somewhat greater one for other people, they do not act wrongly, though if they preferred the greater good, they also would not act wrongly. The resulting view is probably not consequentialist since it does not contain only principles about promoting the good; but it arguably is teleological since its principles all do concern the good in some way.

More radical departures from maximizing may be possible. Teleological theories are commonly contrasted with deontological ones, which say an act can be wrong even if it has the best consequences. Thus, a deontological theory can say it is wrong to kill an innocent person even if that will prevent five other innocent people from being killed because doing so violates a moral constraint against killing; it can likewise contain constraints against lying, promise- breaking, and so on. A deontological theory is clearly nonconsequentialist, and it is also nonteleological if its constraints are independent of the good, say, if it contains independent, underived prohibitions of killing and lying. But some deontologists, who call their view Thomist, do connect constraints to the good. They start by identifying certain states of affairs as intrinsically good, say, pleasure, knowledge, and freedom. But they then claim that alongside a duty to promote these goods is a separate and stronger duty to respect them, which means not choosing against or intentionally destroying them. This second duty grounds constraints against killing, which destroys good human life; lying, which aims at the opposite of knowledge; and more.

But Thomists such as John Finnis (1980) call their view teleological since it is centered on goods that can and should be promoted. The same could not be said of Kantian deontologies, which ground constraints in respect for a value that is located in persons rather than in states of affairs and is not to be promoted since there is no duty to increase the number of valuable persons. But Thomist deontology shares enough assumptions with paradigmatically teleological theories that it arguably, if not uncontroversially, belongs in the category. (If so, deontological ethics contrasts with consequentialism but not necessarily with teleology.)

Teleological moral theories relate all moral duties to the goodness of states of affairs. They will therefore be rejected by those who think claims about intrinsic goodness are unintelligible or who hold, with Kant (1998), that the fundamental value is that of persons. These are minority views, however. Most philosophers accept as underived such claims as that pain is evil and knowledge good, so there is at least some moral duty to prevent the one and promote the other. The key issue about teleological ethics, then, is whether *all* duties can be related to the good. In addressing this issue, the many forms teleological ethics can take should be remembered. It can value not just pleasure but also, say, equal distribution and virtuous action; it can allow or even require agents to give more weight to some people's good; and it need not demand maximization of the good. But the question remains whether teleological ethics can recognize moral constraints, which can make it wrong to do what has the best effects. Strict consequentialists reject such constraints or claim that belief in them is justified only insofar as it has good consequences. But those who find constraints independently compelling will ask whether teleological ethics can accommodate constraints, as Thomist theories try to do, and, if so, whether it gives them the best explanation. If the answer to both questions is yes, then the teleological approach to ethics can capture a wide range of moral phenomena. If not, it will be unacceptable to those who think it sometimes wrong to do what will promote the most good.

See also Aristotle; Consequentialism; Deontological Ethics; Ethics, History of; Kant, Immanuel; Utilitarianism.

Bibliography

Aristotle, *The Nicomachean Ethics.* Translated by David Ross. Oxford: Oxford University Press, 1980.

Broad, C. D. "Self and Others." In *Broad's Critical Essays in Moral Philosophy*, edited by David R. Cheney. London: Allen & Unwin, 1971, pp. 262–282.

Finnis, John. *Natural Law and Natural Rights.* Oxford: Clarendon Press, 1980.

Frankena, William K. *Ethics.* 2nd ed. Englewood Cliffs, NJ: Prentice-Hall, 1973.

Kant, Immanuel. *Foundations of the Metaphysics of Morals* Translated by Mary Gregor. Cambridge, U.K.: Cambridge University Press, 1998.

Mill, John Stuart. *Utilitarianism* (1861). In *Essays on Ethics, Religion, and Society*, edited by J. M. Robson. Vol. 10 of *Collected Works of John Stuart Mill.* Toronto: University of Toronto Press, 1969, pp. 203–259.

Moore, G. E. *Principia Ethica.* Cambridge, U.K.: Cambridge University Press, 1903.

Rashdall, Hastings. *The Theory of Good and Evil, A Treatise on Moral Philosophy.* 2 vols. London: Oxford University Press, 1907.

Scheffler, Samuel. *The Rejection of Consequentialism: A Philosophical Investigation of the Considerations Underlying Rival Moral Conceptions.* Oxford: Clarendon Press, 1982.

Sidgwick, Henry. *The Methods of Ethics.* 7th ed. London: Macmillan, 1907.

Slote, Michael. *Common-Sense Morality and Consequentialism.* London: Routledge & Kegan Paul, 1985.

Thomas Hurka (2005)

TELEOLOGY

The term *teleology* locates a series of connected philosophical questions. If we grant that there is such a thing as purposive or goal-directed activity (as we must, since, for example, a political campaign aimed at victory represents a clear, uncontroversial case), we may ask the following questions: (1) By what criteria do we identify purposive activity? (2) What is the nature of the systems that exhibit purposive activity? (3) Does the nature of purposive activity require us to employ special concepts or special patterns of description and explanation that are not needed in an account of nonpurposive activity? And if we grant that there are objects and processes which perform functions (again, as we must, since no one would deny, for instance, that the human kidney performs the function of excretion), we may ask: (4) By what criteria do we identify functions? (5) What is the nature of the systems that exhibit functional activity? (6) Does the description of functions require special concepts or special patterns of analysis?

These six questions have been formulated with the help of a distinction between purposive and functional activity. Although the distinction is not always drawn in discussions of teleology, it is desirable for a number of reasons. It seems, at least prima facie, that the criteria of functional activity are quite distinct from the criteria of purposive activity: urine excretion, for example, seems to be a function by virtue of its role in the economy of a living organism, whereas activity seems to be purposive in virtue of the manner in which it is controlled. Thus, it seems at least logically possible that a purposive activity could perform no function, and that a function could be performed without purposive activity. Moreover, in view of this fundamental conceptual difference between purpose and function, we should expect the analysis of purposive and functional activity to show differences in logical pattern. On the other hand, it also seems clear that there are close connections between function and purpose; thus the final question: (7) What is the relation between ascriptions of function and ascriptions of purpose?

PURPOSE ACTIVITY

CRITERIA. A number of writers have proposed definitions of "goal-directed" or "purposive" action that leave open the question whether the action is intentional or in any way involves consciousness. R. B. Braithwaite suggests, as a behavioral criterion of goal-directed activity that either may or may not be goal-intended, "persistence toward the goal under varying conditions." This is a condensed version of very similar criteria offered by R. B. Perry, E. S. Russell, and A. Hofstadter. All presuppose that a goal may be identified and that both persistence and sensitivity to varying conditions may be located by reference to the goal. E. C. Tolman adds the requirement that purposive activity show "docility," that is, some improvement in reaching the goal in the course of successive trials. But docility, however important it may be in the total picture of biological purposiveness, is surely not part of the criterion of purposiveness. Any abilities that are in fact learned could, in logical principle, be innate.

This criterion, in Braithwaite's form, is of course susceptible of considerable refinement; Braithwaite himself (in *Scientific Explanation*), for example, proposes a way of identifying variations in conditions as relevant variations for applying the criterion. Further possible refinements will be discussed in the next section.

The apparent circularity in the criterion—defining "goal-directed" in terms of a "goal"—is not serious. The location of persistence, sensitivity, and a goal may proceed together by a method of successive approximations. For example, a pattern of animal behavior may appear persistent and lead to a tentative identification of a goal, and the identification may be checked by looking for sensitivity to conditions or further evidence of persistence. A hypothesis about any one of the three—goal, persistence, sensitivity—can be confirmed by investigating either of the other two.

It seems clear that there are behavioral criteria for identifying purposive action, not only of human beings but also of other animals and of artifacts such as self-guided missiles. A pilot who watches a rocket approach in spite of his evasive maneuvers would rightly have no doubts about either the goal-directedness of the rocket's movements or the identity of its goal. No doubt the actual criteria of purposiveness that have been proposed suffer various shortcomings. In particular, they seem to lay down a necessary but not a sufficient condition. However, most philosophers would regard the program of seeking behavioral criteria as sound.

NATURE OF SYSTEMS SHOWING PURPOSIVE ACTIVITY. Is it possible for the philosopher, as distinct from the biologist, psychologist, or communications engineer, to say anything illuminating about the nature of the systems—men, mice, and missiles—that engage in purposive activity? He can at least examine more closely the behavioral criteria of purposiveness, in order to see whether there might be covert reference to the nature of the system in the criterias' actual application. A critic of the behavioral criteria might remark that a river is persistent in reaching the sea and is sensitive to the conditions necessary for reaching the sea—it detours all obstacles—but we would not call the flowing of a river purposive, nor would we call the sea or reaching the sea its goal. In short, the critic might say, a river is not the sort of thing to which we ever ascribe purposiveness.

Directive correlation. A number of philosophers, including Braithwaite, Ernest Nagel, George Sommerhoff, and Morton Beckner, have proposed ways of avoiding the difficulty about rivers and the like. Although there are differences in their accounts, they all adopt the strategy of regarding an activity as purposive only when its goal-seeking character is the outcome of relatively independent but dovetailing processes. Sommerhoff, for example, defines "purposive behavior" with the help of a concept he terms "directive correlation." Two variables, such as the position of a moving target and the direction in which an automatic target-tracking mechanism points, are said to be directively correlated with respect to a goal state (in this case, the state in which the mechanism points at the target) whenever: (1) The two variables are independent in the sense that any value of one is compatible with any value of the other; (2) The actual value of both, at a given time, is at least in part causally determined by the prior value of a "coenetic" (steering) variable (in the example, the coenetic variable is the same as one of the directively correlated variables, namely, the position of the moving target); and (3) the causal determination is such that the actual values of the directively correlated variables are sufficient for the realization of the goal state. Sommerhoff then defines "purposive behavior" as directively correlated behavior in which the coenetic variable is identical with one of the directively correlated variables.

Stipulations (2) and (3) make the notion of two processes dovetailing so as to achieve a goal as precise as the notion of causal determination; and stipulation (1) specifies that the processes must be independent. The requirement of independence rules out such cases as the river, for the direction in which a river flows is not independent of the lay of the land.

Sommerhoff's analysis is not without difficulties (see Nagel and Beckner), but it is undoubtedly correct in general approach. A system *S* that could exhibit directive correlation would satisfy a number of prior conceptions about purposive behavior; for instance, that *S* would employ information about its environment, particularly about an aspect of the environment associated with the goal, and that the behavior of *S* would be dependent upon a specialized physical hookup, such as some sort of circuitry.

It is now possible to suggest a schema for constructing a criterion of purposive activity that includes both a necessary and a sufficient condition and that incorporates some reference both to the empirical character of the activity and to the nature of the system that engages in it. Activity is purposive if and only if it exhibits sensitivity and persistence toward a goal as a result of directive correlation.

NEED FOR SPECIAL CONCEPTS OR PATTERNS OF DESCRIPTION AND EXPLANATION. Purposive activity, in the analyses of Braithwaite and Sommerhoff described above, does not involve a special kind of causality but only a special organization of ordinary causal processes. If these analyses are correct, both living organisms and artificial machines are capable of purposive activity. If, therefore, special concepts or patterns of description and explanation are not needed in the case of purposive machines, it would appear that they are equally unnecessary in the case of organisms. Many philosophers have drawn this conclusion, and it must be admitted that accounts like Braithwaite's and Sommerhoff's constitute powerful arguments in its support.

There is room for some doubt, however. Even if we grant that purposive activity can be defined in terms that are equally applicable to organic and inorganic systems, it does not follow that all purposive activity can be explained on the model of inanimate activity. The most serious doubt concerns those purposive activities that may be described as the acts of agents, such as acts deliberately undertaken for the sake of a consciously envisaged end. Suppose, for example, that some or all of these acts of agents are in principle unpredictable—a view accepted by some philosophers. Then, if they can be explained at all, their explanation is essentially post hoc. The pattern of such explanation is not yet properly understood; nevertheless, there is at least some doubt that it can dispense with the conception of following a rule. But these considerations raise questions that cannot be pursued here.

FUNCTIONS

CRITERIA. When we assert truly—for example, that a function of the kidney is the excretion of urine—precisely what relations must hold between the kidney and excretion? It has been proposed, for example by Nagel, that such teleological terms as *purpose* and *function* can be eliminated in the following way: An expression such as "A function of the kidney is the excretion of urine" is translated into the nonteleological expression "The kidney is a necessary (or necessary and sufficient) condition of urine excretion." In general we may interpret Nagel as proposing a translation schema—For "*F* is the function of *A*," write "*A* is a necessary (or necessary and sufficient) condition of *F*"—that dispenses with teleological language and that also provides part of a criterion (a necessary condition) for identifying functions.

At best, however, Nagel's schema must be modified, for the possession of kidneys is neither a necessary nor a sufficient condition of urine excretion. It is obviously not sufficient; but it is also not necessary, since urine can also be excreted by various artificial devices. (If it is objected that these devices are themselves a sort of kidney, then the statement that a kidney is necessary for excretion reduces to a tautology.) Moreover, the translation schema is much less plausible when applied to organic functions that are ordinarily accomplished in distinct ways. Temperature regulation, for example, is a function of man's body hair; but hair is not necessary for heat regulation, since the function may be performed by other physical and physiological mechanisms. When we ascribe a function to the kidney or to body hair, we seem to be saying no more than that these structures contribute to certain processes; we leave open the question whether they are necessary or sufficient for the processes. The relation "contributing to" may be defined without employing teleological language. Let *F* be a process, some or all of which takes place in system *S*; and let *A* be a part of, or a process in, *S*. Finally, let the terms "*S*-like," "*F*-like," and "*A*-like" refer, respectively, to all those entities that answer to the definition of the terms employed in specifying *S*, *F*, and *A*. (In the example "A function of the kidney in vertebrates is the excretion of urine," all vertebrates are *S*-like, all cases of urine excretion are *F*-like, and all kidneys are *A*-like.) Then "*A* of *S* contributes to *F*" if and only if there exist *S*-like systems and states or environments of these *S*-like systems in which *F*-like processes occur and the possession of *A*-like parts or processes is necessary for the occurrence of *F*-like processes.

On this definition, we may say that in general a man's kidney contributes to the excretion of urine and that body hair contributes to heat regulation. And if we adopt the translation schema "For '*F* is the function of *A* in *S*,' write '*A* contributes to *F* in *S*,'" we may say, even in the case of a man whose bad kidneys have been bypassed to an artificial kidney, that the function of his flesh-and-blood kidneys is still the excretion of urine; they merely fail to perform it.

NATURE OF SYSTEMS SHOWING FUNCTIONAL ACTIVITY. Nagel's translation schema and the above modification of it provide a way of translating a teleological statement T_1 into a statement T_2 that does not employ explicitly teleological terms. Therefore, the satisfaction of T_2 by a given *A*, *F*, and *S* is a necessary condition of *F*'s being a function of A. It is, however, not a sufficient condition; we may not in general translate T_2 into T_1. We would not say, for example, that the function of the ground is to hold up the rocks even though, in our technical sense, the ground contributes to the holding up of rocks. It would seem that out of the whole set of "contributing" cases, only a very restricted subset could be regarded as functions.

How may this subset be specified? We ordinarily attribute functions to two sorts of systems, artifacts and living things. We may consider first a simple artifact such as a cooking pan. We ascribe a function to the whole pan: cooking. Moreover, we also ascribe functions to parts and properties of the pan insofar as they contribute to its usefulness in cooking. For example, it is natural to think of the handle as providing a grip, of the rivets as fastening on the handle, and so on. In short, whenever we are prepared to acknowledge a single function F, we are also prepared to acknowledge a hierarchy of functions, with F at the top and the functions at each lower level contributing to all those above them.

The assignment of functions to living organisms proceeds on the same principle. There are two organic processes that are regarded as fundamental, the maintenance of life and reproduction. Alternatively, these two processes may be thought of as contributing to a single process, the maintenance of a species, which stands at the top of all functional hierarchies. The fundamental processes thus play a defining role in the identification of functions. The following schema lays down a necessary and sufficient condition of functional activity: F_1 is a function of A in S if and only if A contributes to F_1 in S; and F_1 is identical with or contributes to F_2 in S, where F_2 is either a purpose for which the artifact S is designed or the process of maintenance of the species of which S is a member.

The concept of an artifact may be interpreted quite broadly in order to include not only things like cooking pans but also all cultural products, such as works of art, language, and legal institutions. It makes sense, for example, on the above analysis and on this interpretation of *artifact*, to ask "What is the function of Ophelia in *Hamlet*?" and "What is the function of verb inflections in Japanese?" The justification for regarding maintenance of the species as a fundamental function, serving a logical role in functional analysis, is examined below.

NEED FOR SPECIAL CONCEPTS OR PATTERNS OF ANALYSIS. The definition of functional activity offered above provides a way of interpreting ascriptions of functions without using explicitly teleological expressions. However, there is a sense in which many of the concepts that are employed in the ascription of functions are implicitly teleological. Consider, for example, the concept of an "escape reaction." It is applied to a great variety of animal movements, such as flying up, forming dense schools, withdrawing into burrows, jumping into water, and gathering under the mother. These diverse reactions probably have no relevant feature in common other than a functional one; they all, in the technical sense, contribute to the avoidance of death by predation. Such functional concepts are common in the theory of animal behavior, in all branches of natural history, in physiology, and indeed in everyday language. The terms that we most commonly use, for example, in describing machines are defined functionally.

The view that teleological language can be eliminated from the language of science may be true; again, the most difficult cases concern human agency. But the program of eliminating teleological expressions even from biological theory must involve more than the elimination of such terms as *function, purpose, goal,* and *in order to.* If there is any point in eliminating these terms, there is just as much point in eliminating all concepts that are defined functionally, for "The function of this movement is to escape from a predator" is equivalent in asserted content to "This movement is an escape reaction." It is obviously true that the movement in question can be described, without employing the term *escape reaction,* as a movement that contributes to the avoidance of a predator. But if we eliminate the term *escape reaction,* we have excised from the language the term that applies not only to this movement but to all the diverse movements, in a variety of taxonomic groups, that serve this function.

The ascription of functions, therefore, does not require either an explicit or an implicit teleological vocabulary. It should be recognized, however, that the elimination of implicitly teleological expressions (concepts that are defined functionally) would result in a language for biological theory that would bear very little resemblance to the existing language.

Moreover, the difference would not be superficial; the rejection of functional concepts would amount to the rejection of a powerful and fruitful conceptual scheme. Our picture of living organisms as organized functional hierarchies is an essential part of the theory of natural selection; it is the foundation of physiology and morphology; and it is the basis of the medical view of disease as derangement of function. It is the fruitfulness of this conceptual scheme, embodied in a network of connected functional concepts, that constitutes the justification for assigning to maintenance of the species its central logical role in the ascription of functions.

RELATION BETWEEN ASCRIPTIONS OF FUNCTION AND OF PURPOSE

We have drawn a sharp distinction between functional activities, which contribute to a "fundamental" process, and purposive activities, which are persistent, flexible patterns of directively correlated behavior. It is clear, however, that function and purpose are closely connected—so closely, indeed, that many writers have failed to see the distinction. These connections may be described as follows:

(*a*) Whenever we construct an artifact as an aid to our own purposive activities, we are willing to ascribe functions to the artifact and to its parts and properties.

(*b*) Many but by no means all organic functions are served by purposive activities. For example, temperature regulation in the mammals involves directive correlation, whereas the excretion of urine does not.

(*c*) Conversely, every organic mechanism that provides an organism with the means of purposive activity serves the function of maintenance of the species. This is an empirical fact. It does not mean, however, that each case of purposive activity, when it occurs, performs a function. A purposive activity that is ordinarily adaptive (functional under normal circumstances) can lead to disaster when the circumstances are abnormal. For example, the homing of a male moth on a female, directed by the attractant secreted by the female, is ordinarily both purposive and functional. But it can lead the moth to his death when the attractant is placed on a surface covered with an insecticide.

See also Braithwaite, Richard Bevan; Functionalism; Functionalism in Sociology; Nagel, Ernest; Organismic Biology; Perry, Ralph Barton; Speculative Systems of History; Teleological Argument for the Existence of God; Teleological Ethics.

Bibliography

Beckner, Morton. *The Biological Way of Thought.* New York: Columbia University Press, 1959.

Braithwaite, R. B. *Scientific Explanation.* Cambridge, U.K.: Cambridge University Press, 1953.

Braithwaite, R. B. "Teleological Explanations." *PAS,* n.s., 47 (1947): i–xx.

Hofstadter, A. "Objective Teleology." *Journal of Philosophy* 38 (2) (January 1941): 29–39.

Nagel, Ernest. "Teleological Explanation and Teleological Systems." In *Readings in the Philosophy of Science,* edited by H. Feigl and M. Brodbeck, 537–558. New York: Appleton-Century-Crofts, 1953. A revised and enlarged version of this article appears in Nagel's *The Structure of Science,* 401–428. New York: Harcourt Brace, 1961.

Perry, R. B. "A Behavioristic View of Purpose." *Journal of Philosophy* 18 (4) (February 1921): 85–105.

Russell, E. S. *The Directiveness of Organic Activities.* Cambridge, U.K.: Cambridge University Press, 1945.

Sommerhoff, George. *Analytical Biology.* London, 1950.

Tolman, E. C. *Purposive Behavior in Animals and Men.* New York: Century, 1932.

Morton Beckner (1967)

TELEOLOGY [ADDENDUM]

Teleological explanations are said to be forward looking. We ask why Lauren is walking and are told her purpose, which is to buy ice cream when she gets to the shop. Or we ask why vertebrates have kidneys and are told their function, which is filtering blood. In both cases, the end explains the means; something at a time is explained by something else at a later time. This inverts the usual order of causal explanations: If Johnny's throwing the ball explains the window breaking, his throwing preceded the breaking.

PURPOSIVE EXPLANATIONS

How does Lauren's purpose explain her walking? Many philosophers would now say that the relation between her purpose and her walking is a special instance of ordinary physical causation. On a standard version of physicalism, an agent's purpose consists of beliefs and desires, which involve brain states that represent what is believed and desired. If Lauren is walking to the shop to buy ice cream, she has both a desire to buy ice cream and a belief that walking to the shop will let her do so. It is not her buying ice cream but her intention to do so that causes her walking, and since her intention precedes her walking, the usual explanatory order is preserved.

Some physicalists question the causal power and explanatory relevance of beliefs and desires. For example, Jaegwon Kim (1998) argues that, given that mental properties cannot be strictly identified with basic physical properties (a thesis of functionalism), they are causally redundant, since basic physical properties suffice to cause behavior. And Jerry Fodor (1991) argues that, given that the contents of beliefs and desires depend on the relations of an agent to his or her environment (the thesis of content externalism), contents do not explain behavior, since an agent's behavior is caused by his or her intrinsic properties. Similar doubts can be raised with regard to the causal power and explanatory relevance of functions. However, by no means is everyone persuaded by these arguments, and their conclusions are anyway consistent with (what Sydney Shoemaker calls) the core realizers of beliefs and desires being the causes of behavior.

FUNCTIONAL EXPLANATIONS

When functions are attributed to artifacts and components of organic systems, we seem to use a teleological notion of what something is for. "The switch has the function of turning on the light" seems equivalent to "The switch is for turning on the light" (that is why it is there). "Pineal glands have the function of secreting melatonin" seems equivalent to "Pineal glands are for secreting melatonin" (that is why they are there). Not all locutions involving the word *function* have this teleological flavor. "X *performs* the function of Z-ing" does not entail "X *has* the function of Z-ing" or "X is there *in order to* Z." So only function ascriptions of the latter kind are relevant here.

Artifact functions depend on the purposes of the people who design, make, or use the artifacts: The switch has the function of turning on the light because someone put it there (or later adapted it) for that purpose. Organic function ascriptions in biology seemed more puzzling once the bearers of the functions were no longer seen as God's artifacts.

However, many philosophers of biology now believe that natural selection can replace God in function ascriptions. A popular view, developed and defended by, among others, Larry Wright (1976), Ruth Millikan (1989), Karen Neander (1991a, 1991b), and Peter Schwartz (2002), is that the biological function of a trait is what that type of trait was selected for. According to this etiological theory of function, the pineal gland has the function of secreting melatonin because that is what pineal glands did that caused them to be preserved and/or proliferated in the population. This gives functional explanations of the teleological variety a parallel form to purposive explanations: They both explicitly refer to an effect of the item being explained, but in doing so they implicitly refer to a past event to explain it (intentional selection for the effect, or natural selection for the effect). Numerous objections to the etiological theory have been made, but while it has not gone entirely unscathed, in the view of most philosophers of biology it remains the theory to beat (although see, e.g., Christopher Boorse [2002], who strongly disagrees).

As with purposes, an important issue is the explanatory role of functions. According to Wright (1976), a trait's function explains why it is there. Robert Cummins (1975) argues against this, that functions explain how systems operate. An overall capacity of a complex system is explained by a functional analysis, which describes the contributing capacities of the parts of the system, and the contributing capacities of each of their parts, in turn. According to Cummins, a function of a component part is its contribution to a capacity under analysis.

A problem with Cummin's account is that it does not account for the normativity of function ascriptions. Function ascriptions are normative (although not prescriptive) in the sense that they permit the possibility of malfunction: For example, my pineal gland could have the function to secrete melatonin and at the same time it could lack the capacity to secrete melatonin because it is malfunctioning. His account also leaves a lot to be determined by the interests of the researcher. Which overall capacity is to be analyzed and in which environment its exercise is to be analyzed is settled by the interests of the researcher. Thus the account is not naturalistic (it makes use of intentional terms). It is also inaccurate. For example, those interested in explaining death by cancer can give a functional analysis of the kind that Cummins describes. But contributions to death by cancer are not normal (proper) functions by virtue of their role in producing death by cancer. These problems suggest that the analysis is at best incomplete as it stands.

While Cummins's (1975) analysis of functions is problematic, he is right about the importance of functional analysis. This has led some to suggest that biology employs two notions of function, with distinct explanatory roles: a teleological notion for teleological explanations and a notion of a contributing capacity for functional analysis. However, this cannot be the right way to understand their respective explanatory roles if the etiological analysis is the correct analysis of functional norms, since physiological biology, which provides functional analyses of living systems, makes important use of the distinction between normal and abnormal functioning in doing so. Neander (1991b) suggests that the teleological/etiological notion of a function permits an idealized functional analysis, the idea being that we describe the functional organization of a normal system (as opposed to the malfunctioning of an abnormal system) by describing the capacities for which each of its parts was selected.

Bibliography

Boorse, Christopher. "A Rebuttal on Functions." In *Functions: New Essays in the Philosophy of Psychology and Biology*, edited by André Ariew, Robert Cummins, and Mark Perlman. New York: Oxford University Press, 2002.

Cummins, Robert. "Functional Analysis." *Journal of Philosophy* 72 (1975): 741–765.

Fodor, Jerry. "A Modal Argument for Narrow Content." *Journal of Philosophy* 88 (1991): 5–26.

Kim, Jaegwon. *Mind in a Physical World.* Cambridge, MA: MIT Press, 1998.

Millikan, Ruth. "In Defense of Proper Functions." *Philosophy of Science* 56 (1989): 288–303.

Neander, Karen. "Functions as Selected Effects." *Philosophy of Science* 58 (1991a): 168–184.

Neander, Karen. "The Teleological Notion of Function." *Australasian Journal of Philosophy* 69 (1991b): 454–468.

Schwartz, Peter. "The Continuing Usefulness Account of Proper Function." In *Functions: New Essays in the Philosophy of Psychology and Biology*, edited by André Ariew, Robert Cummins, and Mark Perlman. New York: Oxford University Press, 2002.

Wright, Larry. *Teleological Explanation.* Berkeley: University of California Press, 1976.

Karen Neander (2005)

TELESIO, BERNARDINO

(1509–1588)

Bernardino Telesio, the Renaissance philosopher, was born at Cosenza, in Calabria, Italy. He studied philosophy, physics, and mathematics at the University of Padua, and received his doctorate in 1535. In Padua he became acquainted with the teaching of Aristotle and the two main Aristotelian schools, the Averroistic and the Alexandrist. Following the trend of the time, he devoted himself especially to the study of nature; but far from accepting the Aristotelian doctrine, he reacted vigorously against it. Telesio pursued his literary activity mostly at Naples, where he was a guest of the Carafa family, and at Cosenza. He enjoyed the friendship of several popes, and Gregory XIII invited him to Rome to expound his doctrine. He never engaged in any formal teaching, for he preferred to discuss his ideas in private conversations with friends.

Telesio is the author of the nine-book *De Rerum Natura Iuxta Propria Principia* (On the Nature of Things According to Their Principles; 1586) and of several philosophical opuscules. He proposed to interpret nature by following the testimony of the senses, rather than to attempt an explanation through the "abstract and preconceived ideas" of the Aristotelians. Nature must be studied in itself and in its own principles, which are matter and the two active forces of heat and cold. Matter is the passive, inert substratum of all physical change and is substantially the same everywhere. Unlike Aristotelian prime matter, which is pure potency, it is concrete and actual, and hence it can be directly perceived by the senses. Heat and cold are the two opposing forces responsible for all natural events; the first is represented by sky and the second by earth. Heat is also the source of life in plants and animals, as well as the cause of biological operations and some of the lower psychological functions in man. The whole of nature is animated and endowed with sensation in varying degrees (panpsychism). In addition to the vital principle there is present in man and animals "spirit," a very subtle material substance that emanates from the warm element and is generated with the body. Spirit is properly located in the brain and has the function of anticipating and receiving sense impressions. It has both an appetitive power and an intellective power of its own that correspond to the sensitive appetite and the cogitative power (*vis cogitativa*) of the Aristotelians.

Besides body and spirit, man has a *mens,* or *anima superaddita,* which is created by God and informs both body and spirit. This is roughly equivalent to the spiritual soul of Platonic -Augustinian tradition, whose operations transcend those of spirit and reach up to the divine. Apart from the natural drive or instinct of self-preservation, which Telesio attributed to all beings—including inorganic matter—man can also strive after union with God and contemplate the divine. This inner tendency of the *mens,* along with the need for proper sanctions in a future life in order to correct injustices, was one of the arguments used by Telesio to prove the immortality of the soul, which is known by revelation but can also be demonstrated by reason.

For Telesio self-preservation was man's supreme good. Just as in man there is a twofold intellect, one pertaining to the spirit and the other to the soul, so also there is in him a twofold appetitive power. The sensitive appetite tends toward temporal goods and its own preservation in this life; rational appetite or will tends toward immortal goods and its own preservation in a future, eternal life. Virtues are powers or faculties that enable man to achieve self-preservation; they are not merely habits, as Aristotle taught. There are virtues of the spirit and virtues of the soul. Among the virtues, sublimity and wisdom occupy a high place. Sublimity is not merely a particular virtue but virtue as a whole. It stands at the summit of all virtues and somehow includes all of them, for it directs all man's operations toward his supreme good. Wisdom helps man to attain to the knowledge of

God as creator of the universe and can reach out to the knowledge of the divine substance itself.

Although Telesio did not specifically treat the problem of God's existence (it was beyond the scope of his study), he touched incidentally upon Aristotle's argument from motion and criticized it on the ground that movement is an intrinsic property of heat, the first active principle of material beings. Accordingly, there is no need for an extrinsic agent to set the bodies in motion. Besides, an immovable mover that sets the heavens in motion, as conceived by Aristotle, is a contradiction. The existence of God is better proved from the wonderful order of the universe, which can only be the work of a divine mind.

As evidenced by this summary exposition of Telesio's thought, it would be wrong to call him a naturalistic philosopher, if the term *naturalism* is taken to mean a purely materialistic approach to reality. In his *De Rerum Natura* Telesio claimed to investigate the nature of things according to their intrinsic principles, and only incidentally spoke of their extrinsic causes. He gave us a philosophy of nature along the general lines of Aristotle's *Physics,* although from a different point of view and following a more scientific method; he did not intend to present a philosophy of reality as a whole. Briefly, he discussed nature or the world as it is in its concrete reality, not as it came about or in reference to the end for which it was made. His approach to man, knowledge, and morality was on the same plane. One should not be surprised, then, to find in his *De Rerum Natura* no special treatment of God, the spiritual soul, man's ultimate end, and other doctrines commonly held by Christian philosophers. His pertinent statements were nevertheless more than sufficient to show the personal convictions of their author. Thus, in his dedicatory letter to Ferdinand Carafa, duke of Nocera, he wrote: "Our doctrine, far from contradicting the senses and Holy Scripture … so agrees with them that it seems to stem directly from these two sources."

Telesio was called "the first of the moderns" by Francis Bacon, who claimed that Telesio was the first to raise the banner against Aristotle. This same phrase has been used in connection with Telesio by some modern historians of philosophy to indicate his revolt against the traditional teaching of the Catholic Church. The truth is that Telesio was neither a mere critic of Aristotle nor an antagonist of the church, to which he always professed loyalty. His modernity consists, rather, in the emphasis he placed on sense experience in the study of nature, thus paving the way for the scientific method of Galileo Galilei and his followers and opening a path in philosophy that was soon to be followed by Tommaso Campanella, Bacon himself, and Thomas Hobbes. It must be admitted that Telesio often discussed scientific problems with a philosophical method. The result was that his *De Rerum Natura,* a pioneering work of unquestionable value, was neither a scientific study nor a philosophical treatise, but a hybrid combination of science and philosophy not quite in agreement with the rigorous empirical method he professed to follow. This weakness in Telesio's system was pointed out by his contemporary Francesco Patrizi, the Neoplatonist.

See also Alexandrian School; Aristotelianism; Aristotle; Averroism; Bacon, Francis; Campanella, Tommaso; Neoplatonism; Patrizi, Francesco; Renaissance.

Bibliography

WORKS BY TELESIO

De Rerum Natura. Naples, 1586. New edition, edited by Vincenzo Spampanato. 3 vols. Vol. I, Modena: Formíggini, 1910; Vol. II, Genoa, 1913; Vol. III, Rome, 1923.

Varii de Naturalibus Rebus Libelli, edited by Antonio Persio. Venice, 1590. Various philosophical opuscules.

Solutiones Thylesii (and two other opuscules). In Francesco Fiorentino, *Bernardina Telesio.* 2 vols. Florence, 1872–1874. Works contained in an appendix.

WORKS ON TELESIO

Abbagnano, Nicola. *Bernardino Telesio.* Milan: Fratelli Bocca, 1941.

Di Napoli, Giovanni. "Fisica e metafisica in Bernardino Telesio." *Rassegna di scienze filosofiche* 6 (1953): 22–69.

Gentile, Giovanni. *Bernardino Telesio.* Bari: Laterza, 1911.

Soleri, Giacomo. *Telesio.* Brescia: Scuola, 1944.

Troilo, Erminio. *Bernardino Telesio.* 2nd ed. Modena, 1924.

Van Deusen, Neil. "The Place of Telesio in the History of Philosophy." *Philosophical Review* 44 (1935): 417–434.

Van Deusen, Neil. *Telesio, the First of the Moderns.* New York, 1932.

Bernardine M. Bonansea, O.F.M. (1967)

TEMPORAL OR TENSE LOGIC

See *Modal Logic*

TENNANT, FREDERICK ROBERT

(1866–1957)

Frederick Robert Tennant, the philosopher of religion and theologian, spent most of his life in Cambridge, England, and was educated at Cambridge University. He was a fellow of Trinity College and university lecturer in the philosophy of religion. His writings are in two main areas. In the strictly theological field he produced several influential studies of the concepts of sin and the fall of man, in which he diverged widely from the traditional Augustinian doctrines. In the philosophy of religion and the philosophy of science (in both of which his thought shows the influence of his Cambridge contemporary James Ward) Tennant's magnum opus is the two-volume *Philosophical Theology,* which develops, from foundations in the sciences, the thesis that there is "a theistic world-view commending itself as more reasonable than other interpretations or than the refusal to interpret, and congruent with the knowledge—i.e. the probability—which is the guide of life and science" (Vol. II, p. 245).

Tennant described his method as empirical rather than a priori. He meant (1) that his epistemology was based on a psychological examination of the cognitive capacities of the human mind, and (2) that his theistic argument was inductive, treating the existence of God as a hypothesis that goes beyond but builds upon the hypotheses of the special sciences.

Tennant argued in *Philosophy of the Sciences* that all knowledge, other than that in logic and mathematics, consists in probable interpretative judgments whose verification to the human mind is ultimately pragmatic. Thus, science and natural theology share a common method and status: "inductive science has its interpretative explanation-principles, … and its faith elements with which the faith of natural theology is, in essence, continuous" (p. 185). So Tennant can speak of theology as "the final link in a continuous chain of interpretative belief" (p. 184) and can say that "theistic belief is but a continuation, by extrapolation, or through points representing further observations, of the curve of 'knowledge' which natural science has constructed" (pp. 185–186). (For Tennant's conception of faith as the volitional element in the acquisition of all knowledge, scientific no less than religious, see the entry FAITH).

Tennant rejected religious experience—both the special experiences of the mystic and the less special religious experience of the ordinary believer—as a valid ground for belief in God, and he rested his entire case upon what he called the wider, or cosmic, teleology.

The version of the Argument to Design in Volume II of Tennant's *Philosophical Theology*—taking account as it does of David Hume's critique of the much simpler arguments of the eighteenth-century teleologists culminating in William Paley's *Natural Theology,* and taking account also of relevant developments in nineteenth-century and early twentieth-century science including the work of Charles Darwin—is probably the strongest presentation that has been written of this type of theistic reasoning. Serious discussions of the Teleological Argument should deal with it in the form provided by Tennant rather than in the relatively cruder versions of earlier centuries or of contemporary popular apologetics.

Tennant begins by making it clear, in accordance with his general theory of knowledge, that the argument is to provide "grounds for reasonable belief rather than rational and coercive demonstration." It employs a concept of probability that is not that of mathematics or logic but "the alogical probability which is the guide of life" and which, Tennant had already claimed in Volume I, is the ultimate basis of all scientific induction.

The argument itself does not rely (as did Paley's) on particular instances of apparent design in nature or on the arithmetical accumulation of these. Tennant allowed that each separate case of adaptation may be adequately explicable in purely naturalistic as well as in teleological terms. But he held that "the multitude of interwoven adaptations by which the world is constituted a theatre of life, intelligence, and morality, cannot reasonably be regarded as an outcome of mechanism, or of blind formative power, or of aught but purposive intelligence." (*Philosophical Theology,* Vol. II, p. 121).

His detailed argument contains the following strands:

(1) The basic instance of order is that the world stands in relation to human thought as something "more or less intelligible, in that it happens to be more or less a cosmos, when conceivably it might have been a self-subsistent and determinate 'chaos' in which similar events never occurred, none recurred, universals had no place, relations no fixity, things no nexus of determination, and 'real' categories no foothold" (p. 82).

(2) The internal and external adaptation of animal organisms can be accounted for in terms of an evolutionary process operating by means of natural selection; but how, other than by a cosmic pur-

pose, is that process itself to be accounted for? Here "The discovery of organic evolution has caused the ideologist to shift his ground from special design in the products to directivity in the process, and plan in the primary collocations" (p. 85).

(3) The emergence of organic life presupposes complex and specific preparatory processes at the inorganic level. Why has a universe of matter produced life and intelligence? If there were millions of universes, we might expect this to happen in a few of them. But there is only one universe. "Presumably the world is comparable with a single throw of dice. And common sense is not foolish in suspecting the dice to have been loaded" (p. 87).

(4) Nature produces in great abundance beauty that seems to exist only for the enjoyment of man. "Theistically regarded, Nature's beauty is of a piece with the world's intelligibility and with its being a theatre for moral life; and thus far the case for theism is strengthened by aesthetic considerations" (p. 93).

(5) Nature has produced man, with his ethical sense. If we judge the evolutionary process not by its roots in the primeval slime but by its fruits in human moral and spiritual experience, we note that "The whole process of Nature is capable of being regarded as instrumental to the development of intelligent and moral creatures" (p. 103).

(6) These five aspects of nature can individually be understood naturalistically. Nevertheless, taken as a whole they suggest a cosmic purpose that has used nature for the production of man. The more we learn of the complex conditions that had to come about before man could exist, "the less reasonable or credible becomes the alternative theory of cumulative groundless coincidence" (p. 106).

Having thus sought to establish theism as the most reasonable explanation of the world as a whole, Tennant discussed the problem of evil considered as challenging the theistic hypothesis, and he offered a theodicy that is typical of the thought of many British theologians on this subject in the twentieth century. This type of theodicy has an ancestry going back through Friedrich Schleiermacher to the early Hellenistic thinkers of the Christian church, especially Irenaeus, and it stands in contrast to the Augustinian and Latin tradition. For Tennant the possibility of the moral evil of sin was involved in the creation of free and responsible personal beings and was justified by the fact that only free persons can be the bearers of moral and spiritual values. Tennant saw the natural evil of pain in its many forms as a necessary concomitant of man's existence in a world that has its own stable structure and laws of operation; and it is justified by the fact that only in such an environment can the higher values of the human personality develop.

The same aspects of Tennant's thought constitute its strength from one philosophical point of view and its weakness from another point of view. He presented theology as an extension of science and theism as a hypothesis that is arguable in essentially the same sort of way as, for example, organic evolution. To some it will seem that by thus assimilating religious to scientific theorizing, Tennant made theology intellectually respectable; and this was his own view of the matter. To others, however, it will seem that Tennant was presenting religious belief in false colors. From their point of view, having excluded the true basis of religious faith in religious experience, Tennant attempted in vain to infer religious conclusions from nonreligious data, and by thus setting theistic belief upon a wrong and inadequate foundation, he has weakened rather than strengthened it.

See also Darwin, Charles Robert; Evil, The Problem of; Faith; Hume, David; Moral Arguments for the Existence of God; Paley, William; Schleiermacher, Friedrich Daniel Ernst; Teleological Argument for the Existence of God.

Bibliography

WORKS BY TENNANT

The Origin and Propagation of Sin. Cambridge, U.K.: Cambridge University Press, 1902.

The Sources of the Doctrines of the Fall and Original Sin. Cambridge, U.K.: Cambridge University Press, 1903.

The Concept of Sin. Cambridge, 1912.

Miracle and Its Philosophical Presuppositions. Cambridge, U.K.: Cambridge University Press, 1925.

Philosophical Theology, 2 vols. Cambridge, U.K.: Cambridge University Press, 1928 and 1930.

Philosophy of the Sciences. Cambridge, U.K.: Cambridge University Press, 1932.

The Nature of Belief. London: Centenary Press, 1943.

Philosophical Theology, Vol. 3. New York: Cambridge University Press, 1968.

WORKS ON TENNANT

Attfield, David. "The Morality of Sins." *Religious Studies* 20 (1984): 227–238.

Broad, C. D. "Frederick Robert Tennant, 1866–1957." *Proceedings of the British Academy* 44 (1960).

Buswell, J. Oliver. *The Philosophies of F. R. Tennant and John Dewey.* New York: Philosophical Library, 1950.

Mellor, D. H. "God and Probability." *Religious Studies* 5 (1968): 223–234.

Scudder, D. L. *Tennant's Philosophical Theology.* New Haven, CT: Yale University Press, 1940.

Smart, Ninian. "F. R. Tennant and the Problem of Evil." In his *Philosophers and Religious Truth.* London: S.C.M. Press, 1964.

Smart, Ninian. *Philosophers and Religious Truth.* New York: Collier, 1969.

Wynn, Mark. *God and Goodness: A Natural Theological Perspective.* London: Routledge, 1999.

John Hick (1967)
Bibliography updated by Christian B. Miller (2005)

TENSE

See *Appendix, Vol. 10*

TERESA OF ÁVILA, ST.

(1515–1582)

St. Teresa of Ávila, the Spanish mystic, was born of an aristocratic family in Ávila. In 1535 she entered a Carmelite convent there and four years later was prostrated by a long illness, probably of psychological origin. However, she had already felt the call to contemplation, and at about the age of forty, after a long struggle, she received a second "conversion," which turned her toward an intense practice of contemplation. Her order was relatively lax in its rules, and she felt impelled to begin a reform. In 1562 a reformed convent was established in Ávila under her direction. After five years, despite ill health and official opposition, she began energetically to spread the reform to other parts of Spain. She died in 1582, after a three-year illness. Her main works were her *Life* (1562–1565), *The Way of Perfection* (1565), and *The Interior Castle* (1577). The first is a full account of her inner experiences, and the last gives a more systematic description of the contemplative life.

Her account of the stages of mysticism, in the *Life*, uses the analogy of watering a garden by various means. Once the weeds have been uprooted, irrigation is needed. Those who bring the water from a well are compared to beginners in prayer and meditation. It is a laborious activity, involving the taming of the senses so that they are no longer distracting. The second stage of meditation is reached with the prayer of quiet. This is compared to irrigating the garden by a waterwheel. The third mode of watering is by a running brook: This corresponds to a state of contemplation in which effort is no longer needed, as if the work were done by the Lord. It is, according to St. Teresa, "a celestial frenzy," in which the faculties of sense perception no longer function. The soul no longer wishes to live in the world but solely in union with God. The intellect is worth nothing, for ordinary modes of understanding are considered irrelevant or nonsensical. In the fourth stage, which is compared to a shower falling on the garden, the soul is totally passive and receptive, all its faculties somehow united with God. The soul cannot properly understand what is occurring, but afterward it is certain that there has been a union with God.

In *The Interior Castle* St. Teresa supplements her earlier account, comparing the contemplative life to entering a castle or palace in which there are many rooms. These are arranged concentrically in six rings of rooms, or "mansions," round an inner chamber where the king lives. To enter this castle, prayer is needed. Ordinary Christians can enter the first three mansions through humility, meditation, and exemplary conduct; and the attainment of the third mansion represents the life achievement of many worthy Christians. But more remains in the spiritual life than such a virtuous existence. The fourth mansion corresponds to the "second water" of St. Teresa's earlier simile. In the fifth the soul seems to be asleep and unconscious both of the external world and of itself (although such language is analogical; the contemplative is not literally asleep). The soul is illuminated in this state by God. The sixth mansion is like a couple's first sight of one another at a betrothal. Finally, the soul enters the holy of holies. It seems as if this place is dark, because of the overpowering strength of the divine light. Here the soul has a direct vision of God, like the beatific vision to be enjoyed hereafter in heaven. Throughout these descriptions St. Teresa makes frequent use of the imagery of love and of marriage. The distinction between the "betrothal" and the "marriage" is found also in the writings of St. John of the Cross, a friend and follower of St. Teresa.

The detail and sensitivity of St. Teresa's autobiographical reports have given her a special importance in the history of mysticism.

See also John of the Cross, St.; Mysticism, History of; Mysticism, Nature and Assessment of; Women in the History of Philosophy.

Bibliography

St. Teresa's works are collected in Spanish as *Obras de Santa Teresa de Jesús*, edited by P. Silverio, 9 vols. (Burgos, 1915–1926); they appear in English as *Complete Works*, translated and edited by E. Allison Peers, 3 vols. (London:

Sheed and Ward, 1946). Also see E. Allison Peers, *Studies of the Spanish Mystics*, Vol. I (London: Sheldon Press, 1927).

OTHER RECOMMENDED WORKS

De Groot, Jean. "Teresa of Avila and the Meaning of Mystical Theology." In *Hispanic Philosophy in the Age of Discovery: Studies in Philosophy and the History of Philosophy*, Vol. 29, edited by Kevin White. Washington DC: Catholic University American Press, 1997.

Fales, Evan. "Scientific Explanations of Mystical Experiences, Part II." *Religious Studies* 32 (3) (1996): 297–313.

Waithe, Mary E. "Roswitha of Gandersheim, Christine Pisan, Margaret More Roper and Teresa of Avila" In *A History of Women Philosophers. Vol. 2: Medieval, Renaissance*. Norwell: Kluwer, 1989.

Ninian Smart (1967)
Bibliography updated by Tamra Frei (2005)

TERRORISM

Terrorism, whether practiced by states, substate groups, or individuals, is found throughout human history. Most historical accounts, however, focus on what they take to be forms of terrorism that are practiced by substate groups and individuals.

During Biblical times, Jewish Sicarii, known for their use of a short sword (sica), struck down rich Jewish collaborators who were opposed to violent resistance against their Roman conquerors. Later, in the eleventh and twelfth centuries, a group of Shiite Moslems, called the Assassins, opposed efforts to suppress their religious beliefs in Sunni-dominated Persia. Using daggers, the Assassins killed prefects, governors, and caliphs in front of many witnesses, thus ensuring their capture and execution because they believed that by their actions they would gain entry into paradise. Eventually, the group was suppressed by the Mongols in the thirteenth century.

In India, from the eleventh century on, a group called the Thugs was active until it was destroyed by the British in the nineteenth century. The Thugs ritually strangled their victims with a silk tie. They claimed allegiance to the goddess Kali, who it is said required them to kill in order to supply her with blood for nourishment.

Following the French Revolution, the Jacobins under Robespierre gave us the very term *terror*, unleashing a Reign of Terror between 1793 and 1794 upon all levels of French society. During this period, those executed included not only those accused of some offense or disloyalty, but sometimes their children, parents, or even grandparents as well.

Yet, it is not clear that all of these historical examples should be regarded, as they usually are, as acts of terrorism. Without a doubt, they are all cases in which terror (intense fear or fright or intimidation) is induced in large groups of people, but terrorism, as many have come to understand it, involves more than just this. First of all, many think that terrorism must have a political purpose—that it must aim to achieve some change in a government or governmental institution or policy. Now, this is true of most of the historical examples just cited, but it is not true of the Thugs of India whose goals were personal and religious rather than political. Second, many also think that terrorism must directly target innocents, a requirement that does not really hold of any of these historical examples except that of the Jacobins. The Sicarii targeted Jewish collaborators who in virtue of their collaboration were clearly not innocent. The Assassins attacked people in positions of political leadership who were responsible for the religious persecution against Shiite Moslems and so were not innocent. So the only really clear example we have here of terrorism is that of Robespierre's Reign of Terror, directed as it was at innocents as well as at those who were considered to be guilty of some offense. However, in the case of Robespierre's Reign of Terror, what we have is an example of state terrorism, not terrorism as practiced by substate groups or individuals.

Since 1983, the U.S. State Department has defined terrorism as follows: "Terrorism is premeditated, politically motivated violence perpetrated against noncombatant targets by subnational groups or clandestine agents, usually intended to influence an audience." In a U.S. State Department document in which this definition is endorsed, there is also a section that discusses state-sponsored terrorism (Office of the Coordinator for Counterterrorism 2001). It is clear, then, that the U.S. State Department does not hold that only subnational groups or individuals can commit terrorist acts; it further recognizes that states can commit terrorist acts as well. So let us offer the following definition of terrorism, which is essentially the same as the U.S. State Department's definition once it is allowed that states, too, can commit terrorist acts and once it is recognized that it is through attempting to elicit terror (that is, intense fear, fright, or intimidation) that terrorists try to achieve their goals. The definition is: "Terrorism is the use or threat of violence against innocent people to elicit terror in them, or in some other group of people, in order to further a political objective."

Using this definition, there is no problem seeing the attacks on New York City and Washington, D.C., particularly the attacks on the World Trade Center, as terrorist acts. Likewise, the bombing of the U.S. embassies in Kenya and Tanzania in 1998 as well as the suicide bombings directed at Israeli civilians are terrorist acts.

But what about the U.S. bombing of a pharmaceutical plant in Sudan with respect to which the United States blocked a United Nation's (U.N.) inquiry and later compensated the owner but not the thousands of victims who were deprived of drugs? Or what about the United States' $4 billion-a-year support for Israel's occupation of Palestinian lands, which began in 1969 and which is illegal, that is, in violation of U.N. resolutions that specifically forbid "the acquisition of territory by force" and which has resulted in many thousands of deaths? Or to go back further: What about U.S. support for the Contras in Nicaragua, and of death squads in El Salvador during the Reagan years, and the use of terrorist counter-city threats of nuclear retaliation during the Cold War and the actual use of nuclear weapons on Hiroshima and Nagasaki at the end of World War II resulting in over 100,000 deaths? Surely, all of these actions also seem to be either terrorist acts or support for terrorist acts according to our definition. How can we tell then, which, if any, of these terrorist acts or support for terrorist acts are morally justified?

Let us address this question from the perspective of the just war theory. In traditional just war theory, two requirements must be met in order to justify going to war. First, there must be a just cause. Second, just means must be used to fight the war. In order for there to be a just cause (1) There must be substantial aggression. (2) Nonbelligerent correctives must be either hopeless or too costly. (3) Belligerent correctives must be neither hopeless nor too costly.

Needless to say, the notion of substantial aggression is a bit fuzzy, but it is generally understood to be the type of aggression that violates people's most fundamental rights. To suggest some specific examples of what is and is not substantial aggression, usually the taking of hostages is regarded as substantial aggression while the nationalization of particular firms owned by foreigners is not so regarded. But even when substantial aggression occurs, frequently nonbelligerent correctives are neither hopeless nor too costly to pursue. And even when nonbelligerent correctives are either hopeless or too costly, in order for there to be a just cause, belligerent correctives must be neither hopeless nor too costly.

Traditional just war theory assumes, however, that there are just causes and goes on to specify just means as imposing two requirements: (1) Harm to innocents should not be directly intended as an end or a means. (2) The harm resulting from the belligerent means should not be disproportionate to the particular defensive objective to be attained. While the just means conditions apply to each defensive action, the just cause conditions must be met by the conflict as a whole.

Given the constraints imposed on just means, one might think that from the perspective of just war theory, acts of terrorism could never be morally justified. But this would require an absolute prohibition on intentionally harming innocents, and such a prohibition would not seem to be justified, even from the perspective of the just war theory. Specifically, it would seem that harm to innocents can be justified for the sake of achieving a greater good when the harm is: (1) trivial (e.g., as in the case of stepping on someone's foot to get out of a crowded subway), (2) easily reparable (e.g., as in the case of lying to a temporarily depressed friend to keep that person from committing suicide), or (3) nonreparable but greatly outweighed by the consequences of the action. Obviously, it is this third category of harm that is relevant to the possible justification of terrorism. But when is intentional harm to innocents nonreparable yet greatly outweighed by the consequences?

Consider the following example often discussed by moral philosophers: A large person who is leading a party of spelunkers gets stuck in the mouth of a cave in which flood waters are rising. The trapped party of spelunkers just happens to have a stick of dynamite with which they can blast the large person out of the mouth of the cave; either they use the dynamite or they all drown, the large person with them. Now, it is usually assumed in this case that it is morally permissible to dynamite the large person out of the mouth of the cave. After all, if that is not done, the whole party of spelunkers will die, the large person with them. So the sacrifice imposed on the large person in this case would not be that great.

But what if the large person's head is outside rather than inside the cave, as it must have been in the previous interpretation of the case. Under those circumstances, the large person would not die when the other spelunkers drowned. Presumably after slimming down a bit, the large person would eventually just squeeze out of the mouth of the cave. In this case, could the party of spelunkers trapped in the cave still legitimately use the stick of dynamite to save themselves rather than the large person?

Suppose there were ten, twenty, 100, or an even a larger number of spelunkers trapped in the cave. At some point, would not the number be sufficiently great that it would be morally acceptable for those in the cave to use the stick of dynamite to save themselves rather than the large person, even if this meant that the large person would be morally required to sacrifice his life? The answer has to be yes, even if you think it has to be a very unusual case when we can reasonably demand that people thus sacrifice their lives in this way.

Is it possible that some acts of terrorism are morally justified in this way? It is often argued that the dropping of atomic bombs on Hiroshima and Nagasaki was so justified. President Truman, who ordered the bombing, justified it on the grounds that it was used to shorten the war. In 1945, the United States demanded the unconditional surrender of Japan. The Japanese had by that time lost the war, but the leaders of their armed forces were by no means ready to accept unconditional surrender. While the Japanese leaders expected an invasion of their mainland islands, they believed that they could make that invasion so costly that the United States would accept a conditional surrender.

Truman's military advisers also believed the costs would be high. The capture of Okinawa had cost almost 80,000 American casualties while almost the entire Japanese garrison of 120,000 men died in battle. If the mainland islands were defended in a similar manner, hundreds of thousands of Japanese would surely have died. During that time, the bombing of Japan would continue, and perhaps intensify, resulting in casualty rates that were no different from those that were expected from the atomic attack. A massive incendiary raid on Tokyo early in March 1945 had set off a firestorm and killed an estimated 100,000 people. Accordingly, Truman's Secretary of State James Byrnes admitted that the two atomic bombs did cause "many casualties, but not nearly so many as there would have been had our air force continued to drop incendiary bombs on Japan's cities" (Byrnes 1947, p. 264). Similarly, Winston Churchill wrote in support of Truman's decision: "To avert a vast, indefinite butchery … at the cost of a few explosions seemed, after all our toils and perils, a miracle of deliverance" (Churchill 1962, p. 634).

Yet the "vast, indefinite butchery" that the United States sought to avert by dropping atomic bombs on Hiroshima and Nagasaki was one that the United States itself was threatening, and had already started to carry out, with its incendiary attack on Tokyo. And the United States itself could have arguably avoided this butchery by dropping its demand for unconditional Japanese surrender. Moreover, a demand of unconditional surrender can almost never be morally justified since defeated aggressors almost always have certain rights that they should never be required to surrender. Hence, the United States' terrorist acts of dropping atomic bombs on Hiroshima and Nagasaki cannot be justified on the grounds of shortening the war and avoiding a vast, indefinite butchery if the United States could have secured those results simply by giving up its unreasonable demand for unconditional surrender. So, it is difficult to see how the dropping of atomic bombs on Hiroshima and Nagasaki could be justified acts of terrorism.

A more promising case for justified terrorism is the counter-city bombing of the British during the early stages of World War II. Early in the war, it became clear that British bombers could fly effectively only at night because too many of them were being shot down during day raids by German antiaircraft fire. In addition, a study done in 1941 showed that of those planes flying at night that were recorded as having actually succeeded in attacking their targets, only one-third managed to drop their bombs within five miles of what they were aiming at. This meant that British bombers flying at night could reasonably aim at no target smaller than a fairly large city. Michael Walzer (1992) argues that under these conditions, the British terror bombing was morally justified because at this early stage of the war, it was the only way the British had left to them to try to avert a Nazi victory. Walzer further argues that the time period when such terror bombing was justified was relatively brief. Once the Russians began to inflict enormous casualties on the German army and the United States made available its manpower and resources, other alternatives opened up. The British, however, continued to rely heavily on terror bombing right up until the end of the war, culminating in the fire-bombing of Dresden in which something like 100,000 people were killed. Nevertheless, for that relatively brief period when Britain had no other way to avert a Nazi victory, Walzer argues, its reliance on terror bombing was morally justified.

Suppose we agree with Walzer that British terror-bombing during the earlier stages of World War II was morally justified. Could there be a comparable moral justification for Palestinian suicide bombings against Israeli civilians? Israel has been illegally occupying Palestinian land since 1969 in violation of U.N. resolutions following the 1967 Arab–Israeli war. Even a return to those 1967 borders, which the U.N. resolutions require, still permits a considerable expansion of Israel's original borders as specified in the mandate of 1947. Moreover, since the Oslo Peace Accords in 1993 until 2001, Israeli settlements doubled in the occupied territories. Under Israel's prime minister Ariel Sharon, some thirty-five new settlements have been established in the occupied territories. In Gaza in 2001, there were 1.2 million Palestinians and 4,000 Israelis, but the Israelis control 40% of the land and 70% of the water. In the West Bank, there were 1.9 million Palestinians and 280,000 Israelis, but the Israelis controlled 37% of the water.

In addition, Israel failed to abide by its commitments under the Oslo Peace Accords to release prisoners, to complete a third redeployment of its military forces, and to transfer three Jerusalem villages to Palestinian control. Moreover, at the Camp David Meeting in 2000, Israel's proposals did not provide for Palestinian control over East Jerusalem upon which 40% of the Palestinian economy depends. Nor did Israel's proposals provide for a right of return or compensation for the half of the Palestinian population that lives in exile, most of them having been driven off their land by Israeli expansion. So the Palestinian cause is arguably a just one, and clearly the Palestinians lack the military resources to effectively resist Israeli occupation and aggression by simply directly attacking Israeli military forces. The Israelis have access to the most advanced U.S. weapons and $4 billion-a-year from the United States to buy whatever weapons they want. The Palestinians have no comparable external support. Under these conditions, is there a moral justification for Palestinian suicide bombers against Israeli civilians? Assuming that the Palestinians lack any effective means to try to end the Israeli occupation or to stop Israel's further expansion into Palestinian territories other than by using suicide bombers against Israeli civilians, why would this use of suicide bombers not be justified in much the same way that Walzer justifies the British terror bombing in the early stages of World War II?

Much depends on what Israel's intentions are. If the Israelis have the ultimate goal of confining most Palestinians to a number of economically nonviable and disconnected reservations, similar to those on which the United States confines American Indian nations, would not the Palestinians have a right to resist that conquest as best they can, even if this involves the use of suicide bombers? Of course, everything here turns on a correct assessment of Israeli intentions and on whether Palestinians (and Israelis) have sufficiently exhausted the use of nonbelligerent correctives. The 2005 political overtures from Sharon might also indicate a new beginning. Only time will tell.

Starting with the just war theory, we have seen that there are morally defensible exceptions to the just means prohibition against directly killing innocents. The cave analogy argument aims to establish that conclusion. British terror bombing at the beginning of World War II, but not the American dropping of atomic bombs on Hiroshima and Nagasaki at the end of that war, seems to provide a real life instantiation of that argument. The Palestinian use of suicide bombers against Israeli civilians may or may not be a contemporary instantiation of that very same argument.

Yet, even if some acts of terrorism can be justified in this manner, clearly, most acts of terrorism cannot be so justified, and clearly, there was no moral justification for the terrorist attacks on New York City and Washington, D.C., particularly the attacks in the World Trade Center. For Americans, no act of terrorism compares with the September 11, 2001 (9/11), morning attacks on the World Trade Center and the Pentagon. Initial estimates put the number of dead from this terrorist attack at more than 5,000, but later the death toll was reduced to around 3,000. Comparisons were made to the Japanese attack on Pearl Harbor in 1941 where 2,403 sailors, soldiers, and civilians died. But the attack on a military outpost far removed from the American heartland is hardly comparable to an attack against targets in its largest city and in its capital. Nor was 9/11 carried out with the weapons of previous adversaries but by commandeering commercial aircraft with knives and box cutters and using them in murderous suicidal missions. So, this terrorism now faced is something new, something different, and, as a consequence, many people around the world feel vulnerable in a way they would have never thought possible before.

Even so, the question remains as to what is the appropriate response to unjustified terrorist acts. According to the just war theory, before using belligerent correctives, one must be sure that nonbelligerent correctives are neither hopeless nor too costly. The three weeks of diplomatic activity that the United States engaged in with the Taliban government of Afghanistan does not appear to have been sufficient to determine whether it was hopeless or too costly to continue to attempt to bring Osama bin Laden before a U.S court, or better, before an international court of law, prior to going to war against Afghanistan. The United States demanded that the Taliban government immediately hand over bin Laden and "all the leaders of Al Qaida who hide in your land" (Bush 2001). But was it reasonable to expect compliance from the Taliban, given that even after the overthrow of the Taliban government and the installation of a more friendly regime, the United States and its allies were still unable several years later to apprehend bin Laden and reduce the frequency of terrorist attacks sponsored by Al Qaida around the world? Was it reasonable for the United States to have expected the Taliban government, with its limited resources and loose control over the country, to have done in three weeks what it was not able to accomplish after several years? Similar and even more telling questions can be raised about the decision to go to war against Iraq as a response to the threat of terrorism.

Terrorism, whether practiced by states, substate groups, or individuals, has a long and varied history. Whereas the practice can be generally condemned, many who condemn it most strongly are themselves engaged in terrorism or support for terrorism. More significantly, in order for responses to terrorism or the threat of terrorism to be morally justified, they must meet the requirements of the just war theory by first exhausting nonbelligerent correctives, and frequently, this is not done.

See also Just War Theory.

Bibliography

Bell, J. Bowyer. *Terror Out of Zion*. New York: St, Martin's Press, 1977.

Bickerton, Ian, and Carla Klausner. *A Concise History of the Arab-Israeli Conflict*. Upper Saddle River, NJ: Prentice Hall, 2002.

Byrnes, James F. *Speaking Frankly*. New York: Harper, 1947.

Crenshaw, Martha, "The Logic of Terrorism." In *Origins of Terrorism: Psychologies, Ideologies, Theologies, States of Mind*. Edited by Walter Reich. New York: Cambridge University Press, 1990.

Henderson, Harry. *Terrorism*. New York: Facts on File, 2001.

Kameel Nasr. *Arab and Israeli Terrorism*. London: McFarland, 1997.

Laquer, Walter. *The Age of Terrorism*. Boston: Little, Brown, 1987.

Malley, Robert, and Hussein Agha, "Camp David: The Tragedy of Errors." *New York Review of Books* 48 (13), 2001.

Nash, Jay Robert. *Terrorism in the 20th Century*. New York: M. Evans, 1998.

Office of the Coordinator for Counterterrorism. *Patterns of Global Terrorism-2000*, 2001.

Rappoport, David. "Religion and Terror: Thugs, Assassins, and Zealots." In *International Terrorism: Characteristics, Causes, Controls*. Edited by Charles Kegley, 147–149. New York: St. Martin's Press, 1990.

Simon, Jeffrey. *The Terrorist Trap*. Bloomington: Indiana University Press, 2001.

Walzer, Michael. *Just and Unjust Wars*, 2nd ed. New York: Basic Books, 1992

James P. Sterba (2005)

TERTULLIAN, QUINTUS SEPTIMIUS FLORENS

(c. 160–c. 220)

Quintus Septimius Florens Tertullian, the African Church Father, was born in Carthage and was converted to Christianity about 193. He made early use of his training in rhetoric and Roman law in two apologetic works, *Ad Nationes* and *Apologeticum*, written in 197. These owe much to earlier Greek Christian apologies and to the writings of Varro, an Augustan polymath who analyzed religion along Stoic lines; *Ad Nationes* seems to have been a first draft of the *Apologeticum*. Tertullian was the first Christian theologian to write in Latin, and most of his works deal with moral and theological issues; all contain elements of polemic either against various aspects of Greco-Roman culture or against Christian heresies. Tertullian's works can be dated by cross-references, allusions to current events, and by his gradual movement toward the ascetic-apocalyptic sect of the Montanists, advocates of the "new prophecy"; he became a Montanist about 206 and later became the leader of a Montanist group in Carthage. Nothing is known of his life after the time of his last literary work, written about 220.

His writings are vigorously, even violently, individualistic in style and often in content; he loved paradox and contradiction, going so far as to claim in *De Carne Christi* (Ch. 5) that the incarnation of Christ "*certum est quia impossibile*" ("is certain because impossible"). This claim seems to be based on a line of argument found in Aristotle's *Rhetoric* (Book 2, Ch. 23, Sec. 22): It is likely that unlikely things should happen. Tertullian's philosophical theology is derived largely from his Greek Christian predecessors (St. Justin Martyr, Tatian, St. Theophilus, Irenaeus); his own contributions are chiefly Stoic in origin. For him philosophy is partly, or sometimes, an enemy of religion ("What does Jerusalem have to do with Athens?"), sometimes an ally ("Seneca is often one of us").

Only two of Tertullian's nonapologetic works are primarily concerned with philosophical themes. One is the early treatise *Adversus Hermogenes*, in which he attacks the doctrine that matter is eternal and claims that Hermogenes derived this belief from Platonic and Stoic sources. His own arguments against the eternity of matter are partly a revision of a lost book by Theophilus, as the common Genesis text indicates. Hermogenes argued that the immutable God cannot have created the world from himself or have begun to create it ex nihilo; therefore he must have made it from matter, to which its imperfections are to be ascribed. God continually "creates," influencing matter as a magnet influences iron. In reply, Tertullian insisted primarily on God's freedom from "necessity." God created by his free will and therefore was not limited by matter.

His other work of philosophical interest is the Montanist treatise *De Anima* (c. 210–213), which is intended to prove that Platonic teaching is false. The soul is actually corporeal and originates from a "soul-producing seed" at the moment of conception. It is not preexistent and does not transmigrate—an argument directed not only against Platonists but also against Christian heretics, chiefly Gnostic. Tertullian also discusses the human embryo and other related topics. His work is largely based on a treatise on the soul by the Greek physician Soranus, who wrote at Rome early in the second century. From Soranus, Tertullian derives most of his discussions of Plato, the Stoics, Aristotle, Heraclitus, and Democritus. Tertullian's importance thus lies in his mediation of earlier conceptions, Christian and pagan alike, and for his translation of Greek ideas into Latin.

See also Apologists; Aristotle; Heraclitus of Ephesus; Leucippus and Democritus; Plato; Platonism and the Platonic Tradition; Stoicism.

Bibliography

TEXTS AND TRANSLATIONS

First modern edition by F. Oehler, 3 vols., Leipzig, 1853–1854; A Reifferscheid et al. (*Corpus Scriptorum Ecclesiasticorum Latinorum* XX, XLVII, LXX. Vienna, 1890–); and E. Dekkers et al. (*Corpus Christianorum*. Series Latina, I–II, Turnhout: Brepols, 1954–).

English translations in *Ante-Nicene Christian Library* VII, XI, XV, XVIII. Edinburgh: T. and T. Clark, 1868–1870.

Castorina, E., ed. *De spectaculis*. Florence, 1961.

Evans, E., ed. *Adversus Praxeam*. London, 1948.

Evans, E., ed. *De carne Christi*. London 1956.

Evans, E., ed. *De resurretione carnis*. London 1960.

Pollmann, K. *Das Carmen adversus Marcionitas: Einleitung, Text, Übersetzung und Kommentar*. Göttingen: Vandenhoeck & Ruprecht, 1991.

Refoulé, R. F. *De praescriptione haereticorum. Sources Chrétiennes* XLVI. Tübingen, 1910; Frankfurt: Minerva, 1968.

Schneider, A., ed. *Ad nations*. Rome, 1968.

Waszink, J. P., ed. *De anima*. Amsterdam, 1947.

STUDIES

Aziza, Claude. *Tertullien et le judaïsme*. Paris: Belles Lettres, 1977.

Barnes, T. D. *Tertullian: A Historical and Literary Study*. Oxford: Clarendon, 1971; rev. ed., 1985.

Braun, R. et al., ed. *Chronica Tertullianea et Cyprianea, 1975–1994: Bibliographie critique de la première littérature latine chrétienne*. Paris, 1999.

Bray, G. *Holiness and the Will of God: Perspectives on the Theology of Tertullian*. London; Atlanta: John Knox Press, 1979.

Dekkers, E. *Tertullianus en de Geschiednis der Liturgie*. Münster, 1947.

Dunn, Geoffrey. *Tertullian*. London: Routledge, 2004.

Fredouille, J. C. *Tertullien et la conversion de la culture antique*. Paris: Études augustiniennes, 1972.

Moingt, J. *Théologie trinitaire de Tertullien*. Théologie 68–70. Paris: Aubier, 1966.

Nisters, B. *Tertullian: Seine Persönlichkeit un sein Schicksal*. Münsterische Beiträge zur Theologie 25 (1950).

O'Malley, T. P. *Tertullian and the Bible*. Latinitas Christianorum Primaeva 21. Utrecht: Dekker & Van de Vegt, 1967.

Osborne, E. F. *Tertullian, First Theologian of the West*. Cambridge, U.K.: Cambridge University Press, 1997.

Questen, J. *Patrology*, II. pp. 246–340. Utrecht: Spectrum Publishers, 1953.

Rankin, D. I. *Tertullian and the Church*. Cambridge, U.K.: Cambridge University Press, U.K., 1995.

Säflund, G. *De Pallio und stilistische Entwicklung Tertullians*. Skrifter utgivna av Svenska Institutet i Rom VIII, Lund: C. W. K. Gleerup, 1955.

Sider, D. *Ancient Rhetoric and the Art of Tertullian*. Oxford: Oxford University Press, 1971.

Vecchiotti, I. *La filosofia di Tertulliano. Un colpo di sonda nella storia del cristianesimo primitivo*. Urbino: Argalìa, 1970.

Robert M. Grant (1967)
Bibliography updated by Scott Carson (2005)

TESTIMONY

The term *testimony* in contemporary analytic philosophy is used as label for the spoken or written word, when this purports to pass on the speaker's or writer's knowledge, conveying factual information or other truth. Testifying, or giving testimony, is a linguistic action, and testimony is its result, an audible speech act of telling or more extended discourse (perhaps recorded), or a legible written text. Interest in the topic has grown rapidly since the publication of C. A. J. Coady's *Testimony: A Philosophical Study* (1992). Testimony in this broad sense includes the central case of one person telling something to another in face-to-face communication, as well as a range of other cases, from public lectures, television and radio broadcasts, and newspapers to personal letters and e-mails, all kinds of purportedly factual books and other publications, and the information recorded in train timetables, birth registers, and official records of many kinds.

PHILOSOPHICAL ISSUES ABOUT TESTIMONY

The key interest of testimony is as a source for individual human knowledge, alongside perception, memory, inference, and intuition. Thus attaining a correct account of its epistemology is the core organizing issue for explanatory philosophical theorizing about testimony. This interlocks with several other issues.

First, there is no believing what one is told, without first understanding it—grasping both content and force of the speech act. And knowledge of what one was told surely rests on knowledge that one was told. Thus an account of testimony needs to be supplemented with an account of linguistic understanding—both its psychology and its epistemology. Understanding in turn cannot be fully explained except as part of the large project of explaining linguistic meaning, the significance of words, which is grasped when a speech act is understood. Second, telling is just one of the many diverse activities that make up the human social institution of language. Why and how it is epistemically justified to believe the purport of a linguistic act of telling turns on the nature of that act. Appreciation of the interpersonal relations involved in linguistic exchange, especially the commitments and norms involved in the making and reception of the speech act of assertion, must inform our account of testimony.

Third, an account of what makes belief acquired from testimony become knowledge will be persuasive only if it instances a convincing general conception of knowledge; and similarly for justified testimonial belief. Fourth, how is testimony best individuated as an epistemic kind? It is clear that the following very broad category is not one about which any interesting generalizations may be made: whatever may, on occasion, be justifiedly inferred by an audience from observing someone assert that *P*. But exactly how narrow the kind is that we should discern as the core case—what we may call knowledge (or justified belief) from testimony—is debatable. In general knowledge from testimony that *P*, there will be knowledge with that same content *P*; but knowledge of an intended message can also be acquired through sarcasm and metaphor, and despite minor linguistic infelicity by the speaker. One may come to know that *P*, where one's knowledge rests essentially on the fact that *S* told one that *P*, but where one's reason for forming belief in what she said is not that one trusts her to know whereof she speaks, but that one has circumstantial evidence that her utterance, though not from knowledge, is nonetheless sure to be true. A speaker, for instance one whose job it is to instruct, may convey empirically well-established facts that she for perverse reasons does not believe. Can others acquire knowledge from her instruction?

These and other problem cases render the precise individuation of our epistemic kind a subtle and debatable matter. Some argue that the core case is confined to when the testifier speaks from her own knowledge, and her audience trusts her to do so, accepting her word for what she tells on that basis. This is argued to be the core case, because in it alone the audience accepts the teller's linguistic act of assertion at face value as what it purports to be, an expression of knowledge. She accepts the warrant to believe on her say-so offered by the teller. But others, considering cases such as those mentioned above, argue for a broader conception, on which it is not necessary that the testifier speak from knowledge in order for one to acquire knowledge from testimony.

THE IDEAL OF EPISTEMIC AUTONOMY VERSUS MODERN RELIANCE ON KNOWLEDGE AT SECONDHAND, FROM TESTIMONY

An individualist strand in Western philosophy castigates belief derived from testimony as epistemically inferior. Plato (in the *Theatetus*) and Augustine (in *De Magistro*) despised its secondhand character and denied that knowledge, as opposed to mere belief, can ever be acquired from it. Rene Descartes (in his *Meditations on First Philosophy*) insisted on building his knowledge afresh from individualist foundations, and John Locke (in his *Essay on the Human Understanding*) rejected "other men's opinions floating in one's brain" as never amounting to knowledge. They were correct that belief derived from testimony is epistemically problematic and arguably inferior in two related respects, entailed by its being knowledge at secondhand.

First, one who forms belief that *P* on trust in another's testimony does not herself possess the evidence for *P*, but instead a second-order warrant. Her own immediate basis for believing *P* is that she trusts her teller to knows whereof she speaks. This entails that the teller, or some other person or group of people upstream of her in a chain of testimony, possesses nontestimonial evidence establishing the truth of *P*. The trusting recipient of testimony is committed to belief in the existence of this evidence, of which she is personally ignorant, and that her informants have evaluated it correctly. Insistence that, for a first-class warrant amounting to knowledge one must possess the evidence for *P* oneself, would rule out all knowledge thus based on trust in the word of others—and hence, in others' honesty and epistemic good judgment.

Second, such trust is epistemically risky. One who testifies that *P* in an act of assertion purports to speak from knowledge. But her own belief may be false: she may have failed to form belief in an epistemically responsible way, or may have been the subject of bad epistemic luck, and may have fallen into honest error. Or she may be insincere, intent on deception. There are many entirely understandable and common human motives for this. Circumstances are many and frequent in which personal advantage may be gained by lying, and it can require altruism or courage to tell the truth in difficult circumstances. These risks incurred in believing what others tell us mean that we should place our trust in the word of others discriminatingly and circumspectly. The epistemically responsible recipient of testimony will be aware of the need for both sincerity and competence about her topic in her source, and her response will be mediated by this.

But the price of maintaining Descartes's ideal of epistemic self-reliance would be infeasibly high, in the condition of extensive division of epistemic labor that characterizes our modern, highly socialized existence. Topics that we know of, for the most part, only from testimony include: all of history, including our own early personal and family history; much of the geography and politics of the contemporary world; nearly all of knowledge in the various specialized domains of human inquiry—the natural and social sciences, humanities, and so forth. In addition, we rely heavily in our daily lives on the fruits of advanced technology, from plumbing and motor mechanics to information technology and dentistry, about which most of us know little. Each one of us would be unimaginably epistemically and practically impoverished without knowledge learned from trust in the testimony of others.

THE TASKS FOR A POSITIVE EPISTEMOLOGY OF TESTIMONY

A more constructive theoretical approach takes the primary task for epistemology to be the following: to explain precisely how and in what circumstances testimony can yield knowledge and justified belief. This task may be subdivided into micro and macro issues. The central case of testimony occurs when one person tells something to another, thereby expressing her knowledge, and the other understands and believes her, taking her word for it. When all goes as it should, knowledge is thereby shared, and by recursion of this mechanism it may be diffused through a community of speakers of a shared language. Our micro question is: How precisely is knowledge spread from teller to audience in this core process? What are the conditions for belief formed in what one is told to be justified, and knowledgeable?

The macro issues are: How pervasive is epistemic dependence on testimony, in the system of empirical belief of each of us? Can this epistemic dependence be eliminated, in principle or in practice? How much of one's belief system would be left, after such pruning? We have already seen that a very great deal of what an individual believes, in our modern society, is learned initially from testimony. This does not entail that these beliefs are still epistemically dependent on testimony, since the believer may later acquire other, independent evidence—for instance, when one sees for oneself a place of which one has previously only read. Support from coherence and inference to the best explanation may sustain a system of belief initially acquired from trust in testimony. But testimony plays a key role in putting in place the framework—of land masses and seas, cities and nations, natural and social history, and so forth, in terms of which we theorize our experiences. Thus the idea of eliminating dependence on testimony is problematic, and it is not clear that we have any beliefs that are entirely free of epistemic dependence on testimony—hence the unlivability of the supposed ideal of epistemic autonomy.

Hume (1777) thought that knowledge could be gained from testimony, but the warrant to believe it came only with empirical evidence of the reliability of testimony as a source. Reid (1764), in contrast, argued that human nature includes two complementary dispositions, to truthfulness and trustfulness, and that this engenders a defeasible a priori warrant to trust others' testimony. Their two views instance what may be called the reductionist versus the anti-reductionist stance regarding our micro question: What is the basis of a hearer's epistemic entitlement to trust what someone tells her? Coady argues against reductionism, in favor of the view that our knowledge from testimony can only be explained by positing an epistemic principle special to testimony. There is an a priori, albeit defeasible, epistemic entitlement to trust any giver of testimony: One may presume true whatever one is told, so long as one is not aware of evidence that defeats one's presupposition of the sincerity and competence of one's informant. Coady advances several arguments for this view. His first main argument is transcendental: We do gain justified belief, and knowledge, from testimony. But it is impossible noncircularly to establish that testimony is generally reliable; therefore (on pain of denying that testimony can yield knowledge) a hearer must be entitled in effect to presume this on no evidence.

His second argument invokes considerations about the interpretation of the language of a community, to argue that the supposition that all reports made in that community are false is incoherent. He suggests that this fact underwrites an epistemic right to trust on no evidence, in the absence of defeaters. Burge (1993) gives another argument for anti-reductionism: Testimony is presumed to come from a rational source, and in the absence of counterevidence, such a source is presumed true. Fricker (in Chakrabarti and Matilal 1994) argues against Coady's transcendental argument, and presses the presumptive case for reductionism, from the epistemic riskiness of trusting others. She argues that epistemic responsibility requires monitoring others for sincerity and competence, and believing what they tell only if there is empirical basis for trusting them.

Further questions include: What is the range of subject matters on which a person may properly defer to the word of another, so that testimony on it may properly be given and accepted? For instance, can one properly accept, even defer to, another's word on moral, or aesthetic matters? Extensive division of epistemic labor characterizes the sciences, and all academic disciplines in which there is a domain of specialized knowledge and inquiry. There are many issues about the nature of trust and epistemic dependence in these specialized epistemic domains. In the sciences, many results depend on collaborative research from large numbers of individuals, members of collaborating research teams. In history, the judicious evaluation of oral and written testimonial sources is methodologically crucial. The status of testimony in formal settings such as legal ones is another area of interest.

See also Augustine, St.; Descartes, René; Epistemology; Hume, David; Inference to the Best Explanation; Intuition; Knowledge and Truth, The Value of; Locke, John; Memory; Perception; Plato; Reid, Thomas.

Bibliography

Adler, Jonathan. *Belief's Own Ethics*. Cambridge, MA: MIT Press, 2002.

Audi, R. *Epistemology: A Contemporary Introduction to the Theory of Knowledge*. London and New York: Routledge, 1998.

Burge, T. "Content Preservation." *Philosophical Review* 102 (1993): 457–488.

Chakrabarti, A., and B. Matilal, eds. *Knowing from Words*. Dordrecht: Kluwer Academic Publishers, 1994.

Coady, C. A. J. *Testimony: A Philosophical Study*. Oxford: Clarendon Press, 1992.

Elgin, Catherine Z. "Take It from Me: The Epistemological Status of Testimony." *Philosophy and Phenomenological Research* 65 (2) (2002): 291–308.

Fricker, E. "Trusting Others in the Sciences: A Priori or Empirical Warrant?" *Studies in History and Philosophy of Science* 33 (2002): 373–383.

Goldman, A. "Experts: Which Ones Should You Trust?" *Philosophy and Phenomenological Research* 63 (1) (2001): 85–110.

Graham, Peter J. "The Reliability of Testimony." *Philosophy and Phenomenological Research* 61 (3) (2000): 695–709.

Hardwig, J. "The Role of Trust in Knowledge." *Journal of Philosophy* 88 (1991): 693–708

Hume, David. *Enquiry concerning Human Understanding* (1777), edited by P. H. Nidditch. Oxford: Clarendon Press, 1975.

Jones, Karen "Second-Hand Moral Knowledge." *Journal of Philosophy* 96 (1999): 55–78.

Lackey, J. "Testimonial Knowledge and Transmission." *Philosophical Quarterly* 49 (1999): 471–490.

Lackey, J., and E. Sosa, eds. *The Epistemology of Testimony*. Oxford, forthcoming.

Reid, Thomas. *An Inquiry into the Human Mind on the Principles of Common Sense* (1764), edited by Derek Brookes. University Park: Pennsylvania State University Press, 1997.

Elizabeth Fricker (1996, 2005)

TETENS, JOHANN NICOLAUS

(1736 or 1738–1807)

Johann Nicolaus Tetens, the German philosopher and psychologist, was born in Tetenbüll, Schleswig, in 1736 or in Tönnig, Schleswig, in 1738, and died in 1807. He studied at the universities of Rostock and Copenhagen and became a *Magister* at Rostock University in 1759. From 1760 until 1765, when he became director of the local Gymnasium, he taught physics at Bützow Academy. He was full professor of philosophy at the University of Kiel from 1776 to 1789, during which period he also carried out an official study of the local hydraulic installations on the North Sea coast. From 1789 until his death he had a brilliant career as a high financial official in Copenhagen.

Tetens was strongly influenced by J. C. Eschenbach, his teacher of philosophy at Rostock. Eschenbach was an eclectic who accepted some Leibnizian and Wolffian tenets but sided with the Pietists against Christian Wolff; nevertheless, he seems to have been influenced more by the Berlin Academy and by John Locke's empiricism than by C. A. Crusius. Tetens likewise was influenced by Locke and, after their publication, by Gottfried Wilhelm Leibniz's *Nouveaux Essais*. Among his contemporaries he was influenced by David Hartley, Abraham Tucker, J. G. Sulzer, Claude-Adrien Helvétius, and Charles Bonnet.

Tetens was one of the first in Germany to discuss David Hume at length. J. H. Lambert's *Architektonik* and Immanuel Kant's *Inaugural Dissertation* later played important roles in the development of Tetens's own views.

Tetens hoped to reform German metaphysics by using the critical approach of the new empirical psychology. He wished to restore metaphysics in a new form that would meet the criticisms based on the skeptical and psychological orientations of the English and French schools, then widely influential in Germany. On the other hand he defended phenomenalism against the adherents of the schools of common sense and of "popular philosophy."

In his first significant work, *Ueber die allgemeine spekulativische Philosophie* (On general speculative philosophy; Bützow and Wismar, 1775; reprinted Berlin, 1913), Tetens discussed the weaknesses of traditional metaphysics and proposed some remedies. He held that to reform metaphysics, the sources and development of metaphysical concepts must be investigated. The means of inquiry was "inner sense," or introspection. He tried to give purely psychological answers to psychophysiological problems on the one hand and to metaphysical problems on the other.

In this spirit, Tetens's major work, *Philosophische Versuche über die menschliche Natur und ihre Entwicklung* (Philosophical essays on human nature and Its development; 2 vols., Leipzig, 1777; reprinted Berlin, 1913), was an extended inquiry into the origin and structure of knowledge. He distinguished three faculties of the human mind: understanding, will, and feeling of pleasures and pains. He stressed the independence of the third faculty from the first two. The three may be reducible to one, but if so, according to Tetens, we cannot know it.

The mind is essentially active. Even sensation implies a reaction of the subject to the thing sensed. There are three fundamental activities of representation: perception, reflection (or abstraction from perceptions), and fiction (or the construction of new ideas out of perceived and abstracted representations).

Relations are established among perceived things by means of "primary original notions of relationships," or "forms"; one such form is causal connection. The three activities of representation together with the forms bring about the "concept of an object." Tetens proposed a rule for deciding whether something exists subjectively or objectively—we attribute a sensation to a thing if the sensation is contained as a part in the entire sensation of the thing.

Tetens distinguished rational knowledge from sensible knowledge by its being general and necessary. Metaphysical first principles are undeniable because they are rooted in the essence of the ego. They are like natural laws to which the intellect is subjected. The intellect—or common sense—and reason are governed by different kinds of laws, and the confusion between the two kinds of laws brings them into conflict.

Tetens discussed with great insight many other extremely complicated problems in metaphysics, ethics, the philosophy of education, and the philosophy of language. His *Philosophische Versuche* exerted a tremendous influence on Kant while he was writing the *Critique of Pure Reason*, and the many similarities between their doctrines are evident. Tetens's doctrines may be compared to Kant's even in their speculative power and importance.

See also Bonnet, Charles; Crusius, Christian August; Empiricism; Hartley, David; Helvétius, Claude-Adrien; Hume, David; Kant, Immanuel; Lambert, Johann Heinrich; Leibniz, Gottfried Wilhelm; Locke, John; Sulzer, Johann Georg; Wolff, Christian.

Bibliography

Brenke, M. *J. N. Tetens' Erkenntnistheorie vom Standpunkte des Kritizismus.* Rostock: Boldt'sche Hofbuchdruckerei, 1901.

Fuchs, Arnold. *J. N. Tetens' pädagogische Anschauungen.* Langensalza, 1918.

Golembski, W. "Die deutsche Aufklärungsphilosophie als Quelle des Transzendentalismus, I, Die Ontologie des J. N. Tetens." *Bulletin International de l'Academie Polonaise des Sciences et des Lettres* (1934): 167–173.

Kuehn, Manfred. "Hume and Tetens." *Hume Studies* 15(2)(1989): 365–375.

Lorsch, J. *Die Lehre vom Gefühl bei Tetens.* Giessen, 1906.

Schinz, M. *Die Moralphilosophie von Tetens.* Leipzig, 1906.

Seidel, Arthur. *Tetens Einfluss auf die kritische Philosophie Kants.* Leipzig, 1932.

Sommer, R. *Grundzüge einer Geschichte des deutschen Psychologie und Aesthetik von Wolff–Baumgarten bis Kant–Schiller*, 260–302. Würzburg, 1892.

Störring, G. *Die Erkenntnistheorie von Tetens.* Leipzig, 1901.

Uebele, W. "Herder und Tetens." *Archiv für Geschichte der Philosophie* 18 (1905): 216–249.

Uebele, W. *J. N. Tetens nach seiner Gesamtentwicklung betrachtet mit besonderer Berücksichtigung des Verhältnisses zu Kant.* Berlin: Reuther and Reichard, 1911.

Giorgio Tonelli (1967)

Bibliography updated by Tamra Frei (2005)

THALES OF MILETUS

(sixth century BCE)

Thales of Miletus is widely depicted in ancient sources as a pioneering rationalist and the founding father of Greek philosophy, science, and mathematics. Famous for ingenuity in many areas, he was also numbered among the seven sages (*Sophoi* or wise men). Evidence for his life and thought is meager and often questionable. Although written work is attested, nothing survives and he probably wrote nothing (Greek script still had limited uses). The earliest extant reports come from the historian Herodotus (c. 484–between 430 and 420 BCE); other evidence derives largely from Aristotle and his younger colleagues, Theophrastus and Eudemus (fourth century BCE). Hence, the reliability of the evidence depends heavily on the accuracy of the information available to them. Their testimony has been challenged by many scholars. But recent studies afford grounds for confidence, in part by tracing how Thales' ideas were transmitted by his intellectual heirs, including his younger compatriots Anaximander and Anaximenes.

Thales is a pivotal figure not unlike Galileo Galilei. Before him come cosmogonic verse (influenced by Near Eastern and Egyptian traditions) and a century of rapid advances in Greek culture, most notably in civic institutions and technology (e.g., building, coinage, and writing). In his wake, empirical inquiry, abstract speculation, and critical debate flower. Although his role in those developments cannot be assessed precisely, it was probably seminal. Early sources tell of travel to Egypt (where Miletus had a major trading depot), regional diplomacy (advocating a federation of Ionian cities to counter aggressive foreign neighbors), and diverse feats of engineering (diverting the course of the Halys River), economics (monopolizing olive presses), and surveying (calculating the height of pyramids and the distance of ships from shore).

Thales' significance for the history of philosophy stems mainly from his insights in three areas: cosmology, astronomy, and geometry. He is best known today for the bold but obscure claim that water is the *archē* (source or basic causal factor) of everything, ostensibly on the grounds that moisture (not water narrowly defined but fluid generally) is both the "seed" (originating source) and "food" (source of growth and sustenance) of all things. What exactly Thales said or meant is unrecoverable. Aristotle, the primary source for these claims, calls him the founder of material explanation: specifying the material constituents responsible for persistence and change. Thales also proposed that the earth floats on water "like wood"; and he attributed earthquakes to the earth's occasional rocking. Related considerations probably included the mobility of water, its exceptional mutability (readily solidifying and vaporizing), and its ubiquity (falling from the sky, emerging from springs, and both surrounding the land and filling its depressions).

Antiquity admired Thales most for his astronomy. Most famous was his alleged prediction of a solar eclipse (securely dated to May 28, 585 BCE) that halted a major foreign battle. The story, which many scholars doubt, appears first in Herodotus, who says only that he forecast the year. But a newly recovered text on papyrus cites the astronomer Aristarchus of Samos (flourished c. 270 BCE) crediting Thales with discovering the cause of solar eclipses by first determining that they occur only at a new moon. Other reports of his stargazing are more credible: charting the periodic rising and setting of prominent stars and star clusters (as in Hesiod's verse, over a century earlier); introduction of a circumpolar constellation (Ursa Minor); and a rough determination of the solstices and equinoxes, which enabled him to correlate the annual cycles of the sun and stars more reliably, thereby improving Greek calendrical schemes. Methodical observation of the horizon was the basis for most of these discoveries, but study of the lunar cycle is also reported.

Several new insights in geometry are ascribed to Thales: the equality of the opposite angles formed by intersecting lines; the equality of the base angles in isosceles triangles; the bisection of circles by their diameters; the congruence of triangles having a side and two angles equal; and the proportionality of similar triangles. The latter two are cited in connection with practical procedures: the former to calculate the distance of ships, the second to calculate the height of pyramids in Egypt. The novelty of his ideas probably lay not in simply enunciating these elementary propositions, nor in their formal proof, but in asserting their universal scope on the basis of ad hoc reasoning or evidence. Other innovative ideas attributed to Thales include the earliest recorded explanation for the Nile's annual flooding (seasonal winds obstruct its flow), a claim that amber and magnets are animate (because they cause motion, though curiously not self-motion), and a claim that all things are full of gods (perhaps because full of water, which exhibits two standard attributes of divinity: it is both deathless and life-giving). Implicit in many of the views attributed to Thales are basic principles of rational inquiry and naturalistic explanation: observation, analysis, abstraction, generalization, and regularity. Provided that some of this evidence is accurate, Thales may reasonably be counted as the first philosopher—well before the word was coined.

See also Anaximander; Anaximenes; Archē; Aristotle; Nomos and Phusis; Pre-Socratic Philosophy; Theophrastus.

Bibliography

TEXTS AND TRANSLATIONS

Diels, Hermann, and Walther Kranz, eds. *Die Fragmente der Vorsokratiker.* 3 vols. 6th ed. Berlin: Weidmann, 1951–1952. The standard (but incomplete) collection of ancient testimony (widely cited as DK or *VS*).

Kirk, Geoffrey S., J. E. Raven, and Malcolm Schofield. *The Presocratic Philosophers.* 2nd ed. New York: Cambridge University Press, 1983. A useful selection of texts with translation and judicious analysis.

STUDIES

Mansfeld, Jaap. "Aristotle and Others on Thales, or The Beginnings of Natural Philosophy." *Mnemosyne* 40 (1987): 109–129. Analyzes Aristotle's testimony.

O'Grady, Patricia F. *Thales of Miletus: The Beginnings of Western Science and Philosophy*. Aldershot, U.K.: Ashgate, 2002. Suggestive but often uncritical discussion.

Panchenko, Dmitri. "Thales and the Origin of Theoretical Reasoning." *Configurations* 3 (1993): 387–414. An incisive case for his philosophical significance.

White, Stephen A. "Thales and the Stars." In *Presocratic Philosophy*, edited by Victor Caston and Daniel W. Graham. Aldershot, U.K.: Ashgate, 2002. A favorable reassessment of evidence for his astronomical study.

Stephen A. White (2005)

THEISM

The central claim of theism is that God exists. According to a standard version of this doctrine, God is omniscient, omnipotent, perfectly good, and the creator of all contingent things. According to more developed versions, God intervenes in the created world in order to answer prayers and perform miracles. Developed versions of theism are often contrasted with deism because deists hold that God created the contingent world but does not subsequently intervene in it.

Various aspects of theism are discussed in the following articles in the Encyclopedia:

> *Agnosticism; Analogy in Theology; Atheism; Common Consent Arguments for the Existence of God; Cosmological Arguments for the Existence of God; Creation and Conservation, Religious Doctrine of; Degrees of Perfection, Argument for the Existence of God; Deism; Epistemology, Religious; Evil, The Problem of; Faith; Fideism; Foreknowledge and Freedom, Theological Problem of; God, Concepts of; Hiddenness of God; Infinity in Theology and Metaphysics; Miracles; Moral Arguments for the Existence of God; Mysticism, Nature and Assessment of; Ontological Argument for the Existence of God; Pantheism; Perfection; Philosophy of Religion; Philosophy of Religion, Problems of; Physicotheology; Popular Arguments for the Existence of God; Providence; Religious Experience; Religious Experience, Argument for the Existence of God; Revelation; Teleological Argument for the Existence of God; Theism, Arguments For and Against.*

THEISM, ARGUMENTS FOR AND AGAINST

Philosophy of religion enjoyed a renaissance in the final third of the twentieth century. Its fruits include important contributions to both natural theology, the enterprise of arguing for theism, and natural atheology, the enterprise of arguing against it. In natural theology philosophers produced new versions of ontological, cosmological, and teleological arguments for the existence of God. In natural atheology problems of evil, which have always been the chief arguments against theism, were much discussed, and philosophers debated proposed solutions to both the logical problem of evil and the evidential problem of evil.

NATURAL THEOLOGY

Building on work by Charles Hartshorne and Norman Malcolm, Alvin Plantinga (1974) formulated a model ontological argument for the existence of God that employs the metaphysics of possible worlds. Let it be stipulated that being unsurpassably great is logically equivalent to being maximally excellent in every possible world and that being maximally excellent entails being omnipotent, omniscient, and morally perfect. The main premise of Plantinga's argument is that there is a possible world in which unsurpassable greatness is exemplified. From these stipulations and this premise he concludes, first, that unsurpassable greatness is exemplified in every possible world and hence in the actual world and, second, that there actually exists a being who is omnipotent, omniscient, and morally perfect and who exists and has these properties in every possible world. The argument is valid in a system of modal logic that can plausibly be claimed to apply correctly to possible worlds. Plantinga reports that he thinks its main premise is true and so considers it a sound argument.

However, he acknowledges that it is not a successful proof of the existence of God. A successful proof would have to draw all its premises from the stock of propositions accepted by almost all sane or rational persons. The main premise of this argument is not of that sort; a rational person could understand it and yet not accept it. In other words, not accepting the argument's main premise is rationally permissible. But Plantinga maintains that accepting that premise is also rationally permissible. Since he regards it as rational to accept the argument's main premise, he holds that the argument shows it to be rational to accept its conclusion. As he sees it, even though his ontological argument does not establish the truth of theism, it does establish the rational permissibility of theistic belief.

According to William L. Rowe (1975), Samuel Clarke has given us the most cogent presentation of the cosmological argument we possess. It has two parts. The first argues for the existence of a necessary being, and the second argues that this being has other divine attributes such as omniscience, omnipotence, and infinite goodness. As Rowe reconstructs it in contemporary terms, the first part of the argument has as its main premise a version of the principle of sufficient reason, according to which every existing thing has a reason for its existence either in the necessity of its own nature or in the causal efficacy of some other beings. It is then argued that not every existing thing has a reason for its existence in the causal efficacy of some other beings. It follows that there exists a being that has a reason for its existence in the necessity of its own nature. Next it is argued that a being that has a reason for its existence in the necessity of its own nature is a logically necessary being. It may then be concluded that there exists a necessary being.

Rowe takes care to ensure that his version of Clarke's argument is deductively valid. What is more, he maintains that the principle of sufficient reason that is its main premise is not known to be false because no one has set forth any convincing argument for its falsity. However, he claims that the argument is not a proof of the existence of a necessary being. As Rowe sees it, an argument is a proof of its conclusion only if its premises are known to be true, and no human knows that the principle of sufficient reason is true. Hence, even if the argument is sound, it is not a proof of its conclusion. Rowe leaves open the possibility that it is reasonable for some people to believe that the argument's premises are true, in which case the argument would show the reasonableness of believing that a necessary being exists. If the second part of the argument made it reasonable to believe that such a necessary being has other divine attributes, then the theist might be entitled to claim that the argument shows the reasonableness of theistic belief. So Rowe invites the theist to explore the possibility that his cosmological argument shows that it is reasonable to believe in God, even though it perhaps fails to show that theism is true.

Richard Swinburne's teleological argument is part of a cumulative case he builds for theism (Swinburne, 1979). Other parts of the case involve arguments from consciousness and morality, from providence, from history and miracles, and from religious experience. Each part of the case is supposed to increase the probability of theism; the case as a whole is supposed to yield the conclusion that, on our total evidence, theism is more probable than not. The existence of order in the universe is supposed to increase significantly the probability of theism, even if it does not by itself render theism more probable than not.

In constructing his teleological argument, Swinburne appeals to general physical considerations rather than specifically biological order. There is a vast uniformity in the powers and liabilities of material objects that underlies the regularities of temporal succession described by the laws of nature. In addition, material objects are made of components of very few fundamental kinds. Either this order is an inexplicable brute fact or it has some explanation. Explanatory alternatives to theism such as the committee of minor deities suggested by David Hume seem to Swinburne less probable than theism, because theism leads us to expect one pattern of order throughout nature, while we would expect different patterns in different parts of the universe if its order were the product of a committee. So the alternatives are that the temporal order of the world has no explanation and that it is produced by God.

It is a consequence of Bayes's theorem that this order increases the probability of theism if and only if it is more probable if God exists than that God does not exist. Swinburne offers two reasons for thinking that the order of the universe is more probable on theism than on its negation. The first is that the order seems improbable in the absence of an explanation and so cries out for explanation in terms of a common source. The second is that there are reasons for God to make an orderly universe: One is that order is a necessary condition of beauty, and there is good reason for God to prefer beauty to ugliness in creating; another is that order is a necessary condition of finite rational agents growing in knowledge and power, and there is some reason for God to make finite creatures with the opportunity to grow in knowledge and power.

The teleological argument plays a limited role in Swinburne's natural theology. Since it is an inductive argument, it does not prove the existence of God. Swinburne does not claim that by itself it shows that theism is more probable than not; nor does he claim that by itself it establishes the rational permissibility of belief in God.

Hence, only modest claims should be made on behalf of these three arguments for theism. Their authors are well aware that they do not prove the existence of God. However, they may show that belief in God is reasonable or contributes to a cumulative case for the rationality of theistic belief.

PROBLEMS OF EVIL

According to J. L. Mackie (1955), the existence of a God who is omniscient, omnipotent, and perfectly good is inconsistent with the existence of evil. If this is correct, we may infer that God does not exist from our knowledge that evil does exist. A solution to this logical problem of evil would be a proof that the existence of God is, after all, consistent with the existence of evil. One way to prove consistency would be to find a proposition that is consistent with the proposition that God exists and that, when conjoined with the proposition that God exists, entails that evil exists. This is the strategy employed in Plantinga's free-will defense against the logical problem of evil (Plantinga, 1974).

The intuitive idea on which the free-will defense rests is simple. Only genuinely free creatures are capable of producing moral good and moral evil. Of course, God could create a world without free creatures in it, but such a world would lack both moral good and moral evil. If God does create a world with free creatures in it, then it is partly up to them and not wholly up to God what balance of moral good and evil the world contains. The gift of creaturely freedom limits the power of an omnipotent God. According to Plantinga, it is possible that every free creature God could have created would produce at least some moral evil. Hence, it is possible that God could not have created a world containing moral good but no moral evil.

Consider the proposition that God could not have created a world containing moral good but no moral evil and yet creates a world containing moral good. The free-will defense claims that this proposition is consistent with the proposition that God is omniscient, omnipotent, and perfectly good. But these two propositions entail that moral evil exists and thus that evil exists. Hence, if the defense's consistency claim is true, the existence of a God who is omniscient, omnipotent, and perfectly good is consistent with the existence of evil. Therefore, the free-will defense is a successful solution of the logical problem of evil if its consistency claim is true. That claim certainly appears to be plausible.

Most philosophers who have studied the matter are prepared to grant that the existence of God is consistent with the existence of evil. The focus of discussion has shifted from the logical to the evidential problem of evil. The evils within our ken are evidence against the existence of God. The question is whether they make theism improbable or render theistic belief unwarranted or irrational.

William L. Rowe (1988) presents the evidential problem of evil in terms of two vivid examples of evil. Bambi is a fawn who is trapped in a forest fire and horribly burned; Bambi dies after several days of intense agony. Sue is a young girl who is raped and beaten by her mother's boyfriend; he then strangles her to death. According to Rowe, no good state of affairs we know of is such that an omnipotent, omniscient being's obtaining it would morally justify that being's permitting the suffering and death of Bambi or Sue. From this premise he infers that no good state of affairs is such that an omnipotent, omniscient being's obtaining it would morally justify that being in permitting the suffering and death of Bambi or Sue. If there were an omnipotent, omniscient, and morally perfect being, there would be some good state of affairs such that the being's obtaining it would morally justify the being's permitting the suffering and death of Bambi or Sue. Hence, it may be concluded that no omnipotent, omniscient, and morally perfect being exists.

The first step in this argument is an inductive inference from a sample, good states of affairs known to us, to a larger population, good states of affairs without qualification. So it is possible that no good state of affairs known to us morally justifies such evils but some good state of affairs unknown to us morally justifies them. But Rowe argues that the inference's premise gives him a reason to accept its conclusion. We are often justified in inferring from the known to the unknown. If I have encountered many pit bulls and all of them are vicious, I have a reason to believe all pit bulls are vicious.

William P. Alston (1991) challenges Rowe's inference. As he sees it, when we justifiably infer from the known to the unknown, we typically have background knowledge to assure us that the known sample is likely to be representative of the wider population. We know, for example, that character traits are often breed-specific in dogs. According to Alston, we have no such knowledge of the population of good states of affairs because we have no way of anticipating what is in the class of good states of affairs unknown to us. He likens Rowe's reasoning to inferring, in 1850, from the fact that no one has yet voyaged to the moon that no one will ever do so.

The disagreement between Rowe and Alston illustrates the lack of a philosophical consensus on a solution to the evidential problem of evil. It is safe to predict continued debate about whether horrible evils such as the suffering and death of Bambi or Sue provide sufficient evidence to show that theistic belief is unjustified or unreasonable.

See also Alston, William P.; Bayes, Bayes' Theorem, Bayesian Approach to Philosophy of Science; Clarke, Samuel; Cosmological Argument for the Existence of God; Evil, The Problem of; Hume, David; Mackie, John Leslie; Malcolm, Norman; Modality, Philosophy and Metaphysics of; Modal Logic; Ontological Argument for the Existence of God; Philosophy of Religion; Plantinga, Alvin; Religious Experience; Teleological Argument for the Existence of God.

Bibliography

Alston, W. P. "The Inductive Argument from Evil and the Human Cognitive Condition." In *Philosophical Perspectives, Vol. 5: Philosophy of Religion,* edited by James E. Tomberlin. Atascadero, CA: Ridgeview, 1991.

Mackie, J. L. "Evil and Omnipotence." *Mind* 64 (1955): 200–212.

Plantinga, A. *The Nature of Necessity.* Oxford: Clarendon Press, 1974.

Rowe, W. L. *The Cosmological Argument.* Princeton, NJ: Princeton University Press, 1975.

Rowe, W. L. "Evil and Theodicy." *Philosophical Topics* 16 (2) (1988): 119–132.

Swinburne, R. *The Existence of God.* Oxford: Clarendon Press, 1979.

Phillip L. Quinn (1996)

THEMISTIUS

(c. 317–c. 385 CE)

Themistius is one of the principal Greek commentators on Aristotle. He was born at Byzantium, the son of a philosopher (Eugenius), and received a traditional education in Greek culture at various locations. In his twenties Themistius established a philosophical school at Constantinople (as Byzantium had by then become), and prepared the paraphrases on several Aristotelian works that represent his main contribution to the ancient philosophical tradition. After about 350 CE he became involved in the political life of the eastern Empire, and served several emperors as an ambassador, administrator, and adviser. This phase of his career is richly documented in his orations, some of which reflect his philosophical interests.

Themistius cannot be easily labeled by his philosophical affiliation. His extant paraphrases of Aristotle's *De anima*, *De caelo*, *Metaphysics* Book 12, *Physics*, and *Posterior Analytics* follow the Aristotelian text closely and are designed to facilitate study. He was clearly influenced by the work of the great Peripatetic commentator Alexander of Aphrodisias. However, at times Themistius reveals some knowledge of the Platonic tradition, notably in his response to Aristotle's account of the intellect in *De anima* Book 3, chapter 5. He is most safely described as a philosophical scholar who absorbed the Platonic tradition without allowing it to dominate his interpretations, as it did in the case of later commentators, notably Simplicius and Philoponus.

Themistius was respected by Aristotelian commentators in later antiquity, in the Arabic, Hebrew, and western medieval Latin tradition, as well as during the Renaissance. Some of his texts are in fact extant only in Arabic. His interpretation of the active intellect was suggestive enough to allow for the notion of the immortality of the individual soul, and, as such, was welcome within the Christian tradition.

See also Aristotle.

Bibliography

Todd, Robert B. "Themistius." *Catalogus Translationum et Commentariorum* 8 (2003): 57–102 (bibliography at 68–72).

Todd, Robert B., trans. *Themistius on Aristotle on the Soul.* Ithaca, NY: Cornell University Press, 1996.

Todd, Robert B., trans. *Themistius on Aristotle Physics 4.* Ithaca, NY: Cornell University Press, 2003.

Vanderspoel, J. *Themistius and the Imperial Court: Oratory, Civic Duty and Paideia from Constantine to Theodosius.* Ann Arbor: University of Michigan Press, 1995.

Robert B. Todd (2005)

THEODICY

See *Evil, The Problem of; Leibniz, Gottfried Wilhelm*

THEODORIC OF CHARTRES

Theodoric of Chartres (or Thierry of Chartres) was a twelfth-century philosopher and younger brother of Bernard of Chartres. He appears first as a master in 1121, when he spoke in support of Peter Abelard at the latter's trial for heresy at Soissons. In the 1130s he was teaching the arts in Paris, and in 1142 he became chancellor at Chartres. He attended the trial of Gilbert of Poitiers at Rheims in 1148 and shortly afterward became a monk. The date of his death is unknown.

Theodoric's rhetorical teaching survives in a commentary on Cicero's *De Inventione.* Three versions of his exposition of Boethius's *De Trinitate* and a fragmentary exposition of Boethius's *De Hebdomadibus* are also extant, as is a commentary on the beginning of the book of Genesis (the *De Sex Dierum Operibus*). In the last-named work Theodoric's Platonizing cosmology and his mathematical bent found their expression. In his *Heptateuch,* a bulky collection of the sources for each of the seven liberal arts, Theodoric revealed his fidelity to the ancients. Grammar was represented by the works of Donatus and Priscian, rhetoric by Cicero, astronomy by Ptolemy; but the place of honor went to Boethius for his writings on music, arithmetic, geometry, and, especially, dialectic. Theodoric reproduced Boethius's translations and commentaries on the whole of Aristotle's *Organon,* with the exception of the *Posterior Analytics.*

Theodoric regarded the arts as the indispensable instrument of philosophy, which consisted of physics, mathematics, and theology. He based his Trinitarian speculation upon arithmetic, applying the Pythagorean-Platonic dialectic of unity-multiplicity to St. Augustine's dictum that the Father is unity, the Son equality, and the Spirit the agreement of unity and equality. Unity can only engender its equality; both are one substance but have different properties and are called persons by the theologians. Theodoric's argument emphasized the unity of the Trinity but made difficult a numerical distinction between the divine persons. The dialectic of unity-multiplicity was perhaps more appropriately used to explain the relationship of the Creator to creation. Unity is God and is immutable and eternal; the principle of multiplicity is the domain of creation. Unity is the *forma essendi* of creatures, their unique and entire being, totally and essentially omnipresent. Things are not pantheistically identified with the One; multiplicity is distinct from, and subordinate to, unity. The divine unity in an ineffable way absorbs the forms of all beings in itself, but only images of these forms are joined to matter. Theodoric's thought here moves close to his brother's theory of native forms.

Although Theodoric stressed the universal causality and omnipresence of the Creator, he presented creation as an ordered system of secondary causes. Matter was created by God from nothing, but the fashioning of the world out of the four elements occurred by the action of the circular motion of heaven and of the diffusion of heat in the underlying elements. The four elements of matter (which Genesis collectively designates by the names of heaven and earth) arranged themselves into four concentric spheres. The heaven of air and fire enveloped the water and Earth and, being supremely light, tended to move by turning about. Fire became ardent and illumined the air and heated the water, vaporizing it to reveal islands on Earth and to incubate life in the water and on land. The mechanistic character of this explanation is supplemented by a recognition of the role of spirit, which fills and animates the world. Through the "seminal reasons" introduced by God into creation, nature is capable of its own continuation after the completion of the work of six days. Theodoric's doctrine of creation represents an adventurous application of the teachings of the Platonic *Timaeus* to the biblical account.

Theodoric was a bold speculator, molded by and helping to mold the Platonic tradition of Latin Christendom. He seems also to have been the first medieval schoolman to have commented on the recently rediscovered *Prior Analytics* and *Sophistic Refutations* of Aristotle. Moreover, it was to him that Hermann of Carinthia sent his translation of Ptolemy's *Planisphere,* just as Bernard of Tours dedicated his *De Mundi Universitate* to Theodoric. Other disciples and admirers included Clarembald of Arras and John of Salisbury and, in the fifteenth century, Nicholas of Cusa.

See also Abelard, Peter; Aristotle; Augustine, St.; Bernard of Chartres; Bernard of Tours; Boethius, Anicius Manlius Severinus; Cicero, Marcus Tullius; Gilbert of Poitiers; John of Salisbury; Matter; Medieval Philosophy; Nicholas of Cusa; Platonism and the Platonic Tradition.

Bibliography

Commentary and text of works by Theodoric are *De Septem Diebus et Sex Operum Distinctionibus,* edited by N. M. Haring, in "The Creation and Creator of the World According to Thierry of Chartres and Clarenbaldus of Arras," in *Archives d'histoire doctrinale et littéraire du moyen âge* 22 (1955): 137–216; and the following additional articles by Haring: "The Lectures of Thierry of Chartres on Boethius' *De Trinitate,*" in *Archives* ... 25 (1958): 113–226; "A Commentary on Boethius' *De Trinitate* by Thierry of Chartres," in *Archives* ... 23 (1956): 257–325; and "Two Commentaries on Boethius (*De Trinitate* and *De Hebdomadibus*) by Thierry of Chartres," in *Archives* ... 27 (1960): 65–136.

Extracts of Theodoric's commentary on Cicero's *De Inventione* were edited by P. Thomas, "Un commentaire du moyen âge sur la rhétorique de Cicéron," in *Mélanges Charles Graux* (Paris, 1884), pp. 41–45; by W. H. D. Suringar, *Historia Critica Scholiastarum Latinorum,* Vol. I (Leiden, 1834), pp. 213–252; and by R. Ellis, "Petronianum," in *Journal of Philology* 9 (1880): 61.

On the above extracts see P. Delhaye, "L'enseignement de la philosophie morale au XIIe siècle," in *Mediaeval Studies* 11 (1949): 77–99, Appendix C, 97–99; and F. Masai, "Extraits du commentaire de Thierry de Chartres au *De Inventione* de Cicéron," in *Scriptorium* 5 (1951): 117–120, 308–309. There is an edition of the prologue to the *Heptateuch* by E. Jeauneau in *Mediaeval Studies* 16 (1954): 171–175; there is a summary of the contents of the prologue in A. Clerval, *Les écoles de Chartres* (Paris, 1895), pp. 220–240.

A biography of Theodoric is A. Vernet, "Une épitaphe inédite de Thierry de Chartres," in *Receuil de travaux offerts à M. Clovis Brunel,* 2 vols. (Paris, 1955), Vol. II, pp. 660–667.

Theodoric's doctrines are discussed in Étienne Gilson, *History of Christian Philosophy in the Middle Ages* (London, 1955), pp. 145–148; J. M. Parent, *La doctrine de la création dans l'école de Chartres* (Paris and Ottawa, 1958), passim; and W. Jansen, *Der Kommentar des Clarenbaldus von Arras zu Boethius "De Trinitate"* (Breslau, 1926), passim.

David Luscombe (1967)

THEOLOGY

See *God, Concepts of; Philosophy of Religion; Philosophy of Religion, History of; Philosophy of Religion, Problems of; Physicotheology; Religion.*

THEOPHRASTUS

(372/1–282/1 BCE)

Born in Eresus on the Aegean island of Lesbos, Theophrastus moved to Athens, studying under Plato briefly and then Aristotle, soon becoming the latter's colleague. In 322/1 BCE he succeeded Aristotle as head of the Lyceum. The picture arising from his extant works is that of a conscientious scholar and researcher, with a marked emphasis on natural philosophy. His place as Aristotle's first successor has for a long time created the impression of a dogmatic and docile pupil, but a comparison with his master is invidious. A more acceptable perspective, established in antiquity (e.g., frag. 72A), is to view his work as trading on the presence of the Aristotelian corpus, while expanding and adjusting even fundamental aspects of the system where required. Exciting recent finds in Arabic and Syriac sources and the new 1992 edition of fragments (edited by Fortenbaugh et al.) have given us a better idea of his learning, independence of thought, and influence (all references to fragments are to 1992). Diogenes Laertius lists some two hundred titles in the Theophrastan corpus (D.L. 5.42–50), and only a fraction of these works survives. Yet what survives is sufficient to reveal him as a clever and productive philosopher and scientist with wide-ranging interests.

LANGUAGE AND LOGIC

Theophrastus made contributions to the theory of the syllogism (e.g., on the relation between the second and third figures), and he revised Aristotle's modal logic, suggesting that the conclusion has the same modality as the weaker premise, not the major premise (a weakest-link principle). He also proposed revising the system of dialectical predication, subsuming the four predicables under definition, perhaps to create "a single universal method" (frag. 124A–B), and he provided us with a definition of the dialectical *topos*" (not found in Aristotle) as an argumentative strategy or principle (frag. 122B). He is said to have introduced a doctrine of hypothetical syllogisms, possibly in collaboration with Eudemus of Rhodes (350–290 BCE). True to his reputation as a good speaker, his comments on language advance grammar and style, and he makes a notable effort to use appropriate language in each field.

PHYSICS AND SCIENCE

Of Theophrastus's work in the sciences, we still have two major works on plant taxonomy (*Enquiry into Plants*) and explanations for plants (*De causis plantarum* [Causes of plants]), famously influential on Carl Linnaeus (1707–1778); nine short tracts on the inanimate (e.g., winds, stones) and physiology (e.g., sweat, dizziness, fatigue); and fragments pertaining to meteorology, biology, epistemology, and psychology.

While maintaining an empiricist outlook, Theophrastus consistently dealt with issues of a fundamental nature (frags. 142–143). He added significantly to the scientific methodology developed by Aristotle. The latter sought to describe a system of argumentation, providing the first attempt at a second-order language of research. This early scientific methodology was a mix of logical principles and rhetorical habits, combining forms of presentation and manipulation with rules of consistency and rigor. Theophrastus also believed in an appropriate method (*oikeios tropos*) for each field of research (*Metaphysics* 9a11).

In line with Peripatetic doctrine, Theophrastus attributed teleological order to nature, "which does nothing in vain" (e.g., *De causis plantarum* 1.1.1, 2.1.1, 4.4.2), though he allowed for exceptions to this general rule (see the next section). Another feature of Theophrastus's approach is his readiness to allow for multiple explanations for physical phenomena (found again in Epicurus in different form), which may signal a growing awareness that a universal theory is unattainable. A correct explanation should give a reason for puzzling facts (*De ventis* [On winds] 59), be coherent (*De odoribus* [On smells] 64), and harmonize with descriptions of the facts (*De causis plantarum* 1.1, 1.21.4). His views thus adumbrate a principle of falsification.

We can reconstruct significant aspects of Theophrastus's epistemology and psychology on the basis of mostly late sources, some going back to his own work *On the Soul*. His empiricist approach is evident in his claims that perception is crucial for knowledge (frags. 301B and 143), and that exceptional clarity (*to enarges*) is a criterion of truth shared by sensation and intellect (frag. 301A). Regarding Aristotle's *On the Soul*, he asked pertinent questions about the process of sensation (e.g., How does the sense organ become like the object? The answer is that the organ receives a universal form). His concerns over Aristotle's notoriously difficult account of intellect (*nous*) (*On the Soul* 3.5) are paraphrased in Themistius (frag. 307A) and the neo-Platonist Priscian (frag. 307B–D). He asked after the nature of intellect in relation to matter (both seem to be "nothing, but potentially all things"), and puzzled over how intellect and object might affect each other.

METAPHYSICS

Theophrastus's extant short tract on metaphysics, now considered to be a complete work, can be seen as a critical evaluation of Aristotle (and others), in particular, on first principles and the unmoved mover. He presented a range of connected problems that he did not always clearly resolve. (This is typical of his *aporetic* [doubt-prone] style, in this case perhaps because *Metaphysics* is an early work or because it is didactic or both.) He also showed himself to be preoccupied with the boundaries of explanation. For instance, he raised questions about what we can assume as fundamental principles and how many there are, and he looked at possible options (one, more than one) and their problems: A universe with one principle cannot be diverse, but a universe with two or more principles might lack coherence. His discussion of what kind of principles he envisages presents two options: Principles are either the ultimate sources of things (a foundationalist position) or else general laws governing everything (in which case, principles are rules of practice). He restricted the number of principles, and the scope of their influence in the physical realm. This allowed him to keep certain accidental occurrences (e.g., thunder, but also evil) outside the range of events with a final cause. Theophrastus's idea of limited teleology and purposiveness (Theophrastus, *Metaphysics* 7a19–b9, 10a21–23) is confirmed in Arabic sources. In his botanical works, however, he tried to accommodate anomalies within the Aristotelian framework (*De causis plantarum* 5). Obviously, Theophrastus's position complicated the Aristotelian position that "nature does nothing in vain."

ETHICS

Our material for Theophrastus's ethical views is rather uneven, ranging from comments on virtue to friendship and natural kinship between animals and humans. Of interest are the excerpts in Porphyry (c. 300 CE), which discuss forms of sacrifice and reasons for vegetarianism (frags. 531, 584). A lost work on friendship was quite influential, and he seems to have come up with new ideas on emotions (frags. 438–448). His collection of character sketches (*Characters*), hugely popular in the eighteenth century, presents psychological profiles in the style of contemporary comedy depicting men with serious character flaws. These profiles perhaps fit into the general framework of Aristotle's ethics. Aristotle's analysis of types (*Nicomachean Ethics* 2) and his doctrine of virtue as a mean or middle between vices help to understand these flaws as concrete examples of Aristotle's more abstract model. Some fragments support such a connection (*Characters*, p. 19). Theophrastus differs from Aristotle at least in focusing on faults and in adopting an anecdotal style of moral instruction.

HISTORY OF PHILOSOPHY (DOXOGRAPHY)

Theophrastus's critical evaluations of earlier philosophers (pre-Socratics, Platonists) are extant in short passages and the treatise *De sensibus* (On sensation), which is believed to be part of a larger work, perhaps his *Physical Opinions* (D.L. 5.48) or his *Reply to Physical Philosophers* (D.L. 5.46, frag. 241A). These comments represent important aspects of his methodology and his influence on the early history of philosophy. Not only do they show a greater awareness of the philosophical enterprise as a continuous discourse by their methodical preservation and assessment of past achievements, but they also illustrate, through his criticisms and convenient organization of materials, the reason for his impact on following ages. Theophrastus's work in this area contributed to the consolidation and preservation of philosophical debates in the Hellenistic schools.

See also Aristotle; Diogenes Laertius; Ethics, History of; Hellenistic Thought; History and Historiography of Philosophy; Logic, History of Metaphysics, History of; Neoplatonism; Peripatetics; Plato; Platonism and the Platonic Tradition; Porphyry; Pre-Socratic Philosophy; Teleology; Themistius; Virtue and Vice.

Bibliography

WORKS BY THEOPHRASTUS

Metaphysics. Translated by W. D. Ross and F. H. Fobes. Oxford, U.K.: Clarendon Press, 1929.

De causis plantarum. 3 vols. Translated by Benedict Einarson and George K. K. Link. Cambridge, MA: Harvard University Press, 1976–1990.

Theophrastus of Eresus: Sources for His Life, Writings, Thought, and Influence. 2 vols, edited and translated by William W. Fortenbaugh, P. M. Huby, R. W. Sharples, and D. Gutas. Leiden, Netherlands: Brill, 1992. Text and translation of sources up to the fourteenth century. References to fragments refer to this work.

Theophrastus of Eresus: Sources on Biology (Texts 328–435). Vol. 5. Commentary by R. W. Sharples. Leiden, Netherlands: Brill, 1995.

Theophrastus of Eresus: Sources on Physics (Texts 137–223). Vol. 3.1. Commentary by R. W. Sharples. Leiden, Netherlands: Brill, 1998.

Theophrastus of Eresus: Sources on Psychology (Texts 265–327). Vol. 4. Commentary by Pamela M. Huby. Leiden, Netherlands: Brill, 1999.

Characters. Translated by Jeffrey Rusten. Together with mimes by Herodas and Sophron and other mime fragments. 3rd ed. Cambridge, MA: Harvard University Press, 2002.

On Sweat; On Dizziness; and On Fatigue, edited by William W. Fortenbaugh, Robert W. Sharples, and Michael G. Sollenberger. Leiden, Netherlands: Brill, 2003.

WORKS ON THEOPHRASTUS

Baltussen, H. *Theophrastus against the Presocratics and Plato: Peripatetic Dialectic in the "De sensibus."* Leiden, Netherlands: Brill, 2000.

Diogenes Laertius. *Lives of Eminent Philosophers*. Bk. 5. Translated by R. D. Hicks. Cambridge, MA: Loeb Classical Library, 1925.

Diogenes Laertius. *The Vita Theophrasti*. Bk 5.36–57, edited by M.G. Sollenberger in *Rutgers Studies in the Classical Humanities* vol. 2, 1985, pp. 1–62.

Fortenbaugh, William W., and Georg Wöhrle, eds. *On the Opuscula of Theophrastus*. Stuttgart, Germany: F. Steiner Verlag, 2002.

Han Baltussen (2005)

THEORIES AND THEORETICAL TERMS

In mathematical logic, a theory is the deductive closure of a set of axioms (that is, the set of all propositions deducible from a set of axioms). In the early- and mid-twentieth century, philosophers of science, under the influence of Bertrand Russell's work in philosophy of language and philosophy of mathematics, attempted rationally to reconstruct scientific knowledge by representing scientific theories with the powerful conceptual tools provided by the theory of formal languages.

THE SYNTACTIC VIEW OF THEORIES

The *syntactic* view of theories (also called the received view) was developed by Rudolf Carnap, Ernest Nagel, Hans Reichenbach, and other logical empiricists. Like David Hume, these philosophers thought that insofar as scientific theories accurately describe the world, they cannot be known a priori, but they also recognized that some elements of our theoretical knowledge seem to be independent of the empirical facts. For example, Isaac Newton's second law states that the force on a body is proportional to the rate of change of its momentum, where the constant of proportionality is the inertial mass. This law cannot be tested in an experiment, because it is part of what gives meaning to the concepts employed to describe the phenomena. Hence, the logical empiricists argued, physical theories can be split into a part that expresses definitions of basic concepts and relations among them, and a part that relates to the world. The former part also includes the purely mathematical axioms of the theory and, trivially, all the logical truths expressible in the language of the theory. This part of the theory is a priori knowledge and concerns matters purely of convention. The factual content of the theory is confined to the latter part, and hence the fundamental empiricist principle that the physical world cannot be known by pure reason is satisfied.

Empiricists argue that meaning must originate in experience, and the logical empiricists used this criterion to criticize speculative metaphysics and to place limits on legitimate scientific theorizing. However, we can have no direct experience of theoretical entities such as neutrinos or theoretical properties such as spin. How can theoretical terms be meaningful? The logical empiricists tried to use logic to show how the theoretical language of science is related to the everyday language used to describe the observable world. They were motivated by the verification principle, according to which a (nontautological) statement is meaningful if and only if it can be verified in the immediacy of experience, and the verifiability theory of meaning, according to which the meaning of particular terms (other than logical constants) is either directly given in experience or consists in how those terms relate to what is directly given in experience.

The idea is that a physical theory will have a canonical formulation satisfying the following conditions:

1. L is a first-order language with identity, and K is a calculus defined for L.

2. The nonlogical terms of L can be partitioned into two disjoint sets, one of which contains the *observation* terms, V_O, and the other of which contains the *theoretical* terms, V_T.

3. There are two sublanguages of L, and corresponding restrictions of K, such that one (L_O) contains no V_T terms and the other (L_T) no V_O terms. These sublanguages together do not exhaust L, of course, since L also contains *mixed sentences.*

4. The observational language L_O is given an *interpretation* in the domain of concrete observable entities, processes, events, and their properties. An interpretation of language L (in the model-theoretic sense used here) attributes a reference to each of the nonlogical terms in L at the metalinguistic level. If the axioms of a theory are true under some interpretation, then that interpretation is a *model* for the theory.

5. The theoretical terms of L are given a *partial interpretation* by means of two kinds of postulates: *theoretical postulates*, which define internal relations among the V_T terms and do not feature V_O terms, and *correspondence rules* or *bridge principles*, which feature mixed sentences and relate the V_T and V_O terms. (These correspondence rules are also known as "dictionaries," "operational definitions," and "coordinative definitions," depending on the author. All these terms designate a set of rules connecting theoretical terms to observable states of affairs.)

The theoretical postulates are the axioms of the theory, and the purely theoretical part of the theory is the deductive closure of these axioms under calculus K. The theory as a whole, TC, is the conjunction of T and C, where T is the conjunction of the theoretical postulates and C is the conjunction of the correspondence rules.

The logical empiricists soon abandoned the attempt to give language L_O an interpretation in terms of immediate experience. It was decided instead that it is just as good to opt for a physicalist language, that is, one that refers only to physical objects, properties, and events (Friedman 1999). Initially, it was required that the theoretical terms of L be given *explicit definitions* (this was Carnap's original goal, but he had abandoned it by the time of his 1936–1937 paper). An example of such a definition of a theoretical term V_T is the following:

$$\forall x(V_T(x) \leftrightarrow [Px \rightarrow Qx]),$$

where P is some preparation of an apparatus (known as a test condition) and Q is some observable response of the apparatus (so P and Q are describable in V_O terms alone). For example, an explicit definition of temperature can be given as follows: Any object x has temperature t if and only if when x is put in contact with a thermometer, it gives a reading of t. If theoretical terms could be so defined, this would show that they are convenient devices, can in principle be eliminated, and need not be regarded as referring to anything in the world (this view is called *semantic instrumentalism*).

It was soon realized that explicit definition of theoretical terms is highly problematic. Perhaps the most serious difficulty is that, according to this definition, if we interpret the conditional in the square brackets as material implication, theoretical terms are trivially applicable when the test conditions do not obtain (because if the antecedent is false, the material conditional is always true). If, in contrast, we interpret the conditional as strict implication, then the theoretical term is applicable only when the test conditions obtain. In other words, either everything never put in contact with a thermometer has temperature t (under material implication), or only those things put in contact with a thermometer are candidates for having temperature t (under strict implication). This is clearly inadequate, since scientists use the language of temperature as if things have a temperature whether anybody chooses to measure it or not.

The natural way to solve this problem is to allow subjunctive assertion in explicit definitions. That is, we define the temperature of object *x* in terms of what would happen if *x* were put in contact with a thermometer. Here temperature is understood as a dispositional property. Unfortunately, this raises further problems. First, unactualized dispositions, such as the fragility of a glass that is never damaged, seem to be unobservable properties, and they give rise to statements whose truth conditions are problematic for empiricists, namely counterfactual conditionals, such as "If the glass had been dropped, it would have broken," where the antecedent is false. Dispositions are also modal, that is, they involve possibility and necessity, and empiricists since Hume have disavowed objective modality. Like laws of nature and causation, dispositions are problematic for empiricists. Second, no one has ever provided explicit definitions for terms like "space-time curvature," "spin," and "electron," whether dispositional or not, and there are no grounds for thinking that they could be.

However, advocates of the syntactic view did not abandon the attempt to anchor theoretical terms to the observable world. This is the point of the correspondence rules that connect the theoretical terms with the observational ones and so ensure their cognitive meaningfulness. They do not define the former in terms of the latter; rather, together with the theoretical postulates, they offer a partial interpretation for them. The correspondence rules are also intended to specify procedures for applying the theory to the phenomena. Theoretical concepts such as those of vital forces and entelechies were criticized by the logical empiricists because their advocates failed to express them in terms of precise, testable laws.

According to the view developed so far, *TC* is fully interpreted only with respect to its V_O terms, which refer to ordinary physical objects (such as ammeters, thermometers, and the like) and their states; the V_T terms are only partially interpreted. The models of *TC* comprise all the possible interpretations of *TC* in which the V_O terms have their normal meanings and under which *TC* is true. The problem for the advocate of the syntactic approach is that there will be many models in general, so there is no unique interpretation for the theory as a whole. Hence, it would seem to make no sense to talk of *TC* being true or false of the world. Hempel (1963) and Carnap (1939) solved this problem by stipulating that *TC* is to be given an intended interpretation; theoretical terms are interpreted as (putatively) referring to the entities, processes, events, and properties appropriate to their normal meanings in scientific (and everyday) use.

Thus, if the meaning of the term "electron," say, derives from the picture of electrons as tiny billiard balls or classical point particles, this picture is important in determining what the theory of electrons refers to. Once the explicit-definition project is abandoned, one must accept that the meanings of theoretical statements lacking testable consequences are nonetheless important in determining the referents of the V_T terms. As Suppe put it, "When I give a semantic interpretation to *TC*, I am doing so relative to the meanings I already attach to the terms in the scientific metalanguage. In asserting *TC* so interpreted, I am committing myself to the meaning of 'electron' and so on, being such that electrons have those observable manifestations specified by *TC*" (1977, p. 92).

This version of the syntactic view is committed to the idea that theoretical terms have excess or surplus meaning over and above the meaning given by the partial interpretation in terms of what can be observed. Herbert Feigl explicitly recognized this in 1950 and was thus led to argue for the view that theoretical terms genuinely refer to unobservable entities (*scientific realism*).

Perhaps the most widespread criticism of the syntactic view is that it relies on the distinction between observational terms and theoretical terms. This distinction is supposed to correspond to a difference in how language works. Observational terms are more or less ostensibly defined and directly refer to observable features of the world, while theoretical terms are indirectly defined and refer to unobservable features of the world. Examples of the former presumably include "red," "pointer," "heavier than"; examples of the latter would include "electron," "charge density," "atom." Putnam (1962/1975) and many others have argued that there is no objective line to be drawn between observational and theoretical language, and that all language depends on theory to a degree. Moreover, eliminating theoretical terms, even if it were possible, would not eliminate talk of the unobservable, because it is possible to talk about the unobservable using V_O terms only, for example, by saying that there are particles that are too small to see. (William Demopoulos has argued that this criticism is irrelevant to the project of offering a rational reconstruction of theories.)

Whether or not the distinction between observational and theoretical terms can be drawn in a nonarbitrary way, the syntactic view also faces criticism concerning the correspondence rules. These rules were supposed to have three functions: (a) to generate (together with the theoretical postulates) a partial interpretation of theoretical terms, (b) to give the theoretical terms cognitive significance by connecting them with what can be observed, (c) to specify how the theory is related to the phenomena. There are several problems concerning (c). First, if the correspondence rules are part of the theory, then whenever a new experimental technique is developed in the domain of the theory and the correspondence rules change to incorporate the new connections between theoretical terms and reality, the theory will change. This is counterintuitive. Another problem, raised by Suppe (1977), is that there are probably an indefinite number of ways of applying a theory, and so there ought to be an indefinite number of correspondence rules, but the formulation of the syntactic view requires that there be only finitely many. Furthermore, theories are often applied to phenomena by means of other theories used to establish a causal connection between the states of affairs described by the theory and the behavior of some measuring apparatus. For example, theories of optics are needed to link the occurrences of line spectra with changes in the energy states of electrons. The correspondence rules in this case will incorporate principles of optics to offer mechanisms and explanations for the behavior of measuring devices. Suppe concludes that correspondence rules are not an integral part of the theory as such but rather are auxiliary assumptions about how the theory is to be applied.

Nancy Cartwright (1983, 1989) and many others have argued that the syntactic view is misleading about how scientific theories are applied, because auxiliary assumptions about background conditions are rarely, if ever, sufficient for deriving concrete experimental predictions from a theory. Rather, these authors argue, the connections between abstract theory and concrete experiment are complex, nondeductive, and involve the use of many theories, models, and assumptions that are not yet part of the original theory.

THE SEMANTIC APPROACH TO SCIENTIFIC THEORIES

According to the semantic or model-theoretic view of theories, theories are better thought of as families of models rather than as partially interpreted axiomatic systems. Theories are "extralinguistic entities which may be described or characterized by a number of different linguistic formulations" (Suppe, p. 221).

To understand the semantic approach, first consider a modification of the syntactic view due to Ernest Nagel (1961) and Mary Hesse (1966). These authors insist that there are always models for a theory, whether true of the world or not. According to Nagel, "An interpretation or model for the abstract calculus … supplies some flesh for the skeletal structure in terms of more or less familiar conceptual or visualizable materials" (p. 90). He is here thinking of models like the billiard-ball model of a gas. This model supplies an iconic representation for the theory of gases (we interpret "gas molecule" as referring to a billiard ball and then picture the gas accordingly). This concrete picture allows the physicist to visualize the system and may also provide heuristic guidance for the future development of the theory. Hesse does not restrict models of theories to those that feature "familiar conceptual or visualizable materials," like the billiard-ball model. She regards mathematical structures specified by the formalism of a theory as a paradigm type of model. Indeed, she goes so far as to say that a model can be "any system, whether buildable, picturable, imaginable, or none of these, which has the characteristic of making a theory predictive" (1966, p. 19). In this she seems right in that many theories of contemporary physics, such as quantum mechanics, do not admit of models consisting of familiar or visualizable materials.

The origins of the semantic approach can be traced to Evert Beth and Patrick Suppes. The latter coined the slogan "[T]he correct tool for philosophy of science is mathematics, not meta-mathematics" (see for example, 1961/1969) and thought of theories as set-theoretic structures. Bas van Fraassen (1980, 1989) further elaborated and generalized Beth's approach: Theories are presented by specifying a class of state spaces with laws of coexistence (synchronic constraints) and laws of succession (diachronic constraints), which together specify the allowable trajectories for systems whose states are represented by parameters located in the state space. Examples of laws of coexistence are Boyle's gas law and the Pauli exclusion principle for energy states of electrons and other fermions; examples of laws of succession include the Schrödinger wave equation in quantum mechanics and Hamilton's equations of motion in classical mechanics.

An advantage claimed for the semantic approach is that it is closer to the practice of science, since scientists do not deduce empirical results directly from theories, but rather use theories in conjunction with models that apply to the system in question. Much of the practice of science concerns the development of new models to extend the domain of application of well-known theories. According to Ron Giere (1988) and Bas van Fraassen (1980, 1989), theories are partly linguistic entities insofar as they include various theoretical hypotheses linking models with systems in the real world, but are nonlinguistic insofar as they essentially involve populations of models. Such models "are the means by which scientists represent the world" (Giere, p. 80). Properly speaking, then, a theory comprises the models it uses and hypotheses that assert a similarity between a real system and some aspects of a model (other aspects are left out because of idealization and approximation).

Giere leaves this relation of similarity unanalyzed. For van Fraassen, the relation between theories and the world is one of isomorphism: "To present a theory is to specify a family of structures, its *models*; and secondly, to specify certain parts of those models (the *empirical substructures*) as candidates for the direct representation of observable phenomena. The structures which can be described in experimental and measurement reports we can call *appearances*: the theory is empirically adequate if it has some model such that all the appearances are isomorphic to empirical substructures of that model" (1980, p. 64). The appearances are the representations of the phenomena, in other words, mathematical models of the data (Suppes 1962).

THE REFERENCE OF THEORETICAL TERMS

Theoretical terms that allegedly refer to unobservable entities cannot be defined ostensively. If the reference of theoretical terms, such as "electron," is fixed by the relevant scientific theory, the sense of such a term fixes its reference (this is called a *descriptivist theory of reference*). Thomas Kuhn (1962) argued that the sense of many scientific terms—terms such as "atom," "electron," "species," and "mass"—has changed considerably during the course of scientific revolutions. If the references of theoretical terms are fixed by the whole of the theories in which they feature, then any change in the latter will result in a change in the former.

In response, Hilary Putnam, in "Explanation and Reference" (1975), advocated a radically different account of the meaning of theoretical terms. He pointed out that most people have no idea how to link many terms with their references but nonetheless successfully refer to particular kinds of things using them. They do so by deferring to experts. For example, most people successfully use the word "platinum" even though lack an explicit definition and have no way to distinguish samples. Only a few experts have detailed criteria.

Putnam advocates a *causal theory of reference* for natural-kind terms. According to this theory, the referent of "water," for example, is whatever causes the experiences that give rise to talk of water. Reference is fixed not by the description associated with a term, but by the cause of the use of the term. This allows for continuity of reference across theory changes. Even though theories about electrons have changed, and hence the meaning of the term "electron" has changed, the term, Putnam argues, has always referred to whatever causes the phenomena that prompted its introduction, such as the conduction of electricity by metals.

THE RAMSEY-SENTENCE APPROACH TO THEORIES

Frank Ramsey argued that the content of a physical theory is captured in its *Ramsey sentence*, the result of taking an axiomatization of the form described above and replacing all the theoretical terms with variables and existentially quantifying over the latter. For example, $\emptyset(O_1, \ldots, O_n; T_1, \ldots, T_m)$ has the Ramsey sentence $\exists t_1, \ldots, \exists t_m \emptyset(O_1, \ldots, O_n; t_1, \ldots, t_m)$. In effect, the Ramsey sentence of a theory is a statement in higher-order logic that says that the theory has a model consistent with a fixed interpretation of the observational terms. Ramsey thus treated theoretical terms as disguised definite descriptions. The Ramsey sentence and the original theory both imply the same observational sentences involving *O*-terms, and hence the factual content of the latter is captured by the former. David Lewis (1970) used Ramsey's method to show how new theoretical terms could be defined in terms of antecedently understood theoretical terms, rather than observational terms.

The Ramsey-sentence approach to theories has been thought to show that scientific knowledge of the unobservable theoretical world is purely structural (Worrall 1989). This raises technical problems discussed in Demopoulos (forthcoming), Demopoulos and Friedman (1985), and Psillos (2000).

See also Philosophy of Science, Problems of; Scientific Realism.

Bibliography

Beth, Evert. "Towards an Up-to-Date Philosophy of the Natural Sciences." *Methodos* 1 (1949): 178–185.

Carnap, Rudolf. *Foundations of Logic and Mathematics.* Chicago; University of Chicago Press, 1939.

Carnap, Rudolf. "Testability and Meaning." *Philosophy of Science* 3 (1936): 419–471; 4 (1937): 1–40.

Cartwright, Nancy. *How the Laws of Physics Lie.* Oxford, U.K.: Oxford University Press, 1983.

Cartwright, Nancy. *Nature's Capacities and Their Measurement.* Oxford, U.K.: Oxford University Press, 1989.

Demopoulos, William. "Carnap's Philosophy of Science." In *The Cambridge Companion to Carnap*, edited by R. Creath and Michael Friedman. Cambridge, U.K.: Cambridge University Press, forthcoming.

Demopoulos, William, and Michael Friedman. "Critical Notice: Bertrand Russell's *The Analysis of Matter: Its Historical Context and Contemporary Interest*." *Philosophy of Science* 52 (1985): 621–639.

Feigl, Herbert. "Existential Hypotheses: Realistic versus Phenomenalistic Interpretations." *Philosophy of Science* 17 (1950): 35–62.

Friedman, Michael. *Reconsidering Logical Positivism*. Cambridge, U.K.: Cambridge University Press, 1999.

Giere, Ronald N. *Explaining Science*. Chicago: University of Chicago Press, 1988.

Hempel, Carl. "Implications of Carnap's Work for Philosophy of Science." In *The Philosophy of Rudolf Carnap*, edited by Paul Schilpp. LaSalle, IL: Open Court, 1963.

Hesse, Mary. *Models and Analogies in Science*. Oxford, U.K.: Oxford University Press, 1966.

Kuhn, Thomas. *The Structure of Scientific Revolutions*. Chicago: University of Chicago Press, 1962.

Lewis, David. "How to Define Theoretical Terms." *Journal of Philosophy* 67 (1970): 427–446.

Nagel, Ernest. *The Structure of Science*. New York: Harcourt, Brace, and World, 1961.

Psillos, Stathis. "Carnap, the Ramsey-Sentence, and Realistic Empiricism." *Erkenntnis* 52 (2000): 253–279.

Putnam, Hilary. "Explanation and Reference." In his *Mind, Language, and Reality*. Vol. 2 of *Philosophical Papers*. Cambridge, U.K.: Cambridge University Press, 1975.

Putnam, Hilary. "What Theories Are Not" (1962). In his *Mathematics, Matter, and Method*. Vol. 1 of *Philosophical Papers*. Cambridge, U.K.: Cambridge University Press, 1975.

Ramsey, Frank Plumpton. "Theories" (1929). In his *Foundations of Mathematics and Other Logical Essays*, edited by R. B. Braithwaite, 212–236. Paterson, NJ: Littlefield and Adams, 1960.

Suppe, Frederick, ed. *The Structure of Scientific Theories*. 2nd ed. Urbana: University of Illinois Press, 1977.

Suppes, Patrick. "A Comparison of the Meaning and Use of Models in Mathematics and the Empirical Sciences" (1961). In his *Studies in the Methodology and Foundations of Science*, 10–23. Dordrecht, Netherlands: Reidel, 1969.

Suppes, Patrick. "Models of Data." In *Logic, Methodology, and the Philosophy of Science*, edited by Ernest Nagel, Patrick Suppes, and Alfred Tarski, 252–267. Stanford, CA: Stanford University Press, 1962.

Van Fraassen, Bas C. *Laws and Symmetry*. Oxford, U.K.: Oxford University Press, 1989.

Van Fraassen, Bas C. *The Scientific Image*. Oxford, U.K.: Oxford University Press, 1980.

Worrall, John. "Structural Realism: The Best of Both Worlds?" *Dialectica* 43 (1989): 99–124.

James Ladyman (2005)

THEORIES OF TYPES

See *Russell, Bertrand Arthur William (section on logic and mathematics); Type Theory*

THEOSOPHY

See *Steiner, Rudolf; Swedenborg, Emanuel*

THINKING

"Thinking" is an essentially human activity occurring in two basic forms. We may think in order to attain knowledge of what is, must, or may be the case; we also may think with a view to making up our mind about what we will or will not do. Following Aristotle, these two forms of thought may be called, respectively, contemplation and deliberation. Both forms may be carried on well or badly, successfully or unsuccessfully, intelligently or stupidly. When contemplation is successful, it terminates in a conclusion; successful deliberation terminates in a decision or resolution. Again following Aristotle, the form of reasoning involved in contemplation may be called theoretical, and the form involved in deliberation may be called practical. Obviously, our day-by-day reasoning in ordinary life is an untidy mixture of both these basic forms.

Less generally, thinking is commonly understood as a largely covert activity, something done mainly *in foro interno*. This activity is also conceived of as intentional in Franz Brentano's sense of "being directed towards an object." For whether we are trying to solve a logical puzzle or are in the process of making up our minds about what to say to a noisy, officious neighbor, we are thinking about something or other. This object (or subject) of our thinking may be either abstract or concrete. We may think about courage, justice, or humanity just as easily as we think about our neighbors and friends, our flowers and the evening sunset. In thinking about these various objects, whether abstract or concrete, we are also necessarily thinking something about them. We think of them as having various features, as doing something or other, or as being related in this or that way to other things of various sorts. For convenience, we may express the last fact about thinking by saying that our specific thoughts have contents as well as objects. We may think that the rain is welcome, that Mary is enchanting, that debts ought to be paid, or that triangularity entails trilaterality.

Another distinctive feature of particular thoughts is that the language used to describe them is nonextensional in a rich sense that is commonly called intentional. As Roderick Chisholm has pointed out, this type of discourse has three distinguishing marks. For one thing, some sentences used to describe thoughts or to ascribe them to thinkers may contain a substantive expression (a name or description) in such a way that neither the sentence nor its negation implies either the existence or the nonexistence of that thing to which the substantive expression truly applies. An example of such a sentence, which illustrates that one may think about nonexisting objects, is "Tommy is thinking about Santa Claus."

Second, a noncompound sentence about thinking may contain a prepositional clause in such a way that neither the sentence nor its negation implies either the truth or the falsity of the propositional clause. An example of such a sentence, emphasizing that one may think what is false, is "It occurred to Jones that demons cause schizophrenia." Finally, a sentence like "Mary thought that the author of *Waverley* wrote *Ivanhoe*" has the peculiarity that although Walter Scott is the author of *Waverley*, one cannot infer that Mary thought that Scott wrote *Ivanhoe*. This last mark of intentionality implies that although things or events have many names and may be described in many different ways, the fact that a person thinks of them in connection with one name or description does not imply that he thinks of them in connection with some other name or description.

From these few remarks about the nonextensional character of discourse about thoughts, several important conclusions about the nature of thinking may immediately be drawn. First, of all the logically equivalent linguistic forms that may be used to describe either the object or the content of a person's thought, only one such form is in most cases strictly applicable. This suggests that thinking something about a particular subject generally involves conceiving of the subject under a certain name or description and attributing something to the subject according to a fairly specific form of attribution. To the extent that the name or description and the attribution are expressible in certain specific words, it will not, in general, be true that an expression or description of the thought in some other words will be equally accurate. The force of this point may be put by saying that at least some thoughts are essentially conceptual, tied to a particular mode of conceiving of a thing or attribute, and felicitously expressed only in specific verbal forms.

Another consequence of these considerations is that certain thoughts have a particular logical form. This emerges not only from the fact that in most thoughts a subject (or object) is in some way characterized, so that the thinking may involve the idea of, schematically, *S*'s being *M*, but also from the possibility that certain logical forms may be involved in a thought while equivalent forms are not. Thus, from "Jones thought that it will rain or snow," it does not follow that Jones thought that it will not both not rain and not snow, even though what is thought in these two cases is logically equivalent by virtue of De Morgan's laws. (One reason that this implication does not hold is that Jones may never have heard of these laws.)

Taking all of what has been said about particular thoughts into account, it appears that as ordinarily conceived, the thoughts involved in both contemplation and deliberation have the following basic features. First, they are characteristically, but perhaps not necessarily, carried on *in foro interno*. Second, they are directed toward an object or a number of objects, and they either attribute something to, or deny something about, this object or objects. Third, the language used to describe them is nonextensional in the sense of possessing at least one of the three intentional marks mentioned above. Fourth, thoughts are often conceived in relation to, and are felicitously expressible by, specific verbal forms; that is, they are often essentially linguistic or conceptual. Finally, particular thoughts have some kind of logical form; they may be categorical, hypothetical, disjunctive, universal, particular, and the like. In general, it may be said that the philosophical task of analyzing the concept of thinking must yield an explanation of exactly what sort of activity thinking is and of how and to what extent it can possess the features just mentioned.

TRADITIONAL THEORIES

A survey of the full range of views on thinking that have been influential in the history of philosophy would reveal, roughly speaking, that most important theories of thinking have been variants of one or more of the following basic views: Platonism, Aristotelianism, conceptualism, imagism, psychological nominalism, and behaviorism. A brief description and criticism of these may thus serve as a useful introduction to the philosophical theory of thinking.

According to the Platonist, thinking is either a dialogue in the soul involving mental words that refer to Forms (such as Redness, Triangularity, Flying) and, possibly, to individuals (such as Socrates) or a spiritual activity of inspecting or recollecting Forms and discerning their natures and interrelations. According to Aristotelianism, thinking is an act of the intellect in which a thing's essence, or intelligible form, actually qualifies the intellect; to think about humanity is for one's intellect to be informed by—literally, to share—the essence humanity. To the extent that one thinks something about humanity—for instance, that it involves animality—one's intellect is also informed by this other essence, the latter being perhaps part of the former.

For conceptualists (the rationalists, for example, and Immanuel Kant) thinking is an activity of bringing concepts or ideas before the mind, these being either innate and applicable to the world in virtue of God's grace (René Descartes, Gottfried Wilhelm Leibniz) or else formed by abstraction from sense experiences and thus actually sharing the abstract features of those experiences (John Locke and, for empirical concepts only, Kant). For imagists (George Berkeley, David Hume) thinking is basically a sequence of episodes involving images; these images are tied to certain "habits," which are the inveterate tendencies of the mind to move from one image to another. To think about triangularity, according to this view, is to imagine some particular triangle while disposed to pass on to other images "of the same sort."

According to the psychological nominalist (such as Thomas Hobbes when he speaks of reasoning) thinking is literally a dialogue in the soul (or, better, in the head) involving the use of verbal images, or mental words, which denote things or classes of things. In this view a complete thought is a mental utterance of a sentence, such as "Tom is tall." Finally, according to behaviorism, thinking is either thoughtful overt speech—thoughtful in the sense that it is in accordance with various principles of relevance, evidence, or inference that the agent is prepared to cite in explanation of his behavior—or a changing series of dispositions to behave intelligently that the agent can at any time avow.

SOME BASIC DIFFICULTIES. One perennial problem peculiar to the Platonic approach is that of accounting for one's ability to learn about the Forms and thus of learning to think. The trouble is that Forms are conceived of as independent of the changing world in which we live, and Plato's suggestion (in the *Phaedo*) that man was born with an ability to "recollect" the Forms experienced in another life is scarcely acceptable to a contemporary thinker. Also, since Forms are conceived of as distinct from the common domain of sense experience, there is a profound difficulty about how to justify knowledge of the Forms. Plato had argued in the *Theaetetus* that true knowledge "can give an account of itself," but it seems that a satisfactory answer has not been given to the question of how agreement in argument or a man's ability to answer objections brought against his view shows knowledge of an independent world of Forms. This problem has been posed more recently, for instance by W. V. Quine, as a demand that the Platonist provide clear, objective criteria for the identity of such strange otherworldly entities as propositions and attributes.

A basic problem for the Aristotelian is to account for the logical form of a thought—that is, for the fact that one may think "If *p* were the case, *q* would be the case" or even "It will either rain or snow." The reason for difficulty here is that there are no intelligible forms corresponding to subjunctive conditionality, to disjunction, or, indeed, to any other logical relation, and it is by no means clear how the intelligible essences that do inform the intellect can be joined to constitute a thought about something conditional or disjunctive. Also, since all general ideas are presumably to be extracted from the sensible forms of experienced objects, thought about what is unobservable, like electrons and negative charges, seems to be impossible as well.

Apart from their highly questionable theories of intelligible essences, one basic drawback common to the Platonic and the Aristotelian views of thinking is their difficulty in accounting for a man's ability to think about particular, nonabstract objects. In the *Sophist*, Plato does, it is true, suggest that some of the mental words of a soul's dialogue may refer to particulars such as Socrates, but his general position is that the objects of thought must be unchanging, intelligible objects, which are universal rather than particular. In arguing that the individuality of a thing is determined by its matter, which is essentially a potentiality rather than an actuality, Aristotle was committed to a similar view, although his medieval heirs argued that particulars could be thoroughly conceived of if, like angels and gods, they constituted the only possible members of a species.

John Duns Scotus, philosophizing as a modified Aristotelian, attempted to get around this difficulty by arguing that particulars are merely congeries of universals. This view, although common in the objective idealism of the nineteenth century, faces a serious problem of distinguishing actual from merely possible particulars or, as Leibniz would have expressed it, of distinguishing a world containing a certain actual particular from a merely possible world containing a "compossible" particular. This Leibnizian type of objection tends to be expressed today by saying that the language used to characterize actual, as opposed to merely possible or fictional, particulars is essentially token reflexive, involving an implicit reference to the speaker: adequate identification of a particular concrete thing cannot be given wholly in context-independent general terms (see Stuart Hampshire and P. F. Strawson).

A difficulty common to conceptualism and Aristotelianism is that in most of their forms they involve an untenable theory of concept formation—namely, abstractionism. As Peter Geach pointed out, this theory fails even for the favorite examples of the abstractionist since one cannot abstract the concept of color from an experience of scarlet, the latter not being redness plus a differentia. Conceptualists also share with Aristotelians the difficulty already noted of giving an adequate account of the logical form of various thoughts. Kant, a conceptualist, went further than most in the attempt, but he was forced to bring in a priori categories and to insist that men are born with an innate ability to think according to such patterns as "All … are …" and "Either … or …." His approach in this regard was unsatisfactory not only because it is out of line with the well-attested fact that one must *learn* to think according to certain patterns but also because there are no special patterns in accordance with which all men *must* think. (On the last point see B. J. Whorf.)

Imagism shares with Aristotelianism and conceptualism the difficulty of accounting for the logical forms of thought, but it faces the added difficulty of explaining our ability to think of things never perceived, like infinity and million-sided polygons. Although psychological nominalism escapes these difficulties with ease, it runs headlong into the objection that we do not constantly mutter words to ourselves throughout every thinking moment. This objection is not meant to imply that we never think in words; its point is, rather, that we do not always do so and that it is not essential to our thinking one thing rather than another that we experience some verbal imagery. The final alternative, behaviorism, is simply Procrustean as a theory of thinking, for it ignores the plain fact that we do commonly think to ourselves *in foro interno*. As a result of this failure, the behaviorist is unable to account satisfactorily for the changes in behavior and behavioral dispositions that are frequently brought about by our silent deliberation and contemplation.

MERITS OF TRADITIONAL THEORIES. Although each theory just discussed has serious drawbacks and can therefore be said to fail in some measure or other, each nevertheless has some hold on the truth. Thus, the Platonist's idea that thinking is a kind of dialogue in the soul is not entirely empty, for while all thinking is not inner speech pure and simple, it is still true that it is generally like inner speech in crucial respects and that it is felicitously expressed in verbal discourse. The implication that thinking may be carried out *in foro interno* and yet not be mere inner speech is also shared by conceptualism and imagism. The latter has the added advantage of accounting for the occasional utility of imagistic thinking, as in pondering the location of a town on a map, the kind of angle formed by certain intersecting lines, and so on (see H. H. Price). Psychological nominalism actually accounts for most features of conceptual thinking except for the possibility of its occurring without verbal imagery. The forms of thought are explained by reference to the forms of the sentences used in inner speech, the object and content of a thought are explained with reference to the words used, and so on.

Behaviorism, finally, although not without its shortcomings, does have the advantage of accounting for the important fact that some episodes of thinking, such as resolves and decisions, essentially involve behavioral dispositions: If a man is not moved, or disposed, to do *A* when he believes he is in circumstances *C*, he is not, *ceteris paribus*, resolved or decided to do *A* in *C*. The crucial importance of this tie-up between certain forms of thought and behavioral dispositions is that it shows how an explanation of behavior in terms of reasons (rather than causes) can be acceptable. Without this tie-up we would have to say that a man's reasons for acting are strictly irrelevant to the question of why he so acted, for the intellect could not then "move a man to act."

TOWARD AN ADEQUATE ACCOUNT

A useful way of working out an account of thinking free from the drawbacks of traditional theories is to examine Gilbert Ryle's influential critique of all theories that insist that thinking must be done *in foro interno*. According to his argument in *The Concept of Mind*, all such theories are based on the mistaken idea that nonhabitual, intelligent human behavior is always guided by silent thought, whose presence explains why the behavior occurs and why it is intelligent. In Ryle's opinion this persistent idea is plainly untenable and leads to a vicious regress. This regress occurs because thinking is itself an activity that is admittedly done well or badly, intelligently or stupidly. This being so, the idea in point would imply that the intelligent character of thinking requires explanation by further thinking, which in turn guides the first thinking and explains why it occurs, why it is intelligent, and the like. Since this further thinking will itself be done well or badly, intelligently or stupidly, it will also require explanation by a third line of thinking and so on without end.

In rejecting this traditional idea, Ryle argues that reference to interior and anterior acts of thinking is not in any way needed for the explanation of most intelligent behavior. In his view a form of behavior, especially verbal behavior, may be regarded as intelligent, thoughtful, or even rational if it is done in accordance with certain principles of inference, evidence, relevance, and so on. That the behavior is in accordance with these principles does not mean that they are rehearsed in thought while the behavior is being carried out. On the contrary, it means only that the behavior conforms to, or is in line with, these principles and that the agent is disposed to cite or at least to allude to them if called upon to explain his behavior. Thus, if a man calculates out loud, then—assuming that this calculation is done in accordance with principles in the above sense—there is no need to introduce any further thought episodes to account for the fact that he arrives at a certain conclusion or resolution; the steps that led him to the conclusion or resolution are already laid bare. If the calculation shows intelligence or ingenuity, it does so by virtue of the relations between the overt steps; going from a premise to a conclusion is not proved reasonable or unreasonable, rational or irrational, by reference to something other than the premise and the conclusion. When we have the premise and the conclusion, we have all we need to decide whether the inference was reasonable. Even if we were to allude to interior steps of reasoning in order to explain a man's actions, we would have to appraise those steps in light of the same principles. Therefore, it may, in fact, be said that purely overt calculation or deliberation is itself a process of thinking and that thinking is not something that is necessarily done silently in the soul. In other words, overt thinking is just as useful a mode of thinking as any other, and there is no need, even no point, in always hunting for hidden acts of thought.

CRITICISM OF RYLE'S APPROACH. Although there is considerable plausibility to Ryle's approach, it must be granted that not all the calculation or deliberation that accounts for a man's actions is done out loud or on paper. In fact, nothing is more obvious than the fact that a good share of one's calculation is not done overtly and that reference to silent thought is constantly and legitimately made in order to account for activities that would otherwise remain inexplicable. Thus, a man may make a move in chess after sitting in silent anguish for long minutes at the board; and the intelligence of this move will remain a stubborn question mark until, perhaps after the game, he outlines the strategy behind it. The same is true in countless other cases. On being asked a question, the mathematics student may close his eyes for a minute before giving the answer, and when the answer is given, he can usually follow it with a proof, a line of reasoning he will claim to recall having thought out *in foro interno*.

Ryle was, of course, aware of these cases in *The Concept of Mind*, and he attempted to account for them by arguing that a man can learn to mutter to himself as well as mutter out loud. Thus, when pressed, Ryle could not entirely dispense with the traditional conception of covert thinking; in regarding it as "inner speech" he was, in fact, squarely in the tradition of Hobbes, and his view is thus subject to the same fundamental difficulty—namely, that to most it seems plainly false that inner speech occurs whenever one can correctly be said to think *in foro interno*.

THE ANALOGY THEORY

Although Ryle's view of thinking does not, as a whole, succeed, in the opinion of the present writer it does come close to the truth. For while silent thought need not be inner speech, it may still be an activity that is at least formally analogous to speech. In what sense "formally analogous"? In the sense in which chess played with pennies and nickels is formally analogous to chess played with standard pieces or in which the Frenchman's "Il pleut" is formally analogous to the Englishman's "It is raining": the same basic moves are made, but the empirical features of the activities are different. Thus, while the thought p is empirically different from the act of saying that p (in that the former need not even involve verbal imagery), it may still be regarded as formally the same: Both are activities that conform to the same principles and have many of the same implications. This sort of formal identity among empirically different activities is, of course, hard to state clearly, but at least an intuitive sense of what is meant by speaking of such an identity can be conveyed by the following analogy. Saying that p is a formal analogue of thinking that p in the way that playing "Texas chess" (with automobiles on certain counties) is a formal analogue of playing ordinary chess (with ivory pieces on checkered boards). What is essential in both cases is that formally analogous activities are carried on in accordance with the same basic principles—the principles or rules of chess, on one hand, and various principles of inference and relevance, on the other.

This theory of thinking, which may be called the analogy theory, does more than merely correct the shortcomings of Ryle's view. It also seems to account for all of the distinctive features of conceptual thinking that were mentioned earlier. Since it also appears to possess none of the drawbacks of traditional theories, it is perhaps the most satisfactory account of thinking yet developed by philosophers.

See also Being; Empiricism; Intention; Universals, A Historical Survey.

Bibliography

CONTEMPORARY DISCUSSIONS

Alston, William P. "The Role of Reason in the Regulation of Belief." In *Rationality in the Calvinian Tradition*, edited by N. Wolterstorff et al. Lanham, MD: University Press of America, 1983.

Bealer, George. "A Theory of Concepts and Concept Possession." *Proceedings of the Tenth Annual SOFIA Conference*, edited by Enrique Villanueva. Atascadero, CA: Ridgeview Press.

Bergmann, Gustav. "Intentionality." In *Meaning and Existence*. Madison: University of Wisconsin Press, 1960.

Chisholm, Roderick. "Sentences about Believing." *PAS* 56 (1955–1956): 125–148.

Chisholm, Roderick, and Wilfrid Sellars. "Intentionality and the Mental." In *Minnesota Studies in the Philosophy of Science*, Vol. II, edited by Herbert Feigl and Grover Maxwell. Minneapolis: University of Minnesota Press, 1958.

Davidson, Donald. "What Thought Requires." In *The Foundations of Cognitive Science*, edited by Joao Branquinho. Oxford: Clarendon Press, 2001.

Gibbard, Allan. "Thoughts and Norms." *Nous Supplement* 13 (2003): 83–98.

Ginnane, W. J. "Thoughts." *Mind* 49 (1960): 372–390.

Hampshire, Stuart. *Thought and Action*. London: Chatto and Windus, 1959.

Harman, Gilbert. *Change in View: Principle of Reasoning*. Cambridge, MA: MIT Press, 1986.

Harman, Gilbert. *Thought*. Princeton, NJ: Princeton University Press, 1973.

Jeffrey, Richard. *The Logic of Decision*. 2nd ed. Chicago: University of Chicago Press, 1983.

Kenny, Anthony. *Action, Emotion, and Will*. London: Routledge and Kegan Paul, 1963.

Lehrer, Keith. *Metamind*. Oxford: Clarendon Press, 1990.

Price, H. H. *Thinking and Experience*. 2nd ed. London: Hutchinson, 1969. An extremely valuable discussion of traditional theories of thinking.

Quine, W. V. *Word and Object*. Cambridge, MA: MIT Press, 1960.

Ryle, Gilbert. *The Concept of Mind*. London: Hutchinson, 1949.

Skyrms, Brian. *The Dynamics of Rational Deliberation*. Cambridge, MA: Harvard University Press, 1990.

Stalnaker, Robert C. *Inquiry*. Cambridge, MA: MIT Press, 1984.

Stein, Edward. *Without Good Reason: The Rationality Debate in Philosophy and Cognitive Science*. Oxford: Oxford University Press, 1996.

Strawson, P. F. *Individuals*. London: Methuen, 1959.

Whorf, B. J. *Language, Thought, and Reality*. Cambridge, MA: Technology Press of Massachusetts Institute of Technology, 1956.

TRADITIONAL THEORIES

Detailed information on traditional theories may be found in F. C. Copleston, *A History of Philosophy*. 7 vols. (New York, 1959). Specific reference may be made, however, to the following classics, which are published in numerous editions: Aristotle, *De Anima* and *Nicomachean Ethics*, Book 5; George Berkeley, *Principles of Human Knowledge*, introduction; René Descartes, *Meditations* and *Principles of Philosophy*; Thomas Hobbes, *Leviathan*, Part I, Ch. 5, and *Elements of Philosophy*, Chs. 2–3; David Hume, *Enquiry concerning Human Understanding*, Secs. 2–4, and *Treatise of Human Nature*, Secs. 1–4; Immanuel Kant, *Critique of Pure Reason* and *Critique of Practical Reason*; G. W. Leibniz, *Leibniz Selections*, edited by P. P. Wiener (New York, 1951); John Locke, *Essay concerning Human Understanding*, Book II, Chs. 1, 2, 7, 8; Plato, *Phaedo, Republic, Sophist*, and *Theaetetus*.

PSYCHOLOGICAL STUDIES

Bartlett, F. C. *Thinking*. London: Allen and Unwin, 1953.

Bruner, J. S., J. J. Goodnow, and G. A. Austin. *A Study of Thinking*. New York: Wiley, 1956.

THE ANALOGY THEORY

Aune, Bruce. *Knowledge, Mind, and Nature: An Introduction to Theory of Knowledge and the Philosophy of Mind*. New York: Random House, 1967. Ch. 8.

Aune, Bruce. "On Thought and Feeling." *Philosophical Quarterly* 13 (1963): 1–12.

Geach, Peter. *Mental Acts*. London, 1957.

Sellars, Wilfrid. "Physical Realism." *Philosophy and Phenomenological Research*15 (1954): 13–32. An illuminating discussion of conceptualism and recent Platonism.

Sellars, Wilfrid. *Science, Perception, and Reality*. London, 1964.

Bruce Aune (1967)
Bibliography updated by Benjamin Fiedor (2005)

THOMAS À KEMPIS

(1379/1380–1471)

Thomas à Kempis, the writer on asceticism and probable author of *The Imitation of Christ,* was born in Kempen, near Düsseldorf, Germany. He belonged to the Brethren of the Common Life, a group that was much influenced by Jan van Ruysbroeck and whose organization centered on the Windesheim community. The major part of Thomas's life was spent at the Augustinian monastery of St. Agnes, near Zwolle.

Thomas's writings on the interior life and ways of practicing virtue are not philosophical or theoretical but are purely practical in intent. This is true also of *The Imitation of Christ,* about whose authorship there has been much dispute. It is not altogether certain that the work, really a set of four treatises, should be attributed to Thomas. The oldest manuscripts date from about 1422 and contain only the first book, and the first complete edition goes back to 1427. Since the work is not quoted earlier than the fifteenth century, it seems likely that it originated during Thomas's lifetime. Moreover, the style is remarkably like that of writings that can certainly be ascribed to him (a statistical investigation has also supported this). For these reasons we can rule out certain speculative attributions (to Jean Gerson and to John Gersen, in the thirteenth century). On the other hand, the first attribution of the book to him occurred rather late, in the second edition of an account of the Windesheim community written in the latter part of the fifteenth century. The fact that Thomas signed a manuscript of the *Imitation* is not conclusive, for he was, like his fellow monks, a copyist and also signed a Bible. But the balance of probability is that Thomas himself compiled the work anonymously, and he certainly incorporated into it materials not original to himself, especially in the first book.

The wide circulation of the book was partly due to the efforts of the copyists at Windesheim, but it was also due to the kind of piety it recommended. The second part of the full title (*Of the Imitation of Christ and of Contempt for All Worldly Vanities*) indicates that its teachings were adapted to the monastic life—and indeed it was primarily intended as a handbook for monks. But its tender concentration on the figure of Jesus made attractive its doctrine of resignation—the surrendering of all worldly concerns to the service of, and imitation of, Christ. Moreover, it gave very concrete guidance on many problems—for example, how to distinguish the results of grace from natural acts and propensities. The most notable feature of the book, however, is its uncompromising and uncomfortable insistence on self-mortification as preparation for grace and the presence of the true Lover of the soul, Christ. The "imitation" of Christ that Thomas recommends is not a simple copying of Jesus but acting by analogy with Jesus, whose life was mainly characterized, according to Thomas, by suffering and self-sacrifice.

The first book has mainly to do with the moral reform of the individual. The second concerns the preparation for the interior or illuminative life. The third consists in a dialogue between Christ and the soul that gives a further exposition of ascetic practices, and one or two passages give a hint of the kind of mystical experience awaiting those who truly love Christ. The fourth book is a manual for those who receive Holy Communion.

There is very little theology in the *Imitation*. Thomas seems to have been reacting against the speculations of academic theology, for he wrote: "Of what use is your highly subtle talk about the blessed Trinity, if you are not humble?" and "I would rather feel compunction than be able to produce the most precise definition of it." The strongly practical bent of the work, in any event, gave it a continuing relevance to the Christian life and enabled it to achieve the status of a classic ranking, in Christian piety, with *Pilgrim's Progress*.

See also Asceticism; Gerson, Jean de; Ruysbroeck, Jan van; Virtue and Vice.

Bibliography

WORKS BY THOMAS

Opera et Libri Vite Fratris Thome a Kempis. Edited by P. Danhausser. Nuremberg: Per Caspar Hochfeder, 1494. Critical edition by M. J. Pohl, 7 vols. Freiburg im Breisgau, 1902–1922.

Prayers and Meditations on the Life of Christ. Translated by William Duthoit London, 1904.

The Founders of the New Devotion. Translated by J. P. Arthur. London, 1905.

The Chronicle of the Canons Regular of Mount St. Agnes. Translated by J. P. Arthur. London: K. Paul, Trench, Trubner, 1906.

Meditations and Sermons on the Incarnation, Life and Passion of Our Lord. Translated by Dom Vincent Scully. London, 1907.

Sermons to the Novices Regular. Translated by Dom Vincent Scully. London: K. Paul, Trench, Trubner, 1907.

The Imitation of Christ. Translated by Ronald Knox and Michael Oakley. New York: Sheed and Ward, 1960. The freshest and most direct translation.

WORKS ON THOMAS

Huijben, Jacques, and Pierre Debougnie. *L'auteur ou les auteurs de L'Imitation.* Louvain, 1957. On the question of authorship of the *Imitation.*

Scully, Dom Vincent. *Life of the Venerable Thomas à Kempis.* London: R. and T. Washbourne, 1901.

Yule, George Udney. *The Statistical Study of Literary Vocabulary.* Cambridge, U.K.: Cambridge University Press, 1944. On the question of the authorship of the *Imitation.*

Ninian Smart (1967)

THOMAS AQUINAS, ST.

(c. 1224–1274)

St. Thomas Aquinas, the Catholic theologian and philosopher, was born at Roccasecca, Italy, the youngest son of Landolfo and Teodora of Aquino. At about the age of five he began his elementary studies under the Benedictine monks at nearby Montecassino. He went on to study liberal arts at the University of Naples. It is probable that Thomas became a master in arts at Naples before entering the Order of Preachers (Dominicans) in 1244. He studied in the Dominican courses in philosophy and theology, first at Paris and, from 1248 on, under Albert the Great at Cologne. In 1252 he was sent to the University of Paris for advanced study in theology; he lectured there as a bachelor in theology until 1256, when he was awarded the magistrate (doctorate) in theology. Accepted after some opposition from other professors as a fully accredited member of the theology faculty in 1257, Thomas continued to teach at Paris until 1259.

Thomas Aquinas then spent almost ten years at various Dominican monasteries in the vicinity of Rome, lecturing on theology and philosophy (including an extensive study of the major works of Aristotle) and performing various consultative and administrative functions in his order. In the fall of 1268 Aquinas returned for his second professorate in theology at the University of Paris. He engaged in three distinct controversies: against a group of conservative theologians who were critical of his philosophic innovations; against certain radical advocates of Aristotelianism or Latin Averroism; and against some critics of the Dominicans and Franciscans and their right to teach at the university. Many of Aquinas's literary works were in process or completed at this time. It is thought that he was provided with secretarial help in this task, partly in view of the fact that his own handwriting was practically illegible. Called back to Italy in 1272, Aquinas taught for a little more than a year at the University of Naples and preached a notable series of vernacular sermons there. Illness forced him to discontinue his teaching and writing toward the end of 1273. Early in 1274 he set out for Lyons, France, to attend a church council. His failing health interrupted the trip at a point not far from his birthplace, and he died at Fossanova in March of that year.

The writings of Thomas Aquinas were produced during his twenty years (1252–1273) as an active teacher. All in Latin, they consist of several large theological treatises, plus recorded disputations on theological and philosophical problems (the "Disputed Questions" and "Quodlibetal Questions"), commentaries on several books of the Bible, commentaries on twelve treatises of Aristotle, and commentaries on Boethius, the pseudo-Dionysius, and the anonymous *Liber de Causis.* There are also about forty miscellaneous notes, letters, sermons, and short treatises on philosophical and religious subjects. Although Aquinas's philosophic views may be found in almost all his writings (thus the "Exposition of the Book of Job" reads like a discussion among philosophers), certain treatises are of more obvious interest to philosophers. These are listed in detail at the end of this entry.

GENERAL PHILOSOPHICAL POSITION

In the main, Aquinas's philosophy is a rethinking of Aristotelianism, with significant influences from Stoicism, Neoplatonism, Augustinism, and Boethianism. It also reflects some of the thinking of the Greek commentators on Aristotle and of Cicero, Avicenna, Averroes, Solomon ben Judah ibn Gabirol, and Maimonides. This may suggest that we are dealing with an eclectic philosophy, but actually Aquinas reworked the speculative and practical philosophies of his predecessors into a coherent view of the subject that shows the stamp of his own intelligence and, of course, the influence of his religious commitment.

One of the broad characteristics of Aquinas's work in philosophy is a temperamental tendency to seek a middle way on questions that have been given a wide range of answers. This spirit of moderation is nowhere better illustrated than in his solution to the problem of universals. For centuries philosophers had debated whether genera and species are realities in themselves (Plato, Boethius, William of Champeaux) or mere mental constructs (Roscelin, Peter Abelard). What made this odd discussion important was the conviction (certainly shared by Aquinas) that these universals (such as humanity, justice, whiteness, dogness) are the primary objects of human understanding. Most thinkers in the Middle Ages felt that if something is to be explained, it must be treated in universal terms. Therefore, the problem of universals was not simply an academic question.

Aquinas's position on this problem is now called moderate realism. He denied that universals are existing realities (and frequently criticized Plato for having suggested that there is a world of intelligible Forms), but he also insisted that men's universal concepts and judgments have some sort of foundation in extramental things. This basis for the universality, say of humanity, would consist in the real similarity found among all individual men. It was not that Aquinas attributed an actual, existent universal nature to all individual men: that would be an extreme realism. Rather, only individuals exist; but the individuals of a given species or class resemble each other, and that is the basis for thinking of them as universally representative of a common nature.

Thomas's spirit of compromise as a philosopher was balanced by another tendency, that toward innovation. His original Latin biographers all stress this feature of his work. Thomas introduced new ways of reasoning about problems and new sources of information, and he handled his teaching in a new way. In this sense Thomas Aquinas was not typical of the thirteenth century and was perhaps in advance of his contemporaries.

FAITH AND RATIONAL KNOWLEDGE

As Aquinas saw it, faith (*fides*) falls midway between opinion and scientific knowledge (*scientia*); it is more than opinion because it involves a firm assent to its object; and it is less than knowledge because it lacks vision. Both are intellectual acts and habits of assent: in the case of faith a person is not sufficiently moved by the object to accept it as true, so, by an act of will, he inclines himself to believe. Knowledge implies assent motivated by a personal seeing of the object without any direct influence from will. Where objects of belief have to do with divine matters that exceed man's natural cognitive capacity, the disposition to believe such articles of religious faith is regarded as a special gift from God. Reason (*ratio*) is another type of intellectual activity: Simple understanding and reasoning differ only in the manner in which the intellect works. Through intellection (understanding) one knows simply by seeing what something means, while through reason one moves discursively from one item of knowledge to another. (These functions of believing and knowing are treated in many places by Aquinas: *Summa Contra Gentiles* III, 147; *In Boethii de Trinitate,* Ques. II and III; *Summa Theologiae* I, Ques. 79–84.)

Aquinas thought that philosophy entailed reasoning from prior knowledge, or present experience, to new knowledge (the way of discovery) and the rational verification of judgments by tracing them back to more simply known principles (the way of reduction). Where the basic principles are grasped by man's natural understanding of his sensory experiences, the reasoning processes are those of natural science and philosophy. If one starts to reason from judgments accepted on religious faith, then one is thinking as a theologian. Questions V and VI of *In Boethii de Trinitate* develop Aquinas's methodology of the philosophical sciences: philosophy of nature, mathematics, and metaphysics. He distinguished speculative or theoretical reasoning from the practical: The purpose of speculation is simply to know; the end of practical reasoning is to know how to act. He described two kinds of theology: The philosophical "theology," metaphysics, which treats divine matters as principles for the explanation of all things, and the theology taught in Scripture, which "studies divine things for their own sakes" (*In Boethii de Trinitate* V, 4 c).

Thus philosophy, for Aquinas, was a natural type of knowledge open to all men who wish to understand the meaning of their ordinary experiences. The "philosophers" whom he habitually cited were the classic Greek, Latin, Islamic, and Jewish sages. Christian teachers mentioned by Aquinas were the "saints" (Augustine, John of Damascus, Gregory, Ambrose, Dionysius, Isidore, and Benedict); they were never called Christian philosophers. The word *theology* was rarely used by Aquinas. In the first question of his *Summa Theologiae* he formally calls his subject sacred doctrine (*sacra doctrina*) and says that its principles, unlike those of philosophy, are various items of religious faith.

Thus, Thomas Aquinas was by profession a theologian, or better, a teacher of sacred doctrine who also studied and wrote about philosophy. He obviously used a good deal of pagan and non-Christian philosophy in all his writings. His own understanding of these philosophies was influenced by his personal faith—as almost any man's judgment is influenced by his stand for or against the claim of religious faith—in this sense Thomism is a "Christian philosophy." Aquinas did not ground his philosophical thinking on principles of religious belief, however, for this would have destroyed his distinction between philosophy and sacred doctrine, as presented in the opening chapters of the first book of *Summa Contra Gentiles.* One of the clearest efforts to maintain the autonomy of philosophy is found in Aquinas's *De Aeternitate Mundi* (about 1270), in which he insists that, as far as philosophical considerations go, the universe might be eternal. As a Christian, he believed that it is not eternal.

Among interpreters of Aquinas there has been much debate whether his commentaries on Aristotle deal with his personal thinking. It is generally agreed even by non-Thomists (W. D. Ross, A. E. Taylor) that these expositions are helpful to the reader who wishes to understand Aristotle. It is not so clear whether the mind of Aquinas is easily discernible in them. One group of Thomists (Étienne Gilson, Joseph Owens, A. C. Pegis) stresses the more obviously personal writings (such as the two *Summa*'s) as bases for the interpretation of his thought; another school of interpretation (J. M. Ramírez, Charles De Koninck, J. A. Oesterle) uses the Aristotelian commentaries as the main sources for Aquinas's philosophic thought.

THEORY OF KNOWLEDGE. The Thomistic theory of knowledge is realistic. (This theory is presented in *Summa Theologiae* I, 79–85; *Quaestiones Disputatae de Veritate* I, II; *In Libros Posteriorum Analyticorum* I, 5; II, 20.) Men obtain their knowledge of reality from the initial data of sense experience. Apart from supernatural experiences that some mystics may have, Thomas limited human cognition to sense perception and the intellectual understanding of it. Sense organs are stimulated by the colored, audible, odorous, gustatory, and tactile qualities of extramental bodies; and sensation is the vital response through man's five external sense powers to such stimulation. Aquinas assumed that one is cognitively aware of red flowers, noisy animals, cold air, and so on. Internal sensation (common, imaginative, memorative, and cogitative functions) works to perceive, retain, associate, and judge the various impressions (phantasms) through which things are directly known. Man's higher cognitive functions, those of understanding, judging, and reasoning, have as their objects the universal meanings that arise out of sense experience. Thus, one sees and remembers an individual apple on the level of sensation—but he judges it to be healthful because it contains vitamins, or for any other general reason, on the level of intellectual knowledge. Universals (health, humanity, redness) are not taken as existing realities but are viewed as intelligibilities (*rationes*) with a basis in what is common to existents. As a moderate realist, Aquinas would resent being classified as a Platonist; yet he would defend the importance of our knowledge of the general and common characteristics of things.

Although human cognition begins with the knowing of bodily things, man can form some intellectual notions and judgments concerning immaterial beings: souls, angels, and God. Aquinas taught that man does this by negating certain aspects of bodies (for instance, a spirit does not occupy space) and by using analogy. When the notion of power is attributed to God, its meaning is transferred from an initially physical concept to the analogous perfection of that which can accomplish results in the immaterial order. Thomas did not think that men, during earthly life, can know the nature of God in any adequate, positive way.

Discursive reasoning was taken as an intellectual process moving from or toward first principles in logical processes of demonstration (the ways of discovery and reduction, described above). In one way, sense experience is the first principle (starting point) for all of man's natural knowledge. This is one aspect of Aquinas's empiricism. Following Aristotle's *Posterior Analytics,* Thomas taught that many sensations combine to form a unified memory, and many memories constitute sense experience. From this manifold of experience, by a sort of sensory induction, there arises within human awareness a beginning (*principium*) of understanding. Such first principles are not demonstrated (they naturally emerge from sense cognition), but they become the roots for consequent intellectual reasoning. A doctor who tries a variety of remedies to treat headaches eventually notices that one drug works well in almost all cases—at some point he grasps the universal "Drug *A* is a general remedy for headache." From this principle he proceeds rationally to order his practice. If he becomes a teacher of medicine, he uses such a theoretical principle to instruct others. This is the basis of the life of reason.

PHILOSOPHY AND THE PHYSICAL WORLD

In his exposition of the *Liber de Causis* (Lect. 1), Aquinas described a sequence of philosophic studies: logic, mathematics, natural philosophy (physics), moral philosophy, and, finally, metaphysics. The first kind of reality examined in this course would be that of the physical world. (At the start of the next century, John Duns Scotus criticized Thomas for attempting to base his metaphysics and his approaches to God on physics.) Interpreters still debate whether Aquinas himself felt that this was the order to be followed in learning philosophy, or whether he was merely reporting one way that the "philosophers" had taught it. In any case, the philosophical study of bodies, of mobile being in the Aristotelian sense, was important to Aquinas. One group of his writings (*De Principiis Naturae,* parts of Book II of the *Summa Contra Gentiles,* the treatise *De Aeternitate Mundi*) offers a quite personal treatment of this world of bodies. Another set of writings (the commentaries on Aristotle's *Physics* and *De Generatione et Corruptione*) shows how indebted Aquinas was to Aristotle in his theory of physical reality.

MATTER AND FORM. The philosophy of nature (*phusis*) was understood as the study of a special kind of beings, those subject to several kinds of change. Physical beings have primary matter as one component and, depending on their species or kind, substantial form as their other integral principle. Neither matter nor form is a thing by itself; matter and form are simply the determinable and determining factors within any existing physical substance. Like Aristotle, Aquinas took it that there are many species of bodily substances: all the different kinds of inanimate material (wood, gold, water, etc.) and all the species of plants and animals. Within each such species there is one specifying principle (the substantial form of wood, potato plant, or dog), and the many individual members of each species are differentiated by the fact that the matter constituting dog *A* could not also constitute dog *B* (so viewed, matter is said to be quantified, or marked by quantity).

CHANGE. Being mobile, physical beings are subject to four kinds of change (*motus*): of place (locomotion), of size (quantitative change), of color, shape, and so on (qualitative change), and of species of substance (generation and corruption, substantial change). Basically, prime matter is that which remains constant and provides continuity during a change from one substance to another. When a pig eats an apple, that part of the apple really assimilated by the pig becomes the very substance of the pig; some factor in the apple, the prime matter, must continue on into the pig. All four types of change are explained in terms of the classic theory of four causes. The final cause is the answer to the question "why" something exists or occurs; the agent or efficient cause is the maker or producer of the change; the material cause is that out of which the change comes; and the formal cause is the specifying factor in any event or existent. So used, "cause" has the broad meaning of raison d'être.

SPACE AND TIME. Certain other points in Aquinas's philosophy of nature further illustrate the influence of Aristotle. Place, for instance, is defined as the "immobile limit of the containing body" (*In IV Physicorum* 6). Moreover, each primary type of body (the four elements still are earth, air, fire, and water) is thought to have its own "proper" place. Thus, the place for fire is "up" and that for earth is "down." Some sort of absolute, or box, theory of space may be presupposed; yet in the same passage Aquinas's discussion of the place of a boat in a flowing river indicates a more sophisticated understanding of spatial relativity. Time is defined, as in Aristotle, as the measure of motion in regard to "before" and "after." Eternity is a type of duration differing from time in two ways: The eternal has neither beginning nor termination, and the eternal has no succession of instants but exists entirely at once (*tota simul*).

ENCOURAGEMENT OF SCIENCE. Doubtless Aquinas's philosophy of the physical world was limited and even distorted by certain views and factual errors derived from Aristotle and from thirteenth-century science. Apart from the mistaken hypothesis that each element has its proper place in the universe, Thomas also used the Eudoxian astronomy, which placed the earth at the center of a system of from 49 to 53 concentric spheres. (Besides the Commentary on *De Caelo* II, 10, and the Commentary on *Meteorologia* II, 10; see *Summa Contra Gentiles* I, 20, and *Summa Theologiae* I, 68, 4 c.) At times Thomas showed an open mind on such questions and an ability to rise above the limitations of his period. His Commentary on Aristotle's *Metaphysics* (Lect. 1 on Book III and Lect. 9 on Book XII) provides a key instance. Pointing out that astronomers differ widely on the number and motions of the planets, Aquinas recommended that one study all the reports and theories of such scientists, even though these scientific explanations are not the last word on the matter and are obviously open to future revision. He further compared the study of physical science to the work of a judge in a court of law. One should listen to, and try to evaluate, all important testimony before attempting to formulate one's own judgment on the problems of contemporary science. This is Aquinas at his best, hardly a philosophical dogmatist.

HUMAN FUNCTIONS AND MAN'S NATURE

Anthropology, or psychology, in the classical sense of the study of man's psyche, forms an important part of Aquinas's philosophy. His view of man owed much to the Aristotelian treatise *On the Soul,* to the Christian Platonism of Augustine and John of Damascus, and to the Bible. This part of Aquinas's thought will be found in *Scriptum in IV Libros Sententiarum* (Commentary on the *Sentences*) I, Dists. 16–27; *Summa Contra Gentiles* II, 58–90; *Quaestio Disputata de Anima*; the *Libros de Anima*; and *Summa Theologiae,* I, 75–90.

Aquinas's usual way of working out his theory of human nature was first to examine certain activities in which man engages, then to reason to the kinds of operative powers needed to explain such actions, and finally to conclude to the sort of substantial nature that could be the subject of such powers. He described the biological activities of man as those of growth, assimilation of food, and sexual reproduction. A higher set of activities included sensory perception, emotive responses to what is perceived, and locomotion: These activities man shares with brute animals. A third group of activities comprises the cognitive functions of understanding, judging, and reasoning, as well as the corresponding appetitive functions of affective inclination toward or away from the objects of understanding. To these various functions Aquinas assigned generic powers (operative potencies) of growth, reproduction, sensory cognition and appetition, physical locomotion, and intellectual cognition and appetition (will).

Reexamining these functional powers in detail, Aquinas distinguished five special sense powers for the cognition of physical individuals: sight, hearing, smell, taste, and touch. These functions and powers are called external because their proper objects are outside the mental awareness of the perceiver: This is essential to epistemological realism. Following these are four kinds of internal sensory activities: the perceptual grasping of a whole object (*sensus communis*), the simple retention of sensed images (imagination), the association of retained images with past time (sense memory), and concrete discrimination or judgment concerning individual things (cogitative sense, particular reason). Still on the level of sensory experience, Aquinas (here influenced by John of Damascus) described two kinds of appetition (emotion): A simple tendency toward or away from what is sensed as good or evil (this affective power is called the concupiscible appetite), and a more complicated sensory inclination to meet bodily threats, obstacles, and dangers by attacking or avoiding them or by putting up with them (this affective power is called irascible appetite). Eleven distinct kinds of sensory passions (emotions) are attributed to these two sensory appetites: love, desire, delight, hate, aversion, and sorrow to the concupiscible; fear, daring, hope, despair, and anger to the irascible. Much of this psychological analysis is quite sophisticated, employing data from Greek, Roman, and early Christian thought and also using the physiological and psychological treatises of Islamic and Jewish scholars. It also forms the basis of the analysis of human conduct in Thomistic ethics.

On the higher level of distinctively human experience, Aquinas found various other activities and powers. These are described in his commentary on Book III of Aristotle's *De Anima,* in the *Summa Contra Gentiles* (II, 59–78), and in Questions 84–85 of the *Summa Theologiae.* The general capacity to understand (*intellectus*) covers simple apprehension, judging, and reasoning. The objects of intellection are universal aspects (*rationes*) of reality. Since universal objects do not exist in nature, Aquinas described one intellectual action as the abstraction of universal meanings (*intentiones*) from the individual presentations of sense experience. This abstractive power is called agent intellect (*intellectus agens*). A second cognitive function on this level is the grasping (*comprehensio*) of these abstracted meanings in the very act of cognition; this activity is assigned to a different power, the possible intellect (*intellectus possibilis*). Thus, there are two quite different "intellects" in Thomistic psychology: One abstracts, the other knows. No special power is required for intellectual memory; the retention of understandings is explained by habit formation in the possible intellect.

WILL. Affective responses to the universal objects of understanding are functions of intellectual appetition. Considered quite different from sensory appetition, this is the area of volition, and the special power involved is the will (*voluntas*). Aquinas distinguished two kinds of volitional functions. First, there are those basic and natural tendencies of approval and affective approach to an object that is judged good or desirable without qualification. In regard to justice, peace, or a perfectly good being, for instance, Aquinas felt that a person's will would be naturally and necessarily attracted to such objects. This natural movement of the will is not free. Second, there are volitional movements toward or away from intellectually known objects that are judged as partly desirable or as partly undesirable. Such movements of will are directed by intellectual judgments evaluating the objects. In this case volition is said to be "deliberated" (specified by intellectual considerations) and free. It is in the act of decision (*arbitrium*) that man is free. Aquinas did not talk about "free will"; the term *libera voluntas* is found only twice in all his works, and then in a nontechnical usage; rather, he spoke of free choice or decision (*liberum arbitrium*). Man, by virtue of his intellectual powers, is free in some of his actions.

SOUL. Although Aquinas sometimes spoke as if these various "powers" of man were agents, he formally stressed the view that it is the whole man who is the human agent. A human being is an animated body in which the psychic principle (*anima*) is distinctive of the species and determines that the material is human. In other words, man's soul is his substantial form. Some of man's activities are obviously very like those of brutes, but the intellectual and volitional functions transcend materiality by virtue of their universal and abstracted character. Aquinas took as an indication of the immateriality of the human soul the fact that it can understand universal meanings and make free decisions. The soul is a real part of man and, being both immaterial and real, it is spiritual. From certain other features of man's higher activities, especially from the unity of conscious experience, Aquinas concluded to the simplicity and integration of man's soul: It is not divisible into parts. This, in turn, led him to the conclusion that the soul is incapable of corruption (disintegration into parts) and thus is immortal.

Since Thomas thought the soul incapable of being partitioned, he could not explain the coming into being of new human souls by biological process. He was thus forced to the view that each rational soul is originated by divine creation from nothing. Human parents are not the total cause of their offspring; they share the work of procreation with God. This view explains why Aquinas put so much stress on the dignity and sanctity of human reproduction, which he regarded as more than a biological function. When he claimed, in his ethics, that the begetting and raising of children is the primary purpose of married life, he was not thinking of simple sexual activity but of a human participation in God's creative function. This does not mean that man is the highest of God's creatures; Aquinas speculated that there are other kinds of purely intellectual beings with activities, powers, and natures superior to those of men. These are angels. Thomas Aquinas is called the Angelic Doctor in Catholic tradition because of his great interest in these purely spiritual but finite beings. They would constitute the highest realm of the universe.

METAPHYSICS AND REAL BEING

Aquinas devoted much thought to the question "What does it mean to be?" Many Thomists think that his greatest philosophical ability was shown in the area of metaphysics. His general theory of reality incorporates much of the metaphysics of Aristotle, and some interpreters have seen Thomistic metaphysics as but a baptized Aristotelianism. Recent Thomistic scholarship has selected two non-Aristotelian metaphysical teachings for new emphasis: the theory of participation and the general influence of Platonic metaphysics (L. B. Geiger, Cornelio Fabro, R. J. Henle), and the primacy of *esse,* the fundamental act of being (Gilson, Jacques Maritain, G. P. Klubertanz). Because *esse,* which simply means "to be," is sometimes translated as "existence," this second point of emphasis is called by some writers the existentialism of Thomistic metaphysics. It has little, however, to do with present-day existentialism. A major treatment of metaphysical problems is to be found in Aquinas's long Commentary on Aristotle's *Metaphysics,* but here again the problem is to decide how much is Thomistic. Some very competent scholars (Pegis, Gilson) regard this work as a restatement of Aristotelianism; others (De Koninck, Herman Reith) consider the Commentary to be a key exposition of Aquinas's own metaphysics. It is admitted by all that there are some explanations in it that are not found in Aristotle.

Metaphysics, for Aquinas, was the effort to understand reality in general, to find an ultimate explanation of the manifold of experience in terms of the highest causes. His predecessors had variously described the subject matter of this study as existing immaterial substances, as the most universal and common aspects of being, as the first causes of all things, and as the divine being in itself. Commenting on these opinions in the prologue to his Commentary on the *Metaphysics,* Aquinas remarked: "Although this science considers these items, it does not think of each of them as its subject; its subject is simply being in general." In this sense, he called the study of being "first philosophy."

ANALOGY. It is distinctive of Aquinas's thought to maintain that all existing realities, from God down to the least perfect thing, are beings—and that "being" has in this usage an analogical and not a univocal meaning. In a famous passage (*In I Sententiarum* 19, 5, 2, ad 1) Aquinas describes three sorts of analogy: one in which a given perfection is present in one item but only attributed to another; one in which one perfection exists in a somewhat different way in two or more items; and one in which some sort of remote resemblance or community is implied between two items which have no identity either in existence or in signification. "In this last way," Aquinas adds "truth and goodness, and all things of this kind, are predicated analogously of God and creatures." In later works the notion of proportionality is introduced to develop the concept of the analogy of being. Vision in the eye is a good of the body in somewhat the same way that vision in the intellect is a good of the soul. Similarly, the act of being in a stone is proportional to the act of being in a man, as the nature of a stone is proportional to the nature of man. Whereas some interpreters feel that the analogy of proportionality is the central type of analogy of being, others insist that Aquinas used several kinds of analogy in his metaphysics.

BEING AND ESSENCE. One early but certainly personal presentation of the metaphysics of Aquinas is to be found in the brief treatise *De Ente et Essentia,* which was strongly influenced by Avicenna. His usage of basic terms of analysis, such as being (*ens*), essence (*essentia*), nature, quiddity, substance, accident, form, matter, genus, species, difference, immaterial substance (*substantia separata*), potency, and act, is clearly but rather statically defined in this *opusculum.* Additional precisions, particularly on the meaning of element, principle, cause, and *esse,* are to be found in the companion treatise, *De Principiis Naturae.* A more dynamic approach to being and its operations is offered in the *Quaestiones Disputatae de Potentia Dei* and in Part I of the *Summa Theologiae.*

Fundamental in the metaphysical thinking of Aquinas is the difference between *what* a being is and the fact *that* it is. The first is a question of essence; the second is the act of being, *esse.* Essences are many (various kinds of things—stones, cows, air, men) and are known through simple understanding, without any necessity of adverting to their existence or nonexistence. For a thing *to be* is entirely another matter; the fact that something exists is noted in human experience by an act of judgment. Many essences of things are material, but there is nothing about *esse* that requires it to be limited to materiality. This proposition (to be is not necessarily to be material) is the "judgment of separation" (*In Boethii de Trinitate* V, 3). Many Thomists now regard it as a fundamental point of departure for Aquinas's metaphysical thinking.

There are also certain most general features of real beings that transcend all division into genera and species; these are convertible with metaphysical being. In other words, they are coextensive and really identical with being. Such transcendentals are thing (*res*), something (*aliquid*), one, true, good, and (according to some interpreters) beautiful. The more important of these transcendentals suggest that every being is internally undivided but externally distinct from all else (*unum*), that every being has some intelligible meaning (*verum*), and that every being is in some way desirable (*bonum*). The theory of transcendentals is much more expanded and stressed in later scholasticism than in Aquinas's own writings. He barely touches upon it in Questions I and XXI of *De Veritate* and in the discussion of God's attributes in *Summa Theologiae* (I, Ques. 6, 11, 16).

POTENCY AND ACT. Potency and act are important principles in Aquinas's metaphysical explanation of the existence and operation of things. In *De Potentia Dei* (I, 1) Aquinas pointed out that the name "act" first designated any activity or operation that occurs. Corresponding to this sort of operational act is a dual meaning of potency (or power). Consider the activity of sawing wood: The passive potency of wood to be cut is required (water, for instance, cannot be sawed); also required is the active potency of the sawyer to do the cutting. In addition, in the same text, Aquinas says that the notion of "act" is transferred to cover the existence of a being. Essential potency, the metaphysical capacity to exist, would correspond to this act of being (*esse*). In this way the theory of act and potency was applied to all levels of being. At the highest level, God was described as Pure Act in the existential order, but this did not prevent Aquinas from attributing to God an active potency for operating.

FINALITY. Still another dimension of metaphysical reality, for Aquinas, was that of finality. He thought of all activities as directed toward some end or purpose, a basic assumption in Aristotle. But Aquinas developed this tendential, vector characteristic of being and applied it to the inclination of possible beings to become actual. The finality of being, in Thomism, is that dynamic and ongoing inclination to be realized in their appropriate perfections that is characteristic of all realities and capacities for action. In this sense the finality of being is an intrinsic perfectionism in the development of all beings. Aquinas also held that all finite beings and events are tending toward God as Final Cause. This is metaphysical finality in the sense of order to an external end. This theme runs through Book III of *Summa Contra Gentiles.*

PHILOSOPHY AND GOD

The consideration of the existence and nature of God was approached by Aquinas both from the starting point of supernatural revelation (the Scriptures), which is the way of the theologian, and from the starting point of man's ordinary experience of finite beings and their operations, which is the way of the philosopher: "The philosophers, who follow the order of natural cognition, place the knowledge of creatures before the divine science; that is, the philosophy of nature comes before metaphysics. On the other hand, the contrary procedure is followed among the theologians, so that the consideration of the Creator precedes the consideration of creatures" (*In Boethii de Trinitate,* Prologue). In the same work (II, 3 c) we are told that the first use of philosophy in sacred doctrine is "to demonstrate items that are preambles to faith, such as those things that are proved about God by natural processes of reasoning: that God exists, that God is one," and so on.

Aquinas recognized two types of demonstration, one moving from cause to effects and the other from effects back to their cause. The arguments that he selected to establish that God exists use the second procedure and are technically called *quia* arguments. In other words, these proofs start with some observed facts of experience (all Aquinas's arguments to God's existence are a posteriori) and conclude to the ultimate cause of these facts. Well aware of his debt to his predecessors, Aquinas outlined three arguments for the existence of God in *De Potentia Dei* (III, 5 c). The first shows that, since the act of being is common to many existents, there must be one universal cause of all (Plato's argument, Aquinas noted); the second argument starts from the fact that all beings in our experience are imperfect, not self-moved, and not the source of their actual being, and the reasoning concludes to the existence of a "mover completely immobile and most perfect" (Aristotle's argument); the third argument simply reasons from the composite nature of finite beings to the necessary existence of a primary being in which essence and the act of existing are identical (Avicenna's proof). Aquinas felt that these two pagan philosophers and an Islamic thinker had successfully established the conclusion "that there is a universal cause of real beings by which all other things are brought forth into actual being."

THE "FIVE WAYS." The most famous of the arguments are the "Five Ways" (*Quinque Viae*) of reasoning to the conclusion that God exists (*Summa Theologiae* I, 2, 3, c). All these ways employ the principle of causality and start from empirical knowledge of the physical world. They are not entirely original with Aquinas, depending not only on Plato, Aristotle, and Avicenna but also on Augustine and especially on Moses Maimonides. The First Way begins with the point that things in the world are always changing or moving and concludes to the existence of one, first, moving Cause. The Second Way argues from the observation of efficient production of things in the universe to the need of an existing, first, efficient Cause. The Third Way reasons from the contingent character of things in the world (none of them has to be) to the existence of a totally different kind of being, a necessary one (which has to be). The Fourth Way argues from the gradations of goodness, truth, and nobility in the things of man's experience to the existence of a being that is most true, most good, and most noble. The Fifth Way starts from the orderly character of mundane events, argues that all things are directed toward one end (the principle of finality), and concludes that this universal order points to the existence of an intelligent Orderer of all things. At the end of his statement of each "way," Thomas simply said, "and this is what all men call God," or words to that effect. Obviously, he presupposed a common meaning of the word *God* in the dictionary or nominal sense. There is disagreement among interpreters as to whether the "ways" are five distinct proofs or merely five formulations of one basic argument. Most Thomists now favor the second view.

Aquinas favored the argument from physical motion (*prima autem et manifestior via est*). The *Summa Contra Gentiles* (I, 13) offers an extended version of this first argument and frankly indicates its relation to the ideas in the last books of Aristotle's *Physics*. The other four ways are but briefly suggested in the *Summa Contra Gentiles*. In another, much neglected, work (*Compendium Theologiae* I, 3) the first way is stated clearly and concisely. Before attempting to establish in detail the various attributes of God, such as divine unity, one should consider whether he exists. Now, all things that are moved must be moved by other things; furthermore, things of an inferior nature are moved by superior beings. (Aquinas's examples are chosen from thirteenth-century physics and astronomy, in which the four basic elements were thought to be under dynamic influence of the stars, and lower celestial bodies were considered to be moved about by those at a greater distance from Earth. How much of the force of this argument may depend on outmoded science is a matter of debate in present-day Thomism.)

Aquinas next argues that the process in which *A* moves *B*, *B* moves *C*, and so on cannot be self-explanatory. His way of saying this is "This process cannot go on to infinity." He concludes that the only possible explanation of the series of physical motions observed in the universe requires the acceptance of the existence of a different sort of "mover"—a being that is not moved by another, in other words, a first mover. This would have to be a real being, of course, and of a quite different nature from bodily things. He eventually suggests that this "first mover existing above all else" is what Christians call God.

In the same passage from the *Compendium*, two other facets of the argument from motion are introduced. First, Aquinas claims that all causes observed as acting in the physical universe are instrumental in character and must be used, as it were, by a primary agent. This primary agent is again another name for God. To suppose that the universe is self-explanatory is, to Aquinas, like thinking that a bed could be constructed by putting the tools and material together, "without any carpenter to use them." This is an important case of the conception of God as a divine craftsman. In the second place, this text suggests briefly that an infinite series of moved movers is an impossibility; the length of the series has nothing to do with its explanatory function, if all its members be finite. Finally, any such series requires a first mover (primary in the sense of causality, not necessarily of chronological priority). This first mover would be a Supreme Being. It is obvious that many of the attributes of God are already implied in the argument for divine existence.

KNOWLEDGE OF GOD. Regarding the nature and attributes of God, Aquinas's greatest emphasis fell on how little we really know about the Supreme Being. In a series of articles (*Summa Theologiae* I, 86–88) on the objects of human knowledge, he reiterated his position that man is naturally equipped to understand directly the natures of material things; further, that man is aware of his own psychic functions as they occur but that all man's understanding of the nature of his own soul, of immaterial substances such as angels, and of infinite immaterial being (God) is achieved by dint of discursive and indirect reasoning. There is, of course, a wide gap between material and immaterial substances. Yet both these types of finite beings fall within the same logical genus, as substances, and thus bodies and created spirits have some aspects in common. On the other hand, God is an immaterial being of an entirely different nature from that of bodies or even of created spirits. Between God and creatures there is no univocal community: That is to say, God does not fall within the same genus, either real or logical, as any other being. Hence, God's nature transcends all species and genera. Man's natural knowledge of God's nature is therefore very imperfect, achieved by negating various imperfections found in finite beings: Thus, God is not in time, not in place, not subject to change, and so on. Furthermore, man may reach some semipositive knowledge of God by way of analogy: Thus, God is powerful but not in the finite manner of other beings; he is knowing, willing, and so on.

PROVIDENCE. Divine providence is that attribute of God whereby he intelligently orders all things and events in the universe. As Aquinas explained it in the *Summa Contra Gentiles* (III), God both establishes the plan (*ratio*) in accord with which all creatures are kept in order and executes this plan through continued governance of the world. Literally, providence means "foresight," and this required Aquinas to face certain problems traditionally associated with any theory of divine foreknowledge. First of all, he insisted that such a view of divine providence does not exclude chance events from the universe. In one sense, a chance event occurs apart from the intention of the agent. However, what is intended by one agent may involve another agent who is unaware of the intention of the first. Hence, a plurality of real but imperfect agents sets the stage for chance: God knows this and permits it to occur.

EVIL. In the *Quaestiones Disputatae de Malo* and elsewhere Aquinas agreed with Augustine that evil (both physical and moral) is a privation of goodness, of perfection, in being or in action. This does not deny the fact that evil really occurs but asserts that it is like a wound in being (the phrase is Maritain's); and, like any defect, evil is important by virtue of what is lacking. As to why a perfectly good God will allow evil to occur, Thomas argued that the possibility of evil is necessary so that many goods may be possible. "If there were no death of other animals, there would not be life for the lion; if there were no persecution from tyrants, there would be no occasion for the heroic suffering of the martyrs" (*Summa Theologiae* I, 22, 2, ad 2).

FREEDOM. Aquinas also did not admit that divine foreknowledge is opposed to the exercise of human freedom. His explanation of this point (in *Summa Theologiae* I, 103, 7 and 8) is complicated and not easy to state briefly. In effect, human freedom does not imply absolute indeterminism (action that is uncaused). What a man does freely is caused by himself, as a knowing and willing agent. God makes man capable of choosing well or ill, permits man to do so freely, and knows what man will accomplish. What appears to be necessitated from one point of view may be quite contingent and free from another viewpoint. From God's vantage point in eternity, human actions are not affairs of past or future but are events within the all-inclusive present of a divine observer who witnesses these events but does not determine them.

ETHICS AND POLITICAL PHILOSOPHY

The foregoing problems and considerations fall within Aquinas's speculative philosophy. His practical philosophy, aimed at the intelligent performance of actions, is divided into ethics, economics (treating problems of domestic life), and politics. In all three areas the thinking is teleological; finality, purposiveness, and the means-end relation all are aspects of Thomistic teleology. Rationally controlled activities must be directed to some goal; they are judged good or bad in terms of their attainment of that goal and in terms of the means by which they attain (or fail to attain) that end.

Aquinas dealt with the theoretical analysis of ethical activities in a long series of works: the *Scriptum in IV Libros Sententiarum,* Book III; *Summa Contra Gentiles* III, 114–138; the *In X Libros Ethicorum; Quaestiones Disputatae de Malo*; and the *Summa Theologiae,* Part II. Most of these works take the approach of moral theology, viewing moral good and evil in terms of accord or discord with divine law, which is revealed in Scripture and developed and interpreted in Christian tradition. Thomas himself did not consider moral theology to be a part of philosophy, and it will not be further considered here, except as throwing incidental light on his ethical position.

VOLUNTARY ACTION. Aquinas's ethics consists of a study of good and evil in human conduct, from the point of view of man's achievement of ultimate happiness. Not all the actions in which man is involved are truly human but only those accomplished under control of man's intellect and will. The primary characteristic of human conduct, according to Aquinas, is not so much freedom as voluntariness. His description of voluntary activity is a development of the teaching of Aristotle. Several factors are required for a voluntary action. There must be sufficient knowledge on the part of a moral agent that a given action is within his power; he cannot be entirely ignorant of the kind of action that he is performing or of the means, circumstances, and end of his action. Violence, under certain conditions, modifies the voluntariness of one's actions—as do certain kinds of uncontrollable feelings. Furthermore, as Aquinas saw it there are two opposites to what is voluntary. The "involuntary" is a contrary: It represents a diminution of voluntariness. Thus, an action that is partly involuntary is also partly voluntary and is, to a greater or lesser extent, imputable to the agent. On the other hand, the "not-voluntary" is the contradictory of what is voluntary, and an agent who is not voluntary is not morally responsible for his action.

NATURAL LAW. Most surveys of ethical theories classify Aquinas's ethics as a natural law theory. He described natural law as a rational participation in the eternal law of God and suggested that all men have a sufficient knowledge of what is morally right (the *justum*) to be able to regulate their own actions. In a famous passage (*Summa Theologiae* I–II, 94, 2) Aquinas explained the way in which he thought that rules of natural law are known. The judgment of *synderesis* (an intellectual quality enabling any man to intuit the first principle of practical reasoning) is simply the proposition "Good should be done and sought after; evil is to be avoided." (Most modern Thomists take this rule as a formal principle in the Kantian sense, requiring further knowledge to fill in the content of specific moral rules.) Aquinas then proceeded to describe three kinds of inclinations natural to man: that of man's substantial nature toward the conservation of its own existence and physical well-being, that of man's animal nature to seek such biological goods as sexual reproduction and the care of offspring, and that of man's reason whereby he tends toward universal goods, such as consideration of the interests of other persons and the avoidance of ignorance. All three kinds of inclinations are presented as natural and good, provided they are reasonably pursued. They form the bases from which one may conclude to a number of rules of natural moral law. Aquinas never attempted to make an exhaustive listing of the precepts of such a law; nor did he consider such a codification advisable.

In point of fact, the natural law approach to moral theory is not the only, and not the best, classification of Aquinas's ethics. Particularly in view of various shifts in the meaning of "law" since the time of Aquinas (notably a growing stress on law as a fiat of legislative will), it can be positively misleading to limit Aquinas's ethics to a natural law position. He defines law in general as "any ordinance of reason that is promulgated for the common good by one who has charge of a community" (*Summa Theologiae* I–II, 90, 4 c). "Reason" is the key word in this definition. Right reason (*recta ratio*) is the justification of ethical judgment in Aquinas's thought. "In the case of volitional activities, the proximate standard is human reason (*regula proxima est ratio humana*) but the supreme standard is eternal law. Therefore, whenever a man's action proceeds to its end in accord with the order of reason and of eternal law, then the act is right; but when it is twisted away from this rightness, then it is called a sin" (21, 1 c).

REASON, GOODNESS, AND JUSTICE. Thomistic ethics requires a person to govern his actions as reasonably as he can, keeping in mind the kind of agent that he is and the position that he occupies in the total scheme of reality. Man's own good is achieved by the governance of his actions and feelings under rational reflection—and God does not require anything else. "For we do not offend God, except by doing something contrary to our own good" (*Summa Contra Gentiles* III, 121–122). It is a part of being reasonable to respect the good of others. The moral good, then, is not so much what men are obligated to do by an all-powerful legislator; rather, it is that which is in accord with the reasonable perfecting of man. In becoming a better agent within himself, man is making himself more fit for ultimate happiness and for the vision of God. This kind of ethics resembles a self-perfectionist theory, without idealist overtones.

Aquinas based much of his teaching on ethical rules on the theory of natural justice found in Book V of the *Nicomachean Ethics*. All things have specific natures that do not change: Dogs are dogs and stones are stones. Certain functions are taken as natural and appropriate to given natures: Eating is an act expected of a dog but not of a stone. Human nature shares certain functions with the higher brutes but is distinguished by the performance of rational activities. Some of these typical functions are always the same in relation to man's nature and ethical rules pertaining to these do not change. Aquinas's example of such an immutable rule of justice is simply "Theft is unjust." Other ethical judgments, however, are not essential to justice (for example, detailed ordinances that contain many variable factors); these secondary rules are by no means absolute and immutable. Examples would be rules concerned with taxation, buying and selling, and other such circumstantially variable regulations. Moral law is composed of both types of rules and is neither absolute nor immutable in all its requirements.

CONSCIENCE. In *De Veritate* (XVII) Aquinas referred to moral conscience as a concrete intellectual judgment whereby the individual agent decides for himself that a given action or feeling is good or bad, right or wrong, to be done or not to be done. Conscience was not considered a special power or moral sense, nor was it viewed as the source of universal moral convictions. For Aquinas it was simply a man's best practical judgment concerning a concrete moral problem. As such, moral conscience is a person's internal guide to good action; one acts immorally in going against his conscience, for it is his best judgment on a matter. If it is not his best judgment, then the person is clearly required to make a better effort to reach a conscientious decision. Reasonable consideration of a proposed action includes thinking of the kind of action that it is (the formal object), the purpose to which it is directed (the end), and the pertinent circumstances under which it is to be performed. These three moral determinants were used by Aquinas to complete the theory of right reasoning in *De Malo* (II, 4 c, ad 2, ad 5).

FAMILY. Aquinas also considered man in his social relations. In the *Summa Contra Gentiles* (III, cc. 122–126) the family is regarded as a natural and reasonable type of small society, designed to provide for the procreation and raising of children and for the mutual good of husband and wife. (The material on matrimony in the so-called *Supplement* to the *Summa Theologiae* was excerpted from Book IV of the *Scriptum in IV Libros Sententiarum* and does not represent Aquinas's mature thought.) The main reason why people get married, Aquinas thought, is to raise children, so his approach to the family was child-oriented. There should be but one husband and wife in a family; they should stay together until the children are fully grown and educated; they should deal honestly and charitably with each other as marriage partners. Many of Aquinas's arguments for monogamy and the indissolubility of the marriage bond are but restatements of similar reasonings in Aristotle's *Politics.*

POLITICAL THEORY. Aquinas's family, living in southern Italy, had been closely allied with the imperial government: His father and at least two of his brothers were in the service of Emperor Frederick II. Aquinas thus grew up with monarchic loyalties. However, early in life he joined the Dominicans, a religious community remarkable for its democratic and liberal practices. As a result Aquinas's political philosophy (in *De Regno,* in *In Libros Politicorum,* and in *Summa Theologiae,* I–II, passim) stressed the ideal of the limited monarchy, or that kind of state which Aristotle had called the *politeia.* The purpose of the state is described as to provide for temporal peace and welfare. Political society is quite different from ecclesiastical society (the church), whose end is otherworldly. Here again Aquinas always stressed the central role of reason: "Divine justice (*ius divinum*) which stems from grace does not cancel human justice which comes from natural reason." There is no detailed theory of government in Aquinas's writings.

ART AND AESTHETICS

In his theory of art Aquinas was quite abstract and intellectualistic, taking Aristotle's *Rhetoric, Poetics,* and *Nicomachean Ethics* (Book VI) as his major sources. He used a new awareness of the spiritual and moral dimensions of the beautiful, found seminally in the mystical Neoplatonism of Dionysius the Pseudo-Areopagite, to develop the fragmentary aesthetics of Aristotelianism. Most of these precisions are found in Aquinas's commentary on the fourth chapter of Dionysius's *De Divinis Nominibus.*

Art is understood to be a special habit, or acquired skill, of the practical intellect, which is simply man's possible intellect applied to problems of action. Prudence, the key practical habit in moral discourse, is defined as right reason in doing things (*recta ratio agibilium*). Similarly, art is defined as right reason in making things (*recta ratio factibilium*). These two practical habits are not confused. Elsewhere it is explained: "The principle of artifacts is the human intellect which is derived by some sort of similitude from the divine intellect, and the latter is the principle of all things in nature. Hence, not only must artistic operations imitate nature but even art products must imitate the things that exist in nature" (*In I Politicorum* 1). Some artifacts are merely useful; others may be beautiful; and still others may exist only in the order of thought (Aquinas took seriously the dictum that logic is an art).

He regarded the beautiful and the good as really identical but insisted that they differ in their formal meanings (*rationes*). Where the good is simply that which all desire, the beautiful is that which gives pleasure when perceived (*quod visum placet*). Three aspects of the beautiful are distinguished: integrity (*integritas sive perfectio*), due proportion (*debita proportio sive consonantia*), and brilliance (*claritas*). Each of these aesthetic factors is taken as capable of variation in degree and appeal.

These notions on the general meaning of Beauty were used not to describe the attraction of a life of sacrifice but of spiritual perfection as a member of a religious community, such as the Dominicans. "In fact," Aquinas wrote, "there are two kinds of beauty. One is spiritual and it consists in a due ordering and overflowing of spiritual goods. Hence, everything that proceeds from a lack of spiritual good, or that manifests intrinsic disorder, is ugly.

Another kind is external beauty which consists in a due ordering of the body" (*Contra Impugnantes Dei Cultum et Religionem* 7, ad 9). He was actually defending the practice of begging, as used in the mendicant orders. Aquinas agreed that there is something distasteful about begging but argued that it is an admirable exercise of humility, when religiously motivated. Here again the concept of purpose, teleological order, is central.

Metaphysical participation recurs as a key theme in Aquinas's discussion of the manner in which the manifold of creation shares in the transcendent beauty of God. All lower beauties are but imperfect manifestations of one highest *pulchritudo.* This is Dionysian mystical aesthetics and is presented in *In Dionysii de Divinis Nominibus* (IV, 5–6).

AUTHORITY AND INFLUENCE

Aquinas has been given a special position of respect in the field of Catholic scholarship, but this does not mean that all Catholic thinkers agree with him on all points. Within three years of his death a number of propositions closely resembling his philosophic views were condemned as errors by Bishop Tempier of Paris. This episcopal condemnation was formally revoked in 1325. Thomistic thought met much criticism in the later Middle Ages. Since the Renaissance nearly all the popes have praised Aquinas's teaching; the one who provided for the first collected edition of his works (St. Pius V) also did the same for St. Bonaventure, a Franciscan, and proclaimed both Doctors of the Church. In the ecclesiastical law of the Catholic Church, revised in 1918, canon 589:1 states that students for the priesthood are required to study at least two years of philosophy and four of theology, "following the teaching of St. Thomas." Further, canon 1366:2 directs professors in seminaries to organize their teaching "according to the method, teaching and principles of the Angelic Doctor."

Actually, Thomism has never been the only kind of philosophy cultivated by Catholics, and from the fourteenth century to the Enlightenment, Thomism was rivaled and sometimes obscured by Scotism and Ockhamism.

In 1879, with the publication of the Encyclical *Aeterni Patris* by Pope Leo XIII, the modern revival of Thomism started. While this document praised Thomism throughout, Pope Leo added this noteworthy qualification: "If there be anything that ill agrees with the discoveries of a later age, or, in a word, improbable in whatever way—it does not enter Our mind to propose that for imitation to our age" (Étienne Gilson, ed., *The Church Speaks to the Modern World,* New York, 1954, p. 50.)

In 1914 a group of Catholic teachers drew up a set of twenty-four propositions that, they felt, embodied the essential points in the philosophy of Aquinas. The Sacred Congregation of Studies, with the approval of Pope Pius X, published these "Twenty-four Theses" as clear expressions of the thought of the holy Doctor. (Original Latin text in *Acta Apostolicae Sedis* 6 [1914]: 384–386; partial English version in Charles Hart, *Thomistic Metaphysics,* Englewood Cliffs, NJ, 1959, passim.)

The first six theses attempt a formulation of the general metaphysical position of Aquinas. All beings are composed of potential and actual principles, with the exception of God, who is pure act. The divine *esse* (act of being) is utterly simple (that is, without parts or constituents) and infinite in every way. Other beings are composite; their acts of existing are limited in character and merely participated. In general, metaphysical being may be understood in terms of analogy: God's being and that of created things do not belong within the same genus, but there is some remote resemblance between divine and nondivine beings. To satisfy competing theories of analogy that developed in Renaissance Thomism, the theses describe this metaphysical analogy in terms of both attribution (following Francisco Suárez) and proportionality (following Cardinal Cajetan). The real distinction between essence and *esse* is stressed in the fifth thesis, while the difference between substance and accidents is stated in the sixth (accidents *exist in* some substance but never, in the natural course of things, exist by themselves). Marking a transition to special metaphysics (cosmology and philosophical psychology), the seventh proposition treats a spiritual creature as composed of essence and *esse,* and also of substance and accidents, but denies that there is any composition of matter and form in spirits.

A series of theses (VIII to XIII) describe bodily beings as constituted of prime matter and substantial form, neither of which may exist by itself. As material, bodies are extended in space and subject to quantification. Matter as quantified is proposed as the principle that individuates bodies. The location of a body in place is also attributed to quantity. Thesis XIII distinguishes nonliving from living bodies and makes the transition to a group of propositions concerned with human nature and its activities. The life principle in any plant or animal is called a soul, but, in the case of the human animal, the soul is found to be a principle of a very special kind. Theses XIV to XXI focus on the vital nature and functions of man. His soul is capable of existing apart from the human body; it is brought into existence directly by God's creative action; it is without constituent parts and so cannot be disintegrated, that is to say, the human soul is immortal. Moreover, man's soul is the immediate source of life, existence, and all perfection in the human body. Subsequent propositions emphasize the higher human functions of cognition and volition, and they distinguish sensitive knowledge of individual bodies and their qualities from intellectual understanding of the universal features of reality. Willing is subsequent to intellectual cognition, and the free character of volitional acts of choice is strongly asserted.

The last three theses offer a summary of Aquinas's philosophic approach to God. The divine existence is neither directly intuited by the ordinary man nor demonstrable on an a priori basis. It is capable of a posteriori demonstration using any of the famous arguments of the Five Ways; these arguments are briefly summarized. Thesis XXIII reaffirms the simplicity of God's being and maintains the complete identity between the divine essence and *esse.* The final thesis asserts the creation by God of all things in the universe and stresses the point that the coming into existence and the motion of all creatures are to be attributed ultimately to God as First Cause.

These twenty-four theses represent a rigid and conservative type of Thomism. Many modern Catholic philosophers, while recognizing that these propositions do express some of the basic themes in the speculative thought of Aquinas, doubt that it is possible to put the wisdom of any great philosopher into a few propositions and prefer to emphasize the open-minded spirit with which Aquinas searched for information among his predecessors and approached the problems of his own day. After all, it was Aquinas who remarked that arguments from authority are appropriate in sacred teaching but are the weakest sort of evidence in philosophic reasoning.

See also Abelard, Peter; Aesthetics, History of; Albert the Great; Aristotelianism; Aristotle; Augustine, St.; Averroes; Avicenna; Being; Boethius, Anicius Manlius Severinus; Bonaventure, St.; Cajetan, Cardinal; Cicero, Marcus Tullius; Duns Scotus, John; Empiricism; Enlightenment; Essence and Existence; Eternal Return; Ethics, History of; Faith; Gilson, Étienne Henry; Ibn Gabirol, Solomon ben Judah; John of Damascus; Liber de Causis; Maimonides; Maritain, Jacques; Metaphysics, History of; Neoplatonism; Ockhamism; Plato; Pseudo-Dionysius; Roscelin; Ross, William David; Scientia Media and Molinism; Scotism; Stoicism; Suárez, Francisco; Taylor, Alfred Edward; Thomism; Universals, A Historical Survey; William of Champeaux.

Bibliography

WORKS BY THOMAS AQUINAS

Collected Editions

Opera Omnia, 25 vols. Parma, 1852–1873. Reprinted, New York, 1948–1950. A noncritical but almost complete edition.

Opera Omnia, 34 vols. Paris, 1871–1882. A noncritical but almost complete edition.

S. Thomae Aquinatis, Opera Omnia. Rome, 1882–. The Leonine Edition is recognized by scholars as the standard edition of the works of Aquinas.

Individual Works

Scriptum in IV Libros Sententiarum (1252–1257). 4 vols, edited by Pierre Mandonnet and M. F. Moos. Paris, 1929–1947. No English version.

De Ente et Essentia (1253). Vol. XLIII of Leonine edition. Translated by Armand Maurer as *On Being and Essence.* Toronto, 1949.

De Principiis Naturae (1253). Vol. XLIII of Leonine edition. Translated by V. J. Bourke in *The Pocket Aquinas,* edited by V. J. Bourke, 61–77. New York: Washington Square Press, 1960.

Contra Impugnantes Dei Cultum et Religionem (1256). Vol. XLI of Leonine edition. Translated by J. Proctor as *An Apology for the Religious Orders.* Westminster, MD, 1950.

Quaestiones Disputatae de Veritate (1256–1259). Vol. XXII of Leonine edition. Translated by R. W, Mulligan et al. as *Truth,* 3 vols. Chicago, 1952–1954.

Quaestiones Quodlibetales (1256–1272). Vol. XXV of Leonine edition. Partially translated by S. Edwards as *Quodlibetal Questions 1 and 2. Medieval Sources in Translation,* Vol. 27. Toronto, 1983.

In Librum Boethii de Trinitate Expositio (1257–1258). Vol. L of Leonine edition. Translated by R. E. Brennan as *The Trinity and the Unicity of the Intellect.* St. Louis, 1946.

In Librum Dionysii de Divinis Nominibus (1258–1265), edited by Ceslas Pera. Turin, 1950. Partially translated by V. J. Bourke in *The Pocket Aquinas,* 269–278. New York: Washington Square Press, 1960.

Summa de Veritate Catholicae Fidei Contra Gentiles (1259–1264), Vols. XIII–XV of the Leonine edition. Rome, 1918–1930. Also published in a one-volume "manual" edition. Turin and Rome, 1934. Translated by A. C. Pegis, J. F. Anderson, V. J. Bourke, and C. J. O'Neil as *On the Truth of the Catholic Faith,* 5 vols. New York, 1955–1957.

De Emptione et Venditione (1263). Vol. XLII of Leonine edition. Translated and edited by Alfred O'Rahilly as "Notes on St. Thomas on Credit." *Irish Ecclesiastical Record* 31 (1928): 164–165. Translation reprinted in *The Pocket Aquinas,* 223–225. New York: Washington Square Press, 1960.

Quaestiones Disputatae de Potentia Dei (1265). Edited by R. M. Spiazzi. Turin, 1949. Translated by Lawrence Shapcote as *On the Power of God.* Westminster, MD: Newman Press, 1952.

Commentaries on Aristotle (1265–1273), listed in next section.

De Regno (1265–1266). Vol. XLII of Leonine edition. Translated by G. B. Phelan and I. T. Eschmann as *On*

Kingship. Toronto: Pontifical Institute of Mediaeval Studies, 1949.

Compendium Theologiae (1265–1269). Vol. XLII of Leonine edition. Translated by Cyril Vollert as *Compendium of Theology.* St. Louis, 1957.

Summa Theologiae (1265–1273). Vols. IV–XII of the Leonine edition. Rome, 1918–1930. Reprinted, Turin, 1934. Translated by the English Dominican Fathers as *The Summa Theologica,* 22 vols. London, 1912–1936. Revision of part of the English Dominican Fathers' translation appears in *Basic Writings of Saint Thomas Aquinas,* edited by A. C. Pegis. New York: Random House, 1945.

Quaestiones Disputatae de Spiritualibus Creaturis (1267). Vol. XXIV of Leonine edition. Translated by John Wellmuth and Mary Fitzpatrick as *On Spiritual Creatures.* Milwaukee, 1949.

Quaestio Disputata de Anima (1269). Vol. XXIV of Leonine edition. Translated by J. P. Rowan as *The Soul.* St. Louis, 1949.

Quaestiones Disputatae de Malo (1269–1272). Vol. XXIII of Leonine edition. Translated by J. and J. Oesterle as *Disputed Questions on Evil.* Notre Dame, IN: University of Notre Dame Press, 1983.

Quaestiones Disputatae de Virtutibus (1269–1272). Edi Vol. XXIV of Leonine edition. Partially translated by J. P. Reid as *The Virtues in General.* Providence, RI, 1951.

In Job Expositio (1269–1272). In Vol. XVII of Leonine edition. Rome, 1962. Translated by A. Damico as *The Literal Exposition on Job: A Scriptural Commentary concerning Providence.* Classics in Religious Studies 7. Atlanta, 1989.

In Evangelium Joannis Expositio (1269–1272), edited by Raphael Cai. Turin, 1952. Partially translated by J. A. Weisheipl and F. R. Larcher as *Commentary on the Gospel of Saint John,* Part I. Albany, NY, 1980.

De Unitate Intellectus (1270). Edited by Vol. XLIII of Leonine edition. Translated by Sister Rose E. Brennan as *The Unicity of the Intellect.* St. Louis: Herder, 1946.

De Substantiis Separatis (1271). Vol. XL of Leonine edition. Translated by F. J. Lescoe as *Treatise on Separate Substances.* West Hartford, CT: Saint Joseph College, 1963.

De Aeternitate Mundi (1271). Vol. XLIII of Leonine edition. Translated by Cyril Vollert as *On the Eternity of the World.* Milwaukee: Marquette University Press, 1964.

In Librum de Causis (1271), edited by H. D. Saffrey. Fribourg, 1954. Translated by V. A. Guagliardo et al. as *Commentary on the Book of Causes.* Thomas Aquinas in Translation Series. Washington, DC, 1996.

Commentaries on Aristotle

In Libros Posteriorum Analyticorum. In Vol. I of the Leonine edition. Rome, 1882. Translated by Pierre Conway. Quebec, 1956.

In Libros de Anima. In Vol. XLV of the Leonine edition. Also edited by R. M. Spiazzi. Turin, 1955. Translated by Kenelm Foster and Silvester Humphries as *Aristotle's De Anima with the Commentary of St. Thomas.* London and New Haven, CT, 1951.

In Libros de Caelo et Mundo. In Vol. III of the Leonine edition. Rome, 1886. Also edited by R. M. Spiazzi. Turin, 1952. No English version.

In X Libros Ethicorum. In Vol. XLVII of the Leonine edition. Also edited by R. M. Spiazzi. Turin, 1949. Translated by C. I. Litzinger as *Commentary on the Nicomachean Ethics,* 2 vols. Chicago: Regnery, 1964.

In Libros de Generatione et Corruptione. In Vol. III of the Leonine edition. Rome, 1886. Also edited by R. M. Spiazzi. Turin, 1952. No English version.

In Libros Peri Hermeneias. In Vol. I of the Leonine edition. Rome, 1882. Also edited by R. M. Spiazzi. Turin, 1955. Translated by Jean Oesterle as *Aristotle on Interpretation—Commentary by St. Thomas and Cajetan.* Milwaukee: Marquette University Press, 1962.

In Libros de Memoria et Reminiscentia, et de Sensu et Sensato. In Vol. XLV of the Leonine edition. Also edited by R. M. Spiazzi. Turin, 1949. No English version.

In XII Libros Metaphysicorum. In Vol. XLVI of the Leonine edition. Also edited by R. M. Spiazzi. Turin, 1950. Translated by J. P. Rowan as *Commentary on the Metaphysics of Aristotle,* 2 vols. Chicago: Regnery, 1961.

In Libros Meteorologicorum. in Vol. III of the Leonine edition. Rome, 1886. Also edited by R. M. Spiazzi. Turin, 1952. No English version.

In VIII Libros Physicorum. In Vol. II of the Leonine edition. Rome, 1884. Also edited by P. M. Maggiolo. Turin, 1954. Translated by R. J. Blackwell and others as *Commentary on Aristotle's Physics.* New Haven, CT: Yale University Press, 1963.

In Libros Politicorum. In Vol. XLVIII of the Leonine edition. Also edited by R. M. Spiazzi. Turin, 1951. Translation of Book III, Lectures 1–6 by E. L. Fortin and Peter D. O'Neill in *Medieval Political Philosophy,* edited by Ralph Lerner and Muhsin Mahdi, 297–334. New York: Free Press of Glencoe, 1963.

WORKS ON THOMAS AQUINAS

Guides

Bergomo, Petri de. *Tabula Aurea in Omnia Opera S. Thomae Aquinatis.* Bologna, 1485. Reprinted in Vol. XXV of *S. Thomae, Opera Omnia.* Parma, 1873.

Busa, Roberto. *Index Thomisticus.* Stuttgart-Bad Cannstatt: Fromann-Holzboog, 1974–1980.

Deferrari, Roy J., Sister M. Inviolata Barry, and Ignatius McGuiness. *A Lexicon of St. Thomas Aquinas, Based on the Summa Theologica and Selected Passages of His Other Works.* Washington, DC: Catholic University of America Press, 1949.

Indices … in Summam Theologiae et Summam Contra Gentiles. In Vol. XVI of the Leonine edition. Reprinted with some omissions in *Editio Leonina Manualis.* Rome, 1948.

Schütz, Ludwig. *Thomas-Lexikon.* Paderborn, 1895. Reprinted New York, 1949.

Studies

Aertsen, Jan. *Nature and Creature: Thomas Aquinas' Way of Thought.* Leiden: Brill, 1988.

Anderson, J. F. *An Introduction to the Metaphysics of St. Thomas Aquinas.* Chicago: Regnery, 1953. Collection of basic texts with clear explanations; useful for the theory of analogy.

Bourke, V. J. *Aquinas' Search for Wisdom.* Milwaukee: Bruce, 1965. A factual biography excluding pious legends and situating Thomas's thought in the context of his life.

Burrell, David. *Knowing the Unknowable God: Ibn Sina, Maimonides, Aquinas.* Notre Dame: University of Notre Dame Press, 1986.

Callahan, Leonard. *A Theory of Esthetic according to St. Thomas.* Washington, DC: Catholic University of America Press, 1927. Rethinks the original theory but also interprets the fragmentary maxims of Aquinas on beauty and art.

Chenu, M. D. *Toward Understanding Saint Thomas.* Chicago: Regnery, 1964. Masterful introduction to the advanced study of the works of Thomas Aquinas.

Copleston, F. C. *Aquinas.* Harmondsworth, U.K.: Penguin, 1955. This is a well-written exposition of the philosophy of Thomas, with some effort to meet the criticisms of British analysts.

Davies, Brian. *The Thought of Thomas Aquinas.* Oxford: Clarendon Press, 1992.

De Koninck, Charles. "Introduction à l'étude de l'âme." *Laval théologique et philosophique* 3 (1947): 9–65. Reprinted in Stanislas Cantin, *Précis de psychologie thomiste.* Quebec, 1948. LXXXIII, 173.

Descoqs, Pedro. *Thomisme et scolastique.* Paris: G. Beauchesne, 1927. Representative Suarezian criticism of the metaphysics of Aquinas; insists that there are other valid positions in philosophy.

Duns Scotus, John. *De Primo Principio.* Translated and edited by Evan Roche. St. Bonaventure, NY: Franciscan Institute, 1949. Important for fourteenth-century criticism by Duns Scotus of the general metaphysics and natural theology of Thomas.

Fabro, Cornelio. *La nozione metafisica di partecipazione secondo S. Tommaso.* Milan, 1939; 2nd ed., Turin, 1950. Outstanding study of the metaphysics of Thomism, stressing the Platonic elements.

Finnis, John. *Aquinas: Moral, Political, and Legal Theory.* New York: Oxford University Press, 1998.

Flannery, Kevin. *Acts Among Precepts: The Aristotelian Structure of Thomas Aquinas's Moral Theory.* Washington DC: Catholic University of America Press, 2001.

Garrigou-Lagrange, Réginald. *Reality: A Synthesis of Thomistic Thought.* St. Louis: Herder, 1950. Adapted from a long article in the *Dictionnaire de théologie catholique,* this work represents a most conservative type of Thomism.

Geiger, L. B. *La participation dans la philosophie de saint Thomas.* Paris, 1942. Excellent discussion of the Platonic themes in Thomas's metaphysics; with Fabro and Geiger it has become clear that Thomism is not a "baptized" Aristotelianism.

Gilby, Thomas. *The Political Thought of Thomas Aquinas.* Chicago: University of Chicago Press, 1958. Work of popularization that offers, however, a rather balanced view of the monarchic and democratic elements in Thomas's ideas on government.

Gilson, Étienne. *The Christian Philosophy of St. Thomas Aquinas.* New York: Random House, 1956. With "Catalogue of St. Thomas's Works" by I. T. Eschmann. A highly esteemed exposition; the French original followed the order of the *Summa Contra Gentiles*; this English revision stresses the idea that Thomism is a Christian philosophy.

Grabmann, Martin. *Die Werke des hl. Thomas von Aquin.* 3rd ed. Münster, 1949. The most complete study of the chronology and authenticity of the writings of Aquinas.

Henle, R. J. *Saint Thomas and Platonism.* The Hague: Nijhoff, 1956. Good example of a careful textual study using the method of parallel passages taken in chronological sequence.

Hughes, Christopher. *On a Complex Theory of a Simple God: An Investigation in Aquinas' Philosophical Theology.* Ithaca: Cornell University Press, 1989.

Jaffa, H. V. *Thomism and Aristotelianism. A Study of the Commentary by Thomas Aquinas on the Nicomachean Ethics.* Chicago: University of Chicago Press, 1952. A sharp criticism of Aquinas as an interpreter of Aristotle's practical philosophy.

Kenny, Anthony, ed. *Aquinas: A Collection of Critical Essays.* Garden City: Doubleday, 1969.

Kenny, Anthony. *Aquinas on Mind.* London: Routledge, 1993.

Klubertanz, G. P. *St. Thomas Aquinas on Analogy.* Chicago: Loyola University Press, 1960. Advanced and difficult study of all that Aquinas has written on metaphysical analogy; stresses the pluralism inherent in the theory: several types of analogy are at work.

Kluxen, Wolfgang. *Philosophische Ethik bei Thomas von Aquin.* Mainz, 1964. Important discussion of the relation between moral theology and ethics.

Kretzmann, Norman. *The Metaphysics of Creation: Aquinas's Natural Theology in Summa Contra Gentiles II.* Oxford: Clarendon Press, 1999.

Kretzmann, Norman. *The Metaphysics of Theism: Aquinas's Natural Theology in Summa Contra Gentiles I.* Oxford: Clarendon Press, 1997.

Kretzmann, Norman, and Stump, Eleonore, eds. *The Cambridge Companion to Aquinas.* Cambridge, U.K.: Cambridge University Press, 1993.

Lonergan, Bernard. *Verbum: Word and Idea in Aquinas.* Edited by David Burrell. Notre Dame, IN: University of Notre Dame Press, 1967.

Maritain, Jacques. *The Angelic Doctor: The Life and Thought of St. Thomas Aquinas,* rev. ed. New York, 1958. Popular work stressing papal approval of Thomistic philosophy and the special status of Aquinas in Catholic educational programs.

Maritain, Jacques. *Art and Scholasticism.* New York: Scribners, 1930. An almost classic account of the aesthetic theory of Thomas, with some adaptation to artistic problems in the twentieth century.

Maurer, Armand, ed. *St. Thomas Aquinas, 1274–1974: Commemorative Studies,* 2 vols. Toronto: Pontifical Institute of Medieaval Studies, 1974.

McInerny, Ralph. *Aquinas and Analogy.* Washington, DC: Catholic University of America Press, 1996.

Meyer, Hans. *The Philosophy of St. Thomas Aquinas.* St. Louis: Herder, 1944. In the guise of an exposition of Aquinas's thought, this is actually a trenchant critique of Thomism.

Oesterle, John A. *Ethics: The Introduction to Moral Science.* Englewood Cliffs, NJ: Prentice-Hall, 1957. Representative textbook emphasizing the autonomy and strictly philosophical character of Thomistic ethics.

Owens, Joseph. *An Elementary Christian Metaphysics.* Milwaukee: Bruce, 1963. Advanced textbook in the tradition of the Christian philosophy interpretation of Aquinas.

Owens, Joseph. *St. Thomas Aquinas on the Existence of God: Collected Papers of Joseph Owens,* edited by John Catan. Albany: State University of New York Press, 1980.

Pasnau, Robert. *Thomas Aquinas on Human Nature: A Philosophical Study of Summa Theologiae Ia 75–89.* Cambridge, U.K.: Cambridge University Press, 2001.

Pieper, Josef. *Guide to Thomas Aquinas.* Translated by Richard and Clara Winston. New York: Pantheon, 1962. A readable and elementary introduction by a noted German Thomist.

Rahner, Karl. *Geist im Welt. Zur Metaphysik der endliche Erkenntnis bei Thomas von Aquin.* Innsbruck and Leipzig, 1939. Outstanding German study of the theory of knowledge.

Ramírez, J. M. *De Auctoritate Doctrinae Sancti Thomae Aquinatis.* Salamanca, 1952. Representative of the well-informed and broadminded views of some Spanish Dominicans on the status of Thomism in Catholic philosophy.

Rommen, Heinrich. *The State in Catholic Thought.* St. Louis: Herder, 1945. Situates Thomistic political philosophy in the broader context of Catholic thinking as a whole.

Reith, Herman. *The Metaphysics of St. Thomas Aquinas.* Milwaukee: Bruce, 1958. Standard exposition, not difficult to read. Includes 200 pages of quotations from many works of Thomas.

Ryan, J. K. "St. Thomas and English Protestant Thinkers." *New Scholasticism* 22 (1) (1948): 1–33; (2) (1948): 126–208. Excellent survey of the reactions to, and criticisms of, Aquinas in post-Reformation British thought.

Smith. Gerard. *Natural Theology: Metaphysics II.* New York: Macmillan, 1951. On Thomas's philosophical approach to God; Ch. 16 discusses divine foreknowledge and human freedom.

Stump, Eleonore. *Aquinas.* London: Routledge, 2003.

Torrell, Jean-Pierre. *Saint Thomas Aquinas,* Vol. 1: *The Person and His Work.* Translated by Robert Royal. Washington, DC: Catholic University of America Press, 1996.

Ude, Johannes. *Die Autorität des hi. Thomas von Aquin als Kirchenlehrer.* Salzburg, 1932. Basic study of the question "Must Catholics agree in philosophy and theology with Thomas Aquinas?" The answer is "No."

Walz, Angelus, *Saint Thomas d'Aquin.* French adaptation by Paul Novarina. Louvain and Paris, 1962. One of the best biographies; this French printing has much more information than the English version, *Saint Thomas Aquinas,* translated by S. T. Bullough. Westminster, MD: Newman Press, 1951.

Westberg, Daniel. *Right Practical Reason: Aristotle, Action, and Prudence in Aquinas.* Oxford: Clarendon Press, 1994.

Wippel, John. *The Metaphysical Thought of Thomas Aquinas: From Finite Being to Uncreated Being.* Washington, DC: Catholic University of America Press, 2000.

Wittmann, Michael. *Die Ethik des hl. Thomas von Aquin.* Munich, 1933. Good historical study of Thomistic ethics in relation to Aristotle, the Stoics, and the Fathers of the Church.

WORKS ON THOMISM

Bourke, V. J. *Thomistic Bibliography, 1920–1940.* St. Louis: Modern Schoolman, 1945.

Bulletin thomiste (since 1921).

Ingardia, Richard. *Thomas Aquinas: International Bibliography 1977–1990.* Bowling Green, OH: Philosophy Documentation Center, 1993.

Mandonnet, Pierre, and Jean Destrez. *Bibliographie thomiste.* Le Saulchoir, Belgium: Revue des Sciences Philosophiques et Thélogiques, 1921; rev. ed., edited by M. D. Chenu. Paris: Vrin, 1960.

Répertoire bibliographique. Annual supplement to *Revue philosophique de Louvain* (Belgium).

Wyser, Paul. *Thomas von Aquin* and *Der Thomismus,* fascicles 13–14 and 15–16 of *Bibliographische Einführungen in das Studium der Philosophie.* Fribourg, Switzerland, 1948ff.

Vernon J. Bourke (1967)
Bibliography updated by Christian B. Miller (2005)

THOMASIUS, CHRISTIAN
(1655–1728)

Christian Thomasius was a philosopher and jurist and the first important thinker of the German Enlightenment. He was born in Leipzig, the son of the Aristotelian philosopher Jakob Thomasius, who had been a teacher of Gottfried Wilhelm Leibniz. Christian, after studying philosophy and law at the universities of Leipzig and Frankfurt an der Oder, began lecturing at Leipzig in 1682. His theological enemies forced him to move in 1690 to the Ritterakademie in Halle. He helped to found the University of Halle, became professor of law there in 1694, and later was Geheimrat (privy counselor) and rector of the university.

LAW AND THEOLOGY

Thomasius followed his father, as well as Hugo Grotius and Samuel von Pufendorf, in the study of natural law. He sought a foundation for law, independent of theology, in man's natural reason. Like Pufendorf he opposed the orthodox Lutheran view that revelation is the source of law and that jurisprudence is subordinate to theology. He held that law is based on common sense and on truths common to all religions. On the other hand, many precepts traditionally held to be absolute were only the result of the historical development of a given nation, subject to change and justifiable only in terms of the characteristics of that nation. Thomasius asserted the right of free and impartial interpretation of the Bible and of God's laws, reacting against orthodox Lutheran exegesis and the intricacies and dogmatism of scholastic theology. He condemned fanaticism and the persecution of heretics and preached toleration of differing religious beliefs.

Thomasius opposed the episcopal system of church government, which asserted the rights of consistories and of theological faculties in church affairs, and supported a territorial system of church government, in which the government would have control of church administration but not of dogma. In dogma neither state nor consistories and faculties should have power; the latter should make decisions concerning dogma, but individual churches and Christians should be free to accept or reject them. Thomasius thus sought to break the power of the governing bodies of the church, which were dominated by intolerant orthodox Lutherans, and to subordinate the church to the government, which by natural law should be supreme within the state. It was these doctrines that forced Thomasius's expulsion from Leipzig and led to his reception at Halle by the Prussian government, which was more liberal in religious matters.

EDUCATION AND THE NATURE OF MAN

Thomasius held that philosophy should be practical and should concentrate on man, his nature, and his needs. He opposed the Aristotelian scholasticism of orthodox Lutheranism because its abstractions and speculative complexities were useless in life. His *Introductio ad Philosophiam Aulicam* (An Introduction to Philosophy for the Courtier; Leipzig, 1688) was in the tradition of Renaissance humanistic pedagogy. It advocated a worldly education intended to produce "courtiers" (politicians, diplomats, and bureaucrats) rather than the "pedantic" scholastic education of the universities. The German states established after the Thirty Years' War were organizing centralized governments and modern administrations on the French model, and they needed officials with the practical education Thomasius advocated. Thomasius's model was the education given in the German *Ritterakademien* (schools for the nobility), and he himself introduced this practical, worldly education into the teaching of the Halle faculty of law.

The *Introductio* was intended as the first of a series of texts furthering Thomasius's educational goals. In it Thomasius advocated eclecticism and disapproved of sectarianism and quarrels between schools of thought. He held that philosophy should be independent of revealed theology and founded on the observation of reality. Metaphysics was harmful and should be confined to a short terminological excursus. For Thomasius theoretical philosophy comprised natural theology, physics, and mathematics. The *Introductio* presented his theory of man and covered psychology and theory of knowledge, knowledge being obtained through the senses only. Thomasius was a nominalist, and he was skeptical about rationally proving God's existence. He closed with a summary of logic, both practical and theoretical. Thomasius continued the educational program of the *Introductio* in his *Einleitung zu der Vernunfft-Lehre* (Introduction to logic; Halle, 1691), *Einleitung zur Sitten-Lehre* (Introduction to ethics; Halle, 1692), *Ausübung der Vernunfft-Lehre* (Practical logic; Halle, 1693), and *Ausübung der Sitten-Lehre* (Practical ethics; Halle, 1696), all of which introduced the use of German into university teaching.

In the *Introductio* and other works Thomasius's eclecticism and opposition to dogmatism, his empiricism, his concentration on description of human nature and the giving of advice for practical behavior, are evident. His eclecticism and opposition to dogmatism was connected with the tradition of Peter Ramus that survived in the school of John Amos Comenius and with Thomasius's philosophical individualism. He often presented his doctrines as only hypothetical and spoke of "my own" philosophy, renouncing absolute truth. Thomasius's concentration on the practical was influenced by such writers as Pierre Charron and Baltasar Gracián. Besides his texts he wrote special works on "prudence" (*Klugheit, prudentia*), giving advice for persons in different situations and positions.

Thomasius held that logic should be simple, should avoid the scholastic syllogistic treatment, and should be based on personal experience. Its goal should be not only the demonstration but also the discovery of truth. In line with his empiricism and opposition to dogmatism, Thomasius wrote much on probability and combined his discussion of logic with psychology and sociology.

Thomasius believed that Christian ethics must be based on rational love. Love, in its different forms, is the basic impulse in man. The will is independent of reason and is the origin of evil.

PIETISM

About 1694 Thomasius underwent a personal religious and philosophical crisis. Influenced by certain Pietist thinkers, he lost faith in the natural goodness and intellectual power of man and held that virtue and truth could be reached only through God's grace, man being otherwise vicious and blind. He solemnly disavowed his former errors in a public confession. By 1705 Thomasius showed a renewed faith in human freedom and goodness and in the natural light. The period from 1694 to 1705 is known as Thomasius's Pietist period, but his acceptance of Pietism was eased by substantial similarities between his own views and those of the Pietists. Both opposed "pedantry," Aristotelianism, Lutheran orthodoxy, the episcopal system of church government, and intolerance;

both were also eclectic and empirical and avoided scholastic abstractions and theological subtleties. A personal acquaintance with the Pietist A. H. Francke played an important part in Thomasius's temporary conversion to other Pietist views.

METAPHYSICS

Thomasius's two works on metaphysics were published at Halle during his Pietist period, the *Confessio Doctrinae Suae* in 1695 and the *Versuch vom Wesen des Geistes* (An Essay on the Essence of Spirit) in 1699. Like Paracelsus, Valentin Weigel, Jakob Boehme, and others before him, Thomasius presented a mystical or theosophical variety of animism or vitalism. The world, both spiritual and material, is animated by a spirit created by God. Truth can be found only in the Bible as made clear by divine illumination. Although such views were held by some Pietists, they were not confined to them, and Thomasius continued to hold them after his Pietist period. Perhaps Thomasius's metaphysics was influenced not only by Pietism but also by the school of Comenius, who influenced Thomasius in other ways, and by the Hermetic school of medicine and chemistry, which had a mystically based experimental attitude. The latter possibility especially would explain Thomasius's combination of empiricism and a mystical metaphysics advanced only as a hypothesis.

INFLUENCE

Thomasius's most important followers were either Pietists or their sympathizers, and his views soon became the official Pietist philosophy. The theologian Joachim Lange in particular stressed Thomasius's Pietism and held that divine illumination was the only source of truth. By 1710 Thomasius's followers had displaced the Aristotelians in nearly all the German universities. Lange led the first attacks against the new doctrines of Christian Wolff, but Thomasius, true to his spirit of toleration, did not participate in the attack. Wolffianism became dominant after 1730, but a few Pietist centers remained. Later, the work of the Pietists A. F. Hoffmann and Christian August Crusius helped to bring about the renewal of German philosophy after 1760, which culminated in the critical philosophy of Immanuel Kant.

See also Aristotelianism; Boehme, Jakob; Charron, Pierre; Comenius, John Amos; Crusius, Christian August; Empiricism; Enlightenment; Gracián y Morales, Baltasar; Grotius, Hugo; Hermeticism; Holism and Individualism in History and Social Science; Kant, Immanuel; Leibniz, Gottfried Wilhelm; Paracelsus; Pietism; Philosophy of Law, History of; Pufendorf, Samuel von; Ramus, Peter; Toleration; Wolff, Christian.

Bibliography

ADDITIONAL WORKS BY THOMASIUS

Institutiones Iurisprudentiae Divinae. Frankfurt and Leipzig, 1688.

Die neue Entfindung einer wohlgegründeten und für das gemeine Wesen höchstnötige Wissenschaft. Das Verborgene des Hertzens anderer Menschen auch wider ihren Willen aus der täglichen Conversation zu erkennen. Halle, 1692.

Kleine deutsche Schriften. Halle, 1701.

Fundamenta Iuris Naturae et Gentium. Halle, 1705.

Kurtzer Entwurff der politischen Klugheit. Halle, 1705.

WORKS ON THOMASIUS

Barnard, F. M. "The Practical Philosophy of Christian Thomasius." *Journal of the History of Ideas* 32 (1971): 221–246.

Battaglia, Felice. *Cristiano Thomasius*. Rome, 1935.

Bienert, Walther. *Der Anbruch der Christlichen deutschen Neuzeit dargestellt an Wissenschaft und Glauben des Christian Thomasius*. Halle: Akademischer, 1934.

Bloch, Ernst. *Christian Thomasius*. Berlin: Aufbau-Verlag, 1953.

Fleischmann, Max, ed. *Christian Thomasius, Leben und Lebenswerk*. Halle: Niemeyer, 1931.

Hunter, Ian. "Christian Thomasius and the Desacralization of Philosophy." *Journal of the History of Ideas* 61(4) (2000): 595–616.

Jaitner, W. R. *Thomasius, Rüdiger, Hoffmann und Crusius*. Bleicherode, 1939.

Kayser, R. *Christian Thomasius und der Pietismus*. Hamburg, 1900.

Link Salinger, R. "Christian Thomasius: Of Moral Philosophy and Natural Law." In *Philosophy and Culture*. Vol 2, edited by Venant Cauchy. Montreal: Montmorency, 1988.

Neisser, Liselotte. *Christian Thomasius und seine Beziehung zum Pietismus*. Munich, 1928.

Schneiders, Werner. *Recht, Moral und Liebe. Untersuchungen zur Entwicklung der Moralphilosophie und Naturrechtslehre des 17 Jahrhunderts bei Christian Thomasius*. Münster, 1961.

Schroder, Peter. "Thomas Hobbes, Christian Thomasius and the Seventeenth-Century Debate on the Church and State." *History of European Ideas* 23(2-4) (1997): 59–79.

Schubert-Fikentscher, Gertrud. *Unbekannter Thomasius*. Weimar: Böhlaus Nachfolger, 1954.

Wolf, Erik. *Grotius, Pufendorf, Thomasius*. Tübingen, 1927.

Giorgio Tonelli (1967)
Bibliography updated by Tamra Frei (2005)

THOMAS OF YORK

(1220/1225–1260/1269)

Thomas of York, the English metaphysician and theologian, joined the Franciscan order by 1245, and he became doctor of theology at Oxford in 1253. He was fifth lecturer to the Oxford Franciscans (1253/1254) and sixth lecturer at the Cambridge convent (1256/1257). Thomas was the protégé of both Adam Marsh and Robert Grosseteste, whose tradition he followed. He wrote a treatise, *Manus Quae contra Omnipotentem* (The hand which is raised against the almighty), supporting St. Bonaventure in the battle between seculars and mendicants at Paris.

His major work, *Sapientiale,* written between 1250 and 1260 and never finished, is the earliest known metaphysical *summa* of the thirteenth century. It makes use of all the major writers of antiquity, as well as the Muslim and Jewish philosophers (particularly Avicebron and Maimonides), the Church Fathers, and his immediate predecessors at Paris and Oxford. Although he presents all the important opinions on each point, he is not a mere compiler but an original and profound philosopher who had mastered the entire corpus of knowledge available.

In the *Sapientiale* he treats all the standard metaphysical problems, both general and specific (a distinction he seems to have been the first to make), from an essentially Augustinian standpoint. His theory of matter is eclectic: There is a universal matter that is pure potentiality, and matter understood simply as privation. Heavenly bodies, for example, lack the second kind. Because in act they are already everything they are capable of becoming, they are free of any privation. He subscribes to a modified form of Grosseteste's light metaphysics, including a form of corporeity that is present in every body. Since form is the principle of individuation, however, there must be a plurality of forms in any given body. (Thomas does not explicitly raise this question, but it is implicit in much that he says.) He is very clear, though, that the soul cannot be a form perfecting that of the body. It is itself composite and is related to the body "as a pilot is to a ship." The soul is able to gain knowledge by abstracting universals from singulars through sense (the complete universal can be known from one singular), but it gains more certain knowledge from above, receiving ideas from Ideas through interior illumination.

Thomas maintained the distinction in creatures between essence and existence, the latter characterized by composition from matter and form, and the mark of a creature's contingency. His emphasis on the contingency of creation prevented his arriving at a clear-cut assertion of the efficacy of natural causes, although he usually seems to favor this position.

Finally, Thomas was a vigorous proponent of what had become the typical Franciscan position since Grosseteste, denying the eternity of the world, of time, of matter, and of motion, and refusing any accommodation to the Aristotelian or Averroistic schools.

See also Augustinianism; Averroism; Bonaventure, St.; British Philosophy; Essence and Existence; Grosseteste, Robert; Ibn Gabirol, Solomon ben Judah; Maimonides; Metaphysics, History of; Patristic Philosophy.

Bibliography

An edition of the *Sapientiale* is being prepared by R. J. O'Donnell, C.S.B. Pending its appearance, see D. E. Sharp, *Franciscan Philosophy at Oxford in the Thirteenth Century* (Oxford: Oxford University Press, 1930), pp. 49–114; Felix Treserra, "De Doctrinis Metaphysicis Fratris Thomae de Eboraco," in *Analecta Sacra Tarraconensis* 5 (1929): 33–102; and A. B. Emden, *A Biographical Register of the University of Oxford to A.D. 1500* (Oxford: Clarendon Press, 1957–1959), Vol. III, pp. 2139–2140.

Richard C. Dales (1967)

THOMISM

The epithet "Thomist" has been applied since the fourteenth century to followers of St. Thomas Aquinas; the earlier "Thomatist," occasionally used, was dropped toward the end of the fifteenth century. The term has a different implication according to the three main historical periods that can be distinguished. First, until the beginning of the 1500s, during a period of vigorous Scholasticism and competition among several schools, Thomism stood in metaphysics for the doctrine of a composition of essence and existence in all created beings; and in noetics it opposed both nominalism and the Neoplatonic concept of illumination by the Ideas. Second, from the sixteenth until the eighteenth century Thomism flourished in the golden age of Spanish Scholasticism. (At this time Thomists unreservedly applied to theology the metaphysical concept of the premotion of all secondary causes by the first cause.) Third, beginning about the middle of the nineteenth century there was a revival of Thomism that was authoritatively endorsed by the Catholic Church. Since then it has been claimed for Thomism that it represents the *philosophia perennis* of the West; Thomists have engaged in many-sided dialogue with thinkers from other traditions and disciplines and have been constructive in applying Thomistic principles to modern social and political problems.

We shall take these periods in order, noting beforehand that a unified philosophy, inspired by the writings of Thomas, persists throughout. In the philosophy of Thomas phenomenology is not divided from ontology; the world is real and composed of many real and distinct things, all deriving from one fount and all related by the analogy of being. Man is a single substance composed of body and soul; his knowledge begins from experience of the material world, and his understanding is developed through reason; his free activity determines his personal and eternal destiny.

THIRTEENTH TO SIXTEENTH CENTURY

When Thomas died in 1274, much of his teaching was still regarded as startling. Despite the affection in which he had been held (this was greater in the faculties of arts than in those of divinity) and despite his writings against the Latin Averroists, there developed a bitter opposition expressed in criticism and censure. It came from the representatives of the traditional Augustinian theology and was reinforced by the Franciscan masters. Conservative, yet by no means obscurantist, they included Thomas in their suspicions of what can be simplified as the "this-worldliness" of the new Aristotelianism. Étienne Tempier, bishop of Paris, was commissioned by Pope John XXII (Peter of Spain, the famous logician, who was an able natural philosopher) to investigate the charges against the new philosophy; he exceeded his instructions and in 1277, in a scissors-and-paste syllabus, he condemned 219 propositions, about a dozen of which can be traced to Thomas. In the same year Robert Kilwardby, the ex-provincial of the English Dominicans and now the archbishop of Canterbury, forbade the teaching of Thomas at Oxford, and his successor, John Peckham, acridly continued the same policy; they led the group called the *Cantuarienses.* As is evidenced in William de La Mare's list of correctives (*correctoria*) issued to be appended to Thomas's writings, many of the points at issue were highly technical, and some of them may now seem even trivial; the debate, much of which Thomas himself anticipated in his *Quaestiones Quodlibetales,* revolves round what to him were contrasts—but to his critics were conflicts—between nature and grace, reason and faith, determinism and freedom, the existence of the universe from eternity and its beginning in time, the soul as biological form and as spirit, and the role of the senses and of divine enlightenment in the acquisition of knowledge.

Although the censures had no force outside Paris and Oxford and the criticisms were more moderate in substance than they were in tone (they judged Thomas to be dangerous rather than heretical), his fellow Dominicans were quick to rally to his defense, to get the condemnations reversed and to correct the corrections, which they called corruptions. Thomas's old master, Albert the Great, so much the leader of the new movement that it has been called Albertino-Thomism, interposed at Paris; Pierre of Conflans, archbishop of Corinth, and Giles of Lessines remonstrated with Kilwardby; and Richard Clapwell, prior of Blackfriars, Oxford, progressively adopted Thomas's positions and stoutly maintained them against Peckham. The school was strengthened by a brilliant group of English and French Dominicans, and it was adopted by the Dominican order at successive general chapters. It could always count on support from the Roman Curia, which was favorably inclined toward Greek philosophy. The Ecumenical Council of Vienne (1311–1312) endorsed man's psychophysical unity, and in 1323 John XXII canonized Thomas and solemnly commended his doctrine. Henceforth he was a received authority.

Among the Thomists of these first fifty years John of Paris and Thomas Sutton were outstanding; other noteworthy teachers were Raymond Martin, a contemporary of Thomas who worked on the frontiers of Arabic science, William of Macclesfield, William of Hothun (archbishop of Dublin), Thomas Joyce (Jorz), Robert of Orford, Rambert of Bologna, Bernard de la Treille (Bernard of Trilia), Hervé de Nedellec, Nicholas Trivet, James of Lausanne, Ptolemy of Lucca, Peter de la Palu, James of Metz (uneasily attached to the school), and Remigio de Girolami, the master of Dante Alighieri. In their hands the distinctions between essence and existence, matter and form, and substance and accident became sharper, although some of these scholars were reluctant to go beyond Aristotle to support, as Thomas did, the concept of an act of a form. Of particular interest is a German group deriving more directly from Albert than from Thomas and imbued with strains of Neoplatonism from Proclus and Avicenna; within this group were Ulrich of Strasbourg, Dietrich of Vrieberg (Freiburg), Berchtold of Mosburg, and, most famous of all, Meister Eckhart, whose Thomism is not generally considered to have been unequivocal. All these men were Dominicans; the secular master Peter of Auvergne and the Augustinian friars Giles of Rome and James of Viterbo can also be ranged with them.

As the later Middle Ages drew on, the enterprise of integrating a wide-ranging philosophy in theology was succeeded by more piecemeal investigations, and the schools settled down to their own party lines with a sharpened logic but some loss of originality. In the rivalry between the Dominicans and the Franciscans, Thomism was matched against Scotism, and this set the tone of its development: In fact, however, as Dominic de Soto later acknowledged, the agreements between the two were more important than their differences. Moderate realism was represented at all the universities and adhered to at Louvain, at Cologne, and later at Heidelberg. Thomism itself must be reckoned a minority movement, and some prominent Dominicans did not belong to the school. Durandus of Saint-Pourçain steadily ran counter to Thomas's teaching, and the Cambridge Dominican Robert Holkot did not fall in with it. A central figure is John Capreolus, called the *Princeps Thomistarum,* whose writings are a mine of information on the disputes with Scotists and Ockhamists. Although Capreolus chose Thomas's "Commentary on the *Sentences*" for his expositions rather than the better organized *Summa Theologiae,* he, together with Serafino Capponi de Porrecta, bequeathed to their order the habit of systematically articulating the whole corpus of Thomas's teaching. Less confined to the classroom and closer to life and the historical movement of ideas was St. Antoninus, archbishop of Florence, the moralist who is a major authority for medieval economics.

The influence of the Renaissance was already beginning to make itself felt, and the first period of Thomism closed nobly in north Italy with Bartholomew of Spina, Crisostomo Javelli, Francis Sylvester (or Ferrariensis), and Thomas de Vio (or Cajetan). The last two, the classical commentators on the *Summa contra Gentiles* and the *Summa Theologiae,* respectively, were friends and opponents, particularly on the metaphysics of analogy. Both were responsive to the renewed vitality of Latin Averroism, and for them the unity of their school lay more in an inner consistency of approach than in a common subscription to a list of propositions, such as marked later Scholasticism when it had retreated or been banished from the profane world into the ecclesiastical academies. Cajetan, the master of a nervous style that fitted the subtle analysis at which he excelled, was a good scholar and a man of affairs. His standing in the school is second only to that of Thomas himself, although there is some question whether he was not a better Aristotelian than a Thomist. It is alleged that his emphasis on existence as the act of substance rather than on *esse* as the act of being may have encouraged the habit of discussing essences apart from existence, which was treated as a predicate.

SIXTEENTH TO NINETEENTH CENTURY

The second period, coterminous with the golden age of Spain, also had its origins in Burgundy and also declined through an inability to adjust to an expanding world outside its frontiers. In the fifteenth century Dominic of Flanders developed Thomas's exposition of the *Metaphysics,* and Peter Crockaert of Brussels, the master of Francisco de Vitoria (the father of international law), was the first of a great line of masters associated with the University of Salamanca. It was the faculty of this university that intervened with the Spanish government to humanize colonial policy. They forsook the crabbed angularities of fifteenth-century Scholasticism for a more flowing baroque style; at the same time, however, they found what they regarded as the formal logic of Aristotle to be a sufficient instrument for their debates, and the advances made on it (the *subtilitates anglicanae*) were neglected. Although they are chiefly famous as Tridentine divines, the theological questions that they considered—the relations of efficacious grace and free will, of authority and conscience—occasioned sustained philosophical discussion.

Among these sixteenth-century authors, the following are well worth study: Melchior Cano for scientific method and Bartholomew de Medina, Dominic de Soto, and Martin de Ledesma for moral theory. Dominic Báñez is much admired for his high Thomism in metaphysics and natural theology. These were Dominicans, but the best-known writer of the group is the Jesuit Francisco Suárez, who is impressive by virtue of the breadth of his interests and the organization of his voluminous writings, although strict Thomists would reckon him an eclectic and would think that he achieved his clarity by too concrete a habit of thought. The Jesuits were at this time taking the lead in higher education, and of all the orders they were the most aware of contemporary scientific research. Courses of philosophy began to be given apart from theology, and the teamwork of the Jesuits at Coimbra produced the volumes titled *Conimbicenses* (1592), and of the Carmelites at Alcalá de Henares those titled *Complutenses* (1624). In twentieth-century Thomistic studies John of St. Thomas perhaps became more influential than Cajetan, and his *Cursus Philosophicus,* digested in Josef Gredt's *Elementa Philosophica,* may be recommended as of lasting value.

Yet by the end of the seventeenth century Thomism was important only in the centers of ecclesiastical learning; it was part of the establishment, more honored, perhaps, than listened to. Its monument is the Casanata Library in Rome, founded with two chairs of Thomist exegesis. Its philosophy served mainly as a prolegomenon to theological studies and was conducted in the "essentialist" temper of Gottfried Wilhelm Leibniz and Christian Wolff. In this spirit Antoine Goudin wrote his significantly titled *Philosophia Juxta D. Thomae Dogmata* (Milan, 1676), which by 1744 had gone through fourteen editions. Salvatore Roselli's six-volume *Summa Philosophiae* (Rome, 1777) was written in response to the reiteration of the Dominican commitment to Thomas's doctrine made by the master general, John Thomas Boxadors. Both works influenced the revival of Thomism in the next century. But few Thomists took part in the dialogue of philosophers from René Descartes to G. W. F. Hegel, and the writings of the school were studied only by those with antiquarian tastes or a special interest in the history of philosophy.

NINETEENTH AND TWENTIETH CENTURIES

The situation began to change about the middle of the nineteenth century. A circle of teachers at Piacenza, Naples, and Rome who were dissatisfied with the eclectic doctrines that then served for clerical studies and were critical of the developed Kantianism of Georg Hermes, the accommodated Hegelianism of Anton Günther, the antirationalism of traditionalism, and the ontologism of Antonio Rosmini began to look to the synthesis of Thomas. The Dominicans themselves had remained faithful to Thomas, but their temper was somewhat rabbinical and concentrated on the letter of the text; and except in Spain and southern Poland they had been scattered in the troubled times after the French Revolution. At the beginning of the nineteenth century a secular canon, Vincenzo Buzzetti, inspired two brothers, Serafino and Domenico Sordi, who later became Jesuits, and Giuseppe Pecci, the brother of the future Leo XIII, to the work of the restoration of Thomism. They were joined by Gaetano Sanseverino, who contributed the five-volume *Philosophia Christiana* (Naples, 1853), and were supported by the influential Jesuit periodical *Civiltá cattolica.* The movement gathered strength with the affirmation of the rights of reason at the First Vatican Council (1869–1870) and with the teaching of two great professors at the Gregorian University, Matteo Liberatore and Josef Kleutgen, and of two Dominican cardinals, the Corsican Thomas Zigliara and the Spaniard Zefirín Gonzales. Finally, Leo Kill's encyclical *Aeterni Patris* (1879) sounded the recall to Thomas's basic doctrines in order to meet modern needs. Succeeding popes have reinforced this recommendation, not without embarrassment to those not wedded to Thomas's system, and even to those Thomists who would not have philosophy inculcated according to administrative needs. In practice, however, and despite the scares of the Modernist movement and the antimetaphysical temper since the 1940s, the injunctions have not proved irksome; and many forward-looking thinkers have discovered that Thomas was a benign and generous patron of their studies.

A history of neo-Thomism—the title is not relished by many in the school who do not see themselves committed to an absolute system—remains to be written. One characteristic of neo-Thomism has been its willingness to assimilate influence from outside its own tradition, which is a tribute to the depth and versatility of its principles. Another is that it has not been preoccupied with ecclesiastical matters; it inspired the social teaching of Leo XIII, with the result that many laypeople and statesmen have consulted it in developing the ideals and practice of Christian democracy. Nor has the conduct of speculation been reserved to clerics, and in the mid-twentieth century Thomism had no names more eminent than those of Jacques Maritain and Étienne Gilson. Although it appeals primarily to Catholics, its adherents are not necessarily Catholics, or even Christians. It presents no fixed image of conformity.

The Spanish works of high Thomism (the names of Norberto del Prado and Jaime Ramírez may be mentioned) have seemed to stand apart from the streams of contemporary thought, and the chief agencies that have taken Thomism into the world debate have been the University of Louvain and the French Dominicans. The Institut Supérieur at Louvain was founded in 1889 by Désiré Mercier, later cardinal, to bridge the gap between modern science and philosophy, particularly with respect to the problem of knowledge. In connection with this effort, the work of Joseph Maréchal was noteworthy. The French Dominicans have made contributions important both in critical research and in the popularization of Thomistic philosophy, and they have been alert to consider the most seemingly disparate interests; their periodicals, the *Revue des sciences philosophiques et théologiques* and the *Revue thomiste,* provide probably the best index to the activities of the school. From the universities of Munich and Münster has come important work, and the names of Martin Grabmann and Otto Geyer are illustrious. Other outstanding figures are Réginald Garrigou-Lagrange of the University of St. Thomas in Rome and R. Welty and I. M. Bocheński of the University of Fribourg. A strong stream of Thomism is evident in the work of A. E. Taylor at Edinburgh, Kenneth Kirke at Oxford, E. L. Mascall at London, and Mortimer Adler at Chicago. Distinguished work comes from the Medieval Institute in Toronto, and there are flourishing centers of Thomistic study in Washington, D.C.; River Forest, Illinois; St. Louis; Montreal; and Sydney. The enumeration, however, is incomplete and perhaps invidious. The bibliographies of the *Bulletin thomiste* bear witness to a worldwide interest in Thomistic thought on the part of both philosophers and theologians.

See also Albert the Great; Aristotle; Augustinianism; Averroism; Avicenna; Báñez, Dominic; Capreolus, John; Cajetan, Cardinal; Dante Alighieri; Descartes, René; Eckhart, Meister; Essence and Existence; Garrigou-Lagrange, Réginald Marie; Giles of Rome; Gilson, Étienne; Hegel, Georg Wilhelm Friedrich; Holkot, Robert; John of Paris; John of St. Thomas; Kilwardby, Robert; Leibniz, Gottfried Wilhelm; Maréchal, Joseph; Maritain, Jacques; Medieval Philosophy; Mercier, Désiré Joseph; Neoplatonism; Ockhamism; Peckham, John; Proclus; Renaissance; Rosmini-Serbati, Antonio; Scientia Media and Molinism; Scotism; Soto, Dominic de; Suárez, Francisco; Taylor, Alfred Edward; Thomas Aquinas, St.; Ulrich (Engelbert) of Strasbourg; Vitoria, Francisco de; Wolff, Christian.

Bibliography

Bourke, V. J. *Thomistic Bibliography, 1920–1940.* St. Louis, 1945.

Dezza, Paolo. *Alle origini del Neotomismo.* Milan: Fratelli, 1940.

Gilson, Étienne. *History of Christian Philosophy in the Middle Ages,* 277–294, 361–436, 471–485. New York: Random House, 1955. This work contains excellent bibliographies.

Mandonnet, Pierre, and Jean Destrez. *Bibliographie thomiste.* Paris, 1921.

Roensch, F. J. *The Early Thomistic School.* Dubuque, IA: Priory Press, 1964.

Wulf, Maurice de. *Histoire de la philosophie médiévale,* 5th ed., Vol. II, 33–51, 112–151, 197–203, 272–277. Louvain: Institut Supérieure de Philosophie, 1925.

Thomas Gilby, O.P. (1967)

THOMISM [ADDENDUM]

The most important development in Thomism since the original entry has been increased interest in St. Thomas Aquinas among philosophers trained in the analytic tradition. The pioneer was Peter Geach, whose essay on "Aquinas" in *Three Philosophers* (1961) has proved to be seminal. Although often critical of what he takes to be Aquinas's positions, Anthony Kenny's numerous publications—covering such diverse philosophical topics as God, mind, and metaphysics—have been influential in making Aquinas more accessible.

The most comprehensive attempt to argue for the contemporary relevance of Aquinas to analytic philosophers is Eleonore Stump's wide-ranging *Aquinas* (2003). The emergence of philosophy of religion as a recognized discipline within analytical philosophy departments has generated greater interest in Aquinas among a wide variety of theists. Norman Kretzmann, in *The Metaphysics of Theism* (1997) and *The Metaphysics of Creation* (1999), has argued that Aquinas's natural theology as developed in the first three books of the *Summa contra gentiles* is the richest and most impressive resource for the development of a contemporary theistic metaphysics. David Burrell has repeatedly argued, especially in *Freedom and Creation in Three Traditions*(1993), that Aquinas is an important resource for philosophy of religion in an ecumenical spirit as modeled on Aquinas's own dialogue with Muslim and Jewish interlocutors.

Interest in Aquinas has also flourished in ethics. Alasdair MacIntyre, in *Three Rival Versions of Moral Inquiry* (1990), argues for the rational superiority of the Thomistic moral tradition to the failed legacy of the Enlightenment project and the incoherence of Friedrich Nietzsche's genealogy of morals, provoking a large body of secondary literature.

Thomists have traditionally sought to extract from Aquinas a natural-law ethic that could provide the foundation for arguments with those who do not share similar theological commitments. John Finnis's work, especially in *Natural Law and Natural Rights* (1980), is the most influential attempt to articulate a Thomistic theory of natural law that is more attractive to those who accept the modern starting point of individual natural rights. Finnis's argument that the first principles of practical reason indicate a number of irreducible and incommensurable goods as integral to human fulfillment has been criticized by other Thomists (for example, Russell Hittinger) on the grounds that it is incompatible with Aquinas's claim that the contemplation of God is constitutive of human flourishing.

It should be noted that Thomists trained in a more classically historical approach to Aquinas have made notable recent contributions. The works of John F. Wippel and W. Norris Clarke in metaphysics are especially important. In noting this other strain within Thomism, we come to the abiding tension between traditional fidelity to the central commitments of Aquinas and the development of insights that can engage contemporary problems and modes of discourse. In the previous generation of Thomists, the battle was over whether Aquinas could be brought into dialogue with post-Kantian German philosophy; now the focus has shifted to analytic philosophy. Traditional Thomists worry that analytic readings of Aquinas distort his thought, through both the failure to understand it in its original context and the imposition of foreign metaphysical and epistemological dogmas. More analytically-minded Thomists worry that traditional approaches to Aquinas render his thought irrelevant.

See also Enlightenment; MacIntyre, Alasdair; Natural Law; Neo-Kantianism; Nietzsche, Friedrich; Thomas Aquinas, St.

Bibliography

Davies, Brian. *The Thought of Thomas Aquinas*. London: Oxford University Press, 1992.

Kerr, Fergus. *After Aquinas: Versions of Thomism*. London: Blackwell, 2002.

Kretzmann, Norman, and Eleonore Stump, eds. *The Cambridge Companion to Aquinas*. Cambridge, U.K.: Cambridge University Press 1993.

Shanley, Brian J. *The Thomist Tradition*. Dordrecht, Netherlands: Kluwer, 2002.

Brian Shanley, O.P. (2005)

THOMSON, JUDITH JARVIS
(1929—)

Judith Jarvis Thomson has made major contributions to moral theory and metaphysics. In addition to several books in these areas, she has written more than seventy articles on a range of topics, including action theory, philosophy of mind, and philosophy of science. She was educated at Barnard College, Cambridge University, and Columbia University, the last awarding her a doctoral degree in 1959. Since 1962, Thomson has taught at the Massachusetts Institute of Technology, where she became a full professor in 1969.

In moral theory, much of Thomson's work concerns what it is to have a moral right. Thomson's 1971 article "A Defense of Abortion"—an important contribution not only to ethics but also to feminist philosophy— revolutionized the abortion debate, which had previously focused largely on the question of whether the fetus has a right to life. Thomson grants, for the sake of argument, that the fetus has a right to life, but argues that it does not follow that abortion is impermissible. She asks you to imagine waking up in the hospital with your kidneys connected to the circulatory system of a famous violinist with a fatal kidney ailment; the violinist will die without the continued use of your body (no one else with the requisite blood type can be found). It is not obvious that you must continue to lend the violinist the support of your body; thus the fact that something has the right to life, together with the fact that it will die without the continued use of your body, does not obviously show that you must continue to lend it that support. Thus, in Thomson's words, "the right to life will not serve the opponents of abortion in the very simple and clear way" they thought it would.

Thomson's views about rights are further developed in her 1976 and 1985 essays "Killing, Letting Die, and the Trolley Problem" and "The Trolley Problem" (among other essays collected in *Rights, Restitution, and Risk* [1986]). These two essays focus on issues surrounding the problem, due to Philippa Foot (1967), of explaining why it would be impermissible for a surgeon to cut up one patient to save five who need organs, but permissible for a trolley driver to divert a runaway trolley onto a track where it will kill one person from a track where it would kill five. Foot's suggestion is that the duty not to kill is more stringent than the duty to save: Whereas the surgeon chooses between killing one and letting five die, and so should let five die, the trolley driver chooses between killing five and killing one, and so should kill one. Thomson objects that Foot's solution cannot account for the fact that it would be permissible for a *bystander* to flip the switch that diverts the trolley from killing the five, even though the bystander, like the surgeon, chooses between killing one and letting five die. Solving this problem—the Trolley Problem—requires a more subtle understanding of what rights are and which we have. Thomson's *The Realm of Rights* (1990) addresses these issues in detail.

Even if we grant that the distinction between killing and letting die does not solve the trolley problem, we may still think that the distinction is morally important. Many philosophers have thought that whether it is depends on what it consists in, metaphysically. Thomson's "Critical Study of Jonathan Bennett's *The Act Itself*" (1996) suggests that the metaphysical distinction is, roughly, that "there is a method in the making," whereas allowing something to happen does not involve bringing it about by any method—"there is no *how* about it." "Physician Assisted Suicide: Two Moral Arguments" (1999) poses a serious challenge to those who think that while it is morally permissible for a doctor to accede to a patient's request to "let nature take its course"—either by not supplying, or by disconnecting life support—it is impermissible for a doctor to supply or administer a lethal drug at the patient's request. Along the way, Thomson makes the point that the killing/letting die distinction might itself be a moral distinction rather than a metaphysical distinction that makes a moral difference. In particular, it might be a necessary condition on an agent's letting someone die that she "have a liberty-right to act as she does."

The second major theme of Thomson's work in moral theory is her anticonsequentialism. One source of support for this comes from what she takes to be the moral theorist's data: our settled moral judgments about particular examples (for example, that the surgeon may not cut up the healthy patient to save five). Another, developed in "The Right and the Good" (1997) and *Goodness and Advice* (2001), is that the consequentialist's basic idea—that morality requires one to act in such a way as to make the world better than it otherwise would have been—is meaningless: there is no such relation as "better than." If there were such a relation, Thomson argues, then we could make sense of the question: Which is better, St. Francis or chocolate? But the question doesn't make sense: The goodness of a saint is an entirely different property from the goodness of chocolate. If all goodness is, as Thomson puts it, "goodness in a way," then the consequentialist owes us an account of what he or she means when he or she says that we ought to act so as to make the world better than it otherwise would have been. Thomson argues that no such account is available.

A third theme in Thomson's work in moral theory is her opposition to expressivist and relativist views about the content of moral claims. In *Moral Relativism and Moral Objectivity* (1996), coauthored with Gilbert Harman, Thomson defends moral objectivism, Harman defends moral relativism, and each replies to the other's arguments. One exchange concerns Harman's influential argument that moral theory cannot be justified in the same way that scientific theory can: our evidence that scientific hypotheses are true is that the truth of those hypotheses would explain what scientists observe, whereas moral hypotheses are explanatorily inert (1977). Thomson replies that our evidence that moral hypotheses are true is that they would be explained *by* observation: the data explain the hypotheses rather than the other way around.

In metaphysics, one strand of Thomson's work concerns questions about the persistence of material objects through change. "Parthood and Identity Across Time" argues against the thesis that objects have, in addition to spatial parts, temporal parts. According to Thomson, that thesis is absurd, because it implies that "[a]s I hold the bit of chalk in my hand, new stuff, new chalk keeps constantly coming into existence *ex nihilo*." "The Statue and the Clay" (1998) concerns the related issue of how artifacts are related to the material of which they are composed. Thomson argues that artifacts are not identical to but rather constituted by quantities of matter, and she provides a much-needed definition of the constitution relation, which previous writers on the topic had left unexplained.

The killing/letting die distinction is at the intersection of metaphysics and moral theory, along with many of Thomson's other interests—including causation, action, and agency. *Acts and Other Events* (1977) concerns events, their causes, and parts, and presents important challenges to rival theories of events and action. "The Time of a Killing" (1971) and "Causation: Omissions" (2001) also address metaphysical issues that bear on moral problems. Indeed, contemporary philosophy is indebted to Thomson for showing that metaphysics and ethics are often so intimately connected.

See also Abortion; Consequentialism; Euthanasia; Feminist Philosophy; Foot, Philippa; Harman, Gilbert; Objectivity in Ethics; Suicide.

Bibliography

WORKS BY JUDITH JARVIS THOMSON

"The Time of a Killing." *Journal of Philosophy* 68 (1971): 115–132.

"Killing, Letting Die, and the Trolley Problem." *The Monist* 59 (1976): 204–217.

Acts and Other Events. Ithaca: Cornell University Press, 1977.

"Parthood and Identity Across Time." *Journal of Philosophy* 80 (1983): 201–219.

"The Trolley Problem." *Yale Law Journal* 94 (1985): 1395–1415.

Rights, Restitution, and Risk. Cambridge, MA: Harvard University Press, 1986.

The Realm of Rights, edited by William Parent. Cambridge, MA: Harvard University Press, 1990.

"Critical Study of Jonathan Bennett's *The Act Itself*." *Nous* 30 (1996): 545–557.

"The Right and the Good." *Journal of Philosophy* 94 (1997): 273–298.

"The Statue and the Clay." *Noûs* 32 (1998): 149–173.

"Physician Assisted Suicide: Two Moral Arguments." *Ethics* 109 (1999): 497–518.

Goodness and Advice. Princeton, NJ: Princeton University Press, 2001.

"Causation: Omissions." *Philosophy and Phenomenological Research*, 2003.

WORKS ABOUT JUDITH JARVIS THOMSON

Bennett, Jonathan. *The Act Itself*. Oxford: Oxford University Press, 1998.

Foot, Philippa. "The Problem of Abortion and the Doctrine of Double Effect." *Oxford Review* (1967): 5–15.

Harman, Gilbert. *The Nature of Morality*. Oxford: Oxford University Press, 1977.

Harman, Gilbert, and Judith Jarvis Thomson. *Moral Relativism and Moral Objectivity*. Oxford: Blackwell, 1996.

Sider, Theodore. *Four-Dimensionalism*. Oxford: Oxford University Press, 2001.

"A Defense of Abortion." *Philosophy and Public Affairs* 1 (1971): 47–66.

Sarah McGrath (2005)

THOREAU, HENRY DAVID

(1817–1862)

Henry David Thoreau once described himself as "a mystic, a transcendentalist, and a natural philosopher." If this description does some justice to the extent of Thoreau's eclecticism, it nevertheless obscures those characteristics that made him important during his lifetime and still remain significant today, for Thoreau was an anarchist and revolutionary who created a highly articulate literature of revolt. Born at Concord, Massachusetts, the son of a pencil maker, Thoreau emerged from Harvard in 1837 with testimonials signed by Dr. George Ripley, Ralph Waldo Emerson, and the president of the university, all of whom attested, in glowing terms, to his moral and intellectual integrity. After a brief skirmish with school teaching, Thoreau became infected with the ideas of the New England transcendentalists, gave up all plans of a regular profession, and devoted himself to literature and the study of nature. His remarkable practical skills and intimate knowledge of the Concord countryside enabled him to earn his living independently, largely through pencil making and surveying, for the rest of his life.

From 1841 to 1843 Thoreau resided with Emerson. This brought his intellectual development roughly into line with the ideas of transcendentalists such as Amos Bronson Alcott, Margaret Fuller, and Ellery Channing, all of whom he came to know well. Thus, philosophically, Thoreau's reaction against the still fashionable sensationalism of John Locke and the theistic utilitarianism of William Paley was aided by ideas derived from the Scottish philosophers of common sense, who, in turn, formed a bridge to the idealism of Samuel Taylor Coleridge, Thomas Carlyle, and the Germans. Emerson also directed Thoreau to the English metaphysical poets and to Johann Wolfgang von Goethe. But despite this deep and undeniable cultural *rapprochement* it would be a misunderstanding to see Thoreau merely as Emerson's most eccentric disciple. Thoreau's individuality was maintained even at the intellectual level. He also studied New England history and legend, the life of the Indian, and early accounts of American travel and exploration; he probably had a better knowledge of the Greek and Latin classics than Emerson and certainly knew more about Oriental scriptures, of which he possessed an excellent collection. Above all, Thoreau's knowledge of natural history, motivated not so much by a desire for scientific understanding as by a need for concrete communion with nature, marks him off from the rest of Emerson's circle.

NATURE AND SOCIETY

Thoreau's writings everywhere bear the stamp of aboriginal practicality that also made him unique as a person. Society and nature were not for Thoreau, as they were for so many romantic thinkers, dialectical opposites whose inner identity was simply in need of philosophical explication. For him they involved a genuine contrast that he had personally experienced as a professional "saunterer" in and around Concord. Nature represented for Thoreau an "absolute freedom and wildness," whereas society provided "a freedom and culture merely civil." In his writing, as in his life, he attempted to implement the view that man should be regarded "as an inhabitant, or a part and parcel of Nature, rather than a member of society." It is only through a sustained involvement with the vast "personality" of nature that man can simplify his existence, clarify his senses, drive life into a corner, and reduce it to its lowest terms, thus achieving in practice a purer and tougher form of that self-reliance extolled, somewhat abstractly, by Emerson.

With these objects in mind, in the spring of 1845 Thoreau began building himself a hut on the shore of Walden Pond, a small lake then about a mile and a half south of Concord village. There he lived alone, with occasional visits to the village and from friends, until September 1847. His mode of life at the pond is described in *Walden, or Life in the Woods* (1854). For Thoreau Walden was an experiment in individualistic anarchism, just as Fruitlands and the Brook Farm community were for other transcendentalists attempts to revert to more "natural" modes of communal existence. But Thoreau had little confidence in collective protests against the existing social order, inspired by the doctrines of François Marie Charles Fourier. For him individual communion with nature was more fundamental than relationships with other men, even in societies where the worse forms of economic alienation have been overcome. For, unlike any social experience, the experience of nature becomes as much a discipline for the moral will as a stimulant to creative imagination. But essentially it is the spontaneity of wildness or nature that is to be favorably contrasted with the politico-economic organization of advanced European and New England societies. For, wrote Thoreau, "all good things are wild and free." The creative spontaneity of nature that is so crucial for man's spiritual well-being is embodied in all enduring products of culture—in the *Iliad* and *Hamlet,* in religious scriptures, in music, and especially in mythologies of all kinds. Commerce—"that incessant business"—and its political manifestations are indeed "vital functions of human society," yet a bare minimum of time should be consciously spent on them. They are "*infra*-human, a kind of vegetation," whose operations, like those of the human body, should be performed for the most part automatically, unconsciously. Far from viewing economic success alone as the sign of achievement or virtue, Thoreau believed that "to have done anything by which you earned money merely is to have been truly idle, or worse."

Despite the acquisitive basis of New England society, Thoreau saw a vision of true freedom in the expansion of the western frontier. For him the West was identical with the wild, and "wildness is the preservation of the world." These ideas, which constitute Thoreau's most persuasive expressions of revolt against bourgeois society, are best seen in his essays "Walking" (1862) and "Life without Principle" (1863).

REVOLUTION AND REFORM

Thoreau's essay "Civil Disobedience" (1849) has been the most influential of his works because of its overt political implications. It was, for example, a reading of this essay in 1907 that helped Mohandas Gandhi develop his own doctrine of passive resistance. Here Thoreau advocates active rebellion against the state. This involves what he calls "action from principle" on the basis of an intuitive perception of what is right, which is roughly equivalent to acting on the dictates of one's own conscience. He boldly asserts that "the only obligation which I have a right to assume is to do at any time what I think right." Action thus motivated "changes things and relations" and is therefore "essentially revolutionary." Radical social reforms, such as the abolition of slavery (for which Thoreau agitated throughout his life), can be effected not by petitions to elected representatives of government or by other indirect democratic means but only when each right-minded individual takes direct action on his own part. This would consist in withdrawing his allegiance "in person and property" from the government that supports or permits the abuse in question. Such is the form of "peaceful revolution" Thoreau himself attempted to put into practice by refusing to pay taxes. Despite its localized New England context and its relative lack of theoretical sophistication, it is possible to see Thoreau's doctrine of civil disobedience as historically linked, through the revolutionary element in European idealism, with the larger protest against the established order represented more notably by Søren Kierkegaard's *The Present Age* (1846) and the *Communist Manifesto* (1847). Like Karl Marx, Thoreau sought the dismantling of existing institutions in an attempt to discover an economy that would provide full human satisfaction. Yet like Kierkegaard he insisted on maintaining the uniqueness of the individual as the ultimate source of value; he attempted, however, to overcome the isolation his radical views forced upon him by means of a dialogue not with God but with nature.

See also Anarchism; Carlyle, Thomas; Channing, William Ellery; Coleridge, Samuel Taylor; Common Sense; Emerson, Ralph Waldo; Fourier, François Marie Charles; Goethe, Johann Wolfgang von; Kierkegaard, Søren Aabye; Locke, John; Marx, Karl; New England Transcendentalism; Paley, William; Sensationalism; Utilitarianism.

Bibliography

PRIMARY WORKS

The most complete edition of Thoreau's works is that published by Houghton Mifflin in 20 volumes: *The Writings of Henry David Thoreau* (Boston, 1906). See also *The Writings of Henry David Thoreau,* edited by Elizabeth Hall Witherall (Princeton, NJ: Princeton University Press, 1981–).

SECONDARY WORKS

H. S. Salt, *Life of Henry David Thoreau* (London: Bentley, 1890; reissued in an abridged version, 1896), is indispensable for an understanding of Thoreau's personality. For other details see Stanley Cavell, *The Senses of Walden,* expanded edition (Chicago: University of Chicago Press, 1980); Robert D. Richardson Jr., *Henry Thoreau: A Life of the Mind* (Berkeley: University of California Press, 1986); Robert Sattelmeyer, *Thoreau's Reading: A Study in Intellectual History with Bibliographical Catalogue* (Princeton, NJ: Princeton University Press, 1988); Leo Stoller, *After Walden: Thoreau's*

Changing Views on Economic Man (Stanford, CA: Stanford University Press, 1957); Floyd Stovall, ed., *Eight American Authors: A Review of Research and Criticism* (New York: Modern Language Association of America, 1956; reprinted, New York: Norton 1963).

Michael Moran (1967)
Bibliography updated by Philip Reed (2005)

THOUGHT, LAWS OF

See *Laws of Thought*

THOUGHT EXPERIMENTS IN SCIENCE

Thought experiments in science are generally characterized by contrast to actual experiments: The former are conducted by engaging in an imaginative act, the latter by manipulating features of the observed world. So if to perform an (actual) scientific experiment is to conduct an empirical test under controlled conditions with the aim of illustrating, supporting, or refuting some scientific hypothesis or theory, then to perform a scientific thought experiment is to reason about an imaginary scenario with a similar aim. In the case of actual experiments, the theory-relevant evidence generally takes the form of data concerning the behavior of the physical world under specific conditions; in the case of thought experiments, the theory-relevant evidence generally takes the form of intuitions (or predictions) concerning such behavior. In both instances, imagining or performing the experiment ostensibly results in new knowledge about contingent features of the natural world. The primary philosophical puzzle concerning scientific thought experiment is how (if at all) contemplation of a merely imaginary scenario can provide this. (Cf. Kuhn 1964/1977.)

TERMINOLOGICAL ISSUES

The earliest uses of the expressions *Gedankenexperiment* and *mit Gedanken experimentieren* seem to be in the writings of the Danish Kantian Hans Christian Örsted (1811) and the German polymath Georg Christoph Lichtenberg (1793) respectively. However, contemporary use of the term stems from its apparently independent coinage by Ernst Mach, who introduced the expression *Gedankenexperiment* in an 1897 essay of the same name, and discussed a number of examples that have remained central to present-day discussions. Though the historical record is a bit unclear on this point (because later editions of works often insert the word where it was not originally used), it seems to have taken roughly four decades following the publication of Mach's essay for the term *thought experiment* to become widespread in scientific circles. In particular, despite his thorough knowledge of Mach's corpus, Einstein seems not to have used the term to describe his own thinking, at least not in his written works. (Cf. Lichtenberg 1793/1983; Mach 1897; Mach 1905/1976; Schildknecht 1990, 147ff; Witt-Hansen 1976).

Despite the absence of a specific term for the technique, the method was widely employed long before it was labeled. Contemplating imaginary cases in order to develop scientific theory was central to the practice of ancient and medieval natural philosophy, despite the apparent absence of any articulated experimental methodology. And it played a crucial role in the development of early modern natural science. Indeed, some have argued that thought experiment was the predominant mode of scientific investigation prior to the scientific revolution (cf. King 1991, Rescher 1991).

This points to a certain ambiguity in the term's application. Given the characterization offered above, it is a bit challenging to distinguish scientific *thought experiment* as such from scientific *thought* in general, because the latter largely consists in reasoning about (less or more detailed) imaginary scenarios as a way of testing or illustrating (more or less tentative) hypotheses. Indeed, nearly every exercise in a standard physics textbook would, by these criteria, count as a thought experiment. As a matter of sociological fact, however, the expression tends to be reserved for cases where a fairly detailed scenario is contemplated in order to invoke intuitions that help to illustrate or support a specific and novel scientific hypothesis, or to refute a specific and otherwise plausible scientific hypothesis. (A parallel set of definitional and historical issues confronts the analogous term in philosophy, where the term "thought experiment" is generally used to refer to the consideration of fairly detailed, often physically unrealized, scenarios in order to invoke intuitions concerning the proper application of some concept.) Perhaps because of these definitional difficulties, philosophical discussions of scientific thought experiment have focused primarily on a small stable of canonical examples. (For a comprehensive bibliography, see Gendler 2000.)

EXAMPLES

Among the three most widely discussed scientific thought experiments in the philosophical literature are Galileo's refutation of the Aristotelian view that heavy bodies fall faster than light ones, Stevin's determination of the

FIGURE 1

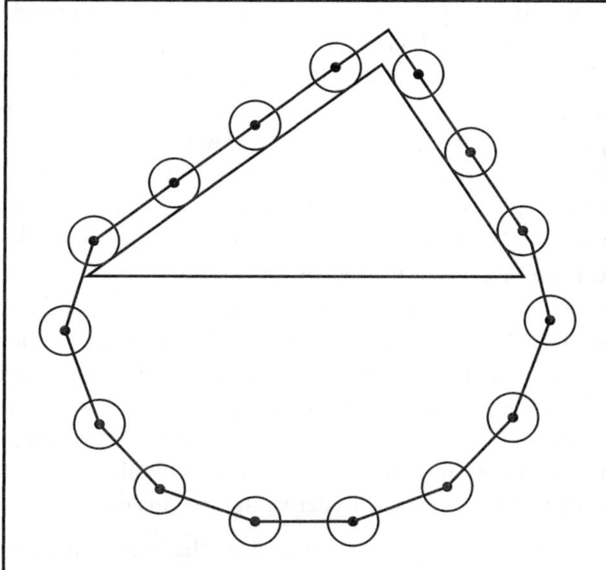

amount of force required to prevent an object from sliding down a frictionless inclined plane, and Einstein's demonstration of the relativity of simultaneity by consideration of the moving train. These exemplify respectively the role of scientific thought experiments in refuting, supporting, and illustrating scientific theories.

In Galileo's *falling body* thought experiment, by which Galileo is said to have refuted the Aristotelian theory that heavier bodies fall faster than lighter ones, Galileo imagines two otherwise similar bodies of differing weights that are strapped together and dropped from a significant height. If one accepts the Aristotelian assumption that natural speed is proportional to weight, and accepts that there is no fact of the matter about whether the strapped body is one entity or two (that is, if one accepts that entification is not physically determined), then it seems that two outcomes are predicted: on the one hand, the lighter body should slow down the heavier whereas the heavier speeds up the lighter, so the combined object should fall with a speed that lies between the natural speeds of its components; on the other hand, because the weight of the two bodies combined is greater than the weight of the heavy body alone, their combination should fall with a natural speed greater than that of the heavy body. Galileo's suggested resolution to the paradox is to assume that the natural speed with which a body falls is independent of its weight, that is, that "both great and small bodies … are moved with like speeds" (Galileo 1638/1989, pp. 107–109; cf. Gendler 1998, 2000).

FIGURE 2

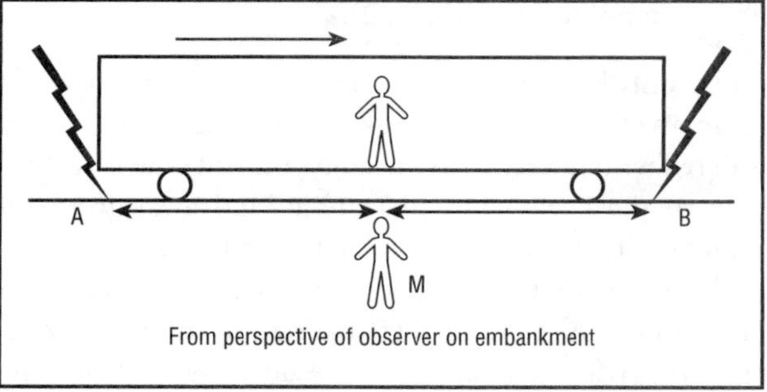

From perspective of observer on embankment

In Stevin's *inclined plane* thought experiment, which served as Mach's original example of the term, Stevinus establishes the amount of force required to prevent an object from sliding down a frictionless inclined plane by imagining a connected string of beads hung across a triangular prism with a horizontal base (as illustrated in figure 1). Consideration of this imaginary setup convinces him that the balls are in a state of equilibrium—that is, that the chain moves neither to the left nor to the right (else, it seems, the system would be in a state of perpetual motion, for because the beads are of equal weight and hung equally along the string, if the current state is one of disequilibrium, so too would be the state into which the system moved as the result of the string sliding.) He next imagines cutting the string at the two lower corners, so that only the beads along the two diagonal planes remain. Given that beads were in equilibrium prior to the cutting, and that the lower part of the loop exerts equal force on both sides of the string, the balls can be expected to remain in equilibrium afterwards. Because the number of beads along each side is proportional to the length of the plane, and because the beads are of equal weight spaced equidistantly, it follows that two bodies on two different, inclined planes are in balance if their weights are proportional to the lengths of the two planes. (Stevin 1955 [1586], pp. 175–179)

In Einstein's *moving train* thought experiment, Einstein illustrates the relativity of simultaneity by imagining a situation in which there are two people, one standing at a point, call it M, along the embankment of a railroad track, the other riding on a train that is moving with respect to the embankment. He then supposes that lightning strikes the embankment at two points, A and B, which are a significant distance from one another, but equidistant from M.

From the perspective of the person standing on the bank, the two flashes occur simultaneously: that is, the ray of light that is emitted from point A reaches M at exactly the same moment as the ray of light that is emitted from point B (see figure 2).

But from the perspective of the person on the moving train, the two flashes are not simultaneous, because (considered with reference to the embankment) she is rushing toward the beam emitted from B, and away from the beam emitted from A. (Note that from her perspective, it is the person on the embankment who is in motion in the direction of A. Note further that neither frame of reference is privileged in any way.) Because the speed of light is constant, the B-light will reach the passenger earlier than the A-light, so from her perspective, the two flashes are not simultaneous: the B-flash occurs first. Einstein concludes: "We thus arrive at the important result: Events which are simultaneous with reference to the embankment are not simultaneous with respect to the train, and *vice versa* … unless we are told the reference-body to which the statement of time refers, there is no meaning in a statement of the time of an event" (Einstein 1961, p. 26).

PHILOSOPHICAL ISSUES

Philosophical discussions of scientific thought experiment have primarily focused on two related questions. The first, which may be called the "what" question, concerns what sort of knowledge one gains from the contemplation of imaginary cases: do they provide one with new knowledge about contingent features of the natural world, or do they instead provide knowledge of some other sort? The second, which might be called the "how" question, concerns the process by which such knowledge is obtained: what, if anything, is epistemically distinctive about the process of thought-experimental reasoning?

THE "WHAT" QUESTION

A strong case can be made for the view that scientific thought experiments do not, in themselves, provide new knowledge about contingent features of the natural world: to the extent that they provide new knowledge, that knowledge concerns necessary truths. So, for example, the reader who works through Einstein's moving train thought experiment does not thereby gain novel knowledge of the (apparently) contingent truth that simultaneity is relative. What one gains instead is new knowledge of the (apparently) necessary truth that, if the speed of light is constant, then simultaneity is relative, which can then be combined with one's antecedent knowledge that the speed of light is constant in order to gain knowledge of the consequent. Likewise in the case of Stevin: What the thought experiment reveals is not the (apparently) contingent fact that the force required to hold a ball in place along an inclined plane is inversely proportional to the length of the plane, but rather to the (apparently) necessary truth that if certain sorts of states are equilibrium states, then the force required is inversely proportional to length. A person combines independent knowledge of this conditional with prior (empirically obtained) knowledge of statics and dynamics, and thereby gains knowledge of the consequent. So too in the Galileo case: What the reader gains is not new knowledge of the (apparently) contingent truth that the speed at which a body falls is independent of its weight, but rather the (apparently) necessary truth that, if entification is not a physically determined matter, then natural speed is independent of weight. And one can combine this conditional knowledge with one's empirically obtained knowledge of the antecedent to derive the conclusion.

Those who wish to challenge this position must argue that it is by engaging in this particular instance of thought-experimental reasoning that knowledge of the relevant contingent antecedent is gained. This is least plausible in the case of illustrative thought experiments that evoke intuitions about highly theoretical properties (e.g., the Einstein case), and most plausible in the case of supportive or refutory thought experiments that evoke physical intuitions (e.g., Galileo, Stevin). So it might be argued that it is precisely by contemplating the imaginary scenario in question that a person might come to know (the contingent fact) that the balls do not move in the Stevin example, or in the Galileo example (the contingent fact) that it is not a physically determined matter whether the strapped objects form one entity or two: though the intuitions evoked by the cases have their ultimate basis in experience (or the accumulated experience encapsulated by evolution [cf. Shepard undated]), the general information they encapsulate was too unsystematized to count as knowledge prior to engaging in the act of directing imagining. Something like this view appears to have been held by Mach, who writes:

> Unquestionably in the assumption from which Stevinus starts, that the endless chain does not move, there is contained primarily only a *purely instinctive* cognition. He feels at once, and we with him, that we have never observed anything like a motion of the kind referred to, that a thing of such a character does not exist. This conviction has so much logical cogency that we accept the conclusion drawn from it respecting the law of equilibrium on the inclined plane without the thought of an objection, although the law, if pre-

> sented as the simple result of an experiment, otherwise put, would appear dubious. (Mach 1976 [1905], p. 34)

THE "HOW" QUESTION

A number of recent discussions of thought-experimental cognition have focused on whether the structured contemplation of imaginary examples produces distinctive sorts of cognitive access to the knowledge they do give (whether or not that knowledge concerns contingent features of the natural world). In a series of widely discussed articles, John Norton (1991, 2002, 2004, and references contained therein) has defended a view that he calls "empiricism" according to which "thought experiments are just ordinary argumentation, disguised in some vivid picturesque or narrative form. As a result," he contends, "they can do nothing more epistemically that can ordinary argumentation" (2002, p. 1). On this view, knowledge obtained through scientific thought experiment is the result of inference from known premises to inductively or deductively implied conclusions: "the actual conduct of a thought experiment consists of the execution of an argument" (Norton 2002, p. 4).

Norton's view has been widely discussed and criticized by those who hold that contemplation of well-articulated specific imaginary cases can give access to inchoate information about patterns of experience to which people lack independent propositional or conceptual access. Some have suggested that thought experiment does this by exploiting the same cognitive mechanisms that mental models do (cf. Nersessian 1993; Miscevic 1992); others have suggested that certain thought experiments work by evoking quasi-sensory intuitions, resulting in new beliefs about contingent features of the natural world that are produced not inferentially, but quasi-observationally (Gendler 2004). Yet others have stressed other aspects of the similarities between thought experiments and actual experiments (for example, their indifference to certain sorts of changes of content but not others), contending that insofar as the latter are not arguments, neither are the former (cf. Arthur 1999, Bishop 1999, Gooding 1992, Sorensen 1992.)

A final contrasting view, advanced in a series of papers and books by James Robert Brown (e.g., Brown 1991, 2002, 2003, 2004, and references contained therein) is that in certain instances (the Galileo case being one) engaging in thought-experimental reasoning provides "*a priori* (though still fallible) knowledge of nature" derived through a process of what Brown terms "platonic insight" (2002, p. 2). "Thought experiments," he writes, "are our telescopes to see into the abstract realm"; by making use of "the mind's eye," they allow us to perceive the laws of nature "*a priori*" (2004, p. 113). The laws in question are necessary rather than contingent, involving "relations between objectively existing abstract entities" (2002, p. 2). Such a view will be appealing only to those who accept Brown's platonist metaphysics along with its corresponding epistemology.

See also Experimentation and Instrumentalism; Scientific Method.

Bibliography

Arthur, Richard. "On Thought Experiments as *A Priori* Science." *International Studies in the Philosophy of Science* 13 (3) (1999): 215–229.

Bishop, Michael. "Why Thought Experiments Are Not Arguments." *Philosophy of Science* 66 (1999): 534–541.

Brown, James Robert. *The Laboratory of the Mind: Thought Experiments in the Natural Sciences.* New York: Routledge, 1991.

Brown, James R. "Thought Experiments." In *The Stanford Encyclopedia of Philosophy (Summer 2002 Edition)*, edited by Edward N. Zalta. Available from http://plato.stanford.edu/archives/sum2002/entries/thought-experiment/.

Brown, J. R. "Why Thought Experiments Transcend Experience." In *Contemporary Debates in Philosophy of Science*, edited by Christopher Hitchcock. Oxford: Blackwell, 2004.

Brown, James Robert. "Peeking into Plato's Heaven." *Philosophy of Science* 71 (2004): 1126–1138.

Einstein, Albert. *Relativity: The Special and General Theory.* New York: Crown Publishers, 1961.

Galilei, Galileo. *Two New Sciences, Including Centers of Gravity and Force of Gravity and Force of Percussion* [1638]. Translated by Stillman Drake. Toronto: Wall & Thompson, 1974. Revised edition, 1989.

Gendler, Tamar Szabó. "Galileo and the Indispensability of Scientific Thought Experiment." *British Journal for the Philosophy of Science* 49 (3) (1998): 397–424.

Gendler, Tamar Szabó. *Thought Experiment: On the Powers and Limits of Imaginary Cases.* New York: Garland Press, 2000.

Gendler, Tamar Szabó. "Thought Experiments Rethought—and Reperceived." *Philosophy of Science* 71 (2004): 1152–1163.

Gooding, David C. "The Cognitive Turn, or, Why Do Thought Experiments Work?" In *Cognitive Models of Science*, edited by Ronald Giere, 45–76. Minneapolis: University of Minnesota Press, 1992.

Hitchcock, Christopher, ed. *Contemporary Debates in Philosophy of Science.* Oxford: Blackwell, 2004.

Horowitz, Tamara, and Gerald Massey, eds. *Thought Experiments in Science and Philosophy.* Savage, MD: Rowman and Littlefield, 1991.

King, Peter. "Mediaeval Thought-Experiments: The Metamethodology of Mediaeval Science." In *Thought Experiments in Science and Philosophy*, edited by Tamara

Horowitz and Gerald Massey, 43–64. Savage, MD: Rowman and Littlefield, 1991.

Kuhn, Thomas. "A Function for Thought Experiments" [1964]. Reprinted in *The Essential Tension*. Chicago: University of Chicago Press, 1977.

Lichtenberg, Georg Christoph. *Schriften und Briefe: Sudelbücher, Fragmente, Fabeln, Verse* (Erster Band), edited by Franz H. Mautner. Frankfurt: Insel Verlag, 1983.

Mach, Ernst. "Über Gedankenexperimente." *Poskes Zeitschrift für den physikalischen und chemischen Unterricht* (January 1897): 1–5.

Mach, Ernst. "Über Gedankenexperimente." *Erkenntnis und Irrtum*, 183–199. Leipzig: Johann Ambrosius Barth,1905. Translation of 1926 edition of *Erkenntinis and Irrtum* by Thomas J. McCormack and Paul Foulkes as "On Thought Experiment." *Knowledge and Error*, 134–147 (Dordrecht, Netherlands: Reidel, 1976).

Miscevic, Nenad. "Mental Models and Thought Experiments." *International Studies in the Philosophy of Science* 6 (3) (1992): 215–226.

Nersessian, Nancy. "In the Theoretician's Laboratory: Thought Experiment as Mental Modeling." *Proceedings of the Philosophy of Science Association* 2 (1993): 291–301.

Norton, John. "Thought Experiments in Einstein's Work." In *Thought Experiments in Science and Philosophy*, edited by Tamara Horowitz and Gerald Massey, 129–148. Savage, MD: Rowman and Littlefield, 1991.

Norton, John. "Why Thought Experiments Do Not Transcend Empiricism." In *Contemporary Debates in Philosophy of Science*, edited by Christopher Hitchcock. Oxford: Blackwell, 2004.

Norton, John. "On Thought Experiments: Is There More to the Argument?" *Philosophy of Science* 71 (2002): 1139–1151.

Rescher, Nicholas. "Thought Experiments in Pre-Socratic Philosophy." In *Thought Experiments in Science and Philosophy*, edited by Tamara Horowitz and Gerald Massey, 31–41. Savage, MD: Rowman and Littlefield, 1991.

Schildknecht, Christiane. *Philosophische Masken: Literarische Formen der Philosophie bei Platon, Descartes, Wolff und Lichtenberg*. Stuttgart, Germany: Metzler, 1990.

Shepard, Roger. "Thought Experiments on Falling Bodies." Available from http://www.cs.northwestern.edu/~paritosh/links/shepard.html

Sorensen, Roy. *Thought Experiments*. New York: Oxford University Press, 1992.

Stevin, Simon. *The Principal Works of Simon Stevin*. Vol. 1: *General Introduction and Mechanics*, [1586], edited by E. J. Dijksterhuis. Amsterdam: C. W. Swets and Zeitlinger, 1955.

Witt-Hansen, Johannes. "H. C. Örsted, Immanuel Kant, and the Thought Experiment." *Danish Yearbook of Philosophy* 13 (1976): 48–65.

Tamar Szabó Gendler (2005)

THUCYDIDES

(460–399 BCE)

Thucydides wrote a history of the epic struggle between Athens and Sparta. His work has proved to be—as he hoped—a "possession for all time," though perhaps not in quite the way he intended. Virtually every age, every occasion, every interpreter, has appropriated a different Thucydides and a different masterpiece. Both the author and the work remain enigmatic.

The reliable biographical details are few, and all derive from his own account. Thucydides son of Olorus was an Athenian, born around 460 BCE. In his analysis of the causes, symptoms, and consequences of the plague that devastated Athens a few years after the outbreak of hostilities with Sparta, Thucydides drew on his own experience of the illness. He was for a time prominent in Athenian public life. During the war, he attained the office of general, one of the very few elected positions in the Athenian democracy (most offices were allocated by lot), and was sent to Thrace, perhaps because of his connections and influence there. In 423 BCE, his fellow citizens banished him for failing to reach the Athenian colony of Amphipolis in time to rescue it from the Spartans. Athens' loss was posterity's gain: Thucydides proceeded to travel the Greek world and gather information for his history from a variety of sources including, as he noted, the Spartans and their allies. He lived to see the end of the war he chronicled, though his narrative breaks off seven years earlier, in 411 BCE.

The history is no less difficult to pin down than the historian, in part because it gives eloquent voice to the various protagonists in the conflict. The history therefore provides ample fodder for a variety of interpretations. Thucydides has been dubbed a scientific historian by some, a dramatist by others. His history is said by some to argue for a realist view of human affairs and international relations, by others to demonstrate the fallacy of such a view.

Thucydides' history is more and other than the sum of its parts. The complexity of his account cannot be reduced; but it can be understood, by taking seriously several considerations. First, Thucydides chose to write history, not tragic poetry, philosophical dialogues, or medical treatises. He explicitly commits himself to giving an accurate account, based on firsthand knowledge or scrupulous inquiry. In the case of the speeches, he states that since it was not possible to "carry them word for word in one's memory," he makes the speakers say what in his judgment is "demanded of them by the various occasions, while adhering as closely as possible to the general sense of what they really said." (1.22.1) In so doing, Thucydides does not abandon history for drama or dogma, but rather insists on the need for and the possibility of rigorously truthful historical interpretation.

Second, certain aspects of human nature (including judgment, passion, chance, the need for security, and the desire for power and gain) form the backbone of Thucydides' attempt to explain and interpret—not merely recount—the events of his time. Different speakers appeal to these concepts in different ways under different circumstances, and so does Thucydides himself when he characterizes the sources and trajectory of Athenian imperial power and the polarization of the Greek world. These building blocks of an intelligible history are therefore not to be seen as static truths, but construed instead in terms of the relationship between actions and contexts over time. It is, for example, not true that the will to power is the fundamental and inexorable force in human affairs, but rather that the will to power leads to greatness for some and security for others until the Greek world is fully polarized, at which point it is essential and possible to exert self-control.

Third, Thucydides was not writing in a vacuum. His decision to write an interpreted history is a response to challenges raised by the experience of democracy. Thucydides' history is intended as a political argument and a political education, and effective as such only to the extent that it is an accurate and intelligible history. Throughout the fifth century the Athenians wrestled with the question of how a polity that gives equal access to decision-making power to all citizens, including those without breeding, education, or property, can possibly achieve order, freedom, or the collective good. Protagoras of Abdera, one of the Sophists, or teachers of the art of politics, argued that participation in democratic practices facilitated self-expression while promoting self-restraint.

By the time of the war, continued reflection on the democratic experience had spawned the view that *Nomos* (law or custom), self-imposed as it was by the people, or by a majority, was in fact an artificial constraint, unrelated to the well-being of any particular citizen. Political deliberation was characterized as a manipulative process designed to advance the interests of some at the expense of others. In response to these challenges to the belief that man's good could be secured through democratic political interaction, some thinkers (Socrates among them) appealed to the force of reason, detached from the realm of politics and persuasion, as the fundamental criterion of the good for man; others (Callicles, in Plato's *Gorgias*) appealed to the force of desire and ambition, likewise detached from social convention. Neither view could accommodate the complexities of the human condition: the real constraints on any person or polity's will to power, and the no less authentic claims of personal needs and passions against the single-minded cultivation of the rational soul.

By the time Thucydides came to write his history, and in part because of the process he charts, the significance of these various aspects of the human experience had become all too evident. He portrays the social and ethical corrosion caused by the polarization of the Greek world, both within and among states, and by war, which he calls a "harsh schoolmaster." Thucydides offers history as a way for people to think and act prudently under such conditions. An interpreted history—which engages the reader's emotions as well as their reason—extends the range of man's experience and cultivates their capacity for judgment under trying circumstances, an appreciation of the need for self-control, and an ability to exercise it.

Historical analysis is most effective when it informs political leadership, as occurred in Athens under the guidance of Pericles (495–429 BCE). As Thucydides portrays him, Pericles sought to educate the Athenians about their real condition, its sources and implications, in such a way as to enable them to anticipate and reconsider their responses. Thucydides acknowledges that this kind of historical leadership did not always work—even when Pericles was alive—and gave way to demagoguery and distortions of the truth after he died. Thucydides himself has acquired a reputation for hostility to democracy because he inclines at times toward institutional substitutes for the dynamic cultivation of judgment through democratic interaction. But his characterization of the respective strengths and weaknesses of the Athenians and the Spartans points to Thucydides' belief that the most admirable polity—the one capable of understanding and responding to the world as it really is—is a democratic polity, like Athens, that cultivates initiative, flexibility, passion, freedom, and is guided by prudent leadership—and by history.

See also Nomos and Phusis; Socrates; Sophists.

Bibliography

Cochrane, C. N. *Thucydides and the Science of History*. New York: Russell & Russell, 1965.

Connor, W. Robert. *Thucydides*. Princeton, NJ: Princeton University Press, 1984.

Cornford, F.M. *Thucydides Mythistoricus*. London: E. Arnold, 1907.

Crane, Gregory. *Thucydides and the Ancient Simplicity: The Limits of Political Realism*. Berkeley: University of California Press, 1998.

Farrar, Cynthia. *Origins of Democratic Thinking: The Invention of Politics in Classical Athens*. Cambridge, U.K., and New York; Cambridge University Press, 1988.

Romilly, Jaqueline de. *Thucydides and Athenian Imperialism*. Translated by Philip Thody. New York: Barnes and Noble, 1963.

Strassler, Robert B., ed. *The Landmark Thucydides: A Comprehensive Guide to the Peloponnesian War*. New York: Free Press, 1996.

Williams, Bernard. *Truth and Truthfulness: An Essay in Genealogy*. Princeton, NJ: Princeton University Press, 2002.

Cynthia Farrar (2005)

THÜMMIG, LUDWIG PHILIPP

(1697–1728)

Ludwig Philipp Thümmig, the German Wolffian philosopher, was professor of philosophy at Halle from 1717 until 1723 when he was expelled with Christian Wolff. On Wolff's recommendation he was appointed professor of philosophy at the Collegium Carolinum in Kassel, but he ended his career as an instructor of pages. His early death prevented him from regaining a decent position when Wolff's fortunes improved.

Thümmig was one of Wolff's earliest pupils, and his *Institutions Philosophiae Wolffianae* (2 vols., Frankfurt and Leipzig, 1725–1726) was intended as a short and more readily understandable presentation, closer to the doctrines of traditional philosophy, of the doctrines presented in Wolff's German works. The work was written in Latin to prevent misunderstandings arising out of Wolff's new German terminology. The order of presentation of the main subjects covered, and the sharp separation between the topics treated in the discussions of the main branches of philosophy, were probably suggested by Wolff and were later adopted by him in his own Latin works. Unlike Wolff in his German works, Thümmig discussed cosmology before psychology, and divided psychology into empirical and rational branches. This order became traditional in the Wolffian school and was adopted by Wolff himself in his Latin works.

Thümmig used the traditional language and manner of exposition to make Wolff's doctrines more acceptable. He introduced non-Wolffian elements into his solution to the problem of preestablished harmony. He also differed from Wolff in regarding the study of natural law as a theoretical science (*scientia legum naturalia*) but ethics and politics as practical sciences whose purpose was to reach an agreement between man's real condition and the natural law.

See also Cosmology; Natural Law; Psychology; Wolff, Christian.

Bibliography

Thümmig's works include *Demonstratio Immortalitas Animae ex Intima Eius Natura Deducta* (Halle, 1721), and *Meletemata Varii et Rarioris Argumenti* (Braunschweig and Leipzig, 1727).

For a discussion of Thümmig, see Max Wundt, *Die deutsche Schulphilosophie im Zeitalter der Aufklärung*, 212–214. (Tübingen: Mohr, 1945).

Giorgio Tonelli (1967)

TILLICH, PAUL

(1886–1965)

Paul Tillich, the German American theologian, was born in Starzeddel in eastern Germany, the son of a Lutheran pastor. He received a theological and philosophical education and was ordained in the Evangelical Lutheran Church in 1912. He served as an army chaplain during World War I and then taught theology and philosophy at Berlin, Marburg, Dresden, and Frankfurt. On Adolf Hitler's advent to power in 1933, Tillich immigrated to the United States, serving as professor of systematic theology and philosophy of religion at Union Theological Seminary from 1933 to 1956. From 1956 until his death he held chairs at Harvard and at the University of Chicago.

ANXIETY

Tillich's religious thought has been enormously influential, particularly in English-speaking countries. He was strongly influenced by existentialism, and he held, as did Søren Kierkegaard, that religious questions are appropriately raised only in relation to problems that are inherent in the "human situation" and that theological claims are not mere responses to theoretical puzzles. Thus, Tillich presents Christian doctrines as resolutions of practical problems. His discussion of anxiety in *The Courage to Be* is a good example of his method. He first analyzes thoroughly and with great sensitivity what he considers the three great anxieties of modern man—the anxiety of death, that of meaninglessness, and that of guilt. These three forms of anxiety are three modes of response to various kinds of threats from nonbeing, threats to which existence as such is subject. As a practical solution to this practical problem, theology presents God. By participating in God, who is the infinite power to resist the threat of nonbeing, man acquires the courage to exist fully, even in the face of such anxiety. Similarly, when a person becomes deeply aware of historical existence as full of ambiguities, he becomes filled with perplexities and despair. The Christian answer is the notion of the Kingdom of God, which is the meaning, fulfillment, and unity of history.

KNOWLEDGE OF REALITY

Tillich's concern was with the religious significance of the "human situation," and he held that religious questions arise out of human problems. In a similar vein, the only basis for an understanding of the ontological structure of reality is the analysis of human existence, of man's encounter with his environment. We can grasp the being of other things only by analogy with man. Tillich, in the first volume of his *Systematic Theology,* sees man as "that being in whom all levels of being are united and approachable." But man is not merely "an outstanding object among other objects." He is the "being who asks the ontological question and in whose self-awareness the ontological answer can be found." Man can proceed in this way "because he experiences directly and immediately the structure of being and its elements"—because "the interdependence of ego-self and world is the basic ontological structure and implies all the others." Man is a self; "therefore selfhood and self-centeredness must be attributed … to all living beings and, in terms of analogy, to all individual *Gestalten* even in the inorganic realm." In accordance with this view, Tillich takes concepts that he supposes to have their primary application to human existence—individualization and participation, dynamics and form, freedom and destiny—and designates them as the elements constituting ontological structure, applying them to being as such.

FAITH

Tillich conceives of faith or, as he calls it, "ultimate concern" as a way of organizing human experience and activity. In his view, faith is an unconditional surrender to something and the willingness to recognize it as an absolute authority; an expectation that one will in some way receive a supreme fulfillment through encounter and commerce with it; a discovery that everything in one's life and one's world is significant only insofar as it is in some way related to it; and experiencing it as holy—that is, reacting to it with an intimate blend of a sense of awe, mystery, and fascination.

Every human being, Tillich believed, has such an ultimate concern, but the objects of the concern vary enormously. Supernatural beings, historical persons whether religious or secular, nations, social classes, political movements, cultural forms like painting and science, material goods, social status—any of these may be the object of an ultimate concern. But despite what Tillich said, it would seem that such orientation around a single object is a rare achievement. Most people, it would seem, have several major interests. Moreover, there is a crucial difference between concern with an object, whether existent or thought to exist, and concern for the realization of some end. The significance of taking an end, like social status, as having authority is not clear. Nevertheless, Tillich's analysis of religiosity is a penetrating one, and it reveals the important resemblances between religiosity and nonreligious modes of personal organization.

GOD

Tillich tried to show that the religious life is more than an organization of human feelings and attitudes and that it involves a reference to a reality outside itself, a reference that can be validated. Although Tillich did not, like Kierkegaard, deny the religious relevance of rational investigation, and although he did think that ontology gives some support to religion, he did not believe in the validity of traditional metaphysical proofs of specifically religious doctrines and in particular of the existence of a personal God. Tillich did not, in fact, accept the notion of a personal deity. For him the doctrine of a supernatural person, like all religious doctrines, is to be conceived as an attempt to symbolize an ultimate reality, "being-itself," which is so ultimate that all that can literally be said about it is that it is ultimate. If the God of theism is a person, the often repeated charge that Tillich is really an atheist thus seems justified; yet Tillich can point out that in the past Christian theology has repeatedly found difficulty in the notion that God is a person in any straightforward or literal sense.

THE ULTIMATE

Tillich defended his view that religious faith is objectively valid by claiming that an ultimate concern must necessarily have what is metaphysically Ultimate as its object. It is not clear, however, that if a concern is ultimate (in the sense of being the dominant interest of a person), the object of the concern is necessarily Ultimate in the relevant sense; that is, that the object of the concern is that on which all else depends for its being. Tillich has argued elsewhere that one can be ultimately concerned only with what is metaphysically Ultimate. Nothing can properly be of ultimate concern unless it is the ultimate determiner of the reality and meaning of our existence, and only being-itself occupies this position. From this conclusion it is only a short step to say that in ultimate concern one is always really concerned with being-itself, whether one realizes it or not.

RELIGIOUS SYMBOLS

But if being-itself is always the object of ultimate concern, what is the status of the various nonultimate entities on which ultimate concern seems to be focused? According to Tillich, as we have seen, the object of an ultimate concern is generally something relatively concrete, such as a person or a social group, and not, at least not consciously, some ineffable metaphysical Ultimate. Tillich claims that these concrete objects function as symbols of the Ultimate. They manifest the Ultimate to those who experience them as holy, and for those persons they *point to* the Ultimate; through them the individual participates in the Ultimate. Thus, ultimate concern has in a sense a double object. Unfortunately, Tillich never gave an intelligible account of these closely interrelated concepts of symbolizing and pointing to, which are so crucial for his position. Pointing to the Ultimate cannot consist in calling the Ultimate to mind, for admittedly most people have no such concept. The main difficulty is that being-itself is given such a fundamental position in Tillich's metaphysical scheme that one necessarily is related to being-itself at every moment in any way in which anyone could conceivably be related to it. Thus, if it is possible to speak of beings participating in being-itself, then each being necessarily so participates at every moment of its existence. There seems to be no room for any special contact with being-itself that could be generated by religious symbols when they are "pointing to it."

DEFENSE OF CHRISTIANITY

As a Christian theologian, Tillich wanted to demonstrate that among ultimate concerns the Christian concern is the most adequate. He sometimes said that some ultimate concerns are "idolatrous" because they are directed at finite objects rather than at the Ultimate. But by his own principles Tillich could not say this, because every case of ultimate concern involves a concrete object that manifests or points to the Ultimate. If it did not so function, it would not be a case of ultimate concern. The only possible way of showing that one ultimate concern is more adequate than another would be to show that it served better as a symbol of being-itself. But since nothing can be said literally about being-itself except that it is Ultimate, a feature that nothing else can share, it is not clear how this could be done. Tillich's own argument for the superiority of Christianity seems itself to be in symbolic terms. He said that by dying on the cross, Jesus Christ, who is the basic symbol of being-itself in Christianity, underlined the fact that symbols have their significance not in themselves but as manifesting the Ultimate.

See also Atheism; Existentialism; Kierkegaard, Søren Aabye; Ontological Argument for the Existence of God; Philosophy of Religion, History of; Philosophy of Religion, Problems of.

Bibliography

WORKS BY TILLICH

Translations of important works include *The Religious Situation,* translated by H. R. Niebuhr (New York: Holt, 1956), and *The Interpretation of History,* translated by N. A. Razetski and E. L. Talmey (New York: Scribners, 1936).

Tillich's magnum opus is *Systematic Theology.* 3 vols. (Chicago: University of Chicago Press, 1951–1963). Vol. I contains most of the philosophically interesting sections. *The Courage to Be* (New Haven, CT: Yale University Press, 1952) is an existentially toned account of the spiritual situation of contemporary man. *The Dynamics of Faith* (New York: Harper, 1957) is the best popular account of Tillich's position. *Biblical Religion and the Search for Ultimate Reality* (Chicago: University of Chicago Press, 1955) defends the thesis that ontological speculation has relevance to biblical religion. *Theology of Culture,* edited by R. C. Kimball (New York: Oxford University Press, 1959), is a collection of Tillich's writings on the mutual relevance of theology and various aspects of culture.

On the notion of a religious symbol, see "The Religious Symbol," in *Journal of Liberal Religion* 2 (1) (Summer 1940): 13–33, and "Theology and Symbolism," in *Religious Symbolism,* edited by F. E. Johnson (New York, 1955), pp. 107–116.

WORKS ON TILLICH

For discussions of Tillich's works, see C. W. Kegley and R. W. Bretall, eds., *The Theology of Paul Tillich* (New York: Macmillan, 1952); W. P. Alston, "Tillich on Idolatry," in *Journal of Religion* 38 (1958): 263–267; Paul Edwards, "Professor Tillich's Confusions," in *Mind* 74 (1965): 192–214; and W. P. Alston, "Tillich's Conception of a Religious Symbol," in *Religious Experience and Truth,* edited by Sidney Hook (New York: New York University Press, 1961), pp. 12–26.

OTHER RECOMMENDED TITLES

Adams, James et al., eds. *The Thought of Paul Tillich.* San Francisco: Harper and Row, 1985.

Crossman, Richard. *Paul Tillich: A Comprehensive Bibliography and Keyword Index of Primary and Secondary Writings in English.* Metuchen, NJ: Scarecrow Press, 1983.

Pauck, Wilhelm, and Marion Pauck. *Paul Tillich: His Life and Thought.* New York: Harper and Row, 1976.

Rowe, William. *Religious Symbols and God: A Philosophical Study of Tillich's Theology.* Chicago: University of Chicago Press, 1968.

Scharlemann, Robert. *Reflection and Doubt in the Thought of Paul Tillich.* New Haven, CT: Yale University Press, 1969.

Thatcher, Adrian. *The Ontology of Paul Tillich.* Oxford: Oxford University Press, 1978.

William P. Alston (1967)
Bibliography updated by Christian B. Miller (2005)

TIME

Time has frequently struck philosophers as mysterious. Some have even felt that it was incapable of rational discursive treatment and that it was able to be grasped only by intuition. This defeatist attitude probably arises because time always seems to be mysteriously slipping away from us; no sooner do we grasp a bit of it in our consciousness than it has slipped away into the past. This entry will argue, however, that this notion of time as something that continually passes is based on a confusion.

ST. AUGUSTINE'S PUZZLES

The apparent mysteriousness of time can make puzzles about time seem more baffling than they are, even though similar ones arise in the case of nontemporal concepts. St. Augustine, in his *Confessions*, asks, "What is time?" When no one asks him, he knows; when someone asks him, however, he does not know. He knows how to use the word "time" and cognate temporal words, such as "before," "after," "past," and "future," but he can give no clear account of this use. Trouble arises particularly from the form in which he puts his question: "What is time?" This looks like a request for a definition, and yet no definition is forthcoming. However, most interesting concepts cannot be elucidated by explicit definitions. Thus, to explain the meaning of the word "length," we cannot give an explicit definition, but we can do things that explain how to tell that one thing is longer than another and how to measure length. In the same way, it is possible to give an account of the use of the word "time" even though it is not possible to do so by giving an explicit definition. In short, this puzzle of St. Augustine's is not of a sort that arises peculiarly in the case of time. Beyond pointing this out, therefore, it is not appropriate here to go further into the matter.

Augustine was also puzzled by how we could measure time. He seems to have been impressed by the lack of analogy between spatial and temporal measurement. For example, one can put a ruler alongside a tabletop, and the ruler and the tabletop are all there at once. However, if one were to measure a temporal process, it would be done by comparing it with some other process, such as the movement of the hand of a watch. At any moment of the comparison, part of the process to be measured has passed away, and part of it is yet to be. It is not possible to get the thing to be measured in front of a person all at once, as one could with the tabletop. Moreover, if two temporal processes are compared—say, a twenty-mile walk last week with a twenty-mile walk today—they are compared with two different movements of a watch hand, whereas two different tabletops are compared with the same ruler. Augustine is led to see a puzzle here because he demands, in effect, that non-analogous things should be talked about as though they were analogous.

In any case, the two things are not, in fact, as non-analogous as they appear to be at first sight. If we pass to a tenseless idiom in which material things are thought of as four-dimensional space-time solids, the difference becomes less apparent. For in the case of the tables we compare two different spatial cross sections of the four-dimensional object that is the ruler with spatial cross sections of the two tables. Augustine seems to have been influenced by the thought that the present is real, although the past and future are not (the past has ceased to exist, and the future has not yet come to be); consequently, the measurement of time is puzzling in a way in which the measurement of space need not be (where the whole spatial object can be present now). This thought—that the present is real in a way in which past and future are not real—is part of the confusion of the flow or passage of time. This is not to say that presentism has not recently been intelligently defended, however implausibly, as by John Bigelow (1996). Apodeictic proof has rarely been possible in metaphysics, and we fall back eventually on trading plausibilities. One of the central objections to presentism is the difficulty it has in analyzing cross-temporal statements such as "Smith will have come before you have finished breakfast." Perhaps the most important objection relates to the explanatory value of four-dimensional space-time in relativity theory to be discussed below.

THE MYTH OF PASSAGE

We commonly think of time as a stream that flows or as a sea over which we advance. The two metaphors come to much the same thing, forming part of a whole way of thinking about time that D. C. Williams has called "the myth of passage"(Williams 1951). If time flows past us or if we advance through time, this would be a motion with respect to a hypertime. For motion in space is motion with respect to time, and motion of time or in time could hardly be a motion in time with respect to time. Ascription of a metric to time is not necessary for the argument, but supposing that time can be measured in seconds, the difficulty comes out clearly. If motion in space is feet per second, at what speed is the flow of time? Seconds per what? Moreover, if passage is of the essence of time, it is presumably the essence of hypertime, too, which would lead one to postulate a hyper-hypertime and so on ad infinitum.

The idea of time as passing is connected with the idea of events changing from future to past. We think of events as approaching us from the future, whereupon they are momentarily caught in the spotlight of the present and then recede into the past. Yet in normal contexts it does not make sense to talk of events changing or staying the same. Roughly speaking, events are happenings to continuants—that is, to things that change or stay the same. Thus, we can speak of a table, a star, or a political constitution as changing or staying the same. But can we intelligibly talk of a change itself as changing or not changing?

It is true that in the differential calculus we talk of rates of change changing, but a rate of change is not the same thing as a change. Again, we can talk of continuants as coming into existence or ceasing to exist, but we cannot similarly talk of a "coming-into-existence" itself as coming into existence or ceasing to exist. It is nevertheless true that there is a special class of predicates, such as "being past," "being present," "being future," together with some epistemological predicates such as "being probable" or "being foreseen," with respect to which we can talk of events as changing. Significantly enough, these predicates do not apply to continuants. We do not, for example, naturally talk of a table or a star as "becoming past" but of its "ceasing to exist." There is something odd about the putative properties of pastness, presentness, futurity, and the like, whereby events are supposed to change. One might conjecture that the illusion of the passage of time arises from confusing the flow of information through our short-term memories with a flow of time itself.

TOKEN-REFLEXIVE EXPRESSIONS. Leaving aside the epistemological predicates, we may suspect that the oddness arises because the words "past," "present," and "future," together with "now" and with tenses, are token-reflexive, or indexical, expressions. That is, these words refer to their own utterance. If italics are allowed to indicate tenselessness in a verb, then if one says, "Caesar *crosses* the Rubicon," the speaker does not indicate whether the crossing is something before, simultaneous with, or after the assertion. Tenseless verbs occur in mathematics where temporal position relative to a person's utterance is not even in question. Thus, we can say, "2 + 2 *is* equal to 4" not because we wish to be noncommittal about the temporal position of 2 + 2 as being 4 but because it has no temporal position at all.

The token-reflexiveness (or more generally the indexicality) of the word "past" can be seen, for example, if a person who said that a certain event *E* is past could equally well have said, "*E is* earlier than this utterance." Similarly, instead of saying, "*E* is present," he could say, "*E is* simultaneous with this utterance," and instead of "*E* is future," he could say, "*E is* later than this utterance." The phrase "*E* was future" is more complicated. It means that if someone had said, "*E* is future" or "*E is* later than this utterance," at some appropriate time earlier than the present utterance (the utterance which we now refer to as "this utterance"), he would have spoken truly. Thus, if we say that in 1939 the battle of Britain was in the future, we are putting ourselves into the shoes of ourselves as we were in 1939, when, given a certain amount of prescience, we might have said truly, "The battle of Britain *is* later than this utterance." Apart from this imaginative projection, we are saying no more than that the battle of Britain *is* later than 1939. Another way of dealing with this problem, one that is preferred by Michael Tooley (1997) would be to interpret the token reflexive expressions as referring not to utterances but to times of utterance.

It follows that there is a confusion in talking of events as changing in respect of pastness, presentness, and futurity. These are not genuine properties, which can be seen if the token-reflexiveness is made explicit. "*E* was future, is present, and will become past" goes over into "*E is* later than some utterance earlier than this utterance, *is* simultaneous with this utterance, and *is* earlier than some utterance later than this utterance." Here the reference is to three different utterances. However, if we allow simultaneity, being later, and being earlier as relations to times as well as events we could render the tensed sentence above by saying, "*E is* later than some time earlier than this utterance, *is* simultaneous with this utterance, and *is* earlier than some time later than this utterance." Also, the troubling sentence "Once there were no utterances" could go over to "There *are* times earlier than this utterance when there were no utterances." A failure to recognize the direct or indirect indexicality of words such as "past," "present," and "future" can lead us to think wrongly of the change from future to past as a genuine change, such as the change in position of a boat that floats down a river.

Nevertheless, there is probably a deeper source of the illusion of time flow. This is that our stock of memories is constantly increasing, and memories are of earlier, not of later, events. It is difficult to state this matter properly because we forget things as well as acquire new memories. With a very old man there may well be a net diminishing of his stock of memories, and yet he does not feel as if time were running the other way. This suggestion is therefore tentative and incompletely worked out. Possibly we confuse a flow of information through our short-term memories with a flow of time itself (Smart 1987). The subordinate question of why our memories are of the past, not of the future, is an extremely interesting question in its own right and will be answered in a later section.

TENSES. Not only words such as "past" and "future" but also tenses can be replaced by the use of tenseless verbs together with the phrase "this utterance." Thus, instead of saying, "Caesar crossed the Rubicon," we could have said, "Caesar *crosses* the Rubicon earlier than this utterance." For the present and future tenses we use "simultaneous with this utterance" and "later than this utterance." Of course, this is not a strict translation. If one person says, "Caesar *crosses* the Rubicon earlier than this utterance," that person refers to his utterance, whereas if another person says, "Caesar crossed the Rubicon," she is implicitly referring to her utterance. Nevertheless, a tensed language is translatable into a tenseless language in the sense that the purposes subserved by the one, in which utterances covertly refer to themselves, can be subserved by the other in which utterances explicitly refer to themselves.

A second qualification must be made. In the case of spoken language the token or "utterance" can be taken to be the actual sounds. In a written language the "token," the configuration of ink marks, is something that persists through time. By "this utterance" we must therefore, in the case of written language, understand the coming-into-existence of the token or perhaps the act of writing it. It has sometimes been objected that this account will not stand because "this utterance" means "the utterance which is *now*," which reintroduces the notion of tense. There does not seem to be any reason, however, why we should accept this charge of circularity. We have as good a right to say that "now" means "simultaneous with this utterance" as our opponent has to say that "this utterance" means "the utterance which is now." The notion of an utterance directly referring to itself does not seem to be a difficult one.

Tenses and their cognates may be seen to be indexical expressions. The truth conditions of sentences containing them cannot be given by translation into a nonindexical language. Nevertheless they can be given in a nonindexical *metalanguage*. The idea derives from Donald Davidson and is advantageous because there is a recursively specifiable infinity of sentences in a language but not of utterances or inscriptions. Equally with the token reflexive account it removes the mystery that one might feel about tenses and cognate expressions.

Tensers, such as Quentin Smith (1993), argue that the words "past," "present" and "future" refer to intrinsic properties of events, though Smith defines "past" and "future" in terms of "present." This makes him in a sense a presentist, though only a mild one as he does not deny the reality of the past and future. Davidson's suggestion for the semantics of tenses is to say that (say) "I will come" is true as (potentially) spoken by person P at time t if and only if P *comes* later than t. As Heather Dyke, in her doughty defense of the token-reflexive approach (Dyke 2002, 2003), has remarked, without the "potentially" (of which critics of modal logic may be suspicious) the Davidsonian schema comes out trivially true in cases where (say) "I will come" is not uttered by P at t. Perhaps one might reply that trivial truth is still truth and so harmless, or one might treat the Davidsonian schema as an idealization. Dyke has urged that one should abandon aspirations of the old token reflexive theory for a translation of tensed sentences into tenseless ones but argue that a tensed sentence states the same fact about the world as can be stated by a tenseless one. Thus she wants a semantics based on tokens of sentences, not sentences, and so abandons recursiveness. A similar appeal to the notion of "fact" is made by D. H. Mellor in his influential *Real Time II* (1998), where he says that ontology can be separated from considerations of semantics. Of course this metaphysical notion of "fact" has been thought problematic, as by Davidson himself. Nevertheless, the difference between the token reflexive account and the metalinguistic one is not of great ontological significance. Dyke contests arguments by Quentin Smith (1993), who has been an immensely prolific defender of the tensed notion of time.

DURATION. The philosophical notion of duration seems to be heavily infected with the myth of passage. Thus John Locke in his *Essay concerning Human Understanding* (1690) says that "duration is fleeting extension" (bk II, ch. 14, paragraph 1). In the early nineteenth century, Henri Bergson (1910, 1911, 1913) made the notion of duration (*durée*) central in his philosophy. According to him, physical time is something spatialized and intellectualized, whereas the real thing, with which we are acquainted in intuition (inner experience), is duration. Unlike physical time, which is always measured by comparing discrete spatial positions—for example, of clock hands—duration is the experienced change itself, the directly intuited nonspatial stream of consciousness in which past, present, and future flow into one another. Bergson's meaning is unclear, partly because he thinks that duration is something to be intuitively—not intellectually—grasped. Duration is closely connected in his thought with memory, for in memory, Bergson says, the past survives in the present. Here he would seem to be open to the objection, urged against him by Bertrand Russell in his *History of Western Philosophy* (1945), that he confuses the memory of the past event with the past event itself, or the thought with that which is thought about.

Even though the Bergsonian notion of duration may be rejected because of its subjectivism and because of its close connection with the notion of time flow or passage, there is nevertheless a clear use of the word "duration" in science and ordinary life. Thus, in talking about the duration of a war, we talk simply about the temporal distance between its beginning and its end.

MCTAGGART ON TIME'S UNREALITY. The considerations thus far adduced may well be illustrated by considering how they bear on John McTaggart Ellis McTaggart's well-known argument for the unreality of time, which was put forward in an article in *Mind* (1908) and in his posthumous *Nature of Existence* (1927). For McTaggart, events are capable of being ordered in two ways. First, they can be ordered in respect to past, present, and future. He calls this ordering of events "the *A* series." Second, events can be ordered in respect to the relations "earlier than" and "later than." He calls this "the *B* series." McTaggart then argues that the *B* series does not by itself give all that is essential to time and that the *A* series is contradictory. Neither leg of his argument can stand criticism. His reason for saying that the *B* series misses the essence of time is that time involves change and yet it always is, was, and will be the case that the Battle of Hastings, say, is earlier than the Battle of Waterloo. It has already been shown, however, that it is not just false but also absurd to talk of events' changing. The Battle of Hastings is not *sempiternally* earlier than the Battle of Waterloo; it simply *is* (tenselessly) earlier than it. The notion of change is perfectly capable of being expressed in the language of the *B* series by saying that events in the *B* series *differ* from one another in various ways. Similarly, the proposition that a thing changes can be expressed in the language of the *B* series by the statement that one spatial cross section of it *is* different from an earlier one, and the proposition that it does not change can be expressed by saying that earlier and later cross sections *are* similar to one another. To express the notion of change, we are therefore *not* forced to say that events change. Nor, therefore, are we forced into referring to the *A* series, into saying that events change (in the only way in which we can plausibly say this) in respect to pastness, presentness, and futurity.

Nevertheless, if we do retreat to the language of the *A* series, we can perfectly well do so without contradiction. Just as McTaggart erred by using tensed verbs when talking of the *B* series, he in effect made the correlative error of forgetting tenses (or equivalent devices) when talking of the *A* series. For the contradiction that he claimed to find in the *A* series is that because any event is in turn future, present, and past, we must ascribe these three incompatible characteristics to it; but an event cannot be future, present, or past *simpliciter* but only with reference to a particular time—for example, one at which it was future, is present, and will be past. If we restore the tenses, the trouble with the *A* series disappears. Unsuccessful though McTaggart's argument is, it provides an excellent case study with which to elucidate the relations between tensed and tenseless language.

SPACE-TIME

The theory of relativity illustrates the advantages of replacing the separate notions of space and time by a unified notion of space-time. In particular, Minkowski showed that the Lorentz transformations of special relativity correspond to a rotation of axes in space-time. He showed how natural the kinematics of special relativity can seem, as opposed to Newtonian kinematics, in which, in effect, we should rotate the time axis without correspondingly rotating the space axes. Since the theory of relativity it has become a commonplace to regard the world as a four-dimensional space-time manifold. Nevertheless, even in the days of Newtonian dynamics, there was nothing to prevent taking this view of the world, even though it would not have been as neat as it is in relativity theory. If we pass to the four-dimensional way of looking at things, it is important not to be confused about certain conceptual matters. Confusion will arise if the tenseless way of talking, appropriate to the four-dimensional picture, is mixed with our ordinary way of talking of things as enduring substances, "the permanent in change."

In ordinary language the word "space" itself is used as the name of a continuant. We can say, for example, that a part of space has become, or has continued to be, occupied. Space-time, however, is a "space" in a tenseless sense of this word, and because time is already in the representation, it is wrong to talk of space-time as itself changing. Thus, in some expositions of relativity it is said that a certain "world line" is a track along which a material body moves or a light signal is propagated. The body or light signal, however, cannot correctly be said to move through space-time. What should be said is that the body or the light signal *lies* (tenselessly) along the world line. To talk of anything's moving through space-time is to bring time into the story twice over and in an illegitimate manner. When we are talking about motion in terms of the space-time picture, we must do so in terms of the relative orientations of world lines. Thus, to say that two particles move with a uniform nonzero relative velocity is expressed by saying that they *lie* (tenselessly) along straight world lines that are at an angle to one another. Similarly, the recent conception of the positron as an electron moving backward in time is misleading because nothing can move, forward or backward, in time. What is meant is that the world lines of a positron and electron, which are produced together or which annihilate one another, can be regarded as a single bent world line, and this may indeed be a fruitful way of looking at the matter.

In popular expositions of relativity we also read of such things as "consciousness crawling up the world line of one's body." This is once more the confusion of the myth of passage and, hence, of the illegitimate notion of movement through space-time. It is instructive to consider how H. G. Wells's time machine could be represented in the space-time picture. A moment's thought should suffice to indicate that it cannot be represented at all. For if a line is drawn extending into the past, this will simply be the representation of a particle that has existed for a long time. It is not surprising that we cannot represent a time machine because the notion of such a machine is an incoherent one. How fast would such a machine flash over a given ten-second stretch? In ten seconds or minus ten seconds? Or what? No sensible answer can be given, for the question is itself absurd. The notion also involves the contradiction, pointed out by D. C. Williams in his article "The Myth of Passage" (1951) that if a person gets into a time machine at noon today, then at 3 a.m., say, that person shall be *both* at 3 p.m. today *and* at, say, a million years ago. There is nevertheless a more consistent notion of time travel though misleadingly so called. A person as a space-time entity might lie along a bent-back world line. It might curve back and then would go back to your great grandmother's time and then a bit forward while you saw your great grandmother. Paradox lurks because if the great grandmother had been shot you would not have existed. David Lewis has proposed a banana skin solution. Since you could not have shot your great grandmother some accident, such as your slipping on a banana skin or your pistol jamming, must have prevented you from harming her. One would wish, however, for a solution of the paradox by reference to the laws of nature.

Though D. H. Mellor ably defends the four-dimensional ontology in his *Real Time II*, he nevertheless says something that may puzzle four-dimensionalists—for example, that a person from birth to death, or a stone over a long period of time, is said to have a certain property at time *t*, but not that a mere time slice or temporal stage of the person or stone has the property. The puzzle is perhaps resolved if we note that Mellor thinks of the thing S as reidentifiable or a sortal as discussed by Peter Strawson. This is understandable because a child could hardly—and an adult could not easily—reidentify the mereological fusion of a bird, a bishop, and Mount Everest. Even so, the four-dimensionalist need not discern a difference between "S is A at *t*" and "S at *t* is A." The time slice may be referred to by reference to the salient four-dimensional object of which it is a slice. Mellor rightly stresses the importance for agency and practical matters of notions of reidentifiable sortals and for the determination of the strengths of beliefs and desires by a method originally due to F. P. Ramsey.

ABSOLUTE AND RELATIONAL THEORIES

Isaac Newton held to an absolute theory of space and time, whereas his contemporary Gottfried Wilhelm Leibniz argued that space and time are merely sets of relations between things that are in space and time. Newton misleadingly and unnecessarily expressed his absolute theory of time in terms of the myth of passage, as when he confusingly said, "Absolute, true and mathematical time, of itself and from its own nature, flows equably without relation to anything external" (*Principia,* in the Scholium to the Definitions of *Mathematical Principles of Natural Philosophy*). The special theory of relativity has made it impossible to consider time as something absolute;

rather, it stands neutrally between absolute and relational theories of space-time. The question as between absolute and relational theories of space-time becomes especially interesting when we pass to the general theory of relativity. According to this theory, the structure of space-time is dependent on the distribution of the matter in the universe. In most forms of the theory there is nevertheless a residual space-time structure that cannot be thus accounted for. A curvature is usually attributed to space-time even in the complete absence of matter, and the inertia of a body, according to this theory, depends in part on this cosmological contribution to the local metrical field and hence not solely on the total mass of the universe, as a purely relational theory would require.

Research on this question is still going on, and until it has been decided, Mach's principle (as Einstein called it), according to which the spatiotemporal structure of the universe depends entirely on the distribution of its matter, will remain controversial. But even if Mach's principle were upheld, it might still be possible to interpret matter, in a metaphysical way, as regions of special curvature of space-time. Graham Nerlich (1994) has given a striking and simple argument against those who, like Leibniz, defend relational theories by asking how one could tell whether everything had not doubled in size. He pointed out that this depends on the assumption that space is Euclidean. Relational theorists usually make the relevant relation that of cause and effect. If this is defined by the use of counterfactual propositions one may object that the murkiness or contextual nature of these contrasts with the absolute theory's reliance on the limpid clarity of geometry. Here I use "absolute" to contrast with 'relational' not as contrasted with "relativistic." An objection to a causal theory of time is that there could be uncaused events and that there are uncountably more space-time points than there are events. Michael Tooley separately assumes an ontology and topology of instants of time, but uses a causal theory to define temporal direction.

TIME AND THE CONTINUUM

An absolute theory of space-time, as envisaged above, need not imply that there is anything absolute about distance (space-time interval). Because of the continuity of space-time, any space-time interval contains as many space-time points as any other (that is, a high infinity of them); space and time do not possess an intrinsic metric, and there must always be an element of convention in definitions of congruence in geometry and chronology, as Adolf Grünbaum has pointed out (Grünbaum1973). This means that the same cosmological facts can be expressed by means of a variety of space-time geometries, provided that they have the same topological structure. (Topology is that part of geometry which treats only of those properties of a figure which remain the same however that figure is transformed into a new one, with the sole restriction that a point transforms into one and only one point and neighboring points transform into neighboring ones. Thus, the surface of a sphere and that of a cube have the same topology, but that of a sphere and that of an infinite plane do not.)

ZENO AND CANTOR. The continuity of space and time can be properly understood only in terms of the modern mathematical theory of infinity and dimensionality. Given the concepts available to him, Zeno rightly rejected the view that an extended line or time interval could be composed of unextended points or instants. (See Aristotle, *Physics* 231a20–231bl8 and *De Generatione et Corruptione*, 316al5–317al7.)

In modern terms it may be said that not even a denumerable infinity of points can make up a nonzero interval. Cantor has shown, however, that there are higher types of infinity than that which belongs to denumerable sets, such as the set of all natural numbers. Cantor showed that the set of real numbers on a line, or segment of a line, is of a higher type of infinity than is the set of natural numbers. Perhaps the right cardinality of "dimensionless points" *can* add up to a nonzero length. This answer is on the right track. Nevertheless, the cardinality of a set of points does not by itself determine dimensionality.

For example, Cantor showed that there is a one-to-one mapping between the points of a plane and the points of a line. However, a mathematical theory of dimension has been developed that accords with our intuitions in assigning 0, 1, 2, 3, and so on, dimensions respectively to points, lines, planes, volumes, and so on, and which also assigns dimensions to other sorts of sets of points. For example, the set of all rational points on a line has dimension 0. So does the set of all irrational points. In these cases an infinity of "unextended points" does indeed form a set of dimension 0. Because these two sets of points together make up the set of points on a line, it follows that two sets of dimension 0 can be united to form a set of dimension 1. Strictly speaking, it is even inaccurate to talk of "unextended points." It is sets of points that have dimension. A line is a set of points, and the points are not parts of the line but members of it. The modern theory of dimension shows that there is no inconsistency in supposing that an appropriate nondenumerable infinity of points makes up a set of greater dimensionality than any finite or denumerable set of points could.

The theory of the continuum implies that if we take away the lower end of a closed interval, what is left is an open interval, an interval without a first point. In fact, Zeno's premises in his paradox of the dichotomy do not lead to paradox at all but are a consistent consequence of the theory of the continuum. Motion is impossible, according to the paradox of the dichotomy, because before one can go from *A* to *B*, one must first get to the halfway mark *C*, but before one can get to *C*, one must get to the halfway mark *D* between *A* and *C*, and so on indefinitely. It is concluded that the motion can never even get started. A similar argument, applied to time intervals, might seem to show that a thing cannot even endure through time. The fallacy in both cases comes from thinking of the continuum as a set of points or instants arranged in succession. For if a continuous interval had to consist of a first, second, third, and so on point or instant, then the dichotomy would provide a fatal objection. However, points or instants do not occur in succession, because to any point or instant there is no *next* point or instant. Such considerations enable us to deal with Zeno's paradox of Achilles and the tortoise, in which similar difficulties are supposed to arise at the *latter* end of an open interval.

KANT'S ANTINOMIES. A related paradox is Kant's first antinomy, in his *Critique of Pure Reason* (1929 [1781]). As was shown by Edward Caird (1889) in his commentary on Kant's *Critique*, the antinomies (or paradoxes which Kant had constructed about space, time, and causality) were as important as Hume's skeptical philosophy in arousing Kant from his "dogmatic slumbers." Kant's first antinomy relates to both space and time; the concentration here is on *Critique* as it relates to time. There are two antithetical arguments. The first states that the world had a beginning in time, whereas the second, with equal plausibility, seems to show that the world had no beginning in time. The first argument begins with the premise that if the world had no beginning in time, then up to a given moment an infinite series of successive events must have passed. But, says Kant, the infinity of a series consists in the fact that it can never be completed. Hence, it is impossible for an infinite series of events to have passed away.

It can be seen that Kant's argument here rests partly on the myth of passage. Kant thinks of the world as having come to its present state through a series of past events, so that an infinite succession would therefore have had to be completed. Otherwise, he would have been just as puzzled about the possibility of an infinite future as about an infinite past, and this does not seem to have been the case. Just as the sequence 0, 1, 2 … can never be completed in the sense that it has no last member, the sequence ——, –2, –1, 0 cannot be completed in the sense that it has no first member. This is not to say, of course, that an infinite set need have either a first or last member. Thus, the set of temporal instants up to, but not including, a given instant, has neither a first nor last member. However, Kant is clearly thinking not of the set of instants but of a sequence of events, each taking up a finite time. The set of instants does not form a sequence because there are no instants that are next to one another. Kant's definition of infinity, besides being objectionably psychologistic, is clearly inapplicable to infinite sets of entities which do not form a sequence, such as the points on a line or a segment of a line. Concerning an infinite set of events which form a sequence, however, Kant is not justified in supposing that its having a last member is any more objectionable than its having a first member. There is a perfect symmetry between the two cases once we rid ourselves of the notion of passage—that is, of the one-way flow of time.

In Kant's antithetical argument, he argues that the world cannot have had a beginning in time, so that, contrary to the thesis of the antinomy, there must have been an infinity of past events. His reason is that if the world had begun at a certain time, all previous time would have been a blank and there would be no reason that the world should have begun at the time it did rather than at some other time. Previously, Leibniz had used the same argument to support a relational theory of time. If time is constituted solely by the relations between events, then it becomes meaningless to ask questions about the temporal position of the universe as a whole or about when it began. In an absolute theory of time (or of space-time) Kant's problem remains, but further discussion of it cannot be pursued here because it would involve a metaphysical discussion of causality and the principle of sufficient reason.

TEMPORAL ASYMMETRY

We have just seen that Kant was puzzled about the infinity of the past in a way in which he was not puzzled about the infinity of the future. Further, it has been suggested that the myth of passage had something to do with this inconsistency. If we reject the notion of passage, we find ourselves with a new, though soluble, problem. This is the apparent temporal asymmetry of the universe, which contrasts sharply with its large-scale spatial symmetry. For example, if we look out at the galaxies, they appear to be distributed evenly in all directions, and yet a time direction seems to be specified by the fact that they are all receding from one another, not approaching one another. On a more mundane level, the temporal asymmetry of the universe is forcibly striking in many ways. For example, there is nothing in our experience analogous to memory but with respect to the future. Nor is there anything like a tape recording or a footprint of the future—that is, there are no *traces* of the future. A memory is indeed a special case of a trace. This asymmetry about traces explains how we can be so confident about the past history of the human race and about the past evolution of living creatures, whereas it would be a bold person who would try to guess the political history of even the next hundred years or the organic evolution of the next few millions. The question "Why are there traces only of the past, not of the future?" is thus a fundamental one.

We must first rule out a purely verbalistic answer to this question. Someone might say that traces are always of the past, never of the future, because it is part of the meaning of the word "trace" that traces are of earlier, not of later, events. This would be to suppose that the earlier question is as stupid as the question "Why are bachelors always male, never female?" This account of the matter is not good enough. Admittedly, in the English language as it is, the expression "female bachelor" is a self-contradictory one. Nevertheless, it is easy to imagine a variant of English in which "bachelor" simply meant "not yet married person" and according to which spinsters could therefore be called "bachelors." For example, if one were to call a spinster a "female analogue" of a bachelor, then it is possible to silence the verbalistic objection to the question about why traces are always of the past, never of the future, by recasting it in the form "Why are there no future analogues of traces?"

TEMPORAL ASYMMETRY AND PHYSICAL LAWS. The temporal directionality of the universe or, at the very least, of the present cosmic era of the universe would therefore appear to be a deep-lying cosmological fact, which is not to be glossed over by verbalistic explanations. How is it to be explained? We must first dismiss the suggestion that the asymmetry lies in the laws of physics. The laws of classical dynamics and electromagnetism, as well as of quantum mechanics, are all expressed by time-symmetrical differential equations. In other words, if $f(t)$ is a solution to these equations, so is $f(-t)$. (Actually to take care of recondite matters, twenty-first century physicists believe not in T symmetry but in CPT symmetry, reversal of time, reversal of charge, and reversal of parity. P symmetry can be thought of as reversal in a space mirror just as C symmetry is a matter of thinking of an antiparticle as a backwards-in-time particle. So CPT symmetry can be thought of as a deeper form of space-time symmetry.)

It follows that if a cinematographic film were taken of any process describable by means of these laws and then run backward, it would still portray a physically possible process. It is true that phenomenological thermodynamics would provide a contrary case, because its second law does contain time explicitly. Thus, if someone put a kettle full of ice on a hot brick, that person finds that the system turns into one in which a kettle full of water sits on a cool brick. A film of this process cannot be reversed to show a process which is possible in phenomenological thermodynamics; we cannot have a system of a kettle filled with water on a cool brick turning into one in which the water has frozen and the brick has become hot. In spite of all this it must still be asserted that the laws of nature are time symmetrical. This is because phenomenological thermodynamics provides only an approximation of the truth (it is refuted by the phenomenon of Brownian motion, for example) and, more importantly, because the detailed explanation of the facts of which phenomenological thermodynamics treats at the surface level is to be found in statistical thermodynamics. Statistical thermodynamics bases itself on the laws of mechanics, which are time symmetrical.

According to statistical thermodynamics, the situation in which the water in the kettle freezes while the brick gets hotter is indeed a physically possible one, though it is an almost infinitely unlikely one. Why it is unlikely has to do not with the laws of nature themselves but with their boundary conditions. There is indeed a puzzle here, because if all the velocities of a closed system are reversed, what results is a configuration that, according to statistical mechanics, is as likely as the original one. Therefore, the process seen on the reversed cinematographic film should be as likely as the original one. The answer to this objection (the reversibility objection) lies in the fact that corresponding to a given macroscopic description (cold kettle on hot brick, say), there is a whole ensemble of possible microstates. It follows that though any microstate is as probable as any other, this is not so with macrostates, and given the information that a body is in a macrostate A, it is highly probable that it will turn into a macrostate B rather than vice versa if B corresponds to an ensemble of microstates which is vastly more numerous than the ensemble of microstates corresponding to *A*.

An analogy with a pack of cards will help to make this clear. Consider a well-shuffled pack of cards. Any order of the cards is as probable as any other provided that the order is precisely described. Given any one such order *P*, it is, of course, just as probable that in shuffling, *P* will turn into the order (call it *Q*) in which the pack is arranged in suits as that *Q* would turn into *P*. But if *P* is described simply as haphazard, there is a vast number of states other than *P* which are also haphazard. Thus, although a shuffling which turns *Q* into *P* is no more probable than one which turns *P* into *Q*, there are far more shufflings which turn *Q* into a state abstractly described as haphazard than there are shufflings which turn a particular haphazard state—say, *P*—into *Q*.

Suppose we started with our cards arranged in suits, the state *Q*. If we shuffled them, they would soon get into what we should call a well-shuffled state. Nevertheless, if we went on shuffling long enough, we should eventually get back to the unshuffled state *Q*. This illustrates the following interesting point. Let us for the moment toy with the almost certainly false cosmological hypothesis that the universe is a finite nonexpanding collection of particles without spontaneous creation or annihilation. Then, just as with our pack of cards, such a universe will eventually return to any given state. The universe will get more and more shuffled until we get the so-called heat death, in which everything is a featureless uniformity and will then become less and less disordered. In the era in which, as we should put it, the universe was getting less disordered, time would seem to run in the opposite direction to that in which it seems to run to us. (Thus, denizens of this era would still say that the universe was getting more disordered.) Indeed, there would be an infinite sequence of cosmic eras, much as is supposed in some Buddhist cosmologies, except that time would seem to run in opposite ways in alternate eras. In a sufficiently large view there would be temporal symmetry in this universe, though not on the scale of any single cosmic era. This is what makes the hypothesis of a finite nonexpanding universe philosophically instructive, even though it is probably contrary to fact.

TRACE FORMATION AND ENTROPY. It is now possible to deal with the formation of traces. Although a wide, relatively isolated part of the universe is increasing in its state of being shuffled, or, to use the more precise notion developed by physicists, in its entropy, subsystems of the wider system may temporally decrease in shuffling, or entropy. Thus, an isolated system, such as that consisting of a cube of ice in a beaker of water, may well have lower entropy than its surroundings. This reduction of entropy is bought at the expense of a more than compensating increase of entropy in the surroundings. There will, for example, be an increase of disorderliness in the system containing the coal and air that react chemically and drive the generators that provide the electric power that drives the refrigerator that makes the ice cube. (The system consisting of coal and oxygen is a more highly ordered one than is that which consists of the ashes and used up air.) Eventually the ice cube melts and becomes indistinguishable from the water in which it floated.

BRANCH SYSTEMS. The formation of a trace is the formation of a subsystem of temporarily lower entropy than that of its surroundings, and the trace is blotted out when the entropy curve of the subsystem rejoins that of the larger system. A footprint in sand is a temporarily highly ordered state of the sand; this orderliness is bought at the expense of an increased disorderliness (metabolic depletion) of the pedestrian who made it, and this extra orderliness eventually disappears as a result of wind and weather. Hans Reichenbach (1956) calls such systems of temporarily lower entropy "branch structures." It is an observable fact, and one to be expected from considerations of statistical thermodynamics, that these branch structures nearly all (in practice, quite all) go in the same direction. This direction defines a temporal direction for the universe or at least for our cosmic era of it.

On investigation it will be seen that all sorts of traces, whether footprints on sand, photographs, fossil bones, or the like, can be understood as traces in this sense. Indeed, so are written records. The close connection between information and entropy is brought out in modern information theory, the mathematics of which is much the same as that of statistical thermodynamics. A coherent piece of prose is an ordered part of the universe, unlike a completely random sequence of symbols.

It is possible that the formation of branch systems may be linked to deeper cosmological facts. Thomas Gold (1958, 1962) has argued persuasively that the formation of such a system is possible only because the universe provides a sink for radiation, and this is possible, again, only because of the mutual recession of the galaxies. It may therefore ultimately be the expansion of the universe that accounts for the direction of time. Beyond noting this interesting suggestion of a link between the small-scale and large-scale structure of the cosmos, we can for our present purposes take the formation of branch systems for granted without linking it to uncertain cosmological speculations.

POPPER'S ACCOUNT. The theory of branch systems outlined above has been developed rigorously by Reichenbach and Grünbaum, whose work partly goes back to that of Ludwig Boltzmann (1895). (A rather similar account of temporal direction has been independently given by O. Costa de Beauregard [1963].) We must now consider a different account of the direction of time, one that was conceived by Karl Raimund Popper.

Slightly changing Popper's example, consider a spherical light wave emitted from a source, as when a small electric bulb is turned on. Consider how this process would look in reverse. We should have a large spherical wave contracting to a point. This would be causally inexplicable. In order to get a spherical light wave coming in from the depths of an infinite space, we should have to suppose a coordinated set of disturbances at every point of a vast sphere, and this would require a deus ex machina. Moreover, this would still not provide the reverse of an outgoing wave expanding indefinitely. Thus, although the contracting wave is as much in accordance with the laws of optics as is the expanding one, it still is not compatible with any physically realizable set of initial conditions. Once more, as with the Reichenbach-Grünbaum solution, it can be seen that temporal asymmetry arises from initial, or boundary, conditions, not from the laws of nature themselves.

Popper's criterion of temporal direction does not shed light on the concept of trace, as does the criterion of branch systems. And traces, particularly memory traces, give us our vivid sense of temporal asymmetry in the world. It is also interesting that if we consider a finite but unbounded nonexpanding universe, a contracting spherical wave would be physically realizable. Just as an expanding series of concentric circles on the earth's surface which have their original center at the North Pole would become a series of circles contracting to the South Pole, so in a symmetrical, finite, but unbounded universe a spherical wave expanding from a center would eventually become a contracting wave, shrinking to the antipodal point of the point of emission. If we included the facts of radiation in our finite nonexpanding universe, we should have to suppose a finite but unbounded space, and Popper's criterion of temporal direction would become inapplicable. Including such facts would therefore also not conflict with our supposition of alternate cosmic eras in such a universe. In such a universe the Reichenbach-Grünbaum account of temporal direction for particular cosmic eras would still be applicable. There are still anthropocentricities to be brought to light, a task which has been impressively achieved by Huw Price in his book *Times Arrow and Archimedes' Point* (1996). He has clearly discussed the time symmetry (or one might say CPT symmetry) of microphysics. On the macro level, causation is at least in our cosmic era asymmetrical because the concept of it is closely related to that of agency and so to the temporal asymmetry of memory traces.

What is presented here is not an analysis of the ordinary language concept of earlier and later. This is learned to some extent ostensively, and we may perfectly well know how to use words such as "earlier" and "later" without knowing anything about entropy or branch systems. As Wittgenstein might have said, "We know the language game." Here the concern is with a deeper problem: what are the general features of the universe which enable us to play the language game? Indeed, if the universe did not contain traces, it would be impossible for there to be any thought at all. It should be noted that Mellor in his aforementioned book rejects the relevance of considerations of entropy and the like and relies on the notion of probability: the cause is an event that raises the objective chance of the event that is the effect. As mentioned above, Tooley also has a causal account. Even so, considerations of entropy could be needed to explain the asymmetry of causation on the macro level. On the micro level, causation is time symmetric and Price has neatly suggested defending locality, and perhaps hidden variables, in quantum mechanics and in the face of John Bell's well-known inequality, by means of backward causation. Curiously, according to Price, Bell had once considered such a solution but had rejected it for dubious philosophical reasons connected with the notion of free will.

COMPROMISE THEORIES

Storrs McCall and Michael Tooley have proposed theories that contain elements of both tensed and tenseless theories. Tooley, in his *Time, Tense, and Causation* (1997), worked out a sophisticated theory that is partly similar to one that C. D. Broad proposed in his *Scientific Thought* (1923). According to this view, only past and future are real and the universe is continually getting bigger as more and more of the future becomes present and past. Tenseless theorists will still see this as open to the objections to notions of time flow and of absolute becoming that were canvassed above. So also will they see McCall's theory according to which reality keeps getting smaller. McCall is inspired by the Everett-Wheeler interpretation of quantum mechanics. Space-time reality is like a giant poplar tree with branches corresponding to possible futures, with trunk, branches of branches, and so on, all pointing up in timelike directions. At every interaction between particles, branches (real possibilities) get lopped off. According to the tenseless theorist, reality must be like a stack of poplar trees, ordered according to the inclusiveness of the sets of branches. The mind boggles. Tooley's (though not McCall's) theory requires an absolute present and Tooley is bold enough to consider modifying special relativity. However, a reconciliation with special relativity could have been acquired at less cost as follows. The equality in all directions of the cosmic background radiation may give an approximation to a preferred frame of reference at each point of space. This will, because of the expansion of the universe, yield a curved hypersurface of cosmic simultaneity. Tooley defends his view of the increase of reality against the objection that it requires a hypertime. However, time travel is not like space travel because we may travel to a place, say the Taj Mahal, where we have not been before. The four-dimensional equivalent of a place is a timelike world-line, which in the example may intersect the world line of the Taj Mahal. The space of commonsense talk and of Newton's *Principia* is a continuant, not like the atemporal space of Euclid. Tooley's cutting off of the future may put in question the explanatory (as opposed to instrumental) value of full Minkowski space, though perhaps less so than presentism.

The tenseless four-dimensional account sits well with mereology, the theory of part and whole. Indeed some philosophical problems come out as easily as shelling peas when one goes four-dimensional. Consider Robert Louis Stevenson's story of Dr. Jekyll and Mr. Hyde, in which the personalities of the virtuous Jekyll and the criminal Hyde alternate in the one body. Mereology distinguishes three objects, the spatiotemporally scattered objects Jekyll and Hyde and the continuous fusion of these two. The problem is not one about identity, which is a clear notion in logic, but about "person" and the problems about these are more legal and psychiatric than philosophical.

CAUSAL THEORIES OF TIME

There are theories of the structure of time, or of space-time, that are based on the notion of causality. Objections to such theories have been made as follows (Smart 1987). How do we deal with points of space-time that are not occupied with events that are neither causes nor effects? Perhaps we could rely on causal connectibility and not on connectedness. Connectibility is a modal notion and so will not be liked by philosophers such as those influenced by W. V. Quine, who are suspicious of modality. In special relativity the notion of connectibility can be defined directly in terms of the geometry of Minkowski space by that of belonging in the same double light cone and then properties of space-time defined by axioms. Still, in face of the beautiful clarity of geometry we may prefer to characterize space-time directly, without trying to define the geometry by reference to causality. Tooley avoids these objections because he has an absolute theory of space-time and uses causality simply to define temporal direction. Possibly some of these objections make difficulty for Mellor who has a relational theory. However his notion of probability is that of objective chance and may depend on a theoretical posit and avoid modality. Tooley also needs a realistic theory of causality which some philosophers will find problematic.

TIME AND FREE WILL: THE SEA FIGHT TOMORROW

It is sometimes thought that the picture of the world as a space-time manifold is incompatible with free will. It is thought that if a single action of one's future actions exists (tenselessly) in the space-time manifold, then it is fated that the person will do this action; one cannot be free not to do it. To evade this conclusion, philosophers have sometimes been inclined to reject the theory of the manifold and also to deny that propositions about the future have to be either true or false. This view can be contested at several levels. First, the fact that this singular future action exists in the space-time manifold does not mean that the person is fated to do it, in the sense that the person comes to do it independently of what it was he or she does in the meantime. It will still be that person's choice. Second, the doctrine of the space-time manifold does not even imply determinism. Determinism asserts that the laws of nature connect earlier and later spatial cross sections of the manifold in a determinate way, whereas indeterminism denies this. Indeterminism is compatible with the theory of the manifold as such but is no friend to free will. Acting by pure chance is not being free. Third, it could be argued that free will is perfectly compatible with determinism anyway. On three counts, therefore, we may assert that the theory of space-time has, in fact, nothing at all to do with the question of free will.

Aristotle canvassed some of these matters in his well-known passage about the sea battle (*De Interpretatione*, ch. 9). Aristotle held that it is necessary that either there will be a sea battle tomorrow or there will not be, but that it is not necessary that there will be a sea battle tomorrow, nor is it necessary that there will not be a sea battle tomorrow. He held, however, that all present and past events are necessary, as are some future ones, such as an eclipse of the moon. It is clear, therefore, that Aristotle's notion of necessity here is not the modern notion of logical necessity. Nor by "necessary" can he even mean "predictable" or "retrodictable." Because past events, though not all retrodictable, may have at least left traces, perhaps Aristotle may have meant by "necessary" something like "knowable in principle." But how about past events whose traces have been blotted out? It is hard to give a coherent interpretation of Aristotle here, and certainly to try to give one would be to go into metaphysical subtleties not especially connected with time. Some commentators have interpreted Aristotle as saying that the proposition "There will be a sea battle tomorrow" is neither true nor false. It would seem, however, that this was not Aristotle's view.

Finally, it must be pointed out that the difference between past and future is misleadingly expressed by the common remark that we can change the future but not the past. It is true that we can affect the future and we cannot affect the past. We cannot, however, *change* the future, for the future is what it will be. If a person decides to take the left-hand fork in a road instead of the right-hand one, that person has not changed the future, for in this case the future *is* that person's going left. To talk of changing the future is indeed to relapse into talking of events changing and of the notion of passage.

See also Causal Approaches to the Direction of Time; Physics and the Direction of Time; Time, Being and Becoming.

Bibliography

GENERAL WORKS

An important book is Hans Reichenbach, *The Philosophy of Space and Time* (New York: Dover, 1958), which is a translation of a book published in German in 1928. Reichenbach partially modified his ideas in this book in his later work *The Direction of Time* (Berkeley: University of California Press, 1957). A wide-ranging book on the philosophy of time is *The Natural Philosophy of Time* by the cosmologist G. J. Whitrow (London: Nelson, 1961). Other important books are Adolf Grünbaum, *Philosophical Problems of Space and Time* (New York: Knopf, 1963), and O. Costa de Beauregard, *La notion du temps* (Paris: Hermann, 1963) and *Le second principe de la science du temps* (Paris: Éditions du Seuil, 1963). See also Adolf Grünbaum's long essay "The Nature of Time" in *Frontiers of Science and Philosophy*, edited by R. G. Colodny (Pittsburgh: University of Pittsburgh Press, 1962).

A valuable essay is Wilfrid Sellars's "Time and the World Order," in *Minnesota Studies in the Philosophy of Science*, vol. 3 (Minneapolis: University of Minnesota Press, 1962). An earlier essay of considerable value is the article "Time" by C. D. Broad in *Encyclopedia of Religion and Ethics*, vol. 12 (Edinburgh and New York: 1921). Several essays of interest are also in *The Problem of Time*, University of California Publications in Philosophy, vol. 18 (Berkeley: University of California, 1935).

A book of readings on space and time is *Problems of Space and Time*, edited and with an introduction by J. J. C. Smart (New York: Macmillan, 1964). The history of philosophical thought about time is presented in M. F. Cleugh, *Time and Its Importance for Modern Thought* (London: Methuen, 1937).

ST. AUGUSTINE'S PUZZLES

Augustine's reflections on time are to be found in his *Confessions*, bk. 11, chaps. 14–28; a good translation is A. C. Outler, *St. Augustine: Confessions and Enchiridion*, vol. 7 of the Library of Christian Classics (Philadelphia: Westminster, 1955). Augustine much influenced Wittgenstein. For evidence of this see Ludwig Wittgenstein, *The Blue and Brown Books*, p. 26 (Oxford: Harper, 1958). W. H. Watson, a physicist who had attended lectures on philosophy by Wittgenstein, quotes a passage from Augustine on time (in order to show what a typical philosophical problem is like) in the first chapter of his *On Understanding Physics* (Cambridge: The University Press, 1938). Part of the article by J. N. Findlay, "Time: A Treatment of Some Puzzles," in *Logic and Language*, first series, edited by A. G. N. Flew (Oxford: Blackwell, 1951), discusses Augustine's puzzles. See also Ronald Suter, "Augustine on Time, With Some Criticisms from Wittgenstein," in *Revue internationale de philosophie* 16 (1962): 319–332.

THE MYTH OF PASSAGE

On the topic of the myth of passage see especially D. C. Williams's brilliant criticism in "The Myth of Passage" in *Journal of Philosophy* 48 (1951): 457–472. In chap. 35 of C. D. Broad, *Examination of McTaggart's Philosophy*, vol. 2, pt. 1 (Cambridge: The University Press, 1938), are relevant arguments against the notion of passage, even though in the end Broad does not free himself from it. An earlier view of Broad's is given in his *Scientific Thought* (London: K. Paul, Trench, Trubne, 1923). On Broad's changing views about time see C. W. K. Mundle, "Broad's Views About Time," in *The Philosophy of C. D. Broad*, edited by P. A. Schilpp (La Salle, IL: Tudor, 1959). A criticism of the notion of passage is in J. J. C. Smart, "The River of Time," in *Essays in Conceptual Analysis*, edited by A. G. N. Flew (London: Macmillan, 1956), and "Spatialising Time" in *Mind* 64 (1955): 239–241. A contrary point of view is defended by A. N. Prior, "Changes in Events and Changes in Things" (The Lindley Lecture, University of Kansas, 1962); "Time After Time," in *Mind* 67 (1958): 244–246; and "Thank Goodness That's Over," in *Philosophy* 34 (1959): 12–17. The last mentioned article defends tensed theories as explaining the difference between our attitudes to past and future pains respectively. A reply by Jonathan Cohen to the last article is to be found in the same volume, and a recent explanation of a biological point of his is in "'Thank Goodness That's Over': The Evolutionary Story," by J. Maclaurin and H. Dyke in *Ratio* 15 (2002): 276–292. Ned Markosian has defended passage in his "How Fast Does Time Pass?" in *Philosophy and Phenomenological Research* 53 (1993): 829–844.

J. McT. E. McTaggart's argument for the unreality of time is to be found in his *Philosophical Studies*, chap. 5 (London: E. Arnold, 1934; originally published as an article in *Mind*, 1908), and in his *Nature of Existence*, vol. 2, chap. 33 (Cambridge: The University Press, 1927). For criticisms of this see C. D. Broad's *Examination of McTaggart's Philosophy*; Paul Marhenke's article in the book *The Problem of Time*; D. W. Gotshalk's "McTaggart on Time" in *Mind* 39 (1930): 26–42; and part of D. F. Pears's article "Time, Truth and Inference," in *Essays in Conceptual Analysis*, edited by A. G. N. Flew. On the other side see Michael Dummett, "A Defense of McTaggart's Proof of the Unreality of Time," in *Philosophical Review* 69 (1960): 497–504; and L. O. Mink, "Time, McTaggart and Pickwickian Language," in *Philosophical Quarterly* 10 (1960): 252–263. A sympathetic and scholarly work on McTaggart is P. T. Geach, *Truth, Love, and Immortality* (London and Berkeley: Hutchinson, 1979).

On tenses and similar token-reflexive expressions see Hans Reichenbach, *Elements of Symbolic Logic*, secs. 50–51 (New York: Macmillan, 1947); Nelson Goodman, *The Structure of Appearance*, chap. 11 (Cambridge, MA: Harvard University Press, 1951); and Bertrand Russell, *An Inquiry into Meaning and Truth*, chap. 7 (New York, 1940). Also see Yehoshua Bar-Hillel, "Indexical Expressions," in *Mind* 63 (1954): 359–379; Jonathan Cohen, "Tense Usage and Propositions," in *Analysis* 11 (1950–1951): 80–87; and R. M. Gale, "Tensed Statements," in *Philosophical Quarterly* 12 (1962): 53–59, together with ensuing discussion notes on this. The article by Sellars, "Time," has much on tenses. Zeno Vendler, "Verbs and Times," in *Philosophical Review* 66 (1957): 143–160, shows that tenses have more functions than one might first suppose. A tense logic is worked out by A. N. Prior in his *Time and Modality* (Oxford: Clarendon, 1957); and R. M. Martin, in his review of this book in *Mind* 68 (1959): 271–275, questions whether this is legitimately part of logic. See also Jonathan Cohen's critical notice of the same book in *Philosophical Quarterly* 8 (1958): 266–271. A tenseless language is advocated by W. V. Quine, *Word and Object*, sec. 36 (Cambridge, MA: Technology Press of the Massachusetts Institute of Technology, 1960). Tensed language is advocated by J. N. Findlay in his article, "An Examination of Tenses," in *Contemporary British Philosophy*, edited by H. D. Lewis (New York: Macmillan, 1956). The token reflexive approach has been well defended by Heather Dyke in several articles, especially "Tokens, Dates and Tenseless Truth Conditions," in *Synthese* (2002): 329–351, and "Tensed Meaning: A Tenseless Account," in the *Journal of Philosophical Research* 28 (2003): 65–81. The tenseless metalinguistic account of the semantics of indexicals is both defended and attacked in articles in *The New Theory of Time*, by L. N. Oaklander and Quentin Smith (New Haven, CT: Yale University Press, 1994). See also J. J. C. Smart, "Time and Becoming," reprinted in his *Essays Metaphysical and Moral* (Oxford: Blackwell, 1987), which contains the conjecture mentioned in the text of a possible source of the illusion of the flow of time. Jeremy Butterfield, in his "Seeing the Present," in *Mind* 93 (1984): 161–176, relates the different ways that common sense sees space and time respectively to the difference between the high velocity of light compared with the timescale of our physiological and electrochemical processes. Also Smart's criticism of causal theories of time and his defense of the reality of the future are reprinted in the same volume. Quentin Smith defends his own tensed theory in his *Language and Time* (New York: Oxford University Press, 1993).

Other articles are R. G. Collingwood, "Some Perplexities About Time," in *PAS* 26 (1925–1926): 135–150; and the symposium "Time and Change" by J. Macmurray, R. G. Braithwaite, and C. D. Broad in *PAS*, Supp., Vol. 8 (1928): 143–188. On the status of the past see A. J. Ayer, "Statements About the Past," in his *Philosophical Essays* (London: Macmillan, 1954).

See also Richard Taylor, "Spatial and Temporal Analogies and the Concept of Identity," in *Journal of Philosophy* 52 (1955): 599–612; and "Moving About in Time" in *Philosophical Quarterly* 9 (1959): 289–301; as well as Bernard Mayo, "Objects, Events, and Complementarity," in *Philosophical Review* 70 (1961): 340–361.

F. H. Bradley's argument for the unreality of space and time is given in his *Appearance and Reality*, 2nd ed., chap. 2 (Oxford: Clarendon, 1930). Henri Bergson's accounts of time and duration are given in his *Time and Free Will* (New York: Macmillan, 1910), *Matter and Memory* (New York: Macmillan, 1911), and *Introduction to Metaphysics* (London: Putnam, 1913). Bertrand Russell in his *History of Western Philosophy* (London: Allen and Unwin, 1945) gives a succinct criticism of Bergson. Like Bergson's, A. N. Whitehead's metaphysics took for granted a form of the myth of passage. His views are to be found especially in *An Enquiry concerning the Principles of Natural Knowledge* (Cambridge: The University Press, 1920), chaps. 3–6, and parts of *Process and Reality* (Cambridge: The University Press, 1929). See also V. C. Chappell, "Whitehead's Theory of Becoming," in *Journal of Philosophy* 58 (1961): 516–528.

SPACE-TIME

Hermann Minkowski's classic paper "Space and Time" can be found in *The Principle of Relativity*, a collection of papers by Einstein and others, translated by W. Perret and G. B. Jeffery, with notes by Arnold Sommerfeld (London: Methuen, 1923). Popular accounts can be found in A. S. Eddington, *Space, Time and Gravitation* (Cambridge: The University Press, 1920), and Moritz Schlick, *Philosophy of Nature*, chap. 7 (New York: Philosophical Library, 1949). Milič Čapek, in his *The Philosophical Impact of Contemporary Physics* (Princeton, NJ: Van Nostrand, 1961), criticizes the theory of the space-time manifold and defends the concept of becoming.

ABSOLUTE AND RELATIONAL THEORIES

A relational theory of space and time is defended by Leibniz. See especially his third and fifth papers in *The Leibniz-Clarke Correspondence*, edited by H. G. Alexander (Manchester: Manchester University Press, 1956) A brilliant argument against Leibniz is in Graham Nerlich, *What Spacetime Explains* (Cambridge, U.K.: Cambridge University Press, 1994). On space-time in the general theory of relativity see Adolf Grünbaum's paper "The Philosophical Retention of Absolute Space in Einstein's General Theory of Relativity" in *Problems of Space and Time*, edited by J. J. C. Smart (New York: Macmillan, 1964), and references given therein. Also see Graham Nerlich, *The Shape of Space*, 2nd ed. (Cambridge, U.K.: Cambridge University Press, 1994). The issue between three and four dimensionalism is thoroughly discussed in Theodore Sider, *Four-Dimensionalism: An Ontology of Persistence and Time* (Oxford: Clarendon, 2001).

TIME AND THE CONTINUUM

A good discussion of the paradoxes of Zeno will be found in Adolf Grünbaum, *Modern Science and Zzeno's Paradoxes* (London: Allen and Unwin, 1968). Since 1951 many articles on Zeno's paradox of Achilles and the tortoise have appeared in *Analysis*. See also V. C. Chappell, "Time and Zeno's Arrow," in *Journal of Philosophy* 59 (1962): 197–213; and Harold N. Lee, "Are Zeno's Paradoxes Based on a Mistake?" in *Mind* 74 (1965): 563–570. Also of interest is Paul Benacerraf, "Tasks, Super-Tasks and the Modern Eleatics," in *Journal of Philosophy* 59 (1962): 765–784. A useful account of Zeno's paradoxes is to be found in Kathleen Freeman, *Pre-Socratic Philosophers: A Companion to Diels, Fragmente der Vorsokratiker*, 3rd ed. (Oxford: Basil Blackwell, 1946).

Kant's antinomies about space and time occur in *The Critique of Pure Reason*. There is a translation of this book by Norman Kemp Smith (London: Macmillan, 1929). Zeno's and Kant's antinomies are discussed by Bertrand Russell in lectures 6 and 7 of *Our Knowledge of the External World* (London: W. W. Norton, 1922). See also C. D. Broad, "Kant's Mathematical Antinomies," in *PAS* 55 (1954–1955): 1–22. The commentary by Edward Caird, mentioned in the present article, is *The Critical Philosophy of Immanuel Kant* (Glasgow: J. Maclehose, 1889).

THE DIRECTION OF TIME

Besides Reichenbach's book *The Direction of Time* and the book by Grünbaum, *Philosophical Problems*, see especially Adolf Grünbaum's paper "Carnap's Views on the Foundations of Geometry" in *The Philosophy of Rudolf Carnap*, edited by P. A. Schilpp (La Salle, IL: Open Court, 1962), which, despite its title, contains a thorough discussion of the present problem, and Grünbaum's essay "The Nature of Time." See also Erwin Schrödinger's fine paper "Irreversibility" in *Proceedings of the Royal Irish Academy* 51 (1950): 189–195; and Norbert Wiener, "Newtonian and Bergsonian Time," which is chap. 1 of *Cybernetics*, 2nd ed. (New York: M.I.T. Press, 1961). Also see Ludwig Boltzmann, "On Certain Questions of the Theory of Gases," in *Nature* 51 (1895): 413–415. Reichenbach's book depends to a great extent on Boltzmann's ideas. There is a readable treatment of some of these issues in the final appendix of Schlick's *Philosophy of Nature*. A different solution to the problem is to be found in notes by K. R. Popper in *Nature* 177 (1956): 538; also vol. 178 (1956): 382; vol. 179 (1957): 1,297; and vol. 181 (1958): 402–403, in connection with which see the note by E. L. Hill and Adolf Grünbaum, in *Nature* 179 (1957): 1,296–1,297. See also O. Costa de Beauregard, "L'Irreversibilité quantique, phénomène macroscopique," in *Louis de Broglie*, edited by A. George (Paris, 1953). Grünbaum has examined Popper's view in his essay "Popper on Irreversibility" in *The Critical Approach to Science and Philosophy: Essays in Honor of Karl Popper*, edited by Mario A. Bunge (New York: Free Press of Glencoe, 1964). There are two beautiful articles titled "The Arrow of Time" by the cosmologist Thomas Gold in *La Structure et l'évolution de l'univers*, proceedings of the eleventh Solvay Conference, pp. 81–91 (Brussels: R. Stoops, 1958), and in *The American Journal of Physics* 30 (1962): 403–410. "The Direction of Time" by Max Black in his *Models and Metaphors* (Ithaca, NY: Cornell University Press, 1962), is written from the point of view that scientific considerations are irrelevant to the problem of the direction of time. D. H. Mellor rejects the relevance of considerations of entropy and statistical mechanics in his *Real Time II* (Cambridge, U.K.: Routledge, 1998). An absolutely outstanding discussion of temporal symmetry and asymmetry in which he identifies unrecognized anthropocentric confusions is Huw Price, *Time's Arrow and Archimedes' Point* (New York: Oxford University Press, 1996).

A readable discussion of the experiment by James H. Christenson, James W. Cronin, Val L. Fitch, and René Turlay, which suggests a possible violation of time symmetry in the laws of nature themselves, can be found in Eugene P. Wigner's article "Violations of Symmetry in Physics" in *Scientific American* 213 (December 1965): 28–42.

TIME AND FREE WILL: THE SEA FIGHT TOMORROW

On fatalism see R. D. Bradley, "Must the Future Be What It Is Going To Be?" in *Mind* 68 (1959): 193–208; Richard Taylor, "Fatalism," in *Philosophical Review* 71 (1962): 56–66, with the discussion on this by Bruce Aune in the same volume, pp. 512–519; and A. J. Ayer, "Fatalism," in his *The Concept of a Person and Other Essays* (London: Macmillan, 1963). On the sea battle see Aristotle, *De Interpretatione*, chap. 9. Extensive notes and a translation can be found in J. L. Ackrill's *Aristotle's Categories and De Interpretation*, vol. 1 of the complete works of Aristotle edited by Jonathan Barnes (Princeton; NJ: Princeton University Press, 1984). This passage has also been translated and discussed by G. E. M. Anscombe in "Aristotle and the Sea-Battle" in *Problems of Space and Time*. See also Colin Strang, "Aristotle and the Sea Battle," in *Mind* 69 (1960): 447–465. Many journal articles on the subject, following on D. C. Williams's interesting "The Sea-Fight Tomorrow," appear in *Structure, Method, and Meaning*, edited by Paul Henle, Horace M. Kallen, and Susanne K. Langer (New York: Liberal Arts Press, 1951). See especially the discussion note "Professor Donald Williams on Aristotle" by Leonard Linsky and the rejoinder by Williams in *Philosophical Review* 63 (1954): 250–255, and Richard Taylor, "The Problem of Future Contingents," and Rogers Albritton's reply in *Philosophical Review* 66 (1957): 1–46. The seventeenth-century English philosopher Thomas Hobbes also wrote on the sea-fight; see his *Works*, edited by William Molesworth, vol. 4, p. 277 (London: J. Bohn, 1839), and discussion by A. G. N. Flew, "Hobbes and the Seafight," *Graduate Review of Philosophy* 2 (1959): 1–5.

Other references are to Storrs McCall, "Objective Time Flow," in *Philosophy of Science* 43 (1976): 337–362; and his "A Dynamic Model of Temporal Becoming," *Analysis* 44 (1984): 172–176; and to McCall's book, *A Model of the Universe: Space-Time, Probability and Decision* (Oxford: Clarendon, 1994). Mellor's *Real Time II* was published in London in 1998. Michael Tooley's *Time, Tense and Causation* was published in Oxford in 1997. See also Michael Tooley, "The Metaphysics of Time" in *The Argument of Time*, edited by Jeremy Butterfield, pp. 21–42 (London: Oxford University

Press, 1999), and "Basic Tensed Sentences and their Analysis" in *Time, Tense, and Reference*, edited by Aleksander Jokic and Quentin Smith, pp. 409–447 (Cambridge, MA: MIT Press, 2003). John Bigelow defends presentism in his "Presentism and Properties," in *Philosophical Perspectives* 10, *Metaphysics* (1996): 35–52.

J. J. C. Smart (1967, 2005)

TIME, BEING, AND BECOMING

The major debate in the philosophy of time, being, and becoming is between defenders of the tenseless theory of time and defenders of the tensed theory of time. During the late twentieth century into the early twenty-first century, the tenseless theory of time was defended by such philosophers as D.H. Mellor, Graham Nerlich, and L. Nathan Oaklander. The tenseless theory implies that temporal features of events consist only of relations of simultaneity, earlier, and later than, and that all events are ontologically equal, regardless of when they occur. The tensed theory, which has many versions, is advocated by such philosophers as William Lane Craig, Quentin Smith, and Michael Tooley. The tensed theory of time implies that some or all of the words *past*, *present*, and *future* are needed to describe time, although what is understood by the words *future*, *present*, and *past*, or by their usage as parts of phrases or sentences (e.g., whether or not they express analyzable or unanalyzable concepts) is a matter that varies among tensed theorists.

THE OLD AND NEW TENSELESS AND TENSED THEORIES OF TIME

For most of the twentieth century, the debate was between defenders of the old tenseless theory of time and defenders of the old tensed theory of time, concerning whether or not tensed sentence tokens are translatable by tenseless sentences. If a tensed sentence token, call it S, such as the sentence token "John was running" can be translated by a tenseless token, such as "John is (tenseless) running earlier than S," then the tensed token S conveys no more temporal information than the tenseless token. Consequently, the defender of the old tenseless theory of time maintained that temporal properties and relations can consist only of the relations of earlier than, later than, and simultaneous with. Some of the main developers of the old tenseless theory are Bertrand Russell (1903, 1906, 1915)—Russell is the first twentieth century defender of the tenseless theory against the tensed theory of time—Hans Reichenbach (1947), J.J.C. Smart (1963, 1966), and Adolf Grünbaum (1973). Smart (1980) was also one of the main founders of the new tenseless theory of time.

Proponents of the old tensed theory of time argued that these sentence tokens cannot be translated. For example, "John (is) running earlier than S" does not convey the temporal information of whether John's running is past, present, or future. Because "John was running" conveys that it is past, this sentence token cannot have the same semantic content (or the same meaning, or express the same proposition) as the tenseless token, and therefore cannot be translated by the tenseless token. Some of the most influential defenders of the old tensed theory of time are C.D. Broad (1923)—who is the first twentieth century defender of the tensed theory and critic of the tenseless theory—A. N. Prior (1967, 1968, 1979), Richard Gale (1962, 1968), and George Schlesinger (1981).

In response to criticisms advanced by the old tensed theory of time, defenders of the tenseless theory largely accepted the argument of Gale and others that tensed sentence tokens cannot be translated by tenseless ones; however, the tenseless theorists now argued that the truth conditions of tensed sentence tokens are tenseless. For example, Mellor (1981) argued that the token S of "John was running" is not translatable by a token "John is (tenseless) running earlier than S", but is true if, and only if, John is (tenseless) running earlier than S. The new tenseless theory of time was in place by 1981, due primarily to the independent work of Mellor (1981) and Smart (1980) (see also Anderson and Faye [1980], Faye [1981], and Oaklander [1984]). The main developments and defenses of various versions of the new tenseless theory from the mid-1980s to the early twenty-first century were made for the most part by L. Nathan Oaklander, but also by Heather Dyke (2002a, 2002b, 2003), Robin Le Poidevin (1992, 2003), Graham Nerlich (1998), L.A. Paul (1997), J. M. Mosersky (2000), and others.

The emergence of the new tenseless theory in the 1980s inspired the new tensed theory of time, whose unifying theme was a criticism of the new tenseless theory and the development of ontologies for a tensed theory that were able to overcome the hurdles set by the new tenseless theorists. Criticisms of one of the two main versions of the new tenseless theory, Mellor's token-reflexive theory, appeared in Graham Priest's (1986, 1987) work, and criticisms of the two main versions of the new tenseless theory (Smart's and Mellor's) appeared in Smith's (1987, 1993) work.

The classification of the new tenseless theories of time into two versions, the token-reflexive version and the date-involving version, was made in the course of Smith's (1987, 1993) criticisms of these theories. One criticism of the former is that the tenseless token-reflexive theory of tensed sentence tokens in natural language is mistaken because (among other reasons) the truth conditions of a tensed sentence token S cannot be about S itself, as well as what S is about. Suppose there are two simultaneous utterances, the utterance U of "The talk will begin in an hour" and the utterance S of "The talk will begin in sixty minutes." These two utterances, given that they occur at the same time, are logically equivalent. It is impossible for the talk to begin in an hour unless it begins in sixty minutes and vice versa. But the token-reflexive truth conditions of S and U are not logically equivalent. U is true if, and only if, the talk begins one hour later than U and S is true if, and only if, the talk begins sixty minutes later than S, whereas because "the talk begins in an hour" and "the talk will begin in sixty minutes" are logically equivalent, it is neither necessary nor sufficient for S's truth that the talk begin one hour later than U. It is not necessary because there is a possible world in which S is true, but in which U is not uttered.

Further, it is sufficient for S's truth that the talk begins one hour later than the time at which U, as a matter of fact, occurs, regardless of whether or not U occurs; if U had not occurred, S would still be true. We have two logically equivalent, simultaneous, tensed sentence tokens that have logically inequivalent truth conditions—which not only fails to explain the logical equivalence of the tensed sentence tokens, but leads to an implicit contradiction. If S and U entail each other, and S and U are each logically equivalent to their respective truth conditions clauses SC and UC, then it follows by the transitivity of logical equivalence that SC and UC are logically equivalent. Because SC and UC are not logically equivalent, SC is not a truth conditions clause for S and UC is not a truth conditions clause for U.

This and other criticisms appear to have motivated an abandonment of the new token-reflexive tenseless theory of time by its originators and developers—Mellor, Oaklander, Paul (1997), Le Poidevin (2003), and so on, as well as by critics who are tensed theorists—Craig (1996, 2000a), Peter Ludlow (1999), and so on. However, Oaklander (2003, 2004), as well as Dyke (2000a, 2002b, 2003), have spent much time developing versions of what Oaklander calls the newer token-reflexive tenseless theory, which they argue are immune to Smith's criticisms. Because Dyke's and Oaklander's theories have not yet been critically evaluated, it must be said that the token-reflexive theory, in its newer version, remains an obstacle in the tensed theorist's path.

The other version of the new tenseless theory of time is the date-theory. This may be criticized by arguing that the new tenseless date-involving truth conditions are neither necessary nor sufficient for the truth of tensed sentence tokens. It appears to be false, for example, that "Jane is running" as uttered at noon on July 1, 1994, is true if, and only if, Jane runs at noon on July 1, 1994. There are possible worlds in which the mentioned sentence utterance, call it U, is true and yet it is false that Jane is running at noon on July 1, 1994.

Suppose, for instance, that times are sets of simultaneous events and that noon on July 1, 1994, refers to the set of simultaneous events that is actually 1,993 years, six months, and twelve hours after the conventionally assigned birth date of Jesus. There is a possible world exactly similar to the actual world except for the fact that the utterance U belongs to a different set of simultaneous events, a set that includes every event included on July 1, 1994, at noon (which means it includes Jane's running), except for some minor difference; say, the set does not include the decision actually made by David to have lunch. Because U occurs simultaneously with Jane's running in this world, U is true; nonetheless, it does not occur at noon on July 1, 1994. Thus date-involving truth conditions do not appear to be necessary for the truth of tensed sentence tokens.

Suppose, in contrast, that one does not reduce times to sets of events, adopting instead a substantival theory that regards times as particulars in their own right, particulars identified by their position in a time sequence, essentially dated (and metricated) in relation to earlier and later times; times may be occupied by events or sets of events, but the times are neither identical with nor necessarily contain their occupants.

The same time (e.g., May 1, 2005, at noon) may have different occupants in different possible worlds. One of the arguments against a substantival version of the tenseless date-theory concerns the date-theory that a sentence token S of "Jane is running" that is uttered at noon on May 1, 2005, is true if, and only if, Jane is (tenseless) running on May 1, 2005, at noon. Suppose Jane is running at this time. Because we are assuming a substantival version of the date-theory, the mentioned time has the essential date property of being May 1, 2005.

In other words, the time is metricated (identified as a part of a sequence of equal-lengthed intervals and assigned a specific ordinal in this sequence, conventionally abbreviated as 5/1/2005) and this metricated time remains identical across possible worlds even if it has different occupants in these worlds. There is a possible world similar to the actual world except that Jane is not running at noon on May 1, 2005, and S does not occupy the time on May 1, 2005, at noon. Instead, S occupies a later time, on May 2, 2005, at noon and Jane is running at noon on May 2, 2005, in this world.

The token S of "Jane is running" on noon, May 2, in this second world is true because S occurs simultaneously with Jane's running. And yet the purported date truth conditions it is supposed to have would imply S is false because it cannot be true unless the date is May 1. But how could the token S of "Jane is running" be false if Jane is running simultaneously with the token S of "Jane is running"? This indicates that the truth condition sentence: "A token S of 'Jane is running' that is uttered at noon on May 1, 2005, is true if, and only if, Jane is (tenseless) running on May 1, 2005 at noon" is false. It is false because the token S is true in the second world even though Jane is not running on May 1 in that world (note that S is here being used in the actual world as a modally stable tag [Marcus 1961] that serves to refer directly to S in both worlds). Thus, the alleged date-involving truth condition sentence does not give us a correct necessary condition ("only if") of S's truth.

Oaklander (1994) responds to these arguments of Smith (1987, 1993) by changing the new date-theory to a still newer date-theory and thus avoids the problem Smith mentions. The newer date-theory, Oaklander says, is that the correct truth condition sentence is that the token S of "Jane is running" uttered at noon on May 1, 2005, in world W, is true at noon on May 1, 2005, in W if, and only if, Jane is (tenseless) running at noon on May 1, 2005, in W." Because the possible world W is mentioned in the truth-condition sentence, the objection based on what occurs in a different possible world is avoided.

This newer theory may seem prima facie plausible. But a closer look shows that, by virtue of being world-indexed, it is irrelevant to the semantic content, truth value, and truth conditions of the token S. If we take any true extensional sentence, such as "The sun is shining on Mount Everest at noon on May 1, 2005," substitute it for the extensional clause after the biconditional, namely, "Jane is (tenseless) running at noon on May 1, 2005," retain the world-index "in W," then we also have a true truth condition sentence for the token S-in-W. If we take any true, contingent, extensional, sentence token T, operate on it to produce the world-indexed operand T-in-W, then T-in-W is necessarily true and fulfills the criteria of being both sufficient and necessary for the truth of S-in-T. But whether or not the sun is shining on Mount Everest has no bearing on the truth or falsity of the sentence token S, which is the sentence token whose truth conditions are being discussed by the tensed theorist and the tenseless theorist. Accordingly, world-indexing the clauses before and after the biconditional does not solve the problem of the truth conditions of a token of "Jane is running" that is uttered at noon on May 1, 2005. We can see that a problem with Oaklander's newer date-theory is that it has, in effect, changed the subject.

The subject is the truth conditions of the non-world-indexed, tensed sentence token, the May 1, 2005, at noon token S, "Jane is running." Oaklander changed the subject to world-indexed sentence tokens, such as the truth conditions of S-in-W, and whether or not the tenseless date-theorist can provide tenseless truth conditions—for S-in-W does nothing to answer Smith's argument that the new tenseless date-theory of time cannot provide satisfactory truth conditions for the tensed sentence token S.

But Oaklander's modal argument is not the only objection that can be brought against Smith's arguments against the new tenseless date-theory of time. Oaklander has advanced further arguments challenging Smith's arguments against the new tenseless date-theory, as have Le Poidevin (2003), Mosersky (2000), L.A. Paul (1997), and Nerlich (1998). Furthermore, arguments in favor of a tensed date-theory have been made by Tooley (1997, 2001, 2003) who also presents arguments against Smith's criticisms of the new date-theory. Whether or not a date-theory of time is viable remains an issue upon which there is as of yet no common consensus.

An equally crucial issue concerns the relation of the new tensed theory of time to the sciences. Smith emphasized (1985, 1993) that the new tensed theorist must show that the crucial sort of scientific theses, the theses predominately found in the central observational part of the sciences, include tensed sentence tokens. These tensed tokens are used to confirm the theoretical claims of the sciences (keeping in mind, of course, the context relativity of the theoretical/observational distinction) and Smith argues that these tensed sentence tokens are logically incoherent if they lack tensed truth conditions.

A long-standing mistake, championed most influentially by Grünbaum, is that tensed statements, if they belong to the sciences, must belong to the theoretical part of physics (specifically, to the basic equations, and the semantic content of the constants and parameters in these equations). This is wrong because the semantic content of the tenses of verbs, and the semantic content of temporal pronouns (*now*, *yesterday*) are essentially observational and by definition belong to the observational, not theoretical, statements in the sciences.

For example, Alexander Friedman's solution to the Einstein equation belongs to the theoretical part of big bang cosmology, but the observational information that the big bang occurred fifteen billion years ago essentially belongs to the observational part of big bang cosmology (see Smith 1985, 1993; Smith and Oaklander 1994). This shows that some of the more superficial evaluations of Smith's *Language and Time* (1993) are mistaken (e.g. the evaluation that it is not based on science but ordinary language analysis of the sort done in the 1950s in England). For it is based, not on ordinary language, but, instead, on the observational part of science, on confirmation theory, logic, and on the deep structure of natural languages (1993, Ch. 6.6) studied in linguistics. However, one of the most conceptually precise and accurate explorations of this notion, Nerlich's *Time and Spacetime* (1998), takes the ingenious route of eliminating the presentness part of the deep structure of a sentence, while still retaining the propositional relation.

Nerlich predicts that Smith will answer his critique by appealing to ordinary language, rather than to science (to which Nerlich appeals). But section 1.5 of *Language and Time* suggests otherwise. Smith would say that he appeals to the conditions in the universe that make true the tensed observation sentence tokens in the observational part of science. What is reported in these observation sentence tokens is the condition that the empirical datum observed is past to some degree or is or will be present in a certain amount of time. Nerlich appeals to the theoretical parts of the special and general theories of relativity. Smith appeals to the tensed observation sentence tokens that confirm the theoretical parts of special and general relativity.

Dennis Sciama (1973, pp. 24–25), for example, made the observation (relative to the observational/theoretical distinction in big bang cosmology): "in its *present* state the universe is far too dilute to be able to thermalize radiation in the time available (10^{10} years) … we conclude that at sometime *in the past* the universe must *have been* sufficiently dense to thermalize radiation.… According to the standard cosmological models the universe thus would require a universal density of at least 10^{-14} gm cm^{-3} (that is about 10^{15} times larger than the *present* mean density. [my italics]" P.A.M. Dirac (1983, p. 47) observes that "the *present* velocity of recession is 10^{-3} [my italics]" I. D. Novikov (1974, p. 273) observes that "the Universe expands isotropically with a high degree of accuracy at *the present time* …This is valid for at least some period in *the past* too." A philosopher of the observational part of science will find that the tense in the verb phrases of the observation sentence tokens are surface manifestations of the deep structure of language, a structure that includes only propositions that have presentness as a part. This deep structure, like Ludlow's (1999) deep structure, is a structure of mind-independent reality. This investigation of the deep structure of scientific observation sentence tokens is a primary task of Smith's *Language and Time.*

The misunderstanding of Smith's work as being ordinary language analysis rather than scientific analysis may be because the tenseless theory is often associated with more scientifically inclined philosophers and the tensed theory with more ordinary language inclined philosophers. This association is largely a myth. Not only Smith but also Storrs McCall (1994), Tooley (1997), Craig (2000b, 2003), Mauro Durato (1995), and many others have developed tensed theories in terms of or in relation to the physical sciences. Many tenseless theorists, such as Mellor (1981), Oaklander (1994, 2003), Dyke (2002), Le Poidevin (1992, 2003), Paul (1997), and others have based their theory in large part on analysis of ordinary language.

DISTINCTIONS BETWEEN TENSED AND TENSELESS EXISTENCE

One of the oldest and most important ontological distinctions in the philosophy of time concerns the "full/empty" versions of the tensed theory of time. Broad's theory (1923) and Tooley's theory (1997, 2001, 2003) imply an empty future and full present and past; that is, the future is nonexistent (nothing exists later than the present time) and the present and past are full (existent). Schlesinger's (1981) theory implies a full future, present, and past and, likewise, McCall's (1994) theory implies a full future, containing real possibilities, and a full present and past; in McCall's theory, the present and past are both real and actualized possibilities, whereas the future consists of real but unactualized possibilities. Bell (1987) articulates a theory with an empty past and Others, such as Prior (1967, 1968), Craig (2000a), John Bigelow (1996), Mark Hinchliff (1996), and Ludlow (1999), hold an empty past, full present, and empty future theory.

Smith and Tooley introduced new but different ways to understand the empty/full ontology. But many philosophers have misunderstood both of their (very different) ontologies to be full, tenseless ontologies. A clarification of their ontologies will be helpful, starting with Smith's ontology.

Most tensed theorists, from 1996 to 2005, (with exceptions, such as Tooley and McCall) call themselves *presentists*. Many of these tensed theorists believe Prior coined this neologism as a name for his theory of temporal solipsism (only what is present is real and possesses properties) and they see themselves as developers of the Priorian tradition. But this widespread belief is because of a misunderstanding of the use of *presentism*. Prior did not coin the neologism *presentist* and never used this word even once in his entire corpus. Nor did Prior's early disciples, such as Genevieve Lloyd (1977; 1978), Ferrel Christensen (1974), and others, use the words *presentism* and *presentist*. Contrary to widespread belief, there was no standard use of this term prior to *Language and Time*, which was published in 1993.

The words *presentism* and *presentist* appear nowhere in philosophy journals and books in the 1950s, 1960s, and 1970s. In the 1980s there were two articles in which *presentism* appears; one by Robert Adams (1986), where he rejects presentism, and in a reply to Adams, where Jonathan Kvanvig (1989) defines *presentism* in a way that contemporary philosophers would call a non-presentist theory. The philosopher who first called himself a presentist and who first called the theory he was advocating presentism was Smith (1993). Far from it being the case that *presentism* was regularly used since Prior's 1950s and 1960s publications, the use of *presentism* did not become widespread until readers of Smith (1993) had time to read the book, write an article, and have it published, that is, with the first post-Smith publications beginning in 1996 (Bigelow 1996, Hintchliff 1996 and others).

By 1997 and 1998 presentism had become the most widely used name of a theory of time (replacing, for example, the names *A-theory*, *tensed theory*, *theory of temporal becoming*, and so on). The false belief that Prior and his 1970s disciples used *presentism* to name Prior's theory partly explains the false belief that Smith misused this word since he had a different theory than Prior. Thus, Smith is typically classified with Tooley and McCall as a contemporary non-presentist who takes tense seriously. The truth is the reverse. Smith correctly used *presentism* and the hundreds of contemporary philosophers who discuss presentism are misusing this word, because of their mistaken belief that it was in wide use prior to Smith (1993) to denote a Priorian version of the tensed theory of time.

The important point is not the mere terminological one that if *presentism* is used accurately (on the causal chain theory of reference), Smith is a presentist, Prior is not a presentist, and the post-1993 philosophers who call themselves presentists are not, in fact, presentists because they do not hold a version of Smith's presentism. The ontologically important issue concerns the presuppositions about the empty/full distinction that led philosophers of time to believe that Smith's presentism was a full tenseless existence theory. Philosophers interpreted him as maintaining that all times exist equally, in an irreducible, tenseless sense of *exists*. But Smith maintained exactly the opposite theory. He held that no times, events, or anything else exist tenselessly; that only one time exists in the present tensed sense; and that past and future times either no longer exist or do not yet exist.

Smith writes: "'x exists'" in the tenseless sense means 'x existed, exists, or will exist' where the middle 'exists' is present tensed … and 'x exists' in the present tensed sense means, or is logically equivalent to, 'x is present' (Smith 1993, p. 165). In fact, Smith argues that there is no tenseless semantic content of *is* or *exists* so that *tenselessly exists* is merely a syntactical string whose semantic content is *existed*, *exists* (present tense), or *will exist*.

This seems to be what post-1993 philosophers meant by their use of *presentism*, so, despite their false beliefs about the correct use of the word *presentism*, it may seem that Smith is a presentist in the same sense in which later philosophers used or misused this word. But there is one main difference: Smith (1993, 2003) argued that past and future tensed sentence tokens can be true in the sense of correspondence only if past and future events presently possess properties of pastness or futurity. Although these past and future events do not exist in the present tense sense of this word, their exemplification of pastness or futurity exists or presently obtains. For the sake of brevity, Smith says that what is past or future may be said to exist in an artifical present tense sense, namely, to presently possess pastness or futurity. If commentators on Smith's ontology distinguished this artificial present tense sense of "exists" from both the natural, genuine present tensed sense of "exists" (is present) and the reductive tenseless use of "exists," all explained in (1993, p. 165), and *if* the philosophers commented that only in the artificial present tense sense of "exists" do all times exist equally, then this would be a correct attribution (even if the artificial sense appears in only three sentences in the book [1993, p.165]. But their criticism is instead based on mistakenly attributing to Smith's times an equal, primitive, tenseless existence and a "spotlight" version of the tensed theory of time, such as Schlesinger (1981) held.

It is noteworthy that both Smith and Prior recognized that pastness and futurity have presentness as part of their meaning, which must be reflected in one's ontology. Both agree with the statement that pastness is (identically) *present* pastness. Using the example of Whitrow's lecture, Prior notes (1979, p. 258): "its pastness is its present pastness, so that although Whitrow's lecture isn't now present and so isn't real, isn't a fact, nevertheless its pastness, its *having* taken place, is a present fact, is a reality, and will be one as long as time lasts." This is also Smith's position, except Smith proceeds to develop an ontological analysis of these statements and Prior does not. Prior merely gives syntactic rules for translating tensed sentences into the syntactically regimented sentences of tense logic (which have operators such as "It was the case that," "It will be the case that," and so on). Peter Ludlow notes (1999, p. 100): "Prior never actually gave a semantics for his tense logic." In addition, Tooley (1997, p. 164) points out some problems with Prior's syntactics for his tense logic. "But, while treating tensed terms as operators on sentences may be convenient for the formulation of a logic of tense, is it also metaphysically perspicuous? I do not believe that it is. In order for a given regimentation of tensed sentences to be metaphysically perspicuous, the syntax needs to reflect the structure that would need to be present in states of affairs to render tensed sentences true." Tooley shows it does not and concludes that the tense-logical reformulation of a natural sentence "does not get one back to the state of affairs in the world that makes the original sentence true. The tense-logical formulation appears, therefore, to leave it completely obscure what sorts of states of affairs are truth-makers for tensed sentences." (Tooley, 1997, p. 166).

More recently, Smith (2002) has developed a different ontology than his (1993), a theory he calls Degree Presentism. This theory implies there are no properties of pastness, presentness, or futurity. Each entity tenselessly stands in a relation to the present of being earlier than it by a certain amount of time, being later than it by an amount of time, or being simultaneous with the present. Only the present exists to the maximal degree. What is earlier or later than the present lacks the amount of existence that is measured by its temporal distance from the present. Something one second earlier than the present is not maximally existent but rather exists to the lower degree of being one second distant from the present.

A recent, non-presentist, tensed account is Tooley's (1997) theory. Here the central ontological claim is that the past and the present are real, but the future is not, while the main semantical claims are, first, that when the terms *past*, *present*, and *future* are used in ordinary sentences, they involve an indexical element that refers directly to the time that the utterance is made; secondly, that there are non-indexical, tensed concepts that are more basic, such as the concepts of being past at time t, or future at time t, or present at time t; and, thirdly, that those more basic tensed concepts can in turn be analyzed. Thus it was claimed, for example, that the sentence "E is (tenseless) present at time t" could be analyzed, using a temporally-indexed notion of actuality, as "E is actual as of time t and nothing later than t is actual as of time t" (Tooley 2003).

The idea that the terms *past*, *present*, and *future*, as used in ordinary sentences, involve an indexical element, and that it is expressions such as *present at time t* that are more basic, suggested to some philosophers that the theory advanced by Tooley was in fact a full tenseless existence theory. For it is often held, by advocates of tensed views, as well as by defenders of tenseless approaches, that the sentence "E lies (tenseless) in the present at time t" is logically equivalent to "E is (tenseless) simultaneous with time t". But these two sentences are, Tooley argues, not equivalent. The reason is that the former, in view of the term *present*, entails the fundamental idea of the tensed theory of time, that time is dynamic, but the latter, which contains instead the word *simultaneous*, does not entail this. For because the sentence "E lies (tenseless) in the present at time t" means the same as "E is actual as of time t, and only times earlier than t are also actual as of t," the truth of this sentence entails an empty future, because it entails that no future state of affairs is actual as of time t (Tooley 2003).

Thus Tooley writes: "The analysis needed here rests upon the claim that the present is the point at which events and states of affairs come into existence, and the basic idea is that, since this view of the present entails that future events and states of affairs are not yet real, an event is present at a given time if and only if the totality of what is actual as of that time does not contain an event or state of affairs that is later than the event in question" (Tooley 2003, p. 438).

But what account can be given of the core notion on which this approach rests—that is, the concept of being actual as of a time? Is it a tensed notion, or a tenseless notion? The most natural view would seem to be that it is a tensed notion. It is true that tensed concepts are typically defined in terms of the concepts of past, present, and future, and such an account entails that the concept of being actual as of a time is not a tensed notion, because it can be argued that it is not analyzable in terms of the concepts of past, present, and future. However, the temporally-relativized concepts of a proposition's being true at a time, and of a state of affairs being actual as of a time are integral to dynamic conceptions of time, and have no place in tenseless approaches. Accordingly, it seems natural to conclude that tensed temporal concepts are best viewed as including both tensed concepts in the narrow sense of concepts involving ideas such as past, present, and future, and also the temporally-indexed concepts of truth and actuality that are crucial for tensed conceptions of time.

Advocates of tenseless approaches to time have argued (Smart 1981, Mellor 1998), however, that the only way one can make sense of such a temporally-indexed notion of actuality is by saying that E is actual as of time t only if E occurs at or earlier than t. If this view is right, then Tooley's approach collapses into a tenseless account. But this criticism would in fact be very wide-ranging indeed, because arguably what is central to any tensed approach to time is the idea that at least some propositions can have different truth values at different times. If this is right, any tensed approach to time requires a temporally-indexed conception of truth, and this combined with a correspondence theory of truth, means that tensed approaches to time need a temporally-indexed conception of actuality. So if the latter can only be understood tenselessly, no tensed theory of time can be correct.

These explanations of Tooley's and others' theories gives a substantive presentation of the novel ideas that are currently under discussion as of 2005. The tensed/tenseless theories and debates are attracting an increasing number of philosophers. The creativity, the new and more complex arguments, and the increasingly precise conceptual distinctions exhibit the advancement or progress of philosophy in a very clear and positive light.

See also Being; Ontology, History of; Prior, Arthur Norman; Reichenbach, Hans; Russell, Bertrand Arthur William; Smart, John Jamieson Carswell; Time.

Bibliography

Adams, Robert. "Time and Thisness." *Midwest Studies in Philosophy* 11 (1986): 315–329.

Anderson, H. B. and J. Faye. "On Future Sea-Battles." In *Studien antik.* Copenhagen: Museum Forlag, 1980.

Bigelow, John. "World Enough for Times." *Nous* 25 (1991): 1–19.

Bigelow, John. "Presentism and Properties." In *Philosophical Perspectives.* Cambridge, MA: Blackwell, 1996.

Broad, C.D. *Examination of McTaggart's Philosophy.* Cambridge, U.K.: Cambridge University Press, 1938.

Broad. C.D. *Scientific Thought.* New York: Harcourt, Brace, and Co., 1923.

Christensen, Ferrel. "McTaggart's Paradox and the Nature of Time." *Philosophical Quarterly* 24 (1974): 289–299.

Craig, William Lane "Presentism: A Defense." In *Time, Tense, and Reference*, edited by A. Jokic and Q. Smith. Cambridge, MA: MIT Press, 2003.

Craig, William Lane. "Tense and the New B-theory of Language." *Philosophy* 71 (1996):5–26.

Craig, William Lane. *The Tensed Theory of Time.* Dordrecht; Boston: Kluwer, 2000a.

Craig, William Lane. *The Tenseless Theory of Time.* Dordrecht; Boston: Kluwer, 2000b.

Dirac, P.A.M. "Fundamental Constansts and Their Development in Time." In *The Physcist's Conception of Nature*, edited by J. Mehra. Dordrecht: Reidel, 1973.

Dyke, Heather. "McTaggart and the Truth About Time." In *Time, Reality, and Experience*, edited by Craig Callender. Cambridge, U.K.: Cambridge University Press, 2002b.

Dyke, Heather. "Tensed Meaning: A Tenseless Account." *Journal of Philosophical Research* 27 (2003): 67–83.

Dyke, Heather. "Tokens, Dates, and Tenseless Truth Conditions." *Synthese*: 131 (2002a): 329–351.

Durato, Mauruce. *Time, Tense and Reality.* Berlin: Spring Verlag, 1995.

Faye, Jan. *An Essay in Natural Philosophy of Time and Causation.* Copenhagen: Forlag, 1981.

Gale, Richard. *The Language of Time.* London: Routledge, 1968.

Gale, Richard. "Tensed Statements." *Philosophical Quarterly* 12 (1962): 53–59.

Geach, Peter."The Perils of Pauline." *The Review of Metaphysics* (1969).

Grünbaum, Adolf. *Philosophical Problems of Space and Time.* Dordrecht; Boston: Reidel, 1973.

Hinchliff, Mark. "McTaggart, Change, and Real Tense." In *The Importance of Time*, edited by L. Nathan Oaklander. Dordrecht; Boston: Kluwer, 2001.

Hinchliff, Mark. "The Puzzle of Change." *Metaphysics: Philosophical Perspectives* (1996): 119–136.

Kripke, Saul. *Naming and Necessity.* Cambridge, MA: Harvard University Press, 1980.

Kvanvig, Jonathan. "Adams on Actualism and Presentism." *Philosophy and Phenomenological Research* 5 (1989): 289–298.

Le Poidevin, R. *Change, Cause, and Contradiction: A Defense of the Tenseless Theory of Time.* Cambridge, MA: MIT Press, 1992.

Le Poidevin, R. "Tenses Need Real Times." In *Time, Tense, and Reference*, edited by Quentin Smith and A. Jokic. Cambridge, MA: MIT Press, 2003.

Levison, Arnold. "Events and Time's Flow." *Mind* 96 (1987): 341–352.

Lloyd, Genevieve. "Tense and Predication." *Mind* 86 (1977): 433–438.

Lloyd, Genevieve. "Time and Existence." *Philosophy* 53 (1978): 215–228.

Ludlow, Peter. *Semantics, Tense, and Time*. Cambridge, MA: MIT Press, 1999.
Ludlow, Peter "Presentism, Triviality, and Varities of Tensions." In *Oxford Studies in Metaphysics*, edited by Dean Zimmerman. Oxford: Clarendon Press, 2004.
Markosian, Ned. "A Defense of Presentism." In *Oxford Studies in Metaphysics*, edited by Dean Zimmerman. Oxford: Oxford University Press, 2004.
Markosian, Ned. "How Fast Does Time Fly?" *Philosophy and Phenomenological Research* 53 (1993): 829–844.
Markosian, Ned. "On Language and the Passage of Time." *Philosophical Studies* 66 (1992): 1–26.
Marcus, Ruth Barcan. "Intensionality in Modal Languages." *Synthese* (1961).
McCall, Storrs. *A Model of the Universe*. Oxford: Oxford University Press, 1994.
Mellor, D. H. *Real Time*. Cambridge, U.K.: Cambridge University Press, 1981.
Mellor, D, H. *Real Time II*. London; New York: Routledge, 1998.
Mosersky, J.M. "Tense and Temporal Semantics." *Synthese* 124 (2000): 257–279.
Nerlich, Graham. "Time as Spacetime." In *Questions of Time and Tense*, edited by Robin Le Poidevin. Oxford: Oxford University Press, 1998.
Novikov, I. D. "Isotropization of of Homogeneous Cosmological Models." In *Confirmation of Cosmological Theories with Observational Data*, edited by M. S. Longair. Dordrect: Reidel, 1974.
Oaklander. L. N. *The Importance of Time*. Dordrecht; Boston: Kluwer, 2001.
Oaklander, L. N. *The Ontology of Time*. Buffalo, NY: Prometheus Books, 2004.
Oaklander, L. N. *Temporal Relations and Temporal Becoming*. Lanham, MD, 1984.
Oaklander, L. N. "Two Versions of the New B-Theory of Language." In *Time, Tense, and Reference*, edited by Quentin Smith and A. Jokic. Cambridge, MA: MIT Press, 2003.
Oaklander, L. N., and Q. Smith, eds. *The New Theory of Time*. New Haven, CT: Yale University Press, 1994.
Paul, L. A. "Truth Conditions of Tensed Sentence Types." *Synthese* 111 (1997): 53–71.
Percival, Phillip. "Presentism." In *Time, Reality, and Experience*, edited by Craig Callender. Cambridge, U.K.: Cambridge University Press, 2002.
Priest, G. "Mellor on Tense." *Analysis* 44 (1986).
Priest, G. "Tense, *Tense*, and TENSE." *Analysis* 46 (1987): 184–187.
Prior, A. N. *Time and Modality*. Oxford. Oxford University Press, 1957.
Prior, A.N. "The Notion of the Present." *Studium Generale* 23 (1979): 245–258.
Prior, A. N. *Papers on Time and Tense*. Oxford: Oxford University Press, 1968.
Prior, A. N. *Past, Present, and Future*. Oxford: Oxford University Press, 1967.
Reichenbach, Hans. *Elements of Symbolic Logic*. New York: Oxford University Press, 1947.
Russell, Bertrand. "Review of Hugh MaColl's Symbolic Logic and its Application." *Mind* 15 (1906): 256–257.
Schlesinger, George. *Aspects of Time*. Indianapolis, IN: Hackett, 1981.
Sciama, Dennis. "The Universe as a Whole." In *The Physcist's Conception of Nature*, edited by J. Mehra. Dordrecht: Reidel, 1973.
Smart, J. J. C. (1971). "Causal Theories of Time." In *Basic Issues in the Philosophy of Time*, edited by E. Freeman and W. Sellars. La Salle: Open Court, 1971.
Smart, J. J. C. *Philosophy and Scientific Realism*. London: Routledge and Kegan Paul, 1963.
Smart, J. J. C. "The Reality of the Future." *Philosophia* 10 (1981) 141–150.
Smart, J. J. C. "The River of Time." In *Essays in Conceptual Analysis*, edited by A. Flew. London: Routledge and Kegan Paul, 1966.
Smart, J. J. C. "Time and Becoming." In *Time and Cause*, edited by P. van Inwagen. Dordrecht, Netherlands: Reidel, 1980.
Sider, Ted. *Four Dimensionalism*. New York: Oxford University Press, 2001.
Smith, Q. "Actuality and Actuality as of a Time." In *The Importance of Time*, edited by L.N. Oaklander. Dordrecht; Boston: Kluwer, 2001.
Smith, Q. *Language and Time*. New York: Oxford University Press, 1993.
Smith, Q. "The Mind-Independence of Temporal Becoming." *Philosophical Studies* (1985).
Smith, Q. "The Multiple Uses of Indexicals." *Synthese* (1989).
Smith, Q. "Problems with the New Tenseless Theory of Time." *Philosophical Studies* (1987).
Smith, Q. "Reference to the Past and Future" In *Time, Tense, and Reference*, edited by Q. Smith and A. Jokic. Cambridge, MA: MIT Press, 2003.
Smith, Q. "Time and Degrees of Existence." In *Time, Reality, and Experience*, edited by Craig Callender. Cambridge, U.K.: Cambridge University Press, 2002.
Smith, Q., and L. N. Oaklander. *Time, Change, and Freedom*. New York: Routledge, 1994.
Tooley, Michael. *Time, Tense, and Causation*. Oxford: Oxford University Press, 1997.
Tooley, Michael. "Response to the Comments on *Time, Tense, and Causation* by Storrs McCall, Nathan Oaklander, and Quentin Smith." In *The Importance of Time*, edited by L.N. Oaklander. Dordrecht; Boston: Kluwer, 2001.
Tooley, Michael. "Basic Tensed Sentences." In *Time, Tense, and Reference*. New York: Routledge, 2003.
Williams, Clifford. "The Date-Analysis of Tensed Sentences." *Australian Journal of Philosophy* 70 (1992): 198–203.
Zimmerman, Dean. "Temporary Intrinsics and Presentism." In *Metaphysics: The Big Questions*, edited by Peter van Inwagen. Malden, MA: Blackwell, 1998.

Quentin Smith (2005)

TIME, CONSCIOUSNESS OF

William James's discussion of the perception of time in *Principles of Psychology* (Vol. I, Ch. 15) provides a convenient starting point for a discussion of the "consciousness of time." James's main concern was to give an empiricist account of our temporal concepts. This is clear from the Lockean question with which he started: "What is the *original* of our experience of pastness, from whence we get the meaning of the term?" (p. 605) and from his answer that the "prototype of all conceived times is the specious present, the short duration of which we are immediately and incessantly sensible" (p. 631). A contemporary empiricist might formulate James's thesis thus: that all other temporal concepts can be defined in terms of the relation "earlier than" and that this relation is sense given or can be ostensively defined so that even if a person does not use the term *specious present*, he is obliged to say that some earlier events are still, in some sense, present to us when we are sensing a later event.

Consider why James used the term *specious present* in describing such facts. He quoted with approval a passage by E. R. Clay, who invented this term; the quotation shows that they both assumed that the philosophically correct use of "present" is to refer to the boundary, conceived of as a durationless instant, between past and future. They pictured time as a line of which the specious present is a segment whose later boundary is the real present and hence concluded that the specious present and its contents are really past. James used two phrases that suggest that the specious present also includes a bit of the future; one, when he said that it has "a vaguely vanishing backward and forward fringe" (p. 613) and, two, when he said that it is "a saddle-back from which we look in two directions into time" (p. 609). This view is implied by nothing else he said, so we shall ignore the paradoxes it would needlessly generate and concentrate on what James said frequently: that we are continuously directly perceiving or intuiting a past duration and its contents.

James illustrated the concept of the specious present by citing experiments carried out by Wilhelm Wundt and his pupil Dietze designed to measure the duration of the longest group of sounds that a person can correctly identify without counting its members. According to Wundt, this duration is 6 seconds; according to Dietze, it is 12 seconds. James equated this period (6 to 12 seconds) with the duration of the specious present (and failed to add the qualification "for hearing"). The ability that Wundt and Dietze were investigating is a familiar one. Hearing a series of sounds as a melody or as a sentence involves recognizing them as forming a temporal pattern, or Gestalt. Another familiar experience is sometimes cited in this context: The chiming of a clock may not be noticed until it has stopped, yet we can still attend to the sounds and, one is inclined to say, inspect them; we can notice facts about them—for example, that there are five or ten chimes. Since James applied the concept of the specious present by reference to such auditory experiences, he was committed to saying that a sound that audibly terminated 5 or 10 seconds ago is still being directly perceived. Now, this seems inconsistent. "I am now directly perceiving (or sensing) *X*" seems to imply "*X* is now present and exists simultaneously with my perceiving (sensing) it."

This criticism was made by H. J. Paton (*In Defence of Reason*, pp. 105–107) against the account of the specious present given by Bertrand Russell and C. D. Broad. Russell and Broad had, however, applied the concept of the specious present differently from James. They appealed to the fact that we see things moving, that we see the second hand of a watch moving in a way that we cannot see the hour hand moving. They took this to imply that we simultaneously sense the second hand (or, rather, the corresponding sensa) occupying a series of adjacent positions. To this Paton replied, "If in a moment I can sense several different positions of the second-hand, then these different positions would be sensed as being all at the same moment.… What I should sense would be not a movement, but a stationary fan covering a certain area and perhaps getting gradually brighter towards one end.… You can't see a sensum that isn't there. If you see it, it is there at the time you see it." Paton concluded that awareness of the positions of the second hand prior to the present instant must be ascribed to memory. Paton, however, overlooked a fact about vision. What he failed to find when he looked at the second hand is found when we look at things that move (traverse a given optical angle) more quickly. If, in the dark, you watch someone rotating a lamp at the appropriate speed, you see a moving ring of light or if, in daylight, you hold a bright object—for instance, a watch—and move it fairly quickly across your visual field while gazing at a point in the middle of its path (place 1), you can still, momentarily, see a streak in place 1 when the watch is seen, out of the corner of your eye, to have halted at place 2. Such facts provide a second way of applying the concept of the specious present.

Our philosophical problem is to analyze and describe the experiences in question in a way that avoids contradictions and which, if we are empiricists, is consistent with saying that temporal relations are given in experience. We shall examine several alternative accounts of the relevant facts but first note that the account one finds appropriate will depend on one's philosophical standpoint, especially concerning the nature of the mind and of perception. Obviously, it makes a difference whether one conceives of the self as, for example, an immaterial substance that transcends time or as a physical organism, whether one holds a realist or a representative theory of perception. Paton assumed, as did Russell and Broad, that what we see are sensa, conceived of as entities numerically distinct from physical objects, and Paton asserted that sensa can exist only at the moment at which they are sensed. Whether this dictum need be accepted will be discussed later.

Our problem is also phenomenological. The specious present doctrine dissolves into a platitude unless we draw a distinction between what is "sensed" (or "immediately experienced" or "directly perceived") and what is "perceived" (or "perceptually accepted, recognized, or judged"). No one doubts that we perceive things changing, that it is correct to speak of "seeing" a thing move, and so on. The phenomenological question is whether, in such cases, the very recent positions or states of things are still being sensed. In posing the problem in this way, we are not committed to a representative theory of perception or to a sensum terminology. As we are using "to sense" and kindred verbs to say that we perceive more than we sense—that we see an orange as juicy and solid when all that we sense is its front surface—does not entail that the things we sense are numerically distinct from the things we perceive—the orange.

ATTEMPTED SOLUTIONS

TIME AS THE FOURTH DIMENSION. A simple solution seems to be open to anyone who accepts the thesis that the physical world is a four-dimensional manifold. If, accordingly, we (learn to) think of physical objects as four-dimensional solids in describing which tenseless verbs must be used, it is a corollary that what is visually sensed is not an instantaneous cross section of the four-dimensional manifold, but a short slice thereof, about one-tenth of a second long in the time dimension. Suppose you see a meteor flash across the sky. If you hold a realist theory of perception, you would say that what you sense is a short slice of the history of the four-dimensional meteor. If you identify conscious states with brain processes, you would say that what you sense is a short slice of certain of your four-dimensional brain cells. And in these sentences "short slice of the history of" would be used literally, since you are presumably following mathematicians such as Hermann Minkowski in treating time as if it were another spatial dimension, which is "at right angles to each of the other three" (whatever this may mean apart from indicating what sort of diagrams to draw).

This account would satisfy the empiricist insofar as it implies that temporal intervals and relations are sense given in the same sense as that in which spatial intervals and relations are sense given. This account, however, does not seem viable. If the physical world were a four-dimensional manifold, it would be logically impossible for its contents—four-dimensional solids—to move or otherwise change unless they did so in a time that is distinct from the one which has been spatialized (and such motion would not concern us since we do not observe motions of four-dimensional solids). The four-dimensional conceptual scheme would permit no use for the basic concepts in terms of which we do (and must?) interpret our experience—notably, our concept of a physical thing as a three-dimensional entity that can move and change, our concept of a physical event as a change in one or more such physical things, and our concept of physical causation as a relation between such physical events.

Now, it is a ground-floor empirical fact that we observe things moving and changing. Anyone who adopts the four-dimensional world theory is therefore obliged to tell us what it is that moves or changes. Since he is treating the physical world as changeless, the only answer he can give is that it is our states of consciousness that change as we become successively aware of adjacent cross sections of the four-dimensional world. But this makes sense only if we, the observers, are not in space-time (and one would still have to acknowledge a [real] time dimension other than the one that has been spatialized, in which our states of consciousness are successive). Our first account of the specious present could be accepted by a dualist if he could show that it is possible to dispense with our concepts of physical things, events, and causes. We may well doubt whether he can do this, for even the physicists cannot formulate many of their questions without using our conceptual scheme.

AUGUSTINE AND BROAD. James followed Clay in assuming that the philosophically correct use of *present* is to refer to a durationless instant. We christen this "the punctiform present (PP) assumption." Anyone who makes this assumption is committed to saying that apart from its later boundary the specious present is really past, and he is thereby disposed to say (1) that the contents of the specious present consist of images or "representations" of what has just been sensed and (2) that what these images represent is known only by memory. Here we have a second way of describing the relevant experiences.

This way of thinking is found in Augustine's classical discussion of time (*Confessions*, Book XI, Secs. 10–28). Augustine claimed that no one would deny that the present has no duration, and surprisingly, until recently no one has. Augustine combined the PP assumption with another that he deemed self-evident—that everything which is past or future does not (now) exist. He proceeded logically to the conclusions that when a person perceives or measures time, what he is attending to is "something which remains fixed in his memory" and therefore that time is not "something objective" (Sec. 27). He ended by, in effect, defining "past" in terms of human memories and "future" in terms of human expectations (Sec. 28). (These conclusions suited Augustine, for his purpose in discussing time was to show that it is meaningless to ask what God was doing before he made heaven and earth; see Secs. 10–13, 30.)

Idealists may be happy to accept Augustine's conclusion that time is unreal (subjective), but many philosophers and psychologists who do not accept this conclusion have found themselves in a quandary as a result of taking for granted Augustine's premises. Their quandary is that however one applies the concept of the specious present, if its contents are described as sensa or images, the sensa or images which a person has at any durationless instant are present at (that is, simultaneous with) that instant, but then whatever relations may hold between such sensa or images, temporal precedence cannot be among them, for this relation holds between things that are not simultaneous. One is then driven to say that awareness of the nontemporal features of one's sensa or images somehow stimulates one to construct ideas of temporal relations that are not sense given. James quoted several psychologists who got into this quandary, but he showed no sign of recognizing its (for him) unacceptable implications—that it obliges one either to deny the objective reality of time or to appeal to an intuition or a priori knowledge of time.

The paradoxical implications of Augustine's premises are clearly exhibited in Broad's account of time in his *Examination of McTaggart's Philosophy*. Broad here abandoned the account of the specious present he had given in *Scientific Thought*, where he had spoken of an event's being present throughout a finite process of sensing. He now asserted that it is only "instantaneous event-particles" which are "present in the strict sense," and he spoke of events (event-particles) becoming (coming into existence) and passing away (ceasing to exist). He was thus committed to the strange metaphysical theory according to which each event-particle is created and annihilated at "successive" instants, and the answer to the question "What exists at present?" would have to be "A set of simultaneous event-particles," though during the time it takes you to utter this phrase, an infinite number of such sets would have been born and died.

Why has the PP assumption been treated as self-evident by so many eminent thinkers? No one has claimed that the correct (strict) use of "here" is to refer to a Euclidean point; why have so many philosophers assumed that the correct (strict) use of "now" or "present" is to refer to a durationless instant? That it rejects, by implication, the PP assumption is a merit of the now popular token-reflexive analysis of sentences containing "now" or "present" or a verb in the present tense. In this analysis "now" is rendered "simultaneous with this utterance," and uttering a sentence takes a second or two. But this analysis is open to two objections: (1) that when one says "It is (now) raining," one is not referring to one's own utterance and (2) that when one refers to "the present war," the duration of the war does not coincide with one's utterance.

To remedy these objections, we need to jettison the traditional oversimplified assumption that the only temporal relations are earlier than, simultaneous with, and later than (the only relations that could hold between durationless instants); we need to recognize the numerous perceptible temporal relations between durations or processes (for example, sounds), the relations that are formally analogous to those that can hold between two segments of varying lengths belonging to the same straight line (coincidence, adjacence, partial and complete overlapping). We may then say "It is (now) raining" equals "The falling of rain (here) overlaps temporally with this" where "this" refers to the duration of the speaker's so-called specious present.

AN EMPIRICIST SOLUTION. The first solution we considered could be accepted only by a dualist who holds that minds are not in space-time (and René Descartes's problems concerning the connection between mind and body would become much more acute, since one's body is being conceived of as a four-dimensional solid). The second solution we considered is consistent only with either a form of idealism that denies the objective reality of time or a form of rationalism which treats our knowledge of time as a priori. If we reject the premises used by Augustine and many others, we can find a solution that is consistent with empiricism and with the views that time order is an objective feature of the world and that we, whatever else we may be, are physical creatures. Consider first the proposition that what is past or future cannot (now) exist. We may reply that "existence" should be predicated, in any tense, only of things (continuants), not of events, which happen or occur, and not of processes, which go on. Admittedly, past or future events are not now happening, and past or future processes are not now going on, but, of course, many of the things, including people, which existed at past times and which will exist at future times exist now.

We must also reject the PP assumption and may define "present" as the duration of the speaker's specious present. But can we, for this purpose, employ either or both of the methods of interpreting "the specious present"? James's method would make the specious present 6 to 12 seconds long; Russell's would make it about one-tenth of a second, so we can scarcely combine these interpretations. In Wundt's experiments, cited by James, the subjects were attending to sounds that had audibly terminated, though they were still presented in the sense that the subject could still "hear" them. If we say that a sound that has audibly terminated is still present, this would be inconsistent, for "it *has* audibly terminated" implies "it is past." We ought surely to describe the duration of the specious present, as interpreted by James, as "the span of immediate memory for hearing," and to call this a *specious* present is appropriate.

Does a similar objection arise if we define "present" as the duration of what is visibly sensed, when, for example, we see a meteor? Can we describe this experience by saying that we simultaneously sense the meteor occupying a series of different places throughout a fraction of a second? Those who accept the PP assumption will say, "No. When the meteor has visibly reached place 2, it is no longer in place 1, where it was one-tenth of a second earlier, and we cannot sense a thing occupying a place in which it no longer is; thus, the fading sensation of the meteor must be ascribed to (immediate) memory." But why the "must"? In discussing such phenomenological problems, for which ordinary language was not designed, it is not decisive to appeal to the "correct" (normal) use of language, but note that "remember" is not used in the way prescribed by our critic. In our earlier example, moving a watch across one's field of vision, we should say that the streak at place 1 is seen, not that it is merely remembered.

The experiences we have in seeing such movements can be described by saying that visual sensations linger and very rapidly fade. (This fact rarely obtrudes on us because we follow a moving object in which we are interested by head or eye movements and do not attend to the resultant blurring of background objects.) But are we obliged to describe the facts by saying that a moving object can be simultaneously seen (sensed) in a series of different positions? We are obliged to do this if we adopt a realist theory of perception. Consider the case of the moving watch. The realist holds that what is sensed is a surface of the watch, and as we conceive such a physical object, it cannot occupy different regions of space at the same time; thus, the realist must describe this experience by saying that, for a very short time, a person still senses (very indistinctly) the watch at place 1 when it has visibly reached place 2. But this argument is not sufficient if one adopts a representative theory of perception, or phenomenalism. For then one may, apparently, say that what one senses is a contemporary instantaneous streaky sensum at place 1.

But can one consistently say this? To say this involves conceiving a sensum as an entity that exists only at a durationless instant. This generates paradox since one will have to say that we falsely believe that we see something moving and that this belief is somehow generated by our sensing a compact series of instantaneous and stationary sensa the later members of which differ in their spatial relations from the earlier; one will also be unable to give an empiricist account of how we come by the notions earlier and later. To try to get out of this quandary, the user of the sensum language may amend his account and say that what we sense is the contemporary instantaneous state of a sensum; then he is conceiving of a sensum as a continuant (albeit a short-lived one)—that is, as something which endures and can change. Those who use sensum language usually do talk of sensa moving and changing.

Since sensa may be and often are conceived of as short-lived continuants, the user of the sensum language is free to drop the PP assumption. The latter implies that the phenomenological objects (images or sensa) which a person has or is aware of at any durationless instant, must be present at—that is, simultaneous with—that instant, and this implies that temporal precedence cannot be sense given. If, however, a sensum is conceived of as a continuant, we may say that the same sensum is present throughout a short period, that successive states or positions of the sensum are present at a given instant, and that a person can still sense a visual sensum where it was one-tenth of a second ago. Paton's statement "You can't sense a sensum that isn't there. If you see it, it is there at the time you see it" was intended to refute the possibility that one can simultaneously sense a sensum occupying a series of adjacent positions, but such dicta cannot be treated as synthetic a priori propositions. Philosophers make the rules of the sensum language as they go along, and there seem to be no clear and accepted rules for translating "visual sensations linger and fade" into this language. If we use this language, we are free to adopt rules that allow empiricists to say what they need to say—that is, that temporal relations between different sensa and different states of the same sensum are sense given.

Few philosophers would now accept Immanuel Kant's view that time (conceived of as an infinite continuum) is an intuited datum or his view that our knowledge of time is a priori (*Critique of Pure Reason*, "Transcendental Aesthetic," II, Sec. 4). Most modern philosophers would agree with James that time is a notion that we construct from temporal relations which are sense given. Such philosophers must surely accept the thesis that temporal relations are sense given within the present and that this duration of which we are in James's words "incessantly sensible" ought to be called "the *conscious* present." Clay and James called this duration "the specious [that is, pseudo] present" because they assumed that only its later boundary should be called "the real present."

FINAL CONSIDERATIONS. The besetting sin of philosophers, scientists, and, indeed, all who reflect about time is describing it as if it were a dimension of space. It is difficult to resist the temptation to do this because our temporal language is riddled with spatial metaphors. This is because temporal relations are formally analogous to spatial relations—for example, the formal resemblance between the overlapping of two sticks and the overlapping of two sounds disposes us to forget that in the latter case "overlapping" is used metaphorically. If we picture the passing of time in terms of movement along a line, we are led to ask "What moves?" and are disposed to answer, like Edmund Husserl, "Events keep moving into the past" and to forget that "move" is now being used metaphorically, that events cannot literally move or change. As J. J. C. Smart asserted, things change, events happen ("The River of Time," *Mind* 58 [1949]: 483–494). Those who spatialize time, conceiving of it as an order in which events occupy different places, are hypostatizing events. The temptation to hypostatize events is presumably the result, at least in part, of the linguistic fact that the terms, which can be said to stand in temporal relations like simultaneous with and earlier than, are event expressions. Those who ponder about time are forever using event expressions as their main nouns, and they frequently seem to forget what events are—changes in three-dimensional things. What we perceive and sense are things changing. Time is a nonspatial order in which things change.

This conclusion is deflationary. Poets, mystics, and metaphysicians naturally prefer more exciting ways of talking about time. It is ironical that although Henri Bergson forcibly criticized the spatialization of time, he based his metaphysical theories largely upon describing time in spatial images and metaphors. Bergson argued that our spatialized concept of time is an intellectual construct which misleadingly represents real concrete time (*durée*), which is grasped by, and belongs only to, inner consciousness (*Time and Free Will*). In describing *durée*, however, he said things that are difficult to reconcile and, in some cases, to interpret at all. *Durée* is said to *flow* (p. 221), yet its different moments are said to *permeate* one another (pp. 110 and 133) and to be *inside* one another (p. 232). Bergson did not recognize that these are as much spatial metaphors as is describing time as linear. It was his own metaphors and his implicit use of the PP assumption that led Bergson to his paradoxical conclusions—for example, that "duration and succession belong not to the external world, but [only] to the conscious mind" (p. 120). We cannot prevent metaphysicians who are so inclined from trying to reduce things to events or processes or to expand things into four-dimensional solids, but such intellectual acrobatics are unnecessary, apart from the paradoxes that they generate. Our consciousness of time's "flow" is our consciousness of things changing.

See also Augustine, St.; Bergson, Henri; Broad, Charlie Dunbar; Consciousness; Consciousness in Phenomenology; Gestalt Theory; Husserl, Edmund; James, William; Kant, Immanuel; McTaggart, John McTaggart Ellis; Russell, Bertrand Arthur William; Smart, John Jamieson Carswell; Space; Wundt, Wilhelm.

Bibliography

The interest of twentieth-century philosophers in time stemmed largely from the writings of Henri Bergson, who held that understanding the nature of time is the key to the main problems of philosophy. His first important book, *Essai sur les données immédiates de la conscience* (Paris: Alcan, 1889), was translated by F. L. Pogson as *Time and Free Will* (New York: Macmillan, 1910). This contains what purports to be a phenomenological description of time consciousness, but from the start Bergson's language is permeated with idealist metaphysics. Edmund Husserl discussed problems concerning awareness of time in his *Vorlesungen zur Phänomenologie des inneren Zeitbewusstseins* (Halle, 1928), which has been translated by J. S. Churchill as *The Phenomenology of Internal Time-Consciousness* (Bloomington: Indiana University Press, 1964). In *An*

Outline of Philosophy (London: Allen and Unwin, 1927), pp. 204–205, and *The Analysis of Mind* (London: Macmillan, 1921), pp. 174–175, Bertrand Russell presented, very briefly, the kind of solution argued for above, but he did not acknowledge any of the difficulties that others have found in this concept. C. D. Broad has made two detailed attempts to analyze the concept of the specious present, in *Scientific Thought* (London: Kegan Paul, 1923), pp. 346–358, and *Examination of McTaggart's Philosophy*, Vol. II (Cambridge, U.K.: Cambridge University Press, 1938), Ch. 35. He used similar diagrams in each book, but what these are said to symbolize differs greatly in each. His earlier account can be criticized for its use of the concept of momentary acts of sensing, but this could have been remedied. In his later account he ended by describing the specious present doctrine as a verbal trick for trying to reconcile contradictory propositions. It looks as if Broad was converted by the sort of criticism made by H. J. Paton in his paper "Self-Identity," *Mind* 38 (1929): 312–329, later reprinted in his *In Defence of Reason* (London and New York: Hutchinson, 1951). J. D. Mabbott criticized his own odd interpretation of the specious present doctrine in "Our Direct Experience of Time," *Mind* 60 (1951): 153–167. C. W. K. Mundle challenged Mabbott's interpretation and discussed several alternatives in "How Specious Is the 'Specious Present'?," *Mind* 63 (1954): 26–48, and later critically examined three different accounts of time contained in Broad's writings in "Broad's Views about Time," in *The Philosophy of C. D. Broad*, edited by P. A. Schilpp (New York: Tudor, 1959). The thesis criticized above, that the physical world should be conceived as a four-dimensional manifold, is argued in J. J. C. Smart's *Philosophy and Scientific Realism* (New York: Humanities Press, 1963).

OTHER RECOMMENDED TITLES

Butterfield, Jeremy. "Seeing the Present." *Mind* 93 (1984): 161–176.

Campbell, John. *Past, Space, and Self*. Cambridge, MA: MIT Press, 1994.

Hestevold, H. Scott. "Passage and the Presence of Experience." *Philosophy and Phenomenological Research* 50 (1990): 537–552.

Hirsh, I. J., and J. E. Sherrick. "Perceived Order in Different Sense Modalities." *Journal of Experimental Psychology* 62 (1961): 423–432.

Le Poidevin, Robin. "The Experience and Perception of Time." In *The Stanford Encyclopedia of Philosophy*. Available from http://www.plato.stanford.edu.

Le Poidevin, Robin, and M. MacBeath. *The Philosophy of Time*. Oxford: Oxford University Press, 1993.

McInerney, P. *Time and Experience*. Philadelphia: Temple University Press, 1991.

Mellor, H. *Real Time II*. London: Routledge, 1998.

Newton-Smith, W. *The Structure of Time*. London: Routledge and Kegan Paul, 1980.

Oaklander, L. Nathan. "On the Experience of Tenseless Time." *Journal of Philosophical Research* 18 (1993): 159–166.

Oaklander, L. Nathan, and Quentin Smith, eds. *The New Theory of Time*. New Haven, CT: Yale University Press, 1994.

Prior, A. N. *Past, Present and Future*. Oxford: Oxford University Press, 1967.

Reichenbach, H. *The Philosophy of Space and Time*. Translated by M. Reichenbach. New York: Dover, 1957.

Russell, Bertrand. "On the Experience of Time." *Monist* 25 (1915): 212–233.

Schlesinger, G. *Aspects of Time*. Indianapolis: Hackett, 1980.

Shoemaker, S. "Time without Change." *Journal of Philosophy* 66 (1969): 363–381.

C. W. K. Mundle (1967)
Bibliography updated by Benjamin Fiedor (2005)

TIME, DIRECTION OF

See *Causal Approaches to the Direction of Time; Physics and the Direction of Time*

TIME IN CONTINENTAL PHILOSOPHY

The attempt to conceive time, time's relation to human experience, and the makeup of the universe is perhaps the central problem of twentieth-century Continental philosophy. Time emerged as a central problem in late nineteenth century German philosophy where temporality became increasingly identified with consciousness and mind. Franz Brentano's work provided an impetus for Edmund Husserl's analyses of *internal time-consciousness*, and Wilhelm Dilthey and Husserl were both influential for Martin Heidegger's fundamental ontology. In France, before these phenomenological approaches had been worked out, Henri Bergson reconceived time in a way that anticipated them and profoundly influenced later French thought.

In general, Bergson calls on metaphysics (that is, Platonism and its latest version in Kant) to embrace the reality of movement, change, becoming, and time. The originality of this thinking consists in differentiating between abstract representations of time and the immediate givenness of *pure duration* in consciousness. In *Time and Free Will* (1910), he distinguishes duration from time understood as a homogeneous medium in which moments are represented as juxtaposed to one another like points on a line. His concern is that this representation of time confuses duration with spatial extension, generating metaphysical problems involving motion (see Zeno's paradoxes) and free will. In duration, Bergson says, moments are not mutually external but interpenetrating (multiplicity); states of consciousness are not separate and distinct but combined and continuous (unity); and actions are not the realization of preexisting possibilities but the fruit of the self's organic evolution through time. Later in the century, Gilles Deleuze will appropriate the Bergsonian concept of heterogeneous and yet continuous multiplicity in his own considerations of time (see below).

In *Matter and Memory* (1991), Bergson's greatest book, he defines duration as the unconscious conservation of memories, which progressively insert themselves into hesitations in the stimulus–response circuits of living bodies. Bergson thus conceives the past as surviving independent of perceived or recollected images, that is, independent of presence. The connection of duration to the past and to anticipated actions transforms duration into the *vital impetus* (*élan vital*), which Bergson presents in *Creative Evolution* (1998). Here he offers an alternative to views of evolution that reduce time to the mechanical realization of preexisting possibilities. Such views treat life as a closed system in which "all is given" (p. 37). The notion that all possibilities are already given renders time meaningless.

After psychology and evolutionary biology, Bergson brings his conception of time to bear on physics. In *Duration and Simultaneity* (1999), he aims to show how duration can resolve the paradoxes surrounding Einstein's special theory of relativity. The concepts of simultaneity and succession presuppose a consciousness in which events are contemporaneous or follow one another. Bergson argues that physicists are incorrect to conclude that a plurality of times exists. Different times assigned to different systems of reference are indeed measurable, but they have no duration other than that of the physicist performing the calculations and therefore no reality. Not surprisingly, Bergson's views have been the center of controversy, and they remain indicative of profound differences between philosophical and scientific ways of conceiving time.

Like Bergson, Husserl originally devoted his attention to describing time as it is given to consciousness, investigating how things and events are represented as continuing over time. How, for instance, is a melody given as a unified object even though its beginning *runs off* into the past before its end arrives? Husserl's response to this question can be found in his lectures *Concerning the Phenomenology of Internal Time Consciousness* (1905). During the period of these lectures, Husserl was developing his phenomenological method of reduction. The objective time of things or events in the world must be suspended or reduced, that is, made relative to consciousness, which, for Husserl, is defined by intentionality. Intentionality turns out to be fundamentally time-consciousness. The appearance of temporal objects (i.e., things identical over time) is analyzed into the contents and the acts of consciousness (the subjective correlates of the contents).

Husserl adopts Brentano's idea that an objective unity in time requires acts of presentation that join its preceding phases with its current phase, for example, the notes of a melody that are sinking away into the past with the note that is heard now. Past notes must be not only retained but also modified so that they are connected to those that follow without being jumbled together. However, Husserl rejects Brentano's claim that the contents of perception, which represents only what is given in the present, are supplemented by imagination, which reproduces those contents with the stamp of having passed. He contends that the consciousness of a note as having just passed is essentially different from recollection or memory, which would rely on an image. In other words, Husserl distinguishes between *retention*, an impressional consciousness that holds on to what was given in perception as it sinks away into the past, and *secondary memory*, a representational consciousness that makes present again what had already run off into the past. He argues that perception of a temporal object, whether enduring unchanged or changing successively, implies different modes of apprehension of the same contents, and retention accounts for the interplay of sameness and difference.

Later, Jacques Derrida will argue that this interplay of sameness and difference blurs Husserl's essential distinction between retention and representation (see below). For Husserl, however, the interplay of sameness and difference also occurs in relation to the future. Like retention, *protention*, the anticipation of what is immediately to come, is a form of impressional (or nonrepresentational) consciousness. Retention and protention constitute the temporal horizon of what is no longer present and what is not yet present for any *primal impression*. These modes of impressional consciousness constitute the temporality of immanent temporal objects. Consciousness of these objects is oriented by a *now-point*, but Husserl maintains that this point is an ideal limit and that the phases of time-consciousness comprise a *living present*.

What Husserl calls the living present implies another and more fundamental level of consciousness: the *absolute flow of time-constituting consciousness*. With regard to a unity constituted in time, we are aware of the threefold temporal intentional dimensions of the object in retention, primal impression, and protention. There is not only the unity of an object through its appearances across time as one and the same object—vertical intentionality—but also the unity of consciousness across the differences in objects that appear for consciousness—transverse intentionality. According to Husserl, the ultimate constituting flow, in which these unities are constituted at once in a double-intentionality, is not itself constituted in time. For this reason, it is difficult to speak of the ultimate ground of temporality as either in time or outside of it, and Husserl refers to it as *quasi*-temporal.

Heidegger's standard criticism is that Husserl, despite the radicality of his descriptions of time-consciousness, never posed the question of the being of consciousness. Therefore, in *Being and Time* (1962), Heidegger reopens "the question about the meaning of being" (p. 2), which has been forgotten since the time of Plato and Aristotle, and approaches time as "the horizon for the understanding of being" (p. 39). To gain access to this horizon, following Husserl, Heidegger engages in a phenomenological analysis of the modes of temporality underlying *existence* (*Dasein*, a term that indicates not only human existence but also being itself). He shows in the first division of *Being and Time* that *Dasein* consists in a structure of care, which intertwines being *ahead of itself*, being *already in the world*, and being *alongside things*. Although anticipated by others, Heidegger's innovation is to show how the past and the future, not the present, define time.

Heidegger begins the second division of *Being and Time* with an analysis of death and finitude and attempts to show how temporality is *the ontological meaning of care*. Because death is *my* death, it makes me break free of inauthentic (group) existence where I do not take responsibility for my possibilities of existence. In contrast, authentic *being-toward-death* is a mode of existence called *anticipatory resoluteness* in which I freely take up my possibilities, opening the horizon of authentic temporality. By *repeating* the existential analysis, Heidegger grounds *Dasein's* ontological structure in temporality. He shows how the originary unity of the structure of care is grounded in the temporal *ecstases* of the future, having-been, and the present. He then distinguishes between the authentic and inauthentic modes of these *ecstases*, contrasting the everyday phenomena of awaiting, *making-present*, and forgetfulness, with the authentic modes of anticipation, the moment (*Augenblick*), and repetition. He also gives a temporal interpretation of structures introduced in the first division—understanding, affectedness (*Befindlichkeit*), falling, and discourse—explicating the temporal conditions for the disclosedness of *Dasein* as being-in-the-world. The temporal interpretation opens the way for a consideration of *Dasein's* historical character.

By means of determining the existential foundation of historical research and historical truth—appropriating Dilthey's idea of hermeneutics—Heidegger shows that our *reckoning* of historical or natural events that occur *in time* is derived from primordial temporality. This derivative character of something being in time leads him to account for phenomena of intratemporality through the temporal structures of *Dasein's* concern with the world, always directed toward a for-the-sake-of-which, that makes measuring time possible. The ordinary understanding of time as an infinite, irreversible sequence of nows originates, Heidegger says, from the *ecstatic-horizonal unity of temporality*.

Heidegger continues the project of *Being and Time* in subsequent lecture courses, including *The Basic Problems of Phenomenology*, which includes a deconstruction of Aristotle's theory of time and an account of how time as it is ordinarily understood presupposes originary temporality. While in *Being and Time* he focuses on the ecstatic character of temporality, the basis of *Dasein's* existence as a *thrown projection*, in *Basic Problems*, he turns his attention to its horizonal schema, or the enclosure of the ecstatic opening. Heidegger focuses especially on the present and its horizon, which he calls *praesens*, to show that Kant understands being on the basis of presence. (A deconstruction of Kant's ontology appears in Heidegger's second book, *Kant and the Problem of Metaphysics* [1929].) For Heidegger, since the ancient Greeks, being has been defined as *ousia*, which he interprets as *constant presence*. Consequently, the relation between being and time has traditionally been understood on the basis of one ecstasis: the present. For Heidegger, a *temporal ontology* is the necessary corrective for this privilege of the present.

In the early 1930s, Heidegger appeals to a notion of the event (*Ereignis*) as a new way to conceive how being comes into presence without recourse to the self-projection of *Dasein*. In this period, Heidegger begins thinking of time in terms of the play of space–time (*Zeitraum*). Much later, he reformulates his approach to temporality in the lecture *On Time and Being* (2002) in which he considers time as the unity of three dimensions of givenness, whose interplay constitutes yet a fourth dimension, which he calls *nearness*. Although Heidegger's thought turns away from *Dasein*, from the human being, toward *Ereignis*, the event of appropriation, the *inner co-belonging* of being and time, remains a fundamental question for him. Indeed, the event of appropriation, for Heidegger, is the event of thinking, which is a kind of memory.

Both Jean-Paul Sartre and Maurice Merleau-Ponty carry Heidegger's project of a phenomenological ontology forward, making temporality integral to their major works. Sartre's *Being and Nothingness* (1993) revolves around the fundamental ontological difference between being-for-itself (Sartre speaks of both consciousness and *Dasein*) and being-in-itself (brute objects). For Sartre, all other accounts of subjectivity (for instance, that of Bergson) have confused the for-itself with the in-itself. Human beings have *no* determining essence; they are *nothing* and therefore they are radically free. Temporality comes into play in this dialectic of being and nothingness because freedom is future oriented. Beginning with the concrete phenomena of *my* particular past, present, and future, Sartre works toward an account of their general form and their unity. He argues that temporality is a structure of being-for-itself that implies separation and synthesis, multiplicity and unity, of the different temporal phases. He dubs this "profound cohesion and dispersion" (p. 195) of temporality a *diasporatic* mode of being-for-itself.

Nevertheless, for Merleau-Ponty, Sartre's idea of a radical voluntarism requires the emphasis of dispersion and separation over cohesion and synthesis. So, in the *Phenomenology of Perception* (1962), Merleau-Ponty develops a phenomenological ontology of time without recourse to Sartre's categories of being-for-itself and being-in-itself. Merleau-Ponty rejects both the early Bergsonian characterization of time as immediately given to consciousness and the Husserlian view that consciousness constitutes time. In order to show how time originates in a synthesis without ever being completely deployed, he directs attention to the "*field of presence* as the primary experience in which time and its dimensions make their appearance" (p. 416). In the primordial field of presence, he says, time is a single thrust, a "bursting forth or dehiscence," and, in Heidegger's words, an *ek-stase*. For Merleau-Ponty, time has a *sense*, which gives it an abiding character (without sense ever being eternal like a Platonic idea).

Merleau-Ponty's concept of sense negotiates the transition from passivity to spontaneity. In opposition to Sartre, therefore, Merleau-Ponty maintains that temporality does not confirm absolute freedom (pure spontaneity) but only the possibilities of commitment and refusal afforded by the historical and corporeal situation. Later, in a sometime bitter debate with Sartre, Merleau-Ponty argues in *Adventures of the Dialectic* (1973) that politics and temporal ontology are interwoven in a way that Sartre misses. He worries that Sartre's early ontology implies that a choice takes place in the instant by fiat, or else it has always already taken place. For Merleau-Ponty, choices, and especially political choices, must repeat a sense given in the past and open a sense continuing into the future.

Despite the dominance of Sartre and Merleau-Ponty's existentialism, Emmanuel Levinas's thought eventually comes to be recognized as providing an important approach to time. Against Bergson's duration, Levinas stresses the instant, an event that comes from the future and is always other than what I have experienced. In *Time and the Other* (1987), he describes this alterity with regard to death, also challenging Heidegger's existential analysis. For Levinas, death is defined not by nothingness but by mystery since it cannot be grasped. Whereas Heidegger allows for a mastery of death and the future in anticipation, Levinas thinks that they are absolutely other. Unlike Heidegger's *Augenblick*, the instant disrupts the solitude and virility of the subject for Levinas, so that time is a relationship with the radically other. In this way, Levinas's discourse of the other moves from ontology to ethics, and in later works, especially *Totality and Infinity* (1969), he continues to consider the ethical significance of time. Like Levinas, Derrida is inspired by the phenomenological approach to time. In *Speech and Phenomena* (1973), Derrida *deconstructs* Husserl's phenomenology of language in the *Logical Investigations* (1901) by means of Husserl's own descriptions of internal time-consciousness. What is at issue is the momentary (and therefore temporal) self-understanding of meaning in an internal dialogue. According to Derrida, with the distinction between expression and indication, Husserl maintains that in an internal dialogue, I understand the meaning of my own expression in the very moment when I speak; there is no mediation of the linguistic phoneme, and no difference between me as speaker and me as hearer, only immediate presence to myself.

Yet, in his early lectures on time-consciousness, Husserl speaks of retention being a *nonperception*. If it is nonperception (without which there could be no living present), retention could not be a pure presence and would have to involve some sort of absence, difference, and mediation. Retention is thus, as Derrida says, *a trace*. This is not a return Brentano's view that imagination lends the experience of time to perception. Rather, Derrida means that the genetic source of the difference between imagination and perception lies in the difference between retentional trace (repetition in the most general sense) and primal impression. The trace implies a kind of spatial distance within my internal dialogue, as if I were speaking not to the one who is closest to me (myself) but to someone else, someone past, someone distant, someone other. Derrida elaborates on the relationship between time and language in "*Ousia* and *Grammē*" (1982), challenging Heidegger's distinction between primordial and derivative temporality and showing how Heidegger's own thought remains oriented by the value of presence.

Finally, Deleuze offers a variety of approaches to time, also influenced by Husserl and Heidegger but especially by Bergson. In *Bergsonism* (1991), he focuses especially on Bergson's concept of duration, defining it as a *qualitative multiplicity* in which there is continuity and heterogeneity. For Deleuze, continuity does not eliminate difference but, rather, makes it be internal (in contrast to Levinas's and Derrida's emphasis on exteriority). Deleuze pushes Bergson's thought further in *Difference and Repetition* (1994), where he discusses three syntheses of time: habit, memory, and the empty form of time. Here he provides his account of the living present, the past in general, and the future as absolutely new (with regard to Friedrich Nietzsche's eternal return). In *The Logic of Sense* (1990), Deleuze opposes thinking of time in terms of the present through the distinction between Chronos and Aion. While Chronos signifies the time of a present that comprehends or mixes together the past and the future, Aion divides the present into the past and the future. As an *instant without thickness*, dividing time in two directions at once, Aion signifies a continuous and heterogeneous multiplicity. Deleuze identifies Aion with the pure, empty form of time that has "unwound its own circle, stretching itself out in a straight line" (p. 165). Later, Deleuze offers commentaries on Bergsonian duration in *Cinema 1: The Movement-Image* (1983) and *Cinema 2: The Time-Image* (1985), and he describes how modern directors achieve a *direct presentation of time*.

In twentieth century Continental philosophy, there have been several major shifts. Bergson challenges thinking of time in terms of space, Husserl describes the quasi-temporal origin of time, and Heidegger calls into question the privilege of presence. Subsequently, Sartre and Merleau-Ponty recognize the need to come to terms with the relation between temporality and sense. The nonpresence of the instant and the trace orient Levinas's and Derrida's thinking, and Deleuze also displaces the time of the present. On the horizon of these philosophies of difference emerging in the 1960s, we find in Michel Foucault and others a renewed concern with *place* that rivals an alleged *temporocentrism* of mainstream Continental philosophy, and it remains to be seen whether time will continue to be a central problem.

See also Aristotle; Bergson, Henri; Brentano, Franz; Deleuze, Gilles; Derrida, Jacques; Dilthey, Wilhelm; Einstein, Albert; Ethics; Foucault, Michel; Heidegger, Martin; Husserl, Edmund; Infinity in Mathematics and Logic; Kant, Immanuel; Levinas, Emmanuel; Merleau-Ponty, Maurice; Nietzsche, Friedrich; Platonism and the Platonic Tradition; Sartre, Jean-Paul.

Bibliography

Ansell Pearson, Keith. *Philosophy and the Adventure of the Virtual: Bergson and the Time of Life*. New York: Routledge, 2002.

Bergson, Henri. *Creative Evolution*. Translated by Arthur Mitchell. Mineola, NY: Dover Publications, 1998 [1907].

Bergson, Henri. *Duration and Simultaneity: Bergson and the Einsteinian Universe*. Translated by Mark Lewis and Robin Durie; edited by Robin Durie. Manchester, U.K.: Clinamen Press, 1999 [1922].

Bergson, Henri. *Matter and Memory*. Translated by N. M. Paul and W. S. Palmer. New York: Zone Books, 1991 [1896].

Bergson, Henri. *Time and Free Will: An Essay on the Immediate Data of Consciousness*. Translated by F. L. Pogson. London: Dover Publications, 1910 [1889].

Brough, John B., and Lester Embree, eds. *The Many Faces of Time*. Dordrecht, MA: Kluwer Academic, 2000.

Carr, David. *Time, Narrative, and History*. Bloomington: Indiana University Press, 1986.

Casey, Edward. *Remembering: A Phenomenological Study*. Bloomington: Indiana University Press, 1987.

Chanter, Tina. *Time, Death, and the Feminine: Reading Levinas with Heidegger*. Stanford, CA: Stanford University Press, 2001.

Dastur, Françoisie. *Heidegger and the Question of Time*. Translated by François Raffoul and David Pettigrew. Atlantic Highlands, NJ: Humanities Press, 1998 [1990].

De Boer, Karin. *Thinking in the Light of Time: Heidegger's Encounter with Hegel*. Albany: State University of New York Press, 2000.

Deleuze, Gilles. *Bergsonism*. Translated by Hugh Tomlinson and Barbara Habberjam. New York: Zone Books, 1991 [1966].

Deleuze, Gilles. *Cinema 1: The Movement-Image*. Translated by H. Tomlinson and B. Habberjam. Minneapolis, MN: Zone Books, 1986 [1983].

Deleuze, Gilles. *Cinema 2: The Time-Image*. Translated by H. Tomlinson and R. Galeta. Minneapolis, MN: Zone Books, 1989 [1985].

Deleuze, Gilles. *Difference and Repetition*. Translated by Paul Patton. New York: Columbia University Press, 1994 [1968].

Deleuze, Gilles. *Logic of Sense*. Translated by Mark Lester and Charles Stivale. New York: Colombia University Press, 1990 [1969].

Derrida, Jacques. "*Ousia* and *Grammē*: Note on a Note from Being and Time." In *Margins of Philosophy*. Translated by

Alan Bass. Chicago: University of Chicago Press, 1982 [1972].

Derrida, Jacques. *Speech and Phenomena, and Other Essays on Husserl's Theory of Signs*. Translated by David Allison. Evanston, IL: Northwestern University Press, 1973 [1967].

Durie, Robin, ed. *Time and the Instant: Essays in the Physics and Philosophy of Time*. Manchester, U.K.: Clinamen Press, 2000.

Gallagher, Shaun. *The Inordinance of Time*. Evanston, IL: Northwestern University Press, 1998.

Heidegger, Martin. *Being and Time*. Translated by J. Macquarrie and E. Robinson. (Especially sections 65, 69, 78–81), New York: Harper, 1962 [1927].

Heidegger, Martin. *Contributions to Philosophy: From Enowning*. Translated by Parvis Emad and Kenneth Maly. Bloomington: Indiana University Press, 1999 [1989].

Heidegger, Martin. *History of the Concept of Time: Prolegomena*. Translated by Theodore Kisiel. (Sections 1–3, 18, 32–36.), Bloomington: Indiana University Press, 1985 [1979].

Heidegger, Martin. *On Time and Being*. Translated by Joan Stambaugh. Chicago: University of Chicago Press, 2002 [1969].

Heidegger, Martin. *The Basic Problems of Phenomenology*. Translated by Albert Hofstadter. Bloomington: Indiana University Press, 1982 [1975]. (Especially sections 19–22).

Heidegger, Martin. *The Concept of Time*. Translated by W. McNeill. Oxford: Blackwell Publishers, 1992 [1989].

Heidegger, Martin. "The Concept of Time in the Science of History" (1915). Translated by H. S. Taylor, H. W. Uffelmann, and J. Van Buren. In *Supplements*, edited by John Van Buren, 49–60. Albany: State University of New York Press, 2002.

Heidegger, Martin. *Kant and the Problem of Metaphysics*. Translated by Richard Taft, Bloomington: Indiana University Press, 1997 [1929].

Husserl, Edmund. *Concerning the Phenomenology of Internal Time Consciousness, Husserliana*. Vol. 10. Translated by John B. Brough; edited by Rudolf Boehm. Dordrecht: Kluwer Academic, 1990 [1928].

Husserl, Edmund. *Die 'Bernauer Manuscripte' über das Zeitbewußtseins (1917/1918), Husserliana*. Vol. 33, edited by R. Bernet and D. Lohmar. Dordrecht: Kluwer Academic, 2001.

Husserl, Edmund. *Logical Investigations*. Vols. 1 and 2. Translated by J. N. Findlay; edited by Dermot Moran. London: Routledge, 2001 [1900/01].

Kisiel, Theodore *The Genesis of Heidegger's Being and Time*. Part III. Berkeley: University of California Press, 1993.

Levinas, Emmanuel. *Time and the Other*. Translated by Richard Cohen. Pittsburgh: Duquesne University Press, 1987 [1947].

Levinas, Emmanuel. *Totality and Infinity*. Translated by Alphonso Lingis. Pittsburgh: Duquesne University Press, 1969 [1961].

McCumber, John *Time in the Ditch: American Philosophy and the McCarthy Era*. Evanston, IL: Northwestern University Press, 2001.

Merleau-Ponty, Maurice. *Adventures of the Dialectic*. Translated by Joseph Bien. Evanston, IL: Northwestern University Press, 1973 [1955].

Merleau-Ponty, Maurice. *Phenomenology of Perception*. Translated by Colin Smith. London: Routledge, 1962 [1945].

Negri, Antonio. *Time for Revolution*. Translated by Matteo Mandarini. London: Continuum International, 2004.

Pöggeler, Otto. "Pathways of 'Time.'" *The Paths of Heidegger's Life and Thought*. Translated by J. Bailiff. Amherst, NY: Humanities Press, 1998.

Protevi, John. *Time and Exteriority*. Lewisburg, PA: Bucknell University Press, 1995.

Ricoeur, Paul. *Time and Narrative*. Vols. 1–3. Translated by Kathleen McLaughlin and David Pellauer. Chicago: University of Chicago Press, 1990 [1983].

Sallis, John. "Time Out…" In *Echoes: After Heidegger*, 44–75. Bloomington: Indiana University Press, 1990.

Sartre, Jean-Paul. *Being and Nothingness*. Translated by Hazel E. Barnes. New York: Washington Square Press, 1993 [1943].

Von Herrmann, Friedrich-Wilhelm. "*Being and Time* and *The Basic Problems of Phenomenology*". Translated by Parvis Emad and Kenneth Maly. In *Reading Heidegger: Commemorations*, edited by John Sallis, 118–135. Bloomington: Indiana University Press, 1993.

Wood, David. "Reiterating the Temporal: Toward a Rethinking of Heidegger on Time." In *Reading Heidegger: Commemorations*, edited by J. Sallis, 136–159. Bloomington: Indiana University Press, 1993.

Wood, David. *The Deconstruction of Time*. Evanston, IL: Northwestern University Press, 2001 [1989].

Heath Massey and Leonard Lawlor (2005)

TIME IN PHYSICS

No one conception of time emerges from a study of physics. One's understanding of physical time changes as science itself changes, either through the development of new theories or through new interpretations of a theory. Each of these changes and resulting theories of time has been the subject of philosophical scrutiny, so there are many philosophical controversies internal to particular physical theories. For instance, the move to special relativity gave rise to debates about the nature of simultaneity within the theory itself, such as whether simultaneity is conventional. Nevertheless, there are some philosophical puzzles that appear at every stage of the development of physics. Perhaps most generally, there is the perennial question, Is there a "gap" between the conception of time as found in physics and the conception of time as found in philosophy?

One can understand all of these changes and controversies as debates over what properties should be attributed to time. The history of the concept of time in physics can then be understood as the history of addition and subtraction of these properties, and the philosophical controversies thus understood as debates about particular additions and subtractions. Just as one may take a set of numbers and impose structure on this set to form the real number line, one may also take the set of moments or events (which will be used interchangeably) and impose various types of structure on this set. Each property attributed to time corresponds to the imposition of a kind of structure upon this set of events, making sense of different claims about time. Let us begin with a bare set of events and successively add structure to this set. In particular, it helps to differentiate *ordering* properties, *topological* properties, and *metrical* properties of time.

ORDER

It seems clear that different times are ordered to some extent. Intuitively, one can give a set an order by making sense of what times are between what other times. The time the cake baked is between the time of mixing the ingredients and the time of eating the cake; eating the cake is between the baking and the feeling full, and so on. One can therefore impose an ordering on this set of events by adding a ternary "between-ness" relation of the form: "x is between y and z" defined for some or all moments in the set. If betweenness is defined for some but not all distinct triples of moments, then it can be said that one has a *partially ordered* set; if betweenness is defined for every triple of the set, then it can be said that one has a *totally ordered* set. Newtonian physics, as will be shown, totally orders classes of simultaneous events. Relativistic physics, by contrast, will only partially order the set of all events.

Between-ness as defined above is not always sufficiently powerful to order topologically nontrivial sets. To see this, consider a circle with four members of the set on it: "1" at twelve o'clock, "2" at three o'clock, "3" at six o'clock, and "4" at nine o'clock. Because the set is closed, 2 is between 1 and 3, between 3 and 4, and between 1 and 4. Consequently, the between-ness relation is blind to the difference between this layout and the same but with "3" at three o'clock and "2" at six o'clock. For such sets more machinery is needed to order the set.

An ordering does not disclose much about the set of moments, $\{t_1, t_2, t_3 \ldots\}$. It does not imply whether t_2 is as far from t_1 as from t_3. Nor does it imply a direction, whether times goes from t_1 to t_3 or t_3 to t_1. Although the baking example suggests a natural direction to the set of times, an ordering is strictly independent of a direction. Nor does the ordering specify the dimensionality of the set or most other properties one normally attributes to time. The next level of structure, topology, will help make sense of some of these attributions to time.

TOPOLOGY

Topological properties are those that are invariant under "smooth" transformations. Technically, these transformations are one-to-one and bicontinuous; and what they leave invariant is the so-called neighborhood structure that is given by picking out a family of open subsets closed under the operations of union and finite intersection. Intuitively, the transformations that leave this structure unchanged correspond to operations such as stretching or shrinking, as opposed to operations such as ripping and gluing. A coffee cup and a doughnut are, topologically speaking, the same shape; if made out of an infinitely pliable rubber, one could be smoothly transformed into the other. Being closed like a circle, having an edge, and being one-dimensional are examples of topological properties. No amount of stretching and shrinking can (for instance) make the circle into a line, make an edge disappear, or make a one-dimensional set two-dimensional.

Many issues in the philosophy of time are in fact questions about the topology of time: is time closed or open? discrete? branching? two-dimensional? oriented (directed)? Formally, the answers to these questions are determined by the topological structure of time.

METRIC

Once topological structure is added to the set of times, most temporal properties are determined. However, there is still a major one remaining: duration. Of the set $\{t_1, t_2, t_3 \ldots\}$ it is still not known whether t_2 is as far from t_1 as it is from t_3—even after all topological properties are specified. The temporal distance between two moments is not a topological invariant, for it can be smoothly stretched or shrunk. To capture the idea of temporal distance, a *metric* must be put on the topological structure. The temporal metric is a function that gives one a number, the temporal distance or duration, between any pair of times. (In relativity what is imposed instead is a *spacetime* metric; see below.)

In principle, an infinite number of possible metrics are mathematically possible. One might choose a metric that makes the duration between 1980 and 1990 twice the duration between 1990 and 2000. However, such a choice would make a mess of almost all of science. It would entail, for instance, that the earth went twice as fast around the sun in the 1990s as it did in the 1980s. One would then have to adjust the rest of physics so as to be compatible with this result. As Hans Reichenbach stresses, there are simpler and more complex choices of temporal metric.

TIME IN CLASSICAL PHYSICS

Time in classical physics is normally assumed to have the ordering, topological, and metrical structure of the real number line. That is, it is one-dimensional, continuous, infinite in both directions, and so on. The temporal metric is just the one used for the real line: between any two times, a and b, the duration is b–a. Time in classical physics does have a number of remarkable properties, of which three will be mentioned here. The first two concern the metrical properties of time, whereas the third is more a property of the dynamics than of time itself.

First, the metric of time is independent of the metric of space. This feature implies that the amount of time between any two events is path-independent: if persons A and B leave an event e_1 and then meet at a later event e_2, the amount of time that has elapsed for A is equal to the amount of time that has elapsed for B. The distinct spatial distances traveled by A and B are irrelevant to how much time has passed between e_1 and e_2.

Second, simultaneity is absolute. Before explaining "absolute," consider the "simultaneous with" relation. For any event e, there is a whole class of events that are simultaneous with e. Indeed, the "simultaneous with" relation is an equivalence relation in classical physics. Equivalence relations are reflexive, symmetric, and transitive; for this example, what is important is that they partition a set into disjoint subsets. Hence the "simultaneous with" relation partitions the set of all events into proper subsets, all of whose members are simultaneous with one another. It is these classes of simultaneous events, rather than the events themselves, that are totally ordered. What is interesting about this partition in classical physics is that it is unique. Classical physics states that every observer, no matter their state of motion, in principle agrees on whether any two events are simultaneous. This observation translates into only one partition (or foliation) being the right one. In this sense simultaneity is absolute—it does not depend on one's frame of reference but is an observer-independent fact of the Newtonian world.

Third, classical physics is time reversal invariant. Consider a sequence of particle positions over time, (x_1,t_1), (x_2,t_2), $(x_3,t_3)\ldots(x_n,t_n)$. The fundamental classical laws of evolution are such that if this sequence is a solution of the laws, then so is the time-reversed sequence $(x_n,t_n)\ldots(x_3,t_3)$, (x_2,t_2), (x_1,t_1). The classical laws are invariant under the transformation of –t for t. This is true also of arbitrarily large multi-particle systems and even of classical fields. If a bull entering a china shop and subsequently breaking vases is a lawful history, then so is a bunch of scattered vase shards spontaneously jumping from the ground and forming perfect vases while a bull backs out of a china shop.

TIME IN SPECIAL RELATIVITY

In classical physics, material processes take place on a background arena of space and time, described above. The move from classical physics to special relativity is usually taken as a change in the background arena from classical space and time to the "spacetime" of Hermann Minkowski. This new entity, spacetime, is fundamental, and space and time only exist in a derivative fashion. On this conception, there is not one metric for time and another for space; rather, there is one spacetime metric supplying spatiotemporal distances between four-dimensional events. These spacetime distances are invariant properties of the spacetime. Time can be decoupled from space only in an observer-dependent way; each distinct possible inertial observer (one who feels no forces) carves up spacetime into space and time in a different way. In a sense, there is no such thing as time in Minkowski spacetime, if by "time" one conceives of something fundamental.

There are, however, two "times" in Minkowski spacetime that correspond to different aspects of classical time, namely, "coordinate" time and "proper" time. Let us take coordinate time first. Think of an arrow in three-dimensional Euclidean space. One can decompose this arrow relative to an arbitrary basis {x,y,z} by measuring how far the arrow extends in the x-direction, how far in the y-direction, and how far in the z-direction, where x, y, and z are perpendicular, and the arrow's base lies at the origin. The same arrow would decompose differently in a different basis {x',y',z'}. As one can decompose a vector in Euclidean space along indefinitely many different bases, so too can one decompose a four-dimensional spacetime vector along many different bases in Minkowski spacetime. Mathematically, coordinate time in special relativity is just one component of an invariant spacetime four-vector, just as y' is one component of a Euclidean spatial vector. In the Euclidean case, the value of the arrow along the first component of the decomposition varies with basis; so too in spacetime, the value of the first component—here, coordinate time—varies with frame of reference.

The second bit of residue of the classical time is the so-called proper time. The proper time is a kind of parameter associated with individual trajectories in spacetime. It is often thought of as a kind of clock tied to an object through its motion. This time is a scalar—that is, just a number—and as such is an invariant of the spacetime. All observers will agree on the value of proper time for A as he travels from e_1 to e_2; all will agree on the value of proper time for B as she travels from e_1 to e_2; and all will agree that these values will not be the same if they take different paths. Unlike with classical time, the temporal distance in Minkowski space is not independent of spatial distance. The amount of time between any two events is path-dependent: if persons A and B leave an event e_1 and then meet at a later event e_2, the amount of time that has elapsed for A is in general not equal to the amount of time that has elapsed for B. Spatial distances can only be completely disentangled from temporal distance in a given inertial frame of reference.

Time in classical physics plays the role of coordinate time and the role of proper time. A little reflection reveals that it can accomplish this task because in classical physics the amount of time between any two events is path-independent.

Three consequences of the shift to special relativity ought to be highlighted. First, simultaneity is not absolute in Minkowski spacetime. Simultaneity is a temporal feature, yet the temporal does not disentangle from the spatial except within an inertial reference frame. What events are simultaneous with one another is observer-dependent. Given spacelike-related events e_1 and e_2, inertial observer A may (rightly) say they are simultaneous whereas inertial observer B, traveling at a constant velocity with respect to A, may (rightly) say e_1 is earlier than e_2. In Minkowski spacetime, they do not disagree over any observer-independent fact of the matter. In terms of the earlier discussion, it can then be said that the "simultaneous with" relation partitions Minkowski spacetime, but only within a frame of reference.

Second, the temporal ordering in Minkowski spacetime is partial, not total. The only temporal ordering that all observers agree on is the ordering among "timelike" events. Timelike related events are those that are in principle connectible by any particle going slower than the speed of light in a vacuum. Think of all the events that can be reached from any given event that way. Consider the event of your elementary school graduation (e_1) and the event of your high school graduation (e_2). Obviously sub-luminal particles could make it from one to the other; for instance, you are a set of such particles. Due to the finite speed of light, however, there are many events that such particles could not reach—for example, whatever was going on at Alpha Centuri simultaneous with (in your reference frame) e_2. What happened on Alpha Centuri simultaneous with e_2 is not an observer-independent fact. But that e_2 follows e_1 is an observer-independent fact. Only the timelike related events are invariantly ordered.

Third, and perhaps most famously, in a sense time passes more slowly for a moving observer than for one at rest. Consider two inertial observers, A and B, traveling at a constant velocity relative to one another, and let a clock be at rest in A's frame. Looking at the ticks of the clock, the special relativistic metric entails that B will conclude that the clock in A's frame is running slow. This effect, known as time dilation, is entirely symmetrical: A would find a clock at rest in B's frame to be running slow, too. Time dilation has many experimentally confirmed predictions, such as that atomic clocks on planes tick slowly relative to clocks on land and that mesons have longer lifetimes than they should from the earth's frame of reference.

TIME IN GENERAL RELATIVITY

General relativity, unlike special relativity, treats the phenomenon of gravitation. It famously does away with Newton's gravitational force, understanding gravitational phenomena as instead a manifestation of spacetime curvature. Loosely put, the idea is that matter curves spacetime and spacetime curvature explains the gravitational aspects of matter in motion. Hence the largest conceptual difference between special and general relativity is that Minkowski spacetime is flat whereas general relativistic spacetimes may be curved in an indefinite number of ways. Otherwise, as regards time, again there is a division between coordinate time and proper time, no privileged foliation of spacetime, only a partial temporal ordering, and the possibility of time dilation.

In terms of the previous division, curvature is a metrical property, so the primary difference between special and general relativity is that the former's metric is merely one of the many possible metrics allowed by the latter. General relativity places various constraints between the spacetime metric, or geometry, and the distribution of matter-energy. Thinking of these constraints as the laws of general relativity, general relativity claims a variety of spacetime geometries are physically possible. Because these different metrics allow and sometimes demand different topologies and even orderings, time may have dramatically different ordering, topological, and metrical properties depending on the spacetime model. Some consequences of this fact are especially worthy of note.

First, there are spacetimes without a single global moment. In special relativity, simultaneity was observer-dependent. Minkowski spacetime could be carved up, or foliated, into a succession of three-dimensional spaces evolving along a one-dimensional time an indefinite number of ways—a distinct foliation for every possible inertial observer. Though this may also be the case in general relativity, there are spacetime models that prohibit even one foliation of spacetime into space and time. The famous Gödel spacetime, named after the great logician Kurt Gödel, is an example of such a spacetime. Due to the effects of curvature, in such spacetimes it is impossible to find even a single global always-spatial three-dimensional surface. There is no global moment of time in such spacetimes. There is no way to conceive of world history, in such a spacetime, as the successive marching of three-dimensional surfaces through time.

Second, perhaps most famously, general relativity has models that permit interesting time travel. In these models a traveler can start off at event e, and by traveling always to the local future (that is, into e's future lightcone), eventually come back to events that are to e's past (that is, in e's past lightcone). Indeed, these models will allow one to travel back to an earlier event: an observer's worldline may intersect e, and then after some proper time has elapsed, intersect e again. These "causal loops" are called closed timelike curves. Of the many models that allow time travel, the Gödel model is again remarkable for it allows the time traveler the fullest menu of possibilities: in the model, it is possible (given enough time and energy) to get from any event e_1 to any other event e_2 on the entire spacetime, including the case where $e_1=e_2$.

Third, whether time is infinite or finite can be an observer-dependent fact. When discussing Minkowski spacetime it was noted that there are different ways to decompose spacetime into space and time; alternatively, there are generally many ways to foliate a spacetime. When nontrivial topologies are considered, there are spacetimes consistent with general relativity that make whether time is infinite or finite a foliation-dependent matter. That is, there are foliations of one and the same spacetime that make time finite and foliations that make time infinite. In spacetimes admitting two such foliations, the age-old question of whether time is finite or infinite would be answered with a convention. In such a world there is no coordinate-independent fact of the matter regarding how long time persists. The universe might last an infinite amount of time according to one coordinization, or language, and a finite amount of time according to another coordinization, or language.

TIME IN FUTURE PHYSICAL THEORIES

As mentioned, because physical theories are always changing, there is no one conception of time emerging from a study of physics. On the horizon of research are the various programs of "quantum gravity," the would-be theory that unifies or at least makes consistent our best theory of matter, quantum field theory, and the best theory of spacetime, general relativity. Though speculative, virtually all of these programs are entertaining dramatic changes for the conception of spacetime, ranging from the idea that spacetime is discrete to the idea that time is an emergent property arising from some more fundamental stuff.

PHILOSOPHICAL CONTROVERSIES

There are many philosophical problems concerning time in physics. Philosophers have discussed the physical possibility of time travel in general relativity, the possibility of discrete time, the nature of time reversal invariance, the possibility of backward causation in physics, such as in the Wheeler-Feynman time-symmetric version of electromagnetism, the possibility of time emerging from something more fundamental in quantum gravity, and more. In addition, it will not be surprising that many topics typically dealt with in the context of space also have temporal counterparts. The absolute-versus-relational debate, famously discussed by Gottfried Leibniz and Samuel Clarke and more than a hundred authors thereafter, is often discussed in the classical context of space; but those arguments apply equally well to the case of time, and in the modern version of the debate, to spacetime. And the many deliberations surrounding the conventionality of the metric apply just as well to the temporal metric as the spatial metric (and of course the spacetime metric). Here the discussion focuses on whether physical time captures all the fundamental properties of time and the so-called problem of the direction of time.

TENSE

In the famous terminology of J. E. McTaggart, the temporal relations of earlier than, later than, and simultaneous with are called "B-properties" and the monadic properties of past-ness, present-ness, and futurity are called "A-properties." Those who argue that the B-properties are the fundamental features of time are dubbed advocates of the "tenseless" theory of time; those who argue that instead the A-properties are fundamental are dubbed advocates of the "tensed" theory of time. Much of the work in philosophy of time, especially throughout the twentieth century, can be described as a debate between tensers and detensers.

Because the categories "tensed" and "tenseless" are broad umbrellas covering many different doctrines, it is probably best not to think of this as one debate. A better way to frame the debate is to conceive it on the model of the debate between mind-body dualists and materialists. Dualists find the description of the mind by the natural sciences to be either incomplete or simply wrong. Various features of mental states—for example, consciousness—are said to be either left out or indescribable by these natural sciences. Materialists counter either by denying the reality of these features or by explaining why the natural sciences do manage to explain such features.

One can conceive the debate regarding time in the same mold. Though the features attributed to time vary with physical theory, some philosophers feel that physical theory has consistently missed out on one or more essential properties of time. Physical theory orders some or all of the events in time, just as the relations of right and left order events in space. In classical (relativistic) physics, for any (some) pair of events, e_1, e_2, physical theory states whether e_1 is earlier, later, or simultaneous with e_2. The theories use relational temporal properties and not monadic ones. One can of course say e_1 is to the past of e_2, but that is just to say that e_1 is earlier than e_2. Physical theory seems to require only tenseless temporal relations. Broadly speaking, the debate is between those who would add some metaphysical feature to time as it is found in science and those who would not. Various arguments are adduced to show that such features are needed or not needed, compatible with science or incompatible, and so on. Consider now three features often felt to be left out by physical time.

THE PRESENT. Physical theory does not identify which time is Now. That is, it judges which events are earlier, later, and simultaneous with which other events, but it fails to mention which among all sets of events are the present ones. Some philosophers argue, based on experience, analysis of ordinary language, or study of puzzles surrounding change, that physical theory misses out on a genuine property of time, Now-ness. Others reply that the idea of a metaphysically special present is wrong-headed. Linguistic features of the now are explained via the properties of indexicals in general. Because one would not reify the here, one should not reify the now. Attempts are then made to show that the language, thought, and behavior attributing objectivity to the present can be explained by facts about human beings and their typical physical environments.

FLOW OR BECOMING. Physical theory also does not describe a property corresponding to the flow of time or to a process of becoming. Again, the different events are ordered, have a certain distance from one another, and so on, but there does not seem to be anything that flows (such as the Now). Nor is there a distinction made among events, such that it makes sense to talk about the Now turning an unreal future real. Again, some philosophers argue, based on experience or the study of various puzzles, that there is genuine becoming in the world. C. D. Broad, for example, proposed a model wherein the past and present are real and the future successively becomes present and hence real.

TIME'S ARROW. If physical time is time-reversal invariant, then nowhere does it distinguish one direction of time. But there are many asymmetric processes: physical ones, such as the radiation and thermodynamic asymmetries; metaphysical ones, such as the asymmetry of causation and of counterfactual dependence; epistemological ones, such as that one typically knows more about the past than the future; and emotional ones, such as that people usually care more about the future than the past. To explain one or more of these asymmetries, some philosophers have posited a directionality to physical time. Others answer that that the physical asymmetries do not themselves need explanation and that they in turn can explain the other asymmetries. To mention one possible sequence of moves, one might try to show that the thermodynamic and radiative temporal asymmetries explain the memory asymmetry (people have memories of the past, not the future), the memory asymmetry explains the knowledge asymmetry, and the knowledge asymmetry explains the psychological asymmetry.

There are also two famous conceptual arguments against the idea that time itself flows (and depending on the model of becoming, against becoming). One, McTaggart's Paradox, claims that the idea of time flowing leads to a logical contradiction. Essential to the idea that time flows, says McTaggart, is the idea that events change their A-properties: for instance, the event of Socrates's death was future, then present, and then past. So every event has all three monadic properties. But this is in straightforward conflict with the claim if an event is future it is not past. McTaggart and his supporters claim that any way of discharging the contradiction by insisting that events are not at the same time past, present, and future leads to infinite regress.

Another argument, by the philosophers C. D. Broad and J. J. C. Smart, begins by noting that change is always the change of some property with respect to time. Movement, for example, is having different locations at different times. So if time flows—if, say, the Present moves—then Broad and Smart suggest that it must be that the Present moves with respect to time. But this time, Smart claims, must be a hyper-time; and if this hyper-time is a kind of time, it must flow with respect to a hyper-hyper-time, and so on. There are too many responses to this argument to consider them all here.

It should not be surprising that considerations from physics enter these debates.

SPECIAL RELATIVITY AND TENSE

Some also argue that a metaphysically distinguished present is inconsistent with special relativity. The reason is obvious: since simultaneity is relative, how can a monadic feature of events such as presentness be frame-dependent? In Minkowski spacetime, there will be cases where for observer O_1, e_1 is present and e_2 is later, whereas for observer O_2, e_2 is present and e_1 is later. Assuming presentness is not frame-dependent, there appears to be a contradiction. This argument, originally made by Hilary Putnam and C. W. Rietdijk, also would affect positions claiming time flows, if the flowing is done by a unique present. Even if correct, by itself this argument does not tell how to arrange the conflict into premises and conclusion. Does relativity disprove the present or does the present disprove relativity? Naturalistically inclined philosophers are loath to consider the latter reading; but strictly speaking, if there were enough prior reason to believe in a privileged present, then alternatives to Minkowski spacetime would need to be considered—such as embedding relativistic phenomena in classical space and time in the manner H. A. Lorentz favored.

GENERAL RELATIVITY AND TENSE

From the perspective of general relativity, the attack on tenses from special relativity seems rather limited. Minkowski spacetime may locally be a good approximation to whatever the true global spacetime is, but strictly speaking special relativity is only valid on planes that are tangent to mere points of the general relativistic geometry. There appears no particular reason to think that general relativity's impact on the tenses debate will mirror special relativity's impact.

As mentioned, general relativity takes from special relativity a division between coordinate time and proper time and only a partial temporal ordering. The question is whether it banishes a privileged foliation of spacetime into space and time. The answer depends on the particular spacetime model and what one means by "privileged." In some models, ones with realistic distributions of matter and energy, one can define a global cosmic time. Cosmic time is defined with respect to the mean motion of matter. The possibility exists of a tenser using cosmic time, which mimics some features of classical time, as the time of becoming, passage, and so on. Challenges to this use include the fact that cosmic time can only be defined in some subset of the solutions to Einstein's field equations, and questions of arbitrariness in the choice of a cosmic time function.

With the possibility of cosmic time in mind, Kurt Gödel argued that general relativity, far from rescuing tenses, in fact showed that time is "ideal," or not fundamental. Reflecting on the odd eponymous spacetime mentioned above, Gödel states that it is obvious that time does not flow in the spacetime he discovered. But that means, Gödel says, that time does not flow in the spacetime of the actual world either. Why? In brief, his idea is that time flow should not be contingent, yet because Gödel spacetime enjoys the same laws of nature as does the actual world, it differs from this world only in the contingent distribution of matter and energy. Indeed, Gödel goes so far as to presume time's flow is essential to time, and hence concludes that Gödel spacetime shows that there is no such thing as time in this world.

THE PROBLEM OF THE DIRECTION OF TIME

So far this entry has described issues concerning time in fundamental or near-fundamental physics. There also exists a philosophical problem arising from an apparent conflict between the way microphysics seems to treat time and the way macroscopic physics treats time. While microphysics may be time reversal invariant, the physics describing macroscopic behavior such as the warming or cooling of bodies to room temperature, the expansion of gases, and so on, is not time reversal invariant. Consider the volume of an initially localized sample of a light gas released in the corner of a room. As time goes on, it will spread through its available volume: (v_1, t_1) (v_2, t_2) (v_3, t_3)…, where $v_3 > v_2 v_1$ and $t_3 > t_2 > t_1$, and so on. While classical mechanics implies that the opposite shrinking process from v_3 to v_1 is lawful, thermodynamics states that it is not.

The science of statistical mechanics seems to reconcile the two by introducing probabilistic considerations: the process from v_3 to v_1 is possible, says statistical mechanics, but highly unlikely, whereas the process from v_1 to v_3 is highly likely. However, statistical mechanics itself is time reversal invariant. It manages to state that evolution from v_3 to v_1 is unlikely and v_1 to v_3 likely. Looked at more closely, however, it implies that *given* v_1, v_3 is more likely in either time direction. In other words, it rightly states that v_3 is a likely state to evolve to, but it also implies that it is a likely state to have evolved from. The second implication is obviously wrong. This problem and related ones occupied many of the founders of statistical physics, including Ludwig Stephan Boltzmann, J. C. Maxwell, Joseph Loschmidt, and Ernest Zermelo. Solutions to the problem seem to require inserting a temporal asymmetry somewhere in the physics, either by assuming temporally asymmetric boundary conditions or by introducing new laws of nature.

See also Philosophy of Physics; Relativity Theory.

Bibliography

Albert, David. *Time and Chance*. Cambridge, MA: Harvard University Press, 2000.

Arntzenius, Frank, and Tim Maudlin. "Time Travel and Modern Physics." In *The Stanford Encyclopedia of Philosophy (Spring 2002 Edition)*, edited by Edward N. Zalta. Available from http://plato.stanford.edu/. Reprinted in *Time, Reality and Experience*, edited by Craig Callender. Cambridge, U.K.: Cambridge University Press, 2002.

Barbour, Julian. *The End of Time*. London: Weidenfeld & Nicholson, 1999.

Broad, C. D. *Examination of McTaggart's Philosophy*, vol. 2, part 1. Cambridge, U.K.: Cambridge University Press, 1983.

Butterfield, Jeremy, ed. *The Arguments of Time*. Oxford: The British Academy, 1999.

Callender, Craig, ed. *Time, Reality and Experience*. Cambridge, U.K.: Cambridge University Press, 2002.

Callender, Craig "Thermodynamic Asymmetry in Time." In *The Stanford Encyclopedia of Philosophy (Spring 2002 Edition)*, edited by Edward N. Zalta. Available from http://plato.stanford.edu/.

Craig, William L. *Time and the Metaphysics of Relativity*. Dordrecht, Netherlands: Kluwer, 2001.

Dainton, Barry. *Time and Space*. Ithaca, NY: McGill-Queen's University Press, 2001.

Dorato, Mauro. *Time and Reality: Spacetime Physics and the Objectivity of Temporal Becoming*. Bologna, Italy: CLUEB, 1995.

Earman, John. "An Attempt to Add a Little Direction to 'The Problem of the Direction of Time.'" *Philosophy of Science* 41 (1974): 15–47.

Earman, John. *Bangs, Crunches, Whimpers and Shrieks*. Oxford: Oxford University Press, 1995.

Einstein, Albert. "On the Electrodynamics of Moving Bodies," as reprinted and translated in *The Principle of Relativity*, 35–65. New York: Dover, 1952.

Friedman, Michael. *Foundations of Space-Time Theories: Relativistic Physics and Philosophy of Science*. Princeton, NJ: Princeton University Press, 1983.

Gödel, Kurt. "A Remark about the Relationship Between Relativity and Idealistic Philosophy." In *Albert Einstein: Philosopher-Scientist*, edited by P. Schilpp, 557–562. La Salle, IL: Open Court, 1949.

Grünbaum, Adolf. "The Meaning of Time." In *Basic Issues in the Philosophy of Time*, edited by E. Freeman and W. Sellars, 195–228. La Salle, IL: Open Court, 1971.

Grünbaum, Adolf. *Philosophical Problems of Space and Time*, (2nd, enlarged edition). Dordrecht, Netherlands: D. Reidel, 1973.

Horwich, P. *Asymmetries in Time: Problems in the Philosophy of Science*. Cambridge, MA: MIT Press, 1987.

Kroes, Peter. *Time: Its Structure and Role in Physical Theories*. Synthese Library, 179. Dordrecht, Netherlands: Kluwer, 1985.

Le Poidevin, Robin, ed. *Questions of Time and Tense*. Oxford: Oxford University Press, 1998.

Le Poidevin, Robin, and Murray McBeath, eds. *The Philosophy of Time*. Oxford: Oxford University Press, 1993.

Lewis, David, "The Paradoxes of Time Travel." In *Philosophical Papers*, vol. 2, edited by David Lewis. Oxford: Oxford University Press, 1986.

McCall, Storrs. *A Model of the Universe*. Oxford: Clarendon Press, 1994.

McTaggart, J. M. E. "The Unreality of Time." *Mind* New Series 68 (1908): 457–484.

Mellor, D. H. *Real Time II*. London: Routledge, 1998.

Minkowski, H. "Space and Time," as reprinted and translated in *The Principle of Relativity*, 73–91. New York: Dover, 1952.

Nerlich, Graham. *What Spacetime Explains*. Cambridge, U.K.: Cambridge University Press, 1994.

Newton-Smith, W. H. *The Structure of Time*. London: Routledge, 1980.

Poincaré, Henri. *Science and Hypothesis*. New York: Dover, 1952.

Price, Huw. *Time's Arrow & Archimedes' Point: New Directions for the Physics of Time*. New York: Oxford University Press, 1996.

Putnam, Hilary. "Time and Physical Geometry." *Journal of Philosophy* 64 (1967): 240–247. Reprinted in Putnam's *Collected Papers*, vol. 1. Cambridge, U.K.: Cambridge University Press, 1975.

Reichenbach, Hans. *The Philosophy of Space and Time*. New York: Dover, 1957.

Reichenbach, Hans. *The Direction of Time*. Berkeley: University of California Press, 1958.

Rietdijk, C. "A Rigorous Proof of Determinism Derived from the Special Theory of Relativity." *Philosophy of Science* 33 (1966): 341–344.

Savitt, Steven, ed. *Time's Arrows Today: Recent Physical and Philosophical Work on the Direction of Time*. Cambridge, U.K.: Cambridge University Press, 1995.

Savitt, Steven. "Being and Becoming in Modern Physics." In *The Stanford Encyclopedia of Philosophy (Spring 2002 Edition)*, edited by Edward N. Zalta. Available from http://plato.stanford.edu/.

Sklar, Lawrence. *Space, Time, and Spacetime*. Berkeley: University of California Press, 1974.

Sklar, Lawrence. "Up, Down, Left and Right, Past and Future." *Nous* 15 (1981): 111–129. Reprinted in *The Philosophy of*

Time, edited by Robin Le Poidevin and Murray McBeath. Oxford: Oxford University Press, 1993.

Smart, J. J. C. *Problems of Space and Time*. London: Macmillan, 1964.

Stein, H. "On Relativity Theory and Openness of the Future." *Philosophy of Science* 58 (1991): 147–167.

Swinburne, Richard. *Space and Time*. London: Macmillan, 1968.

Whitrow, G. *The Natural Philosophy of Time*. Oxford: Oxford University Press, 1961. (2nd edition, 1980.)

Williams, Donald C. "The Myth of Passage." *Journal of Philosophy* 48 (1951): 457–472.

Yourgrau, Palle. *Gödel Meets Einstein: Time Travel in the Gödel Universe*. La Salle, IL: Open Court, 1999.

Craig Callender (2005)

TIMON OF PHLIUS

(320–230 BCE)

Most of Timon's importance rests upon his reputation as a reporter, but he was also responsible for one or two original twists to the philosophy of his master—Pyrrho. He was a literary virtuoso, composing in a variety of verse forms. Seventy-one fragments of his poetry survive in quotations by later writers, sixty-five of them deriving from one work, the *Silloi*, a mock-epic series of lampoons in verse. The majority of them deal with philosophers other than Pyrrho, whom Timon attacks with wit and verve, frequently in pointed parody of Homeric verse; but Timon's purpose is to exalt Pyrrho at their expense: "Truly, no other mortal could rival Pyrrho; such was the man I saw, unproud, and unsubdued by everything which has subdued known and unknown alike, volatile crowds of people, weighed down in all directions by passions, opinion, and vain legislation" (Diels 1901, pgs. 8 and 9).

Timon portrays his hero as a superman: "Old man, how and whence did you find escape from the bondage of opinions and the empty wisdom of the sophists? How did you break the chains of all deception and persuasion? You did not concern yourself with what winds pass over Greece, and from what and into what each thing passes" (Diels 1901, p.48).

This philosophical hagiography deliberately recalls that of Socrates (note the rejection of natural science in the last fragment); Pyrrho is presented as a man apart from and immune to the seductive claims of pseudo-knowledge. But in the verse little of genuine philosophical substance is found, apart from the rejection of anything that smacks of dogmatic opinion: dogma unsupportable by persuasive argument, and the implication that such a rejection brings with it tranquillity.

But Timon also wrote prose works and a crucial report of one of them, *Pytho*, survives in a fragment of the Peripatetic Aristocles (around the first century CE), itself preserved in a text of Eusebius. Timon is reported as saying that anyone seeking happiness should consider these three questions: How are things by nature? What attitude should we adopt toward them? What will be the outcome for those who have this attitude? And he goes on to report (controversially) Pyrrho's answer: Things are indifferent, unmeasurable, and undecidable; neither sensation nor judgment is determinably true or false; and so one should not be opinionated, but be uncommitted and unwavering, saying about everything that it no more is than is not, or that it both is and is not, or that it neither is nor is not. Once accepted, the result is tranquility. In other words, we do not know how things really are; and once we accept that inability, it does not matter. However, Timon's Pyrrho, in contrast with later Pyrrhonians, claimed to be purveying a practical truth, albeit a skeptical one; in his other philosophical poem, *Images*, Timon writes: "The story of the truth has a correct rule, namely the nature of the divine and the good, from which derives the most equable life for man" (Diels 1901, p. 68).

The same poem contained the line: "the appearance prevails everywhere, wherever it comes from" (Diels 1901, p. 70). Here Timon encapsulates the central tenet of later skeptical philosophy, that one can neither question, nor go beyond, the content of appearances. Again anticipating a skeptical topos, in a work *On Sensations*, he wrote "that honey is sweet I do not affirm, but I accept that it appears so" (Diels 1901, p. 74).

In these passages, we may perhaps discern Timon's independent philosophizing; and reports in Sextus attribute views to Timon himself rather than via him to his master. In *Against the Geometers*, Sextus Empiricus attacks geometers on the ultimately Platonic grounds that they assume as firm principles what are in fact mere hypotheses, alluding to Timon's *Against the Physicists* as saying that one should investigate whether anything should be accepted on the basis of a hypothesis. Sextus gives no context; but the title of Timon's volume suggests that he would not have had the geometrical notion specifically in mind, but rather have been more generally concerned with the epistemic status of allegedly explanatory postulates. In this, too, he anticipates characteristic moves of later Pyrrhonism, in particular that encapsulated in the fourth mode of Agrippa.

Timon also dealt with time. Sextus reports that he argued against the indivisibility of the momentary present on the grounds that "no divisible thing such as becoming or perishing, can come to be in an indivisible time" (Diels 1901, p. 76). Change involves a complex of distinct states: They cannot be squeezed into a partless present. That the present was a punctual; *now* was a tenet of Aristotelianism; the idea that no change can occur in a punctual present being a feature of Zeno's arrow paradox. Timon's argument was not, probably, very original in content. But it does show him adopting material supplied by the philosophical tradition and turning it to distinctively skeptical ends, something that was itself distinctive of the later skeptical tradition, and apparently unanticipated by anything we know of in Pyrrho. Thus if Timon's argument was unoriginal, the use to which it was put may well not have been. And herein lies his personal contribution to the development of Greek skepticism.

See also Agrippa; Ancient Skepticism; Pyrrho.

Bibliography

Bett, R. *Pyrrho, His Antecedents, and His Legacy*. Oxford; New York: Oxford University Press, 2000.

Diels, H. *Poetarum Philosophorum Fragmenta*. Berlin: Weidmann, 1901.

Hankinson, R. J.*The Sceptics*. 2nd ed. London; New York: Routledge, 1998.

R. J. Hankinson (2005)

TINDAL, MATTHEW

(1657?–1733)

Matthew Tindal, the English jurist, Whig propagandist, and deist, was born at Beer Ferris, Devonshire, the son of John Tindal, a minister. After an early education in the country, he proceeded to study law at Oxford, first at Lincoln College and later at Exeter College. In 1678 he was elected to a law fellowship at All Souls' College. In 1679 he received the BA and the BCL degrees and in 1685 the DCL. In 1685 he was also admitted as an advocate at Doctors' Commons, a society of ecclesiastical lawyers, with a pension of £200 a year for the remainder of his life. While at Oxford and under the influence of the high churchman George Hickes, he defected from the Church of England and became a Roman Catholic for a brief period, but he recanted in 1688. Soon thereafter, he began to publish a long series of tracts and books, culminating in 1730, when he was over seventy years old, with *Christianity as Old as the Creation.* Frequently called "the deist's Bible," this work elicited more than 150 replies, including Bishop Butler's famous *Analogy of Religion* (1736).

At Oxford, Tindal's enemies accused him of gluttony but granted that he was so abstemious in the drinking of wine that he frequently outsmarted them in argument. Dr. Edmund Gipson, bishop of London, however, won a posthumous "victory" over Tindal when he managed to acquire the manuscript of a second volume of *Christianity as Old as the Creation* and deliberately burned it. The same forged will (probably by Eustace Budgell) that made this action possible also deprived Tindal's nephew of his property.

Tindal died stoically in 1733 and was buried in Clerkenwell Church, London. Without question the most learned of the English deists, Tindal consistently referred to himself as a "Christian deist."

EARLY POLITICAL PUBLICATIONS

Tindal did not begin to publish until he was middle-aged. A first series of tracts, *Essay of Obedience to the Supreme Powers* (1694), *Essay on the Power of the Magistrate and the Rights of Mankind in Matters of Religion* (1697), *The Liberty of the Press* (1698), and *Reasons against restraining the Press* (1704), all showed low church and Miltonic influences. Tindal first gained notoriety with *The Rights of the Christian Church Asserted, against the Romish, and all other Priests who claim an Independent Power over it* (1706), which brought over twenty answers. A sequel, *A Defence of the Rights of the Christian Church* (1709), was condemned by the House of Commons and burned in 1710 by the common hangman. These early works are strongly Whiggish, anti-authoritarian, and anticlerical in tone; they argue for freedom of the press and for general toleration (except for atheists)—principles that were to be even more forcefully urged in *Christianity as Old as the Creation.* For his radical political view that although the magistrate has power to legislate in the area of religion, he has no authority to compel conformity and that persecution of nonconformity not only violates natural law but is also futile, Tindal, like many other deists, was branded by the orthodox as "Spinozan."

"THE DEIST'S BIBLE"

Christianity as Old as the Creation: Or, The Gospel A Republication of the Religion of Nature appeared in 1730 with subsequent editions in 1731, 1732, and 1733; in 1741 it was translated into German by Johann Lorenz Schmidt, a writer in the Leibniz-Wolff tradition. Although the work makes frequent mention of John Locke, it is fundamentally rationalistic, and it is the rationalistic side of Locke that is emphasized—that morality is capable of demonstration and is therefore true, that whatever is known to be true on the basis of reason cannot be falsified by revelation, that the Bible must be read like any other book, that without reason any religion can be held to be true because of the power of tradition.

As is implied by the subtitle, Tindal's thesis is an elaboration of the proposition from Dr. Thomas Sherlock, bishop of Bangor and later of London, quoted on the title page: "The Religion of the Gospel is the true original Religion of Reason and Nature.... And its Precepts declarative of that original Religion, which was as old as the Creation." Citation from the rationalistic orthodoxy of such latitudinarians as Archbishop Tillotson, Samuel Clarke, and Thomas Sherlock, a deceptive device frequently employed by the deists, provides some indication of how close in thought rationalistic orthodoxy and rationalistic deism actually were.

Tindal's use of Sherlock's thesis, developed in a dialogue between *A* (Tindal) and *B* (an objector to, and a questioner of, *A*), is entirely negative. The Scriptures, with all the ambiguities that have confused the Church Fathers, the Schoolmen, and modern theologians, are really a work of supererogation. Although never stated in so many words, it is clear that Tindal's radical anticlericism challenged the validity of all historical religions and established churches.

On the critical and historical side, the Scriptures are examined and attacked by Tindal in great detail to expose the imperfect morality of certain Old Testament heroes and, to some extent, of certain parables of the New Testament. Even worse, according to Tindal, priestcraft and tradition, working together, have corrupted the texts and confused the people. Churches have used the teachings of the New Testament to acquire new members and have then used the teachings of the Old Testament to keep members in line. Tindal was incensed that priests first tempt men to examine their faith and then punish them for so doing if, perchance, their interpretations differ from those established by tradition and authority. This side of Tindal's work greatly influenced Voltaire.

On the philosophical side it is Tindal the rationalist, rather than the critic and moralist, who was the "Christian deist," for Tindal, like Lord Herbert of Cherbury before him, took what Alexander Pope was to call "the high Priori Road." God is conceived of as the God of reason, and because human nature is inalterable, man's reason has known His being and attributes from the beginning of time. Rational man, then, reasons downward from the divine perfections to morality and religion. All men, whether of the highest intellect or the meanest capacity, declares Tindal, are equally capable of knowing the immutable law of nature or reason and the religion of nature. In this respect Tindal is close to the more "orthodox" theologians of the waning rationalist or latitudinarian school in Britain represented by Archbishop Tillotson, Samuel Clarke, and Thomas Sherlock. The book concludes with Tindal's statement of his three basic notions about natural religion. First, there are things that show, by their inner nature, that they are the will of an infinitely wise and good God (for example, the relations between God and man, the immutability of morality). Second, there are things that have no worth in themselves, which are to be considered solely as means (forms of worship, positive regulations and precepts); these are to be used as men see fit in their quest for happiness. Third, there are things (the vested interests of priestcraft, miracles, "enthusiasm") so indifferent that they cannot be considered as either means or ends, and if emphasis is placed on them in religious matters, the worst sort of superstition ensues—and superstition is the enemy of true religion.

Tindal does not consider the fact that many people are totally incapable of right reason, a point that was dutifully reported by many of his opponents. The philosophical argument of Bishop Butler repudiated rationalism as the chimerical building of the world upon hypothesis in the manner of René Descartes. The paradoxical and abusive Bishop Warburton was content to dismiss Tindal's apriorism as "the silliest, and most wretched Error, in an age of Paradoxes." Tindal is the last and most influential of the British deists who sought to keep the movement on a high intellectual level.

See also Butler, Joseph; Clarke, Samuel; Deism; Descartes, René; Locke, John; Patristic Philosophy; Pope, Alexander; Voltaire, François-Marie Arouet de.

Bibliography

There is no collected edition of the works of Tindal. Early documents and "lives" include *A Copy of the will of Dr. Matthew Tindal, with an account of what pass'd concerning the same, between Mrs. Lucy Price, Eustace Budgell esq.; and Mr. Nicholas Tindal* (London, 1733); *Memoirs Of The Life and Writings of Matthew Tindall, LL.D. With A History Of The Controversies Wherein he was Engaged* (London, 1733); and *The Religious, Rational and Moral Conduct of Matthew Tindal, LL.D., late fellow of All Souls', by a member of the same college* (London, 1733).

There are no full-scale modern treatments of Tindal, but the following works are of some importance: Alfred O. Aldridge, "Polygamy and Deism," *Journal of English and Germanic Philology* 48 (1949): 343–360; Rosalie L. Colie, "Spinoza and the Early English Deists," *Journal of the History of Ideas* 20 (1959): 23–46; Arthur Friedman, "Pope and Deism," in *Pope and His Contemporaries: Essays Presented to George Sherburn*, edited by James L. Clifford and Louis A. Landa (Oxford: Clarendon Press, 1949), pp. 89–95; Isabel Rivers, *Reason, Grace, and Sentiment: A Study of the Language of Religion and Ethics in England, 1660–1780*, 2 vols. (Cambridge, U.K.: Cambridge University Press, 1991–2000); Ernest Gordon Rupp, *Religion in England 1688–1791* (Oxford: Clarendon Press, 1986); Ernest Sirluck, "*Areopagetica* and a Forgotten Licensing Controversy," *Review of English Studies* 11 (1960): 260–274; Leslie Stephen, *History of English Thought in the Eighteenth Century*, 2 vols. (Bristol, U.K.: Thoemmes, 1991); Norman L. Torrey, *Voltaire and the English Deists* (New Haven, CT: Yale University Press, 1930), Ch. 5.

See also the general bibliography under the Deism entry.

Ernest Campbell Mossner (1967)
Bibliography updated by Philip Reed (2005)

TOLAND, JOHN

(1670–1722)

John Toland was an English deist, philosopher, diplomat, political controversialist, secular and biblical scholar, and linguist. Christened "Janus Junius" in the Roman Catholic Church, Toland later took the name of John. He was born near Londonderry, Ireland, possibly of partial French extraction. At the age of sixteen he ran away from school to become a Protestant Whig. In 1687 he turned up at Glasgow University and in 1690 was awarded an MA at Edinburgh University. For two years he studied at the University of Leiden under Friedrich Spanheim the younger, and in 1694 he settled at Oxford for some time to carry on research in the Bodleian Library. "The Character you bear in Oxford," he was informed by a correspondent, "is this; that you are a man of fine parts, great learning, and little religion."

The stream of books and pamphlets, mostly anonymous or pseudonymous, that followed has been estimated by various authorities to range from thirty to one hundred. His most famous work, *Christianity not Mysterious: Or, A Treatise Shewing That there is nothing in the Gospel Contrary to Reason, Nor above it: And that no Christian Doctrine can be properly call'd A Mystery*, appeared in 1696, when he was but twenty-five years old, elicited some fifty refutations and prosecution in both England and Ireland. In Ireland it was condemned by Parliament and ordered to be burned by the common hangman; an order was issued for the author's arrest. In England it was presented as a nuisance by the grand jury of Middlesex and roundly denounced in Parliament and in pulpit. In 1697, Toland replied to the Irish condemnation with the *Apology for Mr. Toland* and in 1702 to the English with *Vindicius Liberius: Or, Mr. Toland's Defence of himself.*

POLITICS

Toland's political publications are numerous. He was always the defender of toleration and the opponent of superstition and enthusiasm, a consistent Whig and a Commonwealth man. Outspoken and not very politic, he dedicated several of his tracts to the Whig deist Anthony Collins, who held similar convictions. Among Toland's more important political publications are the *Life of John Milton* (1698) and *Amyntor: Or, a Defence of Milton's Life* (1699), both of which have religious as well as political overtones. In 1701 the *Art of Governing by Parties* and *Anglia Libera: Or, the Limitation and Succession of the Crown of England explain'd and asserted* were published; the latter, supporting the Act of Settlement, was well received by Sophia, electress of Hanover. As a result Toland became secretary to the embassy to Hanover under Lord Macclesfield and presented a copy of the act and the book to Sophia. She was not, however, entirely pleased with his *Reasons for addressing his Majesty to invite into England their Highnesses, the Electress Dowager and the Electoral Prince of Hanover* (1702). Nevertheless, the electress was instrumental in introducing Toland to the court of Berlin and to her daughter Sophia Charlotte, wife of Frederick, the first king of Prussia. For the queen he composed *Letters to Serena* (1704) and *An Account of the Courts of Prussia and Hanover* (1705). At the invitation of the electress, Toland met Gottfried Wilhelm Leibniz and held numerous discussions with him in the presence of the queen. The two philosophers, though disagreeing on certain fundamentals, respected each other, kept up a correspondence for years, and to some extent were mutually influenced.

CAREER

Toland's chaotic career worsened throughout his life. He had early been under the political patronage of the third earl of Shaftesbury and later under that of Robert Harley, Lord Oxford. For the earl of Shaftesbury he had written political tracts, but Toland lost his friendship by publishing one of the earl's works, *An Inquiry concerning Virtue*, without authorization. For Harley he wrote political tracts and brought out an edition of James Harrington's *The Commonwealth of Oceana* with a biography but lost his friendship in 1714 with the *Art of Restoring* and *The Grand Mystery Laid Open*, wherein he implied distrust of his patron's loyalty to the Hanoverian succession. Of necessity, he became a Grub Streeter and lost everything in the South Sea Bubble of 1720. As a result he either wrote or revised someone else's text of *The Secret History of the South-Sea Scheme.* The following year his health went into a rapid decline, abetted by the inept treatment of a physician, which inspired the indomitable Toland, ill as he was, to write a tract titled *Physic without Physicians* ("They learn their Art at the hazard of our lives, and make experiments by our deaths"). In 1722 he died in extreme poverty.

CHRISTIANITY NOT MYSTERIOUS

Like David Hume in "Of Miracles" (1748), Toland found an appropriate quotation for his title page from Archbishop Tillotson: "We need not desire a better Evidence that any Man is in the wrong, than to hear him declare against Reason, and thereby acknowledge that Reason is against him." The first edition appeared anonymously, but the second edition of the same year (1696) bore Toland's name.

Always professing some form of theism here and in subsequent writings, Toland, in his work, has affinities with the rationalistic religious common notions of Lord Herbert of Cherbury and with the empiricism and commonsense approach of John Locke in *An Essay concerning Human Understanding* (1690) and *Reasonableness of Christianity* (1695). He remained, however, fundamentally a rationalist in the line of Giordano Bruno, René Descartes, Benedict de Spinoza, and Leibniz.

Drawing freely upon Lord Herbert, the Cambridge Platonists, and Locke, though without naming names, Toland set out to prove that no Christian doctrine is mysterious—that is, above reason: "Could that Person justly value himself upon his being wiser than his Neighbors, who having infallible Assurance that something call'd a Blictri had a Being in Nature, in the mean time knew not what this Blictri was?" Faith and revelation involve both knowledge and assent, but revelation must rely upon the evidence of faith. In the Gospels, Toland correctly points out, "mystery" does not designate what cannot be known by man but, rather, what is revealed only to the chosen few. Faith, the hallmark of Puritanism, is consequently of no avail without the confirmation of reason.

Like many of the deists Toland argued that priestcraft introduced mysteries and then fostered them by ceremonies and discipline. Unlike Bishop Warburton, that eighteenth-century colossus of controversy who is alleged to have said, "Orthodoxy is my doxy; heterodoxy, another man's doxy," Toland ends *Christianity not Mysterious* with "I acknowledge no Orthodoxy but the Truth."

It was widely believed that Toland was a disciple of Locke, and he had been described to Locke by William Molyneux in 1697 as "a candid Free-Thinker, and a good Scholar." However, when *Christianity not Mysterious* aroused such a stir, Locke, who seems hardly to have realized the logical consequences of his own Arminianism (witness his prolonged controversy with Bishop Stillingfleet), repudiated any approval of his so-called disciple.

BIBLICAL CRITICISM

Oddly enough, Toland's biblical criticism first appears in the seemingly innocuous *Life of John Milton,* wherein, suggesting that the *Eikon Basilike* was not written by Charles I but was a priestly forgery, he proceeds to remark that many supposititious pieces under the name of Christ and his apostles had been accepted in the period of primitive Christianity. Divines rushed in where scholars feared to tread, charging Toland with attacking the authenticity of the Gospels. Toland speedily responded with *Amyntor,* which contains a catalog of apocryphal pieces twenty-two pages in length and is one of the earliest examinations of scriptural canon by an Englishman. Though in no sense definitive, Toland's catalog forced the issues of the canon and of early church history upon the scholars. Christ did not, he declares, institute one religion for the learned and another for the vulgar.

Toland's exploration of early Jewish religion and of the Druids' religion—he was an adept in the Celtic language—led him to the conviction that the simplicity of reason has been corrupted by the machinations of priestcraft. *Letters to Serena* explores somewhat unsystematically the beginnings of religion, examining the origin and force of prejudices, the history of the immortality of the soul among the heathens, the origin of idolatry, and motivations of heathenism. These and other explorations embryonically anticipate Hume in the *Natural History of Religion* (1757) and the *Dialogues concerning Natural Religion* (1779).

Toland argued that belief, prejudice, and superstition are ingrown from infancy. "You may reason yourself into what religion you please; but, pray, what religion will permit you to reason yourself out of it?"

He found a perfect example of surviving simple intuitive religion in a French letter written in 1688 from Carolina: "We know our Saviour's precepts without observing them, and they [the Indians] observe them without knowing him." As Toland put it elsewhere, "Those who live according to Reason … are Christians, tho' they be reputed Atheists." In "Hodegus," an essay of 1720, he interprets Old Testament miracles by a naturalistic method, thereby anticipating Hermann Samuel Reimarus and the German rationalistic school of biblical exegesis.

PHILOSOPHICAL DEVELOPMENT

Toland's rationalism led him to translate and to defend Bruno's Latin treatise of 1514 on the infinite universe and innumerable worlds. In turn, he proceeded into a variety of naturalistic monism, which eventuated in pantheism. In the *Letters to Serena* he attacked Spinoza for his disavowal of the necessity of motion to matter, but in later works he had lavish praise for much of Spinozism. *Socinianism truly stated: being an example of fairdealing in theological Controversy,* a work of 1705 in which is found the first use of the word *pantheist,* is essentially pantheistic.

Toland's final statement, however, if it is to be taken seriously, was published in 1720 in Holland; termed "Cosmopoli," it was issued under the pseudonym Janus Junius Edganesius (indicating Inis-Eogan or Eogani Insuli, the northernmost peninsula of Ireland and the place of Toland's birth). *Pantheisticon: sive Formula celebrandae Sodalitatis,* the work referred to and translated into English in 1751, has been variously interpreted as a serious exposition of the philosophy of pantheism, a literary hoax, a sort of litany in derision of Christian liturgies, a mask to disguise atheism, a modernized version of the secret doctrines of Freemasonry, and a device to stimulate new thinking. The work consists of a dialogue between the president of a pantheistical society which acknowledges no other God than the universe and its members, who respond to his endeavors to inspire them with the love of truth, liberty, and health, cheerfulness, sobriety, temperateness, and freedom from superstition.

It is sufficiently evident that Toland was not a really original thinker but one who reflected many influences. Born Roman Catholic, he became Protestant. He was a latitudinarian, a freethinker, a deist, a materialist, and a pantheist. In a Latin epitaph that he composed for himself, he laid claim to the knowledge often languages. He was a prolific writer on many subjects, sometimes confused and contradictory, sometimes foreshadowing aspects of modern thought. In his life of fifty-two years his restless, inquiring mind was ever active, his accomplishments were manifold, and he was an internationalist of consequence in the Age of Enlightenment.

See also Bruno, Giordano; Cambridge Platonists; Collins, Anthony; Deism; Descartes, René; Enlightenment; Herbert of Cherbury; Hume, David; Leibniz, Gottfried Wilhelm; Locke, John; Materialism; Milton, John; Pantheism; Rationalism; Reimarus, Hermann Samuel; Shaftesbury, Third Earl of (Anthony Ashley Cooper); Spinoza, Benedict (Baruch) de; Stillingfleet, Edward; Toleration.

Bibliography

ADDITIONAL WORKS BY TOLAND

Other works of Toland not named above but worth mentioning include *Adeisidaemon, sive Titus Livius a Superstitione Vindicatus* (The Hague: Thomam Johnson, 1709); *Nazarenus, or Jewish, Gentile, and Mahometan Christianity* (London: J. Brown, 1718); *Tetradymus,* containing "Hodegus," "Clidophorus," "Hypatia," and "Mangoneutes" (London, 1720); and *The Miscellaneous Works of Mr. John Toland, Now first published from his Original Manuscripts,* with a life by Pierre Des Maizeaux, ed., 2 vols. (London, 1747), a reprint, with some additions, of *A Collection of Several Pieces by Mr. John Toland,* 2 vols. (London, 1726).

WORKS ON TOLAND

Champion, Justin. *Republican Learning: John Toland and the Crisis of Christian Culture, 1696–1722.* Manchester, U.K.: Manchester University Press, 2003.

Cragg, G. R. *From Puritanism to the Age of Reason.* Cambridge, U.K.: Cambridge University Press, 1950. Ch. 7.

Daniel, Stephen H. *John Toland: His Method, Manners, and Mind.* Kingston, ON: McGill-Queen's University Press, 1984.

Dyche, Eugene I. "The Life and Works and Philosophical Relations of John (Janus Junius) Toland, 1670–1722." *Abstracts of Dissertations, the University of Southern California,* 64–69. Los Angeles, 1944.

El Nouty, Hassam. "Le Panthéisme dans les lettres françaises au XVIIe siècle: Apercus sur la fortune du mot et de la notion." *Revue des sciences humaines* 97 (1960): 435–457.

Heinemann, F. H. "John Toland and the Age of Enlightenment." *Review of English Studies* 20 (1944): 125–146.

Heinemann, F. H. "John Toland and the Age of Reason." *Archiv für Philosophie* 4 (1950): 35–66.

Heinemann, F. H. "John Toland, France, Holland, and Dr. Williams." *Review of English Studies* 25 (1949): 346–349.

Heinemann, F. H. "Prolegomena to a Toland Bibliography." *Notes and Queries* 185 (1943): 182–186.

Heinemann, F. H. "Toland and Leibniz." *Philosophical Review* 54 (1945): 437–457.

An Historical Account of the Life and Writings of the late eminently famous Mr. John Toland. London, 1722. "By one of his Intimate Friends."

Jacob, Margaret C. *The Radical Enlightenment.* London: Allen and Unwin, 1981.

Lange, Friedrich A. *History of Materialism.* New York: Humanities Press, 1950.

Lantoine, Albert. *Un précurseur de la franc-maçonnerie, J. Toland.* Paris, 1927.

McGuinness, Philip, Alan Harrison, and Richard Kearney, eds. *John Toland's Christianity not Mysterious.* Dublin: Lilliput Press, 1997.

Nourrison, Jean Felix. *Philosophies de la nature. Bacon-Bayle-Toland-Buffon.* Paris, 1887.

Simms, J. G. "John Toland (1670–1722), a Donegal Heretic." *Irish Historical Studies* 16 (1969): 304–320.

Sullivan, Robert E. *John Toland and the Deist Controversy.* Cambridge, MA: Harvard University Press, 1982.

See also the general bibliography under Deism.

Ernest Campbell Mossner (1967)
Bibliography updated by Philip Reed (2005)

TOLERATION

"Toleration" is a policy of patient forbearance in the presence of something that is disliked or disapproved of. Toleration must thus be distinguished from freedom or liberty precisely because it implies the existence of something believed to be disagreeable or evil. When freedom or liberty is said to prevail, no criticism, moral or otherwise, is entailed of the people who are said to be free or of the use to which such people put their freedom. Indeed, there are some writers who would reserve the words *liberty* and *freedom* for the rightful exercise of human choice, thinking, with the poet John Milton, that "only the good man can be free." Toleration, on the other hand, has an element of condemnation built into its meaning. We do not tolerate what we enjoy or what is generally liked or approved of. We speak of freedom of speech, of worship, and of movement—speech, worship, and movement being good or ethically neutral things. But when we speak of toleration, we speak of the toleration of heretics, dissenters, or atheists, all of whom were once thought to be wrongdoers, or we speak of the toleration of prostitution, gambling, or the drug traffic, all of which are still generally regarded as evils. To tolerate is first to condemn and then to put up with or, more simply, to put up with is itself to condemn.

T. S. Eliot once surprised his readers by saying, "The Christian does not wish to be tolerated." He did not mean, as some supposed, that the Christian yearned for martyrdom. He meant that the Christian did not wish to be put up with. The Christian wanted something better—to be respected, honored, loved. And what Eliot said in the name of Christians would doubtless also be said by Jews, Muslims, Mormons, African Americans, or any other minority group that finds itself tolerated by a larger society. Toleration is always *mere* toleration. It is less than equality just as it is distinct from liberty, and it is sharply at variance with fraternity. For these reasons toleration is far from an ideal policy; it is contaminated, so to speak, by that very implication of evil which its meaning contains.

Toleration must also be distinguished from indifference. A man who has no feelings about something is indifferent to it, not tolerant, for if he has no feelings, he cannot be said to dislike or disapprove of it. He cannot claim to put up with what troubles him in no way. It has sometimes been said by critics of religious toleration that such toleration is evidence of indifference to religion and that indifference to religion is bad. Here one must distinguish a logical connection from a historical one. It may well be a historical fact that the growth of religious toleration as a government policy in France and England during the eighteenth century was due to a diminution of religious fervor, to an increase in worldliness, and in a word, to indifference. Even so, however, the toleration must be distinguished from the indifference, for the words have significantly different meanings. There have been many men, like Thomas Hobbes, who were personally indifferent to religion but opposed to religious toleration, and many, like John Locke, who had strong religious beliefs but who favored religious toleration.

ALTERNATIVES TO TOLERATION

The alternative to toleration is often said to be persecution. This is a misleading dichotomy. Persecution is by definition always wrong. Moral condemnation is part of the meaning of the word. Yet who is to say that the alternative to toleration is always a wrong policy? Is the suppression of the drug traffic, for example, wrong? Is it persecution? It would be perverse to say that everything that is not tolerated is persecuted. Persecution is one alternative to toleration. However, there is another alternative which must be expressed in more neutral language, though, of course, it is one of the central difficulties of all social theory that neutral language is not always at one's disposal. Almost all the words we use in discussing social and political problems have a normative element in them. We might be wise, for lack of a better term, to rely on the word *suppression* as the alternative to *toleration.* To ask whether the persecution of religious dissenters was justifiable in thirteenth-century Europe is to prejudice the issue from the outset by speaking of persecution. But one might have an impartial discussion about whether the suppression of religious dissent was justifiable at that time and place, for even those who practiced it would agree to calling it suppression.

Many writers have opposed policies of toleration, but few have ventured to defend intolerance. This is clearly because intolerance in private life is considered a moral defect or weakness, a defect allied to arrogance, narrow-mindedness, and impatience. Hence, intolerance has an unpleasant ring. James Fitzjames Stephen frankly advocated intolerance in opposition to John Stuart Mill's policy of toleration, but though Stephen's arguments were of a kind more likely to appeal to the majority, his success with the public was conspicuously less than Mill's; manifestly, Stephen had made an infelicitous choice of language. Most supporters of what Stephen called intolerance have preferred to speak of order, discipline, authority, or control in putting forward a case for suppression against one of toleration.

PAGAN AND CHRISTIAN ATTITUDES

The central problem of toleration in Western history was for centuries the problem of religious toleration. This is one of the consequences the West has faced because its religion is Christianity. Polytheistic religions are by nature more tolerant. The Greeks, for example, were conservative in the matter of religious ceremonies and institutions, but they admitted a great variety of theological beliefs. Where there were many gods, there could be many dogmas. And although Socrates and the Pythagoreans were persecuted, it was not on religious grounds but because they were accused of threatening the morality and political security of the community. The Romans were less steady in their policy, alternating between policies of general permissiveness and repression of particular sects—notably, but not exclusively, the Christians. Roman toleration was limited by at least one specifically religious notion, namely, the belief that the traditional deities would punish a whole people for the offense of those who failed to worship them.

The early Fathers of the Christian church, having themselves been cruelly persecuted by the Romans, were in favor of religious toleration as a principle. But as soon as Constantine made Christianity a state religion, the pagans, who had once been the persecutors, became the persecuted. Nevertheless, it may be recorded that the Christian repression of paganism never went to the cruel lengths to which Roman repression had gone. St. Augustine, an early advocate of suppressing heretics, went out of his way to say that the death penalty for heresy was wrong. The comparatively few pagans who were put to death by the Christian emperors were usually executed on charges of sorcery rather than of worshiping false gods.

This policy of moderate repression continued throughout the early Middle Ages. In the late Middle Ages, the Renaissance, the Reformation, and the Counter Reformation, toleration was virtually repudiated on principle by European Christians. The few Christians who continued to favor religious toleration are conspicuous for that very reason. They include the Anabaptists in Germany, the Arminians in Holland, Huldrych Zwingli in Switzerland, Sebastian Castellio in France, Socinus in Poland. But the main Protestant churches, whether Lutheran, Calvinist, or Anglican, were not conspicuously more tolerant than the Catholic Church. The Catholic Church's chief instrument of religious discipline was the Inquisition, which freely employed torture as well as the death penalty in its endeavors to recover erring souls for God.

Christian arguments in defense of repression are several. Some writers repeat the old pagan argument that God is offended by heretical practices and is likely to inflict disasters on the whole community as a punishment. Other writers stress the point that heresy is a crime, a form of revolt against lawful authority, a culpable betrayal of promises made (even if only by proxy) at baptism. Crime, it is argued, cannot be tolerated. A more sophisticated argument maintains that the authority of the church is as essential to the continued existence of civil society as is that of the state; hence, those men who defy the church are akin to those who repudiate their duty to the king. Thus, members of such religious sects as the Cathari, Waldenses, and Albigenses are regarded by certain Catholic theorists as seditious rebels who have put themselves in a state of war with the sovereign power. The true religion seals men together in the safety of the commonwealth; dissent and heresy are therefore likely to open the way to anarchy. Furthermore, it is held by all these Christian writers that to tolerate heresy is to do no service to the man concerned, for to leave him alone in his error is to leave him in a state of sin, faced with the prospect of eternal damnation in the life to come. It is thus thought to be no real cruelty to inflict painful penalties, even death itself, on an erring man if by so doing one is sparing him the far greater torments of hell.

PHILOSOPHICAL ARGUMENTS FOR TOLERATION

The philosopher who is best known for having addressed himself to the Christian arguments for suppression was the Englishman John Locke. In the seventeenth century Christians were generally beginning to lose confidence in the old policy of repression, although it was still being practiced. The unity of Christendom was plainly ended and not likely to be recovered. Protestantism in its various forms had come to be almost as great a power in the world as Catholicism. The old notion of one true faith against heresy had lost its meaning. Besides, although Protestantism in its leading forms did not preach toleration, it preached a gospel that led inexorably to the demand for toleration; the Protestant doctrine that every man must be a priest unto himself gave the dissenter just as good grounds as the orthodox believer for claiming that his faith was true. Confidence in the utility—and justice—of suppressing unorthodox opinions was shaken by such writers as Pierre Bayle (1647–1706), who in his *Pensées sur la comète* (1682), argued that morality is independent of religion.

Locke's plea for toleration, set forth in his *Epistola de Tolerantia,* published in 1688, was not the first such plea, but it was the earliest systematic argument in its favor. Locke's first point is that repression is not an effective policy. Force can be used to make a man go through the motions of a given form of Christian worship, but force cannot make a man entertain any faith or belief in the privacy of his soul. What force can do is make a man pretend to be an orthodox believer. And such a policy, says Locke, is not only useless but also morally harmful since it is bound to breed hypocrisy. Locke thus totally rejects the Catholic argument that force—let alone torture and death—can bring any man to salvation.

Second, Locke rejects the traditional argument that a man's obligation to the church is equal to his obligation to the state and that civil society will lapse into anarchy if religious dissent is tolerated. Locke describes the church as a "voluntary society" which has a mission in the world quite independent of the functions of the state. The church exists to save men's souls, and it can fulfill this mission only by persuasion, by essentially nonviolent means. The state, on the other hand, exists to protect men's rights—their lives, liberties, and estates—so that the use of force as an ultimate sanction is a necessary part of the state's function. The state has no concern with the salvation of men's souls, just as the church has no concern with the use of force. Nor has the state any knowledge of what the true religion is. The Persian ruler believes it is Islam; the Spanish ruler believes it is Catholicism; the English king believes it is Anglicanism. They cannot all be right. Therefore, that a religion is established is no evidence that it is the true religion. Each man has his own faith, and every person's conscience is entitled to the same respect.

Locke's theory of toleration was intimately connected with his theory of freedom. Since he held that one of the most fundamental reasons for the existence of the state was the preservation of man's natural right to liberty, he argued that the government was entitled to use force against an individual only when it was necessary to protect the rights of others. Certain things, Locke agreed, could not be tolerated: (1) the propagation of "opinions contrary to human society, or to those moral rules which are necessary to the preservation of civil society"; (2) any claim "to special prerogative opposite to the civil right of the community"; (3) the activity of "persons who are ready on any occasion to seize the government, and possess themselves of the estates and fortunes of their fellow subjects"; (4) transferring allegiance to a foreign prince; and (5) denying the existence of God.

Locke's reason for withholding toleration from atheists was the rather quaint one that a man who did not believe in God could not take a valid oath and that oaths and covenants were "the bonds of human society." Locke was unwilling to extend toleration to Roman Catholics, not on religious grounds but because he held, with some reason, that Roman Catholics were not loyal subjects of the English crown, since they owed their first allegiance to a foreign prince, the pope.

Locke's argument for toleration, which seemed distinctly avant-garde when it was first published, eventually came to be regarded as common sense. Indeed, even Catholic teaching on the subject of toleration moved toward Locke's position. Later Catholic apologists distinguished between (1) theological dogmatic toleration, (2) practical civil toleration, and (3) public political toleration. The first, theological dogmatic toleration, was resisted as firmly as ever. The teaching of the Catholic Church was held to be the absolute and certain truth; thus, to tolerate any opinion at variance with it would be to tolerate falsehood, and the clear duty of the rational mind to uphold truth and deny falsehood imposed an equally categorical duty to deny any religious or moral teaching at variance with the teaching of Rome, which is infallible. However, what is called practical civil toleration was gradually accepted by Catholics. First, it was said to be the Christian's duty to distinguish between the error and the man who erred. Error was always to be opposed, but the man who erred was to be regarded, in full Christian charity, as a fellow man and, therefore, not to be persecuted. On public political toleration, later Catholic theory was somewhat ambiguous. This was because of the need to claim for Catholic minorities in Protestant states the utmost possible toleration without equally committing Catholic governments to tolerating Protestant minorities. Thus, the principle of public political toleration was admitted to vary between its application in a secular state and in a "truly Christian state."

The outstanding exponent of the case for greater toleration in the nineteenth century was John Stuart Mill. In many ways his argument followed the lines laid down by Locke, but Mill put fewer limitations on toleration than did Locke. He was more insistent that the only justification for interfering with any man's liberty was a reasonable assurance that some danger or threat to the liberty of another was involved. Again, where Locke was exclusively concerned with the protection of individual liberty from the interference of state and church, Mill was increasingly concerned with the limitations on human freedom that stemmed from unwritten law—the pressure of convention and public opinion. Mill wanted to see toleration extended from the realm of politics to that of morals and manners, to all self-regarding actions, as he called them. Mill, as a Victorian, lived, of course, in a society that not only frowned on things like free love, adultery, and Sabbath-breaking but also vigorously applied the social sanction of ostracism to any who committed these sins. Mill felt that people were more oppressed and hemmed in by the unwritten laws than they were by laws enforced by the state and that human freedom and variety could not flourish in a repressive atmosphere. Mill demanded toleration because he held that liberty, individuality, and variety were of the highest ethical value; they were what made man "nobler to contemplate."

Mill's ablest critic, James Fitzjames Stephen (in his book *Liberty, Equality, Fraternity,* written in reply to Mill's essay *On Liberty*), argued that intolerance was a necessary preservative of society. The modern liberal state was possible precisely because society was able to discipline itself through unwritten laws. It was a good thing for men to be compelled by social intolerance to keep laws of conduct that the wisdom of the ages had shown to be good. Mill's claim that there was a class of self-regarding actions that had a right to be tolerated because they did not affect others was, in Stephen's view, unfounded; almost everything a man did affected someone else. Suicide, intemperance, debauchery, and so forth were not things that injured the agent alone. The class of self-regarding actions was virtually an empty one. And since almost all conduct was other-regarding, society had a right to interfere as widely as it did. Stephen argued that the general run of men did not have the wit to think out moral codes of their own or the strength of character to obey such codes if they established them. Hence, some form of external sanction was needed if morality was to be upheld. Stephen also rejected Mill's view that variety was a good thing in itself. Goodness, he agreed, was varied, but that did not mean that variety itself was good; a nation in which half the population was criminal would be more diversified than a wholly honest one, but it would not be a better nation. Dissent for its own sake Stephen condemned as frivolous and sentimental Bohemianism. Eccentricity was a mark of weakness rather than of strength; and constraint, far from being an evil, was a great stimulus to exertion. Stephen even held that the intolerance that went with the Puritan spirit had been one of the chief factors enabling England to surge ahead of other nations in making industrial and social progress.

POLITICAL TOLERATION

With the rise of totalitarian governments in the twentieth century, the problem of toleration took on a new aspect. For democratic and freedom-loving governments the toleration of intolerance became an acute problem. In 1936 the British government introduced a ban on political uniforms because of the disturbances caused by Oswald Mosley's fascist movement and its black-shirted adherents; an attempt was made under Harold Wilson's Labour government in 1965 to proscribe acts of racial discrimination. After World War II the United States was troubled by the difficulty of deciding how much toleration could be safely extended to communists when several communists proved to be Russian or Cuban agents and when all communists seemed to have a more pronounced loyalty to the Soviet Union than to the United States. The position of the communists in twentieth-century America was thought to resemble that of the Catholics in seventeenth-century England, and many Americans recalled Locke's view that such persons had forfeited their right to toleration. Other Americans argued that repression was futile; the interdiction of open communist organizations would do little to protect the state from secret and more sinister communist activities. Hence, an abridgment of political toleration would do no good to anyone, for it would simply create martyrs without eliminating spies. Thus, the argument both for and against political toleration in the twentieth century cannot be said to have differed greatly from the debate concerning religious toleration that exercised the minds of earlier generations.

See also Augustine, St.; Bayle, Pierre; Eliot, Thomas Stearns; Freedom; Hobbes, Thomas; Liberty; Locke, John; Mill, John Stuart; Milton, John; Socinianism.

Bibliography

Bonet-Maury, G. *Histoire de la liberté de conscience en France.* Paris: Alcan, 1909.

Budziszewski, J. *True Tolerance: Liberalism and the Necessity of Judgment.* New Brunswick, NJ: Transaction, 1992.

Creighton, M. *Persecution and Tolerance.* London: Longmans Green, 1895.
Devlin, P. A. *The Enforcement of Morals.* London: Oxford University Press, 1965.
Hart, H. L. A. *Law, Liberty and Morality.* London: Oxford University Press, 1963.
Horton, John, and Peter P. Nicholson, eds. *Toleration: Philosophy and Practice.* Aldershot, U.K.: Avebury, 1992.
Jordan, W. K. *The Development of Religious Toleration in England.* London: Allen and Unwin, 1932–1940.
Kamen, Henry Arthur Francis. *The Rise of Toleration.* London: Weidenfeld and Nicolson, 1967.
Kilcullen, John. *Sincerity and Truth: Essays on Arnauld, Bayle, and Toleration.* Oxford: Oxford University Press, 1988.
King, Preston. *Toleration.* London: Allen and Unwin, 1976.
Lecky, W. E. *History of the Rise of Rationalism in Europe.* London: Longmans, 1877.
Lecler, J. *Histoire de la tolérance au siècle de la Réforme.* Paris, 1955.
Locke, John. *Epistola de Tolerantia.* Gouda, 1688.
Luzzatti, L. *La libertà di conscienza.* Milan, 1909.
Mendus, Susan, ed. *Justifying Toleration. Conceptual and Historical Perspectives.* Cambridge, U.K.: Cambridge University Press, 1988.
Mendus, Susan. *Toleration and the Limits of Liberalism.* Atlantic Highlands, NJ: Humanities Press, 1989.
Mendus, Susan, and David Edwards, eds. *On Toleration.* Oxford: Clarendon Press, 1987.
Mill, John Stuart. *On Liberty.* London, 1859.
Newey, Glen. *Virtue, Reason, and Toleration: The Place of Toleration in Ethical and Political Philosophy.* Edinburgh: Edinburgh University Press, 1999.
Rawls, John. *Political Liberalism.* New York: Columbia University Press, 1993.
Ruffini, F. *La libertà religiosa.* Florence, 1901.
Seaton, A. A. *The Theory of Toleration under the Later Stuarts.* Oxford, 1911.
Stephen, J. F. *Liberty, Equality, Fraternity.* London, 1861.
Tinder, Glenn E. *Tolerance and Community.* Columbia: University of Missouri Press, 1995.
Voltaire, F.-M. de. *Traité sur la tolérance.* Paris, 1763.
Wolff, Robert Paul, Herbert Marcuse, and Barrington Moore Jr. *A Critique of Pure Tolerance.* London: Jonathan Cape, 1969.

Maurice Cranston (1967)
Bibliography updated by Philip Reed (2005)

TOLETUS, FRANCIS
(1532–1596)

Francis Toletus, the first important Jesuit philosopher, was born in Córdoba, Spain. He studied philosophy at the University of Valencia and theology at the University of Salamanca under Dominic de Soto. While a professor of philosophy at Salamanca, Toletus entered the Jesuit order (1558). He taught philosophy at the order's Roman College from 1559 to 1563 and theology from 1563 to 1569. In 1593 Toletus became the first Jesuit cardinal. He died in Rome.

Toletus's Latin philosophical works include commentaries on the logic, physics, and psychology of Aristotle; Toletus's commentary on Thomas Aquinas's *Summa* (*Enarratio in Summam Theologiae Divi Thomae*) also contains philosophical material. In all these works his views are Thomistic with many personal modifications. In the theory of knowledge, Toletus taught that individual things are directly apprehended by the intellect, that the primary object of knowledge is a sort of particularized form (*species specialissima*) and not being in general (*Physica,* Venice, 1600, p. 12), that intellectual abstraction is simply a precision from accidents and a consideration of the substance of anything (*De Anima,* Venice, 1575, p. 170), that the agent intellect may be fundamentally the same power as the possible intellect (*De Anima,* Venice, 1586, pp. 144–146). His metaphysics is distinguished by a theory of triple acts in the same being: formal, entitative, and existential (*Physica,* p. 33). The existential act is limited in two ways: by the receptive potency and by its efficient cause (*Enarratio,* Vol. I, p. 118). He denied that essence and existence are really distinct principles (*Physica,* p. 34; *Enarratio,* Vol. I, p. 79), and that matter is pure potency; it has its own actuality (*Physica,* pp. 32–36), but form is the principle of individuation (*De Anima,* p. 163). The number of the categories (ten) in Aristotle's logic is merely probable. It is possible rationally to demonstrate the existence of God but the famous "five ways" of Thomas are incomplete; they do not establish the key attributes of God (*Enarratio,* Vol. I, 69).

See also Aristotle; Epistemology; Epistemology, History of; Soto, Dominic de; Thomas Aquinas, St.; Thomism.

Bibliography

The Latin philosophical works are collected in *Omnia quae Hucusque Extant Opera* (Lyons, 1586). See also *Enarratio in Summam Theologiae Divi Thomae.* 4 vols. (Rome, 1869–1870).
Works on Toletus include L. Morati, "Toledo, Francisco de," *Enciclopedia filosofica* (Venice and Rome, 1957), Vol. IV, cols. 1216–1217 (an excellent entry to which the present account is indebted); C. Giacon, *La seconda scolastica* (Milan: Fratelli Bocca, 1944), pp. 25–44, 51–65.

Vernon J. Bourke (1967)

TOLSTOY, LEV (LEO) NIKOLAEVICH

(1828–1910)

Lev (Leo) Nikolaevich Tolstoy, the renowned Russian novelist, won worldwide fame as a moralist and sage for his antiecclesiastical interpretation of Christianity and fervent preaching of nonviolence. A well-read amateur in philosophy from the age of fifteen, Tolstoy displayed serious philosophical interests in his greatest novel, *War and Peace* (1865–1869), and in 1874 he began an increasingly anguished philosophical and religious quest, seeking a reason for living. His spiritual crisis, dramatically described in *My Confession* (1879), was resolved by a return to the Christian faith of his youth, but in a radically different form based on his reading of selected New Testament texts. The new creed, further elaborated in such works as *What People Live By* (1881) and *What I Believe* (1883), was the foundation for the philosophical and hortatory works on morality, society, and culture that dominated his writing during the last three decades of his life.

PHILOSOPHY OF HISTORY

Tolstoy conceived *War and Peace* as a grand historical narrative embodying conclusions he had reached, partly under the influence of Schopenhauer, concerning causality in history and especially the interplay of freedom, chance, and necessity; the novel's two epilogues address these themes explicitly. It is in the nature of human consciousness, Tolstoy argued, to conceive of oneself and others as free agents whose actions may have a significant impact on the world—in the case of so-called great figures like Napoleon, a determining impact. Yet no individual is more than one node in a vast and unpredictable web of interacting forces, conscious and unconscious, contingent and necessary. Hence individuals cannot with any assurance foresee the effects of their own or others' actions (a point to which Tolstoy returned in his case against violence), and great men do not make history. He delights in describing, for example, how the tide of a decisive battle can be turned by the behavior of a single rank-and-file soldier—although this example undercuts his own arguments against attributing a determining influence to any one person. Tolstoy's philosophy of history is analyzed insightfully in Isaiah Berlin's classic study, *The Hedgehog and the Fox* (1957).

METAPHYSICS AND EPISTEMOLOGY

In *My Confession* Tolstoy expressed his disillusionment with all attempts by human reason, whether philosophical or scientific, to explain how life can have meaning when it inevitably ends in death. Meaning, he decided, can be imparted to a finite life only by linking it with an eternal, infinite reality—by which he meant the spiritual reality of the Christian God—and such union with an infinite deity is achievable only through an act of faith. Though itself "unreasonable," the primitive act of faith answers the ultimate question posed by reason without disqualifying reason from serving as the standard of truth on other questions. Tolstoy accordingly sought to develop something he had dreamed of as early as 1855: a rational religion, one stripped of everything unreasonable, including miracles, sacraments, mysticism, clergy, rituals, special buildings, and dietary rules. Tolstoy's standard of reasonableness proved to be highly fluid and subjective, however. In a Rousseauian spirit he rejected much of modern science and technology as products of false reason, and the mysticism he condemns in some contexts appears to be embraced in others.

Tolstoy's metaphysical views are a form of Christian idealism based on a dualism of matter and spirit. Reality is bifurcated into an infinite, eternal divine world and a finite, temporal material world, with human beings mirroring this division in their possession of a body and a soul. The universal divine reality is manifested in the human soul in the form of love, so that only when people are vehicles of universal love are they living a "true" life, "a life divine and free" (Edie 1976, p. 218). In several respects, however, Tolstoy departed from the commonly accepted Christian versions of this picture, prompting the Russian Orthodox church to excommunicate him in 1901. He opposed Trinitarianism and denied the special divinity of the man Jesus, contending that he was no different in nature from any other son of God. Further, despite frequent references to God as a "Father," Tolstoy did not subscribe to a personal conception of God. His conception, rather, as Richard F. Gustafson has argued in *Leo Tolstoy, Resident and Stranger* (1986), is panentheistic: God is both transcendent and immanent; He is "beyond the world of space and time but includes within Him all the world of space and time" (Gustafson 1986, p. 101). Tolstoy also rejects personal immortality in the sense of an individual life after death, holding rather that individuals attain immortality by merging with the infinite. Gustafson sees the influence of Eastern Christianity in Tolstoy's theology, whereas David Kvitko, in *A Philosophic Study of Tolstoy* (1927), argues that Tolstoy's metaphysical views in general were indebted more to Buddhism than to Christianity. Tolstoy's interest in and extensive knowledge of Chinese philosophy has been well documented by the sinologist Derk Bodde in *Tolstoy and China* (1950).

ETHICS

Tolstoy states that he found the true meaning of Christ's teaching in the Sermon on the Mount as reported in the gospel of Saint Matthew, the text that became the focal point of his thinking about personal and social morality. From the sermon he distilled a moral code consisting of five commandments: first, do not be angry; second, do not lust; third, do not take oaths; fourth, do not resist evil by force; and fifth, love all people, including your enemies. The first, fourth, and fifth commandments are expressions of what, to Tolstoy, was the unique Christian understanding of the universally recognized law of love (the Old Testament's injunction to love one's neighbor as oneself). All the great religions of antiquity, as he explained later in *The Law of Violence and the Law of Love* (1908), considered love a virtue, but only Christianity acknowledged it as a categorical demand, as "the supreme law of human life—i.e., in such a way as not to admit of exceptions in any case" (Edie 1976, p. 217). Christ, in other words, recognized the law as prohibiting *all* use of violence.

Tolstoy was called upon repeatedly to justify his absolutist interpretation of the law, and he did so consistently and with great vigor, not hesitating to condemn violence even when used in self-defense against a mad dog or against a savage who is preparing to slaughter one's children. To support his position he relies not simply on his religious faith but on two philosophical objections to violence that undeniably carry some weight, though perhaps not enough to justify his extreme stance. The first, echoing his skepticism about predictability in *War and Peace*, is that arguments for the use of violence to stop evil rest on the dubious assumption that we can reliably foresee and control the future. The second is that the use of force generates more force in return, making it counterproductive. As the acknowledged prophet of nonviolent resistance, Tolstoy found a devoted disciple in Mohandas Gandhi (with whom he corresponded) and a host of admirers among figures as diverse as Clarence Darrow and Ludwig Wittgenstein.

Tolstoy's second commandment—do not lust—although logically unrelated to the law of love, was advanced with equal maximalism. He treated it as not only a condemnation of extramarital relations but also as a call for celibacy even in marriage. In defending the ideal of universal celibacy he was unmoved by the argument (offered before the development of artificial insemination) that if his ideal were realized, it would mean the end of the human race. His response was, first, that humanly irresistible lapses would more than suffice for the continuation of the species; and second, that in any event, physical extinction would eliminate only the troublesome animal dimension of humanity and thus would be no great loss. Tolstoy's interest in the themes of sexuality and sexual misconduct (to which he himself confessed) gave him literary subjects—especially in later works such as *The Kreutzer Sonata* (1889) and *Resurrection* (1895–1899)—and some awareness of feminist issues.

SOCIAL AND POLITICAL THOUGHT

As the institution that claims a monopoly on the use of violence in society, the state was an obvious target for Tolstoy's moral indignation, and his antistate position ranks as one of the most sweeping in the annals of nonviolent anarchism. He opposed not only serving in the military or the police but also all activity that promotes or supports state force indirectly, such as paying taxes, serving on juries, and holding public office. Moreover, he condemned private ownership and other institutions that are sustained by the threat of state force. Tolstoy saw the gospel injunction against oath-taking (the third of his five commandments) as a recognition of the evils of acknowledging state authority; it confirmed his conviction that there was divine sanction for civil disobedience.

Although Tolstoy himself held a minor position as a justice of the peace in the early 1860s, his other civic activities after his army service (which ended in 1856) were outside any official sphere. In 1859 he founded a school for peasant children on his estate at Iasnaia Poliana and for the next few years devoted much attention to pedagogical theory and practice, producing essays (discussed in Charles Baudouin's *Tolstoi: The Teacher* [1923]) of interest to historians and theorists of education. During the famines of 1873 and 1891–1892, he worked tirelessly in the Russian countryside to organize relief efforts, publicly castigating the tsarist government for its incompetent handling of the crises. Later in the 1890s he provided moral and material support to the *Dukhobors* (literally, "spirit wrestlers"), a Russian sect that attempted to practice Christian anarchism on principles paralleling his own, and he spearheaded the successful drive to arrange for their mass relocation to Canada to escape tsarist persecution. Tolstoy's criticisms and civic initiatives angered the authorities, but he was protected from serious reprisals (other than excommunication) by the enormous popular respect he enjoyed.

AESTHETICS

The most professional and enduring of Tolstoy's philosophical writings, despite its eccentric conclusions, is his book *What Is Art?*, originally published serially in 1897–1898 in the leading Russian journal of philosophy. The work is valued for its systematic approach to aesthetic philosophy, beginning with a critical survey of earlier attempts to define art and ending with a clear and forceful presentation of an expressionist theory centering on the notion of the communication of emotion from artist to audience.

"Art begins," Tolstoy wrote, "when one person, with the object of joining another or others to himself in one and the same feeling, expresses that feeling by certain external indications." The aim is achieved when the feeling is successfully transmitted or, as Tolstoy puts it, when "the spectators or auditors are infected by the feeling which the author has felt." The feeling transmitted, he adds, may be "very strong or very weak, very important or very insignificant, very bad or very good"; any feeling will do as far as art per se is concerned (pp. 121–123). From a strictly aesthetic point of view, then, the worth of art depends simply on its emotional infectiousness, which Tolstoy traced to the individuality, clarity, and sincerity of the feeling conveyed.

Tolstoy is by no means satisfied with a merely aesthetic approach to art, however, and the center of gravity of his treatise soon shifts to the moral demands that art, like every other aspect of culture, must satisfy. Art, according to Tolstoy, must reflect the loftiest religious perception of its time, which means in the modern day that the artist is called upon to communicate feelings flowing from "a perception of our sonship to God and of the brotherhood of man" (p. 240). This does not imply, as some of Tolstoy's critics have charged, that art can be of value only if it transmits specifically religious emotions. Tolstoy indeed esteems religious art as the highest form, but he also strongly commends the whole range of what he calls "universal" art, or art that simply promotes "the loving union of man with man" by transmitting "even the most trifling and simple feelings if only they are accessible to all men without exception, and therefore unite them" (pp. 240–241). What even the most generous critic finds hard to accept, however, is that on Tolstoy's criteria (and by his own admission) simple folk songs are greater music than Beethoven symphonies, and *Uncle Tom's Cabin* is a greater novel than *War and Peace*.

See also Aesthetics, History of; Anarchism; Art, Expression in; Art, Value in; Life, Meaning and Value of; Mysticism, Nature and Assessment of; Schopenhauer, Arthur; Violence; Wittgenstein, Ludwig Josef Johann.

Bibliography

Baudouin, Charles. *Tolstoi: The Teacher*. Translated by Fred Rothwell. New York: Dutton, 1923.

Berlin, Isaiah. *The Hedgehog and the Fox: An Essay on Tolstoy's View of History*. New York: Mentor Books, 1957.

Bodde, Derk. *Tolstoy and China*. Princeton: Princeton University Press, 1950.

Edie, James M., James P. Scanlan, Mary-Barbara Zeldin, and George L. Kline, eds. *Russian Philosophy*. Vol. 2, *The Nihilists; the Populists, Critics of Religion and Culture*. Knoxville, TN: University of Tennessee Press, 1976.

Egan, David R., and Melinda A. Egan, eds. *Leo Tolstoy: An Annotated Bibliography of English-Language Sources to 1978*. Metuchen, NJ: Scarecrow Press, 1979.

Gustafson, Richard F. *Leo Tolstoy, Resident and Stranger: A Study in Fiction and Theology*. Princeton, NJ: Princeton University Press, 1986.

Hopper, Stanley R., ed. *Lift up Your Eyes: The Religious Writings of Leo Tolstoy*. New York: Julian Press, 1960.

Kvitko, David Iur'evich. *A Philosophic Study of Tolstoy*. New York: Author, 1927.

Orwin, Donna Tussing. *Tolstoy's Art and Thought, 1847–1880*. Princeton: Princeton University Press, 1993.

Silbajoris, Rimvydas. *Tolstoy's Aesthetics and His Art*. Columbus, OH: Slavica, 1991.

Tolstoy, Leo. *The Complete Works of Count Tolstoy*. 24 vols, edited and translated by Leo Wiener. Boston: Dana Estes, 1904.

Tolstoy, Leo. *The Kingdom of God Is Within You: Christianity Not as a Mystic Religion but as a New Theory of Life*. Translated by Constance Garnett. Lincoln, Nebraska: University of Nebraska Press, 1984.

Tolstoy, Leo. *My Confession, My Religion*. Midland, MI: Avensblume Press, 1993.

Tolstoy, Leo. *Polnoe sobranie sochinenii* [Complete collected works]. 90 vols. Moscow: Gos. izd. khudozhestvennoi literatury, 1928–1958.

Tolstoy, Leo. *War and Peace*. Translated by Constance Garnett. New York: Modern Library, n.d.

Tolstoy, Leo. *What Is Art?* Translated by Alymer Maude. London: Oxford University Press, n.d.

James P. Scanlan (2005)

TOTALITARIANISM

See *Fascisim*

TOUCH

Two bodies are said to be touching if there is no spatial gap between some point on the surface of one and some point on the surface of the other. If one of the touching bodies is that of a sentient being, it may be aware of certain properties of the other body: for instance, that it is hot or cold, rough or smooth, wet or dry, hard or soft, sweet or sour. The sentient being is said to be aware of an object's sweetness or sourness by taste. (Aristotle attributes our distinguishing taste from touch to the fact that only a part of our flesh is sensitive to flavor.) The remaining properties the sentient being is said, in common speech, to be aware of by touch. Accordingly, touch appears in the traditional list of senses, with sight, hearing, and so on.

ARISTOTLE

Aristotle remarks that in the case of touch the contraries hot-cold, dry-moist, and hard-soft do not seem to have a single subject in the way in which the single subject of the properties acute-grave and loud-soft is sound, which is perceived by hearing. This may lead one to say that there are really a number of different senses that are mistakenly referred to as one sense, touch, perhaps because the body of a sentient being must touch an object in order for it to be aware by any of them of that object's properties. Or one may say that there is a single subject of the different contraries, namely, a material thing, and that there is only one sense, touch, whereby we are aware of the different properties of which the material thing is a subject. If one takes the latter course, it may appear that touch is the only sense whose proper object is the material world.

LOCKE, BERKELEY, AND CONDILLAC

To John Locke, it seemed that "the idea most intimately connected with and essential to body, so as nowhere else to be found or imagined, but only in matter" was the idea of solidity. This idea is received by touch and "arises from the resistance which we find in body to the entrance of any other body into the place it possesses."

As Locke held it to be by touch that we receive the idea of solidity, the idea essential to body, so George Berkeley, in his *Essay towards a New Theory of Vision*, held it to be touch alone that directly acquaints us with the external world. He abandoned this view in *The Principles of Human Knowledge*, maintaining that the objects of touch are as much sensations as are the objects of sight.

Locke regarded solidity as a "simple idea": "If anyone asks me what this solidity is, I send him to his senses to inform him." Later philosophers have tried to explain what is involved in the sensation of solidity. Étienne Bonnot de Condillac distinguished it from the sensations of sound, color, and smell, since a person knows his own body by it. If a person presses his hand against his chest, his hand and chest "will be distinguished from one another by the sensation of solidities which they mutually give each other." Thus, involved in the notion of a sensation of solidity is the notion of the recognition as such of a feeling given to a part of the body. If organic sensations were not localized in the body, a person could never know his own or any other body by touching it, for "it is only with extension that we can construct extension, just as it is only with objects that we can construct objects."

H. H. PRICE

H. H. Price carried the analysis a step further. He divided touch "into three distinct types of sensation: contact sensation proper, muscular sensation, and the sensation of temperature." The perception of solidity involves both contact sensation proper and muscular sensation. The latter is "essentially a modification of the voluminous life-feeling [that] might also be described as our sense of embodiment." Muscular strain is felt at a place in the body and as having vectorial character, that is, originating from or tending toward a certain direction. A person experiences the solidity of something when the resistance he feels on pressing it "is actually felt as coming from within the closed boundary which contact-sensation reveals.… Thus the tactual conception of Matter is strictly speaking tactuo-muscular or contactuo-muscular."

LOCAL SIGN THEORY

The analyses of both Condillac and Price specify organic sensations as being localized. As Condillac expressed it, to know its body the child must "perceive its sensations, not as modifications of its soul, but as modifications of the organs which are their occasional causes." Condillac cannot explain "how the self which is only in the soul appears to be found in the body … it is enough that we observe this fact." The alternatives are either that a person is born with the capacity to locate organic sensations or that he acquires this capacity. Most philosophers hold the capacity to be acquired, although they differ widely in the accounts they give of how it is acquired; whether by the person's learning to interpret some feature of the sensation as a sign of its location (the so-called local sign) or in some other way.

MOVEMENT AND TOUCH

Perhaps the most important recent contribution to the problem of how touch mediates awareness of its objects was made by David Katz in "Der Aufbau der Tastwelt." Summarizing Katz's conclusions, Maurice Merleau-Ponty expresses the crux of the matter as being that "the movement of one's body is to touch what lighting is to vision.… When one of my hands touches the other, the hand that moves functions as subject and the other as object. There are tactile phenomena, alleged tactile qualities, like roughness and smoothness, which disappear completely if the exploratory movement is eliminated. Movement and time are not only an objective condition of knowing touch, but a phenomenal component of tactile data. They bring about the patterning of tactile phenomena, just as light shows up the configuration of a visible surface."

BODY-OBJECT RELATION

With the view that the objects of touch are physical objects may be contrasted the view that we are not aware of the object we touch but of a relation holding between our body and that object. It is a fact that how warm an object feels to an observer depends causally on the warmth of the part of the observer's body with which he is touching it. We notice the temperature of a hand that is colder or warmer than our own. Aristotle explains this in terms of his theory of sensation as the assimilation in form of the organ to the object. D. M. Armstrong mentions it, together with the fact that a person can say immediately with what portion of his body he is in contact with an object perceived by touch, in support of his theory that all immediate tactual perception involves perception of a relation holding between the observer's body and the object he is touching. As evidence for his theory, Armstrong holds that "hardness and softness as immediately perceived by touch, are obviously relative to the hardness or softness of our flesh." It is unclear from this evidence whether Armstrong is justified in claiming more than that how things feel to us depends on the condition of the part of the body with which we feel them.

See also Aristotle; Armstrong, David M.; Berkeley, George; Colors; Condillac, Étienne Bonnot de; Locke, John; Merleau-Ponty, Maurice; Sensa; Sound.

Bibliography

Aristotle. *De Anima.* Book II, Ch. 11.

Armstrong, D. M. *Bodily Sensations.* London and New York: Routledge and Paul, 1962. Chs. 3–5.

Berkeley, George. *An Essay towards a New Theory of Vision.* Dublin, 1709. Secs. 45–49.

Condillac, E. B. de. *Treatise on the Sensations.* Paris and London, 1754. Part II, Chs. 1–5.

Grice, H. P. "Some Remarks about the Senses." In *Analytic Philosophy.* 1st series. Oxford: Blackwell, 1962.

Katz, David. "Der Aufbau der Tastwelt." *Zeitschrift für Psychologie* 11 (1925).

Locke, John. *An Essay concerning Human Understanding.* London, 1690. Book II, Ch. 4.

Merleau-Ponty, Maurice. *Phenomenology of Perception,* 313–317. New York: Humanities Press, 1962.

O'Shaughnessy, B. "The Sense of Touch." *Australasian Journal of Philosophy* 67 (1989): 37–58.

Perkins, M. *Sensing the World.* Indianapolis: Hackett, 1983.

Price, H. H. "Touch and Organic Sensation." *PAS* 44 (1943–1944).

Urmson, J. O. "The Objects of the Five Senses." *Proceedings of the British Academy* 54 (1968): 117–131.

Vesey, G. N. A. *The Embodied Mind.* London: Allen and Unwin, 1965. Ch. 4. Contains an exposition and criticism of the local sign theory and references to other work on the subject.

Warnock, G. J. *Berkeley.* Harmondsworth, U.K., 1953. Ch. 3.

G. N. A. Vesey (1967)
Bibliography updated by Benjamin Fiedor (2005)

TOYNBEE, ARNOLD JOSEPH
(1889–1975)

Arnold Joseph Toynbee was in the twentieth century the foremost contemporary representative of what is sometimes termed "speculative philosophy of history." In some respects he occupied a position analogous to that of Henry Thomas Buckle in the nineteenth century. Like Buckle, he sought to discover laws determining the growth and evolution of civilization and to do so within the context of a wide comparative survey of different historical societies; like Buckle again, the results of his investigation became a storm center of controversy and criticism. To support his hypotheses, Toynbee, however, was able to draw on a vast fund of material of a kind unavailable to his Victorian predecessor, and the imposing examples and illustrations in which his work abounds make Buckle's much-vaunted erudition look strangely threadbare. As a consequence, Toynbee's historical theory is worked out in far greater detail; in fact, it represents a highly articulated and complex structure with many ramifications and appendages. Moreover, the materialist optimism underlying Buckle's linear conception of history as a continuous progressive development is wholly absent from Toynbee's analysis of the rise and decay of different cultures, while, in place of Buckle's positivistic rationalism, there runs through all Toynbee's work, especially his later books, a strain of mysticism and religious idealism.

Toynbee was educated at Balliol College, Oxford, and was a tutor there from 1912 to 1915. Subsequently, he became professor of Byzantine and modern Greek language, literature, and history at London University (1919–1924) and then for thirty years held the post of director of studies in the Royal Institute of International Affairs. He wrote on a wide variety of topics concerning Greek history, international politics, and contemporary affairs, but his main work was his *A Study of History*, the first ten volumes of which were published between 1934 and 1954. As of 1967, two other volumes appeared, the last, titled *Reconsiderations*, being largely an attempt to meet points raised by his numerous critics and, where he has thought it necessary, to qualify previous claims in the light of their objections. Toynbee always listened carefully to those who have disagreed with him, although he has apparently never felt that their observations justified any major revision of his views.

A STUDY OF HISTORY

Toynbee claimed that his project was first suggested to him when, at the beginning of World War I, he became aware of certain striking affinities between the courses taken by the Greco-Roman and modern European civilizations. It occurred to him that similar parallels might be discernible elsewhere, that there is, as he puts it, "a species of human society that we label 'civilisations'" and that the representatives of this species which have thus far appeared on this planet may exemplify in their various histories a common pattern of development. With this idea forming in his mind, Toynbee came across Oswald Spengler's *Decline of the West*, in which he found many of his own intimations affirmed and corroborated. Nevertheless, it seemed to Toynbee that Spengler's account was defective in important ways. The number of civilizations examined (eight) was too small to serve as a basis for safe generalization; little attempt was made to explain why cultures rise and decline in the manner described; and, in general, Spengler's procedure was marred by certain a priori dogmas that distorted his thinking, leading him to display at times a cavalier disregard for the facts. What was required was a more empirical approach, one in which it was clearly recognized that a problem of explanation existed and that the solution of this problem must be in terms of verifiable hypotheses that can stand the test of historical experience.

THE PATTERN OF HISTORY. Toynbee repeatedly referred to his own method as essentially "inductive." His aim (initially, at least) was to "try out the scientific approach to human affairs and to test how far it will carry us." In undertaking this program, he was insistent upon the need to treat as the fundamental units of study "whole societies," as opposed to "arbitrarily insulated fragments of them like the nation-states of the modern West." In contrast with Spengler, he claimed to have identified twenty-one examples (past and present) of the species "civilization," though he admitted that even this number is inconveniently small for his purpose—"the elucidation and formulation of laws." He argued, however, that a significant degree of similarity is discernible between the careers of the societies he examined and compared; certain stages in their respective histories can be seen to conform to a recognizable pattern too striking to be ignored, a pattern of growth, breakdown, and eventual decay and dissolution. Within this pattern certain recurrent "rhythms" may be detected.

When a society is in a period of growth, it offers effective and fruitful responses to the challenges that present themselves; when in decline, on the other hand, it proves incapable of exploiting the opportunities and of withstanding or overcoming the difficulties with which it is confronted. Neither growth nor disintegration, Toynbee holds, is necessarily continuous or uninterrupted. In disintegration, for instance, a phase of rout is frequently succeeded by a temporary rally, followed in turn by a new, more serious relapse. As an example he cited the establishment of a universal state under the Augustan Pax Romana as a period of rally in the career of the Hellenic civilization, coming between a time of troubles which, in the form of revolutions and internecine wars, preceded it and the first stages of the Roman Empire's final collapse, which followed in the third century. Toynbee contended that clearly comparable rout-rally rhythms have manifested themselves in the disintegration of many other civilizations, such as the Chinese, the Sumerian, and the Hindu. In these, too, we encounter the phenomena of increasing standardization and loss of creativity that were apparent when the Greco-Roman society was in decline.

HISTORICAL MODELS. Toynbee's tendency to interpret the history of other civilizations in terms suggested by that of the Hellenic culture is marked, and many of his opponents have claimed that it has led him into imposing artificial schemes upon the past and into postulating parallels by no means borne out by the historical material. In his most recent work Toynbee has shown himself to be sensitive to criticism of this kind. He has maintained, however, that for an investigation of the kind he envisaged it was at least essential to start with a model of some sort, his chief doubts being whether the model he chose was ideally suited to his purpose and whether a future student of the comparative history of civilizations would not be better advised to employ a diversity of specimens, rather than a single example, to guide his inquiries.

However, it is not clear that in proposing this amendment to his original procedure, Toynbee has fully appreciated the principal points at issue. He still seems to be searching for some single pattern of interpretation to which the histories of particular societies can be seen to stand as specimen cases, and in so doing, he overlooks two considerations, both of which have been stressed by various critics.

First, he continues to leave obscure the question of how the identity of a given civilization is to be determined. This is by no means a trivial matter, since in his practice Toynbee has often given the impression of identifying civilizations by reference to the very principles of development that in other places he has claimed to have elicited purely through an empirical survey of their actual careers. He thereby exposes himself to the charge of treating as factual discoveries what are no more than disguised tautologies.

Second, it has been argued that insofar as the term suggests an explanatory device capable of rendering intelligible a certain range of phenomena, Toynbee's references to models in the context cited are misleading. To maintain that a number of other societies have tended to follow a path significantly similar to the course taken by a selected specimen is by itself to explain nothing; at best, it is to point out that there is something *requiring* explanation—namely, the existence of the similarities in question. But although such an objection has force, Toynbee has, in fact, attempted to account for the correlations he believes himself to have discovered. He is not, as some have alleged, content simply to enumerate like instances and has always taken the problem of seeking explanations seriously. Thus, when trying to account for the disintegration of civilizations, he has invoked such notions as the "intractability of institutions" and the "nemesis of creativity," as well as pointing to the development of "internal" and "external" proletariats and of "dominant," as opposed to "creative," minorities.

Whether the explanations he has sought to provide are plausible or convincing is, of course, another matter. Frequently, they seem to involve an appeal to laws too vague to afford adequate support, and at other times Toynbee enlists the services of highly dubious or irrelevant analogies. He also tends to treat literary or folk myths as if they in some way gave evidential backing to his generalizations.

ORDER OR CHAOS. In defending his position, Toynbee has frequently attacked what he calls "antinomian historians," upholders of "the dogma that in history no pattern of any kind is to be found." He has argued that to deny the existence of patterns is implicitly to deny the possibility of writing history, for patterns are presupposed by the whole system of concepts and categories a historian must use if he is to talk meaningfully about the past.

But patterns of what sort? Toynbee sometimes implies that it is essential to choose between two fundamentally opposed views. Either history as a whole conforms to or manifests some unitary order and design, or else it is a "chaotic, disorderly, fortuitous flux" which defies intelligible interpretation. As examples of the first he cites the "Indo-Hellenic" conception of history as "a cyclic movement governed by an Impersonal Law" and the "Judeo-Zoroastrian" conception of it as governed by a supernatural intellect and will. A combination of these ideas appears to underlie Toynbee's own picture of the human past as it finally emerges in *A Study of History*, particularly in the later volumes, where the suggestion that the rise and fall of civilizations may be susceptible to a teleological interpretation is explicitly put forward.

It would seem, however, that Toynbee has posed his dilemma in altogether too simple terms. There are a number of familiar ways in which historians may be said to reduce the material of history to order and coherence, none of which involves the acceptance of all-embracing beliefs regarding the historical process as a whole of the type he instances. Of course, if the notion of the intelligibility of the past is initially defined in a manner that presupposes the validity of such beliefs, it is possible to accuse historians who deny that it is necessary or even legitimate to adopt them of making nonsense of their subject. But why, it may be asked, should such a stipulation be accepted?

REPUDIATION OF OLDER SCHEMES. In fact, Toynbee does not really intend to advance so exclusive a claim. He does not deny that historians may be able to make sense of particular segments of human history without being committed to universalistic positions of the sort mentioned, imperfect and incomplete though such explanations must ultimately be judged to be. He does, however, strongly suggest that the piecemeal approaches and categories of traditional history leave much to be desired, applying to them such terms as *archaic, infantile*, and *crude*. Here, possibly, lies the true source of his objections to "antinomianism." He wishes to condemn the old structures and clichés, the worn axioms unconsciously assumed in conventional historical thought. In particular, he is critical of the lines along which historians have been prone to cut up the past, both geographically and temporally. He distrusts the artificial cohesion they have projected into certain periods through the use of comprehensive simplifying labels like "the Renaissance" and "the Middle Ages," and he questions the unity and self-sufficiency implicit in their conception of "European history."

It is, of course, perfectly acceptable to appraise and seek to revise the conceptual schemes of previous historians in the light of fresh empirical knowledge and discoveries, but it is quite another thing to propound a general theory of historical development which appears in its final form to rely heavily upon extrahistorical considerations and preconceptions of a metaphysical or religious kind. Toynbee has perhaps never sufficiently appreciated the force of this distinction; even so, it would be churlish not to recognize the imaginative fertility, the sheer inventiveness, which is so marked a feature of his system, whatever its shortcomings in other respects. *A Study of History* is rich in methodological suggestions and contains a profusion of original interpretative concepts and frameworks. Whether any of these will be found of value by future historians or social scientists remains to be seen.

FREEDOM AND LAW IN HISTORY

A word may be said about Toynbee's views regarding the future of Western civilization and their relation to his general theory. He frequently speaks as if Western society were in an advanced state of breakdown; at the same time he repeatedly shows himself unwilling to draw the conclusion that it is in fact doomed to final disintegration, and he speaks of the possibility of a "reprieve" granted by God. The "determinism" implicit in his thought when he is seeking to apply "the scientific approach to human affairs" tends thus to conflict with the "libertarian" principles to which he claims to subscribe when discussing the nature of human actions and which are connected with his own metaphysical and religious beliefs. The later volumes of the *Study* display a persistent uneasiness over this apparent contradiction, yet it cannot be said that the efforts he has made in these volumes to reconcile the roles of law and freedom in history have proved satisfactory. Rather, they serve to highlight the logical difficulties that had already revealed themselves at earlier stages in Toynbee's work.

See also Determinism and Freedom; Libertarianism; Philosophy of History; Spengler, Oswald.

Bibliography

WORKS BY TOYNBEE

A Study of History. 12 vols. London: Oxford University Press, 1934–1961.

A Study of History: Abridgment of Volumes I–X, edited by D. C. Somervell. Oxford, Vols. I–VI, 1946; Vols. VII–X, 1957.

Civilisation on Trial. London: Oxford University Press, 1948.

An Historian's Approach to Religion. London: Oxford University Press, 1956.

Experiences. London, New York: Oxford University Press, 1969.

With G. R. Urban. *Toynbee on Toynbee: A Conversation between Arnold J. Toynbee and G.R. Urban*. New York: Oxford University Press, 1974.

Arnold Toynbee, a Selection from His Works. Edited by E. W. F. Tomlin. Oxford, U.K.; New York: Oxford University Press, 1978.

WORKS ON TOYNBEE

Dray, W. H. "Toynbee's Search for Historical Laws." *History and Theory* 1 (1960): 32–54.

Geyl, Pieter. *Debates with Historians*. London, 1955.

McNeill, William Hardy. *Arnold J. Toynbee, a Life*. New York: Oxford University Press, 1989.

Montagu, Ashley, ed. *Toynbee and History: Critical Essays and Reviews*. Boston: Sargent, 1956.

Morton, S. Fiona. *A Bibliography of Arnold J. Toynbee*. Oxford; New York: Oxford University Press, 1980.

Ortega y Gasset, José. *An Interpretation of Universal History*. New York: Norton, 1973.

Samuel, Maurice. *The Professor and the Fossil: Some Observations on Arnold J. Toynbee's "A Study of History."* New York: Knopf, 1956. A criticism of Toynbee's views on the Jews.

Trevor-Roper, H. R. "Arnold Toynbee's Millenium [*sic*]." In his *Men and Events*. New York: Harper, 1957.

Walsh, W. H. "Toynbee Reconsidered." *Philosophy* 38 (1963).

Patrick Gardiner (1967)
Bibliography updated by Michael J. Farmer (2005)

TRACY, DESTUTT DE

See *Destutt de Tracy, Antoine Louis Claude, Comte*

TRADITIONALISM

"Traditionalism" was a philosophy of history and a political program developed by the Counterrevolutionists in France. It was ultramontane in politics and anti-individualistic in epistemology and ethics.

It was the common belief of both those who favored the French Revolution and those who opposed it that the revolution was prepared by the *philosophes.* Voltaire and Jean-Jacques Rousseau were invoked by both parties as having been either the initiators of much-needed reforms or the corrupters of youth. The intellectual differences among the *philosophes* were minimized. The Revolutionary Party believed that Voltaire and Rousseau were the leaders of two schools of thought, both of which removed the seat of authority from the group—society or the nation or the church—to the individual, and that the two schools disagreed only on the question of whether authority was vested in the reason or in feeling (*sentiment*). The Voltairians were said to be individualistic rationalists; the Rousseauists individualistic sentimentalists. In short, the Voltairians were supposed to believe that any individual, by the use of reason alone, could reach all attainable truth in any field; the Rousseauists, that one had only to look into his "heart" to achieve the same result. Oversimplified as this was as history, it was common belief.

The philosophy of Comte Joseph de Maistre (1753–1821) and of his alter ego, Vicomte de Bonald (1754–1840), was developed in conscious reaction to individualism. De Maistre and Bonald were rationalistic, but they maintained that the reason to be trusted was that of the group, not that of the individual. The common reason, like the common sense, was lodged in a superindividual being, manifested in tradition and expressed in language. The superindividual being was the Roman Catholic Church, the authority of which was binding not only on its avowed members, but on all people. The church alone had direct access to the source of truth (God) and for 1,800 years had remained steadfast and unshaken in its dogmas. Since truth must be one and everlasting, the traditionalists were persuaded by a simple conversion of the proposition that where there was a single and everlasting set of ideas, it must be true. "No human institution has lasted eighteen centuries," de Maistre wrote in *Du Pape* (3 vols., Lyons, 1821). Therefore, he inferred, the church must be superhuman or divine.

Human nature can be understood only by seeing humanity as an integral part of the church. The human individual is but a fragment of a whole. He is completely dependent on society for his bodily welfare and even for his thoughts, for his thoughts are internal speech, and no language is either that of a single individual or created by an individual. Combating the theory that language was invented, de Maistre argued, as Rousseau and Thomas Reid had done before him, that thought is required for invention and language must therefore have existed before it could be invented. Language is the thought of the race expressing itself. It is also rational—we cannot express emotions and sensations linguistically. We speak our thoughts; we speak *of* our feelings and emotions. Since the traditionalists were French, they turned to the history of France for their evidence and found it in the antiquity of the Capetian dynasty, founded, in their view, by Louis the Pious in the ninth century, if not by Charlemagne; in the genesis of French from Latin; and in the primacy of Catholicism in France, which was converted from paganism by Dionysius the Areopagite, the first pagan to be converted by St. Paul.

The supremacy of the pope in both religious and secular affairs was emphasized by de Maistre. Although there might be two swords, the spiritual and the temporal, the latter was wielded, in the language of Boniface VIII, at the pleasure and sufferance of the priest (*ad nutum et patientiam sacerdotis*). This factor of the traditionalists' teachings led to ultramontanism, which, when vigorously preached by Hugues Félicité Robert de Lamennais (1782–1854) in the nineteenth century, was condemned by the pope.

Another type of traditionalism was espoused by Pierre-Simon Ballanche (1776–1847). In his major work, *Palingénésie sociale* (1827–1829), Ballanche developed a philosophy of history based on man's fall from primordial innocence. However, he maintained that there could be steady progress toward universal rehabilitation. In upholding the possibility of human progress, Ballanche differed from Bonald and de Maistre, for whom time and change, variety and multiplicity, were inherently evil. To Ballanche they were the only condition of redemption. He was convinced of the ultimate perfection of humankind, at which time all that is potential in the human essence would be realized. All men were to be rehabilitated, regardless of their present merits. There was no eternal hell. Even religion would progress, in that God would reveal its truths bit by bit as humankind became worthy of receiving them. Each man would have to make himself worthy by listening to his heart, an appeal to personal interpretation that was considered heretical.

Although Ballanche agreed with Bonald and de Maistre that the understanding of history could come only from seeing the designs of God in every historical event, he did not believe that government should be theocratic. On the contrary, the two swords must be wielded by two separate powers. The secular power, however, should not be in the hands of the people; they should be permitted to voice their aspirations only so that the sovereign might accept them.

It remained for Lamennais to carry traditionalism to its logical conclusion. Beginning with the strictest form of ultramontanism, he developed into a heresiarch, never realizing that he was moving away from the course of reason. If the pope was the head of the church and the church was superior to the state, then the pope should be recognized as the one sovereign and autonomous being on Earth. The sole test of certitude, Lamennais maintained, lay in the racial reason, and this collective reason was tradition. Tradition gives society its unity, and its unity fosters civilization. However, society to Lamennais was not France; it was humanity. And since civilization was Catholicism, national boundaries were artificial and should be eliminated except for practical purposes. The common sense of humankind, in which he believed as did the Stoics, was nothing that could be substantiated by the reason. It was the reason. One must submit to tradition in order to avoid the divisive effects of sectarianism. When the state put obstacles in the way of such submission, then rebellion was legitimate. However, this involved freedom of conscience, of the press, and of education, if it was to be practiced. It was at this point that Gregory XVI in his encyclical *Mirari Vos* intervened to silence Lamennais.

Traditionalism as a body of doctrine was condemned in 1855 in a decretal against Augustine Bonnetty (1798–1879), a priest. The theory directly condemned was the *fidéisme* of the Abbé Bautain (1796–1867), which Bautain had retracted in 1840. Since the identity of reason, common sense, and tradition demanded prerational assertions, faith seemed to be the only thing left to which the traditionalist might appeal. However, this raised faith to a position above that of reason, contrary to the doctrine of the church. The rationalistic position of the church was confirmed at the third session of the Vatican Council in 1870.

See also Bonald, Louis Gabriel Ambroise, Vicomte De; Conservatism; Lamennais, Hugues Félicité Robert de; Maistre, Comte Joseph de; Philosophy of History; Reid, Thomas; Rousseau, Jean-Jacques; Voltaire, François-Marie Arouet de.

Bibliography

Ballanche, Pierre Simon. *Oeuvres complètes*. 4 vols. Paris, 1830. See especially *Palingénésie sociale* (first published in 2 vols., Paris, 1827–1829); *Le vieillard et le jeune homme* (first published Paris, 1819); *Vision d'Hébal* (first published Paris, 1831).

Berlin, Isaiah. "Joseph de Maistre and the Origins of Fascism." In his *The Crooked Timber of Humanity*, edited by Henry Hardy. New York: Knopf, 1991.

Boas, George. *French Philosophies of the Romantic Period*. Baltimore: Johns Hopkins Press, 1925. Ch. 3.

Denziger, Heinrich. *Enchiridion Symbolorum et Definitionum*, 13th ed. Freiburg, 1921. No. 1613 et seq.; No. 1649 et seq.

Ferraz, Marin. *Histoire de la philosophie en France au XIXe siècle: Traditionalisme et ultramontanisme*. Paris: Didier, 1880.

Gunn, J. Alexander. *Modern French Philosophy*. London: Unwin, 1922. Ch. 7.

Klinck, David. *The French Counterrevolutionary Theorist Louis de Bonald (1754–1840)*. New York: Peter Lang, 1996.

Laski, Harold. *Authority in the Modern State*. New Haven, CT: Yale University Press, 1919. On the condemnation of traditionalism.

Lebrun, Richard. *Joseph de Maistre: An Intellectual Militant*. Kingston: McGill-Queen's University Press, 1988.

Reedy, W. Jay. "The Traditionalist Critique of Individualism in Post-Revolutionary France: The Case of Louis de Bonald." *History of Political Thought* 16 (1) (1995): 49–75.

Stearns, Peter N. *Priest and Revolutionary: Lamennais and the Dilemma of French Catholicism*. New York: Harper and Row, 1967.

George Boas (1967)
Bibliography updated by Philip Reed (2005)

TRAGEDY

The two main strands in the history of philosophical reflection on tragedy, as a genre of art, can both be seen as having their origins in Plato's critique of tragic poetry in the *Republic* and other dialogues. It is there that we find their first sustained philosophical treatment; and with respect to this small part of it, at least, Alfred North Whitehead's characterization of the history of philosophy as a series of footnotes to Plato is not too fanciful.

TRAGEDY AND EMOTION

One strand of thought focuses on the character and value of our experience of tragedy, and can be seen in Plato's charge that tragedy (and indeed mimetic poetry in general) "gratifies and indulges the instinctive desires … with its hunger for tears and for an uninhibited indulgence in grief"; that "it waters [passions] when they ought to be allowed to wither, and makes them control us when we ought, in the interests of our own greater welfare and happiness, to control them" (1987, 606a). Plato's thought that the emotional dimension of our experience of tragedy is particularly significant has been taken up in a variety of directions by other philosophers.

In the *Poetics*, Aristotle argued that tragedy's capacity to arouse the emotions of pity and fear in its audience, so far from rendering it intellectually and morally damaging, is in fact a source of its value: Tragedy aims at emotional effect not for its own sake, or for the sake of gratifying or indulging its audience, he argued, but rather in such a way as to bring about a *catharsis* of the tragic emotions. Precisely what Aristotle meant by *catharsis* is far from clear, and has been the topic of much scholarly debate: The notion has been understood in terms of purgation (of excessive or pathological emotion), of purification, and of intellectual clarification, to mention only some of the most influential of the interpretations that have been offered. Whatever its precise meaning may be, however, it is clear that Aristotle took *catharsis* to be a process or experience that in one way or another is conducive to emotional health or balance, such that our emotional experience of (well-written) tragedy is not indulgently sentimental and opposed to "our better nature," as Plato argued, but is rather an essential element in a fully comprehending attitude to what a work depicts.

Aristotle linked *catharsis* with the pleasure that we take in tragedy: The fact that mention of the former comes at the end of his definition of tragedy suggests that he takes it to be in some sense the goal of works of this sort, and (an appropriate form of) the latter is said to be "what the poet should seek to produce." His defense of the value of our emotional experience of tragedy in terms of *catharsis* is thus at least implicitly a defense of it in terms of tragic pleasure; and a debate related to, and at least as extensive as that concerning the meaning of "*catharsis*," has its origins in his characterization of tragic pleasure as "the pleasure derived from pity and fear by means of imitation [mimesis]" (1967, 1453b). For how is it that one can derive pleasure from what Aristotle himself describes elsewhere (notably in the *Rhetoric*) as painful feelings? This question is a more difficult relative of one prompted by Plato's reference to the fact that "when we hear Homer or one of the tragic poets representing the sufferings of a hero and making him bewail them at length … even the best of us enjoy it" (1987, 605c-d): How is it that in engaging with a work of tragedy one is able, or is enabled by the work, to enjoy the depiction of human suffering?

Debate surrounding these and related questions was particularly prevalent in eighteenth-century British philosophy and criticism, attracting contributions from such figures as Lord Kames, James Beattie, and Joseph Priestley, as well as, more influentially, David Hume, Adam Smith, and Edmund Burke. Some contributors to the debate focus on the question of how one can respond with pleasure to what tragedy depicts: Edmund Burke, for example, in his *A Philosophical Enquiry into the Origin of Our Ideas of the Sublime and the Beautiful*, took the problem to lie in the "common observation" "that objects which in the reality would shock, are in tragical, and such like representations, the source of a very high species of pleasure" (1990, p. 41), and thus in effect construed the problem as one concerning the consistency of one's patterns of response. (As, in a sense, did Plato, though he took the inconsistency between our responses to depictions of suffering in tragedy and our responses to suffering "in reality" to lie not in the fact that the former involve pleasure and the latter "shock" or horror, but rather in that in the former we give vent to our emotions whereas in the latter we strive "to bear them in silence like men.")

Discussions that remain exclusively occupied with the pleasure that Plato holds that one takes in what tragedy depicts often proceed by attempting to resolve the apparent inconsistency in one's patterns of response by pointing to relevant differences between the contexts in question: for example, one's awareness of the fictional status of tragedy, the contribution of artistry, and "aesthetic distance" have all been cited as aspects of our experience of tragedy that are not involved in our experience of actual suffering, the functioning of which explains why pleasure is a characteristic element of the former while typically absent from the latter. However, such discussions risk missing the more difficult issue that arises from Aristotle's characterization of tragic pleasure. For if that characterization is right, the peculiarity of the latter is not simply that it occurs in response to the depiction of things that in other contexts do not give one pleasure, but rather that it is a variety of pleasure that is intimately bound up with painful feeling; as he put it, it is the pleasure "of," or "derived from," such feeling.

The more sophisticated treatments of our emotional experience of tragedy have attempted to address this. Burke, for example, suggested that the apparent inconsistency between one's responses to tragedy and one's responses to actual suffering is illusory; in fact, he held, we are just as disposed to take pleasure in actual sufferings as we are in depictions of suffering, and in both cases our response is based on sympathy, a psychological mechanism that involves pain at the distress of its objects, but also (in order to foster its occurrence) pleasure: "as our Creator has designed we should be united by the bond of sympathy, he has strengthened that bond by a proportional delight" (1990, p. 42). Adam Smith made a similar point when he argued that it is because of its social utility that the experience of sympathy, even when the emotions communicated sympathetically are painful, is naturally pleasurable to human beings.

This account of the matter, though clearly based on a Humean theory of the passions, was rejected by Hume himself, on the grounds that the operation of sympathy is not always pleasurable: If it were, he suggested in a letter to Smith, "an hospital would be a more entertaining place than a ball." (A point anticipated in its spirit if not its tone, by Burke, who suggested that people do indeed find public executions more compelling than "the most sublime and affecting tragedy we have.") Hume's own account of what he described as the seemingly "unaccountable pleasure which the spectators of a well-written tragedy receive from sorrow, terror, anxiety, and other passions that are in themselves disagreeable and uneasy" 1987, p. 216) is by far the most discussed by contemporary contributors to the debate, although it is more interesting as an application of his theory of the passions than it is as an account of our experience of tragedy.

Hume suggested that the spectators' pleasure and their "disagreeable and uneasy" emotions are initially responses to different aspects of a work of tragedy: their distress is a response to what the work depicts, their pleasure a response to the "eloquence" and "genius" with which it depicts it. To leave the matter at that would clearly miss the problem posed by Aristotle's characterization of tragic pleasure. But Hume went on to argue that these responses merge, as the pleasure, which is dominant, overpowers, and somehow "converts" the distress in such as way as to reinforce the former: "The impulse or vehemence, arising from sorrow, compassion, indignation, receives a new direction from the sentiments of beauty. The latter, being the predominant emotion, seize the whole mind, and convert the former into themselves, at least tincture them so strongly as totally to alter their nature" (1987, p. 220). Contemporary discussions of Hume's account have focused on just what this "conversion" of emotion is supposed to involve, for Hume himself was less than clear on the matter. Whatever it does amount to, however, it is clearly dependent on Hume's associationist psychology, and is unlikely to survive the rejection of this.

Philosophical discussion of tragic pleasure, or what scholars often refer to as "the paradox of tragedy," has continued on very much the lines established by eighteenth-century thinkers, though a new slant on the matter (and indeed on the nature of catharsis) has been introduced by philosophers and others influenced by the methods and findings of psychoanalytic theory. It remains a recurring theme in contemporary philosophy of art.

THE PROFUNDITY OF TRAGEDY The second major strand in the history of the philosophy of tragedy is represented in Plato's discussion of the epistemic credentials of tragic poetry, so to speak, where he argued that the tragedian has neither knowledge nor true belief concerning that of which he writes, and (hence) that tragedy cannot be a source of knowledge. Plato's target here is the view that "the tragedians … are masters of all forms of skill, and know all about human excellence and defect and about religion" (1987, 598d-e), or more broadly the thought that tragedy's distinctiveness has to do with its capacity to prompt, and to suggest authoritative answers to, questions of a distinctively ethical sort. Despite Plato's efforts, the appeal of this line of thought survived his critique, not least due to the support that some found for it in Aristotle's claim that "poetry is a more philosophical and more serious business than history" (1987, 1451b), a claim made in the context of his attempt to show that the tragedian's art is, despite Plato's arguments to the contrary, a *technê*, a productive activity that employs rational means or principles in the pursuit of a predetermined practical end. The thought that tragedy is an especially philosophical form of art received its most sustained treatment in nineteenth-century German philosophy and criticism, where versions of it were expounded by Gotthold Lessing, Friedrich Schiller, Friedrich Schlegel, August Wilhelm Schlegel, and Johann Goethe, as well as, and from a philosophical point of view more notably, by Georg Hegel, Arthur Schopenhauer, and Friedrich Nietzsche.

Hegel argued that the business of Classical tragedy—its "essential basis"—is to demonstrate "the validity of the substance and necessity of ethical life" (1975, Vol. 2, p. 1222). It achieves this first by showing the "collision" between different aspects of the ethical that occurs when the latter is fragmented and particularised in human social life: thus he claimed that Sophocles' *Antigone* dramatizes the collision between the authority of the state (represented by Creon) and family love (represented by Antigone). These aspects of ethical life collide because "each of the opposed sides, if taken by itself, has justification; while each can establish the true and positive content of its own aim and character only by denying and infringing the equally justified power of the other" (1975, Vol. 2, p. 1196). The task of tragedy is then to show the "resolution" of conflict of this sort, which it can do in a variety of ways. The most satisfying form of resolution, Hegel claimed, involves the destruction of the characters who embody "false one-sidedness," as happens in *Antigone*, but "the unity and harmony of the entire ethical order" may also be effected and exemplified by the surrender of the hero (as in *Oedipus the King*), the reconciliation of opposing interests (as in the *Eumenides*), or "an inner reconciliation" in the tragic hero himself (as in *Oedipus at Colonus*).

Although he held that tragedy was at its most beautiful in the classical period, Hegel argued that it is in what he called Romantic tragedy that art is at its most philosophical, or, in his terms, comes closest to "bringing to our minds and expressing the Divine, the deepest interests of mankind, and the most comprehensive truths of spirit" (1975, Vol. 1, p. 7). The subject matter of tragedy by this stage of its development is "the subjective inner life of the character," and at its best, which Hegel thought was in Shakespeare's hands, these characters are "concretely human individuals," "free artists of their own selves" (Vol. 2, pp. 1227–1228). Tragedy at this stage represents not collision between particularised ethical powers, as did classical tragedy, but either (and, Hegel claimed, unsatisfactorily) collision between different aspects of a character's personality, or (in what he held are the finest examples of Romantic tragedy) between the character and external circumstances. Tragedy of the latter sort presents the "progress and history of a great soul, its inner development, the picture of its self-destructive struggle against circumstances, events, and their consequences" (Vol. 2, p. 1230).

Hegel's claim that the importance of tragedy lies in its capacity to reveal important truths about the human condition is echoed by Schopenhauer. Indeed, like Hegel, Schopenhauer saw the arts in general as engaged fundamentally in the same task as philosophy; both, as he said, "work at bottom towards the solution of the problem of existence" (1969, Vol. 2, p. 406). Tragedy, Schopenhauer held, is "the summit of poetic art," for in dramatising "the terrible side of life … the unspeakable pain, the wretchedness and misery of mankind, the triumph of wickedness, the scornful mastery of chance, and the irretrievable fall of the just and the innocent," tragedy reveals to us more clearly than anything else the most important feature of reality: "the antagonism of the will with itself" and the fact that "chance and error" are "the rulers of the world" (1969, Vol. 1, pp. 252–253). However, in Schopenhauer's view tragedy is significant not merely because of the importance of what it reveals to us concerning the nature of reality, but also because in the experience of tragedy one may come to recognize the only appropriate response to the terrible truth it presents. This is to adopt an attitude of "resignation": as Schopenhauer put it, "The horrors on the stage hold up to [the spectator] the bitterness and worthlessness of life, and so the vanity of all its efforts and endeavours. The effect of this impression must be that he becomes aware … that it is better to tear his heart away from life, to turn his willing away from it, not to love the world and life" (Vol. 2, p. 435) The greatest tragedies, Schopenhauer said, are those in which this attitude of resignation is not only suggested by a work but also demonstrated by its characters.

If Schopenhauer was less concerned with particular works of tragedy than Hegel, Nietzsche was still less so. In *The Birth of Tragedy*, his infrequent references to particular works of Greek tragedy betray very little of the knowledge of this part of literary history that he surely had; and the Aeschylus, Sophocles, and Euripides whom he discussed in that work figure not as artists in a history of a genre of art, but rather as symbols or personifications of different cultural points or tendencies in Nietzsche's working out of a genealogy of the tragic spirit. The main symbols in this genealogy are those of Dionysus and Apollo, Greek deities whom Nietzsche used creatively to stand for both metaphysical and artistic categories. The Apollonian spirit is that which is concerned with appearances, with the world as composed of individuals; what it offers us is "beautiful illusion" (1993, p.15). The Dionysian spirit is that through which this illusion is shattered, and what is revealed to us reality as it truly is: an endless and pointless struggle of things in flux. As its objects are illusory, the Apollonian vision is too fragile to sustain human beings indefinitely. But with its object of what Nietzsche described as a "witch's brew" of "lust and cruelty" (p. 19) the Dionysian vision is too terrible for human beings to survive. The "supreme goal" of art, Nietzsche claimed, is to allow us to escape this dichotomy.

Art, at its highest, does not attempt to evade the Dionysian truth but rather, by somehow (and in a way that Nietzsche is never very clear about) mediating it through the Apollonian, renders it bearable and even something to be exulted in. Nietzsche suggested that the tragedies of Aeschylus and Sophocles, in which, as he put it, "Dionysus speaks the language of Apollo, but Apollo finally speaks the language of Dionysus" (p. 104) are instances of such art. But he also held that the tragic spirit was almost immediately extinguished in tragedy (in the literary-historical sense), snuffed out by Euripides' rejection of Dionysiac wisdom in favor of Socratic rationality. Nor, he held, is the tragic spirit to be found in post-Renaissance tragedy, in which music, through which the Dionysian wisdom is expressed, plays no substantial role. In fact, Nietzsche believed, at least at the time when he wrote *The Birth of Tragedy*, if not for long afterward, the only art capable of rediscovering the spirit of tragedy is the music-drama of Richard Wagner, the dedicatee of *The Birth of Tragedy*.

The concern with tragedy as a source of insight into problems that are in the broadest sense problems of ethics, which is exhibited in different ways by Hegel, Schopenhauer, and Nietzsche, has been taken up distinctively in contemporary Anglo-American philosophy by Stanley Cavell, who has shown how Shakespearean tragedy can be read as working out problems of skepticism, and as occupied with "how to live at all in a groundless world"; by Martha Nussbaum (1986), who has taken up Hegel's concern with the ethical dilemmas posed in classical tragedy; and by Bernard Williams (1993), who finds in classical tragedy an exploration of the nature of necessity which challenges Kantian conceptions of the voluntary, of obligation, and of responsibility. Here, as in contemporary discussion of the so-called "paradox of tragedy," Plato's fascination with tragedy, though not his condemnation of the art form, lives on.

See also Aristotle; Beattie, James; Burke, Edmund; Cavell, Stanley; Emotion; Goethe, Johann Wolfgang von; Greek Drama; Hegel, Georg Wilhelm Friedrich; Home, Henry; Hume, David; Katharsis; Lessing, Gotthold Ephraim; Nietzsche, Friedrich; Nussbaum, Martha; Plato; Priestley, Joseph; Schiller, Friedrich Wilhelm Joseph von; Schlegel, Friedrich von; Schopenhauer, Arthur; Smith, Adam; Whitehead, Alfred North; Williams, Bernard.

Bibliography

Aristotle. *Poetics*. Translated by Gerald F. Else. Ann Arbor: University of Michigan Press, 1967.

Beistegui, M., and S. Sparks. *Philosophy and Tragedy*. London: Routledge, 2000.

Budd, M. *Values of Art*. London: Allen Lane, 1995.

Bungay, Stephen. *Beauty and Truth: A Study of Hegel's Aesthetics*. New York: Oxford University Press, 1984.

Burke, Edmund. *A Philosophical Enquiry*, edited by Adam Phillips. New York: Oxford University Press, 1990.

Carroll, N. *The Philosophy of Horror, or Paradoxes of the Heart*. New York: Routledge, 1990.

Cavell, Stanley. *Disowning Knowledge in Six Plays of Shakespeare*. Cambridge, U.K.: Cambridge University Press, 1987.

Eaton, Marcia. "A Strange Kind of Sadness." *Journal of Aesthetics and Art Criticism* 41 (1) (1982): 51–63.

Feagin, Susan. "The Pleasures of Tragedy." *American Philosophical Quarterly* 20 (1) (1983): 95–104.

Hegel, G. W. F. *Aesthetics: Lectures on Fine Art*. 2 vols. Translated by T. M. Knox. Oxford: Clarendon Press, 1975.

Hume, David. "Of Tragedy." In *Essays Moral, Literary and Political*, edited by Eugene F. Miller. Indianapolis, IN: Liberty Classics, 1987.

Kuhns, R. *Tragedy: Contradiction and Repression*. Chicago: University of Chicago Press, 1991.

Lamarque, P. "Tragedy and Moral Value." *Australasian Journal of Philosophy* 73 (1995): 239–249.

Levinson, J. "Horrible Fictions." *Journal of Aesthetics and Art Criticism* 49 (1991): 253–258.

Levinson, J. "Music and Negative Emotion." *Pacific Philosophical Quarterly* 63 (1982): 327–346.

Morreall, John. "Enjoying Negative Emotions in Fiction." *Philosophy and Literature* 9 (1) (1985): 95–102.

Neill, A. "Hume's 'Singular Phænomenon.'" *British Journal of Aesthetics* 39 (1999): 112–125.

Neill, A. "'An Unaccountable Pleasure': Hume on Tragedy and the Passions." *Hume Studies* 24 (1998): 335–354.

Nietzsche, Friedrich. *The Birth of Tragedy*. Translated by Shaun Whiteside and edited by Michael Tanner. London: Penguin Books, 1993.

Nussbaum, Martha. *The Fragility of Goodness*. Cambridge, U.K., Cambridge University Press, 1986.

Packer, M. "Dissolving the Paradox of Tragedy." *Journal of Aesthetics and Art Criticism* 47 (1989): 211–219.

Peckham, M. *Beyond the Tragic Vision*. New York: George Braziller, 1962.

Plato. *The Republic*. Translated by Desmond Lee. London: Penguin Books, 1987.

Ridley, A. "Tragedy and the Tender-Hearted." *Philosophy and Literature* 17 (1993): 234–245.

Schier, Flint. "The Claims of Tragedy: An Essay in Moral Psychology and Aesthetic Theory." *Philosophical Papers* 18 (1) (1989): 7–26.

Schier, Flint. "Tragedy and the Community of Sentiment." In *Philosophy and Fiction: Essays in Literary Aesthetics*, edited by Peter Lamarque. Aberdeen: Aberdeen University Press, 1983.

Schopenhauer, Arthur. *The World as Will and Representation*. 2 vols. Translated by E. F. Payne. New York: Dover, 1969.

Williams, Bernard. *Shame and Necessity*. Berkeley: University of California Press, 1993.

Alex Neill (2005)

TRANSCENDENTALISM

See *Kant, Immanuel; Neo-Kantianism; New England Transcendentalism*

TRESCHOW, NIELS
(1751–1833)

Niels Treschow, the Norwegian philosopher, defended a monism strongly influenced by Benedict de Spinoza and Gottfried Wilhelm Leibniz. Treschow was born at Drammen, Norway. He studied at the University of Copenhagen, where he became a professor in 1803. In 1813 he left Denmark to become the first professor of philosophy at the University of Oslo, but he held the post for only one year before entering government service.

Treschow's philosophical views are based on an idea of the unity of all things and on a concept of God similar to that of Spinoza. However, Treschow wanted to combine the idea of God's immanence, the idea that God is in all things, with the idea of God's transcendence, the idea that God is above all things. God is not the unity of all things but rather that which makes all things into a unity; as such, God is not an abstraction but a real individual, "unchangeable, eternal, and independent" (*Om Gud, Idee- og Sandseverdenen*, Vol. I, p. 81). The nature of God is manifest in our consciousness. God, or the One, "stands in the same relation to the manifold produced by it as does our mind to its thoughts, feelings, and decisions" (p. 115). Our consciousness "pictures the Absolute One."

In his psychology also, Treschow tried to uphold a Spinozistic view, opposing the Cartesian dualism of soul and body. "Man may indeed be considered composite," Treschow said, but not a composite of soul and body, for these are both different aspects of the same thing as it is a possible object of the inner and outer sense (see *Om den Menneskelige Natur*, p. 11).

Treschow also commented on the problem of universals and individuals. He criticized the tendency of abstract philosophers to give priority to universals and to regard individual things and events as instances and exemplifications of universals. The concrete individual, he held, is prior in existence and in knowledge. Only individuals exist, and universals are merely means toward the recognition and description of individual things. An individual thing cannot be fully grasped, however, since this would involve recognizing what is at the basis of all its various states, the idea that expresses all these states.

Since only individuals are real, universal concepts, or concepts of species of things, are "artificial," and so also is any classification of things into more or less fixed kinds. The "specific nature of man" is in a way a fiction, but man has developed gradually from some animal in which the specifically human dispositions potentially inhered, and the natural history of man is part of the history of the whole of nature. In his philosophy of history Treschow tried to substantiate his claim that man descended from some species of animal. Humankind's gradual development is due to the interaction of external and internal conditions. The fact that the individual physically and mentally goes through the various phases of the historical development of the species was to Treschow another proof of the primacy of the individual.

See also Cartesianism; Holism and Individualism in History and Social Science; Leibniz, Gottfried Wilhelm; Spinoza, Benedict (Baruch) de; Universals, A Historical Survey.

Bibliography

WORKS BY TRESCHOW

Gives der Noget Begreb Eller Nogen Idee om Enslige Ting? (Are there concepts or ideas about particular things?). Copenhagen, 1804.

Elementer til Historiens Philosophie (Elements of the philosophy of history). Copenhagen, 1811.

Om den Menneskelige Natur, Især fra Dens Aandelige Side (Human nature, especially its mental aspects). Copenhagen, 1812. The first Scandinavian work on empirical psychology.

Om Gud, Idee- og Sandseverdenen (On God and the worlds of ideas and sensations), 3 vols. Christiania, 1831–1833.

WORKS ON TRESCHOW

Høffding, Harald. *Danske Filosofer* (Danish philosophers). Copenhagen, 1909.

Schmidt-Phiseldech, K. *Niels Treschows Historiefilosofi*. Copenhagen, 1933.

Stybe, Svend Erik. "Niels Treschow (1751–1833), A Danish Neoplatonist." *Danish Yearbook of Philosophy* 13 (1976): 29–47.

Svendsen, P. *Gullalderdrøm og Utviklingstro* (The dream of the golden age and the belief in evolution). Oslo, 1940.

Winsnes, A. H. *Niels Treschow. En Opdrager til Menneskelighet* (Niels Treschow. An educator to humanity). Oslo, 1927.

Anfinn Stigen (1967)
Bibliography updated by Tamra Frei (2005)

TROELTSCH, ERNST
(1865–1923)

Ernst Troeltsch, the German theologian and social scientist, was born near Augsburg in Bavaria. He studied Protestant theology at the universities of Erlangen, Göttingen, and Berlin, and after three years as a Lutheran curate in Munich, he returned to the University of Göttingen as a lecturer in theology. He became extraordinary professor at Bonn in 1892, and in 1894 ordinary professor of systematic theology at Heidelberg, a position that he held for twenty-one years. He also served as a member of the Bavarian upper legislative house. In 1915 he moved to a chair of philosophy in the University of Berlin, serving concurrently as a member of the Prussian Landtag and as undersecretary of state for religious affairs.

Troeltsch contributed to the philosophy and sociology of religion and also to cultural and social history, ethics, and jurisprudence. His work raised in many related fields the much-debated questions of the extent and limitations of the historicosociological method. He played a leading role in the clarification of the conception of historicism and made important contributions to the study of methodology in the historical sciences. By recognizing the impact of sociological and historical thinking on the shaping of modern mentality, Troeltsch became involved in the intractable problems of the relation between absolute ethical and religious values and historical relativity. He remained uncompromisingly sincere in revealing the difficulties of this approach and admitted to not being able to surmount them or to reconcile conflicting results in an all-embracing theory.

Troeltsch's intellectual development was bound up with his recognition of the importance of historical change. He chose theology as the field in which, in his own words, "one had access to both metaphysics and the extraordinarily exciting historical problems." The historical theology devoid of metaphysics of his teacher Albrecht Ritschl stimulated him to radical doubt of the validity of Ritschl's own procedure, although with Ritschl Troeltsch accepted the Kantian primacy and underivative character of the basic structure of human morality. He argued that moral awareness was basic to the human constitution and that it was only during the course of historical development that morality and religion became connected and interdependent. To understand Christian ethics as the supreme manifestation of such historical combination was nevertheless his aim in *Grundprobleme der Ethik* (written 1902; in *Gesammelte Schriften*, Vol. II).

Troeltsch was aware of the problems arising from two basic assumptions: (1) the Kantian thesis that the formal necessities and laws of morality are irreducible and (2) the equally basic assumption of materialist ethics that what we study are the manifestations of a grown and growing morality in religious, social, and political consciousness. Thus Immanuel Kant's formalism changed in Troeltsch's hands from a means of critical analysis to an attempt to provide an ontology of personality. The point of reference for an understanding of the moral person is no longer the will as such, but morality as realizing itself through persons in history.

Troeltsch's major work is *Die Soziallehren der christlichen Kirchen und Gruppen* (Tübingen, 1912, translated by Olive Wyon as *The Social Teaching of the Christian Churches*, London and New York, 1931). It is a collection of many detailed studies in Christian social ethics published earlier in the *Archiv für Sozialwissenschaft und Sozialpolitik*, with new chapters on Calvinism, the sects, and mysticism. The work is unified by the sociological formulation of the entire history of the Christian churches.

It is easy to see how Troeltsch maneuvered himself into what has been described as the "crisis of historicism." For despite his insistence on the formal a priori of morality and the necessity of thinking of some values and norms as transcending historical change and accident, Troeltsch could not avoid the suggestion that the explanation of a given phenomenon can be adequately provided only by an account of its genesis.

Troeltsch faced the problems his position posed for Christian ethics and theology, with their claims to historically unique or historically transcendent values. In *Die Trennung von Staat und Kirche* (Separation of state and church) he spoke of the polymorphous truth of the churches. This conception was still present in his later attempts to reconcile the absolutist claims of Christian revelation—which as monomorphous truth belongs strictly to the early church—with the later developments of the three great Christian forms of social expression: the church, the sects, and mysticism.

Troeltsch made reliable and learned contributions to the history of ideas, notably his analysis of the role of Protestantism in the formation of the modern world and his searching studies of the differentiation of Protestantism into Calvinism and Lutheranism with their important differences in ethos. He was in basic agreement with his friend Max Weber, whose theses he summarized and elaborated. His important contributions to the conception of group personalities are generally recognized in sociology, philosophy, and jurisprudence. His work on the great social groups—family, guild, state, and church—owed much to Otto von Gierke's *Genossenschaftsrecht*, but Troeltsch went beyond Gierke's emphasis on corporative formations to a study of their personal aspect.

Troeltsch's political thought emerged from his wide learning in the history of ideas. After World War I he was among those German thinkers who realized that Germany's disastrous estrangement from the West was based on a divergence in political philosophy. He urged a return of German political thinking to the position of the eighteenth-century Enlightenment, before the romantic glorification of the state. He thought that this position was compatible with Western thought, as rooted in Stoic and Christian ethics with their essential respect for the individual person that grew into the modern democratic idea of the rights of man. Troeltsch made the point that German political thinking had yet to learn from the West not to despise arrogantly the serious possibilities of compromise.

In 1922 Troeltsch collected his writings on the philosophy of history under the title *Der Historismus und seine Probleme* (Historicism and its problems). Material toward a projected second volume is contained in *Christian Thought, Its History and Application* (London, 1923, edited by Friedrich von Hügel; published in German under the title *Der Historismus und seine Überwindung*, Berlin, 1924).

See also Enlightenment; Historicism; Kant, Immanuel; Philosophy of Religion; Religion and Morality; Ritschl, Albrecht Benjamin; Weber, Max.

Bibliography

WORKS BY TROELTSCH

Vernunft und Offenbarung bei J. Gerhard und Melanchthon. Göttingen: Vandenhoeck and Ruprecht, 1891.

Die Absolutheit des Christentums und die Religionsgeschichte. Tübingen: Mohr, 1902.

Psychologie und Erkenntnistheorie in der Religionswissenschaft. Tübingen: Mohr, 1905.

Protestantisches Christentum und Kirche in der Neuzeit. Leipzig and Berlin, 1906.

Die Trennung von Staat und Kirche. Tübingen, 1907.

Die Bedeutung des Protestantismus für die Entstehung der modernen Welt. Munich: Oldenbourg, 1911. Translated by W. Montgomery as *Protestantism and Progress*. London: Williams and Norgate, 1912.

Die Bedeutung der Geschichtlichkeit Jesu für den Glauben. Tübingen: Mohr, 1911.

Gesammelte Schriften. 4 vols. Tübingen: Mohr, 1912–1925. Does not contain all the works.

Augustin, die christliche Antike und das Mittelalter. Munich: Oldenbourg, 1915.

Spektator-Briefe, Aufsätze über die deutsche Revolution und die Weltpolitik 1918/1922. Tübingen: Mohr, 1924.

Deutscher Geist und Westeuropa. Tübingen: Mohr, 1925.

Vorlesungen über "Glaubenslehre." Munich: Duncker and Homblot, 1925.

Troeltsch, Ernst. *Writings on Theology and Religion*. Atlanta: John Knox Press, 1977.

Troeltsch, Ernst. *Kritische Gesamtausgabe*. Edited by Friedrich Wilhelm Graf. Berlin; New York: W. de Gruyter, 1998.

WORKS ON TROELTSCH

Alberca, Ignacio Escribano. *Die Gewinnung theologischer Normen aus der Geschichte der Religion bei E. Troeltsch*. Munich: Hueber, 1961.

Bodenstein, Walter. *Neige des Historismus, Ernst Troeltschs Entwicklungsgang*. Gütersloh: Gütersloher Verlagshuas, Gerd Mohn, 1959.

Chapman, Mark D. *Ernst Troeltsch and Liberal Theology: Religion and Cultural Synthesis in Wilhelmine, Germany*. Oxford; New York: Oxford University Press, 2001.

Clayton, John Powell. *Ernst Troeltsch and the Future of Theology*. Cambridge; New York: Cambridge University Press, 1976.

Drescher, Hans-Georg. *Ernst Troeltsch: His Life and Work*. Minneapolis: Fortress Press, 1993.

Gayhart, Bryce A. *The Ethics of Ernst Troeltsch: A Commitment to Relevancy*. Lewiston, NY: E. Mellen Press, 1990.

Graf, Friedrich Wilhelm, and Hartmut Ruddies. *Ernst Troeltsch Bibliographie*. Tübingen: J.C.B. Mohr, 1982.

Kaftan, Theodor. *Ernst Troeltsch*. Schleswig, 1912.

Kasch, Wilhelm F. *Die Socialphilosophie von Ernst Troeltsch*. 1963.

Köhler, Walther. *Ernst Troeltsch*. Tübingen: Mohr, 1941.

Myers, Max A., and Michael R. LaChat. *Studies in the Theological Ethics of Ernst Troeltsch*. Lewiston: E. Mellen Press, 1991.

Ogletree, Thomas W. *Christian Faith and History: A Critical Comparison of Ernst Troeltsch and Karl Barth*. New York: Abingdon Press, 1965.

Pauck, Wilhelm. *Harnack and Troeltsch: Two Historical Theologians*. New York: Oxford University Press, 1968.

Renz, Horst, Friedrich Wilhelm Graf, and Trutz Rendtorff. *Troeltsch-Studien*. Gütersloh: Mohn, 1982.

Rintelen, Fritz-Joachim von. "Der Versuch einer Überwindung des Historismus bei Ernst Troeltsch." *Deutsche Vierteljahrsschrift* 8 (1930): 324–372.

Scheler, Max. "Ernst Troeltsch als Soziologe." *Kölner Vierteljahrshefte für Soziologie* (1923–1924).

Tillich, Paul. "Ernst Troeltsch." *Kant-Studien* 29 (1924): 351–358.

Vermeil, Edmond. *La pensée religieuse d'Ernst Troeltsch*. Paris, 1922.

Wichelhaus, Manfred. *Kirchengeschichtsschreibung und Soziologie im neunzehnten Jahrhundert und bei Ernst Troeltsch*. Heidelberg: Winter, 1965.

Eva Schaper (1967)
Bibliography updated by Michael J. Farmer (2005)

TRUBETSKOI, EVGENII NIKOLAEVICH

(1863–1920)

A Russian philosopher, law specialist, religious and political figure, Evgenii Trubetskoi was a member of one of the oldest aristocratic families of Russia. He received an excellent education, graduating from the Department of Law of Moscow University (1885) and earning a master's degree in philosophy for his work on St. Augustine (1892) and a doctorate for his work on Pope Gregory VII (1897). He taught law and philosophy in Iaroslavl' (1886–1897), Kiev (1897–1905), and Moscow (1905–1917), where he was elected chair of philosophy after the sudden death of its former head, his brother Sergei Trubetskoi (1862–1905). Parallel to his teaching career, he was active in Russian cultural, academic, and political circles. Trubetskoi was one of founders of several philosophical associations (Psychological Society at Moscow University, Vladimir Solov'ev Religious-Philosophical Society, and others); he was a leading figure of the publishing house Put (The Way) and of the group of religious thinkers affiliated with it, who represented the so-called "neo-Slavophile" current in Russian culture. He was one of the founders and leaders of the Constitutional Democratic (Kadet) Party; he was editor in chief (1906–1910) of the liberal-conservative magazine *Moskovsky Ezhenedel'nik* (Moscow weekly); a member of the State Council in 1916–1917; and a participant in the Council of the Russian Orthodox Church in 1917–1918. After the Revolution of 1917 he adopted a sharply anti-Bolshevik stance and joined the White Army. Trubetskoi died in Novorossiysk at the Black Sea, where the defeated army was preparing to leave Russia.

Trubetskoi was a prolific author, whose writings embrace many fields: religion, philosophy, law, and politics. In the last years of his life he wrote valuable studies on Russian icon painting, as well as fairy tales and his memoirs. His main works, in which he presents an original philosophical system, are *Mirosozertsanie V. S. Solov'eva* (V. S. Solov'ëv's world view, 2 vols., Moscow, 1913), *Metafizicheskie predposylki poznaniya* (Metaphysical premises of knowledge, Moscow, 1917), and *Smysl zhizni* (The meaning of life, Moscow, 1918).

His system belongs to the school of Russian religious philosophy founded by Vladimir Solov'ëv and often referred to as "metaphysics of All-Unity." Trubetskoi's place in this school, which includes Pavel Florenskii, Sergei Bulgakov, Lev Karsavin, Nikolai Losskii, and other principal Russian religious thinkers of the twentieth century, is determined by a special attachment of his philosophy to the thought of the founder of the school (this attachment was enhanced by the fact that Trubetskoi and his brother Sergei were close personal friends of Solov'ëv). Other thinkers in the school are more independent of Solov'ëv, adopting from him just a few key ideas, such as "All-Unity," "Sophia the Wisdom of God," or "Godmanhood," and often criticizing him. In the case of Trubetskoi, however, the entire body of his philosophy emerges out of the critical analysis of Solov'ëv's metaphysics.

Trubetskoi defines the message of Solov'ëv's oeuvre as the teaching on "Godmanhood," and reviews all of this vast and heterogeneous work, selecting a certain core that conveys the message rightly and truly. (He leaves out of the core mainly what he calls Solov'ëv's "Utopias": ideas of theocracy, androgynous love, or the absolute nature of the Roman pope's authority). Then he sets the task of developing this core into a systematic philosophy, complementing it with new ideas and concepts. Due to such a method of "immanent critique," his study of Solov'ëv becomes the basis of his own philosophy.

As for new concepts introduced by Trubetskoi, the most important is "Absolute Consciousness," which is his version of Solov'ëv's All-Unity. Each thing or phenomenon is endowed, for Trubetskoi, with its "meaning" or "truth," conceived epistemologically, as a content of a certain consciousness or, in the tradition of Christian Platonism, as "God's idea" of the thing in question; Absolute Consciousness is defined as the set of all such truths. It is structured into the "exoteric" sphere (God's ideas pertaining to the things of the world) and "esoteric" sphere (God's ideas about Himself).

Taking this concept as his point of departure, Trubetskoi develops, first of all, a detailed theory of cognition. In putting the emphasis on cognition, he was influenced by the Western philosophy of his time, dominated as it was by Neo-Kantianism; but at the same time, following the traditional line of Solov'ëv and much of Russian thought in general, he adopts a critical attitude toward both Kant and Neo-Kantianism. Thus the main part of his theory of cognition takes the form of a critical analysis of Kantian epistemology, aiming to disclose implicit "metaphysical (i.e., ontological) premises" in the latter, and to subordinate epistemology to ontology. Attempts of this kind, often described as "the overcoming of Kant," were typical of Russian philosophy of that period and were dubbed "ontological epistemology" by Nikolai Berdiaev. Trubetskoi's theory of cognition is not the most successful of such attempts, since his treatment of such basic concepts as truth and consciousness is clearly in the Kantian line, and his critical attitude is in fact rather superficial.

A devoted Orthodox Christian of traditionalist views, Trubetskoi believed that in trying to describe the inner dynamics of the Absolute, philosophy risks falling into "Gnosticism" and "Schellingianism." Thus his ontology, presented chiefly in his last work *Smysl zhizni* (The meaning of life), is a traditional Christian philosophy of God and world, or theodicy, developed with the aid of Solov'ëvian concepts of Godmanhood and Sophia (the latter is identified by Trubetskoi with the exoteric sphere of Absolute Consciousness). The final goal of the course of the world is the "conversion of everything human and, even more, everything terrestrial, into Godmanhood" (*Smysl zhizni*, p. 225). The attainment of this goal is not, however, guaranteed; Trubetskoi resorts to his sophiology to describe the path toward it, which he calls the "process of Godmanhood."

Because of the existence of evil and the freedom of the will, each creature may or may not approach its ideal image in Sophia; in Trubetskoi's terms, it possesses both "sophianic and antisophianic potentials." Thus he considers various spheres of reality, presenting a detailed classification of sophianic and antisophianic elements in each sphere: For example, light is regarded as sophianic and darkness as antisophianic. While it may be questionable as an ontology, this approach becomes fruitful when applied to phenomena of Russian art and culture; in particular, it serves as the underpinnings for Trubetskoi's interpretation of the Russian icon as "contemplation in colors," which won wide recognition.

While hardly the best-known or most profound example of Russian thought, Trubetskoi's philosophy nonetheless demonstrates typical features of the Russian religious-philosophical renaissance: its origins in Solov'ëv's thought; its leanings toward religious and mystical experience, resulting in a mixture of theological and philosophical discourse; and its striving to combine this discourse with the "last word" in Western philosophy.

See also Berdyaev, Nikolai Aleksandrovich; Bulgakov, Sergei Nikolaevich; Florenskii, Pavel Aleksandrovich; Kant, Immanuel; Karsavin, Lev Platonovich; Losskii, Nikolai Onufrievich; Neo-Kantianism; Russian Philosophy; Schelling, Friedrich Wilhelm Joseph von; Solov'ëv (Solovyov), Vladimir Sergeevich; Trubetskoi, Sergei Nikolaevich.

Bibliography

WORKS BY TRUBETSKOI

Entsiklopediia prava (The encyclopedia of law). St. Petersburg: LAN, 1999.

Icons: Theology in Color. Translated by Gertrude Vakar. New York: St. Vladimir Seminary Press, 1971.

Iz proshlogo: vospominaniia; iz putevykh zametok bezhentsa (From the past: Memoirs; Travel notes of a refugee). Tomsk: Vodolei, 2000.

Mirosozertsanie V. S. Solov'eva (V. S. Solov'ëv's world view). Moscow: Medium, 1995.

Smysl zhizni (The meaning of life). Moscow: Respublika, 1994.

Voina i mirovaia zadacha Rossii (War and Russia's global task). Moscow: I. D. Sytin, 1915.

WORKS ABOUT TRUBETSKOI

Zenkovsky, V. V. *A History of Russian Philosophy*. Translated by George L. Kline. London: Routledge, 2003.

Segey Horujy (2005)

TRUBETSKOI, NIKOLAI SERGEEVICH
(1890–1938)

A Russian linguist, ethnologist, and student of culture, Nicolai Trubetskoi was one of the founders of Eurasianism. His father, Sergei Trubetskoi, was a well-known philosopher and the first elected rector of Moscow University. Although a descendant of an old aristocratic family, he played an outstanding role in the democratization of Russian life. Unfortunately, his life was cut short: He died less than a month after his election at the age of forty-three; the same fatal ailment (heart disease) killed his son, who lived to be only forty-eight.

It is hard to determine to what extent Trubetskoi's family was responsible for his future scholarly and political views, but certain influences are apparent. He grew up in a devout Orthodox family and owed a great deal to his religious upbringing. The history and meaning of Christianity interested both father and son. The same holds for the relations between Christianity and other religions. The least one can say about Trubetskoi's worldview is that it was formed in a highly cultured religious family with a strong interest in Russia's history and destiny.

In 1905, when Trubetskoi was fifteen years old, he published his first article, but his scholarly interests date back to 1903. He was a typical child prodigy and in this respect he continued the tradition of his incredibly gifted family. Trubetskoi's article was published in the prestigious *Etnograficheskoe obozrenie* (Ethnographic review). It treats the Finnish song "Kulto neito" in light of the theory of survivals. His contributions to the same journal appeared regularly until World War I.

Like many of his peers, Trubetskoi did not go to school: His teachers were private tutors. In 1908 he entered Moscow University and declared his major in the philosophical-psychological department. Disappointed with its curriculum, after two semesters he transferred to the Department of Linguistics but never lost interest in philosophy. His indebtedness to Georg Hegel is unmistakable, and in matters of history he was an extreme determinist. However, his Orthodoxy can explain his teleological position as well as his affinity with Hegel. As a prospective philologist Trubetskoi studied old languages and the comparative method. He also continued his studies of non-Indo-European languages and folklore (especially Finno-Ugric and Caucasian).

In 1913 Trubetskoi graduated with a work on the expression of the future in Indo-European and stayed at the university to prepare for advanced exams and eventually to join the faculty. He spent the next year in Leipzig, where he heard the lectures of the greatest comparative scholars of that time. On his return to Moscow, he married Vera Petrovna Bazilevskaia (1892–1965). In 1915 he passed his master's exams and in 1916 received the rank of adjunct professor. The 1917 Bolshevik Revolution found him in the Caucasus, and he never saw Moscow again. He migrated south with the White Army and eventually came to Constantinople. There he received an offer from Sofia University and spent two years as a docent in Bulgaria. In Sofia in 1920, Trubetskoi published his book *Rossiia i chelovechestvo* (Russia and mankind), which inaugurated Eurasianism, a trend that later enjoyed great popularity among the Russian émigrés between two world wars.

The main idea of Eurasianism is that Russia belongs to the East rather than to the West and has little to do with "the Romano-Germanic" world. Trubetskoi's diatribe against the West is oddly at variance with his upbringing, for he was a classic product of European culture, but it accords well with his lifelong interest in non-Indo-European languages and oral tradition and his glorification of the morals of nomadic peoples. It therefore comes as no surprise that his next book bears the title (in translation) *The Legacy of Genghis Khan: A Perspective on Russian History Not from the West but from the East* (1925). Trubetskoi's attack on European ethnocentricity found many supporters and many opponents among his contemporaries, but after World War II his theories merged with those of the anticolonial movement, which explains a renewed interest in them. His Eurasianist works and the trend he initiated have been studied extensively in many countries, and the foundational texts have been translated into several "Romano-Germanic" languages. After the collapse of the Soviet Union, they were also published in Russia.

Trubetskoi's position in Bulgaria was precarious, but an offer from Vienna University to become a professor of Slavic secured his future, and in the autumn of 1922 the most productive period of Trubetskoi's life began. In Vienna he taught all the Slavic languages and literatures, and his lectures, published posthumously, provide a good idea of his activities. Eurasianism too remained at the center of his interests. However innovative his ideas on Russian history and its future and however original his contributions to the study of Russian literature, especially medieval, may be, it is his linguistic work that made him world famous. Trubetzkoi is the founder of a branch of linguistics known as phonology. His main ally in that endeavor was Roman Jakobson, another expatriate from Moscow, who lived in Czechoslovakia. He and Trubetskoi became the main inspiration of a group of linguists known as the Prague Circle.

The focus of phonology is not on the production of the sounds of speech but on their ability to distinguish meaning, form oppositions, and change as elements of a system and a self-regulating code. Sounds viewed from this perspective are called phonemes. Phonology (that is, functional phonetics) served as the basis of what came to be known as structuralism. The conceptual apparatus of phonology was later extended to the other areas of linguistics, mythology, folklore, literary studies, anthropology, psychology, and even geography, with varying success. Although the Prague version of structuralism is not the only one, it is arguably the most influential. Trubetskoi developed his ideas in numerous publications, but his main book appeared posthumously.

On March 13, 1938, German troops occupied Austria. All his life Trubetskoi suffered from various illnesses; the spring of 1938 was an especially hard period for him. The Gestapo subjected him to a long interrogation, and his papers were impounded. The search and the interrogation had a devastating effect on Trubetskoi. Dangerous symptoms developed in his lungs, and on June 25 he died.

See also Eurasianism; Hegel, Georg Wilhelm Friedrich; Phonology; Trubetskoi, Sergei Nikolaevich.

Bibliography

WORKS BY NIKOLAI TRUBETSKOI

Principles of Phonology. Translated by Christiane A. M. Baltaxe. Berkeley: University of California Press, 1969. Originally published as *Grundzüge der Phonologie* (Travaux du cercle linguistique de Prague 7. Prague: Cercle linguistique de Copenhague et Ministè, publ. de la Rèpublique Tcéco-Slovaque, 1939). The book contains a bibliography of Trubetskoi's works through 1968.

Theory and History of Literature. Vol. 72: *Writings on Literature*, edited, translated, and introduced by Anatoly Liberman.

Minneapolis: University of Minnesota Press, 1990. Includes, among others, Trubetzkoy's lectures on Dostoevsky.

WORKS ABOUT NIKOLAI TRUBETSKOI

Liberman, Anatoly, ed. *The Legacy of Genghis Khan and Other Essays on Russia's Identity*. Ann Arbor: Michigan Slavic Publications, 1991. Liberman's postscript contains a detailed biography of Trubetzkoy and an analysis of his Eurasianist works.

Liberman, Anatoly, ed. *Studies in General Linguistics and Language Structure*. Translated by Marvin Taylor and Anatoly Liberman. Durham, NC: Duke University Press, 2001.

Nos. 2–4 contain numerous references to the literature on Trubetzkoi.

Anatoly Liberman (2005)

TRUBETSKOI, SERGEI NIKOLAEVICH

(1862–1905)

Sergei Nikolaevich Trubetskoi was a Russian philosopher, socially conscious essayist, and man of public affairs. After graduating from the historico-philological department of Moscow University in 1885, he remained at the university. In 1890 he defended his master's dissertation, "Metafizika v Drevnei Gretsii" (Metaphysics in ancient Greece), and in 1900 he defended his doctoral dissertation, "Uchenie o Logose v ego istorii" (The doctrine of the logos in its history). From 1900 to 1905 he served as one the editors of the journal *Voprosy filosofii i psikhologii* (Questions of philosophy and psychology). He actively participated in the Zemstvo movement, becoming one of its spiritual leaders. Starting in 1901, at the beginning of the student disturbances, he came out for the institution of university autonomy. After Moscow University was granted autonomy in 1905, he was chosen as its head. However, the wave of disturbances at that time had swamped the university, putting liberal defenders of academic freedoms in a difficult position and leading to Trubetskoi's untimely death.

In his philosophical views Trubetskoi is close to Vladimir Sergeevich Solov'ëv. Like Solov'ëv, Trubetskoi experienced the influence of the Slavophiles, German idealism, and ancient Platonism, uniting Christianity and Platonism in his doctrine. However, Trubetskoi did not share Solov'ëv's mysticism: If for Solov'ëv the central theme was the doctrine of Sophia, Trubetskoi's main work was devoted to the theme of the Logos. And it is not by chance that an early work of Trubetskoi's that was devoted to sophiology remained unfinished; in his works this theme is represented by a theory of the world soul, where Platonism is united with a Kantian doctrine of *a priori* forms of sensation.

TRUBETSKOI'S CONCRETE IDEALISM

Trubetskoi's conceptions received their most complete exposition in his works *O prirode chelovecheskogo soznaniia* (On the nature of human consciousness; 1889–1891) and *Osnovaniia idealizma* (The foundations of idealism; 1896). He called his doctrine *concrete idealism*, in contrast to the abstract idealism of classical German philosophy.

As his starting point, Trubetskoi takes not abstract concept (of the type of Georg Wilhelm Friedrich Hegel's *pure being*) but concrete being, real entity as the subject of all definitions, which reveals thought in this subject. Being necessarily precedes thought; if the contrary is assumed, one arrives at panlogism, that is, at the production from abstract thought of all the abundance of its definitions. According to Trubetskoi the eternal actual consciousness (God) precedes every finite (becoming) consciousness; he thus rejects the pantheistic doctrine of Johann Gottlieb Fichte, Friedrich Wilhelm Joseph von Schelling, and Hegel concerning humanity as the "becoming God" and defends the positions of theism. Attempting to prove that being cannot be reduced to a logical idea and that general concepts are only relations of thought to its object, Trubetskoi at the same time recognizes the spiritual nature of reality, the rational laws of the cosmic Logos according to which both natural life and human life are ordered.

In attempting to remain on the foundation of rationalism, the philosopher, however, does not consider reason to be the sole source of knowledge. Just as in man it is possible to identify three faculties—sense perception, thought, and will—so knowledge, too, is realized with the aid of experience, conditioned by the *a priori* laws of perception (universal sensationalism), with the aid of reason, which reveals the lawful connection of phenomena, the universal correlatedness of that which exists, and finally with the aid of faith, which establishes the reality of the entities one thinks and perceives. The object of faith is an autonomous living power, defined as spirit; faith, according to Trubetskoi, is the recognition of "real entities or subjects independent of us" (1994, p. 671). With this, faith "convinces us of the reality of the external world, of the reality of objects of sense perception and reason" (p. 665).

In contrast to Solov'ëv, Trubetskoi does not identify faith with intellectual intuition or with inspiration: True to Orthodox tradition, he is careful to separate faith from imagination and places the moral or ethical sphere above the aesthetic sphere. Both in God and in humans the foundation of the personality is will; and therefore being is revealed to faith as a faculty of will. However, Trubetskoi does not oppose faith and reason, revelation and speculation, but points to their unity, emphasizing that "the concept of the Logos is connected with Greek philosophy, in which it arose, and with Christian theology, in which it took firm root" (1994, p. 44).

In accordance with this conviction, Trubetskoi devotes his chief historico-philosophical work, *Metaphysics in Ancient Greece* (1890), to Greek philosophy, where the concept of the Logos was formed, and his chief historico-theological work, *The Doctrine of the Logos in Its History*, to the Christian understanding of the Logos, which was developed in the struggle with Judaism and Gnosticism. Greek philosophy, according to Trubetskoi, is one of the spiritual sources of Christianity. It is not antagonistic to Christianity, not the cause of the distortion of the original Evangelical faith, as many Protestant theologians have asserted. Nevertheless, Trubetskoi recognizes the achievements of Protestant scholarship, in particular that of the historical criticism of Adolf Harnack, to whose discoveries he attempts to give his own interpretation, on the basis of the Orthodox patristic tradition. With his thoughts developing in the spirit of this tradition, Trubetskoi displays a critical attitude toward Solov'ëv's theocratic utopia and toward his interpretation of the Bible through the prism of mystical symbolism and Catholic orthodoxy.

THE SOBORNOST (CONCILIAR NATURE) OF CONSCIOUSNESS

In analyzing the nature of human consciousness, Trubetskoi poses the complex philosophical question about the interrelation of the individual and the universal. According to Trubetskoi this question has not been resolved in European philosophy: Neither empiricism nor idealism have been able to explain the nature of consciousness, and therefore the nature of personality has not been understood. The empiricists identified personality with individual internal states of consciousness, with a set of psychical associations (psychologism) that do not have objective logical significance. By contrast, German idealism dissolved personality in a universal principle, making it a disappearing "moment" in the development of the absolute spirit.

According to Trubetskoi the common root of modern European philosophy in its two variants is subjectivism, originating in Protestantism. Having shown that it is impossible to explain consciousness either as a property of the separate empirical individual or as a product of a universal generic principle, Trubetskoi, following the Slavophiles, arrives at the conclusion that the personal, finite consciousness can be understood only if one admits the sobornost (conciliar nature—from "church council") of consciousness, the common or communal nature of the latter. He considers that this is the only way one can explain man's ability to gain universal and necessary knowledge of reality and to gain an understanding of other people and of the surrounding world. Sobornost as the essence of consciousness is conceived by Trubetskoi as guaranteeing the objectivity of knowledge. For him, the premise of this objectivity and therefore of the possibility of communal consciousness (consciousness rooted in sobornost) is the existence of the eternally actual consciousness, that is, the consciousness of the divine person of the Creator.

Sobornost is a kind of perfect society or a "metaphysical socialism." "Individualistic psychology and subjective idealism both lead to the rejection of the individual soul, but metaphysical socialism, the recognition of the sobornost of consciousness, grounds our faith in this soul. If it is grounded abstractly, isolated individuality tends to become a zero, nothing; individuality is preserved and actualized only in society, and in fact only in the perfect society" (1994, p. 577). The perfect society is an ideal toward which humankind strives. This society must be ruled by the law of love, and love is "the unity of all in one, the consciousness of all in oneself and of oneself in all" (p. 592). But such love, according to Trubetskoi, is unrealizable in natural human union. It presupposes the divine-human union, or the Church.

Just as reason is a property of the universal subject, sense perception, too, according to Trubetskoi, should not be considered to belong only to the individual consciousness. There exists a certain universal sense perception whose bearer is the world soul as its subject, distinct from God. Trubetskoi conceives this bearer as a cosmic entity, or as the world in its psychical foundation, thanks to which the world appears as a living and animate organism. Remaining an adherent of the Logos complemented by faith, Trubetskoi is convinced that at the foundation of the world there lies a rational and loving principle, and for this reason the world is essentially good. This is the source of Trubetskoi's optimism, of his energy, and of his indefatigable academic and public activity.

See also Fichte, Johann Gottlieb; Harnack, Carl Gustav Adolf von; Hegel, Georg Wilhelm Friedrich; Idealism;

Platonism and the Platonic Tradition; Schelling, Friedrich Wilhelm Joseph von; Solov'ëv (Solovyov), Vladimir Sergeevich; Trubetskoi, Evgenii Nikolaevich.

Bibliography

WORKS BY TRUBETSKOI

Sobranie sochinenii (Collected works). Vols. 1–6. Moscow, 1906–1912.

Sochineniia (Works). Moscow, 1994.

WORKS ON TRUBETSKOI

Bohachevsky-Chomiak, Martha. *Sergei N. Trubetskoi: An Intellectual among the Intelligentsia in Prerevolutionary Russia*. Belmont, MA: Nordland, 1976.

Elansky, P. P. "Kn. S. N. Trubetskoi i filosofiia" (Prince S. N. Trubetskoi and philosophy). *Mysl' i slovo* (Moscow) (1917).

Gaidenko, P. P. "'Konkretnyi idealizm' S. N. Trubetskogo" (The "Concrete Idealism" of S. N. Trubetskoi). *Voprosy literatury* 9 (1990).

Lopatin, L. M. *Kniaz' S. N. Trubetsk oi i ego obshchee filosofskoe mirosozertsanie* (Prince S. N. Trubetskoi and his general philosophical worldview). Moscow, 1906.

Kotliarevsky, S. A. "Mirosozertsanie kniazia S. N. Trubetskogo" (The worldview of Prince S. N. Trubetskoi). *Voprosy filosofii i psikhologii* 131 (1) (1916).

Rachinsky, G. A. "Religiozno-filosofskie vozzreniia kn. S. N. Trubetskogo" (The religious-philosophical views of Prince of S. N. Trubetskoi). *Voprosy filosofii i psikhologii* 131 (1) (1916).

Sbornik rechei, posviashchennykh pamiati S. N. Trubetskogo (Collection of speeches dedicated to the memory of S. N. Trubetskoi). Moscow, 1909.

Zen'kovskii, V. V. *A History of Russian Philosophy*. 2 vols. Translated by George L. Kline. New York: Columbia University Press, 1953. Originally published in Russian under the title *Istoriia russkoi filosofii* in 1948 and 1950.

P. Gaidenko (2005)
Translated by Boris Jakim

TRUTH

Theories of truth investigate truth as a property of one's thoughts and speech. We attribute truth and falsity to a wide variety of so-called *truth-bearers*: linguistic items (sentences, utterances, statements, and assertions), abstract items (propositions), and mental items (judgments and beliefs). What is the property we are attributing when we call a truth-bearer true? The question is crucial because of truth's involvement in central philosophical claims: For example, it is often said that truth is the aim of science, that the meaning of a sentence is given by the conditions under which it is true, that logical validity is the preservation of truth, or that ethical statements are neither true nor false. A proper understanding of truth promises to illuminate fundamental issues in metaphysics, the philosophy of language, logic, and ethics.

The two traditional theories of truth are the correspondence theory and the coherence theory. Further theories of truth have emerged since the last part of the nineteenth century, most notably the pragmatic theory, the identity theory, and the semantic theory. There has also been a reaction against the idea that truth has a substantive nature to uncover, which has led to markedly increased support for so-called deflationary theories of truth.

A different motivation for theorizing about truth is the challenge posed by the semantic paradoxes, especially the Liar paradox. Theories of truth prompted by the Liar tend to be concerned less with the nature of truth, and more with the logic and semantics of the predicate *true*. There has been surprisingly little contact between these two groups of theories (though see Priest, Beall, and Armour-Garb 2005).

THE CORRESPONDENCE THEORY OF TRUTH

According to the correspondence theory truth consists in correspondence to the facts. A truth-bearer (say, the proposition that snow is white) is true if and only if it corresponds to a fact (that snow is white). Broadly speaking, truth is a relational property between truth-bearers on the one side and the world on the other.

There is the suggestion of the correspondence account in Plato's *Sophist* (263b), where in Theaetetus's presence the Stranger contrasts the true statement "Theaetetus sits" with the false statement "Theaetetus flies": "The true one states about you the things that are as they are … [w]hereas the false statement states about you things different from the things that are." In *Categories* Aristotle writes, "The fact of the being of a man carries with it the truth of the proposition that he is … the truth or falsity of the proposition depends on the fact of the man's being or not being" (14b14–22; see also 4b8). The correspondence idea may also be present in Aristotle's famous definition of truth, "To say of what is that it is, and of what is not that it is not, is true" (*Metaphysics* Γ, 1011b25). Echoes of the Platonic-Aristotelian account are present in the Stoics and medieval philosophers (e.g., St. Thomas Aquinas, William of Ockham, and Jean Buridan), and many modern philosophers from René Descartes onward endorse the correspondence idea, though with little or no discussion.

A classic statement of the correspondence theory is given by G. E. Moore: To say of a given belief that it is true "is to say that there is in the Universe *a* fact to which it corresponds" (1953, p. 302). Moore takes it that we are all perfectly familiar with the relation of correspondence, "That there *is* such a relation, seems to me clear; all that is new about my definitions is that they concentrate attention upon just *that* relation, and make it the essential point in the definitions of truth and falsehood" (p. 304). Moore's remarks bring out both a strength and a weakness of the correspondence theory. The correspondence theory is the most natural account of truth—it seems that no one need deny that a true belief corresponds to how things are. But this raises the suspicion that the correspondence theory is platitudinous—to say that a truth-bearer corresponds to the facts is just an elaborate way of saying that it is true. There is no distinctive theory of truth unless more can be said about the correspondence relation. And Moore admits that he can offer no analysis of it; the best he can do, he says, is to "define it in the sense of pointing out what relation it is, by simply pointing out that it is *the* relation which does hold between this belief, if true, and this fact, and does not hold between this belief and any other fact" (p. 301).

Bertrand Russell (1906–1907, 1912/1959) attempts to shed light on the correspondence relation by arguing for a structural isomorphism or congruence between beliefs and facts. Beliefs and facts are structured complexes, and when a belief-complex is suitably congruent with a fact-complex, the belief is true. Consider Othello's belief that Desdemona loves Cassio. According to Russell, believing is a four-place relation; in the present case it is the cement that unites Othello, Desdemona, the loving relation, and Cassio into one complex whole. The last three items are what Russell calls the *objects* in the belief, and these objects are ordered in a certain way by the believing relation (Othello believes that Desdemona loves Cassio, not that Cassio loves Desdemona). Now consider another complex unity, Desdemona's love for Cassio, composed of the objects in Othello's belief. Here, the loving relation is the cement that binds together Desdemona and Cassio in the same order that they have in Othello's belief. If this complex unity exists, then it "is called the fact corresponding to the belief. Thus a belief is true when there is a corresponding fact, and is false when there is no corresponding fact" (p. 129).

OBJECTIONS TO THE CORRESPONDENCE THEORY

It is central to Russell's elucidation that there is a structural congruence between the content of a true belief and the corresponding fact—for example, between the proposition expressed by the sentence "Desdemona loves Cassio" and the fact that Desdemona loves Cassio. But sentences and the propositions they express come in a variety of logical structures—negations, conditionals, universal generalizations, and so on. Are there, then, "funny facts": negative facts, hypothetical facts, universal facts, and other logically complex facts? It might seem that the real world—the world of dated, particular events and things in specific spatial and temporal orderings—just does not seem able to contain anything of this kind of complexity: negative, universal, or hypothetical situations, for example. We seem to be presented with a dilemma: either facts are too "linguistic," too closely tied to the logical structures of our language, or facts are worldly items that are not structurally congruent with the propositions we express.

Russell (1956) and Ludwig Wittgenstein (1922) go on to develop their philosophy of logical atomism, according to which there are no logically complex facts, only atomic facts. True propositions that are logically simple or atomic correspond to atomic facts, but logically complex true propositions no longer correspond to logically complex facts. Rather, complex propositions are recursively broken down into the simple propositions that compose them, and the truth of complex propositions is ultimately explained via the atomic facts to which true atomic propositions correspond. Difficulties remain, however: certain complex propositions, for example, "because" statements and subjunctives, are resistant to a recursive breakdown into simple components; and we can still ask whether universal facts are required for true universal generalizations, and negative facts for true negations. Despite these well-known problems, versions of logical atomism are not without their supporters (e.g., see Armstrong 1997). In a different vein J. L. Austin avoids "funny facts" by denying that correspondence is a matter of structural congruence, "There is no need whatsoever for the words used in making a true statement to 'mirror' in any way, however indirect, any feature whatsoever of the situation or event" (1999, p. 155)—even a single word or simple phrase can correspond to a complex situation. Rather, correspondence is a correlation that is determined by our linguistic conventions: it is "*absolutely and purely* conventional" (p. 154).

A far-reaching and influential family of objections to the correspondence theory takes issue with a certain distinction of standpoints that the theory seems to imply. There is the standpoint we occupy when we judge, say, that there are cows in the garden, and then there is the standpoint we occupy when we determine whether our judgment is true. When we occupy this latter standpoint, the correspondence theory seems to require us to judge whether our judgment is appropriately related by correspondence to the facts. Gottlob Frege (1999) objects that there really is no further standpoint to take up, and no further judgment to make—rather we should simply verify whether there are cows in the garden. This line of thought leads Frege to the conclusion that truth is undefinable; it also tends toward deflationism, since it may seem that truth drops out of the picture.

According to another line of objection, it is an illusion that we can have access to an unvarnished realm of facts with which to compare our judgment. Our knowledge of the world is mediated by our descriptions, interpretations, and judgments; we cannot step outside our own system of beliefs and compare those beliefs with "bare reality." Since the correspondence theory says that truth consists in correspondence to the facts, and those facts are inaccessible to us, we can never know that a judgment is true, and we are led to skepticism. Those who endorse this line of criticism typically associate the correspondence theory with metaphysical realism and advocate instead some form of antirealism and an "epistemic" account of truth, say, in terms of verification (like the logical positivists) or assertibility (see Dewey 1938, Dummett 1978).

THE COHERENCE THEORY OF TRUTH

If we cannot judge a belief against the facts, perhaps we should judge it against our other beliefs: does it "hang together" with the rest of our beliefs? The coherence theorist says that the truth of a belief consists in its coherence with other beliefs. Given some favored coherent set of beliefs, the truth of any of its members consists in its membership in that set—in this way the skeptic is disarmed, since truth no longer requires access to an independent realm of facts. Versions of the coherence theory have been attributed to Benedict (Baruch) de Spinoza, Immanuel Kant, Johann Gottlieb Fichte, and Georg Wilhelm Friedrich Hegel (see by way of comparison Walker 1989), and the theory was championed by idealists, including Harold H. Joachim (1906) and Brand Blanshard (1939), at the end of the nineteenth century and the beginning of the twentieth. Joachim rejects Descartes' idea that we can know truths individually, "The ideal of knowledge for me is a system, not of *truths*, but of truth"; knowledge of an individual truth "is the smallest and most abstracted fragment of knowledge, a mere mutilated shred torn from the living whole in which alone it possessed its significance" (1906, p. 48). So Joachim advocates a thoroughgoing holistic view of knowledge and of truth, "Truth in its essential nature is that systematic coherence which is the character of a significant whole" (p. 50). The coherence theory was subsequently adopted by some logical positivists, notably Otto Neurath (1959), who, like Joachim, endorsed a holistic view of knowledge and truth, and combined it with the positivists' verificationist doctrine that no sense can be attached to a reality that goes beyond what can be verified or falsified by the empirical methods of science.

There are attractive features of the coherence theory. In favor of holism, we can say that statements like "The Enlightenment brought about the French Revolution" and "Neutrinos lack mass" cannot be understood in isolation from a good deal of history and science; and we do often test the truth of a statement against a large body of background statements. But the coherence theory is a theory of the nature of truth, not a theory of how we test for truth, and as such it has been the target of a number of objections. Russell (1906–1907), Moritz Schlick (1959), and others have argued that an arbitrary set of propositions, say, those of a fairy tale or a good novel, would count as a set of truths as long as the propositions cohere with one another—where coherence is taken in the sense of consistency or compatibility. An appeal to comprehensiveness seems not to help the coherence theorist here: Given a coherent set of propositions however large, there will always be equally large coherent sets incompatible with it (and with each other). And placing restrictions on membership in the favored set—for example, admitting only our actual beliefs, or ideal beliefs held at the end of inquiry—seems to tie truth less to coherence and more to the successful tracking of the facts. A further objection derives from Russell: Suppose we have a large, coherent set of propositions about, say, the nineteenth century, and suppose that we can coherently add the proposition that Bishop Stubbs wore episcopal gaiters. According to the coherence theory this proposition is true, in virtue of its membership in a coherent set. If we protest that we cannot be committed to its truth because we do not know whether it is true or false, then we are using true and false in a way that the coherence theorist does not recognize. The difficulty is compounded if we now run the argument with the proposition that Bishop Stubbs *did not* wear episcopal gaiters (further discussion of the coherence theory can be found in Putnam [1981], Blackburn [1984], Davidson [1984], and Walker [1989]).

THE PRAGMATIC THEORY OF TRUTH

The pragmatic theory of truth is associated primarily with the American pragmatists Charles S. Peirce and William James, and their influence can still be felt in the work of, for example, Richard Rorty (1982) and Robert B. Brandom (1994). According to Peirce we are to understand any idea or object through its practical effects, "Consider what effects, that might conceivably have practical bearings, we conceive the object of our conception to have. Then, our conception of these effects is the whole of our conception of the object" (1955b, p. 31).

Peirce applies his rule to the idea of *reality*: the practical effect that real things have on us "is to cause belief" (1955b, p. 36), and so the question is how to distinguish true belief from false belief. Peirce's answer is that the true beliefs are the ones to which we will all agree, and only the methods of science can realize the hope of reaching this consensus. Peirce writes, "This great hope is embodied in the conception of truth and reality. The opinion which is fated to be ultimately agreed to by all who investigate, is what we mean by the truth, and the object represented in this opinion is the real. That is the way I would explain reality" (p. 38). This is not the independently existing reality associated with the correspondence theory: For Peirce, what is special about science is its ability to settle opinion, and reality is whatever settled opinion says it is.

James applies Peirce's rule directly to truth. The practical effects of true beliefs are successful actions, beneficial dealings with the world; truths are "invaluable instruments of action" (1907, p. 97), truths "*pay*" (p. 104). And so, in accordance with Peirce's rule, truth *is* what is useful, what "works." James places less emphasis than Peirce on consensus and scientific method (indeed, Peirce renamed his theory "pragmaticism" to distance it from James's version). James applies his theory to individuals' beliefs as well as collective beliefs, and religious and metaphysical beliefs as well as empirical ones (e.g., "On pragmatist principles, if the hypothesis of God works satisfactorily in the widest sense of the word, it is true" [p. 143]).

It is standardly objected that we can have beneficial false beliefs and detrimental true beliefs. My false belief that I play the violin beautifully may in fact improve my performance; my true belief that I do not may worsen it. James has the resources for a response. While "the true is only the expedient in our way of thinking," truth is the expedient in a strong sense, "expedient in the long run and on the whole of course" (1907, p. 106). We have to take the long view: I may perform well this time, but overall I will be better served by an accurate assessment of my talents. The long view must be taken not only of individuals' beliefs, but of whole theories—Ptolemaic astronomy was expedient for centuries (p. 107). "The 'absolutely' true, meaning what no farther experience will ever alter, is that ideal vanishing-point towards which we imagine that all our temporary truths will some day converge. … Meanwhile we have to live today by what truth we can get today, and be ready tomorrow to call it falsehood" (pp. 106–107).

Along with a controversial commitment to relativism, James presents here a holistic theme that may suit his pragmatism: It is perhaps more plausible that the truth of an entire system of belief, as opposed the truth of our beliefs taken individually, is a matter of its working for us. Taken this way, pragmatism may be seen as a version of the coherence theory. Still, a basic objection remains: It is plausible that a body of truths should be useful or coherent, but it does not follow that truth *consists in* utility or coherence—a correspondence theorist will say that truths are useful and mutually coherent just because they correspond to the world.

THE IDENTITY THEORY OF TRUTH

Despairing of the correspondence theory, F. H. Bradley wrote, "if we are to advance, we must accept once for all the identification of truth with reality" (1999, pp. 35–36). Here, Bradley seems to embrace the identity theory of truth: a truth does not correspond to a fact, but is identical to a fact (Bradley's view is discussed in Candlish 1995). Another influence is Frege's remark, "A fact is a true thought" (1999, p. 101), though Frege himself did not endorse the identity theory. Versions of the theory are defended by Jennifer Hornsby (1997) and Julian Dodd (2000). The theory may appear counterintuitive: If true mental items—true judgments or true beliefs—are facts, then it seems that the mind contains facts, that mind and world are literally the same. It may also be argued that the theory is unstable, collapsing into deflationism or leading to the elimination of true judgments altogether—"straight to thought's suicide," as Bradley puts it (1893, p. 150).

THE SEMANTIC THEORY OF TRUTH

The semantic theory of truth originates with the mathematician and logician Alfred Tarski (1930–1931/1983, 1999). Tarski sought a *definition* of truth that was formally correct and met the following constraint: It must imply all sentences of the form exemplified by

"Aardvarks amble" is true if and only aardvarks amble,

that is, all sentences of the form: p is true if and only if p. These so-called T-sentences are so basic to truth, Tarski thought, that they must follow logically from any adequate definition—in this way, he said, we do justice to Aristotle's definition (see the previous discussion). Indeed, Tarski regarded each T-sentence as a "partial definition" of truth, and if we were dealing with a finite language (in the sense that it contains only finitely many sentences), we need only list all the associated T-sentences for a complete definition of truth for that language (see 1930–1931/1983, pp. 251–253). But since Tarski was after a definition of truth for formal languages that were infinitary, such a list is not feasible. So instead Tarski provided a recursive definition—not of truth, though, but of the more basic notion of *satisfaction*. In the simplest kind of case, satisfaction is a relation between an object and a predicate—for example, a London bus satisfies the predicate *is red*. Satisfaction is defined recursively, first for predicates (of a given language) that exhibit no logical complexity, and second for those that do. Tarski then defined truth in terms of satisfaction. The result was a definition of truth for formal languages that was formally precise and implied the T-sentences.

It is remarkable that both correspondence theorists and deflationists have found Tarski's account congenial. Correspondence theorists are drawn to satisfaction as a word-world relation and to the possibility that the correspondence relation between a sentence and a fact can be broken down into relations between parts of sentences (predicates and names) and the things they refer to (e.g., Devitt 1991). This raises the hope that correspondence is no more mysterious than the semantic relations between predicates and names and their referents. Deflationists, in particular disquotationalists, are drawn to the idea that the T-sentences say all there is to say about truth, as will be seen later on. Tarski himself emphasized the neutrality of his theory: "We may accept the semantic conception of truth without giving up any epistemological attitude we may have had; we may remain naïve realists, critical realists or idealists, empiricists or metaphysicians—whatever we were before. The semantic conception is completely neutral toward all these issues" (1999, p. 140).

Tarski's aim was not to uncover the nature of truth, but to place the concept of truth beyond suspicion. On the one hand, he thought, truth is fundamental to science, logic, and metamathematics; on the other hand, truth has an "evil reputation" because of its involvement with the Liar paradox. Tarski's aim was to find a way of defining truth in terms that no one could question:

> The definition of truth, or of any other semantic concept, will fulfil what we intuitively expect from every definition; that is, it will explain the meaning of the term being defined in terms whose meaning appears to be completely clear and unequivocal. And, moreover, we have then a kind of guarantee that the use of semantic concepts will not involve us in any contradictions. (1999, p. 127)

Anyone wishing to turn Tarski's definition into a fully general account of truth faces a number of obstacles. Tarski defined truth only for regimented, formal languages, not for natural languages like English; the definition is a definition of truth for a given language, not for truth *simpliciter*; and the definition, according to Hartry Field (1972), fails to explain truth since it merely reduces truth to further semantic notions that are not themselves adequately explained.

DEFLATIONARY THEORIES OF TRUTH

Deflationists say that "substantive" theories of truth—such as the correspondence and coherence theories—are radically misguided: there is no substantive property of truth to theorize about. According to Frank Ramsey truth is *redundant*, "It is evident that 'It is true that Caesar was murdered' means no more than that Caesar was murdered" (1999, p. 106). Truth is less easily eliminated from generalizations like "Everything Socrates says is true," but Ramsey argues that it can be done (p. 106). The word *true* disappears, and any reason to investigate the nature of truth disappears along with it. According to a more sophisticated version of the redundancy theory, the prosentential theory of truth (Grover, Camp, and Belnap 1975), the word *true* is not even a genuine predicate, but a mere component of prosentences. If I say "That is true" in response to a claim of yours, I have produced not a sentence but a prosentence, referring back to your sentence just as the pronoun *he* may refer back to the name *John*. We might think of "That is true" as hyphenated, with no more internal structure than the pronoun *he*. On the prosentential view, *true* does not survive as a discrete property-denoting predicate. P. F. Strawson's (1949) variant of the redundancy theory attributes to *true* a performative role: we use *true* not to pick out a property, but to perform speech-acts such as endorsing, agreeing, and conceding.

Disquotationalists also ascribe to *true* a role different from that of ordinary predicates. According to the disquotational theory of truth—championed by W. V. Quine (1970) and further developed and defended by Field (e.g., see 1994)—to say that a sentence is true is really just an indirect way of saying the sentence itself. There really is no more to the truth of the sentence "Penguins waddle" than is given by the Tarskian T-sentence

> "Penguins waddle" is true if and only if penguins waddle,

and the totality of T-sentences tells the whole story about truth. This prompts the question: Why not dispense with the truth predicate in favor of direct talk about the world? The disquotationalist will respond by pointing to generalizations such as "Every sentence of the form 'p or not p' is true" (see Quine 1970, pp. 10–13). In such a case we could dispense with the truth predicate only if we could produce an infinite conjunction of sentences of the form "p or not p": "Aardvarks amble or aardvarks do not amble, and bison bathe or bison do not bathe, and … ." But we cannot produce infinitely long sentences. So to achieve the desired effect, we generalize over sentences, and then, via the truth-predicate, bring them back down to earth by disquoting them. The truth-predicate is a device for disquotation. Despite surface appearances, *true* does not denote a property or relation—it is a logical device. So there is no property of truth to explore and no work for truth to do beyond its logical role.

The disquotational theory takes the truth-bearers to be sentences, and this raises a concern about the scope of the theory (for further concerns, see David 1994). Suppose that on the authority of others I believe that Dmitri is always right, though I speak no Russian. I say, with apparent understanding, "What Dmitri says is true." But according to disquotationalism understanding what I have said is just a matter of understanding what Dmitri said; and since I cannot understand what Dmitri said, I cannot understand what I have said. Disquotationalists typically relativize their theory to the sentences of a given natural language such as English. And since an English speaker will not understand every sentence of English, some disquotationalists recognize the need to go further and restrict the theory to the sentences of a given speaker's idiolect (those sentences that the speaker understands). This seems to lead us away from the commonsensical notion of truth—ordinarily, it seems, we can apply the notion of truth to foreign sentences, and to sentences of English that we do not yet understand. In short, the concept of truth seems not to depend on the sentences that a speaker happens to understand at a given time. The challenge to the disquotationalist (taken up by Field and others) is to ease the counterintuitive restrictions on disquotational truth in ways that do not compromise the theory.

These difficulties for disquotationalism might motivate a different choice of truth-bearer—propositions instead of sentences. Paul Horwich (1998) presents a *minimal theory of truth*, according to which a complete account of truth is given by the propositional analogues of Tarski's T-sentences:

> The proposition that aardvarks amble is true if and only aardvarks amble; The proposition that bison bathe is true if and only if bison bathe,

and so on, ad infinitum. Far from being restricted to speakers' idiolects, *true* applies to all propositions, including those expressed by sentences we do not understand. But now there is a new set of concerns. First, since we do not understand every proposition, we will understand only a fraction of the axioms that compose the minimal theory—and so our grasp of truth must always remain partial. Second, since the minimal theory describes truth in a piecemeal way, for each proposition individually, it does not include any generalizations about truth. So it may be objected that the theory cannot explain generalizations such as "Only propositions are true"—the theory does not tell us what is not true, so it does not rule out, for example, the absurdity that the Moon is true. (For more on this objection, see Anil Gupta [1993]; Christopher S. Hill [2002] offers a version of minimalism that is responsive to it.) Third, consider the form shared by Horwich's axioms: the proposition that p is true if and only p. To obtain an axiom, we must be careful to replace each occurrence of p by English tokens of the same sentence-type, with the same meaning. But now sentences appear to be back in the picture—together with the substantive semantic notion of meaning, which may not be as free of involvement with truth as minimalism requires.

This last remark relates to a general challenge faced by all forms of deflationism. Deflationists typically focus on uses of *true* such as "'Aardvarks amble' is true," or "Most of what Socrates says is true"—what we may call *first-order* uses, where *true* applies to a particular truth-bearer or a set of truth-bearers. But *true* is also used in other ways: for example, consider the claim that the meaning of a sentence is given by its truth-conditions or the claim that to assert is to put forward as true. These uses of *true*, call them *second order*, purport to explain meaning and assertion. Unlike first-order uses, they do not apply to any particular truth-bearers, and so it is not easy to see how they might be treated as redundant and eliminable or given a merely disquotational role. These second-order uses must be explained. Moreover, the deflationist must show that it is possible to explain meaning and assertion (and many other concepts apparently related to truth, such as validity, belief, verification, explanation, and practical success) in terms that assign to truth a limited logical role or no role at all.

THEORIES OF TRUTH AND THE LIAR

One version of the Liar paradox is generated by the self-referential sentence:

(1) (1) is false.

Suppose that (1) is true, then what it says is the case, and so (1) is false. On the contrary, suppose that (1) is false—then since that is what (1) says it is, (1) is true. A contradiction is reached either way and we are landed in paradox.

Hierarchical theories of truth have perhaps been the orthodox response to the Liar. Let L_0 be a fragment of English that does not contain the predicate *true*. Let true-in-L_0 be the truth predicate for L_0, holding of exactly the true sentences of L_0. If true-in-L_0 is itself a predicate of L_0, then we can construct the Liar paradox in L_0 via the sentence "This sentence is not true-in-L_0." Accordingly, the predicate *true-in-L_0* is confined to a richer *metalanguage* for the *object language* L_0. But on pain of the Liar, this metalanguage cannot contain its own truth predicate; for that a further metalanguage is needed. In this way a hierarchy of languages is generated, each language beyond L_0 containing the truth predicate for the preceding language. By a celebrated theorem of Tarski's (1930–1931/1983), no classical formal language can contain its own truth predicate, and we are led to a hierarchy of formal languages. Some have carried over this result to natural languages as a way of dealing with the Liar, though Tarski did not endorse this move. Russell's hierarchical approach was embodied in his theory of types and orders (1967). It is often complained that hierarchical approaches force an unnatural regimentation on a natural language like English; Russell himself at one time called the approach "harsh and highly artificial."

Another kind of approach abandons classical semantics—usually it is the principle of bivalence ("Every sentence is true or false") that is rejected. If we can motivate the existence of truth-value gaps, then we can say that (1) is neither true nor false and avoid the contradiction. Saul Kripke's (1975) influential theory of truth takes Liar sentences to be "gappy" because they are *ungrounded*: any attempt to evaluate a Liar sentence leads only to sentences involving *true* or *false*—in the case of (1), we are repeatedly led back to (1) itself. Kripke constructs a language that, remarkably, contains its own truth and falsity predicates. It cannot, however, accommodate the predicates "is false or gappy" or "not true"—and so ultimately we cannot dispense with a hierarchy.

The revision theory of truth (Gupta and Belnap 1993) is formally a variant of Kripke's theory, but provides a distinctive way of explaining the meaning of truth. Truth is taken to be a circular concept, and the revision theory describes how its meaning is given by the Tarskian T-sentences via a dynamic process that, through systematic revisions, provides better and better approximations of the extension of *true*.

Contextual theories of truth are motivated by so-called strengthened reasoning about the Liar. Start with a Liar sentence, say,

(2) (2) is not true.

Reasoning in the usual way, we will find that (2) is pathological. But then we may infer

(3) (2) is not true.

Now (2) and (3) are composed of the same words with the same meanings, and yet one is pathological and the other is true. Contextual theorists claim that this change in truth status without a change in meaning is best explained by a contextual shift (compare "I'm hungry" said before dinner and "I'm hungry" said after dessert). Most contextual theories are hierarchical (e.g., Burge 1979, Barwise and Etchemendy 1987), though Keith Simmons (1993) develops a suggestion of Kurt Gödel's, according to which an unstratified concept of truth applies everywhere except for certain singularities.

Any purported solution to the Liar faces the so-called Revenge Liar—a version of the Liar couched in the terms of the solution. Truth-value gap approaches must deal with the Liar sentence "This sentence is false or gappy," hierarchical approaches with "This sentence is not true at any level," and contextual theories with "This sentence is not true in any context." With no agreed-on solution in sight, and with the constant threat of Revenge Liars, some have concluded that we must cut the Gordian knot and embrace the contradictions associated with the Liar. According to dialetheists such as Graham Priest (1987) there are sentences that are both true and false, and among them are the Liar sentences (for critical discussions of dialetheism, see Priest, Beall, and Armour-Garb 2004). Besides meeting the obvious charge of counterintuitiveness, dialetheists must underwrite their theory with a plausible paraconsistent logic (a logic that challenges the principle that everything follows from a contradiction) and ensure that dialetheism is not itself vulnerable to a Revenge Liar.

See also Meaning; Semantics.

Bibliography

Alston, William P. *A Realist Conception of Truth*. Ithaca, NY: Cornell University Press, 1996.

Aristotle. *Categories* and *Metaphysics*. In *The Basic Works of Aristotle*, edited by Richard McKeon. New York: Random House, 1941.

Armstrong, David M. *A World of States of Affairs*. New York: Cambridge University Press, 1997.

Austin, J. L. "Truth." In *Truth*, edited by Simon Blackburn and Keith Simmons, 149–161. New York: Oxford University Press, 1999. Austin's essay originally appeared in *Proceedings of the Aristotelian Society* in 1950.

Barwise, Jon, and John Etchemendy. *The Liar: An Essay on Truth and Circularity*. New York: Oxford University Press, 1987.

Blackburn, Simon. *Spreading the Word: Groundings in the Philosophy of Language*. Oxford, U.K.: Clarendon Press, 1984.

Blackburn, Simon, and Keith Simmons, eds. *Truth*. New York: Oxford University Press, 1999.

Blanshard, Brand. *The Nature of Thought*. London: Allen and Unwin, 1939.

Bradley, F. H. *Appearance and Reality: A Metaphysical Essay*. New York: Macmillan, 1893.

Bradley, F. H. "On Truth and Copying." In *Truth*, edited by Simon Blackburn and Keith Simmons, 31–45. New York: Oxford University Press, 1999. Bradley's essay originally appeared in *Mind* in 1907 and also appeared in *Essays on Truth and Reality* in 1914.

Brandom, Robert B. *Making It Explicit: Reasoning, Representing, and Discursive Commitment*. Cambridge, MA: Harvard University Press, 1994.

Burge, Tyler. "Semantical Paradox." *Journal of Philosophy* 76 (1979): 169–198.

Candlish, Stewart. "The Truth about F. H. Bradley." *Mind* 98 (1989): 331–348.

Candlish, Stewart. "Resurrecting the Identity Theory of Truth." *Bradley Studies* 1 (1995): 116–124.

David, Marian. *Correspondence and Disquotation: An Essay on the Nature of Truth*. New York: Oxford University Press, 1994.

Davidson, Donald. "A Coherence Theory of Truth and Knowledge." In *Truth and Interpretation: Perspectives on the Philosophy of Donald Davidson*, edited by Ernest LePore, 307–319. Oxford, U.K.: Basil Blackwell, 1984.

Davidson, Donald. "The Folly of Trying to Define Truth." *Journal of Philosophy* 93 (1996): 263–279.

Devitt, Michael. *Realism and Truth*. 2nd ed. Oxford, U.K.: Basil Blackwell, 1991.

Dewey, John. *Essays in Experimental Logic*. Chicago: University of Chicago Press, 1916.

Dewey, John. *Logic: The Theory of Inquiry*. New York: Henry Holt, 1938.

Dodd, Julian. *An Identity Theory of Truth*. New York: St. Martin's Press, 2000.

Dummett, Michael. *Truth and Other Enigmas*. Cambridge, MA: Harvard University Press, 1978.

Etchemendy, Jon. "Tarski on Truth and Logical Consequence." *Journal of Symbolic Logic* 53 (1988): 51–79.

Field, Hartry. "Deflationist Views of Meaning and Content." *Mind* 103 (411) (1994): 249–284.

Field, Hartry. "Tarski's Theory of Truth." *Journal of Philosophy* 69 (13) (1972): 347–375.

Frege, Gottlob. "The Thought: A Logical Inquiry." In *Truth*, edited by Simon Blackburn and Keith Simmons, 85–105. New York: Oxford University Press, 1999. Frege's essay was originally published in German in 1918 under the title "Der Gedanke: eine logische Untersuchung." It was also reprinted in English under its current title in the journal *Mind* in 1956.

Grover, D., J. Camp, and N. Belnap. "A Prosentential Theory of Truth." *Philosophical Studies* 27 (1975): 73–125.

Gupta, Anil. "Minimalism." In *Philosophical Perspectives*. Vol. 7: *Language and Logic*, edited by James E. Tomberlin, 359–369. Atascadero, CA: Ridgeview Press, 1993.

Gupta, Anil, and Nuel Belnap. *The Revision Theory of Truth*. Cambridge, MA: MIT Press, 1993.

Hill, Christopher S. *Thought and World*. New York: Cambridge University Press, 2002.

Hornsby, Jennifer. "Truth: The Identity Theory." *Proceedings of the Aristotelian Society* 97 (1997): 1–24.

Horwich, Paul. *Truth*. 2nd ed. New York: Oxford University Press, 1998.

James, William. *The Meaning of Truth: A Sequel to "Pragmatism."* New York: Longmans, Green, 1909.

James, William. *Pragmatism, a New Name for Some Old Ways of Thinking: Popular Lectures on Philosophy*. New York: Longmans, Green, 1907.

Joachim, Harold H. *The Nature of Truth: An Essay*. Oxford, U.K.: Clarendon Press, 1906.

Kirkham, Richard L. *Theories of Truth: A Critical Introduction*. Cambridge, MA: MIT Press, 1992.

Kripke, Saul. "Outline of a Theory of Truth." *Journal of Philosophy* 72 (1975): 690–716.

Martin, Robert L. *Recent Essays on Truth and the Liar Paradox*. New York: Oxford University Press, 1984.

Moore, G. E. *Some Main Problems of Philosophy*. New York: Humanities Press, 1953.

Neurath, Otto. "Protocol Sentences." In *Logical Positivism*, edited by A. J. Ayer, 199–208. Glencoe, IL: Free Press, 1959. Neurath's essay was published in 1932–1933 under the title "Protokollsätze" in the journal *Erkenntnis*.

Peirce, Charles S. "The Fixation of Belief." In *Philosophical Writings of Peirce*, edited by Justus Buchler, 5–22. New York: Dover Publications, 1955a. Peirce's essay originally appeared in *Popular Science Monthly* in 1877.

Peirce, Charles. "How to Make Our Ideas Clear." In *Philosophical Writings of Peirce*, edited by Justus Buchler, 23–41. New York: Dover Publications, 1955b. Peirce's essay originally appeared in *Popular Science Monthly* in 1878.

Plato. *Sophist*. In *The Collected Dialogues of Plato, Including the Letters*, edited by Edith Hamilton and Huntington Cairns. New York: Pantheon Books, 1961.

Priest, Graham. *In Contradiction: A Study of the Transconsistent*. Dordrecht, Netherlands: Nijhoff, 1987.

Priest, Graham, J. C. Beall, and Brad Armour-Garb. *The Law of Non-Contradiction: New Philosophical Essays*. Oxford, U.K.: Clarendon Press, 2004.

Putnam, Hilary. *Reason, Truth, and History*. New York: Cambridge University Press, 1981.

Quine, W. V. *Philosophy of Logic*. Englewood Cliffs, NJ: Prentice-Hall, 1970.

Ramsey, Frank. "Facts and Propositions." In *Truth*, edited by Simon Blackburn and Keith Simmons, 106–107. New York: Oxford University Press, 1999. Ramsey's essay originally published in *Proceedings of the Aristotelian Society* in 1927.

Rorty, Richard. *Consequences of Pragmatism: Essays, 1972–1980*. Minneapolis: University of Minnesota Press, 1982.

Russell, Bertrand. "Mathematical Logic as Based on the Theory of Types." In *From Frege to Gödel: A Source Book in Mathematical Logic, 1879–1931*, edited by Jean van Heijenoort, 150–182. Cambridge, MA: Harvard University Press, 1967. Russell's essay originally published in *American Journal of Mathematics* in 1908.

Russell, Bertrand. "On the Nature of Truth." *Proceedings of the Aristotelian Society* 7 (1906–1907): 28–49.

Russell, Bertrand. "The Philosophy of Logical Atomism," 1918 lectures. In *Logic and Knowledge: Essays, 1901–1950*, edited by Robert Charles Marsh. London: Allen and Unwin, 1956.

Russell, Bertrand. *The Problems of Philosophy* (1912). New York: Oxford University Press, 1959.

Schlick, Moritz. "The Foundation of Knowledge." In *Logical Positivism*, edited by A. J. Ayer, 209–227. Glencoe, IL: Free Press, 1959. Schlick's essay was originally published in German in 1934 under the title "Ueber das Fundament der Erkenntnis" in the journal *Erkenntnis*.

Simmons, Keith. *Universality and the Liar: An Essay on Truth and the Diagonal Argument*. New York: Cambridge University Press, 1993.

Strawson, P. F. "Truth." *Analysis* 9 (6) (1949): 83–97.

Tarski, Alfred. "The Concept of Truth in Formalized Languages" (1930–1931). In *Logic, Semantics, Metamathematics: Papers from 1923 to 1938*. 2nd ed. Translated by J. H. Woodger; edited by John Corcoran. Indianapolis, IN: Hackett, 1983.

Tarski, Alfred. "The Semantic Conception of Truth and the Foundations of Semantics." In *Truth*, edited by Simon Blackburn and Keith Simmons, 115–143. New York: Oxford University Press, 1999. Tarski's essay originally appeared in *Philosophical and Phenomenological Research* in 1944.

Walker, Ralph C. S. *The Coherence Theory of Truth: Realism, Anti-Realism, Idealism*. London: Routledge, 1989.

Wittgenstein, Ludwig. *Tractatus Logico-Philosophicus*. 1921. New York: Harcourt, Brace, 1922.

Keith Simmons (2005)

TRUTH AND FALSITY IN INDIAN PHILOSOPHY

By and large, classical Indian philosophy treats truth within an epistemological context, and different theories of truth are connected with different theories of knowledge. Truth is regarded as a property of cognitions, not of sentences or propositions, although it is presupposed that a true cognition, if appropriately verbalized, would be expressed by a true statement. Cognitions form dispositions or beliefs, but the concept of a belief is also not in the forefront in classical Indian analyses. Modern interpreters tend to use the term *veridicality*, rather than *truth*, because of this focus. Cognitions are episodic psychological events divided into types according to epistemic and other criteria, and perceptual, inferential, testimonial, and hypothetical veridical (true) cognitions are not only the results of processes that are veritable "knowledge sources" (*pramāṇa*) but are also causes of effort and action, including speech. A cognition has objecthood, its indication or intentionality, which is a feature it can share with other cognitions: two people can have the same cognition in this sense. Against such a background, contested issues include, most notably, the nature of veridicality as a cognitive property and the nature of justification, that is, how veridicality is known.

PRECLASSICAL AND EARLY CLASSICAL METAPHYSICS

Classical Indian philosophy proper stretches from about 100 BCE to the modern period (1800s and beyond). Earlier Vedic and Upanishadic thought, along with rejection of a Brahmanic worldview by Buddhists, Jainas, and materialists, sets the stage for the professional reasoners. According to yogis and mystics of an early age (recorded in Upanishads, "mystic treatises," from about 800 BCE) consciousness has lost its native state of bliss and self-awareness. It can be recovered through meditation and various practices of yoga and religious discipline. Buddhist literature develops the theme: The world is a dream from which one needs to awaken to an emptiness brimming with delight and compassion, or, in still later Hindu literature, awaken to one's true self as one with the Absolute Brahman. Nonveridical perception is held up as an analogue to one's everyday lack of awareness of Brahman (*nirvāṇa*).

Brahman is the real, the "truth" in a metaphysical sense, and spiritual knowledge, which is compared to veridical perception and is true in some higher sense of the word. Mystical sublation shows Brahman to be the real (*sat*, being), as a sublating perception shows a rope formerly misperceived as a snake to be the rope that it is. Such reasoning becomes crystallized as the doctrine of two truths common in much Buddhism and Vedānta (i.e., Hindu schools of Upanishadic philosophy). Indeed, Advaita (Nondualist) Vedānta develops a theory of three truths: the true (cognition, or consciousness, of Brahman), the indeterminable (cognition that is true of the world but not of Brahman, for example, a veridical cognition of water), and the false (not true of the world, for example, a dream or mirage). In Buddhism, a four-cornered negation is said to characterize nirvāṇa or speech about nirvāṇa: not F, not not-F, not (F and not-F), and not not (F and not-F). The logic and language of everyday life do not apply.

Metaphysical controversy marks the beginning of classical Indian philosophy, which is defined by texts devoted to systematic presentation of worldviews complete with supporting arguments and attacks on rival theories. Jaina logicians developed a theory of seven-truth perspectives to support their nonabsolutism (*anekāntavāda*) in metaphysics or perspectivalism, the view that truth is relative to a perspective. (Some have seen in this way *ahiṃsā* [non-injury]—the core teaching of Jainism—applied to the life of the mind.) Every philosophy has something to be said for it. Every judgment has a grain of truth, as tied to a particular take on things, but, likewise, the negation of every judgment, and their combination. A fourth *naya* (perspective) is inexpressibility: every cognition has something about it that is paradoxical or ineffable in another fashion. Further combinations result in seven modes.

Jainas aside, disputes between idealists and realists dominate the earlier centuries of classical philosophy. A school of direct realists, Nyāya (Logic), argues that the intentionality of even a nonveridical cognition hits a feature of the world, albeit misplaced. When one misperceives mother-of-pearl as silver, the silver-hood of which one is aware exists elsewhere. Had one not experienced it previously, one would not misperceive in this way ("It's silver"). The mother-of-pearl misperceived as silver is real, and so, too, the silver-ness wrongly indicated. Buddhists and other classical idealists argue, in sharp contrast, that one's desires and interests shape one's perceptions and all determinate cognition. Illusion shows that there are no objects independent of consciousness, since the false is seen to appear as the true.

Regarding the nature of veridicality, realists tend to embrace varieties of a correspondence theory. A cognition is veridical just in case the object cognized is cognized as being some way it is in fact. Whether there need be congruence between the object as qualified (thing-ontological relation-property) and the cognition as structured (qualificandum-qualificative relation-qualifier) was debated for several centuries. Realist camps explain illusion in different ways. Prābhākara Mīmāṃsakas deny that the intentionality of cognitions ever in itself misfires. The problem lies in confusing a perceiving and a remembering occurring at the same time. Nyāya philosophers hold that a nonveridical cognition presents something in some way that it is not, analyzing the error, "That is silver," as perceptual. That is, according to them silver-hood is projected into the sensory flow by a dispositional misfiring, the thing being in fact shell. They say that the view that there are two cognitions occurring simultaneously, a perceiving and a remembering (along with a failure to notice the difference), is wrong for several reasons. A single cognition stream defines a person's mental life. The nonveridical cognition of shell presents the thing perceptually as silver such that one says of the thing in front, "That is a piece of silver," and reaches out to pick it up. The thing perceived as silver motivates one's effort and action (including speech).

Prābhākara Mīmāṃsakas nevertheless join with Nyāya in seeing cognitive objects both as out there in the world and as structured: Property-bearers, which are enduring entities, are qualified by properties, some of which change (e.g., color) and some of which are essential to the thing qualified (e.g., cow-hood or being earthen). Cognition is similarly structured on the Nyāya theory, presenting qualificandum as qualifier. Thus, when there is a match between how an object is presented cognitionwise with the thing as it is in the world, the cognition is true.

Buddhists and other idealists tend to adopt a pragmatic theory. A cognition is veridical just in case it proves workable in helping one get what one wants and avoid what one wants to avoid. Realists agree that cognition is in this way useful and that sometimes one knows that a cognition is true by inferring its truth from the success of the action it guided. But realists see the nature of truth as correspondence. The Buddhists see workability not just as a mark of the truth but as truth itself. One calls cognitions true that make one successful, and false those that lead to frustrated efforts instead. Insofar as cognitive contents or indications are verbalizable, they are useful fictions, since the real is unverbalizable, knowable only through direct perception. Direct perception has unique particulars as object, not the general concepts contemplated by the mind. Concepts are mental constructions, and what one says depends on mental projections on things that are ungeneralizable as things in themselves, as self-characterized particulars (*svalakṣaṇa*).

Later Buddhist logicians use an exclusion theory of concepts (*apoha*) in working out principles of logic and epistemology. The *apoha* theory seems motivated by Buddhist nominalism. A causally ordered series of particulars is conveniently designated a cow, though, strictly speaking, the series is a mental projection on fleeting particulars, none of which is either a cow or a non-cow. Designations exclude the least adequate concepts ("not a non-cow and so a cow"), according to one's desires and purposes; they do not apply directly to things in themselves. This view does not result in skepticism, since from one's everyday perspective truth is unproblematic. One distinguishes the veridical and the nonveridical by their perceived effects, satisfactions, or frustrations of desire through action undertaken on the basis of a belief (or mental construction, *kalpanā*).

GENUINE SOURCES OF KNOWLEDGE AND THEIR IMITATORS

Normative epistemology centers on the distinction between the veritably true cognition and its veritable knowledge source in distinction to the cognition that might seem to be veridical with the right pedigree but is in fact false and unreliable. Some kind of foul-up or deviation is to be suspected in a process resulting in the nonveridical. Though the evaluative paradigm is psychological and causal, inferential fallacies are discovered along with other epistemic faults. Indeed, long lists of fallacies appear in logic textbooks of both Buddhists and Hindus, including a majority of those known to the Aristotelian tradition and modern textbooks of critical reasoning. Veridicality is the ultimate touchstone, and disputants, given their differences on the nature of truth, rather surprisingly agree on fallacies and other concrete patterns of epistemic deficiency. Fallacies include nongenuine provers (*hetvābhāsa*), that is, evidence that seems to indicate a probandum in question but fails to secure the truth.

The distinction between the apparent (but false) and the genuine is made early in a metaphysical context, in the *Nyāyasūtra*, where it is used to refute the illusionist who would deny the reality of everyday objects. Things could be unreal or nonexistent, like dream objects. The epistemologist's knowledge source may itself be an illusion. Vātsyāyana (c. 400) points out in his *Nyāyasūtra* commentary (4.2.34) that the concept of the apparent whatever (as an apparent person that is really a post misperceived in the distance) presupposes the concept of the genuine variety (formed from previous experiences of persons). The apparently F could not be recognized without knowledge of things that are F genuinely. Thus, the concept of the illusory is parasitic on that of the veridical. If all cognitions were false, the cognition of the falsity would also be false. This is nonsense. Falsity requires an appreciation of truth. Thus, there is no reason to think that all objects and knowledge sources could be pretenders.

Despite such metaphysical argument, it is in epistemology where the distinction is most exploited. What is a genuine knowledge source (*pramāṇa*) as distinct from the imitator or pseudo (*ābhāsa*, thus *pramāṇābhāsa*)? People are subject to cognitive error of several types including logical error (*anumānābhāsa*), of which the *hetvābhāsas* (apparent [but false] reasons or provers) are the most discussed. Illusion is apparent (but false) perception (*pratyakṣābhāsa*). Understanding a false statement and being misled by the testimony of the deluded or of a deceiver, which is a form of *śābdābhāsa* (apparent [but false] testimony), will be treated separately later on. In general, if a cognition that appears to be, for example, perceptual from a first-person point of view is nonveridical (however defined), it is no result of perception as a genuine knowledge source, but of a cousin process, a close cousin, perhaps, indistinguishable from the real McCoy by the cognizer at the time. Much effort, under different flags, goes into trying to specify the features of cognitive processes that are marks of the one or the other, the genuine truth-generator or the imitator. The issues are complex, as can be guessed simply from the fact that at least thirty distinct definitions of truth and falsity are examined by late classical philosophers.

FALSE STATEMENTS AS NONGENUINE TESTIMONY

Classical Indian theories of meaning are mainly referentialist, and it is interesting to see how a false statement is analyzed by the classical epistemologists. Such enquiry also connects with questions about the lack, in Indian ontologies, of an exact equivalent of Western philosophy's "proposition." What is said about false claims, statements that seem meaningful but fail to hit the facts? Only the Nyāya view will be laid out; other schools present variations.

A case of *śābdābhāsa* (pseudoknowledge from testimony) may be taken to originate in a false statement of a speaker that a hearer understands and accepts, having no reason not to. As with perceptual cognition where there is no block, testimonial uptake and acceptance are normally fused. A blocker (*pratibandhaka*) would be, for example, the hearer knowing in advance the opposite or knowing the speaker is a liar or deluded, the statement not being syntactically well formed or meeting certain conditions called semantic expectation (one cannot understand the statement, for example, "He wets with fire," since wetting is done only with water). Given no blockage, the false statement has a role in the generation of the hearer's comprehending and accepting cognition, which is false.

Taking the objecthood of that cognition to be the target of inquiry (a homonym misunderstood as well as a lie could constitute the deviant source), the Nyāya philosopher analyzes it in much the same manner as with apparent perception. The way (*prakāra*) that an object, a qualificandum, is being cognized would indicate a qualifier that exists elsewhere than in the thing. The standard realist story about how qualifiers, which are real-world realities, form dispositions (*saṃskāra*), which are inappropriately aroused, is available here as with other forms of cognitive error. The peculiarity of testimonial pseudoknowledge concerns the speaker's statement being a causal factor in the generation of the hearer's nonveridical testimonial cognition. Nevertheless, it is the result—how the hearer understands the statement—that is targeted in the standard account of apparent (but false) testimony.

HOW IS VERIDICALITY KNOWN?

Prominent in classical debates about veridical cognitions and their sources is the issue of how veridicality is known. Prābhākara Mīmāṃsakas and Vedāntins say there is a kind of self-certification (*svataḥprāmāṇya*) at least with respect to certain contents or a cognition's own occurrence. Nyāya philosophers and others say that certification requires apperception, a second-order awareness, and certification by inferential means. The nature of the justificational inferences becomes central. Bhāṭṭa Mīmāṃsakas propose that while every cognition wears veridicality on its face—at least one assumes veridicality as a default—decertification is possible. Vedāntins tend to insist that there is a self that is essentially self-aware and the precondition of all cognition and experience. They view the other-certificationalists (*parataḥprāmāṇyavādin*) as confused about self-knowledge, though they may get the story right about knowledge of the external world, at least provisionally right, until the dawning of spiritual knowledge (*vidyā*).

On all views, confidence in a cognition's truth prompts effort and action; there are differences about whether the confidence has to be in some sense self-conscious. Realists of the two-cognition persuasion on illusion support a self-certificationism by taking a noncongruent correspondence view of the nature of truth. Idealists, too, often attack the qualificandum-qualifier structure supposed by Nyāya.

In Nyāya certification is said to proceed in three ways. First, a knowledge source can be identified by intrinsic features and in relation to a cognition in question as its result. Second, a cognition's veridicality can be certified with respect to its fruit, success of effort and action—a way that is also tied to causal relations and that is accepted by practically all disputants. The third procedure involves typifying. As mentioned, a cognition belongs to a type in virtue of its objecthood, its indicating, for instance, "*a* is F." Such objecthood can be shared with other cognitions, belonging to other people and to the cognizing subject at other times. So once a cognition as specified by its objecthood has been certified, a later cognition known to be a token of that type would also be certified.

Self-certificationists say that certification rides piggyback on apperception or whatever the way it is that a particular cognition is itself cognized. It appears that in this way ethical prescriptions of scripture can be upheld. They require no external justification. Certain Buddhists admit a form of certificational inference that looks like a kind of *a priori* knowledge, whereas Nyāya philosophers view all inference as depending crucially on prior perceptions.

Against the other-certificationists it is argued that, given that veridicality is in question, no certification would be possible, since only a cognition known to be veridical could possibly provide certification. If a certificational inference is required to show that a cognition is veridical, then there would have to be another inference to certify it, and one lands in an impossible regress and skepticism. Without the possibility of knowing that a cognition is veridical, trust in cognition would fly away. However, normally one does trust one's cognition, as is proved by one's behavior. Thus, however a veridical cognition is itself known or cognized, in that way its veridicality is also known, argue the self-certificationists. Other-certificationists respond by agreeing that an assumption of veridicality is a cognitive default, such that a cognition normally would not require certification to spark unhesitating effort and action. A cognition may nevertheless be called into doubt by good reasons, reasons that make one desist and reconsider.

Pseudocertification, on the Nyāya view, is possible but the presumption is also against it. Pseudocertification is certification that seems right from a first-person perspective but is misleading in fact. Apparent certification can be defeated (*bādhita*) by one's coming to learn something that undermines or rebuts a putatively certificational pseudoinference, whereas genuine certification requires that there be no ultimate defeater (*bādhaka*) in fact, that is, that one's evidence for regarding a cognition as veridical would hold no matter what else one comes to know. Established positions (*siddhānta*) serve as winnowing devices, and what one already knows can prevent wrong cognitions from arising. But one is not infallible. Just about any cognition, including an apparent certification, can prove to be wrong. But cognition of a cognition's veridicality, as distinct from a first-order assumption of truth, presents a higher barrier to doubt. Not only would there have to be good reasons to doubt the original cognition but also further reasons to question its certification.

The realist admission of a fallibilism that has few exceptions leaves the door wide open for the Advaitin nonrealist. Late Advaita Vedānta develops its two- or three-truth theory in sophisticated polemics where the Advaitin takes a minimalist position about the Upanishadic truth that Brahman is everything. World description may be left to the realists (science). The way that Brahman is the world is not statable (cognizable) in language that conflicts with statements (cognitions) about everyday things. Realism holds only provisionally.

See also Knowledge in Indian Philosophy; Logic, History of: Logic and Inference in Indian Philosophy; Meditation in Indian Philosophy; Mind and Mental States in Indian Philosophy; Negation in Indian Philosophy; Philosophy of Language in India; Universal Properties in Indian Philosophical Traditions.

Bibliography

Chakrabarti, Arindam. "Telling as Letting Know." In *Knowing from Words: Western and Indian Philosophical Analysis of Understanding and Testimony*, edited by Bimal Krishna Matilal and Arindam Chakrabarti. Dordrecht, Netherlands: Kluwer Academic, 1994.

Chakrabarti, Kisor Kumar. "Some Remarks on Indian Theories of Truth." *Journal of Indian Philosophy* 12 (4) (1984): 339–356.

Ganeri, Jonardon. *Semantic Powers: Meaning and the Means of Knowing in Classical Indian Philosophy*. Oxford, U.K.: Clarendon Press, 1999.

Hayes, Richard P. *Dignāga on the Interpretation of Signs*. Dordrecht, Netherlands: Kluwer Academic, 1987.

Krishna, Daya, et al., eds. *Samvāda: A Dialogue between Two Philosophical Traditions*. New Delhi, India: Indian Council of Philosophical Research, 1991.

Matilal, Bimal Krishna. *The Character of Logic in India*, edited by Jonardon Ganeri and Heeraman Tiwari. Albany: SUNY Press, 1998.

Matilal, Bimal Krishna. "A Realist View of Perception." In *The Philosophy of P. F. Strawson*, edited by Pranab Kumar Sen and Roop Rekha Verma. New Delhi, India: Indian Council of Philosophical Research, 1995.

Mohanty, Jitendra Nath. *Reason and Tradition in Indian Thought: An Essay on the Nature of Indian Philosophical Thinking*. Oxford, U.K.: Clarendon Press, 1992.

Nyāyasūtra (Nyāyadarśanam). With four commentaries, the *Nyāyasūtra-bhāṣya* of Vātsyāyana, the *Nyāyasūtravārttika* of Uddyotakara, the *Nyāyasūtravārttikatātpāryaṭīkā* of Vācaspati Miśra, and the *Vṛtti* of Viśvanātha, edited by A. M. Tarkatirtha, Taranatha Nyayatarkatirtha, and H. K. Tarkatirtha. New Delhi, India: Munshiram Manoharlal, 1985.

Phillips, Stephen H. *Classical Indian Metaphysics: Refutations of Realism and the Emergence of "New Logic."* Chicago: Open Court, 1995.

Phillips, Stephen H., and N.S. Ramanuja Tatacharya. *Epistemology of Perception: Gageśa's "Tattvacintāmaṇi."* Vol. I, *pratyakṣa-khaṇḍa, Introduction, Translation, and Commentary*. New York: American Institute of Buddhist Studies, 2004.

Potter, Karl H. "Does Indian Epistemology Concern Justified True Belief?" *Journal of Indian Philosophy* 12 (4) (1984): 307–328.

Ram-Prasad, Chakravarthi. *Advaita Epistemology and Metaphysics: An Outline of Indian Non-realism*. London: RoutledgeCurzon, 2002.

Rao, Srinivasa. *Perceptual Error: The Indian Theories*. Honolulu: University of Hawaii Press, 1998.

Ruegg, D. Seyfort. "Does the Mādhyamika Have a Thesis and Philosophical Position." In *Buddhist Logic and Epistemology: Studies in the Buddhist Analysis of Inference and Language*, edited by Bimal Krishna Matilal and Robert D. Evans. Dordrecht, Netherlands: D. Reidel, 1986.

Stephen H. Phillips (2005)

TRUTHLIKENESS

Truth is the aim of inquiry. Despite this, progress in an inquiry does not always consist in supplanting falsehoods with truths. The history of science is replete with cases of falsehoods supplanting other falsehoods. If such transitions are to constitute epistemic progress, then it must be possible for one falsehood better to realize the aim of inquiry—be more truthlike, be closer to the truth, or have more verisimilitude—than another. The notion of "truthlikeness" is thus fundamental for any theory of knowledge that endeavors to take our epistemic limitations seriously without embracing epistemic pessimism.

Given that truthlikeness is not only a much-needed notion but rich and interesting, it is surprising that it has attracted less attention than the simpler notion of truth. The explanation is twofold. First, if knowledge requires truth, then falsehoods cannot constitute knowledge. The high value of knowledge has obscured other epistemic values such as the comparative value of acquiring more truthlike theories. Second, if knowledge requires justification, then the notion of probability often takes center stage. There has been a long and deep confusion between the notions of subjective probability (seemingly true) and the notion of truthlikeness (similarity to the truth; Popper, 1972). This, together with the high degree of development of the theory of probability, obscured the necessity for a theory of truthlikeness.

Sir Karl Popper was the first to notice the importance of the notion (1972, chap. 10 and addenda). Popper was long a lonely advocate of both scientific realism and fallibilism: that, although science aims at the truth, most theories have turned out to be false and current theories are also likely to be false. This seems a bleak vision indeed and fails to do justice to the evident progress in science. Popper realized that the picture would be less bleak if a succession of false (and falsified) theories could nevertheless constitute steady progress toward the truth. Further, even if actually refuted by some of the data, the general observational accuracy of a false theory might be good evidence for the theory's approximate truth, or high degree of truthlikeness. That our theories, even if not true, are close to the truth, may be the best explanation available for the accuracy of their observable consequences (Boyd, 1983; Putnam, 1978, chap. 2).

Note that truthlikeness is no more an epistemic notion than is truth. How truthlike a theory is depends only on the theory's content and the world, not on our knowledge. The problem of our epistemic access to the truthlikeness of theories is quite different from the logically prior problem of what truthlikeness consists in.

Popper proposed a bold and simple account of truthlikeness: that theory B is more truthlike than theory A if B entails all the truths that A entails, A entails all the falsehoods that B entails, and either B entails at least one more truth than A or A entails at least one more falsehood than B (Popper, 1972).

This simple idea undoubtedly has virtues. Let the *Truth* be that theory that entails all and only truths (relative to some subject matter). On Popper's account the Truth is more truthlike than any other theory, and that is as it should be. The aim of an inquiry is not just some truth or other. Rather, it is the truth, the whole truth, and nothing but the truth about some matter—in short, the Truth—and the Truth realizes that aim better than any other theory. The account also clearly separates truthlikeness and probability. The Truth generally has a very low degree of (subjective) probability, but it definitely has maximal truthlikeness. Furthermore, the account yields an interesting ranking of truths—the more a truth entails, the closer it is to the Truth.

Popper's account also has some defects. For example, it does not permit any falsehood to be closer to the Truth than any truth. (Compare Newton's theory of motion with denial of Aristotle's theory.) But its most serious defect is that it precludes any false theory being more truthlike than any other (Miller, 1974; Tichý, 1974). The flaw is simply demonstrated. Suppose theory A entails a falsehood, say *f*, and we attempt to improve on A by adding a new truth, say *t*. Then the extended theory entails both *t* and *f* and hence entails their conjunction: *t*&*f*. But *t*&*f* is a falsehood not entailed by A. Similarly, suppose A is false and we attempt to improve it by removing one of its falsehoods, say *f*. Let *g* be any falsehood entailed by the reduced theory B. Then $g \supset f$ is a truth entailed by A but not B. (If B entailed both *g* and $g \supset f$, it would entail *f*.) So truths cannot be added without adding falsehoods, nor falsehoods subtracted without subtracting truths.

Maybe this lack of commensurability could be overcome by switching to quantitative measures of true and false logical content. Indeed, Popper proposed such accounts, but the problem they face is characteristic of the content approach, the central idea of which is that truthlikeness is a simple function of two factors—truth-value and logical content/strength (Kuipers, 1982; Miller, 1978). If truthlikeness were such a function, then among false theories truthlikeness would vary with logical strength alone. There are only two well-behaved options here: Truthlikeness either increases monotonically with logical strength, or else it decreases. But strengthening a false theory does not itself guarantee either an increase or a decrease in truthlikeness. If it is hot, rainy, and windy (h&r&w), then both of the following are logical strengthenings of the false claim that it is cold (~h): It is cold, rainy, and windy (~h&r&w); it is cold, dry, and still (~h&~r&~w). The former involves an increase, and the latter a decrease, in truthlikeness.

A quite different approach takes the likeness in truthlikeness seriously (Hilpinen, 1976; Niiniluoto, 1987; Oddie, 1981; Tichý, 1974, 1976). An inquiry involves a collection of possibilities, or possible worlds, one of which is actual. Each theory selects a range of possibilities from this collection—that theory's candidates for actuality. A proposition is true if it includes the actual world in its range. Each complete proposition includes just one such candidate. The Truth, the target of the inquiry, is the complete true proposition—that proposition that selects the actual world alone. If worlds vary in their degree of likeness to each other, then a complete proposition is the more truthlike the more like actuality is the world it selects. This is a promising start, but we need to extend it to incomplete propositions. The worlds in the range of an incomplete proposition typically vary in their degree of likeness to actuality, and the degree of truthlikeness of the proposition should be some kind of function thereof: average likeness is a simple suggestion that yields intuitively pleasing results. (For a survey, see Niiniluoto, 1987, chap. 6.) The framework can also be used in the analysis of related notions such as approximate truth or closeness to being true (Hilpinen, 1976; Weston, 1992).

There are two related problems with this program. The first concerns the measure of likeness between worlds. It would be a pity if this simply had to be postulated. The second concerns the size and complexity of worlds and the number of worlds that propositions typically select. Fortunately, there is available a handy logical tool for cutting the complexity down to a finite, manageable size (Niiniluoto, 1977; Tichý, 1974, 1976). We can work with kinds of worlds rather than whole words. The kinds at issue are specified by the constituents of first-order logic (Hintikka, 1965), a special case of which are the maximal conjunctions of propositional logic (like h&r&w, ~h&r&w, ~h&~r&~w). Constituents have two nice features. First, each depicts in its surface structure the underlying structure of a kind of world. And, second, like the propositional constituents, they are highly regular in their surface structure, enabling degree of likeness between constituents to be extracted. (The world in which it is cold, rainy, and windy [~h&r&w] is more like the world in which it is hot, rainy, and windy [h&r&w] than it is like the world in which it is cold, dry, and still [~h&~r&~w]. In the propositional case, just add up the surface differences.) Since every statement is logically equivalent to a disjunction of constituents, we have here the elements of a quite general account of truthlikeness, one that can be extended well beyond standard first-order logic (Oddie, 1986, chap. 5).

Not just any features count in a judgment of overall likeness. Such judgments clearly presuppose a class of respects of comparison. The possibilities specified by h&r&w and ~h&r&w differ in one weather respect and agree on two, whereas those specified by h&r&w and ~h&~r&~w differ in all three. But now consider the following two states (where ≡ is the material biconditional): hot ≡ rainy, and hot ≡ windy. The possibility specified by h&r&w can equally be specified by h&(h ≡ r)&(h ≡ w); ~h&r&w by ~h&~(h ≡ r)&~(h ≡ w); and ~h&~r&~w by ~h&(h ≡ r)&(h ≡ w). Counting differences in terms of these new features does not line up with our intuitive judgments of likeness. Unless there is some objective reason for counting the hot-rainy-windy respects rather than the hot-(hot ≡ rainy)-(hot ≡ windy) respects, truthlikeness (unlike truth) seems robbed of objectivity.

This is the main objection to the likeness program (Miller, 1974). If sound, however, it would reach far indeed, for perfectly analogous arguments would establish a similar shortcoming in a host of important notions—similarity in general, structure, confirmation, disconfirmation, fit of theory to data, accuracy, and change (Oddie, 1986, chap. 6). The advocate of the objectivity of such notions simply has to grasp the nettle and maintain that some properties, relations, and magnitudes are more basic or fundamental than others. Realists, of course, should not find the sting too sharp to bear.

See also Aristotle; Confirmation Theory; Newton, Isaac; Philosophy of Science, History of; Philosophy of Science, Problems of; Popper, Karl Raimund; Propositions; Putnam, Hilary; Realism; Truth.

Bibliography

Boyd, R. "On the Current Status of the Issue of Scientific Realism." *Erkenntnis* 19 (1983): 45–90.

Hilpinen, R. "Approximate Truth and Truthlikeness." In *Formal Methods in the Methodology of Empirical Sciences,* edited by M. Przelecki, K. Szaniawski, and R. Wojcicki. Dordrecht: Reidel, 1976.

Hintikka, J. "Distributive Normal Forms in the Calculus of Predicates." In *Formal Systems and Recursive Functions,* edited by J. N. Crossley and M. A. Dummett. Amsterdam: North-Holland, 1965.

Kuipers, T. A. F. "Approaching Descriptive and Theoretical Truth." *Erkenntnis* 18 (1982): 343–387.

Kuipers, T. A. F., ed. *What Is Closer-to-the-Truth?* Amsterdam: Rodopi, 1987.

Miller, D. "Distance from the Truth as a True Distance." In *Essays on Mathematical and Philosophical Logic,* edited by J. Hintikka, I. Niiniluoto, and E. Saarinen. Dordrecht: Reidel, 1978.

Miller, D. "Popper's Qualitative Theory of Verisimilitude." *British Journal for the Philosophy of Science* 25 (1974): 166–177.

Niiniluoto, I. "On the Truthlikeness of Generalizations." In *Basic Problems in Methodology and Linguistics,* edited by R. E. Butts and J. Hintikka. Dordrecht: Reidel, 1977.

Niiniluoto, I. *Truthlikeness.* Dordrecht: Reidel, 1987.

Oddie, G. *Likeness to Truth.* Dordrecht: Reidel, 1986.

Oddie, G. "Verisimilitude Reviewed." *British Journal for the Philosophy of Science* 32 (1981): 237–265.

Popper, K. R. *Conjectures and Refutations,* 4th ed. London, 1972.

Putnam, H. *Meaning and the Moral Sciences.* London: Routledge and Kegan Paul, 1978.

Tichý, P. "On Popper's Definitions of Verisimilitude." *British Journal for the Philosophy of Science* 25 (1974): 155–160.

Tichý, P. "Verisimilitude Redefined." *British Journal for the Philosophy of Science* 27 (1976): 25–42.

Weston, T. "Approximate Truth and Scientific Realism." *Philosophy of Science* 59 (1992): 53–74.

Graham Oddie (1996)

TRUTH-TABLES

See *Logical Terms, Glossary of*

TSCHIRNHAUS, EHRENFRIED WALTER VON

(1651–1708)

Ehrenfried Walter von Tschirnhaus (or Tschirnhausen), the German mathematician and physicist, was born in Kieslingswalde, near Görlitz, and became count of Kieslingswalde and Stolzenberg. He studied mathematics at Görlitz and at the University of Leiden, where the Cartesian philosophers Adriaan Heereboord and Arnold Geulincx were teaching. After serving with the Dutch in 1672 during a war with France, Tschirnhaus studied further in Leiden and in Germany, and in 1674 he traveled to London, Paris, Rome, Sicily, and Malta. He met Benedict de Spinoza in Holland, English scientists in London, and he undoubtedly met Cartesian philosophers and scientists such as Jacques Rohault and Pierre-Sylvain Régis in Paris. Tschirnhaus finally settled down in Kieslingswalde. He established several factories for manufacturing glass and for grinding magnifying glasses, and was associated with J. F. Böttger in the development of Meissen porcelain. Tschirnhaus published various essays on mathematics and optics in the *Acta Eruditorum* from 1682 to 1698, and a philosophical treatise, *Medicina Mentis* (Amsterdam, 1687; 2nd ed. revised, Leipzig, 1695; reprinted with introduction by W. Risse, Hildesheim, 1964), on methodology, logic, and theory of knowledge, which also explained some of his geometrical discoveries.

Medicina Mentis followed Tschirnhaus's scientific interests; but some general features of the treatise were derived from Cartesianism, Spinoza, English empiricism, and, in some respects, from Gottfried Wilhelm Leibniz. Tschirnhaus's "mental medicine" was intended as a method of discovering rational truth as a basis of a happy life. Only true knowledge can tame the passions, which are the source of error and therefore of unhappiness.

Knowledge comes only from the senses, but purely sensible knowledge—which Tschirnhaus called imagination—is passive, approximate, and relative, and must be governed by rigid precepts. Reason abstracts from imagination, producing universal and strict concepts. The intellect considers things "as they exist in themselves"; that is, it penetrates their "real nature" and connects in one whole the real thing and its sensible and abstract representations. Reason operates by analysis, intellect by synthesis.

Only intellectual knowledge can reach truth and be communicated. Falsehood arises when intellect works like imagination. The criterion of truth is "what can be conceived"—that is, ideas insofar as they may be connected or not connected with one another. This criterion does not rest simply on an abstract rule to be applied in each case, but on the possibility of connecting ideas in a comprehensive system. But for Tschirnhaus this system was not, as for the rationalists, a closed and independent cognitive order. He considered the intellectual faculty to be the source of logical truth. But metaphysical truth comes from experience, and it is truth insofar as it has been deduced from experience by reasoning conforming to logical standards, and insofar as it is confirmed "through evident experiments."

Intellectual knowledge operates by elaborating simple concepts, or "definitions"; by deducing simple properties, or "axioms," from them; and by connecting the definitions in all possible ways to produce "theorems." Tschirnhaus held that definition is real. It is a knowledge of causes that enables us to reproduce the object. In its highest stages intellectual knowledge is knowledge of the natural world. Science is a whole, and should conform to the methodological ideal of mathematical clarity. Physics is the foundation of the other sciences. By demonstrating the rationality and necessity of all events, physics leads us to recognize divine providence. Human freedom arises from the command of God.

Although Tschirnhaus's *Medicina Mentis* was quite famous in its own day and its methodology was an important source of Christian Wolff's ideas, it exerted no direct influence on the German Enlightenment.

See also Cartesianism; Empiricism; Geulincx, Arnold; Leibniz, Gottfried Wilhelm; Régis, Pierre-Sylvain; Rohault, Jacques; Spinoza, Benedict (Baruch) de; Wolff, Christian.

Bibliography

Campo, Mariano. *Cristiano Wolff e il razionalismo precritico.* Milan: Vite e pensiero, 1939. Vol. I, Part 1, Ch. 2.

Klüger, Richard. *Die pädagogischen Ansichten des Philosophen Tschirnhaus.* Leipzig, 1913.

Kulstad, Mark A. "Leibniz, Spinoza, and Tschirnhaus: Metaphysics a Trois, 1675–1676." In *Spinoza: Metaphysical Themes*, edited by Olli Koistinen. New York: Oxford University Press, 2002.

Kunze, A. "Lebensbeschreibung des E. W. von Tschirnhaus und Wurdigung seiner Verdienste." *Neues Lausitzer Magazin* 43 (1866).

Radetti, G. "Cartesianesimo e spinozismo nel pensiero di E. W. von Tschirnhaus." *Rendiconti della Classe di Scienze morali, storiche e filologiche della Accademia Nazionale dei Lincei*, Sec. 6, 14 (5 and 6) (1938): 566–601.

Reinhardt, K. *Beiträge zur Lebensgeschichte von E. W. von Tschirnhausen.* Meissen, Germany, 1903.

Schönfeld, Martin. "Dogmatic Metaphysics and Tschirnhaus's Methodology." *Journal of the History of Philosophy* 36 (1) (1998): 57–76.

Van Peursen, C. A. "E. W. Von Tschirnhaus and the "Ars Inveniendi." *Journal of the History of Philosophy* 54 (3) (1993): 395–410.

Verweyen, Johannes. *E. W. von Tschirnhaus als Philosoph.* Bonn, 1906.

Weissenborn, H. *Lebensbeschreibung des E. W. von Tschirnhaus.* Eisenach, Germany, 1866.

Giorgio Tonelli (1967)
Bibliography updated by Tamra Frei (2005)

TUNG CHUNG-SHU

See *Dong Zhongshu*

TURGOT, ANNE ROBERT JACQUES, BARON DE L'AULNE

(1727–1781)

The French statesman, economist, and philosopher of history Anne Robert Jacques Turgot, Baron de l'Aulne, was born in Paris. He began formal theological training in 1743, anticipating a career in the church. As a young scholar at the Sorbonne (1749–1751) he showed brilliant promise in several writings on the philosophy of history. In 1752 he left the service of religion to become a magistrate, and from 1753 to 1761 he fulfilled the legal and administrative duties of a master of requests. His writings in this period included contributions to the *Encyclopédie* in metaphysics, linguistics, science, economics, and political theory, as well as short writings over a similarly broad range of fields, but his contemplated major work on the history of human progress never materialized. From 1761 to 1774 he served as the enlightened intendant (royal administrator) of Limoges; in this period and later, economic subjects predominated in his writings. Appointed minister of marine by Louis XVI in 1774, he was very shortly afterward transferred to the crucial position of comptroller general of finance. In this post Turgot instituted economies, corrected abuses in the taxation system, established free grain trade within France, and suppressed the guilds and the labor services. Opposition at court and in the Parlement of Paris, and the withdrawal of royal support, led to his resignation after twenty months (1776), thus ending the last attempt at thoroughgoing reform of the ancien régime in France before the Revolution.

ECONOMIC AND SOCIAL THEORIES

Turgot's economic theories are expressed most fully in his *Réflexions sur la formation et la distribution des richesses* (1766, published serially 1769–1770; translated as *Reflections on the Formation and the Distribution of Riches*, New York, 1898). In this and other works his basic principles are essentially physiocratic: The sole ultimate source of wealth is land, and only the growth and the unhindered flow of capital can create prosperity. Assuming that the French economy would continue to be largely agrarian, Turgot advocated a gradual simplification and moderation of taxation, looking toward the day when only landowners would be taxed, on the basis of a careful assessment of their profits, and when restrictions and impositions upon commerce and industry might be altogether abolished.

Turgot's general political thought, based on a belief in paternalistic, enlightened monarchy, is of less interest than his two *Lettres à un grand vicaire sur la tolérance* (Letters to a grand vicar on toleration, 1753, 1754; in *Oeuvres*, Vol. I) concerning governmental toleration of religion. In these letters he defended a broad toleration of different faiths but maintained that the state may offer special protection to the "dominant" or most numerous religion, as a useful guide to men in their uncertainties. He nevertheless held that some sects—those too rigid, irrational, morally or socially burdensome, or politically subversive—are not worthy of such protection, but should simply be tolerated; Roman Catholicism, he noted, might be considered by some to be such a sect. The dogma of infallibility is dangerous if it is false, and "it is certainly false or inapplicable when the exercise of infallibility is confided to those who are not infallible, that is to princes and governments" (*Oeuvres,* Vol. I, p. 425). Intolerance, unworthy of a gentle and charitable Christianity, must in any case be eradicated, for the rights of society are not greater than those of individuals, and individual conscience is no proper concern of government.

PHILOSOPHY OF HISTORY

To the philosopher, Turgot's importance may well derive from his early writings on the theory of history, notably his *Tableau philosophique des progrès successifs de l'esprit humain* (Philosophic panorama of the progress of the human mind, 1750; in *Oeuvres,* Vol. I), and his "Plan de deux discours sur l'histoire universelle" (Plan of two discourses on universal history; c. 1750, in *Oeuvres,* Vol. I). Upon the basis of contemporary psychological sensationalism, and with a nod to Providence, Turgot constructed a broad theory of human progress reflecting past theories and foreshadowing later ones.

In contrast to the phenomena of the world of nature, trapped in unprogressive cycles of birth and death, Turgot postulated the infinite variability and indeed the perfectibility of humankind. In the past and in the future, as knowledge and experience accumulate, man's reason, passions, and freedom permit him to escape from the repetitive cycles of external nature. Movement and change give rise to new relationships, and thus all experience is instructive; even passion and error, calamity and evil providentially contribute to humankind's advance. Indeed, the ambitions and the vices of men and the barbarities of warfare, however morally reprehensible, may often rescue humankind from stagnation or mediocrity.

The vital medium of progress, wrote Turgot, is the process of human communication. Ideas deriving from sensations are developed through the use of signs, pictures, and especially language, by which knowledge and experience are transmitted and augmented from generation to generation. Since above all it is the man of genius who can grasp the implications and make articulate the lessons of experience, it is society's duty to encourage natural genius and to heed its advice. "Moral" circumstances, such as the cultivation of genius, are more important in determining the extent and nature of progress than are such physical circumstances as climate.

Progress is uneven throughout man's history. Moreover, it varies necessarily in the different areas and aspects of human activity, such as science, technology, morality, and the arts. Progress in the arts, for example, is always radically limited by the nature of man himself, since the goal of the arts is pleasure alone, whereas speculative scientific knowledge can be as infinite as the natural universe. And each area of activity has its own rules of progress. In his discussion of scientific progress, Turgot suggested three historical stages of development (anticipating Auguste Comte's system): the anthropomorphic or supernatural, the abstract or speculative, and the empirical-mathematical.

For Turgot the broad tempo of progress was increasing in the mid-eighteenth century; indeed, despite instances of momentary or partial decadence, any wholesale retrogression of humankind was now impossible. Surely, he wrote, the general momentum of science, buttressed by mathematics, was irreversible. Yet Turgot, especially in his later years, had frequent doubts, and he was well aware of the forces of error and evil in the world, both in the past and in the happier future. The historical continuity so much stressed in his writings in fact ruled out any immediate, thorough renovation of humankind. Certainly the future would not bring the radical break with a deplorable past that was intimated in the thought of many another writer of the Enlightenment. Because the element of empiricism was seldom wholly absent in Turgot, his historical thought, although undoubtedly optimistic, was never unreservedly utopian.

See also Encyclopédie; Enlightenment; Philosophy of History; Progress, The Idea of.

Bibliography

Turgot's works were published as *Oeuvres de Turgot et documents le concernant,* edited by Gustave Schelle, 5 vols. (Paris: Alcan, 1913–1923). See also: *Turgot on Progress, Sociology, and Economics: A Philosophical Review of the Successive Advances of the Human Mind,* translated and edited by Ronald L. Meek (Cambridge, U.K.: Cambridge University Press, 1973).

For literature on Turgot, see Douglas Dakin, *Turgot and the Ancien Régime in France* (London: Methuen, 1939), which has an extensive bibliography; Edgar Faure, *La disgrâce de Turgot* (Paris: Gallimard, 1961), which also has an extensive bibliography; Philippe Fontaine, "Turgot's 'Institutional Individualism,'" *History of Political Economy* 29 (1) (1997): 1–20; Malcolm Hill, *Statesman of the Enlightenment: The Life of Anne-Robert Turgot* (London: Othila Press, 1999); Frank E. Manuel, *The Prophets of Paris* (Cambridge, MA: Harvard University Press, 1962), Ch. I, pp. 11–51; and Robert Nisbet, "Turgot and the Contexts of Progress," *Proceedings of the American Philosophical Society* 119 (3) (1975): 214–222.

Henry Vyverberg (1967)
Bibliography updated by Philip Reed (2005)

TURING, ALAN M.
(1912–1954)

Alan Mathison Turing was born June 23, 1912, in London and died June 7, 1954, at his home near Manchester. He suffered the conventional schooling of the English upper-middle class, but defeated convention by becoming a shy, eccentric but athletic Cambridge mathematician. The Second World War transformed Turing's life by giving him a crucial role in breaking German ciphers, with particular responsibility for the Atlantic war. Thereafter Turing led the design of electronic computers and the program of artificial intelligence. In 1950 he began another career as a mathematical biologist, but was assailed by prosecution for homosexuality. His last two years, though overshadowed by punishment and security risk status, saw vigorous and defiant work until his death by cyanide poisoning.

Turing's paper *Computing Machinery and Intelligence* appeared in 1950. This, his only contribution to a philosophical journal, was to become one of the most cited. He considered the question "can a machine think" and gave an argument that broke with all previous speculation about homunculi and robots, and from all earlier discussion of mind, matter, freewill, and determinism. It was based on his own elucidation of mathematical computability, as achieved in 1936. It also reflected his unique experience with practical computation.

Turing's computability arose from the long search for a logical basis to mathematics, in which Bertrand Russell had played a prominent part. In 1931 Gödel showed that no formal proof scheme such as Russell had envisaged could encapsulate mathematics. In 1935 Turing seized on the further outstanding question, of whether there could be a definite method for deciding whether a given proposition was susceptible to formal proof. The question turned on finding a definition of "method," and this Turing supplied with his "Turing machine" construction. This was mathematically equivalent to the definition of "effectively calculable" offered by the logician Alonzo Church a little earlier, but Church accepted that Turing's argument gave it a natural and compelling rationale. Their assertions, taken together, are referred to as the Church-Turing thesis. On accepting this thesis, it follows that there is no effective method for deciding provability. Many other mathematical questions of decidability have likewise been resolved.

Turing's thesis was based on analyzing the actions of a human mind when following a rule, and translating it into formal actions of reading and writing. More generally, Turing's formalism was intended to capture what could be carried out by a "purely mechanical process," interpreting this as one that "could be carried out by a machine." Thus Turing found a new connection between the mind and the material world. On the one hand, he gave a new logical analysis of mental operations, but on the other hand, the criterion of "effectiveness" implied something that could be implemented physically.

As mathematics, Turing's argument meant encoding operations *on* symbols *by* symbols, rather as Gödel encoded theorems *about* numbers *by* numbers. Turing exploited this by describing a "universal" machine, which could do the work of any Turing machine. This concept led directly to the modern computer in which program and data are stored and manipulated alike as symbols. In 1936 Turing had no technology for implementing this idea. He did further important work exploring the mathematics of uncomputability, which touched on the role of human intuition in mathematics. He also discussed the foundations of mathematics with Wittgenstein. But then six years of war work brought him back to the "universal machine." He had gained the experience of advanced electronics and hence the means of putting his idea into practice.

Turing's central interest in computing lay in its role in investigating the nature of the mind. He described his post-war computer plan as "building a brain," and asserted with increasing confidence that *any* action of the mind, including creative acts, could be described as computable operations. Turing's sophisticated cryptanalytic work had impressed him with the apparently limitless scope of the computable. He now discounted arguments derived from Gödel's theorem suggesting a noncomputable aspect to the human mind. He emphasized that any computable operation could be implemented on a single universal machine: the computer. Hence, the computer could rival human intelligence.

Turing's 1950 paper summarized these arguments for a wide readership. His underlying view assumed a physical basis for Mind, but rather than argue for this he appealed to an argument from external observation. He held that a computer exhibiting the appearance of intelligence should be credited with intelligence. He thus avoided discussing the reality of consciousness, and sought to sidestep its traditional philosophical primacy. Instead, he illustrated his "imitation game" with a provocatively wide view of "intelligence," and took pleasure in playing the role of a new Galileo, defying orthodox belief in the uniquely human nature of mind.

This "imitation game," the so-called "Turing Test" for intelligence, was not the only content of this paper. He also sketched a constructive program for Artificial Intelligence research, which he saw as a combination of "top-down" methods by programming and "bottom-up" methods using networks capable of developing functions through training. Turing saw self-modification in machines as a key analogy with human mental development. His doubts and reservations centered on the question of defining a valid line separating the mind from the external world with which it interacts.

Turing made a prophecy of progress within fifty years, which though cautiously expressed, still proved over-optimistic. Some artificial intelligence protagonists have come to see Turing's ambitious goal as a distraction from systematic research. But many thinkers have found it vital to continue Turing's arguments. Lucas revived the objection from Gödel's theorem, which Turing had dismissed. Hofstadter and Dennett then vigorously defended Turing's view. A new argument was made by Penrose. This shares with Turing a wholly materialist viewpoint, but holds that there must be uncomputable elements in the physics of the brain, arising from the reduction process of quantum mechanics. A late talk given by Turing indicates that he, too, considered this question, but death cut off the physical investigations he undertook in 1953 and 1954. The relationship of computability to physics, in particular to the material basis of mind, is the central question left by Turing's work.

As a human being Alan Turing was highly willful and far from soulless, yet he sought to mechanize will and mocked the concept of soul. He was highly original and resisted social conformity, yet attempted to explain creativity as a process of learning. Truthfulness was paramount to him, yet he committed himself to state secrets and defined intelligence by imitation. The paradoxical life and death of Alan Turing continue to fascinate.

See also Artificial Intelligence; Church, Alonzo; Computability Theory; Computing Machines; Gödel, Kurt; Logic Machines; Machine Intelligence; Russell, Bertrand Arthur William.

Bibliography

PRIMARY WORKS

The Essential Turing, edited by B. J. Copeland. Oxford: Oxford University Press, 2004.

Collected Works of A. M. Turing, edited by R. O. Gandy et al. Amsterdam: Elsevier, 1992–2001.

SECONDARY WORKS

Diamond, C., ed. *Wittgenstein's Lectures on the Foundations of Mathematics, Cambridge 1939.* Hassocks, U.K.: Harvester, 1976.

Herken, R., ed. *The Universal Turing Machine.* Oxford: Oxford University Press, 1988.

Hofstadter, D. R., and D. C. Dennett. *The Mind's I.* New York: Basic, 1981.

Hodges, A. *Alan Turing: The Enigma.* New York: Simon & Schuster, 1983.

Hodges, A. *Turing: A Natural Philosopher.* London: Routledge, 1997.

Penrose, R. *The Emperor's New Mind.* Oxford: Oxford University Press, 1989.

Teuscher, C., ed. *Alan Turing: Life and Legacy of a Great Thinker.* Berlin: Springer, 2004.

Andrew Hodges (2005)

TURING AND COMPUTABILITY

See *Logic, History of: Modern Logic: Since Gödel: Turing and Computability Theory*

TURING TEST

See *Machine Intelligence; Turing, Alan M.*

TWARDOWSKI, KAZIMIERZ

(1866–1938)

Kazimierz Twardowski had a twofold role in the recent history of philosophy. He had a decisive influence on Polish philosophy in the twentieth century; and at the turn of the twentieth century he contributed to the transformation of European philosophy in its search for new, intellectually responsible methods of philosophical inquiry. His conception of philosophy and his specific contributions to epistemology, philosophical psychology, and theory of science helped to pave the way for the emergence of phenomenology and of some forms of analytic philosophy.

Twardowski was born in Vienna. He studied philosophy at the University of Vienna, where he came under the influence of Franz Brentano. In 1892 he received a PhD degree from the university, and he became a lecturer there in 1894. In 1895 he was appointed to a chair of philosophy at the University of Lwów, where he taught until 1930.

Like Brentano, he wanted philosophy to be scientific, which to him meant a rejection of grandiose but nebulous speculation, an unrelenting war on conceptual confusion and linguistic obscurity, and a painstaking analysis of clearly defined problems, which through elimination of conceptual sloppiness, leads to empirically verifiable conclusions. No wholesale condemnation of metaphysics was intended by these methodological injunctions. Nevertheless, Twardowski was increasingly aware of the boundary beyond which the method of philosophy, as conceived by him, could not reach and beyond which a philosopher qua philosopher should remain silent.

More specifically, the basic philosophical science, avoiding both irresponsible speculation and skepticism, was to be the Brentanist "descriptive psychology," understood as a sort of empirical inquiry, but distinct from experimental psychology. Twardowski, however, went well beyond Brentano and contributed to the demise of psychologistic accounts of meaning and of psychologism in general. In an early and influential book, *Zur Lehre vom Inhalt und Gegenstand der Vorstellungen,* Twardowski introduced a sharp distinction between the mental act, its content, and its object. The distinction between content, which is mental and a part of a person's biography, and object, which is not, was overlooked by Brentano and the early Alexius Meinong but became crucial for Twardowski and led him to a general theory of objects of thought. These ideas influenced Meinong, Edmund Husserl, and to some extent Moritz Schlick, and through them much of early-twentieth-century philosophy. The difficulties of Twardowski's theory of objects, with its attending danger of overpopulating the Platonic heaven, led later to Stanisław Leśniewski's "ontology" and Tadeusz Kotarbiński's "reism." Twardowski's conclusions, far from supporting psychologism, implied a sharp separation of logic and philosophy from psychology. Moreover, the actual procedure of this "psychological investigation" did not look much like psychology either. Phenomenologists have seen in it the germ of the ideas that reappeared both in the later Husserl and in the realist branch of phenomenology. Up to a certain point, it is equally plausible to construe Twardowski's contributions as an early attempt to develop a philosophical psychology, in the sense of an examination of the logical geography of mental concepts.

Twardowski's later work included a further analysis of mental concepts; the formulation of a nonpsychologistic and non-Platonizing account of logic, based on the distinction between acts and their products; the extension of a similar line of reasoning to a general theory and classification of the sciences; and an examination, on several occasions, of various methodological issues of psychology. This included a critique of reductive materialism and a defense of introspection as a source of knowledge. One of his most influential works, "O tak zwanych prawdach względnych," was a lucid critique of relativism.

A strong sense of the scholar's social responsibilities, heightened by the special circumstances of Polish history, led Twardowski to devote more and more time to educational activities, to the detriment of his own work, but to the lasting benefit of Polish philosophy.

As a teacher, Twardowski transformed Polish philosophy and endowed it with a distinct style. He did not preach any particular weltanschauung, and his influence—not unlike that of G. E. Moore—was due less to his specific doctrines than to his way of doing philosophy, his qualities of character, his intellectual integrity, and the impact of his personal example. The school that he created was not linked by a common allegiance to any philosophical creed, but rather by a common acceptance of rigorous standards of professional excellence. Most of his pupils went their own independent ways, representing a wide spectrum of philosophical opinion, but they never ceased to express their gratitude to him. The best-known among them, Jan Łukasiewicz, Leśniewski, Kazimierz Ajdukiewicz, and Kotarbiński, differed from Twardowski methodologically in their emphasis on the philosophical relevance of symbolic logic. Twardowski's influence, transmitted by his numerous students—philosophers and nonphilosophers—went far beyond academic circles and, fostering the ethos of free and responsible inquiry in all areas of intellectual life, became a significant factor in the history of Polish culture.

Twardowski organized the teaching of philosophy in Poland, initiated regular meetings of philosophers, founded the first Polish psychological laboratory (1901), the Polish Philosophical Society (1904), and in 1911 the quarterly journal *Ruch Filozoficzny,* which he edited until his death. In 1935 he became the chief editor of *Studia Philosophica,* a periodical publishing works of Polish philosophers in foreign languages. He was also active as the editor of several different series of original works and translations, many of them inspired by him, such as Władysław Witwicki's masterful translations of Plato.

See also Brentano, Franz; History and Historiography of Philosophy; Husserl, Edmund; Kotarbiński, Tadeusz; Leśniewski, Stanisław; Łukasiewicz, Jan; Meinong, Alexius; Moore, George Edward; Phenomenology; Plato; Schlick, Moritz.

Bibliography

WORKS BY TWARDOWSKI

Idee und Perzeption. Vienna, 1892.

Zur Lehre vom Inhalt und Gegenstand der Vorstellungen. Vienna, 1894.

Wyobrażenia i pojęcia. Lwów, 1898.

"O tak zwanych prawdach względnych," *Księga Pamiątkowa Uniwersytetu Lwowskiego.* Lwów, 1900. Translated into German by M. Wartenberg as "Über sogenannte relative Wahrheiten." *Archiv für systematische Philosophie* 8 (4) (1902): 415–447.

Zasadnicze pojęcia dydaktyki i logiki. Lwów, 1901.

"Über begriffliche Vorstellungen." In *Beilage zum XVI Jahresbericht der Philosophischen Gesellschaft a. d. Universität zu Wien.* Leipzig, 1903.

O filzofji średniowiecznej. Lwów, 1910.

O metodzie psychologji. Warsaw, 1910.

O czynnościach i wytworach. Kraków, 1911.

O psychologji, jej przedmiocie, zadaniach i metodzie. Lwów, 1913.

Rozprawy i artykuły filozoficzne. Lwów, 1927.

Wybrane pisma filozoficzne. Edited by T. Czeżowski. Warsaw: Panstwowe Wydawn, Naukowe, 1965.

WORKS ON TWARDOWSKI

Discussions of Twardowski in English include T. Czeżowski, "Tribute to Kazimierz Twardowski on the 10th Anniversary of His Death," in *Journal of Philosophy* 57 (1960): 209–215; T. Czeżowski, "Kazimierz Twardowski as Teacher," in *Studia Philosophica* 3 (1948): 13–17; J. N. Findlay, *Meinong's Theory of Objects* (London: Oxford University Press, H. Milford, 1933); Roman Ingarden, "The Scientific Activity of Kazimierz Twardowski," in *Studia Philosophica* 3 (1948): 17–30; and Z. A. Jordan, *Philosophy and Ideology* (Dordrecht, Netherlands: Reidel, 1963).

A bibliography of writings by and on Twardowski until 1938, compiled by D. Gromska, can be found in *Ruch Filozoficzny* 14 (1938): 14–39. Additional bibliography can be found in Z. A. Jordan's book.

George Krzywicki-Herburt (1967)

TYCHE

See *Moira/Tychē/Anakē*

TYPE THEORY

Type theory, in one sense, is the view that some category of abstract entities—sets, in the simplest example, but there are analogous views of properties, relations, concepts, and functions—come in a hierarchy of levels, with an entity of one level applying to (having as members, or having as instances, or…) entities only of a lower level. Such a view gives an intuitively comprehensible picture of the universe of abstracta and provides a principled way of avoiding Bertrand Arthur William Russell's Paradox and its analogues. In a second sense, the term refers to any of a wide range of formal axiomatic systems embodying some form of the view. The present entry gives a short history of the view and a brief survey of the systems.

The systems are generally formulated in *many-sorted* quantificational logic, with a separate alphabet of quantified variables ranging over each type of entity. Axiomatically, they incorporate the rules of propositional logic (usually though not always classical) and of quantifier logic, the latter reduplicated for each alphabet of variables. Beyond this the most important axioms postulate the existence entities of the various types. For versions of Simple Type Theory, these are typically unrestricted comprehension principles: For any type, *t*, there is a set (or property, or …) of a higher type containing as members (or having as instances, or …) all the entities of type *t* satisfying an arbitrarily chosen formula of the language. For versions of Ramified Type Theory, this is restricted: Only such entities are postulated as can have their membership (or …) specified by formulas in which certain sorts of variables do not occur. References are given below to works in which precise formulations can be found; Alonzo Church is particularly helpful in this matter.

Type theory as a way of avoiding the set-theoretic paradoxes is one of Russell's great contributions to the study of the foundations of mathematics, but the idea of a hierarchy with sets (or set-like entities …) coming in levels is a bit older. Schroeder had presented a version of it, and Gödel Frege had based his foundational system on it. For Frege, the hierarchy of entities reflected the hierarchy of grammatical categories in an (idealized) language. At the bottom there were *objects*, the referents of singular terms. Predicates (either simple or complex) then stood for *concepts*, which he conceived of as so different from objects that it was an abuse of language to try to say anything of the two together (hence his avowedly nonsensical dictum about the concept horse not being a concept). Linguistic constructions with *blanks* that can be filled by simple or complex predicates—his prime examples were the first-order quantifiers "it holds of every object that it ___" and "it holds of at least one object that it ___"—he construed as a sort of second-level predicate and took to denote second-level concepts: entities as different from (first-level) concepts as they are from objects. And so (in principle; in practice he made little use of higher levels) on up. The grammar of his formal system reflected this: No term or variable for an item of one level was allowed to stand in the positions filled by terms or variables for items of other levels. Had he rested content with this machinery, his formal system would have been a version of (what later came to be called) the Simple Theory of Types and demonstrably consistent.

To carry out his project of giving a logicist foundation for arithmetic, however, he had to prove that there were infinitely many objects, and to do this, he postulated that every concept had an object—its *Werthverlauf*—as a kind of shadow. These objects functioned essentially as sets: Frege was able to define membership by saying that one object was a member of a second iff the second was the *Werthverlauf* of a concept holding of the first. Since a *Werthverlauf* could have any objects whatever—including *Werthverlaufs!*—as members, the derived set theory was untyped. Frege was able to prove in it the existence of an infinite set, and to interpret (a variant of) the Peano axioms for Arithmetic. Russell was able to derive in it his contradiction. (There is a readable account of the derivation of Arithmetic in the untyped set theory in Hatcher 1982.)

Russell was not initially attracted to Frege's linguistic hierarchy. He wanted to formulate a general metaphysical theory and to describe the differences between horses and concepts by denying of the one the very same predicates he affirmed of the other. During his period of experimentation after the discovery of the paradoxes, he toyed with and rejected versions of type theory, finally coming to it by an indirect route.

Sets (Russell said *classes*) themselves—entities satisfying an axiom of extensionality—he was willing to give up as excess ontological baggage. A set is typically defined by giving an open formula that specifies its membership, and Russell preferred to think in terms of nonextensional entities designated by the formulas. He thought of sentences as standing for *propositions*, which he took to be complex entities built up out of the items designated by the words in a sentence in a way that paralleled the syntactic construction of the sentence. The items expressed by open formulas he called *propositional functions*: things which, when given some entity as argument, would yield the proposition that would be expressed by inserting a name of the argument in place of the free variable. Russell's Paradox, however, does not depend on the assumption of extensionality: A *naïve* theory of propositional functions is inconsistent in the same way as naïve set theory. If a consistent theory of propositional functions could be found, however, a theory of sets could be interpreted in it by contextual definition: Statements about sets would be interpreted as statements about propositional functions to which the differences between extensionally equivalent functions were irrelevant. Apparently almost immediately after seeing how to dispense with the strange entities he called *denoting concepts*—"On Denoting" eliminates them by giving a new analysis of the propositions he had thought of as containing them—he thought of what might be called a theory of *virtual* propositional functions, a theory in which, though neither classes nor propositional functions were postulated as entities, statements *apparently* referring to them could be formulated.

On this theory reference to a propositional function (say, *X is a horse*) would be replaced by reference to a pair of entities: one of the propositions that might have been taken as a value of the function (for example, *Bucephalus is a horse*) along with one of the component entities of that proposition (Bucephalus, in this case). The key notion was one of the *substitution* of an entity for one of the constituents of a proposition: Rather than saying that Traveler, for example, satisfies the propositional function *X is a horse*, on the new theory, we will say that the proposition obtained from *Bucephalus is a horse* by substituting Traveler for Bucephalus in it is a true one. (Note that this notion of substitution is not a syntactic one: We are substituting one flesh-and-blood horse for another in a proposition, construed as a complex but nonlinguistic entity. The developed formalization of the theory, of course, has provisions for substitution of names in the sentences expressing propositions!)

Since the place of a variable for propositional functions is taken by two variables for entities (one for a proposition, one for a *designated argument*), and a variable for a higher-level propositional function taking first-level propositional functions will similarly be replaced by three variables and so on, this theory gives the effect of a typed theory of propositional functions: When references to and quantifications over propositional functions are replaced with terms and variables for propositions and other entities recognized by the theory in the way sketched, it will be impossible to say that a higher-level item serves as an argument for a lower! (Russell described the theory in his 1906 essay, which he withdrew before publication. Remarkably, essentially the same system was developed again, apparently independently, several decades later. For discussions of Russell's theory and his reasons for abandoning it, see Peter Hylton [1980] and Gregory Landini [1998].)

Russell took propositions and propositional functions to be the objects of cognitive attitudes and the meanings of linguistic expressions as well as the fundamental objects of mathematics. In trying to formulate a general theory of entities that could serve all these functions, he confronted not only the set-theoretic paradoxes but also those now classed as *semantic* or *intentional*, and they drove him to an even more restrictive form of type theory. This was the *Ramified Theory of Types*, first presented in Russell (1908) (a paper largely recycled in the introduction to *Principia Mathematica* two years later). On this theory there is a kind of double hierarchy. Propositional functions are classified not only by the arguments they take but also by the conceptual resources that go into their definitions: A propositional function can only have arguments of certain lower levels, but two propositional functions taking exactly the same arguments may be of different types if in formulating them (it is best, here, to think of the functions as the meanings of open formulas) one quantifies over entities of a different level.

Start with a domain of nonabstract or nonconceptual entities as a bottom level. The level of a propositional function will be at least one higher than that of its argument (or, in the case of a relational function, the highest level of its arguments). It will only have this minimum level, however, if no quantified variables are used in its formulation that range over entities of a higher level than its arguments, and the general rule is that the level of a propositional function is one greater than the highest level of its arguments or of the entities quantified over in its formulation, whichever is higher. (Propositions, since they do not take arguments, formed a single type on his earlier approaches, but the Ramified Theory divides them into a hierarchy based on the quantifications involved in them. This makes possible a quick dissolution of many semantic paradoxes: When Epimenides says that every proposition asserted by a Cretan is false, he asserts a proposition of a higher level than those he quantifies over, and so his assertion does not cover the proposition he himself has asserted.)

The Ramified Theory, though notationally complicated, has a perspicuous semantic interpretation which make its ontological commitments seem fairly innocent: Kurt Gödel, in a note added to reprintings of his 1944 essay, speaks of it as embodying a strictly nominalistic (or strictly antirealistic) kind of constructivism about abstract entities. From a mathematical point of view, it is a very weak theory: When it is supplemented by an Axiom of Infinity (stating that there are infinitely many objects of the lowest level), it suffices to derive a certain portion of elementary number theory, but only a restricted portion. In order to provide a foundation for classical mathematics, Russell added the Axioms of Reducibility. These maintained the type distinctions of the Ramified Theory (allowing Russell to appeal to them in dealing with the semantic and intentional paradoxes) but postulated the existence of enough *predicative* propositional functions (functions, that is, of the lowest possible level for their arguments) to provide a model of the mathematically stronger Simple Theory of Types, and the mathematical work of *Principia Mathematica* is then essentially conducted in the Simple Theory. (The clearest account of Ramified Type Theory and its use in analyzing the paradoxes is in Church [1976], to which sections 58 and 59 of Church [1956] can serve as an introduction.)

In the early 1920s two alternatives to the Ramified Theory were proposed. One was described in the introduction and appendices Russell wrote for the second edition of *Principia Mathematica* (1925). It was noted by Gödel in 1944, but otherwise seems to have been ignored until the 1990s. On this theory the two factors in the Ramified Theory's classification are separated. Each function has a simple type depending only on the arguments it takes, and also a ramification level determined by what entities are quantified over in its formulation. A function of higher simple type (one, that is, that can take functions as arguments) can be affirmed of any argument of the appropriate simple type, even an argument whose ramification level is higher than its own. Each quantified variable for propositional functions, however, is restricted to range only over functions of a certain ramification level. Gödel (1944) noted that this system was acceptable to the same nominalistic constructivism as Ramified Type Theory. One way of making this precise is that, as shown in A. P. Hazen and J. M. Davoren (2001), the 1925 system, like the Ramified system, can be given a semantics on which quantification over objects other than the basic, bottom-level, ones is interpreted substitutionally.

In Appendix B to the second edition of *Principia Mathematica*, Russell gave what he claimed was a derivation of the principle of mathematical induction in his new system, but the proof contains an essential error. Landini (1996) gives a correct proof of induction but uses an additional extensionality axiom that is not valid on the nominalistic semantics. The exact mathematical strength of the 1925 system, supplemented by an Axiom of Infinity, is not clear: It will not suffice for the full strength of (first-order) Peano Arithmetic, but it may yield a richer fragment of it than the Ramified system.

At about the same time, F. P. Ramsey (1925) proposed abandoning ramification altogether, giving a formulation of the Simple Theory of Types. On this view, the basic objects, or *individuals*, form one type and the types of other entities are defined exclusively by the types of arguments they can take: Properties of individuals will form one type, properties of properties of individuals another, relations between individuals and properties of individuals a third, and so on. The theory need not be extensional: It can allow distinctions between properties holding of exactly the same objects, and both Aldo Bressan (1972) and Montague (cf. Daniel Gallin 1976) developed versions based on modal logic, the first seeking applications in the formalization of physical theory and the second a variety of semantic and conceptual analyses. For mathematical purposes Ramsey assumed extensionality; on this assumption, propositional functions of a single argument amount to sets, those of more than one to *relations-in-extension*. The resulting system is described (and compared with the Ramified Theory) in sections 34–36 of W. V. Quine (1969).

Obviously, Ramsey and those who have followed him have abandoned Russell's attempt to deal with the semantic and intentional paradoxes through type distinctions. Their view was that the set-theoretic paradoxes were adequately handled by the Simple Theory of Types, and the others essentially involved other concepts—semantic or cognitive/epistemological—and were so properly dealt with by separate theories. Alfred Tarski showed that the semantic paradoxes could be avoided by invoking a doctrine of levels of language (clearly foreshadowed by Russell at the end of his introduction to Ludwig Wittgenstein's essay [1921].) Russell seems to have thought the intentional paradoxes were best handled by assimilating them to semantic paradoxes through a kind of *language of thought* idea, which he discussed in Appendix C to the second edition of *Principia Mathematica*.

The extensional Simple Theory of Types, without an axiom of infinity, was proven consistent by Gerhard Gentzen (1936) (one of the successes of Hilbert's Program!). With an axiom asserting the existence of infinitely many individuals, it becomes a usable system of set theory, strong enough to derive most of the mathematics actually used in the natural sciences. As such it was taken as *standard* by many researchers between the publication of *Principia Mathematica* and the 1930s: Gödel (1931) and Tarski (1935) both assume it as their background system. Subsequent set theorists have preferred other axiomatizations, such as Zermelo-Fraenkel set theory, but (as described in sections 37–38 of Quine [1969]), they can be seen as natural generalizations of Simple Type Theory. To get from a system like Ramsey's to one like Zermelo's, one makes five changes:

(1) abandoning relational types (reducing relations to sets by using the Wiener-Kuratowski analysis of ordered pairs),

(2) abandoning the many-sorted formal language, with its separate alphabets of variables ranging over different types of entity, in favor of a description of the whole hierarchy in a first-order language with a single sort of variable,

(3) making the hierarchy cumulative, so a set can have members of any lower level rather than being restricted to members of the immediately preceding level,

(4) allowing sets of infinitely high level, which can have members of all finite levels,

(5) reformulate the axioms to give an elegant systematization of the new framework.

The first is just a simplification, adding nothing to the system. The second would be perverse if we still, like Russell in the first decade of the twentieth century, thought of the entities in the hierarchy as the meanings of expressions in our language, but is natural if we think of them in a Platonistic way as entities independent of our thought or language. The third can be shown to be harmless, and the fourth, though a significant enrichment of the system, is natural after the third. The fifth is not trivial: The resulting systems are stronger than the Type Theory we started with, and would be even if we left out the infinite types. Conceptually, however, the generalized type-theoretic way of thinking about set theory is very satisfying. The stages of George Boolos (1971) are very reminiscent of Russellian types.

Church (1940) makes a different generalization. As Russell's *propositional function* suggests, a property can be thought of as a function mapping arguments (of appropriate type) to propositions (or, assuming extensionality, to truth values). Church assumes two basic types, of individuals and truth values, and represents properties as functions from entities of some type to truth values, and then adds types for other kinds of function: Thus, there is a type of functions from individuals to individuals, a type of functions from individuals to (functions from individuals to individuals), and so on. The formal language embodying this conception is based on a typed version of Church's *lambda calculus*, an elegant notation for the representation of recursive functions. (Montague's intensional logic, mentioned above, is essentially a modal version of Church's system.)

All the type theories mentioned so far have been based on classical logic (or, in modal extensions thereof). The considerations that motivate *intuitionistic logic* are independent of those leading to type theories (recall that Russell's Paradox works in essentially the same way in intuitionistic as in classical logic!), and variants of all of these systems based on intuitionistic logic are possible. They have received some study under the name *theory of species*. Joachim Lambek and P. J. Scott (1986) present what is essentially an intuitionistic variant of the system of Church (1940), showing that it has natural connections with mathematical *category theory*. Per Martin-Löf (1984), with greater philosophical attention to intuitionistic concerns about the meaningfulness of mathematical assertions, has developed fragments of intuitionistic type theory in a series of publications, with Martin-Löf serving as a summary of his work to that point. Since intuitionistic proofs often provide information that can be used to define algorithms, there has been considerable interest in Martin-Löf's and similar systems among computer scientists; Thompson (1991) provides an introduction to the systems and their applications. The area is one of active research by logicians, and efforts to develop more powerful and general theories have encountered difficulties, as witnessed by Thierry Coquand (1994), of a kind that would have been familiar to early twentieth-century researchers in the foundations of mathematics.

See also Epistemology; Frege, Gottlob; Gödel, Kurt; Intuitionism and Intuitionistic Logic; Mathematics, Foundations of; Russell, Bertrand Arthur William.

Bibliography

Boolos, George. "The Iterative Conception of Set." *Journal of Philosophy* 68 (1971): 215–231.

Bressan, Aldo. *A General Interpreted Modal Calculus*. New Haven: Yale University Press, 1972.

Burgess, John, and A. P. Hazen. "Predicative logic and Formal Arithmetic." *Notre Dame Journal of Formal Logic* 39 (1998): 1–17.

Church, Alonzo. "A Formulation of the Simple Theory of Types." *Journal of Symbolic Logic* 5 (1940): 65–68.

Church, Alonzo. "Axioms for Functional Calculi of Higher Order." In *Logic and Art*. Edited by Richard Rudner and Israel Scheffler. Indianapolis, IN: Bobbs Merrill, 1972.

Church, Alonzo. "Comparison of Russell's Resolution of the Semantical Antinomies with That of Tarski." *Journal of Symbolic Logic* 41 (1976): 747–760. Reproduced with revisions in *Recent Essays on Truth and the Liar Paradox*. Edited by R. L. Martin. Oxford: Clarendon Press, 1984.

Church, Alonzo. *Introduction to Mathematical Logic*. Princeton, NJ: Princeton University Press, 1956.

Church, Alonzo. "Russellian Simple Type Theory." *Proceedings and Addresses of the American Philosophical Association* 47 (1974): 21–33.

Church, Alonzo. "Schroeder's Anticipation of the Simple Theory of Types." *Erkenntnis* 10 (1976): 407–411.

Coquand, Thierry. "A New Paradox in Type Theory." In *Logic, Methodology and Philosophy of Science IX*. Edited by Dag Prawitz, Brian Skyrms, and Dag Westerstahl. Amsterdam: North-Holland, 1994.

Fitch, Frederic B. "Propositions as the Only Realities." *American Philosophical Quarterly* 8 (1971): 99–103.

Gallin, Daniel. *Intensional and Higher-order Modal Logic*. Amsterdam: North-Holland, 1976.

Gentzen, Gerhard. "Widerspruchsfreiheit d. Stufenlogik." *Mathematische Zeitschrifft* 41 (1936): 357–366. English translation in *Collected Papers of Gerhard Gentzen*. Edited by M. E. Szabo. Amsterdam: North-Holland, 1969.

Gödel, Kurt. "Russell's Mathematical Logic." In *The Philosophy of Bertrand Russel*. Edited by P. A. Schilpp. Evanston: Northwestern University, 1944.

Gödel, Kurt. "Über formal unentscheidbare Sätze der *Principia Mathematica* und verwandter Systeme I." *Monatshefte für Mathematik und Physik* 38 (1931): 173–198.

Hatcher, William S. *The logical Foundations of Mathematics*. New York: Pergamon Press, 1982.

Hazen, A. P., and J. M. Davoren. "Russell's 1925 Logic." *Australasian Journal of Philosophy* 78 (2001): 534–556.

Hylton, Peter. "Russell's Substitutional Theory." *Synthese* 45 (1980): 1–31.

Lambek, Joachim, and P. J. Scott. *Introduction to Higher Order Categorical Logic*. Cambridge, U.K.: Cambridge University Press, 1986.

Landini, Gregory. "The Definability of the Set of Natural Numbers in the 1925 *Principia Mathematica*." *Journal of Philosophical Logic* 25 (1996): 597–615.

Landini, Gregory. *Russell's Hidden Substitutional Theory*. New York: Oxford University Press, 1998.

Linsky, Bernard. *Russell's Metaphysical Logic*. Stanford, CT: CSLI, 1999.

Martin-Löf, Per. *Intuitionistic Type Theory*. Naples: Bibliopolis, 1984.

Pelham, Judy, and Alasdair Urquhart. "Russellian Propositions." In *Logic, Methodology and Philosophy of Science IX*. Edited by Dag Prawitz, Brian Skyrms, and Dag Westerstahl. Amsterdam: North-Holland, 1994.

Quine, W. V. *Set Theory and its Logic*. Cambridge, MA: Harvard University Press, 1969.

Ramsey, F. P. "The Foundations of Mathematics." *Proceedings of the London Mathematical Society* 25 (1925): 338–384.

Russell, B. A. W. "Mathematical Logic as Based on the Theory of Types." *American Journal of Mathematics* 30 (1908): 222–262.

Russell, B. A. W. "On the Substitutional Theory of Classes and Relations."(Originally written 1906 but withdrawn from publication.) In *Essays in Analysis*. Edited by D. Lackey. London: Allen & Unwin, 1973.

Sambin, Giovanni, and Jan Smith. *Twenty-Five Years of Constructive Type Theory*. Oxford: Oxford University Press, 1998.

Tarski, Alfred. "Der Wahrheitsbegriff in den formalisierten Sprachen." *Studia Philosophica* 1 (1935): 261–405.

Thompson, Simon. *Type Theory and Functional Programming.* Wokingham, U.K.: Addison-Wesley, 1991.

Whitehead, Alfred North and Bertrand Russell. *Principia Mathematica.* Cambridge, U.K.: Cambridge University Press: 1910. Revised edition 1925.

Wittgenstein, Ludwig. "Logisch-Philosophische Abhandlung." *Annalen der Naturphilosophie* 14 (1921): 185–262. Reprinted in book form with facing English translation as *Tractatus-Logico Philosophicus.*

Allen P. Hazen (2005)

UGLINESS

Aesthetics has often been described as the philosophical study of beauty and "ugliness." It is important at the outset to see what is involved in this familiar definition, for it embodies a view of ugliness and of its role within aesthetic theory that has been the major source of contention in historical debates on the concept. The first thing to note about this view is that it takes ugliness to be a category that properly falls within aesthetic theory. Ugliness designates aesthetic disvalue as beauty designates positive aesthetic value. The two therefore constitute a value polarity analogous to right and wrong in ethics or to truth and falsehood in epistemology. Just as the field of ethics comprises responsible human actions of which some are evil and blameworthy, so, among perceptual objects, there are some that have negative aesthetic value. This does not mean that such objects simply lack the characteristics by virtue of which things are beautiful; it means, rather, that they possess recognizable properties that are the opposites of those found in beautiful objects.

The relation between beauty and ugliness has commonly been conceived in hedonistic terms, that is, whereas a beautiful object is a source of pleasure in the spectator, an ugly object arouses its opposite, pain. Plato, in numerous instances, takes beauty to be characteristically pleasurable (*Hippias Major* 297–299, *Philebus* 50–52, *Laws* II). Aristotle perpetuates this view, and in his study of specific art forms (notably tragedy) he holds that it is the proper function of these forms to create pleasure. Yet it is clear in his classic *Poetics* that he is troubled by the seeming conflict between this view of art and the empirical fact that works of art often represent objects and events that are ugly. Aristotle raises the question first in regard to the type of visual art that depicts things "which in themselves we view with pain" (IV). He does not doubt, however, that the painting itself arouses pleasure, a phenomenon that is explained by our intellectual interest in recognizing the object. Comedy, moreover, "imitates" men who are ignoble and therefore ludicrous; and though this is a kind of ugliness, the comedy is, for reasons that Aristotle does not specify, kept from being painful (V). Finally, though the protagonist is a good man who suffers adversity, tragedy is not merely shocking (XIII).

Thus Aristotle initiated the controversy over the "paradox of tragedy" that has survived to the present day. As has been shown, this paradox is not the sole instance of the problem of ugliness in art, but it states the problem most acutely, both because tragedy is almost the only artistic genre whose subject matter is necessarily sorrowful or pathetic and because of the preeminent value that has traditionally been claimed for works in this genre. Why do we esteem narratives of evil and suffering? The poetic values of tragic literature, the ennobling courage of the hero, the insight and wisdom gained by the spectator—these are among the usual solutions of the paradox. All of them consider the ugly as only a single aspect of the work of art, for they all undertake to show that within the work as a whole the ugliness is somehow transcended. Hence they presuppose that some objects, such as the preartistic model of tragic plot, are "painful in themselves," and therefore ugly.

Throughout aesthetic theory, ugliness is discussed mainly by those philosophers who deny precisely this assumption. They wish to hold that ugliness does not exist, and since their thesis runs counter to ordinary belief, they are constrained to justify it. In Augustine, the unreality of ugliness is enjoined by his most fundamental philosophical doctrines. Stated theologically, the world and everything in it have been created by an infinitely good God, as an expression of his goodness; stated metaphysically, existence is not neutral with respect to value and disvalue, but is rather an embodiment, through and through, of positive value. In such a worldview, the apparent presence of evil of any kind poses a problem, and Augustine considers sin and blindness just such problems. But aesthetic disvalue is a particular issue for him because his conception of reality is conspicuously aesthetic. All things are images of the ideas of form and harmony that exist in the mind of God, and together they make up an internally ordered unity. The categories of Greek aesthetic theory are thus writ large in his metaphysics.

To say that a thing can exist at all only if it possesses form, and that, indeed, its existence cannot be conceived of apart from form, implies the solution of Augustine's problem. Objects are beautiful by virtue of their form, but if this is so, then ugliness does not exist, since sheer formlessness cannot exist. The opposite of beauty is not anything real, but merely the absence or "privation" of positive value. But now the argument seems to prove almost too much, for it appears to deny the possibility of the very facts—that is, apparently ugly objects—which gave rise to it in the first place. Augustine therefore employs the notion of "degrees" of value characteristic of metaphysical optimism and idealism. An object may not have the form appropriate to things of its kind, but this lack constitutes a relative deficiency of beauty, not sheer ugliness. Moreover, such objects must be seen not in isolation but as parts of the universe as a whole. Seeming ugliness sets off, and thereby enhances, the beauty of the world. Augustine uses the same argument in the case of objects, such as dangerous animals, which are not in any clear way lacking in form, but are considered ugly because they are displeasing or offensive to the sight.

However, when "form" has been construed less broadly than it was by Augustine, it has been used to differentiate beauty from genuine ugliness. During the sixteenth and seventeenth centuries, numerous treatises were devoted to particular arts, on the model of the *Poetics*. The properties of form that a work must possess in order to achieve beauty are specified precisely and narrowly. These include the "unities" in drama (Pierre Corneille) and the "correct" anatomical proportions in the visual arts (Albrecht Dürer). A work of art that lacks these properties is still recognizably a drama or a sculpture and therefore has some organization or structure. Yet it is not only deficient in beauty but really ugly.

This assured and unequivocal way of distinguishing ugliness was called into question, however, by the rebellion against the "rules" of form that was carried on throughout the eighteenth century. The rules were found to be too parochial and constricting. Yet the distinction between beauty and ugliness might still have been drawn, by reference to felt experience rather than to the object, if the hedonistic theory of value had been consistently preserved. But examination of aesthetic experience (of the sublime) reveals that it engenders feelings that are akin to pain. Sublime objects are overwhelming, menacing, intractable to understanding and control. And yet such experiences, because they are intensely moving, are of great value. Thus, both formalism and hedonism, which had traditionally sustained the duality of beauty-ugliness, are impugned. More fundamentally still, the eighteenth century first established aesthetics as an autonomous and systematic discipline. The question "What counts as a properly aesthetic phenomenon?" was then raised explicitly for the first time. The answer to this question, as we shall see, ultimately determines whether ugliness is a category of aesthetic disvalue. In all these ways, the eighteenth century provided impulse and direction to the vigorous prosecution in recent thought of what was first called, at the close of that century, "the theory of ugliness" (Friedrich von Schlegel, 1797).

According to two of the most influential answers to the question raised above, the aesthetic is to be found either (1) wherever some conceptual theme is embodied in an object that can be grasped by sense and imagination or (2) wherever some sensory structure expresses to the observer its distinctive feeling-quality. Any object of either kind is said to possess beauty. Ugliness, traditionally, is the "opposite" of aesthetic value. But what would be the opposites of these two conceptions of the aesthetic? In the first case, the opposite would be found in some sensory presentation devoid of intellectual significance or, alternatively, in pure concepts, such as certain of those of science and philosophy, which are beyond imagination. Such objects, however, do not exemplify aesthetic disvalue; rather they fall wholly outside of the realm of the aesthetic as it is defined according to this theory. In the second case, similarly, a thing completely lacking any emotional tone—if any such thing exists—is simply nonaesthetic.

This conclusion, however, fails to take into account ugliness in the usual sense—that is, what we perceive as being displeasing or revolting. W. T. Stace, a recent exponent of the first theory mentioned above, which he took over from G. W. F. Hegel, suggests that what is thus excluded from the aesthetic should be called "the unbeautiful"— "the mere negative absence of beauty"—rather than the ugly. Ugliness itself is a "species" of beauty that is present whenever such concepts as evil and disaster enter into the aesthetic object. The pain that such concepts arouse in us is moral, not aesthetic, and it is usually overcome by the aesthetic pleasure we gain from the total object. Bernard Bosanquet develops the second theory, derived from Benedetto Croce, by arguing that most of what is usually found to be ugly is deemed so because of "the weakness of the spectator." Either the work of art makes very great demands on his emotional capacities or, as in satiric comedy, it offends his moral beliefs; the "weakness," however, is remediable. Such a work of art is therefore more properly considered an instance of "difficult beauty" than of ugliness. Are there any objects at all that come within the realm of the aesthetic and are genuinely (or, as Bosanquet says, "invincibly") ugly? Bosanquet is "much inclined" to think that there are none. Given his view that the expressive is the aesthetic, and that "every form expresses" and is therefore beautiful, it is difficult to see how there could be any such object. He holds, however, that ugliness is to be located in what is only incipiently and partially expressive, that is, in a work of art that suggests some feeling but does not coherently elaborate and fulfill the suggestion, as in sentimental or "affected" art.

The traditional polarity of beauty-ugliness marks the distinction between aesthetic value and disvalue. Both the above theories conceive of the aesthetic in such a way that they leave little or no room for disvalue. Yet both Stace and Bosanquet regard the aesthetic experience as pleasurable. At the same time, they want to make room for art that is tragic, demonic, "difficult" (Stace, for example, cites the sculpture of Jacob Epstein). Therefore, as has just been shown, they seek to reconcile the painfulness of such art with the positive value that it necessarily possesses as an aesthetic object. In the case of Bosanquet, however, the question should be raised whether the expression of feeling is universally accompanied by pleasure. Historically, the concept of "expression" has tended to accommodate emotions of every kind within art, even those, as in an art of violence or outrage, which are "darkest." Successful artistic expression can render such emotions more, rather than less, concentrated and painful, and if it be urged that pleasure is taken in the unity and power of the artist's conception, there are, according to Bosanquet's theory, many nonartistic aesthetic objects that are intensely expressive and for which this explanation will not hold. Since there is no necessary or logical connection between "expression" and "pleasingness," it must be decided empirically whether, even when "the weakness of the spectator" is overcome, his experience of the expressive object has a positive hedonic tone. Stace's view that the painfulness of the theme of a work of art is moral, not aesthetic, seems more like definitional legislation than an insight into aesthetic experience. Moral perplexity and frustration are integral to such art as tragedy, and their painfulness enters into our perception of the total work of art. Stace's view, too, is a defense of hedonism. Yet there is no reason a priori to hold to hedonism in aesthetics, and indeed these difficulties cast doubt on such a theory. The term *ugliness*, in the sense of what is preponderantly painful, may still be used to designate one kind of aesthetic object without any implications of disvalue. So considered, "*X* is ugly but aesthetically good" is not self-contradictory and may indeed be something that we want to and have to say. Those modern artists who have vigorously repudiated the pleasingness of beauty as the goal of their creative efforts have made this way of speaking sound less implausible than it once did.

The graver and more basic question is whether ugliness, in the broader sense of negative aesthetic value, is, for aesthetic theory, otiose. Doubtless, we also want to say sometimes that the work of art is bad. Bosanquet, however, takes genuine ugliness to be at least partially expressive, and if we follow this lead, badness must be construed as a deficiency or relatively slight degree of aesthetic goodness. The work achieves less than it promises, the nonartistic object is lacking in vitality or charm. According to this view, then, there is no opposite to aesthetic value, but only, as Augustine said, a "privation" of it. On the other hand, this may be thought to be a gratuitous misreading of those properties that are commonly held to constitute ugliness or that are adduced as reasons for judging a thing ugly. Muddy orchestration or incoherent plot structure are, significantly, opposites to orchestral clarity or unity of plot, and they are equally real and present to awareness. In the absence of compensating virtues, objects that possess them are "positively bad."

No matter whether the denial of negative value should, finally, be tolerated or rejected, it is fair to say that this denial is less vexing in aesthetics than in ethics or epistemology. The explanation lies, in large part, in Bosanquet's notion of "the weakness of the spectator." The determination of beauty and ugliness is much more closely tied to the perceptual and emotional capacities of the spectator and to the attitudes that affect them than it is to moral and cognitive values. This leads us to think that the experience of negative value (though not that of positive value) results from a failure to see what is yet there to be seen. Thus, the transvaluation of what had previously been accounted ugly, which is endemic to the history of art and taste, is characteristically credited with being an enlargement of sympathy and a refinement of discrimination. The more obdurate cognitive and moral judgments of falsehood and evil, however, are not characteristically altered in this way. Can any limits, therefore, be set to what sensibility finds to be aesthetically good? To define the field of the aesthetic in such a way that all things are seen to possess positive value formalizes the endless catholicity of aesthetic interest. Freed from the exigencies of morality and the biases of perceptual habit, the aesthetic approach to the world, at the hypothetical limit, fixes upon any tone or shade the quality of any ambience. In John Keats's words, it "has as much delight in … an Iago as an Imogen." But if everything engages and rewards aesthetic perception, then either "aesthetic disvalue" is a self-contradiction or else it denotes nothing.

See also Aesthetic Qualities; Aesthetics, History of; Aesthetics, Problems of; Aristotle; Augustine, St.; Beauty; Bosanquet, Bernard; Croce, Benedetto; Hegel, Georg Wilhelm Friedrich; Humor; Plato; Pleasure; Schlegel, Friedrich von; Stace, Walter Terence; Tragedy; Visual Arts, Theory of the.

Bibliography

Bosanquet, Bernard. *Three Lectures on Aesthetic*. London, 1923. Lecture III is the starting point for any serious discussion of the problem of ugliness.

Chapman, Emmanuel. *Saint Augustine's Philosophy of Beauty*. New York: Sheed and Ward, 1939. Those of Augustine's writings on aesthetics that have survived are scattered among several different treatises. This convenient volume locates these passages.

Pepper, Stephen C. *The Basis of Criticism in the Arts*. Cambridge, MA: Harvard University Press, 1946. Contrasts the meaning and status of ugliness in some of the major aesthetic theories. In the author's own view, ugliness is a moral rather than an aesthetic category.

Rosenkranz, Karl. *Ästhetik des Hässlichen*. Köenigsberg, 1853. The classic post-Hegelian study of ugliness. Addicted somewhat to multiplying conceptual distinctions but a thoughtful and suggestive analysis. Argues that art would be unduly narrow if it did not include the ugly and that ugliness is not simply a device to enhance beauty.

Santayana, George. *The Sense of Beauty*. New York: Scribners, 1936. An influential contemporary statement of hedonist aesthetics.

Stace, W. T. *The Meaning of Beauty*. London: G. Richards and H. Toulmin, 1929.

Véron, Eugène. *Esthétique*. Paris: C. Reinwald, 1878. Translated by W. H. Armstrong as *Aesthetics*. London: Chapman and Hall, 1879. An early and forceful statement of the theory that the artist seeks emotional self-expression rather than beauty and will therefore exploit rather than mitigate the ugliness of his subject.

OTHER RECOMMENDED WORKS

Coleman, Earle J. "The Beautiful, the Ugly and the Tao." *Journal of Chinese Philosophy* (1991): 213–226.

Devereaux, Mary. "The Ugly." *The American Society for Aesthetics Newsletter*, vol. 24, no. 3 (Winter 2005): 1–2.

Guyer, Paul. "Thomson's Problems with Kant: A Comment on Kant's Problems with Ugliness." *Journal of Aesthetics and Art Criticism*, vol. 50, no. 4 (Fall 1992): 317–319.

Higgins, Lesley Hall. *The Modernist Cult of Ugliness: Aesthetic and Gender Politics*. New York: Palgrave Macmillan, 2002.

Kieran, Matthew. "Aesthetic Value: Beauty, Ugliness and Incoherence." *Philosophy*, vol. 72, no. 281 (1997): 383–399.

McCall, Robert E. "The Metaphysical Analysis of the Beautiful and the Ugly" (with comment by James P. Reilly). *Proceedings and Addresses of the American Philosophical Association*. Vol. 30, 1956, pp. 137–153.

Mesa, James, P. "The Good, the Bad, and the Ugly: The Aesthetic in Moral Imagination." In *Beauty, Art and the Polis*, edited by Alice Ramos, Catholic University of America Press, 2000, pp. 237–244.

Miller, William Ian. *The Anatomy of Disgust*. Harvard University Press, 1998.

Pickford, R. W. "The Psychology of Ugliness." *British Journal of Aesthetics* 9 (1969): 258–270.

Raters, Marie-Luise. "Unbeautiful Beauty in Hegel and Bosanquet." *Bradley Studies*, vol. 7, no. 2 (Autumn 2001): 162–176.

Shier, David. "Why Kant Finds Nothing Ugly." *British Journal of Aesthetics*, vol. 38, no. 4 (1998): 412–418.

Thomson, Garrett. " Kant's Problems with Ugliness." *Journal of Aesthetics and Art Criticism*, vol. 50, no. 2 (Spring 1992): 107–115.

Jerome Stolnitz (1967)
Bibliography updated by Mary Devereaux (2005)

ULRICH (ENGELBERT) OF STRASBOURG

(fl. 1248–1277)

Ulrich (Engelbert) of Strasbourg was a scholastic philosopher and theologian, priest, and author. A member of the Dominican priory at Strasbourg in the German province, Ulrich studied under Albert the Great at Cologne, together with Thomas Aquinas and Hugh of Strasbourg, between 1248 and 1254. During those years Ulrich heard Albert expound the Dionysian corpus and the *Ethics* of Aristotle. As a lecturer in theology at Strasbourg, Ulrich acquired considerable fame for his learning; among his illustrious disciples was Lector John of Fribourg.

The ancient catalogs attribute to Ulrich commentaries on Aristotle's *Metheora* and *De Anima,* Peter Lombard's *Sentences,* and the book of Ecclesiastes. His only extant work, however, is a remarkable compendium of theology titled *De Summo Bono,* planned and probably written in eight books. Only the first book and fragments of others have been published, and the known manuscripts end with Book VI, tr. 5. This compendium was composed between 1262 and 1272 and marks a notable advance over the earlier *summas* of William of Auxerre, Alexander of Hales, and Albert the Great. It is divided into (1) introduction to theology, (2) essence of the supreme Good, (3) Trinity in general, (4) the Father and creation, (5) the Son and incarnation, (6) the Holy Spirit and sanctification, (7) sacraments, and (8) ultimate beatitude.

The doctrinal framework of Ulrich's thought is predominantly Augustinian and Neoplatonic, depending largely on Pseudo-Dionysius, Avicenna, *Liber de Causis,* and Albert. For Ulrich man has a rational predisposition for knowing the existence of God as the supreme cause. This knowledge is rendered more precise, although not comprehensive, by the traditional three ways: (1) negating imperfections found in creatures (for example, as creatures are finite, God is infinite); (2) seeing God as the ultimate cause of all perfections; and (3) recognizing the transcendence of those perfections in God. God created the universe in a hierarchical order ranging from the first luminous intelligence through lesser intelligences, man, animals, plants, elements, and material principles. In all creatures there is a real distinction between essence and existence, and in all material substances there is only one substantial form. Created intellectual substances, seeing the eternal Ideas in God, illuminate lesser intelligences to know truth. The human mind has four immediately evident (*per se nota*) rules by which it can investigate theology, the science of the faith: God is the supreme Truth and cause of all truth; primary Truth can neither deceive nor be deceived, therefore his Word should be believed; we should believe everything clearly revealed by God through his spokesmen; Scripture is true precisely because God gave it to us in that way. Unlike these rules, the articles of faith are not immediately evident, but in the light of faith and these rules, the articles of faith become objects of scientific study.

For five years (1272–1277) Ulrich was provincial of the German province before the General Chapter of Bordeaux assigned him to Paris to lecture on the *Sentences* and to obtain his degree in theology. He died, probably in 1278, before becoming a master; in the manuscripts he is designated a bachelor in theology.

See also Albert the Great; Alexander of Hales; Aristotle; Augustinianism; Avicenna; Medieval Philosophy; Neoplatonism; Peter Lombard; Pseudo-Dionysius; Thomas Aquinas, St.

Bibliography

Daguillon, Jeanne. *Ulrich de Strasbourg, O.P., la "Summa de Bono,"* Lib. I. Paris, 1930. Bibliothèque Thomiste, Vol. XII.

Glorieux, Palémon. *Ulrich de Strasbourg au XIIIe siècle,* 2 vols. Paris, 1933–1934. Vol. I, pp. 145–151.

Grabmann, Martin. "Studien über Ulrich von Strassburg." In *Mittelalterliches Geistesleben; Abhandlungen zur Geschichte der Scholastik und Mystik,* 3 vols. Munich: Hueber, 1926–1956. Vol. I, pp. 147–221.

Quétif, Jacques, and Jacques Échard. *Scriptores Ordinis Praedicatorum Recensiti,* 2 vols. Paris: Lutetiæ Parisiorum, apud J.-B.-C. Ballard, and N. Simart, 1719–1721. Vol. I, p. 256.

Théry, Gabriel. "Originalité du plan de la Summa de Bono d'Ulrich de Strasbourg." *Revue Thomiste* 27 (1922): 276–297.

James A. Weisheipl, O.P. (1967)

ULTIMATE MORAL PRINCIPLES: THEIR JUSTIFICATION

See *Moral Principles: Their Justification*

UNAMUNO Y JUGO, MIGUEL DE

(1864–1936)

The Spanish philosopher of life Miguel de Unamuno y Jugo's concern was neither with the problems of linguistic clarification and conceptual analysis nor with speculative metaphysical constructions but, rather, with coming to terms with life both intellectually and emotionally. The symbols Unamuno used are related to Spanish life and destiny and his way of thinking was Spanish, but his message is universal. He expressed himself symbolically, through poetry, religious writings, and the novel, and through the general evocative and emotive character of his prose. However, his efforts to give literal articulation to the mystery and anguish of his existence make him a philosopher rather than exclusively a novelist or poet. The style of philosophy that Unamuno represents must at all times emanate from the world situation and the life situation of the individual philosopher. It follows that Unamuno's philosophy is to be found not only in his writings but also in his general mode of life, particularly in his conspicuous political actions at a time of serious turmoil in Spain.

In view of this it is quite proper to call Unamuno an existentialist. First, his philosophy clearly wells up from his own human situation in space and time. Second, his writings tend to be emotive rather than intellectual. He wished to express not exact ideas but feelings; and feelings are often more accurately expressed in the turgid and quasi-sentimental language of Unamuno than in logical exegesis. Third, his subject matter was existential—death and anxiety, doubt and faith, guilt and immortality. Fourth, he traced the sources of his thought to such existentialist precursors as Blaise Pascal and Søren Kierkegaard and found kinship with anyone who stressed intuition and subjectivity in the life of man and in the construction of worldviews—with men like Arthur Schopenhauer, Friedrich Nietzsche, and William James. Finally, Unamuno's philosophy, like Kierkegaard's, was deliberately unsystematic, an expression of his wrestling with existence, and any systematic account of that expression must falsify or at least distort the facts of experience.

LIFE

Don Miguel de Unamuno y Jugo was born in the Basque city of Bilbao. He studied philosophy and classics at the University of Madrid and moved to Salamanca in 1891 as professor of Greek at the university there. He was associated with the university for most of the rest of his life, being appointed rector in 1901 and named rector for life in 1934. Unamuno's first published work, *En torno al casticismo* (On purism; 1895), was a historical and political work that questioned and examined the place of Spain in the modern world. His first novel, *Paz en la guerra* (Peace in war; 1897), sometimes called the first existentialist novel, was based on his early memories of the siege of Bilbao in 1873. In the novel *Amor y pedagogía* (Love and pedagogy; 1902) Unamuno tried to show the basic failure of science in dealing with human and humanistic problems. *Amor y pedagogía* describes a man's attempt to educate his family scientifically and the dismal failure of this attempt. *Vida de Don Quijote y Sancho* (*Life of Don Quixote and Sancho*, 1905) foreshadowed many of the themes of Unamuno's masterpiece, *Del sentimiento trágico de la vida en los hombres y en los pueblos*. The *Vida de Don Quijote* is a plea for salvation through the anguish and passion experienced by the man of flesh and blood. *Del sentimiento trágico de la vida* (*The Tragic Sense of Life*), which appeared in 1913, expresses Unamuno's intemperate longing for eternal life and his desperate search for some solace in the exploration of the tension and conflict that exists between faith and reason. The novel *Niebla* (*Mist*) was published in 1914, and in 1917 Unamuno's modern version of the problem of Cain, *Abel Sánchez*, appeared. In 1924 Unamuno was deported to Fuerteventura in the Canary Islands for his unrelenting attack on the totalitarianism of General Primo de Rivera. He managed to escape to France and remained in exile until 1930, when Rivera's dictatorship fell. Unamuno was reinstated as rector of the University of Salamanca the next year.

From 1931 to 1933 Unamuno served in the Cortes, the constituent assembly of the Spanish republic, as an independent Republican deputy. His last and greatest novel appeared in 1933. *San Manuel bueno, mártir* (Saint Emanuel the Good, martyr) describes the agony of a priest who finds it impossible to believe. Unamuno's independence, individualism, and patriotism led to his being dismissed from his rectorship in 1936. He at first favored the nationalists in the Spanish Civil War, but he came to feel that neither side was working for the best interest of either Spain or humanity. During the last year of his life he was under house arrest in Salamanca.

CENTRAL THEMES

To characterize Unamuno's basically unsystematic philosophical position is difficult. A few themes can be isolated from his philosophy, however, and may be generalized as follows:

(1) Unamuno's interest was primarily in the individual rather than in social reality, and thus his philosophy extols the agony and the importance of the individual. In this context Unamuno's Spanishness becomes not a social ideal but the expression of his individuality.

(2) He emphasized the importance of personal integrity. Truthfulness to oneself and total honesty in ideals are the hallmarks of the philosophical man.

(3) He saw his function—and that of philosophers generally—as that of a Socratic gadfly to the community. The philosopher is needed to reawaken us to our genuine nature, to our authentic problems, and to the honest attempts to resolve them.

(4) Much of Unamuno's life was spent in agony over the conflict between faith and reason. Reason alone—which Unamuno invariably associated with skepticism—cannot lead to any kind of fundamentally hopeful knowledge. Faith can do so, but faith exists only in the shadow of the despair that is reason; it has no independent and positive existence. Faith can never totally dispel reason, and reason always leads to despair. The logic of the heart is hopeful and gives meaning to life, but it is never strong enough to fully set aside the darkness of the logic of the head.

(5) Unamuno's general conception of religion was related to the tension between faith and reason. Although Catholicism did not fully satisfy either his emotions or his reason, Unamuno felt that religion is a necessity of life. We must risk faith in the way that Pascal wagered, James willed, and Kierkegaard leaped. We must, for profoundly pragmatic reasons, live as if God does in fact exist.

(6) The above views led to the doctrine that commitment is one of the central features of the authentic life. An authentic life is dedicated to and identified with an ideal, an ideal that genuinely emanates from the depths of each man. The truth of such a commitment can be vindicated and confirmed only by the heart; but since reason casts permanent doubt on that commitment, a blind, courageous leap of faith is needed for authentic human existence.

(7) Life thus becomes a vague, brittle, and tenuous cluster of experiences between two awesome, incomprehensible, and impenetrable barriers of nothingness: birth and death. Only through a foundationless but fervid commitment can man escape, at least temporarily, the despair of meaninglessness.

(8) Unamuno loved Spain and was an impartial observer and recorder of the Spanish temperament. According to Unamuno, the Spaniard—like his paradigm Don Quixote—wants adventures, willingly risks revolution for the establishment of utopian societies, and is impractical. But there is also a practical side to the Spaniard, symbolized by Sancho Panza, which often degenerates into blind formalism, intolerance, religious bigotry, and unprincipled commercialism.

Unamuno's commitment to Spain embraced his commitment to the Catholic Church. However, it was only his heart that pulled him toward the church; his reason pulled him away from it. This excruciating tension between his fervent emotional need and hope for the presence of an enveloping and supporting God and for certainty with respect to the immortality of the soul on the one hand, and the fact that he found this world picture rationally untenable on the other hand, was central to Unamuno's philosophy.

GOD AND EXISTENCE

The problem of human existence, in Unamuno's famous formulation, is *el sentimiento trágico de la vida* (the tragic sense of life); it is the fact that there is sorrow that has no resolution and evil that has no redemption. We should weep, not because it helps but precisely because it avails us nothing. If we recognize the pervasiveness of hopelessness and despair, we can at least experience the brotherhood of man. Without disease or defect (be it sin in paradise, a weak species of apelike man, or immunization—the momentary creation of an illness for the sake of health) there can be no progress. Philosophy in this sense is eminently practical: *Primum vivere, deinde philosophari*—"man philosophizes in order to live." "He philosophizes either in order to resign himself to life or to seek some finality in it, or to distract himself and forget his griefs, or for pastime and amusement" (*The Tragic Sense of Life*, p. 29).

The most attractive solution to the problems of human existence, to "the tragic sense of life," is the hope for eternal life expressed in man's perennial hunger for immortality. This hunger has two dimensions—it refers either to the nondestruction of the soul or to the merger of the soul with the universe or the totality of being. In connection with the first of these dimensions, Unamuno seems to have held that the destruction of a man's consciousness is an a priori impossibility: We cannot even conceive of the nonexistence of consciousness, since that conception is itself an act of consciousness. In connection with the second, he concluded that man is nothing if he is not everything—to exist is yearning to reach all space, all time, all being. To be a man is to seek to become God.

Unless man is God, he is not even man: "Either all or nothing!" was Unamuno's motto.

Catholicism promises immortality, but modern rationalism denies it. As a consequence, fundamental doubt sets in, doubt that is both passionate and rational. Such tense but mature insight, however, does lead to some solace: "But here, in the depths of the abyss, the despair of the heart and of the will and the skepticism of reason meet face to face and embrace like brothers" (ibid., p. 106). Man must reach the depths of despair, doubt, and agony in order to arrive at the solid "foundation upon which the heart's despair must build up its hope." Furthermore, the agony that arises out of the tensions of passionate doubt and total rational skepticism when both are focused on the problem of eternal life may also form "a basis for action and morals."

Tension is the essence of life, and the tension that leads to agony is also the tension that allows man to feel his existence; pure consciousness deserves only suicide. Life, to be felt as real, *as there*, as existing, must be a life of passion. This truth is well illustrated by love, which for Unamuno is basically sexual love. In the tensions and paradoxes of love—as well as in compassion and pity—man experiences the richness, concreteness, and fullness of his existence. Consciousness, in this sense, is knowledge through participation; it is "co-feeling."

The hope for immortality is supported by the notion of God. The traditional arguments for the existence of God prove nothing other than that we have the idea of God. The God who is the idea of excellence and the first mover is a fleshless and passionless abstraction and cannot soothe the anguish of man's existence. This abstraction is not what the heart craves. The strongest conclusion of reason is that we "cannot prove the impossibility of His existence." Belief in God is an expression solely of man's longing for the rich and concrete experience of his existence and of his determination to live by this longing and make it a basis for action. Man's agonizing hunger for the divine—even though it cannot be satisfied directly—leads to hope, faith, and charity, and eventually to his sense of beauty and of goodness.

There are other typically existentialist themes in Unamuno's philosophy:

(1) Man is painfully aware of his contingency. That he exists or that he is the particular person he happens to be is neither necessary nor permanent.

(2) To assuage his anguish, man must feel his existence, even if he is led to suffering. He must learn to experience his uniqueness by expanding the range and the self-consciousness of his perceptions of the world.

(3) All existence is a mystery: Consciousness is a mystery, contingency is a mystery, absurdity is a mystery, and anguish is a mystery.

(4) Love is the basic force of human existence. It encompasses all the conative relations of man to being and enables him to overcome the anguish of his contingency by giving him the rich feeling of his own existence.

(5) The central temporal dimension of human existence is the future, which leads to a desire for immortality and to a concern with death. This focus on the future is expressed in Unamuno's use of *esperar*: It means both the joys of hope and the anguish of eternal waiting. The structure of the future expresses both man's determination to continue to live and his permanent dissatisfaction and despair concerning existence.

(6) Goals are self-created and are permanent commitments.

(7) Finally, Unamuno's views on the nature of language foreshadow those of Maurice Merleau-Ponty and Martin Heidegger. Language is a mode of being. Living, not only knowing, is expressed in certain basic forms, one of which is language. Language thus is not symbolic but the actual embodiment of an idea. Without language an idea could not exist.

EPISTEMOLOGY AND METAPHYSICS

Truth, according to Unamuno, is subjective; it exists only as it is manifested in authentic belief. Belief, in turn, is an expression of man's total being and consequently is realized in action. Objective truth is, strictly speaking, a meaningless conception. Through its identity with belief and action, truth is ultimately an act of will. It is a will to create; and the will as creator wants and loves at the same time. Because of this personal and volitional factor in truth, the opposite of truth is not error but the lie. This subjective view of truth gives a distinct idealistic, even mystical, cast to Unamuno's thought. All knowledge about man and the world is subjective in the sense that it begins with first-person experience. To think of truth as transcending first-person experiences is, strictly speaking, a contradiction, because the very program of transcending first-person experiences is a first-person project and concept and a construction. There is, however, another kind of truth, illustrated by mathematics, which is the function of reason alone, whereas true belief is a function of man's whole being.

Unamuno followed Heraclitus in holding that reality is a state of permanent flux, so that no two experiences are ever the same. There are two metaphysical alternatives. Reality may be a vast sea of consciousness with my subjectivity at the center. There is no easy way to distinguish this consciousness from a mere dream. Its sole foundation is the fact that I experience it and that I will it to be real. Unamuno ultimately rejected this view. The other view is that the focus of our being may be outside ourselves. We may identify ourselves with the realities of other people, with trees, flowers, and mountains. This orientation, to which Unamuno did not accede fully but which he preferred, is close to objective idealism and to naturalism. In either view, man and world are intimately meshed.

See also Common Consent Arguments for the Existence of God; Existentialism; Faith; Heidegger, Martin; Heraclitus of Ephesus; Immortality; James, William; Kierkegaard, Søren Aabye; Life, Meaning and Value of; Love; Merleau-Ponty, Maurice; Nietzsche, Friedrich; Pascal, Blaise; Reason; Schopenhauer, Arthur.

Bibliography

WORKS BY UNAMUNO

En torno al casticismo. Madrid, 1895.

Paz en la guerra. Madrid: F. Fe, 1897; 3rd ed., Madrid, 1931.

Amor y pedagogía. Barcelona, 1902; 2nd ed., Madrid, 1934.

Vida de Don Quijote y Sancho, según Miguel de Cervantes Saavedra, explicada y comentada. Madrid, 1905; 2nd enlarged ed., Madrid, 1914. Translated by H. P. Earle as *Life of Don Quixote and Sancho according to Miguel de Cervantes Saavedra Expounded with Comment*. New York: Knopf, 1927.

Poesías. Bilbao, 1907.

Por tierras de Portugal y España. Madrid, 1911.

Rosario de sonetos líricos. Madrid: Imprenia española, 1911.

Contra esto y aquello. Madrid: Renacimiento, 1912; 4th ed., Buenos Aires: Espasa-Calpe Argentina, 1941.

El espejo de la muerte. Madrid, 1913.

Del sentimiento trágico de la vida en los hombres y en los pueblos. Madrid, 1913. Translated by J. E. Crawford Flitch as *The Tragic Sense of Life in Men and in Peoples*. London, 1921.

Niebla. Madrid, 1914. Translated by Warren Fite as *Mist. A Tragi-comic Novel*. New York, 1928.

Ensayos, 7 vols. Madrid, 1916–1918.

Abel Sánchez. Madrid: Renacimiento, 1917. Translated by Anthony Kerrigan in *Abel Sanchez and Other Stories*. Chicago: Gateway, 1956.

Andanzas y visiones españolas. Madrid: Renacimiento, 1922; 2nd ed., Buenos Aires: Espasa-Calpe Argentina, 1941.

De Fuerteventura á París. Paris: Editorial Excelsior, 1925.

La agonía del cristianismo. Madrid: Renacimiento, 1931. Translated by K. F. Reinhardt as *The Agony of Christianity*. New York: Ungar, 1960.

San Manuel bueno, mártir y tres historias más. Madrid: Espasa-Calpe, 1933.

Epistolario á Clarín. Madrid, 1938.

La ciudad de Henoc. Comentario 1933. Mexico City: Editorial Séneca, 1941.

Obras completas, 7 vols. Edited by Manuel García Blanco. Madrid: Aguado, 1950–1959.

Poems. Translated by Eleanor Turnbull. Baltimore, 1952.

Cancionero, diario poético. Buenos Aires: Losada, 1953.

Teatro. Barcelona, 1954.

España y los españoles. 2 vols. Madrid: A. Aguado, 1955.

Inquietudes y meditaciones. Madrid: A. Aguado, 1957.

Cincuenta poesías inéditas (1899–1927). Madrid: Ediciones de los Papeles de Son Armadans, 1958.

Our Lord Don Quixote: The life of Don Quixote and Sancho, with Related Essays. Princeton, NJ: Princeton University Press, 1967.

Desde el miradol de la guerra. Paris: Centre de recherches hispaniques, 1970.

The Last Poems of Miguel de Unamuno. Princeton, NJ: Princeton University Press, 1974.

Ficciones: Four Stories and a Play. Princeton, NJ: Princeton University Press, 1976.

Escritos socialistas, 1894–1922. Madrid: Ayuso, 1976.

Artículos olvidados sobre españa y la primera guerra mundial. London: Tamesis Book, 1976.

El torno a las artes. Madrid: Espasa-Calpe, 1976.

Crónica política española (1915–1923). Salamanca: Grupo Editorial Ambos Mundos, 1977.

República española y españa republicana (1931–1936). Salamanca: Almar, 1979.

La vida literaria. Madrid: Espasa-Calpe, 1981.

Ensueño de una patria. Valencia: Pre-Textos, 1984.

The Private World: Selections from the Diario Intima and Selected Letters. Princeton, NJ: Princeton University Press, 1985.

Dos articulos y dos discursos. Madrid: Editorial Fundamentos 1986.

El resentimiento trágico de la vida. Madrid: Alianza Editorial, 1991.

Artículos en 'la nación' de buenos aires, 1919–1924. Salamanca: Ediciones Universidad de Salamanca, 1994.

WORKS ON UNAMUNO

Ferrater Mora, José. *Unamuno*. Translated by Philip Silver. Berkeley: University of California Press, 1962.

Meyer, François. *L'ontologie de Miguel de Unamuno*. Paris: Presses Universitaires de France, 1955.

Oromi, Miguel. *Pensamiento filosófico de M. de Unamuno*. Madrid, 1943.

Rudd, Margaret Thomas. *The Lone Heretic*. Austin: University of Texas Press, 1963.

Peter Koestenbaum (1967)
Bibliography updated by Thomas Nenon (2005)

UNCERTAINTY PRINCIPLE

See *Quantum Mechanics*

UNCONSCIOUS

Under the impact of new developments in science, ideas in all fields are undergoing rapid change. This is especially true of the twentieth-century conception of the *unconscious,* the term being used here in a general sense for all those mental processes of which the individual is not aware while they occur in him.

The present interest in the unconscious is a result of the advance of science and psychology since the mid-1800s, and to understand this interest requires some knowledge of the history of ideas. But the timing of this outburst of interest, its intensity (which is greatest in the English-speaking countries and least in Russia and China), and the particular conception of the unconscious that is now dominant are mainly due to one man, Sigmund Freud. His high degree of success in creating widespread appreciation of the power of the unconscious makes the improvement of his conception of it a matter of great importance. Fortunately, a historical survey can not only put recent sectarian conflicts in perspective but can also throw light on aspects of the unconscious that have long been recognized by philosophers and humanists but that receive inadequate emphasis in Freudian theory.

There have been few peoples since, say, 3000 BCE who have not possessed myths expressing a sense of the power of divine or natural agencies to influence the individual without his being aware of that influence. Before the emergence of clear conceptions regarding nature and man there prevailed a sense of the continuity of phenomena, and it was taken for granted that man was part of a totality in which anything might influence anything else. This assumption of continuity is evident in much Eastern thought. Western recognition, from around 1600 CE, of unconscious mental processes, at first philosophical but gradually becoming more scientific, may be superficially regarded as the rediscovery of something that had long been taken for granted in certain Eastern traditions and also in some Greek and Christian writings. Plotinus held that "the absence of a conscious perception is no proof of the absence of mental activity," Augustine was interested in memory as a faculty extending beyond the grasp of the conscious mind, Thomas Aquinas developed a theory of the mind covering "processes in the soul of which we are not immediately aware," and most mystics assumed that insights might be gained by a process of inner reception in which the conscious mind is passive.

But these early ideas lack an essential feature of the modern concept of the unconscious that became possible only after Western thought had set out on the search for precision and scientific validity and, in doing so, had separated the conscious mind from material processes; that is, this became possible only from about 1600 on, or after René Descartes. For the ultimate purpose of the concept of unconscious mental processes is to link conscious awareness and behavior with its background—a system of processes of which one is not immediately aware—and to establish this connection without losing the benefits of scientific precision. Here lies the weakness of the concept of the unconscious: It cannot be made fully acceptable to the scientific age until some science or union of sciences has provided an adequate conception of the unity and continuity of conscious thought, unconscious cerebral processes, physiological changes, and the processes of growth. In fact, the idea of the unconscious (or some equivalent) can acquire scientific status only after a unified picture of the human organism has repaired the intellectual lesions created by Cartesian and other dualistic or specialized methods.

DESCARTES TO FREUD

It is useful, if oversimplified, to consider that Descartes, by his definition of mind as awareness, provoked as a reaction the Western "rediscovery" of unconscious mental processes. During the two and a half centuries between Descartes's *Discourse on Method* (1637) and Freud's first interest in the unconscious, many philosophers, psychologists, biologists, novelists, and poets recognized that mental activity of various kinds occurs without awareness. This view was reached through introspection, through observation, or through attempts to create a theory of the working of the mind. By the last decades of the nineteenth century it was so widespread in Germany and Britain, and to a lesser extent in France, that one can say that by then the existence of the unconscious mind had become a common assumption of educated and psychological discussions; however, its structure, mode of operation, and role in illness were left for the twentieth century to explore.

Here we can consider only a few names out of many, selected either because they were influential or because their ideas represent an advancing understanding.

Our survey opens at the moment when Cartesian thought was acquiring influence. Ralph Cudworth, English divine and philosopher, wrote in 1678:

> There may be some vital energy without clear consciousness or express attention—Our human souls are not always conscious of whatever they have in them—that vital sympathy, by which our soul is united and tied fast to the body, is a thing that we have no direct consciousness of, but only in its effects—There is also a more interior kind of plastic power in the soul … whereby it is formative of its own cogitations, which it itself is not always conscious of. (*True Intellectual System of the Universe,* Book I, Ch. 3)

Many other thinkers of the seventeenth and eighteenth centuries expressed similar ideas, at first mainly in relation to the cognitive aspects, such as perception and memory. Gottfried Wilhelm Leibniz introduced the notion of a quantitative threshold. For him ordinary perceptions were the summation of countless small ones, each of which we are not aware of, because they lie below this threshold.

Two eighteenth-century figures were among the first to direct attention to the emotional aspects of the unconscious mind. Jean-Jacques Rousseau tried to explore the unconscious background of his own temperament and to discover the reason for his fluctuating moods ("It is thus certain that neither my own judgment nor my will dictated my answer, and that it was the automatic consequence of my embarrassment"), and J. G. Hamann, a German religious philosopher, studied the deeper levels of his own mind as evidenced in his experience of conversion, in the emotional life, and in imaginative thinking ("How much more the formation of our own ideas remains secret!").

Between 1750 and 1830 a number of German philosophers and poets increasingly emphasized the emotional and dynamic aspects of the unconscious. Johann Gottfried Herder stressed the role of unconscious mental processes in relation to the imagination, dreams, passion, and illness. Johann Wolfgang von Goethe expressed in poems and *aperçus* his sense of the fertile interplay of conscious and unconscious in the creative imagination, "where consciousness and unconsciousness are like warp and weft." Johann Gottlieb Fichte treated the unconscious as a dynamic principle underlying conscious reason. G. W. F. Hegel based his philosophy on the conception of an unconscious historical process becoming in the individual a partly conscious will. For Friedrich von Schelling unconscious nature becomes conscious in the ego.

Many of the romantic writers and poets, particularly in Germany and England, echoed what was in the air: a vivid sense of the powerful, dark, yet creative aspects of the unconscious mind. Thus, J. P. F. Richter wrote: "The unconscious is really the largest realm in our minds, and just on account of this unconsciousness the inner Africa, whose unknown boundaries may extend far away."

Another sequence of German thinkers made the idea of the unconscious a commonplace of European educated circles by about 1880: Arthur Schopenhauer, C. G. Carus, Gustav Fechner, Eduard von Hartmann, and Friedrich Nietzsche. Schopenhauer took the idea of a mainly unconscious will in nature and in man as his central theme. Carus, physician and friend of Goethe, opened his *Psyche* (1846) with the words: "The key to the understanding of the character of the conscious lies in the region of the unconscious" and presented Goethe's favorable view of the unconscious. Fechner, like Freud (who expressed a debt to him), regarded the mind as an iceberg largely below the surface and moved by hidden currents. He used the concept of mental energy, a topography of the mind, an unpleasure-pleasure principle, and a universal tendency toward stability. Von Hartmann's *Philosophy of the Unconscious* (1869) gave a survey of a vast field of unconscious mental activities, and this book enjoyed a great success in Germany, France, and England. He discussed twenty-six aspects of the unconscious and converted the Goethean ideas of Carus's *Psyche* into a grandiose metaphysical system. Nietzsche, in his penetrating insights into the unconscious, reflected what was already widespread but gave it a new intensity. "The absurd overvaluation of consciousness …. Consciousness only touches the surface …. The great basic activity is unconscious …. Every sequence in consciousness is completely atomistic …. The real continuous process takes place below our consciousness; the series and sequence of feelings, thoughts, and so on, are symptoms of this underlying process …. All our conscious motives are superficial phenomena; behind them stands the conflict of our instincts and conditions."

Nietzsche had cried, "Where are the new doctors of the soul?" Soon after, Freud started on his task: to begin afresh, unprejudiced by all this speculation, and to try to identify the precise structure of unconscious processes and their role in particular mental disturbances, so that lesions of the mind might be repaired by systematic techniques. We are not here concerned with his methods of therapy or with their degree of efficacy but with his steadily developing and often modified theory of the unconscious mind.

Freud was not the first to develop a systematic theory of conflicts in the unconscious. J. F. Herbart had put forward a theory of the operation of unconscious inhibited ideas and their pressure on consciousness, and of the resulting conflict between conscious and unconscious ideas at the threshold of consciousness. But he had little immediate influence. Meanwhile, a school of medical thought was developing in England that treated the patient as a unity, took for granted the interplay of unconscious and conscious, and sought to use this way of thinking in its approach to mental illness. William Hamilton, student of medicine and metaphysics, lectured on the role of the unconscious, particularly in relation to emotions and action, thus providing the background for the psychiatrist H. Maudsley and the naturalist W. B. Carpenter. Maudsley's *The Pathology of Mind* (1879) expresses this English school of thought about the unconscious and is included in the references given by Freud in his *Interpretation of Dreams* (1900), while Carpenter's *Principles of Mental Physiology* (1876) discusses "unconscious cerebration." A group of physicians in Germany were pursuing similar lines of thought, but for these figures and for the French interest in hypnotism, which exerted a strong influence on depth psychology, the reader must turn to histories of psychiatry.

During the 1870s several theories of unconscious organic memory were developed, and between 1880 and 1910 physicians and philosophers in many countries were concerned with various aspects of the unconscious (see references given in the surveys cited below).

FREUD

Sigmund Freud, even late in life, had no idea how extensive attention to the unconscious had been. Today we need to see him in perspective in order to strengthen what was weak in his ideas and so to advance toward a complete theory of the unconscious mind in health as well as in sickness. A more detailed survey of Freudian theory and method is given elsewhere; here we can treat only those aspects of his ideas that are directly relevant to the theory of the unconscious.

For Freud all mental processes are determined by natural laws, ultimately by those governing chemical and physical phenomena; they are associated with quantities of psychic energy that strive toward release and equilibrium; the primary driving force is instinctual energy (libido, a concept that was at first narrowly, then more widely interpreted) expressing an often unconscious wish, and moving from unpleasure to physical pleasure (pleasure principle); the predominant energy is sexual, but other forms are present, and Freud later assumed two basic instincts, sexuality in a broad sense and aggression (Eros and Thanatos). The establishment of civilized life involves restraints on sexual activity, and the unconscious proper (in Freudian theory the accessible unconscious being called the preconscious) consists of instinctual energies, either archaic or repressed during the life of the individual, particularly in childhood (universal incestuous desires of the earliest years, adolescent frustrated dreaming, aggressive impulses, etc.); these are available only through the use of special techniques. A genetic or developmental approach to mental illness is therefore essential. Forgetting is an active process in which painful memories are repressed.

The Freudian unconscious is a pool of mainly repressed energies, distorted by frustration and exerting a stress on conscious reason and its shaping of the patterns of daily life. The strain produced by this stress, present in some degree in all civilized men and women, is seen in neurosis. It is only by exceptional luck in heredity or experience that civilized man can avoid this tragic and potentially universal feature of modern life, the major influence of the unconscious being antagonistic to reason. This doom and neurosis he can escape (wholly, Freud thought at first; later he had doubts) by becoming aware of his situation and gaining insight into the particular traumatic experiences that created his neurosis. Freud began with an unquestioning conviction that insight brought recovery. The interpretation of dreams (which are symptoms and express wish fulfillment) and the process of free association can render accessible the regions of the unconscious producing the neurosis and can make possible a cure. Myths express for communities what dreams do for the individual. Later, Freud developed his ego theory, dividing the mind into three areas: the id, or basic instincts; the ego, or rational part of the mind that deals with reality; and the superego, a differentiated part of the ego that results mainly from the child's self-identification with his parents. This triple division overlaps awkwardly with the unconscious-conscious dichotomy, and here the theory becomes obscure. It left Freud unsatisfied—indeed, late in his life he stated that understanding of the deepest levels of the mind was not yet possible.

These are, in condensed form, the main ideas that make up the core of the Freudian theory of the unconscious, leaving aside his many applications of it. The theory, in its most characteristic form, is a description of the pathology of civilized man, although for Freud this implied little restriction, since all suffer in some degree from the neurosis of civilization.

When this theory is reviewed today, most agree that Freud's general conception of a repressed unconscious, and its relation to child sexuality, aggression, defense mechanisms, sublimation, and so forth, is a permanent contribution of the highest importance. On the other hand, his sharp categories (conscious-unconscious, wishful-realistic, stages of sexual development, etc.) are merely, as he himself recognized, provisional steps toward the truth. But his theory suffers from a more radical weakness than these.

Freud's attitude toward the unconscious has been regarded as biological. But it was not so in a genuine sense, for all viable organisms display an organizing principle, not yet understood, which ensures that everything occurs in support of the continuation of life. This coordinating and formative principle underlies all organic properties, including the processes of the human unconscious, such as the imaginative and inventive faculties without which civilization could not have developed. It has been widely recognized that this factor—although it had been emphasized in earlier views of the unconscious, for example, by Cudworth, Goethe, Fichte, Schelling, Samuel Taylor Coleridge, and Carus—is not adequately represented in the Freudian theory, perhaps because it was neglected by the physicochemical approach to organisms dominant when Freud was shaping his ideas. His theory of the mind is overly analytic or atomistic and must be complemented by a general and powerful principle of coordination.

ADLER, JUNG, AND RANK

The lack of a general principle of coordination was recognized by three of Freud's colleagues, Alfred Adler, Carl Gustav Jung, and Otto Rank, who, from different points of view, stressed the potential integration and self-organizing power either of the unconscious or of the mind as a whole. Adler treated the person as a unity; he did not regard the unconscious-conscious division as basic and held that the inaccessible unconscious contains elements that have never been repressed but are simply not yet understood and are unconsciously assumed in the endeavor to adapt socially and to overcome supposed or real weaknesses.

The individual's aspiration or unconscious need to realize a potential unity was more deeply appreciated by Jung. He created the concept of the collective unconscious, which is not a "group mind" but the deepest level in the individual mind, consisting of potentialities for ways of thinking shared by all men because their genetic constitutions are closely similar and their family and social experiences share certain universal features. In a given society the collective unconscious contains particular traditional symbols or archetypes that organize thought and action. This sociological concept of the deeper mental levels involves a historical background in which ritual, myth, symbol, and religious attitude play organizing and integrating roles that contribute to the strength and stability of the psyche and that are subject to an underlying tendency developing a differentiated unity in the person (individuation). The tension of superficially opposed aspects in the unconscious mind produces autonomous foci of energy, acting as complexes. The ultimate aim for Jung was not discovery of truth but acceptance of the role of deep psychology in the present historical situation: assistance in the search for life-enhancing significance in the fate of living in a scientific age at a time when traditional sources of strength have been weakened but a fully comprehensive scientific truth is not yet in sight. In this search, psychology enters realms that previously belonged to history, philosophy, and religion. Jung's ideas form part of a discursive communication of attitudes, rather than being steps toward an ultimately confirmable theory of unconscious mental processes.

Rank stressed the role of religious and aesthetic traditions in shaping the unconscious, and he saw in the life will a factor making for integration. The writings of these three display agreement that Freud, particularly in his early work, overemphasized the role of genital sexuality, unduly neglected the historical background of the individual unconscious, and failed to allow for the role of factors making for coordination both within each Freudian level of the mind and between the various levels.

THE FUTURE OF THE CONCEPT

It has been observed (by Ira Progoff and others) that, mainly in their later years, Freud, Adler, Jung, and Rank all looked toward a future theory of the mind based on what perhaps can best be called the organic core of the mind (similar to Jung's objective psyche and psychoid) and capable of covering all human mental faculties, man's cultural history, his imagination, his mental illnesses and health. This still lies ahead. It seems that no important basic advance has been made in the theoretical understanding of the unconscious mind since then; certainly no one has yet made a satisfactory synthesis of the reliable features of their views. Thus, there has been a pause in the advance of the theory of subjective deep psychology.

Freud hoped for assistance from the neurophysiology of the brain, but this has not yet come.

We should now consider what the unconscious has stood for in the minds of different groups. The mystics saw it as the link with God; the Christian Platonists as a divine creative principle; the romantics as the connection between the individual and universal powers; the early rationalists as a factor operating in memory, perception and ideas; the postromantics as organic vitality expressed in will, imagination, and creation; dissociated Western man as a realm of violence threatening his stability; physical scientists as the expression of physiological processes in the brain that are not yet understood; monistic thinkers as the prime mover and source of all order and novelty in thought and action; Freud (in his earlier years) as a melee of inhibited memories and desires the main influence of which is damaging; and Jung as a prerational realm of instincts, myths, and symbols often making for stability. It is natural to seek a common principle underlying these partial truths, but we do not possess the unified language in which to express it scientifically.

The formulation of a valid theory of the integrated human mind and of its various pathologies would imply the possibility of a transformation in man and his unconscious toward a more harmonious condition accompanied by the development of a social order that does not bring with it inescapable neurosis. This may seem a distant hope. But recent advances in biology and medicine have opened new vistas of improvement, and no survey of the idea of the unconscious would be complete without a glance into this possible future for theory and practice, for therein may lie the deepest reason for the fascination that the idea has for so wide a public.

This sketch of the idea of the unconscious has neglected its recent applications to religion, art, the history of science, philosophy, literature (Marcel Proust believed that the reality of experience lies in the unconscious), ethics, and justice. In all these realms the main effect has been to broaden, deepen, and loosen traditional conceptions. But the unification of scientific principles, so badly needed today, still lies ahead. In this an improved conception of the unconscious must play a crucial role.

See also Adler, Alfred; Augustine, St.; Carus, Carl Gustav; Cudworth, Ralph; Descartes, René; Fechner, Gustav Theodor; Fichte, Johann Gottlieb; Freud, Sigmund; Goethe, Johann Wolfgang von; Hamann, Johann Georg; Hamilton, William; Hartmann, Eduard von; Hegel, Georg Wilhelm Friedrich; Herbart, Johann Friedrich; Herder, Johann Gottfried; Jung, Carl Gustav; Leibniz, Gottfried Wilhelm; Nietzsche, Friedrich; Proust, Marcel; Psychoanalytic Theories, Logical Status of; Rousseau, Jean-Jacques; Schelling, Friedrich Wilhelm Joseph von; Schopenhauer, Arthur; Thomas Aquinas, St.

Bibliography

HISTORICAL SURVEYS

It is remarkable that no authoritative critical study has yet been made of all ideas of the unconscious from earliest times to the present; the following works are useful historical surveys:

Ellenberger, H. "The Unconscious before Freud." *Bulletin of the Menninger Clinic* 21 (1957): 3.

Margetts, E. L. "Concept of Unconscious in History of Medical Psychology." *Psychiatric Quarterly* 27 (1953): 115.

Whyte, L. L. *The Unconscious before Freud.* New York: Basic, 1960; paperback ed., 1962.

Zilboorg, Gregory. *History of Medical Psychology.* New York: Norton, 1941.

COMMENTARIES

Drews, A. C. H. *Psychologie des Unbewussten.* Berlin, 1924.

Geiger, Moritz. "Fragment über den Begriff des Unbewussten und die psychische Realität." *Jahrbuch für Philosophie und phänomenologische Forschung* 4 (1921): 1–137.

Jones, Ernest. *The Life and Work of Sigmund Freud,* 3 vols. New York: Basic, 1953–1957.

MacIntyre, Alasdair C. *The Unconscious: A Conceptual Analysis.* New York, 1958.

Miller, J. G. *Unconsciousness.* New York, 1942.

Northridge, William L. *Modern Theories of the Unconscious.* London, 1924.

Progoff, Ira. *Death and Rebirth of Psychology.* New York, 1942.

Taylor, W. S. "Psycho-analysis Revised or Psychodynamics Developed?" *American Psychologist* (November 1962): 784.

ORIGINAL WORKS

Carus, C. G. *Psyche.* Pforzheim, 1846; 3rd ed., Stuttgart, 1860.

Cudworth, Ralph. *True Intellectual System of the Universe.* London, 1678.

Freud, Sigmund. *Die Traumdeutung.* Vienna, 1900. Translated by James Strachey as *The Interpretation of Dreams,* in *Standard Edition of the Complete Psychological Works,* James Strachey, general editor, 24 vols. New York, 1953–1964. Vols. IV and V.

Freud, Sigmund. "The Unconscious." In *Collected Papers,* edited by James Strachey, 5 vols. London: Hogarth Press, 1924–1950. Vol. IV, *Papers on Metapsychology and Papers on Applied Psychoanalysis,* p. 98.

Hartmann, Eduard von. *Die Philosophie des Unbewussten,* 3 vols. Berlin, 1869. Translated by W. C. Coupland as *The Philosophy of the Unconscious.* London: K. Paul, Trench, Trubner, 1883.

Jung, C. G. *Über die Psychologie des Unbewussten.* Zürich: Rascher, 1943. Translated by R. F. C. Hull as *Two Essays on Analytical Psychology,* Vol. VII of *Collected Works.* New York, 1953; paperback ed., New York: Meridian, 1956.

Jung, C. G. *Wandlung und Symbole der Libido.* Leipzig, 1912. Translated by Beatrice M. Hinkle as *Psychology of the Unconscious.* London, 1916. Rev. ed. and new translation by R. F. C. Hull from the 4th ed. (1952), *Symbole der Wandlung,* as *Symbols of Transformation,* published as Vol. V of *Collected Works,* Herbert Read et al., eds. London and New York, 1956.

Leibniz, G. W. *Die philosophischen Schriften.* Edited by C. J. Gerhardt, 7 vols. Berlin, 1875–1890. Vol. V, p. 48, Vol. VI, p. 600.

Schopenhauer, Arthur. *Die Welt als Wille und Vorstellung.* Leipzig, 1819. Translated by R. B. Haldane and J. Kemp as *The World as Will and Idea,* 3 vols. London: Trubner, 1883–1886.

Lancelot Law Whyte (1967)

UNDERDETERMINATION THESIS, DUHEM-QUINE THESIS

Underdetermination is a relation between evidence and theory. More accurately, it is a relation between the propositions that express the (relevant) evidence and the propositions that constitute the theory. The claim that evidence underdetermines theory may mean two things: first, that the evidence cannot prove the truth of the theory, and second, that the evidence cannot render the theory probable. Let us call the first deductive underdetermination and the second inductive (or ampliative) underdetermination. Both kinds of claims are supposed to have a certain epistemic implication, namely that belief in theory is never warranted by the evidence. This is the underdetermination thesis.

DEDUCTIVE UNDERDETERMINATION

Deductive underdetermination is pervasive in all interesting cases of scientific theory. If the theory is not just a summary of the evidence, the evidence cannot determine, in the sense of proving, the theory. For instance, no finite amount of evidence of the form Aa_i & Ba_i can entail an unrestricted universal generalization of the form *All A's are B*. Deductive underdetermination rests on the claim that the link between evidence and (interesting) theory is *not* deductive. What is the epistemic problem it is supposed to create? Given that the link is not deductive, it is claimed that we can never justifiably believe in the truth of a theory, no matter what the evidence is. However, it would be folly to think that deductive underdetermination creates a genuine epistemic problem. There are enough reasons available for the claim that belief in theory can be justified even if the theory is not proven by the evidence: Warrant-conferring methods need not be deductive.

Deductive underdetermination speaks against simplistic accounts of the hypothetico-deductive method, which presuppose that the epistemic warrant for a theory is solely a matter of entailing correct observational consequences. Two or more rival theories (together with suitable initial conditions) may entail exactly the same observational consequences. Given the above presupposition, it follows that the observational consequences cannot warrant belief in one theory over its rivals. Though simplistic accounts of the hypothetico-deductive method need to be jettisoned, there are ways to meet the challenge of deductive underdetermination, even if we stay close to hypothetico-deductivism. Since theories entail observational consequences only with the aid of auxiliary assumptions, and since the available auxiliary assumptions may change over time, the set of observational consequences of a theory is not circumscribed once and for all. Hence, even if, for the time being, two (or more) theories entail the same observational consequences, there may be future auxiliary assumptions such that, when conjoined with one of them, they yield fresh observational consequences that can shift the evidential balance in favor of it over its rivals. Besides, a more radical (though plausible) thought is that theories may get (indirect) support from pieces of evidence that do not belong to their observational consequences.

INDUCTIVE UNDERDETERMINATION

Inductive underdetermination takes for granted that any attempt to *prove* a theory on the basis of evidence is futile. Still, it is argued, no evidence can confirm a theory or make it probable, or no evidence can confirm a theory more than its rivals. This claim is rather odd. In all its generality, it is a recapitulation of inductive skepticism. If induction lacks justification, then no inductively established theory is warranted by the evidence. Yet induction does not lack justification. In any case, according to recent externalist-reliabilist theories of justification, belief in theory is justified if induction is reliable; and there is no argument that it is *not*. If inductive scepticism is set aside, inductive underdetermination must relate to problems with the theory of confirmation. For on *any* theory of confirmation, the evidence (even if it is restricted to observational consequences) can render a theory probable or more probable than its rivals. That is, the evidence can raise the probability of a theory. So inductive underdetermination must rest on some arguments that question the confirmatory role of the evidence vis-à-vis the theory. There is a battery of such arguments, but they may be classified under two types.

The first capitalizes on the fact that no evidence can affect the probability of the theory unless the theory is assigned some nonzero initial probability. In fact, given the fact that two or more rival theories are assigned different prior probabilities, the evidence can confirm one more than the others, or even make one highly probable. The challenge, then, is this: Where do these prior probabilities come from? A total denial of the legitimacy of any prior probabilities would amount to inductive skepticism. Inductive underdetermination would be inductive skepticism. The more interesting version of inductive underdetermination does not challenge the need to employ prior probabilities, but rather their epistemic credentials. If, it is argued, prior probabilities have epistemic force, then the evidence can warrant a high degree of belief in a theory (or greater degree of belief in a theory than its rivals). But, it is added, how can prior probabilities have any epistemic force?

The subjective Bayesians' appeal to subjective prior probabilities (degrees of belief) accentuates rather than meets this challenge. Bayesians typically argue that, in the long run, the prior probabilities wash out: even widely different prior probabilities will converge, in the limit, to the same posterior probability, if agents conditionalize on the same evidence. But this is scant consolation because, apart from the fact that in the long-run we are all dead, the convergence-of-opinion theorem holds only under limited and very well-defined circumstances that can hardly be met in ordinary scientific cases. The alternative is to claim that prior probabilities have epistemic force because they express rational degrees of belief, based, for instance, on plausibility or explanatory judgements. This claim faces many challenges, but its defense might well be necessary for blocking the epistemic implications of inductive underdetermination. In its favor, it can be said that rational belief in theory is not solely a matter of looking for strict observational evidence.

The second type of argument rests on the claim that theories that purport to refer to unobservable entities are, somehow, unconfirmable. The problem is supposed to be that since there cannot be direct observational access to unobservable entities, no observational evidence can support the truth of a theory that posits them, and no evidence can support a theory more than others that posit different unobservable entities. The distinctive element of the second type of argument is that the resulting inductive underdetermination is selective. It does *not* deny that observational generalisations can be confirmed. Hence, it does not deny that the evidence can confirm or render probable observational theories. It denies that the same can be the case for theories that refer to unobservable entities.

Even if a sharp distinction between observable and unobservable entities were granted (though it is by no means obvious that it should), this selective inductive underdetermination has a bite only if the methods that lead to, and warrant, belief in observable entities and observational generalizations are different from the methods that lead to, and warrant, belief in theories that posit unobservable entities. Yet the methods are the same. In particular, explanatory considerations play an indispensable role in both cases. In the end, this kind of selective inductive underdetermination undermines itself: it either collapses into inductive skepticism or has no force at all.

EMPIRICAL EQUIVALENCE

It is commonly argued that there can be totally empirically equivalent theories— that is, theories that entail exactly the same observational consequences under any circumstances. In its strong form, this claim (let's call it the Empirical Equivalence Thesis, *EET*) asserts that *any* theory has empirically equivalent rivals (some of which might be hitherto unconceived). *EET* is an entry point for the epistemic thesis of total underdetermination: that there can be no evidential reason to believe in the truth of *any* theory. But there is no formal proof of *EET*, though a number of cases have been suggested ranging from Descartes' "evil demon" hypothesis to the hypothesis that for every theory T there is an empirically equivalent rival asserting that T is empirically adequate yet false, or that the world is *as if* T were true. One can, of course, argue that these rival hypotheses have only philosophical value and drive only an abstract philosophical doubt. In science, it is often hard to come by just one totally empirically adequate theory, much less a bunch of them.

Yet it seems that there is a genuine case of empirical equivalence of theories of quantum mechanics. Alternative interpretations of the quantum-mechanical formalism constitute empirically equivalent but different theories that explain the world according to different principles and mechanisms. The most typical rivalry is between the orthodox understanding of quantum theory—the "Copenhagen interpretation," according to which a particle cannot have a precise position and momentum at the same time—and the Bohmian understanding of quantum theory—the hidden-variables interpretation, according to which particles always have a definite position and velocity, and hence momentum. On Bohm's theory, particles have two kinds of energy: the usual (classical) energy and a "quantum potential" energy. More recently, there have been three particularly well-developed theories (the Bohmian quantum mechanics, the many-worlds interpretation, and the spontaneous-collapse approach) such that there is no observational way to tell them apart. And it seems that there *cannot* be an observational way to tell them apart. This situation is particularly unfortunate, but one may respond that the ensued underdetermination is local rather than global; hence the possible skepticism that follows is local.

The Duhem-Quine thesis has been suggested as an algorithm for generating empirically equivalent theories. Briefly put, this thesis starts with the undeniable premise that all theories entail observational consequences only with the help of auxiliary assumptions and concludes that it is always possible that a theory, together with suitable auxiliaries, can accommodate *any* recalcitrant evidence. A corollary, then, is that for any evidence and any two rival theories T and T', there are suitable auxiliaries A such that T' and A will be empirically equivalent to T (together with its own auxiliaries). Hence, it is argued, no evidence can tell two theories apart. It is questionable that the Duhem-Quine thesis is true. There is no proof that *nontrivial* auxiliary assumptions can always be found.

But let us assume, for the sake of the argument, that it is true. What does it show? Since the Duhem-Quine thesis implies that any theory can be saved from refutation, it does create some genuine problems to a falsificationist (Popperian) account of theory testing— that is, the view that theories are tested by attempting to refute them. If attempted refutations are the sole test for theories, two incompatible theories that are not refuted by the evidence are equally well tested by it. But the Duhem-Quine thesis does not create a similar problem to an inductivist. From the fact that any theory can be suitably adjusted so that it resists refutation it does not follow that all theories are equally well confirmed by the evidence. An inductivist can argue that the empirical evidence does not lend equal inductive support to two empirically congruent theories. It is not necessarily the case that the auxiliary assumptions that are needed to save a theory from refutation will themselves be well supported by the evidence. Since it is reasonable to think that the degree of support of the auxiliary assumptions associated with a theory is reflected in the degree of support of the theory, it follows that not all theories that entail the same evidence are equally well supported by it.

EET has generated much philosophical discussion. An argument favored by the logical positivists is that such cases of total underdetermination are illusions: the rival theories are simply notational variants. This move presupposes that theories are not taken at face value. For anyone who does not subscribe to a verificationist criterion of meaning, this move is moot. It does make sense to say that there *can* be distinct but totally empirically equivalent theories. The hard issue is not to exclude their possibility on a priori grounds but to find ways to distinguish their epistemic worth, should we find ourselves in such a predicament.

Another move, favored by Quine, is to go for pragmatism: The balance is shifted to the theory *we* (our community) favor, simply because it is *our* theory. This raises the spectre of epistemic relativism. Yet another move is to go for skepticism: among rival totally empirically equivalent theories one is true, but we cannot possibly come to know or justifiably believe which this is. This skeptical answer might be supplemented with some differential stance towards the rival theories, but this differential treatment will not be based on epistemic reasons but rather on pragmatic considerations. Indeed, social constructivists have seized upon this in order to claim that social, political, and ideological factors break observational ties among theories: hence, they argue, belief in theory is socially determined.

The general problem with the skeptical move is that it rests on a restricted account of what counts as evidence (or reason) for justified belief; it counts only observations as possible epistemic reason for belief. But rational belief may well be a function of other epistemic reasons—for instance, the theoretical virtues that a theory possesses. This last thought ushers in yet another possibility: that empirically equivalent theories may well differ in their explanatory power. Insofar as explanatory power can offer epistemic credentials to a theory, it can break supposed epistemic ties among totally empirically equivalent rivals. This move makes rational belief a more complex affair and tallies with the intuitions of scientific and common sense. Yet it faces the problem of justifying the claim that theoretical virtues are epistemic reasons— that is, that a virtuous theory (a theory with great explanatory power) is more likely to be true than a less virtuous one.

This is not an unsolvable problem. There are, broadly, two ways to tackle it. One is to argue (rather implausibly) that some theoretical virtues are constitutive marks of truth. The other is to argue for a broad conception of evidence that takes the theoretical virtues to be empirical and contingent marks of truth. A central element in this latter argument is that theories can get extra credence by entailing novel predictions—that is, predictions such that information about the predicted phenomenon was not previously known and not used in the construction of the theory. In the end, the epistemic relations between evidence and theory cannot be exhausted by their logico-semantic relations.

See also Confirmation Theory; Scientific Realism.

Bibliography

Cushing, J. T. *Quantum Mechanics: Historical Contingency and the Copenhagen Hegemony*. Chicago: The University of Chicago Press, 1994.

Devitt, Michael. "Underdetermination and Realism." *Philosophical Issues* 12 (2002): 26–50.

Earman, John. "Underdetermination, Realism, and Reason." *Midwest Studies in Philosophy* 18 (1993): 19–38.

Laudan, Larry. "Demystifying Underdetermination." *Minnesota Studies in the Philosophy of Science* 14 (1990): 267–297.

Newton-Smith, William. "The Underdetermination of Theory by Data." *Aristotelian Society* Suppl. 52 (1978): 71–91.

Psillos, Stathis. *Scientific Realism: How Science Tracks Truth*. London and New York: Routledge, 1999.

Quine, W. V. "On Empirically Equivalent Systems of the World." *Erkenntnis* 9 (1975): 313–328.

Stathis Psillos (2005)

UNITY AND DISUNITY IN SCIENCE

Unity covers a wide range of loosely connected ideas in science, differently analyzed by different interpreters. Generally, they are expressions, or echoes, of the idea that science can succeed in providing one consistent, integrated, simple, and comprehensive description of the world. This entry will provide a historical perspective on such ways of thinking about unity in science. (Readers should bear in mind that the real history is much more complex and interesting than the following microsketch, which is intended only to introduce the leading ideas.)

MECHANISMS AND LAWS

The scientific revolution of the seventeenth century involved consolidation of the "mechanical (or corpuscularian) philosophy" according to which natural phenomena are to be understood in terms of shaped matter in motion, with the natural world likened to a giant mechanism. Natural philosophy could look for unity in this regard by thinking of the parts of the world machine as all governed by the same simple set of rules or laws. Isaac Newton's mechanics could be seen in this regard as a paradigm of unification, showing how the same laws covered motion in both the heavens and on Earth.

But there was a monkey wrench in this mechanist paradigm: Newton's law of gravity involved "action at a distance," inadmissible by most seventeenth-century interpreters as a legitimate mechanical principle. Mechanism required contact action. Newton's official response was that "I make no hypotheses," that is, no hypotheses or speculations about what the underlying real mechanism of gravity might be. Instead, he presented his mechanics as "mathematical only," that is, mathematical principles by which motions can be reliably and accurately described but with no pretense to describing what makes things move as they do. Accordingly, some of Newton's successors thought of unity in theory and in science in terms of a simple set of general, mathematical laws that integrate, by covering, a wide range of phenomena that otherwise might seem independent, and all this without any thought of underlying mechanisms. This will be referred to as the "nomological attitude."

These two ideas, seeing disparate phenomena as manifestation of one underlying mechanism or covered by one set of simple laws, interacted and intertwined during the eighteenth and nineteenth centuries. For example, James Clerk Maxwell worked to treat first electric and magnetic effects and then discovered he could also cover optical phenomena, thinking of all of these first as manifestations of one underlying mechanism, developing the laws that might govern such a mechanism, and then letting go of the postulated underlying mechanism as unverifiable speculation in favor of the general laws that had emerged. Heinrich Rudolf Hertz maintained that Maxwell's theory is Maxwell's equations, and eventually Albert Einstein's special relativity did in the speculated stuff of electromagnetic mechanisms, the luminiferous aether.

The opposition of mechanisms versus laws also played out, with the opposite result, during the second half of the nineteenth century over the issue of atoms. The predictive and explanatory success of chemistry, as well as the nascent kinetic theory (statistical mechanics), emboldened some to see atoms and molecules as real cogs in the cosmic machine. Others scoffed at postulation of things too small to see or individually detect as "metaphysics," not science. Continuum mechanics and even contact action presented severe problems for an atomistic theory. The speculated indivisibility of atoms, though mentioned by some, was not really the issue. Rather, it was whether one could correctly think of the underlying order in terms of discrete parts interacting in something like the mechanist tradition or whether this should be seen, at best, as a kind of pretty imaginative picture, while scientific truth was exhausted by mathematical laws in the nomological tradition.

The issue of atoms came to a head in the first decade of the twentieth century in the work augmented and integrated by Jean-Baptiste Perrin. Perrin catalogued the astonishingly numerous and diverse facts that could be encompassed by postulating atoms: constant ratios in chemistry, relative atomic weighs, diffusion and other fluctuation phenomena, osmotic pressure, behavior of electrolytes, specific heat, behavior of thin materials, even why the sky is blue. Perrin tabled sixteen independent ways of reaching the same estimate of Avogadro's number. Einstein's theory of Brownian motion proved especially effective—in a sense one could "see" the causal effects of individual molecular collisions. A vast range of otherwise diverse observable phenomena were unified in the sense of interpreting them as the manifestation of the properties and behavior of atoms. By 1913 most of the physics community accepted atoms as real.

Electric, magnetic, and optical phenomena unified by Maxwell's laws. Perrin's diverse phenomena unified by postulation of atoms. Though they are in some ways polar attitudes, mechanistic and nomological thinking really cannot operate without one another. To provide unifying explanations, mechanisms need to be governed by laws, and laws, if they are to do more than exhaustively list superficially observable phenomena, must at least have the form of describing some conceptually more economic structure.

REDUCTIONISM

The nineteenth century saw explosive development of the natural sciences, emboldening some toward the end of the century to speculate that physics was almost completed with little left to do but to work out the applications to other natural phenomena. Contrary to what one might have imagined, the shocks of relativity and quantum mechanics in the first quarter of the twentieth century initially encouraged rather than tempered such scientific utopian attitudes. Some strands of positivism in the second quarter of the century described unity of science in terms of unity of language and methods; others took the spirit of unification to its logical extreme, emphasizing axiomatic formulation and developing the idea of reduction of all natural phenomena to "fundamental physics" in the spirit of the logicists' hope of reducing all of mathematics to logic. By the 1950s and 1960s reductionistic thinking had taken a deep hold on much thinking in both philosophy and science, no doubt encouraged by advances within science in subjects such as quantum chemistry and microbiology. Unity now took the form of (expected) chains of reductive definitions, identifying not just complex physical, but biological, psychological, and social phenomena with the behavior of physical parts, everything ultimately to be described in terms of the laws of fundamental physics.

Again a monkey wrench, or this time two, brought the reductionist juggernaut to a halt. In the 1970s and 1980s philosophy of science became acutely aware of difficulties with the whole reductionist program. The reversal began with the collapse of the two show cases: claimed deductive reduction of thermodynamics to statistical mechanics and of Mendelian to molecular genetics. Temperature is in fact realized by mechanisms in addition to mean kinetic energy, and in principle could be realized in indefinitely many ways. There is no neat one trait–one gene correlation and the developmental effects of any one bit of DNA depend, not just on its genetic, but on its overall environmental context. If temperature and genes are multiply realizable by disparate physical constructs, then surely also, for example, are mental states. Higher level objects and phenomena may still all be physically realized, but in such diverse ways that the program of reduction by definitions and deduction loses plausibility. *Unity* no longer seems such an apt term.

This first basis for some kind of disunity was followed in the 1980s and 1990s by a second. Nancy Cartwright, Ronald N. Giere, and others have pointed out that, whatever the ultimate aims of science or of some scientists might be, the science we actually have, now or any time in the foreseeable future, hardly follows the pattern of calculation of phenomena from universally applicable, exact, true laws or of description in terms of mechanisms known or even believed to operate exactly as described. Rather, science uses laws in the construction of idealized models, always limited in scope, and even where they apply never exactly correct. Rather than providing descriptions that set out exactly what the phenomena are, the laws of science are only true, or at least only exactly true, of the idealized models that in turn enable us to understand phenomena and their hidden sources in terms of the idealizations to which the phenomena are similar. For the puny minds of even the best physicists, to understand the fluid properties of water we need to resort to continuum hydrodynamical models, while to understand dispersive phenomena we turn to the discontinuous models of statistical mechanics. "Foundational" theories fare no better. Quantum field theory and general relativity each idealize away from the phenomena of the other, are mutually inconsistent, and have no humanly accessible direct application to most phenomena of human interest. The science we have displays disunity on a grand scale.

UNITY AND DISUNITY IN SCIENCE

Or does it? Few would dispute the claims just listed about science and idealized models. But many challenge the interpretation of these facts as constituting disunity in any weighty sense. Since *unity* and *disunity* have no well-established univocal usage and are susceptible to expropriation as rhetorical weapons by advocates of one or another larger position, we have difficulty in saying just what the issue really is, let alone in resolving it. Yet there are interesting and important issues here, ones that it is suggested we do not understand at all well. For elaboration let us, with hindsight, revisit the unification afforded by the postulation of atoms.

Descriptions of none of the phenomena described as manifestations of the existence and behavior of atoms follow from the bare postulation of atoms alone. We require assumptions, not only about the properties and behavior of atoms but also—for many of the phenomena—about a great deal else. The accounts based on the postulation of atoms hardly constitute the deductions imagined by the reductionists. Rather, they work, often fortuitously, by appealing to a helter-skelter of plausible assumptions, phenomenological observations, disconnected results from other accounts, and a wide range of approximative mathematical methods and experimental techniques from independently practiced fields. Nonetheless, all these accounts have at their core the assumption that material is composed of relatively stable and discrete parts with properties that admit of systematic investigation. In all the admittedly disunified messy process of science the postulation of atoms is doing real and systematic work—we would not have this body of accounts without the postulation of atoms.

This kind of intertheoretic asymmetry occurs broadly. Quantum theory plays a role in understanding chemistry that chemistry does not play in understanding quantum theory, and similarly for chemistry and biology, biology and psychology, and many other pairs of theories and theoretical domains. Clearly, such asymmetry has to do with the circumstance that parts of an object or process play crucial roles in the behavior of the containing whole. But one does not yet understand at all clearly the nature of such intertheoretic relations—reductionism was a vast oversimplification. The mirage of some kind of simple unity was the artifact of imagining that the human mind could get its head around all of the natural world, exactly and, at least potentially, in all its detail. This will not happen, at least not until long after this encyclopedia has become hopelessly out of date. In the mean time we face the complex and interesting challenge of charting the complex interplay of elements of unity and disunity in the science we know.

See also Philosophy of Physics; Reduction; Special Sciences.

Bibliography

Darden, Lindley, and Nancy Maull. "Interfield Theories." *Philosophy of Science* 44 (1977): 43–64

Maudlin, Tim. "On the Unification of Physics." *Journal of Philosophy* 93 (1996): 129–144.

McRae, Robert F. *The Problem of the Unity of the Sciences: Bacon to Kant*. Toronto: University of Toronto Press, 1961.

Morrison, Margaret. *Unifying Scientific Theories: Physical Concepts and Mathematical Structures*. New York: Cambridge University Press, 2000.

Nagel, Ernest. *The Structure of Science: Problems in the Logic of Scientific Explanation*. New York: Harcourt, Brace, 1961.

Oppenheim, Paul, and Hilary Putnam. "The Unity of Science as a Working Hypothesis." In *Minnesota Studies in the Philosophy of Science*. Vol. 2, edited by Herbert Feigl, Michael Scriven, and Grover Maxwell. Minneapolis: Minnesota University Press, 1958.

Wilson, Mark. "Mechanics, Classical." In *The Routledge Encyclopedia of Philosophy*. Vol. 6, edited by Edward Craig, 251–259. London: Routledge, 1998.

Paul Teller (2005)

UNIVERSAL PROPERTIES IN INDIAN PHILOSOPHICAL TRADITIONS

EARLY GRAMMARIANS ON UNIVERSALS OF WORDS AND MEANINGS

In ancient India systematic metaphysics started with a linguistic turn. Ontological concepts and controversies arose in the context of musings on meanings of words and debates on declensions, unlike in ancient Greece, where metaphysics arose out of wondering about numbers, figures, and nature. In Pāṇini's grammar and his early commentaries (between the fourth and second centuries BCE) the three crucial technical terms for a universal—*sāmānya*, *jāti*, and *ākṛti*—were already explicitly in use. Philosophers of language dabbled in metaphysics since Patañjali's "Great Commentary" to Pāṇini's grammar. The device of adding a *tva* or *tā* (roughly equivalent to the English "ness") to any nominal root x, yields, as meaning, the property of being x. From substance (*dravya*) one can thus mechanically abstract substanceness (*dravya-tva*), from real (*sat*) and reality (*sattā*). With this device in place it was natural to make the distinction between an individual substance and the property that makes it what it is, its abstract essence. But even to parse this talk of concrete cows rather than of the bovine essence, the grammarians drew the distinction between talking about one particular cow and talking about any cow or a cow in general (VMB on Pāṇini sutra 1.2.58 and 1.2.64). The distinction between the general and the particular also came up for discussion in the context of the logic of pluralization. What allowed one to say "trees" or "men" instead of using the word for a tree or man as many times as the number of trees one referred to? It must be because the direct meaning of a common noun is the shared universal property of the referents that one could eliminate all but one remaining occurrence of that word, when speaking generally. One could also issue universalizable moral imperatives such as, "A cow ought not to be killed," which, Patañjali jokes, is not obeyed by simply sparing the life of one single cow.

Jāti (a word that, in modern Indian vernaculars, has come to mean "a class," "a caste," or even "a nation")—the Sanskrit counterpart of the Latin "genera"—is used by Pāṇini for a shared property of all the particulars of one natural kind, which serves also to distinguish any one of them from things of other kinds. The particulars are called *vyakti*—a word that etymologically suggests a distinct concrete manifestation of common and uncommon properties. The problem with this universalist theory of meaning—defended by Vajapyāyana—was that when, in a descriptive or prescriptive sentence, the action denoted by the verb has to hook up with what the noun means, it has to be a particular. For, after all, no one can bring cowness, cut the tree-essence, or meet humanity on the street.

Thus, in Indian philosophical semantics the dispute between those who insisted that a word primarily means a universal and their rivals who held that it must be particular substances that are the first meanings of words is at least twenty-two centuries old. The word often used for *universal* by Patañjali was *ākṛti* (literally "shape"), which is more reminiscent of form than a property. In answer to the basic question "What is a word?" Patañjali considers the option, "Is it that which remains non-distinct among distinct individuals, un-torn when individuals are torn down?" and answers, "No, that is not the word, that is only the universal (*ākṛti*).

The need to switch to imperishable universals as meanings was felt both by the grammarians and the Mīmāṃsā school of Vedic hermeneutics for whom the authority of authorless sentences of the Vedas rested on their eternity. The relation between words and objects was said to be entrenched and eternal. If perishable particular horses, cows, humans, and plants were the meanings of words, how could they be the eternally connected meanings of these beginningless Vedic words? The word *gauḥ* (cow) is therefore best taken to be eternally connected to the timeless bovine essence.

The first clear recognition of the need to postulate universals might have come, not so much from the theory of meaning but from reflecting on the generality or repeatability of the audible words themselves. That there could be many pronunciations or distinguishable phonations of the same word was seen to be an unquestionable example of the one-in-many. That naturally went hand in hand with the idea of the real word-type existing timelessly there independently of its temporal perishable token-utterances. Later, in the philosophy of Bhartrhari, sometimes called a linguistic nondualist, word-universals and meaning-universals and one's natural tendency to superimpose the former on the latter were elaborately discussed, because it was easy to confuse them with Bhartrhari's single most important metaphysical concept of a speech-bud or linguistic-potentiality (*sphoṭa*) in all consciousness, where signifier and signified exist undivided, waiting to blossom into articulated structures of sentences.

In the context of interpreting Kātyāyana's aphorism, "the word-meaning-relation being fixed," Patañjali mentions two alternative ways of taking the concepts of form (*ākṛti*) and content or substance (*dravyam*). In the first sense forms are universal properties that remain unchanged while individual material substances come and go, hence the forms must be those fixed meanings. In the second sense, somewhat like René Descartes's lump of wax, the substance continues to exist, retaining its sameness while the structures vary or perish, hence the substance or content must be that fixed meaning. If one defines the universal as the invariant across variations of individuals, then that definition fits both the form (under the first interpretation) as well as the indestructible content (under the second interpretation). One encounters a similar clash of intuitions in Ludwig Josef Johann Wittgenstein's *Tractatus Logico-Philosophicus*, where, about the ultimate constituents of all atomic facts, one finds the remark, "Objects are form and content." This idea of the enduring stuff of changing entities as a ground of sameness, found in early grammarians' and Advaita Vedāta thought, was later on picked up by the Jaina notion of a vertical universal (*ūrdhvata-sāmānya)*, as against the more common property-universal that was termed *horizontal universal* (*tiryak-sāmānya)*.

THE HOT TOPICS FOR DEBATE

Between fifth and fifteenth centuries the debate between mainstream Nyāya-Vaiśeika and Mīmāṃsā realists and Buddhist nominalists raged around the existence of eternal essences. The major points of disputation were:

(1) Must one explain the use of a common noun or the experience of community across a plurality of particulars by postulating a single real property inherent in each of those particulars? (Vaiśeika and Mīmāṃsā said yes with some caveats, and Buddhists said no.)

(2) Is this property totally distinct from the individuals that exemplify it? (Vaiśeika said yes, and Bhāṭṭa Mīmāṃsā said yes and no.)

(3) Does a universal exist only in all its own instances or are universals omnipresent ? (This is a trick question set up by the Buddhist nominalist, answered cautiously by Vaiśeika.)

(4) Do universals have any role in causation? (Vaiśeika said that they can cause one's awareness of them. For Buddhists anything that is eternal must be causally barren, hence nonexistent. For Udayanācārya [tenth-century Nyāya-Vaiśeika] nomic relations of necessary concomitance are ontologically founded on the universals inherent in the causes and effects.)

(5) Can the work that is done by universals be done by relations of resemblance between particulars? (Vaiśeika said no, Jainism and Madhva Vedāta said yes).

THE CLASSICAL NYĀYA-VAIŚEIKA REALISM ABOUT UNIVERSALS

Universals come to occupy a crucial role as the fourth type of real, in the scheme of six basic categories of reals or "things-meant-by-words" (*padārthas*)—notice again the semantic orientation—listed in the Vaiśeika sutras of Kaṇāda. In that canonical scheme, after the three types of unrepeatables—substances, particular qualities, and motions—come common properties. Although substances, qualities, and motions are entities of different types, they share one common property: They are all real. What is this realness that is common to all substances, qualities, and motions? Realness is a generic essence present in many substances, qualities, and motions. It is a universal, the highest one. Then there are less general features as well, the substance-hood shared by all substances, the quality-hood common to all qualities, and the motion-hood inherent in all motions. These second-tier universals are called common-uncommon since they function as defining properties belonging to all the members of the class to be defined, and lacked by all else.

The Vaiśeika sutra's word for universal is *sāmānya*" (the phonetic resemblance with "sameness" may not be entirely accidental), meaning "what is common." The word for an individuator or particularity is *víseṣa*, which means "uncommon feature" or "specialty," the difference-maker. Flower-ness could be a common property, shared by roses, jasmines, and sunflowers. But the same property would be a difference-maker when you compare a rose with fruits, seeds, stones, and animals, since none of these except the rose has flower-ness. Hence, Kaṇāda's aphorism, "Universal and particularity depend upon understanding" (VS:1/2/3).

Commentators hasten to point out that this formulation does not mean that universals are subjective or invented by one's ways of understanding the world. All it means is that one finds out by the verdict of one's understanding whether some property is a pure universal or also a demarcator, as shown earlier.

Four broad arguments are generally proposed by these staunch realists for proving the existence of universal properties:

(1) The evidence of sense-perception is the strongest of all. Unless one is threatened by a logical inconsistency, one must admit some common recurrent entity in each of those many things that sense-perception shows one to be of the same kind. This class-character, the basis for one's sense of sameness (*anugata-pratīti*), is a universal.

(2) The argument from the meaning of general words runs as follows. A learnable common noun such as *bird* can denote an unlimited number of particulars of enormous variety. How the same word with the same meaning can correctly apply to so

many diverse particulars calls for an explanation. The explanation must lie in a distinction between reference (*śakya*) and sense (*śakyatāvacchedaka*). Thanks to the existence of an objective universal, for example, bird-ness, which serves as the same sense, the same word can distributively refer to all birds or any bird. This does not boil down to one of the early extreme views that the bare particular or the pure universal is the primary meaning of a word. It is the balanced view that the meaning of a word is a particular possessing a general property that serves as the common mode of presentation of its unlimited number of referents.

(3) Then one has the argument from lawlike causal connections. Fire is a substance, but when it causes burning, its causal efficacy is not determined by its simply being a substance, for, then any substance would burn. To explain what makes fire—and not any other substance—the cause of burning, one needs to postulate fire-ness as the property that limits the causality of fire toward this effect. With the advent of extremely technical New Nyāya (around the thirteenth century) the need to have limiters (*avacchedaka*) of cause-hood and effect-hood became the standard ground for ontological commitment to universals.

(4) Admission of universals also helped Nyāya solve the problem of justifying the inductive leap from observation of a few cases to a universal generalization covering all cases of a concomitance. The common property observed in a few instances can, as it were, put one in direct perceptual touch with all the other instances where also it inheres, not in their individual details but in a generic way. Here, the universal itself is supposed to play the role of the operative connection between the sense-organ and the apparently unobserved instances of that universal.

With all these supporting arguments for its existence, the precise definition offered by Nyāya-Vaiśeika settled down to this, "A universal is that which, being eternal, is inherent in many." Not any quality inhering in a substance is a universal. A wish inheres in a soul, but it is a short-lived episode, not a universal. Colors are not universals in this system because they are unrepeatable qualities clinging to the particular surfaces. All colors share the universal color-hood. But two red apples have two distinct red colors in them, just as each of them would have a distinct falling-motion when they both fall. A universal must subsist wholly in each of its instances by the special relation of inherence. A universal must be wholly inherent in each of its instances. The word *inherent* must be taken seriously. A single string may be running through many flowers, but it is only in contact with them, the whole string is not inherent in any one of them.

What is inherence? It is a kind of being-in, the converse of which is an intimate "having." Humanity inheres in me, just in case I have humanity. Now, having can be of many kinds. Things have qualities and motions. Wholes have parts. I have a pen in my hand. A rich man has a big house. The logical structure of each of these relations of characterization, constitution, contact, and ownership, however, is utterly different. All four are more or less aptly reportable by the use of the preposition *in* or *of*: the taste is in the apple, the room is or consists in the walls, roof, and floor, the pen is in between the fingers, and the house is of the rich merchant. Still, one initial grouping could be made to clarify their distinct structures. The taste and the room cannot exist without the apple or the room-parts. The taste cannot float about on its own, minus the apple. The room cannot stand independently of the walls. But that pen can easily exist untouched by the hand, and that house can change hands.

So, the first two relations hold between pairs that are "incapable of standing apart from one another" (*ayutasiddha*), whereas the other two relations hold between pairs that are "capable of standing apart from one another" (*yutasiddha*). However tightly my ring is stuck to my finger, it is not inherent in it as inseparably as finger-ness is inherent in my fingers. It is no physical glue but a metaphysical inseparability that joins the goat-ness to the goat, ties up the running and black color of the goat to the goat, as well as binds the goat to its body-parts. The kind of being-inseparably-in that connects the universal to its instances has to be distinguished from the way a berry lies in a bowl. For the sake of economy—the principle of not multiplying entities beyond necessity—the mainstream Nyāya-Vaiśeika metaphysicians posit only one single such relation as enough to link innumerable pairs of universals and particulars, qualities and substances, and wholes and parts. For systemic reasons, this relation is supposed to be eternal as well. And this is inherence (*samavāya*). Even other universal-friendly realists, such as the Bhāṭṭa Mīmāṃsaka, give Vaiśeika a lot of grief over this peculiar theory of the exemplification. The Bhāṭṭas themselves take the relation between a universal and its own exemplifier to be identity-in-difference. The Buddhist logician finds both inherence and identity-in-difference equally unpalatable.

Though one cannot experience Vaiśeika universals by themselves, they are ontologically independent of the particular instances. Even when all cows are destroyed in the world, cow-ness will still be around, for otherwise the possibility of a fresh cow coming to be remains inexplicable.

REAL UNIVERSALS AND TITULAR PROPERTIES: ON BEING A COOK

Though all universals are common features, not all common features corresponding to multiply applicable descriptions are, strictly speaking, universals. Being a Brahman (a member of the highest priestly intellectual class) is taken to be a natural kind by Nyāya-Vaiśeika in the face of vehement opposition by anticaste Buddhists and Jainas. But being a cook is the standard example of a common feature that is not a real universal. The Nyāya-Vaiśeika philosophers suggest six tests that an alleged (semantically suggested) property must pass to count as a genuine universal. These tests or hurdles are called universal-blockers:

(1) If a property has only a single exemplifier, then it is not a universal. "Being the Statue of Liberty" is not a universal, neither is time-hood, because there is no more than one Statue of Liberty, one time.

(2) If two properties have exactly the same extension, for example, the property of being a Homo sapiens and the property humanity, they cannot be two distinct universals.

(3) The domains of two universals can be either completely disjoint or one of them completely included in the other. They cannot be partially intersecting and partially excluding each other. Thus, being material and having a limited size cannot both be universals in Vaiśeika ontology, because while lots of things have both the properties, open space is supposed to be material yet not limited in size, while the internal sense-organ is supposed to be limited in size but immaterial. Whether crosscutting disqualifies both the properties or only one of them, and whether the neat ontological hierarchy that is presupposed by this universal-blocker is integral to a realist metaphysics have been the subject of much contemporary debate (see Shastri 1964, Mukhopadhyaya 1984).

(4) A regress-generating property is not a universal. Universal-hood is not a universal, although all universals seem to have that property in common. Because then one could multiply levels of universals endlessly. Universals do not have further universals in them.

(5) When the nature of a characteristic is to merely distinguish its bearer, for example, one earth-atom, from another particular of that kind, such ultimate individuators should not be brought under a general category of individuator-hood, for that militates against their necessarily unique nature. Failing this test, the alleged generality individuator-ness (*visesatva*) fails to qualify as a universal within Vaiśeika atomism.

(6) The feature must bear inherence and no other relation to its bearer. Inherence-hood is not a universal because, had it been one, it would have to be related by inherence to inherence, which would be absurd. An absence cannot be a universal. Nor could the negativity common to all absences be a universal. Even though every rabbit is hornless, neither the absence of horn itself nor the absence-ness of the absence resides in rabbits or absences by inherence. Besides these, compound properties such as being a sturdy black cow or being either a cow or a buffalo are ruled out because universals are supposed to be simple.

What happens to the properties that, thus, get disqualified by a universal-blocker? They are thrown into the mixed pile of titular, surplus, or imposed properties (*upādhi*). They could still be of much theoretical and practical use. Not only nonnatural generalities like being a New Yorker, but even is-ness, knowability, and positive presence (shared by items of all the six categories—substance, quality, motion, universal, inherence, and final individuator—but not found in absences) are merely titular properties. Knowability and existence (is-ness) are (intensionally) distinct properties, in spite of being equiextensive, because they are not universals.

HOW ARE UNIVERSALS KNOWN?

One needs philosophical reasoning to grasp such deep universals as substance-hood, because many instances of substance-hood, such as time, atoms, other people's souls, are not objects of perception. If the instances are perceptible, the universals must be directly perceptible as well. One sees flower-ness in a flower, just as one sees its hue and smells its fragrance. According to Nyāya epistemology, to see Black Beauty as a horse one must first see its horse-ness (which is a perceived universal, though it is not perceived to be a universal).

But many strong arguments could be given against the perceptibility of universals (NM, ch VII). The following are a couple of examples:

If properties were perceived, one would perceive them even at the time of encountering the first exemplifier, but one does not. Hence properties are abstracted, not seen. Both the premises of this argument, of course, could be questioned. For the empirical knowledge of a common property to dawn gradually, a recognition must take place in the second, third, and subsequent sightings of the instances. To be faithful to the form of that recognition, "I have seen this sort of animal before," is to admit that even in the first instance that sortal property was seen.

Here is another antiperception argument. If properties were objects of perception, they would be causes of perception, but they are not. Therefore, they are not perceived. Again, both the premises are rejected by the Nyāya realists. Pot-ness need not itself reflect light back into the retina for it to be causally relevant to the visual perception of pot-ness. As long as the pot in which it inheres is in contact with the seeing eyes, it has a causally operative connection with the appropriate sense-organ. If, of course, perception is defined as prelinguistic and nonconceptual (as some Buddhists have done) and universals are taken to be word-generated concepts, then to use that definition as an argument for imperceptibility of universals would be crudely question-begging.

With Fregean sensibilities one could propose another quick argument against the perceptibility of universals. Universals are not objects but functions. Therefore, they are not objects of perception. Still, there is a clear shift in the meaning of "object" between the premise and conclusion of this argument. There is a basic (rationalist?) resistance even among realists in the West to admit sense-perception of universals, because universals are supposed to belong to the intelligible realm. In *The Problems of Philosophy* Bertrand Russell claims that one has direct acquaintance with universals, but that acquaintance is not meant to be sensory. It is only David M. Armstrong, whose view about universals comes close to Nyāya-Vaiśeika realism, who seems to have warmed up to the idea of perceiving universals.

ATTACKS FROM THE BUDDHIST NOMINALIST

Vaiśeika's first argument for the existence of universals depends on the generalization, "In every case, the sense of commonness or similarity felt by word-users must be spawned by an objective universal." Surely, this generalization is riddled with counterexamples. One has just seen earlier how people feel a sense of similarity across many cooks, yet the Nyāya-Vaiśeika realists refuse to admit cook-ness as a universal. There is no good reason to posit these weird entities, and every reason to eliminate them. So claimed the Sautrāntika-Yogacara Buddhists, "It does not come there (from another place), it was not there already, nor is it produced afresh, and it has no parts, and even when it is elsewhere it does not leave the previous locus. Amazing indeed is this volley of follies!" (PV 1.152–153).

With this oft-quoted remark Dharmakirti (1994) summarizes his battery of objections against the Nyāya-Vaiśeika theory of universals. How can a universal remain the same while existing in distinct things and places? Does it scatter itself into parts or does it live in its entirety in each instance? When the locus moves, does it move? If cow-ness is everywhere, why is it absent in a horse? If it is only where its instances are now, then how does it travel to a new place when a cow is born there? It does not pervade the place where an individual is located, for then the place itself would be its instance, yet how can it manage to inhere in the individual that occupies that place? If the particular instance is needed as a revealer of the ubiquitous universal, how come one cannot perceive the cow—its revealer—independently of noticing the universal cow-ness? A lamp reveals the preexistent pot in a room, but one does not need to see the pot first before one notices the lamp (PV 156).

Most of these difficulties, the realists retorted, suffer from a category-mistake. They assume that a universal is just another kind of super-particular. But a universal is not a spatiotemporal thing, and that is why multiple-location without divisibility is not a problem for it. In spite of such robust responses Buddhist antirealism about universals became more trenchant in the second millennium until such caustic were remarks directed at the Vaiśeika realists, "One can clearly see five fingers in one's own hand. One who commits oneself to a sixth general entity finger-hood, side by side with the five fingers, might as well postulate a horn on top of one's head."

APOHA SEMANTICS: THE BUDDHIST EXCLUSIONIST ACCOUNT OF CONCEPT-FORMATION

Buddhist logicians have an error-theory about universals and permanent substances. There are nothing but momentary quality-particulars in the world. But the human mind, afflicted by recurrence-wishes and language-generated conventional myths, has a tendency to cluster some of them together first in the fictional form of enduring substantial things and then further classify these "things" into types. This illusion of generality, of course, has some pragmatic value, because, except in contemplative experience, most of one's working cognitions of the world take the form of predictive or explanatory inferences on the basis of these apparently general features and their mutual connections.

When a particular cow (which is a fictional cow-shape superimposed on certain packets of quality-tokens) is seen to be other than all other animals, the original indeterminate (concept-free) perceptual content somehow causally triggers off this difference-obliterating tendency. The particular cow-image is made to "fit" this linguistic and imaginative exclusion from the complementary class of horses, rabbits, pillars, and such things. The specificity of the particular cow—its numerical detailed differences from other cows—is ignored; instead, this mere exclusion from noncows is foisted on to the perceptual content as a predicate. This exclusion masquerades as the universal cow-ness. To take Dharmakirti's (1994) example, the universal antipyretic-ness is a useful figment of imagination. In the external world there is no single shared intrinsic property of different medicinal plants all of which work as fever-reducers, except that they are other than those things that fail to relieve fever. Antipyretic-ness is an erroneous reification of this mere exclusion (*apoha*). This, in a nutshell, is the apoha nominalism of the Yogacara Buddhist logicians.

MILDER NOMINALISMS: RESEMBLANCE THEORIES

In the middle of this great battle between the realists and nominalists, the Jaina syncretists step in with the reconciliatory message that every object of knowledge has an alternatively more-than-one (*anekānta*) nature—particularity and generality are just two of them. One cannot doubt that things do objectively resemble each other. These resemblances are real relations. But both the things and their mutual resemblances are particulars. Nothing has the burden of being repeatable.

The Jainas reject the Buddhist version of nominalism, more or less on the same grounds as Kumārila Bhāṭṭa, the great Mīmāṃsaka, rejected it. Positive predicates, Kumārila had objected, cannot all be given a negative meaning. Since these exclusions are nonentities invented by erroneous imagination, to say that all one's words mean them is to turn all words into empty terms. Indeed, since all exclusions are equally hollow in content, distinguishing one from another would be like trying to distinguish one imaginary nonexistent from another. Only those denials make sense that have something positive to deny. Since all descriptions capture only negations, this theory, ironically, strips one's negations of all meaning, since there is nothing left to deny.

Jaina thinkers reject the exclusionism of the Buddhist but use the Buddhist criticisms to reject the Vaiśeika realism. In its place they propose this resemblance theory. Prabhācandra anticipates the Russellian objection that at least all these resemblance-relations would ultimately need a shared resemblance-universal. His answer to it is that, just as a Vaiśeika final individuator (*víseṣa*) does not need another distinguisher, one resemblance does not need a higher level resemblance or universal to explain why all those resemblances are similar. While accounting for the similarity between ground-level particulars, they also account for their own similarity to each other. Versions of this theory were adopted by followers of Rāmānuja (qualified monist Vedāta) as well as by Madhva (dualist Vedātin) logicians. Vyāsatīrtha of the latter school clarified how a single resemblance can reside, as it were, with one leg in the resembler and with another leg simultaneously in many other similar particulars.

The category of resemblance admitted by these philosophers is different from the resemblance admitted by Prābhākara Mīmāṃsakas, for the latter were realists about universals, while the Jainas and the Madhvas rejected, as logically redundant, both universals and inherence. The only difference between Prābhākara and Vaiśeika as regards universals centers on their conceptions of inherence.

CONTRASTS WITH WESTERN METAPHYSICS OF FORMS AND PROPERTIES

It should be clear by now that there is no core theory of universals shared by all the Indian philosophers. But one can discern five broad features that distinguish the Indian theories of universals from their Western counterparts:

(1) Even the strongest realist position of the Nyāya-Vaiśeika never took the form of the realism of Plato's theory of ideas. Indian realists about universals were equally realists about the perceptible particulars of the external world. Earthly particulars were never thought to be less real copies of thinkable universals, even by those who believed in universals.

(2) Even if one concedes that the Nyāya universals were closer to Aristotle's universal properties, which are immanent in the worldly particulars, Aristotle could never agree that universals are themselves directly perceived, which is the standard Nyāya position.

(3) The peculiar form that nominalism took in the Indian Buddhist theory of word-meanings as exclusions does not have any parallel in the West. One finds an interestingly different counterpart of the Jaina and Madhva theories of resemblance in Nelson Goodman, but exclusion-nominalism remains a unique contribution of Indian Buddhism.

(4) Most Western realist accounts of universals take colors and such qualities, as well as relations such as "being larger than," as paradigm examples of universal properties. In Indian realist thought the distinction between such particular qualities (*guṇa*) and universal properties (*jāti*) has been sacrosanct. It is only recently that the idea of particular qualities is gaining ground in Western analytic metaphysics of tropes. Even relations are not treated as genuine universals by any classical Indian realist.

(5) The controversial and complex theory of inherence as a single concrete connector joining not only universals and their instances but also particular qualities to substances and, most puzzlingly, wholes to their parts is totally foreign to the Western realists.

See also Atomic Theory in Indian Philosophy; Knowledge in Indian Philosophy.

Bibliography

IN SANSKRIT

Udayana. *Kiranavali.* Calcutta, India: Bibliotheca Indica, 1956.

Jayanta Bhāṭṭa. *Nyayamanjari.* Part 2, Chapter 5. Mysore, India: Oriental Research Institute, 1983.

Dharmakirti. *Pramana Varttikam,* edited by Swami Dwarikadas Shastri. Varanasi, India: Bauddhabharati, 1994.

Asoka Pandita. "Samanyadusanadikprasarita." In *Six Buddhist Nyāya Tracts,* edited by Haraprasad Shastri. Calcutta, India: The Asiatic Society, 1989.

Patañjali. *Vyakarana-Mahabhasyam.* Vols. 1–2, edited by Bala Shastri. Delhi, India: Pratibha Prakashan, 2001.

IN ENGLISH

Bhattacharya, Gopinath. "Some Aspects of the 'Universal.'" In *Essays in Analytical Philosophy.* Calcutta, India: Sanskrit Pustak Bhandar, 1989.

Chakrabarti, Kisor. "The Nyaya-Vaisesika Theory of Universals." *Journal of Indian Philosophy* 3 (1975): 363–382.

Dasgupta, Surendranath. *The Mahābhāsya of Patañjali: With Annotations,* edited by Sibajiban Bhattacharyya. New Delhi, India: Indian Council of Philosophical Research, 1991.

Dravid, Raja Ram. *The Problem of Universals in Indian Philosophy.* Delhi, India: Motilal Banarsidass, 1972.

Halbfass, Wilhelm. *On Being and What There Is: Classical Vaiśesika and the History of Indian Ontology.* Albany: SUNY Press, 1992.

Hayes, Richard P. *Dignāga on the Interpretation of Signs.* Dordrecht, Netherlands: D. Reidel, 1988.

Herzberger, Radhika. *Bhartrhari and the Buddhists: An Essay in the Development of Fifth and Sixth Century Indian Thought.* Dordrecht, Netherlands: D. Reidel, 1986.

Mukhopadhyaya, P. K. *Indian Realism.* Calcutta, India: Firma K. L., 1984.

Shastri, Dharmendra Nath. *Critique of Indian Realism.* Agra, India: Agra University, 1964.

Siderits, Mark. "More Things in Heaven and Earth." *Journal of Indian Philosophy* 10 (1982): 187–208.

Arindam Chakrabarti (2005)

UNIVERSALS

See *Universals, A Historical Survey*

UNIVERSALS, A HISTORICAL SURVEY

The word *universal,* used as a noun, has belonged to the vocabulary of English-writing philosophers since the sixteenth century, but the concept of universals, and the problems raised by it, has a far longer history. It goes back through the *universalia* of medieval philosophy to Aristotle's *τὰ καθόλου* and Plato's *εἴδη* and *ἰδέαι*. Indeed, Plato may be taken to be the father of this perennial topic of philosophy, for it is in his dialogues that we find the first arguments for universals and the first discussion of the difficulties they raise. Plato believed that the existence of universals was required not only ontologically, to explain the nature of the world that as sentient and reflective beings we experience, but also epistemologically, to explain the nature of our experience of it. He proposed a solution to his problem, but he also recognized the objections to his particular solution. Ever since, except for intervals of neglect, philosophers have been worrying about the nature and status of universals. No account has yet been propounded that has come near to receiving universal acceptance; this reflects not merely disagreement on the answers to be offered but also, and perhaps more importantly, disagreement on exactly what the questions are that we are, or should be, trying to answer.

That in some sense or other there are universals, and that in some sense or other they are abstract objects—that is, objects of thought rather than of sense perception—no philosopher would wish to dispute; the difficulties begin when we try to be more precise. They may be indicated (although not defined) by the abstract nouns that we use when we think about, for example, beauty, justice, courage, and goodness and, again, by the adjectives, verbs, adverbs, and prepositions that we use in talking of individual objects, to refer to their qualities and to the relations between them. In saying of two or more objects that each is a table, or square, or brown, or made of wood, we are saying that there is something common to the objects, which may be shared by many others and in virtue of which the objects may be classified into kinds. Not merely is such classification possible, for scientific and other purposes; it is unavoidable: All experience is of things as belonging to kinds, however vague and inarticulate the classification may be. Whatever we see (to take sight as an example) we see as *a something*—that is, as an object of a certain kind, as having certain qualities, and as standing in certain relations to other objects—and although every individual object is unique, in that it is numerically distinct from all others, its features are general, in that they are (or might be) repeated in other objects. Even if there were only one red object in the world, we would know what it would be like for there to be others, and we would be able to recognize another if we were to meet with it.

Generality is an essential feature of the objects of experience, recognition of generality is an essential feature of experience itself, and reflection of this generality is shown in the vocabulary of any language, all the words of which (with the exception of proper names) are general. Universals are, by tradition, contrasted with particulars, the general contrasted with the numerically unique, and differing theories of universals are differing accounts of what is involved in this generality and in our experience of it. The leading theories of universals—realism, conceptualism, nominalism, and resemblance theories—can best be explained by an examination of the doctrines of the main exponents. In following that sequence we shall be adhering approximately (although not precisely) to the chronological order in which the rival theories developed, and we shall be historically selective, in that we say almost nothing of the periods in the history of philosophy during which the controversies continued (for example, medieval philosophy) but of which a detailed knowledge is not necessary to a general understanding of the issues involved. The aim here is to present the different views that have been held, not to trace the fortunes of each view throughout the history of the subject.

REALISM

Realist and conceptualist theories of universals are, by long tradition, regarded as opposed because according to realism universals are nonmental, or mind-independent, whereas according to conceptualism they are mental, or mind-dependent. For the realist, universals exist in themselves and would exist even if there were no minds to be aware of them; if the world were exactly what it is now, with the one difference that it contained no minds at all, no consciousness of any kind, the existence of universals would be unaffected. They are public somethings with which we are somehow or other acquainted, and a mindless world would lack not universals but only the awareness of them: They would be available for discovery, even if there were nobody to discover them. For the conceptualist, on the other hand, universals are in the mind in a private sense, such that if there were no minds, there could be no universals, in the same way as there could be no thoughts or imagery or memories or dreams. As will be seen, whatever may be said for or against realism, pure conceptualism cannot be a satisfactory theory, for it is essentially incomplete; it says something about our consciousness of universals but nothing at all about any basis for this consciousness. Consequently, philosophers who have been conceptualists either have been so because they have been interested only in the epistemological question, in the conceptual structure of human thought and experience, or have combined their conceptualism with another theory designed to answer the ontological question—that is, the question what there is in the world corresponding to our mental concepts or ideas, what our concepts are concepts of. The antithesis between the two theories of realism and conceptualism is not, therefore, as clear-cut as it has often been presented to be.

The two main versions of realism are those of Plato and Aristotle. Plato's came first, and the difficulties it raised, some raised by Plato himself, others added by Aristotle, were what led Aristotle to devise his own quite different, but still realist, account. Plato and Aristotle were both realists in that they accorded to universals an existence independent of minds; where they differed was on the nature of the existence and the status that they believed universals to possess.

PLATO. Although it is possible to give, in some detail, a statement of what may be called Plato's theory of universals, and to give it full documentary support by quotations from his writings, we would be mistaken to regard it as a final and fully worked out theory. It was a theory toward which Plato can be seen working his way throughout his philosophical career, not so much by independent arguments as by intertwining strands of thought, all leading in the same general direction. There were a number of facts about the world and our experience of it by which he was impressed and puzzled. His theory evolved as an explanation of them, but he was never satisfied that he had solved his problem. He was his own first critic, and a penetrating one, and to the end of his life he was torn, as is brought out in his dialogue *Parmenides,* between the conviction that his theory was fundamentally correct and the recognition that it posed problems that he found himself unable to solve. It should not be thought, therefore, that he ever produced a final account that he was prepared to rest content with and that needed an Aristotle to find fault with it.

Plato's interest in questions about universals was first aroused by Socrates, by whom he was greatly influenced, whom he introduced as one of the speakers in all his dialogues (with the single exception of *The Laws*), and who in all but the later dialogues appears as the central character actually directing the conversation. Unfortunately, we are presented with difficulties of interpretation, the details of which we shall not enter into here, because our knowledge of Socrates is derived entirely from descriptions given by other writers, one of whom was Plato. Hence arises the problem of deciding which of the doctrines ascribed to "Socrates" in the Platonic dialogues are those of the actual Socrates and which of them are extensions or even entirely new doctrines developed by Plato himself. In general, it is accepted that the "Socrates" of the early dialogues does represent the views, and even more the methods of philosophical inquiry, of Socrates himself but that as time went on Plato more and more used him as the spokesman of Plato's own views, the transitional stage being marked by such dialogues as *Phaedo* and the *Republic.* We may conclude that while Socrates did not explicitly hold a theory of universals (and we have Aristotle's word for it, in *Metaphysics* 1078b, that Socrates did not hold the view Plato put forward), his philosophical questions were such that Plato held they could not be answered except by such a theory; in other words, Plato, in putting a theory of universals into Socrates' mouth, was not attributing it to Socrates as what he had actually expounded but was maintaining it as the logical consequence of Socrates' own arguments: Socrates stopped short of propounding such a theory himself but was logically committed to it.

Socrates' main interest was in the human virtues, and his aim was to secure a satisfactory definition of the virtue under discussion. His questions were all of the form "What is *X*?," where "*X*" stood for beauty, courage, piety, justice, and so on, in one case (*Meno*) even virtue itself. The answers that he received he rejected because they were too narrow or too wide, but more commonly because instead of giving the essential definition of the virtue they gave instances of it or mentioned kinds of it. Thus, it was no answer to the question "What is piety?" to reply that a man is acting piously if he prosecutes a murderer; again, it was no answer to the question "What is virtue?" to reply that the virtue of a man consists in managing a city's affairs capably, that a woman's virtue consists in managing her domestic affairs capably, that there are different virtues for an old man and a young man, for a free man and a slave, and so on. Granted that there are many virtues, what is wanted is the one and the same form that they all have and by which they are virtues. The search, then, is for the single and essential form common to all things of the same kind, by virtue of which they are things of the same kind.

The "things" about which Socrates in fact asked his questions were limited because his philosophical interest was limited, but even he did not confine himself to human conduct. He acknowledged, for instance, that health or size or strength must be the same in all its instances, with the consequence that we answer the question "What is health?" only when we have given the essence of health—that is, what is common and peculiar to all instances of health. Plato took this further and maintained (although not without hesitation) that there must be an essence common to all things of a given kind, whatever that kind was. It would apply not only to abstract virtues, such as justice and courage, but also to natural objects, such as trees, and to artifacts, such as tables. An object would not be a table unless it had the same essence (of tablehood) as all other tables; despite the different shapes and sizes that individual tables may possess, there must be a single form or essence, common to them all, which constitutes their being tables and distinguishes them from other objects, such as chairs or beds. Plato summarized his position in the statement "We are in the habit of postulating one single form for each class of particulars to which we give the same name" (*Republic* 596A). And he held it to be true not only of objects designated by nouns (such as "bed" and "table") but also of attributes or qualities indicated by predicates (such as "beautiful" and "greater than"). As there must be a form or essence of bedhood somehow common to all beds, so there must be a form or essence of beauty (or the beautiful) common to all things that are beautiful.

So far Plato had done nothing more than take over the Socratic contrast between the single general, essential form common to a class of particulars and the particulars themselves and extend it more widely than Socrates had done: He found the same contrast not only in the realms of ethics, aesthetics, and mathematics but also in the everyday world of sense experience. But he went on to ask the questions that Socrates had never asked, namely what are we to say about the relationship between the universal form and its particular manifestations, and what are we to say about the nature and existence of the universal itself? His answer was to develop the theory known as the theory of Forms, according to which each universal is a single substance or Form, existing timelessly and independently of any of its particular manifestations and apprehended not by sense but by intellect. His arguments can be distinguished, although not entirely separated, into two general kinds, metaphysical or ontological and epistemological. If knowledge is to be possible at all (and Plato did not doubt either that it was possible or that in certain spheres it was actual), it must be of what is stable and unchanging.

However, the familiar world of ordinary experience does not meet this requirement, for the one constant and striking feature of all objects (and their qualities) in this world is that they are subject to change and decay: Both natural objects and artifacts come, or are brought, into being, undergo changes throughout their existence, and sooner or later die or disintegrate and disappear. This is the Heraclitean doctrine of flux, which Plato accepted and which he believed required as its counterpart a nonsensible realm of unchanging stability, without which there could be no knowledge. What can be known must be real, unitary, and unchanging: These are the Forms. Particulars are only semireal, real to the extent that in some way or other, or to some degree or other, they manifest the Forms, unreal to the extent that being material, they lack the perfection of pure Forms and are subject to the laws of material change and decay. Thus, Forms are required, to confer on particulars such reality as they do have, to constitute their being what they are and of what kinds they are. A bed is a bed rather than a table because it somehow manifests the Form Bed. A Form is required not only to explain a particular object's being what it is but also to cause its being what it is; the doctrine is thus not merely a logical but a metaphysical doctrine. Plato emphasized this in the analogy of the sun (*Republic* VI), where he compared the chief Form of all, the Form of the Good, with the sun, which as the light-giving and life-giving agent in the physical world is the prime material cause of natural life as well as of our awareness, through our senses, of the material world.

Another consideration that led Plato to suppose the Forms as transcendent substances was the presence of what he thought to be contradictions in the material world: What is real cannot contain contradictions; therefore the material world cannot be more than an appearance of reality. That a single object should be both beautiful (in one respect) and ugly (in another), or large (in comparison with a second object) and at the same time small (in comparison with a third), was enough, in his view, to show that the Forms were more than immanent. Therefore, not only must there be Forms in order to cause particulars to be what they are, but the Forms must be separate from the particulars because they must be free of the imperfection and defectiveness with which particulars are inevitably infected. The Forms are thus not only independent substances but perfect and ideal patterns, which particulars must fall short of.

This comes out especially in the consideration of mathematical (primarily geometrical) and value concepts, namely those of ethics and aesthetics. For a line to be straight or a figure to be circular, there must be the Forms of Straightness and Circularity. But it is well known that no actual line is ever perfectly straight and no figure is ever perfectly circular; however carefully and precisely drawn, it possesses some curves or kinks that more minute scrutiny could disclose. And what we are thinking about when we study or discuss a geometrical theorem is not the diagram of the circle drawn, freehand or mechanically, on the blackboard but the circle represented by the diagram. We thus have both the diagram of the circle, adequate as a diagram but imperfect as a circle, and the perfect Form of Circularity of which it is a diagram. While this gives rise to the question, which cannot be pursued here, whether Plato distinguished between the Form of Circularity (of which there could not be more than one) and a Perfect Circle (of which, if there could be one, there could be more than one—as required by, for example, a theorem involving two intersecting circles), there is no doubt that he did think a Form not only was the perfect pattern, of which a particular was an imperfect manifestation, but also was what the particular would be if, *per impossibile,* it could be perfect. Thus, to take an aesthetic example, Beauty (or the Beautiful) not only is the pattern that beautiful particulars inadequately manifest but also is itself perfectly beautiful; it is a substance possessing in perfection the essence that its derivative particulars possess only partially or in some degree. As Plato came to realize later (*Parmenides* 131ff.), and as

Aristotle repeated, if a Form stands to its particulars as "one over many," and if the Form is an ideal pattern of which the particulars are imperfect copies, then an infinite regress argument (known as the third-man argument) is generated: For the Form to be predicable of itself as well as of its particulars, it must share a character with them; but then there will be a Form of this character; this second Form will be predicable of itself, requiring a third Form of it, a fourth, and so on ad infinitum.

As was indicated above by the geometrical example, Plato believed that his theory of Forms accounted for the possibility of knowledge of universal truths, which was the only kind of knowledge strictly meriting the name. When, by working out or following the proof, we learn that a square constructed on the diagonal of a given square has an area equal to double the area of the given square, we have learned a truth that is necessary and universal. It is not something that happens, as a matter of fact, to be true of the squares in our diagram but might turn out not to be true of some other squares; that is, it is not an empirical generalization that subsequent experience might show to be false as a generalization. We have a piece of a priori knowledge, which no possible experience could affect, namely that if a square has a given area, and if a second square has its sides equal in length to a diagonal of the original square, then the area of the second square must be double the area of the first. Our knowledge is not knowledge of our diagram squares, or any others that we care to draw, for, as we have seen, they are not in fact squares. But it is knowledge, and the only thing, therefore, that it can be knowledge of is the Form Square (or the Square).

What defeated Plato in any attempt to give a complete account of his theory was the problem of describing the relation of Forms to particulars. In different places he spoke of the Forms "being in" their particulars, of particulars "participating in" their forms, and of particulars "copying" their forms. Literal interpretation of any of these phrases gives rise to logical difficulties, and to take them metaphorically is to leave the statement of the theory imprecise and the problem unanswered. In Plato's final writings (*Epistle* VII) on the subject there are signs that he was inclined to think that the fault lay with the inadequacy of language to describe what he wanted to describe, but the trouble is deeper than mere paucity of vocabulary. We can form some kind of a picture of his two worlds if we think of the world of Forms as actually existing somewhere, populated by objects like the Standard Meter and the Standard Pound, and we can then think of actual particulars as being imperfect copies of the originals. But that picture, taken literally, is false, because Plato's Forms do not exist in a place or at a time. The mystery of their "existence" becomes impenetrable when we are asked to use the word *exist* in a way that we are incapable of conceiving. In his theory of Forms, with the Forms not immanent but transcendent, the problem of their relation to particulars becomes not almost impossibly difficult to solve but in principle insoluble.

ARISTOTLE. Aristotle, Plato's pupil and successor, is often regarded as the careful scientific-minded thinker, anxious to restrain philosophy within the range of the observable and to avoid the imaginative speculations of Plato. While this picture is in general correct and in particular fits Aristotle's criticisms of Plato's theory of Forms regarded as universals, his own theory of a Form as the object of a definition that describes a thing's essential nature becomes in the end as obscure as Plato's. His criticism that Plato's theory does nothing to provide a scientific explanation of the nature of things applies equally forcibly to his own theory of essences, and natural science, as we know it, began to progress only when, many centuries later, it liberated itself from this aspect of Aristotelianism.

But Aristotle's theory of universals, which is nowhere fully elaborated and has to be pieced together from different passages, is important, both because it offered an alternative to Plato's and because it is more obviously attractive to common sense. His objections to Plato are numerous and detailed but are not all of equal weight. Basically, apart from the infinite regress argument, which he took over from Plato, they come to two: First, that Plato, by making the Forms perfect, separate substances, introduced an unnecessary and unhelpful duplication, and second, that Plato confused the categories of substance and property. Nothing is accounted for by making the Forms perfect patterns of particulars. To attempt to explain the nature of one set of entities by postulating a second and better set does not solve a problem but merely repeats it at a different level: Whatever the question was that needed to be answered about particulars, it will need to be answered again about the Forms; mere multiplication answers nothing. Second, Plato was guilty of a logical mistake in treating a Form both as an individual substance (which the "separation" thesis requires) and as a property (which it would have to be to be a universal). Substances are individuals and have properties, but they cannot be properties, yet Plato's theory treats them as both.

For Aristotle the only true substances were single individual objects, such as Socrates or this table. (It is true that Aristotle introduced a difficulty by treating genus and species also as substances, for they are what it is the aim of science to know, but they are secondary substances, and the knowledge we may gain of them is knowledge about primary substances—that is, the individual objects met with in experience.) Universals, therefore, are not substances existing independently of particulars. They exist only as common elements in particulars: The universal *X* is whatever is common to, or shared by, all *x*'s; it is what is predicated of the individual. Individual objects are to be classified into kinds according as they share the same property, and the kinds are to be subdivided into genus and species by the differences between more determinate properties. Thus, all colored objects belong to the genus "color" because they all alike have the property of being colored, whereas red objects and green objects belong to different species of the genus, because the first have the property of being colored red and the second have the property of being colored green. One of the primary tasks of natural science is to divide and classify natural objects by genus and species into the real kinds to which, by nature, they belong.

Aristotle's theory is more economical than Plato's, requiring only one world of being instead of two, the contrast between the two theories being indicated by the labels that they later acquired in medieval scholastic philosophy: Plato's was a theory of *universalia ante rem* (universals independent of particulars), and Aristotle's of *universalia in rebus* (universals in things). And with the possible exception of ideal concepts, such as those of geometry, which Plato had argued had no actual instances, Aristotle's account seems better to fit a fact, or what we take to be a fact, of human experience, namely that a particular really is an instance of its universal. Not only should we say that we get our idea of red, for example, from seeing red objects, such as fire engines or ripe tomatoes, but we should also say (except for philosophical theories of perception) that the object really was red, not that (as with Plato) the tomato tried unsuccessfully to be red but that (with Aristotle) it actually was red. The properties that an object has, and that together constitute its nature, its being an object of that kind, whatever that kind may be (for example, whether it is a horse or a table), are really in the object, in some sense of "in." If objects do not and cannot possess any of the characteristics that according to experience and the scrutiny of observation they appear to have, then scientific knowledge becomes either altogether impossible or unrelated to the natural world. Aristotle's view avoids the Platonic paradox that nothing in the observable world can ever be what it seems to be.

The contrast between the two views comes out again in their accounts of how we apprehend universals. They are agreed both that awareness of universals is implicit in ordinary sense experience (for it is this awareness that conditions our experience as being what it is) and that we are aware of universals not by sense itself but by intellect. Plato could not say that we become aware of them by abstraction from particular instances, because they have separate existence and never are more than defectively instantiated: If our concept of *X* were only what we could abstract from imperfect instances, we never could apprehend *X* itself. Therefore there must be some other mode of apprehension, which Plato called ἀνάμνησις (usually translated as "recollection" but less misleadingly interpreted in this context as "recovery"). The human soul has prenatal knowledge of universals and of their mutual relations, and postnatal experience of the ordinary world serves, or may serve, to revive this knowledge in suitable circumstances. Thus, experience does not directly provide us with new apprehensions (of universals) or with new knowledge of necessary truths (connections between universals) but acts as a stimulus to remind us of what we already know but have hitherto in this life forgotten. Plato's argument here, if it is to be regarded as an argument, is a transcendental one (in Immanuel Kant's sense of the word): Our knowledge is a priori, that is, of such a kind that we cannot get it from experience, although we do get it in experience; therefore it must be innate, that is, knowledge of what we originally knew prior to any experience. As a transcendental argument it could be effective only if it could be shown that there was no other possible way of accounting for our apprehension of universals and our knowledge of universal truths. And Aristotle thought that there was another, less fanciful and less speculative way, derived from actual experiences and memories of previous experiences.

Apprehension of a universal, or formation of a concept, is not a sudden once-and-for-all business, given in a single experience, but a gradual process. Sense perception gives rise to memory, and memory conditions subsequent perceptions, so that they are not merely perceptions but recognitions of what is in some degree or other familiar from previous perceptions. Awareness of characteristics thus becomes clearer and more explicit with the growth and variety of experience. By a process of induction, namely intuitive induction, the first primitive awareness of a universal (necessary to any perception) becomes stabilized in the mind, leading ultimately to a clear and articulate concept of it. Thus, for Aristotle, as for Plato, grasp of universals is by the intellect, but it is by the intellect gradually working on what it is at first dimly and indeterminately conscious of in the data of sense perception. A simple example from arithmetic will illustrate his point. As children we learn to count. We get the idea of 2 from being faced with pairs of objects, and we learn that 2 + 2 = 4 from coming to "see," for instance, that two apples plus two other apples are equal in number to four other apples. But we also come, sooner or later, to "see" that the number 2 characterizes any pair of objects, and that 2 + 2 = 4 is a necessary truth, applicable to any two pairs compared with a quartet. We have the power, which becomes actualized in experience, of intuiting clearly the universal in the particular and of intuiting the necessary in the matter of fact; this, for Aristotle, is the beginning of scientific knowledge.

AUGUSTINE. Medieval philosophy was not primarily interested in questions about the nature of human knowledge. But its concern with metaphysics, especially in those aspects that carried theological implications, led to a continuation of the dispute between the two versions of realism and later to a nominalist rejection of both. Platonic realism was championed by St. Augustine, for whom divine illumination performed much the same function as Plato's Form of the Good, rendering intelligible by its light the necessity of eternal truths that the human intellect could grasp. Man is above the beasts, not only because he can acquire, by the mind alone, knowledge of eternal truths, but also because even in sensation he judges of material objects by incorporeal standards: In judging a physical object to be beautiful he implies the objective existence of Beauty, both as a universal and as a standard. Again, the intelligible structure of the temporal world, which the reason of man (but not the senses of the beasts) can grasp, is itself nontemporal; for example, the concepts and truths of mathematics, although empirically applicable, are timeless necessities. Ideas as objective essences are exemplars contained "in the divine intelligence." Thus, Plato's theory of Forms enters theology, and the question arises whether Augustine in his theory of ideas supposed that men were in direct contact with the mind of God. It is fairly clear that he did not but much less clear how he could avoid it.

THOMAS AQUINAS. The leading exponent of Aristotelian realism was Thomas Aquinas, who, although professing the greatest reverence for Augustine, departed widely from Augustine's views. Thomas's metaphysics is, like Aristotle's, teleological, maintaining that the nature of things and events is to be explained in terms of the ends that they serve, and he extended Aristotle's contrasts between potentiality and act, between form and matter, and between essence and existence. Essences are universals, which have no being apart from existence but which are intelligible without the supposition of existence. The existence of things does not follow from their essence—otherwise existence could not be, as it clearly is, contingent. Universals are apprehended directly by the mind, but only in the material things the nature of which they comprise; they are not to be found in themselves, although by the processes of abstraction and comparison the mind can approximate to thinking of them in themselves. The chief follower in the Thomist tradition was John Duns Scotus, who nevertheless rejected much in Thomas, such as the distinction between essence and existence, and followed Avicenna in differentiating between the "thisness" of an individual object (which distinguishes it from other objects of the same kind) and the nature of an individual object (which distinguishes it from objects of other kinds).

CRITICISM OF REALISM. Although each of the two versions of realism received vigorous support in the long disputes of medieval philosophy, and although Augustinianism for a time prevailed, Aristotle's version has had the longer-lasting influence, especially on philosophers brought up in the British tradition of empiricism. That things do have common characters and that the characters are objectively real seems hardly deniable, and this is part of what Aristotle's theory asserts. But although it is more hardheaded than Plato's, it does raise its own difficulties, two of which may be mentioned. First, how much does it in fact explain of what it purports to explain? We do not account for two tables' being tables better by saying that they have a single characteristic (or set of characteristics) in common than by saying that they are both imitations of a single Form. And if what is to be accounted for is rather our ground for saying that they are tables, which is a question not about their being tables but about our justification for believing or claiming to know that they are, then admittedly we are perceptually aware of the characteristics of each, and of their similarity. But is saying that some (or all) of the characteristics of the one table are like (even exactly like) the characteristics of the other what the Aristotelian means to do when he maintains that there is a universal common to them (and any other tables)? This may be doubted, for the Aristotelian asserts that a single universal is present in each of the objects, or that each is an instance of it, all the objects of a given kind sharing in the universal of that kind.

But this is metaphorical talk, and to explain by metaphor is not to explain at all. As a descriptive statement "These two tables are the same shape" is unobjectionable; as an explanatory statement it is less obviously illuminating. Second, Aristotle's supposition that objects belong to real kinds, which are there for us to discover, ignores the fact that distinctions between kinds or classes are not found but made by us, as was later emphasized by John Locke. This difficulty is not fatal to the Aristotelian theory, which could accommodate it by emphasizing different levels of determinacy in a universal or class characteristic, but it leads to the question, pursued by Ludwig Wittgenstein in the twentieth century, whether it is necessary that any single characteristic at all be common to all members of a single class. If it is not necessary, our recognition of objects as belonging to a certain class does not have to depend on the apprehension of a universal shared by all its members, for it may be that nothing, even in the metaphorical sense, is shared. Aristotle's theory, which prima facie has the merits of being simple and realistic, is perhaps both too simple and not realistic enough.

CONCEPTUALISM

As has already been indicated, conceptualism should not be regarded strictly as a rival theory to realism, even if some of its exponents have mistakenly so regarded it. Starting from an extreme Aristotelian position, that everything which exists is particular, conceptualism concentrates on the fact that generality is an essential feature of both experience and language, and it seeks to answer the question how mental concepts are formed, how they can be general if the data of experience from which they are formed are particular, and how words are general in their significance. Nominalism carries the process further by maintaining that only words are general. Both theories, even if they answered their own question satisfactorily, would have to face the question what basis in reality there is for the generalization inherent in experience, thought, and language. Some versions ignore this question altogether; others answer it in terms of the similarities and differences to be found between particulars. The essential difference between the theories of conceptualism and nominalism is that while both profess to answer a question about language—how words are general, or how words have meaning—nominalism does it more economically, without interposing concepts between words and what words stand for. The conceptualist says that a word is general or meaningful because in the mind there is a corresponding general concept; he then has to explain what a general concept is. The nominalist thinks that the meaningfulness of a word can be accounted for without postulating a separate mental entity called a concept.

Conceptualism is primarily associated with the three classical British empiricists, Locke, George Berkeley, and David Hume, all of whom propounded views about what, in the terminology of the time, were called general ideas. They were all empiricists in that they agreed that all ideas, or the elements that ideas are composed of, come from, and can come only from, experience: The mind can work on what is given to it by sense experience but can neither have ideas prior to any experience (a denial of the doctrine of innate ideas and, by implication, of Plato's suggestion of prenatal acquaintance with the Forms) nor create ideas de novo. Thus, the essence of empiricism is the Epicurean doctrine, given fresh impetus in the seventeenth century by Pierre Gassendi, that *nihil est in intellectu nisi prius fuerit in sensu* ("Nothing is in the mind which is not first in the senses").

LOCKE. John Locke was first in the field, with his *Essay on Human Understanding* (1690), a long, rambling, and discursive work composed and revised over many years. Unfortunately, the passages in the *Essay* in which he discussed general ideas, or, as he more commonly and perhaps misleadingly called them, "abstract ideas," are neither so clearly thought out and expressed nor perhaps even so consistent as to save him from varying interpretations. The initial difficulty concerns the word *idea* itself, which is the key word of his philosophy, but which he neither defined nor used so as to escape ambiguity. Sometimes when he spoke of ideas in the mind he appears to have meant mental images such as occur in remembering, imagining, and dreaming; in this view thinking is done in images, which are particular in their occurrence and existence but somehow become general in their use. At other times he meant, or at least has been taken to have meant, that abstract ideas are mental entities different from images. At still other times he showed signs of using the word *idea* not as the name for any mental occurrence at all but as shorthand for the meaning of a word. Thus, the idea of red would be not an image of something red but what we mean by the word *red* or what we think an object to be when we think it is red; to have the idea of red is to be able to use the word *red* correctly and to be able to discriminate correctly between those objects that are red and those that are not. Attention here will be paid mainly to the first view, of ideas as images, for it is a conceptualist view; so would be the second, that general ideas are mental occurrences different from images, but this appears to be a view that Berkeley fathered on Locke rather than one Locke actually held.

According to Locke we form general ideas by a process of abstraction from particular ideas. In two different places he gave what appear to be two different accounts of abstraction. In the *Essay on Human Understanding* (Book III, Ch. 3) he said that a general idea—for example, of man—is formed by leaving out of the particular ideas of various individual men all features that are not common to them all and retaining only what is common to them all. The general idea of animal is arrived at by still further leaving out, "retaining only a body, with life, sense and spontaneous motion, comprehended under the name 'animal.'" If this passage were taken in isolation, regardless of what else Locke said on the matter, there would be something to be said for the Berkeleian interpretation. For Locke appears to have been saying that we start with a number of particular images, each, for example, of a different individual man of our acquaintance, and end with something that is still an image but is now a ghostly general image, characterized not by any of the features that are peculiar to any of the individual men but only by all those that all men share. It was not difficult for Berkeley to ridicule as logically absurd the suggestion of a mental image, all the features of which are (as, in this view, they would be) determinables. In his polemic Berkeley did not consider the possibility that Locke might have been getting at something different, namely that mental images may be indeterminate, so that the logical laws of contradiction and excluded middle do not apply to them; for instance, a mental image of a cloudless night sky is an image of a number of stars but of no precise number.

Locke's other account of abstraction, however, which occurs earlier in the *Essay,* seems to be the one he seriously intended. For he came back to it again later in the work than the passage just discussed, and it may even be that in that passage he thought he was still giving the same view as before. In Book II (Ch. 11, Sec. 9) he thus described abstraction:

> The mind makes the particular ideas, received from particular objects, to become general; which is done by considering them as they are in the mind such appearances—separate from all other existences, and the circumstances of real existence.... This is called *abstraction,* whereby ideas taken from particular things become general representatives of all of the same kind.... Thus, the same colour being observed today in chalk or snow, which the mind yesterday received from milk, it considers that appearance alone, makes it a representative of all of that kind; and having given it the name "whiteness," it by that sound signifies the same quality wheresoever to be imagined or met with; and thus universals, whether ideas or terms are made.

It should be noted, from the last phrase, that Locke was using the word *universal* in the subjective conceptualist way, to indicate a concept or idea, not that of which it is the idea. If there is a problem of objective universals raised by a number of things being "all of the same kind" or "the same quality wheresoever met with," Locke showed no sign here of being troubled by it. He was interested only in the question how we form the general ideas that undoubtedly we do have (for without them thought, language, and even experience as we know it would be impossible) when every idea or image that occurs in our consciousness is a particular occurrent. I cannot form an image of whiteness or of white, only of a white something, such as a piece of white chalk or a white snowball. The general idea is not a different idea from the particular idea, somehow extracted from it. It is the particular idea regarded in a special way. First, the mind attends only to a certain aspect of the idea and ignores the rest; second, it treats the idea in that aspect as representative of everything that is similar in that aspect. If *abstraction* is perhaps not the most happily chosen term here, at least Locke's meaning is clear, and he repeated it several times later. A general idea is not one that has a different kind of existence from particulars; all ideas, he said, are particular in their existence. A general idea is a particular idea, used in respect to some aspect as representative of a class, namely the class of things determined by the aspect attended to; in thinking or talking about whiteness the ideas of the piece of white chalk, the snowball, and the glass of milk will all do equally well.

Just how far Locke regarded himself as committed to ideas as images and how far he would have regarded his account as being philosophical rather than psychological (if he could have been induced to accept the distinction) is hard to say. But it is fairly clear that his account is not philosophically satisfactory. He showed himself to be well aware that the real problem is one concerning the applicability and use of general words or terms. But as must have been obvious to him, significant use of words in speech or writing is not in fact paralleled by a corresponding string of introspectable images. Therefore, at best, his claim that a general word is meaningful because it stands for a general idea would have to involve "stand for" in a dispositional sense; that is, a word is meaningful if a corresponding idea can be found for it. Even then he would be open to the nominalist criticism that nothing is explained simply by duplicating a general word with a general idea. Furthermore, he stressed that almost all thought is verbal: The use of nonverbal imagery in thinking is restricted to a very narrow and primitive level. And, in fact, in the latter part of the *Essay* he showed signs of interpreting ideas not as pictures corresponding to words but as meanings of words, particularly when he was discussing modes—that is, concepts not necessarily used with existential reference. To have an idea, for example, of murder or of gratitude is to understand and use the words *murder* and *gratitude* in a certain way, and to have a correct idea is to understand and use the words in the same way others do. The question whether *A* has shown gratitude in his conduct to *B* is a question not only what *A*'s conduct has been but also whether it sufficiently fits the accepted sense of *gratitude.*

Finally, Locke extended this to all general ideas and rejected the Aristotelian thesis that apprehending universals is apprehending real kinds, or real principles of classification. In maintaining this he was making a move toward a kind of nominalism, for he was emphasizing the fact that concepts, other than those determined by technical or arbitrary definition, are open-ended. We do not find objects and their features divided by nature or God into real and objectively delimited classes; we observe objects and their features, but the distinction between one class and another is something we ourselves make by criteria of convenience and utility. Similarities and differences are there for us to observe; whether the similarities are sufficiently close so that we can place the objects in the same or in different classes is for us to decide. A modern example would be the question whether a machine can think, or whether a computer can remember. Such a question, Locke would insist, is to be answered only by seeing what operations the machine performs and then deciding whether they are sufficiently close to what we mean by *thinking* or *remembering* when we talk of our own activities to make it reasonable, rather than misleading, to describe them in these terms.

A consequence of this kind of conceptualism will be that concepts are not permanently fixed, as on a simple realist theory they would be; a concept is liable to development and change, as fresh experience or changes of view show the need or utility of it. For example, a central question of twentieth- and twenty-first-century sociology, which concerns not only moral outlooks but also legal decisions and the development of law and penal policy, is the question under what conditions a man is to be held not responsible for his physical actions. But the answer to the question is not to be reached simply by determining whether the physical, psychological, and medical facts of a particular case place it inside or outside the accepted scope of responsibility; it also leads to examining the notion of responsibility itself, which in the slow process of time undergoes modification. Experience being ineluctably conceptual, not only are concepts derived from experience, but concepts shape experience itself, as indeed Aristotle had hinted. If there were nothing else valuable in conceptualism, it would be of importance as a corrective to the naïveté of extreme realism, which suggests that all the material of human experience falls into a scheme of pigeonholes or a fixed mold and that the task of inquiry is simply to find out what the scheme or mold is.

BERKELEY. George Berkeley, Locke's immediate successor and fiercest critic, devoted the whole introduction of his main philosophical work, *The Principles of Human Knowledge* (1710), to a violent attack on Locke's theory of abstract ideas, for reasons perhaps not primarily concerned with universals at all. However, it is extremely doubtful whether he had, in fact, either studied Locke carefully enough or interpreted him correctly. Berkeley's own theory of general ideas as particular ideas that become "general by being made to represent or stand for all other particular ideas of the same sort" is expressed in a way that might be a verbatim quotation from Locke himself (cf. Locke, *Essay,* Book III, Ch. 3, Sec. 13: "Ideas are general when they are set up as representatives of many particular things.… [They] are all of them particular in their existence … their general nature being nothing but the capacity they are put into, by the understanding, of signifying or representing many particulars"). And Hume's enthusiastic comment that Berkeley's view of general ideas as particular ideas used generally is "one of the greatest and most valuable discoveries that has been made of late years in the republic of letters" does Hume little credit; his examination of Locke was clearly no more thorough than Berkeley's had been.

If Berkeley had done nothing but propound his account of general ideas, his contribution would have been nil. But, in fact, he did much more. Aware that a central strand in the supposed problem of universals was the fact of language and appreciating the question how sounds made by the human larynx or marks made on paper could be used to convey a meaning (this too had been stressed by Locke), he protested against the simple view of *unum nomen unum nominatum,* that every time the same word is used it is accompanied in the mind by the same idea. First, this is empirically false, as anybody could find out by noticing the many different ideas (images) he might have on the different occasions he used the word; for example, *red* might be accompanied sometimes by an image of a red dress, sometimes by an image of a red apple, a red flower, and so on, which might in any case all be different shades of red. Furthermore, it is not even true that every time a man uses a word that can be accompanied by an image, it is accompanied by one. The actual occurrence of an image, if not necessary, could not help to explain the meaningfulness of a word. Sometimes Berkeley wrote as if an image were necessary in a dispositional sense; a word is significant if a suitable image can be had or produced to correspond to it. Thus, he compared a use of language—for instance, in conversation—to the use of algebraic symbols in a calculation: We can represent a given quantity by the symbol *x*, and we carry out the calculation without all the time thinking of the quantity represented by *x*; what matters is that we can, at any time we want to, replace *x* by the quantity. Similarly, words for the most part, as actually employed, function as cashable counters.

But Berkeley went on to emancipate himself even from this tenuous servitude to ideas as images. He hinted at it when he said that the important thing is the definition of a word, not the occurrence or recurrence of an idea: "It is one thing for to keep a name constantly to the same definition, and another to make it stand every where for the same idea: The one is necessary, the other useless and impracticable." But later he went even further and suggested what can be described as an operational theory of meaning. This is nowhere fully developed, chiefly because he abandoned serious philosophical inquiry while still a young man, but unmistakable indications of it persist throughout his writings.

In the *Principles* they appear in two ways: (*a*) the reminder of the diversity of function of language; and (*b*) the doctrine of "notions." The tendency among philosophers to try to explain the significance of words in terms of corresponding ideas was due to a simple and entirely false view of language, namely that its sole function was informing, or "the communication of ideas"; this made it easier to think of ideas as pictures translated into words by the speaker and retranslated into pictures by the hearer. (The modern television analogy of visual pictures translated into radio signals by the transmitter and retranslated into visual pictures by the receiving set would not be entirely inapt.) But as Berkeley rightly emphasized, to inform is not the function of language, only one of its functions. It has others, "the raising of some passion, the exciting to or deterring from an action, the putting the mind in some particular disposition"—to which we could add still others, such as asking questions, praying, vowing, swearing, making promises, declaring intentions, and expressing wishes or fears.

It is not entirely clear exactly what Berkeley intended the doctrine of "notions" to be. He acknowledged that his own principles did not allow him to say that we have (or can have) ideas of everything we may significantly talk of, because they did not allow him to say that we have ideas of mind or spirit (ideas being passive and mind or spirit being active); yet a man who uses the words *mind* and *spirit* (to which Berkeley added all words denoting relations) is not uttering meaningless gibberish. Therefore, it must be true of at least some words that we "know or understand what is meant" by them although we can have no corresponding ideas. In these cases we have notions. Notions, as they appear in the *Principles,* do not solve any problem (if one exists) regarding how words that cannot be paralleled by ideas can be significant—they merely occur as a label for the fact that there are such words. They are not the answer but appear to be Berkeley's name for the question. If by "having a notion of *x*" he meant "knowing or understanding the meaning of the word *x*, although not being able to have an idea of *x*," then the question how one can know or understand the meaning of an idealess word is not answered by saying that he has a notion, and there is no reason to think that Berkeley deluded himself into supposing that his doctrine of notions actually gave an answer to anything. The *Principles* takes the matter no further than the negative conclusion not only that a word need not be accompanied by an idea but also that some words cannot be. This is the beginning of an admission that the intelligibility of language neither requires nor is illuminated by suppositions about mental imagery.

In a much later work, *Alciphron* (1732), Berkeley returned to the topic and showed how (with the examples of force from physics and grace from theology) although frontal questions such as "What is force?" and "What is grace?" could produce no answer, yet these were genuine concepts, because it was true that the use of them (or of the words *force* and *grace*) could lead to fruitful results. Or again, "the algebraic mark, which denotes the root of a negative square, hath its use in logistic operations, although it be impossible to form an idea of any such quantity." In allowing that a concept could be fertile even though it could not be cashed, Berkeley was at once breaching the walls of strict empiricism and anticipating the theory construction of modern science, particularly of modern physics.

HUME. Immediately after Berkeley came David Hume, the third of the great British empiricists and the one who has had the most lasting influence on subsequent developments in the philosophy of that school. He devoted an early section of his *Treatise of Human Nature* (1739) to the subject of abstract ideas (Book I, Part i, Sec. 7), professing to accept Berkeley's doctrine of general ideas and producing arguments to confirm it. But in fact he was not merely repeating Berkeley's views. He took one step backward in maintaining that the use of every general word must be accompanied by a particular mental idea: "'Tis certain that we form the idea of individuals, whenever we use any general term." But he took several steps forward in suggesting how a given idea can represent others of the same kind—that is, how the idea can become general.

Hume's emphasis on the role of the word was even stronger than Berkeley's had been. Whereas Berkeley had supposed that a word becomes general by its relation to a particular but representative idea, Hume put it the other way round, that a particular idea becomes general by being "annexed to a certain term." "All abstract ideas are really nothing but particular ones … but, being annexed to general terms, they are able to represent a vast variety." Where Berkeley had contented himself with maintaining that an idea became general by representing all ideas of that kind, Hume offered an account of how a particular idea could represent others that were not at the time present to the mind. It did this through custom or habit, by the association of ideas and the association of words. At any given moment a man has only one individual idea before his mind, but because of the resemblances that he has found in his experience, the one individual idea is associated with others of the same kind, which are not actually present to the mind at the time but which would be called up by the stimulus of a suitable experience or a suitable word. Thus, the possession of a general idea or a concept becomes a mental disposition, the readiness, engendered by custom, to have some idea belonging to a given kind, when the appropriate stimulus occurs, and the acquisition of a concept will be the gradual process of (1) learning by experience and habituation to recognize instances and to discriminate between them and instances of a different concept; and (2) having the appropriate associations and dispositions set up in one's mind. To have a concept actually in mind at any given time is to have in mind an individual idea plus the appropriate associative dispositions.

Hume assigned words a key role in his doctrine of association of ideas, supposing that particular ideas, which resemble one another somewhat but not exactly or in all respects, tend to be associated with one another because each is associated with the same general word. The differences between a ripe tomato and a scarlet-painted automobile are more numerous and conspicuous than their similarities, but the idea of the one can readily be associated with that of the other by the fact that the word *red* is used of each, and thus the idea of either could serve as representative of the class of red objects, whatever the variety of objects and the differences between the many shades of red displayed. "A particular idea becomes general by being annex'd to a general term; that is, to a term, which from a customary conjunction has a relation to many other particular ideas, and readily recalls them in the imagination." One could say that according to Hume we learn to think by learning to talk, not the other way round, and that in learning to talk the chief influence is that of custom and association. Here Hume failed, as nominalism also failed, to see that the attempt to account for the generality of an idea in terms of the generality of a word will not do, if taken only as far as he took it. In the sense in which he insisted that every idea is particular, so is every word. Whatever reasons there are for denying the existence of general ideas as distinct from particular ideas will also be reasons for denying the existence of general words as distinct from particular words. Paradoxical though it may seem, the sense in which the word *red* may be said to be general is such that the word *red* cannot occur in any sentences at all, for what occurs in a particular sentence is a particular word *red*. The fourth word in the sentence "Some automobiles are red" may be very like the first word in the sentence "Red tomatoes are ripe," but they are different individual words, occupying different positions in space (as printed). Even in this case they are not exactly alike (for the first does not, and the second does, start with a capital letter), and other "reds" could be even more unlike—for instance, if they were printed in different fonts of type or were written down by different people.

Consideration of this point would have required Hume to say about a word's being general what he (like Locke and Berkeley) said about an idea's being general, namely that it was based on (or constituted by) the resemblance between particulars. (Difficulties in making out somebody's handwriting stem precisely from its deviating more than usual from the familiar resemblances.) Conceptualism therefore comes down, in the persons of these three authors, on the side of resemblance as being the ontological basis of general ideas. All that actually exists is individual; generalization, or concept formation, is possible only to the extent that individual objects and occurrences, their features, and the relations between them display perceptible resemblances to a greater or lesser extent. But Hume offered, or at least hinted at, a more sophisticated version of resemblance. According to Locke, two objects would resemble each other if they possessed certain features in common—that is, if certain features of the one were identical (in an Aristotelian sense) with certain features of the other. Thus, one object possessing features *abcd* would resemble another possessing features *adef,* but less closely than it resembled one possessing features *acdf.* But Hume saw that this raised difficulties for simple (or unanalyzable) ideas or qualities—for example, that "*blue* and *green* are different simple ideas, but are more resembling than *blue* and *scarlet*; tho' their perfect simplicity excludes all possibility of separation or distinction." They may resemble each other "without having any common circumstance the same." The notion of resemblance as an ultimate relation, without requiring that the respect in which two objects resemble each other should be a quality identical in each, propounded here by Hume, has been taken further in later developments of his theory.

NOMINALISM AND RESEMBLANCE

NOMINALIST THEORIES. The nominalist view, that only names (or, more generally, words) are universal, "for the things named are every one of them singular and individual" (Hobbes, *Leviathan,* Ch. 4), has had a very long history. It was the subject of much controversy in medieval philosophy, more for the theological heresies it was believed to engender than on grounds of logic, and it was advanced again in the seventeenth century by Thomas Hobbes.

Of the medievalists mention need be made only of two, one early and the other late. Peter Abelard, although fiercely critical of the extreme nominalism of Roscelin de Compiègne, was strongly influenced by it. For Abelard a universal was not a sound (*vox*), as it was for Roscelin, but a word (*sermo*)—that is, a meaningful sound—and it acquired its meaning from its referential use, the reference being mediated by a general idea that is a composite image. Thus, although Abelard was described by his successors as a nominalist, he was only partly and confusedly so; he could as well be called a conceptualist, or even a moderate realist.

William of Ockham, a polemical figure who was pronounced a heretic and excommunicated, produced a number of logical works in which he developed a battery of arguments against realism and supported a form of nominalism. According to him, universals are terms or signs standing for or referring to individual objects and sets of objects, but they cannot themselves exist. For what exists must be individual, and a universal cannot be that; the mistake of supposing that it could was the fatal contradiction of Platonic realism. And Aristotelian realism was no better, for it involved its own contradiction, that the identical universal should be present in a number of particulars. Real universals are neither possible nor needed. Rather, universals are predicates or meanings, possessing logical status only, required for thought and communication, not naming anything that could possibly exist.

In its extreme form, that there is nothing common to a class of particulars called by the same name other than that they are called by the same name, nominalism is so clearly untenable that it may be doubted whether anybody has actually tried to hold it. If all the individuals (objects, qualities, or whatever they were) called by the same name—for example, "table"—had nothing in common but being called by the same name, no reason could be given why just they and no others had that name, and no reason could be given for deciding whether to include an object in or to exclude it from the class. On a realist view certain objects are called "tables" because they are tables (that is, they partially embody a Platonic Form of tablehood or possess a common Aristotelian feature of tablehood). On an extreme nominalist view they are tables only because they are called "tables," and no answer at all can be given to the question why certain objects are (or are to be) called "tables" and others not. Perhaps the only extreme nominalist has been Humpty Dumpty. ("'When *I* use a word, it means just what I choose it to mean—neither more nor less.' 'The question is,' said Alice, 'whether you *can* make words mean different things.' 'The question is,' said Humpty Dumpty, 'which is to be master—that's all.'") Moderate nominalism, while retaining the view that only words are universals, saves itself from total subjectivity by basing the use of words on the resemblances between things. Hobbes, for example, in the *Leviathan* (Ch. 4) said: "One universal name is imposed on many things, for their similitude in some quality or other accident." So *table* is a universal word, applicable to any individual objects between which a certain resemblance holds. Objects, their qualities, and their relations are all individual, the only thing that is general being the word that is applicable to objects (or qualities, or relations) of a given class in virtue of the resemblances between them.

Nominalism and a conceptualism such as Hume's here converge, differences being in approach and emphasis rather than in substance. And nominalism must in the end reduce itself to a resemblance theory that, if acceptable, finally renders nominalism unnecessary. Nominalism's only reason for insisting on the universality of the word is its denial of the universality of the thing: Things are individuals, and the properties of a thing are individual to it. But the universality of the word depends on resemblances between things; thus, nominalism requires a resemblance theory. However, as was already mentioned in reference to Hume, the nominalist must, to be consistent, go further and recognize that what he says of things, if true of them, must be true of words also, which requires him to make what logicians have called the "type-token" distinction. Any occurrence of the word *red* is individual ("red" as a token), and two occurrences of what would be called the same word ("Red" as a type) are occurrences of the same word only in that they resemble each other in the relevant ways. Thus, the universal word *Red* becomes the class of the resembling individual words "red," "***red***," "RED," and so on, and once the universality of a word has been analyzed along these lines, the reason for saying that only words are universal is gone, for exactly the same account can be given by the resemblance theory of universality in things. Nominalism was able to present the appearance of being a distinct theory of universals only as long as its exponents and critics alike failed to apply to it the type-token distinction. Once that is applied, words are seen to be on all fours with things, and the question becomes, for words as for things, whether generality can be analyzed simply in terms of resemblances between individuals, as Hume suggested. Nominalism not only requires the support of a resemblance theory to explain how a word can have a general use but also, in its only consistent form, is a resemblance theory.

RESEMBLANCE THEORIES. Whether or not Hume actually held what might be described as the pure-resemblance theory, that is the only form of resemblance theory that is distinctive. The version advanced by Locke, and possibly by Berkeley, too, according to which the degree of resemblance between two objects depends on the extent of qualitative identity between them, collapses into a modified Aristotelian realism. Pure resemblance, although allowing that if two objects resemble each other there must be some respect in which they are similar, would deny that this respect is to be regarded as an identical something common to both; not to deny this would be to reintroduce the Aristotelian universal. Red objects are to be called red simply because they resemble each other in a way in which they do not resemble blue objects, or hard objects, or smooth objects, or spherical objects. Nothing is described by saying that the universal red is what is common to any pair of red objects that is not more accurately and less misleadingly described by saying that both are red—that is, resemble each other in respect of each being red. There is a similarity between the red of the one and the red of the other, and the similarity might be anything from being virtually exact (as in two new red postage stamps of the same denomination) to being only approximate and generic (as in two flags of widely different shades of red, one flag, in addition, being bright and new, the other old and faded). The world is made up of individual things and events, with their individual qualities and relations, and with resemblances in different respects and of differing degrees. Were it not for such resemblances (and contrasting differences), concept formation and language would be impossible; indeed, biological survival would be impossible, too. The resemblance theory is metaphysically the most economical, but it has objections to face, notably two: (1) It does not succeed in dispensing with universals in a traditional sense, such as the Aristotelian, because resemblance itself will have to be such a universal, and if it is, there is no ground for denying others. (2) As two objects that resemble each other must be similar in some respect, the respect must be something common to both.

Although these two objections are frequently reiterated, it is not clear that either has great force, as is shown by H. H. Price's detailed discussion in *Thinking and Experience* (1953). The argument that the resemblance theory requires resemblance itself to be a universal in a sense in which the theory denies that there are any universals has been the more persistent; it is particularly associated with Bertrand Russell (although he was not the first to propound it). But although he advanced it in two books widely separated in time, *Problems of Philosophy* (1912) and *An Inquiry into Meaning and Truth* (1940), his confidence seems to have diminished. Originally he maintained a realist theory of universals, of a Platonic kind, and held that it could be proved, at least in the case of relations, that there must be such universals.

> If we wish to avoid the universals *whiteness* and *triangularity,* we shall choose some particular patch of white or some particular triangle, and say that anything is white or a triangle if it has the right sort of resemblance to our chosen particular. But then the resemblance required will have to be a universal.

That is, we could theoretically dispense with universals of quality by analyzing them in terms of relation, and ultimately in terms of the relation of resemblance. The latter we cannot dispense with, for if we say that the resemblance between a pair of similar particulars is itself a particular relation, we shall then have to admit a resemblance between that resemblance relation and the resemblance relation holding between another pair of similar particulars; the only way to save ourselves from an infinite regress (of resemblances between resemblances between resemblances … between resemblance relations) is to admit that "the relation of resemblance must be a true universal. And having been forced to admit this universal, we find that it is no longer worth while to invent difficult and unplausible theories to avoid the admission of such universals as whiteness and triangularity." In this respect, Russell held, the rationalists were right, as against the empiricists like Hume: The existence of real universals has been proved, at least in the case of the relation of resemblance, and no good reason is left for denying it in the case of other relations and of qualities.

Some years later, in *The Analysis of Mind* (1921), Russell showed more hesitation, when he wrote, "I *think* a logical argument could be produced to show that universals are part of the structure of the world." Finally, in the *Inquiry,* after repeating his original argument, he said, "I conclude, therefore, though with hesitation, that there are universals, and not merely general words."

Price seems to have lost confidence in the validity of Russell's proof even more thoroughly, and far more rapidly. In *Thinking and Representation* (1946) he accepted that resemblance has to be a universal and repeated that the most the resemblance theory would have achieved "would be to reduce all other universals to this one relational universal." He went on: "This is a very notorious difficulty, and perhaps by much repetition it has become a bore. Yet I do not think it has ever been answered." But in *Thinking and Experience* (1953) he thought the difficulty could be answered, and he spent several pages answering it. Admittedly, his first argument is hardly convincing, namely that the opponents of the resemblance theory (such as Russell) are begging the question by assuming the very thing that they have to prove, that there are universals: From the fact that the theory analyzes all other alleged universals in terms of resemblance, and that it is ultimate, it does not follow that resemblance is a universal. We cannot answer the question whether there are any universals by replying that even if there are no other universals, resemblance must be one. Against Price here, it may be doubted whether Russell's objection is of this question-begging form. The objection, rather, is that the only way of avoiding the admission of resemblance as a universal leads to a vicious infinite regress. Nevertheless, Russell's objection is invalid, as the next stage of Price's answer shows. It is true that the resemblance theory would have to admit different orders or levels of resemblance, resemblances between pairs of particulars, resemblances between these resemblances, and so on ad infinitum. But there is nothing logically vicious or unintelligible about that. The resemblance that we notice between any pair of similar individuals is as individual as they and as the qualities of each; the resemblance we notice or can find between such a resemblance relation and another resemblance relation holding between another pair of similar individuals is itself individual; the process can be continued as long as patience and imagination hold out. We do not need a real universal of resemblance to stop the regress, simply because the regress does not need to be stopped. The fallacious assumption at the root of this objection to the resemblance theory is not the question-begging assumption that there are universals but the assumption that unless there are, a vicious regress is generated.

The merit of the resemblance theory is that it does not confuse, as the realist theories arguably did, the roles of explanation and description. Why or how tables are tables rather than chairs, and elephants are elephants rather than tigers, is not answered by saying that each is what it is because it instantiates the appropriate universal. The only explaining that has to be done on why a given object is a table is to be done in causal terms. What does have to be explained is something about ourselves, namely how it is that we can (indeed, must) experience, in terms of kinds and generality, that we form concepts, and that we develop language for communication. That experience, thought, and language depend on the use of universals, in some sense, is undeniable, and the explanation of this is to be given by a suitably illuminating description of the world we experience. About ourselves the question of universals is a question of explanation. About our world the question of universals is a question of description, and this the resemblance theory seems adequately, and nontendentiously, to provide.

In the twentieth century, philosophers paid far more attention to actual language and, largely under the influence of Ludwig Wittgenstein, came to appreciate that even if the notion of there being (in some sense) something common to all instances covered by a single general word is true of some words, it is not true of all, and that even the resemblances within a group of things all called by the same general name may be what Wittgenstein called "family resemblances"—the vague and overlapping likenesses that one sees between the different members of a family. His own example is what "we call 'games.'" He meant "board-games, card-games, ball-games, Olympic games, and so on. What is common to them all? Don't say: 'There *must* be something common, or they would not be called "games"'—but *look and see* whether there is anything common to all" (*Philosophical Investigations,* I, Sec. 66). There is nothing common to all games, only "similarities, relationships, and a whole series of them at that." The concept of causality, too, has stubbornly resisted the attempts of philosophers to analyze it, as though there were only one *it* to analyze—although the hint that it really requires the Wittgenstein treatment first came from Aristotle himself.

The history of the subject of universals has come a long way from looking for a general entity for which a general word is to be the name (Plato), via looking for recurring identities (Aristotle), selected identities (Locke), and resemblances (Hume), to looking for varying and overlapping resemblances and recognizing that only vain servitude to a theory insists on trying to find what is common to a whole range of overlaps (Wittgenstein). Furthermore, with the development of semantics it has come to be appreciated that not all general words are, even in a stretched sense, "names" at all. They can be significant for their syntactical function, indicating, for instance, condition or conjunction or contrast ("if," "and," "although") or, again, attitudes, outlooks, or degrees of confidence ("perhaps," "probably," "certainly"). The philosophical history of universals has been plagued by the persistent treatment of words as names, which has been made easier by philosophers' taking as their examples only objects and their qualities. But questions about universals are questions about generality, and generality is the essential feature of all words, not just of those that might plausibly be called names.

See also Abelard, Peter; Aristotle; Augustine, St.; Avicenna; Berkeley, George; Empiricism; Epistemology, History of; Gassendi, Pierre; Hobbes, Thomas; Hume, David; Illumination; Kant, Immanuel; Laws of Nature; Locke, John; Medieval Philosophy; Plato; Properties; Realism; Relations, Internal and External; Roscelin; Russell, Bertrand Arthur William; Semantics; Socrates; Subject and Predicate; Thomas Aquinas, St.; William of Ockham; Wittgenstein, Ludwig Josef Johann.

Bibliography

PLATO AND ARISTOTLE

Plato introduced his theory of Forms into many different dialogues, in particular *Phaedo, Republic,* and *Parmenides*; in the last of these he summarized the trend of his thought in earlier dialogues and subjected it to criticism, which was further developed by Aristotle, as in *Metaphysics* M. Aristotle's own views are briefly indicated in *Posterior Analytics* II, 19. Sir David Ross, in *Plato's Theory of Ideas* (Oxford: Clarendon Press, 1951), provides a useful account and discussion of the development of Plato's views and Aristotle's criticisms.

MEDIEVAL PHILOSOPHY

Some account of medieval philosophy's treatment of the theme of universals is given in Father Frederick Copleston's *A History of Philosophy,* Vols. II and III (London, 1950). A more detailed discussion of the four key figures in the dispute between realism and nominalism—Augustine, Abelard, Thomas, and William of Ockham—is to be found in M. H. Carré's *Realists and Nominalists* (London: Oxford University Press, 1946). *Selections from Mediaeval Philosophers,* edited by Richard McKeon (London, 1928), contains a few relevant passages. Copleston, in his bibliographies, provides references to editions of the full texts, where available, and to the appropriate volumes of J. P. Migne's *Patrologia Latina.*

SEVENTEENTH- AND EIGHTEENTH-CENTURY PHILOSOPHY

Hobbes's few remarks on universals are to be found in his *Elements of Philosophy,* I, 2, and in *Leviathan,* Ch. 4. Locke scattered comments all over his diffuse and repetitious *Essay on Human Understanding,* but the main entries are II, xi, and III, iii. Berkeley devoted the whole of the introduction to his *Principles of Human Knowledge* to the subject and returned to it, in a rather more sophisticated way, in *Alciphron,* 7.4. Hume dispatched it briskly in his *Treatise of Human Nature,* I, i, 17. Thomas Reid, in his *Essays on the Intellectual Powers of Man,* V, 6, subjected the other philosophers to telling criticism and foreshadowed modern tendencies.

RECENT PHILOSOPHY

In *Studies in Philosophy and Psychology,* Vols. XV–XVII (London: Macmillan, 1930), G. F. Stout reprinted three relevant papers, the last criticizing the resemblance theory and advocating the view of a universal as a "distributive unity" of a class. Bertrand Russell followed his paper "On the Relation of Universals and Particulars," in *PAS* (1911–1912), with *Problems of Philosophy* (London: Williams and Norgate, 1912), which contains two chapters on the subject; it is taken up again in *Analysis of Mind* (London: Macmillan, 1921) and *Inquiry into Meaning and Truth* (London: Allen and Unwin, 1940). Russell's views are the subject of an article by O. K. Bouwsma in *Philosophical Review* (1943). Other relevant articles are F. P. Ramsey, "Universals," in *Mind* (1925); A. J. Ayer, "On Particulars and Universals," in *PAS* (1933–1934); R. I. Aaron, "Two Senses of the Word Universal," in *Mind* (1939), and "Our Knowledge of Universals," in *Proceedings of the British Academy* (1944); Morris Lazerowitz, "The Existence of Universals," in *Mind*

(1946); Nelson Goodman and W. V. Quine, "Steps towards a Constructive Nominalism," in *Journal of Symbolic Logic* 12 (1947); W. V. Quine, "On What There Is," in *Review of Metaphysics* (1948–1949); A. N. Prior, in *Mind* (1949); A. C. Lloyd, "On Arguments for Real Universals," in *Analysis* (1951); D. F. Pears, "Universals," in *Philosophical Quarterly* (1950–1951); R. B. Brandt, "The Languages of Realism and Nominalism," in *Philosophy and Phenomenological Research* (1956–1957); Arthur Pap, in *Philosophical Quarterly* (1959–1960); and Renford Bambrough, "Universals and Family Resemblances," in *PAS* 61 (1960–1961). The last paper takes as its point of departure the "family resemblance" account of the use of general words given by Ludwig Wittgenstein in *The Blue and Brown Books* (Oxford: Blackwell, 1958), pp. 17–27, and *Philosophical Investigations* (Oxford: Blackwell, 1953), Secs. 65–77. A general survey of the problems connected with universals is undertaken, at a level of no great philosophical difficulty, by R. I. Aaron in *The Theory of Universals* (Oxford: Clarendon Press, 1952) and, more briefly, by A. D. Woozley in *Theory of Knowledge* (London: Hutchinson's University Library, 1949). Other books, each containing several chapters on the subject, are Nelson Goodman's *Structure of Appearance* (Cambridge, MA: Harvard University Press, 1951), John Holloway's *Language and Intelligence* (London: Macmillan, 1951), and, most detailed of all, H. H. Price's *Thinking and Experience* (Cambridge, MA: Harvard University Press, 1953). Papers by I. M. Bocheński, Alonzo Church, and Nelson Goodman are included in the symposium *The Problem of Universals* (Notre Dame, IN: University of Notre Dame Press, 1956).

A. D. Woozley (1967)

UTILITARIANISM

"Utilitarianism" can most generally be described as the doctrine that states that the rightness or wrongness of actions is determined by the goodness and badness of their consequences. This general definition can be made more precise in various ways, according to which we get various species of utilitarianism.

ACT AND RULE UTILITARIANISM

The first important division is between "act" utilitarianism and "rule" utilitarianism. If, in the above definition, we understand *actions* to mean "particular actions," then we are dealing with the form of utilitarianism called act utilitarianism, according to which we assess the rightness or wrongness of each individual action directly by its consequences. If, on the other hand, we understand *actions* in the above definition to mean "sorts of actions," then we get some sort of rule utilitarianism. The rule utilitarian does not consider the consequences of each particular action but considers the consequences of adopting some general rule, such as "Keep promises." He adopts the rule if the consequences of its general adoption are better than those of the adoption of some alternative rule.

Since, in this context, the word *rule* can be interpreted in two ways, to mean either "possible rule" or "rule actually operating in society," there are actually two species of rule utilitarianism. If we interpret *rule* simply as "possible rule," we get an ethical doctrine strongly resembling that of Immanuel Kant. It is true that Kant is not normally regarded as a utilitarian, but nevertheless a utilitarian strain can be detected in his thought. If we interpret his categorical imperative, "Act only on that maxim through which you can at the same time will that it should become a universal law," as meaning "Act only on that maxim which you would like to see established as a universal law," and if liking here is determined by the individual's feelings as a benevolent man, then we get a version of utilitarianism which may usefully be called Kantianism. It is true that Kant would object to this appeal to feelings of benevolence and would wish to distinguish sharply between *willing* and "*wanting* or *liking.* Nevertheless, it is far from clear how Kant's distinction can be defended; and when he elucidates his general principle by means of examples, he does indeed tend to think in terms of the consequences that we should like to see brought about. However, the word *Kantianism* is used here merely as a useful and perhaps not inappropriate label; whether Kant himself would approve of its present application is not an important issue in the present discussion.

If, in our definition of *utilitarianism,* we interpret the word *rule* as "actual rule," or "rule conventionally operative in society," we get a form of rule utilitarianism that has been propounded in recent times by Stephen Toulmin, who seems mainly concerned with the justification, and in some cases the reform, of rules of conduct that are actually operative in society.

When we think of the writers with whom the term *utilitarianism* is most naturally associated, namely, Jeremy Bentham, J. S. Mill, and Henry Sidgwick, we must think of utilitarianism primarily as act utilitarianism. However, controversy has developed over whether Mill should not rather be interpreted as a rule utilitarian, and there has also been much discussion of the rival claims of act and rule utilitarianism to be viable ethical theories.

R. M. Hare, in his book *Freedom and Reason* (Oxford, 1963), has recently argued that there is no clear distinction between act and rule utilitarianism, since if a certain action is right, it must be the case that any action just like it in relevant respects will also be right. If these respects are then specified in detail, we get a rule of the form "Do actions of this sort." A defender of the distinction between act and rule utilitarianism could reply that since the situations in which actions occur are infinitely variable, and since no two actions have quite the same sorts of consequences, the act utilitarian may not be able to describe the "relevant respects" mentioned above in any less general form than "The action is of the sort that has the best consequences." But if this is so, Hare's principle that if an action is right then any action which is like it in the relevant respects is also right does not yield a sufficiently particular form of rule to justify the assimilation of act and rule utilitarianism.

EGOISTIC AND UNIVERSALISTIC UTILITARIANISM

Act utilitarianism, unlike rule utilitarianism, lends itself to being interpreted either in an egoistic or in a nonegoistic way. Are the good consequences that must be considered by an agent the consequences to the agent himself (his own happiness, for example), or are they the consequences to all humankind or even to all sentient beings? If we adopt the former alternative, we get egoistic utilitarianism; and if we adopt the latter alternative, we get universalistic utilitarianism. Since what is best for me is unlikely to be what is best for everyone, it is clear that there is not only a theoretical but also a practical incompatibility between egoistic and universalistic utilitarianism. This was not always seen by the early utilitarians, who sometimes seem to have confused the two doctrines. There is, in fact, even a pragmatic inconsistency in egoistic utilitarianism, since an egoist, on his own principles, would be unlikely to wish to be seen in his true colors, and so would have no motive for expressing his ethical doctrine. In this entry we shall be concerned with utilitarianism in the universalistic sense.

HEDONISTIC AND IDEAL UTILITARIANISM

Another distinction, which cuts across that between act and rule utilitarianism, is the distinction between hedonistic and ideal utilitarianism. Utilitarianism has been defined above as the view that the rightness or wrongness of an action depends on the total goodness or badness of its consequences. A hedonistic utilitarian will hold that the goodness or badness of a consequence depends only on its pleasantness or unpleasantness. As Bentham put it, quantity of pleasure being equal, pushpin is as good as poetry. An ideal utilitarian, such as G. E. Moore, will hold that the goodness or badness of a state of consciousness can depend on things other than its pleasantness. According to him, the goodness or badness of a state of consciousness can depend, for example, on various intellectual and aesthetic qualities. In his calculations, the ideal utilitarian will be concerned not only with pleasantness and unpleasantness, but also with such things as knowledge and the contemplation of beautiful objects. He may even hold that some pleasant states of mind can be intrinsically bad, and some unpleasant ones intrinsically good. J. S. Mill took up an intermediate position. He held that although pleasantness was a necessary condition for goodness, the intrinsic goodness of a state of mind could depend on things other than its pleasantness, or, as he put it, there are higher and lower pleasures.

It should be noted that we have assumed that the only things that can be intrinsically good or bad are states of consciousness. Other things can of course be extrinsically good or bad. For example, an earthquake is normally extrinsically bad, that is, it causes a state of affairs that is on the whole intrinsically bad. Moreover, a utilitarian can hold that something that is intrinsically bad, such as the annoyance of remembering that we have forgotten to do something, is extrinsically good, for it is a means to a set of consequences that are on balance intrinsically good. G. E. Moore held that states of affairs other than states of consciousness could be intrinsically good or bad. For an ideal utilitarian, this is a theoretically possible contention, but nevertheless, few ideal utilitarians would find the contention a plausible one, and we shall therefore ignore it in this article.

NORMATIVE AND DESCRIPTIVE UTILITARIANISM

Utilitarianism may be put forward either as a system of normative ethics, that is, as a proposal about how we ought to think about conduct, or it may be put forward as a system of descriptive ethics, that is, an analysis of how we do think about conduct. The distinction between normative and descriptive utilitarianism has not always been observed. It is important to bear carefully in mind the distinction between normative and descriptive utilitarianism and to note that objections to descriptive utilitarianism do not necessarily constitute objections to normative utilitarianism.

HISTORICAL REMARKS

Properly speaking, utilitarianism began with Jeremy Bentham (1748–1832), who was a universalistic hedonistic act utilitarian. He put forward his view essentially as normative ethics, but he was unclear about the distinction between normative and factual utterances and may justly be accused of committing what Moore later called the naturalistic fallacy—the fallacy of claiming to deduce ethical principles solely from matters *of* fact. (David Hume had in effect pointed out this fallacy before Bentham's time.)

PRECURSORS OF UTILITARIANISM. Anticipations of Bentham are to be found in the history of ethics. In ancient times Aristippus of Cyrene and Epicurus propounded hedonistic theories. However, their doctrines approximate egoistic rather than universalistic utilitarianism, despite the fact that they were unclear about the difficulty of reconciling the two doctrines and hence tried to have it both ways. The same might be said of Abraham Tucker and William Paley, the more immediate precursors of Bentham, who also injected certain theological conceptions into their systems. The tension between egoistic and universalistic hedonism can also be detected in the eighteenth-century French writer Claude-Adrien Helvétius, who appears to have influenced Bentham; also, the political philosopher William Godwin should be mentioned. David Hume is often classified as a utilitarian, but he used utility not as a normative or even as a descriptive principle, but as an explanatory one: When asked why we approve of certain traits of character, he would point out that they are traits which either are useful or are immediately agreeable. Both because he used the principle of utility in an explanatory way and because he was primarily concerned with the evaluation of traits of character (virtues and vices and the like) rather than with the question of what actions ought to be done, it is not advisable to regard Hume as a utilitarian.

J. S. MILL. As was mentioned above, there has been some controversy over whether J. S. Mill (1806–1873) ought to be regarded as an act utilitarian or as a rule utilitarian. Mill does not make his position on this issue very clear. Probably he was not very well aware of the distinction, and in any case he would probably have thought it a fairly unimportant one, since he was mainly concerned with the opposition between utilitarianism in general and other systems of ethics that were quite nonutilitarian. Although Bentham had on at least one occasion used the word *utilitarian,* it was Mill who introduced it into philosophy. He appropriated it, with some change of meaning, from a passage in the Scottish novelist John Galt's *Annals of the Parish* (Edinburgh, 1821).

SIDGWICK. We can with some confidence classify Mill as a normative utilitarian rather than a descriptive one, but the first utilitarian philosopher who was very explicit on this issue was Henry Sidgwick (1838–1900). Sidgwick understood that there is a distinction between normative and factual sentences, although, like G. E. Moore (1873–1958), he thought that ethical principles could be the objects of intellectual intuition. Sidgwick was a universalistic hedonistic utilitarian, but he was also strongly attracted by the claims of egoism. He saw more clearly than earlier writers that there was a theoretical inconsistency in being both an egoistic and a universalistic utilitarian, and he considered the possibility that there might be theological sanctions that would reconcile the two views, if not in theory, then at least in practice.

LATER UTILITARIANS. Moore and Hastings Rashdall were ideal universalistic utilitarians, although Moore, with his principle of organic unities, and Rashdall, with his importation into the utilitarian calculations of the moral worth of the actions themselves, introduced considerations which, if taken seriously, would seem to vitiate the truly utilitarian character of their theories.

A subtle form of rule utilitarianism of the sort we have called Kantianism was propounded in 1936 by R. F. Harrod. Contemporary writers such as Stephen Toulmin, P. H. Nowell-Smith, John Rawls, K. E. M. Baier, and M. G. Singer have propounded views that either are or approximate rule utilitarianism. R. B. Brandt has been sympathetic to rule utilitarianism and has recently defended a rather subtle and complex version of it.

ANALYSIS AND CRITIQUE

UTILITARIANISM AS A DESCRIPTIVE ETHICS. It is fairly easy to show that both act utilitarianism and rule utilitarianism are inconsistent with usual ideas about ethics, or what can be called the common moral consciousness. For the principles of both systems will in some cases lead us to advocate courses of action that the plain man would regard as wrong. Consider, for example, the case of a secret promise to a dying man. To ease his dying moments, I promise him that I will deliver a hoard of money, which he entrusts to me, to a rich and profligate relative of his. No one else knows either about the promise or the hoard. On utilitarian principles, it would appear that I should not carry out my promise. I can surely put the money to much better use by giving it, say, to a needy hospital. In this way I would do a lot of good and no harm. I do not disappoint the man to whom I made the promise, because he is dead. Nor, by breaking the promise, do I do indirect harm by weakening men's faith in the socially useful institution of promise making and promise keeping, for on this occasion no one knows about the promise. Normally, of course, an act utilitarian will keep a promise even when the direct results are not beneficial, because the indirect effects of sowing mistrust are so harmful. This consideration clearly does not apply in the present instance. The plain man, however, would be quite sure that the promise to the dying man should be kept. In this instance, therefore, we have a clear case in which utilitarianism is inconsistent with the way in which, for the most part, people in fact think about morality.

The rule utilitarian, on the other hand, would probably agree with the plain man in the above case, because he would appeal to the utility of the rule of promise keeping in general, not to the utility of the particular act of promise keeping. Nevertheless, cases can be brought up that will show the incompatibility of even rule utilitarianism with the common moral consciousness. For example, a riot involving hundreds of deaths may be averted only by punishing some innocent scapegoat and calling it punishment. Given certain empirical assumptions, which may perhaps not in fact be true, but which in a certain sort of society might be true, it is hard to see how a rule utilitarian could object to such a practice of punishing the innocent in these circumstances, and yet most people would regard such a practice as unjust. They would hold that a practice of sometimes punishing the innocent would be wrong, despite the fact that in certain circumstances its consequences would be good or that the consequences of any alternative practice would be bad. In this instance, then, there is a conflict between even the rule utilitarian and the plain man. (This is not, of course, to say that in fact, in the world as it is, the rule utilitarian will be in favor of a practice of punishing the innocent, but it can be shown that in a certain sort of world he would have to be.)

ACT UTILITARIANISM AS A SYSTEM OF NORMATIVE ETHICS. Both act and rule utilitarianism fail, then, as systems of descriptive ethics. But act utilitarianism as a system of normative ethics would seem to have certain advantages over both rule utilitarianism and nonutilitarian, or deontological, systems of ethics (a deontological system of ethics is one that holds that an action can be right or wrong in itself, quite apart from consequences). Moreover, the failure of act utilitarianism as a descriptive system is the source of its interest as a possible normative system: If it had been correct as a descriptive system, then the acceptance of it as a normative system would have left most men's conduct unchanged.

No proof of utilitarianism. A system of normative ethics cannot be proved intellectually. Any such "proof" of utilitarianism as was attempted by Bentham or Mill can be shown to be fallacious. (Mill disclaimed the possibility of proof and spoke more vaguely of "considerations capable of determining the intellect," but he presented an attempted proof nonetheless.) Sidgwick and Moore were clearer on this point and saw that ethical principles cannot be deduced from anything else. They appealed instead to intellectual intuition, but recent developments in epistemology and other fields of philosophy have made the notion of intellectual intuition a disreputable one. The tendency among some more recent writers, such as C. L. Stevenson, R. M. Hare, and P. H. Nowell-Smith, has been to regard assertions of ultimate ethical principles and valuations as expressions of feeling or attitude, or as akin to imperatives rather than to statements of fact. In this respect, they develop further the position held much earlier by Hume. Now if we abandon a cognitivist theory about the nature of moral judgments, such as was held by Sidgwick or Moore, and adopt the view that ultimate ethical principles depend only on our attitudes, that is, on what we like or dislike, we must give up the attempt to prove any ethical system, including the act-utilitarian system. We may nevertheless recommend such a system. We may also try to show inconsistencies or emotionally unattractive features of various possible alternative systems.

Appeal to generalized benevolence. In putting forward act utilitarianism as a normative system, we express an attitude of generalized benevolence and appeal to a similar attitude in our audience. (The attitude of generalized benevolence is not the same as altruism. Generalized benevolence is self-regarding, and other-regarding too—I count my happiness neither more nor less than yours.) Of course, we all have in addition other attitudes, self-love, and particular likes and dislikes. As far as self-love is concerned, either this will be compatible with generalized benevolence or it will not. If the former, then self-love does not conflict with act utilitarianism, and if the latter, nevertheless self-love then will be largely canceled out, as among a number of people engaged in discussion.

Arguments against deontological systems. As to particular likes and dislikes, an important case concerns our liking for obeying the rules of some deontological ethics in which we have been raised. However, the following persuasive considerations can be brought up as arguments against the adherent of a deontological system of ethics. It can be urged that although the dictates of a generalized benevolence might quite often coincide with those of an act-utilitarian ethics, there must be cases in which the two would conflict with one another. Would the benevolent and sympathetic persons to whom we conceive ourselves to be appealing be happy about preferring abstract conformity with an ethical rule, such as "Keep promises," to preventing avoidable misery of his fellow creatures?

It will be noticed that the above defense of utilitarianism against deontology is purely persuasive, an appeal to the heart and not to the intellect. It is based on the metaethical view that ultimate ethical principles are expressions of our attitudes and not the findings of some sort of intuition of ethical fact. An intellectualist in metaethics, such as W. D. Ross, could well resist our appeal to feeling by saying that it is possible to see that his deontological principles are correct, and that whether we like them or not is beside the point.

Weakness of rule utilitarianism. In defending act utilitarianism, then, we appeal to feelings, namely, those of generalized benevolence. Since people possess other attitudes too, such as loyalty to a code of morals in which they have brought up, the possession of feelings of generalized benevolence is not a sufficient condition of agreement with the act utilitarian. But it is a necessary condition. Now the rule utilitarian also appeals ultimately to feelings of generalized benevolence. Like the deontologist, however, he is open to the charge of preferring conformity with a rule to the prevention of unhappiness. He is indeed more obviously open to such a charge, since he presumably advocates his rule utilitarian principle because he thinks that these rules conduce to human happiness. He is then inconsistent if he prescribes that we should obey a rule (even a generally beneficial rule) in those cases in which he knows that it will not be most beneficial to obey it. It will not do to reply that in most cases it is most beneficial to obey the rule. It is still true that in some cases it is not most beneficial to obey the rule, and if we are solely concerned with beneficence, in these cases we ought not to obey the rule. Nor is it relevant that it may be better that everybody should obey the rule than that nobody should. That the rule should always be obeyed and that it should never be obeyed are not the only two possibilities. There is the third possibility that sometimes it should be obeyed and sometimes it should not be obeyed.

Hedonistic act utilitarianism. We shall therefore neglect rule utilitarianism as a system of normative ethics, and consider only act utilitarianism, which will be conveniently put forward in a hedonistic form. The reader will easily be able to adapt most of what is said to cover the case of ideal utilitarianism. Indeed, in many cases the differences between hedonistic and ideal utilitarianism are not usually of much practical importance, since the hedonist will usually agree that the states of mind the ideal utilitarian regards as intrinsically good, but which he does not, are nevertheless extrinsically good. Bentham would say that Mill's higher pleasures, if not intrinsically better than the lower ones, are usually more "fecund" of further pleasures. This is not to say, however, that there are no cases in which there would not be a significant difference between hedonistic and ideal utilitarianism.

The act-utilitarian principle can now be put in the following form: "The only reason for performing some action *A*, rather than various alternative actions, is that *A* results in more happiness (or more generally, in better consequences) for all humankind (or perhaps all sentient beings) than will any of these alternative actions." Since this principle expresses an attitude of generalized benevolence, we can expect to find a good deal of sympathy for it among the sort of people with whom it would be profitable to carry on a discussion about ethics. It may therefore be possible to obtain wide assent to the principle, provided that we can develop its implications in a clear and consistent manner and that we can show that certain common objections to utilitarianism are not as valid as they are supposed to be. We have already seen that certain objections, based on "the common moral consciousness," fail because they are valid only against descriptive utilitarianism and not against normative utilitarianism.

Determining consequences. Utilitarianism would be an easier doctrine to state if we could assume that we could always tell with certainty what all the consequences of various possible actions would be, and if we could assume that very remote consequences need not be taken into account. In applying the utilitarian principle, we would simply have to envisage two or more sets of consequences extending into the future, and ask ourselves, as sympathetic and benevolent men, which of these we would prefer. There would be no need for any calculation or for any summation of pleasures. We would simply have to compare two or more possible total situations. Sometimes, indeed, the postulate that we need not consider very remote situations will not be necessary. For example, if it be admitted that, on the whole, people are more happy than not, a man and woman who are left alive as sole representatives of the human race after some atomic holocaust could, as utilitarians, decide to have children in the hope that the world would once more be populated indefinitely far into the future. This is because although the generations will extend indefinitely far into the future, there is reason to believe that each generation will be happy rather than unhappy, while if no children are had, there will be no succeeding generations at all, and so no possibility of happiness accruing in the future. In normal cases, however, we do need to assume that remote consequences can be left out of account. Surely, however, this is a plausible assumption, for on the whole, the goodness and badness of very remote consequences are likely to cancel out. In any case, if this assumption cannot be made, also difficulties will arise for many deontological systems (for example, the system of W. D. Ross), which allow beneficence as one principle among others.

Unfortunately, however, we do not know with certainty what the various possible consequences of our actions will be. This uncertainty would not be so bad provided we could assign numerical probabilities to the various consequences. We could then still employ a method similar to that of envisaging total consequences. A very simplified example may make this clear. Suppose that the only relevant consequences are, on the one hand, a 3/5 probability of Smith's being in some state *S*, and on the other hand, if we do an alternative action, a 2/7 probability of Jones's being in some state *T*. We simply envisage 21 people just like Smith in state *S* as against 10 people just like Jones in state *T*. It should be evident how, in theory at least, this method could be extended to more complex cases. However, numerical probabilities can rarely be assigned to possible future events, and the utilitarian is reduced to an intuitive weighting of various consequences with their probabilities. It is impossible to justify such intuitions rationally, and we have here a serious weakness in utilitarianism. It is true that this weakness also extends to prudential decisions, and most people think that they can make prudential decisions with some rationality. But this is not of much help, since in propounding a normative system we are concerned with what we ought to think, not with how we do think. Utilitarianism is therefore badly in need of support from a theory whereby, at least roughly or in principle, numerical probabilities could be assigned to all types of events.

THE PLACE OF RULES IN ACT UTILITARIANISM. Even the act utilitarian cannot always be weighing up consequences. He must often act habitually or in accordance with rough rules of thumb. However, this does not affect the value of the act-utilitarian principle, which is put forward as a criterion of rational choice. When we act habitually we do not exercise a rational choice, and the utilitarian criterion is not operative. It is, of course, operative when we are deciding, on act-utilitarian principles, the habits or rules of thumb to which we should or should not school ourselves. The act utilitarian knows that he would go mad if he deliberated on every trivial issue, and that if he did not go mad he would at least slow up his responses so much that he would miss many opportunities for probably doing good. He may also school himself to act habitually because he may think that if he deliberated in various concrete situations, his reasoning would be distorted by a selfish bias.

APPLICATIONS

UTILITARIANISM AND GAME THEORY. The act utilitarian will of course use as some of his premises propositions about how other members of the community are likely to act. For example, if certain individuals are adherents of a deontological morality, their actions will tend to be made predictable and their behavior will constitute valuable information for the act utilitarian when he is planning his own actions. Thus, an act utilitarian who has something important to do with his time may be wise to abstain from voting in an election (assuming that there is no legal compulsion to vote), for he will reflect that most people will in fact go to vote and that elections are very rarely decided by a single vote.

But how should the act utilitarian reason if he lives in a society in which everyone else is an act utilitarian? He needs information about what other people will do, but since they reason as he does, what they will do depends on what they think he will do. There is a circularity in the situation that can be resolved only by the technique of the theory of games.

Moral philosophers have commonly failed to give the correct solution to this sort of question. In the case in which the act utilitarian is asking whether he should do an action *A* or not do it, moral philosophers have commonly envisaged only two possibilities: Either everyone does *A* or no one does *A*. They have failed to notice the possibility of what, in the theory of games, is called a mixed strategy. Each act utilitarian can give himself a probability p of doing *A*. Thus, in the case of the voting, each act utilitarian might toss pennies or dice in such a way as to give himself a certain probability p of voting, so that the best possible proportion of people will turn up to vote and a small proportion will be free to do other things. The calculation of p is a simple maximization problem, provided that we know numerical values of the probabilities and numerical values of the various consequences of alternative actions. Of course, this is unlikely to be the case, and the question of a mixed strategy is usually more of theoretical than of practical importance. Moreover, in very many important cases the effect of even a few people acting in a certain way is, in practice, so disastrous that the probability we should give ourselves of acting in this way may be so small that we may as well say, like the rule utilitarians, that we would never do it.

UTILITARIANISM AND PRAISE AND BLAME. Not only do we use moral language to deliberate about what we should do, but we also use moral language to praise people and blame them. Suppose that we use the words "good action" and "bad action" to convey praise and blame, and "right action" and "wrong action" to evaluate what ought to be done. On act-utilitarian principles, then, a right action is one that produces the best consequences. A good action is one that should be praised. Normally we will wish to praise right actions and blame wrong ones, but this is not invariably the case. As Sidgwick has pointed out very clearly, when, as utilitarians, we assess agents and motives as good or bad, the question at issue is not the utility of the actions but the utility of praise or blame of them. Suppose that the only way in which a soldier can save the lives of half a dozen companions is by throwing himself upon a grenade that is about to explode, thus taking upon himself the full impact of the blast and inevitably being killed. The act utilitarian would have to say that the soldier ought to sacrifice himself in this way. Nevertheless, he would not censure the soldier or say that he had acted from a bad motive if he had refrained from this heroic act and his companions had been killed. There is nothing to be gained by censuring someone for lack of extraordinary heroism, and probably much harm in doing so. The act utilitarian should say that the soldier's motive was not a bad one, although his action was as a matter of fact a wrong one.

Consider a case in which an action, normally of trivial import, happens to have very unfortunate consequences. A man with a head cold goes to the office, instead of nursing his illness at home. He is visited by an eminent statesman, who catches the cold and, in consequence, is not quite at his best in carrying out some delicate negotiations. These negotiations fail just by a hairsbreadth, whereas if the statesman had been fully fit they would have succeeded. In consequence, thousands of people die from starvation, a misfortune that would have been avoided if the negotiations had succeeded. These deaths from starvation would therefore not have occurred if the man with a head cold had not gone to his office in an infectious state. Someone may be tempted to argue as follows: "Surely it is not a very wrong action to go to the office suffering from a head cold. In some cases, where important work has to be done, it may even be praiseworthy. But in this case the action had very bad consequences, and so the utilitarian must say that it is very wrong. There must therefore be something wrong with utilitarianism." The utilitarian must reply that the objector is confusing two things, the rightness or wrongness of an action and the praiseworthiness or blameworthiness of it. The action, he can consistently say, was very wrong, but it was not very bad: That is, it ought not to be blamed very much, if at all. If we blame it, we are concerned with the utility of discouraging similar actions on the part of other people, and since going to the office with a head cold is not normally productive of very bad consequences, this action, although in fact very wrong, was not a very bad or blameworthy one.

Another reason why utility (or rightness) of an action does not always coincide with utility of praise or blame of it, and hence with its goodness or badness, is that, as Sidgwick pointed out, although universal benevolence, from the act-utilitarian view, is the ultimate standard of right and wrong, it is not necessarily the best or most useful motive for action. For example, although family affection may not always act in the same direction as generalized benevolence, it very frequently does so, and is a much more powerful motive than the latter. The act utilitarian may well think it useful to praise an action done from family affection in order to strengthen and encourage this motive, even when in fact the action was not generally beneficial.

Similarly, members of a community may act according to some traditional code of rules and may be likely to become simply amoral if a premature attempt is made to convert them to utilitarianism. A utilitarian may well think, therefore, that he ought to support this traditional nonutilitarian code of morals, if its general tendency is at all beneficent. He may therefore apportion praise and blame among members of this community according to whether their actions are in conformity with this code, and not according to whether they are right or wrong from the utilitarian standpoint. The relations between act utilitarianism and the traditional morality of a community in which an act utilitarian may find himself are very complex, and have been quite thoroughly investigated by Sidgwick.

See also Aristippus of Cyrene; Baier, Kurt; Bentham, Jeremy; Brandt, R. B.; Consequentialism; Deontological Ethics; Egoism and Altruism; Epicurus; Game Theory; Godwin, William; Good, The; Happiness; Hare, Richard M.; Hedonism; Helvétius, Claude-Adrien; Hume, David; Kant, Immanuel; Metaethics; Mill, John Stuart; Moore, George Edward; Paley, William; Pleasure; Punishment; Rashdall, Hastings; Rawls, John;

Ross, William David; Sidgwick, Henry; Stevenson, Charles L.

Bibliography

HISTORY OF UTILITARIANISM

For the history of utilitarianism, see especially H. Sidgwick, *Outlines of the History of Ethics* (London, 1946), with an additional chapter by Alban G. Widgery; Ernest Albee, *A History of English Utilitarianism* (New York: Macmillan, 1902); and Leslie Stephen, *The English Utilitarians* (London: Duckworth, 1900), which contains references to the works of Tucker and Paley. The works of Helvétius are not readily accessible, but a list of various editions can be found in the bibliography of Ian Cumming, *Helvétius, His Life and Place in the History of Educational Thought* (London: Routledge and Kegan Paul, 1955).

MAJOR UTILITARIANS

For works by Bentham, see especially his *Fragment on Government and Introduction to the Principles of Morals and Legislation,* edited by Wilfred Harrison (Oxford, 1948), and his *Deontology,* edited by John Bowring (London and Edinburgh, 1843). A very scholarly modern work on Bentham is David Baumgardt, *Bentham and the Ethics of Today, with Bentham Manuscripts—Hitherto Unpublished* (Princeton, NJ: Princeton University Press, 1952). For works by J. S. Mill, see *Utilitarianism, On Liberty, Essay on Bentham, Together with Selected Writings of Jeremy Bentham and John Austin,* edited with an introduction by Mary Warnock (Malden, MA: Blackwell, 2003). M. St. J. Packe, *The Life of John Stuart Mill* (London: Secker and Warburg, 1954), gives evidence on p. 53 (footnote) that Bentham used the word *utilitarian* before Mill. An interesting discussion of Mill's ethical principles is given in Karl Britton, "Utilitarianism: the Appeal to a First Principle," in *PAS* 60 (1959–1960): 141–154. Britton is also the author of an account of Mill's philosophy, *John Stuart Mill* (London: Penguin, 1953). A nineteenth-century criticism of utilitarianism is J. Grote, *An Examination of the Utilitarian Philosophy* (Cambridge, U.K., 1870). For Sidgwick, see his *Methods of Ethics,* 7th ed. (London, 1907), which is discussed by C. D. Broad in *Five Types of Ethical Theory* (London: Kegan Paul, 1930). Godwin's moral philosophy is critically expounded by D. H. Monro in his *Godwin's Moral Philosophy* (London: Oxford University Press, 1953). Ideal utilitarianism may be studied in G. E. Moore, *Principia Ethica* (Cambridge, U.K.: Cambridge University Press, 1903) and *Ethics* (London: Williams and Norgate, 1912), and in H. Rashdall, *Theory of Good and Evil* (Oxford: Clarendon Press, 1907). A sympathetic discussion of utilitarianism will be found in A. J. Ayer's essay "The Principle of Utility," in his *Philosophical Essays* (London: Macmillan, 1954).

RULE AND ACT UTILITARIANISM

Many modern writers have espoused views that can be described as rule utilitarianism. See especially Stephen Toulmin, *The Place of Reason in Ethics* (Cambridge, U.K.: Cambridge University Press, 1951); P. H. Nowell-Smith, *Ethics* (London: Penguin, 1954); J. Rawls, "Two Concepts of Rules," in *Philosophical Review* 64 (1955): 3–32; K. E. M. Baier, *The Moral Point of View* (Ithaca, NY: Cornell University Press, 1958); M. G. Singer, *Generalization in Ethics* (New York: Knopf, 1961). J. O. Urmson, "The Interpretation of the Philosophy of J. S. Mill," in *Philosophical Quarterly* 3 (1953): 33–39, interprets Mill as a rule utilitarian. His view is contested by J. D. Mabbott, "Interpretation of Mill's *Utilitarianism,*" in *Philosophical Quarterly* 6 (1956): 115–120. The issue between act and rule utilitarianism is in effect discussed by A. C. Ewing, "What Would Happen If Everyone Acted Like Me?" in *Philosophy* 28 (1953): 16–29, and by A. K. Stout, "But Suppose Everybody Did the Same?" in *Australasian Journal of Philosophy* 32 (1954): 1–29. J. J. C. Smart, "Extreme and Restricted Utilitarianism," in *Philosophical Quarterly* 6 (1956): 344–354, is a defense of act as against rule utilitarianism. The terms *extreme* and *restricted* are used here instead of the more appropriate words *act* and *rule.* These last were introduced by R. B. Brandt in his *Ethical Theory* (Englewood Cliffs, NJ: Prentice-Hall, 1959), which contains good discussions of act and rule utilitarianism. Brandt has also developed a complex and subtle form of rule utilitarianism in his paper "In Search of a Credible Form of Rule Utilitarianism," in *Morality and the Language of Conduct,* edited by George Nakhnikian and Héctor-Neri Castañeda (Detroit: Wayne State University Press, 1953). See also H. D. Aiken, "The Levels of Moral Discourse," in *Ethics* 62 (1952): 235–248. Rule utilitarianism is criticized by H. J. McCloskey, "An Examination of Restricted Utilitarianism," in *Philosophical Review* 66 (1957): 466–485. A Kantian type of rule utilitarianism is presented by R. F. Harrod, "Utilitarianism Revised," in *Mind* 45 (1936): 137–156, and J. C. Harsanyi, "Ethics in Terms of Hypothetical Imperatives," in *Mind* 67 (1958): 305–316. Jonathan Harrison's article "Utilitarianism, Universalisation and Our Duty to Be Just," in *PAS* 53 (1952–1953): 105–134, discusses important issues and includes a criticism of Harrod.

NEGATIVE UTILITARIANISM

K. R. Popper, *The Open Society and Its Enemies,* 3rd ed., Vol. 1 (London, 1957), Ch. 5, note 6, has put forward some considerations that suggest the possibility of expressing utilitarianism in terms of the prevention of misery rather than in terms of the promotion of happiness, although Popper himself does not seem to be a utilitarian. Such a "negative utilitarianism" has been criticized by R. N. Smart, "Negative Utilitarianism," in *Mind* 67 (1958): 542–543.

EXPOSITIONS AND CRITICISMS

An exposition of act utilitarianism as a normative system is given by J. J. C. Smart, *An Outline of a System of Utilitarian Ethics* (Melbourne: Melbourne University Press and University of Adelaide, 1961). An introductory textbook from an act-utilitarian point of view is C. A. Baylis, *Ethics, the Principles of Wise Choice* (New York: Holt, 1958). There are useful chapters on utilitarianism in John Hospers, *Human Conduct* (New York: Harcourt Brace, 1961). The inconsistency of an egoistic utilitarianism is pointed out by B. H. Medlin, "Ultimate Principles and Ethical Egoism," in *Australasian Journal of Philosophy* 35 (1957): 111–118. J. Rawls, in his article "Justice as Fairness," in *Philosophical Review* 67 (1958): 164–194, holds that one must never act solely to increase the general happiness if in so doing one makes any particular person unhappy. I. M. Crombie, in his article "Social Clockwork and Utilitarian Morality" in

Christian Faith and Communist Faith, edited by D. M. Mackinnon (London: Macmillan, 1953), suggests that a utilitarian could accuse the deontologist of a sort of idolatrous attitude toward rules. Another valuable point made in this article is that utilitarianism is in a certain way a self-correcting doctrine. See also A. I. Melden, "Two Comments on Utilitarianism," in *Philosophical Review* 60 (1951): 508–524; H. W. Schneider, "Obligations and the Pursuit of Happiness," in *Philosophical Review* 61 (1952): 312–319; and S. M. Brown Jr., "Utilitarianism and Moral Obligation," ibid., 299–311, which led to comments by C. A. Baylis and John Ladd, ibid., 320–330. J. O. Urmson, "Saints and Heroes," in *Essays in Moral Philosophy,* edited by A. I. Melden (Seattle: University of Washington Press, 1958), makes some distinctions that he tentatively suggests may be accommodated more easily by a utilitarian than by a nonutilitarian ethics. A pioneering application of the theory of games to problems of moral philosophy is to be found in R. B. Braithwaite, *Theory of Games as a Tool for the Moral Philosopher* (Cambridge, U.K.: Cambridge University Press, 1955).

METAETHICAL THEORIES

For the noncognitivist theories of metaethics of C. L. Stevenson, R. M. Hare, and P. H. Nowell-Smith, see C. L. Stevenson, *Ethics and Language* (New Haven, CT: Yale University Press, 1944); R. M. Hare, *The Language of Morals* (Oxford: Clarendon Press, 1952); and P. H. Nowell-Smith, *Ethics* (London: Penguin, 1954). Hare's sequel, *Freedom and Reason* (Oxford: Clarendon Press, 1963), contains an interesting chapter on utilitarianism.

J. J. C. Smart (1967)

UTILITARIANISM [ADDENDUM]

J. J. C. Smart's advocacy of utilitarianism has been perhaps the most influential since Henry Sidgwick's nearly a century earlier. Nevertheless, there have been some significant developments since Smart's work, outlined here.

Fundamental to Smart's approach is his thesis that there can be no proof of ultimate normative moral principles. In this respect, ultimate normative principles, Smart thinks, are unlike many other kinds of claims. For example, some claims are true because of the definitions of the terms in them ("Bachelors are unmarried"). And, setting aside worries about induction, we observe that some claims are proven false by empirical investigation ("Drinking caffeinated coffee makes you sleepy"), and that other claims are confirmable by empirical investigation ("sugar dissolves in boiling water"). Ultimate normative principles, however, are different. They are not true by definition. They are neither refutable nor confirmable by purely empirical investigation. And ultimate normative principles are *basic,* that is, are not derivable from something deeper. So they cannot be proved, Smart thinks.

Indeed, in Smart's view, to endorse some ultimate moral principle is not to express a cognition, that is, a belief. Smart held that moral judgments essentially express something noncognitive, such as a sentiment, an attitude, or a commitment. So Smart was a noncognitivist in ethics. Yet Smart did think that there is a way of supporting ultimate normative principles—by appeal to generalized benevolence. He meant that we might find certain proposed moral principles attractive from the point of view of impartial concern for all. This point of view accords any benefit or harm to any individual the same weight as it accords to the same size benefit or harm to any other individual. Smart's idea is that, from the point of view of impartial benevolence, utilitarianism is virtually irresistible.

Four years after the publication of Smart's entry in the first edition of this encyclopedia, John Rawls published *A Theory of Justice* (1971). Many of the theses in Rawls's book had been put forward by him or others before, but his book solidified support for many of these theses. The net effect was that Rawls's book changed the landscape in moral and political philosophy.

Rawls's most pervasive influence was in what we might call moral methodology. He championed the search for "reflective equilibrium" between the specific moral judgments that we make after careful reflection and the general moral principles that we affirm after careful reflection. We seek general principles that are consistent with and provide some justification for our more specific judgments. At least to some extent, we are willing to adjust our specific judgments to fit with the best general principles we can find. When specific moral judgments and general principles cohere, we have reflective equilibrium.

This picture of theorizing in normative ethics has been widely accepted by moral philosophers, though the picture has been interpreted in a variety of different ways. One point about it that seems incontrovertible is that achieving reflective equilibrium between one's specific moral judgments and one's more general moral principles hardly proves that the judgments and principles are true. A coherent set of beliefs or commitments can be deeply misguided rather than true. Coherence is not a sufficient condition of truth.

But the consistency of any two beliefs with one another is a necessary condition of their both being true.

So if moral commitments are beliefs, they had better be consistent with one another. Even if moral commitments are not really beliefs but instead are noncognitive states, they are faulty if inconsistent.

As Smart noted, act utilitarianism conflicts with many popular moral commitments. Suppose that we would produce slightly greater net aggregate welfare by, for example, breaking a promise or stealing or framing an innocent person than we would by not doing such a thing. Act utilitarians must favor breaking the promise or stealing or framing an innocent person in such circumstances. But here act utilitarianism seems, to most people, deeply mistaken.

In his entry on this topic in the first edition, Smart replied with a rhetorical question: "Would the benevolent and sympathetic persons to whom we conceive ourselves to be appealing be happy about preferring abstract conformity with an ethical rule, such as 'Keep promises,' to preventing avoidable misery of his fellow creatures?" Part of the rhetorical force of this question comes from the implication that we are here choosing between conforming to a rule when this would benefit no one and breaking a rule when this would prevent avoidable misery.

If such are indeed the circumstances, many people would agree with Smart that it would be right to break the promise, because of the following argument. An action is wrong only if it harms someone. Breaking a promise would, in some cases, harm no one. So, in these cases, breaking a promise could not be wrong. If one could prevent avoidable misery in a way that would not be wrong, then one would be morally required to do so. Thus, in the case posed by Smart, one would be morally required to break the promise.

There are various problems with this argument. For example, there are problems with its first premise, that an action is morally wrong only if it harms someone. Suppose that I broke a promise to you, or stole from you, in a way that harmed no one. Could not such an act be wrong despite the fact that no one was harmed?

Rather than pursue that question, let us turn to the more important question: What about cases where breaking a rule would benefit some people but harm someone else? For instance, we have a rule against framing people, particularly innocent people. Breaking this rule would harm the person framed, but others might benefit. Consider a (very unlikely) situation where for some reason the harm caused to the innocent person is less than the aggregate benefit to others. Now suppose that framing the innocent person would produce at least a little greater net welfare than any alternative possible act. In any such case, act utilitarianism licenses framing the innocent person under such circumstances. Some philosophers try to defend act utilitarianism here by arguing that framing an innocent person could be the lesser of two evils in catastrophic cases. Suppose that the only way of preventing hundreds or thousands or even millions of innocent people from dying is to frame some innocent person for some crime. In such catastrophic cases, many people would admit that morality would reluctantly allow, or even require, framing the innocent person.

But those who admit this need hardly go as far as act utilitarianism does. Act utilitarianism holds that breaking a promise or stealing or injuring or even framing an innocent person is morally right not only when such an act would prevent a catastrophe but also when it would produce only a little greater net aggregate welfare than not performing the act. This act-utilitarian claim is terribly counterintuitive.

This is not the only place where act utilitarianism departs dramatically from our intuitive views. Consider the act-utilitarian view of praise and blame. As Smart explained, act utilitarians since Sidgwick have held that an action is to be praised if and only if praising it maximizes utility, and blamed if and only if blaming it maximizes utility. Act utilitarianism also holds that an action, which might be praised or blamed, is morally right if and only if the action maximizes utility. So what about cases where utility would be maximized if blame were directed at an action that itself maximized utility? Act utilitarianism holds that in such cases the right action should be blamed. Likewise, act utilitarianism can hold that a wrong action (one that failed to maximize utility) should be praised if praising the wrong action would for some reason maximize utility.

Again, these are counterintuitive claims. Common moral awareness sees a much tighter connection between an action's being morally right and its being praiseworthy than act utilitarianism allows. Equally, common moral awareness sees a much tighter connection between an action's being morally wrong and its being blameworthy than act utilitarianism allows.

Another way in which act utilitarianism is counterintuitive has come to light as a result of an article published by Peter Singer in 1971, the same year in which Rawls's book was published. On highly plausible assumptions about the disparity in wealth in the world, the needs of the billion worst off, the diminishing marginal utility of wealth, and the unwillingness of most others to contribute significantly to reducing world poverty, act utilitarianism seems to demand nothing less than huge sacrifices from the average individual in a relatively wealthy country for the sake of helping the poorest in the world. An average individual in a relatively wealthy country could save someone's life by making a small contribution to one of the best relief organizations. That is true of the first contribution an individual might make, but also of each of very many further contributions. True, if most average individuals in wealthy countries made personal contributions to the most efficient poverty-relief organizations, each of them might not need to contribute more than a few percent of annual income. But in fact the average person in the relatively wealthy country knows that most others will not give anything at all. In this context, act utilitarianism makes extreme demands on the average person in relatively wealthy countries.

How far do these demands go? Act utilitarianism requires you to keep making contributions until you reach a point where further contributions on your part fail to maximize net aggregate utility. The most obvious way further contributions could fail to maximize net aggregate utility would be for the harm to you and your dependents to be at least as great as the benefits produced for the recipients of aid. Another way in which further contributions from you could fail to maximize net aggregate utility would be for those contributions to undermine your capacity to make more contributions later. In any case, act utilitarianism seems to require enormous sacrifices from the average person in a relatively wealthy country to rescue the needy of the world. A very high level of personal sacrifice for such a worthy cause is obviously admirable. And *some* level of personal sacrifice for such a worthy cause does seem morally *required*. But the level of sacrifice that is required by morality seems, intuitively, nowhere near as high as act utilitarianism claims it is.

Much of the work on utilitarianism since the publication of Rawls's book has focused on whether any version of the theory has intuitively acceptable implications. For example, Derek Parfit (1984) has sought a utilitarian principle with intuitively acceptable implications about how large the population should be. Again, Fred Feldman (1997) and Shelly Kagan (1999) have suggested supplementing act utilitarianism with a principle of desert: It matters not just how much net benefit is produced but also that benefits go to the deserving rather than to the undeserving. A difficulty with the latter approach, however, is that it appears to presuppose and leave unexplained principles about desert that a different utilitarian approach could easily explain. Why should only those who do certain kinds of acts be punished? Why should those who do certain other kinds of things be praised or otherwise rewarded? Because significant benefits will result from social practices of punishing those who do certain kinds of act and from social practices of praising and rewarding those who do certain other kinds of act. This is a rule-utilitarian explanation.

Indeed, if we are looking for a version of utilitarianism to be in reflective equilibrium with the moral judgments we make after careful reflection, act utilitarianism seems quite inferior to rule utilitarianism. Rule utilitarianism claims that an act is wrong if it is forbidden by rules whose internalization would produce the greatest (expected) utility. Rules that forbid promise breaking, stealing, lying (including framing the innocent), physical attack, and so on, produce greater utility than rules that allow these kinds of acts. So rule utilitarianism has no difficulty explaining why these kinds of acts are wrong.

Smart did not agree. He suggested that most people believe that a practice of framing the innocent would be wrong even in a possible world in which such a practice, as a rule, would maximize utility. But is there an empirically possible world in which not just one instance, but a general *practice*, of framing the innocent would maximize utility? Surely there is not *if* any such practice would have to be publicly known. For if a practice of framing the innocent became publicly known, public confidence in the police and courts would quickly dissipate, with terrible consequences for social order.

This point brings out an important difference between act utilitarianism and rule utilitarianism. Again as Sidgwick (1907) noticed, act utilitarianism might endorse what he called an "esoteric morality," that is, a principle determining right and wrong whose correctness should be known about by less than everyone, perhaps even by only a few. In contrast, rule utilitarians are hostile to the idea of secret rules determining what people are or are not morally allowed to do. As John Harsanyi (1982, 1993) has stressed, rule utilitarianism, in evaluating any proposed code of rules, attaches great importance to the expectations and incentives that would follow from public knowledge of the social acceptance of the rules.

Following Richard Brandt (1979), rule utilitarians have also stressed that the costs of getting a code of rules internalized by new generations of agents must be counted as part of the cost/benefit assessment of that code. The focus here is on new generations so as not to let the cost/benefit assessment of a code be influenced by which rules a society happens to accept already.

As rules become more numerous and complicated and as they demand more self-sacrifice, the costs of getting new generations to internalize them increase. At some point, the costs of yet more rules, or of greater complication, outweigh the benefits. Likewise, at some point the costs of getting new generations to internalize yet more demanding rules about helping the world's needy will outweigh the benefits of having agents willing to make the sacrifices necessary to help. So there are compelling rule-utilitarian reasons to restrict the number, complexity, and demandingness of rules. These restrictions help rule utilitarianism generate rules that accord with our intuitive views and conflict with act-utilitarian demands.

For about thirty years after the publication of Smart's entry in the first edition of this encyclopedia, most philosophers were persuaded by his objection that rule utilitarianism is fatally flawed. Smart wrote, "The rule utilitarian also appeals ultimately to feelings of generalized benevolence. … He is then inconsistent if he prescribes that we should obey a rule (even a generally beneficial rule) in those cases in which he knows that it will *not* be most beneficial to obey it." If what ultimately matters is how well individuals' lives go, why follow a rule when breaking it would maximize how well individuals' lives go? This objection to rule utilitarianism can be formulated as follows:

Premise 1. Rule utilitarians' overarching aim is to maximize utility.

Premise 2. Rule utilitarians endorse what conflicts with that aim, since their theory requires us to follow certain rules even when following those rules would not maximize utility.

Premise 3. It is inconsistent to maintain an overarching aim and then to endorse what conflicts with that aim.

Conclusion. Rule utilitarians are inconsistent.

One rule-utilitarian response to this objection is to reject its second premise. In other words, this response admits that in cases where following some generally beneficial rule would not maximize utility, the rule should not be followed. The suggestion might be that rule utilitarianism itself has a rule for abnormal cases where following the normal rules would not maximize utility. This rule might be, "In such cases, do whatever will maximize utility." But this defense of rule utilitarianism threatens to collapse rule utilitarianism into act utilitarianism. Such a collapse would be fatal to rule utilitarianism. For if rule utilitarianism ends up endorsing the very same acts that act utilitarianism endorses, why bother with rule utilitarianism, since it is the more complicated of these two theories?

A better way to defend rule utilitarianism is to attack the first premise of the objection, by denying that rule utilitarians must have maximizing utility as their overarching aim. Consider moral agents of which the following statements are true:

- Their fundamental moral motivation is to act in ways that are impartially justifiable.
- They believe that acting on impartially justifiable rules is impartially justifiable.
- They believe that rule utilitarianism is the best theory of impartially justifiable rules.

Agents with this psychological profile are rule utilitarians, but these agents do not have maximizing utility as their overarching aim. So rule-utilitarian agents need not be inconsistent.

Even if rule-utilitarian agents need not be inconsistent, is their theory itself nevertheless inconsistent? Rule utilitarianism consists of two principles: the principle that rules should be selected in terms of their expected utility, and the principle that the rules thus selected determine what kinds of acts are morally wrong. These two principles do not conflict with one another. And neither of them expresses an overarching aim to maximize utility. The theory simply does not contain that overarching aim. Thus, rule utilitarianism can consistently require us to follow certain rules even on occasions when following these rules would not maximize utility.

The ultimate justification for rule utilitarianism may come from its ability to provide general principles that accord with our more specific moral judgments. Admittedly, achieving reflective equilibrium between our principles and our more specific moral judgments cannot establish that the principles or judgments are true. Nevertheless, if rule utilitarianism is attractive in its own right, and if it underwrites and ties together all our more specific moral judgments, and it if does this more securely than any rival general principle does, we have good grounds for accepting rule utilitarianism.

But does rule utilitarianism succeed in providing a general principle that underwrites and ties together all our more specific moral judgments? The answer is uncertain. With Smart's objections to rule utilitarianism now answered, the theory is again under development. However, the possibility remains that the theory will be refuted by counterexample. This will happen if it is discovered that the implications of rule utilitarianism for some kind of case are just too counterintuitive, i.e., if they conflict sharply with our very confident convictions about what is morally required in that kind of case.

One area of persistent controversy is over what constitutes the good that the rules should maximize. Many prominent utilitarians have held that utility is a matter exclusively of welfare and that welfare consists exclusively of net pleasure. But many philosophers have held that there is more to welfare than net pleasure. Some, for example, have held that making significant achievements, obtaining important knowledge, and having deep friendships constitute benefits to the individual, that is, constitute additions to the individual's welfare, beyond whatever pleasure the individual directly or indirectly gets from these things.

There is also controversy about whether rule utilitarianism is right to evaluate rules purely in terms of how much aggregate welfare would result. Many philosophers hold that not only the aggregate amount but also its distribution matters. So, for example, many philosophers hold that an outcome containing greater aggregate welfare might be less good than an alternative containing less aggregate welfare if the worst-off individuals in the outcome with less aggregate welfare are less badly off than are the worst-off in the outcome with greater aggregate welfare. For the sake of illustration, consider an artificially simple example in which the world consists of only two groups of people and only two codes of rules to compare:

First code of rules

	Units of welfare	
	Per person	Per group
10,000 people in group A	1	10,000
100,000 people in group B	10	1,000,000
Total welfare for both groups		1,010,000

Second code of rules

	Units of welfare	
	Per person	Per group
10,000 people in group A	8	80,000
100,000 people in group B	9	900,000
Total welfare for both groups		980,000

Such examples exert strong pressure on us to accept that benefits to worse-off individuals should be accorded more importance than the same-size benefits to the better-off. Philosophers who accept this often call themselves rule consequentialists instead of rule utilitarians.

An as yet unresolved difficulty is whether rule utilitarianism retains its fundamental impartiality if, in the cost/benefit assessment of rules, benefits to the worst-off are accorded more importance than the same-size benefits to the better-off. Certainly, one of the chief attractions of utilitarianism is its fundamental impartiality. This is not something to be jettisoned lightly.

See also Bentham, Jeremy; Brandt, R. B.; Consequentialism; Mill, John Stuart; Sidgwick, Henry; Smart, John Jamieson Carswell; Teleological Ethics.

Bibliography

Adams, R. M. "Motive Utilitarianism." *Journal of Philosophy* 73 (1976): 467–481.

Bailey, James Wood. *Utilitarianism, Institutions, and Justice.* New York: Oxford University Press, 1997.

Bales, R. E. "Act-Utilitarianism: Account of Right-Making Characteristics or Decision-Making Procedure?" *American Philosophical Quarterly* 8 (1971): 257–265.

Brandt, Richard B. "Some Merits of One Form of Rule-Utilitarianism" (1967). In his *Morality, Utilitarianism, and Rights,* 111–136. New York: Cambridge University Press, 1992.

Brandt, Richard B. *A Theory of the Good and the Right.* Oxford, U.K.: Oxford University Press, 1979.

Brink, David O. *Moral Realism and the Foundations of Ethics.* New York: Cambridge University Press, 1989.

Broome, John. *Weighing Goods.* Oxford, U.K.: Blackwell Publishers, 1991.

Crisp, Roger. *Mill on Utilitarianism.* London: Routledge, 1997.

Cullity, Garrett. *The Demands of Affluence.* Oxford, U.K.: Oxford University Press, 1994.

Feldman, Fred. *Utilitarianism, Hedonism, and Desert: Essays in Moral Philosophy.* New York: Cambridge University Press, 1997.

Foot, Philippa. "Utilitarianism and the Virtues." *Mind* 94 (1985): 196–209.

Griffin, James. *Well-Being: Its Meaning, Method, and Moral Importance.* Oxford: Oxford University Press, 1987.

Hardin, Russell. *Morality within the Limits of Reason.* Chicago: University of Chicago Press, 1988.

Hare, R. M. *Moral Thinking.* Oxford, U.K.: Oxford University Press, 1981.

Harsanyi, John. *Essays on Ethics, Social Behaviour, and Scientific Explanation.* Dordrecht, Netherlands: Reidel, 1976.

Harsanyi, John. "Expectation Effects, Individual Utilities, and Rational Desires." In *Rationality, Rules, and Utility: New Essays on the Moral Philosophy of Richard Brandt,* edited by Brad Hooker, 115–126. Boulder, CO: Westview Press, 1993.

Harsanyi, John. "Morality and the Theory of Rational Behaviour." In *Utilitarianism and Beyond,* edited by Amartya Sen and Bernard Williams, 39–62. Cambridge, U.K.: Cambridge University Press, 1982.

Harsanyi, John. "Rule Utilitarianism and Decision Theory." *Erkenntnis* 11 (1977): 25–53.

Hooker, Brad. *Ideal Code, Real World: A Rule-Consequentialist Theory of Morality*. Oxford, U.K.: Oxford University Press, 2000.

Hooker, Brad, Elinor Mason, and Dale E. Miller, eds. *Morality, Rules, and Consequences*. Lanham, MD: Rowman and Littlefield, 2000.

Jackson, Frank. "Decision-Theoretic Consequentialism and the Nearest and Dearest Objection." *Ethics* 101 (1991): 461–482.

Jamieson, Dale, ed. *Singer and His Critics*. Oxford, U.K.: Blackwell Publishers, 1999.

Johnson, Conrad. *Moral Legislation*. New York: Cambridge University Press, 1991.

Kagan, Shelly. *The Limits of Morality*. Oxford, U.K.: Oxford University Press, 1989.

Kagan, Shelly. "Equality and Desert." In *What Do We Deserve?* edited by Louis Pojman and Owen McLeod, 298–314. New York: Oxford University Press, 1999.

Kelly, Paul J. *Utilitarianism and Distributive Justice: Bentham and the Civil Law*. New York: Oxford University Press, 1990.

Mackie, J. L. "The Disutility of Act-Utilitarianism." *Philosophical Quarterly* 23 (1973): 289–300.

Mackie, J. L. "Morality and the Retributive Emotions" (1982). In his *Persons and Values*, 206–219. New York: Oxford University Press, 1985.

Mason, Elinor. "Can an Indirect Consequentialist Be a Real Friend?" *Ethics* 108 (1998): 386–393.

McNaughton, David, and Piers Rawling. "On Defending Deontology." *Ratio* 11 (1998): 37–54.

Mulgan, Tim. *The Demands of Consequentialism*. Oxford, U.K.: Oxford University Press, 2001.

Murphy, Liam. *Moral Demands in Non-ideal Theory*. New York: Oxford University Press, 2000.

Parfit, Derek. "Equality and Priority." *Ratio* 10 (1997): 202–221.

Parfit, Derek. *Reasons and Persons*. Oxford, U.K.: Oxford University Press, 1984.

Pettit, Philip. "Consequentialism and Moral Psychology." *International Journal of Philosophical Studies* 2 (1994): 1–17.

Pettit, Philip. "The Consequentialist Perspective." In *Three Methods of Ethics*, edited by Marcia Baron, Philip Pettit, and Michael Slote, 92–174. Malden, MA: Blackwell Publishers, 1997.

Railton, Peter. "Alienation, Consequentialism, and the Demands of Morality." *Philosophy and Public Affairs* 13 (1984): 134–171.

Rawls, John. "Outline for a Decision Procedure in Ethics." *Philosophical Review* 60 (1951): 177–197.

Rawls, John. *A Theory of Justice*. Cambridge, MA: Harvard University Press, 1971.

Regan, Donald. *Utilitarianism and Co-operation*. Oxford, U.K.: Oxford University Press, 1980.

Scanlon, T. M. "Contractualism and Utilitarianism." In *Utilitarianism and Beyond*, edited by Amartya Sen and Bernard Williams. Cambridge, U.K.: Cambridge University Press, 1982.

Scheffler, Samuel. *The Rejection of Consequentialism*. Oxford, U.K.: Oxford University Press, 1982. Rev. and exp. ed., 1994.

Sen, Amartya, and Bernard Williams, eds. *Utilitarianism and Beyond*. Cambridge, U.K.: Cambridge University Press, 1982.

Shaw, William. *Contemporary Ethics: Taking Account of Utilitarianism*. Cambridge, MA: Blackwell Publishers, 1999.

Sidgwick, Henry. *Methods of Ethics*. 7th ed. London: Macmillan, 1907.

Singer, Peter. "Famine, Affluence, and Morality." *Philosophy and Public Affairs* 1 (1971): 229–243.

Smart, J. J. C. "Outline of a System of Utilitarian Ethics." In *Utilitarianism: For and Against*, by J. J. C. Smart and Bernard Williams, 3–74. Cambridge, U.K.: Cambridge University Press, 1973.

Streumer, Bart. "Can Consequentialism Cover Everything?" *Utilitas* 15 (2003): 237–247.

Sumner, L. W. *The Moral Foundation of Rights*. New York: Oxford University Press, 1987.

Sumner, L. W. *Welfare, Happiness, and Ethics*. Oxford, U.K.: Oxford University Press, 1996.

Unger, Peter. *Living High and Letting Die: Our Illusion of Innocence*. New York: Oxford University Press, 1996.

Williams, Bernard. "A Critique of Utilitarianism." In *Utilitarianism: For and Against*, by J. J. C. Smart and B. Williams, 77–150. Cambridge, U.K.: Cambridge University Press, 1973.

Williams, Bernard. *Ethics and the Limits of Philosophy*. Cambridge, MA: Harvard University Press, 1985.

Williams, Bernard. *Making Sense of Humanity and Other Philosophical Papers*. New York: Cambridge University Press, 1995.

Williams, Bernard. *Morality: An Introduction to Ethics*. New York: Harper and Row, 1972. See especially the final chapter.

Williams, Bernard. *Moral Luck*. Cambridge, U.K.: Cambridge University Press, 1981.

Wolf, Susan. "Moral Saints." *Journal of Philosophy* 79 (1982): 419–39.

Brad Hooker (2005)

UTOPIAS AND UTOPIANISM

The word *utopia* was invented by Thomas More, who published his famous *Utopia* (in Latin) in 1516. More coupled the Greek words *ou* (no, or not) and *topos* (place) to invent a name that has since passed into nearly universal currency. Further verbal play shows the close relation between utopia and *eutopia*, which means "the good [or happy] place." Through the succeeding centuries this double aspect has marked the core of utopian literature, which has employed the imaginary to project the ideal. (This is not to deny that More's own attitude towards the ideal society he imagined may well have been ambivalent.)

The words utopia and utopian, however, have been put to many uses besides the one suggested by More's book. Common to all uses is reference to either the imaginary or the ideal, or to both. But sometimes the words are used as terms of derision and sometimes with a vagueness that robs them of any genuine usefulness. For example, a proposal that is farfetched or implausible is often condemned as utopian, whether or not the proposal has any idealistic content. In another, closely related pejorative use, utopian designates that which is unacceptably different from the customary or is radical in its demands. The connotation of impossibility or complete impracticality serves to discredit a threatening idealism. Similarly, daydreams and fantasies—psychologically driven and frequently bizarre expressions of private ideals—are called utopian, as if utopia were synonymous with deviant or deranged thinking. Even when the word is used without hostility, its coverage is enormously wide. Almost any expression of idealism—a view of a better life, a statement of basic political commitments, a plea for major reform in one or another sector of social life—can earn for itself the title utopian. Furthermore, all literary depictions of imaginary societies are called utopian, even if they are actually dystopias (bad places) that represent some totalitarian or fiendish horror, or are primarily futuristic speculations about technical and scientific possibilities that have no important connection to any idealism.

Much historical experience is reflected in this variety of usage. Indeed, the ways in which utopia (and utopian) are used can be symptomatic of prevailing attitudes towards social change in general. Nevertheless, clarity could be served if we see the core of utopianism as speculation, in whatever literary form, about ideal societies and ideal ways of life for whole populations, in which perfection, defined in accordance with common prepossessions and not merely personal predilections, is aimed at. Perfection is conceived of as harmony, the harmony of each person with himself or herself and with the rest of society. (If there must always be war, then utopian war is waged only against outsiders.) The tradition of utopian thought, in this core sense, is thus made up of elaborated ideas, images, and visions of social harmony.

Not discussed in this entry is dystopian speculation in many genres about the near or distant future, in which the condition of human life is degraded or deformed. In many cases, dystopia shares with utopia a total vision of an imaginary society; but a deliberate hell, not a planned heaven. What brings such a condition into being is zeal to maintain the power of the ruling group, not the project of human well-being. An oppressive and tenacious dictatorship holds sway. The most famous example is the sadistic dystopia of George Orwell's *Nineteen Eighty-Four* (1949).

INSPIRATION OF UTOPIANISM

The forerunners of the utopian tradition are the fables and myths of the golden age, the Garden of Eden, or some benign state of nature. These inherited stories, although of considerable antiquity, look back to some even more remote time in the misty past when harmony was allegedly the normal condition of life. Remorse or nostalgia is the usual accompaniment of these stories. Reality is not what it was, and worldly good sense holds that it is not likely that life will ever be again what it was—except perhaps through some divine intercession.

An uncontrived harmony characterized the primal felicity. Simple people led lives as simple as themselves; because human nature was undeveloped, they were easily made content. If the glories and pleasures of civilization were missing, so were its artificialities, corruptions, and physical and psychological sufferings. Whenever disgust or disenchantment with civilization has become acute, these old stories are retold in order to expose the faults of civilization. But apart from their role in this fundamentally self-conscious method of striking at an existing order, these stories are primarily interesting as repositories of the age-old longings of ordinary humanity. All that the world is not is summed up in short and supposedly seductive descriptions. Sometime long ago, when people were still in touch with their uncontaminated nature, they lived without domination, irrational inequality, scarcity, brutalizing labor, warfare, and the tortures of conscience; they lived without disharmony in any form. The good life is, in the first instance, defined by the absence of these things. Although fondness for an early simplicity may seem regressive—an ignoble attachment to a primitive and subhuman harmony—a principal impetus for utopianism is undeniably to be found here.

The later tradition not only fills out the picture that is only a sketch in the old myths, but more important, transcends the old myths. Whatever wistfulness for the golden age may be present, there is general agreement that primal harmony cannot be regained. The condition of harmony, which defines the good life, must be civilized. It may be more or less complex, more or less scientific, more or less abundant, more or less hierarchical, more or less free, but it must be organized and institutionally articulated (and almost always governed). Throughout the utopian tradition, reality is not defied to the extent of wishing away the idea of a settled society. In Plato's *Republic*, Socrates can dwell only briefly on the excellence of an amiably anarchic rusticity (no war, no class-strife, no politics, no meat-eating, no philosophy or sciences or high art) before his admirer Glaucon, with the stinging phrase "city of pigs," forces him to turn his thoughts to the ideal city (the city of justice, which is founded on the initial unjust act of taking land from others). This transition can be taken as typical of utopianism as a whole.

VARIETIES OF UTOPIANISM

Even with a scrupulous adherence to the definition of utopianism as the succession of ideas, images, and visions of social harmony, the relevant texts are extremely numerous. The main types of utopias include, first, and most properly utopian, descriptions of imaginary societies held to be perfect or much closer to perfection than any society in the real world. They are located in the past, present, or future and are contained in treatise, novel, story, or poem with varying degrees of detailed specification and imaginative inventiveness.

The second type of utopia—closely allied to the first—is found in those works of political theory in which reflection on the fundamental questions of politics leads the theorist beyond politics to consider the social and cultural presuppositions of the ideal political order and the ends of life which that political order (placed in a certain social and cultural setting) can and should facilitate. Whereas the political theorist comes to the forms and purposes of all institutional life by way of political concerns and, as it were, incidentally, the intentionally utopian writer, with Thomas More as the model, works out from the start a comprehensive view of the ideal society and its way of life, a view in which political forms need not be of central importance. Some works of political theory—Plato's *Republic*, for example—so capably discuss nonpolitical matters that they fit into either category.

Those philosophies of history that culminate in a vision of achieved perfection are a third cluster of writings that are not imaginary projections of the ideal but display instead metaphysical optimism of a total kind. These are the theories of inevitable progress created by such thinkers as the Marquis de Condorcet, Herbert Spencer, and Karl Marx. Marx, for one, indignantly fought against inclusion in the utopian tradition because he presented himself as an antiutopian realist blessed with unique insight into the nature of the historical process and its necessary workings carried even to the future, not as an idealist preaching to the world an ahistorical conception of the ideal. For all that, others have taken his writings as belonging in the utopian tradition. Roughly, the same holds for Spencer and some other philosophers of history. No list of the major sources of utopian literature would be acceptable without theorists of inevitable progress.

Fourth are those works—sometimes called philosophical anthropologies—in which the writer attempts not only to isolate the instincts, traits, and capacities that are peculiar to humanity among all species in nature, but also to specify what is genuinely human rather than merely conventional, and what human growth and fuller realization would be. These discourses are not always consciously utopian; they may be directed to individual reformation or to preparation for the afterlife. Furthermore, the discussion may be carried on without reference to concrete social practices and institutions. That is, philosophical anthropologies aim to assess the various kinds of human activity, the various pleasures open to human beings, or the various styles of life made possible by advancing civilization or cumulatively progressive science. A few examples are Schiller's *On the Aesthetic Education of Man* (1795), Ernst Bloch's *The Principle of Hope* (1955–1959), Herbert Marcuse's *Eros and Civilization* (1955), and Norman O. Brown's *Love's Body* (1966). But despite the abstract quality of philosophical anthropology, and whatever the intentions of a given writer, it would be unduly constrictive to omit altogether this literature from an account of utopianism. When its idealism is manifest, philosophical anthropology is thus highly relevant to or allied with utopianism.

In the fifth group are prophecies of profound alteration for the better in human existence made by religious groups, statements of purpose made by revolutionary groups, and blueprints offered by individuals, sects, and secular associations. Obviously, not all activist and reformist political and religious groups have sought to remake society completely, in conformity with the utopian aim of harmony. Nevertheless, many groups have not been satisfied merely to speculate about the ideal society but have sought to realize it, either by persuasion or violence. Examples are the sixteenth-century Anabaptist millenarian, or chiliastic, movements in Europe, radical Protestant groups in the English civil war in the middle of the seventeenth century, and some of the marginal radical figures in the French Revolution, such as Gracchus Babeuf. And in the nineteenth century, especially in the United States, small bands of eager people, religious or simply high-minded, formed utopian communities on unoccupied land, enclaves in isolation from the larger society. Some residues continued to exist after the nineteenth century. In the second half of the twentieth century, for example, a few communal utopian experiments in the United States were inspired by *Walden Two*

(1948), the utopian novel by B. F. Skinner, a behavioral psychologist.

CAUSES OF UTOPIANISM

The literature of social harmony is thus extensive and diverse. Some periods and some cultures have been richer in utopianism than others. The question therefore arises as to why some persons become utopian in their thought or, more rarely, in their action. What causes the desire for change to be absolute, the character of idealism to be extreme and uncompromising, the passion for harmony so averse to the normal condition of dispute and dissonance? Several answers are found scattered in the history of utopianism; some indicate urgency, others do not.

First, some intellectuals simply need to invent worlds. The construction of a utopia, even if only on paper, is a godlike act and resembles the creation of a fictional world by the nonutopian novelist. A utopia can thus be an effort at mastering the complexity of social phenomena; part of the effort consists of rearranging social phenomena to form a more rational or beautiful pattern. In short, one impulse that sustains utopianism, from Plato to the latest science fiction, is to give imagination free rein. This is serious intellectual playfulness. (The same could be said about philosophers of inevitable progress, howsoever they present their optimism.)

Another cause is the desire for moral clarity. In the course of carrying one's demands on social reality as far as possible, one may achieve a fixed—potentially rigid—position in relation to that reality. As a consequence, reality can be constantly put to the test. To the utopian writer, improvisation that allows purposes to emerge from the onrush of experience or waits for new means to suggest or impose new ends is nothing more than a passive or complacent or naive immersion in reality or a confused and unprepared reception of it. Although utopian writers may do nothing to improve society, they may still deem it worthwhile to preserve the concept of the ideal. This may be thought desirable even in comparatively decent societies; to insist on the distinction between the acceptable and the ideal can have a chastening influence on those who govern as well as on those who happily go along. The utopian writer in all varieties of utopianism promotes dissatisfaction and self-criticism, with the risk, of course, of simultaneously provoking a reinvigorated defense of the status quo.

A further cause of utopian thought—and one that lacks the quality of comparative detachment present in the two preceding ones—is the wish to subject society to a total indictment. What is involved here is not a sense that things could be, or may always be, much better than they are but that everything, or nearly everything, is intolerable—inhumanly oppressive—and deserves to go under. There is the direct, unappeasable indictment of established institutions, the way of Jean-Jacques Rousseau in his discourses, William Blake in some of his long poems, Marx and Engels in *The Communist Manifesto*, or D. H. Lawrence in his two books on the unconscious. In works of this sort hatred of social reality may be stronger than love of any alternative; the positive utopianism may be only implicit.

Other works propose, in contrast, that existing social conditions are a spurious utopia: the mass pleasures, whether technological or licentious, provided by affluent society block the way to a genuine transformation of the human condition into a genuine utopia. Such was the theme of the Frankfurt School of social critique in the middle third of the twentieth century. The indictment of society is indirect when the utopianism is explicit and the practices of the ideal society are sketched. And because the main aim is to indict, the practices of the ideal society are, at least in large part, the contradiction of those in existence. The utopian imagination in these instances is hemmed in by the grave defects of the real world; the urge is strong to replace them by conditions that in no way resemble them or to discredit them intellectually. Utopian writing so motivated may blend into radical satire aimed at the status quo and produce a work as great as Jonathan Swift's *Gulliver's Travels* (1726). Or it may produce works such as William Morris's *News from Nowhere* (1891) that are plainly archaistic and may expose themselves to the charge of immaturity or irrelevance. Almost all utopian works contain curiosities and excesses, which may often be explained as compensatory responses to especially terrible features of the real world.

A similar cause of utopian thought is tactical. There are times when it may appear to those bent on reforming society that overstatement is necessary for some degree of success. That is, utopian works need not harbor utopian intentions or even an abstract utopian commitment. Although writers may lavish great energy on making their utopias plausible and attractive, they may aspire only to contribute to the gradual and partial amelioration of their societies. By painting fair pictures of felicity and suggesting that the world is, as presently made up, remote from that felicity, they may encourage an innovating spirit. At the same time, these utopias will give at least guidelines for reform. There may be no real expectation that the utopia will ever fully materialize or, indeed, that pure felicity can be had on any terms. Nevertheless, without that exaggeration, less-than-utopian reform would perhaps be too modest or too slow. Much depends on the persuasiveness of the writer's scheme. For that reason the utopias of reform tend to be less free in their speculation and are content to suggest the completion of certain good tendencies in the real world rather than trying to overturn it theoretically. Edward Bellamy's *Looking Backward, 2000–1887* (1888) is an example of this tactic.

The last cause of utopian thought is the most obvious—the conviction that the whole truth about human well-being in a setting of social harmony is known, can be imparted, and should be acted on. There is, of course, a wide variety in the historical situations that call forth such an overweening attitude. But if some radical Protestant groups (such as the German Anabaptists of the sixteenth century), some utopian movements of the nineteenth century (such as those inspired by the Comte de Saint-Simon, Charles Fourier, and Robert Owen), and those Marxists who are quasi-utopian are exemplary, there must be a sense of deep, intolerable wrong. There must also be a sense of enormous possibility, of not only righting the wrong but also going beyond to perfection itself, and either an overpowering group- or self-confidence or the conviction that the utopian leaders and their following are the instruments of some higher will or the culmination of some impersonal process. The word *messianism* perhaps best summarizes some manifestations of this utopian spirit.

USES OF UTOPIANISM

Apart from their place in history, of what use are the works of utopianism? When utopian writings are deliberate constructions of whole societies, readers may think that utopianism is simply a scattering of uninhabited palaces—grand imaginary structures that may amuse realists if not filling them with contempt. But utopianism is more than its core, the deliberate constructions made by the imagination. The utopian aspiration is found in various modes of writing, and is sometimes oblique or even hidden. Is there, however, something of enduring value, in all these modes, even the deliberate constructions, apart from any question of application? There are, in fact, several benefits conferred by utopianism.

As already noted, a cause of utopian writing is playful delight in the act of imagining new kinds of social reality. This delight can be answered by the pleasure the reader takes in the results of that playfulness. The standards for judging utopianism (in any of its modes) from this point of view are primarily aesthetic—plausible novelties in the projected way of life, clever and ingenious details, daring departures from customary practices. The inner coherence of the utopian ideal matters more than any closeness to probability, although naturally too much strain on belief weakens the pleasure. Admiration for the skill of the utopian writer may be mixed with appreciation for being allowed to contemplate what it would mean to live other lives. No stimulus to make one's own better need be felt. This may make the utopian enterprise somewhat precious, but it can be a source of guiltless satisfaction even to the most conservative temperaments. The utopian works of H. G. Wells are famous for their power to gratify the taste for sampling different worlds, however else they may instruct.

A second use of utopianism is as a record of human aspiration. For the record to be complete, many other kinds of utterance must be consulted, but the various modes of utopianism supply a valuable indication. They are peculiarly vivid forms taken by changeable human longings underlain by permanent human wants. Read with due allowance for their often lopsided or eccentric quality, they will shed vivid light on their times. The desperation of a given historical period, together with the limits of its hopefulness, may emerge from a study of its utopian writings. The abundance or paucity of utopian writing is itself an aid to understanding a period.

Third is the contribution of several modes of utopian literature to general sociology. The great constructed utopias—Plato's *Republic* and *Laws*, the relevant parts of Aristotle's *Politics*, More's *Utopia*, Tommaso Campanella's *The City of the Sun* (1623), Morelly's *Code de la nature* (1755), the writings of Saint-Simon and Fourier (early nineteenth century), H. G. Wells's *A Modern Utopia* (1905)—incorporate a great deal of sociological wisdom. Common to these and other utopias is the idea of the integration of social institutions in its most intense version, utopian harmony. To utopian writers no habit or practice seems innocent of significance for the proper maintenance of the utopian society. Utopian writers are therefore constantly pointing out connections between things that appear unrelated. Part of utopian analysis consists in the attempt to identify the major elements of society and to demonstrate how they act on one another and how each must be adjusted to the others if the best possible world is to be attained. For all their care, utopian writers commit a radical abstraction when they create their images of perfection, but this is the price paid by all general sociology, including that which is wholly neutral and descriptive.

The last use of utopianism is moral. Utopian literature (including the literature relevant or allied to it) is a repository of reflection on human nature. Although not directly concerned to expose frailty, to scrutinize motives, and to astonish with cynical revelations, utopian literature has in it much hard psychological intelligence. Utopian writers disagree among themselves on the extent to which human nature is reformable, but rarely is this problem treated lightly. Indeed, it is usually acknowledged as the problem requiring the deepest study; it is also the source of the greatest hesitation. The principal mission of utopianism is to encourage the hope that human nature is changeable for the better beyond the limits assigned by worldly pessimism or theological despair. That the real world, despite its amazing pluralist variety, still does not exhaust the possibilities of human nature is the heart of utopianism. The long series of utopian texts enlarge the world by suggesting new character types and new social milieus in which these types could emerge. They also enlarge the world by their claim that the societies of the world ignore, repress, distort, or destroy human potentialities that have not yet been fulfilled.

It is true that the concept of harmony rules out some segment of the spectrum of human nature. The essence of antiutopianism is the charge that any imaginable utopia, like any generous philosophical anthropology, actually impoverishes human nature by not allowing scope to those traits—wildness, excess, discontent, perversity, risk-taking, heroism—that threaten harmony. If therefore the precondition of a harmonious life is the thorough manageability of people, allegedly for their own good, human nature must suffer a terrible diminution. Such diminution is the awful hidden human sacrifice that utopianism exacts with a good conscience. What intensity of experience, what craving for more than satisfaction, what passion for the unknown and the unlimited, would be left? Humanity should always face difficulties that are impossible or nearly impossible to overcome.

For many people, perhaps most, utopia can and does already appear in experiences and temporary conditions, in moments and episodes, in the world as it is. Each person's utopia is different from everyone else's. Utopia cannot be an uninterrupted and common way of life for a whole society. The only genuine utopia is actual life, and every proposed utopia is a dystopia. The critique of utopianism is without doubt a rich field and numbers Friedrich Nietzsche and Fyodor Dostoyevsky among its luminaries. A shrewd and witty antiutopian satire is Aldous Huxley's novel *Brave New World* (1932). A related antiutopian theme is that utopias are often driven by a strong passion for equality that threatens to efface all that is fine or rare in life or that can be created by or appeal to only a few. Utopias level society and thus work to make people more or less uniform and interchangeable; preaching individual expressive growth, utopias often destroy the social and psychological conditions of such growth. Utopian harmony is only monotonous.

In rebuttal, utopian writers and their sympathizers are proud to confine their imagination to the realm of the largest happiness. Within that realm, utopians say, much more human excellence is possible than many people commonly think. That would be proven, if only the world, or a part of it, could be transformed or would become more permissive. Without subscribing to any set of specific utopian ideas, one can appreciate—at least to a moderate extent—the efforts of utopian writers to rescue this sentiment from the disparagement of those who believe, explicitly or not, that pain not only will but should remain, if not definitive of the human condition, then its substratum.

See also Civil Disobedience; Cosmopolitanism; Multiculturalism; Postcolonialism; Republicanism.

Bibliography

Buber, Martin. *Paths in Utopia*. 1949. Translated by R. F. C. Hull. Boston: Beacon, 1970.

Bury, J. B. *The Idea of Progress*. 1932. New York: Dover, 1955.

Cioran, E. M. *History and Utopia*. 1960. Translated by Richard Howard. New York: Seaver Books, 1987.

Claeys, Gregory, and Lyman Tower Sargent, eds. *The Utopia Reader*. New York: New York University Press, 1999.

Cohn, Norman. *The Pursuit of the Millennium*. 2nd edition. 1957. New York: Oxford University Press, 1970.

Gray, Alexander. *The Socialist Tradition, Moses to Lenin*. London: Longman's Green, 1946.

Horsburgh, H. J. N. "The Relevance of the Utopian." *Ethics* 67 (1957): 127–138.

Kateb, George, ed. *Utopia*. New York: Atherton, 1971.

Kateb, George. *Utopia and Its Enemies*. 2nd edition. New York: Schocken, 1972.

Lovejoy, Arthur O., et al., eds. *A Documentary History of Primitivism*. 1935. New York: Octagon Books, 1965.

Mannheim, Karl. *Ideology and Utopia*. 1929, 1936. Translated by Louis Wirth and Edward Shils. New York: Harcourt, Brace, 1968.

Manuel, Frank E., ed. *Utopias and Utopian Thought*. Boston: Beacon, 1966.

Manuel, Frank. E., and Fritzie P. Manuel, eds. *French Utopias*. New York: Free Press, 1966.

Manuel, Frank E., and Fritzie P. Manuel. *Utopian Thought in the Western World*. Cambridge, MA: Harvard University Press, 1979.

More, Thomas. *Utopia*, edited and translated with an introduction by David Wootton. Indianapolis: Hackett, 1999.

Mumford, Lewis. *The Transformations of Man*. New York: Harper, 1956.

Negley, Glen. *Utopian Literature: A Bibliography*. Lawrence, KS: Regents Press of Kansas, 1978.

Negley, Glenn, and J. Max Patrick, eds. *The Quest for Utopia*. New York: H. Schuman, 1952.

Noyes, John Humphrey. *History of American Socialisms*. 1870. New York: Dover, 1961.

Polak, Fred L. *The Image of the Future*. 1961. 2 vols. Translated by Elsie Boulding. New York: Elsevier, 1973.

Popper, Karl. *The Open Society and Its Enemies*. 5th edition. 2 vols. Princeton, NJ: Princeton University Press, 1966.

Sargent, Lyman Tower. *British and American Utopian Literature 1516–1975: An Annotated Chronological Bibliography*. New York: Garland, 1988.

Thrupp, Sylvia, ed. *Millennial Dreams in Action*. New York: Schocken, 1970.

George Kateb (1967, 2005)

VACUUM AND VOID

See *Quantum Mechanics*

VAGUENESS

A term is vague if, and only if, it is capable of having borderline cases. All borderline cases are inquiry-resistant: Senator Hillary Clinton is a borderline case of "chubby" because, given her constitution, no amount of conceptual or empirical investigation can settle the question of whether or not she is chubby. Notice that this is not vagueness in the sense of being underspecific. If her spokesperson states that the senator weighs between 100 and 200 pounds, reporters will complain that the assertion is too obvious to be informative—not that the matter is indeterminate.

Typically, borderline cases lie between clear negative cases and clear positives. Moreover, the transition from clear to borderline cases will itself be unclear. If one thousand women queue in order of weight, there is no definite point at which the definitely non-chubby end and the borderline chubby begin. In addition to this second order vagueness: There is third order vagueness: There is no definite point at which the definitely definite cases end and the indefinitely definite ones begin.

Vagueness is responsible for Eubulides' 2,400-year-old sorites paradox. This conceptual slippery slope argument can be compactly formulated with the help of mathematical induction:

> Base step: A collection of 1 million grains of sand is a heap.
>
> Induction step: If a collection of n grains of sand is a heap, then so is a collection of $n - 1$ grains.
>
> Conclusion: One grain of sand is a heap.

Long dismissed as a sophism, the sorites began to acquire respect in the 1970s. By 1990, its status was comparable to Eubulides' other underestimated paradox, the liar.

Eubulides may have intended the sorites to support Parmenides' conclusion that all is one. For one solution is to deny the base step on the grounds that there really are no heaps. Since a sorites paradox can be formulated for any vague predicate for ordinary items (cloud, chair), the solution only generalizes by a rejection of common sense. In any case, a few contemporary metaphysicians have championed this radical position. A less strident group hopes that the sorites will be rendered obsolete by science's tendency to replace vague predicates by precise ones.

VIEWS ON VAGUENESS

C. S. Pierce was the first philosopher to propose that logic be revised to fit vagueness. Pierce developed a form of many-valued logic. "Hillary Clinton is chubby" is assigned a degree of truth between 1 (full truth) and 0 (full falsehood), say .5. Truth-values of compound statements are then calculated on the basis of rules. Disjunctions are assigned the same truth value as their highest disjunct. Conditionals count as fully true only when the antecedent has a truth-value at least as high as the consequent. This "fuzzy logic" undermines the induction step of the sorites. As the progression heads into the borderline zone, the consequent has a value a bit lower than the antecedent. Although a small departure from full truth is normally insignificant, the sorites accumulates marginal differences into a significant difference.

Supervaluationists deny that borderline statements have any truth-value at all. Words mean what we intend them to mean. Since there has been no practical need to decide every case, our words are only partially meaningful. We are free to fill in the gaps as we go along. If a statement would come out true regardless of how the gaps were filled, then we are entitled to deem the statement as actually true. This modest departure from truth-functionality lets the supervaluationists count "Clinton is chubby" or "Clinton is not chubby" as true even though neither disjunct has a truth-value. Indeed, all the tautologies of classical logic will be endorsed by this principle. All the contradictions will be likewise rejected. This suggests a solution to the sorites paradox. For every precisification of "heap" makes the induction step come out false.

Supervaluationism resonates with the use theory of meaning. If a term gets its meanings from linguistic practices, then the incompleteness of those practices will generate semantic gaps. In his work, Derek Parfit (1984) provides the example of a club that stops meeting. After a while, some of the members of the club start meeting again. Is this a new club or has the old club been revived? Parfit maintains this question is empty; there is no true answer or false answer. There might have been a correct answer if the founders had written a constitution that specified the conditions under which the club persists. But the club was an informal institution. Parfit believes our concept of personhood has a similar level of informality. There is vagueness as to when a fetus develops into a person, vagueness as to when brain damage suffices to end a person, and vagueness as to whether a person survives various hypothetical processes such as teletransportation.

Vagueness raises a methodological issue in philosophical analysis. What should be done with borderline cases? In his work, Nelson Goodman (1951) states a good theory is entitled to decide these "don't care" cases. To the victor go the spoils! Others are more sympathetic to the principle of coordinated indeterminacy; we should prefer theories that preserve gaps.

Aristotle postulated we should not demand more precision than the subject matter allows. But Goodman's argument is suspicious of any *a priori* assessment of how much precision is permitted. Just as we may be surprised to find that an apparently determinate question lacks a determinate answer (such as "What time is at the North Pole?"), we may be surprised that an apparently indeterminate question has a determinate answer. For instance, Ernst Mach dismissed the question "Is heat the absence of coldness or is coldness the absence of heat?" as a scholastic quibble. Atomists later showed that coldness is the absence of heat.

Israel Scheffler (2001) traced the belief that there are empty questions to the analytic-synthetic distinction. After all, a borderline case is supposed to be semantically indeterminate. We are supposedly unable to conceive of how the addition of a single grain could turn a non-heap into a heap. Scheffler believes that rejection of analytic-synthetic distinction would prevent intellectualism defeatism. In his work, he urges philosophers to stick to classical logic and persist with inquiry.

Epistemicists embraced Scheffler's logical conservatism but offered a new foundation for defeatism. They said vagueness is ignorance. "Clinton is chubby" has an *unknowable* truth-value. Consequently, the induction step of the sorites is plain false; there is an n such that n grains of sand make a heap but $n - 1$ does not. So there is no need to change logic. Instead we should change our beliefs about language.

The basic objection to epistemicism is that it requires a linguistic miracle. How could our rough and ready practices ensure a threshold for "heap" and "chubby"? Given that the threshold for "heap" exists, what explains our ignorance of it?

Timothy Williamson (1994) answers that knowledge requires a margin for safety. Suppose case n is an F and case $n + 1$ is a non-F that is indistinguishable from case n. The correctness of your belief that n is an F would then be a matter of luck. Since knowledge is incompatible with luck, you would not really know that n is an F. So given that there is a threshold for F-ness, you cannot know it. In his work, Williamson reconciles ignorance with the use theory of meaning by emphasizing the chaotic complexity of linguistic practice. Our computational resources are not sufficient to settle all cases.

Is Williamson's ignorance too relativistic? Parfit's intuition is that no amount of investigation can settle the question of whether the club is old or new—not merely that no amount of *human* investigation is enough. If Williamson were right, then extraterrestrial anthropologists could figure out whether Parfit's club was new by applying their superior intellects. Indeed, since there is variation in human cognition, Williamson's account seems to permit borderline status to vary a bit from speaker to speaker. Supervaluationists and fuzzy logicians claim an advantage because their borderline cases are absolute.

Roy Sorensen (2001) suggests that the epistemicist can model absolute borderline cases with truth-maker gaps. A truth-maker is a state of affairs that makes a proposition true. All contingent propositions that are definitely true have truth-makers. But some truths lack truth-makers. Applying a predicate to a borderline case yields a proposition with a free-floating truth-value. Since we can learn the truth-values of contingent propositions only through connections with their truth-makers, indefinite truths are absolutely unknowable. Since there are borderline cases of "has a truth-maker" there will also be absolute higher order vagueness.

See also Fuzzy Logic; Goodman, Nelson; Many-Valued Logics; Parfit, Derek; Peirce, Charles Sanders.

Bibliography

Evans, Gareth, "Can There Be Vague Objects?" *Analysis* 38 (1978): 208.

Fine, Kit, "Vagueness, Truth, and Logic." *Synthese* 30 (1975): 265–300.

Goodman, Nelson. *The Structure of Appearance*. New York: Bobbs-Merrill, 1951.

Parfit, Derek.*Reasons and Persons*. Oxford: Clarendon, 1984.

Sheffler, Israel. *Beyond the Letter*. London: Routledge, 1979.

Sorensen, Roy. *Vagueness and Contradiction*. New York: Oxford University Press, 2001.

Wheeler, Samuel. "Megarian Paradoxes as Eleactic Arguments." *American Philosophical Quarterly* 20 (1983): 287–295.

Williamson, Timothy. *Vagueness*. London: Routledge 1994.

Roy Sorensen (1996, 2005)

VAIHINGER, HANS
(1852–1933)

Hans Vaihinger, the German philosopher of the "as if," was born in a devout home near Tübingen. Although he developed unorthodox religious views at an early age, he attended the Theological College of the University of Tübingen. Vaihinger wanted to be a man of action, but his extreme nearsightedness forced him into scholarly pursuits. He regarded the contrast between his physical constitution and the way he would like to live as irrational, and his defective vision made him sensitive to other frustrating aspects of existence.

Vaihinger eventually became a professor of philosophy at Halle, but failing vision necessitated his giving up his duties in 1906. He then turned to completing his most important work, *Die Philosophie des Als-Ob* (Berlin, 1911; translated by C. K. Ogden as *The Philosophy of "As If,"* New York, 1924), which had been started in 1876. The volume went through many editions and made the philosophy of fictions well known. Vaihinger also achieved renown as an Immanuel Kant scholar and founded the journal *Kant-Studien.* He also founded (with Raymund Schmidt) the *Annalen der Philosophie,* a yearbook concerned with the "as if" approach. He was much interested in the theory of evolution and emphasized the biological function of thought. On occasion he expressed himself sharply. For example, when quite young he defined humankind as "a species of monkey suffering from megalomania." This resulted in considerable controversy, and Vaihinger later seemed to regret this definition, although he still found some merit in it.

GENERAL POINT OF VIEW

In many ways Vaihinger was attracted to apparent inconsistencies. Although he held theological doctrines to be false in any literal or factual sense, Vaihinger, somewhat like George Santayana, found considerable aesthetic and ethical merit in Christian doctrines. Both idealism and materialism interested him, but he found either alone to be unsatisfactory. Indeed, he regarded the problem of the relation of matter to mind as logically insoluble. He was much influenced by Kant and emphasized the importance of categories supplied by the mind in the perception of objects; yet he wanted to modify Kant in a more materialistic and empirical direction.

Vaihinger's urge to absorb elements of apparently conflicting approaches is illustrated by the label he chose for his philosophy: idealistic positivism or positivist idealism. He was impressed by F. A. Lange's *History of Mate-*

rialism and respected both Lange's Kantian views and his great knowledge of the natural sciences. But even Lange's neo-Kantianism needed to be made more empirical and positivistic, in Vaihinger's view. This was to be achieved by recognizing the necessity and utility of acting on the basis of fictions that are known to be false.

Vaihinger praised Arthur Schopenhauer's pessimism and irrationalism. Too many philosophers (especially G. W. F. Hegel) had believed that the ideal of philosophy was to furnish a rational explanation for everything. But for Vaihinger both nature and history contain many irrational elements, and he regarded Schopenhauer as one of the few philosophers sincere enough to emphasize that irrationality.

Vaihinger maintained that pessimism gives moral strength, enables one to endure life, and helps to develop a more objective view of the world. He emphasized that in his opinion the difficulties of Germany, and especially its defeat in World War I, were largely attributable to the prevailing optimism of German idealism. He saw a close relation between philosophy and practical politics, arguing that a "rational pessimism" might have prevented the war.

FICTIONS

The Platonic myths were the first stimuli to Vaihinger's eventual theory of fictions. Later, Kant's antinomies also were influential. Lange had said, "Man *needs* to supplement reality by an ideal world of his own creation"; Vaihinger expanded this view and applied it to science, metaphysics, theology, social ideals, and morality. Fictions are not to be mistaken for true propositions, for fictions are known to be false. They contradict observed reality or are self-contradictory, and so they falsify experience. Something can work *as if* true, even though false and recognized as false.

Vaihinger distinguished his philosophy from any pragmatism that holds that a statement is true if it is useful in practice. In contrast, he argued: "An idea whose theoretical untruth or incorrectness, and therewith its falsity, is admitted, is not for that reason practically valueless and useless; for such an idea, in spite of its theoretical nullity may have great practical importance" (*The Philosophy of "As If,"* p. viii). Nevertheless, he admitted that in practice pragmatism and fictionalism had much in common, especially in their acknowledgment of the significance of heuristic ideals.

Nor can fictionalism be identified with any variety of skepticism. Vaihinger interpreted skepticism as the doubting of some view. Fictionalism does not doubt the correctness of its fictions; it knows them to be wrong. Vaihinger thought that the label "skepticism" was applied to his philosophy because of its views on God and immortality. He suggested that the label "relativism" (in the sense of opposition to absolutism) better fitted his views.

FICTIONS AND HYPOTHESES. Vaihinger distinguished between hypotheses and fictions. Methodologically they are very different, but they are similar in form and hard to separate in practice. According to Vaihinger, a hypothesis is "directed toward reality" and is subject to verification, but fictions are never verifiable, for they are known to be false. In the case of a number of competing hypotheses, the most probable is selected, but in the case of a number of competing fictions, the most expedient is chosen. Vaihinger held that to treat "Man is descended from the lower mammals" as a hypothesis is to say that we believe that if we had lived at the appropriate time, we would have perceived the ancestors of man, that we may still find the remains of those ancestors, and so on. In contrast, Johann Wolfgang van Goethe's notion of an animal archetype of which all known animal species are modifications was a fiction. Goethe did not believe the archetype had ever existed; he was saying that all animals could be regarded as if they were modifications of the single type.

Goethe's fiction was of considerable value despite its falsity, since it suggested a new classificatory system and had heuristic value for Darwin's later theory. Hypotheses, then, are constructed with the hope of verification, but "the fiction is a mere auxiliary construct, a circuitous approach, a scaffolding afterwards to be demolished." Thus, what is untenable as a hypothesis, especially if exceptions to it are discovered, may be useful as a fiction. Hypotheses are verified by experience, but fictions are justified by the services they render, by their utility.

CHARACTERISTICS OF FICTIONS. Fictions have four general characteristics: (1) They either deviate from reality or are self-contradictory. (2) They disappear either in the course of history or through logical operations and are used only provisionally. (3) The users of a fiction normally are consciously aware that the fiction lays no claim to being true; frequently in the history of thought, however, the first users of a fiction mistake it for a hypothesis. (4) Fictions are the means to some definite end; fictions lacking that expediency are mere subjective fancies.

THE UTILITY OF FICTIONS. Vaihinger adopted a basically biological account of the utility of fictions and made lengthy comparisons of psychical and physical processes, holding that the same general notion of utility applies in both cases. He specifically mentioned "ready adaptation to circumstances and environment," the maintenance of a "successful reaction" to external impulses and influences, and "the adoption and acceptance or the repulsion of new elements." A Kantian emphasis also appears in this context. The psyche is not a receptacle into which sense impressions are poured but is, rather, a "*formative force,* which independently changes what has been appropriated." It is also assimilative and constructive. Logical thought, using fictions, "is an active appropriation of the outer world."

EXAMPLES OF FICTIONS. Vaihinger discussed in great detail specific fictions used in diverse realms of discourse. God and immortality have already been mentioned. It may be a great convenience to act as if the cosmos were orderly and created by an all-powerful and all-good God and as if man were immortal. The virgin birth is another "beautiful, suggestive and useful myth." Vaihinger agreed with Kant that despite the scientific difficulties of the notion, it has practical utility as an excellent symbol of humankind triumphantly resisting evil and raising itself above temptation. In science the atom is a fiction. Both those who defended the literal reality of the atom and the early positivists who rejected its reality on the grounds that atomic theory was internally contradictory were mistaken. The atom is, rather, "a group of contradictory concepts which are necessary in order to deal with reality."

A materialistic notion of the world is false if taken as a hypothesis but is a necessary and useful fiction. Materialism, Vaihinger held, simplifies our notion of the external world and helps to bolster a scientific outlook. Natural scientists carry on their work as if an external material world existed independently of perceiving subjects, and thus science can "proceed on the basis of relations far simpler than those actually presented to a careful observation of reality itself" (ibid., p. 200). The notion of a vital force in biology, while full of difficulties, may have some use as a fiction. Vaihinger regarded such a fiction as "an abbreviation for the sum of all the causes that determine the phenomena of life" (ibid., p. 212). It enables us to express some matters in a simpler way than we otherwise could. To cite one final example, doctrines in social theory, such as the notion of an original social contract, may be helpful. An extremely complicated situation can be grasped by adopting a fiction that deliberately substitutes for "the complete range of causes and facts" a part of that range.

Vaihinger's theory of fictions can be regarded as a denial of the view of W. K. Clifford and others that belief should always be proportionate to the evidence. Intellectually, practically, and morally we need false but expedient fictions to cope with the world. Many traditional philosophic views are mistaken in that they confuse the human need for certain doctrines with the truth of those doctrines; but various forms of skepticism, positivism, and materialism are wrong in assuming that because certain doctrines are false, they should be eliminated.

THEORY OF MIND

According to Vaihinger, all knowledge "is a reduction of the unknown to the known, that is to say a comparison." He held that there are limitations to all thought, although he did not wish to lament them; we cannot leap out of our skins and somehow attain what we cannot attain. These limitations apply not only to man but also to "the highest Mind of all," and they come about because thought originated as a means to an end. The end is to serve the will to live.

THE PURPOSE OF THOUGHT. Vaihinger held that "the test of the correctness of a logical result lies in *practice,* and the purpose of thought must be sought not in the reflection of a so-called objective world, but in rendering possible the calculation of events and of operations upon them" (ibid., p. 5). The purpose of thought is not correspondence with an assumed objective reality; nor is it the theoretical reconstruction of an outer world within consciousness; nor is it the comparison of things and logical constructs. It is pragmatic in the sense that successful logical products enable us to "*calculate events that occur without our intervention.*"

Vaihinger maintained that nature proceeds entirely according to "hard and unalterable laws … but thought is an adaptable, pliant, and adjustable organic function." Very probably the most elementary physical processes contain certain strivings. In organic beings, those strivings develop into impulses. Man, in his evolutionary development from the animals, has had those impulses transformed into will and action. Thus ideas, judgments, and conclusions act as means of survival.

SENSELESS PROBLEMS. Vaihinger put great stress on what he termed the "Law of the Preponderance of the Means over the End." According to this law, the well-adapted means to a specific end everywhere have a tendency to become independent and ends in themselves. Thus the mind sets itself impossible problems that cannot be solved, even by "the highest Mind of all," just because no mind was developed for those purposes. Eventually "emancipated thought" sets for itself senseless problems, among which Vaihinger listed questions about the origin of the world, the formation of matter, the origin of motion, the meaning of the world, and the purpose of life. He gave particular attention to the relation of mind and matter. His philosophy was admittedly inconsistently dualistic; on the one hand it reduced all reality to sensations, and on the other it reduced all reality to matter. But Vaihinger insisted that no logical, rational unification is possible through any philosophy and that the question of the relation of mind to matter is as senseless as that of the purpose of existence.

However, a nonrational solution is possible to the various world-riddles: "in intuition and in experience all this contradiction and distress fades into nothingness." Experience and intuition, Vaihinger said, are "higher than all human reason," and we do not "understand the world when we are pondering over its problems, but when we are doing the world's work." Experience and intuition give us the harmonious unity that reason cannot supply. Philosophers are especially prone to torture themselves with unanswerable questions; the wise man is content if life is successful on the level of practice. Shifts, probably unwarranted, in the meaning of such terms as *understand* occur here, but Vaihinger's main point seems to be that there are nonrational solutions to questions which have no rational answers.

THOUGHT AND REALITY. Subjective events alter reality either by adding to it or by subtracting from it. Yet correct practical results are frequently obtained, and in that sense "thought tallies with reality." Hence, both what Vaihinger called logical optimism, the assumption that thought mirrors reality, and logical pessimism, the assumption that thought is always deceptive, need to be avoided. Senseless questions will not be answered in the future by some new philosophic synthesis but, rather, are explained by "looking backwards," by discovering their psychological origin.

RELIGION

Vaihinger's views on religion illustrate his general reluctance to accept either alternative of some of the traditional philosophic polarities. His early rationalistic, ethical theism later developed into a variety of pantheism. His pantheism then became, during his stay at Tübingen, a kind of Kantian agnosticism and then something close to Schopenhauerian atheism. Vaihinger saw no need to adopt a negative view toward the historical forms of the church and its various dogmas. But even though he regarded many Christian doctrines as fictions of considerable ethical and aesthetic value, doubt entered. For example, although he thought it was a fiction satisfying to many to take the world as if created, or at least regulated, by "a more perfect Higher Spirit," he further insisted that a supplementary fiction was necessary, holding that the "order created by the Higher Divine Spirit had been destroyed by some hostile force."

Vaihinger believed Friedrich Carl Forberg's views on religion were overly neglected. He agreed with Forberg that "theoretical atheism" was harmless and that everyone should have "an attack" of such atheism at least once, in order to find out whether he desired the good for its own sake or merely for some advantage either in this world or in a future world. On the other hand, Vaihinger deplored "practical atheism," understood as the failure to act so as to make the world better. Religion became a mode of behavior rather than the acceptance of certain theoretical views.

Vaihinger held, in agreement with Forberg, that the striving toward the kingdom of God is what matters, not the achieving of it. In fact, it is very likely that the kingdom of God is an actual impossibility. The man who neglects none of his duties to his fellows and helps to further the common good, even though convinced that the world is filled with wickedness and stupidity, practices true religion. Religion is not the belief in the kingdom of God but the attempt to make it come about while recognizing its impossibility. Vaihinger argued that this was the general view of Kant. He believed that this religion not only had warmth and poetry but also "represents in its radical form the highest point to which the human mind, or rather the human heart, is capable of raising itself."

See also Clifford, William Kingdon; Fictionalism; Goethe, Johann Wolfgang van; Hegel, Georg Wilhelm Friedrich; Idealism; Kant, Immanuel; Lange, Friedrich Albert; Materialism; Neo-Kantianism; Pantheism; Pessimism and Optimism; Pragmatism; Santayana, George; Schopenhauer, Arthur.

Bibliography

Additional works by Vaihinger are *Hartmann, Dühring und Lange* (Iserlohn: J. Baedecker, 1876); *Kommentar zu Kants Kritik der reinen Vernunft,* 2 vols. (Leipzig, 1881–1892); *Nietzsche als Philosoph* (Berlin: Reuther and Reichard, 1902); and *Die Philosophie in der Staatsprüfung* (Berlin: Reuther and Reichard, 1906).

The English translation by C. K. Ogden of *The Philosophy of "As If"* was made from the sixth German edition, specially revised by Vaihinger for the English-speaking philosophical world; it also contains a lengthy and helpful autobiography of Vaihinger that emphasizes the intellectual origins of his views.

See also W. Del Negro, "Hans Vaihinger's philosophisches Werk mit besonderer Berücksichtigung seiner Kantforschung," in *Kant-Studien* (1934): 316–327.

Rollo Handy (1967)

VAILATI, GIOVANNI

(1863–1909)

Giovanni Vailati, the Italian analytical philosopher and historian of science, was born at Crema, Lombardy. He studied engineering and mathematics at the University of Turin, where he later became an assistant to Giuseppe Peano (1892) and Vito Volterra (1895) and lectured on the history of mechanics (1896–1899). In 1899 he resigned his university post to be free for independent work, earning his living by teaching mathematics in high schools. By the end of his life Vailati's ideas were internationally recognized; some of his writings had been translated into English, French, and Polish, and he was personally acquainted with many of the important scholars of his time. He was forgotten after his death, however, and only since the late 1950s has he received renewed attention.

The main feature of Vailati's thought is his methodological and linguistic approach to philosophical problems. Rather than propounding anything resembling a doctrine, Vailati presented concrete examples of how to apply his new methods. He left no complete book, but only some two hundred essays and reviews on a great number of problems in several academic disciplines. The best way to indicate the range of his philosophical interests is, therefore, to report the titles of his most important essays in philosophy. In chronological order, they are "The Importance of Investigating the History of the Sciences" (its bearing on the understanding of scientific method); "Deductive Method as a Tool for Inquiry"; "Questions of Words in the History of Science and Culture" (on semantical problems); "The Difficulties that Impair Any Attempt Rationally to Classify the Sciences"; "The Logical Bearing of Brentano's Classification of Mental Facts"; "The Applicability of the Concepts of Cause and Effect in Historical Sciences"; "The Most Modern Definition of Mathematics" (Bertrand Russell's); "The Role of Paradoxes in Philosophy"; "The Tropes of Logic" (in which the important point is made that induction cannot be grounded, because if it were grounded, it would become deduction); "The Hunt for Antitheses" (an attack on the philosophical tendency toward unification and a defense of analysis); "The Distinction between Knowing and Willing"; "The Search for the Impossible" (which contains an assessment of G. E. Moore's *Principia Ethica* and an acceptance of his method); "Pragmatism and Mathematical Logic"; "Toward a Pragmatic Analysis of Philosophical Terminology"; "A Handbook for Liars" (a review of Giuseppe Prezzolini's *The Art of Persuading*); and "The Grammar of Algebra" (containing a comparison of the syntax of ordinary language with that of algebra).

Vailati's next important work, "Language as an Obstacle to the Elimination of Illusory Contrasts," is possibly his most concentrated inquiry into the relation between speech and thought and into the influence of speech on thought. Finally should be mentioned the papers Vailati wrote with his pupil, Mario Calderoni—"The Origins and Fundamental Idea of Pragmatism," "Pragmatism and Various Ways to Say Nothing," and "The Arbitrary in the Operation of the Mental Life." To all these articles Vailati brought a sense of humor; independence of judgment; a mind as cautious, matter-of-fact, and candid as one could wish for in a philosopher; complete control of mathematics, symbolic logic, and the history of the subject being examined; and an extremely concentrated style.

PHILOSOPHY

For Vailati, philosophy is no superscience that can teach scientists what they should do. It cannot make discoveries; it can only prepare the intellectual climate and furnish some of the necessary tools. It is a neutral enterprise that can receive contributions from people holding different personal beliefs and conceptions. It should avoid the struggle between systems which, "let us hope, will some day end like the reported fight between the two lions who ate one another up leaving only their tails on the ground" (*Scritti*, p. 652). As it has no special field of its own, philosophy should not construct any special language or resort to any jargon but should take into account what is already present in language. When a philosopher wants to ban a problematic term to avoid a related problem, he deludes himself; and when he substitutes for an ordinary-language term a technical term of his own or one drawn from a special science, his policy reminds one of "the advice given to children in jest that one can catch a bird by putting salt on its tail" (ibid., p. 315). The right policy consists in correcting the use of the ordinary term—in using it "technically," if you like, but in a technical use as near as possible to its ordinary use. On the other hand, Vailati denounced as misleading similarity in verbal form or in grammar as contrasted with similarity in thought. He defended the independence of the philosopher with respect to usage as such.

Vailati wrote his most rewarding pages on such subjects as definitions, the difference between statements and other types of sentences, the logic of dispositional expressions versus categorical ones, axioms and postulates, deduction and induction, and the use of experiments. Also of importance are several papers on analytical ethics.

Vailati held that "opinions, whether true or false, are always *facts,* and as such they deserve and require to be made the object of research and verification" (ibid., p. 65). Semantically, this is possible because we can understand and talk about sentences of which it cannot be said that they are either true or false. Indeed, "the question of determining *what we mean* when we propound a given proposition is entirely different from the question of deciding *whether it is true or false*" (ibid., p. 923). On the other hand, mere understanding should not be confounded with scientific method, nor does the study of all that can be significantly said supply us with criteria for assessing truth and falsity. One cannot even begin to deal with the question whether a sentence is true or false before settling the question of what is meant by it. But to decide truth or falsity one must connect present and future experiences in terms of prevision, and propositions and facts in terms of intersubjective verification, both in science and in philosophy. In both "it must be demanded of anybody who advances a thesis that he be capable of indicating the facts which according to him should obtain (or have obtained) if his thesis were true, and also their difference from other facts which according to him would obtain (or have obtained) if it were not true" (ibid., p. 790).

VAILATI'S "PRAGMATISM"

Vailati was a liberal analytical philosopher of the kind that has flourished in England and the United States since World War II. However, he is usually referred to as the chief Italian "Peircean," or "logical," pragmatist. He was indeed one of the first to read Charles Sanders Peirce correctly and to carefully distinguish his thought from William James's. But Vailati's thought was too complex and his acquaintance with the history of ideas too thorough, and the concept of pragmatism is itself too manifold, to call him only a pragmatist. Although he stressed the importance of Peirce, he traced Peirce's ideas back to George Berkeley and even to Plato's *Theaetetus,* claiming that Socrates was presented in that work as "defending against Protagoras the thesis now supported by Peirce under the name of 'pragmatism'" (ibid., p. 921). If Vailati was impressed by Peirce's criteria for meaning and truth, he was equally impressed by Peano's work in mathematical logic, Ernst Mach's principle of the economy of thought, Moore's approach to ethics and Russell's to mathematics, Franz Brentano's classification of mental phenomena, the Gottfried Wilhelm Leibniz revival (to which Vailati contributed), and James's conception of consciousness.

Vailati did not possess Peirce's speculative power and overwhelming originality, but neither did he share the American's ontological troubles and commitments, and he gave his own researches a more empirical and methodological bent. By "pragmatism" Vailati meant mainly a new freedom of thought, a refusal to subscribe to any given doctrine, a willingness to use new intellectual techniques, and a cooperative attitude toward philosophical problems. He possessed new methods and new ways of thought which were neither positivistic nor idealistic; and he needed a new banner under which to fight his intellectual battle within Italian philosophy, which was then in the process of passing over from nineteenth-century positivism to the neoidealism of Benedetto Croce and Giovanni Gentile. Vailati's very individual position within that process helps to account for the long silence about his work, some other reasons being the scattered nature of his publications, the fact that he was in advance of his time, and the intervention of World War I and Italian fascism.

HISTORICAL WORK

As a historian Vailati dealt chiefly with mechanics, logic, and geometry. He made important contributions to the study of post-Aristotelian Greek mechanics, of Galileo Galilei's forerunners, of definition in Plato and Euclid, of the influence of mathematics on logic and epistemology, and of Gerolamo Saccheri's work in logic and in non-Euclidean geometry. He gave a remarkable representation (much more than a translation) of Book A of Aristotle's *Metaphysics.* He was particularly interested in the dialectic of continuity and change, in how "the same" problems are faced and solved in different ways in different periods; which, owing to his constant interest in language, meant that he traced the history of the relations between concepts and terms.

Vailati's work as a historian and as an analytical philosopher were closely interwoven; they are two applications of the same attitudes and methods. He saw the difference between theoretical and historical research not so much in their subject matters as in their approach to their subject matters. Philosophers and scientists, he held, should cooperate in historical research and remember that no history is complete unless the social background of ideas is taken into account. In science, past results are not "destroyed" by new ones, for new results make old ones even more important in the very process of superseding them. "Every error shows us a rock to be avoided, while not every discovery shows us a path to be followed" (ibid., p. 65). By his awareness of the importance and his command of the methodology of historical research, Vailati avoided the abstract ahistorical atmosphere and the scientifically biased attitude of many logical positivists.

LOGIC

Vailati wrote some early papers in symbolic logic, but he was chiefly interested in the function of logic within philosophy. He attacked confusions between logic and psychology and between logic and epistemology.

CORRESPONDENCE

Vailati's thought cannot be completely evaluated until the hundreds of letters he wrote to Mach, Brentano, Peano, Croce, Volterra, Giovanni Papini, Prezzolini, Giovanni Vacca, and many others, are published. Many concern topics not dealt with in the *Scritti.* These letters constitute one of the last large scientific correspondences of the eighteenth-century kind. They will throw new light on the intellectual history of Europe around 1900 and possibly establish connections hitherto unnoticed or only suspected.

See also Berkeley, George; Brentano, Franz; Croce, Benedetto; Galileo Galilei; Gentile, Giovanni; Geometry; Induction; James, William; Language and Thought; Leibniz, Gottfried Wilhelm; Logic, History of; Mach, Ernst; Moore, George Edward; Papini, Giovanni; Peano, Giuseppe; Peirce, Charles Sanders; Plato; Pragmatism; Propositions; Scientific Method; Semantics; Socrates.

Bibliography

Vailati's manuscripts (some still unpublished) and many of the letters he received are in the Institute for the History of Philosophy of the State University of Milan. The only almost-complete edition of his papers is the *Scritti* (Florence, 1911), which was followed by two anthologies: *Gli strumenti della conoscenza,* edited by Mario Calderoni (Lanciano, 1911), and *Il pragmatismo,* edited by Giovanni Papini (Lanciano, 1911). *Il pragmatismo* includes a completion of Vailati's notes for a book on pragmatism. Some of his best essays were first reprinted in *Il metodo della filosofia,* edited by Ferruccio Rossi-Landi (Bari, 1957), and in *Scritti di metodologia scientifica e di analisi del linguaggio,* edited by M. F. Sciacca (Milan, 1959). Complete collections of the philosophical papers and of the correspondence are in preparation.

The first contemporary scholar to point out Vailati's importance was Eugenio Garin, in 1946; see his *Cronache di filosofia italiana* (Bari: Laterza, 1955), Ch. 5, Sec. 5. See also Ferruccio Rossi-Landi's introduction to *Il metodo della filosofia*; Rossi-Landi's "Materiale per lo studio di Vailati, in *Rivista critica di storia della filosofia* 12 (1957): 468–485 and 13 (1958): 82–108, with extensive bibliographies and an attempt to classify all of Vailati's papers; and Rossi-Landi's "Some Modern Italian Philosophers," in *Listener* 17 (1450 and 1451) (1957): 59–61 and 97–98. The most complete study is a special issue of the *Rivista critica di storia della filosofia* 18 (1963): 273–523, which contains essays by twenty authors.

Ferruccio Rossi-Landi (1967)

VALENTINUS AND VALENTINIANISM

Valentinus (mid-2nd century CE) was the founder of what came to be one of the most influential Gnostic sects of heretical Christianity. Little can be known with certainty about either his life or his teachings, apart from what has been preserved for us in the writings of the church fathers, much of which is reported only very sketchily, with a view toward refutation. The discovery, in 1945, of important Coptic texts at Nag Hammadi has improved our understanding of his thought, but the texts discovered there (principally the so-called *Evangelium Veritatis* [Gospel of truth]) represent the thought of the various schools drawing inspiration from his teachings and cannot reasonably be attributed to Valentinus himself. St. Irenaeus (*Adversus Haereseis* I) and others assert that he was a native of Egypt, where he is said to have studied under Theodas, alleged to have been a pupil of St. Paul, but reports of both the connection to Egypt and to St. Paul may be motivated by a desire to put him into a certain tradition, whether mystical or theological. St. Irenaeus also reports that he lived in Rome during three pontificates (Hyginus, 136–140; Pius, 140–155; Anicetus, 155–166), and Tertullian (*Adversus Valentinianos*) says that he was in communion until he was passed over for the episcopacy (possibly in favor of Pius, though this is not clear), whereupon he left the church. Tertullian also mentions large numbers of followers (*frequentissimum plane collegium inter haereticos, Adv. Val.* I), some of whom appear to have founded movements of their own, for example, Theodotus, Heracleon, Florinus, Ptolemaeus, and Marcus—these last two serving as particular targets for St. Irenaeus.

The philosophical and theological system of Valentinus bears some similarities to Platonism, though it has also been suggested, with much less plausibility, that his system was founded upon principles drawn from the Ophites, a Gnostic sect particularly devoted to the role of the serpent as metaphor and, in some cases, object of worship. If there were Pythagorean elements, as has also been suggested, they have been very cleverly disguised. Like Pythagoreanism, however, we may say that Valentinianism as we know it comes primarily from the writings of his disciples (and from his critics among the fathers) rather than from any writings of his own that have come down to us. It is possible to divide his followers into two "schools," one in the East (the "Anatolian" or "Oriental") and one in the West (the "Italian"). It has been alleged by some scholars that the Eastern school better preserved the teachings of Valentinus himself, but of course in the absence of empirical data it is impossible to make such a judgment without begging the question. More is said about the connection to Platonism below.

The Valentinians posit a primal being, Bythos (from the Greek *buthos*, "the depth," or "abyss"), who existed before all else, though in some sources he is portrayed as eternally coexisting with the Silence or Contemplation that is his thought. From this primordial pair arose, by emanation, three "syzygies" (Greek *suzugia*, "pair"), pairs of beings known as "aeons" (Greek *aiôn*, literally "age" or "generation" but also personified as a title for a divine being), which may have been conceived as aspects of divinity, though this interpretation possibly reflects a Trinitarian influence that may have been alien to Valentinus. (Some evidence suggests that Valentinus tried to remain in communion with the church, in which case he may have tried to formulate his ideas in a manner conducive to orthodoxy; on the other hand, the refutations of his followers would have been put into the terms and relations most natural to the orthodox writers of the refutations.)

The syzygies themselves represent cosmological opposites such as male and female, and it may be this aspect of the system that has suggested to some a Pythagorean influence. From this first triad of syzygies emanate other aeons, until there are thirty in all. These fifteen syzygies of thirty aeons make up the so-called *pleroma* (Greek *plêrôma*, "fullness," or "satiety"), a realm of immaterial, spiritual being. The last aeon to arise by emanation from the original triad is Sophia who, being farthest from the source of Being, managed through weakness to fall into sin and produce an offspring, Achamoth. If we care to take the comparisons with Platonic metaphysics seriously, we may note that Achamoth appears to represent a metaphysical principle of mimesis, for it creates a rival world, the *kenoma* (Greek *kenôma* "emptiness," or "vacuum"), in imitation of the *pleroma*, and a rival being, the Demiurge, in imitation of Bythos.

The Demiurge is clearly intended to be the God of the Old Testament, since he sets about creating the heavens and the earth of Genesis and everything in them. In particular, he creates humankind out of matter (Greek *hulê*) by imparting into it something of his own psychic substance (Greek *psukhê*). In addition to these two aspects of humankind, the "psychic" and the "hylic," a third, spiritual element, the "pneumatic" (Greek *pneuma*), was incorporated into our nature, apparently without the Demiurge's knowledge.

As in other Gnostic systems, humankind falls into classes that depend upon the degree to which members of the class have access to the saving knowledge (Greek *gnôsis*) that will enable them to escape the temporally finite material existence of the *kenoma* and enter into the eternal bliss of the *pleroma*. In the Valentinian system there are three classes: the *pneumatikoi* (that is, the Valentinians themselves) represent the spiritual, or highest, class, to whom full *gnôsis* has been given; the lowest class, the *hulikoi*, are those whose material aspect dominates and who are thus doomed never to escape from the *kenoma* and who will be destroyed along with it at the end of time; somewhere between lie the *psukhikoi*, or "psychics," the non-Valentinian Christians who can attain a kind of pseudo-salvation by means of faith and good works that will enable them to enter into the same plane of existence as the Demiurge. Christ is an aeon among the original thirty who unites himself (either at conception or at baptism) with the human Jesus of Nazareth (who is present only in a docetic sense), who is then the first to bring *gnôsis* to the rest of humankind.

Apart from the role of the Christ aeon and Jesus of Nazareth, there is little here to suggest Christian origins, in spite of Valentinus's reported desire to remain in communion with the orthodox church, and this fact has prompted some scholars to suggest that the Valentinians were, in fact, merely borrowing from pagan versions of Gnosticism. However, as with the connections to the Ophites, the Platonists, and the Pythagoreans, this is mere speculation. The evidence regarding Valentinus himself is so thin, and that regarding the Valentinian schools so varied and contradictory, that it is quite difficult, if not impossible, to make any clear and non-circular case for the influences and origins of any aspect of the system as a whole. At best, similarities to other philosophical systems can be noted, but it is difficult to draw any secure conclusions about influences. The putative connection to Platonism, for example, clearly lies in the positing of two "realms," one ideal and the other material, with different sorts of beings inhabiting each and the material representing a kind of "falling away" from the ideal; but this kind of metaphysical system can be found in Jewish thought that either predates or is fully independent of Platonism. Of greater significance would seem to be Achamoth as a principle of mimesis, but that construal of his role in the system is already an interpretation beyond what can be found in the actual Valentinian texts, and it cannot serve to establish a definite link with Platonist thought. Similarly, it is perhaps tempting to see Pythagorean "dyads" in the Valentinian syzygies, but mere parallelism is insufficient to establish genuine borrowing.

See also Gnosticism; Platonism and the Platonic Tradition; Pythagoras and Pythagoreanism.

Bibliography

TEXTS AND TRANSLATIONS

Clement of Alexandria. *Stromateis*, edited by J. Ferguson. Washington, DC: Catholic University Press of America, 1991.

The Facsimile Edition of the Nag Hammadi Codices. Department of Antiquities, Arab Republic of Egypt in Conjunction with UNESCO. Leiden: E. J. Brill, 1972–1984.

Foester, W., and R. McL. Wilson, eds. *Gnosis: A Selection of Gnostic Texts.* Oxford: Clarendon Press, 1972–1974.

Hippolytus. *Refutatio omnium Haeresium*, edited by M. Marcovich.Berlin: De Gruyter, 1986.

Irenaeus. *Adversus omnes Haereses* (*Elegkos kai Anatropê tês Pseudônumou Gnôseôs*), editions by A. Stieren (Leipzig: T. O. Weigel, 1848–1853) and W. Harvey (Cambridge: Cambridge University Press, 1857); critical text by A. Rousseau, L. Doutreleau, et al. (*Sources Chrétiennes*, 100, 152 f., 210 f., 263 f., and 293 f. Paris: Éditions du Cerf, 1965–1982).

Layton, Bentley. *The Gnostic Scriptures: A New Translation with Annotations and Introductions.* London: SCM, 1987.

Nag Hammadi Studies. Leiden: E. J. Brill, 1975– (for main editions of texts).

Robinson, James M., ed. *The Nag Hammadi Library in English.* Leiden and New York: E. J. Brill, 1977, 1996.

Tertullian. *Adversus Valentinianos*, edited by J.-C. Fredouille, *Sources Chrétiennes* 280, 281. Paris: Éditions du Cerf, 1980–1981.

Völker, W. *Quellen zur Geschichte der christlichen Gnosis.* Tübingen: Mohr, 1932, esp. pp. 57–141.

STUDIES

Barc, Bernard. *Colloque international sur les textes de Nag Hammadi.* Québec: Presses de l'Université Laval, 1981.

Bermejo Rubio, Fernando. *La escisión imposible: Lectura del gnosticismo valentiniano.* Salamanca: Universidad Pontificia, 1998.

Cross, F. L., ed. *The Jung Codex.* London: Mowbray, 1955.

Davison, J. E. "Structural Similarities and Dissimilarities in the Thought of Clement of Alexandria and the Valentinians." *Second Century* 3 (1983): 201–217.

Dawson, David. *Allegorical Readers and Cultural Revision in Ancient Alexandria.* Berkeley: University of California Press, 1992.

DeConick, April D. "The Great Mystery of Marriage: Sex and Conception in Ancient Valentinian Traditions." *Vigiliae Christianae* 57 (2003): 307–342.

Desjardins, Michel. "Reconstructing Valentinian Families." In *Religionswissenschaft in Konsequenz: Beiträge im Anschluss an Impulse von Kurt Rudolph*, edited by Rainer Flasche et al. Münster: LIT Verlag, 2000.

Desjardins, Michel. *Sin in Valentinianism.* Atlanta, GA: Scholars Press, 1990.

Desjardins, Michel. "The Sources for Valentinian Gnosticism. A Question of Methodology." *Vigiliae Christianae* 40 (1986): 342–347.

Edwards, Mark J. "Gnostics and Valentinians in the Church Fathers." *Journal of Theological Studies* 40 (1989): 26–47.

Good, D. J. "Sophia in Valentinianism." *Second Century* 4 (1984): 193–201.

Holzhausen, Jens. "Irenäus und die valentinianische Gnosis." *Vigiliae Christianae* 55 (2001): 341–355.

Layton, Bentley. *The Rediscovery of Gnosticism.* Proceedings of the International Conference on Gnosticism at Yale, New Haven, CT, March 28–31, 1978. Leiden: E. J. Brill, 1980.

Markschies, Christoph Johannes. *Valentinus Gnosticus?: Untersuchungen zur valentinianischen Gnosis: mit einem Kommentar zu den Fragmenten Valentins.* Tübingen: Mohr, 1991.

McGuire, Anne M. "Valentinus and the *Gnostike Hairesis*: Irenaeus, *Haer*. I.XI.l and the Evidence of Nag Hammadi, XVIII,1." *Studia Patristica* 18, Papers of the Ninth International Conference on Patristic Studies, Oxford, 1983, edited by Elizabeth A. Livingstone, 247–252. Kalamazoo, MI: Cistercian Publications, 1985.

Pagels, Elaine. "Irenaeus, the 'Canon of Truth', and the 'Gospel of John'": 'Making a Difference'; Through Hermeneutics and Ritual." *Vigiliae Christianae* 56 (2002): 339–371.

Pagels, Elaine. "A Valentinian Interpretation of Baptism and Eucharist, and its Critique of Orthodox Sacramental Theology and Practice." *Harvard Theological Review* 65 (1972): 153–170.

Poirier, Paul-Hubert. "Pour une histoire de la lecture pneumatologique de Gn 2, 7." *Revue des Études Augustiniennes* 40 (1994): 1–22.

Quispel, Gilles. "The Original Doctrine of Valentinus the Gnostic." *Vigiliae Christianae* 50 (1996): 327–352.

Quispel, Gilles. "Valentinus and the *Gnostikoi*." *Vigiliae Christianae* 50 (1996): 1–4.

Sagnard, Francois. *La Gnose valentinienne et le témoignage de Saint Iréneé.* Paris: J. Vrin, 1947.

Simonetti, Manlio. "Valentinus gnosticus." *Cassiodorus* 1 (1995): 197–205.

Stead, G. C. "The Valentinian Myth of Sophia." *Journal of Theological Studies* 20 (1969): 75–104.

Townsley, A. L. "St. Irenaeus' Knowledge of Presocratic Philosophy." *Rivista di Storia e Letteratura Religiosa* 12 (1976): 374–379.

Scott Carson (2005)

VALÉRY, PAUL

(1871–1945)

As a law student in Montpellier, Valéry published poems and befriended such influential authors as André Gide and Stéphane Mallarmé. As a result of a personal crisis in 1892, he resolved to abandon literature and devote himself to his autodidactical pursuit of knowledge. While serving in the Ministry of War, and then as private secretary to a powerful businessman, Valéry found time to read and write. In 1894 he began the first of some 261 notebooks in which he developed his matinal reflections for over fifty years. At Gide's instigation Valéry began to prepare a volume of poems, and ended up writing *La jeune parque* (The young fate) (1917), a hermetic allegory of consciousness that established him as an eminent French poet. In 1927 Valéry was elected as a member of the French Academy. He went on to lecture and write about an astounding array of topics, including science, history, architecture, dance, the visual arts, literature, politics, globalization, modern warfare, psychology, and moral philosophy. His achievement includes volumes of poetry, melodramas written to the music of Arthur Honnegger, philosophical dialogues, and numerous collections of essays and aphorisms. A chair in poetics was created for Valéry at the Collège de France in 1936.

Valéry's relation to philosophy was ambivalent. The philosopher, he ironizes, is a "specialist of the universal" (*Oeuvres*, vol. 1, p. 1235). And the universal is only what is "grossier" (coarse or crude) enough to be so (*Oeuvres*, vol. 2, p. 881). The philosopher is an artist who does not admit it. Every abstract theory is at bottom a fragment of an autobiography. Words that serve people perfectly well in ordinary transactions become the object of infernal, Sisyphean labors when philosophers wrongheadedly take words as ends instead of means and look for their ultimate meanings. Words are like a board thrown across an abyss; we can cross over if we move quickly, but not if we linger and test the board's strength. As the past no longer exists, the idea of historical truth is problematic. Origins are elusive, and "everything begins as an interruption" (*Oeuvres*, vol. 2, p. 881).

In spite of his misgivings about philosophical generalizations, Valéry did elaborate various philosophical theses, especially in aesthetics. He critiques inspirationist models of artistic creation; moments of inspiration can only produce fragments. The making of artworks is always a combination of deliberate and spontaneous processes, only their proportion varies. Appreciating a work requires the imaginative reconstruction of the creative process. Yet the creator's thoughts about a work's meaning have no special privilege. In literature, language is an end in itself. Poetry is to prose as dancing is to walking. To describe or sum up a work—in five hundred words or more—is necessarily to fail to convey what is most essential to it.

See also Aesthetics, History of; Aesthetics, Problems of; Philosophy of Language.

Bilbiography

PRIMARY WORKS

The Collected Works of Paul Valéry, edited by Jackson Mathews. 15 vols. Princeton, NJ: Princeton University Press, 1956–1975.

Oeuvres, edited by Jean Hytier. 2 vols. Paris: Gallimard, 1957–1960.

Cahiers. 29 vols. Paris: Centre National de la Recherche Scientifique, 1957–1961.

SECONDARY WORKS

"Selected Bibliography." Valéry Studies, University of Newcastle upon Tyne. Available from http://www.paulvalery.org.

Paisley Livingston (2005)

VALLA, LORENZO

(1407–1457)

Lorenzo Valla, the Italian humanist, is best known as the man who exposed the Donation of Constantine and thus undermined a leading argument for papal sovereignty in the secular realm. This fact and the reputation for hedonism derived from his youthful work *De Voluptate* (On pleasure) have conspired to invest Valla with an air of disrepute that he probably does not deserve. In particular, this reputation does not do justice to Valla's efforts on behalf of a return to the spirit of the Gospel or to his respect for Paul and the early Greek and Latin Church Fathers, in which he clearly anticipates later developments. Nor does it recognize his passion for historical truth and for the defense of plain speaking against what he regarded as metaphysical obscurity and verbalizing. Valla was perhaps the most versatile of the humanists; he initiated a series of attacks upon Scholastic logic, theology, and law, in addition to his contributions to historical and textual criticism.

Valla was above all a brilliant philologian and a staunch champion of the new humanities; most of his writing is best understood from this point of view. Valla was born in Rome. He learned Latin and Greek there and perhaps in Florence, and he spent three formative years, from 1431 to 1433, teaching rhetoric at the University of Pavia. Pavia was a lively center of humanists, and it may have been here that Valla heard the discussions of ancient ethics that prompted him to write the earliest of his extant works, the dialogue generally known under the title "On Pleasure" (Valla actually called it "On the True Good"). Several versions of this dialogue appeared, with the speeches variously assigned to different contemporaries of Valla. Contrary to a widespread impression, Valla does not directly endorse Epicurean ethics in the work; he permits speakers to present Stoic and Epicurean ethics and then, in the person of a third speaker, criticizes their views from a Christian standpoint. This third speaker clearly represents the convictions of Valla himself. The Stoic spokesman presents a defense of Stoic *honestas* or virtue, together with a quite un-Stoic complaint against nature, "which has made men so prone to vice." An Epicurean replies, at much greater length, in defense of nature and "utility." Utility is equated with pleasure and described as a mistress among her handmaidens, the virtues, rather than as a harlot among honest matrons. The third speaker criticizes both of his predecessors and argues that the true Christian should disregard the goals of this life and concentrate on the joys that await him in Heaven. However, this speaker accepts without challenge the equating of "the useful" with pleasure; he insists only that the pleasures a Christian should pursue are not those of this world. Thus, despite his rejection of Epicurean morality, Valla's description of heavenly pleasures is more graphic than we are accustomed to expect from a Christian writer. Renaissance joie de vivre is allowed to assert itself only in a future life. Does Valla depart radically from earlier Christian doctrine, or does he simply make explicit what would constitute the traditional Christian hope if it were spelled out? Obviously there is room for disagreement here, but there can be no disagreeing with the view of the eminent historian Eugenio Garin that Valla's work on pleasure represents a major Renaissance document.

After sojourns in various Italian cities, Valla entered the service of King Alfonso of Aragon, with whom he remained from 1435 to 1448. During this time in Naples, and probably in connection with Alfonso's quarrels with the pope, Valla wrote his most renowned work—his exposure as a forgery of the supposed Donation of the Emperor Constantine of the Western Empire to Pope Sylvester. Although he was anticipated in this by several earlier writers, among them Nicholas of Cusa, Valla's treatise stands out as a very effective piece of historical criticism and, incidentally, a strong plea for the spiritual purity of the Holy See. In view of the latter it should not appear surprising that Valla was later accepted into the pontifical secretariat and spent the remaining years of his life in Rome. The genuineness of Valla's respect for historical truth and his scorn for superstition is shown in such statements as this in the treatise on the Donation: "A Christian man who calls himself the son of light and truth ought to be ashamed to utter things that not only are not true but are not even likely."

While with King Alfonso, Valla also wrote a work on free will, *De Libero Arbitrio*, in which he takes issue with Boethius's treatment of free will in the *Consolation of Philosophy*. In his dialogue Valla distinguishes God's foreknowledge, which cannot be said to be the cause of our volitions, from his will. God's accurate prediction that Judas will become a traitor does not excuse Judas. But Valla refuses to deal with the further question of whether God's will, which cannot be denied, takes away human choice. The divine will, he argues, is known neither to men nor to angels; we stand by faith, not by the probability of reasons.

A similar reluctance to engage in argumentative philosophizing appears in the treatise *Dialectic*, an attack upon conventional Aristotelian logic, printed a half-century after Valla's death. Valla here pleads for the elimination of empty subtleties and vain word-juggling. "Let us conduct ourselves more simply and more in line with natural sense and common usage," he says. "Philosophy and dialectic … ought not to depart from the most customary manner of speaking." Valla's treatment of the Aristotelian categories is not without interest. The Latin word for entity (*entitas*), for example, is simply a coinage of a participle from the verb "to be" that does not occur in standard Latin and hence ought to be regarded with suspicion. To say that a stone is an entity (*lapis est ens*) amounts to no more than saying that it is a thing (*res*), which is perfectly satisfactory and more clear. Therefore, Aristotle's metaphysics, which deals with "being qua being," is meaningless, suggesting as it does that what "is" is "able not to be." Having protested the positing of mysterious entities, quiddities, and essences and having equated substances with bodies or things, Valla then reduces the remaining nine categories of Aristotle to two: quality and action. Definitions, according to Valla, are explications of all the qualities and actions that are present in a thing. In the course of his exposition, Valla has occasion to challenge the validity of many scholastic distinctions: for example, those between the concrete and the abstract, between matter and form, and so on. Unsatisfactory as Valla's own offerings may be (they are not clearly dedicated to the solution of any specific philosophical problems), nevertheless it must be admitted that a fresh consideration of technical terms was certainly called for at the time and was eventually carried through by later critics.

Valla displays great sensitivity to nuances of meaning in his *Elegantiae Linguae Latinae* (Elegancies of the Latin language), in which he makes careful analyses of the usage of many Latin terms. Critics have observed that Valla's own style was not as elegant as it could have been, but his advice was widely consulted.

Valla was often accused of bad form in his attacks on people and schools of thought, but one must recall that invectives and ad hominem attacks were the order of the day. In the Renaissance professional rivalry did not bother to conceal itself under polite or semipolite discussions of issues. Valla defended himself against the charge of malevolence and vindictiveness in a letter to Giovanni Serra, in which he concludes: "I do not censure all authors, but only a few, … not all philosophers but some from all sects, not the best but the worst, not impudently but calmly, ready to accept correction should it prove valid."

See also Aristotelianism; Aristotle; Epicureanism and the Epicurean School; Hedonism; Humanism; Italian Philosophy; Nicholas of Cusa; Renaissance; Stoicism.

Bibliography

Valla's works were collected in an edition that was published in Basel (1540). It has been reproduced, along with some treatises and letters missing from the earlier edition, in an edition with an introduction by Eugenio Garin (Turin, 1962). The standard biography is still Girolamo Mancini's *Vita di Lorenzo Valla* (Florence, 1891). Valla's treatise on free will is available in English in *The Renaissance Philosophy of Man*, edited by Ernst Cassirer, Paul Oskar Kristeller, and John H. Randall Jr. (Chicago: University of Chicago Press, 1948). *The Treatise of Lorenzo Valla on the Donation of Constantine* has been translated by C. B. Coleman (New Haven, CT: Yale University Press, 1922). The treatise on pleasure was published under the title *De verro falsoque bono* by Maristella De Panizza Lorch (Bari, Italy: Adriatica, 1970).

OTHER RECOMMENDED WORKS

Camporeale, Salvatore I. "Lorenzo Valla's 'Oratio' on the Pseudo-Donation of Constantine: Dissent and Innovation in Early Renaissance Humanism." *Journal of the History of Ideas* 57 (1) (1996): 9–26.

Connell, William J. "Lorenzo Valla: A Symposium." *Journal of the History of Ideas* 57 (1) (1996): 1–7.

Jardine, Lisa. "Lorenzo Valla: Academic Skepticism and the New Humanist Dialectic." In *The Skeptical Tradition*, edited by Myles Burnyeat. Berkeley: University of California Press, 1983.

Jardine, Lisa. "Lorenzo Valla and the Intellectual Origins of Humanist Dialectic." *Journal of the History of Philosophy* 15 (1977): 143–164.

Johnson, Lawrence J. "The Linguistic Imperialism of Lorenzo Valla and the Renaissance Humanists." *Interpretation* 7 (1978): 29–49.

Monfasani, John. "Lorenzo Valla and Rudolph Agricola." *Journal of the History of Philosophy* 28 (2) (1990): 181–200.

Monfasani, John. "Was Lorenzo Valla an Ordinary Language Philosopher?" *Journal of the History of Ideas* 50 (1989): 309–323.

Paganini, Gianni. "Hobbes, Valla and the Trinity." *British Journal for the History of Philosophy* 11 (2) (2003): 183–218.

Synan, Edward A. "Boethius, Valla, and Gibbon." *Modern Schoolman* 69 (3–4) (1992): 475–491.

Trinkaus, Charles. "Lorenzo Valla on the Problem of Speaking about the Trinity." *Journal of the History of Ideas* 57 (1) (1996): 27–53.

Neal W. Gilbert (1967)
Bibliography updated by Tamra Frei (2005)

VALUE AND VALUATION

The terms *value* and *valuation* and their cognates and compounds are used in a confused and confusing but widespread way in our contemporary culture, not only in economics and philosophy but also and especially in other social sciences and humanities. Their meaning was once relatively clear and their use limited. *Value* meant the worth of a thing, and *valuation* meant an estimate of its worth. The worth in question was mainly economic or quasi economic, but even when it was not, it was still worth of some sort—not beauty, truth, rightness, or even goodness. The extension of the meaning and use of the terms began in economics, or political economy, as it was then called. *Value* and *valuation* became technical terms central to that branch of economics which was labeled the theory of value. Then German philosophers, especially Rudolf Hermann Lotze, Albrecht Ritschl, and Friedrich Nietzsche, began to take the notion of value and values in a much broader sense and to give it primary importance in their thinking.

Philosophers from the time of Plato had discussed a variety of questions under such headings as the good, the end, the right, obligation, virtue, moral judgment, aesthetic judgment, the beautiful, truth, and validity. In the nineteenth century the conception was born—or reborn, because it is essentially to be found in Plato—that all these questions belong to the same family, since they are all concerned with value or what ought to be, not with fact or what is, was, or will be. All these questions, it was believed, may not only be grouped under the general headings of value and valuation but are better dealt with and find a more systematic solution if they are thought of as parts of a general theory of value and valuation that includes economics, ethics, aesthetics, jurisprudence, education, and perhaps even logic and epistemology. This conception matured in the 1890s in the writings of Alexius Meinong and Christian von Ehrenfels, two Austrian followers of Franz Brentano. Through them and through others like Max Scheler and Nicolai Hartmann, two twentieth-century German followers of Edmund Husserl (himself influenced by Brentano), the idea of a general theory of value became popular on the Continent and in Latin America. It had some influence in Great Britain, in the works of Bernard Bosanquet, W. R. Sorley, J. M. Mackenzie, John Laird, and J. N. Findlay, but rather less than elsewhere, for, on the whole, British philosophers have held to more traditional terms such as *good* and *right.* But it received an excited welcome in the United States just before and after World War I. The idea was introduced by Hugo Münsterberg and W. M. Urban, taken up by Ralph Barton Perry, John Dewey, D. H. Parker, D. W. Prall, E. W. Hall, and others, and later refurbished by S. C. Pepper and Paul W. Taylor. This wide-ranging discussion in terms of *value, values,* and *valuation* subsequently spread to psychology, the social sciences, the humanities, and even to ordinary discourse.

PHILOSOPHICAL USAGES

The uses of *value* and *valuation* are various and conflicting even among philosophers, but they may perhaps be sorted out as follows. (1) *Value* (in the singular) is sometimes used as an abstract noun (*a*) in a narrower sense to cover only that to which such terms as *good, desirable,* or *worthwhile* are properly applied and (*b*) in a wider sense to cover, in addition, all kinds of rightness, obligation, virtue, beauty, truth, and holiness. The term can be limited to what might be said to be on the plus side of the zero line; then what is on the minus side (bad, wrong, and so forth) is called disvalue. *Value* is also used like *temperature* to cover the whole range of a scale—plus, minus, or indifferent; what is on the plus side is then called positive value and what is on the minus side, negative value.

In its widest use *value* is the generic noun for all kinds of critical or pro and con predicates, as opposed to descriptive ones, and is contrasted with existence or fact. The theory of value, or axiology, is the general theory of all such predicates, including all the disciplines mentioned above. The classic example in English of this approach is the work of R. B. Perry. In its narrower use, *value* covers only certain kinds of critical predicates and is contrasted with descriptive predicates and even with other critical ones like rightness and obligation. In this case the theory of value, or axiology, is a part of ethics, rather than the other way around. The work of C. I. Lewis is the best example of the narrower approach.

Those who take the wider approach sometimes distinguish "realms of value"; Perry and Taylor, for example, list eight of these: morality, the arts, science, religion, economics, politics, law, and custom or etiquette. Even when *value* is used in the narrower sense, several meanings of the term, or kinds of value, are sometimes distinguished. (The narrower distinctions may also be recognized by those who use value in the wider sense.) These meanings correspond to the senses or uses of *good,* which G. H. von Wright prefers to call "forms" or "varieties of goodness." Many classifications of kinds of value, or forms of goodness, have been proposed. Lewis distinguishes (*a*) utility or usefulness for some purpose; (*b*) extrinsic or instrumental value, or being good as a means to something desirable or good; (*c*) inherent value or goodness, such as the aesthetic value of a work of art in producing good experiences by being contemplated or heard; (*d*) intrinsic value, or being good or desirable either as an end or in itself, which is presupposed by both (*b*) and (*c*); (*e*) contributory value, or the value that an experience or part of an experience contributes to a whole of which it is a part (not a means or an object). A stick of wood may be useful in making a violin, a violin may be extrinsically good by being a means to good music, the music may be inherently good if hearing it is enjoyable, the experience of hearing it may be intrinsically good or valuable if it is enjoyable for its own sake, and it may also be contributively good if it is part of a good evening or weekend.

Dewey, however, attacks the distinction between means and ends while stressing the notion of total value or goodness on the whole—goodness when all things are considered. To Lewis's list of kinds of value, some writers, W. D. Ross for instance, would add moral value, the kind of value or goodness that belongs to a virtuous man, to good motives, or to morally approved traits of character. Von Wright distinguishes instrumental goodness (a good knife), technical goodness (a good driver), utilitarian goodness (good advice), hedonic goodness or pleasantness (a good dinner), and welfare (the good of man). He also mentions moral goodness but argues that it is a subform of utilitarian goodness; Ross would deny this.

(2) *Value* as a more concrete noun—for example, when we speak of "a value" or of "values"—is often used (*a*) to refer to what is valued, judged to have value, thought to be good, or desired. The expressions "his values," "her value system," and "American values" refer to what a man, a woman, and Americans value or think to be good. Such phrases are also used to refer to what people think is right or obligatory and even to whatever they believe to be true. Behind this widespread usage lies the covert assumption that nothing really has objective value, that *value* means being valued and *good* means being thought good. But the term *value* is also used to mean (*b*) what has value or is valuable, or good, as opposed to what is regarded as good or valuable. Then *values* means "things that have value," "things that are good," or "goods" and, for some users, also things that are right, obligatory, beautiful, or even true.

In both usage (*a*) and usage (*b*) it is possible to distinguish different kinds of values, corresponding to the different kinds of value or forms of goodness mentioned above. It is also common to distinguish more or less clearly between material and spiritual values or among economic, moral, aesthetic, cognitive, and religious values.

Some philosophers, especially those influenced by Scheler and Hartmann, think of *value* as a general predicate like "color," which subsumes more specific value predicates analogous to "red" or "yellow." They call these more specific value predicates "values" (*Werte, valeurs*). Just as "a color" does not mean "a thing that has color" but a particular color like red, so "a value" does not mean "a thing that has value" but a particular kind of value, like pleasure value or courage value. These philosophers call a thing that is good "a good" or "a value carrier," not "a value." Since the adjective *valuable* simply means "having value" or "being good" in some sense (or, perhaps better, "having a considerable amount of value"), much of the above will apply to it, mutatis mutandis.

(3) *Value* is also used as a verb in such expressions as "to value," "valuating," and "valued." *Valuing* is generally synonymous with *valuation* or *evaluation* when these are used actively to mean the act of evaluating and not passively to mean the result of such an act. But sometimes *valuation* and *evaluation* are used to designate only a certain kind of valuing, namely, one that includes reflection and comparison. In either case *valuation* may be, and is, used in wider or narrower senses corresponding to the wider and narrower uses of *value.* For Dewey and Richard M. Hare it covers judgments about what is right, wrong, obligatory, or just, as well as judgments about what is good, bad, desirable, or worthwhile. For Lewis *valuation* covers only the latter use. The expression "value judgment" is also used in both of these ways. Among the writers who distinguish two main kinds of normative discourse, evaluating and prescribing, some, like Taylor, classify judgments of right and wrong as well as judgments of good and bad under evaluations and judgments, using *ought* under prescriptions; others put judgments of right and wrong under prescriptions.

Dewey always distinguishes two senses of "to value." It means either (*a*) to prize, like, esteem, cherish, or hold dear, or (*b*) to apprize, appraise, estimate, evaluate, or valuate. In the second sense reflection and comparison are involved; in the first sense they are not. In the first sense, he seems to regard mere desiring or liking as a form of valuing. Others often follow him in this, but some writers limit valuing to acts in which something is not merely desired or liked but judged to be good or to have value. Even Perry, who holds that the statement "*X* is good" = "*X* has positive value" = "*X* is an object of favorable interest," insists that we must distinguish between desiring *X* and judging *X* to have value, which would be judging *X* to be desired.

Thus, words such as *value* and *valuation* may be, and are, used in a variety of ways, even when they are used with some care—which is, unfortunately, not often the case both in and out of philosophy. In using the terms, one should choose a clear and systematic scheme and use it consistently. Because of the ambiguity and looseness that the terms often engender, it would seem advisable to use them in their narrower senses or not at all, keeping to more traditional terms such as *good* and *right,* which are better English, whenever possible.

PHILOSOPHICAL THEORIES

Philosophical theories of value and valuation, whether conceived in the wider or in the narrower manner and whether formulated in the traditional or in the newer "value" vocabulary, have been of two sorts. Normative theories make value judgments or valuations; they tell us what is good or what has value, what is bad, and so on. Metanormative theories analyze value, valuation, and good; they neither make value judgments in this way nor tell us what is good or has value. Instead, they define what goodness and value are and what it means to say that something is good or has value. Sometimes philosophers also offer descriptive generalizations about what is valued or regarded as good in some culture or group of cultures, and explanatory theories about why this is so valued or regarded (David Hume, Moritz Schlick, F. C. Sharp, John Ladd). However, this is usually ancillary to their discussions of normative or metanormative questions. In themselves such descriptive and explanatory theories belong to anthropology, psychology, and sociology, not to philosophy. Recently, many analytical philosophers have been maintaining that even normative theories, however important they may be, have no place in philosophy proper, where theories of value and valuation should be limited to metanormative questions.

NORMATIVE THEORIES. In the broader conception, a normative theory of value must show, at least in general outline, what is good, bad, better, and best, and also what is right, obligatory, virtuous, and beautiful. In the narrower conception, normative theories of value have usually addressed themselves primarily to the question of what is good in itself or as an end or what has intrinsic value, an approach that Dewey has persistently attacked. They ask not what goodness and intrinsic value are but what the good is, what has value for its own sake, what is to be taken as the end of our pursuit or as the criterion of intrinsic worth.

Some theories have answered that the end or the good is pleasure or enjoyment or, alternatively, that the criterion of intrinsic value is pleasantness or enjoyableness. More accurately, they say that only experiences are intrinsically good, that all experiences that are intrinsically good are pleasant and vice versa, and that they are intrinsically good because and only because they are pleasant. These are the hedonistic theories of value, held by such thinkers as Epicurus, Hume, Jeremy Bentham, J. S. Mill, Henry Sidgwick, von Ehrenfels, Meinong (at first), and Sharp. There are also quasi-hedonistic theories in which the end or the good is said to be not pleasure but something very similar, such as happiness, satisfaction, or felt "satisfactoriness," to use Lewis's term. Examples are to be found in the writings of Dewey, Lewis, Parker, P. B. Rice, and perhaps Brand Blanshard.

Antihedonistic theories are of two kinds. Some agree that there is, in the final analysis, only one thing that is good or good-making but deny that it is pleasure or any other kind of feeling. Aristotle says it is eudaemonia (excellent activity); Augustine and Thomas Aquinas, communion with God; Benedict de Spinoza, knowledge; F. H. Bradley, self-realization; Nietzsche, power. Others, such as Plato, G. E. Moore, W. D. Ross, Laird, Scheler, Hartmann, and Perry, are more "pluralistic," holding that there are a number of things that are good or good-making in themselves. They differ in their lists but all include two or more of the following: pleasure, knowledge, aesthetic experience, beauty, truth, virtue, harmony, love, friendship, justice, freedom, self-expression. Of course, hedonists and other "monistic" thinkers may also regard such things as intrinsically good, but only if and because they are pleasant, self-realizing, or excellent.

METANORMATIVE THEORIES. The scope of metanormative theories may also be inclusive or limited, but both kinds will pose similar questions and offer similar answers. Their questions and answers have been variously stated in the formal or material mode, or the linguistic or nonlinguistic, but they will not be classified here.

One question or group of questions posed by metanormative theories concerns the nature of value and valuation: what is goodness or value? what is the meaning or use of *good?* what is valuing? what are we doing or saying when we make a value judgment? A subquestion here is what moral value and evaluation are, and how they are distinct from nonmoral value and valuation, if at all. Another question or set of questions has to do with the justification or validity of value judgments and normative theories: can they be justified or established with any certainty by some kind of rational or scientific inquiry? can they be shown to have objective validity in any way? if so, how? what is the logic of reasoning in these matters, if there is one? Here a subquestion is what is the logic of moral justification or reasoning, if there is one, and is it in any way distinctive. Beyond this there is an even more "meta" level of questioning: what is the nature of a metanormative theory, and how can it be defended? This last problem, as well as the subquestions just mentioned, has frequently been discussed in the twentieth century and earlier but will not be considered here.

In reply to the first question or group of questions, some philosophers have held that terms like *value* and *good* stand for properties; that in value judgments we are ascribing these properties to objects or kinds of objects (including activities and experiences), although we may also be taking pro or con attitudes toward them; and that, therefore, value judgments are descriptive or factual in the sense of truly or falsely ascribing properties to things. They are therefore cognitivists or descriptivists in value theory. Of these the naturalists add that the property involved is a natural or empirical one, which can be defined. Aristotle, von Ehrenfels, and Perry claim that value is the relational property of being an object of desire or interest (an interest theory of value); Parker, that it is the satisfaction of desire (another interest theory of value); Lewis and Rice (as well as the early Meinong), that it is the quality of being, enjoyed or enjoyable in some way (the affective theory of value). George Santayana seems sometimes to hold one of these views, sometimes another, and sometimes to regard value as an indefinable natural quality ascribed to what we desire or enjoy.

Other cognitivists add that value or goodness is a metaphysical property that can neither be observed by or in ordinary experience nor made an object of empirical science. Examples of metaphysical definitions are being truly real (Neoplatonists), being ontologically perfect (Hegelian idealists), or being willed by God (theologians). Still others assert that intrinsic goodness or value is an indefinable nonnatural or nonempirical quality or property different from all other descriptive or factual ones (they even describe it as being nondescriptive or nonfactual). These philosophers are called intuitionists or nonnaturalists (Plato, Sidgwick, Moore, Ross, Laird, Scheler, Hartmann, and perhaps the later Meinong). They all hold that value belongs to objects independently of whether we desire, enjoy, or value them, and even independently of God's attitude toward them—as some metaphysical theorists and naturalists also do. Meinong, Scheler, Hartmann, and Hall contend that value is intuited through the emotions even though it is objective; Sidgwick, Ross, Laird, and others, that it is an object of intellectual intuition.

In the mid-twentieth century many writers, both analytical philosophers and existentialists, have taken the position that value terms do not stand for properties, natural or nonnatural, and that value judgments are not property-ascribing statements but have some other kind of meaning or function. These writers have therefore been called noncognitivists or antidescriptivists. Their positive theories are varied. Some argue that value judgments are wholly or primarily embodiments or expressions of attitude, emotion, or desire, and/or instruments for evoking similar reactions in others (A. J. Ayer, Bertrand Russell, Charles L. Stevenson). Others maintain that this account of value terms and judgments is inadequate and that value judgments are to be thought of as prescriptions, recommendations, acts of grading, or simply as valuations, not something else (Hare, Taylor, Stephen E. Toulmin, Patrick H. Nowell-Smith, R. W. Sellars, and J. O. Urmson).

Whether value judgments are susceptible to being justified or proved, and, if so, how, depends very considerably on the position taken in answer to the questions regarding the meaning of *good.* Some value judgments are derivative—for instance, the conclusion of the following inference:

What is pleasant is good.
Knowledge is pleasant.
Therefore, knowledge is good.

The real question is about the justification of basic or nonderivative value judgments. According to the intuitionist, such judgments cannot be justified by argument, but they do not need to be, since they are intuitively known or self-evident. According to the naturalist, they can be established either by empirical evidence (in Perry's view, by empirical evidence about what is desired) or by the very meaning of the terms involved (analytically or by definition). According to the metaphysical and theological axiologist, they can be established either by metaphysical argument, or by divine revelation, or by definition. Noncognitivists, being of many persuasions, have various views about justification. Some extreme emotivists and existentialists assert or imply that basic value judgments are arbitrary, irrational, and incapable of any justification (Ayer and Jean-Paul Sartre). Others believe that there are intersubjectively valid conventions, like "What is pleasant is good," which warrant our arguing from certain considerations to conclusions about what is good (Toulmin). Still others contend, in different ways, that attitudes, recommendations, commitments, conventions, and, hence, value judgments may be rational or justified, even if they cannot be proved inductively or deductively (Hare, Taylor, J. N. Findlay, and, up to a point, Stevenson).

See also Aesthetic Experience; Aristotle; Augustine, St.; Ayer, Alfred Jules; Beauty; Bentham, Jeremy; Blanshard, Brand; Bosanquet, Bernard; Bradley, Francis Herbert; Brentano, Franz; Dewey, John; Ehrenfels, Christian Freiherr von; Epicurus; Freedom; Good, The; Hare, Richard M.; Hartmann, Nicolai; Hume, David; Husserl, Edmund; Justice; Lewis, Clarence Irving; Lotze, Rudolf Hermann; Love; Meinong, Alexius; Mill, John Stuart; Moore, George Edward; Nietzsche, Friedrich; Perry, Ralph Barton; Plato; Pleasure; Ritschl, Albrecht Benjamin; Ross, William David; Russell, Bertrand Arthur William; Santayana, George; Sartre, Jean-Paul; Scheler, Max; Schlick, Moritz; Sellars, Roy Wood; Sidgwick, Henry; Spinoza, Benedict (Baruch) de; Stevenson,

Charles L.; Thomas Aquinas, St.; Truth; Virtue and Vice; Wright, Georg Henrik von.

Bibliography

INTRODUCTIONS

Frankena, William K. *Ethics.* Englewood Cliffs, NJ: Prentice-Hall, 1963. Elementary and systematic.

Frondizi, Risieri. *What Is Value?* Translated by Solomon Lipp. La Salle, IL, 1963. A useful elementary historical and critical work.

Nowell-Smith, Patrick H. *Ethics.* London: Penguin, 1954. A British systematic and analytical approach.

SYSTEMATIC DISCUSSIONS AND HISTORY

Blanshard, Brand. *Reason and Goodness.* New York: Macmillan, 1961. Scholarly and clear.

Laird, John. *The Idea of Value.* Cambridge, U.K.: Cambridge University Press, 1929. Scholarly and complex.

USAGES OF TERMS

Garnett, A. Campbell. *The Moral Nature of Man.* New York: Ronald Press, 1952. Ch. 4 is a useful, clear critique of prevailing semantic confusion.

Lepley, Ray, ed. *The Language of Value.* New York: Columbia University Press, 1957.

Lepley, Ray, ed. *Value: A Cooperative Inquiry.* New York: Columbia University Press, 1949. Both this and the following work illustrate usages, and both contain some good essays by Americans.

CONTINENTAL EUROPEAN WORKS

Ehrenfels, Christian von. *System der Werttheorie,* 2 vols. Leipzig: Reisland, 1897–1898. An early theory of value.

Hartmann, Nicolai. *Ethics,* 3 vols. Translated by Stanton Coit. London, 1932. An elaborate example of German intuitionism.

Meinong, Alexius. *Psychologisch-ethische Untersuchungen zur Werttheorie.* Graz, 1894. Another early theory of value and valuation.

Von Wright, Georg H. *The Varieties of Goodness.* London: Routledge and Kegan Paul, 1963. One of the latest theories of value.

BRITISH WORKS

Findlay, John N. *Values and Intentions.* New York: Macmillan, 1961. A value theory influenced by both British and Continental writers.

Hare, Richard M. *The Language of Morals.* Oxford: Clarendon Press, 1952. An imperativist analysis of value judgments.

Moore, G. E. *Principia Ethica.* Cambridge, U.K.: Cambridge University Press, 1903. A famous early analytical approach.

Urmson, J. O. "On Grading." *Mind* 59 (1950). A later analytical approach.

AMERICAN WORKS

Dewey, John. *Theory of Valuation.* Chicago: University of Chicago Press, 1939. A brief statement of the instrumentalist theory of values.

Lewis, C. I. *An Analysis of Knowledge and Valuation.* La Salle, IL: Open Court, 1946. A variation of a pragmatic theory.

Perry, Ralph B. *General Theory of Value.* New York: Longmans, Green, 1926. A classic work.

Perry, Ralph B. *Realms of Value.* Cambridge, MA: Harvard University Press, 1954. Restatement of Perry's value theory; applications to various fields.

Stevenson, Charles L. *Ethics and Language.* New Haven, CT: Yale University Press, 1944. An emotive theory.

Taylor, Paul W. *Normative Discourse.* Englewood Cliffs, NJ: Prentice-Hall, 1961. "The first fullscale attempt to use the 'informal logic' approach in general theory of value" (preface, p. xi).

William K. Frankena (1967)

VALUE AND VALUATION [ADDENDUM]

The ambiguities in the use of *value* and related words that William Frankena acutely summarized persist. But there has been some further work on value, especially in the narrow ethical sense of what is desirable or worth pursuing, that deserves comment. Some of the most interesting recent research has been by psychologists.

In relation to aesthetic value, psychologists have investigated how the kinds of experiences that we think point toward aesthetic value in their objects are produced. The psychology of identification with characters in fiction has been a fertile subject. So has the role of the unexpected (or not entirely expected) in appreciation of music. In all of this, there has been a tendency to connect aesthetic value with the quality of experiences that works of art (or beauties in nature) provide to those who are prepared to respond to them.

In relation to value in the narrow ethical sense of what is desirable or worth pursuing, much psychological research has investigated what people find satisfying in the present, or what they can be expected to find satisfying later (when they experience it), or what they prefer for the future. The evidence can seem telling, and yet many philosophers would want to distinguish sharply between what people like or prefer on one hand, and what has or would have value in their lives on the other.

There is the further complication that what has value in one life might have less or more within the context of a different kind of life. A kind of experience could be wonderful in one life and routine in another. C. I. Lewis (1883–1964) spoke of contributory value within a context. This suggests a contrast between instrumental value—the value that something causally has as a means to something else—and two kinds of noninstrumental value. One, which might be termed intrinsic, is a fixed value (regardless of context) that something has because of what it is. The other is a noninstrumental value that depends on context.

How relevant is psychological research to judgments of what has value in a life? This is a vexed issue, one that connects with the long-standing philosophical problem of the relation between facts and ethical values (in various senses of value). This is sometimes spoken of as the problem of the *is* and the *ought*.

PSYCHOLOGICAL RESEARCH ON SUBJECTIVE WELL-BEING. The term *well-being* is sometimes used as a translation of Aristotle's *eudaemonia*, his term for the consortium of values in a desirable kind of life. Your subjective well-being is what you would estimate as the degree of desirability in the life you have. Many people tend to assume that their subjective well-being would go up sharply if they got a great deal more money, or if they were much luckier in getting what they wanted (and as a result had much more pleasure). Recent psychological research has tended to undermine these assumptions.

Australian work on the *hedonic treadmill* has shown that, while the subjective well-being of lottery winners can be expected to go up for a short period, it then tends to return to roughly the pre-lottery levels. This is because of adaptation: After a while it simply takes more to satisfy the newly wealthy person. Conversely, people who have been rendered paraplegic in their youth, tend after a while to return to prior levels of satisfaction in life. It takes less to give them pleasure.

There are exceptions to this. People who become paraplegic at an advanced age are much less likely to bounce back. Also there is evidence to suggest that newly raised levels of satisfaction that are linked to sense of self are more likely to persist. Mihaly Csikszentmihalyi has outlined a broad class of exceptions, having to do with experiences of losing oneself in a sequence of skilled activity. His subjects report these as continuing to be peak experiences. This lends psychological support to arguments like that of Plato's *Philebus*, that not all pleasures are alike and that some should be assigned much higher value than others.

Happiness is sometimes regarded as an index of the desirability of a life. Michael Argyle's data show that factors important to happiness cannot easily be reducible to pleasure. The element of one's attitude toward oneself, and toward the life they lead, is prominent in this. Someone who is very lucky in getting pleasures might all the same dislike themselves and not be happy.

Much of this psychological evidence can seem telling, especially in undermining simple views of what might make a life desirable. But it still can seem an open question whether a life that is happy and involves high subjective well-being is really a desirable one. What of someone who has an accident, as a result undergoes a right-side frontal lobotomy (becoming an idiot), and then is happy as can be? We tend to pity (rather than envy) such a person. Many of us also would not envy the sadist who has a very lucky run of victims. Conversely, could the life of someone who does not have an especially great amount of pleasure and is not unusually happy in any normal sense (e.g., Ludwig Wittgenstein) be unusually desirable? Norman Malcolm gives as words of the dying Wittgenstein, "Tell them I've had a wonderful life."

Even if satisfaction is not an index of the desirability of a life, it could be a factor. Many philosophers from Confucius and Aristotle on have taken it as obvious that a desirable kind of life must have at least a moderate degree of inner satisfaction. Even if psychological data do not entail judgments of value, one could hold that they can count in favor of certain judgments. Many philosophers, following Stephen Toulmin (b. 1922), have insisted that there can be reasons in support of ethical conclusions. If so, it is plausible to hold that psychological data often do provide reasons.

CAN A JUDGMENT OF VALUE BE CORRECT? One powerful reply to any line of thought that holds that psychological data provide evidence of what is desirable in life is this: Ethical judgments, including those of value in the narrow sense, it will be said, merely express the attitude of the person who accepts them. There is no truth here about something that is objectively the case.

One way of considering this issue is by examining degrees and kinds of objectivity. This is central to David Hume's essay *The Sceptic*. Richard W. Miller (b. 1945), like Hume, has examined differences between ethical and aesthetic objectivity.

There also has been a frontal assault on the notion that ethical judgments (including judgments of value) can have opinion-independent correctness. This was developed by A. J. Ayer and Charles Stevenson, and subsequently has been refined by Bernard Williams and Gilbert Harman. One argument for it is this. We can know that something is the case only if that it is the case plays a causal role in our coming to believe that it is. Scientific knowledge meets this requirement. But our ethical judgments can be causally explained without bringing in any alleged fact that they are correct. They can be explained in terms of a collection of personal and social factors, including temperament, upbringing, acculturation, and so on. Hence there are no ethical facts, and certainly no opinion-independent facts about what really is a desirable kind of life.

A variety of issues are relevant. There is the nature (and perhaps the legitimacy) of the fact-value contrast. A naturalist in ethics need not take it as expressing any deep truth. There also are philosophers (e.g., P. F. Strawson and Bede Rundle) who have insisted on the interpretative elements in anything that we would term a fact, so that a fact is not anything in the world. It might generally be the case that what is judged to be a value also has an interpretative element, and, if so, an ethical judgment that encapsulated a very widely shared interpretation might look like a fact. G. E. M. Anscombe maintained that it was a *brute fact* that she owed her grocer money for potatoes that he had delivered at her request.

There also is the matter of the causal analysis of how people come to have the ethical beliefs they have. Plainly, factors such as upbringing and acculturation normally have a very large role, and it may be that often they are the whole story. But there are occasions when someone who has been brought up with a certain ethical view of *X* actually experiences *X*, and feels forced to change her or his mind. *X* might be a social practice that one had been taught was perfectly acceptable, but, looked at closely, seemed disgusting. Or *X* might be a highly recommended way of life, but after you have entered onto it seems somehow lacking. How thorough a knowledge do we have of the causation (all the causal factors) in such cases?

Sometimes people do have a sense that the cause of their rejecting, say, slavery was that it simply turned out to be disgusting—or that the recommended way of life just did not seem all that good, at least for them. They think, in short, that their changed opinion was caused by a sense of what ethically was the case. Can such a judgment about a causal relation have any validity? It can be plausible to hold that sometimes people do have an immediate awareness of a causal relation that does not require derivation from a covering generalization. Anscombe gives the example in *Intention* of knowing that one's fright was caused by the horrid face at the window.

DETERMINING WHAT IS DESIRABLE IN LIFE. If it is the case that some judgments of value in the narrow sense are better than others, then it is natural to ask how these can be arrived at or grounded. Many philosophers, as different from one another as Aristotle, Friedrich Nietzsche, and G. E. Moore have offered answers. Aristotle provides general considerations determining what can count as eudaemonia. The nature of humans as rational is given weight, as is the desirability of a life not far from what one imagines as the life of the gods.

Moore's nomination of intuition as the source of judgments of goodness is a way of saying that there is no strictly rational procedure. Nevertheless the final chapter of *Principia Ethica* contains a list of what seemed to him to be factors that would have a high degree of value. These include consciousness of Beauty and personal affection for someone worthy of it. James Griffin (b. 1933) also has provided a provisional list of major *prudential* values, approximating major noninstrumental values that can be attained. These include accomplishment, autonomy and liberty, understanding, enjoyment, and deep personal relations.

Both Moore's and Griffin's lists emerge as results of general reflection, doubtless with personal experience as part of its base. It is possible though to be highly skeptical of generalization about value. One can hold that the nuances of individual cases that fit under a general heading can make a major difference to the values. This is a point made in the "On the Three Evils" section of Nietzsche's *Thus Spake Zarathustra*, and echoed in Albert Camus's (1913–1960) *The Myth of Sisyphus*.

Along these lines, you could think it possible that something might contribute more (or less) of noninstrumental value in your life than something of the same general description would to someone else's life. Besides this, you can doubt that some familiar claims about what contributes noninstrumental value to lives have much validity for the general run of cases. Is there any way to arrive at a well-based answer to such questions?

One reply is this: A person can be in a good position to make a judgment about the noninstrumental value of *X* in a particular life, or the noninstrumental value *X* tends to have in lives in general, if you have a very good idea of what it is like to have *X* in a life. This could be the result of close observation of someone in whose life *X* is a part. Also, biographies and literary works, if they can be trusted, might sometimes provide such an idea.

The most common route though is to have experienced *X* in one's own life. This can be compared to being an eyewitness to an event. Some eyewitnesses are more reliable than others, and no eyewitness is guaranteed never to make mistakes. But to be an eyewitness is to be in a better position to know what happened than would otherwise be the case. Similarly, to have experienced *X* in your life is generally to be in a better position to judge the noninstrumental value of *X*—at least in the context of the one life you know best. Mistakes are possible; but so also (if this line of thought is sound) is knowledge, and the knowledge may well be particular rather than general.

See also Good, The; Intrinsic Value; Value and Valuation.

Bibliography

DETERMINING WHAT IS DESIRABLE IN LIFE

Griffin, James. *Well-Being: Its Meaning, Measurement, and Moral Importance.* Oxford, U.K.: Clarendon Press, 1986. A nuanced and subtle study of value and issues related to value which repays repeated readings.

Kupperman, Joel. "The Epistemology of Noninstrumental Value." In *Philosophy and Phenomenological Research*, 66 (2005). A defense of claims that there can be knowledge of non-instrumental value.

FACT AND VALUE

Anscombe, G. E. M. "On Brute Facts." In *Analysis*, 18 (1958): 69–72. A strong attempt to undermine the widely assumed opposition between facts and values.

Rundle, Bede. *Facts.* London, 1993. Am examination of facts that is subversive of some widely accepted philosophical ideas.

OBJECTIVITY AND CORRECTNESS IN JUDGMENTS OF VALUE

Harman, Gilbert. *The Nature of Morality: An Introduction to Ethics.* New York: Oxford University Press, 1977. This contains an argument for relativism, presented with some panache.

Miller, Richard W. "Three Versions of Objectivity: Aesthetic, Moral, and Scientific." In *Aesthetics and Ethics*, edited by Jerrold Levinson. Cambridge, U.K.: Cambridge University Press, 1998: 26–58. An exceptionally careful and nuanced discussion of varieties of objectivity.

Williams, Bernard. "The Truth in Relativism." In *Moral Luck: Philosophical Papers, 1973–1980.* Cambridge, U.K.; New York: Cambridge University Press, 1981. A subtle and provocative attack on some ideas of objective truth in ethics.

PSYCHOLOGICAL INVESTIGATIONS

Argyle, Michael. *The Psychology of Happiness* London; New York: Methuen, 1987.A clear account of factors relevant to happiness.

Brickman, P., D. Coates, and R. Janoff-Bulman, "Lottery Winners and Accident Victims: Is Happiness Relative?" In *Journal of Personality and Social Psychology*, 37 (1978): 287–302. The classic study of the hedonic treadmill.

Csikszentmihalyi, Mihaly. *Flow: the Psychology of Optimal Experience.* New York: Harper & Row, 1990. A study of experiences that are prized in people's lives.

Kahneman, Daniel. "Objective Happiness." In *Well-Being: the Foundations of Hedonic Psychology*, edited by D. Kahneman, E. Diener, and N. Schwartz. New York: Russell Sage Foundation, 1999. A strong general account of recent research.

Oatley, Keith, and Mitra Gholamain. "Emotions and Identification: Connectionsbetween Readers and Fiction." In *Emotion and the Arts*, edited by Mette Hjort and Sue Laver. New York, 1997. A fine example of psychological investigaton that sheds light on the production of aesthetic value.

Joel J. Kupperman (2005)

VALUE JUDGMENTS

See *Value and Valuation*

VALUE OF KNOWLEDGE AND TRUTH, THE

See *Knowledge and Truth, The Value of*

VAN FRAASSEN, BAS

(1941–)

Bas van Fraassen was born in Goes, in the Netherlands, on April 5. He lived in Holland until he was fifteen years old, when he moved with his family to Canada. After finishing his undergraduate studies in philosophy (with honors) at the University of Alberta in 1963, he went to the University of Pittsburgh for his Ph.D., which he completed in 1966 with a dissertation on the causal theory of time that was supervised by Adolf Grünbaum. He taught at Yale University, the University of Toronto, and the University of Southern California before moving to Princeton University, where he has been a Professor of Philosophy since 1982.

Van Fraassen has made seminal contributions to several areas of philosophy, and his work can be roughly divided into three major "periods": (i) the philosophical logic phase (1966–1979); (ii) the constructive empiricist period (1980–1993); and (iii) the empirical stance phase (1994 to the present). But throughout these periods, there has been a unified vision underlying his approach, with two crucial features: (a) the search for an empiricist (antirealist and, in a sense, antimetaphysical) approach to science and philosophy more generally; and (b) an attempt to preserve through this empiricism "classical" features of the domain under consideration—by taking scientific theories literally, retaining classical logic whenever possible, and resisting the need for introducing causally irrelevant items (such as possible worlds).

In the philosophical logic phase, this vision is articulated through the development of several proposals guided by techniques from philosophical logic. For instance, van Fraassen's method of supervaluations provides a way of retaining classical logic (or, at least, classical logic's theorems), even in the presence of truth-value gaps. This method can then be used to accommodate logical paradoxes, such as the Liar ("This sentence is not true"). Van Fraassen's early work on space-time theories also illustrates the empiricist component of the vision, with the development of interpretations of space-time theories that do not presuppose the existence of absolute space (1970). Moreover, in his development of a semantics for free logic, van Fraassen assumed only existing individuals in the domain, thereby avoiding a commitment to nonexistent objects that early work in the area had presupposed. Finally, van Fraassen's early theory of meaning relations among predicates and modality does not involve any commitment to real modalities in nature.

Several of these problems can be approached from a unified perspective with the development of constructive empiricism (van Fraassen 1980). This is a view about the aim of science: the search for empirically adequate theories. The constructive empiricist articulates something novel: an empiricist alternative to scientific realism that avoids the early pitfalls of logical positivism. As opposed to logical positivism, the constructive empiricist takes scientific theories literally; there's no attempt to reformulate such theories in some formal language. And as opposed to scientific realism, the constructive empiricist puts forward an interpretation of science in which scientific theories need not be true to be good, as long as they are empirically adequate (and informative). To flesh out the proposal, van Fraassen argues that it is possible to make sense of scientific methodology from this viewpoint, and highlights, in particular, the crucial role played by models in scientific theorizing. He develops a new version of the semantic approach to scientific theories, insisting that to present a theory is to specify a class of models rather than to provide a list of axioms in a formalized language. As opposed to earlier positivist proposals, van Fraassen's work articulates a theory of the pragmatics of explanation that does not require scientific theories to be true for them to be explanatory. He also advances a new interpretation of probability that is compatible with the rejection of real modalities in nature.

Constructive empiricism's lack of commitment to metaphysically dubious notions (at least from an empiricist perspective)—such as laws of nature, possible worlds, and real modalities in nature—is developed further in van Fraassen's book *Laws and Symmetry* (1989). The book argues that attempts to characterize the notion of law of nature are doomed to failure because either they are unable to justify the inference from *It is a law that P* to *P*, or they fail to identify the features that make *P* a law in the first place. As an alternative, van Fraassen suggests that many roles that traditional philosophical proposals have assigned to laws of nature can be accommodated without commitment to the latter—provided we examine the role played by symmetry (roughly, transformations that leave certain structures invariant). A detailed case for this proposal in the context of quantum mechanics and a thorough development of an empiricist view of quantum theory is then articulated in *Quantum Mechanics: An Empiricist View* (1991).

After the development of the details of constructive empiricism, a more general question arises: How is it possible to be an empiricist instead of just developing an empiricist approach to science? To elaborate a broader perspective on empiricism that includes constructive empiricism as a particular case is a major goal of van Fraasen's empirical stance (2002). Instead of articulating empiricism as a doctrine (a set of beliefs), van Fraassen insists that empiricism should be conceptualized as a stance: an attitude, an epistemic policy. This move has several advantages. First, it avoids the incoherence of certain earlier empiricist proposals that failed to meet their own empiricist standards and ended up being meaningless or lacking any content. Second, the move also provides a novel way of understanding our practice, in particular the role of experience in our epistemic life, and how to make sense of scientific revolutions as a decision problem. The crucial features of van Fraassen's earlier works are also found here, notably in the development of an empiricist perspective that preserves the "classical" features of the phenomena under consideration.

See also Empiricism; Laws of Nature; Liar Paradox, The; Logical Paradoxes; Philosophy of Science, Problems of; Pragmatics; Presupposition; Realism.

Bibliography

Churchland, P. M., and C. A. Hooker, eds. *Images of Science: Essays on Realism and Empiricism, with a Reply by Bas C. van Fraassen*. Chicago: The University of Chicago Press, 1985.

van Fraassen, B. C. *The Empirical Stance*. New Haven, CT: Yale University Press, 1991.

van Fraassen, B. C. *An Introduction to the Philosophy of Time and Space*. New York: Random House, 1970.

van Fraassen, B. C. *Laws and Symmetry*. Oxford: Clarendon Pres, 1989.

van Fraassen, B. C. *Quantum Mechanics: An Empiricist View*. Oxford: Clarendon Press, 1991.

van Fraassen, B. C. *The Scientific Image*. Oxford: Clarendon Press, 1980.

Otávio Bueno (2005)

VANINI, GIULIO CESARE

(1584 or 1585–1619)

Giulio Cesare Vanini was born in Taurisano, in the province of Lecce, Italy, in 1584 or early in 1585. After completing a course of study in law in Naples, he proceeded to Padua to study theology. He entered the order of the Carmelites, and he visited various Italian cities—Venice, Genoa, and perhaps Bologna—and traveled in Germany, England, and France. In 1612, in England, he abjured, but, having aroused suspicion because of his ideas, he moved on again. In 1615, in Lyon, he published his *Amphitheatrum Aeternae Providentiae* (published by the widow of Antoine De Harsy), and in 1616, in Paris, the dialogues, in four books, *De Admirandis Naturae Reginae Deaeque Mortialium Arcanis* (published by Adrian Périer). Both works were given the regular permission of the ecclesiastical authorities but nevertheless aroused suspicions. Vanini then went to Toulouse, where he taught and practiced medicine. In August 1618 he was arrested by the Inquisition. He was condemned, and then in February 1619 burned to death after horrible torture.

Vanini's work, which shows repeatedly a kinship with that of Averroes, reflects above all the influence of the writers of the fifteenth and sixteenth centuries, among whom he had a particular predilection for Pietro Pomponazzi, whom he called his master, the prince of the philosophers of his century, and a second Averroes ("in his body Pythagoras would have placed the spirit of Averroes"). Next to Pomponazzi he placed Girolamo Cardano, Julius Caesar Scaliger, and numerous others, whom he drew from freely. His liberal use of other sources, long passages of which he inserted, even verbatim, into his own works, has caused several recent historians to speak of plagiarism and of writings that are "devoid of originality and scientific integrity." In reality, his attitude toward using the writings of others was common in his time; the present-day preoccupation with the citation of sources did not exist (certain Latin writings of Giordano Bruno are a case in point). Furthermore, the writings from which Vanini borrowed generally underwent a marked transformation in his pages.

Intensely critical of all revealed religions (his "atheism" stemmed from this), Vanini believed strongly in the divinity of nature and in the immanence of God in nature, which is eternal and eternally regulated by strict laws ("Natura Dei facultas, imo Deus ipse"). He held that the world is without origin, at least so far as could be established by natural religion. The human spirit is material, the soul mortal. Using arguments and themes taken from Cardano, Vanini stated that there is a natural explanation for all supposedly exceptional and miraculous phenomena in universal determinism; and thus, going back to Pomponazzi, he interpreted rationally all the aspects and forms of religious life.

Despite his frequent declaration that, as a Christian, he would continue to accept on faith even that which reason had disproved, the radical bent of Vanini's criticism escaped no one, and, as the seventeenth century progressed, he became almost a symbol of "atheistic and libertine" thought.

See also Atheism; Averroes; Bruno, Giordano; Laws of Nature; Pomponazzi, Pietro.

Bibliography

WORKS BY VANINI

Luigi Corvaglia, ed., *Le opere di Giulio Cesare Vanini e le loro fonti,* 2 vols. (Milan: Società Anonima Editrice Dante Alighieri, 1933–1934), is a reprint of the original editions with the texts of the "sources" printed alongside to show the "plagiarism." See also Guido Porzio, *Le opere di Giulio Cesare Vanini tradotte per la prima volta in italiano con prefazione del traduttore,* 2 vols. (Lecce, Italy, no date; published 1913), which includes biography, documents, complete bibliography.

WORKS ON VANINI

See F. Fiorentino, "Giulio Cesare Vanini e i suoi biografi," in *Studi e ritratti della rinascenza* (Bari, Italy: Laterza, 1911); E. Namer, "Nuovi documenti su Vanini," in *Giornale critico della filosofia italiana* 13 (1932): 161–198; E. Namer, *Documents sur la vie de Jules-César de Taurisano* (Bari, Italy, no date; published 1965); John Owen, *The Skeptics of the Italian Renaissance* (London: Sonnenschein, 1893), pp. 345–419; G. Spini, "Vaniniana," in *Rinascimento* 1 (1950): 71–90; G. Spini, *Ricerca dei libertini* (Rome: Editrice Universale de Roma, 1950), pp. 117–135.

Eugenio Garin (1967)
Translated by Robert M. Connolly

VARISCO, BERNARDINO

(1850–1933)

Bernardino Varisco, the Italian metaphysician, was born at Chiari (Brescia). It was only in the later part of his long life that he developed his philosophy, for he began as a teacher of science and his early outlook was characterized by empiricism and positivism. These views found expression in *Scienza e opinioni* (1901). Thereafter he became interested in the problem of reconciling the scientific and religious ways of understanding the world and moved into metaphysics. In 1906 he was appointed professor of theoretical philosophy at the University of Rome, where he remained until his retirement in 1925. His metaphysic was a philosophy of spirit in the manner of Gottfried Wilhelm Leibniz and Rudolf Hermann Lotze and won him a considerable reputation in Italy and elsewhere.

The empiricism of Varisco's earlier phase was still apparent in the approach that he employed in constructing his distinctive philosophy. His starting point is the given fact of a plurality of conscious subjects. Each of these has its own private perspective upon the world, and each is also a spontaneous center of activity. In the personal subject, a high level of rationality and self-consciousness has been reached, but this is surrounded by an extensive penumbra of subconsciousness. Varisco thinks of conscious life as shading off imperceptibly into lower levels. Below the level of man's personal existence there is animal life, and it is argued that this in turn shades off into so-called inanimate existence. Thus, Varisco arrives at a kind of monadology, or panpsychism. Reality is made up of an infinite number of subjects, although at the level of inanimate nature these subjects are very primitive and have nothing like the self-consciousness of the personal human subject.

Varisco's metaphysic has a dynamic aspect, for these subjects are in constant action and interaction. The variations set up are of two kinds. Some arise from spontaneous activity in the subjects themselves, and in this way Varisco provides for freedom and for what he calls an "alogical" factor in reality. The other kind of variations arises from the mutual interaction of the subjects, and this happens in regular ways, so that the universe has also an ordered, logical character.

The most obscure and presumably the weakest part of Varisco's philosophy is his attempt to move from the plurality of subjects to a unitary reality. His appeal is to the notion of "being," which, implicitly or explicitly, is present in every act of thought whereby a subject grasps an object. Being is identified with the universal subject, with thinking itself in all particular subjects and in the world. In *I massimi problemi,* Varisco says explicitly that the universal subject is a logical conception that falls short of the notion of a personal God, although he believed that teleology and the conservation of value point toward theism. However, in his posthumous *Dall'uomo a Dio* (1939) he completes his pilgrimage from positivism to theism, arguing for a God who limits himself by his creation so that men can cooperate with him in creative activity. Such a view, he believed, supports a religious attitude to life and is especially compatible with Christianity.

See also Empiricism; Leibniz, Gottfried Wilhelm; Lotze, Rudolf Hermann; Metaphysics; Panpsychism; Positivism.

Bibliography

WORKS BY VARISCO

Scienza e opinioni. Rome, 1901.

La conoscenza. Pavia, 1905.

I massimi problemi. Milan, 1910. Translated by R. C. Lodge as *The Great Problems.* London: Allen, 1914.

Conosci te stesso. Milan, 1912. Translated by Guglielmo Salvadori as *Know Thyself.* London: Allen and Unwin, 1915.

Sommario di filosofia. Rome, 1928.

Dall'uomo a Dio. Padua: CEDAM, 1939.

WORKS ON VARISCO

Chiapetta, L. *La teodicea di Bernardino Varisco.* Naples, 1938.

De Negri, E. *La metafisica di Bernardino Varisco.* Florence, 1929.

Drago, P. C. *La filosofia di Bernardino Varisco.* Florence: Monnier, 1944.

Librizzi, C. *Il pensiero di Bernardino Varisco.* Padua: CEDAM, 1942; rev. ed., 1953.

John Macquarrie (1967)

VARONA Y PERA, ENRIQUE JOSÉ

(1849–1933)

Enrique José Varona y Pera was a Cuban philosopher, statesman, and man of letters. Beginning in the mid-1870s, Varona dominated Cuban intellectual life for fifty years. He was a professor of philosophy at the University of Havana, was founding editor of *Revista cubana,* and took an active part in education and politics. A former member of the Spanish Cortes, he became a revolutionary colleague of José Martí, was appointed secretary of public instruction and fine arts after the 1898 revolution, and served as vice-president of Cuba from 1913 to 1917.

Varona, one of the leading Latin American positivists, adapted French positivism and British empiricism to the contemporary sociopolitical and cultural situation of Cuba. Logic, psychology, and ethics were his primary philosophic concerns.

J. S. Mill's analysis of induction served as the basis of Varona's work in logic. As a scientific study of the ways in which man thinks and learns, logic assists in providing methodologies for the particular sciences as well as for the educational process. There are three stages in any mental act: The first and third are directed toward the object of experience, the second consists exclusively of mental activity. Unrelated data are obtained from nature; they are then related significantly in terms of ideal constructs, and the resultant schema is again compared with experience through controlled experimentation.

In psychology the root problem is that of human freedom. Varona subordinated the study of psychology to that of physiology and accepted a strictly deterministic position. However, his concern for the political and cultural independence of Cuba demanded an interpretation of man that provided room for freedom. Although man is not free, the development of intelligence provides him with the ability to avoid being an automaton, to understand the nature of causal determination, and thereby to "train and direct it, which is tantamount to overcoming it."

The proper approach to the study of ethics is genetic. Morality is based on the social nature of man, which, in turn, has its roots in the evolutionary biological process. "Man is not sociable because he is moral.... Man becomes moral by virtue of being sociable" (*Conferencias filosóficas, tercera serie: Moral* [Havana, 1888], p. 10). Just as the biological organism is dependent upon its natural environment, so the human organism is dependent upon its social environment. Such social dependence constitutes social solidarity. Awareness of this dependence and conscious accommodation of the individual to the social milieu constitutes moral behavior.

Throughout Varona's work and especially in a final book of aphorisms, *Con el eslabón* (Manzanillo, 1927), a subtle, penetrating irony concerning the foibles of human thought and existence was evident.

See also Empiricism; Ethics; Latin American Philosophy; Logic, History of; Mill, John Stuart; Positivism; Psychology.

Bibliography

Varona's collected works are *Obras,* 4 vols. (Havana, 1936–1938). Works on Varona include John H. Hershey, "Enrique José Varona, Cuban Positivist," in *Humanist* 3 (January 1944): 164ff.; Medardo Vitier, *La filosofía en Cuba* (Mexico City: Fondo de Cultura Económica, 1948), Ch. 11; and Humberto Piñera Llera, *Panorama de la filosofía cubana* (Washington, DC: Unión Panamericana, 1960), Ch. 5.

Fred Gillette Sturm (1967)

VASCONCELOS, JOSÉ

(1882–1959)

José Vasconcelos, the Mexican politician and philosopher, was born in Oaxaca. Vasconcelos was active in the Mexican revolution, directed the reform of Mexican education as secretary of education in the early 1920s, ran unsuccessfully for the presidency in 1929, and subsequently was exiled for a time. He was rector of the National University of Mexico, visiting professor at the University of Chicago, and director of the Biblioteca Nacional de México. The sources of his philosophy were Pythagoras, Plotinus, Arthur Schopenhauer, Friedrich Nietzsche, A. N. Whitehead, and especially Henri Bergson. Of Latin American philosophers, Vasconcelos is the most original, venturesome, and impassioned.

He called his philosophy aesthetic monism, scientific realism, and organic logic. The system he developed stressed intuition in addition to scientific experience; the particular, concrete, and heterogeneous; organic wholes; the fluid, living, and psychical; and the methods of art rather than mathematics. The true method of philosophy, Vasconcelos claimed, is to understand the particular phenomenon, not by reducing it to the universal but by relating it to other particulars in an organic whole in which unity is achieved without sacrifice of individuality.

The pervasive term in Vasconcelos's theory of reality is energy, which is unformed in its primordial condition but takes on determinate structures in the three phenomenal orders of the atomic, cellular, and spiritual. The transformation in recent physics of the elementary particle from a rigid body to an "individualized dynamic frequency," Vasconcelos held, emphasizes activity and novelty in the atom, which are reminders of spirit. In the cellular order, internal purposes are introduced. Spirit is eminently creative, but its action follows structures, or a priori methods, of logical inference for intellect, of values or norms for will, and of aesthetic unities for feeling. The early thought of Vasconcelos was pantheistic, finding the creative principle in the self-sufficient pervasive energy of the world. His later thought, after he had returned to the Roman Catholic Church, was theistic. It appears that in both periods "spirit," rudimentary or refined, was basic to his view of reality.

In Vasconcelos's aesthetics may be found implications for both reality and the life of spirit. The work of art, an emotionally intuited image, observes principles which, although more lucid in the work itself, have general application in reality. A musical scale is constructed by the musician out of the continuum of natural pitches; its members are discrete tones separated by intervals or jumps. The activity of constructing this scale is analogous to that of intelligence in separating and ordering the objects of sensation; the discontinuity of the tones is similar to that of quantum phenomena in physics. Musical compositions observe three modes of aesthetic unity—melody, harmony, and rhythm—in which the heterogeneous or discontinuous is unified without loss of diversity. A true metaphysics, fortified by modern science, finds the same types of unity in reality, unlike mathematics, which unifies by reduction to homogeneous quantities.

Art, according to Vasconcelos, expresses the transformations of the spirit in the pursuit of value. He distinguished three kinds of art. Apollonian art is formal and intellectual. It can be saved from decay in giganticism or sensuality only by a shift to the Dionysian mode of passionate affirmation of the human will. Dionysian art does not decline; passion either destroys the spirit or saves it by a change to religious ardor. In mystical art, passion is directed from a temporal and human object to an eternal and divine object. Passion need not retreat from fate, as the Greeks thought; as Christianity discovered, it can be fully satisfied in the divine.

A similar conclusion occurs in the ethics of Vasconcelos. A terrestrial ethics, exemplified diversely in empiricism, hedonism, Confucianism, humanism, and socialism, does not take man beyond his animal and human condition. (Apart from this deficiency, a limited socialism stripped of Marxist theory has merit; Vasconcelos was critical of capitalism.) Metaphysical ethics attempts to go further in the name of reason; but the rational universal law of Immanuel Kant is a discipline appropriate for things and not for spirits. The highest ethics is revelatory; it combines transcendence, emotional illumination, and infinite love. Vasconcelos highly praised the wisdom of Buddhism and of Christianity, but he preferred Christianity because of its affirmation of life.

See also Aesthetics, History of; Bergson, Henri; Intuition; Kant, Immanuel; Latin American Philosophy; Nietzsche, Friedrich; Plotinus; Pythagoras and Pythagoreanism; Schopenhauer, Arthur; Scientific Realism; Whitehead, Alfred North.

Bibliography

Principal works by Vasconcelos include *Pitágoras: Una teoría del ritmo* (Havana: El Siglo XX, 1916); *El monismo estético* (Mexico City: Murguia, 1918); *Tratado de metafísica* (Mexico City: México joven, 1929); *Ética* (Madrid: Aguilar, 1932); *Estética* (Mexico City: Botas, 1936); *El realismo científico* (Mexico City: Centro de Estudios Filosóficos de la Facultad de Filosofía y Letras, 1943); and *Lógica orgánica* (Mexico City: Edición de el Colegio Nacional, 1945).

Also see Patrick Romanell, *Making of the Mexican Mind* (Lincoln: University of Nebraska Press, 1952), Ch. 4.

Arthur Berndtson (1967)

VASQUEZ, GABRIEL

(1549–1604)

Gabriel Vasquez, the neo-Scholastic theologian, was born at Villascuela del Haro, Spain, and died at Alcalá. Educated in the Jesuit houses of study in Spain, he taught moral philosophy at Ocaña from 1575 to 1577 and theology at Madrid and Alcalá. Eventually he succeeded Francisco Suárez in the chair of theology at Rome, where he taught from 1585 to 1592. His *Commentaria ac Disputationes in Primam Pattern S. Thomae* (8 vols., Alcalá, 1598–1615), a lengthy commentary on Part I of Thomas Aquinas's *Summa Theologiae*, contains much philosophical speculation. A posthumously published summary of this work, *Disputationes Metaphysicae* (Madrid, 1617), helped to popularize his philosophy.

Vasquez's most influential contribution lies in his distinction between the formal concept in the understanding (a mental entity, or "idea," constituting knowledge, *qualitas ipsa cognitionis*) and the objective concept that is the reality that is known (*res cognita*) through the formal concept (*Commentaria* I, 76, nn. 2–5). Since, in the view of Vasquez, the actual being (*esse*) of the thing that is known is identified with the act whereby it is known (*cognosci*), we may have here one of the sources of idealism in modern philosophy. There is little doubt that René Descartes's Jesuit teachers knew the thought of Vasquez, and hence the Cartesian teaching that ideas are direct objects of knowledge may owe a good deal to Vasquez (see the study by R. Dalbiez). Like Suárez, Vasquez introduced many changes into Thomistic metaphysics. He rejected the view that essence and existence are really distinct, opposed the theory that act is limited by the potency in which it is received, and argued that matter as marked by quantity (*materia signata quantitate*) cannot be the principle that individuates bodily things.

In psychology Vasquez also had teachings that are highly personal. He saw no reason for postulating two intellectual powers in man (agent and possible intellects, in Thomas) and implied that the one understanding can do the work of both. He regarded man as a composite of soul and body, but he treated these two "parts" almost as if they were two different substances joined together by a peculiar sort of metaphysical semireality that he called a "mode." Here again, we may have a source of Descartes's mind-body problem and of the psychophysical parallelism of post-Cartesianism.

In his long discussion of St. Thomas's proofs for the existence of God, Vasquez again showed a critical attitude toward the thought of Thomas. In place of the traditional Five Ways of demonstration (which require the acceptance of a metaphysics of causality), Vasquez described a whole new series of arguments of his own. God's existence is demonstrated from the claim that morality requires it (an argument that reappears in Immanuel Kant) and from various types of "spontaneous assents" based on what one learns from parents, on a survey of the whole of reality (*ex rerum universitate*), and on our knowledge of the divine conservation and governance of the world (*Commentaria* I, 19, nn. 9–12). It is evident that Vasquez's work is one of the reasons that Thomism came to be misunderstood in modern philosophy.

See also Descartes, René; Kant, Immanuel; Scotism; Suárez, Francisco; Thomas Aquinas, St.; Thomism.

Bibliography

Dalbiez, R. "Les sources scolastiques de la théorie cartésienne de l'être objectif." *Revue d'histoire de la philosophie* 3 (1939): 464–472.

Gilson, Étienne. *Études sur le rôle de la pensée médiévale dans la formation du système cartésien*, 203–207. Paris: Vrin, 1930.

Solana, M. *Los grandes escolásticos españoles*, 109–128. Madrid: Ratés, 1928.

Wells, Norman J. "John Poinsot on Created Eternal Truths vs Vasquez, Suarez and Descartes." *American Catholic Philosophical Quarterly* 3 (1968): 425–446.

Vernon J. Bourke (1967)
Bibliography updated by Tamra Frei (2005)

VASUBANDHU

(fl. fourth or fifth century CE)

Vasubandhu was an Indian Buddhist philosopher who made significant contributions to the clarification and development of the Indian Buddhist schools of philosophy traditionally classified as the Vaibhāṣika (or Sarvāstivāda), the Sautrāntika, and the Yogācāra (or Cittamātra). Erich Frauwallner argued (1951), on the basis of a study of Vasubandhu's biographers, Paramārtha (499–569), Bus-ton (1290–1364) and Tāranātha (1575–1634), that there were two Vasubandhus, one who composed Yogācāra works and lived in the fourth century CE, and another who lived in the fifth century CE and composed treatises from the Vaibhāṣika and Sautrāntika points of view. But later studies (Jaini 1959, Anacker 1998) disputed Frauwallner's argument and advanced the hypothesis that there was only one author of these works and that he lived in the fourth century CE According to Buddhist tradition, Vasubandhu was at first an orthodox follower of the Vaibhāṣika school, and, after having allied himself with the Sautrāntika school, was convinced by his half-brother, Asaṇa, to accept the Mahāyāna scriptures (which were not accepted by the Vaibhāṣikas or Sautrāntikas) and to adopt the theses of the Yogācāra school.

VASUBANDHU'S CONTRIBUTIONS TO THE VAIBHĀṢIKA AND SAUTRĀNTIKA PHILOSOPHIES

Vasubandhu's contribution to the Vaibhāṣika philosophy is his masterly treatise the *Abhidharmakośa* (Treasury of knowledge). In this work he sets out in verse theses held in most of the Vaibhāṣika schools. One of the most fundamental of these theses is that what truly exists (that is, what exists apart from being conceived) is a substantially real permanent or impermanent phenomenon (*dharma*) or a collection of substantially real impermanent phenomena that is by convention conceived as a single entity of a certain kind. The treatise as a whole explains the world of conventional phenomena in terms of how its underlying substantially real phenomena are caused to combine and separate to perpetuate our rebirth and suffering and how, by eliminating their causes, our rebirth and suffering can be eliminated.

To this work Vasubandhu added a prose treatise, the *Ātmavādapratiṣedha* (Refutation of the theory of a self). In it he defends the theory of persons of the Vaibhāṣikas, who believe that we, as persons conceived from the first-person singular perspective, suffer and are reborn because we misapprehend ourselves as selves in the sense of being substantially real phenomena. We can become free from rebirth and suffering by realizing that we are not substantially real phenomena. Nonetheless, he believes, we ultimately exist insofar as we are the collections of substantially real impermanent aggregates (*skandhas*) of which our bodies and mental states are composed; only these aggregates are found, by direct perception and correct inference, to be the phenomena on the basis upon which we conceive ourselves as persons. Vasubandhu then presents objections to the theories of persons held in the unorthodox Vaibhāṣika school called the Vātsīputrīya and in the Hindu school called the Vaiśeṣika. According to the Vātsīputrīyas, we ultimately exist without being collections of such phenomena, and according to the Vaiśeṣikas, we ultimately exist as permanent and partless substantially real phenomena. Vasubandhu claims that the Vātsīputrīyas' arguments for their theory are inconsistent with other theses they should, as Vaibhāṣikas, accept, and argues that their theory, like that of the Vaiśeṣikas, has the absurd consequence that we are completely different from, and so causally unrelated to, our aggregates.

In reply to the objections of the Vātsīputrīyas and Vaiśeṣikas—that the Vaibhāṣika theory of persons implies that we are not the same over time, do not possess mental states, and so on— Vasubandhu explains how, in spite of our reducibility to collections of impermanent aggregates, we are said to be the same over time, to possess mental states, and so on. Vasubandhu also briefly rejects the thesis of Nāgārjuna, the founder of the Mādhyamika school of Indian Buddhist philosophy, that nothing is substantially real, which, he believes, implies that we do not ultimately exist at all, since we could not in that case be reducible in existence to collections of substantially real phenomena.

Vasubandhu's most important contribution to the development of the Sautrāntika school was the *Abhidharmakośabhāṣya* (Commentary on the treasury of knowledge), a prose commentary on the verses in the *Abhidharmakośa.* In this work he adopts the Sautrāntika project of correcting the ontological excesses of the Vaibhāṣika school by showing that they are not supported by Buddhist scriptures. Although Vasubandhu accepts the Vaibhāṣika thesis that what exists is either a substantially real phenomenon or a collection of substantially real impermanent phenomena, he argues that the Vaibhāṣikas introduce more substantially real phenomena than are needed in order to explain how suffering and rebirth arise and are eliminated. For instance, he rejects the Vaibhāṣika explanation of how substantially real phenomena that have occurred in the past or will occur in the future can be apprehended if they do not ultimately exist at the time they are being apprehended. Their explanation is that substantially real phenomena ultimately exist in the past, present, and future insofar as they possess a real nature (*svabhāva*) by virtue of which they can be identified by themselves; they are said to be past phenomena when they have already exercised their characteristic causal power, to be present phenomena when they are exercising it, and to be future phenomena when they have not yet exercised it. Vasubandhu's basic objection to this explanation is that it unnecessarily introduces into their basic ontology past and future substantially real phenomena, because it is possible to apprehend substantially real phenomena that have ceased to exist and have not yet come to exist.

Among the many other theses of the Vaibhāṣikas he rejects are the theses: (i) that there can be a cause that is simultaneous with or can follow its effect (he claims that a cause must always precede its effect), (ii) that a future result of an action must occur in the same person who performed the action because there is present in the continuum of the person's aggregates of body and mind a separate substantially real phenomenon that causes the retention of the seed the action produces in the same causal continuum (he claims that the retention of the seed is due to the causal relationship between the phenomena in the continuum), and (iii) that an impermanent phenomenon can exist for more than an instant (he believes that an impermanent phenomenon by nature ceases to exist as soon as it arises).

It may have been during his Sautrāntika period (though some scholars think it was when he had already become a follower of the Yogācāra movement) that Vasubandhu wrote a number of treatises on logic in which he presents revisions and clarifications of forms of argument used by Indian philosophers in debate. In the *Vādavidhi* (The way of argument), part of which has survived, Vasubandhu anticipates some of the views of the Buddhist logician Dignāga, a circumstance that perhaps explains why he is sometimes said to be one of Dignāga's teachers.

VASUBANDHU'S CONTRIBUTIONS TO YOGĀCĀRA PHILOSOPHY

One of Vasubandhu's earliest contributions to the clarification and development of Yogācāra thought may be the *Pañcaskandhakaprakaraṇa* (A treatise on the five aggregates), which is an attempt to improve upon Asaṇa's account of the five aggregates in the *Abhidharmasammucaya* (Compendium of knowledge). In the *Karmasiddhaprakaraṇa* (A treatise on the establishment of Karma), Vasubandhu argues that the workings of the law of actions and their results are not correctly explained by the orthodox Vaibhāṣikas or by the Vātsīputrīyas and that the law's explanation requires reference to the Yogācāra theory that there is, apart from the six types of consciousnesses that are associated with the six types of organs of cognition, a storehouse consciousness (*ālayavijñāna*) that carries the seeds of all experiences and that this consciousness is not the substantially real self that we misapprehend it to be.

In the *Triṃśikākārikāvṛtti* (Thirty verse treatise) and the *Trisvabhāvanirdeśa* (Teaching on the three natures), Vasubandhu explains how consciousness functions in terms of its three natures. He argues that persons and other phenomena are just ever-changing manifestations of consciousness, which is itself a beginningless sequence of momentary mental states that takes three different forms. Its most basic form is that of the storehouse consciousness, which is a beginningless sequence of mental states in which is stored the seeds that are produced by actions and give rise to their results. In dependence upon this sequence as an underlying support, it takes the forms of the afflicted mind (*kliṣṭamanas*), which is a sequence of minds that misapprehend the first sequence as a substantially real self, and of a sequence of six organ-dependent cognitions of objects. All three of these ever-changing forms of consciousness, Vasubandhu adds, are mental constructions and are to be eliminated on the path to Buddhahood.

The conceptual framework Vasubandhu uses to explain how mental constructions can cease to exist is that consciousness possesses three natures (*svabhāvas*). They are its nature of being dependent upon causes and conditions (*paratantra*), its nature of falsely appearing to be divided into a mind that grasps an object and an object that is grasped by it (*parikalpita*), and its thoroughly established nature (*pariniṣpannasvabhāva*) of not in fact being divisible into a mind that grasps an object and an object that is grasped by it. To become free from mental constructions and the rebirth and suffering they occasion, we need to realize in what way consciousness, in relation to its possession of these three natures, is without a nature (*niḥsvabhāvatā*). In relation to consciousness possessing the nature of appearing to be divided into a mind that grasps an object and an object that is grasped by it, consciousness is by its own nature without such a nature. In relation to consciousness possessing the nature of being dependent upon causes and conditions, consciousness is without a nature by virtue of which it could come to be by itself. In relation to consciousness possessing a thoroughly established nature, consciousness is without a nature by virtue of which it is divisible into a mind that grasps an object and an object that is grasped by it. To become free of rebirth and suffering and become a Buddha, Vasubandhu explains, we need to enter into a state of consciousness that is free from all mental constructions.

In Vasubandhu's *Viṃśatikākārikāvṛtti* (Twenty verse treatise) and his own commentary on it, he answers objections to the central theses of the Yogācāra philosophy. He says that the things we believe to exist apart from mind (that is, the things we believe to be external objects) are mere mental constructions (*vijñaptimātra*), because what does not exist apart from mind appears, because of the constructive activity of mind, to exist apart from mind, just as what does not exist apart from sight appears, because of an eye disorder, to exist apart from sight. In reply to the objection that if there are no external objects, perceptions cannot be distinguished from one another and the same objects cannot be perceived by different persons, he argues that perceptions in dreams differ from one another in spite of lacking external objects as causes and that many different persons perceive the same objects as a result of similar actions performed in the past. He also argues that the suffering that is experienced by beings in the hell realms is not produced by external objects, because otherwise the hell-guardians, who are said in scripture not to suffer in these realms, would suffer along with those reborn in those realms. He adds that there can be no atoms of which external objects are composed, since they could not possess different sides as parts and so could not occupy space and be combined to compose external objects, which are said to occupy space.

Vasubandhu also composed many commentaries on Yogācāra treatises and Mahāyāna scriptures. Important among those that have survived (either in Sanskrit or in Tibetan or Chinese) are the *Madhyāntavibhāgabhāṣya* (Commentary on the separation of the middle from the extremes), the *Mahāyānasūtrālaṃkārabhāṣya* (Commentary on the ornament of the Mahāyāna Sūtras), the *Mahāyānasaṃgrahabhāṣya* (Commentary on the compendium of Mahāyāna), and the *Dharmadharmatāvibhāgavṛtti* (Commentary on the distinction between phenomena and their true nature).

See also Buddhism; Buddhism—Schools; Causation in Indian Philosophy; Indian Philosophy; Logic, History of: Logic and Inference in Indian Philosophy; Nāgārjuna; Self in Indian Philosophy.

Bibliography

Anacker, Stefan. *Seven Works of Vasubandhu, The Buddhist Psychological Doctor*. Delhi: Motilal Banarsidass, 1998.

Duerlinger, James. *Indian Buddhist Theories of Persons: Vasubandhu's "Refutation of the Theory of a Self."* Curzon Critical Studies in Buddhism Series. London and New York: RoutledgeCurzon, 2003.

Frauwallner, Erich. *On the Date of the Buddhist Master of the Law, Vasubandhu*. Rome: Serie Orientale Roma, III, 1951.

Jaini, Padmanabh S. "On the Theory of the Two Vasubandhus." *Bulletin of the London School of Oriental and African Studies* 22 (1959): 48–53.

Kochumuttom, Thomas A. *A Buddhist Doctrine of Experience: A New Translation and Interpretation of the Works of Vasubandhu the Yogācārin.* Delhi: Motilal Banarsidass, 1982.

Lusthaus, Dan. *Buddhist Phenomenology: A Philosophical Investigation of Yogācāra Buddhism and the Ch'eng Wei-shih Lun.* Curzon Critical Studies in Buddhism Series. London: RoutledgeCurzon, 2002.

Potter, Karl H. *Encyclopedia of Indian Philosophies.* Vol. 3, *Buddhist Philosophy from 100 to 350 A.D.* Delhi: Motilal Banarsidass, 1999.

Pruden, Leo. M. *Abhidharmakośabhāṣyam by Louis de La Vallée Poussin.* 4 vols. Berkeley: Asian Humanities Press, 1990.

Stcherbatsky, Theodore. *The Central Conception of Buddhism and the Meaning of the Word "Dharma."* Delhi: Motilal Banarsidass, 1970.

Wood, Thomas E. *Mind Only: A Philosophical and Doctrinal Analysis of the Vijñānavāda.* Delhi: Motilal Banarsidass, 1994.

James Duerlinger (2005)

VAUVENARGUES, LUC DE CLAPIERS, MARQUIS DE

(1715–1747)

The French moralist and epigrammatist Luc de Clapiers, marquis de Vauvenargues, was born at Aix-en-Provence. He early revealed a lofty character that despised egotism and pettiness. Ambitious for glory, he became an army officer at the age of seventeen, despite a weak physique. He served throughout the Italian campaign of 1734. The later German campaign of 1741, especially the harsh retreat from Prague, ruined his health, forcing him to retire at the age of twenty-six. His hope of a career in diplomacy was dashed by lack of fortune and protection. While vainly waiting at Aix for replies to his petitions for appointment to a post, he contracted a severe case of smallpox that left him disfigured and sickly. His last years were spent in Paris, in unhappy poverty and solitude (despite Voltaire's admiration), but he endured the injustice of men and events with stoic resignation rather than with bitterness. During this period he wrote his *Introduction à la connaissance de l'esprit humain* (Paris, 1746; augmented edition, 1747), which included the supplement "Réflexions et maximes." He also wrote character sketches in the fashion of Jean de La Bruyère, although less brilliantly, and *Réflexions sur divers auteurs*, a work of generally sound and objective criticism. He is particularly known for his maxims.

Vauvenargues's life and writings are characterized by their contradictions rather than by their consistency. Weak in health, he had a proud, heroic soul; poverty-stricken, he refused to consider gainful work out of aristocratic prejudice and a dislike for restraint. A lover of peace, he praised war and the martial virtues; opposed to ethical absolutes, he considered greatness of soul and action to be absolute virtues. Extremely unhappy and frustrated in life, his writings are resolutely optimistic; almost without friends, his correspondence reveals a noble ideal of friendship. Inclined to sentiment, he was from youth enamored of Plutarch, Seneca, and the Stoic attitudes.

Vauvenargues was a vigorous but not a profound or systematic thinker. He is notable for his incisive insights and formulations, principally in regard to character and moral ideals. He was a deist and not a Christian; but, believing religion necessary to social order, he opposed the propaganda of the *philosophes.* His philosophy, however, was secular in spirit, concerned with the problem of human nature and of what men should be and how they should live. He defended the worth of human nature both against the pessimism of the Christian doctrine of original sin and the corrosive cynicism of Duc François de La Rochefoucauld. Like other thinkers of his time, he justified the passions. Following Benedict de Spinoza, he divided the passions into two kinds, according to their motivation: "They have their principle in the love of being [and desire for its] perfection, or in the feeling of its imperfection or withering." However, he warned against submitting to a single dominating passion. In a phrase that calls to mind both Blaise Pascal and Reinhold Niebuhr, Vauvenargues said of man, "The feeling of his imperfection makes his eternal torture." Although he believed that man's need for greatness and importance is laudable, he also maintained that men should respond with charity to the needs of others. Vauvenargues's moments of humanitarianism, however, were devoid of sentimentalism.

Vauvenargues wished to defend the value of self-interest, which is naturally a good, and also to preserve the ethical character of acts. He adopted two main approaches. Before Jean-Jacques Rousseau did, Vauvenargues distinguished between *amour propre* and *amour de nous-mêmes. Amour de nous-mêmes* allows us to seek happiness outside ourselves: "One is not his own unique object." There is, then, a difference between the satisfaction of *amour propre* and its sacrifice. Against those who held that all acts are motivated by self-interest Vauvenargues maintained that it is absurd to call sacrifice of life, for example, an act of self-interest, for in such an act we consider ourselves as the least part of the whole and lose everything. Still combating La Rochefoucauld, Vauvenargues also argued that the criterion of acts is their effect on others; acts are virtuous if they tend to the good of all, even if they also satisfy self-interest. This definition opened a line of argument that had dangerous consequences in the hands of the materialists: (1) If each man must satisfy his self-interest where he can, men may be considered "fortunately born" or "unfortunately born" but not responsible for their acts. (2) Ethical and political considerations became fused, and eventually, with Rousseau, Johann Gottlieb Fichte, and G. W. F. Hegel, this led to the concept of the "ethical state." How should acts be judged? "Reason deceives us more often than the heart," declared Vauvenargues; like Rousseau, he trusted the "first impulse."

Vauvenargues believed that in regard to happiness, too, each man must follow his fated way; no philosophical formula can guide him. But he did offer one principle: "There is no enjoyment except in proportion as one acts, and our soul possesses itself truly only when it exerts itself completely." To give up action is to fall into nothingness. Existence is a function of becoming. Vauvenargues satirized pitilessly both the indolent and those who engage in aimless agitation. Activity, courage, glory, and ambition summarize his ideal of life and his concept of virtue. Greatness of soul is consistent with evil, as in Catiline; all depends on character and education. The great soul does not care about public esteem; true glory is an intimate feeling, self-satisfying to the point where it may paradoxically disdain action.

Although Vauvenargues was not interested in political philosophy, he did argue against the notion that men are, or may be naturally, politically or socially equal: "Law cannot make men equal in spite of nature." Hierarchy, in all respects, is inevitable.

Vauvenargues frequently espoused contradictory views. Although he developed no important theoretical positions, he occupies a leading rank in the long line of what the French term "moralists," excelling in psychological portraits and the striking but abstract formula of the maxim.

See also Ethics, History of; Fichte, Johann Gottlieb; Hegel, Georg Wilhelm Friedrich; La Bruyère, Jean de; La Rochefoucauld, Duc François de; Niebuhr, Reinhold; Pascal, Blaise; Plutarch of Chaeronea; Rousseau, Jean-Jacques; Seneca, Lucius Annaeus; Spinoza, Benedict (Baruch) de; Stoicism; Voltaire, François-Marie Arouet de.

Bibliography

Vauvenargues's works were published in a collected edition as *Oeuvres completes*, in 4 vols. (Paris, 1821); his moral works were published as *Oeuvres morales*, in 3 vols. (Paris, 1874).

For literature on Vauvenargues, see F. Vial, *Une philosophie et une morale du sentiment: Luc de Clapiers, marquis de Vauvenargues* (Paris: Droz, 1938), and G. Lanson, *Le Marquis de Vauvenargues* (Paris: Hachette, 1930).

OTHER RECOMMENDED WORKS

Fine, Peter M. *Vauvenargues and La Rochefoucauld.* Manchester, U.K.: Manchester University Press, 1974.

Meagher, Paul. "Vauvenargues' Quest for a New Moral Philosophy." *Lumen* 13 (1994): 125–136.

L. G. Crocker (1967)
Bibliography updated by Tamra Frei (2005)

VAZ FERREIRA, CARLOS

(1872–1958)

Carlos Vaz Ferreira, the Uruguayan educator and philosopher, was born in Montevideo. He became a professor of philosophy and rector at the University of Montevideo and played a prominent part in the theory and administration of primary and secondary education in Uruguay. He wrote voluminously and was a popular lecturer. As a result, he was for several decades a major intellectual force in his country. At various times and in various respects, he was influenced by Herbert Spencer, J. S. Mill, William James, and Henri Bergson, without full commitment to any of them.

Vaz Ferreira was impressed by the fluid complexity of experience, thought, and reality. Words and logical forms impose false precision and system on the contents of thought. The remedy is not a flight from reason but the development of a plastic reason close to experience, life, and instinct, alert to degrees of probability and unwilling to assent beyond the warrant of the question and evidence. The formulation and disposition of metaphysical questions requires the highest degree of caution, but metaphysics is both legitimate and necessary. It is impossible to move far in science without running into metaphysical questions, and it is necessary to cultivate metaphysics in order to understand the symbolic and limited nature of science and to counteract the bad metaphysics that comes into being when metaphysics is neglected. Vaz Ferreira was critical of positive religion but was sympathetic to religion as the emotional apprehension of a possible transcendent being.

The ethics of Vaz Ferreira showed the same skepticism fused with marked human warmth and moral insight. Ethical principles cannot be stated without exceptions or descent into casuistry. Ideals clash and choices are usually between alternatives that contain some evil. An ethically sensitive person therefore is more subject than others to doubt, crisis, and remorse: satisfied conscience is more readily found in those who have a narrow awareness and ready formulas. But an ethically sensitive person may exemplify the perfection of individual morality, in which are combined a feeling for each individual act and a care for all possible results. Vaz Ferreira held that there has been moral progress in the course of history: Ideals have been added from time to time, more persons now share to some degree in all ideals, and there is greater resistance to evil.

See also Appearance and Reality; Bergson, Henri; Experience; James, William; Latin American Philosophy; Metaphysics; Mill, John Stuart.

Bibliography

Vaz Ferreira's principal works include *Los problemas de la libertad* (Problems of liberty; Montevideo, 1907); *Conocimiento y acción* (Knowledge and action; Montevideo: Mariño y Caballero, 1908); *Moral para intelectuales* (Ethics for intellectuals; Montevideo, 1909); *El pragmatismo* (Montevideo, 1909); *Lógica viva* (Living logic; Montevideo, 1910); *Sobre los problemas sociales* (On social problems; Montevideo, 1922); *Fermentario* (Montevideo, 1938).

See also Arturo Ardao, *Introducción a Vaz Ferreira* (Montevideo: Barreiro y Ramos, 1961).

Arthur Berndtson (1967)

VEBLEN, THORSTEIN BUNDE
(1857–1929)

Thorstein Bunde Veblen, the American economist and social theorist, is perhaps best known for his ironic style, a style that was at one with his life. Although he is still thought of abroad as the most influential American social scientist, among social scientists in America his influence has almost vanished. He is virtually unknown to college students, even if a scattered lot of Veblen's concepts—most obviously, "conspicuous consumption"—are unwittingly part of their speech and analyses.

Born on a Wisconsin farm, Veblen developed the most comprehensive and penetrating analysis of American industrial society in the early twentieth century. He emphasized qualitative relationships in the historical process, and his aim was an inclusive theory of social change. However, the largest number of those who have walked in Veblen's footsteps are known for quantitative, essentially unhistorical, often antitheoretical investigations. Where his followers have not deviated from his work in these ways, they have in another: Veblen called for, if he did not usually practice, dispassionate social analysis; many of his most fervent disciples are also quite fervent in their social analyses.

Like his contemporary, Charles S. Peirce, Veblen was a scholar of great intellectual achievement whose academic career was, at best, undistinguished. He took his doctorate in philosophy at Yale, whence he moved to Cornell to study economics. In a year he moved to the new University of Chicago, where he taught, and he also edited the *Journal of Political Economy.* Before long acrimony between Veblen and the administration over his academic and social nonconformity developed to a point where the happiest step for all concerned was for Veblen to leave Chicago. That experience, added to by similar ones at his next teaching post at Stanford, prompted Veblen to write one of his most scathing, if also very useful and sound, books: *The Higher Learning in America: A Memorandum on the Conduct of Universities by Businessmen* (New York, 1918). The original subtitle, abandoned for one reason or another, was "A Study in Total Depravity."

Stanford and Veblen failed to cement relations, and Veblen drifted to the University of Missouri, where he was sheltered by the eminent economist Herbert Davenport. Lectures at the New School for Social Research in New York City, and a brief interlude with the federal government, for which he wrote memoranda connected with World War I, ended Veblen's professional career. The department of economics at Cornell chose to add him to its faculty but that wish was denied by the university administration. Veblen spent his last few years unproductively, in a cabin in the Stanford hills, where he died, embittered against society.

The prime influences on Veblen appear to have been David Hume, Charles Darwin, and Karl Marx—although the influence of each was much transmuted by the mind and the circumstances of Veblen. The skepticism of Hume and the evolutionary approach of Darwin combined with the American scene to impel Veblen to launch a barrage of telling criticism (in essays in *The Place of Sci-*

ence in Modern Civilization, New York, 1919) at what he took to be the metaphysical, teleological, and optimistic qualities of Marxian analysis. But Veblen was not so much a critic as an adaptor of Marx, and his own works may be looked at most usefully in that light.

Darwinian concepts aside, the starting point of Veblen's analysis of society and of social change was fundamentally Marxian. The relationship of tension and change that Marx attributed to the conflict between "the forces of production" and "the mode of production" are present in Veblen's close equivalents, technology and institutions. For both men this relationship deserves and requires investigation within a framework of history (for Marx) or the genetic process (for Veblen).

But if the starting point for Veblen was the same as that of Marx, it was also there that basic similarities ended. For Marx the nineteenth-century assumptions of rationality went unquestioned, but for Veblen those assumptions were high on the list of matters to be investigated. As a consequence Veblen believed that a theory of social change required the integration of social psychology (and the psychology of related matters, such as nationalism and patriotism) with economics, politics, and history. Stemming from this is another difference: For Marx there were "general laws of motion of capitalist society" discoverable by the investigator; for Veblen those general laws had to be so qualified by national and cultural differences that it was not only plausible but also probable that capitalism would work out differently in different nations. Thus the very general quality of the conclusions to be found in *Capital,* when compared with Veblen's differing expectations for capitalism in Great Britain and Germany (in *Imperial Germany and the Industrial Revolution,* New York, 1915) and in the United States (in *The Theory of Business Enterprise,* New York, 1904, and in *Absentee Ownership,* New York, 1923). The point is illustrated by Veblen's findings about Japan and Germany, which (with much prescience) he saw as facing very much the same future despite their very different economic histories. For Veblen the decisive factors for the two nations were those making for extreme nationalism and social irrationality, moving them in much the same direction at much the same speed.

There is a final and striking difference between Marx and Veblen. In addition to his role as a social scientist, Marx was a political activist and propagandist, and his scientific writings were integrally connected with his political aims, concerning which Marx was optimistic. Veblen was politically aloof, except for a few periods such as his wartime propagandistic activity, and his role was that of Cassandra. Marx saw the class struggle as the means by which the contradictions between the forces and the mode of production would one day necessarily bring about the desired socialist society. Although Veblen would have found that socialist society less repulsive than the capitalist society he analyzed, his mood was gloomy and his vision apocalyptic, as suggested in one of his better-known but by no means unrepresentative observations in *The Instinct of Workmanship* (New York, 1914, p. 25): "history records more frequent and more spectacular instances of the triumph of imbecile institutions over life and culture than of peoples who have saved themselves alive out of a desperately precarious institutional situation, such, for instance, as now faces the people of Christendom."

Veblen's critical energies were spent most persistently in attacking the business system and nationalism, in that order. But he reserved his most savage wit for organized religion, which he considered a special—and the most successful—form of salesmanship (see the appendix to Ch. 11 of *Absentee Ownership*), manned by mental defectives whose business it is "to promise everything and deliver nothing."

See also Darwin, Charles Robert; Hume, David; Marx, Karl; Nationalism; Peirce, Charles Sanders; Philosophy of Social Sciences.

Bibliography

Of Veblen's 11 books, his first, *The Theory of the Leisure Class* (New York: Macmillan, 1899), was the most influential and most fundamental. See also *The Engineers and the Price System* (1919; New York: Harcourt Brace, 1963).

For the definitive biography of Veblen, see Joseph Dorfman, *Thorstein Veblen and His America* (New York: Viking Press, 1934).

For a more recent account of Veblen as an economist, see Douglas Dowd, *Thorstein Veblen* (New York: Washington Square Press, 1964). See also David Riesman, *Thorstein Veblen, a Critical Interpretation* (New York: Scribners, 1953; 2nd ed., 1960). Riesman is one of Veblen's severer critics.

ADDITIONAL SOURCES

Diggins, John P. *The Bard of Savagery: Thorstein Veblen and Modern Social Theory.* New York: Seabury Press, 1978.

Qualey, Carlton C., ed. *Thorstein Veblen; the Carleton College Veblen Seminar Essays.* New York: Columbia University Press, 1968.

Tilman, Rick. *The Intellectual Legacy of Thorstein Veblen.* Westport, CT: Greenwood Press, 1996.

Douglas F. Dowd (1967)
Bibliography updated by Philip Reed (2005)

VECCHIO, GIORGIO DEL

See *Del Vecchio, Giorgio*

VEDA

See *Indian Philosophy*

VEDANTA

See *Indian Philosophy*

VENN, JOHN

(1834–1923)

The British logician John Venn was born at Drypool, Hull, the elder son of the Reverend Henry Venn, a prominent evangelical divine. After early education at Highgate and Islington proprietary schools, he entered Gonville and Caius College, Cambridge, in 1853. On graduating Sixth Wrangler in 1857, he became a fellow and remained on the foundation for sixty-six years, until his death. During the last twenty years of his residence he was also president of the college. Venn took orders in 1858 and served as a curate in parishes near London before returning to Cambridge as college lecturer in moral sciences in 1862. He married in 1867. In 1869 he was Hulsean lecturer and published thereafter a work titled *On Some Characteristics of Belief* (London, 1870), but contact with Henry Sidgwick and other Cambridge agnostics, plus the reading of Augustus De Morgan, George Boole, J. Austin, and J. S. Mill had the effect of transferring his interests from theology almost wholly to logic, and in 1883 he gave up his orders without altogether withdrawing from the church. In the same year he became a fellow of the Royal Society and took the degree of doctor of science.

Venn was among those responsible for the development of the moral sciences tripos at Cambridge and in the course of his teaching published successively the three works by which he is now remembered: *The Logic of Chance* (London, 1866; 3rd ed., 1888); *Symbolic Logic* (London, 1881; 2nd ed., 1894); and *The Principles of Empirical or Inductive Logic* (London, 1889; 2nd ed., 1907). In 1888 he presented his extensive collection of books on logic to the university library, and he turned in later years to antiquarian pursuits, writing the history of his college and his family and collaborating with his son, J. A. Venn, in the preparation of Part I of *Alumni Cantabrigienses* (4 vols., London, 1922). Venn was an accomplished linguist and throughout most of his long life an active botanist and mountaineer. In addition to designing a simple mechanical contrivance to illustrate his well-known logical diagrams, he is said to have invented a very successful machine for bowling at cricket.

Venn has no strong claim to be regarded as an original thinker. His general position in philosophy was that of an orthodox, though unusually cautious and skeptical, empiricist. Outside the fields of logic and methodology he contributed little of importance, and even within them his role was essentially that of a critic and expositor of ideas first mooted by other men. In that capacity, however, his writings are marked by an acumen, learning, and lucidity that rank them among the best productions of their day. Within its limits, therefore, his reputation is still a high one.

LOGIC

Venn was a follower of Boole and to a lesser extent of Mill and a defender of both against the criticisms of William Stanley Jevons on the one hand and of the idealist logicians on the other. His *Symbolic Logic* is an attempt to show not merely that the Boolean algebra "works" but also that it is in the main line of historical tradition and that its supposedly mathematical obscurities are in fact intelligible from a purely logical point of view. Like De Morgan, he is aware of the element of convention in the choice of a logical standpoint and hence of the possibility of alternative versions of the basic propositional forms. He thus contrasts the four Aristotelian (or "predicative") types of proposition with the eight forms of Sir William Hamilton (which reduce on analysis to the five possible relations of inclusion and exclusion between pairs of classes), and compares them both with the fifteen possibilities that arise on his own "existential" view, based on the emptiness or occupancy of the four "compartments" marked out by a pair of terms and their negatives. Unlike some of his predecessors, he sees the difference as one of convenience rather than correctness, and so finds it unnecessary to dispute the merits of the older logic in order to vindicate the claims of the new. A similar tolerance is apparent in his treatment of the vexed issue concerning the "existential import" of propositions, where, after careful discussion, he opts for the presumption that universal propositions do not imply the existence of members in the subject class—a view that the great majority of writers from J. M. Keynes onward have since found reason to accept. Less open-minded, perhaps, is his attitude to Jevons's reforms of the Boolean calculus; but he made several improvements of his own, notably in the writing of particular propositions as inequations, and, by the introduction of his diagrammatic methods, he did more than anyone else to render the workings of that calculus intelligible to the nonmathematical mind.

PROBABILITY

The Logic of Chance is also a work of much value to those embroiled in the mathematical complications of the theory of probability. The rationalistic handling of this subject by earlier writers was not to Venn's taste, and he recognized more clearly than they did the difficulties of relating their a priori computations to the realities of uncertain reasoning in everyday life. Following the suggestions of Leslie Ellis, he therefore identifies the probability of events not with the amount of belief it is rational to have in them but with their statistical frequency of occurrence in the generic class of events to which they belong. He assumes, that is, that the world contains series of resembling events in which individual irregularity in the possession of properties is combined with aggregate regularity "in the long run." The assignment of probability to a type of event is thus a mere matter of ascertaining the relative frequency with which it tends, increasingly, to occur as the series is extended to large numbers; and this is, in principle, not a subjective affair but a perfectly empirical and objective type of inquiry into the properties of a certain kind of group. To define probability in this way is, as Venn realized, to restrict it more narrowly than is usually done. No meaning can properly be attached to the probability of a single event, and the notion becomes equally inapplicable to the large range of judgments expressing partial belief (in theories and the like) that had hitherto been dealt with under this head. There are difficulties, moreover (as he also recognized), in assuming that observed frequencies are a reliable clue to "long-run" or "limiting" frequencies—that it is possible, in effect, on inductive grounds to arrive at such long-run frequencies by means of sample observations, however extended. For such a conclusion can itself be only probable, and that in a sense which Venn does not offer to define. Thus a knowledge of statistical frequency, even if obtainable, would be no sufficient ground for preferring one expectation to another. Probability, as Venn conceives it, is clearly not the guide of life.

SCIENTIFIC METHOD

The frequency theory of probability has had able defenders since Venn's time and is now less vulnerable to criticism. His version of it remains, however, the classical one, and the majority of later exponents acknowledge their debt to him. By comparison, the scientific methodology set forth in *Empirical Logic* has suffered somewhat from its association with that of Mill, on which it is largely modeled and whose conclusions it largely accepts. Venn differs from Mill chiefly in setting greater store by laws of coexistence than by laws of causal succession. The idea of causation he considers too crude and popular in conception to be of much use in science, and he is accordingly skeptical as to the value of the inductive methods. So far from being a reliable instrument for the discovery of causes, Mill's canons of induction are effective, he thinks, only where the conditions of the problem and its possible solutions have been narrowly circumscribed in advance, and under ordinary circumstances this can seldom be done. Inductive procedures are thus by no means so conclusive as Mill supposed, though we are not therefore justified in assuming, with Jevons, that they can be rationalized by appeal to the calculus of probability. Judgments of probability themselves make use of induction, and the two must therefore be kept, so far as possible, distinct. More generally, the use of formal methods in the classification, ordering, and prediction of natural phenomena can never be more than approximate, owing to the number of simplifying assumptions necessary before it can get under way. Venn's subsidiary discussions of definition, division, hypothesis, measurement, and so on, are similarly concerned to stress the difficulties of applying principles to cases and the amount that is taken for granted in doing so. Though less closely acquainted than some other writers with the details of scientific practice, he is also less liable than most to mistake the logic of science for a description of its technique.

See also Austin, John; Boole, George; British Philosophy; De Morgan, Augustus; Hamilton, William; Jevons, William Stanley; Logic Diagrams; Logic, History of; Mill, John Stuart; Mill's Methods of Induction; Probability and Chance; Sidgwick, Henry.

Bibliography

Venn has been somewhat neglected by historians of philosophy and no comprehensive study of him exists. For a serviceable brief account, see J. A. Passmore, *A Hundred Years of Philosophy* (London: Duckworth, 1957), pp. 134–136. His views on probability are most fully criticized in J. M. Keynes, *Treatise on Probability* (London: Macmillan, 1921).

P. L. Heath (1967)

VERIFIABILITY PRINCIPLE

The most distinctive doctrine of the logical positivists was that for any sentence to be cognitively meaningful it must express a statement that is either analytic or empirically verifiable. It was allowed that sentences may have "emotive," "imperative," and other kinds of meaning (for example, "What a lovely present!" or "Bring me a glass of water!") even when they have no cognitive meaning, that is, when they do not express anything that could be true or false, or a possible subject of knowledge. But—leaving aside sentences expressing analytic statements—for a sentence to have "cognitive," "factual," "descriptive," or "literal" meaning (for example, "The sun is 93 million miles from the earth") it was held that it must express a statement that could, at least in principle, be shown to be true or false, or to some degree probable, by reference to empirical observations. The iconoclasm of the logical positivists was based on this criterion of meaning, for according to the verifiability principle a great many of the sentences of traditional philosophy (for example, "Reality is spiritual," "The moral rightness of an action is a nonempirical property," "Beauty is significant form," "God created the world for the fulfillment of his purpose") must be cognitively meaningless. Hence, like Ludwig Wittgenstein in the *Tractatus Logico-Philosophicus*, they held that most of the statements to be found in traditional philosophy are not false but nonsensical. The verifiability principle, it was maintained, demonstrates the impossibility of metaphysics, and from this it was concluded that empirical science is the only method by which we can have knowledge concerning the world.

The verifiability principle stands historically in a line of direct descent from the empiricism of David Hume, J. S. Mill, and Ernst Mach. It has some affinities with pragmatism and operationalism, but it differs from them in some important respects. Pragmatism, as presented by C. S. Peirce, William James, and John Dewey, is the view that the "intellectual purport" of any symbol consists entirely in the practical effects, both on our conduct and on our experiences, that would follow from "acceptance of the symbol." This view, unlike the verifiability principle, makes the meaning of a sentence relative to certain human interests and purposes and to the behavior adopted for the realization of these purposes. Operationalism, as held by P. W. Bridgman and others, is the view that the meaning of a term is simply the set of operations that must be performed in order to apply the term in a given instance. Thus, according to this view, the meaning, or rather *a* meaning, of the term *length* is given by specifying a set of operations to be carried out with a measuring rod. Moritz Schlick and other logical positivists sometimes said that the meaning of a sentence is the method of its verification. But, unlike the advocates of operationalism, they meant by "the method of verification" not an actual procedure but the logical possibility of verification. The verifiability principle had among its immediate antecedents Schlick's *Allgemeine Erkenntnislehre* (Berlin, 1918) and Rudolf Carnap's *Der logische Aufbau der Welt* (Berlin, 1928). It was first formulated explicitly by Friedrich Waismann in his "Logische Analyse des Wahrscheinlichkeitsbegriffs" (1930) and subsequently by Schlick, Carnap, Otto Neurath, Hans Reichenbach, Carl Hempel, A. J. Ayer, and other logical positivists in numerous publications.

PROBLEMS RAISED BY THE PRINCIPLE

The controversial questions concerning the principle are: (1) What is it to be applied to—propositions, statements or sentences? (2) Is it a criterion for determining what the meaning of any particular sentence is, or is it simply a criterion of whether a sentence is meaningful? (3) What is meant by saying that a statement is verifi*able*, or falsifi*able*, even if in practice it has not been, and perhaps cannot be, verified, or falsified? (4) What type of statement directly reports an empirical observation, and how do we ascertain the truth-value of such a statement? (5) Is the principle itself either analytic or empirically verifiable, and if not, in what sense is it meaningful? (6) Is the question that the principle is intended to answer (that is, the question "By what general criterion can the meaning or the meaningfulness of a sentence be determined?") a logically legitimate question?

WHAT IS THE PRINCIPLE TO BE APPLIED TO? In some of the earlier formulations of the verifiability principle it is presented as a criterion for distinguishing between meaningful and meaningless propositions. However, in an accepted philosophical usage, every proposition is either true or false, and hence a fortiori a proposition cannot be meaningless. To meet this point some of the later exponents of the principle say that a grammatically well-formed indicative sentence, whether it is cognitively meaningful or not, expresses a "statement"; the term *proposition* is retained for what is expressed by a cognitively meaningful sentence—that is, propositions are treated as a subclass of statements. The verifiability principle is then presented as a criterion for distinguishing between meaningful and meaningless statements. This procedure, however, presupposes a usage for "cognitively meaningful sentence," and indeed it is sentences that are normally said to be meaningful or not.

Consequently, in still other formulations the principle is presented as applying directly to sentences; the objection to this is that sentences are not normally said to be true or false, and hence they are not said to be verifiable or falsifiable.

In order to meet these difficulties, sentences, statements, and propositions may be distinguished in the following way: A sentence, as we shall understand it, belongs to a particular language, it is meaningful or not, but it is not properly said to be true or false, or to stand in logical relations to other sentences, or to be verifiable or falsifiable. A statement is what is expressed in certain circumstances by an indicative sentence, and the same statement may be expressed by different sentences in the same or in different languages; a statement is properly said to be true or false, it does stand in logical relations to other statements, and it is verifiable or falsifiable. What can or cannot be said of statements applies equally to propositions, except that a proposition cannot be meaningless, that is, it cannot be expressed by a meaningless sentence.

For convenience we shall sometimes speak of sentences as being verifiable or not, and of statements as being meaningful or not. But, more strictly, we shall understand the verifiability principle as claiming that the cognitive meaning or meaningfulness of a *sentence* is to be determined by reference to the verifiability (or falsifiability) of the *statement* expressed by the sentence.

A CRITERION OF MEANING OR MEANINGFULNESS? The earliest presentations of the verifiability principle identified the meaning of a sentence with the logical possibility of verifying the corresponding statement, and apparently, in the last analysis, with the occurrence of certain experiences. This has some initial plausibility in the case of "empirical sentences," that is, sentences containing, apart from nondescriptive expressions, only empirical predicates (for example, "red," "round," "middle C"). An empirical predicate is, by definition, one that stands for a property that can be observed or experienced. Consequently, in the case of such a sentence as "This is red," there is a natural tendency to say that the meaning of the sentence is given by the experience that would verify it. The meaning is understood by anyone who can use the sentence for the purpose of identifying red objects when he sees them and cannot be understood by anyone who cannot identify red objects. It might be argued that a congenitally blind person could be said to understand the sentence "This is red" if he were able to identify red objects in some other way, by touch, for example. But in that case, an early adherent of the verifiability principle might reply, the predicate "red" has, for the person in question, not a visual but a tactual meaning. Our ability to understand empirical predicates, he might say, is plainly restricted by our capacity for sensory discrimination. For example, a person may be able to give a verbal definition of "C♭" as "the note midway between the notes designated by 'C' and 'C♯'"; but there is an important sense in which he does not know what "C♭" means if he is not able to discriminate quarter tones. It may be fairly objected, however, that this argument rests on the ambiguities of the words *meaning, stands for*, and *designates*; for example, the sense in which a term may be said to have a "tactual meaning" if it designates something tactual is not the sense in which a sentence may have a "cognitive or factual meaning." Moreover, it cannot be correct to identify the meaning of a sentence with the experiences that would verify it, for the characteristics that can be appropriately attributed to an experience cannot be appropriately attributed to the meaning of a sentence, nor conversely—for example, the meaning of a sentence does not occur at a particular time or with a certain intensity, as does an experience. And finally, if the meaning of a sentence were identified with the experiences of a particular person, the verifiability principle would result in a radical form of solipsism.

To meet these objections some other early formulations of the principle identified the meaning of a statement with that of some finite conjunction of statements directly reporting empirical observations. As will appear in more detail later, there are two main replies to this: (1) there are many types of statement whose meaning is not equivalent to that of any finite conjunction of observation statements, and (2) to identify the meaning of one statement with that of another is simply to say that the two statements have the same meaning, and this is not to explain or to give the meaning of the original statement.

For the foregoing reasons, it cannot be held that the verifiability principle is a criterion for determining the *meaning* of any particular sentence. In its later formulations it is presented simply as a criterion for determining whether a sentence is cognitively or factually *meaningful.*

STRONG VERIFIABILITY. In their early formulations Waismann, Schlick, and others held that the cognitive meaning of a sentence is determined completely by the experiences that would verify it conclusively. According to Waismann, for example, in "Logische Analyse des Wahrscheinlichkeitsbegriffs," "Anyone uttering a sentence must know in which conditions he calls the statement true or false; if he is unable to state this, then he does not know what he has said. A statement which cannot be verified conclusively is not verifiable at all; it is just devoid of any meaning." This was sometimes called the requirement of "strong verifiability." It says, in effect, that for any statement *S* to be cognitively meaningful there must be some finite consistent set of basic observation statements $O_1 \cdots O_n$, such that *S* entails and is entailed by the conjunction of $O_1 \cdots O_n$. The principal objections to this requirement are: (1) a strictly universal statement, that is, a statement covering an unlimited number of instances (for example, any statement of scientific law), is not logically equivalent to a conjunction of any finite number of observation statements and hence is not conclusively verifiable; (2) any singular statement about a physical object can in principle be the basis of an unlimited number of predictions and hence is not conclusively verifiable; (3) statements about past and future events, and statements about the experiences of other people, are not conclusively verifiable; (4) even if an existential statement (for example, "Red things exist" or "At least one thing is red") is verifiable in the required sense, its denial cannot be verifiable in this sense, for its denial (for example, "Red things do not exist" or "Everything is nonred") is a strictly universal statement. Hence, the requirement of strong verifiability would have the strange consequence that the denial of an existential statement would never be meaningful, and this would involve the rejection of the fundamental logical principle that if a statement *S* is true, then not-*S* is false, and that if *S* is false, then not-*S* is true; (5) if a statement *S* is meaningful by the present requirement and *N* is any meaningless statement, then the molecular statement *S or N* must be meaningful; (6) the present requirement presupposes that observation statements are conclusively verifiable, for unless this is so, no statement at all, not even a statement that is logically equivalent to a finite conjunction of observation statements, will be conclusively verifiable—or cognitively meaningful.

FALSIFIABILITY. It was sometimes suggested that conclusive falsifiability rather than conclusive verifiability should be the criterion of a cognitively meaningful statement. The criterion of conclusive falsifiability says, in effect, that a statement *S* is meaningful if and only if not-*S* is conclusively verifiable. Consequently, objections analogous to those already considered still apply: (1) existential statements are not conclusively falsifiable, for if *S* is an existential statement, not-*S* is a strictly universal statement; (2) even if a universal statement is conclusively falsifiable, its denial is not conclusively falsifiable, since its denial is an existential statement. Hence, the present criterion would have the consequence that the denial of a universal statement would never be meaningful, and again this would involve the rejection of the fundamental principle of logic mentioned before; (3) the present criterion is open to the special objection that a universal statement (for example, "Whatever is pure water boils at 100° C.") would be meaningful, that is, conclusively falsifiable, only if the corresponding negative existential statement (for example, "There is an instance of pure water that does not boil at 100° C.") were assertable, and a fortiori meaningful; but this negative existential statement would be meaningful, that is, conclusively falsifiable, only if the corresponding universal statement were assertable, and a fortiori meaningful. To escape from this circle it would be necessary to have a different and independent criterion of significance for either universal or existential statements; (4) if *S* is meaningful by the present requirement and *N* is any meaningless statement, then *S and N* must be meaningful; (5) again, the present requirement presupposes that basic observation statements are conclusively verifiable.

CONFIRMABILITY. To meet the preceding difficulties the later formulations of the verifiability principle require of a meaningful statement that it should be related to a set of observation statements in such a way that they provide not conclusive verifiability but simply some degree of evidential support for the original statement. This was sometimes called the requirement of "weak verifiability." It says that for any statement *S* to be cognitively meaningful there must be some set of basic observation statements $O_1 \cdots O_n$ such that *S* entails $O_1 \cdots O_n$ and that $O_1 \cdots O_n$ confirms, or gives some degree of probability to, S. A formulation of this kind was given by Ayer in the first edition of *Language, Truth and Logic* (1936). He held that a statement is verifiable, and hence meaningful, if one or more observation statements can be deduced from it, perhaps in conjunction with certain additional premises, without being deducible from these other premises alone. The qualification concerning additional premises is introduced to allow, among other things, theoretical statements in science to be verifiable.

But this formulation, as Ayer recognizes in the second edition of his book, permits any meaningless statement to be verifiable. For if *N* is any meaningless statement and *O* some observation statement, then from *N* together with the additional premise *if N then O* the observation statement *O* can be deduced, although *O* cannot be deduced from the additional premise alone. To meet objections of this kind Ayer introduces a number of conditions; he says (1) "a statement is directly verifiable if it is either itself an observation-statement, or is such that in conjunction with one or more observation-statements it entails at least one observation-statement which is not deducible from these other premises alone," and (2) "a statement is indirectly verifiable if it satisfies the following conditions: First, that in conjunction with certain other premises it entails one or more directly verifiable statements that are not deducible from these other premises alone; and secondly, that these other premises do not include any statement that is not either analytic, or directly verifiable, or capable of being independently established as indirectly verifiable."

These conditions are designed inter alia to prevent obviously meaningless statements from being verifiable simply by occurring as components of verifiable molecular statements as in the objection to the requirement of strong verifiability (see above), and the objection to the requirement of conclusive falsifiability. The conditions are, however, insufficient for this purpose. As Hempel remarks, according to the present formulation if S is meaningful, then S *and* N will be meaningful, whatever statement N may be. And Alonzo Church has shown that given any three observation statements O_1, O_2, and O_3, no one of which entails either of the others, and any statement N, it is possible to construct a molecular statement from which it follows that either N or not-N is verifiable. Such a molecular statement is one of the form $(\sim O_1 \cdot O_2) \vee (O_3 \cdot \sim N)$. For $(\sim O_1 \cdot \sim O_2) \vee (O_3 \cdot \sim N)$ together with O_1 entails O_3, and so the molecular statement is directly verifiable; but N together with $(\sim O_1 \cdot O_2) \vee (O_3 \cdot \sim N)$ entails O_2, and therefore N is indirectly verifiable. Alternatively, $(\sim O_1 \cdot O_2) \vee (O_3 \cdot \sim N)$ may by itself entail O_2, and in that case $\sim N$ and O_3 also entail O_2, and therefore $\sim N$ is directly verifiable.

Difficulties of the kind raised by Hempel and Church obtain when a component of a molecular statement is superfluous as far as the verifiability of the molecular statement is concerned, that is, when the inclusion or exclusion of the component makes no difference to the verifiable entailments of the molecular statement. To eliminate components of this kind, R. Brown and J. Watling have proposed that for a molecular statement to be verifiable, either directly or indirectly, it must contain "only components whose deletion leaves a statement which entails verifiable statements not entailed by the original statement, or does not entail verifiable statements entailed by the original statement." This stipulation is designed to ensure that every component of a verifiable molecular statement either is independently verifiable (that is, "entails verifiable statements not entailed by the original statement") or else contributes to the meaning of the molecular statement in such a way that the molecular statement entails verifiable statements not entailed by any of its components (that is, any of the components alone "does not entail verifiable statements entailed by the original statement"). The intention of these stipulations is to ensure that a meaningless statement cannot occur as a component of a verifiable molecular statement and derive verifiability from the statement in which it occurs.

In two important articles titled "Testability and Meaning" (1936–1937), Carnap distinguished the testing of a sentence from its confirmation; a sentence is "testable" if we know of a particular procedure (for example, the carrying out of certain experiments) that would confirm to some degree either the sentence or its negation. A sentence is "confirmable" if we know what kind of evidence would confirm it, even though we do not know of a particular procedure for obtaining that evidence. Carnap considers four different criteria of significance—complete testability, complete confirmability, degree of testability, and degree of confirmability. All of these exclude metaphysical statements as being meaningless. The fourth criterion is the most liberal and admits into the class of meaningful statements empirical statements of the various kinds that were excluded by the requirement of conclusive verifiability or the requirement of conclusive falsifiability.

Each of Carnap's criteria determines a more or less restrictive form of empiricist language, and this, according to his view, is the same thing as a more or less restrictive form of empiricism. Carnap is largely concerned in these articles with giving a technical account of the formal features of such languages. One of the most serious difficulties he encounters is that of giving a satisfactory account of confirmability. His procedure is, in effect, to regard as cognitively meaningful all and only those statements that can be expressed in a formalized empiricist language.

Similarly, Hempel, in his article "Problems and Changes in the Empiricist Criterion of Meaning" (1950), discussed the proposal that a sentence has cognitive meaning if and only if it is translatable into an empiricist language. A formalized language is characterized by enumerating the formation and transformation rules of its syntax and the designation rules for the terms of its basic vocabulary. An empiricist language is one in which the basic vocabulary consists exclusively of empirical terms. As Hempel explains, dispositional terms may be introduced by means of "reduction sentences," and the theoretical constructs of the more advanced sciences (for example, "electrical field," "absolute temperature," "gravitational potential") can be accommodated by allowing the language to include interpreted deductive systems.

Hempel claims for his criterion that it avoids many of the difficulties of the earlier formulations of the verifiability principle. The logic of a formalized language may ensure that no universal or existential statement is excluded from significance merely on account of its universal or existential form and also that for every significant statement its denial is also significant. The vocabulary and syntax of a formalized empiricist language ensures that no meaningless statement will be admitted as significant, even by occurring as a component of a verifiable molecular statement.

Nevertheless, leaving purely formal objections aside, the main difficulty of both Carnap's and Hempel's treatment of the verifiability principle is that of giving an adequate characterization of an empiricist language. An "empirical term" or an "observation predicate" is one that designates a property that is in principle observable, even though in fact it is never observed by anyone. But if the property has never in fact been observed, how are we to know that it is observable?

It may be said that a basic observation statement "*Pa*," asserting that an object *a* has the observable property *P*, is meaningful only if the experiences that would verify the statement could occur. But "could" here cannot mean "factually could," since we can speak meaningfully of occurrences that are factually impossible. Apparently what is meant is that the experiences in question must be logically possible. But then it seems that the only sense that can be given to saying that the *experiences* are logically possible is that the statement "*Pa*" is contingent. However, in "*Pa*" the object *a* is simply named or referred to, and the property *P* ascribed to it—and it seems that every statement of this form must be contingent. Thus, unless a further explanation of the expression "observation predicate" is forthcoming, we have no way of distinguishing between those basic observation statements that are meaningful and those that are not.

OBSERVATION STATEMENTS. Schlick, in an early article titled "A New Philosophy of Experience," claimed that to understand a proposition we must be able to indicate exactly the particular circumstances that would make it true and those that would make it false. "Circumstances" he defined as facts of experience; and thus it is experience that verifies or falsifies propositions. An obvious objection to this view is that sense experience is essentially private, and hence apparently the cognitive meaning of every statement must be essentially private. Schlick attempted to avoid this objection by distinguishing between the content and form of experience. The content, he said, is private and incommunicable—it can only be lived through. But the form of our experiences, he claimed, is expressible and communicable, and this is all that is required for scientific knowledge. However, Schlick's distinction between content and form cannot save his view from the objection of solipsism; for if the meaning of every descriptive expression is to be found, in the last analysis, in private experience, then this is so not only for qualitative words but also for the relational words that are supposed to describe the form of experience.

Thus, the first problem concerning statements reporting empirical observations is that they should be expressible in such a way that their meaning is not private to any one observer. The logical possibility of verifying a given statement can then be explained without mentioning the experiences of any particular person or indeed the experiences of anyone at all. If basic observation statements can be formulated in the required way, they express logically possible evidence, and hence any statement suitably related to a set of observation statements is verifiable in principle, even though no one is ever in a position to have the relevant experiences, that is, to verify the statement in question.

In order to achieve this result some adherents of the verifiability principle regard certain statements describing physical objects as basic (for example, "This is a black telephone"); others attempt to achieve the same result while still regarding sense-datum or phenomenal statements as basic (for example, "Here now a black patch" or "This seems to be a telephone"). In either case, there is the difficulty of explaining how these statements are related to the experiences that would verify them.

The question whether a statement reporting an empirical observation is conclusively verifiable is, as we have seen, of importance for the criterion of conclusive verifiability and for that of conclusive falsifiability. It has also been thought to be of importance for the criterion of weak verifiability or confirmability, for, it has been said, unless basic statements are certain, or in some sense incorrigible, no other statement can be even probable or confirmable. Finally, as we noted before, there is also the problem of explaining what is meant by saying that a basic observation statement is verifiable in principle, that is, that certain experiences are logically possible, if in fact the experiences in question never occur.

IS THE PRINCIPLE ITSELF MEANINGFUL? It is sometimes objected that the verifiability principle itself, according to the criterion it lays down, must be either analytic or empirically verifiable if it is to be cognitively meaningful. But if it is analytic, then it is tautological and uninformative; at best it only exemplifies a proposed use of the terms "cognitive meaning" and "understanding." And if it is empirically verifiable, then it is a contingent statement about the ordinary use or some technical use of these terms and at best is only confirmable to some degree by the relevant evidence. In either case, it is objected, the principle cannot be the decisive criterion of cognitive meaning that its adherents suppose it to be.

One reply to this objection is that a criterion that determines a certain class of statements cannot have the same logical status as the statements in question. For example, the statement that expresses the principle of causality in effect determines a class of statements, namely, the class of causal statements, but obviously it is not itself a causal statement. Similarly, the verifiability principle, which claims to delimit the class of cognitively meaningful statements, cannot be expected to have the same logical status as the statements it delimits.

In order to understand the status of the verifiability principle, in the form in which it was held by the logical positivists, the following considerations are relevant: (1) They claimed that an essential difference between their empiricism and the earlier empiricism of Hume, Mill, and Mach was that it was based not on any particular psychological assumptions but only on considerations of logic. They may have believed that it is factually impossible for us to have experiences radically different in kind from those that we now have, but they did not present the verifiability principle as stating or implying this. But then, if the possibility of mystical or religious experiences is allowed, it seems that at least some metaphysical statements are verifiable and therefore meaningful. This conclusion has been accepted by some later adherents of the verifiability principle, but it is evident that the logical positivists wished to present their criterion of meaning in such a way that it would exclude all metaphysical statements from the class of meaningful statements.

(2) It might be argued, as Ayer once did, that it is meaningful to say that mystics have unusual experiences, but that nevertheless we can have no grounds for supposing that their experiences are relevant to the truth or falsity of any statement of fact, since we have no grounds for thinking that the "object" of such experiences could be described in ordinary empirical terms. The statement "Mystics have experiences that they report by the sentence 'Reality is One'" is empirically verifiable in the ordinary way. But the statement "Reality is One" is not empirically verifiable in the ordinary way. To this, however, the mystic may reply that he can describe in ordinary empirical terms the kind of preparation or discipline he recommends, and if we are not willing to carry out the appropriate procedure we are simply refusing to consider the possibility of verifying mystical statements. The antimetaphysical import of the verifiability principle, he may say, is apparently based on the assumption that we cannot have experiences radically different in kind from those that we now have.

(3) Some of the logical positivists (Schlick, the early Ayer) claimed that the verifiability principle is in effect a statement of the sense of "cognitive or factual meaning" and "understanding" that is actually accepted in everyday life. Schlick, for example, said that the verifiability principle is "nothing but a simple statement of the way in which meaning is actually assigned to propositions, both in everyday life and in science. There never has been any other way, and it would be a grave error to suppose that we believe we have discovered a new conception of meaning that is contrary to common opinion and which we want to introduce into philosophy" ("Meaning and Verification"). But, as we have seen, if the verifiability principle is simply a contingent statement about a certain linguistic usage, its logical status cannot justify the degree of confidence that its adherents place in it.

(4) Finally, the principle has been regarded as a recommendation or a decision concerning the use of the expression "factually meaningful statement." It has been claimed that this decision prevents radical intellectual confusion and that it promotes clarity in the discussion of many philosophical questions. Carnap and Ayer, among others, have taken this view of the status of the verifiability principle. It should be noted that this does not imply that the principle is regarded as an analytic or necessarily true statement. A principle that expresses a linguistic recommendation is no doubt closely related to a corresponding analytic statement, but the recommendation itself is not tautological and uninformative. A recommendation or a decision has a different logical status; it is not successful by being true or unsuccessful by being false.

MORE RECENT CRITICISMS. Following the later work of Wittgenstein it is now widely held among philosophers that to ask whether a sentence is meaningful is simply to ask whether the words that compose the sentence are used according to the rules or practice of a language. Understanding a word, it is said, does not involve "knowing what the word stands for" or "being able to recognize what the word designates"; it involves only the ability to use the word in accordance with certain linguistic rules. Furthermore, the rules governing the correct use of different kinds of words differ enormously, and hence there is not just one way of misusing the words that occur in a sentence and thereby rendering the sentence meaningless. Each of the sentences "I do not exist," "The round square feels depressed," "Nonbeing is infinitely perfect," and "The Absolute enters into but transcends all change" involves a violation of one or more linguistic rules, but of quite different rules. Consequently, it is said, it is not possible to give a general criterion of the meaningfulness of a sentence. The verifiability principle is an attempt to answer the question "Under what conditions is a sentence cognitively or factually meaningful?," but this question, according to the view now widely held, is not one to which it is possible to give an answer that is both general and informative. Two further criticisms are made of the verifiability principle: (1) the principle, it is said, is not at all a criterion of the meaningfulness of a sentence but simply a characterization of an "empirical sentence," (2) the principle confuses the question of whether a sentence is meaningful with the different question of whether the statement it expresses can be known to be true or false. These more recent objections to the verifiability principle occur in most post-Wittgensteinian discussions of the topic of meaning. A useful summary of the arguments is given by J. L. Evans in "On Meaning and Verification."

Truth theory of meaning. It is convenient to begin by examining the second of these two further criticisms. It is concerned with the fact that one component of the verifiability principle is the thesis that the meaning of a statement is given by its truth conditions. This idea, which may be called "the truth theory of meaning," had been employed and stated by philosophers before the discussions of the Vienna circle. It is assumed, for example, by Bertrand Russell in his theory of descriptions. And Wittgenstein, in the *Tractatus*, said explicitly, "To understand a proposition means to know what is the case if it is true."

The formal correctness of this view can be seen from the following definition of the meaning of a statement in terms of its truth conditions. "*Die Sonne scheint* means *that the sun is shining* $=_{\text{Df}}$ *Die Sonne scheint* is true if, and only if, the sun is shining"; in general, "*S* means *that p* $=_{\text{Df}}$ *S* is true if, and only if, *p*." Nevertheless, it has to be admitted that the truth theory provides no effective clarification of the notion of cognitive or factual meaning. For even if the truth conditions of a statement *S* can be enumerated exhaustively in terms of a finite conjunction of observation statements $O_1 \ldots O_n$ (and, as we have seen, in very many cases this cannot be done) this entitles us to assert only that *S* and $O_1 \ldots O_n$ have the same meaning. But this does not clarify what the meaning of *S* is, or what it is for *S* to be meaningful. To say simply that two statements have the same meaning is not to say what either statement means or what it is for either statement to be meaningful.

For the kind of clarification that is being sought we now need a different and independent explanation of the meaning of an observation statement. Furthermore, the definition of the meaning of a statement in terms of its truth conditions provides no clarification unless the notion of truth is further explained. The truth of a statement can be defined in terms of its meaning in the following way. "*Die Sonne scheint* is true $=_{\text{Df}}$ *Die Sonne scheint* means *that the sun is shining*, and the sun is shining"; in general "*S* is true $=_{\text{Df}}$ *S* means *that p*, and *p*." But obviously it would be circular to employ this definition of truth in an attempt to clarify the notion of cognitive meaning. The two preceding definitions show, however, that there is a close connection between the notion of cognitive or factual meaning and the notion of truth. And hence, in reply to the second of the two further criticisms of the verifiability principle mentioned above, it may be argued that there must be a close connection between understanding a sentence as expressing a statement of fact and its being possible for one to know whether the statement is true or false.

Meaning and experience. The first of the two further criticisms of the verifiability principle is concerned with the fact that another component of the principle is the thesis that the truth conditions of a statement can be known only by reference to experience. This is the traditional doctrine of empiricism or positivism. The logical positivists (with the exception of Neurath, Carnap, and others, who at one time adopted a "coherence theory" of truth) held this view on the grounds that there are only two ways in which the truth-value of a statement can be ascertained, either a priori or a posteriori. According to their doctrine, if a statement can be known to be true a priori, then it is analytic and tautological and hence not a statement of fact. Therefore, if a statement is a statement of fact, it cannot be known a priori—its truth-value can be ascertained only by reference to experience. The simple dichotomy (either a priori or a posteriori) on which this argument is based has been criticized in more recent philosophy. W. V. Quine, for example, maintains that for the most part the statements that compose the corpus of knowledge have their truth-values determined by linguistic and pragmatic considerations, as well as by the occurrence of certain sensory experiences. He allows, however, that statements "on the periphery" have their truth-values determined by experience. Thus, even in a more qualified version of empiricism the difficulty still remains of making clear what it is to know that a statement is true "by reference to experience."

Nevertheless, the criticism of the verifiability principle now being considered admits that for a sentence to be an "empirical sentence" it must express a statement that is in some sense verifiable, that is, the truth conditions of which can be known by reference to experience. And it may be argued that the grounds on which this is admitted are such that they compel a similar admission for every sentence that can be understood as expressing a statement of fact. It is evident that if a form of language can be used to describe the world—that is, to make statements—its rules cannot be wholly syntactical, that is, of the kind that govern simply the formation and transformation of sentences in the language. For the language to be descriptive it must also have semantic rules, for example, rules that relate the use of its basic predicates to certain states of affairs in the world. Semantic rules may be said to govern directly the use of basic predicates and to govern indirectly, via definitions and other syntactical means, the use of nonbasic predicates. The more detailed analysis of a semantic rule—that is, an account of how such rules function in a language—is a difficult matter that we need not attempt here. For our present purpose it is sufficient to note that it would be a contradiction to say that a language was descriptive but had no semantic rules; similarly, it would be a contradiction for someone to say that he could understand a sentence as expressing a statement although he had not been able to ascertain the semantic rules of the language in which the sentence was expressed.

We can now see why many present-day philosophers say that the verifiability principle is simply a characterization of an empirical sentence. If a sentence is used to describe an experienceable state of the world, then the semantic rules governing its predicates relate those predicates, directly or indirectly, to that state of the world. It follows that the sentence expresses a statement that is in principle verifiable. But consider the position of a philosopher who maintains that he uses certain sentences to make statements about the world, although these statements are not verifiable in any sense at all. This position seems to be simply incoherent. If the sentences in question express statements, the use of the predicates that occur in them must be governed by semantic rules; how can these rules be known or explained to anyone else if the states of affairs which the sentences are supposed to describe are not experienceable in any way at all? The philosopher in question may eventually admit that the relevant states of the world are, after all, experienceable—but intuitively or by some other special kind of experience. This, apparently, would be a psychological claim, to the effect that we are capable of types of experience other than those we usually associate with the normal functioning of our sense organs. The onus of proof to show that such experiences are possible plainly rests upon the philosopher in question. But even if such experiences do occur, and are of such a kind that they can be associated, via semantic rules, with the descriptive expressions of a language, this will not provide an exception to the requirement laid down by the verifiability principle—it will, in fact, be simply an extension of that requirement to types of sentences that formerly could not be understood as expressing statements of fact.

For a further examination of this question, it would seem that the correct approach would be to give a completely general analysis of "knowing the use of a predicate." Such an analysis cannot be given here, but the following outline may be suggested. In the case of a basic predicate it may be held that (1) an essential part of the use of the predicate is to identify a property, (2) an ability to use the predicate to identify the relevant property does not constitute knowing its use, unless the user also knows what the ability consists in, and (3) the user cannot be said to know this if it is impossible for him to have any kind of experience of the property in question.

Thus, to revert to the first and main criticism of the verifiability principle, it may be admitted that to ask whether a sentence is meaningful is to ask whether the constituent words are used according to the rules of a language. And it may be admitted that the rules governing the use of different kinds of words differ immensely and that there is not just one way in which a sentence can be meaningless. Nevertheless, if the foregoing remarks are correct, a sentence cannot be understood as expressing a statement unless the use of the descriptive expressions that occur in it are governed by semantic rules; and these rules cannot be known or explained to anyone else unless it is possible for the users of the language to have some kind of experience of the states of the world to which the descriptive expressions in question are related. These requirements are, perhaps, all that is essential in the claim made by the verifiability principle in its later formulations.

See also Basic Statements; Logical Positivism.

Bibliography

FORMULATIONS AND FAVORABLE DISCUSSIONS

Ayer, A. J. *Language, Truth and Logic*. London: Gollancz, 1936; 2nd ed., 1946.

Ayer, A. J. "Logical Positivism—A Debate" (with F. C. Copleston). In *A Modern Introduction to Philosophy*, edited by Paul Edwards and Arthur Pap. Glencoe, IL: Free Press, 1957; 2nd ed., rev., New York, 1965.

Ayer, A. J. "The Principle of Verifiability." *Mind* 45 (1936).

Ayer, A. J. "Verification and Experience." *PAS* 37 (1936–1937). Reprinted in *Logical Positivism*, edited by A. J. Ayer. Glencoe, IL: Free Press, 1959.

Brown, R., and J. Watling. "Amending the Verification Principle." *Analysis* 11 (1950–1951).

Carnap, Rudolf. "Testability and Meaning." *Philosophy of Science* 3 (1936): 419–471; 4 (1937): 1–40. Reprinted in *Readings in the Philosophy of Science*, edited by Herbert Feigl and May Brodbeck, 47–92. New York: Appleton-Century-Crofts, 1953.

Hempel, C. G. "The Concept of Cognitive Significance: A Reconsideration." *Proceedings of the American Academy of Arts and Sciences* 80 (1951): 61–77.

Hempel, C. G. "Problems and Changes in the Empiricist Criterion of Meaning." *Revue internationale de philosophie* 4 (1950): 41–63. Reprinted in *Semantics and the Philosophy of Language*, edited by Leonard Linsky. Urbana: University of Illinois Press, 1952. Also reprinted in *Logical Positivism*, edited by Ayer (see above).

Reichenbach, Hans. "The Verifiability Theory of Meaning." *Proceedings of the American Academy of Arts and Sciences* 80 (1951). Reprinted in *Readings in the Philosophy of Science*, edited by Herbert Feigl and May Brodbeck. New York: Appleton-Century-Crofts, 1953.

Schlick, Moritz. "Form and Content." Three lectures given in London in 1932. Reprinted in *Gesammelte Aufsätze*.

Schlick, Moritz. "Meaning and Verification." *Philosophical Review* 45 (1936): 339–368. Reprinted in *Gesammelte Aufsätze* and in *Readings in Philosophical Analysis*, edited by Herbert Feigl and Wilfrid Sellars. New York: Appleton-Century-Crofts, 1949.

Schlick, Moritz. "A New Philosophy of Experience." *Publications in Philosophy of the College of the Pacific*, No. 1. Stockton, CA, 1932. Reprinted in *Gesammelte Aufsätze 1926–1936*. Vienna: Gerold, 1938.

Schlick, Moritz. "Positivismus und Realismus." *Erkenntnis* 3 (1932–1933): 1–31. Reprinted in *Gesammelte Aufsätze* and translated in Ayer, ed., *Logical Positivism* (see above).

Waismann, Friedrich. "Logische Analyse der Wahrscheinlichkeitsbegriffs." *Erkenntnis* 1 (1930–1931).

Whiteley, C. H. "On Meaning and Verifiability." *Analysis* (1938–1939).

Whiteley, C. H. "On Understanding." *Mind* 58 (1949).

CRITICISMS

Barnes, W. H. F. "Meaning and Verifiability." *Philosophy* 14 (1939).

Berlin, Isaiah, "Verification." *PAS* 39 (1938–1939).

Church, Alonzo. Review of Ayer's *Language, Truth and Logic*, 2nd ed. *Journal of Symbolic Logic* 14 (1949).

Copleston. F. C. "Logical Positivism—A Debate" (with A. J. Ayer). In *A Modern Introduction to Philosophy*, edited by Edwards and Pap (see above).

Copleston, F. C. "A Note on Verification." *Mind* 59 (1950). Reprinted, with "A Further Note on Verification," in *Contemporary Philosophy*. London: Burns and Oates, 1956.

Ducasse, C. J. "Verification, Verifiability, and Meaningfulness." *Journal of Philosophy* 33 (1936): 230–236.

Evans, J. L. "On Meaning and Verification." *Mind* 62 (1953): 1–19.

Ewing, A. C. "Meaninglessness." *Mind* 46 (1937): 347–364.

Kneale, W. C. "Verifiability." *PAS*, Supp. 19 (1945).

Lazerowitz, Morris. "The Positivistic Use of 'Nonsense.'" *Mind* 57 (1946). Reprinted in *The Structure of Metaphysics*.

Lazerowitz, Morris. "The Principle of Verifiability." *Mind* 46 (1937): 372–378.

Lazerowitz, Morris. "Strong and Weak Verification." *Mind* 48 (1939) and 59 (1950). Reprinted in *The Structure of Metaphysics*. London: Routledge and Paul, 1955.

Lewis, C. I. "Experience and Meaning." *Philosophical Review* 43 (1934). Reprinted in *Readings in Philosophical Analysis*, edited by Herbert Feigl and May Sellars. New York: Appleton-Century-Crofts, 1953.

O'Connor, D. J. "Some Consequences of Professor Ayer's Verification Principle." *Analysis* 10 (1949–1950).

Russell, Bertrand. *An Inquiry into Meaning and Truth*. New York: Norton, 1940.

Russell, Bertrand. "On Verification." *PAS* 38 (1937–1938): 1–15.

Stace, W. T. "Metaphysics and Meaning." *Mind* 44 (1935): 417–438. Reprinted in *A Modern Introduction to Philosophy*, edited by Paul Edwards and Arthur Pap. Glencoe, IL: Free Press, 1957; 2nd ed., New York, 1965.

Stebbing, L. Susan. "Communication and Verification." *PAS*, Supp. 13 (1934).

Waismann, Friedrich. "Language Strata." In *Logic and Language*, edited by A. G. N. Flew. 2nd series. Oxford: Blackwell, 1953.

Waismann, Friedrich. "Verifiability." *PAS*, Supp. 19 (1945): 119–150. Reprinted in *Logic and Language*, edited by A. G. N. Flew. 1st series. Oxford, 1951.

Warnock, G. J. "Verification and the Use of Language." *Revue internationale de philosophie* 5 (1951): 307–322. Reprinted in *A Modern Introduction to Philosophy*, edited by Paul Edwards and Arthur Pap. Glencoe, IL: Free Press, 1957; 2nd ed., New York, 1965.

Wisdom, John. "Metaphysics and Verification." *Mind* 47 (1938): 452–498. Reprinted in *Philosophy and Psycho-analysis*. Oxford: Blackwell, 1953.

Wisdom, John. "Note on the New Edition of Professor Ayer's *Language, Truth and Logic*." *Mind* 57 (1948). Reprinted in *Philosophy and Psycho-analysis*.

RELATED DISCUSSIONS

Alston, W. P. "Pragmatism and the Verifiability Theory of Meaning." *Philosophical Studies* 6 (1955).

Bridgman, P. W. "Operational Analysis." *Philosophy of Science* 5 (1938).

Grice, H. P. "Meaning." *Philosophical Review* 46 (1957): 377–388.

Heath, A. E. "Communication and Verification." *PAS*, Supp. 13 (1934).

MacKinnon, D. M. "Verifiability." *PAS*, Supp. 19 (1945).

Morris, C. W. "The Concept of Meaning in Pragmatism and Logical Positivism," in *Proceedings of the Eighth International Congress of Philosophy* (1934). Prague, 1936.

Nagel, Ernest. "Verifiability, Truth, and Verification." *Journal of Philosophy* 31 (1934): 141–148. Reprinted in *Logic without Metaphysics*. Glencoe, IL: Free Press, 1956.

Nelson, E. J. "The Verification Theory of Meaning." *Philosophical Review* 43 (1954).

OTHER RECOMMENDED TITLES

Bealer, George. "The Incoherence of Empiricism." *The Aristotelian Society*, Supp. 66 (1992): 99–138. Reprinted in *Rationality and Naturalism*, edited by S. Wagner and R. Warner. Notre Dame, IN: University of Notre Dame Press, 1993.

Coffa, Alberto. *The Semantic Tradition from Kant to Carnap*. Cambridge, U.K.: Cambridge University Press, 1991.

Cohen, Jonathan. "Is a Criterion of Verifiability Possible?" *Midwest Studies in Philosophy* 5 (1980): 347–352.

Dummett, Michael. "The Metaphysics of Verificationism." In *The Philosophy of A. J. Ayer*, edited by Lewis Hahn. La Salle, IL: Open Court, 1992.

Edington, D. "The Paradox of Knowability." *Mind* 94 (1985): 557–568.

Feigl, H. "The Weiner Kreis in America." In *The Intellectual Migration*, edited by D. Fleming and B. Bailyn. Cambridge, MA: Harvard University Press, 1969.

Hempel, Carl. *Aspects of Scientific Explanation*. New York: Free Press, 1965.

Johnston, Mark. "Verificationism as Philosophical Narcissism." In *Philosophical Perspectives, 7: Language and Logic*, edited by James Tomberlin. Atascadero, CA: Ridgeview Press, 1993.

Okasha, Samir. "Verificationism, Realism, and Scepticism." *Erkenntnis* 55 (2001): 371–385.

Quine, W. V. O. "Two Dogmas of Empiricism." In *From a Logical Point of View: Nine Logico-Philosophical Essays*. Cambridge, MA: Harvard University Press, 1980.

Smart, J. J. C. "Verificationism." In *Cause, Mind, and Reality: Essays Honoring C. B. Martin*. Norwell, MA: Kluwer, 1989.

R. W. Ashby (1967)
Bibliography updated by Benjamin Fiedor (2005)

VERIFIABILITY PRINCIPLE [ADDENDUM]

The doctrines associated with the slogan that meaning is the mode of verification continued to develop in the last four decades of the twentieth century. While the exact formulation of the principle was itself controversial, the essential idea was to link semantic and epistemic concerns by letting the meaning of an expression be its role within an empirical epistemology. At the same time the fortunes of logical empiricism, the movement associated with verificationism, changed substantially as well. First, as philosophers who conspicuously did not identify themselves with logical empiricism moved to center stage, the movement as a separately identifiable phenomenon virtually ceased to exist. This did not dispose of verificationism, however, for often the later philosophers' views were strikingly similar to the logical empiricism that they supposedly replaced, just as the criticisms of logical empiricism were often pioneered by the logical empiricists themselves. The second major change in the fortunes of this view was the renewal of interest in the history of philosophy of science, especially in the histories of the logical empiricists themselves. Now freed from the myopia that comes from being part of the fray, philosophers were able to explore the roots of logical empiricism, what held it together as a movement, which of its doctrines were central or peripheral, and even which views look more plausible in hindsight than they did before their systematic interconnection could be appreciated.

One root of verificationism lies in the increasing professionalization of both the sciences and philosophy around the turn of the twentieth century. The sciences tended to emphasize the importance of empirical investigation, to explore its scope and limits, and to deplore as metaphysical any claims not based on evidence. Correspondingly, many philosophers claimed for themselves a nonempirical source of knowledge concerning things higher or deeper than mere observation could reveal, that is, concerning metaphysics. Logical empiricism grew out of methodological discussions within science rather than philosophy, and many of its central proponents were trained in the sciences. True, logical empiricism made special accommodation for the a priori domains of mathematics and logic. But these were technical subjects of use within the sciences and for which there were increasingly well-developed modes of conflict resolution. Moreover, the way in which the accommodation was reached, namely through the logical analysis of language, especially the language of science, comported well with a basic empiricism and provided no comfort to traditional philosophy.

A second root of verificationism lies in Bertrand Russell's reaction to the paradox that bears his name (viz., a contradiction that arises when sets can contain themselves) and in Ludwig Wittgenstein's further elaboration of a related idea. In order to avoid the paradox, Russell had restricted the grammar so that apparent assertions of sets containing themselves were no longer well formed. Similarly, Wittgenstein emphasized that some combinations of words were neither true nor false but just nonsensical; they were, he said, metaphysical. This seemed to offer the ideal diagnosis of the sought-after distinction: Scientifically respectable claims were either empirically meaningful in virtue of having some appropriate relation to the observations that would be the source of their justification, or else they were true in virtue of the language itself; traditional metaphysics, by contrast, was simply unintelligible. Phrased in this way, the verifiability principle leaves as a separate question the issue of what the appropriate relation to observation would be.

It has also become clearer what the logical status of the principle itself is. Initially, these philosophers could imagine that they were saying something about language in general or about the language of science. But as it became apparent that there were alternative languages to be considered, it became obvious that the principle could be put as a proposal for a language or as an analytic or empirical claim either about a particular language or about a range of languages. Perhaps the dominant form of the principle is as a proposal for a language to explicate the linguistic practices that are already largely in place in the sciences. As a proposal, it is not a claim, and hence neither true nor false, but not thereby unintelligible. If the proposal is adopted, the corresponding claim about the language that has those rules would be analytic. There would also be the empirical claim that we had adopted such a language and even empirical claims about that language if it were specified as, say, the language that is now used in contemporary physics.

So construed, many of the objections that were first made to the principle (and which continued to be made through the period in question) can be seen to be wrongheaded. The most persistent of these criticisms is that the principle renders itself an unintelligible claim. Whether construed as a proposal, as an analytic claim, or as an empirical one, this is just a (willful) misunderstanding. The same can be said for the criticism that it renders all philosophy meaningless. Equally misguided is the repeated objection that the principle cannot be right because we can understand a sentence without knowing whether it is true. Obviously, the principle in no way denies this truism.

Potentially more serious is the idea that all attempts to specify the principle have failed and are thus likely to continue to do so. Reinforcing this idea are papers by Carl Gustav Hempel (1950, 1965) that, while they are not really histories, strike many readers as signed confessions of complicity in a series of disasters. In defense of the principle it must be said that, except for those immediately around Wittgenstein, complete verifiability was virtually never at issue. Even in the *Aufbau*, where the general question is raised many times, all but one formulation are much more liberal. Similarly, strict falsifiability was never proposed as a criterion of meaningfulness. Concerning the more fertile ground of confirmation and disconfirmation, the difficulties seem to have arisen because the formulations tried both to link semantic and epistemic concerns *and* to specify a complete theory of confirmation. This latter task is so difficult that we should not expect early success nor conclude from failure that the enterprise is misguided—any more than we give up physics simply because we still lack the final theory.

There were, of course, other sources of difficulty. Many attempts, such as A. J. Ayer's, tried to apply a criterion of meaningfulness at the level of whole sentences even though those sentences could contain meaningless parts. More successful in this regard was Rudolf Carnap's "Methodological Character of Theoretical Concepts" (1956), which applied the criterion at the level of primitive terms. In a paper that was famous despite being unpublished for many years, David Kaplan (1975) provided two counterexamples to Carnap's criterion. These examples were widely regarded as decisive, but Richard Creath (1976) showed that one of the examples missed its mark and the criterion could be patched in a natural way so as to avoid the other. Less easily dismissed is W. Rozeboom's (1960) criticism that Carnap's criterion ties meaningfulness to a particular theory when it should apply only to the language. Finally, Carnap's criterion, like many others, seems to presuppose that the theory/observation distinction can be drawn at the level of vocabulary. There came to be general agreement that this presupposition is mistaken and distorts any criterion based on it. In fairness, it must be admitted that some theory/observation distinction is essential to a healthy empiricism and that Carnap was from the very beginning fully aware of the limitations of formulating the distinction in this way. Finding a satisfactory way is still an unsolved problem.

W. V. O. Quine is often associated with the demise of logical empiricism, and his "Two Dogmas of Empiricism" (1951) is often thought to have rejected verificationism decisively. It would be more accurate to say that he rejected the idea that individual sentences could be separately confirmed, but he did not resist linking meaningfulness with confirmation holistically construed. Indeed, his demand that behavioral criteria be provided for analyticity to render it intelligible is exactly parallel to Carnap's demand for correspondence rules to render theoretical terms meaningful. Moreover, Quine's argument from the indeterminacy of translation to the unintelligibility of interlinguistic synonymy makes sense only if meaning and confirmation are somehow linked as in the verifiability principle.

So what then of this link between semantic and epistemic issues? At least there is much to be said for it. A theory of meaning should give accounts of meaningfulness (having a meaning), of synonymy (having the same meaning), and of understanding (knowing the meaning). The verifiability principle provides *a* way of doing these things not provided by simply identifying various entities as "the meanings" of expressions. Moreover, it provides *a* defense against wholesale skepticism by tying what we know to how we know. And finally, it provides *a* way of dealing with the so-called a priori by making those claims knowable in virtue of knowing the meanings of the expressions involved. No doubt there are others ways, perhaps even equally systematic ways, of accomplishing these ends, and no doubt these other paths should be investigated as well. But the basic idea behind the verifiability principle, namely that semantical and epistemic questions should be linked, is far from refuted, and its promise is far from exhausted.

See also Analyticity; Ayer, Alfred Jules; Carnap, Rudolf; Empiricism; Epistemology; Hempel, Carl Gustav; Language; Meaning; Philosophy; Philosophy of Science, History of; Philosophy of Science, Problems of; Quine, Willard Van Orman; Russell, Bertrand Arthur William; Semantics; Skepticism, History of; Verifiability Principle; Wittgenstein, Ludwig Josef Johann.

Bibliography

Antony, Louise. "Can Verificationists Make Mistakes?" *American Philosophical Quarterly* 24 (1987): 225–236.

Ayer, A. J. *Language, Truth and Logic.* London: Gollancz, 1936.

Ayer, A. J. "The Principle of Verifiability." *Mind* 45 (1936): 199–203.

Bercic, Boran. "On the Logical Status of the Principle of Verifiability." *Synthesis Philosophica* 15 (2000): 9–26.

Carnap, R. "The Methodological Character of Philosophic Problems." In *The Foundations of Science and the Concepts of Psychology and Psychoanalysis*, edited by H. Feigl and M. Scriven. Minneapolis, 1956.

Carnap, R. "On the Character of Philosophic Problems." Translated by W. M. Malisoff. *Philosophy of Science* 1 (1934): 5–19.

Carnap, R. "On the Use of Hilbert's ϵ-Operator in Scientific Theories." In *Essays on the Foundations of Mathematics*, edited by Y. Bar-Hillel et al. Jerusalem: Magnes Press, Hebrew University, 1961.

Coffa, Alberto. *The Semantic Tradition from Kant to Carnap.* Cambridge, U.K.: Cambridge University Press, 1991.

Cohen, Jonathan. "Is a Criterion of Verifiability Possible?" *Midwest Studies in Philosophy* 5 (1980): 347–352.

Creath, R. "On Kaplan on Carnap on Significance." *Philosophical Studies*30 (1976): 393–400.

Creath, R. "Was Carnap a Complete Verificationist in the *Aufbau?*" *PSA* 1 (1982): 384–393.

Dummett, Michael. "The Metaphysics of Verificationism." In *The Philosophy of A. J. Ayer*, edited by Lewis Hahn. La Salle, IL: Open Court, 1992.

Glymour, C. *Theory and Evidence.* Princeton, NJ: Princeton University Press, 1980.

Hempel, Carl. *Aspects of Scientific Explanation.* New York: Free Press, 1965.

Hempel, C. G. "Problems and Changes in the Empiricist Criterion of Meaning," *Revue internationale de philosophie* 4 (1950): 41–63.

Johnston, Mark. "Verificationism as Philosophical Narcissism." In *Philosophical Perspectives, 7: Language and Logic*, edited by James Tomberlin. Atascadero, CA: Ridgeview Press, 1993.

Kaplan, D. "Significance and Analyticity: A Comment on Some Recent Proposals of Carnap." In *Rudolf Carnap, Logical Empiricist: Materials and Perspectives*, edited by J. Hintikka. Dordrecht: Holland, 1975.

Moser, Paul K. "Epistemology (1900–Present)." In *Routledge History of Philosophy*, Vol. 10: *Philosophy of the English Speaking World in the 20th Century*, edited by John Canfield. London: Routledge, 1996.

Okasha, Samir. "Verificationism, Realism, and Scepticism." *Erkenntnis* 55 (2001): 371–385.

Quine, W. V. O. "Things and Their Place in Theories." In his *Theories and Things.* Cambridge, MA: Harvard University Press, 1981.

Quine, W. V. O. "Two Dogmas of Empiricism." *Philosophical Review* 60 (1951): 20–43. Reprinted in his *From a Logical Point of View: Nine Logico-Philosophical Essays.* Cambridge, MA: Harvard University Press, 1980.

Quine, W. V. O. *Word and Object.* Cambridge, MA: MIT Press, 1960.

Rozeboom, W. "A Note on Carnap's Meaning Criterion." *Philosophical Studies* 11 (1960): 33–38.

Richard Creath (1996)

Bibliography updated by Benjamin Fiedor (2005)

VICO, GIAMBATTISTA

(1668–1744)

Born in Naples, Italy, in 1668, Giambattista Vico is best known for his critique of the Cartesian method and his philosophy of history. Beyond these areas, he is also known for contributions to linguistic theory, legal history, and cultural anthropology. Many have construed Vico as an eighteenth-century thinker who expressed the germ of ideas more fully developed in the nineteenth century. Thus, for example, Karl Löwith understands Vico's master work *The New Science* to anticipate "not only fundamental ideas of Herder and Hegel, Dilthey and Spengler, but also the more particular discoveries of Roman history by Niebuhr and Mommsen, the theory of Homer by Wolf, the interpretation of mythology by Bachofen, the reconstruction of ancient life through etymology by Grimm, the historical understanding of laws by Savigny, of the ancient city and of feudalism by Fustel de Coulanges, and of the class struggles by Marx and Sorel" (1949, p. 115).

The familiar picture of Vico as the "great anticipator" contains some truth. More recent scholarship, in contrast, has tried to understand Vico as a thinker in his own right. The result has been a proliferation of different and often incompatible interpretations. These include views of Vico as a pioneer of contemporary hermeneutics; a creator of the modern social sciences; an architect of a uniquely Christian synthesis of philosophy and poetry; an advocate of a naturalistic Epicureanism thinly disguised as orthodox piety; a proponent of a Counter-Enlightenment approach to politics; and an author of a "genealogy of morals" that exposes the roots of modern secularism in pagan idolatry, divination, and sacrifice.

Rather than comment on rival interpretations of Vico, I here invite the reader to consider some aspects of what Vico himself regards as a continuous project of thought. This project begins with the works he published in 1709 and 1710 (*On the Study Methods of Our Time* and *On the Most Ancient Wisdom of the Italians*), runs through his jurisprudential writings from 1720 to 1722 (*Universal Right*), and concludes with the three major versions of *The New Science* (1725, 1730, 1744).

ANTI-CARTESIAN WRITINGS

In 1709 Vico published a version of the inaugural oration he delivered at the University of Naples in the preceding year, under the title *De nostri temporis studiorum ratione* (*On the Study Methods of Our Time*). In that work, which does not mention Descartes by name, Vico considered the art of "criticism" (*critica*), juxtaposing it with the art of "topics" (*topica*). Characteristic of criticism, in Vico's sense of the term, is a "dry and attenuated method of argumentation" that he associated with the Stoics and their then contemporary counterparts. Vico chided critics for wanting to purify, from even the suspicion of falsehood, their first truths, which they took to exist "above, outside of and beyond all images of bodies" (1990, Vol. 1, p. 104). His argument against criticism involves two main claims. The first claim is that to prioritize criticism in the education of children is unwise. Youths taught not to accept anything unless it can be certified by a rationalistic standard will have bad memories, impoverished imaginations, and a knack for rashly entering into "astonishing and unaccustomed ventures" (1990, Vol. 1, p. 104). The second claim is that criticism is poorly suited to discover truth. Because "the invention of arguments is prior by nature in the judgment of truth" (1990, Vol. 1, p. 106), criticism has no work to do unless the mind has investigated and brought to light the full range of relevant possibilities. The success of this prior investigation, Vico thought, depends upon the exercise of memory and imagination, especially in assisting the mind as it runs through the commonplaces. These mental capacities, Vico argued, are smothered by premature indoctrination in criticism, but can be developed through an immersion in topics.

In *On the Study Methods of Our Time* (1709/1988), Vico protests against what he regards as the domination of Cartesian criticism, but he does not oppose it as such. In *On the Most Ancient Wisdom of the Italians*, a work published a year later, 1710, he became more explicit in his opposition to Descartes. In that work, Vico charged Descartes with dogmatism, attributing to him the desire to consider all truths doubtful until metaphysically established by the principle "Cogito, ergo sum" ("I think; therefore I am"). Vico argued that, contrary to how he presented himself, Descartes is far from original. He noted that the use of the evil genius was anticipated by the Stoic in Cicero's *Academia* (45 BCE), and that the *cogito* principle was already enunciated by the slave Sosia in Plautus's *Amphitryo* (186 BCE). Vico does not claim that the *cogito* principle is false; he merely holds, "It is an ordinary cognition that happens to any unlearned person such as Sosia, not a rare and exquisite truth that requires such deep meditation by the greatest of philosophers to discover it" (1971, p. 73). The *cogito* principle is not only hackneyed, according to Vico; it is also unable to meet the skeptic's argument. For the *cogito* principle to provide knowledge of the nature of the mind, it would have to grasp the causes of thought (for Vico, as for Aristotle, knowledge is knowledge of causes). According to Vico, the *cogito* principle furnishes only consciousness (*conscientia*) of thinking, without illuminating its causes, and thereby fails to provide knowledge (*scientia*).

Like Francis Bacon before him and Immanuel Kant after him, Vico sought a middle path between dogmatism and skepticism. Against the skeptics, whom he represented as tracing absence of knowledge to a universal ignorance of causes, Vico pointed to domains in which we possess knowledge of the causes of things, because we originate them ourselves. His examples were synthetic geometry, painting, sculpture, ceramics, architecture—crafts in which skepticism has no application, unlike those of rhetoric, politics, and medicine, which are "conjectural" arts in that they do not teach the forms by which their subject matter is created. Vico formulated a second argument, more theological in character, against the skeptics. Although skeptics properly observe that we do not know the causes of things that we are merely acquainted with (here we have consciousness or awareness, but not knowledge), it does not follow that these things lack causes. The pertinent question, according to Vico, is not "Do they have causes?" but "Where are the causes located?" If the causes are truly unknown, as the skeptic argues, they cannot be within us. But they must exist somewhere, in some locus or receptacle outside the self. This locus Vico named the "comprehension of causes, in which is contained all genera, or all forms, through which all effects are given" (1971, p. 75). Since this "comprehension" is infinite and necessarily prior to finite body, it is nothing other than God, "and indeed the God whom we Christians profess" (1971, p. 75).

In place of the *cogito* principle, Vico proposed his own version of a first truth, crystallized in his principle "Verum et factum convertuntur" ("The true and the made are convertible") (1971, p. 63). Although Vico claimed to derive the *verum-factum* principle philologically, he also understood it to be the core of a new anti-Cartesian epistemology and metaphysics. The core of the new metaphysics was that to know something is to make it, where making is collecting or gathering elements into a whole. Strictly speaking, only God conforms to the *verum-factum* principle, because he uniquely contains "the elements of things, extrinsic and intrinsic alike" (1971, p. 63). Because God makes elements and contains them within himself, he can arrange them perfectly, with utter precision and control. God's understanding of the elements of things is self-knowledge. Human beings, by contrast, do not possess such understanding of the elements. Since the human mind does not contain the elements of things within itself, it thinks about them through representations, at one remove, as it were. "Thought [*cogitatio*] is therefore proper to the human mind, but understanding [*intelligentia*] proper to the divine mind" (1971, p. 63). Human thinking, Vico concluded, should be understood as "participation in reason" (1971, p. 63). Thus, in contrast to the dogmatists, who exalt human truth, Vico downgraded it. Unlike the skeptics, however, he did not intend to deny its claims altogether: "Humanity is neither nothing, nor everything" (1971, p. 81).

A final dimension of Vico's early polemic is what might be called his "genealogical" critique of Descartes. In the second of two responses to Cartesian critics, Vico suggested that Descartes maliciously neglected ancient philosophers to promote his own doctrines. He was even so bold as to suggest that Descartes was an intellectual tyrant: "Descartes has done what those who have become tyrants have always been wont to do. They came to power proclaiming the cause of freedom. But once they are assured of power, they become worse tyrants than their original oppressors" (1971, p. 167). Vico unmasked Descartes's appeal to the natural light of reason as an excuse to avoid the labor of erudition and to avoid reading texts in the original languages. Vico also indicted Descartes for concealing the nature of his sources. In wanting his readers to believe that he had no significant predecessors or important teachers, Descartes "gathers the fruit of that plan of wicked politics, to destroy completely those men through whom one has reached the peak of power" (1971, p. 167). Descartes's Machiavellian cunning inspired him to lie about his origins: "Although he can dissimulate the fact with the greatest art in what he says, he was versatile in every sort of philosophy" (1971, p. 167). As an alternative to what he regarded as the uncandid fable of Descartes's *Discourse on the Method*, Vico proposed his own *Autobiography* where he sought to "narrate plainly and step by step the entire series of Vico's studies with the candor proper to a historian" (1990, Vol. 1, p. 7).

THE TURN TO HISTORY

In 1716, Vico began producing philosophical history, composing (though hampered by a severe cramp in his left arm) *The Life of Antonio Carafa* (which only appears in the eight-volume collection of Vico's work published by Laterza called *Opere di G. B. Vico*). At that time he discovered *On the Law of War and Peace*, by the Dutch jurist Hugo Grotius (1583–1645). Impressed with Grotius's work, Vico made him the last of his "four authors." The first three authors whom Vico privileged in his *Autobiography* were Plato, Cornelius Tacitus (c. 56–c. 120), and Francis Bacon. Vico associates Plato with "universal knowledge" that contemplates "man as he ought to be" (1990, Vol. 1, p. 29). The Roman historian Tacitus, by contrast, offered "counsels of utility" pertaining to "man as he is" (1990, Vol. 1, p. 29). Uniting Platonic "esoteric wisdom" and Tacitean "vulgar wisdom" is Bacon, "at one and the same time a universal man in theory and in practice" (1990, Vol. 1, p. 30). Despite his ambition, Bacon failed intellectually to encompass "the universe of cities and the course of all times, or the extent of all nations" (1990, Vol. 1, p. 44). Grotius, however, "embraces in a system of universal law the whole of philosophy and philology" (1990, Vol. 1, p. 44). Vico described his own ambition in similar terms. He sought to reconcile "the best philosophy, that of Plato made subordinate to the Christian religion," with a type of philology that "contains within itself the history of languages and the history of things " (1990, Vol. 1, p. 45).

To bring this reconciliation about, Vico began researching the history of Roman law after reading and annotating Grotius. The first fruit of this inquiry was several volumes collected under the title of *Diritto Universale* (*Universal Right*; 1720–1722/2000). Vico's occasion for writing this work was his desire to demonstrate his qualifications for a chair in law at the University of Naples paying six times as much as his position in rhetoric, which he would hold for most of his life. The intellectual wellspring for the work was Vico's desire to address the question whether justice is natural or merely conventional. Vico reduced contemporary answers to this question to two positions. First, there was the stance that he associated with "the skeptics," a category that included Epicurus, Niccolò Machiavelli, Thomas Hobbes, Benedict de Spinoza, and Pierre Bayle. Their common argument is that justice is not natural, but rooted in fear, chance, or necessity. Second, Vico considered the possibility that justice is grounded in the social nature of humans as a necessary condition for maintaining social order. This was the strategy of Grotius, who claimed to treat the rational basis of law in a quasi-mathematical manner, abstracting from particulars. Vico faults Grotius for excessive abstraction. Rather than bring his profound philological learning to bear in his attempt to counter the reduction of justice to expediency, Grotius depended on abstract and rationalistic arguments that are not persuasive against the skeptics. The positive aim of the *Universal Right* is to replace Grotius's system with a new conception that places particular facts and universal truths in a more illuminating relationship.

This attempt required Vico to turn his attention to the history of legal concepts, particularly the law of nations. Against Grotius's tendency to treat the law of nations (*ius gentium*) and natural law (*ius naturale*) as if they were not only distinct but also separate and autonomous, Vico attempted to exhibit natural law as present within the law of nations, which in time becomes civil law (*ius civile*). This attempt required Vico to argue that natural law has a dual origin: a metaphysical origin in eternal truth and a historical origin in the customs of human society. These dual sources can ultimately be traced to a single origin, God, whom the work identified as the "one principle and one end of universal law" (1974, p. 341). Vico ordered the volumes of the *Universal Right* according to a tripartite scheme intended to reflect the "origin" of divine and human things, their "cycle" (progress and return), and their "constancy."

Vico began the *Universal Right* with a brief consideration of trinitarian theology, followed by an exploration of the virtue possible for fallen humanity. In terms reminiscent of Augustine, Vico made the following identifications: "The force of truth [*vis veri*], or human reason is virtue insofar as it fights self-love [*cupiditas*]; the same virtue is justice insofar as it directs and equalizes utilities" (1974, p. 57). To support his antiskeptical contention that "right is in nature," Vico argued that humans are naturally social, despite their love of self. Although humanity is fallen, it possesses certain "affections" that manifest themselves in facial expressions, which are the beginnings of "expressive language" (1974, p. 59). To recognize distress in the face of another and to acknowledge this pain are natural to humans: "Man differs from animate brutes not only by reason and language, but also by his countenance" (1974, p. 59). From such commiseration in humankind, Vico infers that prior to any calculation of self-interest, "man will bring help to men" (1974, p. 59). Hence, society is natural to human beings and is made possible by sharing advantages.

Here one can perceive how historical consciousness enters into Vico's thinking about justice. The question "Does right exist in nature?" becomes a question about the social nature of humankind, which in turn Vico resolves into a historical inquiry about human nature in the primal state. To anchor in history his conviction that justice is natural, and thereby remedy what he regards as the chief failing of Grotius's natural law, Vico is driven to a philosophical and philological investigation of human origins.

How can Vico reconcile the claim that our concept of justice is, in some sense, subject to historical development, with an affirmation of its eternity and immutability? Vico addresses this question in the chapter of the *Universal Right* with the long title "Utility [*utilitas*] Is the Occasion, Nobility [*honestas*] Is the Cause, of Right [*ius*] and Human Society" (1974, p. 61). Historical occasions are not the cause or sufficient reason of the idea of justice, because "flux cannot generate the eternal, as bodies cannot generate anything above body" (1974, p. 61). Hence justice cannot be reduced to what promotes the advantage or interest of particular individuals; neither the first nor final cause of justice is utility. Yet occasions when issues of advantage and interest arise arouse the "will to justice." Through the pursuit of their own advantage, "men, naturally social and divided, weak and needy from original sin, are brought to cultivate society, that is, to celebrate their social nature" (1974, p. 61). Vico concludes, "As the body is not the cause but the occasion by which the idea of truth is aroused in the mind of men, so utility of the body is not the cause but the occasion by which the will to justice is aroused in the soul" (1974, p. 61).

Vico's use of Nicolas de Malebranche's distinction between cause and occasion protects him from reducing justice to the merely conventional. It does so, however, by elevating instances that would strike some as mere historical accident to the rank of the philosophically significant "occasions" on which human knowledge of justice depends. If Vico is to make this high valuation of occasion and custom plausible, he must construct a historical narrative that depicts how equity (*aequum bonum*) expanded over time, and yet maintain the eternity of the concept. Vico attempted this task in the long section of the first part of the *Universal Right*, which purports to describe the cycle of universal right. To provide additional confirmation of his findings, both philosophical and philological, he added a second volume to the work, titled *De constantia jurisprudentis* (On the Constancy of the Jurisprudent). The first chapter of this work begins with the declaration "a new science is attempted" (*nova scientia tentatur*), and marks the transition to the final phase of his thought, contained in *The New Science.*

VICO'S NEW SCIENCE

The composition of the *Universal Right* established Vico as an erudite scholar, but it did not win him the law chair that he sought. Deciding to compose in the language of his countrymen, rather than that of the university, Vico wrote, in 1725, the first part of his autobiography and a first draft of *The New Science.* Now lost, this draft assumed the form of a negative critique of the "improbabilities, absurdities, and impossibilities that his predecessors had rather imagined than thought out" (1990, Vol. 1, p. 54). Because Vico could not afford to print the work as it stood, he decided to rewrite it using a "positive method that would be more concise and thus more efficacious" (1990, Vol. 1, p. 54). The result of this effort is the first version of *The New Science* (1725/1984). Its full title indicates the continuity with his previous work: *Principles of a New Science of the Nature of Nations, from Which Are Derived New Principles of the Natural Law of Peoples.*

In the subsequent versions of *The New Science* (1730, 1744), Vico placed less emphasis on the specifically political problematic. His larger aim was to achieve a new understanding of the origins of human culture. Vico thought that prior attempts to achieve this goal were vitiated by methodological errors characteristic of both philosophers and philologists. Philosophers, Vico argued, confuse their own refined natures with that of the first humans, who were necessarily simple and crude. They project their own "esoteric wisdom" and mental habits onto the primitive mind, which is not capable of advanced conceptual thinking. This projection is rooted in the "conceit of scholars," the habit of supposing that what contemporary thinkers know "is as old as the world" (*The New Science*, para. 127). Yet philologists (poets, historians, orators, grammarians) are no more helpful for understanding human origins, according to Vico. This is not only because they lack access to relevant data, but also because they are susceptible to the "conceit of nations"—the prejudice that "before all other nations, [one's own nation] invented the comforts of human life and that its remembered history goes back to the very beginning of the world" (*The New Science*, para. 125). Against the background of this twin failure, Vico concluded, "We must reckon as if there were no books in the world" (*The New Science*, para. 330).

Vico's attempt to transcend philosophy and philology assumed the form of a system that aspires to contain the virtues and avoid the vices of each. In its final exposition in 1744, the system began with a chronological table that outlines "the world of the ancient nations," followed by an enumeration of 114 "axioms" that purport to organize the material of the chronological table into a coherent whole. Against the inclination to despair that any recovery of remote human origins is possible, Vico proposed "the eternal and never failing light of a truth beyond all question: that the world of civil society has certainly been made by men, and that its principles are therefore to be found within the modifications of our own human mind" (*The New Science*, para. 331). Vico was pessimistic about the ultimate intelligibility of the world of nature, "which since God made it, He alone knows" (*The New Science*, para. 330). The civil world, however, is eminently knowable: "Since men made it, men could come to know it" (*The New Science*, para. 331). Here Vico reformulated the *verum-factum* principle that he articulated in the *Ancient Wisdom* of 1710. From the *verum-factum* principle, Vico went on to identify three "universal and eternal principles (such as every science must have) on which all nations were founded and still preserve themselves" (*The New Science*, para. 332). These are religion, marriage, and burial. The core of *The New Science* is the attempt to read human culture as the exhibition of these principles in a variety of guises, mutually ordered by what Vico called a "divine legislative mind" and, more simply, "Providence" (*The New Science*, para. 133).

Vico's emphasis on Providence is appropriate, because it is the first and principal "aspect" of the final version of *The New Science.* Vico lists seven aspects of his total conception: (1) "a rational civil theology of divine providence," (2) a "philosophy of authority," (3) a "history of human ideas," (4) "a philosophical criticism that grows out of the history of ideas," (5) "an ideal eternal history traversed in time by the histories of all nations," (6) "a system of the natural law of the peoples," (7) "principles of universal history" (*The New Science*, paras. 385–399).

The New Science is known both for its method of investigation and its substantive conclusions. Regarding method, Vico proclaimed his desire to begin where his subject matter begins, with the assumption that the nature (*natura*) of civil phenomena is intelligible only through their birth (*nascimento*). If there are several possible ways of conceiving the history of an idea or institution, Vico argued that we should focus on the possibility whose manner is most orderly and conducive to the preservation of the human race. Such an "order of things cannot be approached directly, but must be sought through the "order of ideas" and "order of language." As a preliminary to accomplishing the goal of the new science, to disclose the necessary substructure of the civil world, Vico asked the reader whether he can imagine more, fewer, or different causes than the ones he finds. Near the end of the section "Method" of Book 1, Vico declared that his aim was to clean, piece together, and restore "the great fragments of antiquity, hitherto useless to science because they lay begrimed, broken, and scattered" (*The New Science*, para. 357). The light shed by excavation and reconstruction would enable him, Vico thought, to trace "all the effects narrated by certain history" to their originating institutions, "as to their necessary causes" (*The New Science*, para. 358). Not all readers have found persuasive Vico's claim to strict logical necessity. Rather than defend the claim, many contemporary interpreters have advanced the weaker argument that a Viconian perspective is able to render intelligible aspects of the civil world (especially myth, custom, law, poetry) that would otherwise remain obscure.

The content of Vico's new science resists summary description. Its basic scheme is the division of human history into three periods: the age of gods, the age of heroes, and the age of humankind. In the age of gods, "every gentile nation had its Jove" (*The New Science*, para. 193). In every pagan culture, the sky came to be identified as a god who speaks in the language of lightning and thunder. "Jove" was the work of the "theological poets," who created the "first divine fable" and believed it themselves. The practical effect of Jove was to settle the wandering first humans and to set up a system of primitive religion based on divination and sacrifice. Vico's attitude toward primitive religion was complex. The fables created (or "feigned") by the theological poets were based on a "credible impossibility: it is impossible that bodies should be minds, yet it was believed that the thundering sky was Jove" (*The New Science*, para. 383). Yet Vico's attitude toward pagan religion is not one of enlightened condescension. "Through the thick clouds of those first tempests, intermittently lit by those flashes, they made out this great truth: that divine providence watches over the welfare of all mankind" (*The New Science*, para. 385). Thus ran Vico's partial defense of the primitive mind: It apprehended a truth, even if in distorted fashion, that later philosophers (especially the Epicureans and their then contemporary counterparts) altogether missed.

In the age of gods, primitive humans are incapable of proper political organization. There were no cities, only families governed by the "cyclopean paternal authority" of the fathers. The heroic age began with the founding of the cities, prompted by the need of family fathers to unite for the sake of self-defense against their increasingly resentful slaves (the "*famuli*"). Nominating one of their number as king, the fathers generated "severe aristocratic commonwealths" (*The New Science*, para. 663). Vico's narrative of the genesis of heroic commonwealths from the "state of the families" was a polemic directed against Hobbes and "the three princes of natural law," whom he identified as Grotius, the English jurist John Selden (1584–1654), and the German natural-law philosopher Samuel von Pufendorf. Based on neither contract nor self-interest, heroic commonwealths were essentially religious in character. Viewing themselves as descendants of the gods, the heroes secure their dominance through myths that define the plebeians as less than fully human (because they were not of divine descent), and thereby exclude them from citizenship. Toward heroic civil institutions as well, Vico's attitude was complex. On the one hand, he appreciated the gravity and reverence characteristic of aristocratic virtue, especially as expressed in Roman jurisprudence. On the other hand, he sympathized with the plebeians and their struggle for liberty and equality. As with the age of gods, determining Vico's judgment about the merits of the heroic age is a difficult matter of interpretation.

What prompted the transition from the heroic to the human age was the increase in self-knowledge on the part of the plebeians, as encoded in the poetic character of the Athenian lawgiver Solon (c. 630–c. 560 BCE). Once they came to fully recognize their equal humanity, the plebeians began to demand participation in civil society. At this point human nature became "benign," as exemplified by the Roman general Scipio Africanus (236–184 or 183 BCE), the Athenian statesman Aristides the Just (c. 530–c. 468 BCE), and Socrates. The form of government changed from aristocratic to democratic, issuing in "free popular commonwealths." Initially, this appeared to be progress. Philosophy (enabled by the trope of irony) came onto the scene, leading to a purification of the "vulgar wisdom" that developed in the divine and heroic ages. But the "political philosophy" of Plato and Aristotle, of which Vico approved, gave way to "monastic or solitary philosophy," as represented by the Stoics and the Epicureans. "As the popular states become corrupt, so also did the philosophies. They descended to skepticism. Learned fools fell to calumniating the truth" (*The New Science*, para. 1102). In the first phase of the human age, humans were "benign," but their quest for pleasure and luxury led them to become "delicate" and finally "dissolute" (*The New Science*, para. 242). Under the influence of radically antitraditional philosophy that sets itself against "common sense," the citizens, growing ever more atomistic, eventually become "aliens in their own nations" (*The New Science*, para. 1008). Vico indicated three remedies to the problem of social fragmentation: monarchy, conquest by more unified nations, and destruction followed by a return to the age of gods.

Vico's philosophy of decline appears inextricably linked to the decline of philosophy. According to one twentieth-century student of Vico, the last phase of the age of men is a condition where "thought still rules, but a thought which has exhausted its creative power and only constructs meaningless networks of artificial and pedantic distinctions" (Collingwood 1946, p. 67). This is the condition of "beasts made more inhuman by the barbarism of reflection than the first men had been made by the barbarism of sense" (*The New Science*, para. 1006). Yet along with the fatalistic strain of Vico's view of history, one must consider his evident belief in the power of his new science to inspire a rapprochement between philology and philosophy, tradition and reason, politicians and academics. Is such an equilibrium possible? If so, what form would it take? For both students of Vico and social philosophers, these questions remain.

See also Aristotle; Bachofen, Johann Jakob; Bacon, Francis; Bayle, Pierre; Cartesianism; Cicero, Marcus Tullius; Dilthey, Wilhelm; Epicureanism and the Epicurean School; Grotius, Hugo; Hegel, Georg Wilhelm Friedrich; Herder, Johann Gottfried; Hobbes, Thomas; Homer; Kant, Immanuel; Machiavelli, Niccolò; Malebranche, Nicolas; Marx, Karl; Myth; Niebuhr, Reinhold; Philosophy of History; Philosophy of Language; Plato; Pufendorf, Samuel von; Savigny, Friedrich Karl von; Sociology of Knowledge; Socrates; Sorel, Georges; Spengler, Oswald; Stoicism.

Bibliography

WORKS BY VICO

On the Study Methods of Our Time (1709). Translated by Elio Gianturco. Ithaca, NY: Cornell University Press, 1990.

On the Most Ancient Wisdom of the Italians (1710). Translated by L. M. Palmer. Ithaca, NY: Cornell University Press, 1988.

Universal Right (1720–1722). Translated by Giorgio Pinton and Margaret Diehl. Amsterdam: Rodopi, 2000.

The New Science of Giambattista Vico (1725–1744). Translated by Thomas G. Bergin and Max H. Fisch. Ithaca, NY: Cornell University Press, 1984.

The Autobiography of Giambattista Vico (1725–1731) Translated by Max Harold Fisch and Thomas Goddard Bergin. Ithaca, NY: Cornell University Press, 1944.

Opere di G. B. Vico. 8 vols. Edited by Fausto Nicolini. Bari, Italy: Laterza, 1911–1941.

Opere filosofiche. Edited by Paolo Cristofolini. Florence, Italy: Sansoni, 1971.

Opere giuridiche. Edited by Paolo Cristofolini. Florence, Italy: Sansoni, 1974.

Opere. 2 vols. Edited by Andrea Battistini. Milan, Italy: Mondadori, 1990.

WORKS ON VICO

Adams, H. P. *The Life and Writings of Giambattista Vico*. London: George Allen and Unwin, 1935.

Amerio, Franco. *Introduzione allo studio di G. B. Vico*. Turin, Italy: Societa Editrice Internazionale, 1947.

Bedani, Gino. *Vico Revisted: Orthodoxy, Naturalism, and Science in the "Scienza Nuova."* New York: St. Martin's Press, 1989.

Berlin, Isaiah. *Vico and Herder*. London: Hogarth Press, 1976.

Botturi, Francesco. *La sapienza della storia: Giambattista Vico e la filosofia pratica*. Milan, Italy: Università Cattolica del Sacro Cuore, 1991.

Collingwood, Robin. *The Idea of History*. Oxford: Clarendon Press, 1946.

Croce, Benedetto. *The Philosophy of Giambattista Vico*. Translated by R. G. Collingwood. New York: Russell and Russell, 1964.

Hösle, Vittorio. *Introduzione a Vico: La scienza del mondo intersoggettivo*. Milan, Italy: Guerni e Associati, 1997.

Lachterman, David. "Mathematics and Nominalism in Vico's *Liber Metaphysicus*." In *Sachkommentar xu G. Vico's Liber*

Metaphysicus, edited by Stephan Otto and Helmut Viechtbauer, 47–85. Munich: Wilhelm Fink Verlag, 1985.

Lilla, Mark. *G. B. Vico: The Making of an Anti-modern*. Cambridge, MA: Harvard University Press, 1993.

Löwith, Karl. *Meaning in History*. Chicago: University of Chicago Press, 1949.

Mazzotta, Giuseppe. *The New Map of the World: The Poetic Philosophy of Giambattista Vico*. Princeton, NJ: Princeton University Press, 1999.

Milbank, John. *The Religious Dimension in the Thought of Giambattista Vico, 1668–1744*. Lewiston, NY: Edwin Mellen Press, 1991.

Miner, Robert. *Vico, Genealogist of Modernity*. Notre Dame, IN: University of Notre Dame Press, 2002.

Mooney, Michael. *Vico in the Tradition of Rhetoric*. Princeton, NJ: Princeton University Press, 1985.

Pompa, Leon. *Vico: A Study of the "New Science."* 2nd. ed. Cambridge, U.K.: Cambridge University Press, 1985.

Schaeffer, John. *Sensus Communis: Vico, Rhetoric, and the Limits of Relativism*. Durham, NC: Duke University Press, 1990.

Verene, Donald Philip. *Vico's Science of Imagination*. Ithaca, NY: Cornell University Press, 1981.

Robert C. Miner (2005)

VIENNA CIRCLE, THE

See *Logical Positivism*

VIOLENCE

"Violence" is derived from the Latin *violentia*, "vehemence," which itself comes from *vis* (force) + *latus* (to carry) and means, literally, intense force. Violence shares its etymology with violate, "injure." *Violence* is used to refer to swift, extreme force (e.g., a violent storm) and to forceful injurious violation (e.g., rape, terrorism, war).

Violence has received some philosophical consideration since ancient times, but only since the twentieth century has the concept of violence itself been of particular concern to philosophers. Perhaps this is due to the exponential growth in the efficiency of and access to the means of violence in the modern era, to the unprecedented carnage the twentieth century saw, or to the emergence of champions of nonviolence such as Mohandas Gandhi and Martin Luther King Jr. Beyond clarifying the concept of violence, philosophical argument has turned to the moral and cultural justifiability of violence to achieve personal, social, or political ends.

Philosophers do not achieve consensus about the concept. Often, violence is taken to consist in overt physical manifestations of force. These may be on the scale of individuals (e.g., mugging) or of nations (e.g., war). In its primary use *violence* refers to swift, extreme physical force typically involving injury and violation to persons or property. There is increasing philosophical interest in a wider use of the term extending beyond the overtly physical to covert, psychological, and institutional violence. In this broader sense racism, sexism, economic exploitation, and ethnic and religious persecution all are possible examples of violence; that is, all involve constraints that injure and violate persons, even if not always physically.

Concerning the moral and political justifiability of using violence to achieve personal or social ends, again philosophers disagree. Some have taken violence to be inherently wrong (e.g., murder), while most have taken it to be an open question whether violence is normatively justifiable. Terrorism presents a special case. It is aimed at randomly selected innocent victims in an effort to create general fear, thus sharpening focus on the terrorists' cause or demands. This random targeting of innocents accounts for the near universal moral condemnation of terrorism, despite the dominant view that violence in general is not inherently wrong.

Arguments purporting to justify violence do not value it in itself but as a means to an end sufficiently good to outweigh the evils of the injury or violation involved. Often, such justifiable violence is seen as a necessary means to important ends; that is, the good achieved by justifiable violence could not be achieved without it. Arguments challenging the justifiability of violence tend to reject the claim to necessity, arguing for nonviolent means, or to deny the claim that violation and injury are outweighed by the ends achieved. Such arguments may be against violence per se or merely against particular violent acts.

Georges Sorel's *Reflections on Violence* (1908) is the earliest extensive philosophical work devoted to the subject. While Karl Marx saw a role for violence in history, it was secondary to the contradictions inherent in collapsing systems. Sorel synthesizes Marx's proletarianism, Pierre-Joseph Proudhon's anarchism and Henri Bergson's voluntarism, defending revolutionary trade unionism in its efforts to destroy the existing institutional order. Sorel advocates the violent general strike as the means of class warfare against the state and owners of industry.

In *On Violence* (1970) Hannah Arendt reviews the twentieth-century apologists for violence in an effort to explain the increasing advocacy of violence, especially by the new left. She questions Mao Zedong's "Power grows out of the barrel of a gun" and articulates the position that power and violence are opposites. For Arendt the extreme of violence is one against all while the extreme of power is all against one. Power is acting in concert with others while violence is acting with implements against others. Loss of power leads some to try to replace it with violence. But violence is the opposite of power and cannot stand in its stead. Arendt concedes that violence can be justified but insists that it is only in defense against clear, present, immediate threats to life where the violence does not exceed necessity and its good ends are likely and near.

Newton Garver's "What Violence Is" (1975) extends the discussion to covert, psychological, and institutional violence. According to Garver, "Any institution which systematically robs certain people of rightful options generally available to others does violence to those people" (p. 420). Despite his sympathy with nonviolence, Garver claims that it is not a viable social goal. Violence between nations may be reduced but not eliminated.

See also Anarchism; Arendt, Hannah; Bergson, Henri; King, Martin Luther; Marx, Karl; Pacifism; Proudhon, Pierre-Joseph; Racism; Sexism; Social and Political Philosophy; Sorel, Georges; Voluntarism.

Bibliography

Arendt, H. *On Violence.* New York: Harcourt Brace, 1970.

Corlett, J. Angelo. *Terrorism: A Philosophical Analysis.* Dordrecht: Kluwer Academic, 2003.

Cotta, S. *Why Violence? A Philosophical Interpretation.* Gainesville, FL: University Presses of Florida, 1985.

Garver, N. "What Violence Is." In *Today's Moral Problems,* edited by R. Wasserstrom. New York: Macmillan, 1975.

Gray, G. *On Understanding Violence Philosophically.* New York: Harper and Row, 1970.

Holmes, R. L. "Violence and the Perspective of Morality." In *On War and Morality.* Princeton, NJ: Princeton University Press, 1989.

Honderich, Ted. *Violence for Equality: Inquiries in Political Philosophy.* Harmondsworth, U.K.: Penguin, 1980.

Reitan, Eric. "The Moral Justification of Violence: Epistemic Considerations." *Social Theory and Practice* 28 (3) (2002): 445–464.

Schaffer, J. A., ed. *Violence: Award Winning Essays in the Council for Philosophical Studies Competition.* New York: McKay, 1971.

Sorel, G. *Reflections on Violence* (1908). Translated by T. E. Hulme and J. Roth. Glencoe, IL: Free Press, 1950.

Weber, Samuel, and Hent de Vries, eds. *Violence, Identity, and Self-Determination.* Stanford, CA: Stanford University Press, 1997.

Wolff, R. P. "On Violence." *Journal of Philosophy* 66 (1969): 601–616.

Duane L. Cady (1996)
Bibliography updated by Philip Reed (2005)

VIRTUE AND VICE

Assuming that human agents possess settled dispositions or character traits, some of which are especially deemed worthy of praise while others deserve blame or reproach, moral philosophers have long treated the first sort under the category "virtue" and their opposites under the general term "vice." The *fin-de-siecle* revival of the virtue tradition in normative ethics as a third force, alongside Kantianism and consequentialism, has resulted in focused attention by theorists of all persuasions on the nature and proper role of virtues and vices in any comprehensive treatment of morality. Thus, two consequentialists (Driver 2001, Hurka 2001) have produced full-length treatments of the virtues, and there has been a growing appreciation of the key role of virtue in Immanuel Kant's ethics (Herman 1993, O'Neill 1996, Wood 1999). While the attention to virtue among Kantians and neo-Kantians is not too surprising, since much of Kant's later work was devoted to working out the important role that virtue and character play in morality (the weighty concluding section of the 1797 *Metaphysics of Morals* is rightly titled "The Doctrine of Virtue"), the consequentialist turn to virtue is, perhaps, more surprising. Jeremy Bentham, for example, gave a rather rude treatment of virtue in his *Deontology*, as recently described by Julia Annas (2002).

AN EMPIRICAL CHALLENGE TO TRAITS OF CHARACTER

This recent consequentialist vindication of virtue can involve a considerable departure from the paradigmatic picture of virtues and vices as traits of character, however. Tom Hurka (2001), for example, defines moral virtues and vices as responsive *attitudes* taken up toward intrinsic goods and evils, in explicit opposition to the view going back to Aristotle that treats them as stable dispositions or persisting states of persons. In this identification Hurka is acknowledging a controversy stemming from certain results in social psychology that some philosophers have taken to rule out on empirical grounds any robust conception of personality traits. Extreme situationists argue on the basis of considerable experimental evidence that the layperson's readiness to attribute to themselves and others robust character traits that are stable across situations, both over time and in various circumstances, and that can be used to predict behavior, is undermined by what has been termed "the power of the situation."

In experiments no longer permitted by twenty-first-century ethical guidelines, subjects were duped into administering what they were led to believe were severe electric shocks to their "victims" or invited to "role-play" as prison guards to such an extent that the subsequent sadistic behavior caused the researchers to abort the exercise. In addition, we have increasing evidence from developments at prisons in Iraq and other places around the world that average American young people, in stressful environments, can engage in dehumanizing practices that shock almost all of us. Gilbert Harman, considering both experimental and real-life examples of such catastrophic character failure, has forcefully pressed the negative implications he sees for the very foundations of virtue theory: "I myself think it is better to abandon all thought and talk of character and virtue. I believe that ordinary thinking in terms of character traits has had disastrous effects on people's understanding of each other. … I think we need to get people to stop doing this. We need to convince people to look at situational factors and to stop explaining things in terms of character traits. We need to abandon all talk of virtue and character, not find a way to save it by reinterpreting it" (1999/2000, p. 224).

Such a sweeping dismissal of all talk of character traits is, arguably, an overly simplified reading of the relevant personality studies (see Matthews, Deary, and Whiteman 2003 for a synthesis of the empirical evidence favoring interactionism, the view that behavior is a function of both personality differences and situational influences). Yet even the more balanced presentation of a similar skepticism in John Doris's 2002 study surely calls for critical appraisal by virtue theorists of any normative persuasion. Annas (2002), Swanton (2003), and other virtue ethicists have responded to the challenge. There is also room for more detailed treatments integrating social psychology, personality theory, and ethical theory, preferably by collaborating researchers with relevantly different research interests and, perhaps, in newly designed psychological experiments designed to test for cross-situational attribution of virtues and vices (see Cawley, Martin, and Johnson 2000).

The exploration of this basic challenge to virtue theory promises to carry on the pioneering work of Owen Flanagan, who first brought philosophers' attention to the situationist challenge and who championed what he labeled the "Principle of Minimal Psychological Realism": "Make sure when constructing a moral theory or projecting a moral ideal that the character, decision processing, and behavior prescribed are possible, or are perceived to be possible, for creatures like us" (1991, p. 32). This call for ethicists to take note of social-scientific findings dovetails nicely with recent philosophical calls for naturalist or science-friendly approaches to the philosophy of mind, epistemology, and metaphysics. The principle is best thought of as giving contemporary substance to the familiar principle that "ought" implies "can."

VIRTUE THEORY AS DISTINCT FROM VIRTUE ETHICS

A distinction should be drawn, then, between virtue theory taken quite generally and virtue ethics proper, where virtue theory covers any theoretical treatment of the nature of virtue and vice, even if their role in the theory is not central, and virtue ethics privileges them in some way or other. In Christine Swanton's self-consciously pluralistic conception (2003), virtue ethics, like consequentialism, should be seen as a broad genus encompassing various species. Thus, alongside the familiar neo-Aristotelian varieties of virtue ethics (Foot 2001, Hursthouse 1999), there is room for Michael Slote's "agent-based" account (1992), which opposes the neo-Aristotelian emphasis on the agent's happiness and well-being (*eudaimonia*) as grounding the goodness of virtue insofar as its presence helps the agent to flourish in a social context, in favor of the view that various inner traits and motives are admirable on their own. James Martineau thus joins Friedrich Nietzsche in the pluralist pantheon of virtue ethicists, alongside Thomas Aquinas and David Hume and their Greek and Roman forebears.

Any version of virtue ethics gives primacy of place to moral character over action, to the aretaic over the deontic, and sees the individual's development of virtues and elimination of vices as the best assurance that good deeds (right actions) will be forthcoming. Thus, for the virtue ethicist, the familiar bumper sticker's call for "*random* acts of kindness" seems incoherent as well as quixotic. If people cultivate the virtue of kindness, they can be reliably counted on to perform kind actions in a variety of circumstances, to adjust their reactions to others' needs consistently and appropriately, by expressing a suitable interpersonal sensitivity, rather than by following formulaic prescriptions or rules for conduct. An honest person, for example, will not only tell the truth when called upon to do so but will also not shade it or allow others to dissemble. The honest person will not resent just criticism, abide flattery, envy rogues and rascals alike, or engage in any number of sharp practices in business dealings.

Dishonest people, in contrast, will predictably exhibit the opposite sorts of behavioral tendencies. They will lie when convenient, cheat on their taxes, allow others to think them more deserving than they truly are, overlook mistakes on restaurant checks that are in their favor, and so on. For both the virtuous and the vicious, then, character structures will be expressed in a variety of ways and across a variety of circumstances, although some core traits will remain at the center of the individual's personality.

COMPARING VIRTUE AND VICE

It may be thought that a certain asymmetry will be found when comparing virtue and vice, with the former, perhaps, more predictable in its natural expression than the latter. A coward, it may be thought, might not run from some dangers and might not fear a wide range of things. Perhaps the Falstaffian figure that comes to mind is just a stereotype, and real cowards are much more selective in avoiding danger, rhetorical war hawks avoiding the draft by enrolling in college, perhaps, but not avoiding the most intimidating teachers or toughest courses.

This impression might simply reflect the fact that virtue theorists say much more about positive traits and much less about negative ones. It is the virtues, after all, that the theorist is trying to inculcate; detailed descriptions of the vices are often left out or given short shrift. The theorist accentuates the positive, perhaps. Aristotle, in his general theory of the virtues as the means between vices on both sides, one of excess and the other of deficiency, had a great deal to say about the vices and saw them as having the same psychological structures in the soul as the virtues. For him, vices were equally "settled dispositions" (*hexeis*), results of the wrong sort of habituation as opposed to the right kind. In departing from Aristotle in this regard, owing to our relative disenchantment with his general theory of excellence (*aretē*) as a mean, we moderns may well have tended to downplay the phenomenology of vice.

Tom Hurka's categorization of the range of vices (2001), from the *pure* ones (e.g., malice, *Schadenfreude*, sadism) at one end of the spectrum, through those of *indifference* (e.g., callousness, sloth, smugness), to the mildest forms at the other end, which he calls vices of *disproportion* (e.g., foolhardiness, avarice, intemperance), is a welcome reminder of the richness of our moral vocabulary and of the basic symmetry to be found when comparing virtue and vice. They both come in various forms and degrees, and can be similarly graphed by intensity and the relative value of their respective objects and fields. One important vice, hypocrisy in all of its manifestations, is the subject of the 2004 book by Bela Szabados and Eldon Soifer, who treat it from Kantian, consequentialist, and virtue ethicist perspectives. The philosophical fortunes of vice are thus on the rise.

THE PROBLEM OF VAGUENESS IN APPEALS TO VIRTUE

Critics of virtue ethics as a serious competitor in normative ethical theory have found it wanting in its vague decision procedure for deciding difficult cases. Moreover, by comparison with consequentialism and deontology, virtue ethics has made few contributions to the field of applied ethics. As for the last charge, the scene is shifting a great deal, since it is common these days to have virtue ethics treated alongside its more familiar predecessors with equal billing, as it were, in textbooks. In the subfield of professional ethics, Justin Oakely and Dean Cocking (2001) have deployed the resources of virtue ethics, comparing them favorably with Kantian and utilitarian approaches. The idea of a good general practitioner, whether in law, medicine, or business, is ripe for development along the lines of virtue ethics. Oakley and Cocking address a number of difficult issues from this angle in the course of their book.

One chief worry is the seeming vagueness of the advice to follow the example of the ideally virtuous person, especially in displaying the exquisite sensitivity to concrete detail supposedly exhibited by the practically wise (*phronimos*), which moral particularists and antitheorists tend to highlight. John McDowell (1998) and Martha Nussbaum (1986), among others working within the Aristotelian framework, have stressed the advantages of thinking of moral choice as uncodifiable, as the product of particular judgments made on the spot by individuals who embody the relevant virtues and are thereby in a better position than others to rightly perceive and assess the immediate needs of the situation. A virtuous friend, for example, is in the best position to give painful yet necessary advice to an individual, at the right time, with the right affect, neither too forcefully nor unclearly phrased, with due allowance for the receptivity and ability of the other to listen and take it in at that time. Similarly, the temperate person hits the right target in choosing bodily pleasures, adjusting intake by giving due attention to the situation (e.g., a party or a wake) and its demands (e.g., the need to stay alert and focused versus an opportunity to relax).

Christine Swanton (2003) has developed this ancient target analogy so favored by Aristotle and the Stoics in compelling fashion. She defines a virtuous act as one that hits the target of the relevant virtue, and she stresses the vicissitudes and complexities of "moral archery." Imagine that you are at a conference where you spot a stranger with some command of English who cannot (as you can) fully appreciate the sophisticated and scintillating philosophical discussion going on. You decide to devote your energies to the apparent needs of the stranger, leave the meeting room and make conversation, only to discover that this is more difficult than you imagined, definitely not enjoyable, and, the truth be told, perhaps not as helpful to the other as you had hoped. He could just as easily have spent time at the book exhibit while you stayed in the session, and you could have met him there in due time. The point is that while a kind person might have impressions calling for an expression of virtue, the exact specification of what is kind in the precise circumstances is not at all clear in advance or even *in situ*. Even the ideal moral archer may miss the target for reasons extremely hard to calculate in advance. Nonetheless, sensitivity to the particular environment is the distinct strength of the ideally virtuous agent.

Against this sort of appeal James Griffin has forcefully replied, citing the implausibility of "an ideally virtuous person, whose dispositions are in perfect balance and who therefore is better able to perceive situations correctly, including features that general principles often fail to capture. This is another piece of over-ambition in ethical theory" (1996, p. 115). While Griffin's complaint stems from his general pessimism about the ambitions of a normative theory to take us deeply into the solution of practical moral problems, virtue ethicists do have a special responsibility to be more precise than they have been.

Rosalind Hursthouse (1999) has been quite sensitive to this particular charge and has emphasized that the alleged imprecision of virtue ethics is in part an artifact of the fact that most ethicists are so familiar with, and not explicit about, the basic principles of the main normative theories on offer. Consider the following principles (one for virtue ethics, one for consequentialism, and one for deontology):

> (VEP) An action is right if and only if (iff) it is what a virtuous agent, acting in character, would do in the circumstances.
>
> (CP) An action is right iff it promotes the best consequences.
>
> (DP) An action is right iff it accords with a correct moral rule or principle.

Since ways of filling out the consequentialist and deontological proposals come so readily to mind, we can immediately think of various ways to give more substance and specificity to (CP) and (DP). For example, in the consequentialist case we envisage utilitarian attention to quantity and quality of pleasure, satisfaction of preferences, or maximization of happiness These criteria are applied to acts themselves or to rules for choosing acts as in versions of rule utilitarianism. In the deontological case, we think of moral rules and principles, such as being commanded by God or in accord with natural law, licensed by the categorical imperative, responsive to the formula of humanity, chosen by free agents in an ideal initial bargaining position, etc.

Because ethicists since the enlightenment have been unaccustomed to filling in the details of any virtue theory, (VEP) can seem hopelessly vague to those whose historical perspective begins more or less with Kant. Hursthouse argues that when the most basic principles are staked out as starkly and simply as above, (VEP) has as much clearly marked precision as (DP) and (CP). As we become accustomed to the workings of the moral imagination of those at home with the virtues, we will find it easier to fill in (VEP) with alternative specifications, compare the advantages of each, and weigh and balance the strengths and weaknesses of a variety of historical and contemporary proposals of virtue theorists. Perhaps it will also be easier to see how society at large harbors and encourages various vices and character defects in our social, political, and personal lives. Surely, greed and ruthlessness in business and carelessness of citizens in rich nations lead people to ignore the needs of the planet and its less fortunate inhabitants, and hence lead to poverty and environmental degradation.

One attractive feature of a virtue-theoretical approach to morality is the fact that most communities around the world, however different they are in culture and religion and a myriad other ways, tend to organize their early moral education of children around the promotion of virtue and the avoidance of vice. It may well be that, in trying to reach across cultural divides to find a common moral vocabulary with which to address the pressing moral issues of global reach, we would do well to supplement the categories so familiar since the Enlightenment in the West (e.g., duty, utility, costs versus benefits) with the highly nuanced and richly textured vocabulary of virtue and vice.

See also Evil; Moral Psychology; Virtue Ethics.

Bibliography

Annas, Julia. "Should Virtue Make You Happy?" *Apeiron* 35 (4) (2002): 1–19.

Cawley, Michael J., James E. Martin, and John A. Johnson. "A Virtues Approach to Personality." *Personality and Individual Differences* 28 (2000): 997–1013.

Crisp, Roger, ed. *How Should One Live? Essays on the Virtues.* Oxford, U.K.: Clarendon Press, 1996.

Doris, John. *Lack of Character: Personality and Moral Behavior.* New York: Cambridge University Press, 2002.

Driver, Julia. *Uneasy Virtue.* New York: Cambridge University Press, 2001.

Flanagan, Owen. *Varieties of Moral Personality: Ethics and Psychological Realism.* Cambridge, MA: Harvard University Press, 1991.

Foot, Philippa. *Natural Goodness.* New York: Oxford University Press, 2001.

Griffin, James. *Value Judgement: Improving Our Ethical Beliefs.* Oxford, U.K.: Clarendon Press, 1996.

Harman, Gilbert. "Moral Philosophy Meets Social Psychology: Virtue Ethics and the Fundamental Attribution Error." *Proceedings of the Aristotelian Society* 99 (1999): 315–331.

Harman, Gilbert. "The Nonexistence of Character Traits." *Proceedings of the Aristotelian Society* 100 (1999/2000): 223–226.

Herman, Barbara. *The Practice of Moral Judgment.* Cambridge, MA: Harvard University Press, 1993.

Hooker, Brad, and Margaret Little, eds. *Moral Particularism.* Oxford, U.K.: Clarendon Press, 2000.

Hurka, Thomas. *Virtue, Vice, and Value.* New York: Oxford University Press, 2001.

Hursthouse, Rosalind. *On Virtue Ethics.* New York: Oxford University Press, 1999.

McDowell, John. *Mind, Value, and Reality.* Cambridge, MA: Harvard University Press, 1998

Matthews, Gerald, Ian J. Deary, and Martha Whiteman. *Personality Traits.* 2nd ed. New York: Cambridge University Press, 2003.

Nussbaum, Martha. *The Fragility of Goodness: Luck and Ethics in Greek Tragedy and Philosophy.* New York: Cambridge University Press, 1986.

Oakley, Justin, and Dean Cocking. *Virtue Ethics and Professional Roles.* New York: Cambridge University Press, 2001.

O'Neill, Onora. "Kant's Virtues." In *How Should One Live? Essays on the Virtues*, edited by Roger Crisp. Oxford, U.K.: Clarendon Press, 1996.

Sherman, Nancy. *Making a Necessity of Virtue: Aristotle and Kant on Virtue.* New York: Cambridge University Press, 1997.

Slote, Michael. *From Morality to Virtue.* New York: Oxford University Press, 1992.

Swanton, Christine. *Virtue Ethics: A Pluralistic View.* New York: Oxford University Press, 2003.

Szabados, Bela, and Eldon Soifer. *Hypocrisy: Ethical Investigations.* Peterborough, ON: Broadview Press, 2004.

Wood, Allen W. *Kant's Ethical Thought.* New York: Cambridge University Press, 1999.

Lawrence J. Jost (2005)

VIRTUE EPISTEMOLOGY

"Virtue epistemology" has a narrow and a broad sense. In the narrow sense, the central claim of virtue epistemology is that, perhaps with some minor qualifications aside, knowledge is true belief resulting from intellectual virtue. On this view, the intellectual virtues are stable dispositions for arriving at true beliefs and avoiding false beliefs. Put another way, the intellectual virtues are reliable dispositions: either reliable powers, such as accurate perception and sound reasoning, or reliable character traits, such as intellectual honesty and intellectual carefulness.

In the broad sense, virtue epistemology is the position that the intellectual virtues are the appropriate focus of epistemological inquiry, whether or not knowledge can be defined in terms of such virtues, and whether or not such virtues can be understood as dispositions toward true belief. In this broad sense, the intellectual virtues continue to be understood as excellences of cognitive agents, but it is left open whether such excellences make the agent reliable, and whether the agent's being reliable is even relevant in the most important kinds of epistemic evaluations.

A number of claims have been made on behalf of virtue epistemology. As noted, virtue epistemologists claim that the resources of virtue theory can help to explicate a range of important kinds of epistemic evaluation. They have also claimed that virtue epistemology can provide an adequate response to skepticism, that it can solve Gettier problems, that it can contribute to a unified theory of value across epistemology and ethics, and that it can overcome the debates between internalism and externalism and between foundationalism and coherentism.

One issue that has been much discussed in the literature concerns the nature of the intellectual virtues. More specifically, it concerns the relationship between the intellectual virtues and the moral virtues. On one side of this debate are those who think that the intellectual virtues are much like the moral virtues. On this view, the intellectual virtues are such character traits as intellectual courage, intellectual honesty, and intellectual carefulness. For example, Linda Zagzebski (1996) takes Aristotle's account of the moral virtues as her model for the intellectual virtues, arguing that Aristotle was mistaken to insist on a strong distinction here. Other virtue epistemologists, such as Ernest Sosa, follow Aristotle in thinking of the intellectual virtues as reliable powers or abilities. Thus Aristotle took intuition into first principles and demonstrative reason to be paradigmatic intellectual virtues. Updating Aristotle's list of the virtues, Sosa considers reliable perception and various sorts of sound inductive reasoning too to be paradigmatic epistemic virtues.

Despite these differences among virtue epistemologists, there are points in common as well. For one, all virtue epistemologists begin with the assumption that epistemology is a normative discipline. The main idea of virtue epistemology is to understand the kind of normativity involved in a virtue-theoretic model of knowledge. This idea is best understood in terms of a thesis about the direction of analysis. Just as virtue theories in ethics try to understand the normative properties of actions in terms of the normative properties of moral agents, so virtue epistemology tries to understand the normative properties of beliefs in terms of the normative properties of cognitive agents. Hence virtue theories in epistemology have been described as person-based rather than belief-based, just as virtue theories in ethics have been described as person-based rather than act-based.

VIRTUE AND KNOWLEDGE

A major motivation for applying virtue theory to the theory of knowledge is that the position explains a wide range of our pretheoretical intuitions about who knows and who does not. Thus suppose we think of intellectual virtues as reliable powers, and we think of knowledge as true belief grounded in such powers. This would explain why beliefs caused by clear vision, mathematical intuition, and reliable inductive reasoning typically have positive epistemic value, and why beliefs caused by wishful thinking, superstition, and hasty generalization do not. Namely, the former beliefs are grounded in intellectual virtues, whereas the latter beliefs are not. Another advantage of a virtue approach is that it seems to provide the theoretical resources for answering important kinds of skepticism. For example, by making epistemic evaluation depend on instancing the intellectual virtues, the approach potentially explains how justified belief and knowledge are possible for beings like us, and even if we cannot rule out skeptical possibilities involving evil demons or brains in vats. The idea is that actually instancing the virtues is what gives rise to knowledge, even if we would not have the virtues, or they would not have their reliability, in certain nonactual situations.

THE ANALYSIS OF KNOWLEDGE. In 1963, Edmund Gettier wrote a short paper purporting to show that knowledge is not true justified belief. His argument proceeded by way of counterexamples, each of which seemed to show that a belief can be both true and justified and yet not amount to knowledge. Here are two examples in the spirit of Gettier's originals:

Case 1. On the basis of excellent reasons, *S* believes that her coworker Mr. Nogot owns a Ford: Nogot testifies that he owns a Ford, and this is confirmed by *S*'s own relevant observations. From this *S* infers that someone in her office owns a Ford. As it turns out, *S*'s evidence is misleading, and Nogot does not in fact own a Ford. However, another person in *S*'s office, Mr. Havit, does own a Ford, although *S* has no reason for believing this (Lehrer 1965).

Case 2. Walking down the road, *S* seems to see a sheep in the field and on this basis believes that there is a sheep in the field. However, owing to an unusual trick of the light, *S* has mistaken a dog for a sheep, and so what she sees is not a sheep at all. Nevertheless, unsuspected by *S*, there *is* a sheep in another part of the field (Chisholm 1977).

In both cases the relevant belief seems justified, at least in senses of justification that emphasize the internal or the subjective, and in both cases the relevant belief is true. Yet in neither case would we be inclined to judge that *S* has knowledge. From the perspective of virtue theory, there is a natural way to think about the two cases. It is natural to distinguish between achieving some end by luck or accident, and achieving the end through the exercise of one's abilities (or virtues). This suggests the following difference between Gettier cases and cases of knowledge. In Gettier cases, *S* believes the truth, but only by accident. In cases of knowledge, however, it is no accident that *S* believes the truth. Rather, in cases of knowledge, *S*'s believing the truth is the result of *S*'s own cognitive abilities—believing the truth can be credited to *S*. To put this another way, in cases of knowledge, *S* believes the truth because *S* is intellectually virtuous. Below are four formulations of this idea:

> We have reached the view that knowledge is true belief out of intellectual virtue, belief that turns out right by reason of the virtue and not just by coincidence. (Sosa 1991)

> Knowledge is a state of true belief arising out of acts of intellectual virtue. (Zagzebski 1996)

> When a true belief is achieved non-accidentally, the person derives epistemic credit for this that she would not be due had she only accidentally happened upon a true belief.... The difference that makes a *value* difference here is the variation in the degree to which a person's abilities, powers, and skills are causally responsible for the outcome, believing truly that *p*. (Riggs 2002)

> When we say that *S* knows *p*, we imply that it is not just an accident that *S* believes the truth with respect to *p*. On the contrary, we mean to say that *S* gets things right with respect to *p* because *S* has reasoned in an appropriate way, or perceived things accurately, or remembered things well, etc. We mean to say that getting it right can be put down to *S*'s own abilities, rather than to dumb luck, or blind chance, or something else. (Greco 2004)

More needs to be said here. In particular, virtue theorists must provide an account of the difference between getting things right by accident and getting things right because one believes out of epistemic virtue. The four quotations above imply that the distinction involves the notions of cause and causal explanation: in cases of knowledge, *S*'s believing the truth is caused by (or explained by) the fact that *S* believes out of epistemic virtue. But these key notions are difficult, and there is no agreement among virtue theorists about how they should be understood.

SKEPTICISM. The problem of skepticism has received sustained attention in the theory of knowledge. Skepticism is best thought of as a theoretical problem, rather than as a practical problem or an existential problem. The problem is not that we might not know what we think we know. Neither is it that we cannot act until skeptical doubts have been adequately laid to rest. Rather, skeptical arguments constitute theoretical problems in the following sense: they begin from premises that seem eminently plausible, and proceed by seemingly valid reasoning to conclusions that are outrageously implausible. The task for a theory of knowledge is to identify some mistake in the skeptical argument and to replace it with something that is theoretically more adequate. It has been argued that a virtue-theoretic approach promises resources for doing just this. To see how, it will be helpful to consider two skeptical arguments.

The first belongs to a family of skeptical arguments, all of which claim that our knowledge of the world depends on how things appear through the senses, and that there is no good inference from how things appear to how things actually are. Here is the argument put formally:

1. All of our beliefs about the world depend, at least in part, on how things appear to us via the senses.

2. The nature of this dependency is broadly evidential: the fact that things in the world appear in a certain way is often our reason for thinking that they are that way.

3. Therefore, if I am to know how things in the world actually are, it must be via some good inference from how things appear to me. (By 1, 2)

4. But there is no good inference from how things appear to how things are.

5. Therefore, I cannot know how things in the world actually are. (By 3, 4)

The argument is a powerful one. Premises (1) and (2) say only that our beliefs about the world depend for their evidence on how things appear to us. That seems undeniable. Premise (4) is the only remaining independent premise, but there are good reasons for accepting it. One reason is that there seems to be no noncircular argument from appearance to reality. This is because any such argument would have to include a premise about the reliability of sensory appearances, but it is hard to see how that such a premise could be justified without relying on sensory appearances to make the case. Second, even if we could formulate a noncircular argument from appearances to reality, no such inference would be psychologically plausible, since we do not make inferences when we form beliefs about objects on the basis of sensory appearances. This is because an inference takes us from belief to belief, but we typically do not have beliefs about appearances. In the typical case, we form our beliefs about objects in the world without forming beliefs about appearances at all, much less by inferring beliefs about the world from beliefs about appearances.

Something in the skeptical argument is not innocent, of course. Here is a suggestion on what it is. The skeptical argument begins with the claim that beliefs about the world depend for their evidence on how things appear, and it concludes from this that knowledge of the world requires a good inference from appearances to reality. But this line of reasoning depends on an implicit assumption: that sensory appearances ground beliefs about the world by means of an inference. It is perhaps at this point that the skeptical reasoning is mistaken, and virtue theory gives us resources for saying why.

Let us define an inference as a movement from premise beliefs to a conclusion belief on the basis of their contents and according to a general rule. According to virtue theory, this is one way that knowledge can be grounded, since making a reliable inference (one in which the general rules used are good ones) is one way of virtuously forming a belief. But it is not the only way. For example, perceptual beliefs are reliably, and therefore virtuously, formed, but not by means of a general rule taking one from belief to belief. When one forms a perceptual belief about the world, one does not begin with a belief about how things appear and then infer a belief about objects in the world. Rather, the process is more direct than that. In a typical case, one reliably moves from appearances to reality without so much as a thought about the appearances themselves, and without doing anything like following a rule of inference. Put simply, our perceptual powers are not reasoning powers. Rather, they are intellectual virtues in their own right, and therefore capable of grounding knowledge directly.

Consider now a different line of skeptical reasoning. René Descartes believes that he is sitting by the fire in a dressing gown. Presumably, he has this belief because this is how things are presented to him by his senses. However, Descartes reasons, things could appear to him just as they do even if he were in fact not sitting by the fire, but were instead sleeping or mad or the victim of a deceiving demon. Again, the point is not that these other possibilities are practical possibilities, or that they are in some sense causes for concern. Rather, the possibilities point to a theoretical problem: On the one hand, it seems that good evidence must rule out alternative possibilities. On the other hand, it seems that Descartes's evidence does not rule out the alternative possibilities in question. But then how can Descartes know that he is sitting by the fire?

Once more it has been argued that a virtue approach has the resources for solving the problem. As stated above, intellectual virtues, including our perceptual powers and our reasoning abilities, may be thought of as intellectual powers or abilities. Yet in general, abilities and powers can achieve success only in relevantly close possible worlds. In other words, to say that someone has an ability to achieve *X* (hitting baseballs, for example) is to say that he would be successful in achieving *X* in a range of situations relevantly similar to those in which he typically finds himself. But then possibilities that do not occur in relevantly similar situations, like the extreme possibilities of skeptical arguments, do not count in determining whether a person has some ability in question. For example, it does not count against Babe Ruth's ability to hit baseballs that he cannot hit them in the dark. Likewise, it does not count against our perceptual powers that we cannot discriminate real fires from demon-induced hallucinations. Accordingly, virtue theory explains why our inability to rule out Descartes's possibility of a demon is irrelevant to whether we have knowledge. Namely, knowledge is true belief grounded in intellectual virtue. The fact that our intellectual faculties would be unreliable in worlds where demons induce perceptions is irrelevant to whether they count as epistemically virtuous in the actual world.

NONTRADITIONAL PROBLEMS

As noted above, a number of virtue epistemologists are interested in traditional problems of epistemology, such as the analysis of knowledge, the nature of epistemic justification, and the problem of skepticism. These philosophers argue that a virtue approach in epistemology provides new insights into old problems. A second camp explicitly advocates a shift away from the traditional problems of epistemology and argues that a virtue approach is the best vehicle for achieving the new focus. These theorists agree that the intellectual virtues should play a central role in epistemology, but they prefer to ask different questions and engage in different projects.

Lorraine Code (1984, 1987) argues for the importance of epistemic responsibility, or the responsibility to know well. Code thinks that such responsibility is related, but not reducible, to our moral responsibility to live well. Redirecting epistemology in this way, she argues, constitutes a more adequate development of the initial insights of virtue epistemology. This is because, in part, the notion of responsibility emphasizes the active nature of the knower, as well as the element of choice involved in the knower's activity. Only an active, creative agent can be assessed as responsible or irresponsible, as having fulfilled obligations to fellow inquirers, and so on. Moreover, placing emphasis on virtue and responsibility has consequences for both how epistemology should be conducted and the kind of epistemological insights to be expected. Echoing a point by Alasdair MacIntyre, Code argues that an adequate understanding of what it is to be virtuous requires placing virtuous selves in the unity of thick narratives. A consequence of this is that we should not expect to describe tidy conditions for justification and knowledge. The relevant criteria for epistemic evaluation are too varied and complex for that, and so any simple theory of knowledge will distort rather than adequately capture those criteria. This does not mean, however, that insight into the nature and conditions of justification and knowledge is impossible. Rather, such insight is to be gained by narrative history rather than theory construction of the traditional sort.

James Montmarquet (1987, 1993) investigates the topic of doxastic responsibility, or the kind of responsibility for beliefs that can ground moral responsibility for actions. Often enough, the morally outrageous actions of tyrants, racists, and terrorists seem perfectly reasonable, even necessary, in the context of their distorted belief systems. To find their actions blameworthy, we have to find their beliefs blameworthy as well, it would seem. A virtue account, Montmarquet argues, provides what we are looking for. Precisely because it understands justification in terms of epistemically virtuous behavior, in such an account, justified (and unjustified) beliefs can be under a person's control. And this allows relevant beliefs to become appropriate objects of blame and praise.

A common objection to this sort of view, and to virtue accounts in general, is that judgments of responsibility are inappropriate in the cognitive domain. The idea is that judgments of praise and blame presuppose voluntary control, and that we lack such control over our beliefs. Montmarquet responds to this objection by distinguishing between a weak and a strong sense of voluntary control. Roughly, a belief is voluntary in the weak sense if it is formed in circumstances that allow virtuous belief formation. This kind of voluntariness amounts to freedom from interference or coercion. A belief is voluntary in the strong sense (again roughly) if it is fully subject to one's will. Montmarquet concedes that responsibility requires weak voluntary control, but argues that we often have this kind of control over our beliefs. On the other hand, we do not typically have strong voluntary control over our beliefs, but responsibility does not require it.

Finally, Jonathan Kvanvig (1992) has argued for a more radical departure from traditional epistemological concerns. According to Kvanvig, traditional epistemology is dominated by an "individualistic" and "synchronic" conception of knowledge. From the traditional perspective, an important task is to specify the conditions under which individual *S* knows proposition *p* at time *t*. Kvanvig argues that this perspective should be abandoned in favor of a new social and genetic approach. Whereas the traditional perspective focuses on questions about justified belief and knowledge of individuals at particular times, a new genetic epistemology would focus on the cognitive life of the mind as it develops within a social context. In the new perspective, questions concerning individuals are replaced with questions concerning the group, and questions concerning knowledge at a particular time are abandoned for questions about cognitive development and learning. Kvanvig argues that virtues are central within the new perspective in at least two ways. First, epistemic virtues are essential to understanding the cognitive life of the mind, particularly the development and learning that takes place over time through mimicking and imitating virtuous agents. Second, in a social and genetic approach, epistemic virtues play a central role in characterizing cognitive ideals. For example, a certain structuring of information is superior, Kvanvig argues, if an epistemically virtuous person would come to possess such a structure in appropriate circumstances.

See also Aristotle; Code, Lorraine; Descartes, René; MacIntyre, Alasdair; Skepticism, Contemporary; Sosa, Ernest.

Bibliography

Axtell, Guy. "Epistemic-Virtue Talk: The Reemergence of American Axiology?" *Journal of Speculative Philosophy* 10 (3) (1996): 172–198.

Axtell, Guy, ed. *Knowledge, Belief, and Character*. Lanham, MD: Rowman and Littlefield, 2000.

Axtell, Guy. "Recent Work in Virtue Epistemology." *American Philosophical Quarterly* 34 (1) (1997): 410–430.

Axtell, Guy. "The Role of the Intellectual Virtues in the Reunification of Epistemology." *Monist* 81 (3) (1998): 488–508.

Chisholm, Roderick. *Theory of Knowledge*. 2nd ed. Englewood Cliffs, NJ: Prentice-Hall, 1977.

Code, Lorraine. *Epistemic Responsibility*. Hanover, NH: Published for Brown University Press by University Press of New England, 1987.

Code, Lorraine. "Toward a 'Responsibilist' Epistemology." *Philosophy and Phenomenological Research* 45 (1) (1984): 29–50.

DePaul, Michael, and Linda Zagzebski, eds. *Intellectual Virtue: Perspectives from Ethics and Epistemology*. Oxford, U.K.: Oxford University Press, 2004.

Fairweather, Abrol, and Linda Zagzebski, eds. *Virtue Epistemology: Essays on Epistemic Virtue and Responsibility*. Oxford, U.K.: Oxford University Press, 2001.

Gettier, Edmund. "Is Justified True Belief Knowledge?" *Analysis* 23 (1963): 121–123.

Goldman, Alvin. "Epistemic Folkways and Scientific Epistemology." In his *Liaisons: Philosophy Meets the Cognitive and Social Sciences*. Cambridge, MA: MIT Press, 1992.

Greco, John. "Knowledge as Credit for True Belief." In *Intellectual Virtue: Perspectives from Ethics and Epistemology*, edited by Michael DePaul and Linda Zagzebski. Oxford, U.K.: Oxford University Press, 2004.

Greco, John. *Putting Skeptics in Their Place*. New York: Cambridge University Press, 2000.

Greco, John, ed. *Sosa and His Critics*. Oxford, U.K.: Blackwell, 2004.

Greco, John. "Virtue Epistemology." In *The Stanford Encyclopedia of Philosophy*, Fall 1999, edited by Edward N. Zalta. Available from http://plato.stanford.edu/.

Greco, John. "Virtues in Epistemology." In *The Oxford Handbook of Epistemology*, edited by Paul Moser. Oxford, U.K.: Oxford University Press, 2002.

Hookway, Christopher. "Cognitive Virtues and Epistemic Evaluations." *International Journal of Philosophical Studies* 2 (2) (1994): 211–227.

Kvanvig, Jonathan. *The Intellectual Virtues and the Life of the Mind*. Savage, MD: Rowman and Littlefield, 1992.

Lehrer, Keith. "Knowledge, Truth, and Evidence." *Analysis* 25 (1965): 168–175.

Lehrer, Keith. *Theory of Knowledge*, 2nd ed. Boulder, CO: Westview Press, 2000.

Montmarquet, James. "Epistemic Virtue." *Mind* 96 (1987): 482–497.

Montmarquet, James. *Epistemic Virtue and Doxastic Responsibility*. Lanham, MD: Rowman and Littlefield, 1993.

Plantinga, Alvin. *Warrant and Proper Function*. Oxford, U.K.: Oxford University Press, 1993.

Riggs, Wayne. "Reliability and the Value of Knowledge." *Philosophy and Phenomenological Research* 64 (1) (2002): 79–96.

Sosa, Ernest. "Beyond Internal Foundations to External Virtues." In *Epistemic Justification: Internalism vs. Externalism, Foundations vs. Virtues*, by Laurence BonJour and Ernest Sosa. Oxford, U.K.: Blackwell, 2003.

Sosa, Ernest, "Intellectual Virtue in Perspective." In his *Knowledge in Perspective*. Cambridge, U.K.: Cambridge University Press, 1991.

Sosa, Ernest. *Knowledge in Perspective*. Cambridge, U.K.: Cambridge University Press, 1991.

Sosa, Ernest. "The Raft and the Pyramid: Coherence versus Foundations in the Theory of Knowledge." *Midwest Studies in Philosophy* 5 (1980): 3–25.

Zagzebski, Linda. *Virtues of the Mind*. Cambridge, U.K.: Cambridge University Press, 1996.

Zagzebski, Linda. "What Is Knowledge?" In *The Blackwell Guide to Epistemology*, edited by John Greco and Ernest Sosa. Oxford, U.K.: Blackwell, 1999.

John Greco (1996, 2005)

VIRTUE ETHICS

In 1930 C. D. Broad first proposed to divide ethical theories into two classes, teleological and deontological, thereby introducing a dichotomy that quickly became standard in ethics. Teleological theories were defined as ones that hold that the moral rightness of an action is always determined by its tendency to promote certain consequences deemed intrinsically good; deontological theories, as ones that deny this claim. Broad's dichotomy was widely accepted as being exhaustive, but in fact there are two fundamental classes of normative moral judgments that do not fit easily into it. First, it focuses on rightness or obligation, excluding moral judgments concerning what is admirable, good, excellent, or ideal. Second, it concerns only actions and their consequences, saying nothing about moral judgments concerning persons, character, and character traits.

The contemporary movement known as virtue ethics is usually said to have begun in 1958 with Elizabeth Anscombe's advice to do ethics without the notion of a "moral ought." Although her own critique of moral-obligation concepts (viz., that they have meaning only within religious frameworks that include the notion of a divine lawgiver) did not gain widespread acceptance among secular ethicists, her constructive proposal to look for moral norms not in duty concepts but within the virtues or traits of character that one needs to flourish as a human being quickly caught on. Soon thereafter philosophers such as Alasdair MacIntyre, Philippa Foot, Edmund Pincoffs, and many others began to articulate and defend a third option in normative ethics: one whose chief concern was not a theory of morally right action but rather those traits of character that define the morally good or admirable person.

Phrases such as "revival of" or "return to" often precede mention of virtue ethics in contemporary discussions, and it is generally true that questions about the virtues occupy a much more prominent place in ancient and medieval moral philosophy than in moral theories developed since the Enlightenment. But it is important to note that the conscious awareness of virtue ethics as a distinct way of theorizing about ethics arose from within contemporary Anglo American ethical theory. Virtue ethics took root as a reaction against the underlying common assumptions of both teleological and deontological ethical theories and has achieved its greatest critical success as a protest against these accepted ways of doing normative ethics. Accordingly, one can view virtue ethics as having two complementary aspects: a critical program that presents a critique of the prevailing assumptions, methods, and aspirations of normative teleological and deontological moral theories; and a constructive program, in which an alternative virtue-oriented normative moral conception is developed and defended.

THE CRITICAL PROGRAM

At this first level virtue theorists are not necessarily committed to defending a full-scale alternative to existing ethical theory programs but rather to showing why such approaches are systematically unable to account satisfactorily for moral experience. Major criticisms made by virtue theorists against their opponents include the following.

OVERRELIANCE ON RULE MODELS OF MORAL CHOICE. Utilitarians and Kantians, it is held, both mistakenly view universal and invariable principles and laws as being exhaustive of ethics. But real-life moral exemplars do not simply deduce what to do from a hierarchy of timeless, universal principles and rules. They possess sound judgment skills that enable them to respond appropriately to the nuances of each particular situation in ways that go beyond mere mechanical application of rules.

OVERLY RATIONALISTIC ACCOUNTS OF MORAL AGENCY. Traditional moral theorists, it is held, too often assign a merely negative role in the moral life for desires and emotions. However, morally admirable people are not simply people who do their duty, but people who do so with the right kinds of emotions. Additionally, though many teleologists and deontologists do acknowledge the importance of motives in ethics, they typically mislocate them in abstractions such as "the greatest happiness principle" or "the moral law" rather than in particular persons and our relationships to them.

FORMALISM. Mainstream teleological and deontological theorists tend to focus exclusively on conceptual analyses of their favored duty-concepts and then on logical arguments based on such analyses. Additionally, they tend to view moral questions as arising only when an individual agent is trying to decide what to do in certain problematic situations. These methodological commitments result in a view of morality that is impoverished and overly restrictive. Virtue theorists, on the other hand, are much more open to drawing connections between morality and other areas of life such as psychology, anthropology, history, art, and culture. Their long-term agent-perspective also enables them to correctly view moral deliberation and choice as involving much more than snapshot decisions.

THE CONSTRUCTIVE PROGRAM

In offering their alternative, virtue theorists face the fundamental task of showing how and why a virtue-oriented conception of ethics is superior to its act- and duty-based competitors. In what ways is moral experience better understood once virtue-concepts become the primary tools of analysis? Here one may distinguish two general tendencies: Radical virtue ethics attempts to interpret moral experience and judgment without employing duty-concepts at all (or at least by claiming that such concepts are always derivable from more fundamental ones concerning good people—for example, "morally right" acts might be defined simply as those acts performed by moral exemplars); moderate virtue ethics seeks to supplement standard act approaches with an account of the virtues. The former approach tends to view teleological and deontological ethical theories as totally misguided; the latter sees them merely as incomplete. Major issues confronting constructive virtue ethics programs include the following.

DEFINING MORAL VIRTUE. What counts as a moral virtue and why? Is there any plausible way to distinguish between moral and nonmoral virtues? How exactly do virtues relate to actions, reasons, principles, rules, desires, emotions? Are virtues beneficial to their possessors, and, if so, are they too self-centered to count as moral traits?

JUSTIFYING THE VIRTUES. How can we establish the validity of those character traits defined as moral virtues, once the option of appealing to the value of the acts that the virtues tend to encourage is ruled out? Traditionally, moral virtues have been defined as traits that human beings need in order to live well or flourish. But does the idea of flourishing provide solid enough ground on which to base the moral virtues? Is it still possible to speak accurately of *a* single human function, or is human life more variously textured than the classical picture allows? How and why is evidence of flourishing necessarily evidence of moral virtuousness? On the other hand, if one declines to issue pronouncements about "the human *telos*" and instead opts for a softer, more pluralistic functionalism that seeks to define virtues in terms of different kinds of human purposes or practices, can one still arrive at a substantive notion of the virtues that holds that they are more than local cultural products?

APPLYING THE VIRTUES. How do the virtues relate to one another in real life? Is there anything to the ancient "unity of virtues" thesis (which, on the Aristotelian model, views *phronesis* or practical wisdom as generating and uniting all of the moral virtues), or does it make sense to hold that a person might possess one moral virtue such as courage and nevertheless lack others? How many different moral virtues are there? Are some more fundamental than others? Can they be ranked in order of importance? Do virtues ever conflict with one another? What kinds of specific practical guidance do we get from the virtues, especially in cases where they appear to conflict with one another (e.g., honesty vs. kindness, love vs. fidelity)?

It should come as no surprise that radical virtue-ethics approaches have attracted far fewer followers than more moderate versions and that the critical program has had a much stronger influence on contemporary ethical theory than has the constructive program. Those who turn to late-twentieth-century work in virtue ethics in hopes of finding greater consensus on either theoretical or normative issues than exists among ethical theorists elsewhere are bound to be disappointed. Still, it is no small sign of virtue ethics's success that contemporary ethical theorists of all persuasions are addressing questions of character, agency, and motivation as never before—and that there now exist greater realism and humility among contemporary philosophers concerning how ethical theory should proceed and what it might reasonably accomplish.

See also Anscombe, Gertrude Elizabeth Margaret; Broad, Charlie Dunbar; Consequentialism; Deontological Ethics; Kant, Immanuel; Metaethics; Utilitarianism.

Bibliography

Annas, Julia. "Virtue Ethics." In *The Oxford Companion to Ethical Theory*, edited by David Copp. Oxford: Oxford University Press, 2004.

Anscombe, G. E. M. "Modern Moral Philosophy." *Philosophy* 33 (1958): 1–19. Reprinted in her *Collected Philosophical Papers*. Vol. 3. Minneapolis, 1981.

Aristotle. *Nicomachean Ethics*.

Broad, C. D. *Five Types of Ethical Theory*. London: Kegan Paul, 1930. See pp. 206–207 for Broad's division of ethical theories into deontological and teleological.

Flanagan, O., and A. O. Rorty, eds. *Identity, Character, and Morality: Essays in Moral Psychology*. Cambridge, MA: MIT Press, 1990. Nineteen commissioned essays; see esp. part 5.

Foot, Philippa. *Natural Goodness*. Oxford: Oxford University Press, 2001.

Foot, Philippa. *Virtues and Vices*. Berkeley: University of California Press, 1978. Reprinted in *Virtues and Vices and Other Essays in Moral Philosophy*. Oxford: Oxford University Press, 2002.

French, P. A., T. E. Uehling, and H. K. Wettstein, eds. *Ethical Theory: Character and Virtue*. Midwest Studies in Philosophy. Vol. 13. Notre Dame, IN: University of Notre Dame Press, 1988. Twenty-nine commissioned essays.

Hursthouse, Rosalind. *On Virtue Ethics*. Oxford: Oxford University Press, 1999.

Johnson, Robert. "Virtue and Right." *Ethics* 115 (2003): 810–834.

Kruschwitz, R. B., and R. C. Roberts, eds. *The Virtues: Contemporary Essays in Moral Character*. Belmont, CA: Wadsworth, 1987. Seventeen essays. The first anthology on the topic. Includes an extensive bibliography of relevant works published up to 1985.

MacIntyre, A. *After Virtue*. 2nd ed. Notre Dame, IN: University of Notre Dame Press, 1984.

MacIntyre, A. *Dependent Rational Animals*. Chicago and La Salle, IL: Open Court, 1999.

McDowell, John. *Mind, Value, and Reality*. Cambridge, MA: Harvard University Press, 1998.

Philosophia 20 (1990). Double issue on virtue, with special reference to Philippa Foot's work. Thirteen commissioned essays.

Pincoffs, E. L. *Quandaries and Virtues*. Lawrence: University Press of Kansas, 1986.

Slote, M. *From Morality to Virtue*. New York: Oxford University Press, 1992.

Slote, M. *Morals from Motives*. Oxford: Oxford University Press, 2001.

Sreenivasan, Gopal. "Errors about Errors: Virtue Theory and Trait Attribution." *Mind* 111 (2002): 47–68.

Statman, D., ed. *Virtue Ethics*. Edinburgh: Edinburgh University Press, 1996.

Swanton, Christine. *Virtue Ethics: A Pluralistic View*. Oxford: Oxford University Press, 2003.

Wallace, J. *Virtues and Vices*. Ithaca, NY: Cornell University Press, 1978.

Robert B. Louden (1996)
Bibliography updated by Rosalind Hursthouse (2005)

VISUAL ARTS, THEORY OF THE

There are competing views on what qualifies photographs, paintings, sculpture, and architecture as visual arts. This entry focuses on theories of vision and their implications for claims about each of these four art forms. There is also debate over whether it is desirable to identify these major categories of art in terms of particular sense modalities. What is partly at issue is whether vision and visual experience are isolated from other sense modalities. The status of photography, painting, sculpture, and architecture as major art forms is by no means beyond challenge; they, along with their paradigm cases, exhibit considerable variation within and across cultures, and through time.

PHOTOGRAPHY

Photography, like vision, seems to have an especially intimate connection with the world by virtue of a causal or "mechanical" process that is describable in purely physical terms. Interestingly, this alleged mechanical connection has also been responsible for the lion's share of skepticism about whether photography is indeed an art. The basic idea is that the appearance of a photograph is, like visual experience itself, dependent in a special way on the presence of the targeted object or scene. The claim is not (necessarily) that a photograph looks like the object or scene in the world, but rather that the way the photograph looks is, in an important way, independent of intentions or other mental states of the photographer, even if the photographed scenes are staged or an object's appearance is manipulated or disguised. The possibilities for manipulation and disguise, in fact, motivate a distinction, fundamental to most theories of photography as an art, between what is *photographed* and what the photograph is a *picture* of, that is, what it pictorially represents. For example, a photograph of the forequarters of a jackrabbit, suitably enlarged, cropped, and merged with a photograph of the hindquarters of an antelope may end up as a picture of a fictional animal, a "jackelope." What is photographed is due to a process independent of a photographer's mental states, while what is pictured is conceived as dependent at least in part on the artist's intentions or cultural context.

Kendall Walton has argued that the viewer of a photograph literally sees the object that has been photographed (commonly known as the transparency thesis), that a photograph's transparency constitutes one type of photographic realism, and that this realism accounts for a significant part of a photograph's power. Walton claims that, just as telescopes enable us to see things far away, photographs enable us to see things in the past. However, one may accept the relevance of what is photographed to the work's content but reject the claim that photographs are transparent, that is, that one *sees* the object or scene. For example, in one account of what it is to see something, one's visual experience provides information about the spatial location of the viewer, so-called egocentric spatial information, in relation to what is seen. Since neither photographs nor paintings provide such information, it is concluded that neither is transparent. Some allege that photographs may provide such information, such as information that the viewer of the photograph is at that time standing where the photographer was when he or she took the photograph. Others object that, even though seeing generally carries egocentric spatial information, it does not always do so, such as when one sees something in a series of mirrors.

Options multiply. Some allege that one does not see actual objects or scenes in mirrors, but only their reflections. A variant view takes the relevant concept to be what can generally be expected from a given type of perceptual process, rather than what it always provides (Cohen and Meskin 2004). The crucial point for this view is that it is reasonable to expect egocentric spatial information from vision but not from photographs or paintings. Further, it needs to be acknowledged that what can reasonably be expected may vary in relation to context and an individual's powers or background of experience. The increasing ease with which digital images can be manipulated in fact makes it reasonable to be skeptical about many of their alleged information-bearing properties.

Some art photographers, not surprisingly, have made the alleged realism and associated power of photography part of the subject matter of their work. Jerry Uelsmann's combinations of photographs within the same image give them a surreal and sometimes mystical character. Zeke Berman constructs and photographs little stage sets that create visual ambiguities in the photograph's pictorial space. Manipulated photographs of fantastical animals are part of installations designed by Joan Fontcuberta and Pere Formiguera as a send-up of the supposed objectivity of photographic documentation in ethnological and anthropological studies. Artists may also use photographs of some objects—qua photographs of those objects—as materials for making pictures having a different content, connecting with a general question in the visual arts over whether and how the character of the materials artists use affect the content or significance of the work.

Suppose, for the sake of argument, that the way the objects in a photograph look is dependent on the presence of the objects in front of the camera at a given time. Nigel Warburton (1988) criticizes this "snapshot" account of seeing on the grounds that, in ordinary seeing, visual experiences of an object change as the object and viewer move in relation to each other. Warburton concludes that, because photographs—like paintings—do not have this property, viewers of the photograph do not literally see the objects photographed. The relevant visual concern then becomes how one looks at something rather than what one sees, which in turn raises questions about relationships among vision, space, and time that are relevant to all of the visual arts.

PAINTING

Painting is sometimes thought to be the visual art par excellence. Confusingly, however, the term *painting* is frequently used to indicate drawings, prints, collage, and almost any other method or materials used to create something that, crudely put, can be hung on a wall. Literally construed, paintings are composed of paint; how artists work with different physical materials, such as paint, to make art would seem to be relevant, even central, to appreciating them. Paintings, broadly construed, may also pictorially represent things, arguably in virtue of the two-dimensional array of line, shape, and color, abstracted from whatever medium is used. The development of various technologies to mass-produce two-dimensional arrays raises the question whether merely being a two-dimensional array is enough to warrant status as art.

Paintings and drawings are plausibly thought of as physical objects; prints, such as Rembrandt's *Medea* (1648), are not. Jerrold Levinson (1996, p. 131) calls prints (and other types of art) that have many impressions, such that no individual impression is identical with the work itself, "multiples." But not all prints are multiples. Monoprints, like paintings and drawings, are singular because they are, by definition, produced by a process in which only one physical object can count as a genuine exemplar (to use Levinson's terminology) of the work. Photographs, depending on what photographic process is used, may also be multiple or singular.

These ontological differences have implications for whether one can see the (allegedly) visual work of art. Impressions of a print can be seen, but the print itself, as opposed to its exemplars, cannot be seen (or, less precisely, it can be seen only "in" or "through" impressions of it). Prints may also have multiple states—stages in the printmaking process—some of which may be considered to be works in themselves and each of which may have multiple impressions. Prints may be grouped together as a suite, such as the four plates of Hogarth's *The Analysis of Beauty*, raising the possibility that the set constitutes the work of art. Even if one accepts impressions of prints as works of art in their own right, they are still impressions of a print, which is not itself a physical object.

Other media, such as mosaics, introduce further complications, and may undermine the precision of the singular/multiple distinction. Tesserae can be mass-produced and combined formulaically to cover a surface with a pattern or image, which would seem to make them multiples, though mosaics of this type are rarely considered works of art. Highly sophisticated forms, such as those that evolved under the rule of Justinian, by contrast, have greater claim to be singular works of art. They are products of a workshop tradition very similar to that which persisted for centuries in Europe for painting. The master was responsible for the overall design and implementation of its most important components, such as the figures, especially faces and hands; assistants provided backgrounds and possibly drapery. Rubens's assistants painted large portions of works that we identify as singular works by Rubens; Constable's *Salisbury Cathedral* was so popular that he painted seven of them. Are they copies of a single work—a sort of prototype that cannot itself be seen—or seven different paintings that are visually virtually identical?

Titles are linguistic entities that may be given by painters themselves, making them clearly part of the artwork, though only debatably part of the painting. An inscription of the painting's title—or of other words, for that matter—in the painting itself may be a visually significant property of the painting, but as a linguistic entity or property, it is generally nonvisual. The caveat is necessary since some types of linguistic inscriptions—calligraphy, for example—have visually significant properties. But a painting may have a title that is not inscribed and hence not at all visible, yet is still part of the work.

Singular works of visual art, such as paintings and drawings, are physical objects, but this does not preclude them from having representational and expressive qualities, or from playing a role in a culture and in history, including the history of art. Many artifacts—furniture, tools, and televisions—have functions. Paintings are artifacts with the function of providing certain kinds of visual experiences. Nelson Goodman trenchantly criticizes the idea that pictures show us "the way things look." Richard Wollheim argues that the crucial visual experience is what one can *see in* a painting. As he puts it, "The marked surface must be the conduit along which the mental state of the artist makes itself felt within the mind of the spectator if the result is to be that the spectator grasps the meaning of the picture" (1987, p. 22). The artist's hand is to guide the perceiver's eye; how an artist works with the physical materials, as a medium, is essential to the painting's meaning.

Making a work of art, however, may require more than what a lone painter can do or what any given viewer can see in what is created. Arthur Danto proposes that even ordinary objects can be "transfigured" into art by the existence of a theory and history of art, which is something "the eye cannot descry" (1960, p. 580). The art world of the mid-twentieth century subsumed not only painted surfaces but also commonplace objects, visually indistinguishable from ordinary, everyday objects or real things, into the category of art. Everyday artifacts can constitute a medium, not merely materials, for making art, standing alone or as part of a construction or installation.

A contrasting view proposes that visual works of art are pure appearances and denies that any of them, not merely multiples, are physical objects. These virtual objects, as Susanne Langer characterizes them, are "created solely for the eye" (1953, p. 10), and as such have no practical purpose or function dependent on the physical characteristics of their constitutive materials. Clive Bell's (1958) concept of significant form as line, color, their relationship, and a sense of space also depends on the purely visual, independent of both concepts and use. Both take the value of the visual arts to be in the visual experience one has in the presence of a work. Neither view accommodates the attribution of different contents to objects that are visually indistinguishable, something that Wollheim and Danto, in their different ways, are at pains to allow.

Visual experience is not merely ocular. Paintings, drawings, prints, and even photographs may be created with the expectation that perceivers' visual experiences will not be isolated from other sense modalities any more than from their concepts and beliefs. At a minimum, as Wollheim points out, we see with an *embodied* eye: at a distance and from a given (literal) point of view. The interplay of figure and ground is not merely visual, but relates to experiences of physical proximity and distance. Volumes and shapes are apprehensible by both vision and touch. Studies show that congenitally blind subjects can identify the content of raised line drawings of outline shape, contour, and even vanishing-point perspective. Paul Crowther (2002) goes further, taking the relevant connections to be not only between vision and touch, but between visual and motor *exploration* of the world and of the work. Past actions, including working with the relevant types of materials, affect visual experience. Chinese calligraphy, for example, is a semi-pictorial, linguistic inscription, and part of the tradition of appreciating it is to mimic making the brushstrokes in the air, using memory and imagination.

SCULPTURE

Sculptures and paintings relate differently to the space around them, depending on what one takes to be the paradigm cases of each. Suppose we take paintings that employ vanishing-point perspective, where there is a point internal to the space represented in the picture from which things are shown (its so-called "internal depiction point"), as its paradigm cases (Hopkins 2004). Such painting, like vision, is perspectival in that it organizes what it represents from a particular point of view. Sculpture in the round, by contrast, occupies a space that is continuous with that of the perceiver. It organizes the space around it, drawing on the perceiver's and the represented object's potential for movement and action. It has no internal depiction point, and hence is not perspectival. Tactile and somatosensory phenomena have a more obvious role to play in the appreciation of sculpture in the round, something that may be seen as a resource that enhances its power, or as an appeal to the "lower senses" as compared with the cognitively more esteemed sense of sight.

Sculpture might seem to be by definition three-dimensional, and visible as such, though the existence of multiples confounds this simple requirement, as they do with paintings and prints. Cast sculptures are multiples; one sees the exemplars, such as Rodin's *The Thinker*, but not the work itself. Cast and molded pieces are routinely hand-worked in various ways—painted, appliquéd, carved, and so on—motivating the acceptance of such pieces as works themselves rather than merely as exemplars of a type that cannot itself be seen. Installation art that is to be installed differently in different sites also challenges the idea that one sees the work rather than a particular installation of it.

An alternative strategy for distinguishing sculpture from pictures takes the sculptural to be a property of a work rather than sculpture as a category of art, so that a single work may have both sculptural and pictorial properties (Koed 2005). The basic idea is that materials—which can include paint—are treated as a sculptural medium when their three-dimensionality is used for representational purposes. For example, Paleolithic cave paintings are sculptural in exploiting protrusions from the cave wall to emphasize the swell of a bison's forequarters, and pictorial in exploiting line and color, applied to the surface of the cave wall, to represent a particular, or a particular type of, animal.

Bas-relief, including painted bas-relief, as a mode of representation, may actually have a closer connection with ordinary vision than either vanishing-point perspective painting or sculpture in the round, and hence is arguably a better candidate for being a paradigm case of visual art than painting or sculpture. Sculpture in the round exploits a crucial feature of ordinary vision that pictures do not, that is, one's visual experience changes as one moves around the object (except *per accidens*, as when looking at a sphere in a cylindrical room). However, sculpture accomplishes this by replicating, or at least approximating, the three-dimensional shape of an object rather than by representing it. One could say it presents, rather than represents, the shape of the object. In contrast, when pictures represent the shape of an object, they do not generate the changes in visual experience that ordinary seeing does as the perceiver moves about (except again, *per accidens*, as with pictures of relatively flat objects, such as pieces of paper). Visual experiences of bas-relief, however, change in relevant ways as one changes physical position in relation to the relief, though the relief does not replicate the shape that the represented object has in the round (again, except accidentally). Indeed, a low relief representation of a relatively flat object, such as a piece of paper, may have greater physical depth than both what it represents and three-dimensional representations of it. Bas-relief, within the requisite distance, also enhances without replicating the visual experiences of three-dimensional form and depth that are due to binocular disparity.

Installation art can be treated as a form of sculpture in an "expanded field " (Krauss 1983), though the relationship of sculpture to its surrounding spaces is better illuminated by contrasting it with installation art. Artists have control over the entire designated space for their installations, rather than merely over the construction of individual objects. A good case can be made for installation art as a distinct category of art, one where the artist has control over the entire space that the installation occupies, in contrast to a type of art such as sculpture, where the work may be seen as controlling the space that surrounds it. Video installations employing speech and music are certainly not merely visual and are probably best grouped with other video art and film. Further, the status of the objects within installations—and some installations contain no objects at all—is different from sculpture because the space of the installation is exploited in a variety of ways and is often treated as a gray area between life and art. Perceivers may be required to "complete" the work, for example, by stepping on a switch that turns on a light, as one engages in the semi-voyeuristic activity of viewing Marcel Duchamp's *Étant donnés*. Installations often create environments that prompt self-consciousness or reflection on one's habitual actions or role as viewer.

The continuity of the installation space with lived space can be facilitated by the use of everyday objects and by invitations to treat the material components of the piece in ways ordinarily forbidden with art, such as when museum-goers are invited to walk on Carl Andre's 144 zinc squares. The use of ephemeral materials, such as banana peels, critiques the timelessness associated with traditional sculpture in the round by creating objects that one is not merely to see but to see deteriorate over time. Museums routinely display, for our visual delectation, objects that were created to be used and not merely looked at, such as illuminated manuscripts, ceramics, and furniture, which may already show signs of deterioration and wear, itself a candidate for visual appreciation, as with the Japanese *sabi* aesthetic developed by the sixteenth-century tea master Rikyu.

ARCHITECTURE

One could develop a theory of architecture as a purely visual art by separating its form from its function; alternatively, one might posit the appearance of functionality, apprehended by the imagination, as the object of experience when treating architecture as a purely visual art. A more promising approach takes functionality as integrating one's experience of form, just as pictorial content informs one's appreciation of a painting. Deep traditions in architectural theory see it as structuring, in a positive way, how one lives and works. Architecture, as an art—though not as a purely visual art—is thus conceived and evaluated by its contribution to, or inhibition of, domestic life or commercial work. If architecture is the attempt to build well, it will accommodate and fulfill purposes that are partly informed by individual needs and desires, and partly by cultural and social realities.

Herbert Read takes the monument—a solid, sculptured edifice—as a paradigm category of visual art, attenuating toward sculpture in one direction and architecture in another. Monuments, like architecture, have functions, so his typology of visual art does not provide any assistance on how to reconcile a work's function with its status as a visual art. But it does provide a way of thinking of something built, as opposed to something sculpted, as an organic whole. A striking example is the Rajrani Temple in Bhubaneswar, a solid temple with no interior. Its inverse is exemplified by cave temples of Ajanta and the Kailasanatha at Ellora, which are not so much built as carved out of "living" rather than dismembered chunks of rock. Its sculpture is subservient to, and inseparable from, the temple's overall form. As one conceptually pulls sculpture away from the monument, however, it goes through a phase that makes it vulnerable to the charge that it is mere decoration, as in Robert Venturi's characterization of architecture as a "decorated shed," which simultaneously ridicules both the structure and its ornament. Thinking of architecture in this way invites the question "What needs to be added to a building to make it architecture?", which has as little promise as the fundamental question in philosophy of architecture as does "What needs to be added to a set of lines, shapes, and colors to make it a picture?" in philosophy of painting.

A recurrent issue in the philosophy of the visual arts is whether visually indistinguishable replicas have any status as art, let alone the same status, or meanings, as what they replicate. In architecture, the replica takes the form of the historic reconstruction of a building or a set of buildings. As with painting, one must ask from what vantage point, and to whom, the buildings are supposedly visually indistinguishable. Supposing that the relevant view is from the street, some cities have ordinances that allow the gutting of a building's interior, provided that the building's facade is preserved. Some designated historic districts in cities in the United States prohibit indistinguishable replicas or restorations, to ensure that anyone with even a minimally informed eye will know that whatever looks like an original will in fact be one. In contrast, the inauthenticity of the prettified "reconstruction" of a colonial village at Williamsburg, Virginia, has been criticized, even ridiculed, by comparing it with the deliberate artifice of the "leisure entertainment" of Disneyland. But Disneyland's "Main Street," it should be noted, is sometimes identified as installation art. It is a site for various ordinary activities, but different enough not to be confused with everyday life. Modified reconstructions that are altered to be economic, practical, and family-friendly are commonly criticized for the same reasons as copies or forgeries of paintings: they are not visually the same.

See also Art, Definitions of; Art, Ontology of; Art, Performance in; Art, Representation in.

Bibliography

Bell, Clive. *Art* (1913). New York: Putnam, 1958.

Berger, John. *Ways of Seeing*. London: British Broadcasting Company and Penguin Books, 1972.

Cohen, Jonathan, and Aaron Meskin. "On the Epistemic Value of Photographs." *Journal of Aesthetics and Art Criticism* 62 (2) (2004): 197–210.

Crowther, Paul. *The Transhistorical Image: Philosophizing Art and Its History*. Cambridge, U.K.: Cambridge University Press, 2002.

Currie, Gregory. "Photography, Painting and Perception." *Journal of Aesthetics and Art Criticism* 49 (1) (1991): 23–29.

Danto, Arthur, and Sidney Morgenbesser, eds. *Philosophy of Science*. New York: Meridian Books, 1960.

Graham, Gordon. "Architecture." In *Oxford Handbook of Aesthetics*, edited by Jerrold Levinson, 555–571. New York: Oxford University Press, 2003.

Hopkins, Robert. "Painting, Sculpture, Sight, and Touch." *British Journal of Aesthetics* 44 (2) (2004): 149–166.

Hopkins, Robert. *Picture, Image, and Experience*. Cambridge, U.K.: Cambridge University Press, 1998.

Koed, Eric. "Sculpture and the Sculptural." *Journal of Aesthetics and Art Criticism* 63 (2) (2005): 147–154.

Krauss, Rosalind. "Sculpture in the Expanded Field." In *The Anti-Aesthetic: Post Modern Culture*, edited by Hal Foster, 31–42. London and Sydney: Pluto Press, 1983.

Langer, Susanne. *Feeling and Form*. New York: Scribners, 1953.

Levinson, Jerrold. "Titles." *Journal of Aesthetics and Art Criticism* 44 (1) (1995): 29–39. Reprinted in *Music, Art, and Metaphysics*, 159–178. Ithaca, NY: Cornell University Press, 1990.

Levinson, Jerrold. "The Visual Work of Art." In *The Dictionary of Art*. London: Macmillan, 1996. Reprinted in *The Pleasures of Aesthetics*, 129–137. Ithaca, NY: Cornell University Press, 1996.

Lopes, Dominic McIver. "Art Media and the Sense Modalities: Tactile Pictures." *Philosophical Quarterly* 47 (189) (1997): 425–440.

Margolis, Joseph. "Painting." In *The Blackwell Guide to Aesthetics*, edited by Peter Kivy, 215–229. Malden, MA: Blackwell Publishing, 2004.

Maynard, Patrick. "Drawing and Shooting: Causality in Depiction." *Journal of Aesthetics and Art Criticism* 44 (1) (1985): 115–129.

Maynard, Patrick. *The Engine of Visualization: Thinking Through Photography*. Ithaca, NY: Cornell University Press, 1997.

Mey, Kerstin. "Sculpture." In *Encyclopedia of Aesthetics*. Vol. 4, edited by Michael Kelly. New York: Oxford University Press, 1998.

Read, Herbert. *The Art of Sculpture*. Princeton, NJ: Princeton University Press, 1961.

Rosenthal, Mark. *Understanding Installation Art: From Duchamp to Holzer*. Munich, Berlin, London, New York: Prestel, 2003.

Savedoff, Barbara E. *Transforming Images: How Photography Complicates the Picture*. Ithaca, NY: Cornell University Press, 2000.

Scruton, Roger. *The Aesthetics of Architecture*. Princeton, NJ: Princeton University Press, 1979.

Venturi, Robert. *Learning from Las Vegas*. Cambridge, MA: MIT Press, 1977.

Walton, Kendall. "Transparent Pictures: On the Nature of Photographic Realism." *Critical Inquiry* 11 (1984): 246–276.

Warburton, Nigel. "Seeing through 'Seeing Through Photographs.'" *Ratio* n.s. 1 (1988): 64–74.

Wollheim, Richard. *Art and Its Objects*. 2nd ed. Cambridge, U.K.: Cambridge University Press, 1980.

Wollheim, Richard. *Painting as an Art*. Princeton, NJ: Princeton University Press, 1987.

Susan L. Feagin (2005)

VITALISM

"Vitalism" is primarily a metaphysical doctrine concerning the nature of living organisms, although it has been generalized, by Henri Bergson for example, into a comprehensive metaphysics applicable to all phenomena. We shall examine vitalism only as a theory of life.

There have been three general answers to the question "What distinguishes living from nonliving things?" The first, and currently most fashionable, answer is "A complex pattern of organization in which each element of the pattern is itself a nonliving entity." In this view, a living organism, and each of its living parts, is exhaustively composed of inanimate parts; and these parts have no relations except those that are also exhibited in inanimate systems. The second answer is "The presence in living systems of emergent properties, contingent upon the organization of inanimate parts but not reducible to them." This answer resembles the first in acknowledging that a living system is exhaustively composed of nonliving parts; it holds, however, that the parts have relations in the living system that are never exhibited in inanimate systems. The third, and least fashionable, answer is "The presence in living systems of a substantial entity that imparts to the system powers possessed by no inanimate body." This is the position of vitalism. It holds, first, that in every living organism there is an entity that is not exhaustively composed of inanimate parts and, second, that the activities characteristic of living organisms are due, in some sense, to the activities of this entity.

THE VITAL ENTITY

The vital entity that animates an organism may, for brevity, be termed its "Life"—a usage that is in fact supported by vitalistic writings. The first thesis of vitalism may be stated as: The Life of an organism is substantial, but it is not—or at least not totally—made up of nonliving substance.

To say that the Life is substantial is to indicate that it has always been conceived more or less closely in accordance with an available doctrine concerning the nature of substance. All vitalists have, for example, held that the Life of an organism is a particular, not a universal; that it is the subject of predicates and not only a predicate; and that it is an agent possessing some degree of autonomy with respect to the body it animates. Most, but not all, vitalists have also maintained that Life, or at least an aspect of it, is capable of existence apart from its organism.

NAÏVE VITALISM

In addition to regarding Life as a substance, all vitalists have adopted a model that helps to specify the sort of substance it is. It may be helpful at this point to distinguish between naive and critical vitalism. Naive vitalism is embedded in common sense in much the same way as a version of mind-body dualism: everyday speech, common maxims, and habitual metaphors all suggest and support it. This type of vitalism, for example, is simply the most direct and literal interpretation of such expressions as "He lost his life," "a lifeless corpse," "A cat has nine lives," and "Scientists will someday create life in the test tube." When the average man thinks about the nature of life at all, he is likely to be guided by these and similar expressions. Naive vitalism has been and indeed still is the popular doctrine. The model of Life adopted by the naive vitalist is the most familiar one available; Life is regarded as a material substance, usually as a fluid body.

In the most primitive forms of vitalism, the Life is flatly identified with a material fluid, the breath, or the blood. This view just misses materialism; it is vitalistic only because the fluid is assigned properties unlike those of any other material body, for example, the power of sensation. Slightly less primitive is the view that Life is a fluid like the blood, only invisible and rather more fiery. The doctrine of the spirits as it occurs in Galen and his successors is an example of this sort of vitalism. The process of etherealizing the Life culminates in the view that it is a fluid but one that is assigned no properties other than its power of animating an organism. This is still a prevalent view and was present, for example, in Mary Shelley's *Frankenstein.*

CRITICAL VITALISM

Although it has conceptual and historical roots in the material substance models, critical vitalism is far more sophisticated. Its various versions have been elaborated by professional philosophers and biologists; indeed, its two outstanding exponents, Aristotle and the twentieth-century biologist and philosopher Hans Driesch, were professionals in both fields. Aristotle's writings, especially his treatises *On the Soul* and *On the Generation of Animals,* are the standard works of vitalistic doctrine. In them Aristotle established four traditions that, it can be said, virtually determined the course of subsequent critical vitalism: he identifies what has been called here the Life of an organism with its psyche; he locates purposive activity, organic unity, and embryological development as the phenomena that vitalism must take most seriously; he argues that the activities of the part must be understood by reference to the form of the whole and that morphogenesis must be understood by reference to the form of the adult; and finally, he describes the manner of the psyche's influence on its organism as formal, not efficient, causation. In short, critical vitalism after Aristotle takes the soul as the model of the Life and attributes to Life the power of achieving and maintaining organic form.

NATURE AND HISTORY. Vitalism was defined above as a metaphysical doctrine in the sense that it is formulated with a degree of vagueness sufficient to exempt it from empirical refutation. However, this is not to say that vitalism has no implications concerning matters of fact. By means of very plausible arguments, vitalists have derived empirical consequences, some of which have been falsified and some verified. For example, it was argued that since the Life is the blood, a transfusion of blood into a corpse would bring it to life. This experiment failed, but the failure obviously did not refute every version of vitalism or even the doctrine that the Life is the blood. More seriously, Driesch argued that if vitalism is true, then a bit of embryonic tissue that ordinarily develops into a particular organ ought to be capable of developing into other organs. It does happen that some embryonic tissue has this capability. But although Driesch cites such an experiment, he did not actually predict its results. Had they been unfavorable, Driesch would still have had a way to save vitalism. For although he is willing to set limits to the regulative powers of the Life, he gives no antecedent specification of these limits.

In short, vitalism is irrefutable. When this is coupled with the tendency to describe the Life in terms that are among the most problematical in philosophy, it is easy to see that vitalism is subject to the worst aspects of intellectual obscurantism. Its leading exponents, for instance, William Harvey, Georg Stahl, G. L. L. Buffon, Caspar Wolff, J. F. Blumenbach, Lorenz Oken, and K. E. von Baer, represent no improvement upon Aristotle either in the philosophical elaboration of vitalism or in its application to biological phenomena. The long period from Aristotle to Driesch, on the contrary, was characterized by confused invasions of naive vitalism; by the proliferation of such ad hoc entities as life forces, formative impulses, generative fluids, animal heat, and animal electricity; and by the merging of vitalistic thought with other fragments of biological metaphysics, such as the doctrine that living things are arranged along a linear scale corresponding to degrees of perfection (the *scala naturae*), and the archetypal conceptions of organic form. Moreover, vitalism showed a curious tendency to come out on the losing side of biological controversy: After Charles Darwin, it was anti-Darwinian; and it supported the view that organic syntheses could be effected only in a living organism. It also supported the useless and misleading conception of a primordial living substance, the protoplasm, a term and idea that unfortunately still survive.

HANS DRIESCH. After Bergson, Hans Driesch is the best-known twentieth-century vitalist. (Bergson will not be considered here since his biological views are intelligible only as an application of his more general metaphysics.) Driesch's position may be described as Aristotelianism painstakingly applied to modern findings—some of them the result of his own laboratory researches—in physiology and embryology. He also provides three empirical proofs of vitalism.

Driesch defines vitalism as "the theory of the autonomy of the processes of life." It is doubtful that this rules out any biological theories at all, but it does locate Driesch's major concern. He explicitly distinguishes between vitalism and animism, but he does not define *animism.* The term seems to be roughly equivalent to naive vitalism. He also considers vitalistic the view that the parts of an organic system can be understood only by reference to the form of the whole—a view that might preferably be classified as "organismic." But the latter distinction had not been clearly drawn in Driesch's time; he is quite correct in assuming that organismic biology is closer to the vitalistic tradition than, for example, Cartesian mechanism is.

According to Driesch, the Life of an organism is a substantial entity, an entelechy. Driesch employs this term as a mark of respect for Aristotle, although he does not use it with Aristotle's meaning. For Driesch, the entelechy is an autonomous, mindlike, nonspatial entity that exercises control over the course of organic processes; it is not actuality or activity in Aristotle's sense.

Driesch admits that the laws of physics and chemistry apply to organic changes. There is even a sense in which everything that happens in the organism is subject to physicochemical explanation. We may consider, for example, the first division of a fertilized ovum into two blastomeres (daughter cells). Even this relatively simple event can be analyzed as a complex sequence of cooperating chemical syntheses and mechanical movements resulting in, among other things, the duplication of the nucleus, the migration of the daughter nuclei into the opposite sides of the egg, and the formation of a cell membrane between them. Each step in each sequence is a physicochemical event and could be, at least in principle, described and explained as such. But chemistry and physics cannot explain why the steps occur when and where they do. Thus—and on this point some interpretation is necessary—although each event that constitutes first cleavage is physicochemical, it is subject only to post hoc explanation in physicochemical terms. The state of the egg and its environment at time t does not determine what events will begin at later time $t + dt$. But the latter events, after they have occurred, can be exhibited as consequences of events that ended at t. The state of the egg at t determines a range of possibilities; the entelechy influences the course of cleavage, in Driesch's terms, selectively "suspending" and "relaxing the suspension" of these possibilities.

An analogy may shed some light on this doctrine. Suppose that a person's voluntary acts are undetermined, at least at the physicochemical level; that for example, whether or not I clench my fist is not decided by the laws of physics and chemistry. Then the constitution of my body at a given time presents two possibilities, both within my organic capacity: to clench my fist or not. My choice to clench it is analogous to the action of an entelechy. The clenching could not by hypothesis have been predicted on physicochemical grounds, but after its occurrence it can be explained as the outcome of a sequence of physical and chemical events.

Driesch conceives of the laws of nature as placing constraints on the possible activities of a system. For example, the first principle of energetics (thermodynamics) states simply that whatever happens, energy is conserved, but conservation of energy is compatible with any number of actual changes in the system. The entelechy operates in the region of possibilities left open by the operation of laws. Driesch favors a particular metaphor: the entelechy is like an artist who gives form to a material medium, the medium itself both providing possibilities and presenting limitations.

There are, according to Driesch, three "empirical proofs" of vitalism.

(1) In 1888 the German biologist Wilhelm Roux performed the following experiment. Just after the first cleavage of a frog's egg he killed one blastomere with a hot needle. He allowed the other to develop, and it formed a half embryo, resembling a normal embryo that had been cut in two. Roux concluded that the egg is essentially a machine; after cleavage half its parts are in each blastomere.

Driesch performed a similar experiment in 1891 with the eggs of a sea urchin. He separated the blastomeres after first cleavage but found that instead of forming a half embryo, each blastomere developed into a perfect but half-sized larva. This result, Driesch argued, is incompatible with Roux's theory of the successive subdivision of the germ machinery. No machine that could build an organism could possibly build the same organism after it was chopped in two.

Subsequent embryologists have multiplied cases similar to that of Driesch's urchin eggs. Parts of embryos often can generate other than their normal parts. Driesch assigns the term *harmonious equipotential system* to wholes whose parts cooperate in the formation of an organic unity, if the parts themselves also have the potentiality of forming other parts of the unity. The existence of harmonious equipotential systems constitutes the first proof of vitalism.

(2) The formation of a whole sea urchin larva from a single blastomere—one that under ordinary circumstances would form one half of the larva—also provides an illustration of what Driesch calls a "complex equipotential system," that is, a system in which a part, the blastomere, forms a whole, the larva, when it would ordinarily form only a part. The existence of complex equipotential systems provides the second proof.

(3) The third proof is the existence of agency; its paradigm is deliberate human action. The action of an entelechy has been compared to conscious choice, and, indeed, Driesch regards human agency as a special mode of the entelechy's regulation of living processes. But agency characterizes other vital processes as well, especially embryological development. Unfortunately, his definition of agency as "an individual 'answer' to an individual stimulus—founded upon an historical basis" is not made clear.

Vitalism is not a popular theory among biologists, for many reasons apart from its affinity with various lost causes. The successful elucidation of various pieces of biological machinery (for example, the rather successful models of cleavage that at least outline a possible chemical explanation of equipotentiality) have rendered Driesch's first and second proofs rather suspect and, in general, have fostered confidence in the future of nonvitalist theory. There have been numerous philosophical criticisms of vitalism, most of them centering on the rather obvious point that vitalism provides nothing more than pseudoexplanation. The strongest case for vitalism can be summarized as follows: With respect to invulnerability to criticism, vitalism and its most plausible alternatives are in exactly the same position. The various lines of contemporary argument against the possibility of accounting for human agency on an inorganic model lend some support to the vitalist contention that physics and chemistry extend over only some aspects of organic activity.

See also Aristotelianism; Aristotle; Bergson, Henri; Buffon, Georges-Louis Leclerc, Comte de; Darwin, Charles Robert; Driesch, Hans Adolf Eduard; Harvey, William; Materialism; Oken, Lorenz; Organismic Biology; Philosophy of Biology; Stahl, Georg Ernst.

Bibliography

Agar, W. E. *A Contribution to the Theory of Living Organisms,* 2nd ed. Melbourne, 1951.

Aristotle. *The Works of Aristotle Translated into English,* 11 vols. Edited by J. A. Smith and W. D. Ross. Oxford: Clarendon Press, 1908–1952. See *De Generatione Animalium* (Vol. II) and *De Anima* (Vol. III).

Bergson, Henri. *Creative Evolution.* Translated by Arthur Mitchell. New York: Holt, 1911.

Driesch, Hans. *The History and Theory of Vitalism.* London: Macmillian, 1914.

Driesch, Hans. *The Science and Philosophy of the Organism.* London: A. and C. Black, 1908.

Schlick, Moritz. *Philosophy of Nature.* New York: Philosophical Library, 1949. A classic critique of vitalism.

Schubert-Soldern, Rainer. *Mechanism and Vitalism: Philosophical Aspects of Biology.* Translated by C. E. Robin. Notre Dame, IN: University of Notre Dame Press, 1962.

Morton O. Beckner (1967)

VITORIA, FRANCISCO DE

(1492/1493–1546)

Francisco de Vitoria, the political and legal philosopher and theologian, was born in Vitoria, capital of the Basque province of Álava, Spain. While still a boy, he joined the Dominican order in Burgos, and in 1509 or 1510 he was sent to the Collège Saint-Jacques in Paris, where he finished his courses in the humanities and went on to study philosophy and theology. While a student of theology, he directed an edition of the *Secunda Secundae* ("Second Part of the Second Part" of the *Summa*) of St. Thomas Aquinas. The date of his ordination is unknown. From 1516 to 1522 or 1523 he taught theology in the *écoles majeures* of the Collège Saint-Jacques and edited the *Sermones Dominicales* of Peter of Covarrubias, the *Summa Aurea* of St. Antoninus of Florence, and the *Diccionario moral* of Peter Bercherio. He obtained the licentiate and doctorate in theology in 1522. After teaching theology at St. Gregory's monastery in Valladolid from 1523 to 1526, he won by competition the "chair of prime," the most important chair of theology, at the University of Salamanca and held it until his death. Melchior Cano, Mancio, Ledesma, Tudela, Orellana, and Barron, among others, were his disciples. Vitoria helped to formulate the imperial legislation regarding the newly discovered American territories.

With the exception of the prologues to his editions of the works mentioned, Vitoria published nothing during his lifetime. His works include *lecturas* (his class lectures as preserved in the notes taken by his disciples), many of which have been published recently; *relectiones* (extraordinary lectures, which are summaries or popularizations of his ordinary lectures), published for the first time in 1557; and several writings on different topics. Vitoria is famous chiefly for his *relectiones*, the most important of which are *De Potestate Civili, De Potestate Ecclesiae Prior, De Potestate Ecclesiae Posterior, De Potestate Papae et Concilii*, and, particularly, *De Indis* and *De Iure Belli.*

According to Vitoria, political society (*respublica*) is a perfect, self-sufficient society, a moral and juridical person. It is a natural, not a conventional, society. In other words, it is required by nature and has its end set by nature. Actual states are the result of positive human acts, but men are obliged by natural law to live in some form of political society, outside of which no good or full human life is possible. The end of society is twofold: to promote the common good and virtuous life of its citizens and to protect their rights. The proximate origin of political society is the will of families. Authority is an essential property of the state, for without it the organic unity of the citizens and their activity, necessary for the attainment of the common temporal good, would be impossible. Like every natural right, authority derives ultimately from nature's author and resides originally in the body politic. However, since political society is incapable of exercising public authority directly, it must transfer it to one or several rulers. Particular forms of government depend on the will of the citizens. The absolutely best form is monarchy, "for the whole world is most wisely ruled by one Prince and Lord." The reason behind this claim is that monarchy, better than any other form, creates and preserves the necessary unity of social action without unduly curtailing the citizen's freedom; "freedom in monarchy," Vitoria remarked, "is no less than in democracy, wherein discussions and seditions, inimical to liberty, are the unavoidable result of the participation of many in government."

Beyond individual states there is a larger society, the international society constituted by the whole human family. It, too, is natural and necessary, although less strictly so, for the satisfaction of man's needs and the development and perfection of his faculties. International society possesses its own authority, which is immanent in the whole of humankind. From this universal authority derive the laws that establish the rights and correlative duties of the different states. The sum of these laws forms the *ius gentium*, which is partly made up of conclusions drawn from the principles of natural law by natural reason and partly of positive customs and treaties among nations. Vitoria established the chief rights of every nation, whether great or small, as the right to existence; the right to juridical equality; the right to independence (except where a nation is juridically and politically so immature as to be incapable of self-rule, in which case a more civilized nation may temporarily administer it under mandate or keep it in trusteeship); the right to free communication and trade, denial of which by another nation could justify war; and the right—and the duty—of every state to intervene in defense of nations victimized by domestic tyrants or threatened or attacked by stronger nations.

War is licit as a last resort, according to Vitoria, when all other means of persuasion have failed. The cause that justifies a war, whether defensive or offensive, is the violation of a right. An essential condition for the licitness of a war is that the evils resulting from it will not be greater than the good intended. Defensive war can be justly undertaken by any person; offensive war can be launched only by public authority. The ruler waging a just war is invested with power by human society. Just as the state has the power to punish criminals among its citizens, so humankind has the power to punish a nation guilty of injustice. All means necessary for the attainment of victory are permissible in a just war. Once victory is achieved, the conquering nation should exercise its rights over the conquered with moderation and Christian charity.

The thesis that Vitoria was the founder of modern international law has been definitively established by numerous scholars. It was officially acknowledged in 1926, when the Dutch Association of Grotius gave the University of Salamanca a gold medal coined to honor Vitoria as the founder of international law. Also in 1926 the Asociación Francisco de Vitoria was founded in Spain for the purpose of studying and spreading Vitoria's ideas through publications, conferences, and special courses at the University of Salamanca.

See also Authority; Peace, War, and Philosophy; Philosophy of Law, History of; Thomas Aquinas, St.

Bibliography

WORKS BY VITORIA

Commentarios á la "Secunda Secundae" de Santo Tomás, 5 vols. Edited by Vicente Beltrán de Heredia. Salamanca, 1932–1935.

Relectiones Theologicae, 3 vols. Edited and translated into Spanish by Luis G. Alonso Getino. Madrid, 1933–1936. There is an English translation and photographic reproduction of the 1696 edition of *Relectiones* in the series Classics of International Law. Washington, DC, 1917.

WORKS ON VITORIA

Beltrán de Heredia, Vicente. *Francisco de Vitoria*. Barcelona: Editorial Labor, 1939.

Beltrán de Heredia, Vicente. "Vitoria (François de)." In *Dictionnaire de théologie catholique*. Vol. XV, cols. 3117–3133.

Brady, Bernard V. "An Analysis of the Use of Rights Language in Pre-Modern Catholic Social Thought." *Thomist* 57 (1) (1993): 97–121.

Davis, G. Scott. "Conscience and Conquest: Francisco De Vitoria on Justice in the New World." *Modern Theology* 13 (4) (1997): 475–500.

Doyle, John P. "Vitoria on Choosing to Replace a King." In *Hispanic Philosophy in the Age of Discovery: Studies in Philosophy and the History of Philosophy*, Vol. 29, edited by Kevin White. Washington DC: Catholic University American Press, 1997.

Getino, Luis G. Alonso. *El maestro fray Francisco de Vitoria: su vida, su doctrina y su influencia*. Madrid, 1930.

Giacon, Carlo. *La seconda scolastica*, Vol. I: *I grandi commentatori di San Tommaso*, 163–213. Milan: Fratelli Bocca, 1944.

Hartigan, Richard S. "Francesco De Vitoria and Civilian Immunity." *Political Theory* 1 (1973): 79–91.

Morris, John F. "The Contribution of Francisco De Vitoria to the Scholastic Understanding of the Principle of the Common Good." *Modern Schoolman* 78 (1) (2000): 9–33.

Naszályi, Aemilius. *Doctrina Francisci de Vitoria de Statu*. Rome, 1937.

Reichberg, Gregory M. "Francisco De Vitoria, De Indis and De Iure Belli Relectiones (1557): Philosophy Meets War." In *The Classics of Western Philosophy: A Reader's Guide*, edited by Jorge J. E. Gracia. Malden, MA: Blackwell Publishing, 2003.

Sanchez Sorondo, Marcelo. "Vitoria: The Original Philosopher of Rights." In *Hispanic Philosophy in the Age of Discovery: Studies in Philosophy and the History of Philosophy*, Vol. 29, edited by Kevin White. Washington DC: Catholic University American Press, 1997.

Scott, James Brown. *The Spanish Origin of International Law*, Vol. I: *Francisco de Vitoria and His Law of Nations*. Oxford: Clarendon Press, 1934.

Soder, Josef. *Die Idee der Völkergemeinschaft. F. de Vitoria und die philosophischen Grundlagen des Völkerrechts*. Frankfurt am Main: Metzner, 1955.

Solana, Marcial. *Historia de la filosofía española*, 3 vols., Vol. III, 43–91. Madrid: Real Academia de Ciencias Exactas, Físicas y Naturales, 1941.

Truyol y Serra, Antonio. *Los principios del derecho público en Francisco de Vitoria*. Madrid, 1946.

Felix Alluntis, O.F.M. (1967)

Bibliography updated by Tamra Frei (2005)

VIVES, JUAN LUIS

(1492–1540)

Juan Luis Vives, the Spanish humanist, was born in Valencia and died in Bruges. Considerably younger than such scholars as Desiderius Erasmus, Guillaume Budé, and John Colet, Vives deserves an honorable place among them for his moral seriousness, sincerity of religious belief, promotion of education, and social concern, as manifested in projects for the promotion of peace and the relief of the poor. In many of these respects Vives is approached only by his nearer contemporary, Thomas More; his character emerges very favorably from any comparison with the earlier group. His efforts to secure patronage from the nobility did not blind him to the plight of those more needy than he, nor did he engage in the acrimonious personal quarrels that marred the character of some humanists.

Vives was a fine scholar and an excellent writer. After initial schooling in Spain he went to Paris to attend the university. Here he found still active a school of terminist logicians and physicists whose influence extended, so Vives tells us, to all the higher faculties. The earlier Oxford and Paris developments in logic and physics were being studied by teachers under the influence of the Scottish philosopher and theologian John Major. But the new learning was gaining favor, and there were signs among both students and teachers of dissatisfaction with the nominalist approach. Two of Vives's own teachers, Gaspar Lax and John Dullaert, told him that they were sorry that they had wasted so much time on "useless little questions." The "little questions" concerned such issues as the logical analysis of signification and of inference, as well as the quantification of physical phenomena. The complaint voiced by Vives and by many other humanists concerned not so much the intrinsic value of these discussions as the fact that they were permitted to invade all other fields of learning, often to the exclusion of the proper subject matter. Vives particularly disliked the petty vindictiveness and personal egoism displayed by younger men who delighted in scoring points over older opponents. When Vives returned to the University of Paris after his sojourn at Louvain, he expected to meet with a cool reception because of his book *Adversus Pseudodialecticos* (Against the pseudo dialecticians; 1520), in which he sharply criticized the academic climate at the university. To his surprise, he was warmly received, as he told Erasmus in a letter of 1520, and was assured that terminist quibbling was no longer tolerated in nonlogical discussions.

Vives's criticism of school philosophy was one of the more moderate and informed humanist attacks. He held Aristotle and the other ancients in high regard but deplored the failure of their followers to observe nature afresh. Vives condemned the undue humility of those who claimed to be only "dwarfs, standing on the shoulders of giants": If we cannot see farther than our predecessors, he insists, it is not because we are dwarfs and they giants but because we are lying prostrate on the ground, having given up the search for the truth. Vives insists as strongly as did Lorenzo Valla that philosophical terminology should not be artificial; the usage of such ancient writers as Cicero and Seneca should be taken as models. Philosophers should not depart too far from the speech of the people. Vives admitted, however, that it may occasionally be necessary for philosophers to coin terms of their own as well as to clarify those in ordinary usage.

Vives's own philosophy may be characterized as Augustinian in its general outlines, with eternal salvation and the vision of God overriding lesser concerns. It is in the light of this general orientation that his much discussed "empiricism" must be evaluated. Of all things on Earth, it is man's own soul that it most behooves him to know, by means of direct observation. But undue curiosity concerning other things, especially concerning their "inner natures and causes," is out of place and, indeed, impious. To inquire too curiously into the elements, the forms of living beings, or the number, magnitude, disposition, and powers of natural objects is to "tear the seventh veil." Such an attitude is certainly not favorable to purely theoretical scientific inquiry. But Vives's central concern is with man's felicity, and only to the extent that inquiry into nature serves to promote man's felicity is it admissible as part of the curriculum of studies. This curriculum would stress the useful arts, to the analysis of which Vives devoted great attention. In common with humanists in general, Vives stressed the utility of the arts and insisted that they must be systematized or brought into rules and precepts so as to be applicable to the purposes of ordinary life. Inordinate attention to their logical analysis must be curtailed; instead, students are to be constantly reminded of the empirical origins of useful knowledge. In his discussion of method in the arts, Vives explicitly drew on Galen as well as on suggestions in Aristotle.

Neither history nor theology is an art from this standpoint, since neither subject has been reduced to rules. Vives was impatient with the school theology of his time; he found little of value in the controversies between Scotists and Thomists and disliked their fanaticism: "They would accuse each other of heresy if it were not for the mellowing effect of the customs of the school." It has been aptly remarked that Vives's religious thought has close affinities with northern Pietism as exemplified by the Brethren of the Common Life, the movement that left such an impression on Erasmus. In keeping with this is Vives's obvious sympathy for the common people, a note conspicuously absent from the writings of many other humanists.

On a few points Vives specifically rejected Platonism—for example, in maintaining that God does not require divine Ideas and that we do not have reminiscences of Ideas from our past lives. Vives prefers to explain the insights of Plato's doctrine of reminiscence by means of certain natural relationships between the human mind and "those first true seeds of knowledge whence all the rest of our knowledge springs," called anticipations by the Stoics. This Stoic doctrine merges easily in Vives's thought, as in that of many of his contemporaries, with an appeal to common sense (*sensus communis*), which here takes on its modern flavor. Common sense furnishes us with an argument for God's existence, there being no people so benighted as to be completely destitute of some knowledge, however dim, of God. Human minds, furthermore, are all informed with the need to worship God, but what form this worship takes is a matter of human persuasion. Here we may trace the influence of Florentine Platonism, with which Vives was quite familiar. Perhaps from the same source is Vives's often repeated assertion that nothing would be more wretched than man if his actions aimed only at earthly ends. He condemns the vices of pleasure (*voluptas*) and pride (*superbia*) as roundly as any other medieval writer. Pride is responsible for the "frenzied craving for knowledge" shown by some men who are anxious to appear distinguished among their fellow men. Only piety, however, can permanently satisfy man and give him rest.

See also Aristotle; Cicero, Marcus Tullius; Colet, John; Erasmus, Desiderius; Galen; Humanism; Major, John; More, Thomas; Pietism; Platonism and the Platonic Tradition; Scotism; Seneca, Lucius Annaeus; Stoicism; Thomism.

Bibliography

Vives's writings, with the exception of his commentaries on Augustine's *City of God*, were collected by Mayáns y Ciscar, 8 vols. (Valencia, 1782). The biography by Adolfo Bonilla y San Martín, *Luis Vives y la filosofía del renacimiento* (Madrid, 1903), is reliable but not too detailed. See also *Vives: On Education, a translation of the De Tradendis Disciplinis*, translated by Foster Watson (Cambridge, U.K., 1913), and Vives's *De Anima et Vita*, edited by M. Sancipriano (Florence, 1954).

OTHER RECOMMENDED WORKS

Hidalgo Serna, Emilio. "'Ingenium' and Rhetoric in the Work of Vives." *Philosophy and Rhetoric* 16 (1983): 228–241.

Noreña, Carlos G. *Juan Luis Vives and the Emotions*. Carbondale: Southern Illinois University Press, 1989.

Noreña, Carlos G. *Studies in Spanish Renaissance Thought*. The Hague: Martinus Nijhoff, 1975.

Noreña, Carlos. "Was Juan Luis Vives a Disciple of Erasmus?" *Journal of the History of Philosophy* 7 (1969): 263–272.

Neal W. Gilbert (1967)
Bibliography updated by Tamra Frei (2005)

VLASTOS, GREGORY
(1907–1991)

Gregory Vlastos led a revival of interest in ancient philosophy and was the first American scholar to deploy the methods of analytic philosophy in this area. Best known for his work on the philosophy of Socrates, he also published widely on Plato and on topics in pre-Socratic philosophy. Before turning to ancient philosophy, he published works in social and political theory, and his writings on justice continue to be influential.

He was born in the Greek community of Istanbul, raised as a Protestant, and educated at Roberts College (an American-sponsored institution of secondary and higher education in Istanbul). He took a bachelor of divinity degree in 1929 from the Chicago Theological Seminary and proceeded to Harvard University, where, after studying philosophy under Raphael Demos and Alfred North Whitehead, he was awarded his PhD in 1931. In that year he took a position at the Queen's University in Kingston, Ontario. He served in the Canadian Air Force during World War II. In 1948, he joined the Sage School of Philosophy at Cornell. In 1954–1955, he was a member at the Institute for Advanced Study in Princeton and, in 1955, joined the Department of Philosophy at Princeton University, which he served for many years as Stuart Professor and then chairman. He was president of the Eastern Division of the American Philosophical Association in 1965–1966. In 1976, he moved to the University of California at Berkeley, where he remained until his death.

Vlastos had a huge influence on the next generation of scholars of ancient philosophy, which has been led in the United States largely by his students, proteges, and members of the seminars he conducted for young college teachers. Many of these became highly distinguished: Richard Kraut, Terence Irwin, A. P. D. Mourelatos, Alexander Nehamas, Gerasimos Santas, and Nicholas Smith, to name a few.

Vlastos began the revolution in Platonic studies with his article, "The Third Man Argument in the *Parmenides*" (1954), which rendered the argument in formal terms and ignited a debate (joined by such notable philosophers as Peter Geach and Wilfrid Sellars) over both the soundness of the argument and its purpose. Vlastos concluded that the argument revealed Plato's "honest perplexity" about the theory of forms. Vlastos held a developmental view of Plato: Early dialogues (those with affinities to the *Apology*) were mainly innocent of metaphysics, middle dialogues (such as the *Republic*) were committed to a theory of the degrees of reality, and later dialogues showed Plato to be critical toward his former metaphysical theories.

On the theory of forms in Plato, Vlastos wrote a number of important papers, of which "Degrees of Reality in Plato" (1965) is the most famous. He explained, in a way that has been the basis for most subsequent work in this area, what Plato could mean by saying that a form was more real than its sensible instances: The form is cognitively more dependable.

Vlastos brought attention to Plato's writings about love and friendship, raising the question whether an individual person could be an object of love on the Platonic theory, which seems to place the Form of Beauty itself at the apex of love. Vlastos saw that Plato represented Socrates as a teacher who failed more often than he succeeded, and, in a famous essay, he attributed Socrates' failure to an inability to respond to his students with love ("The Paradox of Socrates," 1971).

Drawn early to Socrates' single-minded devotion to the care of the soul, Vlastos brought out the problem in Socrates' doctrine of the unity of virtue: Why, if they are one, do they have different definitions? His solution was that the virtues are not strictly identical, but biconditionally related in such a way that having any virtue implies having the others.

During his Berkeley period he generated his most influential work—a set of articles and a book about the Platonic Socrates that defined the subject for the next generation of scholars. He established a method for identifying the philosophy of Socrates, taking Plato's works to reflect the philosophy of Socrates insofar as they are compatible with Plato's *Apology of Socrates*, which he supposed to be an adequate historical guide on philosophical points.

In one of his most influential pieces, "The Socratic Elenchus" (1983), Vlastos identified the method Socrates uses in certain early dialogues as elenchus (a kind of cross-examination), about which Vlastos asked the question that has been fundamental to subsequent research. Socrates, he pointed out, depends on the elenchus for both negative conclusions, refuting the bogus knowledge-claims of others, and, for positive results, supporting his own ethical views. Yet the method seems to have no foundation aside from the assent of Socrates' interlocutors. Vlastos suggested that the method winnows out the interlocutors' false views, leaving ones that are likely to be true, thus providing credibility for those views that fall short of certainty, but nevertheless provide practical grounds for Socrates' moral teaching. Socrates' disclaimer of knowledge was not a lie, as many believed in antiquity, but a case of what Vlastos called "complex irony": the complex truth behind it is that Socrates lacks certainty, while maintaining what Vlastos called "elenctic knowledge," knowledge supported by the elenchus. In this way Vlastos introduced a new understanding of Socratic irony, which was to give a title to his last book.

Just before his death, in *Socrates, Ironist and Moral Philosopher* (1991), Vlastos brought together his conclusions about Socrates, of which the most important was that Socrates was a trend-setting innovator in moral theory, as "the first to establish the eudaimonist foundation of ethical theory," and, moreover, "the founder of the non-instrumentalist form of eudaimonism held in common by … all Greek moral philosophers except the Epicureans" (1991, p. 10). Even more revolutionary, according to Vlastos, Socrates rejected the traditional morality of retaliation, the idea that justice requires people to harm their enemies.

Vlastos had a gift for identifying questions of interpretation that drew other philosophers into discussion, both of his proposed answers and of the questions themselves. He never ceased to express a love for his subject that was infectious and has been passed down to subsequent generations of scholars. Whether or not the answers he gave will survive the test of scholarly debate, his questions will continue to define that debate.

See also Eudaimonia; Justice; Plato; Socrates.

Bibliography

WORKS BY GREGORY VLASTOS

"The Third Man Argument in the *Parmenides*." *Philosophical Review* 63 (1954): 319–349.

"The Paradox of Socrates." In *The Philosophy of Socrates: A Collection of Critical Essays*. Garden City: Anchor Books, 1971, pp 1–21.

Platonic Studies. 2nd ed. Princeton, NJ: Princeton University Press, 1981. Contains, among other essays, these that are cited in this article: "Degrees of Reality in Plato" (1965), "The Individual as Object of Love in Plato" (1969), and "The Unity of the Virtues in the *Protagoras*" (1971).

"The Socratic Elenchus." *Oxford Studies in Ancient Philosophy* 1 (1983): 27–58.

"Socrates' Disavowal of Knowledge." *Philosophical Quarterly* 35 (1985): 1–31.

Socrates: Ironist and Moral Philosopher. Ithaca, NY: Cornell University Press, 1991.

Socratic Studies, edited by Myles Burnyeat. Cambridge, U.K.: Cambridge University Press, 1994. Contains, among other essays, these that are cited in this article: "The Socratic Elenchus: Method is All" (revised from the 1983 paper), and "Socrates Disavowal of Knowledge" (revised from the 1985 paper).

Studies in Greek Philosophy. 2 vols, edited by Daniel W. Graham. Princeton, NJ: Princeton University Press, 1995.

WORKS ABOUT GREGORY VLASTOS

Annas, Julia. *The Morality of Happiness*. New York: Oxford University Press, 1993.

Irwin, Terence. *Plato's Ethics*. New York: Oxford University Press, 1995.

Paul Woodruff (2005)

VOID

See *Quantum Mechanics*

VOLITION

The action of opening a door by pushing on it is composed of the agent's action of voluntarily exerting force with his or her arm and hand plus that action's causing the door to open. Is the voluntary exertion of arm and hand similarly composed of an action producing a result? There is a clear candidate here for the role of result—namely, the limb's exerting force. It could have exerted exactly the same force, by means of just the same muscle contractions, without the agent's voluntarily exerting the force with it. So the exerting of force by the limb is only a part of the whole action. But does the remainder consist of this part's being caused by action of the agent? Philosophers disagree on the answer to this question. Section I below offers one way of spelling out an affirmative answer (which is developed more fully in Ginet [1990, ch. 2]). Section II briefly sketches some alternative views.

SECTION I

When one voluntarily exerts force with a limb, the action that causes the limb to exert force is a mental action, which, following an old tradition in philosophy and psychology, is called *volition*. We view such exertions as voluntary because we experience them as directly under our control. This is most clear in those cases of voluntary exertion where we have to concentrate on what we are doing with the body—such as my experience of trying an unfamiliar dance movement with my left leg. Here my attention is focused on my exertion with the leg. I note just how I am trying to exert it and just how the exertion feels. This contrasts with my moving my left leg in the course of walking along enjoying a fine day, where I do not attend at all to my exertion with the leg. I do it, as we say, "automatically," perhaps without even noting that I am now exerting that leg. But the difference is between these cases should not be exaggerated. It is not at all like the difference between one of the foregoing experiences and an exertion of my body that I experience as purely involuntary, such as the movement of my lower leg in response to a sharp tap just below the kneecap. In this last case, though I experience the leg's exertion, I do not experience it as something that I voluntarily determine. But my experience of voluntary exertions, even when it is most nonattentive, is colored with the sense of my making them happen.

I experience my voluntary acts as the specific exertions they are—at least in those respects that I voluntarily determine. If in walking I had made an appreciably different movement with my leg at one point than the one I actually made—taking a much longer step, say, than the one I actually took—my experience of making the movement would have been correspondingly different, whether or not I was attending to the experience.

The normal subjective experience of voluntarily exerting the body in a certain way is a compound of two significantly different parts. There is, first, a perceptual aspect. One perceives the exertion in a certain direct way, not visually or by feeling it with some other part of one's body. But the experience of voluntary exertion is more than the direct perception of the exertion. I could feel my arm exerting force in just the same way it does when I thrust it upward without experiencing this exertion as something I make happen. I could experience it as something that just happens to me, unconnected with my will, while at the same time perceiving the exertion of the arm as just like one I might have produced voluntarily. The voluntariness of the experience of voluntary exerting is a further part of it, distinct from the perceptual part, an aspect that would be more conspicuous by its absence than it is by its presence.

It is this nonperceptual part of the experience that is volition. This part could occur all by itself, unaccompanied by perception of exertion. It could seem to me that I voluntarily exert a force upward with my arm without at the same time having the sense that I feel the exertion happening. The arm feels paralyzed and anaesthetized.

Neither sort of impoverished experience—seeming to feel an exertion without seeming voluntarily to make it or seeming voluntarily to make it without seeming to feel it—happens very often. But both do in fact occasionally occur. And we know enough about how our experience depends on what happens in our neural system to know how it is possible in principle to produce either sort. Seeming to make an exertion without seeming to feel it could be produced by depriving a subject of the input neural capacity to perceive the exertion while leaving unimpaired their output neural capacity to make the exertion. And we could produce the experience of seeming to feel a given sort of exertion while lacking the sense that it is voluntary by giving to the perceptual system of a subject who is not trying to make any exertion the same neural input that causes a subject to feel that sort of exertion when he or she makes it voluntarily.

The mental action of volition is not an antecedent of the experience of voluntarily exertion, not a prior mental occurrence that triggers the whole package of the exertion and the experience of it. Rather it is that *part* of the experience whose presence is what makes the exertion seem voluntary and whose absence would make it seem involuntary.

Volition is the means by which I cause my body's exertion when I voluntarily exert it. For my volition counts as my trying to exert it—that is, as my trying to cause it to exert. So when I succeed, it is by this trying, this volition, that I cause it.

Volition resembles certain other mental actions (such as deciding) in having intentional content. The volition involved in my voluntarily exerting a certain force with my arm is volition to exert that sort of force. Its being a volition to exert a certain force with my arm is not a matter of what it causes but an intrinsic property of the mental act itself, in the same way that it is an intrinsic property of a certain act of deciding that it is a deciding to raise my arm.

Volition is an intentional mental occurrence whose content (or object) does not go beyond exerting force with one's body in the immediate present. Occurrent intention and occurrent desire are other sorts of intentional mental occurrences whose contents are not so restricted. Volition to exert in a certain way is not a kind of occurrent desire to exert in that way. For one thing, volition is action and not desire; not even occurrent desire is action. For another thing, it is possible to have volition to exert a certain way without at the time in any way desiring or intending to exert in that way. This would happen, for example, if I were sure that my arm is paralyzed and tried to exert it just to see what it is like to experience inefficacious volition. If I were mistaken about my arm's being paralyzed, I would exert it voluntarily but not intentionally. This shows also that volition to exert in a certain way is not a kind of decision or intention to exert in that way.

Volition differs from deciding also in not being a single-shot mental act with a static content. Volition is a fluid mental activity whose content is continually changing. At each moment, it is concerned only with bodily exertion in the immediate present. I can all at one time decide to swim another length of the pool, but I cannot all at one time have the volition to make the whole sequence of bodily exertions involved in turning a doorknob and pulling the door open, any more than I can perform that sequence of exertions all at one time. Volition is part of the experience of voluntary exertion and its content, unlike the content of a decision or intention, is as much tied to the immediate present as is voluntary exertion itself.

As we approach an instant, the content of volitional activity approaches an unchanging, frozen proposition about the immediate present. What I will at a particular moment is to exert at that moment a determinate degree of force in a determinate direction with one or more parts of my body. I do not will to *move* my body. The content of volition at a moment is not concerned with movement, which takes time, but only with exertion of directed force at that moment. Temporally extended movements are the objects of intentions rather than volitions. Volitions do not plan ahead, not even a little bit. Volitions do not *plan* at all. They *execute* (or try to execute). I have an intention as to what course of movement my body is to take over the next few moments, and in light of that intention I go through a certain course of volitional activity over the period of the movement, willing at each point, in light of my perceptions, the directed force needed at that point to keep the movement on the path prescribed by my intention. Volition is analogous to steering with a steering wheel rather than to steering with buttons that trigger preset patterns of movement. If there are mental triggers of sequences of voluntary exertion (as there may be in familiar, practiced movements), the volitional activity is not the trigger but rather part of what is triggered.

When I exert voluntarily, my volition is not just that my body exert but that I exert with my body. I will not just exerting but exerting caused by me. I will that my willing—this very volition of whose content we speak—cause the exertion. The content must refer to the volition of which it is the content and say that this volition is to cause the body to exert in a certain way.

The content of my volition at an instant could be expressed by me in a proposition of the following form: "I will that this willing cause my bodily part B to exert force of degree F in direction D." Here F is a certain range of degrees of force. and D is a certain range of directions. What I will is never absolutely precise with respect to the degree or direction of the force. When I begin to move a lever, the degree and direction of the force exerted by my arm, as measurable by a precision instrument, could vary within certain limits and still fit the content of my volition. Gaining more finely tuned control of one's body is at least partly a matter of becoming able to will contents that are more determinate.

SECTION II

Several philosophers have put forward accounts of voluntary bodily action that incorporate something like volition but differ from the foregoing account of it in one way or another. Hugh McCann (1972, 1974, 1976 [all reprinted in McCann 1998]) presents an account that is nearly the same as the foregoing one. One minor difference is that on McCann's view, volition (willing) to exert entails intending to exert. John Searle (1983) gives to something he calls *intention in action* a role similar to the one given volition in the foregoing account in that it is the initial part, rather than a cause or accompaniment, of an action. But it differs in that an intention is not an action, whereas a volition is. Alvin Goldman (1976) gives the name "volition" to a certain kind of *occurrent desire*, but an occurrent desire is also not an action. Wilfrid Sellars (1976) gives the name to an *occurrent intention* or *decision* to act in a certain way; a decision is, like volition, a mental action, but a decision is intrinsically an intention to exert the body in a certain way, whereas a volition is not.

Larry Davis (1979) uses "volition" to name not a conscious mental activity of which we are directly aware but a functionally defined subconscious mental process that is not part of our experience but is posited by theory as that which causes the bodily exertion and the agent's belief that he or she is acting. Frederick Adams and Alfred Mele hold that "the major functional roles ascribed to volition are nicely filled by a triad composed of intention, trying, and information feedback" (1992, p. 323). Trying to A, on their account, "is an event or process that has A-ing as a goal and is initiated and (normally) sustained by a pertinent intention. Successful tryings to A, rather than causing A-ings, are A-ings." So, on their view, in one's voluntary exertion with one's limb, the trying to exert that is involved is to be identified not with a mental action that causes the exertion but with the whole voluntary exertion. There is no mental part of the action that causes the rest. Mele does hold (2002) that any action must have a proximal mental cause—namely, an intention to act straightaway.

According to Timothy O'Connor (2000), an action of a person involves *agent causation*. The mark of an action is that the agent, the enduring entity that is the person, and not any mental or other event causes the event parts of action. The initial event the agent causes in voluntarily exerting in a certain way could, on this view, be volition as characterized in section I above, but O'Connor himself takes it to be an "executive state of intention" to act in that way (p. 72).

The *tryings* of Jennifer Hornsby (1980) are mental actions and, in her account of action, play a role in causing bodily events analogous to that played by volition in the foregoing account. But on her account the momentary content of a trying can specify a temporally extended sequence of bodily exertion and even external consequences of these (for example, the content can be to open a door). This and the fact that for her a trying implies intending or desiring the content of the trying make her tryings significantly different from the volitions described section I.

See also Determinism, A Historical Survey; Goldman, Alvin; Searle, John; Sellars, Wilfrid.

Bibliography

Adams, Frederick, and Alfred R. Mele. "The Intention/Volition Debate." *Canadian Journal of Philosophy* 22 (1992): 323–338.

Davis, Lawrence. *Theory of Action*. Englewood Cliffs, NJ: Prentice-Hall, 1979.

Ginet, Carl. *On Action*. New York: Cambridge University Press, 1990.

Goldman, Alvin. "The Volitional Theory Revisited." In *Action Theory*, edited by Myles Brand and Douglas Walton. Dordrecht: D. Reidel, 1976.

Hornsby, Jennifer. *Actions*. London: Routledge & Kegan Paul, 1980.

James, William. "The Will." Chap. 27 in *Principles of Psychology*. 2 vols. Mineola, NY: Dover Publications, 1950.

Libet, Benjamin, Anthony Freeman, and Keith Sutherland, eds. *The Volitional Brain: Towards a Neuroscience of Free Will*. Imprint Academic, 1999.

McCann, Hugh. "Is Raising One's Arm a Basic Action?" *Journal of Philosophy* 68 (1972): 235–250.

McCann, Hugh. "Trying, Paralysis, and Volition." *Review of Metaphysics* 28 (1976): 423–442.

McCann, Hugh. "Volition and Basic Action." *Philosophical Review* 83 (1974): 451–473.

McCann, Hugh. *The Works of Agency*. Ithaca, NY: Cornell University Press, 1998.

Mele, Alfred. *Motivation and Agency*. New York: Oxford University Press, 2003.

O'Connor, Timothy. *Persons and Causes: The Metaphysics of Free Will*. New York: Oxford University Press, 2000.

Searle, John. *Intentionality*. Cambridge, U.K.: Cambridge University Press, 1983.

Sellars, Wilfrid. "Volitions Re-Affirmed." In *Action Theory*, edited by Myles Brand and Douglas Walton. Dordrecht: D. Reidel, 1976.

Carl Ginet (2005)

VOLNEY, CONSTANTIN-FRANÇOIS DE CHASSEBOEUF, COMTE DE

(1757–1820)

Constantin-François de Chasseboeuf, comte de Volney, the French *philosophe* and historian, was born in Anjou. He early showed a scholarly disposition, and at fifteen he asked for Hebrew lessons in order to verify translations of the Bible. Inheriting independent wealth, he left for Paris at seventeen, turned down his father's plea to study law, and, interested in the relation between the moral and the physical aspects of man, chose medicine instead. He also pursued his study of history and languages, and he became involved in the polemics and ideological struggles of the time. In 1783 he gave himself the name Volney and left for Egypt and Syria "to acquire new knowledge and embellish the rest of my life by an aura of respect and esteem." After eight months in a Coptic monastery, devoted to mastering Arabic, he spent three and a half years traveling on foot throughout Egypt and Syria. The resulting *Voyage en Égypte et Syrie* (1787) is his most enduring production. A remarkable travel book, it differs from those of the romantic travelers (such as François René de Chateaubriand) by its impersonality and its careful, objective account of physical, political, and moral conditions. It was used as a guide by Napoleon Bonaparte's armies.

After his return to France, his prestige assured, he was placed in charge of commercial relations with Corsica and, on the outbreak of the Revolution, was elected a representative of the third estate. His revolutionary career was quite distinguished; he defended civil rights and freedoms, attacked the church strongly, and later opposed the excesses of the Jacobins. In 1792 he bought land in Corsica and showed how products of the New World could be successfully transplanted. There he met and became friendly with Napoleon, whose greatness he foresaw. Forced to leave because of unrest in Corsica, he subsequently spent ten months in prison, falsely accused of being a royalist, until he was released after the ninth of Thermidor. Appointed professor of history in the new École Normale, he developed a critical methodology for historical investigation. When that institution was suppressed in 1795, he went to the United States. Well received by George Washington, he was happy at first. John Adams, however, was unforgiving of Volney's severe criticisms of his political writings, and he felt an animosity toward the French as a result of the XYZ Affair. In addition, a theological quarrel with Joseph Priestley, who was then in America, did not dispose Adams favorably toward visiting philosophers. Accused of being a secret agent, Volney was forced to leave America in 1798, but by then he had traveled all over the country. In 1803 he published *Tableau du climat et du sol des États-Unis d'Amérique*, an objective description famous for its picture of Niagara Falls; in the preface he told of his persecutions.

Back in France, Volney cooperated in Napoleon's coup of the 18th Brumaire and was named senator. However, he frequently opposed Napoleon's dictatorial tendencies, and he also opposed the Concordat of 1801. Napoleon ridiculed him along with his whole group of *idéologues* (including Pierre Cabanis and Comte Antoine Destutt de Tracy), but he later made Volney a count. Volney, however, supported the Restoration and was rewarded with a peerage. Volney was known for his independence and for his ill-tempered, overbearing character.

WORKS

Volney's most famous work is *Les ruines, ou Méditations sur les révolutions des empires* (1791), a work conceived in Benjamin Franklin's study in Paris. Widely read and admired during his lifetime and later, it now seems a shallow piece of rhetoric. It was much read in English, under the title *The Ruins of Empires* (1792). The author contemplates the ruins of Palmyra and wonders how powerful empires, seemingly destined to last forever, succumbed to the universal law of change and destruction. A belated example of "philosophic" polemics, *Les ruines* promoted deism by a comparative study of religious doctrines and practices, preached tolerance and free inquiry, the unalienable rights of men and peoples, and the right of self-government. Some ethical ideas were sketched, which Volney developed in *La loi naturelle*. Thus, man in the state of nature "did not see at his side beings descended from the heavens to inform him of his needs which he owes only to his senses, to instruct him of duties which are born solely of his needs."

Even more interesting as a reflection of moderate views held by *philosophes* at the end of the century is Volney's *La loi naturelle, ou Catéchisme du citoyen français* (1792). In this work he affirmed a natural law given by God, but this natural law is essentially physical ("the regular and constant order by which God rules the universe"). The moral aspect of natural law is only an extension of the biological requirement for self-preservation and "perfection" on the part of the individual and the species. Consequently, morals could become an exact science. In this work, as in *Les ruines*, Volney praised the harmony and order of relationships in the universe, declaring that man is no exception to their rule; yet within this impersonal natural law he discerned purpose and final causes, namely, the happiness and perfection of the individual. Physical suffering has a useful natural function, and the advantage of greater sensitivity in man is compensated by the disadvantage of greater suffering. Law is a command (or prohibition) followed by reward or punishment. Moral law depends on general and constant rules of conduct that inhere in the order of things. Moral law is not obvious; rather, it forms "in its developments and consequences, a complex ensemble that requires the knowledge of many facts and all the sagacity of reasoning." The basic principle of natural law is self-preservation, not happiness, which is "an article of luxury." Pleasure and pain are the mechanisms by which natural law works. Men are aware of these laws only in society. Life in society is man's true natural state, since it is necessary for his self-preservation; in what is called the state of nature, man was only a miserable brute. Volney's formulations reveal the infiltration of naturalistic viewpoints into natural law theory. The whole moral dimension of human life is reduced to a basic biological law, and all of morality is based on narrow utilitarian values.

Volney was also the author of works on biblical chronology (hostile to orthodox interpretations) and on ancient history. He proposed a universal alphabet and the study of culture through language.

See also Cabanis, Pierre-Jean Georges; Chateaubriand, François René de; Deism; Destutt de Tracy, Antoine Louis Claude, Comte; Franklin, Benjamin; Laws of Nature; Priestley, Joseph.

Bibliography

Volney's complete works were published as *Oeuvres complètes* in 8 volumes (Paris, 1821) and in 11 volumes (Brussels, 1822).

For literature on Volney, see J. Barni, *Les moralistes français au XVIIIe siècle* (Paris, 1873); J. Gaulmier, *Volney* (Paris, 1959); and A. Picavet, *Les idéologues* (Paris, 1891).

See also Counihan, Roberat D., "The Political Philosophy of Volney: Case History of French Revolutionary Intellectualism" (MA thesis; University of North Carolina, Chapel Hill, 1969).

L. G. Crocker (1967)

VOLSKI, STANISLAV

(1880–1936?)

Stanislav Volski was the assumed name of Andrei Vladimirovich Sokolov, the Russian Marxist journalist and philosopher. Volski studied at Moscow University but was expelled in 1899. He was active in the Bolshevik faction until March 1917, when he broke with V. I. Lenin. In 1909 Volski published the only pre-Soviet book-length treatise on Marxist ethical theory, but its "Nietzschean" individualism had little impact on the development of Marxism-Leninism. In the 1920s and 1930s Volski was reduced to the status of literary popularizer and translator. The date and circumstances of his death are still unknown.

According to Volski, class solidarity and discipline are tactically essential to victory in the class struggle, but all binding norms will vanish with the defeat of capitalism. Under socialism individuals will be "freed from the numbing pattern of coercive norms" and from the "idea of duty," the "inevitable companion of bourgeois society" (*Filosofiya Borby,* p. 272).

Volski saw societies as weapons that individuals use in their struggle with nature. Typically, in bourgeois societies (based on fixed division of labor), individuals are free to develop only within the narrow confines of their occupational specialties. As a result they are self-alienated, conformist, and myopic. But in socialist society (based on variable division of labor), harmoniously self-determining individuals will grow into unique selfhood as ends in themselves. Their absolute value as persons will not be a formal postulate or imperative, as was claimed by the Russian Kantian Marxists, but rather a goal to be achieved by free struggle and social creativity. In this process "the socialization of methods is accompanied by an individualization of goals" (ibid., p. 300). "Struggle," Volski declared, "is the joy of being," and "socialism is freedom of struggle; everything that increases struggle is good, everything that diminishes it is bad" (ibid., pp. 306, 302).

Assimilating Friedrich Nietzsche's insight that "enemy" means not "villain," but "opponent," Volski claimed that I should grant full freedom to the individual whose ideal is inimical to mine and that I should strive to make him an "integral personality," working with him to remove external obstacles to our sharp and clear collision. In struggling with me, he enriches me, enlivening my highest values. "Of all those who surround me, … the most precious, most essential is he with whom I struggle for life and death." He is both friend and enemy, and we share the "morality of 'friend-enemies'—the morality of the future" (ibid., pp. 310, 311).

See also Lenin, Vladimir Il'ich; Marxist Philosophy; Nietzsche, Friedrich; Russian Philosophy; Socialism.

Bibliography

Filosofiya Borby: Opyt Postroyeniya Etiki Marksizma (The philosophy of struggle: an essay in Marxist ethics). Moscow, 1909.

Sotsialnaya Revolyutsiya na Zapade i v Rossi (The social revolution in the West and in Russia). Moscow, 1917.

"Volski." In *Bolshaya Sovetskaya Entsiklopediya* (Great Soviet encyclopedia), 1st ed. Moscow, 1929. Vol. XIII, Cols. 66–67.

George L. Kline (1967)

VOLTAIRE, FRANÇOIS-MARIE AROUET DE
(1694–1778)

François-Marie Arouet de Voltaire encapsulates the spirit of the French Enlightenment in both his refusal to develop a philosophical system and his clear concern for social and political issues. But he is also representative of the eighteenth century in his deep attachment to John Locke's epistemological thought, his emphasis on the limited nature of human understanding, and his commitment to popularizing philosophy, especially by handling it through the medium of novels and tales in which irony often functions as an ad hominem argument. It is thus that he fulfilled the role of philosopher and that his philosophy met the needs of his times, times characterized by a break with seventeenth-century dogmatism and an intensification of the critique of the political and religious spheres aiming to bring forth a morality on the human scale, centered on the values of tolerance and respect for others. Those values were soon to bear fruit in the doctrine of the Rights of Man.

Born in Paris to an established bourgeois Parisian family, François-Marie Arouet, who took the name Voltaire in 1718, received a sound education from his Jesuit teachers at the Collège Louis-le-Grand and soon managed to make his way into the most brilliant Parisian intellectual milieu of his time. There, he gave evidence of his poetic talent and satiric verve—the latter cost him a brief exile to the Netherlands in 1713 and periods of imprisonment in the Bastille in 1717–1718. In the years that followed, he issued an epic poem, *Henriade* (1723), celebrating the tolerance of King Henry IV of France and entrenching his literary prestige on the Parisian intellectual scene. A romantic quarrel with the chevalier de Rohan in 1726 resulted in Voltaire's being exiled to England, where he lived until 1728, taking advantage of the circumstances to improve his English and absorb English culture, especially in the field of philosophy. During this period, he read William Shakespeare, deepened his knowledge of Locke and Isaac Newton, became familiar with Deism, and made the acquaintance of Jonathan Swift, Alexander Pope, John Gay, and doubtless George Berkeley. This sojourn also enabled him to take a detached perspective on French intellectual, political, and religious life.

On his return to France, he published *Temple du goût* (1733), which anticipates his praise for French classicism in 1751 in *Siècle de Louis XIV*; *Épître à Uranie* (1732), an early challenge to the notion of divine goodness; and the famous *Lettres philosophiques* (1734), which contain the essentials of the philosophical plan he subsequently sought to carry out. These were followed by *Remarques sur les pensées de Pascal* (1734). The publication of *Lettres philosophiques*, which discredited the regime under which France was governed by contrasting it to the more liberal English model, resulted in exile once again, this time to the home of Madame du Châtelet in Lorraine. Voltaire took advantage of this extended retreat (1734–1749)—which was broken up by excursions to Paris and Sceaux to advance his candidacy for official positions (historiographer royal in 1745 and election to the Académie française in 1746)—to produce the some fifty tragedies and comedies that won him literary renown; gather together documents on history; work on philosophy (*Traité de métaphysique* dates from 1734); and publish his *Éléments de la philosophie de Newton* (1738), on the thinker with whose approach to physics Voltaire's metaphysical theism was in sympathy.

After Madame du Châtelet's death in 1749 and a brief stay in Paris, Voltaire went into voluntary exile at the court of Frederick II of Prussia, with whom he had been corresponding for years. It was during his Prussian period, in 1751, that he published *Siècle de Louis XIV*. A quarrel with Frederick about a diatribe against Pierre-Louis Moreau de Maupertuis published by Voltaire led to his departure from Berlin in 1753. He went to Paris and from there to Geneva, Switzerland, where he settled in 1755. His Geneva period saw the start of his collaboration on the *Encyclopédie*, the publication of his *Essai sur les moeurs* (1756), and the production of works, like the celebrated *Candide*, that were increasingly critical of established religion. To protect himself against possible reprisal, Voltaire decided in 1760 to permanently settle in Ferney, France, which sits near the French-Swiss border. It was here that he became truly celebrated and his home took its place among the most fertile centers of intellectual activity of the time, thanks to his sustained correspondence with the elite of Europe, including Catherine II of Russia. Here, too, he wrote many novels and tales that enhanced his fame and he took up his role as the opponent of injustice, defending victims of intolerance and fanaticism. A case in point is his well-known struggle on behalf of the Protestant merchant Jean Calas, who was unjustly condemned, tortured, and executed.

Voltaire's struggles to promote religious tolerance cannot be viewed separately from his all-out attack on Catholicism in many vigorously worded pamphlets such as *Sermon des Cinquante* (1762), *Questions sur les miracles* (1765), and *Examen important de Milord Bolingbroke, ou le tombeau du fanatisme* (1767). However, it was his battles in defense of justice that won him a special place in the hearts of his contemporaries, who gave him a triumphant welcome on his return to Paris in 1778 to present the last of his tragedies, *Irène*. Voltaire died in Paris on May 30, 1778, aged eighty-four. The clergy of that city refused to give him a Christian burial, so his body was transported to the Abbey of Scellières, near Troyes. Subsequently, during the Revolutionary period, his remains were returned to Paris and buried in the Pantheon.

PHILOSOPHY

Although he was fully familiar with the French tradition, especially Michel Eyquem de Montaigne, Pierre Gassendi, René Descartes, and Pierre Bayle, thinkers with a common interest in skepticism, following his stay in London Voltaire drew the essentials of his philosophical position from the English tradition. From Locke's thought, he adopted the critique of the notion of innate ideas; the role assigned to philosophical inquiry as the means for best determining the faculties and limits of human understanding; and the acceptance of the unknowable nature of the essence of things. These precepts set him on the road to ontological skepticism. Doubt regarding external things was mirrored by doubt about human interiority, concerning that it is possible to believe that its distinguishing constituent, thought, is nothing more than a product of matter. Locke had indicated the possibility of "thinking matter" and Voltaire gives him a degree of credit for this but does not attempt to decide the question, because, as he says in *Le philosophe ignorant* (1767), one's knowledge of substance, whether material or spiritual, is not a given:

> Once again, what I am saying is not that it is matter that thinks in us; I am saying, with [Locke], that it does not behoove us to state it is impossible for God to cause matter to think, that it is absurd to state this, and that it is not up to earthworms to limit the power of the Supreme Being. (Art. 29; in *Oeuvres complètes*, ed. Moland, vol. 26).

Is Voltaire duping his readers here to lead them toward atheism? Not at all. His invocation of the divine is sincere and flows from his engagement with English thought. For it is from Newton that he drew the notion that the universe is a manifestation of the existence of God and that gravitational physics appears to prove that matter submits to the laws decreed by its creator. In response to criticism of Newton that characterized gravitational attraction as an occult quality of a kind equivalent to the notorious Cartesian vortices, Voltaire bent to the task of showing that an unknown cause can be proven to exist from its effects. Thus, even if attraction is not a perceivable thing, it is nevertheless the case that its existence is a true fact, because it is possible to prove its effects and calculate its proportions, even while acknowledging that this phenomenon's ends are hidden from one and known to God alone. Along the road to probabilistic knowledge of the natural order, Newton had opened up a way by proposing a procedure featuring the integrity and prudence implied by the watchword *hypothesis non fingo* (I feign no hypotheses). Allying Locke with Newton thus led Voltaire to a theistic vision consisting, on the one hand, of admitting the existence of God, conceived as the sole necessary being—but without saying anything about God's attributes nor the ends of God's creation—while on the other hand admitting the existence of a finite and contingent matter that requires divine aid to be set in motion.

METAPHYSICS

THE ONTOLOGICAL STATUS OF REALITY. Anticipating the definition of metaphysics proposed by Étienne Bonnot de Condillac in his *Essai sur l'origine des connaissances humaines* (1746), in which "ambitious metaphysics," which presumes to discover all and know all, is distinguished from "restrained metaphysics," which contains its inquiries within the limits of the weaknesses of the human mind, Voltaire, following in Locke's footsteps, conceives of metaphysics as a naturally limited science whose methods can only be founded on empiricism. As he wrote to Frederick II, "Metaphysics, in my opinion, is made up of two things, the first what all men of good sense know, the second what they will never know." In this light, Voltaire's skepticism can be termed *Zetetic* (to make use of an ancient term): that is, it is perennially in search of truth, even though truth is by nature destined to escape it, and it perennially revisits its own assumptions, accepting that over time some of its initial convictions will be subjected to critique or abandoned.

If there is one point on which Voltaire's position was to remain unchanged, it is surely the existence of two opposed substances: God and matter. His conviction on this score led him to oppose both the materialists and Berkeley's immaterialism. Still, Voltaire's conception of the relationship between these two substances underwent continuous change. The existence of matter appears obvious, at least in its phenomenal manifestation: it is sufficient to allow objects to take their effect on the senses to be persuaded of their presence. Belief in the existence of God rests on two banal proofs, recalled in *Traité de métaphysique*: the proof from ultimate causation (God is the architect of a world that acknowledges its Demiurge) and the proof *a contingentia mundi*, according to which the ultimate reason for things can only be found in a necessary Being who constitutes the ultimate explanation for them. (Voltaire subsequently abandoned the latter proof, retaining only the teleological one.) There flows from this the existence of this necessary Being, conceived as infinite, whose infinity is expressed through its eternity, immensity, and omnipotence. One can see why Voltaire opposed materialism all his life: it appeared to him to be an untenable form of reductionism, as well as to confuse two distinct levels by ascribing the quality of necessity to necessarily contingent matter.

Having acknowledged the existence of two substances, it is necessary to consider their relationship and in particular the two delicate matters of creation and of the existence of evil. The problem of creation is presented as early as *Traité de métaphysique* in the form of a set of alternatives: Either God drew the world out of nothingness or else he drew the world out of himself. The first alternative is doubtful: How can something be drawn from nothing? The second is equally so: It comes down to conceiving the world as a part of the divine essence. Logically, then, one must conclude that the world has eternal existence, but that would presuppose an eternity other than divine eternity.

The hypothesis of God's freedom makes it possible to settle this question: It is because God is free that he created the world at the moment he wished to. However, this brings one back to the first difficulty, that of creation ex nihilo, which was deemed untenable from the outset. As early as the *Éléments* in 1738, Voltaire had turned to the concept of divine decree to reconsider the idea of the existence of necessary and eternal matter. In *Tout en Dieu*, he explains the eternity of matter with a simple argument: Since God is the first cause and every cause has effects, one can conclude that God has been acting for all eternity and therefore that the material world is eternal. In 1768, in *Philosophe ignorant*, Voltaire was to reach the inevitable conclusion implied by this argument when he reasoned that the world is a form of eternal emanation from God, while guarding against pantheistic slippage and definitively rejecting the Christian concept of creation ex nihilo.

THE PHENOMENAL STATUS OF REALITY So much for relations between God and the material world. What of the more specific relationship between the soul and the body? First, it is necessary to be able to be sure of the existence of the soul. Now, if God has the power to give to matter the possibility of thought, why would he burden himself with useless substance? Called on to choose between pure idealism and strict materialism, Voltaire preferred to invoke his ignorance of this subject and to maintain doubt, "because it is just as presumptuous to say that a body organized by God Himself cannot receive the thought of God Himself as it is ridiculous to say that spirit cannot think" (*Philosophe ignorant*, art. 29; in *Oeuvres complètes*, ed. Moland, vol. 26). It is easy to foresee that doubt would also prevail on the question of the form taken by human freedom, which may in reality consist of pure material determinism or be a reflection within one of divine freedom.

In fact, over time, Voltaire did come close to a deterministic position that led him, in the name of the principle of parsimony (which makes it superfluous to hypothesize a soul acting on the body), to explain the process of cognition wholly in materialist terms and to deny the Cartesian concepts of liberty of indifference and free will. Thus, in the entry on freedom in the *Dictionnaire philosophique*, *freedom* is defined strictly in negative terms, as the ability to do what one wishes, or rather as will that is determined by the set of causes that constitute the world —causes that ultimately refer to a prime mover that is their reason. The materialism that makes it possible to describe the order of the world and the laws of that order, and thus human actions as a part of it, must always be framed as being dependent on a spiritual principle that is alone capable of explaining its proper functioning. This accounts for Voltaire's glowing praise of Nicolas Malebranche in *Tout en Dieu*, since occasionalism is the system that provides the most correct explanation for the interactions that occur in the world, which at bottom have only one true cause: God.

PHILOSOPHICAL OPTIMISM

Whereas Voltaire's position on the question of creation and divine and human freedom evolved only somewhat, there is one problem in connection with which his intellectual evolution was radical, that of the existence of evil. In his early writings, he seems not to grasp the real difficulty posed by the existence of physical and moral suffering (and in this he is close to Pope and Gottfried Wilhelm Leibniz), making it vanish by adopting the perspective of the whole: If, since God himself is good, the organization of the universe as a whole is good, then the evil that one sees appearing here and there is justified at the holistic level. Indeed, it may not even be evil, since the notion of evil is always relative and its existence undoubtedly has a function, that of revealing the beauty of the whole, just as shadows are necessary to accentuate the effects of light in a picture.

But the 1755 Lisbon earthquake played for Voltaire the role that Auschwitz and Dachau played for philosophers in the second half of the twentieth century: it was a revelation of evil that is absolute because wholly gratuitous. *Poème sur le désastre de Lisbonne* (1756) and *Candide* (1759) show Voltaire attaining awareness of the positive existence of evil, evil that appears to have no possible justification. And yet God exists and, as a free being, he must be responsible for the disasters caused by the natural laws that he has willed. Must one therefore assign the fault to God, which would constitute true blasphemy? Voltaire is unafraid to affirm precisely that: since evil exists, it must be necessary that this be so, with evil being a necessary condition of divine action. In contrast to Leibniz, who claims to justify the existence of evil and thus rescue the principle of God's goodness, Voltaire seeks to excuse God by showing that undoubtedly he did his best but did not create the best of all possible worlds, and by acknowledging that the ultimate explanation for the reality of evil exceeds the bounds of one's understanding.

RELIGION AND ETHICS

If one restricts oneself to the etymological significance of the word *religion*, which evokes the linking of individuals to one another, Voltaire must be said not to have had a religion, because for him the relationship with the divine is strictly personal and requires no collective rite. But if one agrees to conceive of religion as a specific relationship linking the human to the divine, Voltaire was a fully religious person. To be religious is, for Voltaire to worship God as the reasonable cause of everything that happens; to thank him for having allowed one to benefit from it and marvel at it; and not to seek to adopt the divine perspective and claim thereby to understand its decrees, but to wish humbly to understand why something that happens in one way does not happen in another. It is thus up to reason to lead one to the Supreme Being, which is itself universal reason, and not up to faith, which wraps things up in mystery and relies on miracles to better subordinate weak minds and enable priests to exercise power over them. Voltaire's theism is in no sense a natural theology; but it aims to be a purified form of natural religion, along the lines set down by Herbert of Cherbury, and is wholly opposed to both positive religion and atheism.

Voltaire's opposition to atheism is categorical and rests on a simple argument: The laws of the physical world are so reasonable that they necessarily presuppose an intelligent artisan. His opposition to established religion is equally categorical. His celebrated watchword, "*Écrasez l'infâme* (Erase the infamy)," is a reminder of how violently he struggled against Christianity, especially toward the end of his life, when fear of political power, the enforcer of religious power, had diminished in him. His exasperation was directed less against the message of Christ, which he incorporated into a universalist conception of human values, than against what the church as an institution had done with that message and against the methods it had used to disseminate it (e.g., superstition, the worship of relics, faith in miracles, the establishment of the Inquisition, and incitement to fanaticism).

In his struggle against "*l'infâme*," he used every available weapon and did not hesitate to borrow alike from Christians and atheists, skeptics and deists,—those of their arguments that seemed to him the strongest. Over the course of this long struggle, Voltaire's immense erudition stood him in good stead, and he was effective at searching out the most convincing reasoning wherever necessary, turning to the European scholarship of previous centuries as well as to his contemporaries. He invoked Italian (Giordano Bruno and Giulio Cesare Vanini), English (John Toland, Anthony Collins, Matthew Tindal, Thomas Woolston, Henry St. John Bolingbroke, and Thomas Chubb), German (Henricus Cornelius Agrippa von Nettesheim, and Desiderius Erasmus), and French writers (Théophile de Viau, Jacques Vallée des Barreaux, François de La Mothe Le Vayer, Charles de Marguetel de Saint-Denis [Seigneur de Saint-Évremond], Pierre Bayle, and Julien Offray de La Mettrie).

In 1762, Voltaire went so far as to publish a long extract from the *Testament* of Jean Meslier, a text that was extremely hard on Christianity, written by one who knew it well because he had served it for many years as the curé of Étrépigny, France. Voltaire took care to touch up the text perceptibly, with a view to preserving natural religion and keeping only those criticisms that targeted revealed religion. Why preserve natural religion and not be satisfied with an internal religion that would amount at bottom to a system of morality? This is accounted for by Voltaire's anthropological pessimism. Human beings would not respect the rules of morality if there was no religion to bring those rules before their consciences. In truth, religion and morality are one and the same, as is to be inferred from a formulation found in chapter 4 of the *Oreilles du comte de Chesterfield et le chapelain Goudman* (1775): "Let us do our duty to God, let us worship Him, let us be just: that is what our true praise and true prayers consist of." (*Oeuvres complètes*, ed. Moland, vol. 39). In other words, religion is the morality of the weak and morality the religion of the strong. It would be possible to do without religion if everyone was wise and respected the moral law engraved in every heart. But that is not the case, and that is why religion retains its usefulness, as does the notion of punishment and reward following death, which alone can serve to temper bad inclinations and make social life not only possible but indeed agreeable.

But what morality is one speaking of, and how does Voltaire picture it? On this score, it is possible to draw an analogy between the natural world and the moral world. Just as the laws of the natural world can be uncovered by one who applies one's intelligence to the matter, those of the moral world are unveiled if one takes the trouble to reflect on them; and in light of such reflection, they lead one to distinguish right from wrong. What makes it possible to differentiate morality from particular systems of ethics specific to a given people is its universality, that it transcends not just borders but centuries. The beauty of a moral act does not change with time; the truth of moral values is not subject to relativism. Thus, it will always be right to defend the poor and the oppressed and always wrong to condemn without proof. That is how setting an example of virtue by practicing it confers a kind of immortality. In the West, Socrates exemplifies this truth; in the East, Confucius. At bottom, in the eyes of Voltaire (who on this score is heir to the Greeks), a philosopher's value resides more in the way he or she has lived life than in the system he or she has sought to build.

JUSTICE AND TOLERATION

Voltaire's involvement in social issues can be explained on the basis of his philosophical convictions. Since moral law exists, it must operate to the benefit of others and rest on the justice one owes to other natural beings, human beings in particular. In fact, virtue is nothing more than beneficence directed toward one's neighbor. The inverse is also true: Vice is malice directed toward that same neighbor. In this connection, nothing aroused greater indignation in Voltaire than the excesses of religious fanaticism. Under the Ancien Régime, these excesses were tolerated politically, the government often serving as an accomplice to them and never as the detached judge of collective passions or of the crying injustices to which such passions gave rise. In the manner of an anthropologist, Voltaire ascribed the weakness for fanaticism to Westerners only, ever concerned to seek the welfare of others even at their own expense and seeing in Easterners a willingness to be satisfied with complete indifference to their neighbors.

In light of these views, it is possible to understand Voltaire's militant stance in favor of enlightened despotism: It is the corollary of his anthropological pessimism, requiring a strong but just prince to ensure that the diverse factions that constitute the state do not destroy each other. For Voltaire was not just a philosopher; he was also a historian, and he knew that, because human beings prey on each other, barbarity is always at the gates, bringing the possibility of massacres in its train. Voltaire sought to serve as the unquiet watchman of the Enlightenment, to ensure that the light shed by his times should not be swallowed up in total darkness.

Voltaire played this role of watchman by defending unjustly accused contemporaries, as witness his efforts on behalf of Pierre-Paul Sirven, Thomas Arthur Lally, baron De Tollendal, the Chevalier Jean-François de La Barre, and especially Calas *père* and *fils*. With the Calas affair, the most celebrated cause defended by Voltaire, tolerance became his primary concern and, little by little, he let go of reflection in favor of action, conscious that only involvement by philosophers makes the exercise of justice possible and that, without such involvement, justice would remain an abstract notion reigning over a heaven of Platonic ideas.

In *Traité sur la tolérance à l'occasion de la mort de Jean Calas* (1763), one can discern Voltaire's method for bringing about the triumph of a cause that he deems just. This work is a treatise in name only: It brings together an account of the Calas affair with past examples of fanaticism, general historical reflections on tolerance, a dialogue between a dying man and a well man, and a letter to the Jesuit Father Le Tellier, all designed to reveal the possible breakdown of tolerance, before concluding with an account of the most recent decree regarding the Calas family. Making use of all the stylistic resources Voltaire had at his disposal, this work seeks to convince by playing on readers' emotions. Taking readers from laughter to tears, it designedly forces them to pity the Calas family, a technique calculated to bring about awareness of the Calases' true misfortune.

Voltaire undoubtedly realized early on that his struggle would not suffice if it were not backed up by a complete recasting of legislation with a view to limiting injustice. This is what lies behind his strong interest in Cesare Bonesana Beccaria's masterwork, *Essay on Crimes and Punishment*, which he read and commented on with minute attention. His reading of Beccaria led him to believe that only judicial reform would make possible the real-life implementation of Enlightenment ideals. An echo of this concept of judicial reform is found in his *Prix de la justice et de l'humanité* (1777), composed one year before his death. Here, Voltaire advances his vision of a society built on just laws, one that prefers prevention to punishment, tolerance to fanaticism. He lauds the principle that the punishment should fit the crime and criticizes capital punishment and recourse to torture; and he insists the law must have a public nature and must not be obeyed unless it is known to all (as Thomas Hobbes had already stipulated in *Leviathan*). Furthermore, the law must be applied by judges of integrity, chosen on the basis of merit and not by reason of their social origins. In this regard, Voltaire is one of the main sources of inspiration for the ideals of the French Revolution.

HISTORICAL PHILOSOPHY

Voltaire's historical project cannot be dissociated from his philosophical and moral concerns. Once again, an analogy helps clarify the point: Since both the natural world and the moral world are governed by laws, it must also be possible to identify those of the historical world. To do so, a rigorous method is necessary, one that admits only acknowledged facts and repudiates mythical discourse, just as Voltaire undertook to do in his *Histoire de Charles XII* (1739). More than a methodology, historical work must have its own proper end, that of extracting coherent meaning from the mass of historical data. It is for this reason that, in *Siècle de Louis XIV*, Voltaire abandons narrative history (the approach he had taken with *Charles XII*, for example) in favor of a more general historiography—philosophical this time—that seeks to present the state of mind of a century and not to analyze the personal strengths and shortcomings of an individual. In thus depicting a vast panorama of human history, in which individual actions are brought into relation with an organized whole, Voltaire anticipates the Hegelian concept of the spirit of a people (*Volksgeist*).

It is with *Essai sur les moeurs et l'esprit des nations* (1756), however, that Voltaire let go the approach of a history limited to an individual or a century, to seek to extract from a mass of historical data a vision of human becoming made possible by an analysis of the mores and spirit of nations. Thus, rather than perceiving in the long view of history a movement toward salvation, as had Jacques Bénigne Bossuet in his *Discours sur l'histoire universelle*, Voltaire sees in it the immanent progress of civilization founded ultimately on universal morality and rationality. This movement of universal reason, however, does not have the character of necessity, since breaches of universal moral obligation are always possible. The concept of a universal history is merely a way of expressing a finding that one reports on in one's capacity as a historian reflecting on human history as a whole. This finding comes down to the view that it is reasonable to believe that the essence of reason consists of a permanent striving toward the good. As to knowing whether this is really so, and especially whether it will always be so in the future, Voltaire refrains from judgment: here as elsewhere, he adopts the role of skeptic rather than that of dogmatist.

See also Agrippa von Nettesheim, Henricus Cornelius; Atheism; Bayle, Pierre; Berkeley, George; Bolingbroke, Henry St. John; Bossuet, Jacques Bénigne; Bruno, Giordano; Chubb, Thomas; Clandestine Philosophical Literature in France; Collins, Anthony; Condillac, Étienne Bonnot de; Deism; Descartes, René; Enlightenment; Erasmus, Desiderius; Ethics, History of; Gassendi, Pierre; Gay, John; Innate Ideas; La Mettrie, Julien Offray de; La Mothe Le Vayer, François de; Leibniz,

Gottfried Wilhelm; Locke, John; Meslier, Jean; Montaigne, Michel Eyquem de; Newton, Isaac; Pessimism and Optimisim; Philosophy of History; Pope, Alexander; Socrates; Swift, Jonathan; Tindal, Matthew; Toland, John; Vanini, Giulio Cesare; Woolston, Thomas.

Bibliography

WORKS BY VOLTAIRE

Oeuvres complètes. 53 vols., edited by L. Moland. Paris: Garnier frères, 1877–1885.

Voltaire's Correspondence. 135 vols., edited by Theodore Besterman. Geneva, Switzerland: Institut et Musée Voltaire, 1953–1977.

Complete Works of Voltaire. 85 vols., edited by Theodore Besterman, W. H. Barber, and N. Cronk, Geneva, Switzerland: Institut et Musée Voltaire, 1968–2001.

Corpus des notes marginales de Voltaire. 5 vols. Berlin: Akademie-Verlag, 1979–1994.

WORKS ABOUT VOLTAIRE

Besterman, Theodore. *Studies on Voltaire and the Eighteenth Century*. 380 vols. Geneva, Switzerland: Insitut et Musée Voltaire, 1956–2000.

Brooks, Richard A. *Voltaire and Leibniz*. Geneva, Switzerland: Librairie Droz, 1964.

Brumfitt, John H. *Voltaire, Historian*. London: Oxford University Press, 1958.

Carré, Jean Raoul. *Consistance de Voltaire le philosophe*. Paris: Boivin et cie, 1938.

Dédéyan, Charles. *Voltaire et la pensée anglaise*. Paris: Centre de documentation universitaire, 1956.

Gay, Peter. *Voltaire's Politics: The Poet as Realist*. Princeton, NJ: Princeton University Press, 1959.

Goulemot, Jean, André Magnan, and Didier Masseau, eds. *Inventaire Voltaire*. Paris: Gallimard, 1995.

Lanson, Gustave. *Voltaire*. Paris: Hachette et cie, 1906.

Lauer, Rosemary Z. *The Mind of Voltaire: A Study in His "Constructive Deism."* Westminster, MD: Newman Press, 1961.

Lepape, Pierre. *Voltaire le conquérant: Naissance des intellectuels au siècle des Lumières*. Paris: Editions du Seuil, 1994.

Maestro, Marcello T. *Voltaire and Beccaria as Reformers of Criminal Law*. New York: Columbia University Press, 1942.

Martin-Haag, Éliane. *Voltaire: du cartésianisme aux Lumières*. Paris: Vrin, 2002.

McKenna, Antony. *De Pascal à Voltaire: Le rôle des Pensées de Pascal dans l'histoire des idées entre 1670 et 1734*. 2 vols. Oxford, U.K.: The Voltaire Foundation at the Taylor Institution, 1990.

Pellissier, Georges. *Voltaire philosophe*. Paris: A. Colin, 1908.

Pomeau, René. *La religion de Voltaire*. Paris: Librairie Nizet, 1956.

Pomeau, René. *Politique de Voltaire*. Paris: A. Colin, 1963.

Porset, Charles. *Voltaire humaniste*. Paris: Editions maçonniques de France, 2003.

Ridgeway, Ronald S. *La propagande philosophique dans les tragédies de Voltaire*. Geneva, Switzerland: Institut et Musée Voltaire, 1961.

Schwarszbach, Bertram Eugene. *Voltaire's Old Testament Criticism*. Geneva, Switzerland: Librairie Droz, 1971.

Torrey, Norman Lewis. *Voltaire and the English Deists*. New Haven, CT: Yale University Press, 1930.

Trousson, Raymond, Jeroom Vercruysse, and Jacques Lemaire, eds. *Dictionnaire Voltaire*. Paris: Hachette, 1994.

Trousson, Raymond, and Jeroom Vercruysse, eds. *Dictionnaire général de Voltaire*. Paris: Honoré Champion, 2003.

Wade, Ira O. *The Intellectual Development of Voltaire*. Princeton, NJ: Princeton University Press, 1969.

Waterman, Mina. *Voltaire, Pascal, and Human Destiny*. New York: King's Crown Press, 1942.

Sébastien Charles (2005)

VOLUNTARISM

The term *voluntarism* (from the Latin *voluntas,* "will") applies to any philosophical theory according to which the will is prior to or superior to the intellect or reason. More generally, voluntaristic theories interpret various aspects of experience and nature in the light of the concept of the will, or as it is called in certain older philosophies, passion, appetite, desire, or *conatus.* Such theories may be psychological, ethical, theological, or metaphysical.

PSYCHOLOGICAL VOLUNTARISM

Voluntaristic theories of psychology represent men primarily as beings who will certain ends and whose reason and intelligence are subordinate to will. The outstanding classical representatives are Thomas Hobbes, David Hume, and Arthur Schopenhauer. Hobbes, for example, thought that all voluntary human behavior is response to desire or aversion, which he brought together under the name "endeavor"; he based his ethical and political theories chiefly on this claim. Hume maintained that reason has no role whatever in the promptings of the will; that "reason is, and ought only to be the slave of the passions, and can never pretend to any other office than to serve and obey them." Schopenhauer, the outstanding voluntarist of them all, believed that the will is the very nature or essence of man and indeed of everything, identifying it with the "thing-in-itself" that underlies all phenomena.

The point of all such theories can best be appreciated by contrasting them with the more familiar theories of rationalism found, for example, in Plato's dialogues or René Descartes's *Meditations.* Plato thought that men ideally perceive certain ends or goals by their reason and then direct their wills to the attainment of these ends or goals. This is why he thought no man could knowingly will evil. Thus in the *Symposium* he traced the ascent of the soul toward higher and higher ends, the supposition being that these ends are apprehended first by the senses and then ultimately by the pure or unfettered intelligence, which enlists the will or desire for their pursuit. The corruption of a man was for Plato precisely the dominance of the will, that is, of a man's appetites or desires, this being a deviation from what human nature ideally should be. Descartes, similarly, supposed that the understanding first grasps certain ideas or presents certain ends to the mind and that the will then either assents or withholds its assent, thus following rather than directing the understanding.

Voluntarist theories reject this general picture as the reversal of the truth. Ends and goals, according to these theories, become such only because they are willed; they are not first perceived as ends and then willed. Hume in particular maintained that no sense can be made of the idea, so central to Plato's philosophy, of reason directing the passions, or even of its ever conflicting with them. Reason, he argued, is concerned entirely with demonstrations (deduction) or with the relations of cause and effect (induction). In neither case can it give us ends or goals. Mathematics is used in mechanical arts and the like, but always as a means of attaining something that has nothing to do with reason. The computations of a merchant, for example, can be fallacious, but the ends for which they are undertaken can in no sense be fallacious or irrational. They can only be wise or foolish, that is, such as to promote or to frustrate other ends that are again products of the will. Similarly, Hume thought that no discovery of causal connections in nature can by itself have the least influence on the will. Such discoveries can only be useful or useless in enabling men to choose appropriate means to certain ends, which are in no way derived from reason. "It can never in the least concern us to know," Hume said, "that such objects are causes, and such others effects, if both causes and effects be indifferent to us." Reason therefore can never produce actions or impulses, nor can it oppose them. An impulse to act can be opposed only by a contrary impulse, not by reason. There can, accordingly, be no such thing as a conflict between reason and passion, and the only way in which willed behavior can be "irrational" is for it to be based upon some misconception—for instance, on some erroneous conception of what is a fit means to the attainment of an end that is entirely the product of the will.

The theories of other voluntarists do not differ essentially from Hume's theory, although there are differences of emphasis. All agree that men are moved by their impulses, appetites, passions, or wills and that these are incapable of fallacy or error. There is thus no such thing as a rational or irrational will, although one may will imprudently in relation to other things that one wills. J. G. Fichte expressed this idea when he said that a free being "wills because it wills, and the willing of an object is itself the last ground of such willing."

ETHICAL VOLUNTARISM

It is obvious that the voluntarist conception of human nature contains implications of the highest importance for ethics. If ends or goals are entirely products of the will and the will is neither rational nor irrational, then ends themselves cannot be termed either rational or irrational and it becomes meaningless to ask whether this or that end is really good or bad independently of its being willed. Hobbes drew precisely this conclusion. To say that something is good, he said, is to say nothing more than that it is an object of one's appetite, and to say that something is bad is only to say that one has an aversion to it. Good and bad are thus purely relative to desires and aversions, which are, of course, sometimes quite different in different men. Wise behavior, on this conception, can be nothing other than prudence, that is, the selection of appropriate means to the attainment of whatever goals one happens to have. Hobbes thought that there is one goal, however, that is fairly common to all men: the goal of self-preservation. His political philosophy thus consisted essentially of formulas by means of which men can preserve themselves in safety and security within a commonwealth.

Essentially the same ideas were defended by Socrates' contemporary, Protagoras, and are reflected in his maxim that "man is the measure of all things." They also find expression in the philosophy of William James and are, in fact, an important aspect of pragmatism in general. James thought that things are good solely by virtue of the fact that they are "demanded," that is, that someone wants them or lays claim to them, and he noted that such a demand might be for "anything under the sun." Considered apart from the demands of sentient beings, nothing in the universe has any worth whatsoever. Hence James concluded that the only proper ethical maxim is to satisfy as many demands as possible, no matter what these happen to be, but at the "least cost," that is, with the minimum of frustration to other demands. It is clear that within the framework of voluntaristic theories like this, no meaning can be attached to asking what is truly worthy of one's desires, unless this question is interpreted to mean "What is in fact satisfying of one's desires?"; nor does it make sense to seek, as did Immanuel Kant, any metaphysical principles of morals. Truth and falsity in ethics are exhausted in questions as to the truth or falsity of various opinions concerning the utility of proposed means to the achievement of ends, that is, to the satisfaction of appetite, desire, and demand. They have no relevance to any questions concerning ends themselves.

THEOLOGICAL VOLUNTARISM

Just as the theories thus far described give prominence to the human will over human reason, so certain theological conceptions give prominence to the divine will. Perhaps the most extreme form of theological voluntarism is exemplified in the thinking of St. Peter Damian (1007–1072). He maintained that human reason or "dialectic" is worthless in theological matters, for the simple reason that the very laws of logic are valid only by the concurrence of God's will. God is omnipotent, he said, and can therefore render true even those things reason declares to be absurd or contradictory. It is thus idle for philosophers to speculate upon what must be true with respect to divine matters, since these depend only on God's will.

A very similar idea has found expression in many and various forms of fideism, according to which the justification of religious faith is found in the very act of faith itself, which is an act of the will, rather than in rational proof. Thus Søren Kierkegaard described purity of heart as the willing of a single thing and emphatically denied that such notions as reason and evidence have any place in the religious life. William James, following suggestions put forth by Blaise Pascal, similarly justified the will to believe, defending the absolute innocence, under certain circumstances, of religious belief entirely in the absence of evidence. Many contemporary religious leaders, pressing the same notion, give prominence to the idea of religious commitment, suggesting that religion is primarily a matter of the will rather than of reason. This is, in fact, traditional in Christian thought, for even the most philosophical and rationalistic theologians, such as St. Anselm of Canterbury, have almost without exception given priority to the act of faith, maintaining that religious belief should precede rather than follow rational understanding. This idea is expressed in the familiar dictum *credo ut intelligam,* which means "I believe, in order that I may understand."

Perhaps no religious thinker has stressed the primacy of God's will in questions of morality more than Kierkegaard, who seems to have held that the divine will is the only and the ultimate moral justification for any act. Strictly understood, this means that an action that might otherwise be deemed heinous is not so, provided it is commanded by God. In the fourteenth century this was quite explicitly maintained by William of Ockham. William said that the divine will, and not human or divine reason, is the ultimate standard of morality, that certain acts are sins solely because they have been forbidden by God, and other acts are meritorious only because they have been commanded by God. He denied that God forbids certain things because they are sins or commands certain things because they are virtues, for it seemed to him that this would be a limitation upon God's will. There can be, he thought, no higher justification for any act than that God wills it, nor any more final condemnation of an act than that God forbids it. The moral law, accordingly, was for William simply a matter of God's free choice, for God's choice cannot be constrained by any moral law, being itself the sole source of that law. This view is frequently echoed in religious literature but usually only rhetorically.

METAPHYSICAL VOLUNTARISM

A number of thinkers have believed that the concept of the will is crucial to the understanding of law, ethics, and human behavior generally; a few have suggested that it is crucial to the understanding of reality itself. Such suggestions are found in the philosophies of Fichte, Henri Bergson, and others, but in no philosophy does it have such central importance as in that of Arthur Schopenhauer. Schopenhauer thought that will is the underlying and ultimate reality and that the whole phenomenal world is only the expression of will. He described living things as the objectifications of their wills and sought to explain not only the behavior but also the very anatomical structures of plants, animals, and men in terms of this hypothesis. The will was described by Schopenhauer as a blind and all-powerful force that is literally the inexhaustible creator of every visible thing. The sexual appetite, which he considered to be fundamentally the same in all living things, was described by him as a blind urge to live and to perpetuate existence without any goal beyond that, and he denied that it had anything whatever to do with reason or intelligence, being in fact more often than not opposed to them. The religious impulse found in all cultures at all times was similarly explained as the response to a blind and irrational will to possess endless existence. In the growth and development of all living things Schopenhauer discerned the unfolding of the will in nature, wherein certain things appear and transform themselves in accordance with a fairly unvarying pattern and in the face of obstacles and impediments, solely in accordance with what is willed in a metaphysical sense but entirely without any rational purpose or goal. On the basis of this voluntarism, he explained ethics in terms of the feelings of self-love, malice, and compassion, all of which are expressions of the will, and he denied—in sharp contrast to Kant—that morality has anything to do with reason or intelligence. He argued that men have free will only in the sense that every man is the free or unfettered expression of a will and that men are therefore not the authors of their own destinies, characters, or behavior. Like other voluntarists, Schopenhauer thus emphasized the irrational factors in human behavior and, in doing so, anticipated much that is now taken for granted in those sophisticated circles that have come under the influence of modern psychological theories.

See also Anselm, St.; Bergson, Henri; Descartes, René; Determinism, A Historical Survey; Dialectic; Ethics, History of; Fichte, Johann Gottlieb; Fideism; Hobbes, Thomas; Hume, David; James, William; Kant, Immanuel; Kierkegaard, Søren Aabye; Pascal, Blaise; Peter Damian; Plato; Protagoras of Abdera; Schopenhauer, Arthur; Socrates; Volition; William of Ockham.

Bibliography

A good general work on voluntarism that is both historical and critical is Vernon J. Bourke's *Will in Western Thought* (New York: Sheed and Ward, 1964).

Thomas Hobbes's ethical and political theories are developed in his *Leviathan,* of which there are many editions. See also *Body, Man, and Citizen,* a selection from Hobbes's writings edited by Richard S. Peters (New York: Collier, 1962).

David Hume's defense of psychological voluntarism is best expressed in his *Treatise of Human Nature,* Book II, Part 3, especially Section 3; the quotations in this article are taken from L. A. Selby-Bigge's edition of that work (Oxford, 1888 and 1955).

For a fairly concise expression of Schopenhauer's voluntarism, see *The Will to Live,* a collection of his essays edited by R. Taylor (New York, 1962).

J. G. Fichte develops the idea of an active power in nature in the first book of his *The Vocation of Man,* edited by R. M. Chisholm (New York: Liberal Arts Press, 1956). The quotation from Fichte comes from his *The Science of Rights,* translated by A. E. Kroeger (Philadelphia: Lippincott, 1869), p. 193.

One of the clearest ancient defenses of a pragmatic basis of laws and institutions is given in Plato's *Protagoras,* where it is ascribed to Protagoras and criticized by Socrates. William James's ethical voluntarism is developed in his essay "The Moral Philosopher and the Moral Life," and the application of his principles to religious belief is given in his "The Will to Believe," both of which are found in nearly all editions of his popular essays.

The theological voluntarism of St. Peter Damian, as well as William of Ockham's ethical theories, are very well summarized in Frederick Copleston's *History of Philosophy,* Vols. II and III (London, 1950 and 1953). See also Étienne Gilson's *Reason and Revelation in the Middle Ages* (New York: Scribners, 1938) for a clear account of the opposition between rationalism and fideism. Kierkegaard has eloquently expressed the opposition between reason and religion in many writings, but see particularly his *Purity of Heart,* translated by Douglas V. Steere (New York: Harper, 1938).

Richard Taylor (1967)

VYSHESLAVTSEV, BORIS PETROVICH
(1877–1954)

Boris Petrovich Vysheslavtsev, the Russian philosopher and religious thinker, was born in Moscow. He studied at the University of Moscow under the Russian jurist and philosopher P. I. Novgorodtsev and later at the University of Marburg under the neo-Kantians Hermann Cohen and Paul Natorp. Upon the publication in 1914 of his dissertation, *Etika Fikhte* (Fichte's ethics), he received a doctorate from the University of Moscow and in 1917 was made professor of philosophy at that institution. Expelled from the Soviet Union in 1922, he emigrated first to Berlin, then in 1924 to Paris, where he became a professor at the Orthodox Theological Institute and was associated with Nikolai Berdyaev in affairs of the Russian *émigré* press. Prior to World War II Vysheslavtsev was active in the ecumenical movement. From the time of the German occupation of France until his death he lived in Switzerland.

Vysheslavtsev's lifelong concern with the themes of irrationality and the absolute was already evident in his work on Johann Gottlieb Fichte. He there asserted that beyond the sphere of rationality or "system" lies the irrational sphere, infinite and incapable of being systematized. Through the antinomy of these spheres philosophy arrives at recognition of the Absolute as the infinity that transcends the universe and all oppositions, even the opposition between Georg Cantor's "actual" and "potential" infinities. Because the Absolute underlies every rational construction, it is irrational. It cannot be exhausted by any concept but is "the mysterious limitlessness which is revealed to intuition."

According to Vysheslavtsev, the essence of man's ethical and religious life consists in his relation to the Absolute. He explored this relation in subsequent works, principally *Etika preobrazhennogo erosa* (The ethics of transfigured Eros), emphasizing the irrational forces in man and interpreting Christian doctrine in the light of the depth psychology of Carl Jung and the French psychoanalyst Charles Baudouin. Vysheslavtsev argued that moral laws cannot guide human conduct successfully, because they are rational rules directed to the conscious will and are defeated by the "irrational antagonism" that stems from man's subconscious. For moral ideals to be significant and effective they must take possession of the subconscious, which they can do only if they are reached through the sublimation of subconscious impulses. Sublimation, operating through the imagination, transforms man's lower impulses into higher ones and turns his inherent, arbitrary freedom into moral freedom that seeks the good. Such sublimation is aided by divine grace and is possible only where the soul turns freely toward the Absolute. Christian ethics is not an ethics of law but "the ethics of sublimation."

In his later years Vysheslavtsev increasingly concerned himself with social problems and wrote a major work on modern industrial culture, *Krizis industrial'noi Kul'tury* (The crisis of industrial culture), and a trenchant philosophical critique of Soviet Marxism, *Filosofskaia nishcheta marksizma* (The philosophical poverty of Marxism).

See also Absolute, The; Berdyaev, Nikolai Aleksandrovich; Cantor, Georg; Cohen, Hermann; Fichte, Johann Gottlieb; Jung, Carl Gustav; Natorp, Paul; Rationality; Russian Philosophy.

Bibliography

WORKS BY VYSHESLAVTSEV

The Eternal in Russian Philosophy. Translated by Penelope V. Burt. Grand Rapids, MI, and Cambridge, U.K.: Eerdmans, 2002.

Etika Fikhte (Fichte's ethics). Moscow, 1914.

Etika preobrazhennogo erosa (The ethics of transfigured eros). Moscow: Respublika, 1994.

Khristianstvo i sotsial'nyi vopros (Christianity and the social question). Paris: YMCA Press, 1929.

Krizis industrial'noi kul'tury: marksizm, neosotsializm, neoliberalizm (The crisis of industrial culture: Marxism, neosocialism, neoliberalism). New York: Chalidze Publications, 1982.

Serdtse v Khristianskoy i Indiyskoy Mistike (The heart in Christian and Indian mysticism). Paris: YMCA Press, 1929.

Filosofskaia nishcheta marksizma (The philosophical poverty of Marxism). Frankfurt am Main: Posev, 1957.

Zwei Wege der Erlosung: Erlosung als Losung des tragischen Widerspruchs (Two paths of salvation: Salvation as resolution of the tragic contradiction). Zurich: Rhein-Verlag, 1937.

WORKS ON VYSHESLAVTSEV

Beliaev, M. M., et al. *O Rossii i russkoi filosofskoi kul'ture: filosofy russkogo posleoktiabr'skogo zarubezh'ia* (Russia and Russian philosophical culture: The philosophers of the Russian post-October emigration). Moscow: Nauka, 1990.

Kline, G. L. "A Philosophical Critique of Soviet Marxizm." *Review of Metaphysics*, 9 (1955) 1: 90–105.

Redlikh, Roman, ed. *Dialektika Vysheslavtseva* (Vysheslavtsev's dialectic). Frankfurt am Main: Posev, 1973.

V. V. Zenkovsky. "B. P. Vysheslavtsev, kak Filosof" (B. P. Vysheslavtsev as philosopher). *Novy Zhurnal*, 15 (1955): 249–261.

V. V. Zenkovsky. *Istoriya Russkoy Filosofii*. 2 vols. Paris, 1948–1950. Translated by G. L. Kline as *A History of Russian Philosophy*, 2 vols., New York and London, 1953.

James P. Scanlan (1967)
Bibliography updated by Vladimir Marchenkov (2005)

WAHLE, RICHARD

(1857–1935)

Richard Wahle, the Austrian philosopher and psychologist, was born in Vienna. He was appointed Privatdozent in philosophy at the University of Vienna in 1885. A decade later he was called to a professorship in philosophy at the University of Czernowitz, where he taught until 1917. From 1919 to 1933 he again lectured at the University of Vienna. Possessed of originality and an unusually lively style, he published a number of books in the fields of psychology, general philosophy, and ethics.

Wahle is known especially for his relentlessly sharp critique of traditional philosophy, particularly of metaphysics, which he regarded as "one of the most dangerous breeding-places of empty phrases." An absolute, true knowledge, of the sort to which metaphysics aspires, cannot exist. For all knowledge consists in nothing more than that "an image (or idea) is given in dependence on the self"; a reality existing in itself can never be known. Against the traditional philosophical and metaphysical "delusion of knowledge," Wahle set his own positivistic "philosophy of occurrences," according to which the "given" constitutes the sole admissible point of departure for philosophical thought. What are empirically given to us, however, are only freely suspended, surfacelike, passive, powerless "occurrences" (the contents of perception and imagination) that are the effects of unknown "really operative, powerful substantial primitive factors," which remain forever hidden and are in principle unknowable. Wahle's epistemological standpoint, described also as "antisubjectivist product-objectivism" or "agnostic product-realism," lies beyond the antitheses of materialism and spiritualism, realism and idealism (or phenomenalism), objectivism and subjectivism. He regarded all of these positions as false because things are neither essence nor appearance but simply complexes of "occurrences," and the subjective and the objective are identical inasmuch as only neutral "occurrences" are given to us. Thus Wahle's antimetaphysical and skeptical agnosticism leads from illusory knowledge to genuine ignorance, which is the only attainable goal for philosophy.

As a psychologist, Wahle firmly rejected any kind of metaphysics of the soul, as well as faculty psychology and the depth psychology of the unconscious (psychoanalysis). A satisfactory explanation of mental processes, he held, can result only from connecting them with the corresponding physiological prerequisites. There are no independent psychical unities (like the ego), forces, acts, or powers; they appear to exist only because of an inexact style of expression. For example, the ego is neither substance nor force; it is not an independent, simple, active thing at all but only a designation for a certain sphere of occurrences. Similarly, the will is said to be "the reflex action become stable under the accompaniment of images following a concurrence of reflex movements" (*Über den Mechanismus des geistigen Lebens,* p. 371).

Wahle attached special value to obtaining as penetrating an analysis as possible of those mental happenings that proceed essentially in "additive series." In such happenings, besides association, the "constellation" (the state of excitation of the brain at the given moment) is particularly significant. Organic sensations and bodily determinations, as well as the motor system, also play an important part in the processes of thinking, feeling, and willing. Wahle saw in the operations of the brain the antecedents or representatives of conscious processes; to the momentary molecular change of an entire specific brain region corresponds a concrete peculiarity of the given image. The brain, however, is not the "cause" of the mental occurrences or experiences but only the "necessary co-occurrence" of any such occurrence. Both psychopathological phenomena and the origin and formation of character can be understood only physiologically, more particularly from the more or less disturbed (in the case of psychopathology) or undisturbed (in the case of character formation) combined action of a very few elementary brain functions.

Wahle's reflections on the philosophy of culture and history were tinged with skepticism and pessimism, as was his conception of the intellectual capacity and ethical worth of man. Whatever meaning there is in life derives from the existence of love, joy, and pain. Life's highest wisdom is embodied in fulfilling the challenge to be happy with a modesty that is noble, free of illusion, and resigned.

See also Agnosticism; Ethical Subjectivism; Idealism; Metaphysics; Objectivity in Ethics; Pessimism and Optimism; Phenomenalism; Psychoanalysis; Psychology; Realism; Skepticism, History of; Unconscious.

Bibliography

WORKS BY WAHLE

Das Ganze der Philosophic und ihr Ende. Vienna and Leipzig, 1894.

Über den Mechanismus des geistigen Lebens. Vienna and Leipzig, 1906.

Josua. Munich, 1912. A second edition was published in 1928.

Die Tragikomödie der Weisheit. Vienna and Leipzig, 1915; 2nd ed., 1925.

Entstehung der Charaktere. Munich: Drei Masken, 1928.

Grundlagen einer neuen Psychiatrie. Vienna, 1931.

Fröhliches Register der paar philosophischen Wahrheiten (Cheerful catalog of the few philosophical truths). Vienna and Leipzig, 1934.

WORKS ON WAHLE

Flinker, Friedrich. *Die Zerstörung des Ich. Eine kritische Darlegung der Lehre Richard Wahles.* Vienna and Leipzig, 1927.

Hochfeld, Sophus. *Die Philosophie Richard Wahles und Johannes Rehmkes Grundwissenschaft.* Potsdam, 1926.

Franz Austeda (1967)
Translated by Albert E. Blumberg

WALLACE, ALFRED RUSSEL

(1823–1913)

Alfred Russel Wallace, the English naturalist and coformulator with Charles Darwin of the theory of natural selection, was born at Usk, Monmouthshire. He was largely self-educated, having left school at fourteen to serve as a surveyor's assistant with his brother. Like many of his contemporaries he acquired an early taste for the study of nature. But he also read widely and was influenced by the works of Alexander von Humboldt, Thomas Malthus, and Charles Lyell, as Darwin was. In 1844, while teaching school at Leicester, he met the naturalist H. W. Bates (1825–1892), who introduced him to scientific entomology. The two men later embarked on a collecting trip to the Amazon, where Wallace remained for four years examining the tropical flora and fauna.

In 1854, after a brief visit to England, Wallace set out by himself for the Malay Archipelago. He subsequently wrote an account of this trip, *The Malay Archipelago* (London, 1869), which is a fascinating narrative. When he returned in 1862, he had become a convinced evolutionist and was known in scientific circles for his formulation of the theory of natural selection. Another of his scientific contributions was "Wallace's line," a zoogeographical boundary he drew in 1863 to separate Indian and Australian faunal regions, and which was assumed to pass through the middle of the archipelago.

The rest of Wallace's long life was spent in England, except for a lecture tour of the United States in 1887 and short visits to the Continent. Darwin, Lyell, Thomas Henry Huxley, John Tyndall, and Herbert Spencer were among his most intimate friends. He wrote extensively on a wide variety of subjects, but biological interests remained central to his outlook and are reflected in such books as *The Geographical Distribution of Animals* (London and New York, 1876), *Darwinism* (London and New York, 1889), *Man's Place in the Universe* (London and New York, 1903), and *The World of Life* (London and New York, 1910).

Wallace first thought of the theory of natural selection in February 1858, when he was ill with a fever at Ternate in the Moluccas. The occasion gave him time to reflect on the mechanism by which species might be altered. He outlined the theory rapidly in a paper, "On the Tendency of Varieties to Depart Indefinitely from the Original Type," and sent it to Darwin, who saw that Wallace had hit upon exactly the theory that he himself had formed and privately written down in 1842. With characteristic generosity he proposed that Wallace's outline should be published immediately. Lyell, however, urged a compromise that resulted in a joint communication from Darwin and Wallace that was read at the Linnaean Society on July 1, 1858. The two men thus received equal credit for the new doctrine, although Darwin was actually the pioneer. The joint communication created no stir at the meeting. However, it was later clearly recognized as a revolutionary document that demolished forever the ancient idea of the fixity of species by formulating a scientific theory of how species change and how their adaptations are secured at each stage of the process.

When Darwin published his famous books, the accord between him and Wallace began to disappear. The view expressed in *The Origin of Species* that evolution required the operation of factors of a Lamarckian as well as of a selective sort was unacceptable to Wallace. For him "natural selection is supreme" and is the sole means of modification, except in the case of man. Hence he became, like August Weissmann, an apostle of neo-Darwinism. This led him to hold that every phenotypic character of an organism must be useful to that organism in the struggle for life; the principle of utility is of universal application.

With regard to human evolution Wallace differed from Darwin in affirming that man's mental powers, especially "the mathematical, musical and artistic faculties," have not been developed under the law of natural selection. These faculties point to the existence in man of something that he has not derived from his animal progenitors, "something which we may best refer to as being of a spiritual essence." It came into action when man appeared on the evolutionary stage. As he grew older, Wallace put more and more emphasis on the spiritual agency, so that in *The World of Life* it is described as "a Mind not only adequate to direct and regulate all the forces at work in living organisms, but also the more fundamental forces of the whole material universe." For many years Wallace was interested in spiritualism and psychical research. A pamphlet that he published in 1866, *The Scientific Aspect of the Supernatural,* discussed such matters as clairvoyance, apparitions, animal magnetism, and the problem of miracles. It was clear that he took them seriously, and they influenced his general outlook. All this was far removed from anything Darwin was prepared to countenance.

Apart from the theory of natural selection, Wallace's most enduring work was his *Geographical Distribution of Animals.* He also made acute judgments on anthropological matters, such as the evolutionary significance of the human brain and human intelligence. Thus he contended that the brain is a specialized organ that has freed man from the dangers of specialization by vastly increasing his adaptability and that man's intelligence has allowed him to evolve without undergoing major somatic changes. Yet despite Wallace's fertility in producing ideas and his command of a wide array of facts, he never quite succeeded in relating the two. His ideas were not carefully analyzed or tested. At bottom he was a naturalist, with a deep love of nature and an inexhaustible passion for collecting.

See also Darwin, Charles Robert; Darwinism; Evolutionary Theory; Huxley, Thomas Henry; Malthus, Thomas Robert; Naturalism; Philosophy of Biology.

Bibliography

ADDITIONAL WORKS BY WALLACE

Contributions to the Theory of Natural Selection. New York: Macmillan, 1870.

My Life: A Record of Events and Opinions. New York: Dodd Mead, 1905.

WORKS ON WALLACE

Eiseley, Loren. *Darwin's Century.* Garden City, NY: Doubleday, 1958.

George, Wilma Beryl. *Biologist Philosopher: A Study of the Life and Writings of Alfred Russel Wallace.* New York: Abelard-Schuman, 1964.

Hogben, L. T. *A. R. Wallace.* London: Society for Promoting Christian Knowledge, 1918.

Marchant, J. *A. R. Wallace: Letters and Reminiscences.* London: Cassell, 1916.

T. A. Goudge (1967)

WANG BI
(226–249 CE)

Third-century Chinese philosopher Wang Bi (226–249 CE) achieved fame as an interpreter of the *Laozi* and the *Yijing* (Classic of changes), whose radical reformulation of the concept of Dao as nonbeing (*wu*) helped spark a new current of thought called *Xuanxue* (Learning of the mysterious), sometimes translated as "neo-Daoism." To Wang, Confucius, Laozi, and the other sages of old had discerned the true meaning of Dao as the root of all beings. This was misunderstood, which necessitated a reinterpretation of the classical heritage.

Wang probed the basis of interpretation and argued that words do not fully express meaning. This was a major debate in early medieval Chinese philosophy. Against earlier commentators who reduced meaning to reference, Wang believed that words are necessary but insufficient for understanding and sought to uncover the fundamental ideas that unite the classics. Famously, Wang declared that words must be forgotten before meaning can be understood.

From this hermeneutical perspective, Wang approaches the meaning of Dao, bringing into view both its transcendence and creative power. According to the *Laozi* (also known as *Daodejing*, the "Classic of the Way and Virtue"), Dao is nameless and formless; yet, it is also the beginning of all things. To Wang, this encapsulates the mystery (*xuan*) of Dao and discloses the central insight that "all beings originate from nonbeing" (*Laozi* commentary, chs. 1, 40).

The *Laozi* states, "Dao gives birth to one," which produces "two" and the rest of creation (ch. 42). Whereas commentators before Wang generally took this to mean that the Dao produced the original "vital energy" (*qi*), which in turn generated the yin and yang energies, Wang focused on the logic of creation. The many can be traced to "one" in the sense of a necessary ontological foundation, but "one" does not refer to any agent or substance. The ground of beings cannot be itself a being; otherwise, infinite regress cannot be overcome. "Beginning" is not a temporal reference but indicates logical priority. "One" is but another term for Dao and should be understood metaphysically as "nonbeing"; "it is not a number," as Wang asserts in his commentary to the *Yijing*, but that which makes possible all numbers and functions. Nonbeing—literally "not having" any property of being—is not a "something" of which nothing can be said; rather, it is a negative concept that sets the Dao categorically apart from the domain of beings and in so doing preserves the transcendence of Dao without compromising its creative power.

The Daoist world reflects a pristine order. This is to be understood in terms of constant principles (*li*) that govern the universe. They do not derive from an external source, but in the light of nonbeing can only be said to be "naturally so" (*ziran*), which Wang describes as "an expression for the ultimate" (*Laozi* commentary, ch. 25). Similarly, human nature should be viewed as "one," understood as what is true (*zhen*) in human beings.

The concept of *ziran* also sets the direction of Daoist ethics and politics. Effortlessly and spontaneously, nature accomplishes its myriad tasks and provides for all beings. In principle, the human world should also be naturally simple, noncontentioius, and self-sufficient. If present realities deviate from this order, it is imperative to recover what is true, to reorient human thinking and action by realizing *ziran*, and in this sense to return to Dao. This is how Wang interprets the key Daoist concept of nonaction (*wuwei*).

Nonaction does not mean total inaction or any esoteric technique to get things done; instead it is a mode of being characterized by the absence of desires, which corrupt one's nature. This, too, follows from the analysis of nonbeing. Genuine well-being can only be measured by the extent to which one is not being fettered by desires, or not having the kind of interest-seeking thought/action that invariably precipitates disorder. Nonaction acts constantly to diminish desires—and to diminish any false sense of self that engenders desires—until one reaches the tranquil depth of emptiness and quiescence. This defines not only the goal of self-cultivation but also that of government.

The order of nature encompasses the family and the state. Their hierarchical structure is rooted in the principles governing the Daoist world. The key to Daoist government lies in "honoring the root and putting to rest the branches." At the policy level, this means not burdening the people with excessive taxation, heavy punishment, and war, which Wang considered the bane of Chinese politics. Following nonaction, the ruler needs only to ensure that obstructions to human flourishing are removed. At a deeper level, desires must be put to rest so that the root may grow; that is, the ruler must embrace emptiness and enable those under the spell of desires to reclaim their true nature.

To many of Wang's contemporaries, the ideal reign of *ziran* can only be realized by a sage, who is utterly different from ordinary human beings in that he is endowed with an extraordinarily pure *qi*-constitution and is inherently without desires and emotions. Wang Bi, however, argued that the sage is different from ordinary human beings only in terms of his profound "spirituality and enlightenment." In his humanity, the sage "cannot be without sorrow and pleasure to respond to things," but he is not burdened by them. Sage nature signifies complete self-realization.

While standing under tradition—whether in hermeneutics, metaphysics, or concerning the nature of the sage—Wang came to understand it anew. The philosophy of nonbeing made a strong impact on the development of Buddhist philosophy. The concept of *li* (principle) played a pivotal role in later neo-Confucian philosophy. In both instances, Wang's contribution is substantial.

See also Chinese Philosophy: Daoism; Guo Xiang.

Bibliography

Chan, Alan K. L. *Two Visions of the Way*. Albany: State University of New York Press, 1991.

Lynn, Richard J., tr. *The Classic of Changes: A New Translation of the* I Ching *as Interpreted by Wang Bi*. New York: Columbia University Press, 1994.

Lynn, Richard J., tr. *The Classic of the Way and Virtue: A New Translation of the* Tao-te ching *of Laozi as Interpreted by Wang Bi*. New York: Columbia University Press, 1999.

Wagner, Rudolf G. *A Chinese Reading of the Daodejing: Wang Bi's Commentary on the Laozi with Critical Text and Translation*. Albany: State University of New York Press, 2003.

Wagner, Rudolf G. *The Craft of a Chinese Commentator: Wang Bi on the Laozi*. Albany: State University of New York Press, 2000.

Wagner, Rudolf G. *Language, Ontology, and Political Philosophy in China: Wang Bi's Scholarly Exploration of the Dark (Xuanxue)*. Albany: State University of New York Press, 2003.

Alan K. L. Chan (2005)

WANG CHONG

(c. 27–100)

Historically speaking, Wang Chong is one of the best-known thinkers of Han China (221 BCE–220 CE), but the significance of his ideas is far less certain. Wang's native province of Guiji stood on the southeast margins of the Han Empire. Although once studying in the capital Luoyang, he remained basically an obscure local figure. He wrote several books and the most important and only surviving one is the *Lunheng*. This book was not known to the national elite community until the late second century, since then being recognized as a major intellectual work.

Modern opinions split on the nature of the *Lunheng*. Many believe the book reveals Wang as an iconoclast and skeptic who courageously denounced the Confucian orthodoxy and prevalent superstitions. Some, in contrast, consider him a mere rhetorician whose inconsistent arguments seek to justify the existence of people like himself, namely, conceited scholar–officials suffering world failures. The truth probably lies somewhere in between.

Consisting of eighty-five chapters and covering many subjects, the *Lunheng* is not easy to characterize. "*Lun*" means discourse while "*heng*" signifies to weigh or to measure. Wang Chong took the title to mean *discourses as measurements*. This book was thus purported to be a critique of common beliefs. Wang's most obvious target is the so-called theory of "interaction between Heaven and Man." This theory maintains that Heaven regulates, and acts in response to, human behavior. Early Han proponents of Confucianism relied heavily on this theory in their attempt to construct a doctrine as the orthodox ideology for both the state and society. They depicted Heaven as the guardian of Confucian values. It, for instance, punishes human misconduct, particularly that of rulers, by either generating anomalous natural phenomena or bringing down disasters. Wang denied categorically that Heaven was possessed of a will or that the world had any purpose. His critique went beyond a particular theory of heaven. He was deeply opposed to magic itself, especially the kind we now call *sympathetic magic*. This is by no means trivial considering the fact that magic and magical thinking dominated Han life. Wang also found fault with sagely figures, such as Confucius and Mencius. All these critiques earned him the reputation as a great rationalist. There may be some truth to this seemingly anachronistic representation. Wang actually described his project as one to make distinctions between the real and the fanciful although his basis for making such distinctions is sometimes alien to us today.

The *Lunheng* contains evident contradictions in its arguments. The most controversial part of this book is its discussion concerning fate. Whereas denying the existence of a heavenly will, Wang insisted upon predetermined fate. He contended that all human conditions were unavoidable and that the events of an individual's life were in no way related to that person's quality or conduct. He developed complex theories of fate, not unlike a modern economist trying to decipher the invisible hand working in the financial market. Wang's ideas on this subject were unconvincing to many and opened the door to the charge that his philosophical contentions were largely self-serving.

In terms of writing style in the *Lunheng*, Wang has been accused of being unstructured and redundant. But Wang can be very witty. To give just one example, a famous moral tale relates that upon hearing her husband was killed in war, a woman wailed with such a grief that a city wall collapsed. To this Wang asks: If one cries at water and fire in a state of true grief, can the water be roused to extinguish the fire? In this regard, Wang may be considered a minor Voltaire of early China.

It is easily noticeable that Wang attacked fiercely certain ideas and sayings associated with Confucianism not long after it emerged as the state orthodoxy for the first time in Chinese history. Yet that impression can be misleading. Wang's true target was what he saw as the fanciful thoughts of his time, some of which were used to establish the authority of Confucianism. He had no quarrel with core Confucian values, and indeed promoted the position of Confucian scholars in his book. Despite his rather modest agenda, *xuanxue*—antitraditionalists who arose a century after his death—drew on the *Lunheng* for inspiration. In this peculiar way, Wang helped to bring about a major change in the history of Chinese philosophy.

See also Chinese Philosophy; Confucius; Determinism, A Historical Survey; Mencius; Voltaire, François-Marie-Arouet de.

Bibliography

Fung, Yu-lan. *A History of Chinese Philosophy*. Vol. 2 Translated by Derk Bodde. Princeton, NJ: Princeton University Press, 1953.

Satō, Kyōgen. *Ronkō no kenkyū*. Tokyo: Sōbunsha, 1981.

Wang, Ch'ung. *Lun-heng*. 2 vols. Translated by Alfred Forke. Leipzig: 1907–1911. Reprinted, New York: Paragon Book Gallery, 1962.

Jo-shui Chen (2005)

WANG FUZHI

(1619–1692)

Wang Fuzhi was a Chinese philosopher in the late neo-Confucian School. After his initial attempt to resist the Manchu invasion of China had failed, he devoted the rest of his life to the reinterpretation of Chinese philosophical classics and the development of his own philosophical view. The last seventeen years of his life were spent as a hermit at the foot of a barren mountain which he named "the boat mountain" (*chuanshan*); hence his well-known alias: Wang Chuanshan. His copious works were first published posthumously by his son. Most notable among his works are: *Du Sishu Daquan Shuo* (Discourse on reading the great collection of commentaries on the four books), *Zhouyi Waizhuan* (External commentary on the book of changes), *Zhouyi Neizhuan* (Internal commentary on the book of changes), *Du Tongjian Lun* (A treatise on reading Tongjian), and *Zhuangzi Zhengmeng Zhu* (Commentary on Zhang Zai's zhengmeng).

Wang Fuzhi's metaphysics places the cosmic principle (*li*) in the midst of cosmic energy (force; *qi*), thereby denying any transcendent status of the cosmic principle. The universe is constituted by *qi*, which develops in accordance with a certain order. According to Wang Fuzhi, this order does not exist prior to the development of *qi*; it is simply "the way things are" as well as "the way things ought to be" for cosmic energy. *Qi* is self-regulating in virtue of this internal cosmic principle; therefore, *qi* is not a blind force. Wang Fuzhi not only acknowledges the orderliness of *qi*, but also recognizes the all-encompassing nature of *qi*. The universe is filled with *qi* from time immemorial; cosmic states are simply the different developmental stages of *qi*. When *qi* condenses, it composes myriad things; when material objects disintegrate, everything returns to the rarified form of *qi*. In this respect, his metaphysics follows directly from that of Zhang Zai.

In addition to advocating the unity between principle and *qi*, Wang Fuzhi also espouses the unity between Dao and concrete things (*qi*—a different word from the cosmic energy *qi*). Dao is the way particular things are and the way they ought to be. According to Wang Fuzhi, Dao does not have any a priori status; it does not exist independently of concrete things. In other words, Dao is postdevelopmental in the production of concrete things, just as cosmic principle (*li*) is postdevelopmental in the activities of *qi*. To Wang Fuzhi, only the concrete cosmic energy (*qi*), and the concrete objects composed of *qi*, are real. His metaphysics has often been interpreted as a form of materialism and realism.

Because *qi* constantly evolves and transforms itself, the universe perpetually generates and renews itself. When applied to the human world, this cosmology entails that human history is not predetermined. Wang Fuzhi's philosophy of history is modernistic in spirit, for he holds that the modern is more advanced than the ancient; ancient laws and morals do not necessarily apply to the contemporary world. To find the best way to govern, people need to deal with the present context and understand the present societal needs. A good ruler is one who understands and aims to meet his or her people's wants and desires. Following Mencius, Wang Fuzhi argues that people's common desire is nothing but the satisfaction of their basic needs in life. These desires are natural to human beings; they are thus not morally blameworthy.

Wang Fuzhi rejects Buddhists' renouncement of human desires; he also criticizes the Cheng-Zhu School's doctrine that one needs to extinguish human desires in order to exemplify the Heavenly principle. He advocates the unity of the Heavenly principle and human desires: the principle of heaven lies in nothing but what the people desire in common. An ideal state of the world is reached when all people can have their basic desires satisfied. To Wang Fuzhi, human history is simply a reflection of human nature; human politics is solely determined by what the people want in common. This view reaffirms the Confucian humanism underlined in classic Confucianism.

See also Chinese Philosophy: Confucianism.

Bibliography

MAJOR WORKS BY WANG FUZHI

Zhouyi waizhuan (External commentary on the book of changes), 1655.

Laozi yan (Extended interpretation on Laozi), 1655.

Shangshu yinyi (The extended meaning of the book of history), 1663.

Du Sishu daquan shuo (Discourse on reading the great collection of commentaries on the four books), 1665.

Chunqiu shilun (A general treatise on Chun Qiu), 1668.

Liji zhangju (A textual annotation on the book of rites), 1673–1677.

Zhouyi daxiang jie (Interpretation on the images of the book of changes), 1676.

Siwen lu (Record of thoughts and questions), post 1677.

Zhangzi Zhengmeng zhu (Commentary on Zhang Zai's zhengmeng), post 1677.

Sishu xunyi (A contemporary interpretation of the meaning of the four books), 1679.

Zhuangzi jie (Interpretation on Zhuangzi), 1681.

Zhouyi neizhuan (Internal commentary on the book of changes), 1685.

Du Tongjian lun (A treatise on reading Tongjian), 1687–1691.

Song lun (A treatise on the Song dynasty), 1691.

WORKS ON WANG FUZHI

Black, Alison Harley. *Man and Nature in the Philosophical Thought of Wang Fu-Chih*. Publications on Asia of the Henry M. Jackson School of International studies, No 41. Seattle, WA: University of Washington Press. 1989.

Hou, Wai-lu, and Chi-chih Chang. "Philosophical thought of Wang Fu-chih." *Chinese Studies in History and Philosophy* 1 (Spring 1968): 12–28

Liu, JeeLoo. "Is Human History Predestined in Wang Fuzhi's Cosmology?" *Journal of Chinese Philosophy*28(3), 2001, 321–337.

Liu, JeeLoo. "Wang Fuzhi." In *The Encyclopedia of Chinese Philosophy*, edited by Antonio S. Cua. New York: Routledge, 2003, 748–755.

McMorran, Ian. "Late Ming Criticism of Wang Yang-Ming: The Case Of Wang Fu-Chih." *Philosophy East & West* 23, 1973, 91–102.

McMorran, Ian. *The Passionate Realist: An Introduction to the Life and Political Thought of Wang Fuzhi, (1619–1692)*. Hong Kong: Sunshine, 1992.

Teng, S.Y. "Wang Fu-chih's Views on History and Historical Writing." *Journal of Asian Studies* 28, 111–123.

Wright, Kathleen. "The Fusion of Horizons: Hans-Georg Gadamer and Wang Fu-Chih." *Continental Philosophy Review* 33 (3), 2000: 345–358.

Zhang, Jiemo. "On the Aesthetic Significance of Wang Fuzhi's Theory of the Unity of Poetry and Music, with Criticisms of Certain Biases." *Chinese Studies in Philosophy* 21(3), Spring 1990, 26–53.

Jeeloo Liu (2005)

WANG SHOU-JEN

See *Wang Yang-ming*

WANG YANG-MING

(1472–1529)

Wing-tsit Chan reminds the reader that "the philosophy of Wang Yang-ming is a vigorous philosophy born of serious searching and bitter experience" (1963, Chan's introduction, p. ix). Wang's doctrine of the unity of knowledge and action, for example, may be regarded as a forceful and concise way of stating the unity of his life and teaching during his formative years. For Wang, learning to become a sage involved a serious and resolute commitment to Dao or *ren* (humanity)—the ideal of "forming one body" with all things in the universe. Says Wang: "The great man regards Heaven, Earth, and the myriad things as one body (*yiti*). Moreover, the *ren*-person also forms one body with plants, stones, tiles, mountains, and rivers" (1963, p. 272).

Alternatively, one may characterize Wang's vision of the highest good as an ideal of the universe as a harmonious moral community. A commitment to the vision of *ren* is a commitment to the task of clarifying the concrete significance of the vision—an ideal theme rather than an ideal norm as a basis for deriving precepts. An ideal theme is a unifying perspective, a point of orientation, not a fixed principle of conduct. For expressing his vision Wang sometimes used the term Dao (way) instead of *ren*. Dao and *ren* differ in the direction of stress. On the one hand, *ren* stresses the significance of Wang's moral vision as residing in affectionate human relationships, a habitat that is capable of indefinite expansion and ultimately embraces the whole universe. Dao, on the other hand, stresses the ongoing course of changing circumstances that calls for an exercise of the agent's sense of rightness (*yi*). The unlimited possibilities of the concrete significance of Dao cannot be exhausted with any claim to finality (*dao wu zhongqiong*). Notably Wang sometimes uses the term *tianli* (heavenly principle, pattern, rationale) to express his vision of the highest good. *Tianli* is inherent in *xin* (heart/mind); often it is obscured by the presence of selfish desires.

Except for its ethical significance, Wang shows little interest in the pursuit of factual knowledge. Unlike Zhu Xi (1130–1200), who emphasizes the significance of *li* (principle, pattern, or rationale) in the investigation of things (*gewu*) in the Great Learning, Wang focuses instead on the rectification of the mind (*zhengxin*) that deviates from his moral vision. Rectification of the mind involves, in particular, an acknowledgment of the unity of moral knowledge and action (*zhixing heyi*), an enlargement of the scope of moral concern in the light of the vision of *ren*, rather than extensive acquisition of factual knowledge.

Wang's doctrine of the unity of knowledge and action is sometimes stated as the unity of moral learning and action (*xuexing heyi*). Wang's discussion involves two different senses of *zhi*, corresponding to two senses of knowledge. For convenience, this entry will use the distinction between prospective and retrospective moral knowledge—that is, knowledge acquired anterior or prior to action and knowledge posterior to action.

Prospective moral knowledge, for the most part, is a product of learning, an acknowledgment of the projective significance of the standards embedded in the various notions of Confucian virtues. Prospective moral knowledge is implicit in Wang's compendious remark that "knowledge is the direction of action and action is the effort of knowledge" (1963, p. 11) As prospective knowledge, and by virtue of its cognitive content, it provides a direction or a leading idea (*zhuyi*) for actual conduct. Another compendious remark appears to make use of both prospective and retrospective senses of moral knowledge: "knowledge is the beginning of action and action is the completion of knowledge" (1963, p. 11). Wang's emphasis on personal realization of his moral vision is an emphasis on retrospective moral knowledge. For Wang, the transition from prospective to retrospective knowledge involves a variety of intellectual acts (inquiry, understanding, sifting, or discrimination) and volitional acts (involving resolution, intention, moral desire, and the purity of moral motives in the endeavor to achieve the ideal of *ren*). More especially, in his mature thought, Wang constantly focused on extending *liangzhi*, commonly rendered as "innate or intuitive knowledge of the good."

Liangzhi, in the sense of the ability of moral discrimination, while basic, cannot capture the depth of Wang's concern in his teaching of extending *liangzhi*. While the human mind is in the rudimentary sense consciousness, without a commitment to the vision of *ren*—alternatively to Dao or *tianli*—it would be indifferent to moral concern. Possessed of *liangzhi*, the human mind as informed by the vision will be distinctively marked as moral consciousness. As Wang was wont to say, it is *liangzhi* that manifests *tianli* or *liangzhi* that manifests Dao. As the intrinsic quality (*benti*) of the moral mind, *liangzhi* is "naturally intelligent, clear and unbeclouded" (1963, p. 274). This notion of *liangzhi* as the seat of moral consciousness does involve *liangzhi* in the sense of moral discrimination, and significantly stresses the exercise of clear intelligence in discerning the moral import of particular situations. As embodying the concern for *tianli*, *liangzhi* is properly considered a personal standard; that is, a standard for making autonomous judgment of the moral quality of thought and actions, as well as feelings. Thus Wang's notion of *liangzhi* cannot be understood apart from his vision and confidence in the mind as possessing its own capability of realizing the vision.

Liangzhi, being an active concern of the moral mind with *tianli*, clearly involves the determination to its actualization. As embodying this active concern with *tianli*, *liangzhi* cannot be rendered as *intuition*, as this term is used in Ethical Intuitionism. Genuine perplexity arises in changing or exigent circumstances, where established standards do not provide clear guidance (Cua 1982, ch. 3). While *liangzhi* is inherent in all minds, the distinguishing characteristic of the sage lies in his or her attitude toward study and reflection. As invested with *tianli*, *liangzhi* is indeed a standard, but it does not issue recipes for coping with changing circumstances. Wang believed that *liangzhi* can provide unerring guidance, but it is unclear how he could account for failure in extending *liangzhi* and the relation between moral and factual knowledge. Focus on the nature of retrospective moral knowledge and experience may provide a critical point of departure for developing the notion of *liangzhi* in Confucian ethics.

See also Confucianism; Zhu Xi.

Bibliography

Chang, Carsun. *The Development of Neo-Confucian Thought.* Vol. 2. New York: Bookman Associates, 1962.

Ching, Julia. *To Acquire Wisdom: The Way of Wang Yang-ming.* New York: Columbia University Press, 1976.

Cua, A. S. "Between Commitment and Realization: Wang Yang-ming's Vision of the Universe as a Moral Community." *Philosophy East and West* 43 (4) (1993): 611–49.

Cua, A. S. *Moral Vision and Tradition: Essays in Chinese Ethics.* Washington, DC: The Catholic University of America Press, 1998.

Cua, A. S. *The Unity of Knowledge and Action: A Study in Wang Yang-ming's Moral Psychology*. Honolulu: University Press of Hawaii, 1982.

Deustch, Elliot, et al. "Proceedings of East-West Philosophers' Conference on Wang Yang-ming: A Comparative Study." *Philosophy East and West* 23 (1, 2) (1973).

Tu, Wei-ming. *Neo-Confucian Thought in Action: Wang Yang-ming's Youth (1472–1509)*. Berkeley: University of California Press, 1976.

Wang Yang-ming. *Instructions for Practical Living and Other Neo-Confucian Writings.* Translated by Wing-tsit Chan. New York: Columbia University Press, 1963.

Wang Yang-ming. *The Philosophical Letters of Wang Yang-ming.* Translated by Julia Ching. Columbia: University of South Carolina Press, 1972.

Antonio S. Cua (2005)

WAR

See *Peace, War, and Philosophy*

WATSUJI TETSURŌ

(1889–1960)

Watsuji Tetsurō, the best philosopher of ethics of modern Japan, was known also for his studies of cultural history. He was born in Himeji and died in Tokyo. Watsuji's work can be divided into three categories: his early literary efforts, his philological and historical studies, and his works on an ethical system. Gifted with literary talent, he wrote some short novels and a play while still studying philosophy, but these had no great success. Among his early philosophical essays are those on Friedrich Nietzsche (Tokyo, 1913) and on Søren Kierkegaard (Tokyo, 1915). His cult of ancient Greece, manifested in *Gūzō saikō* (The revivals of the idols; Tokyo, 1918), developed into an interest in the cultural history of his own country. His first work on this subject was *Nihon kodai bunka* (Ancient Japanese culture; Tokyo, 1920). Japanese culture and character were to be the subject of his constant study, as was attested by his *Nihon seishin-shi* (The history of Japanese spirit; 2 vols., Tokyo, 1926, 1934). Meanwhile, his other studies, based on philological research, covered the textual questions about Homer, primitive Christianity, early Buddhism, and Confucius. While these works differ in scientific value, they contain many insights and reveal him as more a litterateur than an expert philologist and historian. This is obvious in his well-known *Fūdo* (Tokyo, 1934; translated as *A Climate,* 1961), a work of psychological intuition and deep sensibility rather than a scientific or philosophical study of the conditioning effect of climate on culture.

A turning point in his career was his appointment as assistant professor of ethics at Kyoto University (1925). Out of his lectures at Kyoto grew his *Ningengaku toshite no rinrigaku* (Ethics as anthropology), a treatise of systematic ethics, initiated in 1931. Watsuji's ethic was designed as a Japanese system based upon the essential relationships of man to man, man to family, and man to society. In contrast with the private, individual ethics of the West, his ethic sees man as involved in community and society. *Rinri* (ethics) in Sino-Japanese characters meant for him the principle (*ri*—or *li* in Chinese) of companionship (*rin*). Furthermore, he introduced the Buddhist dialectic elements (negation of negation) to show how the individual is absorbed into the whole. It is true that in postwar years he rewrote the parts of his ethics concerning the state and the emperor. Yet his achievement was that he systematized—although in Western categories—a traditional ethics that is a substantial part of the ethos of Japan and also of China. His attitude toward East-West contacts may be surmised from his *Sakoku Nihon no higeki* (National seclusion, Japan's tragedy; Tokyo, 1951). His two-volume *Nihon rinri shisō-shi* (History of Japanese ethical thought; Tokyo, 1952) is a major contribution to the subject. Western philosophers who had a great influence upon Watsuji were Edmund Husserl and Martin Heidegger.

See also Buddhism; Confucius; Ethics, History of; Heidegger, Martin; Homer; Husserl, Edmund; Japanese Philosophy; Kierkegaard, Søren Aabye; Nietzsche, Friedrich.

Bibliography

Japanese primary sources include *Watsuji Tetsurō zenshū* (The complete works of Watsuji Tetsurō), 27 vols. (Tokyo: Iwanami Shoten, 1961–1992), and *Jijoden no kokoromi* (An attempt in autobiography; Tokyo, 1961).

Watsuji's *Fūdo* has been translated into English as *A Climate* by G. Bownas (Tokyo, 1961). A discussion of his work may be found in G. K. Piovesana, *Recent Japanese Philosophical Thought, 1862–1962* (Tokyo: Enderle Bookstore, 1963), pp. 131–145.

Gino K. Piovesana, S.J. (1967)

WAYLAND, FRANCIS

(1796–1865)

Francis Wayland, the American Baptist clergyman, educator, and moral philosopher, was one of the central figures in the modification of American collegiate education. As president of Brown University (1827–1855), he introduced proposals to ease the rigidity of the classical curriculum by an approximation of the later elective system. With his mentor, Eliphalet Nott of Union College, Schenectady, New York, Wayland approved of the substitution of modern language study for at least some of the required Greek and Latin, encouraged training in science and its practical application, and advocated a more professional faculty employed for longer terms. To some degree his interest in these reforms was the result of his Jeffersonian philosophy of democracy. He was completely in accord with Thomas Jefferson's insistence that a republican government can flourish only if the voters are well educated. He argued, too, that native talent was widely diffused and should be given the opportunity to develop through education.

Philosophically, Wayland was a naive realist of the Scottish school of philosophy. His theory of knowledge was basically Lockean sensationalism supported by a faculty psychology. Knowledge is gained by a combination of experience and intuition, leading to inductive generalizations whose certainty he did not question. Ultimately Wayland's epistemology rests upon a theistic assumption, that there is a correspondence between what man finds in the universe and what God put there for man to find. However, Wayland's most important contribution to American philosophic development was moral rather than epistemological. His textbook, *The Elements of Moral Science,* first published in 1835, was very widely used and served as a model for many imitators. In this book Wayland departed from the William Paley form of utilitarian ethics that had been taught in the colleges and introduced an ethical position more dependent upon the deontological position characteristic of Bishop Butler. The Enlightenment emphasis on the rights of man was subordinated to a philosophicoreligious stress upon ethics as a system of duties. The moral quality of an action is declared to reside in its intention rather than in its consequences.

Wayland's moral theory led him to an increasing rejection of the institution of slavery. At first he found intolerable only the thought of being himself a slave owner; later he came to feel that all property in human beings was intolerable. From a mildly antislavery position in 1835, he moved to vigorous abolitionism and support of the Union cause in the Civil War. To at least some of the Southern defenders of slavery, Wayland became the archenemy, particularly because of his insistence that the Scriptures cannot be used to support the institution of slavery. Wayland's exchange of letters with Richard Fuller, a Southern clergyman, published as *Domestic Slavery Considered as a Scriptural Institution* (New York and Boston, 1845), presents the arguments on both sides most effectively.

See also Butler, Joseph; Enlightenment; Jefferson, Thomas; Paley, William; Philosophy of Education, History of; Realism.

Bibliography

Wayland's *The Elements of Moral Science* has appeared in the John Harvard Library (Cambridge, MA: Belknap Press of Harvard University Press, 1963) with an extended introduction by the editor, J. L. Blau. Wayland's other major works are *The Elements of Political Economy* (New York: Leavitt Lord, 1837), *Thoughts on the Present Collegiate System in the United States* (Boston: Gould, Kendall and Lincoln, 1842), and *The Elements of Intellectual Philosophy* (Boston and New York, 1854). For discussions of Wayland see J. L. Blau, *Men and Movements in American Philosophy* (Englewood Cliffs, NJ: Prentice-Hall, 1952) and Wilson Smith, *Professors and Public Ethics* (Ithaca, NY: American Historical Association and Cornell University Press, 1956).

J. L. Blau (1967)

WEAKNESS OF THE WILL

The primary philosophical topic explored under the rubric "weakness of the will" is roughly what Aristotle called *akrasia*. This classical Greek term is formed from the alpha privative (basically, a negation sign) and *kratos*, meaning "strength" or "power." The power at issue is the power to control oneself in the face of actual or anticipated temptation. So *akrasia* is deficient self-control. Self-control, in this sense, may be understood as constituted primarily by a robust capacity to see to it that one does what one believes to be best on the whole when tempted to do otherwise. The self-controlled person, Aristotle writes, "is in such a state as … to master even those [temptations of a certain kind] by which most people are defeated," and the akratic person "is in such a state as to be defeated even by those … which most people master" (*Nicomachean Ethics* 1150a11–13).

In Plato's *Protagoras*, Socrates says that the common view about akratic action is that "many people who know what it is best to do are not willing to do it, though it is in their power, but do something else" (352d). Here he raises (among other issues) the central question in subsequent philosophical discussion of *akrasia*: Is strict akratic action possible? Strict akratic action may be defined as free, intentional action that is contrary to a conscious belief that the agent has at the time to the effect that it would be best to *A* (or best not to *A*)—best from the perspective of his own values, desires, beliefs, and the like, as opposed, for example, to a common evaluative perspective that he does not endorse. In this entry, I call beliefs with all the properties just mentioned *P beliefs*.

A feature of paradigmatic strict akratic actions that is typically taken for granted and rarely made explicit is that the *P* beliefs with which they conflict are rationally acquired. In virtue of clashing with the agent's rationally acquired *P* beliefs, akratic actions are subjectively irrational (to some degree, if not without qualification). There is a failure of coherence in the agent of a kind directly relevant to assessments of the agent's rationality. This kind of failure would be exhibited, for example, by a student who freely goes to a party tonight even though he or she has a *P* belief that it would be best not to go and to study instead.

To some theorists (e.g., R. M. Hare, Socrates, and Gary Watson), the threat that strict akratic action poses to our ability to make sense of human action seems so severe that they deem strict akratic action conceptually or psychologically impossible. Many others, including Donald Davidson, Alfred Mele, David Pears, and Amelie Rorty, try to accommodate strict akratic action in a general theory of human action.

SKEPTICISM ABOUT STRICT AKRATIC ACTION

For the purposes of this entry, it may be assumed (*P1*) that people sometimes act freely and (*P2*) that people sometimes perform intentional actions that are contrary to their *P beliefs*. Some compulsive hand-washers or crack cocaine addicts may occasionally confirm *P2*. But acting contrary to one's *P* belief is not sufficient for acting akratically; one's action must also be free. Some philosophers argue that strict akratic action is impossible because actions contrary to the agent's *P* beliefs are necessarily unfree.

Assumptions *P1* and *P2* and the following assertion form a consistent triad: (*UF*) All actions contrary to the agent's *P* belief are unfree. How might a philosopher try to defend *UF* while granting *P1* and *P2*? Here is a sketch of one such defense (Harepresents a similar argument in chapter 5):

Argument A

A1. Having a *P* belief that it is best to *A* now is conceptually sufficient for having an intention to *A* now.

A2. Any agent who intends to *A* now but does not *A* now is unable to *A* now.

A3. Such an agent, being unable to *A* now, is compelled to perform—and therefore unfreely performs—whatever pertinent intentional action he now performs.

Premise *A2* is falsified by simple counterexamples. A professional pitcher who intends to throw a pitch in the strike zone may accidentally miss even though he was able to do what he intended. Of course, the failures in alleged strict akratic actions may be different in important ways, and it may be claimed that *A2* simply needs to be revised to capture the difference. One likely suggestion is that in alleged strict akratic actions, the failure involves a change of intention—for example, a change from intending to study to intending to attend a party—whereas the pitcher's failure does not. Now, either the change of intention is paired with a corresponding change of belief or it is not. If there is a change of belief that matches the change of intention—for example, a change to believing that it would be better to attend the party—then the agent does not act contrary to his current *P* belief in executing that intention. But it is assumed that some actions are contrary to their agents' current *P* beliefs, and the skeptic is supposed to be arguing that all such actions are unfree. So suppose that the change of intention is not paired with a corresponding change of belief and that the agent's *P* belief persists. Then *A1* is false. It is falsified by an agent who had intended in accordance with a *P* belief but no longer so intends even though the belief persists.

A1 is in dire straits anyway, given *P2*. Consider compulsive hand-washers or crack cocaine addicts who believe that it is best not to wash their hands now or not to use crack now, but who do so anyway—intentionally and unfreely. If *A1* is true, they are intentionally washing their hands or using crack while intending not to do so. Although this may be conceptually possible—for example, perhaps an agent with a split brain may intend not to *A* while also intending to *A* and acting on the latter intention—it is a highly implausible hypothesis about representative cases of the kind at issue. A much more plausible hypothesis is that although the troubled agents believe that it would be best not to wash their hands now or not to use crack now, they lack a corresponding intention and instead intend to do what they are doing.

A3 also is problematic. Bob has been dieting and believes it best to order a low-calorie salad for lunch today. Unfortunately, he is tempted by several other items on the menu, including a hamburger, a steak, and a pork sandwich. He orders the steak. Even if Bob was unable to order the salad, we would need an argument that he was compelled to order the steak—that, for example, ordering the burger was not a live option.

Gary Watson offers the following argument for *UF*:

Argument B

B1. An agent's succumbing to a desire contrary to his *P* belief cannot be explained by his choosing not to resist nor by his making a culpably insufficient effort to resist.

B2. Only one explanation remains: The agent was unable to resist.

So *UF*. All actions contrary to the agent's *P* belief are unfree.

Watson argues that an agent's choosing not to resist cannot explain strict akratic action, for to make such a choice "would be to change" one's *P* belief (p. 337). For example, "The weak drinker's failure to resist her desire to drink is a failure to implement her choice not to drink. To choose not to implement this choice would be to change her original judgment, and the case would no longer be a case of failure to implement a judgment" (pp. 336–337). Watson also contends that an insufficient effort cannot be due to a belief that the effort is not worth the trouble, since the belief that it is worth the trouble is implicit in the violated *P* belief (p. 338). Nor, he argues, can the insufficient effort be explained by a misjudgment of "the amount of effort required," for misjudgment is "a different fault from weakness of will" (p. 338).

In some alleged instances of strict akratic action, agents believe that it would be best to *A*, choose accordingly, and then backslide while retaining that belief. In others, agents with the same *P* belief do not choose accordingly; they do not make the transition from belief to intention. Although Watson has the former kind of case in mind, it is useful to attend to a case of the latter kind. Imagine, if you can, that a drinker, Drew, who has had one shot of bourbon and needs to drive home soon, believes that it would be best to switch now to coffee but neither chooses nor intends to do so and intentionally drinks another bourbon. The reader is not asked to imagine that Drew akratically drinks the second bourbon; it is left open that she drinks it unfreely. If Drew can believe that it would be best not to drink a second bourbon without choosing accordingly, then she can fail "to resist her desire to drink" without there being any failure on her part "to implement her choice not to drink." If she makes no such choice, she does not fail to implement it. And if there is no such failure of implementation, then the reason Watson offers for maintaining that the agent "change[d] her original judgment" is undercut.

A scenario in which a belief-matching choice is made will be discussed shortly. The plausibility of scenarios of the present sort deserves a bit more attention now. Consider the following story. On New Year's Eve, Joe, a smoker, is contemplating kicking the habit. Faced with the practical question of what to do about his smoking, he is deliberating about what it would be best to do about it. He is convinced that it would be best to quit smoking sometime, but he is unsure whether it would be best to quit soon. Joe is under a lot of stress, and he worries that quitting smoking now might drive him over the edge. Eventually, he judges that it would be best to quit by midnight. But he is not yet settled on quitting. Joe tells his partner, Jill, that he has decided that it would be best to stop smoking, beginning tonight. Jill asks, "So is that your New Year's resolution?" Joe sincerely replies, "Not yet; the next hurdle is to decide to quit. If I can do that, I'll have a decent chance of kicking the habit."

This story at least has the appearance of coherence. Seemingly, although Joe decides that it would be best to quit smoking, he may or may not choose (i.e., form the intention) to quit. Watson offers no argument for the incoherence of stories of this kind. (It has not been claimed that Joe is a free agent.)

If Drew can fail to resist her desire for a second bourbon without changing her belief about what it is best to do, what about Lucy, who, like Drew, takes another bourbon despite believing that it would be best to switch now to coffee, but, unlike Drew, chooses to switch now to coffee when she makes her judgment? Watson would say (*W1*) that Lucy's "failure to resist her desire to drink [a second bourbon] is a failure to implement her choice not to drink," (*W2a*) that "to choose not to implement this choice [is] to change her original judgment," (*W2b*) that to choose not to resist her desire to drink a second bourbon is to change that judgment, and (*W3*) that Lucy's drinking the second bourbon is therefore not a strict akratic action, since it is not contrary to her *P* belief (pp. 336–337). Is *W2a* or *W2b* true? Watson offers no argument for either, and some stories in which analogues of both are false certainly seem coherent.

Here is one such story. Alex's friend, Bob, has proposed that they affirm their friendship by becoming blood brothers, since Alex is about to go away to prep school. The ceremony involves the boys' cutting their own right palms with a pocket knife and then shaking hands so that their blood will mingle. Alex is averse to cutting himself, but he carefully weighs his reasons for accepting the proposal against his competing reasons (including his aversion), and he judges that it would be best to accept the proposal and to perform the ceremony at once. He chooses, accordingly, to cut his hand with the knife straightaway. Without considering that he may find the task difficult, he grasps the knife and moves it toward his right palm with the intention of drawing blood. However, as he sees the knife come very close to his skin, he intentionally stops because of his aversion. He chooses not to implement his original choice just now, and he chooses not to resist his aversion further just now. Alex abandons his original choice. But he has not changed his mind about what it is best to do, and he is upset with himself for chickening out. (Soon, Alex resolves to try again, this time without looking. The second attempt succeeds.)

If this story is incoherent, Watson should explain why. If he were to assent to *A1*, he could appeal to it here: since Alex no longer intends to cut his hand straightaway, it would follow that he no longer believes that it would be best to cut it straightaway. But Watson rejects *A1* to accommodate compulsives who act contrary to a *P* belief.

EXPLAINING STRICT AKRATIC ACTION

Imagine that although Jack believes that it would be better to study tonight for tomorrow's test than to attend a friend's party, he goes to the party and does not study. To the extent that his belief is sensitive to his motivational states (e.g., his desire to get a decent grade on the test), it has a motivational dimension. That helps explain why strict akratic action is regarded as theoretically perplexing. How, some philosophers wonder, can the motivation that is directly associated with a belief of this kind—in this case, Jack's motivation to study—be outstripped by competing motivation, especially when the competing motivation (a desire to have fun tonight) has been taken into account in arriving at the belief?

One answer (defended in Mele 1987) rests partly on the following two theses and on various arguments for those theses.

> *P* beliefs normally are formed at least partly on the basis of our evaluation of the objects of our desires (i.e., the desired items).
>
> The motivational force of our desires does not always match our evaluation of the objects of our desires.

If both theses are true, it should be unsurprising that sometimes, although we believe it better to *A* than to *B*, we are more strongly motivated to *B* than to *A*. Given how our motivation stacks up, it should also be unsurprising that we *B* rather than *A*.

Thesis 1 is a major plank in a standard conception of practical reasoning. In general, when we reason about what to do, we inquire about what it would be best, or better, or good enough, to do, not about what we are most strongly motivated to do. When we ask such questions while having conflicting desires, our answers typically rest significantly on our assessments of the objects of our desires—which may be out of line with the motivational force of those desires, if thesis 2 is true.

Thesis 2 is confirmed by common experience and thought experiments and has a foundation in empirical studies. Desire-strength is influenced not only by our evaluation of the objects of desires, but also by such factors as the perceived proximity of prospects for desire-satisfaction, the salience of desired objects in perception or in imagination, and the way we attend to desired objects (as Ainslie, Metcalfe and Mischel, and others have observed). Factors such as these need not have a matching effect on assessment of desired objects.

Empirical studies of the role of representations of desired objects in impulsive behavior and delay of gratification (reviewed in Mele 1995) provide ample evidence that our representations of desired objects have two important dimensions, a motivational and an informational one. Our *P* beliefs may be more sensitive to the informational dimension of our representations than to the motivational dimension, with the result that such beliefs sometimes recommend actions that are out of line with what we are most strongly motivated to do at the time. If so, strict akratic action is a real possibility—provided that at least some intentional actions that conflict with agents' *P* beliefs at the time of action are freely performed. To be sure, it has been argued that no such actions can be free, but, as the preceding section indicates, representative arguments for that thesis are unpersuasive.

Unless a desire of ours is irresistible, it is up to us, in some sense, whether we act on it, and it is widely thought that relatively few desires are irresistible. Arguably, in many situations in which we act against our *P* beliefs, we could have used our resources for self-control in effectively resisting temptation. Normal agents can influence the strength of their desires in a wide variety of ways. For example, they can refuse to focus their attention on the attractive aspects of a tempting course of action and concentrate instead on what is to be accomplished by acting as they judge best. They can attempt to augment their motivation for performing the action judged best by promising themselves rewards for doing so. They can picture a desired item as something unattractive—for example, a wedge of chocolate pie as a wedge of chewing tobacco—or as something that simply is not arousing. Desires normally do not have immutable strengths, and the plasticity of motivational strength is presupposed by standard conceptions of self-control. Occasionally, we act contrary to our *P* beliefs, and it is implausible that, in all such cases, we are unable to act in accordance with those beliefs.

The key to understanding strict akratic action is a proper appreciation of the point that the motivational force or causal strength of a motivational attitude need not be in line with the agent's evaluation of the object of that attitude. Our *P* beliefs are based, in significant part, on our assessments of the objects of our desires; and when assessment and motivational force are not aligned, we may believe it better to *A* than to *B* while being more strongly motivated to *B* than to *A*. If while continuing to have that belief, we freely do *B*, our action is strictly akratic.

See also Aristotle; Davidson, Donald; Hare, Richard M.; Plato; Power; Socrates.

Bibliography

Ainslie, George. *Breakdown of Will*. Cambridge, U.K.: Cambridge University Press, 2001.

Aristotle. *Nicomachean Ethics*. In *The Complete Works of Aristotle: The Revised Oxford Translation,* edited by Jonathan Barnes. Princeton, NJ: Princeton University Press, 1984.

Charlton, William. *Weakness of Will*. Oxford: Basil Blackwell, 1988.

Davidson, Donald. *Essays on Actions and Events*. Oxford: Clarendon Press, 1980.

Dunn, Robert. *The Possibility of Weakness of Will*. Indianapolis, IN: Hackett, 1987.

Hare, R. M. *Freedom and Reason*. Oxford: Oxford University Press, 1963.

Mele, Alfred R. *Autonomous Agents: From Self-Control to Autonomy*. New York: Oxford University Press, 1995.

Mele, Alfred R. *Irrationality: An Essay on Akrasia, Self-Deception, and Self-Control*. New York: Oxford University Press, 1987.

Metcalfe, Janet, and Walter Mischel. "A Hot/Cool-System Analysis of Delay of Gratification: Dynamics of Willpower." *Psychological Review* 106 (1999): 3–19.

Pears, David. *Motivated Irrationality*. Oxford: Oxford University Press, 1984.

Plato. *Protagoras*. Translated by C. C. W. Taylor. Oxford: Clarendon Press, 1976.

Rorty, Amelie. "Where Does the Akratic Break Take Place?" *Australasian Journal of Philosophy* 58 (1980): 333–346.

Watson, Gary. "Skepticism about Weakness of the Will." *Philosophical Review* 86: 316–339.

Alfred R. Mele (2005)

WEBER, ALFRED

(1868–1958)

The German sociologist and philosopher of history Alfred Weber, like his older brother Max, studied law and political economy in preparation for a legal career and later changed to sociology and university teaching. Alfred Weber's academic career began in 1899 at the University of Berlin and continued at the University of Prague (1904), where he came into contact with Tomáš Masaryk, then professor of sociology. From 1907 to 1933, Weber held a professorship at Heidelberg; in 1933 he resigned at the rise of the Hitler regime. It was due largely to him that the Heidelberg Institute of Social Sciences became one of the chief centers of sociopolitical research during the Weimar Republic, and under his direction it regained its renown after World War II.

Having established his reputation as an economic sociologist by the publication in 1909 of his work on the location of industry (*Über den Standort der Industrien*), Weber turned to historical and cultural-sociological studies, culminating in his main work, *Kulturgeschichte als Kultursoziologie* (1935). In this work he attempted to discover by sociological analysis the chief structural constituents of the historical process. These constituents he distinguished as the social process, the civilization process, and the culture process; although he distinguished between them, he emphasized their relatedness within the diverse constellations of a given historical continuum. By "social process" Weber understood the reoccurrence of certain societal sequences that, notwithstanding individual variations, reveal sufficient uniformity to provide the basis for a comparative study of different peoples. As an example of such a social process, Weber cited the succession from kinship organization to territorial groupings in diverse sociohistorical entities. The "civilization process" was for him essentially the growth of knowledge concerning the techniques of controlling natural and material forces. Weber regarded the discovery of these techniques as a continuous and cumulative progress permitting, by virtue of the transferability of such knowledge, an element of homogeneity amid the otherwise heterogeneous sociohistorical circumstances.

Weber's main attention was focused on the "culture process," which he did not regard as transferable. Culture can be understood only by recognizing the historical uniqueness of each case, since culture derives from the creative spontaneity of man, which in turn is the expression of an "immanent transcendence" that is not susceptible to the generalizing methods of science. There can therefore be no causal laws in the domain of culture. To assert their existence seemed to Weber no less mistaken than Herbert Spencer's "wrong-headed social evolutionism" (*Farewell to European History,* p. 49). Like Johann Gottfried Herder, for whom he had a profound admiration, Weber deplored what he called the Enlightenment's "dogmatic progressivism" as a "dangerous sort of optimism" (loc. cit.). The progressivist, evolutionary thesis stemmed, in Weber's opinion, from confusing the culture process with the civilization process, thus misconceiving the nature of culture, for culture does not follow any definite or lineal order of development but occurs sporadically, defying the causal determinism that operates in the realms of science and technology.

Weber's theory of immanent transcendentalism also colored his political views. In place of state socialism (whether of the Bismarckian or the Marxist-Leninist kind), he advocated a "debureaucratized" form of "free socialism," under which man's functional role within the social system would never be that of a mere functionary whose inner sense of right and wrong could be made subservient to reasons of state.

Weber's insistence on viewing the historical world of man as a realm where transcendental but (in contrast to G. W. F. Hegel) immanent determinants are at least as decisive as empirical or material factors reveals not only his fundamental disagreement with the Marxist school of historical determinism but also his most significant point of departure from the sociological methodology of his older brother. Unlike Max Weber, Alfred Weber could not conceive of a meaningful sociological interpretation or explanation of human thought or action that aimed to dispense with a value-oriented perspective.

Alfred Weber may possibly have exaggerated the difference between his methodological approach and that of his brother; it may well be true to say with Arnold Brecht that it is a difference of degree rather than of kind, that Alfred Weber was a latent and partisan relativist and Max Weber an overt and neutral one (*Political Theory,* Princeton, NJ, 1959, p. 278). Be that as it may, Alfred Weber's stress on a specifically historicocultural approach to sociology, no less than his denial of the validity of the naturalistic method in the sphere of human affairs, contributed to the relative lack of understanding of his theories by many contemporary sociologists.

Whatever the ultimate assessment of Alfred Weber as a sociologist, his penetrating insight into the forces that shape human history and his uncompromising adherence to the principle of individual social responsibility place him high in the tradition of thinkers of integrity in scholarship and in action.

See also Enlightenment; Functionalism in Sociology; Hegel, Georg Wilhelm Friedrich; Herder, Johann Gottfried; Masaryk, Tomáš Garrigue; Philosophy of History; Weber, Max.

Bibliography

WORKS BY WEBER

Über den Standort der Industrien. Tübingen, 1909. Translated by C. J. Friedrich as *Theory of the Location of Industries.* Chicago: University of Chicago Press, 1929.

Gedanken zur deutschen Sendung. Berlin: Fischer, 1915.

"Prinzipielles zur Kultursoziologie." *Archiv für Sozialwissenschaft und Sozialpolitik* 47 (1920–1921): 1–49. Translated by G. H. Weltner and C. F. Hirschman as *Fundamentals of Culture-Sociology.* New York, 1939.

Die Not der geistigen Arbeiter. Munich, 1923.

Deutschland und die europäische Kulturkrise. Berlin: Fischer, 1924.

Die Krise des modernen Staatsgedankens in Europa. Stuttgart: Deutsche Verlags-Anstalt, 1925.

Ideen zur Staats- und Kultursoziologie. Karlsruhe: Braun, 1927.

Kulturgeschichte als Kultursoziologie. Leiden: Sijthoff, 1935.

Das Tragische und die Geschichte. Hamburg: Govert, 1943.

Abschied von der bisherigen Geschichte. Hamburg: Claassen and Goverts, 1946. Translated by R. F. C. Hull as *Farewell to*

European History. New Haven, CT: Yale University Press, 1948.

Der dritte oder der vierte Mensch. Munich: Piper, 1953.

Einführung in die Soziologie. Munich: Piper, 1955.

WORKS ON WEBER

Barnes, H. E., and Howard Becker. *Social Thought from Lore to Science,* 2 vols. New York: Heath, 1938. Vol. II, Ch. 20.

Colvin, Milton. "Alfred Weber—The Sociologist as a Humanist." *American Journal of Sociology* 65 (1959): 166–168.

Neumann, Sigmund. "Alfred Weber's Conception of Historico-Cultural Sociology." In *An Introduction to the History of Sociology,* edited by H. E. Barnes, 353–361. Chicago: University of Chicago Press, 1948.

Salomon, Albert. "The Place of Alfred Weber's *Kultursoziologie* in Social Thought." *Social Research* 3 (1936): 494–500.

Frederick M. Barnard (1967)

WEBER, MAX

(1864–1920)

Max Weber, the German sociologist, historian, and philosopher, was raised in Berlin. His father was a lawyer and National Liberal parliamentary deputy, his mother a woman of deep humanitarian and religious convictions. The Weber household was a meeting place for academics and liberal politicians. From 1882 to 1886 Weber studied law at the universities of Heidelberg, Berlin, and Göttingen, except for a year of military training. His doctoral dissertation (1889) was on medieval commercial law, and he continued his researches into legal history with a study of Roman agrarian law. In 1890 he was commissioned by the Verein für Sozialpolitik to investigate the social and economic plight of the east German agricultural worker. Between 1894 and 1897 he was professor of economics, first at Freiburg, then at Heidelberg. During the next four years, however, a severe nervous illness forced him into academic retirement and kept him from productive work. His health never recovered sufficiently for him to resume an academic career, and he spent the years preceding World War I mainly at Heidelberg as a private scholar, although he became associate editor of the *Archiv für Sozialwissenschaft und Sozialpolitik* in 1903. During the war he was director of army hospitals at Heidelberg. As a consultant to the German armistice commission at Versailles he helped to draw up the memorandum on German war guilt; he also advised the commission that prepared the first draft of the Weimar constitution. Late in the war, Weber had accepted a temporary teaching post at the University of Vienna, and in 1919 he became professor of economics at Munich. He died shortly thereafter.

SOCIOLOGY, POLITICS, ETHICS, AND ECONOMICS

Weber was attracted to practical politics as well as to scholarship, and he had a vivid sense of the political and cultural significance of historical and sociological investigations. Nevertheless, he insisted that these two "callings" must be kept apart, for both political and academic reasons. His east German agrarian studies had convinced him that the decline of the *Junkers* as a positive political force made it necessary to foster a professional class of politicians who could direct the German administrative machine. He condemned Otto von Bismarck for having failed to cultivate such a class and for thus paving the way for the political dilettantism to which Weber attributed most of the weaknesses of German diplomacy. He also argued that scientific and philosophical inquiries into social phenomena were not capable of settling disputes about ethical and cultural values, commitment to which was a sine qua non of worthwhile political activity. Empirical scientific investigation could lead to the discovery of the ultimate motives of human behavior, which would serve as a preliminary to an adequate causal explanation of historical events; it could demonstrate the means necessary to given ends; and it could show otherwise unsuspected by-products of alternative policies. Philosophical analysis could lay bare the conceptual structure of various evaluative systems, place them with respect to other possible ultimate values, and delimit their respective spheres of validity. But such studies could not show that any particular answers to evaluative questions were correct. Weber pointed out that an evaluative choice does not depend merely on technical considerations applied to given ends; it is inherent in the very nature of the criteria used to discuss such questions that dispute about those criteria is both possible and necessary. There would be something incoherent in the idea that such disputes could ever be definitively settled.

Weber argued that the blurring by academic writers of the distinction between fact and value characteristically led to two unwarranted prejudices. First, because of the academic's duty to examine all sides of any question, he was likely to develop a predilection for the middle course, although a compromise "*is not by a hairbreadth more scientifically true* than the most extreme ideals of the parties of the left or right." Second, because the scientific investigator's methods were peculiarly well adapted to discovering the probable results of policies, he was likely to think that a policy's value must also be settled by reference to results. But, Weber argued, policies could be rational, not merely in the sense of adapting means to ends (*zweckrational*), but also in the sense that they consistently and genuinely express the attachment to certain values of an agent who is indifferent to the achievement or nonachievement of further ends (*wertrational*).

Weber denied that any form of social activity could be purely economic. All activities have an economic aspect insofar as they face scarcity of resources and thus involve planning, cooperation, and competition. But economic considerations alone cannot explain the particular direction taken by any social activity or movement; for this, other values have to be taken into consideration. Further, the sociologist's own culturally conditioned values are already involved in the way in which he has isolated an intelligible field of study from the infinite complexity of social life. Hence, there is a certain subjectivity of value at the very foundations of social scientific inquiry, but this need not damage the objectivity of the results of such inquiry.

VERSTEHEN AND CAUSAL EXPLANATION

Social phenomena involve the actions of agents who themselves attach a sense (*Sinn*) to what they are doing. Correspondingly, sociology requires an understanding (*Verstehen*) of the sense of what is being studied. Without it, Weber argued, the sociologist would not even be in a position to describe the events he wants to explain. In this respect Weber was squarely in the tradition of G. W. F. Hegel, Wilhelm Dilthey, and Heinrich Rickert, but he developed these philosophical ideas into a methodology and applied it to a vast spectrum of empirical data.

Verstehen is particularly susceptible to the investigator's subjective bias, and the sense of unfamiliar forms of activity is likely to be interpreted by reference to what is familiar, but perhaps only superficially similar. Weber therefore thought that *Verstehen* must be supplemented by what he sometimes seemed to regard as a distinct method of inquiry, causal explanation. He argued that causal explanations in sociology are, as such, completely naturalistic and that the social sciences are distinguished by the addition of *Verstehen.* He did not always see clearly that a method which is to serve as a check on rashly subjective misinterpretations of the sense of an activity must itself be capable of producing more correct interpretations. Nor did he always understand that what he called causal explanation, therefore, must itself already involve the concept of *Verstehen.*

This point can be illustrated by Weber's treatment of authority (*Herrschaft*). As a prelude to a causal treatment, he tried to define authority naturalistically in terms of statistical laws expressing "the probability that a command with a given specific content will be obeyed by a given group of persons." The presence of expressions such as "command" and "obeyed" in this definition shows that it already presupposes *Verstehen.* This continues to hold for Weber's further treatment of the various types of legitimation in terms of which he classified authority: the traditional, the rational (bureaucratic), and the charismatic (involving attachment to the person of a powerful individual leader—Weber regarded charismatic authority as a principal source of social change). Here, as elsewhere in his work, the appeal to statistical laws must be understood as ancillary to the process of arriving at an adequate *Verstehen* and not as belonging to a distinct method of causal inquiry.

THE "IDEAL TYPE"

Both *Verstehen* and causal explanation are again involved in Weber's account of the use of "ideal types" in historical and sociological inquiries. Whereas a purely classificatory concept is reached by abstraction from a wide range of phenomena with differing individual characteristics, an ideal type is intended to illuminate what is peculiar to a given cultural phenomenon. Its most characteristic use is in connection with types of rational behavior. The ideal type is a model of what an agent would do if he were to act completely rationally according to the criteria of rationality involved in his behavior's sense. On the one hand, the ideal type facilitates *Verstehen* in that, although not itself a description of reality, it provides a vocabulary and grammar for clear descriptions of reality. On the other hand, although the ideal type is not itself a causal hypothesis, it is an aid to the construction of such hypotheses for the explanation of behavior that deviates from the ideal-typical norm. Weber regarded the three forms of authority (traditional, rational, and charismatic) as well as the theory of the market in economics as ideal types. The most succinct and celebrated application of the concept, as well as of most of his other methodological ideas, is to be found in *The Protestant Ethic and the Spirit of Capitalism.* In this work Weber argued that the development of European capitalism could not be accounted for in purely economic or technological terms but was in large part the result of the ascetic secular morality associated with the twin emphases in Calvinistic theology on predestination and salvation.

See also Authority; Determinism, A Historical Survey; Dilthey, Wilhelm; Hegel, Georg Wilhelm Friedrich; Philosophy of Social Sciences; Rickert, Heinrich.

Bibliography

WORKS BY WEBER

Gesammelte Aufsätze zur Religionssoziologie. 3 vols. Tübingen: Mohr, 1920–1921. Vol. I, Part 1, translated by Talcott Parsons as *The Protestant Ethic and the Spirit of Capitalism.* London: Allen and Unwin, 1930.

Gesammelte politische Schriften. Munich: Drei Masken, 1921.

Gesammelte Aufsätze zur Wissenschaftslehre. Tübingen: Mohr, 1922.

Wirtschaft und Gesellschaft. Tübingen: Mohr, 1922. 2nd ed., 2 vols. Tübingen, 1925. Part 1 translated by A. M. Henderson and Talcott Parsons as *The Theory of Social and Economic Organization.* Glencoe, IL, 1947. Vol. II, pp. 735ff., translated by Don Martindale and Gertrude Neuwirth as *The City.* New York: Free Press, 1958. Selections (chiefly from Ch. 7) in *Max Weber on Law in Economy and Society,* translated by E. A. Shils and Max Rheinstein. Cambridge, MA: Harvard University Press, 1954.

Wirtschaftsgeschichte. Munich: Duncker and Humblot, 1923. Translated by F. H. Knight as *General Economic History.* London: Allen and Unwin, 1927.

Gesammelte Aufsätze zur Soziologie und Sozialpolitik. Tübingen: Mohr, 1924.

From Max Weber: Essays in Sociology. Translated by H. H. Gerth and C. Wright Mills. New York: Oxford University Press, 1946.

Schriften zur theoretischen Soziologie, zur Soziologie der Politik und Verfassung. Frankfurt: Schauer, 1947.

On the Methodology of the Social Sciences. Translated and edited by E. A. Shils and H. A. Finch. Glencoe, IL: Free Press, 1949.

WORKS ON WEBER

Antoni, Carlo. *Dallo storicismo alla sociologia.* Florence, 1940. Translated by H. V. White as *From History to Sociology.* Detroit, MI: Wayne State University Press, 1959.

Aron, Raymond. *Essai sur la théorie de l'histoire dans l'Allemagne contemporaine.* Paris: Vrin, 1938.

Aron, Raymond. *La sociologie allemande contemporaine.* Paris: Alcan, 1935. Translated by M. Bottomore and T. Bottomore as *Modern German Sociology.* London, 1957.

Beetham, David. *Max Weber and the Theory of Modern Politics,* 2nd ed. Cambridge, U.K.: Polity Press, 1985.

Behnegar, Nasser. *Leo Strauss, Max Weber, and the Scientific Study of Politics.* Chicago: University of Chicago Press, 2003.

Bendix, Reinhard. *Max Weber. An Intellectual Portrait.* London: Heinemann, 1960.

Diggins, John P. *Max Weber: Politics and the Spirit of Tragedy.* New York: Basic, 1996.

Henrich, Dieter. *Die Einheit der Wissenschaftslehre Max Webers.* Tübingen, 1952.

Käsler, Dirk. *Max Weber: An Introduction to His Life and Work.* Translated by Philippa Hurd. Chicago: University of Chicago Press, 1988.

Lennert, Rudolf. *Die Religionstheorie Max Webers.* Stuttgart, 1935.

Mayer, J. P. *Max Weber and German Politics.* London: Faber and Faber, 1944.

Parsons, Talcott. *The Structure of Social Action.* New York: McGraw-Hill, 1937.

Scaff, Lawrence. *Fleeing the Iron Cage: Culture, Politics, and Modernity in the Thought of Max Weber.* Berkeley: University of California Press, 1989.

Swedberg, Richard. *Max Weber and the Idea of Economic Sociology.* Princeton, NJ: Princeton University Press, 2000.

Weber, Marianne. *Max Weber. Ein Lebensbild.* Tübingen: Mohr, 1926.

Peter Winch (1967)
Bibliography updated by Philip Reed (2005)

WEIL, SIMONE

(1909–1943)

The French author and mystic Simone Weil was born in Paris into a well-to-do family of distinguished intellectuals. During her lifetime she published only articles, dealing mainly with political and social issues, in obscure syndicalist sheets. Her uncompromising dedication to the search for truth and social justice as a way of life made her a significant though much debated personality. She lived a life of stringent deprivation. In spite of ill health she worked in factories, joined the anti-Franco volunteers in Spain, and worked as a farm laborer in the south of France after the 1940 defeat. After 1942 she lived in exile in New York and then in England. Jewish by birth, she wished to partake fully in the suffering of the victims of Nazism, and she allowed herself to die of hunger.

While in her twenties she was trained by Alain (Émile Auguste Chartier) in philosophy and logic. She had a voracious, relentless mind, and her studies included Greek, Latin, Sanskrit, several modern languages, philosophy, Western and Oriental religions, science, mathematics, and literature. Her writings are primarily based on textual comment and syncretic, ahistoric, and controversial interpretations. Her thought is rooted in Platonic and Stoic philosophy reinterpreted in terms of an apparently genuine mystical experience—in 1938 Weil experienced a moment of supernatural revelation and union with Christ. It gave her a mystical sense of vocation as possessor of a truth that she was delegated to transmit.

The bulk of her work, touching on the social, moral, aesthetic, and religious facets of life, was posthumously published. The published works combine fragments, more or less consistently developed and sometimes rather speciously selected, from her notebooks, letters, articles, and memoranda. The three-volume *Cahiers* (two volumes in the English translation) gives the integral but still fragmentary manuscript text from which the first published volumes were drawn.

A systematic interpretation of her work is problematical and, besides, could do her sometimes brilliant, sometimes obscure, paradoxical writing scant justice. Her thought is concentrated in two areas, the social and metaphysical, linked by her special concept of the human person. In a universe ruled by an iron, impersonal necessity, the human being shows an ineradicable expectation of goodness that is the sacred part of the human person. Society, the collective in whatever form, is the "large animal" offering the individual a false transcendency. Modern industrial society uproots but offers no values corresponding to the sacred aspirations of the individual. Not until labor and thought coincide and work is reintegrated into the spiritual edifice of society will the individual regain a sense of freedom, dignity, and community.

Central to Weil's thought is the fundamental human frustration caused by the inherent contradiction between two forces—the rigorous mechanical necessity at work in the universe and the inner expectation of good. Weil developed her metaphysics from this central conflict. She presents a dialectic of divine creation and voluntary personal "decreation" or disindividualization whereby the creature relinquishes the particular and becomes annihilated in divine love through methodical destruction of the self. The destruction of the self is to be attained first by rigorous use of discursive reason pushed to its ultimate limits, at which point there will remain only a wall of unpassable contradictions representing the absurdities of the human condition. The second step is the way of the mystics and involves nondiscursive disciplines—attention, waiting, "transparency," an inner void, and silence followed by certainty. Both methods of approach are apparent in her writing. Her God is impersonal and passive because all-loving. Only through a voluntary withdrawal of God could the act of creation take place. Evil, felt by man as suffering and apprehended by the understanding as the incomprehensible, is the paradoxical lot of the creature because of the nature of the initial act of finite creation by the infinite being.

See also Mysticism, History of; Mysticism, Nature and Assessment of; Platonism and the Platonic Tradition; Stoicism; Women in the History of Philosophy.

Bibliography

WORKS BY WEIL

For bibliographies see *Selected Essays, 1934–1943*, translated by Richard Rees (London: Oxford University Press, 1962), pp. 228–229, and Michel Throut, *Essai de bibliographie des écrits de Simone Weil*, Vol. 26, *Archives des lettres modernes* (October 1959, Paris).

The notebooks have been published in French as *Cahiers*, 3 vols. (Paris: Plon, 1951, 1953, 1956), and in English translation by Arthur F. Wills as *The Notebooks of Simone Weil*, 2 vols. (New York: Putnam, 1956).

The published selections of her writings include *La pesanteur et la gràce* (Paris: Plon, 1946), translated by Emma Craufurd as *Gravity and Grace* (London: Routledge, 1952); *L'enracinement* (Paris: Gallimard, 1949), translated by Arthur F. Wills as *The Need for Roots* (New York: Putnam, 1952); *Attente de Dieu* (Paris: La Colombe, 1950), translated by Emma Craufurd as *Waiting for God* (New York: Putnam, 1951); *La connaissance surnaturelle* (Paris: Gallimard, 1950); *La condition ouvrière* (Paris: Gallimard, 1951); *Lettre à un religieux* (Paris: Gallimard, 1951), translated by Arthur F. Wills as *Letter to a Priest* (London: Routledge, 1953); *Intuitions pré-chrétiennes* (Paris: La Colombe, 1951), parts of which have been selected, edited, and translated by Elisabeth Geissbuhler as *Intimations of Christianity among the Ancient Greeks* (London: Routledge, 1957); *La source grecque* (Paris: Gallimard, 1953); and *Écrits de Londres* (Paris: Gallimard, 1957).

Additional Works

Oppression et liberté. Paris: Gallimard, 1955.

Écrits de Londres et dernières lettres. Paris: Gallimard, 1957.

Leçons de philosophies (Roanne 1933–1934). Edited by Anne Reynaud. Paris: Plon, 1959.

Essai biographique et critique. Paris: Presses Universitaires de France, 1960.

Écrits historiques et politiques. Paris: Gallimard, 1960.

Pensées sans ordre concernant l'amour de Dieu. Paris: Gallimard, 1962.

Sur la science. Paris: Gallimard, 1966.

Réflexions sur les causes de la liberté et de l'oppression sociale. Paris: Gallimard, 1980.

Œuvres completes. 6 vols. Paris: Gallimard, 1989–1994.

Additional Translations

First and Last Notebooks. Translated by Richard Rees. London: Oxford University Press, 1970.

Formative Writings: 1929–1941. Edited and translated by Dorothy Tuck McFarland and Wilhelmina Van Ness. Amherst: University of Massachusetts Press, 1987.

Gateway to God. Edited by David Raper. Glasgow: Collins, Fontana, 1974.

The Iliad, or, The Poem of Force. Translated by Mary McCarthy. Wallingford, PA: Pendle Hill, 1956.

Lectures on Philosophy. Translated by H. Price. Cambridge: Cambridge University Press, 1978.

On Science, Necessity, and the Love of God. Collected, translated, and edited by Richard Rees. London: Oxford University Press, 1968.

Oppression and Liberty. Translated by Arthur Wills and John Petrie. Amherst: University of Massachusetts Press, 1973.

Seventy Letters. Translated by Richard Rees. London: Oxford University Press, 1965.
Simone Weil, an Anthology. Wallingford, PA: Pendle Hill, 1956.
The Simone Weil Reader. Edited by George A. Panichas. New York: David McKay, 1977.

WORKS ON WEIL

Allen, Diogenes, and Eric O. Springsted. *Spirit, Nature and Community: Issues in the Thought of Simone Weil*. Albany: State University New York Press, 1994.
Anderson, David. *Simone Weil*. London: SCM Press, 1971.
Bell, Richard H., ed. *Simone Weil's Philosophy of Culture*. Cambridge, U.K.: Cambridge University Press, 1993.
Blum, Lawrence, and Victor Seidler. *A Truer Liberty: Simone Weil and Marxism*. London: Routledge and Kegan Paul, 1989.
Cabaud, Jacques. *Simone Weil: A Fellowship in Love*. New York: Channel Press, 1964.
Coles, Robert. *Simone Weil: A Modern Pilgrimage*. Reading, MA: Addison-Wesley, 1987.
Davy, Marie-Magdeleine. *The Mysticism of Simone Weil*. Translated by Cynthia Rowland. Boston: Beacon Press, 1951.
Dietz, Mary G. *Between the Human and the Divine: The Political Thought of Simone Weil*. Otowa, NJ: Rowman & Littlefield, 1988.
Dunaway, John M., and Eric O. Springsted. *The Beauty That Saves: Essays on Aesthetics and Language in Simone Weil*. Macon, GA: Mercer University Press, 1966.
Fiori, Gabriella. *Simone Weil: An Intellectual Biography*. Translated by Joseph R. Berrigan. Athens: University of Georgia Press, 1989.
Gray, Francine du Plessix. *Simone Weil*. New York: Viking, 2001.
Kempfer, G. *La philosophie mystique de Simone Weil*. Paris: La Colombe, 1960.
Little, J. P. *Simone Weil: Waiting on Truth*. Oxford: St. Martin's Press, 1988.
Malan, I. R. *L'enracinement de Simone Weil*. Paris: Didier, 1961.
McClellan, David. *Utopian Pessimist—The Life and Thought of Simone Weil*. New York: Poseidon Press, 1990.
McFarland, Dorothy Tuck. *Simone Weil*. New York: Unger, 1983.
Moulakis, Anthanasios. *Simone Weil and the Politics of Self-Denial*. Translated by Ruth Hein. Columbia: University of Missouri Press, 1998.
Nevin, Thomas. *Simone Weil, Portrait of a Self-Exiled Jew*. Chapel Hill: University of North Carolina Press, 1991.
Perrin, J. M., and Gustave Thibon. *Simone Weil as We Knew Her*. Translated by Emma Craufurd. London: Routledge and Kegan Paul, 1953.
Pétrement, Simone. *Simone Weil: A Life*. New York: Pantheon, 1976.
Rees, Richard. *Simone Weil: A Sketch for a Portrait*. Carbondale: Southern Illinois University Press, 1966.
Rhees, Rush. *Discussions of Simone Weil*. Edited by D. Z. Phillips. Albany: State University of New York Press, 1998.
Springsted, Eric O. *Simone Weil and the Suffering of Love*. Cambridge, U.K.: Cowley, 1986.
Veto, Miklos. *The Religious Metaphysics of Simone Weil*. Translated by Joan Dargan. Albany: State University of New York Press, 1994.
Winch, Peter. *Simone Weil: "The Just Balance."* Cambridge, U.K.: Cambridge University Press, 1980.

Germaine Brée (1967)
Bibliography updated by Thomas Nenon (2005)

WELL-BEING

See *Eudaimonia; Happiness; Self-Interest.*

WESTERMARCK, EDWARD ALEXANDER
(1862–1939)

Edward Alexander Westermarck is best known as an anthropologist and sociologist; he is important in philosophy, however, as an exponent of a subjectivist theory of ethics, which he illustrated and supported by a survey of the actual variations in moral ideas. He himself made it clear in *Memories of My Life* that his interest in the sociology of morals arose from a concern with the philosophical question of the status of moral judgments and not vice versa.

Westermarck was born in Helsinki, Finland, of Swedish ancestry and was educated at the University of Helsinki. After 1887 he lived partly in England and partly in Finland, but he also made lengthy visits to Morocco from 1897 on. He was lecturer in sociology at the University of London from 1903 and professor of sociology there from 1907 to 1930; professor of practical philosophy at the University of Helsinki from 1906 to 1918; and professor of philosophy at the Academy of Abo from 1918. Westermarck did not marry, and his life was spent mainly in research, writing, and university teaching. On occasion, however, he joined other Finnish intellectuals in defense of their country's national interests, and he took a leading part in the founding of people's high schools for the Swedish-speaking population of Finland and of the Swedish university at Abo in Finland, of which he became the first rector in 1918.

As an undergraduate Westermarck became (and thereafter remained) an agnostic. The theme of his last book, *Christianity and Morals,* is that the moral influence of Christianity has been, on the whole, bad rather than good. He found German metaphysics distasteful but was attracted by English empiricism, especially that of J. S. Mill and Herbert Spencer. This interest, together with the aim of using the library of the British Museum, attracted Westermarck to England. Through an interest in evolution he was led to the investigation of the history of marriage, which was to be the subject of his first book. Though much of his later work was based on his own observations and personal knowledge of Morocco, all Westermarck's early anthropological research was carried out in the reading room of the British Museum. On each topic that he studied, he painstakingly collected an enormous volume of data from a wide range of sources. His aim was never merely to amass evidence, however, but to draw general conclusions from it. In *The History of Human Marriage,* for example, he rejected the widely accepted theory of primitive promiscuity or communal marriage, severely criticizing the use of supposed "survivals" as evidence for it and showing that the actual evidence pointed to the extreme antiquity of individual marriage. And throughout this work evolution by natural selection is used as a guiding principle in forming theories and explanations.

Westermarck's second and longest work, *The Origin and Development of the Moral Ideas,* written from 1891 to 1908, is partly philosophical and partly sociological. He began by propounding the subjectivist view of ethics presupposed in the whole plan of the investigation. No ethical principles are objectively valid; moral judgments are based not on the intellect but on emotions; there can be no moral truths. "Consequently the object of scientific ethics cannot be to fix rules for human conduct … its task can be none other than to investigate the moral consciousness as a fact." Thus, he discussed the nature and origin of the specifically moral emotions and the analysis of moral concepts, and he carefully examined and attempted to explain the conflicting tendencies to pass moral judgments on overt acts or exclusively on the will.

The bulk of this work treats the moral ideas comparatively and historically in order to confirm this account of the moral consciousness. Westermarck surveyed the varying attitudes and practices of many human societies on such topics as homicide, blood revenge, charity, slavery, truthfulness, altruism, asceticism, regard for the dead, and regard for supernatural beings. This detailed survey showed the continuity between moral and nonmoral retributive emotions and traced the variations in moral ideas to a number of causes.

General conclusions do not readily emerge from this mass of information, but some widely held views are conclusively proved to be false. There is no simple path of moral advance through history; many of the sentiments and rules that we associate with moral refinement are found in primitive peoples, while more barbarous views and practices have sometimes accompanied the advance of civilization. Nevertheless, Westermarck did indicate a few main trends that he expected to continue—the expansion of the altruistic sentiment, the increasing influence on moral judgments of reflection as opposed to sentimental likes and dislikes, and the restricting of religion to the function of supporting ordinary moral rules as opposed to special religious duties.

Ethical Relativity is Westermarck's most exclusively philosophical work. It repeated much from the early chapters of *The Origin and Development of the Moral Ideas,* but it argued more directly for the subjectivist view of ethics and replied to such critics of the earlier work as G. E. Moore, Hastings Rashdall, and William McDougall. Westermarck began by saying that if moral judgments state objective truths, there must be considerations by which their truth can be established, but he showed that typical ethical theories, including hedonism, utilitarianism, evolutionary ethics, rationalism, and the various accounts of a special "moral faculty," are quite unable to defend their basic principles. He recognized that the variability of moral judgments did not in itself disprove objectivism, but he argued that the persistent disagreement even on fundamental principles among the most thoughtful of moral specialists tells strongly against every form of intuitionism. He admitted that our ordinary moral judgments make a claim to objectivity, but he rightly insisted that this does not show that any judgments have objective validity. Our moral judgments result from the "objectivizing" of moral emotions, this being just one example of "a very general tendency to assign objectivity to our subjective experience." This point is of radical importance, for it undermines all attempts to support ethical objectivism by appealing to the meaning of moral terms and incidentally reveals Westermarck's firm grasp of essentials that are often obscured by the current preoccupation with the use of ethical language.

To the argument that the subjectivist theory is fatal to our spiritual convictions and aspirations, Westermarck replied that a scientific theory would not be invalidated even if it were shown to be harmful and that in any case subjectivism, by making people more tolerant and more critically reflective, is likely to do more good than harm. In reply to McDougall he defended his view that there are distinguishable moral emotions, marked off by apparent impartiality.

An important part of *Ethical Relativity* and the earlier work is the analysis of particular moral concepts to show exactly how they are related to emotions. Among other things Westermarck insisted that although the concept of "moral goodness" is based on approval, those of "right," "ought," and "duty" rest not on approval but on disapproval, of what ought not to be done or ought not to be omitted.

Westermarck admitted that the variability of moral judgments is due largely to differences in knowledge and beliefs, especially religious beliefs, and that insofar as variability can be thus explained, it is not evidence against the objective validity of ethics. However, some variations—in particular, in the breadth of the altruistic sentiment—are due to emotional differences. The gradual extension of morality until it enjoins respect for all humankind and even for animals is due to the expansion of this altruistic sentiment, not to reason or religion. Not only particular moral judgments, but also the broader features of normative theories, are explained by the emotional basis of ethics. This applies not only to various hedonistic views, which are obviously linked to the source of the moral emotions in pleasure and pain, but also to the ethics of Immanuel Kant, which Westermarck criticized very thoroughly, concluding that "in his alleged dictates of reason the emotional background is transparent throughout" (p. 289).

Westermarck's ethical subjectivism belongs to a persistent, though often unpopular, tradition in philosophy. He himself particularly commended Adam Smith's *Theory of Moral Sentiments.* Westermarck's own chief contributions are his stress on "objectivization," his careful analysis of moral concepts in relation to the emotions, and his moderate and cautious use of the argument from the variability of moral judgments, backed by immense evidence of this variability. His criticism of many contrary views and his defense of his own theory against contemporary critics are also effective, though he did not develop very far the logical and epistemological considerations that tell against the objectivist view of ethics. He formulated his account with considerable care. By making it clear that moral judgments do not report the feelings of the speaker or of anyone else and that moral terms are not necessarily simply expressive of the immediate feelings of the speaker, he protected his view against the stock objections to cruder versions of subjectivism, and he left room for the part played by social demand and custom in the genesis of morality. His formulations are, perhaps, still open to more refined objections, for to give any adequate account of moral concepts is a difficult task. There are also difficulties in his theory of the moral emotions. Nevertheless, some contemporary moral philosophers believe that Westermarck's views on ethics are substantially correct and that he made an important contribution to the development and defense of views of this kind.

See also Ethical Subjectivism; Ethics and Morality; Ethics, History of; Kant, Immanuel; McDougall, William; Mill, John Stuart; Moore, George Edward; Rashdall, Hastings; Smith, Adam.

Bibliography

WORKS BY WESTERMARCK

The Origin and Development of the Moral Ideas, 2 vols. London: Macmillan, 1906–1908.

The History of Human Marriage, 5th ed., 3 vols. London: Macmillan, 1921.

The Goodness of Gods. London: Watts, 1926.

A Short History of Marriage. New York: Macmillan, 1926.

Memories of My Life. London: Allen and Unwin, 1929.

Early Beliefs and Their Social Influence. London: Macmillan, 1932.

Ethical Relativity. London: Kegan Paul, 1932.

Three Essays on Sex and Marriage. London: Macmillan, 1934.

The Future of Marriage. London: Macmillan, 1936.

Christianity and Morals. London: Kegan Paul, 1939.

WORKS ON WESTERMARCK

Discussions of Westermarck's philosophical views can be found in Paul Edwards's *The Logic of Moral Discourse* (Glencoe, IL: Free Press, 1955), pp. 46–50, 61–64; G. E. Moore's *Philosophical Studies* (London: Routledge, 1922), pp. 332–336; and L. A. Reid's review of Westermarck's *Ethical Relativity,* in *Mind* 42 (1933): 85–94.

J. L. Mackie (1967)

WEYL, (CLAUS HUGO) HERMANN

(1885–1955)

(Claus Hugo) Hermann Weyl, the German-American mathematician, physicist, and philosopher of science, was born in Elmshorn, Germany, and died in Zürich. He studied at Munich and received his Ph.D. in 1908 from Göttingen, where he was Privatdozent from 1910 to 1913. He taught at the Eidgenossische Technische Hochschule in Zürich from 1913 to 1930, lecturing at Princeton in 1928-1929. He taught at Göttingen again from 1930 to 1933 and then returned to Princeton, remaining at the Institute for Advanced Study until 1953, when he became emeritus. He became a naturalized citizen in 1939. In 1925 he received the Lobachevski Prize for his research in geometrical theory. Weyl received many honorary degrees and was a member of numerous scientific societies and a civilian member of the Office of Scientific Research and Development in 1944.

Weyl's *Raum, Zeit, Materie* (Berlin, 1918; translated by H. L. Brose from the 4th German edition as *Space-Time-Matter,* London, 1922) is a classic in relativity theory. Weyl also made significant contributions to the formalization of quantum theory (*Gruppentheorie und Quantenmechanik,* Leipzig, 1928; translated by H. P. Robertson as *Theory of Groups and Quantum Mechanics,* London, 1931). Perhaps his most important contribution of philosophical interest in this book was his attempted solution to the problem of a unified field theory in relativity. Such a theory would ultimately express in one general invariant mathematical tensor equation or law the characteristics of gravitational, electric, and magnetic fields, and show the so-called elementary particles (such as electrons or protons) as derivative from that equation. That is, the discontinuous "particles" would be generated and controlled by the continuous unified field. In 1950, in a new preface to *Space-Time-Matter,* Weyl wrote that after his own first attempt at formulating such a theory, "Quite a number of unified field theories have sprung up in the meantime. They are all based on mathematical speculation and, as far as I can see, none has had a conspicuous success." He explained that "a unitary field theory … should encompass at least three fields: electromagnetic, gravitational, and electronic. Ultimately the wave fields of other elementary particles will have to be included too, unless quantum physics succeeds in interpreting them all as different quantum states of one particle." (In quantum theory all particles have associated wave fields.) No such theory has as yet been successfully formulated, despite even Albert Einstein's final heroic and desperate attempts along this line.

Weyl also showed the validity in general relativity of a variational principle of least action. He dealt in some detail with the problem of action at a distance by examining and defining more precisely the notion of gravitational waves propagated at a finite speed (the speed of light), as is held in general relativity, in contrast to the older Newtonian theory of an infinite or indefinitely high speed for all gravitational influences. Weyl also espoused a cosmological model in which all observers located on different galaxies anywhere would have equivalent overall views of the universe.

Weyl's *Das Kontinuum* (Leipzig, 1918) consists, first, of a logical and mathematical analysis of groups and functions and deals with such questions as the axiomatic method (in the manner of David Hilbert), the natural numbers (including Richard's antinomy), and the iteration and substitution principles of formal mathematical systems. Second, Weyl analyzed the concept of number in general, in conjunction with the notion of the continuum: the logical foundations of the infinitesimal calculus, with applications to spatial and temporal continua, magnitudes and measures, curves and surfaces. In all of this he explicitly used the ideas of Georg Cantor, Bertrand Russell, A. N. Whitehead, Jules Henri Poincaré, Augustin-Louis Cauchy, Richard Dedekind, Gottlob Frege, Ernst Zermelo, and Henri Bergson. Throughout, he attempted to distinguish the abstract, idealized, schematized ("objective") mathematical continua of space and time from the intuitive, phenomenal ("subjective") space and time personally and immediately experienced by each individual. Weyl acknowledged a debt to the ideas of Bergson concerning "duration" as given in phenomenal or intuitive time.

Weyl's definitive work in the philosophy of science, *Philosophie der Mathematik und Naturwissenschaft* (Munich, 1927; translated by O. Helmer, revised and augmented, as *Philosophy of Mathematics and Natural Science,* Princeton, NJ, 1949), dealt with pure and applied mathematics. In pure mathematics, he discussed mathematical logic and axiomatics, number theory and the continuum, the infinite, and geometry. In the natural sciences, he explained basic questions concerning space, time, and the transcendental world, with special concern for the epistemological problem of subject and object. The transcendental world is, of course, the Kantian idea with Weyl's added notion that this world might be knowable by the physicist. But the question of knowing was precisely the epistemological problem that troubled Weyl, as will be seen below.

In this work Weyl also discussed methodological problems in the theory of measurement and in the formation of scientific concepts and theories. Finally, he attempted to offer a general "physical picture of the world" in the course of analyzing the ideas of matter and causality.

The first German edition of *Philosophy of Mathematics and Natural Science* was written just before the broader philosophical implications of quantum theory had been recognized; hence Weyl added several appendices to the English edition in which he coped with the newer problems. In Appendix C he declared that "whatever the future may bring, the road will not lead back to the old classical scheme." Thus, Weyl had no real hope that a classical mechanical model would ever again be established as the basis of objective reality, and he explicitly emphasized that in quantum theory the relations between subject and object "are more closely tied together than classical physics had recognized." Weyl's notion of the vagueness of the distinction between subject and object in quantum theory has deeper metaphysical implications, of which fact he was clearly aware. How could we know the real world apart from our interactions with it and apart from the consequent indeterminacy in such "knowledge"? What, then, is the physical "object" apart from our subjective knowledge of it?

Weyl's final work was *Symmetry* (Princeton, NJ, 1952), published on the eve of his retirement from the institute. In it Weyl related the precise geometrical concept of symmetry to the vaguer artistic ideas of proportion, harmony, and beauty. In this account he was sensitive to the ideas of Plato and other great Greek classical aestheticians. His illustrated survey ranged from Sumerian art forms through the ancient Greeks and the medievals, and down to contemporary physicists, crystallographers, and biologists, briefly mentioning modern women's fashions.

See also Bergson, Henri; Cantor, Georg; Confirmation Theory; Frege, Gottlob; Hilbert, David; Mathematics, Foundations of; Philosophy of Science, History of; Philosophy of Science, Problems of; Plato; Poincaré, Jules Henri; Relativity Theory; Russell, Bertrand Arthur William; Whitehead, Alfred North.

Bibliography

Other works by Weyl of interest to philosophers of science are: *Die Idee der Riemannschen Fläche* (Leipzig, 1913); *The Classical Groups* (Princeton, NJ: Princeton University Press, 1939); *Algebraic Theory of Numbers* (Princeton, NJ: Princeton University Press, 1940); *Metamorphic Functions and Analytic Curves* (Princeton: Princeton University Press, 1943); and *The Structure and Representation of Continuous Groups* (Princeton: Princeton University Press, 1955).

For further works by Weyl and for works on him, see *Biographical Memoirs of the Fellows of the Royal Society* 3 (1957): 305–328.

Carlton W. Berenda (1967)

WHATELY, RICHARD

(1787–1863)

Richard Whately, the English logician, was a fellow of Oriel College and archbishop of Dublin. In 1860 Augustus De Morgan said of Whately that "to him is due the title of the restorer of logical study in England." Between 1826, the year Whately's *Elements of Logic* was published, and 1860, George Boole, De Morgan, and John Stuart Mill were writing. It is therefore natural to expect to find adumbrations of their work in Whately, but in his systematic and formal treatment of logic there are remarkably few. Mill did mention that Whately revived the discussion of connotative terms (called attributive by Whately). Whately's section on "the drift of propositions," which is original and perceptive, was ignored until the twentieth century. Yet this is all that was original, and it is to be found only in later editions.

This systematic section was based on Henry Aldrich's cram book, *Artis Logicae Compendium,* published in 1691 and still used at Oxford in Whately's day. The section was conservative. All propositions were considered to be subject–copula–predicate in form. All arguments were held to be reducible to syllogisms and syllogisms to be based on the *dictum de omni et nullo,* for this is the dictum of the first figure, and the other figures reduce to the first. Modal and hypothetical propositions were squeezed into subject–copula–predicate form. Disjunctives were reduced to hypotheticals and then treated as such.

Why, then, did De Morgan regard Whately as the "restorer of logical study in England"? The book was something of a best seller and the style, roughly Gilbert Ryle vintage 1826, is excellent. But this was not enough.

Whately's achievement was not so much in logic as in moral metalogic; he explained what logicians should have been doing. When he wrote, nearly 250 years after Francis Bacon, no British philosopher had made a convincing reply to the charges leveled against logic from the time of the Renaissance. The case was lost by default, and the status of logic sank so far that it ceased to be something a philosophical system must make room for, as geometry was, and became something that must accommodate itself to the convenience of the system. Therefore, logic had been continually rewritten to suit current philosophical speculation. The status of logic could not be restored until the subject matter was defined, the rewriting ended, and the charges against it answered.

Logic, said Whately, is "entirely conversant about language," and it is only as reasoning is expressed in language that logic can study it. He was not concerned with whether reasoning can be carried out some other way—by, say, "abstract ideas." This delimitation of the subject for investigation was neutral and did not necessitate subscribing to the nominalism Whately took over from Thomas Hobbes.

Once the subject was delimited, the charges against logic could be more effectively answered. Whately granted the common objection, voiced by John Locke, that man argued correctly before syllogism was heard of;

nevertheless, putting arguments in logical form provides a test of validity. This test applies in all fields. There is no logic peculiar to science or religion. Induction is not a new method of reasoning, as Bacon claimed. Induction means, first, a form of argument; but inductions of this sort are syllogistic. Induction also means generalizing from instances. This is not the province of logic, and logic cannot guarantee the truth of premises so reached. While it is true that in syllogism the conclusion contains nothing that is not in the premises, this does not render it futile, as George Campbell and others had held. "It is peculiarly creditable to Adam Smith and Malthus, that the data from which they drew such important conclusions had been in everyone's hands for centuries" (Whately, *Elements of Logic,* Book IV, Ch. 2, Sec. 4).

By example as well as by argument Whately combated the view that "logic is the Art of bewildering the learned by frivolous subtleties." He illustrated points and drew exercises from discussions in science, sociology, and religion, and thus exhibited logic in use.

Whately's *Elements of Rhetoric* (London, 1828) dealt with the effectiveness of arguments, but it also contains interesting material on such subjects as plausibility and argument from analogy. *Historic Doubts Relative to Napoleon Buonaparte* (London, 1819) is a witty and attractive reductio ad absurdum of David Hume's short way with miracles. Whately edited and annotated works of William Paley and Bacon, noting the naturalistic fallacy in Paley. He also wrote much on questions of the day relating to Ireland and on religion and economics.

See also Bacon, Francis; Boole, George; De Morgan, Augustus; Fallacies; Hobbes, Thomas; Hume, David; Induction; Logic, History of; Logic, Traditional; Malthus, Thomas Robert; Mill, John Stuart; Paley, William; Smith, Adam.

Bibliography

In addition to the works cited in the text, see E. J. Whately, *Life and Correspondence of Richard Whately, D.D.*, 2 vols. (London: Longmans, Green, 1866).

Mary Prior (1967)

WHEWELL, WILLIAM
(1794–1866)

William Whewell, the British philosopher and historian of science, was born in Lancaster. He spent the greater part of his life at Trinity College, Cambridge, as an undergraduate, fellow, and tutor, and finally as master of Trinity from 1841 until his death. He twice served as vice chancellor of Cambridge University, and he also taught mineralogy and later (1838–1855) moral philosophy.

Whewell's output was exceptional both in its abundance and in its diversity. Save for a dozen papers on the tides (1833–1850), however, his scientific works were devoted not so much to research as to teaching (*Mechanical Euclid,* Cambridge, U.K., 1837) or popularization and to apologetics (*Astronomy and General Physics,* London, 1833; *Plurality of Worlds,* London, 1853). In addition to his scientific writings he published a number of works in moral philosophy (*Elements of Morality, Including Polity,* 2 vols., London, 1845; *Lectures on Systematic Morality,* London, 1846; *Lectures on the History of Moral Philosophy in England,* London, 1852) and pedagogy (*Principles of English University Education,* London, 1837; *Of a Liberal Education,* London, 1845). He also produced editions, with prefaces, notes, and in some instances translations, of works by Isaac Newton, Joseph Butler, Hugo Grotius, Plato, and others, as well as sermons, poetry, and occasional or polemical essays.

However, his principal work—in length, scope, and the central position it occupies in his thought—is constituted by the *History of the Inductive Sciences, from the Earliest to the Present Time* (3 vols., London, 1837) and the *Philosophy of the Inductive Sciences, Founded upon Their History* (London, 1840). The former, one of the first general histories of natural science, is erudite yet perfectly readable. The latter, revised and enlarged for its third edition, was published in three parts under separate titles: *History of Scientific Ideas* (2 vols., London, 1858); *Novum Organon Renovatum* (London, 1858); and *On the Philosophy of Discovery* (London, 1860).

According to Whewell, the theory of induction, which had been examined to the point of exhaustion after Francis Bacon formulated it as a program for future science, should be taken up again in view of the fact that the sciences called inductive have been actually established. Notwithstanding the opinions of the "writers of authority" invoked by J. S. Mill, the word *induction* can now validly signify only one thing: the method of construction employed in those sciences that all modern thinkers agree to call inductive. And the only means of becoming acquainted with this method is to see it at work in history. (This is the source of the close connection between the two works, the *History* and the *Philosophy,* which matured simultaneously over a period of many years.)

INDUCTION AND HISTORY

The study of history reveals an inductive process that does not resemble the generalizing argument of the logicians. In the first place, the induction practiced by the scientist is not reasoning that is valid *vi formae* (by virtue of its form). It is quite another way of arriving at truth: a venturesome course taken by the mind, which, as if deciphering a cryptogram, tests or tries out various hypotheses in turn, until by a "happy guess" it hits upon the relevant idea. The question therefore is not under what conditions this procedure is logically correct—it never is—but simply whether its result is sound. Care and rigor assert themselves in the experimental control of the inductive proposition, and not in its elaboration, which allows great freedom to the imagination. It is fruitless to try to set up an "inductive logic" that is symmetrical with deductive logic and that formulates canons analogous to those of the syllogism.

In the second place, scientific induction consists not in generalizing the observed facts but in colligating them, in binding them together by the intelligible unity of a new conception. Finding this conception requires the initiative of genius. Generalization comes afterward; the decisive discovery is the forging of the idea. Once this idea has taught us how to read experience, it becomes incorporated into experience; and it seems to us that we see it there. Thus, the contribution of the mind to knowledge is ignored: this is the source of the empiricist error. One forgets that the facts have little by little been given form by ideas and that the facts of today (such as the fact that the earth revolves) are the hypotheses of yesterday; our facts are realized theories.

INDUCTION AND IDEAS

Whewell's epistemological analyses have a general philosophical import; indeed, they furnish an indispensable basis for the theory of knowledge. Whewell was one of the first to whom the thought occurred that such a theory could rely validly only on the history of the sciences, examining how this exemplary form of knowledge had developed. Such an examination seemed to him to justify what one might call an inductive rationalism. All knowledge requires an ideal element just as much as an empirical one. By reason of this "fundamental antithesis" Whewell's philosophy at one and the same time is, in contrast with that of the apriorists, a philosophy of induction, and in contrast with that of the empiricists, a philosophy of the idea. Even the experimental sciences rest on certain axioms whose character as necessary truths—acknowledged to the point that one cannot distinctly conceive their negation—can be explained only by the presence in our mind of certain "fundamental ideas." Number, space, time, cause, medium, polarity, affinity, symmetry, resemblance, final cause—new ideas are added to those that precede as one descends the ladder of the sciences. It was this notion that largely inspired Antoine Cournot.

But such a rationalism, stamped with the influence of Immanuel Kant, is by no means bound up with a deductive idealism. The fundamental ideas are illuminated for us only progressively, in the course of our effort to interpret experience. They become elements of the structure of reason; and the principles that they govern pass little by little, as they are better understood, from the status of happy guesses to that of necessary truths that education then makes permanent in the public mind. Through this bold conception of how self-evidence develops, the theory of fundamental ideas is joined with the theory of induction, the idea as category with the idea as hypothesis. Here there would have been a prefiguring of modern theories of the self-construction of the reason had not theological preoccupations led Whewell to locate these "fundamental ideas," from all eternity, in the divine understanding. As a result the apparent invention of these ideas by man is ultimately reduced to a simple discovery.

Although Whewell's authority was recognized, his philosophy was received only with reservation. His theory of fundamental ideas ran counter to the empiricist tradition, and freethinkers regarded the theological setting of the theory as an anachronism. The logicians, for their part, complained that Whewell's theory of induction had altered the sense of the word by wrongly assimilating inductive method to the method of hypothesis and that it had neglected the question of proof. In all these respects Mill was his typical opponent. It is worth remarking, however, that neither he nor the other critics attacked Whewell's most daring and most novel notions, the interesting nature of which seems to have escaped them: the incorporation of ideas into the facts and the development of self-evidence.

See also Bacon, Francis; Butler, Joseph; Cournot, Antoine Augustin; Epistemology; Epistemology, History of; Grotius, Hugo; Induction; Kant, Immanuel; Mill, John Stuart; Newton, Isaac; Philosophy of Science, History of Plato.

Bibliography

In addition to Whewell's works cited in the text, see I. Todhunter, *William Whewell, an Account of His Writings with Selections from His Literary and Scientific Correspondence,* 2 vols. (London: Macmillan, 1876), and Mrs. Stair Douglas, *The Life and Selections from the Correspondence of William Whewell* (London, 1879).

For further information on Whewell's philosophy, see M. R. Stoll, *Whewell's Philosophy of Induction* (Lancaster, 1929); Robert Blanché, *Le rationalisme de Whewell* (Paris: Alcan, 1935); C. J. Ducasse, "Whewell's Philosophy of Scientific Discovery," in *Philosophical Review* 60 (1951): 56–69 and 213–234; and Silvestro Marcucci, *L'"idealismo" scientifico di William Whewell* (Pisa: Istituto di Filosofia, 1963).

Robert Blanché (1967)
Translated by Albert E. Blumberg

WHICHCOTE, BENJAMIN
(1609–1683)

Benjamin Whichcote, the guiding spirit of the Cambridge Platonists, was born at Whichcote Hall, Stoke, Shropshire, of "an ancient and honourable family." He was admitted to Emmanuel College, Cambridge, in 1626 and in 1633 was elected a fellow of Emmanuel. Whichcote was renowned as a college tutor for the number and the character of his pupils, who included John Smith and John Worthington, and for the personal attention he paid to them. Ordained deacon and priest in 1636, he was in the same year appointed Sunday afternoon lecturer at Trinity Church in Cambridge, a post he held for nearly twenty years and by virtue of which he exerted considerable influence on the moral and religious life of Cambridge. At a time of violent, dogmatic theological controversy, his sermons were a fervent plea for liberality and toleration. It was his habit to speak from notes; he introduced into pulpit oratory a new, vigorous, colloquial, epigrammatic style in contrast to the traditional formal discourse. Various versions of his Sunday lectures, reconstructed from notes, were published after his death in 1683 and constitute his most substantial work.

In 1643 he temporarily left Cambridge to become rector of North Cadbury in Somerset, where he married. The following year he was invited back to Cambridge to become provost of King's College, the former provost having been ejected by the Puritan Parliament. He accepted only after great hesitation and secured special provision for the support of the former provost. Alone among the newly appointed heads of colleges, he refused to subscribe to the National Covenant, by which he would have sworn to support Calvinist forms of church government and doctrine. He secured a similar exemption for the fellows of his college. In 1650 he was elected vice-chancellor of the university.

His influence at Cambridge was now at its height and aroused considerable alarm among his more orthodox Calvinist colleagues. Especially alarmed was his former tutor at Emmanuel, Anthony Tuckney. In July 1651 Whichcote preached a commencement sermon as vice-chancellor that provoked a lively controversy between Whichcote and Tuckney in the form of letters. Tuckney accused Whichcote of laying too much stress on reason and too little on faith, of being unduly influenced by pagan ideas and by the Dutch Arminians, of being too tolerant of unorthodoxy. In reply Whichcote denied that it is possible to emphasize reason unduly, reason being "the candle of the Lord." Faith not founded on reason was mere superstition. His own ideas, he maintained, derived from meditation rather than from reading; he knew little or nothing, he said, of the Arminians (this is scarcely credible) but was not ashamed of having learned from Plato. As for tolerance, the Christian's duty is to regard with charity the views of other Christians, however mistaken he takes them to be, and to minimize rather than to exaggerate differences. Reason, tolerance, the minimizing of differences—these qualities were characteristic of Whichcote personally and were central to his moral and religious outlook.

With the restoration of Charles II, Whichcote was dismissed as provost of King's College. He complied with the Act of Uniformity and was permitted to preach, finally becoming vicar of St. Lawrence Jewry, London, where he is buried. In London as in Cambridge his sermons, especially those he delivered regularly in the City at the Guildhall, attracted congregations considerable in both quality and numbers. He died as a result of a cold contracted while visiting Ralph Cudworth at Cambridge.

Whichcote wrote nothing. He was essentially a teacher who needed the inspiration of an audience that was physically present. His views have to be extracted from his correspondence, his sermons, and the aphorisms set down in his manuscripts. His leading ethical principle was that actions are good and bad, right and wrong, in their own nature, not because they are commanded or forbidden; the goodness of an action derives from its conformity with the nature of things as apprehended by reason. In his own teaching this principle is invoked against the Calvinist doctrine that moral laws are simply expressions of God's will, but his pupils were able to turn these principles against Thomas Hobbes's doctrine that moral laws are expressions of the will of the sovereign. Whichcote initiated the rationalistic tendency in British ethics, which runs through Cudworth, Samuel Clarke, and Richard Price to our own times. But there is nothing dry or formalistic in his rationalism; his emphasis is not on obedience to rules of conduct but on affection and spontaneity. He thought of religion and morality as liberating rather than as imposing rules.

In theology his influence encouraged the development of the characteristically "liberal" point of view, with its emphasis on goodness rather than on creeds. He thought that the Calvinists, in treating as of central importance questions of creeds, government, and ritual, made the same mistake as the high church Anglicans to whom they were so bitterly opposed. These were matters about which men should be left free to differ, choosing whatever forms and formulations help them to live better lives. This was the side of Whichcote's teaching that caught the attention of the third earl of Shaftesbury, who edited a volume of Whichcote's sermons in 1698; historically, it issues in eighteenth-century deism and nineteenth-century liberal theology, as represented, for example, in the work of Matthew Arnold, a great admirer of the Cambridge school.

See also Cambridge Platonists.

Bibliography

In 1685 there appeared in London *Select Notions of that Learned and Reverend Divine of the Church of England, Dr. Whichcote*, described as being "faithfully collected from him by a pupil and particular friend of his"; the *Select Sermons* were edited with a preface by the third earl of Shaftesbury in 1698. *Several Discourses*, edited by John Jeffrey, was published in 1701 (London); Jeffrey also edited the first edition of *Moral and Religious Aphorisms*, published in 1703 (Norwich), and a sermon, *On the True Nature of Peace in the Kingdom or Church of Christ* (1717). The most useful edition of the discourses is *The Works of the Learned Benjamin Whichcote, D.D.* (Aberdeen, 1751); for the aphorisms see *Moral and Religious Aphorisms*, edited by Samuel Salter (London, 1753), which also includes the correspondence with Tuckney. There is a modern edition of the *Aphorisms* with an introduction by Dean Inge (London, 1930). Ernest Trafford Campagnac, *The Cambridge Platonists* (Oxford: Clarendon Press, 1901), contains considerable selections from Whichcote.

OTHER RECOMMENDED WORKS

Davenport, Paul M. *Moral Divinity with a Tincture of Christ: An Interpretation of the Theology of Benjamin Whichcote, Founder of Cambridge Platonism*. The Hague: Martinus Nijhoff, 1972.

Gill, Michael B. "The Religious Rationalism of Benjamin Whichcote." *Journal of the History of Philosophy* 37 (2) (1999): 271–300.

Greene, Robert A. "Whichcote, the Candle of the Lord, and Synderesis." *Journal of the History of Ideas* 52 (4) (1991): 617–644.

Greene, Robert A. "Whichcote, Wilkins, 'Ingenuity,' and the Reasonableness of Christianity." *Journal of the History of Ideas* 42 (1981): 227–252.

Patrides, C. A., ed. *The Cambridge Platonists*. Cambridge, U.K.: Cambridge University Press, 1980.

Roberts, James D. *From Puritanism to Platonism in Seventeenth Century England*. The Hague: Martinus Nijhoff, 1968.

John Passmore (1967)
Bibliography updated by Tamra Frei (2005)

WHITEHEAD, ALFRED NORTH

(1861–1947)

Alfred North Whitehead, the philosopher and mathematician, made one of the outstanding attempts in his generation to produce a comprehensive metaphysical system that would take account of scientific cosmology.

Whitehead was born at Ramsgate on the Isle of Thanet and wrote of his boyhood in a country vicarage on the East Kent coast in the "Autobiographical Notes" (*The Philosophy of Alfred North Whitehead*, pp. 3–14) and, more vividly, in some of the essays in *Essays in Science and Philosophy* (pp. 3–52). The religious (Anglican) background of his home and the experience of companionship with strong characters in a close-knit community made impressions that left their mark on his later philosophy. With these went a Wordsworthian sense of man's continuity with nature. In his education at Sherborne, an ancient public school in Dorset, he was taught the classics and history, less in a detached spirit of scholarship than as exercises in the study of what Michael Oakeshott has called "the practical past"—a living tradition illustrating general ideas and pointing to analogies in contemporary life. This approach to history remained with him and is apparent in his philosophical books, especially *Science and the Modern World* and *Adventures of Ideas*. It is a use of history in the spirit of what Edmund Burke called "philosophic analogy."

Whitehead also learned a good deal of mathematics at Sherborne, and in 1880 he went to Trinity College, Cambridge, with a scholarship in mathematics. In 1884 he was elected to a fellowship at Trinity. Bertrand Russell was his most distinguished pupil, and from 1900 to 1911 they collaborated on the *Principia Mathematica*, which attempted to prove that mathematics could be deduced from premises of formal logic. In his obituary note on

Whitehead, Russell wrote that although one or the other would take primary responsibility for writing some parts, every part was always discussed by both of them, the whole work being a complete collaboration. W. V. Quine, in his essay "Whitehead and the Rise of Modern Logic," called *Principia Mathematica* "one of the great intellectual monuments of all time." (The fourth volume, which Whitehead was to have written on the logical foundations of geometry, never appeared.)

Whitehead resigned his lectureship from Cambridge in 1910 and moved to London. He taught at the University of London until 1914, when he became professor of applied mathematics at the Imperial College of Science and Technology. During this period Whitehead did his most intensive work in the philosophy of science.

In 1924, Whitehead accepted an invitation to a chair in philosophy at Harvard University. He was then sixty-three; the transfer gave him the opportunity to develop his philosophy of science into a full-scale metaphysical philosophy.

Whitehead's work is commonly described as falling into the three periods indicated above: the early years in Cambridge up to 1910, when he was collaborating with Russell on the logical foundations of mathematics; the middle years in London up to 1924, when he was writing on the philosophy of science; and the last years in America, when he wrote first and foremost as a metaphysician. This division can, however, be overstressed. The philosophical interests explicit in his later work can be found implicitly in the earlier work, and some of the general assumptions of Whitehead's logical and mathematical work influence the later philosophy. Rather than as a succession of interests, his thought can best be interpreted as a developing unity. This is the approach of Victor Lowe in the essay "The Development of Whitehead's Philosophy" and in his book *Understanding Whitehead*. Wolfe Mays has remarked that the progression of Whitehead's thought can be looked on as a spiral, returning to certain general notions from different standpoints, rather than as a succession of stages.

LOGICAL FOUNDATIONS OF MATHEMATICS

Whitehead and Russell had been working independently on the logic of mathematics. Russell had become acquainted with the work of Giuseppe Peano in 1900 (Gottlob Frege's work came to their attention shortly after) and was working on *Principles of Mathematics* (Cambridge, U.K., 1903). Since 1891, Whitehead had been working on *A Treatise on Universal Algebra*, for which he was made a fellow of the Royal Society in 1903. In the *Treatise* he developed some ideas of Hermann Grassmann's *Ausdehnungslehre* (theory of extension) of 1844 and 1862, attempting to give a general formal description of addition and multiplication that would hold for all algebras. The *Treatise* was little noticed at the time; it is discussed by Quine in the essay "Whitehead and the Rise of Modern Logic."

In 1906 the Royal Society published Whitehead's memoir *On Mathematical Concepts of the Material World*, in which he put forth an interpretation of concepts formalized in a logico-mathematical scheme as basic notions describing the material world. Whitehead sought to define the concepts of a geometry from which, as a formal system, the theorems of Euclidean geometry can be derived and which can be interpreted by notions of space, time, and matter. At this early stage he was already dissatisfied with the Newtonian scheme of the material world as composed of atoms each occupying a position in absolute space at an absolute time. In *On Mathematical Concepts of the Material World* the ultimate entities that compose the universe are said to be lines of force. A particle is the field of a line of force at a point; particles are thus defined as elements in a field, and a point as not just having simple location in space but as an element in a linear polyadic relation R, so that R (a, b, c) means the points a, b, c are in linear order. This makes the notion of both a point and a particle a vector and not a scalar one.

Whitehead had been impressed as an undergraduate by J. J. Thomson's lecture "The Poynting Flux of Energy in Electrodynamics," describing the transmission of energy with quantitative flow and definite direction (see *Adventures of Ideas*, p. 238); in *The Philosophy of Whitehead* (pp. 235–260) Mays comments on the significance of this notion of the flux of energy for Whitehead's later work, leading to a view of nature as routes of events or occasions inheriting from each other. Lowe says that the developments in physics that interested Whitehead when he wrote the memoir were vector physics, the theories of molecular and submolecular energetic vibration, and the rise of "field" as a basic concept. The influence of all these ideas, generalized in different terminologies, can be seen throughout his work.

PHILOSOPHY OF SCIENCE

The twofold interest in logico-deductive schemes and in empirical interpretations can also be traced throughout Whitehead's work. Indeed, he saw the connection between such schemes and the vague world of our experience as the central problem of philosophy. He sought the connection by describing a logical scheme as a systematic and generalized formulation of relationships crudely observable in experience.

The next link in this line of thought is the development of his method of extensive abstraction. There is an exposition of this in "The Anatomy of Some Scientific Ideas" (*The Organization of Thought*, Ch. 7); it is also discussed in *An Enquiry concerning the Principles of Natural Knowledge* (Part III). The method of extensive abstraction is a topological device by which such geometrical elements as points are defined, through concepts of "whole and part" and "overlapping," as relations between volumes of a certain shape extending over others of like shape—for example, rectangles, circles, or ellipses—so that a pattern like a nest of Chinese boxes is produced:

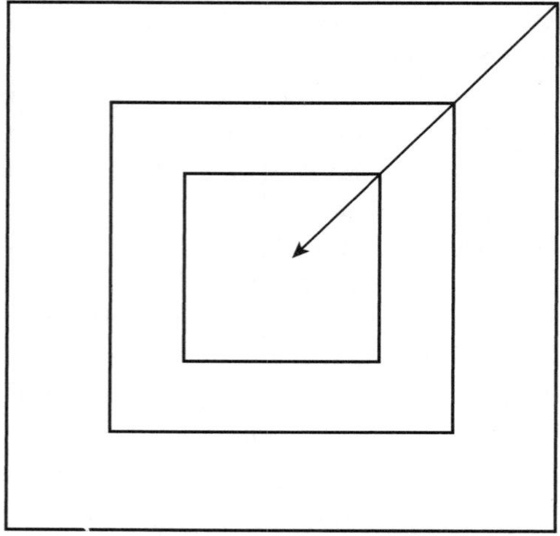

A "point" is not an ideal entity at the center or even an ideal limit of this route of approximation. It is defined as the whole convergent set. Similarly, a straight line can be defined as the direction of a route of overlapping ellipses or oblong rectangles, for example:

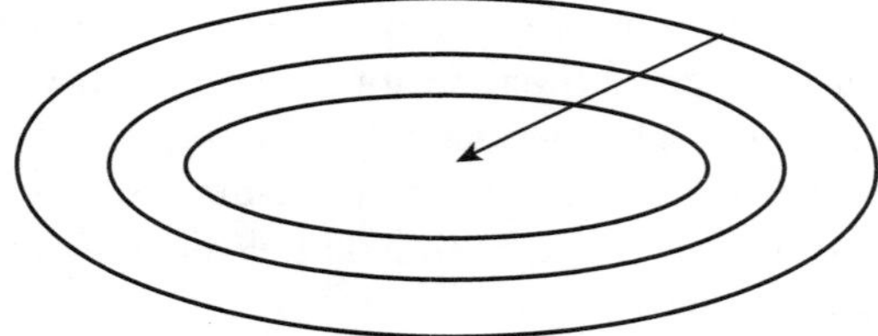

Whitehead looks on this type of definition as having an analogy in a perceived relation. No one can perceive Euclidean points with position and no magnitude or lines with length and no breadth, but volumes extending over other volumes can be perceived. The relations of "extending over" as formulated in the method of extensive abstraction are topological constructs, making precise relations that are also perceptible. This attempt to combine a view of logical schemes as reached from perceived relations with a view of them as theoretical constructs for which interpretations may be sought in experience underlies much of Whitehead's work.

OBJECTS AND EVENTS. A combination of theoretical construction and alleged derivation from experience also appears in Whitehead's analysis of nature in terms of "events" and "objects" given in the books of his middle period, *The Principles of Natural Knowledge* and *The Concept of Nature*. He claimed continually that the starting point is empirical. Just as in his earlier *On Mathematical Concepts of the Material World* he had attacked the notion of atoms externally related to one another in absolute space and time, so in his later analysis of nature (which he defined as "disclosed in sense experience"), he attacked the ultimacy of the Humean analysis of our experience into distinct impressions of sensation, such as visual sensations of colored patches. He believed that our more deep-seated experience was of something going on with spatiotemporal spread. This "passage" of nature could be divided into "events," so that its constituents are thought of not as enduring atoms but as happenings that can be described as events extending over other events. The writing of this article is a slice of the passage of nature, an event extending over the writing of this sentence, which is an event extending over the writing of this word. Thus, we converge by a route of approximation to what is happening here and now (again, an application of the basic notion of a pattern of volumes and durations extending over one another).

Events display recurrent patterns, the forms and properties of which Whitehead called "objects" and, in the later books, "eternal objects." This is his version of the problem of universals as abstract forms of recurrent recognizable characteristics in the passage of nature. The phrase "eternal objects," along with the interest in Plato shown in his later work, particularly in *Process and Reality*, might suggest that Whitehead took a Platonic realist view of a realm of such abstract entities. This is not so; his view was nearer to the Aristotelian one of *universalia in rebus* or, in his own phrase, "seeking the forms in the facts." His "objects" are "ingredients" in the process of events; they are "pure potentials" actualizable in an indefinite number of instances. At the same time he was no nominalist; the objects are more than names for observed resemblances. They are properties and relations that are exemplified in recurrences in patterns that can be precisely formulated.

Different types of objects can be distinguished. First, there is a "sense object"; for example, a color like Cambridge blue is perceived as situated in an event. A sense object requires a relation between a "percipient event," the "situation" to which it is referred, and active and passive conditioning events relating the percipient event to the situation. Second, there is the "perceptual object," a determinate association of sense objects in a series of situations strung together in a continuity and perceived as one prolonged event—for instance, that red and black coat. Perceptual objects can be delusive, as in reflections in mirrors or diffractions in water. Third, "physical objects" are those objects whose relations to events condition the appearance of the perceptual objects, as, for instance, the straight stick that appears bent in water. Fourth, "scientific objects" are inferred, nonperceived objects, such as "electrons," that account for the general properties and relations within events that constitute the situations in which physical objects are ingredients. At the stage of science in which Whitehead was writing he instanced electrons as the ultimate scientific objects. He would no doubt have welcomed the further refinements that have occurred since in discoveries of fundamental particles.

Whitehead would also have seen these developments as supporting his distinction between "uniform" and "nonuniform" objects. A uniform object is located in an event throughout a duration and also characterizes any slice of that duration. Perceptual objects are normally uniform; a bar of iron as perceived in any duration however small is still a bar of iron. A nonuniform object needs a minimum time span in order to be expressed at all; he thought a molecule, for instance, cannot exist in a lesser time than that required by the periodicity of its atomic constituents. Whitehead was impressed by the possibility suggested by the physics of his time that the ultimate scientific objects might be nonuniform rather than uniform. The development of quantum theory reinforced this idea. The notion of atomic events, or "occasions," displaying nonuniform objects and forming continuities through their overlapping so that they produce physical and perceptual objects, becomes a crucial one in Whitehead's later work. The distinctions and relations between different levels of objects are discussed in *The Principles of Natural Knowledge* (Ch. 7) and, more briefly, in the papers "Time, Space and Material" and "Uniformity and Contingency."

RELATIVITY PRINCIPLE. Objects situated in events form patterns among themselves that are constituents in wider patterns, finally dependent on a uniform pervasive pattern that expresses the uniformity of nature as an ongoing passage of related events with spatiotemporal spread. The attempt to unify notions of space, time, and matter, along with his attempt, stemming from *On Mathematical Concepts of the Material World*, to relate these to a set of formal notions underlying a geometry, led Whitehead to have a particular interest in Albert Einstein's general and special theories of relativity. Whitehead published his own alternative in *The Principle of Relativity* (1922). He refused to give a crucial role to special facts, notably the velocity of light, and, unlike Einstein, insisted that space must be "homaloidal" (that is, of uniform spread). His reason for this seems to follow from his view of abstraction, which led him to think that a logico-mathematical scheme of notions must be precisely realized in the physical world. Whitehead also believed that the possibility of measurement depended on exact congruence between one region of space and another, independently of physical bodies. Thus, though there are analogies in their conception of relativity, Whitehead's view depends on there being a noncontingent uniformity in spatial relations and is less open to experimental applications.

Whitehead's theory is set forth in his book *The Principle of Relativity* and in his article "Einstein's Theory: An Alternative Suggestion," contributed to *The Times* in 1920 and reprinted in *The Interpretation of Science*. Whitehead's views on relativity have not, however, been taken up by physicists.

METAPHYSICS

Science and the Modern World (given as Lowell Lectures at Harvard in 1925) is perhaps the most inspired expression of Whitehead's metaphysical philosophy. It is a book in which lucid and illuminating reflections on the history of science in relation to philosophy are interspersed with technically difficult passages; the book might have been written, as one reviewer remarked, by Dr. Jekyll and Mr. Hyde. But the technical passages are less overlaid with idiosyncratic terminology and a labored attempt at producing a system than is *Process and Reality* (1929). Those who find *Process and Reality* excessively forbidding can gain a very fair impression of the best of the later Whitehead by going from *Science and the Modern World* to his last books, *Adventures of Ideas* and *Modes of Thought*.

In *Modes of Thought* the analysis of nature into events and objects becomes an analysis of nature into "actual occasions," understood as unities that synthesize their relations to other occasions in their own "processes of becoming." Such a unity is called a "concrescence of prehensions," from *concrescere*, "to grow together," the end product being something *concretum*, "concrete," and from *prehendere* "to grasp," suggesting an active relationship but not necessarily a conscious awareness (as is suggested by the word *apprehension*).

Instead of events extending over other events Whitehead now spoke of "societies" (also called *nexūs*, the plural of the Latin *nexus*) of actual occasions, which can be structured by subsocieties and which can inherit characteristics from one another in serial order, in which case they are called "enduring objects." "The real actual things that endure [such as stones or animal organisms] are all societies. They are not actual occasions" (*Adventures of Ideas*, p. 262).

This general view of larger units in nature as systems of smaller units with their own inner structure is called "the philosophy of organism." The notion of organism had already been defined in *The Principles of Natural Knowledge* (p. 3) as "the concept of unities functioning and with spatio-temporal extensions," a notion that it is said cannot be expressed in terms of a material distribution at an instant. (The definition of nonuniform objects as needing a time span for their expression may be recalled.) It is suggested that the notion of organism, thus interpreted, could be a unifying one between the physical and biological sciences, physics becoming the study of the smaller and biology of the larger organisms.

PERCEPTION. In the earlier books Whitehead had attacked the "bifurcation of nature" as the kind of view of appearance and reality that assigns secondary qualities such as colors to subjective experience and primary qualities to the physical sphere. Instead of this division he wrote about perception as nature ordered in a perspective from the standpoint of an event within nature itself called the percipient event, all perceived qualities being qualities of nature in that perspective.

In *Science and the Modern World* and in *Symbolism* (1927) the view of perception is developed in terms of what it is to be a percipient event. We start from the notion of an actual occasion as a "prehending" entity in active interaction with its whole environment. The primitive mode of perception is not, Whitehead insisted, an apprehension of clear-cut sense data or Humean "impressions of sensation." Rather, it is a vaguer sense of environing realities pressing in upon us. Whitehead called this "perception in the mode of causal efficacy" and thought that it is mediated primarily through kinesthetic organic sensation. "Philosophers," he said, "have disdained the information about the universe obtained through their visceral feelings, and have concentrated on visual feelings" (*Process and Reality*, p. 169 [184]; references to *Process and Reality* give the page of the Cambridge edition, 1929, followed by the page of the New York edition, 1929). This is a causal, not a phenomenalist, view of perception, in which the functioning of the physiological organism (disregarded by David Hume) is crucial. Environing events are mediated through the organism, becoming finally transmuted into conscious sensations, which are then projected as sensa qualifying regions of the contemporary world (this is called "symbolic reference" and "perception in the mode of presentational immediacy"). Since there is a time lag between the transmission of influences from the environment and the projection of sensa onto the contemporary world (events that are strictly contemporaneous must in Whitehead's view be causally independent), there is always a chance that perception in the mode of presentational immediacy will not give veridical information about the state of the environment, as when we perceive a yellow patch in the sky that we take to be a star, though the star has long since gone out of existence.

In "the mode of causal efficacy" the qualities of environing events are mediated through organic experiences of the percipient's body. The most difficult aspect in Whitehead's theory is the transmutation of an emotional organic experience into a sensum. He found a link in our use of color words such as *red* and *green* to describe certain affective states.

> This notion of the sensa as qualifications of affective tone is a paradox for philosophy, though it is fairly obvious to common sense. A red-irritation is prevalent among nerve-racked people and among bulls. The affective tone of perception in a green woodland in spring can only be defined by the delicate shades of the green. (*Adventures of Ideas*, p. 315)

But can an irritation be "red" except by metaphor (waiving the question of whether bulls do have color vision), and does Andrew Marvell's "green thought in a green shade" mean that "green" characterizes the thought or, rather, that there is an overwhelming awareness of green in the environment?

PROCESS AND REALITY. Whitehead's comprehensive metaphysical philosophy was presented in "An Essay on Cosmology," in *Process and Reality*, based on the Gifford Lectures given at the University of Edinburgh during the 1927–1928 session. Whitehead distinguished cosmology from metaphysics (which he held dealt with the formal character of all facts), maintaining that cosmology described the general characteristics of our "cosmic epoch." That is, it took account of the empirical character of a particular type of world order—in the case of our world order, one characterized by electromagnetic events, dimensions, shapes, and measurability. Laws of nature, Whitehead held, were not part of the ultimate metaphysics of the universe; they could change their character with the rise and fall of different cosmic epochs dominated by different kinds of facts.

Process and Reality is a very difficult book, partly because of its vocabulary and not least when words of ordinary speech, such as *feelings*, are used with special meaning. Its manner of presentation is also difficult; the reader is confronted in the second chapter with the "categoreal [*sic*] scheme," comprising a category of the ultimate, 8 categories of existence, and 27 categories of explanation. He may find it advisable to read on and turn back to the scheme in the hope that what is there set out in summary form may become clearer in the light of the further discussions.

Lowe, in *Understanding Whitehead*, gives what is probably the most balanced presentation of Whitehead's work as a whole. Some of its notions are interpreted by analogy with more traditional metaphysical ones in Ivor Leclerc's *Whitehead's Metaphysics*, where comparison starts from the Aristotelian discussion of what it is to be a complete fact. Some aspects of the notions of "actual entities," "eternal objects," and their relations are considered in detail by William A. Christian in *An Interpretation of Whitehead's Metaphysics*; he has a particular interest in Whitehead's doctrine of God and its resemblance to and difference from more traditional views. The main drawback of these otherwise able books is that they seek to elucidate Whitehead's system in its own terms. It is likely that the contribution of *Process and Reality* can be estimated only if philosophers working independently of direct exegesis find that some of its ideas can be developed, perhaps in different terminology, and put to use in particular philosophical problems. It is likely, too, that these will be ways of thinking that take more account of the philosophy of science and vary more from the main tradition of European metaphysics than do these authors. It is a merit in Mays's book *The Philosophy of Whitehead* that it points out that behind *Process and Reality* lies the influence of Whitehead's early interest in axiomatic systems, as well as in electromagnetic field theories, especially the notion of the flow of energy. The book, however, criticizes Whitehead's realist metaphysical cosmology from the standpoint of a different philosophy of science.

It would be impossible to epitomize *Process and Reality* even in a longer treatment than can be given here. Attention can, however, be called to certain features. There is continuity with lines of thought in the earlier books, but the language becomes more naturally applicable to sentient experience. This is partly due to Whitehead's reading of Henri Bergson, F. H. Bradley, and William James, all of whom influenced him in shaping his own particular form of organic pluralism. It is also, however, due to a deliberate onslaught on the notion of "vacuous actuality," existence entirely devoid of subjective experience. Thus, Whitehead's "actual entities," while still linear events, are presented as processes of self-formation with "subjective aim." Actual entities are "epochal" happenings that take a minimal time span to become and which then perish; they are succeeded by others that conform to them and thus secure the continuity which Whitehead held was necessary if we are to have recognition of enduring objects and the expectation of continuing regularities which he believed to be necessary if induction is to be justified. The overlapping of events by other events in a field becomes the "objectification" of an actual entity in other actual entities, whereby the "feelings" and qualities of one entity are transmitted to others.

The notion of objectification is one of the most difficult of all Whitehead's views, and it is doubtful whether any satisfactory elucidation of it has yet been made. He envisaged objectification as more than a response to a stimulus and more than a causal interaction; in some sense it is a genuine reenactment of the feelings of one actual entity in another, and he maintained that we can experience this transition of feeling. The use of the term *feeling* presents great difficulty. Whitehead used it as a technical term for "the basic generic operation of passing from the objectivity of the data to the subjectivity of the actual entity in question" (*Process and Reality*, p. 55 [65]). This is to maintain that every entity, however lowly, appropriates its responses to the rest of its world in some form of sentient experience, but this does not necessarily involve consciousness. Consciousness he saw as a rare kind of sentience arising within experience; experience does not, as idealists have held, arise within consciousness.

The difficulties in this theory stem partly from Whitehead's insistence that there should not be basically different kinds of entities in the world—organic and inorganic, for instance, or minds and bodies. All entities should display the same general character. He then took certain psychological notions and generalized them (by claiming that consciousness is incidental, not essential) to cover biological and even physical processes.

> I find myself as essentially a unity of emotions, enjoyments, hopes, fears, regrets, valuations of alternatives, decisions—all of them subjective reactions to the environment as active in my nature. My unity—which is Descartes' "*I am*"—is my process of shaping this welter of material into a consistent pattern of feelings. The individual enjoyment is what I am in my role of a natural activity, as I shape the activities of the environment into a new creation, which is myself at this moment; and yet, as being myself, it is a continuation of the antecedent world. (*Modes of Thought*, p. 228)

As a description of the kind of concrescence of prehensions I find myself to be, this is persuasive. Extended downward to describe the inner life of molecules, it strains the imagination. The possibility of making this generalization depends, Whitehead said, on our holding that "the energetic activity considered in physics is the emotional intensity entertained in life" (ibid., p. 232). Thus, Whitehead did not concern himself with the issue of freedom versus determinism as a special problem in human action. Insofar as actual entities conform to their environment and immediate past, there is determinism; insofar as any entity modifies its response through its unique subjective element of feeling, there is freedom. So freedom is a "clutch at novelty" that can appear at any point in nature.

Is it, in fact, possible to make the same general categories cover every kind of existent? Whitehead rejected "emergence" views, according to which different levels of existents may display special irreducible properties. (This view also has its difficulties.) Moreover, when Whitehead made the same "categoreal" characteristics apply to all actualities, it is possible that some of the notions he thus generalized may be of a more abstract type than others with which he connected them; one may suspect, for example, that this is so in the case of energy and emotion. Also, he held that all forms of experience—physiological and psychological and the distinctive kinds of the latter, such as moral, aesthetic, and religious—must be particular exemplifications of the same basic principles. It is by no means evident that a coherent theory of experience must imply this; there may be reasons why the principles of aesthetics, for example, might differ from those of morality or religion.

NATURAL THEOLOGY

Whitehead's interest in religion runs throughout his philosophy and is by no means confined to its later phase, though it is there that he sought to express it in a natural theology. He saw religion as sustaining a sense of the importance of an individual's experience within the social relationships and experience of his life. Beyond this broadly sociological interest, he held that religion was also concerned with permanence amid change. He connected the idea of permanence with the conception of a general ordering of the process of the world that could provide the ground first of "extensive connection," then of all more specific orderings. The ordering of the world, called "the primordial nature of God," has been compared by Mays to a sort of cosmic propositional function, a "form of definiteness" that can then be instantiated by "values," which are actual processes of events. But though Whitehead did indeed speak of the primordial nature of God as a "conceptual prehension" and, as such, "deficient in actuality," the interpretation of it as simply a formal schema omits the point that to Whitehead the notion of "conceptual prehension" includes "appetition," an urge toward the realization of the forms (or eternal objects) so prehended. This drive to realization is said to supply all particular actual entities with their "subjective forms," and God is thus represented as "the principle of concretion" whereby actual processes take their rise. God does not create other actual entities; he provides them with an initial impetus to self-creation. Each actual entity, including God, is a particular outcome of "creativity," which is said to stand for the continual process by which the many elements in the world are synthesized into new unities, each being called a "concrescence," described as a "production of novel togetherness." It is the creative advance into novelty of a pluralistic process. In response to the processes of becoming of the other actual entities of the world, God acquires a "consequent nature," in which they are "objectified" (again this difficult notion of reenactment) in his own self-formation, which appears to be coterminous with the process of nature.

The difficulties in Whitehead's natural theology are great, not least because he used traditional religious language in ways that may suggest misleading analogies. The most perceptive development of his natural theology is that of Charles Hartshorne, especially in *Philosophers Speak of God* (with William L. Reese, Chicago, 1953) and *The Logic of Perfection* (La Salle, IL, 1962). Hartshorne states, however, that his own views in natural theology were taking shape before he came in contact with Whitehead's work, which acted as a reinforcement.

WHITEHEAD'S INFLUENCE

It was suggested above that Whitehead's contribution may best appear if other philosophers find seminal ideas in it that they can develop independently. Hartshorne's work in natural theology may be one example; others would be work on concepts on the border between the physical and biological sciences, such as W. E. Agar's *A Contribution to the Theory of the Living Organism* (Melbourne, 1943), J. H. Woodger's *Biological Principles* (London, 1929), and R. S. Lillie's *General Biology and Philosophy of Organism* (Chicago, 1945). Some sociologists have also found support in Whitehead for views of societies as ongoing processes composed of subsocieties with ramified interrelations. H. H. Price has shown interest in the phenomenology of organic rather than visual sensations (see his paper "Touch and Organic Sensation," *PAS* 44 [1943–1944]: 1–30, especially his treatment of what he calls "bilateral dynamic transactions"). The main influence on contemporary philosophy is no doubt the pioneering logical work of *Principia Mathematica.*

Whitehead received the rare distinction of being awarded the Order of Merit. He had a gift for writing that showed itself at its best in the striking phrase and the vivid metaphor or analogy (some of these have been collected by A. H. Johnson in *The Wit and Wisdom of Alfred North Whitehead*, Boston, 1947). His style is less happy when this very gift of fine writing tempted him to be vaguely grandiose. Hence, rigorous critical interpretation is needed, which is more likely to be rewarding insofar as it leads to more than pure commentary.

See also Logic, History of.

Bibliography

WORKS BY WHITEHEAD

A bibliography of Whitehead's works up to 1941, including articles in journals and references to selected reviews of books, was compiled by Victor Lowe and R. C. Baldwin and is in *The Philosophy of Alfred North Whitehead*, edited by Paul A. Schilpp (Evanston, IL: Northwestern University Press, 1941, 2nd ed., New York: Tudor, 1951). George L. Kline lists Whitehead's works that have been translated into other languages in *Process and Divinity; Philosophical Essays Presented to Charles Hartshorne*, edited by William L. Reese and Eugene Freeman (La Salle, IL: Open Court, 1964), pp. 235–268. A number of essays in this book deal with aspects of Whitehead's work.

Lucien Price's *Dialogues of Alfred North Whitehead* (London, 1961) contains transcripts from memory of some of Whitehead's conversations in his last years. However, the dialogues show the side of Whitehead that came out in conversation with a classical humanist and give little impression of him as a philosopher of science.

Only principal logical and philosophical books and articles are listed below.

A Treatise on Universal Algebra. Cambridge, U.K.: Cambridge University Press, 1898.

On Mathematical Concepts of the Material World. Philosophical Transactions of the Royal Society of London, Series A (1906). Reprinted in *Alfred North Whitehead: An Anthology*, edited by F. S. C. Northrop and Mason W. Gross. Cambridge, U.K.: Cambridge University Press, 1953, pp. 11–82. This book also has extracts from Whitehead's main works and a note on terminology by Gross.

Principia Mathematica, 3 vols. Cambridge, U.K.: Cambridge University Press, 1910–1913. Written with Bertrand Russell.

An Introduction to Mathematics. London: Williams and Norgate, 1911.

The Organization of Thought. London: Williams and Norgate, 1917. This work, with others presented to the Aristotelian Society between 1916 and 1923, has been reprinted in *The Interpretation of Science*, edited by A. H. Johnson. New York: Bobbs-Merrill, 1961. The chief essays are "Space, Time and Relativity" (1915), "Time. Space and Material" (1919), and "Uniformity and Contingency" (1922); the book also contains other occasional papers on the philosophy of science and some occasional addresses given in Whitehead's last years.

An Enquiry concerning the Principles of Natural Knowledge. Cambridge, U.K.: Cambridge University Press, 1919.

The Concept of Nature. Cambridge, U.K.: Cambridge University Press, 1920.

The Principle of Relativity. Cambridge, U.K.: Cambridge University Press, 1922.

Science and the Modern World. New York: Macmillan, 1925.

Religion in the Making. New York: Macmillan, and Cambridge, U.K.: Cambridge University Press, 1926.

Symbolism, Its Meaning and Effect. New York; Macmillan, 1927: Cambridge, U.K.: Cambridge University Press, 1928.

Process and Reality. New York: Macmillan, and Cambridge, U.K.: Cambridge University Press, 1929. Two separate editions.

The Function of Reason. Princeton, NJ: Princeton University Press, 1929.

The Aims of Education and Other Essays. New York: Macmillan, and London: Williams and Norgate, 1929. This includes shorter versions of *The Organization of Thought* and "Space, Time and Relativity," as well as "The Anatomy of Some Scientific Ideas."

Adventures of Ideas. New York: Macmillan, and Cambridge, U.K.: Cambridge University Press, 1933.

Nature and Life. Chicago: University of Chicago Press, and Cambridge, U.K.: Cambridge University Press, 1934. The best general presentation of Whitehead's dissatisfaction with the Newtonian scheme of the material world.

Modes of Thought. New York: Macmillan, and Cambridge, U.K.: Cambridge University Press, 1938.

Essays in Science and Philosophy. New York: Philosophical Library, 1947.

"Immortality" and "Mathematics and the Good," in Schilpp, op. cit. Whitehead's last two lectures.

WORKS ON WHITEHEAD

Haack, S. "Descriptive and Revisionary Metaphysics." *Philosophical Studies* 35 (1979): 361–371.

Hartshorne, Charles. *Whitehead's Philosophy: Selected Essays, 1935–1970.* Lincoln: University of Nebraska Press, 1972.

Leclerc, I., ed. *The Relevence of Whitehead.* New York: Humanities Press, 1961.

Leclerc, I. *Whitehead's Metaphysics: An Introductory Exposition.* 2nd ed. London: Allen & Unwin, 1965.

Lowe, V. *Alfred North Whitehead: The Man and His Work.* 2 vols. Baltimore, MD: The Johns Hopkins University Press, 1985, 1990.

Lowe, V. *Understanding Whitehead.* 2nd ed. Baltimore, MD: The Johns Hopkins University Press, 1966.

Nobo, J. L. *Whitehead's Metaphysics of Extension and Solidarity.* Albany: State University of New York Press, 1986.

Palter, R. M. *Whitehead's Philosophy of Science.* Chicago: University of Chicago Press, 1960.

Quine, W. V. "Whitehead and the Rise of Modern Logic." In *The Philosophy of A. N. Whitehead*, edited by P. A. Schilpp. La Salle, IL: Open Court, 1941.

Ross, Stephen David. *Perspectives in Whitehead's Metaphysics.* Albany: State University of New York Press, 1983.

Russell, Bertrand. "Whitehead and Principia Mathematica." *Mind* 57 (1948): 137–138.

Dorothy M. Emmet (1967)

Bibliography updated by Benjamin Fiedor (2005)

WHY

Lack of clarity about the uses of the word *why* is responsible for confusion on a number of philosophical fronts. In this entry we shall confine ourselves to two groups of topics where greater attention to the proper and improper behavior of this word might well have avoided the adoption of misguided theories. There is, first, the contrast, or the alleged contrast, between the "how" and the "why" and the view, shared by writers of very different backgrounds, that science can deal only with how-questions. Second, there are certain "ultimate" or "cosmic" questions, such as "Why do we exist?" or, more radically. "Why does the world exist?" or "Why is there something rather than nothing?" Some, like Arthur Schopenhauer and Julian Huxley, regard these questions as unanswerable; others, like Étienne Gilson and F. C. Copleston, believe that they can be answered; but whether these questions can be answered or not, it seems to be widely agreed that they are very "deep." These questions, in the words of the British astrophysicist A. C. B. Lovell, raise problems "which can tear the individual's mind asunder" (*The Individual and the Universe,* New York, 1961, p. 125). Speaking of the question "Why is there something rather than nothing?," Martin Heidegger first remarks that it is "the fundamental question of metaphysics" and later adds that "with this question philosophy began and with this question it will end, provided that it ends in greatness and not in an impotent decline" (*An Introduction to Metaphysics,* p. 20).

HOW AND WHY

The contrast between the how and the why has been insisted on for two rather different reasons. Some writers have done so in the interest of religion or metaphysics. Their position seems to be that while science and empirical research generally are competent to deal with how-questions, the very different and much deeper why-questions are properly the concern of religion or metaphysics or both. Thus, in a widely read book the British psychiatrist David Stafford-Clark insists that the confusion between the how and the why is the "fundamental fallacy" behind "the whole idea that science and religion are really in conflict at all" (*Psychiatry Today,* Harmondsworth, U.K., 1952, p. 282). Sigmund Freud in particular is accused of committing this fallacy in his antireligious writings. Stafford-Clark is not at all opposed to Freudian theory so long as it confines itself to the how of psychological phenomena. Psychoanalysis cannot, however, "begin by itself to answer a single question as to why man is so constructed that they should happen in this way" (p. 287). Although he repeatedly expresses his own fervent belief in God, Stafford-Clark unfortunately does not tell us how religion answers the question why man is "constructed" the way he is. Perhaps he would answer it along the lines in which Isaac Newton answered a similar question about the sun. "Why is there one body in our system qualified to give light and heat to all the rest," Newton wrote in his first letter to Richard Bentley, "I know no reason, but because the author of the system thought it convenient" (*Opera,* London, 1779–1785, Vol. IV, pp. 429ff.).

Similar views are found in the writings of many professional philosophers. Thus, writing of Newton's work on gravitation, A. N. Whitehead observes that "he [Newton] made a magnificent beginning by isolating the stresses indicated by his law of gravitation." But Newton "left no hint, why in the nature of things there should be any stresses at all" (*Modes of Thought,* New York and Cambridge, U.K., 1938, pp. 183–184). Similarly, discussing the limitations of science, Gilson declares that "scientists never ask themselves *why* things happen, but *how* they happen.… Why anything at all is, or exists, science knows not, precisely because it cannot even ask the question" (*God and Philosophy,* New Haven, CT, 1959, p.

140). For Gilson the two topics mentioned at the beginning of this entry appear to merge into one. The why of particular phenomena, he seems to argue, cannot be determined unless we answer the question "why this world, taken together with its laws … is or exists" (p. 72).

Among those who have asserted that science can only deal with how-questions there are some who are not at all friendly to metaphysics or religion. These writers usually add to their remarks that science cannot handle why-questions the comment that no other enterprise fares any better. This "agnostic positivism," as we may call it, goes at least as far back as David Hume. We know, he writes, that milk and bread are proper nourishment for men and not for lions or tigers, but we cannot "give the ultimate reason why" this should be so (*An Inquiry concerning Human Understanding,* Sec. IV, Part I). Hume seems to imply that this unhappy state can never be remedied, regardless of the advances of physiology or any other science. Several writers in the second half of the nineteenth century advanced this position under the slogan "The task of science is to describe phenomena, not to explain them." Ernst Mach, Gustav Kirchhoff, and Joseph Petzoldt were among the best-known figures in central Europe who advocated this view. In England, Karl Pearson, its most influential exponent, conceded that there was no harm in speaking of "scientific explanations" so long as *explanation* is used "in the sense of the descriptive-*how*" (*The Grammar of Science,* Everyman edition, 1937, p. 97). We can indeed "describe how a stone falls to the earth, but not why it does" (p. 103). "No one knows why two ultimate particles influence each other's motion. Even if gravitation be analyzed and described by the motion of some simpler particle or ether-element, the whole will still be a description, and not an explanation, of motion. Science would still have to content itself with recording the *how.*" No matter how far physics may progress, the why will "remain a mystery" (p. 105).

It is important to disentangle purely verbal from substantive issues in all of this. Insofar as the various writers we have quoted merely wish to assert that causal statements and scientific laws in general are contingent and not logically necessary propositions, little exception could be taken to their remarks. However, they are, or at least they appear to be, saying a great deal more. They all seem to agree that there is a class of meaningful questions, naturally and properly introduced by the word *why* in one of its senses, which cannot be answered by the use of empirical methods. Writers belonging to the first group claim that the answers can be obtained elsewhere. The agnostic positivists maintain that human beings cannot obtain the answers at all.

It is this substantive issue which we shall discuss here, and it is necessary to point out that there are numerous confusions in all views of this kind. To begin with, although this is the least important observation, *how* and *why* do not always have contrasting functions but are in certain situations used to ask the very same questions. Thus, when we know or believe that a phenomenon, *A,* is the cause of another phenomenon, *X,* but at the same time are ignorant of the "mechanics" of *A*'s causation of *X,* we indifferently use *how* and *why.* We know, for example, that certain drugs cure certain diseases, but our knowledge is in a medical sense "purely empirical." Here we would be equally prepared to say that we do not know "why" the drug produces the cure and that we do not know "how" it does this. Or, to take a somewhat different case, it is widely known that cigarette smoking is causally connected with lung cancer. It is also known that sometimes two people smoke the same amount and yet one of them develops lung cancer while the other one does not. In such a case the question naturally arises why cigarette smoking, if it is indeed the cause at all, leads to cancer in one case but not in the other. And we would be just as ready to express our ignorance or puzzlement by saying that we do not know how it is as by saying that we do not know why it is that smoking produced cancer in the first man but not in the second. In all such cases it is clear that science is in principle competent to deal with the "why" no less than with the "how," if only because they are used to ask the very same questions.

It is undeniable, however, that in certain contexts *how* and *why* are used to ask different questions. This contrast is most obvious when we deal with intentional, or more generally with "meaningful," human actions. What seems far from obvious, what in fact seems plainly false, is that empirical methods are not in principle adequate to determine the answers to why-questions in these contexts. Let us take as our example the theft of the Star of India sapphire and other gems from the Museum of Natural History in New York. We can here certainly distinguish the question why the burglary was committed from the question how it was carried out. The latter question would concern itself with the details of the act—how the thieves got into the building, how they immobilized the alarm system, how they avoided the guards, and so on. The why-question, by contrast, would inquire into the aim or purpose of the theft—were the thieves just out to make a vast amount of money, or were there perhaps some other aims involved, such as proving to rival gangs how skillful they were or showing the incompetence of the police force?

Now, the aim or purpose of a human being is surely not in principle undiscoverable, and frequently we know quite well what it is. The person himself usually, though not always, simply knows what his aim is. An orator, for example, who is advocating a certain policy, ostensibly because it is "for the good of the country," may at the same time know perfectly well that his real aim is personal advancement. It used to be said that in such situations a human being knows his own purpose by means of "introspection," where introspection was conceived of as a kind of "inner sense." This way of talking is not inappropriate to situations in which somebody is confused about his own motives, for then special attention to his own feelings, resembling in some ways the effort to discriminate the detailed features of a physical scene, may well be necessary in order to ascertain his "true" aims.

Much more commonly, however, a human being simply knows what his aims are, and it would be much better to say that he knows this "without observation" than that he knows it by introspection. In order to find out the purpose of somebody else's action, it is in countless instances sufficient to ask the person a direct question about his aim. Where the agent's veracity is suspect or where a person is the victim of self-deception, it is necessary to resort to more elaborate investigations. In the former type of case one might ask the agent all kinds of other questions (that is, questions not directly about the purpose of his action), one might interview his friends and acquaintances and other witnesses of his conduct, one might tap his telephone and employ assorted bugging devices, and one might perhaps go so far as to question him after the administration of "truth" drugs. In the latter type of case it may not be possible to ascertain the real purpose unless the person undertakes psychiatric treatment. While the practical difficulties in the way of discovering the purpose of an action are no doubt insurmountable in many cases of both these types, empirical procedures are clearly in principle adequate to this task.

We also contrast how- and why-questions when the latter are not inquiries into the purpose of any agent. Here, however, *how* has a different meaning from any previously discussed. In all examples so far considered, how-questions were in one way or another causal questions—"How did the thieves carry out their plan of stealing the Star of India?" is a question about the means of achieving a certain goal, and "How is it that smoking produces cancer in one man but not in another?," although not a question about means, is nevertheless about the processes leading to a certain result. These causal "hows" should be distinguished from what one may call the "how" of "state" or "condition." "How cold does it get in New York in the winter?" "How does the decline in his powers manifest itself?" "How is his pain now—is it any better?" are examples of the "how" of state or condition, and it is how-questions of this kind which we contrast with nonteleological why-questions—"Why does it get so cold in New York in the winter?" "Why did his powers decline so early in life?" "Why is his pain not subsiding?"

It is sometimes maintained or implied, as in the remarks of Stafford-Clark quoted earlier, that why-questions are invariably inquiries about somebody's purpose or end—if not the purpose of a human being, then perhaps that of some supernatural intelligence. This is clearly not the case. There can be no doubt that *why* is often employed simply to ask questions about the cause of a phenomenon. Thus the question "Why are the winters in New York so much colder than in Genoa, although the two places are on the same geographical latitude?" would naturally be understood as a request for information about the cause of this climatic difference, and it is not necessary for the questioner to suppose that there is some kind of plan or purpose behind the climatic difference in order to be using the word *why* properly. In saying this, one is not begging any questions against the theory that natural phenomena like the cold of the winter in New York are the work of a supernatural being: One is merely calling attention to what is and what is not implied in the ordinary employment of *why* in these contexts.

Let us briefly summarize the results obtained so far: In some situations *how* and *why* are naturally employed to ask the very same questions; when we deal with intentional human actions, we naturally use *why* to inquire about the purpose or goal of the agent and *how* to learn about the means used to achieve that goal; finally, how-questions are frequently used to inquire about the state or condition of somebody or something, while why-questions inquire about the cause of that state or condition without necessarily implying that any purpose or plans are involved. In all these cases it appears to be in principle possible to answer why-questions no less than how-questions, and this without the aid of religion or metaphysics.

THE THEOLOGICAL "WHY"

Let us turn now to what we earlier called "cosmic" why-questions. Two such cosmic "whys" need to be distinguished, the first of which, for rather obvious reasons, will be referred to as the theological "why." Here the questioner would be satisfied with a theological answer if he found such an answer convincing in its own right. He may or may not accept it as true, but he would not regard it as irrelevant.

Gilson, whose remarks on the limitations of science were quoted earlier, immediately supplies the answer to the "supreme question" which science "cannot even ask." Why anything at all exists must be answered by saying:

> [Each] and every particular existential energy, and each and every particular existing thing depends for its existence upon a pure Act of existence. In order to be the ultimate answer to all existential problems, this supreme cause has to be absolute existence. Being absolute, such a cause is self-sufficient; if it creates, its creative act must be free. Since it creates not only being but order, it must be something which at least eminently contains the only principle of order known to us in experience, namely, thought. (*God and Philosophy,* p. 140)

There is no doubt that many people who ask such questions as "Why does the universe exist?" or "Why are we here?" would also, at least in certain moods, be satisfied with a theological answer, though they would not necessarily accept all the details of Gilson's Thomistic theology. It should be emphasized that one does not have to be a believer in God to be using *why* in this way. The American playwright Edward Albee, for example, once remarked, "Why we are here is an impenetrable question." Everyone in the world, he went on, "hopes there is a God," and he later added, "I am neither pro-God nor anti-God" (*New York Times,* January 21, 1965). Albee's question "Why are we here?" evidently amounts to asking whether there is a God and, if so, what divine purposes human beings are supposed to serve. He does not definitely accept the theological answer, presumably because he feels unsure of its truth, but he does regard it as very much to the point.

It should be observed in passing that people frequently use the word *why* to express a kind of cosmic complaint or bewilderment. In such cases they are not really asking for an answer, theological or otherwise. This use of *why* is in some respects similar to the theological "why" and may not inappropriately be referred to as the quasi-theological "why." A person who is and regards himself as a decent human being, but who is suffering a great deal, might easily exclaim "Why do I have to suffer so much, when so many scoundrels in the world, who never worked half as hard as I, are having such a lot of fun?" Such a question may well be asked by an unbeliever who is presumably expressing his regret that the workings of the universe are not in harmony with the moral demands of human beings. Even when believers ask questions of this kind, it may be doubted that they are invariably requesting information about the detailed workings of the Divine Mind. In the deeply moving first-act monologue of *Der Rosenkavalier,* the Marschallin reflects on the inevitability of aging and death:

> I well remember a girl
> Who came fresh from the convent to be forced
> into holy matrimony.
> Where is she now?
> . . . .
> How can it really be,
> That I was once the little Resi
> And that I will one day become the old
> woman?

How, she exclaims, can something like this be? She is far from doubting the existence of God and proceeds to ask:

> Why does the dear Lord do it?

And worse, if he has to do it in this way:

> Why does He let me watch it happen
> With such clear senses? Why doesn't He hide it
> from me?

The Marschallin obviously does not expect an answer to this question, not, or not merely, because she thinks that the world's metaphysicians and theologians are not quite up to it. She is not, strictly speaking, asking a question but expressing her regret and her feeling of complete helplessness.

However, let us return from the quasi-theological to the theological "why." The difficulties besetting an answer like Gilson's are notorious and need not be reviewed here at length. There are the difficulties, much stressed by recent writers, of saying anything intelligible about a disembodied mind, finite or infinite, and there are further difficulties of talking meaningfully about the creation of the universe. There are the rather different difficulties connected not with the intelligibility of the theological assertions but with the reasoning used to justify them. Schopenhauer referred to all such attempts to reach a final resting place in the series of causes as treating the causal principle like a "hired cab" which one dismisses when one has reached one's destination. Bertrand Russell objects that such writers work with an obscure and objectionable notion of explanation: to explain something, we are not at all required to introduce a "self-sufficient" entity, whatever that may be. Writing specifically in reply to Gilson, Ernest Nagel insists that it is perfectly legitimate to inquire into the reasons for the existence of the alleged absolute Being, the pure Act of existence. Those who reject such a question as illegitimate, he writes, are "dogmatically cutting short a discussion when the intellectual current runs against them" (*Sovereign Reason,* Glencoe, IL, 1954, p. 30). Without wishing to minimize these difficulties, it is important to insist that there is a sense in which the theological why-questions are intelligible. The question can be answered for such a person if it can be shown that there is a God. If not, it cannot be answered. Albee and Gilson, for example, do not agree about the truth, or at any rate the logical standing, of the theological assertion, but they agree that it is relevant to their cosmic why-question. There is thus a sense in which the questioner here knows what he is looking for.

THE SUPERULTIMATE "WHY"

The theological "why" must be distinguished from what we are here going to call the superultimate "why." A person who is using *why* in the latter way would regard the theological answer as quite unsatisfactory, not (or not just) because it is meaningless or false but because it does not answer his question. It does not go far enough. For granting that there is a God and that human beings were created by God to serve certain of his purposes, our questioner would now ask "Why is there a God of this kind with these purposes and not another God with other purposes?" or, more radically, he would ask "Why was there at some time God rather than nothing?" The biblical statement "In the beginning God created heaven and earth," Heidegger explicitly remarks, "is not an answer to … and cannot even be brought into relation with our question." The believer who stops with God is not pushing his questioning "to the very end" (*An Introduction to Metaphysics,* pp. 6–7). (It is not certain how somebody pressing the superultimate why-question would react to the rejoinder of those theologians who maintain that God exists necessarily and that hence the question "Why was there at some time God rather than nothing?" is illegitimate. In all likelihood he would support the view, accepted by the majority of Western philosophers since Hume and Immanuel Kant, that it makes no sense to talk about anything, natural or supernatural, as existing necessarily.)

There are times when most people would regard these superultimate why-questions as just absurd. Stafford-Clark himself speaks with impatience of the "rumination" and the tedious and interminable speculations of obsessional patients. "'Why is the world?' was a question to which one patient could find no answer but from which he could find no relief" (*Psychiatry Today,* p. 112). Yet, at other times, most of us are ready to treat these why-questions as supremely profound, as riddles to which it would be wonderful to have the answer but which, because of our finite intellects, must forever remain unsolved. It is true that certain philosophers, like Friedrich von Schelling and Heidegger, who have frequently been denounced as obscurantists, have laid special emphasis on superultimate why-questions; but it would be a total misunderstanding of the situation to suppose that more empirical philosophers, or indeed ordinary people, are not given to asking them or to treating them with great seriousness. It is almost unavoidable that any reasonably intelligent and reflective person who starts wondering about the origin of the human race, or animal life, or the solar system, or our galaxy and other galaxies, or about the lack of justice in the world, the brevity of life, and seeming absolute finality of death, should sooner or later ask "Why this world and not another—why any world?"

The scientist Julian Huxley is as far removed in temperament and philosophy from Heidegger as anybody could be. Yet he also speaks of the "basic and universal mystery—the mystery of existence in general … why does the world exist?" For Huxley it is science that "confronts us" with this mystery, but science cannot remove it. The only comment we can make is that "we do not know." We must accept the existence of the universe "and our own existence as the one basic mystery" (*Essays of a Humanist,* London, 1964, pp. 107–108). Ludwig Büchner was a materialist and an atheist, and yet he repeatedly spoke of the "inexplicability of the last ground of things." Nor are superultimate why-questions confined to those who do not believe in God or who have no metaphysical system. Schopenhauer was supremely confident that his was the true metaphysic, but he nevertheless remarks in the concluding chapter of his main work that his "philosophy does not pretend to explain the existence of the world in its ultimate grounds.… After all my explanations," he adds, "one may still ask, for example, whence has sprung this will, the manifestation of which is the world.… A perfect understanding of the existence, nature, and origin of the world, extending to its ultimate ground and satisfying all demands, is impossible. So much as to the limits of my philosophy, and indeed of all philosophy" (*The World as Will and Idea,* 3 vols., translated by R. B. Haldane and J. Kemp, London, 1883, Ch. 50)

Similarly, Voltaire, who was a firm and sincere believer in God and who never tired of denouncing atheists as blind and foolish, nevertheless asked, at the end of the article "Why?" in his *Philosophical Dictionary,* "Why is there anything?," without for a moment suggesting that an appeal to God's creation would be a solution. William James, too, although he repeatedly defended supernaturalism, never claimed that it provided an answer to the question "How comes the world to be here at all instead of the non-entity which might be imagined in its place?" Philosophy, in James's opinion, whether it be naturalistic or supernaturalistic, "brings no reasoned solution" to this question, "for from nothing to being there is no logical bridge" (*Some Problems of Philosophy,* New York, 1911, pp. 38–40). "The question of being," he observes later in the same discussion, is "the darkest in all philosophy. All of us are beggars here, and no school can speak disdainfully of another or give itself superior airs" (ibid., p. 46).

Having pointed out how widespread is this tendency to ask and take seriously the superultimate why-question, it is necessary to explain why, in the opinion of a number of contemporary philosophers, it must nevertheless be condemned as meaningless. It is the mark of a meaningful question, it would be urged, that not all answers can be ruled out a priori; but because of the way in which the superultimate why-question has been set up, it is logically impossible to obtain an answer. It is quite clear that the questioner will automatically reject any proposed answer as "not going back far enough"—as not answering his why. "All explanation," in the words of Peter Koestenbaum, an American disciple and expositor of Heidegger, "occurs within that which is to be explained … so the question applies to any possible answer as well" ("The Sense of Subjectivity," p. 54), that is, there cannot be an answer. If, however, a question can be put at all, to quote Wittgenstein,

> then it *can* also be answered … doubt can only exist where there is a question; a question only where there is an answer, and this only where something *can* be *said.* (*Tractatus Logico-Philosophicus,* 6.5 and 6.51)

It must be emphasized that the superultimate "why" does not express ignorance about the "early" history of the universe. Büchner, for example, had no doubt that matter was eternal and that nothing which could be called "creation" had ever occurred; Voltaire similarly had no doubt that the physical universe was created by God and that God had always existed—yet both of them asked the superultimate "why" and regarded it as unanswerable. No doubt, some who have asked superultimate why-questions would, unlike Büchner and Voltaire, declare themselves ignorant of the remote history of the universe, but it is not this ignorance that they are expressing by means of the superultimate "why."

Those who insist that the superultimate why-question is meaningful do not usually deny that it very radically differs from all other meaningful why-questions. To mark the difference they occasionally refer to it by such labels as "mystery" or "miracle." Thus Koestenbaum remarks that "questions of this sort do not lead to answers but to a state of mind that appreciates the miracle of existence," they call attention to "the greatest of all mysteries" (op. cit., pp. 54–55). Heidegger writes that the question "is incommensurable with any other" (*An Introduction to Metaphysics,* p. 4) and subsequently observes that "not only what is asked after but also the asking itself is extraordinary" (ibid., p. 10).

Calling the superultimate why-question a "mystery" or a "miracle" or "incommensurable" or "extraordinary" does not in any way remove the difficulty: It is just one way of acknowledging that there is one. If it is granted that in all other situations a question makes sense only if an answer to it is logically possible, one wonders why this principle or criterion is not to be applied in the present case. If the defender of the meaningfulness of the superultimate why-question admits that in the "ordinary" sense the question is meaningless but that in some other and perhaps deeper sense it is meaningful, one would like to be told what this other and deeper sense is.

The point of the preceding paragraphs is sometimes expressed in a way that is not totally satisfactory. It is maintained that a question does not make sense unless the questioner knows what kind of answer he is looking for. However, while the fact that the questioner knows the "outline" of the answer may be a strong or even conclusive reason for supposing that the question is meaningful, the converse does not hold. One can think of examples in which a question is meaningful although the person asking it did not know what a possible answer would look like. Thus somebody might ask "What is the meaning of life?" without being able to tell us what kind of answer would be relevant and at a later time, after falling in love for the first time, he might exclaim that he now had the answer to his question—that love was the meaning of life. It would be much better to say in such a case that the question, as originally asked, was not clear than to say that it was meaningless. It is not objectionable to condemn a question as meaningless on the ground that the questioner does not know what he is looking for if in the context this is a way of saying that he has ruled out all answers a priori; and very probably those who express themselves in this way do not mean to point to some contingent incapacity on the part of the questioner but, rather, to a disability consequent upon the logical impossibility of obtaining an answer to the question. It is similar to saying that it is inconceivable that 3 plus 2 should equal 6 when we do not mean to assert a contingent fact about a certain incapacity on the part of human beings but, rather, that "3 plus 2 equals 6" is a self-contradiction.

The conclusion that the superultimate why-question is meaningless can also be reached by attending to what has here happened to the word *why.* A little reflection shows that in the superultimate question "why" has lost any of its ordinary meanings without having been given a new one. Let us see how this works when the question is put in the form "Why does the universe exist?" and when the "universe" is taken to include everything that in fact exists. In any of its familiar senses, when we ask of anything, *x,* why it happened or why it is what it is—whether *x* is the collapse of an army, a case of lung cancer, the theft of a jewel, or the stalling of a car—we assume that there is something or some set of conditions, other than *x,* in terms of which it can be explained. We do not know what this other thing is that is suitably related to *x,* but unless it is in principle possible to go beyond *x* and find such another thing, the question does not make any sense. (This has to be slightly modified to be accurate. If we are interested in the "why" of a state of *x* at a certain time, then the answer can certainly refer to an earlier state of *x.* This does not affect the issue here discussed since, in the sense with which we are concerned, reference to an earlier state of *x* is going beyond *x.*) Now, if by "the universe" we mean the totality of things, then our *x* in "Why does the universe exist?" is so all-inclusive that it is logically impossible to find anything which could be suitably related to that whose explanation we appear to be seeking. "The sense of the world," wrote Wittgenstein, "must lie outside the world" (*Tractatus Logico-Philosophicus,* 6.41), but by definition nothing can be outside the world. Heidegger, who avoids the formulation "Why does the universe exist?" and who instead inquires into the why of *das seiende* (the official translation of this term is "the essent," but Koestenbaum and others quite properly translate it as "things"), nevertheless makes it clear that *das seiende* here "takes in everything, and this means not only everything that is present in the broadest sense but also everything that ever was or will be." "Our question," he writes a little later, presumably without seeing the implications of this admission, "reaches out so far that we can never go further" (*An Introduction to Metaphysics,* p. 2).

For anybody who is not clearly aware of what we may call the logical grammar of *why* it is very easy to move from meaningful why-questions about particular things to the meaningless why-question about the universe. This tendency is aided by the picture that many people have of "the universe" as a kind of huge box that contains all the things "inside it." Voltaire's article "Why?," from which we quoted earlier, is a good example of such an illegitimate transition. Voltaire first asks a number of why-questions about specific phenomena, such as

> Why does one hardly ever do the tenth part good one might do? Why in half Europe do girls pray to God in Latin, which they do not understand? Why in antiquity was there never a theological quarrel, and why were no people ever distinguished by the name of a sect?

He then gets more and more philosophical:

> Why, as we are so miserable, have we imagined that not to be is a great ill, when it is clear that it was not an ill not to be before we were born?

A little later we have what may well be a theological "why":

> Why do we exist?

Finally, as if there had been no shift in the meaning of *why* Voltaire asks:

> Why is there anything?

It should be noted that the argument we have just presented is not in any way based on an empiricist meaning criterion or on any question-begging assumptions in favor of naturalism. Anybody who uses the word *universe* in a more restricted sense, so that it is not antecedently impossible to get to an entity that might be the explanation of the universe, may be asking a meaningful question when he asks "Why does the universe exist?" Furthermore, even if *universe* is used in the all-inclusive sense, what we have said does not rule out the possibility that God or various divine beings are part of the universe in this sense. The point has simply been that the word *why* loses its meaning when it becomes logically impossible to go beyond what one is trying to explain. This is a matter on which there need not be any disagreement between atheists and theists or between rationalists and empiricists.

It will be well to bring together the main conclusions of this entry:

(1) There is a sense in which *how* and *why* have roughly the same meaning. In this sense science is perfectly competent to deal with the *why.*

(2) There are certain senses in which *how* and *why* serve to ask distinct questions, but here too both types of questions can in principle be answered by empirical procedures.

(3) One of the cosmic "whys"—what we have called the theological "why"—is used to ask meaningful questions, at least if certain semantic problems about theological utterances are disregarded. It was pointed out, however, that this does not imply that the theological answers are true or well supported.

(4) Some apparent questions introduced by "why" are really complaints and not questions, and for this reason unanswerable.

(5) What we have called the superultimate "why" introduces questions that are devoid of sense, whether they are asked by ordinary people in their reflective moments or by philosophers.

See also Explanation; Gilson, Étienne Henry; Heidegger, Martin; Hume, David; Mach, Ernst; Newton, Isaac; Pearson, Karl; Petzoldt, Joseph; Schelling, Friedrich Wilhelm Joseph von; Schopenhauer, Arthur; Voltaire, François-Marie Arouet de; Whitehead, Alfred North; Wittgenstein, Ludwig Josef Johann.

Bibliography

Wittgenstein returned to a discussion of cosmic why-questions in a lecture given in 1930 which was published for the first time under the title "A Lecture on Ethics," in *Philosophical Review* (1965). He makes it clear that although he regards the questions as nonsensical, he "deeply respects" the tendency to ask such questions. The complete text of Voltaire's article "Why?," sometimes called "The Whys," is available in the six-volume edition of the *Philosophical Dictionary* published in London by J. Hunt and H. L. Hunt in 1824. Views similar to those expressed in the last section of the present article are defended in John Passmore, "Fact and Meaning," in *Thinking and Meaning* (Louvain and Paris, 1963). Jean-Paul Sartre appears to reach similar conclusions in the final section of *Being and Nothingness,* translated by H. E. Barnes (New York: Philosophical Library, 1956).

Heidegger's fullest discussion of the superultimate why-question occurs in Ch. 1 of *Einführung in die Metaphysik* (Tübingen: Niemeyer, 1953), translated by Ralph Manheim as *An Introduction to Metaphysics* (New Haven, CT: Yale University Press, 1959). Koestenbaum's treatment is contained in his "The Sense of Subjectivity," in *Review of Existential Psychology and Psychiatry* 2 (1962): 47–64. Max Scheler discusses the superultimate why-question in his essay "Vom Wesen der Philosophic und der moralischen Bedingung des philosophischen Erkennens," in *Gesammelte Werke,* edited by Maria Scheler, Vol. V (Bern: Francke, 1954). His position seems to be very similar to that of Heidegger and other existentialists. Scheler concludes that "he who has not, as it were, looked into the abyss of the absolute Nothing will completely overlook the eminently positive content of the realization that there is something rather than nothing" (pp. 93–94).

The only detailed attempt to reply to arguments such as those urged in the present entry and to show that the superultimate why-question is meaningful, although it is in principle unanswerable, is found in M. K. Munitz, *The Mystery of Existence* (New York: Appleton-Century-Crofts, 1965). Clearly theological uses of "why" occur in Ch. 7 of Richard Taylor, *Metaphysics* (Englewood Cliffs, NJ: Prentice-Hall, 1963) and in F. C. Copleston's remarks in his debate with A. J. Ayer, "Logical Positivism," in *A Modern Introduction to Philosophy,* edited by Paul Edwards and Arthur Pap, 2nd ed. (New York: Free Press, 1965). There are some interesting remarks on what we have here been calling the quasi-theological "why" in Ch. 14 of S. E. Toulmin, *The Place of Reason in Ethics* (Cambridge, U.K.: Cambridge University Press, 1950).

The general topic of what makes a question meaningful has only very rarely been discussed by philosophers. Rudolf Carnap, in *Der logische Aufbau der Welt,* Part V, Sec. E (Berlin: Weltkreis, 1928; 2nd ed., Hamburg, 1961), and Moritz Schlick, in "Unanswerable Questions?," in *Philosopher* (1935), reprinted in his *Gesammelte Aufsätze* (Vienna: Gerold, 1938), propose empiricistic meaning criteria and conclude that questions that cannot even in principle be answered must be condemned as meaningless. However, as was pointed out in the text, this conclusion does not depend on the adoption of an empiricistic meaning criterion. Thus the phenomenologist Oskar Becker writes that "according to the principle of transcendental idealism a question which is in principle undecidable has no sense—to it there corresponds no possible state of affairs which could supply an answer" ("Beiträge zur phänomenologischen Begründung der Geometrie und ihrer physikalischen Anwendungen," in *Jahrbuch für Philosophie und phänomenologische Forschung* 6 (1923): 412. There are numerous suggestive remarks in Ch. 20 of Friedrich Waismann's posthumously published *The Principles of Linguistic Philosophy* (New York: St. Martin's Press, 1965).

On *how* and *why,* in addition to the works quoted in the text, mention should be made of James Martineau, *Modern Materialism* (New York: Putnam, 1877), where the view is defended that science cannot deal with the "why." Agnostic positivism is defended in E. W. Hobson, *The Domain of Natural Science* (Cambridge, U.K.: Cambridge University Press, 1923). A J. Ayer in the debate with Copleston supports the position that science can handle why-questions so long as they are intelligible.

When we ask why a person acted in a certain way or why he holds a certain belief, we frequently ask for an explanation in terms of reasons. It has been argued by a number of recent writers that such explanations cannot be regarded as a species of causal explanation—at any rate in the sense in which we habitually search for causal explanations in the natural sciences. This topic has not been discussed in the present entry since it is treated at some length elsewhere in this encyclopedia (see the entry Philosophy of History).

Paul Edwards (1967)

WIGGINS, DAVID
(1933–)

David Wiggins was professor of philosophy at Bedford College, London; professor of philosophy at Birkbeck College, London; Wykeham Professor of Logic at Oxford University; and a fellow of New College, Oxford. He has published in metaphysics, philosophy of language, moral and political philosophy, and the history of philosophy. His major works are *Identity and Spatio-temporal Continuity*; *Sameness and Substance*; *Needs, Values, and Truth: Essays in the Philosophy of Value*; and *Sameness and Substance Renewed.*

The most influential part of Wiggins's work has been in metaphysics, where he has developed a fundamentally Aristotelian conception of substance, enriched by insights drawn from Putnam (1975) and Kripke (1980). His works also contain influential discussions of the problem of personal identity, which Wiggins elucidates via a conception that he calls the "Animal Attribute View."

Wiggins's metaphysic of substance embodies several contentions. The first is that a distinction can be drawn between sortal and nonsortal concepts, the former providing answers to the question "What is it?" asked of a substance. If *a* and *b* are the same, there must be an answer to the question "The same what?" This answer can be provided by a sortal concept satisfied by both *a* and *b*. This thesis implies that any substance satisfies at any time some sortal or other.

Wiggins also maintains that any substance must satisfy the same substance sortal throughout its existence, though it will also satisfy various phase sortals that apply to it only at certain stages of its career. For example, "child" is a phase sortal, while "man," Wiggins says, is a substance sortal. Protean change is not possible. Following Quine (1960), some opponents of this view hold that substances are not to be distinguished from events or processes, and can be thought of as having temporal parts. These proponents of "four-dimensionalism," as the doctrine of temporal parts is commonly called, also typically hold that any temporal part of one object and any temporal part of the same or another object can be thought of as constituting a third object (Quine 1960, Lewis 1986). There is, for example, the object consisting of the first decade of Aristotle and the third decade of the Eiffel Tower. This thesis is sometimes referred to as mereological universalism, or unrestricted composition. Wiggins's thesis that any substance must satisfy some one substance sortal throughout its existence is intended to be inconsistent with mereological universalism. More fundamentally, Wiggins argues against four-dimensionalism.

Another significant component of Wiggins's metaphysics is his denial of relative identity. Wiggins maintains that identity is not relative to different sortals, in the sense that *a* and *b* may be the same *f* but different *g*'s. The relative-identity thesis was introduced into modern debate by Peter Geach (1972) and appears to be illustrated by familiar kinds of change. For example, an old general is the same person or human being as the young boy he was, but he is not the same child, since the old general is not a child. Again, if a piece of clay is reshaped to make different statues, it is the same piece of clay throughout, but not the same statue. To deal with such examples, Wiggins appeals to (1) the distinction between phase sortals and substance sortals and (2) the distinction between constitution and identity. The first type of example, he suggests, can be dealt with merely by paying proper attention to tense: The general was the same child as the boy, and the boy will be the same man as the general. In the second type of case he suggests that we must recognize that the piece of clay is distinct from all the statues it successively constitutes. We can correctly say that the clay is at one time a statue of Goliath, say. But this is because one of the meanings of "is" is "constitutes"—a meaning that must be recognized in addition to the "is" of predication and the "is" of identity.

Wiggins opposes relative identity because he sees it as incompatible with Leibniz's Law, the principle that if *a* is identical with *b*, *a* and *b* must share all their properties. Some opponents of Wiggins have criticized his distinction between constitution and identity, which allows the possibility of two things in the same place at the same time (Lewis 1986). Others have questioned his positive argument that Leibniz's Law and relative identity are incompatible. Debate about these matters continues.

One sortal concept to which Wiggins has given special attention is that of a person. In *Identity and Spatio-temporal Continuity* (1967) and its successors, he developed his response to the problem of personal identity originating in the writings of John Locke, with particular reference to the writings of Bernard Williams (1973), Derek Parfit (1984), and Sydney Shoemaker (1963). In response to the famous Reduplication Argument against Lockean accounts of personal identity in terms of consciousness, put forward by Williams, Wiggins insists that the concept of a person, as a genuine sortal concept, must satisfy "the *a* and *b* rule," that whether later *a* is identical with earlier *b* can depend only on facts about *a* and *b* and the relations between them. This entails a rejection of the modified Lockean "best candidate" type of account of personal identity developed by Shoemaker and endorsed by Parfit.

Wiggins also rejects Parfit's thesis that identity is not what matters in survival. Finally, he rejects Locke's distinction between man and person, and endorses the thesis that persons just are animals (more specifically, human beings). Many philosophers have accepted the distinction on the basis of thought experiments in which, for example, brains are transplanted from one skull into another, with consequent transference of memory and character traits. Wiggins suggests that in such cases the same human being (not merely the same person) has different bodies successively. More fundamentally, he denies the real possibility of such cases. In the last position, he is influenced by the work of Kripke and Putnam. In this area too, Wiggins's position remains one of the options subject to current debate and development. The "animalist" position is developed in different ways by van Inwagen (1990) and Olson (1997), and is opposed by Shoemaker (1963).

See also Aristotle; Identity; Kripke, Saul; Leibniz, Gottfried Wilhelm; Lewis, David; Locke, John; Meaning; Parfit, Derek; Personal Identity; Putnam, Hilary; Quine, Willard Van Orman; Shoemaker, Sydney; Williams, Bernard.

Bibliography

Geach, Peter. *Logic Matters*. Oxford, U.K.: Basil Blackwell, 1972.

Kripke, Saul. *Naming and Necessity*. Oxford, U.K.: Basil Blackwell, 1980.

Lewis, David. *On the Plurality of Worlds*. Oxford, U.K.: Basil Blackwell, 1986.

Olson, Eric. *The Human Animal*. Oxford, U.K.: Oxford University Press, 1997.

Parfit, Derek. *Reasons and Persons*. Oxford, U.K.: Clarendon Press, 1984.

Putnam, Hilary. "The Meaning of 'Meaning.'" In his *Mind, Language, and Reality*. Vol. 2 of *Philosophical Papers*. Cambridge, U.K.: Cambridge University Press, 1975.

Quine, Willard Van Orman. *Word and Object*. Cambridge, MA: MIT Press, 1960.

Shoemaker, Sydney. *Self-Knowledge and Self-Identity*. Ithaca, NY: Cornell University Press, 1963.

Van Inwagen, Peter. *Material Beings*. Ithaca, NY: Cornell University Press, 1990.

Wiggins, David. *Identity and Spatio-temporal Continuity*. Oxford, U.K.: Basil Blackwell, 1967.

Wiggins, David. *Needs, Values, and Truth: Essays in the Philosophy of Value*. 2nd ed. Oxford: Blackwell, 1991.

Wiggins, David. *Sameness and Substance*. Oxford, U.K.: Basil Blackwell, 1980.

Wiggins, David. *Sameness and Substance Renewed*. Cambridge, U.K.: Cambridge University Press, 2000.

Williams, Bernard. *Problems of the Self*. Cambridge, U.K.: Cambridge University Press, 1973.

Harold W. Noonan (2005)

WILDE, OSCAR FINGAL O'FLAHERTIE WILLS

(1854–1900)

Born in Dublin to artistically minded parents, Wilde studied for three years at Trinity College in Dublin, and then at Magdalen College in Oxford, where his tutors included the English art critic John Ruskin and the English essayist Walter Pater. At the age of twenty-four he moved to London, where he very quickly became a conspicuous figure on the social scene, celebrated for his wit, personality, and self-consciously foppish dress sense. He married in 1884, had two children, and then, within a couple of years, noticed that he was homosexual. He fell in love with Lord Alfred Douglas in the early 1890s, was repeatedly and publicly denounced by Douglas's father, the Marquess of Queensberry, until eventually Wilde sued for libel, and lost. This led to his trial and conviction for sodomy, and to a sentence of two years' hard labor, which he served first in Wandsworth prison and then in Reading gaol. He was released in 1897, and spent the remaining years of his life as a social outcast in France, cash-strapped and increasingly ill. When he died, he was just forty-six.

Although Wilde is chiefly remembered for his one-liners—not unreasonably, given how good so many of them are—he was a more versatile writer than this fact might suggest. He published prose fiction, including a collection of fairy stories, *The Happy Prince and Other Tales* (1888), and a novel, *The Picture of Dorian Gray* (1891); he published verse, most notably "The Ballad of Reading Gaol" (1898); he dabbled in social commentary of a utopian bent, as seen in "The Soul of Man under Socialism" (1891); and he was a highly successful dramatist, with the best of his plays, *The Importance of Being Earnest* (1894), still being performed regularly in the twenty-first century. He also wrote essays and dialogues on art and art criticism, the most important of which, "The Decay of Lying" and "The Critic as Artist," were among the pieces that he published in 1891, under the title *Intentions*.

Wilde was not a philosopher, and it is an interesting question whether, or to what extent, he can be taken to have contributed to philosophy. His most obvious connection to the subject, after all, is the rather unusual one of being, not the originator of a philosophical position, but the emblem or embodiment of one: Wilde stands for aestheticism in much the way that Lord Byron, for instance, stands for Romanticism. And this is a role that Wilde cultivated assiduously.

The term "aestheticism" refers to a cluster of more or less closely related views (often glossed as "art for art's sake"), rather than to a single theory or system; and many of these views enjoyed wide currency in the second half of the nineteenth century, not least through the writings of Ruskin and Pater. Perhaps the most characteristic tenet of aestheticism is the claim that aesthetic value is independent of and/or superior to other kinds of value. From this standpoint, the preeminently Victorian habit of bringing moral values to bear on the assessment of art—of asking, if not first then certainly foremost, whether such-and-such a work is edifying, say, or is likely to deprave—was point missing and philistine. Instead, the aestheticists insisted, the question should be whether a given work is beautiful. As Wilde put it in the preface to *Dorian Gray*: "There is no such thing as a moral or an immoral book. Books are well written, or badly written. That is all." And this statement means that the artist's task cannot be didactic: "An ethical sympathy in an artist is an unpardonable mannerism of style" (Wilde 1949, p. 5).

Taken in its stronger form—that aesthetic value is both independent of and superior to other kinds of value—the aestheticist tenet prompts a view not merely about art, but also about life. It encourages the thought that one should try to turn oneself into a work of art, to understand oneself in aesthetic terms rather than moral ones, say, and this is a project to which Wilde devoted considerable effort, claiming (to André Gide) that he had put his genius into his life, and only his talent into his work. His dress sense, his manner, and above all his style, were carefully calculated for aesthetic effect: "To me," as a character in *Dorian Gray* says, "Beauty is the wonder of wonders. It is only shallow people who do not judge by appearances. The true mystery of the world is the visible, not the invisible ..." (Wilde 1949, p. 29). And so successful was Wilde in cultivating his public persona that when Gilbert and Sullivan's operetta *Patience* was first performed in 1881, no one doubted after whom the dandified aesthete, Reginald Bunthorne, had been modeled.

"A critic cannot be fair in the ordinary sense of the word," Wilde wrote. "It is only about things that do not interest one that one can give a really unbiassed opinion, which is no doubt the reason why an unbiassed opinion is always absolutely valueless" (Wilde 1907, p. 153). This thought—an outright rejection of the value of disinterestedness in the experience of art—perhaps has a claim to be regarded as Wilde's most original contribution to the philosophy of art, shades of Ruskin notwithstanding. Wilde insisted that "it is only by intensifying his own personality that the critic can interpret the personality and work of others," and even went so far as to accord a higher value to the critic's work than to the artist's (Wilde 1907, p. 127), a relative estimation, incidentally, that proved to be prophetic of much that passed for literary studies in the later twentieth century. Wilde developed some of these thoughts, and they are interesting. But it is hard not to feel that they are, in the end, really only a side product of the much more pressing business of turning his life into art, of striking a stylish pose that should, above all, be effective, even if, as he himself averred, "All art is quite useless" (Wilde 1949, p. 6).

See also Aesthetic Qualities; Aesthetics, History of; Art, Value in; Beauty; Humor; Pater, Walter Horatio; Romanticism; Ruskin, John; Value and Valuation.

Bibliography

WORKS BY OSCAR WILDE

The Artist as Critic: Critical Writings of Oscar Wilde, edited by Richard Ellmann. Englewood Cliffs, NJ: Prentice Hall, 1969.

Intentions. London: The English Library, 1907.

The Annotated Oscar Wilde: Poems, Fiction, Plays, Lectures, Essays, and Letters, edited by H. Montgomery Hyde. New York: Potter, 1982.

The Complete Letters of Oscar Wilde, edited by Merlin Holland and Rupert Hart-Davis. New York: Holt, 2000.

The Picture of Dorian Gray. London: Penguin Books, 1949.

The Picture of Dorian Gray: Authoritative Texts, Backgrounds, Reviews and Reactions, Criticism, edited by Donald L. Lawler. New York: Norton, 1988.

WORKS ABOUT OSCAR WILDE

Bloom, Harold, ed. *Oscar Wilde*. New York: Chelsea, 1985.

Brown, Julia Prewitt. *Cosmopolitan Criticism: Oscar Wilde's Philosophy of Art*. Charlottesville: University of Virginia Press, 1997.

Chai, Leon. *Aestheticism: The Religion of Art in Post-Romantic Literature*. New York: Columbia University Press, 1990.

Cohen, Philip K. *The Moral Vision of Oscar Wilde*. Rutherford, NJ: Fairleigh Dickinson University Press, 1978.

Ellmann, Richard. *Oscar Wilde*. New York: Knopf, 1987.

Eltis, Sos. *Revising Wilde: Society and Subversion in the Plays of Oscar Wilde*. Oxford: Clarendon, 1997.

Freedman, Jonathan, ed. *Oscar Wilde: A Collection of Critical Essays*. Upper Saddle River, NJ: Prentice Hall, 1996.
McCormack, Jerusha, ed. *Wilde the Irishman*. New Haven, CT: Yale University Press, 1998.
Price, Jody. *A Map with Utopia: Oscar Wilde's Theory for Social Transformation*. New York: Peter Lang, 1996.
Raby, Peter, ed. *The Cambridge Companion to Oscar Wilde*. Cambridge, U.K.: Cambridge University Press, 1997.
Schmidgall, Gary. *The Stranger Wilde: Interpreting Oscar*. New York: William Abrahams, 1994.
Shewan, Rodney. *Oscar Wilde: Art and Egoism*. New York: Barnes, 1977.

Aaron Ridley (2005)

WILL

See *Determinism, A Historical Survey*; *Volition*

WILLIAM HEYTESBURY

See *Heytesbury, William*

WILLIAM OF AUVERGNE

(c. 1180–1249)

William of Auvergne (or Paris) was born in Aurillac in the province of Auvergne. He was a master of theology at Paris by 1223 and was consecrated bishop of Paris in 1228. His chief philosophical works are *De trinitate, seu De primo principio* (c. 1223; translated as *The Trinity, or The First Principle*), which presents his metaphysics; *De universo* (c. 1231–1240; translated as *The Universe of Creatures*); and *De anima* (c. 1240; translated as *The Soul*); all parts of his seven-part *Magisterium divinale et sapientiale*. These works were written in a literary and highly personal style influenced by Latin translations of Avicenna.

Reacting to the teaching of many then newly circulating translations of Greek and Arabic texts of metaphysics and natural philosophy, and writing under early-thirteenth-century prohibitions at Paris, William attempted to identify and refute the errors of these works. But he was also greatly influenced by their teachings when they accorded with Christian faith, and incorporated them into an outlook influenced by St. Augustine.

Especially influenced by Avicenna, William was the first Latin thinker to base his metaphysics on Avicenna's distinction between being and essence. According to William, everything that exists is a possible being, whose essence is distinct from its being, or a necessary being, whose essence and being are identical. There must be a single necessary being, God or the first being, from whom existing possible beings receive their being. William described existing possible beings as composed of being and essence, raising the question of whether he, like Aquinas, posited a real distinction of being and essence in creatures. From Boethius, William took a related distinction between being (*esse*) and what a thing is (*quod est*). Identifying what a thing is with its essence, he distinguished beings by participation, whose essence is distinct from their being, from beings by essence, whose being and essence are identical. Beings by participation, he argued, must partake of their being from a unique being by essence, God.

Despite care to avoid the errors of non-Christian thinkers, William himself sometimes treads on dangerous ground. At one point he describes God as the being of everything, suggesting pantheism. At other times, emphasizing God's power in opposition to the necessitarian tendencies of Arabic thought, he writes as though creatures are not genuine causal agents but merely conduits of God's causal power. Such statements, however, probably do not reflect his considered views.

A key error that William identified in Avicenna (misidentified as Aristotle) was his doctrine of creation. According to this doctrine, God does not, as Christians think, create all things freely and contingently from nothing, but necessarily emanates a single intelligence or spiritual being. From this being necessarily emanate in turn further intelligences and the heavenly spheres, a process ending with the emanation of human souls and things of the sublunary world from the tenth intelligence. William took this doctrine to result from an incorrect application of the principle that from what is one, insofar as it is one, comes only one. Drawing on the doctrine of the divine will of the Jewish thinker Avicebron (1021–1058), William argued instead that God created the world not insofar as he is one, but insofar as he is free.

William also attacked Avicenna's and Aristotle's non-Christian doctrine that the world exists without beginning. The first Latin thinker to treat the issue in depth, he refuted a battery of arguments for an eternal world and presented lengthy arguments for its beginning. Several of these arguments, some drawn from the sixth-century Alexandrian thinker John Philoponus, allege that a world without beginning involves paradoxes of infinity, and would be popular with later Franciscan thinkers, including Bonaventure.

William's *The Soul* is the most substantial early-thirteenth-century treatment of the soul. Despite using Aristotle's definition of the soul as the perfection of an organic body potentially having life, William in fact adopted a non-Aristotelian conception of the soul as an incorporeal, indivisible, simple substance, identifying it with the whole human being and treating the body as its prison or cloak. To show the distinctness of soul and body, William used Avicenna's "floating man' argument that someone floating in the air without use of the senses would know the existence of his soul, but not of his body. William rejected a plurality of distinct souls in a human being corresponding to the vegetative, sensitive, and rational vital functions, attributing these functions to a single rational soul. Perhaps the first Latin thinker to hold that souls and angels are wholly immaterial without any kind of matter, William argued at length that the soul survives destruction of the body and is immortal.

In epistemology William was concerned to attack the doctrines of an agent intelligence and an agent intellect. The former doctrine, found in Avicenna, posits that intelligible forms are impressed on the human intellect by the tenth intelligence. William objected that this is incompatible with our need to study to acquire knowledge. The doctrine of an agent intellect, according to William, posits within the human soul two intellects, a receptive or material intellect and an active or agent intellect, which impresses intelligible forms on the material intellect. Noting the popularity of this doctrine in his day, William objected that it is incompatible with the simplicity of the soul and would mean that we know everything that can naturally be known. His positive account of knowledge is unclear, however, being expressed in imprecise and metaphorical terms. It has been suggested that he treated God as an agent intellect. But in fact he held only that God impresses on the human intellect the principles of truth and morality; once these principles are known, the whole soul can acquire scientific knowledge directly without the mediation of any agent intellect within or outside it.

Early to advocate a voluntarist conception of free will, William held that the will is king and noblest power in the soul, with command over its other powers, and is counseled by the intellect. The will itself must be capable of apprehension and cognition if it is not to be blind, and the intellect likewise has a kind of appetite. The will cannot be forced, prevented, or necessitated. William wrote that he was puzzled that Aristotle had not considered the will.

Eminent in his day, William influenced Aquinas's metaphysics of being and essence and Franciscan thinkers' arguments for the beginning of the world. His works survive in many manuscripts, suggesting an influence whose full extent remains to be studied.

See also Agent Intellect; Avicenna; Thomas Aquinas, St.

Bibliography

WORKS BY WILLIAM OF AUVERGNE

De immortalitate animae. In *Des Dominicus Gundissalinus Schrift von der Unsterblichkeit der Seele*, edited by Georg Bülow. Münster, Germany: Aschendorff, 1897.

"Tractatus Magistri Guillelmi Alvernensis *De bono et malo*," edited by J. Reginald O'Donnell. *Mediaeval Studies* 8 (1946): 245–299.

"Tractatus secundus Guillelmi Alvernensis *De bono et malo*," edited by J. Reginald O'Donnell. *Mediaeval Studies* 16 (1954): 219–271.

Opera omnia (1674). 2 vols. Frankfurt am Main: Minerva, 1963.

Il "Tractatus de gratia" di Guglielmo d'Auvergne, edited by Guglielmo Corti. Rome: Lateran University, 1966.

De trinitate, edited by Bruno Switalski. Toronto: Pontifical Institute of Mediaeval Studies, 1976.

The Trinity, or The First Principle. Translated by Roland J. Teske and Francis C. Wade. Milwaukee, WI: Marquette University Press, 1989.

The Immortality of the Soul. Translated by Roland J. Teske. Milwaukee, WI: Marquette University Press, 1991.

The Universe of Creatures. Translated by Roland J. Teske. Milwaukee, WI: Marquette University Press, 1998. A partial translation.

The Soul. Translated by Roland J. Teske. Milwaukee, WI: Marquette University Press, 2000. Contains a full bibliography.

WORKS ON WILLIAM OF AUVERGNE

Caster, Kevin J. "The Distinction between Being and Essence according to Boethius, Avicenna, and William of Auvergne." *Modern Schoolman* 73 (1996): 309–332.

Gilson, Etienne. "La notion d'existence chez Guillaume d'Auvergne." *Archives d'histoire doctrinale et littéraire du moyen âge* 21 (1946): 55–91.

Gilson, Etienne. "Pourquoi saint Thomas a critiqué saint Augustin." *Archives d'histoire doctrinale et littéraire du moyen âge* 1 (1926): 5–127.

Kramp, Josef. "Des Wilhelm von Auvergne 'Magisterium Divinale.'" *Gregorianum* 1 (1920): 538–613; 2 (1921): 42–103, 174–195.

Marrone, Steven P. *William of Auvergne and Robert Grosseteste: New Ideas of Truth in the Early Thirteenth Century*. Princeton, NJ: Princeton University Press, 1983.

Masnovo, Amato. *Da Guglielmo d'Auvergne a S. Tommaso d'Aquino*. 3 vols. 2nd ed. Milan, Italy: Vita et Pensiero, 1946.

Moody, Ernest A. "William of Auvergne and His Treatise *De anima*." In his *Studies in Medieval Philosophy, Science, and Logic*, 1–109. Berkeley: University of California Press, 1975.

Teske, Roland J. "William of Auvergne on the 'Newness' of the Word." *Mediaevalia: Textos e Estudios* 7–8 (1995): 287–302.

Teske, Roland J. "William of Auvergne's Rejection of the Agent Intellect." In *Greek and Medieval Studies in Honor of Leo Sweeney, S.J.*, edited by William J. Carroll and John J. Furlong, 211–235. New York: Peter Lang, 1995.

Valois, Noël. *Guillaume d'Auvergne, évêque de Paris (1228–1249): Sa vie et ses ouvrages*. Paris: Picard, 1880.

Neil Lewis (2005)

WILLIAM OF CHAMPEAUX

(c. 1070–1121)

William of Champeaux, born at Champeaux near Melun, was perhaps a student of Anselm of Laon. William was held in high esteem by his contemporaries for his mastery of grammar, logic, and rhetoric, as well as for theological speculations. By 1100 he was the Master of the Cathedral School associated with Notre Dame in Paris, the most prestigious position available for a philosopher; he held the rank of archdeacon, and was a confidante of Philip I. In this period Peter Abelard was first William's student and then his rival in public debates over philosophy. In 1108, William entered the Abbey of St. Victor newly established outside the walls on Paris, on the south bank of the Seine, and apparently continued to teach while there. In 1114 William was made bishop of Châlons-sur-Marne, a position he held until his death there in 1121.

William's theological views are presented in a compendium of short discussions, each addressed to a particular question: his *Sententiae* (partially printed by Lefèvre). His views on logic, language, metaphysics, and rhetoric are preserved in many manuscripts and by later authors, most notably by Abelard; little of this material has yet been edited or sorted out, and there is no scholarly consensus about which views can reliably be attributed to William, although it seems clear that William lectured and perhaps wrote extensively on the liberal arts. Abelard mentions in passing William's claim that every sentence has both a grammatical and a logical sense (*Logica ingredientibus* 7, Glosses on the "Topics" 271–273); that present-tense sentences about nonexistents should be interpreted figuratively (*Dialectica* 135–136); and that differentiae are only accidentally related to the genera they differentiate (*Dialectica* 541). But the best-known and most widely attested philosophical views of William of Champeaux have to do with the problem of universals.

According to Abelard, William initially held a position known as "material essence realism": One and the same material essence is found in distinct individuals of the same species, which are distinguished from one another by the addition of further forms to the material essence. When challenged by Abelard, William modified his position to hold that the same thing (the material essence) is not literally present in different things; distinct things are called the same "indifferently." This latter position seems to be endorsed in William's discussion of the Trinity in his *Sententiae*. Abelard presents William's positions briefly in his *Historia calamitatum* 65–66, and William's positions along with his criticisms at length in his *Logica ingredientibus* 1, Glosses on the "Isagoge" 11–17 and *Logica nostrorum petitioni sociorum* 512–517. William's replies are not known independently.

See also Abelard, Peter; Propositions; Saint Victor, School of; Universals, A Historical Survey.

Bibliography

SELECTED WORKS

Fredborg, Karin M. "The Commentaries on Cicero's *De inventione and Rhetorica ad Herennium* by William of Champeaux." *Cahiers de l'institut du moyen-âge grec et latin* 17 (1976): 1–39.

Iwakuma, Yukio. "The *Introductiones dialecticae secundum Wilgelmum and secundum magistrum G. Paganellum*." *Cahiers de l'institut du moyen-âge grec et latin* 63 (1993): 45–114.

Iwakuma, Yukio. "William of Champeaux and the *Introductiones*." In *Acts of the 10th European Symposium on Medieval Logic and Semantics*, edited by H. A. G. Braakhuis and C. H. Kneepkens. Leiden: Brill 1996.

Lefèvre, Georges. *Les variations de Guilliame de Champeaux et la question des Universaux*. Lille, France: Université de Lille 1898. Includes William's *Sententiae*.

Marenbon, John. *The Philosophy of Peter Abelard*. Cambridge, U.K.: Cambridge University Press, 1997. Discusses reports of William's teaching in unedited manuscripts.

Mews, Constant. "Logica in the Service of Philosophy: William of Champeaux and His Influence on the Study of Language and Theology in the Twelfth Century." In *Studien zur Abtei Sankt Viktor zu Paris und zu den Viktorinern*, edited by Rainer Berndt (Corpus victorinum. Instrumenta 1), Berlin 2004.

Rosier-Catach, Irène. "Abélard et les grammairiens: sur le verbe substantif et la prédication." *Vivarium* 41 (2003): 175–248.

Peter King (2005)

WILLIAM OF CONCHES

William of Conches, the twelfth-century Chartrain philosopher, was born at Conches in Normandy at the end of the eleventh century. He probably studied under Bernard of Chartres, learning at least grammar from him, and began teaching in the early 1120s. About 1140 William, who was perhaps now in Paris, had John of Salisbury as one of his pupils; John found him perpetuating the spirit of Bernard's own teaching. However, opposition from less lettered philosophers led William to return to his native Normandy under the protection of Duke Geoffrey Plantagenet, whose son, the future Henry II of England, he taught. He died sometime after 1154.

William left glosses on Priscian in both an early and a later version, and recent evidence suggests that he may have written glosses on Juvenal. However, his other surviving writings testify above all to a considerable achievement in philosophy and in scientific thought. They include a commentary on the *Consolation of Philosophy* by Boethius that is dependent on older glosses but is animated by an ampler philosophical and physical interest; glosses upon Macrobius; a first version of a commentary upon the Chalcidian version of Plato's *Timaeus*; and a systematic work, the *Philosophia Mundi,* which ranges widely over the topics of God, the universe, and man. William considers the nature of God and his relationship to creation; he also considers the structure and composition of the universe, the elements, the heavens, motion, and geography. Finally, he examines the biology and psychology of man.

These were all youthful writings, completed by the early 1120s. In a second version of his commentary on the *Timaeus,* William abandoned his former assimilation of the Platonic world soul with the Holy Spirit of Christian doctrine. In the later 1140s he continued to modify youthful theses and produced a masterpiece, the *Dragmaticon Philosophiae,* cast in the form of a dialogue with Duke Geoffrey. In this work, which built upon the earlier *Philosophia Mundi,* William developed his physical and astronomical interests and produced the most up-to-date scientific encyclopedia of the mid-twelfth century. Like the *Philosophia Mundi,* it was widely circulated. Some historians consider William to be the author of the *Moralium Dogma Philosophorum,* an influential collection of moralist citations from Scripture, the Church Fathers, and ancient pagan writers.

Much of William's philosophical effort was directed toward ensuring that Christian theology embraced the study of the universe and of man. He saw in Plato's *Timaeus* a doctrine of creation that helped to explain the account given in the book of Genesis. He identified the Platonic archetypal world with the wisdom of God, the Logos of Christian belief. He firmly underlined St. Paul's teaching on the intelligibility of this world (Romans 1:20). The created universe bears the imprint of its creator, and its harmony reveals the fundamental attributes of God—power, wisdom, and goodness. These aspects of God are commonly signified by the names of three divine persons, but William was preoccupied with the creative activity of the Trinity rather than with the intimate relationships of the divine life. Stressing the cosmological function of the Holy Spirit, William presented the third person of the Trinity as the principle of life that animates the world and, in his earlier writings, as identical with the *anima mundi,* or world soul, of Platonic doctrine. Conservative theological opinion was thereby antagonized.

After 1140 William of St.-Thierry, the Cistercian friend of Bernard of Clairvaux, launched an attack against the grammarian of Conches, as he had earlier against Peter Abelard. He criticized William for following Abelard and for transgressing the limits of theological inquiry set by the fathers of the church. He accused the Chartrain of Sabellianism and of subordinationism in his cosmological interpretation of the Trinity, and of materialism in making God an immanent regulatory principle of the universe. In the *Dragmaticon* William yielded somewhat to these criticisms, but he was also influenced by new translations of Greek and Arabic medical writings. His animistic vision of the universe was now tempered by an increased insistence on the power of secondary causes, of nature itself to sustain the universe in cooperation with God. William arrived at a new sense of the autonomous value of nature, and he offered many new perspectives. On the individual human soul and its faculties he joined the medical theories of the newly translated *Pantegni* of ʿAlī ibn al-ʾAbbas and of the *Isagoge* of Johannitius to the traditional Boethian doctrine. Stimulated by the *Pantegni* as well as by Vergil and Lucretius, he criticized the traditional theory of the four elements as the first principles of things. The Ptolemaic theory of planetary motion appeared in William's *Dragmaticon,* which became a striking witness to the broadening of the contemporary scientific horizon.

See also Abelard, Peter; Bernard of Chartres; Bernard of Clairvaux; Boethius, Anicius Manlius Severinus; Chartres, School of; Creation and Conservation, Religious Doctrine of; God, Concepts of; John of Salisbury; Lucretius; Medieval Philosophy; Plato.

Bibliography

Extracts from the *Commentary on Boethius' Consolation of Philosophy* are in J. M. Parent, *La doctrine de la création dans l'école de Chartres* (Paris: Vrin, 1938), pp. 122–136, and, edited by C. Jourdain, in *Notices et extraits des manuscrits de la Bibliothèque Impériale,* Vol. 20, Part II (Paris, 1862), pp. 40–82.

Glosses on Macrobius' Commentary on the Dream of Scipio is unedited, but see E. Jeauneau in *Archives d'histoire doctrinale et littéraire du moyen âge* 27 (1960): 17–28.

Extracts from *Glosses on Plato's Timaeus* have been edited by V. Cousin, in *Ouvrages inédits d'Abélard* (Paris, 1836), pp. 646–657; by J. M. Parent, op. cit., pp. 137–177; and by T. Schmid, in *Classica et Mediaevalia* 10 (1949): 220–266; there is also an edition of Schmid's version by E. Jeauneau, *Glosae super Platonem* (Paris: J. Vrin, 1965).

Extracts from *Glosses on Priscian,* edited by E. Jeauneau, are in *Recherches de théologie ancienne et médiévale* 27 (1960): 212–247.

Philosophia Mundi may be found in *Patrologia Latina,* edited by J. P. Migne, Vol. 172, Cols. 39–102 (under Honorius Augustodunensis), and in Vol. 90, Cols. 1127–1178 (under Bede).

Dragmaticon Philosophiae, edited by G. Gratarolus, was published under the title of *Dialogus de Substantiis Physicis* (Strasbourg, 1567).

See also *Moralium Dogma Philosophorum,* edited by J. Holmberg (Uppsala: Almqvist and Wiksells, 1929.)

A study of William is T. Gregory, *Anima mundi. La filosofia di Guglielmo di Conches e la scuola di Chartres* (Florence: Sansoni, 1955).

David Luscombe (1967)

WILLIAM OF MOERBEKE

(c. 1215–c. 1286)

William of Moerbeke, one of the most competent and influential translators of Greek philosophical texts in the Middle Ages, was born at Moerbeke, near Ghent. He spent a number of years at the papal court in various Italian cities and also lived for some time in Greece and Asia Minor. His translations of Aristotle and other Greek authors began to appear about 1260. At the court of Pope Urban IV (1261–1264) in Orvieto, he made the acquaintance of his fellow Dominican, Thomas Aquinas, then beginning his series of Aristotelian commentaries, who encouraged him in his project of translating Aristotle. For several years before his death William was archbishop of Corinth.

Despite the claims that have sometimes been made about him, William of Moerbeke was not the first to translate the bulk of the Aristotelian corpus directly from Greek into Latin. It is true that in the twelfth century Western scholars had necessarily depended on translations from the Arabic, made in Spain or Sicily, for their knowledge of Aristotle. In the thirteenth century, however, at least partly as a result of the Fourth Crusade, a wider dissemination of Greek scholarship and easier access to Greek manuscripts encouraged Western translators to work directly from Greek originals, and many new translations came into use in the first half of the century. Thus, William's translation of Aristotle's *Metaphysics,* for example, while it may have been the first complete version, was apparently the third Latin translation to be made from the original text. A translation from Greek into Latin (the so-called *Metaphysica Vetus*) was in use at Paris as early as 1210, some time before the appearance of the *Metaphysica Nova,* based on the Arabic version, and a second translation from the Greek (the *Translatio Media*) seems to have been used by Albert the Great as the basis of his commentary. Many other works of Aristotle were similarly available by the middle of the thirteenth century in translations from the Greek as well as from the Arabic. While the extent of his indebtedness to earlier translators has not yet been precisely determined, William is known to have used some of the existing translations from the Greek in his own work.

Considered in themselves, then, William of Moerbeke's translations of Aristotle must be reckoned a less than revolutionary contribution to Aristotelian studies in the medieval West. It is not even known with certainty how far Thomas Aquinas, the outstanding interpreter of Aristotle in the thirteenth century, made use of his colleague's work. Nevertheless, William's translations of Aristotle and of other Greek philosophers, taken as a whole, can be said to have inaugurated a new phase of Aristotelian scholarship in Latin Christendom.

To begin with, William's new translations and revised versions of Aristotle's works gave the West a much more accurate text of "the Philosopher" than it had hitherto possessed. As a translator he was unquestionably superior in most respects to his predecessors. His strict adherence to the letter of the original text has been stigmatized as slavish, but it made his translations an unrivaled instrument of exact philosophical scholarship in his day.

Furthermore, William's translations of various post-Aristotelian authors helped Western scholars to form a clearer picture of the history of Greek philosophy and of the distinctive traits of Aristotle's doctrine. The Arabic versions of Aristotle's works had reached the West in the company of Neoplatonizing commentaries and Neoplatonic writings falsely attributed to Aristotle. Thanks to William's translations of important commentaries by Alexander of Aphrodisias, Simplicius, Themistius, and

John Philoponus, and of the *Elementatio Theologica* and other works of the Neoplatonist Proclus, the figure of the historical Aristotle stood out much more clearly than before, and Western thinkers were enabled to distinguish more precisely between the Platonic and Aristotelian approaches to philosophy. William's translation of Proclus was especially important in this connection, showing as it did that the influential *Liber de Causis,* far from being a genuine work of Aristotle, was in fact derived from Proclus's *Elementatio Theologica.*

Through his translation of Proclus William also influenced the development of medieval Neoplatonism. The works that he translated gave a fresh stimulus to the Neoplatonic school formed by Ulrich of Strasbourg and other disciples of Albert the Great and through that school helped to shape the mystical doctrine of Meister Eckhart.

See also Albert the Great; Alexander of Aphrodisias; Aristotelianism; Aristotle; Eckhart, Meister; Liber de Causis; Medieval Philosophy; Neoplatonism; Philoponus, John; Proclus; Simplicius; Themistius; Thomas Aquinas, St.; Ulrich (Engelbert) of Strasbourg.

Bibliography

See Martin Grabmann, *Guglielmo di Moerbeke, O.P., il traduttore delle opere di Aristotele* (Rome: Gregorianum, 1946).

Eugene R. Fairweather (1967)

WILLIAM OF OCKHAM
(c. 1285–1349)

William of Ockham, the most influential philosopher of the fourteenth century, apparently was born sometime between 1280 and 1290 at the village of Ockham, in Surrey, near London. Entering the Franciscan order at an early age, he commenced his course of theological study at Oxford in 1309 or 1310, and completed the requirements for the degree of master of theology with the delivery of his lectures on Peter Lombard's *Book of Sentences* in 1318–1319, or, at the latest, 1319–1320. Although an old tradition indicated that he studied under John Duns Scotus, it seems unlikely that he did so, since Duns Scotus left Oxford at the beginning of the century and died in 1308. Ockham's writings show intimate familiarity with the teachings of Duns Scotus, but this is explained by the dominant position Duns Scotus had acquired at Oxford, particularly within the Franciscan order.

Ockham's lectures on the *Sentences* made a profound impression on the students of theology at Oxford, but his new way of treating philosophical and theological questions aroused strong opposition by many members of the theological faculty. Normally the completion of his lectures on the *Sentences,* which gave Ockham the status of a *baccalaureus formatus* or *inceptor,* would have been followed by award to him of a teaching chair in theology. The granting of his teaching license was prevented by the chancellor of the university, John Lutterell, who in 1323 went to the papal court at Avignon to present charges against Ockham of having upheld dangerous and heretical doctrines. Because Ockham's academic career was thus interrupted while he was an *inceptor* awaiting award of the teaching license, he came to be known as "the venerable inceptor"—a title later misconstrued as meaning "founder of nominalism" (*inceptor scholae nominalium*).

Ockham was summoned to Avignon in 1324 to answer the charges against him, and he remained there four years, awaiting the outcome. A commission of theologians appointed by Pope John XXII to examine Ockham's writings submitted two lists of suspect doctrines in 1326, but there is no evidence of any final action having been taken on the charges that, in any case, were relatively mild. Despite the lack of a teaching chair, Ockham was extremely active during these years in developing his theological and philosophical positions, writing treatises and commentaries on logic and physics, a variety of treatises on theological questions, and an important series of quodlibetal questions that, presumably, he debated orally at Oxford or at Avignon.

In 1327, while at Avignon, Ockham became involved in the dispute then raging over the question of apostolic poverty, in which the general of the Franciscan order, Michael of Cesena, took a position opposed by the pope. Asked to study the question, Ockham found that a previous pope, Nicholas III, had made a pronouncement that fully supported the position of Cesena and of the majority of the Franciscans. When this controversy reached a critical stage in 1328, and it became evident that John XXII was about to issue an official condemnation of the position held by the Franciscans, Cesena and Ockham, along with two other leaders of the Franciscan opposition, fled from Avignon and sought the protection of Emperor Louis of Bavaria, who had repudiated the authority of the Avignon papacy in connection with the issue of succession to the imperial crown. Immediately after their flight from Avignon, Ockham and his companions were excommunicated by the pope for their refusal to submit to his authority.

Under the emperor's protection Ockham took up residence in Munich and devoted his full energies to writing a series of treatises on the issue of papal power and civil sovereignty, in which he held that John XXII had forfeited his right to the papal office by reason of heresy. When John XXII died in 1334, Ockham continued his polemic against the succeeding Avignon popes until 1347, when Louis of Bavaria died and the antipapal position became a lost cause. There is evidence that Ockham at that time sought reconciliation with the papal authority and with the rest of his own order, but the outcome is unknown. It is believed that he died in 1349, a victim of the Black Plague that, in the middle of the fourteenth century, took the lives of most of the intellectual leaders of northern Europe and played a major part in bringing about the cultural decline that lasted for more than a century.

WRITINGS

Ockham's writings fall into two distinct groups associated with the two different periods of his career. All of the political and polemical treatises directed against the Avignon papacy were written during his residence in Munich, between 1333 and 1347. Of these treatises many are solely of historical interest; but the lengthy *Dialogus Inter Magistrum et Discipulum,* written between 1334 and 1338, the *Octo Quaestiones Super Potestate ac Dignitate Papali,* written in 1340, and the *Tractatus de Imperatorum et Pontificum Potestate,* composed around 1347, present Ockham's philosophy of church and state and convey his deep-rooted convictions concerning the religious mission of the church.

The nonpolitical writings that embody Ockham's distinctive contributions to philosophy and theology were probably all written while he was at Oxford and at Avignon, between 1317 and 1328. The earliest of these include the lectures on the *Sentences,* a lengthy exposition of Aristotle's *Physics* extant only in manuscript form, and literal commentaries on Porphyry's *Isagoge* and on Aristotle's *Categoriae, De Interpretatione,* and *De Sophisticis Elenchis*; the first three of the commentaries were published at Bologna in 1496 under the title *Expositio Aurea … Super Artem Veterem* (Golden Exposition … of the Ancient Art). Ockham's most important work on logic, completed before he left Avignon, was a systematic treatise titled *Summa Logicae,* extant in several printed editions. An incomplete *Summulae in Libros Physicorum* (also given the title *Philosophia Naturalis*) contains an independent treatment of the subjects dealt with in the first four books of Aristotle's *Physics,* and was printed in several editions, beginning in 1495. In manuscript form only there is a work titled *Quaestiones Super Libros Physicorum,* which was probably one of his later writings; it covers, in the form of disputed questions, most of the topics treated in his earlier literal commentary on the *Physics* but reflects some changes in his views that occurred after the earlier work had been written. Two short compendia of logic, each extant only in a single manuscript version, are believed to be authentic works of Ockham, but they add nothing significant to the doctrines of his *Summa Logicae.*

Of Ockham's theological writings the lectures on the first book of the *Sentences,* known as the *Ordinatio* because Ockham revised and edited them for circulation, are of primary importance. Printed at Lyons in 1495, along with Ockham's lectures on the other three books of the *Sentences,* they are called the *Reportatio* because the text is derived from stenographic versions of the lectures as they were delivered. A modern critical edition of both parts of these lectures on the *Sentences* is very much needed. Of comparable importance for the understanding of Ockham's philosophical and theological doctrines are the quodlibetal questions, printed at Paris in 1487 and again at Strasbourg in 1491 under the title *Quodlibeta Septem.* Three other certainly authentic theological treatises, composed during the Oxford-Avignon period, are the *Tractatus de Corpore Christi* and *Tractatus de Sacramento Altaris,* which have been regularly printed together under the second of these titles, and the *Tractatus de Praedestinatione et de Praescientia Dei et de Futuris Contingentibus,* of which a modern edition, edited by Philotheus Boehner, was published in 1945. The 1495 Lyons edition of Ockham's theological works includes *Centiloquium Theologicum,* whose authenticity has been questioned by many scholars but without decisive evidence. In describing the philosophical doctrines of Ockham, use will be made chiefly of the *Commentary on the Sentences,* the *Summa Logicae,* and the *Quodlibeta Septem.*

CHARACTER OF OCKHAM'S PHILOSOPHY

Ockham's major contributions to the development of late medieval and early modern philosophy were in the areas of epistemology, logic, and metaphysics. His approach to these problems and his concern with them were those of a scholastic theologian, as had been the case with Thomas Aquinas, Duns Scotus, and other leading scholastic thinkers of the thirteenth century.

The basic problem of scholastic theology since the beginning of the thirteenth century had been that of finding a means of accommodating the philosophical system of Aristotle within the dogmatic framework of Christian doctrine. To achieve such an accommodation was a philosophical task because no alteration in the articles of the faith could be allowed, and consequently all elimination of contradictions had to be achieved by internal criticism or reinterpretation of the philosophical assumptions and arguments of Aristotle. Aquinas had sought to achieve an essentially external accord between natural philosophy and Christian theology, such as would leave the Aristotelian system internally intact. The Franciscan theologians, from St. Bonaventure to Duns Scotus, had considered this inadequate and had sought to achieve the required integration of philosophy and theology by exploiting the more Platonic elements of the Aristotelian system, much as the Greek Neoplatonists and the Muslim philosopher Avicenna had done. All of the thirteenth-century syntheses of philosophy and theology involved, in one form or another, the metaphysical and epistemological doctrine of realism—the doctrine that the human intellect discovers in the particulars apprehended by sense experience an intelligible order of abstract essences and necessary relations ontologically prior to particular things and contingent events and that from this order the intellect can demonstrate necessary truths concerning first causes and the being and attributes of God.

EMPIRICISM AND NOMINALISM. Ockham's significance, both as a theologian and as a philosopher, lay in his rejection of the metaphysical and epistemological assumptions of medieval realism, and in his reconstruction of the whole fabric of philosophy on the basis of a radical empiricism in which the evidential base of all knowledge is direct experience of individual things and particular events. The counterpart of this epistemological empiricism was the nominalistic analysis of the semantical structure and ontological commitment of cognitive language that Ockham developed in his logical writings. Ockham's empiricism was not phenomenalistic or subjectivistic, and it could be called a realistic empiricism according to a modern usage of "realism"; it presupposed and was based on the principle that the human mind can directly apprehend existent individuals and their sensible qualities, and that it can also directly apprehend its own acts. Insofar as Ockham is called a nominalist, his doctrine is not to be construed as a rejection of any ontological determination of meaning and truth, but rather as an extreme economy of ontological commitment in which abstract or intensional extralinguistic entities are systematically eliminated by a logical analysis of language.

OCKHAM'S RAZOR. The principle of parsimony, whose frequent use by Ockham gained it the name of "Ockham's razor," was employed as a methodological principle of economy in explanation. He invoked it most frequently under such forms as "Plurality is not to be assumed without necessity" and "What can be done with fewer [assumptions] is done in vain with more"; he seems not to have used the formulation "Entities are not to be multiplied without necessity." The principal use made by Ockham of the principle of parsimony was in the elimination of pseudo-explanatory entities, according to a criterion he expresses in the statement that nothing is to be assumed as necessary, in accounting for any fact, unless it is established by evident experience or evident reasoning, or is required by the articles of faith.

POSITIVE THEOLOGY. As applied by Ockham, the principle of parsimony resulted in an empiricist criterion of evidence that left little room for a natural theology. But since it also reduced physics and cosmology to the status of positive sciences without metaphysical necessity, it left room for a positive theology based on revelation and faith that could no more be refuted than it could be demonstrated by any necessary reasons or observational evidence. Moreover, this positive theology, in which God is conceived as the omnipotent creator of all finite things whose creative and causal action is wholly free and unnecessitated, provided an indirect justification of Ockham's philosophical empiricism, since it demanded a conception of the world of created things as radically contingent in both their existence and their interaction. Ockham made full use of the doctrine of divine omnipotence as an ad hominem argument against those who sought to discredit his philosophical doctrine on theological grounds; philosophically, however, the doctrine was equivalent to the principle that whatever is not self-contradictory is possible, and that what is actual, within the range of the logically possible, cannot be established by reason alone but only by experience.

CRITIQUE OF REALISM

Ockham's epistemology and metaphysics were designed to resolve a basic problem that the Scholastics had inherited from the Greek philosophical tradition and that may be summed up in the paradoxical thesis that the objects of thought are universal, whereas everything that exists is singular and individual. Seeking to overcome this gap between the intelligible and the existent, the earlier

Scholastics had elaborated various forms of the doctrine called moderate realism, according to which there are common natures in individual existing things, distinct from their individuating principles although not separable except in thought. On the psychological side, these doctrines held that the human intellect abstracts, from the particular presentations of sense experience, an intelligible species, or likeness, by means of which it apprehends the common nature apart from the individuating conditions. The varieties of this moderate realism turned on the answer to the question of whether, in an individual, the common nature is (1) really distinct from the individuating principle or (2) "formally distinct," as Duns Scotus proposed or (3) distinct only according to the mode of consideration although involving some "foundation in the thing" for such distinguishability, as Aquinas held.

Ockham considered all forms of this doctrine of common natures in individual things to be self-contradictory and irrational. If the human nature of Socrates is really distinct from Socrates, then it is not Socrates' nature or essence, for a thing cannot be said to be essentially something that it really is not. If the common nature is anything at all, it is either one thing or many things; if one and not many, it is not common but singular, and if not one but many, then each of the many is singular and there is still nothing common.

CRITICISM OF THE SCOTIST VIEW. The answer of Duns Scotus—that the common nature is really identical with, but formally distinct from, the *haecceitas* or individuating differentia that was said to contract the specific nature to singularity—was an attempt to find something intermediate between identity and nonidentity. Ockham argued, against the Scotist thesis, that if the specific nature and the individuating difference are really identical, they cannot be formally distinct; and if they are formally distinct, they cannot be really identical. Duns Scotus had claimed that they are both really identical and formally distinct. Let a and b represent the individual difference and the specific nature, respectively. Then, since a is not formally distinct from a, it follows that if a is identical with b, then b is not formally distinct from a. Similarly, since a is not formally distinct from a, then if b is formally distinct from a, b is not identical with a. In these arguments Ockham employs, with great effectiveness, the principle commonly ascribed to Gottfried Wilhelm Leibniz—that if two things are identical, whatever is true of one is true of the other; and if something is true of one that is not true of the other, they are not identical.

CRITICISM OF THE THOMIST VIEW. The third answer—that the same thing is singular and universal according to different ways of considering it—is ridiculed by Ockham on the ground that what a thing is in itself can in no way depend on how someone thinks of it. "For with the same ease I could say that a man considered in one way is an ass, considered in another way he is an ox, and considered in a third way he is a she-goat" (*Expositio Super VIII Libros Physicorum*, in *Ockham: Philosophical Writings*, edited by Philotheus Boehner, p. 14). Nor can it be said, as Aquinas appears to say in his *De Ente et Essentia*, that the nature or essence of a thing is in itself neither individual nor universal but is made singular by being received in individuating matter and is made universal by being received into the mind. Anything whatsoever, Ockham insists, is one thing and a singular thing by the very fact that it is a thing, and it is impossible that its unity or singularity is due to something added to it.

OCKHAM'S POSITION. It remains, then, that universality and community are properties only of signs—of language expressions and of the acts of thought expressed by them. The problem of universals therefore is not a metaphysical problem of explaining how abstract common natures are individuated to singular existence, nor is it a psychological problem of explaining how the intellect can abstract from the images of sense experience a common nature inherent in the individuals experienced; for there are no common natures to be individuated or to be abstracted. The problem of individuation is a logical problem of showing how general terms are used in propositions to refer to individuals signified by them; this problem is resolved in terms of the quantifying prefixes and other syncategorematic determinants of the referential use of terms in propositions. As an epistemological problem, the problem of universals is that of explaining how experience of individual existing things can give rise to concepts of universal character and to universally quantified propositions that hold for all objects signified by the subject term. The basis of Ockham's answer to these problems is given in his doctrine of intuitive and abstractive cognition.

INTUITIVE AND ABSTRACTIVE COGNITION

The doctrine of intuitive and abstractive cognition is formulated at the beginning of Ockham's *Commentary on the Sentences* in connection with the question of whether evident knowledge of theological truths can be acquired by man in this life. After distinguishing apprehension from judgment as a distinct act of the intellect, and after showing that every act of judgment presupposes an act of apprehension of what is signified by the terms of the proposition expressing such a judgment, Ockham distinguishes two kinds of intellectual apprehension, intuitive cognition and abstractive cognition.

Intuitive cognition is defined as an act of apprehension in virtue of which the intellect can evidently judge that the apprehended object exists or does not exist, or that it has or does not have some particular quality or other contingent condition; in short, an intuitive cognition is an act of immediate awareness in virtue of which an evident judgment of contingent fact can be made.

Abstractive cognition is defined as any act of cognition in virtue of which it cannot be evidently known whether the apprehended object exists or does not exist, and in virtue of which an evident contingent judgment cannot be made. That these two ways of apprehending the same objects are possible is clear from experience; while I am observing Socrates sitting down, I can evidently judge that Socrates is seated, but if I leave the room and then form the judgment that Socrates is seated, it is not evident, and may indeed be false.

The important point in this distinction is that intuitive and abstractive cognition do not differ in the objects apprehended, but solely in the fact that intuitive cognition suffices for making an evident contingent judgment concerning the object apprehended, whereas an abstractive cognition does not. Nor is the distinction one between sensation and thought, for however much it may be true that affection of the senses by the external object is a necessary condition for an intuitive cognition of a sensible object, the intuitive cognition is an intellectual act that is presupposed by the act of judgment whose evidence is derived from it. Neither is the distinction one between direct awareness of the object and awareness of something representing the object in its absence; both kinds of apprehension are directly of the object. It is not even logically necessary that the object of an intuitive cognition be present or actually existent, although if, by the power of God, an intuitive cognition of an object were preserved after the object was removed or destroyed, it would then yield the evident judgment that the object was not present or that it did not exist; for it is self-contradictory, and hence not even within the power of God, for a cognition to yield an evident judgment that an object exists if the object does not exist.

INTUITIVE COGNITION OF NONEXISTENTS. Ockham must admit that an intuitive cognition of a nonexistent object is logically possible because an intuitive cognition, however much it may be caused by the presence of its object, is not identical with its object; hence it is not self-contradictory that it exists without the object's existing. And if we suppose that any effect that can be produced by a created cause can be produced by God without the created cause, this logical possibility could be realized by the power of God. In this way God could, and according to Christian belief did, produce intuitive cognitions of future things and events by which the prophets and saints had evident knowledge of what did not yet exist; and God himself, who apprehends all things intuitively and not abstractively, is aware not only of the things he has created but of all the things he does not choose to create. Thus, an intuitive cognition of a nonexistent object is logically possible, although it is realizable only by the power of God. Without such divine intervention, however, such cognitions can arise only if the object is present to the knower; and the judgments to which intuitive cognitions can give rise, in the natural course of events, are affirmative judgments of present existence and present fact.

INTUITIVE COGNITION OF MENTAL STATES. Ockham does not restrict the objects of intuitive cognition to objects perceptible to the external senses but includes nonsensible actualities that are apprehended introspectively, such as thoughts, volitions, and emotions. Thus the intellect, by reflecting on its own acts, can form evident judgments of the existence of those acts; for example, if I am intuitively aware of Socrates being seated, I can not only judge evidently that Socrates is seated, but I can also give evident assent to the second-order proposition "I evidently know that Socrates is seated." Although Ockham generally holds that the reflexive act is distinct from, and posterior to, the direct act, he speaks as if the evidence of the reflexive act can include that of the direct act.

DERIVATION OF ABSTRACTIVE COGNITIONS. Given an intuitive cognition of some object or event, the intellect thereby acquires an abstractive cognition of the same object or event, which it retains as a *habitus,* or acquired capacity, to conceive the object without any causal concurrence by the object itself; thus, objects that we have experienced intuitively can be apprehended abstractively, the only difference being that the abstractive cognition does not suffice to make evident a contingent judgment concerning the object thought of. If we leave out of account the logically possible case of God's producing an abstractive cognition without a preceding intuitive cognition, the principle holds, according to Ockham, that no abstractive cognition can be had that is not derived from an intuitive cognition of the object or objects conceived. This principle, which corresponds to David Hume's thesis that there is no idea which is not derived from one or more impressions, is basic to Ockham's theory of natural knowledge and its source of evidence.

UNIVERSALITY OF ABSTRACTIVE COGNITION. In his earlier formulation of the doctrine of intuitive and abstractive cognition, Ockham supposed that the abstractive cognition immediately derived from an intuitive cognition is a concept only of the singular object of the intuitive cognition. But in his *Quodlibeta* (Quod. I, q. 13) he states that a simple abstractive cognition cannot be a concept peculiar to one singular object to the exclusion of other objects that would, if apprehended intuitively, yield a wholly similar concept. Thus the universality of the concept, in this later theory, is immediately involved in the transition from intuitive to abstractive cognition. The operation is analogous to that of deriving, from a proposition of the form *Fa,* the open sentence *Fx,* which becomes a general proposition when the free variable *x* is bound by a quantifying prefix. In Ockham's terminology, the abstractive cognition has signification but acquires supposition only by formation of a judgment or proposition.

CONCEPTS. The concept, or universal in the mind, is a cognition of objects in virtue of which it cannot be evidently judged that they exist or do not exist. But what sort of reality is such a cognition or concept? One opinion is that the concept is a mental image or species which, because it is a resemblance of the external objects, causes the intellect to become aware of those objects. But Ockham points out, as Hume did later, that such a species could in no way represent to the intellect the objects of which it is a likeness, unless these objects were already known to it—no more, Ockham says, than a statue of Hercules could represent Hercules, or be recognized as his likeness, if the viewer had never seen Hercules.

In his *Commentary on the Sentences* Ockham mentions three theories of the concept as "probable" or tenable. According to the first theory, the concept is not a reality existing in the mind or outside the mind but is the being conceived of the external objects, the *esse obiectivum* of the objects—a view that was held by Peter Aureol and had adherents down to the time of René Descartes, who in the *Meditations* used this notion of the "objective being" of the concept in proving God's existence from his idea of God. Of the concept thus conceived, Ockham says that its being is its being understood—*eorum esse est eorum cognosci.* A second theory supposes that the concept is a real quality in the soul, used by the intellect for the individuals of which it is a concept, just as a general term in a proposition is used for the individuals of which it is a sign. A third theory, which Ockham finally adopted, is that the concept is merely the act of understanding the individual things of which it is said to be a concept. This theory is preferred on grounds of economy, for inasmuch as any of the theories requires that the intellect apprehend the extramental individuals, this function can be satisfied by the act of understanding without need of any other mental vehicle serving as surrogate for the objects.

Generality of concepts. The question may well be raised of how a concept derived from intuitive apprehension of a single object can constitute an act of understanding a definite set of objects—not any objects whatsoever but just those objects to which the concept is applicable or which, if directly experienced, would elicit that concept. Why should an intuitive cognition of Socrates yield a general concept applicable to just those individuals of which it is true to say "This is a man"? Ockham says that this is because the objects are similar, on which account the abstractive concept elicited by experience of one of the objects is ipso facto a concept of all similar objects. The realist might well insist that Ockham, in supposing this similarity in things, is covertly reintroducing the doctrine of common natures; but Ockham replies that similar individuals are similar by reason of what each individual is in itself, and not by reason of anything common. Two things are similar, for example, in being singular things, but this is not because there is one singularity common to the two things. Thus a concept can be a single act of understanding many individuals that are similar, without being an act of understanding anything other than just those individuals themselves. Again the analogy with the open sentence *Fx* is suggested, for if we should ask what things satisfy this function, the answer is that it is any of those things such that *Fx* holds for it. The obvious circularity of this question and answer indicates that any explanation that can be given of the fact that things are conceived in a universal manner by intelligent beings must itself use such universal concepts and thereby must presuppose the fact to be explained.

Concepts as natural signs. In this account Ockham describes concepts as natural signs whose relation to the things conceived is established not by human choice but by the fact that an act of understanding has no content other than the objects understood and arises in the first instance only through direct experience of such objects. Ockham seems to recognize the futility of seeking to account for the possibility of knowledge as such by means of a particular branch of knowledge like physics or psychology; "*natura occulte operatur in universalibus* [nature works in a hidden manner in the case of universals]," he remarks, and is content to leave it at that.

LOGIC AND THEORY OF SCIENCE

Although the human intellect, according to Ockham, can directly apprehend and conceive the individual things that exist independently of our thought, the objects of knowledge (in the sense of *scire*) are propositions, formed within our minds by operations we freely perform by combining concepts derived from intuitive cognitions of things. Only propositions can be true or false, and since knowledge is of the true, its objects are propositions—complexes of signs put together by us. Logic is concerned with these ways of putting concepts together, insofar as these operations affect the truth or falsity of the resultant propositions.

Ockham was skilled in the formal logic developed in the arts faculties of the universities on foundations laid in the twelfth century by Peter Abelard, and represented in the thirteenth century by the treatises of the so-called terminist logicians William of Sherwood and Peter of Spain. The distinctive feature of this logic was its use of the concept of the supposition of terms in formulating the syntactical and semantical properties of cognitive language. In his *Summa Logicae* Ockham systematized the contributions of his predecessors in a reformulation of the whole content of Aristotelian logic on semantical foundations of a purely extensional character. These foundations, exhibited in his analysis of the signification of terms and of the truth conditions of propositions, reveal the ontological basis of his empiricist theory of knowledge and of scientific evidence. Some preliminary distinctions made at the beginning of Ockham's work on logic are important for understanding this analysis.

LOGIC AS A SCIENCE OF LANGUAGE. Logic, as a *scientia sermocinalis,* or science of language, deals with language as a system of signs that can be used in making true or false statements about things signified by those signs. The expressions of spoken and written language are instituted by convention to signify what is naturally signified (or intended) by acts of thought constituting the "inner discourse of the soul." Logic studies the properties of language expressions insofar as they embody the logically essential functions of mental discourse. Medieval logicians distinguished language signs into two basically different types: categorematic signs, which have independent meaning and can function as subjects and predicates of propositions, and syncategorematic signs, which have no independent meaning but exercise various logical functions with respect to the categorematic signs.

This important distinction corresponds to that made in modern logic between descriptive signs and logical signs. The categorematic signs, normally called terms, were divided into two distinct and nonoverlapping semantical types: terms of first intention, which signify things that are not language signs, and terms of second intention, which signify language signs or the concepts expressed by them, as signs. This distinction corresponds to that now made between the descriptive signs of the object language and the descriptive signs of the metalanguage. In Ockham's view, most of the metaphysical labyrinths in which the thirteenth-century Scholastics became entangled, such as the problem of universals in re, arose from the logical mistake of construing terms of second intention as terms of first intention; thus, because the term *man* is predicable of (or inheres in) the singular names "Socrates" and "Plato," they supposed that what is signified by the term *man* is some single reality that inheres in the individuals named by the names "Socrates" and "Plato."

SUPPOSITION. "Supposition" is defined by Ockham as the use of a categorematic term, in a proposition, for some thing or things—normally, for the thing or things it signifies. But terms can be used nonsignificatively as names of the concepts they express or as names of the spoken or written words of which they are instances. When used nonsignificatively as the name of the word, they were said to have material supposition; when used nonsignificatively as naming the concept expressed by the word, they were said to be used with simple supposition; but when used significatively for the things signified by them and understood by the concept or act of understanding expressed by them, they were said to be used in personal supposition. The earlier terminist logicians, who were metaphysical realists, had construed simple supposition as the use of a term for the universal nature that they supposed to exist in the individuals denoted by the term in its personal supposition—which is why they called this use simple (or absolute) supposition. But Ockham, who held that universality is a property only of concepts or language signs, rejected this interpretation and construed simple supposition as the use of a term for the concept or mental intention expressed by it.

The ontological foundations of Ockham's logic are exhibited in his analysis of the terms of first intention that Aristotle classified, in his *Categoriae,* as so many different ways of signifying "primary substances"—that is, concrete individuals. The terms Aristotle grouped under the category of substance, as signifying beings qua beings according to what they essentially are, were said by Ockham to be absolute terms, terms that signify nothing other than the individuals for which they can stand when used in propositions with personal supposition. The concrete terms of the so-called categories of accident, which are predicable of substance terms but signify them only as "of such quality," as "so big," or as "in such a place," were called by Ockham connotative terms—terms that refer obliquely to something other than the thing or things for which they can stand, and imply some contingent factual condition determining the range of objects for which the term can stand. The oblique reference may be to a part or parts of the object directly denotable by the term, to a quality of the object, or to some other thing or things with respect to which the denoted thing stands in some contingent relation—for instance, the term *father* stands for one thing by referring to another thing (a child) and implying that the child was generated by the person who is directly designated by the term *father.*

NOMINALISM. Ockham's nominalism consists in his refusal to construe abstract terms as names of entities distinct from the individual things signified by absolute terms. The realists, while conceding that the concrete forms of connotative terms stand for substances, held that their oblique reference is to entities distinct from these substances but inhering in them—these distinct entities are directly named by the abstract forms of such connotative terms. Thus the term *father,* in their view, connotes an entity called fatherhood and implies that it inheres in the thing denoted by the term *father.* Similarly the term *large,* although predicable of terms signifying substances, was said to connote an entity, distinct from such substances but inhering in them, called quantity or magnitude. Ockham was willing to grant that terms signifying sensible qualities, such as *white, hot,* and *sweet,* connote entities that are distinct from substances and are directly signified by the abstract terms *whiteness, heat,* and *sweetness*; hence he admitted as absolute terms the abstract forms of those qualitative predicates. But in all other cases he held that connotative terms, whether concrete or abstract, signify no entities other than those directly signifiable by substance terms or by these absolute quality terms. What the realists had done, in Ockham's view, was to treat facts about substances as entities distinct from those things, as if the fact that a man is six feet tall is an entity distinct from the man but inhering in him, or as if the fact that Socrates has fathered a son is an entity distinct from Socrates and from his son.

From a logical point of view, Ockham's analysis is a restriction of the domain of reference of terms, or of the domain of objects constituting possible values of the variable of quantification, to individual substances and singular (not common) sensible qualities. Ontologically, this means that the only things that there are, are individual substances and equally individual qualities. All terms that are not direct names (or absolute signs) of these objects are predicate terms which, although referring to no other objects than these, do so by indicating a contingent fact about such objects.

In thus impoverishing the domain of objects of reference, Ockham enriches the domain of truths to be known about these objects. The frequent charge that Ockham atomized the world by refusing to recognize relations as real entities distinct from substances and qualities fails to take account of the fact that the connotative terms relate the individuals by implying factual conditions by which the objects are tied together in an existential sense—something that cannot be done by treating relations as entities distinct from their relata and, in effect, as just another class of substances. From Ockham's point of view, it was the realists who atomized the world by treating all predicates as absolute names.

In rejecting the thesis that predicates designate entities distinct from the individuals denoted by absolute terms, Ockham rejects the interpretation of the affirmative copula as a sign of the inherence of an abstract entity in the individuals denoted by the subject term. The truth condition of an affirmative categorical proposition, in Ockham's interpretation, is that subject and predicate "stand for the same." Thus, in the proposition "Socrates is an animal," it is not indicated that Socrates has animality or that animality inheres in Socrates, but it is indicated that the individual denoted by the name "Socrates" is an individual for which the term *animal* stands and which it signifies. In universally quantified propositions, the affirmative copula indicates that every individual for which the subject term stands is something for which the predicate term stands; and in particular, or existentially quantified, propositions, the affirmative copula indicates that there is at least one individual signified by the subject term that is also signified by the predicate term.

This analysis of general propositions corresponds closely to the modern formulas $(x)Fx \supset Gx$ and $(\exists x)Fx \cdot Gx$, except that the medieval analysis requires existential import as part of the truth condition of the universal affirmative and does not require existential import as a truth condition of the particular negative. In order for subject and predicate to stand for the same, there must be something they stand for; but it is not required that they stand for something in order that they not stand for the same thing. Ockham skillfully carried out the formal development of truth rules for propositions of more complex forms and for various modalities and used them in formulating inference rules both for syllogistic arguments and for arguments based on truth-functional relations between unanalyzed propositions.

SCIENTIFIC KNOWLEDGE. The Aristotelian dictum that science is of the universal was accepted by Ockham in the sense that scientific knowledge is of propositions composed of universal terms, quantified universally for all the individuals signified by the subject term and having the properties of necessity and evidence. Strictly speaking, scientific knowledge is only of demonstrable conclusions evident by reason of indemonstrable, necessary, and evident premises from which they are logically deducible. But Ockham extends the notion of *scientia,* defined as evident grasp of a proposition that is true, to include the indemonstrable premises of demonstrations and also to include evident knowledge of contingent propositions in virtue of intuitive cognition.

EVIDENCE AND SELF-EVIDENCE. Since, for Ockham, the universal propositions of scientific demonstrations are formed only from concepts by which things are apprehended abstractively and without evidence of their existence, the question of what kind of evidence such propositions can have is a crucial question for him. This problem reduces to that of the evidence of the indemonstrable premises of the sciences. Aristotle's characterization of such premises as necessary, self-evident (*per se nota*), and primary could not be accepted by Ockham without considerable qualification. First of all, he says that no such propositions are necessary as assertoric categorical propositions, but are necessary only if they are construed as conditionals or as propositions concerning the possible (*de eo quod potest esse*). Second, he distinguishes between two kinds of evidence that such propositions, construed as conditionals or as of the mode of possibility, may have: the proposition may be evident by the meaning of its terms (*per se nota*) or evident by experience (*nota per experientiam*). The first kind of evidence is obtained through the premises of mathematical demonstrations and by those premises of the natural sciences that are analytically evident by the definition of the terms. But in every natural or physical science there are premises that are not *per se nota* but are established by generalization from singular contingent propositions evident by intuitive cognition; such are the premises that state causal laws or correlate dispositional properties with their commensurately universal subject terms.

INDUCTION. What justifies the passage from singular propositions evident by direct experience to universal propositions affirmed for all possible cases? How does evident knowledge that this particular wood is combustible, acquired by direct observation of its burning, allow us to know that any piece of wood, if subjected to fire in the presence of air, will burn? Ockham invokes as justification for such generalized propositions a rule of induction, described as a *medium extrinsecum,* that corresponds to the principle of the uniformity of nature—that all individuals of specifically similar nature (*eiusdem rationis*) act or react in similar manner to similar conditions. He regards this principle as analytically evident from the meaning of "similar nature"; but since it is logically possible, and hence possible by the power of God, that an effect can be produced without its natural cause, the application of this rule of induction in establishing general premises or laws on the basis of experience of particular cases is valid only within the general hypothesis of the common course of nature (*ex suppositione communis cursus naturae*). Consequently, the evidence of such premises of the natural or positive sciences is not absolute but hypothetical. It should be further noted that Ockham, and his contemporaries as well, drew a sharp distinction between what comes to be by nature and what comes to be by the action of voluntary intelligent agents, both man and God. The principle that like causes produce like effects under like conditions is considered valid only on the supposition that no voluntary agencies are involved.

There is a marked analogy between Ockham's view of the evidential status of the premises of the empirical sciences and that of the premises of positive (or revealed) theology. In the one case their evidence is conditional on the hypothesis of a common course of nature, and in the other on the hypothesis of a revealed order of grace freely (and hence not necessarily) provided by God for the salvation of human souls. Neither hypothesis is logically or metaphysically necessary, and each is, in its own domain, used as a methodological principle pragmatically justified by its fruitfulness. What corresponds to Pelagianism in theology is dogmatic Aristotelianism in natural philosophy, and Ockham takes due precautions against both.

METAPHYSICS AND THEOLOGY

Ockham's metaphysics is primarily a critique of the traditional metaphysical doctrines of his scholastic predecessors. Most of these doctrines represent, in Ockham's view, confusions of logical and physical concepts or of ways of signifying things and the things signified. Such is the case with the supposed distinction, in things, between their essence and their existence, and with the distinction between potential and actual being; to say that something exists does not mean that there is something which is of itself nonexistent to which existence is added, and to say that something exists potentially does not mean that "something which is not in the universe, but can exist in the universe, is truly a being" (*Summa Logicae Pars Prima,* 1951, p. 99, ll. 55–58). These are distinctions between two modalities of statements, assertoric and *de possibili,* and not between things denoted by the terms of statements. The old issue of whether "being" is predicated univocally, equivocally, or analogically of substances and accidents, and of God and creatures, is resolved by saying that in the sense in which "being" is equivalent to "something," it is predicated in the same way of everything there is; but if "univocal" is taken as meaning that the term signifies everything according to a single determinate concept, the term *being* is equivocal and has as many meanings as there are kinds of things. The first sense is like saying $(x)(x = x)$; the second, or equivocal use, is indicated if we say "*to be a man* is not *to be white.*"

SUBSTANCE. The term *substance,* for Ockham, has the sense of Aristotle's primary substance, or ὑποκείμενον, rather than the sense of intelligible essence, or τὸ τί ἦν εἶναι. Basically, substance is conceived as the individual subject or substratum of qualities, and with regard to corporeal substances Ockham indicates that we are aware of substances only as the subject of sensible qualities. Thus he says that "no external corporeal substance can be naturally apprehended in itself, by us, however it may be with respect to the intellect itself or any substance which is of the essence of the knower" (*Commentary on the Sentences* I, d. 3, q. 2), and he adds that "substance is therefore understood in connotative and negative concepts, such as 'being which subsists by itself,' 'being which is not in something else,' 'being which is a subject of all accidents,' etc." (ibid.). These remarks suggest that the general terms of the category of substance are not as absolute as Ockham elsewhere supposes, and that the only nonconnotative concept is the transcendental concept "being" or "thing"; on this basis, general names are eliminated in favor of connotative predicates, proper names are eliminated in favor of descriptive phrases, and the whole category of substance is reduced to the referential function expressed in language by the phrase "thing such that … ," or by what is equivalent to the bound variable of quantification. Historically, Ockham's conception of substance as the posited (or "supposited") referent of the connotative predicates points toward John Locke's "something I know not what" characterization of substance; similarly, Ockham's treatment of sensible qualities as entities distinct from substances (and by the power of God separable, as in the Sacrament of the Altar), along with his contention that quantitative predicates signify nothing other than substances having parts outside of parts, pointed the way to the seventeenth-century treatment of qualities as secondary and quantitative attributes as primary.

MATTER AND FORM. With respect to the notion of cause, Ockham effected a considerable modification of the traditional Aristotelian doctrine. The intrinsic causes, matter and form, were construed physically rather than metaphysically; matter is not, for Ockham, a pure potentiality but is actual in its own right as body having spatially distinguishable parts, its extension being, in the scholastic terminology, the form of corporeity. The concept of form likewise is understood physically in the sense of μορφή rather than of εἶδος, and tends to be understood as shape and structure of the material parts. This is shown in Ockham's rejection of the notion of a form of the whole (*forma totius*) and in his thesis that a whole is its parts. Many pages of Ockham's works are devoted to the thesis, defended with an almost ferocious intensity, that quantity is not any entity other than substance (or quality), but is substance or sensible qualities as divisible into parts, or as numerable. This doctrine clearly suggests the later view that the primary qualities signified by quantity terms constitute the real essence of substances.

EFFICIENT CAUSES. The tendency toward a more mechanistic theory of natural substances and events is evident in Ockham's treatment of efficient causality. He says that one thing is said to be cause of another if, when it is present, the effect follows, and when it is not present, the effect does not occur. Such a causal relation can be known only by experience, and it is impossible to deduce a priori, from knowledge of one thing, that something else must result from it. This is so on the general epistemological principle that from the cognition of one thing we cannot acquire "first knowledge" of another thing which is really distinct from it but must have intuitive cognition of the latter in itself. Hence the knowledge that one thing is the cause of another, or that something is caused by some other definite thing, is acquired only if we have intuitive cognition of each of the two things and repeated experience of their concomitance or sequence.

Like Hume, Ockham bases our knowledge of causal relations on experience alone and rejects the doctrine that the effect is virtually in its cause and deducible from the essential nature of the cause. But he is not skeptical with regard to the objectivity of causation; his point is that the only evidence we have of causal connections is experience of observed sequences. Although we cannot establish the causal relations between things a priori, and must accept the principle of the uniformity of nature as an act of faith, Ockham's faith in this principle appears to be as firm as his faith in the revealed doctrines of theology. In his *Summulae Physicorum* (II, c. 12) he says: "Leaving out of consideration all free and voluntary agencies, whatever happens by [natural] causes occurs of necessity and inevitably, and nothing of that sort occurs by chance" (1637 ed., p. 14).

FINAL CAUSES. The Aristotelian doctrine that nature acts for an end is interpreted by Ockham as a pure metaphor. In his *Quodlibeta* (Quod. IV, qq. 1 and 2) he states that it cannot be shown by any self-evident premises or by experience that any effect whatsoever has a final cause, whether distinct from the agent or not distinct from the agent; for that which acts by necessity of nature acts uniformly under like conditions, and it cannot be shown that it does so because of some end desired or aimed at. We speak of natural processes as having ends, not because the agents are really "moved by desire" but simply because natural bodies under similar conditions are observed to act in determinate ways, as if aiming at an end. But such language is purely metaphorical.

In applying his strict criteria of evidence to the doctrines of Aristotelian physics and cosmology, Ockham shows that many principles which Aristotle took to be necessary and self-evident are not. The arguments that celestial bodies have no matter and are ingenerable and incorruptible, that there cannot be a plurality of worlds, and that action at a distance is impossible were held by Ockham to be inconclusive and nonevident. Although Ockham was not concerned with establishing a new physics and cosmology to replace that of Aristotle, his critical treatment of Aristotle's arguments and his constant insistence on the possibility of different theories equally capable of accounting for the facts to be explained were influential in creating the intellectual environment in which later fourteenth-century philosophers explored new physical theories and laid some of the foundations for the scientific revolution of the seventeenth century.

THEOLOGICAL KNOWLEDGE. As a theologian, Ockham was concerned with the question of the cognitive status of theology. The thirteenth-century Scholastics had, for the most part, characterized theology as a science, on the ground that it contains truths which are necessary and "in themselves" evident, even though most of them are not evident to man in his present condition. The question of how we can know that a proposition is evident-in-itself, when it is not evident to us, was answered by saying that a person who does not know geometry may yet be fully assured that a theorem which is an object of belief to him is an object of scientific knowledge to the expert mathematician. Thus, Aquinas said that the articles of faith from which the theologian demonstrates his conclusions are accepted as evident in the light of a higher science (that of God), much as the astronomer accepts the theorems of geometry as premises for his astronomical reasonings but nevertheless demonstrates the conclusions of astronomy in a scientific manner.

Ockham, in a question of his *Commentary on the Sentences* (Prologue, q. 7), examines this and other similar arguments and rejects them as invalid. Every truth evidently known, he says, is either self-evident (*per se nota*), deduced from such, or is evident from intuitive cognition; but the articles of faith are not evidently knowable by man in any of these ways in his present life, for if they were, they would be evident to infidels and pagans, who are not less intelligent than Christians. But this is not the case. Furthermore, it cannot be maintained that theology is a science because it carries out valid processes of deduction of conclusions from the premises accepted on faith, for conclusions cannot be any more evident than the premises from which they are derived.

IMPOSSIBILITY OF NATURAL THEOLOGY. Ockham subjects the *prolegomena fidei*, or propositions about God held to be evidently knowable on natural grounds, to the criteria of evidence and proof that pertain to the natural or philosophical sciences. The issue of whether there is a natural theology as a part of philosophy reduces to the question of whether, from analytic premises evident from the meaning of the terms or from empirical evidence provided by direct experience of the object of theology, such a science is possible. It is conceded by all that man, in his present life, does not have intuitive cognition of God—not, certainly, by getting a degree in theology. But Ockham had argued, with respect to any naturally acquired knowledge, that it is only by intuitive cognition of an object that we can evidently judge that it exists—and the only objects of which we can have simple abstractive concepts are those we have experienced intuitively or those specifically similar to them. From this it follows that we cannot have any simple and proper concept of God nor any direct evidence of his existence. Can we, then, from concepts derived from experience of other things, form a complex concept or description uniquely applicable to God and prove that an object satisfying this nominal definition exists?

CRITIQUE OF PROOFS FOR GOD'S EXISTENCE. Ockham admits that a descriptive concept of God can be formed from the concept of "being" or "thing" in its univocal (but empty) sense, along with such connotative or negative terms as "nonfinite," "uncaused," and "most perfect." But proving that there exists an object so describable is another matter. The arguments by which his predecessors had attempted to prove God's existence are examined by Ockham with great thoroughness in his *Commentary on the Sentences,* in the *Quodlibeta,* and in the possibly inauthentic *Centiloquium Theologicum.* St. Anselm's so-called Ontological Argument is analyzed (and shown to consist of two different arguments) but is rejected as invalid; and the old arguments from degrees of perfection are disposed of without difficulty.

It is chiefly the causal arguments, in the form used by Duns Scotus, that Ockham takes seriously; and these he examines with extraordinary care because of the way in which Duns Scotus used the concept of infinity in formulating them. Ockham's great logical skill is revealed at its best in his patient and remorseless untangling of the subtleties of the Scotist arguments. Those involving final causality are shown to have no force in themselves, so that the main issues are faced in the arguments from efficient causes. The thesis that there cannot be an infinite regress in the order of efficient causes is rejected as nonevident if the causes are successive in a temporal sense, but Ockham is willing to grant that there cannot be an infinite regress of "conserving causes," since these would have to exist simultaneously. Ockham does, therefore, allow that the existence of at least one conserving cause can be proved if it is granted that there are things whose existence is dependent on conservation by something else; but he immediately points out that we could not prove that there is only one such conserving cause, nor could we prove that the celestial spheres are not sufficient to account for the conservation of the things in the world. Thus the value of this argument for theological purposes is very slight indeed. It is also clear that a natural theology, in the sense involving strictly scientific or evident demonstrations, is completely ruled out by Ockham's basic epistemological principles.

He is willing to concede that it is "probable" that there is one supreme being, that this being is the cause of at least part of the movements and order of the world, and that this being is of an intellectual nature; but since Ockham defines "probable," following Aristotle's *Topics,* as an argument or premise that appears to be true to everyone, to the majority, or to the wisest, all this means is that most people, and the philosophers of old, have believed that there is a deity of this sort.

POSITIVE THEOLOGY. To conclude, from Ockham's merciless criticism of alleged proofs of theological beliefs, that he was an unbeliever and a religious skeptic would be a mistake—although some have drawn this conclusion. There is much evidence in Ockham's writings of an intense loyalty to the Christian faith and of full commitment to the articles of faith as divinely revealed. What Ockham appears to have found objectionable in the theological work of his contemporaries was their attempt to prove what cannot be proved and their loading of theology with pseudo explanations that merely blunted and obscured the tremendous implications of the fundamental articles of the Christian faith. The omnipotence of God and his absolute freedom are the two articles of Christian belief that Ockham never loses sight of; and in his internal treatment of the content of Christian doctrine, just as in his internal treatment of natural philosophy, Ockham invokes these articles of faith as justification for an empiricist or positivistic position. Just as the hypothesis of the common course of nature is a methodological postulate of physical explanation, so the order of grace as set up in the sacramental system and laws of the church is accepted as a postulate of the Christian life; but just as God is not bound or obligated by the order of nature he has established, so he is not bound or obligated by the order of grace he has established as the "common way" of salvation of souls. Neither order is necessary in itself or a necessary consequence of God's being or essence; the utter contingency of the created world, whose existence and order is a sheer fact without any metaphysical ground of necessity, is for Ockham a consequence of the omnipotence and absolute freedom of God that cannot, and should not, be softened or obscured by attempts to construe it in terms of the metaphysics of pagans and infidels.

ETHICAL AND POLITICAL DOCTRINES

In contrast with most of the thirteenth-century scholastic doctors, Ockham made little attempt to formulate a rational psychology or theory of the human soul. In his *Quodlibeta* (Quod. I, q. 10) he raises the question of whether it can be demonstrated that the intellective soul is a form of the body. Since the Council of Vienne had ruled a few years before that this Thomist doctrine was *de fide* (although the formulation was ambiguous enough to allow some latitude), Ockham was not as critical of it as he might otherwise have been. He points out that a person following natural reason would no doubt suppose that his own acts of understanding and of will, of which he has intuitive cognition, are acts of his substantial being or form; however, he would not suppose this to be an incorruptible form separable from his body but rather an extended and corruptible form like that of any other material body. If, however, we must understand by "intellective soul" an immaterial and incorruptible form that exists as a whole in the whole body and as a whole in each part, "it cannot be evidently known by reason or experience that such a form exists in us, nor that the understanding proper to such a substance exists in us, nor that such a soul is a form of the body. Whatever the Philosopher thought of this does not now concern me, because it seems that he remains doubtful about it wherever he speaks of it. These three things are only matters of belief" (Quod. I, q. 10).

Ockham thought that the Franciscan doctrine of a plurality of forms in the human being is more probable on natural grounds than the doctrine of a single form; indeed, if matter has its own corporeal form (*forma corporeitatis*) as extended substance, the sensitive soul would be a distinct form of organization of this matter; and the intellectual soul, if immortal and incorruptible, might well be in the organic body as a pilot is in his boat. But the only evident knowledge we have of ourselves as minds is the intuitive cognition of our acts of thinking and willing, and the subject of these acts is not apprehended directly as a substance or form. Nor is the faculty psychology elaborated by the earlier Scholastics, with its distinctions of active and passive intellect and of really distinct powers within the soul, evident or necessary. We are aware of the soul only as that which thinks and wills; and since the person who thinks is not other than the person who wills, the terms *intellect* and *will* refer to precisely the same subject, and not to distinct entities or faculties within that subject.

FREE WILL. If it is only by intuitive cognition of our own acts that we are aware of ourselves as intelligent beings, it is only in this way that we are aware of ourselves as voluntary agents free to choose between opposite actions. Ockham defines freedom (*libertas*) as "that power whereby I can do diverse things indifferently and contingently, such that I can cause, or not cause, the same effect, when all conditions other than this power are the same" (Quod. I, q. 16). That the will is free, he says, cannot be demonstratively proved by any reason, "because every reason proving this assumes something equally unknown as is the conclusion, or less known." Yet this freedom can be evidently known by experience, he says, because "a man experiences the fact that however much his reason dictates some action, his will can will, or not will, this act" (Quod. I, q. 16).

This liberty of will, for Ockham, is the basis of human dignity and of moral goodness and responsibility, more than the power of thinking—although the two are mutually involved. The seat of morality is in the will itself, Ockham says, "because every act other than the act of will, which is in the power of the will, is only good in such manner that it can be a bad act, because it can be done for an evil end and from an evil intention" (Quod. III, q. 13). Also, every action, other than the act of willing itself, can be performed by reason of natural causes and not freely, and every such action could be caused in us by God alone instead of by our will; consequently, the action in itself is neither virtuous nor vicious, except by denomination from the act of the will. Not even Immanuel Kant was more concerned to distinguish morality from legality, or the good will from the right action. Ockham had, in Peter Abelard, a medieval precedent for this emphasis.

FREE WILL AND GOD'S FOREKNOWLEDGE. Having thus affirmed the total freedom and integrity of the human will, Ockham was faced with the problem of reconciling this with the doctrine of divine foreknowledge of future contingent events, among which the decisions of the human will must be counted. The answer, apparently considered sufficient by Aquinas, that God sees, in one eternal glance, all the decisions of each soul, now and to come, is not sufficient for Ockham. God's intellect is not distinct from his will and his omnipotent causality of all things; hence, says Ockham, "either the determination or production of the created will follows the determination [of the divine will], or it does not. If it does, then the created will acts just as naturally as any natural cause … and thus, the divine will being determined, the created will acts accordingly and does not have the power of not acting accordingly, and consequently no act of the created will is to be imputed to it" (*Commentary on the Sentences,* d. 38, q. 1). Ockham considers the problem of how God knows, with certainty and from all eternity, the contingent and free decisions of the human will, an insoluble problem; for both the freedom of the human will and the power of God to know all contingent acts of created beings must be conceded. "It is impossible," he says, "for any [created] intellect, in this life, to explain or evidently know how God knows all future contingent events" (d. 38, q. 1).

PROBLEM OF EVIL. While recognizing the Aristotelian conception of natural good and of virtuous choices in accordance with right reason, Ockham is primarily concerned with the theological norm of moral goodness, which is the will of God expressed in the commandments of both the Old Testament and the New Testament, whereby man is obligated (but not coerced) to love and obey God above all else. Thus, what God wills man to do of man's free will defines the right, and disobedience to God's will defines sin. This provides a solution of the old problem of evil, or of God as cause of the sinful acts of man; for since moral evil is the doing of the opposite of what one is obligated to do, and since God is not obligated to any act, it is impossible for God to sin by his causal concurrence in the production of an act sinfully willed by the creature. But Ockham raises an interesting paradox in this connection by supposing that God might command a man to hate him (or to disobey him). To obey God is to love God, and to love God is to do his will; but if it is God's will that I do not do his will, I do his will if I don't, and don't do it if I do. Hence, this command is impossible for a creature to fulfill; and although there would seem to be no patent self-contradiction in supposing that God could issue such a command, it would seem to be self-contradictory, and hence impossible, for God to will that this command be fulfilled.

GOD'S FREEDOM. Although Ockham recognizes that God has established laws binding the Christian to live in a certain way as a member of the church, participant in its sacraments, and believer in its articles of faith, this fact imposes no obligation on God either to bestow eternal life on the Christian who obeys God's precepts and loves him above all else, or to withhold eternal life from those who do not follow God's laws and love him above all else. "It is not impossible," Ockham says, "that God could ordain that a person who lives according to right reason, and does not believe anything except what is conclusive to him by natural reason, should be worthy of eternal life" (*Commentary on the Sentences* III, q. 8). Similarly, although according to the established order an infused grace is required for a man to be eligible for acceptance by God, Ockham insists that God is not necessitated, by reason of such a created grace given to a man, to confer eternal life on him—"always contingently and freely and mercifully and of his own graciousness he beatifies whomsoever he chooses … purely from his kindness he will freely give eternal life to whomsoever he will give it" (*Commentary on the Sentences* I, d. 17, q. 1).

What is distinctive of Ockham's theological point of view is its emphasis on the freedom and spontaneous liberality of God and on the "givenness" of the world that God creates. This stands in sharp contrast to the Muslim characterization of God as the necessary being whose act is equally necessary and therefore determinant of necessity in all that occurs in the created world. Ockham's doctrine of divine omnipotence is not to be understood, as some have done, on the analogy of an oriental potentate issuing arbitrary commands as a pure display of power; rather, it is grounded in the conception of a goodness that is purely spontaneous and unnecessitated, whose gift of existence to creatures and of freedom of choice to man is a perfectly free gift with no strings attached. Ockham's theology of divine liberty and liberality is the complement of his philosophy of radical contingency in the world of existing finite beings and of the underivability of matters of fact from any a priori necessity.

CHURCH AND STATE. Ockham's political and polemical writings on the issue of papal power eloquently convey the thesis that the law of God is the law of liberty and not one of oppression or coercion. The treatise *De Imperatorum et Pontificum Potestate* (On the Power of Emperors and Popes), dealing with the papal claim to plenitude of power, makes this very clear. Christ, in instituting the church, did not give Peter a plenitude of power that would give him the right to do everything not explicitly forbidden by divine or natural law; rather, Peter was given a limited and defined sphere of authority and power. Therefore, Ockham argues, the pope has no authority to deprive any human being of his natural rights or of the rights and liberties given to man by God. "As Christ did not come into the world in order to take away from men their goods and rights, so Christ's vicar, who is inferior and in no way equal to him in power, has no authority or power to deprive others of their goods and rights" (*De Imperatorum …*, p. 10, ll. 12–15). Ockham specifies three of these inalienable rights: first, all those rights that non-Christians justly and admittedly enjoyed before the coming of Christ—for any of these rights to be taken from Christians by papal authority would be to make the liberty of Christians less than that of pagans and infidels;

second, the disposition of temporal things belongs not to the papal authority but to the laity, according to the words of Christ that the things that are Caesar's should be rendered unto Caesar; third, although the pope is charged with the teaching of God's word, maintenance of divine worship, and provision of such things as are necessary for the Christian in his quest for eternal life, the pope has no power to command or requisition those things that are not necessary to this end, "lest he should turn the law of the Gospels into a law of slavery."

On the important question of who is to be the judge of what is necessary for the legitimate ends of the church, Ockham holds that this cannot be the prerogative of the pope, of those under his command, or of the civil rulers. The ultimate decision should be sought in the Gospel, interpreted not by the clergy alone but by "the discretion and counsel of the wisest men sincerely zealous for justice without respect to persons, if such can be found—whether they be poor or rich, subjects or rulers" (*De Imperatorum…*, p. 27, ll. 17–20). This not very practical proposal nevertheless suggests that the membership of the Christian community as private individuals, rather than as officeholders, constitutes the true church. Yet Ockham is not, like Marsilius of Padua, against the principle of the pope as head of the church and vicar of Christ; he only seeks safeguards against abuse of the papal office and illegitimate assumption of tyrannical powers by holders of that office. Legitimate sovereignty, whether papal or civil, is not despotism; the dominion a master has over a slave is not the kind of authority exercised legitimately by a king, pope, or bishop. A pope may turn out to be a heretic and may be deposed—not by the emperor but only by a general council of the church. The imperial power derives from God, not directly but by way of the people who confer upon the emperor his power to legislate; the imperial power is not, as the popes had claimed, derived from the papacy. Ockham's political theory, insofar as it was formulated at all in his polemical writings, was not secularist or anticlerical; it was against absolutism in either church or state and much concerned that the "law of force," which is characteristic of the civil state, should not be adopted by the papal authority, lest the law of God, which is a law of liberty, be corrupted and degraded by temporal ambitions and lust for power.

See also Abelard, Peter; Anselm, St.; Aristotle; Avicenna; Bonaventure, St.; Degrees of Perfection, Argument for the Existence of God; Descartes, René; Determinism, A Historical Survey; Duns Scotus, John; Empiricism; Evil, The Problem of; Hume, David; Induction; Intentionality; Leibniz, Gottfried Wilhelm; Logic, History of; Marsilius of Padua; Medieval Philosophy; Neoplatonism; Ockhamism; Ontological Argument for the Existence of God; Peter Aureol; Peter Lombard; Peter of Spain; Realism; Semantics, History of; Socrates; Thomas Aquinas, St.; Universals, A Historical Survey; William of Sherwood.

Bibliography

WORKS BY OCKHAM

The critical editions of Ockham's works are in three series:

Opera Theologica (*Op. Theol.*). 10 vols., edited by Gedeon Gál et al. St. Bonaventure, NY: Franciscan Institute Publications, 1967–1986.

Opera Philosophica (*Op. Phil.*). 7 vols., edited by Gedeon Gál et al. St. Bonaventure, NY: Franciscan Institute Publications, 1974–1988.

Opera Politica (*Op. Pol.*). 4 vols., edited by H. S. Offler. Vol. I–III. Manchester, U.K.: Manchester University Press; Vol. IV, Oxford: Oxford University Press, 1940–1997 (incomplete).

The main works are:

Scriptum in Librum Primum Sententiarum (*Ordinatio*), edited by Gedeon Gál, Stephen Brown, Jerry I. Etzkorn, and Francis E. Kelley. *Op. Theol* I–IV, 1967–1979.

Quaestiones in Libros Secundum, Tertium et Quartum Sententiarum (*Reportatio*), edited by Gedeon Gál, Rega Wood, Jerry I. Etzkorn, Francis E. Kelley, and Romuald Green. *Op. Theol.* V–VII, 1981–1984.

Quodlibeta Septem, edited by Joseph C. Wey. *Op. Theol.* IX, 1980. English translation by Alfred J. Freddoso and Francis E. Kelley, *Quodlibetal Questions.* 2 vols. New Haven, CT: Yale University Press, 1991.

Summa Logicae, edited by Philotheus Boehner, Gedeon Gál, and Stephen Brown. *Op. Phil.* I, 1974. English translation of Part I by Michael J. Loux, *Ockham's Theory of Terms.* Notre Dame, IN: University of Notre Dame Press, 1974. English translation of Part II by Alfred J. Freddoso and Henry Schuurman, *Ockham's Theory of Propositions,* Notre Dame, IN: University of Notre Dame Press, 1980.

Expositio in Librum Porphyrii De Praedicabilibus, edited by Ernest A. Moody. In *Op. Phil.* II, 1978: 8–131. English translation by Eike-Henner W. Kluge, " William of Ockham's Commentary on Porphyry. " *Franciscan Studies* 33 (1973): 171–254, and 34 (1974): 306–382.

Tractatus de Praedestinatione et de Praescientia Dei Respectu Futurorum Contingentium, edited by Philotheus Boehner and Stephen Brown. In *Op. Phil.* II, 1978: 505–539. English translation by Marilyn McCord Adams and Norman Kretzmann, *Predestination, God's Foreknowledge and Future Contingents.* New York: Appleton-Century-Crofts; 2nd ed., 1983.

Expositio in Libros Physicorum Aristotelis, edited by Vladimir Richter et al. *Op. Phil.* IV–V, 1985.

Brevis Summa Libri Physicorum, edited by Stephen Brown. In *Op. Phil.* VI, 1984: 1–134. English translation by Julian Davies, *Ockham on Aristotle's Physics.* St. Bonaventure, NY: Franciscan Institute, 1989.

Opus Nonaginta Dierum, edited by H. S. Offler and J. G. Sikes, in *Op. Pol.* I, 2nd ed., 1974: 287–368, and *Op. Pol.* II, 1963: 375–858. English translation by John Kilcullen and John Scott, *The Work of Ninety Days.* CD-ROM, Bowling Green, OH: Philosophy Documentation Center.

Breviloquium de Principatu Tyrannico, edited by H. S. Offler, in *Op. Pol.* IV, 1997: 79–277. English translation by John Kilcullen, *A Short Discourse on Tyrannical Government.* Cambridge, U.K.: Cambridge University Press, 1992.

Dialogus, edited by and English translation by John Kilcullen et al. in progress on the web. Available from http://www.britac.ca.uk/pubs/dialogus/ockdial.html.

A Letter to the Friars Minor and Other Writings. English translation by John Kilcullen of selected political writings from Ockham. Cambridge, U.K.: Cambridge University Press, 1995.

On the Power of Emperors ad Popes (*De Imperatorum et Pontificum Potestate*), edited by and English translation by Annabel S. Brett. Bristol, U.K.: Thoemmes Press for the University of Durham, 1998.

WORKS ON OCKHAM

Abbagnano, Nicola. *Guglielmo di Ockham.* Lanciano, Italy: Carabba, 1931.

Adams, Marilyn McCord. *William Ockham.* 2 vols. Notre Dame, IN: University of Notre Dame Press, 1987.

Baudry, L. *Guillaume d'Occam.* Vol. I: *L'homme et les oeuvres.* Paris, 1950. Contains extensive bibliography of works on Ockham; full information on Ockham's published and unpublished works will be found on pp. 273–294.

Baudry, L. *Lexique philosophique de Guillaume d'Ockham.* Paris, 1958.

Baudry, L. *Le Tractatus de Principiis Theologiae attribué à G. d'Occam.* Paris, 1936.

Beckmann, Jan P. *Ockham-Bibliographie 1900–1990.* Hamburg: Felix Meiner, 1992.

Biard, Joël. *Guillaume d'Ockham. Logique et philosophie.* Paris: P.U.F., 1997.

Biard, Joël. *Logique et théorie du signe au XIVe siècle.* Paris: Vrin, 1989.

Boehner, Philotheus. *Collected Articles on Ockham.* St. Bonaventure, NY, 1956.

Courtenay, William J. *Schools and Scholars in Fourteenth-Century England.* Princeton, NJ: Princeton University Press, 1987.

Federhofer, Franz. *Die Erkenntnislehre des Wilhelm von Ockham.* Munich, 1924.

Freppert, Lucan. *The Basis of Morality according to William Ockham.* Chicago: Franciscan Herald Press, 1988.

Goddu, André. *The Physics of William of Ockham.* Leiden: Brill, 1984.

Gottfried, Martin. *Wilhelm von Ockham.* Berlin: de Gruyter, 1949.

Guelluy, Robert. *Philosophie et théologie chez Guillaume d'Ockham.* Louvain and Paris, 1947.

Hochstetter, Erich. *Studien zur Metaphysik und Erkenntnislehre Wilhelms von Ockham.* Berlin, 1927.

Holopainen, Taina M. *William of Ockham's Theory of the Foundations of Ethics.* Helsinki: Luther-Agricola Society, 1991.

Lagarde, Georges de. *La naissance de l'esprit laïque au déclin du moyen âge,* Vols. IV–VI. Paris, 1942–1946.

Leff, Gordon. *William of Ockham. The Metamorphosis of Scholastic Discourse.* Manchester, U.K.: Manchester University Press, 1975.

Maurer, Armand. *The Philosophy of William of Ockham in the Light of Its Principles.* Toronto: Pontifical Institute of Mediaeval Studies, 1999.

McGrade, Arthur Stephen. *The Political Thought of William of Ockham.* Cambridge, U.K.: Cambridge University Press, 1974.

Michon, Cyrille. *Nominalisme. La théorie de la signification d'Occam.* Paris: Vrin, 1994.

Moody, E. A. *The Logic of William of Ockham.* New York and London: Sheed and Ward, 1935.

Moody, E. A. *Truth and Consequence in Medieval Logic.* Amsterdam, 1953.

Moser, Simon. *Grundbegriffe der Naturphilosophie bei Wilhelm von Ockham.* Innsbruck, 1932.

Panaccio, Claude. *Le discours intérieur. De Platon à Guillaume d'Ockham.* Paris: Éd. du Seuil, 1999.

Panaccio, Claude. *Les mots, les concepts et les choses. La sémantique de Guillaume d'Occam et le nominalisme d'aujourd'hui.* Montréal: Bellarmin, and Paris: Vrin, 1992.

Panaccio, Claude. *Ockham on Concepts.* Aldershot, U.K.: Ashgate, 2004.

Scholz, Richard. *Wilhelm von Ockham als politischer Denker und sein Breviloquium de Principatu Tyrannico.* Leipzig: Hiersemann, 1944.

Shapiro, Herman. *Motion, Time and Place according to William Ockham.* St. Bonaventure, NY, 1957.

Spade, Paul Vincent, ed. *The Cambridge Companion to Ockham.* Cambridge, U.K.: Cambridge University Press, 1999.

Spade, Paul Vincent. *Lies, Language and Logic in the Late Middle Ages.* London: Variorum Reprints, 1988.

Spade, Paul Vincent. *Thoughts, Words and Things. An Introduction to Late Mediaeval Logic and Semantic Theory.* Available from http://www.pvspade.com/Logic/index.html, 1996.

Tachau, Katherine H. *Vision and Certitude in the Age of Ockham.* Leiden: Brill, 1988.

Vasoli, Cesare. *Guglielmo d'Occam.* Florence, 1953. Contains an extensive bibliography of works on Ockham.

Vignaux, Paul. *Justification et prédestination au XIVe siècle.* Paris: Leroux, 1934.

Vignaux, Paul. "Nominalisme" and "Occam." In *Dictionnaire de théologie catholique.* 15 vols. Paris, 1903–1950. Vol. XI, cols. 733–789 and 864–904.

Vignaux, Paul. *Le nominalisme au XIVe siècle.* Montreal, 1948.

Webering, Damascene. *The Theory of Demonstration according to William Ockham.* St. Bonaventure, NY: Franciscan Institute, 1953.

Wolter, Allan B. et al. *William of Ockham (1285–1347). Commemorative Issue.* 3 vols. *Franciscan Studies* 44–46 (1984–1986).

Wood, Rega. *Ockham on the Virtues.* West Lafayette, IN: Purdue University Press, 1997.

Zuidema, Sytse. *De Philosophie van Occam in Zijn Commentaar op de Sententien,* 2 vols. Hilversum, Netherlands, 1936.

Ernest A. Moody (1967)
Bibliography updated by Claude Panaccio (2005)

WILLIAM OF SHERWOOD

(1200/1210–1266/1271)

William of Sherwood, or Shyreswood, was an English logician. All that is known for certain of William of Sherwood's life is that in 1252 he was a master at Oxford, that he became treasurer of the cathedral church of Lincoln soon after 1254, that he was rector of Aylesbury and of Attleborough, that he was still living in 1266, and that he was dead in 1271. From references in his works, however, and from the fact that his logic almost certainly had a direct influence on the logical writings of Peter of Spain, Lambert of Auxerre, Albert the Great, and Thomas Aquinas, all of whom were at Paris around the same time, it seems undeniable that he taught logic there from about 1235 to about 1250.

William's impact on his contemporaries went unacknowledged except by Roger Bacon, who, in his *Opus Tertium* (1267), described him as "much wiser than Albert [the Great]; for in *philosophia communis* no one is greater than he." Bacon's phrase *philosophia communis* must refer to logic; no other kind of work can be definitely attributed to William, and his logical works certainly were influential. They consist of an *Introductiones in Logicam,* a *Syncategoremata,* a *De Insolubilibus* (on paradoxes of self-reference), an *Obligationes* (on rules of argument for formal disputation), and a *Petitiones Contrariorum* (on logical puzzles arising from hidden contrariety in premises). Only the first two were ever published; they are longer and far more important than the last three. A commentary on the *Sentences,* a *Distinctiones Theologicae,* and a *Conciones* (a collection of sermons) have also been attributed to William, though their authenticity is seriously questioned.

The *Introductiones* consists of six treatises, the first four and the last one of which correspond (very broadly) to Aristotle's *De Interpretatione, Categories, Prior Analytics, Topics,* and *Sophistical Refutations,* in that order. The third treatise contains the earliest version of the mnemonic verses for the syllogism "Barbara, Celarent …," and there are other interesting minor innovations in those treatises. The most important novelties are concentrated in the fifth treatise, "Properties of Terms"; it contains the logico-semantical inquiries that gave the terminist logicians their name. William recognizes four properties of terms—*significatio, suppositio, copulatio,* and *appellatio.* The last three may be very broadly described as syntax-dependent semantical functions of a term's *significatio,* which is its meaning in the broadest sense.

In order to distinguish such medieval contributions from strictly Aristotelian logic, thirteenth-century philosophers spoke of them as *logica moderna.* When William wrote, *logica moderna* was thought of as having two branches, *proprietates terminorum* and *syncategoremata.* In his separate treatise on the latter, William investigates the semantical and logical properties of such syncategorematic words as *every, except, only, is, not, if, or, necessarily.* Both branches may be said to be concerned with the points of connection between syntax and semantics and with the effect those points have on the evaluation of inferences. William's treatment of both is marked by a concern with the philosophical problems to which they give rise.

The ingredients of the *logica moderna* certainly antedate William's writings, but his may very well be the earliest full-scale organization of those elements in the way that became characteristic of medieval logic after his time.

See also Albert the Great; Aristotle; Bacon, Roger; Logic, History of; Medieval Philosophy; Peter of Spain; Semantics, History of; Thomas Aquinas, St.

Bibliography

Martin Grabmann has edited *Die Introductiones in logicam des Wilhelm von Shyreswood, Literarhistorische Einleitung und Textausgabe* in *Sitzungsberichte der Bayerischen Akademie der Wissenschaften, Philosophische-historische Abteilung,* Jahrgang 1937, Vol. 10 (Munich, 1937). Norman Kretzmann has translated *William of Sherwood's Introduction to Logic* (Minneapolis: University of Minnesota Press, 1966), and J. Reginald O'Donnell has edited "The Syncategoremata of William of Sherwood" in *Medieval Studies* 3 (1941): 46–93.

Norman Kretzmann (1967)

WILLIAMS, BERNARD

(1929–2003)

Bernard Arthur Owen Williams, an English philosopher, was educated at Balliol College, Oxford, and received his BA in 1951. He was a Fellow of All Souls College, Oxford, and went on to teach at New College, Oxford, University College London, and Bedford College, London, before moving in 1967 to Cambridge as Knightbridge Professor and Fellow of King's College; he was Provost of King's from 1979 to 1987. In 1988 he became a professor at Berkeley, then in 1990 was appointed White's Professor of Moral Philosophy at Oxford. An English public figure as well as a distinguished thinker, he was chairperson of the

Committee on Obscenity and Film Censorship and served on the Royal Commission on Gambling, the Labour Party's Commission on Social Justice, and the Independent Inquiry into the Misuse of Drugs Act, as well as on the Board of the English National Opera. He was knighted in 1999.

Williams was a brilliant and versatile contributor to many branches of philosophy and its history. Trained in classics, he wrote about Plato and Aristotle, and also, in *Shame and Necessity*, about the ethical consciousness of classical Greece as revealed in its literature, law, and culture. He wrote an important book about René Descartes, and was profoundly drawn to the work of Friedrich Nietzsche. But his main contributions are his own ideas about knowledge, truth, reality, the self, ethics, and morality.

Williams did not offer a systematic philosophical theory and was distrustful of such theories; instead he tried to bring clarity and a recognition of complexity and historical contingency to a number of central philosophical problems. A theme throughout his work was how to combine the point of view of the individual with the conception of the world encouraged by the scientific ideal of objectivity and its kin. An early example is his paper, *The Self and the Future*, about the problem of personal identity over time, which showed that the first-person conception of the self is more favorable to a physical condition of personal identity than to a condition based on psychological similarity.

In his book on Descartes, he introduced the fruitful notion of the absolute conception of reality—a conception that would be free of every contingency of the human perspective and would therefore describe the world as it is in itself, not merely as it appears to us—, or the world that is there anyway, as he put it. This conception drives the pursuit of scientific objectivity, but also raises the question whether humans can reasonably hope to approach it. Williams thought the view *sub specie aeternitatis* was a reasonable goal for science, but rejected its authority for ethics.

He used the term *ethics* for the general topic of how to live, and *morality* for the special type of modern theory of right and wrong that is based on some form of impartiality or universalizability over all persons. Impartial morality, he argued in *Ethics and the Limits of Philosophy* and elsewhere, does not have an adequate basis in human motivation for the authority it claims over the individuals to whom it is addressed. The appropriate standpoint for assessing human conduct is *from here* not from an external vantage point assumed to be the same for everyone.

Williams held more generally that all reasons for action are internal reasons, by which he meant reasons derived from some desire or interest already present in the agent's subjective motivational set. External reasons, such as those Kant imagined the categorical imperative to provide, do not exist. It follows that moral requirements in particular must be rooted in already existing desires and commitments, and that they may be less than universal in their application. Williams also embraced a qualified relativism, whereby we can morally appraise only forms of life that constitute real options for us: It makes no sense for us to judge either right or wrong the moral beliefs of a medieval samurai, for example.

He had a large impact on moral philosophy through his claim that impersonal morality undermines the integrity of individual life by requiring us to detach from our most fundamental projects and personal commitments, the things that give life its substance and make it worth living. Utilitarianism does this by asking that we regard the attainment of our own aims simply as part of the general welfare, and ourselves as instruments of the universal satisfaction system. But Kantian universalisability, too, requires us to act on our deepest commitments only under the authorization of the higher-order principle that anyone in our situation may do the same—for example, rescue one's own child from drowning rather than a stranger. This, said Williams, is one thought too many. The core of personal life cannot survive subordination to the impersonal standpoint. The exploration of this critique and responses to it have become a focal point of moral theory.

Williams was skeptical about what he called the morality system, and of ethical theory, but he was not a moral skeptic: Morality, he thought, should seek confidence rather than theoretical foundations, and he himself held strong moral views. He believed that ethical judgments were often supported by less universal, more local grounds—particularly judgments involving thick moral concepts like cruelty, courage and chastity. But he drew the corollary that ethical knowledge expressed by those concepts can be lost if the practices and forms of life that underlie them disappear.

Williams formulated the important concept of moral luck, a term he invented for the phenomenon of our moral vulnerability to factors that are not under our control, so that what we are guilty of may depend partly on the actual, and not merely the foreseeable, results of our choices. This possibility was strenuously denied by Kant, but it is central to the moral content of tragedy, one of Williams's great subjects. He rejected the ideal of finding principles of choice which would guarantee that if we follow them, we will have no reason to reproach ourselves later, whatever happens.

His final book, *Truth and Truthfulness*, pursued the reconciliation of his commitment to objectivity about factual, scientific, and historical truth with his resistance to the claims of objectivity in ethics. He attacked general postmodernist skepticism about truth, explained the vital moral importance of respect for factual truth, especially in politics, and analyzed the historical development of our ideas about truth, lying, and authenticity, starting with an imagined prehistory and then proceeding from the ancient world to the present.

See also Aristotle; Descartes, René; Ethics, History of; Kant, Immanuel; Nietzsche, Friedrich; Personal Identity; Plato; Truth; Utilitarianism.

Bibliography

PRIMARY WORKS

Morality: An Introduction to Ethics. New York: Harper & Row, 1972.

Problems of the Self; Philosophical Papers, 1956–1972. Cambridge U.K.: Cambridge University Press, 1973.

"A Critique of Utilitarianism." In *Utilitarianism; For and Against*, by J. J. C. Smart and Bernard Williams. Cambridge U.K.: Cambridge University Press, 1973.

Descartes: the Project of Pure Inquiry. Hassocks, U.K.: Harvester Press, 1978.

Moral Luck: Philosophical Papers, 1973–1980. Cambridge, U.K.; New York: Cambridge University Press, 1981.

Ethics and the Limits of Philosophy. Cambridge, MA: Harvard University Press, 1985.

Shame and Necessity. Berkeley: University of California Press, 1993.

Making Sense of Humanity and Other Philosophical Papers, 1982–1993. Cambridge, U.K.; New York: Cambridge University Press, 1995.

Truth and Truthfulness: An Essay in Genealogy. Princeton NJ: Princeton University Press, 2002.

Thomas Nagel (2005)

WILSON, EDWARD O.

(1929–)

Edward O. Wilson was born in Birmingham, Alabama, on June 10. His first degree was in biology from the University of Alabama. He moved north to Harvard as a graduate student, remaining there for the rest of his working life, first as a doctoral student, then as a junior fellow, and next as a member of the department of biology (later the department of organismic biology), retiring 2000 as a University Professor. Wilson is married with one child. He has received much acclaim, including the Pulitzer Prize for nonfiction (twice), the Craaford Prize of the Swedish Academy of Science, membership in the National Academy of Sciences, and fellowship in the Royal Society.

Wilson's abiding passion has been the world of ants. He has authored books on their nature, their behavior, and their classification. His *magnum opus* is *The Ants* (1990), jointly authored with Bert Holldöbler. This book won Wilson one of his Pulitzer Prizes. Another of Wilson's interests, arising from the ant studies, has been biogeography, the study of the distributions of organisms. With the late Robert MacArthur, in the 1960s, Wilson proposed an important theory of island flora and fauna, arguing that immigration and emigration and extinction eventually reach equilibrium. The ants also led naturally to an interest in chemical communication, with Wilson studying the use of pheromones for information transmission.

From here, Wilson was led into more general issues pertaining to social behavior, and a trilogy ensued. First there was *The Insect Societies* (1971), in which Wilson considered what we now know about the insects and their behaviors, paying special reference to the so-called social insects (especially the hymenoptera: the ants, the bees, and the wasps). Next came *Sociobiology: The New Synthesis* (1978), a book that popularized the term "sociobiology" (meaning the study of social behavior from an evolutionary perspective), in which Wilson extended and developed his thinking, covering the whole of the animal kingdom, including our own species. Finally there was *On Human Nature* (1978), written in a somewhat more popular fashion, and for which Wilson won the other of his Pulitzer Prizes. In this final book of the trilogy, Wilson turned exclusively to humankind, arguing that much that we know about the evolution of social behavior in other animals applies almost equally to humans.

Wilson's forays into human sociobiology were highly controversial. Some critics contended that in the guise of objective science, he simply defended conservative views of society, while social scientists argued that he had no feeling for the subtleties and ranges of human culture. Wilson defended and extended his thinking, pointing out that taking a biological perspective does not at once commit one to a hard-line deterministic position. It has never been his position that the genes are the sole causal factor behind human nature. It is just that biology must be accorded equal causal weight in human affairs alongside the environment and culture.

More and more, through the 1980s, Wilson turned to philosophical questions. With respect to the theory of knowledge (epistemology), Wilson stresses the interconnected nature of our understanding. He wants to show that everything can be explained in just a few basic principles. The Victorian polymath William Whewell, in his *The Philosophy of the Inductive Sciences*, spoke of the highest kind of knowledge as being that which connects together the most disparate areas of science. Whewell spoke of such connection as a "consilience of inductions," and this phrase prompted Wilson to call one of his books *Consilience* (1998), referring to its plea that we bind together all aspects of human knowledge.

Along with epistemology, ethics has always been an interest of Wilson's. His hero in this field is Herbert Spencer, and although Wilson would not want to associate himself with the negative connotations of attempts to link evolution and morality—especially with so-called Social Darwinism—Wilson stands right in the tradition of those who argue that morality is and must be based in human nature as created and preserved by evolution. What is of great importance to Wilson is the need to be sensitive to the environment around us. He speaks of "biophilia," the human love of nature. He believes that we need nature not just to sustain us but also because, in a totally artificial world, we humans would wither and die. Our evolution has tied us to both physical and psychological needs of other organisms. This means that the Wilsonian categorical imperative focuses on biodiversity. In a world without many species, humans are condemned. Following his own prescriptions, for the past decade Wilson has been ardently committed to the preservation of the Brazilian rain forests.

Like Spencer and all other traditional thinkers of this ilk, Wilson turns to notions of progress to link evolution and ethics. Most particularly, he denies that the evolutionary process is one of aimless meandering. Rather, Wilson interprets it as showing an upward rise, from lesser to greater, with humans at the top. Wilson's thinking on this point is part and parcel of his feelings about ultimate questions. An intensely religious man who lost his faith in Christianity in his teens, Wilson was able to replace it with a new religion: Darwinism. He sees religion as an essential part of human culture, binding the tribe together, but he argues that this religious cohesion can endure in the modern age only with the propagation of new "myths" (his word). This is the essential message of Wilson's *On Human Nature* (1978). This is the story of evolution with the philosophical foundation of materialism. For Wilson, science, ethics, and religion are as one. They make for the ultimate consilience.

See also Darwinism; Evolutionary Ethics; Materialism; Organismic Biology; Philosophy of Biology; Whewell, William.

Bibliography

The key books by Wilson include the work on biogeography coauthored with Robert MacArthur, *The Theory of Island Biogeography* (Princeton, NJ: Princeton University Press, 1967); the trilogy *The Insect Societies* (Cambridge, MA: Harvard University Press, 1971); *Sociobiology: The New Synthesis* (Cambridge, MA: Harvard University Press, 1975); *On Human Nature* (Cambridge, MA: Harvard University Press, 1978); the coauthored work with Bert Holldöbler, *The Ants* (Cambridge, MA: Harvard University Press, 1990); *The Diversity of Life* (Cambridge, MA: Harvard University Press, 1992); and *Consilience* (New York: Knopf, 1998). The work by William Whewell that so influenced Wilson is *The Philosophy of the Inductive Sciences* (London, 1840; London: Cass, 1967). A more detailed overview of Wilson's work and thinking can be found in Michael Ruse, *Mystery of Mysteries: Is Evolution a Social Construction?* (Cambridge, MA: Harvard University Press, 1999). Also informative, not only about Wilson but about his various colleagues, friends, and enemies, is his autobiography *Naturalist* (Washington, DC: Island Press, 1994).

Michael Ruse (2005)

WINCKELMANN, JOHANN JOACHIM
(1717–1768)

Johann Joachim Winckelmann, the German art historian and founder of scientific archaeology, was born at Stendal in Prussia. After early schooling in Stendal and Berlin, he studied theology and classics at Halle and mathematics and medicine at Jena. He held a series of minor positions and then became a librarian at Nöthnitz, near Dresden, where he met many artists and critics who stimulated his interest in the fine arts. Influenced by the papal nuncio in Dresden, Winckelmann became a Catholic; and in 1755, after the publication of his first important work, *Gedanken über die Nachahmung der griechischen Werke in der Malerei und Bildhauerkunst* (Thoughts on the imitation of Greek works in painting and sculpture; Dresden and Leipzig, 1754), he went to Rome on a royal subsidy. In Rome he was supported by various high churchmen. In 1758 he visited Naples, Herculaneum, and Pompeii and spent a longer period in Florence. In 1760 he became librarian and surveyor of antiquities to Cardinal Albani and wrote his *Anmerkungen über die Baukunst der Alten* (Remarks on the architecture of the ancients; Leipzig, 1762). In 1763 he was appointed general surveyor of antiquities for Rome and Latium. While general surveyor he published *Abhandlung über die Fähigkeit der Empfindung des Schönen in der Kunst und dem Unterricht in derselben* (Treatise on the power of feeling beauty and on teaching it; Dresden, 1764); *Geschichte der Kunst des Alterthums* (History of ancient art; Dresden, 1764); and *Versuch einer Allegorie, besonders für die Kunst* (An essay on allegory, especially for art; Dresden, 1766). In 1768 Winckelmann was murdered in an inn at Trieste.

Winckelmann was the founder of classical archaeology and of art history. He was the first person to consider a work of art not only as an item of contemplative pleasure and imitation or as an object of erudite commentary and psychological characterization, but as a creation of a particular nation and period with its own special geographical, social, and political conditions, which expresses the style of the spirit of the milieu as a whole.

Winckelmann's aesthetic theory is found mostly in scattered remarks in his works on ancient art, and his ideas were constantly evolving. They were methodological by-products of his work as a historian systematizing the history of ancient art. For these reasons any reconstruction of Winckelmann's aesthetic doctrines is controversial. These views were nevertheless systematized by his contemporaries, and extended from ancient art to literature both ancient and modern.

Winckelmann was dissatisfied with all received definitions of beauty, and he held that beauty is indefinable—that it is one of the greatest mysteries of nature, and beyond the limits of human understanding. (There is nevertheless an absolute standard of taste. But this cannot be deduced; it must be grasped through a deeper insight into actual works of art.) One general characteristic of beauty is proportion; but to dead proportion must be added living form.

Expression (*Ausdruck*) is a lower stage of beauty. It is a lively imitation of both the soul and the body as passive and active. Pure beauty is reached through the stillness of this feeling of life. The highest stage of beauty arises from the unification of expression and pure beauty in grace. By this unity beauty becomes an appearance of divinity in the representation of a sensible object. The unity of a work of art arises mainly from simplicity (*Einfalt*) and measure (*Mässigung*), or the harmony of opposing traits—for instance, understanding and passion. This process of unification corresponds to the rise from sensible to ideal beauty, or from the imitation of nature to the creation of a higher nature. The observation of nature gives us the means of overcoming spurious standards of beauty and a set of samples to be used by the intellect in creating the higher nature.

Beauty is felt by the senses, but it is understood and created by the intellect (*Verstand*)—which is the faculty of ideas as well as of distinct concepts. The "ideal" (*Das Ideale*), or "spirit" (*Geist*), is the most important and controversial notion in Winckelmann's aesthetics. One kind of ideal is created when an artist combines in one unique whole elements of beauty among different natural objects—for example, by constructing a perfect female figure from separate parts imitating parts of different real women, each of which is the most perfect of its kind. A superior kind of ideal arises when the choice of parts is directed not only by a feeling for proportion, but by a supernatural idea translated into matter—for example, the superhuman perfection of a particular human type or quality such as the combination of attractive manhood and pleasing youthfulness in the Apollo del Belvedere, or of enormous pain in a great soul in the Laocoön. The second kind of ideal is not abstracted from experience, but is derived from an intuition of the beauty of God himself. It is realized through a creative process like that of God creating his own image in man. Ideal beauty of the second kind must show "noble simplicity and quiet greatness" (*edle Einfalt und stille Grösse*). Immanuel Kant later systematized this double conception in his *Critique of Judgment.*

Because beauty in its highest form is spiritual, it must suggest a deeper ethical meaning. These ethical thoughts are the content of real art. Art makes them intuitively known through allegory. Nature also presents allegories to man; and man himself spoke through images before he spoke in rational language. Painting, sculpture, and poetry all express through allegory invisible things; and thus allegory is the foundation of the unity of the different fine arts.

Simplicity, or unity, gives distinctness (*Deutlichkeit*) to a work of art. Winckelmann held therefore that there is an intuitive, or sensible, distinctness, whereas the then current psychology admitted only intellectual distinctness and allowed only clarity to sensibility. Kant, later, was the first to introduce the concept of intuitive distinctness into the theory of knowledge.

Winckelmann saw in Greek art the standard of ideal beauty. The Greek man was the most spiritually and ethically balanced, and therefore the most physically perfect, because of various climatic, geographical, historical, social, and political conditions. Greek artists could therefore use the most beautiful human specimens as models, and they should be imitated by modern artists. Imitation of nature and imitation of the Greeks is the same thing.

See also Aesthetic Judgment; Aesthetics, History of; Art, Value in; Beauty; Kant, Immanuel.

Bibliography

WORKS BY WINCKELMANN

Monumenti antichi inediti, 2 vols. Rome, 1767.

Werke, 12 vols. Edited by Joseph Eiselein. Donaueschingen, 1825–1829.

Werke. Edited by W. Rehm and H. Diepolter. Berlin, 1952–. Critical edition.

Kleine Schriften und Briefe. Edited by W. Senf. Weimar: H. Böhlaus Nachfolger, 1960.

WORKS ON WINCKELMANN

Aron, Erich. *Die deutsche Erweckung des Griechentums durch Winckelmann und Herder.* Heidelberg, 1929.

Baumecker, Gottfried. *Winckelmann in seinen Dresdner Schriften.* Berlin: Junker and Dünnhaupt, 1933.

Curtius, Ludwig. *Winckelmann und seine Nachfolge.* Vienna: Schroll, 1941.

Hatfield, H. C. *Winckelmann and His German Critics, 1755–1781.* New York: King's Crown Press, 1943.

Justi, Carl. *Winckelmann und seine Zeitgenossen,* 3 vols. Leipzig, 1866–1873; 4th ed. Leipzig: Koehler and Amelang, 1943.

Rehm, W. *Winckelmann und Lessing.* Berlin, 1941.

Vallentin, Berthold. *Winckelmann.* Berlin: Bondi, 1931.

Zbinden, W. *Winckelmann.* Bern, 1935.

Giorgio Tonelli (1967)

WINDELBAND, WILHELM

(1848–1915)

The German philosopher and historian of philosophy Wilhelm Windelband was born in Potsdam and educated at Jena, Berlin, and Göttingen. He taught philosophy at Zürich, Freiburg im Breisgau, Strasbourg, and Heidelberg. He was a disciple of Rudolf Hermann Lotze and Kuno Fischer and was the leader of the so-called southwestern German (or Baden) school of neo-Kantianism. He is best known for his work in history of philosophy, to which he brought a new mode of exposition—the organization of the subject by problems rather than by chronological sequence of individual thinkers. As a systematic philosopher he is remembered for his attempt to extend the principles of Kantian criticism to the historical sciences, his attempt to liberate philosophy from identification with any specific scientific discipline, and his sympathetic appreciation of late nineteenth-century philosophy of value.

Windelband believed that whereas the various sciences (mathematical, natural, and historical) have specific objects and limit their investigations to determined areas of the total reality, philosophy finds its unique object in the knowledge of reality provided by these various disciplines taken together as a whole. The task of philosophy, he held, was to explicate the a priori bases of science in general. The aim of philosophy was to show not how science is possible but why there are many different kinds of science; the relationships that obtain between these various sciences; and the nature of the relation between the critical intelligence—the knowing, willing, and feeling subject—and consciousness in general.

According to Windelband, both the triumphs and the limitations of contemporary philosophical thought had their origins in Immanuel Kant's thought. Kant had established the dogma that all knowledge must be of the type provided by the natural sciences. But, Windelband held, if knowledge is limited to only that which can be contained within the categories as set forth in the *Critique of Pure Reason,* then the kinds of activities associated with the will and the emotions—that is to say, the subjects of Kant's second and third critiques—are removed from the province of knowledge. The inadequacies of the Kantian identification of knowledge in general with natural scientific knowledge alone had been demonstrated by the post-Kantian idealists, who sought to construct a theory of knowledge capable of appreciating "the needs of modern culture, and … the historical material of ideas" (*History of Philosophy,* p. 569). Idealism failed, however, because it ended by hypostatizing a spiritual sphere that presumably was separate from the world of matter and that operated according to principles utterly different from those which science explicated in general causal laws. Thus, whereas Kantianism had failed to include ethics and aesthetics within the domain of scientific philosophy, idealism failed to provide a place for those aspects of the world revealed by the natural sciences and eternally established as causally determined. It thus appeared to late nineteenth-century thinkers that there were at least two levels of reality, one spiritual and historical, the other material and determined; and it seemed that knowledge itself, far from being one, was at least twofold. On the one hand, it was empirical and discovered laws; on the other hand, it was rational and revealed the essential freedom behind the laws. Such at least had been the contention of Wilhelm Dilthey and the neo-idealists. As long as this division persisted, Windelband held, pessimism, the denial of philosophy, must flourish also.

The way out of the difficulty was to be provided by a fundamental reappraisal in philosophy, a reconsideration of modern thought ab initio. For Windelband this meant primarily an attempt to find a way to apply the technique of transcendental deduction to the historical as well as the physical sciences. It also meant liberation from the notion that natural science was the archetype of all knowledge.

In an early address, "Was ist Philosophie?" (1882), Windelband distinguished between theoretical judgments (*Urteile*) and critical judgments (*Beurteilungen*). The former expressed the "mutual implicativeness" (*Zusammengehörigkeit*) of two "representational contents" (*Vorstellungsinhalte*); the latter expressed the relation between the judging consciousness (*beurteilenden Bewusstsein*) and the object represented (see *Präludien,* Vol. I, p. 29). Theoretical judgments are judgments of fact and are always positive; their purpose is to extend the limits of knowledge in a given science. Critical judgments, however, can be either positive or negative, and they express the position assumed by the subject when a given theoretical judgment is endowed with a status as means to some end.

The individual sciences expand the series of theoretical judgments; philosophy examines the relations between the ability of individual consciousness to render judgments and that "consciousness in general" (*Bewusstsein überhaupt*) which is the intuited basis of every critical judgment. Philosophy, then, "has its own proper field and its own problem in those values of universal validity that are the organizing principles for the functions of culture and civilization and for all the particular values of life. But it will describe and explain those values only that it may give an account of their validity; it treats them not as facts but as norms" (*History of Philosophy,* pp. 680–681). The various sciences are concerned with facts, which they organize in different ways according to the ends for which those facts are "constructed." Philosophy, however, is concerned with the processes by which events attain the status of facts for particular sciences.

Critical judgments, then, are rendered in respect not of what is but of what ought to be; in accordance not with laws but with norms. There is a "normative consciousness" (*Normalbewusstsein*) presupposed by philosophy; this "normative consciousness" is *in abstracto* the same as that which, *in concreto,* underlies every scientific, moral, and aesthetic experience. It is not to be thought of as either a metaphysical or a psychological entity. It is, rather, merely the "sum-total of the inter-connections and relations between existents" (*Logic,* p. 59). These relations "are not themselves existents, either as things, as states, or as activities; they can only become 'actual' as the content of the psychical functions of knowing.... In itself the realm of the valid is nothing else than the form and order under which that which exists is determined" (ibid.). It follows, then, that "this whole is closed to our knowledge; we shall never know more than a few fragments of it, and there is no prospect of our ever being able to patch it together out of the scraps that we can gather" (ibid., p. 65). Therefore, philosophy cannot end in science or in any practical rule of life; it can only point the attention of humanity to the sensed "principles of absolute judgment" that are presupposed in every human confrontation of the world in scientific, moral, and aesthetic experience.

Windelband regarded as baseless every attempt to distinguish between the different disciplines that constitute science on the basis of a presumed essential difference between their objects. The disciplines are distinguished only by their methods, which are in turn functions of the ends or values informing them as instruments of culture. In the address "Geschichte und Naturwissenschaften" (1894), he distinguished between the natural sciences and the historical sciences, and he argued that the natural sciences aim at the construction of general laws and "explain" an event by identifying it as an instance of a general law. Historical sciences, on the other hand, are individualizing; they concentrate on specific events and attempt to determine their specific physiognomy or form. Natural science Windelband termed *nomothetic*; historical science, *idiographic.* But, he added, any given object could be studied by both kinds of science. A mental event, if viewed under the aspect of physical causality—as an instance of the working of some general law—was a natural event. That same mental event, described in its individuality and valued for its deviation from the class to which it belonged, became an object of the idiographic sciences. Positivists erred in holding that every event must be viewed nomothetically, just as idealists erred in thinking that certain kinds of events cannot be so viewed. The total picture of the world that consciousness is in principle able to construct can be constructed only through the use of both kinds of investigation. No single event can be deduced from general laws, and no law can be framed out of the contemplation of a single event. "Law and event remain together as the ultimate, incommensurable limits of our representation of the world" (*Präludien,* Vol. II, p. 160).

See also Consciousness; Dilthey, Wilhelm; Fischer, Kuno; History and Historiography of Philosophy; Idealism; Kant, Immanuel; Lotze, Rudolf Hermann; Neo-Kantianism.

Bibliography

WORKS BY WINDELBAND

Die Lehre vom Zufall. Berlin, 1870.

Präludien: Aufsätze und Reden zur Einführung in die Philosophie, 2 vols. Freiburg im Breisgau, 1884; 5th ed., Tübingen, 1914.

Lehrbuch der Geschichte der Philosophic. Tübingen, 1892; 14th ed., revised by Heinz Heimsoeth, Tübingen, 1948. Translated by J. H. Tufts as *History of Philosophy.* New York: Macmillan, 1893; 2nd ed., New York: Macmillan, 1901.

"Die Prinzipien der Logik." In *Enzyklopädie der philosophischen Wissenschaften,* by Wilhelm Windelband and Arnold Ruge. Tübingen, 1912. Translated by B. E. Meyer as *Logic.* London: Macmillan, 1913.

"Geschichtsphilosophie: Eine Kriegsvorlesung, Fragment aus dem Nachlass." Edited by Wolfgang Windelband and Bruno Bauch. *Kantstudien, Ergänzungshefte im Auftrag der Kantgesellschaft* (38) (1916): 5–68.

WORKS ON WINDELBAND

Collingwood, R. G. *The Idea of History,*165–168. Oxford: Clarendon Press, 1946.

Gronau, G. "Die Kultur und Wertphilosophie Wilhelm Windelbands." In *Die Philosophie der Gegenwart.* Langensalza, 1922.

Rickert, Heinrich. *Wilhelm Windelband.* Tübingen, 1915.

Rossi, Pietro. *Lo storicismo tedesco contemporaneo,*149–207. Turin: Einaudi, 1956.

Hayden V. White (1967)

WISDOM

"Wisdom" in its broadest and commonest sense denotes sound and serene judgment regarding the conduct of life. It may be accompanied by a broad range of knowledge, by intellectual acuteness, and by speculative depth, but it is not to be identified with any of these and may appear in their absence. It involves intellectual grasp or insight, but it is concerned not so much with the ascertainment of fact or the elaboration of theories as with the means and ends of practical life.

WISDOM LITERATURE

Concern with the art of living long preceded formal science or philosophy in human history. All ancient civilizations seem to have accumulated wisdom literatures, consisting largely of proverbs handed down from father to son as the crystallized results of experience. Perhaps the most ancient known collection of these sayings is the Egyptian "Wisdom of Ptah-hotep," which comes down from about 2500 BCE. The writings of Confucius (sixth century BCE) and Mencius (fourth century BCE), though more sophisticated, are still concerned chiefly with the Dao, the good or normal human life. The early writers of India held views at once more speculative and more disillusioned than those of China; both Buddhists and Hindus found the greatest happiness of man in deliverance from the grinding round of suffering and death and in absorption into ātman or nirvāṇa, where personality and struggle alike disappear. But large parts of the Bhagavad-Gita and the Dhammapada, two classics among the scriptures of India, are devoted to maxims and counsels for the conduct of life.

Of far greater influence in the West has been the wisdom literature of the Hebrew people, which consists of the more philosophical parts of the Old Testament and the Apocrypha. Perhaps the most important of these are the books of Job, Proverbs, and Psalms and the apocryphal book called The Wisdom of Solomon. There is no certain knowledge of who wrote any of them; they are probably the work of many men, extending over centuries. They differ strikingly from the writings of Greek and Chinese moralists in the closeness with which morality is identified with religion. The Hebrew sages were all monotheists who held that God fashioned the world but remained outside it; he had made his will known in the law delivered to Moses. This law set the standard and pattern of goodness for all time; the good man will make it his study and seek to conform his life to it. At the same time these sages reduced the miraculous element in Jewish history; they made no claim to being inspired themselves, and inclining, indeed, to assume that the sole motive of conduct was self-advantage, they offered their prudential maxims as not only conforming to the divine law but as also the product of good sense and sound reason. There is very little evidence that they were affected by Greek thought, though Greek influence must have flowed around them after the conquests of Alexander. It is possible that in their cool and reasonable note, contrasting so sharply with the visionary fervor of the prophets, there is an echo of the reflective thought of Greece.

The Greeks had a wisdom literature of their own that long preceded the appearance of their great philosophers. Hesiod (eighth century BCE) and Theognis (sixth century BCE) summed up in poetic form the maxims of traditional morality. Pythagoras (sixth century BCE), a curious combination of mathematician and religious seer, seems to have found in philosophy the guide of practical life. This view was further developed by the Sophists, who, at a time when libraries and universities were unknown, undertook to instruct young men in the arts, theoretical and practical, that were most likely to lead to success. In their emphasis on success, however, there was something skeptical and cynical; the art of life tended in their teaching to become the sort of craft that enabled one by clever strategy to achieve place and power.

THE GREEK CONCEPTION

The first full statement and embodiment of the classic Greek conception of wisdom came with Socrates (c. 470–399 BCE), who insisted that virtue and knowledge were one, that if men failed to live well, it was through ignorance of what virtue really was. He had no doubt that if men knew what virtue was, they would embody it in their conduct. Thus, he set himself to define the major virtues with precision. His method was to consider particular instances of them and bring to light the features they had in common; this would give the essence and true pattern of the virtue in question. He did not profess to be satisfied with the results of his inquiries, but his acuteness and thoroughness made him the first of the great theoretical moralists, and the courage with which he carried his principles into both life and death gave him a unique place in Western history.

The stress on wisdom was maintained by his disciple Plato. For Plato there are three departments of human nature, which may be described as the appetites, directed to such ends as food and drink; the distinctively human emotions, such as courage and honor; and reason. Of these reason is the most important, for only as impulse and feeling are governed by it will conduct be saved from chaos and excess; indeed, in such government practical wisdom consists. In one respect Aristotle carried the exaltation of reason further than Plato; in addition to this practical wisdom, he recognized another and purely intellectual virtue, the wisdom that pursues truth for its own sake and without reference to practice. In this pursuit, which can be followed effectively only by the philosopher, lay the highest and happiest life.

It was among the Stoics, however, that guidance by reason was most seriously and widely attempted. In the thought of the Roman emperor Marcus Aurelius (121–180 CE), both nature and human nature are determined by causal law, and the wrongs and insults that other men inflict on us are therefore as inevitable as the tides. The wise man will understand this inevitability and not waste his substance in futile indignation or fear. He will conform himself to nature's laws, recognize that passion is a symptom of ignorance, free himself from emotional attachments and resentments, and live as far as he can the life of a "passionless sage." The account given by Marcus Aurelius in his famous journal of his struggle to order his practice and temper by this ideal of austere rationality has made his little book a classic of pagan wisdom.

MODERN PHILOSOPHERS

The opinions of modern philosophers on the meaning of wisdom are too various for review here. But it can be noted of these thinkers, as it was of Marcus Aurelius, that their standing as purveyors or exemplars of wisdom bears no fixed relation to their eminence as philosophers. If their chief work lies, as Immanuel Kant's does, in the theory of knowledge, or as John McTaggart Ellis McTaggart's does, in technical metaphysics, it may have no obvious bearing on practical life. Furthermore, by reason of an unhappy temperament, some philosophers of name and influence, such as Jean-Jacques Rousseau, have been far from notable exemplars of wisdom in either controversy or conduct. On the other hand, there are thinkers who have shown in their writing, and sometimes also in their lives, so large a humanity and good sense that they have been held in especial esteem for their wisdom whether or not they have been of high philosophical rank. Michel Eyquem de Montaigne and Ralph Waldo Emerson are examples on one level; John Locke, Bishop Butler, John Stuart Mill, and Henry Sidgwick are examples from a more professional level. Among technical thinkers of the first rank, a figure who has left a deep impression for a wisdom serene and disinterested, though a little above the battle, is the famous philosopher of Amsterdam, Benedict de Spinoza (1632–1677).

COMPONENTS OF WISDOM

Are there any traits uniformly exhibited by the very diverse minds that by general agreement are wise? Two traits appear to stand out—reflectiveness and judgment.

REFLECTIVENESS. By reflectiveness is meant the habit of considering events and beliefs in the light of their grounds and consequences. Conduct prompted merely by impulse or desire is notoriously likely to be misguided, and this holds true of both intellectual and practical conduct. Whether a belief is warranted must be decided by the evidence it rests on and the implications to which it leads, and one can become aware of these only by reflection. Similarly, whether an action is right or wrong depends, at least in part, on the results that it produces in the way of good and evil, and these results can be taken into account only by one who looks before he leaps. Common sense, with its rules and proverbs, no doubt helps, but it is too rough and general a guide to be relied on safely; and the reflective man will have at his command a broader view of grounds and consequences, causes and effects. He will more readily recognize the beliefs of superstition, charlatanism, and bigotry for what they are because he will question the evidence for them and note that when reflectively developed, they conflict with beliefs known to be true. In the same way he will be able to recognize some proposals for action as rash, partisan, or shortsighted because certain consequences have been ascribed to them falsely and others have been ignored. In some activities wisdom consists almost wholly of such foresight. A general, for example, is accounted wise if he can foresee in detail how each of the courses open to him will affect the prospects of victory.

JUDGMENT. There is a wisdom of ends as well as of means, which is here denoted by "judgment." The goal of the general—namely, victory—is laid down for him, but the ordinary man needs the sort of wisdom that can appraise and choose his own ends. The highest wisdom of all, Plato contended, is that required by the statesman, who is called upon to fix both the goals toward which society strives and the complex methods by which it may most effectively move toward them. Unfortunately, at this crucial point where the ends of life are at issue, the sages have differed profoundly. Some, like Epicurus and Mill, have argued for happiness; others, like the Christian saints, for self-sacrificing love; others, such as Friedrich Nietzsche, for power. Many philosophers of the twentieth century came to hold that this conflict is beyond settlement by reason, on the ground that judgments of good and bad are not expressions of knowledge at all but only of desire and emotion. For these thinkers there is properly no such thing as wisdom regarding intrinsic goods; knowledge is confined to means.

Whatever the future of this view, common opinion is still at one with the main tradition of philosophy; it regards the judgment of values as a field in which wisdom may be preeminently displayed. It must admit, however, that this judgment is of a peculiar kind; it seems to be intuitive in the sense that it is not arrived at by argument nor easily defended by it. One may be certain that pleasure is better than pain and yet be at a loss to prove it; the insight seems to be immediate. And where immediate insights differ, as they sometimes do, the difference appears to be ultimate and beyond remedy. Must such wisdom end in dogmatic contradiction and skepticism?

That it need not do so will perhaps be evident from a few further considerations. First, differences about intrinsic goods may be due to mere lack of knowledge on one side or the other. The Puritans who condemned music and drama as worthless could hardly have excluded them if they had known what they were excluding; in these matters wider experience brings an amended judgment. Second, what appears to be intuitive insight may express nothing more than a confirmed habit or prejudice. Where deep-seated feelings are involved, as in matters of sex, race, or religion, the certainty that belongs to clear insight may be confused with the wholly different certainty of mere confidence or emotional conviction. Fortunately, Sigmund Freud and others have shown that these irrational factors can be tracked down and largely neutralized. Third, man's major goods are rooted in his major needs, and since the basic needs of human nature are everywhere the same, the basic goods are also the same. No philosophy of life that denied value to the satisfactions of food or drink or sex or friendship or knowledge could hope to commend itself in the long run.

It should be pointed out, finally, that the judgment of the wise man may carry a weight out of all proportion to that of anything explicit in his thought or argument. The decisions of a wise judge may be implicitly freighted with experience and reflection, even though neither may be consciously employed in the case before him. Experience, even when forgotten beyond recall, leaves its deposit, and where this is the deposit of long trial and error, of much reflection, and of wide exposure in fact or imagination to the human lot, the judgment based on it may be more significant than any or all of the reasons that the judge could adduce for it. This is why age is credited with wisdom; years supply a means to it whether or not the means is consciously used. Again, the individual may similarly profit from the increasing age of the race; since knowledge is cumulative, he can stand on the shoulders of his predecessors. Whether individual wisdom is on the average increasing is debatable, but clearly the opportunity for it is. As Francis Bacon, a philosopher whose wisdom was of the highest repute, remarked, "We are the true ancients."

See also Bacon, Francis; Butler, Joseph; Confucius; Emerson, Ralph Waldo; Epicurus; Freud, Sigmund; Locke, John; Marcus Aurelius Antoninus; McTaggart, John McTaggart Ellis; Mencius; Mill, John Stuart; Montaigne, Michel Eyquem de; Nietzsche, Friedrich; Philosophy; Plato; Pythagoras and Pythagoreanism; Sidgwick, Henry; Spinoza, Benedict (Baruch) de; Socrates; Stoicism.

Bibliography

For proverbial wisdom see Archer Taylor, *The Proverb* (Cambridge, MA: Harvard University Press, 1931), and—old but suggestive—R. C. Trench, *Proverbs and Their Lessons* (London and New York, 1858).

For the problems of determining right and wrong, see any first-rate work on ethics, such as Henry Sidgwick, *The Methods of Ethics,* 7th ed. (Chicago: University of Chicago Press, 1962).

For an analysis of reflection, see, for example, John Dewey, *How We Think* (Boston: Heath, 1910).

For the place of reason in valuation, see L. T. Hobhouse, *The Rational Good* (New York: Holt, 1921), or Brand Blanshard, *Reason and Goodness* (New York: Macmillan, 1961).

For some useful popular works see T. E. Jessop, *Reasonable Living* (London, 1948); H. C. King, *Rational Living* (New York, 1912); and A. E. Murphy, *The Uses of Reason* (New York: Macmillan, 1943).

Brand Blanshard (1967)

WISDOM, (ARTHUR) JOHN TERENCE DIBBEN

(1904–1993)

(Arthur) John Terence Dibben Wisdom, the British analytic philosopher, was closely associated with Ludwig Wittgenstein, whose chair in philosophy at Cambridge he held. Wisdom became professor of philosophy there in 1952. He took his B.A. degree at Cambridge in 1924 and his M.A. there in 1934.

The philosophical problem on which Wisdom wrote the most is the question of what the nature of philosophy is, and his writings reflect his changing views concerning the proper answer to this question. His writings can be divided into two groups: those through 1934, putting forward one answer to the question, and those after 1936, consisting of successive attempts to make clear a quite different view of the nature of philosophy, along with applications of this new approach to a number of familiar first-level philosophical problems.

LOGICAL CONSTRUCTIONS

Wisdom's first book, *Interpretation and Analysis* (1931), compares Jeremy Bentham's notion of a "fiction" with Bertrand Russell's idea of a logical construction—a central notion of British philosophizing in the 1920s and 1930s. According to the theory of logical constructions, to say that a kind of entity *X* is a logical construction out of entities of kind *Y* is to say that statements about entities of kind *X* are translatable into statements about entities of kind *Y,* the *Y*'s being "more ultimate," "more fundamental," than the *X*'s. (It was often said to be less misleading to say, not "*X*'s are logical constructions," but "'*X*' is an incomplete symbol.") Thus, for example, it was said that nations, which are, after all, a kind of "abstraction," are logical constructions out of their nationals, and this meant that statements about, for example, England and France are translatable into statements about Englishmen and Frenchmen. The translation was to be performed not merely by replacement of the words—for "England is a monarchy" does not mean the same as "Englishmen are a monarchy"—but also by changing the predicates, and no doubt the new predicates would be more complicated. Nevertheless, a fact about England is not something "over and above" a fact or set of facts about Englishmen. And other things, too, were said to be logical constructions: propositions were said to be logical constructions out of sentences, people out of mental and bodily events, material objects (including human bodies) out of sense data, and so on. Indeed, Russell and others used the notion very widely; Ockham's razor (according to which "entities must not be multiplied beyond necessity") was given the modern form: supposedly transcendent or abstract entities are everywhere to be regarded as logical constructions out of the more concrete entities given in sense experience. This procedure has the advantage of explicitly blocking a mistaken inference that may arise, for example, from George Berkeley's analysis of a material object as a "congeries of ideas" (for "ideas," read "sense data"). Analyzing it in this way suggests, for example, that the apple I hold in my hand is made of sense data and that I would be eating sense data if I ate the apple. But to say that the apple is a *logical* construction out of sense data is only to say that statements about it are translatable into statements about sense data.

G. E. Moore had written (in "A Defense of Common Sense") that the work of the philosopher was not to find out whether this or that (supposed) matter of fact really was a fact but rather to find the analysis of what we know in knowing the things we do unquestionably know. Thus, I know for certain that I have two hands, but what is the analysis of what I know in knowing this? The followers of Russell and the early Wittgenstein ("logical atomists," as they have been called) saw their task as the analysis of such statements into "atomic statements," which are logically and epistemologically fundamental; they sought to provide translations of statements containing the expression "*X*" into statements that do not contain "*X*," thus justifying the claim that *X*'s are logical constructions.

The first exhaustive treatment of this central notion is to be found in Wisdom's series of five articles titled

"Logical Constructions," which appeared in successive issues of *Mind* from 1931 to 1933. The first three of these essays discuss the relation between sentences in general and the facts expressed by them; the governing idea comes from Wittgenstein's *Tractatus,* where a sentence (on Wisdom's interpretation) is said to be a picture of the fact it expresses. Wisdom tries to bring out precisely what this comes to, in the case not only of such "simple" sentences as "Wisdom killed Al Capone" but also of negations, generalizations, and compound sentences. The fourth and fifth essays are concerned more specifically with logical constructions: How precisely is the analysandum (for example, a statement about sense data) related on the one hand to the fact it pictures and on the other hand to the analysans (a statement about an external object) and the fact it pictures?

In the last of the five essays philosophy is identified with analysis, which is said to provide the required translations. Philosophical propositions are thus verbal (that is, about words), differing only in aim or intention from those of writers of dictionaries: "The philosophical intention is clearer insight into the ultimate structure" of facts, and "philosophic progress does not consist in acquiring knowledge of new facts but in acquiring new knowledge of facts."

The essays "Ostentation" (1933) and "Is Analysis a Useful Method in Philosophy?" (1934) also deal with logical constructions.

THE NEW APPROACH TO PHILOSOPHY

Wittgenstein, who had been away from Cambridge since before World War I, returned there in 1929; his writings from then on show a gradual change in his conception of the nature of philosophy and of language. Wisdom himself returned to Cambridge in 1934 (he had for some years been teaching philosophy at St. Andrews University in Scotland), and his thinking was then strongly influenced by the new view of philosophy being worked out by Wittgenstein. Wisdom's essay "Philosophical Perplexity" (1936) shows that by 1936 a striking change had taken place,

No doubt many within the analytic movement had felt uneasiness about its program, and there had been criticism of the movement from its beginnings, but this was the first appearance in print of an alternative to the earlier reductive account of what philosophers are and ought to be doing. (Wittgenstein's writings of the period were not published until much later, after his death.)

According to the new conception of philosophy (set out briefly in "Philosophical Perplexity" and in greater detail in "Metaphysics and Verification," 1938), philosophical claims are answers to questions of the forms "What are *X*'s?," "What is it to know that here is an *X*?," "Are there any *X*'s?," "Is there any such thing as knowing that here there is an *X*?," where "*X*" is replaced by some very general term such as "material object," "soul," or "causal connection." Answers to the first pair of questions are of two and only two forms: the reductive (*X*'s are logical constructions out of *Y*'s; knowledge that here is an *X* is really knowledge about *Y*'s), and the transcendentalist (*X*'s are unanalyzable, are ultimate; knowledge that here is an *X* is unique, a special way of knowing appropriate only to *X*'s). A philosopher's answers to the second pair of questions will be connected with his answers to the first pair—for example, a reductionist is less likely to be a skeptic (although some have been both reductionists and skeptics with respect to, say, material objects), whereas a transcendentalist is more likely to fall into skepticism.

In view of their form, answers to the first pair of questions are apt to appear to be strictly definitional (as when one says "Fathers are male parents"), and answers to the second pair may appear to be making straightforward empirical points (as when one says what goes on inside Earth). But the philosopher does neither of these things. A philosophical question arises out of a dissatisfaction with the "categories of being" (in the formal mode, "kinds of statement") implicit in our ordinary way of talking. Reductive answers to the first pair of questions and skeptical answers to the second pair are disguised proposals of alternative categorizations; transcendentalist answers to the first pair of questions and nonskeptical answers to the second pair are disguised proposals that we retain the categorizations already marked in the language. The various answers all bring home to us the likenesses and differences between "categories of being" that are either concealed by or implicit in our ordinary way of talking.

Consider, for example, a certain kind of skepticism about material objects. The skeptic says, "We don't really know that there is cheese on the table" and "It would be well if we prefixed every remark about material things with 'probably.'" Such skepticism draws our attention to a likeness shared by all statements about material objects and to a difference between all such statements on the one hand and statements about sensations on the other. The skeptic forces us to see that if a man makes a statement about a material object—whatever the object, whatever the circumstances—then it always makes sense for us to say "But perhaps he is mistaken"; whereas if he says he is having this or that sensation or sense experience, it would not make sense to say this of him. Ordinary language conceals this, for we ordinarily mark a difference among material-object statements; we say that some are at best probable (such as reports about what is going on inside Earth) and that others (such as reports about what is going on inside our fists) are as certain as any statement about a sensation or experience. Of course the job remains of showing why it strikes the skeptic—and us—as important to mark what is pointed to in his claim.

Consider the reductionist view of material objects (see "Metaphysics and Verification"). The reductionist says, "Material objects are logical constructions out of sense data." He draws our attention to a likeness between material-object statements and a certain kind of statement about sense data, a likeness in their mode of verification; if you have already found out that this has, does, and will continue to appear to be (say) a bit of cheese, then there is nothing further to do in the way of finding out whether or not it is a bit of cheese. Ordinary language conceals this likeness, for our ordinary use of the words is such that it is simply false to say that "This is a bit of cheese" means the same as "This has, does, and will appear to be a bit of cheese." Or, as it might be put, the reductionist draws our attention to a likeness between the statement "A material-object statement means the same as a certain complex sense-datum statement" and ordinary statements of the form "'*X*' means the same as '*Y*'" that we would unhesitatingly accept as true; and a difference between it and many ordinary statements of the form "'*X*' means the same as '*Y*'" that we would unhesitatingly reject as false.

Whether a philosophical claim is true is not the important question; what we should do with respect to a philosophical question about the nature of *X*'s and our knowledge of *X*'s is to bring out in full all the features of *X*'s that incline one to opt for this or that philosophical answer—thereby bringing out the relevant likenesses and differences between *X*'s (or statements about *X*'s) and other kinds of entities (or kinds of statements). In this way we obtain that illumination of the category of *X*'s which alone can answer the dissatisfaction that was expressed in our philosophical question.

Any account of the nature of a philosophical claim is itself a philosophical claim (for example, an answer to the question "What are philosophical claims?") and is itself to be dealt with in this way. In the essays already mentioned Wisdom also tries to bring out the likenesses and differences between philosophical claims and other kinds of claims that have been stressed by those who supposed that philosophical claims tell us facts about the world and by those who said that these claims are merely verbal.

"OTHER MINDS"

The papers mentioned so far are primarily concerned with expounding Wisdom's new view of the nature of philosophy, and the first-level philosophical claims considered there appear for the most part as examples; by contrast, his series of papers titled "Other Minds" (which appeared in successive issues of *Mind* between 1940 and 1943) is concerned mainly with the first-level questions relating to our knowledge of other minds, and the second-level question on the nature of philosophy is discussed largely in order to shed light on the first-level questions. His aim in these papers is to bring out all the problems that issue in the question "Do we ever know what anyone else is thinking, feeling, experiencing …?" and to give them the sort of treatment he has said a philosophical problem calls for. Roughly, papers I and II bring out the likenesses and differences between statements about other minds and statements about invisible currents flowing through wires; III compares the philosopher's and the plain man's use of "It's at best probable" and "We know by analogy"; IV and V deal with telepathy and extra or extended ways of knowing in general; VI and VII show what considerations rule out the possibility that one should have "direct" knowledge of the sensations of others—that is, knowledge of the kind one has of one's own sensations (this is done by showing what makes a statement be a statement that is not merely about one's own sensations); and VIII deals with the status of the statement "No one has any knowledge at all apart from knowledge as to his own sensations of the moment."

The difference in conception of the nature of philosophy between Wisdom's later work and, for example, the "Logical Constructions" papers has often been discussed. It is therefore worth mentioning that there is also considerable continuity. As previously noted, Wisdom had earlier thought of "the philosophical intention [as] clearer insight into the ultimate structure" of facts; in "Philosophical Perplexity" he still regarded it as a search for "illumination of the ultimate structure of facts." He did not, in this paper of 1936 or in any of his later works, regard philosophy as merely the study either of the workings of language for its own sake or of the confusions of ordinary language. The analogy he later drew between philosophy and psychoanalysis led many people to think he regarded philosophy as strictly a kind of therapy. But this was never his view, and indeed one may regard his successive efforts to characterize the philosophical enterprise as attempts to bring out just what sort of insight and understanding the philosopher does provide (see, for example, "Gods" and "Philosophy, Metaphysics and Psychoanalysis").

WISDOM AND WITTGENSTEIN

It is dangerous to talk about the conception of philosophy held by the later Wittgenstein—there are very few remarks on the nature of philosophy in Wittgenstein's posthumously published *Philosophical Investigations,* and those he does make are obscure. Nevertheless, Wittgenstein's manner of dealing with philosophical problems there suggests that Wisdom differs from him at least in his attitude toward philosophy. While Wisdom always acknowledged his great debt to Wittgenstein, he says of him in "Philosophical Perplexity," "He too much represents [philosophical theories] as merely symptoms of linguistic confusion. I wish to represent them as also symptoms of linguistic penetration." And he reminds us repeatedly that we are not to take his work as representing Wittgenstein's own views.

In sum, Wisdom's view is that the goal of philosophy is an understanding of just what philosophers have at all times sought to understand—"time and space, good and evil, things and persons." In making their case, philosophers have always appealed to linguistic usage—in "The Metamorphosis of Metaphysics" (reprinted in *Paradox and Discovery*) Wisdom brings out the similarity between contemporary linguistic philosophy and older forms of speculative philosophy. But he also reminds us that good philosophy of any age gives us a clearer view not merely of how we may go wrong in our talking and thinking but of how we may go right.

See also Analysis, Philosophical; Bentham, Jeremy; Berkeley, George; Logic, History of; Moore, George Edward; Other Minds; Russell, Bertrand Arthur William; Wittgenstein, Ludwig Josef Johann.

Bibliography

WORKS BY WISDOM

Interpretation and Analysis. London: K. Paul, Trench, Trubner, 1931.

"Logical Constructions." *Mind* 40–42 (1931–1933).

Problems of Mind and Matter. Cambridge, U.K.: Cambridge University Press, 1934. A work of the same period as the "Logical Constructions" papers; it is concerned with perception and with the relation between a man's body and mind in virtue of which it is true to say that that body and mind are his body and mind.

Other Minds. Oxford: Blackwell, 1952. Contains the eight papers that originally appeared in *Mind,* 1940–1943, as well as a symposium contribution titled "Other Minds" that was originally published in *PAS* supp. 20 (1946) and "The Concept of Mind" and "Metaphysics," the presidential address to the meeting of the Aristotelian Society, November 1950.

Philosophy and Psychoanalysis. Oxford: Blackwell, 1953. Contains "Ostentation," "Is Analysis a Useful Method in Philosophy?," "Philosophical Perplexity," "Metaphysics and Verification," "Gods," "Philosophy, Metaphysics and Psychoanalysis," and other articles and reviews.

Paradox and Discovery. Oxford: Blackwell, 1965. Contains "The Metamorphosis of Metaphysics," "A Feature of Wittgenstein's Technique," "The Logic of God," "Paradox and Discovery," and other short pieces.

WORKS ON WISDOM

Gasking, D. A. T. "The Philosophy of John Wisdom, I and II." *Australasian Journal of Philosophy* (1954).

Passmore, John. *A Hundred Years of Philosophy,* 367–368, 434–438. London: Duckworth, 1957.

Urmson, J. O. *Philosophical Analysis,* 76–85, 169–182. Oxford: Clarendon Press, 1956.

Judith Jarvis Thomson (1967)

WITTGENSTEIN, LUDWIG JOSEF JOHANN

(1889–1951)

Ludwig Josef Johann Wittgenstein, the Austrian-British philosopher, was born in Vienna, the youngest of eight children. Ludwig's paternal grandfather, a convert from Judaism to Protestantism, had been a wool merchant in Saxony before moving to Vienna. Ludwig's father, Karl Wittgenstein, had, as a strong-willed boy, rebelled against a classical education, running away to America when he was seventeen. After two years he returned to Vienna and underwent a brief training in engineering. He went to work as a draftsman, designed and largely directed the construction of a steel-rolling mill, became its manager, in ten years' time was the head of a large steel company, and subsequently organized the first cartel of the Austrian steel industry. Ludwig's mother was the daughter of a Viennese banker. She was a Roman Catholic, and Ludwig was baptized in the Catholic Church. Ludwig had four brothers and three sisters; all the children were generously endowed with artistic and intellectual talent. Their mother was devoted to music, and their home became a center of musical life. Johannes Brahms was a frequent visitor and a close friend of the family. One of Ludwig's brothers, Paul, became a distinguished pianist.

Ludwig was educated at home until he was fourteen. He was an indifferent student, and apparently his greatest interest was in machinery; a sewing machine that he constructed was much admired. His parents decided to send him to a school at Linz, in Upper Austria, that provided preparation in mathematics and the physical sciences rather than a classical education. After three years at Linz, Wittgenstein studied mechanical engineering for two years at the Technische Hochschule at Charlottenburg, in Berlin. He left this school in the spring of 1908 and went to England. In the summer of 1908 he experimented with kites at a kite-flying station in Derbyshire. That fall he registered as a research student of engineering at the University of Manchester. He engaged in aeronautical research for three years and designed a jet-reaction engine and a propeller.

Wittgenstein's interest began to shift to pure mathematics and then to the philosophical foundations of mathematics. He chanced upon Bertrand Russell's *Principles of Mathematics* and was greatly excited by it. He decided to give up engineering and to study with Russell at Cambridge. At the beginning of 1912 he was admitted to Trinity College, where he remained for the three terms of 1912 and the first two terms of 1913. Under Russell's supervision he applied himself intensively to logical studies and made astonishing progress. Soon he was engaged in the research that culminated in the logical ideas of the *Tractatus.*

Wittgenstein's most intimate friend during those early years at Cambridge was David Pinsent, a fellow student, to whom he later dedicated the *Tractatus.* When they met in the spring of 1912, Wittgenstein, in addition to studying logic, was doing experiments in the psychological laboratory on rhythm in music. He and Pinsent were united by strong musical interests. They had a repertoire of forty of Franz Schubert's songs, whose melodies Wittgenstein would whistle while Pinsent accompanied him on the piano. Wittgenstein could play the clarinet and had an excellent memory for music and an unusual gift for sight-reading. He retained a deep interest in music throughout his life; in his philosophical writings there are many allusions to the nature of musical understanding.

In 1912, Wittgenstein was doing his first extensive reading in philosophy, and according to Pinsent he expressed "naive surprise" that the philosophers whom he had "worshipped in ignorance" were after all "stupid and dishonest and make disgusting mistakes!" He and Pinsent made holiday junkets to Iceland and Norway, Wittgenstein paying all expenses. Pinsent found Wittgenstein a difficult companion: irritable, nervously sensitive, often depressed. But when he was cheerful he was extremely charming. Sometimes he was depressed by the conviction that his death was near at hand and that he would not have time to perfect his new ideas in logic, sometimes by the thought that perhaps his logical work was of no real value. Even so, his general frame of mind was less morbid than before he had come to Cambridge. For a number of years previously there had hardly been a day, he told Pinsent, in which he had not thought of suicide "as a possibility." Coming to study philosophy with Russell had been his "salvation."

Wittgenstein worked with fierce energy at his logical ideas. In the spring of 1913 he submitted to hypnosis with the hope that in the hypnotic trance he could give clear answers to questions about difficulties in logic. He entertained a plan of going to live in seclusion in Norway for some years, devoting himself to logical problems. The reasons he gave to Pinsent were that he could do better work in the absence of all distractions, but he also said that "he had no right to live in a world" where he constantly felt contempt for other people and irritated them by his nervous temperament. Wittgenstein acted on his plan and lived in Norway from the latter part of 1913 until the outbreak of World War I. He stayed on a farm at Skjolden and later built a hut, where he lived in complete seclusion.

During this period Wittgenstein corresponded with Russell. His letters were warmly affectionate and were full of the excitement of his logical discoveries. However, he expressed the conviction that he and Russell had such different "ideals" that they were not suited for true friendship. Two people can be friends, he said, only if both of them are "pure," so that they can be completely open with one another without causing offense. A relationship founded on "hypocrisy" is intolerable. He and Russell should break off entirely or else limit their communications to their logical work. Both of them have weaknesses, but especially himself: "My life is *full* of the most hateful and petty thoughts and acts (this is *no* exaggeration)." "Perhaps you think it is a waste of time for me to think about myself; but how can I be a logician if I am not yet a man! *Before everything else* I must become pure."

When war broke out Wittgenstein entered the Austrian Army as a volunteer. He served in an artillery group on a vessel on the Vistula and later in an artillery workshop at Kraków. He was ordered to an officers' training school and subsequently served on the eastern front and later with mountain artillery in the southern Tyrol. During these years he continued to work at his book, writing down his philosophical thoughts in notebooks that he carried in his rucksack. He completed the book in August 1918; when he was taken prisoner by the Italians in November, he had the manuscript with him. From his prison camp near Monte Cassino he wrote to Russell, to whom the manuscript was subsequently delivered by diplomatic courier through the offices of a mutual friend, J. M. Keynes.

While serving on the eastern front Wittgenstein bought at a bookshop in Galicia a copy of one of Lev Tolstoy's works on the Gospels, which apparently made a deep impression on him. In the prison camp in Italy he read a standard version of the Gospels, possibly for the first time, and is reported to have been disturbed by much that he found in it and to have questioned its authenticity, perhaps because of the differences from Tolstoy's version.

Wittgenstein was anxious to have his book, *Logisch-Philosophische Abhandlung,* published immediately. Shortly after his release from imprisonment and his return to Vienna, in August 1919, he offered it to a publisher. He believed that his book finally solved the problems with which he and Russell had struggled. From Russell's letters, however, he concluded that Russell had not understood his main ideas, and he feared that no one would. He and Russell met in Holland in December 1919 to discuss the book. Russell undertook to write an introduction for it, but the following May, Wittgenstein wrote to Russell that the introduction contained much misunderstanding and he could not let it be printed with his book. Subsequently the publisher with whom he had been negotiating rejected the book. Wittgenstein wrote to Russell, in July 1920, that he would take no further steps to have it published and that Russell could do with it as he wished. The German text was published in 1921 in Wilhelm Ostwald's *Annalen der Naturphilosophie.* The following year it was published in London with a parallel English translation, under the title *Tractatus Logico-Philosophicus.* A new and improved English translation was published in 1961.

Most of the notebooks used in the preparation of the *Tractatus* were destroyed on Wittgenstein's order. Three of them, however, from the years 1914–1916, were accidentally preserved and were published in 1961 with a parallel English translation. The notebooks present a vivid picture of the intensity of Wittgenstein's struggles with the problems of the *Tractatus,* and they sometimes help to show what the problems were.

Soon after his return to civilian life Wittgenstein decided to become a schoolteacher. He attended a teacher-training course in order to receive a certificate, and in the fall of 1920 he began teaching classes of children aged nine and ten in the village of Trattenbach in Lower Austria. He was an exacting teacher. He did not get on with his colleagues and was often depressed. When he was transferred to another village he was somewhat happier, for one of the teachers, Rudolf Koder, was a talented pianist. The two of them devoted many afternoons to music, Wittgenstein playing the clarinet or whistling. He remained a schoolteacher until 1926. In 1924 he prepared a dictionary of six thousand to seven thousand words for the use of pupils in the elementary schools of the Austrian villages; this small book was published in 1926.

When his father died, in 1913, Wittgenstein inherited a large fortune. In the summer of the following year he wrote to Ludwig von Ficker, editor of the literary review *Der Brenner,* proposing to send a large sum of money to be distributed among needy Austrian poets and artists. The poets Rainer Maria Rilke and Georg Trakl received sizable gifts of money from this anonymous source. Upon his return to civilian life after the war, Wittgenstein gave his fortune to two of his sisters. Part of the reason for this action was that he did not want to have friends for the sake of his money, but undoubtedly it was largely due to his inclination toward a simple and frugal life.

During his years as a teacher, until Frank Ramsey visited him in 1923, Wittgenstein probably gave no thought to philosophy. Ramsey, a brilliant young mathematician and philosopher at Cambridge, had just completed a review of the *Tractatus* and was eager to discuss the book with its author. He found Wittgenstein living in extreme simplicity in a small village. In explaining his book, to which he was willing to devote several hours a day for a fortnight or more, Wittgenstein would become very excited. He told Ramsey, however, that he would do no further work in philosophy because his mind was "no longer flexible." He believed that no one would understand the *Tractatus* merely by reading it but that some day some person would, independently, think those same thoughts and would derive pleasure from finding their exact expression in Wittgenstein's book.

After his resignation as a schoolteacher in 1926, Wittgenstein inquired at a monastery about the possibility of entering upon monastic life, but he was discouraged by the father superior. In the summer of that year he worked as a gardener's assistant with the monks at Hütteldorf, near Vienna. Meanwhile, one of his sisters had commissioned the architect Paul Engelmann to build a mansion for her in Vienna. Engelmann, a friend of Wittgenstein's, proposed to him that they undertake it jointly. Wittgenstein agreed and actually became the directing mind in the project, which occupied him for two years. The building has been described by G. H. von Wright as "characteristic of its creator. It is free from all decoration and marked by a severe exactitude in measure and proportion. Its beauty is of the same simple and static kind that belongs to the sentences of the *Tractatus.*" During the same period Wittgenstein did some work in sculpture.

Moritz Schlick, a professor in Vienna, had been deeply impressed by the *Tractatus.* He managed to establish contact with Wittgenstein and apparently prevailed upon him to attend one or two meetings of the group founded by Schlick, known as the Vienna circle. Subsequently Schlick and Friedrich Waismann paid visits to Wittgenstein, in which he expounded some ideas that were passed on to other members of the circle.

In January 1929 he returned to Cambridge to devote himself again to philosophy. What produced this renewal of interest is unknown, but it is said that it was provoked by a lecture he heard L. E. J. Brouwer give in Vienna in 1928 on the foundations of mathematics. Wittgenstein found he would be eligible to receive the Ph.D. degree from Cambridge if he submitted a dissertation, whereupon he submitted the *Tractatus.* Russell and G. E. Moore were appointed to give him an oral examination, which they did in June 1929. Moore found the occasion "both pleasant and amusing." Trinity College granted Wittgenstein a research fellowship. At this time he published a short paper, "Some Remarks on Logical Form," which he soon came to think was weak and confused. This paper and the *Tractatus* were the sole philosophical writings of his that were published in his lifetime.

Wittgenstein began to give lectures in January 1930. He remained at Cambridge until the summer of 1936, when he went to live for a year in his hut in Norway and to begin writing the *Philosophical Investigations.* In 1937 he returned to Cambridge and two years later succeeded Moore to the chair of philosophy.

Wittgenstein's lectures made a powerful impression on his auditors. They were given without notes or preparation. Each lecture was new philosophical work. Wittgenstein's ideas did not come easily. He carried on a visible struggle with his thoughts. At times there were long silences, during which his gaze was concentrated, his face intensely alive, and his expression stern, and his hands made arresting movements. His hearers knew that they were in the presence of extreme seriousness, absorption, and force of intellect. When he spoke his words did not come fluently, but they came with force and conviction. His face was remarkably mobile and expressive when he talked. His eyes were often fierce, and his whole personality was commanding. His lectures moved over a wide range of topics and were marked by great richness of illustration and comparison. Wittgenstein attacked philosophical problems energetically, even passionately. Unlike many other philosophers, who really want to retain the problems rather than to solve them, Wittgenstein's desire was to clear them up, to get rid of them. He exclaimed to a friend: "My father was a business man and I am a business man too!" He wanted his philosophical work to be businesslike, to settle things.

When he was not working at philosophy Wittgenstein could sometimes, with a friend, put on a charming mood of mock seriousness in which he said nonsensical things with utmost gravity. These lighthearted moments were, however, comparatively infrequent. Most commonly his thoughts were somber. He was dismayed by the insincerity, vanity, and coldness of the human heart. He was always troubled about his own life and was often close to despair. Human kindness and human concern were for him more important attributes in a person than intellectual power or cultivated taste. He had an acute need for friendship, and his generosity as a friend was striking. At the same time it was not easy to maintain a friendly relationship with him, for he was easily angered and inclined to be censorious, suspicious, and demanding.

In World War II Wittgenstein found it impossible to remain a spectator. He obtained a porter's job at Guy's Hospital in London and worked there from November 1941 to April 1943. He was then transferred to the Royal Victoria Infirmary in Newcastle, where he served as a "lab boy" in the Clinical Research Laboratory until the spring of 1944. He impressed the doctors for whom he worked by the prolonged and concentrated thought he gave to their medical problems. This hard thinking would often result in a new way of looking at the problems. At Newcastle, Wittgenstein devised a simple technique for estimating the area of war wounds that proved of value in determining their treatment.

In 1944 he resumed his lectures at Cambridge. But he became increasingly dissatisfied with his role as a teacher. He feared that his influence was positively harmful. He was disgusted by what he observed of the half understanding of his ideas. "The only seed I am likely to sow is a jargon," he said. He strongly disliked universities and academic life. He felt an increasing need to live alone, perhaps occasionally seeing a friend, and to devote his remaining energies (for several years he had been repeatedly unwell) to finishing the *Investigations.*

In the fall of 1947 he finally resigned his chair. He sought a secluded life, first in the Irish countryside near Dublin, then in an isolated cottage on the west coast of Ireland. He worked hard when his health permitted it. In the summer of 1949 he went to spend three months with a friend in the United States. Upon his return to England, in the fall, he was discovered to have cancer. He wrote that he was not shocked by this news because he had no wish to continue living. During part of 1950 he visited his family in Vienna, then went to Oxford to live with a friend, and afterward made a trip to Norway. In 1951 he moved to the home of his physician in Cambridge. Wittgenstein had expressed an aversion to spending his last days in a hospital, and his doctor had invited him to come to his own home to die. Wittgenstein was deeply grateful for this offer. Knowing that death was imminent, he continued hard at work. The philosophical thoughts that he wrote in his notebooks at this time are of the highest quality.

On April 27 he was taken violently ill. When his doctor informed him that the end had come he said, "Good!" His last words, before he lost consciousness, were "Tell them I've had a wonderful life!" He died on April 29, 1951.

THE *TRACTATUS*

The *Tractatus* is a comprehensive work of extreme originality, yet it is less than eighty pages long. It is arranged as a series of remarks numbered in decimal notation. The following propositions are distinguished by their numbering as the primary theses of the book:

(1) The world is everything that is the case.

(2) What is the case, the fact, is the existence of states of affairs.

(3) A logical picture of facts is a thought.

(4) A thought is a sentence with a sense.

(5) A sentence is a truth-function of elementary sentences.

(6) The general form of a truth-function is $[\bar{p},\bar{\xi},N(\bar{\xi})]$.

(7) Whereof one cannot speak, thereof one must be silent.

Erik Stenius has perceptively remarked that the book has a "musical" structure and that the numbering brings out a "rhythm of emphasis": these seven main propositions are "forte" places in the rhythm.

THE PICTURE THEORY. In a notebook Wittgenstein wrote (*Notebooks,* p. 39): "My *whole* task consists in explaining the nature of sentences." (The German *Satz* will be translated sometimes as "sentence," sometimes as "proposition.") What makes it possible for a combination of words to represent a fact in the world? How is it that by producing a sentence I can say something—can tell someone that so-and-so is the case?

Wittgenstein's explanation consists in the striking idea that a sentence is a picture. He meant that it is literally a picture, not merely like a picture in certain respects. Apparently this thought first occurred to him during the war, when he saw in a magazine an account of how a motorcar accident was represented in a law court by means of small models (see *Notebooks,* p. 7). So he said: "A proposition is a picture of reality. A proposition is a model of reality as we think it to be" (*Tractatus,* 4.01). The dolls and toy cars could be manipulated so as to depict different ways in which the accident might have taken place. They could be used to construct different propositions about the accident—to put forward different accounts, different models of what took place. Wittgenstein's general conception was that when we put a sentence together we construct a model of reality. "In a proposition a situation is, as it were, put together experimentally" (4.031).

One would not normally think that a sentence printed on a page is a picture. According to the *Tractatus* it really is a picture, in the ordinary sense, of what it represents. Wittgenstein conceived the proof of this to be that although words we have not previously encountered have to be explained to us, when we meet for the first time a sentence that is composed of familiar words, we understand the sentence without further explanation. "I understand a sentence without having had its sense explained to me" (4.021). This can appear to one as a remarkable fact. If it is a fact, the only possible explanation would be that a sentence shows its sense. It shows how things are if it is true (4.022). This is exactly what a picture does. A sentence composed of old words is able to communicate a new state of affairs by virtue of being a picture of it.

In any picture, according to the *Tractatus,* there has to be a one-to-one correspondence between the elements of a picture and the things in the state of affairs its represents. If one element of a picture stands for a man and another for a cow, then the relationship between the picture elements might show that the man is milking the cow. A picture is a fact, namely the fact that the picture elements are related to one another in a definite way. A picture fact shows that the things the picture elements stand for are related in the same way as are the picture elements.

Since a sentence is held to be a picture, there must be as many elements to be distinguished in it as in the state of affairs it portrays. The two must have the same logical or mathematical multiplicity. Again, this does not seem to be true of our ordinary sentences. For Wittgenstein this meant not that it is not true but that our sentences possess a concealed complexity that can be exhibited by analysis.

According to the *Tractatus* a picture must have something in common with what it pictures. This common thing is the picture's "form of representation." There are different kinds of pictures, different pictorial notations, different methods of projection. But all pictures must have in common with reality the same logical form in order to be able to picture reality at all, either truly or falsely. This logical form, also called "the form of reality," is defined as the possibility that things in the world are related as are the elements of the picture (2.18, 2.151). Sentences, since they are pictures, have the same form as the reality they depict.

WHAT CANNOT BE SAID. A picture can depict reality, but it cannot depict its own form of representation. It depicts (represents) its subject from "outside," but it cannot get outside itself to depict its own form of representation. A picture of another form might depict the representational form of a given picture; for instance, a picture in sound might depict the representational form of a picture in color. But in order for the one to represent the form of the other, there must be something that is the same in both. "There must be something identical in a picture and what it depicts, to enable the one to be a picture of the other at all" (2.161). Therefore, logical form, the form of reality, which all pictures must possess, cannot be depicted by any picture.

This consideration must apply to sentences, too. We make assertions by means of sentences. With a sentence we say something. We say how things are. Things in the world are related in a certain way, and we try to describe that. But we cannot describe how our sentences succeed in representing reality, truly or falsely. We cannot say what the form of representation is that is common to all sentences and that makes them pictures of reality. We cannot say how language represents the world. We cannot state in any sentence the pictorial form of all sentences. "What can be said can only be said by means of a sentence, and so nothing that is necessary for the understanding of *all* sentences can be said" (*Notebooks,* p. 25).

This doctrine implies that in a sense one cannot say what the meaning of a sentence is. With regard to the sentence "*a* is larger than *b,*" one can explain to a person what "*a*" and "*b*" each refer to and what "larger" means, but there is not a further explanation to give him, namely what "*a* is larger than *b*" means. We understand the elements of a sentence, and we see how they are combined. But we cannot say what this combination means. Yet we grasp its meaning. In some sense we know what it means, because the sentence shows its meaning. Anything that can be said can be said clearly, but not everything that is understood can be said. In a letter to Russell, Wittgenstein remarked that his "main contention" was this distinction between what can be said in propositions—that is, in language—and what cannot be said but can only be shown. This, he said, was "the cardinal problem of philosophy."

THE NATURE OF THOUGHT. The picture theory of propositions is at the same time an account of the nature of thought. Wittgenstein said: "A thought is a sentence with a sense" (*Tractatus,* 4). This implies that thinking is impossible without language. Since a thought is a sentence and a sentence is a picture, a thought is a picture. The totality of true thoughts would be a true picture of the world.

The view that a thought is a sentence seems to imply that the words of a sentence could be the constituents of a thought. But in a letter written to Russell shortly after the *Tractatus* was completed, Wittgenstein explicitly denied this. A thought consists not of words "but of psychical constituents that have the same sort of relation to reality as words. What those constituents are I don't know." "I don't know *what* the constituents of a thought are but I know *that* it must have such constituents which correspond to the words of Language" (*Notebooks,* pp. 130, 129). It would appear from these remarks that Wittgenstein's view was not that a thought and a sentence with a sense are one and the same thing but that they are two things with corresponding constituents of different natures. Each of these two things is a picture. "Thinking is a kind of language. For a thought too is, of course, a logical picture of a sentence, and therefore it just is a kind of sentence" (*Notebooks,* p. 82).

To say that a state of affairs is conceivable (thinkable) means that we can make a picture of it (*Tractatus,* 3.001). A thought "contains" the possibility of a state of affairs, for the logical form of the thought is the possibility that things in the world are combined in the way the constituents of the thought are combined. Whatever is conceivable is possible. In a spoken or written sentence a thought is "made perceptible to the senses." All thoughts can be stated in sentences; what cannot be stated cannot be thought.

A consequence of these views is that the form of representation of propositions (the form of reality, logical form), which cannot be stated, also cannot be thought. Language shows us something we cannot think. A function of philosophy is to indicate (*bedeuten*) what cannot be said (or thought) by presenting clearly what can be said. According to the *Tractatus,* therefore, there is a realm of the unthinkable that, far from being a mere wind egg, is the foundation of all language and all thought. In some way we grasp this foundation of thought (what we do here cannot really be said); it is mirrored in our thoughts, but it cannot be an object of thought.

Obviously the *Tractatus* is a thoroughly metaphysical work; this is not a minor tendency of the book. Yet it was once widely regarded as being antimetaphysical in its outlook. There is some excuse for this interpretation, since at the end of the book Wittgenstein said that the correct philosophical method would be to prove to anyone who wants to say something metaphysical that he has failed to give a meaning to certain signs in his sentences (6.53). But Wittgenstein did not reject the metaphysical; rather, he rejected the possibility of stating the metaphysical.

NAMES AND OBJECTS. The conception of propositions, and therefore of language, in the *Tractatus* rests on the notion of a name. This is defined as a "simple sign" employed in a sentence. A simple sign is not composed of other signs, as, for example, the phrase "the king of Sweden" is. The word *John* would satisfy this requirement of a simple sign. But a further requirement of a name is that it should stand for a simple thing, which is called an "object." According to the *Tractatus* the object for which a name stands is the meaning of the name (3.203). It is easy to determine whether a sign is composed of other signs but not whether it stands for something simple.

Wittgenstein conceived of objects as absolutely simple and not merely as simple relative to some system of notation. "Objects make up the substance of the world. That is why they cannot be composite.... Substance is what exists independently of what is the case.... Objects are identical with the fixed, the existent.... The configuration of objects is the changing, the mutable" (2.021, 2.024, 2.027, 2.0271).

A name is not a picture of the object it stands for, and therefore a name does not say anything. A picture in language—that is, the sentence—can be formed only by a combination of names. This combination pictures a configuration of objects. The combination of names is like a *tableau vivant* (4.0311). (One might think here, for example, of a group of people posed to represent *The Last Supper*). A name is a substitute for an object, and a combination of names portrays a configuration of objects—that is, a state of affairs (*Sachverhalt*).

A reader of the *Tractatus* will be perplexed to know what examples of names and of objects would be. No examples are given. It is said that names occur only in "elementary" propositions, but there are no examples of the latter notion. Wittgenstein was not able to come to any conclusion about examples. The *Notebooks* show that he was very vexed by this problem. He struggled with the question of whether "points of the visual field" might be simples (see, for example, p. 45). Sometimes he wondered whether any ordinary name whatsoever might not be a "genuine" name. And he wondered whether his watch might not be a "simple object" (*Notebooks,* pp. 60–61). His final conviction that there are absolutely simple objects was purely a priori. He wrote in his notes:

> It seems that the idea of the *simple* is already to be found contained in that of the complex and in the idea of analysis, and in such a way that we come to this idea quite apart from any examples of simple objects, or of propositions which mention them, and we realize the existence of the simple object—*a priori*—as a logical necessity. (*Notebooks,* p. 60)

The "logical necessity" arises from the requirement that propositions have a definite sense. "The demand for simple things is the demand for definiteness of sense" (*Notebooks,* p. 63). As it is put in the *Tractatus,* "The requirement that simple signs be possible is the requirement that sense be definite" (3.23). An indefinite sense would be no sense at all. A proposition might be ambiguous, but the ambiguity would be between definite alternatives: either this or that.

The sentences of everyday language are in perfect logical order. This order rests on the simples—that which is fixed, unchangeable, hard (*das Harte: Notebooks,* p. 63). The simples and their configurations—that is what order is. Wittgenstein said: "Our problems are not abstract, but perhaps the most concrete that there are" (*Tractatus,* 5.5563).

ELEMENTARY PROPOSITIONS. A combination of genuine names is an elementary proposition. It is not analyzable into other propositions. "It is obvious that the analysis of propositions must bring us to elementary propositions which consist of names in immediate combination" (4.221). An elementary proposition shows (represents) a certain configuration of simple objects.

The picture theory is meant to hold for all genuine propositions, not merely for elementary propositions. Wittgenstein said without qualification: "A proposition is a picture of reality" (4.01, 4.021). Elementary and nonelementary propositions are equally pictures: the difference is that in an elementary proposition the pictorial nature is manifest. "It is *evident* that we perceive (*empfinden*) an elementary proposition as the picture of a state of affairs" (*Notebooks,* p. 25). But Wittgenstein admitted that most sentences do not seem to be pictures.

> At first sight a sentence—one set out on the printed page, for example—does not seem to be a picture of the reality with which it is concerned. But no more does musical notation at first sight seem to be a picture of music, nor our phonetic notation (letters) to be a picture of our speech. And yet these sign-languages prove to be pictures, even in the ordinary sense, of what they represent. (*Tractatus,* 4.011)

All genuine propositions, according to the *Tractatus,* are analyzable into elementary propositions. This analysis of our ordinary propositions, with their complicated modes of symbolizing—their various "methods of projection"—will make manifest their concealed pictorial nature. In his introduction to the *Tractatus,* written for the first English edition, Russell said:

> Mr. Wittgenstein is concerned with the conditions for a logically perfect language—not that any language is logically perfect, or that we believe ourselves capable, here and now, of constructing a logically perfect language, but that the whole function of language is to have meaning, and it only fulfils this function in proportion as it approaches to the ideal language which we postulate.

That this is an incorrect account of the *Tractatus* is sufficiently shown by Wittgenstein's remark "All the propositions of our everyday language are actually in perfect logical order, just as they are" (5.5563). The analysis achieved by the philosophical logician will not create order where previously there was no order; instead, it will make evident what is already there.

Every genuine proposition has one and only one complete analysis into elementary propositions (3.25). This is so even if every fact consists of infinitely many states of affairs and every state of affairs is composed of infinitely many simple objects (4.2211). The completely analyzed proposition will consist of simple names; the meaning of each simple name will be a simple object; the particular way in which the names are combined in the proposition will say that the simple objects in the world are related in the same way. To understand the completely analyzed proposition one need only understand the names—that is, know what objects they stand for. What their combination means will be immediately evident. Understanding a proposition requires merely understanding its constituents (4.024).

As Rush Rhees has remarked, the idea that there are elementary propositions is not an arbitrary assumption. Wittgenstein was trying to solve the question of how language and thought can be related to reality. His basic intuition was that language pictures reality. If this is so, then among the sentences of language there must be some that show their sense immediately, which, of course, does not mean that their truth is self-evident. Wittgenstein had no criteria for identifying elementary propositions and could give no general account of their subject matter. But if his intuition was right, then there must be elementary propositions—that is, propositions that show their sense immediately and of which all other propositions are "truth-functions." If this were not so, no sentence could say anything or be understood (Rush Rhees, "The *Tractatus*: Seeds of Some Misunderstandings," pp. 218–219).

THEORY OF TRUTH-FUNCTIONS. A truth-function of a single proposition *p* is a proposition whose truth or falsity is uniquely determined by the truth or falsity of *p*; for example, *not-p* (*p* is false) is a truth-function of *p.* A truth-function of two propositions *p, q* is a proposition whose truth or falsity is uniquely determined by the truth or falsity of *p, q*; for instance, "*p, q* are both true" is a truth-function of *p, q.* According to the *Tractatus* (5) every genuine proposition is a truth-function of elementary propositions. (It is an interesting and difficult question whether this doctrine follows from the picture theory or, on the other hand, is even compatible with it.) If two nonelementary propositions *r* and *s* are truth-functions of some of the same elementary propositions, then *r* and *s* will be internally related: For instance, one of them may logically follow from the other, or they may be contradictories or contraries of each other. If we see the internal structure of two propositions, we know what logical relations hold between them. We do not need, in addition, a knowledge of logical principles. We can actually do without the formal principles of logic, "for in a suitable notation we can recognize the formal properties of propositions by mere inspection of the propositions themselves" (6.122).

Wittgenstein employed a technique (known as the method of truth tables) for making manifest the truth conditions of a proposition that is a truth-function of other propositions—that is, for exhibiting the relation between the truth or falsity of the latter and the truth or falsity of the former.

There are two limiting cases among the possible groupings of truth conditions of propositions. One case would be when a proposition was true for all truth possibilities of the elementary propositions; this proposition is called a tautology. The other would be when a proposition was false for all the truth possibilities; this proposition is called a contradiction. Although it is convenient to refer to tautologies and contradictions as "propositions," they are actually degenerate cases, not genuine propositions. They are not pictures of reality. They do not determine reality in any way. They have no truth conditions, since a tautology is *un*conditionally true and a contradiction *un*conditionally false. Wittgenstein compared a genuine proposition, a picture, to "a solid body that restricts the freedom of movement of others." In contrast a tautology (for example, "He is here, or he is not here") "leaves open to reality the whole of logical space." No restriction is imposed on anything. A contradiction (for example, "He is here, and he is not here") "fills the whole of logical space and leaves no point of it for reality" (4.461, 4.462, 4.463).

According to the *Tractatus* the so-called propositions of logic, logical truths, principles of logic are all tautologies. They express no thoughts. They say nothing. We could do without them. But they are not nonsense, for the fact that a certain combination of propositions yields a tautology reveals something about the structures of the constituent propositions. "That the propositions of logic are tautologies *shows* the formal—logical—properties of language, of the world" (6.12).

NECESSITY. Wittgenstein's picture theory and his explanation of logical truth lead to an interesting doctrine of necessity and also to a denial of any knowledge of the future. Genuine propositions say only how things are, not how things must be. The only necessity there can be is embodied in tautologies (and the equations of mathematics). Neither tautologies nor equations say anything about the world. Therefore, there is no necessity in the world. "Outside of logic everything is accidental" (6.3). One proposition can be inferred from another proposition only if there is an internal, structural connection between them. The existence of one state of affairs cannot be inferred from the existence of another, entirely different, state of affairs (5.135). But that is what an inference to a future state of affairs would have to be. Thus Wittgenstein declared that we do not know whether the sun will rise tomorrow (6.36311).

WILL AND ACTION. If we conceive of an act of will (a volition) as one occurrence and the transpiring of what is willed as an entirely different occurrence, it follows from the foregoing doctrines that there can be, at most, a merely accidental correlation between one's will and what happens in the world. I cannot make anything happen—not even a movement of my body. "The world is independent of my will" (6.373). In his notes Wittgenstein gave this idea dramatic expression: "I cannot bend the happenings of the world to my will: I am completely powerless" (*Notebooks,* p. 73).

ETHICS. According to the picture theory a proposition and its negation are both possible; which one is true is accidental. Wittgenstein drew the conclusion that there can be no propositions of ethics. His thought here was that if anything has value, this fact cannot be accidental: the thing must have that value. But everything in the world is accidental. Therefore there is no value in the world. "In the world everything is as it is, and everything happens as it does happen: *in* it no value exists—and if it did, it would have no value" (*Tractatus,* 6.41).

This view is an absolute denial not of the existence of value but of its existence in the world. Propositions can state only what is in the world. What belongs to ethics cannot be stated; it is "transcendental" (6.421). The world, and what is in the world, is neither good nor evil. Good and evil exist only in relation to the subject (the ego). But this "subject" to which Wittgenstein referred is also "transcendental." It is not in the world but is a "limit" of the world (5.5632).

THE MYSTICAL. In the view of the *Tractatus* there are a variety of things that cannot be stated: the form of representation of propositions, the existence of the simple objects that constitute the substance of the world, the existence of a metaphysical subject, of good and evil—these things are all unsayable. Wittgenstein seems to have believed that we have thoughts on these matters only when we view the world as a limited whole. This latter experience is what he called "the mystical" (6.45).

Although one cannot say anything on these metaphysical topics included in the mystical, this is not because they are absurd but because they lie beyond the reach of language. "Unsayable things do indeed exist" (*Es gibt allerdings Unaussprechliches*: 6.522). This itself is something unsayable. It is one of those sentences of his own of which Wittgenstein declared that although they can produce philosophical insight, they are actually nonsensical and eventually must be "thrown away" (6.54). The final proposition of the book ("Whereof one cannot speak, thereof one must be silent") is not the truism one might take it to be, for it means that there is a realm about which one can say nothing.

THE *TRACTATUS* AND LOGICAL POSITIVISM. The *Tractatus* exerted a considerable influence on the so-called Vienna circle of logical positivism. Moritz Schlick, the leader of this movement, declared that the *Tractatus* had brought modern philosophy to a "decisive turning point." It is true that there is some agreement between the predominant views of the Vienna circle and the positions of the *Tractatus*—for example, that all genuine propositions are truth-functions of elementary propositions, that logical truths are tautologies and say nothing, and that philosophy can contain no body of doctrine but is an activity of clarifying thoughts.

But there are fundamental differences. The Vienna circle did not adopt the picture theory of propositions, which is the central idea of the *Tractatus.* A conspicuous doctrine of the circle was that all genuine propositions are reducible to propositions that report "direct perception" or what is "immediately given in experience." This doctrine is not found in the *Tractatus.* A corollary to it is the famous positivist thesis "The meaning of a statement is its method of verification." But the topic of verification is not even brought into the *Tractatus.* The only proposition there that seems to resemble this thesis is the following: "To understand a proposition means to know what is the case if it is true" (4.024). Even here nothing is explicitly said about verification, and a comment immediately following this remark shows that Wittgenstein was not thinking about verification. A proposition, he said, "is understood by anyone who understands its constituents." That is to say, if you understand the words in a sentence, you thereby understand the sentence. There is no mention of a requirement that you must know how to verify what it says.

As previously noted, Wittgenstein was tempted by the suggestion that "points in the visual field" are examples of the simples out of which all meaning is composed. But the final view of the *Tractatus* is that the simples are fixed, immutable things, which exist "independently of what is the case." If so, they cannot be described by propositions and cannot be given in experience. The *Tractatus* does not contain, therefore, an empiricist theory of meaning. What it holds is that to understand any sentence one must know the references of the names that compose it; that is all. When you understand a sentence you know how reality is constituted if the sentence is true, regardless of whether you know how to verify what it says. The picture theory is not a verification theory of meaning. It is ironical that the role of verification in meaning and understanding receives much attention in Wittgenstein's later philosophy, which obviously is not positivistic, but none at all in the reputedly positivistic *Tractatus.*

Logical positivism and the author of the *Tractatus* were both opposed to metaphysics, but in different ways. For positivism there is nothing at all behind metaphysical propositions except possibly their authors' emotions. "Metaphysicians are musicians without musical ability," said Rudolf Carnap. In the view of the *Tractatus* one may gain insights into the presuppositions and limits of language, thought, and reality. These metaphysical insights cannot be stated in language, but if they could be, they would be true insights and not mere muddles or expressions of feeling.

The foregoing sketch of the *Tractatus* has omitted many of its important topics. Wittgenstein wrote in his notes, "My work has extended from the foundations of logic to the nature of the world." In his preface to the *Tractatus* he expressed the opinion that he had obtained the final solution of the problems treated in the book, but he added that one value of his work is that "it shows how little is achieved when these problems are solved."

THE "NEW" PHILOSOPHY

In 1929, Wittgenstein returned to Cambridge, after an absence of more than fifteen years, to resume philosophical research and to lecture. From then until his death he did a huge amount of writing. Among the first works of this period were two large typescript volumes. One, which was composed in the period 1929–1930, has been published under the title *Philosophische Bemerkungen.* The other is a systematic work of nearly 800 typewritten pages written between 1930 and 1932. In both of these volumes Wittgenstein reexamined the problems of the

Tractatus and revised what he had written there. This led him to questions he had not previously considered. Perhaps it can be said that he found that the logical investigations of the *Tractatus* and its supreme problem of the relation of language to reality had drawn him more and more into questions in the philosophy of psychology. These volumes seem to show that the change from the *Tractatus* to the *Philosophical Investigations* was an intensive but continuous development rather than a sudden revolution.

In 1933–1934, Wittgenstein dictated to his students a set of notes that came to be called the *Blue Book,* and in 1934–1935 he dictated another set, later known as the *Brown Book.* (Although Wittgenstein always wrote in German, the *Blue Book* and the *Brown Book* were dictated in English.) Both circulated widely in typescript, and Wittgenstein's new ideas began to create a stir. The *Blue Book* is clear and lively and is perhaps the beginner's best introduction to Wittgenstein. Nevertheless, it is a comparatively superficial work; Wittgenstein never regarded it as more than a set of class notes. The *Brown Book,* on the other hand, he regarded for a short time as a draft of something that might be published. He worked at a revision but gave it up in 1936, when he began to write the *Philosophical Investigations.* Wittgenstein refrained from publishing the *Investigations* during his lifetime, but his explicit wish was that it be published posthumously, a wish that he probably did not have with respect to any of the rest of the voluminous work he produced between 1929 and 1951.

The *Philosophical Investigations* was published in 1953 in two parts. Part I was written in the period 1936–1945 and Part II between 1947 and 1949. Concurrently with the *Investigations,* Wittgenstein did other writing, which was closely related to the topics of the *Investigations* or even overlapped it. From the years 1937 to 1944 there are extensive manuscripts on the philosophy of logic and mathematics. *Remarks on the Foundations of Mathematics,* published in 1956, consists of selections, made by the editors, from this material. A quantity of writing in the form of loose notes, probably from the years 1947 to 1949, is of the same subject matter and quality as the latter part of Part I of the *Investigations.* Wittgenstein's last manuscript notebooks, from the years 1949 to 1951, treating questions about belief, doubt, knowledge, and certainty, also contain much material that should eventually be published.

PHILOSOPHICAL INVESTIGATIONS

Wittgenstein believed that the *Investigations* could be better understood if one saw it against the background of the *Tractatus.* A considerable part of the *Investigations* is an attack, either explicit or implicit, on the earlier work. This development is probably unique in the history of philosophy—a thinker producing, at different periods of his life, two highly original systems of thought, each system the result of many years of intensive labors, each expressed in an elegant and powerful style, each greatly influencing contemporary philosophy, and the second being a criticism and rejection of the first.

Apparently it is possible for a serious student of Wittgenstein to form the impression that "the *Investigations* basically contains an application of the main ideas of the *Tractatus* to several concrete problems, the only difference being the use of language-games instead of the language of the natural sciences which formed the theoretical background of the *Tractatus.*" This view is thoroughly mistaken, as will be seen.

THE WHOLE OF LANGUAGE. It is held in the *Tractatus* that any proposition presupposes the whole of language. "If objects are given, then at the same time we are given *all* objects. If elementary propositions are given, then at the same time *all* elementary propositions are given" (5.524). "If all objects are given, then at the same time all *possible* states of affairs are also given" (2.0124). An elementary proposition is a combination of names, and in order to understand the proposition one must in some sense "know" the objects for which the names stand. In understanding any proposition at all one must know some objects, and therefore, as stated, one must know all objects and all possibilities. Any proposition whatsoever carries with it the whole of "logical space." This view is connected with the idea that there is an essence of propositions. The essence of propositions is "the essence of all description, and thus the essence of the world" (5.4711). The essence of propositions is the same as "the universal form of proposition" (*Die allgemeine Satzform*). That there is a universal form of proposition is proved by the fact that all possibilities—i.e., all forms of proposition—"must be *foreseeable*" (*Notebooks,* p. 89; *Tractatus,* 4.5).

The *Investigations* emphatically rejects the idea that each proposition carries with it the whole of language. A sentence does presuppose a "language game," but a language game will be only a small segment of the whole of language. An example of a language game is the following, which appears at the beginning of the *Investigations* (Sec. 2): There are a builder and his helper. The building materials are blocks, pillars, slabs, and beams. The two men have a language consisting of the words *block, pillar, slab, beam.* The builder calls out one of the words and the helper brings the building material that he has learned to bring at that call. Wittgenstein called the words and the actions with which they are joined a language game (*Sprachspiel*). He said that it is complete in itself and could even be conceived to be the entire language of a tribe. If we think it is incomplete we are only comparing it with our more complex language. In the *Brown Book* there is the analogy of someone's describing chess without mentioning pawns. As a description of chess it is incomplete, yet we can also say that it is a complete description of a simpler game (*Blue and Brown Books,* p. 77). This simpler game does not presuppose chess, nor does the part played, for example, by the word *block* in the game of Sec. 2 imply its use in descriptions or questions.

According to the *Tractatus* every form of proposition can be anticipated because a new form of proposition would represent a new combination of simple objects in logical space. It would be like grouping the pieces on a chessboard in a new way. It would be a different arrangement of what you already have. But in Wittgenstein's later philosophy a new language game would embody a new "form of life," and this would not merely be a rearrangement of what was there before. Suppose the people of a certain tribe use language to describe events that are occurring or have occurred (such as men walking, running, or fighting, or the weather), or that they believe have occurred, but they do not have any imaginative use of language. They do not lie, pretend, make supposals, or engage in any imaginative play. Nor does any behavior of pretending occur: the children do not ever, for example, walk on all fours and growl as if they were lions. These people would not understand kidding. If one of us said to them something obviously false and then laughed, they would not know how to take it. (We should remember that among ourselves we differ greatly in our responsiveness to joking and pretense.) What these people lack is not words but the behavior and reactions that enter into the language games of imagination. Are they capable of foreseeing a use of language to convey a play of imagination? They do not even understand it when they encounter it. A new use of language embedded in a new form of life could not be anticipated, any more than could the rise of nonobjective painting.

THE ESSENCE OF LANGUAGE. The *Tractatus* assumes that there is a universal form of language, just as it assumes (6.022) that there is a universal form of number—that which is common to all numbers. The *Investigations* rejects this assumption. There is nothing common to the various forms of language that makes them language. There is not something common to all language games, just as there is not something common to all games. We are asked to consider the various kinds of games there are (for example, board games, card games, ball games) and the variety within each kind. If we pick out a feature common to two games we shall find that it is absent from some other place in the spectrum of games. Not all games are amusing, not all involve winning or losing, not all require competition between players, and so on. What makes all of them games, what gives unity to those activities, is not some feature present in all games but a multitude of relationships "overlapping and criss-crossing." Wittgenstein employed the analogy of a family resemblance. One can often see a striking resemblance between several generations of the same family. Studying them at close hand one may find that there is no feature common to all of the family. The eyes or the build or the temperament are not always the same. The family resemblance is due to many features that "overlap and criss-cross." The unity of games is like a family resemblance. This is also the case with sentences, descriptions, and numbers.

> Why do we call something a "number": Well, perhaps because it has a—direct—relationship with several things that have hitherto been called number; and this can be said to give it an indirect relationship to other things we call the same name. And we extend our concept of number as in spinning a thread we twist fibre on fibre. And the strength of the thread does not reside in the fact that some one fibre runs through its whole length, but in the overlapping of the fibres. (Sec. 67)

One of the remarkable features of the *Investigations* is the detail and ingenuity of Wittgenstein's examination of some sample concepts (*reading, deriving, being guided*: Secs. 156–178) in order to bring out the variety of cases that fall under them and to prove that they are not united by an essence. If these concepts do not have an essential nature, then neither do the concepts of *description, proposition,* and *language.* The *Tractatus* was wrong in a most fundamental assumption.

ABSOLUTE SIMPLES. The *Tractatus* held that the ultimate elements of language are names that designate simple objects. In the *Investigations* it is argued that the words *simple* and *complex* have no absolute meaning. It has to be laid down, within a particular language game, what is to be taken as simple and what composite. For example, is one's visual image of a tree simple or composite? The question makes no sense until we make some such stipulation as that if one sees merely the trunk, it is simple, but if one sees trunk and branches, it is composite.

> But isn't a chess board, for instance, obviously, and absolutely composite?——You are probably thinking of the composition out of thirty-two white and thirty-two black squares. But could we not also say, for instance, that it was composed of the colours black and white and the schema of squares? And if there are quite different ways of looking at it, do you still want to say that the chessboard is absolutely "composite"? ... Is the colour of a square on a chessboard simple, or does it consist of pure white and pure yellow? And is white simple, or does it consist of the colours of the rainbow?——Is this length of 2 cm. simple, or does it consist of two parts, each 1 cm. long? But why not of one bit 3 cm. long, and one bit 1 cm. long measured in the opposite direction? (Sec. 47)

By such examples Wittgenstein tried to show that the ideas of "simple" and "complex" are necessarily relative to a language game. The notion of a simplicity that is not relative but absolute, because all of language is based on it, is a philosophical "super-concept." We have an image but we do not know how to apply it: we do not know what would be an example of an absolute simple.

In the *Tractatus* the existence of simple objects was conceived as following from the requirement that the sense of sentences be definite. In the *Investigations* this requirement is regarded as another philosophical illusion. We have imagined an "ideal" of language that will not satisfy actual needs. A sharp boundary has not been drawn between, for example, games and activities that are not games. But why should there be one in general? Precision and exactness are relative to some particular purpose. The guests are to arrive exactly at one o'clock, but this notion of exactness would not employ the instruments and measurements of an observatory. "No *single* ideal of exactness has been laid down; we do not know what we should be supposed to imagine under this head" (Sec. 88). Losing sight of the fact that there are different standards of exactness for different purposes, we have supposed that there is a certain state of complete exactness underneath the surface of our everyday speech and that logical analysis can bring it to light. We have supposed, therefore, that a proposition would have one and only one complete analysis.

In searching for the ideal of perfect exactness we become dissatisfied with ordinary words and sentences. We do not find in actual language the pure and clear-cut structure that we desire. The more closely we examine actual language, the sharper becomes the conflict between it and our philosophical ideal. The latter now begins to seem empty. We do not even understand how it could be realized in actual language. We have been bewitched by a picture. Instead of trying to perceive in our language a design too fine to grasp, we need to see more clearly what is really there. We should abandon preconceived ideas and hypotheses and turn to description, the purpose of which will be to remove our philosophical perplexities. The substitution of description for analysis, and the new conception that nothing is hidden, is a major change from the *Tractatus.*

MEANING AS USE. If the picture theory is the central feature of the *Tractatus,* it is important to see how Wittgenstein's new thinking judged that theory. Surprisingly, there is not much explicit discussion of it, and the remarks that do occur are usually enigmatic. But if we take a long view of the new philosophy, there can be no question that it rejects the picture theory. In the later work as well as the earlier, Wittgenstein was concerned with the question, How can a sentence say something; how can language represent reality? The first sentence of the *Blue Book* is "What is the meaning of a word?" and it might equally well have been "What is the meaning of a sentence?" Both philosophical systems are centered on the same question, but the answer given in the second is entirely different. Instead of holding that a sentence has meaning or sense because it is a picture, the *Investigations* says that the meaning of a sentence is its "use" (*Gebrauch*) or "employment" (*Verwendung*) or "application" (*Anwendung*).

Some readers of Wittgenstein have doubted that he spoke of the use of a sentence, and others have thought that in any case it is wrong to speak this way. There is no question on the first point. Wittgenstein spoke of the "use" of a sentence in many passages. For example: "But doesn't the fact that sentences have the same sense consist in their having the same *use*?" (*Investigations,* Sec. 20); there are "countless different kinds of use of what we call 'symbols,' 'words,' 'sentences'" (Sec. 23).

The other objection may be important. Some philosophers want to say that a sentence cannot have a use. Words have a use; we learn the use of words, not of sentences. We understand sentences without having their sense explained to us, because we understand the use of the words that compose them.

What is espoused here is really the ground of the picture theory of the *Tractatus* (cf. *Tractatus,* 4.021, 4.026, 4.027). In the *Investigations* there is more than one objection to the above argument. Wittgenstein denied that we always understand a sentence, even if it is a grammatically correct sentence whose words we do understand. If someone says, for example, that the sentence "This is here" (saying which, he points to an object in front of him) makes sense to him, "then he should ask himself in what special circumstances this sentence is actually used. There it does make sense" (Sec. 117). "A philosopher says that he understands the sentence 'I am here,' that he means something by it, thinks something—even when he doesn't think at all how, on what occasions, this sentence is used" (Sec. 514). Wittgenstein was saying that these sentences have sense only in special circumstances; in other circumstances we do not understand them—that is, we do not know what to do with them.

The view of the *Tractatus* is entirely different. An elementary sentence is a combination of names, and if we know what the names refer to, then we understand the sentence, for it shows its sense. "Circumstances" have nothing to do with it. The *Investigations* regards this view as absurd. What does the sentence "I am here" show? Certainly it does not show its use. What can it mean to say that it shows its sense? A significant sentence is a tool with which a certain job is done. By looking at a sentence you cannot always tell whether it is a tool and, if it is, what job it is used for. The *Investigations* denies the claim that was the basis of the picture theory, namely that "we understand the sense of a propositional sign without its having been explained to us" (*Tractatus,* 4.02).

In holding that (in many cases) the meaning of an expression is its use, Wittgenstein was not declaring that the words *meaning* and *use* are general synonyms. By the "use" of an expression he meant the special circumstances, the "surroundings," in which it is spoken or written. The use of an expression is the language game in which it plays a part. Some readers have arrived at the mistaken idea that by the "use" of an expression Wittgenstein meant its ordinary or its correct use: They have thought that he was an "ordinary-language philosopher." But Wittgenstein studied any use of language, real or imaginary, that may illuminate a philosophical problem. Often he invented language games that corresponded to no actual use of language (see, for example, *Blue and Brown Books,* pp. 103–104, 110). The language games are "*objects of comparison* which are meant to throw light on the facts of our language by way not only of similarities, but also of dissimilarities" (*Investigations,* Sec. 130).

The *Tractatus* holds that language is ultimately composed of names, that the meaning of a name is a simple object, and that the sense of a sentence arises from the names that compose it. One name stands for one thing, another for another thing, and the combination pictures a state of affairs (4.0311). Thus, naming is prior to the sense of sentences (although it is also said that a name has meaning only in a sentence: 3.3). A sentence says something because it is composed of names that stand for things. In the *Investigations* two objections are made against this notion of the priority of names. First, the meaning of a word is never the thing, if there is one, that corresponds to the word (Sec. 40). Second, before one can find out what a name stands for one must already have mastered the language game to which the name belongs. In order to learn the name of a color, a direction, a sensation, one must have some grasp of the activities of placing colors in an order, of reading a map, of responding to the words, gestures, and behavior that are expressions of sensation. Merely pointing at something and saying a word achieves nothing. The kind of use the word will have, the special circumstances in which it will be said, must be understood before it can even be a name.

One could say that the *Tractatus* conceives of a significant sentence as having the nature of a mechanism. If the parts fit, then the whole thing works: you have a picture of reality. If the parts do not fit, they are like cogwheels that do not mesh. There is, as it were, a clash of meanings. But in the *Investigations* we read: "When a sentence is called senseless, it is not as it were its sense that is senseless" (Sec. 500). If someone said to us, for example, "My head is asleep," we should be perplexed. It would be no help if he said: "You know what it is for an arm or a leg to be asleep. I have the same thing, except that it is my head." Here we do not know what the "same" is. It is not that we see that the meaning of "head" is incompatible with the meaning of "asleep." We do not perceive a clash of meanings. But we do not know what behavior and circumstances go with this sentence. It is not that we see that it cannot have a use (because the words do not fit together). The fact is that it does not have a use: we do not know in what circumstances one should say it. "Look at the sentence as an instrument, and at its sense as its employment!" (Sec. 421). Instead of the fundamental notion being the right combination of words and the sense of the sentence being explained in terms of it, it is the other way around: whether the sentence has an "employment" (*Verwendung*) is what is fundamental.

This would be our only criterion for whether there is a sense-making combination of parts.

One additional criticism of the picture theory will be noted. Suppose that a sentence were a picture. There would still be a question of how we should apply the picture. If someone showed you a drawing of a cube and told you to bring him one of those things, you might in good faith bring him a triangular prism instead of a cube. More than one way of taking the drawing was possible. It suggests a cube, but it is possible to interpret the drawing differently. A picture represents an old man walking up a steep path leaning on a stick. But could it not also represent him as sliding down the hill in that position? For us it is more natural to take it in the first way, but the explanation of this does not lie in anything intrinsic to the picture. A picture of a green leaf might be understood to be a representation of the color green, or of a specific shade of green, or of leaf shape in general, or of a particular shape of leaf, or of foliage in general, and so on. How a picture is used will determine what it is a picture of. It cannot, therefore, be a fundamental explanation of the sense of sentences to say that they are pictures. Wittgenstein hinted that the picture theory is plausible because we tend to think of portraits that hang on our walls and are, as it were, "idle." If we consider instead an engineer's machine drawing or an elevation with measurements, then the activity of using the picture will be seen to be the important thing (Sec. 291).

LOGICAL COMPULSION. Our discussion may suggest the following view: How a word, sentence, or picture is interpreted determines what use is made of it. How a man responds to an order, for example, depends on how he understands it, and whether the one who gave the order will be satisfied with that response will depend on what he meant by it. If someone understands the algebraic formula determining a numerical series, then he will know what numbers should occur at various places in the expansion of the series. What a person deduces from a proposition will depend entirely on his understanding of the proposition. Wittgenstein once wrote (in a pre-*Tractatus* notebook): "What propositions follow from a proposition must be completely settled before that proposition can have a sense" (*Notebooks,* p. 64). By virtue of grasping the meaning or sense of an expression we know how to employ it: we know when to say it and what action it calls for. Instead of meaning being identical with use, it comes before use, and use is based on it. When you hear a sentence and understand it or give an order and mean it, the action required in responding to the sentence or obeying the order is already, in a queer sense, taken in your mind. In your act of meaning or understanding, "your mind as it were flew ahead and took all the steps" before they were taken physically (*Investigations,* Sec. 188). In taking, or accepting, those physical steps, you would be ratifying what has already transpired in your mind. To do differently would be inconsistent with the previous mental act. Consistency, rationality, requires you to take these steps or draw these conclusions. Understanding carries compulsion with it.

This idea of "logical compulsion" is vigorously attacked in the *Investigations* and in Wittgenstein's writings on the foundations of mathematics. Was Wittgenstein rejecting deductive reasoning and logical necessity? No. He was rejecting this picture of logical necessity, namely that when I have understood a proposition and there is a question of what follows from it, I have to deduce such-and-such consequences because it was already settled in my understanding of the proposition that it would have those consequences. Wittgenstein's criticism of this imagery creates a continuity between his philosophy of psychology and his philosophy of logic. A part of his criticism could be put as follows: Suppose that two people, *A* and *B,* have received the same instruction in elementary arithmetic. They have been given the same rules and illustrations and have worked through the same examples. Later, when they are required to perform some arithmetical operation, *A* does it right and *B* wrong, although *B* thinks he has done it correctly. We shall say that *A* understood the problem and *B* did not. What does this come to? It could have been that the sole difference between them was that *A* wrote down correct numbers and *B* incorrect ones. If this fact is our criterion of a difference of understanding, then it is wrongheaded to postulate a difference of understanding to explain the fact that *A* and *B* wrote down different answers.

The inclination to insert an act or state of understanding as an intermediary between, for example, hearing an order and executing it is an example of what is called in the *Brown Book* (*Blue and Brown Books,* p. 143) "a general disease of thinking." It consists in always looking for (and "finding") mental states and acts as the sources of our actions. Other examples of this inclination are thinking that one must know where one's pain is before one can point to the place, thinking that we call various shades of red by the name "red" because we see something in common in all of them, thinking that we speak of "looking in our memory for a word" and of "looking in the park for a friend" because we have noticed a similarity between the two cases.

The assumption of mental states to explain our actions comes from a "one-sided diet." If we let our view range over the family of cases of "differences of understanding," we shall discover some in which the only difference between two people who understood a certain proposition differently consists in their having drawn different conclusions from it.

Must we believe, then, that our understanding does not reach beyond the particular training we received and the examples we studied? No. There is a good sense in which it reaches beyond, for we do go on to apply rules in new cases in what we agree is the same way we were taught. Does this agreement have to be explained by the fact that our understanding has penetrated to the essence of the examples? No. This agreement is one of the "extremely general facts of nature" (*Investigations,* pp. 56, 230) that underlie our concepts. We do handle new cases in the same way. If this strikes us as mysterious, it is a symptom of our confusion. We are trying to imagine that the future steps are taken in the mind, "in a queer sense," before they are taken in reality—as if the mind were a machine that already contained its future movements (*Investigations,* Secs. 193–195).

Wittgenstein was saying that our understanding of a rule is not a state that forces us to apply the rule in a particular way. Someone who has received the ordinary instruction in arithmetic or chess and has applied it normally in the past could go on in the future in a different way but still be a rational person. Perhaps he could even give a reasonable defense of his divergence.

If this is true, it makes it seem that there are no rules, for a rule forbids some things and requires others. It appears that anything goes, anything can be justified. But then understanding, meaning, language itself all crumble away because they imply rules.

Wittgenstein was not denying, however, that there are rules and that we follow them. He held that the way a rule is applied in particular cases determines its meaning. A rule, as it is formulated in a sentence, "hangs in the air" (*Investigations,* Sec. 198). What puts it on the ground, gives it content, is what we say and do in actual cases. And on this there is overwhelming agreement: we nearly always say and do the same. It is this agreement that determines whether a particular action is in accordance with a rule. Rather than to say that we agree because we follow rules, it is more perceptive to say that our agreement fixes the meaning of the rules, defines their content. In a sense the content of the rules grows as our practice grows. Instead of thinking of humankind as coerced by the rules of logic and mathematics, we should consider that human practice establishes what the rules are.

PRIVATE RULES. The idea that the content of a rule can be fixed only by a practice provides a transition to one of the most subtle topics of the *Investigations,* namely the treatment of "private language." The conception that a significant sentence is a picture was replaced in Wittgenstein's thought by the conception that the sense of a sentence is determined by the circumstances in which it is uttered. Swinging a stick is a strike and pushing a piece of wood is a move—in the circumstances of games. Likewise, saying some words is making a decision—in certain circumstances. In one set of circumstances saying a particular sentence would be asserting something; in other circumstances saying those same words would be asking a question; in still others it would be repeating what someone had said.

This is a difficult conception to grasp. We feel a strong inclination to say that the only thing that determines the sense of what someone says is what goes on in his mind as he says it. As John Locke put it, "Words, in their primary or immediate signification, stand for nothing but *the ideas in the mind of him that uses them.*" Whether some words you uttered expressed a question or an assertion is solely a matter of whether there was a question or an assertion in your mind. What the occasion was, what happened before and after, what persons were present—those circumstances are irrelevant to the sense of your words. The only "circumstance" that matters is the mental occurrence at the time of utterance.

Wittgenstein fought hard and resourcefully against this objection. One technique he used was to describe different cases of deciding, asserting, intending, expecting, and so on. The purpose of this was to show that when one utters some words that express, for instance, a decision, one cannot pick out anything that occurred (for example, a thought, an image, some spoken words, a feeling) such that one wants to call that the act of deciding.

This technique, although powerful, may provoke the response that the only thing proved is the intangibility, the indescribability, of the mental phenomenon in question. William James remarked about the intention of saying a thing before one has said it: "It is an entirely definite intention, distinct from all other intentions, an absolutely distinct state of consciousness, therefore; and yet how much of it consists of definite sensorial images, either of words or of things? Hardly anything!" This intention has "a nature of its own of the most positive sort, and yet what can we say about it without using words that belong to the later mental facts that replace it? The intention *to-say-so-and-so* is the only name it can receive" (*Principles of Psychology,* New York, 1890, Vol. I, p. 253). Likewise, the decision to stay an hour longer cannot be expressed in any other words than those, yet it is a quite definite mental occurrence; one knows it is there!

Wittgenstein opposed this conception not with further description but with an argument. It is the following: If a decision or expectation or sensation were a state or event that was logically independent of circumstances, then no one, not even the subject of the supposed event, could ever determine that it had occurred. First, how would one learn what, for example, deciding is? Since circumstances are supposed to be irrelevant, one could not learn it by observing other people. Apparently one would have to learn what deciding is from one's own case. But as Wittgenstein remarked: "If I know it only from my own case, then I know only what *I* call that, not what anyone else does" (*Investigations,* Sec. 347). Thus it would be unverifiable whether two people refer to the same phenomenon by the word *deciding.* But worse is to come. One could not even take comfort in the thought "At least I know what *I* call 'deciding.'" You might believe that you have always called the same thing by that name. Yet nothing could determine that this belief was right or wrong. Perhaps the private object constantly changes but you do not notice the change because your memory constantly deceives you (*Investigations,* p. 207)! The idea that you might have a language with logically private rules—that is, rules that only you could understand because only you could know to what the words refer—is a self-contradictory idea. Following a rule implies doing the same, and what "the same" is can only be defined by a practice in which more than one person participates.

Wittgenstein's rejection of the intrinsically private, inner object is a consequence of his new conception of meaning. Language requires rules, and following a rule implies a customary way of doing something. It could not be that only once in the history of humankind was a rule followed (Sec. 199). An expression has a meaning only if there is a regular, a uniform, connection between saying the expression and certain circumstances. When we call something measuring, for example, a part of the uniformity we require is a constancy in the results of measurement (Sec. 242). A person can be guided by a signpost only if there is a regular way of responding to signposts. The meaning of an expression is its use—that is to say, the language game in which it occurs—that is to say, the uniform relation of the expression to certain circumstances. Wittgenstein made explicit the connection between this view of the nature of meaning and his attack on "private" mental contents when he said that following a rule is a practice and therefore one cannot follow a rule "privately" (Sec. 202).

See also Brouwer, Luitzen Egbertus Jan; Existence; James, William; Keynes, John Maynard; Language; Logical Positivism; Logic, History of; Mathematics, Foundations of; Moore, George Edward; Number; Ostwald, Wilhelm; Proper Names and Descriptions; Propositions; Ramsey, Frank Plumpton; Rilke, Rainer Maria (René); Russell, Bertrand Arthur William; Schlick, Moritz; Thinking; Tolstoy, Lev (Leo) Nikolaevich; Volition; Wright, Georg Henrik von.

Bibliography

WORKS BY WITTGENSTEIN

Tractatus Logico-Philosophicus. London: Routledge, 1922. Contains the German text of *Logisch-Philosophische Abhandlung,* with English translation on facing pages, and an introduction by Bertrand Russell. Republished with a new translation by D. F. Pears and B. F. McGuinness. London: Routledge and Paul, 1961.

"Some Remarks on Logical Form." *PAS* supp. 9 (1929): 162–171.

Philosophical Investigations. Edited by G. E. M. Anscombe, Rush Rhees, and G. H. von Wright, translated by G. E. M. Anscombe. Oxford: Blackwell, 1953. Contains German text of *Philosophische Untersuchungen,* with English translation on facing pages.

Remarks on the Foundations of Mathematics. Edited by G. E. M. Anscombe, Rush Rhees, and G. H. von Wright, translated by G. E. M. Anscombe. Oxford: Blackwell, 1956. Parallel German and English texts.

The Blue and Brown Books: Preliminary Studies for the Philosophical Investigations. Oxford: Blackwell, 1958. With a preface by Rush Rhees.

Notebooks 1914–1916. Edited by G. E. M. Anscombe and G. H. von Wright, translated by G. E. M. Anscombe. Oxford: Blackwell, 1961. Parallel German and English texts.

Philosophische Bemerkungen. Frankfurt, 1964.

"A Lecture on Ethics." *Philosophical Review* 74 (1965). A paper delivered at Cambridge in 1929 or 1930.

WORKS ON WITTGENSTEIN

Biography

Gasking, D. A. T., and A. C. Jackson. "Ludwig Wittgenstein," memorial notice. *Australasian Journal of Philosophy* 29 (1951).

Malcolm, Norman. *Ludwig Wittgenstein: A Memoir.* London: Oxford University Press, 1958.

Russell, Bertrand. "Ludwig Wittgenstein," memorial notice. *Mind* 60 (1951).

Ryle, Gilbert. "Ludwig Wittgenstein," memorial notice. *Analysis* 12 (1951).

Von Wright, G. H. "Ludwig Wittgenstein: A Biographical Sketch," Malcolm, op. cit.

Wisdom, John. "Ludwig Wittgenstein, 1934–1937." *Mind* 61 (1952).

Tractatus

Anscombe, G. E. M. *An Introduction to Wittgenstein's Tractatus.* London: Hutchinson University Library, 1959.

Black, Max. *A Companion to Wittgenstein's Tractatus.* Ithaca, NY: Cornell University Press, 1964.

Colombo, G. C. M. Critical introduction and notes to the Italian translation of the *Tractatus.* Milan and Rome, 1954.

Daitz, E. "The Picture Theory of Meaning." In *Essays in Conceptual Analysis,* edited by Antony Flew. London: Macmillan, 1956.

Griffin, James. *Wittgenstein's Logical Atomism.* Oxford: Clarendon Press, 1964.

Hartnack, Justus. *Wittgenstein og den moderne Filosofi.* Copenhagen, 1960. Translated into German as *Wittgenstein und die moderne Philosophie.* Stuttgart, 1962.

Hintikka, Jaakko. "On Wittgenstein's Solipsism." *Mind* 67 (1958).

Keyt, David. "A New Interpretation of the *Tractatus* Examined." *Philosophical Review* 74 (1965).

Keyt, David. "Wittgenstein's Notion of an Object." *Philosophical Quarterly* 13 (1963).

Maslow, Alexander. *A Study in Wittgenstein's Tractatus.* Berkeley: University of California Press, 1961.

Pitcher, George. *The Philosophy of Wittgenstein.* Englewood Cliffs, NJ: Prentice-Hall, 1964.

Ramsey, F. P. Critical notice of the *Tractatus.* In *The Foundations of Mathematics,* edited by R. F. Braithwaite. London: K. Paul, Trench, Trubner, 1931.

Rhees, Rush. "Miss Anscombe on the *Tractatus.*" *Philosophical Quarterly* 10 (1960).

Rhees, Rush. "The *Tractatus*: Seeds of Some Misunderstandings." *Philosophical Review* 72 (1963).

Russell, Bertrand. "The Philosophy of Logical Atomism." In *Logic and Knowledge,* edited by R. C. Marsh, London: Allen and Unwin, 1956.

Schlick, Moritz. "The Turning Point in Philosophy." In *Logical Positivism,* edited by A. J. Ayer. Glencoe, IL: Free Press, 1959.

Stenius, Eric. *Wittgenstein's Tractatus.* Ithaca, NY: Cornell University Press, 1960.

Wienpahl, Paul D. "Wittgenstein and the Naming Relation." *Inquiry* 7 (1964).

Blue and Brown Books, Investigations, Remarks on the Foundations of Mathematics

Albritton, Rogers. "On Wittgenstein's Use of the Term 'Criterion.'" *Journal of Philosophy* 56 (22) (1959).

Ayer, A. J. "Privacy." *Proceedings of the British Academy* 45 (1959).

Ayer, A. J., and Rush Rhees. "Can There Be a Private Language?" PAS supp. 28 (1954). Symposium.

Bambrough, Renford. "Universals and Family Resemblances." *PAS* 61 (1960–1961).

Bouwsma, O. K. "The Blue Book." *Journal of Philosophy* 58 (6) (1961).

Buck, R. C. "Non-other Minds." In *Analytical Philosophy,* edited by R. J. Butler. Oxford: Blackwell, 1962.

Carney, J. D. "Private Language: The Logic of Wittgenstein's Argument." *Mind* 69 (1960).

Cavell, Stanley. "The Availability of Wittgenstein's Later Philosophy." *Philosophical Review* 71 (1962).

Chihara, C. S. "Mathematical Discovery and Concept Formation." *Philosophical Review* 72 (1963).

Chihara, C. S. "Wittgenstein and Logical Compulsion." *Analysis* 21 (1961).

Cook, J. W. "Wittgenstein on Privacy." *Philosophical Review* 74 (1965).

Cowan, J. L. "Wittgenstein's Philosophy of Logic." *Philosophical Review* 70 (1961).

Dummett, Michael. "Wittgenstein's Philosophy of Mathematics." *Philosophical Review* 68 (1959).

Feyerabend, Paul K. "Wittgenstein's *Philosophical Investigations.*" *Philosophical Review* 64 (1955).

Fodor, J. A., and J. J. Katz. "The Availability of What We Say." *Philosophical Review* 72 (1963).

Gasking, D. A. T. "Avowals." In *Analytical Philosophy,* edited by R. J. Butler. Oxford: Blackwell, 1962.

Hardin, C. L. "Wittgenstein on Private Languages." *Journal of Philosophy* 56 (1959).

Hartnack, Justus. *Wittgenstein og den moderne Filosofi,* see above.

Kreisel, Georg. "Wittgenstein's *Remarks on the Foundations of Mathematics.*" *British Journal for the Philosophy of Science* 9 (1958).

Kreisel, Georg. "Wittgenstein's Theory and Practice of Philosophy." *British Journal for the Philosophy of Science* 11 (1960).

Malcolm, Norman. "Behaviorism as a Philosophy of Psychology." In *Behaviorism and Phenomenology,* edited by T. W. Wann. Chicago: William Marsh Rice University by the University of Chicago Press, 1964.

Malcolm, Norman. *Dreaming.* New York: Humanities Press, 1959.

Malcolm, Norman. *Knowledge and Certainty.* Englewood Cliffs, NJ: Prentice-Hall, 1963. See "Wittgenstein's *Philosophical Investigations*" and "Knowledge of Other Minds."

Moore, G. E. "Wittgenstein's Lectures in 1930–1933." In *Philosophical Papers.* New York: Macmillan, 1959.

Nell, E. J. "The Hardness of the Logical 'Must.'" *Analysis* 21 (1961).

Pitcher, George. *The Philosophy of Wittgenstein.* Englewood Cliffs, NJ: Prentice-Hall, 1964.

Rhees, Rush. Preface to *The Blue and Brown Books.* Oxford: Blackwell, 1958.

Rhees, Rush. "Some Developments in Wittgenstein's View of Ethics." *Philosophical Review* 74 (1965).

Rhees, Rush. "Wittgenstein's Builders." *PAS* 60 (1959–1960).

Strawson, P. F. Critical notice of *Philosophical Investigations. Mind* 63 (1954).

Thomson, Judith J. "Private Languages." *American Philosophical Quarterly* 1 (1964).

Waismann, Friedrich. "Notes on Talks with Wittgenstein." *Philosophical Review* 74 (1965).

Wellman, Carl. "Our Criteria for Third-Person Psychological Sentences." *Journal of Philosophy* 58 (1961).

Wellman, Carl. "Wittgenstein and the Egocentric Predicament." *Mind* 68 (1959).

Wellman, Carl. "Wittgenstein's Conception of a Criterion." *Philosophical Review* 71 (1962).

Wisdom, John. "A Feature of Wittgenstein's Technique." *PAS* supp. 35 (1961).

Wisdom, John. *Philosophy and Psychoanalysis.* Oxford, 1953.

Norman Malcolm (1967)

WITTGENSTEIN, LUDWIG JOSEF JOHANN [ADDENDUM 1]

Of Ludwig Josef Johann Wittgenstein's philosophical writings available in print, by far the greater part was published after the 1967 *Encyclopedia of Philosophy.* The year 1967 also saw the publication on microfilm of Wittgenstein's *Nachlass.* In addition to the *Nachlass* itself and the posthumously published material from it, there has become available since 1967 a considerable body of Wittgenstein's letters, records of conversations with him, and notes taken by students at his lectures. Altogether, vastly more material is available to the student of Wittgenstein than there was in the mid-1960s. The *Tractatus* and the *Philosophical Investigations* remain, however, the central works for anyone trying to understand Wittgenstein's philosophy. The other writings do give a far fuller understanding of how Wittgenstein's later thought developed; they make clear important continuities between earlier and later work that had been difficult to see earlier. The recognition of these continuities can, for example, be seen in several of the essays in Peter Winch (1969), including Winch's own introductory essay on the unity of Wittgenstein's philosophy. Hidé Ishiguro (1969), in that volume, established that Wittgenstein's connection between meaning and use was not new in his later philosophy. He had always tied meaning to use; what was new in the later work, Ishiguro argued, was the willingness to consider a great variety of different kinds of use besides stating of facts; and Winch notes also the importance in Wittgenstein's later work of the idea that what we call "stating a fact" can itself be many different sorts of thing. A very important continuity noted by Anthony Kenny (1973) lies in Wittgenstein's conception of philosophy itself, including the contrast he made between philosophy and natural science, and the central role he gave to descriptions (rather than proofs) within philosophy.

The material written in the late 1940s and just before Wittgenstein's death shows how Wittgenstein's thought developed after the completion of what was published as Part I of *Philosophical Investigations.* He mentioned to friends his intention (never carried out) of replacing much of what is in the last thirty pages or so of Part I with what is in Part II, along with related material (subsequently published as *Remarks on Philosophical Psychology* and *Last Writings on Philosophical Psychology,* Vol. 1). His comment helps make clear how he saw the investigations of psychological concepts that occupy so much of Part II of the *Investigations* and of the related manuscripts. He is not turning away from the central questions about language in the *Investigations* to new and unrelated topics. Those questions themselves led him repeatedly into detailed examination of such matters as how what is going on in our minds bears on whether we speak with understanding or rather only as parrots might. The late writings show also his concern with the question, important to him from the 1930s onward, how what is given in experience is relevant to the concepts we grasp. These issues are closely related also to the investigations in *Remarks on Colour* (1977), drawn from manuscripts from the last eighteen months of Wittgenstein's life.

Wittgenstein was greatly stimulated by G. E. Moore's attempts to reply to skeptical arguments by asserting things he took it to be plain that he knew (for example, that Earth had existed for a long time) and by Moore's discussion of the paradoxical character of saying "I believe he has gone out, but he has not." Moore's paradox about belief provides a focus for some of Wittgenstein's discussions of psychological concepts in Part II of the *Investigations* and the related manuscripts. Moore's commonsense response to skepticism provided the impetus for Wittgenstein's treatment of skepticism and knowledge in *On Certainty.* He criticized Moore for having misunderstood the concept of knowledge on the model of that of belief and doubt; and indeed *On Certainty* is to some degree continuous with Wittgenstein's other discussions of psychological concepts. But it also stands on its own as an investigation of how certainty forms a part of our various language games and of the role played in those language games by empirical propositions that are not questioned. Wittgenstein's methods in *On Certainty* have been applied by other philosophers in discussions of religious and ethical claims, but he himself does not attempt to apply general principles about doubt, certainty, or knowledge to ethics or religion. (Some of his views about ethics and religion, as well as about art and other topics, have been gathered from various manuscripts and published in *Culture and Value.*)

There is a group of questions about how Wittgenstein saw the relation between facts and the language games in which we are engaged and about how far his approach, in his later philosophy, involves some kind of idealism or relativism. Do facts exercise any sort of control on the character of our concepts? If there were people who engaged in language games very different from ours—if there were, for example, people who thought one could travel to the moon while in a dream—would we be in a position to criticize such people as fundamentally in error? Several of Wittgenstein's works published after 1967 are particularly relevant to these questions, including *On Certainty, Zettel* (a collection of remarks Wittgenstein had cut from various manuscripts, mostly from the late 1940s), and Wittgenstein's "Remarks on Frazer's *Golden Bough*" (included in Wittgenstein, 1993). Wittgenstein's discussions of mathematics also bear directly on the question how free we are in our development of concepts: What would we be getting wrong if our mathematics, or our logic, were very different? In these discussions Wittgenstein is frequently responding to Gottlob Frege's conception of objectivity in logic and mathematics.

RECEPTION OF WITTGENSTEIN'S PHILOSOPHY

Philosophers are far from agreement on how Wittgenstein's philosophical achievements can be assimilated or indeed whether they should be. There are many philosophers who regard Wittgenstein's influence as pernicious and who think that the best response to his philosophy is to ignore it. This view rests sometimes on the idea that his philosophy developed to meet his personal needs and is irrelevant to the genuine interests of contemporary philosophy. A second kind of response to Wittgenstein involves making a sharp distinction between, on the one hand, the important philosophical claims and arguments that are thought to be in his work or implied by it and, on the other, his own understanding of his philosophy as not involving disputable theses or explanations and as aiming to dissolve philosophical problems rather than to find the correct answers. If that distinction is made, it may then be held that we should simply ignore his views about philosophy (which it may also be held are inconsistent with his own practice) and should instead pay attention to the theses and arguments (on which, on this view, his reputation must properly rest). Philosophers who read Wittgenstein in this way do not agree among themselves whether the theses in question are true, the arguments sound; nor do they agree about what the extractible theses are supposed to be. Thus, for example, those who ascribe to him theses about the necessary conditions for a language disagree about whether these conditions include the necessity that a speaker of any language have been at least at some time a member of a community of speakers. A third distinct kind of response to Wittgenstein takes seriously his conception of philosophical problems as dependent upon our misunderstandings of the workings of our language; they arise when language is allowed to go "on holiday." And so any adequate approach to these problems depends on coming to see how we are led into them; it will not issue in solutions that leave unchanged our idea of the problems themselves. Finally, some elements of Wittgenstein's approach to philosophical problems, and his criticisms of standard philosophical moves in response to them, have also been treated as important and interesting by those who, like Richard Rorty, wish to see analytical philosophy replaced by some other kind of intellectual activity.

The philosophical disputes about Wittgenstein's work have been focused to a considerable degree on the issues discussed by Norman Malcolm in the original *Encyclopedia* piece, including the relation between meaning and use, the possibility of a private language, and the objectivity of rules. Much recent controversy has been inspired by the writings of Michael Dummett and Saul Kripke. Dummett reads Wittgenstein as putting forward an antirealist theory of meaning; Kripke has argued that Wittgenstein in the *Investigations* presents a new skeptical problem and a skeptical solution to it. Responses to Dummett and Kripke have made clear the importance of understanding Wittgenstein's aims, his desire to show how our misconceptions can make something perfectly ordinary appear problematic; thus, it is the step in our arguments at which the ordinary first appears problematic that we fail to note, and to which we need to attend.

See also Analysis, Philosophical; Dummett, Michael Anthony Eardley; Frege, Gottlob; Kripke, Saul; Malcolm, Norman; Meaning; Moore, George Edward; Philosophy; Rorty, Richard; Skepticism, History of.

Bibliography

WORKS BY WITTGENSTEIN

Philosophical Remarks. Edited by R. Rhees; translated by R. Hargreaves and R. White. Oxford, 1964; 2nd ed., Oxford: Blackwell, 1975.

Zettel. Edited by G. E. M. Anscombe and G. H. von Wright; translated by G. E. M. Anscombe. Oxford: Blackwell, 1967; 2nd ed., 1981.

On Certainty. Edited by G. E. M. Anscombe and G. H. von Wright; translated by G. E. M. Anscombe and D. Paul. Oxford: Blackwell, 1969.

Proto-tractatus. Edited by B. F. McGuinness, T. Nyberg, and G. H. von Wright; translated by D. F. Pears and B. F. McGuinness. Ithaca, NY: Cornell University Press, 1971.

Philosophical Grammar. Edited by R. Rhees; translated by A. Kenny. Oxford: Blackwell, 1974.

Remarks on Colour. Edited by G. E. M. Anscombe; translated by L. McAlister and M. Schättle. Oxford: Blackwell, 1977.

Remarks on the Foundations of Mathematics. Edited by G. H. von Wright, R. Rhees, and G. E. M. Anscombe; translated by G. E. M. Anscombe, 3rd ed. Cambridge, MA: MIT Press, 1978.

Culture and Value. Edited by G. H. von Wright; translated by P. Winch. Oxford: Blackwell, 1980.

Remarks on the Philosophy of Psychology. Vol. 1, edited by G. E. M. Anscombe and G. H. von Wright; translated by G. E. M. Anscombe. Vol. 2, edited by G. H. von Wright and H. Nyman; translated by C. G. Luckhardt and M. A. E. Aue. Chicago: University of Chicago Press, 1980.

Last Writings on the Philosophy of Psychology. Edited by G. H. von Wright and H. Nyman; translated by C. G. Luckhardt and M. A. E. Aue. 2 vols. Chicago: University of Chicago Press, 1982–1992.

Werkausgabe. 8 vols. Frankfurt, 1989.

Philosophical Occasions, 1912–1951. Edited by J. Klagge and A. Nordmann. Indianapolis: Hackett, 1993. Contains all Wittgenstein's shorter published writings; some letters and records of lectures; also a full account of the Wittgenstein *Nachlass.*

Wiener Ausgabe. Edited by M. Nedo. 22 vols. Vienna: Springer-Verlag, 1993–.

The Published Works of Ludwig Wittgenstein. Edited by H. Kaal and A. McKinnon. Electronic text database.

LECTURES AND CONVERSATIONS

Wittgenstein's Lectures, Cambridge, 1930–1932. Edited by D. Lee. Totowa, NJ: Rowman and Littlefield, 1980.

Wittgenstein's Lectures, Cambridge, 1932–1935. Edited by A. Ambrose. Totowa, NJ: Rowman and Littlefield, 1979.

Wittgenstein's Lectures on the Foundations of Mathematics, Cambridge, 1939. Edited by C. Diamond. Ithaca, NY: Cornell University Press, 1976; Chicago: University of Chicago Press, 1989.

Wittgenstein's Lectures on Philosophical Psychology 1946–47. Edited by P. T. Geach. Chicago: University of Chicago Press, 1988.

Wittgenstein and the Vienna Circle: Conversations Recorded by Friedrich Waismann. Edited by B. F. McGuinness; translated by J. Schulte and B. F. McGuinness. New York: Barnes and Noble, 1979.

WORKS ON WITTGENSTEIN

Anscombe, G. E. M. "The Question of Linguistic Idealism." In *From Parmenides to Wittgenstein.* Minneapolis: University of Minnesota Press, 1981.

Canfield, J. V., ed. *The Philosophy of Wittgenstein.* 15 vols. New York: Garland, 1986. Comprehensive collection of over 250 articles.

Cavell, S. *The Claim of Reason.* Oxford: Clarendon Press, 1979.

Conant, J. "Kierkegaard, Wittgenstein, and Nonsense." In *Pursuits of Reason,* edited by T. Cohen et al. Lubbock: Texas Tech University Press, 1993.

Diamond, C. *The Realistic Spirit: Wittgenstein, Philosophy, and the Mind.* Cambridge, MA: MIT Press, 1991.

Dummett, M. *Truth and Other Enigmas.* London: Duckworth, 1978.

Goldfarb, W. "I Want You to Bring Me a Slab: Remarks on the Opening Sections of the *Philosophical Investigations.*" *Synthese* 56 (1983).

Goldfarb, W. "Kripke on Wittgenstein on Rules." *Journal of Philosophy* 82 (1985).

Hacker, P. M. S. *Insight and Illusion: Themes in the Philosophy of Wittgenstein.* Oxford, 1972; rev. 2nd ed., Oxford: Clarendon Press, 1986.

Holtzman, S. H., and Leich, C. M., eds. *Wittgenstein: To Follow a Rule.* London: Routledge and Kegan Paul, 1981.

Ishiguro, H. "Use and Reference of Names." In *Studies in the Philosophy of Wittgenstein,* edited by P. Winch. London: Routledge and Kegan Paul, 1969.

Kenny, A. *Wittgenstein.* Cambridge, MA: Harvard University Press, 1973.

Kripke, S. *Wittgenstein on Rules and Private Language.* Cambridge, MA: Harvard University Press, 1982.

Malcolm, N. *Nothing Is Hidden: Wittgenstein's Criticism of His Early Thought.* Oxford: Blackwell, 1986.

McDowell, J. *Selected Papers,* Vol. 1. Cambridge, MA, 1996.

McGuinness, B. F. *Wittgenstein, a Life: Young Ludwig: 1889–1921.* Berkeley: University of California Press, 1988.

Monk, R. *Ludwig Wittgenstein: The Duty of Genius.* New York: Free Press, 1990.

Pears, D. F. *The False Prison.* 2 vols. Oxford: Clarendon Press, 1987–1988.

Rhees, R. *Discussions of Wittgenstein.* London: Routledge and Kegan Paul, 1970.

Shanker, S. G., ed. *Ludwig Wittgenstein: Critical Assessments.* 4 vols. London: Croom Helm, 1986. Comprehensive collection of 104 articles.

Shanker, V. A., and S. G. Shanker. *A Wittgenstein Bibliography.* London: Croom Helm, 1986. Covers primary sources and over 5,400 items on Wittgenstein.

Sluga, H., and D. Stern, eds. *Cambridge Companion to Wittgenstein.* Cambridge, U.K.: Cambridge University Press, 1996. Includes a full bibliography of Wittgenstein's writings and good selective bibliography of secondary literature.

Winch, P., ed. *Studies in the Philosophy of Wittgenstein.* London: Routledge and Kegan Paul, 1969.

Wright, C. *Wittgenstein on the Foundations of Mathematics.* Cambridge, MA: Harvard University Press, 1980.

Cora Diamond (1996)

WITTGENSTEIN, LUDWIG [ADDENDUM 2]

Although aesthetics was a subject of deep and lifelong importance to Ludwig Wittgenstein, he wrote very little directly on the topic. He did, however, write remarks on the visual arts, literature and poetry, architecture, and especially music throughout his multifarious writings on the philosophies of language, mind, mathematics, psychology, and philosophical method. A number of these remarks, including some from his more personal notebooks, are collected in *Culture and Value*, and scholars have the collected notes from a course of lectures he gave in Cambridge in 1938. In those lectures Wittgenstein was quick to differentiate between types of questions, particularly between questions of empirical psychology and aesthetic questions (he said that, while he was interested in scientific issues, only conceptual and aesthetic issues could truly grip him).

He also looked, with at the time unprecedented detail, into the nuances of humankind's actual critically descriptive aesthetic language, showing how remote such context-specific articulations are from questions of the highest level of aesthetic generality, e.g. "What is Beauty?" He also showed how particularized aesthetic judgments can be supported by reasons as they emerge within a particularized context of aesthetic perception and evaluation, but *without* recourse to a more general theory that underwrites the judgment. Wittgenstein also investigated, and underscored the importance of, the contextual backdrop and the artistic tradition from which a work emerges; aesthetic reasoning, he suggested, very often proceeds by comparative juxtaposition, not by a form of deductive argumentation from general principles (and yet it is, in a full-blooded sense, reasoning nonetheless).

Scholars also have the record by G. E. Moore of Wittgenstein's lectures of 1930–1933, a document that has been of particular value to those working in the philosophy of criticism. In them, Wittgenstein made one link between the philosophies of language and of art explicit, developing a similarity between the meaning of the word "game" and the word "art." Like the class of all games, he suggested, art has no single essence, common property, or unitary feature present in all cases and by virtue of which the object in question is justifiably characterized as a work of art. This thought, along with the writings in his *Philosophical Investigations* concerning "family resemblance" concepts, i.e. concepts or classes whose members may exhibit some overlapping characteristics but no one defining feature in common, generated the view (articulated in the writings in the 1950s of Morris Weitz, William Kennick, and others) that art is itself an "open concept."

As such, it would prove intrinsically resistant to any traditional or essence-capturing definition; writers on aesthetics of the period frequently endorsed an "anti-essentialism" on these grounds. But this led, in turn, to the counter-argument (beginning with Maurice Mandelbaum) that the defining feature making essentialistic definition possible after all may not be an exhibited property, specifically that it may be relational in nature (just as it is a relational, ascertainable, and category-membership-determining fact about a person that she is or is not a grandmother, but this will not be a visually discernible or "exhibited" property). This was followed in turn by institutional theories of art (developed, in very different ways, by Arthur Danto and George Dickie, among others) designed to capture art's essence, the single property that at bottom makes it what it is. Debate about the viability, the general applicability, and the degree of illumination provided by such accounts, continues to the present.

Other strands of Wittgenstein's philosophy as they relate to aesthetic considerations have also been taken up since the 1950s and 1960s and continue into the early twenty-first century. These include studies in the 1970s and 1980s of the significance of Wittgenstein's remarks on aspect-perception and "seeing-as" in connection with problems of the visual discernment of representational content in a marked surface (by Richard Wollheim, who amended the concept to that of "seeing-in," and by others) and in connection with the perception of expressive properties and the use of expressive predicates (by Benjamin Tilghman and others). Others have continued to explore areas that extend well beyond the quite narrow issue of definition versus anti-essentialism (mistakenly, and ironically, regarded by many as the essence of the significance of Wittgenstein's later philosophical writings for aesthetic understanding). These include studies, in the 1990s to the 2000s, of the significance of Wittgenstein's remarks on "language-games" and a "form of life" in his philosophy of language for literary language as well as, conversely, the value of literary cases for work in the philosophy of language, studies of his remarks on music, studies of the complex interrelations between philosophical conceptions of linguistic meaning and aesthetic theory, studies of the relations between ethical and aesthetic values, studies of the legacy of romanticism in relation to Wittgenstein's later thought, studies of Wittgenstein's writings on self-reference and self-description for questions concerning autobiographical language and self-knowledge, and assessments of Wittgenstein's writings for literary aesthetics. Taken as a whole, late-twentieth-century and early-twenty-first-century work on Wittgenstein's aesthetics has shown that the focus on definition was only one aspect among many.

See also Aesthetics, History of; Art, Expression in; Art, Representation in; Danto, Arthur; Moore, George Edward; Visual Arts, Theory of the; Wollheim, Richard.

Bibliography

WORKS BY LUDWIG WITTGENSTEIN

Philosophical Investigations. 3rd ed. Translated by G. E. M. Anscombe. New York: Blackwell, 1968.

Lectures and Conversations on Aesthetics, Psychology, and Religious Belief. Edited by Cyril Barrett. Berkeley: University of California Press, 1972.

Culture and Value. Edited by G. H. von Wright. Translated by Peter Winch. Chicago: University of Chicago Press, 1980.

WORKS ABOUT LUDWIG WITTGENSTEIN

Allen, Richard, and Malcolm Turvey, eds. *Wittgenstein, Theory, and the Arts*. New York: Routledge, 2001.

Cavell, Stanley. *Must We Mean What We Say?: A Book of Essays*. New York: Cambridge University Press, 1976.

Dauber, Kenneth, and Walter Jost, eds. *Ordinary Language Criticism: Literary Thinking after Cavell after Wittgenstein*. Evanston, IL: Northwestern University Press, 2003.

Eldridge, Richard. *Leading a Human Life: Wittgenstein, Intentionality, and Romanticism*. Chicago: University of Chicago Press, 1997.

Elton, William, ed. *Aesthetics and Language*. Oxford: Blackwell, 1954.

Hagberg, Garry L. *Art as Language: Wittgenstein, Meaning, and Aesthetic Theory*. Ithaca, NY: Cornell University Press, 1995.

Hagberg, Garry L. *Meaning and Interpretation: Wittgenstein, Henry James, and Literary Knowledge*. Ithaca, NY: Cornell University Press, 1994.

Kennick, William E. "Does Traditional Aesthetics Rest on a Mistake?" *Mind* 67 (3) (July 1958): 317–334.

Lewis, Peter B., ed. *Wittgenstein, Aesthetics, and Philosophy*. Burlington, VT: Ashgate, 2004.

Mandelbaum, Maurice. "Family Resemblances and Generalization concerning the Arts." *American Philosophical Quarterly* 12 (3) (1965): 219–228.

Moore, George Edward. "Wittgenstein's Lectures, 1930–1933." In *Philosophical Papers*, 252–324. London: Allen & Uwin, 1959.

Tilghman, B. R. *But Is It Art? The Value of Art and the Temptation of Theory*. Oxford and New York: Basil Blackwell, 1984.

Tilghman, B. R. *Wittgenstein, Ethics, and Aesthetics: The View from Eternity*. Albany: State University of New York Press, 1991.

Weitz, Morris. "The Role of Theory in Aesthetics." *Journal of Aesthetics and Art Criticism* 15 (1) (September 1956): 27–35.

Wollheim, Richard. *Arts and Its Objects*. New York: Cambridge University Press, 1992.

Garry L. Hagberg (2005)

WODEHAM, ADAM

(c. 1298–1358)

Adam Wodeham studied theology with Walter Chatton. The man he held in high esteem, his friend and mentor, was, however, William Ockham. All three men were Englishmen and fellow Franciscans. But whereas Chatton systematically opposed Ockham's views, Wodeham rose to Ockham's defense. As a teacher of theology himself, Wodeham lectured on Peter Lombard's *Sentences*. He did so three times, in London, Norwich (c. 1330), and Oxford (1332). The text of only the last two lectures survive, and only the second has been printed in a modern critical edition. Wodeham developed his own philosophical and theological doctrines by rethinking those of Ockham, some of which he considerably altered. This entry mentions only his most original contributions to philosophy proper.

LANGUAGE AND THOUGHT

Wodeham agreed with Ockham that the languages humans speak derive their meaningfulness from an intrinsically significant mental language, common to all intellects. The terms of that language are concepts. Concepts are acts of apprehending individual things. Some are singular, by which a given individual thing is apprehended, as when we see a thing or remember one we have earlier seen. Others are general, as, for example, the concept corresponding to the word "rose," by which we apprehend all actual and possible roses indiscriminately. Mental sentences too are acts of apprehension. When we form a mental sentence, however, we apprehend a thing of a different sort, Wodeham thought, namely a state of affairs. For example, a rose being a flower is apprehended not by a concept, but by the mental correlate of "a rose is a flower." Concepts and mental sentences are to be regarded as signifying those very things we apprehend by them.

ONTOLOGY

Wodeham's ontology is thus twofold. It contains a restricted ontology of concrete individuals, a strictly nominalist ontology, but in its full extension it also includes states of affairs, and therefore abstract things. Accordingly, Wodeham regarded words such as "being," "thing" and "something" as having two senses. In one sense of "thing," only concrete individuals, actual or possible, are things. In another sense, states of affairs, though they are abstract entities, are things, whether they obtain or can obtain, or not. Wodeham recognized both affirmative and negative states of affairs. Discussing Augustine, he remarks that the person who prefers not to exist over existing in misery can be correctly described as preferring one thing over another, though both things are states of affairs, one negative, the other affirmative.

BELIEF AND KNOWLEDGE

Much of our intellectual activity consists in forming beliefs. We form a belief when we judge a state of affairs to obtain. We cannot form a belief, then, unless we first form a mental sentence by which we apprehend the relevant state of affairs. In some cases, it appears to us that the state of affairs we are considering obtains. The mental sentence by which we are apprehending it is then called "evident." Whenever we form an evident mental sentence, we tend to judge accordingly. There are, however, as Wodeham notes, degrees of evidence. At its lower degree, the evidence of a mental sentence is potentially outweighed by reasons we have or might have to dissent or doubt. We then judge accordingly only if we fail to bring these reasons to mind. At its higher degree, by contrast, the evidence of a mental sentence cannot be outweighed by any reasons to the contrary, and we are therefore compelled to judge accordingly. The sentence "If equals are subtracted from equals, the remainders are equal" has this degree of evidence, whereas the sentence "This boat is moving" has the lower degree of evidence. Wodeham assumed that if a mental sentence has the higher degree of evidence, its truth is guaranteed. On this assumption, he rules that only beliefs caused by mental sentences that have the higher degree of evidence (or that follow just as evidently from such sentences) are acts of knowledge. All other beliefs, whatever their cause, are matters of fallible opinion or perhaps of faith, but not of knowledge.

INFLUENCE

Wodeham's views, in particular on ontology, were extremely influential. In reaction to them, Parisian scholars of the mid-fourteenth century divided into two camps: those who recognized states of affairs and those who denied them. John Buridan was their most prominent opponent. He rejected, therefore, Wodeham's semantics of sentences, though not his semantics of terms. Authors who recognized the existence of states of affairs in addition to that of concrete individuals include Gregory of Rimini and Nicolas Oresme.

See also Chatton, Walter; Ockhamism; William of Ockham.

Bibliography

WORKS BY WODEHAM

Adam Goddam super quattuor libros sententiarum. Edited by John Major. Paris: P. le Preux, 1512. Contains Wodeham's Oxford lectures abbreviated (in c. 1375) by Henry Totting de Oyta, who inserted in the text comments of his own.

Lectura secunda in librum primum sententiarum. Edited by Rega Wood and Gedeon Gál. St. Bonaventure, NY: Franciscan Institute, 1990. Contains Wodeham's Norwich lectures.

Tractatus de indivisibilibus. Edited by Rega Wood. Dordrecht, Netherlands: Kluwer, 1998. Discusses alternative conceptions of the structure of the continuum as they connect with alternative attempts to solve the paradoxes of the infinite.

WORKS ON WODEHAM

Courtenay, William. *Adam Wodeham: An Introduction to His Life and Writings.* Leiden, Netherlands: Brill, 1978. Contains valuable historical and manuscript information.

Gál, Gedeon. "Adam Wodeham's Question on the 'Complexe Significabile' as the Immediate Object of Scientific Knowledge." *Franciscan Studies* 37 (1977): 66–102. This article revealed Wodeham as the source of Gregory of Rimini's theory of propositionally signifiable things—that is, of states of affairs.

Karger, Elizabeth. "Adam Wodeham on the Intentionality of Cognitions." In *Ancient and Medieval Theories of Intentionality*, edited by D. Perler. Leiden, Netherlands: Brill, 2001.

Karger, Elizabeth. "Ockham and Wodeham on Divine Deception as a Skeptical Hypothesis." *Vivarium* 42 (2) (2004): 225–236.

Karger, Elizabeth. "William of Ockham, Walter Chatton and Adam Wodeham on the Objects of Knowledge and Belief." *Vivarium* 33 (2) (1995): 171–196.

Sylla, Edith Dudley. "God, Indivisibles and Logic in the Later Middle Ages: Adam Wodeham's Response to Henry of Harclay." *Medieval Philosophy and Theology* 7 (1) (1998): 69–87.

Elizabeth Karger (2005)

WOLFF, CHRISTIAN

(1679–1754)

Christian Wolff was a rationalist polymath and an influential leader of the early German Enlightenment. He was born in Breslau into an impoverished family of leather workers. In his academic career, he gained renown by teaching mathematics and became famous for systematizing and updating the German philosopher and mathematician Gottfried Wilhelm Leibniz. Wolff pioneered socio-economics, framed the idea of subsidiarity (the EU welfare model), and made lasting contributions to international law. He developed German into a philosophical language (e.g., coining *Begriff*), created a terminology still in use in the twenty-first century (e.g., "monism" and "dualism"), and dominated continental thought before Immanuel Kant in Germany, Switzerland, Poland, Southeast Europe, and Russia. In his philosophical work, he revived ontology as a systematic framework for the empirical sciences, and expanded the geometric method, a mathematical design for rational thought and conceptual reasoning. He advanced the first formal theory of evolution and defined the ecological and cosmological notion of a world as a network of worldlines (*nexus rerum*). Like Leibniz, he sided with the Jesuit accommodation in the Rites Controversy (1610–1724). Unlike Leibniz, he openly declared himself a neo-Confucian in the textual tradition of Zhu Xi (1130–1200).

This bold move resulted in his exile in 1723 and spawned the Pietism Controversy 1723–1740. His Christian critics denounced him as a pagan, "Spinozist," and atheist, while Thomasius attacked him as a "new, insolent Confucian" in 1726. His pupils lost teaching posts in Prussia and Swabia; his texts were outlawed at Halle in 1723 and in Prussia in 1729. His opponents were Christian fundamentalists influenced by Martin Luther, Philipp Jakob Spener, and John Calvin. They relented in the 1730s, when it became undeniable that Wolff accommodated mainstream opinions and retracted his provocative metaphysical claims. But he never retracted his arguments for academic freedom, especially as a freedom from religious dogma. He was celebrated as "the teacher of Germany" (*praeceptor Germaniae*) who yielded to his critics by choosing Sir Isaac Newton over Leibniz and Christ over Confucius, while preserving the unity of his system of ideas in a reformulated encyclopedic Latin oeuvre.

At Marburg, he served an enlightened Calvinist ruler, the Landgrave of Hesse-Cassel. He was invited to join Utrecht University and to lead Russia's and Prussia's academies. After the coronation of Frederick II, he left for a royal welcome in Berlin in 1740. His return to Halle, which was condoned by the king, was seen as a cultural feat for Prussia and was a legal victory for reason. The elector of the Holy Roman Empire and founder of the Bavarian Academy elevated him to nobility. Baron Wolff died on his estate (*Rittergut*) near Leipzig in 1754. He was the chief German thinker after Leibniz and before Kant.

CONTEXT, WORK, AND IMPACT

Wolff was born January 24, 1679, in the capital of Silesia (Breslau, present-day Wroclaw), in the Protestant northeast of Hapsburg, Austria (present-day Poland). He was the only survivor of six children by a tanner. Following his father's wishes, he attended Breslau's Lutheran School and majored in divinity at Jena in 1699. He changed his course of studies to mathematics and went to Leipzig to earn his magister degree in 1702. With a thesis on ethics according to the mathematical method, he won a magister legens in 1703, entitling him to teach. He taught mathematics as an adjunct professor at Leipzig and joined the staff of *Acta Eruditorum*, the first academic journal in Germany, published in Leipzig. For the *Acta*, he wrote as a specialist in mathematics but soon branched out to other fields, such as military architecture natural history, and natural philosophy. In 1706, for instance, Wolff reviewed the *Optics* (1704) by Newton (1642–1727) and the expanded *True Physics* (1705) by Newton's student John Keill (1671–1721). The Swedish invasion of Saxony in 1706 (Great Northern War 1700–1721) made Wolff leave Leipzig; Gottfried Wilhelm Baron von Leibniz (1646–1716) helped him to find employment at Halle University as a professor of mathematics. In 1709, he established himself as an expert in the quantitative dynamics of gases (with *Aerometry*).

With these credentials in natural philosophy, Wolff taught logic (1709), next ontology, and eventually ethics—in violation of administrative rules, because philosophy classes had been the exclusive turf of the theology faculty. Despite resistance by the Pietist mayor August Hermann Francke (1663–1727) and the evangelical theologian Joachim Lange (1670–1744), Wolff taught outside his area until 1723. In 1709, he was elected to the Royal Society, and in 1711 to the Berlin Academy.

With the four-volume *Foundations of All Exact Sciences* (1710), Wolff made a name for himself as the leading author of up-to-date German textbooks on the new quantitative sciences. In 1711 he wrote an anonymous review of a handbook (1710) by François Noël on China's geography and astronomy and on Chinese measurements for *Acta Eruditorum*. In 1712 he anonymously contributed to *Acta* a review on Alexandre [sic: François] Noël's translation of six Confucian classics. He wrote the four-volume *Elements of Universal Mathematics* (1713–1715), the so-called *German Logic* (*Rational Thoughts on the Forces of the Human Mind*, 1713), and a *Mathematical Dictionary* (1716). Staying in Halle, he declined calls to Marburg (1714), Wittenberg (1715), Jena (1716), and Leipzig (1716). In 1715 he became court councilor (*Hofrat*) and also professor of physics at Halle; Peter I (the Great, 1672–1725) asked him to serve as a tsarist advisor in St Petersburg. In 1718 he defended Confucian secular humanism and supported Chinese morals in *Reason of Wolff's Classes in Mathematics and Global Philosophy* (Ratio praelectionum Wolfianarum [in] mathesin & philosophiam universam).

In 1719 he published *German Metaphysics (Rational Thoughts on God, World, Human Soul, and All Things in General)*, his best-known work. It was read as a revolutionary and secular system; it was a best-seller and the program for a new philosophical network. His Swabian pupil Georg Bernhard Bilfinger (1693–1750) called the network the "Leibnizian-Wolffian School Philosophy."

Although this label irritated Wolff, Bilfinger was being honest. Leibniz was Wolff's most famous mentor, from whom he appropriated main ideas of the monadology and natural dynamics. He also followed Leibniz's rational theodicy. Later, however, Wolff's Leibnizian label turned into a misnomer. Spurred into action by the angry ideological critique of these subversive ideas, and their negative repercussions, Wolff spoke out against them and distanced himself from the deeper implications of ideas such as "monad" and "preestablished harmony." Most students who followed him in this moderation fared well nationally. Others, who resisted this about-face and insisted on the revolutionary significance of Leibniz's ideas in their Wolffian integration, found themselves marginalized (even by Wolff) or driven into exile. Bilfinger, exiled to Russia, was the most radical early interpreter who was not rejected by the later Wolff.

The Leibnizian-Wolffian School Philosophy grew to include female naturalists and free-thinkers, such as the karmic pantheist Johanna Charlotte Unzer (b. Ziegler 1725–1782); among its supporters abroad was the later Newtonian Gabrielle de Châtelet (1706–1749). Early continental feminists celebrated Wolff. Early (male, German) members were known as the textbook authors. The School Philosophy bred a new generation of Enlightenment thinkers, such as the poet and philosopher Johann Christoph Gottsched (1700–1766), and it culminated in the work of Alexander Gottlieb Baumgarten (1714–1762). Baumgarten's *Metaphysica* (1739) was the definitive textbook (used by Kant), and his *Aesthetica* (1750) was the historic Wolffian basis of modern aesthetics.

In 1719 Halle University elected Wolff to serve as its provost (*prorektor*). In 1721 he ended the two-year term with *Speech on the Morals of the Chinese*, a public address to an audience of more than a thousand. He refused to submit the text to the next provost (Lange) for religious scrutiny, which prompted the Pietists to conspire at the royal court. Around the same time, Wolff wrote German *Ethics* (1720), *Politics* (1721), *Physics* (1723), *Teleology* (1724), and *Physiology* (1725).

On November 8, 1723, King Frederick William I (r. 1713–1740) sentenced Wolff to death but granted his exile from Prussia if he left within two days. He fled to Marburg, called by Landgrave Charles I of Hesse (1654–1730). He took the mathematics and physics chair held by Denis Papin (1647–c. 1712), who had co-invented the steam engine with Leibniz (1690). Tsarina Catherine (1684–1727, Empress 1725) offered Wolff the vice presidency of the Russian Academy (in 1723 and 1725). By 1728 his fame had vastly increased the student numbers at Marburg, but he remained a target of Pietists and Calvinists.

Wolff qualified his early liberal challenges in detailed replies to critics (*Schutzschriften* to Lange and Johann Budde in 1724; *Notes to Tübingen Theology* in 1725). He moderated his secular ontology with *Comments to German Metaphysics* in 1724, published his own edition of the speech on Confucius (*Oratio de Sinarum philosophia practica* in 1726, with Bilfinger), and fought for academic freedom (*Preliminary Discourse on Philosophy* in 1728). In 1729 fundamentalists succeeded in having all his works declared illegal in Prussia.

While Wolff taught in Hesse, he was made honorary professor of the Russian Academy at St. Petersburg in 1725. Writing now for a wider European audience, he reformulated his views in a Latin series, with *Rational Philosophy or Logic* (1728; its preface is the *Preliminary Discourse on Philosophy as Such*, which he expanded into a separate work), followed by *First Philosophy or Ontology* in 1730, *General Cosmology* in 1731, *Empirical Psychology* in 1732, and *Rational Psychology* in 1734. *Natural Theology* (1736–1737) and *Global Practical Philosophy* (1738–1739) completed the group. The Latin series replaced the German textbooks, and the new set reveals his rejection of charges of paganism and "free-thinking." These works allowed Wolff's mainstream academic acceptance.

In 1733, the French Academy elected Wolff to one of its eight foreign members. Lobbied by a Wolffian (a warrior, Prince Leopold of Anhalt-Dessau 1676–1747), Frederick William I of Prussia certified Wolff at Marburg as a state counselor of Hesse, now ruled by Frederick I (1676–1751, king of Sweden since 1720; landgrave of Hesse since 1730). In 1734 Prussia rescinded the 1723 arrest warrant; Frankfurt at the Oder offered him a position; the Prussian Academy offered him the vice-presidency; and Halle University allowed his return. He stayed at Marburg until 1740, with students such as Mikhail Lomonossov (1711–1765), the founder of Moscow University (1755).

In 1740, Frederick II (the Great, 1712–1786) promoted Wolff to Prussian privy counselor, offered him the presidency of the Academy, and welcomed him back to Halle as an interdisciplinary professor of mathematics, law, and public policy. Meanwhile, the Leibnizian-

Wolffian School Philosophy had evolved to the leading cultural movement of the German Age of Reason. With the foundation of debate clubs such as the Society of the Friends of Truth (1736, which coined the slogan *sapere aude!*—dare to understand!) and the creation of a host of journals, the rational matrix of the early Enlightenment framed by Wolff had spread into the civil and public sphere of continental Europe. His students, driven from Prussia, taught in other parts of Germany, in Bavaria, Switzerland, Austria, Italy, and Russia.

The 1740 coronation of Frederick II was a pivotal event in Wolff's lifetime. Frederick was an avowed agnostic, who had been imprisoned by his Pietist father Frederick William I. The coronation of the jailed "atheist" was a triumph for the Enlightenment. Frederick's alliance with Wolff was a cultural feat for Prussia and signaled the better protection of academic freedom, the first political harbinger of Germany's later division of church and state.

Back in Halle, Wolff served as the university chancellor in 1743. There he developed a system of natural law (*Natural Law*, 8 vol., 1740–48) and outlined a theory of international law (*International Law*, 1749), which he grounded on natural law (*Principles of Natural and International Law*, 1750). In 1752 he was elected to the Italian Academy in Bologna. His final works were *Moral Philosophy* (1750–1753) and *Economics* (1754–1755). This late series repeats his early praise for the Mandarin-run welfare state of China as an exemplary administrative framework and informed Prussian political economy until 1786, when Frederick's successor returned to more parochial Lutheran values. Political economy had been taught since the creation of cameral chairs by Frederick William I, for training Prussia's tax revenue administrators (a century before the field was read at Oxford).

On September 10, 1745, Wolff was made imperial baron of the Holy Roman Empire (*Reichsfreiherr*) by his pupil Maximilian Joseph III (1727–1777), the enlightened Bavarian king (elector since 1745), who founded the Academy of Sciences at Munich, which later advanced stellar optics, helioscopy, and spectral analysis (e.g., Fraunhofer, 1814). Wolff acquired the feudal seat Klein-Dölzig in Saxony in 1748 and retired from teaching. He had single-handedly changed the German and East European landscape of legal, secular, and social thought—the thrust of his arguments had been so persuasive that they were seen as mainstream a mere generation after they had been first branded as extreme.

Baron Wolff died on his estate near Leipzig on April 9, 1754. His Leibnizian-Wolffian School, then the popular German philosophy, was already besieged by the critiques of the young Pietist theologian Christian August Crusius (1715–1775), whose philosophical tracts appeared in the 1740s. The Lisbon tsunami (November 1, 1755), the worst tectonic disaster in recorded European history, with 70,000 deaths, was internationally seen as a refutation of Leibniz's theodicy of the "best of all possible worlds" and turned Wolff's metaphysical framework, with its optimistic, anthropocentric outlook, into the butt of skeptical mockery.

Wolff advanced the continental Age of Reason and systematized early modern thought. Georg Friedrich Wilhelm Hegel (1770–1831), Karl Marx (1818–83), and Friedrich Nietzsche (1844–1900) dismissed him as an obsolete thinker. Kant (1724–1804), who called him the greatest of all German philosophers, joined Wolff's metaphysical viewpoint to its logical opposite, Humean skepticism, as the dialectic field for the collective "critical path of reason" (1781). Wolff created the grammar for the social sciences, integrated law and economics, and built the foundation (partly with his work on architecture and design, and partly via Gottsched and Baumgarten) for the later discipline of aesthetics.

INFLUENCES ON WOLFF

The earliest influences informing Wolff's intellectual development were Christian theology and the literary Baroque. His father, Christoph Wolff, had intellectual aspirations, and his family followed the Lutheran faith. His birth place Breslau was multidenominational, a regional result of the settlements after the Thirty Years War (1618–1648). In this Protestant city, which involved western Calvinist and eastern Jewish communities, he attended the Lutheran gymnasium (senior high school or community college) and distinguished himself in debates with students from the Roman Catholic school run by the Jesuit order. Wolff's rector was the poet Gryphius (1616–1684), a Baroque student of Martin Opitz's earlier *Book of German Poetry* (1624). Gryphius worked for a linguistic and cultural renewal of Germany, devastated by the genocide. His critique of protestant Aristotelianism, as a reactionary paradigm, exposed Wolff to problems of scholastic authority and to intolerant flaws in the campus doctrine.

In Jena and Leipzig, Wolff reacted to Gryphius' critique by turning to the so-called renegades of his day, René Descartes (1596–1650), Ehrenfried Walter v. Tschirnhaus (1651–1708), and Leibniz. Wolff proposed settling neo-scholastic issues by constructing a new design of conceptual analysis and logical deduction, which he applied to formal, natural, and moral philosophy. In Jena, he studied the geometric method by Erhard Weigel (1625–1699) and a similar method proposed by Descartes. In Leipzig, he studied Tschirnhaus' art of invention (*ars invenienda*), a version of the geometric method influenced by optical ideas of Baruch Spinoza (1632–1677) and by catoptrics and dioptrics, the calculus of mirror reflection and lens refraction. Tschirnhaus used his art of invention for the reverse chemical engineering of Chinese porcelain (1708). Wolff applied the geometric method to conceptual reasoning, sharing Tschirnhaus' and Spinoza's hope that the free-spirited rational quests for scientific discovery would create civil happiness.

In Leipzig and Halle, Wolff interpreted Leibniz's monadology as a system of reflective substances. These ultimate and indivisible points are nature's energetic sources of material arrays; twenty-first-century scholars might call such monads powerpoints. Wolff shared Leibniz's interest in Chinese ontology and understood this model of reality as a rational matrix of interactive objects. Yet Wolff was not sure about the depth of physical interaction, repeatedly changing his mind over whether the energetic reciprocity of nature extends to the free powerpoints in the foundational Leibnizian monadology.

In Marburg, he rejected Leibniz's preestablished harmony and studied physical influx, a model of causation proposed by the Spanish scholastic Francisco Suárez (1548–1617). In 1724 he argued that influxionist causal processes govern the natural elements, only to change his mind again and to become ultimately noncommittal about any rational account of natural causes.

In 1726 he appropriated the principle of decorum from his ex-colleague Christian Thomasius (1655–1728). For Thomasius, the decorum was the rational ground of any good legislation. Thomasius defined it as the form of fair distribution and equated it with the Golden Rule (using it for legal briefs against witch trials and in defense of free sexual liaisons). Wolff read the principle of decorum in a wider sense, as the basic way of civil progress and as a human mirror of cosmic development. He identified it with the convergent arrows of civilization and evolution that are tipped toward perfection. This near-mystical reading of the decorum Wolff claimed as his own, but he acknowledged its previous account in the Book of Rites (*Li Ji*; especially *Da Xue* or "Great Learning" and *Zhong Yong* or "Doctrine of the Mean"). Wolff's principle of decorum (flat out rejected by Thomasius in 1726) was informed by Bilfinger and by the Jesuits Philippe Couplet, Athanasius Kircher, and Noël.

Wolff was also influenced by Lange, Hugo Grotius (1583–1645), and John Locke (1632–1704). Lange's attacks prompted him to retract some of his ontological claims for a metaphysical skepticism compatible with Lutheran doctrine. Wolff's caution was influenced by Newton's rules for philosophy (1687) and by Locke's empiricism. Locke was systematically used by the Pietists to shore up their fundamentalism against rationalist claims. Yielding to English and Saxon critics, Wolff rejected Leibniz's dynamics for Newton's mechanics, thus supporting the majority opinion of the day. But he did not entirely retract his earlier views. The theory of natural law, as developed above all by Grotius (see the subtitle of Wolff's *Reason* [1718; 2nd ed. 1735]), allowed him to make his rational point, while diplomatically avoiding farther and more controversial implications of the same ideas.

MATHEMATICS AND LOGIC

Wolff's initial series of mathematical works are systematic expositions of the scientific knowledge of the day, reflecting the state of the art in geometry, arithmetic, and algebra, as well as of the newly advanced calculus (following Leibniz, not Newton, as nineteenth-century mathematicians would do after Wolff as well). Wolff's mathematical works (1710–1716) do not give much space to statistics and stochastic. In part, this neglect had a historical reason. The revolutionary advances in the theory of probability (e.g., Jakob Bernoulli's *Ars coniectandi*, 1713) were made when part of this series was already in press. Moreover, the physical significance of probabilistic tools was shown later (e.g., by Daniel Bernoulli's *Hydrodynamica*, 1733), and only after Wolff had published his logics (1713 and 1728). While Johann Bernoulli (1667–1748) had written on waves, curves, and integrals earlier, Wolff apparently did not know what to make of it.

Wolff's methodological ideal is Euclidean geometry, an axiomatic and deductive system, which was to him the perfect science of nature. He trusted that all natural events, however vague, incoherent, or ambiguous they may seem, express invariant rational patterns, which one should be able to determine as clear and distinct truths. Probabilistic tools fail to reveal such geometric exactitude, and this is a sign of the limitation of the tools, and not the real limit of the events modeled by them. Wolff's nature is rationally ordered; its ways are logical; and science is "the art of demonstration" (*Logic* vii § 1).

Wolff's scientific works were without equal; they democratically addressed a general readership and popularized science in Germany. The *Foundations*, for instance, is a survey of mathematics, geography, mechanics, hydraulics, ballistics, war tactics, fortress design (*Fes-*

tungsbau), and civil architecture. These textbooks were used in Germany for decades; in the Balkans, such as Romania, and in Eastern Europe, such as the Ukraine, these texts were taught well into the nineteenth century. Wolff pioneered the distinction of pure and applied research; he stressed their equal significance, and he saw in mathematics the common denominator of all science.

Wolff regards logic as a system of universal relations, in contrast to Thomasius, Locke, and Lange (who looked at logic either with Christian disdain or as synonymous with natural sense). Against Arnauld's *Logic* (1662), Wolff argued that conceptual organization is not just a mnemonic tool or a *palais de mémoire* for arranging and retrieving stores of knowledge, but also the mirror of the order of nature (1713). The function of Wolff's logic is the theoretical clarification of natural data and the practical enlightenment of secular reason.

The early Wolff discussed logic together with psychology (1713); later, he joined logic to ontology (1728). Wolff's logic involves concepts, propositions, and the map of syllogistic arguments. The logic of scientific discovery works with definitions, laws, and experience. Since the truth-content of propositions and their relations reflect the cosmos, truth is inseparable from the order of events in physical and ultimate reality. As science is the art of demonstration, logic is the art of invention (*ars invenienda*) in scientific work. Propositions can serve as hypotheses that support deductive networks of explanations, and they are also testable. The value of hypotheses depends on experiments. As positive results make hypotheses probable, negative results call them into question; further data will have to determine whether a hypothesis is to be revised or dismissed.

ONTOLOGY AND METAPHYSICS

Wolff described reality as the sum of observable things, whose actions and properties are ordered by small dynamic elements or substances (*Metaphysics*, 1719). The empirical structure is the world, defined as an interactive, developing web of things (*nexus rerum*), whose natural basis is the ontological system of rationally accessible simple elements. The substantial basis and the objective superstructure are a coherent whole, the order of nature.

The order of nature is ruled by the principle of (the impossibility of) contradiction—it is impossible for something to be and not to be at the same time; existential differences emerge only in time. The history of nature is the logical flow of its causal processes; their beginnings and ends differ, but transitions are lawfully harmonized. This causal logic obeys the principle of sufficient reason.

This order covers all reality. Its ontological basis is Leibniz's array of monads, organic, conscious, and indivisible force points, which function as Aristotelian entelechies, a primordial software of elementary action, material trade, and environmental fate. In the naturally evolving cosmos, all stuff, things, minds, and networks integrate in an ultimate harmonious and spiritual rule. Wolff's metaphysics combines ontology with a system of spirits (rational psychology or the "*pneumatic* of minds"), a system of nature (rational cosmology or the "world-doctrine"), and a system of divinity (rational theology or the "natural God-scholarship"). Being, minds, empirical reality, and supreme law are radically unified in an emphatically coherent, intelligible, and predictable order of nature.

Wolff framed this system as a rational reply to the scientific unifications by Nicolas Copernicus (1473–1543), Galileo (1564–1642), Johannes Kepler (1571–1630), and Descartes. This ontology is a conjectured "final theory" for all future research. Its problem is its unity—if the divine law integrates in natural order, then "God" is at risk of becoming Spinoza's *natura naturans* or turning into a cosmic energy flow.

As God is at risk of being merged with the cosmos in Wolff's system, freedom is at risk of being dissolved in a divinely deterministic blueprint of creative processes. For Wolff, any effect results from a prior sufficient reason according to lawful and rational patterns. But if all that happens is in principle predictable, where will this leave spontaneity, or the causation of willful and free actions?

The standard answer—freedom has its seat in the soul—does not quite map onto Wolff's system because of his Leibnizian leanings. Souls are simple substances, and all such monads strive and reflect in an interplay the steps of which are harmoniously preestablished. Christian critics objected that all humans are sinners; that "sinning" means the buck stops with the blameworthy person; and that God, who created persons, gave them free will. But if all personal actions resulted from a preestablished arrangement by God at creation, God would be guilty of human evil, and persons would be wheels in a world-machine (Lange, *Causa Dei*, 1723). This Pietist objection to Wolff's metaphysics was construed as a political charge that soldiers going AWOL cannot be blamed for desertion, which led the Prussian king to look at Wolff as a traitor to be fired, punished, and exiled.

Wolff's revised causal ontology drops the preestablished harmony of elementary souls for the addition of real interactions on the level of monads (henceforth called only "simple substances"; *Comments to German*

Metaphysics, 1724). Since substances are invested with a spontaneous power, they affect one another, and in this sense one soul can freely lead another soul into sin. Substances also affect things, like bodies, and hence souls can freely sin in their embodiments.

Paradoxically, the result of Wolff's revision is an even tighter rational order of the universe—as empirical structures form a *nexus rerum*, their basis is to be explicated as a network of elements or *nexus elementorum* (*Comments*, 1724). Now everything is purposeful. Nature's order has a supreme and final regularity. Apparent flaws, like evil, are transient and local phenomena but are not integral parts of the design; the general thrust of the natural network mirrors a pervasive goal-directedness. For Wolff, the whole creation reflects its first cause, whose effects are always good to its creatures, particular to humans (*German Teleology*, 1724).

But this revision does not let Wolff's metaphysics off the Spinozist hook. For as nature is a lawfully evolving framework, things are always getting better, and there is no need for a meddling celestial God to perform miracles on Earth. Since miracles break the natural flow, the logic of the cosmic order reveals miracles as making a causal mess—so requiring more miracles (*miraculum restitutionis*), ontological cleaning crews that restore the causal order broken by the initial miracle (*German Metaphysics*, 1719 and *Cosmologia Generalis*, 1731). The Christian notion of God, in its Catholic and Lutheran senses, does not "fit" the Wolffian reality of being, whereas a stipulated rational and dynamic wave-front, benevolently "naturing" nature, is its ontological consequence.

Wolff's identification of this dynamic ordering as the principle of decorum, which "waves" micro- and macroscopic worlds along their inexorable ways toward perfection (preface to *Speech on Chinese*, 1726), triggered another evangelical outcry and more charges of Spinozism, paganism, and atheism. Wolff replied by defining this power as "God" in the standard Lutheran sense (*Detailed News*, 1726).

Still, evangelicals objected to this metaphysics; they disliked Wolff's (qualified) embrace of Newton as early as 1719. (Pietists roundly rejected the content of *Principia* until midcentury.) That Wolff integrated the laws of motion, and included the technical concepts of mass and force (*Ontology*, 1729), made his world-idea seem all the more deterministic, material, and machinelike. As his critics reminded him (such as Lange in *Brief Sketch of the Axioms in Wolff's Philosophy Harmful to Natural and Revealed Religion*, 1736), the issue is over the elementary matrix of causal interplays. Just as Leibniz's preestablished harmony invites the problem of freedom vis-a-vis dogmas of sin, Wolff's interacting monads, the *nexus elementorum* of1724, draw this charge from another angle: If all was lawfully ordered, where would this leave room for surprises, or for human willfulness?

Wolff's final revisions amounted to a withdrawal from any causal claims and to a self-imposed silence on the issue of the behavior of elements. He vetoed identifying substances or souls with monads (*General Cosmology*, 1731 §182). The three possible metaphysical explanations of causal phenomena—physical influx, occasionalism, and preestablished harmony—all have their pros and cons, but which one would really be right no one can say (*Rational Psychology*, 1734). Wolff's order of nature, no matter which logical moves he made, kept provoking political and clerical critique. In 1734, he gave up on first causes and on mind-body interactions.

ETHICS AND AESTHETICS

Wolff's epistemological platform is the Cartesian cogito, the living being full of doubts, or the human power for reasoning things out. In reason, helped by experience and observation, one discovers the laws of nature in their present workings and in their evolutionary thrust toward a perfected state. In a historical sense, natural laws are the forms of progressive realization and organization, ultimately of nature itself. In a semantic sense, these laws, in their worked-out patterns, generate ever richer information or essential being, which is the best reality in perfection. In a practical sense, the laws of nature point to the final form of the natural good. Hence Wolff's practical law of nature is divinely inspired, aesthetically ideal, and morally binding.

If one wonders why beauty and the good should come about, Wolff argued, one will see that both are the clear and distinct ideas that prevail in the self-realization of nature's law. Why should a person be moral? By reason one knows "what the law of nature wants to get"; and "therefore a reasonable human being does not need any additional laws," for the progressively perfecting law of nature is humanity's law in light of reason. (*Ethics* § 23 1720; also *Global Practical Philosophy* § 268 1738).

Regardless of which metaphysical theory suits the causation of free actions best, the power of reason can shed light on the natural law and thus enlighten human choices. This law or decorum is the formal pattern of perfection. The idea of perfection is the declared source ("*fons … mea*") of Wolff's entire practical philosophy (as outlined in the preface of his *Moral Philosophy*, 1750).

Conceptually, perfection is the consensus of variety; Wolff defined consensus dynamically, as the interactive trend toward fair trade. Scientifically, in the twenty-first century, Wolff's idea of the naturally self-perfecting consensus is reflected in the ecological understanding of climax communities, environmental integrity, and biological diversity. Practically, for Wolff, perfection is the categorical duty and the moral imperative—do what makes the state of oneself and others more perfect; refrain from making it less perfect. Thus the natural law commands to work out the state of the art of the commerce of living forces, each of which freely wants to realize its material momentum in an ever more complex nature.

Accordingly, good and evil (just like beauty and ugliness) can be defined over their relative degree of systemic perfection—from the perspective of integrity and design, nasty and repugnant events are imperfect. The duty to realize well-ordered frames and a sustainable consensus, no matter its particular instantiation, has political and civil implications.

The enlightened sovereign regards the state like a house that needs to be built in the best way, through an efficient allocation of essential weights, for the sake of maximal strength of the whole. The ruler ought to order and maintain the best administrative design for the common good or the welfare of the people. The welfare state, whose revenues help weaker social groups for the sake of a tighter social contract, is Wolff's design (*Principles of Natural Law*, 1754 § 1022). It is inspired by the form of Mandarin administration under the neo-Confucian Qing rulers (since 1644). Wolff's take on the natural law is also shaped by Thomasius, Grotius, and Samuel Pufendorf (1632–94). The political task of the ruler is formally equivalent to the aesthetic task of a designer or architect. Architecture is Wolff's ideal art (his focus would provoke later aestheticians to criticize Wolff for roundly neglecting poetics). As architecture points to material blueprints of well-ordered frames that efficiently distribute mass in elegant designs, Wolff's intellectual concern is to advance the art's form and make it more of a science (*Universal Mathematics*, 1713).

Wolff is the father of German aesthetics, but he did not develop a specific theory of art. Instead, he laid its consistent foundation in philosophical terms. He argued for two aspects of the mind, cognitive powers and sentient will, and derived knowledge from sensation. The impressed data are ordered by the mind, and this order reveals a form—in the terms of Arthur Schopenhauer (1788–1860), the arena of appearances displays the handwriting of the natural force or will-to-life. The law of this form is the decorum; this law reveals geometrically and naturally elegant shapes. This design guides cosmic processes toward their historical unfolding into a final state of the art.

This metaphysical concept of perfection is a physically constant cosmological operation. In Wolff's reading, this operation is an evolutionary vector of material interplays toward complexity. Material interplays develop as progressive consensual grids, and the decorum is their entelechy: a rational, benevolent, substantial *conatus.* Wolff's principle (*prima principia decori*) is binding for ethics, politics, economics, and social order. As the decorum is evident to the unbiased observer, specific religions can illustrate it, but theology, whatever its type, is not a privileged perspective. Theology is an "art," but playful arts contain superior information only if they evolve into science. Architecture is about the design of material structures. The perception of good design elicits pleasure. In this Wolffian sense, the good and the beautiful do not depend on God's arbitrary will but instead on the rational order of nature. Monotheistic revelation is not needed; reason is enough.

INFLUENCE

The paradox of Wolff's influence is that he was the most successful early modern German thinker while suffering the same fate as Newton, the leading scientist of the era—his declared ideas were so persuasive that they were not just academically successful but also soon perceived as oddly trivial. Progress after Wolff was made by critique, by integrating Wolff's ideas in larger models. But while Newton remains admired, Wolff was forgotten after two generations. Later thinkers, from Kant to Marx, regarded him as part of the establishment that needed to be overcome. As a result of their intellectual impact, Wolff was not taught in the twentieth century.

In the eighteenth century, Wolff completed the step from the early Enlightenment to the apex of the Age of Reason, an age that culminated in the split of church and state (1740) and in the American (1776) and French (1789) revolutions. At the start of the era, witches were burnt; priests, preachers, and feudal lords reigned supreme; and the commoners had little to say. Wolff's political legacy was the influence on the academies of the day of his philosophical reflections on rational design, on logical reasons, and on the civil merit in questioning authority. For Voltaire (1694–1778), Wolff defined the Enlightenment—"*Federico regnante, Wolfio docente* (Frederick reigns; Wolff teaches)."

The integration of Wolff's liberal humanistic ideas in Prussian governance by Frederick the Great played no small part in Prussia's advancement to a world power. Wolff's system engaged Kant and Hegel, and thus ensured the continuity of continental thought from Spinoza to the present. During his lifetime, his followers were the Leibnizian-Wolffian school philosophers, who discussed *German Metaphysics* and organized an academic network. His system became the paradigm of German thought until the rise of Kant's star in the 1780s. Some students deserted to the Pietists and advanced in Halle. Daniel Strähler (1692–1750) criticized Wolff in his *Examination of Wolff's Rational Thoughts* (1723).

Other disciples, who stuck to their guns, were fired and driven out, such as Christian Gabriel Fischer (1686–1751) from Königsberg and all of Prussia (1725). Ludwig Philipp Thümmig (1697–1728) left with Wolff in 1723, went to Cassel (ruled by the Landgrave of Hesse), and published the first exegesis, *Principles of Wolffian Philosophy* (1725–1726). Wolffians gained nationwide appointments and ruled the intellectual field well into the 1770s. Bilfinger, the author of the *Elucidations* (1725), went to Tübingen. Johann Friedrich Stiebritz (1707–1772) taught at Gießen and Frankfurt, and wrote *Wolffian Thought Condensed* (1744–1745). Johann Franz Coing (1725–1792) went to Marburg in 1753 and wrote *System of God, Human Soul, World, and the First Principles of Human Cognition* (1765). The philologist, literary critic, and playwright Gottsched taught ontology at Leipzig and produced with *First Principles of Human Cognition* (1765), the most celebrated interpretation next to Baumgarten's. Johann Peter Reusch, who went to Jena in 1738, followed suit with *Metaphysical System (1734)*.

The works by Friedrich Christian Baumeister (1709–1795) at Wittenberg and Görlitz, *Elements of Rational Thought* (1735) and *Ontological Primer* (1738), gained wide circulation. Andreas Böhm (1720–1790) at Gießen contributed to the debate with *Metaphysics* (1753). Johann Nikolaus Frobesius (1701–1756) at Helmstedt (whose poet laureate was the female Wolffian Unzer) supplied with *Outline of Wolff's Metaphysics-System* (1730) yet another perspective. Israel Gottlieb Canz (1690–1753) at Tübingen (after Bilfinger was fired on behest of the theologians) contributed to the Jewish reception that influenced Moses Mendelssohn (1729–1786) with *The Use of Leibnizian-Wolffian Thought in Theology* (1728), *All Moral Disciplines* (1739), *Basics of Human Cognition* (1741), and *Elementary Philosophy* (1744). The Pietist Martin Knutzen (1713–1751) at Königsberg contributed *Elements of Rational and Logical Thought* (1744) before parting ways with Wolff over the theological ramifications of causal patterns.

Johann (Jean) Henri Samuel Formey (1711–1797), secretary of the Berlin Academy, thought that Enlightenment should not be a male affair and trained female intellectuals with the six-volume *La Belle Wolffienne* (1741–1753). One result of Formey's work was to create a social space for Unzer, the female thinker of the age. Unzer learnt from the Wolffian Georg Friedrich Meier (1718–1777) and from the psychologists in her family at Halle. She wrote a phenomenology of embodiment based on Wolff and Spinoza (*Outline of Philosophy for Females* (1751; 2nd ed. 1767).

Wolff's influence culminated in Kant. Kant arrived on the scene with a critique of Wolff's Newtonian departure from Leibniz (1749). Later, he integrated Wolff's and Euler's ideas into predictions of Earth's rotational and environmental fate, as well as into the discoveries of the daily rhythm of coastal winds, the coriolis turn of trade winds, and the seasonal cycle of the monsoon (1754–1757). In his critical phase, he denounced Wolff as a "dogmatic philosopher" and regarded him as the polar opposite to Hume; the *Critique* (1781) ends with a proposed middle way (a la Bilfinger) between the two heuristic extremes. Wolff's challenge is the natural law, the decorum, or rite of nature. The effect of Wolff's early *Aerometry* on Kant's rational apercus of climate patterns remains provocative to the twenty-first century, in light of current information on global warming. In modern times, Wolff's impact on the socioeconomic shape of the European Union (Maastricht treaties) is recognized, but his views on natural frames or "houses" (*oikos*), and on their internal dynamic interplays, are not topics of philosophical research.

See also Arnauld, Antoine; Baumgarten, Alexander Gottlieb; Bilfinger, Georg Bernhard; Calvin, John; Confucius; Copernicus, Nicolas; Cosmology; Crusius, Christian August; Descartes, René; Enlightenment; Galileo Galilei; Gottsched, Johann Christoph; Grotius, Hugo; Hegel, Georg Wilhelm Friedrich; Hume, David; Kant, Immanuel; Kepler, Johannes; Knutzen, Martin; Leibniz, Gottfried Wilhelm; Locke, John; Luther, Martin; Marx, Karl; Meier, Georg Friedrich; Mendelssohn, Moses; Monism and Pluralism; Newton, Isaac; Nietzsche, Friedrich; Ontology; Pietism; Schopenhauer, Arthur; Spinoza, Benedict (Baruch) de; Suárez, Francisco; Thomasius, Christian; Thümmig, Ludwig Philipp; Tschirnhaus, Ehrenfried Walter von; Voltaire, François-Marie Arouet de; Women in the History of Philosophy; Zhu Xi (Chu Hsi).

Bibliography

WORKS BY CHRISTIAN WOLFF

Gesammelte Werke [Collected works]. Edited by J. École, H. W. Arndt, C. A. Corr, J. E. Hofmann, and M. Thomann. Hildesheim: Georg Olms, 1965ff. [1965ff.]

All of the following works are contained in Wolff's Gesammelte Werke. *They were originally published at different times and in different cities throughout Germany, as reflected below, but have been gathered together in this modern reprint collection of Wolff's work.* (GW = *Gesammelte Werke*; Roman numerals refer to the German (I) or Latin (II) series in GW; Arabic numerals refer to the volumes in the individual series; a second Arabic numeral after volume number (e.g. 1.1.) refers to an individually released part of the volume.)

Aërometriae Elementa in quibus aliquot aëris vires ac proprietates iuxta methodum Geometrarum demonstrantur [*Aerometry*]. Leipzig, 1709.

Anfangsgründe aller mathematischen Wissenschaften [*Foundations of All Exact Sciences*]. 4 vols. Frankfurt/Leipzig, 1710. In GW I: 12–15.

Elementa matheseos Universae [*Universal Mathematics*]. 1st ed. 2 vol.; 2nd ed. 4 vol. Halle, 1713–1715. In GW II: 29–33.

Vernünftige Gedanken von den Kräften des menschlichen Verstandes und ihrem richtigen Gebrauche in der Erkenntnis der Wahrheit [*German Logic*]. Frankfurt/Leipzig, 1713. In GW I: 1.

Mathematisches Lexicon [*Mathematical Dictionary*]. Leipzig, 1716. In GW I: 11.

Ratio praelectionum Wolfianarum [in] mathesin et philosophiam universam et opus Hugonis Grotii de jure belle et pacis [*Reason of Wolff's Classes*]. Halle, 1718. In GW II: 36.

Vernünftige Gedanken von Gott, der Welt und der Seele des Menschen auch allen Dingen überhaupt [*German Metaphysics*]. Halle, 1719. In GW I: 2.

Vernünftige Gedanken von der Menschen Tun und Lassen zur Beförderung ihrer Glückseligkeit [*German Ethics*]. Frankfurt/Leipzig, 1720. In GW I: 4.

Vernünftige Gedanken von dem gesellschaftlichen Leben der Menschen und insbesondere dem Gemeinwesen zur Beförderung der Glückseligkeit des menschlichen Geschlechts [*German Politics*]. Frankfurt/Leipzig, 1721. In GW I: 5.

Vernünftige Gedanken von den Wirkungen der Natur [*German Physics*]. Halle, 1723. In GW I: 6.

Vernünftige Gedanken von den Absichten der natürlichen Dinge [*German Teleology*]. Frankfurt/Leipzig, 1724. In GW I: 7.

Anmerkungen über die vernünftigen Gedanken von Gott, der Welt und der Seele des Menschen auch allen Dingen überhaupt, zu besserem Verstande und bequemeren Gebrauche derselben [*Comments to German Metaphysics*]. Frankfurt, 1724. In GW I: 3.

Vernünftige Gedanken von dem Gebrauch der Teile in Menschen, Tieren und Pflanzen [*German Physiology*]. Leipzig, 1725. In GW I: 8.

Oratio de Sinarum philosophia practica / Rede über die praktische Philosophie der Chinesen. Frankfurt, 1726. Edited and translated by Michael Albrecht as *Speech on the Morals of the Chinese* (Hamburg: Felix Meiner, 1985).

Ausführliche Nachricht von seinen eigenen Schriften, die er in deutscher Sprache von den verschiedenen Teilen der Weltweisheit herausgegeben, auf Verlangen ans Licht gestellt [*Detailed News*]. Frankfurt, 1726. In GW I: 9.

Discursus praeliminaris de philosophia in genere [*Preliminary Discourse on Philosophy*]. Frankfurt, 1728. In GW II: 1.1.

Philosophia rationalis sive Logica, methodo scientifica pertractata et ad usum scientiarum atque vitae aptata [*Rational Philosophy or Logic*]. Frankfurt, 1728. In GW II: 1.2–3.

Philosophia prima, sive Ontologia, methodo scientifica pertractata qua omnis cognitiones humanae principia continentur [*First Philosophy or Ontology*]. Frankfurt/Leipzig, 1731. In GW II: 3.

Cosmologia generalis, methodo scientifica pertractata qua ad solidam, inprimis Dei atque naturae, cognitionem via sternitur [*General Cosmology*]. Frankfurt/Leipzig, 1731. In GW II: 4.

Psychologia empirica, methodo scientifica pertractata qua ea, quae de anima humana indubia experientiae fide constant, continentur et ad solidam universae philosophiae practicae ac theologiae naturalis tractationem via sternitur [*Empirical Psychology*]. Frankfurt/Leipzig, 1732. In GW II: 5.

Psychologia rationalis, methodo scientifica pertractata qua ea, quae de anima humana indubia experientiae fide innotescunt, per essentiam et naturam animae explicantur, et ad intimiorem naturae ejusque autoris cognitionem profutura proponuntur [*Rational Psychology*]. Frankfurt/Leipzig, 1734. In GW II: 6.

Theologia naturalis, methodo scientifica pertractata [*Natural Theology*]. 2 vols. Frankfurt/Leipzig, 1736–1737. In GW II: 7.1–7.2 and 8.

Philosophia practica universalis, methodo scientifica pertractata [*Global Practical Philosophy*]. 2 vols. Frankfurt/Leipzig, 1738–1739. In GW II: 10–11.

Jus Naturae, methodo scientifica pertractatum [*Natural Law*]. 8 vols. Frankfurt/Leipzig/Halle, 1740–1748. In GW II: 17–24.

Jus Gentium, methodo scientifica pertractatum in quo jus gentium naturale ab eo, quod voluntarii, pactitii et consuetudinarii est, accurate distinguitur [*International Law*]. Halle, 1749. In GW II: 25.

Institutiones juris naturae et gentium in quibus ex ipsa hominis natura continuo nexu omnes obligationes et jura omnia de deducuntur [*Principles of Natural and International Law*]. Halle, 1750. In GW II: 26.

Philosophia moralis sive Ethica, methodo scientifica pertractata [*Moral Philosophy*]. 4 vols. Halle, 1750–1753. In GW II: 12–16.

Oeconomica, methodo scientifica pertractata [*Economics*] 2 vols. Halle, 1754–1755. In GW II: 27–28.

WORKS ABOUT CHRISTIAN WOLFF

Albrecht, Michael. "Einleitung." In *Oratio de Sinarum philosophia practica*, edited by Michael Albrecht. Hamburg: Meiner, 1985.

Arndt, Hans Werner. "Rationalismus und Empirismus in der Erkenntnislehre Christian Wolffs." In *Christian Wolff 1679–1754: Interpretationen zu seiner Philosophie und deren Wirkung*, edited by Werner Schneiders, 31–47. Hamburg: Meiner, 1983.

Backhaus, Jürgen, ed. *Christian Wolff and Law & Economics: The Heilbronn Symposium*. Hildesheim: Olms, 1998.

Backhaus, Jürgen. "Christian Wolff on Subsidiarity, the Division of Labor, and Social Welfare." *European Journal of Law and Economics* 4 (1997): 129–146.

Beck, Lewis White. *Early German Philosophy: Kant and His Predecessors.* Cambridge, MA: Harvard University Press, 1969.

Biller, Gerhard. *Wolff nach Kant: eine Bibliographie.* Hildesheim: Olms, 2004.

Bissinger, Anton. "Zur metaphysischen Begründung der Wolffschen Ethik." In *Christian Wolff 1679–1754: Interpretationen zu seiner Philosophie und deren Wirkung,* edited by Werner Schneiders, 148–160. Hamburg: Meiner, 1983.

Campo, Mariano. *Cristiano Wolff e il razionalismo precritico* (1939). 2 vols. Hildesheim: Olms, 1980.

Corr, Charles A. "Christian Wolff and Leibniz." *Journal of the History of Ideas* 36 (1975): 241–262.

Corr, Charles A. "Introduction." In *Vernünftige Gedanken von Gott, der Welt und der Seele des Menschen, auch allen Dingen überhaupt* [*German Metaphysics*]. Halle, 1719. In GW I: 2.1–47.

Drechsler, Wolfgang. "Christian Wolff (1679–1754): A Biographical Essay." *European Journal of Law and Economics* 4 (1997): 111–128.

École, Jean. "A propos du project de Wolff d'écrire une "Philosophie des Dames." *Studia Leibnitiana* 15 (1983): 46–57.

École, Jean. "La critique wolffienne du spinozisme." *Archives de Philosophie* 46 (1983): 553–567.

École, Jean. *La Métaphysique de Christian Wolff.* 2 vols. Hildesheim: Olms, 1990.

École, Jean. *Nouvelles etudes et nouveaux documents photographiques sur Wolff.* Hildesheim: Olms, 1997.

Heimsoeth, Heinz. "Christian Wolffs Ontologie und die Prinzipienforschung Immanuel Kants." In *Studien zur Philosophie Immanuel Kants: Metaphysische Ursprünge und ontologische Grundlagen,* edited by Heinz Heimsoeth. Kant-Studien Ergänzungsheft 71, Bonn: Bouvier, 1956.

Krause, Günter. "Christian Wolff and the Classics of Scientific Socialism." *European Journal of Law and Economics* 4 (1997): 285–297.

Ludovici, Carl Gustav. *Ausführlicher Entwurf einer vollständigen Historie der Wolffischen Philosophie.* 3 vols. Leipzig, 1736–1737. In *Werke* III: 1. Hildesheim: Olms, 2003.

Philipp, Wolfgang. *Das Werden der Aufklärung in theologiegeschichtlicher Sicht.* Göttingen: Vandenhoeck & Ruprecht, 1957.

Reinert, Erik S., and Arno M. Daastøl. "Exploring the Genesis of Economic Innovations." *European Journal of Law and Economics* 4 (1997): 233–283.

Rutherford, Donald. "Idealism Declined: Leibniz and Christian Wolff." In *Leibniz and His Correspondents,* edited by Paul Lodge, 214–237. Cambridge, U.K.: Cambridge University Press, 2004.

Rudolph, Oliver-Pierre. "Mémoire, réflexion et conscience chez Christian Wolff." *Revue philosophique* 3 (2003): 351–360.

Schneiders, Werner, ed. *Christian Wolff 1679–1754: Interpretationen zu seiner Philosophie und deren Wirkung.* Hamburg: Meiner, 1983.

Schönfeld, Martin. "Christian Wolff and Leibnizian Monads." *Leibniz Society Review* 11 (2002): 81–90.

Schönfeld, Martin. "German Philosophy after Leibniz." In *Companion to Early Modern Philosophy,* edited by Steven Nadler, 545–561 Oxford, U.K.: Blackwell, 2002.

Schönfeld, Martin. *The Philosophy of the Young Kant: The Precritical Project.* New York: Oxford University Press, 2000.

Schönfeld, Martin. "The Tao of Königsberg." *Florida Philosophical Review* 3 (2003): 5–32.

Stolzenberg, Jürgen, and Oliver-Pierre Rudolph, eds. *Christian Wolff und die Europäische Aufklärung. Akten des 1. Internationalen Christian-Wolff-Kongresses, Halle (Saale), 4.–8. April 2004.* Hildesheim: Olms, 2005.

Tonelli, Giorgio. "Der Streit über die Mathematische Methode in der Philosophie in der ersten Hälfte des 18. Jahrhunderts und die Entstehung von Kants Schrift über die 'Deutlichkeit.'" *Archiv für Philosophie* 9 (1959): 37–66.

Tonelli, Giorgio. *Elementi methodologici e metafisici in Kant dal 1747 al 1768.* Turin: Edizione di Filosofia, 1959.

Tonelli, Giorgio. "Wolff, Christian." In *Encyclopedia of Philosophy,* edited by Paul Edwards. 8 vols. New York: Macmillan, 1967.

Vleeschauwer, Herman Jean de. "La genèse de la méthode mathématique de Wolff." *Revue belge de philologie et d'histoire* 11 (1931): 651–677.

Wundt, Wilhelm. *Die deutsche Schulphilosophie im Zeitalter der Aufklärung.* Tübingen: Mohr, 1924.

Zeller, Eduard, "Wolffs Vertreibung aus Halle." In *Vorträge und Abhandlungen,* edited by Eduard Zeller. 2 vols. Leipzig: Fues, 1865.

Martin Schönfeld (2005)

WOLLASTON, WILLIAM

(1659–1724)

Born in 1660 at Coton-Clanford in Staffordshire, England, William Wollaston entered Sidney Sussex College, Cambridge, in 1674 as a pensioner. After receiving his MA in 1681, he took up the post of assistant master of Birmingham Grammar School. In his late twenties he unexpectedly came into a large inheritance and subsequently married a wealthy heiress with whom he had eleven children. Retiring to a life devoted to domestic matters, he began writing treatises on philosophical and ecclesiastical questions. In 1691 his *The Design of Part of the Book of Ecclesiastes* was published. His one important philosophical work, *The Religion of Nature Delineated*, was first published in 1724, with eight more editions following by 1759. Although he wrote many other treatises, he burned most of them toward the end of his life. He died in 1724, wealthy and esteemed. Queen Caroline had a bust of him placed along with those of Isaac Newton, John Locke, and Samuel Clarke in the royal garden at Richmond, England.

Wollaston is often grouped with Clarke as an unflinching defender of the kind of moral rationalism that David Hume, among others, opposed. Clarke, along with many other philosophers of the period, was motivated to write on moral philosophy in reaction to Thomas Hobbes's work, which he regarded as both wrong and dangerous. Wollaston was one of the few who did not join the debate with Hobbes; as a result, his work is, for the period, unusually free of polemics.

WOLLASTON'S CRITERION OF IMMORALITY

Clarke argued that wrong actions are unfit or inappropriate to the real nature and relations of things. At one point he characterizes evildoers as attempting "to make things be what they are not, and cannot be," which he thought was as absurd as trying to change a mathematical truth. Wollaston constructs his entire moral theory around this idea. But unlike Clarke, for whom the basic moral notions are fitness and unfitness, Wollaston argues that moral goodness and evil can be reduced to truth and falsehood.

His argument has two stages. In the first, he argues that we are able to say things not only with words but also with actions. Beginning by defining true propositions as those that "express things as they are," he argues that actions may express, declare, or assert propositions, by which he means something more than that we understand gestures such as laughing, weeping, or shrugging. To use his example, if one group of soldiers fires on another, the first group's actions declare that the second is its enemy. If it turns out that the second group is not the first group's enemy, its declaration is false. Since we can understand actions, they—like sentences—have meaning, and whatever has a meaning is capable of truth and falsity.

Wollaston acknowledges that some actions have only conventional meaning—taking one's hat off when praying is a sign of reverence for Christian men but not for Jewish men. According to him, words always have a conventional meaning. He thinks, however, that many actions have a natural meaning that cannot be changed by agreement or force. For example, by using and disposing of something, I signify that it is mine. If it is not mine, my actions declare something false. When actions have natural meaning, Wollaston maintains that they express propositions more strongly than do mere words.

In the second stage of his argument, Wollaston proposes what he thinks is the basic criterion of immoral actions, "No act of any being, to whom moral good and evil are imputable, that interferes with any true proposition, or denies anything to be as it is, can be right" (1724, p. 13). Since immoral actions deny things to be what they are, they express false propositions. If I break a promise, I falsely declare that I never made one. If I am ungrateful, I falsely assert that I never received favors. To treat things as being what they are not is, for Wollaston, irrational in the sense that it is one of the greatest absurdities, "It is to put bitter for sweet, darkness for light, crooked for straight, etc." (p. 15).

TRUTH, HAPPINESS AND REASON

Wollaston goes on to try to show that "the way to happiness and the practice of reason" come to the same thing: they are both acting in conformity to truth (1724, p. 52). He thinks the nature of human beings is such that aim at their own happiness. Not only is happiness our natural good but we also have a duty to strive for our own happiness as well as the happiness of others. Anticipating Jeremy Bentham, Wollaston defines happiness as the "true quantity of pleasure": pleasures and pains may be measured in terms of their intensity and duration. We are happy when the sum total of pleasures exceeds the sum total of pains. Just as happiness cannot be achieved by anything that interferes with morality (truth), so the practice of truth (acting morally), Wollaston argues, cannot make a person unhappy. Morality and happiness are congruent, if not in this world, then in the afterlife.

Wollaston thinks that we are first and foremost rational creature. On his view, reason—or, more precisely, right reason—enables us to discover truth. When our actions are in accord with right reason, they express truths. To act according to right reason is thus the same as acting according to truth. It is reason's nature to command, he maintains, and as rational creatures, reason ought to govern us. Not only does reason enable us to discover which actions are morally good, but Wollaston also assumes that our motivation to act morally comes from reason. He argues that true happiness can be achieved only by pursuing means that are consistent with our rational nature, concluding that the "truest" definition of morality is "the pursuit of happiness by the practice of truth and reason" (1724, p. 52).

Belief in God underpins Wollaston's moral theory. God is the author of nature, including our nature as rational beings. The truths we should aim to mirror in our actions are God's truths. They are natural, however, because we are able to grasp them by reason unaided by divine revelation. Thus, there is, he claims, such a thing as natural religion.

CRITICISMS OF WOLLASTON

Wollaston is perhaps best known today not because of what he wrote, but because of the criticisms Hume and others brought against his theory. While his theory was popular during his lifetime, it was, and continues to be, subject to misinterpretations and parodies. Some of this was fostered by Wollaston's tendency to state his views in rhetorical or even paradoxical terms, for example, saying that an evildoer "lives a lie" or that "the *true quantity of pleasure* differs not from that *quantity of true pleasure*" (1724, pp. 11, 36). To the annoyance of some commentators, he included many footnotes in which he quotes in the original from Greek, Roman, Hebrew, and Arabic sources.

While many objections to Wollaston are based on misinterpretations of his view, some are so hilarious that they should be taken as parodies rather than as serious criticism. John Clarke (1725), offers the following quip. If expressing truth is our aim, a person should "spend his time in thrumming over such worthy and weighty propositions as these, 'a man's no horse, a horse, no cow, a cow no bull, nor a bull an ass" (p. 19). Hume (1978), following the eighteenth-century sentimentalist Francis Hutcheson (2002), often takes Wollaston's criterion of wrong actions to be the intention to cause false beliefs in others. He illustrates this reading with the absurd example of someone walking by an open window and seeing Hume cavorting with his neighbor's wife and being caused to falsely believe she is his wife. Hume responds that if that is the case, then the wrongdoing is unintentional since the adulterer's intention is to satisfy his lust and passion, not to cause false beliefs in others. Furthermore, if he had taken the precaution of shutting the window, his actions would not have been immoral, since they would not have caused false beliefs in others.

Some criticisms of Wollaston are directed to his view that wrong actions express falsehoods. The most telling is that his criterion is circular. It is wrong for me to take off with your property, Wollaston says, because I falsely declare it to be mine, not yours. But if we ask why this is what my action means, the answer is that the fact that it is yours means that I should not steal it. In every case the truth that is supposedly denied by a wrong action already has moral content. Clarke (1725) was the first to raise the problem of circularity, but the best-known formulation is Hume's (1978). Richard Price, the eighteenth-century rationalist, and J. L. Mackie (1980), the late twentieth-century sentimentalist, offer similar versions.

Both Hume (1978) and Mackie (1980) object to Wollaston's theory on motivational grounds, arguing that reason alone cannot move us. Both also argue that while people often refrain from performing an action because they see that it is unjust or immoral, no one refrains because he or she thinks it expresses a falsehood. Hutcheson (2002) and the twentieth-century philosopher Joel Feinberg (1977) worry that the fact that truth and falsehood do not come in degrees implies that on Wollaston's view "all crimes must be equal." Wollaston foresaw this criticism and argued that an offense increases with the importance of the truth denied. By introducing the idea of the importance of truth, however, Wollaston abandons his claim that conformity to truth is the only criterion of wrongness. Despite these criticisms, however, philosophers such as Feinberg (1977) and Mackie (1980) find Wollaston's idea that actions have meaning to be philosophically interesting.

See also Action; Bentham, Jeremy; Clarke, Samuel; Ethics, History of; Evil; Feinberg, Joel; Hobbes, Thomas; Hume, David; Hutcheson, Francis; Locke, John; Mackie, John Leslie; Newton, Isaac; Price, Richard; Rationalism.

Bibliography

WORKS BY WOLLASTON

The Design of Part of the Book of Ecclesiastes: Or, The Unreasonableness of Men's Restless Contention for the Present Enjoyments, Represented in an English Poem. London: James Knapton, 1691.

The Religion of Nature Delineated. London: n.p., 1724.

WORKS ABOUT WOLLASTON

Clarke, John. *Examination of the Notion of Moral Good and Evil Advanced in the Religion of Nature Delineated.* London: A. Bettesworth, 1725.

Feinberg, Joel. "Wollaston and His Critics." *Journal of the History of Ideas* 38 (1977): 345–352.

Hume, David. *A Treatise of Human Nature.* 2nd ed., edited by L. A. Selby-Bigge. Oxford, U.K.: Clarendon Press, 1978.

Hutcheson, Francis. *An Essay on the Nature and Conduct of the Passions and Affections: With Illustrations on the Moral Sense,* edited by Aaron Garrett. Indianapolis, IN: Liberty Fund, 2002.

Joynton, Olin. "The Problem of Circularity in Wollaston's Moral Philosophy." *Journal of the History of Philosophy* 22 (1984): 435–443.

Mackie, J. L. *Hume's Moral Theory.* London: Routledge and Kegan Paul, 1980.

Tweyman, Stanley. "Truth, Happiness and Obligation: The Moral Philosophy of William Wollaston." *Philosophy* 51 (1976): 35–46.

Charlotte R. Brown (2005)

WOLLHEIM, RICHARD
(1923–2003)

Richard Arthur Wollheim, an English philosopher, was born in London. After service in World War II, where he rose to captain, he returned to Balliol College, Oxford, first to continue the study of history (in which he received a bachelor of arts degree in 1946), then philosophy, politics, and economics (in which he received a bachelor of arts degree in 1948). He was Grote Professor of Philosophy of Mind and Logic at University College London, 1963–1982; professor of philosophy at Columbia University, 1982–1985; Mills Professor of Intellectual and Moral Philosophy at the University of California at Berkeley, 1985–2002; and professor of philosophy and the humanities at the University of California at Davis, 1989–1996. He was elected a fellow of the British Academy in 1972 and of the American Academy of Arts and Sciences in 1986; and was vice-president of the British Society of Aesthetics, 1968–1993, and president, 1993–2003. His writings focused principally on two subjects: art and human psychology. He made outstanding contributions not just to general but also to substantive aesthetics, above all the philosophy of painting. His unrivalled knowledge of psychoanalytic theory enabled him to write a masterly account of Sigmund Freud's thought and endowed his work in the philosophy of mind with its distinctive character. The strength of his contributions to the advancement of psychoanalytic theory were recognized in the profession by the honors accorded him by the British Psychoanalytical Society and the International Psychoanalytical Association, among others. He died in London.

AESTHETICS

Wollheim's aesthetics is marked by its psychological orientation, manifest in his account of the nature of art, artistic meaning, pictorial representation and artistic expression. In his works, Wollheim argued that art is a form of life (in Ludwig Wittgenstein's sense), artistic activity and appreciation requiring the existence of practices and institutions, art being an essentially historical phenomenon, the changes to which it is inevitably subject affecting the conceptual structure that surrounds it. The aim of artists is, he maintained, to endow their work with a meaning determined by the intentions that guide their activity; the distinctive function of the spectator is to grasp that meaning, to retrieve those intentions, which is achieved, if the artist fulfilled them, by engaging with the work and undergoing the experience the artist intended it to provide.

This psychological account of artistic meaning and understanding is applied to the art of painting in what is perhaps Wollheim's masterpiece, *Painting as an Art,* which maintains that great art is, as is the socialism he embraced throughout his life, rooted in the assumption of a common human nature. A painting's meaning (each painting having one and only one meaning), which is visual, is revealed in the experience induced in an adequately sensitive and informed spectator who looks at the surface of the painting as the fulfilled intentions of the artist led him or her to mark it. He distinguished five principal kinds of primary pictorial meaning achievable by a work: representational, expressive, textual, historical, and metaphorical; he identified what he characterized as secondary meaning, which is what the act of giving a picture its primary meaning meant to the artist; and he illustrated these categories with a remarkable series of challenging interpretations of works by some of the painters he most admired.

He elucidated two other central issues, the nature of pictorial representation and of artistic expression, in psychological terms, each exploiting a species of perception. Pictorial representation is a function of "seeing-in," a perceptual experience which consists of two aspects, the configurational being the seeing of a marked surface, the recognitional being the seeing in this surface of something—a plane of color, perhaps—in front of or behind something else. Artistic expression, at least that involved in the art of painting, is a function of "expressive perception," a perceptual experience with three aspects, the first representing the world as "corresponding" to an affective condition, the second being an affect in the viewer that is "of a piece" with the corresponding condition, and the third being a revelation or intimation of the origin, either of the experience itself or of the kind to which it belongs, in so-called "complex" projection.

Wollheim also advanced an account of the ontology of art. He argued that the fundamental distinction within works of art is between individuals and types, some works of art being individuals, the rest types. Furthermore, every work of art belonging to the same art belongs to the same category, type or individual as the case may be, and, for all works of art, the identity of a work of art is determined by the history of its production.

PSYCHOLOGY

His investigation of the question, What is it to lead the life of a person?, claims a fundamental status for the nature of the process that mediates between a person and the life he or she leads—the leading of a life. This process is constituted by interactions between a person's past, present, and future, and to elucidate this Wollheim presented a typology of the mind, distinguishing mental dispositions from mental states, and proceeds to examine their interactions as well as those among the various systems of the mind, the conscious, the preconscious, and the unconscious. The aim is to outline a philosophy of mind of a kind that psychoanalytic theory requires and it is studded with profound observations of human life that even those sceptical of psychoanalysis stand to benefit from. His study of the emotions, which he "repsychologized," attributing to them psychological reality, represents them as mental dispositions that cause their manifestations, assigning them a particular role within the psychology of the person— that of providing the person with an attitude to the world. He sketched and then developed in great detail a characteristic history, one the recognition of which is essential to understanding what an emotion is.

This proceeds from the "originating condition" of emotion—the satisfaction or frustration of a desire, actually or merely believed in or prospective— through the "precipitating factor," to the transformation of the "originating condition," the experience of satisfaction or frustration being "extroverted," the "precipitating factor" being perceived to correspond to the experience and becoming the object of an emotion, and then, finally, to internal and external manifestations of the emotion and other outcomes. Two of the so-called moral emotions, shame and guilt, which are given extended treatment, are represented as deviating from this characteristic history, incorporating the psychoanalytic notion of fantasy as an essential ingredient of their nature.

See also Art, Expression in; Art, Representation in.

Bibliography

WORKS BY RICHARD WOLLHEIM

Sigmund Freud. New York: Viking, 1971.

On Art and the Mind. Cambridge, MA: Harvard University Press, 1974.

Art and Its Objects: With Six Supplementary Essays. 2nd ed. New York: Cambridge University Press, 1980.

The Thread of Life. New York: Cambridge University Press, 1984.

Painting as an Art. London: Thames and Hudson, 1987.

The Mind and Its Depths. Cambridge, MA: Harvard University Press, 1993.

On the Emotions. New Haven, CT: Yale University Press: 1999.

WORKS ABOUT RICHARD WOLLHEIM

Hopkins, Jim, and Anthony Savile, eds. *Psychoanalysis, Mind, and Art: Perspectives on Richard Wollheim.* Cambridge, MA: Blackwell, 1992.

van Gerwen, Rob, ed. *Richard Wollheim on the Art of Painting: Art as Representation and Expression.* New York: Cambridge University Press, 2001.

Malcolm Budd (2005)

WOLLSTONECRAFT, MARY
(1757–1797)

Mary Wollstonecraft has long been recognized as one of the most influential feminist theorists in history, largely through her *Vindication of the Rights of Woman* (1792). Late-twentieth-century scholarship also began to explore her other texts and their significance.

Wollstonecraft's work is a product of the late Enlightenment, emphasizing the need to achieve virtue and progress through development of reason and sensibility. It also reflects ideas of the Dissenters and political radicals who stood among the relatively few English supporters of the French Revolution. Wollstonecraft's early mentors were Richard Price and Joseph Priestley. The circle with whom she continued to associate included writers and artists such as William Blake, Thomas Paine, Henry Fuseli, and William Godwin. Like them, she opposed slavery, standing armies, and many elements of political patriarchy such as primogeniture, aristocracy, and probably monarchy. She shared their critique of the corrupting influence of political and social institutions structured around "unnatural distinctions" based on rank, property, religion, or profession.

Wollstonecraft's most distinctive and well-known contribution was to extend this analysis to demand an end to unnatural distinctions based on sex and family relations. As she wrote in the *Rights of Woman,* if observation could not prove that men had more natural capability for reason than women, they could claim no superiority over women and certainly no right to rule them. In analysis shaped by John Locke and Jean-Jacques Rousseau (but one that attacked Rousseau for his views on women), she concluded that education, experience, and the "present constitution of society," and not nature, created most observed character differences between men and women.

She argued that unnatural distinctions between women and men tended toward the same effects as other unjust power relations: They corrupt the character of all parties to the relationship, rendering the dominant party dependent on its power and making the subordinate party resort to cunning and unvirtuous strategies of self-preservation. In the case of women she pointed to the use of beauty as what might now be called a "weapon of the weak." Unlike better-known democratic theorists of her era, she applied an antipatriarchal analysis commonly used on institutions such as government to the family itself.

She advocated altering the social practices such as dress, courtship, employment, and family relations that had given men power over women and kept both from virtue. She sought expanded work opportunities for women. She proposed development of a public school system educating girls and boys and children of different classes similarly and together, at least for the early years of their schooling, and wanted girls to study subjects that had been forbidden to them. Her final, unfinished novel, *Maria, or the Wrongs of Woman,* underscored the necessity of women's ability to support themselves, divorce, and have rights over their children.

Although she is most famous for her arguments on women's rights, other contributions are worth noting. Her *Vindication of the Rights of Men* (1790) was one of the first attacks on Edmund Burke's *Reflections on the Revolution in France,* and it engaged his work on the sublime and the beautiful, thus integrating aesthetics and politics in a critique of Burke's defense of monarchy, aristocracy, and pomp. Her further exploration of the French Revolution in the *Historical and Moral View of the Origin and Progress of the French Revolution* (1794) contains an underrated inquiry into the nature of political history and the relationship between ideals and human action. Wollstonecraft's *Letters Written during a Short Residence in Sweden, Norway, and Denmark* influenced the early generation of English Romantics, including Samuel Taylor Coleridge, Robert Southey, William Wordsworth, and Percy Bysshe Shelley and his wife, Wollstonecraft's daughter, Mary Shelley.

See also Analytical Feminism; Beauty; Blake, William; Burke, Edmund; Coleridge, Samuel Taylor; Enlightenment; Feminist Ethics; Feminist Philosophy; Godwin, William; Locke, John; Paine, Thomas; Price, Richard; Priestley, Joseph; Rousseau, Jean-Jacques; Shelley, Percy Bysshe; Ugliness; Women in the History of Philosophy.

Bibliography

WORKS BY WOLLSTONECRAFT

The Works of Mary Wollstonecraft. Edited by J. Todd and M. Butler. New York: New York University Press, 1989. Includes all of Wollstonecraft's works (other than letters). Among the most important are:

Mary: A Fiction (1788).

A Vindication of the Rights of Men, in a Letter to the Right Honorable Edmund Burke (1790).

A Vindication of the Rights of Woman with Strictures on Moral and Political Subjects (1792).

An Historical and Moral View of the Origin and Progress of the French Revolution; and the Effect It Has Produced in Europe (1794).

Letters Written during a Short Residence in Sweden, Norway, and Denmark (1796).

Maria, or the Wrongs of Woman (post.).

WORKS ON WOLLSTONECRAFT

Poovey, M. *The Proper Lady and the Woman Writer: Ideology as Style in the Works of Mary Wollstonecraft, Mary Shelley, and Jane Austen.* Chicago: University of Chicago Press, 1984.

Sapiro, V. *A Vindication of Political Virtue: The Political Theory of Mary Wollstonecraft.* Chicago: University of Chicago Press, 1992.

Tomalin, C. *The Life and Death of Mary Wollstonecraft.* New York: Harcourt Brace Jovanovich, 1974.

Virginia Sapiro (1996)

WOMEN IN THE HISTORY OF PHILOSOPHY

The standard twentieth-century histories of European philosophy do not include women as important, original contributors to the discipline's past. Some relegate a few to footnotes; most omit women entirely. Recent research, inspired by the influence of feminist theory, and by a renewed interest in the historiography of philosophy, has uncovered numerous women who contributed to philosophy over the centuries.

Women's representation in philosophy's history was not always as marginal as it came to be by the opening of the twentieth century. For example, in the seventeenth century, Thomas Stanley's history mentioned twenty-four women philosophers of the ancient world, while Gilles Ménage discussed some seventy, including women Platonists, Academicians, Dialecticians, Cyrenaics, Megarians, Cynics, Peripatetics, Epicureans, Stoics, and Pythagoreans. With respect to the moderns, the seventeenth-century treatises of Jean de La Forge and Marguerite Buffet provided doxographies of women philosophers. Even in the nineteenth century, when women were virtually being erased from the standard histories, Lescure, Joël, Foucher de Careil, and Cousin wrote special studies on female philosophers.

Published 1987–1991, *A History of Women Philosophers,* volume 1, *600 BC–500 AD,* edited by Mary Ellen Waithe, has provided a detailed discussion of the following figures: Themistoclea, Theano I and II, Arignote,

Myia, Damo, Aesara of Lucania, Phintys of Sparta, Perictione I and II, Aspasia of Miletus, Julia Domna, Makrina, Hypatia of Alexandria, Arete of Cyrene, Asclepigenia of Athens, Axiothea of Philesia, Cleobulina of Rhodes. Hipparchia the Cynic, and Lasthenia of Mantinea. In addition to the medieval and Renaissance philosophers discussed in the second volume of Waithe's *History* (Hildegard of Bingen, Heloise, Herrad of Hohenbourg, Beatrice of Nazareth, Mechtild of Magdeburg, Hadewych of Antwerp, Birgitta of Sweden, Julian of Norwich, Catherine of Siena, Oliva Sabuco de Nantes Barrera, Roswitha of Gandersheim, Christine de Pisan, Margaret More Roper, and Teresa of Avila), scholars have recently begun to focus attention on such humanist and Reformation figures as Isotta Nogarola, Laura Cereta, Cassandra Fidele, Olimpia Morata, and Caritas Pickheimer.

THE SEVENTEENTH CENTURY

In the early modern period women's initial published philosophical endeavors inserted argumentation into the largely literary genre of the *querelle des femmes,* or woman question. Thus, Marie de Gournay, adopted daughter of Michel Eyquem de Montaigne, in *The Equality of Men and Women* (1622) replaced persuasive force based on example with skeptical and fideistic arguments; Anna Maria van Schurman's *Whether a Maid May Be a Scholar?* (1659) and Sor Juana Inés de la Cruz's "Response to Sor Filotea" (1700) used scholastic models of argumentation to discuss woman's nature and her relation to learning. By 1673, when Bathsua Makin published *An Essay to Revive the Ancient Education of Gentlewomen,* an unbroken, explicitly acknowledged line of influence ran from Gournay through van Schurman to Makin. In the second half of the century, partly in response to the writings of Desiderius Erasmus, Juan Luis Vives, and François de Salignac de La Mothe Fénelon, a number of treatises on the education of girls appeared, stressing its importance for religion and society. Authors included the Port Royal educator Sister Jacqueline Pascal and Madame de Maintenon.

In the second half of the Age of Reason women also produced numerous works on morals and the passions, including the maxims of Marguerite de La Sablière, Marquise de Sablé, and Queen Christina of Sweden. Perhaps the most well-known seventeenth-century woman writer of moral psychology is Madeline de Scudéry, of whom Gottfried Wilhelm Leibniz said that she had "clarified so well the temperaments and the passions in her … conversations on morals."

Another type of philosophical writing by women, the treatment of natural philosophy, begins to appear after 1660. In Paris Jeanne Dumée and, in England, Aphra Behn argued in defense of Nicolas Copernicus. But by far the most prolific female philosopher then was Margaret Cavendish, who published over a half dozen books on natural philosophy in which she advanced a unique combination of hard-nosed materialism together with an organic model of natural change and a denial of mechanism.

Of Anne Conway Leibniz said, "My philosophical views approach somewhat closely those of the late Countess of Conway." Her metaphysical treatise argued against René Descartes, Benedict de Spinoza, and Thomas Hobbes in favor of a monistic vitalism. On the Continent Princess Elisabeth of Bohemia, whose letters to Descartes had exposed the weakness of the latter's published views on mind-body interaction and free will, discussed Conway's philosophy with a Quaker correspondent. Seventeenth-century England also produced Mary Astell, who in the appendix to the *Letters concerning the Love of God* (1695) argued against occasionalism. In *A Serious Proposal to the Ladies, Part II* (1697), Astell offered women a manual for improving their powers of reasoning, a work that was influenced by Descartes and the Port Royal logicians. Damaris Cudworth Masham also argued against occasionalism in *Discourse concerning the Love of God* (1696). In *Occasional Thoughts* (1705) she defended a number of Lockean views on knowledge, education, and the relative merits of reason and revelation. Masham also corresponded with Leibniz on metaphysical issues, especially his views on substance; yet despite this scholarly career, she stood in need of defense against the charge that the arguments addressed to Leibniz could not have been written by a woman. It was Catherine Trotter Cockburn who came to her defense. Cockburn wrote a number of philosophical works, including *A Defence of Mr. Locke's Essay of Human Understanding* (1702) and a vindication of the views of Samuel Clarke.

In France in the final years of the seventeenth century, Gabrielle Suchon published, arguably, the most ambitious philosophical text that had yet been written by a woman on the Continent: *Treatise of Morals and of Politics* (1693), which included book-length treatments of liberty, science, and authority. Excerpts of her work were published in the scholarly journals of the time, but since the *Treatise* was published under a pseudonym, Suchon fell into oblivion by the late eighteenth century. (Anonymous authorship similarly led to Conway's erasure.)

THE EIGHTEENTH CENTURY

In England Catherine Macaulay published a critical treatment of Hobbes's political philosophy and her magnum opus, *Letters on Education* (1790), to which Mary Wollstonecraft explicitly acknowledges her debt in her own *Vindication of the Rights of Woman* (1792). By the end of the century Mary Hays's *Female Biography* (1803) demonstrated that English women were beginning to trace a history of feminist social and political philosophy that reached back about 100 years to Astell. At the turn of the century, with the growing professionalization of philosophy and placement of it over against the belles lettres and religion, women were producing philosophy stripped of its moorings within discussions of the woman question and theology, and written in journalistic style, as evidenced in Mary Shepherd's book-length treatments of causation, skepticism, and knowledge of the external world, with their attendant criticisms of such figures as David Hume and George Berkeley.

In Enlightenment France Anne Dacier published a translation and commentary for the writings of Marcus Aurelius and entered the debate about the ancients versus the moderns in her *The Causes of the Corruption of Taste* (1714). Dacier's salonist friend, the marquise de Lambert, published a number of works on morals, the passions, education, and woman's status, which continued to be published a century later. Sophie de Grouchy, Marquise de Condorcet, added to her translation of Adam Smith's. *Theory of the Moral Sentiments* her own blend of rationalist ethics and moral sentiment theory in her eight letters on sympathy.

Prior to the French Revolution philosophy of education, in particular, critical responses to Jean-Jacques Rousseau's *Émile,* occupied a prominent place in women's philosophical writings, as exemplified in Louise d'Epinay's *The Conversations of Emilie* (1774) and the works of Mme. de Genlis. In addition to her work on education Louise-Marie Dupin also left an extensive manuscript, *Observations on the Equality of the Sexes and of Their Difference,* which she dictated to her secretary, Rousseau. The French Revolution moved the issue of woman's education into the arena of the rights of a woman as a citizen. Perhaps the most famous of these treatises is Olympe de Gouge's *Declaration of the Rights of Woman* (1791).

In the area of natural philosophy there is no question but that Émilie du Châtelet deserves recognition as an important figure of the eighteenth century. Her *Principles of Physics* (1740) and her letters on the "active force" controversy (1742) attempt to reconcile what she takes to be most useful in Newtonian mechanics and Leibnizian philosophy. Du Châtelet also published a *Discourse on Happiness* (1779) and essays on the existence of God, the formation of color, and grammatical structure.

By the end of the century French women were producing broad critiques of culture and the arts, as evidenced in the mathematician Sophie Germain's *General Considerations on the State of the Sciences and Letters* (1833) and Madame de Staël's *On the Influence of the Passions on the Happiness of Individuals and Nations* (1796).

Germany spawned two critical treatments of Immanuel Kant's views on women: the first by an unidentified "Henriette" and the second by Amalia Hoist. In Switzerland Marie Huber's publications included three Enlightenment texts on the principles of natural religion: *The World Unmask'd* (English translation, 1736), *The State of Souls Separated from their Bodies* (English translation, 1736), and *Letters on the Religion Essential to Man* (English translation, 1738).

In Russia Catherine the Great's correspondence with Voltaire was published posthumously. Finally, in Italy Laura Bassi publicly disputed philosophical theses and published five lectures on natural philosophy; Maria Agnesi discussed logic, metaphysics, and Cartesian physics in *Philosophical Propositions* (1738); and Giuseppa Barbapiccola translated and wrote a critical introduction for Descartes's *Principles of Philosophy* (1731).

The information now available about women philosophers and ongoing research on this topic will provide us with a richer picture of philosophy's significant figures, topics, and styles of argumentation. It is to be hoped that future histories of philosophy will reflect this richer panorama of the past.

See also Berkeley, George; Conway, Anne; Copernicus, Nicolas; Descartes, René; Erasmus, Desiderius; Feminist Philosophy; Fénelon, François de Salignac de la Mothe; Gournay, Marie le Jars de; Hildegard of Bingen; Hobbes, Thomas; Hume, David; Hypatia; Kant, Immanuel; Leibniz, Gottfried Wilhelm; Locke, John; Marcus Aurelius Antoninus; Montaigne, Michel Eyquem de; Rousseau, Jean-Jacques; Spinoza, Benedict (Baruch) de; Vives, Juan Luis; Voltaire, François-Marie Arouet de; Wollstonecraft, Mary.

Bibliography

THE SEVENTEENTH CENTURY

Astell, M. *Letters concerning the Love of God between the Author of the Proposal to the Ladies and Mr. John Norris* (London, 1695); *A Serious Proposal to the Ladies Part II: Wherein a*

Method is offer'd for the Improvement of their Minds (London, 1697); *Some Reflections Upon Marriage* (London, 1700); *The Christian Religion as Profess'd by a Daughter of the Church of England* (London, 1705).

Behn, A. "The Translator's Preface." In B. le Bovier de Fontenelle, *A Discovery of New Worlds,* translated by A. Behn (London, 1688).

Cavendish, M. L., Duchess of Newcastle. *Philosophical and Physical Opinions* (London, 1655); *Orations of Divers Sorts* (London, 1662); *Philosophical Letters: or, Modest Reflections upon some Opinions in Natural Philosophy Maintained By Several Famous and Learned Authors of this Age* (London, 1664); *Observations upon Experimental Philosophy* (London, 1666); *Grounds of Natural Philosophy* (London, 1668).

Christina, Queen of Sweden. *L'ouvrage de loisir* (c. 1670–1680) and *Les sentiments héroïques* (c. 1670–1680), with *Réflexions diverses sur la Vie et sur les Actions du Grand Alexandre, Les Vertues et vices de Caesar,* and correspondence, in J. Arckenholtz, *Mémoires concernant Christine, reine de Suède,* 4 vols. (Leipzig, 1751–1760).

Conway, A., Viscountess. *The Principles of the Most Ancient and Modern Philosophy* (Latin translation: Amsterdam, 1690; English retranslation: London, 1692; both reprinted: The Hague, 1982); *The Conway Letters,* edited by M. H. Nicholson and S. Hutton (Oxford: Clarendon Press, 1992).

Dumée, J. *Entretien sur l'opinion de Copernic touchant la mobilité de la terre* (Paris, n.d.); ms. c. 1680, Bibliothèque Nationale Fonds français 1941.

Elisabeth, Princess of Bohemia. Her letters in: *Oeuvres de Descartes,* edited by C. Adam and P. Tannery (Paris, 1897–1913; rev. ed. 1964–1974); N. Malebranche, *Correspondance, actes et documents 1638–1689,* edited by A. Robinet, Vol. 18 (Paris, 1961); *Papers of William Penn,* Vol. 1, edited by M. Dunn and R. Dunn (Philadelphia, 1981).

Gournay, M. le Jars de. *L'egalité des hommes et des femmes* (Paris, 1622); *L'ombre de la Damoiselle de Gournay* (Paris, 1626); *Les advis ou Les presens de la Demoiselle de Gournay* (Paris, 1634).

Juana Inés de la Cruz, Sor. *Carta athenagórica de la madre Juana Inés de la Cruz* (Puebla de los Angeles, 1690); *Fama, y obras póstumas del fenix de Mexico, Decima Musa, Poetisa Americana* (Madrid, 1700); *Obras completas,* edited by A. Méndez Plancarte (A. Salceda), 4 vols. (Mexico City, 1951–1957).

Lettres, Opuscules et Mémoires de Mme. Périer et de Jacqueline, Soeurs de Pascal. Edited by P. Faugère. Paris, 1845.

Maintenon, F. d'Aubigné. *Lettres sur l'éducation des filles,* edited by Th. Lavallée (Paris, 1854); *Entretiens sur l'éducation des filles,* edited by Th. Lavallée (Paris, 1854); *Lettres historiques et édifiantes adressées aux dames de St.-Louis,* edited by Th. Lavallée, 2 vols. (Paris, 1856); *Conseils et instructions aux demoiselles pour leur conduite dans le monde,* 2 vols. (Paris, 1857).

Makin, B. *An Essay to Revive the Antient Education of Gentlewomen.* London, 1673.

Masham, D. C. A *Discourse concerning the Love of God* (London, 1696; French translation, 1705); *Occasional Thoughts in Reference to a Vertuous or Christian Life* (London, 1705); letters to Locke in *The Correspondence of John Locke,* edited by E. S. de Beer, 8 vols. (Oxford, 1976–85); letters to Leibniz in *Die Philosophischen Schriften von Leibniz,* edited by C. I. Gerhardt, 7 vols. (Berlin, 1875–1890).

*Réflexions ou Sentences et Maximes morales de Monsieur de la Rochefoucauld, Maximes de Madame la marquise de Sablé. Pensées diverses de M. L. D. et les Maximes chrétiennes de M***** (Mme. de La Sablière) (Amsterdam, 1705).

Schurman, A. M. van. *Amica dissertatio inter Annam Mariam Schurmanniam et Andr. Rivetum de capacitate ingenii muliebris ad scientias* (Paris, 1638); *Opuscula, hebraea, graeca, latina, gallica, prosaica et metrica* (Leiden, 1648).

Scudéry, M. de. *Discours sur la gloire* (Paris, 1671); *Conversations sur divers sujets,* 2 vols. (Paris, 1680); *Conversations nouvelles sur divers sujets,* 2 vols. (Paris, 1684); *Conversations morales,* 2 vols. (Paris, 1686); *Nouvelles Conversations de morale,* 2 vols. (Paris, 1688); *Entretiens de morale,* 2 vols. (Paris, 1692).

Suchon, G. *Traité de la morale et de la Politique* (Lyon, 1693); *[Traité] Du célibat Volontaire, ou la Vie sans engagement, par Demoiselle Suchon* (Paris, 1700).

THE EIGHTEENTH CENTURY

Agnesi, M. G. *Propositiones Philosophicae.* Milan, 1738.

Barbapiccola, G. E. *I Principii della Filosopfia.* Turin, 1722.

Bassi, L. M. C. *Philosophica Studia* (49 theses disputed for the doctorate; Bologna, 1732); *De acqua corpore naturali elemento aliorum corporum parte universi* (theses for a disputation; Bologna, 1732); the following appear in *De Bononiensi Scientiarum et Artium Instituto atque Academia Commentarii: De aeris compressione* (1745); *De problemate quodam hydrometrico* (1757); *De problemate quodam mechanico* (1757); *De immixto fluidis aere* (1792).

Cockburn, C. Trotter. *The Works of Mrs. Catherine Cockburn, Theological, Moral, Dramatic, and Poetical,* edited by T. Birch. London, 1751.

Dacier, A. L. *Réflexions morales de l'empereur Marc Antonin* (Paris, 1690–1691; English translation: London, 1692); *Des causes de la corruption du goût* (Paris, 1714).

D'Épinay, L. *Les conversations d'Émilie.* Leipzig, 1774; Paris, 1781.

Documents of Catherine the Great: The Correspondence with Voltaire and the Instruction of 1767 in the English text of 1768, edited by W. F. Reddaway. Cambridge, U.K., 1931.

du Châtelet, G. É. Le Tonnelier De Breteuil, Marquise. *Institutions de Physique* (Paris, 1740); *Réponse de Madame**** [du Châtelet] *à la lettre que M. de Mairan … lui a écrite le 18 février sur la question des forces vives* (Brussels, 1741); *Dissertation sur la nature et la propagation du feu* (Paris, 1744); *Principes mathématiques de la philosophie naturelle,* 2 vols. (Paris, 1756); *Réflexions sur le bonheur* in *Opuscules philosophiques et littéraires, la plupart posthumes ou inédits* (Paris, 1796); essays in Ira O. Wade, *Studies on Voltaire with Some Unpublished Papers of Mme du Châtelet* (Princeton, NJ: Princeton University Press, 1947).

Dupin, L. *Portefeuille de Mme Dupin.* Paris, 1884.

Genlis, S. F. du Crest de Saint-Aubin, Comtesse de. *Adèle et Théodore ou lettres sur l'éducation* (Paris, 1782; English translation: London, 1783); *Discours sur la suppression des couvents de religieuses et l'éducation publique des femmes* (Paris, 1790).

Germain, S. *Oeuvres philosophiques de Sophie Germain, suivies de pensées et de lettres inédites.* Paris, 1879; 1896.

Gouges, O. de. *Les droits de la femme* (Paris, [1791]); *Oeuvres*, edited by Groult (Paris, 1986).

Grouchy, S. de, Marquise de Condorcet. *Lettres sur la Sympathie*. In *Théorie des Sentimens Moraux*. Vol. 2. Paris, 1798.

Hoist, A. *Über die Bestimmung des Weibes zur öhern Geistesbildung*. Berlin, 1802.

Huber, M. *Le monde fou préféré au monde sage* (Amsterdam, 1731); *Le systême des anciens et des modernes, … sur l'état des âmes séparées des corps* (London, 1731), both in English translation as *The World Unmask'd, or the Philosopher the greatest Cheat in Twenty Four Dialogues … To which is added, The State of Souls Separated from their Bodies … In Answer to a Treatise entitled, An Enquiry into Origenism* (London, 1736); *Lettres sur la religion essentielle à l'homme, distinguée de ce qui n'en est que l'accessoire* (Amsterdam, 1738; English translation, 1738).

Lambert, A. de. *Réflexions Nouvelles Sur Les Femmes par une Dame de la Cour de France* (Paris, 1727); *Lettres sur la véritable éducation* (Paris/Amsterdam, 1729); *Traité de l'Amitié, Traité de la Vieillesse, Réflexions sur les Femmes, sur le Goût, sur les Richesses* (Amsterdam, 1732); *Oeuvres complètes …* (Paris, 1808).

Macaulay, C. S. *Loose Remarks on Certain Positions to be found in Mr. Hobbes's Philosophical Rudiments of Government and Society* (London, 1767); *Letters on Education* (London, 1790).

Shepherd, M. *An Essay Upon the Relation of Cause and Effect, controverting the Doctrine of Mr. Hume …* (London, 1824); *Essays on the Perception of an External Universe* (London, 1827); "Lady Mary Shepherd's Metaphysics," *Fraser's Magazine for Town and Country* 5 (30) (July 1832).

Staël, G. de. *De l'influence des passions sur le bonheur des individus et de nations*. Paris, 1796.

Wollstonecraft, M. *Thoughts on the Education of Daughters* (London, 1787); *A Vindication of the Rights of Men* (London, 1790); *A Vindication of the Rights of Woman* (London, 1792).

WORKS ON WOMEN PHILOSOPHERS

Albistur, M., and D. Armogathe. *Histoire du féminisme français*. Vol. 1. Paris: Femmes, 1977.

Buffet, M. *Nouvelles observations sur la langue françoise … Avec les éloges d'illustres sçavantes tant anciennes que modernes*. Paris, 1668.

Cousin, V. *Jacqueline Pascal: Premières études sur les femmes illustres et la société du XVIIe siècle*. Paris, 1844. *Madame de Sablé: Nouvelles Etudes sur la société et les femmes illustres du dix-septième siècle*. Paris, 1854. *La société Française au XVIIe Siècle d'après Le Grand Cyrus de Mlle de Scudéry*. 2 vols. Paris, 1858.

Dronke, P. *Women Writers of the Middle Ages*. Cambridge, U.K.: Cambridge University Press, 1984.

Foucher de Careil, L. *Descartes et la Princesse Palatine, ou de l'influence du cartésianisme sur les femmes au XVIIe siècle*. Paris, 1862.

Foucher de Careil, L. *Descartes, la princesse Elisabeth et la reine Christine*. Paris, 1909.

Harth, E. *Cartesian Women*. Ithaca, NY: Cornell University Press, 1992.

Joël, K. *Die Frauen in der Philosophie*. Hamburg, 1896.

King, M. L. *Women of the Renaissance*. Chicago: University of Chicago Press, 1991.

Kristeller, P. O. "Learned Women of Early Modern Italy: Humanists and University Scholars." In *Beyond Their Sex: Learned Women of the European Past*, edited by P. Labalme. New York: New York University Press, 1980.

La Forge, J. de. *Le cercle des femmes sçavantes*. Paris, 1663.

Le Doeuff, M. "Long Hair, Short Ideas." In *The Philosophical Imaginary*. Stanford, CA: Stanford University Press, 1989.

Lescure, M. de. *Les femmes philosophes*. Paris, 1881.

Ménage, G. *Historia mulierum philosopharum*. Lyon, 1690; English translation, 1702; new English ed. by B. Zedler, Lanham, MD: University Press of America, 1984.

Merchant, C. *The Death of Nature: Women, Ecology, and the Scientific Revolution*. San Francisco: Harper and Row, 1980.

O'Neill, E. "Disappearing Ink: Early Modern Women Philosophers and Their Fate in History." In *Philosophy in a Feminist Voice*, edited by J. Kourany. Princeton, NJ: Princeton University Press, 1998.

Schiebinger, L. *The Mind Has No Sex? Women in the Origins of Modern Science*. Cambridge, MA: Harvard University Press, 1989.

Stanley, T. *A History of Philosophy*, 3 vols. London, 1687.

Waithe, M. E., ed. *A History of Women Philosophers*. 3 vols. Dordrecht: Nijhoff, 1987–1991.

Wilson, K., and F. Warnke, eds. *Women Writers of the Seventeenth Century*. Athens: University of Georgia Press, 1989.

Eileen O'Neill (1996)

WOODBRIDGE, FREDERICK JAMES EUGENE

(1867–1940)

Frederick James Eugene Woodbridge, the American educator, was born in Windsor, Ontario, and attended Amherst College, Union Theological Seminary, and the University of Berlin. He taught philosophy at the University of Minnesota (1894–1902) and Columbia University (1902–1937). At Columbia he also served as dean of the faculty of political science, philosophy, and pure science (1912–1929). Like his colleague John Dewey, he had great influence as a teacher. His influence was less widespread than was Dewey's and was more confined to professional philosophers, but it went deep and is clearly responsible for the revival in the United States of Aristotelian trends of thought. His successor at Columbia University as teacher of the history of philosophy, John H. Randall Jr., is a notable instance of his influence.

REALISM AND NATURALISM

In describing his own philosophical position Woodbridge used the terms *realism* and *naturalism*. By *realism* he meant that life and mind are products that develop, here and there, in the course of the manifold developments in the natural world. Mind, life, consciousness, and soul are activities of certain types of bodies; they never appear apart from those bodies, although mind, once it has emerged in Nature, may come to guide and thus to master some of the occurrences in the world about it. Consciousness is an awareness of some of the things in the environment; it salutes, as it were, those things. Consciousness, far from being the source of the objective world, presupposes its existence. In all this realistic position Woodbridge regarded himself, quite correctly, as reaffirming in modern terms some basic themes of Aristotle's metaphysics.

By *naturalism* Woodbridge meant much the same thing as he meant by *realism.* Naturalism, he said, "is an attitude and not a doctrine." Some contemporary writers used the word *Nature* to indicate a norm of perfection that the historical processes in this world seldom bring to fulfillment. Others, especially theologians, used it to connote an inferior mode of being, contrasting it with an allegedly superior spirit or supernature. Woodbridge avoided such implied judgments. He wrote, in a hitherto unpublished letter of July 24, 1939:

> Let Nature be, as I love to put it, heaven and earth, the sea, and all that in them is, and I do not see how one can here complain of ambiguity; there is no mistaking what is named by the name Nature. So now I have adopted the practice of spelling Nature with a big N to indicate that it is a name given and not a predicate with implications. It is a name for the clearly identified subject-matter of all inquiry, so that now we can ask what Nature is and proceed at once to look for answers.

In other writers the word *naturalism* often introduced untested presuppositions and undetected prejudices. Woodbridge took Nature as anything and everything we encounter and want to investigate. He abjured "anticipations of nature" and made no commitments, in advance of careful study and research, as to the "interpretations of nature" that investigation would reveal to be proper and true. Nature is what we find around us, whether we are looking on a top closet shelf, or through telescopic instruments at stellar universes that are distant in both time and space, or at the evidences for ancient cities that long ago disappeared from view. Daily life, technical science, and history alike presuppose Nature; that is, all these kinds of quests for knowledge presuppose simply that there is much to investigate. *Naturalism,* in Woodbridge's sense of the term, is not a thesis about what kind of world we have; it is a summons to unbiased research.

Woodbridge's writings reflect, in their form as well as in their content, the attitude he called naturalism and realism. He had no interest in producing an intricate tome designed systematically to account for the existence of everything. Rather, he wrote outstanding essays, in each of which he pushed some one line of analysis as far as he then could. His interests are revealed by the titles of his essays: "Substance," "Teleology," "Creation," "Structure," "Evolution," "Behaviour," "Sensations," "Mind," and "Man." In these essays he examined the question of what thing or process or aspect of the world we isolate for inspection when we speak, for example, of "substance" or "teleology." The positions these essays expose are consistent enough, to be sure. But no one is a premise from which others are deduced; rather, each is a fresh inquiry into some facet of Nature. Moreover, Woodbridge maintained that all the possible investigations that might be undertaken still would not exhaust the intricacies of Nature. We may reach some profound conclusions, but we can never properly say concerning any or all of our conclusions that we have discovered the whole truth about Nature.

TIME AND CHANGE

The most influential of Woodbridge's writings are his discussions of time and change (see particularly Ch. 2 of *The Purpose of History*). Woodbridge argues that what happens at any time is not simply or wholly the effect of what has already happened; an event is dependent upon its past as the material upon which activity may be expended, but it is also a new and fresh expenditure of activity upon that material. What occurs is reconstruction, transformation, remaking. What was is thus pushed back into the past, and what becomes takes the place of what was. Time does not move from past through present to future; rather, it moves from the possible to the actual, that is, from one of the potentialities of what formerly was to a single actuality that is brought into existence by an action (whether that action be unconscious chance or conscious choice) upon what was. What comes to us from the past offers us opportunities and often imposes cruel limitations, but it does not make our choices for us. Rather, it allows us to realize our ends insofar as we have understanding of the potentialities it contains. History has no one end; it includes many processes with their many, often incompatible, ends. And human choices, insofar as they are intelligent, may well be effective to some degree. A naturalistic theory of Nature thus issues in a humanistic theory of man.

See also Aristotelianism; Aristotle; Consciousness; Dewey, John; Metaphysics; Naturalism; Realism.

Bibliography

WORKS BY WOODBRIDGE

The Purpose of History. New York: Columbia University Press, 1916.

The Realm of Mind. New York: Columbia University Press, 1926.

The Son of Apollo: Themes of Plato. Boston: Houghton Mifflin, 1929.

Nature and Mind. New York: Columbia University Press, 1937. A volume of essays presented to Woodbridge on his seventieth birthday by students, colleagues, and friends; contains a bibliography of his writings.

An Essay on Nature. New York: Columbia University Press, 1940.

Aristotle's Vision of Nature. Edited with an introduction by J. H. Randall Jr. New York: Columbia University Press, 1965.

WORKS ON WOODBRIDGE

Cohen, Morris R. *American Thought,* 315–316. Glencoe, IL: Free Press, 1954.

Cohen, Morris R. Chapter 17, "Later Philosophy," of *Cambridge History of American Literature,* Vol. III, pp. 263–264. Cambridge, U.K.: Cambridge University Press, 1921.

Costello, Harry T. "The Naturalism of Frederick J. E. Woodbridge." In *Naturalism and the Human Spirit,* edited by Y. H. Krikorian, 295–318. New York: Columbia University Press, 1944.

Lamprecht, Sterling P. *Our Philosophical Traditions,* 486–497. New York: Appleton-Century-Crofts, 1955.

Randall, John H., Jr. "Dean Woodbridge." *Columbia University Quarterly* 32 (December 1940): 324–331.

Randall, John H., Jr. "Introduction" and "The Department of Philosophy." In *A History of the Faculty of Philosophy, Columbia University,* 3–57, 102–145. New York: Columbia University Press, 1957.

Sterling P. Lamprecht (1967)

WOODGER, JOSEPH HENRY

(1894–1981)

Joseph Henry Woodger, the British biologist, was born at Great Yarmouth, Norfolk. He was graduated from University College, London, where he studied zoology, and after war service returned there to teach. The rest of his academic career was associated with the University of London, as reader in biology from 1922 to 1947 and professor of biology from 1947 to 1959. In the term of 1949-1950 he was appointed Tarner lecturer at Trinity College, Cambridge, whose philosophers—C. D. Broad, Bertrand Russell, and Alfred North Whitehead—greatly influenced his early outlook. Later, the influence of the logicians Rudolf Carnap and Alfred Tarski can be seen in his writings, some of which are highly formal studies of the language and principles of biology. The chief work of his early period is *Biological Principles* (1929); the two best-known works of his later period are *The Axiomatic Method in Biology* (1937) and *Biology and Language* (1952).

Underlying the whole of Woodger's activities as a philosopher of science is his concern with a single problem generated by "the contrast between the brilliant skill, ingenuity and care bestowed upon observation and experiment in biology, and the almost complete neglect of caution in regard to the definition and use of the concepts in terms of which its results are expressed." The effect of this has been to arrest the development of the life sciences. Hence, in *Biological Principles* Woodger proposed to examine a number of key concepts that have entered into the chronic controversies and antitheses of biology, such as those between mechanism and vitalism, preformation and epigenesis, teleology and causation, structure and function, organism and environment, and body and mind. He employed the techniques of analysis made familiar by the Cambridge philosophers of the time. These techniques required clarity and precision in the use of ordinary English expressions, but no use of logical symbolism was introduced. Woodger showed that many of the traditional disputes arose either from failure to eliminate metaphysical elements from biological topics or from shortcomings in the biologists' language, which was often sloppy and imprecise. Trouble was also caused by the implicit adoption of theories of knowledge that were not critically evaluated. He objected to phenomenalism, for example, because the arguments used by phenomenalists presupposed the very knowledge that they declared unattainable—knowledge about brains and sense organs as physical objects in the world. In his own alternative to phenomenalism, Woodger contended that the existence of such objects is a hypothesis that "seems unavoidable for anyone who does not believe that when he uses language he is always talking to himself" (*Biology and Language,* p. 69).

In his subsequent work Woodger turned to mathematical logic as a means of reconstructing the language of biology. Here he made some pioneer contributions. *The Axiomatic Method in Biology* used the machinery of

Whitehead and Russell's *Principia Mathematica* to construct a logical calculus that could be applied to certain nonmetrical concepts of genetics, embryology, and taxonomy. The standard apparatus of logical constants, logical variables, postulates, and theorems was taken over, and to it was added a set of ten undefined "biological constants" together with postulates concerning them. The resulting axiom system permitted the deduction of a number of consequences in the form of precise specifications of such notions as "gametes," "zygotes," "cell hierarchies," "alleles," and so on. A simplified version of this calculus was given in *The Technique of Theory Construction* (Chicago, 1939), in which a specimen theory that is a fragment of the earlier system was neatly developed.

Biology and Language showed how these matters could be approached from the reverse direction. In a section devoted to the reconstruction of the language of genetics, Woodger began not by axiomatizing the set of genetical statements but by recasting observation records in symbolic form and then introducing piecemeal the technical vocabulary needed to move to successively higher levels of theory. This book went beyond classical symbolic logic in its discussion of the language of evolutionary studies, where Woodger developed a special branch of set theory in order to reconcile the gradualness in evolutionary changes with the demand that passage from one taxonomic category to another must take place in one generation.

Logicians have been more appreciative than biologists of Woodger's "experiments" in applied logistic. The abstract formalisms are clear, rigorous, and interesting as logical exercises. Yet although the claims made for them are modest, it might well be argued that it is premature to produce axiomatizations of existing biological knowledge or even that biology is not the sort of science that can be fully reconstructed in axiomatic terms.

See also Broad, Charlie Dunbar; Carnap, Rudolf; Organismic Biology; Philosophy of Biology; Philosophy of Science; Russell, Bertrand Arthur William; Tarski, Alfred; Whitehead, Alfred North.

Bibliography

WORKS BY WOODGER

Biological Principles. London: K. Paul, Trench, Trubner, 1929.

The Axiomatic Method in Biology. Cambridge, U.K.: Cambridge University Press, 1937.

Biology and Language. Cambridge, U.K.: Cambridge University Press, 1952.

WORKS ON WOODGER

Berkeley, E. C. "Conditions Affecting the Application of Symbolic Logic." *Journal of Symbolic Logic* 7 (1942): 160–168.

Carnap, Rudolf. *Introduction to Symbolic Logic and Its Application,* 213–225. New York: Dover, 1958.

Goudge, T. A. "Science and Symbolic Logic." *Scripta Mathematica* 9 (1943): 69–80.

Gregg, J. R., and F. T. C. Harris, eds. *Form and Strategy in Science: Studies Dedicated to Joseph Henry Woodger on the Occasion of His Seventieth Birthday.* Dordrecht, Netherlands: Reidel, 1964.

T. A. Goudge (1967)

WOOLSTON, THOMAS
(1670–1731)

Thomas Woolston, the English divine, religious controversialist, freethinker, and deist, was born in Northampton, the son of a successful tradesman. After schooling there and at Daventry, he entered Sidney Sussex College, Cambridge, in 1685, the same college from which the deist William Wollaston had graduated a few years earlier. Woolston received the BA in 1689 and the MA in 1692. In 1691 he was made fellow of the college and proceeded to take orders, achieving the BD in 1699. The study of Origen early led him to an allegorical interpretation of the Scriptures. He was subsequently accused of derangement of the mind and in 1720 was deprived of his fellowship. Two years later he retaliated by printing and dedicating to the master of the college *The Exact Fitness of the Time in Which Christ Was Manifested in the Flesh, Demonstrated by Reason, Against the Objections of the Old Gentiles, and of Modern Unbelievers,* a discourse that he had delivered twenty years earlier as a public exercise both in the chapel of the college and in St. Mary's Church. The theme of this work is expressed in the words "The first Reason, why *the then Greatness of the Roman Empire was a fit Circumstance of Time for the Mission of Christ,* is, that He might better manifest his Divine Authority and Commission to the civil Powers of the World."

A long series of heterodox religious pamphlets followed that led to unsuccessful prosecution by the government in 1725 and culminated in 1729 with conviction for blasphemy. Woolston was sentenced to a fine of £100, a year's imprisonment, and security for good behavior during life. Failure to meet the fine brought about confinement until his death in January 1731. Samuel Clarke, the rationalistic theologian, had made unsuccessful efforts to get Woolston released. A five-volume edition of Woolston's *Works* was published in 1733.

Woolston's first ironical application of Origen's allegorical method of scriptural interpretation appeared in 1705 under the title of *The Old Apology for the Truth of the Christian Religion Against the Jews and Gentiles Revived.* His anticlerical campaign, particularly directed at those who refused the allegorical way, inspired a number of tracts. *Four Free-Gifts to the Clergy* (1723–1724) accused the "ministers of the letter" of being worshipers of the apocalyptic beast and ministers of Antichrist. *The Moderator Between An Infidel and an Apostate* with its two supplements, all of 1725, continued the attack, the "infidel" being the greatly admired Anthony Collins and the "apostate" being a literal-minded divine. In reality the tracts are defenses of the freethinking Collins and attacks on the clergy who had abandoned the allegorical methods of the Church Fathers.

Another series of tracts from 1727 to 1729 began with *A Discourse On the Miracles of Our Saviour In View of the Present Controversy Between Infidels and Apostates.* Here again Woolston was the disciple of Collins, who had promised to write on the miracles but had never got around to it. In all events, however, Woolston is much more outspoken than Collins would possibly have been. Each of these six tracts, in which he frequently employs the device of an imaginary friend, a learned rabbi, as interlocutor, is ironically dedicated to a different bishop of the Church of England. It is argued that the only evidence for the messiahship of Jesus is found in the Old Testament prophecies, and both prophecy and fulfillment must be interpreted as parables. Many events of Jesus' life (especially the miracles) are patently absurd if given a literal interpretation. Jesus was a spiritual Messiah, healing distempers of the soul, not of the body. Hell, Satan, and the devils are in reality states of mind. Starting with the minor miracles, Woolston deals with fifteen in all, concluding with the Resurrection.

If all of Woolston's allegorizing be madness, there is yet method in it. A man of considerable learning, Woolston employs a racy, colloquial, and frequently witty style. For example, the rabbi comments, "I can't read the Story [of the apparitions of Jesus after his death] without smiling, and there are two or three Passages in it that put me in Mind of Robinson Cruso's filling his Pockets with Biskets, when he had neither Coat, Waste-coat, nor Breeches on."

Up to the last Woolston consistently denied that he was an infidel, avowing that he was a believer in the truth of Christianity. His faith in Christianity is perhaps still open to question, but it is certain that he was a deist, whether rationalistic or Christian. He was never a religious fanatic. Voltaire was much impressed by Woolston's attacks on the miracles and made much use of them.

On all occasions Woolston defended universal and unbounded religious toleration and freedom of thought and of publication. Conversely, he insisted that a hired and established priesthood is the root of all evil, and he vigorously defended such "freethinkers" as the Quakers. Ironically, he was the victim of the authoritarian principles he had dedicated his life to eradicate.

See also Deism.

Bibliography

See *Life* of Woolston, prefixed to Vol. I of his *Works,* 5 vols. (London, 1733); *The Life of the Reverend Mr. Thomas Woolston* (London, 1733); Norman L. Torrey, *Voltaire and the English Deists* (New Haven, CT: Yale University Press, 1930), Ch. 4. See also the general bibliography under the Deism entry.

Ernest Campbell Mossner (1967)

WORLD SOUL

See *Macrocosm and Microcosm*; *Panpsychism*; *Pantheism*

WRIGHT, CHAUNCEY

(1830–1875)

Chauncey Wright, the American philosopher and mathematician, was born in Northampton, Massachusetts. On the surface, his life was completely uneventful. From 1852 to 1870 he worked as a mathematician for the *Nautical Almanac*; he was twice a lecturer at Harvard College—in psychology in 1870 and in mathematical physics in 1874—and he occasionally tutored private pupils. In 1860 he was elected a fellow of the American Academy of Arts and Sciences, of which he was later secretary. He visited Charles Darwin in England in 1872—the major social event of his life. Between 1864 and 1875 he contributed numerous articles to the *North American Review* and the *Nation.* His longer articles were published posthumously in 1877 under the title *Philosophical Discussions*; his *Letters* appeared in 1878.

Wright was not successful as a lecturer, but he was a splendid tutor, and many interested individuals sought to converse with him. It was through this easy interchange of ideas that men such as Charles Sanders Peirce, William

James, and Oliver Wendell Holmes Jr. came to feel the influence of his philosophy. Wright was the mentor of the Metaphysical Club, which met in Cambridge in the early 1870s and included Peirce, James, and Holmes among its members.

ROLE OF SCIENTIFIC CONCEPTS

Wright was America's first technically proficient philosopher of science. He constantly criticized Herbert Spencer as being ignorant of the nature of scientific inference. Spencer tried to assemble all the results of scientific investigation and to fit them together into a total picture of the universe. However, Wright claimed, the theoretical concepts and principles of science are not simply summaries of events; rather, they are tools for extending our concrete knowledge of nature. Theoretical concepts, he said, are finders, not merely summaries, of truth.

Some commentators point out that this "working hypothesis" notion of scientific principles is similar to John Dewey's instrumentalism. According to Dewey, all ideas are working hypotheses and all thinking is experimental, scientific thinking being only a limiting case in the sense of having ideal controls. Wright, however, did not formulate an instrumental view of mind in anything like this general sense. All he did was to emphasize the "working hypothesis" nature of scientific concepts; he did not generalize this interpretation into an account of all thinking. To say that Wright "prefigured" Dewey's brand of pragmatism can mean no more than that he provided the logic of scientific inference that later philosophers generalized into a pragmatic view of mind.

SCIENTIFIC EXPLANATION

Wright distinguished two types of scientific explanation. First, an event can be explained by stating the cause of its occurrence even when it is not possible to show that the characteristics of the event are resultants of any combination of characteristics of the cause. Second, in cases like the parallelogram of forces, one can explain not only the occurrence of an event but also its characteristics as resultants of some combination of characteristics of its cause. Wright felt that some events could never be explained in this second sense, and hence he was advocating, in an embryonic way, a doctrine of emergence. He also believed that this distinction would allow a universal determinist, or necessitarian, to account for novelty and newness in the universe. Furthermore, he thought it provided the means for formulating an enlightened materialist doctrine—namely, that all mental events can be explained by physical events in the first sense but not in the second sense.

EVOLUTION

Wright analyzed the logical structure of evolutionary thought in his articles "The Limits of Natural Selection" (1870), "The Genesis of Species" (1871), and "Evolution by Natural Selection" (1872). He called these articles his definition and defense of Darwinism, and Darwin was sufficiently impressed to reprint "The Genesis of Species" and distribute it in England. Since Wright was answering specific questions, his essays have a piecemeal quality, but they are filled with enlightening points. Of particular interest are his comparison of explanation in biology with explanation in geophysics, his analyses of "accident" and "species," and his defense of "every event has a cause" as a presupposition of scientific investigation.

COSMOLOGY

In his cosmological essays Wright condemned the nebular hypothesis and criticized Spencer's defense of it. He referred to the production of systems of worlds as "cosmic weather." He believed that cosmic events, like ordinary weather, show on the whole no development or any discernible tendency whatever. In the stellar world there is a doing and undoing without end. Wright based his nondevelopmental view on what he called the principle of countermovements, "a principle in accordance with which there is no action in nature to which there is not some counter-action" (*Philosophical Discussions,* p. 9). He was, obviously, much impressed with the conservation principles of physics. Beginning with his concept of countermovements, and depending primarily upon the first law of thermodynamics and the conservation of angular momentum, he worked out a technical and elaborate hypothesis about the origin of the sun's heat and the positions and movements of planets.

OTHER DOCTRINES

Epistemologically, Wright was in the Humean tradition, but unlike many British empiricists he emphasized the empirical verification of beliefs and was indifferent to the origins of belief. Concerning religion, he was an agnostic. James observed that "never in a human head was contemplation more separated from desire." Wright simply had no desires about God one way or another. In moral philosophy he was a utilitarian, defending, in particular, J. S. Mill's views.

The metaphysical topics that most interested Wright were self-consciousness and a priori knowledge. In *Philosophical Discussions* (pp. 199–266), after sketching a naturalistic account of self-consciousness, Wright tried to show that the notion of substance was meaningless. He believed that ultimate reality consisted of "neutral phenomena" and that the distinction between subject and object is only a classification through observation. Wright's position was essentially a neutral monism and was a precursor of William James's notion of pure experience.

Unlike most nineteenth-century philosophers, Wright did not deny the existence of a priori knowledge. Quite to the contrary, he insisted that all knowledge, even the perception of qualities as well as relations and abstract concepts, has an a priori element, and this element can be explained experientially (*Letters*, pp. 123–135). This analysis is particularly interesting at the present, since we are currently offered various forms of "factual" or "pragmatic" concepts of a priori knowledge.

See also Cosmology; Darwin, Charles Robert; Darwinism; Dewey, John; Evolutionary Theory; Explanation; James, William; Knowledge, A Priori; Mill, John Stuart; Peirce, Charles Sanders; Pragmatism; Utilitarianism.

Bibliography

WORKS BY WRIGHT

Philosophical Discussions. Edited by C. E. Norton. New York: Holt, 1877.

Letters. Edited by J. B. Thayer. Cambridge, MA: Wilson, 1878.

Philosophical Writings. Edited by Edward H. Madden. New York: Liberal Arts Press, 1958.

WORKS ON WRIGHT

Madden, Edward H. *Chauncey Wright.* New York: Washington Square Press, 1964.

Madden, Edward H. *Chauncey Wright and the Foundations of Pragmatism.* Seattle: University of Washington Press, 1963. Contains complete bibliography of articles on Wright.

Edward H. Madden (1967)

WRIGHT, GEORG HENRIK VON

(1916–2003)

Georg Henrik von Wright held the Swedish language chair of philosophy at the University of Helsinki from 1946 through 1948 and from 1952 through 1961; in between he was professor at the University of Cambridge (1948–1951). From 1961 until his retirement he was a research professor in the Academy of Finland. A member of the Swedish-speaking minority in Finland, von Wright lived almost all of his life in Helsinki.According to von Wright, the major influences on his philosophy were Eino Kaila, an important and charismatic figure in Finnish philosophy; G. E. Moore; and Ludwig Wittgenstein.

Kaila sparked von Wright's interest in formal matters and his use of logical methods. Moore's writings may have inspired von Wright's unpretentiousness and unrelenting quest for clarity. Wittgenstein had a profound personal influence on von Wright—he was Wittgenstein's student, then his successor as professor in Cambridge, and finally, with G. E. M. Anscombe and Rush Rhees, one of his literary executors. Yet Wittgenstein's philosophical influences on von Wright's work are less apparent.

Throughout life von Wright combined, to an extent that is not common among today's academic philosophers, two rather different approaches to philosophy: one the passionate commitment of the humanist and the other the detached objectivity of the scholar. The former approach is exemplified by a number of books in Swedish such as *Tanke och förkunnelse* (Thought and prophecy) (1955), *Humanismen som livhsållning* (Humanism as a way of life) (1978), and *Vetenskapen och förnuftet* (Science and reason) (1986). With his largely pessimistic views about the future of humankind, von Wright has won wide public acclaim in the Nordic countries, particularly in Sweden.

In the rest of the world, von Wright is best known for his academic work. He wrote on induction and probability (*The Logical Probability of Induction* [1941]; *A Treatise on Induction and Probability* [1951]) and on ethics (*The Varieties of Goodness* [1963]). But his main reputation lies in modal logic and in the theory of action. In *An Essay in Modal Logic* (1951), von Wright developed his method of distributive normal forms and analyzed a number of modal systems, one of which is nowadays usually referred to the Gödel/Feys/von Wright system T. In this work von Wright recognized the possibility of modal logics of knowledge and belief (that is, logics in which the modal box operator is interpreted as "the agent knows that" or "the agents believes that"); it was he who introduced the terms *epistemic logic* and *doxastic logic*, respectively, for these kinds of logic. This theme was later developed in great detail by von Wright's countryman and one-time student Jaakko Hintikka.

Von Wright's paper "Deontic Logic" in *Mind* (1951) opened up the new field of deontic logic and was the first in a long series of papers and books in which von Wright elaborated and deepened his analysis. One important insight was that the fruitful study of deontic logic requires a logic of action as a basis, and in *Norm and Action* and many later works he tried to lay the foundations of such a logic. He is unique among early action theorists in letting his formal logic of action inform the philosophy of action and vice versa.

According to von Wright, to act is to interfere with the course of nature—to bring about a change, to bring about an event. This view led him to question the relationship between action and causality and eventually convinced him that an explanation of human action in purely causal terms will always leave out something important. In *Explanation and Understanding* (1973), he presented an influential examination of practical syllogisms: although they cannot possess logical validity in the ordinary sense, nevertheless they may be accepted as explanations *ex post actu*.

See also Anscombe, Gertrude Elizabeth Margaret; Ethics, History of; Hintikka, Jaakko; Humanism; Induction; Modal Logic; Moore, George Edward; Probability and Chance; Wittgenstein, Ludwig Josef Johann.

Bibliography

WORKS BY VON WRIGHT

The Logical Problem of Induction. Acta Philosophica Fennica, fasc. 3. Helsinki: Societas Philosophica, 1941.

"Deontic Logic." *Mind* 60 (1951): 1–15.

"An Essay in Modal Logic." *Studies in Logic and the Foundations of Mathematics*. Amsterdam: North-Holland, 1951.

A Treatise on Induction and Probability. International Library of Psychology, Philosophy, and Scientific Method. London: Routledge& Kegan Paul, 1951.

Tanke och förkunnelse (Thought and prophecy). Helsinki: Söderström, 1955.

Norm and Action: A Logical Inquiry. London: Routledge & Kegan Paul, 1963.

The Varieties of Goodness. London: Routledge & Kegan Paul, 1963.

Explanation and Understanding. Ithaca, NY: Cornell University Press; London: Routledge & Kegan Paul, 1971.

Humanismen som livshållning och andra essayer (Humanism as a way of life and other essays). Helsinki: Söderström, 1978.

Vetenskapen och förnuftet: ett försök till orienteering (Science and reason: An attempt at orientation). Helsinki: Söderström, 1986.

BOOKS ABOUT VON WRIGHT

Schilpp, P. A., and L. E. Hahn. *The Philosophy of Georg Henrik von Wright*. Vol. 19 of *The Library of Living Philosophers*. La Salle, IL: Open Court, 1989.

Krister Segerberg (1996, 2005)

WUNDT, WILHELM

(1832–1920)

Wilhelm Wundt, the German philosopher and psychologist who founded the first psychological laboratory and won world fame as a teacher and scholar, was born in Neckarau, a suburb of Mannheim. After studying medicine at the universities of Tübingen, Heidelberg, and Berlin, he was a *Privatdozent* from 1857 to 1864 at the Physiological Institute founded by Hermann von Helmholtz in Heidelberg. At the age of twenty-four he became so severely ill that he was given up by his physicians and remained close to death for several weeks. In this time of crisis he developed his most essential religious and philosophical views, and also his ideas concerning the mental.

In a series of contributions to the theory of sense perception, published between 1858 and 1862, Wundt's interest in psychological problems, an interest derived from his physiological studies, becomes clear. He gave his first psychological lecture in 1862, and in 1863 his *Vorlesungen über die Menschen- und Tier-Seele* (2 vols., Leipzig, 1863, translated by J. G. Creighton and E. B. Titchener as *Lectures on Human and Animal Psychology*, London, 1896). A series of lectures given in 1864 on the fundamentals of physiological psychology was published at Leipzig in 1874 as *Grundzüge der physiologischen Psychologie* (translated by E. B. Titchener as *Principles of Physiological Psychology*, New York, 1904), his chief work. In the same year Wundt was called to the professorship in inductive philosophy at Zürich. In 1875 he accepted a call to Leipzig, where he founded the world's first experimental laboratory in psychology, the Institut für Experimentelle Psychologie, in 1879. Students from many countries throughout the world became devoted disciples and returned home to found similar institutions.

As a young man in Heidelberg, Wundt was a member of the Baden Stände assembly and the presiding officer of the Heidelberg Society for Workingmen's Education; he was in favor of a patriotic socialism. During the Franco-Prussian War of 1870–1871 he served as an army doctor. As an old man he was rector of Leipzig University (1900) and was overwhelmed with national and international honors and titles. Although in his last years he was practically blind, he did not retire from his teaching position until 1917. A philosophical autobiography was prepared for publication in the year of his death in Grossbothen, near Leipzig.

PHILOSOPHY

As a philosopher Wundt was self-taught. He published a system of logic (*Logik,* 2 vols., Stuttgart, 1880–1883; 4th and 5th eds., 3 vols., 1919–1924), a system of ethics (*Ethik,* Stuttgart, 1886; 5th ed., 3 vols., 1923–1924), and a system of philosophy (*System der Philosophie,* Leipzig, 1889; 4th ed., 2 vols., Leipzig, 1919) during the 1880s. He later wrote on historical subjects (*Die Nationen und ihre Philosophie,* 1915; *Leibniz,* 1916). Wundt was a voluntarist and a follower of the German school of idealism; as such he was indebted to Gottfried Wilhelm Leibniz in particular, and also to Arthur Schopenhauer and G. W. F. Hegel. He opposed sensationalism, materialism, and the relativity of values; nevertheless, he drew ideas from contemporary positivism, particularly in his eclectic historicism and his theoretical inclination to a sociological collectivism. This positivist tendency, noticeable until the middle of his career, especially as a kind of defense against metaphysics, was overcome late in his life. Wundt's main concern in logic was exactness in formal derivations; in ethics it was to secure the Leibnizian morality, based on duty, against contemporary utilitarianism and hedonism on the one hand and subjectivism and relativism on the other. Wundt also essentially followed Leibniz in his parallelist treatment of the mind-body problem.

GENERAL PSYCHOLOGY

If in his philosophy Wundt was primarily an eclectic and historical encyclopedist, he demonstrated his originality in psychology, where he achieved worldwide fame as the real founder of the science and its methodology. However, he was far from wanting to destroy the interconnection between psychology and philosophy. He regarded psychology as the common basis for all scientific and cultural knowledge and the bond uniting all the individual sciences, and therefore as the "science directly preparatory to philosophy."

Nevertheless, Wundt resisted "psychologism" as later formulated and criticized by Edmund Husserl—that is, the reduction of cultural organization and normative evaluations to mere mental processes and the relativization of the timelessly valid to the mere here and now in consciousness.

One of Wundt's main concerns was to investigate conscious processes in their own context by experiment and introspection. He regarded both of these as "exact methods," interrelated in that experimentation created optimal conditions for introspection. Where the experimental method failed, Wundt turned to other "objectively valuable aids," specifically to "those products of cultural communal life which lead one to infer particular mental motives. Outstanding among these are speech, myth, and social custom." Wundt's two main fields of investigation and his two main works, the *Physiologische Psychologie* and his *Völkerpsychologie* (Folk psychology, or Psychology of nations; 2 vols., Leipzig, 1904; 3rd ed., 10 vols., Leipzig, 1911–1920), correspond to this methodological division.

As a follower of Leibniz, Wundt maintained a strict psychophysical parallelism in his basic concepts and rejected any form of theory of reciprocal interaction (causation); however, he limited the mental to the realm of conscious events ("the actual"), in what F. A. Lange referred to as "psychology without soul." Experience should be investigated in its context, "as it is actually given to the subject." In contrast with the natural sciences, the subject matter of psychology is "the content of experience in its immediate nature, unmodified by abstraction and reflection." This claim, which in today's terminology is a strictly phenomenological one, was accompanied by a demand for explanations derived from strict necessity and based on as complete an analysis as possible of the direct, complex findings. Wundt modified the categories of explanation by assuming a unique "psychic causality," which he sought to distinguish from scientific or mechanical causality as including motivation. At this point in his thinking, again following Leibniz, he fought against British and French sensationalism and materialism.

Despite his stress on analytic observation, many notions of Wundt's psychology are transitional to the modern *Ganzheitspsychologie* (psychology of totalities, psychology of wholes) of Felix Krueger and others, among them the "principle of creative resultants or synthesis," which allows perception to transcend a mere addition of stimuli; the "unity of the frame of mind"; and the "value-grade of the total," or feeling and emotion. In his theory of the types of feelings Wundt went beyond the narrow dimensions of pleasure and displeasure, and developed the concept of "total feeling." Although Wundt sought to investigate the elements of conscious processes and their connecting forms, he cannot be counted among the classical sensationalist psychologists because his theory of actuality refers to constantly changing processes rather than to static elements.

Wundt designated the basic mental activity "apperception." Apperception is a unifying function that should be understood as an activity of the will. Feelings are attitudes adopted in apperception toward its individual contents. Thus apperception is simultaneously a descriptive and an explanatory concept. It remained for Krueger, Wundt's pupil and his successor at Leipzig, to remove the limitation to the "pure mental actuality" (structural psychology) and thereby pave the way for the psychology of personality.

Many aspects of Wundt's empirical physiological psychology are still fruitful today. Among them are his principles of mutually enhanced contrasts and of assimilation and dissimilation, for instance, in color and form perception, and his advocacy of "objective" methods of expression and of recording results, especially in language. Another is the principle of heterogony of ends, which states that multiply motivated acts lead to unintended side effects, which in turn become motives for new actions.

SOCIAL PSYCHOLOGY

Wundt believed that his principles of physiological psychology were provable and confirmable in the nonexperimental realm of social, developmental, or cultural psychology, which he called *Völkerpsychologie.* In this field sociological considerations, and particularly the encyclopedic presentation of materials from history and from the other *Geisteswissenschaften* (roughly, "cultural and social sciences," or "humanities"), became Wundt's main concern, overshadowing actual psychological questions. The "objective products of the collective intellect" in nations—speech, myth (religion), and social custom (law)—that were the original subjects of *Völkerpsychologie* came in practice to include social structures and the arts. In Wundt's analysis, which he applied to an incredible amount of material and which was necessarily modified by later progress in the cultural and social sciences, the principle of the social, prehistoric, collective determination of intellectual development dominated. Concern with the individual and with individual development was neglected for this sociogenetic problem. There is, besides, a methodological gap between phenomenological and experimental psychology and cultural psychology, as was emphasized by Wilhelm Dilthey and Eduard Spranger, wide enough to endanger the unity of psychology.

Despite the outmoded material it contains, Wundt's gigantic lifework still offers a powerful inspiration that has never been totally exhausted, at least partly because, since his time, psychology and the *Geisteswissenschaften* have continued to move further apart. Felix Krueger said at Wundt's grave, "In him faithfulness to fact was raised to the level of genius." Thoroughness and methodical acuity, combined with universal versatility, created something unique in his work. Wundt has been extolled as the last "polyhistor." Education and aesthetics were the only fields to which he made no contribution. E. G. Boring computed his total published output at 53,000 pages—an entire library. The complete list of his works, published by his daughter Eleonore Wundt in 1926, is a hefty brochure. In both philosophy and psychology Wundt's oscillation between idealistic and positivistic tendencies kept him bound to his time and caused a notable lack of consistency. He was a major pioneer of both scientific and cultural psychology, even though he was unable to integrate them. The unity of all sciences through psychology and the development of philosophy out of psychology remain as transient theoretical postulates unrealizable and unrealized by developments since his death.

See also Apperception; Dilthey, Wilhelm; Geisteswissenschaften; Hegel, Georg Wilhelm Friedrich; Helmholtz, Hermann Ludwig von; Husserl, Edmund; Idealism; Introspection; Krueger, Felix; Lange, Friedrich Albert; Leibniz, Gottfried Wilhelm; Materialism; Mind-Body Problem; Phenomenology; Positivism; Psychology; Schopenhauer, Arthur; Sensationalism; Spranger, (Franz Ernst) Eduard; Voluntarism.

Bibliography

ADDITIONAL WORKS BY WUNDT

Erlebtes und Erkanntes, Selbstbiographie (Things experienced and perceived, autobiography). Stuttgart, 1920.

Wilhelm Wundts Werk, ein Verzeichnis seiner sämtlichen Schriften (Wilhelm Wundt's work, a list of his complete writings). Edited by Eleonore Wundt. Munich: Beck, 1927.

WORKS ON WUNDT

Boring, E. G. *A History of Experimental Psychology,* 2nd ed., 318–347. New York: Appleton-Century-Crofts, 1950.

Heussner, A. *Einführung in Wilhelm Wundts Philosophie und Psychologie.* Göttingen: Vandenhoeck and Ruprecht, 1920.

Hoffmann, Arthur. "Wilhelm Wundt, eine Würdigung." *Beiträge zur Philosophie des deutschen Idealismus* 2 (1922).

König, Edmund. *W. Wundt, Seine Philosophie und Psychologie.* Stuttgart: Frommann, 1901; 3rd ed., 1912.

Nef, Willi. *Die Philosophie Wilhelm Wundts.* Leipzig: Meiner, 1923.

Peters, R. S., ed. *Brett's History of Psychology,* 479–488. London, 1953.

Petersen, Peter. *Wilhelm Wundt und seine Zeit.* Stuttgart. 1925.

A Wilhelm Wundt Archive, established by his daughter in his house at Grossbothen, was transferred to the Psychological Institute of the University of Leipzig at her death and is administered by the institute.

Albert Wellek (1967)
Translated by Tessa Byck

WYCLYF, JOHN

(c. 1320–1384)

John Wyclyf, the scholastic philosopher and ecclesiastical reformer, was born in the north of England, near Richmond. He spent most of his adult life in and around Oxford; he served several parishes as priest and held a series of prebends that gave him a modest income. On several occasions he was asked his opinion in matters of government policy toward the papacy, and he appeared once before Parliament. In 1374 Wyclyf was a member of a royal commission of three that met with representatives of the papal Curia at Bruges to attempt to solve the impasse between England and the papacy over England's refusal to pay the Peter's pence. Later he became an adherent of and adviser to the duke of Lancaster, John of Gaunt, who protected Wyclyf when, under pressure from the English hierarchy, he was charged with heresy. Wyclyf retired, probably on Lancaster's advice, from active public life to his parish at Lutterworth in 1382. In that year he suffered a paralytic stroke but continued his prolific writing until his death, from a second stroke, two years later.

Wyclyf's literary life may be divided into three periods. During the first period, from about 1358 to 1372, he was primarily an academic philosopher, lecturing on logic and metaphysics in orthodox terms. During the second period, from 1372 to 1377 or 1378, he began to apply his realist philosophy to the problems of church and state, an application that resulted in his doctrine of dominion. In the last period, from 1377 or 1378 to 1384, he went much further in his investigation of the basis and structure of the Roman church and came to conclusions quite openly antipapal. During this period papal bulls were aimed against him (1377); he was twice haled before local bodies on orders from Rome; and many of his conclusions were specifically condemned, although he was not personally disciplined. These same conclusions, in addition to many more, were condemned by the Council of Constance in 1415.

Wyclyf's philosophical presuppositions colored all his thought. The transition from one period of his life to another was barely perceptible and he was able, late in his life, to refer to his earlier expressions with few apologies. In the atmosphere of mid-fourteenth-century Oxford, Wyclyf early had to take a position toward the *universalia post rem* of William of Ockham's nominalism, then popular and persuasive. He rejected its priority of the particulars over universals in favor of the older Augustinian tradition of *universalia ante rem.* Once he had accepted this position, he followed it to its logical conclusions and constructed a *summa de ente* in twelve books that, while not so systematic as most other *summae* of the thirteenth and fourteenth centuries, nevertheless dealt in great detail with the salient points of dispute between the nominalists, the *doctores moderni,* as he called them, and the protagonists of universal ideas.

THE *SUMMA DE ENTE*

Following his early works on logic, written probably between 1360 and 1365, Wyclyf's *Summa de Ente* occupied him until at least 1370, when his attention was diverted to theology. The *Summa* in its final form consists of two books of six treatises each. The first book treats being in general, the doctrine of universals, and the nature and function of time. These questions are approached from the point of view of man and his cosmos. The second book is pure theology: God's intellection, his knowledge, his will, the Trinity, his ideas and his power to create outside himself. In Wyclyf's grand design the first book is anthropology and the second book is theology. Universals thus may be considered the human parallel of God's ideas. Knowing only the *Timaeus* of Plato's works, Wyclyf adhered to Plato as he knew him from Augustine. His realism was uncompromising. Universals exist *ante rem,* temporally and logically prior to the particular. "The idea is therefore essentially the divine nature and formally the *ratio* according to which God intelligizes [*intelligit*] creatures." These ideas make up the creative mind of God. In a parallel fashion the universal (on man's level) is its singular. The singular participates in its universal, which is by nature a projection of an idea in the mind of God. As a creation of God's mind, the singular is incapable of annihilation. For God to allow a singular to be annihilated would be to permit the annihilation of a part of himself—an obvious impossibility.

As he articulated this line of thought, Wyclyf was led to examine the church's doctrine of transubstantiation. He reasoned that the church held that in the Eucharist the substance of bread and wine was annihilated. From about 1379 he attacked the doctrine vehemently on purely logical and philosophical grounds. This position in turn was bitterly attacked by orthodox theologians and later formally anathematized at the Council of Constance. In view of his basic realism Wyclyf could not have done otherwise than he did.

THE CHURCH

About 1374 Wyclyf had begun a spirited defense of the doctrine of dominion. This concept of the sanctions of power was rooted in Augustine and had recently been propounded by Richard FitzRalph, archbishop of Armagh in Ireland. Dominion or lordship is founded in grace, and he who is without grace has no proper right to exercise dominion. Applied to the religious hierarchy, it would have deprived many of the higher clergy of their power and emoluments.

In 1378 Wyclyf was led, by an incident involving the theory and practice of sanctuary, to examine the nature of the church and the relations of the papacy with the English crown. In the course of the dispute arising from the publication of his views, he came to the clear conclusion that the pope and the cardinalate were unnecessary and that in England the king should control the church, allowing for counsel and advice of theologians in matters of theology.

Wyclyf was a stout defender of the Pauline-Augustinian doctrine of predestination, which he related to and strengthened with his doctrines of universals and necessity. The implications of predestination did not favor a highly organized ecclesiastical organization; if a believer is predestined by God to salvation from all eternity, the church would soon have no reason for existence. Individualism in religious matters could hardly be tolerated by the establishment.

In the last years of his life Wyclyf composed a second *summa*, a *Summa Theologica*, also in twelve books. Not a *summa* in the thirteenth-century style, it was a series of polemical treatises concerned with problems in church or national polity, in defense of his contested opinions. In presentation he remained a Schoolman to the end, but his ideas were disruptive of the establishment, and opposition, at Oxford and in London, was determined and ruthless. The opposition to his efforts at reform is somewhat surprising, in view of his highly pronounced English nationalism; but English clerics were his bitterest opponents. In Wyclyf's view, his thought and action were consistent and consistently rooted in the doctrine of divine ideas, the creative *rationes* by which the universals existed before the particular and were exhibited in the particular, *essentialiter, formaliter, et eternaliter.*

See also Augustine, St.; Augustinianism; Determinism, A Historical Survey; Medieval Philosophy; Plato; Realism; William of Ockham.

Bibliography

The Wyclif Society published 33 volumes of Wyclyf's works (London, 1883–1922) but omitted some important philosophical treatises. See also S. H. Thomson, *Joh. Wyclif Summe de Ente libb. I et II* (Oxford: Clarendon Press, 1930; reissued Boulder, CO, 1956), a Latin text with critical introduction; and A. D. Breck, ed., *Joh. Wyclyf De Trinitate* (Boulder: University of Colorado Press, 1962).

The standard life of Wyclyf is H. B. Workman, *John Wyclif*, 2 vols. (Oxford: Clarendon Press, 1926). See also K. B. McFarlane, *John Wycliffe and the Beginnings of English Nonconformity* (London: English Universities Press, 1952); and J. A. Robson, *Wyclif and the Oxford Schools* (Cambridge, U.K.: Cambridge University Press, 1961).

S. Harrison Thomson (1967)

XENOPHANES OF COLOPHON

(c. 570 BCE—c.475 BCE)

Like the other founders of Greek philosophy, Xenophanes lived in Ionia and investigated natural phenomena such as the basic substances, the history and structure of the cosmos, and weather phenomena. He is best known for his criticisms of religious beliefs and practices, for his own conception of the divine, and for being the earliest philosopher to discuss epistemological questions. A poet who traveled widely in Greek lands, he composed his philosophical work in verse, presumably for performance, which suggests that his radical theological views were not abhorrent to his audiences. Some forty fragments of his writings survive, more than one hundred lines, far more than what remains from any earlier philosopher.

His *theological* fragments consist in statements that seemingly criticize the anthropomorphic polytheism of Greek tradition and in pronouncements on the true nature of god. He claims that (just like the Greeks) Ethiopians and Thracians believe their gods look like themselves (frag. 16) and that if animals could draw, horses would depict their gods as horses, oxen as oxen, etc. (frag. 15). He reproaches the revered poets Homer and Hesiod for ascribing to the gods actions humans consider immoral (frag. 11). He does not argue that these diverse accounts of the divine are false or even contradictory, but the remark about animals seems intended to ridicule the differing human (including Greek) beliefs about the gods. Nor is the reproach about the gods' behavior an argument, but it further undermines tradition: Greeks not only think the gods are like humans, they think they are immoral too!

Abandoning the Olympian gods led Xenophanes not to atheism but to new opinions on the nature of the divine and a new way of apprehending it. God "always remains in the same place, moving not at all" (frag. 26); "not at all like mortals in body or thought" (frag. 23); "is one, greatest among gods and men, all of him sees, all of him thinks, all of him hears" (frag. 24); "without toil he shakes all things by the thought of his mind" (frag. 25). Fragments 24 and 25 probably assert omniscience and omnipotence. Xenophanes presents a nonanthropomorphic god possessing cognitive abilities corresponding to human ones but far exceeding humans in power. It is a theistic account since "shakes all things" seems to mean that god controls and causes all events in the cosmos. Xenophanes may also have been a monotheist. If so, he was the first Greek to adopt this revolutionary view. The relevant text is fragment 23, whose opening words can be translated either "god is one" or "one god." The next phrase, "greatest among gods and men," suggests a plurality of gods, so the god Xenophanes describes would be the supreme god but not the only one. But it can be objected that his criticisms of the traditional anthropomorphic gods and his belief in a supreme god that governs everything tell against polytheism. This objection is reinforced by the report that he said it is unholy for any god to have a master and that no god is deficient in anything at all (Testimony 32), claims hard to square with a belief that combines polytheism with a single supreme deity. These are strong motives for taking "among gods and men" not to imply polytheism. One way is to take it as a *polar expression*, as if an atheist said that there is no god in heaven or earth, using "in heaven or earth" (ironically) to mean simply "anywhere." But many are dissatisfied by this solution, and there is no consensus on the question of Xenophanes's monotheism.

Xenophanes gives no argument for the existence or the nature of his supreme deity. He seems not to have questioned the existence of the divine. The only reason given for any of its attributes is that "it is not fitting for him to go to different places at different times" (frag. 26). Not tradition or other authority, but Xenophanes' sense of what befits the divine, is his criterion for determining god's nature. In this limited sense we find in Xenophanes the beginnings of rational theology.

Three fragments introduce important issues in epistemology although their meaning is disputed. "By no means did the gods intimate all things to mortals from the beginning, but in time, by searching, they discover better" (frag. 18) may refer specifically to the intellectual progress being made by Xenophanes and his fellow early philosophers and emphasize the importance of empirical work for making advances. Certainly, some of Xenophanes's new ideas on natural phenomena were based in observation and investigation, as opposed to mere theorizing. "No man has seen nor will anyone know the clear truth about the gods and all the things I speak of. For even if someone were to say exactly what has been brought to pass, he still does not know, but belief is fashioned over all things" (frag. 34) distinguishes truth, knowledge, and belief and denies that true beliefs and assertions amount to knowledge. It may indicate a skepticism about the possibility of acquiring knowledge of the subjects studied by the early philosophers. If so, the progress heralded in fragment 18 must fall short of certain knowledge. We must remain with beliefs, which may be better or worse: They may be better or worse supported by investigations, which themselves may be more or less thorough and careful. Fragment 35, which may be the conclusion of Xenophanes's discussion of these topics, advises, with modesty uncharacteristic of the Presocratics: "Let these things be believed as like the truth." Xenophanes's views remain on the level of beliefs; if he has *searched* well, his views will be *better*—possibly true or closer to the truth than conflicting views. But even if they are, they cannot be known to be more like the truth, only believed to be so.

See also Epistemology; Homer; Philosophy of Religion.

Bibliography

TEXTS

Diels, Hermann, and Walther Kranz, eds. *Die fragmente der Vorsokratiker, griechisch und deutsch*. Vol. 1, 6th ed. Berlin: Weidmann, 1951, p. 126–138.

Heitsch, E. *Xenophanes: Die fragmente*. Munich: Artemis, 1983.

Lesher, James H. *Xenophanes of Colophon: Fragments; A Text and Translation with Commentary*. Toronto: University of Toronto Press, 1992.

Studies

Barnes, Jonathan. *The Presocratic Philosophers*. Rev. ed. London: Routledge & Kegan Paul, 1982, p. 82–99, 137–143.

Fränkel, Hermann. "Xenophanesstudien," *Hermes* 60, 1925, p. 174–192. Reprinted in *Wege und Formen frühgriechischen Denkens*. 3rd ed. Munich: Beck, 1968. Translation of part of this paper by M. R. Cosgrove under the title "Xenophanes' Empiricism and his Critique of Knowledge" in *The Pre-Socratics: A Collection of Critical Essays*. Edited by Alexander P. D. Mourelatos. Garden City, NY: Doubleday, 1974, p. 118–131.

Guthrie, W. K. C. *A History of Greek Philosophy*. Vol. 1. Cambridge, U.K.: Cambridge University Press, 1962, p. 360–402.

Kirk, Geoffrey S., John E. Raven, and Malcolm Schofield, eds. *The Presocratic Philosophers: A Critical History with a Collection of Texts*. 2nd ed. Cambridge, U.K.: Cambridge University Press, 1983, p. 163–180.

Richard McKirahan (2005)

XENOPHON
(c. 430 BCE–c. 350 BCE)

Xenophon was an Athenian citizen, soldier, gentleman-farmer, historian, and author of many varied and often graceful prose works. When young he knew Socrates, whom he consulted before joining, in 401, the famous expedition to Persia narrated in his masterpiece, the

Anabasis. Xenophon played a part in leading the defeated remnant back to Greece. Meanwhile, in 399, Socrates had been executed on trumped-up charges. In the subsequent pamphleteering, Xenophon wrote in Socrates' defense. His so-called *Apology of Socrates* is an unconvincing footnote to Plato's; but later he compiled his extensive and valuable *Memorabilia* (Recollections of Socrates) the work that has given Xenophon, not himself a philosopher, considerable importance to all post-Socratic philosophers. In it Xenophon supplemented his defense of Socrates against specific charges (made in a pamphlet by Polycrates) with a more general description of his character as a man, a friend, and a teacher, strongly emphasizing his beneficial influence on all who knew him and, for illustration, recording many conversations in which Socrates' views or methods were displayed. Xenophon claimed to have heard many of these conversations himself; others were reported to him by friends among the original interlocutors. Some longer sequences of conversations follow up related topics, but individual conversations are never sustained as long as even a short Platonic dialogue.

Undeniably, Xenophon's Socrates is less lively in discussion than Plato's and far less impressive in defending his paradoxes. The difference reveals the gulf between Plato and his contemporaries in literary skill and in philosophical understanding. But there is no need to reject Xenophon's testimony, despite persistent attacks by scholars on his honesty. Xenophon's picture of Socrates is his own, drawn from his own and his friends' memories of Socrates, not plagiarized from other "Socratic" writers any more than from Plato; it is authenticated precisely by its failings. Xenophon saw Socrates as a man of enormously strong moral character and a teacher of moral principles revolutionary for their day in their demand for unselfishness and self-control. Xenophon only half understood the philosophical significance of Socrates's views, and for fuller understanding we must turn to Plato; but Xenophon occasionally added important details, and with allowance for his limitations an impression of Socrates can be obtained from him that helps us to discern very generally the area in which Plato was presenting his own arguments and no longer those of Socrates.

Xenophon's Socrates demonstrates repeatedly the practical importance of knowledge. He advises young men ambitious to be generals and politicians to acquire knowledge, and draws analogies to show that all skills must be learned; he discusses their respective skills with a painter, a sculptor, a breastplate maker, and even, humorously, with a courtesan. He does not try, as Plato's Socrates did, to question the significance of the craftsmen's knowledge, but only to show that their knowledge can be usefully increased by deeper understanding of the purposes of their various crafts. In turn, he is suspicious of the purely theoretical study of astronomy and geometry beyond their practical uses. Xenophon stresses, nevertheless, that Socrates himself was not ignorant of theoretical science.

Xenophon does not quote in so many words the Socratic paradox "no one errs voluntarily," but he does state that Socrates did not distinguish knowledge from self-control and identified justice and all other virtues with knowledge; knowledge of justice or piety is what produces the just or pious man. Characteristically, however, he repeatedly shows Socrates warning against "weakness of will," and forgets that in the Socratic view, strictly speaking, this could not occur; his admiration of Socrates' own self-control leads him to praise self-control as an independent virtue.

Xenophon occasionally reproduces a Socratic elenchus, or interrogation demonstrating an interlocutor's ignorance, and comments that Socrates used this method to stimulate moral improvement in his pupils by inducing them to acquire knowledge. Xenophon shows no grasp of elenchus as a philosophical weapon for testing arguments, nor indeed of the Platonic Socrates' insistence that consciousness of one's ignorance may be the best one can achieve. Xenophon's Socrates uses no "irony," but states positive views quite unreservedly. He is interested in definitions and unlike Plato's Socrates confidently provides them; rather surprisingly, he is willing to define *good* and *beautiful* as relative to utility. Perhaps out of many suggestions intended by Socrates to be tentative, or to show the difficulties of definition, Xenophon—in pursuit of certainty—isolated a few solutions as final.

Xenophon at one point describes Socrates' method as "leading the discussion back to its basic premise (*hypothesis*)" by establishing, for example, an agreed general definition of the good citizen before assessing a particular citizen's goodness; he tells us that Socrates regarded agreement in discussion as the best guarantee against error. This account of *hypothesis* is much simpler than Plato's in either *Meno* or *Phaedo*, but it is abundantly exemplified in Plato's early dialogues. Xenophon nowhere ascribes to Socrates any theory of Forms, but he quotes a suggestion of Socrates that etymologically "to perform dialectic" means "to arrange things in classes."

Xenophon's entertaining *Symposium* (Banquet) and *Oeconomicus* (Household management) display Socrates taking part in sustained discussions; but here this is a literary device with no biographical intention, and in any case little is attributed to Socrates. Xenophon's idealizing *Cyropaedia* (Education of Cyrus) shows very slight Socratic influence.

See also Medieval Philosophy; Plato; Socrates; Universals, A Historical Survey.

Bibliography

Xenophon's complete works may be found in both Greek and English in the seven-volume Loeb Classical Library edition (London and New York, 1914–1925). The *Memorabilia* in the Loeb edition, translated by E. C. Marchant, appeared in 1923.

For studies on Xenophon's Socrates, see A. Delatte, *Le troisième Livre des souvenirs socratiques de Xénophon* (Liège: Faculté de Philosophie et Lettres, 1933), and R. Simeterre, *La théorie socratique de la vertuscience selon les "Mémorables" de Xénophon* (Paris, 1938).

David B. Robinson (1967)

XENOPHON [ADDENDUM]

See Appendix, Vol. 10

XUNZI

(fl. 295–238 BCE)

Among the classical Confucian thinkers of the Warring States period (Zhanguo 475–221 BCE), Xunzi plays a commanding role in the systematic development and defense of Confucian Tradition. Xunzi's teachings are contained in the *Xunzi*, compiled by Liu Xiang of the Former Han (206 BCE–8 CE). Although some scholars have questioned the authenticity of some of the essays, this work shows remarkable coherent and reasoned statements of the central aspects of the Confucian ethical and political vision of a harmonious and well-ordered society. Moreover, especially impressive is Xunzi's wide-ranging interest in such timeless issues as the ideal of the good human life, relation between morality and human nature, the nature of deliberation, ethical discourse and argumentation, moral agency and moral knowledge, the ethical significance of honor and shame, ethical uses of historical knowledge, moral education, and personal cultivation. Because of the comprehensive and systematic character of his philosophical concerns, Xunzi is sometimes compared to Aristotle.

Whereas both Mencius and Xunzi are exponents and defenders of Confucius's ideal of well-ordered society, traditional Chinese scholars often distinguish their thought by the contrast between government by *ren* or benevolence and government by *li* (rites, rules of proper conduct). However, for both, the key concepts are *ren*, *yi* (righteousness, rightness, fittingness), and *li*. Xunzi writes:

> The *dao* (Way) of former kings consists of exaltation of *ren* and acting in accord with the Mean. What is meant by the Mean? I answer that: "*li* and *yi*." *Dao* is not the *dao* of Heaven, nor is it the *dao* of the Earth. It is the *dao* that guides humanity, the *dao* embodied in the lives of the paradigmatic individuals. (*ruxiao pian*, ch. 8)

Unlike Mencius, Xunzi was a forceful advocate of abolition of hereditary titles. Even more important, an enlightened ruler will enrich the state and its people with ample surplus to cope with untoward circumstances, protect the country with strong military defense measures in the spirit of *ren*, and promulgate and efficiently administer ethically legitimate laws and institutions. Thus an enlightened ruler is one who is good at organizing the people in society in accordance with the requirements expressed in *ren*, *yi*, and *li*. Some key aspects of Xunzi's philosophy are highlighted below.

Xunzi is best known for his thesis that human nature (or *xing*) is bad (*e*), and that any goodness man experiences is a direct result of activity that is constructive and productive (*wei*). Xunzi appeals to presumably established linguistic usages of *shan* and *e*: "All men in the world, past and present, agree in defining *shan* [goodness] as that which is upright, reasonable, and orderly, and *e* [badness] as that which is prejudiced, irresponsible, and chaotic." (*xing 'e pian*, ch. 23). Xunzi continued: "Now suppose man's nature was in fact intrinsically upright, reasonable, and orderly—then what need would there be for sage kings and *li* [rules of proper conduct] and *yi* [righteousness]?" (*ruxiao pian*, ch. 8).

In light of Xunzi's definitions of *shan* and *e*, it seems clear that these are evaluative terms based on his normative conception of moral and political order. The original human nature (*xing*) is normatively neutral. It consists of feelings (*qing*) such as "love, hate, joy, anger, sorrow, and pleasure," and desires (*yu*), which are responses to the arousal of feelings. What makes these feelings and desires problematic is that in the absence of the guidance of *li* and *yi*, humans tend to pursue their satisfaction without regard to other persons' needs and desires. And given human partiality and scarcity of resources, conflict is inevitable.

Li and *yi* are the products of the constructive activity (*wei*) of the sages. Emphasis on *li* (ritual, rites, rules of proper conduct) is the hallmark of Xunzi's ethics. The *li* are formal prescriptions or rules of proper conduct. Although the *li* represent an established ethical tradition, they do not always provide adequate guidance in dealing with changing circumstances of human life. As markers of Dao (the Way), "the *li* provide models, but no explanations"; their primary function is regulation of conduct—defining the boundaries for the pursuit of desires. Notably, Xunzi also stresses the supportive and ennobling functions. Ultimately, the *li* promote the ennoblement of human characters by investing them with qualities of *ren* (benevolence) and *yi*. For Xunzi, the ultimate end of learning is to become a sage that embodies Dao—that is, *ren*, *yi*, and *li*. Ordinary humans are capable of becoming sages if they make efforts to understand the rationales and practice of these virtues.

Xunzi elaborates a complex theory concerning the capacity for knowing Dao and the significance of ethical commitment to the practice of Dao. Knowing Dao is the precondition to approving the Dao as the guide of human life. Xunzi is insistent that Dao is a whole consisting of many corners (*yu*) or aspects. All humans are liable to *bi* (obscuration, blindness), the beclouding of mind that leads to construing one aspect and ignoring an equally important aspect. Philosophers are especially prone to be victims of *bi*. For example, Mozi was beset by preoccupation with utility and failed to understand the importance of the beauty of form; Zhuangzi was beset by preoccupation with heaven and failed to understand the importance of humanity. Xunzi admits that Dao is a proper subject of discourse, but contentious reasoning must be avoided. The participants in reasoned discourse must be benevolent (*renxin*) and impartial (*gongxin*), and have a learning or receptive attitude (*xuexin*) toward competing views. For the telos in argumentation is to resolve problems of common concern in the light of Dao, not to win in disputation.

See also Confucius; Mencius.

Bibliography

Cua, Antonio S. *Ethical Argumentation: A Study in Hsun Tzu's Moral Epistemology*. Honolulu: University of Hawaii Press, 1985.

Cua, Antonio S. "Ethical Significance of Shame: Insights of Aristotle and Xunzi." *Philosophy East and West* 53 (2) (2003): 147–202.

Cua, Antonio S. "The Ethical and the Religious Dimensions *Li*." *Review of Metaphysics* 55 (3) (2002): 501–549.

Cua, Antonio S. *Human Nature, Ritual, and History: Studies in Xunzi and Chinese Philosophy*. Washington: The Catholic University of America Press, 2005.

Cua, Antonio S. "The Possibility of Ethical Knowledge: Reflections on a Theme in the *Hsün Tzu*." In *Epistemological Issues in Ancient Chinese Philosophy*, edited by Hans Lenk and Gregor Paul. Albany: State University of New York Press, 1993.

Dubs, H. H. *Hsuntze: The Moulder of Ancient Confucianism*. London: Arthur Probsthain, 1927.

Goldin, Paul R. *Rituals of the Way: The Philosophy of Xunzi*. La Salle, IL: Open Court, 1996.

Kline, T. C., and Philip J. Ivanhoe, eds. *Nature, and Moral Agency in the* Xunzi. Indianapolis: Hackett, 2000. Updated bibliography.

Knoblock, John. *Xunzi: A Translation and Study of the Complete Works*. 3 vols. Stanford, CA: Stanford University Press, 1988, 1990, and 1994. Vols. 1 and 3 contain excellent bibliographies.

Lee, Janghee. *Xunzi and Early Chinese Naturalism*. Albany: State University of New York Press, 2005.

Li, Disheng. *Xunzi jishi (Xunzi: An Exegesis)*. Taipei: Xuesheng, 1979.

Machle, Edward J. *Nature and Heaven in the Xunzi*. Albany: State University of New York Press, 1993.

Vittinghoff, Helmolt. "Recent Bibliography in Classical Chinese Philosophy." *Journal of Chinese Philosophy* 28 (1, 2) (2001): 1–208.

YAMAGA SOKŌ

(1622–1685)

Yamaga Sokō was a Japanese Confucianist of the *kogakuha,* or "school of ancient learning," and codifier of the ethics of the military class, *Bushidō,* the "way of the warrior." He was born in Aizu, Fukushima prefecture. At nine he entered the school of Hayashi Razan in Edo (Tokyo), where he learned the official Zhu Xi doctrine. Interested in military science, he became a master of it. He taught it first at the castle of Lord Asano of Akō (Hyogo prefecture) and later in Edo, where the novelty of his advocating the use of firearms attracted many followers. In 1666 he wrote *Seikyō yōroku* (The essence of Confucianism), a blunt critique of Zhu Xi's ideas. For this and for his innovations in military science, he incurred the wrath of his two former teachers, Hayashi and the military expert Hōjō Ujinaga, and was exiled from Edo. For the rest of his life he lived under mild confinement at the castle of Lord Asano, instilling into the samurai of Akō the loyalty that was to make forty-seven of them famous for revenging their lord by slaying the man who had disgraced him and dutifully committing hara-kiri. Their deed and death was immortalized in the drama *Chūshingura.*

In the preface to *Seikyō yōroku,* Yamaga clearly states the program of the "school of ancient learning," adding that the doctrine of Confucius and the ancient sages had been obscured by interpreters and commentators. He dismisses Mencius, Zhu Xi, and Wang Yangming easily; he rejects the "great ultimate" (*taikyoku*) of Zhu Xi as a later Buddhist interpolation in Confucianism. The universe, he holds, is explained by the movement of yin and yang, the passive and active elements, and it has no beginning or end. Human nature is neither good nor bad, but ethically neutral. He stresses self-interest, but he urges that common utility take precedence over it.

The term *Bushidō* is a recent one, coined long after his death, but its meaning is clearly traceable to two of his books, *Shidō* and *Bukyō shōgaku.* His "way of the warrior" consists of ethical norms and practical means of fostering in oneself a sense of loyal duty (*gi*) toward one's lord. Mental training is paramount; serenity, sincerity, magnanimity, introspection, and self-restraint are the virtues to be cultivated. Yamaga praised the ancient Chinese sages but he was a strong nationalist who extolled Japan over China.

See also Chinese Philosophy; Confucius; Hayashi Razan; Human Nature; Japanese Philosophy; Mencius; Wang Yang-ming; Zhu Xi (Chu Hsi).

Bibliography

For Yamaga's works see *Yamaga Sokō zenshū* (Complete works of Yamaga Sokō), edited by Hirose Yutaka, 15 vols. (Tokyo: Iwanami Shoten, 1940). For discussion, see Hori Isao, *Yamaga Sokō* (Tokyo, 1963) and W. T. de Bary, Ryusaku Tsunoda, and Donald Keene, eds., *Sources of Japanese Tradition* (New York: Columbia University Press, 1958), pp. 394–410, which contains selections in translation.

Gino K. Piovesana, S.J. (1967)

YAMAZAKI ANSAI

(1618–1682)

Yamazaki Ansai, the Japanese Confucianist notable for his ethical bent and Confucian rationalization of Shintoism, was raised at Kyoto in a Buddhist monastery. He was so unruly that he was sent to Tosa (now the city of Kōchi) on Shikoku Island, where he came under the influence of Tani Jichu (1598–1649), the originator of the southern branch of the Zhu Xi school of Confucianism in Japan. Having discarded Buddhism, Yamazaki taught Zhu Xi Confucianism in Kyoto and Edo (Tokyo) from 1648. Uncompromising in character, he condescended in 1665 to become the official scholar of Hoshina Masayuki, lord of Aizu (in northeast Japan). At Hoshina's death in 1672 Yamazaki returned to Kyoto and developed his Confucian Shintoism.

Though a stern Confucianist teacher he gathered around him more than six thousand students; among the best were Asami Keisai (1652–1711), Satō Naokata (1650–1719), and Miyake Shōsai (1662–1741). They formed the Kimon or Ansai school. However, Yamazaki's Shintoism held the seed of disharmony; before his death this school split into four. He urged the ethical formula *keinai gigai,* that is, "Devotion within, righteousness without." By "devotion" he meant not simply Confucian self-cultivation but rather a religiously rectified mind related to cosmic reason. By "righteousness" he meant virtue toward others. His maxim, "Learning is knowing and practice," suggests a middle way between overemphasis on mastery of the mind and overemphasis on social virtues.

Yamazaki's Shintoism deserves attention because of its Confucian rationalism and the influence it had in the revival of Shintoist studies in Japan. It is called *Suika Shintō* and elaborates on Confucian cosmogony to explain Japan's mythological creation chronicles. Trying to see a rational core in these legends, he developed the Shinto creed, borrowing from neo-Confucianism. His best pupils, however, did not follow him in his Shintoist phase; and the *kokugakusha,* the "national learning scholars," did not become the purveyors of a rationalized Shintoism. His most lasting impact was made through his popularization of Confucian ethics and indirect fostering of loyalism toward the emperor. This last trend was exemplified in Asami Keisai, Yamagata Daini, and in the school of Mito historians. Yamazaki is, however, given credit for later loyalist and nationalist trends.

See also Buddhism; Chinese Philosophy; Confucius; Japanese Philosophy; Loyalty; Nationalism; Rationalism; Virtue and Vice; Zhu Xi (Chu Hsi).

Bibliography

For Japanese sources, see *Yamazaki Ansai zenshu* (Yamazaki Ansai: complete works), 5 vols. (Nagoya: Hatsubaijo Matsumoto Shoten, 1937), and Bitō Masahide, *Nihon hōken shisōshi kenkyu* (Studies on the history of feudal thought in Japan; Tokyo, 1961), pp. 40–99. An English source is W. T. de Bary, Ryusaku Tsunoda, and Donald Keene, eds., *Sources of Japanese Tradition* (New York: Columbia University Press, 1958), pp. 363–371.

Gino K. Piovesana, S.J. (1967)

YANG XIONG

(53 BCE–18 CE)

Having achieved his youthful ambition to become court poet, Yang Xiong spent his thirties and forties producing the occasional *fu* (rhapsodic poems) the throne required. Sometime around his fiftieth year, perhaps in reaction to the factionalized politics at the capital, Yang came to disparage his own poetic genius, equating the verbal pyrotechnics with childish games injurious to the moral process. In consequence, Yang turned to composing and then defending three works, the *Taixuan jing* (*Canon of Supreme Mystery*; c. 4 CE), the *Fayan* (*Model Sayings*; c. 12 CE), and the *Fangyan* (*Dialect Words*; unfinished?). Creating these new "classics" (*jing*) required greater ingenuity on Yang's part than writing *fu*, for Yang sought to capture both the inner message and the outer form of the canonical works: The *Mystery* was patterned after the *Yijing* (*Classic of Changes*); the *Model Sayings*, after the *Lunyu* (*Analects*); and the *Fangyan* claimed inspiration from the ancient Chou transcriptions of the *Odes* and possibly also the *Erya*, an early word list ascribed to Confucius. By such bold attempts at "renewing the old," Yang would restore the authentic teachings of the sages.

In imitation of the *Yijing*, an abstruse divination text turned philosophical work by the addition of "Ten

Wings," the *Taixuan jing* unfolds on two levels: For the ordinary reader, its divinatory formulae prescribe the virtues of humility, respect, and cautiousness that make for social order and personal safety. More sophisticated readers correlate a series of vignettes drawn from daily life and keyed to the calendar with graphic emblems, cryptic summaries, and Yang's own auto-commentaries to discover the complex relations binding human conduct and preordained fate. In Yang's view, four main factors determine the quality of life: Time, Tools, Position, and Virtue. Although the workings of fate (*ming*)—equated in Yang's work with Time—lie outside human control, time's depredations may be offset to some extent by other factors under better human control. Using the most advanced scientific theories of his time, Yang sketches the finely tuned cycles of yin/yang, and the Five Phases, relating them to decision-making and the hierarchical orders of civilization. In outlining these regularities, Yang touches upon the main topics of Han debate, including the existence of ghosts and providence, the role of divination and the divine, the origins and stages of the universe, and definitions of "good rule."

If the single most important theme of Yang Xiong's *Mystery* is the interaction between human will and divine fate, the *Fayan* sees single-minded devotion to the Good leading to an exquisite appreciation of the social and cosmic orders which itself constitutes the highest happiness of which humans are capable. In its brief dialogues, the *Fayan* constructs a compelling argument in favor of this inherently unprovable assertion by juxtaposing hypothetical cases with the examples of famous men and women, so as to assert three linked propositions: First, a crucial distinction exists between popular "heroes" and current officeholders and the "true" Ru faithful to Confucian ideals who neither pursue material success nor confuse the subtle Way with factual knowledge or rule-making. Second, the very process of learning to intuit the sages' intent so hones the learner's being that it gradually experiences the most exquisite pleasure known to humankind, a kind of moral connoisseurship called "the ultimate in discrimination" (*zhishi*) (chap. 6). Third, this therapeutic and pleasurable journey toward Goodness is the only sure reward for an expenditure of effort, as the pursuit of Goodness is "easy": it entails no trickery or treachery; it imparts mental equilibrium along with an ability to understand and predict human behavior (chaps. 2, 9); and it reveals an entire world marvelously balanced.

Given the broad strokes of the *Mystery* and the sweeping claims of the *Fayan*, some find it hard to place the *Fangyan*, a meticulous record of dialect expressions within the extended Chinese cultural sphere. The melodic patterns of human speech—as well as musical rhythms, the calligraphic forms of written characters, and the geographical configurations of the earth—intimate the divine order. Word patterns in particular fascinate Yang, for "words are the music of the heart-mind (*xin*); and writings, its painting" (*Fayan*, chap. 5). Yang's highest goal was to employ artistic forms to excite the sensibilities so that they might become more receptive to the serious business of moral edification. Therefore, Yang was the first to develop theories of aesthetic concepts and the hermeneutic enterprise, then to demonstrate the emotive power of language through his own rhetorical masterpieces.

During his lifetime, devoted disciples regarded Yang as Master, though some contemporaries mistrusted Yang's incredible versatility. Following his death, Yang was elevated to the pantheon by many. Han Yu (768–842), for example, named Yang Xiong as the single master qualified to "transmit the [Confucian] Way" after Mencius; Sima Guang (1018–1086) went further, insisting that neither Mencius nor Xunzi could compare with Yang. However, some Song thinkers, especially Zhu Xi (1130–1200), condemned Yang for his eclecticism, his arrogance in daring to create classics, his willingness to serve two dynastic courts, and his outright rejection of the Mencian theory of human nature. Only with the Qing Evidential Research movement did interest in Yang's work revive.

See also Aesthetics, History of; Chinese Philosophy; Confucius; Han Yu; Hermeneutics; Mencius; Time; Xunzi; Zhu Xi (Chu Hsi).

Bibliography

WORKS BY YANG XIONG

Fang-yen. Annotated and translated by Paul L. M. Serruys as *The Chinese Dialects of Han Time According to Fang Yen*. Berkeley: University of California Press, 1959.

Fayan yishu. Compiled by Wang Rongbao. Beijing: Zhonghua, 1987.

Taixuan jiaoyi. Compiled by Zheng Wangeng. Beijing: Shifan daxue, 1989. The best edition of the *Taixuan jing*.

Fayan zhu. Annotated by Han Jing. Beijing: Zhonghua, 1992.

The Canon of Supreme Mystery. Translated with commentary by Michael Nylan. Albany: State University of New York Press, 1993.

Fayan. Translated by Michael Nylan. Seattle: University of Washington Press, forthcoming.

WORKS ABOUT YANG XIONG

Knechtges, David R. *The Han Rhapsody: A Study of the fu of Yang Hsiung, 53 B.C.–A.D. 18*. Cambridge, U.K.: Cambridge University Press, 1976.

Pan Ku. *The Han shu Biography of Yang Hsiung (53 B.C.–A.D. 18)*. Translated and annotated by David R. Knechtges. Tempe: Arizona State University Press, 1982.

Michael Nylan (2005)

YANG ZHU

(c. 440–c. 380 BCE)

Not much has been discovered about Yang Zhu the person from the documents that still exist. However, the *Mencius*, the *Xunzi*, the *Hanfeizi*, the *Lushi Chunqiu*, the *Huainanzi*, and the *Lunheng* all confirm that Yang's school was one of the most influential in pre-Qin China. For Mencius, Yang and Mo Di were the most influential thinkers prior to Mencius's time, although he criticized Yang's emphasis on the individual and its anarchist consequence, as well as his selfishness and apathy to the public interest. These criticisms, however, are somewhat misleading for an understanding of the true nature of Yang's thought.

In the past, Chinese intellectuals were led to believe that "Yang Zhu chooses to exist only for his own self, and does nothing for the world, not even by drawing one hair of his" (*Mencius* 3B 9). Yet an unbiased understanding, based on existing texts, reveals that Yang cherished the value of life and the authenticity of self. For example, the Hanfeizi said that Yang was one who "despised things and values life" (*Hanfeizi Jijie*, p. 353). In the *Lushi Chunqiu*, it was said that "Scholar Yang elevates the self" (*Lüshi Chunqiu Jishi*, p. 803). And, according to the *Huainanzi*, "To keep the totality of one's natural life and conserve the authentic of one's self, not to burden one's body with external things. This is that upon which Yangzi stands, yet it is criticized by Mencius" (Liu An 1985, p. 218).

These comments allow us to reread more coherently the *Yang Zhu* and other chapters of the *Liezi*, where many texts related to Yang were presented (even if these works are seen by many scholars as having been forged by later hands). In the *Liezi*, when Yang is asked by Qinzi whether he would agree to lose one hair to help out the whole world, he answers that the "human world is for certain not to be helped out by one hair" (*Liezi*, p. 218). Yang's emphasis is on "keeping the totality of one's natural life" and "conserving the authenticity of one's self," statements that can be understood in reference to his philosophy of body, in which he claims that the appropriate satisfaction of human desires and the economy of energy are essential in attaining the wholeness of one's own life.

Yang's emphasis on the authenticity of self is more understandable to twenty-first century readers: He is more like modern thinkers in that he underlines the autonomy of self in respect to all external determinations. *Autonomy* in this sense means the spontaneous unfolding of one's own nature—a nature not to be determined by external entities, either real or ideal, but to be determined internally by one's own self, which is different from Kant's idea of autonomy as positing norms by one's own free will. With his idea of autonomy, Yang made the distinction between "fled-away-persons" (*dunren*) and "conforming people" (*shunmin*). The *dunren* were escapists from their own natural self in living at the mercy of external factors. By contrast, the *shunmin* were those who did not run after external values and were free with the authenticity of their life, closely related to the self's autonomy.

Yang's philosophical anthropology is somewhat similar to St. Augustine's philosophy in *City of God* and Arnold Gehlen's in *Man, His Nature and Place in the World*. Yang believed that human intellect developed out of biological weakness, and from these weak biological conditions a person "should use things to nourish his own nature, let his own intellect develop without appealing to physical force" (*Liezi*, p. 224). The reason to use human intellect was for the purpose of conserving one's life by using natural resources without the necessity of appealing to physical force when competing with stronger animals. Based on this, Yang developed a philosophy of learning. Beginning with the tenet that life is a basic value, and avoiding losing oneself by embarking upon too many different courses of learning, Yang posited the authenticity of life as the final unity of all learning. The *Shuofu* chapter of the *Liezi* states that, "Because of too many deviations in roads, one can not find one's lost sheep; with too many deviations in learning, the learner would lose his own life" (*Liezi*, p. 254). Yang's pragmatist vision of learning meant to learn for the purpose of conserving life and its development according to self-authenticity, which for him were the ultimate values of human existence.

See also Augustine, St.; Chinese Philosophy; Confucius; Determinism and Freedom; Gehlen, Arnold; Han Fei; Kant, Immanuel; Mencius; Mozi; Xunzi.

Bibliography

Graham, Angus C., trans. *The Book of Lieh-tzŭ*. New York: Columbia University Press, 1990.

Hsü Wei-yü. *Lüshi Chunqiu Jishi* [Collected commentaries on spring and autumn of Mr. Lü]. Vol. 2. Taipei: Shijie Bookstore, 1988.

Liezi. In *Er Shi Er Zi* [Works of twenty-two masters]. Vol. 2. Taipei: Prophet Press, 1976.

Liu An. *Huainanzi* [The book of masters of Huainan]. Annotated by Gao Yu. Taipei: Shijie Bookstore, 1985.
Mencius. Translated by D. C. Lau. Rev. ed. Hong Kong: Chinese University Press, 2003.
Wang Xianshen. *Hanfeizi Jijie* [Collected explanations of Hanfeizi]. Taipei: Shijie Bookstore, 1988.

Vincent Shen (2005)

ZABARELLA, JACOPO

(1532–1589)

Jacopo Zabarella was one of the leading Aristotelians of the sixteenth century. He taught at the University of Padua for twenty-five years, from 1564 until his death. The fruit of these years of lecturing is contained in his printed works, which include treatises on Aristotelian logic and natural science. His writings in logic, and especially on scientific method, earned Zabarella a reputation as the most outstanding logician of his time; they continued to be read by school philosophers in Germany and Italy for several generations after his death and still command respect as interpretations of Aristotle.

Zabarella proceeds in characteristic scholastic fashion, examining and resolving, independently of each other, a sequence of issues. In the process he canvasses the views of an impressive number of predecessors among the Latins and seems fully conversant with Greek philosophy, including the Greek commentators on Aristotle. The doctrines discussed by Zabarella range, as is usual with scholastic writers, over an immense amount of material, basically that presented by Aristotle in his *Organon* and in the *Libri Naturales*. As a philosopher Zabarella is willing to leave certain arguments to the theologians—for example, whether God could have created prime matter without form. "My advice is to dispute in Aristotelian, not theological, fashion," he remarks. This does not mean, however, that Zabarella was not willing to consider and even to endorse arguments of a strictly philosophical nature presented by theologians; hence, the names of Thomas Aquinas, John Duns Scotus, Gregory of Rimini, and many others frequently occur in his works, along with the appeals to Averroes so frequent among Italian philosophers of his time. Analysis of the arguments advanced by predecessors constitutes one part of Zabarella's presentation (*ratio*); he also appeals to experience (*experientia*), his own or that of most people. Thus, he mentions having climbed the highest hill in the vicinity of Padua, seeing clouds below, and learning when he descended in the evening that it had rained in the valley during the day. But there is no reference to controlled experiment in his writings; in this respect he remained a bookish philosopher, like most university professors of his time.

No one has followed Zabarella carefully through the maze of his discussions in order to secure a clear view of his total thought. The studies we have are partial and will doubtless require revision in the light of increased knowledge of the whole tradition he represents. Nevertheless, some of his conclusions can be definitely stated.

Zabarella regards Aristotle's science as perfect with respect to structure and form, imperfect only with regard to its subject matter. He compares Aristotle's writings on natural science with Euclid's *Elements* and suggests that the philosopher of nature can easily derive theorems of physics from the principles contained in them. Zabarella does not envisage the possibility that Aristotle's approach might be supplemented by mathematics. The fourteenth-century attempts at quantification in physics originating at Paris and Oxford had been transported to Italy by such teachers as Paul of Venice, but Zabarella does not seem aware of these developments. He did not welcome novel hypotheses, preferring, for example, to stand by Aristotle's explanation that the movement of projectiles can be attributed to pushing by the surrounding air (*antiperistasis*). Zabarella rejects the view that the "preceding motion is the cause of the greater velocity of the following motion."

In his discussions of the heavens, Zabarella betrays no concern with the Copernican theory published during his youth. He seems slightly dubious about the epicycles of the astronomers, but in this he was no doubt simply reflecting the doubts of Averroes. Zabarella endorses the view, also derived from Averroes, that the "confused" knowledge of the world supplied by the natural scientist must be made "distinct" by the metaphysician. For example, he concedes that the argument, "Since there is eternal movement, there must be an eternal mover," may be established by the natural scientist, whose bailiwick is the consideration and causal explanation of things in motion. But consideration of immaterial substances in themselves (the "eternal motors") must be left to the metaphysician.

Contemporaries had raised a difficulty in connection with certain mutually canceling actions in nature ("reactions"), which seemed to them to defy the Aristotelian dictum "Nature never does anything in vain." Zabarella points out that such mutual frustration nevertheless does not frustrate nature in general, since all things turn out according to the law of universal nature (*ex lege naturae universalis*).

Another question much discussed in scholastic physics concerned the elements in what we would call chemical compounds (called "mixtures" by the Schoolmen). Do they persist in existence after losing their sensible identity as elements and becoming part of the compound? Various solutions had been proposed to this problem; Zabarella accepts that of Averroes—the same "reality" of the elementary forms of matter is in the elements and in the mixture, but their "formality" is changed.

In Aristotelian metaphysics and philosophy the distinction between matter and form is crucial and difficult, especially in its application to human beings. School philosophers of Zabarella's time exercised a great deal of ingenuity in order to make sense of the Aristotelian doctrine that the soul is the form of the body. There were two main opinions: one, that the soul is a "form giving being" to man; the other, that the soul is merely a "form assisting" in man's operation, much as a sailor presides over the operation of an already formed ship. Zabarella chooses the former interpretation, although not without vacillation.

On another much disputed question, concerning the perception of sense qualities, Zabarella endorses the view of Albert the Great that there is no need to postulate an "active sense" (*sensus agens*); certain sensed qualities have it in themselves to multiply their "spiritual" species in the medium, in contrast to such other qualities as heat, which really produce their counterparts in the medium and in the sense of touch.

Zabarella decisively rejects the Averroist thesis of the unity of the intellect, insisting that the intellect is multiplied according to the number of individual men. The intellect is the form of man; since it is not itself "in act," it is able to receive all things spiritually and hence is capable of knowing all things.

LOGIC

Zabarella's most original contributions lie in his logical works. The nature of logic and its relation to other disciplines were controversial matters even in antiquity, and these controversies were renewed during the Renaissance. Zabarella sides with the Greek commentators on Aristotle in maintaining that logic is not strictly a part of philosophy but an instrumental discipline furnishing other arts and sciences with tools of inquiry. Two of these tools are order and method. Order is an intellectual habit that teaches us how to dispose suitably the parts of any given discipline so that we can learn it more easily. Method is also an intellectual instrument producing knowledge of the unknown from that which is known, but it permits us to draw syllogistic inferences. The nature of both order and method must be clarified by an analysis of their objectives: ease of learning in the case of order, perfect knowledge (*cognitio*) in the case of method.

These analyses are set forth in Zabarella's treatise *De Methodis* (On methods), in which he challenges two schools of thought prevalent in his time. One, drawn from Neoplatonic commentators on Aristotle, held that there are four methods employed in the arts and sciences: demonstrative, definitive, divisive, and resolutive. The other, advocated by medical men and drawn from Galen, held that there are three orders of teaching any discipline. Zabarella presents a simplified version, reducing the number of orders and methods to two. Contemplative disciplines are transmitted by the compositive order, practical or operative disciplines by the resolutive, which begins with the end to be achieved in any pursuit and reasons backward to an initial step in its direction.

This was traditional Aristotelian doctrine, but Zabarella's elaboration of compositive and resolutive methods was more original. In the natural sciences there are two things to be studied, substances and accidents. Substances can be investigated only by the resolutive method, which begins with sensible effects and "resolves" them into their causes. We know substances when we possess definitions of them, but these definitions, contrary to received opinion, are not "methods." Accidents, on the other hand, can be demonstrated by the demonstrative or compositive method once the principles discovered by the resolutive method are available.

In his work "On the Regress," Zabarella analyzes a special form of demonstration in which "the cause and the effect reciprocate, and the effect is more known to us than the cause." The best example of such a regress is to be found, Zabarella tells us, in Aristotle's *Physics*. We know in a confused way that where there is generation, there is matter, but only demonstration makes it clear to us why matter is the cause of generation. We must make use of a "mental examination," which tells us that matter is "that which is apt to receive all forms and privations."

Zabarella reaffirms man's central place in the universe; the operation of the most outstanding part of man is his highest perfection, and this is to be found in contemplation. Man is of a middle nature; he is the most noble animal, created in the image of God, but there is also a sense in which he is ignoble and imperfect, the sense in which we say, "To sin is human" or "After all, he is only a man." Such concern for placing man in nature probably echoes fifteenth-century humanism.

See also Albert the Great; Aristotelianism; Aristotle; Averroes; Duns Scotus, John; Galen; Gregory of Rimini; Humanism; Logic, History of; Paul of Venice; Scientific Method; Thomas Aquinas, St.

Bibliography

None of Zabarella's works has been translated into English, and this is unfortunate, since he ranks high as an expositor of Aristotle. Furthermore, copies of his *Opera Logica* (published first in Venice, 1578, but many times thereafter) are hard to obtain. The same may be said of his *De Rebus Naturalibus* (Venice, 1590) and his commentaries on the *Physics* and *De Anima*. A modern edition of the *De Methodis* and other logical works would be welcome and would furnish us with one of the most sophisticated expositions of school logic and thinking concerning scientific method to be given during the Renaissance.

For studies on Zabarella, see Ernst Cassirer, *Das Erkenntnis problem in der Philosophie und Wissenschaft der neueren Zeit* (Berlin: Cassirer, 1906), Vol. I, pp. 134–141; John Herman Randall Jr., *The School of Padua and the Emergence of Modern Science* (Padua, 1961), pp. 49–63 (gives ample quotations in Latin); N. W. Gilbert, *Renaissance Concepts of Method* (New York: Columbia University Press, 1960), Ch. 7; J. J. Glanville, "Zabarella and Poinsot on the Object and Nature of Logic," in *Readings in Logic*, edited by R. Houde (Dubuque, IA: Brown, 1958); Riccardo Pozzo, ed., *The Impact of Aristotelianism on Modern Philosophy (Studies in Philosophy and the History of Philosophy, Vol. 39)* (Washington DC: Catholic University of America Press, 2004); and William A. Wallace, "Circularity and the Paduan 'Regressus': From Pietro D'abano to Galileo Galilei." *Vivarium* 33(1)(1995): 76–97.

Neal W. Gilbert (1967)
Bibliography updated by Tamra Frei (2005)

ZARATHUSTRA

See *Zoroastrianism*

ZEN

See *Buddhism—Schools: Chan and Zen*

ZEN'KOVSKII, VASILII VASIL'EVICH

(1881–1962)

Vasilii Vasil'evich Zen'kovskii, a Russian philosopher and theologian, was born in Proskurov into the family of a teacher. Zen'kovskii studied natural sciences, history, and philology at Kiev University. In 1913–1914 he continued his education in Germany, Austria, and Italy. Following his return to Russia he was appointed a professor of psychology at Kiev University (1915–1919). In 1919 he immigrated to Yugoslavia, where he worked as a professor at the University of Belgrade (1920–1923). In 1923 he moved to Czechoslovakia, where he became the director of the Academy of Education in Prague (1923–1926). In 1926 he settled in France, where he was a professor of the Theological Academy in Paris until his death. In 1944 he was elected as dean of the academy. Like many Russian intellectuals of the time, Zen'kovskii went through a spiritual crisis in his youth. He became an atheist when he was fifteen years old, but later returned to the church and dedicated all of his life to developing and promoting Christian philosophy and education. In 1942 he was ordained to Orthodox Christian priesthood.

PHILOSOPHY

Zen'kovskii belongs to a pleiad of prominent Russian thinkers who carried on Russia's intellectual tradition after the 1917 Communist Revolution and continued it outside the homeland despite the hardships of emigration. In the history of Russian thought Zen'kovskii is best known for his two-volume classic *Istoriia russkoi filosofii* (History of Russian philosophy; 1948–1950), which still remains an unsurpassed contribution to the field. He also authored many works in philosophy, theology, psychology, pedagogy, and literary history that left a notable mark on Russian culture. Overall, his philosophical system may be described as "Orthodox universalism" (Sapov 1995) or, in Zen'kovskii's own words, as an "experiment in Christian philosophy."

Zen'kovskii began his scholarly career with the study of psychic causality. He was interested in the phenomenon of religious consciousness, more particularly in the origin of the idea of God in the human mind. According to Zen'kovskii neither the social nor the subconscious sphere could produce in human consciousness such an idea that had its true roots in the mystical experience of the interconnection between the human being and the divine realm. He points out that some people apparently lack this inner vision, and as a result they advance theories that reduce religious experience to other forms of human activity, as was the case, for example, with Karl Marx, Émile Durkheim, or Sigmund Freud.

In his epistemological views Zen'kovskii rejects the autonomy and self-sufficiency of human reason. He develops a "Christocentric understanding of knowledge," which postulates that Christ as divine Logos (John 1:1) represents the ultimate generating and regulating power of human intellectual activities. More specifically, as Vadim Sapov notes, Zen'kovskii defends the "concept of 'ecclesial reason,' according to which one should search for the metaphysical basis of knowledge in the notion of the Church" (1995, p. 204) as the living body of Christ.

In his youth Zen'kovskii was to a considerable extent influenced by the nineteenth-century Russian philosophers Lev Mikhailovich Lopatin and Vladimir Sergeevich Solov'ëv (Solovyov), and his ontology also bears certain similarities to the Solov'ëvian tradition. Zen'kovskii combines here the elements of philosophy and theology by focusing on the concept of creation. He develops his own version of Sophiology that represents a variation of the Sophiological teachings of Solov'ëv and later of Sergei Nikolaevich Bulgakov and that centers around the notion of Sophia or God's Wisdom as the bridge between the creator and the creatures. In his Sophiological doctrine Zen'kovskii distinguishes between "ideas in God" and "ideas in the world" or between divine and created Sophia. Divine Sophia stands for God's plan of creation, while created Sophia represents the ideal foundation of the universe itself. Divine and created aspects of Sophia are connected with each other as the archetype and its image or Logos.

The concept of human personhood occupies the central place in Zen'kovskii's philosophical system. Every human being, in his view, is unique and experiences a different combination of genetic, social, and spiritual influences. Acts of freedom that are rooted in the metaphysical depth of one's self also constitute an inalienable part of the human person. Without divine grace such freedom, however, almost inevitably leads humanity to evil. The original sin that limits the creative potential of free will finds its manifestation in the "split between reason and heart." Hence, the purpose of human life consists in the restoration of lost spiritual wholeness through the church. Accordingly, the main task of any pedagogical efforts must be directed to helping the young generation in its efforts toward such a spiritual transformation.

THEOLOGICAL TEACHINGS

Zen'kovskii's theological teachings are collected in his *Apologetika* (Apologetics; 1957), which aims at defending Christian worldview against the challenges of modern culture and science. Here as elsewhere it is hard to dissociate Zen'kovskii's religious views from his philosophical argumentation. The work addresses a variety of issues from the dogmatic question of creation to the controversial problem of freedom. When facing the paradox of freedom versus evil, Zen'kovskii joins many other Russian thinkers, including Nikolay Aleksanrovich Berdyayev, in arguing that human freedom is totally unrestricted. In *Apologetics* he points out that "freedom is a true freedom only if it is unlimited—in it is God's likeness" (1997, p. 406). He adds, however, that, the "Lord can commit to death, total destruction those individuals who resist a complete harmonization of being" (p. 229).

While Berdyayev in his philosophy questions divine omnipotence to proclaim the ultimate power of freedom, Zen'kovskii believes in the all-powerful God but seems to undermine God's all-goodness by forecasting a complete extermination of the wicked in the future. He refers to the authority of the Bible, according to which the "second death, i.e. annihilation awaits those who will not want to come back to God" (1997, p. 302). This interpretation reveals some of the aspects of Zen'kovskii's Orthodox Christian thought that today's readers may find rather conservative, if not fundamentalist.

See also Berdyaev, Nikolai Aleksandrovich; Bulgakov, Sergei Nikolaevich; Determinism and Freedom; Durkheim, Émile; Freedom; Freud, Sigmund; Lopatin, Lev Mikhailovich; Marx, Karl; Philosophy of Religion, History of; Russian Philosophy; Solov'ëv (Solovyov), Vladimir Sergeevich.

Bibliography

WORKS BY ZEN'KOVSKII

Problema psikhicheskoi prichinnosti (The problem of psychic causality). Kiev, Russia: 1914.

Russkie mysliteli i Evropa (Russian thinkers and Europe). Paris: YMCA Press, 1926.

Dar svobody (The gift of freedom). Paris: 1928.

Problema vospitaniia v svete khristianskoi antropologii (The problem of education in the light of Christian anthropology). Paris: YMCA Press, 1934.

Istoriia russkoi filosofii. 2 vols. Paris: YMCA Press, 1948–1950.

Osnovy khristianskoi filosofii (Principles of Christian philosophy). Moscow: Kanon, 1997.

WORKS ON ZEN'KOVSKII

Lossky, N. O. *History of Russian Philosophy*. New York: International Universities Press, 1951.

Sapov, Vadim. "Zen'kovskii, Vasilii Vasil'evich." In *Russkaia filosofiia. Malyi entsyklopedicheskii slovar'* (Russian philosophy: A small encyclopedic dictionary), edited by A. I. Aleshin, 202–205. Moscow: "Nauka," 1995.

Mikhail Sergeev (2005)

ZENO OF CITIUM

(334–262/1 BCE)

Zeno, creator of the philosophical system that became known as Stoicism, was born probably in 334 BCE in Citium, a coastal settlement in southeastern Cyprus, whih was largely Hellenized by that time. His family may well have been of Phoenician origin (as was a significant minority of the population). At the age of twenty-two, he left for Athens. There he spent the next decade or so studying philosophy with various teachers. In time a group formed round Zeno himself; and because these "Zenonians" met in a public colonnade named the Painted Stoa, they came to be called Stoics. Zeno evidently established a prominent position in Athenian society. In his later years Antigonus Gonatas, the Macedonian monarch, attempted without success to attract him to his court, while the Athenians themselves voted him public honors in both life and death, particularly because of the exemplary moral example he had set. "More self-controlled than Zeno" became the benchmark phrase. He died in 262/1 BCE.

Zeno's philosophical hero was Socrates. The Stoics, so Philodemus tells us, were prepared to be known as "Socratics"; and Stoicism is best understood as a theoretical articulation of Socrates' intellectualist ethics, buttressed by a monistic metaphysics that is at once materialist and pantheist. Zeno's early attraction to the Socrates portrayed in Xenophon's *Memorabilia* is attested to in an anecdote that associates it with the influence exercised over him by his first teacher, the Cynic philosopher Crates. He appears to have cultivated a Cynicizing image in his own lifestyle. Zeno was noted for frugality, stamina, unsociability—and a Laconic sharpness in repartee. His *Republic*, the first book he wrote, constituted a critique of Plato's great work so uncompromisingly Cynic that Stoics of Cicero's time tried either to disown or to bowdlerize it.

Here Zeno rejects the need for an elaborate educational system; he sweeps away institutions such as temples, law courts, gymnasia; he abolishes coinage. Women are to wear the same clothing as men. Any man may mate with any woman: Gone is all Plato's sexual regulation. Gone, too, is Plato's insistence on a rigidly stratified class structure. All that is required for true citizenship is virtue. Single-minded Cynic rejection of every conventional value is the short way to acquire that, and thus to help build a community of the virtuous in the here and now. But Zeno also invoked a more positive and distinctively Socratic idea in this context. Eros—the god of erotic love—was to be the deity presiding over Zeno's city, bringing it friendship, freedom, and concord. The wise and virtuous will, like Socrates, seek out young people whose physical attractions indicate a propensity to virtue. By such relationships the bonds of society are to be forged.

Like all Zeno's writings, the *Republic* is now lost. Quite a number of other book titles are preserved, indicating a much wider range of philosophical preoccupations than are typical of the Cynics or of Socrates himself. Extended verbatim quotations are rare, but doctrines and especially definitions are cited in a variety of later classical authors. From these it is clear that the main structure of Stoic ethics was already articulated in Zeno's own pioneering work. Thus he endorses the Socratic idea that virtue is exclusively a matter of knowledge and wisdom, and that because it is, on its own, sufficient for happiness, the human goal consists in living in accordance with virtue. More innovative is Zeno's way of explaining what it means to be wise, and how in living wisely a person "follows nature." He took an expression in common moral discourse—*kathêkon*: what is incumbent upon me, my duty. Although (or perhaps in part because) it had never received any previous philosophical attention, he made it elemental within his own ethics. By a characteristic piece of etymologizing, *kathêkon* is explained as behavior that "comes in accordance with" the nature of a human being, or more generally an animal or plant of a particular kind. In a human it is what reason enjoins or forbids. Virtue or excellence in a person accordingly consists in "reason consistent and firm and unchangeable," and "living consistently" is by the same token the human goal: *eurhoia biou*, "success in life" (but etymologically its "life's smooth current").

Virtue is therefore not an ideal remote from everyday life but something focused on duties that are incumbent upon the ordinary person: honoring parents, serving country, spending time with friends, taking proper care of your health. An unqualified Cynic might have regarded most such things as indifferent to happiness. Zeno did not flatly disagree. But at this point he made another innovative move, decisive for the shape of Stoic ethics and for attacks upon it, ancient and modern. Some things indifferent for happiness (such as natural ability, beauty, health, wealth) are "preferred," like favorites at court, as according with nature; others (such as their opposites) not, as contrary to nature. Ordinarily reason will enjoin behavior designed to secure those that are preferred. But not always. Self-mutilation may be in order if the only alternative is military service with a tyrant in an unjust cause. What really matters for happiness is listening to right reason and acting accordingly, even if it is only the perfectly rational or wise person—the "sage"—who manages to do that with complete consistency. Consequently it is paradoxically the sage alone who is truly rich, strong, beautiful, and so on.

Knowledge, too, was, in Zeno's assessment, commonly accessible, not the preserve of philosophy or the sciences. Like the Socratic Stilpo, another of his teachers, Zeno rejected Platonic universals. As in ethics, so in epistemology he introduced fresh vocabulary to express the new idea he wanted to make fundamental: *katalêpsis*, "cognitive grasp." All of us—wise or wretched fools (which is what we are if we do not attain virtue and wisdom)—have a reliable basis for navigating the world we inhabit: sensory impressions conveying a grasp of reality that could not be wrong. Zeno used his hands to illustrate the point. An open palm represents what it is to receive an impression. Closing the fingers a little signifies assent. Clenching the fist is *katalêpsis*: Assent that is unquestionably right. The need for a concept of secure rational understanding—*epistêmê*—on the Platonic model is not denied. Zeno illustrated this by clasping his clenched right fist tightly and forcibly with his left hand. The point? Contra Plato, there can be no secure understanding without the kind of cognitive grasp of the sensible world that is made available to everyone by a providential Nature.

Belief in a providential nature—which the Stoics identified with God and Zeus and Fate—was something Zeno found Socrates arguing in Xenophon's *Memorabilia* (1.4, 4.3), most compellingly in the inference that, just as the physical stuff we are made of is supplied by the world about us, so our intelligence must derive from a cosmic intelligence. Zeno had studied logic with the dialectician Diodorus Cronus (author of the famous Master Argument) and formulated a pithy syllogism to express the point in causal and biological terms:

> What emits seed of something rational is itself rational.
> But the world emits seed of something rational.
> Therefore the world is rational.

Zeno seems to have considered the Socratic provenance of this line of reasoning particularly significant. But he was also anxious to claim the support of the entire philosophical tradition so far as he could. He exploited Plato's *Timaeus* (29B–30B) to argue:

> The rational is superior to the nonrational.
> But nothing is superior to the world.
> Therefore the world is rational.

The same was true, he argued, of "intelligent" and "ensouled."

From the Academic philosopher Polemo, yet another of his teachers, Zeno may have learned to find in the *Timaeus* something no less important: the duality of God and matter that he made fundamental to his own monistic metaphysics. But for theory about the cosmos, no previous philosopher was more important to him than Heraclitus. It must have been his reading of Heraclitus that convinced Zeno that nature was to be understood in terms of fire—its methodical crafting of the coming into being of things, its transformations, and the periodic cosmic holocausts it fuels. The richness of the Heraclitean resonances in Stoicism is now most apparent in the *Hymn to Zeus* of Zeno's pupil and successor as head of the school, Cleanthes.

See also Cicero, Marcus Tullius; Cleanthes; Cynics; Diodorus Cronus; Epistemology; Heraclitus of Ephesus; Logic, History of; Philodemus; Plato; Socrates; Stoicism; Xenophon.

Bibliography

BOOKS

Arnim, Hans von, ed. *Stoicorum Veterum Fragmenta. Vol. I: Zeno et Zenonis Discipuli*. Leipzig: Teubner, 1903.

Diogenes Laertius. *Lives of Eminent Philosophers*. 2 vols. Translated by R. D. Hicks. Cambridge, MA: Harvard University Press, 1925.

Pearson, A. C. *The Fragments of Zeno and Cleanthes*. Cambridge, U.K.: Cambridge University Press, 1891.

Scaltsas, Theodore, and Andrew S. Mason, eds. *The Philosophy of Zeno: Zeno of Citium and His Legacy*. Larnaka: The Municipality of Larnaka, 2002.

Schofield, Malcolm. *The Stoic Idea of the City*. 2nd edition. Chicago: The University of Chicago Press, 1999.

CHAPTER ARTICLES

Decleva Caizzi, F. "The Porch and the Garden: Early Hellenistic Images of the Philosophical Life." In *Images and Ideologies: Self-Definition in the Hellenistic World*, edited by Anthony W. Bulloch, Eric S. Gruen, Anthony A. Long, and Andrew Stewart. Berkeley: University of California Press, 1993.

Schofield, Malcolm. "Cicero, Zeno of Citium, and the Vocabulary of Philosophy." In *Le Style de la Pensée: Receuil de Textes en Hommage à Jacques Brunschwig*, edited by M. Canto-Sperber and P. Pellegrin. Paris: Les Belles Lettres, 2002.

Sedley, David N. "The Origins of Stoic God." In *Traditions of Theology: Studies in Hellenistic Theology*, edited by Dorothea Frede and André Laks. Leiden: Brill, 2002.

JOURNAL ARTICLES

Dorandi, Tiziano. "Filodemo, Gli Stoici (P.Herc. 155 e 339)." *Cronache Ercolanesi* 12 (1982): 91–133.

Long, Anthony A. "Socrates in Hellenistic Philosophy." *Classical Quarterly* 38 (1988): 150–71.

Mansfeld, Jaap. "Diogenes Laertius on Stoic Philosophy." *Elenchos* 7 (1986): 295–382.

Schofield, Malcolm. "The Syllogisms of Zeno of Citium." *Phronesis* 28 (1983): 31–58.

Malcolm Schofield (2005)

ZENO OF ELEA

c. 490–430 BCE

According to Plato (*Parmenides* (127A–C), Zeno was born around 490 BCE. He was a citizen of Elea, a Greek city in southern Italy with which Parmenides was also associated. Little is known about his life. The setting of Plato's *Parmenides* is a visit Zeno and Parmenides made to Athens in Socrates' youth (around 450 BCE), but since the conversation in that dialogue between Parmenides and Socrates certainly did not take place, there is no strong reason to believe that the visit did either. According to tradition, Zeno died heroically defying a tyrant in Elea. Philosophically he was a follower of Parmenides, whose doctrines he defended by arguing against opposing views; hence Aristotle called him the father of dialectic. Although Zeno wrote a book containing forty arguments against plurality. very little of his writing remains; approximately twenty lines of quotations, supplemented by relatively scanty testimonia. We have information about a dozen of his arguments. Under these circumstances, Zeno's immense influence on the history of philosophy is all the more remarkable.

Plato, our earliest witness, depicts Zeno as defending Parmenides' views against people who ridiculed Parmenides on the grounds that his views have absurd consequences. Zeno paid them back in their own coin, pursuing implications of the opposing views, which he showed have consequences even more absurd than those the opponents claimed to follow for Parmenides (*Parmenides* 128C–D). Zeno's book comprised a series of polemical arguments that employed the strategy *reductio ad absurdum* against the claim that there exists more than one thing (ibid. 128B–D).

Although Plato's account fits some of Zeno's arguments, it does not hold for them all. Several argue that motion cannot exist, another that the senses fail to discern the truth, another that things do not have locations. And so it is unclear how reliable Plato (whose reports of some other early philosophers are unreliable) is as a source on Zeno. Some scholars deny that Parmenides was a monist at all, or in the relevant sense, and some have held that some of Zeno's arguments tell as strongly against Parmenides' monism as they do against his opponents' pluralism. If this is correct, then Plato's account of Zeno's arguments is wholly misguided. Others have also argued that Zeno is better defined as a proto-sophist, a paradox-monger who constructed ingenious arguments with perverse conclusions, without any philosophical commitments at all.

Despite these concerns, the text of this encyclopedia follows the traditional view that Parmenides believed that there exists only one entity, which is motionless and changeless (it has other attributes as well); that the human senses are entirely deceptive as a source of knowledge of reality; and that Zeno defended this theory through arguments that derive absurd consequences not only from the assumption that there exists a plurality of entities but also from the assumptions that motion and change exist, and other assumptions that humans make about the world. Plato's account is taken to be essentially correct; when it states that Zeno defended Parmenides' view that there is just one thing, it is quoting this core Parmenidean thesis as a shorthand method of referring to the entire theory.

Scholars have disputed the identity of Parmenides' opponents against whom Zeno directed his arguments. Some held that they were the Pythagoreans, but the case collapsed for lack of evidence. Others have suggested that the opponents were not actual objectors but any possible objectors, that Zeno constructed a series of arguments that systematically refuted all possible alternative theories—for example, the theory that motion is continuous and also the theory that motion is discrete—but that interpretation failed for the same reason. What remains is the most natural interpretation, that Parmenides' opponents were people (ordinary folk and philosophers as well) who found Parmenides' views obviously, radically, and amusingly wrong because they conflict so strongly with humankind's most deeply held beliefs about the world.

The Zenonian legacy is a number of arguments known as paradoxes because of their implausible conclusions. Many of them have the form of an antinomy, which is a special kind of *reductio* argument. Zeno proves a thesis by demonstrating that its contradictory has incompatible consequences. Since the consequences cannot both be true, the contradictory of the original thesis is false, so the thesis itself is true. As a matter of fact, Zeno's arguments do not contain the final move, which is characteristic of reductio arguments: they stop when they have shown that the contradictory of the thesis is false and do not draw the inference that the thesis itself is true. It has therefore been claimed that the arguments are not reductio arguments at all. But this criticism affects only the form, not the intent of the argument; they are reductio arguments in spirit if not in letter.

ARGUMENTS AGAINST PLURALITY

Several of Zeno's arguments against plurality survive. They include the argument of both like and unlike; the argument of both large and small; and the argument of both limited and unlimited.

ARGUMENT OF BOTH LIKE AND UNLIKE. The first argument against plurality is as follows: (a) If things are many, they must be both like and unlike; but (b) what is like cannot be unlike and what is unlike cannot be like; therefore (c) there cannot be many things (*Parmenides* 127D). The meaning of (a) is unclear: In what way are many things both like and unlike? One attempt to explicate it as follows. If there are many things, each of them is like itself in that everything that is true of it is true of it. This is trivially true. But if one thing (A) is counted as like another (B) only if everything that is true of A is true of B and/or vice versa, and if A is unlike B if and only if A is not like B (i.e., "like" and "unlike" are contradictories, as (b) indicates), then *any* two things are unlike one another.

For example, even if A and B are as alike as two peas in a pod, A will be unlike B because it is true of A that it is A but it is not true of B that it is A. Following this interpretation, which places a very strong condition on things being "like," (a) is true but (b) is false, so it follows that the alleged impossibility is not impossible at all. For impossibility to occur, the things would have to be both like and unlike the same thing (whereas here A is like one thing (A) and unlike something else (B)). Further, they would have to be both like and unlike the same thing in the same respect (since A can be like B in color but unlike B in weight) and at the same time (since A can be like B in color at one time but not another). The paradox fails on the interpretation given. It also fails if one admits a weaker condition for one thing being like another. For example, if one counts A as like B if at least one thing true of A is also true of B, so that A will be unlike B only if nothing true of A is true of B, the alleged impossibility again proves perfectly possible, since the only way something can be both like and unlike is by being like one thing and unlike something else. Other attempts to reconstruct the argument have been proposed, but none has yet succeeded in making it plausible, so it seems likely that Zeno's first argument is fallacious.

ARGUMENT OF BOTH LARGE AND SMALL. Two of Zeno's surviving five fragments contain parts of a different and more complex argument against plurality. The argument claims that if things are many, they are both large and small: (a) so large that they are infinite and (b) so small that they have no size. The argument consists of two separate parts, one showing that things are large and one that they are small. It is an antinomy, but in this case Zeno argues that each branch of the antinomy is subject in its own right to a serious objection.

The entire argument for (a) has survived, but only part of the argument for (b). The proof of (b) came first, and the part that is reported is as follows: "Nothing has size because each of the many things is the same as itself and one." Zeno then argues that anything without size, thickness, or bulk does not exist: "If it is added to something else that exists, it will not make it any larger. For if it were of no size and were added, what it is added to cannot increase in size. It follows immediately that what is added is nothing. But if when it is subtracted the other thing is no smaller, and it is not increased when it is added, clearly the thing added or subtracted is nothing." (DK 29B2) This argument holds for three-dimensional bodies (though not for other kinds of things: I do not become larger by becoming happier, though one might say that happiness is added to me), so it is reasonable to take Zeno as arguing against the kind of pluralism that supposes that there exists a plurality of bodies (physical pluralism). What is missing is a reason to hold that "nothing has size because each of the many things is the same as itself and one."

The argument for (a) states: "If it exists, each thing must have some size and thickness, and a part of it must be apart from the rest. And the same reasoning holds for the part that is in front: that too will have size and part of it will be in front. Now to say this once is the same as to keep saying it forever. No such part of it will be last, nor will there be one part unrelated to another. Therefore, if there are many things they must be both small and large; so small as not to have size, but so large as to be unlimited." (DK 29B1) The first claim follows from (b). Zeno proceeds on the assumption that size implies divisibility: any body can be divided into spatially distinct parts, each of which is itself a body. This in turn entails divisibility without limit: the process of subdividing never reaches an end, so the parts are so large as to be unlimited.

Most scholars believe that the argument claims to prove that the size of the totality of the parts is infinitely large. If so, it is fallacious. All it proves is that number of the parts is infinitely large, and as the series 1/2 + 1/4 + 1/8 + … (whose sum is 1) shows, the sum of an infinite series need not be infinite. In the present case, the size of the totality of the parts remains equal to the size of the original whole. But if we adopt another interpretation the argument is valid. Since the argument focuses not on the size of the parts, but on the process and the products of division, the problem it raises concerns not the size of the totality of the parts but the possibility of completing the division. According to this interpretation, Zeno is demonstrating a difficulty in ordinary notions of physical bodies and spatial extension. People think that bodies are divisible and Zeno points out there is no reason to postulate that divisibility is impossible beyond some minimum size. It follows that bodies are infinitely divisible: even a small body is large enough to have an infinite number of parts. This conclusion is surprising enough to be worthy of Zeno.

The account of division just given suggests a way to supply the missing step in the argument for (b). How does the innocuous fact that something is the same as itself and one imply that it has no size? Perhaps it is because being "one" entails having no parts—otherwise it would be many. Since (as the process of division shows) anything with size can be divided into parts, only something without size will have no parts and so be "one." And then the argument for (b) comes into play.

ARGUMENT OF BOTH LIMITED AND UNLIMITED. The argument is: "(a) If there are many things, they must be just as many as they are, neither more nor less. But if they are just as many as they are, they must be limited. (b) If there are many things, the things that exist are unlimited, since between things that exist there are always others, and still others between those. Therefore the things that exist are unlimited." (DK 29B3) Branch (a) of this antinomy amounts to the claims that any plurality of things consists of a definite number of things and that any definite number is limited. The latter of these is equivalent to the claim that there is no such thing as a definite unlimited number. It has been objected that this last claim is false, since some infinite collections are pluralities that in a relevant way are definite and yet not "just as many as they are." But Zeno did not have the modern understanding of the infinite available to him, and the notion of "unlimited" with which he was working (in which the word means "inexhaustible" or "endless") makes it reasonable, even truistic, to say that an unlimited collection of things has no definite number. The former claim, that every plurality contains a definite number of things, as at least superficially plausible, which is enough to launch the paradox. Whether or not it is true will depend on how an individual counts the things in question (and perhaps their parts as well—see the paradox of both large and small), which Zeno does not specify.

Branch (b) can be interpreted in several ways, some of them anachronistic (for example, that the plurality in question is not three-dimensional objects but mathematical points on a line) and some open to obvious objections (for example, if Zeno is talking about three-dimensional objects that can touch one another, it is just false that there are always other objects in between). The source for this argument suggests a more interesting approach, saying: "In this way he proved the quantity unlimited on the basis of bisection." (Simplicius, *In Physica* 140, 33). Simplicius need not have quoted all the Zenonian text he had access to, and since he quoted part of the argument he could very well have known the rest of it. In the kind of division referred to, an object is first cut in half, then one of the halves is cut in half, and so on ad infinitum. If there are two adjacent objects A and B, this argument can be used to prove not that A and B have other objects in between them, but that there is no part of A nearest to B. If A is adjacent to B on the left, then the right half of A (which is itself a part of A) is in some sense nearer to B than A is, and so is the right half of that half, and so on. The point is the same as that of the argument discussed above: when A is divided in this way it turns out to have an unlimited number of parts. And again, this conclusion follows validly if one assumes certain views about physical bodies and spatial extension.

ARGUMENTS AGAINST MOTION

Four of Zeno's arguments against motion were particularly difficult to refute, according to Aristotle, who summarized them and offered solutions. They are the Dichotomy (or the Stadium); the Achilles; the Flying Arrow; and the Moving Rows. The following exposition is based mainly on Aristotle's penetrating discussion.

THE DICHOTOMY (OR THE STADIUM). This paradox argues that motion does not exist because it requires something impossible to happen. In order to cross a stadium from the starting line (A) to the finish line (B), after setting out one must reach A_1, the midpoint of the interval AB, before reaching B, then A_2, the midpoint of the interval A_1B, and so on. Each time one reaches the midpoint of an interval one still has another interval to cross with a midpoint of its own. There is an infinite number of intervals to cross. But it is impossible to cross an infinite number of intervals. Therefore one cannot reach the finish line.

The backbone of the argument lies in the following claims. (a) To move any distance one must always cross half the distance; (b) there is an infinite number of half-distances; (c) it is impossible to get completely through an infinite number of things one by one in a finite time; therefore (d) it is impossible to move any distance.

Aristotle, the primary source for the paradox, discusses the paradox several times in *Physics* (233a21, 239b9, 263a4). He rejects the inference to (d) on the grounds that the time of the motion is not finite, but infinite. Not that he supposes that every motion takes an infinite length of time; rather, as he has argued elsewhere in the *Physics* (6, 1–2), time is divisible in the same way that the distance traversed is divisible. If it takes a minute to cross the whole distance, it takes half a minute to cross the first half-distance, a quarter of a minute to cross the second half-distance, and so on. As the distances become smaller so does the time required to cross them, and the time interval required for the whole movement can be divided into the same number of subintervals as the number of subintervals into which the distance of the whole movement can be divided. So the time (just like the distance) is infinite in one respect (Aristotle calls this "infinite by division") and finite in another ("in extent").

Aristotle, however, does not stop here. He observes, "This solution is sufficient to use against the person who raised the question … but insufficient for the facts of the matter and the truth" (*Physics* 263a15), and then proceeds to discuss a deeper issue that the paradox raises: whether it is possible at all to perform an infinite number of acts, even the acts of getting through the sequence of decreasing time intervals. Granted that if one can do it, it will take a finite time, but can we do it at all?

Aristotle's solution to this stronger version of the paradox relies on his distinction between the actual infinite and the potential infinite. It is impossible to complete an actually infinite number of tasks, but possible to complete tasks that are potentially infinite. A line or a time-interval contains a potentially infinite number of points or instants. A point is actualized by stopping there; an instant is actualized by stopping then. Crossing the distance by making a single continuous movement does not actualize any of the midpoints. Hence, according to Aristotle's analysis, motion is possible because it does not involve completing an infinite number of tasks. Aristotle's final position on the paradox is that (d) does not follow from (a) (b) and (c), and Zeno committed an elementary blunder in supposing that it does, and moreover that (b) is true only if taken to claim that there is a potentially infinite number of half-distances, whereas (c) is true only if taken to refer to an actually infinite number of things and additionally if the proviso "in a finite time" is deleted.

THE ACHILLES. This paradox too argues against the possibility of motion. The swiftest runner (Achilles) gives the slowest (traditionally a tortoise, although no mention of the reptile occurs in Aristotle's account) a head start. But then he cannot catch up. He must first reach the tortoise's starting point (A), by which time the tortoise will have moved ahead some distance, however small, to another point (A_1). Getting to A proves to be only the first stage of a longer race. In the second stage of the race Achilles must reach A_1, but by then, the tortoise will have gone ahead an even smaller distance, to A_2, and so on. Each time Achilles reaches the point from which the tortoise has started, the tortoise is no longer there, so Achilles never catches up.

Aristotle observes, "This is the same argument as the Dichotomy, but it differs in not dividing the magnitude in half": Achilles runs more than twice as fast as the tortoise. Therefore, on the basis of his analysis of the Dichotomy argument, Aristotle thinks that the Achilles goes as follows: (a) To catch up with the tortoise, Achilles must always reach the point from which the tortoise started; (b) There is an infinite number of such starting points; (c) It is impossible to get completely through an infinite number of things one by one in a finite time; Therefore (d) Achilles cannot catch up with the tortoise. Unlike the Dichotomy, this argument does not conclude with the statement that motion is impossible. However, since the nature of motion implies that a faster runner will eventually catch up with a slower one, Zeno's conclusion that this cannot happen *entails* that motion cannot exist. According to Aristotle's analysis, though (which remains the dominant interpretation), the Achilles is fallacious since it commits the same mistake as the Dichotomy.

However, Aristotle's own statement of the Achilles (*Physics* 239b14) suggests that this interpretation is mistaken. The passage reads: "The slower will never be caught by the swiftest. For the pursuer must first reach the point from which the pursued departed, so that the slower must always be some distance in front." This summary says nothing about there being an infinite number of starting points or about the impossibility of performing an infinite number of tasks, or performing them in a finite time. Rather, the paradox turns on the words "always" and "never," which points to a different interpretation of the argument: (a) Achilles catches up with the tortoise when he reaches the point where the tortoise then is; (b) each time, before catching the tortoise, Achilles must reach the point from which the tortoise started; (c) when Achilles reaches the point from which the tortoise started, the tortoise has moved ahead; therefore, (d) the tortoise is always some distance ahead of Achilles [from (b and c)]; therefore (e) Achilles never catches up [from (d)].

This argument is different from the Dichotomy argument and is not open to the same objection. Where the Dichotomy is based on the impossibility of performing an infinite number of tasks, the Achilles turns on the words "always" and "never." The Achilles challenges the existence of motion if (e) is taken to assert that there is no time at which is it true that Achilles reaches the point where the tortoise then is; and this is in fact is the natural way to understand (e). But if in (e) "never" means "there is no time at which is it true that… " then in order for the argument to go through, (d) "always" must correspondingly mean "at all times is it true that … ." So, (d) must be taken to claim that the tortoise is ahead of Achilles at all times. In faact, this is a valid inference: If the tortoise is always (in this sense of "always') ahead, then Achilles never (in the corresponding sense of "never") catches up. But (d) appears obviously false, since faster things do in fact catch up with slower things. In the argument, (d) follows from (b) and (c), but these premises do not entail that the tortoise is ahead of Achilles at all times (as is needed for the argument to go through to (e)), only that the tortoise is still ahead at every time during the race. For example, if the tortoise's head start is nine miles and its speed is 1 m.p.h. while Achilles' speed is 10 m.p.h, then Achilles catches up with the tortoise at the end of one hour. During the race—before the hour is over—Achilles is always catching up and the tortoise is always ahead. But the scope of "always" is restricted to the time during which Achilles has not yet caught up; it does not have unrestricted scope ("at all times") as is needed for (d) to entail (e). As was noted above, (e) will follow only if there is no time at which it is true that Achilles has caught up, and the argument—in particular (b) and (c)—has given no reason to believe this.

THE FLYING ARROW. Aristotle's summary is as follows: If everything is always at rest when it is in a space equal to itself, and what is moving is always at an instant, the moving arrow is motionless" (*Physics* 239b5). The argument is incomplete as it stands and has been completed in various ways, one of which is the following: (a) Whenever something is in a space equal to itself, it is at rest (from Aristotle's summary); (b) an arrow is in a space equal to itself at each instant of its flight (supplemented); therefore (c) an arrow is at rest at each instant of its flight [from (a) and (b)]; (d) what is moving is always at an instant (from Aristotle's summary); therefore (e) during the whole of its flight the arrow is at rest [from (c) and (d)].

Aristotle objects: the argument "follows from assuming that time is composed of instants; if this is not conceded, the deduction will not go through" (*Physics* 239b31). This fastens on the move from (d) to (e). Aristotle's view of time, that it is not composed of instants, defeats the paradox. It can also be objected (again on Aristotelian grounds, see *Physics* 6, 3) that rest and motion take place over time intervals, not at instants. Motion requires occupying different places at different times; it is measured by the distance covered in an interval of time; nothing can move in an instant or for an instant. Likewise, rest is properly understand as the absence of motion: something is at rest during a time interval when it is not in motion. It makes no more sense to speak of rest in an instant or for an instant than it does to say that it is moving in or for an instant. This constitutes an objection to (c).

Another objection concerns (a), which implies that something in motion is not in a space equal to itself. But what does this mean? When is the moving thing not occupying a space equal to itself, and in what way? Two possible answers to the first of these questions are that it does not occupy a space equal to itself over the entire duration of its motion and (ii) at an instant during its motion. On interpretation (i) the idea is that in its motion the arrow occupies different positions at different instants and the sum (in some sense of the word) of those positions is larger than any of the individual positions. If the arrow initially occupies position AB (extending from point A to point B) and ends up at position CD (where the distance from C to D is equal to the distance from A to B), then the distance from A to D is equal to the space the arrow is in during the whole of its flight, and the distance from A to D is larger than the distance from A to B. Conversely, during any period when the arrow is at rest, it will be in a space equal to itself. Interpretation (i) makes sense of (a), but if make the argument invalid. Because (a) concerns motion and rest over the duration of the motion, which is an interval of time, not at an instant, and it is in general illegitimate to infer a conclusion about the behavior of something at individual instants in an interval from its ehavior during the interval as a whole, or vice versa. Consquently the inferences to (c) and (e) are invalid. On interpretation (ii) the move to (c) is valid, but there is no obvious reason why Zeno should have thought or should have expected anyone to agree that things change size during their motion, so that at any instant of its flight an arrow is larger or smaller than when it is at rest. Thus the argument fails: On one interpretation (i) it is invalid and on another (ii), although valid, it contains an unacceptable premise.

THE MOVING ROWS. Aristotle reports this argument as follows: "The fourth argument concerns equal bodies moving in a stadium alongside equal bodies in the opposite direction, the one group moving from the end of the stadium, the other from the middle, at equal speed. [Zeno] claims in this argument that it follows that half the time is equal to the double. … Let A's represent the equal stationary bodies, B's the bodies beginning from the middle, equal in number and size to the A's, and C's the bodies beginning from the end, equal in number and size to these and having the same speed as the B's. It follows that the first B is at the end at the same time as the first C, as the B's and C's move alongside one another, and the first C has come alongside all the B's but the first B has come alongside half the A's. And so the time is half. For each of them is alongside each thing for an equal time. It follows simultaneously that the first B has moved alongside all the C's, for the first C and the first B will be at the opposite ends simultaneously, because both have been alongside the A's for an equal amount of time" (*Physics* 239b33).

In discussing this passage, Simplicius, in *Physics* 1016, 19, provides diagrams to illustrate the starting position and the finish:

DIAGRAM 1: Starting position:

```
            A A A A
D   B B B B →            E
              ← C C C C
```

DIAGRAM 2: Finishing position:

```
            A A A A
D           B B B B      E
            C C C C
```

The kernel of the argument is as follows: (a) The time it takes the first B to have come alongside four C's is equal to the time it takes the first B to have come alongside two A's; (b) the first B is alongside each A and also alongside each C for the same amount of time; (c) but during its motion B is alongside two A's and B is alongside four C's; therefore (d) the total time B is alongside the A's is half the total time B is alongside the C's [from (b) and (c)]; therefore (e) half the time is equal to the double [from (a) and (d)]. Here "the double" refers to the time taken in being alongside the four C's; it means "the double of half the time," not "the double of the whole time." (Another iteration of the argument will yield the conclusion that half the whole time equals double the whole time.)

Aristotle claims the argument is based on an elementary mistake: "The mistake is in thinking that an equal magnitude moving with equal speed takes an equal time in moving alongside something in motion as it does in moving alongside something at rest" (*Physics* 240a1). Thus, (b) is false, and consequently so are (d) and (e). Aristotle's analysis is correct if Zeno is treating the motion of extended bodies over a continuous magnitude. But could Zeno have committed so gross a blunder?

An influential interpretation acquits Zeno of this charge. Zeno is arguing not against the ordinary view of time (and perhaps space and motion as well) as being continuous, but against another possible view, that they are discrete: there are "atoms" of time and space, and motion proceeds in atomic "jumps," going from one atomic location to the next from one atomic instant to the next. Either something is moving or it is not; if it is moving, it is in successive locations at successive instants, if it is not, it is in the same location at successive instants. By hypothesis the B's and the C's are moving. One instant after the instant they occupy the starting position (Diagram 1) they will occupy the position illustrated in Diagram 3:

DIAGRAM 3: Position after one step:

```
            A A A A
D       B B B B →          E
          ← C C C C
```

One instant later, they will occupy the position illustrated in Diagram 2. And contrary to what happens if space and time are continuous, there is no instant at which the lead B is next to the lead C (as in Diagrams 4 and 5).

DIAGRAM 4: This position does not occur:

```
              A A A A
D       B B B B →          E
            ← C C C C
```

DIAGRAM 2: Nor does this position:

```
              A A A A
D         B B B B →        E
            ← C C C C
```

Those who hold this interpretation have claimed the Moving Rows argument to be Zeno's most sophisticated argument and one that tells decisively against the view that time and space are atomic. But there are two obstacles to it. First, it conflicts with Aristotle's statement of the argument, which states that "each of them is alongside each thing for an equal time"; as just noted the lead B is never alongside the lead C. Second, there is no evidence in favor of it. Our sources give no hint that the bodies are atomic bodies or the times are atomic instants and there is no reason to think that such a theory of space and time had been considered by anyone as early as Zeno. The only reason given to support this interpretation is that Zeno was too clever to make the mistake that Aristotle finds—an assessment that is refuted by the equally elementary mistake diagnosed in the paradox of like and unlike.

TWO MORE PARADOXES

Zeno did not limit himself to arguments against the existence of plurality and motion. Two other arguments—the Millet Seed and the Place of Place—survive that challenge other deeply held beliefs.

THE MILLET SEED. This argument apparently criticizes the senses, therefore supporting Parmenides' view that the senses are radically unreliable. It is preserved in the form of a dialogue between Zeno and Protagoras (Simplicius, *In Physica*, 1108.18). In essence it states: (a) One millet seed or one ten-thousandth of a millet seed does not make a sound when it falls; (b) a bushel of millet seeds makes a sound when it falls; (c) there is a ratio between the bushel of millet seeds and one millet seed or one ten-thousandth of a millet seed; (d) the sounds made by the bushel, the millet seed, and the ten-thousandth of a millet seed have the same ratios as the ratios identified in (c); therefore (e) a millet seed makes a sound when it falls, and so does one ten-thousandth of a millet seed [from (b) and (d)]. (e) contradicts (a), which depends on the evidence of hearing. Therefore, hearing is unreliable.

Aristotle rebuts the paradox by saying that a threshold of force is needed to produce sound, and that the force of one millet seed falling is below the threshold. Other solutions suggest themselves as well.

THE PLACE OF PLACE. This argument is reported in several sources, including Aristotle's *Physics* (209a23, 210b22) and Simplicius's *In Physica*. Its essence is as follows: (a) Everything that exists is in a place; therefore (b) place exists; therefore (c) place is in a place [from (a) and (b)]; (d) but this goes ad infinitum. Therefore (e) place does not exist.

Aristotle and his followers rebutted the argument by denying (a): not everything that exists is in a place, "for no one would say that health or courage or ten thousand other things were in a place" (Eudemus, quoted in Simplicius *In Physica* 563.25); and "nothing prevents the first place from being in something else, but not in it as in a place" (Aristotle, *Physics* 210b24). One can grant that a three-dimensional object has a place without conceding that its place is the kind of thing that can have a place. Alternatively one might accept the reasoning through (d) but deny that (d) entails (e). Not all infinite regresses are vicious.

CONCLUSION

The present treatment has offered versions of the most important of Zeno's surviving arguments and has suggested ways to refute them. This follows the tradition in discussing Zeno and the other Eleatic philosophers that has been dominant since Plato (*Sophist* 258B–D). Aristotle employed this practice and not just as a matter of historical interest. His philosophical method required him to take his predecessors' views into account and find solutions for puzzles and problems they presented, and his views on place, time, motion, and the infinite were framed with Zeno's paradoxes in mind. Philosophical interest in Zeno was renewed (notably by Bertrand Russell) after the modern conception of the infinite had been elaborated; once again contemporary philosophical tenets were employed to refute the paradoxes (principally the Dichotomy, the Achilles, and the Flying Arrow) and the challenge they present to ordinary views of space, time, and motion, and once again the discussion went beyond what Zeno proposed and encompassed related puzzles that his paradoxes suggested.

This astonishing ability to invent exciting and fruitful paradoxes is not Zeno's only contribution to philosophy. If Parmenides was the first pre-Socratic philosopher to employ deductive arguments, Zeno was the first to do so in prose, and his fragments show that he made great advances over Parmenides in the clarity of his reasoning and the complexity of his arguments. Also noteworthy is his use of deductions to point out the danger of maintaining familiar beliefs without examining them. These contributions easily outweigh any errors one may (frequently by employing concepts, distinctions and proof techniques that were not developed for centuries or millennia after Zeno's time) detect in his arguments.

See also Aristotle; Dialectic; Infinity in Mathematics and Logic; Logic, History of; Logical Paradoxes; Melissus of Samos; Motion; Parmenides of Elea; Plato; Russell, Bertrand Arthur William; Set Theory; Simplicius; Socrates.

Bibliography

PRIMARY TEXTS

Caveing, Maurice. *Zénon d'Élée. Prolégomènes aux doctrines du continu.* Paris: Vrin, 1982.

Diels, Hermann, and Walther Kranz. *Die Fragmente der Vorsokratiker.* 5th ed. Dublin and Zurich: Weidmann, 1951.

Lee, H. D. P. *Zeno of Elea.* Cambridge, U.K.: Cambridge University Press, 1936.

Untersteiner, Mario. *Zenone. Testimonianze e Frammenti.* Florence: La Nuova Italia, 1963.

SECONDARY TEXTS

Barnes, Jonathan. *The Presocratic Philosophers.* 2nd ed. Boston: Routledge & Kegan Paul, 1982.

Black, Max. "Achilles and the Tortoise." *Analysis* 11 (1951): 91–101.

Dillon, John. "More Evidence on Zeno of Elea?" *Archiv für Geschichte der Philosophie* 58 (1976): 221–222.

Dillon, John. "New Evidence on Zeno of Elea?" *Archiv für Geschichte der Philosophie* 56 (1974): 127–131.

Fränkel, Hermann. "Zeno of Elea's Attacks on Plurality." *American Journal of Philology* 63 (1942): 1–25, 193–206.

Furley, David. *Two Studies in the Greek Atomists.* Princeton, NJ: Princeton University Press, 1967.

Grünbaum, Adolf. *Modern Science and Zeno's Paradoxes.* Middletown, CT: Wesleyan University Press, 1967.

Guthrie, W. K. C. *A History of Greek Philosophy*, Vol. 2: *The Presocratic Tradition from Parmenides to Democritus.* Cambridge, U.K.: Cambridge University Press, 1965.

Hinton, J. M., and C. B. Martin. "Achilles and the Tortoise." *Analysis* 14 (1954): 56–68.

Kirk, G. S., and J. E. Raven. *The Presocratic Philosophers.* Cambridge, U.K.: Cambridge University Press, 1957.

Kirk, G. S., J. E. Raven, and M. Schofield. *The Presocratic Philosophers.* 2nd ed. Cambridge, U.K.: Cambridge University Press, 1982.

Lear, Jonathan. "A Note on Zeno's Arrow." *Phronesis* 26 (1981): 91–104.

McKirahan, Richard D. "La dichotomie de Zénon chez Aristote." In *Qu'est-ce que la philosophie présocratique*, edited by André Laks and Claire Louguet, 465–496. Villeneuve d'Ascq (Nord): Presses Universitaires du Septentrion, 2002.

McKirahan, Richard D. "Zeno." In *The Cambridge Companion to Early Greek Philosophy*, edited by A. A. Long, 134–158. Cambridge, U.K.: Cambridge University Press, 1999.

Owen, G. E. L. "Zeno and the Mathematicians." *Proceedings of the Aristotelian Society* 58 (1957–58): 199–222.

Russell, Bertrand. *Our Knowledge of the External World.* Chicago: Open Court, 1914.

Ryle, Gilbert. *Dilemmas.* Cambridge, U.K.: Cambridge University Press.

Salmon, Wesley, ed. *Zeno's Paradoxes*. New York: Bobbs-Merrill, 1970.

Solmsen, Friedrich. "The Tradition about Zeno of Elea Re-Examined." *Pronesis* 16 (1971): 116–141.

Sorabji, Richard. *Time, Creation, and the Continuum: Theories in Antiquity and the Early Middle Ages*. Ithaca, NY: Cornell University Press, 1983.

Tannery, Paul. *Pour l'histoire de la science*. Hellène. Paris: Alcan, 1887.

Thomas, L. E. "Achilles and the Tortoise." *Analysis* 12 (1952): 92–94.

Vlastos, Gregory. "A Note on Zeno's Arrow." *Phronesis* 11 (1966): 3–18.

Vlastos, Gregory. "Plato's Testimony concerning Zeno of Elea." *Journal of Hellenic Studies* 95 (1975): 136–162.

Vlastos, Gregory. "A Zenonian Argument against Plurality." In *Essays in Ancient Greek Philosophy*, edited by John P. Anton and George L. Kustas, 119–144. Albany: State University of New York Press, 1971.

Vlastos, Gregory. "Zeno of Elea." In *Encyclopedia of Philosophy*, 1st ed., edited by Paul Edwards, 369–379. New York: Macmillan, 1967.

Vlastos, Gregory. "Zeno's Race Course: With an Appendix on the Achilles." *Journal of the History of Philosophy* 4 (1966): 95–108.

Richard McKirahan (2005)

ZENO'S PARADOXES

See *Infinity in Mathematics and Logic*; *Zeno of Elea*

ZHANG ZAI

(1020–1077)

Born into a family from Kaifeng in Henan Province, Zhang Zai, styled Zihou, lived in a small town called Hengqu of Mei County in modern Shaanxi Province for the major part of his life and hence was known as Hengqu. After a few years of strenuous study of Daoism and Buddhism, he was encouraged by Fan Zhongyan to study *Zhongyong* (The doctrine of the mean) when he was only 21. He thus left Daoism and Buddhism behind and returned to the Confucian classics in a quest for a philosophy of the Confucian Way (*dao*). Like Zhou Dunyi, Zhang Zai finally set his mind on the *Yijing* (Book of changes) and change (*yi*) as the very essence of the Way. Zhang Zai's main work was *Zheng meng* (Rectifying the obscure), in which he developed his metaphysics of vital energy (*qi*). In this treatise he became the first philosopher to expound on vital energy as the essence of the Way and thus provide a systematic foundation for understanding and developing the cosmology and ontology of change in the Confucian tradition. Included in *Zheng meng* is the noteworthy essay "Ximing" (Western inscription), which gives a deeply felt statement of his view on the cosmos, human life, and ideal Confucian practice.

In comparison with Zhou Dunyi, who developed a cosmology of change in terms of the abstract notions of the great ultimate (*taiji*) and rationality (*li*), Zhang Zai sought a more unified and yet more detailed description of the formation and transformation of all things in the world in terms of vital energy. Zhang Zai's metaphysics of the ubiquitous vital energy both inspires and justifies his theory of the human mind as endowed with both cognitive and ethical capacity. Like Zhou, Zhang Zai applied his cosmology to his life and strove to be a Confucian sage. In his mind, the ideal of a Confucian sage was to let morality guide one's heart and mind on earth (and to prepare for heaven) while following the teachings of past sages, all in hopes of improving the destiny of the living and establishing a peace that would last for generations.

In his metaphysics of vital energy and dialectics of the transformation of vital energy, Zhang Zai conceives of vital energy as primarily subsisting in the great void (*taixu*) and as the primordial source of the generation of things in the world. The great void gives rise to vital energy, which differentiates yin and yang and the five powers (*wuxing*), which then gives rise to all the things in the world. In this process of generation, rationality (*li*), as the order and form of things, arises naturally from the vital energy. Unlike Zhu Xi (1130–1200) after him, Zhang Zai never views rationality as an autonomous or independent category of reality. Instead, he regards rationality as always inherent in the vital energy, and he regards all things as transformations of the vital energy, which alone determines the formation and destruction of things.

In his reflections on human nature, Zhang Zai distinguishes between the nature of heaven and earth (*tiandi zhi xing*) and the nature of temperament and desires (*qizhi zhi xing*) of a person. The former is rooted in the primary unformed vital energy, and the latter arises from the formed body of a person. The moral virtue in a person consists in grasping one's primary nature and controlling one's secondary nature.

In connection with this distinction of two natures, Zhang Zai also makes a distinction between knowledge of virtues (*dexing zhi zhi*) and knowledge of seeing and hearing (*jianwen zhi zhi*). The first sort of knowledge comes not from seeing and hearing but from reflection on the nature of heaven and earth until one sees the functions and powers of the Way and understands how one embodies these functions and powers and can channel them to transform oneself into a virtuous sage. For Zhang Zai, cultivating one's nature not only opens one's mind to understanding and knowledge of the ultimate reality but also leads to human goodness (*ren*). When the mind understands ultimate reality, it can unify and command one's nature and emotions, because it can relate to and embody ultimate reality as the ultimate ground of unity and integration.

In conclusion, Zhang Zai's philosophy, as presented in his essay "Ximing," embodies a deep cosmic piety of the Confucian tradition that is both ethical and religious in spirit. In lieu of an explicit organized religion, Confucianism reaches for a cosmic sentiment of piety rooted in self-cultivation of a human-cosmic bond that would transcend and dissolve the problems of life and death. Hence Zhang Zai's final statement in "Ximing": "In life I feel at ease; in death I will be at peace"

See also Cheng Hao; Cheng Yi; Chinese Philosophy: Confucius; Shao Yong; Zhou Dunyi.

Bibliography

Zhang Zai. *Zhang Zai ji*. Beijing: Zhonghua shuju, 1978. Contains *Zheng meng* (Rectifying the obscure), *Jingxue li ku* (Treasury of li in the Confucian classics), *Hengqu "Yi" shuo* (Zhang Zai's discourse on the *Yijing*). This is best edition of Zhang Zai's work.

Chung-ying Cheng (2005)

ZHOU DUNYI

(1017–1073)

Zhou Dunyi was the first eleventh-century Chinese thinker who argued for the inseparability of metaphysics and ethics. His two works—*Taiji tushuo* (An Explanation of the Diagram of the Great Ultimate) and *Tongshu* (Penetrating the Book of Changes)—were major neo-Confucian writings on the metaphysical nature of moral cultivation.

In the *Taiji tushuo*, Zhou Dunyi comments on the Diagram of the Great Ultimate (*Taiji tu*). The Diagram, created by the Daoist Chen Tuan (c. 906–989), consists of five circles. The top circle is an empty one, symbolizing the universe as a self-generative and self-reproducing entity. The second circle contains intermixing semi-circles of dark and light colors, with the dark color representing the *yin* (the yielding cosmic force) and the light color the *yang* (the active cosmic force). The third circle is a group of five small circles, each represents one of the Five Phases (*wu xing*)—water, fire, wood, metal, and earth. Describing biological reproduction, the fourth circle depicts how the *yin* moves the female, and the *yang* the male. Building on the fourth circle, the fifth circle likens the process by which the myriad beings are produced through the union of the two sexes.

For Zhou, the Diagram of the Great Ultimate is a graphic depiction of the two-way flow between the whole and the part, the one and the many. Reading from the top to the bottom, the Diagram shows how the one gives rise to the many. It explains the ways in which the intermixing of the *yin* and *yang* creates the Five Phases and the multitude of beings. However, reading from the bottom to the top, the Diagram describes how the many are in fact one. It traces the steps by which the myriad beings are derived from the Five Phases and the *yin* and *yang*. No matter whether it is from one to many or from many to one, the Diagram shows that the universe is an organic system wherein part and whole play equal role. On this basis, Zhou explains the metaphysical nature of moral cultivation. He suggests that human beings, given their sensibility and consciousness, are free to decide whether they are active participants or stubborn obstructers of the universe's self-renewal. Hence, daily moral practices are as much metaphysical as ethical, involving a conscious decision to render human activities to be a part of the universe's self-regeneration.

In the *Tongshu*, Zhou Dunyi further explains the metaphysical nature of moral cultivation. According to Zhou, there are two reasons why the innate human goodness is called sincerity (*cheng*). First, the innate human goodness, although available to every human being, is hidden. One has to uncover it by being honest and true to oneself. Second, because all beings in this universe are intricately connected as a family of beings, to be true to oneself requires being true to others. Thus sincerity has to be rooted in altruism. For Zhou, Yan Hui (Confucius's favorite student) is a prime example of the cultivation of sincerity. Materially, Yan Hui was in an uninviting situation—having only a single bamboo dish of rice, a single gourd dish of drink, and living in a mean narrow lane. But spiritually, Yan Hui was always upbeat because he had developed a noble state of mind that linked him to the universe.

In paying tribute to Yan Hui, Zhou Dunyi in effect redefines the Confucian learning. In earlier times, learning was understood by Confucian scholars as being a loyal government official. Hence, successful prime ministers (such as Yi Yin of the Shang Dynasty in the seventeenth century BCE) were considered to be exemplary students of Confucius. By promoting Yan Hui as the true student of Confucius, Zhou sees learning as an individual quest for broadening the mind. A learned person, then, is not just a person of action; he is also a person of the right mind, who recognizes the inherent connections among all beings in this universe. By focusing on the cultivation of the mind, Zhou helps to distinguish neo-Confucianism from Classical Confucianism.

See also Cheng Hao; Cheng Yi; Confucius; Shao Yong; Zhang Zai; Zhu Xi.

Bibliography

Chan, Wing-tsit, tr. *A Source Book in Chinese Philosophy.* Princeton, NJ: Princeton University Press, 1963.

Fung, Yu-lan. *A History of Chinese Philosophy.* Vol. 2. Translated by Derk Bodde. Princeton, NJ: Princeton University Press, 1953.

Graham, A. C. *Two Chinese Philosophers: Ch'eng Ming-tao and Ch'eng Yi-chuan.* La Salle, IL: Open Court, 1992.

Huang Zongxi. *Song Yuan xue'an* [Intellectual Biographies of Song and Yuan Dynasties]. Taibei: Taiwan Zhonghua shuju reprint.

Mou Zongsan. *Xinti yu xingti* [The Substance of the Mind and the Substance of Human Nature]. Vol. 1. Taibei: Zhengzhong shuju, 1969.

Tu, Wei-ming. *Confucian Thought: Selfhood as Creative Transformation.* Albany: State University of New York Press, 1985.

Zhou Dunyi. *Zhou Dunyi ji* [Collected Works of Zhou Dunyi]. Beijing: Zhonghua shuju, 1990.

Tze-ki Hon (2005)

ZHUANGZI

(b. 369 BCE)

Zhuangzi, the greatest Daoist next to Laozi, was also known by his private name, Zhou. Not much is known about his life except that he was a minor government official at one time and that he later declined a prime ministership in the state of Chu to retain his freedom. Although Zhuangzi and Mencius were contemporaries, they were not acquainted with each other's teachings. Zhuangzi advanced the concept of Dao and gave Daoism a dynamic character. To him, Dao as Nature is not only spontaneity but also a constant flux, for all things are in a state of perpetual "self-transformation," each according to its own nature and in its own way. If there is an agent directing this process, there is no evidence of it. Things seem to develop from simple to higher life and finally to man, but man will return to the simple stuff, thus completing a cycle of transformation.

In this unceasing transfiguration, things appear and disappear. In such a universe "time cannot be recalled" and things move like "a galloping horse." They seem to be different, some large and some small, some beautiful and some ugly, but Dao equalizes them as one. This is Zhuangzi's famous doctrine of the "equality of all things." According to it, reality and unreality, right and wrong, life and death, beauty and ugliness, and all conceivable opposites are reduced to an underlying unity. This is possible because all distinctions and oppositions are merely relative, because they are the result of a subjective point of view, because they mutually cause each other, and because opposites are resolved in Dao. By the doctrine of "mutual causation" Zhuangzi meant that a thing necessarily produces its opposite; for instance, "this" implies "that," life ends in death, construction requires destruction, and so forth. By the resolution of opposites Zhuangzi meant that a thing and its opposite, both being extremes, need to be synthesized. But the synthesis is itself an extreme that requires a synthesis. At the end Dao will synthesize all, in a dialectic manner not unlike that of G. W. F. Hegel.

In Zhuangzi's philosophy the pure man abides in the great One, wherein he finds purity and peace. He becomes a "companion of Nature" and does not substitute the way of man for the way of Nature. He rejects all distinctions and seeks no self, fame, or success. He seeks "great knowledge," which is all-embracing and extensive, and discards "small knowledge," which is partial and discriminative. He "fasts in his mind" and "sits down and forgets everything"—especially the so-called humanity and righteousness of hypocritical society; he "travels in the realm of infinity." In this way he cultivates "profound virtue," and achieves a "great concord" with Dao. Herein he finds spiritual peace and "emancipation."

Both the mystical and fatalistic elements are obvious, and in these Zhuangzi went beyond Laozi. He was also more transcendental, for while Laozi's chief concern was how to govern, Zhuangzi's primary interest was to "roam beyond the mundane world," in spite of the fact that his ideal being is "sagely within" and "kingly without," that is, both transcendental and mundane. Nevertheless, Zhuangzi stresses the individual more than does Laozi. To be in accord with Dao, everything must nourish its own nature and follow its own destiny. The eagle should rise to the clouds, but the dove should hop from treetop to treetop. If a man were to shorten the crane's neck because it is long or to lengthen the duck's leg because it is short, that would be interfering with Nature. Spiritual freedom and peace can be achieved only through knowing one's own nature and capacity and being able to adapt oneself to the universal process of transformation. Although the ultimate goal is oneness with Dao, one's individuality is to be clearly recognized. Individual differences are not to be taken as basis for discrimination, but neither are they to be denied or ignored. This respect for individual nature and destiny eventually led to the emphasis on the particular nature in neo-Daoism.

See also Chinese Philosophy; Hegel, Georg Wilhelm Friedrich; Laozi; Mencius.

Bibliography

Available in English is *Chuang Tzu*, translated by Herbert A. Giles (London: Allen and Unwin, 1961); the authorship of this work is a very controversial matter. Most scholars accept the first seven chapters, the so-called inner chapters, as authentic and the remaining 26 chapters as later additions, either partly or in whole dating from the third to the first century BCE. Selections have been translated in Wing-tsit Chan, *A Source Book in Chinese Philosophy* (Princeton, NJ: Princeton University Press, 1963). See also Fung Yu-lan, *A Short History of Chinese Philosophy* (New York: Macmillan, 1948).

Fung, Yu-lan. *A Taoist Classic: Chuang-tzu*; A New Selected Translation with an Exposition of the Philosophy of Kuo Hsiang. Beijing, Foreign Language Press, 1998.

Graham, Angus C. *The Inner Chapters*. Boston: Unwin Paperbacks, 1989.

Kjellberg, Paul and Ivanhoe, Philip J. eds. *Essays on Skepticism, Relativism, and Ethics in the Zhuangzi*. Albany: State University of New York Press, 1996.

Mair, Victor Mair ed. *Experimental Essays on Chuang-tzu*. Honolulu: University of Hawaii Press, 1983.

Mair, Victor. *Wandering on the Way: Early Taoist Tales and Parables of Chuang Tzu*. Honolulu: University of Hawaii Press, 1998.

Watson, Burton. *The Complete Works of Chuang Tzu*. New York: Columbia University Press, 1968.

Wu, Kuang-ming. *Chuang Tzu: World Philosopher at Play*. American Academy of Religion, Studies in Religion, 26. New York: Crossroad, 1982.

Wing-tsit Chan (1967)
Bibliography updated by Huichieh Loy (2005)

ZHU XI (CHU HSI)
(1130–1200)

Zhu Xi was a leading scholar, thinker, and teacher of the revival of philosophical Confucianism known at the time as *Daoxue* (learning of the way), often referred to as neo-Confucianism. The prolific author of texts synthesizing the views of his immediate predecessors and reinterpreting the classical canon, Zhu Xi attained a status in the Chinese tradition comparable to that of Thomas Aquinas in the European world. Zhu's influence has been even more pervasive and long-lived, however; from 1313 until their abolition in 1905, China's civil service examinations took Zhu's commentaries to be the authoritative interpretations of the classics. Hence for nearly a millennium every literate individual in China had at least some familiarity with Zhu's teachings.

Zhu was born into turbulent times. In 1127 Jurchen people conquered northern China. Zhu's father was among many who protested the humiliating peace treaty that China was forced to accept, and he was demoted to a rural position in Anhui, where Zhu was born. Zhu took up his father's politics as he matured, committing himself to the hawkish group that wanted to take back the north. Partly out of disenchantment with the regime's failure to follow such policies, Zhu never played a significant role in the national bureaucracy despite having passed the highest-level civil service exam and having received his *jinshi* degree at the age of nineteen.

At first Zhu was quite eclectic in his intellectual and spiritual interests, but several encounters in his twenties with the staunch Confucian Li Tong (1095–1163) convinced him to commit himself wholeheartedly to the Confucianism associated with two celebrated thinkers from the eleventh century, the brothers Cheng Hao (1032–1085) and Cheng Yi (1033–1107). Over much of the rest of his life, Zhu held sinecure positions as a temple guardian and devoted himself to study, writing, and teaching. He produced a huge corpus of essays and commentaries that, together with the voluminous recorded and published conversations between Zhu and his students, articulated and defended a creative synthesis that has come to define mainstream neo-Confucianism.

Zhu's philosophical system was the product of the range of interlocking areas his writings encompassed: ontology, cosmology, nature (human and otherwise), psychology, epistemology, moral cultivation, ethics, and politics. In addition, despite his distance from national politics, he was deeply concerned with the practical import of his views; among other things, he worked to revitalize independent academies and advocated a form of village self-government known as a "community compact." Like most long-lived and prolific thinkers, Zhu revised his outlook over time, and many expressions of his ideas are highly contextual, depending on the circumstances he was addressing.

The central concepts in Zhu's ontology are *li* (pattern or principle) and *qi* (material force). Zhu saw that the patterns followed by one thing or in one affair interact with those of countless others, as when the unchecked growth of one tree stunts the growth of others nearby, and argued that there is an all-encompassing *li* in accord with which the myriad subsidiary patterns are able to develop in order and harmony. *Li* are the patterns underlying the constant change of the psychological and material world; *qi* is the dynamic stuff of which this world is composed. *Qi*, in turn, can be analyzed as either *yin* or *yang*, depending on whether it is contracting or expanding, soft or hard, dark or light, and so on. Each thing or affair has its own *li*, which in one sense can be understood as the possibilities for that thing: the patterns of change it can instantiate. Zhu held that the patterns followed by one thing interact with those of countless others, as when the unchecked growth of one tree stunts the growth of others nearby; he argued that there is an all-encompassing *li* in accord with which the myriad subsidiary patterns are able to develop in order and harmony.

From the human perspective, this all-encompassing *li* is called "moral pattern (*yi li*)"; applied to the cosmos, it is "nature's pattern (*tian li*)." Zhu believed *li* to have logical priority over *qi* but to have no existence independent of *qi*. He borrowed the term "Great Ultimate (*taiji*)" from Zhou Dunyi (1017–1073) to refer to the source of all creativity, the not-yet-material totality of all patterns in which *qi* has yet to be differentiated into *yin* and *yang*. The ideas of unceasing creativity and its original goodness lie at the heart of Zhu's metaphysics.

The view that nature has at its core goodness, harmony, creativity, and order applies equally to humans and to the cosmos at large. Zhu developed ideas of Cheng Yi and others to explain how we can be said to have good natures yet regularly have problematic thoughts and feelings. He also discussed the things we need to do to realize the pure goodness of our original natures. One core idea is that problems occur when our "unactualized (*weifa*)" minds become "actualized (*yifa*)" via our real and imperfect bodies and their desires. Our moral natures themselves have some reality, as can be seen by the near-ubiquitous spontaneous compassionate response we have to the suffering of innocents, but our *qi*—the psycho-physical reality of our emotions, habits, and so on—is not, except in sages, purely expressive of the equilibrium in our unactualized minds.

What is to be done? Zhu believed that education should begin with a period of "lesser learning" in which one learns good habits without delving into the reasoning that justifies them. In the subsequent "greater learning," one continues to nurture the "reverence (*jing*)" for moral pattern while beginning to investigate the theoretical grounding of those patterns. This "investigation of things (*gewu*)," which relied in part on a controversial redaction of the brief classic text *Greater Learning*, was the subject of much subsequent debate. Zhu seems to have had two kinds of investigation foremost in mind: the patterns observed in peoples' interactions with one another and the patterns instantiated by ancient sages and worthies, as recorded in the classics and histories. Indeed, reading was a central focus of his teaching, just as textual scholarship was a central focus of his scholarship. Zhu believed that without reference to external models of proper patterns, students would be too easily misled by introspection into their own reactions and motivations, which might be clouded by the impurities of one's *qi*. The goal of Zhu's teachings was practical: Given the centrality of "benevolence (*ren*)" in the life of the morally worthy person (and in the acme of human personality, the sage), he sought to motivate people to improve themselves by the most reliable method.

See also Cheng Hao; Cheng Yi; Chinese Philosophy; Confucius; Cosmology; Ontology, History of; Thomas Aquinas, St.; Zhou Dunyi.

Bibliography

ORIGINAL SOURCES

A great deal of work has been done since 1990 in compiling modern editions of Zhu's corpus. Most comprehensive is the *Complete Works of Zhu Xi* (*Zhuzi Quanshu*) from Shanghai Classics Press and Anhui Education Press; the first volumes began to appear in 2002. In 1996 Sichuan Education Press published *Collected Works of Zhu Xi* (*Zhu Xi Ji*) in ten volumes, which contains all of Zhu's formal writings. In addition, there are numerous editions of Zhu's collected sayings (*Zhuzi Yulei*) and other monographs available.

TRANSLATIONS

Daniel Gardner has provided perhaps the best introduction to Zhu's thought by translating selections from Zhu's conversations about learning, in *Learning to Be a Sage* (Berkeley: University of California Press, 1990). Further depth is provided by Allen Wittenborn's excellent, complete translation of Zhu's *Further Reflections on Things at Hand* (Lanham, MD: University Press of America, 1991). Wing-tsit Chan's translations are still quite helpful; see both the section on Zhu in his *Sourcebook in Chinese Philosophy* (Princeton, NJ: Princeton University Press, 1963) and the numerous comments from Zhu included in the important collection of earlier neo-Confucian writings that Zhu coedited, *Reflections on Things at Hand* (New York: Columbia University Press, 1967).

SECONDARY STUDIES

The closest thing to a general, book-length study of Zhu in English is Julia Ching, *The Religious Thought of Chu Hsi* (Oxford: Oxford University Press, 2000). Donald Munro's *Images of Human Nature* (Princeton, NJ: Princeton University Press, 1988) critically engages a range of Zhu's ideas by focusing on the images he uses to structure his thinking. The best work in English on the intellectual context in which Zhu's ideas developed is Hoyt Tillman, *Confucian Discourse and Chu Hsi's Ascendancy* (Honolulu, University of Hawaii Press, 1992). There are also a handful of more specialized monographs and many articles devoted to Zhu; a particularly high-quality collection of the latter is Wing-tsit Chan, ed., *Chu Hsi and Neo-Confucianism* (Honolulu, 1986). Chan's *Chu Hsi: New Studies* (Honolulu, 1989) also contains a wide range of helpful essays. Finally, Chinese-language studies of Zhu are flourishing. Two particularly important works are Chen Lai, *A Study of Zhu Xi's Philosophy* (*Zhu Xi zhexue yanjiu*) (Beijing, 1988) and Yu Yingshi, *Zhu Xi's Historical World* (*Zhu Xi de lishi shijie*) (Taibei, 2003).

Stephen C. Angle (2005)

ZIEHEN, THEODOR

(1862–1950)

Theodor Ziehen, the German psychologist and philosopher, was born in Frankfurt am Main and served as professor of psychiatry at the universities of Jena, Utrecht, Halle, and Berlin. He lived as a private scholar in Wiesbaden from 1912 to 1917, when he returned to teaching as professor of philosophy and psychology at the University of Halle. He retired in 1930.

Ziehen's viewpoint in epistemology is in the broadest sense positivistic. Knowledge must start with that which is experientially given, which Ziehen termed "becomings" (*gignomene*). From this "gignomenal principle" follows the "principle of immanence," according to which there is no such thing as metaphysical knowledge of the transcendental, and therefore it is nonsensical to want to know that which is not given. The first task of philosophy thus consists in seeking the laws of all that is given (the "positivistic" or "nomistic" principle). According to Ziehen, such a "gignomenological" investigation leads to the conclusion that the traditional antithesis between the subjective, mental world of consciousness and the objective, material external world is inadmissible because the given is "psychophysically neutral." We must, however, distinguish two kinds of law-governed relations: The *gignomene* are to be called mental insofar as they are considered with regard to their "parallel components" (the mental, subjective ingredients of experiences, which parallel certain physiological processes); and the *gignomene* are to be understood as physical insofar as attention is fixed on their "reduction ingredients" ("reducts"), which are subject to causal laws.

Thus, Ziehen did not distinguish in the customary manner between material and mental reality; rather, he sought to understand the structure of the given, which he claimed to be the sole reality, in terms of two kinds of regularities—causal laws and parallel laws. Viewed from this "binomistic" standpoint, which assumes a twofold conformance to law in the given, real things appear as possibilities of perception, as potential perceptions, as "virtual reducts" that are both "transgressive" and "intramental." They lie beyond the boundaries of the individual content of consciousness, but they are nevertheless not situated "behind" experience but are immanent in it. Thus, real things represent certain aspects of experience that are determined by the causal type of laws. The processes governed by causal law ("the laws of nature") go along specific paths with a specific velocity; through the parallel laws that direct mental life, the *gignomene* are transformed into individual experiences.

Thus, for Ziehen psychology stood in contrast with the other natural sciences—the causal sciences—as the science of the "parallel component" of the given. Ziehen combated what he considered to be mythologizing faculty psychology, including Wilhelm Wundt's theory of apperception. He advocated a physiologically oriented, analytic, serial, or associationist approach to the subject. To association he added a second factor regulating the course of consciousness—the "constellation." A constellation arises at a given time from the mutual inhibition and stimulation of ideas, and it selects from the many ideas that are associated and, hence, ready for reproduction. In addition to association and constellation, Ziehen assumed three other basic mental functions—synthesis, analysis, and comparison.

Besides the causal laws and the parallel laws, Ziehen assumed a third, more general kind of regularity—conformity to logical laws—common to and set above the two other kinds of laws.

Ziehen also wrote on the philosophy of religion. He identified God with the regularity governing the world. God must be thought of as the essence or embodiment of "regularity in general"; as the totality of logical regularity, of natural laws, and of the laws of mental and spiritual life. It would be an inadmissible anthropomorphism to look beyond the regularities for a personal source of them.

See also Basic Statements; Epistemology; Laws of Nature; Philosophy of Religion; Positivism; Psychology; Wundt, Wilhelm.

Bibliography

WORKS BY ZIEHEN

Leitfaden der physiologischen Psychologie. Jena, Germany: Fischer, 1891; 12th ed., 1924.

Erkenntnistheorie auf psychophysiologischer und physikalischer Grundlage. Jena, Germany: Fischer, 1913; 2nd ed., published as *Erkenntnistheorie,* 2 parts, 1934–1939.

Die Grundlagen der Psychologic, 2 vols. Leipzig and Berlin: Teubner, 1915.

Lehrbuch der Logik. Bonn: A. Marcus and E. Weber, 1920.

Autobiography in *Die Philosophie der Gegenwart in Selbstdarstellungen,* Vol. IV. Edited by Raymond Schmidt. Leipzig: Meiner, 1923.

Vorlesungen über die Ästhetik, 2 parts. Halle: Niemeyer, 1923–1925.

Die Grundlagen der Religionsphilosophie. Leipzig, 1928.

WORKS ON ZIEHEN

Graewe, H. "Theodor Ziehen zum 90. Geburtstag." *Die Pyramide* (Innsbruck) (11) (1952): 201–202.

Peters, Wilhelm. "Theodor Ziehen zum 70. Geburtstag." *Kant-Studien* 37 (1932): 237–240.

Ulrich, Martha. "Der Ziehen'sche Binomismus und sein Verhältnis zur Philosophie der Gegenwart." *Kant-Studien* 25 (1921): 366–395.

Franz Austeda (1967)
Translated by Albert E. Blumberg

ZOROASTRIANISM

"Zoroastrianism," for more than a thousand years the dominant religion of Persia, is founded on the teachings of the prophet Zarathustra. (Zoroaster is an often used version of his name, and from it the name of the religion is derived; this version reflects ancient Greek transliteration.) Four main stages in the religion's history can be distinguished: the early faith as promulgated by Zarathustra himself; the religion of the Persian Empire under Darius I (who ruled 521–486 BCE) and his Achaemenid successors; its renewal under the Arsacid (250 BCE–226 CE) and Sassanian (226–641) dynasties; and the late period, when the religion was swamped by Islam but continued as the faith of a minority, some of whom settled in India and are known as Parsis (literally "Persians").

SCRIPTURES

The scriptures are known as the Avesta (or Zend-Avesta) and consist of various hymns, treatises, and poems. They comprise the Yasna, a collection of liturgical writings that contains the important Gāthās (literally "songs"), possibly written by Zarathustra himself; the Yashts, hymns to various divinities; and the Vendidād, which contains prescriptions for rituals of purification and so on. Many of these writings belong to a period when Zoroastrianism had become overlaid by polytheistic elements; some may date from as late as the fourth century, although the majority were composed much earlier. From the fourth century a further and extensive set of writings, which expressed the reformed theology of the Sassanian period, was compiled in the later language of Pahlavi.

ZARATHUSTRA AND HIS TEACHING

There is considerable dispute and uncertainty about the date and place of the prophet's life. Although Greek sources mention dates of up to several thousand years BCE, the most plausible theories are that he lived in the tenth or ninth century BCE or in the sixth or fifth. Although certain evidence points to his having lived in eastern Iran, the language of the Gāthās has been found to belong to northwest Iran. According to the traditions surrounding Zarathustra's life, he converted King Vishtaspa (Hystaspes in Greek transliteration), which proved decisive for the spread of the new religion. Vishtaspa ruled parts of eastern Iran and was the father of Darius the Great, a strong exponent and protector of the faith. These facts lend some support to the hypothesis that Zarathustra lived at the later date and in eastern Iran.

Although traditional accounts of Zarathustra's life are heavily overlaid by legend, it is probable that he was the son of a pagan priest of a pastoral tribe. At the age of thirty or a little later, he had a powerful religious experience, probably of a prophetic nature, analogous to the inaugural visions of such Old Testament prophets as Isaiah. He is reported to have encountered the angel Vohu Manah ("Good Thought"), who took him to the great spirit Ahura-Mazda ("The Wise Lord"), Zarathustra's name for God. Other revelations combined to induce him to preach a purified religion, combating the existing Persian polytheism, which had similarities to the Vedic religion of India. At first he met with considerable opposition, but the conversion of Vishtaspa paved the way for Zarathustra's wide influence, despite the king's later defeat in war and the occupation of his capital. Zarathustra is said to have been killed at the age of seventy-seven during Vishtaspa's defeat, but according to later accounts, he died while performing the fire sacrifice, an important element in the new cultus.

Zarathustra's God had the attributes of a sky god, like the Indian god Varuna. Both were ethical and celestial and were worshiped by the Indo-European Mitanni of the mountainous region to the north of the Mesopotamian plain during the latter part of the second millennium BCE. Zarathustra strongly denounced the cult of the gods of popular religion, equating such beings with evil spirits who seduced men from the worship of the one Spirit. The belief in the malicious opposition to the purified religion that he preached and the incompatibility of Ahura-Mazda's goodness with the creation of evil led Zarathustra to conceive of a cosmic opposition to God. He mentions Drūj ("The Lie"), an evil force waging war against Ahura-Mazda. From this early concept developed the later Zoroastrian theology of dualism.

Although Zarathustra attacked the existing religion, he also compromised with it. A slight concession to polytheism was involved in the doctrine of the Amesha-Spentas ("Immortal Holy Ones"), such as Dominion and Immortality, which were personified qualities of Ahura-Mazda. It is probable that Zarathustra was making use of certain aspects of the existing mythology and transforming them into attributes and powers of God. He seems to have used the fire sacrifice, a prominent feature of later and modern Zoroastrianism, transforming what had previously been part of the fabric of the polytheistic cultus. Zarathustra's fire sacrifice was also related in origin to the ritual surrounding the figure of Agni (Fire) in ancient Indian religion.

He preached an ethic based on the social life of the husbandman, the good man being one who tends his cattle and tills the soil in a spirit of peace and neighborliness. The good man must also resist worshipers of the *daevas* (gods), who, together with the evil spirit opposed to Ahura-Mazda, threaten the farmer's livelihood. These ideas probably reflected the social conditions of Zarathustra's time and country, when there was a transition from the nomadic to the pastoral life. The *daeva*-worshipers would then represent bands of nomadic raiders, and the new purified religion would be a means of cementing a settled, pastoral fabric of society. One of the Gāthās is a dialogue in which there figures a mysterious being called the Ox Soul, who complains of the bad treatment meted out to cattle upon the earth. The angel Vohu Manah promises that they will be protected by Zarathustra, who prays earnestly to Ahura-Mazda for assistance. These connections between the new religion and a settled cattle-raising society later became obscured when Zoroastrianism became the religion of the Persian Empire and when they were no longer relevant.

The moral life, however, was not confined to neighborliness and resistance to evil *daeva*-worshipers. It was part of a much wider cosmic struggle, in which the good man participates in the battle of Ahura-Mazda against the evil Angra Mainyu, the chief agent of The Lie (in later language, these were called, respectively, Ormazd and Ahriman). The battle will consummate in a final judgment, involving the resurrection of the dead and the banishment of the wicked to the regions of punishment. This notion of a general judgment was supplemented by a dramatic picture of the individual's judgment. He must cross to Ahura-Mazda's paradise over the narrow bridge called Chinvat. If his bad deeds outweigh his good ones, he will topple into the dreadful, yawning abyss. Some of this Zoroastrian eschatology came to influence Jewish eschatology, partly through the contact with Persia consequent to the Exile and partly because of the succeeding Persian suzerainty over Israel. Zoroastrianism, therefore, indirectly influenced Christianity.

DEVELOPMENT OF RITUAL

When Zoroastrianism came to be the dominant religion of the Persian Empire during the Achaemenid dynasty, there was an increasing trend toward restoring the cult of lesser deities. This was a partial consequence of the adoption of Zoroastrianism as the state cult. Artaxerxes II, for instance, caused images of the goddess Anahita (connected in origin to Ishtar, the Babylonian fertility deity) to be set up in the chief cities of the empire. The cultus came to be administered, in some areas at least, by the priestly class known as the Magi, from which term the word *magic* is derived; the Magi also came to figure in Christian legend about the birth of Christ. This priestly class was probably of Median origin. At first, the Magi had opposed the new faith, but after having adopted it, they began to change its character by importing extensive magical and ritual practices into it. Thus, the later portions of the Avesta contain spells and incantations. Further, the Gāthās were no longer treated simply as expressing Zarathustra's religion and teachings but as having intrinsic magical powers. Their proper repetition could combat the evil powers by which men were beset. However, the full history of the development of Zoroastrianism toward a ritualistic cult has never been fully disentangled, partly because of the intervening changes brought about in the late fourth century BCE by Alexander's conquest of the Persian Empire and its subsequent division among Greek dynasties. This Hellenistic period, lasting until the Parthian era in the second century BCE (begun by Mithridates I of the Arsacid dynasty), saw further syncretism, an offshoot of which was Mithraism, the cult of Mithra or Mithras, which later became important in the Roman Empire as a mystery religion.

DEVELOPMENT OF COSMOLOGY

While Zarathustra had stressed the ethical dimension of religion and the Mazdaism, as Zoroastrianism was later called, of the Achaemenid period had emphasized its ritual dimension, the reformed Zoroastrianism established in the Sassanian period displayed a strong interest in the doctrinal dimension of the faith. It is chiefly in this phase of Zoroastrianism that we discover a speculative interest in the workings of the universe. A theory of history was worked out that divided historical time into four eras, each lasting 3,000 years. In the first era, God brings into existence the angelic spirits and *fravashis,* which are the eternal prototypes of creatures (and, preeminently, of human beings). Since Ahura-Mazda creates by means of thought and since he foresees Angra Mainyu, the latter comes into existence. During the second period, the primeval man, Gayomard, and the primeval Ox (the prototype of the animal realm) exist undisturbed, but at the beginning of the third epoch the Evil Spirit, Angra Mainyu, succeeds in attacking and destroying them. From the seed of these two primeval beings men and animals arise, and there is a mixture of good and evil in the world. The last era begins with Zarathustra's mission; it will culminate in the final divine victory, which will occur partly through the agency of Soshyans, a semidivine savior. The universe will then be restored to an everlasting purified state in which the saved, now immortal, sing the praises of Ahura-Mazda. In this theory of history, the individual's life is linked to the unfolding cosmic drama.

The theory, while assigning the final victory to God, allows the nature and scale of the Evil One's operations to be alarming. Further, if Angra Mainyu arises through the thought of Ahura-Mazda, then evil comes from the Creator. This put the Zoroastrian theologians in a dilemma, and so attempts were made to work out doctrines that would more consistently explain the existence of evil. For instance, the movement known as Zurvanism held that both Ahura-Mazda and Angra Mainyu issued from a first principle, Zurvān (Infinite Time). Zurvān is beyond good and evil; only with the realm of finite time is the contrast between good and evil meaningful. On the other hand, Zurvān, the Supreme Being, dwells in an eternal state, raised beyond the conflicts and contrasts that exist in the temporal world.

INFLUENCE AND SURVIVAL

Elements of Zoroastrian teaching and mythology entered into Mithraism and Manichaeanism, and its eschatology had a marked influence on the Judeo-Christian tradition. However, the Muslim conquest of Persia in the seventh century largely destroyed the religion in its home country. Its survival in India was due to the Zoroastrians who emigrated in order to escape Muslim persecution. This Parsi community, centered chiefly on the west coast in and around Bombay, has maintained the cultus and interprets the faith in a strictly monotheistic sense. Their emphasis on education has given them an influence out of all proportion to their numbers.

See also Cosmology; Dualism in the Philosophy of Mind; Evil, The Problem of; Freud, Sigmund; Mani and Manichaeism.

Bibliography

Duchesne-Guillemin, J. *Zoroastre.* Paris: Maisonneuve, 1948.

Ghirshman, R. *Iran.* Baltimore, 1954.

Modi, J. J. *Religious Ceremonies and Customs of the Parsis,* 2nd ed. London, 1954.

Zaehner, R. C. *The Dawn and Twilight of Zoroastrianism.* London: Weidenfeld and Nicolson, 1961.

Zaehner, R. C. *Zurvān: A Zoroastrian Dilemma.* Oxford: Clarendon Press, 1955.

Zend-Avesta. Translated by J. Darmesteter in *Sacred Books of the East,* edited by F. Max Müller. Oxford: Clarendon Press, 1883.

RECOMMENDED READING

Boyce, Mary. *A History of Zoroastrianism.* 3 vols. Leiden: Brill, 1975–1982.

Boyce, Mary. *A Persian Stronghold of Zoroastrianism.* Oxford: Clarendon Press, 1977.

Boyce, Mary. *Zoroastrians, Their Beliefs and Practices,* reprint edition. London: Routledge, 2001.

Clark, Peter. *Zoroastrianism: An Introduction to an Ancient Faith.* Brighton, UK, and Portland, OR: Sussex Academic Press, 1998.

Hinnells, John. *Zoroastrian and Parsi Studies: Selected Works of John Hinnells.* Burlington, VT: Ashgate, 2000.

Insler, S. H. *The Gāthās of Zarathustra.* Leiden: Brill, 1975.

Kriwaczek, Paul. *In Search of Zarathustra: The First Prophet and the Ideas that Changed the World.* New York: Knopf, 2003.

Mahalingam, Indira, and Brian Carr, eds. *Companion Encyclopedia of Asian Philosophy.* London: Routledge, 1997.

Ninian Smart (1967)

Bibliography updated by Christian B. Miller (2005)

ZUBIRI, XAVIER
(1898–1983)

Xavier Zubiri, the Spanish Christian ontologist, was born in San Sebastián. He was professor of the history of philosophy in Madrid from 1926 to 1936 and in Barcelona from 1940 to 1942, after an absence abroad during the Spanish Civil War. He then left university teaching to give well-attended "private courses" in Madrid. His influence in Spain has been out of all proportion to the scanty amount of his published work.

Zubiri has been called a Christian existentialist, and indeed that is one aspect of his effort to synthesize neoscholastic theology with certain contemporary philosophies (those of Edmund Husserl, Martin Heidegger, and José Ortega y Gasset) and with modern science. To achieve this harmonizing of separate disciplines, Zubiri undertook studies in theology, philosophy, and natural science that could well have occupied three scholarly lives. He took a doctorate of theology in Rome and of philosophy in Madrid (where he studied under Ortega) before attending Heidegger's lectures in Freiburg and studying physics, biology, and Asian languages in various European centers. He translated into Spanish not only metaphysical works by Heidegger but also texts on quantum theory, atomic science, and mathematical physics generally.

From this extensive study Zubiri concluded that positive science and Catholic philosophy were separate points of view concerning the same reality. The philosopher-theologian cannot dispute, correct, or complete anything in science, but neither does he have to accept the philosophical opinions of scientists. The connection between these two parallel approaches to reality is simply that the sciences always leave us metaphysically hungry and with the feeling that they have not exhausted all the possibilities of knowledge, so they impel us to turn to philosophy. It is only when we come to philosophy in this way that it is really valuable; any philosophy that is undertaken without being forced upon us by scientific study is insipid.

What the sciences must get from philosophy, Zubiri claims, is an idea of nature, a theory of being to delimit their ontological horizons. They cannot themselves build such an idea out of positive facts, although they can criticize and reject unsuitable concepts of nature offered by philosophers. Aristotle provided an idea of nature adequate for the founding of physics, and Scholasticism did the same for modern science: Without John Duns Scotus and William of Ockham, Galileo Galilei's work would have been impossible. Physics is again in crisis, facing problems that cannot be solved by physicists, logicians, or epistemologists but only by ontologists, who can supply a fresh idea of nature within which quantum physics can progress.

In his philosophy of existence, Zubiri accepts the "radical ontological nullity" of man, who is nothing apart from the tasks he has to wrestle with. It is in dealing with his tasks that man comes to be. His nature consists in the mission of being sent out into existence to realize himself as a person. These views Zubiri read into Heidegger and Ortega, but he added a doctrine of "religation." (*Religation* was coined by Zubiri from the Latin *religare*, "to tie," which may also be the root of "religion.") According to this doctrine, we are not simply thrown into existence, as atheistic existentialists say, but are impelled into it by something that we feel all the time as an obligation, a force imposing on us the task of choosing and realizing ourselves. That something is deity, to which we are bound, or tied. Religation, the relation to deity, is the "fundamental root of existence" and the "ontological structure of personality."

See also Aristotle; Duns Scotus, John; Existentialism; Galileo Galilei; Heidegger, Martin; Husserl, Edmund; Ortega y Gasset, José; Philosophy of Science, History of; William of Ockham.

Bibliography

Zubiri's works include *Ensayo de una teoría fenomenológica del juicio*, a doctoral thesis on Husserl (Madrid, 1923); *Naturaleza, historia, Dios* (Madrid, 1944); *Sobre la esencia* (Madrid, 1962); and *Cinco lecciones de filosofía* (Madrid: Sociedad de Estudios y Publicaciones, 1963).

For commentary on Zubiri, see Luis Diez del Corral et al., *Homenaje a Xavier Zubiri* (Madrid, 1963), and Julián Marías, "Xavier Zubiri," in *La escuela de Madrid* (Buenos Aires, 1959).

OTHER WORKS BY ZUBIRI

Inteligencia sentiente. Inteligencia y realidad. Madrid: Alianza Editorial/Sociedad de Estudios y Publicaciones, 1980.

Inteligencia y Logos. Madrid Alianza Editorial/Sociedad de Estudios y Publicaciones, 1982.

Siete ensayos de Antropología filosófica. Bogotá: Ed. Universidad de Santo Tomás, 1982.

Inteligencia y Razón. Madrid: Alianza Editorial/Sociedad de Estudios y Publicacione, 1983.

Sobre el hombre. Madrid: Alianza Editorial/Sociedad de Estudios y Publicacione, 1986.

El problema filosófico de la historia de las religions. Madrid: Alianza Editorial/Sociedad de Estudios y Publicacione, 1993.

Los problemas fundamentales de la metafísica occidental. Madrid: Alianza Editorial/Sociedad de Estudios y Publicacione, 1994.

Espacio. Materia. Tiempo. Madrid: Alianza Editorial/Fundación Xavier Zubiri, 1996.

Sobre el problema de la filosofía. Madrid: Alianza Editorial/Fundación Xavier Zubiri, 1996.

El problema teologal del hombre: Cristianismo. Madrid: Alianza Editorial/Fundación Xavier Zubiri, 1997.

El hombre y la verdad. Madrid: Alianza Editorial/Fundación Xavier Zubiri, 1999.

Primeros escritos (1921-1926). Madrid: Alianza Editorial/Fundación Xavier Zubiri, 1999.

TRANSLATIONS

On Essence. Washington, DC: Xavier Zubiri Foundation of North America, 1980.

Nature, History, God. Washington, DC: Xavier Zubiri Foundation of North America, 1981.

Man and God. Washington, DC: Xavier Zubiri Foundation of North America, 1997.

The Philosophical Problem of the History of Religions. Washington, DC: Xavier Zubiri Foundation of North America, 1999.

Sentient Intelligence. Washington, DC: Xavier Zubiri Foundation of North America, 1999.

The Dynamic Structure of Reality. Champagne: University of Illinois Press, 2003.

OTHER

A complete bibliography of Zubiri's writings, the English translations of those writings, and literature on Zubiri is maintained by the Xavier Zubiri Foundation of North America at www.zubiri.org.

Neil McInnes (1967)

Bibliography updated by Thomas Nenon (2005)